5 REASONS

to buy your textbooks and course materials at

CENGAGE**brain**.com

1 **SAVINGS:**
Prices up to 75% off, daily coupons, and free shipping on orders over $25

2 **CHOICE:**
Multiple format options including textbook, eBook and eChapter rentals

3 **CONVENIENCE:**
Anytime, anywhere access of eBooks or eChapters via mobile devices

4 **SERVICE:**
Free eBook access while your text ships, and instant access to online homework products

5 **STUDY TOOLS:**
Study tools* for your text, plus writing, research, career and job search resources
availability varies

Find your course materials and start saving at:
www.cengagebrain.com

Engaged with you.
www.cengage.com

QUICK START GUIDE

1. To get started, navigate to www.cengagebrain.com and select "Register a Product."

A new screen will appear prompting you to add a Course Key. A Course Key is a code given to you by your instructor — this is the first of two codes you will need to access MindTap. Every student in your course section should have the same Course Key.

2. Enter the Course Key and click "Register."

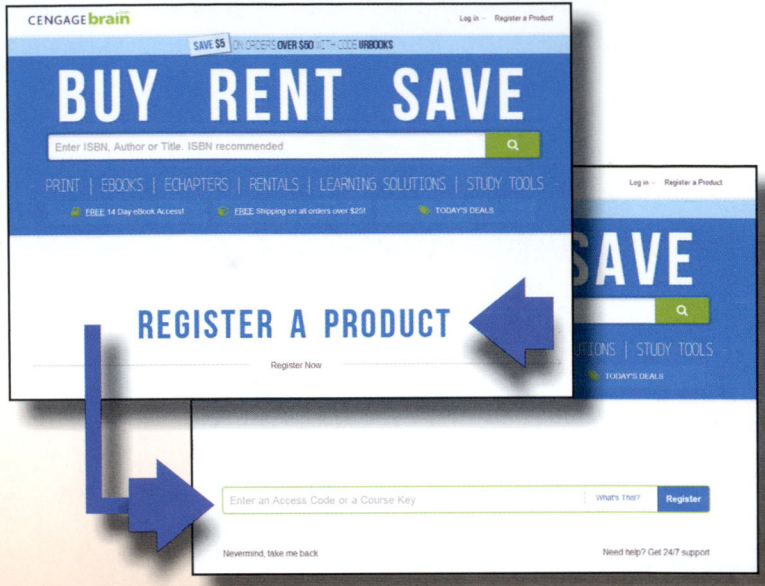

If you are accessing MindTap through your school's Learning Management System, such as BlackBoard or Desire2Learn, you may be redirected to use your Course Key/Access Code there. Follow the prompts you are given and feel free to contact support if you need assistance.

3. Confirm your course information above and proceed to the log in portion below.

If you have a CengageBrain username and password, enter it under "Returning Students" and click "Login." If this is your first time, register under "New Students" and click "Create a New Account."

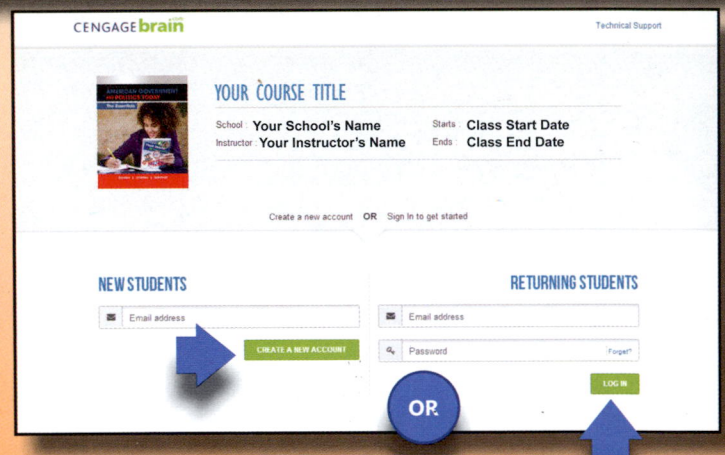

4. Now that you are logged in, you can access the course for free by selecting "Start Free Trial" for 20 days or enter in your Access Code.

Your Access Code is unique to you and acts as payment for MindTap. You may have received it with your book or purchased separately in the bookstore or at www.cengagebrain.com. Enter it and click "Register."

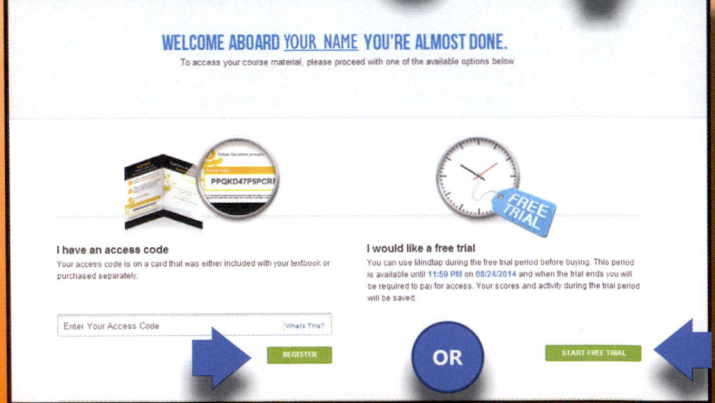

NEED HELP?

For CengageBrain Support: Login to **Support.Cengage.com**. Call **866-994-2427** or access our **24/7 Student Chat!** Or access the **First Day of School PowerPoint Presentation** found at **www.cengagebrain.com**.

EIGHTH EDITION

WORLD HISTORY

WILLIAM J. DUIKER
The Pennsylvania State University

JACKSON J. SPIELVOGEL
The Pennsylvania State University

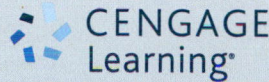

CENGAGE
Learning®

Australia • Brazil • Mexico • Singapore • United Kingdom • United States

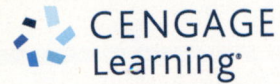

CENGAGE Learning®

World History, **Eighth Edition**
William J. Duiker and Jackson J. Spielvogel

Product Team Manager: Cara St. Hilaire

Senior Content Developer:
  Margaret McAndrew Beasley

Associate Content Developer: Cara Swan

Product Assistant: Andrew Newton

Media Developer: Kate MacLean

Marketing Development Manager:
  Kyle Zimmerman

Senior Content Project Manager: Carol Newman

Senior Art Director: Cate Rickard Barr

Manufacturing Planner: Sandee Milewski

IP Analyst: Alexandra Ricciardi

IP Project Manager: Amber Hosea

Production Service/Compositor: Cenveo
  Publisher Services

Text Designer: Shawn Girsberger

Cover Designer: Sarah Bishins

Cover Image: 'Saruwaka Cho, Yoru Shibai,' 1856
  (1925). Saruwaka Street, Yedo, with theatres,
  in light of the full moon. No 90 of 'The
  Hundred Views of Yedo.' A print from *The
  Colour Prints of Hiroshige* by Edward F
  Strange, by Cassell and Company Limited,
  London, New York, Toronto and Melbourne,
  1925. ©The Print Collector/HIP/The Image
  Works

For product information and technology assistance, contact us at **Cengage Learning Customer & Sales Support, 1-800-354-9706.**

For permission to use material from this text or product, submit all requests online at **www.cengage.com/permissions**. Further permissions questions can be e-mailed to **permissionrequest@cengage.com**.

Library of Congress Control Number: 2014936314

Student Edition
ISBN: 978-1-305-09120-7

Cengage Learning
20 Channel Center Street
Boston, MA 02210
USA

Cengage Learning is a leading provider of customized learning solutions with office locations around the globe, including Singapore, the United Kingdom, Australia, Mexico, Brazil, and Japan. Locate your local office at **www.cengage.com/global**.

Cengage Learning products are represented in Canada by Nelson Education, Ltd.

To learn more about Cengage Learning Solutions, visit **www.cengage.com**.

Purchase any of our products at your local college store or at our preferred online store **www.cengagebrain.com**.

Printed in the United States of America
Print Number: 02   Print Year: 2015

ABOUT THE AUTHORS

WILLIAM J. DUIKER is liberal arts professor emeritus of East Asian studies at The Pennsylvania State University. A former U.S. diplomat with service in Taiwan, South Vietnam, and Washington, D.C., he received his doctorate in Far Eastern history from Georgetown University in 1968, where his dissertation dealt with the Chinese educator and reformer Cai Yuanpei. At Penn State, he has written widely on the history of Vietnam and modern China, including the widely acclaimed *Communist Road to Power in Vietnam* (revised edition, Westview Press, 1996), which was selected for a Choice Outstanding Academic Book Award in 1982–1983 and 1996–1997. Other recent books are *China and Vietnam: The Roots of Conflict* (Berkeley, 1987), *U.S. Containment Policy and the Conflict in Indochina* (Stanford, 1995), *Sacred War: Nationalism and Revolution in a Divided Vietnam* (McGraw-Hill, 1995), and *Ho Chi Minh* (Hyperion, 2000), which was nominated for a Pulitzer Prize in 2001. Although his research specialization is in the field of nationalism and Asian revolutions, his intellectual interests are considerably more diverse. He has traveled widely and has taught courses on the history of communism and non-Western civilizations at Penn State, where he was awarded a Faculty Scholar Medal for Outstanding Achievement in the spring of 1996. In 2002 the College of Liberal Arts honored him with an Emeritus Distinction Award.

TO YVONNE,
FOR ADDING SPARKLE TO THIS BOOK AND TO MY LIFE
W.J.D.

JACKSON J. SPIELVOGEL is associate professor emeritus of history at The Pennsylvania State University. He received his Ph.D. from The Ohio State University, where he specialized in Reformation history under Harold J. Grimm. His articles and reviews have appeared in such journals as *Moreana*, *Journal of General Education*, *Catholic Historical Review*, *Archiv für Reformationsgeschichte*, and *American Historical Review*. He has also contributed chapters or articles to *The Social History of the Reformation*, *The Holy Roman Empire: A Dictionary Handbook*, *Simon Wiesenthal Center Annual of Holocaust Studies*, and *Utopian Studies*. His work has been supported by fellowships from the Fulbright Foundation and the Foundation for Reformation Research. At Penn State, he helped inaugurate the Western civilization course as well as a popular course on Nazi Germany. His book *Hitler and Nazi Germany* was published in 1987 (seventh edition, 2014). He is the author of *Western Civilization*, published in 1991 (ninth edition, 2015). Professor Spielvogel has won five major university-wide teaching awards. During the year 1988–1989, he held the Penn State Teaching Fellowship, the university's most prestigious teaching award. In 1996, he won the Dean Arthur Ray Warnock Award for Outstanding Faculty Member and in 2000 received the Schreyer Honors College Excellence in Teaching Award.

TO DIANE,
WHOSE LOVE AND SUPPORT MADE IT ALL POSSIBLE
J.J.S.

BRIEF CONTENTS

CONTENTS

PART III   THE EMERGENCE OF NEW WORLD PATTERNS (1500–1800)   386

14   NEW ENCOUNTERS: THE CREATION OF A WORLD MARKET   388

15   EUROPE TRANSFORMED: REFORM AND STATE BUILDING   418

16   THE MUSLIM EMPIRES   446

MAPS

CHRONOLOGIES

FEATURES

DOCUMENTS

(continued on page 953)

PREFACE

For several million years after primates first appeared on the surface of the earth, human beings lived in small communities, seeking to survive by hunting, fishing, and foraging in a frequently hostile environment. Then suddenly, in the space of a few thousand years, there was an abrupt change of direction as humans in a few widely scattered areas of the globe began to master the art of cultivating food crops. As food production increased, the population in those areas rose correspondingly, and people began to congregate in larger communities. Governments arose to provide protection and other needed services to the local population. Cities appeared and became the focal point of cultural and religious development. Historians refer to this process as the beginnings of civilization.

For generations, historians in Europe and the United States pointed to the rise of such civilizations as marking the origins of the modern world. Courses on Western civilization conventionally began with a chapter or two on the emergence of advanced societies in Egypt and Mesopotamia and then proceeded to ancient Greece and the Roman Empire. From Greece and Rome, the road led directly to the rise of modern civilization in the West.

There is nothing inherently wrong with this approach. Important aspects of our world today can indeed be traced back to these early civilizations, and all human beings the world over owe a considerable debt to their achievements. But all too often this interpretation has been used to imply that the course of civilization has been linear, leading directly from the emergence of agricultural societies in ancient Mesopotamia to the rise of advanced industrial societies in Europe and North America. Until recently, most courses on world history taught in the United States routinely focused almost exclusively on the rise of the West, with only a passing glance at other parts of the world, such as Africa, India, and East Asia. The contributions made by those societies to the culture and technology of our own time were often passed over in silence.

Two major reasons have been advanced to justify this approach. Some people have argued that it is more important that young minds understand the roots of their own heritage than that of peoples elsewhere in the world. In many cases, however, the motivation for this Eurocentric approach has been the belief that since the time of Socrates and Aristotle, Western civilization has been the main driving force in the evolution of human society.

Such an interpretation, however, represents a serious distortion of the process. During most of the course of human history, the most advanced civilizations have been in East Asia or the Middle East, not in the West. A relatively brief period of European dominance culminated with the era of imperialism in the late nineteenth century, when the political, military, and economic power of the advanced nations of the West spanned the globe. During recent generations, however, that dominance has gradually eroded, partly as a result of changes taking place in Western societies and partly because new centers of development are emerging elsewhere on the globe—notably in Asia, especially with the growing economic strength of China and India.

World history, then, has been a complex process in which many branches of the human community have played an active part, and the dominance of any one area of the world has been a temporary rather than a permanent phenomenon. It will be our purpose in this book to present a balanced picture of this story, with all respect for the richness and diversity of the tapestry of the human experience. Due attention must be paid to the rise of the West, of course, since that has been the most dominant aspect of world history in recent centuries. But the contributions made by other peoples must be given adequate consideration as well, not only in the period prior to 1500, when the major centers of civilization were located in Asia, but also in our own day, where a multipolar picture of development is clearly beginning to emerge.

Anyone who wishes to teach or write about world history must decide whether to present the topic as an integrated whole or as a collection of different cultures. The world that we live in today, of course, is in many respects an interdependent one in terms of economics as well as culture and communications, a reality that is often expressed by the phrase "global village." The convergence of peoples across the surface of the earth into an integrated world system began in early times and intensified after the rise of capitalism in the early modern era. In recognition of this trend, historians trained in global history, as well as instructors in the growing number of world history courses, have now begun to speak and write of a "global approach" that gives less attention to the study of individual civilizations and focuses instead on the "big picture" or, as the world historian Fernand Braudel termed it, interpreting world history as a river with no banks.

On the whole, this development is to be welcomed as a means of bringing the common elements of the evolution of human society to our attention. But this approach also involves two problems. For the vast majority of their time on earth, human beings have lived in partial or virtually total isolation from each other. Differences in climate, location, and geographic features have created human societies very different from each other in culture and historical experience. Only in relatively recent times (the commonly accepted date has long been the beginning of the age of European exploration at the end of the fifteenth century, but some would now push it back to the era of the Mongol Empire or even earlier) have cultural interchanges begun to create a common "world system," in which events taking place in one part of the world are rapidly transmitted throughout the globe, often with momentous consequences. In recent generations, of course, the process of global interdependence has been proceeding even more rapidly. Nevertheless, even now the process is by no means complete, as ethnic and regional differences continue to exist and to shape the course of world history. The tenacity of these differences and sensitivities is reflected not only in the rise of internecine conflicts in such divergent areas as Africa, India, and eastern Europe but also in the emergence in recent years of such regional organizations as the African Union, the Association for the Southeast Asian Nations, and the European Union.

The second problem is a practical one. College students today often are not well informed about the distinctive character of civilizations such as China and India and, without sufficient exposure to the historical evolution of such societies, will assume all too readily that the peoples in these countries have had historical experiences similar to ours and will respond to various stimuli in a similar fashion to those living in western Europe or the United States. If it is a mistake to ignore those forces that link us together, it is equally a mistake to underestimate those factors that continue to divide us and to differentiate us into a world of diverse peoples.

Our response to this challenge has been to adopt a global approach to world history while at the same time attempting to do justice to the distinctive character and development of individual civilizations and regions of the world. The presentation of individual cultures is especially important in Parts I and II, which cover a time when it is generally agreed that the process of global integration was not yet far advanced. Later chapters adopt a more comparative and thematic approach, in deference to the greater number of connections that have been established among the world's peoples since the fifteenth and sixteenth centuries. Part V consists of a series of chapters that center on individual regions of the world while at the same time focusing on common problems related to the Cold War and the rise of global problems such as overproduction and environmental pollution.

We have sought balance in another way as well. Many textbooks tend to simplify the content of history courses by emphasizing an intellectual or political perspective or, most recently, a social perspective, often at the expense of sufficient details in a chronological framework. This approach is confusing to students whose high school social studies programs have often neglected a systematic study of world history. We have attempted to write a well-balanced work in which political, economic, social, religious, intellectual, cultural, and military history are integrated into a chronologically ordered synthesis.

Features of the Text

To enliven the past and let readers see for themselves the materials that historians use to create their pictures of the past, we have included **primary sources** (boxed documents) in each chapter that are keyed to the seven major themes of world history and relate to the surrounding discussion in the text. The documents include examples of the religious, artistic, intellectual, social, economic, and political aspects of life in different societies and reveal in a vivid fashion what civilization meant to the individual men and women who shaped it by their actions. A question at the end of each box helps to guide students in analyzing the documents. The Opposing Viewpoints feature (see full description later in the Preface) provides additional primary source materials.

Each chapter includes a **lengthy introduction and conclusion** to help maintain the continuity of the narrative and to provide a synthesis of important themes. Anecdotes in the chapter introductions dramatically convey the major theme or themes of each chapter. A **timeline** at the end of each chapter enables students to see the major developments of an era at a glance and within cross-cultural categories, while the more **detailed chronologies** interspersed within the narrative reinforce the events discussed in the text.

Updated maps and extensive illustrations serve to deepen the reader's understanding of the text. **Map captions** are designed to enrich students' awareness of the importance of geography to history, and numerous **spot maps** enable students to see at a glance the region or subject being discussed in the text. Map captions also include a question to guide students' reading of the map. To facilitate understanding of cultural movements, illustrations of artistic works discussed in the text are placed near the discussions. **Chapter outlines and focus questions, including Critical Thinking and new Connections to Today questions**, at the beginning of each chapter give students a useful overview and guide them to the main subjects of each chapter. The focus questions are then repeated at the beginning of each major section in the chapter. A **glossary of important terms** (boldfaced in the text when they are introduced and defined) is provided at the back of the book to maximize reader comprehension. A **guide to pronunciation** is now provided in parentheses in the text, following the first mention of a complex name or term.

Comparative Essays, keyed to the seven major themes of world history (see p. xxxi), enable us to draw more concrete comparisons and contrasts across geographic, cultural, and chronological lines. **Comparative Illustrations**, also keyed to the seven major themes, continue to be a feature in each chapter. Both the Comparative Essays and the Comparative Illustrations conclude with focus questions to help students develop their analytical skills. We hope that the Comparative Essays and the Comparative Illustrations will assist instructors who wish to encourage their students to adopt a comparative approach to their understanding of the human experience.

The **Film & History** feature, now appearing in many chapters, presents a brief analysis of the plot as well as the historical significance, value, and accuracy of popular films. New features have been added on films such as *Gladiator*, *The Young Victoria*, *Persepolis*, and *The Iron Lady*.

The **Opposing Viewpoints** feature, which has proven popular with reviewers and their students since its introduction in the sixth edition, presents a comparison of two or three primary sources to facilitate student analysis of historical documents. This feature has been expanded and now appears in almost every chapter. Focus questions are included to help students evaluate the documents.

New end-of-chapter elements, first added in the seventh edition, provide study aids for class discussion, individual review, and/or further research. The **Chapter Summary** is illustrated with thumbnail images of chapter illustrations and combined with a **Chapter Timeline**. A **Chapter Review**, which includes **Upon Reflection** essay questions and a list of **Key Terms**, assists students in studying the chapter. **Suggested Readings** (annotated bibliographies) highlight the most recent literature on each period and also give references for some of the older, "classic" works in each field.

New to This Edition

After reexamining the entire book and analyzing the comments and reviews of many colleagues who have found the book to be a useful instrument for introducing their students to world history, we have also made a number of other changes for the eighth edition.

We have continued to strengthen the global framework of the book, but not at the expense of reducing the attention assigned to individual regions of the world. New material has been added to most chapters to help students be aware of similar developments globally, including new comparative sections.

The enthusiastic response to the primary sources (boxed documents) led us to evaluate the content of each document carefully and add new documents throughout the text, including new comparative documents in the **Opposing Viewpoints** feature.

The **Suggested Reading** sections at the end of each chapter have been thoroughly updated and are organized under subheadings to make them more useful. New illustrations were added to every chapter. **Chapter Notes** have now been placed at the end of each chapter.

A new focus question entitled **Connections to Today** has been added at the beginning of each chapter to help students appreciate the relevance of history by asking them to draw connections between the past and the present.

New **historiographical subsections** (often marked by headings in question format), which examine how and why historians differ in their interpretation of specific topics, have also been added. To keep up with the ever-growing body of historical scholarship, new or revised material has been added throughout the book on many topics (see specific notes below).

Chapter-by-Chapter Content Revisions

Chapter 1 New and revised material on religion in Neolithic societies and the role of ritual in ancient Egypt; new Opposing Viewpoints features, "The Great Flood: Two Versions," and "The Governing of Empires: Two Approaches"; new historiographical subsection, "What Were the Causes of Civilization?"

Chapter 2 Two new documents, "In the Beginning" and "A Singular Debate"; new information on early forms of currency in India.

Chapter 3 New opening vignette on Qin dynasty; new document, "The Mandate of Heaven" in ancient China; new information on early writing and currency. Addition of material and document "A Prescription for the Emperor" on Han dynasty (moved from Chapter 5 and revised).

Chapter 4 New and revised material on the following: the role of the phalanx and colonies in the rise of democracy in Greece, helots and women in Sparta, the political system in Sparta, Sophocles, and sports and violence in ancient Greece; new documents, "Sophocles: 'The Miracle of Man'" and "Relations Between Greeks and Non-Greeks."

Chapter 5 The section on Han China has been moved back to Chapter 3; new material on the following: Roman children and early Christianity, especially Christian women; new subsection: "The Struggle of the Orders: Social Division in the Roman Republic"; new subsection: "The Nature of Roman Imperialism"; new subsection: "Prosperity in the Early Empire: Trade with China and India," focusing on the Silk Road and contact between Romans and Chinese; new section, "A Comparison of the Roman and Han Empires"; new document, "The Assassination of Julius Caesar"; new Opposing Viewpoints feature, "Women in the Roman and Han Empires"; new Comparative Illustration, "Emperors, West and East."

Chapter 6 Revised opening vignette on the first arrivals in the Americas; new document "Aztec Religion Through Spanish Eyes"; added material on early civilizations in South America.

Chapter 7 New document "The Spread of the Muslim Faith" on the meaning of *jihad* in the Qur'an; new material on Arab science and philosophy, the arrival of the Turks in the Middle East, and early Arab seafaring technology.

Chapter 8 Two new documents "A Chinese View of Africa" and "The Slave Trade in Ancient Africa"; enhanced treatment of West Africa.

Chapter 9 Two new documents, "Chinese Traders in the Philippines" and "The Spread of Buddhism in Southeast Asia"; new historiographical interpretation question, "The Indian Economy: Promise Unfulfilled?"; added information on the Kushan state.

Chapter 10 Two new documents, "Choosing the Best and Brightest" and "Proper Etiquette in Tang Dynasty China"; added material on Chinese cartography and trade relations.

Chapter 11 New document, "A Plea to the New Emperor"; updated information on Korea.

Chapter 12 New material on the *missi dominici*, the role of peasant women, commercial capitalism, and women in medieval cities; new document, "Pollution in a Medieval City"; new Opposing Viewpoints feature, "Two Views of Trade and Merchants"; new historiographical subsection, "What Was the Significance of Charlemagne?"

Chapter 13 New section, "Women in the Byzantine Empire"; new material on Italian Renaissance art; new subsection, "Machiavelli and Political Power in the Renaissance"; new Opposing Viewpoints feature, "The Renaissance Prince: The Views of Machiavelli and Erasmus."

Chapter 14 Two new documents, "Dividing up the Spoils of Exploration" and "Idolaters and Heathens in Old Siam";

revised Opposing Viewpoints feature, "The March of Civilization"; added material on cartography and navigation, and the "maroon" slave communities in the Americas.

Chapter 15 New material on Judith Leyster; new documents, "Queen Elizabeth I: 'I Have the Heart of a King'" and "The King's Day Begins"; new historiographical subsection, "Was There a Military Revolution?"

Chapter 16 New historiographical subsection, "The Ottoman Empire: A Civilization in Decline?"; new material on Indian textile industry.

Chapter 17 New Opposing Viewpoints feature, "Some Confucian Commandments"; new document, "A Plea for Women's Education"; revised opening vignette; revised material on Chinese and Japanese foreign trade; new material on galleon and impact of silver in China; references to Yi Dynasty changed to Choson Dynasty.

Chapter 18 New material on the following: a consumer revolution in the eighteenth century and the finances of the French court; new document, "The State of French Finances."

Chapter 19 New material on Indian cotton trade and famine and the impact of overpopulation; new document, "The Great Irish Potato Famine."

Chapter 20 New material on the following: the lower classes and prostitution, mass leisure and mass consumption, Caspar David Friedrich and Romanticism, and Post-Impressionism; new documents, "Prostitution in Victorian London" and "Flaubert and an Image of Bourgeois Marriage."

Chapter 21 New document, "Tragedy at Caffard Cove"; revised sections on British reforms in India and direct and indirect rule in Africa.

Chapter 22 New Opposing Viewpoints feature, "Practical Learning or Confucian Essence: The Debate over Reform"; two new documents, "The Roots of Rebellion in Qing China" and "Program for Reform in Japan"; revised section on the decline of the Qing Dynasty.

Chapter 23 New material on the following: impact of conflict between the Great Powers during the age of imperialism and French African troops in Europe; new material in and reorganization of section on "The Great Depression"; new subsection, "The Social Impact of Total War"; new focus questions for section on "War and Revolution"; new document, "The Decline of European Civilization."

Chapter 24 New opening vignette; new document, "The Zionist Case for Palestine"; new Film & History feature, "*Lawrence of Arabia* (1962)"; revised section on post–World War I Japan.

Chapter 25 New material on the following: Nazi culture and totalitarianism; new Film & History feature: "*Triumph of the Will* (1934)"; new document, "Heinrich Himmler: 'We Had the Moral Right'"; new historiographical section, "The Retreat from Democracy: Did Europe Have Totalitarian States?"

Chapter 26 Revised Map 26.1 to include dates for revolts; added material on Cold War, Korea, and Vietnam; new Film & History feature, "*Doctor Strangelove* (1964)."

Chapter 27 New document "Václav Havel: A Call for a New Politics"; substantially revised material on social and cultural conditions in eastern Europe; updated and revised coverage of conditions in contemporary China.

Chapter 28 New material on the following: France, Germany, Great Britain, Russia, and Latin America; new material in "Varieties of Religious Life"; new Film & History feature, "*The Iron Lady* (2011)"; new document, "A Child's Account of the Shelling of Sarajevo."

Chapter 29 New opening vignette; two new documents, "The Arab Case for Palestine" and Osama bin Laden's "I Accuse!"; updated material on conditions in contemporary Africa, and discussion of Arab Spring; new material on Turkey.

Chapter 30 Two new documents, "Japan Renounces War" and "Return to the Motherland"; revised and updated material on all countries; added Film & History feature, "*Gandhi* (1982)" (moved from Chapter 24).

Because courses in world history at American and Canadian colleges and universities follow different chronological divisions, the text is available in both one-volume comprehensive and two-volume versions to fit the needs of instructors. Teaching and learning ancillaries include the following.

Instructor Resources

MindTap[TM] MindTap for *World History* is a personalized, online digital learning platform providing students with an immersive learning experience that builds critical thinking skills. Through a carefully designed chapter-based learning path, MindTap allows students to easily identify the chapter's learning objectives, complete reading activities organized into short, manageable blocks, and test their content knowledge with Aplia[TM] Critical Thinking Activities developed for the most important concepts in each chapter (see Aplia description below).

- *Setting the Scene:* Each chapter of the MindTap begins with a brief video that introduces the chapter's major themes in a compelling, visual way that encourages students to think critically about the subject matter.
- *Aplia:* The Aplia Critical Thinking assignments will include at least one map-based exercise, one primary source–based exercise, and an exercise summarizing the content and themes of the chapter.
- *Reflection Activity:* Every chapter ends with an assignable, gradable reflection activity, intended as a brief writing assignment to be shared with the class as an online discussion, through which students can apply a theme or idea they've just studied.

MindTap also provides a set of web applications known as MindApps to help you create the most engaging course for your students. The MindApps range from ReadSpeaker (which reads the text out loud to students) to Kaltura (allowing you to insert inline video and audio into your curriculum) to ConnectYard (allowing you to create digital "yards" through social media—all without "friending" your students). MindTap for *World History* goes well beyond an eBook, a homework solution/digital supplement, a resource center website, or a Learning Management System. It is truly a

Personal Learning Experience that allows you to synchronize the text reading and engaging assignments. To learn more, ask your Cengage Learning sales representative to demo it for you, or go to www.Cengage.com/MindTap.

Aplia^TM Aplia is an online interactive learning solution that improves comprehension and outcomes by increasing student effort and engagement. Founded by a professor to enhance his own courses, Aplia provides automatically graded assignments with detailed, immediate explanations on every question. The interactive assignments have been developed to address the major concepts covered in *World History* and are designed to promote critical thinking and engage students more fully in learning. Question types include questions built around animated maps, primary sources such as newspaper extracts, or imagined scenarios, like engaging in a conversation with a historical figure or finding a diary and being asked to fill in some blanks; more in-depth primary source question sets address a major topic with a number of related primary sources and questions that promote deeper analysis of historical evidence. Many of the questions incorporate images, video clips, or audio clips. Students get immediate feedback on their work (not only what they got right or wrong, but why), and they can choose to see another set of related questions if they want more practice. A searchable eBook is available inside the course as well so that students can easily reference it as they work. Map-reading and writing tutorials are also available to get students off to a good start.

Aplia's simple-to-use course management interface allows instructors to post announcements, upload course materials, host student discussions, e-mail students, and manage the gradebook. A knowledgeable and friendly support team offers assistance and personalized support in customizing assignments to the instructor's course schedule. To learn more and view a demo for this book, visit www.aplia.com.

Instructor Companion Website This website is an all-in-one resource for class preparation, presentation, and testing for instructors. Accessible through Cengage.com/login with your faculty account, you will find an Instructor's Manual, PowerPoint presentations (descriptions below), and test bank files (please see Cognero description).

Instructor's Manual For each chapter, this manual contains chapter outlines, lecture suggestions, primary source discussion questions, student research topics, and web and video resources.

PowerPoint® Lecture Tools These presentations are ready-to-use, visual outlines of each chapter. They are easily customized for your lectures. There are presentations of only lectures or only images, as well as combined lecture and image presentations. Also available is a per-chapter JPEG library of images and maps.

Test Bank Cengage Learning Testing, powered by Cognero®, for *World History* was prepared by Kathleen Addison of

California State University, Northridge, and is accessible through Cengage.com/login with your faculty account. This test bank contains multiple-choice and essay questions for each chapter. Cognero® is a flexible, online system that allows you to author, edit, and manage test bank content for *World History*, eighth edition. Create multiple test versions instantly and deliver them through your LMS from your classroom, or wherever you may be, with no special installs or downloads required.

The following format types are available for download from the Instructor Companion Site: Blackboard, Angel, Moodle, Canvas, and Desire2Learn. You can import these files directly into your LMS to edit, manage questions, and create tests. The test bank is also available in PDF format from the Instructor Companion Website.

MindTap Reader for World History MindTap Reader is an eBook specifically designed to address the ways students assimilate content and media assets. MindTap Reader combines thoughtful navigation ergonomics, advanced student annotation, note-taking, search tools, and embedded media assets such as video and MP3 chapter summaries, primary source documents with critical thinking questions, and interactive (zoomable) maps. Students can use the eBook as their primary text or as a multimedia companion to their printed book. The MindTap Reader eBook is available within the MindTap found at www.cengagebrain.com.

CourseReader CourseReader is an online collection of primary and secondary sources that lets you create a customized electronic reader in minutes. With an easy-to-use interface and assessment tool, you can choose exactly what your students will be assigned—simply search or browse Cengage Learning's extensive document database to preview and select your customized collection of readings. In addition to print sources of all types (letters, diary entries, speeches, newspaper accounts, etc.), their collection includes a growing number of images and video and audio clips. Each primary source document includes a descriptive headnote that puts the reading into context and is further supported by both critical thinking and multiple-choice questions designed to reinforce key points. For more information, visit www.cengage.com/coursereader.

Reader Program Cengage Learning publishes a number of readers, some containing exclusively primary sources, others containing a combination of primary and secondary sources, and some designed to guide students through the process of historical inquiry. Visit Cengage.com/history for a complete list of readers.

Cengagebrain.com Save your students time and money. Direct them to www.cengagebrain.com for choice in formats and savings and a better chance to succeed in your class. Cengagebrain.com, Cengage Learning's online store, is a single destination for more than 10,000 new textbooks, eTextbooks, eChapters, study tools, and audio supplements. Students have the freedom to purchase a-la-carte exactly what they need when they need it. Students can save 50 percent on the electronic textbook and can pay as little as $1.99 for an individual eChapter.

Custom Options Nobody knows your students like you, so why not give them a text that is tailored to their needs? Cengage Learning offers custom solutions for your course—whether it's making a small modification to *World History* to match your syllabus or combining multiple sources to create something truly unique. You can pick and choose chapters, include your own material, and add additional map exercises along with the Rand McNally Atlas to create a text that fits the way you teach. Ensure that your students get the most out of their textbook dollar by giving them exactly what they need. Contact your Cengage Learning representative to explore custom solutions for your course.

Student Resources

MindTap Reader MindTap Reader is an eBook specifically designed to address the ways students assimilate content and media assets. MindTap Reader combines thoughtful navigation ergonomics, advanced student annotation, note-taking, search tools, and embedded media assets such as video and MP3 chapter summaries, primary source documents with critical thinking questions, and interactive (zoomable) maps. Students can use the eBook as their primary text or as a multimedia companion to their printed book. The MindTap Reader eBook is available within the MindTap found at www.cengagebrain.com.

Reader Program Cengage Learning publishes a number of readers, some containing exclusively primary sources, others containing a combination of primary and secondary sources, and some designed to guide students through the process of historical inquiry. Visit Cengage.com/history for a complete list of readers.

Cengagebrain.com Save time and money! Go to www.cengagebrain.com for choice in formats and savings and a better chance to succeed in your class. Cengagebrain.com, Cengage Learning's online store, is a single destination for more than 10,000 new textbooks, eTextbooks, eChapters, study tools, and audio supplements. Students have the freedom to purchase a-la-carte exactly what they need when they need it. Students can save 50 percent on the electronic textbook and can pay as little as $1.99 for an individual eChapter.

Writing for College History, 1e [ISBN: 9780618306039] Prepared by Robert M. Frakes, Clarion University. This brief handbook for survey courses in American history, Western Civilization/European history, and world civilization guides students through the various types of writing assignments they encounter in a history class. Providing examples of student writing and candid assessments of student work, this text focuses on the rules and conventions of writing for the college history course.

The History Handbook, 2e [ISBN: 9780495906766] Prepared by Carol Berkin of Baruch College, City University of New York, and Betty Anderson of Boston University. This book teaches students both basic and history-specific study skills such as how to read primary sources, research historical topics, and correctly cite sources. Substantially less expensive than comparable skill-building texts, *The History Handbook* also offers tips for Internet research and evaluating online sources.

Doing History: Research and Writing in the Digital Age, 2e [ISBN: 9781133587880] Prepared by Michael J. Galgano, J. Chris Arndt, and Raymond M. Hyser of James Madison University. Whether you're starting down the path as a history major or simply looking for a straightforward and systematic guide to writing a successful paper, you'll find this text to be an indispensable handbook to historical research. This text's "soup to nuts" approach to researching and writing about history addresses every step of the process, from locating your sources and gathering information, to writing clearly and making proper use of various citation styles to avoid plagiarism. You'll also learn how to make the most of every tool available to you—especially the technology that helps you conduct the process efficiently and effectively.

The Modern Researcher, 6e [ISBN: 9780495318705] Prepared by Jacques Barzun and Henry F. Graff of Columbia University. This classic introduction to the techniques of research and the art of expression is used widely in history courses, but is also appropriate for writing and research methods courses in other departments. Barzun and Graff thoroughly cover every aspect of research, from the selection of a topic through the gathering, analysis, writing, revision, and publication of findings, presenting the process not as a set of rules but through actual cases that put the subtleties of research in a useful context. Part One covers the principles and methods of research; Part Two covers writing, speaking, and getting one's work published.

ACKNOWLEDGMENTS

BOTH AUTHORS GRATEFULLY ACKNOWLEDGE that without the generosity of many others, this project could not have been completed.

William Duiker would like to thank Kumkum Chatterjee and On-cho Ng for their helpful comments about issues related to the history of India and premodern China. His long-time colleague Cyril Griffith, now deceased, was a cherished friend and a constant source of information about modern Africa. Art Goldschmidt has been of invaluable assistance in reading several chapters of the manuscript, as well as in unraveling many of the mysteries of Middle Eastern civilization. He has benefited from comments by Charles Ingrao on Spanish policies in Latin America, and from Tony Hopkins and Dan Baugh on British imperial policy. Dale Peterson has been an unending source of useful news items. Finally, he remains profoundly grateful to his wife, Yvonne V. Duiker, Ph.D. She has not only given her usual measure of love and support when this appeared to be an insuperable task, but she has also contributed her own time and expertise to enrich the sections on art and literature, thereby adding life and sparkle to this edition, as well as the earlier editions, of the book. To her, and to his daughters Laura and Claire, he will be forever thankful for bringing joy to his life.

Jackson Spielvogel would like to thank Art Goldschmidt, David Redles, and Christine Colin for their time and ideas. Daniel Haxall of Kutztown University provided valuable assistance with materials on postwar art, popular culture, Postmodern art and thought, and the digital age. He is especially grateful to Kathryn Spielvogel for her work as editorial associate. Above all, he thanks his family for their support. The gifts of love, laughter, and patience from his daughters, Jennifer and Kathryn; his sons, Eric and Christian; his daughters-in-law, Liz and Laurie; and his sons-in-law, Daniel and Eddie, were especially valuable. He also wishes to acknowledge his grandchildren, Devyn, Bryn, Drew, Elena, Sean, Emma, and Jackson, who bring great joy to his life. Diane, his wife and best friend, provided him with editorial assistance, wise counsel, and the loving support that made a project of this magnitude possible.

Thanks to Cengage's comprehensive review process, many historians were asked to evaluate our manuscript. We are grateful to the following for the innumerable suggestions that have greatly improved our work. Members of this edition's Editorial Review Board (asterisked) deserve our particular thanks.

Joe Fuhrmann
Murray State University

Robert Gerlich
Loyola University

Marc J. Gilbert
North Georgia College

William J. Gilmore-Lehne
Richard Stockton College of New Jersey

Richard M. Golden
University of North Texas

Candice Goucher
Washington State University—Vancouver

Joseph M. Gowaskie
Rider College

Jonathan Grant
Florida State University

Don Gustafson
Augsburg College

Deanna Haney
Lansing Community College

Jason Hardgrave
University of Southern Indiana

Jay Harmon
Catholic High School

Ed Haynes
Winthrop College

Robert Henry
Grossmont College

Marilynn Jo Hitchens
University of Colorado—Denver

Tamara L. Hunt
University of Southern Indiana

*Charles Keller
Southern Arkansas University

Linda Kerr
University of Alberta at Edmonton

David Koeller
North Park University

Zoltan Kramar
Central Washington University

Douglas Lea
Kutztown University

David Leinweber
Emory University

Thomas T. Lewis
Mount Senario College

Craig A. Lockard
University of Wisconsin—Green Bay

George Longenecker
Norwich University

Norman D. Love
El Paso Community College

*Andrew Lowder
Lord Fairfax Community College

Robert Luczak
Vincennes University

*Yuxin Ma
University of Louisville

Aran MacKinnon
State University of West Georgia

Matthew Maher
Metropolitan State College of Denver

Patrick Manning
Northeastern University

*Maxim Matusevich
Seton Hall University

Eric Mayer
Victor Valley College

Dolores Nason McBroome
Humboldt State University

John McDonald
Northern Essex Community College

Andrea McElderry
University of Louisville

Jeff McEwen
Chattanooga State Technical Community College

Margaret McKee
Castilleja High School

Nancy McKnight
Stockton High School

Robert McMichael
Wayland Baptist University

David L. McMullen
University of North Carolina at Charlotte

John A. Mears
Southern Methodist University

Cristina Mehrtens
University of Massachusetts, Dartmouth

David A. Meier
Dickinson State University

Marc A. Meyer
Berry College

Stephen S. Michot
Mississippi County Community College

John Ashby Morton
Benedict College

William H. Mulligan
Murray State University

Henry A. Myers
James Madison University

Marian P. Nelson
University of Nebraska at Omaha

Sandy Norman
Florida Atlantic University

Patrick M. O'Neill
Broome Community College

Roger Pauly
University of Central Arkansas

Norman G. Raiford
Greenville Technical College

Jane Rausch
University of Massachusetts—Amherst

Michael Redman
University of Louisville

Dianna K. Rhyan
Columbus State Community College

Merle Rife
Indiana University of Pennsylvania

Patrice C. Ross
Columbus State Community College

John Rossi
LaSalle University

Eric C. Rust
Baylor University

Maura M. Ryan
Springbrook High School

Jane Samson
University of Alberta

Keith Sandiford
University of Manitoba

Anthony R. Santoro
Christopher Newport University

Elizabeth Sarkinnen
Mount Hood Community College

Pamela Sayre
Henry Ford College

Bill Schell
Murray State University

Linda Scherr
Mercer County Community College

Robert M. Seltzer
Hunter College

Patrick Shan
Grand Valley State University

David Shriver
Cuyahoga Community College

Brett Shufelt
Copiah-Lincoln Community College

David Simonelli
Youngstown State University

Amos E. Simpson
University of Southwestern Louisiana

Wendy Singer
Kenyon College

Christopher Sleeper
MiraCosta College

Marvin Slind
Washington State University

Paul Smith
Washington State University

Matthew Sneider
University of Massachusetts, Dartmouth

John Snetsinger
California Polytechnic State University

George Stow
LaSalle University

John C. Swanson
Utica College of Syracuse

Patrick Tabor
Chemeketa Community College

Anara Tabyshalieva
Marshall University

Tom Taylor
Seattle University

John G. Tuthill
University of Guam

Salli Vaegis
Georgia Perimeter College

Joanne Van Horn
Fairmont State College

Gilmar Visoni
Queensborough Community College

Peter von Sivers
University of Utah

*Michael Walker
Utah Valley University

Christopher J. Ward
Clayton College and State University

Walter Ward
Georgia State University

Pat Weber
University of Texas—El Paso

*Lucius Wedge
Walsh University

Douglas L. Wheeler
University of New Hampshire

David L. White
Appalachian State University

Elmira B. Wicker
Southern University—Baton Rouge

Glee Wilson
Kent State University

Laura Matysek Wood
Tarrant County College

*Joseph Yick
Texas State University—San Marcos

Harry Zee
Cumberland County College

*Colleen Shaughnessy Zeena
Salem State University

The authors are truly grateful to the people who have helped us to produce this book. We especially want to thank Clark Baxter, whose faith in our ability to do this project was inspiring. Margaret McAndrew Beasley thoughtfully, wisely, efficiently, and cheerfully guided the overall development of the eighth edition. We also thank Brooke Barbier for her suggestions and valuable insights. Abbie Baxter provided valuable assistance in suggesting illustrations and obtaining permissions for the illustrations. Anne Talvacchio was as cooperative and cheerful as she was competent in matters of production management.

A NOTE TO STUDENTS ABOUT LANGUAGE AND THE DATING OF TIME

One of the most difficult challenges in studying world history is coming to grips with the multitude of names, words, and phrases in unfamiliar languages. Unfortunately, this problem has no easy solution. We have tried to alleviate the difficulty, where possible, by providing an English-language translation of foreign words or phrases, a glossary, and a pronunciation guide. The issue is especially complicated in the case of Chinese because two separate systems are commonly used to transliterate the spoken Chinese language into the Roman alphabet. The Wade-Giles system, invented in the nineteenth century, was the more frequently used until recent years, when the pinyin system was adopted by the People's Republic of China as its own official form of transliteration. We have opted to use the latter, as it appears to be gaining acceptance in the United States.

In our examination of world history, we also need to be aware of the dating of time. In recording the past, historians try to determine the exact time when events occurred. World War II in Europe, for example, began on September 1, 1939, when Adolf Hitler sent German troops into Poland, and ended on May 7, 1945, when Germany surrendered. By using dates, historians can place events in order and try to determine the development of patterns over periods of time.

If someone asked you when you were born, you would reply with a number, such as 1996. In the United States, we would all accept that number without question because it is part of the dating system followed in the Western world (Europe and the Western Hemisphere). In this system, events are dated by counting backward or forward from the birth of Jesus Christ (assumed to be the year 1). An event that took place 400 years before the birth of Christ would most commonly be dated 400 B.C. (before Christ). Dates after the birth of Christ are labeled as A.D. These letters stand for the Latin words *anno Domini,* which mean "in the year of the Lord" (the year since the birth of Christ). Thus, an event that took place 250 years after the birth of Christ is written A.D. 250. It can also be written as 250, just as you would not give your birth year as "A.D. 1996" but simply as "1996."

Many historians now prefer to use the abbreviations B.C.E. ("before the common era") and C.E. ("common era") instead of B.C. and A.D. This is especially true of world historians who prefer to use symbols that are not so Western or Christian oriented. The dates, of course, remain the same. Thus, 1950 B.C.E. and 1950 B.C. refer to the same year, as do A.D. 40 and 40 C.E. In keeping with the current usage by world historians, this book uses the terms B.C.E. and C.E.

Historians also make use of other terms to refer to time. A decade is 10 years, a century is 100 years, and a millennium is 1,000 years. The phrase "fourth century B.C.E." refers to the fourth period of 100 years counting backward from 1, the assumed date of the birth of Christ. Since the first century B.C.E. would be the years 100 B.C.E. to 1 B.C.E., the fourth century B.C.E. would be the years 400 B.C.E. to 301 B.C.E. We could say, then, that an event in 350 B.C.E. took place in the fourth century B.C.E.

The phrase "fourth century C.E." refers to the fourth period of 100 years after the birth of Christ. Since the first period of 100 years would be the years 1 to 100, the fourth period or fourth century would be the years 301 to 400. We could say, then, for example, that an event in 350 took place in the fourth century. Likewise, the first millennium B.C.E. refers to the years 1000 B.C.E. to 1 B.C.E., and the second millennium C.E. refers to the years 1001 to 2000.

The dating of events can also vary from people to people. Most people in the Western world use the Western calendar, also known as the Gregorian calendar after Pope Gregory XIII, who refined it in 1582. The Hebrew calendar uses a different system in which the year 1 is the equivalent of the Western year 3760 B.C.E., once calculated to be the date of the creation of the world, according to the Old Testament. Thus, the Western year 2013 corresponds to the year 5773 on the Jewish calendar. The Islamic calendar begins year 1 on the day Muhammad fled from Mecca, which is the year 622 on the Western calendar.

THEMES FOR UNDERSTANDING WORLD HISTORY

As they pursue their craft, historians often organize their material on the basis of themes that enable them to ask and try to answer basic questions about the past. Such is our intention here. In preparing the eighth edition of this book, we have selected several major themes that we believe are especially important in understanding the course of world history. These themes transcend the boundaries of time and space and have relevance to all cultures since the beginning of the human experience.

In the chapters that follow, we will refer to these themes frequently as we advance from the prehistoric era to the present. Where appropriate, we shall make comparisons across cultural boundaries or across different time periods. To facilitate this process, we have included a Comparative Essay in each chapter that focuses on a particular theme within the specific time period discussed in that section of the book. For example, the Comparative Essays in Chapters 1 and 6 deal with the human impact on the natural environment during the premodern era, while those in Chapters 22 and 30 discuss the issue during the age of imperialism and in the contemporary world. Each Comparative Essay is identified with a particular theme, although it should be noted that many essays deal with several themes at the same time.

We have sought to illustrate these themes through the use of Comparative Illustrations in each chapter. These illustrations are comparative in nature and seek to encourage the reader to think about thematic issues in cross-cultural terms, while not losing sight of the unique characteristics of individual societies. Our seven themes, each divided into two subtopics, are listed below.

 1. Politics and Government The study of politics seeks to answer certain basic questions that historians have about the structure of a society: How were people governed? What was the relationship between the ruler and the ruled? What people or groups of people (the political elites) held political power? What actions did people take to guarantee their security or change their form of government?

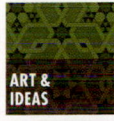 **2. Art and Ideas** We cannot understand a society without looking at its culture, or the common ideas, beliefs, and patterns of behavior that are passed on from one generation to the next. Culture includes both high culture and popular culture. High culture consists of the writings of a society's thinkers and the works of its artists. A society's popular culture is the world of ideas and experiences of ordinary people. Today, the media have embraced the term *popular culture* to describe the current trends and fashionable styles.

 3. Religion and Philosophy Throughout history, people have sought to find a deeper meaning in human life. How have the world's great religions, such as Hinduism, Buddhism, Judaism, Christianity, and Islam, influenced people's lives? How have they spread to create new patterns of culture in other parts of the world?

 4. Family and Society The most basic social unit in human society has always been the family. From a study of family and social patterns, we learn about the different social classes that make up a society and their relationships with one another. We also learn about the role of gender in individual societies. What different roles did men and women play in their societies? How and why were those roles different?

 5. Science and Technology For thousands of years, people around the world have made scientific discoveries and technological innovations that have changed our world. From the creation of stone tools that made farming easier to advanced computers that guide our airplanes, science and technology have altered how humans have related to their world.

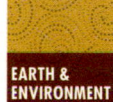 **6. Earth and the Environment** Throughout history, peoples and societies have been affected by the physical world in which they live. Climatic changes alone have been an important factor in human history. Through their economic activities, peoples and societies, in turn, have also made an impact on their world. Human activities have affected the physical environment and even endangered the very existence of entire societies and species.

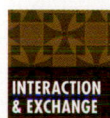 **7. Interaction and Exchange** Many world historians believe that the exchange of ideas and innovations is the driving force behind the evolution of human societies. Knowledge of agriculture, writing and printing, metalworking, and navigational techniques, for example, spread gradually from one part of the world to other regions and eventually changed the face of the entire globe. The process of cultural and technological exchange took place in various ways, including trade, conquest, and the migration of peoples.

The First Civilizations and the Rise of Empires (Prehistory to 500 C.E.)

FOR HUNDREDS OF THOUSANDS of years, human beings lived in small groups or villages, seeking to survive by hunting, fishing, and foraging in an often hostile environment. Then, in the space of a few thousand years, an abrupt change occurred as people in a few areas of the globe began to master the art of cultivating food crops. As food production increased, the population in these areas grew, and people began to live in larger communities. Cities appeared and became centers of cultural and religious development. Historians refer to these changes as the beginnings of civilization.

How and why did the first civilizations arise? What role did cross-cultural contacts play in their development? What was the nature of the relationship between these permanent settlements and nonagricultural peoples living elsewhere in the world? Finally, what brought about the demise of these early civilizations, and what legacy did they leave for their successors in the region? The first civilizations that emerged in Mesopotamia, Egypt, India, and China in the fourth and third millennia B.C.E. all shared a number of basic characteristics. Perhaps most important was that each developed in a river valley that was able to provide the agricultural resources needed to maintain a large population.

The emergence of these sedentary societies had a major impact on the social organizations, religious beliefs, and ways of life of the peoples living in them. As population increased and cities sprang up, centralized authority became a necessity. And in the cities, new forms of livelihood arose to satisfy the growing demand for social services and consumer goods. Some people became artisans or merchants, while others became warriors, scholars, or priests. In some cases, the early cities reflected the hierarchical character of the society as a whole, with a central royal palace surrounded by an imposing wall to separate the rulers from the remainder of the urban population.

Although the emergence of the first civilizations led to the formation of cities governed by elites, the vast majority of the population consisted of peasants or slaves working on the lands of the wealthy. In general, rural peoples were less affected by the changes than their urban counterparts. Farmers continued to live in simple mud-and-thatch huts, and many continued to face legal restrictions on their freedom of action and movement. Slavery was common in virtually all ancient societies.

Within these civilizations, the nature of social organization and relationships also began to change. As the concept of private property spread, people were less likely to live in large kinship groups, and the nuclear family became increasingly prevalent. Gender roles came to be differentiated, with men working in the fields or at various specialized occupations and women remaining in the home. Wives were less likely to be viewed as partners than as possessions under the control of their husbands.

These new civilizations were also the sites of significant religious and cultural developments. All of them gave birth to new religions that sought to explain and even influence the forces of nature. Winning the approval of the gods was deemed crucial to a community's success, and a professional class of priests emerged to handle relations with the divine world.

Writing was an important development in the evolution of these new civilizations. Eventually, all of them used writing as both a means of communication and an avenue of creative expression.

From the beginnings of the first civilizations around 3000 B.C.E., the trend was toward the creation of larger territorial states with more sophisticated systems of control. This process reached a high point in the first millennium B.C.E. Between 1000 and 500 B.C.E., the Assyrians and Persians amassed empires that encompassed large areas of the Middle East. The conquests of Alexander the Great in the fourth century B.C.E. created an even larger, if short-lived, empire that soon divided into four kingdoms. Later, the western portion of these kingdoms, along with the Mediterranean world and much of western Europe, fell subject to the mighty empire of the Romans. At the same time, much of India became part of the Mauryan Empire. Finally, in the last few centuries B.C.E., the Qin and Han dynasties of China governed a unified Chinese empire.

At first, these new civilizations had relatively little contact with peoples in the surrounding regions. But regional trade had started to take hold in the Middle East, and probably in southern and eastern Asia as well, at a very early date. As the population increased, the volume of trade rose with it, and the new civilizations moved outward to acquire new lands and access needed resources. As they expanded, they began to encounter peoples along the periphery of their empires.

Little evidence has survived to know the nature of these first encounters, but it is likely that the results varied according to time and place. In some cases, the growing civilizations found it relatively easy to absorb isolated communities of agricultural or food-gathering peoples that they encountered. Such was the case in southern China and southern India. But in other instances, notably among the nomadic or seminomadic peoples in the central and northeastern parts of Asia, the problem was more complicated and often resulted in bitter and extended conflict.

Over a long period of time, contacts between these nomadic or seminomadic peoples and settled civilizations gradually developed. Often the relationship, at least at the outset, was mutually beneficial, as each needed goods produced by the other. Nomadic peoples in Central Asia also served as an important link for goods and ideas transported over long distances between sedentary civilizations as early as 3000 B.C.E. Overland trade throughout southwestern Asia was already well established by the third millennium B.C.E.

Eventually, the relationship between the settled peoples and the nomadic peoples became increasingly tense. Where conflict occurred, the governments of the sedentary civilizations used a variety of techniques to resolve the problem, including negotiations, conquest, or alliance with other pastoral peoples to isolate their primary tormentors.

In the end, these early civilizations collapsed not only as a result of nomadic invasions but also because of their own weaknesses, which made them increasingly vulnerable to attacks along the frontier. Some of their problems were political, and others were related to climatic change or environmental problems.

The fall of the ancient empires did not mark the end of civilization, of course, but rather served as a transition to a new stage of increasing complexity in the evolution of human society. ◆

Early Humans and the First Civilizations

Excavation of Warka showing the ruins of Uruk

© Nik Wheeler/CORBIS

CHAPTER OUTLINE AND FOCUS QUESTIONS

The First Humans

Q How did the Paleolithic and Neolithic Ages differ, and how did the Neolithic Revolution affect the lives of men and women?

The Emergence of Civilization

Q What are the characteristics of civilization, and what are some explanations for why early civilizations emerged?

Civilization in Mesopotamia

Q How are the chief characteristics of civilization evident in ancient Mesopotamia?

Egyptian Civilization: "The Gift of the Nile"

Q What are the basic features of the three major periods of Egyptian history? What elements of continuity are evident in the three periods? What are their major differences?

New Centers of Civilization

Q What was the significance of the Indo-Europeans? How did Judaism differ from the religions of Mesopotamia and Egypt?

The Rise of New Empires

Q What methods and institutions did the Assyrians and Persians use to amass and maintain their respective empires?

CRITICAL THINKING

Q In what ways were the civilizations of Mesopotamia and Egypt alike? In what ways were they different? What accounts for the similarities and differences?

CONNECTIONS TO TODAY

Q What lessons can you learn from the decline and fall of early civilizations in Mesopotamia, Egypt, Assyria, and Persia, and how do those lessons apply to today's civilizations?

IN 1849, A DARING YOUNG ENGLISHMAN made a hazardous journey into the deserts and swamps of southern Iraq. Braving high winds and temperatures that reached 120 degrees Fahrenheit, William Loftus led a small expedition southward along the banks of the Euphrates River in search of the roots of civilization. As he said, "From our childhood we have been led to regard this place as the cradle of the human race."

Guided by native Arabs into the southernmost reaches of Iraq, Loftus and his small band of explorers were soon overwhelmed by what they saw. He wrote, "I know of nothing more exciting or impressive than the first sight of one of these great piles, looming in solitary grandeur from the surrounding plains and marshes." One of these piles, known to the natives as the mound of Warka, contained the ruins of Uruk, one of the first cities in the world and part of the world's first civilization.

Southern Iraq, known to the ancient Greeks as Mesopotamia, was one of the areas in the world where civilization began. In the fertile valleys of large rivers—the Tigris and Euphrates in Mesopotamia, the Nile in

Egypt, the Indus in India, and the Yellow River in China—intensive agriculture became capable of supporting large groups of people. In these regions, civilization was born. The first civilizations emerged in western Asia (now known as the Middle East) and Egypt, where people developed organized societies and created the ideas and institutions that we associate with civilization.

Before considering the early civilizations of western Asia and Egypt, however, we must briefly examine our prehistory and observe how human beings made the shift from hunting and gathering to agricultural communities and ultimately to cities and civilization. ◄━

The First Humans

 FOCUS QUESTION: How did the Paleolithic and Neolithic Ages differ, and how did the Neolithic Revolution affect the lives of men and women?

Historians rely mostly on documents to create their pictures of the past, but no written records exist for the prehistory of humankind. In their absence, the story of early humanity depends on archaeological and, more recently, biological information, which anthropologists and archaeologists use to formulate theories about our early past. Although modern science has given us more precise methods for examining prehistory, much of our understanding of early humans still relies on considerable conjecture.

The earliest humanlike creatures—known as **hominids**—lived in Africa some 3 to 4 million years ago. Called Australopithecines (aw-stray-loh-PITH-uh-synz), or "southern apemen," by their discoverers, they flourished in eastern and southern Africa and were the first hominids to make simple stone tools. Australopithecines may also have been bipedal—that is, they may have walked upright on two legs, a trait that would have enabled them to move over long distances and make use of their arms and legs for different purposes.

In 1959, Louis and Mary Leakey discovered a new form of hominid in Africa that they labeled *Homo habilis* ("skillful human"). The Leakeys believed that *Homo habilis*, which had a brain almost 50 percent larger than that of the Australopithecines, was the earliest toolmaking hominid. Their larger brains and ability to walk upright allowed these hominids to become more sophisticated in searching for meat, seeds, and nuts for nourishment.

A new phase in early human development occurred around 1.5 million years ago with the emergence of *Homo erectus* ("upright human"). A more advanced human form, *Homo erectus* made use of larger and more varied tools and was the first hominid to leave Africa and move into Europe and Asia.

The Emergence of *Homo sapiens*

Around 250,000 years ago, a crucial stage in human development began with the emergence of *Homo sapiens* (HOH-moh SAY-pee-unz) ("wise human being"). The first anatomically modern humans, known as *Homo sapiens sapiens* ("wise, wise human being"), appeared in Africa between 200,000 and 150,000 years ago. Recent evidence indicates that they began to spread outside Africa around 70,000 years ago. Map 1.1 shows probable dates for different movements, although many of these are still controversial.

These modern humans, who were our direct ancestors, soon encountered other hominids, such as the Neanderthals, whose remains were first found in the Neander valley in Germany. Neanderthal remains have since been found in both Europe and western Asia and have been dated to between 200,000 and 30,000 B.C.E. Neanderthals relied on a variety of stone tools and were the first early people to bury their dead. By 30,000 B.C.E., *Homo sapiens sapiens* had replaced the Neanderthals, who had largely become extinct.

THE SPREAD OF HUMANS: OUT OF AFRICA OR MULTIREGIONAL? The movements of the first modern humans were rarely sudden or rapid. Groups of people advanced beyond their old hunting grounds at a rate of only 2 to 3 miles per generation. This was enough, however, to populate the world in some tens of thousands of years. Some scholars, who advocate a multiregional theory, have suggested that advanced human creatures may have emerged independently in different parts of the world, rather than in Africa alone. But the latest genetic, archaeological, and climatic evidence strongly supports the out-of-Africa theory as the most likely explanation of human origin. In any case, by 10,000 B.C.E., members of the *Homo sapiens sapiens* species could be found throughout the world. By that time, it was the only human species left. All humans today, be they Europeans, Australian Aborigines, or Africans, belong to the same subspecies of human being.

The Hunter-Gatherers of the Paleolithic Age

One of the basic distinguishing features of the human species is the ability to make tools. The earliest tools were made of stone, and so this early period of human history (c. 2,500,000–10,000 B.C.E.) has been designated the **Paleolithic Age** (*paleolithic* is Greek for "old stone").

For hundreds of thousands of years, humans relied on gathering and hunting for their daily food. Paleolithic peoples had a close relationship with the world around them, and over a period of time, they came to know which plants to eat and which animals to hunt. They did not know how to grow crops or raise animals, however. They gathered wild nuts, berries, fruits, and a variety of wild grains and green plants. Around the

✦ CHRONOLOGY	The First Humans
Australopithecines	Flourished c. 3–4 million years ago
Homo habilis	Flourished c. 1–4 million years ago
Homo erectus	Flourished c. 100,000–1.5 million years ago
Neanderthals	Flourished c. 200,000–30,000 B.C.E.
Homo sapiens sapiens	Emerged c. 200,000 B.C.E.

MAP 1.1 The Spread of _Homo sapiens sapiens_. _Homo sapiens sapiens_ spread from Africa beginning about 70,000 years ago. Living and traveling in small groups, these anatomically modern humans were hunter-gatherers. © 2016 Cengage Learning

 Given that some diffusion of humans occurred during ice ages, how would such climate change affect humans and their movements, especially from Asia to Australia and Asia to North America?

world, they captured and consumed various animals, including buffalo, horses, bison, wild goats, reindeer, and fish.

The gathering of wild plants and the hunting of animals no doubt led to certain patterns of living. Archaeologists and anthropologists have speculated that Paleolithic people lived in small bands of twenty to thirty individuals. They were nomadic, moving from place to place to follow animal migrations and vegetation cycles. Hunting depended on careful observation of animal behavior patterns and required a group effort for success. Over the years, tools became more refined and more useful. The invention of the spear and later the bow and arrow made hunting considerably easier. Harpoons and fishhooks made of bone increased the catch of fish.

Both men and women were responsible for finding food—the chief work of Paleolithic people. Since women bore and raised the children, they generally stayed close to the camps, but they played an important role in acquiring food by gathering berries, nuts, and grains. Men hunted for wild animals, an activity that often took them far from camp. Because both men and women played important roles in providing for the band's survival, many scientists believe that a rough equality existed between men and women. Indeed, some speculate that both men and women made the decisions that governed the activities of the Paleolithic band.

Some groups of Paleolithic peoples found shelter in caves, but over time, they also created new types of shelter. Perhaps the most common was a simple structure of wood poles or sticks covered with animal hides. Where wood was scarce, Paleolithic hunter-gatherers might use the bones of mammoths for the framework and cover it with animal hides. The systematic use of fire, which archaeologists believe began around 500,000 years ago, made it possible for the caves and human-made structures to have a source of light and heat. Fire also enabled early humans to cook their food, making it taste better, last longer, and in the case of some plants, such as wild grains, easier to chew and digest.

The making of tools and the use of fire—two important technological innovations of Paleolithic peoples—remind us how crucial the ability to adapt was to human survival. Changing physical conditions during periodic ice ages posed a considerable threat to human existence. Paleolithic peoples used their technological innovations to change their physical environment. By working together, they found a way to survive. And by passing on their common practices, skills, and material products to their children, they ensured that later generations, too, could survive in a harsh environment.

But Paleolithic peoples did more than just survive. The cave paintings of large animals found in southwestern France and northern Spain bear witness to the cultural activity of Paleolithic peoples. A cave discovered in southern France in 1994—known as the Chauvet (shoh-VAY) cave after the leader of the expedition that found it—contains more than three hundred paintings of lions, oxen, owls, bears, and other animals. Most of these are animals that Paleolithic people did not hunt, which suggests to some scholars that the paintings were made for religious or even decorative purposes. The discoverers were overwhelmed by what they saw: "There was a moment of ecstasy.... They overflowed with joy and

Paleolithic Cave Painting: The Chauvet Cave. Cave paintings of large animals reveal the cultural creativity of Paleolithic peoples. This scene is part of a mural in a large underground chamber at Vallon-Pont-d'Arc, France, discovered in December 1994. It dates from around 30,000–28,000 B.C.E. and depicts aurochs (long-horned wild oxen), horses, and rhinoceroses. To make their paintings, Paleolithic artists used stone lamps that burned animal fat to illuminate the cave walls and mixed powdered minerals with animal fat to create red, yellow, and black pigments. Some artists even made brushes out of animal hairs with which to apply the paints.

emotion in their turn…. These were moments of indescribable madness."[1]

The Neolithic Revolution, c. 10,000–4000 B.C.E.

The end of the last ice age around 10,000 B.C.E. was followed by what is called the **Neolithic Revolution**, a significant change in living patterns that occurred in the New Stone Age (*neolithic* is Greek for "new stone"). The name "New Stone Age" is misleading, however. Although Neolithic peoples made a new type of polished stone axes, this was not the most significant change they introduced.

AN AGRICULTURAL REVOLUTION   The biggest change was the shift from gathering plants and hunting animals for sustenance (food gathering) to producing food by systematic agriculture (food production; see Map 1.2). The planting of grains and vegetables provided a regular supply of food, while the domestication of animals, such as sheep, goats, cattle, and pigs, added a steady source of meat, milk, and fibers such as wool for clothing. Larger animals could also be used as beasts of burden. The growing of crops and the taming of food-producing animals created a new relationship between humans and nature. Historians like to speak of this as an agricultural revolution. Revolutionary change is dramatic and requires great effort, but the ability to acquire food on a regular basis gave humans greater control over their environment. It enabled them to give

up their nomadic ways of life and begin to live in settled communities. The increase in food supplies also led to a noticeable expansion of the population.

The shift from hunting and gathering to food producing was not as sudden as was once believed, however. The **Mesolithic Age** ("Middle Stone Age," c. 10,000–7000 B.C.E.) saw a gradual transition from a food-gathering and hunting economy to a food-producing one and witnessed a gradual domestication of animals as well. Likewise, the movement toward the use of plants and their seeds as an important source of nourishment was not sudden. Moreover, throughout the Neolithic period, hunting and gathering as well as nomadic herding remained ways of life for many people around the world.

Systematic agriculture developed independently in different areas of the world between 8000 and 5000 B.C.E. Inhabitants of the Middle East began cultivating wheat and barley and domesticating pigs, cattle, goats, and sheep by 8000 B.C.E. From the Middle East, farming spread into southeastern Europe and, by 4000 B.C.E., was well established in central Europe and the coastal regions of the Mediterranean. The cultivation of wheat and barley also spread from western Asia into the Nile Valley of Egypt by 6000 B.C.E. and soon moved up the Nile to other areas of Africa, especially Ethiopia. In the woodlands and tropical forests of West Africa, a separate agricultural system emerged, based on the cultivation of tubers or root crops such as yams. The cultivation of wheat and barley also moved eastward into the highlands of northwestern and central India between 7000 and 5000 B.C.E. By 5000 B.C.E., rice was being cultivated in southeastern Asia, and from there it spread into southern China. In northern China, the cultivation of millet and the domestication of pigs and dogs seem well established by 6000 B.C.E. In the Western Hemisphere, Mesoamericans (inhabitants of present-day Mexico and Central America) domesticated beans, squash, and maize (corn) as well as dogs and fowl between 7000 and 5000 B.C.E. (see the Comparative Essay "From Hunter-Gatherers and Herders to Farmers" on p. 7).

NEOLITHIC FARMING VILLAGES   The growing of crops on a regular basis gave rise to more permanent settlements, which historians refer to as Neolithic farming villages or towns. Although Neolithic villages appeared in Europe, India, Egypt, China, and Mesoamerica, the oldest and most extensive ones were located in the Middle East. Jericho, in Canaan near the Dead Sea, was in existence by 8000 B.C.E. and covered several acres by 7000 B.C.E. It had a wall several feet thick that enclosed houses made of sun-dried mudbricks. Çatal Hüyük (chaht-ul hoo-YOOK), located in modern Turkey, was an even larger community. Its walls enclosed 32 acres, and its population probably reached six thousand inhabitants during its high point from 6700 to 5700 B.C.E. People lived in simple mudbrick houses that were built so close to one another that there were few streets. To get to their homes, people would walk along the rooftops and enter the house through a hole in the roof.

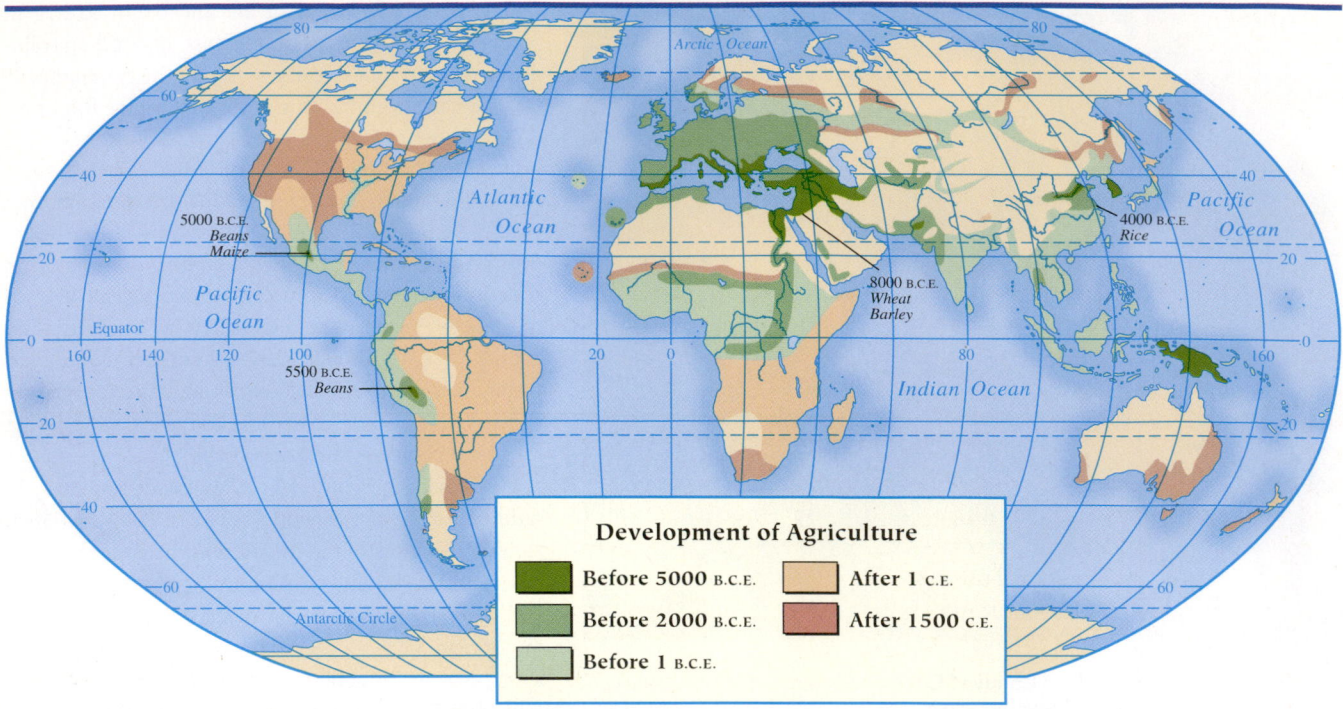

MAP 1.2 The Development of Agriculture. Agriculture first began between 8000 and 5000 B.C.E. in four different parts of the world. It allowed the establishment of permanent settlements where crops could be grown and domesticated animals that produced meat and milk could be easily tended. © 2016 Cengage Learning

Q *What geographic and human factors might explain relationships between latitude and the beginning of agriculture?*

Archaeologists have discovered twelve cultivated products in Çatal Hüyük, including fruits, nuts, and three kinds of wheat. People grew their own food and stored it in storerooms in their homes. Domesticated animals, especially cattle, yielded meat, milk, and hides. Food surpluses also made it possible for people to engage in activities other than farming. Some people became artisans and made weapons and jewelry that were traded with neighboring peoples.

Religious shrines housing figures of gods and goddesses have been found at Çatal Hüyük, as have a number of female statuettes. Molded with noticeably large breasts and buttocks, these "earth mothers" perhaps symbolically represented the fertility of both "our mother" earth and human mothers. The shrines and the statues point to the important role of religious practices in the lives of these Neolithic peoples.

CONSEQUENCES OF THE NEOLITHIC REVOLUTION The Neolithic agricultural revolution had far-reaching consequences. Once people settled in villages or towns, they built houses for protection and other structures for the storage of goods. As organized communities stored food and accumulated material goods, they began to engage in trade. In the Middle East, for example, the new communities exchanged such objects as shells, flint, and semiprecious stones. People also began to specialize in certain crafts, and a division of labor developed. Pottery was made from clay and baked in fire to make it hard. The pots were used for cooking and to store grains. Woven baskets were also used for storage. Stone

tools became refined as flint blades were used to make sickles and hoes for use in the fields. Obsidian—a volcanic glass that was easily flaked—was also used to create very sharp tools. In the course of the Neolithic Age, many of the food plants still in use today began to be cultivated. Moreover, vegetable fibers from such plants as flax and cotton were used to make thread that was woven into cloth.

The change to systematic agriculture in the Neolithic Age also had consequences for the relationship between men and women. Men assumed the primary responsibility for working in the fields and herding animals, jobs that kept them away from the home. Women remained behind, grinding grain into flour, caring for the children, weaving cloth, making cheese from milk, and performing other household tasks that required considerable labor. In time, as work outside the home was increasingly perceived as more important than work done in the home, men came to play the more dominant role in human society, which gave rise to the practice of **patriarchy** (PAY-tree-ark-ee), or a society dominated by men, a basic pattern that has persisted to our own times.

Other patterns set in the Neolithic Age also proved to be enduring elements of human history. Fixed dwellings, domesticated animals, regular farming, a division of labor, men holding power—all of these are part of the human story. For all of our scientific and technological progress, human survival still depends on the growing and storing of food, an accomplishment of people in the Neolithic Age. The Neolithic Revolution was truly a turning point in human history.

From Hunter-Gatherers and Herders to Farmers

EARTH & ENVIRONMENT

About ten thousand years ago, human beings began to practice the cultivation of crops and the domestication of animals. The exact time and place that crops were first cultivated successfully is uncertain. The first farmers undoubtedly used simple techniques and still relied primarily on other forms of food production, such as hunting, foraging, and pastoralism (herding). The real breakthrough came when farmers began to cultivate crops along the floodplains of river systems. The advantage was that crops grown in such areas were not as dependent on rainfall and therefore produced a more reliable harvest. An additional benefit was that the sediment carried by the river waters deposited nutrients in the soil, enabling the farmer to cultivate a single plot of land for many years without moving to a new location. Thus, the first truly sedentary societies were born.

The spread of river valley agriculture in various parts of Asia and Africa was the decisive factor in the rise of the first civilizations. The increase in food production in these regions led to a significant growth in population, while efforts to control the flow of water to maximize the irrigation of cultivated areas and to protect the local inhabitants from hostile forces outside the community provoked the first steps toward cooperative activities on a large scale.

The need to oversee the entire process brought about the emergence of an elite that was eventually transformed into a government.

We shall investigate this process in the next several chapters as we explore the rise of civilizations in the Mediterranean, the Middle East, South Asia, China, and the Americas. We shall also raise a number of important questions: Why did human communities in some areas that had the capacity to support agriculture not take the leap to farming? Why did other groups that had managed to master the cultivation of crops not take the next step and create large and advanced societies? Finally, what happened to the existing communities of hunter-gatherers who were overrun or driven out as the agricultural revolution spread throughout the world?

Over the years, a number of possible explanations, some of them biological, others cultural or environmental, have been advanced to answer such questions. According to Jared Diamond, in *Guns, Germs, and Steel: The Fates of Human Societies*, the ultimate causes of such differences lie not within the character or cultural values of the resident population but in the nature of the local climate and topography. These influence the degree to which local crops and animals can be put to human use and then be transmitted to adjoining regions. In Mesopotamia, for example, the widespread availability of edible crops, such as wheat and barley, helped promote the transition to agriculture in the region. At the same time, the absence of land barriers between Mesopotamia and its neighbors to the east and west facilitated the rapid spread of agricultural techniques and crops to climatically similar regions in the Indus River valley and Egypt.

Erich Lessing/Art Resource, NY

Q *What role did the development of agriculture play in the emergence of civilization?*

Women's Work. This rock painting from a cave in modern-day Algeria, dating from around the fourth millennium B.C.E., shows women harvesting grain.

Between 4000 and 3000 B.C.E., significant technical developments began to transform the Neolithic towns. The invention of writing enabled records to be kept, and the use of metals marked a new level of human control over the environment and its resources. Already before 4000 B.C.E., artisans had discovered that metal-bearing rocks could be heated to liquefy the metal, which could then be cast in molds to produce tools and weapons that were more useful than stone instruments. Although copper was the first metal to be used for producing tools, after 4000 B.C.E., metalworkers in western Asia discovered that a combination of copper and tin produced bronze, a much harder and more durable metal than copper. Its widespread use has led historians to call the period from around 3000 to 1200 B.C.E. the Bronze Age; thereafter, bronze was increasingly replaced by iron.

At first, Neolithic settlements were hardly more than villages. But as their inhabitants mastered the art of farming, more complex human societies gradually emerged. As wealth increased, these societies sought to protect it from being plundered by outsiders and so began to develop armies and to build walled cities. By the beginning of the Bronze Age, the concentration of larger numbers of people in river valleys was leading to a whole new pattern for human life.

The Emergence of Civilization

 FOCUS QUESTION: What are the characteristics of civilization, and what are some explanations for why early civilizations emerged?

As we have seen, early human beings formed small groups that developed a simple culture that enabled them to survive. As human societies grew and developed greater complexity, civilization came into being. A **civilization** is a complex culture in which large numbers of people share a variety of common elements. Historians have identified a number of basic characteristics of civilization, including the following:

1. *An urban focus.* Cities became the centers for political, economic, social, cultural, and religious development. The cities that emerged were much larger than the Neolithic towns that preceded them.

2. *New political and military structures.* An organized government bureaucracy arose to meet the administrative demands of the growing population, and armies were organized to gain land and power and for defense.

3. *A new social structure based on economic power.* While kings and an upper class of priests, political leaders, and warriors dominated, there also existed large groups of free common people (farmers, artisans, craftspeople) and, at the very bottom of the social hierarchy, a class of slaves.

4. *The development of more complexity in a material sense.* Surpluses of agricultural crops freed some people to work in occupations other than farming. Demand among ruling elites for luxury items encouraged the creation of new products. And as urban populations exported finished goods in exchange for raw materials from neighboring populations, organized trade grew substantially.

5. *A distinct religious structure.* The gods were deemed crucial to the community's success, and a professional priestly class, serving as stewards of the gods' property, regulated relations with the gods.

6. *The development of writing.* Kings, priests, merchants, and artisans used writing to keep records.

7. *New forms of significant artistic and intellectual activity.* For example, monumental architectural structures, usually religious, occupied a prominent place in urban environments.

Early Civilizations Around the World

The first civilizations that developed in Mesopotamia and Egypt will be examined in detail in this chapter. But civilizations also developed independently in other parts of the world. Between 3000 and 1500 B.C.E., the valleys of the Indus River in India supported a flourishing civilization that extended hundreds of miles from the Himalayas to the coast of the Arabian Sea (see Chapter 2). Two major cities—Harappa and Mohenjo-Daro—were at the heart of this advanced civilization, which flourished for hundreds of years. As in the city-states that arose in Mesopotamia and along the Nile, the Harappan economy was based primarily on farming, but Harappan civilization also carried on extensive trade with Mesopotamia. Textiles and food were imported from the Mesopotamian city-states in exchange for copper, lumber, precious stones, cotton, and various types of luxury goods.

Another river valley civilization emerged along the Yellow River in northern China about four thousand years ago (see Chapter 3). Under the Shang dynasty of kings, which ruled from 1570 to 1045 B.C.E., this civilization contained impressive cities with huge city walls, royal palaces, and large royal tombs. A system of irrigation enabled early Chinese civilization to maintain a prosperous farming society ruled by an aristocratic class whose major concern was war.

Scholars have long believed that civilization emerged only in four areas—the fertile river valleys of the Tigris and Euphrates, the

Statue from Ain Ghazal. This life-size statue made of plaster, sand, and crushed chalk was discovered in 1984 at Ain Ghazal, an archaeological site near Amman, Jordan. Dating from around 6500 B.C.E., it is among the oldest known statues of the human figure. Although it appears lifelike, its features are too generic to be a portrait of a particular individual. The purpose of this sculpture and the reason for its creation may never be known.
Erich Lessing/Art Resource, NY

Harappa and Mohenjo-Daro

The Yellow River, China

Central Asian Civilization

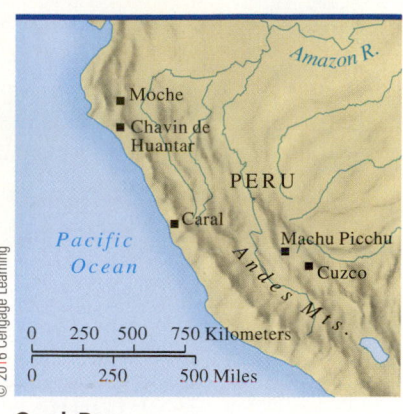

Caral, Peru

Nile, the Indus, and the Yellow River—that is, in Southwest Asia, Egypt, India, and China. Recently, however, archaeologists have discovered other early civilizations. One of these flourished in Central Asia (in what are now the republics of Turkmenistan and Uzbekistan) around four thousand years ago. People in this civilization built mudbrick buildings, raised sheep and goats, had bronze tools, used a system of irrigation to grow wheat and barley, and developed a writing system.

Another early civilization was discovered in the Supe River valley of Peru. At the center of this civilization was the city of Caral, which flourished around 2600 B.C.E. It contained buildings for officials, apartment buildings, and grand residences, all built of stone. The inhabitants of Caral also developed a system of irrigation by diverting a river more than a mile upstream into their fields. This Peruvian culture reached its height during the first millennium B.C.E. (see Chapter 6).

What Were the Causes of Civilization?

Why civilizations developed remains difficult to explain. Since civilizations developed independently in different parts of the world, can general causes be identified that would tell us why all of these civilizations emerged? A number of possible explanations have been suggested. One theory maintains that challenges forced human beings to make efforts that resulted in the rise of civilization. Some scholars have argued that material forces, such as the accumulation of food surpluses, made possible the specialization of labor and development of large communities with bureaucratic organization. But some areas were not naturally conducive to agriculture. Abundant food could be produced only through a massive human effort

to manage the water, an undertaking that required organization and bureaucratic control and led to civilized cities. Other historians have argued that nonmaterial forces, primarily religious, provided the sense of unity and purpose that made such organized activities possible. Finally, some scholars doubt that we will ever discover the actual causes of early civilization.

Civilization in Mesopotamia

Q **FOCUS QUESTION:** How are the chief characteristics of civilization evident in ancient Mesopotamia?

The Greeks called the valley between the Tigris and Euphrates Rivers Mesopotamia (mess-uh-puh-TAY-mee-uh), the land "between the rivers." The region receives little rain, but the soil of the plain of southern Mesopotamia was enlarged and enriched over the years by layers of silt deposited by the two rivers. In late spring, the Tigris and Euphrates overflow their banks and deposit their fertile silt, but since this flooding depends on the melting of snows in the upland mountains where the rivers begin, it is irregular and sometimes catastrophic. In such circumstances, farming could be accomplished only with human intervention in the form of irrigation and drainage ditches. A complex system was required to control the flow of the rivers and produce the crops. Large-scale irrigation made possible the expansion of agriculture in this region, and the abundant food provided the material base for the emergence of civilization in Mesopotamia.

The City-States of Ancient Mesopotamia

The creators of the first Mesopotamian civilization were the Sumerians (soo-MER-ee-unz or soo-MEER-ee-unz), a people whose origins remain unclear. By 3000 B.C.E., they had established a number of independent cities in southern Mesopotamia, including Eridu, Ur, Uruk, Umma, and Lagash (see Map 1.3). As the cities expanded, they came to exercise political and economic control over the surrounding countryside, forming city-states, which were the basic units of Sumerian civilization.

CHRONOLOGY	The Birth of Early Civilizations
Egypt	c. 3100 B.C.E.
Mesopotamia	c. 3000 B.C.E.
India	c. 3000 B.C.E.
Peru	c. 2600 B.C.E.
China	c. 2000 B.C.E.
Central Asia	c. 2000 B.C.E.

MAP 1.3 The Ancient Near East. The Fertile Crescent encompassed land with access to water. Employing flood management and irrigation systems, the peoples of the region established civilizations based on agriculture. These civilizations developed writing, law codes, and economic specialization.

Q *What geographic aspects of the Mesopotamian city-states made conflict between them likely?*

SUMERIAN CITIES Sumerian cities were surrounded by walls. Uruk, for example, was encircled by a wall 6 miles long with defense towers located every 30 to 35 feet along it. City dwellings, built of sun-dried bricks, included both the small flats of peasants and the larger dwellings of the civic and priestly officials. Although Mesopotamia had little stone or wood for building purposes, it did have plenty of mud. Mudbricks, easily shaped by hand, were left to bake in the hot sun until they were hard enough to use for building. People in Mesopotamia were remarkably innovative with mudbricks, inventing the arch and the dome and constructing some of the largest brick buildings in the world.

The most prominent building in a Sumerian city was the temple, which was dedicated to the chief god or goddess of the city and often built atop a massive stepped tower called a **ziggurat** (ZIG-uh-rat). The Sumerians believed that gods and goddesses owned the cities, and much wealth was used to

build temples as well as elaborate houses for the priests and priestesses who served the deities. Priests and priestesses, who supervised the temples and their property, had great power. In fact, historians believe that in the early stages of certain city-states, priests and priestesses may have had an important role in governance. The Sumerians believed that the gods ruled the cities, making the state a **theocracy** (government by a divine authority). Ruling power, however, was primarily in the hands of worldly figures known as kings.

KINGSHIP Sumerians viewed kingship as divine in origin—kings, they believed, derived their power from the gods and were the agents of the gods. As one person said in a petition to his king, "You in your judgment, you are the son of Anu [god of the sky]; your commands, like the word of a god, cannot be reversed; your words, like rain pouring down from heaven, are without number."[2] Regardless of their origins,

The "Royal Standard" of Ur. This detail is from the "Royal Standard" of Ur, a box dating from around 2700 B.C.E. that was discovered in a stone tomb from the royal cemetery of the Sumerian city-state of Ur. The scenes on one side of the box depict the activities of the king and his military forces. Shown in the bottom panel are four Sumerian battle chariots. Each chariot held two men, one who held the reins and the other armed with a spear for combat. A special compartment in the chariot held a number of spears. The charging chariots are seen defeating the enemy. In the middle band, the Sumerian soldiers round up the captured enemies. In the top band, the captives are presented to the king, who has alighted from his chariot and is shown standing above all the others in the center of the panel.

kings had power—they led armies and organized workers for the irrigation projects on which Mesopotamian farming depended. The army, the government bureaucracy, and the priests and priestesses all aided the kings in their rule. Befitting their power, Sumerian kings lived in large palaces with their wives and children.

ECONOMY AND SOCIETY The economy of the Sumerian city-states was primarily agricultural, but commerce and industry became important as well. The people of Mesopotamia produced woolen textiles, pottery, and metalwork. The Sumerians imported copper, tin, and timber in exchange for dried fish, wool, barley, wheat, and metal goods. Traders traveled by land to the eastern Mediterranean in the west and by sea to India in the east. The introduction of the wheel, which had been invented around 3000 B.C.E. by nomadic people living in the region north of the Black Sea, led to carts with wheels that made the transport of goods easier.

Sumerian city-states probably contained four major social groups: elites, dependent commoners, free commoners, and slaves. Elites included royal and priestly officials and their families. Dependent commoners included the elites' clients, who worked for the palace and temple estates. Free commoners worked as farmers, merchants, fishers, scribes, and craftspeople. Probably 90 percent or more of the population were farmers. Slaves belonged to palace officials, who used them in building projects; to temple officials, who used mostly female slaves to weave cloth and grind grain; and to rich landowners, who used them for agricultural and domestic work.

Empires in Ancient Mesopotamia

As the number of Sumerian city-states grew and the states expanded, new conflicts arose as city-state fought city-state for control of land and water. The fortunes of various city-states rose and fell over the centuries. The constant wars, with their burning and sacking of cities, left many Sumerians in deep despair, as is evident in the words of this Sumerian poem from the city of Ur:

> Ur is destroyed, bitter is its lament.
> The country's blood now fills its holes like hot bronze in a mold.
> Bodies dissolve like fat in the sun.
> Our temple is destroyed, the gods have abandoned us, like
>   migrating birds.
> Smoke lies on our city like a shroud.[3]

THE AKKADIAN EMPIRE Located in the flat land of Mesopotamia, the Sumerian city-states were also open to invasion. To the north of the Sumerian city-states were the Akkadians (uh-KAY-dee-unz). We call them a Semitic people because of the type of language they spoke (see Table 1.1). Around 2340 B.C.E., Sargon, leader of the Akkadians, overran the Sumerian city-states and established a dynastic empire. Sargon used the former rulers of the conquered city-states as his governors. His power was based on the military, namely, his standing army of 5,400 men. Sargon's empire, including all of Mesopotamia as well as lands westward to the Mediterranean, inspired generations of Near Eastern leaders to emulate his accomplishment. Even in the first millennium B.C.E., Sargon

TABLE 1.1	Some Semitic Languages	
Akkadian	Assyrian	Hebrew
Arabic	Babylonian	Phoenician
Aramaic	Canaanitic	Syriac

NOTE: Languages in italic type are no longer spoken.

was still remembered in chronicles as a king of Akkad who "had no rival or equal, spread his splendor over all the lands, and crossed the sea in the east. In his eleventh year, he conquered the western land to its furthest point, and brought it under his sole authority."[4] Attacks from neighboring hill peoples eventually caused the Akkadian empire to fall, and its end by 2100 B.C.E. brought a return to independent city-states and the conflicts between them. It was not until 1792 B.C.E. that a new empire came to control much of Mesopotamia under Hammurabi (ham-uh-RAH-bee), who ruled over the Amorites or Old Babylonians, a large group of Semitic-speaking seminomads.

HAMMURABI'S EMPIRE Hammurabi (1792–1750 B.C.E.) employed a well-disciplined army of foot soldiers who carried axes, spears, and copper or bronze daggers. He learned to divide his opponents and subdue them one by one. Using such methods, he gained control of Sumer and Akkad, creating a new Mesopotamian kingdom. After his conquests, he called himself "the sun of Babylon, the king who has made the four quarters of the world subservient," and established a new capital at Babylon.

Hammurabi, the man of war, was also a man of peace. A collection of his letters, found by archaeologists, reveals that he took a strong interest in state affairs. He built temples, defensive walls, and irrigation canals; encouraged trade; and brought about an economic revival. Indeed, Hammurabi saw himself as a shepherd to his people: "I am indeed the shepherd who brings peace, whose scepter is just. My benevolent shade was spread over my city. I held the people of the lands of Sumer and Akkad safely on my lap."[5] After his death, however, a series of weak kings were unable to keep Hammurabi's empire united, and it finally fell to new invaders.

Hammurabi's Empire

- Hammurabi's empire
- Sumerian civilization

THE CODE OF HAMMURABI: SOCIETY IN MESOPOTAMIA
Hammurabi is best remembered for his law code, a collection of 282 laws. Although many scholars today view Hammurabi's collection less as a code of laws and more as an attempt by Hammurabi to portray himself as the source of justice to his people, the code still gives us a glimpse of the Mesopotamian society of his time (see the box "The Code of Hammurabi" on p. 13).

The Code of Hammurabi reveals a society with a system of strict justice. Penalties for criminal offenses were severe and varied according to the social class of the victim. A crime against a member of the upper class (a noble) by a member of the lower class (a commoner) was punished more severely than the same offense against a member of the lower class. Moreover, the principle of "an eye for an eye, a tooth for a tooth" was fundamental to this system of justice. This meant that punishments should fit the crime: "If a freeman has destroyed the eye of a member of the aristocracy, they shall destroy his eye" (Code of Hammurabi, No. 196). Hammurabi's code also had an impact on legal ideas in Southwest Asia for hundreds of years, as the following verse from the Hebrew Bible (Leviticus 24:19–20) demonstrates: "If anyone injures his neighbor, whatever he has done must be done to him: fracture for fracture, eye for eye, tooth for tooth. As he has injured the other, so he is to be injured."

The largest category of laws in the Code of Hammurabi focused on marriage and the family. Parents arranged marriages for their children. After marriage, the parties involved signed a marriage contract; without it, no one was considered legally married. While the husband provided a bridal payment to the bride's parents, the woman's parents were responsible for a dowry to the new husband.

As in many patriarchal societies, women possessed far fewer privileges and rights in the married relationship than men. A woman's place was in the home, and failure to fulfill her expected duties was grounds for divorce. If she was not able to bear children, her husband could divorce her. Furthermore, a wife who was a "gadabout, … neglecting her house [and] humiliating her husband, shall be prosecuted" (No. 143). We do know that in practice not all women remained at home. Some worked in the fields and others in business, where they were especially prominent in running taverns.

Women were guaranteed some rights, however. If a woman was divorced without good reason, she received the dowry back. A woman could seek a divorce and get her dowry back if her husband was unable to show that she had done anything wrong. In theory, a wife was guaranteed the use of her husband's legal property in the event of his death. A mother could also decide which of her sons would receive an inheritance.

Sexual relations were strictly regulated as well. Husbands, but not wives, were permitted sexual activity outside marriage. A wife and her lover caught committing adultery were pitched into the river, although if the husband pardoned his wife, the king could pardon the guilty man. Incest was strictly forbidden. If a father had incestuous relations with his daughter, he would be banished. Incest between a son and his mother resulted in both being burned.

Fathers ruled their children as well as their wives. Obedience was duly expected: "If a son has struck his father, they shall cut off his hand" (No. 195). If a son committed a serious enough offense, his father could disinherit him, although fathers were not permitted to disinherit their sons arbitrarily.

The Code of Hammurabi

FAMILY & SOCIETY

ALTHOUGH IT IS NOT THE EARLIEST MESOPOTAMIAN LAW CODE, Hammurabi's is the most complete. The code emphasizes the principle of retribution ("an eye for an eye") and punishments that vary according to social status. Punishments could be severe. The following selections illustrate these concerns.

The Code of Hammurabi

25. If fire broke out in a free man's house and a free man, who went to extinguish it, cast his eye on the goods of the owner of the house and has appropriated the goods of the owner of the house, that free man shall be thrown into that fire.

129. If the wife of a free man has been caught while lying with another man, they shall bind them and throw them into the water. If the husband of the woman wishes to spare his wife, then the king in turn may spare his subject.

131. If a free man's wife was accused by her husband, but she was not caught while lying with another man, she shall make affirmation by god and return to her house.

196. If a free man has destroyed the eye of a member of the aristocracy, they shall destroy his eye.

198. If he has destroyed the eye of a commoner or broken the bone of a commoner, he shall pay one mina of silver.

199. If he has destroyed the eye of a free man's slave or broken the bone of a free man's slave, he shall pay one-half his value.

209. If a free man struck another free man's daughter and has caused her to have a miscarriage, he shall pay ten shekels of silver for her fetus.

210. If that woman has died, they shall put his daughter to death.

211. If by a blow he has caused a commoner's daughter to have a miscarriage, he shall pay five shekels of silver.

212. If that woman has died, he shall pay one-half mina of silver.

213. If he struck a free man's female slave and has caused her to have a miscarriage, he shall pay two shekels of silver.

214. If that female slave has died, he shall pay one-third mina of silver.

 What do these points of law from the Code of Hammurabi reveal to you about Mesopotamian society?

Source: Pritchard, James B., ed., *Ancient Near Eastern Texts Relating to the Old Testament*, 3rd Edition with Supplement. Copyright © 1950, 1955, 1969, renewed 1978 by Princeton University Press.

The Culture of Mesopotamia

A spiritual worldview was of fundamental importance to Mesopotamian culture. To the peoples of Mesopotamia, the gods were living realities who affected all aspects of life. It was crucial, therefore, that the correct hierarchies be observed. Leaders could prepare armies for war, but success really depended on a favorable relationship with the gods. This helps explain the importance of the priestly class and is the reason why even the kings took great care to dedicate offerings and monuments to the gods.

THE IMPORTANCE OF RELIGION The physical environment had an obvious impact on the Mesopotamian view of the universe. Ferocious floods, heavy downpours, scorching winds, and oppressive humidity were all part of the Mesopotamian climate. These conditions and the resulting famines easily convinced Mesopotamians that this world was controlled by supernatural forces and that the days of human beings "are numbered; whatever he may do, he is but wind," as *The Epic of Gilgamesh* put it. In the presence of nature, Mesopotamians could easily feel helpless, as this poem relates:

> *The rampant flood which no man can oppose,*
> *Which shakes the heavens and causes earth to tremble,*
> *In an appalling blanket folds mother and child,*
> *Beats down the canebrake's full luxuriant greenery,*
> *And drowns the harvest in its time of ripeness.*[6]

The Mesopotamians discerned cosmic rhythms in the universe and accepted its order but perceived that it was not completely safe because of the presence of willful, powerful cosmic powers that they identified with gods and goddesses.

With its numerous gods and goddesses animating all aspects of the universe, Mesopotamian religion was a form of **polytheism**. The four most important deities were An, god of the sky and hence the most important force in the universe; Enlil (EN-lil), god of wind; Enki (EN-kee), god of the earth, rivers, wells, and canals as well as inventions and crafts; and Ninhursaga (nin-HUR-sah-guh), a goddess associated with soil, mountains, and vegetation, who came to be worshiped as a mother goddess, a "mother of all children," who manifested her power by giving birth to kings and conferring the royal insignia on them.

Human relationships with the gods were based on subservience since, according to Sumerian myth, human beings were created to do the manual labor the gods were unwilling to do for themselves. Moreover, humans were insecure because they could never predict the gods' actions. But humans did attempt to relieve their anxiety by discovering the intentions of the gods through **divination**.

Divination took a variety of forms. A common form, at least for kings and priests who could afford it, involved killing animals, such as sheep or goats, and examining their livers or other organs. Supposedly, features seen in the organs of the sacrificed animals foretold events to come. Thus, one

	star	?sun over horizon	?stream	ear of barley	bull's head	bowl	head + bowl	lower leg	?shrouded body
Pictographic sign, c. 3100 B.C.E.									
Interpretation	star	?sun over horizon	?stream	ear of barley	bull's head	bowl	head + bowl	lower leg	?shrouded body
Cuneiform sign, c. 2400 B.C.E.									
Cuneiform sign, c. 700 B.C.E. (turned through 90°)									
Phonetic value*	dingir, an	u_4, ud	a	še	gu_4	nig_2, ninda	ku_2	du, gin, gub	lu_2
Meaning	god, sky	day, sun	water, seed, son	barley	ox	food, bread	to eat	to walk, to stand	man

*Some signs have more than one phonetic value and some sounds are represented by more than one sign; for example, u_4 means the fourth sign with the phonetic value *u*.

From Cultural Atlas of Mesopotamia & the Ancient Near East by Michael Roaf/Courtesy Andromeda Oxford Limited, Oxford, England

The Development of Cuneiform Writing. This chart shows the evolution of writing from pictographic signs around 3100 B.C.E. to cuneiform signs by about 700 B.C.E. Note that the sign for *star* came to mean "god" or "sky." Pictographic signs for *head* and *bowl* came eventually to mean "to eat" in their simplified cuneiform version.

handbook states that if the animal organ has shape *x*, the outcome of the military campaign will be *y*. The Mesopotamian arts of divination arose out of the desire to discover the purposes of the gods. If people could decipher the signs that foretold events, the events would be predictable and humans could act wisely.

THE CULTIVATION OF WRITING AND SCIENCES The realization of writing's great potential was another aspect of Mesopotamian culture. The oldest Mesopotamian texts date to around 3000 B.C.E. and were written by the Sumerians, who used a **cuneiform** ("wedge-shaped") system of writing. Using a reed stylus, they made wedge-shaped impressions on clay tablets, which were then baked or dried in the sun. Once dried, these tablets were virtually indestructible, and the several hundred thousand that have been found so far have been a valuable source of information for modern scholars. Sumerian writing evolved from pictures of concrete objects to simplified and stylized signs, leading eventually to a phonetic system that made possible the written expression of abstract ideas.

Mesopotamian peoples used writing primarily for record keeping, but cuneiform texts were also used in schools set up to teach the cuneiform system of writing. The primary goal of scribal education was to produce professionally trained scribes for careers in the temples and palaces, the military, and government service. Pupils were male and primarily from wealthy families.

Writing was important because it enabled a society to keep records and maintain knowledge of previous practices and events (see the Comparative Illustration "Early Writing" on p. 15). Writing also made it possible for people to communicate ideas in new ways, which is especially evident in the most famous piece of Mesopotamian literature, *The Epic of Gilgamesh*, an epic poem that records the exploits of a legendary king of Uruk. Gilgamesh (GILL-guh-mesh), wise, strong, and perfect in body, part man and part god, befriends a hairy beast named Enkidu. Together they set off in pursuit of heroic deeds. When Enkidu dies, Gilgamesh experiences the pain of mortality and begins a search for the secret of immortality. He finds Utnapishtim, who was granted immortality by the gods after he survived the Great Flood sent by the gods to destroy humankind (see Opposing Viewpoints "The Great Flood: Two Versions" on p. 16). Utnapishtim tries to help Gilgamesh gain immortality, but his efforts fail, and Gilgamesh remains mortal. The desire for immortality, one of humankind's great searches, ends in complete frustration. "Everlasting life," as this Mesopotamian epic makes clear, is only for the gods.

Mesopotamians also made outstanding achievements in mathematics and astronomy. In math, the Sumerians devised a number system based on 60, using combinations of 6 and 10 for practical solutions. Geometry was used to measure fields and erect buildings. In astronomy, the Sumerians made use of units of 60 and charted the heavenly constellations. Their calendar was based on twelve lunar months and was brought into harmony with the solar year by adding an extra month from time to time.

Egyptian Civilization: "The Gift of the Nile"

 FOCUS QUESTIONS: What are the basic features of the three major periods of Egyptian history? What elements of continuity are evident in the three periods? What are their major differences?

"The Egyptian Nile," wrote one Arab traveler, "surpasses all the rivers of the world in sweetness of taste, in length of course and usefulness. No other river in the world can show such

14 ■ **CHAPTER 1** Early Humans and the First Civilizations

RMN-Grand Palais/Art Resource, NY

© Sandro Vannini/CORBIS

Erich Lessing/Art Resource, NY

ART & IDEAS

COMPARATIVE ILLUSTRATION

Early Writing. Pictured at the left is the upper part of the cone of Uruinimgina, covered in cuneiform script from an early Sumerian dynasty. The first Egyptian writing was also pictographic, as shown in the hieroglyphs in the detail from the mural in the tomb of Ramesses I at the top right. In Central America, the Mayan civilization had a well-developed writing system, also based on hieroglyphs, as seen at the right in the text carved on a stone platform in front of the Palace of the Large Masks in Kabah, Mexico.

What common feature is evident in these early writing systems? How might you explain that?

a continuous series of towns and villages along its banks." The Nile River was crucial to the development of Egyptian civilization (see the box "The Significance of the Nile River and the Pharaoh" on p. 17). Egypt, like Mesopotamia, was a river valley civilization.

The Impact of Geography

The Nile is a unique river, beginning in the heart of Africa and coursing northward for thousands of miles. It is the longest river in the world. The Nile was responsible for creating an area several miles wide on both banks of the river that was fertile and capable of producing abundant harvests. The "miracle" of the Nile was its annual flooding. The river rose in the summer from rains in Central Africa, crested in Egypt in September and October, and left a deposit of silt that enriched the soil. The Egyptians called this fertile land the "Black Land" because it was dark in color from the silt and the crops that grew on it so densely. Beyond these narrow strips of fertile fields lay the deserts (the "Red Land"). About 100 miles before it empties into the Mediterranean, the river splits into two major branches, forming the delta, a

triangular-shaped territory called Lower Egypt to distinguish it from Upper Egypt, the land upstream to the south (see Map 1.4). Egypt's important cities developed at the tip of the delta. Even today, most of Egypt's people are crowded along the banks of the Nile River.

Unlike Mesopotamia's rivers, the flooding of the Nile was gradual and usually predictable, and the river itself was seen as life-enhancing, not life-threatening. Although a system of organized irrigation was still necessary, the small villages along the Nile could create such systems without the massive state intervention that was required in Mesopotamia. Egyptian civilization consequently tended to remain more rural, with many small population centers congregated along a narrow band on both sides of the Nile.

The surpluses of food that Egyptian farmers grew in the fertile Nile Valley made Egypt prosperous. But the Nile also served as a unifying factor in Egyptian history. In ancient times, the Nile was the fastest way to travel through the land, making both transportation and communication easier. Winds from the north pushed sailboats south, and the current of the Nile carried them north.

OPPOSING ✕ VIEWPOINTS
The Great Flood: Two Versions

BOTH THE MESOPOTAMIAN POEM, *THE EPIC OF GILGAMESH*, AND THE HEBREW BIBLE (OLD TESTAMENT) include accounts of a great flood. In the first selection, taken from the *The Epic of Gilgamesh*, Utnapishtim tells Gilgamesh the story of how he survived the flood unleashed by the gods to destroy humankind. Utnapishtim recounts how the god Ea advised him to build a boat and how he came to land the boat at the end of the flood. The second selection is the account of the great flood that appears in the book of Genesis in the Hebrew Bible. The biblical Noah appears to be a later version of the Mesopotamian Utnapishtim.

The Epic of Gilgamesh

In those days the world teemed, the people multiplied, the world bellowed like a wild bull, and the great god was aroused by the clamor. Enlil heard the clamor and he said to the gods in council, "The uproar of mankind is intolerable and sleep is no longer possible by reason of the babel." So the gods agreed to exterminate mankind. Enlil did this, but Ea [Sumerian Enki, god of the waters] because of his oath warned me in a dream … "tear down your house and build a boat, abandon possessions and look for life, despise worldly goods and save your soul alive. Tear down your house, I say, and build a boat…. Then take up into the boat the seed of all living creatures…." [Utnapishtim did as he was told, and then the destruction came.]

For six days and six nights the winds blew, torrent and tempest and flood overwhelmed the world, tempest and flood raged together like warring hosts. When the seventh day dawned the storm from the south subsided, the sea grew calm, the flood was stilled; I looked at the face of the world and there was silence, all mankind was turned to clay. The surface of the sea stretched as flat as a rooftop; I opened a hatch and the light fell on my face. Then I bowed low, I sat down and I wept, the tears streamed down my face, for on every side was the waste of water. I looked for land in vain, but fourteen leagues distant there appeared a mountain, and there the boat grounded; on the mountain of Nisir the boat held fast, she held fast and did not budge.

… When the seventh day dawned I loosed a dove and let her go. She flew away, but finding no resting-place she returned. Then I loosed a swallow, and she flew away but finding no resting-place she returned. I loosed a raven, she saw that the waters had retreated, she ate, she flew around, she cawed, and she did not come back. Then I threw everything open to the four winds, I made a sacrifice and poured out a libation on the mountain top.

Genesis 6:11–15, 17–19; 7:24; 8:3, 13–21

Now the earth was corrupted in God's sight and was full of violence. God saw how corrupt the earth had become, for all the people on earth had corrupted their ways. So God said to Noah, "I am going to put an end to all people, for the earth is filled with violence because of them. I am surely going to destroy both them and the earth. So make yourself an ark of cypress wood: make rooms in it and coat it with pitch inside and out…. I am going to bring flood waters on the earth to destroy all life under the heavens, every creature that has the breath of life in it. Everything on earth will perish. But I will establish my covenant with you, and you will enter the ark— you and your sons and your wife and your sons' wives with you. You are to bring into the ark two of all living creatures, male and female, to keep them alive with you…."

The waters flooded the earth for a hundred and fifty days…. By the first day of the first month of Noah's six hundred and first year, the water had dried up from the earth. Noah then removed the covering from the ark and saw that the surface of the ground was dry…. Then God said to Noah, "Come out of the ark, you and your wife and your sons and their wives. Bring out every kind of living creature that is with you—the birds, the animals, and all the creatures that move along the ground—so they can multiply on the earth and be fruitful and increase in number upon it." So Noah came out, together with his sons and his wife and his sons' wives … [and all the animals]. Then Noah built an altar to the Lord and, taking some of all the clean animals and clean birds, he sacrificed burnt offerings on it. The Lord smelled the pleasing aroma and said in his heart, "Never again will I curse the ground because of man, even though every inclination of his heart is evil from childhood. And never again will I destroy all living creatures, as I have done."

 What does the selection from The Epic of Gilgamesh *tell you about the relationship between the Mesopotamians and their gods? How might you explain the similarities and differences between this account and the biblical flood story in Genesis?*

Sources: From *The Epic of Gilgamesh* translated by N. K. Sandars (Penguin Classics 1960, Third Edition 1972). *The Holy Bible, New International Version*®, NIV® Copyright © 1973, 1978, 1984, 2011 by Biblica, Inc.® Used by permission. All rights reserved worldwide.

The Significance of the Nile River and the Pharaoh

RELIGION & PHILOSOPHY

TWO OF THE MOST IMPORTANT SOURCES OF LIFE for the ancient Egyptians were the Nile River and the pharaoh. Egyptians perceived that the Nile made possible the abundant food that was a major source of their well-being. This *Hymn to the Nile*, probably from the nineteenth and twentieth dynasties in the New Kingdom, expresses the gratitude Egyptians felt for the great river.

Hymn to the Nile

Hail to you, O Nile, that issues from the earth and
    comes to keep Egypt alive! …
He that waters the meadows which Re created, in
    order to keep every kid alive.
He that makes to drink the desert and the place
    distant from water: that is his dew coming down
    from heaven….
The lord of fishes, he who makes the marsh-birds to
    go upstream….
He who makes barley and brings emmer [wheat] into
    being, that he may make the temples festive.
If he is sluggish, then nostrils are stopped up, and
    everybody is poor….
When he rises, then the land is in jubilation, then
    every belly is in joy, every backbone takes on
    laughter, and every tooth is exposed.
The bringer of good, rich in provisions, creator of all
    good, lord of majesty, sweet of fragrance….
He who makes every beloved tree to grow, without
    lack of them.

The Egyptian king, or pharaoh, was viewed as a god and the absolute ruler of Egypt. His significance and the gratitude of the Egyptian people for his existence are evident in this hymn from the reign of Sesotris III (c. 1880–1840 B.C.E.).

Hymn to the Pharaoh

He has come to us, he has taken the land of the well,
    the double crown [crown of Upper and Lower Egypt] is
        placed on his head.
He has come, he has united the two lands.
    he has joined the kingdom of the upper land with the lower.
He has come, he has ruled Egypt,
    he has placed the desert in his power.
He has come, he has protected the two lands,
    he has given peace in the two regions.
 He has come, he has made Egypt to live,
    he has destroyed its afflictions.
He has come, he has made the aged to live,
    he has opened the breath of the people.
He has come, he has trampled on the nations,
    he has smitten the [enemies], who knew not his terror.
He has come, he has protected his frontier,
    he has rescued the robbed.

How do these two hymns underscore the importance of the Nile River and the institution of the pharaoh to Egyptian civilization?

Sources: Pritchard, James B., ed., *Ancient Near Eastern Texts Relating to the Old Testament*, 3rd Edition with Supplement. Copyright © 1950, 1955, 1969, renewed 1978 by Princeton University Press. W. M. Flinders-Petrie, *A History of Egypt*, Fifth Edition (Methuen & Co.: London, 1903), Vol. 1, p. 183.

Unlike Mesopotamia, which was subject to constant invasion, Egypt had natural barriers that fostered isolation, protected it from invasion, and gave it a sense of security. These barriers included deserts to the west and east; cataracts (rapids) on the southern part of the river, which made defense relatively easy; and the Mediterranean Sea to the north. These barriers, however, were effective only when combined with Egyptian fortifications at strategic locations. Nor did these barriers prevent the development of trade. Indeed, there is evidence of very early trade between Egypt and Mesopotamia.

The regularity of the Nile floods and the relative isolation of the Egyptians created a sense of security and a feeling of changelessness. To the ancient Egyptians, when the Nile flooded each year, "the fields laugh, and people's faces light up." Unlike people in Mesopotamia, Egyptians faced life with a spirit of confidence in the stability of things. Ancient Egyptian civilization was characterized by a remarkable degree of continuity for thousands of years.

The Old and Middle Kingdoms

Modern historians have divided Egyptian history into three major periods, known as the Old Kingdom, the Middle Kingdom, and the New Kingdom. These were periods of long-term stability characterized by strong monarchical authority, competent bureaucracy, freedom from invasion, much construction of temples and pyramids, and considerable intellectual and cultural activity. But between the periods of stability were intervals known as the Intermediate Periods, characterized by weak political structures and rivalry for leadership, invasions, a decline in building activity, and a restructuring of society.

THE OLD KINGDOM According to the Egyptians' own tradition, their land consisted initially of numerous populated areas ruled by tribal chieftains. Around 3100 B.C.E., the first Egyptian royal dynasty, under a king called Menes, united Upper and Lower Egypt into a single kingdom. Henceforth,

MAP 1.4 Ancient Egypt. Egyptian civilization centered on the life-giving water and flood silts of the Nile River, with most of the population living in Lower Egypt, where the river splits to form the Nile delta. Most of the pyramids, built during the Old Kingdom, are clustered south and west of Cairo.

Q *How did the lands to the east and west of the river help to protect Egypt from invasion?*

Significance of the Nile River and the Pharaoh" on p. 17): "What is the king of Upper and Lower Egypt? He is a god by whose dealings one lives, the father and mother of all men, alone by himself, without an equal."[7] In obeying their king, subjects helped maintain the cosmic order. A breakdown in royal power could only mean that citizens were offending divinity and weakening the universal structure. Among the various titles of Egyptian kings, that of **pharaoh** (originally meaning "great house" or "palace") eventually came to be the most common.

Although they possessed absolute power, Egyptian kings were supposed to rule not arbitrarily but according to set principles. The chief principle was called *Ma'at* (MAH-ut), a spiritual precept that conveyed the ideas of truth and justice and especially right order and harmony. To ancient Egyptians, this fundamental order and harmony had existed throughout the universe since the beginning of time. Pharaohs were the divine instruments who maintained it and were themselves subject to it.

Although theoretically absolute in their power, in practice Egyptian kings did not rule alone. Initially, members of the king's family performed administrative tasks, but by the fourth dynasty, a bureaucracy with regular procedures had developed. Especially important was the office of vizier, "steward of the whole land." Directly responsible to the king, the vizier was in charge of the bureaucracy. For administrative purposes, Egypt was divided into provinces, or *nomes* as they were later called by the Greeks— twenty-two in Upper Egypt and twenty in Lower Egypt. A governor, called by the Greeks a *nomarch*, was head of each nome and was responsible to the king and vizier. Nomarchs, however, tended to build up large holdings of land and power within their nomes, creating a potential rivalry with the pharaohs.

the king would be called "king of Upper and Lower Egypt," and a royal crown, the Double Crown, was created, combining the White Crown of Upper Egypt and the Red Crown of Lower Egypt. Just as the Nile served to unite Upper and Lower Egypt physically, the king served to unite the two areas politically.

The Old Kingdom encompassed the fourth through eighth dynasties of Egyptian kings, lasting from around 2575 to 2125 B.C.E. It was an age of prosperity and splendor, made visible in the construction of the greatest and largest pyramids in Egypt's history. The capital of the Old Kingdom was located at Memphis, south of the delta.

Kingship was a divine institution in ancient Egypt and formed part of a universal cosmic scheme (see the box "The

THE MIDDLE KINGDOM Despite the theory of divine order, the Old Kingdom eventually collapsed, ushering in a period of disarray. Finally, a new royal dynasty managed to pacify all Egypt and inaugurated the Middle Kingdom, a period of stability lasting from around 2010 to 1630 B.C.E. Egyptians later portrayed the Middle Kingdom as a golden age, a clear indication of its stability. Several factors contributed to its vitality. The nome structure was reorganized. The boundaries of each nome were now settled precisely, and the obligations of the nomes to the state were clearly delineated. Nomarchs were confirmed as hereditary officeholders but with the understanding that their duties must be performed faithfully. These included the collection of taxes for the state and the recruitment of labor forces for royal projects, such as stone quarrying.

The Middle Kingdom was characterized by a new concern of the pharaohs for the people. In the Old Kingdom, the pharaoh had been viewed as an inaccessible god-king. Now he was portrayed as the shepherd of his people with the responsibility to build public works and provide for the public welfare. As one pharaoh expressed it, "He [a particular god] created me as one who should do that which he had done, and to carry out that which he commanded should be done. He appointed me herdsman of this land, for he knew who would keep it in order for him."[8]

Society and Economy in Ancient Egypt

Egyptian society had a simple structure in the Old and Middle Kingdoms; basically, it was organized along hierarchical lines with the god-king at the top. An upper class of nobles and priests aided the king and participated in the elaborate rituals of life that surrounded the pharaoh. This ruling class ran the government and managed its own landed estates, which provided much of its wealth.

Below the upper classes were merchants and artisans. Merchants engaged in an active trade up and down the Nile as well as in town and village markets. Some merchants also engaged in international trade; the king sent them to Crete and Syria, where they obtained wood and other products. Expeditions traveled into Nubia for ivory and down the Red Sea to Punt for incense and spices. Eventually, trade links were established between ports in the Red Sea and countries as far away as the Indonesian archipelago. Egyptian artisans made an incredible variety of well-built and beautiful goods: stone dishes; painted boxes made of clay; wooden furniture; gold, silver, and copper tools and containers; paper and rope made of papyrus; and linen clothes.

By far the largest number of people in Egypt simply worked the land. In theory, the king owned all the land but granted portions of it to his subjects. Large sections were in the possession of nobles and the temple complexes. Most of the lower classes were serfs, or common people bound to the land, who cultivated the estates. They paid taxes in the form of crops to the king, nobles, and priests; lived in small villages or towns; and provided military service and forced labor for building projects.

The Culture of Egypt

Egypt produced a culture that dazzled and awed its later conquerors. The Egyptians' technical achievements, especially visible in the construction of the pyramids, demonstrated a measure of skill unequaled in the world at that time. To the

The Making of Jewelry. In ancient Egypt, people used jewelry for self-adornment as well as a mark of social status. This photo of a wall fragment from a tomb in Thebes around 1400 B.C.E. shows jewelers and metal craftsmen at work. At the top, jewelers are seen drilling holes in hard-stone beads with three or four bow drills. The beads were then polished and strung in collars, as seen in the lower panel.
The Trustees of the British Museum/Art Resource, NY

Egyptians, all of these achievements were part of a cosmic order suffused with the presence of the divine.

SPIRITUAL LIFE IN EGYPTIAN SOCIETY The Egyptians had no word for religion because it was an inseparable element of the entire world order to which Egyptian society belonged. Egypt was part of the universal cosmic scheme, and the pharaoh was the divine being whose function was to maintain Egypt's stability within the cosmic order.

This perspective helps explain the importance of ritual in ancient Egypt. Through their rituals, Egyptians worked to maintain the cosmic order by appeasing the gods and goddesses who controlled the universe. Egyptian ritual ceremonies focused on an image of a deity, providing it with food and sustenance and thereby performing an act of ritual worship to appease the god. The pharaoh was at the heart of Egypt's ritual life. He supervised the sacred ceremonies that were performed in the temples, although it was the pharaoh's religious deputies—the priests—who executed the daily ceremonies.

The Egyptians had a remarkable number of gods associated with heavenly bodies and natural forces, hardly unusual in view of the importance to Egypt's well-being of the sun, the river, and the fertile land along its banks. The sun was the source of life and hence worthy of worship. A sun cult developed, and the sun god took on different forms and names, depending on his specific role. He was worshiped as Atum in human form and also as Re, who had a human body but the head of a falcon. The pharaoh took the title of "Son of Re" because he was regarded as the earthly embodiment of Re.

River and land deities included Osiris (oh-SY-russ) and Isis (Y-sis) with their child Horus, who was related to the Nile and to the sun as well. Osiris became especially important as a symbol of resurrection or rebirth. A famous Egyptian myth told of the struggle between Osiris, who brought civilization to Egypt, and his evil brother Seth, who killed him, cut his body into fourteen parts, and tossed them into the Nile River. Isis, the faithful wife of Osiris, found the pieces and, with help from other gods, restored Osiris to life. As a symbol of resurrection and as judge of the dead, Osiris took on an important role for the Egyptians. By identifying with Osiris, one could hope to gain new life just as Osiris had done. The dead, embalmed and mummified, were placed in tombs (in the case of kings, in pyramidal tombs), given the name of Osiris, and by a process of magical identification became Osiris. Like Osiris, they could then be reborn. The flood of the Nile and the new life it brought to Egypt were symbolized by Isis gathering all of the parts of Osiris together and were celebrated each spring in the Festival of the New Land.

Later Egyptian spiritual practice began to emphasize morality by stressing the role of Osiris as judge of the dead. The dead were asked to give an account of their earthly deeds so that Osiris could determine whether they deserved a reward. At first, the Osiris cult was reserved for the very wealthy, who could afford to take expensive measures to preserve the body after death. During the Middle Kingdom, however, the cult became "democratized" and was extended to all Egyptians who aspired to an afterlife.

THE PYRAMIDS   One of the great achievements of Egyptian civilization, the building of pyramids, occurred in the time of the Old Kingdom. Pyramids were built as part of a larger complex of buildings dedicated to the dead—in effect, a city of the dead. The area included a large pyramid for the king's burial, smaller pyramids for his family, and *mastabas*, rectangular structures with flat roofs, as tombs for the pharaoh's noble officials.

The tombs were well prepared for their residents, their rooms furnished and stocked with numerous supplies, including chairs, boats, chests, weapons, games, dishes, and a variety of foods. The Egyptians believed that human beings had two bodies, a physical one and a spiritual one they called the *ka*. If the physical body was properly preserved (by mummification) and the tomb was furnished with all the objects of regular life, the *ka* could return, surrounded by earthly comforts, and continue its life despite the death of the physical body.

To preserve the physical body after death, the Egyptians practiced mummification, a process of slowly drying a dead body to prevent it from decomposing. Special workshops, run by priests, performed this procedure, primarily for the wealthy families who could afford it. According to an ancient Greek historian who visited Egypt around 450 B.C.E., "The most refined method is as follows: first of all they draw out the brain through the nostrils with an iron hook.… Then they make an incision in the flank with a sharp Ethiopian stone through which they extract all the internal organs."[9] The liver, lungs, stomach, and intestines were placed in four special jars that were put in the tomb with the mummy. The priests then covered the corpse with a natural salt that absorbed the body's water. Later, they filled the body with spices and wrapped it with layers of linen soaked in resin. At the end of the process, which took about seventy days, a lifelike mask was placed over the head and shoulders of the mummy, which was then sealed in a case and placed in its tomb.

Pyramids were tombs for the mummified bodies of the pharaohs. The largest and most magnificent of all the pyramids was built under King Khufu. Constructed at Giza around 2540 B.C.E., this famous Great Pyramid covers 13 acres, measures 756 feet at each side of its base, and stands 481 feet high (see the Comparative Illustration "The Pyramid" in Chapter 6 on p. 161). Its four sides are almost precisely oriented to the four points of the compass. The interior included a grand gallery to the burial chamber, which was built of granite with a lidless sarcophagus for the pharaoh's body. The Great Pyramid still stands as a visible symbol of the power of Egyptian kings and the spiritual conviction that underlay Egyptian society. No pyramid built later ever matched its size or splendor. The pyramid was not only the king's tomb; it was also an important symbol of royal power. It could be seen from miles away, a visible reminder of the glory and might of the ruler who was a living god on earth.

ART AND WRITING   Commissioned by kings or nobles for use in temples and tombs, Egyptian art was largely functional. Wall paintings and statues of gods and kings in temples served a strictly spiritual purpose. They were an integral part of the performance of ritual, which was thought necessary to preserve the cosmic order and hence the well-being of Egypt. Likewise, the mural scenes and sculptured figures found in the tombs had a specific function: they were supposed to assist the journey of the deceased into the afterworld.

Egyptian art was also formulaic. Artists and sculptors observed a strict canon of proportions that determined both form and presentation. This canon gave Egyptian art a distinctive appearance for thousands of years. Especially characteristic was the convention of combining the profile, semiprofile, and frontal views of the human body in relief work and painting in order to represent each part of the body accurately. The result was an art that was highly stylized yet still allowed distinctive features to be displayed.

Writing emerged in Egypt during the first two dynasties. The Greeks later called Egyptian writing **hieroglyphics** (HY-uh-roh-glif-iks), meaning "priest-carvings" or "sacred writings." Hieroglyphs were signs that depicted objects and had a sacred value at the same time. Although hieroglyphs were later simplified into two scripts for writing purposes, they never developed into an alphabet. Egyptian hieroglyphs were initially carved in stone, but later the two simplified scripts were written on papyrus, a paper made from the reeds that grew along the Nile. Most of the ancient Egyptian literature that has come down to us was written on papyrus rolls and wooden tablets.

Disorder and a New Order: The New Kingdom

The Middle Kingdom came to an end around 1650 B.C.E. with the invasion of Egypt by a people from western Asia known to the Egyptians as the Hyksos. The Hyksos used horse-drawn war chariots and overwhelmed the Egyptian soldiers, who fought from donkey carts. For almost a hundred years, the Hyksos ruled much of Egypt, but the conquered took much from their conquerors. From the Hyksos, the Egyptians learned to use bronze in making new farming tools and weapons. They also mastered the military skills of the Hyksos, especially the use of horse-drawn war chariots.

THE EGYPTIAN EMPIRE Eventually, a new line of pharaohs—the eighteenth dynasty—made use of the new weapons to throw off Hyksos domination, reunite Egypt, establish the New Kingdom (c. 1539–1069 B.C.E.), and launch the Egyptians along a new militaristic and imperialistic path, characterized by the development of a more professional army. During the period of the New Kingdom, Egypt assembled an empire and became the most powerful state in the Middle East.

Massive wealth aided the power of the New Kingdom pharaohs. The Egyptian rulers showed their wealth by building new temples. Queen Hatshepsut (hat-SHEP-soot) (c. 1503–1480 B.C.E.), in particular, one of the first women to become pharaoh in her own right, built a great temple at Deir el Bahri (dayr ahl BAH-ree) near Thebes. As pharaoh, Hatshepsut sent out military expeditions, encouraged mining, fostered agriculture, and sent a trading expedition up the Nile. Hatshepsut's official statues sometimes show her clothed and bearded like a king. She was referred to as "His Majesty." Hatshepsut was succeeded by her nephew, Thutmosis (thoot-MOH-suss) III (c. 1480–1450 B.C.E.), who led seventeen military campaigns into Syria and Canaan and even reached the Euphrates River. Egyptian forces occupied Canaan and Syria and also moved westward into Libya.

AKHENATEN AND RELIGIOUS CHANGE The eighteenth dynasty was not without its troubles, however. Amenhotep (ah-mun-HOH-tep) IV (c. 1353–1336 B.C.E.) introduced the worship of Aten, god of the sun disk, as the supreme god and, later in his reign, as the only god. In the pharaoh's eyes, he and Aten had become co-rulers of Egypt. Changing his own name to Akhenaten (ah-kuh-NAH-tun) ("servant of Aten"), the pharaoh closed the temples of other gods and especially endeavored to lessen the power of the priesthood dedicated to the god Amon-Re at Thebes. Akhenaten strove to reduce the priests' influence by replacing Thebes as the capital of Egypt with Akhetaten (ah-kuh-TAH-tun) ("horizon of Aten"), a new city located at modern Tell el-Amarna, 200 miles north of Thebes. The pharaoh decreed that Akhetaten, not Thebes, would be his final resting place.

Akhenaten's attempt at religious change failed. It was too much to ask Egyptians to give up their traditional ways and beliefs, especially since they saw the destruction of the old gods as subversive of the very cosmic order on which Egypt's survival and continuing prosperity depended. Moreover, the priests at Thebes were unalterably opposed to the changes, which had diminished their influence and power. At the same time, Akhenaten's preoccupation with religion caused him to ignore foreign affairs and led to the loss of both Syria and Canaan. Akhenaten's changes were soon undone after his death by those who influenced his successor, the boy-pharaoh Tutankhamun (too-tang-KAH-mun) (c. 1332–1322 B.C.E.). Tutankhamun returned the government to Thebes and restored the old gods. The Aten experiment had failed to take hold, and the eighteenth dynasty itself soon came to an end.

DECLINE OF THE EGYPTIAN EMPIRE The nineteenth dynasty managed to restore Egyptian power one more time. Under Ramesses (RAM-uh-seez) II (c. 1279–1213 B.C.E.), the Egyptians went on the offensive, regained control of Canaan, and restored Egypt as an imperial power. During his long sixty-seven year reign, Ramesses II provided visible demonstrations of his power by constructing mammoth new temple buildings, many of which were characterized by colossal statues of himself.

After the death of Ramesses II, struggles for the throne weakened the government, and new invasions in the thirteenth century by the "Sea Peoples," as the Egyptians called them, destroyed Egyptian power in Canaan and drove the Egyptians back within their old frontiers. The days of

Bildarchiv Steffens/The Bridgeman Art Library

Statues of Ramesses II at Abu Simbel. After being driven out of Canaan and Syria by the Hittites, the Egyptian empire grew to power one final time under Ramesses II. He succeeded in reconquering Canaan but was unable to restore the boundaries of the previous empire. The massive Temple of Ramesses II, located at Abu Simbel, was carved out of a cliff of Nubian sandstone. The giant statues represent Ramesses II.

Egyptian empire were ended, and the New Kingdom itself expired with the end of the twentieth dynasty in 1069 B.C.E. For the next thousand years, despite periodical revivals of strength, Egypt was dominated by Libyans, Nubians, Assyrians, Persians, and finally Macedonians, after the conquest of Alexander the Great (see Chapter 4). In the first century B.C.E., Egypt became a province in Rome's mighty empire.

Daily Life in Ancient Egypt: Family and Marriage

Ancient Egyptians had a very positive attitude toward daily life on earth and followed the advice of the wisdom literature, which suggested that people marry young and establish a home and family. Monogamy was the general rule, although a husband was allowed to keep additional wives if his first wife was childless. Pharaohs were entitled to harems; the queen, however, was acknowledged as the "great wife," with a status higher than that of the other wives. The husband was master in the house, but wives were very much respected and in charge of the household and the education of the children. From a book of wise sayings (which the Egyptians called "instructions") came this advice:

> If you are a man of standing, you should found your household and love your wife at home as is fitting. Fill her belly; clothe her back. Ointment is the prescription for her body. Make her heart glad as long as you live. She is a profitable field for her lord. You should not contend with her at law, and keep her far from gaining control.... Let her heart be soothed through what may accrue to you; it means keeping her long in your house.[10]

Women's property and inheritance remained in their hands, even in marriage. Although most careers and public offices were closed to women, some women did operate businesses. Peasant women worked long hours in the fields and at numerous domestic tasks. Upper-class women could function as priestesses, and a few queens, such as Hatshepsut, even became pharaohs in their own right.

Parents arranged marriages. The primary concerns were family and property, and the chief purpose of marriage was to produce children, especially sons. From the New Kingdom came this piece of wisdom: "Take to yourself a wife while you are [still] a youth, that she may produce a son for you."[11] Daughters were not slighted, however. Numerous tomb paintings show the close and affectionate relationship parents had with both sons and daughters. Marriages could and did end in divorce, which was allowed, apparently with compensation for the wife. Adultery, however, was strictly prohibited, with stiff punishments—especially for women, who could have their noses cut off or be burned at the stake.

The Spread of Egyptian Influence: Nubia

The civilization of Egypt had an impact on other peoples in the lands of the eastern Mediterranean. Egyptian products have been found in Crete and Cretan products in Egypt (see Chapter 4). Egyptian influence is also evident in early Greek statues. The Egyptians also had an impact to the south in Nubia (the northern part of modern Sudan). In fact, some archaeologists have recently suggested that the African kingdom of Nubia may have arisen even before the kingdoms of Egypt.

It is clear that contacts between the upper and lower Nile had been established by the late third millennium B.C.E., when Egyptian merchants traveled to Nubia to obtain ivory, ebony, frankincense, and leopard skins. A few centuries later, Nubia had become an Egyptian tributary. At the end of the second millennium B.C.E., Nubia profited from the disintegration of the Egyptian New Kingdom to become the independent state of Kush. Egyptian influence continued, however, as Kushite culture borrowed extensively from Egypt, including religious beliefs, the practice of interring kings in pyramids, and hieroglyphs.

Erich Lessing/Art Resource, NY

Nubians in Egypt. During the New Kingdom, Egypt expanded to include Canaan and Syria to the north and the kingdom of Nubia to the south. Nubia had emerged as an African kingdom around 2300 B.C.E. Shown in a fourteenth-century B.C.E. painting from an Egyptian official's tomb in Nubia are Nubians arriving in Egypt with bags and rings of gold. Nubia was a major source of gold for the Egyptians.

But in the first millennium B.C.E., Kush also had a direct impact on Egypt. During the second half of the eighth century B.C.E., Kushite monarchs took control of Egypt and formed the twenty-fifth dynasty of Egyptian rulers. It was not until 663 B.C.E.that the last Kushite ruler was expelled from Egypt. During this period, the Kushite rulers of Egypt even aided the Israelites in their struggle with the Assyrians (see "The Hebrews: The 'Children of Israel'" later in this chapter).

Although its economy was probably founded primarily on agriculture and animal husbandry, Kush developed into a major trading state in Africa that endured for hundreds of years. Its commercial activities were stimulated by the discovery of iron ore in a floodplain near the river at Meroë. Strategically located at the point where a land route across the desert to the south intersected the Nile River, Meroë eventually became the capital of a new state. In addition to iron products, Kush and Meroë supplied goods from Central and East Africa, notably ivory, gold, ebony, and slaves, to the Romans, Arabia, and India. At first, goods were transported by donkey caravans to the point where the river north was navigable. By the last centuries of the first millennium B.C.E., however, the donkeys were being replaced by camels, newly introduced from the Arabian peninsula.

New Centers of Civilization

 FOCUS QUESTIONS: What was the significance of the Indo-Europeans? How did Judaism differ from the religions of Mesopotamia and Egypt?

Mesopotamia and Egypt have dominated our story of civilization so far, but significant developments were also taking place on the fringes of these civilizations. Farming had spread into the Balkan peninsula of Europe by 6500 B.C.E., and by 4000 B.C.E., it was well established in southern France, central Europe, and the coastal regions of the Mediterranean. Although migrating farmers from the Anatolian peninsula may have brought some farming techniques into Europe, some historians believe that the Neolithic peoples of Europe domesticated animals and began to farm largely on their own.

One outstanding feature of late Neolithic Europe was the erection of **megaliths** (*megalith* is Greek for "large stone"). Radiocarbon dating, a technique that allows scientists to determine the age of objects, shows that the first megalithic structures were constructed around 4000 B.C.E., more than a thousand years before the great pyramids were built in Egypt. Between 3200 and 1500 B.C.E., standing stones, placed in circles or lined up in rows, were erected throughout the British Isles and northwestern France. Other megalithic constructions have been found as far north as Scandinavia and as far south as the islands of Corsica, Sardinia, and Malta. Archaeologists have demonstrated that the stone circles were used as observatories to detect not only such simple astronomical phenomena as the midwinter and midsummer sunrises but also such sophisticated phenomena as the major and minor standstills of the moon.

Nomadic Peoples: Impact of the Indo-Europeans

On the fringes of civilization lived nomadic peoples who depended on hunting and gathering, herding, and sometimes a bit of farming for their survival. Most important were the

Steve Vidler/SuperStock

Stonehenge. The Bronze Age in northwestern Europe is known for its megaliths, large standing stones. Between 3200 and 1500 B.C.E., standing stones, placed in circles or lined up in rows, were erected throughout the British Isles and northwestern France. The most famous of these megalithic constructions is Stonehenge in England.

TABLE 1.2 Some Indo-European Languages

SUBFAMILY	LANGUAGES
Indo-Iranian	*Sanskrit*, Persian
Balto-Slavic	Russian, Serbo-Croatian, Czech, Polish, Lithuanian
Hellenic	Greek
Italic	*Latin*, Romance languages (French, Italian, Spanish, Portuguese, Romanian)
Celtic	Irish, Gaelic
Germanic	Swedish, Danish, Norwegian, German, Dutch, English

NOTE: Languages in italic type are no longer spoken.

© 2016 Cengage Learning

pastoral nomads who on occasion overran civilized communities and forged their own empires. Pastoral nomads domesticated animals for both food and clothing and moved along regular migratory routes to provide steady sources of nourishment for their animals.

The Indo-Europeans were among the most important nomadic peoples. These groups spoke languages derived from a single parent tongue. Indo-European languages include Greek, Latin, Persian, Sanskrit, and the Germanic and Slavic tongues (see Table 1.2). The original Indo-European-speaking peoples were probably based in the steppe region north of the Black Sea or in southwestern Asia, in modern Iran or Afghanistan, but around 2000 B.C.E., they began to move into Europe, India, and western Asia. The domestication of horses and the importation of the wheel and wagon from Mesopotamia facilitated the Indo-European migrations to other lands (see Map 1.5).

THE HITTITES One group of Indo-Europeans who moved into Asia Minor and Anatolia (modern Turkey) around 1750 B.C.E. coalesced with the native peoples to form the Hittite kingdom, with its capital at Hattusha (Bogazköy in modern Turkey). Between 1600 and 1200 B.C.E., the Hittites formed their own empire in western Asia and even threatened the power of the Egyptians.

The Hittites were the first of the Indo-European peoples to make use of iron, enabling them to construct weapons that were stronger and cheaper to make because of the widespread availability of iron ore. During its height, the Hittite Empire also demonstrated an interesting ability to assimilate other cultures into its own. In language, literature, art, law, and religion, the Hittites borrowed much from Mesopotamia as well as from the native peoples they had subdued. Recent scholarship has stressed the important role of the Hittites in transmitting Mesopotamian culture, as they transformed it, to later civilizations in the Mediterranean area, especially to the Mycenaean Greeks (see Chapter 4).

MAP 1.5 The Spread of the Indo-Europeans. From their probable homeland in the steppe region north of the Black Sea, Indo-European-speaking peoples moved eventually into Europe, India, and western Asia. The languages shown on the map are all Indo-European languages (see Table 1.2).

Q *How do you explain the movements of the Indo-European-speaking peoples?*

Territorial States in Western Asia: The Phoenicians

During its heyday, the Hittite Empire was one of the great powers in western Asia. Constant squabbling over succession to the throne, however, tended to weaken royal authority at times. Especially devastating, however, were attacks by the Sea Peoples from the west and aggressive neighboring tribes. By 1190 B.C.E., Hittite power had come to an end. The destruction of the Hittite kingdom and the weakening of Egypt around 1200 B.C.E. left no dominant powers in western Asia, allowing a patchwork of petty kingdoms and city-states to emerge, especially in the area of Syria and Canaan. The Phoenicians (fuh-NEE-shunz) were one of these peoples.

A Semitic-speaking people (see Table 1.1 on p. 12), the Phoenicians lived in the area of Canaan along the Mediterranean coast on a narrow band of land 120 miles long. Their newfound political independence after the demise of Hittite and Egyptian power helped the Phoenicians expand the trade that was already the foundation of their prosperity. The chief cities of Phoenicia—Byblos, Tyre, and Sidon—were ports on the eastern Mediterranean, but they also served as distribution centers for the lands to the east in Mesopotamia. The Phoenicians themselves produced a number of goods for foreign markets, including purple dye, glass, wine, and lumber from the famous cedars of Lebanon. In addition, the Phoenicians improved their ships and became great international sea traders. They charted new routes, not only in the Mediterranean but also in the Atlantic Ocean, where they reached Britain and sailed south along the west coast of Africa. The Phoenicians established a number of colonies in the western Mediterranean, including settlements in southern Spain, Sicily, and Sardinia. Carthage, the Phoenicians' most famous colony, was located on the north coast of Africa.

Culturally, the Phoenicians are best known as transmitters. Instead of using pictographs or signs to represent whole words and syllables as the Mesopotamians and Egyptians did, the Phoenicians simplified their writing by using twenty-two different signs to represent the sounds of their speech. These twenty-two characters or letters could be used to spell out all the words in the Phoenician language. Although the Phoenicians were not the only people to invent an alphabet, theirs would have special significance because it was eventually passed on to the Greeks. From the Greek alphabet was derived the Roman alphabet that we still use today (Table 1.3 shows the derivation of the letters A to F). The Phoenicians achieved much while independent, but they ultimately fell subject to the Assyrians and Persians.

The Hebrews: The "Children of Israel"

To the south of the Phoenicians lived another group of Semitic-speaking people known as the Hebrews. Although they were a minor factor in the politics of the region, their **monotheism**—belief in but one God—later influenced both Christianity and Islam and flourished as a world religion in its own right. The Hebrews had a tradition concerning their origins and history that was eventually written down as part of the Hebrew Bible, known to Christians as the Old Testament. Describing them as a nomadic people, the Hebrews' own tradition states that they were descendants of the patriarch Abraham, who had migrated from Mesopotamia to the land of Canaan, where the Hebrews became identified as the "Children of Israel." Moreover, according to tradition, a drought in Canaan caused many Hebrews to migrate to Egypt, where they lived peacefully until they were enslaved by pharaohs who used them as laborers on building projects. The Hebrews remained in bondage until Moses led his people out of Egypt in the well-known "exodus," which some historians believe occurred in the first half of the thirteenth century B.C.E. According to the biblical account, the Hebrews then wandered for many years in the desert until they entered Canaan. Organized into twelve tribes, the Hebrews became embroiled in conflict with the Philistines, who had settled along the coast of Canaan but were beginning to move inland.

TABLE 1.3   **The Phoenician, Greek, and Roman Alphabets**

| Phoenician | | | Greek | | | Roman | |
Phoenician	Phoenician Name	Modern Symbol	Early Greek	Classical Greek	Greek Name	Early Latin	Classical Latin
K	'aleph	'	A	A	alpha	A	A
ʝ	beth	B	8	B	beta		B
ʌ	gimel	G	1	Γ	gamma		C
◿	daleth	D	△	△	delta	◖	D
F	he	H	ʒ	E	epsilon	Ⅎ	E
ʏ	waw	W	ʔ		digamma	ʔ	F

Source: Andrew Robinson, *The Story of Writing* (London, 1995), 170.

Many scholars today doubt that the biblical account reflects the true history of the early Israelites. They argue that the early books of the Bible, written centuries after the events described, preserve only what the Israelites came to believe about themselves and that recent archaeological evidence often contradicts the details of the biblical account. Some of these scholars have even argued that the Israelites were not nomadic invaders but indigenous peoples in the Canaanite hill country. What is generally agreed, however, is that between 1200 and 1000 B.C.E., the Israelites emerged as a distinct group of people, possibly organized into tribes or a league of tribes.

WAS THERE A UNITED KINGDOM OF ISRAEL? According to the Hebrew Bible, the Israelites established a united kingdom of Israel beginning with Saul (c. 1020–1000 B.C.E.), who supposedly achieved some success in the ongoing struggle with the Philistines. But after his death, a brief period of anarchy ensued until one of Saul's lieutenants, David (c. 1000–970 B.C.E.), reunited the Israelites, defeated the Philistines, and established control over all of Canaan. Among David's conquests was the city of Jerusalem, which he supposedly made into the capital of a united kingdom.

According to the biblical account, David's son Solomon (c. 970–930 B.C.E.) did even more to strengthen royal power. He expanded the political and military establishments and extended the trading activities of the Israelites. Solomon is portrayed as a great builder who was responsible for the Temple in the city of Jerusalem. The Israelites viewed the Temple as the symbolic center of their religion and hence of the kingdom of Israel itself. Under Solomon, ancient Israel supposedly reached the height of its power.

The accuracy of this biblical account of the united kingdom of Israel under Saul, David, and Solomon has recently been challenged by a new generation of archaeologists and historians. Although they mostly accept Saul, David, and Solomon as historical figures, they view them more as chief warlords than as kings. If a kingdom of Israel did exist during these years, it was not as powerful or as well organized as the Hebrew Bible says. Furthermore, they argue, there is no definitive archaeological evidence that Solomon built the Temple in Jerusalem.

THE KINGDOMS OF ISRAEL AND JUDAH There may or may not have been a united kingdom of Israel, but after the death of Solomon, tensions between northern and southern tribes in Israel led to the establishment of two separate kingdoms—the kingdom of Israel, composed of the ten northern tribes, with its capital eventually at Samaria, and the southern kingdom of Judah, consisting of two tribes, with its capital at Jerusalem (see Map 1.6). In 722 or 721 B.C.E., the Assyrians (uh-SEER-ee-unz) destroyed Samaria, overran the kingdom of Israel, and deported many Hebrews to other parts of the Assyrian Empire. These dispersed Hebrews (the "ten lost tribes") merged with neighboring peoples and gradually lost their identity.

The southern kingdom of Judah was also forced to pay tribute to Assyria but managed to retain its independence as Assyrian power declined. A new enemy, however, appeared on the horizon. The Chaldeans (kal-DEE-unz) defeated

MAP 1.6 The Israelites and Their Neighbors in the First Millennium B.C.E. After the death of Solomon, tensions between the tribes in Israel led to the creation of two kingdoms—a northern kingdom of Israel and a southern kingdom of Judah. With power divided, the Israelites could not resist invasions that dispersed many of them from Canaan. Some, such as the "ten lost tribes," never returned. Others were sent to Babylon but were later allowed to return under the rule of the Persians.

Q *Why was Israel more vulnerable to the Assyrian Empire than Judah was?*

Assyria, conquered the kingdom of Judah, and completely destroyed Jerusalem in 586 B.C.E. Many upper-class people from Judah were deported to Babylonia; the memory of their exile is still evoked in the stirring words of Psalm 137:

> By the rivers of Babylon, we sat and wept when we remembered Zion….
> How can we sing the songs of the Lord while in a foreign land?
> If I forget you, O Jerusalem, may my right hand forget its skill.
> May my tongue cling to the roof of my mouth if I do not remember you,
> If I do not consider Jerusalem my highest joy.[12]

But the Babylonian captivity of the people of Judah did not last. A new set of conquerors, the Persians, destroyed the Chaldean kingdom and allowed the people of Judah to return to Jerusalem and rebuild their city and Temple. The revived kingdom of Judah remained under Persian control until the

Prisoners from Judah. The Assyrians overran the kingdom of Israel in 722 or 721 B.C.E., destroyed the capital city of Samaria, and then began an assault on the kingdom of Judah. In this eighth-century B.C.E. relief from the palace of Sennacherib at Nineveh, Assyrian soldiers are seen impaling Jewish prisoners after their conquest of the fortified town of Lachish in Judah in 701 B.C.E.

conquests of Alexander the Great in the fourth century B.C.E. The people of Judah survived, eventually becoming known as the Jews and giving their name to Judaism, the religion of Yahweh (YAH-way), the Israelite God.

THE SPIRITUAL DIMENSIONS OF ISRAEL The spiritual perspective of the Israelites evolved over time. Early Israelites probably worshiped many gods, including nature spirits dwelling in trees and rocks. For some Israelites, Yahweh was the chief god of Israel, but many, including kings of Israel and Judah, worshiped other gods as well. It was among the Babylonian exiles in the sixth century B.C.E. that Yahweh—the God of Israel—came to be seen as the only God. After these exiles returned to Judah, their point of view eventually became dominant, and pure monotheism came to be the major tenet of Judaism.

According to the Hebrew conception, there is but one God, called Yahweh, who created the world and everything in it. Yahweh ruled the world and was subject to nothing. This omnipotent creator was not removed from the life he had created, however, but was a just and good God who expected goodness from his people. If they did not obey his will, they would be punished. But he was primarily a God of mercy and love: "The Lord is gracious and compassionate, slow to anger and rich in love. The Lord is good to all; he has

compassion on all he has made."[13] Each individual could have a personal relationship with this being.

Three aspects of the Hebrew religious tradition had special significance: the covenant, the law, and the prophets. The Israelites believed that during the exodus from Egypt, when Moses, according to biblical tradition, led his people out of bondage and into the Promised Land, God made a covenant or contract with the tribes of Israel, who believed that Yahweh had spoken to them through Moses (see the box "The Covenant and the Law: The Book of Exodus" on p. 28). The Israelites promised to obey Yahweh and follow his law. In return, Yahweh promised to take special care of his chosen people, "a peculiar treasure unto me above all people."

This covenant between Yahweh and his chosen people could be fulfilled, however, only by obedience to the law of God. Most important were the ethical concerns that stood at the center of the law. Sometimes these took the form of specific standards of moral behavior: "You shall not murder. You shall not commit adultery. You shall not steal."[14] True freedom consisted of following God's moral standards voluntarily. If people chose to ignore the good, suffering and evil would follow.

The Israelites believed that certain religious teachers, called prophets, were sent by God to serve as his voice to his people (see the box "Three Hebrew Prophets: Micah, Isaiah, and Amos" on p. 29). The golden age of prophecy began in the mid-eighth century B.C.E. and continued during the time when the people of Israel and Judah were threatened by Assyrian and Chaldean conquerors. The "men of God" went through the land warning the Israelites that they had failed to keep God's commandments and would be punished for breaking the covenant: "I will punish you for all your iniquities."

Out of the words of the prophets came new concepts that enriched the Jewish tradition. The prophets embraced a concern for all humanity. All nations would someday come to the God of Israel: "All the earth shall worship thee." This vision encompassed the elimination of war and the establishment of peace for all nations. In the words of the prophet Isaiah, "He will judge between the nations and will settle disputes for many people. They will beat their swords into plowshares and their spears into pruning hooks. Nation will not take up sword against nation, nor will they train for war anymore."[15]

Although the prophets developed a sense of universalism, the demands of the Jewish religion (the need to obey God) eventually encouraged a separation between the Jews and their non-Jewish neighbors. Unlike most other peoples of the Middle East, Jews could not simply be amalgamated into a community by accepting the gods of their conquerors and their neighbors. To remain faithful to the demands of their God, they might even have to refuse loyalty to political leaders.

The Rise of New Empires

 FOCUS QUESTION: What methods and institutions did the Assyrians and Persians use to amass and maintain their respective empires?

Small and independent states could exist only as long as no larger state dominated western Asia. New empires soon arose, however, and conquered vast stretches of the ancient world.

The Covenant and the Law: The Book of Exodus

RELIGION & PHILOSOPHY

ACCORDING TO THE BIBLICAL ACCOUNT, it was during the exodus from Egypt that the Israelites supposedly made their covenant with Yahweh. They agreed to obey their God and follow his law. In return, Yahweh promised to take special care of his chosen people. This selection from the biblical book of Exodus describes the making of the covenant and God's commandments to the Israelites.

Exodus 19:1–8

In the third month after the Israelites left Egypt—on the very day—they came to the Desert of Sinai. After they set out from Rephidim, they entered the desert of Sinai, and Israel camped there in the desert in front of the mountain. Then Moses went up to God, and the Lord called to him from the mountain, and said, "This is what you are to say to the house of Jacob and what you are to tell the people of Israel: 'You yourselves have seen what I did to Egypt, and how I carried you on eagles' wings and brought you to myself. Now if you obey me fully and keep my covenant, then out of all nations you will be my treasured possession. Although the whole earth is mine, you will be for me a kingdom of priests and a holy nation.' These are the words you are to speak to the Israelites." So Moses went back and summoned the elders of the people and set before them all the words the Lord had commanded him to speak. The people all responded together, "We will do everything the Lord has said." So Moses brought their answer back to the Lord.

Exodus 20:1–3, 7–17

And God spoke all these words, "I am the Lord your God, who brought you out of Egypt, out of the land of slavery. You shall have no other gods before me.... You shall not misuse the name of the Lord your God, for the Lord will not hold anyone guiltless who misuses his name. Remember the Sabbath day by keeping it holy. Six days you shall labor and do all your work, but the seventh day is a Sabbath to the Lord your God. On it you shall not do any work, neither you, nor your son or daughter, nor your manservant or maidservant, nor your animals, nor the alien within your gates. For in six days the Lord made the heavens and the earth, the sea, and all that is in them, but he rested on the seventh day. Therefore the Lord blessed the Sabbath day and made it holy. Honor your father and your mother, so that you may live long in the land the Lord your God is giving you. You shall not murder. You shall not commit adultery. You shall not steal. You shall not give false testimony against your neighbor. You shall not covet your neighbor's house. You shall not covet your neighbor's wife, or his manservant or maidservant, his ox or donkey, or anything that belongs to your neighbor."

What was the nature of the covenant between Yahweh and the Israelites? What was its moral significance for the Israelites? How does it differ from Hammurabi's code, and how might you explain those differences?

Source: *The Holy Bible, New International Version*®, NIV® Copyright © 1973, 1978, 1984, 2011 by Biblica, Inc.® Used by permission. All rights reserved worldwide.

The Assyrian Empire

The first of these empires was formed in Assyria, located on the upper Tigris River, an area that brought it into both cultural and political contact with southern Mesopotamia. The Assyrians were a Semitic-speaking people who exploited the use of iron weapons, first developed by the Hittites, to establish an empire that by 700 B.C.E. included Mesopotamia, parts of the Iranian Plateau, sections of Asia Minor, Syria, Canaan, and Egypt down to Thebes (see Map 1.7). Ashurbanipal (ah-shur-BAH-nuh-pahl) (669–627 B.C.E.) was one of the strongest Assyrian rulers, but during his reign it was already becoming apparent that the Assyrian Empire was greatly overextended. Moreover, subject peoples, such as the Babylonians, greatly resented Assyrian rule and rebelled against it. Soon after Ashurbanipal's reign, the Assyrian Empire began to disintegrate. The capital city of Nineveh fell to a coalition of Chaldeans and Medes in 612 B.C.E., and in 605 B.C.E., the rest of the empire was finally divided between the two powers.

At its height, the Assyrian Empire was ruled by kings whose power was considered absolute. Under their leadership, the empire came to be well organized. Local officials were directly responsible to the king. The Assyrians also developed an efficient system of communication to administer their empire more effectively. A network of staging posts was established throughout the empire that used relays of horses (mules or donkeys in mountainous terrain) to carry messages. The system was so effective that a provincial governor anywhere in the empire (except Egypt) could send a question and receive an answer from the king in his palace within a week.

The Assyrians' ability to conquer and maintain an empire was due to a combination of factors. Over many years of practice, the Assyrians developed effective military leaders and fighters. They were able to enlist and deploy troops numbering in the hundreds of thousands, although most campaigns were not on such a large scale. Size alone was not decisive, however. The Assyrian army was well organized and disciplined. It included a standing army of infantry as its core, accompanied by cavalry and horse-drawn war chariots that were used as mobile platforms for shooting arrows. In addition to fighting set battles on open ground, the Assyrian army

Three Hebrew Prophets: Micah, Isaiah, and Amos

RELIGION & PHILOSOPHY

THE HEBREW PROPHETS WARNED THE ISRAELITES that they must obey God's commandments or face punishment for breaking their covenant with God. These selections from the prophets Micah, Isaiah, and Amos make clear that God's punishment would fall on the Israelites for their sins. Even the Assyrians, as Isaiah indicated, would be used as God's instrument to punish them.

Micah 6:9–16

Listen! The Lord is calling to the city—and to fear your name is wisdom—"Heed the rod and the One who appointed it. Am I still to forget, O wicked house, your ill-gotten treasures … ? Shall I acquit a man with dishonest scales, with a bag of false weights? Her rich men are violent; her people are liars and their tongues speak deceitfully. Therefore, I have begun to destroy you, to ruin you because of your sins. You will eat but not be satisfied; your stomach will still be empty. You will store up but save nothing, because what you save I will give to the sword. You will plant but not harvest; you will press olives but not use the oil on yourselves, you will crush grapes but not drink the wine…. Therefore I will give you over to ruin and your people to derision; you will bear the scorn of the nations."

Isaiah 10:1–6

Woe to those who make unjust laws, to those who issue oppressive decrees, to deprive the poor of their rights and withhold justice from the oppressed of my people, making widows their prey and robbing the fatherless. What will you do on the day of reckoning, when disaster comes from afar? To whom will you run for help? Where will you leave your riches? Nothing will remain but to cringe among the captives or fall among the slain. Yet for all this, his anger is not turned away, his hand is still upraised. "Woe to the Assyrian, the rod of my anger, in whose hand is the club of my wrath! I send him against a godless nation, I dispatch him against a people who anger me, to seize loot and snatch plunder, and to trample them down like mud in the streets."

Amos 3:1–2

Hear this word the Lord has spoken against you, O people of Israel—against the whole family I brought up out of Egypt: "You only have I chosen of all the families of the earth; therefore I will punish you for all your sins."

 What did the Hebrew prophets see as the chief transgressions of the Israelites? What do these selections tell you about the nature of the Israelites as a "chosen" people?

was also capable of waging guerrilla warfare in the mountains and laying siege to cities.

Another factor in the effectiveness of the Assyrian military machine was its use of terror as an instrument of warfare. As a matter of regular policy, the Assyrians laid waste to the land in which they were fighting, smashing dams, looting and destroying towns, setting crops on fire, and cutting down trees, particularly fruit trees. They were especially known for committing atrocities on their captives. King Ashurnasirpal (ah-shur-NAH-zur-pahl) recorded this account of his treatment of prisoners:

> 3000 of their combat troops I felled with weapons…. Many of the captives taken from them I burned in a fire. Many I took alive; from some of these I cut off their hands to the wrist, from others I cut off their noses, ears and fingers; I put out the eyes of many of the soldiers…. I burned their young men and women to death.[16]

After conquering another city, the same king wrote, "I fixed up a pile of corpses in front of the city's gate. I flayed the nobles, as many as had rebelled, and spread their skins out on the piles…. I flayed many within my land and spread their skins out on the walls."[17] It should be noted that this policy of extreme cruelty to prisoners was not used against all enemies but was primarily reserved for those who were already part of the empire and then rebelled against Assyrian rule (see Opposing Viewpoints "The Governing of Empires: Two Approaches" on p. 31).

ASSYRIAN SOCIETY Assyrian deportation policies created a polyglot society in which ethnic differences were not very important. What gave identity to the Assyrians themselves was their language, although even that was akin to the language of their southern neighbors in Babylonia, who also spoke a Semitic tongue. Religion was also a cohesive force. Assyria was literally "the land of Ashur," a reference to its chief god. The king, as Ashur's representative on earth, provided a final unifying focus.

Agriculture formed the principal basis of Assyrian life. Assyria was a land of farming villages with relatively few significant cities, especially in comparison to southern Mesopotamia. Unlike the river valleys, where farming required the minute organization of large numbers of people to control irrigation, Assyrian farms received sufficient moisture from regular rainfall.

Trade was second to agriculture in economic importance. For internal trade, metals—including gold, silver, copper, and bronze—were used as a medium of exchange. Various agricultural products also served as a form of payment or exchange. Because of their geographic location, the Assyrians served as intermediaries and participated in an international

MAP 1.7 **The Assyrian and Persian Empires.** Cyrus the Great united the Persians and led them in a successful conquest of much of the Near East, including most of the lands of the Assyrian Empire. By the time of Darius, the Persian Empire was the largest the world had yet seen.

Q *Based on your examination of this map of the Assyrian and Persian Empires, what do you think would be the challenges of governing a large empire?*

trade, importing timber, wine, and precious metals and stones while exporting textiles produced in palaces, temples, and private workshops.

ASSYRIAN CULTURE The Assyrians assimilated much of Mesopotamian civilization and saw themselves as guardians of Sumerian and Babylonian culture. Assyrian kings also tried to maintain old traditions when they rebuilt damaged temples by constructing the new buildings on the original foundations rather than in new locations.

Among the best-known objects of Assyrian art are the relief sculptures found in the royal palaces in three of the Assyrian capital cities, Nimrud, Nineveh, and Khorsabad. These reliefs, which were begun in the ninth century B.C.E. and reached their high point in the reign of Ashurbanipal in the seventh, depicted two different kinds of subject matter: ritual or ceremonial scenes revolving around the king and scenes of hunting and war. The latter show realistic action scenes of the king and his warriors engaged in battle or hunting animals, especially lions. These images depict a strongly masculine world where discipline, brute force, and toughness are the enduring values—indeed, the very values of the Assyrian military monarchy.

The Persian Empire

After the collapse of the Assyrian Empire, the Chaldeans, under their king Nebuchadnezzar (neb-uh-kud-NEZZ-ur) II (605–562 B.C.E.), made Babylonia the leading state in western Asia. Nebuchadnezzar rebuilt Babylon as the center of his empire, giving it a reputation as one of the great cities of the ancient world. But the splendor of Chaldean Babylonia proved to be short-lived when Babylon fell to the Persians in 539 B.C.E.

The Persians were an Indo-European-speaking people who lived in southwestern Iran. Primarily nomadic, the Persians were organized into tribes until the Achaemenid (ah-KEE-muh-nud) dynasty managed to unify them. One of the dynasty's members, Cyrus (559–530 B.C.E.), created a powerful Persian state that rearranged the political map of western Asia.

CYRUS THE GREAT In 550 B.C.E., Cyrus extended Persian control over the Medes, making Media the first Persian **satrapy** (SAY-truh-pee), or province. Three years later, Cyrus defeated the prosperous Lydian kingdom in western Asia Minor, and Lydia became another Persian satrapy. Cyrus's forces then went on to conquer the Greek city-states that had been established on the Ionian coast. Cyrus then turned eastward, subduing the

OPPOSING ✕ VIEWPOINTS

The Governing of Empires: Two Approaches

POLITICS & GOVERNMENT

BOTH THE ASSYRIANS AND THE PERSIANS CREATED LARGE EMPIRES that encompassed large areas of the ancient Near East. Although both Assyrian and Persian rulers used military force and violence to attain their empires, their approaches to conquest and ruling sometimes differed. Assyrian rulers were known for their terror tactics and atrocities, as described in the first two selections. Although the kings of Persia also used terror when needed, they also had a reputation for less cruelty and more tolerance. Especially noteworthy was Cyrus, as is evident in this selection from a decree (known as the Cyrus Cylinder) that he issued in 538 B.C.E. The propaganda value of his words is also apparent, however.

King Sennacherib (704–681 B.C.E.) Describes His Siege of Jerusalem (701 B.C.E.)

As to Hezekiah, the Jew, he did not submit to my yoke, I laid siege to 46 of his strong cities, walled forts and to the countless small villages in their vicinity, and conquered them by means of well-stamped earth-ramps, and battering-rams brought thus near to the walls combined with the attack by foot soldiers, using mines, breaches as well as sapper work. I drove out of them 200,150 people, young and old, male and female, horses, mules, donkeys, camels, big and small cattle beyond counting, and considered them booty. Himself I made a prisoner in Jerusalem, his royal residence, like a bird in a cage. I surrounded him with earthwork in order to molest those who were leaving his city's gate.

King Ashurbanipal (669–627 B.C.E.) Describes His Treatment of Conquered Babylon

I tore out the tongues of those whose slanderous mouths had uttered blasphemies against my god Ashur and had plotted against me, his god-fearing prince; I defeated them completely. The others, I smashed alive with the very same statues of protective deities with which they had smashed my own grandfather Sennacherib—now finally as a belated burial sacrifice for his soul. I fed their corpses, cut into small pieces, to dogs, pigs, … vultures, the birds of the sky and also to the fish of the ocean. After I … thus made quiet again the hearts of the great gods, my lords, I removed the corpses of those whom the pestilence had felled, whose leftovers after the dogs and pigs had fed on them were obstructing the streets, filling the places of Babylon, and of those who had lost their lives through the terrible famine.

The Cyrus Cylinder

I am Cyrus, king of the world, great king, legitimate king, king of Babylon, king of Sumer and Akkad, king of the four corners of the earth.…

When I entered Babylon as a friend and when I established the seat of the government in the palace of the ruler under jubilation and rejoicing, Marduk, the great lord [the chief Babylonian god], caused the magnanimous inhabitants of Babylon to love me, and I was daily endeavoring to worship him. My numerous troops walked around in Babylon in peace. I did not allow anybody to terrorize any place of the country of Sumer and Akkad. I strove for peace in Babylon and in all his other sacred cities. As to the inhabitants of Babylon … I brought relief to their dilapidated housing, putting thus an end to their main complaints.…

As to the region from as far as Ashur and Susa … I returned to these sacred cities on the other side of the Tigris, the sanctuaries of which have been ruins for a long time, the images which used to live therein and established for them permanent sanctuaries. I also gathered all their former inhabitants and returned to them their dwellings.

Both Ashurbanipal and Cyrus entered Babylon as conquerors. How did their treatment of the conquered city differ? How do you explain the differences? Which method do you think was more effective? Why?

Sources: Pritchard, James B., ed., *Ancient Near Eastern Texts Relating to the Old Testament*, Third Edition with Supplement. © 1950, 1955, 1969, renewed 1978 by Princeton University Press. Reprinted by permission of Princeton University Press.

eastern part of the Iranian Plateau, Sogdia, and even western India. His eastern frontiers secured, Cyrus entered Mesopotamia in 539 and captured Babylon (see Map 1.7). His treatment of Babylonia showed remarkable restraint and wisdom. Babylonia was made into a Persian province under a Persian **satrap** (SAY-trap), or governor, but many government officials were kept in their positions. Cyrus took the title "King of All, Great King, Mighty King, King of Babylon, King of the Land of Sumer and Akkad, King of the Four Rims [of the earth], the Son of Cambyses the Great King, King of Anshan"[18] and insisted that he stood in the

King Ashurbanipal's Lion Hunt. This relief, sculpted on alabaster as a decoration for the Assyrian northern palace in Nineveh, depicts King Ashurbanipal engaged in a lion hunt. Lion hunts were not conducted in the wild but were held under controlled circumstances: the king and his retainers faced lions released from cages in an arena. The scene was intended to glorify the king as the conqueror of the king of beasts. Relief sculpture, one of the best-known forms of Assyrian art, reached its zenith under Ashurbanipal just before the Assyrian Empire began its rapid disintegration.

ancient, unbroken line of Babylonian kings. By appealing to the vanity of the Babylonians, he won their loyalty. Cyrus also issued an edict permitting the Jews, who had been brought to Babylon in the sixth century B.C.E., to return to Jerusalem with their sacred objects and to rebuild their Temple as well.

To his contemporaries, Cyrus deserved to be called Cyrus the Great. The Greek historian Herodotus recounted that the Persians viewed him as a "father," a ruler who was "gentle, and procured them all manner of goods."[19] Cyrus must have been an unusual ruler for his time, a man who demonstrated considerable wisdom and compassion in the conquest and organization of his empire (see Opposing Viewpoints "The Governing of Empires: Two Approaches" on p. 31). He won approval by using not only Persians but also native peoples as government officials in their own states. Unlike the Assyrian rulers of an earlier empire, he had a reputation for mercy. Medes, Babylonians, and Jews all accepted him as their legitimate ruler. Indeed, the Jews regarded him as the anointed one of God: "I am the Lord who says of Cyrus, 'He is my shepherd and will accomplish all that I please'; he will say of Jerusalem, 'Let it be rebuilt'; and of the Temple, 'Let its foundations be laid.' This is what the Lord says to his anointed, to Cyrus, whose right hand I take hold of to subdue nations before him."[20]

EXPANDING THE EMPIRE Cyrus's successors extended the territory of the Persian Empire. His son Cambyses (kam-BY-seez) (530–522 B.C.E.) undertook a successful invasion of Egypt. Darius (duh-RY-uss) (521–486 B.C.E.) added a new Persian province in western India that extended to the Indus River and moved into Europe proper, conquering Thrace and making the Macedonian king a vassal. A revolt of the Ionian Greek cities in 499 B.C.E. resulted in temporary freedom for these communities in western Asia Minor. Aid from the Greek mainland, most notably from Athens, encouraged the

Ionians to invade Lydia and burn Sardis, center of the Lydian satrapy. This event led to Darius's involvement with the mainland Greeks. After reestablishing control of the Ionian Greek cities, Darius undertook an invasion of the Greek mainland, which culminated in the Athenian victory in the Battle of Marathon, in 490 B.C.E. (see Chapter 4).

GOVERNING THE EMPIRE By the reign of Darius, the Persians had assembled the largest empire the world had yet seen. It not only included all the old centers of power in Egypt and western Asia but also extended into Thrace and Asia Minor in the west and into India in the east. For administrative purposes, the empire had been divided into approximately twenty satrapies. Each province was ruled by a satrap, literally a "protector of the kingdom." Satraps collected tributes, were responsible for justice and security, raised military levies for the royal army, and normally commanded the military forces within their satrapies. In terms of real power, the satraps were miniature kings who created courts imitative of the Great King's.

An efficient system of communication was crucial to sustaining the Persian Empire. Well-maintained roads facilitated the rapid transit of military and government personnel. One in particular, the so-called Royal Road, stretched from Sardis, the center of Lydia in Asia Minor, to Susa, the chief capital of the Persian Empire. Like the Assyrians, the Persians established staging posts equipped with fresh horses for the king's messengers.

THE GREAT KING In this vast administrative system, the Persian king occupied an exalted position. Although not considered a god in the manner of an Egyptian pharaoh, he was nevertheless the elect one or regent of the Persian god Ahuramazda (uh-HOOR-uh-MAHZ-duh) (see the next section, "Persian Religion"). All subjects were the king's servants, and he was the source of all justice, possessing the power of life and death over

Werner Forman/Art Resource, NY

everyone. Persian kings were largely secluded and not easily accessible. They resided in a series of splendid palaces. Darius in particular was a palace builder on a grand scale.

The policies of Darius also tended to widen the gap between the king and his subjects. As the Great King himself said of all his subjects, "What was said to them by me, night and day it was done."[21] Over a period of time, the Great Kings in their greed came to hoard immense quantities of gold and silver in treasuries located in the capital cities. Both their hoarding of wealth and their later over-taxation of their subjects were crucial factors in the ultimate weakening of the Persian Empire.

In its heyday, however, the empire stood supreme, and much of its power depended on the military. By the time of Darius, the Persian monarchs had created a standing army of professional soldiers. This army was truly international, composed of contingents from the various peoples who made up the empire. At its core was a cavalry force of ten thousand and an elite infantry force of ten thousand Medes and Persians known as the Immortals because they were never allowed to fall below ten thousand in number. When one was killed, he was immediately replaced.

PERSIAN RELIGION Of all the Persians' cultural contributions, the most original was their religion, **Zoroastrianism**. According to Persian tradition, Zoroaster (ZOR-oh-ass-tur) was born in 660 B.C.E. After a period of wandering and solitude, he experienced revelations that caused him to be revered as a prophet of the "true religion." His teachings were eventually written down in the third century B.C.E. in the *Zend Avesta*, the sacred book of Zoroastrianism.

Zoroaster's spiritual message was basically monotheistic. To Zoroaster, the religion he preached was the only perfect one, and Ahuramazda was the only god. Ahuramazda ("Wise Lord") was the supreme deity, "creator of all things." According to Zoroaster, Ahuramazda also possessed qualities that all humans should aspire to, such as good thought, right action, and piety. Although Ahuramazda was supreme, he was not unopposed; this gave a dualistic element to Zoroastrianism. At the beginning of the world, the good spirit of Ahuramazda was opposed by the evil spirit, later identified as Ahriman.

Gianni Dagli Orti/The Art Archive/Picture Desk

Darius, the Great King. Darius ruled the Persian Empire from 521 to 486 B.C.E. He is shown on his throne in Persepolis, the new capital city he built. In his right hand, Darius holds the royal staff; with his left, he grasps a lotus blossom with two buds, a symbol of royalty.

Humans also played a role in this cosmic struggle between good and evil. Ahuramazda, the creator, gave all humans free will and the power to choose between right and wrong. The good person chooses the right way of Ahuramazda. Zoroaster taught that there would be an end to the struggle between good and evil. Ahuramazda would eventually triumph, and at the last judgment at the end of the world, the final separation of good and evil would occur. Individuals, too, would be judged. Each soul faced a final evaluation of its actions. The soul of a person who had performed good deeds would achieve paradise; but if deeds had been evil, the person would be thrown into an abyss of torment. Some historians believe that Zoroastrianism, with its emphasis on good and evil, heaven and hell, and a last judgment, had an impact on Christianity, a religion that eventually surpassed it in significance.

CHRONOLOGY	Early Empires
The Assyrians	
Height of power	700 B.C.E.
Ashurbanipal	669–627 B.C.E.
Fall of Nineveh	612 B.C.E.
Assyrian Empire destroyed	605 B.C.E.
The Persians	
Unification under Achaemenid dynasty	600s B.C.E.
Persian control over Medes	550 B.C.E.
Conquests of Cyrus the Great	559–530 B.C.E.
Cambyses and conquest of Egypt	530–522 B.C.E.
Reign of Darius	521–486 B.C.E.

CHAPTER SUMMARY

Humanlike creatures first emerged in Africa around 3 to 4 million years ago. Over a period of time, Paleolithic people learned to create sophisticated tools, to use fire, and to adapt to and even change their physical world. They were primarily nomads, who hunted animals and gathered wild plants for survival. The agricultural revolution of the Neolithic Age, which began around 10,000 B.C.E., dramatically changed human patterns of living. The growing of food on a regular basis and the taming of animals enabled humans to stop their nomadic ways and settle in permanent settlements, which gave rise to more complex human societies.

These more complex human societies, which we call the first civilizations, emerged around 3000 B.C.E. in the river valleys of Mesopotamia, Egypt, India, and China. An increase in food production in these regions led to a significant growth in human population and the rise of cities. The peoples of Southwest Asia and Egypt developed cities and struggled with the problems of organized states as they moved from individual communities to larger territorial units and eventually to empires. They invented writing to keep records and created literature. They constructed monumental buildings to please their gods, give witness to their power, and preserve their culture. They developed new political, military, social, and religious structures to deal with the basic problems of human existence and organization. These first civilizations left detailed records that allow us to view how they grappled with

three of the fundamental problems that humans have pondered: the nature of human relationships, the nature of the universe, and the role of divine forces in that cosmos.

By the middle of the second millennium B.C.E., much of the creative impulse of the Mesopotamian and Egyptian civilizations was beginning to wane. Around 1200 B.C.E., a number of small states emerged, but all of them were eventually overshadowed by the rise of the great empires of the Assyrians and Persians. The Assyrian Empire was the first to unite almost all of the ancient Middle East. Even larger, however, was the empire of the Great Kings of Persia. The many years of peace that the Persian Empire brought to the Middle East facilitated trade and the general well-being of its peoples. It is no wonder that many peoples expressed their gratitude for being subjects of the Great Kings of Persia. Among these peoples were the Hebrews, who created no empire but nevertheless left an important spiritual legacy. The embrace of monotheism created in Judaism one of the world's greatest religions, one that went on to influence the development of both Christianity and Islam.

CHAPTER TIMELINE

CHAPTER REVIEW

Upon Reflection

Q What achievements did early humans make during the Paleolithic and Neolithic Ages, and how did those achievements eventually make possible the emergence of civilization?

Q What roles did geography, environmental conditions, religion, politics, economics, and women and families play in the civilizations of Southwest Asia and Egypt?

Q Compare and contrast the administrative and military structures and the attitudes toward subject peoples of the Assyrian and Persian Empires.

Key Terms

hominids (p. 3)
Paleolithic Age (p. 3)
Neolithic Revolution (p. 5)
Mesolithic Age (p. 5)
patriarchy (p. 6)
civilization (p. 8)
ziggurat (p. 10)
theocracy (p. 10)
polytheism (p. 13)
divination (p. 13)
cuneiform (p. 14)
pharaoh (p. 18)
hieroglyphics (p. 20)
megalith (p. 23)
monotheism (p. 25)
satrapy (p. 30)
satrap (p. 31)
Zoroastrianism (p. 33)

Suggested Reading

THE PREHISTORIC WORLD For a brief but sound survey, see **I. Tattersall,** *The World from Beginnings to 4000 B.C.E.* (Oxford, 2008). Also of considerable value in examining the prehistory of humankind is **S. Mithen,** *After the Ice: A Global Human History, 20,000–5000 B.C.* (Cambridge, Mass., 2006). On the role of women in prehistory, see **J. M. Adovasio, O. Soffer, and J. Page,** *The Invisible Sex: Uncovering the True Roles of Women in Prehistory* (New York, 2007).

ANCIENT NEAR EAST A very competent general survey of the ancient Near East is **M. Van de Mieroop,** *A History of the Ancient Near East, ca. 3000–323 B.C.,* 2nd ed. (Oxford, 2006). For a detailed survey, see **A. Kuhrt,** *The Ancient Near East, c. 3000–330 B.C.,* 2 vols. (London, 1996). On the economic and social history of the ancient Near East, see **D. C. Snell,** *Life in the Ancient Near East* (New Haven, Conn., 1997).

ANCIENT MESOPOTAMIA A beautifully illustrated survey of ancient Mesopotamia can be found in **M. Roaf,** *Cultural Atlas of Mesopotamia and the Ancient Near East* (New York, 1996). For a summary of the historical and archaeological evidence on the Sumerians, see **H. Crawford,** *Sumer and the Sumerians,* 2nd ed. (Cambridge, 2004). On daily life, see **S. Bertman,** *Handbook to Life in Ancient Mesopotamia* (New York, 2003).

ANCIENT EGYPT For an excellent introduction to ancient Egypt, see **T. Wilkinson,** *The Rise and Fall of Ancient Egypt* (New York, 2010). Daily life in ancient Egypt can be examined in **R. David,** *Handbook to Life in Ancient Egypt* (New York, 1998). On the interaction of the Egyptians with the Nubians and other peoples in Africa south of Egypt, see **D. B. Redford,** *From Slave to Pharaoh: The Black Experience of Ancient Egypt* (Baltimore, 2004).

ANCIENT ISRAEL There is an enormous literature on ancient Israel. For an important revisionist view on the archaeological aspects, see **I. Finkelstein and N. Silberman,** *The Bible Unearthed: Archaeology's New Vision of Ancient Israel* (New York, 2002). For a historical narrative, see the survey by **H. Shanks,** *Ancient Israel: A Short History from Abraham to the Roman Destruction of the Temple,* rev. ed. (Englewood Cliffs, N.J., 1998). On the controversies surrounding the history of the Israelites, see **J. M. Golden,** *Ancient Canaan and Israel* (Oxford, 2004).

THE ASSYRIAN AND PERSIAN EMPIRES A detailed account of Assyrian political, economic, social, military, and cultural history is **H. W. F. Saggs,** *The Might That Was Assyria* (London, 1984). On the Persian Empire, see **L. Allen,** *The Persian Empire* (Chicago, 2005). On the history of Zoroastrianism, see **S. A. Nigosian,** *The Zoroastrian Faith: Tradition and Modern Research* (New York, 1993).

Chapter Notes

1. J. M. Chauvet et al., *Dawn of Art: The Chauvet Cave* (New York, 1996), pp. 49–50.
2. Quoted in A. Kuhrt, *The Ancient Near East, c. 3000–330 B.C.* (London, 1995), vol. 1, p. 68.
3. Quoted in Michael Wood, *Legacy: The Search for Ancient Cultures* (New York, 1995), p. 34.
4. Quoted in M. Van de Mieroop, *A History of the Ancient Near East, ca. 3000–323 B.C.* (Oxford, 2004), p. 69.
5. Quoted in ibid., p. 106.
6. Quoted in T. Jacobsen, "Mesopotamia," in H. Frankfort et al., *Before Philosophy* (Baltimore, 1949), p. 139.
7. Quoted in M. Covensky, *The Ancient Near Eastern Tradition* (New York, 1966), p. 51.
8. Quoted in B. G. Trigger et al., *Ancient Egypt: A Social History* (Cambridge, 1983), p. 74.

9. Quoted in R.-M. Hagen and R. Hagen, *Egypt: People, Gods, Pharaohs* (Cologne, 2002), p. 148.

10. J. B. Pritchard, *Ancient Near Eastern Texts*, 3rd ed. (Princeton, N.J., 1969), p. 413.

11. Ibid., p. 420.

12. Psalms 137:1, 4–6.

13. Psalms 145:8–9.

14. Exodus 20:13–15.

15. Isaiah 2:4.

16. Quoted in H. W. F. Saggs, *The Might That Was Assyria* (London, 1984), p. 261.

17. Ibid., p. 262.

18. Quoted in J. M. Cook, *The Persian Empire* (New York, 1983), p. 32.

19. Herodotus, *The Persian Wars*, trans. G. Rawlinson (New York, 1942), p. 257.

20. Isaiah, 44:28, 45:1.

21. Quoted in Cook, *The Persian Empire*, p. 76.

MindTap is a fully online, highly personalized learning experience built upon Cengage Leaning content. MindTap combines student learning tools—readings, multimedia, activities, and assessments—into a singular Learning Path that guides students through their course.

Krishna and Arjuna preparing for battle

Ancient India

CHAPTER OUTLINE AND FOCUS QUESTIONS

The Emergence of Civilization in India: Harappan Society

Q What were the chief features of Harappan civilization, and in what ways was it similar to the civilizations that arose in Egypt and Mesopotamia?

The Aryans in India

Q What were some of the distinctive features of the class system introduced by the Aryan peoples, and what effects did it have on Indian civilization?

Escaping the Wheel of Life: The Religious World of Ancient India

Q What are the main tenets of Brahmanism and Buddhism? How did they differ, and how did each religion influence Indian civilization?

The Exuberant World of Indian Culture

Q In what ways did the culture of ancient India resemble and differ from the cultural experience of ancient Mesopotamia and Egypt?

CRITICAL THINKING

Q What role did geography and the local environment play in affecting the nature of the first civilization that developed in the South Asian subcontinent? In what ways were these factors different from those that affected the civilizations discussed in Chapter 1?

CONNECTIONS TO TODAY

Q How would you compare the class system in ancient India as described in the *Law of Manu* with that of the United States at the present time? What do you think accounts for the differences?

ARJUNA WAS DESPONDENT as he prepared for battle. In the opposing army were many of his friends and colleagues, some of whom he had known since childhood. In despair, he turned for advice to Krishna (KHRISH-nuh), his chariot driver, who, unknown to Arjuna (ahr-JOO-nuh), was an incarnation of the Indian deity Vishnu (VISH-nu). "Do not despair of your duty," Krishna advised his friend.

> To be born is certain death;
> to the dead, birth is certain.
> It is not right that you should sorrow
> for what cannot be avoided....
> If you do not fight this just battle
> you will fail in your own law
> and in your honor,
> and you will incur sin.

Krishna's advice to Arjuna is contained in the Bhagavad Gita (bah-guh-vahd GEE-tuh), one of India's most sacred classical writings, and reflects one of the key tenets in Indian philosophy—the belief in reincarnation, or rebirth of the soul. It also points up the importance of doing one's duty without regard for the consequences. Arjuna was a warrior, and according to Aryan (AR-ee-un) tribal tradition, he was obliged to follow the code of his class. "There is more joy in doing one's own duty badly," advised Krishna, "than in doing another man's duty well."

In advising Arjuna to fulfill his obligation as a warrior, the author of the Bhagavad Gita, writing around the second century B.C.E. about a battle that took place almost a thousand years earlier, was by implication urging all readers to adhere to their own responsibility as members of one of India's major classes. Henceforth, this hierarchical vision of a society divided into groups, each with clearly distinct roles, would become a defining characteristic of Indian history.

The Bhagavad Gita is part of a larger work, called the Mahabharata (muh-hahb-huh-RAH-tuh), that deals with the early history of the Aryan peoples who entered India from beyond the mountains north of the Khyber Pass between 1500 and 1000 B.C.E. When the Aryans, a pastoral people speaking an Indo-European language, arrived in India, the subcontinent had had a thriving civilization for almost two thousand years. The Indus Valley civilization, although not as well known in the West as the civilizations of Mesopotamia and Egypt, was just as old, and its political, social, and cultural achievements were equally impressive. That civilization, known to historians by the names of its two major cities, Harappa (huh-RAP-uh) and Mohenjo-Daro (moh-HEN-joh-DAH-roh), emerged in the late fourth millennium B.C.E., flourished for more than a thousand years, and then came to an abrupt end about 1500 B.C.E. It was soon replaced by a new society dominated by the Aryan peoples. The new civilization that emerged represented a rich mixture of the two cultures—Harappan and Aryan—and evolved over the next three thousand years into what we know today as India. ❦

The Emergence of Civilization in India: Harappan Society

 FOCUS QUESTION: What were the chief features of Harappan civilization, and in what ways was it similar to the civilizations that arose in Egypt and Mesopotamia?

Like the civilizations of Mesopotamia and Egypt, the earliest civilizations in India arose in river valleys and were shaped, in part, by their environment. Thus, from its beginnings, Indian civilization has been intimately associated with the geography of the subcontinent.

A Land of Diversity

India was and still is a land of diversity. This diversity is evident in its languages and cultures as well as in its physical characteristics. India possesses an incredible array of languages. It has a deserved reputation, along with the Middle East, as a cradle of religion. Two of the world's major religions, Hinduism and Buddhism, originated in India, and a number of others,

including Sikhism and Islam (the latter of which entered the South Asian subcontinent in the ninth or tenth century C.E.), continue to flourish there.

In its size and geographical complexity, India seems more like a continent than a nation. That complexity begins with the physical environment. The Indian subcontinent, shaped like a spade hanging from the southern ridge of Asia, is composed of a number of core regions. In the far north are the Himalayan and Karakoram mountain ranges, home of the highest peaks in the world. Directly to the south of the Himalayas and the Karakoram range is the rich valley of the Ganges, India's "holy river" and one of the core regions of Indian culture. To the west is the Indus River valley. Today, the latter is a relatively arid plateau that forms the backbone of the modern state of Pakistan, but in ancient times it enjoyed a more balanced climate and served as the cradle of Indian civilization.

South of India's two major river valleys lies the Deccan, a region of hills and an upland plateau that extends from the Ganges Valley to the southern tip of the Indian subcontinent. The interior of the plateau is relatively hilly and dry, but the eastern and western coasts are occupied by lush plains, which have historically been among the most densely populated regions of India. Off the southeastern coast is the island known today as Sri Lanka. Although Sri Lanka is now a separate country quite distinct politically and culturally from India, the island's history is intimately linked with that of its larger neighbor.

In this vast region live a rich mixture of peoples: people speaking one of the languages in the Dravidian family, who may have descended from the Indus River culture that flourished at the dawn of Indian civilization more than four thousand years ago; Aryans, descended from the pastoral peoples who flooded southward from Central Asia in the second millennium B.C.E.; and hill peoples, who may be the descendants of the first migrants passing through the area and hence may have been the earliest inhabitants of all. Although today this beautiful mosaic of peoples and cultures has been broken up into a number of separate independent states, the region still possesses a coherent history that is recognizably Indian.

Harappan Civilization: A Fascinating Enigma

In the 1920s, archaeologists discovered the existence of agricultural settlements dating back more than six thousand years in the lower Indus River valley in modern Pakistan. Those small mudbrick villages eventually gave rise to the sophisticated human communities that historians call Harappan civilization. Although today the area is relatively arid, during the third and fourth millennia B.C.E., it evidently received much more abundant rainfall, and the valleys of the Indus River and its tributaries supported a thriving civilization that may have covered a total area of more than 600,000 square miles, from the Himalayas to the Indian Ocean. More than seventy sites have been unearthed since the area was discovered in the 1850s, but the main sites are at the two major cities, Harappa, in the Punjab, and Mohenjo-Daro, nearly 400 miles to the south near the mouth of the Indus River (see Map 2.1).

MAP 2.1 **Ancient Harappan Civilization.** This map shows the location of the first civilization that arose in the Indus River valley, which today is located in Pakistan.

Q *Based on this map, why do you think Harappan civilization resembled the civilizations of Mesopotamia and Egypt?*

POLITICAL AND SOCIAL STRUCTURES In several respects, Harappan civilization closely resembled the cultures of Mesopotamia and the Nile Valley. Like them, it probably began in tiny farming villages scattered throughout the river valley, some dating back to as early as 6500 or 7000 B.C.E. These villages thrived and grew until by the middle of the third millennium B.C.E. they could support a privileged ruling elite living in walled cities of considerable magnitude and affluence. The center of power was the city of Harappa, which was surrounded by a brick wall over 40 feet thick at its base and more than 3.5 miles in circumference. The city was laid out on an essentially rectangular grid, with some streets as wide as 30 feet. Most buildings were constructed of kiln-dried mudbricks and were square in shape, reflecting the grid pattern. At its height, the city may have had as many as 80,000 inhabitants, making it as large as some of the most populous Sumerian urban centers.

Both Harappa and Mohenjo-Daro were divided into large walled neighborhoods, with narrow lanes separating the rows of houses. Houses varied in size, with some as high as three stories, but all followed the same general plan based on a square courtyard surrounded by rooms. Bathrooms featured an advanced drainage system, which carried wastewater out to drains located under the streets and thence to sewage pits beyond the city walls. But the cities also had the equivalent of the modern slum. At Harappa, tiny dwellings for workers have been found near metal furnaces and the open areas used for pounding grain.

Mohenjo-Daro: Ancient City on the Indus. One of the two major cities of the ancient Indus River civilization was Mohenjo-Daro (below). In addition to rows of residential housing, it had a ceremonial center with a royal palace and a sacred bath that was probably used by the priests to achieve ritual purity. The bath is reminiscent of water tanks in modern Hindu temples, such as the Meenakshi Temple in Madurai (right), where the faithful wash their feet prior to religious devotion. Water was an integral part of Hindu temple complexes, where it symbolized Vishnu's cosmic ocean and the concept of ritual purity. Water was a vital necessity in India's arid climate.

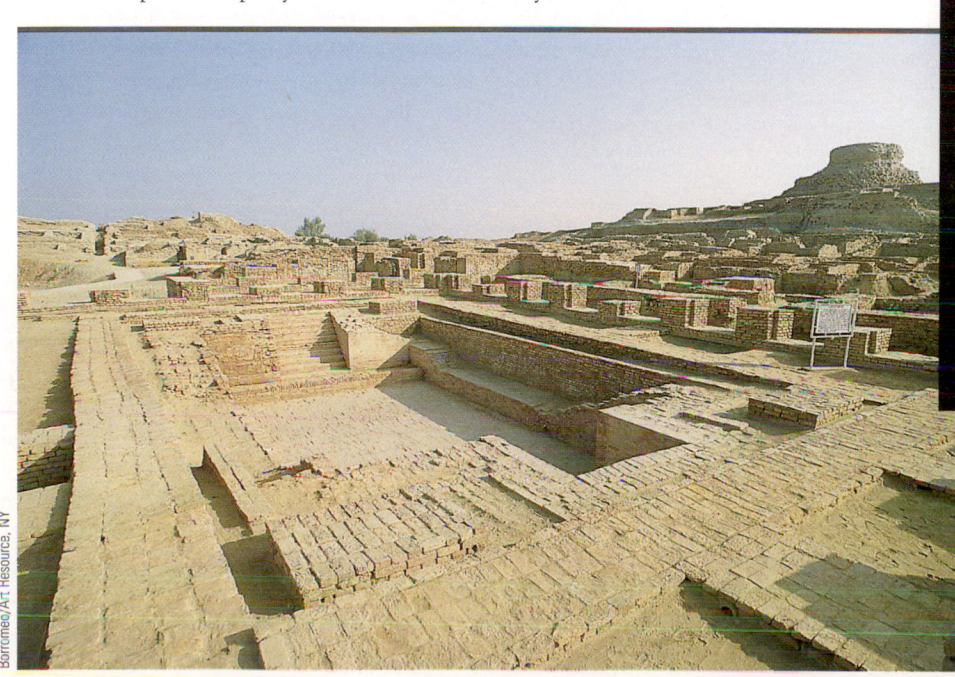

Unfortunately, Harappan writing has not yet been deciphered, so historians know relatively little about the organization of the Harappan state. Recent archaeological evidence suggests, however, that unlike its contemporaries in Egypt and Sumer, Harappa was not a centralized monarchy with a theocratic base but a collection of more than 1,500 towns and cities loosely connected by ties of trade and alliance and ruled by a coalition of landlords and rich merchants. There were no royal precincts or imposing burial monuments, and there are few surviving stone or terra-cotta images that might represent kings, priests, or military commanders. It is possible that religion had advanced beyond the stage of spirit worship to belief in a single god or goddess of fertility. Presumably, priests at court prayed to this deity to maintain the fertility of the soil and guarantee the annual harvest.

As in Mesopotamia and Egypt, the Harappan economy was based primarily on agriculture. Wheat, barley, rice, and peas were apparently the primary crops. The presence of cotton seeds at various sites suggests that the Harappan peoples may have been the first to master the cultivation of this useful crop and possibly introduced it, along with rice, to other societies in the region. But Harappa also developed an extensive trading network that extended to Sumer and other civilizations to the west. Textiles and foodstuffs were apparently imported from Sumer in exchange for metals such as copper, lumber, precious stones, and various types of luxury goods. Much of this trade was conducted by ship via the Persian Gulf, although some undoubtedly went by land.

HARAPPAN CULTURE Archaeological remains indicate that the Indus Valley peoples possessed a culture as sophisticated in some ways as that of the Sumerians to the west. Although Harappan architecture was purely functional and shows little artistic sensitivity, the aesthetic quality of some of the pottery and sculpture is superb. Harappan painted pottery, wheel-turned and kiln-fired, rivals equivalent work produced elsewhere. Sculpture, however, was the Harappans' highest artistic achievement. Some artifacts possess a wonderful vitality of expression. Fired clay seals show a deft touch in carving animals such as elephants, tigers, rhinoceroses, and antelope, and figures made of copper or terra-cotta show a lively sensitivity and a sense of grace and movement that is almost modern.

A Mother Goddess. Between 2600 and 1900 B.C.E., Harappan craftsmen created a variety of terra-cotta objects, including whimsical toy animals, whistles, and tops, as well as dice, for children. Most remarkable, perhaps, are the numerous female figurines, such as the one shown here, with wide hips, bejeweled breasts, fan-shaped headdresses, and numerous strands of necklaces. Sharing their physical attributes with fertility deities in other early civilizations, these mother goddesses represent an idealized form of feminine beauty, which became a recurring feature of Indian art through the ages.

© DeA Picture Library/Art Resource, NY

Writing was another achievement of Harappan society and dates back at least to the beginning of the third millennium B.C.E. (see the Comparative Essay "Writing and Civilization" on p. 41). Unfortunately, the only surviving examples of Harappan writing are the pictographic symbols inscribed on clay seals. The script contained more than four hundred characters, but most are too stylized to be identified by their shape, and as noted earlier, scholars have been unable to decipher them. There are no apparent links with Mesopotamian scripts, although, as in Mesopotamia, the primary purpose of writing may have been to record commercial transactions. Until the script is deciphered, much about the Harappan civilization must remain, as one historian termed it, a fascinating enigma.

THE COLLAPSE OF HARAPPAN CIVILIZATION

One of the great mysteries of Harappan civilization is how it came to an end. Archaeologists working at Mohenjo-Daro have discovered signs of first a gradual decay and then a sudden destruction of the city and its inhabitants around 1500 B.C.E. Many of the surviving skeletons have been found in postures of running or hiding, reminiscent of the ruins of the Roman city of Pompeii, destroyed by the eruption of Mount Vesuvius in 79 C.E.

These tantalizing signs of flight before a sudden catastrophe once led scholars to surmise that the city of Mohenjo-Daro (the name was applied by archaeologists and means "city of the dead") and perhaps the remnants of Harappan civilization were destroyed by the Aryans, pastoral peoples from the north who arrived in the subcontinent around the middle of the second millennium B.C.E. Although the Aryans were considered to be less sophisticated culturally than the Harappans, like many nomadic peoples they excelled at the art of war. As in Mesopotamia and the Nile Valley, contacts between pastoral and agricultural peoples proved unstable and often ended in armed conflict. Today, however, historians are doubtful that the Aryan peoples were directly responsible for the final destruction of Mohenjo-Daro. More likely, Harappan civilization had already fallen on hard times, perhaps as a result of climatic change in the Indus Valley. Archaeologists have found clear signs of social decay, including evidence of trash in the streets, neglect of public services, and overcrowding in urban neighborhoods. Mohenjo-Daro itself may have been destroyed by an epidemic or by natural phenomena such as floods, an

Writing and Civilization

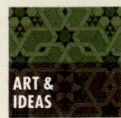

ART & IDEAS

In the year 3250 B.C.E., King Scorpion of Egypt issued an edict announcing a major victory for his army over rival forces in the region. Inscribed in limestone on a cliff face in the Nile River valley, that edict is perhaps the oldest surviving historical document in the world today.

According to prehistorians, human beings invented the first spoken language about 50,000 years ago. As human beings spread from Africa to other continents, that initial language gradually fragmented and evolved into innumerable separate tongues. By the time the agricultural revolution began about 10,000 B.C.E., there were perhaps nearly twenty distinct language families in existence around the world.

During the later stages of the agricultural revolution, the first writing systems also began to emerge in various places around the world (see Map 2.2). The first successful efforts were apparently achieved in Mesopotamia and Egypt, but knowledge of writing soon spread to peoples along the shores of the Mediterranean and in the Indus River valley in South Asia. Wholly independent systems were also invented in China and Mesoamerica. Writing was used for a variety of purposes. King Scorpion's edict suggests that one reason was to enable a ruler to communicate with his subjects on matters of official concern. In other cases, the purpose was to enable human beings to communicate with supernatural forces. In China and Egypt, for example, priests used writing to communicate with the gods. In Mesopotamia and in the Indus River valley, merchants used writing to record commercial and other legal transactions. Finally, writing was also used to present ideas in new ways, giving rise to such early Mesopotamian literature as *The Epic of Gilgamesh*.

How did these early written languages evolve into the complex systems in use today? In almost all cases, the first systems consisted of pictographs, pictorial images of various concrete objects such as trees, water, cattle, body parts, and the heavenly bodies. Eventually, the pictographs became more stylized to facilitate transcription—much as we often use a cursive script instead of block printing today. Finally, and most important for their future development, these

pictorial images began to take on specific phonetic meanings so that they could represent sounds in the written language. Most sophisticated written systems eventually evolved to a phonetic script, based on an alphabet of symbols to represent all sounds in the spoken language, but others went only part of the way by adding phonetic signs to the individual character to suggest pronunciation while keeping the essence of the original pictograph to indicate meaning. Most of the latter systems, such as hieroglyphics in Egypt and cuneiform in Mesopotamia, eventually became extinct, but the ancient Chinese writing system survives today, in greatly altered form.

 What are the various purposes for which writing systems were developed in the ancient world? What appears to have been the initial purpose for the development of the Harappan script?

Scala/Art Resource, NY

Harappan Seals. The Harappan peoples, like their contemporaries in Mesopotamia, developed a writing system to record their spoken language. Unfortunately, it has not yet been deciphered. Most extant examples of Harappan writing are found on fired clay seals depicting human figures and animals. These seals have been found in houses and were probably used to identify the owners of goods for sale. Other seals may have been used as amulets or have had other religious significance. Several depict religious figures or ritualistic scenes of sacrifice.

earthquake, or a shift in the course of the Indus River. If that was the case, any migrating peoples arrived in the area after the greatness of Harappan civilization had already passed.

WHO WERE THE ARYANS? Historians know relatively little about the origins and culture of the Aryans. The traditional view is that they were Indo-European-speaking peoples who inhabited vast areas in the steppes north and east of the Black and Caspian Seas. The Indo-Europeans were pastoral peoples who migrated from season to season in search of fodder for their herds. Historians have credited them with a number of

technological achievements, including the invention of horse-drawn chariots and the stirrup, both of which were eventually introduced throughout much of the Eurasian supercontinent.

Whereas many other Indo-European-speaking peoples moved westward and eventually settled throughout Europe, the Aryans moved south across the Hindu Kush into the plains of northern India. Between 1500 and 1000 B.C.E., they gradually advanced eastward from the Indus Valley, across the fertile plain of the Ganges, and later southward into the Deccan Plateau. Eventually, they extended their political mastery over the entire subcontinent and its Dravidian-speaking

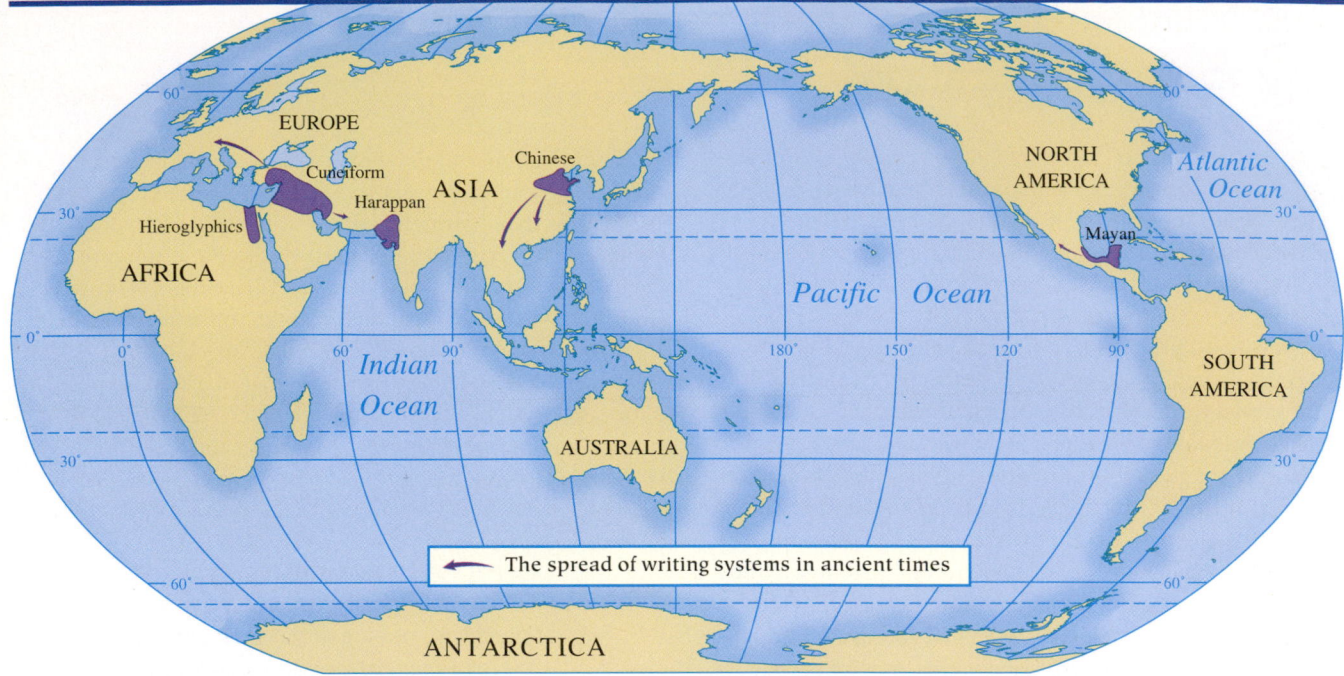

MAP 2.2 Writing Systems in the Ancient World. One of the chief characteristics of the first civilizations was the development of a system of written communication. © 2016 Cengage Learning

 Based on the Comparative Essay on p. 41, in what ways were these first writing systems similar, and how were they different?

inhabitants, although the indigenous culture survived to remain a prominent element in the evolution of traditional Indian civilization.

In recent years, a new theory has been proposed by some Indian historians, who contend that the Aryan peoples did not migrate into the Indian subcontinent from Central Asia, but were in fact descendants of the indigenous population that had originally created the Indus River civilization. Most scholars, however, continue to support the migration hypothesis, although the evidence is not conclusive. They point out that the spoken language of the Aryan people, known as Sanskrit, is widely recognized as a branch of the Indo-European family of languages. Moreover, the earliest account produced by the Aryan people themselves, known as the Rig Veda (RIK VAY-duh) (see the next section), describes a culture based primarily on pastoralism, a pursuit not particularly suited to the Indus River valley. A definitive solution to the debate will have to await further evidence.

The Aryans in India

 FOCUS QUESTION: What were some of the distinctive features of the class system introduced by the Aryan peoples, and what effects did it have on Indian civilization?

After they settled in India, the Aryans gradually adapted to the geographic realities of their new homeland and abandoned the

pastoral life for agricultural pursuits. They were assisted by the introduction of iron, which probably came from the Middle East, where it had been introduced by the Hittites (see Chapter 1) about 1500 B.C.E. The invention of the iron plow, along with the development of irrigation, allowed the Aryans and their indigenous subjects to clear the dense jungle growth along the Ganges River and transform the Ganges Valley into one of the richest agricultural regions in South Asia. The Aryans also developed their first writing system, based on the Aramaic script of the Middle East, and were thus able to transcribe the legends that previously had been passed down from generation to generation by memory (see the box "Writing and Civilization" on p. 41). Most of what is known about the early Aryans is based on oral traditions passed on in the Rig Veda, an ancient work that was written down after the Aryans arrived in India (it is one of several Vedas, or collections of sacred instructions and rituals).

From Chieftains to Kings

As in other Indo-European societies, each of the various Aryan tribes was led by a chieftain, called a **raja** (RAH-juh), who was assisted by a council of elders composed of other leading members of the community; like them, he was normally a member of the warrior class, called the *kshatriya* (kshuh-TREE-yuh). The chief derived his power from his ability to protect his people from rival groups, a skill that was crucial in the warring kingdoms and shifting alliances that were typical of early Aryan society. Though the rajas claimed

In the Beginning

RELIGION & PHILOSOPHY

AS THE INDIANS BEGAN TO SPECULATE about the nature of the cosmic order, they came to believe in the existence of a single monistic force in the universe, a form of ultimate reality called *Brahman*. Today the early form of Hinduism is sometimes called Brahmanism. In the Upanishads (oo-PAHN-ih-shahds), the concept began to emerge as an important element of Indian religious belief. It was the duty of the individual self—called the *Atman*—to achieve an understanding of this ultimate reality so that after death the self would merge in spiritual form with *Brahman*. Sometimes *Brahman* was described in more concrete terms as a creator god—eventually known as Vishnu—but more often in terms of a shadowy ultimate reality. In the following passage from the Upanishads, the author speculates on the nature of ultimate reality.

The Upanishads

In the beginning …, this world was just being, one only, without a second. Some people, no doubt, say: "In the beginning …, this world was just nonbeing, one only, without a second; from that nonbeing, being was produced." But how indeed … could it be so? How could being be produced from nonbeing? …

In the beginning this world was being alone, one only, without a second. Being thought to itself: "May I be many, may I procreate." It produced fire. That fire thought to itself: "May I be many, may I procreate." It produced water. Therefore, whenever a person grieves or perspires, then it is from fire [heat] alone that water is produced. That water thought to itself: "May I be many, may I procreate." It produced food; it is from water alone that food for eating is produced…. That divinity (Being) thought to itself: "Well, having entered into these three divinities [fire, water, and food] by means of this living self, let me develop names and forms."

How would you compare this passage from the Upanishads with the accounts about the origins of life from Egyptian and Hebrew sources as cited in Chapter 1?

Source: From *The Upanishads*, tr. Juan Mascaro. Viking Press, 1965.

---

to be representatives of the gods, they were not viewed as gods themselves.

As Aryan society grew in size and complexity, the chieftains began to be transformed into kings, usually called **maharajas** (mah-huh-RAH-juhs) ("great rajas"). Nevertheless, the tradition that the ruler did not possess absolute authority remained strong. Like all human beings, the ruler was required to follow the *dharma* (DAR-muh), a set of laws that set behavioral standards for all individuals and classes in Indian society.

THE IMPACT OF THE GREEKS While competing groups squabbled for precedence in India, powerful new empires were rising to the west. First came the Persian Empire of Cyrus and Darius. Then came the Greeks. After two centuries of sporadic rivalry and warfare, the Greeks achieved a brief period of regional dominance in the late fourth century B.C.E. with the rise of Macedonia under Alexander the Great. Alexander had heard of the riches of India,

Alexander the Great's Movements in Asia

and in 330 B.C.E., after conquering Persia, he launched an invasion of the east (see Chapter 4). In 326, his armies arrived in the plains of northwestern India and the Indus River valley. They departed almost as suddenly as they had come, leaving in their wake Greek administrators and a veneer of cultural influence that would affect the area for generations to come.

The Mauryan Empire

The Alexandrian conquest was a brief interlude in the history of the Indian subcontinent, but it played a formative role, for on the heels of Alexander's departure came the rise of the first dynasty to control much of the region. The founder of the new state, who took the royal title Chandragupta Maurya (chun-druh-GOOP-tuh MOWR-yuh) (324–301 B.C.E.), drove out the Greek administrators that Alexander had left behind and solidified his control over the northern Indian plain. He established the capital of his new Mauryan Empire at Pataliputra (pah-tah-lee-POO-truh) (modern Patna) in the Ganges Valley (see Map 2.3 on p. 55). Little is known of his origins, although some sources say he had originally fought on the side of the invading Greek forces but then angered Alexander with his outspoken advice.

Little, too, is known of Chandragupta Maurya's empire. Most accounts of his reign rely on the scattered remnants of a lost work written by Megasthenes (muh-GAS-thuh-neez), a Greek ambassador to the Mauryan court, in about 302 B.C.E. Chandragupta Maurya was apparently advised by a brilliant court official named Kautilya (kow-TIL-yuh), whose name has been attached to a treatise on politics called the *Arthasastra*. The work actually dates from a later time, but it may well reflect Kautilya's ideas.

Although the author of the *Arthasastra* follows Aryan tradition in stating that the happiness of the king lies in the happiness of his subjects, the treatise also asserts that when the sacred law of the *dharma* and practical politics collide, the latter must take precedence: "Whenever there is disagreement between history and sacred law or between evidence and sacred law, then the matter should be settled in accordance with sacred law. But whenever sacred law is in conflict with rational law, then reason shall be held authoritative."[1] The *Arthasastra* also emphasizes ends rather than means, achieved results rather than the methods employed. For this reason, it has often been compared to Machiavelli's famous political treatise of the Italian Renaissance, *The Prince*, written more than a thousand years later (see Chapter 15).

As described in the *Arthasastra*, Chandragupta Maurya's government was highly centralized and even despotic: "It is power and power alone which, only when exercised by the king with impartiality, and in proportion to guilt, over his son or his enemy, maintains both this world and the next."[2] The king possessed a large army and a secret police responsible to his orders (according to the Greek ambassador Megasthenes, Chandragupta Maurya was chronically fearful of assassination, a not unrealistic concern for someone who had allegedly come to power by violence). Reportedly, all food was tasted in his presence, and he made a practice of never sleeping twice in the same bed in his sumptuous palace. To guard against corruption, a board of censors was empowered to investigate cases of possible malfeasance and incompetence within the bureaucracy.

The ruler's authority beyond the confines of the capital may often have been limited, however. The empire was divided into provinces that were ruled by governors. At first, most of these governors were appointed by and reported to the ruler, but later the position became hereditary. The provinces themselves were divided into districts, each under a chief magistrate appointed by the governor. At the base of the government pyramid was the village, where the vast majority of the Indian people lived. The village was governed by a council of elders; membership in the council was normally hereditary and was shared by the wealthiest families in the village.

Caste and Class: Social Structures in Ancient India

When the Aryans arrived in India, they already possessed a social system based on a ruling warrior class and other groupings characteristic of a pastoral society. In the subcontinent, they encountered peoples living by farming or, in some cases, by other pursuits such as fishing, hunting, or food gathering. Although the immediate consequences of this mixture of cultures are still unclear, the ultimate result was the emergence of a set of social institutions that continues to have relevance down to the present day.

THE CLASS SYSTEM At the crux of the social system was the concept of a hierarchical division of society that placed each individual within a ritual framework that defined the person's occupation and status within the broader community. In part, this division may have been an outgrowth of attitudes held by the Aryan peoples with regard to the indigenous population. The Aryans, who followed primarily pastoral pursuits, tended to look askance at their new neighbors, who lived by tilling the soil. Further, the Aryans, a mostly light-skinned people, were contemptuous of the indigenous peoples, who were darker. Light skin came to imply high status, whereas dark skin suggested the opposite.

The concept of color, however, was only the physical manifestation of a division that took place in Indian society on the basis of economic functions. Indian classes (called **varna**, literally, "color," and commonly but mistakenly translated as "castes" in English) did not simply reflect an informal division of labor. Instead, at least in theory, they were a set of rigid social classifications that determined not only one's occupation but also one's status in society and one's hope for ultimate salvation (see "Escaping the Wheel of Life" later in this chapter). There were five major *varna* in Indian society in ancient times (see the box "Social Classes in Ancient India" on p. 45). At the top were two classes, collectively viewed as the aristocracy, which represented the ruling elites in Aryan society prior to their arrival in India: the priests and the warriors.

The priestly class, known as the **brahmins**, was usually considered to be at the top of the social scale. Descended from seers who had advised the ruler on religious matters in Aryan tribal society—*brahmin* meant "one possessed of **Brahman**" (BRAH-mun), a term for the supreme god—they were eventually transformed into an official class after their religious role declined in importance. Megasthenes described this class as follows:

> From the time of their conception in the womb they are under the care and guardianship of learned men who go to the mother and … give her prudent hints and counsels, and the women who listen to them most willingly are thought to be the most fortunate in their offspring. After their birth the children are in the care of one person after another, and as they advance in years their masters are men of superior accomplishments. The philosophers reside in a grove in front of the city within a moderate-sized enclosure. They live in a simple style and lie on pallets of straw and [deer] skins. They abstain from animal food and sexual pleasures, and occupy their time in listening to serious discourse and in imparting knowledge to willing ears.[3]

The second class was the *kshatriya*, the warriors. Although often listed below the *brahmins* in social status, many *kshatriyas* were probably descended from the ruling warrior class in Aryan society prior to the conquest of India and thus may have originally ranked socially above the *brahmins*, although they were ranked lower in religious terms. Like the *brahmins*, the *kshatriyas* were originally identified with a single occupation—fighting—but as the character of Aryan society changed, they often switched to other forms of employment. At the same

Social Classes in Ancient India

FAMILY & SOCIETY

THE *LAW OF MANU* IS A SET OF BEHAVIORAL NORMS that, according to tradition, were prescribed by India's mythical founding ruler, Manu. The treatise was probably written in the first or second century B.C.E. The following excerpt describes the various social classes in India and their prescribed duties. Many scholars doubt that the social system in India was ever as rigid as it was portrayed here, and some suggest that upper-class Indians may have used the idea of *varna* to enhance their own status in society.

The *Law of Manu*

For the sake of the preservation of this entire creation, the Exceedingly Resplendent One [the Creator of the Universe] assigned separate duties to the classes which had sprung from his mouth, arms, thighs, and feet.

Teaching, studying, performing sacrificial rites, so too making others perform sacrificial rites, and giving away and receiving gifts—these he assigned to the [brahmins].

Protection of the people, giving away of wealth, performance of sacrificial rites, study, and nonattachment to sensual pleasures—these are, in short, the duties of a *kshatriya*.

Tending of cattle, giving away of wealth, performance of sacrificial rites, study, trade and commerce, usury, and agriculture—these are the occupations of a *vaisya*.

The Lord has prescribed only one occupation [*karma*] for a *sudra*, namely, service without malice of even these other three classes.

Of created beings, those which are animate are the best; of the animate, those which subsist by means of their intellect; of the intelligent, men are the best; and of men, the [brahmins] are traditionally declared to be the best.

The code of conduct—prescribed by scriptures and ordained by sacred tradition—constitutes the highest *dharma;* hence a twice-born person, conscious of his own Self [seeking spiritual salvation], should be always scrupulous in respect of it.

 Based on this description, how does the class system in ancient India compare with social class divisions in other societies in Asia? Why do you think the class system, as described here, developed in India? What is the difference between the class system (varna) and the jati (discussed later in this chapter)?

Source: Manu Smrti 3.55–57: Ed. J. Jolly. London: Trubner, 1887 (Trubner Oriental Series)

---

time, new families from other classes were sometimes tacitly accepted into the ranks of the warriors.

The third-ranked class in Indian society was the **vaisya** (VISH-yuh) (literally, "commoner"). The *vaisyas* were usually viewed in economic terms as the merchant class. Some historians have speculated that the *vaisyas* were originally guardians of the tribal herds but that after settling in India, many moved into commercial pursuits. Megasthenes noted that members of this class "alone are permitted to hunt and keep cattle and to sell beasts of burden or to let them out on hire. In return for clearing the land of wild beasts and birds which infest sown fields, they receive an allowance of corn from the king.

CHRONOLOGY	Ancient India
Harappan civilization	c. 2600–1900 B.C.E.
Arrival of the Aryans	c. 1500 B.C.E.
Life of Gautama Buddha	c. 560–480 B.C.E.
Invasion of India by Alexander the Great	326 B.C.E.
Mauryan dynasty founded	324 B.C.E.
Reign of Chandragupta Maurya	324–301 B.C.E.
Reign of Ashoka	269–232 B.C.E.
Collapse of Mauryan dynasty	183 B.C.E.
Rise of Kushan kingdom	c. first century C.E.

They lead a wandering life and dwell in tents."[4] Although this class was ranked below the first two in social status, it shared with them the privilege of being considered "**twice-born**," a term referring to a ceremony at puberty whereby young males were initiated into adulthood and introduced into Indian society. After the ceremony, male members of the top three classes were allowed to wear the "sacred thread" for the remainder of their lives.

Below the three "twice-born" classes were the **sudras** (SOO-druhs *or* SHOO-druhs), who represented the great bulk of the Indian population. The *sudras* were not considered fully Aryan, and the term probably originally referred to the indigenous population. Most *sudras* were peasants or artisans or worked at other forms of manual labor. They had only limited rights in society. In recent years, DNA samples have revealed that most upper-class South Indians share more genetic characteristics with Europeans than their lower-class counterparts do, a finding that supports the hypothesis that the Aryans established their political and social dominance over the indigenous population.

At the lowest level of Indian society, and in fact not even considered a legitimate part of the class system, were the untouchables (also known as outcastes or **pariahs**). The untouchables probably originated as a slave class consisting of prisoners of war, criminals, ethnic minorities, and other groups considered outside Indian society. Even after slavery was outlawed, the untouchables were given menial and degrading tasks that other Indians would not accept, such as collecting trash, handling dead bodies, or serving as butchers or tanners. One historian estimates that they may have accounted for a little more than 5 percent of the total population of India in antiquity.

The lives of the untouchables were extremely demeaning. They were regarded as being not fully human, and their very presence was considered polluting to members of the other *varna*. No Indian would touch or eat food handled or prepared by an untouchable. Untouchables lived in ghettos and, according to a foreign observer, were required to tap two sticks together to announce their approach when they traveled outside their quarters so that others could avoid them.

Technically, these class divisions were absolute. Individuals supposedly were born, lived, and died in the same class. In practice, upward or downward mobility probably took place, and there was undoubtedly some flexibility in economic functions. But throughout most of Indian history, class taboos remained strict. Members generally were not permitted to marry outside their class (although in practice, men were occasionally allowed to marry below their class but not above it). At first, attitudes toward the handling of food were relatively loose, but eventually that taboo grew stronger, and social mores dictated that sharing meals and marrying outside one's class were unacceptable.

THE JATI The people of ancient India did not belong to a particular class as individuals but as part of a larger kin group commonly referred to as the *jati* (JAH-tee) (in Portuguese, *casta*, which evolved into the English term *caste*), a system of extended families that originated in ancient India and still exists in somewhat changed form today. Although the origins of the *jati* system are unknown (there are no indications of strict class distinctions in Harappan society), the *jati* eventually became identified with a specific kinship group living in a specific area and carrying out a specific function in society. Each *jati* was identified with a particular *varna*, and each had its own separate economic function.

Jatis were thus the basic social organization into which traditional Indian society was divided. Each *jati* was composed of hundreds or thousands of individual nuclear families and was governed by its own council of elders. Membership in this ruling council was usually hereditary and was based on the wealth or social status of particular families within the community.

In theory, each *jati* was assigned a particular form of economic activity. Obviously, though, not all families in a given *jati* could take part in the same vocation, and as time went on, members of a single *jati* commonly engaged in several different lines of work. Sometimes an entire *jati* would have to move its location in order to continue a particular form of activity. In other cases, a *jati* would adopt an entirely new occupation in order to remain in a certain area. Such changes in habitat or occupation introduced the possibility of movement up or down the social scale. In this way, an entire *jati* could sometimes engage in upward mobility, even though

that normally was not possible for individuals, who were tied to their class identity for life.

The class system in ancient India may sound highly constricting, but there were persuasive social and economic reasons why it survived for so many centuries. In the first place, it provided an identity for individuals in a highly hierarchical society. Although an individual might rank lower on the social scale than members of other classes, it was always possible to find others ranked even lower. Class was also a means for new groups, such as mountain tribal people, to achieve a recognizable place in the broader community. Perhaps equally important, the *jati* was a primitive form of welfare system. Each *jati* was obliged to provide for any of its members who were poor or destitute. It also provided an element of stability in a society that all too often was in a state of political turmoil.

Daily Life in Ancient India

Beyond these rigid social stratifications was the Indian family. Not only was life centered around the family, but the family, not the individual, was the most basic unit in society.

THE FAMILY The ideal social unit was an extended family, with three generations living under the same roof. It was essentially patriarchal, except along the Malabar coast, near the southwestern tip of the subcontinent, where a matriarchal form of social organization prevailed down to modern times. In the rest of India, the oldest male traditionally possessed legal authority over the entire family unit.

The family was linked together in a religious sense to its ancestral members by a series of commemorative rites. Family ceremonies were conducted to honor the departed and to link the living and the dead. The male family head was responsible for leading the ritual. At his death, his eldest son had the duty of conducting the funeral rites.

The importance of the father and the son in family ritual underlined the importance of males in Indian society. Male superiority was expressed in a variety of ways. Women could not serve as priests (although some were accepted as seers), nor were they normally permitted to study the Vedas. In general, males had a monopoly on education, since the primary goal of learning to read was to conduct family rituals. In high-class families, young men, after having been initiated into the sacred thread, began Vedic studies with a **guru** (teacher). Some then went on to higher studies in one of the major cities. The goal of such an education might be either professional or religious. Such young men were not supposed to marry until after twelve years of study.

MARRIAGE In general, only males could inherit property, except in a few cases when there were no sons. According to law, a woman was always considered a minor. Divorce was prohibited, although it sometimes took place. According to the *Arthasastra*, a wife who had been deserted by her husband could seek a divorce. Polygamy was fairly rare and apparently occurred mainly among the higher classes, but husbands were permitted to take a second wife if the first was barren. Producing children was an important aspect of marriage, both because children provided security for their parents in old age and because they were a physical proof of male potency. Child marriage was common for young girls, whether because of the desire for children or because daughters represented an economic liability to their parents. But perhaps the most graphic symbol of women's subjection to men was the ritual of *sati* (suh-TEE) (often written *suttee*), which encouraged the wife to throw herself on her dead husband's funeral pyre. The Greek visitor Megasthenes reported "that he had heard from some persons of wives burning themselves along with their deceased husbands and doing so gladly; and that those women who refused to burn themselves were held in disgrace."[5] All in all, it was undoubtedly a difficult existence. According to the *Law of Manu*, an early treatise on social organization and behavior in ancient India, probably written in the first or second century B.C.E., a woman was subordinated to men throughout her life—first to her father, then to her husband, and finally to her sons:

> She should do nothing independently
>   even in her own house.
> In childhood subject to her father,
>   in youth to her husband,
> and when her husband is dead to her sons,
>   she should never enjoy independence....
> Though he be uncouth and prone to pleasure,
>   though he have no good points at all,
> the virtuous wife should ever
>   worship her lord as a god.[6]

THE ROLE OF WOMEN At the root of female subordination to the male was the practical fact that as in most agricultural societies, men did most of the work in the fields. Females were viewed as having little utility outside the home and indeed were considered an economic burden, since parents were obliged to provide a dowry to acquire a husband for a daughter. Female children also appeared to offer little advantage in maintaining the family unit, since they joined the families of their husbands after the wedding ceremony.

Despite all of these indications of female subjection to the male, there are numerous signs that in some ways women often played an influential role in Indian society, and the code of behavior set out in the *Law of Manu* stressed that they should be treated with respect (see the box "The Position of Women in Ancient India" on p. 48). Indians appeared to be fascinated by female sexuality, and tradition held that women often used their sexual powers to achieve domination over men. The author of the Mahabharata, a vast epic of early Indian society, complained that "the fire has never too many logs, the ocean never too many rivers, death never too many living souls, and fair-eyed woman never too many men." Despite the legal and social constraints, women often played an important role within the family unit, and many were admired and honored for their talents. It is probably significant that paintings and sculpture from ancient and medieval India frequently show women in a role equal to that of men,

Female Earth Spirit. This earth spirit, carved on a gatepost of the Buddhist stupa at Sanchi 2,200 years ago, illustrates how earlier representations of the fertility goddess were incorporated into Buddhist art. Women were revered as powerful fertility symbols and considered dangerous when menstruating or immediately after giving birth. Voluptuous and idealized, the earth spirit was believed to be able to cause a tree to blossom by wrapping her leg around its trunk or even merely touching a branch with her arm.

and the tradition of the henpecked husband is as prevalent in India as in many Western societies today.

The Economy

The arrival of the Aryans did not drastically change the economic character of Indian society. Not only did most Aryans eventually take up farming, but it is likely that agriculture expanded rapidly under Aryan rule with the invention of the iron plow and the spread of northern Indian culture into the Deccan Plateau. One consequence of this process was to shift the focus of Indian culture from the Indus Valley farther eastward to the Ganges River valley, which even today is one of the most densely populated regions on earth. The flatter areas in the Deccan Plateau and in the coastal plains were also turned into cropland.

INDIAN FARMERS For most Indian farmers, life was harsh. Among the most fortunate were those who owned their own land, although they were required to pay taxes to the state.

The Position of Women in Ancient India

FAMILY & SOCIETY

THE AMBIVALENT ATTITUDE TOWARD WOMEN IN ANCIENT INDIA is evident in this passage from the *Law of Manu*, which states that respect for women is the responsibility of men. At the same time, it also makes clear that a woman's place is in the home.

The *Law of Manu*

Women must be honored and adorned by their father, brothers, husbands, and brother-in-law who desire great good fortune.

Where women, verily, are honored, there the gods rejoice, where, however they are not honored, there all sacred rites prove fruitless.

Where the female relations live in grief—that family soon perishes completely; where, however, they do not suffer from any grievance—that family always prospers....

The father who does not give away his daughter in marriage at the proper time is censurable; censurable is the husband who does not approach his wife in due season; and after the husband is dead, the son, verily is censurable, who does not protect his mother.

Even against the slightest provocations should women be particularly guarded; for unguarded they would bring grief to both the families.

Regarding this as the highest *dharma* of all four classes, husbands though weak, must strive to protect their wives.

His own offspring, character, family, self, and *dharma* does one protect when he protects his wife scrupulously....

The husband should engage his wife in the collections and expenditure of his wealth, in cleanliness, in *dharma*, in cooking food for the family, and in looking after the necessities of the household....

Women destined to bear children, enjoying great good fortune, deserving of worship, the resplendent lights of homes on the one hand and divinities of good luck who reside in the houses on the other—between these there is no difference whatsoever.

 How do these attitudes toward women compare with those we have encountered in the Middle East and North Africa?

Source: Manu Smrti 3.55–57: Ed. J. Jolly. London: Trubner, 1887 (Trubner Oriental Series)

Many others were sharecroppers or landless laborers. They were subject to the vicissitudes of the market and often paid exorbitant rents to their landlord. Concentration of land in large holdings was limited by the tradition of dividing property among all the sons, but large estates worked by hired laborers or rented out to sharecroppers were not uncommon, particularly in areas where local rajas derived much of their wealth from their property.

Another problem for Indian farmers was the unpredictability of the climate. India is in the monsoon zone. The monsoon is a seasonal wind pattern in southern Asia that blows from the southwest during the summer months and from the northeast during the winter. The southwest monsoon, originating in the Indian Ocean, is commonly marked by heavy rains. When the rains were late, thousands starved, particularly in the drier areas, which were especially dependent on rainfall. Strong governments attempted to deal with such problems by building state-operated granaries and maintaining the irrigation works, but strong governments were rare, and famine was probably all too common. The staple crops in the north were wheat, barley, and millet, with wet rice common in the fertile river valleys. In the south, grain and vegetables were supplemented by various tropical products, cotton, and spices such as pepper, ginger, cinnamon, and saffron.

TRADE AND MANUFACTURING By no means were all Indians farmers. As time passed, India became one of the most advanced trading and manufacturing civilizations in the ancient world. After the rise of the Mauryas, India's role in regional trade began to expand, and the subcontinent became a major transit point in a vast commercial network that extended from the rim of the Pacific Ocean to the Middle East and the Mediterranean Sea. This regional trade went both by sea and by camel caravan. Maritime trade across the Indian Ocean may have begun as early as the fifth century B.C.E. It extended eastward as far as Southeast Asia and China and southward as far as the straits between Africa and the island of Madagascar. Westward to Egypt went spices, teakwood, perfumes, jewels, textiles, precious stones and ivory, and wild animals. In return, India received gold, tin, lead, and wine. The subcontinent had become a major crossroads of trade in the ancient world.

India's expanding role as a manufacturing and commercial hub was undoubtedly a spur to the growth of the state. Under Chandragupta Maurya, the central government became actively involved in commercial and manufacturing activities. It owned mines and land and undoubtedly earned massive profits from its role in regional commerce. Separate government departments were established for trade, agriculture, mining, and the manufacture of weapons, and the movement of private goods was vigorously taxed. Nevertheless, a significant private sector also flourished; it was dominated by great caste guilds, which monopolized key sectors of the economy. A money economy probably came into operation during the second century B.C.E., when copper and gold coins were introduced from the Middle East. This in turn led to the

COMPARATIVE ILLUSTRATION

INTERACTION & EXCHANGE

The First Money. Before the invention of metal coins, many societies used items from nature like beads or shells as an early form of currency. Cowry shells (left photo) have been found in coastal areas throughout the Indian Ocean; their use later spread to China and as far as Africa, where they continued to be used until the early modern era. The first metal coins appeared around 500 B.C.E., when Greek communities along the Turkish coast began to mint silver coins decorated with portraits of rulers or deities. The practice spread to Central and South Asia in the fourth century B.C.E. with the armies of Alexander the Great. After his departure, Hellenistic kingdoms founded in the region minted beautiful silver and gold coins in the Greek style and carried them southward with the Greco-Bactrian invasion of northwest India (symbolized by the elephant headdress on King Demetrius I in the right photo) in 180 B.C.E. From that time on, metal coins were used for most important transactions in South Asian societies, with cowry shells used for items of lesser value.

Q *How does the monetary system used in ancient India compare with that practiced in ancient societies in the Mediterranean and the Middle East?*

development of banking. But village trade continued to be conducted by means of cowry shells (highly polished shells used as a medium of exchange throughout much of Africa and Asia) or barter throughout the ancient period.

Escaping the Wheel of Life: The Religious World of Ancient India

Q FOCUS QUESTIONS: What are the main tenets of Brahmanism and Buddhism? How did they differ, and how did each religion influence Indian civilization?

Like Indian politics and society, Indian religion is a blend of Aryan and Dravidian culture. The intermingling of those two civilizations gave rise to an extraordinarily complex set of religious beliefs and practices, filled with diversity and contrast. Out of this cultural mix came two of the world's great religions, Buddhism and Hinduism, and several smaller ones, including Jainism and Sikhism. Early Aryan religious beliefs, however, are known to historians as **Brahmanism**. In time, Brahmanical beliefs and practices would give rise to Hinduism, as will be discussed in Chapter 9. Here we will focus on the earliest religious traditions and on the origins of Buddhism.

Brahmanism

Evidence about the earliest religious beliefs of the Aryan peoples comes primarily from sacred texts such as the Vedas, four collections of hymns and religious ceremonies transmitted by memory through the centuries by Aryan priests. Many of these religious ideas were probably common to all of the Indo-European peoples before their separation into different groups at least four thousand years ago. Early Aryan beliefs were based on the common concept of a pantheon of gods and goddesses representing great forces of nature similar to the immortals of Greek mythology. The Aryan ancestor of the Greek father-god Zeus, for example, may have been the deity known in early Aryan tradition as Dyaus (see Chapter 4).

The parent god Dyaus was a somewhat distant figure, however, who was eventually overshadowed by other, more functional gods possessing more familiar human traits. For a while, the primary Aryan god was the great warrior god Indra. Indra summoned the Aryan tribal peoples to war and was represented in nature by thunder. Later, Indra declined in importance and was replaced by Varuna, lord of justice. Other gods and goddesses represented various forces of nature or the needs of human beings, such as fire, fertility, and wealth.

The concept of sacrifice was a key element in Aryan religious belief in Vedic times. As in many other ancient cultures, the practice may have begun as human sacrifice, but later animals were used as substitutes. The priestly class, the *brahmins*, played a key role in these ceremonies.

Another element of Indian religious belief in ancient times was the ideal of *asceticism*. Although there is no reference to such practices in the Vedas, by the sixth century B.C.E., self-discipline or subjecting oneself to painful stimuli had begun to replace sacrifice as a means of placating or communicating with the gods. Apparently, the original motive for asceticism was to achieve magical powers, but later, in the Upanishads—a set of commentaries on the Vedas compiled in the sixth century B.C.E.—it was seen as a means of spiritual meditation that would enable the practitioner to reach beyond material reality to a world of truth and bliss beyond earthly joy and sorrow. It is possible that another motive was to permit those with strong religious convictions to communicate directly with metaphysical reality without having to rely on the priestly class at court.

Asceticism, of course, has been practiced in other religions, including Christianity and Islam, but it seems particularly identified with Hinduism, the religion that emerged from the early Indian religious tradition. Eventually, asceticism evolved into the modern practice of body training that we know as *yoga* ("union"), which is accepted today as a meaningful element of Hindu religious practice.

REINCARNATION Another new concept that probably began to appear around the time the Upanishads were written was **reincarnation**. This is the idea that the individual soul is reborn in a different form after death and progresses through several existences on the wheel of life until it reaches its final destination in a union with the Great World Soul, *Brahman*. Because life is harsh, this final release is the objective of all living souls. From this concept comes the term *Brahmanism*, referring to the early Aryan religious tradition.

A key element in this process is the idea of **karma**—that one's rebirth in a next life is determined by one's actions (*karma*) in this life (see Opposing Viewpoints "The Search for Truth" on p. 51). Hinduism, as it emerged from Brahmanism, placed all living species on a vast scale of existence, including the four classes and the untouchables in human society. The current status of an individual soul, then, is not simply a cosmic accident but the inevitable result of actions that that soul has committed in its past existence.

At the top of the scale are the *brahmins*, who by definition are closest to ultimate release from the law of reincarnation. The *brahmins* are followed in descending order by the other classes in human society and the world of the beasts. Within the animal kingdom, an especially high position is reserved for the cow, which even today is revered by Hindus as a sacred beast. Some scholars have speculated that the unique role played by the cow in Hinduism derives from the value of cattle in Aryan pastoral society. But others have pointed out that cattle were a source of both money and food and suggest that the cow's sacred position may have descended from the concept of the sacred bull in Harappan culture.

The concept of *karma* is governed by the *dharma*, or the law. A law regulating human behavior, the *dharma* imposes different requirements on different individuals depending on their

The Searcher. In their search for truth and the ultimate reality, some early followers of Brahmanism embarked on a lifelong retreat from the material world. The holy scripture for such early ascetics was the Upanishads, a collection of writings dating from the middle of the first millennium B.C.E. extolling a life of privation and self-denial. The practice continues today, as this photograph of an Indian mendicant wandering in the mountains of the Deccan Plateau attests.

© William J. Duiker

status in society. Those high on the social scale, such as *brahmins* and *kshatriyas*, are held to a stricter form of behavior than *sudras* are. The *brahmin*, for example, is expected to abstain from eating meat, because that would entail the killing of another living being, thus interrupting its *karma*.

How the concept of reincarnation originated is not known, although it was apparently not unusual for early peoples to believe that the individual soul would be reborn in a different form in a later life. In any case, in India the concept may have had practical causes as well as consequences. In the first place, it tended to provide religious sanction for the rigid class divisions that had begun to emerge in Indian society after the arrival of the Aryans, and it provided moral and political justification for the privileges of those on the higher end of the scale.

At the same time, the concept of reincarnation provided certain compensations for those lower on the ladder of life. For example, it gave hope to the poor that if they behaved properly in this life, they might improve their condition in the next. It also provided a means for unassimilated groups such as ethnic minorities to find a place in Indian society while at the same time permitting them to maintain their distinctive way of life.

OPPOSING ✕ VIEWPOINTS

The Search for Truth

RELIGION & PHILOSOPHY

AT THE TIME THE RIG VEDA WAS ORIGINALLY COMPOSED IN THE SECOND MILLENNIUM B.C.E., *brahmins* at court believed that the best way to communicate with the gods was through sacrifice, a procedure that was carried out through the intermediation of the fire god Agni. The first selection is an incantation uttered by priests at the sacrificial ceremony.

By the middle of the first millennium B.C.E., however, the tradition of offering sacrifices had come under attack by opponents, who argued that the best way to seek truth and tranquility was by renouncing material existence and adopting the life of a wandering mendicant. In the second selection, from the Mundaka Upanishad, an advocate of this position forcefully presents his views. The similarity with the fervent believers of early Christianity, who renounced the corrupting forces of everyday life by seeking refuge in isolated monasteries in the desert, is striking.

The Rig Veda

I extol Agni, the household priest, the divine minister of the sacrifice, the chief priest, the bestower of blessings.

May that Agni, who is to be extolled by ancient and modern seers, conduct the gods here.

Through Agni may one gain day by day wealth and welfare which is glorious and replete with heroic sons.

O Agni, the sacrifice and ritual which you encompass on every side, that indeed goes to the gods.

May Agni, the chief priest, who possesses the insight of a sage, who is truthful, widely renowned, and divine, come here with the gods.

O Agni, O Angiras ["messenger"], whatever prosperity you bring to the pious is indeed in accordance with your true function.

O Agni, illuminator of darkness, day by day we approach you with holy thought bringing homage to you.

Presiding at ritual functions, the brightly shining custodian of the cosmic order [*rta*], thriving in your own realm.

O Agni, be easy of access to us as a father to his son. Join us for our well-being.

The Mundaka Upanishad

Unsteady, indeed, are those boats in the form of sacrifices, eighteen in number, in which is prescribed only the inferior work. The fools who delight in this sacrificial ritual as the highest spiritual good go again and again through the cycle of old age and death.

Abiding in the midst of ignorance, wise only according to their own estimate, thinking themselves to be learned, but really obtuse, these fools go round in a circle like blind men led by one who is himself blind.

Abiding manifoldly in ignorance they, all the same, like immature children think to themselves: "We have accomplished our aim." Since the performers of sacrificial ritual do not realize the truth because of passion, therefore, they, the wretched ones, sink down from heaven when the merit that qualified them for the higher world becomes exhausted.

Regarding sacrifice and merit as most important, the deluded ones do not know of any other higher spiritual good. Having enjoyed themselves only for a time on top of the heaven won by good deeds [sacrifice, etc.] they reenter this world or a still lower one.

Those who practice penance [*tapas*] and faith in the forest, the tranquil ones, the knowers of truth, living the life of wandering mendicancy—they depart, freed from passion, through the door of the sun, to where dwells verily … the imperishable Soul [*atman*].

Having scrutinized the worlds won by sacrificial rites, a *brahmin* should arrive at nothing but disgust. The world that was not made is not won by what is done [i.e., by sacrifice]. For the sake of that knowledge he should go with sacrificial fuel in hand as a student, in all humility to a preceptor [*guru*] who is well versed in the [Vedic] scriptures and also firm in the realization of Brahman.

Unto him who has approached him in proper form, whose mind is tranquil, who has attained peace, does the knowing teacher teach, in its very truth, that knowledge about Brahman by means of which one knows … the only Reality.

 In which passages in these two documents do you find a reference to the idea of karma? Which document makes use of the concept, and how? What role does asceticism play in these documents?

Source: From *Sources of Indian Tradition*, Vol. 1, 2e, by Ainslee Embree. Copyright © 1988 by Columbia University Press.

The ultimate goal of achieving "good" *karma*, as we have seen, was to escape the cycle of existence. To the sophisticated, the nature of that release was a spiritual union of the individual soul with the Great World Soul, *Brahman*, described in the Upanishads as a form of dreamless sleep, free from earthly desires.

Popular Religion

Little is known about the religious beliefs of the vast majority of the Indian people during this formative stage in South Asian society. In all likelihood, popular religion during the first millennium B.C.E. was a distant reflection of its counterpart in India today, which is peopled with a multitude of very human gods and goddesses. It has been estimated that the Hindu pantheon contains more than 33,000 deities. Only a small number are primary ones, however, notably the so-called trinity of gods: Brahman the Creator, Vishnu the Preserver, and Shiva (SHIV-uh) (originally the Vedic god Rudra) the Destroyer. Although Brahman (sometimes in his concrete form called Brahma) is considered to be the highest god, Vishnu and Shiva take precedence in the devotional exercises of many Hindus, who can be roughly divided into Vishnuites and Shaivites. In addition to the trinity of gods, all of whom have wives with readily identifiable roles and personalities, there are countless minor deities, each again with his or her own specific function. A notable example is Ganesha, described in Indian literature as a son of Shiva who was accidentally beheaded by his father in a fit of anger. When Shiva repented of his action, he provided his son with the head of an elephant. Even today the widely revered Ganesha is often viewed as the god of good fortune.

The rich variety and the earthy character of many of these deities are somewhat misleading, however, for Hindus regard the multitude of gods simply as different manifestations of one ultimate reality. The various deities also provide a way for ordinary Indians to personify their religious feelings. Even though some individuals among the early Aryans attempted to communicate with the gods through animal sacrifice or asceticism, most Indians undoubtedly sought to satisfy their own individual religious needs through devotion, which they expressed through ritual ceremonies and offerings at a temple. Such offerings were not only a way of seeking salvation but also a means of satisfying all the aspirations of daily life.

Over the centuries, Indian religious belief changed radically from its origins in Aryan pastoral society. An early belief in deities representing forces of nature gradually gave way to a more elitist system, with a priestly class at court performing sacrifices in order to obtain heavenly favors. During the first millennium B.C.E., religious belief began to evolve into a more personal experience, with an emphasis on ethics as a means of obtaining a union between the individual soul (**Atman**) and the ultimate reality (*Brahman*).[7]

Such a concept, however, was probably too ethereal for the average Indian, who looked for a more concrete form of heavenly salvation, a place of beauty and bliss after a life of disease and privation. In later centuries, the Brahmanical beliefs and practices of early Aryan society would gradually be replaced by a more popular faith that would henceforth become known as Hinduism. We will discuss that transformation in Chapter 9.

Buddhism: The Middle Path

In the sixth century B.C.E., a new doctrine appeared in northern India that would eventually begin to rival the popularity of Brahmanical beliefs throughout the subcontinent. This new doctrine was called **Buddhism**.

THE LIFE OF SIDDHARTHA GAUTAMA The historical founder of Buddhism, Siddhartha Gautama (si-DAR-tuh GAW-tuh-muh) (c. 560–480 B.C.E.), was a native of a small kingdom in the foothills of the Himalaya Mountains in what is today southern Nepal. He was born in the mid-sixth century B.C.E., the son of a ruling *kshatriya* family (see the Comparative Illustration "The Buddha and Jesus" on p. 60). According to tradition, the young Siddhartha was raised in affluent surroundings and trained, like many other members of his class, in the martial arts. On reaching maturity, he married and began to raise a family. At the age of twenty-nine, however, he suddenly discovered the pain of illness, the sorrow of death, and the degradation caused by old age in the lives of ordinary people and exclaimed, "Would that sickness, age, and death might be forever bound!" From that time on, he decided to dedicate his life to determining the cause and seeking the cure for human suffering.

The Three Faces of Shiva. In the first centuries C.E., Hindus began to adopt Buddhist rock art. One outstanding example is at the Elephanta Caves, near the modern city of Mumbai (Bombay). Dominating the cave is this 18-foot-high triple-headed statue of Shiva, representing the Hindu deity in all his various aspects. The central figure shows him in total serenity, enveloped in absolute knowledge. The angry profile on the left portrays him as the destroyer, struggling against time, death, and other negative forces. The right-hand profile shows his loving and feminine side in the guise of his beautiful wife, Parvati.
© William J. Duiker

To find the answers to these questions, Siddhartha abandoned his home and family and traveled widely. At first he tried to follow the model of the ascetics, but he eventually decided that self-mortification did not lead to a greater understanding of life and abandoned the practice. Then one day after a lengthy period of meditation under a tree, he achieved enlightenment as to the meaning of life and spent the remainder of his life preaching it. His conclusions, as embodied in his teachings, became the philosophy (or as some would have it, the religion) of Buddhism. According to legend, the Devil (the Indian term is *Mara*) attempted desperately to tempt him with political power and the company of beautiful girls. But Siddhartha Gautama resisted:

> *Pleasure is brief as a flash of lightning*
> *Or like an autumn shower, only for a moment....*
> *Why should I then covet the pleasures you speak of?*
> *I see your bodies are full of all impurity:*
> *Birth and death, sickness and age are yours.*
> *I seek the highest prize, hard to attain by men—*
> *The true and constant wisdom of the wise.*[8]

BUDDHISM AND BRAHMANISM How much the modern doctrine of Buddhism resembles the original teachings of Siddhartha Gautama is open to debate, for much time has elapsed since his death and original texts relating his ideas are lacking. Nor is it certain that Siddhartha even intended to found a new religion or doctrine. In some respects, his ideas could be viewed as a reformist form of Brahmanism, designed to transfer responsibility from the priests to the individual, much as the sixteenth-century German monk Martin Luther saw his ideas as a reformation of Christianity (see Chapter 15). Siddhartha accepted much of the belief system of Brahmanism, if not all of its practices. For example, he accepted the concept of reincarnation and the role of *karma* as a means of influencing the movement of individual souls up and down the scale of life. He praised nonviolence and borrowed the idea of living a life of simplicity and chastity from the ascetics. Moreover, his vision of metaphysical reality—commonly known as **Nirvana**—is closer to the Aryan concept of *Brahman* than it is to the Christian concept of heavenly salvation. Nirvana, which involves an extinction of selfhood and a final reunion with the Great World Soul, is sometimes likened to a dreamless sleep or to a kind of "blowing out" (as of a candle). Buddhists occasionally remark that someone who asks for a description does not understand the concept.

At the same time, the new doctrine differed from existing practices in a number of key ways. In the first place, Siddhartha denied the existence of an individual soul. To him, the concept of *Atman*—the individual soul—meant that the soul was subject to rebirth and thus did not achieve a complete liberation from the cares of this world. In fact, Siddhartha denied the ultimate reality of the material world in its entirety and taught that it was an illusion that had to be transcended. Siddhartha's idea of achieving Nirvana was based on his conviction that the pain, poverty, and sorrow that afflict human beings are caused essentially by their attachment to the things of this world. Once worldly cares are abandoned, pain and sorrow can be overcome. With this knowledge comes *bodhi*, or

wisdom (source of the term *Buddhism* and the familiar name for Gautama the Wise: Gautama Buddha).

Achieving this understanding is a key step on the road to Nirvana, which, as in Brahmanism, is a form of release from the wheel of life. According to tradition, Siddhartha transmitted this message in a sermon to his disciples in a deer park at Sarnath, not far from the modern city of Varanasi (Benares). Like so many messages, it is deceptively simple and is enclosed in four noble truths: life is suffering, suffering is caused by desire, the way to end suffering is to end desire, and the way to end desire is to avoid the extremes of a life of vulgar materialism and a life of self-torture and to follow the **Middle Path**. Also known as the Eightfold Way, the Middle Path calls for right knowledge, right purpose, right speech, right conduct, right occupation, right effort, right awareness, and right meditation (see the box "How to Achieve Enlightenment" on p. 54).

Another characteristic of Buddhism was its relative egalitarianism. Although Siddhartha accepted the idea of reincarnation (and hence the idea that human beings differ as a result of *karma* accumulated in a previous existence), he rejected the division of humanity into rigidly defined classes based on previous reincarnations and taught that all human beings could aspire to Nirvana as a result of their behavior in this life—a message that likely helped Buddhism win support among people at the lower end of the social scale.

In addition, Buddhism was much simpler than existing beliefs. Siddhartha rejected the panoply of gods that had become identified with Brahmanism and forbade his followers to worship his person or his image after his death. In fact, many Buddhists view Buddhism as a philosophy rather than a religion.

After Siddhartha Gautama's death in 480 B.C.E., dedicated disciples carried his message the length and breadth of India. Buddhist monasteries were established throughout the subcontinent, and temples and **stupas** (STOO-puhs) (stone towers housing relics of the Buddha) sprang up throughout the countryside.

Women were permitted to join the monastic order but only in an inferior position. As Siddhartha had explained, women are "soon angered," "full of passion," and "stupid": "That is the reason ... why women have no place in public assemblies ... and do not earn their living by any profession." Still, the position of women tended to be better in Buddhist societies than it was elsewhere in ancient India

JAINISM During the next centuries, Buddhism began to compete actively with the existing Aryan beliefs, as well as with another new faith known as Jainism. **Jainism** (JY-ni-zuhm) was founded by Mahavira (mah-hah-VEE-ruh), a contemporary of Siddhartha Gautama. Resembling Buddhism in its rejection of the reality of the material world, Jainism was more extreme in practice. Where Siddhartha Gautama called for the "middle way" between passion and luxury on one extreme and pain and self-torture on the other, Mahavira preached a doctrine of extreme simplicity to his followers, who kept no possessions and relied on begging for a living. Some even rejected clothing and wandered through the world naked. Perhaps because of its insistence on a life of poverty, Jainism failed to attract enough adherents to become a major doctrine and

How to Achieve Enlightenment

RELIGION & PHILOSOPHY

ONE OF THE MOST FAMOUS PASSAGES in Buddhist literature is the sermon at Sarnath, which Siddhartha Gautama delivered to his followers in a deer park outside the holy city of Varanasi (Benares), in the Ganges River valley. Here he set forth the key ideas that would define Buddhist beliefs for centuries to come. During an official visit to Sarnath nearly three centuries later, Emperor Ashoka ordered the construction of a stupa (reliquary) in honor of the Buddha's message.

The Sermon at Benares

Thus have I heard. Once the Lord was at Varanasi, at the deer park called Isipatana. There he addressed the five monks:

"There are two ends not to be served by a wanderer. What are these two? The pursuit of desires and the pleasure which springs from desire, which is base, common, leading to rebirth, ignoble, and unprofitable; and the pursuit of pain and hardship, which is grievous, ignoble, and unprofitable. The Middle Way of the Tathagata avoids both these ends. It is enlightened, it brings clear vision, it makes for wisdom and leads to peace, insight, enlightenment, and Nirvana. What is the Middle Way? ... It is the Noble Eightfold Path—Right Views, Right Resolve, Right Speech, Right Conduct, Right Livelihood, Right Effort, Right Mindfulness, and Right Concentration. This is the Middle Way....

"And this is the Noble Truth of Sorrow. Birth is sorrow, age is sorrow, disease is sorrow, death is sorrow; contact with the unpleasant is sorrow, separation from the pleasant is sorrow, every wish unfulfilled is sorrow—in short all the five components of individuality are sorrow.

"And this is the Noble Truth of the Arising of Sorrow. It arises from craving, which leads to rebirth, which brings delight and passion and seeks pleasure now here, now there—the craving for sensual pleasure, the craving for continued life, the craving for power.

"And this is the Noble Truth of the Stopping of Sorrow. It is the complete stopping of that craving, so that no passion remains, leaving it, being emancipated from it, being released from it, giving no place to it.

"And this is the Noble Truth of the Way which Leads to the Stopping of Sorrow. It is the Noble Eightfold Path—Right Views, Right Resolve, Right Speech, Right Conduct, Right Livelihood, Right Effort, Right Mindfulness, and Right Concentration."

 How did Siddhartha Gautama reach the conclusion that the "four noble truths" were the proper course in living a moral life? How do his ideas compare with the commandments that God gave to the Israelites (see Chapter 1)?

Source: Samyutta Nikaya (ed. Leon Feer and C. A. F. Rhys Davids), 6 vols. London: Oxford, 1884–1904 (Pali Text Society), p. 5.421 ff.

Symbols of the Buddha. Early Buddhist sculptures depicted the Buddha only through visual symbols that represented his life on the path to enlightenment. In this relief from the stupa at Bharhut, carved in the second century B.C.E., we see four devotees paying homage to the Buddha, who is portrayed as a giant wheel dispensing his "wheel of the law." The riderless horse on the left represents Siddhartha Gautama's departure from his father's home as he set out on his search for the meaning of life.

never received official support. According to tradition, however, Chandragupta Maurya accepted Mahavira's doctrine after abdicating the throne and fasted to death in a Jain monastery.

ASHOKA, A BUDDHIST MONARCH Buddhism received an important boost when Ashoka (uh-SHOH-kuh), the grandson of Chandragupta Maurya, converted to Buddhism in the third century B.C.E. Ashoka (r. 269–232 B.C.E.) is widely considered the greatest ruler in the history of India. By his own admission, as noted in rock edicts placed around his kingdom, Ashoka began his reign conquering, pillaging, and killing, but after his conversion to Buddhism, he began to regret his bloodthirsty past and attempted to rule benevolently.

Ashoka directed that banyan trees and shelters be placed along the road to provide shade and rest for weary travelers. He sent Buddhist missionaries throughout India and ordered the erection of stone pillars with official edicts and Buddhist inscriptions to instruct people in the proper way (see Map 2.3 and illustration "The Lions of Sarnath" below). In time, much of the population living under Mauryan rule may have converted to Buddhism (see the box "A Singular Debate" on p. 56). According to tradition, his son converted the island of Sri Lanka to Buddhism, and the peoples there accepted a tributary relationship with the Mauryan Empire.

AFTER ASHOKA: THE RULE OF THE FISHES After Ashoka's death in 232 B.C.E., the Mauryan Empire began to decline. In 183 B.C.E., the last Mauryan ruler was overthrown by one of his military commanders, and India began to fragment into separate states. A number of new kingdoms, some of them perhaps influenced by the memory of the Alexandrian conquests, arose along the fringes of the subcontinent in Bactria, known today as Afghanistan. In the first century C.E., Indo-European-speaking peoples fleeing from the nomadic Xiongnu (SHYAHNG-noo) warriors in Central Asia seized power in the area and proclaimed the new Kushan (koo-SHAHN) kingdom (see Chapter 9). For the next two centuries, the Kushans extended their political sway over northern India as far as the central Ganges Valley, while other kingdoms scuffled for predominance elsewhere on the subcontinent. India would not see unity again for another five hundred years.

© 2016 Cengage Learning

MAP 2.3 The Empire of Ashoka. Ashoka, the greatest Indian monarch, ruled over much of the subcontinent in the third century B.C.E. This map shows the extent of his empire and the locations of the pillar edicts that were erected along major trade routes.

Q *Why do you think the pillars and rocks were placed where they were?*

The Lions of Sarnath. Their beauty and Buddhist symbolism make the Lions of Sarnath the most famous of the capitals topping Ashoka's pillars. Sarnath was the holy site where the Buddha first preached, and these roaring lions echo the proclamation of Buddhist teachings to the four corners of the world. The wheel not only represents the Buddha's laws but also proclaims Ashoka's imperial legitimacy as the enlightened Indian ruler.

A Singular Debate

ONE OF THE KEY POINTS OF CONTENTION between advocates of Brahmanism and Buddhism was the belief on the part of the former that members of the highest social class—the Brahmins—were purer than those lower on the social scale, based on their past actions (*karma*). Siddhartha Gautama, however, had argued that all humans were inherently equal at birth and could obtain Nirvana—the state of release from earthly cares—as a consequence of their behavior in this life.

In this passage from the *Tripitaka* (Three Baskets), a collection of Buddhist writings collated by Theravada Buddhists on the island of Sri Lanka, Siddhartha Gautama confronts a devotee of Brahmanism and demonstrates the superiority of Buddhist teachings. Whether the debate actually took place is unlikely, and the date of the passage is uncertain, but it effectively singles out one of the key points of difference between the two teachings.

The Tripitaka

Once when the Lord was staying at Savatthi there were five hundred brahmans from various countries in the city … and they thought: "This ascetic Gautama preaches that all four classes are pure. Who can refute him?"

At that time there was a young brahman named Assalayana in the city, … a youth of sixteen, thoroughly versed in the Vedas … and in all brahmanic learning. "He can do it!", thought the brahmans, and so they asked him to try; … he agreed, and so, surrounded by a crowd of brahmans, he went to the Lord, and, after greeting him, sat down and said:

"Brahmans maintain that only they are the highest class, and the others are below them. They are white, the others black; only they are pure, and not the others. Only they are the true sons of Brahma, born from his mouth, born of Brahma, creations of Brahma, heirs of Brahma. Now what does the worthy Gautama say to that?"

"Do the brahmans really maintain this Assalayana, when they're born of women just like anyone else, of brahman women who have their periods and conceive, give birth and nurse their children, just like any other women?"

"For all you say, this is what they think.…"

…

"Again if a man is a murderer, a thief, or an adulterer, or commits other grave sins, when his body breaks up on death does he pass on to purgatory if he's a kshatriya, vaishya, or shudra, but not if he's a brahman?"

"No, Gautama. In such a case, the same fate is in store for all men, whatever their class."

…

"And is a brahman capable of developing a mind of love without hate or ill will, but not a man of the other classes?"

"No, Gautama. All four classes are capable of doing so."

"Can only a brahman go down to a river and wash away dust and dirt, and not men of the other classes?"

"No, Gautama. All four classes can."

…

"Suppose there are two young brahman brothers, one a scholar and the other uneducated. Which of them would be served first at memorial feasts, festivals, and sacrifices, or when entertained as guests?"

"The scholar, of course; for what great benefit would accrue from entertaining the uneducated one?"

"But suppose the scholar is ill-behaved and wicked, while the uneducated one is well-behaved and virtuous?"

"Then the uneducated one would be served first, for what great benefit would accrue from entertaining an ill-behaved and wicked man?"

"First, Assalayana, you based your claim on birth, then you gave up birth for learning, and finally you have come round to my way of thinking, that all four classes are equally pure!"

At this Assalayana sat silent … his shoulders hunched, his eyes cast down, thoughtful in mind, and with no answer at hand.

 What arguments does the Brahmanic scholar present to Siddhartha Gautama? How does the latter respond?

Source: Ainslee T. Embree (ed.), *Sources of Indian Tradition*, volume I (New York: Columbia University Press, 1988), pp. 140–141.

Several reasons for India's failure to maintain a unified empire have been proposed. Some historians suggest that a decline in regional trade during the first millennium C.E. may have contributed to the growth of small land-based kingdoms, which drew their primary income from agriculture. The tenacity of the Aryan tradition, with its emphasis on tribal rivalries, may also have contributed. Although the Mauryan rulers tried to impose a more centralized organization, clan loyalties once again came to the fore after the collapse of the Mauryan dynasty. Furthermore, the behavior of the ruling class was characterized by what Indians call the "rule of the fishes," which glorified warfare as the natural activity of the king and the aristocracy. The *Arthasastra*, which set forth a model of a centralized Indian state, assumed that war was the "sport of kings." Still, this was not an uneventful period in the history of India, as Indo-Aryan ideas continued to spread southward and both Brahmanism and Buddhism evolved in new directions.

The Exuberant World of Indian Culture

 FOCUS QUESTION: In what ways did the culture of ancient India resemble and differ from the cultural experience of ancient Mesopotamia and Egypt?

Few cultures in the world are as rich and varied as that of India. Most societies excel in some forms of artistic and literary achievement and not in others, but India has produced great works in almost all fields of cultural endeavor—art and sculpture, science, architecture, literature, and music.

Literature

The earliest known Indian literature consists of the four Vedas, which were passed down orally from generation to generation until they were finally written down after the Aryans arrived in India. The Rig Veda dates from the second millennium B.C.E. and consists of more than a thousand hymns that were used at religious ceremonies. The other three Vedas were written considerably later and contain instructions for performing ritual sacrifices and other ceremonies. The Brahmanas and the Upanishads served as commentaries on the Vedas.

The language of the Vedas was **Sanskrit** (SAN-skrit), one of the Indo-European family of languages. After the arrival of the Aryans in India, Sanskrit gradually declined as a spoken language and was replaced in northern India by a simpler tongue known as **Prakrit** (PRAH-krit). Nevertheless, Sanskrit continued to be used as the language of the bureaucracy and of literary expression for many centuries after that and, like Latin in medieval Europe, served as a common language of communication between various regions of India. In the south, a variety of Dravidian languages continued to be spoken.

As early as the fifth century B.C.E., Indian grammarians had codified Sanskrit to preserve the authenticity of the Vedas for the spiritual edification of future generations. A famous grammar written by the scholar Panini in the fourth century B.C.E. set forth four thousand grammatical rules prescribing the correct usage of the spoken and written language. This achievement is particularly impressive in that Europe did not have a science of linguistics until the nineteenth century, when it was developed partly as a result of the discovery of the works of Panini and later Indian linguists.

After the development of a writing system in the first millennium B.C.E., India's holy literature was probably inscribed on palm leaves stitched together into a book somewhat similar to the first books produced on papyrus or parchment in the Mediterranean region. Also written for the first time were India's great historical epics, the Mahabharata and the Ramayana (rah-mah-YAH-nah). Both of these epics may have originally been recited at religious ceremonies, but they are essentially histories that recount the martial exploits of great Aryan rulers and warriors.

The Mahabharata, consisting of more than 90,000 stanzas, was probably written about 100 B.C.E. and describes in great detail a war between cousins for control of the kingdom nine hundred years earlier. Interwoven in the narrative are many fantastic legends of the gods. Above all, the Mahabharata is a tale of moral confrontations and an elucidation of the ethical precepts of the *dharma*. The most famous section of the book is the so-called Bhagavad Gita, a sermon by the legendary Indian figure Krishna on the eve of a major battle. In this sermon, as mentioned at the beginning of this chapter, Krishna sets forth one of the key ethical maxims of Indian society: in taking action, one must be indifferent to success or failure and consider only the moral rightness of the act itself.

The Ramayana, written at about the same time, is much shorter than the Mahabharata. It is an account of a semilegendary ruler named Rama (RAH-mah) who, as a result of a palace intrigue, is banished from the kingdom and forced to live as a hermit in the forest. Later he fights the demon-king of Sri Lanka, who has kidnapped his beloved wife, Sita (SEE-tuh). Like the Mahabharata, the Ramayana is strongly imbued with religious and moral significance. Rama is portrayed as the ideal Aryan hero, a perfect ruler and an ideal son, while Sita projects the supreme duty of female chastity and wifely loyalty to her husband. The Ramayana is a story of the triumph of good over evil, duty over self-indulgence, and generosity over selfishness. It combines filial and erotic love, conflicts of human passion, character analysis, and poetic descriptions of nature (see the box "Rama and Sita" on p. 58).

The Ramayana also has all the ingredients of an enthralling adventure: giants, wondrous flying chariots, invincible arrows and swords, and magic potions and mantras. One of the real heroes of the story is the monkey-king Hanuman, who flies from India to Sri Lanka to set the great battle in motion. It is no wonder that for millennia the Ramayana has remained a favorite among Indians of all age groups, often performed at festivals today and inspiring a hugely popular TV version produced in recent years.

Architecture and Sculpture

After literature, the greatest achievements of early Indian civilization were in architecture and sculpture. Some of the earliest examples of Indian architecture stem from the time of Emperor Ashoka, when Buddhism became the religion of the state. Until the time of the Mauryas, Aryan buildings had been constructed of wood. With the rise of the empire, stone began to be used as artisans arrived in India seeking employment after the destruction of the Persian Empire by Alexander. Many of these stone carvers accepted the patronage of Emperor Ashoka, who used them to spread Buddhist ideas throughout the subcontinent.

There were three main types of religious structures: the pillar, the stupa, and the rock chamber. As noted earlier, during Ashoka's reign, many stone columns were erected alongside roads to commemorate the events in the Buddha's life and mark pilgrim routes to holy places. Weighing up to 50 tons each and rising as high as 32 feet, these polished sandstone pillars were topped with a carved capital, usually depicting lions uttering the Buddha's message. Ten remain standing today (a photograph of one of these pillars appears in the Comparative Illustration "The Stele" on p. 233).

Rama and Sita

ART & IDEAS

OVER THE AGES, THE CONCLUSION OF THE INDIAN EPIC known as the Ramayana has been the focus of considerable debate. After a long period of captivity at the hands of the demon Ravana, Sita is finally liberated by her husband, King Rama. Although the two have a joyful reunion, the people of Rama's kingdom voice suspicions that she has been defiled by her captor, and Rama is forced to banish her to a forest, where she gives birth to twin sons. The account reflects the belief, expressed in the *Arthasastra*, that a king must place the needs of his subjects over his personal desires. Here we read of Rama's anguished decision as he consults with his brother, Lakshmana.

By accepting banishment, Sita bows to the authority of her husband and the established moral order. Subservient and long-suffering, she has been lauded as the ideal heroine and feminine role model, imitated by generations of Indian women. At the close of the Ramayana, Rama decides to take Sita back "before all my people." She continues to feel humiliated, however, and begs Mother Earth to open up and swallow her.

The Ramayana

"A king must be blameless."

"Such words pierce my heart," said Lakshmana. "Fire himself proved her innocent. She is fired gold, poured into golden fire!"

Rama said, "Lakshmana, consider what is a king. Kings cannot afford blame. Ill fame is evil to kings; they above all men must be beyond reproach.... See into what a chasm of sorrow a King may fall...."

Lakshmana said, "Gradually everything seems to change again, and even an Emperor must pay his way through life."

Rama faced his brother. "It must be! It's all the same, can't you see? Where there is growth there is decay; where there is prosperity there is ruin; and where there is birth there is death."

Lakshmana sighed hopelessly. "Well, what will you do?"

"Sita expects to go to the forests tomorrow. Let Sumantra the Charioteer drive you both there, and when you arrive by the river Ganga abandon her."

"She will die. Your child will die!"

"No," said Rama. "I command you! Not a word to anyone."

Lakshmana said, "Surely a king is remote and lonely, and very far from reason. We cannot speak to you...."

Rama said, "Each person can be told what he will understand of the nature of the world, and no more than that—for the rest, take my word...."

Sita was forever beautiful. Wearing her ornaments she turned slowly around and looked at every person there. "Rama, let me prove my innocence, here before everyone."

"I give my permission," said Rama.

Then Sita stepped a little away from him and said, "Mother Earth, if I have been faithful to Rama take me home, hide me!"

Earth rolled and moved beneath our feet. With a great rumbling noise the ground broke apart near Sita and a deep chasm opened, lighted from below with bright lights like lightning flashes, from the castles of the Naga serpent kings....

On that throne sat Mother Earth. Earth was not old, she was fair to look on, she was not sad but smiling. She wore flowers and a girdle of seas. Earth supports all life, but she feels no burden in all that. She is patient. She was patient then, under the Sun and Moon and through the rainfalls of countless years. She was patient with seasons and with kings and farmers; she endured all things and bore no line of care from it.

But this was the end of her long patience with Rama. Earth looked at her husband Janaka and smiled. Then she stretched out her arms and took her only child Sita on her lap. She folded her beautiful arms around her daughter and laid Sita's head softly against her shoulder as a mother would. Earth stroked her hair with her fair hands, and Sita closed her eyes like a little girl.

The throne sank back underground and they all were gone; the Nagas dove beneath the ground and the crevice closed gently over them, forever.

 How does this story reflect some of the basic values of traditional Indian civilization? Why do you think it was necessary for the story to have an unhappy ending, unlike Homer's epic The Odyssey, which ends with the return of the hero Odysseus to his wife, Penelope, after many arduous travels?

Source: From *The Ramayana* by R. K. Narayan. Viking Books, 1972.

A stupa was originally meant to house a relic of the Buddha, such as a lock of his hair or a branch of the famous Bodhi tree (the tree beneath which Siddhartha Gautama had first achieved enlightenment), and was constructed in the form of a burial mound (the pyramids in Egypt also derived from burial mounds). Eventually, the stupa became a place for devotion and the most familiar form of Buddhist architecture. Stupas rose to considerable heights and were surmounted with a spire, possibly representing the stages of existence en route to Nirvana. According to legend, Ashoka ordered the construction of 84,000 stupas throughout India to promote the Buddha's message. A few survive today, including the famous stupa at Sanchi, begun under Ashoka and completed two centuries later.

The final form of early Indian architecture is the rock chamber carved out of a cliff on the side of a mountain. Ashoka began the construction of these chambers to provide rooms

Sanchi Gate and Stupa. Constructed during the reign of Emperor Ashoka in the third century B.C.E., the stupa at Sanchi was enlarged over time, eventually becoming the greatest Buddhist monument on the Indian subcontinent. Originally intended to house a relic of the Buddha, the stupa became a holy place for devotion and a familiar form of Buddhist architecture. Sanchi's four elaborately carved stone gates, each more than 40 feet high, tell stories of the Buddha set in joyful scenes of everyday life. Christian churches would later similarly portray events in the life of Jesus to instruct the faithful.

to house monks or wandering ascetics and to serve as halls for religious ceremonies. The chambers were rectangular, with pillars, an altar, and a vault, reminiscent of Roman basilicas in the West. The three most famous chambers of this period are at Bhaja, Karli, and Ajanta (uh-JUHN-tuh); the last one contains twenty-nine rooms.

All three forms of architecture were embellished with detailed reliefs and freestanding statues of deities, other human figures, and animals that are permeated with a sense of nature and the vitality of life. Many reflect an amalgamation of popular and sacred themes, of Buddhist, Vedic, and pre-Aryan religious motifs, such as male and female earth spirits. Until the second century C.E., Siddhartha Gautama was represented only through symbols, such as the wheel of life, the Bodhi tree, and the footprint, perhaps because artists deemed it improper to portray him in human form, since he had escaped his corporeal confines into enlightenment. After the spread of Mahayana Buddhism in the second century, when the Buddha was no longer portrayed as a teacher but rather as a god, his image began to appear in stone as an object for divine worship (see the Comparative Illustration "The Buddha and Jesus" on p. 60).

By this time, India had established its own unique religious art. The art is permeated by sensuousness and exuberance and is often overtly sexual. These scenes are meant to express otherworldly delights, not the pleasures of this world. The sensuous paradise that adorned the religious art of ancient India represented salvation and fulfillment for the ordinary Indian.

A Carved Chapel. Carved out of solid rock cliffs during the Mauryan dynasty, rock chambers served as meditation halls for traveling Buddhist monks. Initially, they resembled freestanding shrines of wood and thatch from the Vedic period but evolved into magnificent chapels carved deep into the mountainside, such as the chapel at Ajanta shown here. Working downward from the top, stonecutters removed tons of rock, and sculptors embellished and polished the interior. Notice the rounded vault and multicolumned sides reminiscent of Roman basilicas in the West.

COMPARATIVE ILLUSTRATION

RELIGION & PHILOSOPHY

The Buddha and Jesus. As Buddhism evolved, transforming Siddhartha Gautama, known as the Buddha, from mortal to god, Buddhist art changed as well. Statuary and relief panels began to illustrate the story of his life. At the left, in a frieze from the second century C.E., the infant Siddhartha is seen emerging from the hip of his mother, Queen Maya. Although dressed in draperies that reflect Greek influences from Alexander the Great's brief incursion into northwestern India, her sensuous stance and the touching of the tree evoke the female earth spirit of traditional Indian art. On the right is a Byzantine painting depicting the infant Jesus with his mother, the Virgin Mary, dating from the sixth century C.E. Notice that a halo surrounds the head of both the Buddha and Jesus. The halo—a circle of light—is an ancient symbol of divinity. In Hindu, Greek, and Roman art, the heads of gods were depicted emitting sunlike divine radiances. Early kings adopted crowns made of gold and precious gems to symbolize their own divine authority.

Q *What similarities and differences do you see in these depictions of the mothers of key religious figures?*

Science

Our knowledge of Indian science is limited by the paucity of written sources, but it is evident that ancient Indians had amassed an impressive amount of scientific knowledge in a number of areas. Especially notable was their work in mathematics, where they devised the numerical system that we know as Arabic numbers and use today, and in astronomy, where they charted the movements of the heavenly bodies and recognized the spherical nature of the earth at an early date. Their ideas of physics were similar to those of the Greeks; matter was divided into the five elements of earth, air, fire, water, and ether. Many of their technological achievements are impressive, notably the quality of their textiles and the massive stone pillars erected during the reign of Ashoka. As noted, the pillars weighed up to 50 tons each and were transported many miles to their final destination.

CHAPTER SUMMARY

While the peoples of North Africa and the Middle East were actively building the first civilizations, a similar process was getting under way in the Indus River valley. Much has been learned about the nature of the Indus Valley civilization in recent years, but the lack of written records limits our understanding. How did the Harappan people deal with the fundamental human problems mentioned at the close of Chapter 1? The answers remain tantalizingly elusive.

As often happened elsewhere, however, the collapse of Harappan civilization did not lead to the total disappearance of its culture. The new society that eventually emerged throughout the subcontinent after the coming of the Aryans was an amalgam of two highly distinctive cultures, each of which made a significant contribution to the politics, social institutions, and creative impulse of ancient Indian civilization.

With the rise of the Mauryan dynasty in the fourth century B.C.E., the distinctive features of a great civilization begin to be clearly visible. It was extensive in its scope, embracing the entire Indian subcontinent and eventually, in the form of Buddhism and Hinduism, spreading to China and Southeast Asia. But the underlying ethnic, linguistic, and cultural diversity of the Indian people posed a constant challenge to the unity of the state. After the collapse of the Mauryas, the subcontinent would not come under a single authority again for several hundred years.

In the meantime, another great experiment was taking place far to the northeast, across the Himalaya Mountains. Like many other civilizations of antiquity, the first Chinese state was concentrated on a major river system. And like them, too, its political and cultural achievements eventually spread far beyond their original habitat. In the next chapter, we turn to the civilization of ancient China.

CHAPTER TIMELINE

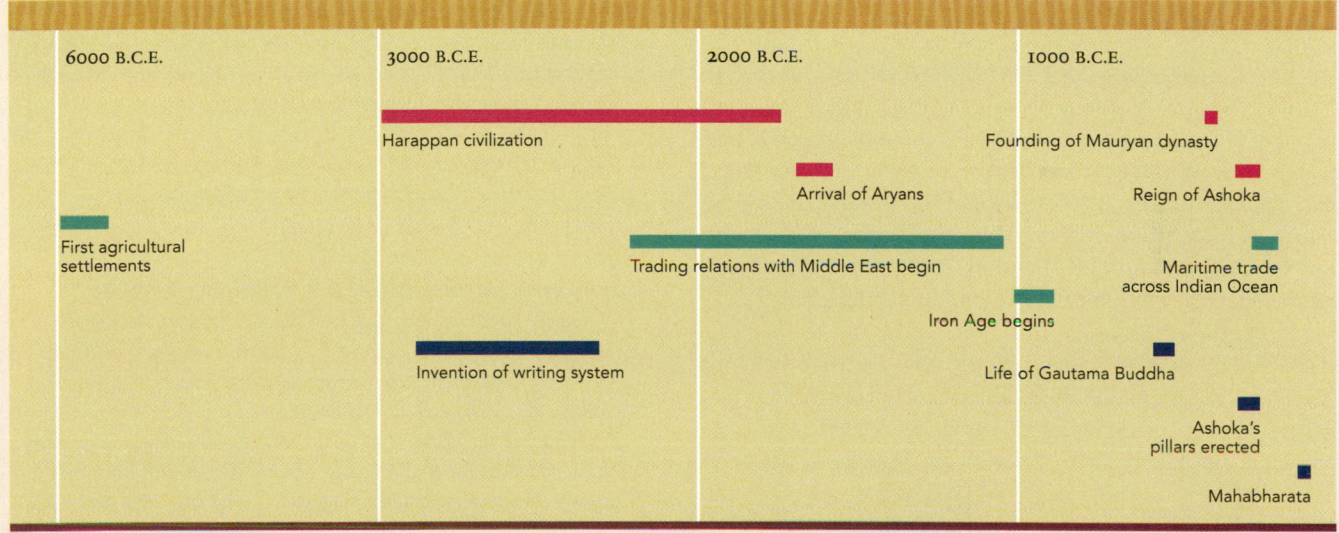

| 6000 B.C.E. | 3000 B.C.E. | 2000 B.C.E. | 1000 B.C.E. |

Harappan civilization

Arrival of Aryans

Founding of Mauryan dynasty

Reign of Ashoka

First agricultural settlements

Trading relations with Middle East begin

Maritime trade across Indian Ocean

Iron Age begins

Invention of writing system

Life of Gautama Buddha

Ashoka's pillars erected

Mahabharata

CHAPTER REVIEW

Upon Reflection

Q What is the debate over the origins of the Aryan peoples, and why do many historians of India consider it to be such an important question?

Q Why was Buddhism able to make such inroads among the Indian people at a time when Brahmanical beliefs had long been dominant in the subcontinent?

Q What were some of the main characteristics of Indian politics and government during the first millennium B.C.E., and how can they be compared and contrasted with those of ancient Egypt and Mesopotamia?

Key Terms

Suggested Reading

THE EMERGENCE OF CIVILIZATION IN INDIA: GENERAL WORKS Several standard histories of India provide a good overview of the ancient period. One of the most readable and reliable is **S. Wolpert**, *New History of India*, 7th ed. (New York, 2003). Also see **B. Metcalf and T. Metcalf**, *A Concise History of India* (Cambridge, 2001). **R. Thapar**, *Early India: From the Origins to* AD *1300* (London, 2002), provides an excellent review of recent scholarship by an Indian historian.

HARAPPAN SOCIETY Because of the relative paucity of archaeological exploration in South Asia, evidence for the Harappan period is not as voluminous as for areas such as Mesopotamia and the Nile Valley. Some of the best work has been written by scholars who actually worked at the sites. One fine account is **J. M. Kenoyer**, *Ancient Cities of the Indus Valley Civilization* (Karachi, 1998). Commercial relations between Harappa and its neighbors are treated in **S. Ratnagar**, *Encounters: The Westerly Trade of the Harappan Civilization* (Oxford, 1981).

For information on the invention of the first writing systems, see **J. T. Hooker, ed.**, *Reading the Past: Ancient Writing from Cuneiform to the Alphabet* (London, 1990), and **A. Hurley**, *The Alphabet: The History, Evolution, and Design of the Letters We Use Today* (New York, 1995).

ESCAPING THE WHEEL OF LIFE: THE RELIGIOUS WORLD OF ANCIENT INDIA There are a number of good books on the introduction of Buddhism into Indian society. The Buddha's ideals are presented in **P. Williams (with A. Tribe)**, *Buddhist Thought: A Complete Introduction to the Indian Tradition* (London, 2000). Also see **J. Strong**, *The Buddha: A Short Biography* (Oxford, 2004).

On the early development of Hinduism, see **E. Bryant**, *The Quest for the Origins of Vedic Culture* (Oxford, 2001), and **V. Narayan**, *Hinduism* (Oxford, 2004). For a comparative treatment, see **K. Armstrong**, *The Great Transformation: The Beginning of Our Religious Traditions* (New York, 2006).

THE EXUBERANT WORLD OF INDIAN CULTURE There are a number of excellent surveys of Indian art, including the concise *Indian Art*, rev. ed. (London, 1997), by R. Craven. See also **V. Dehejia**, *Devi: The Great Goddess* (Washington, D.C., 1999) and *Indian Art* (London, 1997).

Numerous editions of Sanskrit literature are available in English translation. Many are available in the multivolume Harvard Oriental Series. For a shorter annotated anthology of selections from the Indian classics, consult **S. N. Hay, ed.**, *Sources of Indian Tradition*, 2 vols. (New York, 1988). On the role played by women writers in ancient India, see **S. Tharu and K. Lalita, eds.**, *Women Writing in India: 600 B.C. to the Present*, vol. 1 (New York, 1991).

Chapter Notes

1. Quoted in R. Lannoy, *The Speaking Tree: A Study of Indian Culture and Society* (London, 1971), p. 318.
2. The quotation is from ibid., p. 319. Note also that the *Law of Manu* says that "punishment alone governs all created beings.... The whole world is kept in order by punishment, for a guiltless man is hard to find."
3. Strabo's *Geography*, bk. 15, quoted in M. Edwardes, *A History of India: From the Earliest Times to the Present Day* (London, 1961), p. 55.
4. Ibid., p. 54.
5. Ibid., p. 57.
6. From the *Law of Manu*, quoted in A. L. Basham, *The Wonder That Was India* (London, 1961), pp. 180–181. © 1961 Pan Macmillan, London.
7. According to historian Karen Armstrong, the gradual shift from rites to ethics was a characteristic of many belief systems during what historians call the "Axial Age" in the middle of the first millennium B.C.E., when the focus of religious belief began to shift from the priestly classes to the common people. On the Axial Age, see Chapter 4.
8. Quoted in A. K. Coomaraswamy, *Buddha and the Gospel of Buddhism* (New York, 1964), p. 34.

MindTap is a fully online, highly personalized learning experience built upon Cengage Leaning content. MindTap combines student learning tools—readings, multimedia, activities, and assessments—into a singular Learning Path that guides students through their course.

3

China in Antiquity

The First Emperor of Qin

Image Asset Management Ltd./Alamy

CHAPTER OUTLINE AND FOCUS QUESTIONS

The Dawn of Chinese Civilization

Q How did geography influence the civilization that arose in China?

The Zhou Dynasty

Q What were the major tenets of Confucianism, Legalism, and Daoism, and what role did each play in political and philosophical debates during the Zhou dynasty?

The First Chinese Empire: The Qin Dynasty

Q How did the first emperor of the Qin dynasty transform the political, social, and economic institutions of early China?

The Glorious Han Dynasty (202 B.C.E.–221 C.E.)

Q To what degree did the Han dynasty turn to Confucianism as an ideology of the state?

Daily Life in Ancient China

Q What were the key aspects of social and economic life in early China?

Chinese Culture

Q What were the chief characteristics of the Chinese arts and writing system? How did they differ from those in Egypt and Mesopotamia?

CRITICAL THINKING

Q The civilization of ancient China resembled those of its contemporaries in Mesopotamia and North Africa in several respects, but the contrasts were equally significant. What were some of these differences, and how might geography and the environment have contributed to them?

CONNECTIONS TO TODAY

Q Which aspects of Confucian thought as depicted in the *Analects* appear to have particular relevance in today's world? What lessons can we learn today from the teachings of Master Kung?

HIS AMBITION WAS limitless. After mounting the throne of his native state of Qin at the age of thirteen, he immediately set out to conquer all the neighboring states in the region and unite all of China under his rule. Having achieved that objective in the year 221 B.C.E., he then sought to create a highly regimented society according to his own plan. Potential rivals were executed, and their writings were destroyed. Peasants and workers were organized to serve the interests of the state, and thousands of laborers were mobilized to build a gigantic mausoleum, guarded by thousands of molded terra-cotta warriors, to provide for his afterlife. But the vaulting ambitions of the ruler known as Qin Shi Huangdi (chin shee hwang-DEE), or the First Emperor of Qin—as he styled himself—were ultimately destined to be thwarted. After he died at the age of forty-nine in

210 B.C.E., Qin Shi Huangdi's dynasty rapidly fell apart. But although the Qin dynasty was broadly reviled by later generations of historians as an unfortunate aberration in the long course of Chinese history, his legacy lived on in the form of a strong and centralized empire that survived over two millennia and has traditionally been viewed as one of the greatest civilizations in the course of human history. ✦

The Dawn of Chinese Civilization

 FOCUS QUESTION: How did geography influence the civilization that arose in China?

According to a familiar legend, Chinese society was founded by a series of rulers who brought the first rudiments of civilization to the region nearly five thousand years ago. The first was Fu Xi (foo SHEE), the ox-tamer, who "knotted cords for hunting and fishing," domesticated animals, and introduced the beginnings of family life (for an explanation regarding the translation of the Chinese written language, see "A Note to Students About Language and the Dating of Time" on p. xxxii). The second was Shen Nong (shun NOONG), the divine farmer, who "bent wood for plows and hewed wood for plowshares." He taught the people the techniques of agriculture. Last came Huang Di (hwahng DEE), the Yellow Emperor, who "strung a piece of wood for the bow, and whittled little sticks of wood for the arrows." Legend credits Huang Di with creating the Chinese system of writing, as well as with inventing the bow and arrow.[1] Modern historians, of course, do not accept the literal accuracy of such legends but view them instead as part of the process whereby early peoples attempt to make sense of the world and their role in it. Nevertheless, such re-creations of a mythical past often contain an element of truth. Although there is no clear evidence that the "three sovereigns" actually existed, their achievements do symbolize some of the defining characteristics of Chinese civilization: the interaction between nomadic and agricultural peoples, the importance of the family as the basic unit of Chinese life, and the development of a unique system of writing.

The Land and People of China

Although human communities have existed in China for several hundred thousand years, the first *Homo sapiens* arrived in the area sometime after 40,000 B.C.E. as part of the great migration out of Africa. At least as early as the eighth millennium B.C.E., the early peoples living along the riverbanks of northern and central China began to master the cultivation of crops. A number of these early agricultural settlements were in the neighborhood of the Yellow River, where they gave birth to two Neolithic societies known to archaeologists as the **Yangshao** (yahng-SHOW ["ow" as in "how"]) and the **Longshan** (loong-SHAHN) cultures (sometimes identified in terms of their pottery as the painted and black pottery cultures, respectively). Similar communities began to appear in the Yangzi Valley in central China and along the coast to the south. The southern settlements were based on the cultivation of rice, which had been introduced in China as early as the sixth millennium B.C.E., rather than dry crops such as millet, barley, and wheat (the last was an import from the Middle East in the second millennium B.C.E.), but they were as old as those in the north. Thus, agriculture, and perhaps other elements of early civilization, may have developed spontaneously in several areas of China rather than radiating outward from one central region.

At first, these simple Neolithic communities were hardly more than villages, but as the inhabitants mastered the rudiments of agriculture, they gradually gave rise to more sophisticated and complex societies. In a pattern that we have already seen elsewhere, civilization gradually spread from these nuclear settlements in the valleys of the Yellow and Yangzi Rivers to other lowland areas of eastern and central China. The two great river valleys, then, can be considered the core regions in the development of Chinese civilization (see Map 3.1).

Although these densely cultivated valleys eventually became two of the great food-producing areas of the ancient world, China is more than a land of fertile fields. In fact, only 12 percent of the total land area is arable, compared with 23 percent in the United States. Much of the remainder consists of mountains and deserts that ring the country on its northern and western frontiers.

This often arid and forbidding landscape is a dominant feature of Chinese life and has played a significant role in Chinese history. The geographic barriers served to isolate the Chinese people from advanced agrarian societies in other parts of Asia. The frontier regions in the Gobi (GOH-bee) Desert, Central Asia, and the Tibetan plateau were sparsely inhabited by peoples of Mongolian, Indo-European, or Turkish extraction. Most were pastoral societies, and like the contacts between other ancient river valley civilizations and their neighbors, relations between the Chinese and the steppe peoples were intermittent and frequently unstable. Sometimes the two sides engaged in productive trade relations, swapping grain and manufactured goods for hides and other animal products. On other occasions, however, mutual suspicion and contrasting interests led to conflict. Although less numerous than the Chinese, many of the peoples along the frontiers possessed impressive skills in war and were sometimes aggressive in seeking wealth or territory in the settled regions south of the Gobi Desert. Over the next two thousand years, the northern frontier became one of the great fault lines of conflict in Asia as Chinese armies attempted to protect precious farmlands from marauding peoples from beyond the frontier. In turn, nomadic peoples often took offense at Chinese efforts to encroach on their grazing lands. When China was unified and blessed with capable rulers, it could usually keep the nomadic intruders at bay and even bring them under a loose

© 2016 Cengage Learning

MAP 3.1 Neolithic China. Like the ancient civilizations that arose in North Africa and western Asia, early Chinese society emerged along the banks of two major river systems, the Yellow and the Yangzi. China was separated from the other civilizations by snow-capped mountains and forbidding deserts, however, and thus was compelled to develop essentially on its own, without contacts from other societies going through a similar process.

Q *Based on the discussions in the preceding chapters, what are the advantages and disadvantages of close contact with other human societies?*

form of Chinese administration. But in times of internal weakness, China was vulnerable to attack from the north, and on several occasions, nomadic peoples succeeded in overthrowing native Chinese rulers and setting up their own dynastic regimes.

From other directions, China normally had little to fear. To the east lay the China Sea, a lair for pirates and the source of powerful typhoons that occasionally ravaged the Chinese coast but otherwise rarely a source of concern. South of the Yangzi River was a hilly region inhabited by a mixture of peoples of varied linguistic and ethnic stock who lived by farming, fishing, or food gathering. They were gradually absorbed in the inexorable expansion of Chinese civilization.

The Shang Dynasty

Historians of China have traditionally dated the beginning of Chinese civilization to the founding of the Xia (shee-AH) dynasty more than four thousand years ago. Although the precise date for the rise of the Xia is in dispute, recent archaeological evidence confirms its existence. Legend maintains that the founder was a ruler named Yu, who is also credited with introducing irrigation and draining the floodwaters that periodically threatened to inundate the North China plain. The Xia dynasty was replaced by a second dynasty, the Shang

(SHAHNG), around the sixteenth century B.C.E. The late Shang capital at Anyang (ahn-YAHNG), just north of the Yellow River in north-central China, has been excavated by archaeologists. Among the finds were thousands of so-called oracle bones, ox and chicken bones or turtle shells that were used by Shang rulers for divination and to communicate with the gods. The inscriptions on these oracle bones—a form of pictographic writing similar to those we have encountered in Egypt and Mesopotamia—are the earliest known form of Chinese writing and provide much of our information about the beginnings of civilization in China. They describe a culture gradually emerging from the Neolithic to the early Bronze Age.

POLITICAL ORGANIZATION China under the Shang dynasty was a predominantly agricultural society ruled by an aristocratic class whose major occupation was war and control over key resources such as metals and salt. One ancient chronicler complained that "the big affairs of state consist of sacrifice and soldiery."[2] Combat was carried on by means of two-horse chariots. The appearance of chariots in China in the mid-second millennium B.C.E. coincides roughly with similar developments elsewhere, leading some historians to suggest that the Shang ruling class may originally have invaded China from elsewhere in Asia. But items found in Shang burial mounds are similar to Longshan pottery, implying that the Shang ruling elites were linear descendants of the indigenous Neolithic peoples in the area. If that was the case, the Shang may have acquired their knowledge of horse-drawn chariots through contact with the peoples of neighboring regions.

Some recent support for that assumption has come from evidence unearthed in the sandy wastes of Xinjiang (SHIN-jyahng), China's far-northwestern province. There archaeologists have discovered corpses dating back as early as the second millennium B.C.E. with physical characteristics resembling those of Europeans. They are also clothed in textiles similar to those worn at the time in central Asia and eastern Europe, suggesting that they may have been members of a migration by Indo-European peoples from areas much farther to the west. If that is the case, they were probably familiar with advances in chariot making that occurred a few hundred years earlier in southern Russia and Kazakhstan (ka-zak-STAN or kuh-zahk-STAHN). By about 2000 B.C.E., spoked wheels were being deposited at grave sites in Ukraine and also in the Gobi Desert, just north of the great bend of the Yellow River.

COMPARATIVE ILLUSTRATION

RELIGION & PHILOSOPHY

The Afterlife and Prized Possessions. Like the pharaohs in Egypt, Chinese rulers filled their tombs with prized possessions from daily life. It was believed that if a tomb was furnished and stocked with supplies, including chairs, boats, chests, weapons, games, and dishes, the spiritual body could continue its life despite the death of the physical body. In the photo on the left, we see the remains of a chariot and horses in a burial pit in China's Hebei province that dates from the early Zhou dynasty. The lower photo on the right shows a small boat from the tomb of Tutankhamun in the Valley of the Kings in Egypt. The tradition of providing items of daily use for the departed continues today in Chinese communities throughout Asia. The papier-mâché vehicle in the photo at the upper right will be burned so that it will ascend in smoke to the world of the spirits.

Q *How did ancient Chinese tombs compare with the tombs of Egyptian pharaohs? What do the differences tell you about these two societies? What do all of the items shown here have in common?*

It is thus likely that the new technology became available to the founders of the Shang dynasty and may have aided their rise to power in northern China.

The Shang king ruled with the assistance of a central bureaucracy in the capital city. His realm was divided into a number of territories governed by aristocratic chieftains, but the king appointed these chieftains and could apparently depose them at will. He was also responsible for the defense of the realm and controlled large armies that often fought on the fringes of the kingdom. The transcendent importance of the ruler was graphically displayed in the ritual sacrifices undertaken at his death, when hundreds of his retainers were buried with him in the royal tomb.

As the inscriptions on the oracle bones make clear, the Shang ruling elite believed in the existence of supernatural forces and thought that they could communicate with those forces to obtain divine intervention on matters of this world. In fact, the main purpose of the oracle bones seems to have been

Shang China

to communicate with the gods. Supreme among the heavenly forces was the sky god, known as Di. Evidence from the oracle bones also suggests that the king was already being viewed as an intermediary between heaven and earth. An early Shang character for king (王) consists of three horizontal lines connected by a single vertical line; the middle horizontal line represents the king's place between human society and the divine forces in nature.

The early Chinese also had a clear sense of life in the hereafter. Though some of the human sacrifices discovered in the royal tombs were presumably intended to propitiate the gods, others were meant to accompany the king or members of his family on the journey to the next world (see the Comparative Illustration "The Afterlife and Prized Possessions" above). From this conviction would come the concept of **veneration of ancestors** (mistakenly known in the West as "ancestor worship") and the practice, which continues to the present

The Use of Metals

SCIENCE & TECHNOLOGY

Around 6000 B.C.E., people in western Asia discovered how to use metals. They soon realized the advantage of using metal instead of stone to make both tools and weapons. Metal could be shaped more precisely, allowing artisans to make more refined tools and weapons with sharper edges and more regular shapes. Copper, silver, and gold, which were commonly found in their elemental form, were the first metals to be used. These were relatively soft and could be easily pounded into different shapes. But an important step was taken when people discovered that a rock that contained metal could be heated to liquefy the metal (a process called smelting). The liquid metal could then be poured into molds of clay or stone to make precisely shaped tools and weapons.

Copper was the first metal to be used in making tools. The first known copper smelting furnace, dated to 3800 B.C.E., was found in the Sinai. Within the next century, artisans in

Ancient Bronze Ritual Object. This ritual wine vessel was recently unearthed from a tomb dating back to the middle of the second millennium B.C.E. It is one of the earliest such bronze objects that have been excavated in China.
© William J. Duiker

western Asia discovered that tin could be added to copper to make bronze. Bronze has a lower melting point that makes it easier to cast, but it is also a harder metal than copper and corrodes less. Eventually the technique spread eastward, and by 1400 B.C.E., the Chinese were making bronze decorative objects as well as battle-axes and helmets. The widespread use of bronze has led historians to speak of the period from around 3000 to 1200 B.C.E. as the Bronze Age, although this is somewhat misleading in that many peoples continued to use stone tools and weapons even after bronze became available.

But there were limitations to the use of bronze. Tin was not as available as copper, so bronze tools and weapons were expensive. After 1200 B.C.E., bronze was increasingly replaced by iron, which was probably first used around 1500 B.C.E. in western Asia, where the Hittites made weapons from it. Between 1500 and 600 B.C.E., ironmaking spread across Europe, North Africa, and Asia. Bronze continued to be used, but mostly for jewelry and other domestic purposes. Iron was used to make tools and weapons with sharp edges. Because iron weapons were cheaper than bronze ones, more warriors could be armed, and wars could be fought on a larger scale.

Iron was handled differently from bronze: it was heated until it could be beaten into a desired shape. Each hammering made the metal stronger. This wrought iron, as it was called, was typical of iron manufacturing in the West until the late Middle Ages. In China, however, the use of heat-resistant clay in the walls of blast furnaces raised temperatures to 1,537 degrees Celsius, enabling artisans already in the fourth century B.C.E. to liquefy iron so that it too could be cast in molds. Europeans would not develop such blast furnaces until the fifteenth century C.E.

 What were the advantages of making objects out of bronze versus iron in the ancient world? Which metal ultimately triumphed in China?

day in many Chinese communities, of burning replicas of physical objects to accompany the departed on their journey to the next world.

SOCIAL STRUCTURES In the Neolithic period, the farming village was apparently the basic social unit of China, at least in the core region of the Yellow River valley. Villages were organized by clans rather than by nuclear family units, and all residents probably took the common clan name of the entire village. In some cases, a village may have included more than one clan. At Banpo, an archaeological site near the modern city of Xian (shih-AHN) that dates back at least seven thousand years, the houses in the village are separated by a ditch,

which some scholars think may have served as a divider between two clans. The individual dwellings at Banpo housed nuclear families, but a larger building in the village was apparently used as a clan meeting hall. The clan-based origins of Chinese society may help explain the continued importance of the joint family in traditional China, as well as the relatively small number of family names in Chinese society. Even today there are only about four hundred commonly used family names in a society of more than one billion people, and a colloquial expression for the common people in China today is "the old hundred names."

By Shang times, the classes were becoming increasingly differentiated. It is likely that some poorer peasants did not own their farms but were obliged to work the land of the chieftain and other elite families in the village. The aristocrats not only made war and served as officials (indeed, the first Chinese character for *official* originally meant "warrior"), but they were also the primary landowners. In addition to the aristocratic elite and the peasants, there were a small number of merchants and artisans, as well as slaves, probably consisting primarily of criminals or prisoners taken in battle.

The Shang are perhaps best known for their mastery of the art of casting bronze. Utensils, weapons, and ritual objects made of bronze (see the Comparative Essay "The Use of Metals" on p. 67) have been found in royal tombs in urban centers throughout the area known to be under Shang influence. It is also clear that the Shang had achieved a fairly sophisticated writing system that would eventually spread throughout East Asia and evolve into the written language that is still used in China today.

THE SHANG DYNASTY: CHINA'S "MOTHER CULTURE"?

Until recently, the prevailing wisdom among historians—both Chinese and non-Chinese—was that the Yellow River valley was the ancient heartland of Chinese civilization and that technological and cultural achievements gradually radiated from there to other areas in East Asia. Here, it was thought, occurred the first technological breakthroughs, including the development of a writing system, advanced farming techniques, and the ability to make bronze ritual vessels. Supporting this idea was the fact that the first significant archaeological finds in China, including the last Shang capital at Anyang, were made in that region.

Today, this **diffusion hypothesis**, as it is sometimes called, is no longer so widely accepted. The remains of early agricultural communities have now been unearthed in the Yangzi River valley and along the southern coast, and a rich trove of bronze vessels has been discovered in grave sites in central Sichuan (suh-CHWAHN) province. Such finds suggest that although the Yellow River civilization may have taken the lead in some areas, such as complex political organization and the development of writing, similar advances were already occurring in other parts of China, suggesting that communication between regions was already well under way.

The Zhou Dynasty

Q **FOCUS QUESTIONS:** What were the major tenets of Confucianism, Legalism, and Daoism? What role did each play in political and philosophical debates during the Zhou dynasty?

In the eleventh century B.C.E., the Shang dynasty was overthrown by an aggressive young state located to the west of Anyang, the Shang capital, and near the great bend of the Yellow River as it begins to flow directly eastward to the sea. The new dynasty, which called itself the Zhou, survived for about eight hundred years, making it the longest-lived dynasty in the history of China. According to tradition, the last of the Shang rulers was a tyrant who oppressed the people (Chinese sources assert that he was a degenerate who built "ponds of wine" and ordered the composing of lustful music that "ruined the morale of the nation"),[3] leading the ruler of the principality of Zhou to revolt and establish a new dynasty.

The Zhou located their capital in their home territory, near the present-day city of Xian. Later they established a second capital city at modern Luoyang (LWOH-yahng), farther to the east, to administer new territories captured from the Shang. This established a pattern of eastern and western capitals that would endure off and on in China for nearly two thousand years.

Political Structures

The Zhou dynasty (1045–221 B.C.E.) adopted the political system of its predecessors, with some changes. The Shang practice of dividing the kingdom into a number of territories

Early Writing. Although the origins of the Chinese character remain shrouded in mystery, the first extant texts that can be clearly deciphered date from the late Shang dynasty and were inscribed on tortoise shells and chicken bones. Eventually, however, characters became increasingly stylized and began to be engraved on metal objects. The text shown here was engraved on a bronze bowl that was commonly used for ritual purposes and dates back to the early Zhou era. The text itself describes the results of an administrative meeting that took place at the royal court in the city of Chengzhou.

The Mandate of Heaven

POLITICS & GOVERNMENT

WHEN THE RULERS of the rising state of Zhou over-threw the last king of the Shang (Yin) dynasty in the middle of the eleventh century B.C.E., they declared the founding of a new dynasty with its capital located near the Yellow River in Central China. To justify their action, they issued an official decree asserting that the mandate of Heaven—according to which each ruling family was anointed by Heaven provisional on its ability to govern by virtue and wisdom—had been passed from one dynastic family to another, as the Shang had previously replaced their predecessors, the Xia.

Such, at any rate, is the historical account presented in the ancient Chinese classic known as the *Book of History* (*Shujing*), a collection of sayings and documents compiled sometime during the Zhou dynasty (1045–221 B.C.E.). The concept of the mandate of Heaven gradually evolved into an essential element in Chinese political culture over the next two millennia.

The *Book of History*

Ah! August Heaven, High God, has changed his principal son and has revoked the Mandate of this great state of Yin. When a king receives the Mandate, without limit is the grace thereof, but also without limit is the anxiety of it. Ah! How can he fail to be reverently careful!

Heaven has rejected and ended the Mandate of this great state of Yin. Thus, although Yin has many former wise kings in Heaven, when their successor kings and successor people undertook their Mandate, in the end wise and good men lived in misery. Knowing that they must care for and sustain their wives and children, they then called out in anguish to Heaven and fled to places where they could not be caught. Ah! Heaven too grieved for the people of all the lands, wanting, with affection, in giving its Mandate to employ those who are deeply committed. The king should have reverent care for this virtue.

Look at the former peoples of ancient times, the Xia. Heaven guided, indulged, and cherished them, so that they would strive to understand what Heaven favors, but by this time they have let their Mandate fall to the ground. Now look at the Yin; Heaven guided them, stayed near them, nourished them, so that they would strive to comprehend what Heaven favors; but now they have let their Mandate fall to the ground.

Now a young son succeeds to the throne; let him not, then, neglect the aged and experienced. Not only do they comprehend the virtue of our men of old—nay, more, they are sometimes able to comprehend counsels that come from Heaven.

Ah! Even though it be that the king is young, he is [Heaven's] principal son. Let him be grandly able to be in harmony with the little people. In the present time of grace, the king must not dare to be slow, but should be prudently apprehensive about what the people say....

Dwelling in this new city, now let the king just earnestly have reverent care for his virtue. If it is virtue that the king uses, he may pray Heaven for an enduring Mandate. As he functions as king, let him not, because the common people stray and do what is wrong, then presume to govern them by harsh capital punishments; in this way he will achieve much. In being king, let him take his position in the primacy of virtue. The little people will then pattern themselves on him throughout the world; the king will then become illustrious.

How would you compare the advice in this statement with that provided by the author of the Arthasastra *in Chapter 2 (see page 44)? Are there any key differences?*

Source: From *Sources of Chinese Tradition*, 2nd edition, Vol. 1, by Wm. T. DeBary and Irene Bloom. Copyright © 1999 Columbia University Press. Reprinted with permission of the publisher.

governed by officials appointed by the king was continued under the Zhou. At the apex of the government hierarchy was the Zhou king, who was served by a bureaucracy of growing size and complexity. It now included several ministries responsible for rites, education, law, and public works. Beyond the capital, the Zhou kingdom was divided into a number of principalities, governed by members of the hereditary aristocracy, who were appointed by the king and were at least theoretically subordinated to his authority.

THE MANDATE OF HEAVEN But the Zhou kings also introduced some innovations. According to the *Rites of Zhou*, one of the oldest surviving documents on statecraft, the Zhou dynasty ruled China because it possessed the **mandate of Heaven**. According to this concept, Heaven (now viewed as an impersonal law of nature rather than as an anthropomorphic deity) maintained order in the universe through the Zhou king, who thus ruled as a representative of Heaven but not as a divine being. The king, who was selected to rule because of his talent and virtue, was then responsible for governing the people with compassion and efficiency (see the box "The Mandate of Heaven" above). It was his duty to appease the gods in order to protect the people from natural calamities or bad harvests. But if the king failed to rule effectively, he could, theoretically at least, be overthrown and replaced by a new ruler. As noted earlier, this idea was used to justify the Zhou conquest of the Shang. Eventually, the concept of the heavenly mandate would become a cardinal principle of Chinese statecraft.[4] Each founder of a new dynasty would routinely assert that he had earned the mandate of Heaven, and who could disprove it except by overthrowing the king? As a pragmatic Chinese proverb put it, "He who wins is the king; he who loses is the rebel."

In asserting that the ruler had a direct connection with the divine forces presiding over the universe, Chinese tradition reflected a belief that was prevalent in all ancient civilizations. But whereas in some societies, notably in Mesopotamia and Greece (see Chapter 4), the gods were seen as capricious and not subject to human understanding, in China, Heaven was viewed as an essentially benevolent force devoted to universal harmony and order that could be influenced by positive human action. Was this attitude a consequence of the fact that China, though subject to some of the same climatic vicissitudes that plagued other parts of the world, experienced a somewhat more predictable and beneficial environment than regions like the Middle East?

Later Chinese would regard the period of the early Zhou dynasty, as portrayed in the *Rites of Zhou* (which, of course, is no more an unbiased source than any modern government document), as a golden age when there was harmony in the world and all was right under Heaven. Whether the system functioned in such an ideal manner, of course, is open to question. In any case, the golden age did not last, whether because it never existed in practice or because of the increasing complexity of Chinese civilization. Perhaps, too, its disappearance was a consequence of the intellectual and moral weakness of the rulers of the Zhou royal house.

By the sixth century B.C.E., the Zhou dynasty began to decline. As the power of the central government disintegrated, bitter internal rivalries arose among the various principalities, where the governing officials had succeeded in making their positions hereditary at the expense of the king. As the power of these officials grew, they began to regulate the local economy and seek reliable sources of revenue for their expanding armies, such as a uniform tax system and government monopolies on key commodities such as salt and iron. A century later, the Zhou rulers had lost all pretense of authority, and China was divided into a cauldron of squabbling states, an era known to Chinese historians as the "Period of the Warring States" (see "The First Chinese Empire: The Qin Dynasty" later in this chapter).

Economy and Society

During the Zhou dynasty, the essential characteristics of Chinese economic and social institutions began to take shape. The Zhou continued the pattern of land ownership that had existed under the Shang: the peasants worked on lands owned by their lord but also had land that they cultivated for their own use. The practice was called the **well-field system** because the Chinese character for "well" (井) calls to mind the division of land into nine separate segments. Each peasant family tilled an outer plot for its own use and joined with other families to work the inner one for the hereditary lord. How widely this system was used is unclear, but it represented an ideal described by Confucian scholars of a later day. As the following passage from *The Book of Songs* indicates, the life of the average farmer was a difficult one. The "big rat"

is probably the government or a lord who has imposed high taxes on the peasants.

> Big rat, big rat,
> Do not eat my millet!
> Three years I have served you,
> But you will not care for me.
> I am going to leave you
> And go to that happy land;
> Happy land, happy land,
> Where I will find my place.[5]

Trade and manufacturing were carried out by merchants and artisans, who lived in walled towns under the direct control of the local lord. Merchants did not operate independently but were considered the property of the local lord and on occasion could even be bought and sold like chattels. A class of slaves performed a variety of menial tasks and perhaps worked on local irrigation projects. Most of them were probably prisoners of war captured during conflicts with the neighboring principalities. Scholars do not know how extensive slavery was in ancient times, but slaves probably did not constitute a large portion of the total population.

The period of the later Zhou, from the sixth to the third century B.C.E., was an era of significant economic growth and technological innovation, especially in agriculture (see the Comparative Illustration "Early Agricultural Technology" on p. 71). During that time, large-scale water control projects were undertaken to regulate the flow of rivers and distribute water evenly to the fields, as well as to construct canals to facilitate the transport of goods from one region to another. Perhaps the most impressive technological achievement of the period was the construction of a massive water control project on the Min River, a tributary of the Yangzi. This system of canals and spillways, put into operation by the state of Qin a few years prior to the end of the Zhou dynasty, diverted excess water from the river into the local irrigation network and watered an area populated by as many as 5 million people. The system is still in use today, more than two thousand years later.

Food production was also stimulated by a number of advances in farm technology. By the mid-sixth century B.C.E., the introduction of iron had led to the development of iron plowshares, which permitted deep plowing for the first time. Other innovations dating from the later Zhou were the use of natural fertilizer, the collar harness, and the technique of leaving land fallow to preserve or replenish nutrients in the soil. By the late Zhou dynasty, the cultivation of wet rice had become one of the prime sources of food in China. Although rice was difficult and time-consuming to produce, it replaced other grain crops in areas with a warm climate because of its good taste, relative ease of preparation, and high nutritional value.

The advances in agriculture, which enabled the population of China to rise as high as 20 million people during the late Zhou era, were also undoubtedly a major factor in the growth of commerce and manufacturing. During the late Zhou, economic wealth began to replace noble birth as the prime source of power and influence. Tools made of iron became more common, and trade developed in a variety of useful commodities, including cloth, salt, and manufactured goods.

COMPARATIVE ILLUSTRATION

Early Agricultural Technology. For centuries, farmers across the globe have adopted various techniques to guarantee the flow of adequate amounts of water for their crops. One of the most effective ways to irrigate fields in hilly regions is to construct terraces to channel the flow of water from higher elevations. Shown on the right is a hillside terrace in northern China, an area where dry crops such as oats and millet have been cultivated since the sixth millennium B.C.E. The illustration on the left shows a terraced hillside in the southwestern corner of the Arabian peninsula. Excavations show that despite dry conditions through much of the peninsula, terraced agriculture has been practiced in mountainous parts of the region for as long as five thousand years.

Q *In what other areas of the Middle East is irrigated agriculture practiced?*

One of the most important items of trade in ancient China was silk. There is evidence of silkworms being raised as early as the Neolithic period. Remains of silk material have been found on Shang bronzes, and a large number of fragments have been recovered in tombs dating from the mid-Zhou era. Silk cloth was used not only for clothing and quilts but also to wrap the bodies of the dead prior to burial. Fragments have been found throughout Central Asia and as far away as Greece, suggesting that the famous Silk Road stretching from Central China westward to the Middle East and the Mediterranean Sea was in operation as early as the fifth century B.C.E.

Initially, however, jade was probably a more important item of trade carried along the Silk Road. Blocks of the precious stone were mined in the mountains of northern Tibet as early as the sixth millennium B.C.E. and began to appear in China during the Shang dynasty. Praised by Confucius as a symbol of purity and virtue, jade assumed an almost sacred quality among Chinese during the Zhou dynasty.

With the development of trade and manufacturing, China began to move toward a money economy. The first form of money, as in much of the rest of the world, may have been cowries or other seashells (the Chinese character for goods or property contains the ideographic symbol for "shell" 貝), but by the Zhou dynasty, pieces of iron shaped like a knife or round coins with a hole in the middle so they could be carried in strings of a thousand were being used. Most ordinary Chinese, however, simply used a system of barter. Taxes, rents, and even the salaries of government officials were normally paid in grain.

The Hundred Schools of Ancient Philosophy

In China, as in other great river valley societies, the birth of civilization was accompanied by the emergence of an organized effort to comprehend the nature of the cosmos and the role of human beings within it. Speculation over such questions began in the very early stages of civilization and culminated at the end of the Zhou era in the "hundred schools" of ancient philosophy, a wide-ranging debate over the nature of human beings, society, and the universe.

EARLY BELIEFS The first hint of religious belief in ancient China comes from relics found in royal tombs of Neolithic times. By then, the Chinese had already developed a religious sense beyond the primitive belief in the existence of spirits in nature. The Shang had begun to believe in the existence of one transcendent god, known as Shang Di, who presided over all the forces of nature. As time went on, the Chinese concept of religion evolved from a vaguely anthropomorphic god to a somewhat more impersonal symbol of universal order known as Heaven (*Tian*). There was also much speculation among Chinese intellectuals about the nature of the cosmic order. One of the earliest ideas was that the universe was divided into two primary forces of good and evil, light and dark, male and female, called the *yang* and the *yin*, represented symbolically by the sun (*yang*) and the moon (*yin*). According to this theory, somewhat reminiscent

A Ritual Jade Object. Jade has been prized, in the words of a Han dynasty writer, as "the fairest of stones" since the dawn of Chinese civilization. Noted for its hardness and purity of color, it is considered symbolic of many of the finest human virtues and has been found in royal tombs dating back to the period before the rise of the Shang dynasty. Whereas early examples were of relatively simple design, such as ceremonial axes and stone circles, eventually jade appeared in increasingly intricate forms. Shown here is a Zhou dynasty stone circle with a hole in the center—symbolizing Heaven—and surmounted by an elaborately carved dragon.

© William J. Duiker

of the religion of Zoroastrianism in Persia, life was a dynamic process of interaction between the forces of *yang* and *yin*. Early Chinese could only attempt to understand the process and perhaps to have some minimal effect on its operation. They could not hope to reverse it. It is sometimes asserted that this belief has contributed to the heavy element of fatalism in Chinese popular wisdom. The Chinese have traditionally believed that bad times will be followed by good times and vice versa.

The belief that there was some mysterious "law of nature" that could be interpreted by human beings led to various attempts to predict the future, such as the Shang oracle bones and other methods of divination. Philosophers invented ways to interpret the will of nature, while shamans, playing a role similar to the *brahmins* in India, were employed at court to assist the emperor in his policy deliberations until at least the fifth century C.E. One of the most famous manuals used for this purpose was the *Yi Jing*, known in English as the *Book of Changes*.

CONFUCIANISM Efforts to divine the mysterious purposes of Heaven notwithstanding, Chinese thinking about metaphysical reality also contained a strain of pragmatism, readily apparent in the ideas of the great philosopher Confucius. Confucius (*Kung fuci*, or "Master Kung") was born in the state of Lu, in the modern province of Shandong (SHAHN-doong), in 551 B.C.E. After reaching maturity, he apparently hoped to find employment as a political adviser in one of the principalities into which China was divided at that time, but he had little success in finding a patron. Nevertheless, his ideas, as contained in the *Analects* and other works attributed to him, made an indelible mark on Chinese history and culture (see the box "The Wit and Wisdom of Confucious" on p. 73).

In conversations with his disciples contained in the *Analects*, Confucius often adopted a detached and almost skeptical view of Heaven. "If you are unable to serve men," he commented on one occasion, "how can you serve the spirits? If you don't understand life, how can you understand death?" In many instances, he appeared to advise his followers to revere the deities and the ancestral spirits but to keep them at a distance. Confucius believed it was useless to speculate too much about metaphysical questions. It was better by far to assume that there was a rational order to the universe and then concentrate on ordering the affairs of this world.[6]

Confucius's interest in philosophy, then, was essentially political and ethical. The universe was constructed in such a way that if human beings could act harmoniously in accordance with its purposes, their own affairs would prosper. Much of his concern was with human behavior. The key to proper behavior was to behave in accordance with the **Dao** (DOW) (Way). Confucius assumed that all human beings had their own *Dao*, depending on their individual role in life, and it was their duty to follow it. Even the ruler had his own *Dao*, and he ignored it at his peril, for to do so could mean the loss of the mandate of Heaven. The idea of the *Dao* is reminiscent of the concept of *dharma* in ancient India and played a similar role in governing the affairs of society.

Two elements in the Confucian interpretation of the *Dao* are particularly worthy of mention. The first is the concept of duty. It was the responsibility of all individuals to subordinate their own interests and aspirations to the broader need of the family and the community. Confucius assumed that if each individual worked hard to fulfill his or her assigned destiny, the affairs of society as a whole would prosper as well. In this respect, it was important for the ruler to set a good example. If he followed his "kingly way," the beneficial effects would radiate throughout society.

The second key element is the idea of humanity, sometimes translated as "human-heartedness." This concept involves a sense of compassion and empathy for others. It is similar in some ways to Christian concepts, but with a subtle twist. Where Christian teachings call on human beings to "behave toward others as you would have them behave toward you," the Confucian maxim is put in a different way: "Do not do unto others what you would not wish done to yourself." To many Chinese, this attitude symbolizes an element of tolerance in the Chinese character that has not always been practiced in other societies.[7]

The Wit and Wisdom of Confucius

RELIGION & PHILOSOPHY

THE ANALECTS (LUN YU), a collection of sayings supposedly uttered by the ancient Chinese philosopher Confucius and drawn up after his death by his disciples, is considered to be a primary source for the Master's ideas and thought. The degree to which the collection provides an accurate account of his remarks on various subjects has long been a matter of debate among specialists. Some scholars argue that the sayings in the *Analects* reflect the views of his followers two centuries after his death in the fifth century B.C.E. more than they do those of Confucius himself.

Whatever the truth of this contention, the sayings in the *Analects* are generally accepted to be representative of Confucius's own views and have provided moral and philosophical guidance to countless generations of Chinese over the centuries. As such, they have played a major role in shaping the lives and culture of the Chinese people. Presented here are a number of familiar passages from the *Analects* on a variety of subjects.

The Confucian *Analects*

On Human Nature

17.2. By their nature, men are quite similar; in practice, they become far apart.

17.3. Only the wisest and the most ignorant of men cannot be changed.

16.9. Confucius said: Those born with innate knowledge are the highest of men; those who become learned are next in line; those who study but fail to learn follow; those who are ignorant yet do not study are the lowest of men.

On Morality

4.5. All men desire wealth and honor. But unless they can be achieved by virtuous means, they should not be sought after.

4.16. The moral man seeks righteousness; the immoral man seeks profit.

6.28. The virtuous man thinks of the needs of others before those of his own; he seeks to benefit others before himself.

15.23. Tzu Kung [one of the Master's disciples] asked if there was one word that could be applied as a standard for virtuous behavior. Confucius replied: It is reciprocity; do not do unto others what you would not wish done to yourself.

On Filial Piety

2.6. What is filial piety? Confucius said: Parents are concerned when their children become ill.

2.5. [Asked about filial piety] Confucius replied: It consists in not being disobedient; when they are alive, parents should be served according to the rules of propriety; after their death, they should be buried correctly and sacrifices should be carried out in a proper manner.

4.18. Confucius said: When serving one's parents, it is permissible to remonstrate with them, but in a respectful manner; if they do not agree, one should not oppose their wishes and even accept punishment without complaint.

On Education

2.15. Study without thought is a waste of time; thought without study is dangerous.

8.12. It is rare to find a man who has studied for three years without making progress.

On Government

2.3. If the government seeks to rule by decrees and the threat of punishment, the people will have no sense of shame; but if they are governed by virtue and a sense of propriety, they will feel shame and seek to behave correctly.

13.6. If its conduct is correct, a government can succeed without issuing directives; if not, directives will not be obeyed.

12.7. Confucius said: Without the confidence of the people, government cannot succeed.

On Religion

13.3. With regard to what he does not know, the superior man reserves judgment.

7.20. The Master did not comment on the supernatural, on feats of strength, on disorder, and on the spirits.

6.20. To meet one's human obligations, to respect the spirits but maintain distance from them, such indeed may be called wisdom.

11.11. [Asked about serving the spirits of the departed], Confucius replied: If you are unable to serve men, how can you serve the spirits? If you don't understand life, how can you understand death?

 Confucius is viewed by some observers as a reformer, and by others as a conservative. Based on the information available to you in this chapter, how would you classify his ideas, as expressed in the Analects?

Source: *The Four Books: Confucian Analects*, by James Legge (Hong Kong: The International Publication Society, n.d.). Translation by William J. Duiker and © 2011 William J. Duiker.

Confucius may have considered himself a failure because he never attained the position he wanted, but many of his contemporaries found his ideas appealing, and in the generations after his death, his message spread widely throughout China. Confucius was an outspoken critic of his times and lamented the disappearance of what he regarded as the golden age of the early Zhou. One classical source quoted him as follows:

> The practice of the Great Way, the illustrious men of the Three Dynasties—these I shall never know in person. And yet they inspire my ambition. When the Great Way was practiced, the world was shared by all alike. The worthy and the able were promoted to office and practiced good faith and lived in affection. There they did not regard as parents only their own parents, or as sons only their own sons. The aged found a fitting close to their lives, the robust their proper employment; the young were provided with an upbringing and the widow and widower, the orphaned and the sick, with proper care. Men had their talks and women their hearths. They hated to see goods lying about in waste, yet they did not hoard them for themselves; they disliked the thought that their energies were not fully used, yet they used them not for private ends. Therefore all evil plotting was prevented and thieves and rebels did not arise, so that people could leave their outer gates unbolted. This was the age of Grand Unity.[8]

Yet Confucius was not just another disgruntled Chinese conservative mourning the passing of the good old days; rather, he was a revolutionary thinker, many of whose key ideas looked forward rather than backward. Perhaps his most striking political idea was that the government should be open to all men of superior quality, not limited to those of noble birth. As one of his disciples reports in the *Analects*, "The Master said, by their nature, men are quite similar; in practice, they become far apart."[9] Confucius undoubtedly had himself in mind as one of those "superior" men, but the rapacity of the hereditary lords must have added strength to his convictions.

The concept of rule by merit was, of course, not an unfamiliar idea in the China of his day; the *Rites of Zhou* had clearly stated that the king deserved to rule because of his talent and virtue, not as the result of noble birth. In practice, however, aristocratic privilege must often have opened the doors to political influence, and many of Confucius's contemporaries must have regarded his appeal for government by talent as both exciting and dangerous. Confucius did not explicitly question the right of the hereditary aristocracy to play a leading role in the political process, nor did his ideas have much effect in his lifetime. Still, they introduced a new concept that was later implemented in the form of a bureaucracy selected through a civil service examination (see Chapter 10).

Confucius's ideas, passed on to later generations through the *Analects* as well as through writings attributed to him, had a strong impact on Chinese political thinkers of the late Zhou period, a time when the existing system was in disarray and open to serious question. But as with most great thinkers, Confucius's ideas were sufficiently ambiguous to be interpreted in contradictory ways. Some, like the philosopher Mencius (MEN-shuss) (370–290 B.C.E.), stressed the humanistic side of Confucian ideas, arguing that human beings were by nature good and hence could be taught their civic responsibilities by example. He also stressed that the ruler had a duty to govern with compassion:

> Here is the way to win the empire: win the people and you win the empire. Here is the way to win the people: win their hearts and you win the people. Here is the way to win their hearts: give them and share with them what they like, and do not do to them what they do not like. The people turn to a humane ruler as water flows downward or beasts take to wilderness.[10]

Here is a prescription for political behavior that could win wide support in our own day. Other thinkers, however, rejected Mencius's rosy view of human nature and argued for a different approach (see Opposing Viewpoints "A Debate over Good and Evil" on p. 75).

LEGALISM A school of thought that became quite popular during the "hundred schools" era in ancient China was the philosophy of **Legalism**. Taking issue with the view of Mencius and other disciples of Confucius that human nature was essentially good, the Legalists argued that human beings were by nature evil and would follow the correct path only if coerced by harsh laws and stiff punishments. These thinkers were referred to as the School of Law because they rejected the Confucian view that government by "superior men" could solve society's problems and argued instead for a system of impersonal laws.

The Legalists also disagreed with the Confucian belief that the universe has a moral core. They therefore argued that only firm action by the state could bring about social order. Fear of harsh punishment, more than the promise of material reward, could best motivate the common people to serve the interests of the ruler. Because human nature was essentially corrupt, officials could not be trusted to carry out their duties in a fair and even-handed manner, and only a strong ruler could create an orderly society. All human actions should be subordinated to the effort to create a strong and prosperous state subject to his will.

DAOISM One of the most popular alternatives to **Confucianism** was the philosophy of **Daoism** (DOW-iz-uhm) (frequently spelled Taoism). According to Chinese tradition, the Daoist school was founded by a contemporary of Confucius popularly known as Lao Zi (LOW ["ow" as in "how"] dzuh), or the Old Master. Many modern scholars, however, are skeptical that Lao Zi actually existed.

Obtaining a clear understanding of the original concepts of Daoism is difficult because its primary document, a short treatise known as the *Dao De Jing* (DOW deh JING) (sometimes translated as *The Way of the Tao*), is an enigmatic book whose interpretation has baffled scholars for centuries. The opening line, for example, explains less what the *Dao* is than what it is not: "The Tao [Way] that can be told of is not the eternal Tao. The name that can be named is not the eternal name."[11]

Nevertheless, the basic concepts of Daoism are not especially difficult to understand. Like Confucianism, Daoism does not anguish over the underlying meaning of the cosmos.

OPPOSING ✕ VIEWPOINTS

A Debate over Good and Evil

RELIGION & PHILOSOPHY

DURING THE LATTER PART OF THE ZHOU DYNASTY, one of the major preoccupations of Chinese philosophers was to determine the essential qualities of human nature. In the *Analects*, Confucius was cited as asserting that humans' moral instincts were essentially neutral at birth; their minds must be cultivated to bring out the potential goodness therein. In later years, the master's disciples elaborated on this issue. The great humanitarian philosopher Mencius maintained that human nature was essentially good. But his rival Xunzi (SHYOON-zuh) took the opposite tack, arguing that evil is inherent in human nature and could be eradicated only by rigorous training at the hands of an instructor. Later, Xunzi's views would be adopted by the Legalist philosophers of the Qin dynasty, although his belief in the efficacy of education earned him a place in the community of Confucian scholars.

The Book of Mencius

Mencius said, … "The goodness of human nature is like the downward course of water. There is no human being lacking in the tendency to do good, just as there is no water lacking in the tendency to flow downward. Now by striking water and splashing it, you may cause it to go over your head, and by damming and channeling it, you can force it to flow uphill. But is this the nature of water? It is the force that makes this happen. While people can be made to do what is not good, what happens to their nature is like this.…

"All human beings have a mind that cannot bear to see the sufferings of others.…

"Here is why.… Now, if anyone were suddenly to see a child about to fall into a well, his mind would always be filled with alarm, distress, pity, and compassion. That he would react accordingly is not because he would use the opportunity to ingratiate himself with the child's parents, nor because he would seek commendation from neighbors and friends, nor because he would hate the adverse reputation. From this it may be seen that one who lacks a mind that feels pity and compassion would not be human; one who lacks a mind that feels shame and aversion would not be human; one who lacks a mind that feels modesty and compliance would not be human; and one who lacks a mind that knows right and wrong would not be human.

"The mind's feeling of pity and compassion is the beginning of humaneness; the mind's feeling of shame and aversion is the beginning of rightness; the mind's feeling of modesty and compliance is the beginning of propriety; and the mind's sense of right and wrong is the beginning of wisdom."

The Book of Xunzi

Human nature is evil; its goodness derives from conscious activity. Now it is human nature to be born with a fondness for profit. Indulging this leads to contention and strife, and the sense of modesty and yielding with which one was born disappears. One is born with feelings of envy and hate, and, by indulging these, one is led into banditry and theft, so that the sense of loyalty and good faith with which he was born disappears. One is born with the desires of the ears and eyes and with a fondness for beautiful sights and sounds, and by indulging these, one is led to licentiousness and chaos, so that the sense of ritual, rightness, refinement, and principle with which one was born is lost. Hence, following human nature and indulging human emotions will inevitably lead to contention and strife, causing one to rebel against one's proper duty, reduce principle to chaos, and revert to violence. Therefore one must be transformed by the example of a teacher and guided by the way of ritual and right before one will attain modesty and yielding, accord with refinement and ritual and return to order. From this perspective it is apparent that human nature is evil and that its goodness is the result of conscious activity.

Mencius said, "Now human nature is good, and [when it is not] this is always a result of having lost or destroyed one's nature." I say that he was mistaken to take such a view. Now, it is human nature that, as soon as a person is born, he departs from his original substance and from his rational disposition so that he must inevitably lose and destroy them. Seen in this way, it is apparent that human nature is evil.

 What arguments do these two Confucian thinkers advance to support their point of view about the essential elements of human nature? In your view, which argument is more persuasive?

Source: Excerpt from William Theodore de Bary and Irene Bloom, *Sources of Chinese Tradition*, Vol. I, 2nd ed (New York, 1999). Copyright © 1999 by Columbia University Press.

Rather, it attempts to set forth proper forms of behavior for human beings here on earth. In most other respects, however, Daoism presents a view of life and its ultimate meaning that is almost diametrically opposed to that of Confucianism. Whereas Confucian doctrine asserts that it is the duty of human beings to work hard to improve life here on earth,

The Daoist Answer to Confucianism

RELIGION & PHILOSOPHY

THE *DAO DE JING* (*The Way of the Tao*) is the great classic of philosophical Daoism (Taoism). Traditionally attributed to the legendary Chinese philosopher Lao Zi (Old Master), it was probably written during the era of Confucius. This opening passage illustrates two of the key ideas that characterize Daoist belief: it is impossible to define the nature of the universe, and inaction (not Confucian action) is the key to ordering the affairs of human beings.

The Way of the Tao

The Tao that can be told of is not the eternal Tao;
The name that can be named is not the eternal name.
The Nameless is the origin of Heaven and Earth;
The Named is the mother of all things.

Therefore let there always be nonbeing, so we may see their
    subtlety.
And let there always be being, so we may see their outcome.
The two are the same,
But after they are produced, they have different names.
They both may be called deep and profound.
Deeper and more profound,
The door of all subtleties!
When the people of the world all know beauty as beauty,
There arises the recognition of ugliness.

When they all know the good as good,
There arises the recognition of evil.
Therefore:
Being and nonbeing produce each other;
Difficult and easy complete each other;
Long and short contrast each other;
High and low distinguish each other;
Sound and voice harmonize each other;
Front and behind accompany each other.

Therefore the sage manages affairs without action
And spreads doctrines without words.
All things arise, and he does not turn away from them.
He produces them but does not take possession of them.
He acts but does not rely on his own ability.
He accomplishes his task but does not claim credit for it.
It is precisely because he does not claim credit that his
    accomplishment remains with him.

 What is Lao Zi, the presumed author of this document, trying to express about the basic nature of the universe? Based on the Confucian Analects and The Way of the Tao, how do you think the Chinese attempted to understand the order of nature through their philosophies?

Source: From *The Way of Lao Tzu* (Tao-te Ching), by Wing-Tsit Chan, trans. Copyright © 1963 by Macmillan College Publishing Company, Inc.

Daoists contend that the true way to interpret the will of Heaven is not action but inaction (*wu wei*). The best way to act in harmony with the universal order is to act spontaneously and let nature take its course (see the box "The Daoist Answer to Confucianism" above).

Such a message could be very appealing to people who were uncomfortable with the somewhat rigid flavor of the Confucian work ethic and preferred a more individualistic approach. This image would eventually find graphic expression in Chinese landscape painting, which in its classic form

Topham/The Image Works

Lao Zi and Confucius. Little is known about the life of Lao Zi (shown on the left in the illustration), and it is unlikely that he and Confucius ever met. According to tradition, though, the two held a face-to-face meeting. The discussion must have been interesting, for their views about the nature of reality were diametrically opposed. Nevertheless, the Chinese have managed to preserve both traditions, perhaps a reflection of the dualities represented in the Chinese approach to life. A similar duality existed among Platonists and Aristotelians in ancient Greece (see Chapter 4).

The Art of War

POLITICS & GOVERNMENT

WITH THE POSSIBLE EXCEPTION of the nineteenth-century German military strategist Carl von Clausewitz, there is probably no more famous or respected writer on the art of war than the ancient Chinese thinker Sun Tzu (SOON dzuh). Yet surprisingly little is known about him. Recently discovered evidence suggests that he lived in the fifth century B.C.E., during the chronic conflict of the Period of Warring States, and that he was an early member of an illustrious family of military strategists who advised Zhou rulers for more than two hundred years. But despite the mystery surrounding his life, there is no doubt of his influence on later generations of military planners. Among his most avid followers in our day have been the revolutionary leaders Mao Zedong and Ho Chi Minh, as well as the Japanese military strategists who planned the attacks on Port Arthur and Pearl Harbor.

The following brief excerpt from his classic, *The Art of War*, provides a glimmer into the nature of his advice, still so timely today.

Selections from Sun Tzu

Sun Tzu said:

"In general, the method for employing the military is this: … Attaining one hundred victories in one hundred battles is not the pinnacle of excellence. Subjugating the enemy's army without fighting is the true pinnacle of excellence.…

"Thus the highest realization of warfare is to attack the enemy's plans; next is to attack their alliances; next to attack their army; and the lowest is to attack their fortified cities.

"This tactic of attacking fortified cities is adopted only when unavoidable. Preparing large movable protective shields, armored assault wagons, and other equipment and devices will require three months. Building earthworks will require another three months to complete. If the general cannot overcome his impatience but instead launches an assault wherein his men swarm over the walls like ants, he will kill one-third of his officers and troops, and the city will still not be taken. This is the disaster that results from attacking [fortified cities].

"Thus, one who excels at employing the military subjugates other people's armies without engaging in battle, captures other people's fortified cities without attacking them, and destroys others people's states without prolonged fighting. He must fight under Heaven with the paramount aim of 'preservation.' …

"In general, the strategy of employing the military is this: If your strength is ten times theirs, surround them; if five, then attack them; if double, then divide your forces. If you are equal in strength to the enemy, you can engage him. If fewer, you can circumvent him. If outmatched, you can avoid him.…

"Thus, there are five factors from which victory can be known:

"One who knows when he can fight, and when he cannot fight, will be victorious.
"One who recognizes how to employ large and small numbers will be victorious.
"One whose upper and lower ranks have the same desires will be victorious.
"One who, fully prepared, awaits the unprepared will be victorious.
"One whose general is capable and not interfered with by the ruler will be victorious.

"These five are the Way (Tao) to know victory.…

"Thus it is said that one who knows the enemy and knows himself will not be endangered in a hundred engagements. One who does not know the enemy but knows himself will sometimes be victorious, sometimes meet with defeat. One who knows neither the enemy nor himself will invariably be defeated in every engagement."

 Why are the ideas of Sun Tzu about the art of war still so popular among military strategists after 2,500 years? How might he advise U.S. and other statesmen to deal with the problem of international terrorism today?

Source: From *Sun Tzu: The Art of War*, Ralph D. Sawyer (Boulder: Westview Press, 1994), pp. 177–179.

---

would depict naturalistic scenes of mountains, water, and clouds and underscore the fragility and smallness of individual human beings.

Daoism achieved considerable popularity in the waning years of the Zhou dynasty. It was especially popular among intellectuals, who may have found it appealing as an escapist antidote in a world characterized by growing disorder.

POPULAR BELIEFS Daoism also played a second role as a framework for popular spiritualistic and animistic beliefs among the common people. Popular Daoism was less a philosophy than a religion; it comprised a variety of rituals and behaviors that were regarded as a means of achieving heavenly salvation or even a state of immortality on earth. Daoist sorcerers practiced various types of exercises for training the mind and body in the hope of achieving power, sexual prowess, and long life. It was primarily this form of Daoism that survived into a later age.

The philosophical forms of Confucianism and Daoism did not provide much meaning to the mass of the population, for whom philosophical debate over the ultimate meaning of life was less important than the daily struggle for survival. Even among the elites, interest in the occult and in astrology was high, and many royal courts included a hereditary astrologer to help predict the intentions of the heavenly forces. Throughout the ancient period, magico-religious ideas coexisted with interest in natural science and humanistic philosophy.

For most Chinese, Heaven was not a vague, impersonal law of nature, as it was for many Confucian and Daoist intellectuals. Instead, it was a terrain peopled with innumerable gods and spirits of nature, both good and evil, who existed in trees, mountains, and streams as well as in heavenly bodies. As human beings mastered the techniques of farming, they called on divine intervention to guarantee a good harvest. Other gods were responsible for the safety of fishers, transportation workers, or prospective mothers.

Another aspect of popular religion was the belief that the spirits of deceased human beings lived in the atmosphere for a time before ascending to heaven or descending to hell. During that period, surviving family members had to care for the spirits through proper ritual, or they would become evil spirits and haunt the survivors.

Thus, in ancient China, human beings were offered a variety of interpretations of the nature of the universe. Confucianism satisfied the need for a rational doctrine of nation building and social organization at a time when the existing political and social structure was beginning to disintegrate. Philosophical Daoism provided a more sensitive approach to the vicissitudes of fate and nature and a framework for a set of diverse animistic beliefs at the popular level. But neither could satisfy the deeper emotional needs that sometimes inspire the human spirit. Neither could effectively provide solace in a time of sorrow or the hope of a better life in the hereafter. Something else would be needed to fill the gap.

The First Chinese Empire: The Qin Dynasty

Q FOCUS QUESTION: How did the first emperor of the Qin dynasty transform the political, social, and economic institutions of early China?

During the last two centuries of the Zhou dynasty (the fourth and third centuries B.C.E.), the authority of the king became increasingly nominal, and several of the small principalities

into which the Zhou kingdom had been divided began to evolve into powerful states that presented a potential challenge to the Zhou ruler himself. Chief among these were Qu (CHOO) in the central Yangzi Valley, Wu (WOO) in the Yangzi delta, and Yue (yoo-EH) along the southeastern coast. At first, their mutual rivalries were held in check, but by the late fifth century B.C.E., competition intensified into civil war, giving birth to the so-called Period of the Warring States (see the box "The Art of War" on p. 77). Powerful principalities vied with each other for preeminence and largely ignored the now purely titular authority of the Zhou court (see Map 3.2). New forms of warfare also emerged with the invention of iron weapons and the introduction of the foot soldier. Cavalry, too, made its first appearance, armed with the powerful crossbow. Cities were now threatened by larger and more competent armies. When they sought to protect themselves by erecting high walls, their opponents countered by developing new techniques in siege warfare.

Eventually, the relatively young state of Qin (CHIN), located in the original homeland of the Zhou, emerged as a key player in these conflicts. By the mid-fourth century B.C.E., it had become a major force in the contest for hegemony in late-Zhou China by adopting a number of reforms in agriculture, government administration, military organization, and fiscal policy. As a result of policies put into effect by the

MAP 3.2 China During the Period of the Warring States. From the fifth to the third centuries B.C.E., China was locked in a time of civil strife known as the Period of the Warring States. This map shows the Zhou dynasty capital at Luoyang, along with the major states that were squabbling for precedence in the region.

Q *Why did most of the early states emerge in areas adjacent to China's two major river systems, the Yellow and the Yangzi?*

adviser Shang Yang (SHAHNG yahng) in the mid-fourth century B.C.E., Qin society was ruled with ruthless efficiency. In the words of Sima Qian (SUH-mah chee-AHN), a famous historian of the Han dynasty:

> He commanded that the people be divided into tens and fives and that they supervise each other and be mutually liable. Anyone who failed to report criminal activity would be chopped in two at the waist, while those who reported it would receive the same reward as that for obtaining the head of an enemy.[12]

Benefiting from a strong defensive position in the mountains to the west of the great bend of the Yellow River, as well as from their control of the rich Sichuan plains, the Qin gradually subdued their main rivals through conquest or diplomatic maneuvering. In 221 B.C.E., the Qin ruler declared the establishment of a new dynasty, the first truly unified government in Chinese history.

The Qin Dynasty (221–206 B.C.E.)

One of the primary reasons for the triumph of the Qin was probably the character of the Qin ruler, known to history as Qin Shi Huangdi, or the First Emperor of Qin. A man of forceful personality and immense ambition, Qin Shi Huangdi had ascended to the throne of Qin in 246 B.C.E. at the age of thirteen. Described by the Han dynasty historian Sima Qian as having "the chest of a bird of prey, the voice of a jackal, and the heart of a tiger," the new king found the Legalist views of his adviser Li Su (lee SUH) all too appealing. In 221 B.C.E., Qin Shi Huangdi defeated the last of his rivals and founded a new dynasty with himself as emperor.

The Qin Empire, 221–206 B.C.E.

© 2016 Cengage Learning

POLITICAL STRUCTURES The Qin dynasty transformed Chinese politics. Philosophical doctrines that had proliferated during the late Zhou period were prohibited, and Legalism was adopted as the official ideology. Those who opposed the policies of the new regime were punished and sometimes executed, while books presenting ideas contrary to the official orthodoxy were publicly put to the torch, perhaps the first example of book burning in history (see the box "Memorandum on the Burning of Books" on p. 80).

Legalistic theory gave birth to a number of fundamental administrative and political developments, some of which would survive the Qin and serve as a model for future dynasties. In the first place, unlike the Zhou, the Qin was a highly centralized state. The central bureaucracy was divided into three primary ministries: a civil authority, a military authority, and a censorate, whose inspectors surveyed the efficiency of officials throughout the system. This would later become standard administrative procedure for future Chinese dynasties.

Below the central government were two levels of administration: provinces and counties. Unlike the Zhou system, officials at these levels did not inherit their positions but were appointed by the court and were subject to dismissal at the emperor's whim. A penal code provided for harsh punishments for all wrongdoers. Officials were watched by the censors, who reported directly to the throne. Those guilty of malfeasance in office were executed.

SOCIETY AND THE ECONOMY Qin Shi Huangdi, who had a passion for centralization, unified the system of weights and measures, standardized the monetary system and the written forms of Chinese characters, and ordered the construction of a system of roads extending throughout the empire. He also attempted to eliminate the remaining powers of the landed aristocrats and divided their estates among the peasants, who were now taxed directly by the state. He thus eliminated potential rivals and secured tax revenues for the central government.

Members of the aristocratic clans were required to live in the capital city at Xianyang (shi-AHN-yahng), just north of modern Xian, so that the court could monitor their activities. Such a system may not have been advantageous to the peasants in all respects, however, since the central government could now collect taxes more effectively and mobilize the peasants for military service and for various public works projects.

The Qin dynasty was equally unsympathetic to the merchants, whom it viewed as parasites. Private commercial activities were severely restricted and heavily taxed, and many vital forms of commerce and manufacturing, including mining, wine making, and the distribution of salt, were placed under a government monopoly.

Qin Shi Huangdi was equally aggressive in foreign affairs. His armies continued the gradual advance to the south that had taken place during the final years of the Zhou dynasty, extending the border of China to the edge of the Red River in modern Vietnam. To supply the Qin armies operating in the area, a canal was dug that provided direct inland navigation from the Yangzi River in central China to what is now the modern city of Guangzhou (gwahng-JOE) (Canton) in the south.

BEYOND THE FRONTIER: THE NOMADIC PEOPLES AND THE GREAT WALL The main area of concern for the Qin emperor, however, was in the north, where a nomadic people, known to the Chinese as the Xiongnu (SHYAHNG-noo) and possibly related to the Huns (see Chapter 5) or to Indo-European-speaking people in the area, had become increasingly active in the area of the Gobi Desert. The area north of the Yellow River had been sparsely inhabited since prehistoric times. During the Qin period, the climate of northern China was somewhat milder and moister than it is today, and parts of the

Memorandum on the Burning of Books

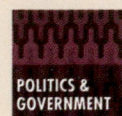

POLITICS & GOVERNMENT

LI SU, who is quoted in the following passage, was a chief minister of the First Emperor of Qin. An exponent of Legalism, Li Su hoped to eliminate all rival theories of government. His recommendation to the emperor on how to accomplish this was recorded by the Han dynasty historian Sima Qian. The emperor approved the proposal and ordered all books contrary to the spirit of Legalist ideology to be destroyed on pain of death. Fortunately, some texts were preserved by being hidden or even memorized by their owners and were thus available to later generations. For centuries afterward, the First Emperor of Qin and his minister were singled out for criticism because of their intolerance and their effort to control the minds of their subjects. Totalitarianism, it seems, is not a modern concept.

Sima Qian, *Historical Records*

In earlier times the empire disintegrated and fell into disorder, and no one was capable of unifying it. Thereupon the various feudal lords rose to power. In their discourses they all praised the past in order to disparage the present and embellished empty words to confuse the truth. Everyone cherished his own favorite school of learning and criticized what had been instituted by the authorities. But at present Your Majesty possesses a unified empire, has regulated the distinctions of black and white, and has firmly established for yourself a position of sole supremacy. And yet these independent schools, joining with each other, criticize the codes of laws and instructions. Hearing of the promulgation of a decree, they criticize it, each from the standpoint of his own school. At home they disapprove of it in their hearts; going out they criticize it in the thoroughfare. They seek a reputation by discrediting their sovereign; they appear superior by expressing contrary views, and they lead the lowly multitude in the spreading of slander. If such license is not prohibited, the sovereign power will decline above and partisan factions will form below. It would be well to prohibit this.

Your servant suggests that all books in the imperial archives, save the memoirs of Ch'in, be burned. All persons in the empire, except members of the Academy of Learned Scholars, in possession of the *Book of Odes*, the *Book of History*, and discourses of the hundred philosophers should take them to the local governors and have them indiscriminately burned. Those who dare to talk to each other about the *Book of Odes* and the *Book of History* should be executed and their bodies exposed in the marketplace. Anyone referring to the past to criticize the present should, together with all members of his family, be put to death. Officials who fail to report cases that have come under their attention are equally guilty. After thirty days from the time of issuing the decree, those who have not destroyed their books are to be branded and sent to build the Great Wall. Books not to be destroyed will be those on medicine and pharmacy, divination by the tortoise and milfoil, and agriculture and arboriculture. People wishing to pursue learning should take the officials as their teachers.

 Why did the Legalist thinker Li Su believe that his proposal to destroy dangerous ideas was justified? Are there examples of similar thinking in our own time? Are there occasions when it might be permissible to outlaw unpopular ideas?

Source: Excerpt from *Sources of Chinese Tradition*, by William Theodore de Bary, pgs. 154–155. Copyright © 1960 by Columbia University Press. Reprinted with the permission of the publisher.

region were heavily forested. The local population probably lived by hunting and fishing, practicing limited forms of agriculture, or herding animals such as cattle or sheep.

As the climate gradually became drier, people were forced to rely increasingly on animal husbandry as a means of livelihood. Their response was to master the art of riding on horseback and to adopt the nomadic life. Organized loosely into communities consisting of a number of kinship groups, they ranged far and wide in search of pasture for their herds of cattle, goats, or sheep. As they moved seasonally from one pasture to another, they often traveled several hundred miles carrying their goods and their circular felt tents, called *yurts*.

But the new way of life presented its own challenges. Increased food production led to a growing population, which in times of drought outstripped the available resources. Rival groups then competed for the best pastures. After they mastered the art of fighting on horseback in the middle of the first millennium B.C.E., territorial warfare became commonplace throughout the entire frontier region, from the Pacific Ocean to Central Asia.

By the end of the Zhou dynasty in the third century B.C.E., the nomadic Xiongnu had unified many of the groups operating in the region and began to pose a serious threat to the security of China's northern frontier. A number of Chinese principalities in the area began to build walls and fortifications to keep them out, but warriors on horseback possessed significant advantages over the infantry of the Chinese.

Qin Shi Huangdi's answer to the problem was to introduce mounted archers into his military units stationed in the north to counter nomad attacks while strengthening the walls to keep the marauders out. In Sima Qian's words:

> First Emperor of the [Qin] … seized control of all the lands south of the Yellow River and established border defenses along the river, constructing forty-four walled district cities

overlooking the river and manning them with convict laborers transported to the border for garrison duty. Thus, he utilized the natural mountain barriers to establish the border defenses, scooping out the valleys and constructing ramparts and building installations at other points where they were needed. The whole line of defenses stretched over ten thousand *li* [a *li* is one-third of a mile]. …[13]

Today, of course, we know Qin Shi Huangdi's project as the Great Wall, which extends nearly 4,000 miles from the sandy wastes of Central Asia to the sea. It is constructed of massive granite blocks, and its top is wide enough to serve as a roadway for horse-drawn chariots (see Chapter 10). Although the wall that appears in most photographs today was built 1,500 years after the Qin, during the Ming dynasty, some of the walls built by the Qin remain standing. Their construction was a massive project that required the efforts of thousands of laborers, many of whom met their deaths there and, according to legend, are buried within the wall.

THE FALL OF THE QIN   The Legalist system put in place by the First Emperor of Qin was designed to achieve maximum efficiency as well as total security for the state. It did neither. Qin Shi Huangdi was apparently aware of the dangers of factions within the imperial family and established a class of **eunuchs** (castrated males) who served as personal attendants for himself and female members of the royal family. The original idea may have been to restrict the influence of male courtiers, and the eunuch system later became a standard feature of the Chinese imperial system. But as confidential advisers to the royal family, eunuchs were in a position of influence. The rivalry between the "inner" imperial court and the "outer" court of bureaucratic officials led to tensions that persisted until the end of the imperial system.

By ruthlessly gathering control over the empire into his own hands, Qin Shi Huangdi had hoped to establish a rule that, in the words of Sima Qian, "would be enjoyed by his sons for ten thousand generations." In fact, his centralizing zeal alienated many key groups. Landed aristocrats and Confucian intellectuals, as well as the common people, groaned under the censorship of thought and speech, harsh taxes, and forced labor projects. "He killed men," recounted the historian, "as though he thought he could never finish, he punished men as though he were afraid he would never get around to them all, and the whole world revolted against him."[14] Shortly after the emperor died in 210 B.C.E., the dynasty descended into factional rivalry, and four years later it was overthrown.

The Glorious Han Dynasty
(202 B.C.E.–221 C.E.)

Q **FOCUS QUESTION:** To what degree did the Han dynasty turn to Confucianism as an ideology of the state?

The fall of the Qin dynasty in 206 B.C.E. was followed by a brief period of civil strife as aspiring successors competed for hegemony. Out of this strife emerged one of the greatest and most durable dynasties in Chinese history—the Han (HAHN). The Han dynasty would later become so closely identified with the advance of Chinese civilization that even today the Chinese sometimes refer to themselves as "people of Han" and to their language as the "language of Han."

The founder of the Han dynasty was Liu Bang (lyoo BAHNG), a commoner of peasant origin who would be known historically by his imperial title of Han Gaozu (HAHN gow-DZOO), or Exalted Emperor of Han. Under his strong rule and that of his successors, the new dynasty quickly moved to consolidate its control over the empire and promote the welfare of its subjects. Efficient and benevolent, at least by the standards of the time, Gaozu maintained the centralized political institutions of the Qin but abandoned its harsh Legalistic approach to law enforcement. Han rulers discovered in Confucian principles a useful foundation for the creation of a new state philosophy. Under the Han, Confucianism, supplemented by elements from the surviving classics of the "hundred schools" period, began to take on the character of an official ideology (see the box "A Prescription for the Emperor" on p. 82).

Confucianism and the State

The integration of Confucian doctrine with Legalist institutions, creating a system generally known as **State Confucianism**, took a while to accomplish. At first, the founding emperor Han Gaozu departed from the Qin policy of centralized rule by rewarding some of his key allies with vast fiefdoms, restricting his own territory to lands around the new capital of Chang'an (CHENG-AHN). But chronic unrest throughout the countryside eventually forced a change in policy. By the mid-second century B.C.E., the influence of unruly aristocratic forces had been curbed, and once again power was concentrated at the imperial court.

Once this was accomplished, the Han rulers sought to restore key components of the Qin system of centralized government. For example, they borrowed the tripartite division of the central government into civilian and military authorities and a censorate. The government was headed by a "grand council" including representatives from all three segments of government. The Han also retained the system of local government, dividing the empire into provinces and districts.

Finally, the Han sought to apply the Qin system of selecting government officials on the basis of merit rather than birth. Shortly after founding the new dynasty, Han Gaozu decreed that local officials would be asked to recommend promising candidates for public service. Thirty years later, in 165 B.C.E., the first known **civil service examination** was administered to candidates for positions in the bureaucracy. Shortly after that, an academy was established to train candidates. The first candidates were almost all from aristocratic or other wealthy families, and the Han bureaucracy itself was still dominated by the traditional hereditary elite. Still, the principle of selecting officials on the basis of talent had been established and would eventually become standard practice. By the end of the first century B.C.E., as many as 30,000 students were enrolled at the academy.

A Prescription for the Emperor

POLITICS & GOVERNMENT

JIA YI (JYAH YEE) (201–168? B.C.E.) was a counselor to Emperor Wendi (wen-DEE) (r. 181–157 B.C.E.), one of the early rulers of the Han dynasty. His words of advice to his sovereign, excerpted in this selection, bear witness to the strong tradition of popular sovereignty in Confucian thought that had earlier been expressed by the well-known fourth-century B.C.E. philosopher Mencius. Following Mencius's example, Jia Yi declared that the desires of the people should be paramount in forming the basis of government. In his opinion, a ruler who did not defer to the wishes of his subjects did not merit the mandate of Heaven. Jia's views on the role of the supernatural in human affairs are particularly striking, as he declared that it was not the will of Heaven, but good or bad deeds undertaken here on earth, that brought fortune or misfortune to the people of China.

"People Are in Every Way the Root"

It is said that in government, the people are in every way the root (base). For the state, the ruler, and the officials, the people constitute the root. Thus the security of the state or its endangerment depends on them [the people]; the prestige of the ruler or his disgrace depends on them; and the honor of the officials or their debasement is contingent on them. This is what is meant by saying the people are in every way the root. Then again, it is said that in government, the people constitute in every way the mandate. For the state, the ruler, and the officials all depend on the people for their mandate. The life or death of the state depends on the people, the vision or blindness of the ruler depends on them, and whether officials are respected or not depends on them. This is why the people are in every way the mandate....

Still further it is said that the people are the power on which the state, the ruler, and the officials all depend for their power. If victory is won, it is because the people want to be victorious; if an attack succeeds, it is because the people want it so; if defense succeeds, it is because the people want to survive.... If the people are fearful of the enemy, they will surely retreat and defeat will surely come. Disaster and fortune, as we see, are determined not in Heaven but by the officers and the people....

Good deeds will in the end bring good fortune, and bad deeds will inevitably bring misfortune. Those who are blessed by Heaven need not thank Heaven, and those who suffer from natural disasters need not blame Heaven, for it is all one's own doing.... Heaven will present good fortune to the virtuous and disaster to those who deprive the people. Even the lowest of people should not *be slighted, and the most foolish among them should not be taken advantage of.* Thus, throughout history, those who oppose the people sooner or later are defeated by the people.... How can anyone think of behaving with arrogance and self-deception? The enlightened ruler and the noble person will vie to practice good when they perceive it, and they will treat evil like an enemy if they hear of it.

 Are Jia Yi's views implicit in the teachings of Confucius, as expressed in the Analects and other sources discussed in this chapter? How do his views compare with the advice offered to rulers in other ancient societies?

Source: From *Sources of Chinese Tradition*, 2nd edition, Vol. 1, by Wm. T. DeBary and Irene Bloom. Copyright © 1999 Columbia University Press. Reprinted with permission of the publisher.

Driven by government policies that used tax incentives to promote large families, the population of the empire increased rapidly—by some estimates rising from about 20 million to more than 60 million at the height of the dynasty—creating a growing need for a large and efficient bureaucracy to maintain the state in proper working order. Unfortunately, the Han were unable to resolve all of the problems left over from the past. Factionalism at court remained a serious problem and undermined the efficiency of the central government. Equally important, despite their efforts, the Han rulers were never able to restrain the great aristocratic families, who continued to play a dominant role in political and economic affairs. The failure to curb the power of the wealthy clans eventually became a major factor in the collapse of the dynasty.

The Economy

Han rulers unwittingly contributed to their own problems by adopting fiscal policies that led eventually to greater concentration of land in the hands of the wealthy. They were aware that a free peasantry paying taxes directly to the state would both limit the wealth and power of the great noble families and increase the state's revenues. The Han had difficulty, however, in preventing the recurrence of the economic inequities that had characterized the last years of the Zhou. Land taxes were not especially high but had to be paid in cash rather than in grain to make collection easier. In years of bad harvests, poor farmers were unable to pay their taxes and were forced to sell their land and become tenant farmers, paying rents of up to half the annual harvest. Although food production increased steadily due to the application of natural fertilizer and the use of iron tools that brought new lands under the plow, the trebling of the population under the early Han eventually reduced the average size of a family's farm plot to about one acre per person, barely enough for survival.

Farm families also faced a number of other exactions, including compulsory military service for adult males and forced labor of up to one month annually. As rural protests escalated during the first decades of Han rule, the imperial government finally ended military conscription and began to rely on professional armies, recruited primarily among non-Chinese minorities living along the periphery of the empire. That strategy, however, would eventually lead to its own problems (see "The Decline and Fall of the Han" later in this chapter).

MANUFACTURING AND TRADE Although such economic problems contributed to the eventual downfall of the dynasty, in general the period of the early Han was one of unparalleled productivity and prosperity, marked by a major expansion of trade, both domestic and foreign. This was not necessarily due to official encouragement. In fact, the Han were as suspicious of private merchants as their predecessors had been and levied stiff taxes on trade in an effort to limit commercial activities. Merchants were also subject to severe social constraints. They were disqualified from seeking office, restricted in their place of residence, and generally viewed as parasites providing little true value to Chinese society.

The state itself directed much trade and manufacturing; it manufactured weapons, for example, and operated shipyards, granaries, and mines. The system of roads was expanded and modernized, and new bridges, rest houses, and post stations for changing horses were added. Unlike the Romans, however (see Chapter 5), the Han rulers relied on waterways for the bulk of their transportation needs. To supplement the numerous major rivers crisscrossing the densely populated heartland of China, new canals were dug to facilitate the moving of goods from one end of the vast empire to the other.

The Han dynasty also began to move cautiously into foreign trade, mostly with neighboring areas in Central and Southeast Asia, although trade relations were established with countries as far away as India and the Mediterranean, where active contacts were maintained with the Roman Empire. Some of this long-distance trade was carried by sea through southern ports like Guangzhou (gwahng-JOE), but more was transported by overland caravans on the Silk Road (see the next section and Chapter 10) and other routes that led westward into Central Asia.

New technology contributed to the economic prosperity of the Han era. Significant progress was achieved in such areas as textile manufacturing, water mills, and iron casting; skill at ironworking led to the production of steel a few centuries later. Paper was invented under the Han, and the development of the rudder and fore-and-aft rigging permitted ships to sail into the wind for the first time. Thus equipped, Chinese merchant ships carrying heavy cargoes could sail throughout the islands of Southeast Asia and into the Indian Ocean.

Imperial Expansion and the Origins of the Silk Road

The Han emperors continued the process of territorial expansion and consolidation that had begun under

the Zhou and the Qin. Han rulers, notably Han Wudi (HAHN woo-DEE), or "Martial Emperor of Han," who ruled from 141 to 87 B.C.E., successfully completed the assimilation into the empire of the regions south of the Yangzi River, including the Red River delta in what is today northern Vietnam. Han armies also marched westward as far as the Caspian Sea, pacifying nomadic tribal peoples and extending China's boundary far into Central Asia (see Map 3.3).

The latter project apparently was originally planned as a means to fend off pressure from the nomadic Xiongnu peoples, who periodically threatened Chinese lands from their base area north of the Great Wall. In 138 B.C.E., Han Wudi dispatched the courtier Zhang Qian (JANG chee-AHN) on a mission westward into Central Asia to seek alliances with peoples living in the area against the common Xiongnu menace. Zhang Qian returned home with ample information about political and economic conditions in Central Asia. The new knowledge permitted the Han court to establish the first Chinese military presence in the area of the Taklimakan (tah-kluh-muh-KAHN) Desert and the Tian Shan (TEE-en SHAHN) (Heavenly Mountains). Eventually, this area would become known to the Chinese people as Xinjiang, or "new region."

Chinese commercial exchanges with peoples in Central Asia now began to expand dramatically. Eastward into China came grapes, precious metals, glass objects, and horses from Persia and Central Asia. Horses were of particular significance because Chinese military strategists had learned of the importance of cavalry in their battles against the Xiongnu and sought the sturdy Ferghana horses of Bactria to increase their own military effectiveness. In return, China exported goods, especially silk, to countries to the west.

Making Paper. One of China's most important contributions to the world was the invention of paper during the Han dynasty. Although the first known use of paper for writing dates back to the first century B.C.E., paper was also used for clothing, wrapping materials, military armor, and toilet tissue. It was even suggested to a prince in 93 B.C.E. that he use a paper handkerchief. Paper was made by pounding fibers of hemp and linen. Then the crushed fibers were placed on a flat meshed surface and soaked in a large vat. After the residue dried, it was peeled away as a sheet of paper, seen piled at the right in this eighteenth-century painting.

MAP 3.3 The Han Empire. This map shows the territory under the control of the Han Empire at its greatest extent during the first century B.C.E. Note the Great Wall's placement relative to nomadic peoples.

Q *How did the expansion of Han rule to the west parallel the Silk Road?*

Silk, a filament recovered from the cocoons of silkworms, had been produced in China since the fourth millennium B.C.E. Eventually, knowledge of the wonder product reached the outside world, and Chinese silk exports began to rise dramatically. By the second century B.C.E., the first items made from silk reached the Mediterranean Sea, stimulating the first significant contacts between China and Rome, its great counterpart in the west (see Chapter 5). The bulk of the trade went overland through Central Asia (thus earning this route its modern name, the Silk Road), although significant exchanges also took place via the maritime route (see Chapter 9). Silk became a craze among Roman elites, leading to a vast outflow of silver from Rome to China and provoking the Roman emperor Tiberius to grumble that "the ladies and their baubles are transferring our money to foreigners."

The silk trade also stimulated a degree of mutual curiosity between China and other civilizations farther to the west. Roman authors such as Pliny the Elder and the geographer Strabo (who speculated that silk was produced from the leaves of a "silk tree") wrote of a strange land called "Seres" far to the east, while Chinese sources mentioned the empire of "Great Qin" at the far end of the Silk Road to the west. Of more immediate consequence was the increased communication that took place with societies in the South Asian subcontinent. The Han dynasty's adoption of Confucianism did not have much direct impact on the religious beliefs of the Chinese people, who continued to worship the pantheon of local deities and spirits of nature connected with popular Daoism. But in the first century C.E., a new salvationist faith appeared on the horizon as merchants from Central Asia brought Buddhist teachings to China for the first time. At first, its influence was limited, as no Buddhist text was translated into Chinese until the fifth century C.E. But the terrain was ripe for the introduction of a new religion into China, and the first Chinese monks departed for India shortly after the end of the Han dynasty.

The Decline and Fall of the Han

In 9 C.E., the reformist official Wang Mang (wahng MAHNG), who was troubled by the plight of the peasants, seized power from the Han court and declared the foundation of the Xin (SHEEN) (New) dynasty. The empire had been crumbling for decades. As frivolous or depraved rulers amused themselves with the pleasures of court life, the power and influence of the central government began to wane, and the great noble families filled the vacuum, amassing vast landed estates and transforming free farmers into tenants. Wang Mang tried to confiscate the great estates, restore the ancient well-field system, and abolish slavery. In so doing, however, he alienated powerful interests, who conspired to overthrow him. In 23 C.E., beset by administrative chaos and a collapse of the frontier defenses, Wang Mang was killed in a coup d'état.

For a time, strong leadership revived some of the glory of the early Han. (Chinese historians refer to the period after the Wang Mang revolt as the Later Han dynasty.) The court did attempt to reduce land taxes and carry out land resettlement programs. The growing popularity of nutritious crops like rice, wheat, and soybeans, along with the introduction of new crops such as alfalfa and grapes, helped boost food production. But the great landed families' firm grip on land and power continued. Weak rulers were isolated within their imperial chambers and dominated by eunuchs and other powerful court insiders. Official corruption and the concentration of land in the hands of the wealthy led to widespread peasant unrest.

The Han also continued to have problems with the Xiongnu beyond the Great Wall to the north. Professional armies recruited from among non-Chinese peoples along the periphery of the empire proved to be unreliable in both performance and loyalty. After attempts to pacify the Xiongnu leaders through negotiations failed to resolve the situation, Han rulers turned once again to military force. The threat from the north did not abate until the end of the first century C.E., when the alliance among the various nomadic groups fractured into disunity. The respite proved to be short-lived, however, as raids on Chinese territory continued intermittently up to the end of the dynasty, sometimes reaching almost to the gates of the capital city.

Buffeted by insurmountable problems within and without, in the late second century C.E., the dynasty entered a period of inexorable decline. The population, which had been estimated at about 60 million in China's first census in the year 2 C.E., had shrunk to less than one-third that number two hundred years later. In the early third century C.E., the dynasty was finally brought to an end when power was seized by Cao Cao (TSOW tsow), a general known to later generations as one of the main characters in the famous Chinese epic *The Romance of the Three Kingdoms*. But Cao Cao was unable to consolidate his power, and China entered a period of almost constant anarchy and internal divisions, compounded by invasions of northern nomadic peoples. The next great dynasty did not arise until the beginning of the seventh century, four hundred years later.

Daily Life in Ancient China

 Q FOCUS QUESTION: What were the key aspects of social and economic life in early China?

Few social institutions have been as closely identified with China as the family. As in most agricultural civilizations, the family served as the basic economic and social unit in society. In traditional China, however, it took on an almost sacred quality as a microcosm of the entire social order.

CHRONOLOGY Ancient China

Xia dynasty	?–c. 1570 B.C.E.
Shang dynasty	c. 1570–c. 1045 B.C.E.
Zhou dynasty	c. 1045–221 B.C.E.
Life of Confucius	551–479 B.C.E.
Period of the Warring States	403–221 B.C.E.
Life of Mencius	370–290 B.C.E.
Qin dynasty	221–206 B.C.E.
Life of the First Emperor of Qin	259–210 B.C.E.
Han Dynasty	202 B.C.E.–221 C.E.

The Role of the Family

In Neolithic times, the farm village, organized around the clan, was the basic social unit in China, at least in the core region of the Yellow River valley. Even then, however, the smaller family unit was becoming more important, at least among the nobility, who attached considerable significance to the veneration of their ancestors.

During the Zhou dynasty, the family took on increasing importance, in part because of the need for cooperation in agriculture. Rice had become the primary crop along the Yangzi River and in the provinces to the south because of its taste, its productivity, and its high nutrient value. But the cultivation of rice is highly labor-intensive. The seedlings must be planted in several inches of water in a nursery bed and then transferred individually to the paddy beds, which must be irrigated constantly. During the harvest, the stalks must be cut and the kernels carefully separated from the stalks and husks. As a result, children—and the labor they supplied—were considered essential to the survival of the family, not only during their youthful years but also later, when sons were expected to provide for their parents. Loyalty to family members came to be considered even more important than loyalty to the broader community or the state. Confucius commented that it is the mark of a civilized society that a son should protect his father even if the latter has committed a crime against the community.

At the crux of the concept of family was the idea of **filial piety**, which called on all members of the family to subordinate their personal needs and desires to the patriarchal head of the family. More broadly, it created a hierarchical system in which every family member had a place. All Chinese learned the **five relationships** that were the key to a proper social order. The son was subordinate to the father, the wife to her husband, the younger brother to the older brother, and all were subject to their king. The final relationship was the proper one between friend and friend. Only if all members of the family and the community as a whole behaved in a properly filial manner would society function effectively.

A stable family system based on obedient and hardworking members can serve as a bulwark for an efficient government, but putting loyalty to the family and the clan over loyalty to the state can also present a threat to a centralizing monarch.

For that reason, the Qin dynasty attempted to destroy the clan system in China and assert the primacy of the state. Legalists even imposed heavy taxes on any family with more than two adult sons in order to break down the family concept. The Qin reportedly also originated the practice of organizing several family units into larger groups of five and ten families that would exercise mutual control and surveillance. Later dynasties continued the practice under the name of the **Bao-jia** (BOW-jah ["ow" as in "how"]) **system**.

But the efforts of the Qin to eradicate or at least reduce the importance of the family system ran against tradition and the dynamics of the Chinese economy, and under the Han dynasty, which followed the Qin, the family revived and increased in importance. With official encouragement, the family system began to take on the character that it would possess until our own day. The family was not only the basic economic unit; it was also the basic social unit for education, religious observances, and training in ethical principles.

Lifestyles

We know much more about the lifestyle of the elites than that of the common people in ancient China. The first houses for the former were probably constructed of wooden planks, but later Chinese mastered the art of building in tile and brick. By the first millennium B.C.E., most public buildings and the houses of the wealthy were probably constructed in this manner. The latter often had several wings surrounding a central courtyard to provide space for several generations under one roof, a style that continued down to modern times. By the second century B.C.E., most Chinese, however, probably lived in simple houses of mud, wooden planks, or brick with thatch or occasionally tile roofs. But in some areas, especially the loess (LESS) (a type of soil common in North China) regions of northern China, cave dwelling remained common down to modern times. The most famous cave dweller of modern times was Mao Zedong, who lived in a cave in Yan'an (yuh-NAHN) during his long struggle against Chiang Kai-shek.

Chinese houses usually had little furniture; most people squatted or sat with their legs spread out on the packed-mud floor. Chairs were apparently not introduced until the sixth or seventh century C.E. Clothing was simple, consisting of cotton trousers and shirts in the summer and wool or burlap in the winter.

The staple foods were millet in the north and rice in the south. Other common foods were wheat, barley, soybeans, mustard greens, and bamboo shoots. In early times, such foods were often consumed in a porridge, but by the Zhou dynasty, stir-frying in a wok was becoming common. When possible, the Chinese family would vary its diet of grain foods with vegetables, fruit (including pears, peaches, apricots, and plums), and fish or meat; but for most, such additions to the daily plate of rice, millet, or soybeans were a rare luxury.

Alcohol in the form of ale was drunk at least by the higher classes and by the early Zhou era had already begun to inspire official concern. According to the *Book of History*, "King Wen admonished … the young nobles … that they should not ordinarily use spirits; and throughout all the states he required that they should be drunk only on occasion of sacrifices, and that then virtue should preside so that there might be no drunkenness."[15] For the poorer classes, alcohol in any form was probably a rare luxury. Chinese legend hints that tea—a plant originally found in upland regions in southern China and Southeast Asia—was introduced by the mythical emperor Shen Nong. In fact, however, tea drinking did not become widespread in China until around 500 C.E. By then tea was lauded for its medicinal qualities and its capacity to soothe the spirit.

Cities

With the rise to power of the Qin, cities began to take on the central importance they would hold through later Chinese history. Urban centers were divided into neighborhoods—perhaps a forerunner of the grid pattern assumed by imperial cities under later dynasties—as a means of facilitating control over the population. As mentioned earlier, landed aristocrats, many of them former opponents of the Qin, were forcibly resettled in the new capital of Xianyang—a pattern that we shall see repeated, notably in France and Japan, in later centuries. Their villas and gardens aped the splendor of the imperial palace, which formed the centerpiece of the urban landscape.

Under the Qin and the Han, as never before, cities became the cultural hub of Chinese society, although their residents made up only a tiny proportion of the total population. In the crowded streets, haughty nobles sought to avoid rubbing shoulders with commoners, while merchants, workers, wandering gangs, and prostitutes relentlessly imitated the mannerisms of the elite. As a poem of the time satirically noted:

> In the city, if they love to have their hair dressed up high,
> Then everywhere else they dress their hair an inch higher.
> In the city, if they love to enlarge their eyebrows,
> Then everywhere else they will make their eyebrows cover half their foreheads.
> In the city, if they love large sleeves,
> Then everywhere else they will use up whole bolts of silk.[16]

The Humble Estate: Women in Ancient China

Male dominance was a key element in the social system of ancient China. As in many traditional societies, the male was considered of transcendent importance because of his role as food procurer or, in the case of farming communities, food producer. In ancient China, men worked in the fields and women raised children and served in the home. This differential in gender roles goes back to prehistoric times and is embedded in Chinese creation myths. According to legend, Fu Xi's wife Nu Wa (noo WAH) assisted her husband in organizing society by establishing the institution of marriage and the family. Yet Nu Wa was not just a household drudge. After Fu Xi's death, she became China's first female sovereign.

During ancient times, women apparently did not normally occupy formal positions of authority, but they often became a force in politics, especially at court, where wives of the ruler or other female members of the royal family were often influential in palace intrigues. Such activities were frowned on, however, as the following passage from *The Book of Songs* attests:

> *A clever man builds a city,*
> *A clever woman lays one low;*
> *With all her qualifications, that clever woman*
> *Is but an ill-omened bird.*
> *A woman with a long tongue*
> *Is a flight of steps leading to calamity;*
> *For disorder does not come from heaven,*
> *But is brought about by women.*
> *Among those who cannot be trained or taught*
> *Are women and eunuchs.*[17]

The nature of gender relationships was also graphically demonstrated in the Chinese written language. The character for man (男) combines the symbols for strength and rice field, while the character for woman (女) represents a person in a posture of deference and respect. The character for peace (安) is a woman under a roof. A wife is symbolized by a woman with a broom. Male chauvinism has deep linguistic roots in China.

Confucian thought, while not denigrating the importance of women as mothers and homemakers, accepted the dual roles of men and women in Chinese society. Men governed society. They carried on family ritual through the veneration of ancestors. They were the warriors, scholars, and ministers. Their dominant role was firmly enshrined in the legal system. Men were permitted to have more than one wife and to divorce a spouse who did not produce a male child. Women were denied the right to own property, and there was no dowry system in ancient China that would have provided the wife with a degree of financial security from her husband and his family. However, there were exceptions, including Ban Zhao (bahn ZHOW), who, although a woman, was one of the most prominent historians of the Han dynasty. But even she conceded that a woman's role in China was to be "humble, yielding, respectful and reverential" in her dealings with others. As the third-century C.E. poet Fu Xuan (foo SHWAHN), a woman, lamented:

> *How sad it is to be a woman*
> *Nothing on earth is held so cheap.*
> *No one is glad when a girl is born.*
> *By her the family sets no store.*
> *No one cries when she leaves her home*
> *Sudden as clouds when the rain stops.*[18]

Chinese Culture

 Q **FOCUS QUESTIONS:** What were the chief characteristics of the Chinese arts and writing system? How did they differ from those in Egypt and Mesopotamia?

Modern knowledge about artistic achievements in ancient civilizations is limited because often little has survived the ravages of time. Fortunately, many ancient civilizations, such as Egypt and Mesopotamia, were located in relatively arid areas where many artifacts were preserved, even over thousands of years. In more humid regions, such as China and South Asia, the cultural residue left by the civilizations of antiquity has been adversely affected by climate.

As a result, relatively little remains of the cultural achievements of the prehistoric Chinese aside from Neolithic pottery and the relics found at the site of the Shang dynasty capital at Anyang. In recent years, a rich trove from the time of the Qin Empire has been unearthed near the tomb of Qin Shi Huangdi near Xian and at Han tombs nearby. But little remains of the literature of ancient China and almost none of the painting, architecture, and music.

Metalwork and Sculpture

Discoveries at archaeological sites indicate that ancient China was a society rich in cultural achievement. The pottery found at Neolithic sites such as Longshan and Yangshao exhibits a freshness and vitality of form and design, and the ornaments, such as rings and beads, show a strong aesthetic sense.

BRONZE CASTING   The pace of Chinese cultural development began to quicken during the Shang dynasty, which ruled in northern China from the sixteenth to the eleventh century B.C.E. At that time, objects cast in bronze began to appear. Various bronze vessels were produced for use in preparing and serving food and drink in the ancestral rites. Later vessels were used for decoration or for dining at court.

The method of casting used was one reason for the extraordinary quality of Shang bronze work. Bronze workers in most ancient civilizations used the lost-wax method, in which a model was first made in wax. After a clay mold had been formed around it, the model was heated so that the wax would melt away, and the empty space was filled with molten metal. In China, clay molds composed of several sections were tightly fitted together prior to the introduction of the liquid bronze. This technique, which had evolved from ceramic techniques used during the Neolithic period, enabled the artisans to apply the design directly to the mold and thus contributed to the clarity of line and rich surface decoration of the Shang bronzes.

Bronze casting became a large-scale business, and more than ten thousand vessels of an incredible variety of form and design survive today. Factories were located not only in the Yellow River valley but also in Sichuan province, in southern China. The art of bronze working continued into the Zhou dynasty, but the quality and originality declined. The Shang bronzes remain the pinnacle of creative art in ancient China.

One reason for the decline of bronze casting in China was the rise in popularity of iron. Ironmaking developed in China around the ninth or eighth century B.C.E., much later than in the Middle East, where it had been mastered almost a thousand years earlier. Once familiar with the process, however, the Chinese quickly moved to the forefront. Ironworkers in Europe and the Middle East, lacking the technology to

A Shang Wine Vessel. Used initially as food containers in royal ceremonial rites during the Shang dynasty, Chinese bronzes were the product of an advanced technology unmatched by any contemporary civilization. This wine vessel displays a deep green patina as well as a monster motif, complete with large globular eyes, nostrils, and fangs, typical of many Shang bronzes. Known as the *taotie* (TOW-tee-YUH ["ow" as in "how"]), this fanciful beast is normally presented in silhouette as two dragons face to face so that each side forms half of the mask. Although the *taotie* presumably served as a guardian force against evil spirits, scholars are still not aware of its exact significance for early Chinese peoples.

© William J. Duiker

achieve the high temperatures necessary to melt iron ore for casting, were forced to work with wrought iron, a cumbersome and expensive process. By the fourth century B.C.E., the Chinese had invented the technique of the blast furnace, powered by a worker operating a bellows. They were therefore able to manufacture cast iron ritual vessels and agricultural tools centuries before an equivalent technology appeared in the West.

Another reason for the deterioration of the bronze-casting tradition was the development of cheaper materials such as lacquerware and ceramics. Lacquer, made from resins obtained from the juices of sumac trees native to the region, had been produced since Neolithic times, and by the second century B.C.E. it had become a popular method of applying a hard coating to objects made of wood or fabric. Pottery, too,

had existed since early times, but technological advances led to the production of a high-quality form of pottery covered with a brown or gray-green glaze, the latter known popularly as celadon. By the end of the first millennium B.C.E., both lacquerware and pottery had replaced bronze in popularity, much as plastic goods have replaced more expensive materials in our own time. This trend continued into the Han dynasty, as bronze was increasingly replaced by iron as the medium of choice. Less expensive to produce, iron was better able to satisfy the growing popular demand during a time of increasing economic affluence. Also during the Han, painting—often in the form of wall frescoes—became increasingly popular in the homes and tombs of the wealthy, although little has survived the ravages of time.

THE FIRST EMPEROR'S TOMB In 1974, in a remarkable discovery, farmers digging a well about 35 miles east of Xian unearthed a number of terra-cotta figures in an underground pit about one mile east of the burial mound of the First Emperor of Qin. Chinese archaeologists sent to work at the site discovered a vast terra-cotta army that they believed was a recreation of Qin Shi Huangdi's imperial guard, which was to accompany the emperor on his journey to the next world.

One of the astounding features of the terra-cotta army is its size. The army is enclosed in four pits that were originally encased in a wooden framework, which has disintegrated. More than a thousand figures have been unearthed in the first pit, along with horses, wooden chariots, and seven thousand bronze weapons. Archaeologists estimate that there are more than six thousand figures in that pit alone.

Equally impressive is the quality of the work. Slightly larger than life size, the figures were molded of finely textured clay and then fired and painted. The detail on the uniforms is realistic and sophisticated, but the most striking feature is the individuality of the facial features of the soldiers. Apparently, ten different head shapes were used and were then modeled further by hand to reflect the variety of ethnic groups and personality types in the army.

The discovery of the terra-cotta army also shows that the Chinese had come a long way from the human sacrifices that had taken place at the death of Shang sovereigns more than a thousand years earlier. But the project must have been ruinously expensive and is additional evidence of the burden the Qin ruler imposed on his subjects. One historian has estimated that one-third of the national income in Qin times may have been spent on preparations for the ruler's afterlife. The emperor's mausoleum has not yet been unearthed, but it is enclosed in a mound nearly 250 feet high surrounded by a rectangular wall extending for nearly 4 miles. According to the Han historian Sima Qian, the ceiling was a replica of the heavens, while the floor contained a relief model of the entire Qin kingdom, with rivers flowing in mercury. According to tradition, traps were set within the mausoleum to prevent intruders, and the workers applying the final touches were buried alive in the tomb with its secrets.

The Tomb of Qin Shi Huangdi. The First Emperor of Qin ordered the construction of an elaborate mausoleum, an underground palace complex protected by an army of terra-cotta soldiers and horses to accompany him on his journey to the afterlife. This massive formation of six thousand life-size armed soldiers, discovered accidentally by farmers in 1974, reflects Qin Shi Huangdi's grandeur and power.

Language and Literature

Precisely when writing developed in China cannot be determined, but certainly by Shang times, as the oracle bones demonstrate, the Chinese had developed a simple but functional script. Like many other languages of antiquity, it was primarily ideographic and pictographic in form. Symbols, usually called characters, were created to represent an idea or to form a picture of the object to be represented. For example, the Chinese characters for mountain (山), the sun (日), and the moon (月) were meant to represent the objects themselves. Other characters, such as "big" (大) (a man with his arms outstretched), represent an idea. The character for "east" (東) symbolizes the sun coming up behind the trees.

Each character, of course, would be given a sound by the speaker when pronounced. In other cultures, this process led to the abandonment of the system of ideographs and the adoption of a written language based on phonetic symbols. The Chinese language, however, has never entirely abandoned its original ideographic format, although the phonetic element has developed into a significant part of the individual character. In that sense, the Chinese written language is virtually unique in the world today.

One reason the language retained its ideographic quality may have been the aesthetics of the written characters. By the time of the Qin dynasty, if not earlier, the written language came to be seen as an art form as well as a means of

Mesopotamian Cuneiform					
Egyptian Hieroglyphics					
Oracle Bone Script					
Modern Chinese	日	山	水	男	女
	sun	hill	water	man	woman

Pictographs in Ancient Cultures. Virtually all written language evolved from pictographs—representations of physical objects that were eventually stylized and tied to sounds in the spoken language. This chart shows pictographs that originated independently in three ancient cultures and the stylized modern characters into which the Chinese oracle pictographs evolved.

communication, and calligraphy became one of the most prized forms of painting in China.

Even more important, if the written language had developed in the direction of a phonetic alphabet, it could no longer have served as the written system for all the peoples of the expanding Chinese civilization. Although the vast majority spoke a tongue derived from a parent Sinitic language (a system distinguished by variations in pitch, a characteristic that gives Chinese its lilting quality even today), the languages spoken in various regions of the country differed from each other in pronunciation and to a lesser degree in vocabulary and syntax; for the most part, they were (and are today) mutually unintelligible.

The Chinese answer to this problem was to give all the spoken languages the same writing system. Although any character might be pronounced differently in different regions of China, that character would be written the same way (after the standardization undertaken under the Qin). Written characters could therefore be read by educated Chinese from one end of the country to the other. This became the language of the bureaucracy and the vehicle for the transmission of Chinese culture from the Great Wall to the southern border and beyond. The written language was not identical to the spoken form, however; it eventually evolved its own vocabulary and grammatical structure, and as a result, users of written Chinese required special training.

The earliest extant form of Chinese literature dates from the Zhou dynasty. It was written on silk or strips of bamboo and consisted primarily of historical records such as the *Rites of Zhou*, philosophical treatises such as the *Analects* and *The Way of the Tao*, and poetry, as recorded in *The Book of Songs* and the *Song of the South*. In later years, when Confucian principles had been elevated to a state ideology, the key works identified with the Confucian school were integrated into a set of so-called Confucian Classics. These works became required reading for generations of Chinese schoolchildren and introduced them to the forms of behavior that would be required of them as adults.

By the Han dynasty, there was considerable experimentation with new forms of expression in literature. Poetry and philosophical essays continued to be popular, but historical writing became the primary form of literary creativity. Historians such as Sima Qian and Ban Gu (the dynasty's official historian and the older brother of the female historian Ban Zhao) wrote works that became models for later dynastic histories. These historical works combined political and social history with biographies of key figures. Like so much literary work in China, their primary purpose was moral and political—to explain the underlying reasons for the rise and fall of individual human beings and dynasties.

Music

From early times in China, music was viewed not just as an aesthetic pleasure but also as a means of achieving political order and refining the human character. In fact, music may have originated as an accompaniment to sacred rituals at the royal court. According to the *Historical Records*, written during the Han dynasty, "When our sage-kings of the past instituted rites and music, their objective was far from making people indulge in the … amusements of singing and dancing…. Music is produced to purify the heart, and rites introduced to rectify the behavior."[19] Eventually, however, music began to be appreciated for its own sake as well as to accompany singing and dancing.

A wide variety of musical instruments were used, including flutes, various stringed instruments, bells and chimes, drums, and gourds. Bells cast in bronze were first used as musical instruments in the Shang period; they were hung in rows and struck with a wooden mallet. The finest were produced during the mid-Zhou era and are considered among the best examples of early bronze work in China. Some weighed more than two tons and, in combination, covered a range of several octaves. Bronze bells have not been found in any other contemporary civilization and are considered one of the great cultural achievements of ancient China. The largest known bell dating from the Roman Empire, for example, is less than 3 inches high.

By the late Zhou era, bells had begun to give way as the instrument of choice to strings and wind instruments, and the purpose of music shifted from ceremony to entertainment. This led conservative critics to rail against the onset of an age of debauchery.

Ancient historians stressed the relationship between music and court life, but it is highly probable that music, singing, and dancing were equally popular among the common people. The *Book of History*, purporting to describe conditions in the late third millennium B.C.E., suggests that ballads emanating from the popular culture were welcomed at court. Nevertheless, court music and popular music differed in several respects. Among other things, popular music was more likely to be motivated by the desire for pleasure than for the purpose of law and order and moral uplift. Those differences continued to be reflected in the evolution of music in China down to modern times.

CHAPTER SUMMARY

Of the great classical civilizations discussed in Part I of this book, China was the last to come into full flower. By the time the Shang began to emerge as an organized state, the societies in Mesopotamia and the Nile Valley had already reached an advanced level of civilization. Unfortunately, not enough is known about the early stages of these civilizations to allow us to determine why some developed earlier than others, but one likely reason for China's comparatively late arrival was that it was virtually isolated from other emerging centers of culture elsewhere in the world and thus was compelled to develop essentially on its own. Only at the end of the first millennium B.C.E. did China come into regular contact with other civilizations in South Asia, the Middle East, and the Mediterranean.

Once embarked on its own path toward the creation of a complex society, however, China achieved results that were in all respects the equal of its counterparts elsewhere. By the rise of the first unified empire in the late third century B.C.E., the state extended from the edge of the Gobi Desert in the north to the subtropical

regions near the borders of modern Vietnam in the south. Chinese philosophers had engaged in debate over intricate questions relating to human nature and the state of the universe, and China's artistic and technological achievements—especially in terms of bronze casting and the terra-cotta figures entombed in Qin Shi Huangdi's mausoleum—were unsurpassed throughout the world.

Meanwhile, another great civilization was beginning to take form on the northern shores of the Mediterranean Sea. Unlike China and the other ancient societies discussed thus far, this new civilization in Europe was based as much on trade as on agriculture. Yet the political and cultural achievements of ancient Greece were the equal of any of the great human experiments that had preceded it and soon began to exert a significant impact on the rest of the ancient world.

CHAPTER TIMELINE

5000 B.C.E.	2000 B.C.E.	1500 B.C.E.	1000 B.C.E.	500 B.C.E.	250 B.C.E.	1 C.E.

Shang Dynasty — Zhou Dynasty — Qin Dynasty — Han Dynasty

First settled agriculture — Bronze Age begins — Invention of the iron plow — Paper invented

Life of Confucius — Hundred Schools of Thought — Arrival of Buddhism

CHAPTER REVIEW

Upon Reflection

Q What were some of the key contributions in political structures, social organization, and culture that the Shang dynasty bequeathed to its successor, the Zhou dynasty? Does the Shang deserve to be called the "mother culture" of China?

Q What kinds of relationships did the Chinese people have with the pastoral peoples living along the frontier? How did these relationships compare with those experienced by advanced societies in North Africa and Western Asia?

Q What contributions did the ancient Chinese people make in the field of metallurgy? How do their achievements compare with developments in ancient Egypt and the Middle East?

Key Terms

Yangshao (p. 64)
Longshan (p. 64)
veneration of ancestors (p. 66)
diffusion hypothesis (p. 68)
mandate of Heaven (p. 69)
well-field system (p. 70)
Dao (p. 72)
Legalism (p. 74)
Confucianism (p. 74)
Daoism (p. 74)
eunuchs (p. 81)
State Confucianism (p. 81)
civil service examination (p. 81)
filial piety (p. 85)
five relationships (p. 85)
Bao-jia system (p. 86)

Suggested Reading

THE DAWN OF CHINESE CIVILIZATION   For an authoritative overview of the ancient period, see **M. Loewe** and **E. L. Shaughnessy,** *The Cambridge History of Ancient China from the Origins of Civilization to 221 B.C.* (Cambridge, 1999).

The period of the Neolithic era and the Shang dynasty has received increasing attention in recent years. For an impressively documented and annotated overview, see **K. C. Chang et al.,** *The Formation of Chinese Civilization: An Archaeological Perspective* (New Haven, Conn., 2005), and **R. Thorp,** *China in the Early Bronze Age* (Philadelphia, 2005). Also see **D. Keightley,** *The Ancestral Landscape: Time, Space, and Continuity in Late Shang China* (Berkeley, Calif., 2005).

THE ZHOU, QIN, AND HAN DYNASTIES   The Zhou and Qin dynasties have also received considerable attention. The former is exhaustively analyzed in **Cho-yun Hsu and J. M. Linduff,** *Western Zhou Civilization* (New Haven, Conn., 1988). **N. Di Cosmo,** *Ancient China and Its Enemies: The Rise of Nomadic Power in East Asian History* (Cambridge, 2002) traces China's relations with some of its neighbors. On bronze casting, see **E. L. Shaughnessy,** *Sources of Eastern Zhou History* (Berkeley, Calif., 1991). For recent treatments of the tumultuous Qin dynasty, see **M. Lewis,** *The Early Chinese Empires: Qin and Han* (Cambridge, Mass., 2007), and **C. Holcombe,** *The Genesis of East Asia, 221 B.C.–A.D. 907* (Honolulu, 2001).

The philosophy of ancient China has attracted considerable attention from Western scholars. For excerpts from all the major works of the "hundred schools," consult **W. T. de Bary and I. Bloom, eds.,** *Sources of Chinese Tradition*, vol. 1 (New York, 1999). On Confucius, see **B. W. Van Norden, ed.,** *Confucius and the Analects: New Essays* (Oxford, 2002).

Environmental issues are explored in **M. Elvin,** *The Retreat of the Elephants: An Environmental History of China* (New Haven, Conn., 2004).

CHINESE CULTURE   For an introduction to classical Chinese literature, consult **V. H. Mair, ed.,** *The Columbia Anthology of Traditional Chinese Literature* (New York, 1994), and **S. Owen, ed.,** *An Anthology of Chinese Literature: Beginnings to 1911* (New York, 1996). For a comprehensive introduction to Chinese art, consult **M. Sullivan,** *The Arts of China*, 4th ed. (Berkeley, Calif., 1999), with good illustrations in color. Also of interest is **P. B. Ebrey,** *The Cambridge Illustrated History of China* (Cambridge, 1999). On some recent finds, consult **J. Rowson,** *Mysteries of Ancient China: New Discoveries from the Early Dynasties* (New York, 1996). On Chinese music, see **J. F. So, ed.,** *Music in the Age of Confucius* (Washington, D.C., 2000).

Chapter Notes

1. *Book of Changes*, quoted in Chang Chi-yun, *Chinese History of Fifty Centuries*, vol. 1, *Ancient Times* (Taipei, 1962), pp. 15, 31, and 65.

2. Ibid., p. 381.

3. Quoted in E. N. Anderson, *The Food of China* (New Haven, Conn., 1988), p. 21.

4. According to Chinese tradition, the *Rites of Zhou* was written by the duke of Zhou himself near the time of the founding of the Zhou dynasty. However, modern historians believe that it was written much later, perhaps as late as the fourth century B.C.E.

5. From *The Book of Songs*, quoted in S. de Grazia, ed., *Masters of Chinese Political Thought: From the Beginnings to the Han Dynasty* (New York, 1973), pp. 40–41.

6. *Confucian Analects* (Lun Yu), ed. J. Legge (Taipei, 1963), 11:11 and 6:20. Author's translation.

7. Ibid., 15:23.

8. *Book of Rites*, sec. 9, quoted in W. T. de Bary et al., eds., *Sources of Chinese Tradition* (New York, 1960), p. 192.

9. *Confucian Analects*, 17:2.

10. *Book of Mencius* (Meng Zi), 4A:9, quoted in de Bary, *Sources of Chinese Tradition*, p. 93.

11. Quoted in ibid., p. 51.

12. M. Lewis, *The Early Chinese Empires: Qin and Han* (Cambridge, Mass., 2007), p. 31, citing *Shiji* 68, pp. 2230, 2232.

13. B. Watson, *Records of the Grand Historian of China* (New York, 1961), vol. 2, pp. 155, 160.

14. Ibid., pp. 32, 53.

15. C. Waltham, *Shu Ching: Book of History* (Chicago, 1971), p. 154.

16. Lewis, *Early Chinese Empires*, p. 85.

17. Quoted in H. A. Giles, *A History of Chinese Literature* (New York, 1923), p. 19.

18. Waley, ed., *Chinese Poems* (London, 1983), p. xx.

19. Chang Chi-yun, *Chinese History*, vol. 1, p. 183.

MindTap is a fully online, highly personalized learning experience built upon Cengage Leaning content. MindTap combines student learning tools—readings, multimedia, activities, and assessments—into a singular Learning Path that guides students through their course.

The Civilization of the Greeks

A bust of Pericles

CHAPTER OUTLINE AND FOCUS QUESTIONS

Early Greece

Q How did the geography of Greece affect Greek history in terms of politics, military developments, and the economy? Who was Homer, and why was his work used as the basis for Greek education?

The Greek City-States (c. 750–c. 500 B.C.E.)

Q What were the chief features of the *polis*, or city-state, and how did the city-states of Athens and Sparta differ?

The High Point of Greek Civilization: Classical Greece

Q What did the Greeks mean by *democracy*, and in what ways was the Athenian political system a democracy? What effect did the two great conflicts of the fifth century—the Persian Wars and the Peloponnesian War—have on Greek civilization?

The Rise of Macedonia and the Conquests of Alexander

Q How was Alexander the Great able to amass his empire, and what was his legacy?

The World of the Hellenistic Kingdoms

Q How did the political, economic, and social institutions of the Hellenistic world differ from those of Classical Greece?

CRITICAL THINKING

Q In what ways did the culture of the Hellenistic period differ from that of the Classical period, and what do those differences suggest about society in the two periods?

CONNECTIONS TO TODAY

Q What are the similarities and differences between ancient Athenian democracy and modern democracy in the United States?

DURING THE ERA OF CIVIL WAR in China known as the Period of the Warring States, a civil war also erupted on the northern shores of the Mediterranean Sea. In 431 B.C.E., two dramatically different Greek city-states— Athens and Sparta—fought for domination of the Greek world. The people of Athens felt secure behind their walls and, in the first winter of the war, held a public funeral to honor those who had died in battle. On the day of the ceremony, the citizens of Athens joined in a procession, with the relatives of the dead wailing for their loved ones. As was the custom in Athens, one leading citizen was asked to address the crowd, and on this day it was Pericles who spoke to the people. He talked about the greatness of Athens and reminded the Athenians of the strength of their political system: "Our constitution," he said, "is called a democracy because power is in the hands not of a minority but of the whole people. When it is a question of settling private disputes, everyone is equal before the law.... Just as our political life is free and open, so is our day-to-day life in our relations with each other…. Here each individual is interested not only in his own affairs but in the affairs of the state as well."

In this famous funeral oration, Pericles gave voice to the ideals of democracy and the importance of the individual, ideals that were quite different from those of some other ancient societies, in which the individual was subordinated to a larger order based on obedience to an exalted emperor. The Greeks asked some basic questions about human life: What is the nature of the universe? What is the purpose of human existence? What is our relationship to divine forces? What constitutes a community? What constitutes a state? What is true education? What are the true sources of law? What is truth itself, and how do we realize it? Not only did the Greeks provide answers to these questions, but they also created a system of logical, analytical thought to examine them. Their answers and their system of rational thought laid the intellectual foundation for Western civilization's understanding of the human condition.

The remarkable story of ancient Greek civilization begins with the arrival of the Greeks around 1900 B.C.E. By the eighth century B.C.E., the characteristic institution of ancient Greek life, the *polis*, or city-state, had emerged. Greek civilization flourished and reached its height in the Classical era of the fifth century B.C.E., but the inability of the Greek city-states to end their fratricidal warfare eventually left them vulnerable to the Macedonian king Philip II and helped bring an end to the era of independent Greek city-states.

Although the city-states were never the same after their defeat by the Macedonian monarch, this defeat did not end the influence of the Greeks. Philip's son Alexander led the Macedonians and Greeks on a spectacular conquest of the Persian Empire and opened the door to the spread of Greek culture throughout the Middle East. ❧

Early Greece

 FOCUS QUESTIONS: How did the geography of Greece affect Greek history in terms of politics, military developments, and the economy? Who was Homer, and why was his work used as the basis for Greek education?

Geography played an important role in Greek history. Compared to Mesopotamia and Egypt, Greece occupied a small area, a mountainous peninsula that encompassed only 45,000 square miles of territory, about the size of the state of Louisiana. The mountains and the sea were especially significant. Much of Greece consists of small plains and river valleys surrounded by mountain ranges 8,000 to 10,000 feet high. The mountains isolated Greeks from one another, causing Greek communities to follow their own separate paths and develop

their own ways of life. Over a period of time, these communities became so fiercely attached to their independence that they were willing to fight one another to gain advantage. No doubt the small size of these independent Greek communities fostered participation in political affairs and unique cultural expressions, but the rivalry among them also led to the bitter warfare that ultimately devastated Greek society.

The sea also influenced Greek society. Greece had a long seacoast, dotted by bays and inlets that provided numerous harbors. The Greeks also inhabited a number of islands to the west, south, and east of the Greek mainland. It is no accident that the Greeks became seafarers who sailed out into the Aegean and Mediterranean Seas to make contact with the outside world and later to establish colonies that would spread Greek civilization throughout the Mediterranean region.

Topography helped determine the major territories into which Greece was ultimately divided (see Map 4.1). South of the Gulf of Corinth was the Peloponnesus (pell-uh-puh-NEE-suss), virtually an island attached by a tiny isthmus to the mainland. Consisting mostly of hills, mountains, and small valleys, the Peloponnesus was the location of Sparta, as well as the site of Olympia, where athletic games were held. Northeast of the Peloponnesus was the Attic peninsula (or Attica), the home of Athens, hemmed in by mountains to the north and west and surrounded by the sea to the south and east. Northwest of Attica was Boeotia (bee-OH-shuh) in central Greece, with its chief city of Thebes (THEEBZ). To the north of Boeotia was Thessaly, which contained the largest plains and became a great producer of grain and horses. To the north of Thessaly lay Macedonia, which was not of much importance in Greek history until 338 B.C.E., when a Macedonian king Philip II conquered the Greeks.

Minoan Crete

The earliest civilization in the Aegean region emerged on the large island of Crete, southeast of the Greek mainland. A Bronze Age civilization that used metals, especially bronze, in making weapons had been established there by 2800 B.C.E. This civilization was discovered at the turn of the twentieth century by the English archaeologist Arthur Evans, who named it "Minoan" (mih-NOH-uhn) after Minos (MY-nuss), a legendary king of Crete. In language and religion, the Minoans were not Greek, although they did have some influence on the peoples of the Greek mainland.

Evans's excavations on Crete unearthed an enormous palace complex at Knossus (NOSS-suss), near modern Iràklion (Heracleion), that was most likely the center of a far-ranging "sea empire," probably largely commercial. We know from the archaeological remains that the people of Minoan Crete were accustomed to sea travel and had made contact with the more advanced civilization of Egypt. Egyptian products have been found in Crete and Cretan products in Egypt. Minoan Cretans also had contacts with and exerted influence on the Greek-speaking inhabitants of the Greek mainland.

The Minoan civilization reached its height between 2000 and 1450 B.C.E. The palace at Knossus, the royal seat of the

MAP 4.1 **Ancient Greece (c. 750–338 B.C.E.).** Between 750 and 500 B.C.E., Greek civilization witnessed the emergence of the city-state as the central institution in Greek life and the Greeks' colonization of the Mediterranean and Black Seas. Classical Greece lasted from about 500 to 338 B.C.E. and encompassed the high points of Greek civilization in arts, science, philosophy, and politics, as well as the Persian Wars and the Peloponnesian War.

Q *How does the geography of Greece help explain the rise and development of the Greek city-state?*

kings, was an elaborate structure that included numerous private living rooms for the royal family and workshops for making decorated vases, ivory figurines, and jewelry. Even bathrooms with elaborate drains, like those found at Mohenjo-Daro in India, were part of the complex. The rooms were decorated with brightly colored frescoes showing sporting events and nature scenes. Storerooms in the palace held enormous jars of oil, wine, and grain, paid as taxes in kind to the king.

The centers of Minoan civilization on Crete eventually suffered a collapse. Many historians believe that a tsunami triggered by a powerful volcanic eruption on the island of Thera was responsible for destroying towns and ships on the north coast of Crete, while volcanic ash devastated the land. Although people began to rebuild, there is evidence that mainland Greeks, known as the Mycenaeans, invaded and pillaged many centers, including Knossus, which was destroyed around 1450 B.C.E.

The First Greek State: Mycenae

The term *Mycenaean* (my-suh-NEE-un) is derived from Mycenae (my-SEE-nee), a remarkable fortified site excavated by the amateur German archaeologist Heinrich Schliemann (HYN-rikh SHLEE-mahn) starting in 1870. Mycenae was one center in a Mycenaean Greek civilization that flourished between 1600 and 1100 B.C.E. The Mycenaean Greeks were part of the Indo-European family of peoples (see Chapter 1) who spread from their original location into southern and western Europe, India, and Persia. One group entered

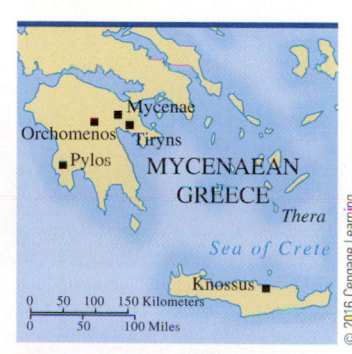

Minoan Crete and Mycenaean Greece

the territory of Greece from the north around 1900 B.C.E. and eventually managed to gain control of the Greek mainland and develop a civilization.

Mycenaean civilization, which reached its high point between 1400 and 1200 B.C.E., consisted of a number of powerful monarchies centered in fortified palace complexes. Like Mycenae itself, the palaces were built on hills and surrounded by gigantic stone walls. These various centers of power probably formed a loose confederacy of independent states, with Mycenae the strongest.

The Mycenaeans were above all a warrior people who prided themselves on their heroic deeds in battle. Archaeological evidence indicates that the Mycenaean monarchies also developed an extensive commercial network. Mycenaean pottery has been found throughout the Mediterranean basin, in Syria and Egypt to the east and Sicily and southern Italy to the west. But some scholars also believe that the Mycenaeans, led by Mycenae itself, spread outward militarily, conquering Crete and making it part of the Mycenaean world. The most famous of all their supposed military adventures has come down to us in the epic poetry of Homer (discussed later in this chapter). Did the Mycenaean Greeks, led by Agamemnon, king of Mycenae, sack the city of Troy on the northwestern coast of Asia Minor around 1250 B.C.E.? Scholars have debated this question ever since Schliemann began his excavations in 1870. Some believe that Homer's account does have a basis in fact, although there is little archaeological evidence to support it.

By the late thirteenth century, Mycenaean Greece was showing signs of serious trouble. Mycenae itself was burned around 1190 B.C.E., and other Mycenaean centers show a similar pattern of destruction as new waves of Greek-speaking invaders moved into Greece from the north. By 1100 B.C.E., the Mycenaean culture was coming to an end, and the Greek world was entering a new period of considerable insecurity.

The Greeks in a Dark Age (c. 1100–c. 750 B.C.E.)

After the collapse of Mycenaean civilization, Greece entered a difficult era of declining population and falling food production. Because of the difficult conditions and our lack of knowledge about the period, historians refer to it as the Dark Age. Not until 850 B.C.E. did farming—and Greece itself—revive.

During the Dark Age, large numbers of Greeks left the mainland and migrated across the Aegean Sea to various islands and especially to the southwestern shore of Asia Minor, a strip of territory that came to be called Ionia (y-OH-nee-uh). Two other major groups of Greeks settled in established parts of Greece. The Aeolian (ee-OH-lee-un) Greeks of northern and central Greece colonized the large island of Lesbos and the adjacent territory of the mainland. The Dorians (DOR-ee-unz) established themselves in southwestern Greece, especially in the Peloponnesus, as well as on some of the south Aegean islands, including Crete.

As trade and economic activity began to recover, iron replaced bronze in the construction of weapons, making them affordable for more people. At some point in the eighth century B.C.E., the Greeks adopted the Phoenician alphabet to give themselves a new system of writing. And near the very end of the Dark Age appeared the work of Homer, who has come to be viewed as one of the greatest poets of all time.

HOMER AND HOMERIC GREECE The *Iliad* and the *Odyssey*, the first great epic poems of early Greece, were based on stories that had been passed down from generation to generation. It is generally assumed that Homer made use of these oral traditions to compose the *Iliad*, his epic poem of the Trojan War. The war was sparked by Paris, a prince of Troy, who kidnapped Helen, wife of the king of the Greek state of Sparta, outraging all the Greeks. Under the leadership of the Spartan king's brother, Agamemnon of Mycenae, the Greeks attacked Troy. After ten years of combat, the Greeks finally sacked the city. The *Iliad* is not so much the story of the war itself, however, as it is the tale of the Greek hero Achilles (uh-KIL-eez) and how the "wrath of Achilles" led to disaster. The *Odyssey*, Homer's other masterpiece, is an epic romance that recounts the journeys of one of the Greek heroes, Odysseus, from the fall of Troy until his eventual return to his wife, Penelope, twenty years later.

Although the *Iliad* and the *Odyssey* supposedly deal with the heroes of the Mycenaean age of the thirteenth century B.C.E., many scholars believe that they really describe the social conditions of the Dark Age. According to the Homeric view, Greece was a society based on agriculture in which a landed warrior-aristocracy controlled much wealth and exercised considerable power. Homer's world reflects the values of aristocratic heroes.

A Mycenaean Death Mask. This death mask of thin gold was one of several found by Heinrich Schliemann in his excavation of Grave Circle A at Mycenae. These masks are similar to the gold mummy masks used in Egyptian royal tombs. Schliemann claimed—incorrectly—that he had found the mask of Agamemnon, king of Mycenae in Homer's *Iliad*.

Homer's Ideal of Excellence

FAMILY & SOCIETY

THE *ILIAD* AND THE *ODYSSEY*, which the Greeks believed were written by Homer, were used as basic texts for the education of Greeks for hundreds of years during antiquity. This passage from the *Iliad*, describing a conversation between Hector, prince of Troy, and his wife, Andromache, illustrates the Greek ideal of gaining honor through combat. At the end of the passage, Homer also reveals what became the Greek attitude toward women: they are supposed to spin and weave and take care of their households and children.

Homer, *Iliad*

Hector looked at his son and smiled, but said nothing. Andromache, bursting into tears, went up to him and put her hand in his. "Hector," she said, "you are possessed. This bravery of yours will be your end. You do not think of your little boy or your unhappy wife, whom you will make a widow soon. Some day the Achaeans [Greeks] are bound to kill you in a massed attack. And when I lose you I might as well be dead.... I have no father, no mother, now.... I had seven brothers too at home. In one day all of them went down to Hades' House. The great Achilles of the swift feet killed them all....

"So you, Hector, are father and mother and brother to me, as well as my beloved husband. Have pity on me now; stay here on the tower; and do not make your boy an orphan and your wife a widow...."

"All that, my dear," said the great Hector of the glittering helmet, "is surely my concern. But if I hid myself like a coward and refused to fight, I could never face the Trojans.... Besides, it would go against the grain, for I have trained myself always, like a good soldier, to take my place in the front line and win glory for my father and myself...."

As he finished, glorious Hector held out his arms to take his boy. But the child shrank back with a cry to the bosom of his girdled nurse, alarmed by his father's appearance. He was frightened by the bronze of the helmet and the horsehair plume that he saw nodding grimly down at him. His father and his lady mother had to laugh. But noble Hector quickly took his helmet off and put the dazzling thing on the ground. Then he kissed his son, ... and prayed to Zeus and the other gods: "Zeus, and you other gods, grant that this boy of mine may be, like me, preeminent in Troy; as strong and brave as I; a mighty king of Ilium. May people say, when he comes back from battle, 'Here is a better man than his father.' Let him bring home the bloodstained armor of the enemy he has killed, and make his mother happy."

Hector handed the boy to his wife.... She was smiling through her tears, and when her husband saw this he was moved. He stroked her with his hand and said, "My dear, I beg you not to be too much distressed. No one is going to send me down to Hades before my proper time. But Fate is a thing that no man born of woman, coward, or hero can escape. Go home now, and attend to your own work, the loom and the spindle, and see that the maidservants get on with theirs. War is men's business; and this war is the business of every man in Ilium, myself above all."

What important ideals for Greek men and women are revealed in this passage from the Iliad*? How do the women's ideals compare with those for ancient Indian and Chinese women?*

Source: From *The Iliad* by Homer, translated by E. V. Rieu (Penguin Classics 1950). Copyright © 1950 the Estate of E. V. Rieu.

HOMER'S ENDURING IMPORTANCE This, of course, explains the importance of Homer to later generations of Greeks. Homer did not so much record history as make it. The Greeks regarded the *Iliad* and the *Odyssey* as authentic history. They gave the Greeks an idealized past, somewhat like the concept of the golden age in ancient China, with a legendary age of heroes, and the poems came to be used as standard texts for the education of generations of Greek males. As one Athenian stated, "my father was anxious to see me develop into a good man ... and as a means to this end he compelled me to memorize all of Homer."[1] The values Homer inculcated were essentially the aristocratic values of courage and honor (see the box "Homer's Ideal of Excellence" above). It was important to strive for the excellence befitting a hero, which the Greeks called *arete*. In the warrior-aristocratic world of Homer, *arete* is won in a struggle or contest. Through his willingness to fight, the hero protects his family and friends, preserves his own honor and his family's, and earns his reputation.

In the Homeric world, aristocratic women, too, were expected to pursue excellence. Penelope, for example, the wife of Odysseus (oh-DISS-ee-uss), the hero of the *Odyssey*, remains faithful to her husband and displays great courage and intelligence in preserving their household during her husband's long absence. Upon his return, Odysseus praises her for her excellence: "Madame, there is not a man in the wide world who could find fault with you. For your fame has reached heaven itself, like that of some perfect king, ruling a populous and mighty state with the fear of god in his heart, and upholding the right."[2]

To later generations of Greeks, these heroic values formed the core of aristocratic virtue, a fact that explains the tremendous popularity of Homer as an educational tool. Homer gave to the Greeks a single universally accepted model of heroism, honor, and nobility. But in time, as a new world of city-states emerged in Greece, new values of cooperation and community also transformed what the Greeks learned from Homer.

The Greek City-States (c. 750–c. 500 B.C.E.)

 FOCUS QUESTION: What were the chief features of the *polis*, or city-state, and how did the city-states of Athens and Sparta differ?

During the Dark Age, Greek villages gradually expanded and evolved into independent city-states. In the eighth century B.C.E., Greek civilization burst forth with new energies, beginning the period that historians have called the Archaic Age of Greece. Two major developments stand out in this era: the evolution of the city-state, or what the Greeks called a *polis* (plural, *poleis*), as the central institution in Greek life and the Greeks' colonization of the Mediterranean and Black Seas.

The *Polis*

In the most basic sense, a *polis* (POH-liss) could be defined as a small but autonomous political unit in which all major political, social, and religious activities were carried out at one central location. The *polis* encompassed a town or city or even village and its surrounding countryside. But each had a central place where the citizens of the *polis* could assemble for political, social, and religious activities. In some *poleis*, this central meeting point was a hill, like the Acropolis in Athens, which could serve as a place of refuge during an attack and later at some sites came to be the religious center on which temples and public monuments were erected. Below the acropolis would be an *agora*, an open space that served both as a market and as a place where citizens could assemble.

Poleis varied greatly in size, from a few square miles to a few hundred square miles. They also varied in population. Athens had a population of about 250,000 by the fifth century B.C.E. But most *poleis* were much smaller, consisting of only a few hundred to several thousand people.

Although our word *politics* is derived from the Greek term *polis*, the *polis* itself was much more than a political institution. It was a community of citizens in which all political, economic, social, cultural, and religious activities were focused. As a community, the *polis* consisted of citizens with political rights (adult males), citizens with no political rights (women and children), and noncitizens (slaves and resident aliens). All citizens of a *polis* possessed rights, but these rights were coupled with responsibilities. The Greek philosopher Aristotle argued that the citizen did not just belong to himself: "We must rather regard every citizen as belonging to the state." However, the loyalty that citizens had to their city-states also had a negative side. City-states distrusted one another, and the division of Greece into fiercely patriotic independent units helped bring about its ruin.

A NEW MILITARY SYSTEM: THE GREEK WAY OF WAR As the *polis* developed, so did a new military system. In earlier times, wars in Greece had been fought by aristocratic cavalry soldiers—nobles on horseback. These aristocrats, who were large landowners, also dominated the political life of their *poleis*. But by the end of the eighth century B.C.E., a new military order came into being that was based on **hoplites** (HAHP-lyts), heavily armed infantrymen who wore bronze or leather helmets, breastplates, and greaves (shin guards). Each carried a round shield, a short sword, and a thrusting spear about 9 feet long. Hoplites advanced into battle as a unit, shoulder to shoulder, forming a **phalanx** (a rectangular formation) in tight order, usually eight ranks deep. As long as the hoplites kept their order, were not outflanked, and did not break, they either secured victory or, at the very least, suffered no harm. The phalanx was easily routed, however, if it broke its order. Thus, the safety of the phalanx depended above all on the solidarity and discipline of its members. As one seventh-century B.C.E. poet noted, a good hoplite was "a short man firmly placed upon his legs, with a courageous heart, not to be uprooted from the spot where he plants his legs."[3]

The hoplite force had political as well as military repercussions. The aristocratic cavalry was now outdated. Since each hoplite provided his own armor, men of property, both aristocrats and small farmers, made up the new phalanx. Those who could become hoplites and fight for the state could also challenge aristocratic control. Thus, the development of the hoplite and phalanx became an important factor in the rise of democracy in Greece.

In the world of the Greek city-states, war became an integral part of the Greek way of life. The Greek philosopher Plato described war as "always existing by nature between every Greek city-state."[4] The Greeks created a tradition of warfare that became a prominent element of Western civilization. For example, the Greeks devised excellent weapons and body armor, making effective use of technological improvements. Greek armies included a wide number of citizen-soldiers, who gladly accepted the need for training and discipline, giving them an edge over their opponents' often far-larger armies of mercenaries. Moreover, the Greeks displayed a willingness to engage the enemy head-on, thus deciding a battle quickly and with as few casualties as possible. Finally, the Greeks demonstrated the effectiveness of heavy infantry in determining the outcome of a battle. All these features of Greek warfare remained part of Western warfare for centuries.

Colonization and the Growth of Trade

Between 750 and 550 B.C.E., large numbers of Greeks left their homeland to settle in distant lands. The growing gulf between rich and poor, overpopulation, and the development of trade were all factors that spurred the establishment of colonies.

Each colony was founded as a *polis* and was usually independent of the mother *polis* (the *metropolis*) that had established it.

The Hoplite Forces. The Greek hoplites were infantrymen equipped with large round shields and long thrusting spears. In battle, they advanced in tight phalanx formation and were dangerous opponents as long as this formation remained unbroken. This vase painting from the seventh century B.C.E. shows two groups of hoplite warriors engaged in battle. The piper on the left is leading another line of soldiers preparing to enter the fray.

In the western Mediterranean, new Greek settlements were established along the coastline of southern Italy, southern France, eastern Spain, and northern Africa west of Egypt. To the north, the Greeks set up colonies in Thrace, where they sought good agricultural lands to grow grains. Greeks also settled along the shores of the Black Sea and secured the approaches to it with cities on the Hellespont and Bosporus, most notably Byzantium, site of the later Constantinople (Istanbul). In establishing these settlements, the Greeks spread their culture throughout the Mediterranean basin. Moreover, colonization helped the Greeks foster a greater sense of Greek identity. Before the eighth century, Greek communities were mostly isolated from one another, and many neighboring states were on unfriendly terms. Once Greeks from different communities went abroad and found peoples with unfamiliar languages and customs, they became more aware of their own linguistic and cultural similarities.

Colonization also led to increased trade and industry. The Greeks on the mainland sent their pottery, wine, and olive oil to the colonized areas; in return, they received grains and metals from the west and fish, timber, wheat, metals, and slaves from the Black Sea region. In many *poleis*, the expansion of trade and industry created a new group of rich men who perceived that the decisions of the *polis* could affect their businesses. They now desired new political privileges but found them impossible to gain because of the power of the ruling aristocrats. This desire for change soon led to political crisis in many Greek states.

Tyranny in the Greek *Polis*

The aspirations of the new industrial and commercial groups laid the groundwork for the rise of **tyrants** in the seventh and sixth centuries B.C.E. They were not necessarily oppressive or wicked, as the modern English word *tyrant* connotes. Greek tyrants were rulers who came to power in an unconstitutional way; a tyrant was not subject to the law. Many tyrants were actually aristocrats who opposed the control of the ruling aristocratic faction in their cities. The support for the tyrants, however, came from the new rich who made their money in trade and industry, as well as from poor peasants who were becoming increasingly indebted to landholding aristocrats. Both groups were opposed to the domination of political power by aristocratic **oligarchies** (*oligarchy* means "rule by the few").

Once in power, the tyrants built new marketplaces, temples, and walls that not only glorified the city but also enhanced their own popularity. Tyrants also favored the interests of merchants and traders. Despite these achievements, however, **tyranny** was largely extinguished by the end of the sixth century B.C.E. Greeks believed in the rule of law, and tyranny made a mockery of that ideal.

Although tyranny did not last, it played a significant role in the evolution of Greek history by ending the rule of narrow aristocratic oligarchies. Once the tyrants were eliminated, the door was opened to the participation of new and more people in governing the affairs of the community. Although this trend culminated in the development of democracy in some communities, in other states expanded oligarchies of one kind or another managed to remain in power. Greek states exhibited considerable variety in their governmental structures; this can perhaps best be seen by examining the two most famous and most powerful Greek city-states, Sparta and Athens.

Sparta

Located in the southeastern Peloponnesus, Sparta, like other Greek states, faced the need for more land. Instead of sending its people out to found new colonies, the Spartans conquered the neighboring Laconians and later, beginning around 730 B.C.E., undertook the conquest of neighboring Messenia despite its larger size and population. Messenia possessed a large, fertile plain ideal for growing grain. After its conquest in the seventh century B.C.E., the Messenians, like the Laconians earlier, were reduced to serfdom—they were known as **helots** (HEL-uts), a name derived from a Greek word for "capture"—and forced to work for the Spartans. But the helots drastically outnumbered the Spartan citizens (some estimates are ten to one) and constantly threatened to revolt. To ensure control over them, the Spartans made a conscious decision to create a military state.

THE NEW SPARTA   Between 800 and 600 B.C.E., the Spartans instituted a series of reforms that are associated with the name of the lawgiver Lycurgus (ly-KUR-guss) (see the box "The Lycurgan Reforms" on p. 101). Although historians are not sure that Lycurgus ever existed, there is no doubt about the result of the reforms that were made: the lives of Spartans were now rigidly organized and tightly controlled (to this day, the word *spartan* means "highly self-disciplined"). Boys were taken from their mothers at the age of seven and put under control of the state. They lived in military-style barracks, where they were subjected to harsh discipline to make them tough and given an education that stressed military training and obedience to authority. At twenty, Spartan males were enrolled in the army for regular military service. Although allowed to marry, they continued to live in the barracks and ate all their meals in public dining halls with their fellow soldiers. Meals were simple; the famous Spartan black broth consisted of a piece of pork boiled in blood, salt, and vinegar, causing a visitor who ate in a public mess to remark that he now understood why Spartans were not afraid to die. At thirty, Spartan males were recognized as mature and allowed to vote in the assembly and live at home, but they remained in military service until the age of sixty.

While their husbands remained in military barracks until age thirty, Spartan women lived at home. Because of this separation, Spartan women had greater freedom of movement. Permitted to own and inherit land, Spartan women had greater power in the household than was common for women elsewhere in Greece and could even supervise large estates. They were encouraged to exercise and remain fit to bear and raise healthy children. Like the men, Spartan women engaged in athletic exercises in the nude. Many Spartan women upheld the strict Spartan values, expecting their husbands and sons to be brave in war. The story is told that as a Spartan mother was burying her son, an old woman came up to her and said, "You poor woman, what a misfortune." "No," replied the mother, "because I bore him so that he might die for Sparta, and that is what has happened, as I wished."[5]

THE SPARTAN STATE   The so-called Lycurgan reforms also reorganized the Spartan government, creating an oligarchy. Two kings from different families were primarily responsible for military affairs and served as the leaders of the Spartan army on its campaigns. A group of five men, known as the *ephors* (EFF-urz), were elected each year and were responsible for the education of youth and the conduct of all citizens. A council of elders, composed of the two kings and twenty-eight male citizens over the age of sixty, decided on the issues that would be presented to an assembly. This assembly of all male citizens did not debate but only voted on the proposals put before it by the council of elders. The assembly also elected the council of elders and the ephors.

To make their new military state secure, the Spartans deliberately turned their backs on the outside world. Foreigners, who might bring in new ideas, were discouraged from visiting Sparta. Nor were Spartans, except for military reasons, allowed to travel abroad, where they might pick up new ideas dangerous to the stability of the state. Likewise, Spartan citizens were discouraged from studying philosophy, literature, or the arts—subjects that might encourage new thoughts. The art of war was the Spartan ideal, and all other arts were frowned on.

In the sixth century, Sparta used its military might and the fear it inspired to gain greater control of the Peloponnesus by organizing an alliance of almost all the Peloponnesian states. Sparta's strength enabled it to dominate this Peloponnesian League and determine its policies. By 500 B.C.E., the Spartans had organized a powerful military state that maintained order and stability in the Peloponnesus. Raised from early childhood to believe that total loyalty to the Spartan state was the basic reason for existence, the Spartans viewed their strength as justification for their militaristic ideals and regimented society.

Athens

By 700 B.C.E., Athens had established a unified *polis* on the peninsula of Attica. Although early Athens had been ruled by a monarchy, by the seventh century B.C.E. it had fallen under the control of its aristocrats. They possessed the best land and controlled political and religious life by means of a council of

The Lycurgan Reforms

FAMILY & SOCIETY

To maintain their control over the helots, the Spartans instituted the reforms that created their military state. In this account of the lawgiver Lycurgus, the Greek historian Plutarch discusses the effect of these reforms on the treatment and education of boys.

Plutarch, *Lycurgus*

Lycurgus was of another mind; he would not have masters bought out of the market for his young Spartans, … nor was it lawful, indeed, for the father himself to breed up the children after his own fancy; but as soon as they were seven years old they were to be enrolled in certain companies and classes, where they all lived under the same order and discipline, doing their exercises and taking their play together. Of these, he who showed the most conduct and courage was made captain; they had their eyes always upon him, obeyed his orders, and underwent patiently whatsoever punishment he inflicted; so that the whole course of their education was one continued exercise of a ready and perfect obedience. The old men, too, were spectators of their performances, and often raised quarrels and disputes among them, to have a good opportunity of finding out their different characters, and of seeing which would be valiant, which a coward, when they should come to more dangerous encounters. Reading and writing they gave them, just enough to serve their turn; their chief care was to make them good subjects, and to teach them to endure pain and conquer in battle. To this end, as they grew in years, their discipline was proportionately increased; their heads were close-clipped, they were accustomed to go barefoot, and for the most part to play naked.

After they were twelve years old, they were no longer allowed to wear any undergarments; they had one coat to serve them a year; their bodies were hard and dry, with but little acquaintance of baths and unguents; these human indulgences they were allowed only on some few particular days in the year. They lodged together in little bands upon beds made of the rushes which grew by the banks of the river Eurotas, which they were to break off with their hands with a knife; if it were winter, they mingled some thistledown with their rushes, which it was thought had the property of giving warmth. By the time they were come to this age there was not any of the more hopeful boys who had not a lover to bear him company. The old men, too, had an eye upon them, coming often to the grounds to hear and see them contend either in wit or strength with one another, and this as seriously … as if they were their fathers, their tutors, or their magistrates; so that there scarcely was any time or place without someone present to put them in mind of their duty, and punish them if they had neglected it.

[Spartan boys were also encouraged to steal their food.] They stole, too, all other meat they could lay their hands on, looking out and watching all opportunities, when people were asleep or more careless than usual. If they were caught, they were not only punished with whipping, but hunger, too, being reduced to their ordinary allowance, which was but very slender, and so contrived on purpose, that they might set about to help themselves, and be forced to exercise their energy and address. This was the principal design of their hard fare.

What does this passage from Plutarch's account of Lycurgus reveal about the nature of the Spartan state? Why would the entire program have been distasteful to the Athenians?

Source: From Plutarch, *The Lives of the Noble Grecians and Romans*, translated by John Dryden, and revised by Arthur Hugh Clough. (New York: Modern Library).

nobles, assisted by a board of nine officials called archons. Although there was an assembly of full citizens, it possessed few powers.

Near the end of the seventh century B.C.E., Athens faced political turmoil because of serious economic problems. Increasing numbers of Athenian farmers found themselves sold into slavery when they were unable to repay loans they had obtained from their aristocratic neighbors, pledging themselves as collateral. Repeatedly, there were cries to cancel the debts and give land to the poor.

THE REFORMS OF SOLON The ruling Athenian aristocrats responded to this crisis by choosing Solon (SOH-lun), a reform-minded aristocrat, as sole archon in 594 B.C.E. and giving him full power to make changes. Solon canceled all land debts, outlawed new loans based on humans as collateral, and freed people who had fallen into slavery for debts. He refused, however, to carry out land redistribution and hence failed to deal with the basic cause of the economic crisis.

Like his economic reforms, Solon's political measures were also a compromise. Though by no means eliminating the power of the aristocracy, they opened the door to the participation of new people, especially the nonaristocratic wealthy, in the government. But Solon's reforms, though popular, did not solve Athens's problems. Aristocratic factions continued to vie for power, and the poorer peasants resented Solon's failure to institute land redistribution. Internal strife finally led to the very institution Solon had hoped to avoid—tyranny. Pisistratus (puh-SIS-truh-tuss), an aristocrat, seized power in 560 B.C.E. Pursuing a foreign policy that aided Athenian trade,

Pisistratus remained popular with the mercantile and industrial classes. But the Athenians rebelled against his son and ended the tyranny in 510 B.C.E. Although the aristocrats attempted to reestablish an aristocratic oligarchy, Cleisthenes (KLYSS-thuh-neez), another aristocratic reformer, opposed this plan and, with the backing of the Athenian people, gained the upper hand in 508 B.C.E.

THE REFORMS OF CLEISTHENES Cleisthenes created the Council of Five Hundred, chosen by lot by the ten tribes in which all citizens had been enrolled. The council was responsible for the administration of both foreign and financial affairs and prepared the business that would be handled by the assembly. This assembly of all male citizens had final authority in the passing of laws after free and open debate; thus, Cleisthenes's reforms had reinforced the central role of the assembly of citizens in the Athenian political system.

The reforms of Cleisthenes created the foundations for Athenian democracy. More changes would come in the fifth century, when the Athenians themselves would begin to use the word *democracy* to describe their system (from the Greek words *demos*, "people," and *kratia*, "power"). By 500 B.C.E., Athens was more united than it had been and was on the verge of playing a more important role in Greek affairs.

Foreign Influence on Early Greek Culture

As the Greeks moved out into the eastern Mediterranean, they came into increased contact with the older civilizations of the Near East and Egypt, which had a strong impact on early Greek culture. The Greeks adopted new gods and goddesses as well as new myths—such as the story of the flood—from Mesopotamian traditions. Greek pottery in the eighth and seventh centuries began to use new motifs—such as floral designs—borrowed from the Near East. Greek sculpture, particularly that of the Ionian Greek settlements in southwestern Asia Minor, demonstrates the impact of the considerably older Egyptian civilization. There we first see the life-size stone statues of young male nudes known as *kouros* (KOO-rohss) figures. The *kouros* bears a strong resemblance to Egyptian statues of the New Kingdom. The figures are not realistic but stiff, the face bearing the hint of a smile; one leg is advanced ahead of the other, and the arms are held rigidly at the sides of the body.

Greek literature was also the beneficiary of a Greek alphabet that owed much to the Phoenicians (see Chapter 1). The Greeks adopted some of the twenty-two Phoenician consonants as Greek consonants and used other symbols to represent vowel sounds, which the Phoenicians did not have. In the process, the Greeks created a truly phonetic alphabet, probably between 800 and 750 B.C.E., thus making the Greek language easier to read and write than Egyptian hieroglyphics and Mesopotamian cuneiform. Greek could be used to record

The Metropolitan Museum of Art/Art Resource, NY

Scala/Art Resource, NY

Kouros. On the left is a statue of a young male nude from around 600 B.C.E., making it an early example of Greek *kouros* sculpture. Such statues, which were placed in temples along with companion figures of clothed young women, known as *korai*, were meant to be representations of the faithful dedicated to the gods. At the right is an early-seventh-century B.C.E. statue of an Egyptian nobleman. Clearly, Egyptian sculpture had a strong influence on Greek art. Unlike the Egyptians, however, Greek sculptors preferred depicting male figures in the nude.

laws and commercial transactions and to write the poetry, philosophical treatises, and other literary works that distinguish Greek culture.

The High Point of Greek Civilization: Classical Greece

 FOCUS QUESTIONS: What did the Greeks mean by *democracy*, and in what ways was the Athenian political system a democracy? What effect did the two great conflicts of the fifth century—the Persian Wars and the Peloponnesian War—have on Greek civilization?

Classical Greece is the name given to the period of Greek history from around 500 B.C.E. to the conquest of Greece by the Macedonian king Philip II in 338 B.C.E. Many of the cultural contributions of the Greeks occurred during this period. The age began with a mighty confrontation between the Greek states and the mammoth Persian Empire.

The Challenge of Persia

As the Greeks spread throughout the Mediterranean, they came into contact with the Persian Empire to the east (see Chapter 1). In his play *The Persians*, the Greek playwright Aeschylus reflected what some Greeks perceived to be the essential difference between themselves and the Persians. The Persian queen, curious to find out more about the Athenians, asks, "Who commands them? Who is shepherd of their host?" The chorus responds: "They are slaves to none, nor are they subject."[6] Thus, at least, some Greeks saw the struggle with the Persians as a contest between freedom and slavery. To the Greeks, a person was a citizen of the state, not a subject.

The Ionian Greek cities in western Asia Minor had already fallen subject to the Persian Empire by the mid-sixth century B.C.E. An unsuccessful revolt by the Ionian cities in 499 B.C.E.—assisted by the Athenian navy—led the Persian ruler Darius (duh-RY-uss) to seek revenge by attacking the mainland Greeks. In 490 B.C.E., the Persians landed an army on the plain of Marathon, only 26 miles from Athens. The Athenians and their allies were clearly outnumbered, but led by Miltiades (mil-TY-uh-deez), one of the Athenian leaders who insisted on attacking, the Greek hoplites charged across the plain of Marathon and crushed the Persian forces.

Xerxes (ZURK-seez), the new Persian monarch after the death of Darius in 486 B.C.E., vowed revenge and planned to invade. In preparation for the attack, some of the Greek states formed a defensive league under Spartan leadership. The Athenians, in the meantime, had acquired a new leader, Themistocles (thuh-MISS-tuh-kleez), who persuaded his fellow citizens to pursue a new military policy, namely, the development of a navy. By the time of the Persian invasion in 480 B.C.E., the Athenians had produced a fleet of about two hundred vessels, primarily triremes (TRY-reemz) (ships with three banks of oars).

Xerxes led a massive invasion force into Greece: close to 150,000 troops, almost seven hundred naval ships, and hundreds of supply ships to keep the large army fed. The Greeks tried to delay the Persians at the pass of Thermopylae (thur-MAHP-uh-lee), along the main road into central Greece. A Greek force numbering close to nine thousand, under the leadership of the Spartan king, Leonidas, and his contingent of three hundred Spartans, held off the Persian army for two days. The Spartan troops were especially brave. When told that Persian arrows would darken the sky in battle, one Spartan warrior supposedly responded, "That is good news. We will fight in the shade!" Unfortunately for the Greeks, a traitor told the Persians how to use a mountain path to outflank the Greek force. The Spartans fought to the last man.

The Athenians, now threatened by the onslaught of the Persian forces, abandoned their city. While the Persians sacked and burned Athens, the Greek fleet remained offshore near the island of Salamis (SAH-luh-miss) and challenged the Persian navy to fight. Although the Greeks were outnumbered, they managed to outmaneuver the Persian fleet and utterly defeated it. A few months later, early in 479 B.C.E., the Greeks formed the largest Greek army seen up to that time and decisively defeated the Persian army at Plataea (pluh-TEE-uh),

northwest of Attica. The Greeks had won the war and were now free to pursue their own destiny.

The Growth of an Athenian Empire in the Age of Pericles

After the defeat of the Persians, Athens took over the leadership of the Greek world by forming a defensive alliance against the Persians called the Delian League in the winter of 478–477 B.C.E. Its main headquarters was on the island of Delos, but its chief officials, including the treasurers and commanders of the fleet, were Athenian. Under the leadership of the Athenians, the Delian League pursued the attack against the Persian Empire. Virtually all of the Greek states in the Aegean were liberated from Persian control. Arguing that the Persian threat was now over, some members of the Delian League wished to withdraw. But the Athenians forced them to remain in the league and to pay tribute. In 454 B.C.E., the Athenians moved the treasury of the league from Delos to Athens. By controlling the Delian League, Athens had created an empire.

At home, Athenians favored the new imperial policy, especially after 461 B.C.E., when politics came to be dominated by a political faction led by a young aristocrat named Pericles (PER-i-kleez). Under Pericles, who remained a leading figure in Athenian politics for more than three decades, Athens embarked on a policy of expanding democracy at home and its new empire abroad. This period of Athenian and Greek history, which historians have subsequently labeled the Age of Pericles, witnessed the height of Athenian power and the culmination of its brilliance as a civilization.

During the Age of Pericles, the Athenians became deeply attached to their democratic system. The sovereignty of the people was embodied in the assembly, which consisted of all male citizens over eighteen years of age. In the 440s, that was probably a group of about 43,000. Not all attended, however, and the number present at the meetings, which were held every ten days on a hillside east of the Acropolis, seldom reached 6,000. The assembly passed all laws and made final decisions on war and foreign policy.

Routine administration of public affairs was handled by a large body of city magistrates, usually chosen by lot without regard to class and usually serving only one-year terms. This meant that many male citizens held public office at some time in their lives. A board of ten officials known as generals (*strategoi* [strah-tay-GOH-ee]) was elected by public vote to guide affairs of state, although their power depended on the respect they had earned. Generals were usually wealthy aristocrats, even though the people were free to select

Athenian Democracy: The Funeral Oration of Pericles

POLITICS & GOVERNMENT

IN HIS *HISTORY OF THE PELOPONNESIAN WAR*, the Greek historian Thucydides presented his reconstruction of the eulogy given by Pericles in the winter of 431–430 B.C.E. to honor the Athenians killed in the first campaigns of the Great Peloponnesian War. It is a magnificent, idealized description of Athenian democracy at its height.

Thucydides, *History of the Peloponnesian War*

Our constitution is called a democracy because power is in the hands not of a minority but of the whole people. When it is a question of settling private disputes, everyone is equal before the law; when it is a question of putting one person before another in positions of public responsibility, what counts is not membership of a particular class, but the actual ability which the man possesses. No one, so long as he has it in him to be of service to the state, is kept in political obscurity because of poverty. And, just as our political life is free and open, so is our day-to-day life in our relations with each other. We do not get into a state with our next-door neighbor if he enjoys himself in his own way, nor do we give him the kind of black looks which, though they do no real harm, still do hurt people's feelings. We are free and tolerant in our private lives; but in public affairs we keep to the law. This is because it commands our deep respect.

We give our obedience to those whom we put in positions of authority, and we obey the laws themselves, especially those which are for the protection of the oppressed, and those unwritten laws which it is an acknowledged shame to

break.... Here each individual is interested not only in his own affairs but in the affairs of the state as well: even those who are mostly occupied with their own business are extremely well-informed on general politics—this is a peculiarity of ours: we do not say that a man who takes no interest in politics is a man who minds his own business; we say that he has no business here at all. We Athenians, in our own persons, take our decisions on policy or submit them to proper discussions: for we do not think that there is an incompatibility between words and deeds; the worst thing is to rush into action before the consequences have been properly debated.... Taking everything together then, I declare that our city is an education to Greece, and I declare that in my opinion each single one of our citizens, in all the manifold aspects of life, is able to show himself the rightful lord and owner of his own person, and do this, moreover, with exceptional grace and exceptional versatility. And to show that this is no empty boasting for the present occasion, but real tangible fact, you have only to consider the power which our city possesses and which has been won by those very qualities which I have mentioned.

 In the eyes of Pericles, what are the ideals of Athenian democracy? In what ways does Pericles exaggerate his claims? Why would the Athenian passion for debate described by Pericles have been distasteful to the Spartans? On the other hand, how does eagerness for discussion perfectly suit democracy?

Source: From *The History of the Peloponnesian War* by Thucydides, translated by Rex Warner. Copyright © Rex Warner 1954.

---

otherwise. The generals could be reelected, enabling individual leaders to play an important political role. Pericles's frequent reelection (fifteen times) as one of the ten generals made him one of the leading politicians between 461 and 429 B.C.E.

Pericles expanded the Athenians' involvement in democracy, which is what by now the Athenians had come to call their form of government (see the box "Athenian Democracy: The Funeral Oration of Pericles" above). Power was in the hands of the people; male citizens voted in the assemblies and served as jurors in the courts. Lower-class citizens were now eligible for public offices formerly closed to them. Pericles also introduced state pay for officeholders, including the widely held jury duty. This meant that even poor citizens could afford to participate in public affairs and hold public office. Nevertheless, although the Athenians developed a system of government that was unique in its time in which citizens had equal rights and the people were the government, aristocrats continued to hold the most important offices, and many people, including women, slaves, and foreigners residing in Athens, were not given the same political rights.

Under Pericles, Athens became the leading center of Greek culture. The Persians had destroyed much of the city during the Persian Wars, but Pericles used the treasury money of the Delian League to set in motion a massive rebuilding program. New temples and statues soon made the greatness of Athens more visible. Art, architecture, and philosophy flourished, and Pericles broadly boasted that Athens had become the "school of Greece." But the achievements of Athens alarmed the other Greek states, especially Sparta, and soon all of Greece was confronting a new war.

The Great Peloponnesian War and the Decline of the Greek States

During the forty years after the defeat of the Persians, the Greek world came to be divided into two major camps: Sparta and its supporters and the Athenian maritime empire. Sparta and its allies feared the growing Athenian Empire. Then, too, Athens and Sparta had created two very different kinds of societies, and neither state was able to tolerate the other's system. A series of disputes finally led to the outbreak of war in 431 B.C.E.

At the beginning of the war, both sides believed they had winning strategies. The Athenians planned to remain behind the protective walls of Athens while the overseas empire and the navy would keep them supplied. Pericles knew that the Spartans and their allies could beat the Athenians in open battles, which was the chief aim of the Spartan strategy. The Spartans and their allies invaded Attica and ravaged the fields and orchards, hoping that the Athenians would send out their army to fight beyond the walls. But Pericles was convinced that Athens was secure behind its walls and stayed put.

In the second year of the war, however, plague devastated the crowded city of Athens and wiped out possibly one-third of the population. Pericles himself died the following year (429 B.C.E.), a severe loss to Athens. Despite the losses from the plague, the Athenians fought on in a struggle that dragged on for another twenty-seven years. A final crushing blow came in 405 B.C.E., when the Athenian fleet was destroyed at Aegospotami (ee-guh-SPOT-uh-my) on the Hellespont. Athens was besieged and surrendered in 404. Its walls were torn down, the navy was disbanded, and the Athenian Empire was no more. The great war was finally over.

The Great Peloponnesian War weakened the major Greek states and destroyed any possibility of cooperation among the states. The next seventy years of Greek history are a sorry tale of efforts by Sparta, Athens, and Thebes, a new Greek power, to dominate Greek affairs. Focused on their petty wars, the Greek states remained oblivious to the growing power of Macedonia to their north.

The Culture of Classical Greece

Classical Greece was a period of remarkable intellectual and cultural growth throughout the Greek world, and Periclean Athens was the most important center of Classical Greek culture.

THE WRITING OF HISTORY History as we know it, as the systematic analysis of past events, was introduced to the Western world by the Greeks. Herodotus (huh-ROD-uh-tuss) (c. 484–c. 425 B.C.E.) wrote *History of the Persian Wars*, which is commonly regarded as the first real history in Western civilization. The central theme of Herodotus's work was the conflict between the Greeks and the Persians, which he viewed as a struggle between freedom and despotism. Herodotus traveled extensively and questioned many people to obtain his information. He was a master storyteller and sometimes included considerable fanciful material, but he was also capable of exhibiting a critical attitude toward the materials he used.

Thucydides (thoo-SID-uh-deez) (c. 460–c. 400 B.C.E.) was a better historian by far; indeed, he is considered the greatest historian of the ancient world. Thucydides was an Athenian and a participant in the Peloponnesian War. He had been elected a general, but a defeat in battle led the fickle Athenian assembly to send him into exile, which gave him the opportunity to write his *History of the Peloponnesian War*.

Unlike Herodotus, Thucydides was not concerned with underlying divine forces or gods as explanatory causal factors in history. He saw war and politics in purely rational terms, as the activities of human beings. He examined the causes of the Peloponnesian War in a clear, methodical, objective fashion, placing much emphasis on accuracy and the precision of his facts. As he stated:

> With regard to my factual reporting of the events of the war I have made it a principle not to write down the first story that came my way, and not even to be guided by my own general impressions; either I was present myself at the events which I have described or else I heard of them from eyewitnesses whose reports I have checked with as much thoroughness as possible.[7]

Thucydides also provided remarkable insight into the human condition. He believed that political situations recur in similar fashion and that the study of history is therefore of great value in understanding the present.

GREEK DRAMA Drama as we know it in Western culture was originated by the Greeks. Plays were presented in outdoor theaters as part of religious festivals. The plays followed a fairly stable form. Three male actors who wore masks acted all the parts. A chorus, also male, spoke lines that explained what was going on. Action was very limited because the emphasis was on the story and its meaning.

The first Greek dramas were tragedies, plays based on the suffering of a hero and usually ending in disaster. Aeschylus (ESS-kuh-luss) (525–456 B.C.E.) is the first tragedian whose plays are known to us. As was customary in Greek tragedy, his plots are simple, and the entire drama focuses on a single tragic event and its meaning. Greek tragedies were sometimes presented in a trilogy (a set of three plays) built around a common theme. The only complete trilogy we possess, called the *Oresteia* (uh-res-TY-uh), was written by Aeschylus. The theme of this trilogy is derived from Homer. Agamemnon, the king of Mycenae, returns a hero from the defeat of Troy. His wife, Clytemnestra, avenges the sacrificial death of her daughter Iphigenia by murdering Agamemnon, who had been responsible for Iphigenia's death. In the second play of the trilogy, Agamemnon's son Orestes avenges his father by killing his mother. Orestes is then pursued by the avenging Furies, who torment him for killing his mother. Evil acts breed evil acts, and suffering is one's lot, suggests Aeschylus. But Orestes is put on trial and acquitted by Athena, the patron goddess of Athens. Personal vendetta has been eliminated, and law has prevailed.

The most successful writer of Greek tragedies was the Athenian playwright Sophocles (SAHF-uh-kleez) (c. 496–406 B.C.E.), whose most famous work was *Oedipus the King*. In this play, the oracle of Apollo foretells that a man (Oedipus) will kill his own father and marry his mother. Despite all attempts at prevention, the tragic events occur. Although it appears that Oedipus suffered the fate determined by the gods, Oedipus also accepts that he himself as a free man must bear responsibility for his actions: "It was Apollo, friends, Apollo, that brought this bitter bitterness, my sorrows to completion. But the hand that struck me was none but my own."[8]

In *Antigone* (an-TIG-oh-nee), the daughter of Oedipus is caught in the dilemma of following her religious obligations to

The Amphitheater at Epidaurus. The photo shows the ancient Greek amphitheater at Epidaurus in the eastern Peloponnesus. It held eighteen thousand onlookers for the theatrical presentations and athletic games that were part of the religious festivals dedicated to Asclepius, the god of healing. The inset photo shows an example of a tragic theatrical mask worn by actors. Since Greek dramas used three male actors who might play several roles, masks were necessary to distinguish the characters.

bury the body of her brother Polynices (pol-ee-NICE-eez), who has died in an attempt to seize the throne of Thebes. Antigone's uncle, Cleon, the king of Thebes, however, has forbidden his burial as a traitor to the state. Should Antigone adhere to her principles and fulfill her obligation to the gods by burying her brother or face death by defying the authority of the state? In this confrontation between Cleon and Antigone, Sophocles bears witness to the complexity of human existence (see the box "Sophocles: 'The Miracle of Man'" on p. 107).

Another outstanding Athenian tragedian, Euripides (yoo-RIP-uh-deez) (c. 485–406 B.C.E.), moved beyond his predecessors by creating more realistic characters. His plots also became more complex, with a greater interest in real-life situations. Euripides was controversial because he questioned traditional moral and religious values. For example, he was critical of the traditional view that war was glorious. Instead, he portrayed war as brutal and barbaric.

Greek tragedies dealt with universal themes still relevant to our day. They probed such problems as the nature of good and evil, the rights of the individual, the nature of divine forces, and the nature of human beings. Over and over, the tragic lesson was repeated: humans were free and yet could operate only within limitations imposed by the gods. Striving to do the best may not always gain a person success in human terms but is nevertheless worthy of the endeavor. Greek pride in human accomplishment and independence was real. As the chorus chants in Sophocles's *Antigone*: "Is there anything more wonderful on earth, our marvelous planet, than the miracle of man?"[9]

Greek comedy developed later than tragedy. The plays of Aristophanes (ar-is-STAH-fuh-neez) (c. 450–c. 385 B.C.E.), who used both grotesque masks and obscene jokes to entertain the Athenian audience, are examples of Old Comedy. But comedy in Athens was also more clearly political than tragedy. It was used to attack or savagely satirize both politicians and intellectuals. Of special importance to Aristophanes was his opposition to the Peloponnesian War.

THE ARTS: THE CLASSICAL IDEAL The artistic standards established by the Greeks of the Classical period have largely dominated the arts of the Western world. Greek art was concerned with expressing eternally true ideals. Its subject matter was basically the human being, expressed harmoniously as an object of great beauty. The Classical style, based on the ideals of reason, moderation, symmetry, balance, and harmony in all things, was meant to civilize the emotions.

In architecture, the most important form was the temple dedicated to a god or goddess. At the center of Greek temples were walled rooms that housed the statues of deities and treasuries in which gifts to the gods and goddesses were safeguarded. These central rooms were surrounded by a screen of columns that made Greek temples open structures rather than closed ones. The columns were originally made of wood but were changed to marble in the fifth century B.C.E.

Some of the finest examples of Greek Classical architecture were built in fifth-century Athens. The most famous building, regarded as the finest example of the Classical Greek temple,

Sophocles: "The Miracle of Man"

RELIGION & PHILOSOPHY

IN *ANTIGONE*, Sophocles presents a thoughtful analysis of the painful dilemmas in human existence. In one outstanding passage, the chorus expresses an exalted message on human resourcefulness and the achievements of human beings.

Sophocles, *Antigone*

Is there anything more wonderful on earth,
Our marvelous planet,
Than the miracle of man!
With what arrogant ease
He rides the dangerous seas,
From the waves' towering summit
To the yawning trough beneath.
The earth mother herself, before time began,
The oldest of the ageless gods,
Learned to endure his driving plough,
Turning the earth and breaking the clods
Till by the sweat of his brow
She yielded up her fruitfulness....

He has mastered the mysteries of language:
And thought, which moves faster than the wind,
He has tamed, and made rational.
Political wisdom too, all the knowledge
Of people and States, all the practical

Arts of government he has studied and refined,
Built cities to shelter his head
Against rain and anger and cold
And ordered all things in his mind.
There is no problem he cannot resolve
By the exercise of his brains or his breath,
And the only disease he cannot salve
Or cure, is death.

In action he is subtle beyond imagination,
Limitless is his skill, and these gifts
Are both enemies and friends,
As he applies them, with equal determination,
To good or evil ends.
All men honor, and the State uplifts
That man to the heights of glory, whose powers
Uphold the constitution, and the gods, and their laws.
His city prospers. But if he shifts
His ground, and takes the wrong path,
Despising morality, and blown up with pride,
Indulges himself and his power, at my hearth
May he never warm himself, or sit at my side.

Q What is Sophocles's view of humans and their accomplishments? What are the limitations to these human accomplishments?

Source: From Sophocles, *Antigone*, trans. Don Taylor (London: Methuen, 2006), pp. 17–18.

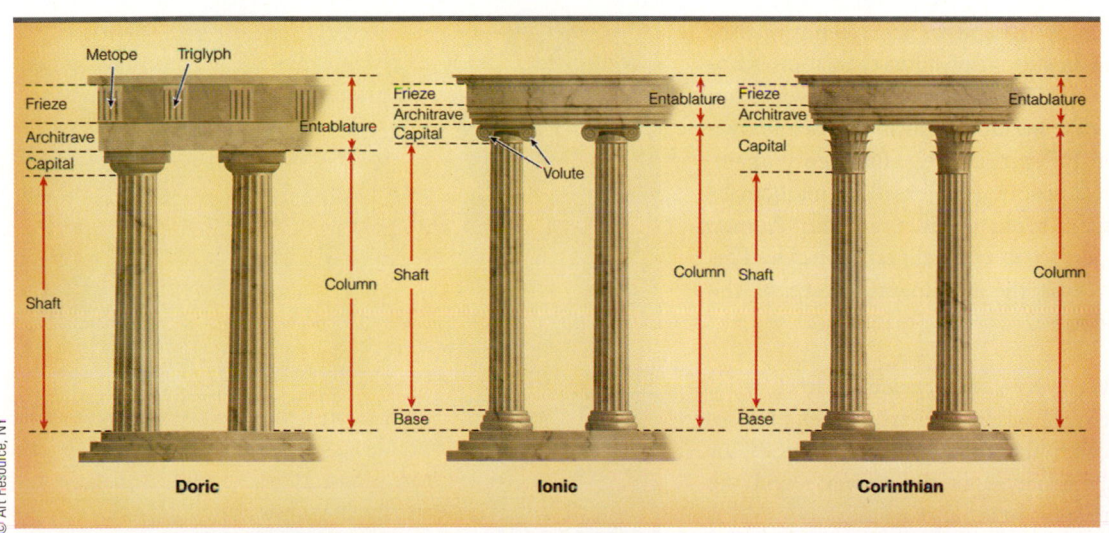

© Art Resource, NY

Doric, Ionic, and Corinthian Orders. The Greeks used columns of different shapes and sizes in their temples. The Doric order, which consisted of thick, fluted columns with simple capitals (the decorated tops of the columns), developed first in the Dorian Peloponnesus. The Greeks considered the Doric order grave, dignified, and masculine. The Ionic style was first developed in western Asia Minor and consisted of slender columns with spiral-shaped capitals. The Greeks characterized the Ionic order as slender, elegant, and feminine. Corinthian columns, with their more detailed capitals modeled after acanthus leaves, came later, near the end of the fifth century B.C.E.

Adam Crowley/Photodisc/Getty Images

The Parthenon. The arts in Classical Greece were designed to express the eternal ideals of reason, moderation, symmetry, balance, and harmony. In architecture, the most important form was the temple, and the classic example of this kind of architecture is the Parthenon, built between 447 and 432 B.C.E. Located on the Acropolis in Athens, the Parthenon was dedicated to Athena, the patron goddess of the city, but it also served as a shining example of the power and wealth of the Athenian Empire.

was the Parthenon, built between 447 and 432 B.C.E. Consecrated to Athena, the patron goddess of Athens, the Parthenon was also dedicated to the glory of the city-state and its inhabitants. The Parthenon typifies the principles of Classical architecture: calmness, clarity, and the avoidance of superfluous detail.

Greek sculpture developed a Classical style that differed significantly from the artificial stiffness of the figures of earlier times, which had been influenced by Egyptian sculpture. Statues of the male nude, the favorite subject of Greek sculptors, now exhibited more relaxed attitudes; their faces were self-assured, their bodies flexible and smooth-muscled. Although the figures possessed natural features that made them lifelike, Greek sculptors sought to achieve not realism but a standard of ideal beauty. Polyclitus (pahl-ee-KLY-tuss), a fifth-century sculptor, wrote a treatise (now lost) on a canon of proportions that he illustrated in a work known as the *Doryphoros* (doh-RIF-uh-rohss). His theory maintained that the use of ideal proportions, based on mathematical ratios found in nature, could produce an ideal human form, beautiful in its perfected and refined features. This search for ideal beauty was the dominant feature of the Classical standard in sculpture.

THE GREEK LOVE OF WISDOM *Philosophy* is a Greek word that originally meant "love of wisdom." Early Greek philosophers were concerned with the development of critical or rational thought about the nature of the universe and the place of divine forces and souls in it.

Scala/Art Resource, NY

Doryphoros. This statue, known as the *Doryphoros*, or spear carrier, is by the fifth-century B.C.E. sculptor Polyclitus, who believed it illustrated the ideal proportions of the human figure. Classical Greek sculpture moved away from the stiffness of earlier figures but retained the young male nude as the favorite subject. The statues became more lifelike, with relaxed poses and flexible, smooth-muscled bodies. The aim of sculpture, however, was not simply realism but rather the expression of ideal beauty.

COMPARATIVE ESSAY

The Axial Age

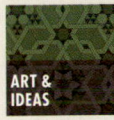

By the fourth century B.C.E., important regional civilizations existed in China, India, Southwest Asia, and the Mediterranean. During their formative periods between 700 and 300 B.C.E., all were characterized by the emergence of religious and philosophical thinkers who established ideas—or "axes"—that remained the basis for religions and philosophical thought in those societies for hundreds of years. Hence, some historians have referred to the period when these ideas developed as "the Axial Age."

During the fifth and fourth centuries in Greece, the philosophers Socrates, Plato, and Aristotle not only proposed philosophical and political ideas crucial to the Greek world and later to Roman and Western civilization but also conceived of a rational method of inquiry that became important to modern science. By the seventh century B.C.E., concepts of monotheism had developed in Persia through the teachings of Zoroaster and in Canaan through the Hebrew prophets. In Judaism, the Hebrews developed a world religion that influenced the later religions of Christianity and Islam.

During the sixth century, two major schools of thought—Confucianism and Daoism—emerged in China. Both sought to spell out the principles that would create a stable order in society. And although their views of reality were diametrically opposed, both came to have an impact on Chinese civilization that lasted into the twentieth century.

Two of the world's greatest religions, Hinduism and Buddhism, began in India during the Axial Age. Hinduism was an outgrowth of the religious beliefs of the Aryan peoples who settled in India. These ideas were expressed in the sacred texts known as the Vedas and in the Upanishads, which were commentaries on the Vedas compiled in the sixth century B.C.E. With its belief in reincarnation, Hinduism provided justification for India's rigid class system. Buddhism was the product of one man, Siddhartha Gautama, known as the Buddha, who lived in the sixth century B.C.E. The Buddha's simple message of achieving wisdom created a new spiritual philosophy that would rival Hinduism. Although a product of India, Buddhism also spread to other parts of the world.

Although these philosophies and religions developed in different areas of the world, they had some features in common. Like the Chinese philosophers Confucius and Lao Tzu, the Greek philosophers Plato and Aristotle had different ideas about the nature of reality. Thinkers in India and China also developed rational methods of inquiry similar to those of Plato and Aristotle. And regardless of their origins, when we speak of Judaism, Hinduism, Buddhism, Confucianism, Daoism, or Greek philosophical thought, we realize that the ideas of the Axial Age not only spread around the world at different times but are also still an integral part of our world today.

 What do historians mean when they speak of the Axial Age? What do you think could explain the emergence of similar ideas in different parts of the world during this period?

Philosophers in the Axial Age. This mosaic from Pompeii re-creates a gathering of Greek philosophers at the school of Plato.

Much of early Greek philosophy focused on the attempt to explain the universe on the basis of unifying principles. Many Greeks, however, were simply not interested in such speculations. The **Sophists** were a group of philosophical teachers in the fifth century B.C.E. who rejected such speculation as foolish. Like their near contemporary Confucius in China (see Chapter 3), they argued that understanding the universe was beyond the reach of the human mind (see the Comparative Essay "The Axial Age" above). It was more important for individuals to improve themselves, so the only worthwhile object of study was human behavior. The Sophists were wandering scholars who sold their services as professional teachers to the young men of Greece, especially those of Athens. The Sophists stressed the importance of **rhetoric** (the art of persuasive oratory) in winning debates and swaying an audience, a skill that was especially valuable in democratic Athens. Unlike Confucius, however, the Sophists tended to be skeptics who questioned the traditional values of their societies. To the Sophists, there was no absolute right or wrong. True wisdom consisted of being able to perceive and pursue one's own good. Many people, however, viewed the Sophists as harmful to society and considered their ideas especially dangerous to the values of young people.

In Classical Greece, Athens became the foremost intellectual and artistic center. Its reputation is perhaps strongest of all in philosophy. Socrates, Plato, and Aristotle raised basic questions that have been debated for two thousand years, for the most part the very same philosophical questions we wrestle with today.

Socrates (SAHK-ruh-teez) (469–399 B.C.E.) left no writings, but we know about him from his pupils. Socrates was a stonemason whose true love was philosophy. He taught a number of pupils, but not for pay, because he believed that the goal of education was to improve the individual. His approach, still known as the **Socratic method**, employs a question-and-answer technique to lead pupils to see things for themselves using their own reason. Socrates believed that all knowledge is within each person; only critical examination was needed to call it forth. This was the real task of philosophy, since "the unexamined life is not worth living."

Socrates questioned authority and criticized some traditional Athenian values, and this soon led him into trouble. Athens had had a tradition of free thought and inquiry, but its defeat in the Peloponnesian War had created an environment intolerant of open debate and soul-searching. Socrates was accused of corrupting the youth of Athens by his teaching. An Athenian jury convicted him and sentenced him to death.

One of Socrates's disciples was Plato (PLAY-toh) (c. 429–347 B.C.E.), considered by many the greatest philosopher of Western civilization. Unlike his master Socrates, who wrote nothing, Plato wrote a great deal. He was fascinated with the question of reality: How do we know what is real? According to Plato, a higher world of eternal, unchanging Ideas or Forms has always existed. To know these Forms is to know truth. These ideal Forms constitute reality and can be apprehended only by a trained mind—which, of course, is the goal of philosophy. The objects that we perceive with our senses are simply reflections of the ideal Forms. They are shadows; reality is in the Forms themselves.

Plato's ideas of government were set out in his dialogue titled *The Republic*. Based on his experience in Athens, Plato had come to distrust the workings of democracy. It was obvious to him that individuals could not attain an ethical life unless they lived in a just and rational state. In *The Republic*, he constructed such an ideal state, in which the population was divided into three basic groups. At the top was an upper class, a ruling elite, the philosopher-kings: "Unless … political power and philosophy meet together …, there can be no rest from troubles … for states, nor yet, as I believe, for all mankind."[10] The second group consisted of the courageous; they would be the warriors who protected the society. All the rest made up the masses, essentially people driven not by wisdom or courage but by desire. They

would be the producers—the artisans, tradespeople, and farmers. Contrary to common Greek custom, Plato also believed that men and women should have the same education and equal access to all positions.

Plato established a school at Athens known as the Academy. One of his pupils, who studied there for twenty years, was Aristotle (AR-iss-tot-ul) (384–322 B.C.E.), who later became a tutor to Alexander the Great. Aristotle did not accept Plato's theory of ideal Forms. Instead, he believed that by examining individual objects, we can perceive their form and arrive at universal principles, but these principles do not exist as a separate higher world of reality beyond material things; rather they are a part of things themselves. Aristotle's interests, then, lay in analyzing and classifying things based on thorough research and investigation. His interests were wide-ranging, and he wrote treatises on an enormous number of subjects: ethics, logic, politics, poetry, astronomy, geology, biology, and physics.

Like Plato, Aristotle wished for an effective form of government that would rationally direct human affairs. Unlike Plato, he did not seek an ideal state based on the embodiment of an ideal Form of justice but tried to find the best form of government by a rational examination of existing governments. For his *Politics*, Aristotle examined the constitutions of 158 states and arrived at general categories for organizing governments. He identified three good forms of government: monarchy, aristocracy, and constitutional government. But based on his examination, he warned that monarchy can easily turn into tyranny, aristocracy into oligarchy, and constitutional government into radical democracy or anarchy. He favored constitutional government as the best form for most people.

Aristotle's philosophical and political ideas played an enormous role in the development of Western thought during the Middle Ages (see Chapter 12). So did his ideas on women. Aristotle maintained that women were biologically inferior to men: "A woman is, as it were, an infertile male. She is female in fact on account of a kind of inadequacy." Therefore, according to Aristotle, women must be subordinated to men, not only in the community but also in marriage: "The association between husband and wife is clearly an aristocracy. The man rules by virtue of merit, and in the sphere that is his by right; but he hands over to his wife such matters as are suitable for her."[11]

Greek Religion

As was the case throughout the ancient world, religion played an important role in Greek society and was intricately connected to every aspect of daily life; it was both social and practical. Public festivals, which originated from religious practices, served specific functions: boys were prepared to be warriors, girls to be mothers. Because religion was related to every aspect of life, citizens had to have a proper attitude toward the gods. Religion was a civic cult necessary for the well-being of the state. Temples dedicated to a god or goddess were the major buildings in Greek cities.

The poetry of Homer gave an account of the gods that provided Greek religion with a definite structure. Over a period of time, all Greeks came to accept a basic polytheistic religion with twelve chief gods who supposedly lived on Mount Olympus, the highest mountain in Greece. Among the twelve were Zeus (ZOOSS), the chief deity and father of the gods; Athena, goddess of wisdom and crafts; Apollo, god of the sun and poetry; Aphrodite, goddess of love; and Poseidon, brother of Zeus and god of the seas and earthquakes. Although the twelve Olympian gods were common to all Greeks, each *polis* usually singled out one of the twelve as a guardian deity for the community. Athena was the patron goddess of Athens, for example.

Because the Greeks wanted the gods to look favorably on their activities, ritual assumed enormous proportions in Greek religion. Prayers were often combined with gifts to the gods based on the principle "I give so that you, the gods, will give in return." Ritual meant sacrifices, whether of animals or agricultural products. Animal sacrifices were burned on an altar in front of a temple or on a small altar in front of a home.

As another practical side of Greek religion, Greeks wanted to know the will of the gods. To do so, they made use of the *oracle*, a sacred shrine dedicated to a god or goddess who revealed the future. The most famous was the oracle of Apollo at Delphi, located on the side of Mount Parnassus, overlooking the Gulf of Corinth. At Delphi, a priestess listened to questions while in a state of ecstasy that was believed to be induced by Apollo. Her responses were interpreted by the priests and given in verse form to the person asking questions. Representatives of states and individuals traveled to Delphi to consult the oracle of Apollo. States might inquire whether they should undertake a military expedition; individuals might raise such questions as "Heracleidas asks whether he will have offspring from the wife he has now." Responses were often enigmatic and at times even politically motivated. Croesus (KREE-suss), the king of Lydia in Asia Minor who was known for his incredible wealth, sent messengers to the oracle at Delphi, asking whether he should go to war with the Persians. The oracle replied that if Croesus attacked the Persians, he would destroy a mighty empire. Overjoyed to hear these words, Croesus made war on the Persians but was crushed. A mighty empire was indeed destroyed—his own.

Festivals also developed as a way to honor the gods and goddesses. Some of these (the Panhellenic celebrations) came to have international significance and were held at special locations, such as those dedicated to the worship of Zeus at Olympia or to Apollo at Delphi. The great festivals incorporated numerous events in honor of the gods, including athletic competitions to which all Greeks were invited.

According to tradition, such athletic games were first held at the Olympic festival in 776 B.C.E. and then held every four years thereafter to honor Zeus. Initially, the Olympic contests consisted of foot races and wrestling, but later boxing, javelin throwing, and various other contests were added. Competitions were always between individuals, not groups. The Greeks looked upon winning athletes as great heroes and often rewarded them with parades, as well as money and free rents for life.

Olympic games were not without danger to the participants. Athletes competed in the nude, and rules were rather relaxed. Wrestlers, for example, were allowed to gouge eyes and even pick up their competitors and bring them down head first onto a hard surface. Boxers wrapped their hands and forearms with heavy leather thongs, making their blows damaging. Some athletes were killed during the games. Given the hatred that often existed between city-states in ancient Greece, their deaths were not always accidental.

The Greek Olympic games came to an end in 393 C.E., when a Christian Roman emperor banned them as pagan exercises. Fifteen hundred years later, the games were revived through the efforts of a French baron, Pierre de Coubertin (PYAYR duh koo-ber-TANH). In 1896, the first modern Olympic games were held in Athens, Greece.

Life in Classical Athens

The *polis* was above all a male community: only adult male citizens took part in public life. In Athens, this meant the exclusion of women, slaves, and foreign residents, or roughly 85 percent of the total population in

Olympic Victors. Athletic games were a feature of festivals honoring Greek gods and goddesses. Those at the Olympic festival honoring Zeus were especially prominent. This 1813 engraving of a decoration on an ancient Greek red-figure vase portrays the victors in the Olympic games being offered a laurel wreath and headband by Victory, personified as a woman.

Attica. There were probably 150,000 citizens in Athens, of whom about 43,000 were adult males who exercised political power. Resident foreigners, who numbered about 35,000, received the protection of the laws but were also subject to some of the responsibilities of citizens, namely, military service and the funding of festivals. The remaining social group, the slaves, numbered around 100,000. Most slaves in Athens worked in the home as cooks and maids or toiled in the fields. Some were owned by the state and worked on public construction projects.

ECONOMY AND LIFESTYLE The Athenian economy was based largely on agriculture and trade. Athenians grew grains, vegetables, and fruit for local consumption. Grapes and olives were cultivated for wine and olive oil, which were used locally and also exported. The Athenians raised sheep and goats for wool and dairy products. Because of the size of the population in Attica and the lack of abundant fertile land, Athens had to import 50 to 80 percent of its grain, a staple in the Athenian diet. Trade was thus very important to the Athenian economy. Perhaps that is one reason why the Greeks were among the first to mint silver coins.

The Athenian lifestyle was basically simple. Athenian houses were furnished with necessities bought from artisans, such as beds, couches, tables, chests, pottery, stools, baskets, and cooking utensils. Wives and slaves made clothes and blankets at home. The Athenian diet was rather plain and relied on such basic foods as barley, wheat, millet, lentils, grapes, figs, olives, almonds, bread made at home, vegetables, eggs, fish, cheese, and chicken. Olive oil was widely used, not only for eating but also for burning in lamps and rubbing on the body after washing and exercise. Although country houses kept animals, they were used for reasons other than their flesh: oxen for plowing, sheep for wool, and goats for milk and cheese.

FAMILY AND RELATIONSHIPS The family was a central institution in ancient Athens. It was composed of husband, wife, and children (a nuclear family), although other dependent relatives and slaves were regarded as part of the family economic unit. The family's primary social function was to produce new citizens. Strict laws enacted in the fifth century stipulated that a citizen must be the offspring of a legally acknowledged marriage between two Athenian citizens whose parents were also citizens.

Adult female citizens could participate in most religious cults and festivals but were otherwise excluded from public life. They could not own property beyond personal items and always had a male guardian. An Athenian woman was expected to be a good wife. Her foremost obligation was to bear children, especially male children who would preserve the family line. A wife was also to take care of her family and her house, either doing the household work herself or supervising the slaves who did the actual work (see Opposing Viewpoints "Women in Athens and Sparta" on p. 113).

Women were kept under strict control. Because they were married at fourteen or fifteen, they were taught about their responsibilities at an early age. Although many managed to learn to read and play musical instruments, they were not given any formal education. And women were expected to remain at home out of sight unless attending funerals or festivals. If they left the house, they were to be accompanied. A woman working alone in public was either poverty-stricken or not a citizen.

Male homosexuality was also a prominent feature of Athenian life. The Greek homosexual ideal was a relationship between a mature man and a young male. It is most likely that this was an aristocratic ideal and not one practiced by the common people. While the relationship was frequently physical, the Greeks also viewed it as educational. The older male (the "lover") won the love of his "beloved" through his value as a teacher and the devotion he demonstrated in training his charge. In a sense, this love relationship was seen as a way of initiating young males into the male world of political and military dominance. The Greeks did not feel that the coexistence of homosexual and heterosexual predilections created any special problems for individuals or their society.

The Metropolitan Museum of Art/Art Resource, NY

Women in the Loom Room. In Athens, women were citizens and could participate in religious cults and festivals, but they had no rights and were barred from political activity. Women were thought to belong in the house, caring for the children and the needs of the household. A principal activity of Greek women was the making of clothes. This vase shows two women working on a warp-weighted loom.

OPPOSING ⤫ VIEWPOINTS

Women in Athens and Sparta

FAMILY & SOCIETY

IN CLASSICAL ATHENS, A WOMAN'S PLACE WAS IN THE HOME. She had two major responsibilities as a wife—bearing and raising children and managing the household. In the first selection, from a dialogue on estate management, Xenophon (ZEN-uh-fuhn) relates the instructions of an Athenian to his new wife. Although women in Sparta had the same responsibilities as women in Athens, they assumed somewhat different roles as a result of the Spartan lifestyle. The second, third, and fourth selections demonstrate these differences as seen in the accounts of three ancient Greek writers.

Xenophon, *Oeconomicus*

[Ischomachus addresses his new wife:] For it seems to me, dear, that the gods with great discernment have coupled together male and female, as they are called, chiefly in order that they may form a perfect partnership in mutual service. For, in the first place that the various species of living creatures may not fail, they are joined in wedlock for the production of children. Secondly, offspring to support them in old age is provided by this union, to human beings, at any rate. Thirdly, human beings live not in the open air, like beasts, but obviously need shelter. Nevertheless, those who mean to win stores to fill the covered place, have need of someone to work at the open-air occupations; since plowing, sowing, planting and grazing are all such open-air employments; and these supply the needful food. For he made the man's body and mind more capable of enduring cold and heat, and journeys and campaigns; and therefore imposed on him the outdoor tasks. To the woman, since he had made her body less capable of such endurance, I take it that God has assigned the indoor tasks. And knowing that he had created in the woman and had imposed on her the nourishment of the infants, he meted out to her a larger portion of affection for newborn babes than to the man....

Your duty will be to remain indoors and send out those servants whose work is outside, and superintend those who are to work indoors, and to receive the incomings, and distribute so much of them as must be spent, and watch over so much as is to be kept in store, and take care that the sum laid by for a year be not spent in a month. And when wool is brought to you, you must see that cloaks are made for those that want them. You must see too that the dry corn is in good condition for making food. One of the duties that fall to you, however, will perhaps seem rather thankless: you will have to see that any servant who is ill is cared for.

Xenophon, *Constitution of the Spartans*

First, to begin at the beginning, I will start with the begetting of children. Elsewhere those girls who are going to have children and are considered to have been well brought up are nourished with the plainest diet which is practicable and the smallest amount of luxury good possible; wine is certainly not allowed them at all, or only if well diluted. Just as the majority of craftsmen are sedentary, the other Greeks expect their girls to sit quietly and work wool. But how can one expect girls brought up like this to give birth to healthy babies? Lycurgus considered slave girls quite adequate to produce clothing, and thought that for free women the most important job was to bear children. In the first place, therefore, he prescribed physical training for the female sex no less than for the male; and next, just as for men, he arranged competitions of racing and strength for women also, thinking that if both parents were strong their children would be more robust.

Aristotle, *Politics*

Now, this license of the [Spartan] women, from the earliest times, was to be expected. For the men were absent from home for long periods of time on military expeditions, fighting the war against the Argives and again against the Arkadians and Messenians.... And nearly two-fifths of the whole country is in the hands of women, both because there have been numerous heiresses, and because large dowries are customary. And yet it would have been better to have regulated them, and given none at all or small or even moderate ones. But at present it is possible for a man to give an inheritance to whomever he chooses.

Plutarch, *Lycurgus*

Since Lycurgus regarded education as the most important and finest duty of the legislator, he began at the earliest stage by looking at matters relating to marriages and births. For he exercised the girls' bodies with races and wrestling and discus and javelin throwing, so that the embryos formed in them would have a strong start in strong bodies and develop better, and they would undergo their pregnancies with vigor and would cope well and easily with childbirth. He got rid of

(continued)

daintiness and sheltered upbringing and effeminacy of all kinds, by accustoming the girls no less than the young men to walking naked in processions and dancing and singing at certain festivals, when young men were present and watching. The nudity of the girls had nothing disgraceful in it for modesty was present and immorality absent, but rather it made them accustomed to simplicity and enthusiastic as to physical fitness, and gave the female sex a taste of noble spirit, in as much as they too had a share in valor and ambition.

 In what ways were the lifestyles of Athenian and Spartan women the same? In what ways were they different? How did the Athenian and Spartan views of the world shape their conceptions of gender and gender roles, and why were those conceptions different?

Sources: From *Ancient Greece: Social and Historical Documents from Archaic Times to the Death of Socrates*, edited by Matthew Dillon and Lynda Garland. London: Routledge, 1994, pp. 393–95. Copyright © 1994 Matthew and Lynda Garland. From *Aristotle, A Treatise on Government*, trans. William Ellis (J. M. Dent & Sons Ltd.: London, 1912), p. 1270a. From *Ideal Commonwealths: Plutarch's Lycurgus*, ed. Henry Morley, 5th ed. (George Rutledge and Sons, Limited, London, 1890).

The Rise of Macedonia and the Conquests of Alexander

 FOCUS QUESTION: How was Alexander the Great able to amass his empire, and what was his legacy?

While the Greek city-states were continuing to fight each other, to their north a new and ultimately powerful kingdom was emerging in its own right. Its people, the Macedonians, were mostly rural folk, organized in tribes, not city-states, and were viewed as barbarians by their southern neighbors, the Greeks. Not until the end of the fifth century B.C.E. did Macedonia emerge as an important kingdom. But when Philip II (359–336 B.C.E.) came to the throne, he built an efficient army and turned Macedonia into the strongest power of the Greek world—one that was soon drawn into the conflicts among the Greeks.

The Athenians at last took notice of the new contender. Fear of Philip led them to ally with a number of other Greek states and confront the Macedonians at the Battle of Chaeronea (ker-uh-NEE-uh), near Thebes, in 338 B.C.E. The Macedonian army crushed the Greeks, and Philip was now free to consolidate his control over the Greek peninsula. The Greek states were joined together in an alliance that we call the Corinthian League because they met at Corinth. All members took an oath of loyalty: "I swear by Zeus, Earth, Sun, Poseidon, Athena, Ares, and all the gods and goddesses. I will abide by the peace, and I will not break the agreements with Philip the Macedonian, nor will I take up arms with hostile intent against any one of those who abide by the oaths either by land or by sea."[12] Philip insisted that the Greek states end their bitter rivalries and cooperate with him in a war against Persia. Before Philip could undertake his invasion of Asia, however, he was assassinated, leaving the task to his son Alexander.

Alexander the Great

Alexander was only twenty when he became king of Macedonia. He had in many ways been prepared to rule by his father, who had taken Alexander along on military campaigns and had given

him control of the cavalry at the important battle of Chaeronea. After his father's assassination, Alexander moved quickly to assert his authority, securing the Macedonian frontiers and smothering a rebellion in Greece. He then turned to his father's dream, the invasion of the Persian Empire.

Alexander the Great. This marble head of Alexander the Great was made in the second or first century B.C.E. The long hair and tilt of his head reflect the description of Alexander in the literary sources of the time. Alexander claimed to be descended from Heracles, a Greek hero worshiped as a god, and when he proclaimed himself pharaoh of Egypt, he gained recognition as a living deity. It is reported that one statue, now lost, showed Alexander gazing at Zeus. At the base of the statue were the words "I place the earth under my sway; you, O Zeus, keep Olympus."

ALEXANDER'S CONQUESTS There is no doubt that Alexander was taking a chance in attacking the Persian Empire, which was still a strong state. In the spring of 334 B.C.E., Alexander entered Asia Minor with an army of 37,000 men. About half were Macedonians, the rest Greeks and other allies. The cavalry, which would play an important role as a strike force, numbered about 5,000.

Alexander's first confrontation with the Persians, at a battle at the Granicus River in 334 B.C.E., almost cost him his life but resulted in a major victory. By the following spring, the entire western half of Asia Minor was in Alexander's hands (see Map 4.2). Meanwhile, the Persian king, Darius III, mobilized his forces to stop Alexander's army. Although the Persian troops outnumbered Alexander's, the Battle of Issus (ISS-uss) was fought on a narrow field that canceled the advantage of superior numbers and resulted in another Macedonian success. After his victory at Issus in 333 B.C.E., Alexander turned south, and by the winter of 332, Syria, Palestine, and Egypt were under his domination. He took the traditional title of pharaoh of Egypt and founded the first of a series of cities named after him (Alexandria) as the Greek administrative capital of Egypt. It became (and remains today) one of the most important cities in Egypt and in the Mediterranean world.

In 331 B.C.E., Alexander renewed his offensive, moved into the territory of the ancient Mesopotamian kingdoms, and fought a decisive battle with the Persians at Gaugamela (gaw-guh-MEE-luh), northwest of Babylon. After his victory, Alexander entered Babylon and then proceeded to the Persian capitals at Susa and Persepolis, where he acquired the Persian treasuries and took possession of vast quantities of gold and silver. By 330, Alexander was again on the march, pursuing Darius. After Darius was killed by one of his own men, Alexander took the title and office of Great King of the Persians.

But Alexander was not content to rest with the spoils of the Persian Empire. Over the next three years, he moved east and northeast, as far as modern Pakistan. By the summer of 327 B.C.E., he had entered India, which at that time was divided into a number of warring states. In 326 B.C.E., Alexander and his armies arrived in the plains of northwestern India. At the Battle of the Hydaspes River, Alexander won a brutally fought battle (see the box "Alexander Meets an Indian King" on p. 116). When Alexander made clear his determination to march east to conquer more of India, his soldiers, weary of campaigning year after year, mutinied and refused to go on. Reluctantly, Alexander turned back, leading his men across the arid lands of southern Persia. Conditions in the desert were appalling; the

MAP 4.2 The Conquests of Alexander the Great. In just twelve years, Alexander the Great conquered vast territories. Dominating lands from west of the Nile to east of the Indus, he brought the Persian Empire, Egypt, and much of the Middle East under his control.

Q *Approximately how far did Alexander and his troops travel during those twelve years?*

Alexander Meets an Indian King

POLITICS & GOVERNMENT

IN HIS CAMPAIGNS IN INDIA, Alexander fought a number of difficult battles. At the Battle of the Hydaspes River, he faced a strong opponent in the Indian king Porus. After defeating Porus, Alexander treated him with respect, according to Arrian, Alexander's ancient biographer.

Arrian, *The Campaigns of Alexander*

Throughout the action Porus had proved himself a man indeed, not only as a commander but as a soldier of the truest courage. When he saw his cavalry cut to pieces, most of his infantry dead, and his elephants killed or roaming riderless and bewildered about the field, his behavior was very different from that of the Persian King Darius: unlike Darius, he did not lead the scramble to save his own skin, but so long as a single unit of his men held together, fought bravely on. It was only when he was himself wounded that he turned the elephant on which he rode and began to withdraw…. Alexander, anxious to save the life of this great soldier, sent … [to him] an Indian named Meroes, a man he had been told had long been Porus's friend. Porus listened to Meroes's message, stopped his elephant, and dismounted; he was much distressed by thirst, so when he had revived himself by drinking, he told Meroes to conduct him with all speed to Alexander.

Alexander, informed of his approach, rode out to meet him…. When they met, he reined in his horse, and looked at his adversary with admiration: he was a magnificent figure of a man, over seven feet high and of great personal beauty; his bearing had lost none of its pride; his air was of one brave man meeting another, of a king in the presence of a king, with whom he had fought honorably for his kingdom.

Alexander was the first to speak. "What," he said, "do you wish that I should do with you?" "Treat me as a king ought," Porus is said to have replied. "For my part," said Alexander, pleased by his answer, "your request shall be granted. But is there not something you would wish for yourself? Ask it." "Everything," said Porus, "is contained in this one request."

The dignity of these words gave Alexander even more pleasure, and he restored to Porus his sovereignty over his subjects, adding to his realm other territory of even greater extent. Thus, he did indeed use a brave man as a king ought, and from that time forward found him in every way a loyal friend.

What do we learn from Arrian's account about Alexander's military skills and Indian methods of fighting?

Source: From *The Campaigns of Alexander* by Arrian, translated by Aubrey de Selincourt. Viking Press, 1976.

---

blazing sun and lack of water led to thousands of deaths before Alexander and his remaining troops reached Babylon. Alexander planned still more campaigns, but in June 323 B.C.E., weakened from wounds, fever, and probably excessive alcohol consumption, he died at the age of thirty-two (see the Film & History feature "*Alexander* (2004)" on p. 117).

THE LEGACY: WAS ALEXANDER GREAT? Alexander is one of the most puzzling significant figures in history. Historians relying on the same sources draw vastly different pictures of him. For some, his military ability, extensive conquests, and creation of a new empire alone justify calling him Alexander the Great. Other historians also praise Alexander's love of Greek culture and his intellectual brilliance, especially in matters of warfare. In the lands that he conquered, Alexander attempted to fuse the Macedonians, Greeks, and Persians into a new ruling class. Did he do this because he was an idealistic visionary who believed in a concept of universal humanity, as some suggest? Or was he merely trying to bolster his power and create an autocratic monarchy?

Those historians who see Alexander as aspiring to autocratic monarchy present a very different portrait of him as a ruthless Machiavellian. One has titled his biography *Alexander the Great Failure*. These critics ask whether a man who slaughtered indigenous peoples, who risked the lives of his soldiers for his own selfish reasons, whose fierce temper led him to kill his friends, and whose neglect of administrative duties weakened his kingdom can really be called great.

But how did Alexander view himself? We know that he sought to imitate Achilles, the warrior-hero of Homer's *Iliad*. Alexander kept a copy of the *Iliad*—and a dagger—under his pillow. He also claimed to be descended from Heracles, the Greek hero who came to be worshiped as a god.

CHRONOLOGY	The Rise of Macedonia and the Conquests of Alexander
Reign of Philip II	359–336 B.C.E.
Battle of Chaeronea; Philip II conquers Greece	338 B.C.E.
Reign of Alexander the Great	336–323 B.C.E.
Alexander invades Asia; Battle of Granicus River	334 B.C.E.
Battle of Issus	333 B.C.E.
Battle of Gaugamela	331 B.C.E.
Fall of Persepolis, the Persian capital	330 B.C.E.
Alexander enters India	327 B.C.E.
Battle of Hydaspes River	326 B.C.E.
Death of Alexander	323 B.C.E.

Alexander (2004)

Alexander is a product of director Oliver Stone's lifelong fascination with Alexander, the king of Macedonia who conquered the Persian Empire in the fourth century B.C.E. and launched the Hellenistic era. Stone's epic film cost $150 million, which resulted in an elaborate and in places visually beautiful film. Narrated by the aging Ptolemy (Anthony Hopkins), Alexander's Macedonian general who took control of Egypt after his death, the film tells the story of Alexander (Colin Farrell) through an intermix of battle scenes, scenes showing the progress of Alexander and his army through the Middle East and India, and flashbacks to his early years. Stone portrays Alexander's relationship with his mother, Olympias (Angelina Jolie), as instrumental in his early development while also focusing on his rocky relationship with his father, King Philip II (Val Kilmer). The movie elaborates on the major battle at Gaugamela in 331 B.C.E., where the Persian leader Darius is forced to flee, and then follows Alexander as he conquers the rest of the Persian Empire and continues east into India. After his troops begin to mutiny, Alexander returns to Babylon, where he dies on June 10, 323 B.C.E.

The enormous amount of money spent on the film enabled Stone to achieve a stunning visual spectacle, but as history, the film leaves much to be desired. The character of Alexander is never developed in depth. He is shown at times as a weak character who is plagued by doubts over his decisions and often seems obsessed with his desire for glory. Alexander is also portrayed as an idealistic leader who believed that the people he conquered wanted change, that he was "freeing the people of the world," and that Asia and Europe would grow together into a single entity. But was Alexander an idealistic dreamer, as Stone apparently believes, or was he a military leader who, following the dictum that "fortune favors the bold," ran roughshod over the wishes of his soldiers in order to follow his dream and was responsible for mass slaughter in the process? The latter is a perspective that Stone glosses over, but Ptolemy probably expresses the more realistic notion that "none of us believed in his dream." The movie also does not elaborate on Alexander's wish to be a god. Certainly, Alexander aspired to divine honors; at one point he sent instructions to the Greek cities to "vote him a god." Stone's portrayal of Alexander is perhaps most realistic in presenting his drinking binges and his bisexuality, which was common in the Greco-Roman world. The movie shows not only his marriage to Roxane (Rosario Dawson), daughter of a Bactrian noble, but also his love for his lifelong companion, Hephaestion (Jared Leto), and his sexual relationship with the Persian male slave Bagoas (Francisco Bosch).

The film contains a number of inaccurate historical details. Alexander's first encounters with the Persian royal princesses and Bagoas did not occur when he entered Babylon for the first time. Alexander did not kill Cleitas in India, and he was not wounded in India at the Battle of the Hydaspes River but at the siege of Malli. Specialists in Persian history have also argued that the Persian military forces were much more disciplined than they are depicted in the film.

The Kobal Collection at Art Resource, NY

Alexander (Colin Farrell) reviews his troops before the Battle of Gaugamela.

Regardless of his ideals, motives, or views about himself, one fact stands out: Alexander ushered in a completely new age, the Hellenistic era. The word *Hellenistic* is derived from a Greek word meaning "to imitate Greeks." It is an appropriate way, then, to describe an age that saw the extension of the Greek language and ideas to the non-Greek world of the Middle East. Alexander's destruction of the Persian monarchy created opportunities for Greek engineers, intellectuals, merchants, soldiers, and administrators.

Those who followed Alexander and his successors participated in a new political unity based on the principle of monarchy. His successors used force to establish military monarchies that dominated the Hellenistic world after his death. Autocratic power became a regular feature of those Hellenistic monarchies and was part of Alexander's political legacy to the Hellenistic world. His vision of empire no doubt inspired the Romans, who were, of course, Alexander's real heirs.

But Alexander also left a cultural legacy. As a result of his conquests, Greek language, art, architecture, and literature spread throughout the Middle East. The urban centers of the Hellenistic Age, many founded by Alexander and his successors, became springboards for the diffusion of Greek culture. While the Greeks spread their culture in the east, they were also inevitably influenced by eastern ways. Thus, Alexander's legacy included one of the basic characteristics of the Hellenistic world: the clash and fusion of different cultures.

The World of the Hellenistic Kingdoms

 FOCUS QUESTION: How did the political, economic, and social institutions of the Hellenistic world differ from those of Classical Greece?

The united empire that Alexander created by his conquests disintegrated after his death. All too soon, Macedonian military leaders were engaged in a struggle for power, and by 301 B.C.E., all hope of unity was dead.

Hellenistic Monarchies

Eventually, four Hellenistic kingdoms emerged as the successors to Alexander (see Map 4.3). In Macedonia, the struggle for power led to the extermination of Alexander the Great's dynasty. Not until 276 B.C.E. did Antigonus Gonatus (an-TIG-oh-nuss guh-NAH-tuss), the grandson of one of Alexander's generals, succeed in establishing the Antigonid (an-TIG-uh-nid) dynasty as rulers of Macedonia and Greece. Another Hellenistic kingdom emerged in Egypt, where a Macedonian general named Ptolemy (TAHL-uh-mee) established himself as king in 305 B.C.E., initiating the Ptolemaic (tahl-uh-MAY-ik) dynasty of pharaohs. A third Hellenistic kingdom came into being in 230 B.C.E. when Attalus I declared himself king of Pergamum (PURR-guh-mum) in Asia Minor and established the Attalid (AT-uh-lid) dynasty.

THE SELEUCID KINGDOM AND INDIA By far the largest of the Hellenistic kingdoms was founded by the general Seleucus (suh-LOO-kuss), who established the Seleucid dynasty of Syria, which controlled much of the old Persian Empire from Turkey in the west to India in the east. The Seleucids, however, found it increasingly difficult to maintain control of the eastern territories. In fact, the Indian ruler Chandragupta

■ Antigonid kingdom	■ Pergamene kingdom
■ Ptolemaic kingdom	■ Seleucid kingdom
■ Aetolian League	■ Achaean League
	■ Mauryan Empire

MAP 4.3 The World of the Hellenistic Kingdoms. Alexander died unexpectedly at the age of thirty-two and did not designate a successor. After his death, his generals struggled for power, eventually establishing four monarchies that spread Hellenistic culture and fostered trade and economic development.

 Which kingdom encompassed most of the old Persian Empire?

Maurya (chun-druh-GOOP-tuh MOWR-yuh) created a new Indian state, the Mauryan Empire, in 324 B.C.E. (see Chapter 2) and drove out the Seleucid forces. His grandson Ashoka (uh-SHOH-kuh) extended the empire to include most of India. A pious Buddhist, Ashoka sought to convert the remaining Greek communities in northwestern India to his religion.

The Seleucid rulers maintained relations with the Mauryan Empire. Trade was fostered, especially in such luxuries as spices and jewels. Seleucus also sent Greek and Macedonian ambassadors to the Mauryan court. Best known of these was Megasthenes (muh-GAS-thuh-neez), whose report on the people of India remained one of the West's best sources of information until the Middle Ages.

Political Institutions

The Hellenistic monarchies created a semblance of stability for several centuries, even though Hellenistic kings refused to accept the status quo and periodically engaged in wars to alter it. At the same time, an underlying strain always existed between the new Greco-Macedonian ruling class and the native populations. Together these factors created a certain degree of tension that was never truly ended until the Roman state to the west stepped in and imposed a new order.

Although Alexander the Great had apparently planned to fuse Greeks and easterners—he used Persians as administrators, encouraged his soldiers to marry easterners, and did so himself—Hellenistic monarchs who succeeded him relied primarily on Greeks and Macedonians to form the new ruling class. Even those easterners who did advance to important administrative posts had learned Greek (all government business was transacted in Greek) and had become Hellenized in a cultural sense. The Greek ruling class was determined to maintain its privileged position.

Hellenistic Cities

Cities played an especially important role in the Hellenistic kingdoms. Throughout his conquests, Alexander had founded new cities and military settlements, and Hellenistic kings did likewise. The new population centers varied considerably in size and importance. Military settlements were meant to maintain order and might consist of only a few hundred men strongly dependent on the king. But there were also new independent cities with thousands of inhabitants. Alexandria in Egypt was the largest city in the Mediterranean region by the first century B.C.E. Seleucus was especially active in founding new cities, according to one ancient writer:

> The other kings have exulted in destroying existing cities; he, on the other hand, arranged to build cities which did not yet exist. He established so many … that they were enough to carry the names of towns in Macedonia as well as the names of those in his family…. One can go to Phoenicia to see his cities; one can go to Syria and see even more.[13]

Hellenistic rulers encouraged a massive spread of Greek colonists to the Middle East because of their intrinsic value to the new monarchies. Greeks (and Macedonians) provided not only recruits for the army but also a pool of civilian administrators and workers who contributed to economic development. Even architects, engineers, dramatists, and actors were in demand in the new Greek cities. Many Greeks and Macedonians were quick to see the advantages of moving to the new urban centers and gladly sought their fortunes in the Middle East. The Greek cities of the Hellenistic era were the chief agents in the spread of Greek culture in the Middle East—as far, in fact, as modern Afghanistan and India.

The Greeks' belief in their own cultural superiority provided an easy rationalization for their political dominance of the eastern cities (see the box "Relations Between Greeks and Non-Greeks" on p. 120). But Greek control of the new cities was also necessary because the kings frequently used the cities as instruments of government, enabling them to rule considerable territory without an extensive bureaucracy. At the same time, for security reasons, the Greeks needed the support of the kings. After all, the Hellenistic cities were islands of Greek culture in a sea of non-Greeks.

The Importance of Trade

Agriculture was still of primary importance to both the native populations and the new Greek cities of the Hellenistic world. The Greek cities continued their old agrarian patterns. A well-defined citizen body owned land and worked it with the assistance of slaves. But these farms were isolated units in a vast area of land ultimately owned by the king or assigned to large estate owners and worked by native peasants dwelling in villages.

Commerce expanded considerably in the Hellenistic era. Indeed, trading contacts linked much of the Hellenistic world. The decline in the number of political barriers encouraged more commercial traffic. Although Hellenistic monarchs still fought wars, the conquests of Alexander and the policies of his successors made possible greater trade between east and west. Two major trade routes connected the east with the Mediterranean. The major route proceeded by sea from India to the Persian Gulf and then up the Tigris River to Seleucia on the Tigris. Overland routes from Seleucia then led to Antioch and Ephesus. A southern route also began by sea from India but went around Arabia and up the Red Sea to Petra and later Berenice. Caravan routes then led overland to Coptos on the Nile, thence to Alexandria and the Mediterranean.

An incredible variety of products were traded: gold and silver from Spain; salt from Asia Minor; timber from Macedonia; ebony, gems, ivory, and spices from India; frankincense (used on altars) from Arabia; slaves from Thrace, Syria, and Asia Minor; fine wines from Syria and western Asia Minor; olive oil from Athens; and numerous exquisite foodstuffs, such as the famous prunes of Damascus. The greatest trade, however, was in the basic staple of life—grain.

Social Life: New Opportunities for Women

The development of the kingdom as the focus of political life in the Hellenistic era resulted in fewer restrictions on the role

Relations Between Greeks and Non-Greeks

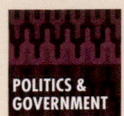

POLITICS & GOVERNMENT

THE RELATIONSHIP BETWEEN THE GREEK CONQUERORS and the native peoples of the Near East was often a difficult one. Although a number of native people learned Greek to advance their economic and political careers, they were often not treated as equals by the dominant Greek minority. The following documents reveal two facets of the problem. The first one is by a native complaining about his treatment by the Greeks. The second document reveals the dangers Greeks sometimes experienced from local peoples.

Letter to Zenon

To Zenon, greeting. You do well if you are healthy. I too am well. You know that you left me in Syria with Krotos and I did everything that was ordered with respect to the camels and was blameless towards you. When you sent a order to give me pay, he gave nothing of what you ordered. When I asked repeatedly that he give me what you ordered and Krotos gave me nothing, but kept telling me to remove myself…. So I wrote to you that you might know that Krotos was the cause of it. When you sent me again to Philadelphia to Jason, although I do everything that is ordered, for nine months now he gives me nothing of what you ordered me to have, neither oil nor grain,…. And I am toiling away both summer and winter. And he orders me to accept sour wine for my ration. Well, they have treated me with scorn because I am a "barbarian." I beg you therefore, if it seems good to

you, to give them orders that I am to obtain what is owing and that in future they pay me in full, in order that I may not perish of hunger because I do not know how to speak Greek.

Letter to Dionysios

To Dionysios from Ptolemaios…. Being outrageously wronged and often put in danger of my life by the below-listed cleaners from the sanctuary, I am seeking refuge with you thinking that I shall thus particularly receive justice. For in the 21st year, they came to the sanctuary, in which I have been for the aforesaid years, some of them holding stones in their hands, others sticks, and tried to force their way in, so that with this opportunity they might plunder the temple and kill me because I am a Greek, attacking me in concerted fashion. And when I made it to the door of the temple before them and shut it with a great crash, and ordered them to go away quietly, they did not depart; but they struck Diphilos, one of the servants, who showed his indignation at the way they were behaving in the sanctuary, robbing him outrageously and attacking him violently and beating him, so that their illegal violence was made obvious to everybody.

What do these documents reveal about the problems that arise in the relationship between conquerors and the conquered?

Source: From Roger S. Bagnall and Peter Derow, editors, *The Hellenistic Period* (Oxford: Blackwell Publishing, 2004), pp. 230–231, 232.

---

of women. In many cities, for example, women of all classes had a new freedom of movement. However, the most notable gains, especially for upper-class women, came in the economic realm. Documents show increasing numbers of women involved in managing slaves, selling property, and making loans. Even then, legal contracts made by women had to include their official male guardians. Only in Sparta were women free to control their own economic affairs. Many Spartan women were noticeably wealthy; females owned 40 percent of Spartan land.

Spartan women, however, were an exception, especially on the Greek mainland. Women in Athens, for example, still remained highly restricted and supervised. Although a few philosophers welcomed female participation in men's affairs, many philosophers rejected equality between men and women and asserted that the traditional roles of wives and mothers were most satisfying for women. And although they were now less restricted, peasant women experienced no real benefit from this freedom because they were still subject to a lifetime of hard work. The large group of women who were condemned to the practice of prostitution faced an even harsher reality.

But the opinions of philosophers did not prevent upper-class women from making gains in areas other than the economic sphere. New possibilities for females arose when women in some areas of the Hellenistic world were allowed to pursue education in the traditional fields of literature, music, and even athletics. Education, then, provided new opportunities for women: female poets appeared in the third century B.C.E., and there are instances of women involved in both scholarly and artistic activities.

The creation of the Hellenistic monarchies, which represented a considerable departure from the world of the city-state, also gave new scope to the role played by the monarchs' wives, the Hellenistic queens. In Macedonia, a pattern of alliances between mothers and sons provided openings for women to take an active role in politics, especially in political intrigue. In Egypt, opportunities for royal women were even greater because the Ptolemaic rulers reverted to an Egyptian custom of kings marrying their own sisters. Of the first eight Ptolemaic rulers, four wed their sisters. Ptolemy II and his sister-wife Arsinoë (ahr-SIN-oh-ee) II were both worshiped as gods in their lifetimes. Arsinoë played an energetic role in government and was involved in the expansion of the Egyptian navy. She was also the first Egyptian queen whose portrait appeared on coins with that of her husband.

Culture in the Hellenistic World

Although the Hellenistic kingdoms encompassed vast territories and many diverse peoples, the diffusion of Greek culture throughout the Hellenistic world provided a sense of unity. The Hellenistic era was a period of considerable accomplishment in many areas—literature, art, science, and philosophy. Although these achievements occurred throughout the Hellenistic world, certain centers, especially the great cities of Alexandria and Pergamum, stood out. In both cities, cultural developments were encouraged by the rulers themselves. Rich Hellenistic monarchs had considerable resources with which to patronize culture.

NEW DIRECTIONS IN LITERATURE AND ART The Hellenistic Age produced an enormous quantity of literature, most of which has not survived. Hellenistic monarchs, who held literary talent in high esteem, subsidized writers on a grand scale. The Ptolemaic rulers of Egypt were particularly lavish. The combination of their largesse and a famous library with more than 500,000 scrolls drew a host of scholars and authors to Alexandria, including a circle of poets. Theocritus (thee-AHK-ruh-tuss) (c. 315–250 B.C.E.), originally a native of the island of Sicily, wrote "little poems" known as *idylls* dealing with erotic subjects, lovers' complaints, and pastoral themes expressing love of nature and appreciation of nature's beauties.

In the Hellenistic era, Athens remained the theatrical center of the Greek world. Tragedy had fallen by the wayside, but a new style of comedy came to the fore. New Comedy completely rejected political themes and sought only to entertain and amuse. The Athenian playwright Menander (muh-NAN-dur) (c. 342–291 B.C.E.) was perhaps the best representative of New Comedy. Plots were simple: typically, a hero falls in love with a not-really-so-bad prostitute, who turns out eventually to be the long-lost daughter of a rich neighbor. The hero marries her, and they live happily ever after.

In addition to being patrons of literary talent, the Hellenistic monarchs were eager to spend their money to beautify and adorn the cities within their states. The founding of new cities and the rebuilding of old ones provided numerous opportunities for Greek architects and sculptors. The buildings of the Greek homeland—gymnasia, baths, theaters, and, of course, temples—lined the streets of these cities.

Both Hellenistic monarchs and rich citizens patronized sculptors. Thousands of statues, many paid for by the people honored, were erected in towns and cities all over the Hellenistic world. Sculptors traveled throughout this world, attracted by the material rewards offered by wealthy patrons. As a result, Hellenistic sculpture was characterized by a considerable degree of uniformity. Hellenistic artistic styles even affected artists in India (see the Comparative Illustration "Hellenistic Sculpture and a Greek-Style Buddha" on p. 122). While maintaining the technical skill of the Classical period,

Hellenistic sculptors moved away from the idealism of fifth-century classicism to a more emotional and realistic art, seen in numerous statues of old women, drunkards, and little children at play.

A GOLDEN AGE OF SCIENCE The Hellenistic era witnessed a more conscious separation of science from philosophy. In Classical Greece, what we would call the physical and life sciences had been divisions of philosophical inquiry. Nevertheless, by the time of Aristotle, the Greeks had already established an important principle of scientific investigation: empirical research, or systematic observation as the basis for generalization. In the Hellenistic Age, the sciences tended to be studied in their own right.

One of the traditional areas of Greek science was astronomy, and two Alexandrian scholars continued this exploration. Aristarchus (ar-iss-TAR-kus) of Samos (c. 310–230 B.C.E.) developed a *heliocentric* view of the universe, contending that the sun and the fixed stars remain stationary while the earth rotates around the sun in a circular orbit. He also argued that the earth rotates around its own axis. This view was not widely accepted, and most scholars clung to the earlier *geocentric* view of the Greeks, which held that the earth was at the center of the universe. Another astronomer, Eratosthenes

Old Market Woman. Unlike the sculptors of the Classical Greek era, Hellenistic sculptors were no longer interested in capturing ideal beauty but moved toward a more emotional and realistic art. This statue of an old market woman is typical of this trend. She is seen carrying chickens and a basket of fruit. Haggard and mired in poverty, she struggles just to go on living.

COMPARATIVE ILLUSTRATION

Hellenistic Sculpture and a Greek-Style Buddha. Greek architects and sculptors were highly valued throughout the Hellenistic world. Shown on the left is a terra-cotta statuette of a draped young woman, made as a tomb offering near Thebes, probably around 300 B.C.E.

The incursion of Alexander into western India resulted in some Greek cultural influences there, especially during the Hellenistic era. During the first century B.C.E., Indian sculptors in Gandhara, which today is part of Pakistan, began to make statues of the Buddha in a style that combined Indian and Hellenistic artistic traditions, as in the stone sculpture of the Buddha on the right. Note the wavy hair topped by a bun tied with a ribbon, also a feature of earlier statues of Greek deities. This Buddha is also seen wearing a Greek-style toga. Left image: Gianni Dagli Orti/The Art Archive at Art Resource, NY; right image: Borromeo/Art Resource, NY

Q *How do you explain the influence of Hellenistic styles in India? What can you conclude from this example about the influence of conquerors on conquered people?*

(er-uh-TAHSS-thuh-neez) (c. 275–194 B.C.E.), determined that the earth was round and calculated its circumference at 24,675 miles—within 200 miles of the actual figure.

A third Alexandrian scholar was Euclid (YOO-klid), who lived around 300 B.C.E. He established a school in Alexandria but is primarily known for his work titled *Elements*. This was a systematic organization of the fundamental elements of geometry as they had already been worked out; it became the standard textbook of plane geometry and was used up to modern times.

By far the most famous scientist of the period was Archimedes (ahr-kuh-MEE-deez) (287–212 B.C.E.) of Syracuse. Archimedes was especially important for his work on the geometry of spheres and cylinders and for establishing the value of the mathematical constant pi. Archimedes was also a practical inventor. He may have devised the so-called Archimedean screw, used to pump water out of mines and to lift irrigation water. During the Roman siege of Syracuse, he constructed a number of devices to thwart the attackers. According to Plutarch's account, the Romans became so frightened "that if they did but see a little rope or a piece of wood from the wall, instantly crying out, that there it was again, Archimedes was about to let fly some engine at them, they turned their backs and fled."[14] Archimedes's accomplishments inspired a wealth of semilegendary stories. Supposedly, he discovered specific gravity by observing the water he displaced in his bath and became so excited by his realization that he jumped out of the water and ran home naked, shouting, "Eureka!" ("I have found it!"). He is said to have emphasized the importance of levers by proclaiming to the king of Syracuse, "Give me a lever and a place to stand, and I will move the earth." The king was so impressed that he encouraged Archimedes to lower his sights and build defensive weapons instead.

PHILOSOPHY: NEW SCHOOLS OF THOUGHT While Alexandria and Pergamum became the renowned cultural centers of the Hellenistic world, Athens remained the prime center for philosophy. After Alexander the Great, the home of Socrates, Plato, and Aristotle continued to attract the most illustrious philosophers from the Greek world, who chose to establish their schools there. New schools of philosophical thought reinforced Athens's reputation as a philosophical center.

Epicurus (ep-i-KYOOR-uss) (341–270 B.C.E.), the founder of **Epicureanism** (ep-i-kyoo-REE-uh-ni-zum), established a school in Athens near the end of the fourth century B.C.E. Epicurus believed that human beings were free to follow self-interest as a basic motivating force. Happiness was the goal of life, and the means to achieve it was the pursuit of pleasure, the only true good. But the pursuit of pleasure was not meant in a physical, hedonistic sense (as our word *epicurean* has come to mean). Pleasure was not satisfying one's desire in an active, gluttonous fashion but rather freedom from emotional turmoil, freedom from worry—the freedom that came from a mind at rest. To achieve this kind of pleasure, one had to free oneself from public affairs and politics. But this was not a renunciation of all social life, for to Epicurus, a life could be complete only when it was based on friendship. His own life in Athens was an embodiment of his teachings. Epicurus and his friends created their own private community where they could pursue their ideal of true happiness.

Another school of thought was **Stoicism** (STOH-i-siz-um), which became the most popular philosophy of the Hellenistic world and later flourished in the Roman Empire as well. It was the product of a teacher named Zeno (ZEE-noh) (335–263 B.C.E.), who came to Athens and began to teach in a public colonnade known as the Painted Portico (the *Stoa Poikile*—hence the name *Stoicism*). Like Epicureanism, Stoicism was concerned with how individuals find happiness. But Stoics took a radically different approach to the problem. To them, happiness, the supreme good, could be found only by living in harmony with the divine will, by which people gained inner peace. Life's problems could not disturb these people, and they could bear whatever life offered (hence our word *stoic*). Unlike Epicureans, Stoics did not believe in the need to separate oneself from the world and politics. Public service was regarded as noble, and the real Stoic was a good citizen and could even be a good government official.

Both Epicureanism and Stoicism focused primarily on human happiness, and their popularity would suggest a fundamental change in the Greek lifestyle. In the Classical Greek world, the happiness of individuals and the meaning of life were closely associated with the life of the *polis*. One found fulfillment in the community. In the Hellenistic kingdoms, the sense that one could find satisfaction and fulfillment through life in the *polis* had weakened. People sought new philosophies that offered personal happiness, and in the cosmopolitan world of the Hellenistic states, with their mixture of peoples, a new openness to thoughts of universality could also emerge. For some people, Stoicism embodied this larger sense of community. The appeal of new philosophies in the Hellenistic era can also be explained by the apparent decline in certain aspects of traditional religion.

RELIGION IN THE HELLENISTIC WORLD When the Greeks spread throughout the Hellenistic kingdoms, they took their gods with them. But over a period of time, there was a noticeable decline in the vitality of the traditional Greek religion, which left Greeks receptive to the numerous religious cults of the eastern world. The eastern religions that appealed most to Greeks, however, were the **mystery religions**. What was the source of their attraction?

Mystery cults, with their secret initiations and promises of individual salvation, were not new to the Greek world. But the Greeks of the Hellenistic era were also strongly influenced by eastern mystery cults, such as those of Egypt, which offered a distinct advantage over the Greek mystery religions. The latter had usually been connected to specific locations (such as Eleusis), which meant that a would-be initiate had to undertake a pilgrimage in order to participate in the rites. In contrast, the eastern mystery religions were readily available since temples to their gods and goddesses were located throughout the Greek cities of the east. All of the mystery religions were based on the same fundamental premises. Individuals could pursue a path to salvation and achieve eternal life by being initiated into a union with a savior god or goddess who had died and risen again.

The Egyptian cult of Isis (Y-sis) was one of the most popular mystery religions. Isis was the goddess of women, marriage, and children; as one of her hymns states, "I am she whom women call goddess. I ordained that women should be loved by men: I brought wife and husband together, and invented the marriage contract. I ordained that women should bear children."[15] Isis was also portrayed as the giver of civilization, who had brought laws and letters to all humankind. The cult of Isis offered a precious commodity to its initiates— the promise of eternal life. In many ways, the cult of Isis and the other mystery religions of the Hellenistic era helped pave the way for Christianity.

CHAPTER SUMMARY

Unlike the great centralized empires of the Persians and the Chinese, ancient Greece consisted of a large number of small, independent city-states, of which the most famous were Sparta, a militaristic *polis* ruled by an oligarchy, and Athens, which became known for its democratic institutions despite the fact that many slaves and women had no political rights. Despite the small size of their city-states, these ancient Greeks created a civilization that was the fountainhead of Western culture. Socrates, Plato, and Aristotle established the foundations of Western philosophy. Western literary forms are largely derived from Greek poetry and drama. Greek notions of harmony, proportion, and beauty have remained the touchstones for all subsequent Western art. A rational method of inquiry, so important to modern science, was conceived in ancient Greece. Many political terms are Greek in origin, and so too are concepts of the rights and duties of citizenship, especially as they were conceived in Athens, the first great democracy the world had seen. Especially during the Classical era of the fifth century B.C.E., a century that began with the Persian Wars, the Greeks raised and debated the fundamental questions

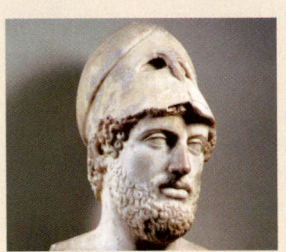

about the purpose of human existence, the structure of human society, and the nature of the universe that have concerned thinkers ever since.

But the growth of an Athenian Empire in that same century led to a mighty conflict with Sparta—the Great Peloponnesian War—that resulted in the weakening of the Greek city-states and opened the door to an invasion by Philip II of Macedonia that put an end to their freedom in 338 B.C.E. But Greek culture did not die, and a new age, known as the Hellenistic era, eventually came into being.

That era began with the conquest of the Persian Empire by Alexander the Great, the young successor to his father, Philip II. Though a great military leader, Alexander was not a good political administrator. He failed to establish any definite structure for the empire he had conquered, and four Hellenistic kingdoms eventually emerged as his successors. The society that emerged within those kingdoms is known as *Hellenistic*, meaning Greek-like or in imitation of the Greeks. The Greek language became the dominant one as Greek ideas became influential. Greek merchants, artists, philosophers, and soldiers found opportunities and rewards throughout the Near East, now a world of kingdoms rather than independent city-states.

The Hellenistic period was, in its own way, a vibrant one. New cities arose and flourished. New philosophical doctrines—such as Epicureanism and Stoicism—captured the minds of many. Significant achievements occurred in literature and science, and Greek culture spread throughout the Near East, making an impact wherever it was carried. Although the Hellenistic era achieved a degree of political stability, by the late third century B.C.E., signs of decline were beginning to multiply, and the growing power of Rome eventually endangered the Hellenistic world.

CHAPTER TIMELINE

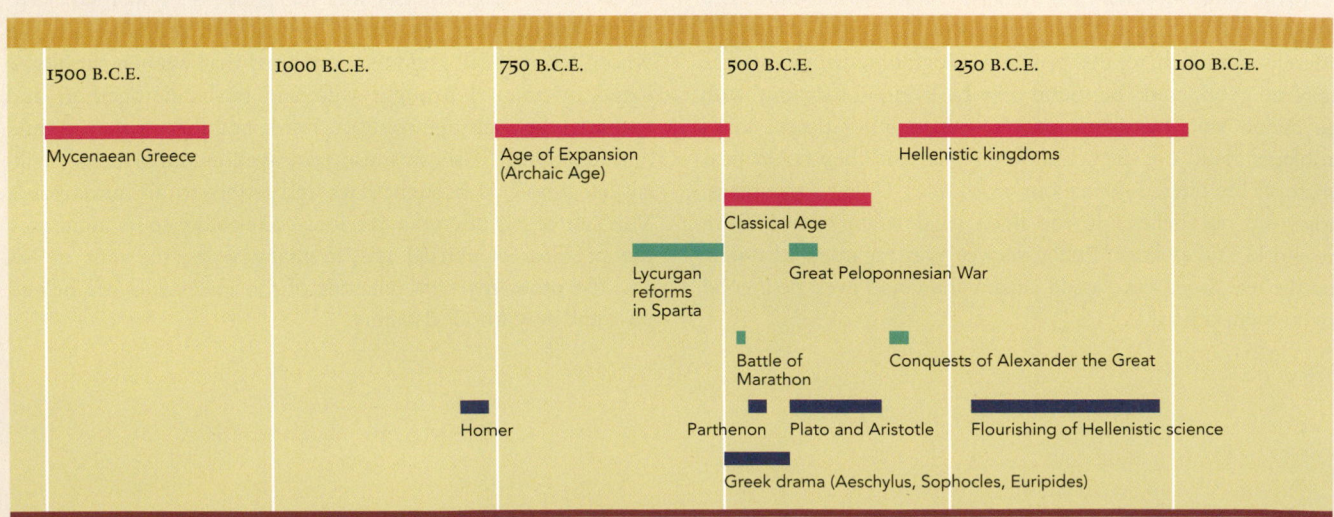

CHAPTER REVIEW

Upon Reflection

Q   What was the *polis*, and why do many historians consider it an important development in the political history of Western civilization?

Q   The Classical Age in Greece is known for its literary, artistic, and intellectual achievements. What basic characteristics of Greek culture are reflected in the major achievements of the Greeks in the writing of history, drama, the arts, and philosophy? What universal human concerns did these same achievements reflect?

Q   What were the main achievements of the Hellenistic kingdoms, and why did they fail to bring any lasting order to the lands of the Near East?

Key Terms

polis (p. 98)
hoplites (p. 98)
phalanx (p. 98)
tyrants (p. 99)
oligarchies (p. 99)
tyranny (p. 100)
helots (p. 100)
Sophists (p. 109)
rhetoric (p. 109)
Socratic method (p. 110)
Epicureanism (p. 122)
Stoicism (p. 123)
mystery religions (p. 123)

Suggested Reading

GENERAL WORKS   A good general introduction to Greek history is **S. B. Pomeroy et al.,** *Ancient Greece: A Political, Social, and Cultural History,* 2nd ed. (New York, 2008). On the Greek way of war, see **V. D. Hanson,** *The Wars of the Ancient Greeks,* rev. ed. (London, 2006).

EARLY GREEK HISTORY   Early Greek history is examined in **J. Hall,** *History of the Archaic Greek World, c. 1200–479 B.C.* (London, 2006). On Sparta, see **P. Cartledge,** *The Spartans* (New York, 2003). On early Athens, see **R. Osborne,** *Demos* (Oxford, 1985). The Persian Wars are examined in **P. Green,** *The Greco-Persian Wars* (Berkeley, Calif., 1996).

CLASSICAL GREECE   A general history of Classical Greece can be found in **P. J. Rhodes,** *A History of the Greek Classical World, 478–323 B.C.* (London, 2006). For a recent account of the Great Peloponnesian War, see **D. Kagan,** *The Peloponnesian War* (New York, 2003).

GREEK CULTURE AND SOCIETY   For a history of Greek art, see **M. Fullerton,** *Greek Art* (Cambridge, 2000). On Greek philosophy, a detailed study is available in **W. K. C. Guthrie,** *A History of Greek Philosophy,* 6 vols. (Cambridge, 1962–1981). On the family and women, see **S. Blundell,** *Women in Ancient Greece* (Cambridge, Mass., 1995).

THE HELLENISTIC ERA   For a general introduction, see **P. Green,** *The Hellenistic Age: A Short History* (New York, 2007). The best general survey of the Hellenistic era is **G. Shipley,** *The Greek World After Alexander, 323–30 B.C.* (New York, 2000). There are considerable differences of opinion on Alexander the Great. Good biographies include **P. Cartledge,** *Alexander the Great* (New York, 2004); **N. G. L. Hammond,** *The Genius of Alexander the Great* (Chapel Hill, N.C., 1997); and **G. M. Rogers,** *Alexander* (New York, 2004). On the various Hellenistic monarchies, see the collection of essays in **C. Habicht,** *Hellenistic Monarchies* (Ann Arbor, Mich., 2006).

HELLENISTIC CULTURE   For a general introduction to Hellenistic culture, see **J. Onians,** *Art and Thought in the Hellenistic Age* (London, 1979). On various facets of Hellenistic religion, see **A. Tripolitis,** *Religions of the Hellenistic-Roman Age* (Ann Arbor, Mich., 2001).

Chapter Notes

1. Xenophon, *Symposium,* trans. O. J. Todd (New York, 1946), III, 5.
2. Homer, *Odyssey,* pp. 290–291.
3. Quoted in T. R. Martin, *Ancient Greece* (New Haven, Conn., 1996), p. 62.
4. Quoted in V. D. Hanson, *The Wars of the Ancient Greeks,* rev. ed. (London, 2006), p. 14.
5. These words from Plutarch are quoted in E. Fantham et al., *Women in the Classical World* (New York, 1994), p. 64.
6. Aeschylus, *The Persians,* in *The Complete Greek Tragedies,* vol. 1, ed. David Grene and Richard Lattimore (Chicago, 1959), p. 229.
7. Thucydides, *The Peloponnesian War,* trans. R. Warner (New York, 1954), p. 24.
8. Sophocles, *Oedipus the King,* trans. D. Grene (Chicago, 1959), pp. 68–69.
9. Sophocles, *Antigone,* trans. D. Taylor (London, 1986), p. 146.
10. Plato, *The Republic,* trans. F. M. Cornford (New York, 1945), pp. 178–179.
11. Quotations from Aristotle are in S. Blundell, *Women in Ancient Greece* (Cambridge, Mass., 1995), pp. 106, 186.
12. Quoted in S. B. Pomeroy et al., *Ancient Greece: A Political, Social, and Cultural History* (Oxford, 1999), p. 390.
13. Quoted in G. Shipley, *The Greek World After Alexander, 323–30 B.C.* (London, 2000), p. 304.
14. Plutarch, *Life of Marcellus,* trans. J. Dryden (New York, n.d.), p. 378.
15. Quoted in W. W. Tarn, *Hellenistic Civilization* (London, 1930), p. 324.

 MindTap

MindTap is a fully online, highly personalized learning experience built upon Cengage Leaning content. MindTap combines student learning tools—readings, multimedia, activities, and assessments—into a singular Learning Path that guides students through their course.

The Roman World Empire

Horatius defending the bridge, as envisioned by Tommaso Laureti, a sixteenth-century Italian painter.

Musei Capitolini, Rome, Italy/Giraudon/The Bridgeman Art Library

CHAPTER OUTLINE AND FOCUS QUESTIONS

Early Rome and the Republic

Q What policies and institutions help explain the Romans' success in conquering Italy? How did Rome achieve its empire from 264 to 133 B.C.E., and what problems did Rome face as a result of its growing empire?

The Roman Empire at Its Height

Q What were the chief features of the Roman Empire at its height in the second century C.E.?

Crisis and the Late Empire

Q What reforms did Diocletian and Constantine institute, and to what extent were the reforms successful? What role did the Germanic tribes play in the Late Roman Empire?

Transformation of the Roman World: The Development of Christianity

Q What characteristics of Christianity enabled it to grow and ultimately to triumph as the official religion of the Roman Empire?

A Comparison of the Roman and Han Empires

Q In what ways were the Roman Empire and the Han Chinese Empire similar, and in what ways were they different?

CRITICAL THINKING

Q Compare and contrast the Roman Empire and Han Chinese Empire in regard to dynastic rule, bureaucratic government, trade, the military, and imperial expansion.

CONNECTIONS TO TODAY

Q What lessons does the fall of the Roman Republic offer to the United States today?

AT THE BEGINNING of the first millennium C.E., almost 50 percent of the world's population lived in one of two mighty world empires—the Han and Roman Empires. They were the largest political entities the world had yet seen. The Han Empire (see Chapter 3) extended from Central Asia to the Pacific Ocean; the Roman Empire encompassed the lands around the Mediterranean, parts of the Middle East, and western and central Europe. Although there were no diplomatic contacts between the two civilizations, the two great empires were linked commercially.

Roman history is the remarkable story of how a group of Latin-speaking people, who established a small community on a plain called Latium in central Italy, went on to conquer all of Italy and then the entire Mediterranean world. Why were the Romans able to do this? Scholars do not really know all the answers, but the Romans had their own explanation. Early Roman history is filled with legendary tales of the heroes who made

Rome great. One of the best known is the story of Horatius at the bridge.

Threatened by attack from the neighboring Etruscans, Roman farmers abandoned their fields and moved into the city, where they would be protected by the walls. One weak point in the Roman defenses, however, was a wooden bridge over the Tiber River. Horatius was on guard at the bridge when a sudden assault by the Etruscans caused many Roman troops to throw down their weapons and flee. Horatius urged them to make a stand at the bridge; when they hesitated, he told them to destroy the bridge behind him while he held the Etruscans back. Astonished at the sight of a single defender, the confused Etruscans threw their spears at Horatius, who caught them on his shield and barred the way. By the time the Etruscans were about to overwhelm the lone defender, the Roman soldiers had brought down the bridge. Horatius then dived fully armed into the water and swam safely to the other side through a hail of arrows. Rome had been saved by the courageous act of a Roman who knew his duty and was determined to carry it out. Courage, duty, determination—these qualities would serve the many Romans who believed that it was their divine mission to rule nations and peoples. As one orator proclaimed, "By heaven's will my Rome shall be capital of the world."[1]

Early Rome and the Republic

Q **FOCUS QUESTIONS:** What policies and institutions help explain the Romans' success in conquering Italy? How did Rome achieve its empire from 264 to 133 B.C.E., and what problems did Rome face as a result of its growing empire?

Italy is a peninsula extending about 750 miles from north to south (see Map 5.1). It is not very wide, however, averaging about 120 miles across. The Apennines form a ridge down the middle of Italy that divides west from east. Nevertheless, Italy has some fairly large fertile plains that are ideal for farming. Most important are the Po River valley in the north; the plain of Latium (LAY-shee-um), on which Rome was located; and Campania to the south of Latium. To the east of the Italian peninsula is the Adriatic Sea and to the west the Tyrrhenian Sea, bounded by the large islands of Corsica and Sardinia. Sicily lies just west of the "toe" of the boot-shaped Italian peninsula.

Geography had an impact on Roman history. Although the Apennines bisected Italy, they were less rugged than the mountain ranges of Greece and did not divide the peninsula into small isolated communities. Italy also possessed considerably more productive agricultural land than Greece, enabling it to support a large population. Rome's location was favorable from a geographic perspective. Located 18 miles inland on the Tiber River, Rome had access to the sea and yet was

MAP 5.1 Ancient Italy. Ancient Italy was home to several groups. Both the Etruscans in the north and the Greeks in the south had a major influence on the development of Rome.

 Once Rome conquered the Etruscans and other local groups, what aspects of the Italian peninsula helped make it defensible against outside enemies?

far enough inland to be safe from pirates. Built on seven hills, it was easily defended. Because the Tiber could be readily forded, Rome became a natural crossing point for north-south traffic in western Italy. All in all, Rome had a good central location in Italy from which to expand.

Moreover, the Italian peninsula juts into the Mediterranean, making Italy an important crossroads between the western and eastern ends of the sea. Once Rome had unified Italy, involvement in Mediterranean affairs was natural. And after the Romans had conquered their Mediterranean empire, governing it was made easier by Italy's central location.

Early Rome

According to Roman legend, Rome was founded by twin brothers, Romulus and Remus, in 753 B.C.E., and archaeologists have found that by around that time, a village of huts had been built on the tops of Rome's hills. The early Romans, basically a pastoral people, spoke Latin, which, like Greek, belongs to the Indo-European family of languages (see Table 1.2 in Chapter 1). The Roman historical tradition also maintained that early Rome (753–509 B.C.E.) had been under the control of seven kings and that two of the last three had been Etruscans (i-TRUSS-kunz), people who lived north of Rome in Etruria. Historians believe that the king list may have some historical accuracy. What is certain

Cincinnatus Saves Rome: A Roman Morality Tale

POLITICS & GOVERNMENT

THERE IS PERHAPS NO BETTER ACCOUNT of how the virtues of duty and simplicity enabled good Roman citizens to prevail during the travails of the fifth century B.C.E. than Livy's account of Cincinnatus (sin-suh-NAT-uss). He was chosen dictator, supposedly in 457 B.C.E., to defend Rome against the attacks of the Aequi (EYE-kwee or EE-kwy). The position of dictator was a temporary expedient used only in emergencies; the consuls would resign, and a leader with unlimited power would be appointed for a specified period (usually six months). In this account, Cincinnatus did his duty, defeated the Aequi, and returned to his simple farm in just fifteen days.

Livy, *The Early History of Rome*

The city was thrown into a state of turmoil, and the general alarm was as great as if Rome herself were surrounded. Nautius was sent for, but it was quickly decided that he was not the man to inspire full confidence; the situation evidently called for a dictator, and, with no dissentient voice, Lucius Quinctius Cincinnatus was named for the post.

Now I would solicit the particular attention of those numerous people who imagine that money is everything in this world, and that rank and ability are inseparable from wealth: let them observe that Cincinnatus, the one man in whom Rome reposed all her hope of survival, was at that moment working a little three-acre farm … west of the Tiber, just opposite the spot where the shipyards are today. A mission from the city found him at work on his land—digging a ditch, maybe, or plowing. Greetings were exchanged, and he was asked—with a prayer for divine blessing on himself and his country—to put on his toga and hear the Senate's instructions. This naturally surprised him, and, asking if all were well, he told his wife Racilia to run to their cottage and fetch his toga. The toga was brought, and wiping the grimy sweat from his hands and face he put it on; at once the envoys from the city saluted him, with congratulations, as Dictator, invited him to enter Rome, and informed him of the terrible danger of Municius's army. A state vessel was waiting for him on the river, and on the city bank he was welcomed by his three sons who had come to meet him, then by other kinsmen and friends, and finally by nearly the whole body of senators. Closely attended by all these people and preceded by his lictors he was then escorted to his residence through streets lined with great crowds of common folk who, be it said, were by no means so pleased to see the new Dictator, as they thought his power excessive and dreaded the way in which he was likely to use it.…

[Cincinnatus proceeds to raise an army, march out, and defeat the Aequi.]

In Rome the Senate was convened by Quintus Fabius the City Prefect, and a decree was passed inviting Cincinnatus to enter in triumph with his troops. The chariot he rode in was preceded by the enemy commanders and the military standards, and followed by his army loaded with its spoils.… Cincinnatus finally resigned after holding office for fifteen days, having originally accepted it for a period of six months.

 What values did Livy emphasize in his account of Cincinnatus? How important were those values to Rome's success? Why did Livy say he wrote his history?

Source: From *The Early History of Rome* by Livy, translated by Aubrey de Selincourt (Penguin Classics, 1960).

---

is that Rome did fall under the influence of the Etruscans for about a hundred years during the period of the kings and that by the beginning of the sixth century, under Etruscan influence, Rome began to emerge as a city. The Etruscans were responsible for an outstanding building program. They constructed the first roadbed of the chief street through Rome, the Sacred Way, before 575 B.C.E. and oversaw the development of temples, markets, shops, streets, and houses. By 509 B.C.E., supposedly when the monarchy was overthrown and a republican form of government was established, a new Rome had emerged, essentially a result of the fusion of Etruscan and native Roman elements.

The Roman Republic

The transition from monarchy to a republican government was not easy. Rome felt threatened by enemies from every direction and, in the process of meeting these threats, embarked on a military course that led to the conquest of the entire Italian peninsula.

THE ROMAN CONQUEST OF ITALY At the beginning of the Republic, Rome was surrounded by enemies, including the Latin communities on the plain of Latium. If we are to believe Livy (LIV-ee), one of the chief ancient sources for the history of the early Roman Republic, Rome was engaged in almost continuous warfare with these enemies for the next hundred years. In his account, Livy provided a detailed narrative of Roman efforts. Many of his stories were legendary in character; writing in the first century B.C.E., he used his stories to teach Romans the moral values and virtues that had made Rome great. These included tenacity, duty, courage, and especially discipline (see the box "Cincinnatus Saves Rome: A Roman Morality Tale" above).

By 338 B.C.E., Rome had crushed the Latin states in Latium. During the next fifty years, the Romans waged a successful struggle with hill peoples from central Italy and then came into direct contact with the Greek communities. The Greeks had arrived on the Italian peninsula in large numbers during the age of Greek colonization (750–550 B.C.E.; see Chapter 4). Initially, the Greeks settled in southern Italy and then crept around the coast and up the peninsula. They also occupied the eastern two-thirds of Sicily.

The Greeks had much influence on Rome. They cultivated olives and grapes, passed on their alphabet, and provided artistic and cultural models through their sculpture, architecture, and literature. By 267 B.C.E., the Romans had completed the conquest of southern Italy by defeating the Greek cities. After crushing the remaining Etruscan states to the north in 264 B.C.E., Rome had conquered most of Italy.

To rule Italy, the Romans devised the Roman Confederation in 338 B.C.E. Under this system, Rome allowed some peoples—especially the Latins—to have full Roman citizenship. Most of the remaining communities were made allies. They were free to run their own local affairs but were required to provide soldiers for Rome. Moreover, the Romans made it clear that loyal allies could improve their status and even have hope of becoming Roman citizens. The Romans had found a way to give conquered peoples a stake in Rome's success.

In the course of their expansion throughout Italy, the Romans had pursued consistent policies that help explain their success. The Romans were superb diplomats who excelled in making the correct diplomatic decisions. While firm and even cruel when necessary—rebellions were crushed without mercy—they were also shrewd in extending their citizenship and allowing autonomy in domestic affairs. In addition, the Romans were not only good soldiers but also persistent ones. The loss of an army or a fleet did not cause them to quit but spurred them on to raise new armies and build new fleets. Finally, the Romans had a practical sense of strategy. As they conquered, the Romans established colonies—fortified towns—at strategic locations throughout Italy. By building roads to these settlements and connecting them, the Romans created an impressive communications and military network that enabled them to rule effectively and efficiently (see the Comparative Illustration "Roman and Chinese Roads" on p. 130). By insisting on military service from the allies in the Roman Confederation, Rome essentially mobilized the entire military manpower of all Italy for its wars.

THE ROMAN STATE After the overthrow of the monarchy, Roman nobles, eager to maintain their position of power, established a republican form of government. The chief executive officers of the Roman Republic were the **consuls** (KAHN-sulls) and **praetors** (PREE-turs). Two consuls, chosen annually, administered the government and led the Roman army into battle. The office of praetor was created in 366 B.C.E. The praetor was in charge of civil law (law as it applied to Roman citizens), but he could also lead armies and govern Rome when the consuls were away from the city. As the Romans' territory expanded, they added another praetor to judge cases in which one or both people were noncitizens. The Roman state also had a number of administrative officials who handled specialized duties, such as the administration of financial affairs and supervision of the public games of Rome.

The Roman **senate** came to hold an especially important position in the Roman Republic. The senate or council of elders was a select group of about three hundred men who served for life. The senate could only advise the magistrates, but this advice was not taken lightly and by the third century B.C.E. had virtually the force of law.

The Roman Republic had a number of popular assemblies. By far the most important was the **centuriate assembly**. Organized by classes based on wealth, it was structured in such a way that the wealthiest citizens always had a majority. This assembly elected the chief magistrates and passed laws. Another assembly, the **council of the plebs**, came into being in 471 B.C.E.

The Roman Republic, then, witnessed the interplay of three major elements. Two consuls and later other elected officials served as magistrates and ran the state. An assembly of adult males (the centuriate assembly), controlled by the wealthiest citizens, elected these officials, while the senate, a small group of large landowners, advised them. Thus, the Roman state was an aristocratic republic controlled by a relatively small group of privileged people.

THE STRUGGLE OF THE ORDERS: SOCIAL DIVISIONS IN THE ROMAN REPUBLIC The most noticeable element in the social organization of early Rome was the division between two groups—the patricians and the plebeians. The **patricians** were descendants of the original senators appointed during the period of the kings and were great landowners, who constituted an aristocratic governing class. Only they could be consuls, magistrates, and senators. Through their patronage of large numbers of dependent clients, they controlled the centuriate assembly and many other facets of Roman life. The **plebeians** constituted the considerably larger group of non-patrician large landowners, less wealthy landholders, artisans, merchants, and small farmers. Although they, too, were citizens, they did not have the same rights as the patricians. Both patricians and plebeians could vote, but only the patricians could be elected to governmental offices. Both had the right to make legal contracts and marriages, but intermarriage between patricians and plebeians was forbidden. At the beginning of the fifth century B.C.E., the plebeians began to seek both political and social equality with the patricians.

The struggle between the patricians and plebeians dragged on for hundreds of years, but the plebeians ultimately were successful. The council of the plebs, a popular assembly for plebeians only, was created in 471 B.C.E., and new officials, known as **tribunes of the plebs**, were given the power to protect plebeians against arrest by patrician magistrates. A new law allowed marriages between patricians and plebeians, and in the fourth century B.C.E., plebeians were permitted to become consuls. Finally, in 287 B.C.E., the council of the plebs received the right to pass laws for all Romans.

COMPARATIVE ILLUSTRATION

Roman and Chinese Roads. The Romans constructed a remarkable system of roads. After laying a foundation of gravel, which allowed for drainage, the Roman builders topped it with flagstones, closely fitted together. Unlike other peoples who built similar kinds of roads, the Romans did not follow the contours of the land but made their roads as straight as possible to facilitate communications and transportation, especially for military purposes. Seen here (above) is a view of the Via Appia (Appian Way), built in 312 B.C.E. to make it easy for Roman armies to march from Rome to the newly conquered city of Capua, a distance of 152 miles (shown on the map). By the beginning of the fourth century C.E., the Roman Empire contained 372 major roads covering 50,000 miles.

Like the Roman Empire, the Han Empire relied on roads constructed with stone slabs for the movement of military forces (right). The First Emperor of Qin was responsible for the construction of 4,350 miles of roads, and by the end of the second century C.E., China had almost 22,000 miles of roads. Although roads in both the Roman and Chinese Empires were originally constructed for military purposes, they came to be used for communications and commercial traffic as well; however, unlike the Romans, the Han emperors used waterways for most of their transportation needs.

 What was the importance of roads to the Roman and Han Empires?

The struggle between the patricians and plebeians, then, had a significant impact on the development of the Roman state. Plebeians could now hold the highest offices of state, they could intermarry with the patricians, and they could pass laws binding on the entire Roman community. Theoretically, by 287 B.C.E., all Roman citizens were equal under the law, and all could strive for political office. But in reality, as a result of the right of intermarriage, a select number of patrician and plebeian families formed a new senatorial aristocracy that came to dominate the political offices. The Roman Republic had not become a democracy.

The Roman Conquest of the Mediterranean (264–133 B.C.E.)

After their conquest of the Italian peninsula, the Romans found themselves face to face with a formidable Mediterranean power—Carthage (KAHR-thij). Founded around 800 B.C.E. on the coast of North Africa by Phoenicians, Carthage had flourished and assembled an enormous empire in the western Mediterranean. By the third century B.C.E., the Carthaginian Empire included the coast of northern Africa, southern Spain, Sardinia, Corsica, and western Sicily. The presence

MAP 5.2 **Roman Conquests in the Mediterranean, 264–133** B.C.E. Beginning with the Punic Wars, Rome expanded its holdings, first in the western Mediterranean at the expense of Carthage and later in Greece and western Asia Minor.

Q *What aspects of Mediterranean geography, combined with the territorial holdings and aspirations of Rome and the Carthaginians, made the Punic Wars more likely?*

of Carthaginians in Sicily, so close to the Italian coast, made the Romans apprehensive. In 264 B.C.E., the two powers began a lengthy struggle for control of the western Mediterranean (see Map 5.2).

THE PUNIC WARS In the First Punic (PYOO-nik) War (the Latin word for Phoenician was *Punicus*), the Romans resolved to conquer Sicily. The Romans—a land power—realized that they could not win the war without a navy and promptly developed a substantial naval fleet. After a long struggle, a Roman fleet defeated the Carthaginian navy off Sicily, and the war quickly came to an end. In 241 B.C.E., Carthage gave up all rights to Sicily and had to pay an indemnity. Sicily became the first Roman province.

Carthage vowed revenge and extended its domains in Spain to compensate for the territory lost to Rome. When the Romans encouraged one of Carthage's Spanish allies to revolt against Carthage, Hannibal (HAN-uh-bul), the greatest of the Carthaginian generals, struck back, beginning the Second Punic War (218–201 B.C.E.).

This time, the Carthaginian strategy aimed at bringing the war home to the Romans and defeating them in their own backyard. Hannibal crossed the Alps with an army of 30,000

to 40,000 men and inflicted a series of defeats on the Romans. At Cannae (KAH-nee) in 216 B.C.E., the Romans lost an army of almost 40,000 men. The Romans seemed on the brink of disaster but refused to give up, raised yet another army, and began to reconquer some of the Italian cities that had gone over to Hannibal's side. More important, the Romans pursued a strategy aimed at undermining the Carthaginian Empire in Spain. By 206 B.C.E., the Romans had pushed the Carthaginians out of Spain.

The Romans then took the war directly to Carthage, forcing the Carthaginians to recall Hannibal from Italy. At the Battle of Zama (ZAH-muh) in 202 B.C.E., the Romans crushed Hannibal's forces, and the war was over. By the peace treaty signed in 201 B.C.E., Carthage lost Spain, which became another Roman province. Rome had become the dominant power in the western Mediterranean.

Fifty years later, the Romans fought their third and final struggle with Carthage. A technical breach in the peace treaty gave the Romans the opportunity to carry out a policy advocated by a number of Romans, especially the conservative politician Cato, who ended every speech he made to the senate with the words, "And I think Carthage must be destroyed." In 146 B.C.E., Carthage was destroyed. For ten days, Roman

The Destruction of Carthage

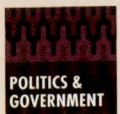

POLITICS & GOVERNMENT

THE ROMANS USED A TECHNICAL BREACH of Carthage's peace treaty with Rome to undertake a third and final war with Carthage (149–146 B.C.E.). Although Carthage posed no real threat to Rome's security, the Romans still remembered the traumatic experiences of the Second Punic War, when Hannibal had ravaged much of their homeland. The city was razed, the survivors sold into slavery, and the land turned into a province. In this passage, the historian Appian of Alexandria describes the final destruction of Carthage by the Romans under the command of Scipio Aemilianus (SEE-pee-oh ee-mil-YAY-nuss).

Appian, *Roman History*

Then came new scenes of horror. The fire spread and carried everything down, and the soldiers did not wait to destroy the buildings little by little, but pulled them all down together. So the crashing grew louder, and many fell with the stones into the midst dead. Others were seen still living, especially old men, women, and young children who had hidden in the inmost nooks of the houses, some of them wounded, some more or less burned, and uttering horrible cries. Still others, thrust out and falling from such a height with the stones, timbers, and fire, were torn asunder into all kinds of horrible shapes, crushed and mangled. Nor was this the end of their miseries, for the street cleaners, who were removing the rubbish with axes, mattocks, and boat hooks, and making the roads passable, tossed with these instruments the dead and the living together into holes in the ground, sweeping them along like sticks and stones or turning them over with their iron tools, and man was used for filling up a ditch. Some were thrown in head foremost, while their legs, sticking out of the ground, writhed a long time. Others fell with their feet downward and their heads above ground. Horses ran over them, crushing their faces and skulls, not purposely on the part of the riders, but in their headlong haste. Nor did the street cleaners either do these things on purpose; but the press of war, the glory of approaching victory, the rush of the soldiery, the confused noise of heralds and trumpeters all round, the tribunes and centurions changing guard and marching the cohorts hither and thither—all together made everybody frantic and heedless of the spectacle before their eyes.

Six days and nights were consumed in this kind of turmoil, the soldiers being changed so that they might not be worn out with toil, slaughter, want of sleep, and these horrid sights....

Scipio, beholding this city, which had flourished 700 years from its foundation and had ruled over so many lands, islands, and seas, as rich in arms and fleets, elephants, and money as the mightiest empires, but far surpassing them in hardihood and high spirit ... now come to its end in total destruction—Scipio, beholding this spectacle, is said to have shed tears and publicly lamented the fortune of the enemy. After meditating by himself a long time and reflecting on the inevitable fall of cities, nations, and empires, as well as of individuals, upon the fate of Troy, that once proud city, upon the fate of the Assyrian, the Median, and afterwards of the great Persian empire, and, most recently of all, of the splendid empire of Macedon, either voluntarily or otherwise the words of the poet [Homer, *Iliad*] escaped his lips:

> The day shall come in which our sacred Troy
> And Priam, and the people over whom
> Spear-bearing Priam rules, shall perish all.

Being asked by Polybius in familiar conversation (for Polybius had been his tutor) what he meant by using these words, Polybius says that he did not hesitate frankly to name his own country, for whose fate he feared when he considered the mutability of human affairs. And Polybius wrote this down just as he heard it.

What does the description of Rome's destruction of Carthage reveal about the nature of Roman imperialism? What features seem more rhetorical than realistic? Why?

Source: From *Appian: Roman History*, Vol. 1, trans. by Horace White, Cambridge, Mass.: Harvard University Press, 1912.

---

soldiers burned and pulled down all of the city's buildings (see the box "The Destruction of Carthage" above). The inhabitants—50,000 men, women, and children—were sold into slavery. The territory of Carthage became a Roman province called Africa.

THE EASTERN MEDITERRANEAN During its struggle with Carthage, Rome also had problems with the Hellenistic states in the eastern Mediterranean, and after the defeat of Carthage, Rome turned its attention there. In 148 B.C.E., Macedonia was made a Roman province, and two years later, Greece was placed under the control of the Roman governor of Macedonia. In 133 B.C.E., the king of Pergamum deeded his kingdom to Rome, giving Rome its first province in Asia. Rome was now master of the Mediterranean Sea.

THE NATURE OF ROMAN IMPERIALISM Rome's empire was built in three stages: the conquest of Italy, the conflict with Carthage and expansion into the western Mediterranean, and the involvement with and domination of the Hellenistic kingdoms in the eastern Mediterranean. The Romans did not possess a master plan for the creation of an empire. Much of

CHRONOLOGY	The Roman Conquest of Italy and the Mediterranean
Conquest of Latins completed	340 B.C.E.
Creation of the Roman Confederation	338 B.C.E.
First Punic War	264–241 B.C.E.
Second Punic War	218–201 B.C.E.
Battle of Cannae	216 B.C.E.
Roman seizure of Spain	206 B.C.E.
Battle of Zama	202 B.C.E.
Third Punic War	149–146 B.C.E.
Macedonia made a Roman province	148 B.C.E.
Destruction of Carthage	146 B.C.E.
Kingdom of Pergamum to Rome	133 B.C.E.

historians have suggested, that at some point a group of Roman aristocratic leaders emerged who favored expansion both for the glory it offered and for the economic benefits it provided. Certainly, by the second century B.C.E., aristocratic senators perceived new opportunities for lucrative foreign commands, enormous spoils of war, and an abundant supply of slave labor for their growing landed estates. By that same time, as the destruction of Carthage indicates, Roman imperialism had become more arrogant and brutal as well. Rome's foreign success also had enormous repercussions for the internal development of the Roman Republic.

THE ROMAN ARMY By the fourth century B.C.E., the Roman army consisted of four legions, each made up of four thousand to five thousand men; each legion had about three hundred cavalry and the rest infantry. In the early Republic, the army was recruited from citizens between the ages of eighteen and forty-six who had the resources to equip themselves for battle. Since most of them were farmers, they enrolled only for a year, campaigned during the summer months, and returned home in time for the fall harvest. Later, during the Punic Wars of the third century B.C.E., the period of service had to be extended, although this was resisted by farmers whose livelihoods could be severely harmed by a long

their expansion was opportunistic; once involved in a situation that threatened their security, the Romans did not hesitate to act. And the more they expanded, the more threats to their security appeared on the horizon, involving them in yet more conflicts. Indeed, the Romans liked to portray themselves as declaring war only for defensive reasons or to protect allies. That is only part of the story, however. It is likely, as some

Roman Legionaries. The Roman legionaries, famed for their courage and tenacity, made possible Roman domination of the Mediterranean Sea. At the time of the Punic Wars, a Roman legionary wore chain-mail armor and a plumed helmet and carried an oval shield, as in the bronze statue from the second or first century B.C.E. shown at the left. Heavy javelins and swords were their major weapons. This equipment remained standard until the time of Julius Caesar. The illustration on the right shows a Roman legion on the march from Trajan's column, erected in the second century C.E.

Left image: Gianni Dagli Orti/The Art Archive at Art Resource, NY; right image: Roger-Viollet/The Image Works absence. Nevertheless, after the disastrous Battle of Cannae in 216 B.C.E., the Romans were forced to recruit larger armies, and the number of legions rose to twenty-five. Major changes in recruitment would not come until the first century B.C.E. with the military reforms of Marius (see "Growing Inequality and Unrest" and "A New Role for the Roman Army" in the next section).

The Decline and Fall of the Roman Republic (133–31 B.C.E.)

By the middle of the second century B.C.E., Roman domination of the Mediterranean Sea was complete. Yet the process of creating an empire had weakened the internal stability of Rome, leading to a series of crises that plagued the Republic for the next hundred years.

GROWING INEQUALITY AND UNREST By the second century B.C.E., the senate had become the effective governing body of the Roman state. It comprised three hundred men, drawn primarily from the landed aristocracy; they remained senators for life and held the chief magistracies of the Republic. The senate directed the wars of the third and second centuries and took control of both foreign and domestic policy, including financial affairs.

Of course, these aristocrats formed only a tiny minority of the Roman people. The backbone of the Roman state and army had traditionally been the small farmers. But over time, many small farmers had found themselves unable to compete with large, wealthy landowners and had lost their lands. By taking over state-owned land and by buying out small peasant owners, these landed aristocrats had amassed large estates, called *latifundia* (lat-i-FOON-dee-uh), that used slave labor. Thus, the rise of the *latifundia* contributed to a decline in the number of small farmers. Since the latter group traditionally provided the foundation of the Roman army, the number of men available for military service declined. Moreover, many of these small farmers drifted to the cities, especially Rome, forming a large class of landless poor.

Some aristocrats tried to remedy this growing economic and social crisis. Two brothers, Tiberius and Gaius Gracchus (ty-BEER-ee-uss and GY-uss GRAK-us), came to believe that the underlying cause of Rome's problems was the decline of the small farmer. To help the landless poor, they bypassed the senate by having the council of the plebs pass land reform bills that called for the government to reclaim public land held by large landowners and to distribute it to landless Romans. Many senators, themselves large landowners whose estates included broad tracts of public land, were furious. A group of senators took the law into their own hands and murdered Tiberius in 133 B.C.E. Twelve years later, Gaius suffered the same fate. The attempts of the Gracchus brothers to bring reforms had opened the door to further violence. Changes in the Roman army soon brought even worse problems.

A NEW ROLE FOR THE ROMAN ARMY In the closing years of the second century B.C.E., a Roman general named Marius (MAR-ee-uss) began to recruit his armies in a new way. The Roman army had traditionally been a conscript army of small farmers who were landholders. Marius, who held the consulship from 104 to 100 B.C.E., recruited volunteers from both the urban and rural poor who possessed no property. These volunteers swore an oath of loyalty to the general, not the senate, and thus constituted a professional-type army that might no longer be subject to the state. Moreover, to recruit these men, the generals would promise them land, forcing the generals to play politics in order to get laws passed that would provide the land promised to their veterans. Marius had created a new system of military recruitment that placed much power in the hands of the individual generals.

Lucius Cornelius Sulla was the next general to take advantage of the new military system. The senate had given him command of a war in Asia Minor, but when the council of the plebs tried to transfer command of this war to Marius, a civil war broke out. Sulla won and seized Rome itself in 82 B.C.E., conducting a reign of terror to wipe out all opposition. Then Sulla restored power to the hands of the senate and eliminated most of the powers of the popular assemblies. Sulla hoped that he had created a firm foundation for the traditional Republic governed by a powerful senate, but his real legacy was quite different from what he had intended. His example of using an army to seize power would prove most attractive to ambitious men.

THE COLLAPSE OF THE REPUBLIC For the next fifty years, Roman history was characterized by two important features: the jostling for dominance of a number of powerful individuals and the civil wars generated by their conflicts. Three individuals came to hold enormous military and political power—Crassus (KRASS-uss), Pompey (PAHM-pee), and Julius Caesar. Crassus was known as the richest man in Rome and led a successful military command against a major slave rebellion. Pompey had returned from a successful military command in Spain in 71 B.C.E. and had been hailed as a military hero. Julius Caesar also had a military command in Spain. In 60 B.C.E., Caesar joined with Crassus and Pompey to form a coalition that historians call the First Triumvirate (*triumvirate* means "three-man rule").

The combined wealth and influence of these three men was enormous, enabling them to dominate the political scene and achieve their basic aims: Pompey received a command in Spain, Crassus a command in Syria, and Caesar a special military command in Gaul (modern France). When Crassus was killed in battle in 53 B.C.E., his death left two powerful men with armies in direct competition. Caesar had conquered all of Gaul and gained fame, wealth, and military experience as well as an army of seasoned veterans who were loyal to him. When leading senators endorsed Pompey as the less harmful to their cause and voted for Caesar to lay down his command and return as a private citizen to Rome, Caesar refused. He chose to keep his army and moved into Italy illegally by crossing the Rubicon, the river that formed the southern boundary of his province. Caesar marched on Rome and defeated the forces of Pompey and his allies, leaving Caesar in complete control of the Roman government.

The Assassination of Julius Caesar

POLITICS & GOVERNMENT

WHEN IT BECAME APPARENT THAT JULIUS CAESAR had no intention of restoring the Republic as they conceived it, about sixty senators, many of them his friends or pardoned enemies, formed a conspiracy to assassinate the dictator. Gaius Cassius and Marcus Brutus, who led the plot, naively imagined that this act would restore the traditional Republic. The conspirators set the Ides of March (March 15) of 44 B.C.E. as the date for the assassination. Caesar was in the midst of preparations for a campaign in the eastern part of the empire. Although warned about a plot against his life, he chose to disregard it. This account of Caesar's death is taken from his biography by the Greek writer Plutarch.

Plutarch, *Life of Caesar*

Fate, however, is to all appearance more unavoidable than unexpected. For many strange prodigies and apparitions are said to have been observed shortly before this event.... One finds it also related by many that a soothsayer bade him [Caesar] prepare for some great danger on the Ides of March. When this day was come, Caesar, as he went to the senate, met this soothsayer, and said to him mockingly, "The Ides of March are come," who answered him calmly, "Yes, they are come, but they are not past...."

All these things might happen by chance. But the place which was destined for the scene of this murder, in which the senate met that day, was the same in which Pompey's statue stood, and was one of the edifices which Pompey had raised and dedicated with his theater to the use of the public, plainly showing that there was something of a supernatural influence which guided the action and ordered it to that particular place. Cassius, just before the act, is said to have looked toward Pompey's statue, and silently implored his assistance.... When Caesar entered, the senate stood up to show their respect to him, and of Brutus's confederates, some came about his chair and stood behind it, others met him, pretending to add their petitions to those of Tillius Cimber, in behalf of his brother, who was in exile; and they followed him with their joint applications till he came to his seat. When he sat down, he refused to comply with their requests, and upon their urging him further began to reproach them severely for their demand, when Tillius, laying hold of his robe with both his hands, pulled it down from his neck, which was the signal for the assault. Casca gave him the first cut in the neck, which was not mortal nor dangerous, as coming from one who at the beginning of such a bold action was probably very much disturbed; Caesar immediately turned about, and laid his hand upon the dagger and kept hold of it. And both of them at the same time cried out, he that received the blow, in Latin, "Vile Casca, what does this mean?" and he that gave it, in Greek to his brother, "Brother, help!" Upon this first onset, those who were not privy to the design were astonished, and their horror and amazement at what they saw were so great that they dared not fly nor assist Caesar, nor so much as speak a word. But those who came prepared for the business enclosed him on every side, with their naked daggers in their hands. Which way soever he turned he met with blows, and saw their swords leveled at his face and eyes, and was encompassed like a wild beast in the toils on every side. For it had been agreed they should each of them make a thrust at him, and flesh themselves with his blood: for which reason Brutus also gave him one stab in the groin. Some say that he fought and resisted all the rest, shifting his body to avoid the blows, and calling out for help, but that when he saw Brutus's sword drawn, he covered his face with his robe and submitted, letting himself fall, whether it were by chance or that he was pushed in that direction by his murderers, at the foot of the pedestal on which Pompey's statue stood, and which was thus wetted with his blood. So that Pompey himself seemed to have presided, as it were, over the revenge done upon his adversary, who lay here at his feet, and breathed out his soul through his multitude of wounds, for they say he received three-and-twenty. And the conspirators themselves were many of them wounded by each other while they all leveled their blows at the same person.

 What does this account of Caesar's assassination reveal about the character of Julius Caesar? Based on this selection, what lessons did Classical historians intend their readers to take from their accounts of great and dramatic political events?

Source: From *The Lives of the Noble Grecians and Romans* by Plutarch, translated by John Dryden and edited by Arthur H. Clough.

Caesar was officially made **dictator** in 47 B.C.E. and three years later was named dictator for life. Realizing the need for reforms, he gave land to the poor and increased the senate to nine hundred members. By filling it with many of his supporters and increasing the membership, he effectively weakened the power of the senate. He also reformed the calendar by introducing the Egyptian solar year of 365 days (with later changes in 1582, it became the basis of our own calendar).

Caesar planned much more in the way of building projects and military adventures in the east, but in 44 B.C.E., a group of leading senators assassinated him (see the box "The Assassination of Julius Caesar" above).

Within a few years after Caesar's death, two men had divided the Roman world between them—Octavian (ahk-TAY-vee-un), Caesar's grandnephew and adopted son, took the western portion and Antony, Caesar's ally and assistant, the eastern half. But the empire of the Romans, large as it was, was still too small for two masters, and Octavian and Antony eventually came into conflict. Antony allied himself closely with the Egyptian queen, Cleopatra VII. At the Battle of Actium in Greece in 31 B.C.E., Octavian's forces smashed the army and navy of Antony and Cleopatra, who both fled to Egypt, where they committed suicide a year later. Octavian, at the age of thirty-two, stood supreme over the Roman world. The civil wars had ended. And so had the Republic.

The Roman Empire at Its Height

 FOCUS QUESTION: What were the chief features of the Roman Empire at its height in the second century C.E.?

With the victories of Octavian, peace finally settled on the Roman world. Although civil conflict still erupted occasionally, the new imperial state constructed by Octavian experienced remarkable stability for the next two hundred years. The Romans imposed their peace on the largest empire established in antiquity.

The Age of Augustus
(31 B.C.E.–14 C.E.)

In 27 B.C.E., Octavian proclaimed the "restoration of the Republic." He understood that only traditional republican forms would satisfy the senatorial aristocracy. At the same time, Octavian was aware that the Republic could not be fully restored. Although he gave some power to the senate, in fact, Octavian became the first Roman emperor. The senate awarded him the title of Augustus, "the revered one"—a fitting title, in view of his power, that had previously been reserved for gods. Augustus proved highly popular, but the chief source of his power was his continuing control of the army. The senate also gave Augustus the title of *imperator* (im-puh-RAH-tur), or commander in chief. *Imperator* is Latin for our word *emperor*.

Augustus maintained a standing army of twenty-eight legions, or about 150,000 men (a legion was a military unit of about 5,000 troops). Only Roman citizens could be legionaries, while subject peoples could serve as auxiliary forces, which numbered around 130,000 under Augustus. Augustus was also responsible for setting up a **praetorian guard** of roughly 9,000 men who had the important task of guarding the emperor. Eventually, the praetorian guard would play a weighty role in making and deposing emperors.

While claiming to have restored the Republic, Augustus inaugurated a new system for governing the provinces. Under the Republic, the senate had appointed the governors of the provinces. Now certain provinces were given to the emperor, who assigned deputies known as legates to govern them. The senate continued to name the governors of the remaining provinces, but the authority of Augustus enabled him to overrule the senatorial governors and establish a uniform imperial policy (see the box "The Achievements of Augustus" on p. 137).

Scala/Art Resource, NY

Augustus. Octavian, Caesar's adopted son, emerged victorious from the civil conflict that rocked the Republic after Caesar's assassination. The senate awarded him the title Augustus. This marble statue from Prima Porta, an idealized portrait, is based on Greek rather than Roman models. The statue was meant to be a propaganda piece, depicting a youthful general addressing his troops. At the bottom stands Cupid, the son of Venus, goddess of love, meant to be a reminder that the Julians, Caesar's family, claimed descent from Venus, thus emphasizing the ruler's divine background.

Augustus also stabilized the frontiers of the Roman Empire. He conquered the central and maritime Alps and then expanded Roman control of the Balkan peninsula up to the Danube River. His attempt to conquer Germany failed when three Roman legions, led by a general named Varus, were massacred in 9 C.E. by a coalition of German tribes. His defeats in Germany taught Augustus that Rome's power was not unlimited and also devastated him; for months, he would beat his head on a door, shouting, "Varus, give me back my legions!"

Augustus died in 14 C.E. after dominating the Roman world for forty-five years. He had created a new order while placating the old by restoring traditional values, a fitting combination for a leader whose favorite maxim was "make haste slowly." By the time of his death, his new order was so well established

The Achievements of Augustus

POLITICS & GOVERNMENT

THIS EXCERPT IS TAKEN FROM A TEXT WRITTEN BY AUGUSTUS and inscribed on a bronze tablet at Rome. Copies of the text in stone were displayed in many provincial capitals. Called "the most famous ancient inscription," the *Res Gestae* of Augustus summarizes his accomplishments in three major areas: his offices, his private expenditures on behalf of the state, and his exploits in war and peace. Though factual in approach, it is a highly subjective account.

Augustus, *Res Gestae*

Below is a copy of the accomplishments of the deified Augustus by which he brought the whole world under the empire of the Roman people, and of the moneys expended by him on the state and the Roman people, as inscribed on two bronze pillars set up in Rome.

1. At the age of nineteen, on my own initiative and at my own expense, I raised an army by means of which I liberated the Republic, which was oppressed by the tyranny of a faction [Mark Antony and his supporters]....

2. Those who assassinated my father [Julius Caesar, his adoptive father] I drove into exile, avenging their crime by due process of law; and afterwards when they waged war against the state, I conquered them twice on the battlefield.

3. I waged many wars throughout the whole world by land and by sea, both civil and foreign, and when victorious I spared all citizens who sought pardon....

5. The dictatorship offered to me ... by the people and the senate, both in my absence and in my presence, I refused to accept....

17. Four times I came to the assistance of the treasury with my own money, transferring to those in charge of the treasury 150,000,000 sesterces. And in the consulship of Marcus Lepidus and Lucius Arruntius I transferred out of my own patrimony 170,000,000 sesterces to the soldiers' bonus fund, which was established on my advice for the purpose of providing bonuses for soldiers who had completed twenty or more years of service....

22. I gave a gladiatorial show three times in my own name, and five times in the names of my sons or grandsons; at these shows about 10,000 fought....

25. I brought peace to the sea by suppressing the pirates. In that war I turned over to their masters for punishment nearly 30,000 slaves who had run away from their owners and taken up arms against the state....

26. I extended the frontiers of all the provinces of the Roman people on whose boundaries were peoples not subject to our empire....

27. I added Egypt to the empire of the Roman people....

35. When I held my thirteenth consulship, the senate, the equestrian order, and the entire Roman people gave me the title of "father of the country" and decreed that this title should be inscribed in the vestibule of my house, in the Julian senate house, and in the Augustan Forum.... At the time I wrote this document I was in my seventy-sixth year.

What were the achievements of Augustus? To what extent did these accomplishments create the "job" of being emperor? In what sense could this document be called a piece of propaganda?

Source: From *Roman Civilization*, Vol. I, by Naphtali Lewis and Meyer Renhold. Copyright © 1955 Columbia University Press. Reprinted by permission of the publisher.

---

that few agitated for an alternative. Indeed, as the Roman historian Tacitus (TASS-i-tuss) pointed out, "Practically no one had ever seen truly Republican government.... Political equality was a thing of the past; all eyes watched for imperial commands."[2] The Republic was now only a memory—and given its last century of warfare, an unpleasant one at that. The new order was here to stay.

The Early Empire (14–180)

There was no serious opposition to Augustus's choice of his stepson Tiberius (ty-BEER-ee-uss) as his successor. By his actions, Augustus established the Julio-Claudian dynasty; the next four successors of Augustus were related either to his own family or that of his wife, Livia.

Several major tendencies emerged during the reigns of the Julio-Claudians (14–68 C.E.). In general, more and more of the responsibilities that Augustus had given to the senate tended to be taken over by the emperors, who also instituted an imperial bureaucracy, staffed by talented freedmen, to run the government on a daily basis. As the Julio-Claudian successors of Augustus acted more openly as real rulers rather than "first citizens of the state," the opportunity for arbitrary and corrupt acts also increased. Nero (NEE-roh) (54–68), for example, freely eliminated people he wanted out of the way, including his own mother, whose murder he arranged. Without troops, the senators proved unable to oppose these excesses, but the Roman legions finally revolted. Abandoned by his guards, Nero chose to commit suicide by stabbing himself in the throat after uttering his final words, "What an artist the world is losing in me!"

THE FIVE GOOD EMPERORS (96–180) Many historians regard the *Pax Romana* (PAKS *or* PAHKS ro-MAH-nuh) (the "Roman peace") and the prosperity it engendered as the chief benefits of Roman rule during the first and second centuries C.E. These benefits were especially noticeable during the reigns of the five so-called **good emperors**. These rulers treated the ruling classes with respect, maintained peace in the empire, and supported generally beneficial domestic policies. Though absolute monarchs, they were known for their tolerance and diplomacy. By adopting capable men as their sons and successors, the first four of these emperors reduced the chances of succession problems.

Under the five good emperors, the powers of the emperor continued to expand at the expense of the senate. Increasingly, imperial officials appointed and directed by the emperor took over the running of the government. The good emperors also extended the scope of imperial administration to areas previously untouched by the imperial government. Trajan (TRAY-jun) (98–117) implemented an alimentary program that provided state funds to assist poor parents in raising and educating their children.

The good emperors were widely praised for their extensive building programs. Trajan and Hadrian (HAY-dree-un) (117–138) were especially active in constructing public works—aqueducts, bridges, roads, and harbor facilities—throughout the provinces and in Rome. Trajan built a new forum in Rome to provide a setting for his celebrated victory column. Hadrian's Pantheon, a temple of "all the gods," is one of the grandest ancient buildings surviving in Rome (see the illustrations for the Pantheon on p. 141).

FRONTIERS AND THE PROVINCES Although Trajan extended Roman rule into Dacia (modern Romania), Mesopotamia, and the Sinai peninsula (see Map 5.3), his successors recognized that the empire was overextended and returned to Augustus's policy of defensive imperialism. Hadrian withdrew Roman forces from much of Mesopotamia. Although he retained Dacia and Arabia, he went on the defensive in his frontier policy by reinforcing the fortifications along a line connecting the Rhine and Danube Rivers and building a defensive wall 80 miles long across northern Britain to keep the Scots out of Roman Britain. By the end of the second century, the Roman forces were established in permanent bases

© 2016 Cengage Learning

MAP 5.3 The Roman Empire from Augustus Through Trajan (14–117). Augustus and later emperors continued the expansion of the Roman Empire, adding more resources but also increasing the tasks of administration and keeping the peace. Compare this map with Map 5.2.

Q *Which of Trajan's acquisitions were relinquished during Hadrian's reign?*

behind the frontiers. But when one frontier was attacked, troops had to be drawn from other frontiers, leaving them vulnerable to attack.

At its height in the second century C.E., the Roman Empire was one of the greatest states the world had seen. It covered about 3.5 million square miles and had a population, like that of Han China, estimated at more than 50 million. While the emperors and the imperial administration provided a degree of unity, considerable leeway was given to local customs, and the privileges of Roman citizenship were extended to many people throughout the empire. In 212, the emperor Caracalla (kar-uh-KAL-uh) completed the process by giving Roman citizenship to every free inhabitant of the empire. Latin was the language of the western part of the empire, while Greek was used in the east. Roman culture spread to all parts of the empire and freely mixed with Greek culture, creating what has been called Greco-Roman civilization.

The administration and cultural life of the Roman Empire depended greatly on cities and towns. A provincial governor's staff was not large, so it was left to local city officials to act as Roman agents in carrying out many government functions, especially those related to taxes. Most towns and cities were not large by modern standards. The largest was Rome, but there were also some large cities in the east: Alexandria in Egypt numbered more than 300,000 inhabitants. In the west, cities were usually small, with only a few thousand inhabitants. Cities were important in the spread of Roman culture, law, and the Latin language, and they resembled one another with their temples, markets, amphitheaters, and other public buildings.

The process of Romanization in the provinces was reflected in significant changes in the governing classes of the empire. In the course of the first century, there was a noticeable decline in the number of senators from Italian families. By the end of the second century, Italian senators made up less than 50 percent of the total. Increasingly, the Roman senate was being recruited from wealthy provincial families. The provinces also provided many of the legionaries for the Roman army and, beginning with Trajan, supplied many of the emperors.

PROSPERITY IN THE EARLY EMPIRE: TRADE WITH CHINA AND INDIA The Early Empire was a period of considerable prosperity. Internal peace resulted in unprecedented levels of trade. Merchants from all over the empire came to the chief Italian ports of Puteoli on the Bay of Naples and Ostia at the mouth of the Tiber River. Long-distance trade beyond the Roman frontiers also developed during the Early Empire. Economic expansion in both the Roman and Chinese Empires helped foster the growth of this trade. Although both empires built roads chiefly for military purposes, the roads also came to facilitate trade. Moreover, by creating large empires, the Romans and Chinese not only established internal stability but also pacified bordering territories, thus reducing the threat that bandits posed to traders. As a result, merchants developed a network of trade routes that brought these two great empires into commercial contact.

Most important was the overland Silk Road, a regular caravan route between West and East (see Chapter 3). Silk, a filament recovered from the cocoons of silkworms, had been produced in China since the fourth millennium B.C.E. Eventually, knowledge of this special product reached the outside world, and Chinese silk exports began to rise. By the second century B.C.E., the first clothing made from silk reached the Mediterranean Sea, stimulating the contacts between China and the Roman Empire. The bulk of the trade went overland through Central Asia (thus earning this route its modern name, the Silk Road). By the first century C.E., large quantities of silk were being delivered to markets in Rome through the Silk Road trade. Silk became a craze among Roman elites, leading to a vast outflow of silver from Rome to China and causing the Roman scholar Pliny the Elder to remark that the Roman treasury was being depleted because wealthy Roman women were purchasing so much silk clothing.

The silk trade also stimulated a degree of mutual curiosity between the two great empires but not much mutual knowledge. The Roman geographer Strabo wrote of a strange land called "Seres" far to the east, while Chinese sources mentioned the empire of "Great Qin" at the far end of the Silk Road to the west. So far as is known, no personal or diplomatic contacts between the two civilizations ever took place. But two great empires at either extreme of the Eurasian supercontinent had for the first time been linked in a commercial relationship.

Trade in the Roman Empire.
Trade was an important ingredient in the prosperity of the Early Roman Empire. Although Roman roads were excellent, most goods traveled by boat throughout the Mediterranean and beyond. This third-century C.E. Roman mosaic from Sousse, Tunisia, shows workers unloading a cargo of iron ore from a ship.

After the takeover of Egypt in the first century C.E., Roman merchants also began an active trade with India, from where they received precious pearls as well as pepper and other spices used in the banquets of the wealthy. The Romans even established a trading post in southern India where their merchants built warehouses and docks.

PROSPERITY IN THE EARLY EMPIRE: INDUSTRY AND FARMING Increased trade helped stimulate manufacturing. The cities of the east still produced the items made in Hellenistic times. The first two centuries of the empire also witnessed the high point of industrial development in Italy. Some industries became concentrated in certain areas, such as bronze work in Capua and pottery in Arretium in Etruria. Other industries, such as brick making, were pursued in rural areas as by-products of large landed estates.

Despite the profits from trade and commerce, agriculture remained the chief pursuit of most people and the underlying basis of Roman prosperity. Although the large *latifundia* still dominated agriculture, especially in southern and central Italy, small peasant farms continued to flourish, particularly in Etruria and the Po Valley. Although large estates depended on slaves for the raising of sheep and cattle, the lands of some *latifundia* were also worked by free tenant farmers who paid rent in labor, produce, or sometimes cash.

Despite the prosperity of the Roman world, an enormous gulf existed between rich and poor. The development of towns and cities, so important to the creation of any civilization, is based largely on the agricultural surpluses of the countryside. In ancient times, the margin of surplus produced by each farmer was relatively small. Therefore, the upper classes and urban populations had to be supported by the labor of a large number of agricultural producers, who never found it easy to produce much more than they needed for themselves. In lean years, when there were no surpluses, the townspeople often took what they wanted, leaving little for the peasants.

Culture and Society in the Roman World

One of the notable characteristics of Roman culture and society is the impact of the Greeks. Greek ambassadors, merchants, and artists traveled to Rome and spread Greek thought and practices. After their conquest of the Hellenistic kingdoms, Roman generals shipped Greek manuscripts and artworks back to Rome. Multitudes of educated Greek slaves labored in Roman households. Rich Romans hired Greek tutors and sent their sons to Athens to study. As the Roman poet Horace (HOR-uss) said, "Captive Greece took captive her rude conqueror." Greek thought captivated Roman minds, and the Romans became willing transmitters of Greek culture.

ROMAN LITERATURE The high point of Latin literature was reached in the Age of Augustus, often called the golden age of Latin literature. The most distinguished poet of the Augustan Age was Virgil (VUR-jul) (70–19 B.C.E.). The son of a small landholder in northern Italy, he welcomed the rule of Augustus and wrote his greatest work in the emperor's honor. Virgil's masterpiece was the *Aeneid*, an epic poem clearly intended to rival the

work of Homer. The connection between Troy and Rome is made in the poem when Aeneas, a hero of Troy, survives the destruction of that city and eventually settles in Latium—establishing a link between Roman civilization and Greek history. Aeneas is portrayed as the ideal Roman—his virtues are duty, piety, and faithfulness. Virgil's overall purpose was to show that Aeneas had fulfilled his mission to establish the Romans in Italy and thereby start Rome on its divine mission to rule the world.

> Let others fashion from bronze more lifelike,
>   breathing images—
> For so they shall—and evoke living faces from marble;
> Others excel as orators, others track with their
>   instruments
> The planets circling in heaven and predict when
>   stars will appear.
> But, Romans, never forget that government is your
>   medium!
> Be this your art:—to practice men in the habit of peace,
> Generosity to the conquered, and firmness against
>   aggressors.[3]

As Virgil expressed it, ruling was Rome's gift.

ROMAN ART The Romans were also dependent on the Greeks for artistic inspiration. The Romans developed a taste for Greek statues, which they placed not only in public buildings but also in their private houses. The Romans' own portrait sculpture was characterized by an intense realism that included even unpleasant physical details. Wall paintings and frescoes in the homes of the rich realistically depicted landscapes, portraits, and scenes from mythological stories.

The Romans excelled in architecture, a highly practical art. Although they continued to adapt Greek styles and made use of colonnades and rectangular structures, the Romans were also innovative. They made considerable use of curvilinear forms: the arch, vault, and dome. The Romans were also the first people in antiquity to use concrete on a massive scale. By combining concrete and curvilinear forms, they were able to construct huge buildings—public baths, such as those of Caracalla, and amphitheaters capable of seating 50,000 spectators. These large buildings were made possible by Roman engineering skills. These same skills were put to use in constructing roads, aqueducts, and bridges: a network of 50,000 miles of roads linked all parts of the empire, and in Rome, almost a dozen aqueducts kept the population of one million supplied with water.

ROMAN LAW One of Rome's chief gifts to the Mediterranean world of its day and to later generations was its system of law. Rome's first code of laws was the Twelve Tables of 450 B.C.E., but that was designed for a simple farming society and proved inadequate for later needs. So, from the Twelve Tables, the Romans developed a system of civil law that applied to all Roman citizens. As Rome expanded, problems arose between citizens and noncitizens and also among noncitizen residents of the empire. Although some of the rules of civil law could be used in these cases, special rules were often needed. These rules gave rise to a body of law known as the

© PictureNet/Corbis

© David Buffington/Photodisc/Getty Images

The Pantheon. Shown here is the Pantheon, one of Rome's greatest buildings. Constructed of brick, six kinds of concrete, and marble, it is a stunning example of the Romans' engineering skills. The outside porch of the Pantheon contains eighteen Corinthian columns made of granite, but it is the inside of the temple that amazes onlookers. The interior is a large circular space topped by a huge dome. A hole in the center of the roof is the only source of light. The dome, built up layer by layer, was made of concrete, weighing 10 million pounds. The walls holding the dome are almost 20 feet thick.

law of nations, defined as the part of the law that applied to both Romans and foreigners. Under the influence of Stoicism, the Romans came to identify their law of nations with **natural law**, a set of universal laws based on reason. This enabled them to establish standards of justice that applied to all people.

These standards of justice included principles that we would immediately recognize. A person was regarded as innocent until proved otherwise. People accused of wrongdoing were allowed to defend themselves before a judge. A judge, in turn, was expected to weigh evidence carefully before arriving at a decision. These principles lived on long after the fall of the Roman Empire.

THE ROMAN FAMILY At the heart of the Roman social structure stood the family, headed by the *paterfamilias* (pay-tur-fuh-MEE-lee-uss)—the dominant male. The household also included the wife, sons with their wives and children, unmarried daughters, and slaves. Like the Greeks, Roman males believed that females needed male guardians. The *paterfamilias* exercised that authority; on his death, sons or nearest male relatives assumed the role of guardians.

Fathers arranged the marriages of daughters. In the Republic, women married "with legal control" passing from father to husband. By the mid-first century B.C.E., the dominant practice had changed to "without legal control," which meant that married daughters officially remained within the father's legal power. Since the fathers of most married women died sooner or later, not being in the "legal control" of a husband made possible independent property rights that forceful women could translate into considerable power within the household and outside it.

Like the Greeks, the Romans did not always raise all the children born into their families. Not only were deformed children abandoned to die of exposure, but infant mortality rates were high—as many as half of all infants did not survive into childhood. Nevertheless, upper-class families did take good care of their surviving children. The father was largely responsible for providing for the education of his children. Roman boys learned reading and writing, moral principles and family values, law, and physical training to prepare them to be soldiers. Girls learned at home what they needed to know to be good wives and mothers.

The end of childhood for Roman males came at the age of sixteen, when a young man exchanged his purple-edged toga for a plain white toga—the toga of manhood—and soon after began his career. For Roman girls, childhood ended at age fourteen, the common age of marriage. Although some Roman doctors warned that early pregnancies could be dangerous for young girls, early marriages persisted because women died at a

Childhood in the Roman World. This illustration, a scene from a third-century sarcophagus, shows an idealized version of an upper-class child's life: he is depicted being breast-fed by his mother, being held by his father, playing in a small chariot pulled by a goat, and reciting to his father.

relatively young age. A good example is Tullia, Cicero's beloved daughter. She was married at sixteen, widowed at twenty-two, remarried one year later, divorced at twenty-eight, remarried at twenty-nine, and divorced at thirty-three. She died at thirty-four, which was not unusually young for women in Roman society.

By the second century C.E., significant changes were occurring in the Roman family. The *paterfamilias* no longer had absolute authority over his children; he could no longer sell his children into slavery or have them put to death. Moreover, the husband's absolute authority over his wife had also disappeared, and by the late second century, women were no longer required to have guardians.

Upper-class Roman women in the Early Empire had considerable freedom and independence (see Opposing Viewpoints "Women in the Roman and Han Empires" on p. 143). They had acquired the right to own, inherit, and dispose of property. Upper-class women could attend races, the theater, and events in the amphitheater, although in the latter two places they were forced to sit in separate female sections. Women still could not participate in politics, but the Early Empire saw a number of important women who influenced politics through their husbands or sons, including Livia, the wife of Augustus, and Plotina, the wife of Trajan.

SLAVES AND THEIR MASTERS Although slavery was a common institution throughout the ancient world, no people possessed more slaves or relied so much on slave labor as the Romans eventually did. Slaves were used in many ways in Roman society. The rich owned the most and the best. In the late Roman Republic, it became a badge of prestige to be attended by many slaves. Greek slaves were in much demand as tutors, musicians, doctors, and artists. Roman businessmen would employ them as shop assistants or craftspeople. Slaves were also used as farm laborers; in fact, huge gangs of slaves worked the large landed estates under pitiful conditions. Many slaves of all nationalities were used as menial household workers, such as cooks, waiters, cleaners, and gardeners. Contractors used slave labor to build roads, aqueducts, and other public structures.

The treatment of Roman slaves varied. There are numerous instances of humane treatment by masters and even reports of slaves who protected their owners from danger out of gratitude and esteem. But slaves were also subject to severe punishments, torture, abuse, and hard labor that drove some to run away,

despite stringent laws against aiding a runaway slave. Some slaves revolted against their owners and even murdered them, causing some Romans to live in unspoken fear of their slaves (see the box "The Roman Fear of Slaves" on p. 144).

Near the end of the second century B.C.E., large-scale slave revolts occurred in Sicily, where enormous gangs of slaves were subjected to horrible working conditions on large landed estates. The most famous uprising on the Italian peninsula occurred in 73 B.C.E. Led by a gladiator named Spartacus (SPAR-tuh-kuss), the revolt broke out in southern Italy and involved 70,000 slaves. Spartacus managed to defeat several Roman armies before being trapped and killed in southern Italy in 71 B.C.E. Six thousand of his followers were crucified, the traditional form of execution for slaves.

IMPERIAL ROME At the center of the colossal Roman Empire was the ancient city of Rome. A true capital city, Rome had the largest population of any city in the empire, close to one million by the time of Augustus. Only Chang'an (CHENG-AHN), the imperial capital of the Han Empire in China, had a comparable population during this time.

An enormous gulf existed between rich and poor in the city of Rome. While the rich had comfortable villas, the poor lived in apartment blocks called *insulae*, which might be six stories high. Constructed of concrete, they were often poorly built and prone to collapse. The use of wooden beams in the floors and movable stoves, torches, candles, and lamps for heat and light created a constant danger of fire. Once started, fires were extremely difficult to put out. The famous conflagration of 64, which Nero was unjustly accused of starting, devastated a good part of the city. Besides the hazards of collapse and fire, living conditions were miserable. High rents forced entire families into one room. In the absence of plumbing and central heating, conditions were so uncomfortable that poorer Romans spent most of their time outdoors in the streets.

Though the center of a great empire, Rome was also a great parasite. Beginning with Augustus, the emperors accepted responsibility for providing food for the urban populace, with about 200,000 people receiving free grain. But even the free grain did not relieve the grim condition of the poor. Early in the second century C.E., a Roman doctor claimed that rickets was common among the city's children.

Women in the Roman and Han Empires

FAMILY & SOCIETY

THE TWO EXCERPTS BELOW ARE TAKEN FROM THE WORKS OF WRITERS IN TWO OF THE ANCIENT WORLD'S GREAT EMPIRES: one is a male philosopher living in the Roman Empire and the other is a female writer in Han China. Although they reflect different cultures, they have similar ideas about the role and education of women. Gaius Musonius Rufus was a philosopher who taught Stoicism in Rome in the first century C.E. His students wrote down some of his philosophical opinions. The excerpt here is taken from his thoughts on whether women should study philosophy. Ban Zhao was a well-educated woman from a prominent aristocratic family. She wrote *Admonitions for Women* as a guide for upper-class women in the proper performance of their wifely duties.

Gaius Musonius Rufus, "That Women Too Should Study Philosophy"

When he was asked whether women ought to study philosophy, he began to answer.... Women have received from the gods the same ability to reason that men have.... Likewise women have the same senses as men, sight, hearing, smell, and the rest.... Since that is so, why is it appropriate for men to seek out and examine how they might live well, that is, to practice philosophy, but not women? ...

Let us consider in detail the qualities that a woman who seeks to be good must possess, for it will be apparent that she could acquire each of these qualities from the practice of philosophy.

In the first place a woman must run her household and pick out what is beneficial for her home and take charge of the household slaves.... Next a woman must be chaste, and capable of keeping herself free from illegal love affairs, ... and not enjoy quarrels, not be extravagant or occupied with her appearance.... There are still other requirements: she must control anger, and not be overcome by grief, and be stronger than every kind of emotion....

[When asked if sons and daughters should be given the same education, he replied,] There are not different sets of virtues for men and women. First, men and women both need to be sensible.... Second, both need to live just lives.... Third, a wife ought to be chaste, and so should a husband....

Well, then, suppose someone says, "Do you think that men ought to learn spinning like women and that women ought to practice gymnastics like men?" No, that is not what I suggest. I say that because in the case of the human race, the males are naturally stronger, and the women weaker, appropriate work ought to be assigned to each, and the heavier task be given to the stronger, and the lighter to the weaker. For this reason, spinning is more appropriate work for women than for men, and household management. Gymnastics are more appropriate for men than for women, and outdoor work likewise.... Some tasks are more appropriate for one nature, others for the other. For that reason some jobs are called men's work, and others women's....

Without philosophy no man and no woman either can be well educated. I do not mean to say that women need to have clarity with or facility in argument, because they will use philosophy as women use it.... My point is that women ought to be good and noble in their characters, and that philosophy is no other than the training for that nobility.

Ban Zhao, *Admonitions for Women*

Let a woman modestly yield to others; let her respect others, let her put others first, herself last. Should she do something good, let her not mention it; should she do something bad, let her not deny it. Let her bear contempt; let her even endure when others speak or do evil to her....

Let a woman retire late to bed, but rise early to her duties; let her not dread tasks by day or night. Let her not refuse to perform domestic duties whether easy or difficult. That which must be done, let her finish completely, tidily and systematically....

Let a woman be composed in demeanor and upright in bearing in the service of her husband. Let her live in purity and quietness and keep watch over herself. Let her not love gossip and silly laughter. Let her cleanse, purify and arrange in order the wine and the food for the offerings to the ancestors....

Now examine the gentlemen of the present age. They only know that wives must be controlled and that the husband's authority must be maintained. They therefore teach their boys to read books and study histories.... Yet only to teach men and not to teach women—is this not ignoring the reciprocal relation between them? Book learning begins at the age of eight, and at the age of fifteen one goes off to school. Why, however, should this principle not apply to girls as well as boys....

In womanly behavior there are four things ... womanly virtue, womanly speech, womanly appearance, and womanly work.

To guard carefully her chastity, to control circumspectly her behavior, in every motion to exhibit modesty, ... : this may be called womanly virtue.

To choose her words with care, to avoid vulgar language, to speak at appropriate times, and not to be offensive to others may be called womanly speech.

To wash and scrub dirt and grime, to keep clothes and ornaments fresh and clean, to wash the head and bathe the body regularly, ... may be called womanly appearance.

With wholehearted devotion to sew and weave, not to love gossip and silly laughter, to prepare the wine and food for serving guests may be called womanly work.

Q *What are the views of Gaius Musonius Rufus and Ban Zhao on the responsibilities of a woman? In what ways do they agree? In what ways do they disagree? How do you explain the differences? From your point of view, what are the strengths and weaknesses in each argument?*

Sources: Lefkowitz, Mary R. and Maureen B. Fant, eds. *Women's Life in Greece and Rome: A Source Book in Translation*, 2nd ed. pp. 50–54 © 1992 M. B. Fant and M. R. Lefkowitz. Reprinted with permission of Johns Hopkins University Press and Bloomsbury Academic. From *Sources of Chinese Tradition*, 2nd edition, Vol. 1, by Wm. T. DeBary and Irene Bloom. Copyright © 1999 Columbia University Press. Reprinted with permission of the publisher.

The Roman Fear of Slaves

FAMILY & SOCIETY

THE LOWEST STRATUM OF THE ROMAN POPULATION consisted of slaves. They were used extensively in households, at the court, as artisans in industrial enterprises, as business managers, and in numerous other ways. Although some historians have argued that slaves were treated more humanely during the Early Empire, these selections by the Roman historian Tacitus and the Roman statesman Pliny indicate that slaves still rebelled against their masters because of mistreatment. Many masters continued to live in fear of their slaves, as witnessed by the saying "As many enemies as you have slaves."

Tacitus, *The Annals of Imperial Rome*

Soon afterwards the City Prefect, Lucius Pedanius Secundus, was murdered by one of his slaves [in 61 C.E.]. Either Pedanius had refused to free the murderer after agreeing to a price, or the slave, in a homosexual infatuation, found competition from his master intolerable. After the murder, ancient custom required that every slave residing under the same roof must be executed. But a crowd gathered, eager to save so many innocent lives; and rioting began. The senatehouse was besieged. Inside, there was feeling against excessive severity, but the majority opposed any change. Among the latter was Gaius Cassius Longinus, who when his turn came spoke as follows....

"An ex-consul has been deliberately murdered by a slave in his own home. None of his fellow-slaves prevented or betrayed the murderer, though the senatorial decree threatening the whole household with execution still stands. Exempt them from the penalty if you like. But then, if the City Prefect was not important enough to be immune; who will be? Who will have enough slaves to protect him if Pedanius's four hundred were too few? Who can rely on his household's help if even fear for their own lives does not make them shield us?"

[The sentence of death was carried out.]

Pliny the Younger to Acilius

A shocking affair, worthy of more publicity than a letter can bestow, has befallen Larcius Macedo, a man of praetorian rank, at the hands of his own slaves. He was known to be an over-bearing and cruel master, and one who forgot—or rather remembered too keenly—that his own father had been a slave. He was bathing at his villa near Formiae, when he was suddenly surrounded by his slaves. One seized him by the throat, another struck him on the forehead, and others smote him in the chest.... When they thought the breath had left his body they flung him on to the hot tiled floor to see if he was still alive. Whether he was insensible, or merely pretended to be so, he certainly did not move, and lying there at full length, he made them think that he was actually dead. At length they carried him out, as though he had been overcome by the heat, and handed him over to his more trusty servants, while his women ran shrieking and wailing to his side. Aroused by their cries and restored by the coolness of the room where he lay, he opened his eyes and moved his limbs, betraying thereby that he was still alive, as it was then safe to do so. His slaves took to flight; most of them have been captured, but some are still being hunted for. Thanks to the attentions he received, Macedo was kept alive for a few days and had the satisfaction of full vengeance before he died, for he exacted the same punishment while he still lived as is usually taken when the victim of a murder dies. You see the dangers, the affronts and insults we are exposed to, and no one can feel at all secure because he is an easy and mild-tempered master....

What do these texts reveal about the practice of slavery in the Roman Empire? What were Roman attitudes toward the events discussed in these documents?

Sources: From *The Annals of Imperial Rome* by Tacitus, translated by Michael Grant (Penguin Classics, 1956, Sixth revised edition 1989). From *Readings in Ancient History*, Hutton Webster (D.C. Health and Co.: Boston 1919), p. 245.

In addition to food, entertainment was also provided on a grand scale for the inhabitants of Rome. The poet Juvenal (JOO-vuh-nul) said of the Roman masses, "But nowadays, with no vote to sell, their motto is 'Couldn't care less.' Time was when their plebiscite elected generals, heads of state, commanders of legions: but now they've pulled in their horns, there's only two things that concern them: Bread and Circuses."[4] The emperor and other state officials provided public spectacles as part of the great festivals—most of them religious in origin—celebrated by the state. The festivals included three major types of entertainment. At the Circus Maximus, horse and chariot races attracted hundreds of thousands, while dramatic and other performances were held in theaters. But the most famous of all the public spectacles were the gladiatorial shows.

THE GLADIATORIAL SHOWS The gladiatorial shows were an integral part of Roman society. They took place in amphitheaters. Perhaps the most famous was the amphitheater known as the Colosseum, constructed in Rome to seat 50,000 spectators. In most cities and towns, amphitheaters were the biggest buildings, rivaled only by the circuses (arenas) for races and the public baths.

Gladiatorial games were held from dawn to dusk (see the Film & History feature "*Gladiator* (2000)" on p. 145). Contests to the death between trained fighters formed the central focus

Gladiator (2000)

The film *Gladiator*, directed by Ridley Scott, is a fictional story set in the Roman Empire near the end of the second century C.E. In the movie, Emperor Marcus Aurelius (Richard Harris) informs his son Commodus (Joaquin Phoenix) that he intends to turn over imperial power to his successful and respected general, Maximus (Russell Crowe), in the hope that this decent and honest man can restore the Roman senate and revive the Republic. Commodus reacts by killing his father, assuming the position of emperor, and ordering the deaths of Maximus, his wife, and son. Maximus escapes but returns too late to Spain to save his wife and child. He is captured and then sold into slavery to Proximo (Oliver Reed), who trains him to be a gladiator. Maximus is eventually sent to Rome, where he becomes a superhero in the gladiatorial games in the Roman Colosseum, all the while awaiting an opportunity to avenge the death of his wife and son by killing Commodus. Maximus becomes involved in a plot with Lucilla (Connie Nielsen), the emperor's sister, and Gracchus (Derek Jacobi), a Roman senator, to rejoin his army, march on Rome, and overthrow the emperor. When Commodus discovers the plot, he challenges the captured Maximus to a duel in the Colosseum but stabs him first to ensure his own success. Despite his injury, Maximus kills the emperor in combat.

Gladiator is a relatively exciting story, but how much of it is based on historical facts? With the exception of Marcus Aurelius, Commodus, and Lucilla, all of the characters are fictional. Marcus Aurelius was a kind emperor with a love of philosophy and died in 180, probably from plague, and certainly not by his son's hands, as depicted in the film. Commodus ruled from 180 to 192, although he was only eighteen when he became emperor, not in his late twenties as in the movie; and he had blond hair, not dark hair. Commodus was an unstable and cruel young man who was strongly attracted to gladiatorial contests. He was obsessed with performing in the arena, especially with slaughtering animals. He was not killed in the Colosseum, however, but strangled by his wrestling partner on the last day of 192.

Contrary to the movie, Marcus Aurelius had no intention of restoring the Republic; by 180, most Romans had become well accustomed to the empire. In fact, Marcus Aurelius had already made his son

Commodus a joint ruler in 177. Nor had Marcus Aurelius banned gladiatorial games, as the movie claims. And although Commodus's sister Lucilla did enter into a plot with some senators to assassinate her brother, the plot of 182 failed, and the conspirators, including Lucilla, were executed.

Although *Gladiator* shows little concern for historical facts, the movie did demonstrate that many people are still interested in ancient history. It became one of the highest earning films of 2000 and won numerous awards including Academy Awards for Best Picture and Best Actor for Russell Crowe. Moreover, the film helped to renew interest in Roman history—sales of biographies of historical Roman figures and of Marcus Aurelius's *Meditations* increased noticeably in the years after the movie was released.

Maximus (Russell Crowe) triumphs in the Roman Colosseum.

DreamWorks/Courtesy Everett Collection

of these games, but the games included other forms of entertainment as well. Criminals of all ages and both genders were sent into the arena without weapons to face certain death from wild animals who would tear them to pieces. Numerous types of animal contests were also held: wild beasts against each other, such as bears against buffaloes; staged hunts with men shooting safely from behind iron bars; and gladiators in the arena with bulls, tigers, and lions. It is recorded that five

The Eruption of Mount Vesuvius

FAMILY & SOCIETY

PLINY THE YOUNGER, an upper-class Roman who rose to the position of governor of Bithynia in Asia Minor, wrote a letter to the Roman historian Tacitus, describing the death of his uncle, Pliny the Elder, as a result of the eruption of Mount Vesuvius. At Tacitus's request, Pliny wrote another letter describing his own experiences during the massive eruption.

Pliny, Letter to Cornelius Tacitus

You say that the letter which I wrote to you at your request, describing the death of my uncle, has made you anxious to know not only the terrors, but also the distress I suffered while I remained behind at Misenum [a town near Pompeii]....

For many days previous there had been slight shocks of earthquake, which were not particularly alarming, because they are common enough in Campania. But on that night the shocks were so intense that everything round us seemed not only to be disturbed, but to be tottering to its fall. My mother rushed into my bedchamber, just as I myself was getting up in order to arouse her, if she was still sleeping....

It was now the first hour of the day, but the light was still faint and weak.... Soon a black, fearful cloud of fiery vapor descended upon the earth and ... covered the whole bay.... Then my mother prayed, entreated, and commanded me to fly as best I could, saying that I was young and could escape, while she was old and infirm, and would not fear to die, if only she knew that she had not been the cause of my death. I replied that I would not save myself unless I could save her too, and so, after taking tight hold of her hand, I forced her to quicken her steps. She reluctantly obeyed, accusing herself for retarding my flight. Then the ashes began to fall, but not thickly.

I looked back, and a dense blackness was rolling up behind us, which spread itself over the ground and followed like a torrent. "Let us turn aside," I said, "while we can still see, lest we be thrown down in the road and trampled on in the darkness by the thronging crowd."

We were considering what to do, when the blackness of night overtook us, not that of a moonless or cloudy night, but the blackness of pent-up places which never see the light. You could hear the wailing of women, the screams of little children, and the shouts of men. Some were trying to find their parents, others their children, others their wives, by calling for them and recognizing them by their voices alone. Some were commiserating their own lot, others that of their relatives, while some again prayed for death in sheer terror of dying. Many were lifting up their hands to the gods, but more were declaring that now there were no longer any gods, and that this night would last forever, and be the end of all the world. Nor were there wanting those who added to the real perils by inventing new and false terrors, for some said that part of Misenimi was in ruins and the rest in flames, and though the tale was untrue, it found ready believers.

A gleam of light now appeared, which seemed to us not so much daylight as a token of the approaching fire. The latter remained at a distance, but the darkness came on again, and the ashes once more fell thickly and heavily. We had to keep rising and shaking the latter off us, or we should have been buried by them and crushed by their weight....

At length the blackness became less dense, and dissipated, as it were, into smoke and cloud. Then came the real light of day.... Our still trembling eyes saw that everything had been transformed, and covered with a deep layer of ashes, like snow. Making our way back to Misenum, we refreshed our bodies as best we could, and passed an anxious, troubled night, hovering between hope and fear....

 What do you think were the reactions of upper-class Romans to this event? How do you think lower-class Romans reacted?

Source: From *Readings in Ancient History*, Hutton Webster (D.C. Health and Co.: Boston 1919), p. 249.

---

thousand beasts were killed in one day of games when Emperor Titus inaugurated the Colosseum in 80 C.E.

These bloodthirsty spectacles were extremely popular with the Roman people. But the gladiatorial games served a purpose beyond mere entertainment. Like the other forms of public entertainment, the games fulfilled both a political and a social function. Certainly, the games served to divert the idle masses from political unrest. It was said of the emperor Trajan that he understood that although the distribution of grain and money satisfied the individual, spectacles were necessary for the "contentment of the masses."

DISASTER IN SOUTHERN ITALY Gladiatorial spectacles were contrived by humans, but the Roman Empire also experienced some spectacular natural disasters. One of the greatest was the eruption of Mount Vesuvius (vuh-SOO-vee-uss) on August 24, 79 C.E. Although known to be a volcano, Vesuvius was thought to be extinct, its hillsides green with flourishing vineyards. Its eruption threw up thousands of tons of lava and ash. Toxic fumes killed many people, and the nearby city of Pompeii (pahm-PAY) was quickly buried under volcanic ash. To the west, Herculaneum (hur-kyuh-LAY-nee-um) and other communities around the Bay of Naples were submerged beneath a mud flow (see the box "The Eruption of Mount Vesuvius" above). Not for another 1,700 years were systematic excavations begun on the buried towns. Through examination of their preserved remains, archaeologists have been able to reconstruct the everyday life and art of these Roman towns. Their discovery in the eighteenth century was an important force in stimulating both scholarly and public interest in Classical antiquity and helped give rise to the Neoclassical style of that century.

Crisis and the Late Empire

 FOCUS QUESTIONS: What reforms did Diocletian and Constantine institute, and to what extent were the reforms successful? What role did the Germanic tribes play in the Late Roman Empire?

During the reign of Marcus Aurelius, the last of the five good emperors, a number of natural catastrophes struck Rome. To many Romans, these natural disasters seemed to portend an ominous future for Rome. New problems arose soon after the death of Marcus Aurelius in 180.

Crises in the Third Century

In the course of the third century, the Roman Empire came near to collapse. Military monarchy under the Severan rulers (193–235), which restored order after a series of civil wars, was followed by military anarchy. For the next fifty years (235–284), the empire was mired in the chaos of continual civil war. Contenders for the imperial throne found that bribing soldiers was an effective way to become emperor. In these five decades, there were twenty-seven emperors, only four of whom did not meet a violent end. At the same time, the empire was beset by a series of invasions, no doubt exacerbated by the civil wars. In the east, the Sassanid (suh-SAN-id) Persians made inroads into Roman territory. Germanic tribes also poured into the empire. Not until the end of the third century were most of the boundaries restored.

Invasions, civil wars, and plague came close to causing an economic collapse of the Roman Empire in the third century. There was a noticeable decline in trade and small industry, and the labor shortage caused by the plague affected both military recruiting and the economy. Farm production deteriorated significantly as fields were ravaged by invaders or, even more often, by the defending Roman armies. The monetary system began to collapse as a result of debased coinage and inflation. Armies were needed more than ever, but financial strains made it difficult to pay and enlist more soldiers. By the mid-third century, the state had to hire Germans to fight under Roman commanders.

The Late Roman Empire

At the end of the third and beginning of the fourth centuries, the Roman Empire gained a new lease on life through the efforts of two strong emperors, Diocletian (dy-uh-KLEE-shun) and Constantine (KAHN-stun-teen). Under their rule, the empire was transformed into a new state, the so-called Late Empire, distinguished by a new governmental structure, a rigid economic and social system, and a new state religion—Christianity (see "Transformation of the Roman World: The Development of Christianity" later in this chapter).

THE REFORMS OF DIOCLETIAN AND CONSTANTINE Both Diocletian (284–305) and Constantine (306–337) extended imperial control by strengthening and expanding the administrative bureaucracies of the Roman Empire. A hierarchy of officials exercised control at the various levels of government. The army was enlarged, and mobile units were set up that could be quickly moved to support frontier troops when the borders were threatened.

Constantine's biggest project was the construction of a new capital city in the east, on the site of the Greek city of Byzantium on the shores of the Bosporus. Eventually renamed Constantinople (modern Istanbul), the city was developed for defensive reasons and had an excellent strategic

Location of Constantinople, the "New Rome"

location. Calling it his "New Rome," Constantine endowed the city with a forum, large palaces, and a vast amphitheater.

The political and military reforms of Diocletian and Constantine also greatly increased two institutions—the army and the civil service—that drained most of the public funds. Though more revenues were needed to pay for the army and the bureaucracy, the population was not growing, so the tax base could not be expanded. To ensure the tax base and keep the empire going despite the shortage of labor, the emperors issued edicts that forced people to remain in their designated vocations. Basic jobs, such as baker or shipper, became hereditary. The fortunes of free tenant farmers also declined. Soon they found themselves bound to the land by large landowners who took advantage of depressed agricultural conditions to enlarge their landed estates.

In general, the economic and social policies of Diocletian and Constantine were based on an unprecedented degree of control and coercion. Though temporarily successful, such authoritarian polices in the long run stifled the very vitality the Late Empire needed to revive its sagging fortunes.

THE END OF THE WESTERN EMPIRE Constantine had reunited the Roman Empire and restored a semblance of order. After his death, however, the empire continued to divide into western and eastern parts, which had become two virtually independent states by 395. In the course of the fifth century, while the empire in the east remained intact under the Roman emperor in Constantinople, the administrative structure of the empire in the west collapsed and was replaced by an assortment of Germanic kingdoms. The process was a gradual one, beginning with the movement of Germans into the empire.

Although the Romans had established a series of political frontiers along the Rhine and Danube Rivers, Romans and Germans often came into contact across these boundaries.

Until the fourth century, the empire had proved capable of absorbing these people without harm to its political structure. In the late fourth century, however, the Germanic tribes came under new pressure when the Huns, a fierce tribe of nomads from the steppes of Asia who may have been related to the Xiongnu (SHYAHNG-noo), the invaders of the Han Empire in China, moved into the Black Sea region, possibly attracted by the riches of the empire to its south. One of the groups displaced by the Huns was the Visigoths (VIZ-uh-gahthz), who moved south and west, crossed the Danube into Roman territory, and settled down as Roman allies. But the Visigoths soon revolted, and the Roman attempt to stop them at Adrianople in 378 led to a crushing defeat for Rome.

Increasing numbers of Germans now crossed the frontiers. In 410, the Visigoths sacked Rome. Vandals poured into southern Spain and Africa, Visigoths into Spain and Gaul. The Vandals crossed into Italy from North Africa and ravaged Rome again in 455. By the middle of the fifth century, the western provinces of the Roman Empire had been taken over by Germanic peoples who set up their own independent kingdoms. At the same time, a semblance of imperial authority remained in Rome, although the real power behind the throne tended to rest in the hands of important military officials known as masters of the soldiers. These military commanders controlled the government and dominated the imperial court. In 476, Odoacer (oh-doh-AY-sur), a new master of the soldiers, himself of German origin, deposed the Roman emperor, the boy Romulus Augustulus (RAHM-yuh-lus ow-GOOS-chuh-luss). To many historians, the deposition of Romulus signaled the end of the Roman Empire in the west. Of course, this is only a symbolic date, as much of direct imperial rule had already been lost in the course of the fifth century.

WHAT CAUSED THE FALL OF THE WESTERN ROMAN EMPIRE? The end of the Roman Empire in the west has given rise to numerous theories that attempt to provide a single, all-encompassing reason for the "decline and fall of the Roman Empire." These include the following: Christianity's emphasis on a spiritual kingdom undermined Roman military virtues and patriotism; traditional Roman values declined as non-Italians gained prominence in the empire; lead poisoning caused by water pipes and cups made of lead resulted in a mental decline; plague decimated the population; Rome failed to advance technologically because of slavery; and Rome was unable to achieve a workable political system. There may be an element of truth in each of these theories, but all of them have also been challenged. History is an intricate web of relationships, causes, and effects. No single explanation will ever suffice to explain historical events. One thing is clear, however. Weakened by a shortage of manpower, the Roman army in the west was simply not able to fend off the hordes of people invading Italy and Gaul. In contrast, the Eastern Roman Empire, which would survive for another thousand years, remained largely free from invasion.

Transformation of the Roman World: The Development of Christianity

 FOCUS QUESTION: What characteristics of Christianity enabled it to grow and ultimately to triumph as the official religion of the Roman Empire?

The rise of Christianity marked a fundamental break with the dominant values of the Greco-Roman world. To understand the rise of Christianity, we must first examine both the religious environment of the Roman world and the Jewish background from which Christianity emerged.

The Religious World of the Roman Empire

The Roman state religion focused on the worship of a pantheon of Greco-Roman gods and goddesses, including Juno, the patron goddess of women; Minerva, the goddess of craftspeople; Mars, the god of war; and Jupiter Optimus Maximus (JOO-puh-tur AHP-tuh-muss MAK-suh-muss) ("best and greatest"), who became the patron deity of Rome and assumed a central place in the religious life of the city. The Romans believed that the observance of proper ritual by state priests brought them into a right relationship with the gods, thereby guaranteeing security, peace, and prosperity, and that their success in creating an empire confirmed that they enjoyed the favor of the gods. As the first-century B.C.E. politician Cicero claimed, "We have overcome all the nations of the world because we have realized that the world is directed and governed by the gods."[5]

The polytheistic Romans were extremely tolerant of other religions. They allowed the worship of native gods and goddesses throughout their provinces and even adopted some of the local deities. In addition, beginning with Augustus, emperors were often officially made gods by the Roman senate, thus bolstering support for the emperors (see the Comparative Essay "Rulers and Gods" on p. 149).

The desire for a more emotional spiritual experience led many people to the mystery religions of the Hellenistic east, which flooded into the western Roman world during the Early Empire. The mystery religions offered their followers entry into a higher world of reality and the promise of a future life superior to the present one.

The Jewish Background

In addition to the mystery religions, the Romans' expansion into the eastern Mediterranean also brought them into contact with the Jews. Roman involvement with the Jews began in 63 B.C.E., and by 6 C.E., Judaea (which embraced the old Jewish kingdom of Judah) had been made a province and placed under the direction of a Roman procurator. But unrest continued, augmented by divisions among the Jews themselves. One group, the Essenes, awaited a Messiah who would

COMPARATIVE ESSAY

Rules and Gods

RELIGION & PHILOSOPHY

All of the world's earliest civilizations believed that there was a close relationship between rulers and gods. In Egypt, pharaohs were considered gods whose role was to maintain the order and harmony of the universe in their own kingdom. In the words of an Egyptian hymn, "What is the king of Upper and Lower Egypt? He is a god by whose dealings one lives, the father and mother of all men, alone by himself, without an equal." In Mesopotamia, India, and China, rulers were thought to rule with divine assistance. Kings were often seen as rulers who derived their power from the gods and acted as the agents or representatives of the gods. In ancient India, rulers claimed to be representatives of the gods because they were descended from Manu, the first man who had been made a king by Brahman, the chief god. Many Romans believed that their success in creating an empire was a visible sign of divine favor.

Their supposed connection to the gods also caused rulers to seek divine aid in the affairs of the world. This led to the art of divination, an organized method to discover the intentions of the gods. In Mesopotamian and Roman society, one form of divination involved the examination of the livers of sacrificed animals; features seen in the livers were interpreted to foretell events to come. The Chinese used oracle bones to receive advice from supernatural forces that were beyond the power of human beings. Questions for the gods were scratched on turtle shells or animal bones, which were then exposed to fire. Shamans examined the resulting cracks on the surface of the shells or bones and interpreted their meaning as messages from supernatural forces. The Greeks divined the will of the gods by use of the oracle, a sacred shrine dedicated to a god or goddess who revealed the future in response to a question.

Underlying all of these divinatory practices was a belief in a supernatural universe, that is, a world in which divine forces were in charge and on which humans were dependent for their own well-being. It was not until the Scientific Revolution of the modern world that many people began to believe in a natural world that was not governed by spiritual forces.

 What role did spiritual forces play in early civilizations?

Vishnu. Brahman the Creator, Shiva the Destroyer, and Vishnu the Preserver are the three chief Hindu gods of India. Vishnu is known as the Preserver because he mediates between Brahman and Shiva and thus maintains the stability of the universe.

Fitzwilliam Museum, University of Cambridge, UK/The Bridgeman Art Library

save Israel from oppression, usher in the kingdom of God, and establish paradise on earth. Another group, the Zealots, were militant extremists who advocated the violent overthrow of Roman rule. A Jewish revolt in 66 C.E. was crushed by the Romans four years later. The Jewish Temple in Jerusalem was destroyed, and Roman power once more stood supreme in Judaea.

The Rise of Christianity

Jesus of Nazareth (c. 6 B.C.E.–c. 29 C.E.) was a Palestinian Jew who grew up in Galilee, an important center of the militant Zealots. Jesus's message was simple. He reassured his fellow Jews that he did not plan to undermine their traditional religion. What was important was not strict adherence to the letter of the law but the transformation of the inner person: "So in everything, do to others what you would have them do to you, for this sums up the Law and the Prophets."[6] God's command was simply to love God and one another: "Love the Lord your God with all your heart and with all your soul and with all your mind and with all your strength. The second is this: Love your neighbor as yourself."[7] In his teachings, Jesus presented the ethical concepts—humility, charity, and brotherly love—that would form the basis of the value system of medieval Western civilization.

To the Roman authorities of Palestine, however, Jesus was a potential revolutionary who might transform Jewish expectations of a messianic kingdom into a revolt against Rome. Therefore, Jesus found himself denounced on many sides, and the procurator Pontius Pilate ordered his crucifixion. But that did not solve the problem. A few loyal followers of Jesus spread the story that Jesus had overcome death, had been resurrected, and had then ascended into heaven. The belief in Jesus's resurrection became an important tenet of Christian doctrine. Jesus was now hailed as "the anointed one" (*Christus* in Greek), the Messiah who would return and usher in the kingdom of God on earth.

Christianity began, then, as a religious movement within Judaism and was viewed that way by Roman authorities for many decades. One of the prominent figures in early

Jesus and His Apostles. Pictured is a fourth-century C.E. fresco from a Roman catacomb depicting Jesus and his apostles. Catacombs were underground cemeteries where early Christians buried their dead. Christian tradition holds that in times of imperial repression, Christians withdrew to the catacombs to pray and hide.

Christianity, however, Paul of Tarsus (c. 5–c. 67), believed that the message of Jesus should be preached not only to Jews but to Gentiles (non-Jews) as well. Paul taught that Jesus was the savior, the son of God, who had come to earth to save all humans, who were all sinners as a result of Adam's sin of disobedience against God. By his death, Jesus had atoned for the sins of all humans and made possible their reconciliation with God and hence their salvation. By accepting Jesus as their savior, they too could be saved.

The Spread of Christianity

Christianity spread slowly at first. Although the teachings of early Christianity were mostly disseminated by preaching, written materials also appeared. Among them were a series of epistles (letters) written by Paul outlining Christian beliefs for different Christian communities. Some of Jesus's disciples may also have preserved some of the sayings of the master in writing and would have passed on personal memories that became the basis of the written *gospels*—the "good news" concerning Jesus—of Matthew, Mark, Luke, and John, which by the end of the first century C.E. had become the authoritative record of Jesus's life and teachings and formed the core of the New Testament. Recently, some scholars have argued that other gospels, such as that of Thomas, were rejected because they deviated from the beliefs about Jesus held by the emerging church leaders.

Although Jerusalem was the first center of Christianity, its destruction by the Romans in 70 C.E. dispersed the Christians and left individual Christian churches with considerable independence. By 100, Christian churches had been established in most of the major cities of the east and in some places in the western part of the empire. Many early Christians came from the ranks of Hellenized Jews and the Greek-speaking populations of the east. But in the second and third centuries, an increasing number of followers came from Latin-speaking peoples.

Initially, the Romans did not pay much attention to the Christians, whom they regarded as simply another Jewish sect. As time passed, however, the Roman attitude toward Christianity began to change. The Romans tolerated other religions as long as they did not threaten public order or public morals. Many Romans came to view Christians as harmful to the Roman state because they refused to worship the state gods and emperors. Nevertheless, Roman persecution of Christians in the first and second centuries was only sporadic and local, never systematic. In the second century, Christians were largely ignored as harmless (see Opposing Viewpoints "Roman Authorities and a Christian on Christianity" on p. 151). By the end of the reigns of the five good emperors, Christians still represented a small minority within the empire, but one of considerable strength.

THE TRIUMPH OF CHRISTIANITY Christianity grew slowly in the first century, took root in the second, and by the third had spread widely. Why was the new faith able to attract so many followers? First, the Christian message had much to offer the Roman world. The promise of salvation, made possible by Jesus's death and resurrection, made a resounding impact on a world full of suffering and injustice. Christianity seemed to imbue life with a meaning and purpose beyond the simple material things of everyday reality. Second, Christianity seemed familiar. It was regarded as simply another mystery religion, offering immortality as the result of the sacrificial death of a savior-god. At the same time, it offered more than the other mystery religions did. Jesus had been a human figure, not a mythological one, and people could relate to him. Finally, Christianity fulfilled the human need to belong. Christians formed communities bound to one another in which people could express their love by helping each other and offering assistance to the poor, sick, widowed, and orphaned. Christianity satisfied the need to belong in a way that the huge, impersonal, and remote Roman Empire never could.

Christianity proved attractive to all classes. The promise of eternal life was for all—rich, poor, aristocrats, slaves, men, and women. Christianity emphasized a sense of spiritual equality for all people. Many women, in fact, found that

OPPOSING ✕ VIEWPOINTS

Roman Authorities and a Christian on Christianity

RELIGION & PHILOSOPHY

AT FIRST, ROMAN AUTHORITIES WERE UNCERTAIN HOW TO DEAL WITH THE CHRISTIANS. In the second century, Christians were often viewed as harmless and yet were subject to persecution if they persisted in their beliefs. Pliny was governor of the province of Bithynia in northwestern Asia Minor (present-day Turkey). He wrote to the emperor for advice about how to handle people accused of being Christians. Trajan's response reflects the general approach toward Christians by the emperors of the second century. The final selection is taken from *Against Celsus*, written about 246 by Origen of Alexandria. In it, Origen defended the value of Christianity against Celsus, a philosopher who had launched an attack on Christians and their teachings.

An Exchange Between Pliny and Trajan

Pliny to Trajan

It is my custom. Sir, to refer to you in all cases where I do not feel sure, for who can better direct my doubts or inform my ignorance? I have never been present at any legal examination of the Christians, and I do not know, therefore, what are the usual penalties passed upon them or the limits of those penalties, or how searching an inquiry should be made.... In the meantime, this is the plan which I have adopted in the case of those Christians who have been brought before me. I ask them if they are Christians. If they say they are, then I repeat the question a second and a third time, warning them of the penalties it entails, and if they still persist, I order them to be taken away to prison. For I do not doubt that, whatever the character of the crime may be which they confess, their pertinacity and inflexible obstinacy certainly ought to be punished.

As is usually the way, the very fact of my taking up this question led subsequently to a great increase of accusations, and a variety of cases were brought before me.... So I postponed my examination, and immediately consulted you.

The matter seems to me worthy of your consideration, especially as there are so many people involved in the danger. Many persons of all ages, and of both sexes alike, are being brought into peril of their lives by their accusers, and the process will go on. For the contagion of this superstition has spread, not only through the free cities, but into the villages and the rural districts.

Trajan to Pliny

You have adopted the proper course, my dear Pliny, in examining into the cases of those who have been denounced to you as Christians, for no hard and fast rule can be laid down to meet a question of such wide extent. The Christians are not to be hunted out. If they are brought before you and the offense is proved, they are to be punished, but with this reservation—that if anyone denies that he is a Christian and makes it clear that he is not, by offering prayers to our deities, then he is to be pardoned because of his recantation, however suspicious his past conduct may have been. But pamphlets published anonymously must not carry any weight whatever, no matter what the charge may be, for they are not only a precedent of the very worst type but they are not in consonance with the spirit of our age.

Origen, *Against Celsus*

[Celsus] says that Christians perform their rites and teach their doctrines in secret, and they do this with good reason to escape the death penalty that hangs over them. He compares the danger to the risks encountered for the sake of philosophy as by Socrates.... I reply to this that in Socrates's cases the Athenians at once regretted what they had done, and cherished no grievance against him.... But in the case of the Christians the Roman Senate, the contemporary emperors, the army, ... and the relatives of believers fought against the gospel and would have hindered it; and it would have been defeated by the combined force of so many unless it had overcome and risen above the opposition by divine power, so that it has conquered the whole world that was conspiring against it....

He [also] ridicules our teachers of the gospel who try to elevate the soul in every way to the Creator of the universe.... He compares them [Christians] to ... the most obtuse yokels, as if they called children quite in infancy and women to evil practices, telling them to leave their father and teachers and to follow them. But let Celsus ... tell us how we make women and children leave noble and sound teaching, and call them to wicked practices. But he will not be able to prove anything of any kind against us. On the contrary, we deliver women from licentiousness and from perversion caused by their associates, ... while we make boys self-controlled when they come to the age of puberty and burn with desires for sexual pleasure, showing them not only the disgrace of their sins, but also what a state these pleasures produce in the souls of bad men, and what penalties they will suffer and how they will be punished.

 What were Pliny's personal opinions of Christians? Why was he willing to execute them? What was Trajan's response, and what were its consequences for the Christians? What major points did Origen make about the benefits of the Christian religion? Why did the Roman authorities consider these ideas dangerous to the Roman state?

Source: From *Readings in Ancient History*, Hutton Webster (D.C. Health and Co.: Boston 1919), p. 250. From Origen, *Contra Celsum*. Trans. Henry Chadwick. Copyright © 1953 Cambridge University Press.

Christianity offered them new roles and new forms of companionship with other women. Christian women fostered the new religion in their homes and preached their convictions to other people in their towns and villages. Many also died for their faith. Perpetua was an aristocratic woman who converted to Christianity. Her pagan family begged her to renounce her new faith, but she refused. Arrested by the Roman authorities, she chose instead to die for her faith and was one of a group of Christians who were slaughtered by wild beasts in the arena at Carthage on March 7, 203.

Moreover, the sporadic persecution of Christians by the Romans in the first and second centuries not only did little to stop the growth of Christianity, but in fact served to strengthen it as an institution in the second and third centuries by causing it to become more organized. Crucial to this change was the emerging role of the bishops, who began to assume more control over church communities. The Christian church was creating a well-defined hierarchical structure in which the bishops and clergy were salaried officers separate from the laity or regular church members.

As the Christian church became more organized, some emperors in the third century responded with more systematic persecutions, but their schemes failed. The last great persecution was at the beginning of the fourth century, but by that time, Christianity had become too strong to be eradicated by force. After Constantine became the first Christian emperor, Christianity flourished. Although Constantine was not baptized until the end of his life, in 313 he issued the Edict of Milan officially tolerating Christianity. Under Theodosius (thee-uh-DOH-shuss) the Great (378–395), it was made the official religion of the Roman Empire. In less than four centuries, Christianity had triumphed.

A Comparison of the Roman and Han Empires

 FOCUS QUESTION: In what ways were the Roman Empire and the Han Chinese Empire similar, and in what ways were they different?

At the beginning of the first millennium C.E., two great empires—the Roman Empire in the West and the Han Empire in the East—dominated large areas of the world. Although there was little contact between them, the two empires exhibited some remarkable similarities. Both lasted for centuries, and both were extremely successful in establishing centralized control (see the Comparative Illustration "Emperors, West and East" on p. 153). Both built elaborate systems of roads in order to rule efficiently and relied on provincial officials, and especially on towns and cities, for local administration. Architectural features found in the capital cities of Rome and Chang'an were also transferred on a smaller scale to provincial towns and cities. In both empires, settled conditions led to a high level of agricultural production that sustained large populations, estimated at between 50 and 60 million in each empire. Although both empires

expanded into areas with different languages, ethnic groups, and ways of life, they managed to extend their legal and political institutions, their technical skills, and their languages throughout their empires. In this way, they integrated local communities into a common political and cultural framework.

The Roman and Han Empires also had similar social and economic structures. The family stood at the heart of the social structure, and the male head of the family was all-powerful. The family also inculcated the values that helped make the empires strong—duty, courage, obedience, and discipline. The wealth of both societies also depended on agriculture. Although a free peasantry provided a backbone of strength and stability in each empire, wealthy landowners were able to gradually convert the free peasants into tenant farmers and thereby ultimately to undermine the power of the imperial governments.

Of course, there were also significant differences. The empires came into existence in different ways. Han China inherited an ideal of imperial culture on which to build. The Romans, on the other hand, began with a small city-state ruled collectively by its prominent citizens. As the Romans expanded throughout Italy and the Mediterranean, they eventually created a single imperial state.

There were also economic and social differences. Merchants were more highly regarded and allowed more freedom in Rome than they were in China. One key reason for this difference is that whereas many inhabitants of the Roman Empire depended to a considerable degree on commerce to obtain such staples as wheat, olives, wine, cloth, and timber, the vast majority of Chinese were subsistence farmers whose needs—when they were supplied—could normally be met by the local environment. As a result, there was undoubtedly less social mobility in China than in Rome, and many Chinese peasants spent their entire lives without venturing far beyond the village gate.

Another difference is that over the four hundred years of the empires' existence, Chinese imperial authority was far more stable. With a more cohesive territory and a strong dynastic tradition, Chinese rulers could easily pass on their authority to other family members. In contrast in the Roman Empire, political instability was a chronic problem, at least in some periods. Although Roman emperors were accorded divine status by the Roman senate after death, accession to the Roman imperial throne depended less on solid dynastic principles and more on pure military force.

Despite the differences, one major inescapable similarity remains: both empires eventually faced overwhelming problems. Both suffered from overexpansion, and both fortified their long borders with walls, forts, and military garrisons to guard against invasions of nomadic people. Both empires were periodically beset by invasions of nomadic peoples: the Han dynasty was weakened by the incursions of the Xiongnu, and the Western Roman Empire eventually collapsed in the face of incursions by the Germanic peoples.

Nevertheless, one inescapable difference between these two contemporary empires also remains. Although the Han

POLITICS & GOVERNMENT

COMPARATIVE ILLUSTRATION

Emperors, West and East. Two great empires with strong central governments dominated much of the ancient world—the Roman Empire in the West and the Han Empire in the East. Shown here are two emperors from these empires. The Roman emperor Hadrian, who ruled from 117 to 138, was the third of the five good emperors. He had been adopted by the emperor Trajan to serve as his successor. Hadrian was a strong and intelligent ruler who took his responsibilities seriously. Between 121 and 132, he visited all of the provinces in the empire. Liu Bang (lyoo BAHNG) came from the peasant class, but through his military prowess, he defeated all rivals in the civil wars that followed the death of the First Emperor of Qin. Liu Bang, who is known historically by his title of Han Gaozu (HAHN gow-DZOO), was the first emperor of the Han dynasty, which ruled China for four hundred years. He won the support of his subjects by reducing their tax burden. He was also responsible for bringing China back under central control but was killed in a frontier battle in 195 B.C.E.

Q *What similarities do you see in the lives of these two rulers?*

dynasty collapsed, the Chinese imperial tradition, along with the class structure and set of values that sustained that tradition, survived, and the Chinese Empire, under new dynasties, continued well into the twentieth century as a single political entity. In stark contrast, the Roman Empire in the west collapsed and lived on only as an idea.

CHAPTER SUMMARY

Sometime in the eighth century B.C.E., a group of Latin-speaking people built a small community called Rome on the Tiber River in Italy. Between 509 and 264 B.C.E., this city expanded and brought almost all of Italy under its control. During this time of conquest, Rome also developed the political institutions of a republic ruled by an aristocratic oligarchy. Between 264 and 133 B.C.E., Rome expanded to the west and east and became master of the Mediterranean Sea and its surrounding territories, creating one of the largest empires in antiquity. In the second century B.C.E., the conservative, traditional values of Rome declined as affluence and individualism increased. After 133 B.C.E.,

Rome's republican institutions proved inadequate for the task of ruling an empire, and after a series of bloody civil wars, Augustus created a new order that established a Roman imperial state.

The Roman Empire experienced a lengthy period of peace and prosperity between 14 and 180. During this *Pax Romana*, trade flourished and the provinces were governed efficiently. In the course of the third century, however, the empire came near to collapse due to invasions, civil wars, and economic decline. At the same time, a new religion—Christianity—was spreading throughout the empire and slowly gained acceptance. The response to the crises of the third century and the rise of

Christianity gradually brought a transformation of the Roman Empire in the fourth and fifth centuries. Although the emperors Diocletian and Constantine brought new life to the so-called Late Empire, their efforts only shored up the empire temporarily. Beginning in 395, the empire divided into western and eastern parts, and in 476, the Roman Empire in the west came to an end.

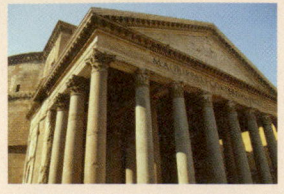

Although the Roman Empire in the west collapsed and lived on only as an idea, Roman achievements were bequeathed to the future. The Romance languages of today (French, Italian, Spanish, Portuguese, and Romanian) are based on Latin. Western practices of impartial justice and trial by jury owe much to Roman law. As great builders, the Romans left monuments to their skills throughout Europe, some of which, such as aqueducts and roads, are still in use today. Aspects of Roman administrative practices survived in the Western world for centuries. The Romans also preserved the intellectual heritage of the Greco-Roman world of antiquity. Nevertheless, although many aspects of the Roman world would continue, the heirs of Rome went on to create new civilizations—European, Islamic, and Byzantine—that would mark yet another stage in the development of human society.

The Han dynasty also created one of the greatest empires in antiquity. Like the Roman Empire, the Han Empire left a rich legacy to its successors. The Confucian institutions and principles enshrined during the long years of Han rule survived several centuries of internal division and eventually re-emerged as the governing doctrine of later Chinese empires down to the twentieth century.

CHAPTER TIMELINE

CHAPTER REVIEW

Upon Reflection

Q Was the fall of the Roman Republic due to systemic institutional weaknesses or the personal ambitions of generals and politicians? Explain your answer.

Q In what ways was the rule of the Roman emperors in the first and second centuries C.E. an improvement over the Republic of the first century B.C.E.? In what ways was their rule not an improvement over the last century of the Republic?

Q In what ways were the Roman and Han imperial systems of government alike? In what ways were they different?

Key Terms

consuls (p. 129)
praetors (p. 129)
senate (p. 129)
centuriate assembly (p. 129)
council of the plebs (p. 129)
patricians (p. 129)
plebeians (p. 129)
tribunes of the plebs (p. 129)
latifundia (p. 134)
dictator (p. 135)
praetorian guard (p. 136)
Pax Romana (p. 137)
good emperors (p. 138)
natural law (p. 141)
paterfamilias (p. 141)

Suggested Reading

GENERAL SURVEYS OF ROMAN HISTORY   For a general account of Roman history, see **M. T. Boatwright, D. J. Gargola, and R. J. A. Talbert,** *The Romans: From Village to Empire* (New York, 2004); and **G. Woolf,** *Rome: An Empire's Story* (New York, 2012). Good surveys of the Roman Republic include **M. H. Crawford,** *The Roman Republic*, 2nd ed. (Cambridge, Mass., 1993), and **C. S. Mackay,** *Ancient Rome: A Military and Political History* (Cambridge, 2004). The history of early Rome is well covered in **T. J. Cornell,** *The Beginnings of Rome: Italy and Rome from the Bronze Age to the Punic Wars (c. 1000–264 B.C.)* (London, 1995). An excellent account of the basic problems of the late Republic can be found in **M. Beard and M. H. Crawford,** *Rome in the Late Republic* (London, 1984). Also valuable is **E. Hildinger,** *Swords Against the Senate: The Rise of the Roman Army and the Fall of the Republic* (Cambridge, Mass., 2002).

EARLY ROMAN EMPIRE   A good survey of the Early Roman Empire is **M. Goodman,** *The Roman World, 44 B.C.–A.D. 180* (London, 1997). See also **R. Mellor,** *Augustus and the Creation of the Roman Empire* (Boston, 2005), for a brief history with documents.

ROMAN SOCIETY AND CULTURE   On Roman art and architecture, see **F. S. Kleiner,** *A History of Roman Art* (Belmont, Calif., 2006). On the Roman family, see **S. Dixon,** *The Roman Family* (Baltimore, 1992). On slavery, see **K. R. Bradley,** *Slavery and Society at Rome* (New York, 1994). On the gladiators, see **F. Meijer,** *The Gladiators: History's Most Deadly Sport* (Boston, 2005).

LATE ROMAN EMPIRE   On the crises of the third century, see **D. S. Potter,** *The Roman Empire at Bay, A.D. 180–395* (New York, 2004). On the Late Roman Empire, see **S. Mitchell,** *History of the Later Roman Empire, A.D. 284–641* (Oxford, 2006). On the collapse of the Roman Empire, see **P. Heather,** *The Fall of the Roman Empire: A New History of Rome and the Barbarians* (New York, 2006). For a general introduction to early Christianity, see **J. Court and K. Court,** *The New Testament World* (Cambridge, 1990).

THE HAN EMPIRE   For a comparison of the Roman and Han Empires, see **W. Scheidel, ed.,** *Rome and China: Comparative Perspectives on Ancient World Empires* (Oxford, 2007).

Chapter Notes

1. Livy, *The Early History of Rome*, trans. A. de Selincourt, 1:16. The words were spoken by Julius Proculus, reportedly relaying to the Roman assembly a message from Romulus, one of Rome's founders, who appeared to him in a dream.
2. Tacitus, *The Annals of Imperial Rome*, trans. M. Grant (Harmondsworth, England, 1964), p. 31.
3. Virgil, *The Aeneid*, trans. C. Day Lewis (Garden City, N.Y., 1952), p. 154.
4. Juvenal, *The Sixteen Satires*, trans. P. Green (New York, 1967), p. 207.
5. Quoted in C. Starr, *Past and Future in Ancient History* (Lanham, Md., 1987), pp. 38–39.
6. Matthew 7:12.
7. Mark 12:30–31.

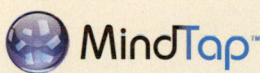 MindTap™

MindTap is a fully online, highly personalized learning experience built upon Cengage Learning content. MindTap combines student learning tools—readings, multimedia, activities, and assessments—into a singular Learning Path that guides students through their course.

New Patterns of Civilization (500–1500 C.E.)

BY THE BEGINNING of the first millennium C.E., many of the great states of the ancient world were in decline; some were even at the point of collapse. On the ruins of these ancient empires, new patterns of civilization began to take shape between 400 and 1500 C.E. In some cases, these new societies were built on the political and cultural foundations laid down by their predecessors. The Tang Dynasty in China and the Guptas in India both looked back to the ancient period to provide an ideological model for their own time. The Byzantine Empire carried on parts of the Classical Greek tradition while also adopting the powerful creed of Christianity from the Roman Empire. In other cases, new states incorporated some elements of the former classical civilizations while heading in markedly different directions, as was the case with the Arabic states in the Middle East and the new European civilization of the Middle Ages. In Europe, however, the Renaissance, which began in the fifteenth century, sought to bring about a revival of parts of the old Greco-Roman culture.

During this period, a number of significant forces were at work in human society. The accoutrements of a more technologically advanced society gradually spread from the heartland regions of the Middle East, the Mediterranean basin, the South Asian subcontinent, and China into new areas of the world—sub-Saharan Africa, central and western Europe, Southeast Asia, and even the islands of Japan, off the eastern edge of the Eurasian landmass. Across the oceans, unique but advanced civilizations continued to take shape in isolation in the Americas. In the meantime, the vast migrations of peoples continued, leading not only to bitter conflicts but also to increased interchanges of technology and ideas. The result was the transformation of separate and distinct cultures and civilizations into an increasingly complex and vast world system embracing not only technology and trade but also ideas and religious beliefs.

As had been the case during antiquity, the Middle East was at the heart of this activity. The Arab empire, which took shape after the death of the Prophet Muhammad in the early seventh century, brought a measure of renewed stability to the region and provided the key link in the revived trade routes that threaded their way throughout Africa and much of the Eurasian supercontinent. The new religion of Islam became the cement that held the disparate peoples of the region together. Muslim traders—both Arab and Berber—opened contacts with West African societies south of the Sahara, while their ships followed the monsoon winds eastward as far as the Spice Islands in Southeast Asia. Traders from Central Asia, some of them Muslim, carried goods back and forth along the Silk Road between the Middle East and China. For the next several hundred years, the great cities of the Middle East—Mecca, Damascus, and Baghdad—became among the wealthiest in the known world.

Islam's contributions to the human experience during this period were cultural and technological as well as economic. Muslim philosophers preserved the works of the ancient

Greeks for posterity, Muslim scientists and mathematicians made new discoveries about the nature of the universe and the human body, and Muslim cartographers and historians mapped the known world and speculated about the fundamental forces in human society.

But the Middle East was not the only or necessarily even the primary contributor to world trade and civilization during this period. While the Arab empire became the linchpin of trade between the Mediterranean and eastern and southern Asia, another center of primary importance in world trade was emerging in East Asia, focused on China. China had been a major participant in regional trade during the Han dynasty, when its silks were already being transported to Rome via Central Asia, but its role had declined after the fall of the Han. Now, with the rise of the great Tang and Song Dynasties, China reemerged as a major commercial power in East Asia, trading by sea with Southeast Asia and Japan and by land with the nomadic peoples of Central Asia.

Like the Middle East, China was also a prime source of new technology. From China came paper, printing, the compass, and gunpowder. The double-hulled Chinese junks that entered the Indian Ocean during the Ming Dynasty were slow and cumbersome but extremely seaworthy and capable of carrying substantial quantities of goods over long distances. Many inventions arrived in Europe by way of India or the Middle East, and their Chinese origins were therefore unknown in the West.

Increasing trade on a regional or global basis also led to the exchange of ideas. Buddhism was brought to China by merchants, and Islam first arrived in sub-Saharan Africa and the Indonesian archipelago in the same manner. Merchants were not the only means by which religious and cultural ideas spread, however. Sometimes migration, conquest, or relatively peaceful processes played a part. The case of the Bantu-speaking peoples in Central Africa is apparently an example of peaceful expansion; and while Islam sometimes followed the path of Arab

warriors, they seldom imposed their religion by force on the local population. In some instances, as with the Mongols, the conquerors made no effort to convert others to their own religions. By contrast, Christian monks, motivated by missionary fervor, converted many of the peoples of central and eastern Europe. Roman Catholic monks brought Latin Christianity to the Germanic and western Slavic peoples, and monks from the Byzantine Empire largely converted the southern and eastern Slavic populations to Eastern Orthodox Christianity.

Another characteristic of the period between 500 and 1500 C.E. was the almost constant migration of nomadic and seminomadic peoples. Dynamic forces in the Gobi Desert, Central Asia, the Arabian peninsula, and Central Africa provoked vast numbers of peoples to abandon their homelands and seek their livelihood elsewhere. Sometimes the migration was peaceful. More often, however, migration produced political instability and sometimes invasion and subjugation. As had been the case during antiquity, the most active source of migrants was Central Asia. The region later gave birth to the fearsome Mongols, whose armies advanced to the gates of central Europe and conquered China in the thirteenth century. Wherever they went, they left a trail of enormous destruction and loss of life. Inadvertently, the Mongols were also the source of a new wave of epidemics that swept through much of Europe and the Middle East in the fourteenth century. The spread of the plague—known at the time as the Black Death—took much of the population of Europe to an early grave.

But there was another side to the era of nomadic expansion. Even the invasions of the Mongols—the "scourge of God," as Europeans of the thirteenth and fourteenth centuries called them—had constructive as well as destructive consequences. After their initial conquests, for a brief period of three generations, the Mongols provided an avenue for trade throughout the most extensive empire (known as the *Pax Mongolica*) the world had yet seen. ◆

Warriors raiding a village to capture prisoners for the ritual of sacrifice

Sef/Art Resource, NY

The Americas

CHAPTER OUTLINE
AND FOCUS QUESTIONS

The Peopling of the Americas

Q Who were the first Americans, and when and how did they come?

Early Civilizations in Central America

Q What were the main characteristics of religious belief in early Mesoamerica?

The First Civilizations in South America

Q What role did the environment play in the evolution of societies in the Americas?

Stateless Societies in the Americas

Q What were the main characteristics of stateless societies in the Americas, and how did they resemble and differ from the civilizations that arose there?

CRITICAL THINKING

Q In what ways were the early civilizations in the Americas similar to the civilizations discussed in Part I, and in what ways were they unique?

CONNECTIONS TO TODAY

Q Do the environmental problems encountered by pre-Columbian societies in the Americas have relevance today? Why or why not?

IN THE SUMMER OF 2001, a powerful hurricane swept through Central America, destroying houses and flooding villages all along the Caribbean coast of Belize and Guatemala. Farther inland, at the archaeological site of Dos Pilas (dohs PEE-las), it uncovered new evidence concerning a series of dramatic events that had taken place nearly 1,500 years earlier. Beneath a tree uprooted by the storm, archaeologists discovered a block of stones containing hieroglyphics that described a brutal war between two powerful city-states of the area, a conflict that ultimately contributed to the decline and fall of Mayan civilization, perhaps the most advanced society then in existence throughout Central America.

Mayan civilization, the origins of which can be traced back to about 500 B.C.E., was not as old as some of its counterparts that we have discussed in Part I of this book. But it was the most recent version of a whole series of human societies that had emerged throughout the Western Hemisphere as early as the third millennium B.C.E. Although these early societies are not yet as well known as those of ancient Egypt, Mesopotamia, and India, evidence is accumulating that advanced civilizations had existed in the Americas thousands of years before the arrival of Hernando Cortés and the Spanish conquistadors in 1519. ◀

The Peopling of the Americas

 FOCUS QUESTION: Who were the first Americans, and when and how did they come?

The Maya (MY-uh) were only the latest in a series of sophisticated societies that had sprung up at various locations in North and South America since human beings first crossed the Bering Strait several millennia earlier. Most of these early peoples, today often referred to as **Amerindians**, lived by hunting and fishing or by food gathering. But eventually organized societies, based on the cultivation of agriculture, began to take root in Central and South America. One key area of development was on the plateau of central Mexico. Another was in the lowland regions along the Gulf of Mexico and extending into modern Guatemala. A third was in the central Andes Mountains, adjacent to the Pacific coast of South America. Others were just beginning to emerge in the vast Amazon River basin and in the river valleys and Great Plains of North America.

For two thousand years, these societies developed in isolation from their counterparts elsewhere in the world. This lack of contact with other human populations deprived them of access to technological and cultural developments taking place in Africa, Asia, and Europe. They did not know of the wheel, for example, and their written languages were rudimentary compared to those in complex civilizations elsewhere around the globe. They did not benefit from the presence of the horse (which had died out in the Americas thousands of years previously) and of other draft animals such as the ox and the water buffalo. Still, in many respects, their cultural achievements were the equal of those realized elsewhere. When the first European explorers arrived in the region at the turn of the sixteenth century, they described much that they observed in glowing terms.

The First Americans

When the first human beings arrived in the Western Hemisphere has long been a matter of conjecture. In the centuries following the voyages of Christopher Columbus (1492–1504), speculation centered on the possibility that the first settlers to reach the American continents had crossed the Atlantic Ocean. Were they the lost tribes of Israel? Were they Phoenician seafarers from Carthage? Were they refugees from the legendary lost continent of Atlantis? In all cases, the assumption was that they were relatively recent arrivals.

By the mid-nineteenth century, under the influence of the Darwinian concept of evolution, a new theory developed. It proposed that the peopling of America had taken place much earlier as a result of the migration of small groups across the Bering Strait, at a time when the area was a land bridge uniting the continents of Asia and North America. Recent evidence, including numerous physical similarities between most early Americans and contemporary peoples living in northeastern Asia, has confirmed this hypothesis. The debate on

when the migrations began continues, however. The archaeologist Louis Leakey, one of the pioneers in the search for the origins of humankind in Africa, suggested that the first hominids may have arrived in America as long as 100,000 years ago. Most scholars today, however, estimate that the first Americans were *Homo sapiens sapiens* who crossed from Asia by foot between 10,000 and 15,000 years ago in pursuit of herds of bison and caribou that moved into the area in search of grazing land at the end of the last ice age. Some suggest that early migrants from Asia may have followed a maritime route down the western coast of the Americas, supporting themselves by fishing and feeding on other organisms floating in the sea.

In recent years, a number of fascinating new possibilities have opened up. A number of sites discovered at such disparate locations as Cactus Hill in Virginia, Buttermilk Creek in Texas, and Paisley Cave in Oregon show signs of human habitation as long as 15,000 years ago. Other recent discoveries raise the possibility that some early settlers may have originally come from Africa or from the South Pacific rather than from Asia. The question has not yet been answered definitively.

Nevertheless, it is now generally accepted that human beings were living in the Americas at least 15,000 years ago. They gradually spread throughout the North American continent and had penetrated almost to the southern tip of South America by about 11,000 B.C.E. These first Americans were hunters and food gatherers who lived in small nomadic communities close to the sources of their food supply. Although it is not known when agriculture was first practiced, beans and squash seeds have been found at sites that date back at least 10,000 years, implying that farming arose in America almost as early as in the Middle East. The cultivation of maize (corn), and perhaps other crops as well, appears to have been under way as early as 5000 B.C.E. in the Tehuacán (teh-hwah-KAHN) Valley in central Mexico. Archaeologists have traced the ancestry of corn back at least 9,000 years to a wild Mexican grass called teosinte (tay-oh-SIN-tee). Through a lengthy process of experimentation, local farmers transformed it into a highly productive food crop that enabled the rise of the first civilizations in the Americas. A similar process may have occurred in the lowland regions near the modern city of Veracruz and in the Yucatán (yoo-kuh-TAHN) peninsula farther to the east. There, in the region that archaeologists call Mesoamerica, one of the first civilizations in the Americas began to appear.

Early Civilizations in Central America

 FOCUS QUESTION: What were the main characteristics of religious belief in early Mesoamerica?

The first signs of civilization in Mesoamerica appeared at the end of the second millennium B.C.E., with the emergence of what is called Olmec (AHL-mek *or* OHL-mek) culture in the hot and swampy lowlands along the coast of the Gulf of Mexico south of Veracruz (see Map 6.1).

© 2016 Cengage Learning

MAP 6.1 Early Mesoamerica. Mesoamerica was home to some of the first civilizations in the Western Hemisphere. This map shows the major urban settlements in the region.

Q *What types of ecological areas were most associated with Olmec, Mayan, and Aztec culture?*

The Olmecs: In the Land of Rubber

Olmec civilization was characterized by intensive agriculture along the muddy riverbanks in the area and by the carving of stone ornaments, tools, and monuments at sites such as San Lorenzo and La Venta. The site at La Venta contains a ceremonial precinct with a 30-foot-high earthen pyramid, the largest of its date in all Mesoamerica. The Olmec peoples organized a widespread trading network, carried on religious rituals, and devised an as yet undeciphered system of hieroglyphics that is similar in some respects to later Mayan writing (see "Mayan Hieroglyphs and Calendars" later in this chapter) and may be the ancestor of the first true writing systems in the Americas.

Olmec society apparently consisted of several classes, including a class of skilled artisans who produced a series of massive stone heads, some of which are more than 10 feet high. The Olmec peoples supported themselves primarily by cultivating crops, such as corn and beans, but also engaged in fishing and hunting. The Olmecs apparently played a ceremonial game on a stone ball court, a ritual that would later be widely practiced throughout the region (see "The Maya" later in this chapter). The ball was made from the sap of a local rubber tree, thus providing the name *Olmec*: "people of the land of rubber."

Trade between the Olmecs and their neighbors was apparently quite extensive, and rubber was one of the products most desired by peoples in nearby regions. It was used not only for the manufacture of balls, but also for rubber bands and footwear, as the Olmec learned how to mix the raw latex (the sap of the rubber tree) with other ingredients to make it more supple.

Eventually, Olmec civilization began to decline, and it apparently collapsed around the fourth century B.C.E. During its heyday, however, it extended from Mexico City to El Salvador and perhaps to the shores of the Pacific Ocean.

The Zapotecs

Parallel developments were occurring at Monte Albán (MON-tee ahl-BAHN), on a hillside overlooking the modern city of Oaxaca (wah-HAH-kuh), in central Mexico. Around the middle of the first millennium B.C.E., the Zapotec (zah-puh-TEK) peoples created an extensive civilization that flourished for several hundred years in the highlands. Like the Olmec sites, Monte Albán contains a number of temples and pyramids, but they are located in much more awesome surroundings on a massive stone terrace atop a 1,200-foot-high mountain overlooking the Oaxaca valley. The majority of the population, estimated at about 20,000, dwelled on terraces cut into the sides of the mountain known to local residents as Danibaan, or "sacred mountain."

The government at Monte Albán was apparently theocratic, with an elite class of nobles and priests ruling over a population composed primarily of farmers and artisans. Like the Olmecs, the Zapotecs devised a written language that has not been deciphered. Zapotec society survived for several centuries following the collapse of the Olmecs, but Monte Albán was abandoned for unknown reasons in the late eighth century C.E.

Teotihuacán: America's First Metropolis

The first major metropolis in Mesoamerica was the city of Teotihuacán (tay-oh-tee-hwah-KAHN), capital of an early state about 30 miles northeast of Mexico City that arose around the third century B.C.E. and flourished for nearly a millennium until it collapsed under mysterious circumstances about 800 C.E. Along the main thoroughfare were temples and palaces, all dominated by the massive Pyramid of the Sun (see the Comparative Illustration "The Pyramid" on p. 161), under which archaeologists have discovered the remains of sacrificial victims, probably put to death during the dedication of the structure. In the vicinity are the remains of a large market where goods from distant regions as well as agricultural produce grown by farmers in the vicinity were exchanged. The products traded included cacao, rubber, feathers, and various types of vegetables and meat. Pulque (POOL-kay), a liquor extracted from the agave (uh-GAH-vee) plant, was used in religious ceremonies. An obsidian mine nearby may explain the location of the city; obsidian is a volcanic glass that was prized in Mesoamerica for use in tools, mirrors, and the blades of sacrificial knives.

Most of the city consisted of one-story stucco apartment compounds; some were as large as 35,000 square feet, sufficient to house more than a hundred people. Each apartment was divided into several rooms, and the compounds were covered by flat roofs made of wooden beams, poles, and stucco. The compounds were separated by wide streets laid out on a rectangular grid and were entered through narrow alleys.

Living in the fertile Valley of Mexico, an upland plateau surrounded by magnificent snowcapped mountains, the

RELIGION & PHILOSOPHY

The Pyramid. The building of monumental structures known as pyramids was characteristic of a number of civilizations that arose in antiquity. The pyramid symbolized the link between the world of human beings and the realm of deities and was often used to house the tomb of a deceased ruler. Shown here are two prominent examples. The upper photo shows the pyramids of Giza, Egypt, built in the third millennium B.C.E. and located near the modern city of Cairo. The second photo shows the Pyramid of the Sun at Teotihuacán, erected in central Mexico in the fifth century C.E. Similar structures of various sizes were built throughout the Western Hemisphere. The concept of the pyramid was also widely applied in parts of Asia. Scholars still debate the technical aspects of constructing such pyramids.

Q *How do the pyramids erected in the Western Hemisphere compare with similar structures in other parts of the world? What were their symbolic meanings to the builders?*

PATSTOCK/age fotostock/SuperStock

SuperStock

Claire L. Duiker

The Grand Plaza at Monte Albán. On the crest of a hilltop at Monte Albán, not far from the modern town of Oaxaca, the Zapotec peoples constructed this grand plaza around the seventh century C.E. In the vicinity are a palace, a ball court, three temple complexes, an observatory, and a majestic pyramid. As in other Mesoamerican cities such as Teotihuacán, Tikal, Palenque, and Chichén Itzá, these religious sites functioned as immense stage sets where the entire community could observe and participate in the dramas and sacrificial rituals of their cultures. The use of poetry, music, and dance to dramatize human fears and hopes was a universal phenomenon in all ancient societies.

inhabitants of Teotihuacán probably obtained the bulk of their wealth from agriculture. At that time, the valley floor was filled with swampy lakes containing the water runoff from the surrounding mountains. The combination of fertile soil and adequate water made the valley one of the richest farming areas in Mesoamerica.

Sometime during the eighth century C.E., perhaps because of drought or the overcultivation of the land, the wealth and power of the city began to decline, and eventually its ruling class departed, with the priests carrying stone images of local deities on their backs. The next two centuries were a time of troubles throughout the region as principalities fought over limited farmland. The problem was later compounded when peoples from surrounding areas, attracted by the rich farmlands, migrated into the Valley of Mexico and began to compete for territory with small city-states already established there. As the local population expanded, farmers began to engage in more intensive agriculture. They drained the lakes to build *chinampas* (chee-NAM-pahs), swampy islands crisscrossed by canals that provided water for their crops and easy transportation to local markets for their excess produce.

The Olmecs: Mother Culture or First Among Equals?

What were the relations among these early societies in Mesoamerica? Trade contacts were quite active, as the Olmecs exported rubber to their neighbors in exchange for salt and obsidian. During its heyday, Olmec influence extended throughout the region, leading some historians to surmise that it was a "mother culture," much as the Shang Dynasty was once thought to be in ancient China (see Chapter 3).

A seventh-century B.C.E. pyramid recently unearthed in the southern Mexican state of Chiapas (chee-AH-pahs) contained tomb objects that bore some resemblance to counterparts in the Olmec site of La Venta, but also displayed characteristics unique to the Zoque (ZOH-kay) culture that was prevalent in that region at the time. Some scholars point to such indigenous elements to suggest that perhaps the Olmec were merely first among equals. This issue has not yet been resolved.

The Maya

Far to the east of the Valley of Mexico, another major civilization had arisen in what is now the state of Guatemala and the Yucatán peninsula. This was the civilization of the Maya ("those who grow maize" in the Mayan language), which was older and just as sophisticated as the society at Teotihuacán.

ORIGINS It is not known when human beings first inhabited the Yucatán peninsula, but peoples contemporaneous with the Olmecs were already cultivating such crops as corn, yams, and manioc in the area during the first millennium B.C.E. As the population increased, an early civilization began to emerge along the Pacific coast directly to the south of the peninsula and in the highlands of modern Guatemala. Contacts were already established with the Olmecs to the west.

Since the area was a source for cacao trees and obsidian, the inhabitants soon developed relations with other early civilizations in the region. Cacao trees (whose name derives from the Mayan word *kakaw*) were the source of chocolate, which was drunk as a beverage by the upper classes, while cocoa beans, the fruit of the cacao tree, were used as currency in

Chocolate: Sacred Drink of Mesoamerica. The Maya recorded religious rites, as well as scenes of daily life, on polychrome clay vessels. Used in ritual ceremonies dedicated to their deities, these vessels contained a foamy chocolate beverage called *kakaw*, from which we derive the word *cacao*, the tree that produces the cocoa beans from which chocolate is made. After the Mayan civilization declined, chocolate (*xocoatl*, or "bitter water," in the Aztec language) continued to be used as a sacred beverage by other Mesoamerican peoples. In this image, a Mayan palace servant is apparently preparing cups of the heavenly nectar to use in a religious ceremony in one of the Mayan city-states.

Werner Forman Archive/The Bridgeman Art Library

markets throughout the region. A fermented beer was produced from the pulp of the fruit. The chocolate consumed in ancient Mesoamerican cultures was roasted and had a bitter taste. The flavor survives today in a classic sauce—mole (moh-LAY)—that includes unsweetened chocolate and chili peppers among its ingredients and is served with poultry and other meats. Chocolate did not develop its familiar sweet taste until the seventeenth century when cocoa beans were brought to Europe and sugar and milk were added.

As the population in the area increased, the inhabitants began to migrate into the central Yucatán peninsula and farther to the north. The overcrowding forced farmers in the lowland areas to shift from slash-and-burn cultivation to swamp agriculture of the type practiced in the lake region of the Valley of Mexico. By the middle of the first millennium C.E., the entire area was honeycombed with a patchwork of small city-states competing for land and resources. The largest urban centers such as Tikal (tee-KAHL) may have had 100,000 inhabitants at their height and displayed a level of technological and cultural achievement that was unsurpassed in the region. By the end of the third century C.E., Mayan civilization had begun to enter its classical phase.

POLITICAL STRUCTURES The power of Mayan rulers was impressive. One of the monarchs at Copán (koh-PAHN)—known to scholars as "18 Rabbit" from the hieroglyphs composing his name—ordered the construction of a grand palace requiring more than 30,000 person-days of labor. Around the ruler was a class of aristocrats whose wealth was probably based on the ownership of land farmed by their poorer relatives. Eventually, many of the nobles became priests or scribes at the royal court or adopted honored professions as sculptors or painters. As the society's wealth grew, so did the role of artisans and traders, who began to form a small middle class.

The majority of the population on the peninsula, however (estimated at roughly 3 million at the height of Mayan prosperity), were farmers. They lived on their *chinampa* plots or on terraced hills in the highlands. Houses were built of adobe and thatch and probably resembled the houses of the majority of the population in the area today. There was a fairly clear-cut division of labor along gender lines. The men were responsible for fighting and hunting, the women for home-making and the preparation of cornmeal, the staple food of much of the population.

Some noblewomen, however, seem to have played important roles in both political and religious life. In the seventh century C.E., for example, Pacal (pa-KAL) became king of Palenque (pah-LEN-kay), one of the most powerful of the Mayan city-states, through the royal line of his mother and grandmother, thereby breaking the patrilineal descent twice. His mother ruled Palenque for three years and was the power behind the throne for her son's first twenty-five years of rule. Pacal legitimized his kingship by transforming his mother into a divine representation of the "first mother" goddess.

MAYAN RELIGION Like some of the early religious beliefs in Asia and the Mediterranean, Mayan religion was polytheistic. Although the names were different, Mayan gods shared many of the characteristics of deities of nearby cultures. The supreme god was named Itzamna (eet-SAHM-nuh) ("Lizard House"). Viewed as the creator of all things, he was credited with bringing the knowledge of maize, cacao, medicine, and writing to the Mayan people.

A Mayan Bloodletting Ceremony. The Mayan elite drew blood at various ritual ceremonies. Here we see Lady Xok, the wife of a king of Yaxchilian, passing a rope pierced with thorns along her tongue in a bloodletting ritual. Above her, the king holds a flaming torch. This vivid scene from an eighth-century C.E. palace lintel demonstrates the excellence of Mayan stone sculpture as well as the sophisticated weaving techniques shown in the queen's elegant gown.

The Creation of the World: A Mayan View

RELIGION & PHILOSOPHY

POPUL VUH (PUH-PUL VOO**),** a sacred work of the ancient Maya, is an account of Mayan history and religious beliefs. No written version in the original Mayan script is extant, but shortly after the Spanish conquest, it was written down in Quiché (kee-CHAY) (the spoken language of the Maya), using the Latin script, apparently from memory. This version was later translated into Spanish. The following excerpt from the opening lines of Popul Vuh recounts the Mayan myth of the creation.

Popul Vuh: The Sacred Book of the Maya

This is the account of how all was in suspense, all calm, in silence; all motionless, still, and the expanse of the sky was empty.

This is the first account, the first narrative. There was neither man, nor animal, birds, fishes, crabs, trees, stones, caves, ravines, grasses, nor forests; there was only the sky.

The surface of the earth had not appeared. There was only the calm sea and the great expanse of the sky.

There was nothing brought together, nothing which could make a noise, nor anything which might move, or tremble, or could make noise in the sky.

There was nothing standing; only the calm water, the placid sea, alone and tranquil. Nothing existed.

There was only immobility and silence in the darkness, in the night. Only the Creator, the Maker, Tepeu, Gucumatz, the Forefathers, were in the water surrounded with light. They were hidden under green and blue feathers, and were therefore called Gucumatz. By nature they were great sages and great thinkers. In this manner the sky existed and also the Heart of Heaven, which is the name of God and thus He is called.

Then came the word. Tepeu and Gucumatz came together in the darkness, in the night, and Tepeu and Gucumatz talked together. They talked then, discussing and deliberating; they agreed, they united their words and their thoughts.

Then while they meditated, it became clear to them that when dawn would break, man must appear. Then they planned the creation, and the growth of the trees and the thickets and the birth of life and the creation of man. Thus it was arranged in the darkness and in the night by the Heart of Heaven who is called Huracan.

The first is called Caculha Huracan. The second is Chipi-Caculha. The third is Raxa-Caculha. And these three are the Heart of Heaven.

So it was that they made perfect the work, when they did it after thinking and meditating upon it.

 What similarities and differences do you see between this account of the beginning of the world and those of other ancient civilizations?

Source: From Popul-Vuh, *The Sacred Book of the Ancient Quiche Maya,* translated by Adrian Recinos. Copyright © 1950 by the University of Oklahoma Press.

Deities were ranked in order of importance and had human characteristics, as in ancient Greece and India. Some, like the jaguar god of night, were evil rather than good. Many of the nature deities may have been viewed as manifestations of one supreme godhead (see the box "The Creation of the World: A Mayan View" above). As at Teotihuacán, human sacrifice (normally by decapitation) was practiced to propitiate the heavenly forces.

Mayan cities were built around a ceremonial core dominated by a central pyramid surmounted by a shrine to the gods. Nearby were other temples, palaces, and a sacred ball court. Like many of their modern counterparts, Mayan cities suffered from urban sprawl, with separate suburbs for the poor and the middle class, and even strip malls stretched along transportation routes, where merchants hawked their wares to pedestrians passing by.

The ball court was a rectangular space surrounded by vertical walls with metal rings through which the contestants attempted to drive a hard rubber ball. Although the rules of the game are only imperfectly understood, it apparently had religious significance, and the vanquished players were sacrificed in ceremonies held after the close of the game. Most of the players were men, although there may have been some women's teams. Similar courts have been found at sites throughout Central and South America, with the earliest, located near Veracruz, dating back to around 1500 B.C.E.

MAYAN HIEROGLYPHS AND CALENDARS The Mayan writing system, developed during the mid-first millennium B.C.E., was based on hieroglyphs that remained undeciphered until scholars recognized that symbols appearing in many passages represented dates in the Mayan calendar (see the box "A Sample of Mayan Writing" on p. 165). This elaborate calendar, which measures time back to a particular date in August 3114 B.C.E., required a sophisticated understanding of astronomical events and mathematics to compile. Starting with these known symbols as a foundation, modern scholars have gradually deciphered the script. Like the scripts of the Sumerians and ancient Egyptians, the Mayan hieroglyphs were both ideographic and phonetic and were becoming more phonetic as time passed.

The responsibility for compiling official records in the Mayan city-states was given to a class of scribes, who wrote on deerskin or strips of tree bark. Unfortunately, virtually all such records have fallen victim to the ravages of a humid climate or were deliberately destroyed by Spanish missionaries after their arrival in the sixteenth century. As one Spanish bishop remarked at the time, "We found a large number of books in these characters and, as they contained nothing in which there were not to be seen superstition and lies of the devil, we burned them all, which they regretted to an amazing degree, and which caused them much affliction."[1]

A Sample of Mayan Writing

ART & IDEAS

THE MAYA WERE THE ONLY MESOAMERICAN PEOPLE to devise a complete written language. Although the origins of the Mayan writing system are unknown, many specialists believe that it may have emerged from scripts invented earlier by the neighboring Zapotecs or Olmecs and that the Maya learned of these experiments through contacts with these peoples in the first millennium B.C.E.

Like the Sumerian and Egyptian scripts, the Mayan system was composed of a mixture of ideographs and phonetic symbols, which were written in double columns to be read from left to right and top to bottom. The language was rudimentary in many ways. It had few adjectives or adverbs, and the numbering system used only three symbols: a shell for zero, a dot for one, and a bar for five.

During the classical era from 300 to 900 C.E., the Maya used the script to record dynastic statistics with deliberate precision, listing the date of the ruler's birth, his accession to power, and his marriage and death while highlighting victories in battle, the capture of prisoners, and ritual ceremonies. The symbols were carved on stone panels, stelae, and funerary urns or were painted with a brush on folding-screen books made of bark paper; only four of these books from the late period remain extant today. A sample of Mayan hieroglyphs is shown below.

 How do Mayan glyphs compare with the early forms of writing in Egypt, China, and Mesopotamia? Consider purpose, ease of writing, and potential for development into a purely phonetic system.

From *Atlas of Ancient America* by Michael Coe, Dean Snow and Elizabeth Benson/Courtesy of Michael Coe.

"birth of . . ."

"death of . . ."

"accession of . . ."

warfare

chucah "he captured . . ."

"captor of . . ."

bloodletting rite

As a result, almost the only surviving written records dating from the classical Mayan era are those that were carved in stone. One of the most important repositories of Mayan hieroglyphs is at Palenque, an archaeological site deep in the jungles in the neck of the Mexican peninsula, considerably to the west of the Yucatán (see Map 6.2). In a chamber located under the Temple of Inscriptions, archaeologists discovered a royal tomb and a massive limestone slab covered with hieroglyphs. By deciphering the message on the slab, archaeologists for the first time identified a historical figure in Mayan history. He was the ruler named Pacal, known from his glyph as "The Shield"; Pacal ordered the construction of the Temple of Inscriptions in the mid-seventh century, and it was his body that was buried in the tomb at the foot of the staircase leading down into the crypt.

As befits their intense interest in the passage of time, the Maya also had a sophisticated knowledge of astronomy and kept voluminous records of the movements of the heavenly bodies (according to some knowledgeable observers, Mayan pyramids, known as *huacas*, were situated to observe the stars). There

A Ball Court. Throughout Mesoamerica, a dangerous game was played on ball courts such as this one. A large ball of solid rubber was propelled from the hip at such tremendous speed that players had to wear extensive padding. The game had religious significance and was not just an athletic contest. The court is thought to have represented the cosmos and the ball the sun, and the losers were sacrificed to the gods in postgame ceremonies. The game is still played today in parts of Mexico (without the sacrifice, of course).

MAP 6.2 The Maya Heartland. During the classical era, Mayan civilization was centered on modern-day Guatemala and the lower Yucatán peninsula. After the ninth century, new centers of power like Chichén Itzá and Uxmal began to emerge farther north.

Q *What factors appear to have brought an end to classical Mayan civilization?*

Scholars once believed that the Maya were a peaceful people who rarely engaged in violence. Now, however, it is thought that rivalry among Mayan city-states was endemic and often involved bloody clashes. Scenes from paintings and rock carvings depict a society preoccupied with war and the seizure of captives for sacrifice. The conflict mentioned at the beginning of this chapter is but a recent example. During the seventh century C.E., two powerful city-states, Tikal and Calakmul (kah-lahk-MOOL), competed for dominance throughout the region, setting up puppet regimes and waging bloody wars that wavered back and forth for years but ultimately resulted in the total destruction of Calakmul at the end of the century.

THE MYSTERY OF MAYAN DECLINE Sometime in the eighth or ninth century, the classical Mayan civilization in the central Yucatán peninsula began to decline. At Copán, for example, it ended abruptly in 822 C.E., when work on various stone sculptures ordered by the ruler suddenly ceased. The end of Palenque soon followed, and the city of Tikal was abandoned by 870 C.E. Whether the decline was caused by overuse of the land, incessant warfare, internal revolt, or a natural disaster such as a volcanic eruption is a question that has puzzled archaeologists for decades. Recent evidence supports the theory that overcultivation of the land due to a growing population gradually reduced crop yields. A long drought, which lasted throughout most of the ninth and tenth centuries C.E., may have played a major role, although the city-state of Tikal, blessed with fertile soil and the presence of nearby Lake Petén, does not appear to have suffered from a lack of water. In general, though, as arable land and water became increasingly scarce, conflict among the various mini-states in the region may have intensified, accelerating the process leading to a final collapse.

Whatever the case, cities such as Tikal and Palenque were abandoned to the jungles. In their place, newer urban centers in the northern part of the peninsula, such as Uxmal (oosh-

were practical reasons for their concern. The arrival of the planet Venus in the evening sky, for example, was a traditional time to prepare for war. The Maya also devised the so-called Long Count, a system of calculating time based on a lunar calendar that called for the end of the current cycle of 5,200 years in the year 2012 of the Western solar-based Gregorian calendar.

Mayan Temple at Tikal. This eighth-century temple, peering over the treetops of a jungle at Tikal, represents the zenith of the engineering and artistry of the Mayan peoples. Erected to house the body of a ruler, such pyramidal tombs contained elaborate works of jade jewelry, polychrome ceramics, and intricate bone carvings depicting the ruler's life and various deities. This temple dominates a great plaza that is surrounded by a royal palace and various religious structures.

MAHL) and Chichén Itzá (chee-CHEN eet-SAH), continued to prosper, although the level of cultural achievement in this postclassical era did not match that of previous years. According to local history, this latter area was taken over by peoples known as the Toltecs (TOHL-teks), led by a man known as Kukulcan (koo-kul-KAHN), who migrated to the peninsula from Teotihuacán in central Mexico sometime in the tenth century. Some scholars believe this flight was associated with the legend of the departure from that city of Quetzalcoatl (KWET-sul-koh-AHT-ul), a deity in the form of a feathered serpent who promised that he would someday return to reclaim his homeland.

The Toltecs apparently controlled the upper peninsula from their capital at Chichén Itzá for several centuries, but this area was less fertile and more susceptible to drought than the earlier regions of Mayan settlement, and eventually they too declined. By the early sixteenth century, the area was divided into a number of small principalities, and the cities, including Uxmal and Chichén Itzá, had been abandoned.

The Aztecs

Among the groups moving into the Valley of Mexico after the fall of Teotihuacán were the Mexica (meh-SHEE-kuh). No one knows their origins, although folk legend held that their original homeland was an island in a lake called Aztlán. From that legendary homeland comes the name *Aztec*, by which they are known to the modern world. Sometime during the early twelfth century, the Aztecs left their original habitat and, carrying an image of their patron deity, Huitzilopochtli (WEET-see-loh-POHSHT-lee), began a lengthy migration that climaxed with their arrival in the Valley of Mexico sometime late in the century.

Less sophisticated than many of their neighbors, the Aztecs were at first forced to seek alliances with stronger city-states.

They were excellent warriors, however, and (like Sparta in ancient Greece and the state of Qin in Zhou dynasty China) theirs had become the dominant city-state in the lake region by the early fifteenth century. Establishing their capital at Tenochtitlán (teh-nahch-teet-LAHN), on an island in the middle of Lake Texcoco (tess-KOH-koh), they set out to bring the entire region under their domination (see Map 6.3).

For the remainder of the fifteenth century, the Aztecs consolidated their control over much of what is modern Mexico, from the Atlantic to the Pacific Ocean and as far south as the Guatemalan border. The new kingdom was not a centralized state but a collection of semiautonomous territories. To provide a unifying focus for the kingdom, the Aztecs promoted their patron god, Huitzilopochtli, as the guiding deity of the entire population, which now numbered several million.

POLITICS Like all great empires in ancient times, the Aztec state was authoritarian. Power was vested in the monarch, whose authority had both a divine and a secular character. The Aztec ruler claimed descent from the gods and served as an intermediary between the material and the metaphysical worlds. Unlike many of his counterparts in other ancient civilizations, however, the monarch did not obtain his position by a rigid law of succession. On the death of the ruler, his successor was selected from within the royal family by a small group of senior officials, who were also members of the family and were therefore eligible for the position. Once placed on the throne, the Aztec ruler was advised by a small council of lords, headed by a prime minister who served as the chief executive of the government, and a bureaucracy. Beyond the capital, the power of the central government was limited. Rulers of territories subject to the Aztecs were allowed considerable autonomy in return for paying tribute, in the form of goods or captives, to the central government. The most important government officials in the provinces were the tax collectors, who collected the tribute.

MAP 6.3 The Valley of Mexico Under Aztec Rule. The Aztecs were one of the most advanced peoples in pre-Columbian Central America. Their capital at Tenochtitlán—Tlaltelolco (tuh-lahl-teh-LOH-koh)—was located at the site of modern-day Mexico City. Of the five lakes shown here, only Lake Texcoco remains today.

Q *What forms of agriculture were practiced in the Valley of Mexico, and why?*

They used the threat of military action against those who failed to carry out their tribute obligations and therefore, understandably, were not popular with the taxpayers. According to Bernal Díaz, a Spaniard who recorded his impressions of Aztec society during a visit in the early sixteenth century:

> All these towns complained about Montezuma [Moctezuma, the Aztec ruler] and his tax collectors, speaking in private so

---

CHRONOLOGY Early Mesoamerica

Arrival of human beings in America	At least 15,000 years ago
Agriculture first practiced	c. 8000 B.C.E.
Rise of Olmec culture	1200 B.C.E.
End of Olmec era	Fourth century B.C.E.
Origins of Mayan civilization	First millennium C.E.
Teotihuacán civilization	c. 300 B.C.E.–800 C.E.
Classical era of Mayan culture	300–900 C.E.
Tikal abandoned	870 C.E.
Migration of Mexica to Valley of Mexico	Late 1100s
Kingdom of the Aztecs	1300s–1400s

---

that the Mexican ambassadors should not hear them, however. They said these officials robbed them of all they possessed, and that if their wives and daughters were pretty they would violate them in front of their fathers and husbands and carry them away. They also said that the Mexicans [that is, the representatives from the capital] made the men work like slaves, compelling them to carry pine trunks and stone and firewood and maize overland and in canoes, and to perform other tasks, such as planting maize fields, and that they took away the people's lands as well for the service of their idols.[2]

SOCIAL STRUCTURES Positions in the government bureaucracy were the exclusive privilege of the hereditary nobility, all of whom traced their lineage to the founding family of the Aztec clan. Male children in noble families were sent to temple schools, where they were exposed to a harsh regimen of manual labor, military training, and memorization of information about Aztec society and religion. On reaching adulthood, they would select a career in the military service, the government bureaucracy, or the priesthood. As a reward for their services, senior officials received large estates from the government, and they alone had the right to hire communal labor.

The remainder of the population consisted of commoners, indentured workers, and slaves. Most indentured workers were landless laborers who contracted to work on the nobles' estates, while slaves served in the households of the wealthy. Slavery was not an inherited status, and the children of slaves were considered free citizens. Commoners might sell themselves into slavery when in debt and then later purchase their freedom.

The vast majority of the population consisted of commoners. All commoners were members of large kinship groups called *calpullis* (kal-PUL-eez). Each *calpulli*, often consisting of as many as a thousand members, was headed by an elected chief, who ran its day-to-day affairs and served as an intermediary with the central government. Each *calpulli* was responsible for providing taxes (usually in the form of goods) and conscript labor to the state.

Each *calpulli* maintained its own temples and schools and administered the land held by the community. Farmland within the *calpulli* was held in common and could not be sold, although it could be passed down within the family. In the cities, each *calpulli* occupied a separate neighborhood, where its members often performed a particular function, such as metalworking, stonecutting, weaving, carpentry, or commerce. Apparently, a large proportion of the population engaged in some form of trade, at least in the densely populated Valley of Mexico, where an estimated half of the people lived in an urban environment. Many farmers, who cultivated their crops in *chinampas* as their predecessors had for centuries, brought their goods to the markets via the canals and sold them directly to retailers (see the box "Markets and Merchandise in Aztec Mexico" on p. 169).

The *calpulli* compounds themselves were divided into smaller family units. Individual families lived in small flat-roofed dwellings containing one or two rooms. Each house was separate from its neighbors and had direct access to the surrounding streets and canals. The houses of farmers living

© 2016 Cengage Learning

Markets and Merchandise in Aztec Mexico

INTERACTION & EXCHANGE

ONE OF OUR MOST VALUABLE DESCRIPTIONS of Aztec civilization is *The Conquest of New Spain*, written by Bernal Díaz, a Spaniard who visited Mexico in 1519. In the following passage, Díaz describes the great market at Tenochtitlán.

Bernal Díaz, *The Conquest of New Spain*

Let us begin with the dealers in gold, silver, and precious stones, feathers, cloaks, and embroidered goods, and male and female slaves who are also sold there. They bring as many slaves to be sold in that market as the Portuguese bring Negroes from Guinea. Some are brought there attached to long poles by means of collars round their necks to prevent them from escaping, but others are left loose. Next there were those who sold coarser cloth, and cotton goods and fabrics made of twisted thread, and there were chocolate merchants with their chocolate. In this way you could see every kind of merchandise to be found anywhere in New Spain, laid out in the same way as goods are laid out in my own district of Medina del Campo, a center for fairs, where each line of stalls has its own particular sort. So it was in this great market. There were those who sold sisal cloth and ropes and the sandals they wear on their feet, which are made from the same plant. All these were kept in one part of the market, in the place assigned to them, and in another part were skins of tigers and lions, otters, jackals, and deer, badgers, mountain cats, and other wild animals, some tanned and some untanned, and other classes of merchandise.

There were sellers of kidney beans and sage and other vegetables and herbs in another place, and in yet another they were selling fowls, and birds with great dewlaps, also rabbits, hares, deer, young ducks, little dogs, and other such creatures. Then there were the fruiterers; and the women who sold cooked food, flour and honey cake, and tripe, had their part of the market. Then came pottery of all kinds, from big water jars to little jugs, displayed in its own place, also honey, honey paste, and other sweets like nougat. Elsewhere they sold timber too, boards, cradles, beams, blocks, and benches, all in a quarter of their own.

Then there were the sellers of pitch pine for torches, and other things of that kind, and I must also mention, with all apologies, that they sold many canoe loads of human excrement, which they kept in the creeks near the market. This was for the manufacture of salt and the curing of skins, which they say cannot be done without it. I know that many gentlemen will laugh at this, but I assure them it is true. I may add that on all the roads they have shelters made of reeds or straw or grass so that they can retire when they wish to do so, and purge their bowels unseen by passersby, and also in order that their excrement shall not be lost.

Which of the items offered for sale in this account might also have been available in a market in Asia, Egypt, or Europe? What types of goods mentioned here appear to be unique to the Americas?

Source: From *The Conquest of New Spain* by Bernal Díaz. Copyright © 1975. (Harmondsworth: Penguin), pp. 232–233.

---

on the *chinampas* were set on raised dirt platforms built above the surrounding fields to prevent flooding.

Gender roles within the family were rigidly stratified. Male children were trained for war and were expected to serve in the army on reaching adulthood. Women were expected to work in the home, weave textiles, and raise children, although, like their brothers, they were permitted to enter the priesthood. According to Bernal Díaz, a female deity presided over the rites of marriage. As in most traditional societies, chastity and obedience were desirable female characteristics. Although women in Aztec society enjoyed more legal rights than women in some other traditional civilizations, they were still not equal to men. Women were permitted to own and inherit property and to enter into contracts. Marriage was usually monogamous, although noble families sometimes practiced **polygyny** (having more than one wife at a time). Wedding partners were normally selected from within the lineage group but not the immediate family. As in most societies at the time, parents usually selected their child's spouse, often for purposes of political or social advancement.

Classes in Aztec society were rigidly stratified. Commoners were not permitted to enter the nobility, although some occasionally rose to senior positions in the army or the priesthood

as the result of exemplary service. As in medieval Europe, such occupations often provided a route of upward mobility for ambitious commoners. A woman of noble standing would sometimes marry a commoner because the children of such a union would inherit her higher status, and she could expect to be treated better by her husband's family, who would be proud of the marriage relationship.

LAND OF THE FEATHERED SERPENT: AZTEC RELIGION AND CULTURE The Aztecs, like their contemporaries throughout Mesoamerica, lived in an environment populated by a multitude of gods. Scholars have identified more than a hundred deities in the Aztec pantheon; some of them were nature spirits, like the rain god, Tlaloc (tuh-lah-LOHK), and some were patron deities, like the symbol of the Aztecs themselves, Huitzilopochtli. A supreme deity, called Ometeotl (oh-met-tee-AH-tul), represented the all-powerful and omnipresent forces of the heavens, but he was rather remote, and other gods, notably the feathered serpent Quetzalcoatl, had a more direct impact on the lives of the people. Representing the forces of creation, virtue, and learning and culture, Quetzalcoatl bears a distinct similarity to Shiva in Hindu belief.

According to Aztec tradition, this godlike being had left his homeland in the Valley of Mexico in the tenth century, promising to return in triumph (see "The Mystery of Mayan Decline" earlier in this chapter).

Aztec cosmology was based on a belief in the existence of two worlds, the material and the divine. The earth was the material world and took the form of a flat disk surrounded by water on all sides. The divine world, which consisted of both heaven and hell, was the abode of the gods. Human beings could aspire to a form of heavenly salvation but first had to pass through a transitional stage, somewhat like Christian purgatory, before reaching their final destination, where the soul was finally freed from the body. To prepare for the final day of judgment, as well as to help them engage in proper behavior through life, all citizens underwent religious training at temple schools during adolescence and took part in various rituals throughout their lives. The most devout were encouraged to study for the priesthood. Once accepted, they served at temples ranging from local branches at the *calpulli* level to the highest shrines in the ceremonial precinct at Tenochtitlán. In some respects, however, Aztec society may have been undergoing a process of secularization. By late Aztec times, athletic contests at the ball court had apparently lost some of their religious significance. Gambling was increasingly common, and wagering on the results of the matches was widespread. One province reportedly sent 16,000 rubber balls to the capital city of Tenochtitlán as its annual tribute to the royal court.

Aztec religion contained a distinct element of fatalism that was inherent in the creation myth, which described an unceasing struggle between the forces of good and evil throughout the universe. This struggle led to the creation and destruction of four worlds, or suns. The world was now living in the time of the fifth sun. But that world, too, was destined to end with the destruction of this earth and all that is within it:

> Even jade is shattered,
> Even gold is crushed,
> Even quetzal plumes are torn....
> One does not live forever on this earth:
> We endure only for an instant![3]

In an effort to postpone the day of reckoning, the Aztecs practiced human sacrifice. The Aztecs believed that by appeasing the sun god, Huitzilopochtli, with sacrifices, they could delay the final destruction of their world. Victims were prepared for the ceremony through elaborate rituals and then brought to the holy shrine, where their hearts were ripped out of their chests and presented to the gods as a holy offering. It was an honor to be chosen for sacrifice, and captives were often used as sacrificial victims, since they represented valor, the trait the Aztecs prized most (see the box "Aztec Religion Through Spanish Eyes" on p. 171).

ART AND CULTURE Like the art of the Olmecs, most Aztec architecture, art, and sculpture had religious significance. At the center of the capital city of Tenochtitlán was the sacred precinct, dominated by the massive pyramid dedicated to Huitzilopochtli and the rain god, Tlaloc. According to Bernal Díaz, at its base the pyramid was equal to the plots of six large European town houses and tapered from there to the top, which was surmounted by a platform containing shrines to the gods and an altar for performing human sacrifices. The entire pyramid was covered with brightly colored paintings and sculptures.

Although little Aztec painting survives, it was evidently of high quality. Díaz compared the best work with that of Michelangelo. Artisans worked with stone and with soft metals such as gold and silver, which they cast using the lost-wax technique. They did not have the knowledge for making implements in bronze or iron, however. Stoneworking consisted primarily of representations of the gods and bas-reliefs depicting religious ceremonies. Among the most famous is the massive disk called the Stone of the Fifth Sun, carved for use at the central pyramid at Tenochtitlán.

The Aztecs had devised a form of writing based on hieroglyphs that represented an object or a concept. The symbols had no phonetic significance and did not constitute a writing system as such but could give the sense of a message and were probably used by civilian or religious officials as notes or memorandums for their orations. Although many of the notes simply recorded dates in the complex calendar that had evolved since Olmec times, others provide insight into the daily lives of the Aztec peoples. A trained class of scribes carefully painted the notes on paper made from the inner bark of fig trees. Unfortunately, many of these notes were destroyed by the Spaniards as part of their effort to eradicate all aspects of Aztec religion and culture.

The Stone of the Fifth Sun. This basalt disk, which weighs 26 tons, recorded the Aztec view of the cosmos. It portrays the perpetual struggle between forces of good and evil in the universe; in the center is an intimidating image of the sun god clutching human hearts with his talons. Having previously traversed the creation and destruction of four worlds, the Aztecs believed they were living in the world of the fifth and final sun—hence this stone carving, which was found in the central pyramid at Tenochtitlán.

Werner Forman/Art Resource, NY

Aztec Religion Through Spanish Eyes

RELIGION & PHILOSOPHY

WHEN THE FIRST EUROPEAN EXPLORERS arrived in Mexico in the early sixteenth century, they reported their impressions of Aztec society in diaries and letters to their compatriots back home. The following passage from Father Diego Duran's *The Aztecs: The History of the Indies of New Spain* describes the ritual of human sacrifice as a central part of Aztec religion. The Aztecs believed that only the gift of human hearts would appease their god Huitzilopochtli and prevent him from bringing disaster to their civilization. Although some modern-day scholars doubt the accuracy of such reports, it is now widely accepted that human sacrifice was a common practice in many Amerindian societies, as it had once been in other parts of the world as well.

Diego Duran, *The Aztecs: The History of the Indies of New Spain*

When the day of the feast arrived, Moteczoma and Tlacaelel blackened their bodies with soot and applied it in such a way that it caught the light.... They placed crowns of fine feathers, adorned with gold and precious stones, upon their heads, and on each arm they wore a sheath of gold reaching from the elbow to the shoulder. On their feet were richly worked jaguar skin sandals, inlaid with gold and gems. They also were robed in splendid royal mantles.... Jeweled plugs were attached to holes in their noses, and both these lords carried flint knives in their hands.

The king and Tlacaelel now appeared before the assembly and went to stand upon the stone which was the likeness and image of the sun, one having ascended by one staircase and the other by another. The five priests of sacrifice followed them. They were to hold down the feet, hands and heads of the victims, and they were painted all over with red ocher, even their loincloths and tunics. Upon their heads they wore paper crowns surmounted by little shields which hung to the middle of their foreheads, also painted in ocher. On the top of their heads they wore long stiff feathers which had been tied to their hair and which stood straight up. On their feet were very common, worthless sandals....

The five priests entered and claimed the prisoner who stood first in the line at the skull rack. Each prisoner they took to the place where the king stood and, when they had forced him to stand upon the stone which was the figure and likeness of the sun, they threw him upon his back. One took him by the right arm, another by the left, one by his left foot, another by his right, while the fifth priest tied his neck with a cord and held him down so that he could not move.

The king lifted the knife on high and made a gash in his breast. Having opened it he extracted the heart and raised it high with his hand as an offering to the sun. When the heart had cooled he tossed it into the circular depression, taking some of the blood in his hand and sprinkling it in the direction of the sun. In this way the sacrificers killed four, one by one; then Tlacaelel came and killed another four in his turn. And so, four by four, the prisoners were slain, till every last man that had been brought from the Mixteca had perished.

 What other societies encountered in this book engaged in human sacrifices as an aspect of their religious practices?

Source: From Diego Duran, *The Aztecs: The History of the Indies of New Spain*, Doris Heyden and Fernando Horcasitas, trans. (New York: Orion Press, 1964), pp. 120–121.

Jade and Gold Funeral Masks. Early civilizations in the Americas, as elsewhere, often placed precious artifacts in the royal tombs of their deceased rulers. The jade and gold mined in Mesoamerica and the continent of South America were transformed into stunning burial masks, as seen here. The jade funeral mask of Lord Pacal (left), a seventh-century ruler of Palenque, was placed in his tomb in the hope that its spiritual energy would propel Pacal into the afterlife, thereby merging him with the divine in the Mayan cosmos. The hammered gold mask from the Chimor culture (right), successors to the Moche civilization in what is present-day Peru, is reminiscent of the famous death mask found at Mycenae, in central Greece (see Chapter 4).

The First Civilizations in South America

 FOCUS QUESTION: What role did the environment play in the evolution of societies in the Americas?

South America is a vast continent, characterized by extremes in climate and geography. The north is dominated by the mighty Amazon River, which flows through dense tropical rain forests carrying a larger flow of water than any other river system in the world (see Map 6.4). Farther to the south, the forests are replaced by prairies and steppes stretching westward to the Andes Mountains, which extend the entire length of the continent, from the Isthmus of Panama to the Strait of Magellan. Along the Pacific coast, on the western slopes of the mountains, are some of the driest desert regions in the world.

South America has been inhabited by human beings for more than 12,000 years. Wall paintings discovered at the so-called Cavern of the Painted Rock in the Amazon region suggest that Stone Age peoples were living in the area at least 11,000 years ago, and a site at Monte Verde, along the central coast of Chile, has been dated to 10,500 B.C.E. Early peoples lived by hunting, fishing, and food gathering, but there are indications that irrigated farming was being practiced on the western slopes of the Andes Mountains more than 5,000 years ago.

Caral

By the third millennium B.C.E., complex societies had begun to emerge in the coastal regions of modern-day Peru and Ecuador. Some settlements were located along the coast, but the remnants of farming communities watered by canals have also been found in the valleys of rivers flowing down from the Andes Mountains. Fish, reeds, and various other maritime products were traded to inland peoples for agricultural produce, wool, and salt.

The most vivid example of this process can be seen along the Pacific coast of modern-day Peru. By 3500 B.C.E.—more than a thousand years earlier than the earliest known cities in Mesoamerica—the first urban settlements appeared in the region. At Caral, a highly publicized site located 14 miles inland from the coast, the remnants of a 4,500-year-old city sit on the crest of a 60-foot-high plateau just above the fertile valley of the Supe River. Several pyramids similar to those built in Mesoamerica were erected at the site, along with plazas, sunken altars, residential areas, and structures that were evidently used for astronomical observation. Nearly twenty similar settlements are scattered over an area of 66 hectares on both sides of the Supe River as it makes it way westward to the sea.

The inhabitants of these ancient settlements raised squash, beans, and tomatoes in the river valley below, and provided such agricultural produce, as well as cotton and salt, to fishing communities along the nearby coast, where the cotton material was used to make fishnets. In return, they received maritime products and reeds for baskets. They were sophisticated farmers, as evidenced by the remnants of ancient irrigation canals found in the vicinity. Some maritime trade was apparently conducted along the Pacific coast, as evidenced by the presence of *Spondylus* shells from Ecuador (used for religious ceremonies) and various plants not found in the vicinity (see the Comparative Illustration "Aspero and Caral" on p. 173).

The exact nature of these early communities is not yet clear. Indeed, it is not known whether these early settlements were actual villages or merely ceremonial centers, although there is convincing evidence of the existence of distinct social classes, a ruling elite, specialized labor, and organized religious beliefs, as well as cultural activities such as music and crafts. There are even indications of the appearance of a primitive writing system (see "Inka Culture" later in this chapter).

Although the reasons for eventual decline are not yet clear, this culture apparently reached its height during the first millennium B.C.E. with the emergence of the Chavín style, named for a site near the modern city of Chavín de Huantar (chah-VEEN day HWAHN-tahr). The ceremonial precinct at the site contained an impressive stone temple

MAP 6.4 Early Peoples and Cultures of Central and South America. This map shows regions of early human settlements in Central and South America. Urban conglomerations appear in Mesoamerica (see inset) and along the western coast of South America.

 Why do you think urban centers appeared in these areas?

© Yvonne V. Duiker

© William J. Duiker

INTERACTION
& EXCHANGE

COMPARATIVE ILLUSTRATION

Aspero and Caral. Archaeologists today debate whether maritime or river valley communities were the most prevalent antecedents of modern urban centers of civilization. Along the Pacific coast of South America in what today is the state of Peru, the answer apparently was both. On a desolate plateau just adjacent to the fertile banks of the Supe River, the ceremonial center of Caral (right) began to emerge at least 5,000 years ago. A few miles to the west, peoples living along the coast established their own settlement, known as Aspero (left), based on the fruits of the sea. For centuries, the two settlements survived in a symbiotic relationship, providing each other with foodstuffs and articles of daily use necessary for their survival. Together they composed one of the oldest centers of civilization in South America, if not in the world at large.

 What specific kinds of goods were exchanged between these two communities during their heyday? Can you think of other civilizations where a similar relationship existed?

complete with interior galleries, a stone-block ceiling, and a system of underground canals that probably channeled water into the temple complex for ceremonial purposes. The structure was surrounded by stone figures depicting various deities and two pyramids. Evidence of metallurgy has also been found, with objects made of copper and gold. Another impressive technological achievement was the building in 300 B.C.E. of the first solar observatory in the Americas in the form of thirteen stone towers on a hillside north of Lima, Peru.

Moche

Chavín society had broken down by 200 B.C.E., but early in the first millennium C.E., another advanced civilization appeared in northern Peru, in the valley of the Moche River, which flows from the foothills of the Andes into the Pacific Ocean. It occupied an area of more than 2,500 square miles, and its capital city, large enough to contain more than 10,000 people, was dominated by two massive adobe pyramids nearly 100 feet high. The larger one, known today as the Pyramid of the Sun, covered a total of 15 acres. The other, built on the side of a mountain and known as the Pyramid of the

A Mind-Changing Experience. For thousands of years, peoples living in the Andes Mountains have chewed the leaf of the coca plant to relieve hunger, restore energy, and cure bodily ailments. At ceremonies held in local temples throughout the region, shamans often engaged in this practice to communicate with the spirits or with the ancestors of their constituents. This terra-cotta object, dating from the first millennium C.E. and unearthed in present-day Ecuador, shows a user entering a trance and having an "out-of-body" experience, as his alter ego emerges full-blown from the top of his head. The concentrated paste of the coca plant is used today in the manufacture of cocaine.

William J. Duiker

Moon, was adorned with painted murals depicting battles, ritual sacrifices, and various local deities.

Artifacts found at Moche (moh-CHAY), especially the metalwork and stone and ceramic figures, exhibit a high quality of artisanship. They were imitated at river valley sites throughout the surrounding area, which suggests that the influence of the Moche rulers may have extended as far as 400 miles along the coast. The artifacts also indicate that the people at Moche, like those in Central America, were preoccupied with warfare. Paintings and pottery as well as other artifacts in stone, metal, and ceramics frequently portray warriors, prisoners, and sacrificial victims. The Moche were also fascinated by the heavens, and much of their art consisted of celestial symbols and astronomical constellations.

ENVIRONMENTAL PROBLEMS The Moche River valley is extremely arid, normally receiving less than an inch of rain annually. The peoples in the area compensated by building a sophisticated irrigation system to carry water from the river to the parched fields. At its zenith, Moche culture was spectacular. By the eighth century C.E., however, the civilization was in a state of collapse, the irrigation canals had been abandoned, and the remaining population had left the area and moved farther inland or suffered from severe malnutrition.

What had happened to bring Moche culture to this untimely end? Archaeologists speculate that environmental

CHRONOLOGY Early South America	
Monte Verde	10,500 B.C.E.
First organized societies in the Andes	c. 3500 B.C.E.
Agriculture first widely practiced	c. 3200 B.C.E.
Founding of Caral	c. 2500 B.C.E.
Chavín style	First millennium B.C.E.
Moche civilization	c. 150–800 C.E.
Wari culture	c. 500–1000 C.E.
Civilization of Chimor	c. 1100–1450
Inka takeover in central Andes	1400s

disruptions, perhaps brought on by changes in the temperature of the Pacific Ocean known as **El Niño**, led to alternating periods of drought and flooding of coastal regions, which caused the irrigated fields to silt up (see the Comparative Essay "History and the Environment" on p. 175). The warm water created by El Niño conditions also killed local marine life, severely damaging the local fishing industry.

WARI AND CHIMOR A few hundred miles to the south of Moche, a people known as the Wari (WAH-ree) culture began to expand from their former home in the Andes

Nazca Lines. The so-called Nazca Lines, a series of large geometric shapes etched on the parched soil of hillsides south of modern-day Lima, Peru, are one of the most enduring mysteries in the archaeology of Latin America. The purpose of these patterns (formally known as geoglyphs) has inspired widespread debate, with some observers even suggesting that they were drawn by aliens from outer space. Most scholars today, however, believe that they represent pathways worn in the soil by the Nazca peoples (contemporaries of the Moche culture in the first millennium C.E.) as they performed their religious rituals. Some of the geoglyphs, as shown here, take the shape of fantastic birds and animals.

History and the Environment

EARTH & ENVIRONMENT

In *The Decline and Fall of the Roman Empire,* published in 1788, the British historian Edward Gibbon raised a question that has fascinated historians ever since: What brought about the collapse of that once powerful civilization that dominated the Mediterranean region for more than five centuries? Traditional explanations have centered on political or cultural factors, such as imperial overreach, moral decay, military weakness, or the impact of invasions. Recently, however, some historians have suggested that environmental problems, such as poisoning due to the use of lead water pipes and cups, the spread of malaria, or a lengthy drought in wheat-growing regions in North Africa, might have at least contributed to Rome's collapse.

The current interest in the impact of the environment on the Roman Empire reflects a growing awareness among historians that environmental conditions may have been a key factor in the fate of several of the great societies in the ancient world. Climatic changes or natural disasters almost certainly led to the decline and collapse of Harappan civilization in the Indus River valley. In the Americas, massive flooding brought about by the El Niño effect (environmental conditions triggered by changes in water temperature in the Pacific Ocean) appears to be one possible cause for the collapse of the Moche civilization in what is today Peru, while drought and overcultivation of the land are often cited as reasons for the decline of the Maya in Mesoamerica.

Climatic changes continued to affect the fate of nations and peoples in later eras as well. Drought conditions and overuse of the land may have led to the gradual decline of Mesopotamia as a focal point of advanced civilization in the Middle East, while soil erosion and colder conditions doomed an early attempt by the Vikings to establish a foothold in Greenland and North America.

Sometimes the problems were self-inflicted, as on Easter Island, a remote outpost in the Pacific Ocean, where Polynesian settlers migrating from the west about 900 C.E. may have denuded the landscape that by the fifteenth century, what had been a reasonably stable and peaceful society had descended into civil war and cannibalism.

Climatic changes, of course, have not always been detrimental to the health and prosperity of human beings. A warming trend that took place at the end of the last ice age eventually made much of the world more habitable for farming peoples about ten thousand years ago. The effects of El Niño may be beneficial to people living in some areas and disastrous in others. But human misuse of land and water resources is always dangerous to settled societies, especially those living in fragile environments.

 Many ancient civilizations throughout the world were weakened or destroyed by changes taking place in the environment. What are some examples in the pre-Columbian Americas?

© William J. Duiker

The Royal Palace at Chan Chan. Chan Chan was the capital of the state of Chimor, which flourished along the coast of Peru at the end of the first millennium C.E. The kingdom eventually declined under the impact of heavy rains and floods that accompanied a period of El Niño conditions. The palace has been restored, but now its sun-dried bricks must be protected from occasional bouts of heavy rainfall.

foothills and established communities along the coast in the vicinity of modern Lima, Peru. As the state of Moche declined, the Wari gradually spread northward in the eighth century and began to occupy many of the urban sites in the Moche valley. According to some scholars, they may even have made use of the Moche's sacred buildings and appropriated their religious symbolism. In the process, the Wari created the most extensive land empire yet seen in South America. In the end, however, they too succumbed to the challenge posed by unstable environmental conditions.

Around 1100, a new power, the kingdom of Chimor (chee-MAWR), with its capital at Chan Chan (CHAHN CHAHN), at the mouth of the Moche River, emerged in the area. Built almost entirely of adobe, Chan Chan housed an estimated 30,000 residents in an area of more than 12 square miles that included a number of palace compounds surrounded by walls nearly 30 feet high. One compound contained an intricate labyrinth that wound its way progressively inward until it ended in a central chamber, probably occupied by the ruler. Like the Moche before them, the people of Chimor—the Chimú (chee-MOO)—relied on irrigation to funnel the water from the river into their fields. An elaborate system of canals brought the water through hundreds of miles of hilly terrain to the fields near the coast. Nevertheless, by the fifteenth century, Chimor, too, had disappeared, a victim of floods and a series of earthquakes that destroyed the intricate irrigation system that had been the basis of its survival.

These early civilizations in the Andes were by no means isolated from other societies in the region. As early as 2000 B.C.E., local peoples had been venturing into the Pacific Ocean on wind-powered rafts constructed of balsa wood. By the late first millennium C.E., seafarers from the coast of Ecuador had established a vast trading network that extended southward to central Peru and as far north as western Mexico, more than 2,000 miles away. Items transported included jewelry, beads, and metal goods. In all likelihood, technological exchanges were an important by-product of the relationship.

Transportation by land, however, was more difficult. Although roads were constructed to facilitate communication between communities, the forbidding terrain in the mountains was a serious obstacle, and the only draft animal on the entire continent was the llama, which is considerably less hardy than the cattle, horses, and water buffalo used in much of Asia. Such problems undoubtedly hampered the development of regular contacts with distant societies in the Americas, as well as the exchange of goods and ideas that had lubricated the rise of civilizations from China to the Mediterranean Sea.

The Inka

The Chimor kingdom was eventually succeeded in the late fifteenth century by an invading force from the mountains far to the south. In the late fourteenth century, the Inka were a small community in the area of Cuzco (KOOS-koh),

Gianni Dagli Orti/The Art Archive at Art Resource, NY

Paracas Royal Mummy. The ancient residents of coastal Chile developed complex methods for mummifying their dead more than four thousand years ago, and this practice continued up through Inka times. In Peru, the Paracas (pah-RAH-kus) culture (200 B.C.E.–500 C.E.) bundled up its rulers in extensive layers of sumptuously embroidered textiles. The body was placed in the fetal position, adorned with articles of value such as a crown of feathers, animal skins, and gold and bone jewelry. The mummy was then interred in a chamber with other deceased members of the community. Food offerings of maize and peanuts accompanied the mummy for sustenance in the afterlife.

a city located at an altitude of 10,000 feet in the mountains of southern Peru. In the 1440s, however, under the leadership of their powerful ruler Pachakuti (pah-chah-KOO-tee) (sometimes called Pachacutec, or "he who transforms the world"), the Inka launched a campaign of conquest that eventually brought the entire region under their authority. Under Pachakuti and his immediate successors, Topa Inka (TOH-puh INK-uh) and Huayna Inka (WY-nuh INK-uh) (the word *Inka* means "ruler"), the boundaries of the empire were extended as far as Ecuador, central Chile, and the edge of the Amazon basin.

THE FOUR QUARTERS: INKA POLITICS AND SOCIETY

Pachakuti created a highly centralized state (see Map 6.5). With a stunning concern for mathematical precision, he divided his empire, called Tahuantinsuyu (tuh-HWAHN-tin-SOO-yoo), or "the world of the four quarters," into provinces and districts. Each province contained about ten thousand residents (at least in theory) and was ruled by a governor related to the royal family. Excess inhabitants were transferred to other locations.

© 2016 Cengage Learning

MAP 6.5 The Inka Empire About 1500 C.E. The Inka were the last civilization to flourish in South America before the arrival of the Spanish. The impressive system of roads constructed to facilitate communication shows the extent of Inka control throughout the Andes Mountains.

Q *In what modern countries was the Inka state located?*

The capital of Cuzco was divided into four quarters, or residential areas, and the social status and economic functions of the residents of each quarter were rigidly defined.

The state was built on forced labor. Often entire communities of workers were moved from one part of the country to another to open virgin lands or engage in massive construction projects. Under Pachakuti, Cuzco was transformed from a city of mud and thatch into an imposing metropolis of stone. The walls, built of close-fitting stones without the use of mortar, were a wonder to early European visitors. The most impressive structure in the city was a temple dedicated to the sun. According to a Spanish observer, "All four walls of the temple were covered from top to bottom with plates and slabs of gold."[4] Equally impressive are the ruins of the abandoned city of Machu Picchu (MAH-choo PEE-choo), built on a lofty hilltop far above the Urubamba River.

Another major construction project was a system of 24,800 miles of highways and roads that extended from the border of modern Colombia to a point south of modern Santiago, Chile. Two major roadways extended in a north-south direction, one through the Andes Mountains and the other along the coast, with connecting routes between them. Rest houses and storage depots were placed along the roads. Suspension bridges made of braided fiber and fastened to stone abutments on opposite banks were built over ravines and waterways. Use of the highways was restricted to official and military purposes. Trained runners carried messages rapidly from one way station to another, enabling information to travel up to 140 miles in a single day.

In rural areas, the population lived mainly by farming. In the mountains, the most common form was terraced agriculture, watered by irrigation systems that carried precise amounts of water into the fields, which were planted with maize, potatoes, and other crops. The plots were tilled by collective labor regulated by the state. Like other aspects of Inkan society, marriage was strictly regulated, and men and women were required to select a marriage partner from within the immediate tribal group. For women, there was one escape from a life of domestic servitude: fortunate maidens were selected to serve as "chosen virgins" in temples throughout the country (see the box "Virgins with Red Cheeks" on p. 178). Noblewomen were eligible to compete for service in the Temple of the Sun at Cuzco, while commoners might hope to serve in temples in the provincial capitals. Punishment for breaking the vow of chastity was harsh, and few evidently took the risk.

INKA CULTURE Like many other civilizations in pre-Columbian Latin America, the Inka state was built on war. Soldiers for the 200,000-man Inka army, the largest and best armed in the region, were raised by universal male conscription. Military units were moved rapidly along the highway system and were bivouacked in the rest houses located along the roadside. Because the Inka had no wheeled vehicles, supplies were carried on the backs of llamas. Once an area was placed under Inka authority, the local inhabitants were instructed in the Quechua (KEH-chuh-wuh) language, which became the lingua franca of the state, and were introduced to the state religion. The Inka had no writing system but kept records using a system of knotted strings called *quipu* (KEE-poo), maintained by professionally trained officials, that were able to record all data of a numerical nature. What could not be recorded in such a manner was committed to memory and then recited when needed. The practice was apparently not invented by the Inka. Fragments of *quipu* have been found at Caral and dated at approximately five thousand years ago. Nor apparently was the experiment limited to the Americas. A passage in the Chinese classic *The Way of the Tao* declares, "Let the people revert to communication by knotted cords."

As in the case of the Aztecs and the Maya, the lack of a fully developed writing system did not prevent the Inka from realizing a high level of cultural achievement. Most of what survives was recorded by the Spanish and consists of entertainment for the elites. The Inka had a highly developed tradition of court theater, including both tragic and comic works. There was also some poetry, composed in blank verse and often accompanied by music played on reed instruments.

Virgins with Red Cheeks

FAMILY & SOCIETY

A LETTER FROM A PERUVIAN CHIEF to King Philip III of Spain written four hundred years ago gives us a firsthand account of the nature of traditional Inkan society. The purpose of author Huaman Poma was both to justify the history and culture of the Inka peoples and to record their sufferings under Spanish domination. In his letter, Poma describes Inkan daily life from birth to death in minute detail. He explains the different tasks assigned to men and women, beginning with their early education. Whereas boys were taught to watch the flocks and trap animals, girls were taught to dye, spin, and weave cloth and perform other domestic chores. Most interesting, perhaps, was the emphasis that the Inka placed on virginity, as is evident in the document presented here. The Inka's tradition of temple virgins is reminiscent of similar practices in ancient Rome, where young girls from noble families were chosen as priestesses to tend the sacred fire in the Temple of Vesta for thirty years. If an Inkan temple virgin lost her virginity, she was condemned to be buried alive in an underground chamber.

Huaman Poma, Letter to a King

During the time of the Incas certain women, who were called *accla* or "the chosen," were destined for lifelong virginity. Mostly they were confined in houses and they belonged to one of two main categories, namely sacred virgins and common virgins.

The so-called "virgins with red cheeks" entered upon their duties at the age of twenty and were dedicated to the service of the Sun, the Moon, and the Day-Star. In their whole life they were never allowed to speak to a man.

The virgins of the Inca's own shrine of Huanacauri were known for their beauty as well as their chastity. The other principal shrines had similar girls in attendance. At the less important shrines there were the older virgins who occupied themselves with spinning and weaving the silklike clothes worn by their idols. There was a still lower class of virgins, over forty years of age and no longer very beautiful, who performed unimportant religious duties and worked in the fields or as ordinary seamstresses.

Daughters of noble families who had grown into old maids were adept at making girdles, headbands, string bags, and similar articles in the intervals of their pious observances.

Girls who had musical talent were selected to sing or play the flute and drum at Court, weddings and other ceremonies, and all the innumerable festivals of the Inca year.

There was yet another class of *accla* or "chosen," only some of whom kept their virginity and others not. These were the Inca's beautiful attendants and concubines, who were drawn from noble families and lived in his palaces. They made clothing for him out of material finer than taffeta or silk. They also prepared a maize spirit of extraordinary richness, which was matured for an entire month, and they cooked delicious dishes for the Inca. They also lay with him, but never with any other man.

According to this selection, one of the chief duties of a woman in Inkan society was to spin and weave. In what other traditional societies was textile making a woman's work? Why do you think this was the case?

Source: From *Letter to a King* by Guaman Poma de Ayala. Translated and edited by Christopher Dilke. Published by E. P. Dutton, New York, 1978.

Mireille Vautier/Alamy

The *Quipu*. Not having a writing system, the Inka tallied the various data of their kingdom on strands of knotted yarn. Highly skilled and esteemed, official secretaries recorded population census data, crop and household inventories, government inspector reports, crime investigations, taxes, legal decisions and contracts, and all the official statistics of the realm by an intricate system of tying knots on a circular grouping of strings of yarn. The use of knotted yarn as a means of recording data was apparently not unique to the Inka.

Jim Zuckerman/Corbis

Machu Picchu. Situated in the Andes in modern Peru, Machu Picchu reflects the glory of Inka civilization. To farm such rugged terrain, the Inka constructed terraces and stone aqueducts. To span vast ravines, they built suspension bridges made of braided fiber and fastened them to stone abutments on the opposite banks. The most revered of the many temples and stone altars at Machu Picchu was the thronelike "hitching post of the sun," so called because of its close proximity to the sun god.

Stateless Societies in the Americas

Q **FOCUS QUESTION:** What were the main characteristics of stateless societies in the Americas, and how did they resemble and differ from the civilizations that arose there?

Beyond Central America and the high ridges of the Andes Mountains, on the Great Plains of North America, along the Amazon River in South America, and on the islands of the Caribbean Sea, other communities of Amerindians were also beginning to master the art of agriculture and to build organized societies.

Although human beings had occupied much of the continent of North America during the early phase of human settlement, the switch to farming as a means of survival did not occur until the third millennium B.C.E. at the earliest, and much later in most areas of the continent. Until that time, most Amerindian communities lived by hunting, fishing, or foraging. As the supply of large animals began to diminish, they turned to smaller game and to fishing and foraging for wild plants, fruits, and nuts.

The Eastern Woodlands

It was probably during the third millennium B.C.E. that peoples in the Eastern Woodlands (the land in eastern North America

from the Great Lakes to the Gulf of Mexico) began to cultivate indigenous plants for food in a systematic way. As wild game and food became scarce, some communities began to place more emphasis on cultivating crops. This shift first occurred in the Mississippi River valley from Ohio, Indiana, and Illinois down to the Gulf of Mexico. Among the most commonly cultivated crops were maize, squash, beans, and various grasses.

As the population in the area increased, people began to congregate in villages, and sedentary communities began to develop in the alluvial lowlands, where the soil could be cultivated for many years at a time because of the nutrients deposited by the river water.

Village councils were established to adjudicate disputes, and in a few cases, several villages banded together under the authority of a local chieftain. Urban centers began to appear, some of them inhabited by ten thousand people or more. At the same time, regional trade increased. The people of the **Hopewell culture** in Ohio ranged from the shores of Lake Superior to the Appalachian Mountains and the Gulf of Mexico in search of metals, shells, obsidian, and manufactured items to support their economic needs and religious beliefs.

Cahokia

At the site of Cahokia, near the modern city of East Saint Louis, Illinois, archaeologists found a burial mound more than 98 feet high with a base larger than that of the Great Pyramid in Egypt. A hundred smaller mounds were also found in the vicinity. The town itself, which covered almost 300 acres and was surrounded by a wooden stockade, was apparently the administrative capital of much of the surrounding territory until its decline in the 1200s. With a population of more than 20,000, it was reportedly the largest city in North America until Philadelphia surpassed that number in the early nineteenth century. Cahokia carried on extensive trade with other communities throughout the region, and there are some signs of regular contacts with the civilizations in Mesoamerica, such as the presence of ball courts in the Central American style. But wars were not uncommon, leading the Iroquois, who inhabited much of the modern states of Pennsylvania and New York as well as parts of southern Canada, to create a tribal alliance called the League of Iroquois.

The Ancient Pueblo Peoples

West of the Mississippi River basin, most Amerindian peoples lived by hunting or food gathering. During the first millennium C.E., knowledge of agriculture gradually spread up the rivers to the Great Plains, and farming was practiced as far west as southwestern Colorado, where an agricultural community was established in an area extending from northern New Mexico and Arizona to southwestern Colorado and parts of southern Utah. Although they apparently never discovered the wheel or used beasts of burden, these Ancient Pueblo peoples (formerly known by the Navajo name "Anasazi," or "alien ancient ones") created a system of roads that facilitated an extensive exchange of technology, products, and ideas throughout the region. By the ninth century, they had mastered the art of irrigation, which allowed them to expand their productive efforts to squash and beans, and had established an important urban center at Chaco Canyon, in southern New Mexico, where they built a walled city with dozens of three-story adobe communal houses, today called **pueblos**, with timbered roofs. Community religious functions were carried out in two large circular chambers called *kivas* (KEE-vuhs). Clothing was made from hides or cotton cloth. At its height, **Pueblo Bonito** contained several hundred compounds housing several thousand residents.

In the mid-twelfth century, the Ancient Pueblo peoples moved north to Mesa Verde, in southwestern Colorado. At first, they settled on top of the mesa, but eventually they expanded onto the cliffs of surrounding canyons.

Sometime during the late thirteenth century, however, Mesa Verde was also abandoned, and the inhabitants migrated southward. Their descendants, the Zuni and the Hopi, now occupy pueblos in central Arizona and New Mexico (thus leading them to adopt their new name). For years, archaeologists surmised that a severe drought was the cause of the migration, but new evidence has raised doubts that decreasing rainfall, by itself, was a sufficient explanation. An increase in internecine warfare, perhaps brought about by climatic changes, may also have played a role in the decision to relocate. Some archaeologists point to evidence that cannibalism was practiced at Pueblo Bonito and suggest that migrants from the south may have arrived in the area, provoking bitter rivalries within Ancient Pueblo society. In any event, with increasing aridity and the importation of the horse by the Spanish in the sixteenth century, hunting revived, and mounted nomads like the Apache and the Navajo came to dominate much of the Southwest. Prior to their relocation, however, the Pueblo Bonito peoples maintained commercial contacts

Cliff Palace at Mesa Verde. Mesa Verde is one of the best-developed sites of the Ancient Pueblo peoples in southwestern North America. At one time they were farmers who tilled the soil atop the mesas, but eventually they were forced to build their settlements in more protected locations. At Cliff Palace, shown here, adobe houses were hidden on the perpendicular face of the mesa. Access was achieved only by a perilous descent via indented finger- and toeholds on the rock face.

Jason Langley/AGE Fotostock

with their counterparts in Mexico and even as far south as the Pacific Coast of South America.

South America: The Arawak

East of the Andes Mountains in South America, other Amerindian societies were beginning to make the transition to agriculture. Perhaps the most prominent were the Arawak (AR-uh-wahk), a people living along the Orinoco River in modern Venezuela. Having begun to cultivate manioc (a tuber also known as *cassava* or *yuca*, the source of tapioca) along the banks of the river, they gradually migrated down to the coast and then proceeded to move eastward along the northern coast of the continent. Some occupied the islands of the Caribbean Sea. In their new island habitat, they lived by a mixture of fishing, hunting, and cultivating maize, beans, manioc, and squash, as well as other crops such as peanuts, peppers, and pineapples. As the population increased, a pattern of political organization above the village level appeared, along with recognizable social classes headed by a chieftain (*cacique*) whose authority included control over the economy. The Arawak practiced human sacrifice, and some urban centers contained ball courts, suggesting the possibility of contacts with Mesoamerica.

Eventually, new peoples from South America began to migrate into the islands of the Caribbean Sea. Known as Caribs, they tended to be more warlike than their predecessors and often drove the previous arrivals to seek refuge on islands farther to the north. A Carib community survives today on the island of Dominica, in the Lesser Antilles.

In most such societies, where clear-cut class stratifications had not as yet taken place, men and women were considered of equal status. Men were responsible for hunting, warfare, and dealing with outsiders, while women were accountable for the crops, the distribution of food, maintaining the household, and bearing and raising the children. Their roles were complementary and were often viewed as a divine division of labor. In such cases, women in the stateless societies of North America held positions of greater respect than their counterparts in the river valley civilizations of the ancient world.

Amazonia

Substantial human activity was also apparently taking place in the Amazon River valley. Scholars have been skeptical that advanced societies could take shape in the region because the soil was believed to lack adequate nutrients to support a large population. Recent archaeological evidence, however, suggests that in some areas where decaying organic matter produces a rich soil suitable for farming—such as the region near the modern river port of Santarem—large agricultural societies may once have existed. More information about this previously unknown culture must await further archaeological evidence.

CHAPTER SUMMARY

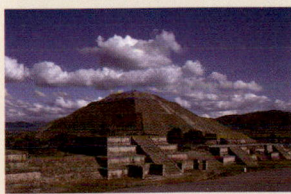

The first human beings did not arrive in the Americas until quite late in the prehistorical period. For the next several millennia, their descendants were forced to respond to the challenges of the environment in total isolation from other parts of the world. Nevertheless, around 5000 B.C.E., farming settlements began to appear in river valleys and upland areas in both Central and South America. Not long afterward—as measured in historical time—organized communities embarked on the long march toward creating advanced technological societies. Although the total number of people living in the Americas is a matter of debate, estimates range from 10 million to as many as 90 million people.

What is perhaps most striking about the developments in the Western Hemisphere is how closely they paralleled those of other civilizations. Irrigated agriculture, long-distance trade, urbanization, and the development of a writing system were all hallmarks of the emergence of advanced societies of the classical type.

Some of the parallels, of course, were less appealing. States in the Western Hemisphere were every bit as addicted to warfare as their counterparts elsewhere. The widespread use of human sacrifice is reminiscent of similar practices in other ancient societies. Not much is yet known about relations between men and women in the Americas, but it appears that gender roles were as sharply delineated there as in much of Asia and the Mediterranean world.

In some respects, the societies that emerged in the Americas were not as advanced technologically as their counterparts elsewhere. They were not familiar with the process of smelting iron, for example, and they had not yet invented wheeled vehicles. Their writing systems were still in their infancy. Several possible reasons have been advanced to explain this technological gap. Geographic isolation—not only from people of other continents but also, in some cases, from each other—deprived them of the diffusion of ideas that had enabled other societies to learn from their neighbors. Contacts among societies in the Americas were made much more difficult because of the topography and the diversity of the environment.

In some ways, too, they were not as blessed by nature. As the sociologist Jared Diamond has pointed out, the Americas did not possess many indigenous varieties of edible grasses that could encourage hunter-gatherers to take up farming. Nor were there abundant large mammals that could easily be domesticated for food and transport (horses had disappeared from the Western Hemisphere before the arrival of *Homo sapiens sapiens* at the end of the last ice age). It was not until the arrival of the Europeans that such familiar attributes of civilization became widely available for human use in the Americas.[5]

These disadvantages can help explain some of the problems that the early peoples of the Americas encountered in their efforts to master their environments. It is interesting to note that the spread of agriculture and increasing urbanization had already begun to produce a rising incidence of infectious diseases. It is also significant that in the Americas, as elsewhere, many of the first civilizations formed by the human species appear to have been brought to an end as much by environmental changes and disease as by war. In the next chapter, we shall return to Asia, where new civilizations were in the process of replacing the ancient empires.

CHAPTER TIMELINE

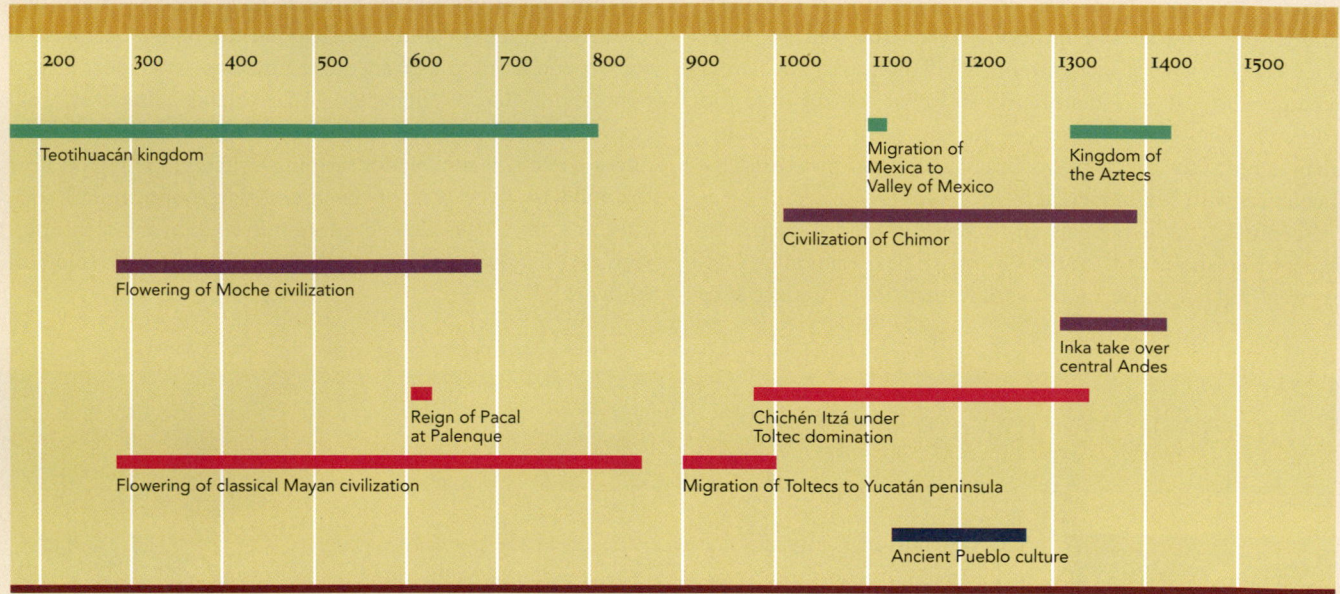

CHAPTER REVIEW

Upon Reflection

Q How did geographic and climatic factors affect the rise and fall of early societies in the Americas? Were similar factors at work among contemporary societies in other parts of the world?

Q What are some of the reasons advanced for the collapse of Mayan civilization in the late first millennium C.E.? Which do archaeologists find the most persuasive?

Q What common features linked the emerging societies in the Americas during the pre-Columbian period? Does it appear that technological and cultural achievements passed from one society to another as frequently as in other parts of the world?

Key Terms

Amerindians (p. 159)
chinampas (p. 162)
calpullis (p. 168)
polygyny (p. 169)
El Niño (p. 174)
quipu (p. 177)
Hopewell Culture (p. 179)
pueblos (p. 180)
Pueblo Bonito (p. 180)

Suggested Reading

EARLY CIVILIZATIONS OF THE AMERICAS For a profusely illustrated and informative overview of the early civilizations of the Americas, see **M. D. Coe** and **R. Koontz**, *Mexico: From the Olmecs to the Aztecs*, 6th ed. (New York, 2008). A fascinating recent account that covers the entire pre-Columbian era is **C. Mann,** *1491: New Revelations of the Americas Before Columbus* (New York, 2006). Also see **W. Polk,** *The Birth of America* (New York, 2006).

MAYAN CIVILIZATION On Mayan civilization, see **D. Webster,** *The Fall of the Ancient Maya: Solving the Mystery of the Maya Collapse* (London, 2002), and **J. Sabloff,** *The New Archeology and the Ancient Maya* (New York, 1990). For a provocative study of religious traditions in a comparative context, see **B. Fagan,** *From Black Land to Fifth Sun* (Reading, Mass., 1998).

ANCIENT SOUTH AMERICA A worthy account of developments in South America is **G. Bawden,** *The Moche* (Oxford, 1996). On the Inka, see **N. Thomson,** *A Sacred Landscape: The Search for Ancient Peru* (Woodstock, N.Y., 2006).

ART, CULTURE, AND THE ENVIRONMENT OF THE ANCIENT AMERICAS On the art and culture of the ancient Americas, see **M. E. Miller,** *Maya Art and Architecture* (London, 1999); **E. Pasztory,** *Pre-Columbian Art* (**Cambridge, 1998**); and **M. Léon-Portilla** and **E. Shorris,** *In the Language of Kings* (New York, 2001). Writing systems are discussed in **M. Coe,** *Breaking the Maya Code* (New York, 1992), and **G. Upton,** *Signs of the Inka Quipu* (Austin, Tex., 2003).

For a treatment of the role of the environment, see **B. Fagan,** *Floods, Famine, and Emperors: El Niño and the Fate of Civilizations* (New York, 1999), and **J. Diamond,** *Collapse: How Societies Choose to Fail or Succeed* (New York 2005).

Chapter Notes

1. Quoted in S. Morley and G. W. Brainerd, *The Ancient Maya* (Stanford, Calif., 1983), p. 513.
2. B. Díaz, *The Conquest of New Spain* (Harmondsworth, England, 1975), p. 210.
3. Quoted in M. D. Coe, D. Snow, and E. P. Benson, *Atlas of Ancient America* (New York, 1988), p. 149.
4. G. de la Vega (El Inca), *Royal Commentaries of the Incas and General History of Peru*, pt. 1, trans. H. V. Livermore (Austin, Tex., 1966), p. 180.
5. J. Diamond, *Guns, Germs, and Steel: The Fates of Human Societies* (New York, 1997), pp. 187–188.

MindTap is a fully online, highly personalized learning experience built upon Cengage Leaning content. MindTap combines student learning tools—readings, multimedia, activities, and assessments—into a singular Learning Path that guides students through their course.

Ferment in the Middle East: The Rise of Islam

Muhammad rises to heaven

CHAPTER OUTLINE AND FOCUS QUESTIONS

The Rise of Islam

Q What were the main tenets of Islam, and how does the religion compare with Judaism and Christianity?

The Arab Empire and Its Successors

Q Why did the Arabs undergo such a rapid expansion in the seventh and eighth centuries, and why were they so successful in creating an empire?

Islamic Civilization

Q What were the main features of Islamic society and culture during its era of early growth?

CRITICAL THINKING

Q In what ways did the arrival of Islam change or maintain the political, social, and cultural conditions that had existed in the area before Muhammad?

CONNECTIONS TO TODAY

Q Do the tactics and the motives that led to the crusades provide any lessons for the conduct of foreign policy by the United States and its allies toward the Middle East today? If so, what are those lessons?

IN THE YEAR 570, in the Arabian city of Mecca, there was born a child named Muhammad (moh-HAM-id *or* muh-HAHM-ud) whose life changed the course of world history. The son of a merchant, Muhammad grew to maturity in a time of transition. The Roman Empire, which had once been able to impose its hegemony over the Middle East, was only a distant memory. The region was now divided into many squabbling states, and the people adhered to many different faiths.

According to tradition, the young Muhammad became deeply concerned at the corrupt and decadent society of his day and took to wandering in the hills outside the city to meditate on the conditions of his time. On one of these occasions, he experienced visions that he was convinced had been inspired by Allah (AH-lah). Muslims believe that this message was conveyed to him by the angel Gabriel, who commanded Muhammad to preach the revelations that he would be given. Eventually, they would be transcribed into the Qur'an (kuh-RAN *or* kuh-RAHN)—the holy book of Islam—and provide inspiration to millions of people throughout the world. According to popular belief, Gabriel also took Muhammad, mounted on his faithful steed Buraq, on a mystical "night journey" to heaven, where Allah introduced him to paradise and hell so that on his return to earth he could instruct the faithful on their prospects in the next world (see the illustration above).

Within a few decades of Muhammad's death, the Middle East was united once again. The initial triumph may have been primarily political and military, based on the transformative power of a dynamic new religion that inspired thousands of devotees to extend their faith to neighboring regions. In any event, Islamic beliefs and culture exerted a powerful influence in all areas occupied by Arab armies. Initially, Arab beliefs and customs, as reflected through the prism of Muhammad's teachings, transformed the societies and cultures of the peoples living in the new empire. But eventually, the distinctive political and cultural forces that had long characterized the region began to reassert themselves. Factional struggles led to the decline and then the destruction of the empire.

Still, the Arab conquest left a powerful legacy that survived the decline of Arab political power. The ideological and emotional appeal of Islam remained strong throughout the Middle East and eventually extended into areas not occupied by Arab armies, such as the Indian subcontinent, Southeast Asia, and sub-Saharan Africa. ◄

The Rise of Islam

 FOCUS QUESTION: What were the main tenets of Islam, and how does the religion compare with Judaism and Christianity?

The Arabs were a Semitic-speaking people of southwestern Asia with a long history. They were mentioned in Greek sources of the fifth century B.C.E. and even earlier in the Old Testament. The Greek historian Herodotus had applied the name *Arab* to the entire peninsula, calling it Arabia. In 106 B.C.E., the Romans extended their authority to the Arabian peninsula, transforming it into a province of their growing empire.

During Roman times, the region was inhabited primarily by the **Bedouin** (BED-oo-un *or* BED-wuhn) Arabs, nomadic peoples who came originally from the northern part of the peninsula. Bedouin society was organized on a tribal basis. The ruling member of the tribe was called the *sheikh* (SHAYK *or* SHEEK) and was selected from one of the leading families by a council of elders called the *majlis* (MAHJ-liss). The *sheikh* ruled the tribe with the consent of the council. Each tribe was autonomous but felt a general sense of allegiance to the larger unity of all the clans in the region.

In early times, the Bedouins had supported themselves primarily by sheepherding or by raiding passing caravans, but after the domestication of the camel during the second millennium B.C.E., the Bedouins began to participate in the caravan trade themselves and became major carriers of goods between the Persian Gulf and the Mediterranean Sea.

The Arabs of pre-Islamic times were polytheistic, with a supreme god known as Allah presiding over a community of spirits. It was a communal faith, involving all members of the tribe, and had no priesthood. Spirits were believed to inhabit natural objects, such as trees, rivers, and mountains, while the supreme deity was symbolized by a sacred stone. Each tribe possessed its own stone, but by the time of Muhammad, a massive black meteorite, housed in a central shrine called the Ka'aba (KAH-buh) in the commercial city of Mecca, had come to possess especially sacred qualities.

In the fifth and sixth centuries C.E., the economic importance of the Arabian peninsula began to increase. As a result of the political disorder in Mesopotamia—a consequence of the constant wars between the Eastern Roman (Byzantine) and Sassanian Persian Empires—and in Egypt, the trade routes that ran directly across the peninsula or down the Red Sea became increasingly perilous, and a third route, which passed from the Mediterranean through Mecca to Yemen and then by ship across the Indian Ocean, became more popular. The communities in that part of the peninsula benefited from the change and took a larger share of the caravan trade between the Mediterranean and the countries on the other side of the Indian Ocean. As a consequence, relations between the Bedouins of the desert and the increasingly wealthy merchant class of the towns began to become strained.

The Ka'aba in Mecca. The Ka'aba, the shrine containing a black meteorite in the Arabian city of Mecca, is the most sacred site of the Islamic faith. Wherever Muslims pray, they are instructed to face Mecca; each thus becomes a spoke of the Ka'aba, the holy center of the wheel of Islam. All Muslims are encouraged to visit the Ka'aba, now dwarfed by skyscrapers erected to provide temporary housing for the faithful, at least once in their lifetime if they are able to do so. Called the *hajj*, this pilgrimage to Mecca represents the ultimate in spiritual fulfillment for every Muslim.

MAP 7.1 The Middle East in the Time of Muhammad. When Islam began to spread throughout the Middle East in the early seventh century, the dominant states in the region were the Roman Empire in the eastern Mediterranean and the Sassanian Empire in Persia.

 What were the major territorial divisions existing at the time and the key sites connected to the rise of Islam?

The Role of Muhammad

Into this world came Muhammad (also known as Mohammed), a man whose spiritual visions unified the Arab world (see Map 7.1) with a speed no one would have suspected possible. Unfortunately, there is almost no verifiable evidence relating to Muhammad's life. As a result, historians must rely on a limited number of sources, including the Qur'an and testimonials about his life by his followers (the *Hadith*). These sources were extensively revised after his death, however, and may have been shaped so as to favor the interests of his successors. Consequently, to many historians of the Middle East, the first years of Islam remain a matter of debate and conjecture.

Born in Mecca to a merchant family and orphaned at the age of six, Muhammad (570–632) grew up to become a caravan manager and eventually married a rich widow, Khadija (kah-DEE-juh), who was also his employer. A member of the local Hashemite (HASH-uh-myt) clan of the Quraishi (koo-RY-shee) tribe, he lived in Mecca as a merchant for several years but, according to tradition, was apparently troubled by the growing gap between the Bedouin values of honesty and generosity and the acquisitive behavior of the affluent commercial elites in the city. Deeply concerned, he began to visit the nearby hills to meditate in isolation. It was there that he encountered the angel Gabriel, who commanded him to preach the revelations that he would be given.

It is said that Muhammad was acquainted with Jewish and Christian beliefs and came to believe that while Allah had already revealed himself in part through Moses and Jesus—and thus through the Hebraic and Christian traditions—the final revelations were now being given to him. Out of his revelations, which were eventually dictated to scribes, came the Qur'an (meaning "recitation"; also spelled Koran), the holy scriptures of Islam (meaning "submission," implying submission to the will of Allah). The Qur'an contained the guidelines by which followers of Allah, known as Muslims (practitioners of Islam), were to live. Like the Christians and the Jews, Muslims (also known as Moslems) were a "people of the Book," believers in a faith based on scripture.

Muslims believe that after returning home, Muhammad set out to comply with Gabriel's command by preaching to the residents of Mecca about his revelations. At first, many were convinced that he was a madman or a charlatan. Others were likely concerned that his vigorous attacks on traditional beliefs and the corrupt society around him might severely shake the social and political order. After three years of proselytizing, he had only thirty followers.

Discouraged, perhaps, by the systematic persecution of his followers, which was allegedly undertaken with a brutality reminiscent of the cruelties suffered by early Christians, as well as the failure of the Meccans to accept his message, in 622

The Message (Muhammad: The Messenger of God) (1976)

Over the years, countless commercial films depicting the early years of Christianity have been produced in Hollywood. In contrast, cinematic portrayals of the birth of other world religions such as Buddhism, Hinduism, and Islam have been rare. In the case of Islam, the reluctance has been based in part on Muslims' traditional prohibition against depicting the face and figure of the Prophet Muhammad. Reactions to depictions of the Prophet in European media in recent years have demonstrated that this issue remains highly sensitive in Muslim communities worldwide.

In the 1970s, a Syrian-American filmmaker, Moustapha Akkad, himself a Muslim, was dismayed at the widespread ignorance of the tenets of Islam in Western countries. He therefore sought to produce a full-length feature film on the life of Muhammad for presentation in Europe and the United States. Failing to obtain financial help from U.S. sources, he sought aid abroad and finally won the support of the Libyan leader Muammar Qaddafi, and the film was released in both English and Arabic versions in 1976.

The film seeks to present an accurate and sympathetic account of the life of the Prophet from his spiritual awakening in 610 to his return to Mecca in 630. To assuage Muslim concerns, neither the figure nor the voice of Muhammad appears in the film. None of his wives, daughters, or sons-in-law appear onscreen. The narrative is carried on through the comments and actions of his friends and disciples, notably the Prophet's uncle Hamza, ably played by the American veteran actor Anthony Quinn.

The film, shot on location in Libya and Morocco, is a sometimes moving account of the emergence of Islam in

Hamza, Muhammad's uncle (left, played by Anthony Quinn), is shown defending Muhammad's followers in the early years of Islam.

John Bryson/Time Life Pictures/Getty Images

early-seventh-century Arabia. Although it does not dwell on the more esoteric aspects of Muslim beliefs, it stresses many of the humanistic elements of Islam, including respect for women and opposition to slavery, as well as the equality of all human beings in the eyes of God. Muhammad and his followers are shown as messengers of peace who are aroused to violence only in order to protect themselves from the acts of their enemies.

Though slow-moving in spots and somewhat lengthy in the manner of the genre, *The Message* (also known as *Muhammad: Messenger of God*) is beautifully filmed and contains a number of stirring battle scenes. Viewers come away with a fairly accurate and sympathetic portrait of the life of the Prophet and his message to the faithful.

Muhammad and some of his closest supporters (mostly from his own Hashemite clan) left the city and retreated north to the rival city of Yathrib, later renamed Medina (muh-DEE-nuh), or "city of the Prophet." That flight, known in history as the **Hegira** (huh-JY-ruh *or* HEH-juh-ruh) (*Hijrah*), marks the first date on the official calendar of Islam. At Medina, Muhammad failed in his original purpose—to convert the Jewish community in Medina to his beliefs. But he was successful in winning support from many residents of the city as well as from Bedouins in the surrounding countryside. From this mixture, he formed the first Muslim community—the *umma* (UM-mah). Returning to his birthplace at the head of a considerable military force, Muhammad conquered Mecca and converted the townspeople to the new faith. In 630, he made a symbolic visit to the Ka'aba, where he declared it a sacred shrine of Islam and ordered the

destruction of the idols of the traditional faith (see the Film & History feature "*The Message (Muhammad: The Messenger of God)* (1976)" above).

The Teachings of Muhammad

Like Christianity and Judaism, Islam is monotheistic. Allah is the all-powerful being who created the universe and everything in it. Islam is also concerned with salvation and offers the hope of an afterlife. Those who hope to achieve it must subject themselves to the will of Allah. Unlike Christianity, Islam makes no claim to the divinity of its founder. Muhammad, like Abraham, Moses, and other figures of the Old Testament, was a prophet, but he was also a man like other men. Because, according to the Qur'an, earlier prophets had corrupted his revelations, Allah sent his complete revelation through Muhammad.

"Draw Their Veils over Their Bosoms"

RELIGION & PHILOSOPHY

BEFORE THE ISLAMIC ERA, many upper-class women greeted men on the street, entertained their husband's friends at home, went on pilgrimages to Mecca, and even accompanied their husbands to battle. Such women were neither veiled nor secluded. Muhammad, however, specified that his own wives, who (according to the Qur'an) were "not like any other women," should be modestly attired and should be addressed by men from behind a curtain. Over the centuries, Muslim theologians, fearful that female sexuality could threaten the established order, interpreted Muhammad's references to "modest attire" and curtains to mean that all Muslim women should remain in segregated seclusion and conceal their bodies. In fact, one strict scholar in fourteenth-century Cairo went so far as to prescribe that, ideally, a woman should leave her home only three times in her life: on entering her husband's home after marriage, after the death of her parents, and after her own death.

In traditional Islamic societies, veiling and seclusion were more prevalent among urban women than among their rural counterparts. The latter, who worked in the fields and rarely saw people outside their extended family, were less restricted. In this excerpt from the Qur'an, women are instructed to "guard their modesty" and "draw veils over their bosoms." Nowhere in the Qur'an, however, does it stipulate that women should be sequestered or covered from head to toe.

Qur'an, Sura 24: "The Light"

*And say to the believing women
That they should lower*

*Their gaze and guard
Their modesty: that they
Should not display their
Beauty and ornaments except
What [must ordinarily] appear
Thereof: that they should
Draw their veils over
Their bosoms and not display
Their beauty except
To their husbands, their fathers,
Their husbands' fathers, their sons,
Their husbands' sons,
Their brothers or their brothers' sons,
Or their sisters' sons,
Or their women, or the slaves
Whom their right hands
Possess, or male servants
Free of physical needs,
Or small children who
Have no sense of the shame
Of sex; and that they
Should not strike their feet
In order to draw attention
To their hidden ornaments.*

 How does the role of women in Islam compare with what we have seen in other traditional societies, such as India, China, and the Americas?

Source: The Holy Quran, 24:32.

At the heart of Islam is the Qur'an, with its basic message that there is no God but Allah and Muhammad is his Prophet. Consisting of 114 *suras* (SUR-uhz) (chapters) drawn together by a committee established after Muhammad's death, the Qur'an is not only the sacred book of Islam but also an ethical guidebook and a code of law and political theory combined.

As it evolved, Islam developed a number of fundamental tenets. Of primary importance is the need to obey the will of Allah. This means following a basic ethical code that consists of what are popularly termed the **Five Pillars of Islam**: belief in Allah and Muhammad as his Prophet; standard prayer five times a day and public prayer on Friday at midday to worship Allah; observance of the holy month of **Ramadan** (RAH-muh-dan), including fasting from dawn to sunset; making a pilgrimage—known as the *hajj* (HAJ)—to Mecca at least once in one's lifetime, if possible (see the Film & History feature *"The Message"*); and giving alms, called *zakat* (zuh-KAHT), to the poor and unfortunate. The faithful who observe the law are guaranteed a place in an eternal paradise (a vision of a luxurious and cool

garden shared by some versions of Eastern Christianity) with the sensuous delights so obviously lacking in the Arabian desert.

Islam is not just a set of religious beliefs but a way of life as well. After the death of Muhammad, a panel of Muslim scholars, known as the **ulama** (OO-luh-mah or oo-LAH-muh), drew up a law code, called the **Shari'a** (shah-REE-uh), to provide believers with a set of prescriptions to regulate their daily lives. Much of the *Shari'a* was drawn from existing legal regulations or from the **Hadith** (hah-DEETH), a collection of the sayings of the Prophet that was used to supplement the revelations contained in the holy scriptures.

Believers are subject to strict behavioral requirements. In addition to the Five Pillars, Muslims are forbidden to gamble, eat pork, drink alcoholic beverages, or engage in dishonest behavior. Sexual mores are also strict. Contacts between unmarried men and women are discouraged, and ideally, marriages are arranged by the parents (see the box "Draw Their Veils over Their Bosoms" above). In accordance with Bedouin custom, polygyny is permitted, but Muhammad attempted to limit the practice by restricting males to no more than four wives.

The degree to which the traditional account of the exposition and inner meaning of the Qur'an can stand up to historical analysis is a matter of debate. As explained earlier, the circumstances surrounding the life of Muhammad and his role in founding the religion of Islam remain highly speculative, and many Muslims may be concerned that the consequences of rigorous examination might undercut key tenets of the Muslim faith. One problem is that the earliest known versions of the Qur'an available today do not contain the diacritical marks that modern Arabic uses to clarify meaning, so much of the sacred text is ambiguous and open to varying interpretations.

The Arab Empire and Its Successors

 Q FOCUS QUESTION: Why did the Arabs undergo such a rapid expansion in the seventh and eighth centuries, and why were they so successful in creating an empire?

The death of Muhammad presented his followers with a dilemma. Although Muhammad had not claimed divine qualities, Muslims saw no separation between political and religious authority. Submission to the will of Allah meant submission to his Prophet, Muhammad. According to the Qur'an, "Whoso obeyeth the messenger obeyeth Allah."[1] Muhammad's charismatic authority and political skills had been at the heart of his success. But Muslims have never agreed on whether he named a successor, and although he had several daughters, he left no sons. In the male-oriented society of his day, who would lead the community of the faithful?

Shortly after Muhammad's death, a number of his closest followers selected Abu Bakr (ah-boo BAHK-ur), a wealthy merchant from Medina who was Muhammad's father-in-law and one of his first supporters, as **caliph** (KAY-liff) (*khalifa*, literally "successor"). The caliph was the temporal leader of the Islamic community and was also considered, in general terms, to be a religious leader, or **imam** (ih-MAHM). Under Abu Bakr's prudent leadership, the movement succeeded in suppressing factional tendencies among some of the Bedouin tribes in the peninsula and began to direct its attention to wider fields. Muhammad had used the Arabic tribal custom of the *razzia* (RAZZ-ee-uh), or raid, in the struggle against his enemies. Now his successors turned to the same custom to expand the authority of the movement.

When historians of the Middle East today discuss the expansion of Islam after the death of Muhammad, the Arabic term *jihad* (jee-HAHD) is often used to describe the process. The word appears in the Qur'an on several occasions, and it appears to have had multiple meanings, much as the word *crusade* does in English. Sometimes *jihad* is used in the sense of "striving in the way of the Lord," as a means of exhorting believers to struggle against the evil within themselves. In other cases, however, it has been translated as "holy war," justifying hostile action against the enemies of Islam. In that sense, the word can be used to describe the expansion of the world of Islam into the realm of the unbelievers (see the box "The Spread of the Muslim Faith" on p. 190). Many Islamic terrorist movements of the present day clearly view *jihad* in the latter sense, an interpretation that many other Muslims vigorously reject. Because the word is so heavily laden with emotional connotations, it clearly should be used sparingly and with care.

Creation of an Empire

Once the Arabs had become unified under Muhammad's successor, they began directing against neighboring peoples the energy they had formerly directed against each other. The Byzantine and Sassanian Empires were the first to feel the strength of the newly united Arabs, now aroused to a peak of zeal by their common faith. In 636, the Muslims defeated the Byzantine army on the Yarmuk (yahr-MOOK) River, north of the Dead Sea. Four years later, they took possession of the Byzantine province of Syria. In 640, they conquered Cairo. To the east, the Arabs defeated a Persian force in 637 and then went on to conquer the entire empire of the Sassanids by 650. In the meantime, the rest of Egypt and other areas of North Africa were also brought under Arab authority (see Chapter 8).

What accounts for this rapid expansion of the Arabs after the rise of Islam in the early seventh century? Historians have proposed various explanations, ranging from a prolonged drought on the Arabian Peninsula to the desire of Islam's leaders to channel the energies of their new converts. Others have suggested that the Byzantine Empire had been weakened by a plague epidemic that had not affected the desert regions farther to the east. Still another hypothesis is that the expansion was deliberately planned by the ruling elites in Mecca to extend their trade routes and bring surplus-producing regions under their control. Whatever the case, Islam's ability to unify the Bedouin peoples certainly played a role. Although the Arab triumph was made substantially easier by the ongoing conflict between the Byzantine and Persian Empires, which had weakened both powers, the strength and mobility of the Bedouin armies with their much vaunted cavalry should not be overlooked. Led by a series of brilliant generals, the Arabs assembled a large, highly motivated army whose valor was enhanced by the belief that Muslim warriors who died in battle were guaranteed a place in paradise.

Once the army had prevailed, Arab civilian administration of the conquered areas was applied. Although early sources often portrayed the conquest in violent terms, many historians today portray the process as generally, but not universally, tolerant. Sometimes, due to a shortage of trained Arab administrators, government was left to local officials. Conversion to Islam was usually voluntary in accordance with the maxim in the Qur'an that "there shall be no compulsion in religion."[2] Those who chose not to convert, however, were required to submit to Muslim rule and to pay a head tax in return for exemption from military service, which was required of all Muslim males. Under such conditions, the local populations often regarded Arab rule as preferable to Byzantine rule or that of the Sassanid dynasty in Persia. Furthermore, the simple and direct character

The Spread of the Muslim Faith

RELIGION & PHILOSOPHY

LIKE CHRISTIANITY, Islam is not an exclusive religion, intended solely for members of a particular social or ethnic group, but is universalist in form, with all humans eligible to join the ranks of the believers. As a result, the sacred books of both religions—the Bible and the Qur'an—contain passages that encourage the spread of faith by whatever means are necessary and appropriate. In this selection from the Qur'an, Muslims are called upon to take part in the proselytizing effort, sometimes known in Arabic as *jihad*. While the vast majority of Muslims today believe that conversion to Islam should only take place by peaceful means, militants cite this passage from Chapter 47 as justification for their decision to make war on "unbelievers."

The Qur'an: Chapter 47, "Muhammad, Revealed at Medina"

Allah will bring to nothing the deeds of those who disbelieve and debar others from His path. As for the faithful who do good works and believe in what is revealed to Muhammad—which is the truth from their Lord—He will forgive them their sins and ennoble their state.

This, because the unbelievers follow falsehood, while the faithful follow the truth from their Lord. Thus Allah coins their sayings for mankind.

When you meet the unbelievers in the battlefield strike off their heads and, when you have laid them low, bind your captives firmly. Then grant them their freedom or take ransom from them, until War shall lay down her armour.

Thus shall you so. Had Allah willed, He could Himself have punished them; but He has ordained it thus that He might test you, the one by the other.

As for those who are slain in the cause of Allah, He will not allow their works to perish. He will vouchsafe them guidance and ennoble their state; He will admit them to the Paradise He has made known to them.

Believers, if you help Allah, Allah will help you and make you strong. But the unbelievers shall be consigned to perdition. He will bring their deeds to nothing. Because they opposed His revelations, He will frustrate their works.

Have they never journeyed through the land and seen what was the end of those who have gone before them? Allah destroyed them utterly. A similar fate awaits the unbelievers because Allah is the protector of the faithful; because the unbelievers have no protector.

Allah will admit those who embrace the true faith and do good works to gardens watered by running streams. The unbelievers take their fill of pleasure and eat as the beasts eat: but Hell shall be their home....

This is the Paradise which the righteous have been promised. There shall flow in it rivers of unpolluted water, and rivers of milk forever fresh; rivers of delectable wine and rivers of clearest honey. They shall eat therein of every fruit and receive forgiveness from their Lord. Is this like the lot of those who shall abide in Hell forever and drink scalding water which will tear their bowels? ...

Know that there is no god but Allah. Implore Him to forgive your sins and to forgive the true believers, men and women. Allah knows your busy haunts and resting places.

 According to this passage, what is the fate of those who adhere to the teachings of the Prophet Muhammad? How should unbelievers be treated?

Source: From *The Koran*, trans. N. J. Dawood (Penguin Classics, 1956, 5th rev. ed. 1990). Copyright © N. J. Dawood.

---

of the new religion and its egalitarian qualities (all people were viewed as equal in the eyes of Allah) were very likely attractive to peoples throughout the region.

The Rise of the Umayyads

The main challenge to the growing empire came from within. Some of Muhammad's followers had not agreed with the selection of Abu Bakr as the first caliph and promoted the candidacy of Ali, Muhammad's cousin and son-in-law, as an alternative. Ali's claim was ignored by other leaders, however, and after Abu Bakr's death, the office passed to Umar (oo-MAR), another of Muhammad's followers. In 656, Umar's successor, Uthman (ooth-MAHN), was assassinated, and Ali, who happened to be in Medina at the time, was finally selected for the position. But according to tradition, Ali's rivals were convinced that he had been implicated in the death of his predecessor,

and a factional struggle broke out within the Muslim leadership. In 661, Ali himself was assassinated, and Mu'awiya (moo-AH-wee-yah), the governor of Syria and one of Ali's chief rivals, replaced him in office. Mu'awiya thereupon made the caliphate (KAY-luh-fayt) hereditary in his own family, called the Umayyads (oo-MY-ads), who were a branch of the Quraishi clan. The new caliphate, with its capital at Damascus, remained in power for nearly a century.

The factional struggle within Islam did not bring an end to Arab expansion. At the beginning of the eighth century, new attacks were launched at both the western and the eastern ends of the Mediterranean world (see Map 7.2). Arab armies advanced across North Africa, and conquered the Berbers, a primarily pastoral people living along the Mediterranean coast and in the mountains in the interior. Muslim fleets attacked several islands in the eastern Mediterranean. Then, around 710, Arab forces, supplemented by Berber allies under their

MAP 7.2 **The Expansion of Islam.** This map traces the expansion of the Islamic faith from its origins in the Arabian peninsula. Muhammad's followers carried the religion as far west as Spain and southern France and eastward to India and Southeast Asia.

Q *In which of these areas is the Muslim faith still the dominant religion?*

commander, Tariq (tuh-REEK), crossed the Strait of Gibraltar and occupied southern Spain (thus the modern name of the Rock of Gibraltar—*Jebel Tariq*, or "Tariq's Mountain"). The Visigothic kingdom, already weakened by internecine warfare, quickly collapsed, and by 725, most of the Iberian Peninsula had become a Muslim state with its center in Andalusia (an-duh-LOO-zhuh). Seven years later, an Arab force, making a foray into southern France, was defeated by the army of Charles Martel between Tours (TOOR) and Poitiers (pwah-TYAY). For the first time, Arab horsemen had met their match, in a disciplined Frankish infantry. Some historians think that internal exhaustion would have forced the invaders to retreat even without their defeat at the hands of the Franks, the Germanic people who had established a kingdom in what is now France. In any event, the Battle of Tours (or Poitiers) would be the high-water mark of Arab expansion in Europe.

As Islamic power spread westward into the Mediterranean basin, the primary adversary for Arab forces was the Byzantine Empire. Because the Byzantines possessed a powerful fleet, many of the battles would inevitably take place at sea. Initially, the Arab ships would be at a substantial disadvantage, since the peoples of the peninsula—lacking protected harbors and sources of wood and iron for ships—had little experience at sea. They were quick to learn, however (see "The Wealth of Araby: Trade and Cities in the Middle East" later in this chapter), and were soon competing on an equal basis with their opponents. Before the end of the seventh century, Arab fleets were able to seize a number of islands in the Mediterranean. In 717, a Muslim force launched an attack on Constantinople with the hope of destroying the Byzantine Empire. But the Byzantines' use of Greek fire, a petroleum-based compound containing quicklime and sulfur, destroyed the Muslim fleet, thereby saving the empire and indirectly Christian Europe, since the fall of Constantinople would have opened the door to an Arab invasion of eastern Europe. The Byzantine Empire and Islam now established an uneasy frontier in southern Asia Minor.

Arab power also extended to the east, consolidating Islamic rule in Mesopotamia and Persia and northward into Central Asia. But factional disputes continued to plague the empire. Many Muslims of non-Arab extraction resented the favoritism toward Arabs shown by local administrators. In some cases, resentment led to revolt, as in Iraq, where Ali's second son, Hussein, disputed the legitimacy of the Umayyads and incited his supporters—to be known in the future as **Shi'ites** (SHEE-yts) (from the Arabic phrase *shi'at Ali*, "partisans of Ali")—to rise up against Umayyad rule in 680. Hussein's forces were defeated, and with the death of Hussein in the battle, a schism between Shi'ite and **Sunni** (SOON-nee) (usually translated "orthodox") Muslims had been created that continues to this day.

Umayyad rule created resentment, not only in Mesopotamia but also in North Africa, where Berber resistance continued, especially in the mountainous areas south of the coastal plains. According to critics, the Umayyads may have contributed to their own demise by their decadent behavior. One caliph allegedly swam in a pool of wine and then imbibed enough of the contents to lower the level significantly. Finally, in 750, a revolt led by Abu al-Abbas (ah-boo al-ah-BUSS), a descendant of Muhammad's uncle, led to the overthrow of the Umayyads and the establishment of the Abbasid (uh-BAH-sid *or* AB-uh-sid) dynasty (750–1258) in what is now Iraq.

The Abbasids

The Abbasid caliphs brought political, economic, and cultural change to the world of Islam. While seeking to implant their own version of religious orthodoxy, they tried to break down the distinctions between Arab and non-Arab Muslims. All Muslims were now allowed to hold both civil and military offices. This change helped open Islamic culture to the influences of the occupied civilizations. Some Arabs began to intermarry with the peoples they had conquered. In many parts of the Islamic world, notably North Africa and the eastern Mediterranean, most Muslim converts began to consider themselves Arabs. In 762, the Abbasids built a new capital city at Baghdad, on the Tigris River far to the east of the Umayyad capital at Damascus. The new capital was strategically positioned to take advantage of river traffic to the Persian Gulf and also lay astride the caravan route from the Mediterranean to Central Asia. The move eastward allowed Persian influence to come to the fore, encouraging a new cultural orientation. Under the Abbasids, judges, merchants, and government officials, rather than warriors, were regarded as the ideal citizens.

ABBASID RULE The new Abbasid caliphate experienced a period of splendid rule well into the ninth century. Best known of the caliphs of the time was Harun al-Rashid (hah-ROON al-rah-SHEED) (r. 786–809), or Harun "the Upright," whose reign is often described as the golden age of the Abbasid caliphate. His son al-Ma'mun (al-muh-MOON) (r. 813–833) was a patron of learning who founded an astronomical observatory and established a foundation for translating Classical Greek works (see "Philosophy and Science" later in this chapter). This was also a period of growing economic prosperity. The Arabs had conquered many of the richest provinces of the Roman Empire and now controlled the routes to the east (see Map 7.3). Baghdad became the center

MAP 7.3 The Abbasid Caliphate at the Height of Its Power. The Abbasids arose in the eighth century as the defenders of the Muslim faith and established their capital at Baghdad. With its prowess as a trading state, the caliphate was the most powerful and extensive state in the region for several centuries. The "Zaidi imams" indicated on the map were a group of dissident Shi'ites who established an independent kingdom on the southern tip of the Arabian peninsula.

Q *Which of the major urban centers shown on this map were under the influence of Islam?*

of an enormous commercial market that extended into Europe, Central Asia, and Africa, greatly adding to the wealth of the Islamic world and promoting an exchange of culture, ideas, and technology from one end of the known world to the other. Paper was introduced from China and eventually passed on to North Africa and Europe. Crops from India and Southeast Asia, including rice, sugar, sorghum, and cotton, moved toward the west, while glass, wine, and indigo dye were introduced into China.

Under the Abbasids, the caliphs became more regal. More kings than spiritual leaders, described by such august phrases as the "caliph of God," they ruled by autocratic means similar to those used by the kings and emperors in neighboring civilizations. A thirteenth-century Chinese author, who compiled a world geography based on accounts by Chinese travelers, left the following description of one of the later caliphs:

> The king wears a turban of silk brocade and foreign cotton stuff [buckram]. On each new moon and full moon he puts on an eight-sided flat-topped headdress of pure gold, set with the most precious jewels in the world. His robe is of silk brocade and is bound around him with a jade girdle. On his feet he wears golden shoes.... The king's throne is set with pearls and precious stones, and the steps of the throne are covered with pure gold.[3]

As the caliph took on more of the trappings of a hereditary autocrat, the bureaucracy assisting him in administering the expanding empire grew more complex as well. The caliph was advised by a council—called a *diwan* (di-WAHN)—headed by a prime minister, known as a **vizier** (veh-ZEER) (*wazir*). The caliph did not attend meetings of the *diwan* in the normal manner but sat behind a screen and then communicated his divine will to the vizier. Some historians have ascribed the change in the caliphate to Persian influence, which permeated the empire after the capital was moved to Baghdad. Persian influence was indeed strong (the mother of the caliph al-Ma'mun, for example, was a Persian), but more likely, the increase in pomp and circumstance was a natural consequence of the growing power and prosperity of the empire.

INSTABILITY AND DIVISION Nevertheless, an element of instability lurked beneath the surface. The lack of spiritual authority may have weakened the caliphate and given impetus to potential rivals, and disputes over the succession were common. At Harun's death, the rivalry between his two sons, Amin and al-Ma'mun, led to civil war and the destruction of Baghdad. As described by the tenth-century Muslim historian al-Mas'udi (al-muh-SOO-dee), "Mansions were destroyed, most remarkable monuments obliterated; prices soared.... Brother turned his sword against brother, son against father, as some fought for Amin, others for Ma'mun. Houses and palaces fueled the flames; property was put to the sack."[4]

Wealth contributed to financial corruption. By awarding important positions to court favorites, the Abbasid caliphs began to undermine the foundations of their own power and eventually became mere figureheads. Under Harun al-Rashid, members of his Hashemite clan received large pensions from the state treasury, and his wife Zubaida (zoo-BY-duh) reportedly spent huge sums while shopping on a pilgrimage to Mecca. One powerful family, the Barmakids, amassed vast wealth and power until Harun al-Rashid eliminated the entire clan in a fit of jealousy.

The life of luxury enjoyed by the caliph and other political and economic elites in Baghdad seemingly undermined the stern fiber of Arab society as well as the strict moral code of Islam. Strictures against sexual promiscuity were widely ignored, and caliphs were rumored to maintain thousands of concubines in their harems. Divorce was common, homosexuality was widely practiced, and alcohol was consumed in public despite Islamic law's prohibition against imbibing spirits.

The Great Mosque of Samarra. The ninth-century mosque of Samarra, located north of Baghdad in present-day Iraq, is the largest mosque in the Islamic world. Rising from the center of the city of Samarra, the capital of the Abbasids for over half a century and one of the largest cities of its time, the imposing tower shown here is 156 feet in height. Its circular ramp may have inspired artists in medieval Europe as they imagined the ancient cultures of Mesopotamia. As a twelfth-century Muslim adventurer noted in his account, *The Travels of Ibn Jubayr*, "Pleased is he who looks upon it." Although the mosque is now in ruins, its spiral tower still signals the presence of Islam to the faithful across the broad valley of the Tigris and Euphrates Rivers.

The process of disintegration was accelerated by changes that were taking place within the armed forces and the bureaucracy of the empire. Given the shortage of qualified Arabs for key positions in the army and the administration, the caliphate began to recruit officials from among the non-Arab peoples in the empire, such as Persians and Turks from Central Asia. These people gradually became a dominant force in the army and administration.

Environmental problems added to the regime's difficulties. The Tigris and Euphrates river system, lifeblood of Mesopotamia for three millennia, was beginning to silt up. Bureaucratic inertia now made things worse, as many of the country's canals became virtually unusable, leading to widespread food shortages.

The fragmentation of the Islamic empire accelerated in the tenth century. Morocco became independent, and in 973, a new Shi'ite dynasty under the Fatimids (FAT-uh-mids) was established in Egypt with its capital at Cairo. With increasing disarray in the empire, the Islamic world was held together only by the common commitment to the Arabic language and the Qur'an.

THE SELJUK TURKS In the eleventh century, the Abbasid caliphate faced yet another serious threat in the form of the Seljuk (SEL-jook) Turks. When the nomadic Xiongnu Empire fell apart early in the first millennium C.E. (see Chapter 3), Turkish-speaking people in the area gradually migrated westward into Xinjiang and Central Asia. Some of them converted to Islam in the process. Eventually, one group, known as the Seljuk Turks, began to serve as military mercenaries for the Abbasid caliphate, where they were known for their ability as mounted archers. Moving gradually into Persia and Armenia as the Abbasids weakened, the Seljuk Turks grew in number until by the eleventh century, they were able to occupy the eastern provinces of the Abbasid Empire. In 1055, a Turkish leader captured Baghdad and assumed command of the empire with the title of **sultan** (SUL-tun) ("holder of power"). While the Abbasid caliph remained the chief representative of Sunni religious authority, the real military and political power of the state was in the hands of the Seljuk Turks. The latter did not establish their headquarters in Baghdad, which now entered a period of decline. As the historian Khatib Baghdadi (kah-TEEB bag-DAD-ee) described:

> There is no city in the world equal to Baghdad in the abundance of its riches, the importance of its business, the number of its scholars and important people, the distinctions of its leaders and its common people, the extent of its palaces, inhabitants, streets, avenues, alleys, mosques, baths, docks and caravansaries, the purity of its air, the sweetness of its water, the freshness of its dew and its shade, the temperateness of its summer and winter, the healthfulness of its spring and fall, and its great swarming crowds. The buildings and the inhabitants were most numerous during the time of Harun al-Rashid, when the city and its surrounding areas were full of cooled rooms, thriving places, fertile pastures, rich watering-places for ships. Then the riots began, an uninterrupted series of misfortunes befell the inhabitants, its flourishing conditions came to ruin to such extent that, before our time and the century

preceding ours, it found itself, because of the perturbation and the decadence it was experiencing, in complete opposition to all capitals and in contradiction to all inhabited countries.[5]

Baghdad would revive, but it would no longer be the "Gift of God" of Harun al-Rashid.

By the last decades of the eleventh century, the Seljuks were exerting military pressure on Egypt and the Byzantine Empire. In 1071, when the Byzantines foolishly challenged the Turks, their army was routed at Manzikert (MANZ-ih-kurt), near Lake Van in eastern Turkey, and the victors took over much of the Anatolian peninsula (see Map 7.4). In dire straits, the Byzantine Empire turned to the west for help, setting in motion the papal pleas that led to the **crusades** (see the next section).

In Europe, and undoubtedly within the Muslim world itself, the arrival of the Turks was initially regarded as a disaster. The Turks were viewed as barbarians who destroyed civilizations and oppressed populations. In fact, in many respects, Turkish rule in the Middle East was probably beneficial. After converting to Islam, the Turkish rulers temporarily brought an end to the fraternal squabbles between Sunni and Shi'ite Muslims while supporting the Sunnis. They put their energies into revitalizing Islamic law and institutions and provided much-needed political stability to the empire, which helped restore its former prosperity. Under Seljuk rule, Muslims began to organize

Frontier between the Byzantine and Abbasid empires, c. 930

Areas of Anatolia occupied by the Abbasids in 1070

Areas of Anatolia occupied by the Seljuk Turks in the early thirteenth century

© 2016 Cengage Learning

MAP 7.4 The Turkish Occupation of Anatolia. This map shows the expansion of Turkic-speaking peoples into the Anatolian peninsula. The Seljuk Turks seized much of the peninsula after the Battle of Manzikert in 1071. In the late thirteenth century, Seljuk power collapsed and was replaced by another Turkic-speaking people, the Ottoman Turks, who began to consolidate their power in the northwestern part of Anatolia. The Ottomans established their capital at Bursa in 1335 and eventually at Constantinople in 1453 (see Chapter 16).

Q *What role did the expansion of the Seljuk Turks play in the origins of the crusades?*

themselves into autonomous brotherhoods, whose relatively tolerant practices characterized Islamic religious attitudes until the end of the nineteenth century, when increased competition with Europe led to confrontation with the West.

Seljuk political domination over the old Abbasid Empire, however, provoked resentment on the part of many Persian Shi'ites, who viewed the Turks as usurping foreigners who had betrayed the true faith of Islam. Among the regime's most feared enemies was Hasan al-Sabahh (hah-SAHN al-SAH-bah), a Cairo-trained Persian who formed a rebel group, popularly known as "assassins" (guardians), who for several decades terrorized government officials and other leading political and religious figures from their base in the mountains south of the Caspian Sea. Like their modern-day equivalents, the members of the terrorist organization known as al-Qaeda, Sabahh's followers were highly motivated and were adept at infiltrating the enemy's camp to carry out their clandestine activities. The organization was finally eliminated by the invading Mongols in the thirteenth century.

The Crusades

Just before the end of the eleventh century, the Byzantine emperor Alexius I desperately called for assistance from other Christian states in Europe to protect his empire against the invading Seljuk Turks. As part of his appeal, he said that the Muslims were desecrating Christian shrines in the Holy Land and molesting Christian pilgrims en route to the shrines. In actuality, the Muslims had never threatened the shrines or cut off Christian access to them. But tension between Christendom and Islam was on the rise, and the Byzantine emperor's appeal received a ready response in Europe. Beginning in 1096 and continuing into the thirteenth century, a series of Christian raids on Islamic territories known as the crusades brought the Holy Land and adjacent areas on the Mediterranean coast from Antioch to the Sinai Peninsula under Christian rule (see Chapter 12).

At first, Muslim rulers in the area were taken aback by the invading crusaders, whose armored cavalry presented a new challenge to local warriors, and their response was ineffectual. The Seljuk Turks by that time were preoccupied with events taking place farther to the east and took no action themselves. But in 1169, Sunni Muslims under the leadership of Saladin (SAL-uh-din *or* Salah al-Din), vizier to the last Fatimid caliph, brought an end to the Fatimid dynasty. Proclaiming himself sultan,

Saladin succeeded in establishing his control over both Egypt and Syria, thereby confronting the Christian states in the area with united Muslim power on two fronts. In 1187, Saladin's army invaded the kingdom of Jerusalem and destroyed the Christian forces concentrated there. Further operations reduced Christian occupation in the area to a handful of fortresses along the northern coast. Unlike the Christians of the First Crusade, who had slaughtered much of the population of Jerusalem when they captured the city (see the box "The Siege of Jerusalem: A Christian Perspective" on p. 196), Saladin did not permit a massacre of the civilian population and even tolerated the continuation of Christian religious services in conquered territories. For a time, Christian occupation forces even carried on a lively trade relationship with Muslim communities in the region.

The Christians returned for another try a few years after the fall of Jerusalem, but the campaign succeeded only in securing some of the coastal cities. Although the Christians would retain a toehold on the coast for much of the thirteenth century (Acre, their last stronghold, fell to the Muslims in 1291), they were no longer a significant force in Middle Eastern affairs. In retrospect, the crusades had only minimal importance in the history of the Middle East, although they may have served to unite the forces of Islam against the foreign invaders, thus creating a residue of distrust toward Christians that continues to

Michael Nicholson/Corbis

The Medieval Castle. Beginning in the eighth century, Muslim rulers began to erect fortified stone castles in the desert. So impressed were the crusaders from Europe by the innovative defenses that they encountered in Muslim castles that they began to incorporate similar features in their own European fortifications, which had previously been made of wood. In twelfth-century Syria, the crusaders constructed the imposing citadel known as the Krak des Chevaliers (Castle of the Knights) on the foundation of a Muslim fort. This new model of a massive fortress of solid masonry set off with rounded towers to deflect missiles soon spread to Europe, where it became the standard means of defending cities and castles from enemy attack.

The Siege of Jerusalem: A Christian Perspective

DURING THE FIRST CRUSADE, Christian knights laid siege to Jerusalem in June 1099. The following excerpt is taken from an account by Fulcher of Chartres, who accompanied the crusaders to the Holy Land.

Fulcher of Chartres, *Chronicle of the First Crusade*

Then the Franks entered the city magnificently at the noonday hour on Friday, the day of the week when Christ redeemed the whole world on the cross. With trumpets sounding and with everything in an uproar, exclaiming: "Help, God!" they vigorously pushed into the city, and straightway raised the banner on the top of the wall. All the heathen, completely terrified, changed their boldness to swift flight through the narrow streets of the quarters. The more quickly they fled, the more quickly they put to flight.

Count Raymond and his men, who were bravely assailing the city in another section, did not perceive this until they saw the Saracens [Muslims] jumping from the top of the wall.

Seeing this, they joyfully ran to the city as quickly as they could, and helped the others pursue and kill the wicked enemy.

Then some, both Arabs and Ethiopians, fled into the Tower of David; others shut themselves in the Temple of the Lord and of Solomon, where in the halls a very great attack was made on them. Nowhere was there a place where the Saracens could escape swordsmen.

On the top of Solomon's Temple, to which they had climbed in fleeing, many were shot to death with arrows and cast down headlong from the roof. Within this Temple, about ten thousand were beheaded. If you had been there, your feet would have been stained up to the ankles with the blood of the slain. What more shall I tell? Not one of them was allowed to live. They did not spare the women and children.

 What happened to the inhabitants of Jerusalem when the Christian knights captured the city? How do you explain the extreme intolerance and brutality of the Christian knights?

Source: Fulcher of Chartres, Chronicle of the First Crusade. From *The First Crusade: The Chronicle of Fulcher of Chartres and Other Source Materials*, 2nd ed. Ed. Edward Peters (University of Pennsylvania Press, 1998), pp. 90–91.

---

resonate through the Islamic world today. Far more important in their impact were the Mongols, a pastoral people who swept out of the Gobi Desert in the early thirteenth century to seize control over much of the known world (see Chapter 10). Beginning with the advances of Genghis Khan (JING-uss *or* GENG-uss KAHN) in northern China, Mongol armies later spread across Cetral Asia, and in 1258, under the leadership of Hulegu (HOO-lay-goo), brother of the more famous Khubilai Khan (KOO-bluh KAHN), they seized Persia and Mesopotamia, bringing an end to the caliphate at Baghdad.

The Mongols

Unlike the Seljuk Turks, the Mongols were not Muslims, and they found it difficult to adapt to the settled conditions that they found in the major cities in the Middle East. Their treatment of the local population in conquered territories was brutal (according to one historian, after conquering a city, they wiped out not only entire families but also their household pets) and destructive to the economy. Cities were razed to the ground, and dams and other irrigation works were destroyed, reducing prosperous agricultural societies to the point of mass starvation. The Mongols advanced as far as the Red Sea, but their attempt to seize Egypt failed, in part because of the effective resistance posed by the Mamluks (MAM-looks) (or Mamelukes, a Turkish military class originally composed of slaves), who had recently overthrown the administration set up by Saladin and seized power for themselves.

Eventually, the Mongol rulers in the Middle East began to assimilate the culture of the peoples they had conquered. Mongol elites converted to Islam, Persian influence became predominant at court, and the cities began to be rebuilt. By the fourteenth century, the Mongol empire had begun to split into separate kingdoms and then to disintegrate. In the meantime, however, the old Islamic empire originally established by the Arabs in the seventh and eighth centuries had long since come to an end. The new center of Islamic civilization was in Cairo, now about to promote a renaissance in Muslim culture under the sponsorship of the Mamluks.

To the north, another new force appeared on the horizon with the rise of the Ottoman Turks on the Anatolian peninsula. In 1453, Sultan Mehmet II seized Constantinople and brought an end to the Byzantine Empire. Then the Ottomans began to turn their attention to the rest of the Middle East (see Chapter 16).

Andalusia: A Muslim Outpost in Europe

After the decline of Baghdad, perhaps the brightest star in the Muslim firmament was in Spain, where a member of the Umayyad dynasty had managed to establish himself after his family's rule in the Middle East had been overthrown in 750 C.E. Abd al-Rathman (AHB-d al-rahkh-MAHN) had escaped the carnage in Damascus and made his way to Spain, where Muslim power had recently replaced that of the Visigoths. By 756, he had legitimized his authority in southern Spain—known to the Arabs as *al-Andaluz* and to Europeans as Andalusia—and taken the title of *emir* (EH-meer) (commander), with his capital at Córdoba (KOR-duh-buh). There he and his successors sought to build a vibrant new center for Islamic culture in the region. With the primacy of Baghdad now at an end, Andalusian rulers established a new caliphate in 929 (see the box "A Pilgrimage to Mecca" on p. 197).

A Pilgrimage to Mecca

RELIGION & PHILOSOPHY

THE PILGRIMAGE TO MECCA, one of the Five Pillars of Islam, is the duty of every Muslim. Ibn Jubayr, a twelfth-century Spanish Muslim who was an ardent proponent of the view that Andalusian Islam had now become the leading force in global Islam with the decline of the Abbasids, left a description of his trip in his journal. The work is famous for its vivid and abundant detail. In this almost lyrical passage, Ibn Jubayr tells of reaching his final destination, the Ka'aba at Mecca, containing the Black Stone. The Qarmata were an extremist religious sect in ninth- and tenth-century Mesopotamia.

Ibn Jubayr, *The Travels of Ibn Jubayr*

The blessed Black Stone is encased in the corner [of the Ka'aba] facing east. The depth to which it penetrates it is not known, but it is said to extend two cubits into the wall. Its breadth is two-thirds of a span, its length one span and a finger joint. It has four pieces, joined together, and it is said that it was the Qarmata—may God curse them—who broke it. Its edges have been braced with a sheet of silver whose white shines brightly against the black sheen and polished brilliance of the Stone, presenting the observer a striking spectacle which will hold his gaze. The Stone, when kissed, has a softness and moistness which so enchants the mouth that he who puts his lips to it would wish them never to be removed. This is one of the special favors of Divine Providence, and it is enough that the Prophet—may God bless and preserve him—declare it to be a covenant of God on each. May God profit us by the kissing and touching of it. By His favor may all who yearn fervently for it be brought to it. In the sound piece of the stone, to the right of him who presents himself to kiss it, is a small white spot that shines and appears like a mole on the blessed surface. Concerning this white mole, there is a tradition that he who looks upon it clears his vision, and when kissing it one should direct one's lips as closely as one can to the place of the mole.

What are the other Pillars of Islam? How does each task contribute to making a good Muslim?

Source: Excerpt from *The Travels of Ibn Jubayr*, J. R. C. Broadhurst trans., (London: Jonathan Cape Ltd., 1952).

Now that the seizure of Crete, Sardinia, Sicily, and the Balearic Islands had turned the Mediterranean Sea into a Muslim lake, Andalusia became part of a vast trade network that stretched all the way from the Strait of Gibraltar to the Red Sea and beyond. Valuable new agricultural products were introduced to the Iberian Peninsula, including cotton, sugar, olives, citrus, and the date palm.

Andalusia also flourished as an artistic and intellectual center. The court gave active support to writers and artists, creating a brilliant culture focused on the emergence of three world-class cities—Córdoba, Seville, and Toledo. Intellectual leaders arrived in the area from all parts of the Islamic world, bringing their knowledge of medicine, astronomy, mathematics, and philosophy. With the establishment of a paper factory near Valencia, the means of disseminating such information dramatically improved, and the libraries of Andalusia became the wonder of their time (see "Philosophy and Science" later in this chapter). Other wonders of the East that now began to become known in western Europe were glass mirrors and the private bath.

One major reason for the rise of Andalusia as a hub of artistic and intellectual activity was the atmosphere of tolerance in social relations fostered by the state. Although Islam was firmly established as the official faith and non-Muslims were required to pay a special tax and prohibited from proselytizing for their faith, the policy of *convivéncia* (con-vee-VEN-cee-uh) (commingling) provided an environment in which many Christians and Jews were able to maintain their religious beliefs and even obtain favors from the court.

A TIME OF TROUBLES Unfortunately, the primacy of Andalusia as a cultural center was short-lived. By the end of the tenth century, factionalism was beginning to undermine the foundations of the emirate. In 1009, the royal palace at Córdoba was totally destroyed in a civil war. Twenty years later, the caliphate itself disappeared as the emirate dissolved into a patchwork of city-states.

In the meantime, the Christian kingdoms that had managed to establish themselves in the north of the Iberian Peninsula were consolidating their position and beginning to expand southward. In 1085, Alfonso VI, the Christian king of Castile, seized Toledo, one of Andalusia's main intellectual centers. The new rulers continued to foster the artistic and intellectual activities of their predecessors, leading eventually to the spread of such ideas northward to the great cities and universities of central and western Europe. To recoup their losses, the Muslim rulers in Seville called on fellow Muslims,

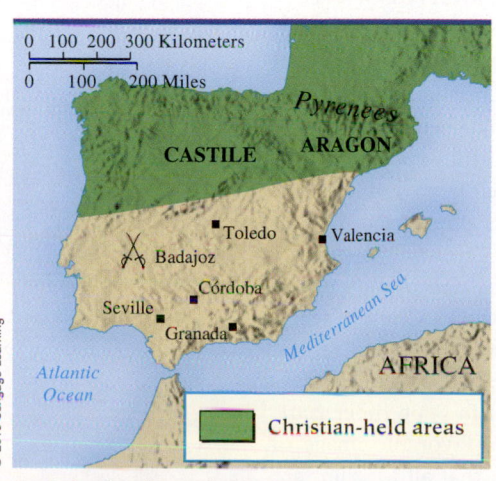

Spain in the Eleventh Century

0 100 200 300 Kilometers
0 100 200 Miles

Pyrenees

CASTILE   ARAGON

Toledo
Badajoz   Valencia
Córdoba
Seville   *Mediterranean Sea*
Granada

Atlantic Ocean

AFRICA

□ Christian-held areas

© 2016 Cengage Learning

The Alhambra in Granada. Islamic civilization reached its zenith with the fourteenth-century castle known as the Alhambra, in southern Spain (left). Sitting high above the city of Granada, the castle is forbidding from the exterior, but behind its walls lies a magical world. The Lion Court (right) in the ruler's private quarters is world renowned for its lion fountain and surrounding arcade with elegant columns and carvings. Like the Hindus in India, the Muslims of the Middle East and Spain lived in a hot, dry climate, making water a highly prized commodity both literally and psychologically.

the Almoravids (al-MOR-uh-vids)—a Berber dynasty in Morocco—for help in halting the Christian advance. Berber mercenaries defeated Castilian forces at Badajoz (bah-duh-HOHZ) in 1086 but then remained in the area to establish their own rule over remaining Muslim-held areas in southern Spain.

A warrior culture with little tolerance for heterodox ideas, the Almoravids quickly brought an end to the era of religious tolerance and intellectual achievement. But the presence of Andalusia's new warlike rulers was unable to stem the tide of Christian advance. In 1215, Pope Innocent III called for a new crusade to destroy Muslim rule in southern Spain. Over the next two hundred years, Christian armies advanced relentlessly southward, seizing the cities of Seville and Córdoba. But a single redoubt of Abd al-Rathman's glorious achievement remained: the remote mountain city of Granada (greh-NAH-duh), with its imposing hilltop fortress, the Alhambra (al-HAM-bruh).

MOORISH SPAIN: AN ERA OF "CULTURAL TOLERANCE"?

In standard interpretations of European history, Western historians have usually described the *Reconquista* (ray-con-KEES-tuh) (reconquest) of southern Spain by the Christian kingdoms in the north as a positive development that freed the Spanish people from centuries of oppressive Muslim rule. In recent years, however, it has become fashionable to point to the Moorish era in Spain (the term *Moors* is often used to refer to the Muslims in Spain) as a period of "cultural tolerance," a time of diversity that was followed by the bloody era of the Spanish Inquisition, when the Catholic Church persecuted Muslims, Jews, and Christian heretics for their refusal to accept the true faith. This interpretation has been especially popular since the terrorist attacks in September 2001, as revisionist scholars seek to present a favorable image of Islam to counter the popular perception that all Muslims are sympathetic to terrorism against the West.

Some historians, however, argue that this portrayal of the Moorish era as a period of "cultural tolerance" overstates the case. They point out that even under the relatively benign rule of Abd al-Rathman true religious tolerance was never achieved and that, in any case, any such era came to end with the arrival of the Almoravids and the Almohads (AL-moh-hads), a Berber dynasty that supplanted the Almoravids in Andalusia in the twelfth century. For historian J. S. Elliot, the era was, at best, one of "cultural interaction," which was eventually followed by a hardening of attitudes on both sides of the cultural spectrum.

CHRONOLOGY Islam: The First Millennium

Life of Muhammad	570–632
Flight to Medina	622
Conquest of Mecca	630
Fall of Cairo	640
Defeat of Persians	650
Election of Ali to caliphate	656
Muslim entry into Spain	c. 710
Abbasid caliphate	750–1258
Construction of city of Baghdad	762
Reign of Harun al-Rashid	786–809
Umayyad caliphate in Spain	929–1031
Founding of Fatimid dynasty in Egypt	973
Capture of Baghdad by Seljuk Turks	1055
Seizure of Anatolia by Seljuk Turks	1071
First Crusade	1096
Saladin destroys Fatimid kingdom	1169
Mongols seize Baghdad	1258
Ottoman Turks capture Constantinople	1453

Sage Advice from Father to Son

POLITICS & GOVERNMENT

TAHIR IBN HUSAYN (tah-HEER IB-un HOO-sayn) was born into an aristocratic family in Central Asia and became a key political adviser to al-Ma'mun, the Abbasid caliph of Baghdad in the early ninth century. Appointed in 821 to a senior position in Khurusan (kor-uh-SAHN), a district near the city of Herat in what is today Afghanistan, he wrote the following letter to his son, giving advice on how to wield authority most effectively. The letter so impressed al-Ma'mun that he had it widely distributed throughout his bureaucracy.

Letter of Tahir ibn Husayn

Look carefully into the matter of the land-tax which the subjects have an obligation to pay.... Divide it among the taxpayers with justice and fairness with equal treatment for all. Do not remove any part of the obligation to pay the tax from any noble person just because of his nobility or any rich person because of his richness or from any of your secretaries or personal retainers. Do not require from anyone more than he can bear, or exact more than the usual rate....

[The ruler should also devote himself] to looking after the affairs of the poor and destitute, those who are unable to bring their complaints of ill-treatment to you personally and those of wretched estate who do not know how to set about claiming their rights.... Turn your attention to those who have suffered injuries and their orphans and widows and provide them with allowances from the state treasury, following the example of the Commander of the Faithful, may God exalt him, in showing compassion for them and giving them financial support, so that God may thereby bring some alleviation into their daily lives and by means of it bring you the spiritual food of His blessing and an increase of His favor. Give pensions from the state treasury to the blind, and give higher allowances to those who know of the Qur'an, or most of it by heart. Set up hospices where sick Muslims can find shelter, and appoint custodians for these places who will treat the patients with kindness and physicians who will cure their illnesses....

Keep an eye on the officials at your court and on your secretaries. Give them each a fixed time each day when they can bring you their official correspondence and any documents requiring the ruler's signature. They can let you know about the needs of the various officials and about all the affairs of the provinces you rule over. Then devote all your faculties, ears, eyes, understanding and intellect, to the business they set before you: consider it and think about it repeatedly. Finally take those actions which seem to be in accordance with good judgment and justice.

How does Tahir's advice compare with that given in the political treatise Arthasastra, *discussed in Chapter 2? Would his advice serve as an effective model for political leadership today?*

Source: H. Keller (ed.), Ibn Abi Tahir Kitab Baghdad (Leipzig, 1908), cited in H. Kennedy, *When Baghdad Ruled the Muslim World: The Rise and Fall of Islam's Greatest Dynasty* (Cambridge, MA, 2004), pp. 204–205.

If there was an era of religious diversity in Spain under Muslim rule, it was all too brief.

Islamic Civilization

FOCUS QUESTION: What were the main features of Islamic society and culture during its era of early growth?

As Thomas Lippman, author of *Understanding Islam*, has remarked, the Muslim religion is based on behavior as well as belief. Although this generalization applies in broad terms to most major religions, it seems to be particularly true of Islam. To be a Muslim is not simply to worship Allah but also to live according to his law as revealed in the Qur'an, which is viewed as fundamental and immutable doctrine, not to be revised by human beings.

Thus, in Islamic society, there is no rigid demarcation between church and state, between the sacred and the secular. As Allah has decreed, so must human beings behave. Therefore, Islamic doctrine must be consulted to determine questions of politics, economic behavior, civil and criminal law, and social ethics.

Of course, to live entirely by God's law is difficult, if not impossible. Moreover, many issues of social organization and human behavior were not addressed in the Qur'an or in the *Hadith* or *Shari'a*. There was therefore some room for differing interpretations of holy scripture in accordance with individual preference and local practice. Still, the Islamic world is and has probably always been more homogeneous in terms of its political institutions, religious beliefs, and social practices than most of its contemporary civilizations.

Political Structures

For early converts, establishing political institutions and practices that conformed to Islamic doctrine was a daunting task. In the first place, the will of Allah, as revealed to his Prophet, was not precise about the relationship between religious and political authority, simply decreeing that human beings should "conduct their affairs by mutual consent." On a more practical plane, establishing political institutions for a large and multicultural empire presented a challenge for the Arabs, whose own political structures were relatively rudimentary and relevant only to small pastoral communities (see the box "Sage Advice from Father to Son" above).

During the life of Muhammad, the problem could be avoided, since he was generally accepted as both the religious and the political leader of the Islamic community—the *umma*. His death, however, raised the question of how a successor should be chosen and what authority that person should have. As we have seen, Muhammad's immediate successors were called caliphs. Their authority was purely temporal, although they were also considered in general terms to be religious leaders, with the title of *imam*. At first, each caliph was selected informally by leading members of the *umma*. Soon succession became hereditary in the Umayyad clan, but their authority was still qualified, at least in theory, by the idea that they should consult with other leaders.

The Wealth of Araby: Trade and Cities in the Middle East

As we have noted, the Abbasid era was probably one of the most prosperous periods in the history of the Middle East. Trade flourished, not only in the Islamic world but also with China (now in a period of efflorescence during the Tang and Song Dynasties; see Chapter 10), with the Byzantine Empire, and with the trading societies in Southeast Asia (see Chapter 9). Trade goods were carried both by ship and by the "fleets of the desert," the camel caravans that traversed the arid land from Morocco in the far west to the countries beyond the Caspian Sea. From West Africa came gold and slaves; from China, silk and porcelain; from East Africa, gold, ivory, and rhinoceros horn; and from the lands of South Asia, sandalwood, cotton, wheat, sugar, and spices. Within the empire, Egypt contributed grain; Iraq, linens, dates, and precious stones; Spain, leather goods, olives, and wine; and western India, pepper and various textile goods. The exchange of goods was facilitated by the development of banking and the use of currency and letters of credit (see the Comparative Essay "Trade and Civilization" on p. 201).

One of the key reasons for the Arab empire's emergence as a major participant in the regional trade network was its success in mastering the latest in naval technology. Arab ships—with hulls of teakwood and lateen sails appropriate for the sailing conditions in the Indian Ocean and beyond—were guided to their destinations by the astrolabe (an invention of the Greeks) and the compass (invented in China). Soon Muslim fleets were a familiar feature in the sea lanes from the western Mediterranean to the coast of southern China. In the process, Muslim merchants gradually replaced their Jewish or Persian counterparts in port cities throughout the region.

Under these conditions, urban areas flourished. While the Abbasids were in power, Baghdad was probably the greatest city in the empire, but after the rise of the Fatimids in Egypt, the focus of trade shifted to Cairo, described by the traveler Leo Africanus as "one of the greatest and most famous cities in all the whole world, filled with stately and admirable palaces and colleges, and most sumptuous temples."[6] Other great commercial cities included Basra at the head of the Persian Gulf, Aden at the southern tip of the Arabian peninsula, Damascus in modern Syria, and Marrakech in Morocco. In the cities, the inhabitants were generally segregated by religion, with Muslims, Jews, and Christians living in separate neighborhoods. But all were equally subject to the most common threats to urban life— fire, flood, and disease.

The most impressive urban buildings were usually the palace for the caliph or the local governor and the great mosque. Houses were often constructed of stone or brick on a timber frame. The larger houses were often built around an interior

The Dhow: Workhorse of the Indian Ocean. The dhow, a generic term for various types of sailing ships found in the Arabian Sea or along the east coast of Africa, has been the classic vessel for transporting goods in the Indian Ocean for over two millennia. Their lateen sails and narrow hulls composed of teak planking make them ideal for catching the monsoon winds that blow seasonally across the ocean between the Asian landmass and the coast of East Africa. The medieval painting on the left by an unknown artist is somewhat stylized but the resemblance to modern-day vessels is clear, although many of the latter (like the cargo vessel plying the waters off the city of Dubai shown at the right) are motorized and thus no longer subject to the whims of the yearly monsoon winds. Wind-powered vessels of this type, however, remain common throughout the region.

Trade and Civilization

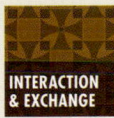

INTERACTION & EXCHANGE

In 2002, archaeologists unearthed the site of an ancient Egyptian port city on the shores of the Red Sea. Established sometime during the first millennium B.C.E., the city of Berenike linked the Nile River valley with ports as far away as the island of Java in Southeast Asia. The discovery of Berenike is only the latest piece of evidence confirming the importance of interregional trade in the ancient world. The exchange of goods between far-flung societies became a powerful engine behind the rise of advanced civilizations throughout the ancient world. Raw materials such as copper, tin, and obsidian; items of daily necessity such as salt, fish, and other foodstuffs; and luxury goods including gold, silk, and precious stones passed from one end of the Eurasian supercontinent to the other, across the desert from the Mediterranean Sea to sub-Saharan Africa. A similar network extended throughout much of the Americas. Less well known but also important was the maritime trade that stretched from the Mediterranean across the Indian Ocean to port cities on the distant coasts of Southeast and East Asia.

During the first millennium C.E., the level of interdependence among human societies intensified as three major trade routes—across the Indian Ocean, along the Silk Road, and by caravan across the Sahara—created the framework of a single system of trade. The new global network was not only commercial but informational as well, transmitting technology and ideas, such as the emerging religions of Buddhism, Christianity, and Islam, to new destinations.

There was a close relationship between missionary activities and trade. Buddhist merchants first brought the teachings of Siddhartha Gautama to China, and Muslim traders carried Muhammad's words to Southeast Asia and sub-Saharan Africa. Indian traders carried Hindu beliefs and political institutions to Southeast Asia.

What caused the rapid expansion of trade during this period? One key factor was the introduction of technology to facilitate transportation. The development of the compass, improved techniques in mapmaking and shipbuilding, and greater knowledge of wind patterns all contributed to the expansion of maritime trade. Caravan trade, once carried by wheeled chariots or on the backs of oxen, now used the camel as the preferred beast of burden through the deserts of Africa, Central Asia, and the Middle East.

Another reason for the expansion of commerce during this period was the appearance of several multinational empires that created zones of stability and affluence in key areas of the Eurasian landmass. Most important were the emergence of the Abbasid Empire in the Middle East and the prosperity of China during the Tang and Song Dynasties (see Chapter 10). The Mongol invasions in the thirteenth

Arab traders in a caravan.

century temporarily disrupted the process but then established a new era of stability that fostered long-distance trade throughout the world.

The importance of interregional trade as a crucial factor in promoting the growth of human civilizations can be highlighted by comparing the social, cultural, and technological achievements of active trading states with those communities that have traditionally been cut off from contacts with the outside world. We shall encounter many of these communities in later chapters. Even in the Western Hemisphere, where regional trade linked societies from the great plains of North America to the Andes Mountains in present-day Peru, geographic barriers limited the exchange of inventions and ideas, placing these societies at a distinct disadvantage when the first contacts with peoples across the oceans occurred at the beginning of the modern era.

 What were the chief factors that led to the expansion of interregional trade during the first millennium C.E.? What role did Islamic peoples play in this process?

courtyard where the residents could retreat from the dust, noise, and heat of the city streets. Sometimes domestic animals such as goats or sheep would be stabled there. The houses of the wealthy were often multistoried, with balconies and windows covered with latticework to provide privacy. The poor in both urban and rural areas lived in simpler houses composed of clay or unfired bricks. The Bedouins lived in tents that could be dismantled and moved according to their needs.

The Arab empire was clearly more urbanized than most other areas of the known world at the time. Yet the bulk of the population continued to live in the countryside, supported by farming or herding animals. Farm productivity increased steadily throughout much of the empire, aided by reservoirs, new crops, and advanced water management techniques such as underground irrigation canals that had first been invented in the region thousands of years previously. During the early stages, most of the farmland was owned by independent peasants, but eventually some concentration of land in the hands of wealthy owners began to take place. Some lands were owned by the state or the court and were cultivated by slave labor, but plantation agriculture was not as common as it would be later in many areas of the world. In the valleys of rivers such as the Tigris, the Euphrates, and the Nile, the majority of the farmers were probably independent peasants. A Chinese account described life along the Nile:

> The peasants work their fields without fear of inundation or droughts; a sufficiency of water for irrigation is supplied by a river whose source is not known. During the seasons when no cultivation is in progress, the level of the river remains even with the banks; with the beginning of cultivation it rises day by day. Then it is that an official is appointed to watch the river and to await the highest water level, when he summons the people, who then plough and sow their fields. When they have had enough water, the river returns to its former level.[7]

Eating habits varied in accordance with economic standing and religious preference. Muslims did not eat pork, but those who could afford it often served other meats, including mutton, goat, poultry, or fish. Fruit, spices, and various sweets were delicacies. The poor were generally forced to survive on boiled millet or peas with an occasional lump of meat or fat. Bread—white or whole meal—could be found on tables throughout the region except in the deserts, where boiled grain was the staple food. Pasta was probably first introduced to the Italians by Arab traders operating in Sicily.

Islamic Society

In some ways, Arab society was probably one of the most egalitarian of its time. Both the principles of Islam, which held that all were equal in the eyes of Allah, and the importance of trade to the prosperity of the state certainly contributed to this egalitarianism. Although there was a fairly well defined upper class, consisting of the ruling families, senior officials,

tribal elites, and the wealthiest merchants, there was no hereditary nobility as in many contemporary societies, and merchants enjoyed a degree of respect that they did not receive in Europe, China, or India.

Not all benefited from the high degree of social mobility in the Islamic world, however. Slavery was widespread. Since a Muslim could not be enslaved, the supply came from sub-Saharan Africa or from non-Islamic populations elsewhere in Asia. Most slaves were employed in the army (which was sometimes a road to power, as in the case of the Mamluks) or as domestic servants, who were occasionally permitted to purchase their freedom. The slaves who worked the large estates experienced the worst living conditions and rose in revolt on several occasions.

The Islamic principle of human equality also fell short, as in most other societies of its day, in the treatment of women. Although the Qur'an instructed men to treat women with respect, and women did have the right to own and inherit property, the male was dominant in Muslim society. Polygyny was permitted, and the right of divorce was in practice restricted to the husband, although some schools of legal thought permitted women to stipulate that their husband could have only one wife or to seek a separation in certain specific circumstances. Adultery and homosexuality were stringently forbidden (although such prohibitions were frequently ignored in practice), and Islamic custom required that women be cloistered in their homes and prohibited from social contacts with males outside their own family.

A prominent example of this custom is the harem, introduced at the Abbasid court during the reign of Harun al-Rashid. Members of the royal harem were drawn from non-Muslim female populations throughout the empire. The custom of requiring women to cover virtually all parts of their body when appearing in public was common in urban areas and continues to be practiced in many Islamic societies today. It should be noted, however, that these customs owed more to traditional Arab practice than to Qur'anic law (see the box "The Gift of the Robe" on p. 203).

The Culture of Islam

The Arabs were heirs to many elements of the remaining Greco-Roman culture of the Roman Empire, and they assimilated Byzantine and Persian culture just as readily. In the eighth and ninth centuries, numerous Greek, Syrian, and Persian scientific and philosophical works were translated into Arabic and eventually found their way to Europe. As the chief language in the southern Mediterranean and the Middle East, Arabic became an international language. Later, Persian and Turkish also came to be important in administration and culture.

The spread of Islam led to the emergence of a new culture throughout the Arab empire. This was true in all fields of endeavor, from literature to art and architecture. But pre-Islamic traditions were not extinguished and frequently combined with Muslim motifs, resulting in creative works of great imagination and originality.

The Gift of the Robe

IBN BATTUTA (IB-un ba-TOO-tuh) (1304–1377), a travel writer born in the Moroccan city of Tangier, is often described as the Muslim equivalent of his famous Italian counterpart Marco Polo. Over the course of a quarter of a century, he voyaged widely throughout Africa and Asia, logging over 75,000 miles in the process. The fascinating personal account of his travels is a prime source of information about his times. In the excerpt presented here, he describes a visit to the city of Balkh (BAHLK), one of the fabled caravan stops on the Silk Road as it passed through Central Asia.

The Travels of Ibn Battuta

After a journey of a day and a half over a sandy desert in which there was no house, we arrived at the city of Balkh, which now lies in ruins. It has not been rebuilt since its destruction by the cursed Jengiz Khān. The situation of its buildings is not very discernible, although its extent may be traced. It is now in ruins, and without society.

Its mosque was one of the largest and handsomest in the world. Its pillars were incomparable: three of which were destroyed by Jengiz Khān, because it had been told him, that the wealth of the mosque lay concealed under them, provided as a fund for its repairs. When, however, he had destroyed them, nothing of the kind was to be found: the rest, therefore he left as they were.

The story about this treasure arose from the following circumstance. It is said, that one of the Califs of the house of Abbas was very much enraged at the inhabitants of Balkh, on account of some accident which had happened, and, on this account, sent a person to collect a heavy fine from them. Upon this occasion, the women and children of the city betook themselves to the wife of their then governor, who, out of her own money, built this mosque; and to her they made a grievous complaint. She accordingly sent to the officer, who had been commissioned to collect the fine, a robe very richly embroidered and adorned with jewels, much greater in value than the amount of the fine imposed. This, she requested might be sent to the Calif as a present from herself, to be accepted instead of the fine. The officer accordingly took the robe, and sent it to the Calif; who, when he saw it, was surprised at her liberality, and said: This woman must not be allowed to exceed myself in generosity. He then sent back the robe, and remitted the fine. When the robe was returned to her, she asked, whether a look of the Calif had fallen upon it; and being told that it had, she replied: No robe shall ever come upon me, upon which the look of any man, except my own husband, has fallen. She then ordered it to be cut up and sold; and with the price of it she built the mosque, with the cell and structure in the front of it. Still, from the price of the robe there remained a third, which she commanded to be buried under one of its pillars, in order to meet any future expenses which might be necessary for its repairs. Upon Jengiz Khān's hearing this story, he ordered these pillars to be destroyed; but, as already remarked, he found nothing.

 Would a Muslim observer have considered the actions of the governor's wife described here to be meritorious? Why or why not?

Source: S. Lee (trans.), *The Travels of Ibn Battuta in the Near East, Asia, and Africa, 1325–1354* (Mineola, NY, 2004), pp. 93–94.

PHILOSOPHY AND SCIENCE During the centuries following the rise of the Arab empire, it was the Islamic world that was most responsible for preserving and spreading the scientific and philosophical achievements of ancient civilizations. At a time when ancient Greek philosophy was largely unknown in Europe, key works by Aristotle, Plato, and other Greek philosophers were translated into Arabic and stored in a "house of wisdom" in Baghdad, where they were read and studied by Muslim scholars. Eventually, many of these works were translated into Latin and were brought to Europe, where they exercised a profound influence on the later course of Christianity and Western philosophy.

The process began in the sixth century C.E., when the Byzantine ruler Justinian (see Chapter 13) shut down the Platonic Academy in Athens, declaring that it promoted heretical ideas. Many of the scholars at the Academy fled to Baghdad, where their ideas and the Classical texts they brought with them soon aroused local interest and were translated into Persian or Arabic. Later such works were supplemented by acquisitions in Constantinople and possibly also from the famous library at Alexandria.

The academies where such translations were carried out—often by families specializing in the task—were not true universities like those that would later appear in Europe but were private operations under the sponsorship of a great patron, many of them highly cultivated Persians living in Baghdad or other major cities. Dissemination of the translated works was stimulated by the arrival of paper in the Middle East, brought by Buddhist pilgrims from China passing along the Silk Road. Knowledge of the new technique of block printing—also a recent invention in China (see Chapter 10)—arrived in the Middle East at this time as well. Paper was much cheaper to manufacture than papyrus, and by the end of the eighth century, the first paper factories were up and running in Baghdad. Libraries and booksellers soon appeared, leading one recent scholar to suggest that Abbasid society was the first "book culture."

What motives inspired this ambitious literary preservation project? At the outset, it may have simply been an effort to

The image shows Arabic calligraphy at the top.

Preserving the Wisdom of the Greeks.
After the fall of the Roman Empire, the philosophical works of ancient Greece were virtually forgotten in Europe or were banned as heretical by the Byzantine Empire. It was thanks to Muslim scholars, who stored copies and translations in libraries in Baghdad, Alexandria, and elsewhere in the Arab world, that many Classical Greek writings survived. Here young Muslim scholars are being trained in the Greek language so that they can translate Classical Greek literature into Arabic. Later the works were translated back into Western languages and served as the catalyst for an intellectual revival in medieval and Renaissance Europe.

provide philosophical confirmation for existing religious beliefs as derived from the Qur'an. Perhaps, also, the purpose was to train administrators for newly conquered lands in Europe by acquainting them with conditions in those areas. Eventually, however, more adventurous minds began to use the Classical texts not only to seek greater knowledge of the divine will but also to seek a better understanding of the laws of nature.

Such was the case with the physician and intellectual Ibn Sina (IB-un SEE-nuh) (980–1037), known in the West as Avicenna (av-i-SENN-uh), who in his own philosophical writings cited Aristotle to the effect that the world operated not only at the will of Allah but also by its own natural laws, laws that could be ascertained by human reason. Avicenna, a native of Balkh, was once imprisoned as punishment for publishing heterodox ideas, but the popularity of his writings caused them to spread nonetheless throughout the Islamic world and beyond.

Although Islamic scholars are justly praised for preserving much of Classical knowledge for the West, they also made considerable advances of their own. Nowhere is this more evident than in mathematics and the natural sciences. Islamic scholars adopted and passed on the numerical system of India, including the use of zero, and a ninth-century Persian mathematician founded the mathematical discipline of algebra (al-jabr, "the reduction"). Simplified "Arabic" numerals had begun to replace cumbersome Roman numerals in Italy by the thirteenth century.

In astronomy, Muslims set up an observatory at Baghdad to study the position of the stars. They were aware that the earth was round and in the ninth century produced a world map based on the tradition of the Greco-Roman astronomer Ptolemy (see the Comparative Illustration "A Twelfth-Century Map of the World" on p. 205). Aided by the astrolabe, an instrument designed to enable sailors to track their position

by means of the stars, Muslim fleets and caravans opened up new trading routes connecting the Islamic world with other civilizations, and Muslim travelers such as al-Mas'udi and Ibn Battuta provide modern readers with their most accurate descriptions of political and social conditions throughout the Middle East.

Muslim scholars also made many new discoveries in optics and chemistry and, with the assistance of texts on anatomy by the ancient Greek physician Galen (c. 180–200 C.E.), developed medicine as a distinctive field of scientific inquiry. Avicenna compiled a medical encyclopedia that, among other things, emphasized the contagious nature of certain diseases and showed how they could be spread by contaminated water supplies. After its translation into Latin, Avicenna's work became a basic medical textbook for medieval European university students.

Ultimately, though, the spurt of interest in Classical philosophy and science throughout much of the Muslim world proved somewhat abortive. The suggestion that reason could build a bridge to faith aroused the ire of traditional Muslim scholars, and although Classical works by such ancient writers as Euclid, Ptolemy, and Archimedes continued to be translated, the influence of Greek philosophy began to wane in Baghdad by the end of the eleventh century and did not recover. At the same time, the new technique of printing did not spread, perhaps because it allegedly lacked the aesthetic qualities of cursive script or was viewed as inappropriate for the dissemination of the words of Allah.

A similar pattern occurred in Spain, where philosophers such as Averroës (uh-VERR-oh-eez), whose Arabic name was Ibn Rushd (IB-un RUSH-ed or IB-un RUSHT), and Maimonides (my-MAH-nuh-deez) (Musa Ibn Maymun, a Jew who often wrote in Arabic) undertook their own translations and wrote in support of Avicenna's defense of the role of human reason. Both were born in Córdoba in the early

COMPARATIVE ILLUSTRATION

A Twelfth-Century Map of the World.

SCIENCE & TECHNOLOGY

The twelfth-century Muslim geographer Al-Idrisi received his education in the Spanish city of Córdoba while it was under Islamic rule. Later he served at the court of the Norman king of Sicily, Roger II, where he created an atlas of the world based on Arab and European sources. In Muslim practice at the time, north and south were inverted from modern practice. Al-Idrisi's map, shown above, depicts the world as it was known at that time, stretching from the Spanish peninsula on the right to the civilization of China on the far left. It is also a testimonial to the vast extension of the power and influence of Islam in the five centuries since the death of Muhammad in 632. Maps drawn by Al-Idrisi's European contemporaries were still highly stylized, with the Christian holy city of Jerusalem placed at the center of the world, as in the map shown at the left.

Q *How much of the world shown on the map above was explored by Muslim fleets?*

twelfth century but were persecuted for their ideas by the Almohads, who had replaced the Almoravids in Andalusia, and both men ended their days in exile in North Africa.

By then, however, Christian rulers such as Alfonso X in Castile and Frederick II in Sicily were beginning to sponsor their own translations of Classical Greek works from Arabic into Latin, whence they made their way to the many new universities sprouting up all over western Europe. The end result of this period of cultural interaction would be an intellectual revolution that would transform the world of medieval Europe to its very core.

ISLAMIC LITERATURE The literature of the Middle East is diverse, reflecting the many distinct cultures of the region. The Arabic and Persian works in particular represent a significant contribution to world literature. Arabic poetry prior to Muhammad extolled the Bedouin experience of tribal life, courage in battle, hunting, sports, and respect for the animals of the desert, especially the camel (see the box "Love for a Camel" on p. 206). Pre-Muslim Persia also boasted a long literary tradition, most of it oral and later written down using the Arabic alphabet. Lacking the desert tradition of the Arabs, Persian writers focused on legends of past kings, Zoroastrian religious themes, romances, fables, and folktales. The transcendent literary monument of early Persian literature is *The Book of Lords*, an early-sixth-century compilation of poetry about Persian myths and legendary heroes.

Islam brought major changes to the culture of the Middle East, not least to literature. Muslims regarded the Qur'an as their greatest literary work, but pre-Islamic traditions

Love for a Camel

ART & IDEAS

EARLY ARABIC POETRY focused on simple pleasures, such as wine, women, song, and the faithful camel. This excerpt is from a longer work by the sixth-century Arab poet Tarafah (tah-RAH-fuh). Tarafah was one of a group of seven poets called the "suspended ones." Their poems, having won a prize in an annual competition, were suspended on a wall for all to read.

The Ode of Tarafah

Ah, but when grief assails me, straightway I ride it off
    mounted on my swift, lean-flanked camel, night and day
    racing, …
Her long neck is very erect when she lifts it up, calling to mind
    the rudder of a Tigris-bound vessel. Her skull is most like
    an anvil, the junction of its two halves meeting together as
    it might be on the edge of a file.
Her cheek is smooth as Syrian parchment, her split lip a
    tanned hide of Yemen, its slit not bent crooked; her eyes are
    a pair of mirrors, sheltering in the caves of her brow-bones,
    the rock of a pool's hollow, …
I am at her with the whip, and my she-camel quickens pace
    what time the mirage of the burning stone-tract shimmers;

elegantly she steps, as a slave-girl at a party will
    sway, showing her master skirts of a trailing
    white gown.
I am not one that skulks fearfully among the hilltops, but
    when the folk seek my succor I gladly give it; if you look
    for me in the circle of the folk you'll find me there, and
    if you hunt me in the taverns there you'll catch me.
Come to me when you will, I'll pour you a flowing cup,
    and if you don't need it, well, do without and good luck
    to you!
Whenever the tribe is assembled you'll come upon me at
    the summit of the noble House, the oft-frequented;
    my boon-companions are white as stars, and a
    singing-wench comes to us in her striped gown or
    her saffron robe, wide the opening of her collar, delicate her
    skin to my companions' fingers, tender her nakedness.
When we say, "Let's hear from you," she advances to us
    chanting fluently, her glance languid, in effortless song.

 Q How does this poem celebrate the secular aspects of life?

Source: Excerpt from *The Seven Odes*, translated by A. J. Arberry, copyright by George Allen & Unwin Ltd.

---

continued to influence writers throughout the region. Poetry is the Persian art par excellence. *The Book of Kings*, a ten-volume epic poem by the Persian poet Ferdowzi (fur-DOW-see) (940–1020), is one of the greatest achievements of Persian literature. It traces the history of the country from legendary times to the arrival of Islam. Iranian schoolchildren still learn its verses, which serve to reaffirm pride in their ancient heritage. But love poetry remained popular. One notable example was Rabe'a of Qozdar (rah-BAY-uh of kuz-DAHR), Persia's first known woman poet, whose writings in the second half of the tenth century expressed her anguish at the suffering love brings.

In the West, the most famous works of Middle Eastern literature are undoubtedly the *Rubaiyat* of Omar Khayyam (OH-mar ky-YAHM) and *Tales from 1001 Nights* (also called *The Arabian Nights*). Although these two works are not especially popular with Middle Eastern readers, they appealed to the taste of nineteenth-century Europeans, who developed a taste for stories set in exotic foreign places—a classic example of the tendency of Western observers to regard the customs and cultures of non-Western societies as strange or exotic.

Omar Khayyam's poetry, which he often composed orally over wine at a neighborhood tavern, is simple and down to earth. Key themes are the impermanence of life, the impossibility of knowing God, and disbelief in an afterlife. Among his most popular verses is the famous couplet: "Here with a loaf of bread beneath the bough, / A flask of wine, a book of verse, and thou." Ironically, recent translations of his work appeal to modern attitudes of skepticism and minimalist simplicity that may make him even more popular in the West:

In youth I studied for a little while;
Later I boasted of my mastery.
Yet this was all the lesson that I learned:
We come from dust, and with the wind are gone....
Drink wine by moonlight, darling, for the moon
Will shine long after this, and find us not.[8]

Like Omar Khayyam's verse, *The Arabian Nights* was loosely translated into European languages and adapted to Western tastes. A composite of folktales, fables, and romances of Indian and indigenous origin, the stories interweave the natural with the supernatural. The earliest stories were told orally and were later transcribed, with many later additions, in Arabic and Persian versions. The famous story of Aladdin and the Magic Lamp, for example, was an eighteenth-century addition. Nevertheless, *The Arabian Nights* has entertained readers for centuries, allowing them to enter a land of wish fulfillment through extraordinary plots, sensuality, comic and tragic situations, and a cast of unforgettable characters.

Sadi (sah-DEE) (1210–1292), considered the Persian Shakespeare, remains to this day the favorite author in Iran. His *Rose Garden* is a collection of entertaining stories written in prose sprinkled with verse. He is also renowned for his sonnetlike love poems, which set a model for generations to come. Sadi was a master of the pithy maxim:

> A cat is a lion in catching mice
> But a mouse in combat with a tiger.
>
> He has found eternal happiness who lived a good life,
> Because, after his end, good repute will keep his name alive.
>
> When thou fightest with anyone, consider
> Whether thou wilt have to flee from him or he from thee.[9]

Such maxims are typical of the Middle East, where the proverb, a one-line witty observation on the vagaries of life, has long been popular. Proverbs are not only a distinctive feature of Middle Eastern verse, especially Persian, but are also a part of daily life—a scholar recently recovered more than four thousand in one Lebanese village, including the following: "He who has money can eat sherbet in Hell." From Persia comes the cynical aphorism: "Trust in God, but tie up your camel."

Some Arabic and Persian literature reflected the deep spiritual and ethical concerns of the Qur'an. The thirteenth-century poet Rumi (ROO-mee), for example, embraced **Sufism** (SOO-fiz-uhm), a form of religious belief that called for a mystical relationship between Allah and human beings (the term *Sufism* stems from the Arabic word for "wool," referring to the rough wool garments that its adherents wore). Converted to Sufism by a wandering dervish (dervishes, from the word for "poor" in Persian, sought to achieve a mystical union with Allah through dancing and chanting in an ecstatic trance), Rumi abandoned orthodox Islam to embrace God directly through ecstatic love. Realizing that love transcends intellect, he sought to reach God through a trance attained by the whirling dance of the dervish, set to mesmerizing music. As he twirled, the poet extemporized some of the most passionate lyrical verse ever conceived. His faith and art remain an important force in Islamic society today.

The Islamic world also made a major contribution to historical writing, another discipline that was stimulated by the introduction of paper manufacturing. The first great Islamic historian was al-Mas'udi. Born in Baghdad in 896, he wrote about both the Muslim and the non-Muslim world, traveling widely in the process. His *Meadows of Gold* is the source of much of our knowledge about the golden age of the Abbasid caliphate. Translations of his work reveal a wide-ranging mind and a keen intellect, combined with a human touch that practitioners of the art in our century might find reason to emulate. Equaling al-Mas'udi in talent and reputation was the fourteenth-century historian Ibn Khaldun (IB-un kal-DOON). Combining scholarship with government service, Ibn Khaldun was one of the first historians to attempt a philosophy of history.

ISLAMIC ART AND ARCHITECTURE The art of Islam is a blend of Arab, Turkish, and Persian traditions. Although local influences can be discerned throughout the region, the Arabs, with their new religion and their writing system, served as a unifying force. Fascinated by the mathematics and astronomy they inherited from the Romans or the Babylonians, they developed a sense of rhythm and abstraction that found expression in their use of repetitive geometric ornamentation. The Turks made their own contribution with the use of abstraction in figurative and nonfigurative designs, while the Persians added their lyrical poetic mysticism.

The ultimate expression of Islamic art is to be found in magnificent architectural monuments beginning in the late seventh century. The first great example is the Dome of the Rock, built in 691 to proclaim the spiritual and political legitimacy of the new religion to the ancient world. Set in the sacred heart of Jerusalem on Muhammad's holy rock and touching both the Western Wall of the Jews and the city's

Scala/Art Resource, NY

The Dome of the Rock. One of the first architectural structures in the Islamic world, as well as one of the finest, the Dome of the Rock is topped with an opulent golden dome that still dominates the skyline of Jerusalem. Built by seventh-century artisans proficient in the Byzantine style, it boasts colored marble columns, glass and tile mosaics, and inscriptions from the Qur'an. Beneath the structure is a rock reputed to be the site of Adam's burial place, as well as the spot where Abraham prepared to sacrifice his son as recounted in the Bible. According to Muslims, the Prophet Muhammad began his night journey to heaven here. This magnificent building symbolizes the presence of Islam in a city historically identified with Judaism and Christianity.

oldest Christian church, the Dome of the Rock remains one of the most revered Islamic monuments. Constructed on Byzantine lines with an octagonal shape and marble columns and ornamentation, the interior reflects Persian motifs with mosaics of precious stones. Although rebuilt several times and incorporating influences from both East and West, this first monument to Islam represents the birth of a new art.

At first, desert Arabs, whether nomads or conquering armies, prayed in an open court, shaded along the *qibla* (KIB-luh) (the wall facing the holy city of Mecca) by a thatched roof supported by rows of palm trunks. There was also a ditch where the faithful could wash off the dust of the desert prior to prayer. As Islam became better established, enormous mosques, such as the one earlier discussed at Samarra (see the illustration "The Great Mosque of Samarra" on p. 193), were constructed, but they were still modeled on the open court, which would be surrounded on all four sides with pillars supporting a wooden roof over the prayer area facing the *qibla* wall. Set in that wall was a niche, or **mihrab** (MEER-uhb), containing a decorated panel pointing to Mecca and representing Allah.

No discussion of mosques would be complete without mentioning the famous ninth-century mosque at Córdoba in southern Spain, which is still in remarkable condition. Its 514 columns supporting double horseshoe arches transform this architectural wonder into a unique forest of trees pointing upward, contributing to a light and airy effect. The unparalleled sumptuousness and elegance make the Córdoba mosque one of the wonders of world art, let alone Islamic art.

Since the Muslim religion combines spiritual and political power in one, palaces also reflected the glory of Islam. Beginning in the eighth century with the spectacular castles of Syria, the rulers constructed large brick domiciles reminiscent of Roman design, with protective walls, gates, and baths. With a central courtyard surrounded by two-story arcades and massive gate-towers, they resembled fortresses as much as palaces. The most impressive remaining Islamic palace is the fourteenth-century Alhambra in Spain. The extensive succession of courtyards, rooms, gardens, and fountains created a fairytale castle perched high above the city of Granada. Every inch of surface is decorated in intricate floral and semiabstract patterns; much of the decoration is done in carved plasterwork so fine that it resembles lace (see the illustration "The Qur'an as Sculptured Design" on p. 209).

The Recycled Mosque. The Great Mosque at Córdoba was erected on the site of a Christian church built by the Visigoths. Earlier the same site had been dedicated to the Roman god Janus. In the eighth century, the Muslims incorporated parts of the Visigothic church into their new mosque, aggrandizing it over the centuries. After the Muslims were driven from Spain, the mosque reverted to Christianity, and in 1523, a soaring cathedral sprouted from its spine (shown below). Inside, the mosque and the cathedral seem to blend well aesthetically, a prototype for harmonious religious coexistence. In the interior, a series of arched columns provide the entire structure with an effect of mass as well as lightness (upper photo). Throughout history, societies have all too often destroyed past architectural wonders, robbing older marble glories to erect new marvels. It is rare and wonderful that the Great Mosque has survived as a testimonial to the continuing struggle to achieve religious tolerance.

The Qur'an as Sculptured Design. Muslim sculptors and artists, reflecting the traditional view that any visual representation of the Prophet Muhammad was blasphemous, turned to geometric patterns, as well as to flowers and animals, as a means of fulfilling their creative urges. The predominant motif, however, was the reproduction of Qur'anic verses in the Arabic script. Calligraphy, which was almost as important in the Middle East as it was in traditional China, used the Arabic script to decorate all of the Islamic arts, from painting to pottery, tile and ironwork, and wall decorations such as this carved plaster panel in a courtyard of the Alhambra palace in Spain. Since a recitation from the Qur'an was an important component of the daily devotional activities for all practicing Muslims, elaborate scriptural panels such as this one perfectly blended the spiritual and the artistic realms.

Since antiquity, one of the primary occupations of women has been the spinning and weaving of cloth to make clothing and other useful items for their families. In the Middle East, this skill reached an apogee in the art of the knotted woolen rug. Originating in the pre-Muslim era, rugs were initially used to insulate stone palaces against the cold as well as to warm shepherds' tents. Eventually, they were applied to religious purposes, since every practicing Muslim is required to pray five times a day on clean ground. Small rugs served as prayer mats for individual use, while larger and more elaborate ones were given by rulers as rewards for political favors. Bedouins in the Arabian desert covered their sandy floors with rugs to create a cozy environment in their tents.

In villages throughout the Middle East, the art of rug weaving has been passed down from mother to daughter over the centuries. Girls as young as four years old took part in the process by helping to spin and prepare the wool shorn from the family sheep. By the age of six, girls would begin their first rug, and before adolescence, their slender fingers would be producing fine carpets. Skilled artisanship represented an extra enticement to prospective bridegrooms, and rugs often became an important part of a woman's dowry to her future husband. After the wedding, the wife would continue to make rugs for home use, as well as for sale to augment the family income. Eventually, rugs began to be manufactured in workshops by professional artisans, who reproduced the designs from detailed painted diagrams.

Representation of the Prophet Muhammad, in painting or in any other art form, has traditionally been strongly discouraged. Although no passage of the Qur'an forbids representational painting, the *Hadith* warned against any attempt to imitate God through artistic creation or idolatry, and this has been interpreted as an outright ban on any such depictions. Accordingly, with the exception of Persian miniatures, where an earlier style involving human representation survived for a while, most decorations on all forms of Islamic art consisted of Arabic script and natural plant and figurative motifs. Repeated continuously in naturalistic or semiabstract geometrical patterns called arabesques, these decorations completely covered the surface and left no area undecorated. This dense decor was also evident in brick, mosaic, and stucco ornamentation and culminated in the magnificent tile work of later centuries.

CHAPTER SUMMARY

After the collapse of Roman power in the west, the Eastern Roman Empire, centered on Constantinople, continued in the eastern Mediterranean and eventually emerged as the unique Christian civilization known as the Byzantine Empire, which flourished for hundreds of years. One of the greatest challenges to the Byzantine Empire, however, came from a new force—Islam—that blossomed in the Arabian peninsula and spread rapidly throughout the Middle East. In the eyes of some Europeans during the Middle Ages, the Arab empire was a malevolent force that posed a serious threat to the security of Christianity. Their fears were not entirely misplaced, for within a century after the death of Islam's founder, Muhammad, Arab armies overran Christian states in North Africa and the Iberian Peninsula, and Turkish Muslims moved eastward onto the fringes of the Indian subcontinent.

William J. Duiker

But although the teachings of Muhammad brought war and conquest to much of the known world, they also brought hope and a sense of political and economic stability to peoples throughout the region. Thus, for many people in the medieval Mediterranean world, the arrival of Islam was a welcome event. Islam brought a code of law and a written language to societies that had previously lacked them. Finally, by creating a revitalized trade network stretching from West Africa to East Asia, it established a vehicle for the exchange of technology and ideas that brought untold wealth to thousands and a better life to millions.

Like other empires in the region, the Arab empire did not last. It fell victim to a combination of internal and external pressures, and by the end of the thirteenth century, it was no more than a memory. But it left a powerful legacy in Islam, which remains one of the great religions of the world. In succeeding centuries, Islam began to penetrate into new areas beyond the edge of the Sahara and across the Indian Ocean into the islands of the Indonesian archipelago.

CHAPTER TIMELINE

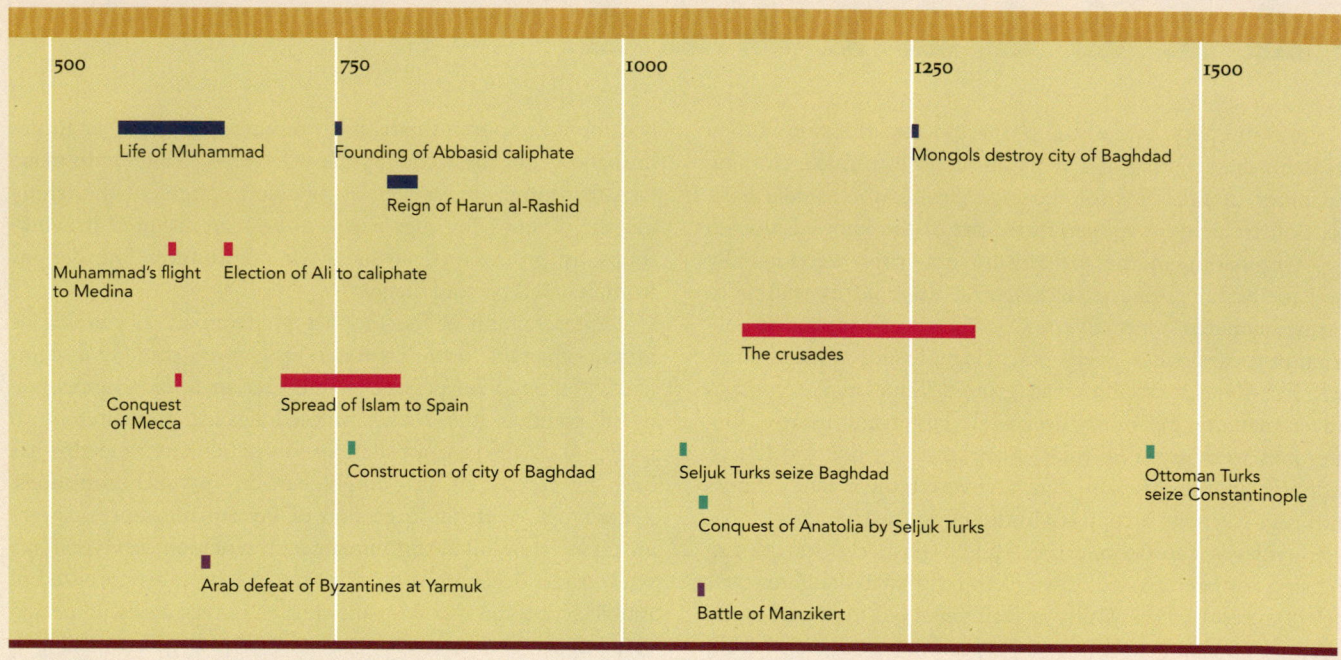

CHAPTER REVIEW

Upon Reflection

Q By what process was Arab power expanded throughout the Middle East and North Africa in the years following the death of Muhammad? What was the impact of that expansion on the subject peoples?

Q What role did the Abbasid Empire play in promoting the establishment of a trade network extending from East Asia to the Mediterranean Sea and beyond? Is it reasonable to say that the Muslim world was the linchpin of global trade during this period?

Q What circumstances do some historians refer to when they say that the Muslim governments in Spain provided an example of religious tolerance?

Key Terms

Bedouin (p. 185)
sheikh (p. 185)
majlis (p. 185)
Hegira (p. 186)
umma (p. 186)
Five Pillars of Islam (p. 188)
Ramadan (p. 188)
ulama (p. 188)
Shari'a (p. 188)
Hadith (p. 188)
caliph (p. 189)
imam (p. 189)
jihad (p. 189)

Shi'ites (p. 191)
Sunni (p. 192)
vizier (p. 193)
sultan (p. 194)
crusades (p. 194)
emir (p. 196)
Sufism (p. 207)
mihrab (p. 208)

Suggested Reading

THE RISE OF ISLAM   Standard works on the rise of Islam include **J. Bloom** and **S. Blair,** *Islam: A Thousand Years of Faith and Power* (New Haven, Conn., 2002), and **J. L. Esposito, ed.,** *The Oxford History of Islam* (New York, 1999). Also see **K. Armstrong,** *Islam: A Short History* (New York, 2000). **F. Donner,** *Muhammad and the Believers: At the Origins of Islam* (Cambridge, Mass., 2010), and **K.-H. Ohlig** and **G.-R. Puin, eds.,** *The Hidden Origins of Islam* (Amherst, N.Y., 2008) adopt a revisionist stance in approaching the early years of Islam. For a standard and laudatory biography of the Prophet, see **K. Armstrong,** *Muhammad: A Prophet for Our Time* (New York, 2006).

Specialized works on various historical periods are numerous. For a view of the crusades from an Arab perspective, see **C. Hillenbrand,** *The Crusades: Islamic Perspectives* (New York, 2001). In *God of Battles: Christianity and Islam* (Princeton, N.J., 1998), **P. Partner** compares the expansionist tendencies of the two great religions. The rise of Arab sea power is analyzed in **G. F. Hourani,** *Arab Seafaring* (Princeton, N.J., 1995).

ABBASID EMPIRE   On the Abbasid Empire, see **H. Kennedy's** highly readable *When Baghdad Ruled the Muslim World: The Rise and Fall of Islam's Greatest Dynasty* (Cambridge, Mass., 2004) and *The Great Arab Conquests: How the Spread of Islam Changed the World We Live In* (Philadelphia, 2007). Christian-Muslim contacts are discussed in **S. O'Shea,** *Sea of Faith: Islam and Christianity in the Medieval Mediterranean World* (New York, 2006). **D. L. Lewis,** in *God's Crucible: Islam and the Making of Europe, 570-1215* (New York, 2008), argues that by preserving the wisdom of the Greeks, Islam saved Medieval Europe from collapse.

SPAIN UNDER ISLAM   On Spain during the Abbasid era, see **M. Menocal's** elegant study, *Ornament of the World: How Muslims, Jews, and Christians Created a Culture of Tolerance in Medieval Spain* (New York, 2002), and **R. Fletcher,** *The Cross and the Crescent: Christianity and Islam from Muhammad to the Reformation* (New York, 2005).

WOMEN   On women, see **F. Hussain, ed.,** *Muslim Women* (New York, 1984), and **G. Nashat** and **J. E. Tucker,** *Women in the Middle East and North Africa* (Bloomington, Ind., 1998).

ISLAMIC ART   For the best introduction to Islamic art, consult **J. Bloom** and **S. Blair,** *Islamic Arts* (London, 1997).

Chapter Notes

1. M. M. Pickthall, trans., *The Meaning of the Glorious Koran* (New York, 1953), p. 89.
2. Quoted in T. W. Lippman, *Understanding Islam: An Introduction to the Moslem World* (New York, 1982), p. 118.
3. F. Hirth and W. W. Rockhill, trans., *Chau Ju-kua: His Work on the Chinese and Arab Trade in the Twelfth and Thirteenth Centuries, Entitled "Chu-fan-chi"* (New York, 1966), p. 115.
4. al-Mas'udi, *The Meadows of Gold: The Abbasids*, ed. P. Lunde and C. Stone (London, 1989), p. 151.
5. Quoted in G. Wiet, *Baghdad: Metropolis of the Abassid Caliphate*, trans. S. Feiler (Norman, Okla., 1971), pp. 118–119.
6. L. Africanus, *The History and Description of Africa and of the Notable Things Therein Contained* (New York, n.d.), pp. 820–821.
7. Hirth and Rockhill, *Chau Ju-kua*, p. 116.
8. E. Yarshater, ed., *Persian Literature* (Albany, N.Y., 1988), pp. 154–159.
9. E. Rehatsek, trans., *The Gulistan or Rose Garden of Sa'di* (New York, 1964), pp. 65, 67, 71.

MindTap is a fully online, highly personalized learning experience built upon Cengage Leaning content. MindTap combines student learning tools—readings, multimedia, activities, and assessments—into a singular Learning Path that guides students through their course.

Early Civilizations in Africa

The Temple at Great Zimbabwe

Nick Greaves/Alamy

CHAPTER OUTLINE AND FOCUS QUESTIONS

The Emergence of Civilization

Q How did the advent of farming and pastoralism affect the various peoples of Africa? How did the consequences of the agricultural revolution in Africa compare with its consequences in Eurasia and America?

The Coming of Islam

Q What effects did the coming of Islam have on African religion, society, political structures, trade, and culture?

States and Noncentralized Societies in Central and Southern Africa

Q What role did migration play in the evolution of early African societies? How did the impact of these migrations compare with similar population movements elsewhere?

African Society

Q What role did lineage groups, women, and slavery play in African societies? In what ways did African societies in various parts of the continent differ? What accounted for these differences?

African Culture

Q What are some of the chief characteristics of African sculpture and carvings, music, and architecture, and what purpose did these forms of creative expression serve in African society?

CRITICAL THINKING

Q In what parts of Africa did the first states and city-states emerge? What conditions led to their appearance?

CONNECTIONS TO TODAY

Q How does the discussion in the Comparative Essay "The Migration of Peoples" in this chapter relate to migratory movements of people around the world today? Is large-scale migration a natural process? If so, should it be allowed to run its course, or should it be restricted in some ways?

IN 1871, THE GERMAN EXPLORER Karl Mauch began to search southern Africa's central plateau for the colossal stone ruins of a legendary lost civilization. In late August, he found what he had been looking for. He recorded the moment in his diary: "Presently I stood before it and beheld a wall of a height of about 20 feet of granite bricks. Very close by there was a place where a kind of footpath led over rubble into the interior. Following this path I stumbled over masses of rubble and parts of walls and dense thickets. I stopped in front of a towerlike structure. Altogether it rose to a height of about 30 feet." Mauch was convinced that "a civilized nation must once have lived here." Like many other nineteenth-century Europeans, however, Mauch was equally convinced that the Africans who had lived there could never have built such splendid structures as the ones he had found at Great Zimbabwe. To Mauch and other archaeologists, Great Zimbabwe must have been the work of "a northern race closely akin to the Phoenician and Egyptian." It was not until the twentieth century that Europeans would overcome their prejudices and finally admit that Africans south of Egypt had also developed advanced civilizations with spectacular achievements.

The continent of Africa has played a central role in the long evolution of humankind. It was in Africa that the first hominids appeared more than 3 million years ago. It was probably in Africa that the immediate ancestors of modern human beings—*Homo sapiens*—emerged. The domestication of animals and perhaps the initial stages of the agricultural revolution may have occurred first in Africa. Certainly, one of the first states appeared in Africa, in the Nile Valley in the northeastern corner of the continent, in the form of the kingdom of the pharaohs. Recent evidence suggests that Egyptian civilization was significantly influenced by cultural developments taking place to the south, in Nubia, in modern Sudan. Egypt in turn exercised a profound influence on scientific and cultural developments throughout the eastern Mediterranean region, including the civilization of the Greeks.

After the decline of the Egyptian empire during the first millennium B.C.E., the focus of social change began to shift from the lower Nile Valley to other areas of the continent: to West Africa, where a series of major trading states began to take part in the caravan trade with the Mediterranean through the vast wastes of the Sahara; to the region of the upper Nile River, where the states of Kush and Axum dominated trade for several centuries; and to the eastern coast from the Horn of Africa (formally known as Cape Guardafui) to the straits between the continent and the island of Madagascar, where African peoples began to play an active role in the commercial traffic in the Indian Ocean. In the meantime, a gradual movement of agricultural peoples brought Iron Age farming to the central portion of the continent, leading eventually to the creation of several states in the Congo River basin and the plateau region south of the Zambezi River.

Thus, since ancient times, the peoples of Africa have played a significant role in the changing human experience. Yet the landmass of Africa is so vast and its topography so diverse that communication within the continent and between Africans and peoples living elsewhere in the world has often been more difficult than in many other regions. As a consequence, while some parts of the continent were directly exposed to the currents of change sweeping across Eurasia and were influenced by them to varying degrees, other regions were virtually isolated from the "great tradition" cultures discussed in Part I of this book and, like the cultures of the Americas, developed in their own directions, rendering generalizations about Africa difficult, if not impossible, to make.

The Emergence of Civilization

 Q FOCUS QUESTIONS: How did the advent of farming and pastoralism affect the various peoples of Africa? How did the consequences of the agricultural revolution in Africa compare with its consequences in Eurasia and America?

After Asia, Africa is the largest of the continents (see Map 8.1). It stretches nearly 5,000 miles from the Cape of Good Hope in the south to the Mediterranean in the north and extends a similar distance from Cape Verde on the west coast to the Horn of Africa on the Indian Ocean.

The Land

Africa is as physically diverse as it is vast. The northern coast, washed by the Mediterranean Sea, is mountainous for much of its length. South of the mountains lies the greatest desert on earth, the Sahara, which stretches from the Atlantic to the Indian Ocean. To the east is the Nile River, heart of the ancient Egyptian civilization. Beyond that lies the Red Sea, separating Africa from Asia.

The Sahara acts as a great divide separating the northern coast from the rest of the continent. Africa south of the Sahara contains a number of major regions. In the west is the so-called hump of Africa, which juts like a massive shoulder into the Atlantic Ocean. Here the Sahara gradually gives way to grasslands in the interior and then to tropical rain forests along the coast. This region, dominated by the Niger River, is rich in natural resources and was the home of many ancient civilizations.

Far to the east, bordering the Indian Ocean, is a very different terrain of snowcapped mountains, upland plateaus, and lakes. Much of this region is grassland populated by wild beasts, which has caused many Westerners to view it as "safari country." Here, in the East African Rift Valley in the lake district of modern Kenya, early hominids began their long trek toward civilization several million years ago.

Directly to the west lies the Congo basin, with its rain forests watered by the mighty Congo River. The forests of equatorial Africa then fade gradually into the hills, plateaus, and deserts of the south. This rich land contains some of the most valuable mineral resources known today.

The First Farmers

It is not certain when agriculture was first practiced on the continent of Africa. Until recently, historians assumed that crops were first cultivated in the lower Nile Valley (the northern part near the Mediterranean) about seven or eight thousand years ago, when wheat and barley were introduced, possibly from the Middle East. Eventually, as explained in Chapter 1, this area gave rise to the civilization of ancient Egypt.

Recent evidence, however, suggests that this hypothesis may need some revision. South of Egypt, near the junction of

MAP 8.1 **Ancient Africa.** Modern human beings, the primate species known as *Homo sapiens*, first evolved on the continent of Africa. Some key sites of early human settlement are shown on this map.

Q *Which are the main river systems on the continent of Africa?*

(see the illustration that accompanies the Comparative Essay "The Migration of Peoples" on p. 218) show that by the fourth millennium B.C.E. fishing and pastoralism in the heart of the Sahara were being supplemented by the limited cultivation of grain crops, including a drought-resistant form of dry rice.

Thus, the peoples of northern Africa, from Nubia westward into the heart of the Sahara, were among the earliest in the world to adopt settled agriculture as a means of subsistence. Shards of pottery found at archaeological sites in the area suggest that they were also among the first to manufacture clay pots, which allowed them to consume their cereals in the form of porridge rather than as bread baked from flour. By 5000 B.C.E., they were cultivating cotton plants for the purpose of manufacturing textiles.

After 3000 B.C.E., the desiccation (drying up) of the Sahara intensified, and the lakes began to dry up, forcing many local inhabitants to migrate eastward toward the Nile River and southward into the grasslands. As a result, farming began to spread into the savannas on the southern fringes of the desert and eventually into the tropical forest areas to the south, where crops were no longer limited to drought-resistant cereals but could include tropical fruits and tubers. In the meantime, the foundation was being laid for the emergence of an advanced civilization in Egypt along the banks of the Nile River (see Chapter 1).

Axum and Meroë

To the south of Egypt in Nubia, the kingdom of Kush had emerged as a major trading state by the end of the second millennium B.C.E. (see Chapter 1). Kush adopted many of its political institutions and much of its culture from the kingdom of the pharaohs farther to the north and—at a time of Egyptian weakness in the eighth century B.C.E.—even managed to seize the city of Memphis and much of the Nile River Delta. Eventually, however, the Kushite rulers were driven out of lower Egypt and forced to retreat back to their original habitat in Nubia, where a new capital was established at Meroë (MER-oh-ee *or* MER-uh-wee), near the Fourth Cataract in the great bend of the Nile River.

The new capital was located near extensive iron deposits and, once smelting techniques had been developed, iron

the White Nile and the Blue Nile, is an area historically known as Nubia (see Chapter 1). By the ninth millennium B.C.E., peoples living in this area began to domesticate animals, first wild cattle and then sheep and goats, which had apparently originated in the Middle East. In areas where the climate permitted, they supplemented their diet by gathering wild grains and soon learned how to cultivate grains such as sorghum and millet, while also growing gourds and melons.

Eventually, the practice of agriculture began to spread westward across the Sahara. At that time, the world's climate was much cooler and wetter than it is today, but a warm, humid climate prevailed in parts of the Sahara, creating lakes and ponds, as well as vast grasslands (known as savannas) replete with game. Hence, indigenous peoples living in the area were able to provide for themselves by hunting, food gathering, and fishing. By the seventh and sixth millennia B.C.E., however, conditions were becoming increasingly arid, forcing them to find new means of support. Rock paintings found in what are today some of the most uninhabitable parts of the region

The Pyramids at Meroë. The kingdom of Kush borrowed much of its culture from the Egyptian empire to the north, while placing its own imprint on all imports. Kushite rulers, for example, modeled their political institutions after those of the pharaohs, but governmental authority was somewhat more centralized, and monarchical power was apparently limited by the influence of priests and the local aristocracy. The pyramids at Meroë, on the banks of the Nile River, are another example. Younger, smaller, unpointed at the top, and more standardized in size and shape than their famous counterparts at Giza, they remain a dramatic reminder of the glory of ancient Kush.

evidently provided the basis for much of the area's growing prosperity. Meroë eventually became a cultural center and a major trading hub for iron goods and other manufactures for the entire region. The prosperity of the area is attested to by the remnants of a number of pyramids, similar in design but smaller in size than their Egyptian counterparts, which were constructed to serve as tombs for the deceased rulers of the ruling dynasty. Recently, other pyramids, some as short as 3 feet high, have been located along the banks of the river, suggesting that local elites mimicked the ruling family in what one archaeologist called "the democratization of pyramids."

By the third century C.E., however, a competitor to Meroë's regional economic prominence began to arise a few hundred miles to the southeast, in the mountainous highlands of what today is known as Ethiopia. The founders of Axum (AHK-soom) claimed descent from migrants who arrived in Africa from the kingdom of Saba (SAH-buh) (also known as Sheba), across the Red Sea on the southern tip of the Arabian peninsula. During antiquity, Saba was a major trading state, serving as a transit point for goods carried from South Asia into the lands surrounding the Mediterranean. Biblical sources credited the "queen of Sheba" with vast wealth and resources. In fact, much of that wealth had originated much farther to the east and passed through Saba en route to the countries adjacent to the Mediterranean. Whether migrants from Saba were responsible for founding Axum is sheer conjecture, but a similarity in architectural styles suggests that there probably was some form of relationship between the two states.

After Saba declined, perhaps because of the desiccation of the Arabian Desert, Axum survived for centuries. Like Saba,

Axum owed much of its prosperity to its location on the commercial trade route between India and the Mediterranean, and ships from Egypt stopped regularly at the port of Adulis (a-DOO-luss) on the Red Sea. Axum exported ivory, frankincense, myrrh, and slaves, while its primary imports were textiles, metal goods, wine, and olive oil. For a time, Axum competed for control of the ivory trade with the neighboring state of Meroë, and hunters from Axum armed with imported iron weapons scoured the entire region for elephants. Probably as a result of this competition, in the fourth century C.E., the Axumite ruler, claiming he had been provoked, launched an invasion of Meroë and conquered it, creating an empire that, in the view of some contemporaries, rivaled those of Rome and Persia (see Map 8.2).

One of the most distinctive features of Axumite civilization was its religion. Originally, the rulers of Axum (who claimed descent from King Solomon through the visit of the queen of Sheba to Israel in biblical times) followed the religion of Saba. But in the fourth century C.E., Axumite rulers adopted Christianity,

MAP 8.2 Ancient Ethiopia and Nubia. The first civilizations to appear on the African continent emerged in the Nile River valley. Early in the first century C.E., the state of Axum emerged in what is today the state of Ethiopia.

Q *Where are the major urban settlements in the region, as shown on this map?*

Beyond the Pillars of Hercules

INTERACTION & EXCHANGE

THE FIRST SUGGESTION that seafarers could pass from the Atlantic to the Indian Ocean around the southern tip of Africa came from the Greek historian Herodotus, who lived during the fifth century B.C.E. In the following passage from his *History of the Persian Wars*, Herodotus describes a voyage by Phoenician sailors around the continent of Africa [known here as Libya] that was recounted to him during his visit to Egypt. The reference to the position of the sun reflects a phenomenon that could have occurred only if the Phoenicians were sailing south of the equator. The Pillars of Hercules was the Greek name for what is known today as the Strait of Gibraltar, separating the continents of Africa and Europe at the western entrance to the Mediterranean Sea.

Herodotus, *History of the Persian Wars*

For my part I am astonished that men should ever have divided Libya, Asia, and Europe as they have, for they are exceedingly unequal. Europe extends the entire length of the other two, and for breadth will not even (as I think) bear to be compared to them. As for Libya, we know it to be washed on all sides by the sea, except where it is attached to Asia.

This discovery was first made by Necos, the Egyptian king, who on desisting from the canal which he had begun between the Nile and the Arabian gulf, sent to sea a number of ships manned by Phoenicians, with orders to make for the Pillars of Hercules, and return to Egypt through them, and by the Mediterranean. The Phoenicians took their departure from Egypt by way of the Erythraean sea, and so sailed into the southern ocean. When autumn came, they went ashore, wherever they might happen to be, and having sown a tract of land with corn, waited until the grain was fit to cut. Having reaped it, they again set sail; and thus it came to pass that two whole years went by, and it was not till the third year that they doubled the Pillars of Hercules, and made good their voyage home. On their return, they declared—I for my part do not believe them, but perhaps others may—that in sailing round Libya they had the sun upon their right hand. In this way was the extent of Libya first discovered.

Why does Herodotus's reference to the position of the sun during the voyage appear to validate the fact that they had sailed south of the equator?

Source: *The History of Herodotus*, George Rawlinson, ed., Vol. III (New York: D. Appleton and Company, 1889), pp. 28–29.

Frans Lemmens/Corbis

Fleets of the Desert. Since the dawn of history, caravans have transported food and various manufactured articles southward across the Sahara in exchange for salt, gold, copper, skins, and slaves. Once carried on by donkey carts, the trade expanded dramatically with the introduction of the one-humped camel into the region from the Arabian peninsula. Unlike most draft animals, the camel can go great distances without water, a scarce item in the desert.

Nok Pottery Head. The Nok peoples of the Niger River are the oldest known culture in West Africa to have created sculpture. This is a typical terra-cotta head of the Nok culture produced between 500 B.C.E. and 200 C.E. Discovered by accident in the twentieth century by tin miners, these heads feature perforated eyes set in triangles or circles, stylized eyebrows, open thick lips, broad noses with wide nostrils, and large ears. Perhaps the large facial openings permitted the hot air to escape as the heads were fired. Although the function of these statues is not known for certain, they were likely connected with religious rituals or devotion to ancestors.

possibly as the result of contacts with Egypt. This commitment to the Egyptian form of Christianity—often called **Coptic** (KAHP-tik) from the local language of the day—was retained even after the collapse of Axum and the expansion of Islam through the area in later centuries. Later, Axum (renamed Ethiopia) would be identified by some Europeans as the "hermit kingdom" and the home of Prester John, a legendary Christian king of East Africa.

The Sahara and Its Environs

Meroë and Axum were part of the ancient trading network that extended from the Mediterranean Sea to the Indian Ocean and were affected in various ways by the cross-cultural contacts that took place throughout that region. Elsewhere in Africa, somewhat different patterns prevailed; they varied from area to area, depending on the geography and climate.

Historians do not know when goods first began to be exchanged across the Sahara in a north-south direction, but during the first millennium B.C.E., the commercial center of Carthage on the Mediterranean had become a focal point of the trans-Saharan trade. The **Berbers**, a pastoral people of North Africa (see Chapter 7), served as intermediaries, carrying food products and manufactured goods from Carthage across the desert and exchanging them for salt, gold and copper, skins, various agricultural products, and perhaps slaves. Carthaginian fleets had for centuries also been actively searching for markets along the east African coast (see the box "Beyond the Pillars of Hercules" on p. 216).

This trade initiated a process of cultural exchange that would exert a significant impact on the peoples of tropical Africa. Among other things, it may have spread the knowledge of iron-working south of the desert. Although historians once believed that ironworking knowledge reached sub-Saharan Africa from Meroë in the first centuries C.E., recent finds suggest that the peoples along the Niger River were smelting iron five or six hundred years earlier. Some scholars believe that the technique developed independently there, but others surmise that it was introduced by the Berbers, who had learned it from the Carthaginians.

Whatever the case, the **Nok** (NAHK) **culture** in northern Nigeria eventually became one of the most active iron-working societies in Africa. Excavations have unearthed numerous terra-cotta and metal figures, as well as stone and iron farm implements, dating back as far as 500 B.C.E. The remains of smelting furnaces confirm that the iron was produced locally.

Early in the first millennium C.E., the introduction of the camel from across the Red Sea in the Middle East provided a major stimulus to the trans-Saharan trade. With its ability to store considerable amounts of food and water, the camel was far better equipped to handle the arduous conditions of the desert than the donkey and the wheeled cart, which had been used previously. The camel caravans of the Berbers, arduously threading their way from the shores of the Mediterranean through the heart of the Sahara, became so essential to the local trade network that they became known as the "fleets of the desert."

THE GARAMANTES Not all the peoples involved in trade across the Sahara were nomadic. Recent exploratory work in the Libyan Desert has revealed the existence of an ancient kingdom that for over a thousand years transported goods between societies along the Mediterranean Sea and sub-Saharan West Africa. The Garamantes (gar-uh-MAN-teez), as they were known to the Romans, carried salt, glass, metal, olive oil, and wine southward in return for gold, slaves, and various tropical products. To provide food for their communities in the heart of the desert, they constructed a complex irrigation system consisting of several thousand miles of underground channels. The technique is reminiscent of similar systems in Persia and Central Asia (see Chapter 7). Scholars believe that the kingdom declined as a result of the fall of the Roman Empire, which led to a drop in the exchange of goods throughout the area, and the desiccation of the desert. As the historian Felipe Fernández-Armesto has noted in his provocative study

The Migration of Peoples

INTERACTION & EXCHANGE

About 50,000 years ago, a small band of humans crossed the Sinai Peninsula from Africa and began to spread out across the Eurasian supercontinent. Thus began a migration of peoples that continued with accelerating speed throughout the ancient era and beyond. By 40,000 B.C.E., their descendants had spread across Eurasia as far as China and eastern Siberia and had even settled the distant continent of Australia.

Who were these peoples, and what provoked their decision to change their habitat? Undoubtedly, the first migrants were foragers or hunters in search of wild game, but with the advent of agriculture and the domestication of animals about 12,000 years ago, other peoples began to migrate vast distances in search of fertile farming and pasturelands.

The ever-changing climate was undoubtedly a major factor driving the process. Beginning in the fourth millennium B.C.E., the drying up of rich pasturelands in the Sahara forced the local inhabitants to migrate eastward toward the Nile River valley and the grasslands of East Africa. At about the same time, Indo-European-speaking farming peoples left the region of the Black Sea and moved gradually into central Europe in search of new farmlands. They were eventually followed by nomadic groups from Central Asia who began to occupy lands along the frontiers of the Roman Empire, while other bands of nomads threatened the plains of northern China from the Gobi Desert. In the meantime, Bantu-speaking farmers had migrated from the Niger River southward into the rain forests of Central Africa and beyond. Similar movements took place in Southeast Asia and the Americas.

This steady flow of migrating peoples often had a destabilizing effect on sedentary societies in their path. Nomadic incursions represented a constant menace to the security of China, Egypt, and the Roman Empire and ultimately brought them to an end. But these vast movements of peoples often had beneficial effects as well, spreading new technologies and means of livelihood. Although some migrants, like the Huns, came for plunder and left havoc in their wake, other groups, like the Celtic peoples and the Bantus, prospered in their new environments.

The most famous of all nomadic invasions is a case in point. In the thirteenth century C.E., the Mongols left

Erich Lessing/Art Resource, NY

Rock Paintings of the Sahara. Even before the Egyptians built their pyramids at Giza, other peoples far to the west in the vast wastes of the Sahara were creating their own art forms. These rock paintings, some of which date back to the fourth millennium B.C.E. and are reminiscent of similar examples from Europe, Asia, and Australia, provide a valuable record of a society that supported itself by a combination of farming, hunting, and herding animals. After the introduction of the horse from Arabia around 1200 B.C.E., subsequent rock paintings depicted chariots and horseback riding. Eventually, camels began to appear in the paintings, a consequence of the increasing desiccation of the Sahara.

their homeland in the Gobi Desert, advancing westward into the Russian steppes and southward into China and Central Asia, leaving death and devastation in their wake. At the height of their empire, the Mongols controlled virtually all of Eurasia except its western and southern fringes, thereby creating a zone of stability in which a global trade and informational network could thrive that stretched from China to the shores of the Mediterranean.

 What have been some of the key reasons for the migration of large numbers of people throughout human history? Is the process still under way in our own day?

A Chinese View of Africa

THIS PASSAGE FROM CHAU JU-KUA'S thirteenth-century treatise on geography describes various aspects of life along the eastern coast of Africa in what is now Somalia, including the urban architecture. The author was an inspector of foreign trade in the city of Quanzhou (sometimes called Zayton) on the southern coast of China. His account was compiled from reports of seafarers. Note the varied uses that the local people make of a whale carcass.

Chau Ju-kua on East Africa

The inhabitants of the Chung-li country [the Somali coast] go bareheaded and barefooted; they wrap themselves in cotton stuffs, but they dare not wear jackets, for the wearing of jackets and turbans is a privilege reserved to the ministers and the king's courtiers. The king lives in a brick house covered with glazed tiles, but the people live in huts made of palm leaves and covered with grass-thatched roofs. Their daily food consists of baked flour cakes, sheep's and camel's milk. There are great numbers of cattle, sheep, and camels....

There are many sorcerers among them who are able to change themselves into birds, beasts, or aquatic animals, and by these means keep the ignorant people in a state of terror. If some of them in trading with some foreign ship have a quarrel, the sorcerers pronounce a charm over the ship so that it can neither go forward nor backward, and they only release the ship when it has settled the dispute. The government has formally forbidden this practice.

When one of the inhabitants dies, and they are about to bury him in his coffin, his kinsfolk from near and far come to condole. Each person, flourishing a sword in his hand, goes in and asks the mourners the cause of the person's death. If he was killed by the hand of man, each one says, we will revenge him on the murderer with these swords. Should the mourners reply that he was not killed by any one, but that he came to his end by the will of Heaven, they throw away their swords and break into violent wailing.

Every year there are driven on the coast a great many dead fish measuring two hundred feet in length and twenty feet through the body. The people do not eat the flesh of these fish, but they cut out their brains, marrow, and eyes, from which they get oil. They mix this oil with lime to caulk their boats, and use it also in lamps. The poor people use the ribs of these fish to make rafters, the backbones for door leaves, and they cut off vertebrae to make mortars with.

 What does this passage offer in terms of information about housing and consumption habits in East Africa?

Source: *Chau Ju-Kua: His Work on the Chinese and Arab Trade in the Twelfth and Thirteenth Centuries, entitled Chu-fan-chi,* translated from the Chinese and annotated by Friedrich Hirth and W. W. Rockhill. (St. Petersburg. Printing Office of the Imperial Academy of Sciences, Vass. Ostr., Kinth Liao, 12. 1911), pp. 130–131.

Civilizations, advanced societies do not easily thrive in desert conditions.[1]

East Africa

South of Axum, along the shores of the Indian Ocean and in the inland plateau that stretches from the mountains of Ethiopia through the lake district of Central Africa, lived a mixture of peoples. Some originally depended on hunting and food gathering, whereas others followed pastoral pursuits.

Beginning in the third millennium B.C.E., farming peoples speaking dialects of the Bantu (BAN-too) family of languages began to migrate from their original homeland in what today is Nigeria (see the Comparative Essay "The Migration of Peoples" on p. 218). Eventually, they reached East Africa, where they may have been responsible for introducing the widespread cultivation of crops and knowledge of ironworking, although there are signs of some limited iron smelting in the area before their arrival.

The Bantu settled in rural communities based on subsistence farming. The primary crops were millet and sorghum, along with yams, melons, and beans. In addition to stone implements, they often used iron tools, usually manufactured in a local smelter, to till the land. Some people kept domestic animals such as cattle, sheep, goats, or chickens or supplemented their diets by hunting and food gathering. Because the population was minimal and an ample supply of cultivable land was available, most settlements were relatively small, although there was apparently a readily visible set of class distinctions within the local population (see the box "A Chinese View of Africa" above).

As early as the era of the New Kingdom in the second millennium B.C.E., Egyptian ships had plied the waters off the East African coast in search of gold, ivory, palm oil, and perhaps slaves. By the first century C.E., the region was an established part of a trading network that included the Mediterranean and the Red Sea. In that century, a Greek seafarer from Alexandria wrote an account of his travels down the coast from Cape Guardafui (GWAR-duh-fwee *or* GWAR-duh-foo-ee) at the tip of the Horn of Africa to the Strait of Madagascar (ma-duh-GAS-kur), thousands of miles to the south. Called the *Periplus* (PER-ih-pluss), this work provides descriptions of the peoples and settlements along the African coast and the trade goods they supplied.

According to the *Periplus,* the port of Rhapta (RAHP-tuh) (probably modern Dar es Salaam) was a commercial metropolis, exporting ivory, rhinoceros horn, and tortoise shell and importing glass, wine, grain, and metal goods such as weapons and tools. The identity of the peoples taking part in this trade is not clear, but it seems likely that the area was inhabited primarily by a mixture of local peoples supplemented by a small number of immigrants from the Arabian peninsula. Out of this mixture would eventually emerge a cosmopolitan **Swahili** (swah-HEE-lee) culture (see "East Africa: The Land of the Zanj" later in this chapter) that continues to exist in coastal areas today. Beyond Rhapta was "unexplored ocean." Some contemporary observers believed that the Indian and Atlantic Oceans were connected (see the box "Beyond the Pillars of Hercules" on p. 216). Others were convinced that the Indian Ocean was an enclosed sea and that the continent of Africa could not be circumnavigated. Adverse winds and currents from the straits dividing Madagascar from Africa down to the southern tip of the continent made sailing conditions difficult.

Trade across the Indian Ocean and down the coast of East Africa, facilitated by the monsoon winds, would gradually become one of the most lucrative sources of commercial profit in the ancient and medieval worlds. Although the origins of the trade remain shrouded in mystery, traders eventually came by sea from as far away as the mainland of Southeast Asia. Early in the first millennium C.E., Malay (mah-LAY) peoples bringing cinnamon to the Middle East began to cross the Indian Ocean directly and landed on the southeastern coast of Africa. Eventually, a Malay settlement was established on the island of Madagascar, where the population is still of mixed Malay-African origin. Historians suspect that Malay immigrants were responsible for introducing such Southeast Asian foods as the banana and the yam to Africa, although recent archaeological evidence suggests that such plants may have arrived in Africa as early as the third millennium B.C.E. The banana, with its high yield and ability to grow in uncultivated rain forest, became the preferred crop of many Bantu peoples.

The Coming of Islam

 Q **FOCUS QUESTION:** What effects did the coming of Islam have on African religion, society, political structures, trade, and culture?

As Chapter 7 described, the rise of Islam during the first half of the seventh century C.E. had ramifications far beyond the Arabian peninsula. Arab armies swept across North Africa, incorporating it into the Arab empire and isolating the Christian state of Axum to the south. Although East Africa and West Africa south of the Sahara were not occupied by the Arab forces, Islam eventually penetrated these areas as well.

African Religious Beliefs Before Islam

When Islam arrived, most African societies already had well-developed systems of religious belief. Like other aspects of African life, early African religious beliefs varied from place to place, but certain characteristics appear to have been shared by most African societies. One of these common features was **pantheism**, belief in a single creator god from whom all things came. Sometimes the creator god was accompanied by a whole pantheon of lesser deities. The Ashanti (uh-SHAN-tee *or* uh-SHAHN-tee) people of Ghana (GAH-nuh) in West Africa believed in a supreme being called Nyame (NY-AH-may), whose sons were lesser gods. Each son served a different purpose: one was the rainmaker, another was the source of compassion, and a third was responsible for the sunshine. This heavenly hierarchy paralleled earthly arrangements: worship of Nyame was the exclusive preserve of the king through his priests; lesser officials and the common people worshiped Nyame's sons, who might intercede with their father on behalf of ordinary Africans.

Belief in an afterlife was closely connected to the importance of ancestors and the **lineage group**, or clan, in African society. Each lineage (LIH-nee-ij) group could trace itself back to a founding ancestor or group of ancestors. These ancestral souls would not be extinguished as long as the lineage group continued to perform rituals in their name. The rituals could also benefit the lineage group on earth, for the ancestral souls, being closer to the gods, had the power to influence the lives of their descendants, for good or evil.

Such beliefs were challenged but not always replaced by the arrival of Islam. In some ways, the tenets of Islam were in conflict with traditional African beliefs and customs. Although the concept of a single transcendent deity presented no problems in many African societies, Islam's rejection of spirit worship and a priestly class ran counter to the beliefs of many Africans and was often ignored in practice. Similarly, as various Muslim travelers observed, Islam's insistence on the separation of the sexes contrasted with the relatively informal relationships that prevailed in many African societies and was probably slow to take root. In the long run, imported ideas were synthesized with indigenous beliefs to create a unique brand of Africanized Islam.

The Arabs in North Africa

In 641, Arab forces advanced into Egypt, seized the delta of the Nile River, and brought two centuries of Byzantine rule to an end. To guard against attacks from the Byzantine fleet, the Arabs eventually built a new capital at Cairo, inland from the previous Byzantine capital of Alexandria, and began to consolidate their control over the entire region.

On their arrival in Egypt, the Arab conquerors were probably welcomed by many, if not the majority, of the local inhabitants. Although Egypt had been a thriving commercial center under the Byzantines, the average Egyptian had not shared in this prosperity. Tax rates were generally high, and Christians were subjected to periodic persecution by the Byzantines, who viewed the local Coptic faith and other sects in the area as heresies. Although the new rulers continued to obtain much of their revenue from taxing the local farming population, tax rates were generally lower than they had been under the corrupt Byzantine government, and conversion to Islam brought exemption from taxation. During the next generations, many Egyptians converted to the Muslim faith, but Islam did not move into the upper Nile Valley until several hundred years later. As Islam spread southward, it was adopted by many lowland peoples, but it had less success in the mountains of Ethiopia, where Coptic Christianity continued to win adherents.

In the meantime, Arab rule was gradually being extended westward along the Mediterranean coast. When the Romans conquered Carthage in 146 B.C.E., they had called their new province Africa, thus introducing a name that would eventually be applied to the entire continent. After the fall of the Roman Empire, much of the area had reverted to the control of local Berber chieftains, but the Byzantines captured Carthage in the mid-sixth century C.E. In 690, the city was seized by the Arabs, who then began to extend their control over the entire area, which they called *al-Maghrib* (al-MAH-greb) ("the west").

At first, the local Berber peoples resisted their new conquerors. The Berbers were tough fighters, and for several generations, Arab rule was limited to the towns and lowland coastal areas. But Arab persistence eventually paid off, and by the early eighth century, the entire North African coast as far west as the Strait of Gibraltar was under Arab rule. The Arabs were now poised to cross the strait and expand into southern Europe and to push south beyond the fringes of the Sahara.

The Spread of Islam in Africa

resins such as frankincense and myrrh, and slaves. Slaves came primarily from the south, where Axum had been attempting to subjugate restive tribal peoples living in the Amharic (am-HAR-ik) plateau beyond its southern border (see the box "Beware the Troglodytes!" on p. 222).

Beginning in the twelfth century, however, relations between Axum and its neighbors deteriorated as the Muslim states along the coast began to move inland to gain control over the growing trade in slaves and ivory. Axum responded with force and at first had some success in reasserting its hegemony over the area. But in the early fourteenth century, the Muslim state of Adal (a-DAHL), located at the juncture of the Indian Ocean and the Red Sea, launched a new attack on the Christian kingdom.

Axum also underwent significant internal change during this period. The Zagwe (ZAH-gweh) dynasty, which seized control of the country in the mid-twelfth century, centralized the government and extended the Christian faith throughout the kingdom, now known as Ethiopia (see the Comparative Illustration "Rock Architecture" on p. 223). Military commanders or civilian officials who had personal or kinship ties with the royal court established vast landed estates to maintain security and facilitate the collection of taxes from the local population. In the meantime, Christian missionaries established monasteries and churches to propagate the faith in

The Kingdom of Ethiopia: A Christian Island in a Muslim Sea

By the end of the sixth century C.E., the kingdom of Axum, long a dominant force in the trade network through the Red Sea, was in a state of decline. Overexploitation of farmland had played a role in the process, as had a shift in trade routes away from the Red Sea to the Arabian peninsula and Persian Gulf. By the beginning of the ninth century, the capital had been moved farther into the mountainous interior, and Axum was gradually transformed from a maritime power into an isolated agricultural society.

The rise of Islam on the Arabian peninsula hastened this process, as the Arab world increasingly began to serve as the focus of the regional trade passing through the area. By the eighth century, a number of Muslim trading states had been established on the African coast of the Red Sea, a development that contributed to the transformation of Axum into a landlocked society with primarily agricultural interests. At first, relations between Christian Axum and its Muslim neighbors were relatively peaceful, as the larger and more powerful Axumite kingdom attempted with some success to compel the coastal Islamic states to accept a tributary relationship. Axum's role in the local commercial network temporarily revived, and the area became a prime source for ivory, gold,

CHRONOLOGY	Early Africa
Origins of agriculture in Africa	c. 9000–5000 B.C.E.
Desiccation of the Sahara begins	c. 5000 B.C.E.
Kingdom of Kush in Nubia	c. 1070 B.C.E.–350 B.C.E.
Iron Age begins	c. Sixth century B.C.E.
Beginning of trans-Saharan trade	c. First millennium B.C.E.
Rise of Meroë	c. 300 B.C.E.
Rise of Axum	First century C.E.
Arrival of Malays on Madagascar	Second century C.E.
Arrival of Bantu in East Africa	Early centuries C.E.
Conquest of Meroë by Axum	Fourth century C.E.
Origins of Ghana	Fifth century C.E.
Arab takeover of lower Nile Valley	641 C.E.
Development of Swahili culture	c. First millennium C.E.
Spread of Islam across North Africa	Seventh century C.E.
Spread of Islam in Horn of Africa	Ninth century C.E.
Decline of Ghana	Twelfth century C.E.
Kingdom of Zimbabwe	c. 1100–c. 1450
Establishment of Zagwe dynasty in Ethiopia	c. 1150
Rise of Mali	c. 1250

Beware the Troglodytes!

IN AFRICA, as elsewhere, relations between pastoral peoples and settled populations living in cities or in crowded river valleys were frequently marked by distrust and conflict. Such was certainly the case in the city of Meroë in the upper Nile Valley, where the residents viewed the nomadic peoples in the surrounding hills and deserts with a mixture of curiosity and foreboding. In the following selection, the second century B.C.E. Greek historian Agatharchides (a-ga-THAR-kuh-deez) describes the so-called Troglodyte (TRAH-gluh-dyt) people living in the mountains east of the Nile River.

On the Erythraean Sea

Now, the Troglodytes are called "Nomads" by the Greeks and live a wandering life supported by their herds in groups ruled by tyrants. Together with their children they have their women in common except for the one belonging to the tyrant. Against a person who has sexual relations with her the chief levies as a fine a specified number of sheep.

This is their way of life. When it is winter in their country—this is at the time of the Etesian winds—and the god inundates their land with heavy rains, they draw their sustenance from blood and milk, which they mix together and stir in jars which have been slightly heated. When summer comes, however, they live in the marshlands, fighting among themselves over the pasture. They eat those of their animals that are old and sick after they have been slaughtered by butchers whom they call "Unclean."

For armament the tribe of Troglodytes called Megabari have circular shields made of raw ox-hide and clubs tipped with iron knobs, but the others have bows and spears.

They do not fight with each other, as the Greeks do, over land or some other pretext but over the pasturage as it sprouts up at various times. In their feuds, they first pelt each other with stones until some are wounded. Then for the remainder of the battle they resort to a contest of bows and arrows. In a short time many die as they shoot accurately because of their practice in this pursuit and their aiming at a target bare of defensive weapons. The older women, however, put an end to the battle by rushing in between them and meeting with respect. For it is their custom not to strike these women on any account so that immediately upon their appearance the men cease shooting.

They do not, he says, sleep as do other men. They possess a large number of animals which accompany them, and they ring cowbells from the horns of all the males in order that their sound might drive off wild beasts. At nightfall, they collect their herds into byres and cover these with hurdles made from palm branches. Their women and children mount up on one of these. The men, however, light fires in a circle and sing additional tales and thus ward off sleep, since in many situations discipline imposed by nature is able to conquer nature.

Q *Does the author of this passage describe the customs of the Troglodytes in an impartial manner, or do you detect a subtle attitude of disapproval or condescension?*

Source: Agatharchides of Cnidus, *On the Erythraen Sea*, trans. S. Burstein (London, 1989), fragments 62-64, as cited in S. Burstein (ed.), *Ancient African Civilizations: Kush and Axum* (Princeton, 1998), pp. 47–50.

---

outlying areas. Close relations were reestablished with leaders of the Coptic church in Egypt and with Christian officials in the Holy Land. This process was continued by the Solomonids (sah-luh-MAHN-idz), who succeeded the Zagwe dynasty in 1270. But by the early fifteenth century, the state had become deeply involved in an expanding conflict with Muslim Adal to the east, a conflict that lasted for over a century and gradually took on the characteristics of a holy war.

East Africa: The Land of the Zanj

The rise of Islam also had a lasting impact on the coast of East Africa, which the Greeks had called Azania and the Arabs called Zanj (ZANJ) referring to the "burnt

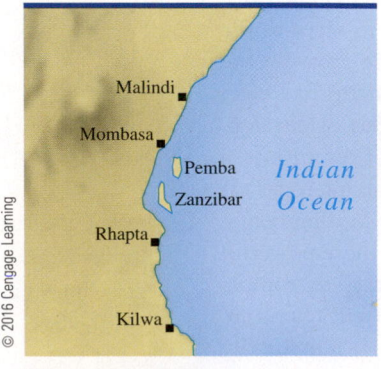

The Swahili Coast

© 2016 Cengage Learning

skin" of the indigenous population. According to Swahili oral traditions, during the seventh and eighth centuries peoples from the Arabian peninsula and the Persian Gulf began to settle at ports along the coast and on the small islands offshore. Then, in the middle of the tenth century, a Persian from the city of Shiraz sailed to the area with his six sons. As his small fleet stopped along the coast, each son disembarked on one of the coastal islands and founded a small community; these settlements eventually grew into important commercial centers including Mombasa (mahm-BAH-suh), Pemba (PEM-buh), Zanzibar (ZAN-zi-bar) (literally, "the coast of the Zanj"), and Kilwa (KIL-wuh). Although this oral tradition may underestimate the indigenous population's growing involvement in local commerce, it also reflects the degree to which African

William J. Duiker

Werner Forman/Art Resource, NY

COMPARATIVE ILLUSTRATION

Rock Architecture. As we have seen, one of the earliest forms of religious architecture in India was the rock temple (see Chapter 2). One of the most famous examples is the eighth-century temple at Ellora, in central India. Named after Shiva's holy mountain in the Himalayas, the temple is approximately the size of the Parthenon in Athens but was literally carved out of a hillside, with its exquisite sculptures open to the sky (left).

This form of architecture also found expression in parts of Africa. In 1200 C.E., Christian monks in Ethiopia began to construct a remarkable series of eleven churches carved out of solid volcanic rock (right). After a 40-foot trench was formed by removing the bedrock, the central block of stone was hewed into the shape of a Greek cross; then it was hollowed out and decorated. These churches, which are still in use today, testify to the fervor of Ethiopian Christianity, which plays a major role in preserving the country's cultural and national identity.

Q *Why do you think some early cultures made frequent use of the concept of rock architecture, while others did not? Why do you think the process was discontinued?*

merchants—who often served as middlemen between the peoples of the interior and the traders arriving from ports all around the Indian Ocean—saw themselves as part of an international commercial network.

In any case, by the ninth and tenth centuries, a string of trading ports had appeared stretching from Mogadishu (moh-guh-DEE-shoo) (today the capital of Somalia) in the north to Kilwa (south of present-day Dar es Salaam) in the south. Kilwa became especially important because it was near the southern limit for a ship hoping to complete the round-trip journey in a single season. Goods such as ivory, gold, and rhinoceros horn were exported across the Indian Ocean to countries as far away as China, while imports included iron goods, glassware, Indian textiles, and Chinese porcelain. Merchants in these cities often amassed considerable profit, as

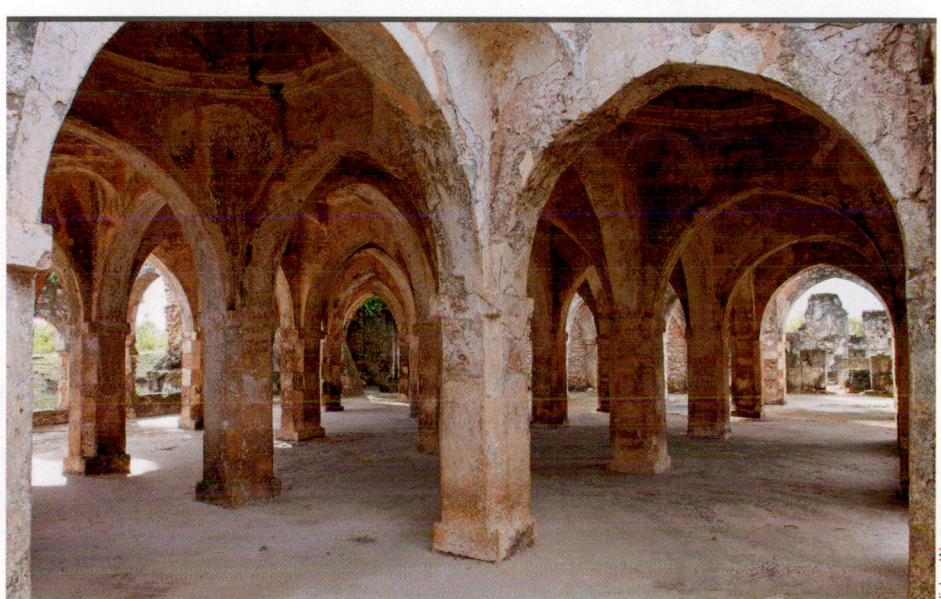

Xinhua/Alamy

The Great Mosque of Kilwa. The city of Kilwa, located on an island south of the present-day city of Dar es Salaam, was a longtime major center of Muslim culture along the coast of East Africa, and its mosque was one of the most impressive stone structures on the entire African continent. Today the city has been abandoned, but the ruins of its mosque serve as a testimonial to the renowned achievements of Swahili civilization, which was vividly described by such tireless Muslim travelers as al-Mas'udi and Ibn Battuta.

evidenced by their lavish stone palaces, some of which still stand in the modern cities of Mombasa and Zanzibar. Though now in ruins, Kilwa was one of the most magnificent cities of its day. The fourteenth-century Arab traveler Ibn Battuta (IB-un ba-TOO-tuh) described it as "amongst the most beautiful of cities and most elegantly built. All of it is of wood, and the ceilings of its houses are of *al-dis* [reeds]."[2] One particularly impressive structure was the Husini Kubwa (hoo-SEE-nee KOOB-wuh), a massive palace with vaulted roofs capped with domes and elaborate stone carvings, surrounding an inner courtyard. Ordinary townspeople and the residents in smaller towns did not live in such luxurious conditions, of course, but even so, affluent urban residents lived in spacious stone buildings, with indoor plumbing and consumer goods imported from as far away as China and southern Europe.

Most of the coastal states were self-governing, although sometimes several towns were grouped together under a single dominant authority. Government revenue came primarily from taxes imposed on commerce. Some trade went on between these coastal city-states and the peoples of the interior, who provided gold and iron, ivory, and various agricultural goods and animal products in return for textiles, manufactured articles, and weapons. Relations apparently varied, and the coastal merchants sometimes resorted to force to obtain goods from the inland peoples. A Portuguese visitor recounted that "the men [of Mombasa] are oft-times at war and but seldom at peace with those of the mainland, and they carry on trade with them, bringing thence great store of honey, wax, and ivory."[3]

By the twelfth and thirteenth centuries, a cosmopolitan culture, eventually known as Swahili, from the Arabic *sahel* (sah-HEL), meaning "coast," began to emerge throughout the seaboard area. Intermarriage between the small number of immigrants and the local population eventually led to the emergence of a ruling class of mixed heritage, some of whom had Arab or Persian ancestors. By this time, too, many members of the ruling class had converted to Islam. Middle Eastern urban architectural styles and other aspects of Arab culture were implanted within a society still predominantly African. Arabic words and phrases were combined with Bantu grammatical structures to form a distinct language, also known as Swahili; it is the national language of Kenya and Tanzania today.

The States of West Africa

During the eighth century, merchants from the Maghrib began to carry Muslim beliefs to the savanna areas south of the Sahara. At first, conversion took place on an individual basis and primarily among local merchants, rather than through official encouragement. The first rulers to convert to Islam were the royal family of Gao (GAH-oh) at the end of the tenth century. Five hundred years later, most of the population in the grasslands south of the Sahara had accepted Islam.

The expansion of Islam into West Africa had a major impact on the political system. By introducing Arabic as the first written language in the region and Muslim law codes and administrative practices from the Middle East, Islam provided local rulers with the tools to increase their authority and the efficiency of their governments. Moreover, as Islam gradually spread throughout the region, a common religion united previously diverse peoples into a more coherent community.

When Islam arrived in the grasslands south of the Sahara, the region was beginning to undergo significant political and social change. As a partial consequence of the initiation of a new wet phase throughout the region in the early fourth century, a number of major trading states were in the making, and they eventually transformed the Sahara into one of the leading avenues of world trade, crisscrossed by caravan routes leading to destinations as far away as the Atlantic Ocean, the Mediterranean, and the Red Sea (see Map 8.3).

GHANA The first of these great commercial states was Ghana, which emerged in the fifth century C.E. in the upper Niger Valley, a grassland region between the Sahara and the tropical forests along the West African coast. (The modern state of Ghana, which takes its name from this early trading society, is located in the forest region to the south.) The majority of the people in the area were farmers living in villages under the authority of a local chieftain. Gradually, these local communities were united to form the kingdom of Ghana.

Zanzibar: Entrepôt of East Africa. The island of Zanzibar was one of the most important trading posts along the coast of East Africa. It was not only an active entrepôt for exchanging goods between inland areas in the continent of Africa and regions throughout the Indian Ocean, but also a center of the mixed Afro-Arabian Swahili culture that flourished up and down the coast. Dhows of all types arrived in the harbor from locations throughout the Indian Ocean. Larger vessels, as shown in Chapter 7, travelled from as far away as the Arabian peninsula, India, and Southeast Asia. Smaller ones, such as this trim little sailing craft in the harbor of Zanzibar, plied the waters along the coast of East Africa. Such ships are still common throughout the region, although many of the larger ships have abandoned the sail for more modern means of locomotion.

MAP 8.3 Trans-Saharan Trade Routes. Trade across the Sahara began during the first millennium B.C.E. With the arrival of the camel from the Middle East, trade expanded dramatically.

Q *What were the major cities involved in the trade, as shown on this map?*

Although the people of the region had traditionally lived from agriculture, a primary reason for Ghana's growing importance was gold. The heartland of the state was located near one of the richest gold-producing areas in all of Africa. Ghanaian merchants transported the gold to Morocco, whence it was distributed throughout the known world. The exchange of goods became quite ritualized. As the ancient Greek historian Herodotus relates:

> The Carthaginians also tell us that they trade with a race of men who live in a part of Libya beyond the Pillars of Heracles [the Strait of Gibraltar]. On reaching this country, they unload their goods, arrange them tidily along the beach, and then, returning to their boats, raise a smoke. Seeing the smoke, the natives come down to the beach, place on the ground a certain quantity of gold in exchange for the goods, and go off again to a distance. The Carthaginians then come ashore and take a look at the gold; and if they think it represents a fair price for their wares, they collect it and go away; if, on the other hand, it seems too little, they go back aboard and wait, and the natives come and add to the gold until they are satisfied. There is perfect honesty on both sides; the Carthaginians never touch the gold until it equals in value what they have offered for sale, and the natives never touch the goods until the gold has been taken away.[4]

Later, Ghana became known to Arabic-speaking peoples in North Africa as "the land of gold." Actually, the name was misleading, for the gold did not come from Ghana but from a neighboring people, who sold it to merchants from Ghana.

Eventually, other exports from Ghana found their way to the bazaars of the Mediterranean coast and beyond—ivory, ostrich feathers, hides, leather goods, and ultimately slaves. The origins of the slave trade in the area probably go back to the first millennium B.C.E., when Berber tribesmen seized African villagers in the regions south of the Sahara and sold

them to buyers in Europe and the Middle East. In return, Ghana imported metal goods (especially weapons), textiles, horses, and salt.

Much of the trade across the desert was still conducted by the nomadic Berbers, but Ghanaian merchants played an active role as intermediaries, trading tropical products such as bananas, kola nuts, and palm oil from the forest states of Guinea along the Atlantic coast to the south. By the eighth and ninth centuries, much of this trade was conducted by Muslim merchants, who purchased the goods from local traders (using iron and copper coins or cowrie shells from Southeast Asia as the primary means of exchange) and then sold them to Berbers, who carried them across the desert. The merchants who carried on this trade often became quite wealthy and lived in splendor in cities like Saleh (SAH-luh), the capital of Ghana. So did the king, of course, who taxed the merchants as well as the farmers and the producers.

Like other West African monarchs, the king of Ghana ruled by divine right and was assisted by a hereditary aristocracy composed of the leading members of the prominent clans, who also served as district chiefs responsible for maintaining law and order and collecting taxes. The king was responsible for maintaining the security of his kingdom, serving as an intermediary with local deities, and functioning as the chief law officer to adjudicate disputes. The kings of Ghana did not convert to Islam themselves, although they welcomed Muslim merchants and apparently did not discourage their subjects from adopting the new faith (see the box "Royalty and Religion in Ghana" on p. 226).

MALI The empire of Ghana flourished for several hundred years, but by the twelfth century, weakened by ruinous wars with Berber marauders, it had begun to decline. The downfall of Ghana was a partial consequence of the emergence of the powerful Almoravid (al-MOR-uh-vid) dynasty in Morocco. The Almoravids were not only active in protecting the Moorish kingdoms in Andalusia (see Chapter 7), but also began to expand their activities southward in the desert from their new capital of Marrakech (mar-uh-KESH), a trading center founded in the eleventh century at a caravan stop near the Atlas Mountains. Attacks by mounted Berber forces on the weakening state of Ghana began shortly after, and it collapsed by the end of the following century.

In the ashes of the kingdom of Ghana rose a number of new trading societies, including large territorial empires like Mali (MAHL-ee) and Songhai (song-GY) in the west, Kanem-Bornu (KAH-nuhm-BOR-noo) in the east, and small commercial city-states like the Hausa states, located in what is today northern Nigeria (see Map 8.4).

Royalty and Religion in Ghana

RELIGION & PHILOSOPHY

AFTER ITS FIRST APPEARANCE IN WEST AFRICA in the decades following the death of Muhammad, Islam competed with indigenous African religions for followers. Eventually, several local rulers converted to the Muslim faith. This passage by the Arab geographer al-Bakri (al-BAHK-ree) reflects religious tolerance in the state of Ghana during the eleventh century under a non-Muslim ruler with many Muslim subjects.

Al-Bakri's Description of Royalty in Ghana

The king's residence comprises a palace and conical huts, the whole surrounded by a fence like a wall. Around the royal town are huts and groves of thorn trees where live the magicians who control their religious rites. These groves, where they keep their idols and bury their kings, are protected by guards who permit no one to enter or find out what goes on in them.

None of those who belong to the imperial religion may wear tailored garments except the king himself and the heir-presumptive, his sister's son. The rest of the people wear wrappers of cotton, silk or brocade according to their means. Most of the men shave their beards and the women their heads.

The king adorns himself with female ornaments around the neck and arms. On his head he wears gold-embroidered caps covered with turbans of finest cotton. He gives audience to the people for the redressing of grievances in a hut around which are placed 10 horses covered in golden cloth. Behind him stand 10 slaves carrying shields and swords mounted with gold. On his right are the sons of vassal kings, their heads plaited with gold and wearing costly garments. On the ground around him are seated his ministers, whilst the governor of the city sits before him. On guard at the door are dogs of fine pedigree, wearing collars adorned with gold and silver. The royal audience is announced by the beating of a drum, called *daba*, made out of a long piece of hollowed-out wood. When the people have gathered, his coreligionists draw near upon their knees sprinkling dust upon their heads as a sign of respect, whilst the Muslims clap hands as their form of greeting.

 Why might an African ruler find it advantageous to adopt the Muslim faith? What kinds of changes would the adoption of Islam entail for the peoples living in West Africa?

Source: Adapted from translation quoted in J. S. Trimingham, *A History of Islam and West Africa*, copyright 1970 by Oxford University Press.

The greatest of the empires that emerged after the destruction of Ghana was Mali. Extending from the Atlantic coast inland as far as the trading cities of Timbuktu (tim-buk-TOO) and Gao on the Niger River, Mali built its wealth and power on the gold trade. But the heartland of Mali was situated south of the Sahara in the savanna region, where there was sufficient moisture for farmers to grow such crops as sorghum, millet, and rice. The farmers lived in villages ruled by a local chieftain, called a *mansa* (MAHN-suh), who served as both religious and administrative leader and was responsible for forwarding tax revenues from the village to higher levels of government.

The primary wealth of the country was accumulated in the cities. Here lived the merchants, who were primarily of local origin, although many were now practicing Muslims.

A Great Gate at Marrakech. The Moroccan city of Marrakech, founded in the ninth century C.E., was a major northern terminus of the trans-Saharan trade and one of the chief commercial centers in pre-modern Africa. Widely praised by such famous travelers as Ibn Battuta, the city was an architectural marvel in that all its major public buildings were constructed of red sandstone. Shown here is the Great Gate to the city, through which camel caravans passed en route to and from the vast desert. In the Berber language, Marrakech means "pass without making a noise," a necessity for caravan traders who had to be alert to the danger of thieves in the vicinity.

William J. Duiker

MAP 8.4 **The Emergence of States in Africa.** By the end of the first millennium C.E., organized states had begun to appear in various parts of Africa. The extensive empires of Ghana, Mali, and Songhai emerged at different times and did not exist simultaneously.

Q *Why did organized states appear at these particular spots and not in other areas of Africa?*

Commercial activities were taxed but were apparently so lucrative that both the merchants and the kings prospered. One of the most powerful kings of Mali was Mansa Musa (MAHN-suh MOO-suh) (r. 1312–1337), whose primary contribution to his people was probably not economic prosperity but the Muslim faith. Mansa Musa strongly encouraged the building of mosques and the study of the Qur'an in his kingdom and imported scholars and books to introduce his subjects to the message of Allah.

The city of Timbuktu ("well of Bouctu," a Taureg woman who lived in the area) is the most storied of the cities that emerged under the kingdom of Mali. It was founded by Berber tribal groups in 1100 C.E. as a seasonal camp for caravan traders on the Niger River. Under Mansa Musa and his successors, the city gradually emerged as a major intellectual and cultural center in West Africa and the site of a renowned mosque, as well as schools of Islamic law, literature, and the sciences. Still, it was trade that drove the commerce of the city. As one Muslim historian later commented, "For Timbuktu, the great wealth was from salt.... Timbuktu would never have grown as important as it did if it hadn't been the main entrepôt for the merchants of Djenné, which sent here a large number of businessmen and men of letters."[5]

Mansa Musa. Mansa Musa, king of the West African state of Mali, was one of the richest and most powerful rulers of his day. During a famous pilgrimage to Mecca, he arrived in Cairo with a hundred camels laden with gold and gave away so much gold that its value depreciated there for several years. To promote the Islamic faith in his country, he bought homes in Cairo and Mecca to house pilgrims en route to the holy shrine, and he brought back to Mali a renowned Arab architect to build mosques in the trading centers of Gao and Timbuktu. His fame spread to Europe as well, evidenced by this Spanish map of 1375, which depicts Mansa Musa seated on his throne in Mali, holding an impressive gold nugget.

States and Noncentralized Societies in Central and Southern Africa

 FOCUS QUESTIONS: What role did migration play in the evolution of early African societies? How did the impact of these migrations compare with similar population movements elsewhere?

In the southern half of the African continent, from the great basin of the Congo River to the Cape of Good Hope, states formed somewhat more slowly than in the north. Until the eleventh century C.E., most of the peoples in this region lived in what are sometimes called **noncentralized societies**, characterized by autonomous villages organized by clans and ruled by a local chieftain or clan head. Beginning in the eleventh century, in some parts of southern Africa, these independent villages gradually began to consolidate. Out of these groupings came the first states.

The Congo River Valley

One area where this process occurred was the Congo River valley, where the combination of fertile land and nearby deposits of copper and iron enabled the inhabitants to enjoy an agricultural surplus and engage in regional commerce. Two new states in particular underwent this transition. Sometime during the fourteenth century, the kingdom of Luba (LOOB-uh) was founded in the center of the continent, in a rich agricultural and fishing area near the shores of Lake Kisale. Luba had a relatively centralized government, in which the king appointed provincial governors, who were responsible for collecting tribute from the village chiefs. At about the same time, the kingdom of Kongo was formed just south of the mouth of the Congo River on the Atlantic coast.

These new states were primarily agricultural, although both had a thriving manufacturing sector and took an active part in the growing exchange of goods throughout the region. As time passed, both began to expand southward to absorb the mixed farming and pastoral peoples in the area of modern Angola. In the drier grassland area to the south, other small communities continued to support themselves by herding, hunting, or food gathering. A Portuguese sailor who encountered them in the late sixteenth century reported:

> These people are herdsmen and cultivators.... Their main crop is millet, which they grind between two stones or in wooden mortars to make flour.... Their wealth consists mainly in their huge number of dehorned cows.... They live together in small villages, in houses made of reed mats, which do not keep out the rain.[6]

Zimbabwe

Farther to the east, the situation was somewhat different. In the grassland regions immediately to the south of the Zambezi (zam-BEE-zee) River, a mixed economy involving farming, cattle herding, and commercial pursuits had begun to develop during the early centuries of the first millennium C.E. Characteristically, villages in this area were constructed inside walled enclosures to protect the animals at night. The most famous of these communities was Zimbabwe (zim-BAHB-way), located on the plateau of the same name between the Zambezi and Limpopo Rivers. From the twelfth century to the middle of the fifteenth, Zimbabwe was the most powerful and most prosperous state in the region and played a major role in the gold trade with the Swahili trading communities on the eastern coast.

The ruins of Zimbabwe's capital, known as Great Zimbabwe (*Zimbabwe* means "stone house" in the Bantu language), provide a vivid illustration of the kingdom's power and influence. Strategically situated between substantial gold reserves to the west and a small river leading to the coast, Great Zimbabwe was well placed to benefit from the expansion of trade between the coast and the interior. The town sits on a hill overlooking the river and is surrounded by stone walls, which enclosed an area large enough to hold over ten thousand residents. Like the Inka in South America (see Chapter 6), the local people stacked stone blocks without mortar to build their walls. The houses of the wealthy were built of cement on stone foundations, while those of the common people were of dried mud with thatched roofs. In the valley below is the royal palace, surrounded by a stone wall 30 feet high (see the illustration on the opening page of this chapter). Artifacts found at the site include household implements and ornaments made of gold and copper, as well as jewelry and porcelain imported from China.

Most of the royal wealth probably came from two sources: the ownership of cattle and the king's ability to levy heavy taxes on the gold that passed through the kingdom en route to the coast. By the middle of the fifteenth century, however, the city was apparently abandoned, possibly because of environmental damage caused by overgrazing. With the decline of Zimbabwe, the focus of economic power began to shift northward to the valley of the Zambezi River.

Southern Africa

South of the East African plateau and the Congo basin is a vast land of hills, grasslands, and arid desert stretching almost to the Cape of Good Hope at the tip of the continent. As Bantu-speaking farmers spread southward during the final centuries of the first millennium B.C.E., they began to encounter Neolithic peoples in the area who still lived primarily by hunting and foraging.

Available evidence suggests that early relations between these two peoples were relatively harmonious. Intermarriage between members of the two groups was apparently not unusual, and many of the hunter-gatherers were gradually absorbed into what became a dominantly Bantu-speaking pastoral and agricultural society that spread throughout much of southern Africa during the first millennium C.E.

THE KHOI AND THE SAN Two such peoples were the Khoi (KOI) and the San (SAHN). The two were related because of their language, known as Khoisan (KOI-sahn), distinguished by the use of "clicking" sounds. The Khoi were herders, while the San were hunter-gatherers who lived in small family communities of twenty to twenty-five members throughout southern Africa from Namibia in the west to the Drakensberg Mountains near the southeastern coast. Archaeologists have studied rock paintings found in caves throughout the area in their efforts to learn more about the early life of the San. These multicolored paintings, which predate the coming of the Europeans, were drawn with a brush made of small feathers fastened to a reed. They depict various aspects of the San's lifestyle, including their hunting techniques and religious rituals.

Africa: A Continent Without History?

Until the second half of the twentieth century, the prevailing view among Western historians was that Africa was a continent without history, a land of scattered villages isolated from the main currents of world affairs. But in the decades after the end of World War II, a new generation of historians trained in African studies, spurred on in part by the appearance in 1959 of Basil Davidson's path-breaking work, *Lost Cities of Africa*, began to contest that view. Their studies have demonstrated that throughout history not only were many African societies actively in contact with peoples beyond their shores, but also that they created a number of advanced civilizations of their own.

Although the paucity of written sources continues to be a challenge for historians, other sources have been used with increasing success to throw light on the African historical experience. African peoples were at the forefront of the agricultural revolution in the ninth and eighth millennia B.C.E., and although some parts of the continent remained isolated from the main currents of world history, a number of other African societies began as early as the first millennium C.E. to play an active role in the expanding global trade network, which stretched from the Mediterranean Sea deep into the Sahara. Another major commercial trade route ran from the Arabian peninsula down the coast of East Africa along the shores of the Indian Ocean. Thus, it is becoming increasingly clear that from the dawn of history the peoples of Africa have made a significant contribution to the human experience.

African Society

 FOCUS QUESTIONS: What role did lineage groups, women, and slavery play in African societies? In what ways did African societies in various parts of the continent differ? What accounted for these differences?

As noted earlier, generalizing about social organization, cultural development, and daily life in traditional Africa is difficult because of the extreme diversity of the continent and its inhabitants. One-quarter of all the languages in the world are spoken in Africa, and five of the major language families are located there. Ethnic divisions are equally pronounced. Because many of these languages did not have a system of writing until fairly recently, historians must rely on accounts by occasional visitors, such as al-Mas'udi and Ibn Battuta. Such travelers,

however, tended to come into contact mostly with the wealthy and the powerful, leaving us to speculate about what life was like for ordinary Africans during this early period.

Urban Life

African towns often began as fortified walled villages and gradually evolved into larger communities serving several purposes. Here, of course, were the center of government and the teeming markets filled with goods from distant regions. Here also were artisans skilled in metalworking or woodworking, pottery making, and other crafts. Unlike the rural areas, where a village was usually composed of a single lineage group or clan, the towns drew their residents from several clans, although individual clans usually lived in their own compounds and were governed by their own clan heads.

In the states of West Africa, the focal point of the major towns was the royal precinct. The relationship between the ruler and the merchant class differed from the situation in most Asian societies, where the royal family and the aristocracy were largely isolated from the remainder of the population. In Africa, the chasm between the king and the common people was not so great. Often the ruler would hold an audience to allow people to voice their complaints or to welcome visitors from foreign countries. In the city-states of the East African coast, the rulers were often wealthy merchants who, as in the case of the town of Kilwa, "did not possess more country than the city itself."[7]

This is not to say that the king was not elevated above all others in status. In wealthier states, the walls of the audience chamber would be covered with sheets of beaten silver and gold, and the king would be surrounded by hundreds of armed soldiers and some of his trusted advisers. Nevertheless, the symbiotic relationship between the ruler and merchant class served to reduce the gap between the king and his subjects. The relationship was mutually beneficial, since the merchants received honors and favors from the palace while the king's coffers were filled with taxes paid by the merchants. Certainly, it was to the king's benefit to maintain law and order in his domain so that the merchants could ply their trade. As Ibn Battuta observed, among the good qualities of the peoples of West Africa was the prevalence of peace in the region. "The traveler is not afraid in it," he remarked, "nor is he who lives there in fear of the thief or of the robber by violence."[8]

Village Life

The vast majority of Africans lived in small rural villages. Their identities were established by their membership in a nuclear family and a lineage group. At the basic level was the nuclear family of parents and preadult children; sometimes it included an elderly grandparent and other family dependents as well. They lived in small, round huts constructed of packed mud and topped with a conical thatch roof. In most African societies, these nuclear family units were combined into larger kinship communities known as households or lineage groups.

The lineage group was similar in many respects to the clan in China or the *jati* in India in that it was normally based on kinship ties, although sometimes outsiders such as friends or

Women and Islam in North Africa

FAMILY & SOCIETY

IN MUSLIM SOCIETIES IN NORTH AFRICA, as else-where, women were required to cover their bodies to avoid tempting men, but Islam's puritanical insistence on the separation of the sexes contrasted with the relatively informal relationships that prevailed in many African societies. In this excerpt from *The History and Description of Africa*, Leo Africanus describes the customs along the Mediterranean coast of Africa. A resident of Spain of Muslim parentage who was captured by Christian corsairs in 1518 and later served under Pope Leo X, Leo Africanus undertook many visits to Africa.

Leo Africanus, *The History and Description of Africa*

Their women (according to the guise of that country) go very gorgeously attired: they wear linen gowns dyed black, with exceeding wide sleeves, over which sometimes they cast a mantle of the same color or of blue, the corners of which mantle are very [attractively] fastened about their shoulders with a fine silver clasp. Likewise they have rings hanging at their ears, which for the most part are made of silver; they wear many rings also upon their fingers. Moreover they usually wear about their thighs and ankles certain scarfs and rings, after the fashion of the Africans. They cover their faces with certain masks having only two holes for the eyes to peep out at. If any man chance to meet with them, they presently hide their faces, passing by him with silence, except it be some of their allies or kinsfolks; for unto them they always [uncover] their faces, neither is there any use of the said mask so long as they be in presence. These Arabians when they travel any journey (as they oftentimes do) they set their women upon certain saddles made handsomely of wicker for the same purpose, and fastened to their camel backs, neither be they anything too wide, but fit only for a woman to sit in. When they go to the wars each man carries his wife with him, to the end that she may cheer up her good man, and give him encouragement. Their damsels which are unmarried do usually paint their faces, breasts, arms, hands, and fingers with a kind of counterfeit color: which is accounted a most decent custom among them.

 Which of the practices described here are dictated by the social regulations of Islam? Does the author approve of the behavior of African women as described in this passage?

Source: From *The History and Description of Africa*, by Leo Africanus (New York: Burt Franklin), pp. 158–159.

---

other dependents may have been admitted to membership. Throughout the precolonial era, lineages served, in the words of one historian, as the "basic building blocks" of African society. The authority of the leading members of the lineage group was substantial. As in China, the elders had considerable power over the economic functions of the other people in the group, which provided mutual support for all members.

A village would usually be composed of a single lineage group, although some communities may have consisted of several unrelated families. At the head of the village was the familiar "big man," who was often assisted by a council of representatives of the various households in the community. Often the "big man" was believed to possess supernatural powers, and as the village grew in size and power, he might eventually be transformed into a local chieftain or monarch.

The Role of Women

Although generalizations are risky, we can say that women were usually subordinate to men in Africa, as in most early societies. In some cases, they were valued for the work they could do or for their role in increasing the size of the lineage group. Polygyny was not uncommon, particularly in Muslim societies. Women often worked in the fields while the men of the village tended the cattle or went on hunting expeditions. In some communities, the women specialized in commercial activities. In one area in southern Africa, young girls were sent into the mines to extract gold because of their smaller physiques.

But there were some key differences between the role of women in Africa and elsewhere. In many African societies, lineage was **matrilinear** rather than **patrilinear**. As Ibn Battuta observed during his travels in West Africa, "A man does not pass on inheritance except to the sons of his sister to the exclusion of his own sons."[9] He said he had never encountered this custom before except among the unbelievers of the Malabar coast in India. Women were often permitted to inherit property, and the husband was often expected to move into his wife's house.

Relations between the sexes were also sometimes more relaxed than in China or India, with none of the taboos characteristic of those societies. Again, in the words of Ibn Battuta, himself a Muslim:

> With regard to their women, they are not modest in the presence of men, they do not veil themselves in spite of their perseverance in the prayers.… The women there have friends and companions amongst men outside the prohibited degrees of marriage [that is, other than brothers, fathers, or other closely related males]. Likewise for the men, there are companions from amongst women outside the prohibited degrees. One of them would enter his house to find his wife with her companion and would not disapprove of that conduct.[10]

When Ibn Battuta asked an African acquaintance about these customs, the latter responded, "Women's companionship with men in our country is honorable and takes place in a good way: there is no suspicion about it. They are not

The Slave Trade in Ancient Africa

FAMILY & SOCIETY

THE PRACTICE OF SLAVERY WAS COMMON throughout the African continent from ancient times, but information on the nature of the slave trade is relatively difficult to find. The following document is a contract for the purchase of a Nubian slave girl in sixth-century C.E. Egypt. Behind the legal terminology contained in the contract, probably a consequence of the adoption of Roman law in pre-Muslim Egypt, lies the poignant reality of a young Nubian girl, and perhaps her future children as well, sold into a lifetime of slavery. Tragically, the traffic in slaves continues in the region today as Muslim traders launch periodic raids on Christian villages in the southern Sudan.

Sale of a Nubian Slave Girl

Greeting. We acknowledge that we the aforementioned Pathermuthis and Anatolios, through this our written contract of sale, of our own free will and with voluntary intent and irrevocable and sincere resolution, with steadfast conscience, with correct intention, without any fraud or intimidation or violence or deceit or constraint of any bad faith or deception, that we have sold to you, the aforementioned most well-born Isidora, … the girl who belongs to us and who has come to us … from the other slave-traders of the Aithiopians, the black slave, Atalous by name, now renamed by you Eutukhia, about twelve years old more or less, an Aloan by race, which

afore-mentioned black slave not being previously mortgaged for any principal sum whatsoever or for any business or agreement or afflicted by any old injury or leprosy or beating or concealed ailment, … for the mutually agreed, approved, resolved between us, full and just price [of] … four gold solidi, of full weight, on the Alexandrian standard, which afore-mentioned price at once we, the vendors, Pathermuthis and Anatolios, have been paid by you … for you to possess and to control and to own with every right of ownership, to acquire, to possess, to use her and, with God willing, her children, to manage and to administer concerning her, to sell, to put up as security, to give away, to exchange as dowry and to give … and to give to your children and descendants, to leave behind and to transmit to your testamentary heirs, successors, and legal heirs, and in general to do and perform with her all such acts as the laws enjoin upon absolute owners to do with their own property unhindered and unimpeded, from now for ever, this perpetual warranty and clearance of title and defense of the present sale in regard to every warranty falling on us, the vendors.

Based on what you have learned in this and previous chapters, to what sorts of duties would a young slave like Isidora be assigned? Did she have the option at some future date to obtain her freedom?

Source: Reprinted from Richard Holton Pierce, "A Sale of an Alodian Slave Girl: a Reexamination of Papyrus Strassburg Inv. 1404," *Symbolae Osloenses* 70 (1995): 159-164, by permission of the publisher (Taylor & Francis Ltd, http://www.tandf.co.uk/journals).

---

like the women in your country." Ibn Battuta noted his astonishment at such a "thoughtless" answer and did not accept further invitations to visit his friend's house.[11]

Such informal attitudes toward the relationship between the sexes were not found everywhere in Africa and were probably curtailed as many Africans converted to Islam (see the box "Women and Islam in North Africa" on p. 230). But it is a testimony to the tenacity of traditional customs that the relatively puritanical views about the role of women in society brought by Muslims from the Middle East made little impression even among Muslim families in West Africa.

Slavery

African slavery is often associated with the period after 1500. Indeed, the slave trade did reach enormous proportions in the seventeenth and eighteenth centuries, when European slave ships transported millions of unfortunate victims abroad to Europe or the Americas (see Chapter 14).

Slavery did not originate with the coming of the Europeans, however. It had been practiced in Africa since ancient times and probably originated when prisoners of war were forced into perpetual servitude. Slavery was common in ancient Egypt and became especially prevalent during the New Kingdom, when slaving expeditions brought back thousands

of captives from the upper Nile to be used in labor gangs, for tribute, and even as human sacrifices (see the box "The Slave Trade in Ancient Africa" above).

Slavery persisted during the early period of state building, well past the tenth century C.E. Berber tribes may have regularly raided agricultural communities south of the Sahara for captives who were transported northward and eventually sold throughout the Mediterranean. Some were enrolled as soldiers, while others, often women, were put to work as domestic servants in the homes of the well-to-do. The use of captives for forced labor or exchange was apparently also common in African societies farther to the south and along the eastern coast.

Life was difficult for the average slave. The least fortunate were probably those who worked on plantations owned by the royal family or other wealthy landowners. Those pressed into service as soldiers were sometimes more fortunate, since in Muslim societies in the Middle East, they might at some point win their freedom. Many slaves were employed in the royal household or as domestic servants in private homes. In general, these slaves probably had the most tolerable existence. Although they ordinarily were not permitted to purchase their freedom, their living conditions were often decent and sometimes practically indistinguishable from those of the free individuals in the household. In some societies in North Africa, slaves reportedly made up as much as 75 percent of the entire population. Elsewhere, the percentage was much lower, in some cases less than 10 percent.

African Culture

 FOCUS QUESTION: What are some of the chief characteristics of African sculpture and carvings, music, and architecture, and what purpose did these forms of creative expression serve in African society?

In early Africa, as in much of the rest of the world at the time, creative expression, whether in the form of painting, literature, or music, was above all a means of serving religion and the social order. Though to the uninitiated a wooden mask or the bronze and iron statuary of southern Nigeria is simply a work of art, to the artist it was often a means of expressing religious convictions and communal concerns. Indeed, some African historians reject the use of the term *art* to describe such artifacts because they were produced for spiritual or moral rather than aesthetic purposes.

Painting and Sculpture

The oldest extant art forms in Africa are rock paintings. The most famous examples are in the Tassili Mountains in the central Sahara, where the earliest paintings may date back as far as 5000 B.C.E., though the majority are a millennium or so younger. Some of the later paintings depict the two-horse chariots used to transport goods prior to the introduction of the camel. Rock paintings are also found elsewhere in the continent, including the Nile Valley and eastern and southern Africa. Those of the San peoples of southern Africa are especially interesting for their illustrations of ritual ceremonies in which village shamans induce rain, propitiate the spirits, or cure illnesses.

More familiar, perhaps, are African wood carvings and sculpture. The remarkable statues, masks, and headdresses were carved from living trees, after the artist had made a sacrifice to the tree's spirit. These masks and headdresses were worn by costumed singers and dancers in performances to the various spirits, revealing the identification and intimacy of the African with the natural world. In Mali, for example, the 3-foot-tall Ci Wara (chee WAH-rah) headdresses, one female, the other male, expressed meaning in performances that celebrated the mythical hero who had introduced agriculture.

In the thirteenth and fourteenth centuries C.E., metal workers at Ife (EE-fay) in what is now southern Nigeria produced handsome bronze and iron statues using the lost-wax method, in which melted wax in a mold is replaced by molten metal. The Ife sculptures may in turn have influenced artists in Benin (bay-NEEN), in West Africa, who produced equally impressive works in bronze during the same period. The Benin sculptures include bronze heads, relief plaques depicting life at court, ornaments, and figures of various animals.

Westerners once regarded African wood carvings and metal sculpture as a form of "primitive art," but the label is not appropriate. The metal sculpture of Benin, for example,

African Metalwork. The rulers of emerging West African states frequently commissioned royal artifacts to adorn their palaces and promote their temporal grandeur. Elaborate stools, weaponry, shields, and sculpted heads of members of the royal family served to commemorate the ruler's reign and preserve his memory for later generations. This regal thirteenth-century brass head attests to the technical excellence and sophistication of Ife metalworkers. The small holes along the scalp and the mouth permitted either hair, a veil, or a crown to be attached to the head, which itself was often attached to a wooden mannequin dressed in elaborate robes for display during memorial services.

is highly sophisticated, and some of the best works are considered masterpieces. Such works were often created by artists in the employ of the royal court.

Music

Like sculpture and wood carving, African music and dance often served a religious function. With their characteristic heavy rhythmic beat, dances were a means of communicating with the spirits, and the frenzied movements that are often identified with African dance were intended to represent the spirits acting through humans.

African music during the traditional period varied from one society to another. A wide variety of instruments were used, including drums and other percussion instruments, xylophones, bells, horns and flutes, and stringed instruments like the fiddle, harp, and zither. Still, the music throughout the continent had sufficient common characteristics to justify a few generalizations. In the first place, a strong rhythmic pattern was an important feature of most African music, although the desired effect was achieved through a

Werner Forman/Art Resource, NY

William J. Duiker

Borromeo/Art Resource, NY

ART & IDEAS

COMPARATIVE ILLUSTRATION

The Stele. A stele is a stone slab or pillar, usually decorated or inscribed and placed upright. Stelae were often used to commemorate the accomplishments of a ruler or significant figure. Shown at the left is the tallest of the Axum stelae still standing, in present-day Ethiopia. The stone stelae in Axum in the fourth century B.C.E. marked the location of royal tombs with inscriptions commemorating the glories of the kings. An earlier famous stele, seen in the center, is the obelisk at Luxor in southern Egypt. A similar kind of stone pillar, shown at the right, was erected in India during the reign of Ashoka in the third century B.C.E. (see Chapter 2) to commemorate events in the life of the Buddha. Archaeologists have also found stelae in ancient China, Greece, and Mexico.

Q *Why do you think the stele was so widely used during early times as a symbol of royal power?*

wide variety of means, including gourds, pots, bells, sticks beaten together, and hand clapping as well as drums.

Another important feature of African music was the integration of voice and instrument into a total musical experience. Musical instruments and the human voice were often woven together to tell a story, and instruments, such as the famous "talking drum," were often used to represent the voice. Choral music and individual voices were frequently used in a pattern of repetition and variation, sometimes known as "call and response." Through this technique, the audience participated in the music by uttering a single phrase over and over as a choral response to the changing call sung by the soloist. This tradition was carried by slaves to the Americas and survives to this day in the gospel music sung in

many African American congregations. Sometimes instrumental music achieved a similar result.

Much music was produced in the context of social rituals, such as weddings and funerals, religious ceremonies, and official inaugurations. It could also serve an educational purpose by passing on to the young people information about the history and social traditions of the community. In the absence of written languages in sub-Saharan Africa (except for the Arabic script, used in Muslim societies in East and West Africa), music served as the primary means of transmitting folk legends and religious traditions from generation to generation. Oral tradition, which was usually undertaken by a priestly class or a specialized class of storytellers, served a similar function.

Architecture

No aspect of African artistic creativity is more varied than architecture. From the pyramids along the Nile to the ruins of Great Zimbabwe south of the Zambezi River, from the Moorish palaces at Zanzibar to the turreted mud mosques of West Africa, African architecture shows a striking diversity of approach and technique that is unmatched in other areas of creative endeavor.

The earliest surviving architectural form found in Africa is the pyramid. The kingdom of Meroë apparently adopted the pyramidal form from Egypt during the last centuries of the first millennium B.C.E. Although used for the same purpose as their earlier counterparts at Giza, the pyramids at Meroë were distinctive in style; they were much smaller and were topped with a flat platform rather than rising to a point. Remains of temples with massive carved pillars at Meroë also reflect Egyptian influence.

Farther to the south, the kingdom of Axum was developing its own architectural traditions. Most distinctive were the carved stone pillars, known as stelae (STEE-lee; singular STEE-luh) (see the Comparative Illustration "The Stele" on p. 233) that were used to mark the tombs of dead kings. Some stood as high as 100 feet. The advent of Christianity eventually had an impact on Axumite architecture. During the Zagwe dynasty, churches carved out of solid rock were constructed throughout the country. The earliest may have been built in the eighth century C.E. Stylistically, they combined indigenous techniques inherited from the pre-Christian period with elements borrowed from Christian churches in the Holy Land (see the Comparative Illustration "Rock Architecture" on p. 223).

In West Africa, buildings constructed in stone were apparently a rarity until the emergence of states during the first millennium C.E. At that time, the royal palace and other buildings of civic importance were often built of stone or cement, while the houses of the majority of the population continued to be constructed of dried mud. On his visit to the state of Guinea on the West African coast, the sixteenth-century traveler Leo Africanus noted that the houses of the ruler and other elites were built of chalk with roofs of straw. Even then, however, well into the state-building period, mosques were often built of mud.

Along the east coast, the architecture of the elite tended to reflect Middle Eastern styles. In the coastal towns and islands from Mogadishu to Kilwa, the houses of the wealthy were built of stone and reflected Arabic influence. As elsewhere, the common people lived in huts of mud, thatch, or palm leaves. Mosques were normally built of stone.

The most famous stone buildings in sub-Saharan Africa are those at Great Zimbabwe. Constructed without mortar, the outer wall and public buildings at Great Zimbabwe are an impressive monument to the architectural creativity of the peoples of the region.

Literature

Literature in the sense of written works did not exist in sub-Saharan Africa during the early traditional period, except in regions where Islam had brought the Arabic script from

The Mosque at Jenne, Mali. With the opening of the gold fields south of Mali, in present-day Ghana, Jenne (GEN-nay) became an important trading center for gold. Shown here is its distinctive mosque made of unbaked clay without reinforcements. The projecting timbers offer easy access for repairing the mud exterior, as was regularly required. The mosque was built in the fourteenth century and has since been reconstructed.

A West African Oral Tradition

ART & IDEAS

LIKE OTHER GREAT EPICS OF WORLD LITERATURE, the West African *Epic of Son-Jara* describes the ordeals of a male protagonist as he hurdles superhuman obstacles while fulfilling his heroic destiny. It is interesting, however, to observe the role played by women in the epic hero's calamitous journey. Although he is often opposed by evil witches and temptresses, he can also be assisted in foiling his foes by a courageous woman. Penelope in the *Odyssey* outwits her enemies, as does Sita in the Ramayana and Draupadi in the Mahabharata.

In this pivotal passage, Son-Jara's sister, Sugulun Kulunkan, offers to seduce his enemy Sumamuru in order to obtain the Manden secret, or magic spell, needed to control the kingdom of Mali. Sumamuru divulges his all-powerful secret and is rebuked by his mother; both son and mother then disown each other with the trenchant symbols of the slashed breast and cut cloth. After each line of verse recited by the bard, an assistant would respond with the endorsement "true." This practice is perhaps the distant ancestor of today's African American custom, called "call and response," of following each line of religious oratory with "Amen."

The Epic of Son-Jara

Son-Jara's flesh-and-blood sister, Sugulun Kulunkan,
She said, "O Magan Son-Jara,
"One person cannot fight this war.
"Let me go seek Sumamuru.
"Were I then to reach him,
"To you I will deliver him,
"So that the folk of the Manden be yours,
"And all the Mandenland you shield."
Sugulun Kulunkan arose,
And went up to the gates of Sumamuru's fortress:
...
"Come open the gates, Susu Mountain Sumamuru!
"Come make me your bed companion!"
Sumamuru came to the gates:
"What manner of person are you?"
"It is I, Sugulun Kulunkan!"

"Well, now, Sugulun Kulunkan,
"If you have come to trap me,
"To turn me over to some person,
"Know that none can ever vanquish me.
"I have found the Manden secret,
"And made the Manden sacrifice,
"And in five score millet stalks placed it,
"And buried them here in the earth.
"'Tis I who found the Manden secret,
"And made the Manden sacrifice,
"And in a red piebald bull did place it,
"And buried it here in the earth.
"Know that none can vanquish me.
"'Tis I who found the Manden secret
"And made a sacrifice to it,
"And in a pure white cock did place it.
"Were you to kill it,
"And uproot some barren groundnut plants,
"And strip them of their leaves,
"And spread them round the fortress,
"And uproot more barren peanut plants,
"And fling them into the fortress,
"Only then can I be vanquished."
His mother sprang forward at that:
"Heh! Susu Mountain Sumamuru!
"Never tell all to a woman,
"To a one-night woman!
"The woman is not safe, Sumamuru."
Sumamuru sprang towards his mother,
And came and seized his mother,
And slashed off her breast with a knife, magasi!
She went and got the old menstrual cloth.
"Ah! Sumamuru!" she swore.
"If your birth was ever a fact,
"I have cut your old menstrual cloth!"

 What purpose did the call and response serve in such epics? What effect would the technique have on the audience?

Source: From *The Epic of Son-Jura: A West African Tradition*, text by Fa-Digi Sisoko, notes, translation, and new introduction by John William Johnson (Bloomington: Indiana University Press, 1992), pp. 91–92.

the Middle East. But African societies compensated for the absence of a written language with a rich tradition of oral lore. The **bard**, a professional storyteller, was an ancient African institution by which history was transmitted orally from generation to generation. In many West African societies, bards were highly esteemed and served as counselors to kings as well as protectors of local tradition. Bards were revered for their oratory and singing skills, phenomenal memory, and astute interpretation of history. As one African scholar wrote, the death of a bard was equivalent to the burning of a library.

Bards served several necessary functions in society. They were chroniclers of history, preservers of social customs and proper conduct, and entertainers who possessed a monopoly over the playing of several musical instruments, which accompanied their narratives. Because of their unique position above normal society, bards often played the role of mediator between hostile families or clans in a community. They were also credited with possessing occult powers and could read divinations and give blessings and curses. Traditionally, bards also served as advisers to the king, sometimes inciting him to action (such as going to battle) through the passion of their poetry. When captured by the enemy, bards were often treated with respect and released or compelled to serve the victor with their art.

One of the most famous West African poems is *The Epic of Son-Jara*. Passed down orally by bards for more than seven hundred years, it relates the heroic exploits of Son-Jara (sun-GAR-uh) (also known as Sunjata or Sundiata), the founder of Mali's empire and its ruler from 1230 to 1255. Although Mansa Musa is famous throughout the world because of his flamboyant pilgrimage to Mecca in the fourteenth century, Son-Jara is more celebrated in West Africa because of the dynamic and unbroken oral traditions of the West African peoples (see the box "A West African Oral Tradition" on p. 235).

Like the bards, women were appreciated for their story-telling talents, as well as for their role as purveyors of the moral values and religious beliefs of African societies. In societies that lacked a written tradition, women represented the glue that held the community together. Through the recitation of fables, proverbs, poems, and songs, mothers conditioned the communal bonding and moral fiber of succeeding generations in a way that was rarely encountered in the patriarchal societies of Europe, Asia, and the Middle East. Such activities were not only vital aspects of education in traditional Africa but also offered a welcome respite from the drudgery of everyday life and a spark to develop the imagination and artistic awareness of the young. Renowned for its many proverbs, Africa also offers the following: "A good story is like a garden carried in the pocket."

CHAPTER SUMMARY

Thanks to the dedicated work of a generation of archaeologists, anthropologists, and historians, we have a much better understanding of the evolution of human societies in Africa than we did a few decades ago. Intensive efforts by archaeologists have demonstrated beyond reasonable doubt that the first hominids lived there. Recently discovered evidence suggests that farming may have been practiced in Africa more than 11,000 years ago.

Less is known about more recent African history, partly because of the paucity of written records. Still, historians have established that the first civilizations had begun to take shape in sub-Saharan Africa by the first millennium C.E., while the continent as a whole was an active participant in emerging regional and global trade with the Mediterranean world and across the Indian Ocean.

Thus, the peoples of Africa were not as isolated from the main currents of human history as was once assumed. Although the state-building process in sub-Saharan Africa was still in its early stages compared with the ancient civilizations of India, China, and Mesopotamia, in many respects these new states were as impressive and as sophisticated as their counterparts elsewhere in the world.

In the fifteenth century, a new factor was added to the equation. Urged on by the tireless efforts of Prince Henry the Navigator, Portuguese fleets began to probe southward along the coast of West Africa. At first, their sponsors were in search of gold and slaves, but at the end of the century, Vasco da Gama's voyage around the Cape of Good Hope signaled Portugal's determination to dominate the commerce of the Indian Ocean in the future. The new situation posed a challenge to the peoples of Africa, whose nascent states and technology would be severely tested by the rapacious demands of the Europeans (see Chapter 14).

CHAPTER TIMELINE

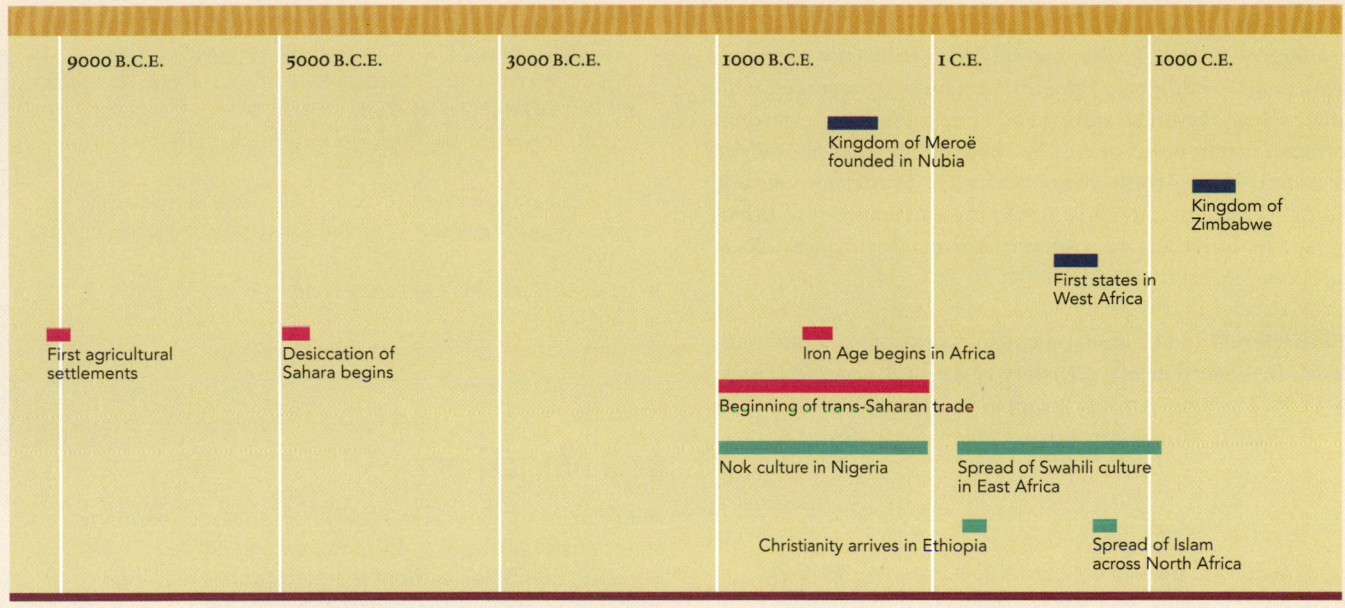

| 9000 B.C.E. | 5000 B.C.E. | 3000 B.C.E. | 1000 B.C.E. | I C.E. | 1000 C.E. |

Kingdom of Meroë founded in Nubia

Kingdom of Zimbabwe

First states in West Africa

First agricultural settlements

Desiccation of Sahara begins

Iron Age begins in Africa

Beginning of trans-Saharan trade

Nok culture in Nigeria

Spread of Swahili culture in East Africa

Christianity arrives in Ethiopia

Spread of Islam across North Africa

CHAPTER REVIEW

Upon Reflection

Q Where and under what conditions was agriculture first practiced on the continent of Africa? What effect did the advent of farming have on the formation of human communities there?

Q Although geographic barriers posed a challenge for African peoples in establishing communications with societies beyond their shores, by the end of the first millennium C.E. the continent had become an active player in the global trade network. What areas of Africa took part in this commercial expansion, and what products were exchanged?

Q The migration of the Bantu-speaking peoples was one of the most extensive population movements in world history. Trace the Bantu migration from its point of origin and discuss how it affected the later history of the continent.

Key Terms

Coptic (p. 217)
Berbers (p. 217)
Nok culture (p. 217)
Swahili (p. 220)
pantheism (p. 220)
lineage group (p. 220)
mansa (p. 226)
noncentralized societies (p. 228)
matrilinear (p. 230)
patrilinear (p. 230)
bard (p. 235)

Suggested Reading

GENERAL SURVEYS Several general surveys provide a useful overview of the early period of African history. The dean of African historians, and certainly one of the most readable, is **B. Davidson.** For a sympathetic portrayal of the African people, see his *African History* (New York, 1968) and *Lost Cities in Africa*, rev. ed. (Boston, 1970). A highly respected recent account is **C. Ehret,** *The Civilizations of Africa: A History to 1800,* 2nd ed. (Charlottesville, Va., 2013). Also see **V. B. Khapoya,** *The African Experience: An Introduction* (Englewood Cliffs, N.J., 1994). **R. O. Collins, ed.,** *Problems in African History: The Precolonial Centuries* (New York, 1993), provides a useful collection of scholarly articles on key issues in precolonial Africa. On the rise of civilizations in Africa, see **F. Fernández-Armesto,** *Civilizations* (New York, 2000). **B. Fagan,** in *The Great Warming: Climate Change and the Rise and Fall of Civilizations* (New York, 2008), relates the rise of states in West Africa to the vagaries of the climate.

SPECIALIZED STUDIES Specialized studies are beginning to appear with frequency on many areas of the continent. For an account of archaeological finds, see **D. W. Phillipson,** *African Archaeology* (Cambridge, 2005). For a more detailed treatment of the early period, see the multivolume *General History of Africa,* sponsored by UNESCO (Berkeley, Calif., 1998). **R. O. Collins** has provided a useful service with his *African History in Documents* (Princeton, N.J., 1990). **C. Ehret,** *An African Classical Age: Eastern and Southern Africa in World History, 1000 B.C. to A.D. 400* (Charlottesville, Va., 1998), applies historical linguistics to make up for the lack of documentary evidence in the precolonial era. For African sources, see **C. Hilliard, ed., *Intellectual Traditions of Pre-Colonial Africa*** (Boston, 1998). Also see **D. A. Welsby, *The Kingdom of Kush: The Napataean Meroitic Empire*** (London, 1996), and **J. Middleton, *Swahili: An African Mercantile Civilization*** (New Haven, Conn., 1992). For a fascinating account of trans-Saharan trade, see **E. W. Bovill, *The Golden Trade of the Moors: West African Kingdoms in the Fourteenth Century*,** 2nd ed. (Princeton, N.J., 1995). On the early history of Ethiopia, see **S. Burstein, ed., *Ancient African Civilizations: Kush and Axum*** (Princeton, N.J., 1998).

AFRICAN ART   For an excellent introduction to African art, see **M. B. Visond et al., *A History of Art in Africa*** (New York, 2001); **R. Hackett, *Art and Religion in Africa*** (London, 1996); and **F. Willet, *African Art*,** rev. ed. (New York, 1993).

Chapter Notes

1. F. Fernández-Armesto, *Civilizations* (London, 2000), pp. 66–68.
2. S. Hamdun and N. King, eds., *Ibn Battuta in Africa* (London, 1975), p. 19.
3. *The Book of Duarte Barbosa* (Nedeln, Liechtenstein, 1967), p. 28.
4. Herodotus, *The Histories*, trans. A. de Sélincourt (Baltimore, 1964), p. 307.
5. Sidi Salem Ould Elhadj, "The Pachalik arma de Tombouctou, 1591-1826," cited in M. de Villiers and S. Hirtle, *Timbuktu: The Sahara's Fabled City of Gold* (New York, 2007), p. 68.
6. C. R. Boxer, ed., *The Tragic History of the Sea, 1589–1622* (Cambridge, 1959), pp. 121–122.
7. Quoted in D. Nurse and T. Spear, *The Swahili: Reconstructing the History and Language of an African Society, 800–1500* (Philadelphia, 1985), p. 84.
8. Hamdun and King, *Ibn Battuta in Africa*, p. 47.
9. Ibid., p. 28.
10. Ibid.
11. Ibid., p. 30.

MindTap is a fully online, highly personalized learning experience built upon Cengage Leaning content. MindTap combines student learning tools—readings, multimedia, activities, and assessments—into a singular Learning Path that guides students through their course.

The Expansion of Civilization in South and Southeast Asia

One of the two massive carved statues of the Buddha formerly at Bamiyan

Thomas J. Abercrombie/National Geographic Creative

CHAPTER OUTLINE AND FOCUS QUESTIONS

The Silk Road

Q What were some of the chief destinations along the Silk Road, and what kinds of products and ideas traveled along the route?

India After the Mauryas

Q How did Buddhism change in the centuries after Siddhartha Gautama's death, and why did the religion ultimately decline in popularity in India?

The Arrival of Islam

Q How did Islam arrive in the Indian subcontinent, and why were Muslim peoples able to establish states there?

Society and Culture

Q What impact did Muslim rule have on Indian society? To what degree did the indigenous population convert to the new religion, and why?

The Golden Region: Early Southeast Asia

Q What were the main characteristics of Southeast Asian social and economic life, culture, and religion before 1500 C.E.?

CRITICAL THINKING

Q New religions had a significant impact on the social and cultural life of peoples living in southern Asia during the period covered in this chapter. What factors caused the spread of these religions in the first place? What changes occurred as a result of the introduction of these new faiths? Were the religions themselves affected by their spread into new regions of Asia?

CONNECTIONS TO TODAY

Q What does the Comparative Essay entitled "Caste, Class, and Family" tell us about the role that nuclear and joint families tend to play in human societies? Do the examples cited provide any lessons for the present day?

WHILE TRAVELING from his native China to India along the Silk Road in the early fifth century C.E., the Buddhist monk Fa Xian (fah SHEE-ahn) stopped en route at a town called Bamiyan (BAH-mee-ahn), a rest stop located deep in the mountains of what is today known as Afghanistan. At that time, Bamiyan was a major center of Buddhist studies, with dozens of temples and monasteries filled with students, all overlooked by two giant standing statues of the Buddha hewn directly out of the side of a massive cliff. Fa Xian was thrilled at the sight. "The law of Buddha," he remarked with satisfaction in his account of the experience, "is progressing and flourishing." He then continued southward to India, where he spent several years visiting Buddhist sites throughout the country. Because little of the literature from that period survives, Fa Xian's observations are a valuable resource for our knowledge of the daily lives of the Indian people.

The India that Fa Xian visited was no longer the unified land it had been under the Mauryan (MOWR-yun) dynasty. The overthrow of the Mauryas in the early second century B.C.E. had been followed by several hundred years of divided rule, when the subcontinent was divided into a number of separate kingdoms and principalities. The dominant force in the north was the

Kushan (KOO-shan) state, established by Indo-European-speaking pastoral peoples who had been driven out of what is now China's Xinjiang province by the Xiongnu in the second or first century B.C.E. (see Chapter 3). The Kushans penetrated into the mountains north of the Indus River, where they eventually formed a kingdom with its capital at Bactria, not far from modern Kabul (KAH-bul). Over the next two centuries, the Kushans established their supremacy along the Indus River and in the central Ganges Valley.

Meanwhile, to the south, a number of kingdoms arose among the Dravidian-speaking peoples of the Deccan Plateau, which had been only partly under Mauryan rule. The most famous of these kingdoms was Chola (CHOH-luh) (sometimes spelled Cola) on the southeastern coast. Chola developed into a major trading power and sent merchant fleets eastward across the Bay of Bengal, where they introduced Indian culture as well as Indian goods to the peoples of Southeast Asia. In the fourth century C.E., Chola was overthrown by the Pallavas (puh-LAH-vuhz), who ruled from their capital at Kanchipuram (KAHN-chee-poo-rum), known today as Kanchi (KAHN-chee), just southwest of modern Chennai (CHEN-ny) (Madras), for the next four hundred years.

The Silk Road

Q **FOCUS QUESTION:** What were some of the chief destinations along the Silk Road, and what kinds of products and ideas traveled along the route?

The Kushan kingdom, with its power base beyond the Khyber Pass in modern Afghanistan, became the dominant political force in northern India in the centuries immediately after the fall of the Mauryas. Prior to being evicted from their original habitat by the Xiongnu, they had engaged in the silk trade with China from their base near Khotan (koh-TAHN), located on the southern route through the Taklimakan (tah-kluh-muh-KAHN) Desert. Now, with their position astride the main trade routes across the northern half of the Indian subcontinent, the Kushans thrived on the commerce that passed through the area (see Map 9.1). The bulk of that trade was between the Roman Empire and China and was transported along the route now known as the Silk Road, one segment of which passed through the mountains northwest of India (see Chapter 10). From there, goods were shipped to Rome through the Persian Gulf or the Red Sea. The importance of the trade with the Mediterranean region is attested to by the fact that gold and silver coins minted by the Kushan state were often imprinted with the figures of Iranian and Greek deities.

Trade between India and Europe had begun even before the rise of the Roman Empire, but it expanded rapidly in the first century C.E., when sailors mastered the pattern of the monsoon winds in the Indian Ocean (from the southwest in the

MAP 9.1 The Kushan Kingdom and the Silk Road. After the collapse of the Mauryan Empire, a new state formed by recent migrants from the north arose north of the Indus River valley. For the next four centuries, the Kushan kingdom played a major role in regional trade via the Silk Road until it declined in the third century C.E.

Q *What were the major products shipped along the Silk Road? Which countries beyond the borders of this map took an active part in trade along the Silk Road?*

summer and the northeast in the winter). Commerce between the Mediterranean and the Indian Ocean, as described in the *Periplus*, a first-century C.E. account by a Greek merchant, was extensive and often profitable, and it resulted in the establishment of several small trading settlements along the Indian coast. Rome imported ivory, indigo, textiles, precious stones, and pepper from India and silk from China. The Romans sometimes paid cash for these goods but also exported silver, wine, perfume, slaves, and glass and cloth from Egypt. Overall, Rome appears to have imported much more than it sold to the Far East.

The Silk Road was a conduit not only of material goods but also of technology and of ideas. The first Indian monks to visit China may have traveled over the road during the second century C.E. By the time of Fa Xian, Buddhist monks from China were beginning to arrive in increasing numbers to visit holy sites in India. The visits not only enriched the study of Buddhism in the two countries but also led to a fruitful exchange of ideas and technological advances in astronomy, mathematics, and linguistics. According to one scholar, the importation of Buddhist writings from India encouraged the development of printing in China, while the Chinese obtained lessons in health care from monks returned from the Asian subcontinent.

A Portrait of Medieval India

INTERACTION & EXCHANGE

MUCH OF WHAT WE KNOW ABOUT LIFE in medieval India comes from the accounts of Chinese missionaries who visited the subcontinent in search of documents recording the teachings of the Buddha. In this selection, the Buddhist monk Fa Xian, who spent several years there in the fifth century C.E., reports on conditions in the kingdom of Mathura (MAH-too-ruh) (Mo-tu-lo), a vassal state in western India that was part of the Gupta Empire. Although he could not have been pleased that the Gupta monarchs in India had adopted the Hindu faith, he found that the people were contented and prosperous except for the outcastes, whom he called Chandalas.

Fa Xian, *The Travels of Fa Xian*

Going southeast … somewhat less than 80 *joyanas* [about 640 miles], we passed very many temples one after another, with some myriad of priests in them. Having passed these places, we arrived at a certain country. This country is called Mo-tu-lo. Once more we followed the Puna river. On the sides of the river, both right and left, are twenty *sangharamas* [monasteries] with perhaps 3,000 priests. The law of Buddha is progressing and flourishing. Beyond the deserts are the countries of western India. The kings of these countries are all firm believers in the law of Buddha. They remove their caps of state when they make offerings to the priests. The members of the royal household and the chief ministers personally direct the food giving; when the distribution of food is over, they spread a carpet on the ground opposite the chief seat (the president's seat) and sit down before it. They dare not sit on couches in the presence of the priests. The rules relating to the almsgiving of kings have been handed down from the time of Buddha till now. Southward from this is the so-called middle country (Madhyadesa). The climate of this country is warm and equable, without frost or snow. The people are very well off, without poll tax or official restrictions. Only those who till the royal lands return a portion of profit of the land. If they desire to go, they go; if they like to stop, they stop. The kings govern without corporal punishment; criminals are fined, according to circumstances, lightly or heavily. Even in cases of repeated rebellion they only cut off the right hand. The king's personal attendants, who guard him on the right and left, have fixed salaries. Throughout the country the people kill no living thing nor drink wine, nor do they eat garlic or onions, with the exception of Chandalas only. The Chandalas are named "evil men" and dwell apart from others; if they enter a town or market, they sound a piece of wood in order to separate themselves; then men, knowing who they are, avoid coming in contact with them. In this country they do not keep swine nor fowls, and do not deal in cattle; they have no shambles [slaughterhouses] or wine shops in their marketplaces. In selling they use cowrie shells. The Chandalas only hunt and sell flesh.

 To what degree do the practices described here appear to conform to the principles established by Siddhartha Gautama in his teachings? Would political advisers such as Kautilya and the Chinese philosopher Mencius have approved of the government's policies?

Source: "Fu-kwo-ki," in Hiuen Tsang, Si-Yu Ki: *Buddhist Records of the Western World*, translated by Samuel Beal (London: Trubner & Co., 1886).

Indeed, the emergence of the Kushan kingdom as a major commercial power was due not only to its role as an intermediary in the Rome-China trade but also to the rising popularity of Buddhism. During the second century C.E., Kanishka (kuh-NISH-kuh), the greatest of the Kushan monarchs, began to patronize Buddhism. Under Kanishka and his successors, an intimate and mutually beneficial relationship was established between Buddhist monasteries and the local merchant community in thriving urban centers like Taxila (tak-SUH-luh) and Varanasi (vah-RAH-nah-see). Merchants were eager to build stupas and donate money to monasteries in return for social prestige and the implied promise of a better life in this world or the hereafter.

For their part, the wealthy monasteries ceased to be simple communities where monks could find a refuge from the material cares of the world; instead they became major consumers of luxury goods provided by their affluent patrons. Monasteries and their inhabitants became increasingly involved in the economic life of society, and Buddhist architecture began to be richly decorated with precious stones and glass purchased from local merchants or imported from abroad. The process was very similar to the changes that would later occur in the Christian church in medieval Europe.

It was from the Kushan kingdom that Buddhism began its long journey across the wastes of Central Asia to China and other societies in eastern Asia. As trade between the two regions increased, merchants and missionaries flowed from Bactria over the trade routes snaking through the mountains toward the northeast. At various stopping points on the trail, pilgrims erected statues and decorated mountain caves with magnificent frescoes depicting the life of the Buddha and his message to his followers. One of the most prominent of these centers was at Bamiyan, not far from modern-day Kabul, where believers carved two mammoth statues of the Buddha out of a sheer sandstone cliff. According to the Chinese pilgrim Fa Xian (see the box "A Portrait of Medieval India" above), when he visited the area in 400 C.E., more than a thousand monks were attending a religious ceremony at the site.

India After the Mauryas

FOCUS QUESTION: How did Buddhism change in the centuries after Siddhartha Gautama's death, and why did the religion ultimately decline in popularity in India?

The Kushan kingdom came to an end under uncertain conditions sometime in the third century C.E. In 320, a new state was established in the central Ganges Valley by a local raja named Chandragupta (chun-druh-GOOP-tuh) (no relation to Chandragupta Maurya, the founder of the Mauryan dynasty). Chandragupta located his capital at Pataliputra (pah-tah-lee-POO-truh), the site of the now decaying palace of the Mauryas. Under his successor, Samudragupta (suh-moo-druh-GOOP-tuh), the territory under Gupta (GOOP-tuh) rule was extended into surrounding areas, and eventually the new kingdom became the dominant political force throughout northern India. It also established a loose suzerainty over the Dravidian state of Pallava to the south, thus becoming the greatest state in the subcontinent since the decline of the Mauryan Empire. Under a succession of powerful, efficient, and highly cultured monarchs, notably Samudragupta (r. 335–375 C.E.) and Chandragupta II (r. 375–415 C.E.), India enjoyed a new "classical age" of civilization (see Map 9.2).

The Gupta Dynasty: A New Golden Age?

Historians of India have traditionally viewed the Gupta era as a time of prosperity and thriving commerce with China, Southeast Asia, and the Mediterranean. Great cities, notable for their temples and Buddhist monasteries as well as for their economic prosperity, rose along the main trade routes throughout the subcontinent. The religious trade also prospered as pilgrims from across India and as far away as China came to visit the major religious centers.

As in the Mauryan Empire, much of the trade in the Gupta Empire was managed or regulated by the government. The Guptas owned mines and vast crown lands and earned massive profits from their commercial dealings. But there was also a large private sector, dominated by *jati* (caste) guilds that monopolized key sectors of the economy. A money economy had probably been in operation since the second century B.C.E., when copper and gold coins had been introduced from the Middle East. This in turn led to the development of banking. Nevertheless, there are indications that the circulation of coins was limited and that cowrie shells continued to be used for local trade. The Chinese missionary Xuan Zang (SHOO-wen ZAHNG), who visited India in the first half of the seventh century, remarked that most commercial transactions were conducted by barter.[1]

But the good fortunes of the Guptas proved to be relatively short-lived. Beginning in the late fifth century C.E., incursions by nomadic warriors from the northwest gradually reduced the power of the empire. Soon northern India was once more divided into myriad small kingdoms engaged in seemingly constant conflict. In the south, however, emerging states like

MAP 9.2 The Gupta Empire. This map shows the extent of the Gupta Empire, the only major state to arise in the Indian subcontinent during the first millennium C.E. The arrow indicates the military campaign into southern India led by King Samudragupta.

 How did the Gupta Empire differ in territorial extent from its great predecessor, the Mauryan Empire?

Chola and Pallava prospered from their advantageous position athwart the regional trade network stretching from the Red Sea eastward into Southeast Asia (see "Foreign Trade" later in this chapter).

CHRONOLOGY Medieval India

Kushan kingdom	c. 150 B.C.E.–c. 200 C.E.
Gupta dynasty	320–600s
Chandragupta I	r. 320–c. 335
Samudragupta	r. 335–375
Chandragupta II	r. 375–415
Arrival of Fa Xian in India	c. 406
First Buddhist temples at Ellora	Seventh century
Travels of Xuan Zang in India	630–643
Conquest of Sind by Arab armies	c. 711
Reign of Mahmud of Ghazni	997–1030
Delhi sultanate	1206–1527
Mongol invasion of northern India	1221
Invasion of Tamerlane	1398

The Transformation of Buddhism

The Chinese pilgrims who traveled to India during the Gupta era encountered a Buddhism that had changed in a number of ways in the centuries since the time of Siddhartha Gautama. They also found a doctrine that was beginning to decline in popularity in the face of the rise of Hinduism, as the Brahmanical religious beliefs of the Aryan people would eventually be called.

The transformation in Buddhism had come about in part because the earliest written sources were transcribed two centuries after Siddhartha's death and in part because his message was reinterpreted as it became part of the everyday life of the people. Abstract concepts of a Nirvana that cannot be described began to be replaced, at least in the popular mind, with more concrete visions of heavenly salvation, and Siddhartha was increasingly regarded as a divinity rather than as a sage.

As a sign of that transformation, the face of the Buddha began to be displayed in sacred sculptures, along with clear suggestions that, like Jesus, he was of divine birth (see the Comparative Illustration "The Buddha and Jesus" on p. 60 in Chapter 2). The Buddha's teachings that all four classes were equal gave way to the familiar Brahmanical conviction that some people, by reason of previous reincarnations, were closer to Nirvana than others.

THERAVADA These developments led to a split in the movement. Purists emphasized what they insisted were the original teachings of the Buddha, describing themselves as the school of **Theravada** (thay-ruh-VAH-duh), or "the teachings of the elders." Followers of Theravada, many of them located in southern India and on the island of Sri Lanka, considered Buddhism a way of life, not a salvationist creed. Theravada stressed the importance of strict adherence to personal behavior and the quest for understanding as a means of release from the wheel of life.

MAHAYANA In the meantime, another interpretation of Buddhist doctrine was emerging in the northwest. Here Buddhist believers, perhaps hoping to compete with other salvationist faiths circulating in the region, began to promote the view that Nirvana could be achieved through devotion and not just through painstaking attention to one's behavior. According to advocates of this school, eventually to be known as **Mahayana** (mah-huh-YAH-nuh) ("greater vehicle"), Theravada teachings were too demanding or too strict for ordinary people to follow and therefore favored the wealthy, who were more apt to have the time and resources to spend weeks or months away from their everyday occupations. Mahayana Buddhists referred to their rivals as **Hinayana** (hee-nuh-YAH-nuh), or "lesser vehicle," because in Theravada fewer would reach enlightenment. Mahayana thus attempted to provide hope for the masses in their efforts to reach Nirvana, but to the followers of Theravada, it did so at the expense of an insistence on proper behavior.

To advocates of the Mahayana school, salvation could also come from the intercession of a **bodhisattva** (boh-duh-SUT-vuh) ("he who possesses the essence of Buddhahood"). According to Mahayana beliefs, some individuals who had achieved *bodhi* and were thus eligible to enter the state of Nirvana after death chose instead, because of their great compassion, to remain on earth in spirit form to help all human beings achieve release from the life cycle. Followers of Theravada, who believed the concept of bodhisattva applied only to Siddhartha Gautama himself, denounced such ideas as "the teaching of demons." But to their proponents, such ideas extended the hope of salvation to the masses. Mahayana Buddhists revered the saintly individuals who, according to tradition, had become bodhisattvas at death and erected temples in their honor where the local population could pray and render offerings. The most famous bodhisattva was Avalokitesvara (uh-VAH-loh-kee-TESH-vuh-rah), a mythic figure whose name in Sanskrit means "Lord of Compassion." Perhaps because of the identification of Avalokitesvara with the concept of mercy, in China he was gradually transformed into a female figure known as Guan Yin (gwahn YIN).

A final distinguishing characteristic of Mahayana Buddhism was its reinterpretation of Buddhism as a religion rather than as a philosophy. Although Mahayana had philosophical aspects, its adherents increasingly regarded the Buddha as a divine figure, and an elaborate Buddhist cosmology developed. Nirvana was not a

Central Asia: Crossroads of Culture. One of the consequences of Alexander the Great's ambition to conquer the known world was the introduction of Greek artistic styles into Central Asia. By the first century C.E., as the Buddhist faith spread throughout the region, freestanding statues of the Buddha in monastic robes reminiscent of Greek togas became increasingly popular. During the Gupta era in northern India (320–600s C.E.), such statues reached a pinnacle of artistic achievement, serving as a model for sculptors from the subcontinent into the islands of Southeast Asia. This fifth-century life-size rendering of the Buddha in red sandstone was found in Mathura, once a thriving religious center in the upper Ganges River valley. Although the head is missing, the portrayal in stone nonetheless displays a unique blend of sensuality and transcendence.

Yvonne V. Duiker

The Education of a *Brahmin*

RELIGION & PHILOSOPHY

ALTHOUGH THE SEVENTH-CENTURY CHINESE TRAVELER Xuan Zang was a Buddhist, he faithfully recorded his impressions of the Hindu religion in his memoirs. Here he describes the education of a *brahmin*, the highest class in Indian society. *Brahmin* youths were educated at what were called *ashramas* (ash-RAHM-uhz), where they received instruction in medicine, science, astronomy, and the Vedas. Their Buddhist counterparts were taught at monasteries, including a famous one at Sarnath, where Siddhartha gave his first sermon.

Xuan Zang, *Records of Western Countries*

The Brahmans study the four *Veda Sastras*. The first is called *Shau* [longevity]; it relates to the preservation of life and the regulation of the natural condition. The second is called *Sse* [sacrifice]; it relates to the [rules of] sacrifice and prayer. The third is called *Ping* [peace or regulation]; it relates to decorum, casting of lots, military affairs, and army regulations. The fourth is called *Shue* [secret mysteries]; it relates to various branches of science, incantations, medicine.

The teachers [of these works] must themselves have closely studied the deep and secret principles they contain, and penetrated to their remotest meaning. They then explain their general sense, and guide their pupils in understanding the words that are difficult. They urge them on and skillfully conduct them. They add luster to their poor knowledge, and stimulate the desponding. If they find that their pupils are satisfied with their acquirements, and so wish to escape to attend to their worldly duties, then they use means to keep them in their power. When they have finished their education, and have attained thirty years of age, then their character is formed and their knowledge ripe. When they have secured an occupation they first of all thank their master for his attention. There are some, deeply versed in antiquity, who devote themselves to elegant studies, and live apart from the world, and retain the simplicity of their character. These rise above mundane presents, and are as insensible to renown as to the contempt of the world. Their name having spread afar, the rulers appreciate them highly, but are unable to draw them to the court. The chief of the country honors them on account of their [mental] gifts, and the people exalt their fame and render them universal homage.... They search for wisdom, relying on their own resources. Although they are possessed of large wealth, yet they will wander here and there to seek their subsistence. There are others who, whilst attaching value to letters, will yet without shame consume their fortunes in wandering about for pleasure, neglecting their duties. They squander their substance in costly food and clothing. Having no virtuous principle, and no desire to study, they are brought to disgrace, and their infamy is widely circulated.

How do the educational practices described here compare with the training provided to young men in other traditional societies in Europe, Asia, and the Americas? What, if anything, was distinctive about the educational system in India?

Source: From Hiuen Tsang, Si-Yu Ki: *Buddhist Records of the Western World*, translated by Samuel Beal (London: Trubner & Co., 1886).

---

form of extinction but a true heaven with many rest stations along the way for the faithful.

Under Kushan rule, Mahayana achieved considerable popularity in northern India and for a while even made inroads in such Theravada strongholds as the island of Sri Lanka (sree LAHN-kuh). But in the end, neither Mahayana nor Theravada was able to retain its popularity in Indian society. By the seventh century C.E., Theravada had declined rapidly on the subcontinent, although it retained its foothold in Sri Lanka and across the Bay of Bengal in Southeast Asia, where it remained an influential force to modern times (see Map 9.3). Mahayana prospered in the northwest for centuries, but eventually it was supplanted by a revived Hinduism and later by a new arrival, Islam. But Mahayana too would find better fortunes abroad, as it was carried over the Silk Road or by sea to China and then to Korea and Japan (see Chapters 10 and 11). In all three countries, Buddhism has coexisted with Confucian doctrine and indigenous beliefs to the present.

The Decline of Buddhism in India

Why was Buddhism unable to retain its popularity in its native India, although it became a major force elsewhere in Asia? Some have speculated that in denying the existence of the soul, Buddhism ran counter to traditional Indian belief. Perhaps, too, one of Buddhism's strengths was also a weakness. In rejecting the class divisions that defined the Indian way of life, Buddhism appealed to those very groups who lacked an accepted place in Indian society, such as the untouchables. But at the same time, it represented a threat to those with a higher status. Moreover, by emphasizing the responsibility of each person to seek an individual path to Nirvana, Buddhism undermined the strong social bonds of the Indian class system.

Perhaps a final factor in the decline of Buddhism was the transformation of Brahmanism into a revised faith known as **Hinduism**. In its early development, Brahmanism had been highly elitist (see box "The Education of a *Brahmin*" above). Not only was observance of court ritual a monopoly of the

© 2016 Cengage Learning

MAP 9.3 The Spread of Religions in Southern and Eastern Asia, 600–1900 C.E. Between 600 and 1900, three of the world's great religions—Buddhism, Hinduism, and Islam—continued to spread from their original sources to various parts of southern and eastern Asia.

Q *Which religion had the greatest impact? How might the existence of major trade routes help explain the spread of these religions?*

brahmin class, but the major route to individual salvation, asceticism, was hardly realistic for the average Indian. In the centuries after the fall of the Mauryas, however, a growing emphasis on devotion—***bhakti*** (BAHK-tee)—as a religious observance brought the possibility of improving one's *karma* by means of ritual acts within the reach of Indians of all classes. Perhaps Hindu devotionalism rose precisely to combat the inroads of Buddhism and reduce the latter's appeal among the Indian population. The Chinese Buddhist missionary Fa Xian reported that mutual hostility between the Buddhists and the *brahmins* in the Gupta era was quite strong:

> Leaving the southern gate of the capital city, on the east side of the road is a place where Buddha once dwelt. Whilst here he bit [a piece from] the willow stick and fixed it in the earth; immediately it grew up seven feet high, neither more nor less. The unbelievers and Brahmans, filled with jealousy, cut it down and scattered the leaves far and wide, but yet it always sprang up again in the same place as before.[2]

For a while, Buddhism was probably able to stave off the Hindu challenge by its own salvationist creed of Mahayana, which also emphasized the role of devotion, but the days of Buddhism as a dominant faith in the subcontinent were numbered. By the eighth century C.E., Hindu missionaries spread throughout southern India, where their presence was spearheaded by new temples dedicated to Shiva at Kanchipuram

(Kanchi), the site of a famous Buddhist monastery, and at Mamallapuram (muh-MAH-luh-poor-um).

When Did the Indians Become Hindus?

When did Brahmanism—the faith originally brought to India by the Aryan peoples in the second millennium B.C.E.—evolve into Hinduism, the religion practiced by the majority of the Indian people today? That question has aroused considerable interest among historians of India in recent years. Of course, the question does not have a single precise answer because the issue is partly a matter of definition and the transition was undoubtedly a gradual process.

Some observers point to the advent of Muslim rule in the northern parts of the subcontinent in the late first millennium C.E. (see "The Arrival of Islam" later in the chapter), when the indigenous people, labeled "Hindus" by the new arrivals, began to develop a greater sense of their distinct ethnic and cultural identity. Others point to the colonial era, when British colonial policies reinforced an Indian sense of being "the Other" and provoked them to come to the defense of their cultural and historical heritage.

Still other historians put the transition in the early centuries of the first millennium C.E., when the Brahmanical emphasis on court sacrifice and asceticism was gradually replaced by a more populist tradition focused on personal worship, known as

William J. Duiker

Mamallapuram Shore Temple. Mamallapuram ("The City of the Great Warrior") was so named by one of the powerful kings of the Pallavan kingdom on the eastern coast of South India. From this port, ships embarked on naval expeditions to Sri Lanka and far-off destinations in Southeast Asia. Although the site was originally identified with the Hindu deity Vishnu, in the eighth century C.E. a Pallavan monarch built this shore temple in honor of Vishnu's rival deity, Shiva. It stands as a visual confirmation of the revival of the Hindu faith in southern India at the time. Centuries of wind and rain have eroded the ornate carvings that originally covered the large granite blocks.

puja (POO-juh), and the achievement of individual goals. In that interpretation, the change from Brahmanism to a faith more accessible to the mass of the population may initially have been stimulated by the egalitarian tendencies of early Buddhism. In any event, by the end of the first millennium C.E., the religious faith originally known as Brahmanism had fought off the challenges of alternative belief systems while transforming itself into the religion of the majority of the Indian people.

The Arrival of Islam

Q **FOCUS QUESTION:** How did Islam arrive in the Indian subcontinent, and why were Muslim peoples able to establish states there?

While India was still undergoing a transition after the collapse of the Gupta Empire, a new and dynamic force in the form of Islam was arising in the Arabian peninsula to the west. As we have seen, during the seventh and eighth centuries, Arab armies carried the new faith westward to the Iberian Peninsula and eastward across the arid wastelands of Persia and into the rugged mountains of the Hindu Kush. Islam first reached India through the Arabs in the eighth century, but a second onslaught in the tenth and eleventh centuries by Turkic-speaking converts had a more lasting effect (see Map 9.3 on p. 245).

Although Arab merchants had been active along the Indian coasts for centuries, Arab armies did not reach India until the

early eighth century. When Indian pirates attacked Arab shipping near the delta of the Indus River, the Muslim ruler in Mesopotamia demanded an apology from the ruler of Sind (SINNED), a Hindu state in the Indus Valley. When the latter refused, Muslim forces conquered lower Sind in 711 and then moved northward into the Punjab (pun-JAHB), bringing Arab rule into the frontier regions of the subcontinent for the first time.

The Empire of Mahmud of Ghazni

For the next three centuries, Islam made no further advances into India. But a second phase began at the end of the tenth century with the rise of the state of Ghazni (GAHZ-nee), located in the area of the old Kushan kingdom in present-day Afghanistan. The new kingdom was founded in 962 when Turkic-speaking slaves seized power from the Samanids, a Persian dynasty. When the founder of the new state died in 997, his son, Mahmud (MAHKH-mood) of Ghazni (r. 997–1030), succeeded him. Brilliant and ambitious, Mahmud used his patrimony as a base of operations for sporadic forays against neighboring Hindu kingdoms to the southeast. Before his death in 1030, he was able to extend his rule throughout the upper Indus Valley and as far south as the Indian Ocean (see Map 9.4). In wealth and cultural brilliance, his court at Ghazni rivaled that of the Abbasid Dynasty in Baghdad. But he was not universally admired. Describing Mahmud's conquests in northwestern India, the contemporary historian al-Biruni (al-buh-ROO-nee) wrote:

> Mahmud utterly ruined the prosperity of the country, and performed wonderful exploits by which the Hindus became like atoms scattered in all directions, and like a tale of old in the mouth of the people. Their scattered remains cherish, of course, the most inveterate aversion towards all Muslims. This is the reason, too, why Hindu sciences have retired far away from those parts of the country conquered by us, and have fled to places which our hand cannot yet reach, to Kashmir, Benares, and other places.[3]

Resistance against the advances of Mahmud and his successors into northern India was led by the Rajputs (RAHJ-pootz), aristocratic Hindu clans who were probably descended from tribal groups that had penetrated into northwestern India from Central Asia in earlier centuries. The Rajputs possessed a strong military tradition and fought bravely, but their military tactics, based on infantry supported by elephants, were no match for the fearsome cavalry of the invaders, whose ability to strike with lightning speed contrasted sharply with the slow-footed forces of their adversaries. Moreover, the incessant squabbling among the Rajput leaders put them at a disadvantage against the single-minded intensity and religious fervor of

MAP 9.4 India, 1000–1200. Beginning in the tenth century, Turkic-speaking peoples invaded northwestern India and introduced Islam to the peoples in the area. Most famous was the empire of Mahmud of Ghazni.

Q *Locate the major trade routes passing through the area. What geographic features explain the location of those routes?*

Mahmud's armies. Although the power of Ghazni declined after his death, a successor state in the area resumed the advance in the late twelfth century, and soon after 1200, Muslim power, in the form of a new Delhi (DEL-ee) sultanate, had been extended over the entire plain of northern India.

The Delhi Sultanate

South of the Ganges River valley, Muslim influence spread more slowly and in fact had little immediate impact. Muslim armies launched occasional forays into the Deccan Plateau, but at first they had little success, even though the area was divided among a number of warring kingdoms, including the Cholas along the eastern coast and the Pandyas (PUHN-dee-ahz) far to the south.

One reason the Delhi sultanate failed to take advantage of the disarray of its rivals was the threat posed by the Mongols on the northwestern frontier (see Chapter 10). Mongol armies unleashed by the great tribal warrior Genghis Khan occupied Baghdad and destroyed the Abbasid caliphate in the 1250s, while other forces occupied the Punjab around Lahore (luh-HOR), from which they threatened Delhi on several occasions. For the next half-century, the attention of the sultanate was focused on the Mongols. That threat finally declined in the early fourteenth century with the gradual breakup of the Mongol Empire, and a new Islamic state emerged in the form of the Tughluq (tug-LUK) dynasty (1320–1413), which extended its power into the Deccan Plateau. In praise of his sovereign, the Tughluq monarch Ala-ud-din (uh-LAH-ud-DEEN), the poet Amir Khusrau (ah-MEER KOOS-roh) exclaimed:

> Happy be Hindustan, with its splendor of religion,
> Where Islamic law enjoys perfect honor and dignity;
> In learning Delhi now rivals Bukhara;
> Islam has been made manifest by the rulers.
> From Ghazni to the very shore of the ocean
> You see Islam in its glory.[4]

Such happiness was not destined to endure, however. During the latter half of the fourteenth century, the Tughluq dynasty gradually fell into decline. In 1398, a new military force crossed the Indus River from the northwest, raided the capital of Delhi, and then withdrew. According to some contemporary historians,

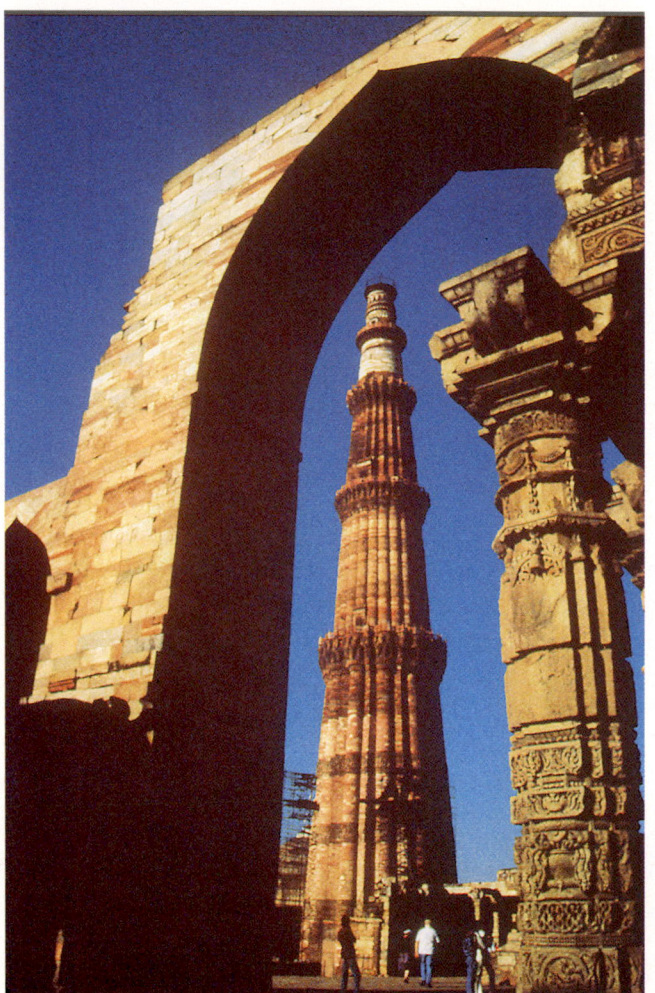

The Kutub Minar. To commemorate their victory in 1192, the Muslim conquerors of northern India constructed a magnificent mosque on the site of Delhi's largest Hindu temple. Much of the material for the mosque came from twenty-seven local Hindu and Jain shrines. Adjacent to the mosque soars the Kutub Minar (KUH-tub mee-NAHR), symbol of the new conquering faith. Originally 238 feet high, the tower's inscription proclaimed its mission to cast the long shadow of Allah over the realm of the Hindus.

as many as 100,000 Hindu prisoners were massacred before the gates of the city. Such was India's first encounter with Tamerlane (TAM-ur-layn).

Tamerlane

Tamerlane (b. 1330s), also known as Timur-i-lang (Timur the Lame), was the ruler of a Mongol khanate based in Samarkand (SAM-ur-kand) to the north of the Pamir (pah-MEER) Mountains. His kingdom had been founded on the ruins of the Mongol Empire, which had begun to disintegrate as a result of succession struggles in the thirteenth century. Tamerlane, the son of a local aristocrat and of mixed Turko-Mongolian heritage, seized power in Samarkand in 1369 and immediately launched a program of conquest. During the 1380s, he brought the entire region east of the Caspian Sea under his authority and then conquered Baghdad and occupied Mesopotamia (see Map 9.5). After his brief foray into northern India, he turned to the west and raided the Anatolian peninsula. Defeating the army of the Ottoman Turks, he advanced almost as far as the Bosporus before withdrawing. "The last of the great nomadic conquerors," as one modern historian described him, died in 1405 in a final military campaign.

The passing of Tamerlane removed a major menace from the diverse states of the Indian subcontinent. But the respite from external challenge was not long. By the end of the fifteenth century, two new challenges had appeared from beyond the horizon: the Mughals, a newly emerging nomadic power beyond the Khyber Pass in the north, and the Portuguese traders, who arrived by sea from the eastern coast of Africa in search of gold and spices. Both, in different ways, would exert a major impact on the later course of Indian civilization.

Society and Culture

 FOCUS QUESTIONS: What impact did Muslim rule have on Indian society? To what degree did the indigenous population convert to the new religion, and why?

The establishment of Muslim rule over the northern parts of the subcontinent had a significant impact on the society and culture of the Indian people.

Religion

Like their counterparts in other areas that came under Islamic rule, some Muslim rulers in India were relatively tolerant of other faiths and used peaceful means, if any, to encourage nonbelievers to convert to Islam. Even the more enlightened, however, could be fierce when their religious zeal was aroused. One ruler, on being informed that a Hindu fair had been held near Delhi, ordered the promoters of the event put to death. Hindu temples were razed, and mosques were erected in their place. Eventually, however, most Muslim rulers realized that not all Hindus could be converted and recognized the necessity of accepting what to them was an alien and repugnant religion.

© 2016 Cengage Learning

MAP 9.5 The Empire of Tamerlane. In the fourteenth century, Tamerlane, a feared conqueror of Mongolian extraction, established a brief empire in Central Asia with his capital at Samarkand.

Q *Which of the states in this map were part of Muslim civilization?*

While Hindu religious practices were generally tolerated, non-Muslims were compelled to pay a tax to the state. Some Hindus likely converted to Islam to avoid paying the tax, but they were then expected to make the traditional charitable contribution required of Muslims in all Islamic societies.

Over time, millions of Hindus did turn to the Muslim faith. Some were individuals or groups in the employ of the Muslim ruling class, such as government officials, artisans, or merchants catering to the needs of the court. But many others were probably peasants from the *sudra* class or even untouchables who found in the egalitarian message of Islam a way of removing the stigma of low-class status in the Hindu social hierarchy.

Seldom have two major religions been so strikingly different. Where Hinduism tolerated a belief in the existence of several deities (although admittedly they were all considered by some to be manifestations of one supreme god), Islam was uncompromisingly monotheistic. Where Hinduism was hierarchical, Islam was egalitarian. Where Hinduism featured a priestly class to serve as an intermediary with the ultimate force of the universe, Islam permitted no one to come

Samarkand, Gem of the Empire. The city of Samarkand has a long history. Originating during the first millennium B.C.E. as a caravan stop on the Silk Road, it was later occupied by Alexander the Great, the Abbasids, and the Mongols before becoming the capital of Tamerlane's expanding empire. Tamerlane expended great sums in creating a city worthy of his imperial ambitions. Shown here is the great square, known as the Registan. Site of a mosque, a library, and a Muslim university, all built in the exuberant Persian style, Samarkand was the jumping-off point for trade with China far to the east.

© William J. Duiker

The Islamic Conquest of India

INTERACTION & EXCHANGE

ONE CONSEQUENCE OF THE MUSLIM CONQUEST of northern India was the imposition of many Islamic customs on Hindu society. In this excerpt, the fourteenth-century Muslim historian Zia-ud-din Barani (ZEE-ah-ud-DIN buh-RAH-nee) describes the attempt of one Muslim ruler, Ala-ud-din, to prevent the use of alcohol and gambling, two practices expressly forbidden in Muslim society. Ala-ud-din had seized power in Delhi from a rival in 1294.

A Muslim Ruler Suppresses Hindu Practices

He forbade wine, beer, and intoxicating drugs to be used or sold; dicing, too, was prohibited. Vintners and beer sellers were turned out of the city, and the heavy taxes which had been levied from them were abolished. All the china and glass vessels of the Sultan's banqueting room were broken and thrown outside the gate of Badaun, where they formed a mound. Jars and casks of wine were emptied out there till they made mire as if it were the season of the rains. The Sultan himself entirely gave up wine parties. Self-respecting people at once followed his example; but the ne'er-do-wells went on making wine and spirits and hid the leather bottles in loads of hay or firewood and by various such tricks smuggled it into the city. Inspectors and gatekeepers and spies diligently sought to seize the contraband and the smugglers; and when seized the wine was given to the elephants, and the importers and sellers and drinkers [were] flogged and given short terms of imprisonment. So many were they, however, that holes had to be dug for their incarceration outside the great thoroughfare of the Badaun gate, and many of the wine bibbers died from the rigor of their confinement and others were taken out half-dead and were long in recovering their health. The terror of these holes deterred many from drinking. Those who could not give it up had to journey ten or twelve leagues [30 to 36 miles] to get a drink, for at half that distance, four or five leagues from Delhi, wine could not be publicly sold or drunk. The prevention of drinking proving very difficult, the Sultan enacted that people might distill and drink privately in their own homes, if drinking parties were not held and the liquor not sold. After the prohibition of drinking, conspiracies diminished.

How does the approach of the ruler described here, a Muslim establishing regulations for moral behavior in a predominantly Hindu society, compare with the approaches adopted by Muslim rulers in African societies as described in Chapter 8?

Source: Excerpt from *A History of India: From the Earliest Times to the Present Day* by Michael Edwardes (London: Thames & Hudson, 1961), p. 108.

---

between believers and their god. Such differences contributed to the mutual hostility that developed between the adherents of the two faiths in the Indian subcontinent, but more mundane issues, such as the Muslim habit of eating beef and the idolatry and sexual frankness of Hindu art, were probably a greater source of antagonism at the popular level (see the box "The Islamic Conquest of India" above).

In other cases, the two peoples borrowed from each other. Some Muslim rulers found the Indian idea of divine kingship appealing. In their turn, Hindu rajas learned by bitter experience the superiority of cavalry mounted on horses instead of elephants, the primary assault weapon in early India. Some upper-class Hindu males were attracted to the Muslim tradition of **purdah** (PUR-duh *or* POOR-duh) and began to keep their women in seclusion (termed locally "behind the curtain") from everyday society. Hindu sources claimed that one reason for adopting the custom was to protect Hindu women from the roving eyes of foreigners. But it is likely that many Indian families adopted the practice for reasons of prestige or because they were convinced that *purdah* was a practical means of protecting female virtue. Adult Indian women had already begun to cover their heads with a scarf during the Gupta era.

All in all, Muslim rule probably did not have a significant impact on the lives of most Indian women (see the Comparative Essay "Caste, Class, and Family" on p. 252). *Purdah* was more commonly practiced among high castes than among the lower castes. Though it was probably of little consolation, relations between the genders were relatively egalitarian in poor and low-class families, as men and women worked together on press gangs or in the fields. Muslim customs apparently had little effect on the Hindu tradition of *sati* (widow burning) (see the box "The Practice of *Sati*" on p. 251). In fact, in many respects, Muslim women had more rights than their Hindu counterparts. They had more property rights than Hindu women and were legally permitted to divorce under certain conditions and to remarry after the death of their husband. The primary role for Indian women in general, however, was to produce children. Sons were preferred over daughters, not only because they alone could conduct ancestral rites but also because a daughter was a financial liability. A father had to provide a costly dowry for his daughter when she married, yet after the wedding, she would transfer her labor and assets to her husband's family. Still, women shared with men a position in the Indian religious pantheon. The cult of the mother-goddess, which had originated in the Harappan era, revived during the Gupta era stronger than ever. The Hindu female deity known as Devi (DAY-vee) was celebrated by both men and women as the source of cosmic power, bestower of wishes, and symbol of fertility.

Overall, the Muslims continued to view themselves as foreign conquerors and generally maintained a strict separation

The Practice of *Sati*

FAMILY & SOCIETY

IN THE COURSE OF HIS EXTENSIVE TRAVELS throughout Africa and Asia, the Muslim diarist Ibn Battuta—whom we first encountered in Chapters 7 and 8—spent several months in Muslim-held territories in India. In the following excerpt, he describes the Hindu practice of *sati*, in which a widow immolates herself on her deceased husband's funeral pyre as a means of expressing her fealty to her lord and master.

The Travels of Ibn Battuta

In this part, I also saw those women who burn themselves when their husbands die. The woman adorns herself, and is accompanied by a cavalcade of the infidel Hindus and Brahmans, with drums, trumpets, and men, following her, both Moslems and Infidels for mere pastime. The fire had been already kindled, and into it they threw the dead husband. The wife then threw herself upon him, and both were entirely burnt. A woman's burning herself, however, with her husband is not considered as absolutely necessary among them, but it is encouraged; and when a woman burns herself with her husband, her family is considered as being ennobled, and supposed to be worthy of trust. But when she does not burn herself, she is ever after clothed coarsely, and remains in constraint among her relations, on account of her want of fidelity to her husband.

The woman who burns herself with her husband is generally surrounded by women, who bid her farewell, and commission her with salutations for their former friends, while she laughs, plays, or dances to the very time in which she is to be burnt.

Some of the Hindus, moreover, drown themselves in the river Ganges to which they perform pilgrimages; and into which they pour the ashes of those who have been burnt. When any one intends to drown himself, he opens his mind on the subject to one of his companions, and says: You are not to suppose that I do this for the sake of any thing worldly; my only motive is to draw near to Kisaī, which is a name of God with them. And when he is drowned, they draw him out of the water, burn the body, and pour the ashes into the Ganges.

 Why do historians evaluate documents such as this one with caution? Are there reasons to doubt the reliability of a report by a Muslim on conditions in Hindu civilization? What evidence do you find in this selection that Ibn Battuta was approaching Hindu society from the perspective of his own experience and applying the values of his own culture?

Source: S. Lee (trans.), *The Travels of Ibn Battuta in the Near East, Asia, and Africa, 1325–1354* (Mineola, NY, 2004), pp. 108–110.

---

between the Muslim ruling class and the mass of the Hindu population. Although a few Hindus rose to important positions in the local bureaucracy, most high posts in the central government and the provinces were reserved for Muslims. Only with the founding of the Mughal Dynasty was a serious effort undertaken to reconcile the differences.

One result of this effort was the religion of the Sikhs (SEEKS *or* see-ikhz) ("disciples"). Founded by the guru Nanak (NAH-nuhk) in the early sixteenth century in the Punjab, Sikhism attempted to integrate the best of the two faiths in a single religion. Sikhism originated in the devotionalist movement in Hinduism, which taught that God was the single true reality. All else is illusion. But Nanak rejected the Hindu tradition of asceticism and mortification of the flesh and, like Muhammad, taught his disciples to participate in the world. Sikhism achieved considerable popularity in northwestern India, where Islam and Hinduism confronted each other directly, and eventually evolved into a militant faith that fiercely protected its adherents against its two larger rivals. In the end, Sikhism did not reconcile Hinduism and Islam but provided an alternative to them.

CLASS AND CASTE One complication for both Muslims and Hindus as they tried to come to terms with the existence of a mixed society was the problem of class and caste (see the Comparative Essay "Caste, Class, and Family" on p. 252). Could non-Hindus form castes, and if so, how were these castes related to the Hindu castes? Where did the Turkic-speaking elites who made up the ruling class in many of the Islamic states fit into the equation?

The problem was resolved in a pragmatic manner that probably followed an earlier tradition of assimilating non-Hindu tribal groups into the system. Members of the Turkic ruling groups formed social groups that were roughly equivalent to the Hindu *brahmin* or *kshatriya* class. During the Delhi sultanate in the north, members of the local Rajput nobility who converted to Islam were occasionally permitted to join such class groupings. Ordinary Indians who converted to Islam also formed Muslim castes, although at a lower level on the social scale. Many who did so were probably artisans who converted en masse to obtain the privileges that conversion could bring.

In most of India, then, Muslim rule did not substantially disrupt the class and caste system, although it may have become more fluid than was formerly the case. One perceptive European visitor in the early sixteenth century reported that in Malabar (MAL-uh-bar), along the southwestern coast, there were separate castes for fishing, pottery making, weaving, carpentry and metalworking, salt mining, sorcery, and labor on the plantations. There were separate castes for doing the laundry, one for the elite and the other for the common people.

Caste, Class, and Family

FAMILY & SOCIETY

Why have men and women played such different roles throughout human history? Why have some societies historically adopted the nuclear family, while others preferred the joint family or the clan? Such questions are controversial and often subject to vigorous debate, yet they are crucial to our understanding of the human experience.

As we know, the first human beings practiced hunting and foraging, living in small bands composed of one or more lineage groups and moving from place to place in search of sustenance. Individual members of the community were assigned different economic and social roles—usually with men as the hunters and women as the food gatherers—but such roles were not rigidly defined. The concept of private property did not exist, and all members shared the goods possessed by the community according to need.

The agricultural revolution brought about dramatic changes in human social organizations. Although women, as food gatherers, may have been the first farmers, men—now increasingly deprived of their traditional role as hunters—began to replace them in the fields. As communities gradually adopted a sedentary lifestyle, women were increasingly assigned to domestic tasks in the home while raising the children. As farming communities grew in size and prosperity, vocational specialization and the concept of private property appeared, leading to the family as a legal entity and the emergence of a class system composed of elites, commoners, and slaves. Women were deemed inferior to men and placed in a subordinate status.

This trend toward job specialization and a rigid class system was less developed in pastoral societies, some of which still practiced a nomadic style of life and shared communal goods on a roughly equal basis within the community. Even within sedentary societies, there was considerable variety in the nature of social organizations. In some areas, the nuclear family consisted of parents and their dependent children. Other societies, however, adopted (either in theory or in

The Good Life. On the walls of the Buddhist temple of Borobudur are a series of bas-reliefs in stone depicting the path to enlightenment. The lower levels depict the pleasures of the material world. Shown here is a woman of leisure, assisted by her maidservants, at her toilette.

practice) the idea of the joint family (ideally consisting of three generations of a family living under one roof) and sometimes, even going a step further, linked several families under the larger grouping of the caste or the clan. Prominent examples of the latter tendency include India and China, although the degree to which reality conformed to such concepts is a matter of debate.

Such large social organizations, where they occurred, often established a rigid hierarchy of status within the community, including the subordination of women. At the same time, they sometimes played a useful role in society, providing a safety net or a ladder of upward mobility for disadvantaged members of the group, as well as a source of stability in societies where legitimate and effective authority at the central level was lacking.

 What were some of the unique aspects of community and family life in traditional India? What do you think accounts for these unique characteristics?

Economy and Daily Life

India's landed and commercial elites lived in the cities, often in conditions of considerable opulence. The rulers possessed the most wealth. One maharaja of a relatively small state in southern India, for example, had more than 100,000 soldiers in his pay along with 900 elephants and 20,000 horses. Another maintained a thousand high-caste women to serve as sweepers of his palace. Each carried a broom and a brass basin containing a

mixture of cow dung and water and followed him from one house to another, plastering the path where he was to tread. Most urban dwellers, of course, did not live in such style. Xuan Zang, the Chinese Buddhist missionary, left us a description of ordinary homes in seventh-century urban areas:

> Their houses are surrounded by low walls.... The earth being soft and muddy, the walls of the towns are mostly built of brick or tiles. The towers on the walls are constructed of

wood or bamboo; the houses have balconies and belvederes, which are made of wood, with a coating of lime or mortar, and covered with tiles. The different buildings have the same form as those in China; rushes, or dry branches, or tiles, or boards are used for covering them. The walls are covered with lime and mud, mixed with cow's dung for purity. At different seasons they scatter flowers about. Such are some of their different customs.[5]

AGRICULTURE The majority of India's population (estimated at slightly more than 100 million by the year 1000), however, lived on the land. Most were peasants who tilled small plots with a wooden plow pulled by oxen and paid a percentage of the harvest to their landlord. The landlord in turn forwarded part of the payment to the local ruler. In effect, the landlord functioned as a tax collector for the king, who retained ultimate ownership of all farmland in his domain. At best, most peasants lived at the subsistence level. At worst, they were forced into debt and fell victim to moneylenders who charged exorbitant rates of interest.

In the north and in the upland regions of the Deccan Plateau, the primary grain crops were wheat and barley. In the Ganges Valley and the southern coastal plains, the main crop was rice. Vegetables were grown everywhere, and southern India produced many spices and fruits, as well as sugarcane and cotton, both of which were gradually transported westward by the Arabs. Although sugarcane was first cultivated in Southeast Asia, the cotton plant apparently originated in the Indus River valley and spread from there. Although some cotton was cultivated in Spain and North Africa by the eighth and ninth centuries, India remained the primary producer of cotton goods. Spices such as cinnamon, pepper, ginger, sandalwood, cardamom, and cumin were also major export products.

FOREIGN TRADE Agriculture, of course, was not the only source of wealth in India. Since ancient times, the subcontinent had served as a major entrepôt for trade between the Middle East and the Pacific basin, as well as the source of other goods shipped throughout the known world. Although civil strife and piracy, heavy taxation of the business community by local rulers to finance their fratricidal wars, and increased customs duties between principalities may have contributed to a decline in internal trade, the level of foreign trade remained high, particularly in the Dravidian-speaking kingdoms in the south and along the northwestern coast, which were located along the traditional trade routes to the Middle East and the Mediterranean Sea. Much of this foreign trade was carried on by wealthy Hindu castes with close ties to the royal courts. But there were other participants as well, including such non-Hindu minorities as the Muslims, the Jews, the Parsis (PAR-seez), and the Jains. The Parsis, expatriates from Persia who practiced the Zoroastrian religion, dominated banking and the textile industry in the cities bordering the Rann of Kutch (RUN of KUTCH). Later they would become a major economic force in the modern city of Mumbai (Bombay). The Jains became prominent in trade and manufacturing even though their faith emphasized simplicity and the rejection of materialism.

According to early European travelers, merchants often lived quite well. One Portuguese observer described the "Moorish" population in Bengal as follows:

> They have girdles of cloth, and over them silk scarves; they carry in their girdles daggers garnished with silver and gold, according to the rank of the person who carries them; on their fingers many rings set with rich jewels, and cotton turbans on their heads. They are luxurious, eat well and spend freely, and have many other extravagances as well. They bathe often in great tanks which they have in their houses. Everyone has three or four wives or as many as he can maintain. They keep them carefully shut up, and treat them very well, giving them great store of gold, silver and apparel of fine silk.[6]

THE INDIAN ECONOMY: PROMISE UNFULFILLED? Outside these relatively small, specialized trading communities, most manufacturing and commerce were in the hands of petty traders and artisans, who were generally limited to local markets. This failure to build on the promise of antiquity has led some historians to ask why India failed to produce an expansion of commerce and growth of cities similar to the developments that began in Europe during the High Middle Ages or even in China during the Song Dynasty (see Chapter 10). Some have pointed to the traditionally low status of artisans and merchants in Indian society, symbolized by the comment in the *Arthasastra* that merchants were "thieves that are not called by the name of thief."[7] Yet commercial activities were frowned on in many areas in Europe throughout the Middle Ages, a fact that did not prevent the emergence of capitalist societies in much of the West.

Another factor may have been the monopoly on foreign trade held by the government in many areas of India. More important, perhaps, was the impact of the class and caste system, which reduced the ability of entrepreneurs to expand their activities and have dealings with other members of the commercial and manufacturing community. Successful artisans, for example, normally could not set up as merchants to market their products, nor could merchants compete for buyers outside their normal area of operations. The complex interlocking relationships among the various classes in a given region were a powerful factor inhibiting the development of a thriving commercial sector in medieval India.

SCIENCE AND TECHNOLOGY Still, Indian thinkers played an important role during this period in promoting knowledge of the sciences throughout the Eurasian world. One example is the fifth-century astronomer Aryabhata (AHR-yuh-BAH-tuh), who accurately calculated the value of pi and measured the length of the solar year at slightly more than 365 days. Indian writings on astronomy, mathematics, and medicine were influential elsewhere in the region, while, as noted in Chapter 7, the Indian system of numbers, including the concept of zero, was introduced into the Middle East and ultimately replaced the Roman numerals then in use in medieval Europe.

The Wonder of Indian Culture

The era between the Mauryas and the Mughals in India was a period of cultural evolution as Indian writers and artists built on the literary and artistic achievements of their predecessors. This is not to say, however, that Indian culture rested on its ancient laurels. To the contrary, it was an era of tremendous innovation in all fields of creative endeavor.

ART AND ARCHITECTURE At the end of antiquity, the primary forms of religious architecture were the Buddhist cave temples and monasteries. The next millennium witnessed the evolution of religious architecture from underground cavity to monumental structure.

The twenty-eight caves of Ajanta (uh-JUHN-tuh) in the Deccan Plateau are among India's greatest artistic achievements. They are as impressive for their sculptures and paintings as for their architecture. Except for a few examples from the second century B.C.E., most of the caves were carved out of solid rock over an incredibly short period of eighteen years, from 460 to 478 C.E. In contrast to the early unadorned temple halls, these caves were exuberantly decorated with ornate pillars, friezes, beamed ceilings, and statues of the Buddha and bodhisattvas. Several caves served as monasteries, which by then had been transformed from simple holes in the wall to large complexes with living apartments, halls, and shrines to the Buddha. Other temples, such as the one at Ellora (eh-LOR-uh), were carved directly out of the mountains (see the Comparative Illustration "Rock Architecture" on p. 223 in Chapter 8).

All of the inner surfaces of the caves, including the ceilings, sculptures, walls, door frames, and pillars, were painted in vivid colors. Perhaps best known are the wall paintings, which illustrate the various lives and incarnations of the Buddha. These paintings are in an admirable state of preservation, making it possible to reconstruct the customs, dress, house interiors, and physical characteristics of the peoples of fifth-century India. Similar rock paintings focusing on secular subjects can be found at Sigiriya (see-gee-REE-uh), a fifth-century royal palace on the island of Sri Lanka. As a defensive measure, the palace was located on top of a gigantic volcanic rock.

Among the most impressive rock carvings in southern India are the cave temples at Mamallapuram (also known as Mahabalipuram), south of the modern city of Chennai (Madras). The sculpture, called *Descent of the Ganges River*, depicts the role played by Shiva in intercepting the heavenly waters of the Ganges and allowing them to fall gently on the earth. Mamallapuram also boasts an eighth-century shore temple

Descent of the Ganges River. One of India's most outstanding sculptures is found at Mamallapuram, an eighth-century Hindu temple on the eastern coast south of Chennai (Madras). This open relief, known as the *Descent of the Ganges River*, is about 20 feet high and 80 feet long. It portrays Shiva's effort to deflect the waters of the heavenly River Ganges on his head to spare the earth from destruction. Although it presents a rich panorama of gods, animals, and men, the gentle elephants in particular delight one and all.

© William J. Duiker

(see the illustration "Mamallapuram Shore Temple" on p. 246), which is one of the earliest surviving freestanding structures in the subcontinent.

From the eighth century until the time of the Mughals, Indian architects built a multitude of magnificent Hindu temples, now constructed exclusively aboveground. Each temple consisted of a central shrine surmounted by a sizable tower, a hall for worshipers, a vestibule, and a porch, all set in a rectangular courtyard that might also contain other minor shrines. Temples became progressively more ornate until the eleventh century, when sculpture began to dominate the structure. The towers became higher and the temple complexes more intricate, some becoming virtual walled compounds set one within the other and resembling small towns.

Among the best examples of temple art are those in the eastern state of Orissa (uh-RIH-suh). The Sun Temple at Konarak (KUH-nar-ek), standing at the edge of the sea and covered with intricate carvings, is generally considered the masterpiece of its genre. Although now in ruins, the Sun Temple still boasts some of India's most memorable sculptures. Especially renowned are the twelve pairs of carved wheels, each 10 feet high, representing the twelve signs of the zodiac.

The greatest example of medieval Hindu temple art, however, is probably Khajuraho (khah-joo-RAH-hoh). Of the original eighty-five temples, dating from the tenth century, twenty-five remain standing today. All of the towers are buttressed at various levels on the sides, giving the whole a sense of unity and creating a vertical movement similar to Mount Kailasa (ky-LAH-suh) in the Himalayas, sacred to Hindus. Everywhere the viewer is entertained by voluptuous temple dancers bringing life to the massive structures. One is removing a thorn from her foot, another is applying eye makeup, and yet another is wringing out her hair.

In the Deccan Plateau, a different style prevailed. The southern temple style was marked by massive oblong stone towers, some 200 feet high. The towers were often covered with a profusion of sculpted figures and were visible for miles. The walls surrounding the temple complex were also surmounted with impressive gate towers, known as *gopuras* (GOH-pur-uhz). Craftsmen in the southern states also won plaudits for the high quality of their bronze statues, many of them portraying Indian deities such as Shiva and Vishnu and designed for use in Hindu religious rituals and ceremonies. Unlike the famous ritual bronzes of ancient China, Indian bronze work relied on the "lost-wax" method described in Chapter 3.

LITERATURE During this period, Indian authors produced a prodigious number of written works, both religious and secular. Indian religious poetry was written in Sanskrit and also in the languages of southern India. As Hinduism was transformed from a contemplative to a more devotional religion, its poetry became more ardent and erotic and prompted a sense of divine ecstasy. Much of the religious verse extolled the lives and heroic acts of Shiva, Vishnu, Rama, and Krishna by repeating the same themes over and over. In the eighth century, a tradition of poet-saints inspired by intense mystical devotion to a particular deity emerged in southern India. Many were women who sought to escape the drudgery of domestic toil through an imagined sexual union with the god-lover. Such was the case for this twelfth-century mystic whose poem expresses her sensuous joy in the physical-mystical union with her god:

> It was like a stream
> running into the dry bed
> of a lake,
> like rain pouring on plants
> parched to sticks.
> It was like this world's pleasure
> and the way to the other,
> both walking towards me.
> Seeing the feet of the master,
> O lord white as jasmine
> I was made worthwhile.[8]

The great secular literature of traditional India was also written in Sanskrit in the form of poetry, drama, and prose. Some of the best medieval Indian poetry is found in single-stanza poems, which create an entire emotional scene in just a few lines. Witness this poem by the poet Amaru (am-uh-ROO):

> We'll see what comes of it, I thought,
>   and I hardened my heart against her.
> What, won't the villain speak to me? She
>   thought, flying into a rage.
> And there we stood, sedulously refusing to look one
>   another in the face,
> Until at last I managed an unconvincing laugh,
>   and her tears robbed me of my resolution.[9]

One of India's most famous authors was Kalidasa (kah-lee-DAH-suh), who lived during the Gupta dynasty. Although little is known of him, including his dates, he probably wrote for the court of Chandragupta II (r. 375–415). Even today, Kalidasa's hundred-verse creation *The Cloud Messenger* remains one of the most popular Sanskrit poems.

In addition to being a poet, Kalidasa was also a great dramatist. He wrote three plays, all dramatic romances that blend the erotic with the heroic and the comic. *Shakuntala*, perhaps the best-known play in all Indian literature, tells the story of a king who, while out hunting, falls in love with the maiden Shakuntala. He asks her to marry him and offers her a ring of betrothal but is suddenly recalled to his kingdom on urgent business. Shakuntala, who is pregnant, goes to him, but the king has been cursed by a hermit and no longer recognizes her. With the help of the gods, the king eventually recalls their love and is reunited with Shakuntala and their son.

Kalidasa was one of the greatest Indian dramatists, but he was by no means the only one. Sanskrit plays typically

William J. Duiker

Dancing Shiva. From the tenth to the twelfth centuries C.E., the southern kingdom of Chola excelled in the use of the lost-wax technique to make portable bronze statues of Hindu gods. Bathed, clothed, and decorated with flowers, these Chola bronzes were then paraded in religious ceremonies. One of the most numerous and iconic of these bronze deities was the dancing Shiva. As shown here, the statue portrays Shiva performing a cosmic dance in which he simultaneously creates and destroys the universe. While his upper right hand creates the cosmos, his upper left hand reduces it in flames. With his right foot, Shiva crushes the back of the dwarf of ignorance. Shiva's dancing statues visually convey to his followers the message of his power and compassion.

contained one to ten acts. They were performed in theaters in the palaces or in court temples by troupes of actors of both sexes who were trained and supported by the royal family. The plots were usually taken from Indian legends of gods and kings. No scenery or props were used, but costumes and makeup were elaborate. The theaters had to be small because much of the drama was conveyed through intricate gestures and dance conventions. There were many different positions for various parts of the body, including one hundred for the hands alone.

Like poetry, prose developed in India from the Vedic period. The use of prose was well established by the sixth and seventh centuries C.E. This is truly astonishing considering that the novel did not appear until the tenth century in Japan and until the seventeenth century in Europe. One of the greatest masters of Sanskrit prose was Dandin (DUN-din), who lived during the seventh century. In *The Ten Princes*, he created a fantastic and exciting world that fuses history and fiction. His keen powers of observation, details of low life, and humor give his writing considerable vitality.

MUSIC Another area of Indian creativity that developed during this era was music. Ancient Indian music had come from the chanting of the Vedic hymns and thus had a strong metaphysical and spiritual flavor. The actual physical vibrations of music (*nada*) were believed to be related to the spiritual world. An off-key or sloppy rendition of a sacred text could upset the harmony and balance of the entire universe.

In form, Indian classical music is based on a scale, called a *raga* (RAH-guh). There are dozens, if not hundreds, of separate scales, which are grouped into separate categories depending on the time of day during which they are to be performed. The performers use a stringed instrument called a *sitar* (si-TAHR) and various types of wind instruments and drums. The performers select a basic *raga* and then are free to improvise the melodic structure and rhythm. A good performer never performs a particular *raga* the same way twice. As with jazz music in the West, the audience is concerned not so much with faithful reproduction as with the performer's creativity.

The Golden Region: Early Southeast Asia

 FOCUS QUESTION: What were the main characteristics of Southeast Asian social and economic life, culture, and religion before 1500 C.E.?

Between China and India lies the region that today is called Southeast Asia. It has two major components: a mainland region extending southward from the Chinese border down to the tip of the Malay Peninsula and an extensive archipelago, most of which is part of present-day Indonesia and the Philippines. Travel among the islands and toward regions to the west, north, and east was not difficult, so Southeast Asia has historically served as a vast land bridge for the movement of peoples between China, the Indian subcontinent, and the more than 25,000 islands of the South Pacific. The first arrival

of humans probably appeared as long as 40,000 years ago, as part of the initial exodus of *Homo sapiens* from Africa. The final destination for some of these peoples was Australia, where their descendants, known today as aborigines, still live.

Mainland Southeast Asia consists of several north-south mountain ranges, separated by river valleys that run in a southerly or southeasterly direction. Several groups of migrants came down the valleys from China in search of new homelands. One of the earliest were **Malayo-Polynesian** (muh-LAY-oh-pah-leh-NEE-zhun) speakers who originated on the island of Taiwan or the southeastern coast of China. Most of them settled in the southern part of the Southeast Asian mainland or on the islands to the south. Then came the Thai (TY) from southwestern China and the Burmese from the Tibetan highlands. Once in Southeast Asia, most of these migrants settled in the fertile deltas of the rivers—the Irrawaddy (ir-uh-WAH-dee) and the Salween (SAL-ween) in Burma, the Chao Phraya (chow PRY-uh) in Thailand, and the Red River and the Mekong (MAY-kahng) in Vietnam—or in lowland areas on the islands to the south.

Although the river valleys facilitated north-south travel on the Southeast Asian mainland, movement between east and west was relatively difficult. The mountains are densely forested and infested with malaria-carrying mosquitoes. Consequently, the lowland peoples in the river valleys were often isolated from each other and had only limited contacts with the upland peoples in the mountains. These geographic barriers may help explain why mainland Southeast Asia is one of the few regions in Asia that was never unified under a single government. Communication among peoples living in the Malay Peninsula and the southern islands, however, was relatively easy.

Given Southeast Asia's location between China and India, it is not surprising that both civilizations influenced developments in the region. In 111 B.C.E., northern Vietnam was conquered by the Han dynasty and remained under Chinese control for more than a millennium, as will be discussed in Chapter 11. The Indian states never exerted much political control over Southeast Asia, but their influence was pervasive nevertheless. The first contacts had taken place by the fourth century B.C.E., when Indian merchants began sailing to Southeast Asia; they were soon followed by Buddhist and Hindu missionaries. Indian influence can be seen in many aspects of Southeast Asian culture, from political institutions to religion, architecture, language, and literature.

Paddy Fields and Spices: The States of Southeast Asia

The traditional states of Southeast Asia can generally be divided between agricultural societies and trading societies. The distinction between farming and trade was a product of the environment. The agricultural societies—notably, Vietnam, Angkor (AN-kor) in what is now Cambodia, and the Burmese state of Pagan (puh-GAHN)—were situated in fertile river deltas that were conducive to the development of a wet rice economy (see Map 9.6). As in India and China, the cultivation of wet rice led to an expanding population and eventually to the formation of states. Although all produced some goods for regional markets, none was tempted to turn to commerce as the prime source of national income. In fact, none was situated astride the main trade routes that crisscrossed the region. Trading societies in the Indonesian archipelago such as Srivijaya and Majapahit, however, were actively involved in the regional trade network from an early time.

THE MAINLAND STATES   One exception to this general rule was the kingdom of Funan (FOO-nan), which arose in the fertile valley of the lower Mekong River in the second century C.E. At that time, much of the regional trade between India and the South China Sea moved across the narrow neck of the Malay Peninsula. With access to copper, tin, and iron, as well as a variety of tropical agricultural products, Funan played an active role in this process, and Oc Eo (ohk-EEOH), on the Gulf of Thailand, became one of the primary commercial ports in the region. Funan declined in the fifth century when trade began to pass through the Strait of Malacca

MAP 9.6 Southeast Asia in the Thirteenth Century. This map shows the major states that arose in Southeast Asia after the year 1000 C.E. Some, such as Angkor and Dai Viet, were predominantly agricultural. Others, such as Srivijaya and Champa, were commercial.

Q *How did geography influence whether states were primarily agricultural or commercial?*

(muh-LAK-uh) and was eventually replaced by the agricultural state of Chenla (CHEEN-luh) and then, three hundred years later, by the great kingdom of Angkor.

Angkor was the most powerful state to emerge in mainland Southeast Asia before the sixteenth century (see the box "The Kingdom of Angkor" on p. 259). The remains of its capital city, Angkor Thom (AN-kor TOHM), give a sense of the magnificence of Angkor civilization. The city formed a square 2 miles on each side. Its massive stone walls were several feet thick and were surrounded by a moat. Four main gates led into the city, which at its height had a substantial population. Recent archaeological evidence suggests that much of the population resided in suburban areas outside the extensive city wall. Like its predecessor, the wealth of Angkor was based primarily on the cultivation of wet rice, which had been introduced to the Mekong River valley from China in the third millennium B.C.E. Other products were honey, textiles, fish, and salt. By the fourteenth century, however, Angkor had begun to decline, a product of incessant wars with its neighbors and the silting up of its irrigation system, and in 1432, Angkor Thom was destroyed by the Thai, who had migrated into the region from southwestern China in the thirteenth century and established their capital at Ayuthaya (ah-yoo-TY-yuh), in lower Thailand, in 1351.

As the Thai expanded southward, however, their main competition came from the west, where the Burmese peoples had formed their own agricultural society in the valleys of the Salween and Irrawaddy Rivers. Like the Thai, they were relatively recent arrivals in the area, having migrated southward from the highlands of Tibet beginning in the seventh century C.E. After subjugating weaker societies already living in the area, in the eleventh century they founded the first great Burmese state, the kingdom of Pagan. Like the Thai, they quickly converted to Buddhism and adopted Indian political institutions and culture. For a while, they were a major force in the western part of Southeast Asia, but attacks from the Mongols in the late thirteenth century (see Chapter 10) weakened Pagan, and the resulting vacuum may have benefited the Thai as they moved into areas occupied by Burmese migrants in the Chao Phraya Valley.

THE MALAY WORLD   In the Malay Peninsula and the Indonesian archipelago, a different pattern emerged. For centuries, this area had been linked to regional trade networks, and much of its wealth had come from the export of tropical products to China, India, and the Middle East. The vast majority of the inhabitants of the region were Malayo-Polynesian-speaking peoples, who, as mentioned earlier, spread from their original homeland in southeastern China into island Southeast Asia and even to more distant locations in the South Pacific, including Tahiti, Hawaii, and Easter Island (see "Expansion into the Pacific" later in this chapter).

Eventually, the islands of the Indonesian archipelago gave rise to two of the region's most notable trading societies—Srivijaya (sree-vih-JAH-yuh) and Majapahit (mah-jah-PAH-hit). Both were major participants in what might be called the "spice road," a maritime equivalent of the Silk Road on the Asian mainland. As the wealth of the Arab empire in the Middle East and then of continental Europe increased, so did the demand for the

Rice Culture in Southeast Asia. Rice was first cultivated in southern Asia seven or eight thousand years ago. It is a labor-intensive crop that requires many workers to plant the seedlings and organize the distribution of water. Initially, the fields are flooded to facilitate the rooting of the rice seedlings and add nutrients to the soil. The upper photo shows terracing on a hillside in Bali, and in the lower photo workers are performing the backbreaking task of transplanting rice seedlings in a flooded field in modern Vietnam.

The significance of rice in Southeast Asia is reflected in the fact that all cultures in the region have traditionally venerated its sacred nature by creating elaborate rituals to the rice goddess. In Indonesia, the worship of Dewi Sri has long been essential to assure a good harvest.

products of Southeast Asia. Merchant fleets from India and the Arabian peninsula sailed to the Indonesian islands to buy cloves, pepper, nutmeg, cinnamon, precious woods, and other exotic products coveted by the wealthy. In the eighth century, Srivijaya, which had been established along the eastern coast of Sumatra around 670, became a powerful commercial state that dominated the trade passing through the Strait of Malacca, at that time the most convenient route from East Asia into the Indian Ocean. The rulers of Srivijaya had helped bring the route to prominence by controlling the pirates who had previously plagued shipping in the strait. Another inducement was Srivijaya's capital at Palembang (pah-lem-BAHNG), a deepwater port where sailors could wait out the monsoon season before making their return voyage. In 1025, however, Chola, one of the kingdoms of southern India and a commercial rival of Srivijaya, inflicted a devastating defeat on the island kingdom. Although Srivijaya survived, it was unable to regain its former dominance, in part because the main trade route had shifted to the east, through the Strait of Sunda (SOON-duh) and directly out into the Indian Ocean. In the late thirteenth century, this shift in trade patterns led to the founding of the new kingdom of Majapahit on the island of Java. In the mid-fourteenth century, Majapahit succeeded in uniting most of the archipelago and perhaps even part of the Southeast Asian mainland under its rule.

THE ROLE OF INDIA Indian influence was evident in all of these societies to various degrees. Based on models from the Dravidian kingdoms of southern India, Southeast Asian kings were believed to possess special godlike qualities that set them apart from ordinary people. In some societies such as Angkor, the most prominent royal advisers constituted a *brahmin* class on the Indian model. In Pagan and Angkor, some division of the population into separate classes based on occupation and ethnic background seems to have occurred, although these divisions do not seem to have developed the rigidity of the Indian class system.

The Kingdom of Angkor

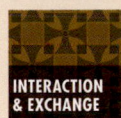

INTERACTION & EXCHANGE

ANGKOR WAS THE GREATEST KINGDOM of its time in Southeast Asia. This passage was written in the thirteenth century by the Chinese customs inspector Chau Ju-kua (zhow RU-gwah), in the city of Quanzhou (CHWAHN-JOE) (sometimes called Zaiton) on the southern coast of China. His account, compiled from reports of seafarers, includes a brief description of the capital city, Angkor Thom, which is still one of the great archaeological sites of the region. Angkor was already in decline when Chau Ju-kua described the kingdom, and the capital was abandoned in 1432.

Chau Ju-kua, *Records of Foreign Nations*

The officials and the common people dwell in houses with sides of bamboo matting and thatched with reeds. Only the king resides in a palace of hewn stone. It has a granite lotus pond of extraordinary beauty with golden bridges, some three hundred odd feet long. The palace buildings are solidly built and richly ornamented. The throne on which the king sits is made of gharu wood and the seven precious substances; the dais is jewelled, with supports of veined wood [possibly ebony]; the screen [behind the throne] is of ivory.

When all the ministers of state have audience, they first make three full prostrations at the foot of the throne; they then kneel and remain thus, with hands crossed on their breasts, in a circle round the king, and discuss the affairs of state. When they have finished, they make another prostration and retire....

[The people] are devout Buddhists. There are serving [in the temples] some three hundred foreign women; they dance and offer food to the Buddha. They are called *a-nan* or slave dancing girls.

As to their customs, lewdness is not considered criminal; theft is punished by cutting off a hand and a foot and by branding on the chest.

The incantations of the Buddhist and Taoist priests [of this country] have magical powers. Among the former those who wear yellow robes may marry, while those who dress in red lead ascetic lives in temples. The Taoists clothe themselves with leaves; they have a deity called P'o-to-li which they worship with great devotion.

[The people of this country] hold the right hand to be clean, the left unclean, so when they wish to mix their rice with any kind of meat broth, they use the right hand to do so and also to eat with.

The soil is rich and loamy; the fields have no bounds. Each one takes as much as he can cultivate. Rice and cereals are cheap; for every tael [1.3 ounces] of lead one can buy two bushels of rice.

The native products comprise elephants' tusks, the *chan* and *su* [varieties of gharu wood], good yellow wax, kingfisher's feathers, ... resin, foreign oils, ginger peel, gold-colored incense, ... raw silk and cotton fabrics.

The foreign traders offer in exchange for these gold, silver, porcelainware, sugar, preserves, and vinegar.

Because of the paucity of written records about Angkor society, documents such as this one from a Chinese source are important for the knowledge they provide about local conditions. What does this excerpt tell us about the political system, religious beliefs, and land use in thirteenth-century Angkor?

Source: Excerpt from Chau Ju-kua: *His Work on the Chinese and Arab Trade in the Twelfth and Thirteenth Centuries*, entitled *Chu-fan-chi*, Friedrich Hirth and W. W. Rockhill, eds., copyright © 1966 by Paragon Reprint.

India also supplied Southeast Asians with a writing system. The societies of the region had no written scripts for their spoken languages before the arrival of the Indian merchants and missionaries. Indian phonetic symbols were borrowed and used to record the spoken language. Initially, Southeast Asian literature was written in the Indian Sanskrit but eventually came to be written in the local languages. At the same time, Southeast Asian authors borrowed popular Indian themes, such as stories from the Buddhist scriptures and tales from the Ramayana.

A popular form of entertainment among the common people, the *wayang kulit* (WAH-yahng KOO-lit), or shadow play, may have come originally from India or possibly China, but it became a distinctive art form in Java and other islands of the Indonesian archipelago. In a shadow play, flat leather puppets were manipulated behind an illuminated screen while the narrator recited tales from the Indian classics. The plays were often accompanied by a gamelan (GA-muh-lan), an orchestra composed primarily of percussion instruments such as gongs and drums that apparently originated in Java.

CHRONOLOGY Early Southeast Asia

Chinese conquest of Vietnam	111 B.C.E.
Arrival of Burmese peoples	c. seventh century C.E.
Formation of Srivijaya	c. 670
Construction of Borobudur	c. eighth century
Creation of Angkor kingdom	c. ninth century
Thai migrations into Southeast Asia	c. thirteenth century
Rise of Majapahit empire	1292
Fall of Angkor kingdom	1432

A Restaurant in Angkor. Most of the carvings found on the walls of the various temples at Angkor portray the victories achieved by Angkor armed forces over their rivals in neighboring countries. A few, however, provide modern visitors with a fascinating indication of the nature of daily life in one of the most spectacular cities of Southeast Asia. Panels illustrate various aspects of life in Angkor society, including fishermen and hunters at work, dog fights, waiters serving their patrons at a local restaurant, and even a woman in the process of childbirth. In the photograph shown here, waiters are serving their patrons at a local restaurant. European historians who contend that the first restaurants were opened in Paris in the eighteenth century should take note.

Daily Life

Because of the diversity of ethnic backgrounds, religions, and cultures, making generalizations about daily life in Southeast Asia during the early historical period is difficult. Nevertheless, it appears that societies in the region did not always apply the social distinctions that prevailed in India. For example, although the local population, as elsewhere, was divided according to a variety of economic functions, the dividing lines between classes were not as rigid and imbued with religious significance as they were in the Indian subcontinent.

SOCIAL STRUCTURES Still, traditional societies in Southeast Asia had some clearly hierarchical characteristics. At the top of the social ladder were the hereditary aristocrats, who monopolized both political power and economic wealth and enjoyed a borrowed aura of charisma by virtue of their proximity to the ruler. Most aristocrats lived in the major cities, which were the main source of power, wealth, and foreign influence. Beyond the major cities lived the mass of the population, composed of farmers, fishers, artisans, and merchants. In most Southeast Asian societies, the vast majority were probably rice farmers, living at a bare level of subsistence and paying heavy rents or taxes to a landlord or a local ruler.

The average Southeast Asian peasant was not actively engaged in commerce except as a consumer of various necessities. But accounts by foreign visitors indicate that in the Malay

world, some were involved in growing or mining products for export, such as tropical food products, precious woods, tin, and precious gems. Most of the regional trade was carried on by local merchants, who purchased products from local growers and then transported them to the major port cities (see the box "Chinese Traders in the Philippines" on p. 261). During the early state-building era, roads were few and relatively primitive, so most of the trade was transported by small boats down rivers to the major ports along the coast. There the goods were loaded onto larger ships for delivery outside the region. Growers of export goods in areas near the coast were thus indirectly involved in the regional trade network but received few economic benefits from the relationship.

As we might expect from an area of such ethnic and cultural diversity, social structures differed significantly from country to country. In the Indianized states on the mainland, the tradition of a hereditary tribal aristocracy was probably accentuated by the Hindu practice of dividing the population into separate classes, called *varna* in imitation of the Indian model. In Angkor and Pagan, for example, the divisions were based on occupation or ethnic background. Some people were considered free subjects of the king, although there may have been legal restrictions against changing occupations. Others, however, may have been indentured to an employer. Each community was under a chieftain, who was in turn subordinated to a higher official responsible for passing on the tax revenues of each group to the central government.

In the kingdoms in the Malay Peninsula and the Indonesian archipelago, social relations were generally less formal. Most of the people in the region, whether farmers, fishers, or artisans, lived in small *kampongs* (KAHM-pahngs) (Malay for "villages") in wooden houses built on stilts to avoid flooding during the monsoon season. Some of the farmers were probably sharecroppers who paid a part of their harvest to a landlord, who was often a member of the aristocracy. But in other areas, the tradition of free farming was strong. In some cases, some of the poorer land belonged to the village as a collective unit and was assigned for use by the neediest families.

WOMEN AND THE FAMILY The women of Southeast Asia during this era have been described as the most fortunate in the world. Although most women worked side by side with men in the fields, as in Africa they often played an active role in trading activities. Not only did this lead to a higher literacy rate among women than among their male counterparts, but it also allowed them more financial independence

Chinese Traders in the Philippines

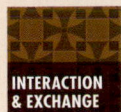

INTERACTION & EXCHANGE

FROM EARLY TIMES, the peoples living in the islands south of the East Asian mainland played an active role in the regional trade network between the Chinese coast and the Indian Ocean. This excerpt from a thirteenth-century Chinese account describes the nature of the commercial exchanges that took place between Chinese merchants and the indigenous population in the Philippine Islands. The author of the account, Chau Ju-kua, was a superintendent of trade in South China. His description of the indigenous peoples in the Philippines is one of the few sources on such communities before the arrival of European ships in the sixteenth century.

A Description of Barbarian Peoples

The country of Ma-i [Philippine archipelago] is to the north of P'o-ni [Borneo]. Over a thousand families are settled together along both banks of a creek (or, gully). The natives cover themselves with a sheet of cotton cloth, or hide the lower part of the body with a loincloth.

There are bronze images of gods, of unknown origin, scattered about in the grassy wilderness. Pirates seldom come to this country.

When trading ships enter the anchorage, they stop in front of the officials' place, for that is the place for bartering of the country. After a ship has been boarded, the natives mix freely with the ship's folk. The chiefs are in the habit of using white umbrellas, for which reason the traders offer them as gifts.

The custom of the trade is for the savage traders to assemble in crowds and carry the goods away with them in baskets; and, even if one cannot at first know them, and can but slowly distinguish the men who remove the goods, there will yet be no loss. The savage traders will after this carry these goods on to other islands for barter, and, as a rule, it takes them as much as eight or nine months till they return, when they repay the traders on shipboard with what they have obtained (for the goods). Some, however, do not return within the proper term, for which reason vessels trading with Ma-i are the latest in reaching home....

The products of the country consist of yellow wax, cotton, pearls, tortoise-shell, medicinal betel-nuts and *yü-ta* cloth

[abaca textiles]; and (the foreign) traders barter for these porcelain, trade-gold, iron censers, lead, coloured glass beads, and iron needles....

The San-sü (or "Three Islands"), belong to the Ma-i; their names are Kia-ma-yen (Calamián Island Group between Mindoro and Palawan), Pa-lau-yu (Palawan), and Pa-ki-nung (Busuanga Island, largest of the Calamián Islands), and each has its own tribes scattered over the islands. When ships arrive there, the natives come out to trade with them; the generic name (of these islands) is San-sü.

Their local customs are about the same as those of Ma-i. Each tribe consists of about a thousand families. The country contains many lofty ridges, and ranges of cliffs rise steep as the walls of a house.

The natives build wattled huts perched in lofty and dangerous spots, and since the hills contain no springs, the women may be seen carrying on their heads two or three jars one above the other in which they fetch water from the streams, and with their burdens mount the hills with the same ease as if they were walking on level ground....

Whenever foreign traders arrive at any of the settlements, they live on board ship before venturing to go on shore, their ships being moored in mid-stream, announcing their presence to the natives by beating drums. Upon this the savage traders race for the ship in small boats, carrying cotton, yellow wax, native cloth, cocoanut-heart mats, which they offer for barter. If the prices (of goods they may wish to purchase) cannot be agreed upon, the chief of the (local) traders must go in person, in order to come to an understanding, which being reached the natives are offered presents of silk umbrellas, porcelain, and rattan baskets; but the foreigners still retain on board one or two (natives) as hostages. After that they go on shore to traffic, which being ended they return the hostages. A ship will not remain at anchor longer than three or four days, after which it proceeds to another place; for the savage settlements along the coast of San-sü are not connected by a common jurisdiction (i.e., are all independent).

 How does the trading process take place in this account? How does each side seek to guarantee satisfaction?

Source: From *Chau Ju-kua, His Work on the Chinese and Arab Trade in the Twelfth and Thirteenth Centuries, entitled Chu-fan-chi*, trans. F. Hirth and W. W. Rockhill (St. Petersburg: Printing Office of the Imperial Academy of Sciences, 1911), pp. 159–162.

than their counterparts in China and India, a fact that was noticed by the Chinese traveler Zhou Daguan (JOE dah-GWAHN) at the end of the thirteenth century: "In Cambodia it is the women who take charge of trade. For this reason a Chinese arriving in the country loses no time in getting himself a mate, for he will find her commercial instincts a great asset."[10]

Although, as elsewhere, warfare was normally part of the male domain, women sometimes played a role as bodyguards as well. According to Zhou Daguan, women were used to protect the royal family in Angkor, as well as in kingdoms located on the islands of Java and Sumatra. While there is no evidence that such female units ever engaged in battle, they did give rise to wondrous tales of "amazon" warriors in the writings of foreign travelers such as the fourteenth-century Muslim adventurer Ibn Battuta.

One reason for the enhanced status of women in traditional Southeast Asia is that the nuclear family was more common than the joint family system prevalent in China and the Indian subcontinent. Throughout the region, wealth in marriage was passed from the male to the female, in contrast to the dowry system applied in China and India. In most societies, virginity was usually not a valued commodity in brokering a marriage, and divorce proceedings could be initiated by either party. Still, most marriages were monogamous, and marital fidelity was taken seriously.

The relative availability of cultivable land in the region may help explain the absence of joint families. Joint families under patriarchal leadership tend to be found in areas where land is scarce and individual families must work together to conserve resources and maximize income. With the exception of a few crowded river valleys, few areas in Southeast Asia had a high population density per acre of cultivable land. Throughout most of the area, water was plentiful, and the land was relatively fertile. In parts of Indonesia, much of the diet could be supplied by the bountiful produce of wild fruit trees—bananas, coconuts, mangoes, and a variety of other tropical fruits.

World of the Spirits: Religious Belief

Indian religions also had a profound effect on Southeast Asia. Traditional religious beliefs in the region took the familiar form of spirit worship and animism that we have seen in other cultures. Southeast Asians believed that spirits dwelled in the mountains, rivers, streams, and other sacred places in their environment. Mountains were probably particularly sacred, since they were considered to be the abode of ancestral spirits, the place to which the souls of all the departed would retire after death.

When Hindu and Buddhist ideas began to penetrate the area early in the first millennium C.E., they exerted a strong appeal among local elites. Not only did the new doctrines offer a more convincing explanation of the nature of the cosmos, but they also provided local rulers with a means of enhancing their prestige and power and conferred an aura of legitimacy on their relations with their subjects. In the Javanese kingdoms and in Angkor, Hindu gods such as Vishnu and Shiva provided a new and more sophisticated veneer for existing beliefs in nature deities and ancestral spirits. In Angkor, the king's duties included performing sacred rituals on the mountain in the capital city; in time, the ritual became a state cult uniting Hindu gods with local nature deities and ancestral spirits in a complex pantheon.

This state cult, financed by the royal court, eventually led to the construction of temples throughout the country. Many of these temples housed thousands of priests and retainers and amassed great wealth, including vast estates farmed by local peasants. It has been estimated that there were as many as 300,000 priests in Angkor at the height of its power. This vast wealth, which was often exempt from taxes, may be one explanation for Angkor's gradual decline in the thirteenth and fourteenth centuries. Initially, the spread of Hindu and Buddhist doctrines was essentially an elite phenomenon. Although the common people participated in the state cult and helped construct the temples, they did not give up their traditional beliefs in local deities and ancestral spirits. A major transformation began in the eleventh century, however, when Theravada Buddhism began to penetrate the mainland kingdom of Pagan from the island of Sri Lanka. From Pagan, it spread rapidly to other areas in Southeast Asia and eventually became the religion of the masses throughout the mainland west of the Annamite Mountains (see the box "The Spread of Buddhism in Southeast Asia" on p. 263).

Theravada's appeal to the peoples of Southeast Asia is reminiscent of the original attraction of Buddhist thought centuries earlier on the Indian subcontinent. By teaching that individuals could seek Nirvana through their own actions rather than through the intercession of the ruler or a priest, Theravada was more accessible to the masses than the state

Sacred Mountain of Bali. In many traditional Asian societies, as in classical Greece, mountains were viewed as the abode of the gods, and temples were built in the shape of a mountain to create an earthly representation of a heavenly paradise. But mountains could hold dangers as well. Such is certainly the case with the Indonesian archipelago in Southeast Asia, an island chain formed by volcanic eruptions along a major fault line in the earth's crust. Shown here is beautiful Mount Agung (AH-goong), on the Indonesian island of Bali, still viewed as the local equivalent of sacred Mount Meru (MAY-roo) in India. In Balinese cosmology, the sea is the home of evil spirits, while humans occupy the profane world in between. An active volcano, Agung erupted in 1964, killing thousands of islanders in a cloud of volcanic ash.

The Spread of Buddhism in Southeast Asia

RELIGION & PHILOSOPHY

LIKE FA XIAN AND XUAN ZANG, I-TSING (635–713) was a Chinese monk who traveled to India in order to study Buddhist teachings. En route home after two decades in South Asia, he stopped at a number of ports in Southeast Asia, including Bhoga (today's Palembang) on the Indonesian island of Sumatra. As this passage indicates, Buddhism had already established a firm beachhead in the region, since many of the local elites had adopted the faith, presumably as a result of contacts with other Buddhist pilgrims and traders from the South Asian subcontinent. Other parts of the region had converted to Brahmanism. Later, both faiths would be replaced by Islam and Christianity.

A Record of the Buddhist Religion as Practised in India and the Malay Archipelago

This [East India] is the place where we embark when returning to China. Sailing from here two months in the south-east direction we come to Ka-cha [Acheh]. By this time a ship from Bhoga [Palembang] will have arrived there. This is generally in the first or second month of the year. But those who go to the Simhala Island [Ceylon] must sail in the south-west direction. They say that the island is 700 yoganas off. We stay in Ka-cha till winter, then start on board ship for the south, and we come after a month to a country of Malayau, which has now become Bhoga; there are many states (under it). The time of arrival is generally in the first or second

month. We stay there till the middle of summer and we sail to the north; in about a month we reach Kwang-fu (Kwang-tung). The first half of the year will be passed by this time.

When we are helped by the power of our (former) good actions, the journey everywhere is as easy and enjoyable as if we went through a market, but, on the other hand, when we have not much influence of Karma, we are often exposed to danger as if (a young one) in a reclining nest. I have thus shortly described the route and the way home, hoping that the wise may still expand their knowledge by hearing more.

Many kings and chieftains in the islands of the Southern Ocean admire and believe (Buddhism), and their hearts are set upon accumulating good actions. In the fortified city of Bhoga Buddhist priests number more than 1,000, whose minds are bent on learning and good practices. They investigate and study all the subjects that exist just as in the Middle Kingdom (Madhya-desa, India); the rules and ceremonies are not at all different. If a Chinese priest wishes to go to the West in order to hear (lectures) and read (the original), he had better stay here one or two years and practice the proper rules and then proceed to Central India.

 Does the author of this account appear to believe that the majority of the population in Acheh consists of fervent disciples of the Buddhist faith? Why or why not?

Source: From I-tsing, A Record of the Buddhist Religion as Practised in India and the Malay Archipelago, *trans. J. Takakusu (Oxford: Clarendon, 1896), pp. xxxiv–xxxv.*

---

cults promoted by the rulers. During the next centuries, Theravada gradually undermined the influence of state-supported religions and became the dominant faith in several mainland societies, including Burma, Thailand, Laos, and Cambodia. In the process, however, it was gradually appropriated by local rulers, who portrayed themselves as "immanent Buddhas," higher than ordinary mortals on the scale of human existence.

Theravada did not penetrate far into the Malay Peninsula or the Indonesian island chain, perhaps because it entered Southeast Asia through Burma farther to the north. But the Malay world found its own popular alternative to state religions when Islam began to enter the area in the thirteenth and fourteenth centuries. Because Islam's expansion into Southeast Asia took place for the most part after 1500, its emergence as a major force in the region will be discussed later in this book (see Chapter 14).

Not surprisingly, Indian influence extended to the Buddhist and Hindu temples of Southeast Asia. Temple architecture reflecting Gupta or southern Indian styles began to appear in Southeast Asia during the first centuries C.E. Most famous is the Buddhist temple at Borobudur (boh-roh-buh-DOOR), in

central Java. Begun in the late eighth century at the behest of a king of Sailendra (SY-len-druh) (an agricultural kingdom based in eastern Java), Borobudur is a massive stupa with nine terraces. Sculpted on the sides of each terrace are bas-reliefs depicting the nine stages in the life of Siddhartha Gautama, from childhood to his final release from the chain of human existence. Surmounted by hollow bell-like towers containing representations of the Buddha and capped by a single stupa, the structure dominates the landscape for miles around.

Second only to Borobudur in technical excellence and even more massive in size are the ruins of the old capital city of Angkor Thom. The temple of Angkor Wat (AN-kor WAHT) is the most famous and arguably the most beautiful of all the existing structures at Angkor Thom. Built on the model of the legendary Mount Meru (the home of the gods in Hindu tradition), it combines Indian architectural techniques with native inspiration in a structure of impressive delicacy and grace.

In existence for more than six hundred years, Angkor Thom serves as a bridge between the Hindu and Buddhist architectural styles. The last of its great temples, known

The Temple of Borobudur. The colossal pyramid temple at Borobudur, on the island of Java, is one of the greatest Buddhist monuments. Constructed in the eighth century C.E., it depicts the path to spiritual enlightenment in stone. Sculptures and relief portrayals of the life of the Buddha at the lower level depict the world of desire. At higher elevations, they give way to empty bell towers (see inset) and culminate at the summit with an empty and closed stupa, signifying the state of Nirvana. Shortly after it was built, Borobudur was abandoned when a new ruler switched his allegiance to Hinduism and ordered the erection of the Hindu temple of Prambanan nearby. Buried for a thousand years under volcanic ash and jungle, Borobudur was rediscovered in the nineteenth century and has recently been restored to its former splendor.

as the Bayon (BAY-on), followed the earlier Hindu model but was topped with sculpted towers containing four-sided representations of a bodhisattva, searching, it is said, for souls to save. Shortly after the Bayon was built, Theravada Buddhist societies in Burma and Thailand began to create a new Buddhist architecture based on the concept of a massive stupa surmounted by a spire. Most famous, perhaps, is the Shwedagon (SCHWEE-da-gahn) Pagoda in Yangon (YAN-gon) (Rangoon), capital of modern Myanmar (Burma), which is covered with gold leaf contributed by devout Buddhists from around the country.

Expansion into the Pacific

One of the great maritime feats of human history was the penetration of the islands of the Pacific Ocean by Malayo-Polynesian-speaking peoples. By 2000 B.C.E., these seafarers had migrated as far as the Bismarck Archipelago, northeast of the island of New Guinea, where they encountered Melanesian peoples whose ancestors had taken part in the first wave of human settlement into the region 30,000 years previously.

From there, the Polynesian peoples—as they are now familiarly known—continued their explorations eastward in large sailing canoes up to 100 feet long that carried more than forty people and many of their food staples, such as chickens, chili peppers, and a tuber called taro, the source of poi. Stopping in Fiji, Samoa, and the Cook Islands during the first millennium C.E., their descendants pressed onward, eventually reaching Tahiti, Hawaii, and even Easter Island, one of the most remote sites of human habitation in the world. Eventually, one group of Polynesians, now known as the Maori (MAU-ree), sailed southwestward from the island of Rarotonga and settled in New Zealand, off the coast of Australia. The final frontier of human settlement had been breached.

Angkor Wat. The Khmer (kuh-MEER) rulers of Angkor constructed a number of remarkable temples and palaces. Devised as either Hindu or Buddhist shrines, the temples also reflected the power and sanctity of the king. This twelfth-century temple known as Angkor Wat is renowned both for its spectacular architecture and for the thousands of fine bas-reliefs relating Hindu legends and Khmer history. Most memorable are the heavenly dancing maidens and the royal processions with elephants and soldiers.

Giant Heads of Easter Island. When the Malayo-Polynesian-speaking peoples spread out from their homeland into the islands of the Pacific, they eventually settled in areas as distant as Hawaii and Easter Island. Some of these peoples first arrived on Easter Island in the fifth century C.E. and soon began to erect giant stone statues. It is thought that they were erected by rival chiefdoms for reasons of prestige. Some scholars estimate that the process of moving the statues from the quarry (shown here) by rolling them on a bed of rounded logs eventually devastated the forests and caused the total erosion of the landscape. As a result, almost the entire population was wiped out.

CHAPTER SUMMARY

During the more than 1,500 years from the fall of the Mauryas to the rise of the Mughals, Indian civilization faced a number of severe challenges. One challenge was primarily external and took the form of a continuous threat from beyond the mountains in the northwest. As a result of the foreign conquest of northern India, Islam was introduced into the region. The new religion soon became a serious rival to traditional beliefs among the people of India. Another challenge had internal causes, stemming from the tradition of factionalism and internal rivalry that had marked relations within the aristocracy since the Aryan influx in the second millennium B.C.E. (see Chapter 2). Despite the abortive efforts of the Guptas, that tradition continued almost without interruption down to the founding of the Mughal Empire in the sixteenth century.

During the same period that Indian civilization faced these challenges at home, it was having a profound impact on the emerging states of Southeast Asia. Situated at the crossroads between two oceans and two great civilizations, Southeast Asia has long served as a bridge linking peoples and

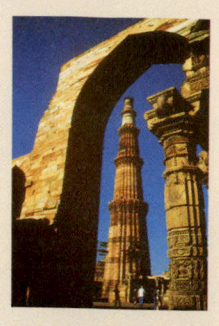

cultures, and as complex societies began to develop in the area, it is not surprising that they were strongly influenced by the older civilizations of neighboring China and India. At the same time, the Southeast Asian peoples put their own unique stamp on the ideas that they adopted and eventually rejected those that were inappropriate to local conditions.

The result was a region characterized by an almost unparalleled cultural richness and diversity, reflecting influences from as far away as the Middle East yet preserving indigenous elements that were deeply rooted in the local culture. Unfortunately, that very diversity posed potential problems for the peoples of Southeast Asia as they faced a new challenge from beyond the

horizon. We shall deal with that challenge when we return to the region later in the book. In the meantime, we must turn our attention to the other major civilization that spread its shadow over the societies of southern Asia—China.

CHAPTER TIMELINE

CHAPTER REVIEW

Upon Reflection

Q How does the religion known today as Hinduism compare in its essential respects with the Brahmanical faith from which it emerged in the first millennium C.E.? What may explain the differences?

Q The Indian social system has been characterized by the existence of extensive lineage groups—known as *jati*—that are larger than the traditional joint and nuclear families found in many other societies. What are the most prominent features of such lineage groups, and why have they endured for so long in Indian society?

Q Many of the states that were formed in Southeast Asia during the first millennium C.E. absorbed strong influences from merchants and missionaries arriving from India. What political, social, and religious characteristics of Indian civilization were adopted by the indigenous states in Southeast Asia, and how were they applied in their new environment?

Key Terms

Theravada (p. 243)
Mahayana (p. 243)
Hinayana (p. 243)
bodhisattva (p. 243)
Hinduism (p. 244)
bhakti (p. 245)
puja (p. 246)
purdah (p. 250)
Malayo-Polynesian (p. 256)

Suggested Reading

GENERAL   The period from the decline of the Mauryas to the rise of the Mughals in India is not especially rich in materials in English. Still, a number of the standard texts on Indian history contain useful sections on the period. Particularly good are **B. and T. Metcalf**, *A Concise History of India* (Cambridge, 2001), and **S. Wolpert**, *India*, 3rd ed. (New York, 2005).

INDIAN SOCIETY AND CULTURE   A number of studies of Indian society and culture deal with this period. See, for example, **R. Thapar**, *Early India, from the Origins to A.D. 1300* (London, 2002), for an authoritative interpretation of Indian culture during the medieval period. On Buddhism, see **H. Akira**, *A History of Indian Buddhism from Sakyamuni to Early Mahayana* (Honolulu, 1990). For traditional accounts of society in both India and Southeast Asia, see **Fa Xian's** *A Record of Buddhistic Kingdoms*, trans. **J. Legge** (Oxford, 1886) and newly issued by Forgotten Books (Lexington, Ky., 2013), and *The Travels of Ibn Battuta in the Near East, Asia and Africa*, trans. **S. Lee** (Mineola, N.Y., 2004).

WOMEN'S ISSUES   For a discussion of women's issues, see **S. Hughes** and **B. Hughes**, *Women in World History*, vol. 1 (Armonk, N.Y., 1995), and **V. Dehejia**, *Devi: The Great Goddess* (Washington, D.C., 1999).

CENTRAL ASIA   For an overview of events in Central Asia during this period, see **D. Christian**, *Inner Eurasia from Prehistory to the Mongol Empire* (Oxford, 1998). On the career of Tamerlane, see **B. F. Manz**, *The Rise and Rule of Tamerlane* (Cambridge, 1989).

MEDIEVAL INDIAN ART   On Indian art during the medieval period, see **V. Dehejia**, *Indian Art* (London, 1997).

EARLY SOUTHEAST ASIA   The early history of Southeast Asia is not as well documented as that of China or India. Except for Vietnam, where histories written in Chinese appeared shortly after the Chinese conquest, written materials on societies in the region are relatively sparse. Historians were therefore compelled to rely on stone inscriptions and the accounts of travelers and historians from other countries. As a result, the history of precolonial Southeast Asia was presented, as it were, from the outside looking in. For an overview of modern scholarship on the region, see **N. Tarling, ed.,** *The Cambridge History of Southeast Asia*, vol. 1 (Cambridge, 1999).

Impressive advances are now being made in the field of prehistory. See **P. Bellwood,** *Prehistory of the Indo-Malaysian Archipelago* (Honolulu, 1997), and **C. Higham,** *The Bronze Age of Southeast Asia* (Cambridge, 1996). Also see the latter's *Civilization of Angkor* (Berkeley, Calif., 2001), which discusses the latest evidence on that major empire. On the region's impact on world history, see the impressive *Strange Parallels: Southeast Asia in Global Context, c. 800–1300*, vol. 1, by **V. Lieberman** (Cambridge, 2003).

Chapter Notes

1. Hiuen Tsiang, *Si-Yu-Ki: Buddhist Records of the Western World*, trans. S. Beal (London, 1982), pp. 89–90.
2. "Fo-Kwo-Ki" (Travels of Fa Xian), ch. 20, p. 43, in ibid.
3. E. C. Sachau, *Alberoni's India* (London, 1914), vol. 1, p. 22.
4. Quoted in S. M. Ikram, *Muslim Civilization in India* (New York, 1964), p. 68.
5. Hiuen Tsiang, *Si-Yu-Ki*, pp. 73–74.
6. D. Barbosa, *The Book of Duarte Barbosa* (Nedeln, Liechtenstein, 1967), pp. 147–148.
7. Quoted in R. Lannoy, *The Speaking Tree: A Study of Indian Culture and Society* (London, 1971), p. 232.
8. Quoted in S. Tharu and K. Lalita, *Women Writing in India*, vol. 1 (New York, 1991), p. 77.
9. Quoted in A. L. Basham, *The Wonder That Was India* (London, 1954), p. 426.
10. Quoted in S. Hughes and B. Hughes, *Women in World History*, vol. 1 (Armonk, N.Y., 1995), p. 217.

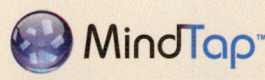
MindTap™

MindTap is a fully online, highly personalized learning experience built upon Cengage Leaning content. MindTap combines student learning tools—readings, multimedia, activities, and assessments—into a singular Learning Path that guides students through their course.

The Flowering of Traditional China

Detail of a Chinese scroll, *Going up the River at the Spring Festival*

Werner Forman/Art Resource, NY

CHAPTER OUTLINE AND FOCUS QUESTIONS

China After the Han

Q Why did China experience several centuries of internal division after the decline of the Han dynasty, and what impact did this period of instability have on Chinese society?

China Reunified: The Sui, the Tang, and the Song

Q What major changes in political structures and social and economic life occurred during the Sui, Tang, and Song Dynasties?

Explosion in Central Asia: The Mongol Empire

Q Why were the Mongols able to amass an empire, and what were the main characteristics of their rule in China?

The Ming Dynasty

Q What were the chief initiatives taken by the early rulers of the Ming Dynasty to enhance the role of China in the world? Why did the imperial court order the famous voyages of Zheng He, and why were they discontinued?

In Search of the Way

Q What roles did Buddhism, Daoism, and Neo-Confucianism play in Chinese intellectual life in the period between the Sui dynasty and the Ming?

The Apogee of Chinese Culture

Q What were the main achievements in Chinese literature and art in the period between the Tang Dynasty and the Ming, and what technological innovations and intellectual developments contributed to these achievements?

CRITICAL THINKING

Q The civilization of ancient China fell under the onslaught of nomadic invasions, as did some of its counterparts elsewhere in the world. But China, unlike other classical empires, was later able to reconstitute itself on the same political and cultural foundations. How do you account for the difference?

CONNECTIONS TO TODAY

Q The Comparative Essay "The Spread of Technology" in this chapter suggests that active participation in the global trade network helped medieval societies compete more effectively in the international marketplace. Do you feel that this argument could be made about societies today?

ON HIS FIRST VISIT to the city, the traveler was mightily impressed. Its streets were so straight and wide that he could see through the city from one end to the other. Along the wide boulevards were beautiful palaces and inns in great profusion. The city was laid out in squares like a chessboard, and within each square were spacious courts and gardens. Truly, said the visitor, this must be one of the largest and wealthiest cities on earth—a city "planned out to a degree of precision and beauty impossible to describe."[1]

The visitor was Marco Polo (MAR-koh POH-loh), and the city was Khanbaliq (kahn-bah-LEEK) (later known as Beijing), capital of the Yuan (YOO-enn *or* YWAHN) dynasty (1279–1368) and one of the great urban centers of the Chinese Empire. Marco Polo was an Italian merchant who had traveled to China in the late thirteenth century and then served as an official at the court of Khubilai Khan (KOO-blah KAHN). Polo's diary, published after his return to Italy almost twenty years later, astonished readers with tales of this magnificent but unknown civilization far to the east. In fact, many of his European contemporaries were skeptical of his claims and suspected that he was a charlatan seeking to win fame and fortune with a fictional account of his travels to fantastic lands. Even today, some observers are skeptical of his claims.

Many contemporary readers of Marco Polo's memoirs in other parts of the world, however, would have found his account of the wonders of the East more credible, for evidence of the greatness of the Chinese Empire—then under the domination of a fearsome Central Asian people called Mongols—was all around them. Indeed, after the decline of the Abbasids in the eleventh and twelfth centuries, China had clearly emerged as the richest and most powerful empire on the Eurasian supercontinent. ✦

China After the Han

 FOCUS QUESTION: Why did China experience several centuries of internal division after the decline of the Han dynasty, and what impact did this period of instability have on Chinese society?

After the collapse of the Han dynasty at the beginning of the third century C.E., China fell into an extended period of division and civil war. Taking advantage of the absence of organized government in China, nomadic forces from the Gobi Desert penetrated south of the Great Wall and established their own rule over northern China. In the Yangzi Valley and farther to the south, native Chinese rule was maintained, but constant civil war and instability led later historians to refer to the period as the "era of the six dynasties."

The collapse of the Han Empire had a marked effect on the Chinese psyche. The Confucian principles that emphasized hard work, the subordination of the individual to community interests, and belief in the essentially rational order of the universe came under severe challenge, and many Chinese began to turn to more messianic creeds that emphasized the supernatural or the promise of earthly or heavenly salvation. Intellectuals began to reject the stuffy moralism and complacency of State Confucianism and sought emotional satisfaction in hedonistic pursuits or philosophical Daoism.

Eccentric behavior and a preference for philosophical Daoism became a common response to a corrupt age. A group of writers known as the "seven sages of the bamboo forest" exemplified the period. Among the best known was the poet Liu Ling (lyoo LING), whose odd behavior is described in this oft-quoted passage:

Liu Ling was an inveterate drinker and indulged himself to the full. Sometimes he stripped off his clothes and sat in his room stark naked. Some men saw him and rebuked him. Liu Ling said, "Heaven and earth are my dwelling, and my house is my trousers. Why are you all coming into my trousers?"[2]

But neither popular beliefs in the supernatural nor philosophical Daoism could satisfy deeper emotional needs or provide solace in time of sorrow or the hope of a better life in the hereafter. Buddhism filled that gap.

Buddhism was brought to China in the first or second century C.E., probably by missionaries and merchants traveling over the Silk Road. The concept of rebirth was probably unfamiliar to most Chinese, and the intellectual hairsplitting that often accompanied discussion of the Buddha's message in India was too esoteric for Chinese tastes. Still, in the difficult years surrounding the decline of the Han dynasty, Buddhist ideas, especially those of the Mahayana school, began to find adherents among intellectuals and ordinary people alike. As Buddhism increased in popularity, it was frequently attacked by supporters of Confucianism and Daoism for its foreign origins. Some even claimed that Siddhartha Gautama had been a disciple of Lao Tzu. But such sniping did not halt the progress of Buddhism, and eventually the new faith was assimilated into Chinese culture, assisted by the efforts of such tireless advocates as the missionaries Fa Xian and Xuan Zang and the support of ruling elites in both northern and southern China (see "The Rise and Decline of Buddhism and Daoism" later in this chapter).

China Reunified: The Sui, the Tang, and the Song

 FOCUS QUESTION: What major changes in political structures and social and economic life occurred during the Sui, Tang, and Song dynasties?

After nearly four centuries of internal division, China was unified once again in 581 when Yang Jian (yahng JEE-YEN), a member of a respected aristocratic family in northern China, founded a new dynasty, known as the Sui (SWAY) (581–618). Yang Jian, who is also known by his reign title of Sui Wendi (SWAY wen-DEE), established his capital at the historic metropolis of Chang'an (CHENG-AHN) and began to extend his authority throughout the heartland of China.

The Sui Dynasty

Like his predecessors, the new emperor sought to create a unifying ideology for the state to enhance its efficiency. But where Liu Bang, the founder of the Han dynasty, had adopted Confucianism as the official doctrine to hold the empire together, Yang Jian turned to Daoism and Buddhism. He founded monasteries for both doctrines in the capital and appointed Buddhist monks to key positions as political advisers.

The Granger Collection, NYC

The Grand Canal. Built over centuries, the Grand Canal is one of the engineering wonders of the world and a crucial conduit for carrying goods between northern and southern China. In this stylized painting, "dragon boats" carry the emperor and his retinue on an inspection tour of the canal and its adjacent territories.

Yang Jian was a builder as well as a conqueror, ordering the construction of a new canal from the capital to the confluence of the Wei and Yellow Rivers nearly 100 miles to the east. His son, Emperor Sui Yangdi (SWAY yahng-DEE), continued the process, and the 1,400-mile-long Grand Canal, linking the two great rivers of China, the Yellow and the Yangzi, was completed during his reign. The new canal facilitated the shipment of grain and other commodities from the rice-rich southern provinces to the densely populated north. The canal also served other purposes, such as speeding communications between the two regions and permitting the rapid dispatch of troops to troubled provinces. Sui Yangdi also used the canal as an imperial highway for inspecting his empire. One imperial procession from the capital to the central Yangzi region was described as follows:

> The emperor caused to be built dragon boats, . . . red battle cruisers, multi-decked transports, lesser vessels of bamboo slats. Boatmen hired from all the waterways . . . pulled the vessels by ropes of green silk on the imperial progress to Chiang-tu [Yangzhou]. The emperor rode in the dragon boat, and civil and military officials of the fifth grade and above rode in the multi-decked transports; those of the ninth grade and above were given the vessels of yellow bamboo. The boats followed one another poop to prow for more than 200 leagues [about 65 miles]. The prefectures and counties through which they passed were ordered to prepare to offer provisions. Those who made bountiful arrangements were given an additional office or title; those who fell short were given punishments up to the death penalty.[3]

Despite such efforts to project the majesty of the imperial personage, the Sui dynasty came to an end immediately after Sui Yangdi's death. The Sui emperor was a tyrannical ruler, and his expensive military campaigns aroused widespread unrest. After his return from a failed campaign against Korea in 618, the emperor was murdered in his palace. One of his generals, Li Yuan (lee YWAHN), took advantage of the instability that ensued and declared the foundation of a new dynasty, known as the Tang (TAHNG). Building on the successes of its predecessor, the Tang lasted for three hundred years, until 907.

The Tang Dynasty

Li Yuan ruled for a brief period and then was elbowed aside by his son, who assumed the reign title Tang Taizong (tahng ty-ZOONG). Under his vigorous leadership, the Tang launched a program of internal renewal and external expansion that would make it one of the greatest dynasties in the long history of China (see Map 10.1). The northwest was pacified and given the name of Xinjiang, or "new region." After a long conflict with Tibet, Chinese control was extended for the first time over that vast and desolate plateau north of the Himalaya Mountains. The southern provinces below the Yangzi were fully assimilated into the Chinese Empire, and the imperial court established commercial and diplomatic relations with the states of Southeast Asia. With reason, China now claimed to be the foremost power in East Asia, and the emperor demanded fealty and tribute from all his fellow rulers beyond the frontier. Korea accepted tribute status and attempted to adopt the Chinese model, and the Japanese dispatched official missions to China to learn more about its customs and institutions (see Chapter 11).

Finally, the Tang Dynasty witnessed a flowering of Chinese culture. Many modern observers feel that the era represents the apogee of Chinese creativity in poetry and sculpture. One reason for this explosion of culture was the influence of Buddhism, which affected art, literature, and philosophy, as well as religion and politics (see the Comparative Illustration "The Two Worlds of Tang China" on p. 272). Monasteries sprang up throughout China, and Buddhist monks served as advisers at the Tang imperial court. The city of Chang'an, now restored to the glory it had known as the capital of the Han dynasty, once again became the seat of the empire. With a population estimated at nearly 2 million, it was possibly the greatest city in the world of its time. The city was filled with temples and palaces, and its markets teemed with goods from all over the known world.

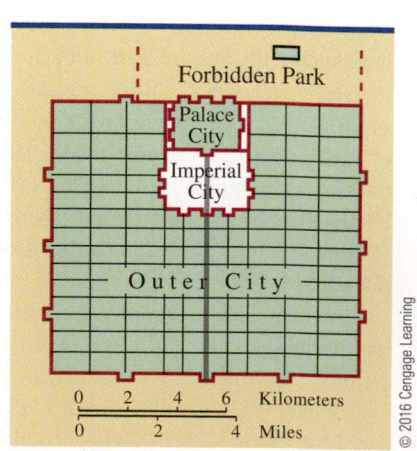

© 2016 Cengage Learning

Chang'an Under the Sui and the Tang

MAP 10.1 China Under the Tang. The era of the Tang Dynasty was one of the greatest periods in the long history of China. Tang influence spread from heartland China into neighboring regions, including Central and Southeast Asia.

Q *Why was the Grand Canal built, and what was its main function during this period?*

But the Tang, like the Han, sowed the seeds of their own destruction. Tang rulers could not prevent the rise of internal forces that would ultimately weaken the dynasty and bring it to an end. Two ubiquitous problems were court intrigues and official corruption. Xuanzong (shyahn-ZOONG) (r. 712–756), one of the great Tang emperors and a renowned patron of the arts, was dominated in later life by one of his favorite concubines, the beautiful Yang Guifei (yahng gway-FAY). One of her protégés, the military adventurer An Lushan (ahn loo-SHAHN), launched a rebellion in 755 and briefly seized the capital of Chang'an. The revolt was eventually suppressed, and Yang Guifei, who is viewed as one of the great villains of Chinese history, was put to death. But Xuanzong, and indeed the Tang Dynasty, never fully recovered from the catastrophe. The loss of power by the central government led to chronic instability along the northern and western frontiers, where local military commanders ruled virtually without central government interference. Climatologists also speculate that a prolonged drought that affected much of the world may have played a role in the decline of the dynasty. It was an eerie repetition of the final decades of the Han.

The end finally came in the early tenth century, when border troubles with northern nomadic peoples called the Khitan (KEE-tan) increased, leading to the final collapse of the dynasty in 907. The Tang had followed the classic Chinese strategy of "using a barbarian to oppose a barbarian" by allying with a trading people called the Uighurs (WEE-gurz), a Turkic-speaking people who

had taken over many of the caravan routes along the Silk Road, against their old rivals. But then another nomadic people called the Kirghiz (keer-GEEZ) defeated the Uighurs and turned on the Tang government in its moment of weakness and overthrew it.

The Song Dynasty

China slipped once again into disunity. This time, the period of foreign invasion and division was much shorter. In 960, a new dynasty, known as the Song (SOONG) (960–1279), rose to power. From the start, however, the Song rulers encountered more problems in defending their territory than their predecessors. Although the founding emperor, Song Taizu (soong ty-DZOO), was able to co-opt many of the powerful military commanders whose rivalry had brought the Tang Dynasty to an end, he was unable to reconquer the northwestern part of the country from the nomadic Khitan peoples. The emperor therefore established his capital farther to the east, at Kaifeng, where the Grand Canal intersected the Yellow River. Later, when pressures from the nomads in the north increased, the court was forced to move the capital even farther south, to Hangzhou (HAHNG-joe), on the coast just south of the Yangzi River delta; the emperors who ruled from Hangzhou are known as the southern Song (1127–1279). The Song also lost control over Tibet. Despite its political and military weaknesses, the dynasty nevertheless ruled during a period of economic

China Reunified: The Sui, the Tang, and the Song ■ **271**

The Art Archive at Art Resource, NY

William J. Duiker

The Two Worlds of Tang China. In Tang Dynasty China, the arts often reflected influences from a wide variety of cultures. On the left is an eighth-century wall painting from a cliffside cave at Dunhuang, a major rest stop on the Silk Road. The portrait of the Buddha clearly reflects Indian influence. The illustration on the right is a stone rubbing of Confucius based on a painting by the Tang Dynasty artist Wu Daozi (woo DOW-zuh) (c. 685–758). Although the original painting is not extant, this block print of a stone copy of Wu Daozi's work, showing Confucius in his flowing robe, reflects the indigenous style for which the painter was famous. It became the iconic portrait of the Master for millions of later Chinese. The Chinese government recently commissioned a copy based on Wu's original painting to serve as the standard portrait of Confucius for people around the world.

Q *How do the two portraits shown here differ in the way their creators seek to present the character and the underlying philosophy of the Buddha and Confucius?*

expansion, prosperity, and cultural achievement and is therefore considered among the more successful Chinese dynasties. The population of the empire had risen to an estimated 40 million people, slightly more than that of the continent of Europe.

Yet the Song were never able to surmount the external challenge from the north, and that failure eventually brought about the end of the dynasty. During its final decades, the Song rulers were forced to pay tribute to the Jurchen (roor-ZHEN) peoples from Manchuria (man-CHUR-ee-uh). In the early thirteenth century, the Song, ignoring precedent and the fate of the Tang, formed an alliance with the Mongols, a new and obscure nomadic people from the Gobi Desert. As under the Tang, the decision proved to be a disaster. Within a few years, the Mongols had become a much more serious threat to China than the Jurchen.

After defeating the Jurchen, the Mongols turned their attention to the Song, advancing on Chinese territory from both the north and the west. By this time, the Song empire had been weakened by internal factionalism and a loss of tax revenues. After a series of river battles and sieges marked by the use of catapults and gunpowder, the Song were defeated, and the conquerors announced the creation of a new Yuan (Mongol) dynasty. Ironically, the Mongols had first learned about gunpowder from the Chinese.

Political Structures: The Triumph of Confucianism

During the nearly seven hundred years from the Sui to the end of the Song, a mature political system based on principles originally established during the Qin and Han Dynasties gradually emerged in China. After the Tang Dynasty's brief flirtation with Buddhism, State Confucianism became the ideological cement that held the system together. The development of this system took several centuries, and it did not reach its height until the period of the Song Dynasty.

EQUAL OPPORTUNITY IN CHINA: THE CIVIL SERVICE EXAMINATION

At the apex of the government hierarchy was the **Grand Council**, assisted by a secretariat and a chancellery; it included representatives from all three authorities—civil, military, and censorate. Under the Grand Council was the Department of State Affairs, composed of ministries responsible for justice, military affairs, personnel, public works, revenue, and rites (ritual). This department was in effect the equivalent of a modern cabinet.

The Tang Dynasty adopted the practice of selecting some officials through periodic civil service examinations. The effectiveness of this merit system was limited, however, because the examination was administered only in the capital city and because the process was dominated by the great aristocratic clans, who had mastered the technique of preparing candidates for the exams. According to one source, fully one-third of those who succeeded on the imperial examinations during the Tang era came from the great families.

The Song were more successful at limiting aristocratic control over the bureaucracy, in part because the power of the nobility had been irreparably weakened during the final years of the Tang Dynasty and did not recover during the interregnum that followed its collapse.

One way of strengthening the power of the central administration was to make the civil service examination system the primary route to an official career (see the box "Choosing the Best and Brightest" on p. 274). To reduce the power of the noble families, relatives of individuals serving in the imperial court, as well as eunuchs, were prohibited from taking the examinations. But if the Song rulers' objective was to make the bureaucracy more subservient to the court, they may have been disappointed. The rising professionalism of the bureaucracy, which numbered about ten thousand in the imperial capital, with an equal number at the local level, provided it with an esprit de corps and an influence that sometimes enabled it to resist the whims of individual emperors.

Under the Song, the examination system attained the form that it would retain in later centuries. In general, three levels of examinations were administered. The first was a qualifying examination given annually at the provincial capital. Candidates who succeeded in this first stage were normally not given positions in the bureaucracy except at the local level. Many stopped at this level and accepted positions as village teachers to train other candidates. Those who wished to secure an official position could take a second examination given at the capital every three years. Some went on to take the final examination, which was given in the imperial palace once every three years. Those who passed were eligible for high positions in the central bureaucracy or for appointments as district magistrates.

During the early Tang, the examinations included questions on Buddhist and Daoist as well as Confucian texts, but by Song times, examinations were based entirely on the Confucian classics (see "Opposing Viewpoints: Action or Inaction: An Ideological Dispute in Medieval China" on p. 275). Candidates were expected to memorize passages and to be able to define the moral lessons they contained. The system guaranteed that successful candidates—and therefore officials—would have received a full dose of Confucian political and social ethics. Whether they followed those ethics, of course, was another matter. Some students brought crib notes into the examination hall (one enterprising candidate concealed an entire Confucian text in the lining of his cloak). For those candidates who succeeded, official arrogance, bureaucratic infighting, corruption, and legalistic interpretations of government regulations were as prevalent in medieval China as in bureaucracies the world over.

The Song authorities tried to open up the system to provide an equal opportunity to the poor as well as to the affluent. Training academies were set up at the provincial and district levels. Without such academies, only individuals fortunate enough to receive training in the classics in family-run schools would have had the expertise to pass the examinations. Still, in most years, the majority of candidates came from the landed gentry, nonaristocratic landowners who controlled much of the wealth in the countryside. Because the gentry prized education and became the primary upholders of the Confucian tradition, they were often called the **scholar-gentry**.

Despite such weaknesses, the civil service examination system was an impressive achievement for its day and probably provided a more efficient government and more opportunity for upward mobility than were found in any other civilization of its time. Most Western governments, for example, began to recruit officials on the basis of merit only in the nineteenth century. Furthermore, by regulating the content of the examinations, the system helped provide China with a cultural uniformity lacking in empires elsewhere in Asia.

The court also attempted to curb official misbehavior through the censorate. Specially trained officials known as censors were assigned to investigate possible cases of official wrongdoing and report directly to the court. The censorate was supposed to be independent of outside pressures to ensure that

CHRONOLOGY Medieval China

Arrival of Buddhism in China	c. first century C.E.
Fall of the Han dynasty	220 C.E.
Sui dynasty	581–618
Tang Dynasty	618–907
Li Bo and Du Fu	700s
Emperor Xuanzong	712–756
Song Dynasty	960–1279
Wang Anshi	1021–1086
Southern Song Dynasty	1127–1279
Life of Genghis Khan	c. 1162–1227
Mongol conquest of China	1279
Reign of Khubilai Khan	1260–1294
Fall of the Yuan dynasty	1368
Ming Dynasty	1369–1644

Choosing the Best and Brightest

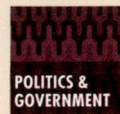

POLITICS & GOVERNMENT

Wang Anshi (WAHNG anh-SHEE) (1021–1086) was a prominent government official in Song Dynasty China. As a senior adviser at court, he sought to implement a series of reforms designed to improve the operations of the Chinese state, and thus improve the well-being of the population. One key tenet of his program was to appoint honest and competent officials to key positions in the bureaucracy. In the great tradition of Chinese statecraft, Wang agreed with the proposition that it was good men, and not just laws, that created the best civil society. Current practice, however, placed primary emphasis on the ability of candidates to memorize passages from the ancient classics. In his view, what was more important was for candidates to understand the general principles of governing and behavior, principles that could be gleaned from the writings of ancient times without the need for rote memorization.

Memorial to Emperor Renzong (1058)

The most urgent need of the present time is to secure capable men. Only when we can produce a large number of capable men in the empire will it be possible to select a sufficient number of persons qualified to serve in the government. And only when we get capable men in the government will there be no difficulty in assessing what may be done, in view of the time and circumstances, and in consideration of the human distress that may be occasioned, gradually to change the decadent laws of the empire in order to approach the ideas of the ancient kings. The empire today is the same as the empire of the ancient kings. There were numerous capable men in their times. Why is there a dearth of such men today? It is because, as has been said, we do not train and cultivate men in the proper way. . . .

What is the way to select officials? The ancient kings selected men only from the local villages and through the local schools. The people were asked to recommend those they considered to be virtuous and able, sending up their nominations to the court, which investigated each one. Only if the men recommended proved truly virtuous and able would they be appointed to official posts commensurate with their individual virtue and ability. Investigation of them did not mean that a ruler relied only upon his own keenness of sight and hearing or that he took the word of one man alone. . . . Having inquired into his actions and utterances, they then tested him in government affairs. What was meant by "investigation" was just that—to test them in government affairs. . . .

Today, although we have schools in each prefecture and district, they amount to no more than school buildings. There are no officers of instruction and guidance; nothing is done to train and develop human talent. Only in the Imperial Academy are officers of instruction and guidance to be found, and even they are not selected with care. The affairs of the court, rites and music, punishment and correction have no place in the schools, and the students pay no attention to them, considering that rites and music, punishment and correction are the business of officials, not something they ought to know about. What is taught to students consists merely of textual exegesis [of the classics].

That, however, was not the way men were taught in ancient times. In recent years, teaching has been based on the essays required for the civil service examinations, but this kind of essay cannot be learned without resorting to extensive memorization and strenuous study, upon which students must spend their efforts the whole day long. Such proficiency as they attain is at best of no use in the government of the empire, and at most the empire can make no use of them. . . .

In addition, candidates are examined in such fields as the Nine Classics, the Five Classics, specialization [in one classic], and the study of law. The court has already become concerned over the uselessness of this type of knowledge and has stressed the need for an understanding of general principles [as set forth in the classics]. . . . When we consider the men selected through "understanding of the classics," however, it is still those who memorize, recite, and have some knowledge of literary composition who are able to pass the examination, while those who can apply them [the classics] to the government of the empire are not always brought in through this kind of selection.

 Does Wang Anshi cite examples from ancient times to strengthen his complaint about the current nature of training for a career in officialdom? Do his criticisms have relevance for our own day?

Source: From *Sources of Chinese Tradition*, Vol. 1, 2nd ed., by William Theodore de Bary and Irene Bloom, pgs. 612–616. Copyright © 1999 Columbia University Press. Reprinted with permission of the publisher.

its members would feel free to report wrongdoing wherever it occurred. In practice, censors who displeased high court officials were often removed or even subjected to more serious forms of punishment, which reduced the effectiveness of the system.

LOCAL GOVERNMENT The Song Dynasty maintained the local government institutions that it had inherited from its predecessors. At the base of the government pyramid was the district (or county), governed by a magistrate. The magistrate, assisted by his staff of three or four officials and several other menial employees, was responsible for maintaining law and order and collecting taxes within his jurisdiction. A district could exceed 100,000 people. Below the district was the basic unit of Chinese government, the village. Because villages were so numerous in China, the central government did not appoint an official at that level

OPPOSING ✕ VIEWPOINTS

Action or Inaction: An Ideological Dispute in Medieval China

RELIGION & PHILOSOPHY

DURING THE INTERREGNUM BETWEEN THE FALL OF THE HAN DYNASTY in 220 C.E. and the rise of the Tang four hundred years later, Daoist critics lampooned the hypocrisy of the "Confucian gentleman" and the Master's emphasis on ritual and the maintenance of proper relations among individuals in society. In the first selection, a third-century Daoist launches an attack on the pompous and hypocritical Confucian gentleman who feigns high moral principles while secretly engaging in corrupt and licentious behavior.

By the eighth century, the tables had turned. In the second selection, Han Yu (hahn YOO) (768–824), a key figure in the emergence of Neo-Confucian thought as the official ideology of the state, responds to such remarks with a withering analysis of the dangers of "doing nothing"—a clear reference to the famous Daoist doctrine of "inaction."

Biography of a Great Man

What the world calls a gentleman [*chun-tzu*] is someone who is solely concerned with moral law [*fa*], and cultivates exclusively the rules of propriety [*ft*]. His hand holds the emblem of jade [authority]; his foot follows the straight line of the rule. He likes to think that his actions set a permanent example; he likes to think that his words are everlasting models. In his youth, he has a reputation in the villages of his locality; in his later years, he is well known in the neighboring districts. Upward, he aspires to the dignity of the Three Dukes; downward, he does not disdain the post of governor of the nine provinces.

Have you ever seen the lice that inhabit a pair of trousers? They jump into the depths of the seams, hiding themselves in the cotton wadding, and believe they have a pleasant place to live. Walking, they do not risk going beyond the edge of the seam; moving, they are careful not to emerge from the trouser leg; and they think they have kept to the rules of etiquette. But when the trousers are ironed, the flames invade the hills, the fire spreads, the villages are set on fire and the towns burned down; then the lice that inhabit the trousers cannot escape.

What difference is there between the gentleman who lives within a narrow world and the lice that inhabit trouser legs?

Han Yu, *Essentials of the Moral Way*

In ancient times men confronted many dangers. But sages arose who taught them the way to live and to grow together. They served as rulers and as teachers. They drove out reptiles and wild beasts and had the people settle the central lands. The people were cold, and they clothed them; hungry, and they fed them. Because the people dwelt in trees and fell to the ground, dwelt in caves and became ill, the sages built houses for them.

They fashioned crafts so the people could provide themselves with implements. They made trade to link together those who had and those who had not and medicine to save them from premature death. They taught the people to bury and make sacrifices [to the dead] to enlarge their sense of gratitude and love. They gave rites to set order and precedence, music to vent melancholy, government to direct idleness, and punishments to weed out intransigence. When the people cheated each other, the sages invented tallies and seals, weights and measures to make them honest. When they attacked each other, they fashioned walls and towns, armor and weapons for them to defend themselves. So when dangers came, they prepared the people; and when calamity arose, they defended the people.

But now the Daoists maintain:

> Till the sages are dead,
> theft will not end . . .
> so break the measures, smash the scales,
> and the people will not contend.

These are thoughtless remarks indeed, for humankind would have died out long ago if there had been no sages in antiquity. Men have neither feathers nor fur, neither scales nor shells to ward off heat and cold, neither talons nor fangs to fight for food. . . .

But now the Daoists advocate "doing nothing" as in high antiquity. Such is akin to criticizing a man who wears furs in winter by asserting that it is easier to make linen, or akin to criticizing a man who eats when he is hungry by asserting that it is easier to take a drink. . . .

This being so, what can be done? Block them or nothing will flow; stop them or nothing will move. Make humans of these people, burn their books, make homes of their dwellings, make clear the way of the former kings to guide them, and "the widowers, the widows, the orphans, the childless, and the diseased all shall have care." This can be done.

Q *How might the author of the first selection have responded to Han Yu's arguments? Which author appears to make the better case for his chosen ideological preference?*

Sources: Excerpt from *Sources of Chinese Tradition*, Vol. 1, 2nd ed., by William Theodore de Bary and Irene Bloom, pgs. 570–573. Copyright © 1999 by Columbia University Press. Reprinted with permission of the publisher. From *Chinese Civilization and Bureaucracy*, by Etienne Balasz. Copyright © 1964 by Yale University Press.

and allowed the villages to administer themselves. Village government was normally in the hands of a council of elders, most often assisted by a chief. The council, usually composed of the heads of influential families in the village, maintained the local irrigation and transportation network, adjudicated local disputes, organized and maintained a militia, and assisted in collecting taxes (usually paid in grain) and delivering them to the district magistrate.

As a rule, most Chinese had little involvement with government matters. When they had to deal with the government, they almost always turned to their village officials. Although the district magistrate was empowered to settle local civil disputes, most villagers preferred to resolve problems among themselves. It was expected that the magistrate and his staff would supplement their income by charging for such services, a practice that reduced the costs of the central government but also provided an opportunity for bribes, a problem that continued to plague the Chinese bureaucracy down to modern times.

The Economy

During the long period between the Sui and the Song, the Chinese economy, like the government, grew considerably in size and complexity. China was still an agricultural society, but major changes were taking place within the economy and the social structure. The urban sector of the economy was becoming increasingly important, new social classes were beginning to appear, and the economic focus of the empire was beginning to shift from the Yellow River valley in the north to the Yangzi River valley in the center—a process that was encouraged both by the expansion of cultivation in the Yangzi delta and by the control exerted over the north by nomadic peoples during the Song.

LAND REFORM The economic revival began shortly after the rise of the Tang. During the long period of internal division, land had become concentrated in the hands of noble families, and most peasants were reduced to serfdom or slavery. The early Tang tried to reduce the power of the landed nobility and maximize tax revenues by adopting the ancient "well-field" system, in which land was allocated to farmers for life in return for an annual tax payment and three weeks of conscript labor.

At first, the new system was vigorously enforced and led to increased rural prosperity and government revenue. But eventually, the rich and the politically influential, including some of the largest Buddhist monasteries, learned to manipulate the system for their own benefit and accumulated huge tracts of land. The growing population, bolstered by a rise in food production and the extended period of social stability, also put steady pressure on the system. Finally, the government abandoned the effort to equalize landholdings and returned the land to private hands while attempting to prevent inequalities through the tax system. The failure to resolve the land problem—along with the climatic changes mentioned earlier—contributed to the fall of the Tang Dynasty in the early tenth century, although the reversion of farmlands to private hands did result in more efficient production in some instances as well as an expansion of the long-distance trade in food products.

The Song tried to resolve the land problem by returning to the successful programs of the early Tang and reducing the power of the wealthy landed aristocrats. During the late eleventh century, the reformist official Wang Anshi (1021–1086) attempted to limit the size of landholdings through progressive land taxes and provided cheap credit to poor farmers to help them avoid bankruptcy. His reforms met with some success, but other developments probably contributed more to the general agricultural prosperity under the Song. These included the opening of new lands in the Yangzi River valley, improvements in irrigation techniques such as the chain pump (a circular chain of square pallets on a treadmill that enabled farmers to lift considerable amounts of water or mud to a higher level), and the introduction of a new strain of quick-growing rice from Southeast Asia, which permitted farmers in warmer regions to plant and harvest two crops each year. It was during the Song Dynasty that rice became the main food crop for the Chinese people.

AN INCREASE IN MANUFACTURING Major changes also took place in the Chinese urban economy, which witnessed significant growth in manufacturing and trade. This process began under the Tang Dynasty, but it was not entirely a product of deliberate state policy. In fact, early Tang rulers shared some of the traditional prejudice against commercial activities that had been prevalent under the Han and enacted a number of regulations that restricted trade and industry. As under the Han, the state maintained monopolies over key commodities such as salt.

Despite the restrictive policies of the state, the manufacturing sector grew steadily larger and more complex, helped by several new technological developments (see the Comparative Essay "The Spread of Technology" on p. 277). During the Tang, the Chinese mastered the art of manufacturing steel by mixing cast iron and wrought iron. The blast furnace was heated to a high temperature by burning coal, which had been used as a fuel in China from about the fourth century C.E. The resulting product was used in the manufacture of swords, sickles, and even suits of armor. By the eleventh century, more than 35,000 tons of steel were being produced annually. The introduction of cotton from India offered new opportunities in textile production. Gunpowder was invented by the Chinese during the Tang Dynasty and used primarily for explosives and a primitive flamethrower; it reached the West via the Arabs in the twelfth century.

THE EXPANSION OF COMMERCE The nature of trade was also changing. In the past, most long-distance trade had been undertaken by state monopolies. By the time of the Song, private commerce was being actively encouraged, and many merchants engaged in shipping as well as in wholesale and retail trade. The construction of the Grand Canal, as well as the expansion of the road system under the Tang, facilitated a dramatic increase in the regional trade network. Guilds began to appear, along with a new money economy. Paper currency began to be used in the eighth and ninth centuries. Credit (at first called "flying money") also made its first appearance during the Tang. With the increased circulation of paper money, banking began to develop as merchants found that strings of

The Spread of Technology

SCIENCE & TECHNOLOGY

From the invention of stone tools and the discovery of fire to the introduction of agriculture and the writing system, mastery of technology has been a driving force in the history of human evolution. But why do some human societies appear to be much more advanced in their use of technology than others? People living on the island of New Guinea, for example, began cultivating local crops like taro and bananas as early as ten thousand years ago but never took the next steps toward creating a complex society until the arrival of Europeans many millennia later. Advanced societies had begun to emerge in the Western Hemisphere during the classical era, but none had discovered the use of the wheel or the smelting of metals for tool making. Writing was in its infancy there.

Technological advances appear to take place for two reasons: need and opportunity. Farming peoples throughout the world needed to control the flow of water, so in areas where water was scarce or unevenly distributed, they learned to practice irrigation to make resources available throughout the region. Peoples living in the Pacific Ocean learned how to read the stars and the ocean currents in order to navigate from island to island. Sometimes, however, opportunity strikes by accident (as in the legendary story of the Chinese princess who dropped a silkworm cocoon in her cup of hot tea, thereby initiating a series of discoveries that resulted in the manufacture of silk) or when new technology is introduced from a neighboring region (as when the discovery of tin in Anatolia launched the Bronze Age throughout the Middle East).

The most important factor enabling societies to keep abreast of the latest advances in technology, it would appear, is participation in the global trade and communications network. In this respect, the relative ease of communications between the Mediterranean Sea and the Indus River valley represented a major advantage for the Abbasid Empire, as the peoples living there had rapid access to all the resources and technological advances in that part of the world. China was more isolated from other major civilizations by distance, but with its size and high level of cultural achievement, it was almost a continent in itself and was able to communicate with countries to the west via the Silk Road and the South China Sea.

Societies that were not linked to this vast network were at an enormous disadvantage in keeping up with new developments in technology. The peoples of New Guinea, at the far end of the Indonesian islands, had little or no contact

The first paper currency. © William J. Duiker

with the outside world. In the Western Hemisphere, a trade network did begin to take shape between societies in the Andes and their counterparts in Mesoamerica. But because of difficulties in communication (see Chapter 6), contacts were more intermittent. As a result, technological developments taking place in distant Eurasia did not reach the Americas until the arrival of the conquistadors.

 In what ways did China contribute to the spread of technology and ideas throughout the world during the period from the Sui dynasty to the beginning of the Ming Dynasty? How did China benefit from the process?

copper coins were too cumbersome for their increasingly complex operations. Unfortunately, early issues of paper currency were not backed by metal coinage and led to price inflation. Equally useful, if more prosaic, was the invention of the abacus, an early form of calculator that simplified the computations needed for commercial transactions.

THE SILK ROAD Long-distance trade, both overland and by sea, expanded under the Tang and the Song. Trade with countries and peoples to the west had been carried on for centuries (see Chapter 3), but it had declined dramatically between the fourth and sixth centuries C.E. as a result of the collapse of the Han and Roman Empires. It began to revive with the rise of the Tang and the simultaneous unification of much of the Middle East under the Arabs. During the Tang era, the route that we call the Silk Road reached its zenith. Along the Silk Road to China came raw hides, furs, and horses. Chinese aristocrats, their appetite for material consumption stimulated by the affluence of Chinese society during much of the Tang and Song periods, were fascinated by the exotic goods and the flora and fauna of the desert and the tropical lands of the South Seas. Much of the trade was carried by the Turkic-speaking Uighurs or Iranian-speaking Sogdians (SAHG-dee-unz) from Central Asia. During the Tang, Uighur caravans of two-humped Bactrian camels (a hardy variety native to Iran and regions to the northeast) carried goods back and forth between China and the countries of South Asia and the Middle East.

In actuality, the Silk Road was composed of a number of separate routes. The first to be used, probably because of the jade found in the mountains south of Khotan (koh-TAHN), ran along the southern rim of the Taklimakan (tah-kluh-muh-KAHN) Desert via Kashgar (KASH-gahr) and thence through the Pamir (pah-MEER) Mountains into Bactria. The first Buddhist missionaries traveled this route between India and China. Eventually, however, this area began to dry up, and traders were forced to seek other routes. From a climatic standpoint, the best route for the Silk Road was to the north of the Tian Shan (TEE-en SHAHN) (Heavenly Mountains), where moisture-laden northwesterly winds created pastures where animals could graze. But the area was frequently infested by bandits who preyed on unwary travelers. Most caravans therefore followed the southern route, which passed along the northern fringes of the Taklimakan Desert to Kashgar and down into northwestern India. Travelers avoided the direct route through the desert (in the Uighur language, the name means "go in and you won't come out") and trudged from oasis to oasis along the southern slopes of the Tian Shan following a route littered by animal bones. The oases were created by the water runoff from winter snows in the mountains and dried up in the searing heat of the desert summer.

The eastern terminus of the Silk Road was the city of Chang'an, perhaps the wealthiest city in the world during the Tang era. The city's days as China's foremost metropolis were numbered, however. Chronic droughts throughout the region made it more and more difficult to supply the city with food, and the growing power of Turkic-speaking peoples such as the Uighurs in the hinterlands made the city increasingly vulnerable to attack by rebel forces. During the later Tang, the imperial court was periodically shifted to the old secondary capital of Luoyang (LWOH-yahng). The Song Dynasty, a product of the steady drift of the national center of gravity toward the south, was forced to abandon Chang'an altogether as a historic symbol of imperial greatness.

THE MARITIME ROUTE The Silk Road was so hazardous that shipping goods by sea became increasingly popular. China had long been engaged in sea trade with other countries in the region, but most of the commerce was originally in the hands of Korean, Japanese, Southeast Asian, or Middle Eastern merchants. Under the Song, however, Chinese maritime trade was stimulated by the invention of the compass and technical

Tang Camel. During the Tang dynasty, trade between China, India, and the Middle East along the famous Silk Road increased rapidly and introduced new Central Asian motifs to Chinese culture. As seen in this sturdy example, the Bactrian two-humped camel played a major role in carrying goods along the trade route, since its ability to withstand long periods without water enabled it to survive the grueling trek across the Central Asian deserts. Created as tomb figures, and therefore preserved for us today, are numerous ceramic studies of horses and camels, along with officials, court ladies, and servants painted in brilliant gold, green, and blue lead glazes.
The Philadelphia Museum of Art/Art Resource, NY

improvements in shipbuilding such as the widespread use of the sternpost rudder and the lug sail (which enabled ships to sail close to the wind). If Marco Polo's observations can be believed, by the thirteenth century, Chinese junks had as many as four masts and could carry several hundred men, many more than contemporary ships in the West. The Chinese governor of Canton in the early twelfth century remarked:

According to the government regulations concerning sea-going ships, the larger ones can carry several hundred men, and the smaller ones may have more than a hundred men on board.... The ships' pilots are acquainted with the configuration of the coasts; at night they steer by the stars, and in the daytime by the Sun. In dark weather they look at the south-pointing needle. They also use a line a hundred feet long with a hook at the end, which they let down to take samples of mud from the sea-bottom; by its appearance and smell they can determine their whereabouts.[4]

A wide variety of goods passed through Chinese ports. The Chinese exported tea, silk, and porcelain to the countries beyond the South China Sea, receiving exotic woods, precious stones, cotton from India, and various tropical goods in exchange. Seaports on the southern China coast exported sweet oranges, lemons, and peaches in return for grapes, walnuts, and pomegranates. The major port of exit in southern China was Canton (also known as Guangzhou), where an estimated 100,000 merchants lived. Their activities were controlled by an imperial commissioner sent from the capital.

Some of this trade was a product of the tribute system, which the Chinese rulers used as an element of their foreign policy. The Chinese viewed the outside world as they viewed their own society—in a hierarchical manner. Rulers of smaller countries along the periphery were viewed as "younger brothers" of the Chinese emperor and owed fealty to him. Foreign rulers who accepted the relationship were required to pay tribute and to promise not to harbor enemies of the Chinese Empire. But the foreign rulers also benefited from the relationship. Not only did it confer legitimacy on them, but they often received magnificent gifts from their "elder brother" as a reward for good behavior. Merchants from their countries also gained access to the vast Chinese market.

Society in Traditional China

These political and economic changes affected Chinese society in several ways during the Tang and Song era. For one thing, it became much more complex. Whereas previously China had been almost exclusively rural, with a small urban class of merchants, artisans, and workers almost entirely dependent on the state, the cities had now grown into an important, if statistically still insignificant, part of the population. Urban life, too, had changed. Cities were no longer primarily administrative centers dominated by officials and their families but now included a much broader mix of officials, merchants, artisans, peddlers, and entertainers. Unlike European cities, however, Chinese cities did not possess special privileges that protected their residents from the rapacity of the central government.

In the countryside, equally significant changes were taking place as the relatively rigid demarcation between the landed aristocracy and the mass of the rural population gave way to a more complex mixture of landed gentry, free farmers, sharecroppers, and landless laborers. There was also a class of "base people," consisting of actors, butchers, and prostitutes, who possessed only limited legal rights and were not permitted to take the civil service examination.

THE RISE OF THE GENTRY   Under the early Tang, powerful noble families not only possessed a significant part of the national wealth, but also dominated high positions in the imperial government, just as they had at the end of the Han dynasty four hundred years earlier. Some Tang rulers, notably Empress Wu Zhao (woo ZHOW) in the late seventh century, sought to limit the power of the great families by recruiting officials through the civil service examinations, but in the end it was the expansion of regional power—often under non-Chinese military governors—after the An Lushan revolt that sounded the death knell to the aristocratic system.

Perhaps the most significant development during the Song Dynasty was the rise of the landed gentry as the most influential force in Chinese society. The gentry class controlled much of the wealth in the rural areas and, under the Song, produced the majority of the candidates for the bureaucracy. By virtue of their possession of land and specialized knowledge of the Confucian classics, the gentry had replaced the aristocracy as the political and economic elite of Chinese society. Unlike the aristocracy, however, the gentry did not form an exclusive class separated by the accident of birth from the remainder of the population. Upward and downward mobility between the scholar-gentry class and the remainder of the population was not uncommon and may have been a key factor in the stability and longevity of the system. A position in the bureaucracy opened the doors to wealth and prestige for the individual and his family, but it was no guarantee of success, and

Court Ladies Preparing Silk. Since antiquity, human beings have fashioned textiles out of hemp, flax, wool, cotton, and silk. The Shang Dynasty produced both hemp and silk cloth, whereas wool was prominent in the Middle East and Greece. Linen, woven in Egypt, was used by the Roman Empire to clothe its army. Fine Indian cotton was introduced to China along the Silk Road, just as Chinese satin was carried by Mongol warriors to Europe, where it was used for making banners. Sometimes the Chinese government demanded bolts of cloth as well as grain as a tax from peasants. Although most silk was produced by peasants as an agricultural by-product, it was also woven by the elegant court ladies of the Song Dynasty, as seen here, and its use as a fabric was restricted to the elite classes until the nineteenth century.

the fortunes of individual families might experience a rapid rise and fall. The soaring ambitions and arrogance of China's landed gentry are vividly described in the following wish list set in poetry by a young bridegroom of the Tang Dynasty:

> Chinese slaves to take charge of treasury and barn,
> Foreign slaves to take care of my cattle and sheep.
> Strong-legged slaves to run by saddle and stirrup when I ride,
> Powerful slaves to till the fields with might and main,
> Handsome slaves to play the harp and hand the wine;
> Slim-waisted slaves to sing me songs, and dance;
> Dwarfs to hold the candle by my dining-couch.[5]

For affluent Chinese in this era, life offered many more pleasures than had been available to their forebears. As a result of increased contacts with the outside world brought about as the result of the rise of the Silk Road and the new maritime routes, the country was much more cosmopolitan than it had been in previous centuries. There were new forms of entertainment, such as playing cards and chess (brought from India, although an early form had been invented in China during the Zhou dynasty); new forms of transportation, such as the paddle-wheel boat and horseback riding (made possible by the introduction of the stirrup); better means of communication (block printing was first invented in the eighth century C.E.); and new tastes for the palate introduced from lands beyond the frontier. Tables and chairs, as well as chopsticks (known in China as "fast ones"), came into common usage in the home during the Song era. Tea had been introduced from the Burmese frontier by monks as early as the Han dynasty, and brandy and other concentrated spirits produced by the distillation of alcohol made their appearance in the seventh century. Tea began to emerge as a national drink and took on ritual significance among intellectuals, poets, and Buddhist monks who believed that it could stimulate the brain cells and focus the mind.

VILLAGE AND FAMILY   The vast majority of the Chinese people still lived off the land in villages ranging in size from a few dozen residents to several thousand. A farmer's life was bounded by his village. Although many communities were connected to the outside world by roads or rivers, most Chinese rarely left the confines of their native village except for an occasional visit to a nearby market town. This isolation was psychological as well as physical, for most Chinese identified with their immediate environment and had difficulty envisioning themselves living beyond the bamboo hedges or mud walls that marked the limit of their horizon.

An even more basic unit than the village in the lives of most Chinese, of course, was the family. The ideal was the joint family with at least three generations under one roof. Because rice farming was heavily labor-intensive, the tradition of the joint family was especially prevalent in the south. When a son married, he was expected to bring his new wife back to live in his parents' home. Often the parents added a new wing to the house for the new family. Women who did not marry remained in the home where they grew up.

Chinese village architecture reflected these traditions. Most family dwellings were simple, consisting of one or at most two rooms. They were usually constructed of dried mud, stone, or brick, depending on available materials and the prosperity of the family. Roofs were of thatch or tile, and the floors were usually of packed dirt. Large houses were often built in a square around an inner courtyard, thus guaranteeing privacy from the outside world.

Within the family unit, the eldest male theoretically ruled as an autocrat. He was responsible for presiding over ancestral rites at an altar, usually in the main room of the house. He had traditional legal rights over his wife, and if she did not provide him with a male heir, he was permitted to take a second wife. She, however, had no recourse to divorce. As the old saying went, "Marry a chicken, follow the chicken; marry a dog, follow the dog." Wealthy Chinese might keep concubines, who lived in a separate room in the house and sometimes competed with the legal wife for precedence.

In accordance with Confucian tradition, children were expected, above all, to obey their parents, who not only determined their children's careers but also selected their marriage partners. Filial piety was viewed as an absolute moral good, above virtually all other moral obligations. Even today, duty to one's parents is considered important in traditional Chinese families, and the tombstones of deceased Chinese are often decorated with tile paintings depicting the filial acts that they performed during their lifetime.

WOMEN IN TANG CHINA   The tradition of male superiority continued from ancient times into the medieval era, especially under the southern Song when it was reinforced by Neo-Confucianism. Female children were considered less desirable than males because they could not undertake heavy work in the fields or carry on the family traditions. Women were not permitted to take the civil service examinations. Poor families often sold their daughters to wealthy villagers to serve as concubines, and female infanticide was not uncommon in times of famine to ensure that there would be food for the remainder of the family. Concubines had few legal rights; female domestic servants, even fewer.

On the surface, conditions improved for women in China during the era of Tang rule, in that a number of court ladies were active in politics, and several were prominent in the entertainment world. Nevertheless, it is doubtful that such limited achievements among the elite trickled down to the mass population (see the box "Proper Etiquette in Tang Dynasty China" on p. 281). In any event, any progress in women's rights was reversed under the Song, when Chinese social customs began to reflect a more rigid interpretation of Confucian orthodoxy. During the Song era, two new practices emerged that changed the equation for women seeking to obtain a successful marriage contract. First, a new form of dowry appeared. Whereas previously the prospective husband offered the bride's family a bride price, now the bride's parents were expected to pay the groom's family a dowry. With the prosperity that characterized Chinese society during much of the Song era, affluent parents sought to buy a satisfactory husband for their daughter, preferably one with a higher social standing and good prospects for an official career.

Proper Etiquette in Tang Dynasty China

DURING THE TANG DYNASTY (618–907), standards for female behavior became highly ritualized, as Confucian social norms, originally codified by the female historian Ban Zhao (Bahn-ZHOW) several hundred years earlier (see Chapter 5), were applied with increasing rigor. Song Ruozhao, (Song Rwo-ZHOW) the daughter of a senior court official, was appointed by Emperor Dezong (Duh-DZONG) (r. 779–805) to instruct the royal princesses in proper etiquette. It was perhaps in this capacity that she—or her older sister Ruohua (Rwo-HWAH)—wrote the influential *Analects for Women*, an instructional pamphlet designed to provide guidance for women in the proper behavior to adopt in various forms of activity.

In some cases, the advice is almost laughingly specific, as when the hostess is instructed to adjust her clothing, place her hands up her sleeves, and walk slowly to the door where, with lowered voice, she invites the guest inside her house. The pamphlet apparently remained in print until the Qing (Ching) Dynasty in the nineteenth century.

Song Ruozhao, *Analects for Women*

Establishing Oneself as a Person

To be a woman, you must first learn how to establish yourself as a person. The way to do this is simply by working hard to establish one's purity and chastity. By purity, one keeps one's self undefiled; by chastity, one preserves one's honor.

When walking, don't turn your head; when talking, don't open your mouth wide; when sitting, don't move your knees; when standing, don't rustle your skirts; when happy, don't exult with loud laughter; when angry, don't raise your voice. The inner and outer quarters are distinct; the sexes should be segregated. Don't peer over the outer wall or go beyond the outer courtyard. If you have to go outside, cover your face; if you peep outside, conceal yourself as much as possible. Do not be on familiar terms with men outside the family; have nothing to do with women of bad character. Establish your proper self so as to become a [true] human being. . . .

Ritual Decorum: Learning Proper Etiquette

To be a woman one must learn the rules of ritual decorum. When you expect a female guest, carefully clean and arrange the furniture and tea implements. When she arrives, take time to adjust your clothing, and then, with light steps and your hands drawn up in your sleeves, walk slowly to the door and with lowered voice, invite her in. Ask after her health and how her family is doing. Be attentive to what she says. After chatting in a leisurely way, serve the tea. When she leaves, send her off in a proper manner. . . .

If you are invited to someone's house, understand your female duties and help with the preparation of the tea. After having talked for a time, rise to leave. Don't overstay your welcome. If your hostess presses you to stay longer to share a meal, conduct yourself with propriety. Don't drink so much that your face turns red and you get sloppy in the handling of your chopsticks. Take your leave before all the food is gone and before you forget your manners. . . .

Serving a Husband

Women leave their families to marry, and the husband is the master of the household [they marry into]. . . . The husband is to be firm, the wife soft; conjugal affections follow from this. While at home, the two of you should treat each other with the formality and reserve of a guest. Listen carefully to and obey whatever your husband tells you. If he does something wrong, gently correct him. Don't be like those women who not only do not correct their husbands but actually lead them into indecent ways. . . . Don't imitate those shrewish wives who love to clash head on with their husbands all the time. Take care of your husband's clothing so that he is never cold in winter, and of his meals so that he never gets thin and sickly from not being fed enough. As a couple, you and your husband share the bitter and the sweet, poverty and riches. In life you share the same bed; in death the same grave. . . .

 Is any of the advice contained in this passage relevant as proper etiquette today? If so, which advice? If not, why?

Source: From *Nu Sishu*, 1854 Japanese edition, cited in William Theodore de Bary and Irene Bloom (eds.), *Sources of Chinese Tradition*, Vol. 1, 2nd ed. (New York: Columbia University Press, 1999), pp. 827–831.

A second source of marital bait during the Song period was the promise of a bride with tiny bound feet. The process of **foot binding**, carried out on girls aged five to thirteen, was excruciatingly painful, as it bent and compressed the foot to half its normal size by imprisoning it in restrictive bandages. But the procedure was often performed by ambitious mothers intent on assuring that their daughters would have the best possible prospects for marriage. A zealous mother would also want her daughter to have a competitive edge in dealing with the other wives and concubines of her future husband. Bound feet represented submissiveness and self-discipline, two of the required attributes of an ideal Confucian wife.

Throughout northern China, foot binding became common under the Song for women of all social classes. It was less widespread in southern China, where the cultivation of wet rice could not be carried out with bandaged feet; there it tended to be limited to the scholar-gentry class. Still, most Chinese women with bound feet contributed to the labor force to supplement

Gianni Dagli Orti/The Art Archive at Art Resource, NY

A Young Chinese Bride and Her Dowry. A Chinese bride had to leave her parental home and move to her husband's house, thereby also transferring her filial allegiance to her in-laws. For this reason, the mother-son relationship was the most important one in a Chinese woman's life. With the expansion of the gentry class during the Song Dynasty, young men who passed the civil service examination became the most sought-after marriage prospects, requiring that the families of young women offer a substantial dowry as an enticement to the groom's family. But some women were destined for more distant homes. In this Persian miniature, a Chinese bride destined to marry a Turkish bridegroom travels along the Silk Road, leading a procession that is transporting her dowry of prized Chinese porcelain to her new home.

the family income. Tattooing the body was also not uncommon, in contrast to earlier times, when it had only been applied to criminals as a means of identification and humiliation.

As in most traditional cultures, there were exceptions to the low status of women in Chinese society. Women had substantial property rights and retained control over their dowries even after divorce or the death of the husband. Women were actively involved in commerce, especially in the major cities, where they ran restaurants and guesthouses, or served as owners or clerks of textile shops catering to female customers. Wives were frequently an influential force in the home, often handling the accounts and taking primary responsibility for raising the children. Some were active in politics. The outstanding example was Wu Zhao (c. 625–c. 706), popularly known as Empress Wu. Selected by Emperor Tang Taizong as a concubine, after his death she rose to a position of supreme power at court. At first, she was content to rule through her sons, but in 690, she declared herself empress of China. To bolster her claim of legitimacy, she cited a Buddhist *sutra* to the effect that a woman would rule the world seven hundred years after the death of Siddhartha Gautama. For her presumption, she has been vilified by later Chinese historians, but she was actually a quite capable ruler, strengthening the civil service examination system and initiating the process of selecting graduates of the examinations for the highest positions in government. During her last years, she reportedly fell under the

influence of courtiers and was deposed in 705, when she was probably around eighty.

Explosion in Central Asia: The Mongol Empire

 FOCUS QUESTION: Why were the Mongols able to amass an empire, and what were the main characteristics of their rule in China?

The Mongols, who succeeded the Song as the rulers of China in the late thirteenth century, rose to power in Asia with stunning rapidity. In the 1160s when Genghis Khan (JING-uss *or* GENG-uss KAHN) (also known as Chinggis Khan), the founder of Mongol greatness, was born, the Mongols were a relatively obscure pastoral people in the area of modern-day Outer Mongolia. Like most of the nomadic peoples in the region, they were organized loosely into clans and tribes and even lacked a common name for themselves. Rivalry among the various tribes over pastureland, livestock, and booty was intense and increased at the end of the twelfth century as a result of a growing population and the consequent overgrazing of pastures. Since they had no source of subsistence besides their herds, the Mongols were, in the words of one historian, in a "state of stress."

This challenge was met by the great Mongol chieftain Genghis Khan (c. 1162–1227), whose original name was Temuchin (TEM-yuh-jin) (or Temujin). When Temuchin was still a child, his father, an impoverished noble of his tribe, was murdered by a rival, and the boy was forced to seek refuge in the wilderness. Described by one historian as tall, adroit, and vigorous, young Temuchin gradually unified the Mongol tribes through his prowess and the power of his personality. In 1206, he was elected Genghis Khan ("universal ruler") at a massive tribal meeting in the Gobi Desert. From that time on, he devoted himself to military pursuits. Mongol nomads were now forced to pay taxes and were subject to military conscription. "Man's highest joy," Genghis Khan reportedly remarked, "is in victory: to conquer one's enemies, to pursue them, to deprive them of their possessions, to make their beloved weep, to ride on their horses, and to embrace their wives and daughters."[6]

The army that Genghis Khan unleashed on the world was not exceptionally large—totaling less than 130,000 in 1227, at a time when the total Mongol population numbered between 1 million and 2 million. But their mastery of military tactics set the Mongols apart from their rivals. Their tireless flying columns of mounted warriors surrounded their enemies and harassed them like cattle, luring them into pursuit and then ambushing them with flank attacks. John Plano Carpini (PLAN-oh car-PEE-nee), a contemporary Franciscan friar, remarked:

As soon as they discover the enemy they charge and each one unleashes three or four arrows. If they see that they can't break him, they retreat in order to entice the enemy to pursue, thus luring him into an ambush prepared in advance.... Their military stratagems are numerous. At the moment of an enemy cavalry attack, they place prisoners and foreign auxiliaries in the forefront of their own position, while positioning the bulk of their own troops on the right and left wings to envelop the adversary, thus giving the enemy the impression that they are more numerous than in reality.[7]

In the years after the election of Temuchin as universal ruler, the Mongols defeated tribal groups to their west and then turned their attention to the non-Chinese kingdoms of northern China. There they discovered that their adversaries were armed with a weapon called a fire-lance, an early form of flamethrower. Gunpowder had been invented in China during the late Tang period, and by the early thirteenth century, a fire-lance had been developed that could spew out flames and projectiles a distance of 30 or 40 yards, inflicting considerable damage on the enemy. The following account of a battle in the 1230s between Mongol forces and the

The Destruction of Baghdad by the Mongols. In 1258, the Mongols attacked the city of Baghdad and brought an end to the Abbasid caliphate, which had prospered for nearly four centuries. Their treatment of the local population was brutal. Cities were razed to the ground, while dams and other irrigation works were destroyed, reducing the people to starvation. In this fourteenth-century miniature, Mongol cavalrymen are seen attacking the troops of the last of the Baghdad caliphs. Two decades later, Mongol warriors defeated the armies of the Song and established the Yuan dynasty in China in 1279.

army of the state of Jin in northern China describes the effects of this weapon:

On the fifth day of the fifth month they sacrificed to Heaven, secretly prepared fire-lances, and embarked 450 Chin soldiers outside the south gate.... During the night they killed the enemy guards outside the dikes, and reached the Wang family temple... . Kuan-Nu divided his small craft into squadrons of five, seven and ten boats, which came out from behind the defenses and caught the Mongols both from front and rear, using the fire-spouting lances. The Mongols could not stand up to this and fled, losing more than 3500 men drowned. Finally their stockades were burnt, and our force returned.[8]

Before the end of the thirteenth century, the fire-lance had evolved into the much more effective handgun and cannon. These inventions came too late to save China from the Mongols, however, and were transmitted to Europe by the early fourteenth century by foreigners employed by the Mongol rulers of China.

While some Mongol armies were engaged in the conquest of northern China, others traveled farther afield and advanced as far as central Europe. Only the death of Genghis Khan in 1227 may have prevented an all-out Mongol attack on western Europe (see the box "A Letter to the Pope" on p. 284). In 1231, the Mongols attacked Persia and then defeated the Abbasids at Baghdad in 1258 (see Chapter 7). Mongol forces attacked the Song from the west in the 1260s and finally defeated the remnants of the Song navy in 1279. Once again, as had occurred after the fall of the Han dynasty, the heartland of China was placed under alien rule.

A Letter to the Pope

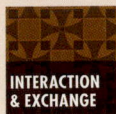

INTERACTION & EXCHANGE

IN 1245, POPE INNOCENT IV dispatched the Franciscan friar John Plano Carpini to the Mongol headquarters at Karakorum to appeal to the great khan Kuyuk (koo-YOOK) to cease his attacks on Christians. After a considerable wait, Carpini was given the following reply, which could not have pleased the pope. The letter was discovered recently in the Vatican archives.

A Letter from Kuyuk Khan to Pope Innocent IV

By the power of the Eternal Heaven, We are the all-embracing Khan of all the Great Nations. It is our command:

This is a decree, sent to the great Pope that he may know and pay heed.

After holding counsel with the monarchs under your suzerainty, you have sent us an offer of subordination, which we have accepted from the hands of your envoy.

If you should act up to your word, then you, the great Pope, should come in person with the monarchs to pay us homage and we should thereupon instruct you concerning the commands of the Yasak.

Furthermore, you have said it would be well for us to become Christians. You write to me in person about this matter, and have addressed to me a request. This, your request, we cannot understand.

Furthermore, you have written me these words: "You have attacked all the territories of the Magyars and other Christians, at which I am astonished. Tell me, what was their crime?" These, your words, we likewise cannot understand. Jenghiz Khan and Ogatai Khakan revealed the commands of Heaven. But those whom you name would not believe the commands of Heaven. Those of whom you speak showed themselves highly presumptuous and slew our envoys. Therefore, in accordance with the commands of the Eternal Heaven the inhabitants of the aforesaid countries have been slain and annihilated. If not by the command of Heaven, how can anyone slay or conquer out of his own strength?

And when you say: "I am a Christian. I pray to God. I arraign and despise others," how do you know who is pleasing to God and to whom He allots His grace? How can you know it, that you speak such words?

Thanks to the power of the Eternal Heaven, all lands have been given to us from sunrise to sunset. How could anyone act other than in accordance with the commands of Heaven? Now your own upright heart must tell you: "We will become subject to you, and will place our powers at your disposal." You in person, at the head of the monarchs, all of you, without exception, must come to tender us service and pay us homage, then only will we recognize your submission. But if you do not obey the commands of Heaven, and run counter to our orders, we shall know that you are our foe.

That is what we have to tell you. If you fail to act in accordance therewith, how can we foresee what will happen to you? Heaven alone knows.

Q *Based on the account given here, what message was the pope seeking to convey to the great khan in Karakorum? What was the nature of the latter's reply?*

Source: From Prawdin, Michael, *The Mongol Empire: Its Rise and Legacy* (Free Press, 1961), pp. 280–281.

By then, the Mongol Empire was quite different from what it had been under its founder. Prior to the conquests of Genghis Khan, the Mongols had been purely nomadic. They spent their winters in the southern plains, where they found suitable pastures for their cattle, and traveled north in the summer to wooded areas where the water was sufficient. They lived in round, felt-covered tents (called yurts), which were lightly constructed so that they could be easily transported. For food, the Mongols depended on milk and meat from their herds and game from hunting.

To administer the new empire, Genghis Khan had set up a capital city at Karakorum (khah-rah-KOR-um), in present-day Outer Mongolia, but prohibited his fellow Mongols from practicing sedentary occupations or living in cities. But under his successors, the Mongols began to adapt to their conquered areas. As one khan remarked, quoting his Chinese adviser, "Although you inherited the Chinese Empire on horseback, you cannot rule it from that position." Mongol aristocrats began to enter administrative positions, while commoners took up sedentary occupations as farmers or merchants.[9]

The territorial nature of the empire also changed. Following tribal custom, at the death of the ruling khan, the territory was distributed among his heirs. The once-united empire of Genghis Khan was thus divided into several separate **khanates** (KHAH-nayts), each under the autonomous rule of one of his sons by his principal wife. One of his sons was awarded the khanate of Chaghadai (chag-huh-DY) in Central Asia with its capital at Samarkand; another ruled Persia from the conquered

The Mongol Conquest of China

Path of Mongol advance

Yellow R.
Chang'an
Kaifeng
Suzhou
Yangtze R.
Hangzhou
SOUTHERN SONG
Canton
South China Sea

0 250 500 750 Kilometers
0 250 500 Miles

© 2016 Cengage Learning

city of Baghdad; a third took charge of the khanate of Kipchak (KIP-chahk), commonly known as the Golden Horde. But it was one of his grandsons, named Khubilai Khan (1215–1294), who completed the conquest of the Song and established a new Chinese dynasty, called the Yuan (from a phrase in the *Book of Changes* referring to the "original creative force" of the universe). Khubilai moved the capital of China northward from Hangzhou to Khanbaliq ("city of the khan"), which was located on a major trunk route from the Great Wall to the plains of northern China (see Map 10.2). Later the city would be known by the Chinese name Beijing (bay-ZHING), or Peking (pee-KING) ("northern capital").

Mongol Rule in China

At first, China's new rulers exhibited impressive vitality. Under the leadership of the talented Khubilai Khan, the Yuan continued to flex their muscles by attempting to expand their empire. Mongol armies advanced into the Red River valley and reconquered Vietnam, which had declared its independence after the fall of the Tang three hundred years earlier. Mongol fleets were launched against Malay kingdoms in Java and Sumatra and also against the islands of Japan. Only the expedition against Vietnam succeeded, however, and even that success was temporary. The Vietnamese counterattacked and eventually drove the Mongols back across the border. The attempted conquest of Japan was even more disastrous, as a massive storm destroyed the Mongol fleet, killing thousands (see Chapter 11). Yuan rulers belatedly discovered that familiar tactics such as cavalry charges and siege warfare were less effective in distant lands composed of unfamiliar terrain.

The Mongols had more success in governing China. After a failed attempt to administer their conquest as they had ruled their own tribal society (some advisers reportedly even suggested that the plowed fields be transformed into pastures), Mongol rulers adapted to the Chinese political system and made use of local talents in the bureaucracy. The tripartite division of the administration into civilian, military, and censorate was retained, as were the six ministries. The civil service system, which had been abolished in the north in 1237 and in the south forty years later, was revived in the early fourteenth

MAP 10.2 Asia Under the Mongols. This map traces the expansion of Mongol power throughout Eurasia in the thirteenth century. After the death of Genghis Khan in 1227, the empire was divided into four separate khanates.

Q *Why was the Mongol Empire divided into four separate khanates?*

century. The state cult of Confucius was also restored, although Khubilai Khan himself remained a Buddhist.

But there were some key differences. Culturally, the Mongols were nothing like the Chinese and remained a separate class with their own laws. The highest positions in the bureaucracy were usually staffed by Mongols. Although some leading Mongols followed their ruler in converting to Buddhism, most commoners retained their traditional religion. Even those who adopted Buddhism chose the Lamaist (LAH-muh-ist) variety from Tibet, which emphasized divination and magic.

Despite these differences, the Mongols were able to rule China for nearly a century. The people of the north, after all, were used to foreign rule, and although those living farther to the south may have resented their alien conquerors, they probably came to respect the stability, unity, and economic prosperity that the Mongols initially brought to China, where they continued the relatively tolerant economic policies of the southern Song. By bringing much of the Eurasian landmass under a single rule, they encouraged long-distance trade, particularly along the Silk Road, now dominated by Muslim merchants from Central Asia. To promote trade, the Grand Canal was extended from the Yellow River to the capital. Adjacent to the canal, a paved highway was constructed that extended all the way from the Song capital of Hangzhou to its Mongol counterpart at Khanbaliq.

The capital was a magnificent city. According to the Italian merchant Marco Polo, who resided there during the reign of Khubilai Khan, it was 24 miles in diameter and surrounded by thick walls of earth penetrated by a dozen massive gates (see the Film & History feature "The Adventures of Marco Polo (1938) and Marco Polo (2007)" on p. 287). He described the old Song capital of Hangzhou as a noble city where "so many pleasures may be found that one fancies himself to be in Paradise."

Ironically, while many of their subjects prospered, the Mongols themselves often did not. Burdened by low wages and heavy military obligations that left them little time for their herds, many Mongol warriors became so impoverished that they were forced to sell their sons and daughters into slavery. In the end, the Yuan fell victim to the same fate that had afflicted other powerful dynasties in China. In fact, it was one of the shortest-lived of the great dynasties, lasting less than a century. Excessive spending on foreign conquest, inadequate tax revenues, factionalism and corruption at court and in the bureaucracy, and growing internal instability, brought about in part by a famine in central China in the 1340s, all contributed to the dynasty's demise.

Khanbaliq (Beijing) Under the Mongols

Khubilai Khan's successors lacked his administrative genius, and by the middle of the next century, the Yuan dynasty in China, like the Mongol khanates elsewhere in Central Asia, had begun to decline rapidly (see Chapter 13).

The immediate instrument of Mongol defeat was Zhu Yuanzhang (JOO yoo-wen-JAHNG), the son of a poor peasant in the lower Yangzi Valley. After losing most of his family in the famine of the 1340s, Zhu became an itinerant monk and then the leader of a gang of bandits. In the 1360s, unrest spread throughout the country, and after defeating a number of rivals, Zhu put an end to the disintegrating Yuan regime and declared the foundation of the new Ming (MING) ("bright") Dynasty (1369–1644).

The Mongols' Place in History

The Mongols were the last, and arguably the greatest, of the nomadic peoples who came thundering out of the steppes of Central Asia, pillaging and conquering the territories of their adversaries. What caused this extraordinary burst of energy, and why were the Mongols so much more successful than their predecessors? Historians are divided. Some have suggested that drought and overpopulation may have depleted the available pasture on the steppes, yet another example of the unseen impact of environmental changes on human history. Others have cited the ambition and genius of Genghis Khan, who was able to arouse a sense of personal loyalty unusual in a society where commitments were ordinarily of a tribal nature. Still others point to his reliance on the organizational unit known as the *ordos* (OR-dohz), described by the historian Samuel Adshead as "a system of restructuring tribes into decimal units whose top level of leadership was organized on bureaucratic lines."[10] Although the *ordos* system had been used by the Xiongnu and other nomadic peoples before them, the Mongols applied it to create disciplined military units that were especially effective against the relatively free-wheeling tactics of their rivals on the steppes and devastating against the relatively immobile armies of the sedentary states in their path. Once organized, the Mongols used their superior horsemanship and blitzkrieg tactics effectively, while taking advantage of divisions within the enemy ranks and borrowing more advanced military technology.

Once in power, however, the Mongols' underlying weaknesses eventually proved fatal. Unlike some of their predecessors, the Mongols had difficulty making the transition from the nomadic life of the steppes to the sedentary life of the villages, and their unwieldy system of royal succession led to instability in their leadership ranks. Still, although the Mongol era was just a brief interlude in the long sweep of human history, it was rich in consequences.

THE MONGOLS: A REPUTATION UNDESERVED? The era of Mongol expansion has usually been portrayed as a tragic period in human history. The Mongols' conquests resulted in widespread death and suffering throughout the world. Nations and empires were humbled, cities destroyed, and

The Adventures of Marco Polo (1938) and Marco Polo (2007)

The famous story of Marco Polo's trip to East Asia in the late thirteenth century has sparked the imagination of Western readers ever since. The son of an Italian merchant from Venice, Polo set off for China in 1270 and did not come back for twenty-four years, traveling east via the Silk Road and returning by sea across the Indian Ocean. Captured by the Genoese in 1298 and tossed into prison, he recounted his experiences to a professional writer known as Rusticello of Pisa. Copies of the resulting book, originally titled *Description of the World*, were soon circulating throughout Europe, and one even found its way into the baggage of Christopher Columbus, who used it as a source for information on the eastern lands he sought during his own travels. Marco Polo's adventures have appeared in numerous languages, thrilling readers around the world, and filmmakers have done their part, producing feature films about his exploits for modern audiences.

Scene from *Adventures of Marco Polo* (1938). Marco Polo (Gary Cooper, gesturing on the right) confers with Kaidu (Alan Hale), leader of the Mongols.

But did Marco Polo actually visit China, or was the book an elaborate hoax? In recent years, some historians have expressed doubts about the veracity of his account. Frances Wood, author of *Did Marco Polo Go to China?* (1996), provoked a lively debate in the halls of academe with her suggestion that he may simply have related tales that he had heard from contemporaries.

Such reservations aside, filmmakers have long been fascinated by Marco Polo's story. The first Hollywood production, *The Adventures of Marco Polo* (1938), starred the prewar screen idol Gary Cooper, with Basil Rathbone as his evil nemesis in China. Like many film epics of the era, it was highly entertaining but was not historically accurate, and it used Western actors in all the main parts. The most recent version, a Hallmark Channel production called *Marco Polo*, appeared in 2007 and starred the young American actor Ian

Somerhalder in the title role. The film is a reasonably faithful rendition of the book, with stirring battle scenes, the predictable "cast of thousands," and a somewhat unlikely love interest between Polo and a Mongolian princess thrown in. Although the lead character is not particularly convincing in the title role—after two grueling decades in Asia, he still bears a striking resemblance to a teenage surfing idol—the producers should be credited for their efforts to portray China as the most advanced civilization of its day. A number of Chinese inventions then unknown in Europe, such as paper money, explosives, and the compass, make their appearance in the film. Emperor Khubilai Khan (played by the veteran actor Brian Dennehy) does not project an imperial presence, however, and is unconvincing when he says that he would prefer someone who can speak the truth to power.

irrigation systems laid waste. Then, just when the ravages of the era appeared to come to an end, bubonic plague, probably carried by lice hidden in the saddlebags of Mongol horsemen, decimated the population of Europe and the Middle East (see Chapter 13). Some regions lost as much as one-third of their population to massacre or starvation.

Few modern historians would dispute the brutality that characterized Mongol expansion. But some now point out that beyond the legacy of death and destruction, the Mongols also brought an era of widespread peace, known as the *Pax*

Mongolica (PAKS *or* PAHKS mahn-GOH-lik-uh), to much of the Eurasian supercontinent and inaugurated what one scholar has described as "the idea of the unified conceptualization of the globe," creating a "basic information circuit" that spread commodities, ideas, and inventions from one end of the Eurasian supercontinent to the other. That being said, there is no denying that the Mongol invasions resulted in widespread suffering and misfortune to millions of people in their path. If there was a Mongol peace, it was, for many, the peace of death. In any event, such conditions were not destined to last.

INTERACTION & EXCHANGE

COMPARATIVE ILLUSTRATION

The Great Walls of China. Although the Great Wall is popularly believed to be more than two thousand years old, the part of the wall that is most frequently visited by tourists today was a reconstruction undertaken during the early Ming Dynasty to protect against invasion from the north. Part of that wall, which was built to protect the imperial capital of Beijing, is shown at the top. The original walls, which stretched from the shores of the Pacific Ocean to the deserts of Central Asia, were often composed of loose stone, dirt, or piled rubble. The section shown in the inset is located north of the Turfan Depression in Xinjiang Province.

Robert Harding Picture Library/SuperStock

William J. Duiker

  What were the major reasons for building the Great Wall? To what degree was the wall successful in achieving these objectives?

The Ming Dynasty

Q **FOCUS QUESTIONS:** What were the chief initiatives taken by the early rulers of the Ming Dynasty to enhance the role of China in the world? Why did the imperial court order the famous voyages of Zheng He, and why were they discontinued?

The Ming inaugurated a new era of greatness in Chinese history. Under a series of strong rulers, China extended its rule into Mongolia and Central Asia. The Ming even briefly reconquered Vietnam, which, after a thousand years of Chinese rule, had reclaimed its independence following the collapse of the Tang Dynasty in the tenth century. Along the northern frontier, the Emperor Yongle (YOONG-luh) (r. 1402–1424) strengthened the Great Wall and pacified the nomadic tribes that had troubled China in previous centuries (see the Comparative Illustration

"The Great Walls of China" above). A tributary relationship was established with the Yi (YEE) Dynasty in Korea.

The internal achievements of the Ming were equally impressive. When they replaced the Mongols in the fourteenth century, the Ming turned to traditional Confucian institutions as a means of ruling their vast empire. These included the six ministries at the apex of the bureaucracy, the use of the civil service examinations to select members of the bureaucracy, and the division of the empire into provinces, districts, and counties. As before, Chinese villages were relatively autonomous, and local councils of elders continued to be responsible for adjudicating disputes, initiating local construction and irrigation projects, mustering a militia, and assessing and collecting taxes.

The society that was governed by this vast hierarchy of officials was a far cry from the predominantly agrarian society that had been ruled by the Han. In the burgeoning cities near the coast and along the Yangzi River valley, factories and workshops were vastly

The World in Chinese Eyes. In 1406 the Chinese admiral Zheng He left the coast of China on the first of his many voyages to the Indian Ocean. He was not sailing into the unknown. Taking advantage of geographical knowledge obtained from Islamic and Mongolian sources, Chinese cartographers of the early Ming era had already produced world maps that included information on the continent of Africa and the vast territories that comprised the Eurasian supercontinent. The earliest of such maps is the *Comprehensive Map of the Great Ming Dynasty.* Drawn up sometime in the fourteenth century, it reflected the knowledge gleaned by seafarers over many generations. In the map shown here, China appears to the right, while the continents of Africa and Europe are compressed on the edge of the map at the far left.

increasing the variety and output of their manufactured goods. The population had doubled, and new crops had been introduced, greatly expanding the food output of the empire.

The Voyages of Zheng He

In 1405, in a splendid display of Chinese maritime might, Emperor Yongle sent a fleet of Chinese trading ships under the eunuch admiral Zheng He (JEHNG-huh) through the Strait of Malacca and out into the Indian Ocean. There they traveled as far west as the east coast of Africa, stopping on the way at ports in South Asia. The size of the fleet was impressive: nearly 28,000 sailors on sixty-two ships, some of them junks larger by far than any other oceangoing vessels the world had yet seen (although the actual size of the larger ships is in dispute). China seemed about to become a direct participant in the vast trade network that extended as far west as the Atlantic Ocean, thereby culminating the process of opening China to the wider world that had begun with the Tang Dynasty.

Why the expeditions were undertaken has been a matter of some debate. Some historians assume that economic profit was the main reason. Others point to Yongle's native curiosity and note that the expedition—and the six others that followed it—returned not only with goods and a plethora of information about the outside world but also with some items

unknown in China (the emperor was especially intrigued by the giraffes brought back from East Africa and placed them in the imperial zoo, where they were identified by soothsayers with the coming of good government). Others speculate that the emperor was seeking to ascertain the truth of rumors that his immediate predecessor, Emperor Jianwen (jee-AHN-wen) (1398–1402), had escaped to Southeast Asia to live in exile.

Whatever the case, the voyages resulted in a dramatic increase in Chinese knowledge about the world and the nature of ocean travel. They also brought massive profits for their sponsors, including individuals connected with Admiral Zheng He at court. This aroused resentment among conservatives within the bureaucracy, some of whom viewed commercial activities with a characteristic measure of Confucian disdain. One commented that an end to the voyages would provide the Chinese people with a respite "so that they can devote themselves to husbandry [agriculture] and schooling."

Shortly after Yongle's death, the voyages were discontinued, never to be revived. The decision had long-term consequences and in the eyes of many modern historians marks a turning inward of the Chinese state, away from commerce and toward a more traditional emphasis on agriculture, away from the exotic lands to the south and toward the heartland of the country in the Yellow River valley.

Ironically, the move toward the Yellow River had been initiated by Yongle himself when he had decided to move the Ming capital from Nanjing (nahn-JING), in central China, where the ships were built and the voyages launched, back to Beijing, where official eyes were firmly focused on the threat from beyond the Great Wall to the north. As a means of reducing that threat, Yongle ordered the resettlement of thousands of families from the fertile Yangzi Valley. The emperor presumably had not intended to set forces in motion that would divert the country from its contacts with the external world. After all, he had been the driving force behind Zheng He's voyages. But the end result was a shift in the balance of power from central China, where it had been since the southern Song Dynasty, back to northern China, where it had originated and would remain for the rest of the Ming era. China would not look outward again for more than four centuries.

WHY WERE ZHENG HE'S VOYAGES ABANDONED? Why the Ming government discontinued Zheng He's explorations and turned its attention back to domestic concerns has long been a quandary. Was it simply a consequence of court intrigues or the replacement of one emperor by another, or were deeper issues involved? Some scholars speculate that the real purpose of the voyages was not economic gain, but "power projection," and that when local rulers throughout the South Seas had been sufficiently

The Way of the Great Buddha

RELIGION & PHILOSOPHY

ACCORDING TO BUDDHISTS, it is impossible to describe the state of Nirvana, which is sometimes depicted as an extinction of self. Yet Buddhist scholars found it difficult to avoid trying to interpret the term for their followers. The following passage by the Chinese monk Shen-Hui (shun-HWEE), one of the leading exponents of Chan Buddhism, dates from the eighth century and attempts to describe the means by which an individual may hope to seek enlightenment. There are clear similarities with philosophical Daoism.

Shen-Hui, *Elucidating the Doctrine*

"Absence of thought" is the doctrine.
"Absence of action" is the foundation.
True Emptiness is the substance.
And all wonderful things and beings are the function.
True Thusness is without thought; it cannot be known through
    conception and thought.
The True State is noncreated—can it be seen in matter and mind?
There is no thought except that of True Thusness.
There is no creation except that of the True State.
Abiding without abiding, forever abiding in Nirvana.
Acting without acting, immediately crossing to the Other Shore.
Thusness does not move, but its motion and functions are
    inexhaustible.
In every instant of thought, there is no seeking; the seeking itself
    is no thought.

Perfect wisdom is not achieved, and yet the Five Eyes all become
    pure and the Three Bodies are understood.
Great Enlightenment has no knowledge, and yet the Six
    Supernatural Powers of the Buddha are utilized and the Four
    Wisdoms of the Buddha are made great.
Thus, we know that calmness is at the same time no calmness,
    wisdom at the same time no wisdom, and action at the same time
    no action.
The nature is equivalent to the void and the substance is
    identical with the Realm of Law.
In this way, the Six Perfections are completed.
None of the ways to arrive at Nirvana is wanting.
Thus, we know that the ego and the dharmas are empty in
    reality and being and nonbeing are both obliterated.
The mind is originally without activity; the Way is always
    without thought.
No thought, no reflection, no seeking, no attainment;
No this, no that, no coming, no going.
With such reality one understands the True Insight [into previous
    and future mortal conditions and present mortal suffering].
With such a mind one penetrates the Eight Emancipations
    [through the eight stages of mental concentration].
By merits one accomplishes the Ten Powers of the Buddha.

 What similarities with philosophical Daoism are expressed in this passage? Compare and contrast the views expressed here with the Neo-Confucian worldview.

Source: Excerpt from *Sources of Chinese Tradition*, by William Theodore de Bary, pgs. 396–397. Copyright © 1960 by Columbia University Press. Reprinted with the permission of the publisher.

---

intimidated to accept a tributary relationship with their "elder brother" in China, the voyages—which had been prohibitively expensive—were no longer necessary. On balance, it seems likely that the voyages were discontinued as the result of internal politics and the inordinate cost of the program.

One recent theory that has gained wide attention and spurred scholarly debate contends that the Chinese fleets did not limit their explorations to the Indian Ocean but actually circled the earth and discovered the existence of the Western Hemisphere. Although that theory has won few scholarly adherents, the voyages, and their abrupt discontinuance, remain one of the most fascinating enigmas in the history of China.

In Search of the Way

 FOCUS QUESTION: What roles did Buddhism, Daoism, and Neo-Confucianism play in Chinese intellectual life in the period between the Sui dynasty and the Ming?

By the time of the Sui dynasty, Buddhism and Daoism had emerged as major rivals of Confucianism as the ruling ideology of the state. But during the last half of the Tang Dynasty,

Confucianism revived and once again became dominant at court, a position it would retain to the end of the dynastic period in the early twentieth century. Buddhist and Daoist beliefs, however, remained popular at the local level.

The Rise and Decline of Buddhism and Daoism

As noted earlier, Buddhism arrived in China with merchants from India and found its first adherents among the merchant community and intellectuals intrigued by the new ideas. During the chaotic centuries following the collapse of the Han dynasty, Buddhism and Daoism appealed to those who were searching for more emotional and spiritual satisfaction than Confucianism could provide. Both faiths reached beyond the common people and found support among the ruling classes as well. The capital of Chang'an even had a small Christian church after Christianity was introduced to China by Syrian merchants in the sixth century C.E.

THE SINIFICATION OF BUDDHISM As Buddhism attracted more followers, it began to take on Chinese characteristics and divided into a number of separate sects (see the box "The Way of the Great Buddha" above). Some, like the **Chan** (Zen in Japanese)

Buddhist Sculpture at Longmen. The Silk Road was an avenue for ideas as well as trade. Over the centuries, Christian, Buddhist, and Muslim teachings came to China across the sandy wastes of the Taklimakan Desert. In the seventh century, the Tang emperor Gaozong (gow-ZOONG) commissioned this massive cliffside carving as part of a large complex of cave art devoted to the Buddha at Longmen (LAHNG-mun) in central China. Bold and grandiose in its construction, this towering statue of the Buddha, surrounded by temple guardians and bodhisattvas, reflects the glory of the Tang Dynasty.

sect, called for mind training and a strict regimen as a means of seeking enlightenment, a technique that reflected Daoist ideas and appealed to many intellectuals. Others, like the **Pure Land** sect, stressed the role of devotion, an approach that was more appealing to ordinary Chinese, who lacked the time and inclination for strict monastic discipline. Still others were mystical sects, like **Tantrism** (TUHN-tri-zem), which emphasized the importance of magical symbols and ritual in seeking a preferred way to enlightenment. Some Buddhist groups, like their Daoist counterparts, had political objectives. The **White Lotus** sect, founded in 1133, often adopted the form of a rebel movement, seeking political reform or the overthrow of a dynasty and forecasting a new era when a "savior Buddha" would come to earth to herald the advent of a new age. Most believers, however, assimilated Buddhism into their daily lives, where it joined Confucian ideology and spirit worship as an element in the highly eclectic and tolerant Chinese worldview.

The burgeoning popularity of Buddhism continued into the early years of the Tang Dynasty. Early Tang rulers lent their support to the Buddhist monasteries that had been established throughout the country. Buddhist scriptures were regularly included in the civil service examinations, and Buddhist and Daoist advisers replaced shamans and Confucian scholar-officials as advisers at court. But ultimately, Buddhism and Daoism lost favor at court and were increasingly subjected to official persecution. Part of the reason was xenophobia. Envious Daoists and Confucianists made a point of criticizing the foreign origins of Buddhist doctrines, which one prominent Confucian scholar characterized as nothing but "silly relics." To deflect such criticism, Buddhists attempted to make the doctrine more Chinese, equating the Indian concept of *dharma* (law) with the Chinese concept of *Dao* (the Way). Emperor Tang Taizong ordered the Buddhist monk Xuan Zang to translate Lao Tzu's classic, *The Way of the Dao*, into Sanskrit, reportedly to show visitors from India that China had its own equivalent to the Buddhist scriptures. But another reason for this change of heart may have been financial. The great Buddhist monasteries had accumulated thousands of acres of land and serfs that were exempt from paying taxes to the state. Such wealth contributed to the corruption of the monks and other Buddhist officials and in turn aroused popular resentment and official disapproval. As the state attempted to eliminate the great landholdings of the aristocracy, the large monasteries also attracted its attention. During the later Tang, countless temples and monasteries were destroyed, and more than 100,000 monks were compelled to leave the monasteries and return to secular life.

BUDDHISM UNDER THREAT There were probably deeper cultural and ideological reasons for the growing antagonism between Buddhism and the state. By preaching the illusory nature of the material world, Buddhism was denying the very essence of Confucian teachings—the necessity for filial piety and hard work. By encouraging young Chinese to abandon their rice fields and seek refuge and wisdom in the monasteries, Buddhism was undermining the foundation stones of Chinese society—the family unit and the work ethic. In the final analysis, Buddhism was incompatible with the activist element in Chinese society, an orientation that was most effectively expressed by State Confucianism. In the competition with Confucianism for support by the state, Buddhism, like Daoism, was almost certain to lose, at least in the more this-worldly, secure, and prosperous milieu of Tang and Song China. The two doctrines continued to win converts at the local level, but official support ceased. In the meantime, Buddhism was under attack in Central Asia as well. In the eighth century, the Uighur kingdom adopted **Manichaeanism** (ma-nuh-KEE-uh-nizm), an offshoot of the ancient Zoroastrian religion with some influence from Christianity. Manichaeanism spread rapidly throughout the area and may have been a reason for the European belief that a Christian king (the legendary Prester John) ruled somewhere in Asia. By the tenth century, however, Islam was beginning to move east along the Silk Road, posing a severe threat to both Manichaean and Buddhist centers in the area. As its lifeline to the Indian subcontinent along the Silk Road was severed, Chinese Buddhism lost access to its spiritual roots and became increasingly subject to the pull of indigenous intellectual and social currents.

The Big Goose Pagoda. When the Buddhist pilgrim Xuan Zang returned to China from India in the mid-seventh century C.E., he settled in the capital of Chang'an, where, under orders from the Tang emperor, he began to translate Buddhist texts in his possession from Sanskrit into Chinese. The Big Goose Pagoda, shown here, was erected shortly afterward to house them. Originally known as the Pagoda of the Classics, the structure consists of seven stories and is more than 240 feet high.

Neo-Confucianism: The Investigation of Things

Into the vacuum left by the decline of Buddhism and Daoism stepped a revived Confucianism. As during the Han dynasty, the teachings of "master Kung" were used to buttress the power and majesty of the state. The emperor continued to be seen as an intermediary between Heaven and earth, while his legitimacy was based not on the hereditary principle but on his talent and virtue, a central component of Confucian doctrine since the era of the "hundred schools" of philosophy in ancient times.

At the same time, however, it was a new form of Confucianism that had been significantly altered by its competition with Buddhist and Daoist teachings. Challenged by Buddhist and Daoist ideas about the nature of the universe, Confucian thinkers began to flesh out the spare metaphysical structure of classical Confucian doctrine with a set of sophisticated theories about the nature of the cosmos and humans' place in it. Although the origins of this effort can be traced to the early Tang period, it

reached fruition during the intellectually prolific Song Dynasty, when it became the dominant ideology of the state.

The fundamental purpose of **Neo-Confucianism**, as the new doctrine was called, was to unite the metaphysical speculations of Buddhism and Daoism with the pragmatic Confucian approach to society. In response to Buddhism and Daoism, Neo-Confucianism maintained that the world is real, not illusory, and that fulfillment comes from participation, not withdrawal.

The primary contributor to this intellectual effort was the philosopher Zhu Xi (JOO SHEE) (see the box "A Confucian Wedding Ceremony" on p. 293). Raised during the southern Song era, Zhu Xi accepted the division of the world into a material world and a transcendent world, called by Neo-Confucianists the **Supreme Ultimate**, or *Tai Ji* (TY JEE). The Supreme Ultimate was roughly equivalent to the *Dao*, or Way, in classical Confucian philosophy. To Zhu Xi, this Supreme Ultimate was a set of abstract principles governed by the law of *yin* and *yang* and the five elements.

Human beings served as a link between the two halves of this bifurcated universe. Although human beings live in the material world, each individual has an identity that is linked with the Supreme Ultimate, and the goal of individual action is to transcend the material world in a Buddhist sense to achieve an essential identity with the Supreme Ultimate. According to Zhu Xi and his followers, the means of transcending the material world is self-cultivation, which is achieved by the "investigation of things."

THE SCHOOL OF MIND During the remainder of the Song Dynasty and into the early years of the Ming, Zhu Xi's ideas became the central core of Confucian ideology and a favorite source of questions for the civil service examinations. But during the mid-Ming era, his ideas came under attack from a Confucian scholar named Wang Yangming (WAHNG yahng-MING). Wang and his supporters disagreed with Zhu Xi's focus on learning through an investigation of the outside world and asserted that the correct way to transcend the material world was through an understanding of self. According to this so-called **School of Mind**, the mind and the universe were a single unit. Knowledge was thus intuitive rather than empirical and was obtained through internal self-searching rather than through an investigation of the outside world. The debate is reminiscent of a similar disagreement between followers of the ancient Greek philosophers Plato and Aristotle. Plato had argued that all knowledge comes from within, while Aristotle argued that knowledge resulted from an examination of the external world. Wang Yangming's ideas attracted many followers during the Ming Dynasty, and the school briefly rivaled that of Zhu Xi in popularity among Confucian scholars. Nevertheless, it never won official acceptance, probably because it was too much like Buddhism in denying the importance of a life of participation and social action.

For the average Chinese, of course, an instinctive faith in the existence of household deities or nature spirits continued to take precedence over the intellectual ruminations of Buddhist monks or Confucian scholars. But a prevailing belief in the concept of

A Confucian Wedding Ceremony

FAMILY & SOCIETY

DURING THE TWELFTH CENTURY, the philosopher Zhu Xi attempted to reinvigorate Confucian teachings in a contemporary setting that would make them more accessible to a broad audience. His goal was militantly Confucian—to combat both popular Buddhist doctrines and the superstitious practices of the common people. With his new moral code, Zhu Xi hoped to put Chinese society back on the Confucian track, with its emphasis on proper behavior. He therefore set forth the proper rituals required to carry out the special days that marked the lives of all Chinese: entry into adolescence, marriage, and funeral and ancestral rites. In the following selection, he prescribes the proper protocol for the Confucian wedding ceremony.

Zhu Xi's *Family Rituals*

4. Welcoming in Person

On the day before the wedding, the bride's family sends people to lay out the dowry furnishings in the groom's chamber. At dawn the groom's family sets places in the chamber. Meanwhile, the bride's family sets up places outside. As the sun goes down, the groom puts on full attire. After the presiding man makes a report at the offering hall, he pledges the groom and orders him to go to fetch the bride. The groom goes out and mounts his horse. When he gets to the bride's home he waits at his place. The presiding man of the bride's family makes a report at the offering hall, after which he pledges the bride and instructs her. Then he goes out to greet the groom. When the groom enters, he presents

a goose. The duenna takes the girl out to climb into the conveyance. The groom mounts his horse and leads the way for the bridal vehicle. When they arrive at his house he leads the bride in and they take their seats. After the eating and drinking are done, the groom leaves the chamber. On reentering, he takes off his clothes and the candles are removed.

5. The Bride Is Presented to Her Parents-in-Law

The next day, having risen at dawn, the bride meets her parents-in-law, who entertain her. Then the bride is presented to the elders. If she is the wife of the eldest son, she serves food to her parents-in-law. Then the parents-in-law feast the bride.

6. Presentation at the Family Shrine

On the third day the presiding man takes the bride to be presented at the offering hall.

7. The Groom Is Presented to the Wife's Parents

The day after that the groom goes to see his wife's parents. Afterward he is presented to his wife's relatives. The bride's family entertains the groom, as in ordinary etiquette.

What was Zhu Xi's apparent purpose in describing proper etiquette in this manner? How would adherence to such rigid rituals contribute to becoming a good Confucian?

Source: Excerpted from *Confucianism and Family Rituals in Imperial China: A Social History of Writing About Rites*, "A Welcoming in Person," translated and edited by P. B. Ebrey. Copyright © Princeton University Press, 1991.

karma and possible rebirth in a next life was one important legacy of the Buddhist connection, while a new manifestation of the Confucian concept of hierarchy was the village god—often believed to live in a prominent tree in the vicinity—who protected the community from wandering evil spirits.

The Apogee of Chinese Culture

FOCUS QUESTION: What were the main achievements in Chinese literature and art in the period between the Tang Dynasty and the Ming, and what technological innovations and intellectual developments contributed to these achievements?

The period between the Tang and the Ming Dynasties was in many ways the great age of achievement in Chinese literature and art. Enriched by Buddhist and Daoist images and themes, Chinese poetry and painting reached the pinnacle of their

creativity. Porcelain emerged as the highest form of Chinese ceramics, and sculpture flourished under the influence of styles imported from India and Central Asia.

Literature

The development of Chinese literature was stimulated by two technological innovations: the invention of paper during the Han dynasty (see Chapter 3) and the invention of woodblock printing during the Tang. At first, paper was used for clothing, wrapping material, toilet tissue, and even armor, but by the first century B.C.E., it was being used for writing as well.

In the seventh century C.E., the Chinese developed the technique of carving an entire page of text into a wooden block, inking it, and then pressing it onto a sheet of paper. Ordinarily, a text was printed on a long sheet of paper like a scroll. Then the paper was folded and stitched together to form a book. The earliest printed book known today is a Buddhist text published in 868 C.E.; it is more than 16 feet long. Although the

Chinese eventually developed movable type as well, block printing continued to be used until relatively modern times because of the large number of Chinese characters needed to produce a lengthy text. Even with printing, books remained too expensive for most Chinese, but they did help popularize all forms of literary writing among the educated elite. Although literature was primarily a male occupation, a few women achieved prominence as a result of their creative prowess.

During the post-Han era, historical writing and essays continued to be favorite forms of literary activity. Each dynasty produced an official dynastic history of its predecessor to elucidate sober maxims about the qualities of good and evil in human nature, and local gazetteers added to the general knowledge about the various regions. Encyclopedias brought together in a single location information and documents about all aspects of Chinese life.

THE IMPORTANCE OF POETRY

But it was in poetry, above all, that Chinese from the Tang to the Ming Dynasties most effectively expressed their literary talents. Chinese poems celebrated the beauty of nature, the changes of the seasons, and the joys of friendship and drink; others expressed sorrow at the brevity of life, old age, and parting. Given the frequency of imperial banishment and the requirement that officials serve away from their home district (an official means of preventing nepotism), it is little wonder that separation was an important theme. Love poems existed but were neither as intense as Western verse nor as sensual as Indian poetry.

The nature of the Chinese language imposed certain characteristics on Chinese poetry, the first being compactness. The most popular forms were four-line and eight-line poems, with five or seven words in each line. Because Chinese grammar does not rely on case or gender and makes no distinction between verb tenses, five-character Chinese poems were not only brief but often cryptic and ambiguous.

Two eighth-century Tang poets, Li Bo (LEE BOH), sometimes known as Li Bai or Li Taibo, and Du Fu, symbolized the genius of the era as well as the two most popular styles. Li Bo was a free spirit. His writing often centered on nature and shifted easily between moods of revelry and melancholy. One of his best-known poems is "Drinking Alone in Moonlight" (see the box "Two Tang Poets" on p. 295).

Where Li Bo was a carefree Daoist, Du Fu was a sober Confucian. His poems often dealt with historical issues or ethical themes, befitting a scholar-official living during the chaotic times of the late Tang. Many of his works reflect a concern with social injustice and the plight of the unfortunate rarely to be found in the writings of his contemporaries. Neither the poetry nor the prose of the great writers of the Tang and Song Dynasties was written for or ever reached the majority of the Chinese population. The millions of Chinese peasants and artisans living in rural villages and market towns acquired their knowledge of Chinese history, Confucian moralisms, and even Buddhist scripture from stories, plays, and songs passed down by storytellers, wandering minstrels, and itinerant monks in a rich oral tradition. One exception is the popular poem "Song of Lasting Pain" by the Tang poet Bo Ju-yi (BOH joo-YEE)

(772–846), whose poignant portrayal of the emperor's consort Yang Guifei resonates among Chinese readers down to the present day.

POPULAR CULTURE

By the Song Dynasty, China had 60 million people, 1 million in Hangzhou alone. With the growth of cities came an increased demand for popular entertainment. Although the Tang Dynasty had imposed a curfew on urban residents, the Song did not. The city gates and bridges were closed at dark, but food stalls and entertainment continued through the night. At fairgrounds throughout the year, one could find comedians, musicians, boxers, fencers, wrestlers, acrobats, puppets and marionettes, shadow plays, and especially storytellers. Many of these arts had come from India centuries before and were now the favorite forms of amusement of the Chinese people.

THE CHINESE NOVEL

During the Yuan dynasty, new forms of literary creativity, including popular theater and the novel, began to appear. The two most famous novels were *Romance of the Three Kingdoms* and *Tale of the Marshes*. The former had been told orally for centuries, appearing in written form during the Song as a scriptbook for storytellers. It was first printed in 1321 but was not published for mass consumption until 1522. Each new edition was altered in some way, making the final edition a composite effort of generations of the Chinese imagination. The plot recounts the power struggle that took place among competing groups after the fall of the Han dynasty. Packed with court intrigues, descriptions of peasant life, and gripping battles, *Romance of the Three Kingdoms* stands as a magnificent epic, China's counterpart to the Mahabharata.

Tale of the Marshes is an often violent tale of outlaw heroes who at the end of the northern Song banded together to oppose government taxes and official oppression. They rob those in power in order to share with the poor. *Tale of the Marshes* is the first prose fiction that describes the daily ordeal of ordinary Chinese people in their own language. Unlike the picaresque novel in the West, *Tale of the Marshes* does not limit itself to the exploits of one hero, offering instead 108 different story lines. This multitude of plots is a natural outgrowth of the tradition of the professional storyteller, who attempts to keep the audience's attention by recounting as many adventures as the market will bear.

Art

Although painting flourished in China under the Han and reached a level of artistic excellence under the Tang, little remains from those periods. The painting of the Song and the Yuan, however, is considered the apogee of painting in traditional China.

Like literature, Chinese painting found part of its inspiration in Buddhist and Daoist sources. Some of the best surviving examples of the Tang period are the Buddhist wall paintings in the caves at Dunhuang (doon-HWAHNG), in Central Asia.

Two Tang Poets

LI BO WAS ONE OF THE GREAT POETS of the Tang Dynasty. The first selection, "Quiet Night Thoughts," is probably the best known poem in China and has been memorized by schoolchildren for centuries. The second poem, "Drinking Alone in Moonlight," reflects the poet's carefree attitude toward life.

Du Fu, Li Bo's prime competitor as the greatest poet of the Tang Dynasty, was often the more reflective of the two. In "Spring Prospect," the poet has returned to his home in the capital after a rebellion against the dynasty has left the city in ruins.

Li Bo, "Quiet Night Thoughts"

Beside my bed the bright moonbeams bound
Almost as if there were frost on the ground.
Raising up, I gaze at the Mountain moon;
Lying back, I think of my old hometown.

Li Bo, "Drinking Alone in Moonlight"

Among the flowers, with a jug of wine,
I drink all alone—no one to share.
Raising my cup, I welcome the moon.
And my shadow joins us, making a threesome.
Alas! the moon won't take part in the drinking,
And my shadow just does whatever I do.
But I'm friends for a while with the moon and my shadow,
And we caper in revels well suited to spring.
As I sing the moon seems to sway back and forth;
As I dance my shadow goes flopping about.
As long as I'm sober we'll enjoy one another,
And when I get drunk, we'll go our own ways:
Forever committed to carefree play,
We'll all meet again in the Milky Way!

Du Fu, "Spring Prospect"

The capital is taken. The hills and streams are left,
And with spring in the city the grass and trees grown dense.
Mourning the times, the flowers trickle their tears;
Saddened with parting, the birds make my heart flutter.
The army beacons have flamed for three months;
A letter from home would be worth ten thousand in gold.
My white hairs I have anxiously scratched ever shorter;
But such disarray! Even hairpins will do no good!

 Historians often contrast these two famous poets in terms of their personalities and their approach to life. Can you see any differences in their points of view as conveyed in these short poems?

These paintings were commissioned by Buddhist merchants who stopped at Dunhuang and, while awaiting permission to enter China, wished to give thanks for surviving the rigors of the Silk Road. The entrances to the caves were filled with stones after the tenth century, when Muslim zealots began to destroy Buddhist images throughout Central Asia, and have only recently been uncovered. Like the few surviving Tang scroll paintings, these wall paintings display a love of color and refinement that are reminiscent of styles in India and Persia (see the Comparative Illustration "The Two Worlds of Tang China" on p. 272).

Daoism ultimately had a greater influence than Buddhism on Chinese painting. From early times, Chinese artists removed themselves to the mountains to write and paint and find the *Dao*, or Way, in nature. In the fifth century, one Chinese painter, too old to travel, began to paint mountain scenes from memory and announced that depicting nature could function as a substitute for contemplating nature itself. Painting, he said, could be the means of realizing the *Dao*. This explains in part the emphasis on nature in traditional Chinese painting. The word for *landscape* in Chinese means "mountain-water," and the Daoist search for balance between earth and water, hard and soft, *yang* and *yin*, is at play in the tradition of Chinese painting. To enhance the effect, poems were added to the paintings, underscoring the fusion of the visual and the verbal in Chinese art. Many artists were proficient in both media, the poem inspiring the painting and vice versa.

To represent the totality of nature, Chinese artists attempted to reveal the quintessential forms of the landscape. Rather than depicting the actual realistic shape of a specific mountain, they tried to portray the "idea" of a mountain. Empty spaces were left in the paintings because in the Daoist vision, one cannot know the whole truth. Daoist influence was also evident in the tendency to portray human beings as insignificant in the midst of nature. In contrast to the focus on the human body and personality in Western art, Chinese art presented people as tiny figures fishing in a small boat, meditating on a cliff, or wandering up a hillside trail, coexisting with but not dominating nature.

The Chinese displayed their paintings on long scrolls of silk or paper that were attached to a wooden cylindrical bar at the bottom. Varying in length from 3 to 20 feet, the paintings

Private Collection/The Bridgeman Art Library

Willows and Distant Mountains. In contrast to the focus on the human personality that is found in Western art, traditional Chinese painting often presented people as the insignificant figures coexisting within the totality of nature. Ma Yuan (1190–1235), descended from a family of painters, continued this long tradition of "mountain-water" landscapes in the painting shown here. Although they are dwarfed by the immensity of the surrounding mountains, these five tiny figures seem in harmony with nature as they go about their daily lives.

were unfolded slowly so that the eye could enjoy each segment, one after the other, beginning at the bottom with water or a village and moving upward into the hills to the mountain peaks and the sky.

By the tenth century, some Chinese painters began to eliminate color from their paintings, preferring the challenge of capturing the distilled essence of the landscape in washes of black ink on white silk. Borrowing from calligraphy, traditionally a sophisticated and revered art, they emphasized the brush stroke and created black-and-white landscapes characterized by a gravity of mood and dominated by overpowering mountains. Other artists turned toward more expressionist and experimental painting. These so-called literati artists were scholars and administrators, highly educated and adept at music, poetry, and painting. For them, the purpose of painting was not representation but expression. No longer did painters wish to evoke the feeling of wandering in nature. Rather, they tried to reveal to the viewer their own mind and feelings. Like many Western painters in the nineteenth and twentieth centuries, many of these artists were misunderstood by the public and painted only for themselves and one another.

Second only to painting in creativity was the field of ceramics, notably the manufacture of porcelain. Made of fine clay baked at unusually high temperatures in a kiln, porcelain was first produced during the period after the fall of the Han and became popular during the Tang era. During the Song, porcelain came into its own. Most renowned perhaps are the celadons (SEH-luh-dahnz), in a delicate gray-green, but Song artists also excelled in other colors and techniques. As in painting, Song delicacy and grace contrasted with the bold and often crude styles popular under the Tang. The translucency of Chinese porcelain resulted from a technique that did not reach Europe until the eighteenth century. During the Yuan and the Ming, new styles appeared. Most notable is the cobalt blue-and-white porcelain usually identified with the Ming Dynasty, which actually originated during the Yuan (see the illustration "World-Class China Ware" in Chapter 17). The Ming also produced a multicolored porcelain—often in green, yellow, and red—covered with exotic designs.

CHAPTER SUMMARY

Traditionally, Chinese historians believed that Chinese history was cyclical, driven by the dynamic interplay of the forces of good and evil, *yang* and *yin*, growth and decay. Beyond the forces of conflict and change lay the essential continuity of Chinese history, based on the timeless principles established by Confucius and other thinkers during the Zhou dynasty in antiquity.

This view of the dynamic forces of Chinese history was long accepted as valid by historians in the West and led many to assert that Chinese history was unique and could not be placed in a European or universal framework. Whereas Western history was linear, leading steadily away from the past, China's always returned to its moorings and was rooted in the values and institutions of antiquity.

In recent years, however, this traditional view of a changeless China has come under increasing challenge from historians who see patterns of change that made the China of the late fourteenth century a very different place from the country that had existed at the rise of the Tang Dynasty in 600. To these scholars, China had passed through its own version of the "middle ages" and was on the verge of beginning a linear evolution into a posttraditional society.

As we have seen, China in the early Ming era was much changed since the end of the Han dynasty more than a thousand years earlier. The industrial and commercial sector had grown considerably in size, complexity, and technological capacity. In the countryside, the concentration of political and economic power in the hands of the aristocracy had been replaced by a more stable and more equitable mixture of landed gentry, freehold farmers, and sharecroppers. The civil service provided an avenue of upward mobility that had not been available under the Han, and the state tolerated a diversity of beliefs that responded to the emotional needs and preferences of the Chinese people. In many respects, China's achievements were unsurpassed throughout the world and marked a major advance beyond antiquity.

Yet there were also some key similarities between the China of the Ming and the China of late antiquity. Ming China was still a predominantly agrarian society, with wealth based primarily on the ownership of land. Commercial activities flourished but remained under a high level of government regulation and by no means represented a major proportion of the national income. China also remained a relatively centralized empire based on an official ideology that stressed the virtue of hard work, social conformity, and hierarchy. In foreign affairs, the long frontier struggle with the nomadic peoples along the northern and western frontiers continued unabated.

Thus, the change that China experienced during its medieval era can probably be best described as one of change within continuity, an evolutionary working out of trends that had first become visible during the Han dynasty or even earlier. The result was a civilization that was the envy of its neighbors and of the known world. It also influenced other states in the region, including Japan, Korea, and Vietnam. It is to these societies along the Chinese rimlands that we now turn.

CHAPTER TIMELINE

CHAPTER REVIEW

Upon Reflection

Q Why is the Tang Dynasty often described as the greatest and most glorious era in Chinese history, and do you think that its reputation is justified?

Q What impact did the era of Mongol rule have on societies that were affected by it? Do you agree that some of the ultimate consequences were beneficial in their effects on world history? If so, why?

Q What are the arguments on both sides of the debate over whether Chinese society underwent fundamental changes during the period discussed in this chapter? Which arguments do you find more persuasive, and why?

Key Terms

Grand Council (p. 273)
scholar-gentry (p. 273)
foot binding (p. 281)
khanates (p. 284)
Chan (p. 290)
Pure Land (p. 291)
Tantrism (p. 291)
White Lotus (p. 291)
Manichaeanism (p. 291)
Neo-Confucianism (p. 292)
Supreme Ultimate (p. 292)
School of Mind (p. 292)

Suggested Reading

GENERAL   For an authoritative overview of the early imperial era in China, see **F. Mote,** *Imperial China* (Cambridge, 1999). A global perspective is presented in **S. A. M. Adshead,** *China in World History* (New York, 2000). For an informative treatment of China's relations with its neighbors, see **C. Holcombe,** *The Genesis of East Asia, 220 B.C.E.–A.D. 907* (Honolulu, 2001).

FROM THE HAN TO THE MING   For a readable treatment of the period from the Han to the Ming Dynasties by reputable scholars, see the several volumes in the series published by the Belknap Press at Harvard: **M. E. Lewis,** *China Between Empires: The Northern and Southern Dynasties* (Cambridge, Mass., 2009) and *China's Cosmopolitan Empire: The Tang Dynasty* (Cambridge, Mass., 2009); **D. Kuhn,** *The Age of Confucian Rule: The Song Transformation of China* (Cambridge, Mass., 2009); and **T. Brook,** *The Troubled Empire: China in the Yuan and Ming Dynasties* (Cambridge, Mass., 2010). Also see **C. Benn,** *China's Golden Age: Everyday Life in the Tang Dynasty* (Oxford, 2004).

MISCELLANEOUS TOPICS   The emergence of urban culture during the Mongol era is analyzed in **C. K. Heng,** *Cities of Aristocrats and Bureaucrats: The Development of Medieval Chinese Cityscapes* (Honolulu, 1999). China's technological achievements are documented in **Deng Yinke,** *Ancient Chi-*

nese Inventions (Cambridge, Mass., 2010) and **S. Winchester,** *The Man Who Loved China* (New York, 2009). On the controversial belief that Chinese fleets circled the globe in the fifteenth century, see **G. Menzies,** *1421: The Year China Discovered America* (New York, 2002). A more judicious approach can be found in **E. Dreyer,** *Zheng He: China and the Oceans in the Early Ming Dynasty, 1405–1433* (New York, 2007).

CENTRAL ASIA   On Central Asia, see **S. A. M. Adshead,** *Central Asia in World History* (New York, 1993), and **E. T. Grotenhuis, ed.,** *Along the Silk Road* (Washington, D.C., 2002). Xuan Zang's journey to India is re-created in **R. Bernstein,** *Ultimate Journey: Retracing the Path of an Ancient Buddhist Monk Who Crossed Asia in Search of Enlightenment* (New York, 2000).

LITERATURE AND ART   Standard treatments of these subjects are **V. Mair,** *The Columbia Anthology of Traditional Chinese Literature* (New York, 1994), and the classic **M. Sullivan,** *The Arts of China,* 4th ed. (Berkeley, Calif., 1999).

Chapter Notes

1. *The Travels of Marco Polo* (New York, n.d.), p. 128.
2. Quoted in A. F. Wright, *Buddhism in Chinese History* (Stanford, Calif., 1959), p. 30.
3. Quoted in A. F. Wright, *The Sui Dynasty* (New York, 1978), p. 180.
4. Chu-yu, *P'ing-chow Table Talks,* quoted in R. Temple, *The Genius of China: 3,000 Years of Science, Discovery, and Invention* (New York, 1986), p. 150.
5. Quoted in E. H. Schafer, *The Golden Peaches of Samarkand: A Study of T'ang Exotics* (Berkeley, Calif., 1963), p. 43.
6. Quoted in J. K. Fairbank, E. O. Reischauer, and A. M. Craig, *East Asia: Tradition and Transformation* (Boston, 1973), p. 164.
7. Quoted in R. Grousset, *L'Empire des Steppes* (Paris, 1939), p. 285.
8. Temple, *Genius of China,* pp. 242–243.
9. A. M. Khazanov, *Nomads and the Outside World* (Cambridge, 1983), p. 241.
10. S. A. M. Adshead, *China in World History* (New York, 2000), p. 132.

MindTap is a fully online, highly personalized learning experience built upon Cengage Learning content. MindTap combines student learning tools—readings, multimedia, activities, and assessments—into a singular Learning Path that guides students through their course.

11

The East Asian Rimlands: Early Japan, Korea, and Vietnam

The Jade Mountain Temple on Returned Sword Lake, Hanoi

© William J. Duiker

CHAPTER OUTLINE AND FOCUS QUESTIONS

Japan: Land of the Rising Sun

Q How did Japan's geographic location affect the course of early Japanese history, and how did it influence the political structures and social institutions that arose there?

Korea: Bridge to the East

Q What were the main characteristics of economic and social life in early Korea?

Vietnam: The Smaller Dragon

Q What were the main developments in Vietnamese history before 1500? Why were the Vietnamese able to restore their national independence after a millennium of Chinese rule?

CRITICAL THINKING

Q How did Chinese civilization influence the societies that arose in Japan, Korea, and Vietnam during their early history?

CONNECTIONS TO TODAY

Q The fact that Japan is an island nation has had a significant effect on how the Japanese people see their role in the world. How do you think the fact that the United States is a continental nation affects the attitude of the American people in today's world?

THERE IS A SMALL body of water in the heart of the Vietnamese national capital of Hanoi (ha-NOY) that is known affectionately to local city-dwellers as Returned Sword Lake. The lake owes its name to a legend that Le Loi (LAY LOY), founder of the later Le (LAY) dynasty in the fifteenth century, drew a magic sword from the lake that enabled him to achieve a great victory over Chinese occupation forces. Thus, to many Vietnamese the lake symbolizes their nation's historical resistance to domination by its powerful northern neighbor.

Ironically, however, a temple that was later erected on tiny Turtle Island in the middle of the lake reflects the strong influence that China continued to exert on traditional Vietnamese culture. After Le Loi's victory, according to the legend, the sword was returned to the water, and the Vietnamese ruler accepted a tributary relationship to his "elder brother," the Chinese emperor in Beijing. China's philosophy, political institutions, and social mores served as hallmarks for the Vietnamese people down to the early years of the twentieth century. That is why Vietnam was for centuries known as "the smaller dragon."

Le Loi's deferential attitude toward his larger neighbor should not surprise us. During ancient times, China was the most technologically advanced society in East Asia. To its north and west were pastoral peoples whose military exploits were often impressive but whose political and cultural attainments were still limited, at least by comparison with the great river valley civilizations of the day. In inland areas south of the Yangzi River were scattered clumps of rice farmers and hill peoples, most of whom had not yet entered the era of state building and had little knowledge of the niceties of Confucian ethics. Along the fringes of Chinese civilization were a number of other agricultural societies that were beginning to follow a pattern of development similar to that of China, although somewhat later in time. One of these was the land of Yueh (YWEH) (Vietnam), where a relatively advanced agricultural civilization had been in existence for several hundred years before the area was finally conquered by the Han dynasty in the second century C.E. Another was in the islands of Japan, where an organized society was beginning to take shape just as Chinese administrators were attempting to consolidate imperial rule over the Vietnamese people. On the Korean peninsula, an advanced Neolithic society had already begun to develop a few centuries earlier.

All of these early agricultural societies were eventually influenced to some degree by their great neighbor, China. Vietnam remained under Chinese rule for a thousand years. Korea retained its separate existence but was long a tributary state of China and in many ways followed the cultural example of its larger patron. Only Japan retained both its political independence and its cultural uniqueness. Yet even the Japanese were strongly influenced by the glittering culture of their powerful neighbor, and today many Japanese institutions and customs still bear the imprint of several centuries of borrowing from China. In this chapter, we will take a closer look at these emerging societies along the Chinese rimlands and consider how their cultural achievements reflected or contrasted with those of the Chinese Empire. ✦

MAP 11.1 **Early Japan.** This map shows key cities in Japan during the early development of the Japanese state.

 Where was the original heartland of Japanese civilization on the main island of Honshu?

Japan: Land of the Rising Sun

 FOCUS QUESTION: How did Japan's geographic location affect the course of early Japanese history, and how did it influence the political structures and social institutions that arose there?

Geography accounts for many of the historical differences between Chinese and Japanese society. Whereas China is a continental civilization, Japan is an island country. It consists of four main islands (see Map 11.1): Hokkaido (hoh-KY-doh) in the north, the main island of Honshu (hahn-SHOO) in the center, and the two smaller islands of Kyushu (KYOO-shoo) and Shikoku (shee-KOH-koo) in the southwest. Its total land area is about 146,000 square miles, about the size of the state of Montana. Japan's main islands are at approximately the same latitude as the eastern seaboard of the United States.

Like the eastern United States, Japan is blessed with a temperate climate. It is slightly warmer on the east coast, which is washed by the Pacific Current sweeping up from the south, and has a number of natural harbors that provide protection from the winds and high waves of the Pacific Ocean. As a consequence, in recent times, the majority of the Japanese people

have tended to live along the east coast, especially in the flat plains surrounding the cities of Tokyo (TOH-kee-oh), Osaka (oh-SAH-kuh), and Kyoto (KYOH-toh). In these favorable environmental conditions, Japanese farmers have been able to harvest two crops of rice annually since early times.

By no means, however, is Japan an agricultural paradise. Like China, much of the country is mountainous, with only about 20 percent of the total land area suitable for cultivation. These mountains are of volcanic origin, since the Japanese islands are located at the juncture of the Asian and Pacific tectonic plates. This location is both an advantage and a disadvantage. Volcanic soils are extremely fertile, which helps explain the exceptionally high productivity of Japanese farmers. At the same time, the area is prone to earthquakes, such as the famous quake of 1923, which destroyed almost the entire city of Tokyo. In 2011, a massive earthquake slightly offshore triggered a tsunami that devastated large areas along the eastern coast of northern Honshu island.

The fact that Japan is an island country has had a significant impact on Japanese history. As we have seen, the continental character of Chinese civilization, with its constant threat of invasion from the north, had a number of consequences for Chinese history. One effect was to make the Chinese more sensitive to the preservation of their culture from destruction at the hands of non-Chinese invaders. As one fourth-century C.E. Chinese ruler remarked when he was forced to move his capital southward under pressure from nomadic incursions, "The King takes All Under Heaven as his home."[1] Proud of their own considerable cultural achievements and their dominant position throughout the region, the Chinese have traditionally been reluctant to dilute the purity of their culture with foreign innovations. Culture more than race is a determinant of the Chinese sense of identity.

By contrast, the island character of Japan probably had the effect of strengthening the Japanese sense of ethnic and cultural

How the Earth Was Formed

RELIGION & PHILOSOPHY

WHEN JAPANESE ACCOUNTS ABOUT THE CREATION of the earth and the emergence of human society began to be recorded in the eighth century C.E., the early chroniclers had already been exposed to Chinese writings on the subject and were very likely influenced by Chinese founding myths such as those we discussed in Chapter 3. Yet there are significant differences in the Japanese approach, which places more emphasis on the role of nature deities than on sage-kings. The Japanese account also links the creation of the Japanese islands directly with the emergence of the imperial line. The following selection is from the *Kojiki* (koh-JIK-ee), an eighth-century chronicle known in English translation as *Records of Ancient Matters*.

Records of Ancient Matters

Now when chaos had begun to condense but force and form were not yet manifest and there was nought named, nought done, who could know its shape? Nevertheless Heaven and Earth first parted, and the Three Deities performed the commencement of creation; yin and yang then developed; and the Two Spirits [Izanagi and Izanami] became the ancestors of all things. Therefore with [Izanagi's] entering obscurity and emerging into light, the sun and moon were revealed by the washing of his eyes; he floated on and plunged into the seawater, and heavenly and earthly deities appeared through the ablutions of his person. So in the dimness of the great commencement, we, by relying on the original teaching, learn the time of the conception of the earth and of the birth of islands; in the remoteness of the original beginning, we, by trusting the former sages, perceive the era of the genesis of deities and of the establishment of men. Truly we do know that a mirror was hung up, that jewels were spat out, and that then a hundred kings succeeded each other; that a blade was bitten and a serpent cut in pieces, so that the myriad deities did flourish. By deliberations in the Tranquil River the empire was pacified; by discussions on the Little Shore the land was purified. Wherefore His Augustness Ho-no-ni-ni-gi [grandson of the sun goddess] first descended to the Peak of Takachi, and the Heavenly Sovereign Kamu-Yamato [Jimmu, the founding emperor of Japan] did traverse the Island of the Dragon-Fly. A weird bear put forth its claws, and a heavenly saber was obtained at Takakura. They with tails obstructed the path and a great crow guided him to Eshinu. Dancing in rows they destroyed the brigands, and listening to a song they vanquished the foeman. Being instructed in a dream, he was reverent to the heavenly and earthly deities and was therefore styled the Wise Monarch; having gazed on the smoke, he was benevolent to the black-haired people, and is therefore remembered as the Emperor-Sage. Determining the frontiers and civilizing the country, he issued laws, reform[ed] the surnames and select[ed] the [clan] names. . . . Though each differed in caution and in ardor, though all were unlike in accomplishments and in intrinsic worth, yet was there none who did not by contemplating antiquity correct manners that had fallen to ruin and, by illumining modern times, repair laws that were approaching dissolution.

 How does this account of the founding of the earth compare with the Mayan creation myth in Popul Vuh, presented in Chapter 6?

Source: From W. de Bary, et al., *Sources of Japanese Tradition (From Earliest Times to 1600)*, vol. I, 2nd ed. (New York, 2001), pp. 15–16.

---

distinctiveness. Although the Japanese view of themselves as the most ethnically homogeneous people in East Asia may not be entirely accurate (the modern Japanese probably represent a mix of peoples, much like their neighbors on the continent), their sense of racial and cultural homogeneity has enabled them to import ideas from abroad without worrying that the borrowings will destroy the uniqueness of their own culture.

A Gift from the Gods: Prehistoric Japan

According to an ancient legend recorded in historical chronicles written in the eighth century C.E., the islands of Japan were formed as a result of the marriage of the god Izanagi (ee-zah-NAH-gee) and the goddess Izanami (ee-zah-NAH-mee). After giving birth to Japan, Izanami gave birth to a sun goddess whose name was Amaterasu (ah-mah-teh-RAH-soo). A descendant of Amaterasu later descended to earth and became the founder of the Japanese nation (see the box "How the Earth Was Formed" above). This Japanese creation myth is reminiscent of similar beliefs in other ancient societies, which often saw themselves as the product of a union of deities. What is interesting about the Japanese version is that it has survived into modern times as an explanation for the uniqueness of the Japanese people and the divinity of the Japanese emperor, who is still believed by some Japanese to be a direct descendant of the sun goddess Amaterasu.

Modern scholars have a more prosaic explanation for the origins of Japanese civilization. According to archaeological evidence, the Japanese islands have been occupied by human beings for at least 100,000 years. The earliest known Neolithic inhabitants, known as the Jomon (JOH-mahn) people (named for the cord pattern of their pottery), lived in the islands as early as 8000 B.C.E. They lived by hunting, fishing, and food gathering.

Agriculture may have appeared in Japan sometime during the first millennium B.C.E., although some archaeologists

The Eastern Expedition of Emperor Jimmu

JAPANESE MYTHS MAINTAINED that the Japanese nation could be traced to the sun goddess Amaterasu, who was the ancestor of the founder of the Japanese imperial family, Emperor Jimmu. This passage from the *Nihon Shoki* (nee-HAHN SHOH-kee) (*Chronicles of Japan*) describes the campaign in which the "divine warrior" Jimmu occupied the central plains of Japan, symbolizing the founding of the Japanese nation. Legend dates this migration to about 660 B.C.E., but modern historians believe that it took place much later (perhaps as late as the fourth century C.E.) and that the account of the "divine warrior" may represent an effort by Japanese chroniclers to find a local equivalent to the sage-kings of prehistoric China.

The Chronicles of Japan

Emperor Jimmu was forty-five years of age when he addressed the assemblage of his brothers and children: "Long ago, this central land of the Reed Plains was bequeathed to our imperial ancestors by the heavenly deities, Takamimu-subi-no-Kami and Amaterasu Omikami.... However, the remote regions still do not enjoy the benefit of our imperial rule, with each town having its own master and each village its own chief. Each of them sets up his own boundaries and contends for supremacy against other masters and chiefs.

"I have heard from an old deity knowledgeable in the affairs of the land and sea that in the east there is a beautiful land encircled by blue mountains. This must be the land from which our great task of spreading our benevolent rule can begin, for it is indeed the center of the universe.... Let us go there, and make it our capital...."

In the winter of that year ... the Emperor personally led imperial princes and a naval force to embark on his eastern expedition.

When Nagasunehiko heard of the expedition, he said: "The children of the heavenly deities are coming to rob me of my country." He immediately mobilized his troops and intercepted Jimmu's troops at the hill of Kusaka and engaged in a battle.... The imperial forces were unable to advance. Concerned with the reversal, the Emperor formulated a new divine plan and said to himself: "I am the descendant of the Sun Goddess, and it is against the way of heaven to face the sun in attacking my enemy. Therefore our forces must retreat to make a show of weakness. After making sacrifice to the deities of heaven and earth, we shall march with the sun on our backs. We shall trample down our enemies with the might of the sun. In this way, without staining our swords with blood, our enemies can be conquered."... So he ordered the troops to retreat to the port of Kusaka and regroup there....

[After withdrawing to Kusaka, the imperial forces sailed southward, landed at a port in the present-day Kita peninsula, and again advanced north toward Yamato.]

The precipitous mountains provided such effective barriers that the imperial forces were not able to advance into the interior, and there was no path they could tread. Then one night Amaterasu Omikami appeared to the Emperor in a dream: "I will send you the Yatagarasu, let it guide you through the land." The following day, indeed, the Yatagarasu appeared flying down from the great expanse of the sky. The Emperor said: "The coming of this bird signifies the fulfillment of my auspicious dream. How wonderful it is! Our imperial ancestor, Amaterasu Omikami, desires to help us in the founding of our empire."

 How does the author of this document justify the actions taken by Emperor Jimmu to defeat his enemies? What evidence does he present to demonstrate that Jimmu had the support of divine forces?

Source: Excerpt from *Sources of Japanese History*, David Lu, ed. (New York: McGraw-Hill, 1974), I, p. 7.

---

believe that the Jomon people had learned to cultivate some food crops considerably earlier than that. By about 400 B.C.E., rice cultivation had been introduced, probably by immigrants from the mainland by way of the Korean peninsula. Until recently, historians believed that these immigrants drove out the existing inhabitants of the area and gave rise to the emerging Yayoi (yah-YOH-ee) culture (named for the site near Tokyo where pottery from the period was found). It is now thought, however, that Yayoi culture was a product of a mixture between the Jomon people and the new arrivals, enriched by imports such as wet rice agriculture, which had been brought by the immigrants from the mainland. In any event, it seems clear that the Yayoi peoples were the ancestors of the vast majority of present-day Japanese.

At first, the Yayoi lived primarily on the southern island of Kyushu, but eventually they moved northward onto the main island of Honshu, conquering, assimilating, or driving out the previous inhabitants of the area, some of whose descendants, known as the Ainu (Y-nyoo), still live in the northern islands. Finally, in the first centuries C.E., the Yayoi settled in the Yamato (YAH-mah-toh) plain in the vicinity of the modern cities of Osaka and Kyoto. Japanese legend recounts the story of a "divine warrior," Jimmu (JIH-moo), who led his people eastward from the island of Kyushu to establish a kingdom in the Yamato plain (see the box "The Eastern Expedition of Emperor Jimmu" above).

In central Honshu, the Yayoi set up a tribal society based on a number of clans, called **uji** (oo-JEE). Each *uji* was ruled by a hereditary chieftain, who provided protection to the local population in return for a proportion of the annual harvest. The population itself was divided between a small aristocratic class and the majority, composed of rice farmers, artisans, and other household servants of the aristocrats. Yayoi society was highly decentralized, although eventually the chieftain of the dominant clan in the Yamato region, who claimed to be descended from the sun goddess Amaterasu, achieved a kind of titular primacy. There is no evidence, however, of a central ruler equivalent in power to the Chinese rulers of the Shang and the Zhou eras.

The Rise of the Japanese State

Although the Japanese had been aware of China for centuries, they paid relatively little attention to their more advanced neighbor until the early seventh century, when the rise of the centralized and expansionistic Tang Dynasty presented a challenge. When the Tang Dynasty began to meddle in the affairs of the Korean peninsula, Yamato rulers sought to deal with the potential threat in two ways. First, they sought alliances with the Korean states (see "The Three Kingdoms" later in this chapter). Second, they attempted to centralize their authority so that they could mount a more effective resistance in the event of a Chinese invasion. The key figure in this effort was Shotoku Taishi (shoh-TOH-koo ty-EE-shee) (572–622), a leading aristocrat in one of the dominant clans in the Yamato region. Prince Shotoku sent missions to the Tang capital of Chang'an to learn about the political institutions already in use in the relatively centralized Tang kingdom (see Map 11.2).

EMULATING THE CHINESE MODEL Shotoku Taishi then launched a series of reforms to create a new system based roughly on the Chinese model. In the so-called seventeen-article

MAP 11.2 Japan's Relations with China and Korea. This map shows the Japanese islands at the time of the Yamato state. Maritime routes taken by Japanese traders and missionaries to China are indicated.

Q *Where did Japanese traders travel after reaching the mainland?*

constitution, he called for the creation of a centralized government under a supreme ruler and a merit system for selecting and ranking public officials (see the box "The Seventeen-Article Constitution" on p. 304). His objective was to limit the powers of the hereditary nobility and enhance the prestige and authority of the Yamato ruler, who claimed divine status and was now emerging as the symbol of the unique character of the Japanese nation. In reality, there is evidence that places the origins of the Yamato clan on the Korean peninsula.

After Shotoku Taishi's death in 622, his successors continued to introduce reforms to make the government more efficient. In the series of so-called **Taika reforms**—*taika* (TY-kuh) means "great change"—that began in the mid-seventh century, the Grand Council of State was established, presiding over a cabinet of eight ministries. To the traditional six ministries of Tang China were added ministers representing the central secretariat and the imperial household. Official communications were to be based on the Chinese written language. The territory of Japan was divided into administrative districts on the Chinese pattern. The rural village, composed ideally of fifty households, was the basic unit of government. The village chief was responsible for "the maintenance of the household registers, the assigning of the sowing of crops and the cultivation of mulberry trees, the prevention of offenses, and the requisitioning of taxes and forced labor." A law code was introduced, and a new tax system was established; now all farmland technically belonged to the state, so taxes were paid directly to the central government rather than through the local nobility, as had previously been the case.

As a result of their new acquaintance with China, the Japanese also developed a strong interest in Buddhism. Some of the first Japanese to travel to China during this period were Buddhist pilgrims hoping to learn more about the exciting new doctrine and bring back scriptures. By the seventh century C.E., Buddhism had become quite popular among the aristocrats, who endowed wealthy monasteries that became active in Japanese politics. At first, the new faith did not penetrate to the masses, but eventually, popular sects such as the Pure Land sect, an import from China, won many adherents among the common people.

THE NARA PERIOD Initial efforts to build a new state modeled roughly after the Tang state were successful. After Shotoku Taishi's death in 622, political influence fell into the hands of the powerful Fujiwara (foo-jee-WAH-rah) clan, which managed to marry into the ruling family and continue the reforms Shotoku had begun. In 710, a new capital, laid out on a grid similar to the great Tang city of Chang'an, was established at Nara (NAH-rah), on the eastern edge of

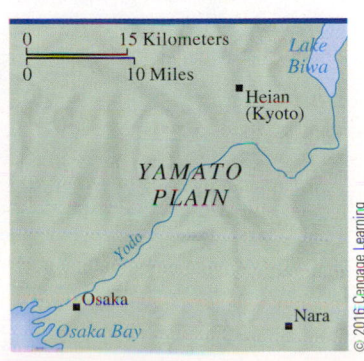

The Yamato Plain

The Seventeen-Article Constitution

THE FOLLOWING EXCERPT from the *Nihon Shoki* (*Chronicles of Japan*) is a passage from the seventeen-article constitution promulgated in 604 C.E. Although the opening section reflects Chinese influence in its emphasis on social harmony, there is also a strong focus on obedience and hierarchy. The constitution was put into practice during the reign of the famous Prince Shotoku.

The Chronicles of Japan

Summer, 4th month, 3rd day [12th year of Empress Suiko, 604 C.E.]. The Crown Prince personally drafted and promulgated a constitution consisting of seventeen articles, which are as follows:

I. Harmony is to be cherished, and opposition for opposition's sake must be avoided as a matter of principle. Men are often influenced by partisan feelings, except a few sagacious ones. Hence there are some who disobey their lords and fathers, or who dispute with their neighboring villages. If those above are harmonious and those below are cordial, their discussion will be guided by a spirit of conciliation, and reason shall naturally prevail. There will be nothing that cannot be accomplished.

II. With all our heart, revere the three treasures. The three treasures, consisting of Buddha, the Doctrine, and the Monastic Order, are the final refuge of the four generated beings, and are the supreme objects of worship in all countries. Can any man in any age ever fail to respect these teachings? Few men are utterly devoid of goodness, and men can be taught to follow the teachings. Unless they take refuge in the three treasures, there is no way of rectifying their misdeeds.

III. When an imperial command is given, obey it with reverence. The sovereign is likened to heaven, and his subjects are likened to earth. With heaven providing the cover and earth supporting it, the four seasons proceed in orderly fashion, giving sustenance to all that which is in nature. If earth attempts to overtake the functions of heaven, it destroys everything. . . . If there is no reverence shown to the imperial command, ruin will automatically result. . . .

VII. Every man must be given his clearly delineated responsibility. If a wise man is entrusted with office, the sound of praise arises. If a wicked man holds office, disturbances become frequent. . . . In all things, great or small, find the right man, and the country will be well governed. . . . In this manner, the state will be lasting and its sacerdotal functions will be free from danger.

 What are the key components of this constitution, the first in the history of Japan? To what degree do its provisions conform to Chinese Confucian principles?

Source: Excerpt from *Sources of Japanese History*, David Lu, ed. (New York: McGraw-Hill, 1974), I, p. 7.

A Worship Hall in Nara. Buddhist temple compounds in Japan traditionally offered visitors an escape from the tensions of the outside world. The temple site normally included an entrance gate, a central courtyard, a worship hall, a pagoda, and a cloister, as well as support buildings for the monks. The pagoda, a multitiered tower, harbored a sacred relic of the Buddha and served as the East Asian version of the Indian stupa. The worship hall corresponded to the Vedic carved chapel. Here we see the Todaiji (toh-DY-jee) worship hall in Nara. Originally constructed in the mid-eighth century C.E., it is reputed to be the largest wooden structure in the world and is the centerpiece of a vast temple complex on the outskirts of the old capital city.

© William J. Duiker

the Yamato plain. The Yamato ruler began to use the title "son of Heaven" in the Chinese fashion. In deference to the belief in the ruling family's divine character, the mandate remained in perpetuity in the imperial house rather than being bestowed on an individual who was selected by heaven because of his talent and virtue, as was the case in China.

Had these reforms succeeded, Japan might have followed the Chinese pattern and developed a centralized bureaucratic government. But as time passed, the central government proved unable to curb the power of the aristocracy. Unlike the situation in Tang China, the civil service examinations in Japan were not open to commoners but were restricted to individuals of noble birth. Leading officials were awarded large tracts of land, and they and other powerful families were able to keep the taxes from the lands for themselves. Increasingly starved for revenue, the central government steadily lost power and influence.

Japan's Warrior Class

POLITICS & GOVERNMENT

THE SAMURAI WAS THE JAPANESE EQUIVALENT of the medieval European knight. Like the knights, the samurai fought on horseback and were expected to adhere to a strict moral code. Although this selection comes from a document dating only to the 1500s, a distinct mounted warrior class had already begun to emerge in Japan as early as the tenth century. This passage shows the importance of hierarchy and duty in a society influenced by the doctrine of Confucius.

The Way of the Samurai

The master once said: . . . Generation after generation men have taken their livelihood from tilling the soil, or devised and manufactured tools, or produced profit from mutual trade, so that people's needs were satisfied. Thus, the occupations of farmer, artisan, and merchant necessarily grew up as complementary to one another. However, the samurai eats food without growing it, uses utensils without manufacturing them, and profits without buying or selling. . . . The samurai is one who does not cultivate, does not manufacture, and does not engage in trade, but it cannot be that he has no function at all as a samurai. . . .

If one deeply fixes [one's] attention on what I have said and examines closely one's own function, it will become clear what the business of the samurai is. The business of the samurai consists in reflecting on his own station in life, in discharging loyal service to his master if he has one, in deepening his fidelity in associations with friends, and, with due consideration of his own position, in devoting himself to duty above all. . . .

The samurai dispenses with the business of the farmer, artisan, and merchant and confines himself to practicing this Way; should there be someone in the three classes of the common people who transgresses against these moral principles, the samurai summarily punishes him and thus upholds proper moral principles in the land. . . . Outwardly he stands in physical readiness for any call to service, and inwardly he strives to fulfill the Way of the lord and subject, friend and friend, father and son, older and younger brother, and husband and wife. Within his heart he keeps to the ways of peace, but without he keeps his weapons ready for use. The three classes of the common people make him their teacher and respect him. By following his teachings, they are enabled to understand what is fundamental and what is secondary.

Herein lies the Way of the samurai, the means by which he earns his clothing, food, and shelter; and by which his heart is put at ease, and he is enabled to pay back at length his obligation to his lord and the kindness of his parents. Were there no such duty, it would be as though one were to steal the kindness of one's parents, greedily devour the income of one's master, and make one's whole life a career of robbery and brigandage. This would be very grievous.

In what ways were the duties of a samurai similar to those of an Indian warrior, as expressed by Krishna in Chapter 2? How do they compare with the responsibilities of a Confucian "gentleman" in China? What might account for the similarities and differences?

Source: From *Sources of Japanese Tradition*, Vol. 2, 2e, pgs. 192–194, by William Theodore de Bary, Carol Gluck, and Arthur E. Tiedemann. Copyright © 2005 by Columbia University Press. Reprinted with permission of the publisher.

THE HEIAN PERIOD The influence of powerful Buddhist monasteries in the city of Nara soon became oppressive, and in 794, the emperor moved the capital to his family's original power base at nearby Heian (hay-AHN), on the site of present-day Kyoto. Like its predecessor, the new capital was laid out in the now familiar Chang'an checkerboard pattern, but on a larger scale than at Nara. Now increasingly self-confident, the rulers ceased to emulate the Tang and sent no more missions to Chang'an. At Heian, the emperor—as the royal line descended from the sun goddess was now styled—continued to rule in name, but actual power was in the hands of the Fujiwara clan, which had managed through intermarriage to link its fortunes closely with the imperial family. A senior member of the clan began to serve as regent (in practice, the chief executive of the government) for the emperor.

What was occurring was a return to the decentralization that had existed prior to Shotoku Taishi. The central government's attempts to impose taxes directly on the rice lands failed, and rural areas came under the control of powerful families whose wealth was based on the ownership of tax-exempt farmland called *shoen* (SHOH-en). To avoid paying taxes, peasants would often surrender their lands to a local aristocrat, who would then allow the peasants to cultivate the lands in return for the payment of rent. To obtain protection from government officials, these local aristocrats might in turn grant title of their lands to a more powerful aristocrat with influence at court. In return, these individuals would receive inheritable rights to a portion of the income from the estate.

With the decline of central power at Heian, local aristocrats tended to take justice into their own hands and increasingly used military force to protect their interests. A new class of military retainers called the **samurai** (SAM-uh-ry) emerged whose purpose was to protect the security and property of their patron (see the box "Japan's Warrior Class" above). They frequently drew their leaders from disappointed aristocratic office seekers, who thus began to occupy a prestigious position in local society, where they often served an administrative as well as a military function. The samurai lived a life of simplicity and self-sacrifice and were expected to maintain an intense and unquestioning loyalty to their lord. Bonds of loyalty were also quite strong among members of the samurai class, and homosexuality was common. Like the knights of medieval Europe, the samurai fought on horseback (although a samurai carried a sword and a bow and arrows rather than lance and shield) and were supposed to live by a strict warrior code, known in Japan as **Bushido** (BOO-shee-doh), or "way of the warrior." As time went on, they became a major force and almost a surrogate government in much of the Japanese countryside.

THE KAMAKURA SHOGUNATE AND AFTER By the end of the twelfth century, as rivalries among noble families led to almost constant civil war, centralizing forces again asserted themselves. This time the instrument was a powerful noble from a warrior clan named Minamoto Yoritomo (mee-nah-MOH-toh yoh-ree-TOH-moh) (1142–1199), who defeated several rivals and set up his power base on the Kamakura (kah-mah-KOO-rah) peninsula, south of the modern city of Tokyo. To strengthen the state, he created a more centralized government—the *bakufu* (buh-KOO-foo *or* bah-KOO-fuh) or "tent government"—under a powerful military leader known as the **shogun** (SHOH-gun) (general). The shogun attempted to increase the powers of the central government while reducing rival aristocratic clans to vassal status. This **shogunate system**, in which the emperor was the titular authority while the shogun exercised actual power, served as the political system in Japan until the second half of the nineteenth century.

The shogunate (SHOH-gun-ut *or* SHOH-gun-ayt) system worked effectively, and it was fortunate that it did, because during the next century, Japan faced the most serious challenge it had confronted yet. The Mongols, who had destroyed the Song Dynasty in China, were now attempting to assert their hegemony throughout all of Asia (see Chapter 10). In 1266, Emperor Khubilai Khan demanded tribute from Japan. When the Japanese refused, he invaded with an army of more than 30,000 troops. Bad weather and difficult conditions forced a retreat, but the Mongols tried again in 1281. An army nearly 150,000 strong landed on the northern coast of Kyushu. The Japanese were able to contain them for two months until virtually the entire Mongol fleet was destroyed by a massive typhoon—a "divine wind," or *kamikaze* (kah-mi-KAH-zee). Japan would not face a foreign invader again until American forces landed on the Japanese islands in the summer of 1945.

Resistance to the Mongols had put a heavy strain on the system, however, and in 1333, the Kamakura Shogunate was overthrown by a coalition of powerful clans. A new shogun, supplied by the Ashikaga (ah-shee-KAH-guh) family, arose in Kyoto and attempted to continue the shogunate system. But the Ashikaga were unable to restore the centralized power of their predecessors. With the central government reduced to a shell, the power of the local landed aristocracy increased to an unprecedented degree. Heads of great noble families, now called **daimyo** (DYM-yoh) ("great names"), controlled vast landed estates that owed no taxes to the government or to the court in Kyoto. As clan rivalries continued, the daimyo relied increasingly on the samurai for protection, and political power came into the hands of a loose coalition of noble families.

By the end of the fifteenth century, Japan was again close to anarchy. A disastrous civil conflict known as the Onin

The Burning of the Palace. The Kamakura era is represented in this action-packed thirteenth-century scene from the *Scroll of the Heiji Period*, which depicts the burning of a retired emperor's palace in the middle of the night. Servants and ladies of the court flee the massive flames; confusion and violence reign. The determined faces of the samurai warriors only add to the ferocity of the attack.

COMPARATIVE ESSAY

Feudal Orders Around the World

POLITICS & GOVERNMENT

When we use the word *feudalism,* we usually think of European knights on horseback clad in armor and wielding a sword and lance. Between 800 and 1500, however, a form of social organization that modern historians have called feudalism developed in different parts of the world. Historians use the term to refer to a decentralized political order in which local lords owed loyalty and provided military service to a king or more powerful lord. In Europe, a feudal order based on lords and vassals arose between 800 and 900 and flourished for the next four hundred years.

In Japan, a feudal order much like that found in Europe developed between 800 and 1500. By the end of the ninth century, powerful nobles in the countryside, while owing a loose loyalty to the Japanese emperor, began to exercise political and legal power in their own extensive lands. To protect their property and security, these nobles retained samurai, warriors who owed loyalty to the nobles and provided military service for them. Like knights in Europe, the samurai followed a warrior code and fought on horseback, clad in armor, but they carried a sword and bow and arrow rather than a sword and lance.

In some respects, the political relationships among the Indian states beginning in the fifth century took on the character of the feudal relationships that emerged in Europe in the Middle Ages. Like medieval European lords, local Indian rajas were technically vassals of the king, but unlike the European situation, the relationship was not a contractual one. Still, the Indian model became highly complex, with vassals characterized as "inner" or "outer," depending on their physical or political proximity to the king, and vassals described as "greater" or "lesser," depending on their power and influence. As in Europe, the vassals themselves often had vassals.

In the Valley of Mexico between 1300 and 1500, the Aztecs developed a political system that bore some similarities to the Japanese, Indian, and European feudal orders. Although the Aztec king was a powerful, authoritarian ruler, the local rulers of lands outside the capital city were allowed considerable freedom. They did pay tribute to the king,

Samurai. During the Kamakura period, painters began to depict the adventures of the new warrior class. Here is an imposing mounted samurai warrior, the Japanese equivalent of the medieval knight in fief-holding Europe. Like his European counterpart, the samurai was supposed to live by a strict moral code and was expected to maintain an unquestioning loyalty to his liege lord. Above all, a samurai's life was one of simplicity and self-sacrifice.

however, and also provided him with military forces. Weapons differed from those used in Europe and Japan: Aztec warriors were armed with sharp knives made of stone and spears of wood fitted with razor-sharp blades cut from stone.

Q *What were the key characteristics of the political order we know as feudalism? To what degree can Japanese conditions be considered "feudal"?*

War (1467–1477) led to the virtual destruction of the capital city of Kyoto and the disintegration of the shogunate. With the disappearance of central authority, powerful aristocrats in rural areas now seized total control over large territories and ruled as independent lords. Territorial rivalries and claims of precedence led to almost constant warfare in this period of "warring states," as it is called (in obvious parallel with a similar era during the Zhou dynasty in China). The trend back toward central authority did not begin until the last quarter of the sixteenth century.

WAS JAPAN A FEUDAL SOCIETY? That question has aroused vigorous debate among historians in recent years. Few would dispute that political, social, and economic conditions in Japan were similar in a number of respects to those in medieval Europe, where the term was first applied (see the Comparative Essay "Feudal Orders Around the World" above as well as Chapter 12). But some European historians worry that the term *feudalism* has been overused; they argue that it should be narrowly defined, based on conditions that existed in Europe during a specific time period.

For the student of world history, the term obviously has some comparative value, in that the broad political and economic conditions that are normally considered to be characteristic of a feudal society can be found in a number of areas around the world. Still, it is important to remember that, under the surface, there were often profound differences between one "feudal" society and another. With that in mind, the term can be a highly useful teaching tool for world historians.

Economic and Social Structures

From the time the Yayoi culture was first established on the Japanese islands, Japan was a predominantly agrarian society. Although Japan lacked the spacious valleys and deltas of the river valley societies, its inhabitants were able to take advantage of their limited amount of tillable land and plentiful rainfall to create a society based on the cultivation of wet rice.

TRADE AND MANUFACTURING As in China, commerce was slow to develop as an independent force in Japan. During ancient times, each *uji* had a local artisan class, composed of weavers, carpenters, and ironworkers, but trade was essentially local and was regulated by the local clan leaders. With the rise of the Yamato state, a money economy gradually began to develop, but most internal trade was still conducted through barter until the twelfth century, when metal coins introduced from China became more popular.

Trade and manufacturing began to develop more rapidly during the Kamakura period, with the appearance of quarterly markets in the larger towns and the emergence of such industries as paper, iron casting, and porcelain. Foreign trade, mainly with Korea and China, began during the eleventh century. Japan exported raw materials, paintings, swords, and other manufactured items in return for silk, porcelain, books, and copper cash. Some Japanese traders were so aggressive in pressing their interests that authorities in China and Korea attempted to limit the number of Japanese commercial missions that could visit each year. Such restrictions were often ignored, however, and encouraged some Japanese traders to turn to piracy.

Significantly, manufacturing and commerce developed rapidly during the more decentralized period of the Ashikaga Shogunate and the era of the warring states, perhaps because of the rapid growth in the wealth and autonomy of local daimyo families. Market towns, now operating on a full money economy, began to appear, and local manufacturers formed guilds to protect their mutual interests. Sometimes local peasants would bring homemade goods, such as silk or hemp clothing, household items, or food, to sell at the markets. In general, however, trade and manufacturing remained under the control of the local daimyo, who would often provide tax breaks to local guilds in return for other benefits. Although Japan remained a primarily agricultural society, it was on the verge of a major advance in manufacturing.

DAILY LIFE One of the first descriptions of the life of the Japanese people comes from a Chinese dynastic history from the third century C.E. It describes lords and peasants living in an agricultural society that was based on the cultivation of wet rice. Laws had been enacted to punish offenders, local trade was conducted in markets, and government granaries stored the grain that was paid as taxes.

Life for the common people probably changed very little over the next several hundred years. Most were peasants, who worked on land owned by their lord or, in some cases, by the state or by Buddhist monasteries. By no means, however, were all peasants equal either economically or socially. Although in ancient times, all land was owned by the state and peasants working the land were taxed at an equal rate depending on the nature of the crop, after the Yamato era, variations began to develop. At the top were local officials, who were often well-to-do peasants. They were responsible for organizing collective labor services and collecting tax grain from the peasants and were in turn exempt from such obligations themselves.

The majority of the peasants were under the authority of these local officials. In general, peasants were free to dispose of their harvest as they saw fit after paying their tax quota, but in practical terms, their freedom was limited. Those

Urban Life in Medieval Japan. Medieval Japan was largely an agricultural society, but had begun to develop trade and manufacturing in growing urban areas. Intraregional trade was transported by horse-drawn carts or by boats on rivers or along the coast. Portrayed here is a detail from a thirteenth-century scroll depicting the bustle and general confusion of the city of Edo (now Tokyo).

CHRONOLOGY	Formation of the Japanese State
Shotoku Taishi	572–622
Era of Taika reforms	Mid-seventh century
Nara period	710–784
Heian (Kyoto) period	794–1185
Murasaki Shikibu	978–c. 1016
Minamoto Yoritomo	1142–1199
Kamakura Shogunate	1185–1333
Mongol invasions	Late thirteenth century
Ashikaga period	1333–1600
Onin War	1467–1477

who were unable to pay the tax sank to the level of *genin* (GAY-nin), or landless laborers, who could be bought and sold by their proprietors like slaves along with the land on which they worked. Some fled to escape such a fate and attempted to survive by clearing plots of land in the mountains or by becoming bandits.

In addition to the *genin*, the bottom of the social scale was occupied by the *eta* (AY-tuh), a class of hereditary slaves who, like the outcasts in India, were responsible for what were considered degrading occupations, such as curing leather and burying the dead. The origins of the *eta* are not entirely clear, but they probably were descendants of prisoners of war, criminals, or mountain dwellers who were not related to the dominant Yamato peoples. As we shall see, the *eta* are still a distinctive part of Japanese society, and although their full legal rights are guaranteed under the current constitution, discrimination against them is not uncommon.

Daily life for ordinary people in early Japan resembled that of their counterparts throughout much of Asia. The vast majority lived in small villages, several of which normally made up a single *shoen*. Housing was simple. Most lived in small two-room houses of timber, mud, or thatch, with dirt floors covered by straw or woven mats—the origin, perhaps, of the well-known *tatami* (tuh-TAH-mee), or woven-mat floor, of more modern times. Their diet consisted of rice (if some was left after the payment of the grain tax), wild grasses, millet, roots, and some fish and birds. Life must have been difficult at best; as one eighth-century poet lamented:

> Here I lie on straw
> Spread on bare earth,
> With my parents at my pillow,
> My wife and children at my feet,
> All huddled in grief and tears.
> No fire sends up smoke
> At the cooking place,
> And in the cauldron
> A spider spins its web.[2]

THE ROLE OF WOMEN Evidence about the relations between men and women in early Japan presents a mixed picture (see the Film & History feature "*Rashomon* (1950)" on p. 310). The Chinese dynastic history reports that "in their meetings and daily living, there is no distinction between... men and women." It notes that a woman "adept in the ways of shamanism" had briefly ruled Japan in the third century C.E. But it also remarks that polygyny was common, with nobles normally having four or five wives and commoners two or three.[3] An eighth-century law code guaranteed the inheritance rights of women, and wives abandoned by their husbands were permitted to obtain a divorce and remarry. A husband could divorce his wife if she did not produce a male child, committed adultery, disobeyed her in-laws, talked too much, engaged in theft, was jealous, or had a serious illness.[4]

When Buddhism was introduced, women were initially relegated to a subordinate position in the new faith. Although they were permitted to take up monastic life—many widows entered a monastery at the death of their husbands—they were not permitted to visit Buddhist holy places, nor were they even (in the accepted wisdom) equal with men in the afterlife. One Buddhist commentary from the late thirteenth century said that a woman could not attain enlightenment because "her sin is grievous, and so she is not allowed to enter the lofty palace of the great Brahma, nor to look upon the clouds which hover over his ministers and people."[5] Other Buddhist scholars were more egalitarian: "Learning the Law of Buddha and achieving release from illusion have nothing to do with whether one happens to be a man or a woman."[6] Such views ultimately prevailed, and women were eventually allowed to participate fully in Buddhist activities in medieval Japan.

Although women did not possess the full legal and social rights of their male counterparts, they played an active role at various levels of Japanese society. Aristocratic women were prominent at court, and some, such as the author known as Lady Murasaki (978–c. 1016), won renown for their artistic or literary talents (see the box "Seduction of the Akashi Lady" on p. 311). Though few commoners could aspire to such prominence, women often appear in the scroll paintings of the period along with men, doing the spring planting, threshing and hulling the rice, and acting as carriers, peddlers, salespersons, and entertainers.

In Search of the Pure Land: Religion in Early Japan

In Japan, as elsewhere, religious belief began with the worship of nature spirits. Early Japanese worshiped spirits called **kami** (KAH-mi) who resided in trees, rivers and streams, and mountains. They also believed in ancestral spirits present in the atmosphere. In Japan, these beliefs eventually evolved into a kind of state religion called **Shinto** (SHIN-toh) (the Sacred Way or Way of the Gods) that is still practiced today. Shinto still serves as an ideological and emotional force that knits the Japanese into a single people and nation.

Shinto does not have a complex metaphysical superstructure or an elaborate moral code. It does require certain ritual acts, usually undertaken at a shrine, and a process of purification, which may have originated in primitive concerns about death, childbirth, illness, and menstruation. This traditional concern about physical purity may help explain the strong

Rashomon (1950)

The Japanese director Akira Kurosawa (ah-KEE-rah KOO-rah-SAW-wah) is one of the most respected filmmakers of the second half of the twentieth century. In a series of films produced after World War II, he sought to evoke the mood of a long-lost era—medieval Japan. The first of his films to attract world attention was *Rashomon* (rah-SHOH-muhn), produced in 1950, in which Kurosawa adopted an unusual technique to explore the ambiguity of truth. The film became so famous that the expression "Rashomon effect" has come to stand for the difficulty of establishing the veracity of an incident.

In the movie, a woman is accosted and raped in a forest glen by the local brigand Tajomaru, and her husband is killed in the encounter. The true facts remain obscure, however, as the testimony of each of the key figures in the story—including the ghost of the deceased—seems to present a different version of the facts. Was the husband murdered by the brigand, or did he commit suicide in shame for failing to protect his wife's virtue? Did she herself kill her husband in anger after he rejected her as soiled goods, or is it even possible that she actually hoped to run away with the bandit?

Although the plot in *Rashomon* is clearly fictional, the film sheds light on several key features of life in medieval Japan. The hierarchical nature of the class system provides a fascinating backdrop, as the traveling couple are members of the aristocratic elite while the bandit—played by the director's favorite actor, Toshiro Mifune (toh-SHEE-roh mi-FOO-neh)—is a rough-hewn commoner. The class distinctions between the two men are evident during their physical confrontation, which involves a lengthy bout of spirited swordplay. A second theme centers on the question of honor. While the husband's outrage at the violation of his wife is quite understandable, his anger is directed primarily at her because her reputation has been irreparably tarnished. She in turn harbors a deep sense of shame that she has been physically possessed by two men, one in the presence of the other.

Over the years, Kurosawa followed his success in *Rashomon* with more films that used themes from

In this scene from Kurosawa's *Rashomon*, the samurai's wife, Masako (Machiko Kyo) pleads with the brigand Tajomaru (Toshiro Mifune).

The Kobal Collection at Art Resource, NY

premodern Japanese history. In *The Seven Samurai* (1954), villagers hire a band of warriors to protect the village from nearby bandits. The warrior-for-hire theme reappears in the satirical film *Yojimbo* (1961), while in *Ran* (1985), the director borrowed a theme from Shakespeare's play *King Lear* by depicting a power struggle among the sons of an aging warlord. Hollywood has in turn paid homage to Kurosawa by producing a number of films that borrow from his work, including *Ocean's Eleven*, *The Magnificent Seven*, and *Hostage*.

Japanese concern for personal cleanliness and the practice of denying women entrance to the holy places.

Another feature of Shinto is its stress on the beauty of nature and the importance of nature itself in Japanese life. Shinto shrines are usually located in places of exceptional beauty and are often dedicated to a nearby physical feature. As time passed, such primitive beliefs contributed to the characteristic Japanese love of nature. In this sense, early Shinto beliefs have been incorporated into the lives of all Japanese.

In time, Shinto evolved into a state doctrine that was linked with belief in the divinity of the emperor and the sacredness of the Japanese nation. A national shrine was established at Ise (EE-say), north of the early capital of Nara, where the emperor annually paid tribute to the sun goddess. But although Shinto had evolved well beyond its primitive origins, like its counterparts elsewhere, it could not satisfy all the religious and emotional needs of the Japanese people. For those needs, the Japanese turned to Buddhism.

As we have seen, Buddhism was introduced into Japan from China during the sixth century C.E. and had begun to spread beyond the court to the general population by the eighth century. As in China, most Japanese saw no contradiction between

Seduction of the Akashi Lady

FAMILY & SOCIETY

OUT OF THE JAPANESE TRADITION of female introspective prose appeared one of the world's truly great novels, *The Tale of Genji*, written around the year 1000 by the diarist and court author Murasaki Shikibu (MOO-rah-SAH-kee SHEE-kee-boo), known as Lady Murasaki. The novel has influenced Japanese writing for more than a thousand years and even today is revered for its artistic refinement and sensitivity. A panoramic portrayal of court life in tenth-century Japan, it traces the life and loves of the courtier Genji as he strives to retain the favor of those in power while simultaneously pursuing his cult of love and beauty. The remarkable character of Genji is revealed to the reader through myriad psychological observations. In this excerpt, Genji has just seduced a lady at court and now feels misgivings at having betrayed his child bride. A *koto* is a Japanese stringed instrument similar to a zither.

Lady Murasaki, *The Tale of Genji*

A curtain string brushed against a koto, to tell him that she had been passing a quiet evening at her music.

"And will you not play for me on the koto of which I have heard so much?" . . .

This lady had not been prepared for an incursion and could not cope with it. She fled to an inner room. How she could have contrived to bar it he could not tell, but it was very firmly barred indeed. Though he did not exactly force his way through, it is not to be imagined that he left matters as they were. Delicate, slender—she was almost too beautiful. Pleasure was mingled with pity at the thought that he was imposing himself upon her. She was even more pleasing than reports from afar had had her. The autumn night, usually so long, was over in a trice. Not wishing to be seen, he hurried out, leaving affectionate assurances behind.

Genji called in secret from time to time. The two houses being some distance apart, he feared being seen by fishers, who were known to relish a good rumor, and sometimes several days would elapse between his visits. . . .

Genji dreaded having Murasaki [his bride] learn of the affair. He still loved her more than anyone, and he did not want her to make even joking reference to it. She was a quiet, docile lady, but she had more than once been unhappy with him. Why, for the sake of brief pleasure, had he caused her pain? He wished it were all his to do over again. The sight of the Akashi lady only brought new longing for the other lady.

He got off a more earnest and affectionate letter than usual, at the end of which he said: "I am in anguish at the thought that, because of foolish occurrences for which I have been responsible but have had little heart, I might appear in a guise distasteful to you. There has been a strange, fleeting encounter. That I should volunteer this story will make you see, I hope, how little I wish to have secrets from you. Let the gods be my judges.

"It was but the fisherman's brush with the salty sea pine.
Followed by a tide of tears of longing."

Her reply was gentle and unreproachful, and at the end of it she said: "That you should have deigned to tell me a dreamlike story which you could not keep to yourself calls to mind numbers of earlier instances.

"Naive of me, perhaps; yet we did make our vows.
And now see the waves that wash the Mountain of Waiting!"

It was the one note of reproach in a quiet, undemanding letter. He found it hard to put down, and for some nights he stayed away from the house in the hills.

 Q *Why does this thousand-year-old passage still resonate with readers today?*

Source: From *The Tale of the Genji* by Lady Murasaki, translated by Edward G. Seidensticker, copyright © 1976 by Edward G. Seidensticker (New York: Alfred A. Knopf).

William J. Duiker

The Ikuta Shinto Shrine in Kobe. Shinto (the Sacred Way) is an indigenous form of spirit worship that originated within the Yayoi culture in ancient Japan. Early Japanese believed in the existence of spirits in nature (*kami*), who served as tutelary guardians for the surrounding population. At first the shrines to such spirits were simple in form and located primarily in forests or mountains, but over time they gradually took on more complex architectural forms. Such is the case with the Ikuta shrine in downtown Kobe. First established early in the first millennium C.E. to provide a site to pay homage to an emanation of the sun goddess Amaterasu, the shrine now contains an impressive worship hall, shown here, set within a beautiful garden with pine trees and flowered bushes. Annual festivals are held here twice a year.

worshiping both the Buddha and their local nature gods (*kami*), many of whom were considered later manifestations of the Buddha. Most of the Buddhist sects that had achieved popularity in China were established in Japan, and many of them attracted powerful patrons at court. Great monasteries were built that competed in wealth and influence with the noble families that had traditionally ruled the country.

Perhaps the two most influential Buddhist sects were the Pure Land (in Japanese, Jodo) sect and **Zen** (in Chinese, Chan or Ch'an). The Pure Land sect, which taught that devotion alone could lead to enlightenment and release, was very popular among the common people, for whom monastic life

was one of the few routes to upward mobility. Among the aristocracy, the most influential school was Zen, which exerted a significant impact on Japanese life and culture during the era of the warring states. With its emphasis on austerity, self-discipline, and communion with nature, Zen complemented many traditional beliefs in Japanese society and became an important component of the samurai warrior's code.

In Zen teachings, there were various ways to achieve enlightenment—*satori* (suh-TAWR-ee) in Japanese. Some stressed that it could be achieved suddenly. One monk, for example, reportedly achieved *satori* by listening to the sound of a bamboo stick striking against roof tiles; another did so by carefully watching the opening of peach blossoms in the spring. But other practitioners, sometimes called adepts, said that enlightenment could come only through studying the scriptures and arduous self-discipline, known as *zazen* (ZAH-ZEN), or "seated Zen." Seated Zen involved a lengthy process of meditation that cleansed the mind of all thoughts so that it could concentrate on the essential.

Sources of Traditional Japanese Culture

Nowhere is the Japanese genius for blending indigenous and imported elements into an effective whole better demonstrated than in the national culture. In such widely diverse fields as art, architecture, sculpture, and literature, the Japanese from early times showed an impressive ability to borrow selectively from abroad without destroying essential native elements.

Growing contact with China during the rise of the Yamato state stimulated Japanese artists. Missions sent to China and Korea during the seventh and eighth centuries returned with examples of Tang literature, sculpture, and painting, all of which influenced the Japanese.

LITERATURE Borrowing from Chinese models was somewhat complicated, however, since the early Japanese had no system for recording their own spoken language and initially adopted the Chinese pictographic language for writing. The challenge was complicated by the fact that spoken Japanese is not part of the Sino-Tibetan family of languages. But resourceful Japanese soon adapted the Chinese written characters so that they could be used for recording the Japanese language. In some cases, Chinese characters were given Japanese pronunciations. But Chinese characters ordinarily could not be used to record Japanese words, which normally contain more than one syllable. Sometimes the Japanese simply used Chinese characters as phonetic symbols that were combined to form Japanese words. Later they simplified the characters into phonetic symbols that were used alongside Chinese characters. This hybrid system continues to be used today.

At first, most educated Japanese preferred to write in Chinese, and a court literature—consisting of essays, poetry, and official histories—appeared in the classical Chinese language. But spoken Japanese never totally disappeared among the educated classes and eventually became the instrument of a unique literature. With the lessening of Chinese cultural influence in the tenth century, Japanese verse resurfaced. Between the tenth and fifteenth centuries, twenty imperial anthologies

Guardian Kings. Larger than life and intimidating in its presence, this thirteenth-century wooden statue departs from the refined atmosphere of the Heian court and pulsates with the masculine energy of the Kamakura period. Placed strategically at the entrance to Buddhist shrines, guardian kings such as this one protected the temple and the faithful. In contrast to the refined atmosphere of the Fujiwara court, the Kamakura era was a warrior's world.

of poetry were compiled. Initially, they were written primarily by courtiers, but with the fall of the Heian court and the rise of the warrior and merchant classes, all literate segments of society began to produce poetry.

Japanese poetry is unique. It expresses its themes in a simple form, a characteristic stemming from traditional Japanese aesthetics, Zen religion, and the language itself. The aim of the Japanese poet was to create a mood, perhaps the melancholic effect of gently falling cherry blossoms or leaves. With a few specific references, the poet suggested a whole world, just as Zen Buddhism sought enlightenment from a sudden perception. Poets often alluded to earlier poems by repeating their images with small changes, a technique that was viewed not as plagiarism but as an elaboration on the meaning of the earlier poem.

By the fourteenth century, the technique of the "linked verse" had become the most popular form of Japanese poetry. Known as *haiku* (HY-koo), it is composed of seventeen syllables divided into lines of five, seven, and five syllables, respectively. The poems usually focused on images from nature and the mutability of life. Often the poetry was written by several individuals alternately composing verses and linking them together into long sequences of hundreds and even thousands of lines. The following example, by three poets named Sogi (SOH-gee), Shohaku (shoh-HAH-koo), and Socho (SOH-choh), is one of the most famous of the period:

> *Snow clinging to slope,*   Sogi
>   *On mist-enshrouded mountains*
>   *At evening time.*
>
> *In the distance flows*   Shohaku
>   *Through plum-scented villages.*
>
> *Willows cluster*   Socho
>   *In the river breeze*
>   *As spring appears.[7]*

Poetry served a unique function at the Heian court, where it was the initial means of communication between lovers. By custom, aristocratic women were isolated from all contact with men outside their immediate family and spent their days hidden behind screens. Some amused themselves by writing poetry. When courtship began, poetic exchanges were the only means a woman had to attract her prospective lover, who would be enticed solely by her poetic art.

During the Heian period, male courtiers wrote in Chinese, believing that Chinese civilization was superior and worthy of emulation. Like the Chinese, they viewed prose fiction as "vulgar gossip." Nevertheless, from the ninth century to the twelfth, Japanese women were prolific writers of prose fiction in Japanese (see the box "Seduction of the Akashi Lady" on p. 311). Excluded from school, they learned to read and write at home and wrote diaries and stories to pass the time. Some of the most talented women were invited to court as authors in residence.

In the increasingly pessimistic world of the warring states of Kamakura (1185–1333), Japanese novels typically focused on a solitary figure who is aloof from the refinements of the court and faces battle and possibly death. Another genre, that of the heroic war tale, came out of the new warrior class. These works described the military exploits of warriors, coupled with an overwhelming sense of sadness and loneliness.

The famous classical Japanese drama known as *No* (NOH) also originated during this period. *No* developed out of a variety of entertainment forms, such as dancing and juggling, that were part of the native tradition or had been imported from China and other regions of Asia. The plots were normally based on stories from Japanese history or legend. Eventually, *No* evolved into a highly stylized drama in which the performers wore masks and danced to the accompaniment of instrumental music. Like much of Japanese culture, *No* was restrained, graceful, and refined.

ART AND ARCHITECTURE In art and architecture, as in literature, the Japanese pursued their interest in beauty, simplicity, and nature. To some degree, Japanese artists and architects were influenced by Chinese forms. As they became familiar with Chinese architecture, Japanese rulers and aristocrats tried

The Golden Pavilion in Kyoto. Gardens, water, and architecture combine to create a magnificent setting for the Golden Pavilion. Constructed in the fourteenth century as a retreat where the shoguns could withdraw from their administrative duties, the pavilion derived its name from the gold foil that covered its exterior. Completely destroyed by an arsonist in 1950 as a protest against the commercialism of modern Buddhism, it was rebuilt and reopened in 1987. The use of water as a backdrop is especially noteworthy in Chinese and Japanese landscapes, as well as in the Middle East.

COMPARATIVE ILLUSTRATION

RELIGION & PHILOSOPHY

In the Garden. In traditional China and Japan, gardens were meant to free the observer's mind from mundane concerns, offering spiritual refreshment in the quiet of nature. Chinese gardens were designed to reconstruct an orderly microcosm of nature, where the harassed Confucian official could find spiritual renewal. Wandering through constantly changing perspectives of ponds, trees, rocks, and pavilions, he could imagine himself immersed in a monumental landscape. In the garden in Suzhou on the left, the rocks represent towering mountains to suggest a Daoist sense of withdrawal and eternity, reducing the viewer to a tiny speck in the grand flow of life.

In Japan, the traditional garden reflected the Zen Buddhist philosophy of simplicity, restraint, allusion, and tranquility. In the garden at the right, at the Ryoanji (RYOH-ahn-jee) temple in Kyoto, the rocks are meant to suggest mountains rising from a sea of pebbles. Such gardens served as an aid to meditation, inspiring the viewer to join with comrades in composing "linked verse" (see the poetry by Sogi, Shohaku, and Socho on p. 313).

Q *How do gardens in traditional China and Japan differ in form and purpose from gardens in Western societies? Why do you think this is the case?*

to emulate the splendor of Tang civilization and began constructing their palaces and temples in Chinese style.

During the Heian period (794–1185), the search for beauty was reflected in various art forms, such as narrative hand scrolls, screens, sliding door panels, fans, and lacquer decoration. As in the case of literature, nature themes dominated—seashore scenes, a spring rain, moon and mist, flowering wisteria and cherry blossoms. All were intended to evoke an emotional response on the part of the viewer. Japanese painting suggested the frail beauty of nature by presenting it on a smaller scale. The majestic mountain in a Chinese painting became a more intimate Japanese landscape with rolling hills and a rice field. Faces were rarely shown, and human drama was indicated by a woman lying prostrate or hiding her face in her sleeve. Tension was shown by two people talking at a great distance or with their backs to one another.

During the Kamakura period (1185–1333), the hand scroll with its physical realism and action-packed paintings of the new warrior class achieved great popularity. Reflecting these chaotic times, the art of portraiture flourished, and a scroll would include a full gallery of warriors and holy men in starkly realistic detail, including such unflattering features as stubble, worry lines on a forehead, and crooked teeth. Japanese sculptors also produced naturalistic wooden statues of generals, nobles, and saints. By far the most distinctive were the fierce heavenly "guardian kings," who still intimidate the viewer today (see the illustration "Guardian Kings" on p. 312).

Zen Buddhism, an import from China in the thirteenth century, also influenced Japanese aesthetics. With its emphasis on immediate enlightenment without recourse to intellectual analysis and elaborate ritual, Zen reinforced the Japanese predilection for simplicity and self-discipline. During this era, Zen philosophy found expression in the Japanese garden, the tea ceremony, the art of flower arranging, pottery and ceramics, and miniature plant display—the famous **bonsai** (bon-SY), literally "pot scenery."

Landscapes served as an important means of expression in both Japanese art and architecture. Japanese gardens were initially modeled on Chinese examples. Early court texts during the Heian period emphasized the importance of including a stream or pond when creating a garden. The landscape surrounding the fourteenth-century Golden Pavilion in Kyoto displays a harmony of garden, water, and architecture that makes it one of the treasures of the world. Because of the shortage of water in the city, later gardens concentrated on rock composition, using white pebbles to represent water (see the Comparative Illustration "In the Garden" above).

Like the Japanese garden, the tea ceremony represents the fusion of Zen and aesthetics. Developed in the fifteenth century, it was practiced in a simple room devoid of external ornament except for a *tatami* floor, sliding doors, and an alcove with a writing desk and asymmetrical shelves. The participants could therefore focus completely on the activity of pouring and drinking tea. "Tea and Zen have the same flavor" goes the Japanese saying. Considered the ultimate symbol of spiritual deliverance, the tea ceremony continues to have great aesthetic value and moral significance today as well as in traditional times.

Japan and the Chinese Model

Few major societies in Asia have been as isolated as Japan. Cut off from the mainland by 120 miles of frequently turbulent ocean, the Japanese had only minimal contact with the outside world during most of their early development.

Whether or not this isolation was ultimately beneficial to Japanese society cannot be determined. On the one hand, lack of knowledge of developments taking place elsewhere probably delayed the process of change in Japan. On the other hand, the Japanese were spared the destructive invasions that afflicted other ancient civilizations. Certainly, once the Japanese became acquainted with Chinese culture at the height of the Tang era, they were quick to take advantage of the opportunity. In the space of a few decades, the young state adopted many aspects of Chinese society and culture and thereby introduced major changes into Japanese life.

Nevertheless, Japanese political institutions failed to follow all aspects of the Chinese pattern. Despite Prince Shotoku's effort to make effective use of the imperial traditions of Tang China, the decentralizing forces in Japanese society remained dominant throughout the period under discussion in this chapter. Adoption of the Confucian civil service examination did not lead to a breakdown of Japanese social divisions; instead, the examination was administered in a manner that preserved and strengthened them. Although Buddhist and Daoist doctrines made a significant contribution to Japanese religious practices, Shinto beliefs continued to play a major role in shaping the Japanese worldview.

Why Japan did not follow the Chinese road to centralized authority has been a subject of debate among historians. Some argue that the answer lies in differing cultural traditions, while others suggest that Chinese institutions and values were introduced too rapidly to be assimilated effectively by Japanese society. One factor may have been the absence of a foreign threat (except for the brief incursion by the Mongols). A recent view holds that diseases (such as smallpox and measles) imported inadvertently from China led to a marked decline in the population of the islands, reducing food output and preventing the population from coalescing in more compact urban centers.

In any event, Japan was not the only society in Asia to assimilate ideas from abroad while at the same time preserving customs and institutions inherited from the past. Across the Sea of Japan to the west and several thousand miles to the southwest, other Asian peoples were embarked on a similar journey. We now turn to their experience.

Korea: Bridge to the East

 FOCUS QUESTION: What were the main characteristics of economic and social life in early Korea?

Few of the societies on the periphery of China have been as directly influenced by the Chinese model as Korea. The relationship between China and Korea has frequently been characterized by tension and conflict, however, and Koreans have often resented what they perceive to be Chinese chauvinism and arrogance.

A graphic example of this attitude has occurred in recent years as officials and historians in both countries have presented differing interpretations of the early history of the Korean people. The Korean peninsula was probably first settled by Altaic-speaking fishing and hunting peoples from neighboring Manchuria during the Neolithic Age. Because the area, which is slightly larger than the state of Minnesota, is relatively mountainous (only about one-fifth of the peninsula is adaptable to cultivation), farming was apparently not practiced until about 2000 B.C.E. At that time, the peoples living in the area began to form organized communities.

It is this period that gives rise to disagreement. In 2004, Chinese official sources claimed that the first organized kingdom in the area, known as Koguryo (koh-GOOR-yoh) (37 B.C.E.–668 C.E.), occupied a wide swath of Manchuria as well as the northern section of the Korean peninsula and was thus an integral part of Chinese history. Korean scholars, basing their contentions on a combination of legend and scattered historical evidence, countered that the first kingdom established on the peninsula, known as Gojoseon (goh-joh-SHAWN), was created by the ruler Dangun (dan-GOON) in 2333 B.C.E., and that both he and his subjects in the surrounding area were ethnically Korean. It was at that time, these scholars maintain, that the Bronze Age got under way in northeastern Asia.

Although this dispute has not yet been resolved, most scholars today do agree that in 109 B.C.E., the northern part of the peninsula came under direct Chinese influence. During the next several generations, the area was ruled by the Han dynasty, which divided the territory into provinces and introduced Chinese institutions. With the decline of the Han in the third

Korea's Three Kingdoms

century C.E., power gradually shifted to local leaders, who drove out the Chinese administrators but continued to absorb Chinese cultural influences. Eventually, three separate kingdoms emerged on the peninsula: Koguryo in the north, Paekche (bayk-JEE) in the southwest, and Silla (SIL-uh) in the southeast.

The Three Kingdoms

From the fourth to the seventh centuries, the three kingdoms were bitter rivals for influence and territory on the peninsula. At the same time, all began to adopt Chinese political and cultural institutions. Koguryo was the first among the kingdoms to introduce Buddhism in the late fourth century C.E. The first Confucian academy on the peninsula was established in the capital at Pyongyang (pyahng-YANG). All three kingdoms also appear

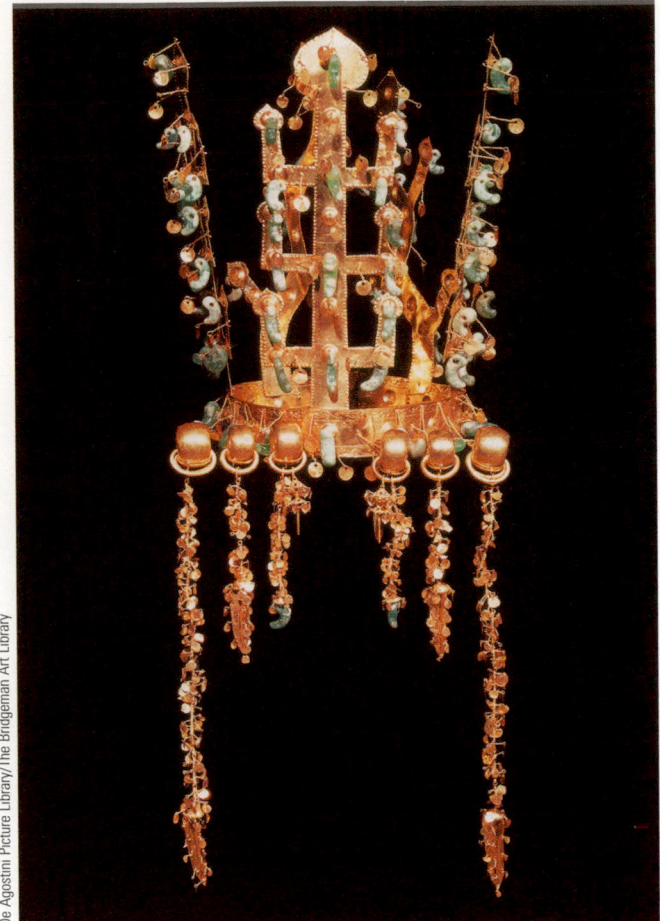

Korean Royal Crown. The Silla Dynasty was renowned for the high quality of its gold, jewelry, crowns, and sword sheaths. Shown here is a jewel-inlaid royal crown of the fifth century C.E. that was excavated from a royal tomb in eastern Korea. Although much Silla artwork reflects Chinese influence, royal crowns located in Silla tombs often contain antler-like motifs, reflecting the animistic traditions of Korea's pre-Chinese past. The comma-shaped jewels symbolize the king's Heaven-sanctioned authority on earth.

to have accepted a tributary relationship with one or another of the squabbling states that emerged in China after the fall of the Han. The kingdom of Silla, less exposed than its two rivals to Chinese influence, was at first the weakest of the three, but eventually it emerged as the dominant power on the peninsula. To pacify the haughty Chinese, who continued to claim a degree of suzerainty with the kingdoms on the peninsula, Silla accepted tributary status under the Tang Dynasty. In the meantime, any remaining Japanese colonies in the south were eliminated.

With the country unified for the first time, the rulers of Silla attempted to use Chinese political institutions and ideology to forge a centralized state. As the state religion, Buddhism grew in popularity, and Korean monks followed the paths of their Japanese counterparts on journeys to Buddhist sites in China. Chinese architecture and art became dominant in the capital at Kyongju (KEE-yahng-joo) and other urban centers, and the written Chinese language became the official means of legal communication. But powerful aristocratic families, long dominant in the southeastern part of the peninsula, were still

The Sokkuram Buddha. As Buddhism spread from India to other parts of Asia, so did the representation of the Buddha in human form. From the first century C.E., statues of the Buddha began to absorb various cultural influences. Some early sculptures, marked by flowing draperies, reflected the Greek culture introduced to India during the era of Alexander the Great. Others were reminiscent of traditional male earth spirits, with broad shoulders and staring eyes. Under the Guptas, artists emphasized the Indian ideal of spiritual and bodily perfection.

As the faith spread along the Silk Road, representations of the Buddha began to reflect cultural influences from Persia and China and eventually from Korea and Japan. Shown here is the eighth-century Sokkuram Buddha, created during the Silla Dynasty. Unable to build structures similar to the cave temples in China and India due to the hardness of the rock in the nearby hills, Korean builders fashioned a small domed cave out of granite blocks, as shown here, and adorned it with a wooden veranda. Today, pilgrims still climb the steep hill to pay homage to this powerful and serene Buddha, one of the finest in Asia.

influential at court. They were able to prevent the adoption of the Tang civil service examination system and resisted the distribution of manorial lands to the poor. But squabbling among noble families steadily increased, and after the assassination of the king of Silla in 780, civil war erupted.

The Rise of the Koryo Dynasty

In the early tenth century, a new dynasty called Koryo (KAWR-yoh) (the root of the modern name of the country in English) arose in the north. The new kingdom adopted Chinese political institutions in an effort to strengthen its power and unify its territory. The civil service examination system was introduced in 958, but as in Japan, the bureaucracy continued to be dominated by influential aristocratic families.

The Koryo Dynasty remained in power for four hundred years, protected from invasion by the absence of a strong dynasty in neighboring China. Under the Koryo, industry and commerce slowly began to develop, but as in China, agriculture was the prime source of wealth. In theory, all land was the property of the king, but in actuality, noble families controlled their holdings. The lands were worked by peasants who were subject to burdens similar to those of European serfs. At the bottom of society was a class of *chonmin* (CHAWN-min), or "base people," composed of slaves, artisans, and other specialized workers.

From a cultural perspective, the Koryo era was one of high achievement. Buddhist monasteries, run by sects introduced from China, including Pure Land and Zen, controlled vast territories, while their monks served as royal advisers at court. At first, Buddhist themes dominated in Korean art and sculpture, and the entire Tripitaka (tri-pih-TAH-kah) (the "three baskets," or sections, of the Buddhist canon) was printed using wooden blocks. Eventually, however, with the appearance of landscape painting and porcelain, Confucian themes began to predominate.

Under the Mongols

Like its predecessor in Silla, the kingdom of Koryo was unable to overcome the power of the nobility and the absence of a reliable tax base. In the thirteenth century, the Mongols seized the northern part of the country and assimilated it into the Yuan empire. The weakened kingdom of Koryo became a tributary of the great khan in Khanbaliq (see Chapter 10).

The era of Mongol rule was one of profound suffering for the Korean people, especially the thousands of peasants and artisans who were compelled to perform conscript labor to help build the ships in preparation for Khubilai Khan's invasion of Japan. On the positive side, the Mongols introduced many new ideas and technology from China and farther afield. The Koryo dynasty had managed to survive, but only by accepting Mongol authority, and when the power of the Mongols declined, the kingdom declined with it. With the rise to power of the Ming in China, Koryo collapsed, and power was seized by the military commander Yi Song-gye (YEE-song-YEE), who declared the founding of the new Choson (also known as Yi [YEE]) Dynasty in 1392. Once again, the Korean people were in charge of their own destiny.

Always aware of potential threats emanating from more powerful neighbors, the Choson kingdom was actively interested in events taking place elsewhere in the region and was

Pulguksa Bell Tower. Among the greatest architectural achievements on the Korean peninsula is the Pulguksa (Monastery of the Land of Buddha), built near Kyongju, the ancient capital of Silla, in the eighth century C.E. Shown here is the bell tower, located in the midst of beautiful parklands on the monastery grounds. In 1966, a scroll was discovered inside a stone stupa adjacent to the monastery. Dating from the early eighth century C.E., it is believed to be the oldest printed text extant in the world today.

The First Vietnam War

POLITICS & GOVERNMENT

IN THE THIRD CENTURY B.C.E., the armies of the Chinese state of Qin (Ch'in) invaded the Red River Delta to launch an attack on the small Vietnamese state located there. As this passage from a Han dynasty philosophical text shows, the Vietnamese were not easy to conquer, and the new state soon declared its independence from the Qin. It was a lesson that was too often forgotten by would-be conquerors in later centuries.

Masters of Huai Nan

Ch'in Shih Huang Ti [the first emperor of Qin] was interested in the rhinoceros horn, the elephant tusks, the kingfisher plumes, and the pearls of the land of Yueh [Viet]; he therefore sent Commissioner T'u Sui at the head of five hundred thousand men divided into five armies. . . . For three years the sword and the crossbow were in constant readiness. Superintendent Lu was sent; there was no means of assuring the transport of supplies so he employed soldiers to dig a canal for sending grain, thereby making it possible to wage war on the people of Yueh. The lord of Western Ou, I Hsu Sung, was killed; consequently, the Yueh people entered the wilderness and lived there with the animals; none consented to be a slave of Ch'in; choosing from among themselves men of valor, they made them their leaders and attacked the Ch'in by night, inflicting on them a great defeat and killing Commissioner T'u Sui; the dead and wounded were many. After this, the emperor deported convicts to hold the garrisons against the Yueh people.

The Yueh people fled into the depths of the mountains and forests, and it was not possible to fight them. The soldiers were kept in garrisons to watch over the abandoned territories. This went on for a long time, and the soldiers grew weary. Then the Yueh came out and attacked; the Ch'in soldiers suffered a great defeat. Subsequently, convicts were sent to hold the garrisons against the Yueh.

 How would the ancient Chinese military strategist Sun Tzu, mentioned in Chapter 3, have advised the Qin military commanders to carry out their operations? Would he have approved of the tactics adopted by the Vietnamese? Why or why not?

Source: From Keith W. Taylor, *The Birth of Vietnam* (Berkeley, 1983), p. 18.

---

quick to follow up on technological advances taking place in China. Koreans were among the first to adopt the new invention of block printing, and Korean cartographers hastened to draw up regional and world maps based on Chinese originals. The famous "Kangnido" world map, produced in Korea in 1402, is considered to be the second oldest surviving map drawn up in Asia (see the illustration "The World in Chinese Eyes" in Chapter 10 on p. 289).

Vietnam: The Smaller Dragon

 FOCUS QUESTIONS: What were the main developments in Vietnamese history before 1500? Why were the Vietnamese able to restore their national independence after a millennium of Chinese rule?

While the Korean people were attempting to establish their own identity in the shadow of the powerful Chinese Empire, the peoples of Vietnam, on China's southern frontier, were seeking to do the same. The Vietnamese (known as the Yueh in Chinese, from the peoples of that name inhabiting the southeastern coast of mainland China) began to practice irrigated agriculture in the flooded regions of the Red River Delta at an early date and entered the Bronze Age sometime during the second millennium B.C.E. By about 200 B.C.E., a young state had begun to form in the area but immediately encountered the expanding power of the Qin dynasty (see Chapter 3). The Vietnamese were not easy to subdue, however, and the collapse of the Qin temporarily enabled them to preserve their independence (see the box "The First Vietnam War" above). Nevertheless, a century later, they were absorbed into the Han Empire.

At first, the Han were satisfied to rule the delta as an autonomous region under the administration of the local landed aristocracy. But Chinese taxes were oppressive, and in 39 C.E., a revolt led by the Trung sisters (widows of local nobles who had been executed by the Chinese) briefly brought Han rule to an end. The Chinese soon suppressed the rebellion, however, and began to rule the area directly through officials dispatched from China. The first Chinese officials to serve in the region became exasperated at the uncultured ways of the locals, who wandered around "naked without shame."[8] In time, however, these foreign officials began to intermarry with the local nobility and form a Sino-Vietnamese ruling class who, though trained in Chinese culture, began to identify with the cause of Vietnamese autonomy.

For nearly a thousand years, the Vietnamese were exposed to the art, architecture, literature, philosophy, and written language of China as the Chinese attempted to integrate the area culturally as well as politically and administratively into their empire. It was a classic example of the Chinese effort to introduce advanced Confucian civilization to the "backward peoples" along the perimeter. To all intents and purposes, the Red River Delta, then known to the Chinese as the "pacified South," or Annam (ahn-NAHM), became a part of China.

A Plea to the New Emperor

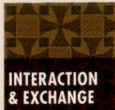

INTERACTION & EXCHANGE

LIKE MANY OTHER SOCIETIES IN PREMODERN East and Southeast Asia, the kingdom of Vietnam regularly paid tribute to the imperial court in China. The arrangement was often beneficial to both sides, as the tributary states received a form of international recognition from the relationship, as well as trading privileges in the massive Chinese market. China, for its part, assured itself that neighboring areas would not harbor dissident elements hostile to its own security.

In this document, contained in a historical chronicle written by Le Tac (LAY-tac) in the fourteenth century, a claimant to the Vietnamese throne seeks recognition in 1295 from the new emperor of the Yuan (Mongol) dynasty in China. Note how the Vietnamese ruler stresses his hope that the new emperor in Beijing, Timur Khan, will adopt a policy of peace and friendship with his southern neighbor. Timur's predecessor, the great Khubilai Khan, had sent Chinese troops to invade Vietnam a few years previously in a bid to place the country back under Chinese rule.

Le Tac, *Essay on Annam*

The Dragon flies in the heavens; new life has come to the Golden Throne. Many embassies have flocked to the Palace to express their sincere congratulations.

One man has ascended the Throne and ten thousand kingdoms are at peace. In great awe I observe that, under His Imperial Majesty's rule, peace and culture flourish within the Empire. His benevolence and virtue permeate the lands beyond the sea as they do at home. Always faithful to the kingly way, He embraces with the same kindness far lands and near. He lays aside military concerns and promotes cultural achievements. He restrains the ardor of his troops and puts an end to all combat. He enlarges His own indulgence and benevolence. He illuminates the virtue and merit of His Ancestors. The sound of thunder has ceased; it has changed into a rain of Imperial blessings. His investiture of tributary kings has been granted with a heavenly generosity. For the people it is a true rebirth, for the Universe a true springtime. I and my people happily live in peace and rejoice to hear the news of His ascendance to the Throne. My glances are directed toward the Northern sky; my heart also turns toward the extreme North, toward the Imperial Dwelling. From this country so remote in the South which I govern, I wish and desire that the longevity of the Emperor may be as great as the mountains of the South are high.

 What message does the new ruler of Vietnam seem to be sending to his counterpart in Beijing? Why does he feel that this message is important in the mutual relations between the two countries?

Source: From Le Tac, An-nam chi-luoc (Hue, University of Hue, 1961), p. 126 [Vietnamese version]; pp. 83–84 [Chinese version]. English translation by T. B. Lam. The translated document appears in Benda and Larkin, *The World of Southeast Asia* (New York: Harper & Row, 1967). pp. 148–149.

The Rise of Great Viet

Despite Chinese efforts to assimilate Vietnam, the Vietnamese sense of ethnic and cultural identity proved inextinguishable, and in 939, the Vietnamese took advantage of the collapse of the Tang Dynasty in China to overthrow Chinese rule.

The new Vietnamese state, which called itself Dai Viet (dy VEE-et) (Great Viet), became a dynamic new force on the Southeast Asian mainland. As the population of the Red River Delta expanded, Dai Viet soon came into conflict with Champa (CHAHM-puh), its neighbor to the south. Located along the central coast of modern Vietnam, Champa was a trading society based on Indian cultural traditons that had been established earlier in 192 C.E. Over the next several centuries, the two states fought on numerous occasions. Finally, in 1471, Dai Viet succeeded in conquering Champa. The Vietnamese then resumed their march southward, establishing agricultural settlements in the newly conquered territory. By the seventeenth century, the Vietnamese had reached the Gulf of Siam.

The Vietnamese faced an even more serious challenge from the north. The Song Dynasty in China, beset with its own problems on the northern frontier, eventually accepted the Dai Viet ruler's offer of tribute status, but later dynasties attempted to reintegrate the Red River delta into the Chinese Empire. The first effort was made in the late thirteenth century by the Mongols, who attempted on two occasions to conquer the Vietnamese. After a series of bloody battles, during which the Vietnamese displayed an impressive capacity for guerrilla warfare, the invaders were driven out (see the box "A Plea to the New Emperor" above). A little over a century later, the Ming Dynasty tried again, and for

The Kingdom of Dai Viet, 1100

© 2016 Cengage Learning

twenty years Vietnam was once more under Chinese rule. In 1428, the Vietnamese evicted the Chinese again, but the experience had contributed to the strong sense of Vietnamese identity.

THE CHINESE LEGACY Despite their stubborn resistance to Chinese rule, after the restoration of independence in the tenth century, Vietnamese rulers quickly discovered the convenience of the Confucian model in administering a river valley society and therefore attempted to follow Chinese practice in forming their own state. The ruler styled himself an emperor like his counterpart to the north (although he prudently termed himself a king in his direct dealings with the Chinese court), adopted Chinese court rituals, claimed the mandate of Heaven, and arrogated to himself the same authority and privileges in his dealings with his subjects. But unlike a Chinese emperor, who had no particular symbolic role as defender of the Chinese people or Chinese culture, a Vietnamese monarch was viewed, above all, as the symbol and defender of Vietnamese independence.

Like their Chinese counterparts, Vietnamese rulers fought to preserve their authority from the challenges of powerful aristocratic families and turned to the Chinese bureaucratic model, including civil service examinations, as a means of doing so. Under the pressure of strong monarchs, the concept of merit eventually took hold, and the power of the landed aristocracy was weakened if not entirely broken. The Vietnamese adopted much of the Chinese administrative structure, including the six ministries, the censorate, and the various levels of provincial and local administration.

Another aspect of the Chinese legacy was the spread of Buddhist, Daoist, and Confucian ideas, which supplemented the traditional belief in nature spirits. Buddhist precepts became popular among the local population, who integrated the new faith into their existing belief system by founding Buddhist temples dedicated to the local village deity in the hope of guaranteeing an abundant harvest. Upper-class Vietnamese educated in the Confucian classics tended to follow the more agnostic Confucian doctrine, but some joined Buddhist monasteries. Daoism also flourished at all levels of society and, as in China, provided a structure for animistic beliefs and practices that still predominated at the village level.

During the early period of independence, Vietnamese culture also borrowed liberally from its larger neighbor. Educated Vietnamese tried their hand at Chinese poetry, wrote dynastic histories in the Chinese style, and followed Chinese models in sculpture, architecture, and porcelain. Many of the notable buildings of the medieval period, such as the Temple of Literature and the famous One-Pillar Pagoda in Hanoi, are classic examples of Chinese architecture.

But there were signs that Vietnamese creativity would eventually transcend the bounds of Chinese cultural norms. Although most classical writing was undertaken in literary Chinese, the only form of literary expression deemed suitable by Confucian conservatives, an adaptation of Chinese written characters, called **chu nom** (CHOO nahm) ("southern characters"), was devised to provide a written system for spoken Vietnamese. In use by the early ninth century, it eventually began to be used for the composition of essays and poetry in the Vietnamese language. Such pioneering efforts would lead in later centuries to the emergence of a vigorous national literature totally independent of Chinese forms.

Society and Family Life

Vietnamese social institutions and customs were also strongly influenced by those of China. As in China, the introduction of

The Temple of Literature, Hanoi. When the Vietnamese regained their independence from China in the tenth century C.E., they retained Chinese institutions that they deemed beneficial. A prime example was the establishment of the Temple of Literature, Vietnam's first university, in 1076. Here sons of mandarins (officials) were educated in the Confucian classics in preparation for an official career. Beginning in the fifteenth century, those receiving doctorates had stelae erected to identify their achievements. Over eighty of these stelae were erected on the school grounds over a space of three hundred years.

© William J. Duiker

The One-Pillar Pagoda, Hanoi. This eleventh-century pagoda was built at the order of a Vietnamese monarch who had dreamed that the Buddhist goddess of mercy, known in China as Guan Yin, while seated on a lotus, had promised him a son. Shortly after the dream the emperor fathered a son. In gratitude he constructed this distinctive pagoda on one pillar, resembling a lotus blossom, the Buddhist symbol of purity, rising out of the mud.

a Confucian system and the adoption of civil service examinations undermined the role of the old landed aristocrats and led eventually to their replacement by the scholar-gentry class. Also as in China, the examinations were open to most males, regardless of family background, which opened the door to a degree of social mobility unknown in most of the other states in the region (see the illustration "The Temple of Literature, Hanoi" on p. 320). Candidates for the bureaucracy read many of the same Confucian classics and absorbed the same ethical principles as their counterparts in China. At the same time, they were also exposed to the classic works of Vietnamese history, which strengthened their sense that Vietnam was a distinct culture similar to, but separate from, that of China.

The vast majority of the Vietnamese people, however, were peasants. Most were small landholders or sharecroppers who rented their plots from wealthier farmers, but large estates were rare due to the systematic efforts of the central government to prevent the rise of a powerful local landed elite.

Family life in Vietnam was similar in many respects to that in China. The Confucian concept of family took hold during the period of Chinese rule, along with the related concepts of filial piety and gender inequality. Perhaps the most striking difference between family traditions in China and Vietnam was that Vietnamese women possessed more rights both in practice and by law. Since ancient times, wives had been permitted to own property and initiate divorce proceedings. One consequence of Chinese rule was a growing emphasis on male dominance, but the tradition of women's rights was never totally extinguished and was legally recognized in a law code promulgated in 1460.

Moreover, Vietnam had a strong historical tradition associating heroic women with the defense of the homeland. The Trung sisters were the first but by no means the only example. In the following passage, a Vietnamese historian of the eighteenth century recounts their story:

> The imperial court was far away; local officials were greedy and oppressive. At that time the country of one hundred sons was the country of the women of Lord To. The ladies [the Trung sisters] used the female arts against their irreconcilable foe; skirts and hairpins sang of patriotic righteousness, uttered a solemn oath at the inner door of the ladies' quarters, expelled the governor, and seized the capital.... Were they not grand heroines?... Our two ladies brought forward an army of all the people, and, establishing a royal court that settled affairs in the territories of the sixty-five strongholds, shook their skirts over the Hundred Yueh [the Vietnamese people].[9]

CHRONOLOGY Early Korea and Vietnam

Foundation of Gojoseon state in Korea	C. 2333 B.C.E.
Chinese conquest of Korea and Vietnam	Second and first centuries B.C.E.
Trung Sisters' Revolt	39 C.E.
Founding of Champa	192
Era of Three Kingdoms in Korea	300s–600s
Restoration of Vietnamese independence	939
Mongol invasions of Korea and Vietnam	1257–1285
Founding of Choson (Yi) Dynasty in Korea	1392
Vietnamese conquest of Champa	1471

CHAPTER SUMMARY

Like many other great civilizations, the Chinese were traditionally convinced of the superiority of their culture and, when the opportunity arose, sought to introduce it to neighboring peoples. Although the latter were viewed in China with a measure of condescension, the adoption of Confucian teachings suggested the possibility of redemption. As the Master had remarked in the *Analects*, "By nature, people are basically alike; in practice they are far apart."[10] As a result, Chinese policies in the region were often shaped by the desire to introduce Chinese values and institutions to non-Chinese peoples living on the periphery.

As this chapter has shown, when conditions were right, China's "civilizing mission" sometimes had some marked success. All three countries that we have dealt with here borrowed liberally from the Chinese model. At the same time, all adapted Chinese institutions and values to the conditions prevailing in their own societies. Though all expressed admiration and respect for China's achievement, all sought to keep Chinese power at a distance.

As an island nation, Japan was the most successful of the three in protecting its political sovereignty and its cultural identity.

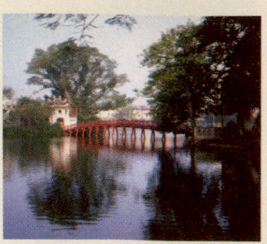

Both Korea and Vietnam were compelled on various occasions to defend their independence by force of arms. That experience may have shaped their strong sense of national distinctiveness, as we shall discuss further in a later chapter.

The appeal of Chinese institutions can undoubtedly be explained by the fact that Japan, Korea, and Vietnam were all agrarian societies, much like their larger neighbor. But it is undoubtedly significant that the aspect of Chinese political culture that was least amenable to adoption abroad was the civil service examination system. The Confucian concept of meritocracy ran directly counter to the strong aristocratic tradition that flourished in all three societies during their early stage of development. Even when the system was adopted, it was put to quite different uses. Only in Vietnam did the concept of merit eventually triumph over that of birth, as strong rulers of Dai Viet attempted to initiate the Chinese model as a means of creating a centralized system of government.

CHAPTER TIMELINE

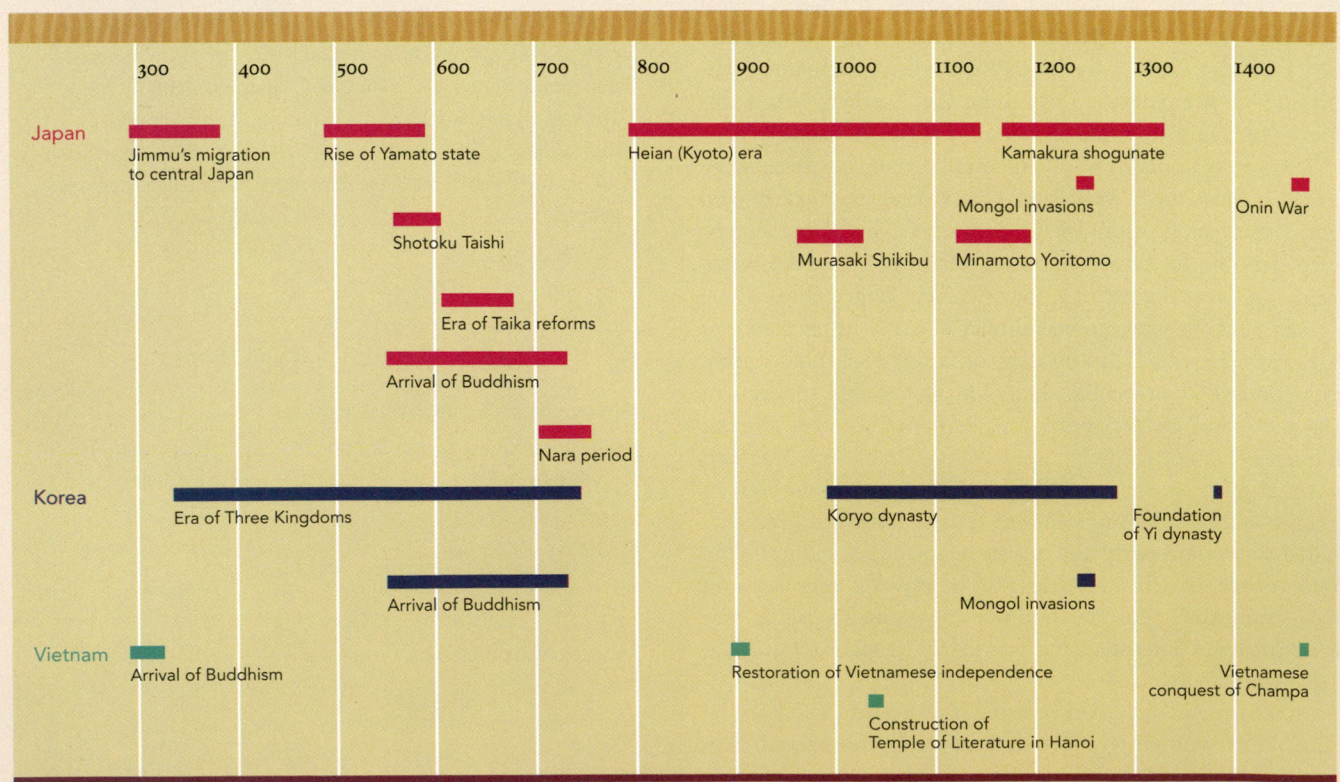

CHAPTER REVIEW

Upon Reflection

Q   To what degree did the institutions and values of medieval Japan conform to the Chinese model? What factors explain the key differences?

Q   How did the Korean peninsula fit into the overall history of East Asia during the period under discussion in this chapter and the previous chapter?

Q   In what ways was Vietnam's relationship with China during the early historical period similar to the relationship between China and the other two major civilizations in the region—Japan and Korea? In what ways was the Vietnamese relationship with China different?

Key Terms

uji (p. 302)
Taika reforms (p. 303)
samurai (p. 305)
Bushido (p. 306)
bakufu (p. 306)
shogun (p. 306)
shogunate system (p. 306)
daimyo (p. 306)
genin (p. 309)
eta (p. 309)
kami (p. 309)
Shinto (p. 309)
Zen (p. 312)
satori (p. 312)
bonsai (p. 314)
chonmin (p. 317)
chu nom (p. 320)

Suggested Reading

RISE OF JAPANESE CIVILIZATION   Some of the standard treatments of the rise of Japanese civilization appear in textbooks dealing with the early history of East Asia. The once-standard text by **J. K. Fairbank, E. O. Reischauer, and A. M. Craig,** *East Asia: Tradition and Transformation* (Boston, 1989), is now considered somewhat out of date, but is still useful and masterfully written. **C. Schirokauer et al.,** *A Brief History of Chinese and Japanese Civilizations* (San Diego, Calif., 2005) is another respected textbook. For recent scholarship on the early period, see the first three volumes of *The Cambridge History of Japan*, ed. **J. W. Hall, M. B. Jansen, M. Kanai,** and **D. Twitchett (Cambridge, 1988).**

EARLY HISTORY OF JAPAN   The best available collection of documents on the early history of Japan is **W. T. de Bary et al., eds.,** *Sources of Japanese Tradition*, vol. 1 (New York, 2001).

For specialized books on the early historical period, see **J. Mass, ed.,** *The Origins of Japan's Medieval World: Courtiers, Clerics, Warriors, and Peasants in the Fourteenth Century*

(Stanford, Calif., 1997); **K. Friday,** *Samurai, Warfare and the State in Early Medieval Japan* (New York, 2004); and **P. Valrey,** *Japanese Culture*, 4th ed. (Honolulu, 2000).

WOMEN'S ISSUES IN EARLY JAPAN   A concise and provocative introduction to women's issues during this period in Japan, as well as in other parts of the world, can be found in **S. S. Hughes and B. Hughes,** *Women in World History* (Armonk, N.Y., 1995). For a tenth-century account of daily life for women at the Japanese court, see **I. Morris, trans. and ed.,** *The Pillow Book of Sei Shonagon* (New York, 1991).

JAPANESE LITERATURE   The best introduction to Japanese literature for college students is still the concise and insightful **D. Keene,** *Seeds in the Heart: Japanese Literature from Earlier Times to the Late Sixteenth Century* (New York, 1993).

KOREA   For an excellent recent survey of Korean history, see **M. J. Seth,** *A Concise History of Korea: From the Neolithic Period Through the Nineteenth Century* (Lanham, Mass., 2006). For documents, see **P. H. Lee,** *Sourcebook of Korean Civilization*, vols. 1 and 2 (New York, 1996).

VIETNAM   Vietnam often receives little attention in general studies of Southeast Asia because it was part of the Chinese Empire for much of the traditional period. For a dated but still useful investigation into the origins of Vietnamese civilization, see **K. W. Taylor,** *The Birth of Vietnam* (Berkeley, Calif., 1983).

Chapter Notes

1.   Cited in C. Holcombe, *The Genesis of East Asia, 221 B.C.–A.D. 907* (Honolulu, 2001), p. 41.
2.   Quoted in D. J. Lu, *Sources of Japanese History*, vol. 1 (New York, 1974), p. 7.
3.   From "The History of Wei," quoted in ibid., p. 10.
4.   From "The Law of Households," quoted in ibid., p. 32.
5.   From "On the Salvation of Women," quoted in ibid., p. 127.
6.   Quoted in B. Ruch, "The Other Side of Culture in Medieval Japan," in K. Yamamura, ed., *The Cambridge History of Japan*, vol. 3, *Medieval Japan* (Cambridge, 1990), p. 506.
7.   Excerpt from *The Cambridge History of Japan*, Vol. III, edited by Koza Yamamura, excerpt from "A Sample of Linked Verse" by H. Paul Verley, from p. 480. Copyright © 1990 Cambridge University Press.
8.   K. W. Taylor, *The Birth of Vietnam* (Berkeley, Calif., 1983), p. 76.
9.   Quoted in ibid., pp. 336–337.
10.   Confucius, *Analects*, 17:2.

MindTap™

MindTap is a fully online, highly personalized learning experience built upon Cengage Leaning content. MindTap combines student learning tools—readings, multimedia, activities, and assessments—into a singular Learning Path that guides students through their course.

The Making of Europe

The coronation of Charlemagne by Pope Leo III, as depicted in a medieval French manuscript

Scala/Art Resource, NY

CHAPTER OUTLINE AND FOCUS QUESTIONS

The Emergence of Europe in the Early Middle Ages

Q What contributions did the Romans, the Christian church, and the Germanic peoples make to the new civilization that emerged in Europe after the collapse of the Western Roman Empire? What was the significance of Charlemagne's coronation as emperor?

Europe in the High Middle Ages

Q What roles did aristocrats, peasants, and townspeople play in medieval European civilization, and how did their lifestyles differ? How did cities in Europe compare with those in China and the Middle East? What were the main aspects of the political, economic, spiritual, and cultural revivals that took place in Europe during the High Middle Ages?

Medieval Europe and the World

Q In what ways did Europeans begin to relate to peoples in other parts of the world after 1000 C.E.? What were the reasons for the crusades, and who or what benefited the most from them?

CRITICAL THINKING

Q In what ways was the civilization that developed in Europe in the Middle Ages similar to those in China and the Middle East? How were they different?

CONNECTIONS TO TODAY

Q Do you think there is a relationship between the crusades in the Middle Ages and contemporary events in the Middle East, including the Persian Gulf War and the activities of al-Qaeda? If so, what do you think the relationship is?

IN 800, CHARLEMAGNE, the king of the Franks, journeyed to Rome to help Pope Leo III, head of the Catholic Church, who was barely clinging to power in the face of rebellious Romans. On Christmas Day, Charlemagne and his family, attended by Romans and Franks, crowded into Saint Peter's Basilica to hear Mass. Quite unexpectedly, according to a Frankish writer, "as the king rose from praying before the tomb of the blessed apostle Peter, Pope Leo placed a golden crown on his head." The people in the church shouted, "Long life and victory to Charles Augustus, crowned by God the great and peace-loving Emperor of the Romans." Seemingly, the Roman Empire in the west had been reborn, and Charles had become the first Roman emperor since 476. But this "Roman emperor" was actually a German king, and he had been crowned by the head of the western Christian church. In truth, the coronation of Charlemagne was a sign not of the rebirth of the Roman Empire but of the emergence of a new European civilization that came into being in western Europe after the collapse of the Western Roman Empire.

This new civilization—European civilization—was formed by the coming together of three major elements: the legacy of the Romans, the Christian church, and the Germanic peoples who moved in and settled the western empire. European civilization developed during a period that historians call the Middle Ages, or the medieval period, which lasted from about 500 to about 1500. To the historians who first used the phrase, the Middle Ages was a middle period between the ancient world and the modern world. During the Early Middle Ages, from about 500 to 1000 C.E., the Roman world of the western empire was slowly transformed into a new Christian European society. ◄

The Emergence of Europe in the Early Middle Ages

Q **FOCUS QUESTIONS:** What contributions did the Romans, the Christian church, and the Germanic peoples make to the new civilization that emerged in Europe after the collapse of the Western Roman Empire? What was the significance of Charlemagne's coronation as emperor?

As we saw in Chapter 10, China descended into political chaos and civil wars after the end of the Han Empire, and it was almost four hundred years before a new imperial dynasty established political order. Similarly, after the collapse of the Western Roman Empire in the fifth century, it would also take hundreds of years to establish a new society.

The New Germanic Kingdoms

The Germanic peoples were an important component of the new European civilization. Already by the third century C.E., they had begun to move into the lands of the Roman Empire. As imperial authority vanished in the fifth century, a number of German kings set up new states. By 500, the Western Roman Empire had been replaced politically by a series of states ruled by German kings.

The fusion of Romans and Germans took different forms in the various Germanic kingdoms. The kingdom of the Ostrogoths (AHSS-truh-gahths) in Italy (see Map 12.1) managed to preserve the Roman tradition of government. After establishing his control over Italy, the Ostrogothic king Theodoric (thee-AHD-uh-rik) (493–526) kept the entire structure of imperial Roman government, although he used separate systems of rule for Romans and Ostrogoths. The Roman population of Italy lived under Roman law administered by Roman officials. The Ostrogoths were governed by their own customs and their own officials.

Like the kingdom of the Ostrogoths in Italy, the kingdom of the Visigoths (VIZ-uh-gahths) in Spain inherited and continued to maintain much of the Roman structure of government. In both states, the Roman population was allowed to maintain Roman institutions while being largely excluded from power as a Germanic warrior caste came to dominate the considerably larger native population. Over a period of time, the Visigoths and the native peoples began to fuse together.

Roman influence was weaker in Britain. When the Roman armies abandoned Britain at the beginning of the fifth century, the Angles and Saxons, Germanic tribes from Denmark and northern Germany, moved in and settled there. Eventually, these peoples succeeded in carving out small kingdoms throughout the island, Kent in southeast England being one of them.

THE KINGDOM OF THE FRANKS One of the most prominent German states on the European continent was the kingdom of the Franks. The establishment of a Frankish kingdom was the work of Clovis (KLOH-viss) (c. 482–511), a member of the Merovingian (meh-ruh-VIN-jee-un) dynasty who became a Catholic Christian around 500. He was not the first German king to convert to Christianity, but the others had joined the Arian (AR-ee-un) sect of Christianity, a group who believed that Jesus had been human and thus not truly God. The Christian church in Rome, which had become known as the Roman Catholic Church, regarded the Arians as heretics, people who believed in teachings different from the official church doctrine. To Catholics, Jesus was human, but of the "same substance" as God and therefore also truly God. Clovis found that his conversion to Catholic Christianity gained him the support of the Roman Catholic Church, which was only too eager to obtain the friendship of a major Germanic ruler who was a Catholic Christian.

By 510, Clovis had established a powerful new Frankish kingdom stretching from the Pyrenees in the west to German lands in the east (modern France and western Germany). After Clovis's death, however, his sons divided his newly created kingdom, as was the Frankish custom. During the sixth and seventh centuries, the once-united Frankish kingdom came to be divided into three major areas: Neustria (NOO-stree-uh), in northern Gaul; Austrasia (awss-TRAY-zhuh), consisting of the ancient Frankish lands on both sides of the Rhine; and the former kingdom of Burgundy.

THE SOCIETY OF THE GERMANIC PEOPLES As Germans and Romans intermarried and began to form a new society, some of the social customs of the Germanic peoples came to play an important role. The crucial social bond among the Germanic peoples was the family, especially the extended family of husbands, wives, children, brothers, sisters, cousins, and grandparents. The German family structure was quite simple. Males were dominant and made all the important decisions. A woman obeyed her father until she married and then fell under the legal domination of her husband. For most women in the new Germanic kingdoms, their legal status reflected the material conditions of their lives. Most women had life expectancies of only thirty or forty years, and perhaps 15 percent of women died in their childbearing years, no doubt due to complications associated with childbirth. For most women, life consisted of domestic labor: providing food and clothing for the household, caring for the children, and assisting with farming chores.

MAP 12.1 **The Germanic Kingdoms of the Old Western Empire.** Germanic tribes filled the power vacuum caused by the demise of the Western Roman Empire, founding states that blended elements of Germanic customs and laws with those of Roman culture, including large-scale conversions to Christianity. The Franks established the most durable of these Germanic states.

Q *How did the movements of Franks during this period correspond to the borders of present-day France?*

a person in monetary terms. That value varied considerably according to social status. An offense against a nobleman, for example, cost considerably more than one against a freeman or a slave.

Germanic law also provided a means of determining guilt or innocence: the ordeal. The ordeal was based on the idea of divine intervention: divine forces (whether pagan or Christian) would not allow an innocent person to be harmed (see the box "Germanic Customary Law: The Ordeal" on p. 327).

The Role of the Christian Church

By the end of the fourth century, Christianity had become the predominant religion of the Roman Empire. As the official Roman state disintegrated, the Christian church played an increasingly important role in the growth of the new European civilization.

THE ORGANIZATION OF THE CHURCH By the fourth century, the Christian church had developed a system of government. A bishop, whose area of jurisdiction was known as a bishopric, or **diocese**, headed the Christian community in each city; the bishoprics of each Roman province were joined together under the direction of an archbishop. The bishops of four great cities—Rome, Jerusalem, Alexandria, and Antioch—held positions of special power in church affairs because the churches in these cities all asserted that they had been founded by the original apostles sent out by Jesus. Soon, however, one of them—the bishop of Rome—claimed that he was the sole leader of the western Christian church. According to church tradition, Jesus had given the keys to the kingdom of heaven to Peter, who was considered the chief apostle and the first bishop of Rome. Subsequent bishops of Rome were considered Peter's successors and came to be known as popes (from the Latin word *papa*, meaning "father"). By the sixth century, the popes had been successful in extending papal authority over the Christian church in the west and converting the pagan peoples of Germanic Europe. Their primary instrument of conversion was the monastic movement.

The German conception of family affected the way Germanic law treated the problem of crime and punishment. In the Roman system, as in our own, a crime such as murder was considered an offense against society or the state and was handled by a court that heard evidence and arrived at a decision. Germanic law was personal. An injury to one person by another could lead to a blood feud in which the family of the injured party took revenge on the family of the wrongdoer. Feuds could involve savage acts of revenge, such as hacking off hands or feet or gouging out eyes. Because this system could easily get out of control, an alternative system arose that made use of a fine called *wergeld* (WUR-geld), which was paid by a wrongdoer to the family of the person injured or killed. *Wergeld*, which literally means "man money," was the value of

Germanic Customary Law: The Ordeal

FAMILY & SOCIETY

IN GERMANIC CUSTOMARY LAW, the ordeal was a means by which accused persons might clear themselves. Although the ordeal took different forms, all involved a physical trial of some sort, such as holding a red-hot iron. It was believed that God would protect the innocent and allow them to come through the ordeal unharmed. This sixth-century account by Gregory of Tours describes an ordeal by hot water.

Gregory of Tours, *An Ordeal of Hot Water* (c. 580)

An Arian presbyter disputing with a deacon of our religion made venomous assertions against the Son of God and the Holy Ghost, as is the habit of that sect [the Arians]. But when the deacon had discoursed a long time concerning the reasonableness of our faith and the heretic, blinded by the fog of unbelief, continued to reject the truth, … the former said: "Why weary ourselves with long discussions? Let acts approve the truth; let a kettle be heated over the fire and someone's ring be thrown into the boiling water. Let him who shall take it from the heated liquid be approved as a follower of the truth, and afterward let the other party be converted to the knowledge of the truth. And do you also understand, O heretic, that this our party will fulfill the conditions with the aid of the Holy Ghost; you shalt confess that there is no discordance, no dissimilarity in the Holy Trinity." The heretic consented to the proposition and they separated after appointing the next morning for the trial. But the fervor of faith in which the deacon had first made this suggestion began to cool through the instigation of the enemy. Rising with the dawn he bathed his arm in oil and smeared it with ointment. But nevertheless he made the round of the sacred places and called in prayer on the Lord….

About the third hour they met in the marketplace. The people came together to see the show. A fire was lighted, the kettle was placed upon it, and when it grew very hot the ring was thrown into the boiling water. The deacon invited the heretic to take it out of the water first. But he promptly refused, saying, "You who did propose this trial are the one to take it out." The deacon all of a tremble bared his arm. And when the heretic presbyter saw it besmeared with ointment he cried out: "With magic arts you have thought to protect yourself, that you have made use of these salves, but what you have done will not avail." While they were thus quarreling there came up a deacon from Ravenna named Iacinthus and inquired what the trouble was about. When he learned the truth he drew his arm out from under his robe at once and plunged his right hand into the kettle. Now the ring that had been thrown in was a little thing and very light so that it was thrown about by the water as chaff would be blown about by the wind; and searching for it a long time he found it after about an hour. Meanwhile the flame beneath the kettle blazed up mightily so that the greater heat might make it difficult for the ring to be followed by the hand; but the deacon extracted it at length and suffered no harm, protesting rather that at the bottom the kettle was cold while at the top it was just pleasantly warm. When the heretic beheld this he was greatly confused and audaciously thrust his hand into the kettle saying, "My faith will aid me." As soon as his hand had been thrust in all the flesh was boiled off the bones clear up to the elbow. And so the dispute ended.

What was the purpose of the ordeal of hot water? What does it reveal about the nature of the society that used it?

Source: From *Translations and Reprints from the Original Sources of European History*, Series I, Vol. 4, No. 4, by A. C. Howland, copyright 1897 by Department of History, University of Pennsylvania Press.

THE MONKS AND THEIR MISSIONS A **monk** (in Latin, *monachus*, meaning "one who lives alone") was a man who sought to live a life divorced from the world, cut off from ordinary human society, in order to pursue an ideal of total dedication to God. As the monastic ideal spread, a new form of **monasticism** based on living together in a community soon became the dominant form. Saint Benedict (c. 480–c. 543), who founded a monastic house for which he wrote a set of rules, established the basic form of monastic life in the western Christian church.

Benedict's rules divided each day into a series of activities, with primary emphasis on prayer and manual labor. Physical work of some kind was required of all monks for several hours a day because idleness was "the enemy of the soul." At the very heart of community practice was prayer, the proper "work of God." Although this included private meditation and reading, all monks gathered together seven times during the day for common prayer and chanting of psalms. The

Benedictine life was a communal one. Monks ate, worked, slept, and worshiped together.

Each Benedictine monastery was strictly ruled by an **abbot**, or "father" of the monastery, who had complete authority over his fellow monks. Unquestioning obedience to the will of the abbot was expected of every monk. Each Benedictine monastery held lands that enabled it to be a self-sustaining community, isolated from and independent of the world surrounding it. Within the monastery, however, monks were to fulfill their vow of poverty: "Let all things be common to all, as it is written, lest anyone should say that anything is his own."[1] Only men could be monks, but women, called **nuns**, also began to withdraw from the world to dedicate themselves to God.

Monasticism played an indispensable role in early medieval civilization. Monks became the new heroes of Christian civilization, and their dedication to God became the highest ideal of Christian life. They were the social workers of their

Saint Benedict. Benedict was the author of a set of rules that was instrumental in the development of monastic groups in the Catholic Church. In this sixth-century Latin manuscript miniature, an abbot is shown offering codes and possessions to Saint Benedict.

communities: monks provided schools for the young, hospitality for travelers, and hospitals for the sick. Monks also copied Latin works and passed on the legacy of the ancient world to the new European civilization. Monasteries became centers of learning wherever they were located, and monks worked to spread Christianity to all of Europe.

Women played an important role in the monastic missionary movement and the conversion of the Germanic kingdoms. Some served as **abbesses** (an abbess was the head of a monastery for nuns, known as a convent); many abbesses came from aristocratic families, especially in Anglo-Saxon England. In the kingdom of Northumbria, for example, Saint Hilda founded the monastery of Whitby in 657. As abbess, she was responsible for making learning an important part of the life of the monastery.

Charlemagne and the Carolingians

During the seventh and eighth centuries, as the kings of the Frankish kingdom gradually lost their power, the mayors of the palace—the chief officers of the king's household—assumed more control of the kingdom. One of these mayors, Pepin (PEP-in or pay-PANH), finally took the logical step of assuming the

Charlemagne's Empire

Legend:
- Frankish kingdom, 768
- Territories gained by Charlemagne

kingship of the Frankish state for himself and his family. Upon his death in 768, his son came to the throne of the Frankish kingdom.

This new king was the dynamic and powerful ruler known to history as Charles the Great (768–814), or Charlemagne (SHAR-luh-mayn) (from the Latin for Charles the Great, *Carolus Magnus*). He was determined and decisive, intelligent and inquisitive, a strong statesman, and a pious Christian. Although unable to read or write himself, he was a wise patron of learning. In a series of military campaigns, he greatly expanded the territory he had inherited and created what came to be known as the Carolingian (kar-uh-LIN-jun) Empire. At its height, Charlemagne's empire covered much of western and central Europe; not until the time of Napoleon in the nineteenth century would an empire of its size be seen again in Europe (see the box "The Achievements of Charlemagne" on p. 329).

Charlemagne continued the efforts of his father in organizing the Carolingian kingdom. Besides his household staff, Charlemagne's administration of the empire depended on the use of counts as the king's chief representatives in local areas. As an important check on the power of the counts, Charlemagne established the *missi dominici* (MISS-ee doh-MIN-i-chee) ("messengers of the lord king"), two men who were sent out to local districts to ensure that the counts were executing the king's wishes. They had the power to remove counts if they were abusing their power, thus making the *missi* an important instrument in bolstering royal power.

WHAT WAS THE SIGNIFICANCE OF CHARLEMAGNE? As Charlemagne's power grew, so did his prestige as the most powerful Christian ruler of what one monk called the "kingdom of Europe." In 800, Charlemagne acquired a new title: emperor of the Romans. The significance of this imperial coronation has been much debated by historians. We are not even sure if the pope or Charlemagne initiated the idea when they met in the summer of 799 in Paderborn in German lands or whether Charles was pleased or displeased.

In any case, Charlemagne's coronation as Roman emperor demonstrated the strength, even after three hundred years, of the concept of an enduring Roman Empire. More important, it symbolized the fusion of Roman, Christian, and Germanic elements. Did this fusion constitute the foundations of European civilization? A Germanic king had been crowned emperor of the Romans by the spiritual leader of western Christendom. Charlemagne

The Achievements of Charlemagne

POLITICS & GOVERNMENT

EINHARD (YN-HART), the biographer of Charlemagne, was born in the valley of the Main River in Germany about 775. Raised and educated in the monastery of Fulda, an important center of learning, he arrived at the court of Charlemagne in 791 or 792. Although he did not achieve high office under Charlemagne, he served as private secretary to Louis the Pious, Charlemagne's son and successor. In this selection, Einhard discusses some of Charlemagne's accomplishments.

Einhard, *Life of Charlemagne*

Such are the wars, most skillfully planned and successfully fought, which this most powerful king waged during the forty-seven years of his reign. He so largely increased the Frank kingdom, which was already great and strong when he received it at his father's hands, that more than double its former territory was added to it.... He subdued all the wild and barbarous tribes dwelling in Germany between the Rhine and the Vistula, the Ocean and the Danube, all of which speak very much the same language, but differ widely from one another in customs and dress....

He added to the glory of his reign by gaining the good will of several kings and nations; so close, indeed, was the alliance that he contracted with Alfonso, King of Galicia and Asturias, that the latter, when sending letters or ambassadors to Charles, invariably styled himself his man.... The Emperors of Constantinople [the Byzantine emperors] sought friendship and alliance with Charles by several embassies; and even when the Greeks [the Byzantines] suspected him of designing to take the empire from them, because of his assumption of the title Emperor, they made a close alliance with him, that he might have no cause of offense. In fact, the power of the Franks was always viewed with a jealous eye, whence the Greek proverb, "Have the Frank for your friend, but not for your neighbor."

This King, who showed himself so great in extending his empire and subduing foreign nations, and was constantly occupied with plans to that end, undertook also very many works calculated to adorn and benefit his kingdom, and brought several of them to completion. Among these, the most deserving of mention are the basilica of the Holy Mother of God at Aix-la-Chapelle [Aachen], built in the most admirable manner, and a bridge over the Rhine River at Mainz, half a mile long, the breadth of the river at this point.... Above all, sacred buildings were the object of his care throughout his whole kingdom; and whenever he found them falling to ruin from age, he commanded the priests and fathers who had charge of them to repair them, and made sure by commissioners that his instructions were obeyed.... Thus did Charles defend and increase as well as beautify his kingdom....

He cherished with the greatest fervor and devotion the principles of the Christian religion, which had been instilled into him from infancy. Hence it was that he built the beautiful church at Aix-la-Chapelle, which he adorned with gold and silver and lamps, and with rails and doors of solid brass. He had the columns and marbles for this structure brought from Rome and Ravenna, for he could not find such as were suitable elsewhere. He was a constant worshiper at this church as long as his health permitted, going morning and evening, even after nightfall, besides attending mass....

He was very forward in caring for the poor, so much so that he not only made a point of giving in his own country and his own kingdom, but when he discovered that there were Christians living in poverty in Syria, Egypt, and Africa, at Jerusalem, Alexandria, and Carthage, he had compassion on their wants, and used to send money over the seas to them.... He sent great and countless gifts to the popes, and throughout his whole reign the wish that he had nearest at heart was to reestablish the ancient authority of the city of Rome under his care and by his influence, and to defend and protect the Church of St. Peter, and to beautify and enrich it out of his own store above all other churches.

 How long did Einhard know Charlemagne? Does this excerpt reflect close, personal knowledge of the man, his court, and his works or hearsay and legend?

Source: From Einhard, *The Life of Charlemagne*, translated by S. E. Turner, pp. 50–54. Copyright © 1960 by The University of Michigan. Translated from the *Monumenta Germanie*.

---

had created an empire that stretched from the North Sea to Italy and from the Atlantic Ocean to the Danube River. This differed significantly from the Roman Empire, which encompassed much of the Mediterranean world. Had a new civilization emerged? And should Charlemagne be regarded, as one of his biographers has argued, as the "father of Europe"?[2]

Other historians argue that there was only a weak sense of community in Europe before 1000. As one has stated, "Europe was not born in the early Middle Ages.... There was no common European culture, and certainly not any Europe-wide economy."[3]

The World of Lords and Vassals

The Carolingian Empire began to disintegrate soon after Charlemagne's death in 814, and less than thirty years later, in 843, it was divided among his grandsons into three major sections: the western Frankish lands, which formed the core of the eventual kingdom of France; the eastern lands, which eventually became Germany; and a "middle kingdom" extending from the North Sea to the Mediterranean. The territories of the middle kingdom became a source of incessant struggle between the other two Frankish rulers and their heirs. At the same time, powerful nobles gained even more dominance in their local territories while the Carolingian rulers fought each other, and incursions by outsiders into various parts of the Carolingian world furthered the process of disintegration.

INVASIONS OF THE NINTH AND TENTH CENTURIES In the ninth and tenth centuries, western Europe was beset by a wave of invasions. Muslims attacked the southern coasts of Europe and sent raiding parties into southern France. The Magyars (MAG-yarz), a people from western Asia, moved into central Europe at the end of the ninth century and settled on the plains of Hungary, launching forays from there into western Europe. Finally crushed at the Battle of Lechfeld (LEK-feld) in Germany in 955, the Magyars converted to Christianity, settled down, and established the kingdom of Hungary.

The most far-reaching attacks of the time came from the Northmen or Norsemen of Scandinavia, also known to us as the Vikings. The Vikings were warriors whose love of adventure and search for booty and new avenues of trade may have spurred them to invade other areas of Europe. Viking ships were the best of the period. Long and narrow with beautifully carved arched prows, the Viking "dragon ships" each carried about fifty men. Their shallow draft enabled them to sail up European rivers and attack places at some distance inland. In the ninth century, Vikings sacked villages and towns, destroyed churches, and easily defeated small local armies. Viking attacks were terrifying, and many a clergyman pleaded with his parishioners to change their behavior and appease God's anger to avert the attacks, as in this sermon by an English archbishop in 1014:

> Things have not gone well now for a long time at home or abroad, but there has been devastation and persecution in every district again and again, and the English have been for a long time now completely defeated and too greatly disheartened through God's anger; and the pirates [Vikings] so strong with God's consent that often in battle one puts to flight ten, and sometimes less, sometimes more, all because of our sins.... We pay them continually and they humiliate us daily; they ravage and they burn, plunder, and rob and carry on board; and lo, what else is there in all these events except God's anger clear and visible over this people?[4]

By the middle of the ninth century, the Norsemen had begun to build winter settlements in different areas of

The Vikings Attack England. The illustration on the left, from an eleventh-century English manuscript, depicts a band of armed Vikings invading England. Two ships have already reached the shore, and a few Vikings are shown walking down a long gangplank onto English soil. On the right is a replica of a well-preserved Viking ship found at Oseberg, Norway. The Oseberg ship was one of the largest Viking ships of its day.

Europe. By 850, groups from Norway had settled in Ireland, and Danes occupied northeastern England by 878. Beginning in 911, the ruler of the western Frankish lands gave one band of Vikings land at the mouth of the Seine (SEN) River, a territory that came to be known as Normandy. This policy of settling the Vikings and converting them to Christianity was a deliberate one; by their conversion to Christianity, the Vikings were soon made a part of European civilization.

THE DEVELOPMENT OF FIEF-HOLDING The disintegration of central authority in the Carolingian world and the invasions by Muslims, Magyars, and Vikings led to the emergence of a new type of relationship between free individuals. When governments ceased to be able to defend their subjects, it became important to find some powerful lord who could offer protection in return for service. The contract sworn between a lord and his subordinate (known as a **vassal**) is the basis of a form of social organization that modern historians called *feudalism*. But feudalism was never a cohesive system, and many historians today prefer to avoid using the term (see the Comparative Essay "Feudal Orders Around the World" in Chapter 11 on p. 307).

With the breakdown of royal governments, powerful nobles took control of large areas of land. They needed men to fight for them, so the practice arose of giving grants of land to vassals who in return would fight for their lord. The Frankish army had originally consisted of foot soldiers, dressed in coats of mail and armed with swords. But in the eighth century, larger horses began to be used, along with the stirrup, which was introduced by nomadic horsemen from Asia. Earlier, horsemen had been throwers of spears. Now they wore armor in the form of coats of mail (the larger horse could carry the weight) and wielded long lances that enabled them to act as battering rams (the stirrups kept them on their horses). For almost five hundred years, heavily armored cavalry, or *knights*, as they were called, dominated warfare in Europe. The knights came to have the greatest social prestige and formed the backbone of the European aristocracy.

Of course, it was expensive to have a horse, armor, and weapons. It also took time and much practice to learn to wield these instruments skillfully from horseback. Consequently, a lord who wanted men to fight for him had to grant each vassal a piece of land that provided for the support of the vassal and his family. In return for the land, the vassal provided his lord with his fighting skills. Each needed the other. In the society of the Early Middle Ages, where there was little trade and wealth was based primarily on land, land became the most important gift a lord could give to a vassal in return for his loyalty and military service.

By the ninth century, the grant of land made to a vassal had become known as a **fief** (FEEF). A fief was a piece of land held from the lord by a vassal in return for military service, but vassals who held such grants of land came to exercise rights of jurisdiction or political and legal authority within these fiefs. As the Carolingian world disintegrated politically under the impact of internal dissension and invasions, an increasing number of powerful lords arose who were now responsible for keeping order.

THE PRACTICE OF FIEF-HOLDING Fief-holding also became increasingly complicated with the development of **subinfeudation** (sub-in-fyoo-DAY-shun). The vassals of a king, who were themselves great lords, might also have vassals who would owe them military service in return for a grant of land taken from their estates. Those vassals, in turn, might likewise have vassals, who at such a level would be simple knights with barely enough land to provide their equipment. The lord-vassal relationship, then, bound together both greater and lesser landowners. At all levels, the lord-vassal relationship was always an honorable relationship between free men and did not imply any sense of servitude.

Fief-holding came to be characterized by a set of practices that determined the relationship between a lord and his vassal. The major obligation of a vassal to his lord was to perform military service, usually about forty days a year. A vassal was also required to appear at his lord's court when summoned to give advice to the lord. He might also be asked to sit in judgment in a legal case, since the important vassals of a lord were peers and only they could judge each other. Finally, vassals were also responsible for aids, or financial payments to the lord on a number of occasions, including the knighting of the lord's eldest son, the marriage of his eldest daughter, and the ransom of the lord's person if he were captured.

In turn, a lord had responsibilities toward his vassals. His major obligation was to protect his vassal, either by defending him militarily or by taking his side in a court of law. The lord was also responsible for the maintenance of the vassal, usually by granting him a fief.

THE MANORIAL SYSTEM The landholding class of nobles and knights contained a military elite whose ability to function as warriors depended on having the leisure time to pursue the arts of war. Landed estates, located on the fiefs given to a vassal by his lord and worked by a dependent peasant class, provided the economic sustenance that made this way of life possible. A **manor** was an agricultural estate operated by a lord and worked by peasants (see Map 12.2). Although a large class of free peasants continued to exist, increasing numbers of free peasants became **serfs**, who were bound to the land and required to provide labor services, pay rents, and be subject to the lord's jurisdiction. By the ninth century, probably 60 percent of the population of western Europe had become serfs.

Labor services involved working the lord's **demesne** (duh-MAYN *or* duh-MEEN), the land retained by the lord, which might consist of one-third to one-half of the cultivated lands scattered throughout the manor. The rest would be used by the peasants for themselves. Building barns and digging ditches were also part of the labor services. Serfs usually worked about three days a week for their lord and paid rents by giving the lord a share of every product they raised.

Serfs were legally bound to the lord's lands and could not leave without his permission. Although free to marry, serfs could not marry anyone outside their manor without the lord's approval. Moreover, lords sometimes exercised public rights or political authority on their lands, which gave them the right to try peasants in their own courts.

MAP 12.2 **A Typical Manor.** The manorial system created small, tightly knit communities in which peasants were economically and physically bound to their lord. Crops were rotated, with roughly one-third of the fields lying fallow (untilled) at any one time, which helped replenish soil nutrients.

 How does the area of the lord's demesne, his manor house, other buildings, garden, and orchard compare with that of the peasant holdings in the village?

Europe in the High Middle Ages

Q **FOCUS QUESTIONS:** What roles did aristocrats, peasants, and townspeople play in medieval European civilization, and how did their lifestyles differ? How did cities in Europe compare with those in China and the Middle East? What were the main aspects of the political, economic, spiritual, and cultural revivals that took place in Europe during the High Middle Ages?

The new European civilization that had emerged in the Early Middle Ages began to flourish in the High Middle Ages (1000–1300). New agricultural practices that increased the food supply spurred commercial and urban expansion. Both lords and vassals recovered from the invasions and internal dissension of the Early Middle Ages, and medieval kings began to exert a centralizing authority. The recovery of the Catholic Church made it a forceful presence in every area of life. The High Middle Ages also gave birth to a cultural revival.

Land and People

In the Early Middle Ages, Europe had a relatively small population of about 38 million, but in the High Middle Ages, the number of people nearly doubled to 74 million. What accounted for this dramatic increase? For one thing, conditions in Europe were more settled and more peaceful after the invasions of the Early Middle Ages had ended. For another, agricultural production surged after 1000.

THE NEW AGRICULTURE During the High Middle Ages, Europeans began to farm in new ways. An improvement in climate resulted in better growing conditions, but an important factor in increasing food production was the expansion of cultivated or arable land, accomplished by clearing forested areas. Peasants of the eleventh and twelfth centuries cut down trees and drained swamps until by the thirteenth century, Europeans had more acreage available for farming than at any time before or since.

Technological changes also furthered the development of farming. The Middle Ages saw an explosion of laborsaving devices, many of which were made from iron, which was mined in different areas of Europe. Iron was used to make scythes, axes, and hoes for use on farms as well as saws, hammers, and nails for building purposes. Iron was crucial in making the *carruca* (kuh-ROO-kuh), a heavy, wheeled plow with an iron plowshare pulled by teams of horses, which could turn over the heavy clay soil north of the Alps.

Besides using horsepower, the High Middle Ages harnessed the power of water and wind to do jobs formerly done by human or animal power. Although the watermill had been invented as early as the second century B.C.E., it did not come into widespread use until the High Middle Ages. Located along streams, watermills were used to grind grain into flour. Often dams were constructed to increase the waterpower. The development of the cam enabled millwrights to mechanize entire industries; waterpower was used in certain phases of cloth production and to run trip-hammers for the working of metals. The Chinese had made use of the cam in operating trip-hammers for hulling rice by the third century C.E. but apparently had not extended its use to other industries.

Where rivers were unavailable or not easily dammed, Europeans developed windmills to use the power of the wind. Historians are uncertain whether windmills were imported into Europe (they were invented in Persia) or designed independently by Europeans. In either case, by the end of the twelfth century, they were beginning to dot the European landscape. The watermill and windmill were the most important devices for the harnessing of power before the invention of the steam engine in the eighteenth century.

The shift from a two-field to a three-field system also contributed to the increase in food production (see the Comparative Illustration "The New Agriculture in the Medieval World" on p. 333). In the Early Middle Ages, peasants had planted one field while another of equal size was allowed to lie fallow (untilled) to regain its fertility. Now estates were divided into three parts. One field was planted in the fall with winter grains, such as rye and wheat, while spring grains, such as oats or barley, and vegetables, such as peas or beans, were planted in the second field.

COMPARATIVE ILLUSTRATION

EARTH & ENVIRONMENT

The New Agriculture in the Medieval World. New agricultural methods and techniques in the Middle Ages enabled peasants in both Europe and China to increase food production. This general improvement in diet was a factor in supporting noticeably larger populations in both areas. Below, a thirteenth-century illustration shows a group of English peasants harvesting grain. Overseeing their work is a bailiff, or manager, who supervised the work of the peasants. To the right, a thirteenth-century painting shows Chinese peasants harvesting rice, which became the staple food in China.

Q *How important were staple foods (such as wheat and rice) to the diet and health of people in Europe and China during the Middle Ages?*

The Art Archive at Art Resource, NY

The Art Archive at Art Resource, NY

The third was allowed to lie fallow. By rotating the use of the fields, only one-third rather than one-half of the land lay fallow at any time. The rotation of crops also kept the soil from being exhausted so quickly, and more crops could now be grown.

DAILY LIFE OF THE PEASANTRY The lifestyle of the peasants was quite simple. Their cottages were built with wood frames with walls made of laths or sticks; the spaces between the laths were stuffed with straw and rubble and then plastered over with clay. Roofs were often thatched with reeds or straw. The houses of poorer peasants consisted of a single room, but others had at least two rooms—a main room for cooking, eating, and other activities and another room for sleeping.

Peasant women occupied an important but difficult position in manorial society. As mothers, they were expected to carry and bear their children, as well as provide for their socialization and religious training. Peasant women also bore responsibility for doing the spinning and weaving that provided the household's clothes, tending the family's vegetable garden and

chickens, and providing the meals. A woman's ability to manage the household might determine whether a peasant family would starve or survive in difficult times. At the same time, peasant women often worked with men in the fields, especially at harvest time. Indeed, as one historian has noted, peasant marriage was an "economic partnership" in which both husbands and wives contributed their own distinctive labor.

Though simple, a peasant's daily diet was adequate when food was available. The staple of the peasant diet, and the medieval diet in general, was bread. Women made the dough for the bread at home and then brought their loaves to be baked in community ovens, which were owned by the lord of the manor. Peasant bread was highly nutritious, containing not only wheat and rye but also barley, millet, and oats, giving it a dark appearance and a very heavy, hard texture. Bread was supplemented by numerous vegetables from the household gardens, cheese from cow's or goat's milk, nuts and berries from woodlands, and fruits, such as apples, pears, and cherries. Chickens provided eggs and sometimes meat.

THE NOBILITY OF THE MIDDLE AGES In the High Middle Ages, European society, like that of Japan during the same period, was dominated by men whose chief concern was warfare. Like the Japanese samurai, many Western nobles loved war. As one nobleman wrote:

> And well I like to hear the call of "Help" and see the wounded fall
> Loudly for mercy praying,
> And see the dead, both great and small,
> Pierced by sharp spearheads one and all.[5]

The men of war were the lords and vassals of medieval society.

The lords were the kings, dukes, counts, barons, and viscounts (and even bishops and archbishops) who had extensive landholdings and wielded considerable political influence. They formed an **aristocracy** or nobility of people who held real political, economic, and social power. Both the great lords and ordinary knights were warriors, and the institution of knighthood united them. But there were also social divisions among them based on extremes of wealth and landholdings.

In the eleventh and twelfth centuries, under the influence of the church, an ideal of civilized behavior called **chivalry** (SHIV-uhl-ree) gradually evolved among the nobility. Chivalry represented a code of ethics that knights were supposed to uphold. In addition to defending the church and the defenseless, knights were expected to treat captives as honored guests instead of throwing them in dungeons. Chivalry also implied that knights should fight only for glory, but the ideals of chivalry were not always taken seriously.

Although aristocratic women could legally hold property, most women remained under the control of men— their fathers until they married and their husbands after that. Nevertheless, these women had many opportunities for playing important roles. Because the lord was often away at war or at court, the lady of the castle had to manage the estate. Households could include large numbers of officials and servants, so this was no small responsibility. Maintaining the financial accounts alone took considerable financial knowledge. The lady of the castle was also responsible for overseeing the food supply and maintaining all the other supplies needed for the smooth operation of the household.

Although women were expected to be subservient to their husbands, there were many strong women who advised and sometimes even dominated their husbands. Perhaps the most famous was Eleanor of Aquitaine (c. 1122–1204). Married to King Louis VII of France, Eleanor accompanied her husband on a crusade, but her alleged affair with her uncle during the crusade led Louis to have their marriage annulled. Eleanor then married Henry, duke of Normandy and count of Anjou (AHN-zhoo), who became King Henry II of England (1154–1189). She took an active role in politics, even assisting her sons in rebelling against Henry in 1173 and 1174 (see the Film & History feature *The Lion in Winter* (1968) on p. 335).

The New World of Trade and Cities

Medieval Europe was overwhelmingly agrarian, with most people living in small villages. In the eleventh and twelfth centuries, however, new elements were introduced that began to transform the economic foundation of European civilization: a revival of trade, the emergence of specialized craftspeople and artisans, and the growth and development of towns.

THE REVIVAL OF TRADE The revival of trade was a gradual process. During the chaotic conditions of the Early Middle Ages, large-scale trade had declined in western Europe except for Byzantine contacts with Italy and the Jewish traders who moved back and forth between the Muslim and Christian worlds. By the end of the tenth century, however, people were emerging in Europe with both the skills and the products for commercial activity. Cities in Italy took the lead in this revival of trade. Venice, for example, emerged as a town by the end of the eighth century, developed a mercantile fleet, and by the end of the tenth century had become the chief western trading center for Byzantine and Islamic commerce.

Flanders as a Trade Center

While the northern Italian cities were busy trading in the Mediterranean, the towns of Flanders were doing likewise in northern Europe. Flanders, the area along the coast of present-day Belgium and northern France, was known for its high-quality woolen cloth. The location of Flanders made it an ideal center for the traders of northern Europe. Merchants from England, Scandinavia, France, and Germany converged there to trade their goods for woolen cloth. Flanders prospered in the eleventh and twelfth centuries, and such Flemish towns as Bruges (BROOZH) and Ghent (GENT) became centers of the medieval cloth trade.

By the twelfth century, a regular exchange of goods had developed between Flanders and Italy, the two major centers of northern and southern European trade. To encourage this trade, the counts of Champagne in northern France began to hold a series of six fairs annually in the chief towns of their territory. At these fairs, northern merchants brought the furs, woolen cloth, tin, and honey of northern Europe and exchanged them for the cloth and swords of northern Italy and the silks, sugar, and spices of the East (see Opposing Viewpoints "Two Views of Trade and Merchants" on p. 336).

As trade increased, both gold and silver came to be in demand at fairs and trading markets of all kinds. Slowly, a money economy began to emerge. New trading companies and banking firms were set up to manage the exchange and sale of goods. New techniques, including double-entry bookkeeping, commercial contracts, and insurance, also appeared

The Lion in Winter (1968)

Directed by Anthony Harvey, *The Lion in Winter* is based on a play by James Goldman, who also wrote the script for the movie and won an Oscar for best adapted screenplay for it. The action takes place in a castle in Chinon, France, over the Christmas holidays in 1183. The setting is realistic: medieval castles had dirt floors covered with rushes, under which lay, according to one observer, "an ancient collection of grease, fragments, bones, excrement of dogs and cats, and everything that is nasty." The powerful but world-weary King Henry II (Peter O'Toole), ruler of England and a number of French lands (the "Angevin Empire"), wants to establish his legacy and plans a Christmas gathering to decide which of his sons should succeed him. He favors his overindulged youngest son John (Nigel Terry), but he is opposed by his strong-willed and estranged wife, Eleanor of Aquitaine (Katharine Hepburn). She has been imprisoned by the king for leading a rebellion against him but has been temporarily freed for the holidays. Eleanor favors their son Richard (Anthony Hopkins), the most military minded of the brothers. The middle brother, Geoffrey (John Castle), is not a candidate but manipulates the other brothers to gain his own advantage. All three sons are portrayed as treacherous and traitorous, and Henry is distrustful of them. At one point, he threatens to imprison and even kill his sons; marry his mistress Alais (Jane Merrow), who is also the sister of the king of France; and have a new family to replace them.

In contemporary terms, Henry and Eleanor are an unhappily married couple, and their family is acutely dysfunctional. Sparks fly as family members plot against each other, using intentionally cruel comments and sarcastic responses to wound each other as much as possible. When Eleanor says to Henry, "What would you have me do? Give up? Give in?" he responds, "Give me a little peace." To which Eleanor replies, "A little? Why so modest? How about eternal peace? Now there's a thought." At one point, John responds to bad news about his chances for the throne with "Poor John. Who says poor John? Don't everybody sob at once. My God, if I went up in flames, there's not a living soul who'd pee on me to put the fire out!" His brother Richard replies, "Let's strike a flint and see." Henry can also be cruel to his sons: "You're not mine! We're not connected! I deny

Eleanor of Aquitaine (Katharine Hepburn) and Henry II (Peter O'Toole) at dinner in Henry's castle in Chinon, France.

you! None of you will get my crown. I leave you nothing, and I wish you plague!"

In developing this well-written, imaginative re-creation of a royal family's hapless Christmas gathering, James Goldman had a great deal of material to use. Henry II was one of the most powerful monarchs of his day, and Eleanor of Aquitaine was one of the most powerful women. She had first been queen of France, but that marriage was annulled. Next she married Henry, who was then count of Anjou, and became queen of England when he became king in 1154. During their stormy marriage, Eleanor and Henry had five sons and three daughters. She is supposed to have murdered Rosamond, one of her husband's mistresses, and aided her sons in a rebellion against their father in 1173, causing Henry to distrust his sons ever after. But Henry struck back, imprisoning Eleanor for sixteen years. After his death, however, Eleanor returned to Aquitaine and lived on to play an influential role in the reigns of her two sons, Richard and John, who succeeded their father.

---

to facilitate the expansion of businesses. All of these new practices were part of a commercial revolution based on the growth of **capitalism**, an economic system in which commerce and industry are controlled by private owners who invest in trade and goods in order to make profits.

TRADE OUTSIDE EUROPE In the High Middle Ages, Italian merchants became even more daring in their trade activities.

They established trading posts in Cairo, Damascus, and a number of Black Sea ports, where they acquired spices, silks, jewelry, dyestuffs, and other goods brought by Muslim merchants from India, China, and Southeast Asia.

The spread of the Mongol Empire in the thirteenth century (see Chapter 10) also opened the door to Italian merchants in the markets of Central Asia, India, and China. As nomads who relied on trade with settled communities, the

Two Views of Trade and Merchants

INTERACTION & EXCHANGE

THE REVIVAL OF TRADE IN EUROPE WAS A GRADUAL PROCESS, but by the High Middle Ages, it had begun to expand dramatically. During the medieval period, trade already flourished in other parts of the world, especially in the Islamic world and in China. Nevertheless, many people in these societies, including rulers, nobles, and religious leaders, had some reservations about the success of merchants. The first selection is taken from an account of the life of Godric, a twelfth-century European merchant who became a saint. The second selection is from the *Prolegomena*, the first part of a universal history written by Ibn Khaldun, a Muslim historian who traveled widely in the Muslim world in the four-teenth century.

Life of Saint Godric

At first, he lived as a peddler for four years in Lincolnshire, going on foot and carrying the smallest wares; then he traveled abroad, first to St. Andrews in Scotland and then for the first time to Rome. On his return, having formed a familiar friend-ship with certain other young men who were eager for mer-chandise, he began to launch upon bolder courses, and to coast frequently by sea to the foreign lands that lay around him. Thus, sailing often to and fro between Scotland and Britain, he traded in many divers wares and, amid these occu-pations, learned much worldly wisdom....

Thus aspiring ever higher and higher, and yearning upward with his whole heart, at length his great labors and cares bore much fruit of worldly gain. For he labored not only as a mer-chant but also as a shipman ... to Denmark and to Flanders and Scotland; in all which lands he found certain rare, and therefore more precious, wares, which he carried to other parts wherein he knew them to be least familiar, and coveted by the inhabi-tants beyond the price of gold itself; wherefore he exchanged these wares for others coveted by men of other lands; and thus he chaffered [traded] most freely and assiduously. Hence he made great profit in all his bargains, and gathered much wealth in the sweat of his brow; for he sold dear in one place the wares which he had bought elsewhere at a small price.

And now he had lived sixteen years as a merchant, and began to think of spending on charity, to God's honor and service, the goods which he had so laboriously acquired. He therefore took the cross as a pilgrim to Jerusalem.... [When he had returned to England] Godric, that he might follow Christ the more freely, sold all his possessions and distributed them among the poor [and began to live the life of a hermit].

Ibn Khaldun, *Prolegomena*

As for trade, although it be a natural means of livelihood, yet most of the methods it employs are tricks aimed at mak-ing a profit by securing the difference between the buying and selling prices, and by appropriating the surplus. This is why [religious] Law allows the use of such methods, which, although they come under the heading of gambling, yet do not constitute the taking without return of other people's goods....

Should their standard of living, however, rise, so that they begin to enjoy more than the bare necessities, the effect will be to breed in them a desire for repose and tranquility. They will therefore cooperate to secure superfluities; their food and clothing will increase in quantity and refinement; they will enlarge their houses and plan their towns for defense. A fur-ther improvement in their conditions will lead to habits of luxury, resulting in extreme refinement in cooking and the preparation of food; in choosing rich clothing of the finest silk; in raising lofty mansions and castles and furnishing them luxu-riously, and so on. At this stage the crafts develop and reach their height. Lofty castles and mansions are built and deco-rated sumptuously, water is drawn to them and a great diver-sity takes place in the way of dress, furniture, vessels, and household equipment. Such are the townsmen, who earn their living in industry or trade.

What did the biographer of Godric and Ibn Khaldun see as valuable in mercantile activity? What reservations did they have about trade? How are the two perspectives alike? How are they different, and how do you explain the differences? What generalizations can you make about Christian and Muslim attitudes toward trade?

Sources: Life of Saint Godric from Reginald of Durham, "Life of St. Godric," in G. G. Coulton, ed., *Social Life in Britain from the Conquest to the Reformation* (Cambridge: Cambridge University Press, 1918), pp. 415–420. From *An Arab Philosophy of History*, ed. and trans. by Charles Issawi. New York: Darwin Press, 1987.

Mongols maintained safe trade routes for merchants moving through their lands. Two Venetian merchants, the brothers Niccolò and Maffeo Polo, began to travel in the Mongol Empire around 1260.

The creation of the crusader states in Syria and Palestine in the twelfth and thirteenth centuries (discussed later in this chapter) was especially favorable to Italian merchants. In return for taking the crusaders to the east, Italian merchant fleets received trading concessions in Syria and Palestine. Venice, for example, which profited the most from this trade, was given a quarter, soon known as "a little Venice in the east," in Tyre on the coast of what is now Lebanon. Such quarters here and in other cities soon became bases for carrying on lucrative trade.

THE GROWTH OF CITIES The revival of trade led to a revival of cities. Towns had greatly declined in the Early Middle Ages, especially in Europe north of the Alps. Old Roman cities continued to exist but had dwindled in size and population. With the revival of trade, merchants began to settle in these old cities, followed by craftspeople or artisans, people who on manors or elsewhere had developed skills and now saw an opportunity to ply their trade and make goods that could be sold by the merchants. In the course of the eleventh and twelfth centuries, the old Roman cities came alive with new populations and growth.

Beginning in the late tenth century, many new cities or towns were also founded, particularly in northern Europe. Usually, a group of merchants established a settlement near some fortified stronghold, such as a castle or monastery. (This explains why so many place names in Europe end in *borough, burgh, burg*, or *bourg*, all of which mean "fortress" or "walled enclosure.") Castles were particularly favored because they were generally located along trade routes; the lords of the castle also offered protection. If the settlement prospered and expanded, new walls were built to protect it.

Although lords wanted to treat towns and townspeople as they would their vassals and serfs, cities had totally different needs and a different perspective. Townspeople needed mobility to trade. Consequently, these merchants and artisans (who came to be called *burghers* or *bourgeois*, from the same root as *borough* and *burg*) needed their own unique laws to meet their requirements and were willing to pay for them. In many instances, lords and kings saw that they could also make money and were willing to sell to the townspeople the liberties they were beginning to demand, including the right to bequeath goods and sell property, freedom from any military obligation to the lord, and written urban laws that guaranteed their freedom. Some towns also obtained the right to govern themselves by choosing their own officials and administering their own courts of law.

Where townspeople experienced difficulties in obtaining privileges, they often swore an oath, forming an association called a **commune**, and resorted to force against their lay or ecclesiastical lords. Communes made their first appearance in northern Italy, in towns that were governed by their bishops, whom the emperors used as their chief administrators. In the eleventh century, city residents swore communal associations with the bishops' noble vassals and overthrew the authority of the bishops by force. Communes took over the rights of government and created new offices for self-rule. Although communes were also sworn in northern Europe, townspeople did not have the support of rural nobles, and revolts against lay lords were usually suppressed. When they succeeded, communes received the right to choose their own officials and run their own cities. Unlike the towns in Italy, however,

where the decline of the emperor's authority ensured that the northern Italian cities could function as self-governing republics, towns in France and England, like their counterparts in the Islamic and Chinese empires, did not become independent city-states but remained ultimately subject to royal authority.

Medieval cities in Europe, then, possessed varying degrees of self-government, depending on the amount of control retained over them by the lord or king in whose territory they were located. Nevertheless, all towns, regardless of the degree of outside control, evolved institutions of government for running the affairs of the community. Only males who were born in the city or had lived there for a specific length of time could be citizens. In many cities, these citizens elected members of a city council who served as judges and city officials and passed laws.

Medieval cities remained relatively small in comparison with either ancient or modern cities (see the Comparative Essay "Cities in the Medieval World" on p. 338). A large trading city might have about 5,000 inhabitants. By 1200, London was the largest city in England with 30,000 people. On the Continent north of the Alps, only a few urban centers of commerce, such as Bruges and Ghent, had populations close to 40,000. Italian cities tended to be larger, with Venice, Florence, Genoa, Milan, and Naples numbering almost 100,000. Even the largest European city, however, seemed small beside the Byzantine capital of Constantinople or the Arab cities of Damascus, Baghdad, and Cairo.

DAILY LIFE IN THE MEDIEVAL CITY Medieval towns were surrounded by stone walls that were expensive to build, so the space within was precious. Consequently, most medieval cities featured narrow, winding streets with houses crowded against each other and second and third stories extending out over the streets. Because dwellings were built mostly of wood before the fourteenth century and candles and wood fires were used for light and heat, fire was a constant threat. Medieval cities burned rapidly once a fire started.

Most of the people who lived in cities were merchants involved in trade and artisans engaged in manufacturing a wide range of products, such as cloth, metalwork, shoes, and leather goods. Generally, merchants and artisans had their own sections within a city. The merchant area included warehouses, inns, and taverns. Artisan sections were usually divided along craft lines. From the twelfth century on, craftspeople began to organize themselves into **guilds**, and by the thirteenth century, there were individual guilds for virtually every craft. Each craft had its own street where its activity was pursued.

The physical environment of medieval cities was not pleasant. They were dirty and smelled of animal and human wastes deposited in backyard privies or on the streets (see the box "Pollution in a Medieval City" on p. 339). The rivers near most cities were polluted with wastes, especially from the tanning and butchering industries. Because of the pollution, cities did not use the rivers for drinking water but relied instead on wells.

Private and public baths also existed in medieval towns. Paris, for example, had thirty-two public baths for men and women. City laws did not allow lepers and people with "bad reputations" to use them. This did not, however, prevent

Cities in the Medieval World

INTERACTION & EXCHANGE

The exchange of goods between societies was a feature of both the ancient and medieval worlds. Trade routes crisscrossed the lands of the medieval world, and with increased trade came the growth of cities. In Europe, towns had dwindled after the collapse of the Western Roman Empire, but with the revival of trade in the eleventh and twelfth centuries, the cities came back to life. This revival occurred first in the old Roman cities, but soon new cities arose as merchants and artisans sought additional centers for their activities. As cities grew, so did the number of fortified houses, town halls, and churches whose towers punctuated the urban European skyline. Nevertheless, in the Middle Ages, cities in western Europe, especially north of the Alps, remained relatively small. Even the larger cities of Italy, with populations of 100,000, seemed insignificant in comparison with Constantinople and the great cities of the Middle East and China.

With a population of possibly 300,000 people, Constantinople, the capital city of the Byzantine Empire (see Chapter 13), was the largest city in Europe in the Early and High Middle Ages, and until the twelfth century, it was Europe's greatest commercial center, important for the exchange of goods between West and East. In addition to palaces, cathedrals, and monastic buildings, Constantinople also had numerous gardens and orchards that occupied large areas inside its fortified walls. Despite the extensive open and cultivated spaces, the city was not self-sufficient and relied on imports of food under close government direction.

As trade flourished in the Islamic world, cities prospered. When the Abbasids were in power, Baghdad, with a population close to 700,000, was probably the largest city in the empire and one of the greatest cities in the world. After the rise of the Fatimids in Egypt, however, the focus of trade shifted to Cairo. Islamic cities had a distinctive physical appearance. Usually, the most impressive urban buildings were the palaces for the caliphs or the local governors and the great mosques for worship. There were also public buildings with fountains and secluded courtyards, public baths, and bazaars. The bazaar, a covered market, was a crucial part of every Muslim settlement and an important trading center where goods from throughout the known world were available. Food prepared for sale at the market was carefully supervised. A rule in one Muslim city stated, "Grilled meats should only be made with fresh meat and not with meat coming from a sick animal and bought for its cheapness." The merchants were among the greatest beneficiaries of the growth of cities in the Islamic world.

During the medieval period, cities in China were the largest in the world. The southern port of Hangzhou had

Robana/British Library Board/Art Resource, NY

Crime and Punishment in the Medieval City. Violence was a common feature of medieval life. Criminals, if apprehended, were punished quickly and severely, and public executions, like the one seen here, were considered a deterrent to crime.

at least a million residents by 1000, and a number of other cities, including Chang'an and Kaifeng, may also have reached that size. Chinese cities were known for their broad canals and wide, tree-lined streets. They were no longer administrative centers dominated by officials and their families but now included a broader mix of officials, merchants, artisans, and entertainers. The prosperity of Chinese cities was well known. Marco Polo, in describing Hangzhou to unbelieving Europeans in the late thirteenth century, said, "So many pleasures can be found that one fancies himself to be in Paradise."

 Based on a comparison of these medieval cities, which of these civilizations do you think was the most advanced? Why?

Pollution in a Medieval City

EARTH & ENVIRONMENT

ENVIRONMENTAL POLLUTION IS NOT NEW. Medieval cities and towns had their own problems with filthy living conditions. This excerpt is taken from an order sent by the king of England to the town of Boutham, a suburb of York, which was then being used by the king as his headquarters in a war with the Scots. It demands rectification of the town's pitiful physical conditions.

The King's Command to Boutham

To the bailiffs of the abbot of St. Mary's, York, at Boutham. Whereas it is sufficiently evident that the pavement of the said town of Boutham is so very greatly broke up that all and singular passing and going through that town sustain immoderate damages and grievances, and in addition the air is so corrupted and infected by the pigsties situated in the king's highways and in the lanes of that town and by the swine feeding and frequently wandering about in the streets and lanes and by dung and dunghills and many other foul things placed in the streets and lanes, that great repugnance overtakes the king's ministers staying in that town and also others there dwelling and passing through; the advantage of more wholesome air is impeded; the state of men is grievously injured, and other unbearable inconveniences and many other injuries are known to proceed from such corruption, to the nuisance of the king's ministers aforesaid and of others there dwelling and passing through, and to the peril of their lives.... The king, being unwilling longer to tolerate such great and unbearable defects there, orders the bailiffs to cause the pavement to be suitably repaired within their liberty before All Saints next, and to cause the pigsties, aforesaid streets and lanes to be cleansed from all dung and dunghills, and to cause proclamation to be made throughout their bailiwick forbidding any one, under pain of grievous forfeiture, to cause or permit their swine to feed or wander outside his house in the king's streets or the lanes aforesaid.

 What does the king's command to Boutham illustrate about the physical environment of medieval cities? What factors or human habits contributed to the degradation of the medieval urban environment?

Source: From *English Historical Documents III*, H. Rothwell, ed. (London: Methuen, 1975).

Snark/Art Resource, NY

Shops in a Medieval Town. Most urban residents were merchants involved in trade and artisans who manufactured a wide variety of products. Master craftsmen had their workshops in the ground-level rooms of their homes. In this illustration, two well-dressed burghers are touring the shopping district of a French town. Tailors, furriers, a barber, and a grocer (from left to right) are visible at work in their shops.

public baths from being known for permissiveness due to public nudity. One contemporary commented on what occurred in public bathhouses: "Shameful things. Men make a point of staying all night in the public baths and women at the break of day come in and through 'ignorance' find themselves in the men's rooms."[6]

In medieval cities, women, in addition to supervising the household, purchasing food and preparing meals, raising the children, and managing the family finances, were also often expected to help their husbands in their trades. Some women also developed their own trades, such as brewing ale or making glass, to earn extra money. When some master craftspeople died, their widows even carried on their trades. Some women in medieval towns were thus able to lead lives of considerable independence and made important contributions to the market economy. Nevertheless, women often made less than men and faced obstacles that kept them from more rewarding opportunities. For example, women in textile production usually were given the most menial jobs. Many were forced to become domestic servants and given room and board in return for cooking, cleaning, and other domestic services.

Evolution of the European Kingdoms

The recovery and growth of European civilization in the High Middle Ages also affected the state. Although lords and vassals seemed forever mired in endless petty conflicts, some medieval kings inaugurated the process of developing new kinds of monarchical states that were based on the centralization of power rather than the decentralized political order that was characteristic of fief-holding. By the thirteenth century, European monarchs were solidifying their governmental institutions in pursuit of greater power.

ENGLAND IN THE HIGH MIDDLE AGES In late September 1066, an army of heavily armed knights under William of Normandy landed on the coast of England, and a few weeks later, on October 14, they soundly defeated King Harold and his Anglo-Saxon foot soldiers in the Battle of Hastings. William (1066–1087) was crowned king of England at Christmastime in London and promptly began a process of combining Anglo-Saxon and Norman institutions that would change England forever. Many of the Norman knights were given parcels of land that they held as fiefs from the new English king. William made all nobles swear an oath of loyalty to him as sole ruler of England and insisted that all people owed loyalty to the king. The Normans also took over existing Anglo-Saxon institutions, such as the office of sheriff. William took a census and more fully developed the system of taxation and royal courts begun by the Anglo-Saxon kings of the tenth and eleventh centuries. All in all, William of Normandy established a strong, centralized monarchy.

The Norman Conquest had numerous repercussions. Because the new king of England was still the duke of Normandy, he was both a king (of England) and at the same time a vassal to a king (of France), but a vassal who was now far more powerful than his lord. This connection with France kept England heavily involved in European affairs throughout the High Middle Ages.

The Norman Conquest of England. The Bayeux (bah-YUH *or* bah-YUR) tapestry, a magnificent wall hanging of woolen embroidery on a linen backing, was made by English needlewomen before 1082 for Bayeux Cathedral. It depicts scenes from the Norman invasion of England. The first segment (left) shows the Norman fleet beginning its journey to England. The second segment (below) shows the Norman cavalry charging the shield wall of the Saxon infantry during the Battle of Hastings.

In the twelfth century, the power of the English monarchy was greatly enlarged during the reign of Henry II (1154–1189; see the Film & History feature *The Lion in Winter* (1968)" on p. 335). The new king was particularly successful in strengthening the power of the royal courts. Henry expanded the number of criminal cases to be tried in the king's court and also devised means for taking property cases from local courts to the royal courts. Henry's goals were clear: expanding the power of the royal courts increased the king's power and, of course, brought revenues into his coffers. Moreover, since the royal courts were now found throughout England, a body of **common law** (law that was common to the whole kingdom) began to replace the different law codes that often varied from place to place.

Henry was less successful at imposing royal control over the church and became involved in a famous struggle between church and state. Henry claimed the right to punish clergymen in the royal courts, but Thomas à Becket, as archbishop of Canterbury, the highest-ranking English cleric, claimed that only church courts could try clerics. Attempts at compromise failed, and the angry king publicly expressed the desire to be rid of Becket: "Who will free me of this priest?" he screamed. Four knights took the challenge, went to Canterbury, and murdered the archbishop in the cathedral. Faced with public outrage, Henry was forced to allow the right of appeal from English church courts to the papal court.

Many English nobles came to resent the growth of the king's power and rose in rebellion during the reign of King John (1199–1216). At Runnymede in 1215, John was forced to accept Magna Carta (Great Charter) guaranteeing feudal liberties. Feudal custom had always recognized that the relationship between king and vassals was based on mutual rights and obligations. Magna Carta gave written recognition to that fact and was used in later years to support the idea that a monarch's power was limited.

During the reign of Edward I (1272–1307), an institution of great importance in the development of representative government—the English Parliament—emerged. Originally, the word *parliament* was applied to meetings of the king's Great Council, in which the greater barons and chief prelates of the church met with the king's judges and principal advisers to deal with judicial affairs. But needing money, in 1295 Edward invited two knights from every county and two residents from each town to meet with the Great Council to consent to new taxes. This was the first Parliament.

Thus, the English Parliament came to be composed of two knights from every county and two burgesses from every borough as well as the barons and ecclesiastical lords. Eventually, the barons and church lords formed the House of Lords; the knights and burgesses, the House of Commons. The Parliaments of Edward I approved taxes, discussed politics, passed laws, and handled judicial business. The law of the realm was beginning to be determined not by the king alone but by the king in consultation with representatives of various groups that constituted the community.

GROWTH OF THE FRENCH KINGDOM The Carolingian Empire had been divided into three major sections in 843. The western Frankish lands formed the core of the eventual kingdom of France. In 987, after the death of the last Carolingian king, the western Frankish nobles chose Hugh Capet (YOO ka-PAY) as the new king, thus establishing the Capetian (kuh-PEE-shun) dynasty of French kings. Although they carried the title of kings, the Capetians had little real power. They controlled as the royal domain only the lands around Paris known as the Île-de-France (EEL-duh-fronhss). As kings of France, the Capetians were formally the overlords of the great lords of France, such as the dukes of Normandy, Brittany, Burgundy, and Aquitaine. In reality, however, many of the dukes were considerably more powerful than the Capetian kings. All in all, it would take the Capetian dynasty hundreds of years to create a truly centralized monarchical authority in France.

The reign of King Philip II Augustus (1180–1223) was an important turning point in the growth of the French monarchy. Philip II waged war against the Plantagenet (plan-TAJ-uh-net) rulers of England, who also ruled the French territories of Normandy, Maine, Anjou, and Aquitaine, and was successful in gaining control of most of these territories, thereby enlarging the power of the French monarchy (see Map 12.3). To administer justice and collect royal revenues in his new territories, Philip appointed new royal officials, thus inaugurating a French royal bureaucracy in the thirteenth century.

Capetian rulers after Philip II continued to add lands to the royal domain. Philip IV the Fair (1285–1314) was especially effective in strengthening the French monarchy. He reinforced the royal bureaucracy and also brought a French parliament into being by asking representatives of the three estates, or classes—the clergy (First Estate), the nobles (Second Estate), and the townspeople (Third Estate)—to meet with him. They did so in 1302, inaugurating the Estates-General, the first French parliament, although it had little real power. By the end of the thirteenth century, France was the largest, wealthiest, and best-governed monarchical state in Europe.

CHRISTIAN RECONQUEST: THE IBERIAN KINGDOMS Much of Spain had been part of the Islamic world since the eighth century. From the tenth century, however, the most noticeable feature of Spanish history was the weakening of Muslim power and the beginning of a Christian reconquest that lasted until the final expulsion of the Muslims at the end of the fifteenth century.

A number of small Christian kingdoms were established in northern Spain in the eleventh century, and within a hundred years, they had been consolidated into the Christian kingdoms of Castile (ka-STEEL), Navarre, Aragon, and Portugal, which first emerged as a separate kingdom in 1139. The southern half of Spain still remained under the control of the Muslims.

But in the thirteenth century, Aragon, Castile, and Portugal made significant conquests of Muslim territory. The Muslims remained ensconced only in the kingdom of Granada in the southeast of the Iberian peninsula, which remained an independent Muslim state until its final conquest by the forces of Ferdinand and Isabella of Aragon and Castile in 1492.

The Spanish kingdoms followed no consistent policy in their treatment of the conquered Muslim population. In Aragon, Muslim farmers continued to work the land but were

MAP 12.3 **Europe in the High Middle Ages.** Although the nobility dominated much of European society in the High Middle Ages, kings began the process of extending their power in more effective ways, creating the monarchies that would form the European states.

Q *Which were the strongest monarchical states by 1300? Why?*

forced to pay very high rents. In Castile, King Alfonso X (1252–1284), who called himself the "King of Three Religions," encouraged the continued development of a cosmopolitan culture shared by Christians, Jews, and Muslims.

THE LANDS OF THE HOLY ROMAN EMPIRE In the tenth century, the powerful dukes of the Saxons became kings of the eastern Frankish kingdom (or Germany, as it came to be called). The best known of the Saxon kings of Germany was Otto I (936–973), who intervened in Italian politics and for his efforts was crowned emperor of the Romans by the pope in 962, reviving a title that had not been used since the time of Charlemagne.

In the eleventh century, German kings created a strong monarchy and a powerful empire by leading armies into Italy. To strengthen their grip, they relied on their ability to control the church and select bishops, whom they could then use as royal administrators. But the struggle between church and state during the reign of Henry IV (1056–1106) weakened the king's ability to use church officials in this way (see "Reform of the

Papacy" later in this chapter). The German kings also tried to bolster their power by using their position as emperors to exploit the resources of Italy. But this strategy tended to backfire; many a German king lost armies in Italy in pursuit of a dream of empire, and no German dynasty demonstrates this better than the Hohenstaufens (hoh-en-SHTOW-fens).

The two most famous members of the Hohenstaufen dynasty, Frederick I Barbarossa (bar-buh-ROH-suh) (1152–1190) and Frederick II (1212–1250), tried to create a new kind of empire. Previous German kings had focused on building a strong German kingdom, but Frederick I planned to get his chief revenues from Italy as the center of a "holy empire," as he called it (hence the name *Holy Roman Empire*). But his attempt to conquer northern Italy ran into severe problems. The pope opposed him, fearful that the emperor wanted to absorb Rome and the Papal States into his empire. The cities of northern Italy, which had become used to their freedom, were also unwilling to be Frederick's subjects. An alliance of these northern Italian cities, with the support of the pope, defeated the emperor's forces in 1176.

The main goal of Frederick II was the establishment of a strong centralized state in Italy dominated by the kingdom in Sicily, which he had inherited from his mother. Frederick's major task was to gain control of northern Italy. In the attempt, however, he became involved in a deadly conflict with the popes, who feared that a single ruler of northern and southern Italy would mean the end of papal power in the center of the peninsula. Furthermore, the northern Italian cities were unwilling to give up their freedom. Frederick nevertheless waged a long and bitter struggle, winning many battles but ultimately losing the war.

The struggle between popes and emperors had dire consequences for the Holy Roman Empire. By spending their time fighting in Italy, the German emperors left Germany in the hands of powerful German lords who ignored the emperor and created their own independent kingdoms. This ensured that the German monarchy would remain weak and incapable of establishing a centralized monarchical state; thus, the German Holy Roman Emperor had no real power over either Germany or Italy. Unlike France and England, neither Germany nor Italy had a centralized national monarchy in the Middle Ages. Both of these regions consisted of many small, independent states, a situation that changed little until the nineteenth century.

THE SLAVIC PEOPLES OF CENTRAL AND EASTERN EUROPE The Slavs were originally a single people in central Europe, but they gradually divided into three major groups: western, southern, and eastern (see Map 12.4). The western Slavs eventually formed the Polish and Bohemian kingdoms. German Christian missionaries converted both the Czechs in Bohemia and the Slavs in Poland by the tenth century. German Christians also converted the non-Slavic kingdom of Hungary, which emerged after the Magyars settled down after their defeat in 955. The Poles, Czechs, and Hungarians all accepted Catholic or western Christianity and became closely tied to the Roman Catholic Church and its Latin culture.

The southern and eastern Slavic populations took a different path: the Slavic peoples of Moravia were converted to the Orthodox Christianity of the Byzantine Empire (see Chapter 13) by two Byzantine missionary brothers, Cyril and Methodius, who began their activities in 863. The southern Slavic peoples included the Croats, Serbs, and Bulgarians. For the most part, they too embraced Eastern Orthodoxy, although the Croats came

to accept the Roman Catholic faith. The adoption of Eastern Orthodoxy by the Serbs and Bulgarians tied their cultural life to the Byzantine state.

The eastern Slavic peoples, from whom the modern Russians and Ukrainians are descended, had settled in the territory of present-day Ukraine and European Russia. There, beginning in the late eighth century, they began to encounter Swedish Vikings who moved down the extensive network of rivers into the lands of the eastern Slavs in search of booty and new trade routes (see the box "A Muslim's Description of the Rus" on p. 344). These Vikings built trading settlements and eventually came to dominate the native peoples, who called them "the Rus" (ROOSS *or* ROOSH), from which the name Russia is derived.

THE DEVELOPMENT OF RUSSIA: IMPACT OF THE MONGOLS A Viking leader named Oleg (c. 873–913) settled in Kiev (KEE-yev) at the beginning of the tenth century and founded the Rus state known as the principality of Kiev. His successors extended their control over the eastern Slavs and expanded the territory of Kiev until it included the area between the Baltic and Black Seas and the Danube and Volga Rivers. By marrying Slavic wives, the Viking ruling class was gradually assimilated into the Slavic population.

MAP 12.4 The Migrations of the Slavs. Originally from east-central Europe, the Slavic people broke into three groups. The western Slavs converted to Catholic Christianity, while most of the eastern and southern Slavs, under the influence of the Byzantine Empire, embraced the Eastern Orthodox faith.

Q *What connections do these Slavic migrations have with what we today characterize as eastern Europe?*

A Muslim's Description of the Rus

FAMILY & SOCIETY

Despite the difficulties that travel presented, early medieval civilization did witness some contact among the various cultures. This might occur through trade, diplomacy, or the conquest and migration of peoples. This document is a description of the Swedish Rus, who eventually merged with the native Slavic peoples to form the principality of Kiev, commonly regarded as the first Russian state. It was written by Ibn Fadlan, a Muslim diplomat sent from Baghdad in 921 to a settlement on the Volga River. His comments on the filthiness of the Rus reflect the Muslim emphasis on cleanliness.

Ibn Fadlan, *The Rus*

I saw the Rus folk when they arrived on their trading mission and settled at the river Atul (Volga). Never had I seen people of more perfect physique. They are tall as date palms, and reddish in color. They wear neither coat nor kaftan, but each man carried a cape which covers one half of his body, leaving one hand free. No one is ever parted from his axe, sword, and knife. Their swords are Frankish in design, broad, flat, and fluted. Each man has a number of trees, figures, and the like from the fingernails to the neck. Each woman carried on her bosom a container made of iron, silver, copper, or gold—its size and substance depending on her man's wealth.

[The Rus] are the filthiest of God's creatures. They do not wash after discharging their natural functions, neither do they wash their hands after meals. They are as lousy as donkeys. They arrive from their distant lands and lay their ships alongside the banks of the Atul, which is a great river, and there they build big houses on its shores. Ten or twenty of them may live together in one house, and each of them has a couch of his own where he sits and diverts himself with the pretty slave girls whom he had brought along for sale. He will make love with one of them while a comrade looks on; sometimes they indulge in a communal orgy, and, if a customer should turn up to buy a girl, the Rus man will not let her go till he has finished with her.

They wash their hands and faces every day in incredibly filthy water. Every morning the girl brings her master a large bowl of water in which he washes his hands and face and hair, then blows his nose into it and spits into it. When he has finished the girl takes the bowl to his neighbor—who repeats the performance. Thus, the bowl goes the rounds of the entire household....

If one of the Rus folk falls sick they put him in a tent by himself and leave bread and water for him. They do not visit him, however, or speak to him, especially if he is a serf. Should he recover he rejoins the others; if he dies they burn him. But if he happens to be a serf they leave him for the dogs and vultures to devour. If they catch a robber they hang him to a tree until he is torn to shreds by wind and weather.

 What was Ibn Fadlan's impression of the Rus? Why do you think he was so critical of their behavior?

Source: From *The Vikings*, by Johannes Bronsted, translated by Kalle Skov (Penguin Books, 1965).

The growth of the principality of Kiev attracted religious missionaries, especially from the Byzantine Empire. One Rus ruler, Vladimir (VLAD-ih-meer) (c. 980–1015), married the Byzantine emperor's sister and in 987 officially accepted Christianity for himself and his people. By the end of the tenth century, Byzantine Christianity had become the model for Russian religious life.

The Kievan Rus state prospered and reached its high point in the first half of the eleventh century. But civil wars and new invasions by Asian nomads caused the principality of Kiev to collapse, and its sack by north Russian princes in 1169 brought an end to the first Russian state, which had remained closely tied to the Byzantine Empire, not to Europe. In the thirteenth century, the Mongols conquered Russia and cut it off even more from Europe.

The Mongols had exploded onto the scene in the thirteenth century, moving east into China and west into the Middle East and central Europe. Although they conquered Russia, they were not numerous enough to settle the vast Russian lands. They occupied only part of Russia but required Russian princes to pay tribute to them. One Russian prince soon emerged as more powerful than the others. Alexander Nevsky (NYEF-skee), prince of Novgorod (NAHV-guh-rahd), defeated a German invading army in northwestern Russia in 1242. His cooperation with the Mongols won him their favor. The khan, leader of the western part of the Mongol Empire, rewarded Alexander Nevsky with the title of grand-prince, enabling his descendants to become the princes of Moscow and eventually leaders of all Russia.

Christianity and Medieval Civilization

Christianity was an integral part of the fabric of European society and the consciousness of Europe. Papal directives affected the actions of kings and princes alike, and Christian teachings and practices touched the lives of all Europeans.

REFORM OF THE PAPACY Since the fifth century, the popes of the Catholic Church had reigned supreme over church affairs. They had also come to exercise control over the territories in central Italy that came to be known as the Papal States, which kept the popes involved in political matters, often at the expense of their spiritual obligations. At the same time, the church became increasingly entangled in the evolving feudal relationships. High officials of the church, such as bishops and abbots, came to hold their offices as fiefs from nobles. As vassals, they were obliged to carry out the usual duties, including military service. Of course, lords assumed the right to choose their vassals and thus came to appoint bishops and abbots. Because lords often chose their vassals from other noble families for political reasons, these bishops and abbots were often worldly figures who cared little about their spiritual responsibilities.

By the eleventh century, church leaders realized the need to free the church from the interference of lords in the appointment of church officials. **Lay investiture** was the practice by which secular rulers both chose nominees to church offices and invested them with (bestowed on them) the symbols of their office. Pope Gregory VII (1073–1085) decided to fight this practice. Gregory claimed that he, as pope, was God's "vicar on earth" and that the pope's authority extended over all of Christendom, including its rulers. In 1075, he issued a decree forbidding high-ranking clerics from receiving their investiture from lay leaders.

Gregory soon found himself in conflict with the German king over his actions. King Henry IV was also a determined man who had appointed high-ranking clerics, especially bishops, as his vassals in order to use them as administrators. Henry had no intention of obeying a decree that challenged the very heart of his administration.

The struggle between Henry IV and Gregory VII, which is known as the Investiture Controversy, was one of the great conflicts between church and state in the High Middle Ages. It dragged on until a new German king and a new pope reached a compromise in 1122 called the Concordat of Worms (kun-KOR-dat of WURMZ *or* VORMPS). Under this agreement, church officials first elected a bishop in Germany. After election, the nominee paid homage to the king as his lord, who then invested him with the symbols of temporal office. A representative of the pope, however, then invested the new bishop with the symbols of his spiritual office.

THE CHURCH SUPREME: THE PAPAL MONARCHY The popes of the twelfth century did not abandon the reform ideals of Pope Gregory VII, but they were more inclined to consolidate their power and build a strong administrative system. During the papacy of Pope Innocent III (1198–1216), the Catholic Church reached the height of its power. At the beginning of his pontificate, in a letter to a priest, the pope made a clear statement of his views on papal supremacy:

> As God, the creator of the universe, set two great lights in the firmament of heaven, the greater light to rule the day, and the lesser light to rule the night, so He set two great dignities in the firmament of the universal church, … the greater to rule the day, that is, souls, and the lesser to rule the night, that is, bodies. These dignities are the papal authority and the royal power. And just as the moon gets her light from the sun, and is inferior to the sun … so the royal power gets the splendor of its dignity from the papal authority.[7]

Innocent III's actions were those of a man who believed that he, as pope, was the supreme judge of European affairs. To achieve his political ends, he did not hesitate to use the spiritual weapons at his command, especially the **interdict**, which forbade priests to dispense the **sacraments** of the church in the hope that the people, deprived of the comforts of religion, would exert pressure against their ruler. Apparently, Pope Innocent's interdicts worked: for example, one of them forced the king of France, Philip Augustus, to take back his wife and queen after Philip had tried to have his marriage annulled.

NEW RELIGIOUS ORDERS AND NEW SPIRITUAL IDEALS Between 1050 and 1150, a wave of religious enthusiasm seized Europe, leading to a spectacular growth in the number of monasteries and the emergence of new monastic orders. Most important was the Cistercian (sis-TUR-shun) order, founded in 1098 by a group of monks dissatisfied with the moral degeneration and lack of strict discipline at their own Benedictine monastery. The Cistercians were strict. They ate a simple diet and possessed only a single robe apiece. More time for prayer and manual labor was provided by shortening the number of hours spent at religious services. The Cistercians played a major role in developing a new, activist spiritual model for twelfth-century Europe. A Benedictine monk often spent hours in prayer to honor God. The Cistercian ideal had a different emphasis: "Arise, soldier of Christ, arise! Get up

A Miracle of Saint Bernard

RELIGION & PHILOSOPHY

SAINT BERNARD OF CLAIRVAUX has been called the most widely respected holy man of the twelfth century. He was an outstanding preacher, wholly dedicated to the service of God. His reputation reportedly influenced many young men to join the Cistercian order. He also inspired myriad stories dealing with his miracles.

A Miracle of Saint Bernard

A certain monk, departing from his monastery ..., threw off his habit, and returned to the world at the persuasion of the Devil. And he took a certain parish living; for he was a priest. Because sin is punished with sin, the deserter from his Order lapsed into the vice of lechery. He took a concubine to live with him, as in fact is done by many, and by her he had children.

But as God is merciful and does not wish anyone to perish, it happened that many years after, the blessed abbot [Saint Bernard] was passing through the village in which this same monk was living, and went to stay at his house. The renegade monk recognized him, and received him very reverently, and waited on him devoutly ... but as yet the abbot did not recognize him.

On the morrow, the holy man said Matins and prepared to be off. But as he could not speak to the priest, since he had got up and gone to the church for Matins, he said to the priest's son, "Go, give this message to your master." Now the boy had been born [mute]. He obeyed the command and feeling in himself the power of him who had given it, he ran to his father and uttered the words of the Holy Father clearly and exactly. His father, on hearing his son's voice for the first time, wept for joy, and made him repeat the same words ... and he asked what the abbot had done to him. "He did nothing to me," said the boy, "except to say, 'Go and say this to your father.'"

At so evident a miracle the priest repented, and hastened after the holy man and fell at his feet saying, "My Lord and Father, I was your monk so-and-so, and at such-and-such a time I ran away from your monastery. I ask your Paternity to allow me to return with you to the monastery, for in your coming God has visited my heart." The saint replied unto him, "Wait for me here, and I will come back quickly when I have done my business, and I will take you with me." But the priest, fearing death (which he had not done before), answered, "Lord, I am afraid of dying before then." But the saint replied, "Know this for certain, that if you die in this condition, and in this resolve, you will find yourself a monk before God."

The saint [eventually] returned and heard that the priest had recently died and been buried. He ordered the tomb to be opened. And when they asked him what he wanted to do, he said, "I want to see if he is lying as a monk or a clerk in his tomb." "As a clerk," they said; "we buried him in his secular habit." But when they had dug up the earth, they found that he was not in the clothes in which they had buried him; but he appeared in all points, tonsure and habit, as a monk. And they all praised God.

What two miracles occur in this tale of Saint Bernard? What does this document reveal about popular religious practices during the Middle Ages?

Source: From *A History of Medieval Europe*, 2e, R. H. C. Davis, Copyright © 1988, pp. 265–266. Reproduced by permission of Taylor & Francis Books UK.

---

off the ground and return to the battle from which you have fled! Fight more boldly after your flight, and triumph in glory!"[8] These were the words of Saint Bernard of Clairvaux (klayr-VOH) (1090–1153), who more than any other person embodied the new spiritual ideal of Cistercian monasticism (see the box "A Miracle of Saint Bernard" above).

Women were also actively involved in the spiritual movements of the age. The number of women joining religious houses grew dramatically in the High Middle Ages. Most nuns were from the ranks of the landed aristocracy. Convents were convenient for families unable or unwilling to find husbands for their daughters and for aristocratic women who did not wish to marry. Female intellectuals found them a haven for their activities. Most of the learned women of the Middle Ages were nuns.

In the thirteenth century, two new religious orders emerged that had a profound impact on the lives of ordinary people. Like their founder, Saint Francis of Assisi (uh-SEE-zee) (1182–1226),

the Franciscans lived among the people, preaching repentance and aiding the poor. Their calls for a return to the simplicity and poverty of the early church, reinforced by their own example, were especially effective and made them very popular.

The Dominican order arose out of the desire of a Spanish priest, Dominic de Guzmán (DAH-muh-nik duh gooz-MAHN) (1170–1221), to defend church teachings from **heresy**—beliefs contrary to official church doctrine. Unlike Francis, Dominic was an intellectual who was appalled by the growth of heresy. He came to believe that a new religious order of men who lived lives of poverty but were learned and capable of preaching effectively would best be able to attack heresy. The Dominicans became especially well known for their roles as the inquisitors of the papal Inquisition.

The Holy Office, as the papal Inquisition was formally called, was a court established by the church to find and try heretics. Anyone accused of heresy who refused to confess

A Group of Nuns. Although still viewed by the medieval church as inferior to men, women were as susceptible to the spiritual fervor of the twelfth century as men, and female monasticism grew accordingly. This manuscript illustration shows at the left a group of nuns welcoming a novice (dressed in white) to their order. At the right, a nun receives a sick person on a stretcher for the order's hospital care.

was considered guilty and was turned over to the state for execution. So were relapsed heretics—those who confessed, did penance, and then reverted to heresy again. Most heretics, however, were put in prison or made to do various forms of penance. To the Christians of the thirteenth century, who believed that there was only one path to salvation, heresy was a crime against God and against humanity. In their minds, force should be used to save souls from damnation.

POPULAR RELIGION IN THE HIGH MIDDLE AGES We have witnessed the actions of popes, bishops, and monks. But what of ordinary clergy and laypeople? What were their religious hopes and fears? What were their spiritual aspirations?

The sacraments of the Catholic Church ensured that the church was an integral part of people's lives, from birth to death. There were (and still are) seven sacraments, administered only by the clergy. Sacraments, such as baptism and the Eucharist (YOO-kuh-rest) (the Lord's Supper), were viewed as outward symbols of an inward grace and were considered imperative for a Christian's salvation. Therefore, the clergy were seen to have a key role in the attainment of salvation.

Other church practices were also important to ordinary people. Saints were seen as men and women who, through their holiness, had achieved a special position in heaven, enabling them to act as intercessors with God. The saints' ability to protect poor souls enabled them to take on great importance at the popular level. Jesus's apostles were, of course, recognized throughout Europe as saints, but there were also numerous local saints who were of special significance to a single area. New cults developed rapidly, especially in the intense religious atmosphere of the eleventh and twelfth centuries. The English, for example, introduced Saint Nicholas,

the patron saint of children, who is known today as Santa Claus.

In the High Middle Ages, the Virgin Mary, the mother of Jesus, occupied the foremost position among the saints. Mary was viewed as the most important mediator with her son, Jesus, the judge of all sinners. Moreover, from the eleventh century on, a fascination with Mary as Jesus's human mother became more evident. A sign of Mary's importance was the growing number of churches all over Europe that were dedicated to her in the twelfth and thirteenth centuries.

Emphasis on the role of the saints was closely tied to the use of relics, which also increased noticeably in the High Middle Ages. Relics were usually the bones of saints or objects intimately connected to saints that were considered worthy of veneration by the faithful. A twelfth-century English monk began his description of the abbey's relics by saying that "there is kept there a thing more precious than gold, … the right arm of St. Oswald…. This we have seen with our own eyes and have kissed, and have handled with our own hands…. There are kept here also part of his ribs and of the soil on which he fell."[9] The monk went on to list additional relics possessed by the abbey, including two pieces of Jesus's swaddling clothes, pieces of Jesus's manger, and part of the five loaves of bread with which Jesus fed five thousand people. Because the holiness of the saint was considered to be inherent in his relics, these objects were believed to be capable of healing people or producing other miracles.

The Culture of the High Middle Ages

The High Middle Ages was a time of extraordinary intellectual and artistic vitality. It witnessed the birth of universities and a building spree that left Europe bedecked with churches and cathedrals.

THE RISE OF UNIVERSITIES The university as we know it—with faculty, students, and degrees—was a product of the High Middle Ages. The word *university* is derived from the Latin word *universitas* (yoo-nee-VAYR-see-tahss), meaning a corporation or guild, and referred to either a corporation of teachers or a corporation of students. Medieval universities were educational guilds or corporations that produced educated and trained individuals.

The first European university appeared in Bologna (boh-LOHN-yuh), Italy, where a great teacher named Irnerius (1088–1125), who taught Roman law, attracted students from all over Europe. Most of them were laymen, usually older individuals who were administrators for kings and princes and were eager

University Students and Violence at Oxford

MEDIEVAL UNIVERSITIES SHARED in the violent atmosphere of their age. Town and gown quarrels often resulted in bloody conflicts, especially during the universities' formative period. This selection is taken from an anonymous description of a student riot at Oxford at the end of the thirteenth century.

A Student Riot at Oxford

They [the townsmen] seized and imprisoned all scholars on whom they could lay hands, invaded their inns [halls of residence], made havoc of their goods and trampled their books under foot. In the face of such provocation the proctors [university officials] sent their assistants about the town, forbidding the students to leave their inns. But all commands and exhortations were in vain. By nine o'clock next morning, bands of scholars were parading the streets in martial array. If the proctors failed to restrain them, the mayor was equally powerless to restrain his townsmen. The great bell of St. Martin's rang out an alarm; oxhorns were sounded in the streets; messengers were sent into the country to collect rustic allies. The clerks [students and teachers], who numbered 3,000 in all, began their attack simultaneously in various quarters. They broke open warehouses in the Spicery, the Cutlery and

elsewhere. Armed with bow and arrows, swords and bucklers, slings and stones, they fell upon their opponents. Three they slew, and wounded fifty or more. One band … took up a position in High Street between the Churches of St. Mary and All Saints', and attacked the house of a certain Edward Hales. This Hales was a longstanding enemy of the clerks. There were no half measures with him. He seized his crossbow, and from an upper chamber sent an unerring shaft into the eye of the pugnacious rector. The death of their valiant leader caused the clerks to lose heart. They fled, closely pursued by the townsmen and country-folk. Some were struck down in the streets, and others who had taken refuge in the churches were dragged out and driven mercilessly to prison, lashed with thongs and goaded with iron spikes.

Complaints of murder, violence and robbery were lodged straightway with the king by both parties. The townsmen claimed 3,000 pounds' damage. The commissioners, however, appointed to decide the matter, condemned them to pay 200 marks, removed the bailiffs, and banished twelve of the most turbulent citizens from Oxford.

 Who do you think was responsible for this conflict between town and gown? Why? Why do you think the king supported the university?

Source: From *The Story of Oxford* by Cecil Headlam, 1907.

---

to learn more about law so that they could apply it in their own jobs. To protect themselves, students at Bologna formed a guild or *universitas*, which was recognized by Emperor Frederick Barbarossa and given a charter in 1158. Kings, popes, and princes soon competed to found new universities, and by the end of the Middle Ages, there were eighty universities in Europe, most of them in England, France, Italy, and Germany (see the box "University Students and Violence at Oxford" above).

University students (all men—women did not attend universities in the Middle Ages) began their studies with the traditional **liberal arts** curriculum, which consisted of grammar, rhetoric, logic, arithmetic, geometry, music, and astronomy. Teaching was done by the lecture method. The word *lecture* is derived from the Latin verb for "read." Before the development of the printing press in the fifteenth century, books were expensive and few students could afford them, so teachers read from a basic text (such as a collection of laws if the subject was law) and then added their explanations. No exams were given after a series of lectures, but when a student applied for a degree, he was given a comprehensive oral examination by a committee of teachers. The exam was taken after a four- or six-year period of study. The first degree a student could earn was a bachelor of arts; later he might receive a master of arts degree.

After completing the liberal arts curriculum, a student could go on to study law, medicine, or theology. This last was the most highly regarded subject at the medieval university. The study of any of these three disciplines could take a decade or more. A student who passed his final oral examinations was granted a doctor's degree, which officially enabled him to teach his subject. Students who received degrees from medieval universities could pursue other careers besides teaching that proved to be much more lucrative. A law degree was necessary for those who wished to serve as advisers to kings and princes. The growing administrative bureaucracies of popes and kings also demanded a supply of clerks with a university education who could keep records and draw up official documents. Universities provided the teachers, administrators, lawyers, and doctors for medieval society.

DEVELOPMENT OF SCHOLASTICISM The importance of Christianity in medieval society made it certain that theology would play a central role in the European intellectual world. Theology, the formal study of religion, was "queen of the sciences" in the new universities.

Beginning in the eleventh century, the effort to apply reason or logical analysis to the church's basic theological doctrines had a significant impact on the study of theology. The philosophical and theological system of the medieval schools is known as **scholasticism** (skoh-LAS-tih-sizm). Scholasticism tried to reconcile faith and reason, to demonstrate that what was accepted on faith was in harmony with what could be learned by reason.

The overriding task of scholasticism was to harmonize Christian teachings with the work of the Greek philosopher Aristotle. In the twelfth century, due largely to the work of Muslim and Jewish scholars in Spain, western Europe was introduced to a large number of Greek scientific and philosophical works, including the works of Aristotle. But Aristotle's works threw many theologians into consternation. Aristotle was so highly regarded that he was called "the philosopher," yet he had arrived at his conclusions by rational thought, not by faith, and some of his doctrines contradicted the teachings of the church. The most famous attempt to reconcile Aristotle and the doctrines of Christianity was that of Saint Thomas Aquinas (uh-KWY-nuss).

Aquinas (1225–1274) is best known for his *Summa Theologica* (SOO-muh tay-oh-LAH-jee-kuh) (*Summa of Theology*—a summa was a compendium of knowledge that attempted to bring together all the received learning of the preceding centuries on a given subject). Aquinas's masterpiece was organized according to the dialectical method of the scholastics. Aquinas first posed a question, cited sources that offered opposing opinions on the question, and then resolved the matter by arriving at his own conclusions. In this fashion, Aquinas raised and discussed some six hundred articles.

Aquinas's reputation derives from his masterful attempt to reconcile faith and reason. He took it for granted that there were truths derived by reason and truths derived by faith. He was certain, however, that the two truths could not be in conflict. The natural mind, unaided by faith, could arrive at truths concerning the physical universe. Without the help of God's grace, however, reason alone could not grasp spiritual truths, such as the Trinity (the manifestation of God in three separate yet identical persons—Father, Son, and Holy Spirit) or the Incarnation (Jesus's simultaneous identity as God and human).

ROMANESQUE ARCHITECTURE   The eleventh and twelfth centuries witnessed an explosion of building, both private and public. The construction of castles and churches absorbed most of the surplus resources of medieval society and at the same time reflected its basic preoccupations, God and warfare. The churches were by far the most conspicuous of the public buildings.

The cathedrals of the eleventh and twelfth centuries were built in the **Romanesque** (roh-man-ESK) style, prominent examples of which can be found in Germany, France, and Spain. Romanesque churches were normally built in the basilica shape used in the construction of churches in the Late Roman Empire. Basilicas were rectangular churches with flat wooden roofs. Romanesque builders made a significant innovation by replacing the flat wooden roof with a long, round stone vault called a barrel vault (or a cross vault where two barrel vaults intersected). Although barrel and cross vaults

Gianni Dagli Orti/The Art Archive at Art Resource, NY

Barrel Vaulting. The eleventh and twelfth centuries witnessed an enormous amount of church construction. Using the basilica shape, master builders replaced flat wooden roofs with long, round stone vaults, known as barrel vaults. As this illustration of a Romanesque church in Vienne, France, indicates, the barrel vault limited the size of a church and left little room in the walls for windows.

were technically difficult to create, they were considered aesthetically more pleasing than flat wooden roofs and were also less apt to catch fire.

Because stone roofs were extremely heavy, Romanesque churches required massive pillars and walls to hold them up. This left little space for windows, and Romanesque churches were correspondingly dark on the inside. Their massive walls and pillars gave Romanesque churches a sense of solidity and almost the impression of a fortress.

THE GOTHIC CATHEDRAL   Begun in the twelfth century and brought to perfection in the thirteenth, the **Gothic** cathedral remains one of the greatest artistic triumphs of the High Middle Ages. Soaring skyward, as if to reach heaven, it was a fitting symbol for medieval people's preoccupation with God.

Two fundamental innovations of the twelfth century made Gothic cathedrals possible. The combination of ribbed vaults and pointed arches replaced the barrel vaults of Romanesque churches and enabled builders to make Gothic churches higher than Romanesque ones. The use of pointed arches and ribbed vaults created an impression of upward movement, a sense of weightless upward thrust that implied the energy of God. Another technical innovation, the flying buttress, a heavy arched pier of stone built onto the outside of the walls,

The Gothic Cathedral. The Gothic cathedral was one of the great artistic triumphs of the High Middle Ages. Shown here is the cathedral of Notre-Dame in Paris. Begun in 1163, it was not completed until the beginning of the fourteenth century.

Chartres Cathedral: Stained-Glass Window. The stained glass of Gothic cathedrals is remarkable for the beauty and variety of its colors. Stained-glass windows depicted a remarkable variety of scenes. The windows of Chartres Cathedral, for example, present the saints, views of the everyday activities of ordinary men and women, and, as in this panel, scenes from the life of Jesus.

made it possible to distribute the weight of the church's vaulted ceilings outward and down and thus eliminate the heavy walls used in Romanesque churches to hold the weight of the massive barrel vaults. Thus, Gothic cathedrals could be built with thin walls containing magnificent stained-glass windows, which created a play of light inside that varied with the sun at different times of the day. The extensive use of colored light in Gothic cathedrals was not accidental but was executed by people who believed that natural light was a symbol of the divine light of God.

The first fully Gothic church was the abbey of Saint-Denis (san-duh-NEE) near Paris, inspired by its famous Abbot Suger (soo-ZHAYR) (1122–1151) and built between 1140 and 1150. By the mid-thirteenth century, French Gothic architecture, most brilliantly executed in cathedrals in Paris (Notre-Dame), Reims, Amiens, and Chartres, had spread to virtually all of Europe.

A Gothic cathedral was the work of the entire community. All classes contributed to its construction. Master masons, who were both architects and engineers, designed them, and stonemasons and other craftspeople were paid a daily wage and provided the skilled labor to build them. A Gothic cathedral symbolized the chief preoccupation of a medieval Christian community, its dedication to a spiritual ideal. As we have observed before, the largest buildings of an era reflect the

values of its society. The Gothic cathedral, with its towers soaring toward heaven, gave witness to an age when a spiritual impulse underlay most aspects of its existence.

Medieval Europe and the World

 FOCUS QUESTIONS: In what ways did Europeans begin to relate to peoples in other parts of the world after 1000 C.E.? What were the reasons for the crusades, and who or what benefited the most from them?

As it developed, European civilization remained largely confined to its home continent, although Europe was never completely isolated. Some Europeans, especially merchants, had contacts with parts of Asia and Africa. The goods of those lands made their way into medieval castles, and the works of Muslim

The First Crusade: The Capture of Jerusalem. Recruited from the noble class of western Europe, the first crusading army had taken Antioch by 1098. Working down the coast of Palestine, the crusaders captured Jerusalem in 1099. Shown here in a fifteenth-century manuscript illustration is a fanciful re-creation of the looting after Jerusalem's capture by the Christian crusaders.

philosophers were read in medieval universities. The Vikings were also daring explorers. After 860, they sailed westward in their long ships across the North Atlantic Ocean, reaching Iceland in 874. Erik the Red, a Viking exiled from Iceland, traveled even farther west and discovered Greenland in 985. Some Vikings even reached North America, landing in Newfoundland, the only known Viking site in North America, but it proved to be short-lived as Viking expansion drew to a close by the tenth century. Only at the end of the eleventh century did Europeans begin their first concerted attempt to expand beyond the frontiers of Europe by conquering the land of Palestine.

The First Crusades

The crusades were based on the idea of a holy war against infidels (unbelievers). Christian wrath against Muslims had already found some expression in the attempt to wrest Spain from the Moors and the success of the Normans in reclaiming Sicily. At the end of the eleventh century, Christian Europe found itself with a glorious opportunity to go after the Muslims when the Byzantine emperor, Alexius I, asked Pope Urban II for help against the Seljuk Turks (see Chapter 13). The pope saw this as a chance to rally the warriors of Europe for the liberation of Jerusalem and the Holy Land of Palestine

from the infidels. The Holy City of Jerusalem had long been the focus of Christian pilgrimages. At the Council of Clermont in southern France toward the end of 1095, Urban challenged Christians to take up their weapons and join in a holy war to recover the Holy Land. The pope promised remission of sins: "All who die by the way, whether by land or by sea, or in battle against the pagans, shall have immediate remission of sins. This I grant them through the power of God with which I am invested."[10] The enthusiastic crowd cried out in response: "It is the will of God, it is the will of God."

The initial response to Urban's speech reveals how appealing many people found this combined call to military arms and religious fervor. A self-appointed leader, Peter the Hermit, who preached of his visions of the Holy City of Jerusalem, convinced a large mob, most of them poor and many of them peasants, to undertake a crusade to liberate the city. One person who encountered Peter described him in these words: "Outdoors he wore a woolen tunic, which revealed his ankles, and above it a hood; he wore a cloak to cover his upper body, a bit of his arms, but his feet were bare. He drank wine and ate fish, but scarcely ever ate bread. This man, partly because of his reputation, partly because of his preaching, [assembled] a very large army."[11]

This "Peasant's Crusade" or "Crusade of the Poor" consisted of a ragtag rabble that moved through the Balkans, terrorizing natives and looting for their food and supplies. Their misplaced religious enthusiasm led to another tragic by-product as well, the persecution of the Jews, long pictured by the church as the murderers of Christ. As a contemporary chronicler described it, "They persecuted the hated race of the Jews wherever they were found." Two bands of peasant crusaders, led by Peter the Hermit, managed to reach Constantinople. The Byzantine emperor wisely shipped them over to Asia Minor, where the Turks massacred the undisciplined and poorly armed mob.

Pope Urban II did not share the wishful thinking of the peasant crusaders but was more inclined to trust knights who had been well trained in the art of war. Three organized crusading bands of noble warriors, most of them French, made their way eastward. The crusading army probably numbered several thousand cavalry and as many as ten thousand infantry. After the capture of Antioch in 1098, much of the crusading host proceeded down the Palestinian coast, evading the well-defended coastal cities, and reached Jerusalem in June 1099. After a five-week siege, the Holy City was taken amid a horrible massacre of the inhabitants—men, women, and children (see the box "The Siege of Jerusalem: A Christian Perspective" in Chapter 7 on p. 196).

After further conquest of Palestinian lands, the crusaders ignored the wishes of the Byzantine emperor and organized four Latin crusader states. Because the crusader kingdoms were surrounded by Muslims hostile to them, they grew increasingly dependent on the Italian commercial cities for supplies from Europe. Some Italian cities, such as Genoa, Pisa, and especially Venice, grew rich and powerful in the process.

But it was not easy for the crusader kingdoms to maintain themselves. Already by the 1120s, the Muslims had begun to strike back. The fall of one of the Latin kingdoms in 1144 led to renewed calls for another crusade, especially from the

Crusader Kingdoms in Palestine

monastic firebrand Saint Bernard of Clairvaux. He exclaimed, "Now, on account of our sins, the enemies of the cross have begun to show their faces.... What are you doing, you servants of the cross? Will you throw to the dogs that which is most holy? Will you cast pearls before swine?"[12] Bernard even managed to enlist two powerful rulers, but their Second Crusade proved to be a total failure.

The Third Crusade was a reaction to the fall of the Holy City of Jerusalem in 1187 to the Muslim forces under Saladin. Now all of Christendom was ablaze with calls for a new crusade. Three major monarchs agreed to lead their forces in person: Emperor Frederick Barbarossa of Germany, Richard I the Lionhearted of England (1189–1199), and Philip II Augustus, king of France. Some of the crusaders finally arrived in the Holy Land by 1189 only to encounter problems. Frederick Barbarossa drowned while swimming in a local river, and his army quickly disintegrated. The English and French arrived by sea and met with success against the coastal cities, where they had the support of their fleets, but when they moved inland, they failed miserably. Eventually, after Philip went home, Richard the Lionhearted negotiated a settlement whereby Saladin agreed to allow Christian pilgrims free access to Jerusalem.

The Later Crusades

After the death of Saladin in 1193, Pope Innocent III initiated the Fourth Crusade. On its way east, the crusading army became involved in a dispute over the succession to the Byzantine throne. The Venetian leaders of the Fourth Crusade saw an opportunity to neutralize their greatest commercial competitor, the Byzantine Empire. Diverted to Constantinople, the crusaders sacked the great capital city of Byzantium in 1204 and set up the new Latin Empire of Constantinople (see Chapter 13). Not until 1261 did a Byzantine army recapture Constantinople. In the meantime, additional crusades were undertaken to reconquer the Holy Land. All of them were largely disasters, and by the end of the thirteenth century, the European military effort to capture Palestine was recognized as a complete failure.

What Were the Effects of the Crusades?

Whether the crusades had much effect on European civilization is debatable. The only visible remains are the European castles that began to incorporate features adopted from fortresses that the crusaders observed in the east (see the illustration "The Medieval Castle" in Chapter 7 on p. 195). Although there may have been some broadening of perspective from

CHRONOLOGY	The Crusades
Pope Urban II's call for a crusade at Clermont	1095
First Crusade	1096–1099
Second Crusade	1147–1149
Saladin's conquest of Jerusalem	1187
Third Crusade	1189–1192
Fourth Crusade—sack of Constantinople	1204
Latin Empire of Constantinople	1204–1261

the exchange between two cultures, the interaction of Christian Europe with the Muslim world was actually both more intense and more meaningful in Spain and Sicily than in the Holy Land.

Did the crusades help stabilize European society by removing large numbers of young warriors who would have fought each other in Europe? Some historians think so and believe that Western monarchs established their control more easily as a result. There is no doubt that the crusades did contribute to the economic growth of the Italian port cities, especially Genoa, Pisa, and Venice. But it is important to remember that the growing wealth and population of twelfth-century Europe had made the crusades possible in the first place. The crusades may have enhanced the revival of trade, but they certainly did not cause it. Even without the crusades, Italian merchants would have pursued new trade contacts with the Eastern world.

Did the crusades have side effects that would haunt European society for generations? Some historians have argued that the crusades might be considered a "Christian holy war," whose memories still trouble the relationship between the Muslim world and the West today. Other historians argue that the early crusaders were motivated as much by economic and political reasons as religious ones.

Another possible side effect is more apparent. The first widespread attacks on the Jews began with the crusades. As some Christians argued, to undertake holy wars against infidel Muslims while the "murderers of Christ" ran free at home was unthinkable. With the crusades, the massacre of Jews became a regular feature of medieval European life.

CHAPTER SUMMARY

After the collapse of the Han Dynasty in the third century C.E., China experienced nearly four centuries of internal chaos until the Tang Dynasty in the seventh century C.E. attempted to follow the pattern of the Han Dynasty and restore the power of the Chinese Empire. The fall of the Western Roman Empire in the fifth century brought a quite different result as three new civilizations emerged out of the collapse of Roman power in the Mediterranean. A new world of Islam emerged in the east; it occupied large parts of the old Roman Empire and created its own flourishing civilization. As we shall see in Chapter 13, the eastern part of the old Roman Empire, increasingly Greek in culture, continued to survive as the Christian Byzantine Empire. At the same time, a new Christian European civilization was establishing its roots in the West. By the eleventh and twelfth centuries, these three heirs of Rome began their own conflict for control of the lands of the eastern Mediterranean.

The coronation of Charlemagne, the descendant of a Germanic tribe converted to Christianity, as emperor of the Romans in 800 symbolized the fusion of the three chief components of the new European civilization: the German tribes, the Roman legacy, and the Christian church. Charlemagne's Carolingian Empire fostered the idea of a distinct European identity. With the disintegration of that empire, however, power fell into the hands of many different lords, who came to constitute a nobility that dominated Europe's political, economic, and social life. But within this world of castles and private power, during the High Middle Ages kings gradually began to develop the machinery of government and accumulate political authority. Although they could not know it then, the actions of these medieval monarchs laid the foundation for the European states that in one form or another have dominated the European political scene ever since.

European civilization began to flourish in the High Middle Ages. The revival of trade, the expansion of towns and cities, and the development of a money economy did not mean the end of a predominantly rural European society, but they did open the door to new ways to make a living and new opportunities for people to expand and enrich their lives. At the same time, the High Middle Ages also gave birth to a cultural revival that led to new centers of learning in the universities, to the use of reason to systematize the study of theology, and to a dramatic increase in the number and size of churches.

The Catholic Church shared in the challenge of new growth by reforming itself and striking out on a path toward greater papal power, both within the church and over European society. The High Middle Ages witnessed a spiritual renewal that enhanced papal leadership and the religious life of the clergy and laity. At the same time, this spiritual renewal also gave rise to the crusading "holy warrior," thereby creating an animosity between Christians and Muslims that still has repercussions to this day.

CHAPTER TIMELINE

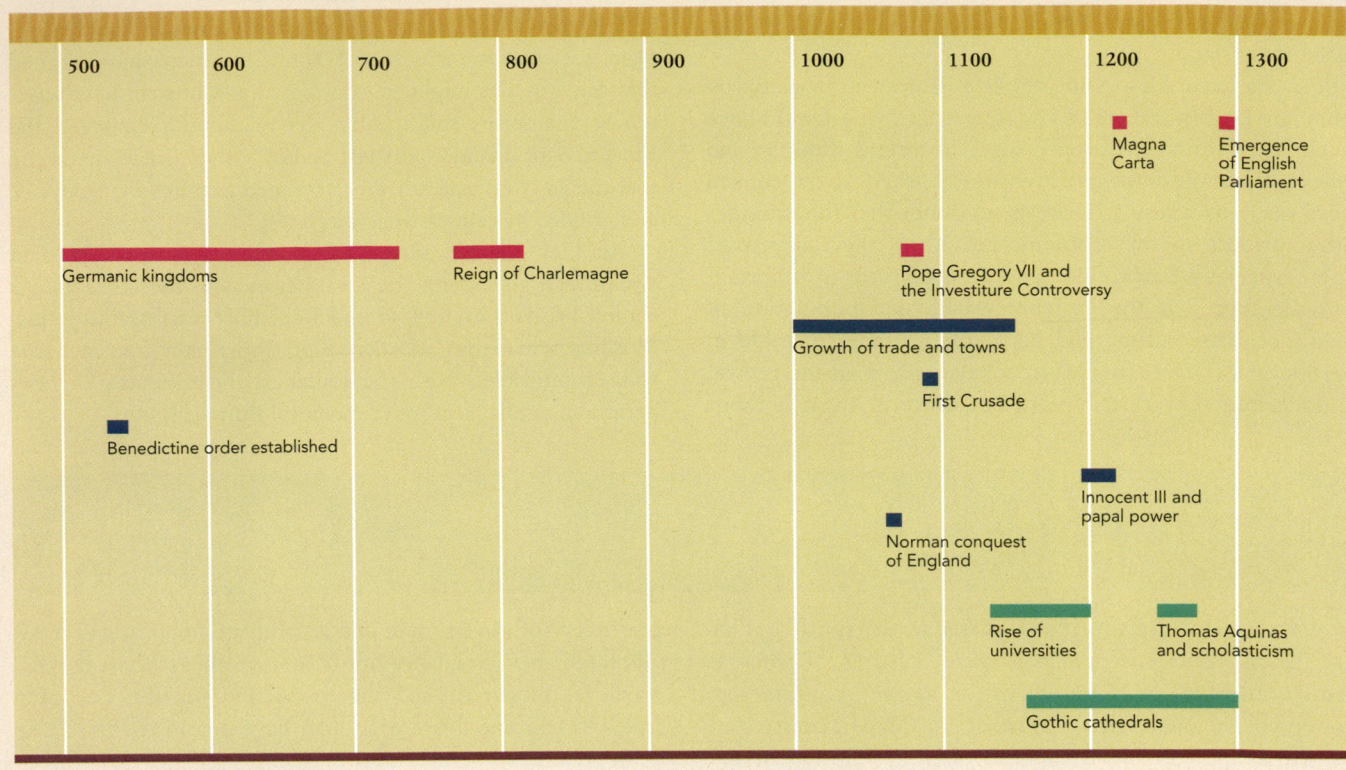

	500	600	700	800	900	1000	1100	1200	1300

Germanic kingdoms

Reign of Charlemagne

Magna Carta

Emergence of English Parliament

Pope Gregory VII and the Investiture Controversy

Growth of trade and towns

Benedictine order established

First Crusade

Innocent III and papal power

Norman conquest of England

Rise of universities

Thomas Aquinas and scholasticism

Gothic cathedrals

CHAPTER REVIEW

Upon Reflection

Q   What impact did the Vikings have on the history and culture of medieval Europe?

Q   How did the revival of trade and cities affect the economy and society of Europe in the High Middle Ages?

Q   The medieval Catholic Church developed in the High Middle Ages at two levels—an institutional level and a popular religion level. What were the most important features of each level?

Key Terms

wergeld (p. 326)
diocese (p. 326)
monk (p. 327)
monasticism (p. 327)
abbot (p. 327)
nuns (p. 327)
abbesses (p. 328)
vassal (p. 331)
fief (p. 331)
subinfeudation (p. 331)
manor (p. 331)

serfs (p. 331)
demesne (p. 331)
aristocracy (p. 334)
chivalry (p. 334)
capitalism (p. 335)
commune (p. 337)
guilds (p. 337)
common law (p. 341)
lay investiture (p. 345)
interdict (p. 345)
sacraments (p. 345)
heresy (p. 346)
liberal arts (p. 348)
scholasticism (p. 349)
Romanesque (p. 349)
Gothic (p. 349)

Suggested Reading

EARLY MIDDLE AGES   For general histories of the Middle Ages, see **J. M. Riddle**, *A History of the Middle Ages, 300–1500* (New York, 2008), and **B. Rosenwein**, *A Short History of the Middle Ages* (Orchard Park, N.Y., 2002). A good history of the Early Middle Ages can be found in **C. Wickham**, *The Inheritance of Rome: A History of Europe from*

400 to 1000 (New York, 2009). On Charlemagne, see **A. Barbero, *Charlemagne: Father of a Continent***, trans. A. Cameron (Berkeley, Calif., 2004).

The Vikings are examined in **M. Arnold, *The Vikings: Culture and Conquest*** (London, 2006). For an important revisionist view of feudalism, see **S. Reynolds, *Fiefs and Vassals*** (Oxford, 1994).

HIGH MIDDLE AGES   For a good introduction to the High Middle Ages, see **W. C. Jordan, *Europe in the High Middle Ages*** (New York, 2003).

Urban history is covered in **D. Nicholas, *The Growth of the Medieval City: From Late Antiquity to the Early Fourteenth Century*** (New York, 1997). On women, see **J. Ward, *Women in Medieval Europe 1200–1500*** (London, 2003). On daily life, see **C. Frugoi, *A Day in a Medieval City***, trans. W. McCuaig (Chicago, 2006).

For a general survey of Christianity in the Middle Ages, see **F. D. Logan, *A History of the Church in the Middle Ages*** (London, 2002). For a superb introduction to early Christianity, see **P. Brown, *The Rise of Western Christendom: Triumph and Adversity, A.D. 200–1000***, 2nd ed. (Oxford, 2002). On the papacy in the High Middle Ages, see **I. S. Robinson, *The Papacy*** (Cambridge, 1990). On monasticism, see **C. H. Lawrence, *Medieval Monasticism***, 3rd ed. (London, 2000), a good general account.

On medieval intellectual life, see **M. L. Colish, *Medieval Foundations of the Western Intellectual Tradition, 400–1400*** (New Haven, Conn., 1997). A good introduction to Romanesque style is **A. Petzold, *Romanesque Art***, rev. ed. (New York, 2003). On the Gothic movement, see **M. Camille, *Gothic Art: Glorious Visions***, rev. ed. (New York, 2003).

MEDIEVAL EUROPE AND THE WORLD   For a detailed survey of the crusades, see **C. Tyerman, *God's War: A New History of the crusades*** (Cambridge, Mass., 2006).

Chapter Notes

1. Quoted in N. F. Cantor, ed., *The Medieval World, 300–1300* (New York, 1963), p. 104.
2. A. Barbero, *Charlemagne: Father of a Continent*, trans. A. Cameron (Berkeley, Calif., 2004), p. 4.
3. C. Wickham, *The Inheritance of Rome: A History of Europe from 400 to 1000* (New York, 2009), p. 4.
4. Quoted in S. Keynes, "The Vikings in England, c. 790–1016," in P. Sawyer, ed., *The Oxford Illustrated History of the Vikings* (Oxford, 1997), p. 81.
5. Quoted in M. Perry, J. Peden, and T. von Laue, *Sources of the Western Tradition*, vol. 1 (Boston, 1987), p. 218.
6. Quoted in J. Gimpel, *The Medieval Machine* (Harmondsworth, England, 1977), p. 92.
7. O. J. Thatcher and E. H. McNeal, eds., *A Source Book for Medieval History* (New York, 1905), p. 208.
8. Quoted in R. H. C. Davis, *A History of Medieval Europe from Constantine to Saint Louis*, 2nd ed. (New York, 1988), p. 252.
9. Quoted in R. Brooke and C. Brooke, *Popular Religion in the Middle Ages* (London, 1984), p. 19.
10. Quoted in Thatcher and McNeal, *Source Book for Medieval History*, p. 517.
11. Quoted in T. Asbridge, *The First Crusade: A New History* (Oxford, 2004), pp. 79–80.
12. Quoted in H. E. Mayer, *The Crusades*, trans. J. Gillingham (New York, 1972), pp. 99–100.

MindTap is a fully online, highly personalized learning experience built upon Cengage Leaning content. MindTap combines student learning tools—readings, multimedia, activities, and assessments—into a singular Learning Path that guides students through their course.

The Byzantine Empire and Crisis and Recovery in the West

Justinian and Theodora

CHAPTER OUTLINE AND FOCUS QUESTIONS

From Eastern Roman to Byzantine Empire

Q How did the Byzantine Empire that had emerged by the eighth century differ from the empire of Justinian and from the Germanic kingdoms in the West? How were they alike?

The Zenith of Byzantine Civilization (750–1025)

Q What were the chief developments in the Byzantine Empire between 750 and 1025?

The Decline and Fall of the Byzantine Empire (1025–1453)

Q What impact did the crusades have on the Byzantine Empire? How and why did Constantinople and the Byzantine Empire fall?

The Crises of the Fourteenth Century in the West

Q What impact did the Black Death have on Europe and Asia in the fourteenth century? What problems did Europeans face during the fourteenth century, and what impact did these crises have on European economic, social, and religious life?

Recovery: The Renaissance

Q What were the main features of the Renaissance in Europe, and how did it differ from the Middle Ages?

CRITICAL THINKING

Q In what ways did the Byzantine, European, and Islamic civilizations resemble and differ from each other? Were their relationships generally based on cooperation or conflict?

CONNECTIONS TO TODAY

Q How is the concept of the Renaissance relevant to the early twenty-first century?

AT THE SAME TIME that medieval European civilization was emerging in the West, the Eastern part of the Late Roman Empire, increasingly Greek in culture, continued to survive. While serving as a buffer between Europe and the peoples to the East, especially the growing empire of Islam, the Late Roman Empire in the East (Byzantine Empire) also preserved the intellectual and legal accomplishments of the Greeks and Romans.

In its early decades, the Eastern Roman Empire was beset by crises. Soon after the beginning of his reign, the emperor Justinian was faced with a serious revolt in the capital city of Constantinople. In 532, two factions, called the Blues and the Greens because they supported chariot teams bearing those colors when they competed in the Hippodrome (a huge amphitheater), joined together and rioted to protest the emperor's taxation policies. The riots soon became a revolt as insurgents burned and looted the center of the city, shouting *"Nika!"* (victory), the word normally used to cheer on their favorite teams.

Aristocratic factions joined the revolt and put forward a nobleman named Hypatius as a new emperor. Justinian seemed ready to flee, but his wife, the empress Theodora, strengthened his resolve by declaring, according to the historian Procopius, "If now, it is your wish to save yourself, O Emperor, there is no difficulty. For we have much money, and there is the sea, here the boats. However, consider whether it will not come about after you have been saved that you would gladly exchange that safety for death. As for myself, I approve a certain ancient saying that royalty is a good burial-shroud."[1] Shamed by his wife's words, Justinian resolved to fight. He ordered troops, newly returned from fighting the Persians, to attack a large crowd that had gathered in the Hippodrome to acclaim Hypatius as emperor. In the ensuing massacre, the imperial troops slaughtered 30,000 of the insurgents, about 5 percent of the city's population. After crushing the Nika Revolt, Justinian began a massive rebuilding program and continued the autocratic reign that established the foundations of the Byzantine Empire (as it came to be known beginning in the eighth century).

Despite the early empire's reversals, the Macedonian emperors in the ninth, tenth, and eleventh centuries enlarged the empire, achieved economic prosperity, and expanded its cultural influence to Eastern Europe and Russia. But after the Macedonian Dynasty ended in 1056 C.E., the empire began a slow but steady decline. Involvement in the crusades proved especially disastrous, leading to the occupation of Constantinople by Western crusading forces in 1204. Byzantine rule was restored in 1261, and the empire survived in a weakened condition for another 190 years until the Ottoman Turks finally conquered it in 1453.

In the fourteenth century, Europe, too, sustained a series of crises and reversals after flourishing during the three centuries of the High Middle Ages. Unlike the Byzantine Empire, however, European civilization rebounded in the fifteenth century, experiencing an artistic and intellectual revival in the Renaissance as well as a renewal of monarchical authority among the Western European states. Europe was poised to begin its dramatic entry into world affairs.

From Eastern Roman to Byzantine Empire

Q **FOCUS QUESTIONS:** How did the Byzantine Empire that had emerged by the eighth century differ from the empire of Justinian and from the Germanic kingdoms in the West? How were they alike?

As noted earlier, the Western and Eastern parts of the Roman Empire began to drift apart in the fourth century. As the Germanic peoples moved into the Western part of the empire

and established various kingdoms over the course of the fifth century, the Late Roman Empire in the East solidified and prospered.

Constantinople, the imperial capital, viewed itself not only as the center of a world empire but also as a special Christian city. The inhabitants believed that the city was under the protection of God and the Virgin Mary. One thirteenth-century Byzantine said: "About our city you shall know: until the end she will fear no nation whatsoever, for no one will entrap or capture her, not by any means, for she has been given to the Mother of God and no one will snatch her out of Her hands. Many nations will break their horns against her walls and withdraw with shame."[2] The Byzantines saw their state as a Christian empire.

The Reign of Justinian (527–565)

In the sixth century, the empire in the East came under the control of one of its most remarkable rulers, the emperor Justinian (juh-STIN-ee-un). As the nephew and heir of the previous emperor, Justinian had been well trained in imperial administration. He was determined to reestablish the Roman Empire in the entire Mediterranean world and began his attempt to reconquer the West in 533.

Justinian's army under Belisarius (bell-uh-SAH-ree-uss), probably the best general of the late Roman world, presented a formidable force. Belisarius sailed to North Africa and quickly defeated the Vandals in two major battles. From North Africa, he led his forces onto the Italian peninsula after occupying Sicily in 535. But it was not until 552 that the Ostrogoths were finally defeated. The struggle devastated Italy, which suffered more from Justinian's reconquest than from all of the previous barbarian invasions.

Justinian has long been criticized for overextending his resources and bankrupting the empire. Historians now think, however, that a devastating plague in 542 and long-term economic factors were far more damaging to the Eastern Roman Empire than Justinian's conquests. Before he died, Justinian appeared to have achieved his goals. He had restored the imperial Mediterranean world; his empire included Italy, part of Spain, North Africa, Asia Minor, Palestine, and Syria (see Map 13.1). But the conquest of the Western empire proved fleeting. Only three years after Justinian's death, another Germanic people, the Lombards, entered Italy. Although the Eastern empire maintained the fiction of Italy as a province, its forces were limited to small pockets here and there.

THE CODIFICATION OF ROMAN LAW Though his conquests proved short-lived, Justinian made a lasting contribution to Western civilization through his codification of Roman law. The Eastern empire was heir to a vast quantity of materials connected to the development of Roman law. These included laws passed by the senate and assemblies, legal commentaries of jurists, decisions of praetors, and the edicts of emperors. Justinian had been well trained in imperial government and was thoroughly acquainted with Roman law. He wished to codify and simplify this mass of materials.

To accomplish his goal, Justinian authorized the jurist Tribonian to make a systematic compilation of imperial edicts.

The Emperor Justinian and His Court. As the seat of late Roman power in Italy, the town of Ravenna was adorned with examples of late Roman art. The Church of San Vitale at Ravenna contains some of the finest examples of sixth-century mosaics. Small pieces of colored glass were set in mortar on the wall to form these figures and their surroundings. The emperor is seen as both head of state (he wears a jeweled crown and a purple robe) and head of the church (he carries a gold bowl symbolizing the body of Jesus).

MAP 13.1 The Eastern Roman Empire in the Time of Justinian. The Eastern Roman emperor Justinian briefly restored much of the Mediterranean portion of the old Roman Empire. His general, Belisarius, conquered the Vandals in North Africa quite easily but wrested Italy from the Ostrogoths only after a long and devastating struggle.

Q *Look back at Map 5.3. What former Roman territories lay outside Justinian's control?*

Theodora and Attendants. This mosaic, located on the south wall of the apse of the Church of San Vitale (Justinian is on the north wall), depicts Theodora and her attendants. Her presence on the wall of this church indicates the important role she played in the late Roman state. At the bottom of her robe is a scene of the Three Wise Men, an indication that Theodora was special enough to have belonged in the company of the three kings who visited the newborn Jesus.

The result was the Code of Law, the first part of the *Corpus Iuris Civilis* (KOR-pus YOOR-iss SIV-i-liss) (Body of Civil Law), completed in 529. Four years later, two other parts of the *Corpus* appeared: the *Digest*, a compendium of writings of Roman jurists, and the *Institutes*, a brief summary of the chief principles of Roman law that could be used as a textbook. The fourth part of the *Corpus* was the *Novels*, a compilation of the most important new edicts issued during Justinian's reign.

Justinian's codification of Roman law became the basis of imperial law in the Byzantine Empire until its end in 1453. More important, however, since it was written in Latin (it was, in fact, the last product of Eastern Roman culture to be written in Latin, which was soon replaced by Greek), it was also eventually used in the West and in fact became the basis of the legal system of all of continental Europe.

THE EMPRESS THEODORA   Theodora (thee-uh-DOR-uh) was the daughter of the "keeper of bears" for the games at Constantinople, who died when Theodora was a child. Theodora followed in her mother's footsteps by becoming an actress, which at that time was considered a lower-class activity. Often actresses also worked as prostitutes, and Theodora was no exception. At the age of twenty-five, she met Justinian, who was forty. His uncle, the emperor Justin, had to change the law to allow an aristocratic senator to marry a woman who had been an actress. After his uncle died in 527, Justinian became emperor and Theodora empress, a remarkable achievement for a woman from the lower classes.

Justinian and Theodora were close and loving companions. She also influenced her husband in both church and state affairs. A strong-willed and intelligent woman, she proved especially valuable in 532, when her steely resolve during the Nika Revolt convinced Justinian to fight and crush the protesters rather than to flee. Theodora also helped establish a number of churches and monasteries, including a convent for former prostitutes.

THE EMPEROR'S BUILDING PROGRAM   After the riots destroyed much of Constantinople, Justinian rebuilt the city and gave it the appearance it would keep for almost a thousand years (see Map 13.2). Earlier, Emperor Theodosius (thee-uh-DOH-shuss) II (408–450) had constructed an enormous defensive wall to protect the capital on its land side. The city was dominated by an immense palace complex, a huge arena known as the Hippodrome, and hundreds of churches. No residential district was particularly fashionable; palaces, tenements, and slums ranged alongside one another. Justinian added many new buildings. His public works projects included roads, bridges, walls, public baths, law courts, and colossal underground reservoirs to hold the city's water supply. He also built hospitals, schools, monasteries, and churches. Churches were his special passion, and in Constantinople he built or rebuilt thirty-four of them. His greatest achievement was the famous Hagia Sophia (HAG-ee-uh soh-FEE-uh), the Church of the Holy Wisdom.

Completed in 537, Hagia Sophia was designed by two Greek scientists who departed radically from the simple, flat-roofed basilica of Western architecture. The center of Hagia Sophia consisted of four huge piers crowned by an enormous dome, which seemed to be floating in space. This effect was

© 2016 Cengage Learning

MAP 13.2 Constantinople. In the Middle Ages, Constantinople was the largest European city and a nexus of trade between East and West. Emperor Justinian oversaw a massive building program that produced important architectural monuments such as Hagia Sophia.

Q *What natural and human-built aspects of the city helped protect it from invasion?*

emphasized by Procopius (pruh-KOH-pee-uss), the court historian, who at Justinian's request wrote a treatise on the emperor's building projects: "From the lightness of the building, it does not appear to rest upon a solid foundation, but to cover the place beneath as though it were suspended from heaven by the fabled golden chain." In part, this impression was created by putting forty-two windows around the base of the dome, which allowed an incredible play of light within the cathedral. Light served to remind the worshipers of God; as Procopius commented:

> Whoever enters there to worship perceives at once that it is not by any human strength or skill, but by the favor of God that this work has been perfected; his mind rises sublime to commune with God, feeling that He cannot be far off, but must especially love to dwell in the place which He has chosen; and this takes place not only when a man sees it for the first time, but it always makes the same impression upon him, as though he had never beheld it before.[3]

As darkness is illuminated by invisible light, so too, it was believed, the world is illuminated by invisible spirit.

The royal palace complex, Hagia Sophia, and the Hippodrome were the three greatest buildings in Constantinople. This last was a huge amphitheater, constructed of brick covered by marble, holding as many as 60,000 spectators. Although gladiator fights were held there, the main events were the chariot races; twenty-four would usually be presented in one day. The citizens of Constantinople were

passionate fans of chariot racing. Successful charioteers were acclaimed as heroes and honored with public statues. Crowds in the Hippodrome also took on political significance. Being a member of the two chief factions of charioteers—the Blues or the Greens—was the only real outlet for political expression. Even emperors had to be aware of their demands and attitudes: the loss of a race in the Hippodrome frequently resulted in bloody riots that could threaten the emperor's power.

A New Kind of Empire

Justinian's accomplishments had been spectacular, but when he died, he left the Eastern Roman Empire with serious problems: too much distant territory to protect, an empty treasury, a smaller population after a devastating plague, and renewed threats to the frontiers. The seventh century proved to be an important turning point in the history of the empire.

PROBLEMS OF THE SEVENTH CENTURY

In the first half of the century, during the reign of Heraclius (he-ruh-KLY-uss *or* huh-RAK-lee-uss) (610–641), the empire faced attacks from the Persians to the East and the Slavs to the north. A new system of defense was put in place, using a new and larger administrative unit, the *theme*, which combined civilian and military offices in the hands of the same person. Thus, the civil governor was also the military leader of the area. Although this innovation helped the empire survive, it also fostered an increased militarization of the empire. By the mid-seventh century, it had become apparent that a restored Mediterranean empire was simply beyond the resources of the Eastern empire, which now increasingly turned its back on the Latin West. A renewed series of external threats in the second half of the seventh century strengthened this development.

The most serious challenge to the empire was the rise of Islam, which unified the Arab tribes and created a powerful new force that swept through the region (see Chapter 7). The defeat of an Eastern Roman army near the Yarmuk River in 636 meant the loss of the provinces of Syria and Palestine. The Arabs also moved into the old Persian Empire and conquered it. An Arab attempt to besiege Constantinople that began in 674 failed, in large part due to the use of Greek fire against the Arab fleets. Greek fire was a petroleum-based compound containing quicklime and sulfur. Because it would burn under water, the Byzantines created the equivalent of modern flamethrowers by using tubes to blow Greek fire onto wooden ships, with frightening effect. Arabs and Eastern Roman forces now faced each other along a frontier in southern Asia Minor.

Interior View of Hagia Sophia. Pictured here is the interior of the Church of the Holy Wisdom in Constantinople (modern Istanbul), constructed under Justinian by Anthemius of Tralles (an-THEE-mee-uss of TRAL-leez) and Isidore of Miletus (IH-zuh-dor of mih-LEE-tuss). Some of the stones used in the construction of the church had been plundered from the famous Classical Temple of Diana, near Ephesus, in Asia Minor (modern Turkey). This view gives an idea of how the windows around the base of the dome produced a special play of light within the cathedral. The pulpits and plaques bearing inscriptions from the Qur'an were introduced when the Turks converted this church to a mosque in the fifteenth century.

Problems also arose along the northern frontier, especially in the Balkans, where an Asiatic people known as the Bulgars had arrived earlier in the sixth century. In 679, the Bulgars defeated the Eastern Roman forces and took possession of the lower Danube valley, setting up a strong Bulgarian kingdom.

By the beginning of the eighth century, the Eastern Roman Empire was greatly diminished in size, consisting only of a portion of the Balkans and Asia Minor. It was now an Eastern Mediterranean state. These external challenges had important internal repercussions as well. By the eighth century, the Eastern Roman Empire had been transformed into what historians call the Byzantine Empire, a civilization with its own unique character that would last until 1453 (Constantinople was built on the site of an older city named Byzantium—hence the name *Byzantine*).

THE BYZANTINE EMPIRE IN THE EIGHTH CENTURY The Byzantine Empire was a Greek state. Justinian's *Corpus Iuris Civilis* had been the last official work published in Latin. Increasingly, Latin fell into disuse as Greek became not only the common language of the Byzantine Empire but its official language as well.

The Byzantine Empire was also a Christian state, built on a faith in Jesus that was shared in a profound way by almost all its citizens. An enormous amount of artistic talent was poured into the construction of churches, church ceremonies, and church decoration. Spiritual principles deeply permeated Byzantine art. The importance of religion to the Byzantines explains why theological disputes took on an exaggerated form. The most famous of these disputes, the so-called iconoclastic controversy, threatened the stability of the empire in the first half of the eighth century.

Beginning in the sixth century, the use of religious images, especially in the form of icons or pictures of sacred figures, became so widespread that charges of idolatry, the worship of images, began to be heard. The use of images or icons had been justified by the argument that icons were not worshiped but were simply used to help illiterate people understand their religion. This argument failed to stop the **iconoclasts**, as the opponents of icons were called.

Iconoclasm was not unique to the Byzantine Empire. In the neighboring Islamic empire, religious art did not include any physical representations of Muhammad (see the Comparative Illustration "Religious Imagery in the Medieval World" on p. 362).

The Byzantine Empire, c. 750

CHRONOLOGY	The Eastern Roman/Byzantine Empire to 750
Justinian codifies Roman law	529–533
Reconquest of Italy by Justinian	535–552
Completion of Hagia Sophia	537
Attacks on the empire in the reign of Heraclius	610–641
Arab defeat of the Byzantines at Yarmuk	636
Defeat by the Bulgars; losses in the Balkans	679
Leo III and iconoclasm	717–741

Art Resource, NY

Erich Lessing/Art Resource, NY

COMPARATIVE ILLUSTRATION

Religious Imagery in the Medieval World. The Middle Ages was a golden age of religious art, reflecting the important role of religion itself in medieval society. These three illustrations show different aspects of medieval religious imagery. In Europe, much Christian art appeared in illuminated manuscripts. The illustration at the top left shows a page depicting the figure of Jesus from *The Book of Kells*, a richly decorated manuscript of the Christian gospels produced by the monks of Iona in the British Isles. Byzantine art was also deeply religious, as was especially evident in icons. At the top right is an icon of the Virgin and Child (Mary and Jesus) from the monastery of Saint Catherine at Mount Sinai in Egypt dating to around the year 600. Painted on wood, this icon shows the enthroned Virgin and Child between Saints Theodore and George with two angels behind them looking upward to a beam of light

Vanni Archive/Art Resource, NY

containing the hand of God. The figures are not realistic; the goal of the icon was to bridge the gap between the divine and the outer material world. Artists in the Muslim world faced a different challenge—Muslims warned against imitating God by creating pictures of living beings, thus effectively prohibiting the representation of humans, especially Muhammad. Islamic religious artists therefore used decorative motifs based on geometric patterns and the Arabic script. The scriptural panel in the lower illustration is an artistic presentation of a verse from the Qur'an, thus blending the spiritual and artistic spheres.

Q *How is the importance of religious imagery in the Middle Ages evident in these three illustrations?*

Iconoclasm would also play a role among some of the new religious groups that emerged in the Protestant Reformation in sixteenth-century Europe (see Chapter 15).

Beginning in 730, the Byzantine emperor Leo III (717–741) outlawed the use of icons. Strong resistance ensued, especially from monks. Leo also used the iconoclastic controversy to add to the prestige of the patriarch of Constantinople, the highest church official in the East and second in dignity only to the bishop of Rome. The Roman popes were opposed to the iconoclastic edicts, and their opposition created considerable dissension between the popes and the Byzantine emperors. Late in the eighth century, the Byzantine rulers reversed their stand on the use of images, but not before considerable damage had been done to the unity of the Christian church. Although the final separation between Roman Catholicism and Greek Orthodoxy (as the Christian church in the Byzantine Empire was called) did not occur until 1054, the iconoclastic controversy was important in moving both sides in that direction.

THE BYZANTINE EMPEROR The emperor occupied a crucial position in the Byzantine state. Portrayed as chosen by God, the Byzantine emperor was crowned in elaborate sacred ceremonies, and his subjects were expected to prostrate themselves in his presence. The wives of the emperors also played significant roles in the court rituals that upheld imperial authority.

The importance of court ritual is apparent in the *Book of Ceremonies*, a tenth-century compendium of imperial ceremonies and court rituals. Court ritual could be very complicated and included a variety of activities. Everyday rituals included the daily opening of the imperial palace: imperial officials, all arranged in order of rank, waited until the palace doors were officially opened; then they marched into the palace in a procession. A similar ceremony was held for the opening of the palace in the afternoon. In addition to these regular daily ceremonies, special ceremonies involving specific rituals were held on many occasions, including the emperor's birthday, the promotion of officials, imperial marriages, and commemorations of important military battles. The emperor was also required to participate in the ceremonies held regularly in the churches on important saints' days and during church festivals.

The power of the Byzantine emperor was considered absolute and was limited in practice only by assassination. A rather unusual ruling class assisted the emperors. Civil servants and high churchmen essentially stemmed from the same ranks of the urban society of Constantinople. They received the same education and often followed the same careers in civil service until they went their separate ways into church and government offices. A strong bureaucracy was one of the most basic features of the Byzantine Empire.

The Byzantine Empire was characterized by what might be called a permanent war economy. Byzantine emperors maintained the late Roman policy of state regulation of economic affairs. Of course, this practice was easy to justify: the survival of the empire depended on careful shepherding of economic resources and the maintenance of the army. Thus, the state encouraged agricultural production, regulated the guilds or corporations responsible for industrial production and the various stages of manufacturing, and controlled commerce by making trade in grain and silk, the two most valuable products, government monopolies.

In addition, because of their many foreign enemies, Byzantine emperors spent considerable energy on war and preparation for war. Manuals on war, providing instruction in the ways of fighting, were a common type of Byzantine literature (see the box "A Byzantine Emperor Gives Military Advice" on p. 364). Byzantine armies, often led by the emperors, were well trained and equipped with the latest weapons. The Byzantines, however, often preferred to secure their goals through diplomacy rather than fighting. Our word *byzantine*—often defined as "extremely complicated" or "carried on by underhanded methods"—stems from the complex and crafty instructions that Byzantine rulers sent to their envoys.

Because the emperor appointed the patriarch, he also exercised control over both church and state. The Byzantines believed that God had commanded their state to preserve the true faith, Orthodox Christianity. Emperor, clergy, and civic officials were all bound together in service to this ideal. It can be said that spiritual values truly held the Byzantine state together.

By 750, it was apparent that two of Rome's heirs, the Germanic kingdoms and the Byzantine Empire, were moving in different directions. Nevertheless, Byzantine influence on the Western world was significant. The images of a Roman imperial state that continued to haunt the West lived on in Byzantium. As noted, the legal system of the West came to owe much to Justinian's codification of Roman law. In addition, the Byzantine Empire served in part as a buffer state, protecting the West for a long time from incursions from the East.

INTELLECTUAL LIFE The intellectual life of the Byzantine Empire was greatly influenced by the traditions of Classical civilization. Scholars actively strived to preserve the works of the ancient Greeks and based a great deal of their own literature on Classical models. Although the Byzantines produced a substantial body of literature, much of it was of a very practical nature, focusing on legal, military, and administrative matters. The most outstanding literary achievements of the empire's early centuries, however, were historical and religious works. Many of the latter were theological treatises, often of an extremely combative nature because of the intense theological controversies. More popular were biographies of saints, which traced the adventures of religious figures who after many struggles achieved a life of virtue.

The empire's best-known historian was Procopius (c. 500–c. 562), court historian during the reign of Justinian. Procopius served as secretary to the great general Belisarius and accompanied him on his wars on behalf of Justinian. Procopius's best historical work, the *Wars*, is a firsthand account of Justinian's wars of reconquest in the Western Mediterranean and his wars against the Persians in the East. Deliberately modeled after the work of his hero, the Greek historian Thucydides (see Chapter 4),

A Byzantine Emperor Gives Military Advice

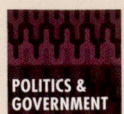

POLITICS & GOVERNMENT

To an empire surrounded by enemies on all sides, military prowess was an absolute necessity. Both Byzantine emperors and the ruling elite, however, also realized that military forces alone would not suffice and consequently fostered the art of diplomacy and military intelligence. This document is from an early-seventh-century work known as the *Strategikon* (stra-TEE-jih-kahn), a manual of strategy written by the emperor Maurice (582–602), himself a strong military leader who led his troops into battle. The work is based on the assumption that a detailed knowledge of the habits and fighting skills of their enemies would give the Byzantines an advantage if they had to fight them.

Maurice, *Strategikon*

The light-haired races [Germanic peoples] place great value on freedom. They are bold and undaunted in battle. Daring and impetuous as they are, they consider any timidity and even a short retreat as a disgrace. They calmly despise death as they fight violently in hand-to-hand combat either on horseback or on foot. If they are hard pressed in cavalry actions, they dismount at a single prearranged sign and line up on foot. Although only a few against many horsemen, they do not shrink from the fight. They are armed with shields, lances, and short swords slung from their shoulders. They prefer fighting on foot and rapid charges.

Whether on foot or on horseback, they draw up for battle, not in any fixed measure and formation, or in regiments or divisions, but according to tribes, their kinship with one another, and common interest. Often, as a result, when things are not going well and their friends have been killed, they will risk their lives fighting to avenge them. In combat they make the front of their battle line even and dense. Either on horseback or on foot they are impetuous and undisciplined in charging, as if they were the only people in the world who are not cowards. They are disobedient to their leaders. They are not interested in anything that is at all complicated and pay little attention to external security and their own advantage. They despise good order, especially on horseback. They are easily corrupted by money, greedy as they are.

They are hurt by suffering and fatigue. Although they possess bold and daring spirits, their bodies are pampered and soft, and they are not able to bear pain calmly. In addition, they are hurt by heat, cold, rain, lack of provisions, especially of wine, and postponement of battle. When it comes to a cavalry battle, they are hindered by uneven and wooded terrain. They are easily ambushed along the flanks and to the rear of their battle line, for they do not concern themselves at all with scouts and the other security measures. Their ranks are easily broken by a simulated flight and a sudden turning back against them....

Above all, therefore, in warring against them one must avoid engaging in pitched battles, especially in the early stages. Instead, make use of well-planned ambushes, sneak attacks, and stratagems. Delay things and ruin their opportunities. Pretend to come to agreements with them. Aim at reducing their boldness and zeal by shortage of provisions or the discomfort of heat or cold. This can be done when our army has pitched camp on rugged and difficult ground. On such terrain this enemy cannot attack successfully because they are using lances. But if a favorable opportunity for a regular battle occurs, line up the army as set forth in the book on formations.

 What did Maurice identify as the strengths and weaknesses of the Germanic peoples? Based on his analysis of their traits, what did he advise his military forces to do if they faced the Germans in battle?

Source: George T. Dennis, trans. *Maurice's Strategikon: Handbook of Byzantine Military Strategy, Book 11* (Philadelphia: University of Pennsylvania Press, 1984), pp. 118–119.

Procopius's narrative features vivid descriptions of battle scenes, clear judgment, and noteworthy objectivity.

LIFE IN CONSTANTINOPLE: THE IMPORTANCE OF TRADE

With a population in the hundreds of thousands, Constantinople was the largest city in Europe during the Middle Ages. Until the twelfth century, Constantinople was also Europe's greatest commercial center. The city was the chief entrepôt for the exchange of products between West and East, and trade formed the basis for its fabulous prosperity. Foreign merchants, however, largely carried on this trade. As one contemporary said:

> All sorts of merchants come here from the land of Babylon, from … Persia, Media, and all the sovereignty of the land of Egypt, from the lands of Canaan, and from the empire of Russia, from Hungary, Khazaria [the Caspian region], and the land of Lombardy and Sepharad [Spain]. It is a busy city, and merchants come to it from every country by sea or land, and there is none like it in the world except Baghdad, the great city of Islam.[4]

Highly desired in Europe were the products of the East: silk from China, spices from Southeast Asia and India, jewelry and ivory from India (used by artisans for church items), wheat and furs from southern Russia, and flax and honey from the Balkans. Many of these Eastern goods were then shipped to the Mediterranean area and northern Europe. Despite the Germanic incursions, trade with Europe did not entirely end.

Moreover, imported raw materials were used in Constantinople for local industries. During Justinian's reign, two Christian monks smuggled silkworms from China to begin a silk industry. The state had a monopoly on the production of silk cloth, and the workshops themselves were housed in Constantinople's royal palace complex. European demand for silk cloth made it the city's most lucrative product. It is interesting to note that the upper classes, including emperors and empresses, were not discouraged from making money through trade and manufacturing. Indeed, one empress even manufactured perfumes in her bedroom.

The Zenith of Byzantine Civilization (750–1025)

 FOCUS QUESTION: What were the chief developments in the Byzantine Empire between 750 and 1025?

In the seventh and eighth centuries, the Byzantine Empire lost much of its territory to Slavs, Bulgars, and Muslims. By 750, the empire consisted only of Asia Minor, some lands in the Balkans, and the southern coast of Italy. Although Byzantium was beset with internal dissension and invasions in the ninth century, it was able to deal with them and not only endured but even expanded, reaching its high point in the tenth century, which some historians have called the golden age of Byzantine civilization.

The Beginning of a Revival

During the reign of Michael III (842–867), the Byzantine Empire began to experience a revival. Iconoclasm was finally abolished in 843, and reforms were made in education, church life, the military, and the peasant economy. There was a noticeable intellectual renewal. But the empire was still plagued by persistent problems. The Bulgars mounted new attacks, and the Arabs continued to harass the periphery. Moreover, a new religious dispute with political repercussions erupted over differences between the pope as leader of the Western Christian church and the patriarch of Constantinople as leader of the Eastern Christian church. Patriarch Photius (FOH-shuss) condemned the pope as a heretic for accepting a revised form of the Nicene Creed stating that the Holy Spirit proceeded from the Father and the Son instead of from the Father alone. A council of Eastern bishops followed Photius's wishes and excommunicated the pope, creating the so-called Photian schism. Although the differences were later papered over, this controversy inserted a greater wedge between the Eastern and Western Christian churches.

The Macedonian Dynasty

The problems that arose during Michael's reign were effectively dealt with by a new dynasty of Byzantine emperors known as the Macedonians (867–1056). The founder of the dynasty, Basil I (867–886), was a Macedonian of uncertain background who came to Constantinople to improve his lot in life. After impressing Emperor Michael III with his wrestling skills, he married the emperor's mistress and was made co-emperor. One year later, he arranged the murder of Michael and then became sole ruler, establishing a dynasty that would last almost two hundred years.

The Macedonian Dynasty managed to hold off Byzantium's external enemies and reestablish domestic order. Supported by the church, the emperors thought of the Byzantine Empire as a continuation of the Christian Roman Empire of late antiquity. Although for diplomatic reasons they occasionally recognized the imperial titles of earlier Western emperors, such as Charlemagne and Otto I, they still regarded them as little more than barbarian parvenus.

ECONOMIC AND RELIGIOUS POLICIES The Macedonian emperors could boast of a remarkable number of achievements in the late ninth and tenth centuries. They worked to strengthen the position of the free farmers, who felt threatened by the attempts of landed aristocrats to expand their estates at the farmers' expense. The emperors were well aware that the free farmers made up the rank and file of the Byzantine cavalry and provided the military strength of the empire. Nevertheless, despite their efforts, the Macedonian emperors found that it was not easy to control the power of the landed nobles, and many free farmers continued to lose their lands to the nobles.

The Macedonian emperors also fostered a burst of economic prosperity by expanding trade relations with Western Europe, especially by selling silks and metalwork, and the city of Constantinople flourished. Foreign visitors continued to be astounded by its size, wealth, and physical surroundings. To Western Europeans, it was the stuff of legends and fables (see the box "A Western View of the Byzantine Empire" on p. 366).

In this period of prosperity, Byzantine cultural influence expanded due to the active missionary efforts of Eastern Byzantine Christians. Eastern Orthodox Christianity was spread to Eastern European peoples, such as the Bulgars and Serbs. Perhaps the greatest missionary success occurred when the prince of Kiev in Russia converted to Christianity in 987. From the end of the tenth century on, Byzantine Christianity became the model for Russian religious life, just as Byzantine imperial ideals came to influence the outward forms of Russian political life.

POLITICAL AND MILITARY ACHIEVEMENTS Under the Macedonian rulers, Byzantium enjoyed a strong civil service, talented emperors, and military advances. Well-educated, competent aristocrats from Constantinople staffed the Byzantine civil service and oversaw the collection of taxes, domestic administration, and foreign policy. At the same time, the Macedonian Dynasty produced some truly outstanding emperors skilled in administration and law, including Leo VI and Constantine VII. Leo VI (886–912), known as Leo the Wise, was an accomplished scholar who composed works on politics

The Byzantine Empire, 1025

© 2016 Cengage Learning

A Western View of the Byzantine Empire

POLITICS & GOVERNMENT

BISHOP LIUDPRAND OF CREMONA undertook diplomatic missions to Constantinople on behalf of two Western kings, Berengar of Italy and Otto I of Germany. This selection is taken from his description of his mission to the Byzantine emperor Constantine VII in 949 as an envoy for Berengar, king of Italy from 950 until his overthrow by Otto I of Germany in 964. Liudprand had mixed feelings about Byzantium: admiration, yet also envy and hostility because of its superior wealth.

Liudprand of Cremona, *Antapodosis*

Next to the imperial residence at Constantinople there is a palace of remarkable size and beauty.... In order to receive some Spanish envoys, who had recently arrived, as well as myself ..., Constantine gave orders that this palace should be got ready....

Before the emperor's seat stood a tree, made of bronze gilded over, whose branches were filled with birds, also made of gilded bronze, which uttered different cries, each according to its varying species. The throne itself was so marvelously fashioned that at one moment it seemed a low structure, and at another it rose high into the air. It was of immense size and was guarded by lions, made either of bronze or of wood covered over with gold, who beat the ground with their tails and gave a dreadful roar with open mouth and quivering tongue. Leaning upon the shoulders of two eunuchs I was brought into the emperor's presence. At my approach the lions began to roar and the birds to cry out, each according to its kind; but I was neither terrified nor surprised, for I had previously made enquiry about all these things from people who were well acquainted with them. So after I had three times [bowed] to the emperor with my face upon the ground, I lifted my head, and behold!

The man whom just before I had seen sitting on a moderately elevated seat had now changed his raiment and was sitting on the level of the ceiling. How it was done I could not imagine, unless perhaps he was lifted up by some such sort of device as we use for raising the timbers of a wine press. On that occasion he did not address me personally, ... but by the intermediary of a secretary he enquired about Berengar's doings and asked after his health. I made a fitting reply and then, at a nod from the interpreter, left his presence and retired to my lodging.

It would give me some pleasure also to record here what I did then for Berengar.... The Spanish envoys ... had brought handsome gifts from their masters to the emperor Constantine. I for my part had brought nothing from Berengar except a letter and that was full of lies. I was very greatly disturbed and shamed at this and began to consider anxiously what I had better do.... It finally occurred to me that I might offer the gifts, which on my account I had brought for the emperor, as coming from Berengar, and trick out my humble present with fine words. I therefore presented him with nine excellent cuirasses, seven excellent shields ..., some swords, spears, and spits, and what was more precious to the emperor than anything, four carzimasia; that being the Greek name for young eunuchs who have had both their testicles and their penis removed. This operation is performed by traders who take the boys into Spain and make a huge profit.

Q *What impressions of the Byzantine court do you get from Liudprand's account? What is the modern meaning of the word* byzantine*? How does this account help explain the modern meaning of the word?*

Source: Excerpt from *Works of Liudprand of Cremona* by F. A. Wright, 1930, Routledge and Kegan Paul Publishers.

---

and theology, systematized rules for regulating both trade and court officials, and arranged for a new codification of all Byzantine law. Constantine VII (945–959) wrote a detailed treatise on foreign policy to instruct his officials, as well as his son, on running the empire wisely. Constantine also worked to reduce the tax burden on the peasants.

In the tenth century, competent emperors combined with a number of talented generals to mobilize the empire's military resources and take the offensive. Especially important was Basil II (976–1025), who campaigned regularly against the Bulgars. Although his first campaign was a failure, he continued his efforts until he defeated the Bulgars and annexed Bulgaria to the empire (see the box "The Achievements of Basil II" on p. 367). After his final victory over the Bulgars in 1014, Basil blinded 14,000 Bulgar captives before allowing them to

return to their homes. The Byzantines went on to add the islands of Crete and Cyprus to the empire and to defeat the Muslim forces in Syria, expanding the empire to the upper Euphrates. By the end of Basil's reign in 1025, the Byzantine Empire was the largest it had been since the beginning of the seventh century.

Women in the Byzantine Empire

In Byzantium, as in European society, women were regarded as inferior to men and, at times, even considered to be the instrument of the devil. In general, women were expected to remain at home. They could leave to shop, visit parents, and take part in civic celebrations, but they were supposed to wear veils on these occasions.

The Achievements of Basil II

POLITICS & GOVERNMENT

BASIL II CAME TO POWER at the age of eighteen and during his long reign greatly enlarged the Byzantine Empire. An alliance with the Russian prince Vladimir was instrumental in bringing Orthodox Christianity to the Russians. We know a great deal about Basil II from an account by Michael Psellus (1018–c.1081), one of the foremost Byzantine historians. He wrote the *Chronographia*, a series of biographies of the Byzantine emperors from 976 to 1078, much of it based on his own observations. In this selection, Psellus discusses the qualities of Basil as a leader.

Michael Psellus, *Chronographia*

In his dealings with his subjects, Basil behaved with extraordinary circumspection. It is perfectly true that the great reputation he built up as a ruler was founded rather on terror than on loyalty. As he grew older and became more experienced he relied less on the judgment of men wiser than himself. He alone introduced new measures, he alone disposed his military forces. As for the civil administration, he governed, not in accordance with the written laws, but following the unwritten dictates of his own intuition, which was most excellently equipped by nature for the purpose....

Having purged the empire of the barbarians [Bulgars] he dealt with his own subjects and completely subjugated them too—I think "subjugate" is the right word to describe it. He decided to abandon his former policy, and after the great families had been humiliated and put on an equal footing with the rest, Basil found himself playing the game of power-politics with considerable success. He surrounded himself with favorites who were neither remarkable for brilliance of intellect, nor of noble lineage, nor too learned.... [W]ith them he was accustomed to share the secrets of state....

By humbling the pride or jealousy of his people, Basil made his own road to power an easy one. He was careful, moreover, to close the exit-doors on the monies contributed to the treasury. So a huge sum of money was built up, partly by the exercise of strict economy, partly by fresh additions from abroad.... He himself took no pleasure in any of it: quite the reverse indeed, for the majority of the precious stones, ... were hidden away in his underground vaults....

On his expedition against the barbarians, Basil did not follow the customary procedure of other emperors, setting out at the middle of spring and returning home at the end of summer. For him the time to return was when the task in hand was accomplished. He endured the rigors of winter and the heat of summer with equal indifference. He disciplined himself against thirst. In fact, all his natural desires were kept under stern control, and the man was as hard as steel.... He professed to conduct his wars and draw up the troops in line of battle, himself planning each campaign, but he preferred not to engage in combat personally. A sudden retreat might otherwise prove embarrassing....

Basil's character was two-fold, for he readily adapted himself no less to the crises of war than to the calm of peace. Really, if the truth be told, he was more of a villain in wartime, more of an emperor in time of peace. Outbursts of wrath he controlled and like the proverbial "fire under the ashes," kept anger hid in his heart, but if his orders were disobeyed in war, on his return to the palace he would kindle his wrath and reveal it. Terrible then was the vengeance he took on the miscreant. Generally, he persisted in his opinions, but there were occasions when he did change his mind.... He was slow to adopt any course of action, but never would he willingly alter the decision, once it was [made]. Consequently, his attitude to friends was unvaried, unless perchance he was compelled by necessity to revise his opinion of them. Similarly, where he had burst out in anger against someone, he did not quickly moderate his wrath. Whatever estimate he formed, indeed, was to him an irrevocable and divinely inspired judgment.

Based on this account, what were the personal qualities that made Basil II successful, and how would you characterize the nature of the Byzantine government? Compare the achievements of Basil II with those of Charlemagne as described by Einhard in "The Achievements of Charlemagne" in Chapter 12 on p. 329. How were the two rulers alike? How were they different? How do you explain the differences?

Source: E. R. A. Sewter, trans. *The Chronographia of Michael Psellus* (Yale University Press, 1953), pp. 23–27.

Women were generally expected to fulfill three major functions: to marry and bear children, to maintain the household, and to weave clothes for their families. Thus, a good wife was seen as a special gift to her husband. Contrary to these ideal female roles, some women in the Byzantine world worked outside the home as artisans and sellers, especially of foodstuffs, in the markets of Constantinople. Others served as midwives, bakers, cooks, and dancers, although some dancers also worked as prostitutes.

Upper-class women had greater opportunities to play important roles in the empire. Some aristocratic wives funded the establishment of monasteries, occupied important positions at court, and patronized the arts. Imperial wives could exercise considerable political power as regents for their sons; some even became empresses in their own right. Irene, for example, served as regent for her son until 797 when she blinded and deposed him; she then ruled in her own right until she was overthrown in 802.

Basil the Bulgar-Slayer. Basil II became known as the Bulgar-slayer after his devastating victory over the Bulgars in 1014. This frontispiece illustration from a religious prayer book shows the warrior Basil standing on top of bodies of the conquered Bulgarians. Both angels and warrior-saints are shown protecting the emperor.

The Decline and Fall of the Byzantine Empire (1025–1453)

Q FOCUS QUESTIONS: What impact did the crusades have on the Byzantine Empire? How and why did Constantinople and the Byzantine Empire fall?

The Macedonian Dynasty of the tenth and eleventh centuries had restored much of the power of the Byzantine Empire; its incompetent successors, however, reversed most of the gains.

New Challenges and New Responses

After the Macedonian Dynasty was extinguished in 1056, the empire was beset by internal struggles for power between ambitious military leaders and aristocratic families who bought the support of the great landowners of Anatolia by allowing them greater control over their peasants. This policy was self-destructive, however, because the peasant-warrior was an important source of military strength in the Byzantine state. By the middle of the eleventh century, the Byzantine army began to decline; with fewer peasant recruits, military leaders also began to rely more on mercenaries.

A CHRISTIAN SCHISM The growing division between the Roman Catholic Church of the West and the Eastern Orthodox Church of the Byzantine Empire also weakened the Byzantine state. The Eastern Orthodox Church was unwilling to accept the pope's claim that he was the sole head of the Christian church. This dispute reached a climax in 1054 when Pope Leo IX and Patriarch Michael Cerularius (sayr-yuh-LAR-ee-uss), head of the Byzantine church, formally excommunicated each other, initiating a schism between the two branches of Christianity that has not been healed to this day.

ISLAM AND THE SELJUK TURKS The Byzantine Empire faced external threats to its security as well. In the West, the Normans were menacing the remaining Byzantine possessions in Italy. A much greater threat, however, came from the world of Islam. By the mid-tenth century, the Islamic empire led by the Abbasid caliphate in Baghdad (see Chapter 7) was disintegrating. An attempt was made around that time to unify the Islamic world under the direction of a Shi'ite Dynasty known as the Fatimids. Originating in North Africa, they conquered Egypt and founded the new city of Cairo as their capital. In establishing a Shi'ite caliphate, they became rivals to the Sunni caliphate of Baghdad and divided the Islamic world.

The Fatimid Dynasty prospered and soon surpassed the Abbasid caliphate as the dynamic center of Islam. Benefiting from their position in the heart of the Nile Delta, the Fatimids played a major role in the regional trade passing from the Mediterranean to the Red Sea and beyond. They were tolerant in matters of religion and created a strong army by using nonnative peoples as mercenaries. One of these peoples, the Seljuk Turks, soon posed a threat to the Fatimids themselves.

A nomadic people from Central Asia, the Seljuk Turks had been converted to Islam. As their numbers increased, they moved into the Eastern provinces of the Abbasid Empire, and in 1055 they captured Baghdad and occupied the rest of the empire. When they moved into Asia Minor—the heartland of the Byzantine Empire and its main source of food and manpower—the Byzantines were forced to react. Emperor Romanus IV led an army of recruits and mercenaries into Asia Minor in 1071 and met Turkish forces at Manzikert (MANZ-ih-kurt), where the Byzantines were soundly defeated. Seljuk Turks then went on to occupy much of Anatolia, where many peasants, already disgusted by their exploitation at the hands of Byzantine landowners, readily accepted Turkish control (see Map 7.4 on p. 194).

A NEW DYNASTY After the loss at Manzikert, factional fighting erupted over the imperial title until Alexius Comnenus (kahm-NEE-nuss) (1081–1118) seized the throne and established a dynasty that breathed new life into the Byzantine Empire. Under Alexius, the Byzantines were victorious on the Greek Adriatic coast against the Normans, defeated their enemies in the Balkans, and stopped the Turks in Anatolia. In the twelfth century, the Byzantine Empire experienced a cultural revival and a period of prosperity, fueled by an expansion of trade. The era was also marked by the increased importance of aristocratic families, especially those from a military background. In fact, Alexius's power was built on an alliance of the Comnenus family with other aristocratic families. But both the Comneni Dynasty and the revival of the twelfth century were ultimately threatened by Byzantium's encounters with crusaders from the West.

Impact of the Crusades

Lacking the resources to undertake additional campaigns against the Turks, Emperor Alexius turned to the West for military assistance and asked Pope Urban II for help against the Seljuk Turks. Instead of the military aid the emperor had expected, the pope set in motion the First Crusade (see Chapter 12), a decision that created enormous difficulties for the Byzantines. To pursue the goal of liberating Palestine from the Muslims, Western crusading armies would have to go through Byzantine lands to reach their objective. Alexius, and especially his daughter, Anna Comnena (who was also the Byzantine Empire's only female historian), were fearful that "to all appearances they were on pilgrimage; in reality they planned to dethrone Alexius and seize the capital."[5]

The Byzantines became cautious; Alexius requested that the military leaders of the First Crusade take an oath of loyalty to him and promise that any territory they conquered would be under Byzantine control. The crusaders ignored the emperor's wishes, and after conquering Antioch, Jerusalem, and additional Palestinian lands, they organized the four crusading states of Edessa, Antioch, Tripoli, and Jerusalem. The Byzantines now had to worry not only about the Turks in Anatolia but also about Westerners in the crusading states. The Second and Third crusades posed similar difficulties for the Byzantine emperors.

With the crusades, the Byzantine Empire also became better acquainted with Westerners and Western customs. In the mid-twelfth century, the Byzantine emperor Manuel I (1140–1183) introduced the Western practice of knightly jousting to the Byzantine aristocracy. The Byzantine emperors also conferred trading concessions on the Italian city-states of Venice, Pisa, and Genoa, and in the course of the century, probably 60,000 Western Europeans came to live in Constantinople. But the presence of Westerners and Western practices also led to a growing hostility. Byzantine writers began to denounce Western attitudes, and Westerners often expressed jealousy of Constantinople's wealth. In 1171, Emperor Manuel I expelled the Venetians and seized their goods and ships, arousing in Venice a desire for revenge that was no doubt a factor in the disastrous Fourth Crusade in 1204.

THE LATIN EMPIRE OF CONSTANTINOPLE

After the death of Saladin in 1193 (see Chapter 7), Pope Innocent III launched the Fourth Crusade. Judging the moment auspicious, Innocent encouraged the nobility of Europe to don the crusader's mantle. The Venetians agreed to transport the crusaders to the East but diverted them from the Holy Land by persuading them to first capture Zara, a Christian port on the Dalmatian coast. The crusading army thus became enmeshed in Byzantine politics.

At the start of the thirteenth century, the Byzantine Empire was experiencing yet another struggle for the imperial throne. One contender, Alexius, son of the overthrown Emperor Isaac II, appealed to the crusaders in Zara for assistance, offering to pay them 200,000 marks in silver (the Venetians were getting 85,000 as a transport fee) and to reconcile the Eastern Orthodox Church with the Roman Catholic Church. The crusade leaders now diverted their forces to Constantinople. When the crusading army arrived, the deposed Isaac II was reestablished with his son, Alexius IV, as co-emperor. Unfortunately, the emperors were unable to pay the promised sum. Relations between the crusaders and the Byzantines deteriorated, leading to an attack on Constantinople by the crusaders in the spring of 1204. On April 12, they stormed and sacked the city (see the box "Christian Crusaders Capture Constantinople" on p. 370). Christian crusaders took gold, silver, jewelry, and precious furs, while the Catholic clergy accompanying the crusaders stole as many relics as they could find.

The Byzantine Empire now disintegrated into a series of petty states ruled by crusading barons and Byzantine princes. The chief state was the new Latin Empire of Constantinople led by Count Baldwin of Flanders as emperor. The Venetians seized the island of Crete and assumed control of Constantinople's trade. Why had the Western crusaders succeeded so easily when Persians, Bulgars, and Arabs had failed for centuries to conquer Constantinople? Although the crusaders were no doubt motivated by greed and a lust for conquest, they were also convinced that they were acting in God's cause. After all, a Catholic patriarch (a Venetian) had now been installed in Constantinople, and the reconciliation of Eastern Orthodoxy with Catholic Christianity had been accomplished. Nor should we overlook the military superiority of the French warriors and the superb organizational skills of the Venetians; together, they formed a powerful and highly effective union.

REVIVAL OF THE BYZANTINE EMPIRE Although he protested the diversion of the crusade from the Holy Land, Pope Innocent III belatedly accepted as "God's work" the conversion of Greek Byzantium to Latin Christianity. Some have argued that Innocent did realize, however, that the use of force to reunite the churches virtually guaranteed the failure of any permanent reunion. All too soon, this proved correct. The West was unable to maintain the Latin Empire, for the Western rulers of the newly created principalities were soon engrossed in fighting each other. Some parts of the Byzantine Empire had managed to survive under Byzantine princes. In 1259, Michael Paleologus (pay-lee-AWL-uh-guss), a Greek military leader, took control of the kingdom of Nicaea in Western Asia Minor, led a Byzantine army to recapture Constantinople two years later, and then established a new Byzantine dynasty, the Paleologi.

The Byzantine Empire had been saved, but it was no longer a Mediterranean power. The restored empire was a badly truncated entity, consisting of the city of Constantinople and its surrounding territory, some lands in Asia Minor, and part of Thessalonica. It was surrounded by enemies—Bulgarians, Mongols, Turks, and Westerners, especially the resentful Venetians. And there was still internal opposition to Michael VIII. But the emperor survived and began a badly needed restoration of Constantinople.

Even in its reduced size, the empire limped along for another 190 years, and Constantinople remained an active economic center. Scholars continued to study the classics, and new churches and monasteries were built. Yet civil strife

Christian Crusaders Capture Constantinople

POLITICS & GOVERNMENT

POPE INNOCENT III INAUGURATED the Fourth Crusade after Saladin's empire began to disintegrate. Tragically, however, the crusading army of mostly French nobles was diverted to Constantinople to intervene in Byzantine politics. In 1204, the Christian crusaders stormed and sacked one of Christendom's greatest cities. This description of the division of the spoils after the conquest of Constantinople is taken from a contemporary account by a participant in the struggle.

Geoffrey de Villehardouin, *The Conquest of Constantinople*

Then it was proclaimed throughout the host by Marquis Boniface of Montferrat, who was lord of the host, and by the barons, and by the doge of Venice, that all the booty should be collected and brought together, as had been covenanted under oath and pains of excommunication. Three churches were appointed for the receiving of the spoils, and guards were set to have them in charge, both Franks [the French] and Venetians, the most upright that could be found.

Then each began to bring in such booty as he had taken and to collect it together. And some brought in loyally, and some in evil sort, because covetousness, which is the root of all evil hindered them. So from that time forth the covetous began to keep things back, and our Lord began to love them less. Ah God! how loyally they had borne themselves up to now! And well had the Lord God shown them that in all things He was ready to honor and exalt them above all people. But often do the good suffer for the sins of the wicked.

The spoils and the booty were collected together, and you must know that all was not brought into the common stock, for not a few kept things back, in spite of the excommunication of the pope. That which was brought to the churches was divided, in equal parts between the Franks and the Venetians, according to the sworn covenant. And you must know further that the pilgrims, after the division had been made, paid out of their share fifty thousand marks of silver to the Venetians, and then divided, at least one hundred thousand marks between themselves, among their own people....

And as to theft, and those who were convicted thereof, you must know that stern justice was meted out to such as were found guilty, and not a few were hanged. The count of St. Paul hung one of his knights, who had kept back certain spoils, with his shield to his neck; but many there were both great and small, who kept back part of the spoils, and it was never known. Well may you be assured that the booty was very great, for if it had not been for what was stolen, and for the part given to the Venetians, there would have been at least four hundred thousand marks of silver, and at least ten thousand horses. Thus were divided the spoils of Constantinople, as you have heard.

Q *What does this document reveal about the crusading ideals and practices of the Europeans?*

Source: From Hutton Webster, *Readings in Medieval and Modern History* (Boston: D. C. Heath & Co., 1917), pp. 116–117.

---

persisted as rival claimants struggled over the throne, and enemies continued to multiply. The threat from the Turks finally doomed the aged empire.

The Ottoman Turks and the Fall of Constantinople

Beginning in northeastern Asia Minor in the thirteenth century, the Ottoman Turks spread rapidly, seizing the lands of the Seljuk Turks and the Byzantine Empire. In 1345, they bypassed Constantinople and pushed into the Balkans. Under Sultan Murad (moo-RAHD), Ottoman forces moved through Bulgaria and into the lands of the Serbs; in 1389, at the Battle of Kosovo (KAWSS-suh-voh), Ottoman forces defeated the Serbs. By the beginning of the fifteenth century, the Byzantine Empire had been reduced to little more than Constantinople,

The Fall of Constantinople, 1453

PONTOON BRIDGE — TURKISH FORCES — TURKISH FORCES — TURKISH FLEET — Bosporus — Golden Horn — ASIA — CHAINS — CITY WALL — Constantinople — Sea of Marmara

0 ___ 2 Kilometers
0 ___ 1 Mile

© 2016 Cengage Learning

now surrounded on all sides by the Ottomans. When Mehmet (meh-MET) II came to the throne in 1451 at the age of only nineteen, he was determined to capture Constantinople and complete the demise of the Byzantine Empire.

The siege began in April when Mehmet moved his army—probably about 80,000 men—within striking distance of the 13-mile-long land walls along the Western edge of the city. The pope and the Italian city-states of Venice and Genoa promised aid, but most of it was too little and too late. The city probably had 6,000 to 8,000 soldiers mobilized for its defense. On April 2, Emperor Constantine XI (1449–1453), the last Byzantine emperor, ordered that a floating chain or boom be stretched across the Golden Horn, the inlet that forms the city's harbor, to prevent a naval attack from the north. Mehmet's forces, however, took control of the tip of the peninsula north of the Golden Horn and then pulled their ships overland across the peninsula

Erich Lessing/Art Resource, NY

The Fall of Constantinople. Few events in the history of the Ottoman Empire are more dramatic than the conquest of Constantinople in 1453. Although the Venetian painter Palma Giovane did not witness the conquest itself, he tried to capture the drama in his opulent reconstruction of the first attack by the Turks on the legendary city. This painting was one of a series done for the Doge's Palace in Venice.

from the Bosporus and placed them into the water behind the chains. The Ottoman fleet in the Horn built a pontoon bridge and set up artillery, forcing the Byzantines to defend the city on all sides.

The Ottomans' main attack, however, came against the land walls. On April 6, the artillery onslaught began. The Ottoman invaders had a distinct advantage with their cannons. One of them, constructed by a Hungarian engineer, had a 26-foot barrel that fired stone balls weighing 1,200 pounds. It took 60 oxen and 2,000 men to pull the great cannon into position. On May 29, Mehmet decided on a final assault, focused against the areas where the walls had been breached. When Ottoman forces broke into the city, the emperor became one of the first casualties. Irregular Ottoman forces began to loot the city before regular troops were able to stop them. About 4,000 defenders were killed, and thousands of the inhabitants were sold into slavery. Early in the afternoon, Mehmet II rode into the city, exalted the power of Allah from the pulpit in the cathedral of Hagia Sophia, and ordered that it be converted into a mosque. He soon began rebuilding the city as the capital of the Ottoman Empire. The Byzantine Empire had come to an end.

CHRONOLOGY The Byzantine Empire, 750–1453	
Revival under Michael III	842–867
Macedonian Dynasty	867–1056
Basil I	867–886
Leo VI	886–912
Constantine VII	945–959
Basil II	976–1025
Schism between Eastern Orthodox Church and Roman Catholic Church	1054
Turkish defeat of the Byzantines at Manzikert	1071
Revival under Alexius Comnenus	1081–1118
Manuel Comnenus	1140–1183
Latin Empire of Constantinople	1204–1261
Revival of Byzantine Empire	1261
Turkish defeat of Serbs at Kosovo	1389
Constantine XI, the last Byzantine emperor	1449–1453
Fall of the empire	1453

The Crises of the Fourteenth Century in the West

 FOCUS QUESTIONS: What impact did the Black Death have on Europe and Asia in the fourteenth century? What problems did Europeans face during the fourteenth century, and what impact did these crises have on European economic, social, and religious life?

At the beginning of the fourteenth century, changes in global weather patterns ushered in what has been called a "little ice age." Shortened growing seasons and disastrous weather conditions, including heavy storms and constant rain, led to widespread famine and hunger. Soon an even greater catastrophe struck.

The Black Death: From Asia to Europe

In the mid-fourteenth century, a disaster known as the **Black Death** struck in Asia, North Africa, and Europe. Bubonic plague was the most common and most important form of plague in the diffusion of the Black Death and was spread by black rats infested with fleas who were host to the deadly bacterium *Yersinia pestis* (yur-SIN-ee-uh PES-tiss).

ROLE OF THE MONGOLS This great plague originated in Asia. After disappearing from Europe and the Middle East in the Middle Ages, bubonic plague continued to haunt areas of southwestern China. In the early 1300s, rats accompanying Mongol troops spread the plague into central China and by 1331 to northeastern China. In one province near Beijing, it was reported that 90 percent of the population died. Overall, China's population may have declined from 120 million in the mid-1300s to 80 million by 1400.

In the thirteenth century, the Mongols had brought much of the Eurasian landmass under a single rule, which in turn facilitated long-distance trade, particularly along the Silk Road, now dominated by Muslim merchants from Central Asia (see Chapter 10). The spread of people and goods throughout this Eurasian landmass also facilitated the spread of the plague.

In the 1330s, the plague had spread to Central Asia; by 1339 it had reached Samarkand, a caravan stop on the Silk Road. From Central Asia, trading caravans brought the plague to Caffa, on the Black Sea, in 1346 and to Constantinople by the following year (see the Comparative Essay "The Role of Disease in History" on p. 373). Its arrival in the Byzantine Empire was noted in a work by Emperor John VI, who lost a son: "Upon arrival in Constantinople she [the empress] found Andronikos, the youngest born, dead from the invading plague, which ... attacked almost all the sea coasts of the world and killed most of their people."[6] By 1348, the plague had spread to Egypt and also to Mecca, Damascus, and other parts of the Middle East. The Muslim historian Ibn Khaldun (IB-un kahl-DOON), writing in the fourteenth century, commented, "Civilization in the East and West was visited by a destructive plague which devastated nations and caused populations to vanish. It swallowed up many of the good things of

civilization and wiped them out."[7] Egypt was particularly devastated by the plague; it has been estimated that the population of Egypt did not return to its pre-1347 level until the nineteenth century.

THE BLACK DEATH IN EUROPE The Black Death of the mid-fourteenth century was the most devastating natural disaster in European history, ravaging Europe's population and causing economic, social, political, and cultural upheaval. Contemporary chroniclers lamented that parents attempted to flee, abandoning their children; one related the words of a child left behind: "Oh father, why have you abandoned me? ... Mother where have you gone?"[8]

The plague reached Europe in October 1347 when Genoese merchants brought it from Caffa to the island of Sicily off the coast of Italy. One contemporary wrote, "As it happened, among those who escaped from Caffa by boat, there were a few sailors who had been infected with the poisonous disease. Some boats were bound for Genoa, others went to Venice and other Christian areas. When the sailors reached these places and mixed with the people there, it was as if they had brought evil spirits with them."[9] The plague quickly spread to southern Italy and then to southern France by the end of the year (see Map 13.3). Diffusion of the Black Death followed commercial trade routes. In 1348, it spread through Spain, France, and the Low Countries and into Germany. By the end of that year, it had moved to England. By the end of the next, the plague had reached northern Europe and Scandinavia. Eastern Europe and Russia were affected by 1351.

Mortality figures for the Black Death were incredibly high. Especially hard hit were Italy's crowded cities, where 50 to 60 percent of the people died. One citizen of Florence wrote, "A great many breathed their last in the public streets, day and night; a large number perished in their homes, and it was only by the stench of their decaying bodies that they proclaimed their deaths to their neighbors. Everywhere the city was teeming with corpses."[10] In England and Germany, entire villages simply disappeared. It has been estimated that out of a total European population of 75 million, as many as 38 million people may have died of the plague between 1347 and 1351.

As contemporaries attempted to explain the Black Death and mitigate its harshness, some turned to extreme sorts of behavior. Many believed that the plague either had been sent by God as a punishment for humans' sins or had been caused by the devil (see Opposing Viewpoints "Causes of the Black Death: Contemporary Views" on p. 375). Some, known as flagellants (FLAJ-uh-lunts), resorted to extreme measures to gain God's forgiveness. Groups of flagellants, both men and women, wandered from town to town, flogging each other with whips to beg the forgiveness of God whom they believed had sent the plague to punish humans for their sinful ways. One contemporary chronicler described a flagellant procession:

> The penitents went about, coming first out of Germany. They were men who did public penance and scourged themselves with whips of hard knotted leather with little iron spikes. Some made themselves bleed very badly between the shoulder blades and some foolish women had cloths ready to catch the blood

The Role of Disease in History

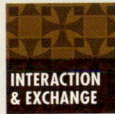

INTERACTION & EXCHANGE

When Hernán Cortés and his fellow conquistadors arrived in Mesoamerica in 1519, the local inhabitants were frightened of the horses and the firearms that accompanied the Spaniards. What they did not know was that the most dangerous enemies brought by these strange new arrivals were invisible—the disease-bearing microbes that would soon kill them by the millions.

Diseases have been the scourge of animal species since the dawn of prehistory, making the lives of human beings, in the words of the English philosopher Thomas Hobbes, "nasty, brutish, and short." With the increasing sophistication of forensic evidence, archaeologists today are able to determine from recently discovered human remains that our immediate ancestors were plagued by such familiar ailments as anemia, arthritis, tuberculosis, and malaria.

With the explosive growth of the human population brought about by the agricultural revolution, the problems posed by the presence of disease intensified. As people began to congregate in villages and cities, bacteria settled in their piles of refuse and were carried by lice in their clothing. The domestication of animals made humans more vulnerable to diseases carried by their livestock. As population density increased, the danger of widespread epidemics increased with it.

As time went on, succeeding generations gradually developed partial or complete immunity to many of these diseases, which became chronic rather than fatal to their victims, as occurred with malaria in parts of Africa, for example, and chickenpox in the Americas. But when a disease was introduced to a particular society that had not previously been exposed to it, the consequences were often devastating. The most dramatic example

Shark/Art Resource, NY

Mass Burial of Plague Victims. The Black Death had spread to northern Europe by the end of 1348. Shown here is a mass burial of victims of the plague in Tournai, located in modern Belgium. As is evident in the illustration, at this stage of the plague, there was still time to make coffins for the victims' burial. Later, as the plague intensified, the dead were thrown into open pits.

was the famous Black Death, the plague that ravaged Europe and China during the fourteenth century, killing one-fourth to one-half of the inhabitants in the affected regions (and even greater numbers in certain areas). Smallpox had the same impact in the Americas after the arrival of Christopher Columbus, and malaria was fatal to many Europeans on their arrival in West Africa. How were these diseases transmitted? In most instances, they followed the trade routes. Such was the case with the Black Death, which was initially carried by fleas living in the saddlebags of Mongol warriors as they advanced toward Europe in the thirteenth and fourteenth centuries and thereafter by rats in the holds of cargo ships. Smallpox and other diseases were brought to the Americas by the conquistadors. Epidemics, then, are a price that humans pay for having developed the network of rapid communication that has accompanied the evolution of human society.

What role has disease played in human history?

and smear it on their eyes, saying it was miraculous blood. While they were doing penance, they sang very mournful songs about the nativity and the passion of Our Lord. The object of this penance was to put a stop to the mortality, for in that time ... at least a third of all the people in the world died.[11]

The flagellants attracted attention and created mass hysteria wherever they went. The Catholic Church, however, became alarmed when flagellant groups began to kill Jews and attack clergy who opposed them. Pope Clement VI condemned the flagellants in October 1349 and urged the public authorities to crush them. By the end of 1350, most of the flagellant movement had been destroyed.

An outbreak of virulent anti-Semitism also accompanied the Black Death. Jews were accused of causing the plague by poisoning town wells. The worst **pogroms** (POH-grums) (massacres) against this minority were carried out in Germany, where

MAP 13.3 Spread of the Black Death. The plague entered Europe through Sicily in 1347 and within three years had killed between one-quarter and one-half of the population. Outbreaks continued into the early eighteenth century, and the European population took two hundred years to return to the level it had reached before the Black Death.

Q *Is there a general pattern between distance from Sicily and the elapsed time before a region was infected with the plague?*

more than sixty major Jewish communities had been exterminated by 1351. Many Jews fled Eastward to Russia and especially to Poland, where the king offered them protection. Eastern Europe became home to large Jewish communities.

Economic Dislocation and Social Upheaval

The deaths of so many people in the fourteenth century had severe economic consequences. Trade declined, and some industries suffered greatly. Florence's woolen industry, one of the giants, had produced 70,000 to 80,000 pieces of cloth in 1338; in 1378, it was yielding only 24,000 pieces.

Both peasants and noble landlords were also affected. A shortage of workers caused a dramatic rise in the price of labor, while the decline in the number of people lowered the demand for food, resulting in falling prices. Landlords were now paying more for labor at the same time that their rental

income was declining. Concurrently, the decline in the number of peasants after the Black Death made it easier for some to convert their labor services to rent, thus freeing them from serfdom. But there were limits to how much the peasants could advance. They faced the same economic hurdles as the lords, who also attempted to impose wage restrictions and reinstate old forms of labor service. New governmental taxes also hurt. Peasant complaints became widespread and soon gave rise to rural revolts.

The English Peasants' Revolt of 1381 was the most prominent. The immediate cause of the revolt was the monarchy's attempt to raise revenues by imposing a poll tax, a flat charge on each adult member of the population. Peasants in Eastern England refused to pay the tax and expelled the collectors forcibly from their villages. Rebellion spread as peasants burned down the manor houses of aristocrats, lawyers, and government officials. Soon, however, the young king, Richard II (1377–1399), with the assistance of aristocrats, arrested hundreds of the rebels

Causes of the Black Death: Contemporary Views

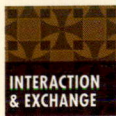

INTERACTION & EXCHANGE

THE BLACK DEATH WAS THE MOST TERRIFYING NATURAL CALAMITY OF THE MIDDLE AGES and affected wide areas of Europe, North Africa, and Asia. People were often baffled by the plague, especially by its causes, and gave widely different explanations. The first selection is taken from the preface to the *Decameron* by the fourteenth-century Italian writer Giovanni Boccaccio (joh-VAH-nee boh-KAH-choh). The other selections are from contemporary treatises that offered widely different explanations for the great plague.

Giovanni Boccaccio, *Decameron*

In the year of Our Lord 1348 the deadly plague broke out in the great city of Florence, most beautiful of Italian cities. Whether through the operation of the heavenly bodies or because of our own iniquities which the just wrath of God sought to correct, the plague had arisen in the East some years before, causing the death of countless human beings. It spread without stop from one place to another, until, unfortunately, it swept over the West. Neither knowledge nor human foresight availed against it.... Nor did humble supplications serve. Not once but many times they were ordained in the form of processions and other ways for the propitiation of God by the faithful, but, in spite of everything, toward the spring of the year the plague began to show its ravages.

On Earthquakes as the Cause of Plague

There is a fourth opinion, which I consider more likely than the others, which is that insofar as the mortality arose from natural causes its immediate cause was a corrupt and poisonous earthy exhalation, which infected the air in various parts of the world and, when breathed in by people, suffocated them and suddenly snuffed them out....

It is a matter of scientific fact that earthquakes are caused by the exhalation of fumes enclosed in the bowels of the earth.

When the fumes batter against the sides of the earth, and cannot get out, the earth is shaken and moves. I say that it is the vapor and corrupted air which has been vented—or so to speak purged—in the earthquake which occurred on St Paul's day, 1347, along with the corrupted air vented in other earthquakes and eruptions, which has infected the air above the earth and killed people in various parts of the world; and I can bring various reasons in support of this conclusion.

Herman Gigas on Well Poisoning

In 1347 there was such a great pestilence and mortality throughout almost the whole world that in the opinion of well-informed men scarcely a tenth of mankind survived.... Some say that it was brought about by the corruption of the air; others that the Jews planned to wipe out all the Christians with poison and had poisoned wells and springs everywhere. And many Jews confessed as much under torture: that they had bred spiders and toads in pots and pans, and had obtained poison from overseas; and that not every Jew knew about this wickedness, only the more powerful ones, so that it would not be betrayed. As evidence of this heinous crime, men say that the bags full of poison were found in many wells and springs, and as a result, in cities, towns and villages throughout Germany, and in fields and woods too, almost all the wells and springs have been blocked up or built over, so that no one can drink from them or use the water for cooking, and men have to use rain or river water instead. God, the lord of vengeance, has not suffered the malice of the Jews to go unpunished. Throughout Germany, in all but a few places, they were burnt. For fear of that punishment many accepted baptism and their lives were spared. This action was taken against the Jews in 1349.

What were the different explanations for the causes of the Black Death? How do you explain the differences, and what do these explanations tell you about the level of scientific knowledge in the Later Middle Ages? Why do you think Jews became scapegoats?

Sources: From *The Decameron* by Giovanni Boccaccio, trans. by Frances Winwar, p. xxii. Reprinted by permission of The Limited Editions Club. From Rosemary Horrox, ed., *The Black Death*, pp. 177–178, 207. Copyright © 1994 University of Manchester Press. Reprinted by permission of the University of Manchester Press.

and ended the revolt. The poll tax was eliminated, however, and in the end most of the rebels were pardoned.

Although the peasant revolts sometimes resulted in short-term gains for the participants, the uprisings were relatively easily crushed and their gains quickly lost.

Accustomed to ruling, the established classes easily combined and stifled dissent. Nevertheless, the revolts of the fourteenth century had introduced a new element to European life; henceforth, social unrest would be a characteristic of European history.

Political Instability

Famine, plague, economic turmoil, and social upheaval were not the only problems of the fourteenth century. War and political instability must also be added to the list. And of all the struggles that ensued, the Hundred Years' War was the most violent.

THE HUNDRED YEARS' WAR In the thirteenth century, England still held one small possession in France known as the duchy of Gascony. As duke of Gascony, the English king pledged loyalty as a vassal to the French king, but when King Philip VI of France (1328–1350) seized Gascony in 1337, the duke of Gascony—King Edward III of England (1327–1377)—declared war on Philip.

The war began in a burst of knightly enthusiasm. The French army of 1337 still relied largely on heavily armed noble cavalrymen, who looked with contempt on foot soldiers and crossbowmen, whom they regarded as social inferiors. The English, too, used heavily armed cavalry, but they relied even more on large numbers of paid foot soldiers. Armed with pikes, many of these soldiers had also adopted the longbow, invented by the Welsh. The longbow had a longer range and greater speed of fire than the crossbow.

The first major battle of the war occurred in 1346 at Crécy (kray-SEE), just south of Flanders. The larger French army followed no battle plan but simply attacked the English lines in a disorderly fashion. The arrows of the English archers decimated the French cavalry. As the chronicler Froissart (frwah-SAR) described it, "The English [with their longbows] continued to shoot into the thickest part of the crowd, wasting none of their arrows. They impaled or wounded horses and riders, who fell to the ground in great distress, unable to get up again without the help of several men."[12] It was a stunning victory for the English and the foot soldier.

The Battle of Crécy was not decisive, however. The English simply did not possess the resources to subjugate all of France, but they continued to try. The English king, Henry V (1413–1422), was especially eager to achieve victory. At the Battle of Agincourt (AH-zhen-koor) in 1415, the heavy, armor-plated French knights attempted to attack across a field turned to mud by heavy rain; the result was a disastrous French defeat and the death of 1,500 French nobles. The English had become the masters of northern France.

The seemingly hopeless French cause fell into the hands of the dauphin (DAH-fin *or* doh-FAN) Charles, the heir to the throne, who governed the southern two-thirds of French lands. Charles's cause seemed doomed until a French peasant woman quite unexpectedly saved the timid monarch. Born in 1412, the daughter of well-to-do peasants, Joan of Arc was a deeply religious person who came to believe that her favorite saints had commanded her to free France. In February 1429, Joan made her way to the dauphin's court and persuaded Charles to allow her to accompany a French army to Orléans (or-lay-AHN). Apparently inspired by the faith of the peasant girl known as "the Maid of Orléans," the French armies found new confidence in themselves and liberated the city. Joan had brought the war to a decisive turning point.

But she did not live to see the war concluded. Captured in 1430, Joan was turned over by the English to the Inquisition, which tried her on charges of witchcraft. In the fifteenth century, spiritual visions were thought to be inspired by either God or the devil. Joan was condemned to death as a heretic and burned at the stake in 1431.

Joan of Arc's accomplishments proved decisive. Although the war dragged on for another two decades, defeats of English armies in Normandy and Aquitaine led to French victory by 1453. Important to the French success was the use of the cannon, a new weapon made possible by the invention of gunpowder. The Chinese had invented gunpower in the tenth century and devised a simple cannon by the thirteenth. The Mongols greatly improved this technology, developing more accurate cannons and cannonballs; both spread to the Middle East in the thirteenth century and to Europe by the fourteenth. The use of gunpowder eventually brought drastic changes to European warfare by making castles, city walls, and armored knights obsolete.

The Battle of Crécy. This fifteenth-century manuscript illustration depicts the Battle of Crécy, the first of several military disasters suffered by the French in the Hundred Years' War, and shows why the English preferred the longbow to the crossbow. At the left, the French crossbowmen stop shooting and prime their weapons by cranking the handle, while English archers continue to shoot their longbows (a skilled archer could launch ten arrows a minute).

POLITICAL DISINTEGRATION By the fourteenth century, the feudal order had begun to break down. With money from taxes, kings could now hire professional soldiers, who tended to be more reliable than feudal knights anyway. Fourteenth-century kings had their own problems as well. Many dynasties in Europe were unable to produce male heirs, while the founders of new dynasties had to fight for their positions as factions of nobles, trying to gain advantages for themselves, supported opposing candidates. Rulers encountered financial problems too. Hiring professional soldiers left them always short of cash, adding yet another element of uncertainty and confusion to fourteenth-century politics.

The Decline of the Church

The papacy of the Roman Catholic Church reached the height of its power in the thirteenth century. But crises in the fourteenth century led to a serious decline for the church. By that time, the monarchies of Europe were no longer willing to accept papal claims of temporal supremacy, as is evident in the struggle between Pope Boniface VIII (1294–1303) and King Philip IV (1285–1314) of France. In his desire to acquire new revenues, Philip claimed the right to tax the clergy of France, but Boniface VIII insisted that the clergy of any state could not pay taxes to their secular ruler without the pope's consent. In no uncertain terms he argued that popes were supreme over both the church and the state.

Philip IV refused to accept the pope's position and sent a small contingent of French forces to capture Boniface and bring him back to France for trial. The pope escaped but soon died from the shock of his experience. To ensure his position and avoid any future papal threat, Philip IV engineered the election of a Frenchman, Clement V (1305–1314), as pope. Using the excuse of turbulence in the city of Rome, the new pope took up residence in Avignon (ah-veen-YOHN) on the East bank of the Rhone River.

From 1305 to 1377, the popes resided in Avignon, leading to an increase in antipapal sentiment. The city of Rome was the traditional capital of the universal church. The pope was the bishop of Rome, and it was unseemly that the head of the Catholic Church should reside in Avignon instead of Rome. Moreover, the splendor in which the pope and cardinals were living in Avignon led to highly vocal criticism of both clergy and papacy. At last, Pope Gregory XI (1370–1378), perceiving the disastrous decline in papal prestige, returned to Rome in 1377.

THE GREAT SCHISM AND CRIES FOR REFORM Gregory XI died in Rome the spring after his return. When the college of cardinals met to elect a new pope, the citizens of Rome, fearful that the French majority would choose another Frenchman who would move the papacy back to Avignon, threatened that the cardinals would not leave Rome alive unless they elected a Roman or an Italian as pope. Wisely, the terrified cardinals duly elected the Italian archbishop of Bari as Pope Urban VI (1378–1389). Five months later, a group of dissenting cardinals—the French ones—declared Urban's election invalid and chose one of their number, a Frenchman, who took the title of Clement VII and promptly returned to Avignon. Because Urban remained in Rome, there were now

two popes, beginning a crisis that has been called the Great Schism of the church.

The Great Schism divided Europe. France and its allies supported the pope in Avignon, whereas France's enemy England and its allies supported the pope in Rome. The Great Schism was also damaging to the faith of Christian believers. The pope was widely believed to be the true leader of Christendom; when both lines of popes denounced the other as the Antichrist, people's faith in the papacy and the church was undermined.

Meanwhile, the crises in the Catholic Church produced cries for reform. The Great Schism led large numbers of churchmen to take up the theory of **conciliarism**, or the belief that only a general council of the church, and not the pope, could bring reform to the church in its "head and members." These cries for change finally led to a church council that met at Constance in Switzerland in 1417. After the competing popes resigned or were deposed, a new pope was elected who was acceptable to all parties.

Although the Council of Constance ended the Great Schism, the council's efforts to reform the church were less successful. By the mid-fifteenth century, the papacy had reasserted its authority and ended the conciliar movement. At the same time, however, as a result of these crises, the church had lost much of its temporal power. Even worse, the papacy and the church had also lost much of their moral prestige.

Recovery: The Renaissance

 FOCUS QUESTION: What were the main features of the Renaissance in Europe, and how did it differ from the Middle Ages?

People who lived in Italy between 1350 and 1550 or so believed that they were witnessing a rebirth of Classical antiquity—the world of the Greeks and Romans. To them, this marked a new age, which historians later called the **Renaissance** (French for "rebirth") and viewed as a distinct period of European history, which began in Italy and then spread to the rest of Europe.

Renaissance Italy was largely an urban society. The city-states became the centers of Italian political, economic, and social life. Within this new urban society, a secular spirit emerged as increasing wealth created new possibilities for the enjoyment of worldly things.

The Renaissance was also an age of recovery from the disasters of the fourteenth century, including the Black Death, political disorder, and economic recession. In pursuing that recovery, Italian intellectuals became intensely interested in the glories of their own past, the Greco-Roman culture of antiquity.

A new view of human beings emerged as people in the Italian Renaissance began to emphasize individual ability. The fifteenth-century Florentine architect Leon Battista Alberti (LAY-un buh-TEESS-tuh al-BAYR-tee) expressed the new philosophy succinctly: "Men can do all things if they will."[13] This high regard for human worth and for individual potentiality gave rise to a new social ideal of the well-rounded personality or "universal person"—*l'uomo universale* (LWOH-moh OO-nee-ver-SAH-lay)—who was capable of achievements in many areas of life.

The Intellectual Renaissance

The emergence and growth of individualism and secularism as characteristics of the Italian Renaissance are most noticeable in the intellectual and artistic realms. The most important literary movement associated with the Renaissance was humanism.

Renaissance humanism was an intellectual movement based on the study of the classics, the literary works of Greece and Rome. Humanists studied the liberal arts—grammar, rhetoric, poetry, moral philosophy or ethics, and history—all based on the writings of ancient Greek and Roman authors. We call these subjects the humanities.

Petrarch (PEE-trark *or* PET-trark) (1304–1374), who has often been called the father of Italian Renaissance humanism, did more than any other individual in the fourteenth century to foster its development. Petrarch sought to find forgotten Latin manuscripts and set in motion a ransacking of monastic libraries throughout Europe. He also began the humanist emphasis on the use of pure Classical Latin. Humanists used the works of Cicero as a model for prose and those of Virgil for poetry. As Petrarch said, "Christ is my God; Cicero is the prince of the language."

In Florence, the humanist movement took a new direction at the beginning of the fifteenth century. Fourteenth-century humanists such as Petrarch had described the intellectual life as one of solitude. They rejected family and a life of action in the community. Now, however, the humanists who worked as secretaries for the city council of Florence took a new interest in civic life. They came to believe that it was the duty of an intellectual to live an active life for one's state. Humanists came to believe that their study of the humanities should be put to the service of the state. It is no accident that humanists served as secretaries in Italian city-states or at courts of princes or popes.

Also evident in the humanism of the first half of the fifteenth century was a growing interest in Classical Greek civilization. One of the first Italian humanists to gain a thorough knowledge of Greek was Leonardo Bruni (leh-ah-NAHR-doh BROO-nee), who became an enthusiastic pupil of the Byzantine scholar Manuel Chrysoloras (man-WEL kriss-uh-LAHR-uss), who taught in Florence from 1396 to 1400.

WAS THERE A RENAISSANCE FOR WOMEN? Historians have disagreed over the benefits of the Renaissance for women. Some maintain that during the Middle Ages upper-class women in particular had greater freedom to satisfy their emotional needs, whereas upper-class women in the Renaissance experienced a contraction of both social and personal options as they became even more subject to male authority. Other historians have argued that although conditions remained bleak for most women, some women, especially those in courtly, religious, and intellectual environments, found ways to develop a new sense of themselves as women. This may be especially true of women who were educated in the humanist fashion and went on to establish literary careers.

Isotta Nogarola (ee-ZAHT-uh noh-guh-ROH-luh), born to a noble family in Verona, mastered Latin and wrote numerous letters and treatises that brought her praise from male Italian intellectuals. Cassandra Fedele (FAY-duh-lee) of Venice, who learned both Latin and Greek from humanist tutors hired by her family, became prominent in Venice for her public recitations of orations. Laura Cereta (say-REE-tuh) was educated in Latin by her father, a physician from Brescia. Laura defended the ability of women to pursue scholarly pursuits (see the box "A Woman's Defense of Learning" on p. 379).

The Artistic Renaissance

Renaissance artists sought to imitate nature in their works of art. Their search for naturalism became an end in itself: to persuade onlookers of the reality of the object or event they were portraying. At the same time, the new artistic standards reflected the new attitude of mind in which human beings became the focus of attention, the "center and measure of all things," as one artist proclaimed.

The frescoes by Masaccio (muh-ZAH-choh) (1401–1428) in Florence have long been regarded as the first masterpieces of Early Renaissance art. With his use of monumental figures, a more realistic relationship between figures and landscape, and the visual representation of the laws of perspective, a new realistic style of painting was born. Onlookers became aware of a world of reality that appeared to be a continuation of their own.

This new Renaissance style was absorbed and modified by other Florentine painters in the fifteenth century. Especially important were two major developments. One emphasized the technical side of painting—understanding the laws of perspective and the geometrical organization of outdoor space and light. The second development was the investigation of movement and anatomical structure. The realistic portrayal of the human nude became one of the foremost preoccupations of Italian Renaissance artists.

A new style in architecture also emerged when Filippo Brunelleschi (fee-LEE-poh BROO-nuh-LESS-kee) (1377–1446), inspired by Roman models, created an interior in the Church of San Lorenzo in Florence that was very different from that of the great medieval cathedrals. San Lorenzo's Classical columns, rounded arches, and coffered ceiling created an environment that did not overwhelm the worshipers physically and psychologically, as Gothic cathedrals did, but comforted them as a space created to fit human, not divine, measurements. Like painters and sculptors, Renaissance architects sought to reflect a human-centered world.

By the end of the fifteenth century, Italian artists had mastered the new techniques for scientific observation of the world around them and were now ready to move into new forms of creative expression. This marked the shift to the High

A Woman's Defense of Learning

ART & IDEAS

AS A YOUNG WOMAN, LAURA CERETA was proud of her learning, but she was condemned by a male world that found it unseemly for women to be scholars. One monk said to her father, "She gives herself to things unworthy of her—namely, the classics." Before being silenced, Laura Cereta wrote a series of letters, including one to a male critic who had argued that her work was so good it could not have been written by a woman.

Laura Cereta, *Defense of the Liberal Instruction of Women*

Your complaints are hurting my ears, for you say publicly and quite openly that you are not only surprised but pained that I am said to show this extraordinary intellect of the sort one would have thought nature would give to the most learned of men—as if you had reached the conclusion, on the facts of the case, that a similar girl had seldom been seen among the peoples of the world. You are wrong on both counts....

I would remain silent, believe me, if you, with your longstanding hostile and envious attitude towards me, had learned to attack me alone.... But I am angry and my disgust overflows. Why should the condition of our sex be shamed by your little attacks? Because of this, a mind thirsting for revenge is set afire.... My cause itself is worthy: I am impelled to show what great glory that noble lineage which I carry in my own breasts has won for virtue and literature—a lineage that knowledge, the bearer of honors, has exalted in every age....

My point is that your mouth has grown foul because you keep it sealed so that no arguments can come of it that might enable you to admit that nature imparts one freedom to all human beings equally—to learn. But the question of my exceptionality remains. And here choice alone, since it is the arbiter of character, is the distinguishing factor. For some women worry about the styling of their hair, the elegance of their clothes, and the pearls and other jewelry they wear on their fingers. Others love to say cute little things, to hide their feelings behind a mask of tranquility, to indulge in dancing, and lead pet dogs around on a leash. For all I care, other women can long for parties with carefully appointed tables, for the peace of mind of sleep, or they can yearn to deface with paint the pretty face they see reflected in their mirrors. But those women for whom the quest for the good represents a higher value restrain their young spirits and ponder better plans. They harden their bodies with sobriety and toil, they control their tongues, they carefully monitor what they hear, they ready their minds for all-night vigils, and they rouse their minds for the contemplation of probity in the case of harmful literature. For knowledge is not given as a gift but by study. For a mind free, keen, and unyielding in the face of hard work always rises to the good, and the desire for learning grows in depth and breadth....

My goodness towards men isn't always rewarded, and you may imagine in your disdain for women that I alone marvel at the felicitousness of having talent.... Do not think, most despicable of men, that I might believe I have fallen out of favor with Jove. I am a scholar and a pupil who has been lulled to sleep by the meager fire of a mind too humble. I have been too much burned, and my injured mind has accumulated too much passion; for tormenting itself with the defending of our sex, my mind sighs, conscious of its obligation. For all things—those deeply rooted inside us as well as those outside us—are being laid at the door of our sex.

 How did Cereta explain her intellectual interests and accomplishments? Why were Renaissance women rarely taken seriously when they sought educational opportunities and recognition for their intellectual talents? Were any of those factors unique to the Renaissance era?

Source: Laura Cereta, "To Biblio Semproni" from *The Collected Letters of a Renaissance Feminist*, ed. and trans. Diana Robin (Chicago, 1997), pp. 74–80 © 1997 The University of Chicago Press. Reprinted by permission of The University of Chicago Press.

Renaissance, which was dominated by the work of three artistic giants, Leonardo da Vinci (leh-ah-NAHR-doh dah VEEN-chee) (1452–1519), Raphael (RAFF-ee-ul) (1483–1520), and Michelangelo (my-kuh-LAN-juh-loh) (1475–1564). Leonardo carried on the fifteenth-century experimental tradition by studying everything and even dissecting human bodies in order to see how nature worked. But Leonardo stressed the need to advance beyond such realism and initiated the High Renaissance's preoccupation with the idealization of nature, an attempt to generalize from realistic portrayal to an ideal form.

At twenty-five, Raphael was already regarded as one of Italy's best painters. He was acclaimed for his numerous madonnas, in which he attempted to achieve an ideal of beauty far surpassing human standards. He is well known for his frescoes in the Vatican Palace, which reveal a world of balance, harmony, and order—the underlying principles of the art of Classical Greece and Rome.

Michelangelo, an accomplished painter, sculptor, and architect, was fiercely driven by a desire to create, and he worked with great passion and energy on a remarkable number of projects. Michelangelo was influenced by Neoplatonism, especially evident in his figures on the ceiling of the Sistine Chapel. These muscular figures reveal an ideal type of human being with perfect proportions. In good Neoplatonic fashion,

Brunelleschi, Interior of San Lorenzo. Cosimo de' Medici contributed massive amounts of money to the rebuilding of the Church of San Lorenzo. As seen in this view of the nave and choir of the church, Brunelleschi's architectural designs were based on the basilica plan borrowed by early Christians from pagan Rome. San Lorenzo's simplicity, evident in its rows of slender Corinthian columns, created a human-centered space.

The State in the Renaissance

In the second half of the fifteenth century, attempts were made to reestablish the centralized power of monarchical governments after the political disasters of the fourteenth century. Some historians called these states the "new monarchies," especially those of France, England, and Spain (see Map 13.4).

THE ITALIAN STATES The Italian states provided the earliest examples of state building in the fifteenth century. During the Middle Ages, Italy had failed to develop a centralized territorial state, and by the fifteenth century, five major powers dominated the Italian peninsula: the duchy of Milan, the republics of Florence and Venice, the Papal States, and the kingdom of Naples.

Milan, Florence, and Venice proved especially adept at building strong, centralized states. Under a series of dukes, Milan became a highly centralized territorial state in which the rulers devised systems of taxation that generated enormous revenues for the government. The maritime republic of Venice remained an extremely

their beauty is meant to be a reflection of divine beauty; the more beautiful the body, the more God-like the figure. Another manifestation of Michelangelo's search for ideal beauty was his *David*, a colossal marble statue commissioned by the government of Florence in 1501 and completed in 1504.

stable political entity governed by a small oligarchy of merchant-aristocrats. Its commercial empire brought in vast revenues and gave it the status of an international power. In Florence, Cosimo de' Medici (KAH-zee-moh duh MED-ih-chee) took control of the merchant oligarchy in 1434. Through lavish patronage and careful courting of political allies, he and

Leonardo da Vinci, *The Last Supper*. Leonardo da Vinci was the impetus behind the High Renaissance concern for the idealization of nature, moving from a realistic portrayal of the human figure to an idealized form. Evident in Leonardo's *Last Supper* is his effort to depict a person's character and inner nature by the use of gesture and movement. Unfortunately, Leonardo used an experimental technique in this fresco, which soon led to its physical deterioration.

Raphael, *Alba Madonna*. Although he died at the age of thirty-seven, Raphael achieved in his own lifetime a fame comparable to that of Michelangelo and Leonardo da Vinci. Raphael sought an idealized beauty that was typical of the High Renaissance. His *Alba Madonna* illustrates his mastery of the Classical principles of balance, harmony, clarity, and rational composition.

National Gallery of Art, Washington DC

Michelangelo, *David*. This statue of David, cut from an 18-foot-high piece of marble, exalts the beauty of the human body and is a fitting symbol of the Italian Renaissance's affirmation of human power. Completed in 1504, *David* was moved by Florentine authorities to a special location in front of the Palazzo Vecchio, the seat of the Florentine government.

Scala/Art Resource, NY

his family dominated the city at a time when Florence was the center of the cultural Renaissance.

As strong as these Italian states became, they still could not compete with the powerful monarchical states to the north and West. Beginning in 1494, Italy became a battlefield for the great power struggle between the French and Spanish monarchies, a conflict that led to Spanish domination of Italy in the sixteenth century.

Italian States in the Renaissance

© 2016 Cengage Learning

MACHIAVELLI AND POLITICAL POWER IN THE RENAISSANCE

No one gave better expression to the Renaissance preoccupation with political power than Niccolò Machiavelli (nee-koh-LOH mahk-ee-uh-VEL-ee) (1469–1527), an Italian who wrote *The Prince* (1513), one of the most influential works on political power in the Western world. Machiavelli's major concerns in *The Prince* were the acquisition, maintenance, and expansion of political power as the means to restore and maintain order. In the Middle Ages, many political theorists stressed the ethical side of a prince's activity—how a ruler ought to behave based on Christian moral principles. Machiavelli bluntly contradicted this approach: "For the gap between how people actually behave and how they ought to behave is so great that anyone who ignores everyday reality in order to live up to an ideal will soon discover he had been taught how to destroy himself, not how to preserve himself."[14] Machiavelli considered his approach far more realistic than that of his medieval forebears. He maintained that political activity should not be restricted by moral considerations. The prince acts on behalf of the state and for the sake of the state must be willing to let his conscience sleep. Machiavelli was among the first Western thinkers to abandon morality as the basis for the analysis of political activity (see Opposing Viewpoints "The Renaissance Prince: The Views of Machiavelli and Erasmus" on p. 383).

WESTERN EUROPE The Hundred Years' War left France prostrate. But it had also engendered a certain degree of French national feeling toward a common enemy that the kings could use to reestablish monarchical power. The development of a French territorial state was greatly advanced by King Louis XI (1461–1483), known as the Spider because of his wily and devious ways. Louis strengthened the use of the *taille* (TY)—an annual direct tax usually on land or property—as a permanent tax imposed by royal authority, giving him a sound, regular source of income, which created the foundations of a strong French monarchy.

The Hundred Years' War had also strongly affected the English. The cost of the war in its final years and the losses to the labor force strained the English economy. At the end of

MAP 13.4 Europe in the Second Half of the Fifteenth Century. By the second half of the fifteenth century, monarchs in Western Europe, particularly France, Spain, and England, had begun the process of modern state building. With varying success, they reined in the power of the church and nobles, increased their ability to levy taxes, and established effective government bureaucracies.

Q *What aspects of Europe's political boundaries help explain why France and the Holy Roman Empire were often at war with each other?*

the war, England faced even greater turmoil when a civil war, known as the War of the Roses, erupted and aristocratic factions fought over the monarchy until 1485, when Henry Tudor established a new dynasty.

As the first Tudor king, Henry VII (1485–1509) worked to establish a strong monarchical government. Henry ended the petty wars of the nobility by abolishing their private armies. He was also very thrifty. By not overburdening the nobility and the middle class with taxes, Henry won their favor, and they provided him much support.

Spain, too, experienced the growth of a strong national monarchy by the end of the fifteenth century. During the Middle Ages, several independent Christian kingdoms had emerged in the course of the long reconquest of the Iberian Peninsula from the Muslims. Two of the strongest were Aragon and Castile. The marriage of Isabella of Castile (1474–1504) and Ferdinand of Aragon (1479–1516) in 1469 was a major step toward unifying Spain. The two rulers worked to strengthen royal control of government. They filled the royal council, which supervised the administration of the government, with middle-class lawyers.

Trained in Roman law, these officials operated on the belief that the monarchy embodied the power of the state. Ferdinand and Isabella also reorganized the military forces of Spain, making the new Spanish army the best in Europe by the sixteenth century.

CENTRAL AND EASTERN EUROPE Unlike France, England, and Spain, the Holy Roman Empire failed to develop a strong monarchical authority. The failure of the German emperors in the thirteenth century ended any chance of centralized authority, and Germany became a land of hundreds of virtually independent states. After 1438, the position of Holy Roman Emperor was held by members of the Habsburg (HAPS-burg) Dynasty. Having gradually acquired a number of possessions along the Danube, known collectively as Austria, the house of Habsburg had become one of the wealthiest landholders in the empire and by the mid-fifteenth century had begun to play an important role in European affairs.

In Eastern Europe, rulers struggled to achieve the centralization of the territorial states. Religious differences troubled the area as Roman Catholics, Eastern Orthodox Christians,

The Renaissance Prince: The Views of Machiavelli and Erasmus

POLITICS & GOVERNMENT

AT THE BEGINNING OF THE SIXTEENTH CENTURY, two writers produced very different views of political power and how a ruler should conduct affairs of state. In this selection from Chapter 17 of *The Prince*, Machiavelli analyzes whether it is better for a ruler to be loved than to be feared. Three years later, the Dutch intellectual Erasmus, leader of the Christian humanists (see Chapter 15), also wrote a treatise on political power, entitled *Education of a Christian Prince*. As is evident in this excerpt from his treatise, Erasmus followed in the footsteps of medieval theorists regarding power by insisting that a true prince should think only of his moral obligations to the people he rules.

Machiavelli, *The Prince* (1513)

This leads us to a question that is in dispute: Is it better to be loved than feared, or vice versa? My reply is one ought to be both loved and feared; but, since it is difficult to accomplish both at the same time, I maintain it is much safer to be feared than loved, if you have to do without one of the two. For of men one can, in general, say this: They are ungrateful, fickle, deceptive and deceiving, avoiders of danger, eager to gain. As long as you serve their interests, they are devoted to you.... But as soon as you need help, they turn against you. Any ruler who relies simply on their promises and makes no other preparations, will be destroyed. For you will find that those whose support you buy, who do not rally to you because they admire your strength of character and nobility of soul, these are people you pay for, but they are never yours, and in the end you cannot get the benefit of your investment. Men are less nervous of offending someone who makes himself lovable, than someone who makes himself frightening. For love attaches men by ties of obligation, which, since men are wicked, they break whenever their interests are at stake. But fear restrains men because they are afraid of punishment, and this fear never leaves them. Still, a ruler should make himself feared in such a way that, if he does not inspire love, at least he does not provoke hatred. For it is perfectly possible to be feared and not hated. You will only be hated if you seize the property or the women of your subjects and citizens. Whenever you have to kill someone, make sure that you have a suitable excuse and an obvious reason; but, above all else, keep your hands off other people's property; for men are quicker to forget the death of their father than the loss of their inheritance....

Erasmus, *Education of a Christian Prince* (1516)

A good prince ... is a living likeness of God, who is at once good and powerful. His goodness makes him want to help all; his power makes him able to do so. On the other hand, an evil prince, who is like a plague to his country, is the incarnation of the devil, who has great power joined with his wickedness. All his resources to the very last, he uses for the undoing of the human race....

[A good prince is one] who holds the life of each individual dearer than his own; who works and strives night and day for just one end—to be the best he can for everyone; with whom rewards are ready for all good men ... for so much does he want to be of real help to his people, without thought of recompense, that if necessary he would not hesitate to look out for their welfare at great risk to himself; who considers his wealth to lie in the advantage of his country; who is ever on the watch so that everyone else may sleep deeply; who grants no leisure to himself so that he may spend his life in the peace of his country; who worries himself with continual cares so that his subjects may have peace and quiet.... He does everything and allows everything that will bring everlasting peace to his country, for he realizes that war is the source of all misfortunes to the state.

 What does Machiavelli have to say about being loved rather than feared? How does this view contrast with that of Erasmus on the characteristics of a good ruler? Which viewpoint do you consider more modern? Why? Which viewpoint do you think is correct? Why?

Sources: Machiavelli, The Prince (1513). From *The Prince* by Machiavelli, translated by David Wootton, pp. 51–52. Copyright © 1995 by Hackett Publishing Company, Inc. Erasmus, Education of a Christian Prince (1516). From *The Education of a Christian Prince*, by Erasmus, translated by L. K. Born. Copyright © 1936 by Columbia University Press.

and other groups, including the Mongols, confronted each other. In Poland, the nobles gained the upper hand and established the right to elect their kings, a policy that drastically weakened royal authority.

Since the thirteenth century, Russia had been under the domination of the Mongols. Gradually, the princes of Moscow rose to prominence by using their close relationship to the Mongol khans to increase their wealth and expand their possessions. During the reign of the great Prince Ivan III (1462–1505), a new Russian state was born. Ivan annexed other Russian principalities and took advantage of dissension among the Mongols to throw off their yoke by 1480.

CHAPTER SUMMARY

After the collapse of Roman power in the West, the Late Roman Empire in the East or the Eastern Roman Empire, centered on Constantinople, continued in the Eastern Mediterranean and eventually emerged as the Byzantine Empire, which flourished for hundreds of years. While a new Christian civilization arose in Western Europe, the Byzantine Empire created its own unique Christian civilization. And while Western Europe struggled in the Early Middle Ages, the Byzantine world continued to prosper and flourish. Especially during the ninth, tenth, and eleventh centuries, under the Macedonian emperors, the Byzantine Empire expanded and achieved an economic prosperity that was evident to foreign visitors who were awed by the size, wealth, and physical surroundings of Constantinople.

During its heyday, Byzantium was a multicultural and multiethnic empire that ruled a remarkable number of peoples who spoke different languages. Byzantine cultural and religious forms spread to the Balkans, parts of central Europe, and Russia. Byzantine scholars eventually spread the study of the Greek language to Italy, fostering the Renaissance humanists' interest in Classical Greek civilization. The Byzantine Empire also interacted with the world of Islam to its East and the new European civilization of the West. Both interactions proved costly and ultimately fatal. Although European civilization and Byzantine civilization shared a common bond in Christianity, it proved incapable of keeping

them in harmony politically. Indeed, the West's crusades to Palestine, ostensibly for religious motives, led to Western control of the Byzantine Empire from 1204 to 1261. Although the empire was restored, it had been significantly weakened and could only limp along until its interaction with its other neighbor—the Muslim world—led to its demise in 1453 when the Ottoman Turks conquered the city of Constantinople and made it the center of their new empire.

While Byzantium was declining in the twelfth and thirteenth centuries, Europe was achieving new levels of growth and optimism. In the fourteenth century, however, Europe too experienced a time of troubles, as it was devastated by the Black Death, economic dislocation, political chaos, and religious decline. But in the fifteenth century, while Constantinople and the remnants of the Byzantine Empire finally fell to the world of Islam, Europe experienced a dramatic revival. Elements of recovery during the Renaissance made the fifteenth century a period of significant artistic, intellectual, and political change in Europe. By the second half of the fifteenth century, as we shall see in the next chapter, the growth of strong, centralized monarchical states made possible the dramatic expansion of Europe into other parts of the world.

CHAPTER TIMELINE

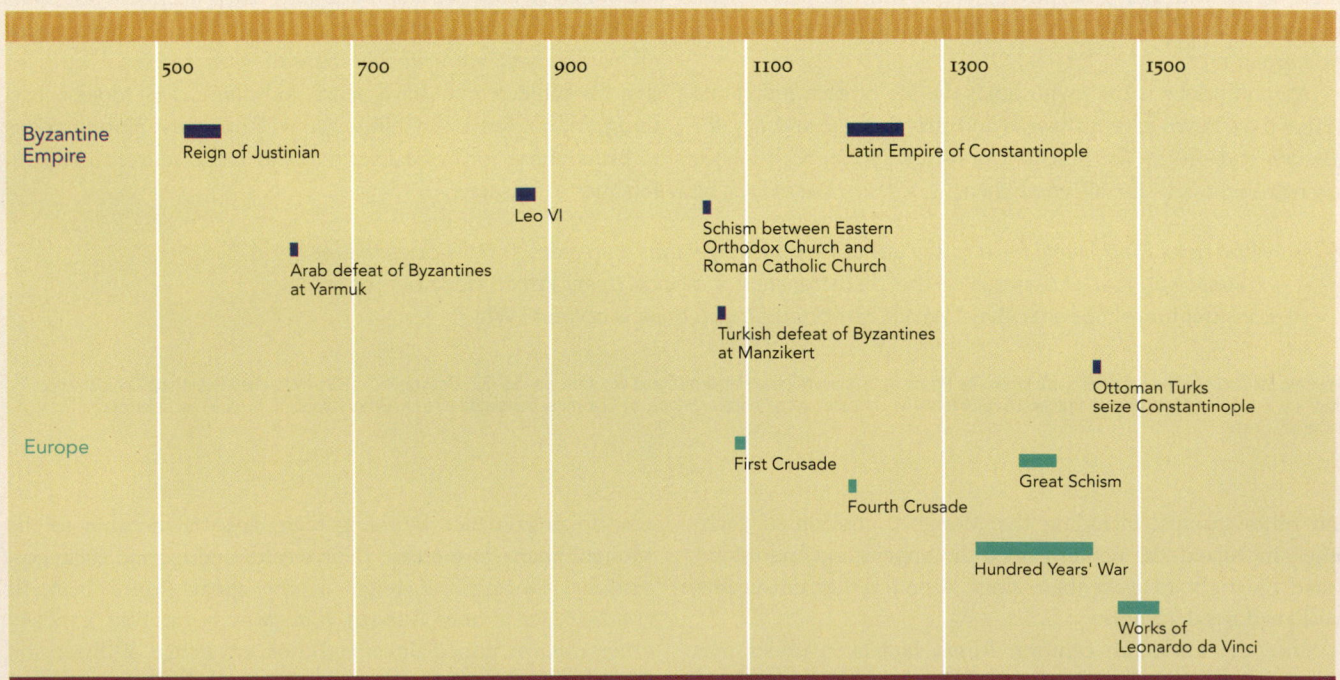

CHAPTER REVIEW

Upon Reflection

Q What were Justinian's major goals, and how did he try to accomplish them? How successful was he in achieving his goals?

Q Why does the chapter use the phrase "zenith of Byzantine civilization" to describe the period from 750 to 1025?

Q What was the relationship between Italian Renaissance humanism and Italian Renaissance art?

Key Terms

iconoclasts (p. 361)
iconoclasm (p. 361)
Black Death (p. 372)
pogroms (p. 373)
conciliarism (p. 377)
Renaissance (p. 377)
Renaissance humanism (p. 378)
taille (p. 381)

Suggested Reading

GENERAL HISTORIES OF THE BYZANTINE EMPIRE For comprehensive surveys of the Byzantine Empire, see **T. E. Gregory, *A History of Byzantium*** (Oxford, 2005), and **W. Treadgold, *A Concise History of Byzantium*** (London, 2001). For a thematic approach, see **A. Cameron, *The Byzantines*** (Oxford, 2006).

THE EARLY EMPIRE (TO 1025) On Justinian, see **J. A. S. Evans, *The Age of Justinian*** (New York, 1996). On Constantinople, see **J. Harris, *Constantinople: Capital of Byzantium*** (London, 2007). Women in the Byzantine Empire are examined in **C. L. Connor, *Women of Byzantium*** (New Haven, Conn., 2004).

THE LATE EMPIRE (1025–1453) The impact of the crusades on the Byzantine Empire is examined in **J. Harris, *Byzantium and the crusades*** (London, 2003). The disastrous Fourth Crusade is examined in **J. Philips, *The Fourth Crusade and the Sack of Constantinople*** (New York, 2004). On the fall of Constantinople, see **D. Nicolle, J. Haldon, and S. Turnbull, *The Fall of Constantinople: The Ottoman Conquest of Byzantium*** (Oxford, 2007).

CRISES OF THE FOURTEENTH CENTURY On the Black Death, see **J. Kelly, *The Great Mortality*** (New York, 2005). A worthy account of the Hundred Years' War is **A. Curry, *The Hundred Years' War***, 2nd ed. (New York, 2004).

THE RENAISSANCE On the Renaissance, see **M. L. King, *The Renaissance in Europe*** (New York, 2004). A brief introduction to Renaissance humanism can be found in **C. G. Nauert Jr., *Humanism and the Culture of Renaissance Europe***, 2nd ed. (Cambridge, 2006). A good survey of Renaissance art is **J. T. Paoletti and G. M. Radke, *Art, Power, and Patronage in Renaissance Italy***, 3rd ed. (Upper Saddle River, N.J., 2003). For a general work on the political development of Europe in the Renaissance, see **C. Mulgan, *The Renaissance Monarchies, 1469–1558*** (Cambridge, 1998).

Chapter Notes

1. Quoted in P. Cesaretti, *Theodora: Empress of Byzantium*, trans. R. M. Frongia (New York, 2004), p. 197.
2. Quoted in J. Harris, *Constantinople: Capital of Byzantium* (New York, 2007), p. 40.
3. Procopius, *Buildings of Justinian* (London, 1897), pp. 9, 6–7.
4. Quoted in Harris, *Constantinople*, p. 118.
5. A. Cameron, *The Byzantines* (Oxford, 2006), p. 45.
6. Quoted in C. S. Bartsocas, "Two Fourteenth-Century Descriptions of the 'Black Death,'" *Journal of the History of Medicine* (October 1966), p. 395.
7. Quoted in M. Dols, *The Black Death in the Middle East* (Princeton, N.J., 1977), p. 270.
8. Quoted in D. J. Herlihy, *The Black Death and the Transformation of the West*, ed. S. K. Cohn Jr. (Cambridge, Mass., 1997), p. 9.
9. Quoted in R. Horrox, *The Black Death* (Manchester, England, 1994), p. 16.
10. G. Boccaccio, *The Decameron*, trans. F. Winwar (New York, 1955), p. xiii.
11. J. Froissart, *Chronicles*, ed. and trans. G. Brereton (Harmondsworth, England, 1968), p. 111.
12. Ibid., p. 89.
13. Quoted in J. Burckhardt, *The Civilization of the Renaissance in Italy*, trans. S. G. C. Middlemore (London, 1960), p. 81.
14. N. Machiavelli, *The Prince*, trans. D. Wootton (Indianapolis, Ind., 1995), p. 48.

MindTap is a fully online, highly personalized learning experience built upon Cengage Leaning content. MindTap combines student learning tools—readings, multimedia, activities, and assessments—into a singular Learning Path that guides students through their course.

HISTORIANS OFTEN REFER to the period from the sixteenth through the eighteenth centuries as the early modern era. During these years, several factors were at work that created the conditions of our own time.

From a global perspective, perhaps the most noteworthy event of the period was the extension of the maritime trade network throughout the entire populated world. Traders from the Middle East had spearheaded the process with their voyages to East Asia and southern Africa in the first millennium C.E., and the Chinese had followed suit with Zheng He's groundbreaking voyages to India and East Africa mentioned in Chapter 10. Then, at the end of the fifteenth century, a resurgent Europe suddenly exploded onto the world scene when the Portuguese discovered a maritime route to the East and the Spanish opened up European contacts with the peoples in the Western Hemisphere. Although the Europeans were late to the game, they were quick learners, and over the next three centuries they gradually managed to dominate shipping on international trade routes.

Some contemporary historians argue that it was this sudden burst of energy from Europe that created the first truly global economic network. Although it is true that European explorers were responsible for opening up communications with the vast new world of the Americas, other historians note that it was the rise of the Arab empire in the Middle East and the Mongol expansion a few centuries later that played the greatest role in creating a widespread communications network that enabled goods and ideas to travel from one end of the Eurasian supercontinent to the other.

Whatever the truth of this debate, there are still many reasons for considering the end of the fifteenth century to be a crucial date in world history. In the first place, it marked the end of the long isolation of the Western Hemisphere from the rest of the inhabited world. In so doing, it led to the creation of the first truly global network of ideas and commodities, which would introduce plants, ideas, and (unfortunately) new diseases to all humanity (see the Comparative Essay "The Columbian Exchange" in Chapter 14). Second, the period gave birth to a stunning increase in trade and manufacturing that stimulated major economic changes not only in Europe but in other parts of the world as well.

The period from 1500 to 1800, then, was an incubation period for the modern world and the launching pad for an era of Western domination that would reach fruition in the nineteenth century. To understand why the West emerged as the leading force in the world at that time, it is necessary to grasp what factors were at work in Europe and why they were absent in other major civilizations around the globe.

Historians have identified improvements in navigation, shipbuilding, and weaponry that took place in Europe in the early modern era as essential elements in the Age of Exploration. As we have seen, many of these technological advances were based on earlier discoveries that had taken place elsewhere—in China, India, and the Middle East—and had then been brought to Europe on Muslim ships or along the trade routes through Central Asia. But it was the capacity and the desire of the Europeans to enhance their wealth and power by making practical use of the discoveries of others that was the significant factor in the equation and enabled them to dominate

The Art Archive/The Picture Desk

international sea lanes and create vast colonial empires in the Western Hemisphere.

European expansion was not fueled solely by economic considerations, however. As in the rise of Islam in the seventh and eighth centuries, religion played a major role in motivating the European Age of Exploration in the early modern era. Although Christianity was by no means a new faith in the sixteenth century (as Islam had been at the moment of Arab expansion), the world of Christendom was in the midst of a major period of conflict with the forces of Islam, a rivalry that had been exacerbated by the conquest of the Byzantine Empire by the Ottoman Turks in 1453.

Although the claims of Portuguese and Spanish adventurers that their activities were motivated primarily by a desire to bring the word of God to non-Christian peoples certainly included a considerable measure of self-delusion and hypocrisy, there seems no reason to doubt that religious motives played a meaningful part in the European Age of Exploration. Religious motives were perhaps less evident in the activities of the non-Catholic powers that entered the competition beginning in the seventeenth century. English and Dutch merchants and officials were more inclined to be motivated purely by the pursuit of economic profit.

While Europe was on the cusp of a dynamic era of political, economic, and cultural expansion, conditions in other parts of the world were less conducive to these economic and political developments. In China, a centralized monarchy was smugly confident of its superiority to all potential rivals and continued to rely on a prosperous agricultural sector as the economic foundation of the empire. In Japan, the powerful Tokugawa Shogunate seized power at the beginning of the seventeenth century, and the era of peace and stability that ensued saw an increase in manufacturing and commercial activity. But Japanese elites, after initially expressing interest in the outside world, abruptly shut the door on European trade and ideas in an effort to protect the "land of the gods" from external contamination.

In the societies of India and the Middle East, commerce and manufacturing had played a vital role since the emergence of the Indian Ocean trade network in the first centuries C.E. But beginning in the eleventh century, the area had suffered through an extended period of political instability, marked by invasions by nomadic peoples from Central Asia. The violence of the period and the local rulers' lack of experience in promoting maritime commerce severely depressed urban manufacturing and trade.

In the early modern era, then, Europe was best placed to take advantage of the technological innovations that had become increasingly available. Whereas other regions were still beset by internal obstacles or had deliberately turned inward to seek their destiny, Europe now turned outward to seek a new and dominant position in the world. This does not imply, however, that significant changes were not taking place in other parts of the world as well, and many of these changes had relatively little to do with the situation in the West. As we shall see, the impact of European expansion on the rest of the world was still limited at the end of the eighteenth century. Although European political authority was firmly established in a few key areas, such as the Spice Islands and Latin America, traditional societies remained relatively intact in most regions of Africa and Asia. And processes at work in these societies were often operating independently of events in Europe and would later give birth to forces that acted to restrict or shape the Western impact. One of these forces was the progressive emergence of centralized states, some of them built on the concept of ethnic unity. ◆

14

New Encounters: The Creation of a World Market

The port of Calicut, India, in the mid-1500s

Mary Evans Picture Library/The Image Works

CHAPTER OUTLINE AND FOCUS QUESTIONS

An Age of Exploration and Expansion

Q How did Muslim merchants expand the world trade network at the end of the fifteenth century?

The Portuguese Maritime Empire

Q Why were the Portuguese so successful in taking over the spice trade?

The Conquest of the "New World"

Q How did Portugal and Spain acquire their empires in the Americas, and how did their methods of governing their colonies differ?

Africa in Transition

Q What were the main features of the African slave trade, and how did European participation in that trade affect traditional African practices?

Southeast Asia in the Era of the Spice Trade

Q What were the main characteristics of Southeast Asian societies, and how were they affected by the coming of Islam and the Europeans?

CRITICAL THINKING

Q Christopher Columbus has recently become a controversial figure in world history. Why do you think this is so, and how would you evaluate his contribution to the modern world?

CONNECTIONS TO TODAY

Q In hindsight, do you think that European explorers can be held accountable for transmitting Old World diseases to the peoples of the Western Hemisphere?

WHEN THE PORTUGUESE FLEET arrived at the town of Calicut (KAL-ih-kuht) (now known as Kozhikode), on the western coast of India, in the spring of 1498, the fleet commander Vasco da Gama (VAHSH-koh dah GAHM-uh) ordered a landing party to go ashore to contact the local authorities. The first to greet them, a Muslim merchant from Tunisia, said, "May the Devil take thee! What brought thee hither?" "Christians and spices," replied the visitors. "A lucky venture, a lucky venture," replied the Muslim. "Plenty of rubies, plenty of emeralds! You owe great thanks to God, for having brought you to a country holding such riches!"[1]

Such words undoubtedly delighted the Portuguese, who explored the immediate vicinity of the town and soon concluded that the local population appeared to be Christians originally converted by the apostle Thomas in the first century C.E. Although it later turned out that they were mistaken—the local faith was a form of Hinduism—their spirits were probably not seriously dampened, for the conversion of the indigenous population was likely of less immediate importance than gold and glory to sailors who had gone through considerable hardship to become the first Europeans since the ancient Greeks to sail across the Indian Ocean. They left two months later with a cargo of spices and the determination to return soon with a second and larger fleet.

Vasco da Gama's maiden voyage to India inaugurated an extended period of European expansion into Asia, led by merchant adventurers and missionaries, that lasted several hundred years and had effects that are still felt today. Eventually, it resulted in a Western takeover of existing trade routes in the Indian Ocean and the establishment of colonies throughout the region, as well as in Africa and Latin America. In later years, Western historians would begin to describe these events as an "Age of Discovery" that significantly broadened the maritime trade network and set the stage for the emergence of the modern world.

In fact, of course, the voyages of Vasco da Gama and his European successors were a "discovery" only in the sense that Europeans for the first time began to take part in a regional trade network that had been in existence for centuries, and was already flourishing at a time when European maritime commerce was still essentially restricted to the Mediterranean Sea and the stormy waters of the North Atlantic Ocean. By the early fifteenth century, Chinese fleets under Zheng He had roamed the Indian Ocean, linking China with societies as distant as the Middle East and the coast of East Africa. By then, ships regularly passed between India, Southeast Asia, eastern Africa, and the Middle East, bringing goods from one part of the region to another. At the same time, Muslim caravans snaked across the Sahara from the Mediterranean to the civilizations that flourished along the banks of the Niger River.

The Europeans, then, were not trailblazers, but latecomers to the process. It was, after all, a Muslim from North Africa who greeted the Portuguese on their first appearance off the coast of India. In this chapter, we turn our attention to the stunning expansion in the scope and volume of commercial and cultural contacts that took place in the generations preceding and following Vasco da Gama's historic voyage to India, as well as to the factors that brought about this expansion. ❦

An Age of Exploration and Expansion

 FOCUS QUESTION: How did Muslim merchants expand the world trade network at the end of the fifteenth century?

Western historians have customarily regarded the voyage of Vasco da Gama as a crucial step in the opening of trade routes to the East. In the sense that the voyage was a harbinger of future European participation in the spice trade, this view undoubtedly has merit. In fact, however, as has been pointed out in earlier chapters, the Indian Ocean had been a busy thoroughfare for centuries. The spice trade had been carried on by sea in the region since the days of the legendary Queen of Sheba, and Arab dhows, Indian sailing ships, and Chinese junks had sailed throughout the

area in search of cloves and nutmeg and other precious items since the Tang Dynasty (see Chapter 10).

Islam and the Spice Trade

By the fourteenth century, a growing portion of the spice trade was being transported in Muslim ships sailing from ports in India or the Middle East. Muslims, either Arabs or Indian converts, had taken part in the Indian Ocean trade for centuries, and by the thirteenth century, Islam had established a presence in seaports on the islands of Sumatra and Java and was gradually moving inland. In 1292, the Venetian traveler Marco Polo observed that Muslims were engaging in missionary activity in northern Sumatra: "This kingdom is so much frequented by the Saracen merchants that they have converted the natives to the Law of Mahomet—I mean the townspeople only, for the hill people live for all the world like beasts, and eat human flesh, as well as other kinds of flesh, clean or unclean."[2]

But the major impetus for the spread of Islam in Southeast Asia came in the early fifteenth century, with the foundation of a new sultanate at Malacca (muh-LAK-uh), on the strait that today bears the same name. The founder was Paramesvara (pahr-uh-muss-VAHR-uh), a vassal of the Hindu state of Majapahit (mah-jah-PAH-hit) on Java, whose original base of operations had been at Palembang (pah-lem-BAHNG), on the island of Sumatra. In 1390, he had moved his base to Tumasik (tuh-MAH-sik) (modern Singapore), at the tip of the Malay Peninsula, hoping to enhance his ability to play a role in the commerce passing through the region. Under pressure from the expanding power of the Thai state of Ayuthaya (ah-yoo-TY-yuh) (see "Southeast Asia in the Era of the Spice Trade" later in this chapter) in the early fifteenth century, Paramesvara moved once again to Malacca. The latter's potential strategic importance was confirmed in the sixteenth century by a visitor from Portugal, who noted that Malacca "is a city that was made for commerce; ... the trade and commerce between the different nations for a thousand leagues on every hand must come to Malacca."[3]

Shortly after its founding, Malacca was visited by a Chinese fleet under the command of Admiral Zheng He (see Chapter 10). To protect his patrimony from local rivals, Paramesvara agreed to become a tributary of the Chinese empire and cemented the new relationship by making an official visit to the Ming imperial court in Beijing. He also converted to Islam, undoubtedly with a view to enhancing Malacca's ability to participate in the trade that passed through the strait, much of which was dominated by Muslim merchants. Blessed by its fortunate location, within a few years, Malacca had become the leading economic power in the region and helped promote the spread of Islam to trading ports

The Strait of Malacca

© 2016 Cengage Learning

throughout the islands of Southeast Asia, including Java, Borneo, Sulawesi (soo-lah-WAY-see), and the Philippines. Adoption of the Muslim faith was eased by the popularity of Sufism, a brand of Islam that expressed a marked tolerance for mysticism and local religious beliefs (see Chapter 7).

The Spread of Islam in West Africa

In the meantime, Muslim commercial and religious influence continued to expand south of the Sahara into the Niger River valley in West Africa. The area had been penetrated by traders from across the Sahara since ancient times, and contacts undoubtedly increased after the establishment of Muslim control over the Mediterranean coastal regions. Muslim traders—first Arabs and later African converts—crossed the desert carrying Islamic values, political culture, and legal traditions along with their goods. The early stage of state formation had culminated with the kingdom of Mali, symbolized by the renowned Mansa Musa, whose pilgrimage to Mecca in the fourteenth century had left an indelible impression on observers (see Chapter 8).

THE EMPIRE OF SONGHAI With the decline of Mali in the late fifteenth century, a new power eventually appeared: the empire of Songhai (song-GY). The founder of Songhai was Sonni Ali (Sonni the Great), a local chieftain from Gao, a major trading entrepôt (ON-truh-poh) on the Niger River east of Timbuktu. After seizing power in 1464, he set out to destroy the remnants of the Mali Empire and restore the formidable empire of his predecessors. Rumored to possess magical powers, Sonni Ali was criticized by Muslim scholars for supporting traditional religious practices, but under his rule, Songhai emerged as a major trading state in the region (see Map 14.1). When he died in 1492, his son ascended to the throne but was deposed shortly thereafter by one of his military commanders, who seized power as king under the name Askia Mohammed (r. 1493–1528).

Under the new ruler, a fervent Muslim, Songhai increasingly relied on Islamic institutions and ideology to strengthen national unity and centralize its authority. Askia Mohammed himself embarked on a pilgrimage to Mecca and was recognized by the caliph of Cairo as the Muslim ruler of the Niger River valley. On his return from Mecca, he tried to revive Timbuktu as a major center of Islamic learning but had less success in converting his predominantly animist subjects. He did preside over a significant increase in trans-Saharan trade in gold, salt, and slaves, which provided a steady source of income to

MAP 14.1 The Songhai Empire. Songhai was the last of the great states to dominate the Niger River valley prior to the European takeover in the nineteenth century.

Q *What were the predecessors of the Songhai Empire in the region? Why is the area so important in African history?*

The City of Timbuktu. The city of Timbuktu sat astride one of the major trade routes that passed through the Sahara between the kingdoms of West Africa and the Mediterranean Sea. Caravans transported food and various manufactured articles southward in exchange for salt, gold, copper, skins, agricultural goods, and slaves. Salt was at such a premium in Timbuktu that a young Moroccan wrote in 1513 that one camel's load brought 500 miles by caravan sold for 80 gold ducats, while a horse sold for only 40 ducats. Timbuktu became a prosperous city and a great center of Islamic scholarship. By 1550, it had three universities connected to its principal mosques and 180 Qur'anic schools. This pen-and-ink sketch was done by the French traveler René Caillie in 1828, when the city was long past its peak of prosperity and renown.

Songhai and other states in the region (see the box "The Great City of Timbuktu" on p. 391). Gold, the source of which was located south of the city of Jenne, was used as the local currency, as well as cowrie shells from the Indian Ocean. Despite the efforts of Askia Mohammed and his successors, however,

The Great City of Timbuktu

INTERACTION & EXCHANGE

AFTER ITS FOUNDING IN THE TWELFTH CENTURY, Timbuktu became a great center of Islamic learning and a fabled city of mystery and riches to Europeans. By the sixteenth century, Timbuktu had become a major commercial center for all trade passing through the Sahara as routes to the gold fields farther to the east declined as a result of Tuareg raids and increasing aridity. This description of the city was written in 1526 by Leo Africanus, a Muslim from the Islamic state of Granada who had once lived in Rome and was one of the great travelers of his time. By then, Timbuktu had become a vibrant multiracial city marked by widespread literacy and tolerant social mores.

Leo Africanus, *History and Description of Africa*

Here are many shops of artificers and merchants, and especially of such as weave linen and cotton cloth. And hither do the Barbary merchants bring cloth of Europe. All the women of this region, except the maid-servants, go with their faces covered, and sell all necessary victuals. The inhabitants, and especially strangers there residing, are exceeding rich, insomuch that the king that now is, married both his daughters to rich merchants. Here are many wells containing sweet water; and so often as the river Niger overfloweth, they convey the water thereof by certain sluices into the town. Corn, cattle, milk, and butter this region yieldeth in great abundance: but salt is very scarce here; for it is brought hither by land from Taghaza which is 500 miles distant. When I myself was here, I saw one camel's load of salt sold for 80 ducats. The rich king of Timbuktu hath many plates and scepters of gold, some whereof weigh 1,300 pounds: and

he keeps a magnificent and well-furnished court. When he travelleth any whither he rideth upon a camel which is led by some of his noblemen; and so he doth likewise when he goeth forth to warfare, and all his soldiers ride upon horses. Whoever will speak unto this king must first fall down before his feet, and then taking up earth must first sprinkle it upon his own head and shoulders: which custom is ordinarily observed by … ambassadors from other princes. He hath always 3,000 horsemen, and a number of footmen that shoot poisoned arrows, attending upon him. They have often skirmishes with those that refuse to pay tribute, and so many as they take, they sell unto the merchants of Timbuktu. Here are very few horses bred, and the merchants and courtiers keep certain little nags which they use to travel upon: but their best horses are brought out of Barbary…. Here are great store of doctors, judges, priests, and other learned men, that are bountifully maintained at the king's cost and charges, and hither are brought divers manuscripts or written books out of Barbary, which are sold for more money than any other merchandise. The coin of Timbuktu is of gold without any stamp or superscription but in matters of small value they use certain shells brought hither out of the kingdom of Persia, 400 of which are worth a ducat: and $6\frac{2}{3}$ pieces of their gold coin weigh an ounce. The inhabitants are people of gentle and cheerful disposition, and spend a great part of the night singing and dancing through all the streets of the city.

What role did the city of Timbuktu play in regional commerce, according to this author? What were the chief means of payment?

Source: From *The History and Description of Africa*, by Leo Africanus (New York: Burt Franklin).

---

centrifugal forces within Songhai, brought on by rivalries at court, chronic drought, and bouts of the plague, led to civil disorder and eventually led to its breakup. The end came in 1591, when Moroccan forces armed with firearms conquered the city of Gao in a bid to gain control over the gold trade in the region. At that point, the city of Timbuktu, and the trade route that had enabled its rise, began a long period of decline, as other forces began to make their entrance into the region.

A New Player: Europe

For almost a millennium, the Catholic states of Europe had largely been confined to the western part of that continent. Their one major attempt to expand beyond those frontiers—the crusades—ultimately had failed. Of course, Europe had never completely lost contact with the outside world. With the revival of trade in the later Middle Ages, European merchants began to travel more frequently to Africa and Asia, much of it driven by a voracious appetite for the spices of the Orient. Nevertheless, their overall contacts with other parts of the world remained limited until the fifteenth century, when Europeans began to

embark on a remarkable series of overseas journeys. What caused European seafarers to undertake such dangerous voyages to the ends of the earth? Two famous early travelers to the lands of the East help to provide us with an explanation.

THE MOTIVES Europeans had long been entranced by legends depicting exotic lands of great riches and magic beyond the rising sun. Such visions had lured the Polos of Venice on their journeys to the fabled Orient (see Chapter 10). Economic motives had been temporarily derailed by the Mongol conquests, but they revived after the Mongol threat to Europe had begun to recede, and Italian merchants from Genoa and Venice took an active part in the spice trade that passed through the Indian Ocean en route to the Caribbean. Access to the riches of the East was interrupted in the fifteenth century, however, by the Ottoman takeover of the Eastern Mediterranean (see Chapter 13). Spices and other precious goods from Asia continued to be transported to Europe via Arab intermediaries but were outrageously expensive. Adventurous Europeans did not hesitate to express their desire to

COMPARATIVE ILLUSTRATION

European Warships During the Age of Exploration. Prior to the fifteenth century, most European ships were either small craft with triangular, lateen sails used in the Mediterranean or slow, unwieldy square-rigged vessels operating in the North Atlantic. By the sixteenth century, European naval architects began to build caravels (left), ships that combined the maneuverability and speed offered by lateen sails (widely used by sailors in the Indian Ocean) with the carrying capacity and seaworthiness of the square-riggers. For a century, caravels were the feared "raiders of the oceans." Eventually, as naval technology progressed, European warships developed in size and firepower, as the illustration of Portuguese carracks on the right shows.

Q *What were the key characteristics of these different types of ships and how did they affect their performance on the high seas?*

share in the wealth. As one Spanish conquistador (kahn-KEESS-tuh-dor) explained, he and his kind went to the Americas to "serve God and His Majesty, to give light to those who were in darkness, and to grow rich, as all men desire to do."[4]

That statement alludes to another major reason for the overseas voyages—religious zeal. John Plano Carpini, the Franciscan friar dispatched in 1245 by the Vatican to the Mongol capital at Karakorum, had initiated the process by appealing to his hosts to convert to the Christian faith. Two centuries later, that crusading mentality reasserted itself in Portugal and Spain, where conflict with regional Muslim powers had intensified religious rivalries. Contemporaries of Prince Henry the Navigator of Portugal, an outspoken advocate of European expansion, said that he was motivated by his zeal to spread the Christian message to pagan peoples beyond the confines of Europe. Although most scholars believe that the religious motive was secondary to economic considerations, it would be foolish to overlook the genuine desire on the part of both explorers and conquistadors, let alone missionaries, to convert the heathen to Christianity. Hernán Cortés (hayr-NAHN kor-TAYSS *or* kor-TEZ), the conqueror of Mexico, asked his Spanish rulers if it was not their duty to ensure that the native Mexicans were "introduced into and instructed in the holy Catholic faith."[5] Thus spiritual and secular motives were closely intertwined in the sixteenth century. No doubt dreams of personal grandeur and glory, along with intellectual curiosity and a spirit of adventure, also played a role in European expansion.

THE MEANS If "God, glory, and gold" were the primary motives, what made the voyages possible? Perhaps first and foremost, by the end of the fifteenth century, European states had achieved a level of knowledge and technology that enabled them to carry out ambitious ocean voyages well beyond the confines of continental Europe. Although the highly schematic and symbolic maps popular in the medieval era (see Chapter 7) were of little help to sailors, detailed charts made by medieval navigators and mathematicians in the thirteenth and fourteenth centuries, known as *portolani* (pohr-tuh-LAH-nee), were more useful. With details on coastal contours, distances between ports (thus the name), and compass readings, they proved of great value for voyages in European waters. But because the *portolani* were drawn on a flat surface and took no account of the curvature of the earth, they were of little use for longer overseas voyages. Only when seafarers began to venture beyond the coasts of Europe did they begin to accumulate information about the actual shape of the earth and how to measure it. By the end of the fifteenth century, cartography had developed to the point that Europeans possessed fairly accurate maps of the known world.

In addition, Europeans had developed remarkably seaworthy ships as well as new navigational techniques. European shipbuilders had mastered the use of the sternpost rudder, an import from China (previous rudders had been located on the right side of the vessel), and had learned how to combine the use of lateen sails (commonly used in the Indian Ocean) with the square rig familiar in northern European waters. With these innovations, they could construct **caravels** (KER-uh-velz), ships mobile enough to sail against the wind and engage in naval warfare and also large enough to be armed with heavy cannons and carry a substantial amount of goods over long distances (see the Comparative Illustration "European Warships During the Age of Exploration" above). Previously, sailors had used a

Principal Voyages of Exploration

A Portuguese expeditions, 1430s–1480s
B Dias, 1487–1488
C da Gama, 1497–1499
D Portuguese voyages to the Orient, 1509–1514
E Columbus's first voyage, 1492

F Columbus's three successive voyages, 1493–1504
G Voyages attended by Vespucci, 1499–1502
H Magellan–del Cano, 1519–1522
I Cabot, 1497

Trade winds	
Areas under Spanish control	Spanish trading cities	Spanish routes
Areas under Portuguese control	Portuguese trading cities	Portuguese routes
	Independent trading cities	Other routes

MAP 14.2 European Voyages and Possessions in the Sixteenth and Seventeenth Centuries. This map indicates the most important voyages launched by Europeans during their momentous Age of Exploration in the sixteenth and seventeenth centuries.

Q *Why did Vasco da Gama sail so far into the South Atlantic on his voyage to Asia?*

quadrant and their knowledge of the position of the polestar to ascertain their latitude. Below the equator, however, this technique was useless. Only with the assistance of new navigational aids such as the compass (a Chinese invention) and the astrolabe, an astronomical instrument reportedly developed from ancient Greek examples by Arab sailors (see Chapter 7), were they able to explore the high seas with confidence.

A final spur to exploration was the growing knowledge of the wind patterns in the Atlantic Ocean (see Map 14.2). The first European fleets sailing southward along the coast of West Africa had found their efforts to return hindered by the strong winds that blew steadily from the north along the coast. During the mid-fifteenth century, however, sailors had learned to tack out into the ocean, where they were able to catch westerly winds in the vicinity of the Azores that brought them back to the coast of western Europe. Christopher Columbus used this technique in his voyages to the Americas,

and others relied on their new knowledge of the winds to round the continent of Africa in search of spices.

The Portuguese Maritime Empire

Q **FOCUS QUESTION:** Why were the Portuguese so successful in taking over the spice trade?

Portugal took the lead when it began exploring the western coast of Africa under the sponsorship of Prince Henry the Navigator (1394–1460). Henry had three objectives: acquiring new trade opportunities for his kingdom (especially in the gold trade with West Africa), weakening the Muslim states in Spain and West Africa, and extending Christianity. In 1419,

© 2016 Cengage Learning

The Trustees of the British Museum/Art Resource, NY

An Ivory Mask from Benin. By the end of the fifteenth century, the West African state of Benin had developed into an extensive and powerful empire enjoying trade with many of its neighbors, as well as with the state of Portugal. With the latter it traded ivory, forest products, and slaves in exchange for textiles and other European manufactured goods. This life-size ivory mask was probably intended to be worn by the king of Benin as a belt ornament in a gesture of gratitude to his mother, who had allegedly used her magical powers to help defeat his enemies. On the crest of the crown are carvings of Portuguese figures, providing one of the first examples in African art of the new trade relationship between that continent and Europe.

he founded a school for navigators on the southwestern coast of Portugal. Shortly thereafter, Portuguese fleets began probing southward along the western coast of Africa in search of gold, which had for centuries been carried northward from its source south of the Sahara. In 1441, Portuguese ships reached the Senegal River, just north of Cape Verde. They found no gold but brought home a cargo of black Africans, most of whom were sold as slaves to wealthy buyers elsewhere in Europe. Within a few years, about a thousand slaves a year were shipped from the area back to Lisbon. Although obtaining slaves had not been one of their original motives for exploring the west coast of Africa, the Portuguese had inadvertently found a way to circumvent the traditional trans-Saharan slave route from Central Africa to the Mediterranean.

Continuing southward, in 1471 the Portuguese discovered a source of gold along the southern coast of the hump of West Africa (an area that would henceforth be known to Europeans as the Gold Coast). A few years later, they established contact with the inland state of Benin, north of the Gold Coast. To facilitate trade in gold, ivory, and slaves (not all slaves were brought back to Lisbon; some were bartered to local merchants for gold), the Portuguese leased land from local rulers and built stone forts along the coast. Trade was slow to develop at first, however, because the Portuguese initially did not have many products that appealed to potential African buyers.

En Route to India

Hearing reports of a route to India around the southern tip of Africa, Portuguese sea captains continued their probing. A few years later, contacts were established with the kingdom of Kongo, near the mouth of the Congo River. Then, in 1487, Bartolomeu Dias (bar-toh-loh-MAY-oo DEE-uhs) took advantage of westerly winds in the South Atlantic to round the Cape of Good Hope, but fearing a mutiny from his crew, he returned home without continuing further. Ten years later, a fleet under the command of Vasco da Gama rounded the cape and stopped at several ports controlled by Muslim merchants along the coast of East Africa, including Sofala, Kilwa, and Mombasa. Then, having located a Muslim navigator who was familiar with seafaring in the region, da Gama's fleet crossed the Arabian Sea and arrived off the port of Calicut, on the southwestern coast of India, on May 18, 1498. The Portuguese crown had sponsored da Gama's voyage with the clear objective of destroying the Muslim monopoly over the spice trade, a monopoly that had been intensified by the Ottoman conquest of Constantinople in 1453 (see Chapter 16). Calicut was a major entrepôt on the long route from the Spice Islands to the Mediterranean Sea, but the ill-informed Europeans believed it was the source of the spices themselves. Purchasing as much in the way of spices as his ships could carry, after three months in India, da Gama set out for home. Although he lost two ships along the way, the remaining vessels returned to Europe with their holds filled with ginger and cinnamon, a cargo that earned the investors a profit of several thousand percent.

The Search for the Source of Spices

During the next years, the Portuguese set out to gain control of the spice trade. In 1510, Admiral Afonso de Albuquerque (ah-FAHN-soh day AL-buh-kur-kee) established his headquarters at Goa (GOH-uh), on the western coast of India south of present-day Mumbai, formerly called Bombay. Over the next few years, they established a series of fortresses and trading posts along the coasts of western India and East Africa in a bid to dominate the trade network of the Indian Ocean. From these ports, the Portuguese raided Arab shippers, provoking the following comment from an Arab source: "[The Portuguese] took about seven vessels, killing those on board and

The Spice Islands

(map labels: Molucca Sea, Tidor, Halmahera, Pacific Ocean, Ceram, Island of New Guinea, Banda Sea, Banda Islands; 0–300 Kilometers, 0–150 Miles)

© 2016 Cengage Learning

The Portuguese Conquest of Malacca

INTERACTION & EXCHANGE

IN 1511, A PORTUGUESE FLEET led by Afonso de Albuquerque attacked the Muslim sultanate at Malacca, on the west coast of the Malay Peninsula. Occupation of the port gave the Portuguese control over the strategic Strait of Malacca and the route to the Spice Islands. In this passage, Albuquerque tells his men the reasons for the attack. Note that he sees control of Malacca as a way to reduce the power of the Muslim world. The relevance of economic wealth to military power continues to underlie conflicts among nations today. The Pacific War in the 1940s, for example, began as a result of a conflict over control of the rich resources of Southeast Asia.

The Commentaries of the Great Afonso de Albuquerque, Second Viceroy of India

Although there be many reasons which I could allege in favor of our taking this city and building a fortress therein to maintain possession of it, two only will I mention to you, on this occasion….

The first is the great service which we shall perform to Our Lord in casting the Moors out of this country…. If we can only achieve the task before us, it will result in the Moors resigning India altogether to our rule, for the greater part of them—or perhaps all of them—live upon the trade of this country and are become great and rich, and lords of extensive treasures…. For when we were committing

ourselves to the business of cruising in the Straits [of the Red Sea], where the King of Portugal had often ordered me to go (for it was there that His Highness considered we could cut down the commerce which the Moors of Cairo, of Mecca, and of Judah, carry on with these parts), Our Lord for his service thought right to lead us hither, for when Malacca is taken the places on the Straits must be shut up, and they will never more be able to introduce their spiceries into those places.

And the other reason is the additional service which we shall render to the King D. Manuel in taking this city, because it is the headquarters of all the spiceries and drugs which the Moors carry every year hence to the Straits without our being able to prevent them from so doing; but if we deprive them of this their ancient market there, there does not remain for them a single port, nor a single situation, so commodious in the whole of these parts, where they can carry on their trade in these things…. I hold it as very certain that if we take this trade of Malacca away out of their hands, Cairo and Mecca are entirely ruined, and to Venice will no spiceries be conveyed except that which her merchants go and buy in Portugal.

What reasons does the author advance to justify his decision to launch an attack on Malacca? How might the ruler of Malacca respond to these reasons?

Source: From *The Commentaries of the Great Afonso Dalboquerque, Second Viceroy of India,* trans. Walter de Gray Birch (London: Printed for the Hakluyt Society, 1880), Vol. III, pp.116–118.

---

making some prisoner. This was their first action, may God curse them."[6] In 1511, Albuquerque attacked Malacca itself (see the box "The Portuguese Conquest of Malacca" above).

For Albuquerque, control of Malacca would serve two purposes. It could help destroy the Arab spice trade network by blocking passage through the Strait of Malacca, and it could also provide the Portuguese with a way station en route to the Spice Islands (known today as the Moluccas) and other points east. After a short but bloody battle, the Portuguese seized the city and put the local Arab population to the sword. They then proceeded to erect the normal accoutrements of the day—a fort, a "factory" (warehouse), and a church.

From Malacca, the Portuguese launched expeditions farther east, to China in 1514 and the Moluccas (muh-LUHK-uhz). There they signed a treaty with a local sultan for the purchase and export of cloves to the European market. Within a few years, they had managed to seize control of much of the spice trade from Muslim traders and had garnered substantial profits for the Portuguese monarchy.

Why were the Portuguese so successful? Basically, it was a matter of guns and seamanship. The first Portuguese fleet to arrive in Indian waters was relatively modest in size. It consisted of three ships and twenty guns, a force sufficient for self-defense and intimidation but not for serious military operations. Most sixteenth-century Portuguese fleets were more heavily armed and were capable of inflicting severe defeats if necessary on local naval and land forces. The Portuguese by no means possessed a monopoly on the use of firearms and explosives, but their highly maneuverable, light ships enabled them to maintain their distance while bombarding the enemy with their powerful cannons. Such tactics gave them a military superiority over lightly armed rivals that they were able to exploit until the arrival of other European forces several decades later.

New Rivals Enter the Scene

Portugal's efforts to dominate the spice trade network were never totally successful, however. After some early disastrous defeats at sea, Muslim rivals sought to recover the initiative, harassing Portuguese fleets from seaports on the Arabian peninsula and the coast of Africa and thereby preventing the latter from obtaining a monopoly on trade within the region. For their part, the Portuguese lacked both the numbers and the wealth to overcome local resistance and colonize the Asian regions. Moreover,

Dividing Up the Spoils of Exploration

INTERACTION & EXCHANGE

WHEN ADVENTURERS FROM PORTUGAL AND SPAIN set off in opposite directions to find a route to the fabled "Spice Islands" on the other side of the globe, they created an awkward dilemma for themselves—how to divide up the territories along the different routes to the East. In the Treaty of Tordesillas, signed in 1494, they agreed to establish a vertical line west of Africa in the middle of the Atlantic Ocean, thus assigning all of the lands to the west to the Spanish, while those to the east were given to Portugal. Most of the Western Hemisphere—except for the eastern hump of the future Brazil—was thus placed in the Spanish sphere of influence.

But what line should be drawn on the other side of the world, where the two journeys would ultimately intersect, presumably somewhere near the Spice Islands themselves? That problem was not resolved in 1494, and as it turned out, domination over the spice trade was the subject of violent dispute involving several European nations over the next three centuries. In the end, ownership over the spice trade was decided at the point of a gun, not by the pen of the diplomat.

The Treaty of Tordesillas (June 7, 1494)

That, whereas a certain controversy exists between the said lords, their constituents, as to what lands, of all those discovered in the ocean sea up to the present day, the date of this treaty, pertain to each one of the said parts respectively; therefore, for the sake of peace and concord, and for the preservation of the relationship and love of the said King of Portugal for the said King and Queen of Castile, Aragon, etc., it being the pleasure of their Highnesses, they their said representatives, acting in their name and by virtue of their powers herein described, covenanted and agreed that a boundary or straight line be determined and drawn north and south, from pole to pole, on the said ocean sea, from the Arctic to the Antarctic pole. This boundary or line shall be drawn straight, as aforesaid, at a distance of three hundred and seventy leagues west of the Cape Verde Islands, being calculated by degrees, or by any other manner as may be considered the best and readiest, provided the distance shall be no greater than abovesaid. And all lands, both islands and mainlands, found and discovered already, or to be found and discovered hereafter, by the said King of Portugal and by his vessels on this side of the said line and bound determined as above, toward the east, in either north or south latitude, on the eastern side of the said bound, provided the said bound is not crossed, shall belong to, and remain in the possession of, and pertain forever to, the said King of Portugal and his successors. And all other lands, both islands and mainlands, found or to be found hereafter, discovered or to be discovered hereafter, which have been discovered or shall be discovered by the said King and Queen of Castile, Aragon, etc., and by their vessels, on the western side of the said bound, determined as above, after having passed the said bound toward the west, in either its north or south latitude, shall belong to, and remain in the possession of, and pertain forever to, the said King and Queen of Castile, Leon, etc., and to their successors.

Q *Why did Spain and Portugal encounter difficulty when seeking to divide up the newly discovered territories in the Pacific Ocean?*

Source: From F. G. Davenport, ed., *European Treaties Bearing on the History of the United States and Its Dependencies to 1648* (Carnegie Institution of Washington: Washington, DC, 1917), p. 95.

---

their massive investments in ships and laborers for their empire (hundreds of ships and hundreds of thousands of workers in shipyards and overseas bases) proved very costly. Disease, shipwrecks, and battles took a heavy toll. The empire was simply too large and Portugal too small to maintain it, and by the end of the sixteenth century, the Portuguese were being severely challenged by European rivals.

THE SPANISH First on the scene was Spain. Queen Isabella of Spain had already signaled her intent to enter the competition in 1492 when she sponsored the voyage of Christopher Columbus into the Atlantic Ocean in search of a westward route to the Indies (see the map "Cape Horn and the Strait of Magellan"). That led to a dispute between the two Iberian nations over the rights to newly conquered

territories. In 1494, in an effort to head off potential conflict between the two countries, the Treaty of Tordesillas (tor-day-SEE-yass) divided the newly discovered world into separate Portuguese and Spanish spheres of influence (see the box "Dividing Up the Spoils of Exploration" above). Thereafter, the route east around the Cape of Good Hope was reserved for the Portuguese, while the route across the Atlantic (except for the eastern hump of South America) was assigned to Spain (see Map 14.2).

Columbus's later voyages eventually convinced influential figures at the Spanish court that the lands he had reached were not the Indies but an unknown land that possessed its own attractions. Still seeking a route to the Spice Islands, in 1519 Spain dispatched a fleet under the command of the Portuguese adventurer Ferdinand Magellan that sailed around the southern tip of

© 2016 Cengage Learning

Cape Horn and the Strait of Magellan

Strait of Magellan
Atlantic Ocean
Tierra del Fuego
Pacific Ocean
Beagle Channel
Cape Horn

0 — 100 Kilometers
0 — 100 Miles

South America, proceeded across the Pacific Ocean, and landed on the island of Cebu in the Philippine Islands. Although Magellan and some forty of his crew were killed there in a skirmish with the local population, one of the two remaining ships sailed on to Tidor, in the Moluccas, and thence around the world via the Cape of Good Hope. In the words of a contemporary historian, having completed the first circumference of the earth, they arrived in Cádiz "with precious cargo and fifteen men surviving out of a fleet of five sail."[7]

As it turned out, the Spanish, who were increasingly preoccupied with the territories newly discovered by Columbus, could not follow up on Magellan's accomplishment, and in 1529 they sold their rights in Tidor to the Portuguese. But Magellan's voyage was not a total loss to the Spanish, who soon managed to consolidate their control over the Philippines and transformed it into a major way station in the carrying trade across the Pacific. Spanish galleons learned to follow the Pacific trade winds by carrying silk and other luxury from China to Acapulco in exchange for silver from the mines of Mexico.

THE ENGLISH AND THE DUTCH The primary threat to the Portuguese toehold in Southeast Asia came from the English and the Dutch. In 1591, the first English expedition to the Indies through the Indian Ocean arrived in London with a cargo of pepper. Nine years later, a private joint-stock company, the East India Company, was founded to provide a stable source of capital for future voyages. In 1608, an English fleet landed at Surat (SOOR-et), on the northwestern coast of India. Trade with Southeast Asia soon followed.

The Dutch, bitter trade rivals to the English, were equally determined to show the flag in the region. Seven years after the first Dutch fleet arrived in India in 1595, the Dutch East India Company (Vereenigde Oost-Indische Compagnie, or VOC) was established under government sponsorship and began to compete actively for access to the spice trade. In 1611, a Dutch fleet made history by sailing directly east on the "roaring forties" (the powerful westerly winds circling the globe at that southern latitude) from South Africa to the Indonesian archipelago. In 1641, the Dutch seized the entrepôt of Malacca, one of the linchpins of Portugal's trading empire in Asia.

The Conquest of the "New World"

 FOCUS QUESTION: How did Portugal and Spain acquire their empires in the Americas, and how did their methods of governing their colonies differ?

Although the Portuguese had successfully defeated their Spanish rivals in obtaining access to the spice trade in the Indies, the latter, aided by their greater resources, were on the verge of establishing a far grander overseas empire.

The Voyages

An important figure in the history of Spanish exploration was an Italian from Genoa, Christopher Columbus (1451–1506). Like many knowledgeable Europeans, Columbus was aware that the world was round, but he was also convinced that the circumference of the earth was smaller than some of his contemporaries believed. He therefore argued that Asia could easily be reached by sailing due west instead of eastward around Africa. After his plan was rejected by the Portuguese, he persuaded Queen Isabella of Castile to finance his exploratory expedition, which left Spain in early August 1492 and reached land somewhere in the islands of the Bahamas ten weeks later. For the next few weeks, his three ships explored the coastline of Cuba and the northern shores of the neighboring island of Hispaniola (his-puhn-YOH-luh *or* ees-pahn-YAH-luh). Columbus believed that he had reached Asia and in three subsequent voyages (1493, 1498, and 1502) sought in vain to find a route through the outer islands to the Asian mainland. In his four voyages, Columbus reached all the major islands of the Caribbean, which he called the Indies, as well as Honduras in Central America.

Although Columbus clung for the rest of his life to his belief that he had reached Asia, other navigators realized that he had discovered a new frontier altogether and joined the race to what Europeans began to call the "New World." A Venetian seafarer, John Cabot, explored the New England coastline of the Americas under a license from King Henry VII of England. The continent of South America was discovered accidentally by the Portuguese sea captain Pedro Cabral (PAY-droh kuh-BRAHL) in 1500. Amerigo Vespucci (ahm-ay-REE-goh vess-POO-chee), a Florentine, accompanied several of Cabral's voyages and wrote a series of letters describing the geography of the lands he observed. The publication of these letters led eventually to the use of the name "America" (after Amerigo) for the new lands.

The Conquests

The newly discovered territories that Europeans referred to as the New World actually contained flourishing civilizations populated by millions of people. But the Americas were new to the Europeans, who quickly saw opportunities for conquest and exploitation. With Portugal clearly in the lead in the race to exploit the riches of the Indies, the importance of these lands was magnified in the minds of the Spanish, especially those who saw a chance to win fame and fortune for themselves and their families.

The Spanish **conquistadors**, as they were called, were a hardy lot of mostly upper-class individuals motivated by a typical sixteenth-century blend of glory, greed, and religious zeal. Their superior weapons, organizational skills, and determination brought them incredible success in their new environment. In 1519, a Spanish expedition under the command of Hernán Cortés landed at Veracruz, on the Gulf of Mexico. Marching to Tenochtitlán (teh-nahch-teet-LAHN) at the head of a small contingent of troops, Cortés received a friendly welcome from the Aztec monarch Moctezuma Xocoyotzin (mahk-tuh-ZOO-muh shoh-koh-YAHT-seen) (often called Montezuma), who initially believed his visitor was a representative of Quetzalcoatl (KWET-sul-koh-AHT-ul), the legendary and godlike feathered serpent of the Amerindian peoples. The king and his subjects were astounded to see men on horseback, for the horse

North Wind/North Wind Picture Archives

guzmā.   mchvacā.

Ibero-Amerikanisches Institut/Art Resource, NY

COMPARATIVE ILLUSTRATION

POLITICS & GOVERNMENT

The Spaniards Conquer a New World. The perspective that the Spanish brought to their arrival in the Americas was quite different from that of the indigenous peoples. In the European painting shown above, the encounter was a peaceful one, and the upturned eyes of Columbus and his fellow voyagers imply that their motives were spiritual rather than material. The image below, drawn by an Aztec artist, expresses a dramatically different point of view, as the Spanish invaders, assisted by their Indian allies, use superior weapons against the bows and arrows of their adversaries to bring about the conquest of Mexico.

Q *What does the Aztec painting presented here show the viewer about the nature of the conflict between the two contending armies?*

had disappeared from the Americas at least ten thousand years earlier.

But tensions soon erupted between the Spaniards and the Aztecs, provoked in part by demands by Cortés that the Aztecs renounce their native beliefs and accept Christianity. When the Spanish took Moctezuma hostage and began to destroy Aztec religious shrines, the local population revolted and drove the invaders from the city. Receiving assistance from the Aztec tribute state of Tlaxcallan (tuh-lah-SKAH-lahn), Cortés managed to fight his way back into the city. Meanwhile, the Aztecs were beginning to suffer the first effects of the diseases brought by the Europeans, which would eventually wipe out the majority of the local population. In a

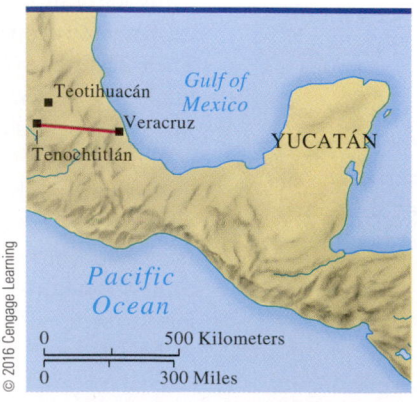

© 2016 Cengage Learning

The Arrival of Hernán Cortés in Mexico

battle that to many Aztecs must have seemed to symbolize the dying of the legendary fifth sun, the Aztecs were finally vanquished (see the box "An Aztec's Lament" on p. 399). Within months, their magnificent city and its temples, believed by the conquerors to be the work of Satan, had been destroyed (see the Comparative Illustration "The Spaniards Conquer a New World" above).

A similar fate awaited the powerful Inka Empire in South America. Between 1531 and 1536, another expedition, led by a hardened and somewhat corrupt soldier, Francisco Pizarro (frahn-SEES-koh puh-ZAHR-oh) (1470–1541), destroyed Inka power high in the Peruvian Andes. The Spanish conquests were undoubtedly facilitated by the prior arrival of European

An Aztec's Lament

INTERACTION & EXCHANGE

THE SPANISH CONQUEST OF MEXICO had an indelible impact on the vanquished local population. Aztec memoirs of the battle were collected by the Spanish a few years after the seizure of Tenochtitlán and were later translated from the original Nahuatl (NAH-waht-ul), the Aztec language, into Spanish or other European languages. In this passage, an Aztec observer describes the enormous sense of sorrow he felt at the tragedy that had befallen his compatriots. Note that the writer concludes that the defeat was ordained by the "Giver of Life" because of his displeasure with the Aztec people.

Flowers and Songs of Sorrow

Nothing but flowers and songs of sorrow
are left in Mexico and Tlatelolco,
where once we saw warriors and wise men.

We know it is true
that we must perish,
for we are mortal men.

You, the Giver of Life,
you have ordained it.

We wander here and there
in our desolate poverty.
We are mortal men.
We have seen bloodshed and pain
where once we saw beauty and valor.

We are crushed to the ground;
we lie in ruins.
There is nothing but grief and suffering
in Mexico and Tlatelolco,
where once we saw beauty and valor.

Have you grown weary of your servants?
Are you angry with your servants,
O Giver of Life?

 How did the author of this selection respond to the destruction of Aztec culture? Does he appear to be angry or resigned? What role did Aztec religion play in shaping his response?

Source: From *The Tears of the Indians*, Bartolomé de Las Casas. Copyright © 1970 by The John Lilburne Company Publishers.

---

diseases, which had decimated the local population. Although it took another three decades before the western part of Latin America was brought under Spanish control, already by 1535, the Spanish had created a system of colonial administration that made the New World—at least in European eyes—an extension of the old.

THE PORTUGUESE IN BRAZIL Although the Spanish had taken the lead in planting their flag in the Western Hemisphere, they were not alone. After the Portuguese sea captain Pedro Cabral inadvertently discovered the eastern coast of Latin America in 1500 while en route to the Indies, the Portuguese crown established the colony of Brazil in the area, basing its claim on the Treaty of Tordesillas, which had allocated that territory to the Portuguese sphere of influence (see the box "Dividing Up the Spoils of Exploration" on p. 396). Like their Spanish rivals, the Portuguese initially viewed their new colony as a source of gold and silver, but they soon discovered that profits could be made in other ways as well. A formal administrative system was instituted in Brazil in 1549, and Portuguese migrants arrived to establish plantations to produce sugar, coffee, and other tropical products for export to Europe.

Governing the Empires

While Portugal set out to strengthen its control over Brazil, Spain began to construct a colonial empire that included Central America, most of South America, and parts of North America. Within the lands of Central and South

CHRONOLOGY	Spanish and Portuguese Activities in the Americas
Christopher Columbus's first voyage to the Americas	1492
Portuguese fleet arrives in Brazil	1500
Columbus's last voyages	1502–1504
Spanish conquest of Mexico	1519–1522
Francisco Pizarro's conquest of the Inkas	1531–1536
Viceroyalty of New Spain established	1535
Formal colonial administrative system established in Brazil	1549

America, a new civilization arose that we have come to call Latin America (see Map 14.3).

Latin America rapidly became a multiracial society. Already by 1501, Spanish rulers allowed intermarriage between Europeans and the inhabitants of the Americas, whom the Europeans called Indians. Their offspring became known as **mestizos** (mess-TEE-zohz). In addition, over a period of three centuries, possibly as many as 8 million African slaves were brought to Spanish and Portuguese America to work the plantations that were established (see "The Slave Trade" later in this chapter). **Mulattoes** (muh-LAH-tohz)—the offspring of Africans and whites—joined mestizos and descendants of whites, Africans, and local Indians to produce a unique multiracial society in Latin America.

MAP 14.3 Latin America from c. 1500 to 1750. From the sixteenth century, Latin America was largely the colonial preserve of the Spanish, although Portugal dominated Brazil. The Latin American colonies supplied the Spanish and Portuguese with gold, silver, sugar, tobacco, cotton, and animal hides.

Q *How do you explain the ability of Europeans to dominate such large areas of Latin America?*

THE STATE AND THE CHURCH IN COLONIAL LATIN AMERICA

Although the colonial empires of Portuguese Brazil and Spanish America lasted more than three hundred years, the difficulties of communication and travel between the Americas and Europe made it virtually impossible for the home-country monarchs to provide close regulation of their empires. This left colonial officials in Latin America with much autonomy in implementing imperial policies. Nevertheless, the Iberians tried to keep the most important posts of colonial government in the hands of Europeans.

To rule their American empires, the kings of Spain and Portugal appointed **viceroys**, who ruled over a bureaucracy staffed primarily by Europeans, known as *peninsulares*. The first Spanish viceroyalty was established for New Spain (Mexico) in

1535. Another was organized in Peru in 1543, and later two additional ones—New Granada and La Plata—were added. Viceroyalties were in turn subdivided into smaller units, where **creoles**—American-born descendants of Europeans—often held prominent positions.

From the beginning, Spanish and Portuguese rulers were determined to convert the indigenous peoples of the Western Hemisphere to Christianity. Catholic missionaries fanned out to different parts of the Spanish Empire, where they brought Indians together into villages where they could be converted to Christianity, taught a trade, and encouraged to grow crops (see the Film & History feature *"The Mission* (1986)" on p. 401). The Catholic Church also built hospitals, orphanages, and schools to instruct Indian students in the rudiments of reading, writing, and arithmetic.

EXPLOITING THE RICHES OF THE AMERICAS The most vital task for administrators in the Americas was to enable the home countries to profit economically from their colonies in Latin America. The chief source of wealth, in the minds of European immigrants, came from the abundant supplies of gold and silver, and they sought the precious metals wherever they went in the Americas. One Aztec observer commented that the Spanish conquerors "longed and lusted for gold. Their bodies swelled with greed, and their hunger was ravenous; they hungered like pigs for that gold."[8] Rich silver deposits were found and exploited in Mexico and in southern Peru (modern Bolivia). When the mines at Potosí (poh-toh-SEE) in Peru were opened in 1545, the value of precious metals imported into Europe quadrupled. It has been estimated that between 1503 and 1650, some 16 million kilograms (17,500 tons) of silver and 185,000 kilograms (200 tons) of gold entered the port of Seville in Spain.

Although the pursuit of gold and silver offered prospects of fantastic financial rewards, agriculture ultimately proved to be a more abiding source of prosperity for Latin America. The American colonies became sources of raw materials for Spain and Portugal as sugar, tobacco, chocolate, precious woods, animal hides, and a number of other natural products made their way to Europe. In turn, the mother countries supplied their colonists with

The Mission (1986)

Directed by Roland Joffé, *The Mission* examines religion, politics, and colonialism in Europe and South America in the mid-eighteenth century. The movie begins with a flashback as Cardinal Altamirano (Ray McAnally) is dictating a letter to the pope to discuss the fate of the Jesuit missions in Paraguay. (The Jesuits were members of the Society of Jesus, a Roman Catholic religious order that was founded in the sixteenth century.) He begins by describing the establishment of a new Jesuit mission (San Carlos) in Spanish territory in the borderlands of Paraguay and Brazil. Father Gabriel (Jeremy Irons) has been able to win over the Guaraní Indians and create a community based on communal livelihood and property (private property has been abolished). The mission includes dwellings for the Guaraní and a church where they can practice their new faith by learning the Gospel and singing hymns. This small band of Jesuits is joined by Rodrigo Mendozo (Robert De Niro), who has been a slave trader dealing in Indians and now seeks to atone for killing his brother in a fit of jealous rage by joining the community at San Carlos. Won over to Father Gabriel's perspective, he also becomes a member of the Jesuit order.

Cardinal Altamirano now travels to South America, sent by a pope anxious to appease the Portuguese monarch over the activities of the Jesuits. Portuguese settlers in Brazil are eager to use the local people as slaves and to confiscate their communal lands and property. In 1750, when Spain agrees to turn over the Guaraní territory in Paraguay to Portugal, the settlers seize their opportunity. Although the cardinal visits a number of missions, including San Carlos, and obviously approves of their accomplishments, his hands are tied by the Portuguese king, who is threatening to disband the Jesuit order if the missions are not closed. The cardinal acquiesces, and Portuguese troops are sent to take over the missions. Although Rodrigo and the other Jesuits join the Guaraní in fighting the Portuguese while Father Gabriel remains nonviolent, all are massacred. The cardinal returns to Europe, dismayed by the murderous activities of the Portuguese but hopeful that the Jesuit order will be spared. All is in vain, however, as the Catholic

monarchs of Europe expel the Jesuits from their countries and pressure Pope Clement XIV into disbanding the Jesuit order in 1773.

In its approach to the destruction of the Jesuit missions, *The Mission* clearly exalts the dedication of the Jesuit order and praises its devotion to the welfare of the Indians. The movie ends with a small group of Guaraní children, now all orphans, picking up a few remnants of debris in their destroyed mission and moving off down the river back into the wilderness to escape enslavement. The final words on the screen illuminate the movie's message about the activities of the Europeans who destroyed the local civilizations in their conquest of the Americas: "The Indians of South America are still engaged in a struggle to defend their land and their culture. Many of the priests who, inspired by faith and love, continue to support the rights of the Indians, do so with their lives," a reference to the ongoing struggle in Latin America against the regimes that continue to oppress the landless masses.

The Jesuit missionary Father Gabriel (Jeremy Irons) with the Guaraní Indians of Paraguay before their slaughter by Portuguese troops.

Warner Brothers/ Everett Collection

manufactured goods (see Map 14.4). Both Spain and Portugal closely regulated the trade of their American colonies to keep others out, but the English and the French eventually became too powerful to be excluded from this lucrative Latin American market.

To produce these goods, colonial authorities initially tried to rely on local sources of human labor. Spanish policy toward the Indians was a combination of confusion, misguided paternalism, and cruel exploitation. Confusion arose over the nature of the Indians. Queen Isabella declared the Indians to be subjects of Castile and instituted the **encomienda system**, under which European settlers received grants of land and could collect tribute from the indigenous peoples and use them as laborers. In return, the holders of an **encomienda** (en-koh-MYEN-duh) were supposed to protect the Indians and supervise

Map content labels:

CANADA, Montreal, Quebec, New York, Boston, Baltimore, Philadelphia, Charleston, New Orleans, Mexico City, MEXICO, Veracruz, Acapulco, Cuba, Puerto Rico, Leeward Is., Cartagena, Panama, Trinidad, New Amsterdam, Guayaquil, PERU, BRAZIL, Pernambuco, Callao, Cuzco, Lima, Bahia, Potosí, Asunción, Rio de Janeiro, São Paulo, Valparaiso, Buenos Aires, Cape Horn

Liverpool, London, Hamburg, Amsterdam, Bordeaux, Le Havre, Marseilles, Azores, Lisbon, RUSSIAN EMPIRE, OTTOMAN EMPIRE, Cairo, Dakar, Accra, Slave Coast, Fernando Po, Zanzibar, Kilwa, Sofala, Mozambique Channel, Cape Town, Cape of Good Hope

Basra, Delhi, Patna, CHINA, Surat, Bombay, INDIA, Calcutta, Masulipatam, Goa, Madras, Cochin, Pondicherry, Canton, Macao, JAPAN, Manila, MALAYA, Malacca, SPICE ISLANDS, SUMATRA, BORNEO, Palembang, Batavia, CELEBES, JAVA

Atlantic Ocean, Pacific Ocean, Indian Ocean

Scale: 0 2,000 4,000 6,000 Kilometers / 0 2,000 4,000 Miles

Legend — Trade winds:

Symbol			
Furs	Silver	Coffee	Tea
Fish	Dyestuffs	Cotton	Silk production
Timber	Gold	Diamonds	Silk textiles
Tobacco	Sugar	Hides	Cotton textiles
Rice	Cacao	Spices	Ivory

MAP 14.4 Patterns of World Trade Between 1500 and 1800. This map shows the major products that were traded by European merchants throughout the world during the era of European exploration.

Q *What were the primary sources of gold and silver, so sought after by Columbus and his successors?*

their spiritual and material needs. In practice, this meant that the settlers were free to implement the system as they pleased. Three thousand miles from Spain, Spanish settlers largely ignored their government and brutally used the Indians to pursue their own economic interests (see Opposing Viewpoints "The March of Civilization" on p. 403). Indians were put to work on sugar plantations and in the lucrative gold and silver mines.

Forced labor, starvation, and especially disease took a fearful toll on Indian lives. With little or no natural resistance to European diseases, the Indians were ravaged by smallpox, measles, and typhus brought by the explorers and the conquistadors. Although scholarly estimates vary drastically, a reasonable guess is that at least half of the local population in some areas died of European diseases. On Hispaniola alone, out of an initial population of 100,000 when Columbus arrived in 1493, only 300 Indians survived by 1570. In 1542, largely in response to the publications of Bartolomé de Las Casas (bahr-toh-loh-MAY day lahs KAH-sahs), a Dominican monk who championed the Indians, the government abolished the *encomienda* system and provided more protection for the Indians. By then, however, the indigenous population had been decimated by disease, causing the Spanish—and eventually the Portuguese as well—to import African slaves to replace the Indians in the sugar fields.

The Competition Intensifies

The success of the Spanish and the Portuguese in exploiting the riches of the Americas soon attracted competition from other European trading states. In 1607, after an abortive effort to establish a base near Cape Hatteras had failed, the English set up its first permanent settlement at Jamestown, near the Chesapeake Bay. Within a few years, other European states had followed suit, and by the end of the seventeenth century, they had occupied much of the eastern seaboard of North America (see Chapter 18).

But the major area of competition was in South America and the Caribbean islands, where the lure of profits from the sugar trade was difficult to resist. The Dutch formed their own West India Company in 1621 to compete with Spanish and Portuguese interests and briefly took control of the sugar plantations on the east coast of Brazil. The French and the English focused their efforts on the Caribbean, where their privateers preyed on Spanish galleons carrying silver from the Americas

OPPOSING ✕ VIEWPOINTS

The March of Civilization

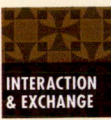

INTERACTION & EXCHANGE

As Europeans began to explore new parts of the world in the fifteenth century, they were convinced that it was their duty to introduce civilized ways to the heathen peoples they encountered. This attitude is reflected in the first selection, which describes the Spanish captain Vasco Núñez de Balboa (BAHS-koh NOON-yez day bal-BOH-uh) in 1513, when from a hill on the Isthmus of Panama he first laid eyes on the Pacific Ocean.

Bartolomé de Las Casas (1474–1566) was a Dominican monk who participated in the conquest of Cuba and received land and Indians in return for his efforts. But in 1514, he underwent a radical transformation that led him to believe that the Indians had been cruelly mistreated by his fellow Spaniards. He spent the remaining years of his life fighting for the Indians. The second selection is taken from his most influential work, *Brevísima Relación de la Destrucción de las Indias*, known to English readers as *The Tears of the Indians*. This work was largely responsible for the reputation of the Spanish conquistadors as cruel and murderous fanatics.

Gonzalo Fernández de Ovieda, *Historia General y Natural de las Indias*

On Tuesday, the twenty-fifth of September of the year 1513, at ten o'clock in the morning, Captain Vasco Núñez, having gone ahead of his company, climbed a hill with a bare summit, and from the top of this hill saw the South Sea. Of all the Christians in his company, he was the first to see it. He turned back toward his people, full of joy, lifting his hands and his eyes to Heaven, praising Jesus Christ and his glorious Mother the Virgin, Our Lady. Then he fell upon his knees on the ground and gave great thanks to God for the mercy He had shown him, in allowing him to discover that sea, and thereby to render so great a service to God and to the most serene Catholic Kings of Castile, our sovereigns....

And he told all the people with him to kneel also, to give the same thanks to God, and to beg Him fervently to allow them to see and discover the secrets and great riches of that sea and coast, for the greater glory and increase of the Christian faith, for the conversion of the Indians, natives of those southern regions, and for the fame and prosperity of the royal throne of Castile and of its sovereigns present and to come. All the people cheerfully and willingly did as they were bidden; and the Captain made them fell a big tree and make from it a tall cross, which they erected in that same place, at the top of the hill from which the South Sea had first been seen.

Bartolomé de Las Casas, *The Tears of the Indians*

There is nothing more detestable or more cruel than the tyranny which the Spaniards use toward the Indians for the getting of pearl. Surely the infernal torments cannot much exceed the anguish that they endure, by reason of that way of cruelty; for they put them under water some four or five ells deep, where they are forced without any liberty of respiration, to gather up the shells wherein the Pearls are; sometimes they come up again with nets full of shells to take breath, but if they stay any while to rest themselves, immediately comes a hangman row'd in a little boat, who as soon as he hath well beaten them, drags them again to their labor. Their food is nothing but filth, and the very same that contains the Pearl, with small portion of that bread which that Country affords; in the first whereof there is little nourishment; and as for the latter, it is made with great difficulty, besides that they have not enough of that neither for sustenance; they lie upon the ground in fetters, lest they should run away; and many times they are drown'd in this labor, and are never seen again till they swim upon the top of the waves; oftentimes they also are devoured by certain sea monsters, that are frequent in those seas. Consider whether this hard usage of the poor creatures be consistent with the precepts which God commands concerning charity to our neighbor....

 Can the sentiments expressed by Vasco Núñez be reconciled with the treatment accorded to the Indians as described by Las Casas? Which selection do you think better describes the behavior of the Spaniards in the Americas? Compare the treatment of the Indians described here with the treatment of African slaves described in the selection "A Slave Market in Africa" on p. 409.

Source: From *The Age of Reconnaissance* by J. H. Parry (International Thomson Publishing, 1969), pp. 233–234. From *The Tears of the Indians*, Bartolomé de Las Casas. Copyright © 1970 by The John Lilburne Company Publishers.

back to Seville. They also competed actively for control of several of the Caribbean islands, where sugar plantations were producing fabulous profits for their new European owners. A number of the islands in the region shifted control several times over the course of the seventeenth and eighteenth centuries.

Christopher Columbus: Hero or Villain?

For centuries, the explorer Christopher Columbus has generally been viewed by most observers in a positive light. By discovering the Western Hemisphere, he opened up the world and laid the foundations for the modern global economy. Recently, however, some historians have begun to challenge the prevailing image of Columbus as a heroic figure in world history and view him instead as a symbol of European colonial repression and a prime mover in the virtual extinction of the peoples and cultures of the Americas (see the Comparative Essay "The Columbian Exchange" on p. 405).

Certainly, they have a point. As we have seen, the immediate consequences of Columbus's voyages were tragic for countless peoples in the Western Hemisphere. And as historical studies have shown, Columbus, who was himself not an entirely sympathetic figure, viewed the indigenous peoples that he encountered with condescension, describing them to his sponsors as naïve innocents who could be exploited for the purpose of bringing wealth and power to Spain. As a consequence, his men frequently treated the local population brutally.

But is it fair to blame Columbus for possessing many of the character traits and prejudices common to his era? To do so is to demand that an individual transcend the limitations of his time and adopt the values of another generation several hundred years into the future—something that few, if any, would be able to achieve. Perhaps it is better to note simply that Columbus and his contemporaries showed relatively little understanding and sympathy for the cultural values of peoples who lived beyond the borders of their own civilization, a limitation that would probably apply to one degree or another to all generations, including our own. Whether Columbus was a hero or a villain will remain a matter of debate. That he and his contemporaries played a key role in the emergence of the modern world is a matter on which there can be no doubt.

Africa in Transition

 FOCUS QUESTION: What were the main features of the African slave trade, and how did European participation in that trade affect traditional African practices?

Although the primary objective of the Portuguese in rounding the Cape of Good Hope was to find a sea route to the Spice Islands, they soon discovered that profits were to be made en route, along the eastern coast of Africa.

The Portuguese in Africa

In the early sixteenth century, a Portuguese fleet commanded by Francisco de Almeida (fran-SEESH-koh duh ahl-MAY-duh) seized a number of East African port cities, including Kilwa, Sofala, and Mombasa, and built forts along the coast in an effort to control the trade in the area. Above all, the Portuguese wanted to monopolize the trade in gold, which was mined in the hills along the upper Zambezi River and then shipped to Sofala on the coast (see Map 14.4 on p. 402 and Chapter 8). For centuries, the gold trade had been monopolized by local Bantu-speaking Shona peoples at Zimbabwe. In the fifteenth century, it had come under the control of a Shona dynasty known as the Mwene Mutapa (MWAY-nay moo-TAH-puh).

The Mwene Mutapa had originally controlled the region south of the Zambezi River and may have been the builders of the impressive city known today as Great Zimbabwe, but sometime in the fifteenth century, they moved northeastward

The War of Jenkin's Ear. In the year 1739, war broke out between the two great naval powers of the day, Great Britain and Spain. Although the conflict was later dubbed "the war of Jenkin's Ear"—in reference to the severing of the ear of a British naval officer by a Spanish soldier—the actual cause was the bitter competition that existed between the two countries over control of trade routes and sources of profit in the Caribbean Sea. After a decade of conflict, the war ended inconclusively. In the painting shown here, a British fleet unsuccessfully attacks a Spanish fortress in the city of Cartagena, in what is today the nation of Colombia. Because of their importance in the production of sugar and other tropical products, the islands of the Caribbean were the cause of frequent disputes among the various European colonial powers in the eighteenth century.

Scala/White Images/Art Resource, NY

COMPARATIVE ESSAY

The Columbian Exchange

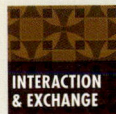

INTERACTION & EXCHANGE

In the Western world, the discovery of the Americas has traditionally been viewed in a largely positive sense, as the first step in a process that expanded the global trade network and eventually led to increased economic well-being and the spread of civilization throughout the world. In recent years, however, that view has come under sharp attack from some observers, who point out that for the peoples of the Americas, the primary legacy of the European conquest was not improved living standards but harsh colonial exploitation and the spread of pestilential diseases that devastated local populations.

Certainly, the record of the European conquistadors leaves much to be desired, and the voyages of Columbus were not of universal benefit to his contemporaries or to later generations. They not only resulted in the destruction of vibrant civilizations in the Americas but also led ultimately to the enslavement of millions of Africans, who were separated from their families and shipped to a far-off world in deplorable, inhuman conditions.

But to focus solely on the evils committed in the name of exploration and civilization misses a larger point and obscures the long-term ramifications of the events taking place. The age of European expansion that began in the fifteenth century was only the latest in a series of population movements that included the spread of nomadic peoples across Central Asia and the expansion of Islam out of the Middle East after the death of the prophet Muhammad. In fact, the migration of peoples in search of a better livelihood has been a central theme in the evolution of the human race since the dawn of prehistory. Virtually all of the migrations involved acts of unimaginable cruelty and the forcible displacement of peoples and societies.

In retrospect, it seems clear that the consequences of such broad population movements are too complex to be summed

The Granger Collection, NYC

A Sugar Plantation. As a result of the growing popularity of sugar in Europe in the sixteenth century, sugar plantations were established in suitable areas throughout the tropical regions of South America and the Caribbean islands. Shown here is a plantation established by the French on the island of Hispaniola. The backbreaking nature of the work is clearly evident, as slaves imported from Africa cut the sugarcane and bring it to the mill for crushing and transformation into raw sugar. Sugar is still grown on a number of islands in the Caribbean, although profit margins are low because of the volatility of the price of sugar.

up in moral or ideological simplifications. The Mongol invasions and the expansion of Islam are two examples of movements that brought benefits as well as costs for the peoples who were affected. By the same token, the European conquest of the Americas not only brought the destruction of cultures and dangerous new diseases but also initiated the exchange of plant and animal species that have ultimately fed millions and been of widespread benefit to peoples throughout the globe. The introduction of the horse, the cow, and various grain crops vastly increased food production in the Americas. The cultivation of corn, manioc, and the potato, all of them products of the Western Hemisphere, has had the same effect in Asia, Africa, and Europe. The **Columbian Exchange**, as it is sometimes labeled, has had far-reaching consequences that transcend facile moral judgments.

The opening of the Americas had other long-term ramifications as well. The importation of vast amounts of gold and silver fueled a price revolution that for years distorted the Spanish economy. At the same time, the increase in liquid capital due to this expansion was a

(continued)

(Comparative Essay continued)

crucial factor in the growth of commercial capitalism that set the stage for the global economy of the modern era. Some have even suggested that the precious metals that flowed into the treasuries of major European trading states may have helped finance the Industrial Revolution (see Chapter 19) that is now spreading rapidly throughout the modern world.

Viewed in that context, the Columbian Exchange, whatever its moral failings, ultimately brought benefits to peoples throughout the world. For some, the costs were high, and it can be argued that the indigenous peoples of the Americas might have better managed the transformation on their own. But the "iron law" of history operates at its own speed and does not wait for laggards. For good or ill, the Columbian Exchange marks a major stage in the transition between the traditional and the modern world.

 How can the costs and benefits of the Columbian Exchange be measured? What standards would you apply in attempting to measure them?

to the valley of the Zambezi. Here they encountered the arriving Portuguese, who had begun to move inland to gain access to the lucrative gold trade and had established ports on the Zambezi River. The Portuguese opened treaty relations with the Mwene Mutapa, and Jesuit priests were eventually posted to the court in 1561. At first, the Mwene Mutapa found the Europeans useful as an ally against local rivals, but by the end of the sixteenth century, the Portuguese had established a protectorate and forced the local ruler to grant title to large tracts of land to European officials and private individuals living in the area. Eventually, those lands would be integrated into the colony of Mozambique. The Portuguese, however, lacked the personnel and the capital to dominate local trade, and in the late seventeenth century, a vassal of the Mwene Mutapa succeeded in driving them from the plateau; his descendants maintained control of the area for the next two hundred years.

North of the Zambezi River, Bantu-speaking peoples were coming under pressure not only from the Portuguese but also from pastoralists migrating southward from the southern Sudan. The latter were frequently aggressive and began to occupy the rift valley and parts of the lake district that had previously been controlled by Bantu-speaking farmers. In some cases, the conflict between farmers and pastoralists was fairly clear-cut. In Rwanda and Burundi, immediately west of Lake Victoria, farming Hutu peoples defended their hilltop communities against roving Tutsi pastoralists occupying the surrounding lowlands.

The Dutch in South Africa

The first Europeans to settle in southern Africa were the Dutch. After an unsuccessful attempt to seize the Portuguese settlement on the island of Mozambique off the East African coast, in 1652 the Dutch set up a way station at the Cape of Good Hope to serve as a base for their fleets en route to the East Indies. At first, the new settlement was intended simply to provide food and other provisions to Dutch ships, but eventually it developed into a permanent colony. Dutch farmers, known as **Boers** and speaking a Dutch dialect that evolved into Afrikaans, began to settle in the sparsely occupied areas outside the city of Cape Town. The temperate climate and the absence of tropical diseases made the territory near the cape almost the only land south of the Sahara that the Europeans found suitable for habitation.

The Dutch, like their chief rivals, the English and the French, also took advantage of the decline of the Songhai Empire to become active in the West African trade in the mid-sixteenth century, encroaching particularly on the Portuguese spheres of influence. During the mid-seventeenth century, the Dutch seized a number of Portuguese forts along the West African coast while at the same time taking over the bulk of the Portuguese trade across the Indian Ocean.

The Slave Trade

The European exploration of the African coastline had little immediate significance for most peoples living in the interior of the continent, except for a few who engaged in direct or indirect trade with the foreigners. But for peoples living on or near the coast, the impact was often great indeed. As the trade in slaves increased during the sixteenth, seventeenth, and eighteenth centuries, thousands and then millions of men, women, and even children were removed from their homes and forcibly exported to plantations in the Western Hemisphere.

THE ARRIVAL OF THE EUROPEANS As we saw in Chapter 8, there were different forms of slavery in Africa before the arrival of the Europeans. For centuries, slaves—often captives seized in battle or in raids between neighboring villages—had been used in many African societies as agricultural laborers, household servants, or concubines. Many served as domestic servants or as wageless workers for the local ruler, and some were permitted to purchase their freedom under certain conditions. After the expansion of Islam south of the Sahara in the eighth century, a vigorous traffic in slaves developed, as Arab merchants traded for slaves along routes snaking across the Sahara or up the Nile River Valley. Under Askia Mohammad and his successors, Songhai became active in the process, launching raids in non-Muslim areas and selling their captives to Arab merchants for shipment to the Middle East, where they were put to use as domestic servants or as workers on plantations throughout the region. Slavery also existed in many European countries, where a few slaves from Africa or Slavic-speaking peoples captured in war in the regions near the Black Sea (the English word *slave* derives from "Slav") were used for domestic purposes or as agricultural workers in the lands adjacent to the Mediterranean. Merchants from Genoa routinely traded captives that had been seized along the coast of the Black Sea to their Arab counterparts in return for spices.

With the arrival of the Europeans in Africa in the fifteenth century, the African slave trade changed dramatically, although the change did not occur immediately. At first, the Portuguese simply replaced European slaves with African ones. During the second half of the fifteenth century, about a thousand slaves were taken to Portugal each year; the vast majority were apparently destined to serve as domestic servants for affluent families throughout Europe. But the discovery of the Western Hemisphere in the 1490s and the subsequent planting of sugarcane in South America and on the islands of the Caribbean changed the situation dramatically.

Cane sugar was native to Indonesia and had first been introduced to Europeans from the Middle East during the crusades. By the fifteenth century, sugar cane was grown (often by slaves from Africa or the region of the Black Sea) in modest amounts on the islands of Cyprus and Sicily and in the southern regions of the Iberian Peninsula. But when the Ottoman Empire seized much of the eastern Mediterranean (see Chapter 16), the Europeans needed to seek out new areas suitable for cultivation. In 1490, the Portuguese established sugar plantations worked by African laborers at São Tomé, an island off the central coast of Africa. Demand increased as sugar gradually replaced honey as a sweetener, especially in northern Europe.

But the primary impetus to the sugar industry came from the colonization of the Americas. During the sixteenth century, plantations were established along the eastern coast of Brazil and on several islands in the Caribbean (see earlier section, "The Competition Intensifies"). Because the cultivation of cane sugar is an arduous process demanding both skill and large quantities of labor, the new plantations required more workers than could be provided by the importation of Europeans (mostly prisoners) or by the Indian population in the Americas, many of whom rapidly died of diseases imported from Europe and Africa. Since the climate and soil of much of West Africa were not especially conducive to the cultivation of sugar (cane sugar requires access to ample water and a frost-free environment), African slaves began to be shipped to Brazil and the Caribbean to work on the plantations. The first were sent from Portugal, but in 1518, a Spanish ship carried the first boatload of African slaves directly from Africa to the Americas.

THE MIDDLE PASSAGE   During the next two centuries, the trade in slaves increased by massive proportions (see Map 14.5). An estimated 275,000 enslaved Africans were exported to other countries during the sixteenth century, more than two-thirds of them to the Americas. The total climbed beyond

MAP 14.5 The Slave Trade. Beginning in the sixteenth century, the trade in African slaves to the Americas became a major source of profit to European merchants. This map traces the routes taken by slave-trading ships, as well as the territories and ports of call of European powers in the seventeenth century.

Q *What were the major destinations for the slave trade?*

© 2016 Cengage Learning

a million in the seventeenth century and jumped to 6 million in the eighteenth century, when the trade spread from West and Central Africa to East Africa. Even during the nineteenth century, when Great Britain and a number of other European countries attempted to end the slave trade, nearly 2 million humans were exported. It has been estimated that altogether as many as 10 million African slaves were transported to the Americas between the early sixteenth and the late nineteenth centuries. As many as 2 million were exported to other areas during the same period.

One reason for these astonishing numbers, of course, was the tragically high death rate. In what is often called the **Middle Passage**, the arduous voyage from Africa to the Americas, losses were frequently appalling. Although figures on the number of slaves who died on the journey are almost entirely speculative, during the first shipments, up to one-third of the human cargo may have died of disease or malnourishment. Even among crew members, mortality rates were sometimes as high as one in four. Later merchants became more efficient and reduced losses to about 10 percent. Still, the future slaves were treated inhumanely, chained together in the holds of ships reeking with the stench of human waste and diseases carried by vermin.

Gateway to Slavery. Of the 12 million slaves shipped from Africa to other parts of the world, some passed through this doorway on Gorée (GOR-ay), a small island in a bay just off the coast of Senegal, near Cape Verde. Beginning in the sixteenth century, European traders shipped Africans from this region to the Americas to be used as slave labor on sugar plantations. Some victims were kept in a prison on the island, which was first occupied by the Portuguese and later by the Dutch, the British, and the French. The sign by the doorway reads, "From this door, they would embark on a voyage with no return, eyes fixed on an infinity of suffering."

Claire L. Duiker

SLAVERY IN THE AMERICAS Ironically, African slaves who survived the brutal voyage fared somewhat better than whites after their arrival. Mortality rates for Europeans in the West Indies were ten to twenty times higher than in Europe, and death rates for those newly arrived in the islands averaged more than 125 per 1,000 annually. But the figure for Africans, many of whom had developed at least a partial immunity to yellow fever, was only about 30 per 1,000.

The reason for the staggering death rates was clearly more than maltreatment, although that was certainly a factor. As we have seen, the transmission of diseases from one continent to another brought high death rates among those lacking immunity. African slaves were somewhat less susceptible to European diseases than the American Indian populations. Indeed, they seem to have possessed a degree of immunity, perhaps because their ancestors had developed antibodies to diseases common to the Old World from the centuries of contact via the trans-Saharan trade. The Africans would not have had immunity to native American diseases, however.

The mortality rates were higher for immigrants than for individuals born in the Americas, who as children gradually developed at least a partial immunity to many diseases. Death rates for native-born slaves tended to be significantly lower than for recent arrivals, which raises the question of why the slave population did not begin to rise after the initial impact of settlement had worn off. The answer appears to be a matter of economics. In the first place, only half as many women were enslaved as men, birthrates for women living in slavery were low, and infant mortality was high. In the second place, as long as the price of slaves was low, many slave owners in the West Indies apparently believed that purchasing a new slave was less expensive than raising a child from birth to working age at adolescence. After the price of slaves began to rise during the eighteenth century, plantation owners started to devote more efforts to replenishing the supply of workers by natural methods.

One of the lesser-known facts about slavery in the Americas is that many Africans did not accept their brutal life on the sugar, cotton, and tobacco plantations and escaped into the wilderness where they set up so-called "maroon" communities safe from control of the European colonial authorities. The most successful such efforts were in Brazil and on the island of Jamaica, where camps for escaped slaves, known as **maroons**, survived for decades carrying out an existence independent of colonial authority. In some cases, maroon communities even won recognition from the local colonial authorities in return for agreeing to return recently escaped slaves to their European masters.

SOURCES OF SLAVES For the most part, Europeans obtained their slaves by traditional means, purchasing them from local African merchants at the infamous slave markets in exchange for gold, guns, or other European manufactured goods such as textiles, copper, or iron utensils (see the box "A Slave Market in Africa" on p. 409). The "third leg" of this so-called **Triangular Trade** took place when slave owners in the Americas paid for their slaves with sugar or its by-products (such as rum and molasses) exported to buyers in Europe. At

A Slave Market in Africa

FAMILY & SOCIETY

TRAFFIC IN SLAVES had been carried on in Africa since the kingdom of the pharaohs in ancient Egypt. But the slave trade increased dramatically after the arrival of European ships off the coast of West Africa. The following passage by a Dutch observer describes a slave market in Africa and the conditions on the ships that carried the slaves to the Americas.

Slavery in Africa: A Firsthand Report

When these slaves come to Fida, they are put in prison all together; and when we treat concerning buying them, they are brought out into a large plain. There, by our surgeons, whose province it is, they are thoroughly examined, even to the smallest member, and that naked too, both men and women, without the least distinction or modesty. Those that are approved as good are set on one side; and the lame or faulty are set by as invalids....

The invalids and the maimed being thrown out, ... the remainder are numbered, and it is entered who delivered them. In the meanwhile, a burning iron, with the arms or name of the companies, lies in the fire, with which ours are marked on the breast. This is done that we may distinguish them from the slaves of the English, French, or others (which are also marked with their mark), and to prevent the Negroes exchanging them for worse, at which they have a good hand.

I doubt not but this trade seems very barbarous to you, but since it is followed by mere necessity, it must go on; but we take all possible care that they are not burned too hard, especially the women, who are more tender than the men.

When we have agreed with the owners of the slaves, they are returned to their prison. There from that time forward they are kept at our charge, costing us two pence a day a slave; which serves to subsist them, like our criminals, on bread and water. To save charges, we send them on board our ships at the very first opportunity, before which their masters strip them of all they have on their backs so that they come aboard stark naked, women as well as men. In this condition they are obliged to continue, if the master of the ship is not so charitable (which he commonly is) as to bestow something on them to cover their nakedness.

You would really wonder to see how these slaves live on board, for though their number sometimes amounts to six or seven hundred, yet by the careful management of our masters of ships, they are so regulated that it seems incredible. And in this particular our nation exceeds all other Europeans, for the French, Portuguese and English slave ships are always foul and stinking; on the contrary, ours are for the most part clean and neat.

The slaves are fed three times a day with indifferent good victuals, and much better than they eat in their own country. Their lodging place is divided into two parts, one of which is appointed for the men, the other for the women, each sex being kept apart. Here they lie as close together as it is possible for them to be crowded.

What is the author's overall point of view toward the institution of slavery? Does he justify the practice? How does he compare Dutch behavior with that of other European countries involved in the slave trade?

Source: From *The Great Travelers*, vol. I, Milton Rugoff, ed. Copyright © 1960 by Simon & Schuster.

---

first, local slave traders obtained their supply from nearby regions, but as demand increased, they had to move further inland to find their victims. In a few cases, local rulers became concerned about the impact of the slave trade on the political and social well-being of their societies (see the box "A Plea Between Friends" on p. 410). As a general rule, however, the local monarchs viewed the slave trade as a source of income, and many launched forays against defenseless villages in search of unsuspecting victims.

Historians once thought that Europeans controlled the terms of the slave trade and were thus able to obtain victims at bargain prices. Recently, however, it has become clear that African intermediaries—private merchants, local elites, and trading state monopolies—were very active in the process and were often able to dictate the price, volume, and availability of slaves to European purchasers. The majority of the slaves sold to European buyers were males; females, who were in great demand in Africa and on the trans-Saharan trade, tended to be reserved for those markets. The slave merchants were often paid in various types of imported goods, including East Asian textiles (highly desired for their bright colors and durability), furniture, and other manufactured products. Until the end of the seventeenth century, the Portuguese preferred gold to slaves and would sometimes pay for the gold by selling slaves to African kingdoms that were short of labor. In fact, not until the beginning of the eighteenth century did slaves surpass gold and ivory as the continent's leading exports.

THE EFFECTS OF THE SLAVE TRADE The effects of the slave trade varied from area to area. It might be assumed that apart from the tragic effects on the lives of individual victims and their families, the practice would have led to the depopulation of vast areas of the continent. This did occur in some areas, notably in modern Angola, south of the mouth of the Congo River, and in thinly populated regions in East Africa, but it was less true in West Africa. There high birthrates were often able to counterbalance the loss of able-bodied adults, and the introduction of new crops from the Americas, such as maize, peanuts, and manioc, led to an increase in food production that made it possible to support a larger population.

A Plea Between Friends

INTERACTION & EXCHANGE

KING AFONSO I OF THE STATE OF KONGO was one of Portugal's chief African allies during the early sixteenth century. A convert to Christianity, he used his relationship with the Portuguese to extend the territory of his kingdom at the expense of neighboring states in the region. Captives obtained during his military campaigns were sold to merchants and then exported abroad as slaves. As the demand for slaves increased, however, traders began to trap and enslave Afonso's own subjects, while flooding the country with goods from abroad that undermined his royal authority.

In this letter, written in 1526, Afonso appealed to his "brother" sovereign, Dom João III, king of Portugal, to prevent such unscrupulous merchants from seizing his subjects and selling them as slaves to European sea captains. The letter is a vivid testimonial to how the slave trade destabilized African societies on or near the coast during the sixteenth and seventeenth centuries.

A Letter to King João

[1526] Sir, your Highness [of Portugal] should know how our Kingdom is being lost in so many ways that it is convenient to provide for the necessary remedy, since this is caused by the excessive freedom given by your factors and officials to the men and merchants who are allowed to come to this Kingdom to set up shops with goods and many things which have been prohibited by us, and which they spread throughout our Kingdoms and Domains in such an abundance that many of our vassals, whom we had in obedience, do not comply because they have the things in greater abundance than we ourselves; and it was with these things that we had them content and subjected under our vassalage and jurisdiction, so it is doing a great harm not only to the service of God, but the security and peace of our Kingdoms and State as well.

And we cannot reckon how great the damage is, since the mentioned merchants are taking every day our natives, sons of the land and the sons of our noblemen and vassals and our relatives, because the thieves and men of bad conscience grab them wishing to have the things and wares of this Kingdom which they are ambitious of; they grab them and get them to be sold; and so great, Sir, is the corruption and licentiousness that our country is being completely depopulated, and Your Highness should not agree with this nor accept it as in your service. And to avoid it we need from those [your] Kingdoms no more than some priests and a few people to teach in schools, and no other goods except wine and flour for the holy sacrament. That is why we beg of Your Highness to help and assist us in this matter, commanding your factors that they should not send here either merchants or wares, because it is *our will that in these Kingdoms there should not be any trade of slaves nor outlet for them.* Concerning what is referred above, again we beg of Your Highness to agree with it, since otherwise we cannot remedy such an obvious damage. Pray Our Lord in His mercy to have Your Highness under His guard and let you do for ever the things of His service. I kiss your hand many times.

At our town of Congo, written on the sixth day of July.
João Teixeira did it in 1526.
The King, Dom Afonso.

[On the back of this letter the following can be read: To the most powerful and excellent prince Dom João, King our Brother.]

 In what ways were the European merchants destabilizing the kingdom of Kongo? What remedy did Afonso propose?

Source: From *The African Past: Chronicles from Antiquity to Modern Times* by Basil Davidson (Boston: Little, Brown and Company, 1964), pp. 191–192.

One of the many cruel ironies of history is that while the institution of slavery was a tragedy for many, it benefited others.

Still, there is no denying the reality that from a moral point of view, the slave trade represented a tragic loss for millions of Africans, not only for the individual victims but also for their families. One of the more poignant aspects of the trade is that as many as 20 percent of those sold to European slavers were children, a statistic that may be partly explained by the fact that many European countries enacted regulations that permitted more children than adults to be transported aboard the ships.

Beyond the effects on individual Africans and their families, the slave trade also had a corrosive impact on the structure of society as a whole. Another consequence of the arrival of the Europeans was the introduction of firearms into the African continent. As the European demand for slaves steadily increased, African slave traders began to use their newly purchased guns to raid neighboring villages in search of captives, initiating a chain of violence that rapidly extended into the interior and created a climate of fear and insecurity throughout the region. Old polities were undermined, and new regimes ruled by rapacious "merchant princes" began to proliferate on the coast.

How did Europeans justify cruelty of such epidemic proportions? In some cases, they rationalized that slave traders were only carrying on a tradition that had existed for centuries throughout the Mediterranean and African world. In others, they eased their consciences by noting that slaves brought from Africa would now be exposed to the Christian

William J. Duiker

Manioc, Food for the Millions. One of the plants native to the Americas that European adventurers would take back to the Old World was manioc (also known as cassava or yuca). A tuber like the potato, manioc is a prolific crop that grows well in poor, dry soils, but it lacks the high nutrient value of grain crops such as wheat and rice and for that reason never became popular in Europe (except as a source of tapioca). It was introduced to Africa in the seventeenth century. Because it flourishes in dry climates and can be preserved easily for consumption at a later date, it eventually became a staple food for up to one-third of the population of that continent. The photo shows a manioc plant growing in East Africa.

faith and would be able to replace American Indian workers, many of whom were considered too physically fragile for the heavy human labor involved in cutting sugarcane.

Political and Social Structures in a Changing Continent

Of course, the Western economic penetration of Africa had other dislocating effects. As in other parts of the non-Western world, the importation of manufactured goods from Europe undermined the foundations of local cottage industries and impoverished countless families. The demand for slaves and the introduction of firearms intensified political instability and civil strife. At the same time, the impact of the Europeans should not be exaggerated. Only in a few isolated areas, such as South Africa and Mozambique, were permanent European settlements established. Elsewhere, at the insistence of African rulers and merchants, European influence generally did not penetrate beyond the coastal regions.

Nevertheless, inland areas were often affected by events taking place elsewhere. In the western Sahara, for example, the

Life of Prince Henry the Navigator	1394–1460
Portuguese ships reach the Senegal River	1441
Bartolomeu Dias sails around the tip of Africa	1487
First boatload of slaves to the Americas	1518
Dutch way station established at the Cape of Good Hope	1652
Ashanti kingdom established in West Africa	1680
Portuguese expelled from Mombasa	1698

diversion of trade routes toward the coast led to the weakening of the old Songhai trading empire and its eventual conquest by a vigorous new Moroccan dynasty in the late sixteenth century. Morocco had long hoped to expand its influence into the Sahara in order to seize control over the commerce in gold and salt, and in 1590, Moroccan forces defeated Songhai's army at Gao, on the Niger River, and then occupied the great caravan center of Timbuktu. Even after the departure of the invaders, Songhai was beyond recovery, and the next two centuries were marked by ongoing strife between divergent states and intense competition between Muslims in the cities and towns and adherents of traditional African religions in rural areas.

European influence had a more direct impact along the coast of West Africa, especially in the vicinity of European forts such as Dakar and Sierra Leone, but no European colonies were established there before 1800. Most of the numerous African states in the area from Cape Verde to the delta of the Niger River were sufficiently strong to resist Western encroachments, and they often allied with each other to force European purchasers to respect their monopoly over trading operations. Some, like the powerful Ashanti kingdom, established in 1680 on the Gold Coast, profited substantially from the rise in seaborne commerce. Some states, particularly along the so-called Slave Coast, in what is now Benin and Togo, or in the densely populated Niger River delta, took an active part in the slave trade. The demands of slavery and the temptations of economic profit, however, also contributed to the increase in conflict among the states in the area.

This was especially true in the region of the Congo River, where Portuguese activities eventually led to the splintering of the state of Kongo and two centuries of rivalry and internal strife among the successor states in the area. A similar pattern developed in East Africa, where Portuguese activities led to the decline and eventual collapse of the Mwene Mutapa. Northward along the coast, in present-day Kenya and Tanzania, African rulers, assisted by Arab forces from Oman and Muscat in the Arabian peninsula, expelled the Portuguese from Mombasa in 1698. Swahili culture now regained some of the dynamism it had possessed before the arrival of Vasco da Gama and his successors. But with much shipping now diverted southward to the route around the Cape of Good Hope, the commerce of the area never completely recovered and was increasingly dependent on the export of slaves and ivory obtained through contacts with African states in the interior.

William J. Duiker

Fort Jesus at Mombasa. Mombasa, a port city on the eastern coast of Africa, was a jumping-off point for the Portuguese as they explored the lands bordering the Indian Ocean. Erected in the early sixteenth century atop a bluff overlooking the harbor, Fort Jesus remained an imposing symbol of European power until 1698, when the Portuguese were expelled by the Arabs. They returned briefly in 1728 but were forced to evacuate a few months later.

Southeast Asia in the Era of the Spice Trade

Q FOCUS QUESTION: What were the main characteristics of Southeast Asian societies, and how were they affected by the coming of Islam and the Europeans?

As we noted earlier, Southeast Asia was affected in various ways by the expansion of the global trade network that began to accelerate in the early fifteenth century with the arrival of Chinese fleets under the command of Admiral Zheng He. Although the Chinese presence soon receded, that of Islam, introduced by merchants from India and the Middle East, now began to make serious inroads, notably in the Malay Peninsula and in coastal regions in the Indonesian archipelago. In 1511, however, the seizure of the Malaccan sultanate by a Portuguese fleet introduced a new threat into the region, while inaugurating a period of intense conflict among various European competitors for access to the spice trade. At first, the rulers of most of the local states in the region were able to fend off these challenges and maintain their independence. As we shall see in a later chapter, however, the reprieve was only temporary.

The Arrival of the West

Where the Portuguese trod, others soon followed. By the early seventeenth century, the Dutch, English, and French had begun to join the scramble for rights to the lucrative spice trade. Within a short time, the Dutch appeared to have the advantage. Formed in 1602, the aggressive and well-financed Dutch East India Company

(Vereenigde Oost-Indische Compagnie, or VOC) possessed ten times the capital of the English East India Company and not only succeeded in elbowing its rivals out of the spice trade but also had begun to consolidate political and military control over the area. On the island of Java, where they established a fort at Batavia (today's Jakarta) in 1619 (see the illustration on p. 387), the Dutch found that it was necessary to bring the inland regions under their control to protect their position on the coast. Rather than establishing a formal colony, however, they tried to rule as much as possible through the local landed aristocracy. On Java and the neighboring island of Sumatra, the VOC established pepper plantations, which soon produced massive profits for Dutch merchants in Amsterdam. Elsewhere they attempted to monopolize the clove trade by limiting cultivation of the crop to one island. By the end of the eighteenth century, the Dutch had succeeded in bringing almost the entire Indonesian archipelago under their control.

The arrival of the Europeans had somewhat less impact on mainland Southeast Asia, where cohesive monarchies in Burma (modern Myanmar), Thailand, and Vietnam resisted foreign encroachment. In addition, the coveted spices did not thrive on the mainland, so the Europeans' efforts there were far less intense than in the islands. The Portuguese did establish limited trade relations with several mainland states, including the Thai kingdom at Ayuthaya, Burma, Vietnam, and the remnants of the old Angkor kingdom in Cambodia. By the early seventeenth century, other European nations had followed and had begun to compete actively for trade and missionary privileges. As was the case elsewhere, the Europeans soon became involved in local factional disputes as a means of obtaining political and economic advantages. In Burma, the English and the French supported rival groups in the internal struggles

CHRONOLOGY The Spice Trade	
Vasco da Gama lands at Calicut in southwestern India	1498
Albuquerque establishes base at Goa	1510
Portuguese seize Malacca	1511
Portuguese ships land in southern China	1514
Magellan's voyage around the world	1519–1522
English East India Company established	1600
Dutch East India Company established	1602
English arrive at Surat in northwestern India	1608
Dutch fort established at Batavia	1619
Dutch seize Malacca from the Portuguese	1641
Burmese sack of Ayuthaya	1767

The Thai Capital at Ayuthaya. The longest-lasting Thai capital was at Ayuthaya, which was one of the finest cities in Asia from the fourteenth century to the eighteenth century. After the Burmese invasion in 1767, most of Ayuthaya's inhabitants were killed, and all official Thai records were destroyed. Here the remains of some Buddhist stupas, erected in a ceremonial precinct in the center of the city, remind us of the greatness of Thai civilization.

accentuated the differences between individual states in the region. Yet beneath these differences was an underlying commonality of life for most people. Despite the diversity of cultures and religious beliefs in the area, Southeast Asians were in most respects closer to each other than they were to peoples outside the region. For the most part, the states and peoples of Southeast Asia were still in control of their own destiny.

RELIGION AND KINGSHIP During the early modern era, both Buddhism and Islam became well established in Southeast Asia, although Christianity began to attract some converts, especially in port cities directly occupied by Europeans, such as Malacca and Batavia, and in the Philippines (see the Comparative Illustration "Malacca: Melting Pot of Asia" on p. 414). Buddhism was dominant in lowland areas on the mainland, from Burma to Viet-

of the monarchy until a new dynasty emerged and threw the foreigners out. A similar process took place at Ayuthaya, which survived the pressure from the Europeans but was eventually destroyed by a Burmese army in 1767.

In Vietnam, the arrival of Western merchants and missionaries coincided with a period of internal conflict among ruling groups in the country. After their arrival in the mid-seventeenth century, the European powers characteristically began to intervene in local politics, with the Portuguese and the Dutch supporting rival factions. By the end of the century, when it became clear that economic opportunities were limited, most European states abandoned their trading stations in the area. French missionaries attempted to remain, but their efforts were hampered by the local authorities, who viewed the Catholic insistence that converts give their primary loyalty to the pope as a threat to the legal status and prestige of the Vietnamese emperor.

State and Society in Precolonial Southeast Asia

Between 1500 and 1800, Southeast Asia experienced the last flowering of traditional culture before the advent of European rule in the nineteenth century. Although the coming of the Europeans had an immediate and direct impact in some areas, notably the Philippines and parts of the Malay world, in most areas Western influence was still relatively limited. Europeans occasionally dabbled in local politics and modified regional trade patterns, but they generally were not a decisive factor in the evolution of local political or social systems.

Nevertheless, Southeast Asian societies were changing in several subtle ways—in their trade patterns, their means of livelihood, and their religious beliefs. In some ways, these changes

nam. At first, Muslim influence was felt mainly on the Malay Peninsula and along the northern coasts of Java and Sumatra, where local merchants encountered their Muslim counterparts from foreign lands on a regular basis. At the same time, traditional religious beliefs continued to survive, especially in inland areas, where the local populations either ignored the new doctrines or integrated them into their traditional forms of spirit worship. Buddhists in rural Burma and Thailand, for example, might also believe in nature spirits. On Java and Sumatra, where Islam was slow to penetrate into the interior, the result was a division between devout Muslims in the cities and essentially animist peasants in the rural villages.

Both Buddhism and Islam brought other changes in their train—temple education for Buddhists and schools for Islamic scholars and new religious and moral restrictions on human behavior such as refraining from eating pork and drinking wine for Muslims (though some foreign Muslims complained that the latter rule was not always followed). Because Islam discouraged the traditional tattooing of the body, Muslim converts turned to the technique of decorating textiles called *batik* (buh-TEEK).

Buddhism and Islam also helped shape Southeast Asian political institutions. As the political systems began to mature, they evolved into four main types: Buddhist kings, Javanese kings, Islamic sultans, and Vietnamese emperors (for Vietnam, which was strongly influenced by China, see Chapter 11). In each case, institutions and concepts imported from abroad were adapted to local circumstances.

The Buddhist style of kingship took shape between the eleventh and the fifteenth centuries as Theravada Buddhism spread throughout the area. It became the predominant political system in the Buddhist states of mainland Southeast Asia—Burma, Ayuthaya, Laos, and Cambodia. Perhaps the

COMPARATIVE ILLUSTRATION

INTERACTION & EXCHANGE

Malacca: Melting Pot of Asia. As the trading port of Malacca changed hands over the course of centuries, its cultural and physical makeup reflected the reality of its complicated history. The remnants of a baroque Portuguese cathedral sit on a bluff overlooking the harbor. A rose-colored Protestant church in Dutch style nestles beneath the hill on the banks of the river (left). Across a small bridge is the Chinatown district, filled with small shops and a Buddhist temple filled with worshipers. Even the local mosque, completed in 1748 and still in use today (right), was built in the Chinese style, with a pagoda serving as a minaret.

Q *How did the spread of Christianity in America and Asia in the sixteenth and seventeenth centuries compare with the expansion of Islam in earlier times?*

most prominent feature of the Buddhist model was the god-like character of the monarch, who was considered by virtue of his *karma* to be innately superior to other human beings and served as a link between human society and the cosmos. Court rituals stressed the sacred nature of the monarch, and even the palace was modeled after the symbolic design of the Hindu universe. In its center was an architectural rendering of sacred Mount Meru, the legendary home of the gods (see the box "Idolaters and Heathens in Old Siam" on p. 415).

The Javanese model was a blend of Buddhist and Islamic political traditions. Like their mainland counterparts, Javanese monarchs possessed a sacred quality and maintained the balance between the sacred and the material world, but as Islam penetrated the Indonesian islands in the fifteenth and sixteenth centuries, the monarchs began to lose their semidivine quality.

The Islamic model was found mainly on the Malay Peninsula and along the coast of the Indonesian archipelago. In this pattern, the head of state was a sultan, who was viewed as a mortal, although he still possessed some magical qualities. The sultan served as a defender of the faith and staffed his bureaucracy mainly with aristocrats, but he also frequently relied on the Muslim community of scholars—the *ulama*—and was expected, at least in theory, to rule according to the *Shari'a*.

ECONOMY AND SOCIETY During the early period of European penetration, the economy of most Southeast Asian societies was based on agriculture, as it had been for thousands of years. Still, by the sixteenth century, commerce was beginning to affect daily life, especially in the cities that were beginning to proliferate along the coasts or on navigable rivers. In part, this was because agriculture itself was becoming more commercialized as cash crops like sugar and spices replaced subsistence farming of rice or other cereals in some areas.

Regional and interregional trade were already expanding before the coming of the Europeans. The central geographic location of Southeast Asia enabled it to become a focal point in

Idolaters and Heathens in Old Siam

RELIGION & PHILOSOPHY

MANY EARLY CHRISTIAN TRAVELERS to the states and societies of southern Asia were offended by the "heathen" religious beliefs and practices that they encountered in the region. In some cases, however, such visitors found much to admire as well. In this account, Joost Schouten, an official of the Dutch East India Company in the early seventeenth century, described what he observed during a visit to Ayuthaya, the capital of the kingdom of Siam in surprisingly favorable terms. Indeed, the sense of tolerance and voluntarism that characterized Buddhist practices at the time continue to be appealing to our modern eyes.

Joost Schouten, *A True Description of the Kingdom of Siam*

The *Siammers*, as also the Neighboring Nations, are all Idolaters and Heathens, so that they have every where great and little Temples and Cloysters for the services of their Gods; and the dwellings of their Priests. These Edifices are builded of Wood and Stone very Artificial and sumptuous, with guilded [gilded] Towers and Pyramids; each of the Temples and Cloysters being filled with an incredible amount of *Idols*, of diverse materials and greatness, gilded, adorned and beautified very rich and admirable; some of the Idols are four, six, eight, and ten fathoms long; In these Temples and Cloysters there are many Priests and Religious Men disciplined, and very obedient to their superiours.... All the Clergy ... are clothed, without any remarkable difference, in yellow linen clothes, having their heads all shorn. The learnedst amongst these are professed Priests.... These are prohibited the natural use of Women, upon pain of being burned; but they may always, and at pleasure upon declaration of their frailty or weakness, quit their frocks, and betake themselves to another life, which happens often amongst them. They live upon the Alms and bounty of

the King and great Ones, as also on the fruit which their Church Lands bring forth; but principally out of the sweet [sweat] and labours of the Commonalty, who unanimously share with them, they sending every morning some Priests and Clerks out of their Cloysters, with begging bags to receive these donations and charity: Besides these Priests, there are a sort of old Nuns shown, lodged in Chappels near the greatest Temples, who assist very devoutly in all their preachings, singings, ceremonies, and other Church services, but all voluntary, being tied to no rules or prescriptions. These Heathens do generally believe, (however differing in many particulars) that there is one upper God, with many lesser Deities in Heaven, who created all things; that the Souls of Men are immortal, and shall be rewarded or punished according to their merits and actions; the good dwelling with the God(s) in bliss, whilest the wicket are tormented by the Devils that seduced them.... The Priests carry themselves very moderately to those of a contrary Religion, condemning no opinions, but believe that all, though of differing tenets, living vertuously, may be saved, all services which are performed with zeal being acceptable to the great God, especially theirs, they being convinced of its truth and innocency. This constancy of theirs makes them not easily to be drawn to any other perswasion, which hath been sufficiently attempted by the *Portugals*, whose industrious Priests omitted nothing for their conversion, and by the Mohametans who are no less zealous in their way, though with little or no success by either of them, and yet the Christians, as also the Mohametans, are both permitted the free exercise of their Religions in their Countrey....

Why does the writer of this document declare that it is difficult to convert the peoples of Siam to other religions, such as Islam or Christianity?

Source: From Francois Caron and Joost Schouten, *A True Description of the Mighty Kingdoms of Japan and Siam* (London: The Argonaut Press, 1935), pp. 104, 106, 109.

a widespread trading network. Spices, of course, were the mainstay of the interregional trade, but other products were exchanged as well. The region exported tin (mined in Malaya since the tenth century), copper, gold, tropical fruits and other agricultural products, cloth, gems, and luxury goods in exchange for manufactured goods, ceramics, and high-quality textiles such as silk from China. Although on balance the region was an importer of manufactured goods, it produced some high-quality goods of its own. The ceramics of Vietnam and Thailand, though not made with the high-temperature firing techniques used in China, were still of good quality. The Portuguese traveler Duarte Barbosa (DWAR-tay bar-BOH-suh) observed that the Javanese were skilled cabinetmakers, weapons manufacturers, shipbuilders, and locksmiths. The royal courts were both the main producers and the primary consumers of luxury goods, most of which were produced by highly skilled slaves in the employ of the court.

In general, Southeast Asians probably enjoyed a somewhat higher living standard than their contemporaries elsewhere in Asia, and hunger was not a widespread problem. Several factors help explain this relative prosperity. In the first place, the region has been blessed with a salubrious climate. The uniformly high temperatures and the abundant rainfall enable farmers to grow two or even three crops each year. Second, although the soil in some areas is poor, the alluvial deltas on the mainland are fertile, and the volcanoes of Sumatra and Java periodically spew forth rich volcanic ash that renews the mineral resources of the soil on both islands. Finally, most of Southeast Asia was relatively thinly populated. According to one estimate, the population of the entire region in 1600 was about 20 million, or about 14 persons per square mile, well below levels elsewhere in Asia. Only in a few areas such as the Red River delta in northern Vietnam was overpopulation a serious problem.

CHAPTER SUMMARY

During the fifteenth century, the pace of international commerce increased dramatically. Chinese fleets visited the Indian Ocean while Muslim traders extended their activities into the Spice Islands and sub-Saharan West Africa. Then the Europeans burst onto the world scene. Beginning with the seemingly modest ventures of the Portuguese ships that sailed southward along the West African coast, the process accelerated with the epoch-making voyages of Christopher Columbus to the Americas and Vasco da Gama to the Indian Ocean in the 1490s. Soon a number of other European states had entered the fray, and by the end of the eighteenth century, they had created a global trade network that distributed foodstuffs, textiles, spices, and precious minerals from one end of the globe to the other.

In less than three hundred years, the expansion of the global trade network changed the face of the world. In some areas, such as the Americas and the Spice Islands, it led to the destruction of indigenous civilizations and the establishment of European colonies. In others, as in Africa, South Asia, and mainland Southeast Asia, it left native regimes intact but had a strong impact on local societies and regional trade patterns. In some areas, it led to an irreversible decline in traditional institutions and values, setting in motion a corrosive process that has not been reversed to this day.

At the time, most European observers viewed the process in a favorable light. Not only did it expand world trade and foster the exchange of new crops and discoveries between the Old and New Worlds, but it also introduced Christianity to "heathen peoples" around the globe. Some modern historians have been much more critical, concluding that European activities during the sixteenth and seventeenth centuries created a "tributary mode of production" based on European profits from unequal terms of trade that foreshadowed the exploitative relationship characteristic of the later colonial period. Other scholars have questioned that contention, however, and argue that although Western commercial operations had a significant impact on global trade patterns, they did not—at least not before the nineteenth century—usher in an era of Western dominance over the rest of the world. Muslim merchants were long able to evade European efforts to eliminate them from the spice trade, and the trans-Saharan caravan trade was relatively unaffected by European merchant shipping along the West African coast.

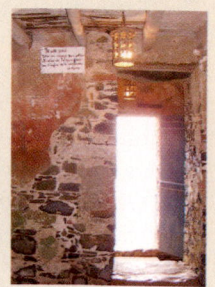

In the meantime, powerful empires continued to hold sway over the lands washed by the Muslim faith. Beyond the Himalayas, Chinese emperors in their new northern capital of Beijing retained proud dominion over all the vast territory of continental East Asia. We shall deal with these regions, and how they confronted the challenges of a changing world, in Chapters 16 and 17.

CHAPTER TIMELINE

CHAPTER REVIEW

Upon Reflection

Q What were some of the key features of the Columbian Exchange, and what effects did they have on the world trade network?

Q How did the expansion of European power during the Age of Exploration compare with the expansion of the Islamic empires in the Middle East a few centuries earlier?

Q Why were the Spanish conquistadors able to complete their conquest of Latin America so quickly when their contemporaries failed to do so in Africa and Southeast Asia?

Key Terms

portolani (p. 392)
caravels (p. 392)
conquistadors (p. 397)
mestizos (p. 399)
mulattoes (p. 399)
viceroys (p. 400)
creoles (p. 400)
encomienda system (p. 401)
encomienda (p. 401)
Columbian Exchange (p. 405)
Boers (p. 406)
Middle Passage (p. 408)
maroons (p. 408)
Triangular Trade (p. 408)

Suggested Reading

EUROPEAN EXPANSION On the technological aspects of European expansion, see **F. Fernandez-Armesto, ed.,** *The Times Atlas of World Exploration* (New York, 1991), and **R. C. Smith,** *Vanguard of Empire: Ships of Exploration in the Age of Columbus* (Oxford, 1993). For an account of advances in mapmaking, see **T. Lester,** *The Fourth Part of the World: The Race to the Ends of the Earth, and the Epic Story of the Map That Gave America Its Name* (New York, 2009). Also see **W. Bernstein's** impressive *A Splendid Exchange: How Trade Shaped the World* (New York, 2008).

COUNTRY-SPECIFIC STUDIES On Portuguese early expansion, see **F. Bethencourt** and **D. Curtis,** *Portuguese Economic Expansion, 1400–1800* (Cambridge, 2007). **J. H. Elliott's** *Empires of the Atlantic World: Britain and Spain in America, 1492–1830* (New Haven, Conn., 2008) is an impressive work by a respected scholar. For a readable account of the conquistadors and their competitors, see is **H. Thomas,** *Conquest: Montezuma, Cortés,* *and the Fall of Old Mexico* (New York, 1993). British activities in Asia are chronicled in **S. Sen,** *Empire of Free Trade: The East India Company and the Making of the Colonial Marketplace* (Philadelphia, 1998), and **Anthony Wild's** elegant work *The East India Company: Trade and Conquest from 1600* (New York, 2000).

THE SPICE TRADE The effects of European trade in Southeast Asia are discussed in **A. Reid,** *Southeast Asia in the Age of Commerce, 1450–1680* (New Haven, Conn., 1989). On the spice trade, see **A. Dalby,** *Dangerous Tastes: The Story of Spices* (Berkeley, Calif., 2000), and **J. Turner,** *Spice: The History of a Temptation* (New York, 2004). The story of sugar is chronicled in **E. Abbott,** *Sugar: A Bittersweet History* (New York, 2008).

THE SLAVE TRADE On the African slave trade, see **J. Campbell,** *Middle Passages: African-American Journeys to Africa, 1787–2005* (New York, 2006) and **F. Knight,** *Working the Diaspora: The Impact of African Labor on the Anglo-American World, 1650–1850* (New York, 2010). **H. Thomas,** *The Slave Trade* (New York, 1997), provides a useful overview.

Chapter Notes

1. From *A Journal of the First Voyage of Vasco da Gama* (London, 1898), cited in J. H. Parry, *The European Reconnaissance: Selected Documents* (New York, 1968), p. 82.

2. H. J. Benda and J. A. Larkin, eds., *The World of Southeast Asia: Selected Historical Readings* (New York, 1967), p. 13.

3. Parry, *European Reconnaissance*, quoting from A. Cortesão, *The Summa Oriental of Tomé Pires* (London, 1944), vol. 2, pp. 283, 287.

4. Quoted in J. H. Parry, *The Age of Reconnaissance: Discovery, Exploration, and Settlement, 1450 to 1650* (New York, 1963), p. 33.

5. Quoted in R. B. Reed, "The Expansion of Europe," in R. DeMolen, ed., *The Meaning of the Renaissance and Reformation* (Boston, 1974), p. 308.

6. K. N. Chaudhuri, *Trade and Civilization in the Indian Ocean: An Economic History from the Rise of Islam to 1750* (Cambridge, 1985), p. 65.

7. Quoted in Parry, *Age of Reconnaissance*, pp. 176–177.

8. Quoted in M. Leon-Portilla, ed., *The Broken Spears: The Aztec Account of the Conquest of Mexico* (Boston, 1969), p. 51.

MindTap is a fully online, highly personalized learning experience built upon Cengage Leaning content. MindTap combines student learning tools—readings, multimedia, activities, and assessments—into a singular Learning Path that guides students through their course.

Europe Transformed: Reform and State Building

A nineteenth-century engraving showing Luther before the Diet of Worms

Art Resource, NY

CHAPTER OUTLINE AND FOCUS QUESTIONS

The Reformation of the Sixteenth Century

Q What were the main tenets of Lutheranism, Calvinism, and Anabaptism, and how did they differ from each other and from Catholicism?

Europe in Crisis, 1560–1650

Q Why is the period between 1560 and 1650 in Europe considered an age of crisis, and how did the turmoil contribute to the artistic developments of the period?

Response to Crisis: The Practice of Absolutism

Q What was absolutism, and what were the main characteristics of the absolute monarchies that emerged in France, Prussia, Austria, and Russia?

England and Limited Monarchy

Q How and why did England avoid the path of absolutism?

The Flourishing of European Culture

Q How did the artistic and literary achievements of this era reflect the political and economic developments of the period?

CRITICAL THINKING

Q What was the relationship between European overseas expansion (as traced in Chapter 14) and political, economic, and social developments in Europe?

CONNECTIONS TO TODAY

Q How does the exercise of state power in the seventeenth century compare with the exercise of state power in the twenty-first century? What, if anything, has changed?

ON APRIL 18, 1521, A LOWLY MONK stood before the emperor and princes of Germany in the city of Worms (VAWRMZ). He had been called before this august diet (a deliberating council) to answer charges of heresy, charges that could threaten his very life. The monk was confronted with a pile of his books and asked if he wished to defend them all or reject a part. Courageously, Martin Luther defended them all and asked to be shown where any part was in error on the basis of "Scripture and plain reason." The emperor was outraged by Luther's response and made his own position clear the next day: "Not only I, but you of this noble German nation, would be forever disgraced if by our negligence not only heresy but the very suspicion of heresy were to survive. After having heard yesterday the obstinate defense of Luther, I regret that I have so long delayed in proceeding against him and his false teaching. I will have no more to do with him." Luther's appearance at Worms set the stage for a serious challenge to the authority of the Catholic Church. This was by no means the first crisis in the church's 1,500-year history, but its consequences were more far-reaching than anyone at Worms in 1521 could have imagined.

After the disintegrative patterns of the fourteenth century, Europe began a remarkable recovery that encompassed a revival of arts and letters in the fifteenth century, known as the Renaissance, and a religious renaissance in the sixteenth century, known as the Reformation. The resulting religious division of Europe (Catholics versus Protestants) was instrumental in triggering a series of wars that dominated much of European history from 1560 to 1650 and exacerbated the economic and social crises that were besetting the region.

One of the responses to the crises of the seventeenth century was a search for order. The most general trend was an extension of monarchical power as a stabilizing force. This development, which historians have called **absolutism** or *absolute monarchy,* was most evident in France during the flamboyant reign of Louis XIV, regarded by some as the perfect embodiment of an absolute monarch.

But absolutism was not the only response to the search for order in the seventeenth century. Other states, such as England, reacted very differently to domestic crisis, and yet another system emerged in which monarchs were limited by the power of their representative assemblies. Absolute and limited monarchy were the two poles of seventeenth-century state building. ◄

The Reformation of the Sixteenth Century

 FOCUS QUESTION: What were the main tenets of Lutheranism, Calvinism, and Anabaptism, and how did they differ from each other and from Catholicism?

The **Protestant Reformation** is the name given to the religious reform movement that divided the Western Christian church into Catholic and Protestant groups. Although the Reformation began with Martin Luther in the early sixteenth century, several earlier developments had set the stage for religious change.

Background to the Reformation

Changes in the fifteenth century—the age of the Renaissance—helped prepare the way for the dramatic upheavals in sixteenth-century Europe.

THE GROWTH OF STATE POWER   In the first half of the fifteenth century, European states had continued the disintegrative patterns of the previous century. In the second half of that century, however, recovery had set in, and attempts had been made to reestablish the centralized power of monarchical governments. To characterize the results, some historians have used the label "Renaissance states"; others have spoken of the **"new monarchies,"** especially those of France, England, and Spain at the end of the fifteenth century (see Chapter 13).

What was new about these Renaissance monarchs was their concentration of royal authority, their attempts to suppress the nobility, their efforts to control the church in their lands, and their desire to obtain new sources of revenue in order to increase royal power and enhance the military forces at their disposal. Like the rulers of fifteenth-century Italian states, the Renaissance monarchs were often crafty men obsessed with the acquisition and expansion of political power. Of course, none of these characteristics was entirely new; a number of medieval monarchs, especially in the thirteenth century, had exhibited them. Nevertheless, the Renaissance period marks a significant expansion of centralized royal authority and a new preoccupation with the acquisition, maintenance, and expansion of political power.

SOCIAL CHANGES IN THE RENAISSANCE   Social changes in the fifteenth century also helped to create an environment in which the Reformation of the sixteenth century could occur. After the severe economic reversals and social upheavals of the fourteenth century, the European economy gradually recovered as manufacturing and trade increased in volume. The Italians and especially the Venetians expanded their wealthy commercial empire, rivaled only by the increasingly powerful Hanseatic (han-see-AT-ik) League, a commercial and military alliance of north German coastal towns. Not until the sixteenth century, when overseas discoveries gave new importance to the states facing the Atlantic, did the Italian city-states begin to suffer from the competitive advantages of the more powerful national territorial states.

As noted in Chapter 12, society in the Middle Ages was divided into three estates: the clergy, or First Estate, whose preeminence was grounded in the belief that people should be guided to spiritual ends; the nobility, or Second Estate, whose privileges rested on the principle that nobles provided security and justice for society; and the peasants and inhabitants of the towns and cities, the Third Estate. Although this social order continued into the Renaissance, some changes also became evident.

Throughout much of Europe, the landholding nobles faced declining real incomes during most of the fourteenth and fifteenth centuries. Many members of the old nobility survived, however, and new blood also infused their ranks. In 1500, the nobles, old and new, who constituted between 2 and 3 percent of the population in most countries, still dominated society, as they had in the Middle Ages, holding important political posts and serving as advisers to the king.

Except in the heavily urban areas of northern Italy and Flanders, peasants made up the overwhelming mass of the Third Estate—they constituted 85 to 90 percent of the total European population. Serfdom had decreased as the manorial system continued its decline. Increasingly, the labor dues owed by peasants to their lord were converted into rents paid in money. By 1500, especially in western Europe, more and more peasants were becoming legally free. At the same time, peasants in many areas resented their social superiors and sought to keep a greater share of the benefits from their labor. In the sixteenth century, the grievances of peasants, especially in Germany, led many of them to support religious reform movements.

Inhabitants of towns and cities, originally merchants and artisans, constituted the remainder of the Third Estate. But by on European intellectual life and thought. Printing from hand-carved wooden blocks had been done in the West since the twelfth century and in China even before that. What was new in the fifteenth century in Europe was multiple printing with movable metal type. The development of printing from movable type was a gradual process that culminated sometime between 1445 and 1450; Johannes Gutenberg (yoh-HAH-nuss GOO-ten-bayrk) of Mainz (MYNTS) played an important role in bringing the process to completion. Gutenberg's Bible, completed in 1455 or 1456, was the first true book produced from movable type.

By 1500, there were more than a thousand printers in Europe, who collectively had published almost 40,000 titles (between 8 million and 10 million copies). Probably half of these books were religious—Bibles and biblical commentaries, books of devotion, and sermons. Next in importance were the Latin and Greek classics, medieval grammars, legal handbooks, and works on philosophy.

The printing of books encouraged scholarly research and the desire to attain knowledge. Printing also stimulated the development of an ever-expanding lay reading public, a development that had an enormous impact on European society. Indeed, without the printing press, the new religious ideas of the Reformation would not have spread as rapidly as they did in the sixteenth century. Moreover, printing allowed European civilization to compete for the first time with the civilization of China.

Harbor Scene at Hamburg. Hamburg was a founding member of the Hanseatic League. This illustration from a fifteenth-century treatise on the laws of the city shows a busy port with ships of all sizes. At the left, a crane is used to unload barrels. In the building at the right, customs officials collect their dues. Merchants and townspeople are shown talking at dockside.

the fifteenth century, the Renaissance town or city had become more complex. At the top of urban society were the patricians, whose wealth from capitalistic enterprises in trade, industry, and banking enabled them to dominate their urban communities economically, socially, and politically. Below them were the petty burghers—the shopkeepers, artisans, guild-masters, and guildsmen—who were largely concerned with providing goods and services for local consumption. Below these two groups were the propertyless workers earning pitiful wages and the unemployed, living squalid and miserable lives. These poor city-dwellers made up 30 to 40 percent of the urban population. The pitiful conditions of the lower groups in urban society often led them to support calls for radical religious reform in the sixteenth century.

THE IMPACT OF PRINTING The Renaissance witnessed the development of printing, which made an immediate impact

PRELUDE TO REFORMATION During the second half of the fifteenth century, the new Classical learning of the Italian Renaissance spread to the European countries north of the Alps and spawned a movement called **Christian humanism** or **northern Renaissance humanism**, whose major goal was the reform of Christianity. The Christian humanists believed in the ability of human beings to reason and improve themselves and thought that through education in the sources of Classical, and especially Christian, antiquity, they could instill an inner piety or an inward religious feeling that would bring about a reform of the church and society. To change society, they must first change the human beings who compose it.

The most influential of all the Christian humanists was Desiderius Erasmus (dez-i-DEER-ee-uss i-RAZZ-mus) (1466–1536), who formulated and popularized the reform program of Christian humanism. He called his conception of religion "the philosophy of Christ," by which he meant that Christianity should be a guiding philosophy for the direction of daily life rather than the system of dogmatic beliefs and practices that the medieval church seemed to stress. In other words, he emphasized inner piety and de-emphasized the external forms of religion (such as the sacraments, pilgrimages, fasts, and relics). To Erasmus, the reform of the church meant spreading an understanding of the philosophy of Jesus, providing enlightened education in the sources of early Christianity, and criticizing the abuses in the church. No doubt his work helped prepare the way for the Reformation; as contemporaries proclaimed, "Erasmus laid the egg that Luther hatched."

CHURCH AND RELIGION ON THE EVE OF THE REFORMATION

Corruption in the Catholic Church was another factor that led people to want reform. Between 1450 and 1520, a series of popes—called the Renaissance popes—failed to meet the church's spiritual needs. The popes were supposed to be the spiritual leaders of the Catholic Church, but as rulers of the Papal States, they were all too often involved in worldly concerns. Julius II (1503–1513), the fiery "warrior-pope," personally led armies against his enemies, much to the disgust of pious Christians, who thought the pope's role was to serve as a spiritual leader. As one intellectual wrote, "How, O bishop standing in the room of the Apostles, dare you teach the people the things that pertain to war?" Many high church officials were also concerned with accumulating wealth and used their church offices as opportunities to advance their careers and their fortunes, and many ordinary parish priests seemed ignorant of their spiritual duties.

While the leaders of the church were failing to meet their responsibilities, ordinary people were clamoring for meaningful religious expression and certainty of salvation. As a result, for some the process of salvation became almost mechanical. As more and more people sought certainty of salvation through veneration of relics (bones or other objects intimately associated with the saints), collections of **relics** grew. Frederick the Wise, elector (one of the seven German princes who chose the Holy Roman Emperor) of Saxony and Martin Luther's prince, had amassed nearly 19,000 relics to which were attached **indulgences** that could reduce a person's time in purgatory by nearly 2 million years. (An indulgence is a remission, after death, of all or part of the punishment due to sin.) Other people sought certainty of salvation in more spiritual terms by participating in the popular mystical movement known as the Modern Devotion, which downplayed religious dogma and stressed the need to follow the teachings of Jesus.

What is striking about the revival of religious piety in the fifteenth century—whether expressed through such external forces as the veneration of relics and the buying of indulgences or the mystical path—was its adherence to the orthodox beliefs and practices of the Catholic Church. The agitation for certainty of salvation and spiritual peace occurred within the framework of the "holy mother Church." But disillusionment grew as the devout experienced the clergy's inability to live up to their expectations. The deepening of religious life, especially in the second half of the fifteenth century, found little echo among the worldly-wise clergy, and this environment helps explain the tremendous and immediate impact of Luther's ideas.

Martin Luther and the Reformation in Germany

Martin Luther (1483–1546) was a monk and a professor at the University of Wittenberg (VIT-ten-bayrk), where he lectured on the Bible. Probably sometime between 1513 and 1516, through his study of the Bible, he arrived at an answer to a problem—the assurance of salvation—that had disturbed him since his entry into the monastery.

Catholic doctrine had emphasized that both faith and good works were required for a Christian to achieve personal salvation. In Luther's eyes, human beings, weak and powerless in the sight of an almighty God, could never do enough good works to merit salvation. Through his study of the Bible, Luther came to believe that humans are saved not through their good works but through faith in the promises of God, made possible by the sacrifice of Jesus on the cross. This doctrine of salvation, or justification by grace through faith alone, became the primary doctrine of the Protestant Reformation (**justification by faith** is the act by which a person is made deserving of salvation). Because Luther had arrived at this doctrine from his study of the Bible, the Bible became for Luther, as for all other Protestants, the chief guide to religious truth.

Luther did not see himself as a rebel, but he was greatly upset by the widespread selling of indulgences. Especially offensive in his eyes was the monk Johann Tetzel, who hawked indulgences with the slogan "As soon as the coin in the coffer [money box] rings, the soul from purgatory springs." Greatly angered, in 1517 he issued a stunning indictment of the abuses in the sale of indulgences, known as the Ninety-Five Theses (see the box "Luther and the Ninety-Five Theses" on p. 422). Thousands of copies were printed and quickly spread to all parts of Germany.

By 1520, Luther had begun to move toward a more definite break with the Catholic Church and called on the German princes to overthrow the papacy in Germany and establish a reformed German church. Through all his calls for change, Luther expounded more and more on his new doctrine of salvation. It is faith alone, he said, not good works, that justifies and brings salvation through Christ.

Unable to accept Luther's ideas, the church excommunicated him in January 1521. He was also summoned to appear before the Reichstag (RYKHSS-tahk) (imperial diet) of the Holy Roman Empire, convened by the newly elected Emperor Charles V (1519–1556). Ordered to recant the heresies he had espoused, Luther refused and made the famous reply that became the battle cry of the Reformation:

> Unless I am convicted by Scripture and plain reason—I do not accept the authority of popes and councils, for they have contradicted each other—my conscience is captive to the Word of God. I cannot and I will not recant anything, for to go against conscience is neither right nor safe. Here I stand, I cannot do otherwise. God help me. Amen.[1]

Members of the Reichstag were outraged and demanded that Luther be arrested and delivered to the emperor. But Luther's ruler, Elector Frederick of Saxony, stepped in and protected him.

Luther and the Ninety-Five Theses

RELIGION & PHILOSOPHY

TO MOST HISTORIANS, the publication of Luther's Ninety-Five Theses marks the beginning of the Reformation. To Luther, they were simply a response to what he considered blatant abuses committed by sellers of indulgences. Although written in Latin, the theses were soon translated into German and disseminated widely across Germany. They made an immense impression on Germans already dissatisfied with the ecclesiastical and financial policies of the papacy.

Martin Luther, Selections from the Ninety-Five Theses

5. The Pope has neither the will nor the power to remit any penalties beyond those he has imposed either at his own discretion or by canon law.

20. Therefore the Pope, by his plenary remission of all penalties, does not mean "all" in the absolute sense, but only those imposed by himself.

21. Hence those preachers of Indulgences are wrong when they say that a man is absolved and saved from every penalty by the Pope's Indulgences. It is mere human talk to preach that the soul flies out [of purgatory] immediately [when] the money clinks in the collection box.

28. It is certainly possible that when the money clinks in the collection box greed and avarice can increase; but the intercession of the Church depends on the will of God alone.

50. Christians should be taught that if the Pope knew the exactions of the preachers of Indulgences, he would rather have the basilica of St. Peter reduced to ashes than built with the skin, flesh, and bones of his sheep [the indulgences that so distressed Luther were being sold to raise money for the construction of the new St. Peter's Basilica in Rome].

81. This wanton preaching of pardons makes it difficult even for learned men to redeem respect due to the Pope from the slanders or at least the shrewd questionings of the laity.

82. For example: "Why does not the Pope empty purgatory for the sake of most holy love and the supreme need of souls? This would be the most righteous of reasons, if he can redeem innumerable souls for sordid money with which to build a basilica, the most trivial of reasons."

86. Again: "Since the Pope's wealth is larger than that of the crassest Crassi of our time, why does he not build this one basilica of St. Peter with his own money, rather than with that of the faithful poor?"

90. To suppress these most conscientious questionings of the laity by authority only, instead of refuting them by reason, is to expose the Church and the Pope to the ridicule of their enemies, and to make Christian people unhappy.

94. Christians should be exhorted to seek earnestly to follow Christ, their Head, through penalties, deaths, and hells.

95. And let them thus be more confident of entering heaven through many tribulations rather than through a false assurance of peace.

 What were the major ideas of Luther's Ninety-Five Theses? Why did they have such a strong appeal in Germany?

Source: From *Martin Luther*, by E. G. Rupp and Benjamin Drewery.

During the next few years, Luther's movement began to grow and spread. As it made an impact on the common people, it also created new challenges. This was especially true of the Peasants' War that erupted in 1524. Social discontent created by their pitiful conditions became entangled with religious revolt as the German peasants looked to Martin Luther for support. But when the peasants took up arms and revolted against their landlords, Luther turned against them and called on the German princes, who in Luther's eyes were ordained by God to maintain peace and order, to crush the rebels. By May 1525, the German princes had ruthlessly suppressed the peasant hordes. By this time, Luther found himself dependent on the state authorities for the growth of his reformed church.

Luther now succeeded in gaining the support of many of the rulers of the three hundred or so German states that made up the Holy Roman Empire. These rulers quickly took control of the churches in their territories. The Lutheran churches in Germany (and later in Scandinavia) became territorial or state churches in which the state supervised the affairs of the church. As part of the development of these state-dominated churches, Luther also instituted new religious services to replace the Catholic Mass. These focused on reading the Bible, preaching the word of God, and singing hymns. Following his own denunciation of clerical celibacy, Luther married a former nun, Katherina von Bora, in 1525. His union provided a model of married and family life for the new Protestant minister.

POLITICS AND RELIGION IN THE GERMAN REFORMATION

From its very beginning, the fate of Luther's movement was closely tied to political affairs. In 1519, Charles I, king of Spain and the grandson of Emperor Maximilian, was elected Holy Roman Emperor as Charles V. Charles V ruled over an immense empire, consisting of Spain and its overseas possessions, the traditional Austrian Habsburg lands, Bohemia, Hungary, the Low Countries, and the kingdom of Naples in southern Italy. Politically, Charles wanted to maintain his enormous empire; religiously, he hoped to preserve the unity of his empire in the Catholic faith. A number of problems, however, kept him preoccupied and cost him both his dream and his health.

Moreover, the internal political situation in the Holy Roman Empire was not in Charles's favor. Although all the German states owed loyalty to the emperor, during the Middle Ages these states had become quite independent of imperial authority. By the time Charles V was able to bring military forces to

A Reformation Woodcut. In the 1520s, after Luther's return to Wittenberg, his teachings began to spread rapidly, ending ultimately in a reform movement supported by state authorities. Pamphlets containing picturesque woodcuts were important in the spread of Luther's ideas. In the woodcut shown here, the crucified Jesus attends Luther's service on the left, while on the right the pope is at a table selling indulgences.

Germany in 1546, Lutheranism had become well established and the Lutheran princes were well organized. Unable to defeat them, Charles was forced to negotiate a truce. An end to religious warfare in Germany came in 1555 with the Peace of Augsburg (OUKS-boork). The division of Christianity was formally acknowledged; Lutheran states were to have the same legal rights as Catholic states. Although the German states were now free to choose between Catholicism and Lutheranism, the peace settlement did not recognize the principle of religious toleration for individuals. The right of each German ruler to determine the religion of his subjects was accepted, but not the right of the subjects to choose their own religion. With the Peace of Augsburg, what had at first been merely feared was now certain: the ideal of Christian unity was forever lost. The rapid spread of new Protestant groups made this a certainty.

The Spread of the Protestant Reformation

Switzerland was home to two major Reformation movements, Zwinglianism and Calvinism. Ulrich Zwingli (OOL-rikh TSFING-lee) (1484–1531) was ordained a priest in 1506 and accepted an appointment as a cathedral priest in the Great Minster of Zürich (ZOOR-ik *or* TSIH-rikh) in 1518. Zwingli's preaching of the Gospel caused such unrest that in 1523 the city council held a public disputation (debate) in the town hall. Zwingli's party was accorded the victory, and over the next two years, evangelical reforms were promulgated in Zürich by a city council strongly influenced by Zwingli. Relics and images were abolished; all paintings and decorations were

removed from the churches and replaced by whitewashed walls. The Mass was replaced by a new liturgy consisting of Scripture reading, prayer, and sermons. Monasticism, pilgrimages, the veneration of saints, clerical celibacy, and the pope's authority were all abolished as remnants of papal Christianity.

As his movement began to spread to other cities in Switzerland, Zwingli sought an alliance with Martin Luther and the German reformers. Although both the German and the Swiss reformers realized the need for unity to defend against the opposition of the Catholic authorities, they were unable to agree on the interpretation of the Lord's Supper, the sacrament of Communion (see Opposing Viewpoints "A Reformation Debate: Conflict at Marburg" on p. 424). Zwingli believed that the scriptural words "This is my body, this is my blood" should be taken figuratively, not literally, and refused to accept Luther's insistence on the real presence of the body and blood of Jesus "in, with, and under the bread and wine." In October 1531, war erupted between the Swiss Protestant and Catholic states. Zürich's army was routed, and Zwingli was found wounded on the battlefield. His enemies killed him, cut up his body, burned the pieces, and scattered the ashes. The leadership of Swiss Protestantism now passed to John Calvin, the systematic theologian and organizer of the Protestant movement.

CALVIN AND CALVINISM John Calvin (1509–1564) was educated in his native France, but after converting to Protestantism, he was forced to flee to the safety of Switzerland. In 1536, he published the first edition of the *Institutes of the Christian Religion*, a masterful synthesis of Protestant thought that

A Reformation Debate: Conflict at Marburg

RELIGION & PHILOSOPHY

DEBATES PLAYED A CRUCIAL ROLE IN THE REFORMATION PERIOD. They were a primary instrument for introducing the Reformation in innumerable cities as well as a means of resolving differences among like-minded Protestant groups. This selection contains an excerpt from the vivacious and often brutal debate between Luther and Zwingli over the sacrament of the Lord's Supper at Marburg in 1529. The two protagonists failed to reach agreement.

The Marburg Colloquy, 1529

The Hessian Chancellor Feige: My gracious prince and lord [Landgrave Philip of Hesse] has summoned you for the express and urgent purpose of settling the dispute over the sacrament of the Lord's Supper.... Let everyone on both sides present his arguments in a spirit of moderation.... Now then, Doctor Luther, you may proceed.

Luther: Noble prince, gracious lord! Undoubtedly the colloquy is well intentioned.... Although I have no intention of changing my mind, which is firmly made up, I will nevertheless present the grounds of my belief and show where the others are in error.... Your basic contentions are these: In the last analysis you wish to prove that a body cannot be in two places at once, and you produce arguments about the unlimited body which are based on natural reason. I do not question how Christ can be God and man and how the two natures can be joined. For God is more powerful than all our ideas, and we must submit to his word.

Prove that Christ's body is not there where the Scripture says, "This is my body!" Rational proofs I will not listen to.... It is God who commands, "Take, eat, this is my body." I request, therefore, valid scriptural proof to the contrary.

Zwingli: I insist that the words of the Lord's Supper must be figurative. This is ever apparent, and even required by the article of faith: "taken up into heaven, seated at the right hand of the Father." Otherwise, it would be absurd to look for him in the Lord's Supper at the same time that Christ is telling us that he is in heaven. One and the same body cannot possibly be in different places....

Luther: I call upon you as before: your basic contentions are shaky. Give way, and give glory to God!

Zwingli: And we call upon you to give glory to God and to quit begging the question! The issue at stake is this: Where is the proof of your position? I am willing to consider your words carefully—no harm meant! You're trying to outwit me.... You'll have to sing another tune.

Luther: You're being obnoxious.

Zwingli: (*excitedly*) Don't you believe that Christ was attempting in John 6 to help those who did not understand?

Luther: You're trying to dominate things! You insist on passing judgment! Leave that to someone else! ... It is your point that must be proved, not mine. But let us stop this sort of thing. It serves no purpose.

Zwingli: It certainly does! It is for you to prove that the passage in John 6 speaks of a physical repast.

Luther: You express yourself poorly and make about as much progress as a cane standing in a corner. You're going nowhere.

Zwingli: No, no, no! This is the passage that will break your neck!

Luther: Don't be so sure of yourself. Necks don't break this way. You're in Hesse, not Switzerland.

 How did the positions of Zwingli and Luther on the sacrament of the Lord's Supper differ? What was the purpose of this debate? Based on this example, why did many Reformation debates lead to further hostility rather than compromise and unity between religious and sectarian opponents? What implications did this have for the future of the Protestant Reformation?

Source: "The Marburg Colloquy," edited by Donald Ziegler, from *Great Debates of the Reformation*, edited by Donald Ziegler, copyright © 1969 by Donald Ziegler.

---

immediately secured his reputation as one of the new leaders of Protestantism.

On most important doctrines, Calvin stood very close to Luther. He adhered to the doctrine of justification by faith alone to explain how humans achieved salvation. But Calvin also placed much emphasis on the absolute sovereignty or all-powerful nature of God—what Calvin called the "power, grace, and glory of God." One of the ideas derived from his emphasis on the absolute sovereignty of God—**predestination**—gave a unique cast to Calvin's teachings. This "eternal decree," as

Calvin called it, meant that God had predestined some people to be saved (the elect) and others to be damned (the reprobate). According to Calvin, "He has once for all determined, both whom He would admit to salvation, and whom He would condemn to destruction."[2] Although Calvin stressed that there could be no absolute certainty of salvation, his followers did not always make this distinction. The practical psychological effect of predestination was to give later Calvinists an unshakable conviction that they were doing God's work on earth, making Calvinism a dynamic and activist faith.

Société de l'Histoire du Protestantisme Français, Paris/Giraudon/The Bridgeman Art Library

John Calvin. After a conversion experience, John Calvin abandoned his life as a humanist and became a reformer. In 1536, Calvin began working to reform the city of Geneva, where he remained until his death in 1564. This sixteenth-century portrait of Calvin pictures him in his study in Geneva.

In 1536, Calvin began working to reform the city of Geneva. He was able to fashion a tightly organized church order that employed both clergy and laymen in the service of the church. The Consistory, a special body for enforcing moral discipline, functioned as a court to oversee the moral life, daily behavior, and doctrinal orthodoxy of Genevans and to admonish and correct deviants. Citizens in Geneva were punished for such varied "crimes" as dancing, singing obscene songs, drunkenness, swearing, and playing cards.

Calvin's success in Geneva enabled the city to become a vibrant center of Protestantism. Following Calvin's lead, missionaries trained in Geneva were sent to all parts of Europe. Calvinism became established in France, the Netherlands, Scotland, and central and eastern Europe, and by the mid-sixteenth century, Calvin's Geneva stood as the fortress of the Reformation.

THE ENGLISH REFORMATION The English Reformation was rooted in politics, not religion. King Henry VIII (1509–1547) had a strong desire to divorce his first wife, Catherine of Aragon, with whom he had a daughter, Mary, but no male heir. The king wanted to marry Anne Boleyn (BUH-lin *or* buh-LIN), with whom he had fallen in love. Impatient with

the pope's unwillingness to grant him an annulment of his marriage, Henry turned to England's own church courts. As archbishop of Canterbury and head of the highest church court in England, Thomas Cranmer ruled in May 1533 that the king's marriage to Catherine was "absolutely void." At the beginning of June, Anne was crowned queen, and three months later, a child was born; much to the king's disappointment, the baby was a girl (the future Queen Elizabeth I).

In 1534, at Henry's request, Parliament moved to finalize the break of the Church of England with Rome. The Act of Supremacy of 1534 declared that the king was "the only supreme head on earth of the Church of England," a position that gave him control of doctrine, clerical appointments, and discipline. Although Henry VIII had broken with the papacy, little change occurred in matters of doctrine, theology, and ceremony. Some of his supporters, including Archbishop Cranmer, sought a religious reformation as well as an administrative one, but Henry was unyielding. But he died in 1547 and was succeeded by his son, the underage and sickly Edward VI (1547–1553), and during Edward's reign, Cranmer and others inclined toward Protestant doctrines were able to move the Church of England (or Anglican Church) in a more Protestant direction. New acts of Parliament gave the clergy the right to marry and created a new Protestant church service.

Edward VI was succeeded by Mary (1553–1558), a Catholic who attempted to return England to Catholicism. Her actions aroused much anger, however, especially when "bloody Mary" burned more than three hundred Protestant heretics. By the end of Mary's reign, England was more Protestant than it had been at the beginning.

THE ANABAPTISTS The Anabaptists were the radical reformers of the Protestant Reformation. To Anabaptists, the true Christian church was a voluntary association of believers who had undergone spiritual rebirth and had then been baptized into the church. Anabaptists advocated adult rather than infant baptism. They also wanted to return to the practices and spirit of early Christianity and considered all believers to be equal. Each church chose its own minister, who might be any member of the community since all Christians were considered priests (though women were often excluded).

Finally, unlike the Catholics and other Protestants, most Anabaptists believed in the complete separation of church and state. Government was to be excluded from the realm of religion and could not exercise political jurisdiction over real Christians. Anabaptists refused to hold political office or bear arms because many took the commandment "Thou shall not kill" literally. Their political beliefs as much as their religious beliefs caused the Anabaptists to be regarded as dangerous radicals who threatened the very fabric of sixteenth-century society. Indeed, the chief thing Protestants and Catholics could agree on was the need to persecute Anabaptists.

The Social Impact of the Protestant Reformation

The Protestants were especially important in developing a new view of the family. Because Protestantism had eliminated

Marriage in the Early Modern World

Marriage is an ancient institution. In China, myths about the beginnings of Chinese civilization maintained that the rite of marriage began with the primordial couple Fuxi and Nugun and that marriage actually preceded such discoveries as fire, farming, and medicine. In the early modern world, family and marriage were inseparable and were at the center of all civilizations.

In the early modern period, the family was still at the heart of Europe's social organization. For the most part, people viewed the family in traditional terms, as a patriarchal institution in which the husband dominated his wife and children. The upper classes in particular thought of the family as a "house," an association whose collective interests were more important than those of its individual members. Parents (especially the fathers) generally selected marriage partners for their children, based on the interests of the family. When the son of a French noble asked about his upcoming marriage, his father responded, "Mind your own business." Details were worked out well in advance, sometimes when children were only two or three years old, and were set out in a legally binding contract. An important negotiating point was the size of the dowry, money presented by the bride's family to the groom upon marriage. The dowry could be a large sum, and all families were expected to provide dowries for their daughters.

Marriage Ceremonies. At the left is a detail of a marriage ceremony in Italy from a fresco painted by Dominico di Bartolo in 1443. At the right is a seventeenth-century Mughal painting showing Shah Jahan, the Mughal emperor (with halo). He is riding to the wedding celebration of his son, who rides before him.

Arranged marriages were not unique to Europe but were common throughout the world. In China, marriages were normally arranged for the benefit of the family, often by a go-between, and the groom and bride were usually not consulted. Frequently, they did not meet until the marriage ceremony. Love was obviously not a reason for marriage and in fact was often viewed as a detriment because it could distract the married couple from their responsibility to the larger family unit. In Japan too, marriages were arranged, often by the heads of dominant families in rural areas, and the new wife moved in with the family of her husband. In India, not only were marriages arranged, but it was not uncommon for women to be married before the age of ten. In colonial Latin America, parents selected marriage partners for their children and often chose a dwelling for the couple as well. In many areas, before members of the lower classes could marry, they had to offer gifts to the powerful noble landowners in the region and obtain their permission. These nobles often refused to allow women to marry in order to keep them as servants.

Arranged marriages were the logical result of a social system in which men dominated and women's primary role was to bear children, manage the household, and work in the field. Not until the nineteenth century did a feminist

Dagli Orti/The Art Archive/The Picture Desk

The Granger Collection, NYC

movement emerge in Europe to improve the rights of women. By the beginning of the twentieth century, that movement had spread to other parts of the world. The New Culture Movement in China, for example, advocated the free choice of spouses. Although the trend throughout the world is toward allowing people to choose their mates, in some areas, especially in rural communities, families remain active in choosing marriage partners.

 In what ways were marriage practices similar in the West and the East during the early modern period? Were there any significant differences?

any idea of special holiness for celibacy and had abolished both monasticism and a celibate clergy, the family could be placed at the center of human life, and a new stress on "mutual love between man and wife" could be extolled (see the Comparative Essay "Marriage in the Early Modern World" on p. 426).

But were doctrine and reality the same? Most often, reality reflected the traditional roles of husband as the ruler and wife as the obedient servant whose chief duty was to please her husband. Luther stated it clearly:

> The rule remains with the husband, and the wife is compelled to obey him by God's command. He rules the home and the state, wages war, defends his possessions, tills the soil, builds, plants, etc. The woman on the other hand is like a nail driven into the wall … so the wife should stay at home and look after the affairs of the household, as one who has been deprived of the ability of administering those affairs that are outside and that concern the state. She does not go beyond her most personal duties.[3]

Obedience to her husband was not a wife's only role; her other important duty was to bear children. To Calvin and Luther, this function of women was part of the divine plan, and for most Protestant women, family life was their only destiny (see the box "A Protestant Woman" on p. 428). Overall, the Protestant Reformation did not noticeably alter women's subordinate place in society.

The Catholic Reformation

By the mid-sixteenth century, Lutheranism had become established in Germany and Scandinavia and Calvinism in Scotland, Switzerland, France, the Netherlands, and eastern Europe. In England, the split from Rome had resulted in the creation of a national church. The situation in Europe did not look particularly favorable for the Roman Catholic Church (see Map 15.1).

MAP 15.1 Catholics and Protestants in Europe by 1560. The Reformation continued to evolve beyond the basic split of the Lutherans from the Catholics. Several Protestant sects broke away from the teachings of Martin Luther, each with a separate creed and different ways of worship. In England, Henry VIII broke with the Catholic Church for political and dynastic reasons.

 Which areas of Europe were solidly Catholic, which were solidly Lutheran, and which were neither?

A Protestant Woman

FAMILY & SOCIETY

IN THE INITIAL ZEAL OF THE PROTESTANT REFORMATION, women were frequently allowed to play untraditional roles. Catherine Zell of Germany (c. 1497–1562) first preached beside her husband in 1527. After the death of her two children, she devoted the rest of her life to helping her husband and their Anabaptist faith. This selection is taken from one of her letters to a young Lutheran minister who had criticized her activities.

A Letter from Catherine Zell to Ludwig Rabus of Memmingen

I, Catherine Zell, wife of the late lamented Mathew Zell, who served in Strasbourg, where I was born and reared and still live, wish you peace and enhancement in God's grace....

From my earliest years I turned to the Lord, who taught and guided me, and I have at all times, in accordance with my understanding and His grace, embraced the interests of His church and earnestly sought Jesus. Even in youth this brought me the regard and affection of clergymen and others much concerned with the church, which is why the pious Mathew Zell wanted me as a companion in marriage; and I, in turn, to serve the glory of Christ, gave devotion and help to my husband, both in his ministry and in keeping his house.... Ever since I was ten years old I have been a student and a sort of church mother, much given to attending sermons. I have loved and frequented the company of learned men, and I conversed much with them, not about dancing, masquerades, and worldly pleasures but about the kingdom of God....

Consider the poor Anabaptists, who are so furiously and ferociously persecuted. Must the authorities everywhere be incited against them, as the hunter drives his dog against wild animals? Against those who acknowledge Christ the Lord in very much the same way we do and over which we broke with the papacy? Just because they cannot agree with us on lesser things, is this any reason to persecute them and in them Christ, in whom they fervently believe and have often professed in misery, in prison, and under the torments of fire and water?

Governments may punish criminals, but they should not force and govern belief, which is a matter for the heart and conscience not for temporal authorities.... When the authorities pursue one, they soon bring forth tears, and towns and villages are emptied.

 What new ideas did Catherine Zell bring to the Reformation? Why did people react so strongly against them?

Source: Excerpt from *Not in God's Image: Women in History From the Greeks to the Victorians* by Julia O'Faolain and Lauro Martines. Copyright © 1973 by Julia O'Faolain and Lauro Martines.

CATHOLIC REFORMATION OR COUNTER-REFORMATION? There is no doubt that the Catholic Church underwent a revitalization in the sixteenth century. But was this reformation a **Catholic Reformation** or a Counter-Reformation? Some historians prefer the term *Counter-Reformation* to focus on the aspects that were a direct reaction against the Protestant movement. Historians who prefer the term *Catholic Reformation* point out that elements of reform were already present in the Catholic Church at the end of the fifteenth century and the beginning of the sixteenth century. Especially noticeable were the calls for reform from the religious orders of the Franciscans, Dominicans, and Augustinians. Members of these groups put particular emphasis on preaching to laypeople. Another example was the Oratory of Divine Love, first organized in Italy in 1497 as an informal group of clergy and laymen who worked to foster reform by emphasizing personal spiritual development and outward acts of charity. The Oratory's members included a Spanish archbishop, Cardinal Ximenes (khee-MAY-ness), who was especially active in using Christian humanism to reform the church in Spain.

No doubt, both positions on the nature of the reformation of the Catholic Church contain elements of truth. The Catholic Reformation revived the best features of medieval Catholicism and then adjusted them to meet new conditions, as is most apparent in the emergence of a new mysticism, closely tied to the traditions of Catholic piety, and the revival of monasticism through the regeneration of older religious orders and the founding of new orders.

THE SOCIETY OF JESUS Of all the new religious orders, the most important was the Society of Jesus, known as the Jesuits, founded by a Spanish nobleman, Ignatius of Loyola (if-NAY-schuss of loi-OH-luh) (1491–1556). Loyola brought together a small group of individuals who were recognized as a religious order by the pope in 1540. The new order was grounded on the principles of absolute obedience to the papacy, a strict hierarchical order for the society, the use of education to achieve its goals, and a dedication to engage in "conflict for God." A special vow of absolute obedience to the pope made the Jesuits an important instrument for papal policy. Jesuit missionaries proved singularly successful in restoring Catholicism to parts of Germany and eastern Europe.

Another prominent Jesuit activity was the propagation of the Catholic faith among non-Christians. Francis Xavier (ZAY-vee-ur) (1506–1552), one of the original members of the Society of Jesus, carried the message of Catholic Christianity to the East. After attracting tens of thousands of converts in India, he

Ignatius of Loyola. The Jesuits became the most important new religious order of the Catholic Reformation. Shown here in a sixteenth-century painting by an unknown artist is Ignatius of Loyola, founder of the Society of Jesus. Loyola is seen kneeling before Pope Paul III, who officially recognized the Jesuits in 1540.

traveled to Malacca and the Moluccas before finally reaching Japan in 1549. He spoke highly of the Japanese: "They are a people of excellent morals—good in general and not malicious."[4] Thousands of Japanese, especially in the southernmost islands, became Christians. In 1552, Xavier set out for China but died of fever before he reached the mainland.

Although conversion efforts in Japan proved short-lived, Jesuit activity in China, especially that of the Italian Matteo Ricci (ma-TAY-oh REE-chee), was more long-lasting. Recognizing the Chinese pride in their own culture, the Jesuits attempted to draw parallels between Christian and Confucian concepts and to show the similarities between Christian morality and Confucian ethics. For their part, the missionaries were much impressed with many aspects of Chinese civilization, and reports of their experiences heightened European curiosity about this great society on the other side of the world.

A REFORMED PAPACY A reformed papacy was another important factor in the development of the Catholic Reformation. The involvement of Renaissance popes in dubious finances and Italian political and military affairs had created numerous sources of corruption. It took the jolt of the Protestant Reformation to bring about serious reform. Pope Paul III (1534–1549) perceived the need for change and took the audacious step of appointing a reform commission to ascertain the church's ills. The commission's report in 1537 blamed the church's problems on the corrupt policies of popes and cardinals. Paul III also formally recognized the Jesuits and summoned the Council of Trent.

THE COUNCIL OF TRENT In March 1545, a group of high church officials met in the city of Trent on the border

CHRONOLOGY	Key Events of the Reformation Era
Luther's Ninety-Five Theses	1517
Excommunication of Luther	1521
Act of Supremacy in England	1534
Pontificate of Paul III	1534–1549
John Calvin's *Institutes of the Christian Religion*	1536
Society of Jesus (Jesuits) recognized as a religious order	1540
Council of Trent	1545–1563
Peace of Augsburg	1555

between Germany and Italy and initiated the Council of Trent, which met intermittently from 1545 to 1563 in three major sessions. The final decrees of the Council of Trent reaffirmed traditional Catholic teachings in opposition to Protestant beliefs. Scripture and tradition were affirmed as equal authorities in religious matters; only the church could interpret Scripture. Both faith and good works were declared necessary for salvation. Belief in purgatory and in the use of indulgences was strengthened, although the selling of indulgences was prohibited.

After the Council of Trent, the Roman Catholic Church possessed a clear body of doctrine and a unified structure under the acknowledged supremacy of the popes. Although the Roman Catholic Church had become one Christian denomination among many, the church entered a new phase of its history with a spirit of confidence.

Europe in Crisis, 1560–1650

 FOCUS QUESTION: Why is the period between 1560 and 1650 in Europe considered an age of crisis, and how did the turmoil contribute to the artistic developments of the period?

Between 1560 and 1650, Europe experienced religious wars, revolutions and constitutional crises, economic and social disintegration, and a witchcraft craze. It was truly an age of crisis.

Politics and the Wars of Religion in the Sixteenth Century

By 1560, Calvinism and Catholicism had become activist religions dedicated to spreading the word of God as they interpreted it. Although their struggle for the minds and hearts of Europeans was at the heart of the religious wars of the sixteenth century, economic, social, and political forces also played important roles in these conflicts.

THE FRENCH WARS OF RELIGION (1562–1598) Religion was central to the French civil wars of the sixteenth century. The growth of Calvinism had led to persecution by the

French kings, but the latter did little to stop the spread of Calvinism. Huguenots (HYOO-guh-nots), as the French Calvinists were called, constituted only about 7 percent of the population, but 40 to 50 percent of the French nobility became Huguenots, including the house of Bourbon (boor-BOHN), which stood next to the Valois (val-WAH) in the royal line of succession. The conversion of so many nobles made the Huguenots a potentially dangerous political threat to monarchical power. Still, the Calvinist minority was greatly outnumbered by the Catholic majority, and the Valois monarchy was staunchly Catholic.

The religious issue was not the only factor that contributed to the French civil wars. Towns and provinces, which had long resisted the growing power of monarchical centralization, were only too willing to join a revolt against the monarchy. So were the nobles, and the fact that so many of them were Calvinists created an important base of opposition to the crown.

For thirty years, battles raged in France between Catholic and Calvinist parties. Finally, in 1589, Henry of Navarre, the political leader of the Huguenots and a member of the Bourbon Dynasty, succeeded to the throne as Henry IV (1589–1610). Realizing, however, that he would never be accepted by Catholic France, Henry converted to Catholicism. With his coronation in 1594, the Wars of Religion had finally come to an end. The Edict of Nantes (NAHNT) in 1598 solved the religious problem by acknowledging Catholicism as the official religion of France while guaranteeing the Huguenots the right to worship and to enjoy all political privileges, including the holding of public offices.

PHILIP II AND MILITANT CATHOLICISM The greatest advocate of militant Catholicism in the second half of the sixteenth century was King Philip II of Spain (1556–1598), the son and heir of Charles V. Philip's reign ushered in an age of Spanish greatness, both politically and culturally. Philip had inherited from his father Spain, the Netherlands, and possessions in Italy and the Americas. To strengthen his control, Philip insisted on strict conformity to Catholicism and strong monarchical authority. Achieving the latter was not an easy task, because each of the lands of his empire had its own structure of government.

The Catholic faith was crucial to the Spanish people and their ruler. Driven by a heritage of crusading fervor, Spain saw itself as a nation of people chosen by God to save Catholic Christianity from the Protestant heretics. Philip II, the "most Catholic king," became the champion of Catholicism throughout Europe. Spain's leadership of a "holy league" against Turkish encroachments in the Mediterranean resulted in a stunning victory over the Turkish fleet in the Battle of Lepanto (LEH-pahn-toh or LIH-pan-toh) in 1571. But Philip's problems with the Netherlands and the English Queen Elizabeth led to his greatest misfortunes.

Philip's attempt to strengthen his control in the Spanish Netherlands, which consisted of seventeen provinces (modern Netherlands and Belgium), soon led to a revolt. The nobles, who stood to lose the most politically, strongly opposed Philip's efforts. Religion also became a major catalyst for rebellion when Philip attempted to crush Calvinism. Violence erupted in 1566, and the revolt became organized, especially in the northern provinces, where the Dutch, under the leadership of William of Nassau, the prince of Orange, offered growing resistance. The struggle dragged on for decades until 1609, when a twelve-year truce ended the war, virtually recognizing the independence of the northern provinces. These seven northern provinces, which called themselves the United Provinces of the Netherlands, became the core of the modern Dutch state.

To most Europeans at the beginning of the seventeenth century, Spain still seemed the greatest power of the age, but the reality was quite different. The Spanish treasury was empty, the armed forces were obsolescent, and the government was inefficient. Spain continued to play the role of a great power, but real power had shifted to England.

THE ENGLAND OF ELIZABETH When Elizabeth Tudor, the daughter of Henry VIII and Anne Boleyn, ascended the throne in 1558, England was home to fewer than 4 million people. Yet during her reign (1558–1603), the small island kingdom became the leader of the Protestant nations of Europe and laid the foundations for a world empire.

Intelligent, cautious, and self-confident, Elizabeth moved quickly to solve the difficult religious problem she inherited from her half-sister, Queen Mary. Elizabeth's religious policy was based on moderation and compromise. She repealed the Catholic laws of Mary's reign, and a new Act of Supremacy designated Elizabeth as "the only supreme governor" of both church and state. The Church of England under Elizabeth was basically Protestant, but it was of a moderate bent that kept most people satisfied.

Elizabeth proved as adept in government and foreign policy as in religious affairs (see the box "Queen Elizabeth I: 'I Have the Heart of a King'" on p. 431). Assisted by competent officials, she handled Parliament with much skill. Caution and moderation also dictated Elizabeth's foreign policy. Nevertheless, Elizabeth was gradually drawn into conflict with Spain. Having resisted for years the idea of invading England as too impractical, Philip II of Spain was finally persuaded to do so by advisers who assured him that the people of England would rise against their queen when the Spaniards arrived. A successful invasion of England would mean the overthrow of heresy and the return of England to Catholicism. Philip ordered preparations for a fleet of warships, the *armada*, to spearhead the invasion of England.

The armada was a disaster. The Spanish fleet that finally set sail had neither the ships nor the manpower that Philip had planned to send. Battered by a number of encounters with the English, the Spanish fleet sailed back to Spain by a northward route around Scotland and Ireland, where it was further pounded by storms. Although the English and Spanish would continue their war for another sixteen years, the defeat of the armada guaranteed for the time being that England would remain a Protestant country.

Queen Elizabeth I: "I Have the Heart of a King"

POLITICS & GOVERNMENT

QUEEN ELIZABETH I RULED ENGLAND from 1558 to 1603 with a consummate skill that contemporaries considered unusual in a woman. Though shrewd and paternalistic, Elizabeth's power, like that of other sixteenth-century monarchs, depended on the favor of her people. When England was faced with the threat of an invasion by the armada of Philip II, Elizabeth sought to rally her troops with a speech in Tilbury, a town on the Thames River. This selection is taken from her speech.

Queen Elizabeth I, Speech at Tilbury

My loving people, we have been persuaded by some, that are careful of our safety, to take heed how we commit ourselves to armed multitudes, for fear of treachery; but I assure you, I do not desire to live to distrust my faithful and loving people. Let tyrants fear; I have always so behaved myself that, under God, I have placed my chiefest strength and safeguard in the loyal hearts and good will of my subjects. And therefore I am come amongst you at this time, not as for my recreation or sport, but being resolved, in the midst and heat of the battle, to live or dies amongst you all; to lay down, for my God, and

for my kingdom, and for my people, my honor and my blood, even the dust. I know I have but the body of a weak and feeble woman; but I have the heart of a king, and of a king of England, too; and think foul scorn that Parma or Spain, or any prince of Europe, should dare to invade the borders of my realms: to which, rather than any dishonor should grow by me, I myself will take up arms; I myself will be your general, judge, and rewarder of every one of your virtues in the field. I know already, by your forwardness, that you have deserved rewards and crowns; and we do assure you, on the word of a prince, they shall be duly paid you. In the mean my lieutenant general shall be in my stead, than whom never princes commanded a more noble and worthy subject; not doubting by your obedience to my general, by your concern in the camp and by your valor in the field, we shall shortly have a famous victory over the enemies of my God, of my kingdom, and of my people.

 What qualities evident in Elizabeth's speech would have endeared her to her listeners? How was her popularity connected to the events of the late sixteenth century?

Source: From Elizabeth I's Speech at Tillbury in 1588 to the troops.

Stapleton Collection/Fine Art/Corbis

Procession of Queen Elizabeth I. Intelligent and learned, Elizabeth Tudor was familiar with Latin and Greek and spoke several European languages. Served by able administrators, Elizabeth ruled for nearly forty-five years and generally avoided open military action against any major power. This picture, painted near the end of her reign, shows the queen in a ceremonial procession.

Economic and Social Crises

The period of European history from 1560 to 1650 witnessed severe economic and social crises as well as political upheaval. Economic contraction began to be evident in some parts of Europe by the 1620s. In the 1630s and 1640s, as imports of silver from the Americas declined, economic recession intensified, especially in the Mediterranean area. Once the industrial and financial center of Europe in the age of the Renaissance, Italy was now becoming an economic backwater.

POPULATION DECLINE Population trends of the sixteenth and seventeenth centuries also reveal Europe's worsening conditions. The population of Europe increased from 60 million in 1500 to 85 million by 1600, the first major recovery of the European population since the devastation of the Black Death in the mid-fourteenth century. By 1650, however, records indicate that the population had declined, especially in central and southern Europe. Europe's longtime adversaries—war, famine, and plague—continued to affect population levels. After the middle of the sixteenth century, another "little ice age," when average temperatures fell, reduced harvests and led to food shortages. Europe's problems created social tensions, some of which became manifested in an obsession with witches.

WITCHCRAFT MANIA Hysteria over witchcraft affected the lives of many Europeans in the sixteenth and seventeenth centuries. Perhaps more than 100,000 people were prosecuted throughout Europe on charges of witchcraft. As more and more people were brought to trial, the fear of witches, as well as the fear of being accused of witchcraft, escalated to frightening levels (see the box "A Witchcraft Trial in France" on p. 433).

Common people—usually those who were poor and without property—were more likely to be accused of witchcraft. Indeed, where lists are available, those mentioned most often are milkmaids, peasant women, and servant girls. In the witchcraft trials of the sixteenth and seventeenth centuries, more than 75 percent of the accused were women, most of them single or widowed and many over fifty years old.

That women should be the chief victims of witchcraft trials was hardly accidental. Nicholas Rémy (nee-koh-LAH ray-MEE), a witchcraft judge in France in the 1590s, found it "not unreasonable that this scum of humanity, i.e., witches, should be drawn chiefly from the feminine sex." To another judge, it came as no surprise that witches would confess to sexual experiences with Satan: "The Devil uses them so, because he knows that women love carnal pleasures, and he means to bind them to his allegiance by such agreeable provocations."[5]

By the mid-seventeenth century, the witchcraft hysteria had begun to subside. As governments grew stronger, fewer magistrates were willing to accept the unsettling and divisive conditions generated by the trials of witches. Moreover, by the end of the seventeenth century and the beginning of the eighteenth, more and more people were questioning their old attitudes toward religion and found it especially contrary to reason to believe in the old view of a world haunted by evil spirits.

ECONOMIC TRENDS IN THE SEVENTEENTH CENTURY In the course of the seventeenth century, new economic trends also emerged. **Mercantilism** is the name historians apply to the economic practices of the seventeenth century. According to the mercantilists, the prosperity of a nation depended on a plentiful supply of bullion (gold and silver). For this reason, it was desirable to achieve a favorable balance of trade in which goods exported were of greater value than those imported, promoting an influx of gold and silver payments that would increase the quantity of bullion. Furthermore, to encourage exports, governments should stimulate and protect export industries and trade by granting trade monopolies, encouraging investment in new industries through subsidies, importing foreign artisans, and improving transportation systems by building roads, bridges, and canals. By imposing high tariffs on foreign goods, they could reduce imports and prevent them from competing with domestic industries. Colonies were also deemed valuable as sources of raw materials and markets for finished goods.

Mercantilist theory on the role of colonies was matched in practice by Europe's overseas expansion. With the development of colonies and trading posts in the Americas and the East, Europeans embarked on an adventure in international commerce in the seventeenth century. Although some historians speak of a nascent world economy, we should remember that local, regional, and intra-European trade still predominated. At the end of the seventeenth century, for example, English imports totaled 360,000 tons, but only 5,000 tons came from the East Indies. What made the transoceanic trade rewarding, however, was not the volume but the value of its goods. Dutch, English, and French merchants were bringing back products that were still consumed largely by the wealthy but were beginning to make their way into the lives of artisans and merchants. Pepper and spices from the Indies, West Indian and Brazilian sugar, and Asian coffee and tea were becoming more readily available to European consumers.

The commercial expansion of the sixteenth and seventeenth centuries was made easier by new forms of commercial organization, especially the **joint-stock company**. Individuals bought shares in a company and received dividends on their investment while a board of directors ran the company and made the important business decisions. The return on investments could be spectacular. During its first ten years, investors received 30 percent annually on their money from the Dutch East India Company, which opened the Spice Islands and Southeast Asia to Dutch activity. The joint-stock company made it easier to raise large amounts of capital for world trading ventures.

Despite the growth of commercial capitalism, most of the European economy still depended on an agricultural system that had experienced few changes since the thirteenth century. At least 80 percent of Europeans still worked on the land. Almost all of the peasants in western Europe were free of serfdom, although many still owed a variety of feudal dues to the nobility. Despite the expanding markets and rising prices, European peasants saw little or no improvement in their lot as they faced increased rents and fees and higher taxes imposed by the state.

A Witchcraft Trial in France

FAMILY & SOCIETY

PERSECUTIONS FOR WITCHCRAFT reached their high point in the sixteenth and seventeenth centuries, when tens of thousands of people were brought to trial. In this excerpt from the minutes of a trial in France in 1652, we can see why the accused witch stood little chance of exonerating herself.

The Trial of Suzanne Gaudry

28 May, 1652.... Interrogation of Suzanne Gaudry, prisoner at the court of Rieux.... During interrogations on May 28 and May 29, the prisoner confessed to a number of activities involving the devil.

Deliberation of the Court—June 3, 1652

The undersigned advocates of the Court have seen these interrogations and answers. They say that the aforementioned Suzanne Gaudry confesses that she is a witch, that she had given herself to the devil, that she had renounced God, Lent, and baptism, that she has been marked on the shoulder, that she has cohabited with the devil and that she has been to the dances, confessing only to have cast a spell upon and caused to die a beast of Philippe Cornié....

Third Interrogation, June 27

This prisoner being led into the chamber, she was examined to know if things were not as she had said and confessed at the beginning of her imprisonment.

—Answers no, and that what she has said was done so by force.

Pressed to say the truth, that otherwise she would be subjected to torture, having pointed out to her that her aunt was burned for this same subject.

—Answers that she is not a witch....

She was placed in the hands of the officer in charge of torture, throwing herself on her knees, struggling to cry, uttering several exclamations, without being able, nevertheless, to shed a tear. Saying at every moment that she is not a witch.

The Torture

On this same day, being at the place of torture.

This prisoner, before being strapped down, was admonished to maintain herself in her first confessions and to renounce her lover.

—Says that she denies everything she has said, and that she has no lover. Feeling herself being strapped down, says that she is not a witch, while struggling to cry ... and upon being asked why she confessed to being one, said that she was forced to say it.

Told that she was not forced, that on the contrary she declared herself to be a witch without any threat.

—Says that she confessed it and that she is not a witch, and being a little stretched [on the rack] screams ceaselessly that she is not a witch.

Asked if she did not confess that she had been a witch for twenty-six years.

—Says that she said it, that she retracts it, crying that she is not a witch.

Asked if she did not make Philippe Cornié's horse die, as she confessed.

—Answers no, crying Jesus-Maria, that she is not a witch.

The mark having been probed by the officer, in the presence of Doctor Bouchain, it was adjudged by the aforesaid doctor and officer truly to be the mark of the devil.

Being more tightly stretched upon the torture rack, urged to maintain her confessions.

—Said that it was true that she is a witch and that she would maintain what she had said.

Asked how long she has been in subjugation to the devil.

—Answers that it was twenty years ago that the devil appeared to her, being in her lodgings in the form of a man dressed in a little cowhide and black breeches....

Verdict

July 9, 1652. In the light of the interrogations, answers, and investigations made into the charge against Suzanne Gaudry,... seeing by her own confessions that she is said to have made a pact with the devil, received the mark from him,... and that following this, she had renounced God, Lent, and baptism and had let herself be known carnally by him, in which she received satisfaction. Also, seeing that she is said to have been a part of nocturnal carols and dances.

For expiation of which the advice of the undersigned is that the office of Rieux can legitimately condemn the aforesaid Suzanne Gaudry to death, tying her to a gallows, and strangling her to death, then burning her body and burying it here in the environs of the woods.

Why were women, particularly older women, especially vulnerable to accusations of witchcraft? What "proofs" are offered here that Suzanne Gaudry had consorted with the devil? What does this account tell us about the spread of witchcraft persecutions in the seventeenth century?

Source: From *Witchcraft in Europe, 1100–1700: A Documentary History* by Alan Kors and Edward Peters, pp. 266–275. Copyright © 1972 by The University of Pennsylvania Press. Reprinted with permission of The University of Pennsylvania Press.

Seventeenth-Century Crises: Revolution and War

During the first half of the seventeenth century, a series of rebellions and civil wars rocked the domestic stability of many European governments. A devastating war that affected much of Europe also added to the sense of crisis.

THE THIRTY YEARS' WAR (1618–1648) The Thirty Years' War began in 1618 in the Germanic lands of the Holy Roman Empire as a struggle between Catholic forces, led by the Habsburg Holy Roman Emperors, and Protestant—primarily Calvinist—nobles in Bohemia who rebelled against Habsburg authority (see Map 15.2). What began as a struggle over religious issues soon became a wider conflict perpetuated by political motivations as both minor and major European powers—Denmark, Sweden, France, and Spain—entered the war. The competition for European leadership between the Bourbon dynasty of France and the Habsburg dynasties of Spain and the Holy Roman Empire was an especially important factor. Nevertheless, most of the battles were fought on German soil.

The war in Germany was officially ended in 1648 by the Peace of Westphalia, which proclaimed that all German states, including the Calvinist ones, were free to determine their own religion. The major contenders gained new territories, and France emerged as the dominant nation in Europe. The more than three hundred entities that made up the Holy Roman Empire were recognized as independent states, and each was given the power to conduct its own foreign policy; this brought an end to the Holy Roman Empire and ensured German disunity for another two hundred years. The Peace of Westphalia made it clear that political motives, not religious convictions, had become the guiding force in public affairs.

MAP 15.2 Europe in the Seventeenth Century. This map shows Europe at the time of the Thirty Years' War (1618–1648). Although the struggle began in Bohemia and much of the fighting took place in the Germanic lands of the Holy Roman Empire, the conflict became a Europe-wide struggle. Compare this map with Map 15.1.

Q *Which countries engaged in the war were predominantly Protestant, which were Catholic, and which were mixed?*

WAS THERE A MILITARY REVOLUTION? By the seventeenth century, war played an increasingly important role in European affairs. Military power was considered essential to a ruler's reputation and power; thus, the pressure to build an effective military machine was intense. Some historians believe that the changes that occurred in the science of warfare between 1560 and 1650 warranted the title of military revolution.

Medieval warfare, with its mounted knights and supplementary archers, had been transformed in the Renaissance by the employment of infantry armed with pikes and halberds (long-handled weapons combining an axe with a spike) and arranged in massed rectangles known as squadrons or battalions. The use of firearms required adjustments to the size and shape of the massed infantry and made the cavalry less effective.

It was Gustavus Adolphus (goo-STAY-vus uh-DAHL-fuss), the king of Sweden (1611–1632), who developed the first standing army of conscripts, notable for the flexibility of its tactics. The infantry brigades of Gustavus's army were composed of equal numbers of musketeers and pikemen, standing six men deep. They employed the salvo, in which all rows of the infantry fired at once instead of row by row. These salvos of fire, which cut up the massed ranks of the opposing infantry squadrons, were followed by a pike charge, giving the infantry a primarily offensive deployment. Gustavus also used his cavalry in a more mobile fashion. After shooting a pistol volley, they charged the enemy with their swords. Additional flexibility was obtained by using lighter artillery pieces that were more easily moved during battle. All of these innovations required coordination, careful training, and better discipline, forcing rulers to move away from undisciplined mercenary forces. Naturally, the success of Gustavus Adolphus led to imitation.

Some historians have questioned the use of the phrase "military revolution" to describe the military changes from 1560 to 1660, arguing instead that military developments were gradual. In any case, for the rest of the seventeenth century, warfare continued to change. Standing armies, based partly on conscription, grew ever larger and more expensive. Standing armies necessitated better-disciplined and better-trained soldiers and led to the education of officers in military schools. Armies also introduced the use of linear rather than square formations to provide greater flexibility and mobility in tactics. There was also an increased use of firearms as the musket with attached bayonet increasingly replaced the pike in the ranks of the infantry. A naval arms race in the seventeenth century led to more and bigger warships or capital ships known as "ships of the line."

Larger armies and navies could be maintained only by levying heavier taxes, making war a greater economic burden and an ever more important part of the early modern European state. The creation of large bureaucracies to supervise the military resources of the state led to growth in the power of state governments.

Response to Crisis: The Practice of Absolutism

 FOCUS QUESTION: What was absolutism, and what were the main characteristics of the absolute monarchies that emerged in France, Prussia, Austria, and Russia?

Many people responded to the crises of the seventeenth century by searching for order. An increase in monarchical power became an obvious means for achieving stability. The result was what historians have called absolutism or absolute monarchy, in which the sovereign power or ultimate authority in the state rested in the hands of a king who claimed to rule by divine right—the idea that kings received their power from God and were responsible to no one but God. Late-sixteenth-century political theorists believed that sovereign power consisted of the authority to make laws, levy taxes, administer justice, control the state's administrative system, and determine foreign policy.

France Under Louis XIV

France during the reign of Louis XIV (1643–1715) has traditionally been regarded as the best example of the practice of absolute or **divine-right monarchy** in the seventeenth century. French culture, language, and manners reached into all levels of European society. French diplomacy and wars overwhelmed the political affairs of western and central Europe. The court of Louis XIV seemed to be imitated everywhere in Europe (see the Comparative Illustration "Sun Kings, West and East" on p. 436).

POLITICAL INSTITUTIONS One of the keys to Louis's power was his control of the central policy-making machinery of government because it was part of his own court and household. The royal court, located in the magnificent palace at Versailles (vayr-SY), outside Paris, served three purposes simultaneously: it was the personal household of the king, the location of central governmental machinery, and the place where powerful subjects came to find favors and offices for themselves and their clients. The greatest danger to Louis's personal rule came from the very high nobles and princes of the blood (the royal princes), who considered it their natural function to assert the policy-making role of royal ministers. Louis eliminated this threat by removing them from the royal council, the chief administrative body of the king, and enticing them to his court, where he could keep them preoccupied with court life and out of politics. Instead of the high nobility and royal princes, Louis relied for his ministers on nobles who came from relatively new aristocratic families. His ministers were expected to be

CHRONOLOGY	Europe in Crisis, 1560–1650: Key Events
Reign of Philip II	1556–1598
French Wars of Religion	1562–1598
Outbreak of revolt in the Netherlands	1566
Defeat of the Spanish armada	1588
Edict of Nantes	1598
Truce between Spain and the Netherlands	1609–1621
Thirty Years' War	1618–1648
Peace of Westphalia	1648

COMPARATIVE ILLUSTRATION

POLITICS & GOVERNMENT

Sun Kings, West and East. At the end of the seventeenth century, two powerful rulers held sway in kingdoms that dominated the affairs of the regions around them. Both rulers saw themselves as favored by divine authority—Louis XIV of France as a divine-right monarch and Kangxi (GANG-zhee) of China as possessing the mandate of Heaven. Thus, both rulers saw themselves not as divine beings but as divinely ordained beings whose job was to govern organized societies. On the left, Louis, who ruled France from 1643 to 1715, is seen in a portrait by Hyacinthe Rigaud (ee-ah-SANT ree-GOH) that captures the king's sense of royal dignity and grandeur. One person at court said of the king: "Louis XIV's vanity was without limit or restraint." On the right, Kangxi, who ruled China from 1661 to 1722, is seen in a portrait that shows him seated in majesty on his imperial throne. A dedicated ruler, Kangxi once wrote, "One act of negligence may cause sorrow all through the country, and one moment of negligence may result in trouble for hundreds and thousands of generations."

Q *Although these rulers practiced very different religions, why did they justify their powers in such a similar fashion?*

subservient: "I had no intention of sharing my authority with them," Louis said.

Court life at Versailles itself became highly ritualized with Louis at the center of it all. The king had little privacy; only when he visited his wife or mother or mistress was he free of the noble courtiers who swarmed about the palace. Most daily ceremonies were carefully staged, including those attending Louis's rising from bed, dining, praying, attending Mass, and going to bed. A mob of nobles aspired to assist the king in carrying out these solemn activities. It was considered a great honor for a noble to be chosen to hand the king his shirt while dressing (see the box "The King's Day Begins" on p. 437). Court etiquette was also a complex matter. Nobles and royal princes were arranged in an elaborate order of seniority and

expected to follow certain rules of precedence. Who could sit down and on what kind of chair was a subject of much debate.

Louis's domination of his ministers and secretaries gave him control of the central policy-making machinery of government and thus authority over the traditional areas of monarchical power: the formulation of foreign policy, the making of war and peace, the assertion of the secular power of the crown against any religious authority, and the ability to levy taxes to fulfill these functions. Louis had considerably less success with the internal administration of the kingdom, however. The traditional groups and institutions of French society—the nobles, officials, town councils, guilds, and representative estates in some provinces—were simply too powerful for the king to have direct control over the lives of his

The King's Day Begins

FAMILY & SOCIETY

THE DUC DE SAINT-SIMON was one of many noble courtiers who lived at Versailles and had firsthand experience of court life there. In his *Memoirs*, he left a controversial and critical account of Louis XIV and his court. In this selection, Saint-Simon describes the scene in Louis's bedroom at the beginning of his day.

Duc de Saint-Simon, *Memoirs*

At eight o'clock the chief valet of the room on duty, who alone had slept in the royal chamber, and who had dressed himself, awoke the King. The chief physician, the chief surgeon, and the nurse (as long as she lived), entered at the same time. The latter kissed the King; the others rubbed and often changed his shirt, because he was in the habit of sweating a great deal. At the quarter, the grand chamberlain was called (or, in his absence, the first gentleman of the chamber), and those who had, what was called the grandes entrées [grand entry]. The chamberlain (or chief gentleman) drew back the curtains which had been closed again, and presented the holy water from the vase, at the head of the bed. These gentlemen stayed but a moment, and that was the time to speak to the King, if any one had anything to ask of him; in which case the rest stood aside. When, contrary to custom, nobody had anything to say, they were there but for a few moments. He who had opened the curtains and presented the holy water, presented also a prayer-book. Then all passed into the cabinet of the council. A very short religious service being over, the King called, they reentered. The same officer gave him his dressing-gown; immediately after, other privilege courtiers entered, and then everybody, in time to find the King putting on his shoes and stockings, for he did almost everything himself and with address and grace. Every other day we saw him shave himself; and he had a little short wig in which he always appeared, even in bed, and on medicine days....

As soon as he was dressed, he prayed to God, at the side of his bed, where all the clergy present knelt, the cardinals without cushions, all the laity remaining standing; and the caption of the guards came to the balustrade during the prayer, after which the king passed into his cabinet.

He found there, or was followed by all who had the entrée, a very numerous company, for it included everybody in any office. He gave orders to each for the day; thus within a half a quarter of an hour it was known what he meant to do; and then all this crowd left directly.

 What were the message and purpose of the royal waking and dressing ceremony for both the nobles and the king? Do you think this account might be biased? Why?

Source: From Bayle St. John, trans., *The Memoirs of the Duke of Saint-Simon on the Reign of Louis XIV and the Regency*, 8th ed. (George Allen: London, 1913), vol. 3, pp. 221–222.

RMN-Grand Palais/Art Resource, NY

Interior of Versailles: The Hall of Mirrors.
Pictured here is the exquisite Hall of Mirrors at Versailles. Located on the second floor, the hall overlooks the park below. Three hundred and fifty-seven mirrors were placed on the wall opposite the windows in order to create an illusion of even greater width. Careful planning went into every detail of the interior decoration. Even the doorknobs were specially designed to reflect the magnificence of Versailles. This photo shows the Hall of Mirrors after the restoration work that was completed in June 2007, a project that took three years, cost 12 million euros (more than $16 million), and included the restoration of the Bohemian crystal chandeliers.

subjects. As a result, control of the provinces and the people was achieved largely by bribing the individuals responsible for carrying out the king's policies.

THE ECONOMY AND THE MILITARY The cost of building palaces, maintaining his court, and pursuing his wars made finances a crucial issue for Louis XIV. He was most fortunate in having the services of Jean-Baptiste Colbert (ZHAHN-bap-TEEST kohl-BAYR) (1619–1683) as his controller general of finances. Colbert sought to increase the wealth and power of France through general adherence to mercantilism, which advocated government intervention in economic activities for the benefit of the state. To decrease imports and increase exports, Colbert granted subsidies to individuals who established new industries. To improve communications and the transportation of goods internally, he built roads and canals. To decrease imports directly, Colbert raised tariffs on foreign goods.

The increase in royal power that Louis pursued led the king to develop a professional army numbering 100,000 men in peacetime and 400,000 in time of war. To achieve the prestige and military glory befitting an absolute king as well as to ensure the domination of his Bourbon dynasty over European affairs, Louis waged four wars between 1667 and 1713. His ambitions roused much of Europe to form coalitions against him to prevent the certain destruction of the European balance of power by Bourbon hegemony. Although Louis added some territory to France's northeastern frontier and established a member of his own Bourbon dynasty on the throne of Spain, he also left France impoverished and surrounded by enemies.

Absolutism in Central and Eastern Europe

During the seventeenth century, a development of great importance for the modern Western world took place with the appearance in central and eastern Europe of three new powers: Prussia, Austria, and Russia.

PRUSSIA Frederick William the Great Elector (1640–1688) laid the foundation for the Prussian state. Realizing that the land he had inherited, known as Brandenburg-Prussia, was a small, open territory with no natural frontiers for defense, Frederick William built an army of 40,000 men, making it the fourth largest in Europe. To sustain the army, Frederick William established the General War Commissariat to levy taxes for the army and oversee its growth. The Commissariat soon evolved into an agency for civil government as well. The new bureaucratic machine became the elector's chief instrument to govern the state. Many of its officials were members of the Prussian landed aristocracy, the Junkers (YOONG-kers), who also served as officers in the all-important army.

In 1701, Frederick William's son Frederick officially gained the title of king. Elector Frederick III became King Frederick I, and Brandenburg-Prussia simply Prussia. In the eighteenth century, Prussia emerged as a great power in Europe.

AUSTRIA The Austrian Habsburgs had long played a significant role in European politics as Holy Roman Emperors. By the end of the Thirty Years' War, the Habsburg hopes of creating an empire in Germany had been dashed. In the seventeenth century, the house of Austria created a new empire in eastern and southeastern Europe.

The nucleus of the new Austrian Empire remained the traditional Austrian hereditary possessions: Lower and Upper Austria, Carinthia, Carniola, Styria, and Tyrol. To these had been added the kingdom of Bohemia and parts of northwestern Hungary. After the defeat of the Turks in 1687 (see Chapter 16), Austria took control of all of Hungary, Transylvania, Croatia, and Slovenia, thus establishing the Austrian Empire in southeastern Europe. By the beginning of the eighteenth century, the house of Austria had assembled an empire of considerable size.

The Austrian monarchy, however, never became a highly centralized, absolutist state, primarily because it contained so many different national groups. The Austrian Empire remained a collection of territories held together by the Habsburg emperor, who was archduke of Austria, king of Bohemia, and king of Hungary. Each of these regions, however, had its own laws and political life.

FROM MUSCOVY TO RUSSIA A new Russian state had emerged in the fifteenth century under the leadership of the principality of Muscovy and its grand dukes. In the sixteenth century, Ivan IV (1533–1584) became the first ruler to take the title of *tsar* (the Russian word for "Caesar"). Ivan expanded the territories of Russia eastward and crushed the power of the Russian nobility. He was known as Ivan the Terrible because of his ruthless deeds, among them stabbing his son to death in a heated argument. When Ivan's dynasty came to an end in 1598, fifteen years of anarchy ensued until the Zemsky Sobor (ZEM-skee suh-BOR), or national assembly, chose Michael Romanov (ROH-muh-nahf) as the new tsar, establishing a dynasty that lasted more than four hundred years. One of its most prominent members was Peter the Great.

Peter the Great (1689–1725) was an unusual character. A strong man towering 6 feet 9 inches tall, Peter enjoyed low humor—belching contests and crude jokes—and vicious punishments, including floggings, impalings, and roastings. Peter got a firsthand view of the West when he made a trip there in 1697–1698 and returned to Russia with a firm determination to westernize Russia. He was especially eager to borrow European technology in order to create the army and navy he needed to make Russia a great power.

As could be expected, one of his first priorities was the reorganization of the army and the creation of a navy. Employing both Russians and Europeans as officers, he conscripted peasants for twenty-five-year stints of service to build a standing army of 210,000 men and at the same time formed the first navy Russia had ever had.

To impose the rule of the central government more effectively throughout the land, Peter divided Russia into provinces. Although he hoped to create a "police state," by which he meant a well-ordered community governed in accordance with law, few of his bureaucrats shared his concept of loyalty to the state. Peter hoped to evoke a sense of civic duty among

Peter the Great as Victor. Peter the Great wished to westernize Russia, especially in the realm of technical skills. His goal was the creation of a strong army and navy and the acquisition of new territory in order to make Russia a great power. Peter the Great is shown here as the victor after his defeat of Sweden in an eighteenth-century portrait attributed to Gottfried Danhauer.

his people, but his own forceful personality created an atmosphere of fear that prevented any such sentiment.

The object of Peter's domestic reforms was to make Russia into a great state and military power. His primary goal was to "open a window to the west," meaning an ice-free port easily accessible to Europe. This could only be achieved on the Baltic, but at that time, the Baltic coast was controlled by Sweden, the most important power in northern Europe. A long and hard-fought war with Sweden won Peter the lands he sought. In 1703, Peter began the construction of a new city, Saint Petersburg, his window to the west and a symbol that Russia was looking westward to Europe. By the time Peter died in 1725, Russia had become a great military power and an important European state.

England and Limited Monarchy

Q FOCUS QUESTION: How and why did England avoid the path of absolutism?

Not all states were absolutist in the seventeenth century. One of the most prominent examples of resistance to absolute monarchy came in England, where king and Parliament struggled to determine the roles each should play in governing England.

Conflict Between King and Parliament

With the death of the childless Queen Elizabeth I in 1603, the Tudor dynasty became extinct, and the Stuart line of rulers was inaugurated with the accession to the throne of Elizabeth's cousin, King James VI of Scotland, who became James I (1603–1625) of England. James espoused the divine right of kings, a viewpoint that alienated Parliament, which had grown accustomed under the Tudors to act on the premise that monarch and Parliament together ruled England as a "balanced polity." Then, too, the **Puritans**—Protestants within the Anglican Church who, inspired by Calvinist theology, wished to eliminate every trace of Roman Catholicism from the Church of England—were alienated by the king's strong defense of the Anglican Church. Many of England's gentry, mostly well-to-do landowners, had become Puritans and formed an important and substantial part of the House of Commons, the lower house of Parliament. It was not wise to alienate these men.

The conflict that had begun during the reign of James came to a head during the reign of his son Charles I (1625–1649). Like his father, Charles believed in divine-right monarchy, and religious differences also added to the hostility between Charles I and Parliament. The king's attempt to impose more ritual on the Anglican Church struck the Puritans as a return to Catholic practices. When Charles tried to force the Puritans to accept his religious policies, thousands of them went off to the "howling wildernesses" of America.

Civil War and Commonwealth

Grievances mounted until England finally slipped into a civil war (1642–1648) won by the parliamentary forces, due largely to the New Model Army of Oliver Cromwell, the only real military genius of the war. The New Model Army was composed primarily of more extreme Puritans known as the Independents, who, in typical Calvinist fashion, believed they were doing battle for God. As Cromwell wrote in one of his military reports, "Sir, this is none other but the hand of God; and to Him alone belongs the glory." We might give some credit to Cromwell; his soldiers were well trained in the new military tactics of the seventeenth century.

Civil War in England

After the execution of Charles I on January 30, 1649, Parliament abolished the monarchy and the House of Lords and proclaimed England a republic or commonwealth. But Cromwell and his army, unable to work effectively with Parliament, dispersed it by force and established a military dictatorship. After Cromwell's death in 1658, the army decided that military rule was no longer feasible and restored the monarchy in the person of Charles II, the son of Charles I.

Restoration and a Glorious Revolution

Charles was sympathetic to Catholicism, and Parliament's suspicions were aroused in 1672 when Charles took the audacious step of issuing the Declaration of Indulgence, which suspended the laws that Parliament had passed against Catholics and Puritans after the restoration of the monarchy. Parliament forced the king to suspend the declaration.

The accession of James II (1685–1688) to the crown virtually guaranteed a new constitutional crisis for England. An open and devout Catholic, his attempt to further Catholic interests made religion once more a primary cause of conflict between king and Parliament. James named Catholics to high positions in the government, army, navy, and universities. Parliamentary outcries against James's policies stopped short of rebellion because members knew that he was an old man and that his successors were his Protestant daughters Mary and Anne, born to his first wife. But on June 10, 1688, a son was born to James II's second wife, also a Catholic. Suddenly, the specter of a Catholic hereditary monarchy loomed large. A group of prominent English noblemen invited the Dutch chief executive, William of Orange, husband of James's daughter Mary, to invade England. William and Mary raised an army and invaded England while James, his wife, and their infant son fled to France. With little bloodshed, England had undergone its "Glorious Revolution."

In January 1689, Parliament offered the throne to William and Mary, who accepted it along with the provisions of a bill of rights (see the box "The Bill of Rights" on p. 441). The Bill of Rights affirmed Parliament's right to make laws and levy taxes. The rights of citizens to keep arms and have a jury trial were also confirmed. By deposing one king and establishing another,

Parliament had destroyed the divine-right theory of kingship (William was, after all, king by grace of Parliament, not God) and asserted its right to participate in the government. Parliament did not have complete control of the government, but it now had the right to participate in affairs of state. Over the next century, it would gradually prove to be the real authority in the English system of **limited (constitutional) monarchy**.

The Flourishing of European Culture

 FOCUS QUESTION: How did the artistic and literary achievements of this era reflect the political and economic developments of the period?

Despite religious wars and the growth of absolutism, European culture continued to flourish. The era was blessed with a number of prominent artists and writers.

Peter Paul Rubens, *The Landing of Marie de' Medici at Marseilles.* The Flemish painter Peter Paul Rubens played a key role in spreading the Baroque style from Italy to other parts of Europe. In *The Landing of Marie de' Medici at Marseilles*, Rubens made a dramatic use of light and color, bodies in motion, and luxurious nudes to heighten the emotional intensity of the scene. This was one of a cycle of twenty-one paintings dedicated to the queen mother of France.

The Bill of Rights

POLITICS & GOVERNMENT

IN 1688, THE ENGLISH EXPERIENCED a bloodless revolution in which the Stuart king, James II, was replaced by Mary, James's daughter, and her husband, William of Orange. After William and Mary had assumed power, Parliament passed the Bill of Rights, which set out the rights of Parliament and laid the foundation for a constitutional monarchy.

The Bill of Rights

Whereas the said late King James II having abdicated the government, and the throne being thereby vacant, his Highness the prince of Orange (whom it hath pleased Almighty God to make the glorious instrument of delivering this kingdom from popery and arbitrary power) did (by the device of the lords spiritual and temporal, and diverse principal persons of the Commons) cause letters to be written to the lords spiritual and temporal, being Protestants, and other letters to the several counties, cities, universities, boroughs, and Cinque Ports, for the choosing of such persons to represent them, as were of right to be sent to parliament, to meet and sit at Westminster upon the two and twentieth day of January, in this year 1689, in order to such an establishment as that their religion, laws, and liberties might not again be in danger of being subverted; upon which letters elections have been accordingly made.

And thereupon the said lords spiritual and temporal and Commons, pursuant to their respective letters and elections, being now assembled in a full and free representation of this nation, taking into their most serious consideration the best means for attaining the ends aforesaid, do in the first place (as their ancestors in like case have usually done), for the vindication and assertion of their ancient rights and liberties, declare:

1. That the pretended power of suspending laws, or the execution of laws, by regal authority, without consent of parliament is illegal.
2. That the pretended power of dispensing with the laws, or the execution of law by regal authority, as it hath been assumed and exercised of late, is illegal.
3. That the commission for erecting the late court of commissioners for ecclesiastical causes, and all other commissions and courts of like nature, are illegal and pernicious.
4. That levying money for or to the use of the crown by pretense of prerogative, without grant of parliament, for longer time or in other manner than the same is or shall be granted, is illegal.
5. That it is the right of the subjects to petition the king, and all commitments and prosecutions for such petitioning are illegal.
6. That the raising or keeping a standing army within the kingdom in time of peace, unless it be with consent of parliament, is against law.
7. That the subjects which are Protestants may have arms for their defense suitable to their conditions, and as allowed by law.
8. That election of members of parliament ought to be free.
9. That the freedom of speech, and debates or proceedings in parliament, ought not to be impeached or questioned in any court or place out of parliament.
10. That excessive bail ought not to be required, nor excessive fines imposed, nor cruel and unusual punishments inflicted.
11. That jurors ought to be duly impaneled and returned, and jurors which pass upon men in trials for high treason ought to be freeholders.
12. That all grants and promises of fines and forfeitures of particular persons before conviction are illegal and void.
13. And that for redress of all grievances, and for the amending, strengthening, and preserving of the laws, parliament ought to be held frequently.

 How did the Bill of Rights lay the foundation for a constitutional monarchy in England?

Source: From *The Statutes: Revised Edition* (London: Eyre & Spotiswoode, 1871), Vol. 2, pp. 10–12.

Art: The Baroque

The artistic movement known as the **Baroque** (buh-ROHK) dominated the Western artistic world for a century and a half. The Baroque began in Italy in the last quarter of the sixteenth century and spread to the rest of Europe and Latin America. Baroque artists sought to harmonize the Classical ideals of Renaissance art with the spiritual feelings of the sixteenth-century religious revival. In large part, Baroque art and architecture reflected the search for power that was characteristic of much of the seventeenth century. Baroque churches and palaces featured richly ornamented facades, sweeping staircases, and an overall splendor meant to impress people. Kings and princes wanted not only their subjects but also other kings and princes to be in awe of their power.

Baroque painting was known for its use of dramatic effects to arouse the emotions. This style was especially evident in the works of Peter Paul Rubens (1577–1640) of Flanders, a prolific artist and an important figure in the spread of the Baroque from Italy to other parts of Europe. In his artistic masterpieces, bodies in violent motion, heavily fleshed nudes, a dramatic use of light and shadow, and rich sensuous pigments converge to express highly intense emotions.

Perhaps the greatest figure of the Baroque was the Italian architect and sculptor Gian Lorenzo Bernini (JAHN loh-RENT-zoh bur-NEE-nee) (1598–1680), who completed Saint Peter's Basilica at the Vatican and designed the vast colonnade enclosing the piazza in front of it. Action, exuberance, profusion, and dramatic effects mark the work of Bernini in the interior of Saint Peter's, where his *Throne of Saint Peter* hovers in midair, held by the hands of the four great doctors of the Catholic Church. Above the chair, rays of golden light drive a mass of clouds and angels toward the spectator. In his most striking sculptural work, the *Ecstasy of Saint Theresa*, Bernini depicts a moment of mystical experience in the life of the sixteenth-century Spanish saint. The elegant draperies and the expression on her face create a sensuously real portrayal of physical ecstasy.

Art: Dutch Realism

A brilliant flowering of Dutch painting paralleled the supremacy of Dutch commerce in the seventeenth century. Wealthy patricians and burghers of Dutch urban society commissioned works of art for their guild halls, town halls, and private dwellings.

Scala/Art Resource, NY

Gian Lorenzo Bernini, *Ecstasy of Saint Theresa*. One of the great artists of the Baroque period was the Italian sculptor and architect Gian Lorenzo Bernini. The *Ecstasy of Saint Theresa*, created for the Cornaro Chapel in the Church of Santa Maria della Vittoria in Rome, was one of Bernini's most famous sculptures. Bernini sought to convey visually Theresa's mystical experience when, according to her description, an angel pierced her heart repeatedly with a golden arrow.

The subject matter of many Dutch paintings reflected the interests of this bourgeois society: portraits of themselves, group portraits of their military companies and guilds, landscapes, seascapes, genre scenes, still lifes, and the interiors of their residences. Unlike Baroque artists, Dutch painters were primarily interested in the realistic portrayal of secular everyday life.

This interest in painting scenes of everyday life is evident in the work of Judith Leyster (LESS-tur) (c. 1609–1660), who established her own independent painting career, a remarkable achievement for a woman in seventeenth-century Europe. Leyster became the first female member of the painters' Guild of Saint Luke in Haarlem, which enabled her to set up her own workshop and take on three male pupils. Musicians playing their instruments, women sewing, children laughing while playing games, and actors performing all form the subject matter of Leyster's portrayals of everyday Dutch life.

A Golden Age of Literature in England

In England, writing for the stage reached new heights between 1580 and 1640. The golden age of English literature is often called the Elizabethan era because much of the English cultural flowering occurred during Elizabeth's reign. Elizabethan literature exhibits the exuberance and pride associated with English exploits at the time (see the box "William Shakespeare: In Praise of England" on p. 443). Of all the forms of Elizabethan literature, none expressed the energy and intellectual versatility of the era better than

National Gallery of Art, Washington, DC

Judith Leyster, *Self-Portrait*. Although Judith Leyster was a well-known artist to her Dutch contemporaries, her fame diminished soon after her death. In the late nineteenth century, a Dutch art historian rediscovered her work. In her *Self-Portrait*, painted in 1635, she is seen pausing in her work in front of one the scenes of daily life that made her such a popular artist in her own day.

William Shakespeare: In Praise of England

ART & IDEAS

WILLIAM SHAKESPEARE is one of the most famous playwrights of the Western world. He was a universal genius, outclassing all others in his psychological insights, depth of characterization, imaginative skills, and versatility. His historical plays reflected the patriotic enthusiasm of the English in the Elizabethan era, as this excerpt from *Richard II* illustrates.

William Shakespeare, *Richard II*

This royal throne of kings, this sceptred isle,
This earth of majesty, this seat of Mars,
This other Eden, demi-Paradise,
This fortress built by Nature for herself
Against infection and the hand of war,
This happy breed of men, this little world,
This precious stone set in the silver sea,
Which serves it in the office of a wall
Or as a moat defensive to a house
Against the envy of less happier lands—
This blessed plot, this earth, this realm, this England,
This nurse, this teeming womb of royal kings,
Feared by their breed and famous by their birth,

Renowned for their deeds as far from home,
For Christian service and true chivalry,
As is the sepulcher in stubborn Jewry [the Holy Sepulcher in
    Jerusalem and the enduring Jewish community there]
Of the world's ransom, blessed Mary's Son—
This land of such dear souls, this dear dear land,
Dear for her reputation through the world,
Is now leased out, I die pronouncing it,
Like a tenement or pelting farm.
England, bound in with the triumphant sea,
Whose rocky shore beats back the envious siege
Of watery Neptune, is now bound in with shame,
With inky blots and rotten parchment bonds.
That England, that was wont to conquer others,
Hath made a shameful conquest of itself.
Ah, would the scandal vanish with my life,
How happy then were my ensuing death!

Q Why is William Shakespeare aptly described as not merely a playwright but a "complete man of the theater"? Which countries might Shakespeare have meant by the phrase "the envy of less happier lands"?

Source: Excerpt from "Richard II" in *Shakespeare: The Complete Works* by G. B. Harrison, copyright © 1968 by Harcourt Brace & Company and renewed 1980 by G. B. Harrison.

---

drama. And no dramatist is more famous or more accomplished than William Shakespeare (1564–1614).

Shakespeare was a "complete man of the theater." Although best known for writing plays, he was also an actor and a shareholder in the chief acting company of the time, the Lord Chamberlain's Company, which played in various London theaters. Shakespeare is to this day hailed as a genius. A master of the English language, he imbued its words with power and majesty. And his technical proficiency was matched by incredible insight into human psychology. Whether writing tragedies or comedies, Shakespeare exhibited a remarkable understanding of the human condition.

CHAPTER SUMMARY

In the last chapter, we observed how the movement of Europeans beyond Europe began to change the shape of world history. But what had made this development possible? After all, the Reformation of the sixteenth century, initially begun by Martin Luther, had brought about the religious division of Europe into Protestant and Catholic camps. By the middle of the sixteenth century, it was apparent that the religious passions of the Reformation era had brought an end to the religious unity of medieval Europe. The religious division (Catholics versus Protestants) was instrumental in beginning a series of religious wars that were complicated by economic, social, and political forces that also played a role.

The crises of the sixteenth and seventeenth centuries soon led to a search for a stable, secular order of politics and made possible the emergence of a system of nation-states in which power politics took on increasing significance. Within those states, there slowly emerged some of the machinery that made possible a growing centralization of power. In those states called absolutist, strong monarchs with the assistance of their aristocracies took the lead in providing the leadership for greater centralization. In this so-called age of absolutism, Louis XIV, the Sun King of France, was the model for other rulers. Strong monarchy also prevailed in central and eastern Europe, where three new powers made their appearance: Prussia, Austria, and Russia.

But not all European states followed the pattern of absolute monarchy. Especially important were developments in England, where a series of struggles between the king and Parliament took place in the seventeenth century. In the long run, the landed aristocracy gained power at the expense of the monarchs, thereby laying the foundations for a constitutional government in which Parliament provided the focus for the institutions of centralized power.

In all the major European states, a growing concern for power and dynamic expansion led to larger armies and greater conflict, stronger economies, and more powerful governments. From a global point of view, Europeans—with their strong governments, prosperous economies, and strengthened military forces—were beginning to dominate other parts of the world, leading to a growing belief in the superiority of their civilization.

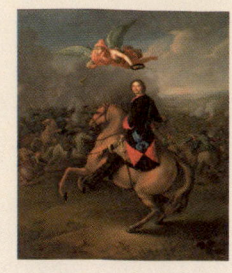

Yet despite Europeans' increasing domination of global trade markets, they had not achieved their goal of diminishing the power of Islam, first pursued during the crusades. In fact, as we shall see in the next chapter, in the midst of European expansion and exploration, three new and powerful Muslim empires were taking shape in the Middle East and South Asia.

CHAPTER TIMELINE

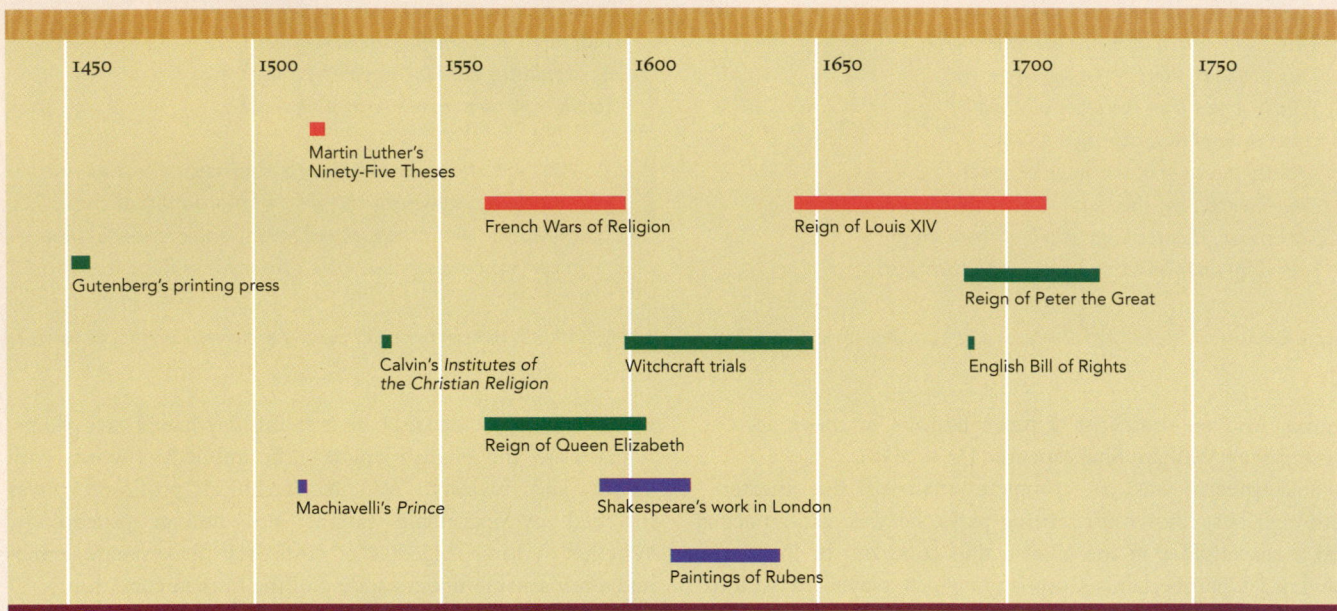

CHAPTER REVIEW

Upon Reflection

Q What role did politics play in the success of the Protestant Reformation?

Q What did Louis XIV hope to accomplish through his domestic and foreign policies? To what extent did he succeed?

Q What role did the gentry play in seventeenth-century England?

Key Terms

absolutism (p. 419)
Protestant Reformation (p. 419)
new monarchies (p. 419)
Christian humanism (northern Renaissance humanism) (p. 420)

relics (p. 421)
indulgences (p. 421)
justification by faith (p. 421)
predestination (p. 424)
Catholic Reformation (p. 428)
mercantilism (p. 432)
joint-stock company (p. 432)
divine-right monarchy (p. 435)
Puritans (p. 439)
limited (constitutional) monarchy (p. 440)
Baroque (p. 441)

Suggested Reading

THE REFORMATION: GENERAL WORKS   A basic survey of the Reformation period is **D. MacCulloch,** *The Reformation*

(New York, 2003). Also see the brief work by **U. Rublack,** *Reformation Europe* (Cambridge, 2005).

THE PROTESTANT AND CATHOLIC REFORMATIONS On Martin Luther's life, see **H. A. Oberman,** *Luther: Man Between God and the Devil* (New York, 1992), and the brief biography by **M. Marty,** *Martin Luther* (New York, 2004). On the English Reformation, see **N. L. Jones,** *English Reformation: Religion and Cultural Adaptation* (London, 2002). On John Calvin, see **W. G. Naphy,** *Calvin and the Consolidation of the Genevan Reformation* (Philadelphia, 2003). A good introduction to the Catholic Reformation can be found in **R. P. Hsia,** *The World of Catholic Renewal, 1540–1770* (Cambridge, 1998).

EUROPE IN CRISIS, 1560–1650 On the French Wars of Religion, see **R. J. Knecht,** *The French Wars of Religion, 1559–1598,* 2nd ed. (New York, 1996). The fundamental study of the Thirty Years' War is now **P. H. Wilson,** *The Thirty Years War: Europe's Tragedy* (Cambridge, Mass., 2009). Witchcraft hysteria can be examined in **R. Briggs,** *Witches and Neighbours: The Social and Cultural Context of European Witchcraft,* 2nd ed. (Oxford, 2002).

ABSOLUTE AND LIMITED MONARCHY A solid and very readable biography of Louis XIV is **J. Levi,** *Louis XIV* (New York, 2004). On the creation of the Austrian state, see **P. S. Fichtner,** *The Habsburg Monarchy, 1490–1848* (New York, 2003). See **P. H. Wilson,** *Absolutism in Central Europe* (New York, 2000), on both Prussia and Austria. On Peter the Great, see **P. Bushkovitz,** *Peter the Great* (Oxford, 2001). On the English Civil War, see **M. A. Kishlansky,** *A Monarchy Transformed* (London, 1996), and **D. Purkiss,** *The English Civil War* (New York, 2006).

EUROPEAN CULTURE For a general survey of Baroque culture, see **F. C. Marchetti et al.,** *Baroque, 1600–1770* (New York, 2005). The literature on Shakespeare is enormous. For a biography, see **S. Greenblatt,** *Will in the World: How Shakespeare Became Shakespeare* (New York, 2005).

Chapter Notes

1. Quoted in R. Bainton, *Here I Stand: A Life of Martin Luther* (New York, 1950), p. 144.

2. J. Calvin, *Institutes of the Christian Religion,* trans. J. Allen (Philadelphia, 1936), vol. 1, p. 228; vol. 2, p. 181.

3. Quoted in B. S. Anderson and J. P. Zinsser, *A History of Their Own: Women in Europe from Prehistory to the Present* (New York, 1988), vol. 1, p. 259.

4. Quoted in J. O'Malley, *The First Jesuits* (Cambridge, Mass., 1993), p. 76.

5. Quoted in J. Klaits, *Servants of Satan: The Age of Witch Hunts* (Bloomington, Ind., 1985), p. 68.

 MindTap™

MindTap is a fully online, highly personalized learning experience built upon Cengage Leaning content. MindTap combines student learning tools—readings, multimedia, activities, and assessments—into a singular Learning Path that guides students through their course.

Turks fight Christians at the Battle of Mohács

The Muslim Empires

CHAPTER OUTLINE AND FOCUS QUESTIONS

The Ottoman Empire

Q What was the ethnic composition of the Ottoman Empire, and how did the government of the sultan administer such a diverse population? How did Ottoman policy in this regard compare with the policies applied in Europe and Asia?

The Safavids

Q What problems did the Safavid Empire face, and how did its rulers attempt to solve them? How did their approaches compare with those in the other Muslim empires?

The Grandeur of the Mughals

Q What role did Islam play in the Mughal Empire, and how did the Mughals' approach to religion compare with that of the Ottomans and the Safavids? What might explain the similarities and differences?

CRITICAL THINKING

Q What were the main characteristics of each of the Muslim empires, and in what ways did they resemble each other? How were they distinct from their European counterparts?

CONNECTIONS TO TODAY

Q How would you compare the position of Islam in the world today with its position in the era described in this chapter?

THE OTTOMAN ARMY, led by Sultan Suleyman the Magnificent, arrived at Mohács, on the plains of Hungary, on an August morning in 1526. The Turkish force numbered about 100,000 men, and its weapons included three hundred new long-range cannons. Facing them was a somewhat larger European force, clothed in heavy armor but armed with only one hundred older cannons, along with a detachment of Hungarian cavalry.

The battle began at noon and was over in two hours. The Hungarian cavalry units had been destroyed, and 20,000 foot soldiers from the European army had drowned in a nearby swamp. The Ottomans had lost fewer than two hundred men. Two weeks later, they seized the Hungarian capital at Buda and prepared to lay siege to the nearby Austrian city of Vienna. Europe was in a panic, but Mohács was to be the high point of Turkish expansion in Europe.

In launching their Age of Exploration, European rulers had hoped that by controlling global markets, they could cripple the power of Islam and reduce its threat to the security of Europe. But the dream of Christian nations to expand their influence around the globe at the expense of their great Muslim rival had not been entirely achieved. On the contrary, the Muslim world, which seemed to have entered a period of decline with the collapse of the Abbasid caliphate during the era of the Mongols, managed to revive in the shadow of Europe's Age of Exploration, a period that witnessed the rise of three great Muslim empires. These powerful Muslim states—of the Ottomans, the Safavids, and the Mughals—dominated the Middle East and the South Asian subcontinent and brought a measure of stability to a region that had been in turmoil for centuries. One of them—the Ottoman Empire—managed to impose its rule over much of eastern Europe and achieve a dominant position in the Mediterranean world.

This stability, however, was not long-lived. By the end of the eighteenth century, much of India and the Middle East had come under severe European pressure and had returned to a state of anarchy. The Ottoman Empire was still substantially intact, but it no longer threatened the Christian nations in Europe, and some observers were convinced that it was in a state of irreversible decline. ◄

The Ottoman Empire

 FOCUS QUESTIONS: What was the ethnic composition of the Ottoman Empire, and how did the government of the sultan administer such a diverse population? How did Ottoman policy in this regard compare with the policies applied in Europe and Asia?

The Ottoman Turks were among the Turkic-speaking nomadic peoples who had spread westward from Central Asia in the ninth, tenth, and eleventh centuries. The first to appear in the Middle East were the Seljuk Turks, who initially attempted to revive the declining Abbasid caliphate in Baghdad. Later they established themselves in the Anatolian peninsula as the successors to the Byzantine Empire. Turks served as warriors or administrators, while the peasants who tilled the farmland were mainly Greek.

The Rise of the Ottoman Turks

In the late thirteenth century, a new group of Turks under the tribal leader Osman (os-MAHN) (r. 1280–1326) began to consolidate power in the northwestern corner of the Anatolian peninsula. That land had been given to them by the Seljuk rulers as a reward for helping drive out the Mongols in the late thirteenth century. At first, the Osman Turks were relatively peaceful and engaged in pastoral pursuits, but as the Seljuk empire began to crumble in the early fourteenth century, the Osman Turks began to expand and founded the Osmanli (os-MAHN-lee) dynasty, with its capital at Bursa (BURR-suh). The Osmanlis later came to be known as the Ottomans.

A key advantage for the Ottomans was their location in the northwestern corner of the peninsula. From there they were able to expand westward and eventually take over the Bosporus and the Dardanelles, between the Mediterranean and the Black Seas. The Byzantine Empire, of course, had controlled the area for centuries, serving as a buffer between the Muslim Middle East and the Latin West. The Byzantines, however, had been severely weakened by the sack of Constantinople in the Fourth Crusade in 1204 and the occupation of much of the empire by western Europeans for the next half century. In 1345, Ottoman forces under their leader Orkhan (or-KHAHN) I (r. 1326–1360)

crossed the Bosporus for the first time to support a usurper against the Byzantine emperor in Constantinople. Setting up their first European base at Gallipoli (gah-LIP-poh-lee) at the Mediterranean entrance to the Dardanelles, Turkish forces expanded gradually into the Balkans and allied with fractious Serbian and Bulgar forces against the Byzantines. In these unstable conditions, the Ottomans gradually established permanent settlements throughout the area, where Turkish provincial governors, called **beys** (BAYS) (from the Turkish *beg*, "knight"), collected taxes from the local Slavic peasants after driving out the previous landlords. The Ottoman leader now began to claim the title of sultan (SUL-tun) or sovereign of his domain.

In 1360, Orkhan was succeeded by his son Murad (moo-RAHD) I, who consolidated Ottoman power in the Balkans, set up a capital at Edirne (eh-DEER-nay) (see Map 16.1), and gradually reduced the Byzantine emperor to a vassal. Murad did not initially attempt to conquer Constantinople because his forces were composed mostly of the traditional Turkish cavalry and lacked the ability to breach the strong walls of the city. Instead, he began to build up a strong military administration based on the recruitment of Christians into an elite guard. Called **janissaries** (JAN-nih-say-reez) (from the Turkish *yeni cheri*, "new troops"), they were recruited from the local Christian population in the Balkans and then converted to Islam and trained as foot soldiers or administrators. One of the major advantages of the janissaries was that they were directly subordinated to the sultanate and therefore owed their loyalty to the person of the sultan. Other military forces were organized by the beys and were thus loyal to their local tribal leaders.

The janissary corps also represented a response to changes in warfare. As the knowledge of firearms spread in the late fourteenth century, the Turks began to master the new technology, including siege cannons and muskets (see the Comparative Essay "The Changing Face of War" on p. 449). The traditional nomadic cavalry charge was now outmoded and was superseded by infantry forces armed with muskets. Thus, the janissaries provided a well-armed infantry that served both as an elite guard to protect the palace and as a means of extending Turkish control in the Balkans. With his new forces, Murad defeated the Serbs at the famous Battle of Kosovo (KAWSS-suh-voh) in 1389 and ended Serbian hegemony in the area.

Expansion of the Empire

Under Murad's successor, Bayazid (by-uh-ZEED) I (r. 1389–1402), the Ottomans advanced northward, annexed Bulgaria, and slaughtered the French cavalry at a major battle on the Danube. A defeat at Ankara (AN-kuh-ruh) at the hands of the Mongol warrior Tamerlane (see Chapter 9) in 1402 proved to be only a temporary setback. When Mehmet (meh-MET) II (r. 1451–1481) succeeded to the throne, he was determined to capture Constantinople. Already in control of the Dardanelles, he ordered the construction of a major fortress on the Bosporus just north of the city, which put the Turks in a position to strangle the Byzantines.

MAP 16.1 The Ottoman Empire. This map shows the territorial growth of the Ottoman Empire from the eve of the conquest of Constantinople in 1453 to the end of the seventeenth century, when a defeat at the hands of Austria led to the loss of a substantial portion of central Europe.

Q *Where did the Ottomans come from?*

THE FALL OF CONSTANTINOPLE The last Byzantine emperor desperately called for help from the Europeans, but only the Genoese came to his defense. With 80,000 troops ranged against only 6,000 to 8,000 defenders, Mehmet laid siege to Constantinople in 1453. In their attack on the city, the Turks made use of massive cannons with 26-foot barrels that could launch stone balls weighing up to 1,200 pounds each. The Byzantines stretched heavy chains across the Golden Horn, the inlet that forms the city's harbor, to prevent a naval attack from the north and prepared to make their final stand behind the 13-mile-long wall along the western edge of the city. But Mehmet's forces seized the tip of the peninsula north of the Golden Horn and then dragged their ships overland across the peninsula from the Bosporus and put them into the water behind the chains. Finally, the walls were breached; the Byzantine emperor died in the final battle (see the box "The Fall of Constantinople" on p. 450). Mehmet II, standing before the palace of the emperor, paused

to reflect on the passing nature of human glory. But it was not long before he and the Ottomans were again on the march.

THE ADVANCE INTO WESTERN ASIA AND AFRICA With their new capital at Constantinople, eventually renamed Istanbul, the Ottoman Turks had become a dominant force in the Balkans and the Anatolian peninsula. They now began to advance to the east against the Shi'ite kingdom of the Safavids (sah-FAH-weeds) in Persia (see "The Safavids" later in this chapter), which had been promoting rebellion among the Anatolian tribal population and disrupting Turkish trade through the Middle East. After defeating the Safavids at a major battle in 1514, Emperor Selim (seh-LEEM) I (r. 1512–1520) consolidated Turkish control over Mesopotamia and then turned his attention to the Mamluks (MAM-looks) in Egypt, who had failed to support the Ottomans in their struggle against the Safavids. The Mamluks were defeated in Syria in 1516; Cairo

COMPARATIVE ESSAY

The Changing Face of War

SCIENCE & TECHNOLOGY

"War," as the renowned French historian Fernand Braudel once observed, "has always been a matter of arms and techniques. Improved techniques can radically alter the course of events." Braudel's remark was directed to the situation in the Mediterranean region during the sixteenth century, when the adoption of artillery changed the face of warfare and gave enormous advantages to the countries—such as the Ottoman Empire—that stood at the head of the new technological revolution in firearms. But it can just as easily be applied to the present day, when potential adversaries possess weapons capable of reaching across oceans and continents.

One crucial aspect of military superiority, of course, lies in the nature of weaponry. From the invention of the bow and arrow to the advent of the atomic era, the possession of superior instruments of war has provided a distinct advantage against a poorly armed enemy. It was at least partly the possession of bronze weapons, for example, that enabled the invading Hyksos to conquer Egypt during the second millennium B.C.E.

Mobility is another factor of vital importance. During the second millennium B.C.E., horse-drawn chariots revolutionized the art of war from the Mediterranean Sea to the Yellow River valley in northern China. Later, the invention of the stirrup enabled mounted warriors to shoot arrows from horseback, a technique applied with great effect by the Mongols as they devastated civilizations across the Eurasian supercontinent.

To protect themselves from marauding warriors, settled societies began to erect massive walls around their cities and fortresses. That in turn led to the invention of siege weapons like the catapult and the battering ram. The Mongols allegedly even came up with an early form of chemical warfare, hurling human bodies infected with the plague into the bastions of their enemies.

The invention of explosives launched the next great revolution in warfare. First used as a weapon of war by the Tang

Roman troops defeating Celtic warriors; from the Great Altar of Pergamum.

© William J. Duiker

Dynasty in China, explosives were brought to the West by the Turks, who used them with great effectiveness in the fifteenth century against the Byzantine Empire. But the Europeans quickly mastered the new technology and took it to new heights, inventing handheld firearms and mounting iron cannons on their warships. The latter represented a significant advantage to European fleets as they began to compete with rivals for control of the Indian and Pacific Oceans.

The twentieth century saw revolutionary new developments in the art of warfare, from armed vehicles to airplanes to nuclear arms. But as weapons grow ever more fearsome, they are more dangerous to use, resulting in the paradox of the Vietnam War, when lightly armed Viet Cong guerrilla units were able to fight the world's mightiest army to a virtual standstill. As the Chinese military strategist Sun Tzu had long ago observed, victory in war often goes to the smartest, not the strongest.

 Why were the Europeans, rather than other peoples, able to make effective use of firearms to expand their influence throughout the world?

---

fell a year later. Now controlling several of the holy cities of Islam, including Jerusalem, Mecca, and Medina, Selim declared himself the new caliph, or successor to Muhammad. During the next few years, Turkish armies and fleets advanced westward along the African coast, occupying Tripoli, Tunis, and Algeria and eventually penetrating almost to the Strait of Gibraltar (see Map 16.1). In their advance, the invaders had

taken advantage of the progressive disintegration of the Nasrid (NAS-rid) dynasty in Morocco, which had been in decline for decades and had lost its last foothold on the European continent when Granada fell to Spain in 1492.

The impact of Turkish rule on the peoples of North Africa was relatively light. Like their predecessors, the Turks were Muslims, and they preferred where possible to administer

The Fall of Constantinople

POLITICS & GOVERNMENT

FEW EVENTS IN THE HISTORY of the Ottoman Empire are more dramatic than the conquest of Constantinople in 1453. In this excerpt, the conquest is described by Kritovoulos, a Greek who later served in the Ottoman administration. Although the author did not witness the conquest itself, he was apparently well informed about the event and provides us with a vivid description.

Kritovoulos, *Life of Mehmed the Conqueror*

[H]e [the Sultan] led them himself. And they, with a shout on the run and with a fearsome yell, went on ahead of the Sultan, pressing on up to the palisade. After a long and bitter struggle they hurled back the Romans [Byzantines] from there and climbed by force up the palisade. They dashed some of their foe down into the ditch between the great wall and the palisade, which was deep and hard to get out of, and they killed them there. The rest they drove back to the gate.

He had opened this gate in the great wall, so as to go easily over to the palisade. Now there was a great struggle there and great slaughter among those stationed there, for they were attacked by the heavy infantry and not a few others in irregular formation, who had been attracted from many points by the shouting. There the Emperor Constantine [Constantine XI Palaeologus], with all who were with him, fell in gallant combat.

The heavy infantry were already streaming through the little gate into the City, and others had rushed in through the breach in the great wall. Then all the rest of the army, with a rush and a roar, poured in brilliantly and scattered all over the City. And the Sultan stood before the great wall, where the standard also was and the ensigns, and watched the proceedings. The day was already breaking....

The soldiers fell on them [the citizens] with anger and great wrath. For one thing, they were actuated by the hardships of the siege. For another, some foolish people had hurled taunts and curses at them from the battlements all through the siege. Now, in general they killed so as to frighten all the City, and to terrorize and enslave all by the slaughter.

When they had had enough of murder, and the City was reduced to slavery, some of the troops turned to the mansions of the mighty, by bands and companies and divisions, for plunder and spoil. Others went to the robbing of churches, and others dispersed to the simple homes of the common people, stealing, robbing, plundering, killing, insulting, taking and enslaving men, women, and children, old and young, priests, monks—in short, every age and class....

After this the Sultan entered the City and looked about to see its great size, its situation, its grandeur and beauty, its teeming population, its loveliness, and the costliness of its churches and public buildings and of the private houses and community houses and those of the officials.... When he saw what a large number had been killed, and the ruin of the buildings, and the wholesale ruin and destruction of the City, he was filled with compassion and repented not a little at the destruction and plundering. Tears fell from his eyes as he groaned deeply and passionately: "What a city we have given over to plunder and destruction."

 What strategy did the Turkish forces use to seize the city of Constantinople? Compare this description of the capture of Constantinople to the description of its capture 250 years earlier described in the box "Christian Crusaders Capture Constantinople" on p. 370. What are the similarities? What are the differences?

Source: From Kritovoulos, *Life of Mehmed the Conqueror*, trans. Charles T. Riggs. © 1954 Princeton University Press. © renewed 1982 Princeton University Press.

---

their conquered regions through local rulers. The central government utilized appointed **pashas** (PAH-shuz) who were directly responsible to Istanbul; the pashas collected taxes, paying a fixed percentage as tribute to the central government, and maintained law and order. The Turks ruled from coastal cities such as Algiers, Tunis, and Tripoli and made no attempt to control the interior beyond maintaining the trade routes through the Sahara to the commercial centers along the Niger River. Meanwhile, local pirates along the Barbary Coast—the northern coast of Africa from Egypt to the Atlantic Ocean—competed with their Christian rivals in raiding the shipping that passed through the Mediterranean.

By the seventeenth century, the links between the imperial court in Istanbul and its appointed representatives in the Turkish regencies in North Africa had begun to weaken. Some of the pashas were dethroned by local elites, while others, such as the bey of Tunis, became hereditary rulers. Even Egypt, whose agricultural wealth and control over the route to the Red Sea made it the most important country in the area to the Turks, gradually became autonomous under a new official class of janissaries. Many of them became wealthy landowners by exploiting their official positions and collecting tax revenues far in excess of what they had to remit to Istanbul. In the early eighteenth century, the Mamluks returned to power, although the Turkish government managed to retain some control by means of a viceroy appointed from Istanbul.

TURKISH EXPANSION IN EUROPE After their conquest of Constantinople in 1453, the Ottoman Turks tried to complete their conquest of the Balkans, where they had been established since the fourteenth century. Although they were successful in taking the Romanian territory of Wallachia (wah-LAY-kee-uh) in 1476, the resistance of the Hungarians initially kept the Turks from advancing up the Danube valley. From 1480 to 1520, internal problems and the need to consolidate their eastern frontiers kept the Turks from any further attacks on Europe.

Suleyman (SOO-lay-mahn) I the Magnificent (r. 1520–1566), however, brought the Turks back to Europe's attention. Advancing up the Danube, the Turks seized Belgrade in 1521 and won a major victory over the Hungarians at the Battle of Mohács (MOH-hach) on the Danube in 1526. Subsequently, the Turks overran most of Hungary, moved into Austria, and advanced as far as Vienna, where they were finally repulsed in 1529. At the same time, they extended their power into the western Mediterranean and threatened to turn it into a Turkish lake until a large Turkish fleet was destroyed by the Spanish at Lepanto in 1571. Despite the defeat, the Turks continued to hold nominal suzerainty over the southern shores of the Mediterranean. One year after Lepanto, the Turks reconstituted their fleet and seized the island of Cyprus. Responding to the joy expressed in Europe over the naval victory at Lepanto, the **grand vizier** (veh-ZEER) (Turkish *vezir*), or chief minister, in Constantinople remarked to the Venetian ambassador, "There is a big difference between our loss and yours. In taking Cyprus, we have cut off one of your arms. In sinking our fleet you only shaved our beard. A lost arm cannot be replaced, but a shorn beard grows back quickly to its prior magnificence."[1]

Although Christians in Europe frequently called for new Crusades against the "infidel" Turks, by the beginning of the seventeenth century the Ottoman Empire was being treated like any other European power by European rulers seeking alliances and trade concessions. During the first half of the seventeenth century, the Ottoman Empire was viewed as a "sleeping giant." Involved in domestic bloodletting and heavily threatened by a challenge from Persia, the Ottomans were content with the status quo in eastern Europe. But under a new line of grand viziers in the second half of the seventeenth century, the Ottoman Empire again took the offensive. By mid-1683, the Ottomans had marched through the Hungarian plain and once again laid siege to Vienna. Repulsed by a mixed army of Austrians, Poles, Bavarians, and Saxons, the Turks retreated and were pushed out of Hungary by a new European coalition. Although they retained the core of their empire, the Ottoman Turks would never again be a threat to Europe and, by the end of the seventeenth and the eighteenth centuries, they faced new challenges from the ever-expanding Austrian Empire in southeastern Europe and the new Russian giant to the north.

The Nature of Turkish Rule

Like other Muslim empires in Persia and India, the Ottoman political system was the result of the evolution of tribal institutions into a sedentary empire. At the apex of the Ottoman system was the sultan, who was the supreme authority in both a political and a military sense. The origins of this system can be traced back to the bey, who was only a tribal leader, a first among equals, who could claim loyalty from his chiefs so long as he could provide booty and grazing lands for his subordinates. Disputes were settled by tribal law; Muslim law was secondary. Tribal leaders collected taxes—or booty—from areas under their control and sent one-fifth on to the bey. Both administrative and military power were centralized under the bey, and the capital was wherever the bey and his administration happened to be.

THE ROLE OF THE SULTAN But the rise of empire brought about changes and an adaptation to Byzantine traditions of rule much as Abbasid political practices had been affected by Persian monarchical tradition at an earlier time in Baghdad. The status and prestige of the sultan now increased relative to the subordinate tribal leaders, and the position took on the trappings of imperial rule. Court rituals were inherited from the Byzantines and Persians, and a centralized administrative system was adopted that increasingly isolated the sultan in his palace. The position of the sultan was hereditary, with a son, although not necessarily the eldest, always succeeding the father. This practice led to chronic succession struggles upon the death of individual sultans, and the losers were often executed (strangled with a silk bowstring) or later imprisoned. Potential heirs to the throne were assigned as provincial governors to provide them with experience.

THE HAREM The heart of the sultan's power was in the Topkapi (tahp-KAH-pee) Palace in the center of Istanbul. Topkapi (meaning "cannon gate") was constructed in 1459 by Mehmet II and served as an administrative center as well as the private residence of the sultan and his family. Eventually, it had a staff of 20,000 employees. The private domain of the sultan was called the **harem** ("sacred place"). Here he resided with his concubines. Normally, a sultan did not marry but chose several concubines as his favorites; they were accorded this status after they gave birth to sons. When a son became a sultan, his mother became known as the queen mother and served as adviser to the throne. This tradition, initiated by the influential wife of Suleyman the Magnificent, often resulted in considerable authority for the queen mother in affairs of state.

Like the janissaries, members of the harem were often of slave origin and formed an elite element in Ottoman society. Since the enslavement of Muslims was forbidden, slaves were taken among non-Islamic peoples. Some concubines were prisoners selected for the position, while others were purchased or offered to the sultan as gifts. They were then trained and educated like the janissaries in a system called *devshirme* (dev-SHEER-may) ("collection"). *Devshirme* had originated in the practice of requiring local clan leaders to provide prisoners to the sultan as part of their tax obligation. Talented males were given special training for eventual placement in military or administrative positions, while their female counterparts were trained for service in the harem, with instruction in reading, the Qur'an, sewing and embroidery, and musical performance. They were ranked according to their status, and some were permitted to leave the harem to marry officials. If they were later divorced, they were sometimes allowed to return to the harem.

Unique to the Ottoman Empire from the fifteenth century onward was the exclusive use of slaves to reproduce its royal heirs. Contrary to myth, few of the women of the imperial harem were used for sexual purposes, as the majority were relatives of the sultan's extended family—sisters, daughters, widowed mothers, and in-laws, with their own personal slaves and entourages. Contemporary European observers compared the atmosphere in the Topkapi harem to a Christian nunnery, with its hierarchical organization, enforced chastity, and rule of silence.

The Sultan's Chambers in Topkapi Palace. After his conquest of Constantinople in 1453, Mehmet II constructed the extensive palace compound known as Topkapi as his royal residence and the seat of the new government. Set on a high promontory overlooking the Bosporus and the Sea of Marmara, this self-contained city housed over four thousand people and included a royal harem, dormitories, libraries, schools, mosques, a hospital, and gardens with fountains. Shown here (left) is the sultan's imperial throne room. The walls of the harem are covered with magnificent tile work designs, including this design of colorful flowers in vases (right).

Because of their proximity to the sultan, the women of the harem often wielded so much political power that the era has been called the "sultanate of women." Queen mothers administered the imperial household and engaged in diplomatic relations with other countries while controlling the marital alliances of their daughters with senior civilian and military officials or members of other royal families in the region. One princess was married seven separate times from the age of two after her previous husbands died either in battle or by execution.

ADMINISTRATION OF THE GOVERNMENT The sultan ruled through an imperial council that met four days a week and was chaired by the grand vizier. The sultan often attended behind a screen, whence he could privately indicate his desires to the grand vizier. The latter presided over the imperial bureaucracy. Like the palace guard, the bureaucrats were not an exclusive group but were chosen at least partly by merit from a palace school for training officials. Most officials were Muslims by birth, but some talented janissaries became senior members of the bureaucracy, and almost all the later grand viziers came from the *devshirme* system.

Recruitment of the Children. The Ottoman Empire, like its Chinese counterpart, sought to recruit its officials on the basis of merit. Through the system called *devshirme* ("collection"), youthful candidates were selected from the non-Muslim population in villages throughout the empire. In this painting, an imperial officer is counting coins to pay for the children's travel expenses to Istanbul, where they will undergo extensive academic and military training. Note the concern of two of the mothers and a priest as they question the official, who undoubtedly underwent the process himself as a child. As they leave their family and friends, the children carry their worldly possessions in bags slung over their shoulders.

Local administration during the imperial period was a product of Turkish tribal tradition and was similar in some respects to fief-holding in Europe. The empire was divided into provinces and districts governed by officials who, like their tribal predecessors, combined both civil and military functions. They were assisted by bureaucrats trained in the palace school in Istanbul. Senior officials were assigned land in fief by the sultan and were then responsible for collecting taxes and supplying armies to the empire. These lands were then farmed out to the local cavalry elite called the *sipahis* (suh-PAH-heez), who obtained their salaries by exacting a tax from all peasants in their fiefdoms. These local officials were not hereditary aristocrats, but sons often inherited their fathers' landholdings, and the vast majority were descendants of the beys who had formed the tribal elites before the imperial period.

Religion and Society in the Ottoman World

Like most Turkic-speaking peoples in the Anatolian peninsula and throughout the Middle East, the Ottoman ruling elites were Sunni Muslims. Ottoman sultans had claimed the title of caliph ("defender of the faith") since the early sixteenth century and thus were theoretically responsible for guiding the flock and maintaining Islamic law, the *Shari'a*. In practice, the sultan assigned these duties to a supreme religious authority, who administered the law and maintained a system of schools for educating Muslims.

Islamic law and customs were applied to all Muslims in the empire. Although most Turkic-speaking people were Sunni Muslims, some communities were attracted to Sufism (see Chapter 7) or other heterodox doctrines. The government tolerated such activities as long as their practitioners remained loyal to the empire, but in the early sixteenth century, unrest among these groups—some of whom converted to the Shi'ite version of Islam—outraged the conservative *ulama* and eventually led to war against the Safavids (see "The Safavids" later in this chapter).

THE TREATMENT OF MINORITIES Non-Muslims—mostly Orthodox Christians (Greeks and Slavs), Jews, and Armenian Christians—formed a significant minority within the empire, which treated them with relative tolerance. Non-Muslims were compelled to pay a head tax (as compensation for their exemption from military service), and they were permitted to practice their religion or convert to Islam (people who were already Muslim were prohibited from adopting another faith). Most of the population in European areas of the empire remained Christian, but in some places, such as the Balkan territory now known as Bosnia and Herzegovina, substantial numbers converted to Islam.

Each religious group within the empire was organized as an administrative unit called a *millet* (mi-LET) ("nation" or "community"). Each group, including the Muslims themselves, had its own patriarch, priest, or grand rabbi who dealt as an intermediary with the government and administered the community according to its own laws. The leaders of the individual *millets* were responsible to the sultan and his officials for the behavior of the subjects under their care and collected taxes for transmission to the government. Each *millet*

CHRONOLOGY The Ottoman Empire

Reign of Osman I	1280–1326
Ottoman Turks cross the Bosporus	1345
Murad I consolidates Turkish power in the Balkans	1360
Ottomans defeat the Serbian army at Kosovo	1389
Tamerlane defeats the Ottoman army at Ankara	1402
Reign of Mehmet II the Conqueror	1451–1481
Turkish conquest of Constantinople	1453
Turks defeat the Mamluks in Syria and seize Cairo	1516–1517
Reign of Suleyman I the Magnificent	1520–1566
Defeat of the Hungarians at Battle of Mohács	1526
Defeat of the Turks at Vienna	1529
Battle of Lepanto	1571
Second siege of Vienna	1683

established its own system of justice, set its own educational policies, and provided welfare for the needy.

Nomadic peoples were placed in a separate *millet* and were subject to their own regulations and laws. They were divided into the traditional nomadic classifications of tribes, clans, and "tents" (individual families) and were governed by their hereditary chiefs, the beys. As we have seen, the beys were responsible for administration and for collecting taxes for the state.

SOCIAL CLASSES The subjects of the Ottoman Empire were also divided by occupation and place of residence. In addition to the ruling class, there were four main occupational groups: peasants, artisans, merchants, and pastoral peoples. The first three were classified as "urban" residents. Peasants tilled land that was leased to them by the state (ultimate ownership of all land resided with the sultan), but the land was deeded to them, so they were able to pass it on to their heirs. They were not allowed to sell the land and thus in practice were forced to remain on the soil. Taxes were based on the amount of land the peasants possessed and were paid to the local sipahis, who held the district in fief.

Artisans were organized according to craft guilds. Each guild, headed by a council of elders, was responsible not only for dealing with the governmental authorities but also for providing financial services, social security, and training for its members. Outside the ruling elite, merchants were the most privileged class in Ottoman society. They were largely exempt from government regulations and taxes and were therefore able in many cases to amass large fortunes. Charging interest was technically illegal under Islamic law, but the rules were often ignored in practice. In the absence of regulations, merchants often established monopolies and charged high prices, which caused them to be bitterly resented by other subjects of the empire.

THE POSITION OF WOMEN Technically, women in the Ottoman Empire were subject to the same restrictions that afflicted their counterparts in other Muslim societies, but their position was ameliorated to some degree by a variety of factors. In the first place, non-Muslims were subject to the laws and customs of their own religions; thus, Orthodox Christian,

Armenian Christian, and Jewish women were spared some of the restrictions applied to their Muslim sisters (although they were then subject to restrictions imposed by their own faith). In the second place, Islamic laws as applied in the Ottoman Empire defined the legal position of women comparatively tolerantly. Women were permitted to own and inherit property, including their dowries. They could not be forced into marriage and in certain cases were permitted to seek a divorce. As we have seen, women often exercised considerable influence in the palace and in a few instances even served as senior officials, such as governors of provinces. The relatively tolerant attitude toward women in Ottoman-held territories has been ascribed by some to Turkish tribal traditions, which took a more egalitarian view of gender roles than the sedentary societies of the region did.

The Ottoman Empire Under Challenge

The Ottoman Empire reached its zenith under Suleyman the Magnificent, often known as Suleyman Kanuni, or "the lawgiver," who launched the conquest of Hungary. But Suleyman also sowed the seeds of later difficulties for his successors. He executed his two most able sons on suspicion of factionalism and was succeeded by Selim II (the Sot, or "the drunken sultan"), the only surviving son and a disaster as ruler.

By the late seventeenth century, the expansionist tendencies of earlier eras had largely disappeared, although the first loss of imperial territory did not occur until 1699, at the Treaty of Karlowitz (KARL-oh-vits), when the Ottomans lost substantial territories in central Europe. Apparently, a number of factors were involved. In the first place, the administrative system inherited from the tribal period began to break down. Although the *devshirme* system of training officials continued to function, *devshirme* graduates were now permitted to marry and inherit property and to enroll their sons in the palace corps. Thus, they were gradually transformed from a meritocratic administrative elite into a privileged and often degenerate hereditary caste. Local administrators were corrupted and taxes rose as the central bureaucracy lost its links with rural areas. The imperial treasury was depleted by constant wars, and transport and communications were neglected. Interest in science and technology, once a hallmark of the Arab empire, had not kept up with developments in Europe. In addition, the empire was increasingly beset by economic difficulties, caused by the diversion of trade routes away from the eastern Mediterranean and the price inflation brought about by the influx of cheap American silver.

Ottoman society was by no means isolated from the outside world. Sophisticated officials and merchants began to mimic the habits and lifestyles of their European counterparts, dressing in the European fashion, purchasing Western furniture and art objects, and ignoring Muslim strictures against the consumption of alcohol and sexual activities outside marriage. During the sixteenth and early seventeenth centuries, coffee and tobacco were introduced into polite Ottoman society, and cafés for the consumption of both began to appear in the major cities (see the box "A Turkish Discourse on Coffee" on p. 455). Such behavior aroused concern in some quarters. One sultan in the early seventeenth century issued a decree prohibiting the consumption of both coffee and tobacco, arguing (correctly, no doubt) that many cafés were nests of antigovernment intrigue. He even began to wander incognito through the streets of Istanbul at night. Any of his subjects detected in immoral or illegal acts were summarily executed and their bodies left on the streets as an example to others.

One of the key weaknesses in Ottoman society after the seventeenth century was that the ruling family lost much of its vitality. Whereas the first sultans reigned twenty-seven years on average, later ones averaged only thirteen years, and the laws of succession appeared to operate against the stability of the state. The throne routinely went to the oldest surviving male, while his rivals were kept secluded in a latticed cage and thus had no governmental experience if they succeeded to rule. Later sultans also became less involved in government, and more power flowed to the office of the grand vizier, called the **Sublime Porte** (PORT), or to eunuchs and members of the harem. Palace intrigue increased as a result.

The Ottoman Empire: A Civilization in Decline?

Over the years, many observers have interpreted the conditions described in the previous section as clear signs that the Ottoman Empire was entering a period of decline, a long slide that ultimately resulted in the collapse of the sultanate in the early twentieth century. Recently, however, some historians—undoubtedly inspired by the desire to discredit the traditional Eurocentric view of history—have taken issue with this paradigm, maintaining that in many respects the empire remained relatively healthy up to the twentieth century and had actually begun to reform itself when World War I broke out in 1914 (see Chapter 24). The debate perhaps hinges more on semantics than on the interpretation of relevant facts. Although some Ottoman rulers made significant efforts during the nineteenth century to initiate reforms in the system, the results were relatively meager, and when war broke out in 1914, the old empire had fallen significantly behind its European counterparts in meeting the challenges of the new century. In that respect, as we shall see, it was hardly alone.

Ottoman Art

The Ottoman sultans were enthusiastic patrons of the arts and maintained large ateliers of artisans and artists, primarily at the Topkapi Palace in Istanbul but also in other important cities of the vast empire. The period from Mehmet II in the fifteenth century to the early eighteenth century witnessed a flourishing of pottery, rugs, silk and other textiles, jewelry, arms and armor, and calligraphy. All adorned the palaces of the new rulers, testifying to their opulence and exquisite taste. The artists came from all parts of the realm and beyond. Besides Turks, there were Persians, Greeks, Armenians, Hungarians, and Italians, all vying for the esteem and generous rewards of the sultans and fearing that losing favor might mean losing their heads! In the second half of the sixteenth century, Istanbul alone listed more than 150 craft guilds, ample proof of the artistic activity of the era.

A Turkish Discourse on Coffee

INTERACTION & EXCHANGE

COFFEE WAS INTRODUCED to Turkey from the Arabian peninsula in the mid-sixteenth century and reportedly came to Europe during the Turkish siege of Vienna in 1527. The following account was written by Katib Chelebi (kah-TEEB CHEL-uh-bee), a seventeenth-century Turkish author who compiled an extensive encyclopedia and bibliography. In *The Balance of Truth*, he described how coffee entered the empire and the problems it caused for public morality. In the Muslim world, as in Europe and later in colonial America, rebellious elements often met in coffeehouses to promote antigovernment activities. Chelebi died in Istanbul in 1657, reportedly while drinking a cup of coffee.

Katib Chelebi, *The Balance of Truth*

[Coffee] originated in Yemen and has spread, like tobacco, over the world. Certain sheikhs, who lived with their dervishes [ascetic followers] in the mountains of Yemen, used to crush and eat the berries … of a certain tree. Some would roast them and drink their water. Coffee is a cold dry food, suited to the ascetic life and sedative of lust….

It came to Asia Minor by sea, about 1543, and met with a hostile reception, *fetwas* [decrees] being delivered against it. For they said, Apart from its being roasted, the fact that it is drunk in gatherings, passed from hand to hand, is suggestive of loose living. It is related of Abul-Suud Efendi that he had holes bored in the ships that brought it, plunging their cargoes of coffee into the sea. But these strictures and prohibitions availed nothing…. One coffeehouse was opened after another, and men would gather together, with great eagerness and enthusiasm, to drink. Drug addicts in particular, finding it a life-giving thing, which increased their pleasure, were willing to die for a cup.

Storytellers and musicians diverted the people from their employments, and working for one's living fell into disfavor. Moreover the people, from prince to beggar, amused themselves with knifing one another. Toward the end of 1633, the late Ghazi Gultan Murad, becoming aware of the situation, promulgated an edict, out of regard and compassion for the people, to this effect: Coffeehouses throughout the Guarded Domains shall be dismantled and not opened hereafter. Since then, the coffeehouses of the capital have been as desolate as the heart of the ignorant…. But in cities and towns outside Istanbul, they are opened just as before. As has been said above, such things do not admit of a perpetual ban.

Why did coffee come to be regarded as a dangerous substance in the Ottoman Empire? Were the authorities successful in suppressing its consumption?

Source: From *The Balance of Truth* by Katib Chelebi, translated by G. L. Lewis, copyright 1927.

ARCHITECTURE By far the greatest contribution of the Ottoman Empire to world art was its architecture, especially the magnificent mosques of the second half of the sixteenth century. Traditionally, prayer halls in mosques were subdivided by numerous pillars that supported small individual domes, creating a private, forestlike atmosphere. The Turks, however, modeled their new mosques on the open floor plan of the Byzantine church of Hagia Sophia (completed in 537), which had been turned into a mosque by Mehmet II, and began to push the pillars toward the outer wall to create a prayer hall with an uninterrupted central area under one large dome. With this plan, large numbers of believers could worship in unison in accordance with Muslim preference. By the mid-sixteenth century, the greatest of all Ottoman architects, Sinan (si-NAHN), began erecting the first of his eighty-one mosques with an uncluttered prayer area. Each was topped by an imposing dome, and often, as at Edirne, the entire building was framed with four towering narrow minarets. By emphasizing its vertical lines, the minarets camouflaged the massive stone bulk of the structure and gave it a feeling of incredible lightness. These four graceful minarets would find new expression sixty years later in India's white marble Taj Mahal (see "Mughal Culture" later in this chapter).

The lightness of the exterior was reinforced in the mosque's interior by the soaring height of the dome and the numerous windows. Added to this were delicate plasterwork and tile decoration that transformed the mosque into a monumental oasis of spirituality, opulence, and power. Sinan's masterpieces, such as the Suleymaniye (soo-lay-MAHN-ee-eh) and the Blue Mosque of Istanbul, were always part of a large socioreligious compound that included a library, school, hospital, mausoleums, and even bazaars, all of equally magnificent construction (see the Comparative Illustration "Hagia Sophia and the Suleymaniye Mosque" on p. 456).

Earlier, the thirteenth-century Seljuk Turks of Anatolia had created beautiful tile decorations with two-color mosaics. Now Ottoman artists invented a new glazed tile art with painted flowers and geometrical designs in brilliant blue, green, yellow, and their own secret "tomato red." Entire walls, both interior and exterior, were covered with the painted tiles, which adorned palaces as well as mosques. Produced at Iznik (the old Nicaea), the distinctive tiles and pottery were in great demand; the city's ateliers boasted more than three hundred artisans in the late sixteenth century.

TEXTILES The sixteenth century also witnessed the flourishing of textiles and rugs. The Byzantine emperor Justinian had introduced the cultivation of silkworms to the West in the sixth century, and the silk industry resurfaced under the Ottomans. Its capital was at Bursa, where factories produced silks

Fergus O'Brien/The Image Bank/Getty Images

William J. Duiker

ART & IDEAS

COMPARATIVE ILLUSTRATION

Hagia Sophia and the Suleymaniye Mosque. The magnificent mosques built under the patronage of Suleyman the Magnificent are a great legacy of the Ottoman Empire and a fitting supplement to Hagia Sophia, the cathedral built by the Byzantine emperor Justinian in the sixth century C.E. Towering under a central dome, these mosques seem to defy gravity and, like European Gothic cathedrals, convey a sense of weightlessness. The Suleymaniye Mosque (left), constructed in the mid-sixteenth century on a design by the great architect Sinan, borrowed many elements from its great predecessor (right) and today is one of the most impressive and most graceful in Istanbul. A far cry from the seventh-century desert mosques constructed of palm trunks, the Ottoman mosques stand among the architectural wonders of the world.

Q *How would you compare the mosques built by the architect Sinan and his successors with the Gothic cathedrals that were being built at the same time in Europe? What do you think accounts for the differences?*

for wall hangings, soft covers, and especially court costumes. Perhaps even more famous than Turkish silk are the rugs. But whereas silks were produced under the patronage of the sultans, rugs were a peasant industry. Each village boasted its own distinctive design and color scheme for the rugs it produced.

© William J. Duiker

The Safavids

Q **FOCUS QUESTIONS:** What problems did the Safavid Empire face, and how did its rulers attempt to solve them? How did their approaches compare with those in the other Muslim empires?

After the collapse of the empire of Tamerlane in the early fifteenth century, the area extending from Persia into Central Asia lapsed into anarchy. The Uzbeks (ooz-BEKS), Turkic-speaking peoples from Central Asia, were the chief political and military force in the area. From their capital at Bokhara

Clothes Make the Man. Having traveled westward from China over the Silk Road, the production of silk got under way in the Ottoman Empire, from which it spread to Europe and Imperial Russia. In the sixteenth and seventeenth centuries, stunning silk caftans such as those shown here radiated Ottoman splendor and power. Their voluminous size, vibrant colors, intricate designs, and sumptuous fabrics aggrandized the wearer—usually a courtier—in both physical and political stature. Magnificent bolts of silk were offered by sultans as diplomatic gifts to solidify political alliances, as well as to reward high officials for their loyalty to the dynasty. To show respect and allegiance during court rituals, officials had to kiss the hem of the sultan's caftan.

(boh-KAHR-uh *or* boo-KAH-ruh), they maintained a semblance of control over the fluid tribal alignments until the emergence of the Safavid Dynasty in Persia at the beginning of the sixteenth century.

The Rise of the Safavids

The Safavid Dynasty was founded by Shah Ismail (IS-mah-eel) (r. 1487–1524), a descendant of Sheikh Safi al-Din (SAH-fee ul-DIN) (hence the name *Safavid*), who traced his origins to Ali, the fourth *imam* of the Muslim faith. In the early fourteenth century, Safi had been the leader of a community of Turkic-speaking people in Azerbaijan, near the Caspian Sea. Safi's community was one of many Sufi mystical religious groups throughout the area. In time, the doctrine spread among nomadic groups throughout the Middle East and was transformed into the more activist Shi'ite faith. Its adherents were known as "red heads" because of their distinctive red cap with twelve folds, meant to symbolize allegiance to the twelve *imams* of the Shi'ite faith.

In 1501, Ismail seized much of the lands of modern Iran and Iraq and proclaimed himself shah of a new Persian state. Baghdad was subdued in 1508, as were the Uzbeks in Bokhara shortly thereafter. Ismail now sent Shi'ite preachers into Anatolia to proselytize and promote rebellion among Turkish tribal peoples in the Ottoman Empire. In retaliation, the Ottoman sultan, Selim I, advanced against the Safavids in Persia

and won a major battle near Tabriz (tah-BREEZ) in 1514. But Selim could not maintain control of the area, and Ismail regained Tabriz a few years later.

The Ottomans returned to the attack in the 1580s and forced the new Safavid shah, Abbas (uh-BAHS) I (r. 1587–1629), to sign a punitive peace in which he acceded to the loss of much territory. The capital was subsequently moved from Tabriz in the northwest to Isfahan (is-fah-HAHN) in the south. Still, it was under Shah Abbas that the Safavids reached the zenith of their glory. He established a system similar to the janissaries in Turkey to train administrators to replace the traditional warrior elite. He also used the period of peace to strengthen his army, now armed with modern weapons, and in the early seventeenth century, he attempted to regain the lost territories. Although he had some initial success, war resumed in the 1620s, and a lasting peace was not achieved until 1638 (see Map 16.2).

Collapse of the Dynasty

Abbas the Great had managed to strengthen the dynasty significantly, and for a time after his death in 1629, it remained stable and vigorous. But succession conflicts plagued the dynasty. Partly as a result, the power of the more militant Shi'ites began to increase at court and in Safavid society at large. The intellectual freedom that had characterized the empire at its height was curtailed under the pressure of religious orthodoxy, and Iranian women, who had enjoyed

MAP 16.2 The Ottoman and Safavid Empires, c. 1683. During the seventeenth century, the Ottoman and Safavid Empires contested vigorously for hegemony in the eastern Mediterranean and the Middle East. This map shows the territories controlled by each state in the late seventeenth century.

Q *Which states shared control over the ancient lands in the Tigris and Euphrates Valleys? In what modern-day countries are those territories?*

The Religious Zeal of Shah Abbas the Great

RELIGION & PHILOSOPHY

SHAH ABBAS I, probably the greatest of the Safavid rulers, expanded the borders of his empire into areas of the southern Caucasus inhabited by Christians and other non-Muslim peoples. After Persian control was assured, he instructed that the local peoples be urged to convert to Islam for their own protection and the glory of God. In this passage, his biographer, the Persian historian Eskander Beg Monshi (es-KAHN-der bayg MAHN-shee), recounts the story of that effort.

Eskander Beg Monshi, "The Conversion of a Number of Christians to Islam"

This year the Shah decreed that those Armenians and other Christians who had been settled in [the southern Caucasus] and had been given agricultural land there should be invited to become Muslims. Life in this world is fraught with vicissitudes, and the Shah was concerned [that] in a period when the authority of the central government was weak, these Christians … might be subjected to attack by the neighboring Lor tribes (who are naturally given to causing injury and mischief), and their women and children carried off into captivity. In the areas in which these Christian groups resided, it was the Shah's purpose that the places of worship which they had built should become mosques, and the muezzin's call should be heard in them, so that these Christians might assume the guise of Muslims, and their future status accordingly be assured.…

Some of the Christians, guided by God's grace, embraced Islam voluntarily; others found it difficult to abandon their Christian faith and felt revulsion at the idea. They were encouraged by their monks and priests to remain steadfast in their faith. After a little pressure had been applied to the monks and priests, however, they desisted, and these Christians saw no alternative but to embrace Islam, though they did so with reluctance. The women and children embraced Islam with great enthusiasm, vying with one another in their eagerness to abandon their Christian faith and declare their belief in the unity of God. Some five thousand people embraced Islam. As each group made the Muslim declaration of faith, it received instruction in the Koran and the principles of the religious law of Islam, and all bibles and other Christian devotional material were collected and taken away from the priests.

In the same way, all the Armenian Christians who had been moved to [the area] were also forcibly converted to Islam.… Most people embraced Islam with sincerity, but some felt an aversion to making the Muslim profession of faith. True knowledge lies with God! May God reward the Shah for his action with long life and prosperity!

How do Shah Abbas's efforts to convert nonbelievers to Islam compare with similar programs by Muslim rulers in India, as described in Chapter 9? What did the author of this selection think about the conversions?

Source: From Eskander Beg Monshi in *History of Shah Abbas the Great*, Vol. II by Roger M. Savory by Westview Press, 1978.

---

considerable freedom and influence during the early empire, were forced to withdraw into seclusion and behind the veil. Meanwhile, attempts to suppress the religious beliefs of minorities led to increased popular unrest. In the early eighteenth century, Afghan warriors took advantage of local revolts to seize the capital of Isfahan, forcing the remnants of the Safavid ruling family to retreat to Azerbaijan, their original homeland. As the Ottomans seized territories along the western border, the empire finally collapsed in 1723. Eventually, order was restored by the military adventurer Nadir Shah Afshar (NAH-der shah ahf-SHAR), who launched an extended series of campaigns that restored the country's borders and even occupied the Mughal capital of Delhi (see "The Shadows Lengthen" later in this chapter).

CHRONOLOGY	The Safavids
Ismail seizes lands of present-day Iran and Iraq and becomes shah of Persia	1501
Ismail conquers Baghdad and defeats the Uzbeks	1508
Reign of Shah Abbas I	1587–1629
Truce achieved between Ottomans and Safavids	1638
Collapse of the Safavid Empire	1723

After his death, the Zand dynasty ruled until the end of the eighteenth century.

Safavid Politics and Society

Like the Ottoman Empire, Persia under the Safavids was a mixed society. The Safavids had come to power with the support of nomadic Turkic-speaking tribal groups, and leading elements from those groups retained considerable influence within the empire. But the majority of the population were Iranian, descendants of migrating peoples who had arrived in the area in the first millennium B.C.E.; most of them were farmers or townspeople, with attitudes inherited from the relatively sophisticated and urbanized culture of pre-Safavid Iran. Faced with the problem of integrating unruly Turkic-speaking tribal peoples with the sedentary Persian-speaking population of the urban areas, the Safavids used the Shi'ite faith as a unifying force (see the box "The Religious Zeal of Shah Abbas the Great" above). The shah himself acquired an almost divine quality and claimed to be the spiritual leader of all Islam. Shi'ism was declared the state religion.

Although there was a landed aristocracy, aristocratic power and influence were firmly controlled by strong-minded shahs, who confiscated aristocratic estates when possible and brought them under the control of the crown. Appointment to senior positions in the bureaucracy was by merit rather than birth.

The Royal Academy of Isfahan. Along with institutions such as libraries and hospitals, theological schools were often included in the mosque compound. One of the most sumptuous was the Royal Academy of Isfahan, built by the shah of Persia in the early eighteenth century. This view shows the large courtyard surrounded by arcades of student rooms, reminiscent of the arrangement of monks' cells in European cloisters.

To avoid encouraging competition between Turkish and non-Turkish elements, Shah Abbas I hired a number of foreigners from neighboring countries for positions in his government.

The Safavid shahs took a direct interest in the economy and actively engaged in commercial and manufacturing activities, although there was also a large and affluent urban bourgeoisie. Like the Ottoman sultan, one shah regularly traveled the city streets incognito to check on the honesty of his subjects. When he discovered that a baker and a butcher were overcharging for their products, he had the baker cooked in his own oven and the butcher roasted on a spit. Although the road system was said to be quite poor, most goods traveled by caravan. The government provided accommodations for weary travelers and, at least in times of strong rulers, kept the roads relatively clear of thieves and bandits.

At its height, Safavid Iran was a worthy successor of the great Persian empires of the past, although it was probably not as wealthy as its neighbors to the east and west, the Mughals and the Ottomans. Hemmed in by the seapower of the Europeans to the south and by the land power of the Ottomans to the west, the Safavids had no navy and were forced to divert overland trade with Europe through southern Russia to avoid an Ottoman blockade. Still, the brocades, carpets, and leather goods of Persia were highly prized throughout the world. A school of philosophy that sought truth in a fusion of rationalist and intuitive methods flourished in the sixteenth and seventeenth centuries, and Safavid science, medicine, and mathematics were the equal of other societies in the region (see the box "Designing the Perfect Society" on p. 460).

Safavid Art and Literature

Persia witnessed an extraordinary flowering of the arts during the reign of Shah Abbas I. His new capital, Isfahan, was a grandiose planned city with wide visual perspectives and a sense of order almost unique in the region. Shah Abbas ordered his architects to position his palaces, mosques, and bazaars around a massive rectangular polo ground. Much of the original city is still in good condition and remains the gem of modern Iran.

Two Lovers. Riza-i-Abbasi (ree-ZAH-yah-BAH-see) (1565–1635), the most renowned painter of the Safavid era, won praise for his exquisite portraits of courtiers and lovers. This delicate painting of a couple embracing conveys passion with a refined elegance. His style influenced later artists, who adapted it to other media, such as dazzling silk fabrics and the Persian carpets still much sought after all over the world. Especially popular were his colorful tile wall decorations depicting scenes of elegant peoples in flowing robes and turbans.

Designing the Perfect Society

POLITICS & GOVERNMENT

IN THE LATE FIFTEENTH CENTURY, the Persian author Muhammad ibn Asad Jalal ud-din al-Dawwani (al-da-WAH-nee) (1427–1501) wrote an essay on the ideal society that was entitled *Jalali's Ethics*. The work later attracted favorable notice at the Mughal court in India and eventually was paraphrased by Emperor Akbar's famous adviser Abu'l Fazl. It thus provides insight into the political and social views of key officials in Safavid Persia, as well as in Mughal India during the reign of its most famous ruler.

Jalali's Ethics

In order to preserve this political equipoise, there is a correspondence to be maintained between the various classes. Like as the equipoise of bodily temperament is affected by intermixture and correspondence of four elements, the equipoise of the political temperament is to be sought for in the correspondence of four classes.

1. *Men of the pen*, such as lawyers, divines, judges, bookmen, statisticians, geometricians, astronomers, physicians, poets. In these and their exertions in the use of their delightful pens, the subsistence of the faith and of the world itself is vested and bound up. They occupy the place in politics that water does among the elements. Indeed, to persons of ready understanding, the similarity of knowledge and water is as clear as water itself, and as evident as the sun that makes it so.

2. *Men of the sword*, such as soldiers, fighting zealots, guards of forts and passes, etc.; without whose exercise of the impetuous and vindictive sword, no arrangement of the age's interests could be effected; without the havoc of whose tempest-like energies, the materials of corruption, in the shape of rebellious and disaffected persons, could never be dissolved and dissipated. These then occupy the place of fire, their resemblance to it is too plain to require demonstration; no rational person need call in the aid of fire to discover it.

3. *Men of business*, such as merchants, capitalists, artisans, and craftsmen by whom the means of emolument and all other interests are adjusted; and through whom the remotest extremes enjoy the advantage and safeguard of each other's most peculiar commodities. The resemblance of these to air—the auxiliary of growth and increase in vegetables—the reviver of spirit in animal life—the medium of the undulation and movement of which all sorts of rare and precious things traverse the hearing to arrive at the headquarters of human nature—is exceedingly manifest.

4. *Husbandmen*, such as seedsmen, bailiffs, and agriculturists—the superintendents of vegetation and preparers of provender; without whose exertions the continuance of the human kind must be cut short. These are, in fact, the only producers of what had no previous existence; the other classes adding nothing whatever to subsisting products, but only transferring what subsists already from person to person, from place to place, and from form to form. How close these come to the soil and surface of the earth—the point to which all the heavenly circles refer—the scope to which all the luminaries of the purer world direct their rays—the stage on which wonders are displayed—the limit to which mysteries are confined—must be universally apparent.

In like manner then as in the composite organizations the passing of any element beyond its proper measure occasions the loss of equipoise, and is followed by dissolution and ruin, in political coalition, no less, the prevalence of any one class over the other three overturns the adjustment and dissolves the junction. Next attention is to be directed to the condition of the individuals composing them, and the place of every one determined according to his right.

 How does the social class system described here compare with the traditional division of classes in premodern Persia?

Source: A. T. Embree (ed.), *Sources of Indian Tradition: From the Beginning to 1800*, Vol. I, 2nd ed. (New York, 1988), pp. 431–432.

The immense mosques are richly decorated with elaborate blue tiles. The palaces are delicate structures with unusual slender wooden columns. These architectural wonders of Isfahan epitomize the grandeur, delicacy, and color that defined the Safavid golden age. To adorn the splendid buildings, Safavid artisans created imaginative metalwork, tile decorations, and original and delicate glass vessels. The ceramics of the period, imitating Chinese prototypes of celadon or blue-and-white Ming design, largely ignored traditional Persian designs.

The greatest area of productivity, however, was in textiles. Silk weaving based on new techniques became a national industry. The silks depicted birds, animals, and flowers in a brilliant mass of color with silver and gold threads. Above all,

carpet weaving flourished, stimulated by the great demand for Persian carpets in the West. Still highly prized all over the world, these seventeenth-century carpets reflect the grandeur and artistry of the Safavid Dynasty.

The long tradition of Persian painting continued into the Safavid era, but changed dramatically in two ways during the second half of the sixteenth century. First, taking advantage of the growing official toleration of portraiture, painters began to highlight the inner character of their subjects. Second, since royal patronage was not always forthcoming, artists sought to attract a larger audience by producing individual paintings that promoted their own distinctive styles and proudly bore their own signature.

The Grandeur of the Mughals

 FOCUS QUESTIONS: What role did Islam play in the Mughal Empire, and how did the Mughals' approach to religion compare with that of the Ottomans and the Safavids? What might explain the similarities and differences?

In retrospect, the period from the sixteenth to eighteenth centuries can be viewed both as a high point of traditional culture in India and as the first stage of perhaps its biggest challenge. The era began with the creation of one of the subcontinent's greatest empires, that of the Mughals (MOO-guls). Mughal rulers, although foreigners and Muslims like many of their immediate predecessors, nevertheless brought India to a peak of political power and cultural achievement. For the first time since the Mauryan dynasty, the entire subcontinent was united under a single government, with a common culture, at least on the surface, that inspired admiration and envy throughout the region.

Babur: Founder of the Mughal Dynasty

When the Portuguese fleet led by Vasco da Gama arrived at the port of Calicut in the spring of 1498 (see Chapter 14), the Indian subcontinent was still divided into a number of Hindu and Muslim kingdoms. But it was on the verge of a new era of unity that would be brought about by a foreign dynasty called the Mughals. Like so many other rulers of northern India, the founders of the Mughal Empire were not natives of India but came from the mountainous region north of the Ganges River. The founder of the dynasty, known to history as Babur (BAH-burr) (1483–1530), had an illustrious pedigree. His father was descended from the great Asian conqueror Tamerlane, his mother from the Mongol conqueror Genghis Khan.

Babur had inherited a fragment of Tamerlane's empire in an upland valley of the Syr Darya (SEER DAHR-yuh) River (see Map 16.2). Driven south by the rising power of the Uzbeks and then the Safavid Dynasty in Persia, Babur and his warriors seized Kabul in 1504 and, thirteen years later, crossed the Khyber Pass into India.

Following a pattern that we have seen before, Babur began his rise to power by offering to help an ailing dynasty against its opponents. Although his own forces were far less numerous than those of his adversaries, he possessed advanced weapons, including artillery, and used them to great effect. His use of mobile cavalry was particularly successful against his enemy's massed forces supplemented by mounted elephants. In 1526, with only 12,000 troops against an enemy force nearly ten times that size, Babur captured Delhi (DEL-ee) and established his power in the plains of northern India. Over the next several years, he continued his conquests in northern India until his death in 1530 at the age of forty-seven.

Babur's success was due in part to his vigor and his charismatic personality, which earned him the undying loyalty of his followers. His son and successor, Humayun (hoo-MY-yoon) (r. 1530–1556), was, in the words of one British historian, "intelligent but lazy." Whether or not this is a fair characterization, Humayun clearly lacked the will to consolidate his father's conquests and the personality to inspire loyalty among his subjects. In 1540, he was forced to flee to Persia, where he lived in exile for sixteen years. Finally, with the aid of the Safavid shah of Persia, he returned to India and reconquered Delhi in 1555 but died the following year in a household accident, reportedly from injuries suffered in a fall after smoking a pipeful of opium.

Humayun was succeeded by his son Akbar (AK-bar) (r. 1556–1605). Born while his father was living in exile, Akbar was only fourteen when he mounted the throne. Illiterate but highly intelligent and industrious, Akbar set out to extend his domain, then limited to the Punjab (puhn-JAHB) and the upper Ganges River valley. "A monarch," he remarked, "should be ever intent on conquest, otherwise his neighbors rise in arms against him. The army should be exercised in warfare, lest from want of training they become self-indulgent."[2] By the end of his life, he had brought Mughal rule to most of the subcontinent, from the Himalaya Mountains to the Godavari (goh-DAH-vuh-ree) River in central India and from Kashmir to the mouths of the Brahmaputra (brah-muh-POO-truh) and the Ganges. In so doing, Akbar had created the greatest Indian empire since the Mauryan dynasty nearly two thousand years earlier (see Map 16.3).

Akbar and Indo-Muslim Civilization

Although Akbar was probably the greatest of the conquering Mughal monarchs, like his famous predecessor Ashoka, he is best known for the humane character of his rule. Above all, he accepted the diversity of Indian society and took steps to reconcile his Muslim and Hindu subjects.

RELIGION AND THE STATE Though raised an orthodox Muslim, Akbar had been exposed to other beliefs during his childhood and had little patience with the pedantic views of Muslim scholars at court. As emperor, he displayed a keen interest in other religions, not only tolerating Hindu practices in his own domains but also welcoming the expression of Christian views by his Jesuit advisers. Akbar put his policy of religious tolerance into practice by taking a Hindu princess as one of his wives, and the success of this marriage may well have had an effect on his religious convictions. He patronized classical Indian arts and architecture and abolished many of the restrictions faced by Hindus in a Muslim-dominated society.

During his later years, Akbar became steadily more hostile to Islam. To the dismay of many Muslims at court, he sponsored a new form of worship called the Divine Faith (*Din-i-Ilahi*), which combined characteristics of several religions with a central belief in the infallibility of all decisions reached by the emperor. Some historians have maintained that Akbar totally abandoned Islam and adopted a Persian model of imperial divinity. But others have pointed out that the emperor was claiming only divine guidance, not divine status, and suggest that the new ideology was designed to cement the loyalty of officials to the person of the monarch. Whatever the case, the new faith aroused deep hostility in Muslim circles and vanished rapidly after his death.

MAP 16.3 The Mughal Empire. This map shows the expansion of the Mughal Empire from the death of Akbar in 1605 to the reign of Aurangzeb at the end of the seventeenth century.

Q *In which cities on the map were European settlements located? When did each group of Europeans arrive, and how did the settlements spread?*

Map labels: Samarkand, AFGHANISTAN, KASHMIR, Kabul, Khyber Pass, Lahore, PERSIA, PUNJAB, TIBET, Delhi, Himalaya Mts., Fatehpur Sikri, Agra, Varanasi (Benares), Patna, Brahmaputra R., Ganges R., RAJPUTS, BENGAL, Dacca, Calcutta, GUJARAT, Diu, Surat, Arabian Sea, Bombay, Godavari R., Bay of Bengal, DECCAN, MARATHAS, MYSORE, Madras, Pondicherry, Calicut, Tranquebar, Cochin, Indian Ocean, SRI LANKA, Colombo, Indus R.

Legend:
— Mughal Empire at Akbar's death, 1605
— Mughal Empire, c. 1700
□ Dutch settlement
■ British settlement
□ Portuguese settlement
■ French settlement

0 250 500 750 Kilometers
0 250 500 Miles

ADMINISTRATIVE REFORMS Akbar also extended his innovations to the imperial administration. The empire was divided into provinces, and the administration of each province was modeled after the central government, with separate departments for military, financial, commercial, and legal affairs. Senior officials in each department reported directly to their counterparts in the capital city of Agra.

Although the upper ranks of the government continued to be dominated by nonnative Muslims, a substantial proportion of lower-ranking officials were Hindus, and a few Hindus were appointed to positions of importance. At first, most officials were paid salaries, but later they were ordinarily assigned sections of agricultural land for their temporary use; they kept a portion of the taxes paid by the local peasants in lieu of a salary. These local officials, known as *zamindars* (zuh-meen-DAHRZ), were expected to forward the rest of the taxes from the lands under their control to the central government, which also derived much of its revenue from the exploitation of substantial crown lands. *Zamindars* often recruited a number of military and civilian retainers and accumulated considerable power in their localities.

The same tolerance that marked Akbar's attitude toward religion and administration extended to the Mughal legal system. While Muslims were subject to the Islamic codes (the *Shari'a*), Hindu law (the *Dharmashastra*) applied to areas settled by Hindus, who after 1579 were no longer required to pay the unpopular *jizya* (JIZ-yuh), or poll tax on non-Muslims. Punishments for crime were relatively mild, at least by the standards of the day, and justice was administered in a relatively impartial and efficient manner.

A HARMONIOUS SOCIETY A key element in Akbar's vision of the ideal social order was the concept of harmony, meaning that each individual and group within the empire would play their assigned role and contribute to the welfare of society as a whole. This concept of social harmony was based in part on his vision of a world shaped by the laws of Islam as transmitted by Muhammad (*Shari'a*), but it also corresponded to the deep-seated indigenous belief in the importance of class hierarchy, as expressed in the Indian class and caste system (see the box "Designing the Perfect Society" on p. 460). In its overall conception, it bears a clear resemblance to the social structure adopted by the Mughals' contemporaries to the west, the Ottoman Empire.

Overall, Akbar's reign was a time of peace and prosperity. Although all Indian peasants were required to pay about one-third of their annual harvest to the state through the *zamindars*, in general the system was applied fairly, and when drought struck in the 1590s, the taxes were reduced or even suspended altogether. Thanks to a long period of relative peace and political stability, commerce and manufacturing flourished. Foreign trade, in particular, thrived as Indian goods, notably textiles, tropical food products, spices, and precious stones, were exported in exchange for gold and silver. Tariffs on imports were low. Much of the foreign commerce was handled by Arab traders, since the Indians, like their Mughal rulers, did not care for travel by sea. Internal trade, however, was dominated by large merchant castes, which also were active in banking and handicrafts.

Akbar's Successors

Akbar died in 1605 and was succeeded by his son Jahangir (juh-HAHN-geer) (r. 1605–1628). During the early years of his reign, Jahangir continued to strengthen central control over the vast empire. Eventually, however, his grip began to

Victoria & Albert Museum, London, UK/The Bridgeman Art Library

The Construction of Fatehpur Sikri. In this contemporary Mughal painting, artisans are completing construction of the Elephant Gate at Akbar's new capital of Fatehpur Sikri (fah-tay-POOR SIK-ree). Because both the Ottoman Empire and Mughal India used Persian as their court language, they learned to appreciate the illuminated manuscript techniques produced by Safavid workshops in Persia and adapted them to their own cultural heritage. Emperor Akbar, the greatest Mughal ruler, enthusiastically embraced the art of bookmaking, peopling his royal workshops with more than one hundred artists. The illustrated manuscripts from Mughal India rival those of Safavid Persia in brilliance and imagination and provide fascinating historical details of military campaigns and court ceremonies, as well as scenes from daily life.

weaken (according to his memoirs, he "only wanted a bottle of wine and a piece of meat to make merry"), and the court fell under the influence of one of his wives, the Persian-born Nur Jahan (NOOR juh-HAHN) (see the box "The Power Behind the Throne" on p. 464). The empress took advantage of her position to enrich her own family and arranged for her niece Mumtaz Mahal (MOOM-tahz muh-HAHL) to marry her husband's third son and ultimate successor, Shah Jahan (r. 1628–1657). When Shah Jahan succeeded to the throne, he quickly demonstrated the single-minded quality of his grandfather (albeit in a much more brutal manner),

bpk, Berlin/Museum fuer Islamische Kunst/Georg Niedermeiser/Art Resource, NY

Jahangir the Magnificent. In 1615, the English ambassador to the Mughal court presented an official portrait of King James I to Shah Jahangir, who returned the favor with a portrait of himself. Thus was established a long tradition of exchanging paintings between the two empires. As it turned out, the practice altered the style of Mughal portraiture, which had previously shown the emperor in action, hunting, participating at official functions, or engaging in battle. Henceforth, portraits of the ruler followed European practice by focusing on the opulence and spiritual power of the empire. In this painting, Jahangir has chosen spiritual over earthly power by offering a book to a sheikh while ignoring the Ottoman sultan, King James I, and the Hindu artist who painted the picture. Even the cherubs, a European artifice, are dazzled by the shah's divine character, which is further demonstrated by an enormous halo.

ordering the assassination of all of his rivals in order to secure his position.

THE REIGN OF SHAH JAHAN During a reign of three decades, Shah Jahan maintained the system established by his predecessors while expanding the boundaries of the empire by successful campaigns in the Deccan Plateau and against Samarkand, north of the Hindu Kush. But Shah Jahan's rule was marred by his failure to deal with the growing domestic problems. He had inherited a nearly empty treasury because of Empress Nur Jahan's penchant for luxury and ambitious charity projects. Though the majority of his subjects lived in grinding poverty, Shah Jahan's frequent military campaigns and expensive building projects put a heavy strain on the imperial finances and compelled him to raise taxes. At the same

The Power Behind the Throne

POLITICS & GOVERNMENT

DURING HIS REIGN AS MUGHAL EMPEROR, Jahangir (1605–1628) was addicted to alcohol and opium. Because of his weakened condition, his Persian wife, Nur Jahan, began to rule on his behalf. She also groomed his young son Khurram to rule as the future emperor Shah Jahan and arranged for him to marry her own niece, Mumtaz Mahal, thereby cementing her influence over two successive Mughal rulers. During this period, Nur Jahan was the de facto ruler of India, exerting her influence in both internal and foreign affairs during an era of peace and prosperity. Although the extent of her influence was often criticized at court, her performance impressed many European observers, as these remarks by an English visitor attest.

Nur Jahan, Empress of Mughal India

If anyone with a request to make at Court obtains an audience or is allowed to speak, the King hears him indeed, but will give no definite answer of Yes or No, referring him promptly to Asaf Khan, who in the same way will dispose of no important matter without communicating with his sister, the Queen, and who regulates his attitude in such a way that the authority of neither of them may be diminished. Anyone then who obtains a favour must thank them for it, and not the King....

Her abilities were uncommon; for she rendered herself absolute, in a government in which women are thought incapable of bearing any part. Their power, it is true, is sometimes exerted in the harem; but, like the virtues of the magnet, it is silent and unperceived. Nur Jahan stood forth in public; she broke through all restraint and custom, and acquired power by her own address, more than by the weakness of Jahangir....

Her former and present supporters have been well rewarded, so that now most of the men who are near the King owe their promotion to her, and are consequently under ... obligations to her.... Many misunderstandings result, for the King's orders or grants of appointments, etc., are not certainties, being of no value until they have been approved by the Queen.

 Based on this description, how does the position that Nur Jahan occupied in Mughal government compare with the roles played by other female political figures in China, Africa, and Europe? What do all of these women have in common?

Source: From *Nur Jahan: Empress of Mughal India* by Ellison Banks Findly. Oxford University Print on Demand, 1993.

---

time, the government did little to improve rural conditions. In a country where transport was primitive (it often took three months to travel the 600 miles between Patna, in the middle of the Ganges River valley, and Delhi) and drought conditions frequent, the dynasty made few efforts to increase agricultural efficiency or to improve the roads or the irrigation network, although a grand trunk road was eventually constructed between the capital Agra (AH-gruh) and Lahore (luh-HOHR), a growing city several hundred miles to the northwest. A Dutch merchant in Gujarat (goo-juh-RAHT) described conditions during a famine in the mid-seventeenth century:

> As the famine increased, men abandoned towns and villages and wandered helplessly. It was easy to recognize their condition: eyes sunk deep in head, lips pale and covered with slime, the skin hard, with the bones showing through, the belly nothing but a pouch hanging down empty, knuckles and kneecaps showing prominently. One would cry and howl for hunger, while another lay stretched on the ground dying in misery; wherever you went, you saw nothing but corpses.[3]

In 1648, Shah Jahan moved his capital from Agra to Delhi and built the famous Red Fort in his new capital city. But he is best known for the Taj Mahal (tahj muh-HAHL) in Agra, widely considered to be the most beautiful building in India, if not in the entire world (see the Comparative Illustration "The Taj Mahal" on p. 470). The story is a romantic one—that the Taj was built by the emperor in memory of his wife Mumtaz Mahal, who had died giving birth to her thirteenth child at the age of thirty-nine. But the reality has a less attractive side: the expense of the building, which employed 20,000 masons over twenty years, forced the government to raise agricultural taxes, further impoverishing many Indian peasants.

THE RULE OF AURANGZEB Succession struggles returned to haunt the dynasty in the mid-1650s when Shah Jahan's illness led to a struggle for power between his sons Dara Shikoh (DA-ruh SHIH-koh) and Aurangzeb (ow-rang-ZEB). Dara Shikoh was described by his contemporaries as progressive and humane, although possessed of a violent temper and a strong sense of mysticism. But he apparently lacked political acumen and was outmaneuvered by Aurangzeb (r. 1658–1707), who had Dara Shikoh put to death and then imprisoned his father in the fort at Agra.

Aurangzeb is one of the most controversial individuals in the history of India. A man of high principle, he attempted to eliminate many of what he considered India's social evils, prohibiting the immolation of widows on their husband's funeral pyre (*sati*), the castration of eunuchs, and the exaction of illegal taxes. With less success, he tried to forbid gambling, drinking, and prostitution. But Aurangzeb, a devout and somewhat doctrinaire Muslim, also adopted a number of measures that reversed the policies of religious tolerance established by his predecessors. The building of new Hindu temples was prohibited, and the Hindu poll tax was restored. Forced conversions to Islam were resumed, and non-Muslims were driven from the court. Aurangzeb's heavy-handed religious policies led to considerable domestic unrest and to a revival of Hindu fervor during the last years of his reign. A number of revolts also broke out against imperial authority.

THE SHADOWS LENGTHEN During the eighteenth century, Mughal power was threatened from both within and without. Fueled by the growing power and autonomy of the local gentry and merchants, rebellious groups in provinces throughout the empire, from the Deccan to the Punjab, began to reassert local authority and reduce the power of the Mughal emperor to that of a "tinsel sovereign." Increasingly divided, India was vulnerable to attack from abroad. In 1739, Delhi was sacked by the Persians, who left it in ashes and carried off its splendid Peacock Throne.

A number of obvious reasons for the virtual collapse of the Mughal Empire can be identified, including the draining of the imperial treasury and the decline in competence of the Mughal rulers. By 1700, the Europeans, who at first were no more than an irritant, had begun to seize control of regional trade routes and to meddle in the internal politics of the subcontinent (see "The Impact of European Power in India" later in the chapter).

It should be noted, however, that even at its height under Akbar, the empire was less a centralized state than a loosely knit collection of heterogeneous principalities held together by the authority of the throne, which tried to combine Persian concepts of kingship with the Indian tradition of decentralized power. Decline set in when centrifugal forces gradually began to predominate over centripetal ones.

Ironically, one element in this process was the very success of the system, which led to the rapid expansion of wealth and autonomous power at the local level. As local elites increased their wealth and influence, they became less willing to accept the authority and financial demands from Delhi. The reassertion of Muslim orthodoxy under Aurangzeb and his successors simply exacerbated the problem by irritating many of the emperor's Hindu subjects. This process was hastened by the growing European military and economic presence along the periphery of the empire.

The Impact of European Power in India

As we have seen, the first Europeans to arrive were the Portuguese. Although they sought to establish a virtual monopoly over regional trade in the Indian Ocean, they did not seek to penetrate the interior of the subcontinent but focused on establishing way stations en route to China and the Spice Islands. The situation changed at the end of the sixteenth century when the English and the Dutch entered the scene. Soon both powers were in active competition with Portugal and with each other for trading privileges in the region (see Opposing Viewpoints "The Capture of Port Hoogly" on p. 466).

Penetration of the new market was not easy for the Europeans because they initially had little to offer their hosts, who had been conducting a thriving trade with peoples throughout the Indian Ocean regional market for centuries. As a result, European merchants focused on taking part in the carrying trade between one Asian port and another. The Portuguese, for example, carried high-quality textile goods from India to Africa in exchange for gold from the mines in Zimbabwe. With their profits, they paid for spices to be transported back to Europe. Eventually, goods such as textiles and spices were paid for with gold and silver bullion mined in Latin America.

The experience of the English was a prime example. When in 1608 the first English fleet arrived at Surat (SOOR-et), a thriving port on the northwestern coast of India, the English request for trading privileges was rejected by Emperor Jahangir, at the suggestion of the Portuguese advisers already in residence at the imperial court. Needing lightweight Indian cloth to trade for spices in the East Indies, the English persisted, and in 1616, they were finally permitted to install their own ambassador at the imperial court in Agra. Three years later, the first English factory, or warehouse, was established at Surat.

During the next several decades, the English presence in India steadily increased as Mughal power waned. By midcentury, additional English trading posts had been established at Bombay ("good bay" in Portuguese) on the west coast of the peninsula, at Fort William (now the great city of Calcutta, recently renamed Kolkata) on the Hoogly River near the Bay of Bengal, and at Madras (muh-DRAS *or* muh-DRAHS) (now Chennai) on the southeastern coast. From there, English ships carried high-quality Indian-made cotton goods back home to the British Isles, where they began to compete effectively with locally produced woolen products, or to the East Indies, where they were bartered for spices to be shipped back to England.

English success in India attracted rivals, including the Dutch and the French. The Dutch eventually abandoned their interests in India to concentrate on the spice trade, but the French were more persistent and seized Madras in 1746. For a brief period, the French competed successfully for trade privileges with the British, but the military genius of Sir Robert Clive (CLYV), an aggressive British administrator and empire builder who eventually became the chief representative of the East India Company in the subcontinent, combined with the refusal of the French government to provide financial support for French actions in India eventually left the latter with only a fort at Pondicherry (pon-dir-CHEH-ree) and a handful of other tiny enclaves on the southeastern coast (see Chapter 18).

In the meantime, Clive began to consolidate British control in Bengal (ben-GAHL), where the local Indian ruler had attacked Fort William and imprisoned the local British population in the infamous Black Hole of Calcutta (an underground prison for holding the prisoners, many of whom died in captivity). In 1757, a small British force numbering about three thousand defeated a Mughal-led army over ten times that size in the Battle of Plassey (see the box "British Victory in India" on p. 520 in Chapter 18). As part of the spoils of victory, the British East India Company exacted from the now-decrepit Mughal court the authority to collect taxes from extensive lands in the area surrounding Calcutta. Less than ten years later, British forces seized the reigning Mughal emperor in a skirmish at Buxar (buk-SAHR), and the British began to consolidate their economic and administrative control over Indian

OPPOSING ✕ VIEWPOINTS

The Capture of Port Hoogly

IN 1632, THE MUGHAL RULER, SHAH JAHAN, ORDERED AN ATTACK on the city of Hoogly (HOOG-lee), a fortified Portuguese trading post on the northeastern coast of India. For the Portuguese, who had profited from half a century of triangular trade between India, China, and various countries in the Middle East and Southeast Asia, the loss of Hoogly at the hands of the Mughals hastened the decline of their influence in the region. Presented here are two contemporary versions of the battle. The first, from the *Padshahnama* (pad-shah-NAHM-uh) (*Book of Kings*), relates the course of events from the Mughal point of view. The second account is by John Cabral, a Jesuit missionary who was resident in Hoogly at the time.

The *Padshahnama*

During the reign of the Bengalis, a group of Frankish [European] merchants … settled in a place one *kos* from Satgaon … and, on the pretext that they needed a place for trading, they received permission from the Bengalis to construct a few edifices. Over time, due to the indifference of the governors of Bengal, many Franks gathered there and built dwellings of the utmost splendor and strength, fortified with cannons, guns, and other instruments of war. It was not long before it became a large settlement and was named Hoogly…. The Franks' ships trafficked at this port, and commerce was established, causing the market at the port of Satgaon to slump…. Of the peasants of those places, they converted some to Christianity by force and others through greed and sent them off to Europe in their ships….

Since the improper actions of the Christians of Hoogly Port toward the Muslims was accurately reflected in the mirror of the mind of the Emperor before his accession to the throne, when the imperial banners cast their shadows over Bengal, and inasmuch as he was always inclined to propagate the true religion and eliminate infidelity, it was decided that when he gained control over this region he would eradicate the corruption of these abominators from the realm.

John Cabral, *Travels of Sebastian Manrique, 1629–1649*

Hugli continued at peace all the time of the great King Jahangir. For, as this Prince, by what he showed, was more attached to Christ than to Mohammad and was a Moor in name and dress only…. Sultan Khurram was in everything unlike his father, especially as regards the latter's leaning towards Christianity…. He declared himself the mortal enemy of the Christian name and the restorer of the law of Mohammad…. He sent a *firman* [order] to the Viceroy of Bengal, commanding him without reply or delay, to march upon the Bandel of Hugli and put it to fire and the sword. He added that, in doing so, he would render a signal service to God, to Mohammad, and to him….

Consequently, on a Friday, September 24, 1632…. all the people [the Portuguese] embarked with the utmost secrecy…. Learning what was going on, and wishing to be able to boast that they had taken Hugli by storm, they [the imperialists] made a general attack on the Bandel by Saturday noon. They began by setting fire to a mine, but lost in it more men than we. Finally, however, they were masters of the Bandel.

 How do these two accounts of the Battle of Hoogly differ? Is there any way to reconcile the two into a single narrative?

Sources: From *King of the World: A Mughal Manuscript from the Royal Library, Windsor Castle*, trans. by Wheeler Thackston, text by Milo Cleveland Beach and Ebba Koch (London: Thames and Hudson, 1997), p. 59.

territory through the surrogate power of the now powerless Mughal court (see Map 16.4).

To officials of the East India Company, the expansion of their authority into the interior of the subcontinent probably seemed like a simple commercial decision, a move designed to seek guaranteed revenues to pay for the increasingly expensive military operations in India. To historians, it marks a major step in the gradual transfer of all of the Indian subcontinent to the British East India Company and later, in 1858, to the British crown. The process was more haphazard than deliberate. Under a new governor general, Warren Hastings, the British attempted to consolidate areas under their control and defeat such rivals as the rising Hindu Marathas (muh-RAH-tuhz), who exploited the decline of the Mughals to expand their own territories in Maharashtra (mah-huh-RAHSH-truh).

THE ECONOMIC CONSEQUENCES OF CONQUEST The British East India Company's takeover of vast landholdings, notably in the eastern Indian states of Orissa (uh-RIH-suh) and

A Pepper Plantation. During the Age of Exploration, pepper was one of the spices most sought by European adventurers. Unlike cloves and nutmeg, it was found in other areas in Asia besides the Indonesian archipelago. Shown here is a French pepper plantation in southern India. Eventually, the French were driven out of the Indian subcontinent by the British and retained only a few tiny enclaves along the coast.

MAP 16.4 India in 1805. By the early nineteenth century, much of the Indian subcontinent had fallen under British domination.

Q *Where was the capital of the Mughal Empire located?*

Bengal, may have been a windfall for enterprising British officials, but it had serious consequences for the Indian economy. In the first place, it resulted in the transfer of capital from the local Indian aristocracy to company officials, most of whom sent their profits back to Britain. Second, it eventually hastened the destruction of India's once healthy textile industry. At first, exports of high-quality Indian cotton goods skyrocketed, as the attractive local muslins and colorful calicoes began to replace the traditional woolen garments previously in fashion in Europe. Eventually, however, rising costs for imported Indian textiles, combined with stiff resistance from the woolen industry, produced dramatic changes in British textile production. Imports of cheap raw cotton from fields newly planted in the Americas, combined with revolutionary new inventions in the spinning and weaving process, transformed the British Isles during the eighteenth century into the center of global textile production. Inexpensive British machine-made textiles were now imported duty-free into India to compete against local goods, many of which were produced on hand looms in Indian villages, thus putting millions out of work.

Finally, British expansion in India hurt the peasants. As the British took over the administration of the land tax, they began to apply British law, which allowed the lands of those unable to pay the tax to be confiscated. In the 1770s, a series of famines led to the death of an estimated one-third of the population in the areas under company administration. The British government attempted to resolve the problem by assigning tax lands to the local revenue collectors (*zamindars*) in the hope of transforming them into English-style rural gentry, but many collectors themselves fell into bankruptcy and sold their lands to absentee bankers while the now landless peasants remained in abject poverty. It was hardly an auspicious beginning to "civilized" British rule.

RESISTANCE TO THE BRITISH As a result of such conditions, Britain's rise to power in India did not go unchallenged. Although Mughal authority was by now virtually moribund, local forces took matters into their own hands. Astute Indian commanders avoided pitched battles with the well-armed British troops but harassed and ambushed them in the manner of guerrillas in our time. Said Haidar Ali (HY-dur AH-lee), one of Britain's primary rivals for control in southern India:

> You will in time understand my mode of warfare. Shall I risk my cavalry which cost a thousand rupees each horse, against your cannon ball which cost two pice? No! I will march your troops until their legs swell to the size of their bodies. You shall not have a blade of grass, nor a drop of water. I will hear of you every time your drum beats, but you shall not know where I am once a month. I will give your army battle, but it must be when I please, and not when you choose.[4]

Unfortunately for India, not all its commanders were as astute as Haidar Ali. In the last years of the eighteenth century, when the East India Company's authority came into the capable hands of Lord Cornwallis and his successor, Lord Mornington, the future marquess of Wellesley, the stage was set for the final consolidation of British rule over the subcontinent.

The Mughal Dynasty: A "Gunpowder Empire"?

To some recent historians, the success of the Mughals, like that of the Ottomans and the Safavids, was due to their mastery of the techniques of modern warfare, especially the use of firearms. In this view, firearms played a central role in the ability of all three empires to overcome their rivals and rise to regional hegemony. Accordingly, some scholars have labeled them "gunpowder empires." Although technical prowess in the art of warfare was undoubtedly a key element in their success, we should not forget that other factors, such as dynamic leadership, political acumen, and the possession of an ardent following motivated by religious zeal (at least in the case of the Safavids in Iran) were equally important in their drive to power and ability to retain it.

In the case of the Mughals, the "gunpowder empire" thesis has been challenged by historian Douglas Streusand, who argues that the Mughals used "the carrot and the stick" to extend their authority, relying not just on heavy artillery but

also on other forms of siege warfare and the offer of negotiations. Once in power, the Mughals created an empire that appeared highly centralized from the outside but was actually a collection of semiautonomous principalities ruled by provincial elites and linked together by the overarching majesty of the Mughal emperor—and not simply by the barrel of a gun. Even today, many Indians regard Akbar as the country's greatest ruler, a tribute not only to his military success but also to the humane policies adopted during his reign.

Society Under the Mughals: A Synthesis of Cultures

The Mughals were the last of the great traditional Indian dynasties. Like so many of their predecessors since the fall of the Guptas nearly a thousand years before, the Mughals were Muslims. But like the Ottoman Turks, the best Mughal rulers did not simply impose Islamic institutions and beliefs on the predominantly Hindu population; they combined Muslim with Hindu and even Persian concepts and cultural values in a unique social and cultural synthesis that even today seems to epitomize the greatness of Indian civilization. The new faith of Sikhism, founded in the early sixteenth century in an effort to blend both faiths (see Chapter 9), undoubtedly benefited from the mood of syncretism promoted by the Mughal court.

To be sure, Hindus sometimes attempted to defend themselves and their religious practices against the efforts of some Mughal monarchs to impose the Islamic religion and Islamic mores on the indigenous population. In some cases, despite official prohibitions, Hindu men forcibly married Muslim women and then converted them to the native faith, while converts to Islam normally lost all of their inheritance rights within the Indian family. Government orders to destroy Hindu temples were often ignored by local officials, sometimes as the result of bribery or intimidation. Although the founding emperor Babur expressed little admiration for the country he had subjected to

✦ CHRONOLOGY	The Mughal Era	
Arrival of Vasco da Gama at Calicut	1498	
Babur seizes Delhi	1526	
Death of Babur	1530	
Humayun recovers throne in Delhi	1555	
Death of Humayun and accession of Akbar	1556	
Death of Akbar and accession of Jahangir	1605	
Arrival of English at Surat	1608	
English embassy to Agra	1616	
Reign of Emperor Shah Jahan	1628–1657	
Foundation of English factory at Madras	1639	
Aurangzeb succeeds to the throne	1658	
Death of Aurangzeb	1707	
Sack of Delhi by the Persians	1739	
French capture Madras	1746	
Battle of Plassey	1757	

his rule, ultimately Indian practices had an influence on the Mughal elites, as many Mughal chieftains married Indian women and adopted Indian forms of dress.

In some areas, Emperor Akbar's tireless effort to bring about a blend of Middle Eastern and South Asian religious and cultural values paid rich dividends, as substantial numbers of Indians decided to convert to the Muslim faith during the centuries of Mughal rule. Some were undoubtedly attracted to the egalitarian characteristics of Islam, but others found that the mystical and devotional qualities promoted by Sufi missionaries corresponded to similar traditions among the local population. This was especially true in Bengal, on the eastern edge of the Indian subcontinent, where Hindu practices were not as well established and where forms of religious devotionalism had long been popular among the population.

THE ECONOMY Although much of the local population in the subcontinent lived in the grip of grinding poverty, punctuated by occasional periods of widespread famine, the first centuries of Mughal rule were in some respects a period of relative prosperity for the region. India was a leading participant in the growing foreign trade that crisscrossed the Indian Ocean from the Red Sea and the Persian Gulf to the Strait of Malacca and the Indonesian archipelago. High-quality cloth from India was especially prized, and the country's textile industry made it, in the words of one historian, "the industrial workshop of the world."

The Shri Mangueshi Temple. Although the Muslim rulers of the Mughal Dynasty controlled the Indian subcontinent for three centuries, the majority of their subjects remained true to their Hindu convictions. This was especially the case in southern parts of the country, where Mughal rule was weak or nonexistent. In the sixteenth century, Hindu believers established the Shri Mangueshi (Shree Man-GWEH-shee) temple in the present-day state of Goa, along the western coast south of Mumbai. When the Portuguese, who had recently conquered the region to serve as the administrative center for their possessions in India, sought to convert the Hindu faithful to Christianity, the temple was moved to its present-day location further inland. The current structure, completed in the mid-eighteenth century, is one of the most revered and beautiful in southern India.

Long-term stability led to increasing commercialization and the spread of wealth to new groups within Indian society. The Mughal era saw the emergence of an affluent landed gentry and a prosperous merchant class. Members of prestigious castes from the pre-Mughal period reaped many of the benefits of the increasing wealth, but some of these changes transcended caste boundaries and led to the emergence of new groups who achieved status and wealth on the basis of economic achievement rather than traditional kinship ties. During the late eighteenth century, this economic prosperity was shaken by the decline of the Mughal Empire and the increasing European presence. But many prominent Indians reacted by establishing commercial relationships with the foreigners. For a time, such relationships often worked to the Indians' benefit. Later, as we shall see, they would have cause to regret the arrangement.

THE POSITION OF WOMEN Deciding whether Mughal rule had much effect on the lives of ordinary Indians is somewhat problematic. The treatment of women is a good example. Women had traditionally played an active role in Mongol tribal society—many actually fought on the battlefield alongside the men—and Babur and his successors often relied on the women in their families for political advice. Women from aristocratic families were often awarded honorific titles, received salaries, and were permitted to own land and engage in business. Women at court sometimes received an education, and Emperor Akbar reportedly established a girls' school at Fatehpur Sikri to provide teachers for his own daughters. Aristocratic women often expressed their creative talents by writing poetry, painting, or playing music. Women of all castes were adept at spinning thread, either for their own use or to sell to weavers to augment the family income. Weaving was carried out in the home by all members of the families of the weaving subcaste. They sold simple cloth to local villages and fine cotton, silk, and wool to the Mughal court. By Akbar's reign, the textile manufacturing was of such high quality and so well established that India sold cloth to much of the world: Arabia, the coast of East Africa, Egypt, Southeast Asia, and Europe.

To a certain degree, these Mughal attitudes toward women may have had an impact on Indian society. Women were allowed to inherit land, and some even possessed *zamindar* rights. Women from mercantile castes sometimes took an active role in business activities. At the same time, however, as Muslims, the Mughals subjected women to certain restrictions under Islamic law. On the whole, these Mughal practices coincided with and even accentuated existing tendencies in Indian society. The Muslim practice of isolating women and preventing them from associating with men outside the

Yvonne V. Duiker

Steve Vidler/SuperStock

© William J. Duiker

COMPARATIVE ILLUSTRATION

The Taj Mahal: Symbol of the Exotic East. The Taj Mahal, completed in 1653, was built by the Mughal emperor Shah Jahan as a tomb to glorify the memory of his beloved wife, Mumtaz Mahal. Raised on a marble platform above the Jumna River, the Taj is dramatically framed by contrasting twin red sandstone mosques, magnificent gardens, and a long reflecting pool that mirrors and magnifies its beauty. The effect is one of monumental size, near blinding brilliance, and delicate lightness, a startling contrast to the heavier and more masculine Baroque style then popular in Europe. The Taj Mahal inspired many imitations around the world, including the Royal Pavilion at Brighton, England (inset at right), constructed in 1815 to commemorate the British victory over Napoleon at Waterloo.

Q *How does Mughal architecture, as exemplified by the Taj Mahal, compare with the mosques erected by architects such as Sinan in the Ottoman Empire?*

home (*purdah*) was adopted by many upper-class Hindus as a means of enhancing their status or protecting their women from unwelcome advances by Muslims in positions of authority. In other ways, Hindu practices were unaffected. The custom of *sati* continued to be practiced despite efforts by the Mughals to abolish it, and child marriage (most women were betrothed before the age of ten) remained common. Women were still instructed to obey their husbands without question and to remain chaste.

Mughal Culture

The era of the Mughals was one of synthesis in culture as well as in politics and religion. The Mughals combined Islamic themes with Persian and indigenous motifs to produce a unique style that enriched and embellished Indian art and culture. The Mughal emperors were zealous patrons of the arts and enticed painters, poets, and artisans from as far away as the Mediterranean. Apparently, the generosity of the Mughals made it difficult to refuse a trip to India. It was said that they would reward a poet with his weight in gold.

ARCHITECTURE Undoubtedly, the Mughals' most visible achievement was in architecture. Here they integrated Persian and Indian styles in a new and sometimes breathtakingly

beautiful form best symbolized by the Taj Mahal, built by the emperor Shah Jahan in the mid-seventeenth century. Although the human and economic cost of the Taj tarnishes the romantic legend of its construction, there is no denying the beauty of the building. It had evolved from a style that originated several decades earlier with the tomb of Humayun, which was built by his widow in Agra in 1565 during the reign of Akbar.

Humayun's mausoleum had combined Persian and Islamic motifs in a square building finished in red sandstone and topped with a dome. The style was repeated in a number of other buildings erected throughout the empire, but the Taj brought the style to perfection. Working with a model created by his Persian architect, Shah Jahan raised the dome and replaced the red sandstone with brilliant white marble. The entire exterior and interior surface is decorated with cut-stone geometric patterns, delicate black stone tracery, or intricate inlay of colored precious stones in floral and Qur'anic arabesques (see the Comparative Illustration "The Taj Mahal: Symbol of the Exotic East" above). The technique of creating dazzling floral mosaics of lapis lazuli, malachite, carnelian, turquoise, and mother-of-pearl may have been introduced by Italian artists at the Mughal court. Shah Jahan had intended to erect a similar building in black marble across the river for his own remains, but the plans were abandoned after he was deposed by his son Aurangzeb. Shah Jahan spent his last years imprisoned in a room in the Red Fort at Agra; from his windows, he could see the beautiful memorial to his beloved wife.

The Taj was by no means the only magnificent building erected during the Mughal era. Akbar, who, in the words of a contemporary, "dresses the work of his mind and heart in the garment of stone and clay," was the first of the great Mughal builders. His first palace at Agra, the Red Fort, was begun in 1565. A few years later, he ordered the construction of a new palace at Fatehpur Sikri, 26 miles to the west. The new palace was built in honor of a Sufi mystic who had correctly forecast the birth of a son to the emperor. In gratitude, Akbar decided to build a new capital city and palace on the site of the mystic's home (see the illustration "The Construction of Fatehpur Sikri" on p. 463). Over a period of fifteen years, from 1571 to 1586, a magnificent new city in red sandstone was constructed. Although the city was abandoned before completion and now stands almost untouched, it is a popular destination for tourists and pilgrims.

PAINTING The other major artistic achievement of the Mughal period was painting. Painting had never been one of the great attainments of Indian culture due in part to a technological difficulty. Paper was not introduced to India from Persia until the latter part of the fourteenth century, so traditionally painting had been done on palm leaves, which had severely hampered artistic creativity. By the fifteenth century, Indian painting had made the transition from palm leaf to paper, and the new medium eventually stimulated a burst of creativity, particularly in the genre of miniatures, or book illustrations.

As in so many other areas of endeavor, painting in Mughal India resulted from the blending of two cultures. While living in exile, Emperor Humayun had learned to admire Persian miniatures. On his return to India in 1555, he invited two Persian masters to live in his palace and introduce the technique. His successor, Akbar, appreciated the new style and popularized it with his patronage. He established a state workshop at Fatehpur Sikri for two hundred artists, mostly Hindus, who worked under the guidance of the Persian masters to create the Mughal school of painting.

The "Akbar style" combined Persian with Indian motifs, such as the use of extended space and the portrayal of humans engaged in physical action, characteristics not usually seen in Persian art. Akbar also apparently encouraged the imitation of European art forms, including the portrayal of Christian subjects, the use of perspective, lifelike portraits, and the shading of colors in the Renaissance style. The depiction of the human figure in Mughal painting outraged orthodox Muslims at court, but Akbar argued that the painter, "in sketching anything that has life … must come to feel that he cannot bestow individuality upon his work, and is thus forced to think of God, the Giver of Life, and will thus increase in knowledge."[5]

Painting during Akbar's reign followed the trend toward realism and historical narrative that had originated in the Ottoman Empire. For example, Akbar had the illustrated *Book of Akbar* made to record his military exploits and court activities. Many of the paintings of Akbar's life portray him in action in the real world. After his death, his son and grandson continued the patronage of the arts.

LITERATURE The development of Indian literature was held back by the absence of printing, which was not introduced until the end of the Mughal era. Literary works were inscribed by calligraphers, and one historian has estimated that the library of Agra contained more than 24,000 volumes. Poetry, in particular, flourished under the Mughals, who established poets laureate at court. Poems were written in the Persian style and in the Persian language. In fact, Persian became the official language of the court until the sack of Delhi in 1739. At the time, the Indians' anger at their conquerors led them to adopt Urdu as the new language for the court and for poetry. By that time, Indian verse on the Persian model had already lost its original vitality and simplicity and had become more artificial in the manner of court literature everywhere.

Another aspect of the long Mughal reign was a Hindu revival of devotional literature, much of it dedicated to Krishna and Rama. The retelling of the Ramayana in the vernacular, beginning in the southern Tamil languages in the eleventh century and spreading slowly northward, culminated in the sixteenth-century Hindi version by the great poet Tulsidas (tool-see-DAHSS) (1532–1623). His *Ramcaritmanas* (RAM-kah-rit-MAH-nuz) presents the devotional story with a deified Rama and Sita. Tulsidas's genius was in combining the conflicting cults of Vishnu and Shiva into a unified and overwhelming love for the divine, which he expressed in some of the most moving of all Indian poetry. The *Ramcaritmanas* has eclipsed its two-thousand-year-old Sanskrit ancestor in popularity and even became the basis of an Indian television series in the late 1980s.

CHAPTER SUMMARY

The three empires discussed in this chapter exhibited a number of striking similarities. First of all, they were Muslim in their religious affiliation, although the Safavids were Shi'ite rather than Sunni, a distinction that often led to mutual tensions and conflict. More important, perhaps, they were all of nomadic origin, and the political and social institutions that they adopted carried the imprint of their preimperial past. Once they achieved imperial power, however, all three ruling

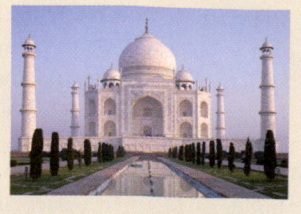

dynasties displayed an impressive capacity to administer a large empire and brought a degree of stability to peoples who had all too often lived in conditions of internal division and war.

The rise of these powerful Muslim states coincided with the opening period of European expansion at the end of the fifteenth century and the beginning of the sixteenth. The military and political talents of these empires helped protect much of the Muslim world from the resurgent forces of Christianity. In fact, the Ottoman Turks carried their empire into the heart of Christian Europe and briefly reached the gates of the great city of Vienna. By the end of the eighteenth century, however, the Safavid Dynasty had imploded, and the powerful Mughal Empire was in a state of virtual collapse. Only the Ottoman Empire was still functioning. Yet it too had lost much of its early expansionistic vigor and was showing signs of internal decay.

The reasons for the decline of these empires have inspired considerable debate among historians. One factor was undoubtedly the expansion of European power into the Indian Ocean and the Middle East. But internal causes were probably more important in the long run. All three empires experienced growing factionalism within the ruling elite, incompetent leadership, and the emergence of divisive forces in the empire at large—factors that have marked the passing of traditional empires since early times. Climate change (the region was reportedly hotter and drier after the beginning of the seventeenth century) may have been a contributing factor. Paradoxically, one of the greatest strengths of these empires—their mastery of gunpowder—may have simultaneously been a serious weakness in that it allowed them to develop a complacent sense of security. With little incentive to turn their attention to new developments in science and technology, they were increasingly vulnerable to attack by the advanced nations of the West.

The Muslim empires, however, were not the only states in the Old World that were able to resist the first outward thrust of European expansion. Farther to the east, the mature civilizations in China and Japan faced down a similar challenge from Western merchants and missionaries. Unlike their counterparts in South Asia and the Middle East, as the nineteenth century dawned, they continued to thrive.

CHAPTER TIMELINE

CHAPTER REVIEW

Upon Reflection

Q How did the social policies adopted by the Ottomans compare with those of the Mughals? What similarities and differences do you detect, and what might account for them?

Q What is meant by the phrase "gunpowder empires," and to what degree did the Muslim states discussed here conform to this description?

Q What role did women play in the Ottoman, Safavid, and Mughal Empires? What might explain the similarities and differences? How did the treatment of women in these states compare with their treatment in other parts of the world?

Key Terms

beys (p. 447)
janissaries (p. 447)
pashas (p. 450)
grand vizier (p. 451)
harem (p. 451)
devshirme (p. 451)
sipahis (p. 453)
millet (p. 453)
Sublime Porte (p. 454)
zamindars (p. 462)

Suggested Reading

CONSTANTINOPLE A dramatic recent account of the Muslim takeover of Constantinople is provided by **R. Crowley** in *1453: The Holy War for Constantinople and the Clash of Islam and the West* (New York, 2005). Crowley acknowledges his debt to the classic by **S. Runciman**, *The Fall of Constantinople, 1453* (Cambridge, 1965).

OTTOMAN EMPIRE Two useful general surveys of Ottoman history are **C. Finkel**, *Osman's Dream: The History of the Ottoman Empire* (Jackson, Tenn., 2006), and **J. Goodwin**, *Lords of the Horizons: A History of the Ottoman Empire* (London, 2002). Also see **C. Findley's** *The Turks in World History* (Oxford, 2005).

For the argument that the decline of the Ottoman Empire was not inevitable, see **E. Karsh et al.**, *Empires of the Sand: The Struggle for Mastery in the Middle East, 1789–1923* (Cambridge, Mass., 2001).

THE SAFAVIDS On the Safavids, see **R. M. Savory**, *Iran Under the Safavids* (Cambridge, 1980). For a thoughtful if scholarly account of the reasons for the rise of the Safavid Empire, see **R. J. Abisaab**, *Converting Persia: Shia Islam and the Safavid Empire, 1501–1736* (London, 2004).

THE MUGHALS For an elegant overview of the Mughal Empire and its cultural achievements, see **A. Schimmel**, *The Empire of the Great Mughals: History, Art and Culture*, trans. **C. Attwood** (London, 2004). The Mughal Empire is analyzed in a broad Central Asian context in **R. C. Foltz**, *Mughal India and Central Asia* (Karachi, 1998).

There are a number of specialized works on various aspects of the period. Economic issues predominate in much recent scholarship. For example, see **O. Prakash**, *European Commercial Enterprise in Pre-Colonial India* (Cambridge, 1998). Finally, **K. N. Chaudhuri**, *Trade and Civilization in the Indian Ocean: An Economic History from the Rise of Islam to 1750* (Cambridge, 1985), views Indian commerce in the perspective of the regional trade network throughout the Indian Ocean.

For treatments of all three Muslim empires in a comparative context, see **J. J. Kissling et al.**, *The Last Great Muslim Empires* (Princeton, N.J., 1996) and **S. Dale**, *The Muslim Empires of the Ottomans, Safavids, and Mughals* (New York, 2010). On the impact of Islam in the subcontinent, see **R. Eaton, ed.**, *Essay on Islam and Indian History* (New Delhi, 2000).

WOMEN OF THE OTTOMAN AND MUGHAL EMPIRES For a detailed presentation of women in the imperial harem, consult **L. P. Peirce**, *The Imperial Harem: Women and Sovereignty in the Ottoman Empire* (Oxford, 1993). The fascinating story of the royal woman who played an important role behind the scenes is found in **E. B. Findly**, *Nur Jahan: Empress of Mughal India* (Oxford, 1993).

ART AND ARCHITECTURE On the art of this era, see **R. C. Craven**, *Indian Art: A Concise History*, rev. ed. (New York, 1997); **J. Bloom** and **S. Blair**, *Islamic Arts* (London, 1997); **M. C. Beach** and **E. Koch**, *King of the World: The Padshahnama* (London, 1997); and **M. Hattstein** and **P. Delius**, *Islam: Art and Architecture* (Königswinter, Germany, 2004).

Chapter Notes

1. Cited in Christophe Courau, "Turquie: Sublime Porte de l'Europe," in *Historia* (October 2005), p. 15.
2. Quoted in V. A. Smith, *The Oxford History of India* (Oxford, 1967), p. 341.
3. Quoted in M. Edwardes, *A History of India: From the Earliest Times to the Present Day* (London, 1961), p. 188.
4. Quoted in ibid., p. 220.
5. Quoted in R. C. Craven, *Indian Art: A Concise History* (New York, 1976), p. 205.

 MindTap™

MindTap is a fully online, highly personalized learning experience built upon Cengage Learning content. MindTap combines student learning tools—readings, multimedia, activities, and assessments—into a singular Learning Path that guides students through their course.

Emperor Kangxi

Hu Weibiao/Panorama/The Image Works

The East Asian World

CHAPTER OUTLINE AND FOCUS QUESTIONS

China at Its Apex

Q Why were the Manchus so successful at establishing a foreign dynasty in China, and what were the main characteristics of Manchu rule?

Changing China

Q How did the economy and society change during the Ming and Qing eras, and to what degree did these changes seem to be leading toward an industrial revolution on the European model?

Tokugawa Japan

Q How did the society and economy of Japan change during the Tokugawa era, and how did Japanese culture reflect those changes?

Korea and Vietnam

Q To what degree did developments in Korea during this period reflect conditions in China and Japan? What were the unique aspects of Vietnamese civilization?

CRITICAL THINKING

Q How did China and Japan respond to the coming of the Europeans, and what explains the differences? What impact did European contacts have on these two East Asian civilizations through the end of the eighteenth century?

CONNECTIONS TO TODAY

Q Can you think of any countries today that actively seek to resist changes influenced by the outside world, as was the case with China during the period discussed in this chapter?

IN DECEMBER 1717, Emperor Kangxi (KANG-shee) returned from a hunting trip north of the Great Wall and began to suffer from dizzy spells. Conscious of his approaching date with mortality—he was now nearly seventy years of age—the emperor called together his sons and leading government officials in the imperial palace and issued an edict summing up his ideas on the art of statecraft. Rulers, he declared, should sincerely revere Heaven's laws as their fundamental strategy for governing the country. Among other things, those laws required that the ruler show concern for the welfare of the people, practice diligence, protect the state from its enemies, choose able advisers, and strike a careful balance between leniency and strictness, principle and expedience. That, he concluded, was all there was to it.[1]

Any potential successor to the throne in Beijing would have been well advised to attend to the emperor's advice. Kangxi was not only one of the longest reigning of all China's rulers but also one of the wisest. His era was one of peace and prosperity, and after half a century of rule, the empire was now at the zenith of its power and influence. As his life approached its end, Heaven must indeed have been pleased at the quality of his stewardship, for the emperor's edict clearly reflected the genius of Confucian teachings at their best and, with its emphasis on prudence, compassion, and tolerance, has a timeless quality that applies to our age as well as to one of the golden ages in the history of China.

There is an element of irony in this remark, since Kangxi, who reigned during one of the most glorious eras in the long history of China, was not Chinese by birth, but a member of the Manchu minority. Under the Ming Dynasty (see Chapter 10), the empire had expanded its borders to a degree not seen since the Han and the Tang Dynasties, and its culture was the envy of its neighbors, earning the admiration of many European visitors, including Jesuit priests and Enlightenment philosophes (see Chapter 18). By the middle of the seventeenth century, however, Ming society was under severe stress, and in the year 1644, the last Ming ruler was overthrown by the Manchus, a semi-pastoral people whose homeland was north of the Great Wall and who created a new dynasty, called the Qing. Kangxi was the greatest of the Qing emperors.

During this extended period of history, China appeared to many observers to be an unchanging society patterned after the Confucian vision of a "golden age" in the remote past. China's rulers, including those of the Qing Dynasty, referred constantly to tradition as a model for imperial institutions and cultural values. Yet although few observers could have been aware of it at the time, China was changing—and rather rapidly. The China of the Han, and even of the Tang and the Song, was a tantalizing vision of the past.

A similar process was under way in neighboring Japan. In the early seventeenth century, the vigorous new Tokugawa (toh-koo-GAH-wah) Shogunate rose to power and managed to revitalize the traditional system in a somewhat more centralized form that enabled it to survive for another 250 years. But major structural changes were taking place in Japanese society, and by the nineteenth century, tensions were growing as the gap between theory and reality widened.

One of the many factors contributing to the quickening pace of change in both countries was contact with the West, which began with the arrival of Portuguese ships in Chinese and Japanese waters in the first half of the sixteenth century. After initially welcoming the new arrivals, Chinese and Japanese rulers soon came to fear the corrosive effects of Western ideas and practices and sought to protect their traditional societies from external intrusion. But neither could forever resist the importunities of Western trading nations, nor were they able to inhibit the societal shifts that were taking place within their borders. When the doors to the West were finally reopened in the mid-nineteenth century, both societies were ripe for radical change. ◄

China at Its Apex

 FOCUS QUESTION: Why were the Manchus so successful at establishing a foreign dynasty in China, and what were the main characteristics of Manchu rule?

In 1514, a Portuguese fleet dropped anchor off the coast of China, just south of the Pearl River estuary and present-day Hong Kong. It was the first direct contact between the Chinese Empire and the West since the arrival of the Venetian adventurer Marco Polo two centuries earlier, and it opened an era that would eventually change the face of China and, indeed, all the world.

The Later Ming

Marco Polo had reported on the magnificence of China after visiting Beijing (bay-ZHING) during the reign of Khubilai Khan, the great Mongol ruler. By the time the Portuguese fleet arrived off the coast of China, of course, the Mongol Empire had long since disintegrated. It had gradually weakened after the death of Khubilai Khan and was finally overthrown in 1368 by a massive peasant rebellion under the leadership of Zhu Yuanzhang (JOO yoo-wen-JAHNG), who had declared himself the founding emperor of a new Ming (Bright) Dynasty (1369–1644), with his capital at Nanjing (nahn-JING) in central China.

As we have seen, the Ming inaugurated a period of territorial expansion westward into Central Asia and southward into Vietnam while consolidating control over China's vast heartland. It had also embarked on a brief era of maritime expansion, when the admiral Zheng He (JEHNG-huh) led a series of voyages that spread Chinese influence far into the Indian Ocean. In 1433, however, those voyages were suddenly discontinued, as the dynasty turned its attention to domestic concerns (see Chapter 10). To underline the new policy, Emperor Yongle (YOONG-luh) transplanted his capital to Beijing, where he ordered the construction of a new imperial home—known as the Imperial City—on the grounds of Khubilai's old palace under the Yuan dynasty.

FIRST CONTACTS WITH THE WEST Despite the Ming's retreat from active participation in maritime trade, when the Portuguese arrived in 1514, China was in command of a vast empire that stretched from the steppes of Central Asia to the China Sea, from the Gobi Desert to the tropical rain forests of Southeast Asia. From the lofty perspective of the imperial throne in Beijing, the Europeans could only have seemed like an unusually exotic form of barbarian to be inserted within the familiar framework of the tributary system, the hierarchical arrangement in which rulers of all other countries were regarded as "younger brothers" of the Son of Heaven. Indeed, the bellicose and uncultured behavior of the Portuguese initially so outraged Chinese officials that they expelled the Europeans. After further negotiations, however, Chinese officials relented and authorized the Portuguese to occupy the tiny territory of Macao (muh-KOW) as a means of retaining sporadic contacts with the Celestial Empire.

The Imperial City in Beijing. During the fifteenth century, the Ming Dynasty erected an immense imperial city on the remnants of the palace of Khubilai Khan in Beijing. Surrounded by 6½ miles of walls, the enclosed compound is divided into a maze of private apartments and offices; it also includes an imposing ceremonial quadrangle with stately halls for imperial audiences and banquets. Because it was off-limits to commoners, the compound was known as the Forbidden City. The fearsome lion shown in the inset, representing the omnipotence of the Chinese Empire, guards the entrance to the private apartments of the palace.

As a result, the arrival of the Portuguese did not have much impact on Chinese society. Direct trade between Europe and China was limited, and Portuguese ships became involved in the regional trade network, carrying silk from China to Japan in return for Japanese silver. Eventually, the Spanish also began to participate, using the Philippines as an anchor in the galleon trade between China and the great silver mines in the Americas.

More influential than trade, perhaps, were the ideas introduced by Christian missionaries, who first received permission to reside in China in the last quarter of the sixteenth century. Among the most active and the most effective were highly educated Jesuits, who were familiar with European philosophical and scientific developments. Court officials were particularly impressed by the visitors' ability to predict the exact time of a solar eclipse, an event that the Chinese viewed with extreme reverence.

Recognizing the Chinese pride in their own culture, the Jesuits attempted to draw parallels between Christian and Confucian concepts (for example, they identified the Western concept of God with the Chinese character for Heaven) and to show the similarities between Christian morality and Confucian ethics. European inventions such as the clock, the prism, and various astronomical and musical instruments impressed Chinese officials, hitherto deeply imbued with a sense of the superiority of Chinese civilization, and helped Western ideas win acceptance at court. An elderly Chinese scholar expressed his wonder at the miracle of eyeglasses:

> White glass from across the Western Seas
> Is imported through Macao:

> Fashioned into lenses big as coins,
> They encompass the eyes in a double frame.
> I put them on—it suddenly becomes clear;
> I can see the very tips of things!
> And read fine print by the dim-lit window
> Just like in my youth.[2]

For their part, the missionaries were much impressed with many aspects of Chinese civilization, and reports of their experiences heightened European curiosity about this great society on the other side of the world (see the box "The Art of Printing" on p. 477). By the late seventeenth century, European philosophers and political thinkers had begun to praise Chinese civilization and to hold up Confucian institutions and values as a mirror to criticize their counterparts in the West.

THE MING BROUGHT TO EARTH During the late sixteenth century, the Ming began to decline as a series of weak rulers led to an era of corruption, concentration of land ownership, and ultimately peasant rebellions and tribal unrest along the northern frontier. The inflow of vast amounts of foreign silver to pay for Chinese goods led to an alarming increase in inflation. Then the arrival of the English and the Dutch, whose ships preyed on the Spanish galleon trade between Asia and the Americas, disrupted the silver trade; silver imports plummeted, severely straining the Chinese economy by raising the value of the metal relative to that of copper. Crop yields declined due to harsh weather—linked to the "little ice age" of the early seventeenth century—and the resulting scarcity made it difficult for the government to provide food in times of

The Art of Printing

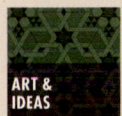

ART & IDEAS

EUROPEANS OBTAINED much of their early information about China from the Jesuits who served at the Ming court in the sixteenth and seventeenth centuries. The Italian Jesuit Matteo Ricci (ma-TAY-oh REE-chee) (1552–1610), who arrived in China in 1601, found much to admire in Chinese civilization. Here Ricci expresses a keen interest in Chinese printing methods, which at that time were well in advance of the techniques used in the West. Later Christian missionaries expressed strong interest in Confucian philosophy and Chinese ideas of statecraft.

Matteo Ricci, *The Diary of Matthew Ricci*

The art of printing was practiced in China at a date somewhat earlier than that assigned to the beginning of printing in Europe, which was about 1405. It is quite certain that the Chinese knew the art of printing at least five centuries ago, and some of them assert that printing was known to their people before the beginning of the Christian era, about 50 B.C.E. Their method of printing differs widely from that employed in Europe, and our method would be quite impracticable for them because of the exceedingly large number of Chinese characters and symbols....

Their method of making printed books is quite ingenious. The text is written in ink, with a brush made of very fine hair, on a sheet of paper which is inverted and pasted on a wooden tablet. When the paper has become thoroughly dry, its surface is scraped off quickly and with great skill, until nothing but a fine tissue bearing the characters remains on the wooden tablet. Then, with a steel graver, the workman cuts away the surface following the outlines of the characters until these alone stand out in low relief. From such a block a skilled printer can make copies with incredible speed, turning out as many as fifteen hundred copies in a single day.... This scheme of engraving wooden blocks is well adapted for the large and complex nature of the Chinese characters, but I do not think it would lend itself very aptly to our European type, which could hardly be engraved upon wood because of its small dimensions.

Their method of printing has one decided advantage, namely, that once these tablets are made, they can be preserved and used for making changes in the text as often as one wishes. Additions and subtractions can also be made as the tablets can be readily patched.... We have derived great benefit from this method of Chinese printing, as we employ the domestic help in our homes to strike off copies of the books on religious and scientific subjects which we translate into Chinese from the languages in which they were written originally. In truth, the whole method is so simple that one is tempted to try it for himself after once having watched the process. The simplicity of Chinese printing is what accounts for the exceedingly large numbers of books in circulation here and the ridiculously low prices at which they are sold.

 How did the Chinese method of printing differ from that used in Europe at that time? What were the advantages of the Chinese system?

Source: From *China in the Sixteenth Century*, by Matthew Ricci, translated by Louis J. Gallagher. Copyright © 1942 and renewed 1970 by Louis J. Gallagher, S. J.

---

imminent starvation. High taxes, necessitated in part because corrupt officials siphoned off revenues, led to rural unrest and violent protests among urban workers. A folk song of the period, addressed to the "Lord of Heaven," complained:

> Old skymaster,
> You're getting on, your ears are deaf, your eyes are gone.
> Can't see people, can't hear words.
> Glory for those who kill and burn;
> For those who fast and read the scriptures,
> Starvation.
> Fall down, old master sky, how can you be so high?
> How can you be so high? Come down to earth.[3]

As always, internal problems were accompanied by disturbances along the northern frontier. Following long precedent, the Ming had attempted to pacify the frontier tribes by forging alliances with them, arranging marriages between them and the local aristocracy, and granting trade privileges. One of the alliances was with the Manchus (man-CHOOZ)—also known as the Jurchen (roor-ZHEN)—the descendants of a non-Chinese people who had briefly established a kingdom in northern China during the early thirteenth century. The Manchus, a mixed agricultural and hunting people, lived northeast of the Great Wall in the area known today as Manchuria (man-CHUR-ee-uh).

At first, the Manchus were satisfied with consolidating their territory and made little effort to extend their rule south of the Great Wall. But during the first decades of the seventeenth century, the problems of the Ming Dynasty began to come to a head. A major epidemic devastated the population in many areas of the country. The suffering brought on by the epidemic helped spark a vast peasant revolt led by the formal postal worker Li Zicheng (lee zuh-CHENG) (1604–1651). With the imperial court now increasingly preoccupied by tribal attacks along the frontier (see Map 17.1), in the 1630s, Li managed to extend the revolt throughout the country, and his forces finally occupied the capital, Beijing, in 1644. The last Ming emperor committed suicide by hanging himself from a tree in the palace gardens.

But the rebels were unable to hold their conquest. Emboldened by the overthrow of the dynasty, the Manchus—now assisted by military commanders who had deserted from the Ming—managed to seize Beijing. Li Zicheng's army

MAP 17.1 China and Its Enemies During the Late Ming Era. During the seventeenth century, the Ming Dynasty faced challenges on two fronts: from China's traditional adversaries, nomadic groups north of the Great Wall, and from new arrivals, European merchants who had begun to press for trading privileges along the southern coast.

Q *How did these threats differ from those faced by previous dynasties in China?*

rapidly disintegrated, and the Manchus declared a new dynasty: the Qing (CHING) (or Pure), which lasted from 1644 until 1911. Once again, China was under foreign rule.

The Greatness of the Qing

The accession of the Manchus to power in Beijing was not universally applauded. Their ruthless policies and insensitivity to Chinese customs soon provoked resistance. Some Ming loyalists fled to Southeast Asia, but others sought to resist the new rulers from inside the country. To make it easier to identify rebels, the government ordered all Chinese to adopt Manchu dress and hairstyles. All Chinese males were to shave their foreheads and braid their hair into a queue (KYOO); those who refused were to be executed. As a popular saying put it, "Lose your hair or lose your head."[4]

But the Manchus eventually proved to be more adept at adapting to Chinese conditions than their predecessors, the Mongols. Unlike the latter, who had tried to impose their own methods of ruling, the Manchus adopted the Chinese political system (although, as we shall see, they retained their distinct position within it) and were gradually accepted by many Chinese as the legitimate rulers of the country.

Like all of China's great dynasties, the Qing was blessed with a series of strong early rulers who pacified the country, rectified many of the most obvious social and economic inequities, and restored peace and prosperity to the country. For the Ming Dynasty, these strong emperors had been Zhu Yuanzhang and Yongle; under the Qing, they would be Kangxi and Qianlong (CHAN-loong). The two Qing monarchs ruled China from the middle of the seventeenth century to the end of the eighteenth and were responsible for much of the greatness of Manchu China.

THE REIGN OF KANGXI Kangxi (r. 1661–1722) was arguably the greatest ruler in Chinese history. Ascending to the throne at the age of seven, he was blessed with diligence, political astuteness, and a strong character and began to take charge of Qing administration while still an adolescent. During the six decades of his reign, Kangxi not only stabilized imperial rule by pacifying the restive peoples along the northern and western frontiers but also managed to make the dynasty acceptable to the general population. As an active patron of arts and letters, he cultivated the support of scholars through a number of major projects.

During Kangxi's reign, the activities of the Western missionaries, Dominicans and Franciscans as well as Jesuits, reached their height. An intellectually curious ruler like the Mughal emperor Akbar, Kangxi was quite tolerant of the Christians, and several Jesuit missionaries became influential at court. Several hundred court officials converted to Christianity, as did an estimated 300,000 among the general population. But the Christian effort was ultimately undermined by squabbling among the Western religious orders over the Jesuit policy of accommodating local beliefs and practices in order to facilitate conversion. The Jesuits had acquiesced to the emperor's insistence that traditional Confucian rituals such as ancestor veneration were civil ceremonies and thus could be undertaken by Christian converts. Jealous Dominicans and Franciscans complained to the pope, who issued an edict ordering all missionaries and converts to conform to the official orthodoxy set forth in Europe. At first, Kangxi attempted to resolve the problem by appealing directly to the Vatican, but the pope was uncompromising. After Kangxi's death, his successor began to suppress Christian activities throughout China.

THE REIGN OF QIANLONG Kangxi's achievements were carried on by his successors, Yongzheng (YOONG-jehng) (r. 1722–1736) and Qianlong (r. 1736–1795). Like Kangxi, Qianlong was known for his diligence, tolerance, and intellectual curiosity, and he too combined vigorous military action

The Temple of Heaven. This temple, located in the capital city of Beijing, is one of the most significant historical structures in China. Built in 1420 at the order of the Ming emperor Yongle, it was the site of the emperor's annual appeal to Heaven for a good harvest. In this important ceremony, the emperor demonstrated to his subjects that he was their protector and would ward off the evil forces in nature. Yongle's temple burned to the ground in 1889 but was immediately rebuilt following the original design.

against the unruly tribes along the frontier with active efforts to promote economic prosperity, administrative efficiency, and scholarship and artistic excellence. The result was continued growth for the Manchu Empire throughout much of the eighteenth century.

But it was also under Qianlong that the first signs of the internal decay of the Manchu Dynasty began to appear. The clues were familiar ones. Qing military campaigns along the frontier were expensive and placed heavy demands on the imperial treasury. As the emperor aged, he became less astute in selecting his subordinates and fell under the influence of corrupt elements at court, including the notorious Manchu official Heshen (HEH-shen). Funds officially destined for military or other official use were increasingly siphoned off by Heshen or his favorites, arousing resentment among military and civilian officials.

Corruption at the center led inevitably to unrest in rural areas, where higher taxes, bureaucratic venality, and rising pressure on the land because of the growing population had produced economic hardship. In central China, discontented peasants who had recently been resettled on infertile land launched a revolt known as the White Lotus Rebellion (1796–1804). The revolt was eventually suppressed, but at great expense.

QING POLITICAL INSTITUTIONS One reason for the success of the Manchus was their ability to adapt to their new environment. They retained the Ming political system with relatively few changes. They also tried to establish their legitimacy as China's rightful rulers by stressing their devotion to the principles of Confucianism. Emperor Kangxi ostentatiously studied the Confucian classics and issued a "sacred edict" that proclaimed to the entire empire the importance of the moral values established by "the Master" (see Opposing Viewpoints "Some Confucian Commandments" on p. 495).

Still, the Manchus, like the Mongols, were ethnically, linguistically, and culturally different from their subject population. The Qing attempted to cope with this reality by adopting a two-pronged strategy. One part of this strategy was aimed at protecting their distinct identity within an alien society. The Manchus, representing less than 2 percent of the entire population, were legally defined as distinct from everyone else in China. The Manchu nobles retained their aristocratic privileges, while their economic base was protected by extensive landholdings and revenues provided from the state treasury. Other Manchus were assigned farmland and organized into eight military units, called **banners**, which were stationed as separate units in various strategic positions throughout China. These "bannermen" were the primary fighting force of the empire. Ethnic Chinese were prohibited from settling in Manchuria and were still compelled to wear their hair in a queue as a sign of submission to the ruling dynasty.

At the same time that the Qing attempted to preserve their identity, they recognized the need to bring ethnic Chinese into the top ranks of imperial administration. Their solution was to create a system, known as **diarchy** (DY-ahr-kee), in which all important administrative positions were shared equally by Chinese and Manchus. Of the six members of the grand secretariat, three were Manchu and three were Chinese. Each of the six ministries had an equal number of Chinese and Manchu members, and Manchus and Chinese also shared responsibilities at the provincial level. Below the provinces, Chinese were dominant. Although the system did not work perfectly, the Manchus' willingness to share power did win the allegiance of many Chinese. Meanwhile, the Manchus themselves, despite official efforts to preserve their separate language and culture, were increasingly assimilated into Chinese civilization.

The new rulers also tinkered with the civil service examination system. In an effort to make it more equitable, quotas were established for each major ethnic group and each province to prevent the positions from being monopolized by candidates from certain provinces in central China that had traditionally produced large numbers of officials. In practice, however, the examination system probably became less equitable during the Manchu era because increasingly positions were assigned to candidates who had purchased their degree instead of competing through the system. Moreover, positions were becoming harder to obtain because their number did not rise fast enough to match the unprecedented increase in population under Qing rule.

CHINA ON THE EVE OF THE WESTERN ONSLAUGHT In some ways, China was at the height of its power and glory in the mid-eighteenth century. But as we have seen, it was also during this period that the first signs of serious trouble for the Qing Dynasty began to appear.

Unfortunately for China, the decline of the Qing occurred just as China's modest relationship with the West was about to give way to a new era of military confrontation and increased pressure for trade. The first challenges came in the north, where Russian traders seeking skins and furs began to penetrate the region between Siberian Russia and Manchuria.

CHRONOLOGY China During the Early Modern Era

Rise of the Ming Dynasty	1369
Voyages of Zheng He	1405–1433
Portuguese arrive in southern China	1514
Matteo Ricci arrives in China	1601
Li Zicheng occupies Beijing	1644
Manchus seize China	1644
Reign of Kangxi	1661–1722
Treaty of Nerchinsk	1689
First English trading post at Canton	1699
Reign of Qianlong	1736–1795
Lord Macartney's mission to China	1793
White Lotus Rebellion	1796–1804

Earlier the Ming Dynasty had attempted to deal with the Russians by the traditional method of placing them in a tributary relationship and playing them off against other non-Chinese groups in the area. But the tsar refused to play by Chinese rules. His envoys to Beijing ignored the tribute system and refused to perform the **kowtow** (the ritual of prostration and touching the forehead to the ground), the classical symbol of fealty demanded of all foreign ambassadors to the Chinese court. Formal diplomatic relations were finally established in 1689, when the Treaty of Nerchinsk (ner-CHINSK), negotiated with the aid of Jesuit missionaries resident at the Qing court, settled the boundary dispute and provided for regular trade between the two countries. Through such arrangements, the Manchus were able not only to pacify the northern frontier but also to extend their rule over Xinjiang (SHIN-jyahng) and Tibet to the west and southwest (see Map 17.2). In the meantime, tributary relations were established with such neighboring countries as Korea, Burma, Vietnam, and Ayuthaya.

Dealing with the foreigners who arrived by sea was more difficult. By the end of the seventeenth century, the English had replaced the Portuguese as the dominant force in European trade. Operating through the East India Company, which served as both a trading unit and the administrator of English territories in Asia, the English established their first trading post at Canton (KAN-tun) in 1699. Over the next decades, trade with China, notably the export of tea and silk to England, increased rapidly. To limit contact between Chinese and Europeans, the Qing licensed Chinese trading firms at Canton to be the exclusive conduit for trade with the West. Eventually, the Qing confined the Europeans to a small island just outside the city walls and permitted them to reside there only from October through March.

For a while, the British tolerated this system, which brought considerable profit to the East India Company and its shareholders. But by the end of the eighteenth century, the British had begun to demand that they be allowed access to other cities along the Chinese coast and that the country be opened to British manufactured goods. The British government and traders alike were restive at the uneven balance of trade between the two countries, which forced the British to ship vast amounts of silver bullion to China in exchange for its silk, porcelain, and tea. In 1793, a mission under Lord Macartney visited Beijing to press for liberalization of trade restrictions. A compromise was reached on the kowtow (Macartney was permitted to bend on one knee, as was the British custom), but Qianlong expressed no interest in British manufactured products (see the box "The Tribute System in Action" on p. 483). An exasperated Macartney compared the Chinese Empire to "an old, crazy, first-rate man-of-war" that had once awed its neighbors "merely by her bulk and appearance" but was now destined under incompetent leadership to be "dashed to pieces on the shore."[5] With his contemptuous dismissal of the British request, the emperor had inadvertently sowed the seeds for a century of humiliation.

MAP 17.2 The Qing Empire in the Eighteenth Century. The boundaries of the Chinese Empire at the height of the Qing Dynasty in the eighteenth century are shown on this map.

What areas were linked in tributary status to the Chinese Empire, and how did they benefit the empire?

Changing China

Q FOCUS QUESTION: How did the economy and society change during the Ming and Qing eras, and to what degree did these changes seem to be leading toward an industrial revolution on the European model?

During the Ming and Qing Dynasties, China remained a predominantly agricultural society; nearly 85 percent of its people were farmers. But although most Chinese still lived in rural villages, the economy was undergoing changes that led to the emergence of a vibrant and rapidly growing industrial and commercial sector. A number of cities, notably along the coast or along the major river systems, began to prosper under the impact of growing contacts between China and the outside world.

The Population Explosion

In the first place, the center of gravity was continuing to shift steadily from the north to the south. In the early centuries of Chinese civilization, the bulk of the population had been located along the Yellow River. Smaller settlements were located along the Yangzi and in the mountainous regions of the south, but the bulk of the population lived in the north. By the Song period, however, that emphasis had begun to shift drastically as a result of climatic changes, deforestation, and continuing pressure from nomads in the Gobi Desert. By the early Qing, the economic breadbasket of China was located along the Yangzi River or in the mountains to the south. One concrete indication of this shift occurred during the Ming Dynasty, when Emperor Yongle ordered the renovation of the Grand Canal to facilitate the shipment of rice from the Yangzi delta to the food-starved north.

Moreover, the population was beginning to increase rapidly. For centuries, China's population had remained within a range of 50 to 100 million, rising in times of peace and prosperity and falling in periods of foreign invasion and internal strife. During the Ming and the early Qing, however, the

European Warehouses at Canton. Aggravated by the growing presence of foreigners in the eighteenth century, the Chinese court severely restricted the movement of European traders in China. They were permitted to live only in a compound near Canton during the seven months of the trading season and could go into the city only three times a month. In this painting, foreign flags (including, from the left, those of the United States, Sweden, Great Britain, and Holland) fly over the warehouses and residences of the foreign community while Chinese sampans and junks sit anchored in the river.

population increased from an estimated 70 to 80 million in 1390 to more than 300 million at the end of the eighteenth century. There were probably several reasons for this population increase: the relatively long period of peace and stability under the early Qing; the introduction of new crops from the Americas, including peanuts, sweet potatoes, and maize; and the planting of a new species of faster-growing rice from Southeast Asia (see the Comparative Essay "Population Explosion" on p. 484).

Of course, this population increase meant much greater pressure on the land, smaller farms, and a razor-thin margin of safety in the event of a natural disaster. The imperial court attempted to deal with the problem through various means, most notably by preventing the concentration of land in the hands of wealthy landowners. Nevertheless, by the eighteenth century, almost all the land that could be irrigated was already under cultivation, and the problems of rural hunger and landlessness were becoming increasingly serious.

Seeds of Industrialization

Another change that took place during the early modern period in China was the steady growth of manufacturing and commerce. Taking advantage of the long era of peace and prosperity, merchants and manufacturers began to expand their operations beyond their immediate provinces. Commercial networks began to operate on a regional and sometimes even a national basis as trade in silk, metal and wood products, porcelain, cotton goods, and cash crops like cotton and tobacco developed rapidly. Foreign trade also expanded after the Ming court in 1567 suspended its prohibition on such activities. In response, Chinese merchants began to set up extensive contacts with countries in Southeast Asia. As Chinese tea, silk, and porcelain became ever more popular in other parts of the world, the trade surplus grew as the country's exports greatly outnumbered its imports. Silver bullion, carried to the Philippines by Spanish galleons from the Americas, flooded into Chinese coffers. As the economy expanded, Chinese officials encouraged the importation of silver as a means of supplementing the inadequate supply of bronze coinage, but eventually the glut of silver in the marketplace caused price distortions that may have contributed to the fall of the Ming Dynasty.

THE QING ECONOMY: READY FOR TAKEOFF? In recent years, a number of historians have suggested that because of these impressive advances, by the end of the eighteenth

The Tribute System in Action

INTERACTION & EXCHANGE

IN 1793, THE BRITISH EMISSARY Lord Macartney visited the Qing Empire to request the opening of formal diplomatic and trading relations between his country and China. Emperor Qianlong's reply, addressed to King George III of Britain, illustrates how the imperial court in Beijing viewed the world. King George could not have been pleased. The document provides a good example of the complacency with which the Celestial Empire viewed the world beyond its borders.

A Decree of Emperor Qianlong

An Imperial Edict to the King of England: You, O King, are so inclined toward our civilization that you have sent a special envoy across the seas to bring to our Court your memorial of congratulations on the occasion of my birthday and to present your native products as an expression of your thoughtfulness. On perusing your memorial, so simply worded and sincerely conceived, I am impressed by your genuine respectfulness and friendliness and greatly pleased.

As to the request made in your memorial, O King, to send one of your nationals to stay at the Celestial Court to take care of your country's trade with China, this is not in harmony with the state system of our dynasty and will definitely not be permitted. Traditionally people of the European nations who wished to render some service under the Celestial Court have been permitted to come to the capital. But after their arrival they are obliged to wear Chinese court costumes, are placed in a certain residence, and are never allowed to return to their own countries. This is the established rule of the Celestial Dynasty with which presumably you, O King, are familiar. Now you, O King, wish to send one of your nationals to live in the capital, but he is not like the Europeans who come to Peking [Beijing] as Chinese employees, live there, and

never return home again, nor can he be allowed to go and come and maintain any correspondence. This is indeed a useless undertaking.

Moreover the territory under the control of the Celestial Court is very large and wide. There are well-established regulations governing tributary envoys from the outer states to Peking, giving them provisions [of food and traveling expenses] by our post-houses and limiting their going and coming. There has never been a precedent for letting them do whatever they like. Now if you, O King, wish to have a representative in Peking, his language will be unintelligible and his dress different from the regulations; there is no place to accommodate him....

The Celestial Court has pacified and possessed the territory within the four seas. Its sole aim is to do its utmost to achieve good government and to manage political affairs, attaching no value to strange jewels and precious objects. The various articles presented by you, O King, this time are accepted by my special order to the office in charge of such functions in consideration of the offerings having come from a long distance with sincere good wishes. As a matter of fact, the virtue and prestige of the Celestial Dynasty having spread far and wide, the kings of the myriad nations come by land and sea with all sorts of precious things. Consequently there is nothing we lack, as your principal envoy and others have themselves observed. We have never set much store on strange or ingenious objects, nor do we need any more of your country's manufactures.

 What reasons did the emperor give for refusing Macartney's request to have a permanent British ambassador in Beijing? How did the tribute system differ from the principles of international relations as practiced in the West?

Source: Reprinted by permission of the publisher from *China's Response to the West: A Documentary Survey, 1839–1923*, by Ssu-yu Teng and John King Fairbank, p. 19, Cambridge, Mass.: Harvard University Press, Copyright © 1954, 1979 by the President and Fellows of Harvard College. Copyright renewed 1982 by Ssu-yu Teng and John King Fairbank.

century China was poised to make the transition from an agricultural to a predominantly manufacturing and commercial economy—a transition that began to take place in western Europe with the onset of the Industrial Revolution at the end of the eighteenth century (see Chapter 19).

Certainly, in many respects, the Chinese economy in the mid-Qing era was as advanced as any of its counterparts around the world. China's achievements in technology over the past centuries were unsurpassed, and the population as a whole was among the most prosperous in the world. A perceptive observer at the time might well have concluded that the Manchu Empire would be highly competitive with the most advanced nations around the globe for the indefinite future.

Nevertheless, a number of factors raise doubts that China in the mid-Qing era was poised to advance rapidly into the industrial age. In the first place, the mercantile class was not as independent in China as in some European societies. Trade and manufacturing in China remained under the firm control of the state. In addition, political and social prejudices against commercial activity remained strong, and the road to success was still seen as resulting from a career in officialdom. Reflecting an ancient preference for agriculture over manufacturing and trade, the state levied heavy taxes on manufacturing and commerce while attempting to keep agricultural taxes low.

To a considerable degree, these views were shared by the population at large, as the scholar-gentry continued to dominate intellectual fashions in China throughout the early Qing

Population Explosion

EARTH & ENVIRONMENT

Between 1700 and 1800, Europe, China, and to a lesser degree India and the Ottoman Empire experienced a dramatic growth in population. In Europe, the population grew from 120 million people to almost 200 million by 1800; in China, from less than 200 million to more than 300 million during the same period.

Four developments in particular contributed to this population explosion. First, better growing conditions, made possible by an improvement in climate, affected wide areas of the world and enabled people to produce more food. Both China and Europe experienced warmer summers beginning in the early eighteenth century. Second, by the eighteenth century, people had begun to develop immunities to the epidemic diseases that had caused widespread loss of life between 1500 and 1700. The increase in travel by ship after 1500 had led to devastating epidemics. For example, the arrival of Europeans in Mexico introduced smallpox, measles, and chickenpox to a native population that had no immunities to European diseases. In 1500, between 11 and 20 million people lived in the area of Mexico; by 1650, only 1.5 million remained. Gradually, however, people developed resistance to these diseases.

A third factor in the population increase was the introduction of new foods. As a result of the Columbian Exchange (see the Comparative Essay "The Columbian Exchange" on p. 405 in Chapter 14), American food crops, such as corn, potatoes, and sweet potatoes, were transported to other parts of the world, where they

became important food sources. China imported a new species of rice from Southeast Asia that had a shorter harvest cycle than existing varieties. These new foods provided additional sources of nutrition that enabled more people to live for a longer time. At the same time, land development and canal building in the eighteenth century enabled government authorities to move food supplies to areas threatened with crop failure and famine.

Finally, the use of new weapons based on gunpowder allowed states to control larger territories and ensure a new degree of order. The early rulers of the Qing Dynasty, for example, pacified the Chinese Empire and ensured a long period of peace and stability. Absolute monarchs achieved similar goals in a number of European states. Less violence resulted in fewer deaths at the same time that an increase in food supplies and a decrease in deaths from diseases were occurring, thus making possible in the eighteenth century the beginning of the world population explosion that persists to this day.

© British Museum, London/The Bridgeman Art Library

Festival of the Yam. The spread of a few major food crops made possible new sources of nutrition to feed more people. The importance of the yam to the Ashanti people of West Africa is evident in this celebration of a yam festival at harvest time in 1817.

Q *What were the main reasons for the dramatic expansion in the world population during the early modern era?*

period. Chinese elites in general had little interest in the natural sciences or economic activities and often viewed them as a threat to their own dominant status within Chinese society as a whole. The commercial middle class, lacking social status and an independent position in society, had little say in intellectual matters and relatively little influence at court.

At the root of such attitudes was the lingering influence of Neo-Confucianism, which remained the official state doctrine in China down to the end of the Qing Dynasty. Although the founding fathers of Neo-Confucianism had originally focused on the "investigation of things," as time passed its practitioners tended to emphasize the elucidation of moral principles rather than the expansion of scientific knowledge. Though the Chinese economy was gradually being transformed from an agricultural to a commercial and industrial

giant, scholars tended to look back to antiquity, rather than to empirical science, as the prime source for knowledge of the natural world and human events. The result was an intellectual environment that valued continuity over change and tradition over innovation.

The Chinese indifference to foreign trade provides a good example. Although the early Ming emperor Yongle had expressed a strong interest in expanding Chinese contacts with the external world (see Chapter 10), his successors tended to focus on internal concerns and for a time even sought to prohibit trade with foreign countries in a bid to bring an end to the chronic pirate attacks taking place along the coast. Interest in geography and the shape of the world also declined, despite advances in map-making as discussed in Chapter 10.

Haggling Over the Price of Tea. An important item in the China trade of the eighteenth and early nineteenth centuries was tea, which had become extremely popular in Great Britain. The painting depicts the various stages of growing, processing, and marketing tea leaves. In the background, workers are removing tender young leaves from the bushes. In the foreground, British and Chinese merchants bargain over the price. After being dried, the leaves are packed into chests and loaded on vessels for shipment abroad.

The Chinese reaction to European clock-making techniques provides an additional case study. In the early seventeenth century, the Jesuit priest Matteo Ricci introduced advanced European clocks driven by weights or springs. The emperor was fascinated and found the clocks more reliable than Chinese timekeepers, but the population at large did not adopt the Western invention. Although European timepieces became a popular novelty at court, the Chinese expressed little curiosity about the technology involved, provoking one European observer to remark that playthings like cuckoo clocks "will be received here with much greater interest than scientific instruments or *objets d'art.*"[6]

Daily Life in Qing China

Despite the changes in the economy, daily life in China under the Ming and early Qing Dynasties continued for the most part to follow traditional patterns.

THE FAMILY Chinese society continued to be organized around the family. As in earlier periods, the ideal family unit in Qing China was the joint family, in which three or four generations lived under the same roof. When sons married, they brought their wives to live with them in their family homestead. Prosperous families would add a separate section to the house to accommodate the new family unit. Unmarried daughters would also remain in the house. Aging parents and grandparents remained under the same roof until they died and were cared for by younger members of the household. This ideal did not always correspond to reality, however, since many families did not possess sufficient land to support a large household. One historian has estimated that only about 40 percent of Chinese families actually lived in joint families.

Still, the family retained its importance in early Qing times for the same reasons as in earlier eras. As a labor-intensive society based primarily on the cultivation of rice, China needed large families to help with the harvest and to provide security for parents too old to work in the fields. Sons were especially prized, not only because they had strong backs but also because they would raise their own families under the parental roof. With few opportunities for employment outside the family, sons had little choice but to remain with their parents and help on the land. Within the family, the oldest male was in charge, and theoretically his wishes had to be obeyed by all family members. These values were reiterated in Emperor Kangxi's Sacred Edict, which listed filial piety and loyalty to the family as its first two maxims.

For many Chinese, the effects of these values were also apparent in the choice of a marriage partner. Arranged marriages were the norm, and the primary consideration in selecting a spouse was whether the union would benefit the family unit as whole. The couple usually had no say in the matter and might not even meet until the marriage ceremony. Not only were romantic feelings between the couple considered unimportant in marriage, but they were often viewed as undesirable because they could draw the attention of the husband and wife away from their primary responsibility to the larger family unit.

Although this emphasis on filial piety might seem to represent a blatant disregard for individual rights, the obligations were not all on the side of the children. The father was expected to provide support for his wife and children and, like the ruler, was supposed to treat those in his care with respect and compassion. All too often, however, the male head of the family was able to exact his privileges without performing his responsibilities in return.

Beyond the joint family was the clan, which was an extended kinship unit consisting of dozens or even hundreds of joint and nuclear families linked by a clan council of elders and a variety of other common social and religious functions.

The clan served several useful purposes. Some possessed lands that could be rented out to poorer families, or richer families within the clan might provide land for the poor. Since there was no general state-supported educational system, sons of poor families might be invited to study in a school established in the home of a more prosperous relative. If the young man succeeded in becoming an official, he would be expected to provide favors and prestige for the clan as a whole.

Like joint families, clans were not universal, and millions of Chinese had none. They may have originated among the great landed families of the Tang era and managed to survive despite periodic efforts by the imperial court to weaken and destroy them. In many cases, clan solidarity was weakened by intralineage conflicts or differing levels of status and economic achievement. Nevertheless, in the early modern period, they were still an influential force at the local level and were particularly prevalent in the south.

THE ROLE OF WOMEN In traditional China, the role of women had always been inferior to that of men. A sixteenth-century Spanish visitor to South China observed that Chinese women were "very secluded and virtuous, and it was a very rare thing for us to see a woman in the cities and large towns, unless it was an old crone."[7] Women were more visible, he said, in rural areas, where they frequently could be seen working in the fields.

The concept of female inferiority had deep roots in Chinese history. This view was embodied in the belief that only a male could carry on sacred family rituals and that men alone had the talent to govern others. Only males could aspire to a career in government or scholarship. Within the family system, the wife was clearly subordinated to the husband. Legally, she could not divorce her husband or inherit property. The husband, however, could divorce his wife if she did not produce male heirs, or he could take a second wife as well as a concubine for his pleasure. Life was especially difficult for a widow: she had to raise her children on a single income or fight off her dead husband's greedy relatives, who would try to coerce her to remarry because, by law, they would then inherit all of her previous property and her original dowry. Female children were also less desirable because of their limited physical strength and because their parents would have to pay a dowry to the parents of their future husbands. Female children normally did not receive an education, and in times when food was in short supply, daughters might even be put to death.

Though women were clearly inferior to men in theory, this was not always the case in practice. Capable women often compensated for their legal inferiority by playing a strong role within the family. Women were often in charge of educating the children and handling the family budget. Some privileged women also received training in the Confucian classics, although their schooling was generally for a shorter time and less rigorous than that of their male counterparts (see the box "A Plea for Women's Education" on p. 487). A few produced significant works of art and poetry.

All in all, however, life for women in traditional China was undoubtedly difficult. In Chinese novels, women were treated as scullery maids or love objects. They were frequently under the domination of both their husband and their mother-in-law, and in some cases the bullying was so brutal that suicide seemed to be the only way out.

Cultural Developments

During the late Ming and early Qing Dynasties, traditional culture in China reached new heights of achievement. With the rise of a wealthy urban class, the demand for art, porcelain, textiles, and literature increased dramatically.

THE RISE OF THE CHINESE NOVEL During the Ming Dynasty, a new form of literature arose that eventually evolved into the modern Chinese novel. Although considered less respectable than poetry and nonfiction prose, these groundbreaking works (often written anonymously or under pseudonyms) were enormously popular, especially among well-to-do urban dwellers.

Written in a colloquial but realistic style, the new fiction produced vivid portraits of Chinese society. Many of the stories sympathized with society's downtrodden—often helpless maidens—and dealt with such crucial issues as love, money, marriage, and power. Adding to the realism were sexually explicit passages that depicted the private side of Chinese life. Readers delighted in sensuous tales that, no matter how pornographic, always professed a moral lesson; the villains were punished and the virtuous rewarded. During the more puritanical Qing era, a number of the more erotic works were censored or banned and found refuge in Japan, where several have recently been rediscovered by scholars.

Gold Vase Plum, known in English translation as *The Golden Lotus*, presents a cutting exposé of the decadent aspects of late Ming society. Considered by many the first realistic social novel—preceding its European counterparts by two centuries—*The Golden Lotus* depicts the depraved life of a wealthy landlord who cruelly manipulates those around him for sex, money, and power. In a rare exception in Chinese fiction, the villain is not punished for his evil ways; justice is served instead by the misfortunes that befall his descendants.

The Dream of the Red Chamber is generally considered China's most distinguished popular novel. Published in 1791, some 150 years after *The Golden Lotus*, it tells of the tragic love of two young people caught in the financial and moral disintegration of a powerful Chinese clan. The hero and the heroine, both sensitive and spoiled, represent the inevitable decline of the Chia family and come to an equally inevitable tragic end, she in death and he in an unhappy marriage to another.

THE ART OF THE MING AND THE QING During the Ming and the early Qing, China produced its last outpouring of traditional artistic brilliance. Although most of the creative work was modeled on past examples, the art of this period is impressive for its technical perfection and impressive quantity.

In architecture, the most outstanding example is the Imperial City in Beijing, which, on the order of Ming emperor Yongle, was constructed on the remnants of the old imperial palace of the Yuan dynasty. His successors continued to add to

A Plea for Women's Education

FAMILY & SOCIETY

As Chinese society evolved under the impact of the economic and social changes that took place during the early Qing era, the role of women in society came under increased scrutiny, and some commentators argued that women should be given an opportunity to play a more active role in society. In this essay, the career official Chen Hongmou (Chehn HOONG-mow) (1696–1771) takes up the case, arguing that women should no longer be cloistered in the home, but should receive an education in the classical texts like their male counterparts. Although Chen did not take issue with the traditional view that women lacked the capacity for deep intellectual thought and achievement, he maintained that an educated woman would be a better daughter, wife, and mother.

Chen Hongmou was a follower of the Song Dynasty neo-Confucian philosopher Zhu Xi (JOO SHEE) (see Chapter 10) and an ardent advocate of seeking practical solutions to problems of governance. His writings on Chinese statecraft were highly influential during the first century of the Qing Dynasty and beyond.

Chen Hongmou, *Jiaonu yigui*

There is no uneducable person in the world. There is also no person whom it is justifiable not to educate. How then can female children alone be excepted? From the moment they grow out of infancy, they are protectively shut up deep within the women's quarters, rather than, like male children, being allowed out into the wider world, to be carefully corrected in their behavior by teachers and friends and to be cultivated by exposure to the classical literary canon. Although parents may love their daughter deeply, they give no more serious thought to her personal development than by providing her with a home, food, and clothing. They teach her to sew, prepare her dowry, and nothing more…. This view that female children need not be educated is a violation of Principle and an affront to the Way….

Now, a woman in her parents' home is a daughter; when she leaves home she becomes a wife; when she bears children she becomes a mother. If she is a worthy daughter, she will become a worthy wife. If she is a worthy wife, she will become a worthy mother. If she is a worthy mother, she will have worthy sons and grandsons. Thus, the process of civilization begins in the women's quarters, and the fortunes of the entire household rest on the pillar of its womenfolk. Female education is a matter of the utmost importance.

Some will object: "But women who can learn to read are few. And if they do become literate, in many cases it will actually hinder their acquisition of proper female virtue." This argument fails to recognize that all women possess a degree of natural intelligence. Even if they cannot learn to master the classics and histories, they nevertheless can get a rough idea of their message…. Moreover, it is evident that in today's world there are already many women with a smattering of learning. They cling fast to the half-baked ideas they have absorbed, cherishing them till their dying day and imparting them to others. Under these circumstances, would it not be better if they [learned to] recite the classical texts in order to get their message right?

Q *What arguments does the author put forth to justify education for women in Qing China? Does he call for equal treatment of the sexes in education? If not, why not?*

the palace, but the basic design has not changed since the Ming era. Surrounded by high walls, the immense compound is divided into a maze of private apartments and offices and an imposing ceremonial quadrangle with a series of stately halls for imperial audiences and banquets. The grandiose scale, richly carved marble, spacious gardens, and graceful upturned roofs also contribute to the splendor of the "Forbidden City."

The decorative arts flourished in this period, especially intricately carved lacquerware and boldly shaped and colored cloisonné (kloi-zuh-NAY *or* KLWAH-zuh-nay), a type of enamelwork in which thin metal bands separate areas of colored enamel. Silk production reached its zenith, and the best-quality silks were highly prized in Europe, where chinoiserie (sheen-wah-zuh-REE *or* shee-nwahz-REE), as Chinese art of all kinds was called, was in vogue. Perhaps the most famous of all the achievements of the Ming era was the blue-and-white porcelain, still prized by collectors throughout the world. Of unsurpassed luminosity, this porcelain was used by Ming emperors to promote the prestige of their opulent and powerful empire. One variety caused such a sensation in the Netherlands that the Dutch began to manufacture their own blue-and-white porcelain at a new factory set up in Delft.

During the Qing Dynasty, Chinese artists produced great quantities of paintings to grace the walls of elite Chinese compounds. The commercial city of Yangzhou (YAHNG-Joh) on the Grand Canal emerged as an active artistic center. Inside the Forbidden City in Beijing, court painters worked alongside Jesuit artists and experimented with Western techniques. In general, however, European art, dismissed by some local artists as "mere craftsmanship," did not greatly influence Chinese painting at this time. Scholarly painters and the literati totally rejected foreign techniques and became obsessed with traditional Chinese styles. As a result, Qing painting became progressively more repetitive and stale. Ironically, the

© William J. Duiker

World-Class China Ware. Ming porcelain was desired throughout the world for its delicate blue-and-white floral decorations. The blue coloring was produced with cobalt that had originally been brought from the Middle East along the Silk Road and was known in China as "Mohammedan blue." In the early seventeenth century, the first Ming porcelain arrived in the Netherlands, where it was called *kraak* because it had been loaded on two Portuguese ships known as carracks seized by the Dutch fleet. It took Dutch artisans more than a century to learn how to produce a porcelain as fine as the examples brought from China.

William J. Duiker

The Ming Tombs: Chinese Feng Shui in Action. When Emperor Yongle moved the capital of China from Nanjing to Beijing in the fifteenth century, the location of the Ming Dynasty's imperial tombs was moved as well. The last thirteen rulers of the dynasty were interred at a new location north of the new Imperial City. The site was selected with care, according to the hallowed principles of *feng shui* (literally "wind and water"), being placed on the southern slope of forested mountains that would protect the site from cold north winds. Entry into the complex took place by a wide avenue lined with stone statues of guardian animals and senior officials. As this statue of a Bactrian camel demonstrates, the lure of the Silk Road still pertained in late Ming Dynasty China.

Qing Dynasty thus represents both the apogee of traditional Chinese art and the beginning of its decline.

Tokugawa Japan

Q **FOCUS QUESTION:** How did the society and economy of Japan change during the Tokugawa era, and how did Japanese culture reflect those changes?

At the end of the fifteenth century, the traditional Japanese system was at a point of near anarchy. With the decline in the authority of the Ashikaga (ah-shee-KAH-guh) Shogunate at Kyoto (KYOH-toh), clan rivalries had exploded into an era of warring states similar to the period of the same name in Zhou dynasty China. Even at the local level, power was frequently diffuse. For a typical daimyo (DYM-yoh) (great lord), the domain had become little more than a coalition of fief-holders held together by a loose allegiance to the manor lord. Prince Shotoku's dream of a united Japan seemed only a distant memory (see Chapter 11). In actuality, Japan was on the verge of an extended era of national unification and peace under the rule of its greatest shogunate, the Tokugawa.

The Three Great Unifiers

The process began in the mid-sixteenth century with the emergence of three very powerful political figures: Oda Nobunaga

(1568–1582), Toyotomi Hideyoshi (1582–1598), and Tokugawa Ieyasu (1598–1616). In 1568, Oda Nobunaga (OH-dah noh-buh-NAH-guh), the son of a samurai (SAM-uh-ry) and a military commander under the Ashikaga Shogunate, seized the imperial capital of Kyoto and placed the reigning shogun under his domination. During the next few years, the brutal and ambitious Nobunaga attempted to consolidate his rule throughout the central plains by defeating his rivals and suppressing the power of the Buddhist estates, but he was killed by one of his generals in 1582 before the process was complete. He was succeeded by Toyotomi Hideyoshi (toh-yoh-TOH-mee hee-day-YOH-shee), a farmer's son who had worked his way up through the ranks to become a military commander. Originally lacking a family name of his own, he eventually adopted the name Toyotomi ("abundant provider") to embellish his reputation for improving the material standards of his domain. Hideyoshi placed his capital at Osaka (oh-SAH-kuh), where he built a castle to accommodate his headquarters, and gradually extended his power outward to the southern islands of Shikoku (shee-KOH-koo) and Kyushu (KYOO-shoo) (see Map 17.3). By 1590, he had persuaded most of the daimyo on the Japanese islands to accept his authority and created a national currency. Then he invaded Korea in an abortive effort to export his rule to the Asian mainland (see "Korea: In a Dangerous Neighborhood" later in this chapter).

Despite their efforts, however, neither Nobunaga nor Hideyoshi was able to eliminate the power of the local daimyo. Both were compelled to form alliances with some daimyo in order to destroy other more powerful rivals. At the conclusion of his conquests in 1590, Toyotomi Hideyoshi could claim to be the supreme proprietor of all registered lands in areas under his authority. But he then reassigned those lands as fiefs to the local daimyo, who declared their allegiance to him. The daimyo in turn began to pacify the countryside, carrying out extensive "sword hunts" to disarm the population and attracting samurai to their service. The Japanese tradition of decentralized rule had not yet been overcome.

After Hideyoshi's death in 1598, Tokugawa Ieyasu (toh-koo-GAH-wah ee-yeh-YAH-soo), the powerful daimyo of Edo (EH-doh)—modern Tokyo—moved to fill the vacuum. Neither Hideyoshi nor Oda Nobunaga had claimed the title of shogun (SHOH-gun), but Ieyasu named himself shogun in 1603, initiating the most powerful and long-lasting of all Japanese shogunates. The Tokugawa rulers completed the restoration of central authority begun by Nobunaga and Hideyoshi and remained in power until 1868, when a war dismantled the entire system. As a contemporary phrased it, "Oda pounds the national rice cake, Hideyoshi kneads it, and in the end Ieyasu sits down and eats it."[8]

Opening to the West

The unification of Japan took place almost simultaneously with the coming of the Europeans. Portuguese traders sailing in a Chinese junk that may have been blown off course by a typhoon had landed on the islands in 1543. Within a few years, Portuguese ships were stopping at Japanese ports on a regular basis to take part in the regional trade between Japan, China, and Southeast Asia. The first Jesuit missionary, Francis Xavier (ZAY-vee-ur), arrived in 1549.

Initially, the visitors were welcomed. Although Japanese leaders were somewhat ambivalent about establishing relations with countries in the outside world, Japanese traders were active in the regional trade network, and when the Ming court sought to prohibit all maritime trade in the 1530s, Japanese merchants countered by engaging in piracy or smuggling along the Chinese coast, despite efforts by leaders in both countries to stop them. The Europeans added a new dimension to the equation. The curious Japanese (the Japanese were "very desirous of knowledge," said Francis Xavier) were fascinated by tobacco, clocks, spectacles, and other European goods, and local daimyo were especially interested in purchasing all types of European weapons and armaments (see the box "A Present for Lord Tokitaka" on p. 490). Oda Nobunaga and Toyotomi Hideyoshi found the new firearms helpful in defeating their enemies and unifying the islands. The effect on Japanese military architecture was particularly striking as local lords began to erect castles on

MAP 17.3 Tokugawa Japan. This map shows the Japanese islands during the long era of the Tokugawa Shogunate. Key cities, including the shogun's capital of Edo (Tokyo), are shown.

Q *Where was the imperial court located?*

MANCHURIA

Hokkaido

Hakodate

Sea of Japan (East Sea)

KOREA

Seoul

Honshu · Nikko

Lake Biwa

Kanto Plain · Edo

Nagoya · Yokohama

Kobe · Kyoto

Himeji · Osaka

Hiroshima

Tsushima

Shimonoseki

Shikoku · Inland Sea

Pacific Ocean

Nagasaki

Kyushu

Kagoshima

East China Sea

© 2016 Cengage Learning

0 100 200 300 Kilometers
0 100 200 Miles

A Present for Lord Tokitaka

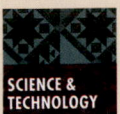

SCIENCE & TECHNOLOGY

THE PORTUGUESE INTRODUCED FIREARMS to Japan in the sixteenth century, and Japanese warriors were quick to explore the possibilities of these new weapons. In this passage, the daimyo of a small island off the southern tip of Japan receives an explanation of how to use the new weapons and is fascinated by the results. Note how Lord Tokitaka (toh-kuh-TAH-kuh) attempts to understand the procedures in terms of traditional Daoist beliefs.

The Japanese Discover Firearms

"There are two leaders among the traders, the one called Murashusa, and the other Christian Mota. In their hands they carried something two or three feet long, straight on the outside with a passage inside, and made of a heavy substance. The inner passage runs through it although it is closed at the end. At its side there is an aperture which is the passageway for fire. Its shape defies comparison with anything I know. To use it, fill it with powder and small lead pellets. Set up a small … target on a bank. Grip the object in your hand, compose your body, and closing one eye, apply fire to the aperture. Then the pellet hits the target squarely. The explosion is like lightning and the report like thunder. Bystanders must cover their ears.… This thing with one blow can smash a mountain of silver and a wall of iron. If one sought to do mischief in another man's domain and he was touched by it, he would lose his life instantly. Needless to say this is also true for the deer and stag that ravage the plants in the fields."

Lord Tokitaka saw it and thought it was the wonder of wonders. He did not know its name at first nor the details of its use. Then someone called it "iron-arms," although it was not known whether the Chinese called it so, or whether it was so called only on our island. Thus, one day, Tokitaka spoke to the two alien leaders through an interpreter: "Incapable though I am, I should like to learn about it." Whereupon, the chiefs answered, also through an interpreter:

"If you wish to learn about it, we shall teach you its mysteries." Tokitaka then asked, "What is its secret?" The chief replied: "The secret is to put your mind aright and close one eye." Tokitaka said: "The ancient sages have often taught how to set one's mind aright, and I have learned something of it. If the mind is not set aright, there will be no logic for what we say or do. Thus, I understand what you say about setting our minds aright. However, will it not impair our vision for objects at a distance if we close an eye? Why should we close an eye?" To which the chiefs replied: "That is because concentration is important in everything. When one concentrates, a broad vision is not necessary. To close an eye is not to dim one's eyesight but rather to project one's concentration farther. You should know this." Delighted, Tokitaka said: "That corresponds to what Lao Tzu has said, 'Good sight means seeing what is very small.'"

That year the festival day of the Ninth Month fell on the day of the Metal and the Boar. Thus, one fine morning the weapon was filled with powder and lead pellets, a target was set up more than a hundred paces away, and fire was applied to the weapon. At first the people were astonished; then they became frightened. But in the end they all said in unison: "We should like to learn!" Disregarding the high price of the arms, Tokitaka purchased from the aliens two pieces of the firearms for his family treasure. As for the art of grinding, sifting, and mixing of the powder, Tokitaka let his retainer, Shinokawa Shoshiro, learn it. Tokitaka occupied himself, morning and night, and without rest in handling the arms. As a result, he was able to convert the misses of his early experiments into hits—a hundred hits in a hundred attempts.

How did Lord Tokitaka use Daoist concepts to explain something unfamiliar to him? What impact did the introduction of firearms have on Japanese society at the time?

the European model. Many of these castles, such as Hideyoshi's castle at Osaka, still exist today.

The missionaries also had some success. Though confused by misleading translations of sacred concepts in both cultures (Francis Xavier was notoriously poor at learning foreign languages), they converted a number of local daimyo, some of whom may have been motivated in part by the desire for commercial profits. By the end of the sixteenth century, thousands of Japanese in the southernmost islands of Kyushu and Shikoku had become Christians. One converted daimyo ceded the superb natural harbor of the modern city of Nagasaki (nah-gah-SAH-kee) to the Society of Jesus, which proceeded to use the new settlement for both missionary and trading purposes. But papal claims to the loyalty of all Japanese Christians and the

European habit of intervening in local politics soon began to arouse suspicion in official circles. Missionaries added to the problem by deliberately destroying local idols and shrines and turning some temples into Christian schools or churches.

EXPULSION OF THE CHRISTIANS Inevitably, the local authorities reacted. In 1587, Toyotomi Hideyoshi issued an edict prohibiting further Christian activities within his domains. Japan, he declared, was "the land of the Gods," and the destruction of shrines by the foreigners was "something unheard of in previous ages." To "corrupt and stir up the lower classes" to commit such sacrileges, he declared, was "outrageous."[9] The parties responsible (the Jesuits) were ordered to leave the country within twenty days. Hideyoshi

William J. Duiker

A Japanese Castle. In imitation of European castle architecture, the Japanese perfected a new type of fortress-palace in the early seventeenth century. Strategically placed high on a hilltop, constructed of heavy stone with tiny windows, and fortified by numerous watchtowers and massive walls, these strongholds were impregnable to arrows and catapults. They served as a residence for the local daimyo, while the castle compound also housed his army and contained the seat of local government. Osaka Castle was built by Toyotomi Hideyoshi essentially as a massive stage set to proclaim his power and grandeur. In 1615, the powerful warlord Tokugawa Ieyasu seized the castle, and it remained in his family's control for nearly 250 years.

was careful to distinguish missionary from trading activities, however, and merchants were permitted to continue their operations (see the box "Toyotomi Hideyoshi Expels the Missionaries" on p. 492).

The Jesuits protested the expulsion, and eventually Hideyoshi relented, permitting them to continue proselytizing as long as they were discreet. But he refused to repeal the edicts, and when the aggressive activities of newly arrived Spanish Franciscans aroused his ire, he ordered the execution of nine missionaries and a number of their Japanese converts. When the missionaries continued to interfere in local politics (some even tried to incite the daimyo in the southern islands against the shogunate government in Edo), Tokugawa Ieyasu completed the process by ordering the eviction of all missionaries in 1612. The persecution of Japanese Christians intensified, leading to an abortive revolt by Christian peasants on the island of Kyushu in 1637, which was bloodily suppressed.

At first, Japanese authorities hoped to maintain commercial relations with European countries even while suppressing the

Western religion, but eventually they decided to regulate foreign trade more closely and closed the two major foreign factories on the island of Hirado (heh-RAH-doh) and at Nagasaki. The sole remaining opening to the West was at the island of Deshima (deh-SHEE-muh *or* den-JEE-muh) in Nagasaki harbor, where in 1609 a small Dutch community was permitted to engage in limited trade with Japan (the Dutch, unlike the Portuguese and the Spanish, had not allowed missionary activities to interfere with their commercial interests). Dutch ships were permitted to dock at Nagasaki harbor only once a year and, after close inspection, were allowed to remain for two or three months. Conditions on the island of Deshima itself were quite confining: the Dutch physician Engelbert Kaempfer complained that the Dutch lived in "almost perpetual imprisonment."[10] Nor were the Japanese free to engage in foreign trade, as the *bakufu* (buh-KOO-foo *or* bah-KOO-fuh)—the central government—sought to restrict the ability of local authorities to carry out commercial transactions with foreign merchants. A small amount of commerce took place with China and other parts of Asia, but Japanese subjects of the shogunate were forbidden to leave the country on penalty of death.

The Tokugawa "Great Peace"

Once in power, the Tokugawa attempted to strengthen the system that had governed Japan for more than three hundred years. They followed precedent in ruling through the *bakufu*, composed now of a coalition of daimyo, and a council of elders. But the system was more centralized than it had been previously. Now the shogunate government played a dual role. It set national policy on behalf of the emperor in Kyoto while simultaneously governing the shogun's own domain, which included about one-quarter of the national territory as well as the three great cities of Edo, Kyoto, and Osaka. As before, the state was divided into separate territories, called domains (*han*), which were ruled by a total of about 250 individual daimyo lords. The daimyo themselves were divided into two types: the *fudai* (FOO-dy) **daimyo** (inside daimyo), who were mostly small daimyo that were directly subordinate to the shogunate, and the *tozama* (toh-ZAH-mah) **daimyo** (outside daimyo), who were larger, more independent lords that were usually more distant from the center of shogunate power in Edo.

DAIMYO AND SAMURAI In theory, the daimyo were essentially autonomous, since they were able to support themselves from taxes on their lands (the shogunate received its own revenues from its extensive landholdings). In actuality, the shogunate was able to guarantee daimyo loyalties by compelling daimyo lords to maintain two residences, one in their own domains and the other at Edo, and to leave their families in Edo as hostages for the daimyo's good behavior. Keeping up two residences also placed the Japanese nobility in a difficult economic position. Some were able to defray the high costs by concentrating on cash crops such as sugar, fish, and forestry products, but most were rice producers, and their revenues remained roughly the same

Toyotomi Hideyoshi Expels the Missionaries

RELIGION & PHILOSOPHY

WHEN CHRISTIAN MISSIONARIES in sixteenth-century Japan began to interfere in local politics and criticize traditional religious practices, Toyotomi Hideyoshi issued an edict calling for their expulsion. In this letter to the Portuguese viceroy in Asia, Hideyoshi explains his decision. Note his conviction that the followers of the Buddha, Confucius, and Shinto all believe in the same God and his criticism of Christianity for rejecting all other faiths.

Toyotomi Hideyoshi, Letter to the Viceroy of the Indies

Ours is the land of the Gods, and God is mind. Everything in nature comes into existence because of mind. Without God there can be no spirituality. Without God there can be no way. God rules in times of prosperity as in times of decline. God is positive and negative and unfathomable. Thus, God is the root and source of all existence. This God is spoken of by Buddhism in India, Confucianism in China, and Shinto in Japan. To know Shinto is to know Buddhism as well as Confucianism.

As long as man lives in this world, Humanity will be a basic principle. Were it not for Humanity and Righteousness, the sovereign would not be a sovereign, nor a minister of a state a minister. It is through the practice of Humanity and Righteousness that the foundations of our relationships between sovereign and minister, parent and child, and husband and wife are established. If you are interested in the profound philosophy of God and Buddha, request an explanation and it will be given to you. In your land one doctrine is taught to the exclusion of others, and you are not yet informed of the [Confucian] philosophy of Humanity and Righteousness. Thus, there is no respect for God and Buddha and no distinction between sovereign and ministers. Through heresies you intend to destroy the righteous law. Hereafter, do not expound, in ignorance of right and wrong, unreasonable and wanton doctrines. A few years ago the so-called Fathers came to my country seeking to bewitch our men and women, both of the laity and clergy. At that time punishment was administered to them, and it will be repeated if they should return to our domain to propagate their faith. It will not matter what sect or denomination they represent—they shall be destroyed. It will then be too late to repent. If you entertain any desire of establishing amity with this land, the seas have been rid of the pirate menace, and merchants are permitted to come and go. Remember this.

What reason did Hideyoshi give for prohibiting the practice of Christianity in Japan? How did his religious beliefs, as expressed in this document, differ from those of other religions like Christianity and Islam?

Source: From *Sources of Japanese Tradition*, Vol. 1, pgs. 316–317, by Ryusaku Tsunoda, William Theodore de Bary, and Donald Keene. Copyright © 1958 Columbia University Press. Reprinted with permission of the publisher.

William J. Duiker

Nijo Palace in Kyoto. When Tokugawa Ieyasu assumed power as shogun of Japan in the early seventeenth century, he retained his headquarters at Edo (modern-day Tokyo), but the imperial court remained in the city of Kyoto. To provide the Tokugawa shoguns with a permanent residence in Kyoto, he ordered the construction of the Nijo palace, an impressive wooden structure decorated with gold leaf and surrounded by two rings of fortifications and a moat. A notable feature of the palace is the so-called "nightingale floor," which is designed to squeak like a bird when walked upon to protect the shogun from a potential assassin.

throughout the period. The daimyo were also able to protect their economic interests by depriving their samurai retainers of their proprietary rights over the land and transforming them into salaried officials. The fief thus became a stipend, and the personal relationship between the daimyo and his retainers gradually gave way to a bureaucratic authority.

The Tokugawa also tinkered with the social system by limiting the size of the samurai class and reclassifying samurai who supported themselves by tilling the land as commoners. In fact, with the long period of peace brought about by Tokugawa rule, the samurai gradually ceased to be a warrior class and were required to live in the castle towns. As a gesture to their glorious past, samurai were still permitted to wear their two swords, and a rigid separation was maintained between persons of samurai status and the nonaristocratic segment of the population. The Jesuit missionary Francis Xavier observed that "on no account would a poverty-stricken gentleman marry with someone outside the gentry, even if he were given great sums to do so."[11]

SEEDS OF CAPITALISM The long period of peace under the Tokugawa Shogunate made possible a dramatic rise in commerce and manufacturing, especially in the growing cities. By the mid-eighteenth century, Edo, with a population of more than one million, was one of the largest cities in the world. The growth of trade and industry was stimulated by a rising standard of living—driven in part by technological advances in agriculture and an expansion of arable land—and the voracious appetites of the aristocrats for new products. The daimyo's need for income also contributed as many of them began to promote the sale of local goods from their domains, such as textiles, forestry products, sugar, and sake (SAH-kee) (fermented rice wine).

Most of this commercial expansion took place in the major cities and the castle towns, where the merchants and artisans lived along with the samurai, who were clustered in neighborhoods surrounding the daimyo's castle. Banking flourished, and paper money became the normal medium of exchange in commercial transactions. Merchants formed guilds not only to control market conditions but also to facilitate government oversight and the collection of taxes. Under the benign, if somewhat contemptuous, supervision of Japan's noble rulers, a Japanese merchant class gradually began to emerge from the shadows to play a significant role in the life of the Japanese nation. Some historians view the Tokugawa era as the first stage in the rise of an indigenous form of capitalism, based loosely on the Western model.

Eventually, the increased pace of industrial activity spread beyond the cities into rural areas. As in Great Britain, cotton was a major factor. Cotton had been introduced to China during the Song Dynasty and had spread to Korea and Japan shortly thereafter. Traditionally, however, cotton cloth had been too expensive for the common people, who instead wore clothing made of hemp. Imports increased during the sixteenth century, however, when cotton cloth began to be used for uniforms, matchlock fuses, and sails. Eventually, technological advances reduced the cost, and specialized communities for producing cotton cloth began to appear in the countryside and were gradually transformed into towns. By the eighteenth century, cotton had firmly replaced hemp as the cloth of choice for most Japanese.

Not everyone benefited from the economic changes of the seventeenth and eighteenth centuries, however, notably the samurai, who were barred by tradition and prejudice from commercial activities. Although some profited from their transformation into a managerial class on the daimyo domains, most still relied on their revenues from rice lands, which were often insufficient to cover their rising expenses; consequently, they fell heavily into debt. Others were released from servitude to their lord and became "masterless samurai." Occasionally, these unemployed warriors—known as *ronin* (ROH-nihn), or "wave men"—revolted or plotted against the local authorities. In one episode, made famous in song and story as "The Forty-Seven *Ronin*," the masterless samurai of a local lord who had been forced to commit suicide by a shogunate official later assassinated the official in revenge. Although their act received wide popular acclaim, the *ronin* were later forced to take their own lives.

CHRONOLOGY	Japan and Korea During the Early Modern Era
First phonetic alphabet in Korea	Fifteenth century
Portuguese merchants arrive in Japan	1543
Francis Xavier arrives in Japan	1549
Rule of Oda Nobunaga	1568–1582
Seizure of Kyoto	1568
Rule of Toyotomi Hideyoshi	1582–1598
Edict prohibiting Christianity in Japan	1587
Japan invades Korea	1592
Death of Hideyoshi and withdrawal of the Japanese army from Korea	1598
Rule of Tokugawa Ieyasu	1598–1616
Creation of Tokugawa Shogunate	1603
Dutch granted permission to trade at Nagasaki	1609
Order evicting Christian missionaries	1612
Yi Dynasty of Korea declares fealty to China	1630s

LAND PROBLEMS The effects of economic developments on the rural population during the Tokugawa era are harder to estimate. Some farm families benefited by exploiting the growing demand for cash crops. But not all prospered. Most peasants continued to rely on rice cultivation and were whip-sawed between declining profits and rising costs and taxes (as daimyo expenses increased, land taxes often took up to 50 percent of the annual harvest). Many were forced to become tenants or to work as wage laborers on the farms of wealthy neighbors or in village industries. When rural conditions in some areas became desperate, peasant revolts erupted. According to one estimate, nearly seven thousand disturbances took place during the Tokugawa era. Peasant disturbances became a more or less routine means of protesting against rising taxes and official corruption or of demanding "benevolence" from the manor lord in times of natural disaster.

Some historians take issue with this grim picture and point out that Japanese peasants did not suffer the same level of hardship as was taking place among their counterparts in neighboring China. In the first place, an increase in the amount of land under cultivation, combined with improved agricultural technology, led to increased yields. Secondly, Japan experienced a relatively low rate of population growth during the Tokugawa era. Although the reasons for that phenomenon are not entirely clear, Honda Toshiaki (HAHN-duh toh-SHEE-ah-kee), a late-eighteenth-century demographer, ascribed the primary cause to a combination of late marriage, abortion, and infanticide. As he described the situation:

> Aware that if they have many children they will not have any property to leave them, [husbands and wives] confer and decide that rather than rear children who in later years will have great difficulty in making a decent living, it is better to take precautions before they are born and not add another mouth to feed. If they do have a child, they secretly destroy it, calling the process by the euphemism of "thinning out."[12]

Life in the Village

The changes that took place during the Tokugawa era had a major impact on the lives of ordinary Japanese. In some respects, the result was an increase in the power of the central government at the village level. The shogunate increasingly relied on Confucian maxims advocating obedience and hierarchy to enhance its authority with the general population. Decrees from the *bakufu* instructed the peasants on all aspects of their lives, including their eating habits and their behavior (see Opposing Viewpoints "Some Confucian Commandments" on p. 495). At the same time, the increased power of the government led to more autonomy from the local daimyo for the peasants. Villages now had more control over their local affairs and were responsible to the central government as much as to the nearby manor lord, although land taxes were still paid to the daimyo.

At the same time, the Tokugawa era saw the emergence of the nuclear family (*ie*) as the basic unit in Japanese society. In previous times, Japanese peasants had few legal rights. Most were too poor to keep their conjugal family unit intact or to pass property on to their children. Many lived at the manorial residence or worked as servants in the households of more affluent villagers. Now, with farm income on the rise, the nuclear family took on the same form as in China, although without the joint family concept. The Japanese system of inheritance was based on primogeniture (pry-moh-JEN-ih-chur). Family property was passed on to the eldest son, although younger sons often received land from their parents to set up their own families after marriage.

THE ROLE OF WOMEN Another result of the changes under the Tokugawa was that women were somewhat more restricted than they had been previously. The rights of females were especially restricted in the samurai class, where Confucian values were highly influential. Male heads of households had broad authority over property, marriage, and divorce; wives were expected to obey their husbands on pain of death. Males often took concubines or homosexual partners, while females were expected to remain chaste. The male offspring of samurai parents studied the Confucian classics in schools established by the daimyo, while females were reared at home, where only the fortunate might receive a rudimentary training in reading and writing Chinese characters. Some women, however, became accomplished poets and painters since, in aristocratic circles, female literacy was prized for enhancing the refinement, social graces, and moral virtue of the home. Under the Tokugawa, it was the obligation of the wife in elite families to reflect her husband's rank and status through a strict code of comportment and dress.

Women were similarly at a disadvantage among the common people. Marriages were arranged, and as in China, the new wife moved in with the family of her husband. A wife who did not meet the expectations of her spouse or his family was likely to be divorced. Still, gender relations were more egalitarian than among the nobility. Women were generally valued as childbearers and homemakers, and both sexes worked in the fields. Coeducational schools were established in villages and market towns, and about one-quarter of the students were female. Poor families, however, often put infant daughters to death or sold them into prostitution and the "floating world" of entertainment (see "The Literature of the New Middle Class" later in this chapter). During the late Tokugawa era, peasant women became more outspoken and active in social protests and in some cases played a major role in provoking demonstrations against government exactions or exploitation by landlords or merchants.

Such attitudes toward women operated within the context of the increasingly rigid stratification of Japanese society. Deeply conservative in their social policies, the Tokugawa rulers established strict legal distinctions between the four main classes in Japan (warriors, artisans, peasants, and merchants). Intermarriage between classes was forbidden in theory, although sometimes the prohibitions were ignored in practice. Below these classes were Japan's outcasts, the *eta* (AY-tuh). Formerly, they were permitted to escape their status, at least in theory. The Tokugawa made their status hereditary and enacted severe discriminatory laws against them, regulating their place of residence, their dress, and even their hairstyles.

Tokugawa Culture

Under the Tokugawa, the tensions between the old society and the emerging new one were starkly reflected in the arena of culture. On the one hand, the classical culture, influenced by Confucian themes, Buddhist quietism, and the samurai warrior tradition, continued to flourish under the patronage of the shogunate. On the other, a vital new set of cultural values began to appear, especially in the cities. This innovative era witnessed the rise of mass entertainment and a popular literature written by and for the townspeople. With the development of woodblock printing in the early seventeenth century, literature became available to the common people, literacy levels rose, and lending libraries increased the accessibility of printed works. In contrast to the previous mood of doom and gloom, the new prose was cheerful and even frivolous, its primary aim being to divert and amuse.

THE LITERATURE OF THE NEW MIDDLE CLASS The best examples of this new urban fiction are the works of Saikaku (Sy-KAH-koo) (1642–1693), considered one of Japan's finest novelists. Saikaku's greatest novel, *Five Women Who Loved Love*, relates the amorous exploits of five women of the merchant class. Based partly on real-life experiences, it broke from the Confucian ethic that stressed a wife's fidelity to her husband and portrayed women who were willing to die for love—and all but one eventually did. Despite the tragic circumstances, the tone of the novel is upbeat and sometimes comic, and the author's wry comments prevent the reader from becoming emotionally involved with the heroines' misfortunes. In addition to heterosexual novels for the merchant class, Saikaku also wrote of homosexual liaisons among the samurai.

OPPOSING ✕ VIEWPOINTS

Some Confucian Commandments

FAMILY & SOCIETY

ALTHOUGH THE QING DYNASTY WAS OF FOREIGN ORIGIN, its rulers found Confucian maxims convenient for maintaining the social order. In 1670, the great emperor Kangxi issued the Sacred Edict to popularize Confucian values among the common people. The edict was read publicly at periodic intervals in every village in China and set the standard for behavior throughout the empire. Like the Qing Dynasty in China, the Tokugawa shoguns attempted to keep their subjects in line with decrees that carefully prescribed all kinds of behavior. Yet a subtle difference in tone can be detected between these two documents. Whereas Kangxi's edict tended to encourage positive behavior, the decree of the Tokugawa Shogunate focused more on actions that were prohibited or discouraged.

Kangxi's Sacred Edict

1. Esteem most highly filial piety and brotherly submission, in order to give due importance to the social relations.
2. Behave with generosity toward your kindred, in order to illustrate harmony and benignity.
3. Show that you prize moderation and economy, in order to prevent the lavish waste of your means.
4. Extirpate strange principles, in order to exalt the correct doctrine.
5. Lecture on the laws, in order to warn the ignorant and obstinate.
6. Labor diligently at your proper callings, in order to stabilize the will of the people.
7. Instruct sons and younger brothers, in order to prevent them from doing what is wrong.
8. Put a stop to false accusations, in order to preserve the honest and good.
9. Fully remit your taxes, in order to avoid being pressed for payment.
10. Remove enmity and anger, in order to show the importance due to the person and life.

Maxims for Peasant Behavior in Tokugawa Japan

1. Young people are forbidden to congregate in great numbers.
2. Entertainments unsuited to peasants, such as playing the samisen or reciting ballad dramas, are forbidden.
3. Staging sumo matches is forbidden for the next five years.
4. The edict on frugality issued by the han at the end of last year must be observed.
5. If a person has to leave the village for business or pleasure, that person must return by ten at night.
6. Father and son are forbidden to stay overnight at another person's house. An exception is to be made if it is to nurse a sick person.
7. Corvée [obligatory labor] assigned by the han must be performed faithfully.
8. Children who practice filial piety must be rewarded.
9. One must never get drunk and cause trouble for others.
10. Peasants who neglect farm work and cultivate their paddies and upland fields in a slovenly and careless fashion must be punished.
11. Fights and quarrels are forbidden in the village.
12. The deteriorating customs and morals of the village must be rectified.
13. Peasants who are suffering from poverty must be identified and helped.
14. This village has a proud history compared to other villages, but in recent years bad times have come upon us. Everyone must rise at six in the morning, cut grass, and work hard to revitalize the village.
15. The punishments to be meted out to violators of the village code and gifts to be awarded the deserving are to be decided during the last assembly meeting of the year.

In what ways did Kangxi's set of commandments conform to the principles of State Confucianism? How do Kangxi's standards compare with those applied in Japan?

Sources: From *Popular Culture in Late Imperial China* by David Johnson et al. Copyright © 1985 The Regents of the University of California. From Chi Nakane and Oishi Shinsabura, *Tokugawa Japan: The Social and Economic Antecedents of Modern Japan* (Japan, University of Tokyo, 1990), pp. 51-52. Translated by Conrad Totman. Copyright 1992 by Columbia University Press.

In the theater, the rise of Kabuki (kuh-BOO-kee) threatened the long dominance of the *No* (NOH) play, replacing the somewhat restrained and elegant thematic and stylistic approach of the classical drama with a new emphasis on violence, music, and dramatic gestures. Significantly, the new drama emerged not from the rarefied world of the court but from the new world of entertainment and amusement (see the Comparative Illustration "Popular Culture: East and West" on p. 496).

Newark Museum/Art Resource, NY

COMPARATIVE ILLUSTRATION

Popular Culture: East and West. By the seventeenth century, a popular culture distinct from the elite culture of the nobility was beginning to emerge in the urban worlds of both the East and the West. At the top is a festival scene from the pleasure district of Kyoto known as the Gion. Spectators on a balcony are enjoying a colorful parade of floats and costumed performers. The festival originated as a celebration of the passing of a deadly epidemic in medieval Japan. On the right below is a scene from the celebration of Carnival on the Piazza Sante Croce in Florence, Italy. Carnival was a period of festivities before Lent, celebrated primarily in Roman Catholic countries. It became an occasion for indulgence in food, drink, games, and practical jokes as a prelude to the austerity of the forty-day Lenten season from Ash Wednesday to Easter.

Scala/Art Resource, NY

 Do festivals such as these still exist in our own day? What purpose might they serve?

Its very commercial success, however, led to difficulties with the government, which periodically attempted to restrict or even suppress it. Early Kabuki was often performed by prostitutes, and shogunate officials, fearing that such activities could have a corrupting effect on the nation's morals, prohibited women from appearing on the stage; at the same time, they attempted to create a new professional class of male actors to impersonate female characters on stage. The decree had a mixed effect, however, because it encouraged homosexual activities, which had been popular among the samurai and in Buddhist monasteries since medieval times. Yet the use of male actors also promoted a greater

emphasis on physical activities such as acrobatics and swordplay and furthered the evolution of Kabuki into a mature dramatic art.

In contrast to the popular literature of the Tokugawa period, poetry persevered in its more serious tradition. Although linked verse, so popular in the fourteenth and fifteenth centuries, found a more lighthearted expression in the sixteenth century, the most exquisite poetry was produced in the seventeenth century by the greatest of all Japanese poets, Basho (BAH-shoh) (1644–1694). He was concerned with the search for the meaning of existence and the poetic expression of his experience. Basho's genius lies in his sudden juxtaposition of a general or eternal condition with an immediate perception, a spark that instantly reveals a moment of truth. Thanks to his love of Daoism and Zen Buddhism, Basho found answers to his quest for the meaning of life in nature, and his poems are grounded in seasonal imagery. The following are among his most famous poems:

> The ancient pond
> A frog leaps in
> The sound of the water.
>
> On the withered branch
> A crow has alighted—
> The end of autumn.

His last poem, dictated to a disciple only three days before his death, succinctly expressed his frustration with the unfinished business of life:

> On a journey, ailing—
> my dreams roam about
> on a withered moor.

Like all great artists, Basho made his poems seem effortless and simple. He speaks directly to everyone, everywhere.

TOKUGAWA ART The arts also reflected the dynamism and changes in Japanese culture under the Tokugawa regime. The shogun's order that all daimyo and their families live every other year in Edo set off a burst of building as provincial rulers competed to erect the most magnificent mansion.

Furthermore, the shoguns themselves constructed splendid castles adorned with sumptuous, almost ostentatious décor and furnishings. And the prosperity of the newly rising merchant class added fuel to the fire. Japanese paintings, architecture, textiles, and ceramics all flourished during this affluent era.

Court painters filled magnificent multipaneled screens with gold foil, which was also used to cover walls and even ceilings. This lavish use of gold foil mirrored the grandeur of the new Japanese rulers but also served a practical purpose: it reflected light in the dark castle rooms, where windows were kept small for defensive purposes. In contrast to the almost gaudy splendors of court painting, however, some Japanese artists of the late sixteenth century returned to the tradition of black ink wash. No longer copying the Chinese, these masterpieces expressed Japanese themes and techniques. In *Pine Forest* by Tohaku (toh-HAH-koo), a pair of six-panel screens depicting pine trees, 85 percent of the paper is left blank, suggesting mist and the quiet of an autumn dawn.

Although Japan was isolated from the Western world during much of the Tokugawa era, Japanese art was enriched by ideas from other cultures. Japanese pottery makers borrowed both techniques and designs from Korea to produce handsome ceramics. The passion for "Dutch learning" inspired Japanese to study Western medicine, astronomy, and languages and also led to experimentation with oil painting and Western ideas of perspective and the interplay of light and dark. Some painters depicted the "southern barbarians," with their strange ships and costumes, large noses, and plumed hats. Europeans desired

Arrival of the Portuguese at Nagasaki. Portuguese traders, dressed in billowing pantaloons and broad-brimmed hats, landed in Japan by accident in 1543. In a few years, they were arriving regularly, taking part in a regional trade network involving Japan, China, and Southeast Asia. In these panels done in black lacquer and gold leaf, we see a late-sixteenth-century Japanese interpretation of the landing of Portuguese merchants at Nagasaki. Normally, Japanese screens are read from right to left, but this one is read left to right. Having arrived by ship, the Portuguese proceed in splendor to the Jesuit priests waiting in a church on the right.

One of the *Fifty-Three Stations of the Tokaido Road*. This block print by the famous Japanese artist Ando Hiroshige shows the movement of goods along the main trunk road stretching along the east coast from Kyoto to Edo in mid-nineteenth-century Japan. With gentle humor, in a series of color prints Hiroshige portrayed the customs of travelers passing through various post stations along the road. These romantic and somewhat fanciful scenes, very popular at the time, evoke an idyllic past, filling today's viewer with nostalgia for the old Japan.

Japanese lacquerware and metalwork, inlaid with ivory and mother-of-pearl, and especially the ceramics, which were now as highly prized as those of the Chinese.

Perhaps the most famous of all Japanese art of the Tokugawa era is the woodblock print. Genre painting, or representations of daily life, began in the sixteenth century and found its new mass-produced form in the eighteenth-century woodblock print. The now literate mercantile class was eager for illustrated texts of the amusing and bawdy tales that had circulated in oral tradition. At first, these prints were done in black and white, but later they included vibrant colors. The self-confidence of the age is dramatically captured in these prints, which represent a collective self-portrait of the late Tokugawa urban classes. Some prints depict entire city blocks filled with people, trades, and festivals, while others show the interiors of houses; thus, they provide us with excellent visual documentation of the times. Others portray the "floating world" of the entertainment quarter, with scenes of carefree revelers enjoying the pleasures of life.

One of the most renowned of the numerous block-print artists was Utamaro (OO-tah-mah-roh) (1754–1806), who painted erotic and sardonic women in everyday poses, such as walking down the street, cooking, or drying their bodies after a bath. Hokusai (HOH-kuh-sy) (1760–1849) was famous for *Thirty-Six Views of Mount Fuji*, a new and bold interpretation of the Japanese landscape. Finally, Ando Hiroshige

(AHN-doh hee-roh-SHEE-gay) (1797–1858) developed the genre of the travelogue print in his *Fifty-Three Stations of the Tokaido Road*, which presented ordinary scenes of daily life, both in the country and in the cities, all enveloped in a lyrical, quiet mood.

Why did a new popular culture begin to appear in Tokugawa Japan while traditional values continued to prevail in neighboring China? One factor was the rapid growth of the cities as the main point of convergence for all the dynamic forces taking place in Japanese society. But other factors may have been at work as well. Despite the patent efforts of the Tokugawa rulers to promote traditional Confucian values, Confucian doctrine had historically occupied a relatively weak position in Japanese society. In China, the scholar-gentry class served as the defenders and propagators of traditional orthodoxy, but the samurai, who were steeped in warrior values and had little exposure to Confucian learning, did not play a similar role in Japan. Tokugawa policies also contributed. Whereas the scholar-gentry class in Qing China continued to reside in the villages, serving as members of the local council or as instructors in local schools, the samurai class in Japan was deliberately isolated from the remainder of the population by government fiat and class privilege. The result was an ideological and cultural vacuum that would eventually be filled by the growing population of merchants and artisans in the major cities.

Korea and Vietnam

 FOCUS QUESTIONS: To what degree did developments in Korea during this period reflect conditions in China and Japan? What were the unique aspects of Vietnamese civilization?

On the fringes of the East Asian mainland, two of China's close neighbors sought to preserve their fragile independence from the expansionistic tendencies of the powerful Ming and Qing Dynasties.

Korea: In a Dangerous Neighborhood

While Japan under the Tokugawa Shogunate moved steadily out from the shadows of the Chinese Empire by creating a unique society with its own special characteristics, the Choson Dynasty in Korea continued to pattern itself, at least on the surface, after the Chinese model. The dynasty had been founded by the military commander Yi Song Gye (YEE song yee) in the late fourteenth century and immediately set out to establish close political and cultural relations with the Ming Dynasty. From their new capital at Seoul (SOHL), located on the Han (HAHN) River in the center of the peninsula, the Choson rulers accepted a tributary relationship with their powerful neighbor and engaged in the wholesale adoption of Chinese institutions and values. As in China, the civil service examinations tested candidates on their knowledge of the Confucian classics, and success was viewed as an essential step toward upward mobility.

There were differences, however. As in Japan, the dynasty continued to restrict entry into the bureaucracy to members of the aristocratic class, known in Korea as the *yangban* (YAHNG-ban) (or "two groups," civilian and military). At the same time, the peasantry remained in serflike conditions, working on government estates or on the manor holdings of the landed elite. A class of slaves, called *chonmin* (CHAWN-min), labored on government plantations or served in certain occupations, such as butchers and entertainers, considered beneath the dignity of other groups in the population.

Eventually, Korean society began to show signs of independence from Chinese orthodoxy. In the fifteenth century, a phonetic alphabet for writing the Korean spoken language (*hangul*) was devised. Although it was initially held in contempt by the elites and used primarily as a teaching device, eventually it became the medium for private correspondence and the publishing of fiction for a popular audience. At the same time, changes were taking place in the economy, where rising agricultural production contributed to a population increase and the appearance of a small urban industrial and commercial sector, and in society, where the long domination of the *yangban* class began to weaken. As their numbers increased and their power and influence declined, some *yangban* became merchants or even moved into the ranks of the peasantry, further blurring the distinction between the aristocratic class and the common people.

Meanwhile, the Choson Dynasty faced continual challenges to its independence from its neighbors. Throughout much of the sixteenth century, the main threat came from the north, where Manchu forces harassed Korean lands just south of the Yalu (YAH-loo) River (see Map 17.3 on p. 489). By the 1580s, however, the larger threat came from the east in the form of a newly united Japan. During much of the sixteenth century, leading Japanese daimyo had been involved in a protracted civil war, as Oda Nobunaga, Toyotomi Hideyoshi, and Tokugawa Ieyasu strove to solidify their control over the islands. Of the three, only Hideyoshi lusted for an empire beyond the seas. Although born to a commoner family, he harbored visions of grandeur and in the late 1580s announced plans to attack the Ming Empire. When the Korean king Sonjo (SOHN-joe) (1567–1608) refused Hideyoshi's offer of an alliance, in 1592 the latter launched an invasion of the Korean peninsula.

At first the campaign went well, and Japanese forces, wreaking death and devastation throughout the countryside, advanced as far as the Korean capital at Seoul. But eventually the Koreans, under the inspired leadership of the military commander Yi Sunshin (YEE-soon-SHIN) (1545–1598), who designed fast but heavily armed ships that could destroy the more cumbersome landing craft of the invading forces, managed to repel the attack and safeguard their independence. The respite was brief, however. By the 1630s, a new threat from the Manchus had emerged from across the northern border. A Manchu force invaded northern Korea in the 1630s and eventually compelled the Choson Dynasty to promise allegiance to the new imperial government in Beijing. Korea was relatively untouched by the arrival of European merchants and missionaries, although information about Christianity was brought to the peninsula by Koreans returning from tribute missions to China, and a small Catholic community was established there in the late eighteenth century.

Vietnam: The Perils of Empire

Vietnam—or Dai Viet (dy VEE-et), as it was known at the time—managed to avoid the fate of many of its neighbors during the seventeenth and eighteenth centuries. Isolated from the major maritime routes that passed through the region, the country was only peripherally involved in the spice trade with the West and did not suffer the humiliation of losing territory to European colonial powers. In fact, Dai Viet had followed an imperialist path of its own, defeating the trading state of Champa to the south in 1471 and imposing its suzerainty over the rump of the old Angkor empire—today known as Cambodia. The state of Dai Viet then extended from the Chinese border to the shores of the Gulf of Siam.

But expansion undermined the cultural integrity of traditional Vietnamese society, as those migrants who settled in the marshy Mekong River delta developed a "frontier spirit" far removed from the communal values long practiced in the old national heartland of the Red River valley. By the

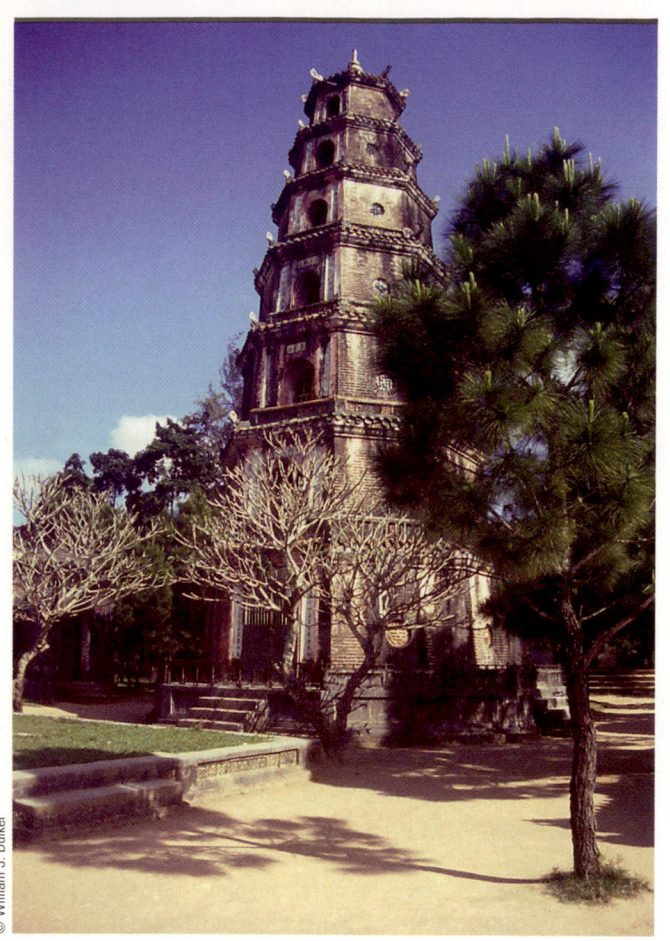

seventeenth century, a civil war had split Dai Viet into two squabbling territories in the north and south, providing European powers with the opportunity to meddle in the country's internal affairs to their own benefit. In 1802, with the assistance of a French adventurer long active in the region, a member of the southern royal family managed to reunite the country under the new Nguyen (NGWEN) dynasty, which lasted until 1945.

To placate China, the country was renamed Vietnam (South Viet), and the new imperial capital was placed in the city of Hué (HWAY), a small river port roughly equidistant from the two rich river valleys that provided the country with its chief sustenance, wet rice. The founder of the new dynasty, who took the reign title of Gia Long, fended off French efforts to promote Christianity among his subjects and sought to promote traditional Confucian values among an increasingly diverse population.

The Thien Mu Pagoda in Hué. When the Nguyen dynasty came to power in Vietnam in 1802, it sought to bolster its legitimacy among the population by adhering to a highly traditional form of Confucian orthodoxy. The most visible manifestation of this policy was the new imperial palace at Hué, modeled after its counterpart in Beijing. In 1968, the palace complex was heavily damaged by the fighting between U.S. and North Vietnamese forces during the Tet offensive. It is now being restored as a national landmark. Adjacent to the palace is the beautiful Thien Mu pagoda, on the banks of the Perfume River. Shown here, the pagoda attests to the continuing influence of Buddhist beliefs in Vietnamese society.

CHAPTER SUMMARY

When the first European ships began to appear off the coasts of China and Japan in the course of the sixteenth century, the new arrivals were welcomed, if only as curiosities. Eventually, several European nations established trade relations with the nations in the region, and Christian missionaries of various religious orders were active in both countries and in Korea and Vietnam as well. But their welcome was short-lived. Europeans eventually began to be perceived as detrimental to law and order, and during the seventeenth century, the majority of the foreign merchants and missionaries were evicted from all four countries. From that time until the beginning of the nineteenth century, the nations of East Asia were relatively little affected by events taking place beyond their borders.

That fact led many observers to assume that the societies of East Asia were essentially

stagnant, characterized by agrarian institutions and values reminiscent of those of the feudal era in Europe. As we have seen, however, that picture is misleading, for conditions in the region, and especially in China and Japan, were evolving and by the early nineteenth century were quite different from what they had been three centuries earlier.

Ironically, these changes were especially marked in Tokugawa Japan, a seemingly "closed" country, but one where traditional classes and institutions were under increasing strain, not only from the emergence of a new merchant class but also from the centralizing tendencies of the powerful Tokugawa Shogunate. On the mainland as well, the popular image in the West of a "changeless China" was increasingly divorced from reality, as social and economic conditions were marked by a growing complexity, giving birth to tensions that by the middle of the nineteenth century would strain the Qing Dynasty to its very core.

By the beginning of the nineteenth century, then, powerful tensions, reflecting a growing gap between the ideal and reality, were at work in Chinese and Japanese society. Under these conditions, both countries were soon forced to face a new challenge from the aggressive power of an industrializing Europe.

CHAPTER TIMELINE

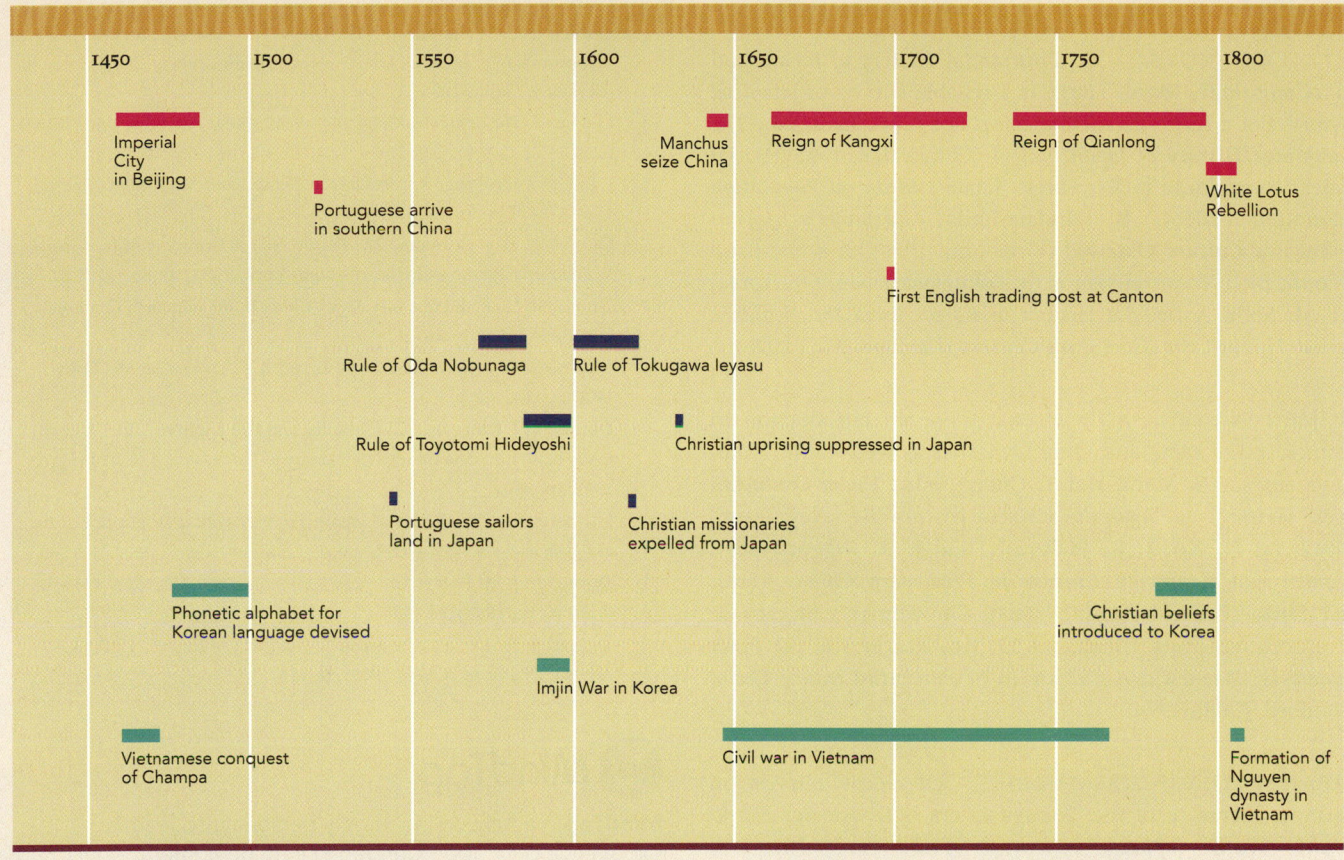

| | 1450 | 1500 | 1550 | 1600 | 1650 | 1700 | 1750 | 1800 |

Imperial City in Beijing

Portuguese arrive in southern China

Manchus seize China

Reign of Kangxi

Reign of Qianlong

White Lotus Rebellion

First English trading post at Canton

Rule of Oda Nobunaga

Rule of Tokugawa Ieyasu

Rule of Toyotomi Hideyoshi

Christian uprising suppressed in Japan

Portuguese sailors land in Japan

Christian missionaries expelled from Japan

Phonetic alphabet for Korean language devised

Christian beliefs introduced to Korea

Imjin War in Korea

Vietnamese conquest of Champa

Civil war in Vietnam

Formation of Nguyen dynasty in Vietnam

CHAPTER REVIEW

Upon Reflection

Q What factors at the end of the eighteenth century might have served to promote or to impede China's transition to an advanced industrial and market economy? Which factors do you think were the most important? Why?

Q Some historians have declared that during the Tokugawa era the Japanese government essentially sought to close the country to all forms of outside influence. Is that claim justified? Why or why not?

Q What was the nature of Sino-Korean relations during the early modern era? How did they compare with Chinese policies toward Vietnam?

Key Terms

banners (p. 479)
dyarchy (p. 480)
kowtow (p. 480)
fudai **daimyo** (p. 491)
tozama **daimyo** (p. 491)

ronin (p. 493)
yangban (p. 499)

Suggested Reading

CHINA UNDER THE MING AND QING DYNASTIES   Reliable surveys with a readable text are **T. Brook,** *The Troubled Empire: China in the Yuan and Ming Dynasties* (Cambridge, Mass., 2010), and **W. Rowe,** *China's Last Empire: Great Qing* (Cambridge, Mass., 2009). For fascinating vignettes of Chinese social conditions, see **J. Spence,** *Return to Dragon Mountain: Memories of a Late Ming Man* (New York, 2007) and *Treason by the Book* (New York, 2001).

   L. Brockey, *Journey to the East: The Jesuit Mission to China, 1579–1724* (Cambridge, Mass., 2007), is an account of China's first encounter with Europe. For a defense of Chinese science, see **B. Elman,** *On Their Own Terms: Science in China, 1550–1900* (Cambridge, Mass., 2005).

CHINESE LITERATURE AND ART   The best surveys of Chinese literature are **S. Owen,** *An Anthology of Chinese Literature: Beginnings to 1911* (New York, 1996), and **V. Mair,**

The Columbia Anthology of Traditional Chinese Literature (New York, 1994). For a comprehensive introduction to the Chinese art of this period, see **M. Sullivan**, *The Arts of China*, 4th ed. (Berkeley, Calif., 1999), and **C. Clunas**, *Art in China* (Oxford, 1997).

JAPAN AND KOREA   **C. Totman**, *A History of Japan*, 2nd ed. (Cambridge, Mass., 2005), is a reliable survey of Japanese history. For a more detailed analysis, see **J. W. Hall, ed.,** *The Cambridge History of Japan*, vol. 4 (Cambridge, 1991). Social issues are explored in **W. Farris,** *Japan's Medieval Population* (Honolulu, 2006). **B. Bodart-Baily,** *Kaempfer's Japan: Tokugawa Culture Observed* (Honolulu, 1999), is a first-hand account by a Western visitor to Tokugawa Japan. On Korea, see **M. Seth,** *A Concise History of Korea: From the Neolithic Period Through the Nineteenth Century* (Lanham, Md., 2006).

WOMEN IN CHINA AND JAPAN   For an introduction to women in the Ming and Qing Dynasties as well as the Tokugawa era, see **S. Mann** and **Y. Cheng, eds.,** *Under Confucian Eyes: Writings on Gender in Chinese History* (Berkeley, Calif., 2001) and **D. Ko, J. K. Haboush,** and **J. R. Piggott, eds.,** *Women and Confucian Culture in Premodern China, Korea, and Japan* (Berkeley, Calif., 2003). On women's literacy in seventeenth-century China, see **D. Ko,** *Teachers of the Inner Chambers: Women and Culture in Seventeenth-Century China* (Stanford, Calif., 1994).

JAPANESE LITERATURE AND ART   Of specific interest on Japanese literature of the Tokugawa era is **D. Keene,** *World Within Walls: Japanese Literature of the Pre-Modern Era, 1600–1867* (New York, 1976). For the most comprehensive and accessible overview of Japanese art, see **P. Mason,** *Japanese Art* (New York, 1993).

Chapter Notes

1. J. D. Spence, *Emperor of China: Self-Portrait of K'ang Hsi* (New York, 1974), pp. 143–144.

2. Quoted in R. Strassberg, *The World of K'ang Shang-jen: A Man of Letters in Early Ch'ing China* (New York, 1983), p. 275.

3. Quoted in F. Wakeman Jr., *The Great Enterprise: The Manchu Reconstruction of Imperial Order in Seventeenth-Century China* (Berkeley, Calif., 1985), p. 16.

4. L. Struve, *The Southern Ming, 1644–1662* (New Haven, Conn., 1984), p. 61.

5. J. L. Cranmer-Byng, *An Embassy to China: Lord Macartney's Journal, 1793–1794* (London, 1912), p. 340.

6. Quoted in D. J. Boorstin, *The Discoverers: A History of Man's Search to Know His World and Himself* (New York, 1983), p. 63.

7. Quoted in C. R. Boxer, ed., *South China in the Sixteenth Century* (London, 1953), p. 265.

8. Quoted in C. Nakane and S. Oishi, eds., *Tokugawa Japan* (Tokyo, 1990), p. 14.

9. Quoted in J. Elisonas, "Christianity and the Daimyo," in J. W. Hall, ed., *The Cambridge History of Japan*, vol. 4 (Cambridge, 1991), p. 360.

10. E. Kaempfer, *The History of Japan: Together with a Description of the Kingdom of Siam, 1690–1692*, vol. 2 (Glasgow, 1906), pp. 173–174.

11. Quoted in J. H. Parry, *European Reconnaissance: Selected Documents* (New York, 1968), p. 144.

12. Quoted in D. Keene, *The Japanese Discovery of Europe, 1720–1830*, rev. ed. (Stanford, Calif., 1969), p. 114.

MindTap is a fully online, highly personalized learning experience built upon Cengage Learning content. MindTap combines student learning tools—readings, multimedia, activities, and assessments—into a singular Learning Path that guides students through their course.

The West on the Eve of a New World Order

The storming of the Bastille

CHAPTER OUTLINE AND FOCUS QUESTIONS

Toward a New Heaven and a New Earth: An Intellectual Revolution in the West

Q Who were the leading figures of the Scientific Revolution and the Enlightenment, and what were their main contributions?

Economic Changes and the Social Order

Q What changes occurred in the European economy in the eighteenth century, and to what degree were these changes reflected in social patterns?

Colonial Empires and Revolution in the Americas

Q What colonies did the British and French establish in the Americas, and how did their methods of administering their colonies differ?

Toward a New Political Order and Global Conflict

Q What do historians mean by the term *enlightened absolutism*, and to what degree did eighteenth-century Prussia, Austria, and Russia exhibit its characteristics?

The French Revolution

Q What were the causes, the main events, and the results of the French Revolution?

The Age of Napoleon

Q Which aspects of the French Revolution did Napoleon preserve, and which did he destroy?

CRITICAL THINKING

Q In what ways were the American Revolution, the French Revolution, and the seventeenth-century English revolutions alike? In what ways were they different?

CONNECTIONS TO TODAY

Q What are the similarities and differences between the French Revolution and contemporary revolutions?

IN PARIS ON THE MORNING of July 14, 1789, a mob of eight thousand men and women in search of weapons streamed toward the Bastille (bass-STEEL), a royal armory filled with arms and ammunition. The Bastille was also a state prison, and although it held only seven prisoners at the time, in the eyes of these angry Parisians, it was a glaring symbol of the government's despotic policies. The armory was defended by the marquis de Launay (mar-KEE duh loh-NAY) and a small garrison of 114 men. The attack began in earnest in the early afternoon, and after three hours of fighting, de Launay and the garrison surrendered. Angered by the loss of ninety-eight of their members, the victorious mob beat de Launay to death, cut off his head, and carried it aloft in triumph through the streets. When King Louis XVI was told the news of the fall of the Bastille by the duc de La Rochefoucauld-Liancourt (dook duh lah-RUSH-foo-koh-lee-ahn-KOOR), he exclaimed, "Why, this is a revolt." "No, Sire," replied the duc. "It is a revolution."

The French Revolution of 1789 was a key factor in the emergence of a new world order. Historians have often considered the eighteenth century the final phase of an old

Europe that would be forever changed by the violent upheaval and reordering of society associated with the French Revolution. Before the Revolution, the old order—still largely agrarian, dominated by kings and landed aristocrats, and grounded in privileges for nobles, clergy, towns, and provinces—seemed content to continue a basic pattern that had prevailed since medieval times. As the century drew to a close, however, a new intellectual ethos based on rationalism and secularism emerged, and demographic, economic, social, and political patterns were beginning to change in ways that proclaimed the arrival of a new and more modern order.

The French Revolution demolished the institutions of the old regime and established a new order based on individual rights, representative institutions, and a concept of loyalty to the nation rather than to the monarch. The revolutionary upheavals of the era, especially in France, gave rise to new liberal and national political ideals, summarized in the French revolutionary slogan "Liberty! Equality! Fraternity!" that transformed France and then spread to other European countries and the rest of the world. ✦

Toward a New Heaven and a New Earth: An Intellectual Revolution in the West

 FOCUS QUESTION: Who were the leading figures of the Scientific Revolution and the Enlightenment, and what were their main contributions?

In the seventeenth century, a group of scientists set the Western world on a new path known as the **Scientific Revolution**, which exposed Europeans to a new way of viewing the universe and their place in it. The Scientific Revolution affected only a small number of Europe's educated elite. But in the eighteenth century, this changed dramatically as a group of intellectuals popularized the ideas of the Scientific Revolution and used them to undertake a dramatic reexamination of all aspects of life. The widespread impact of these ideas on their society has caused historians ever since to call the eighteenth century in Europe the Age of Enlightenment.

The Scientific Revolution

The Scientific Revolution ultimately challenged conceptions and beliefs about the nature of the external world that had become dominant by the Late Middle Ages.

TOWARD A NEW HEAVEN: A REVOLUTION IN ASTRONOMY

The philosophers of the Middle Ages had used the ideas of Aristotle, Ptolemy (the greatest astronomer of antiquity, who lived in the second century C.E.), and Christianity to form the Ptolemaic (tahl-uh-MAY-ik) or **geocentric theory** of the universe. In this conception, the universe was seen as a series of concentric spheres with a fixed or motionless earth at its center. Composed of material substance, the earth was imperfect and constantly changing. The spheres that surrounded the earth were made of a crystalline, transparent substance and moved in circular orbits around the earth. The heavenly bodies, which in 1500 were believed to number ten, were pure orbs of light, embedded in the moving, concentric spheres. Working outward from the earth, the first eight spheres contained the moon, Mercury, Venus, the sun, Mars, Jupiter, Saturn, and the fixed stars. The ninth sphere imparted to the eighth sphere of the fixed stars its daily motion, while the tenth sphere was frequently described as the prime mover that moved itself and imparted motion to the other spheres. Beyond the tenth sphere was the Empyrean Heaven—the location of God and all the saved souls. Thus, God and the saved souls were at one end of the universe, and humans were at the center. They had power over the earth, but their real purpose was to achieve salvation.

Nicolaus Copernicus (NEE-koh-lowss kuh-PURR-nuh-kuss) (1473–1543), a native of Poland, was a mathematician who felt that Ptolemy's geocentric system failed to accord with the observed motions of the heavenly bodies and hoped that his **heliocentric** (sun-centered) **theory** would offer a more accurate explanation. Copernicus argued that the sun was motionless at the center of the universe. The planets revolved around the sun in the order of Mercury, Venus, the earth, Mars, Jupiter, and Saturn. The moon, however, revolved around the earth. Moreover, what appeared to be the movement of the sun around the earth was really explained by the daily rotation of the earth on its axis and the journey of the earth around the sun each year. But Copernicus did not reject the idea that the heavenly spheres moved in circular orbits.

Johannes Kepler (yoh-HAHN-us KEP-lur) (1571–1630) took the next step in destroying the geocentric conception and supporting the Copernican system. A brilliant German mathematician and astronomer, Kepler arrived at laws of planetary motion that confirmed Copernicus's heliocentric theory. In his first law, however, he contradicted Copernicus by showing that the orbits of the planets around the sun were not circular but elliptical, with the sun at one focus of the ellipse rather than at the center.

Kepler's work destroyed the basic structure of the Ptolemaic system. People could now think in new terms of the actual paths of planets revolving around the sun in elliptical orbits. But important questions remained unanswered. For example, what were the planets made of? An Italian scientist achieved the next important breakthrough to a new cosmology by answering that question.

Galileo Galilei (gal-li-LAY-oh GAL-li-lay) (1564–1642) taught mathematics and was the first European to make systematic observations of the heavens by means of a telescope, inaugurating a new age in astronomy. Galileo turned his telescope to the skies and made a remarkable series of discoveries: mountains on the moon, four moons revolving around Jupiter, and sunspots. Galileo's observations seemed to destroy yet another aspect of the traditional cosmology in that the universe seemed to be composed of material similar to that of earth rather than a perfect and unchanging substance.

Medieval Conception of the Universe. As this sixteenth-century illustration shows, the medieval cosmological view placed the earth at the center of the universe, surrounded by a series of concentric spheres. The earth was imperfect and constantly changing, whereas the heavenly bodies that surrounded it were perfect and incorruptible. Beyond the tenth and final sphere was heaven, where God and all the saved souls were located. (The circles read, from the center outward: 1. Moon, 2. Mercury, 3. Venus, 4. Sun, 5. Mars, 6. Jupiter, 7. Saturn, 8. Firmament (of the Stars), 9. Crystalline Sphere, 10. Prime Mover; and around the outside, Empyrean Heaven—Home of God and All the Elect, that is, saved souls.) Image Select/Art Resource, NY

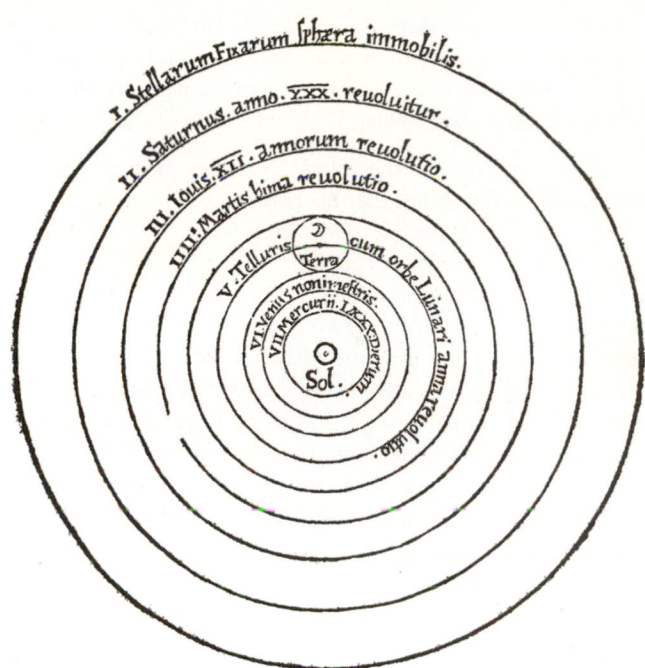

The Copernican System. The Copernican system was presented in *On the Revolutions of the Heavenly Spheres*, published shortly before Copernicus's death. As shown in this illustration from the first edition of the book, Copernicus maintained that the sun was the center of the universe and that the planets, including the earth, revolved around it. Moreover, the earth rotated daily on its axis. (The circles read, from the center outward: Sun; VII. Mercury, orbit of 80 days; VI. Venus; V. Earth, with the moon, orbit of one year; IIII. Mars, orbit of 2 years; III. Jupiter, orbit of 12 years; II. Saturn, orbit of 30 years; I. Immobile Sphere of the Fixed Stars.) Image Select/Art Resource, NY

Galileo's revelations, published in *The Starry Messenger* in 1610, made Europeans aware of a new picture of the universe. But the Catholic Church condemned Copernicanism and ordered Galileo to abandon the Copernican thesis. The church attacked the Copernican system because it threatened not only Scripture but also an entire conception of the universe. The heavens were no longer a spiritual world but a world of matter.

By the 1630s and 1640s, most astronomers had come to accept the new heliocentric conception of the universe. Nevertheless, no one yet had explained motion in the universe and tied together the ideas of Copernicus, Galileo, and Kepler. This would be the work of an Englishman who has long been considered the greatest genius of the Scientific Revolution.

Isaac Newton (1642–1727) taught at Cambridge University, where he wrote his major work, *Mathematical Principles of Natural Philosophy*, known simply as the *Principia* (prin-SIP-ee-uh) by the first word of its Latin title. In the first book of the *Principia*, Newton defined the three laws of motion that govern the planetary bodies, as well as objects on earth. Crucial to his whole argument was the universal law of gravitation, which explained why the planetary bodies did not go off in straight lines but continued in elliptical orbits about the sun. In mathematical terms, Newton explained that every object in the universe is attracted to every other object by a force called gravity.

Newton had demonstrated that one mathematically proven universal law could explain all motion in the universe. At the same time, the Newtonian synthesis created a new cosmology in which the universe was seen as one huge, regulated machine that operated according to natural laws in absolute time, space, and motion. Newton's **world-machine** concept dominated the modern worldview until the twentieth century, when Albert Einstein's concept of relativity created a new picture of the universe.

TOWARD A NEW EARTH: DESCARTES AND RATIONALISM

The new conception of the universe contained in the cosmological revolution of the sixteenth and seventeenth centuries inevitably had an impact on the Western view of humankind. Nowhere is this more evident than in the work of the French philosopher René Descartes (ruh-NAY day-KART) (1596–1650). The starting point for Descartes's new system was doubt. As Descartes explained at the beginning of his most famous work, *Discourse on Method*, written in 1637, he decided to set aside all that he had learned and begin again. One fact seemed to Descartes beyond doubt—his own existence:

> I immediately became aware that while I was thus disposed to think that all was false, it was absolutely necessary that I who thus thought should be something; and noting that this truth *I think, therefore I am*, was so steadfast and so assured that the

suppositions of the skeptics, to whatever extreme they might all be carried, could not avail to shake it, I concluded that I might without scruple accept it as being the first principle of the philosophy I was seeking.[1]

With this emphasis on the mind, Descartes asserted that he would accept only things that his reason said were true.

From his first postulate, Descartes deduced an additional principle, the separation of mind and matter. Descartes argued that since "the mind cannot be doubted but the body and material world can, the two must be radically different." From this came an absolute dualism between mind and matter, or what has also been called **Cartesian dualism**. Using mind or human reason and its best instrument, mathematics, humans can understand the material world because it is pure mechanism, a machine that is governed by its own physical laws because it was created by God—the great geometrician.

Descartes's separation of mind and matter allowed scientists to view matter as dead or inert, as something that was totally separate from themselves and could be investigated independently by reason. The split between mind and body led Westerners to equate their identity with mind and reason rather than with the whole organism. Descartes has rightly been called the father of modern **rationalism**.

EUROPE, CHINA, AND SCIENTIFIC REVOLUTIONS An interesting question that arises is why the Scientific Revolution occurred in Europe and not in China. In the Middle Ages, China had been the most technologically advanced civilization in the world. After 1500, that distinction passed to the West (see the Comparative Essay "The Scientific Revolution" on p. 507). Historians are not sure why. Some have contrasted the sense of order in Chinese society with the competitive spirit existing in Europe. Others have emphasized China's ideological viewpoint that favored living in harmony with nature rather than trying to dominate it. One historian has even suggested that China's civil service system drew the "best and the brightest" into government service, to the detriment of other occupations.

Background to the Enlightenment

The impetus for political and social change in the eighteenth century stemmed in part from the **Enlightenment**. The Enlightenment was a movement of intellectuals who were greatly impressed with the accomplishments of the Scientific Revolution. When they used the word *reason*—one of their favorite words—they were advocating the application of the **scientific method** to the understanding of all life. All institutions and all systems of thought were subject to the rational, scientific way of thinking if people would only free themselves from the shackles of past, worthless traditions, especially religious ones. If Isaac Newton could discover the natural laws regulating the world of nature, they too, by using reason, could find the laws that governed human society. This belief in turn led them to hope that they could make progress toward a better society than the one they had inherited.

Reason, natural law, hope, progress—these were the buzzwords in the heady atmosphere of eighteenth-century Europe.

Major sources of inspiration for the Enlightenment were Isaac Newton and his fellow Englishman John Locke (1632–1704). Newton had contended that the world and everything in it worked like a giant machine. Enchanted by the grand design of this world-machine, the intellectuals of the Enlightenment were convinced that by following Newton's rules of reasoning, they could discover the natural laws that governed politics, economics, justice, and religion.

John Locke's theory of knowledge also made a great impact. In his *Essay Concerning Human Understanding*, written in 1690, Locke denied the existence of innate ideas and argued instead that every person was born with a *tabula rasa* (TAB-yuh-luh RAH-suh), a blank mind:

> Let us then suppose the mind to be, as we say, white paper, void of all characters, without any ideas. How comes it to be furnished? Whence comes it by that vast store which the busy and boundless fancy of man has painted on it with an almost endless variety? Whence has it all the materials of reason and knowledge? To this I answer, in one word, from experience.... Our observation, employed either about external sensible objects or about the internal operations of our minds perceived and reflected on by ourselves, is that which supplies our understanding with all the materials of thinking.[2]

By denying innate ideas, Locke's philosophy implied that people were molded by their environment, by whatever they perceived through their senses from their surrounding world. Thus, by altering the environment and subjecting people to proper influences, they could be changed and a new society created. And how should the environment be changed? Newton had paved the way: reason enabled enlightened people to discover the natural laws to which all institutions should conform.

The Philosophes and Their Ideas

The intellectuals of the Enlightenment were known by the French term *philosophes* (fee-loh-ZAHFS), although they were not all French and few were philosophers in the strict sense of the term. The **philosophes** were literary people, professors, journalists, economists, political scientists, and, above all, social reformers. They came from both the nobility and the middle class, and a few even stemmed from lower-middle-class origins. Although it was a truly international and cosmopolitan movement, the Enlightenment also enhanced the dominant role being played by French culture; Paris was its recognized capital. Most of the leaders of the Enlightenment were French. The French philosophes, in turn, affected intellectuals elsewhere and created a movement that touched the entire Western world, including the British and Spanish colonies in America (see Map 18.1). (The terms *British* and *Great Britain* came to be used after 1707 when the United Kingdom of Great Britain came into existence, uniting the governments of England and Scotland, as well as Wales, which had been joined to England previously.)

To the philosophes, the role of philosophy was not just to discuss the world but to change it. To the philosophes, reason

The Scientific Revolution

SCIENCE & TECHNOLOGY

When Catholic missionaries arrived in China in the sixteenth century, they marveled at the sophistication of Chinese civilization and its many accomplishments, including woodblock printing and the civil service examination system. In turn, their hosts were impressed with European inventions such as the spring-driven clock and eyeglasses.

It is not surprising that visitors from the West were impressed with what they saw in China, for that country had long been at the forefront of human achievement. After the sixteenth century, however, Europe would take the lead in the advance of science and technology, a phenomenon that would ultimately bring about the Industrial Revolution and set in motion a transformation of human society.

Why did Europe suddenly become the engine for rapid change in the seventeenth and eighteenth centuries? One factor was the change in the European worldview, the shift from a metaphysical to a materialist perspective and the growing inclination among European intellectuals to question first principles. In contrast to China, where, for example, the "investigation of things" proposed by Song Dynasty thinkers had been used to analyze and confirm principles first established by Confucius and his contemporaries, empirical scientists in early modern Europe rejected received religious ideas, developed a new conception of the universe, and sought ways to improve material conditions around them.

The telescope—a European invention.

Iberfoto/The Image Works

Why were European thinkers more interested in practical applications of their discoveries than their counterparts elsewhere? No doubt the literate mercantile and propertied elites of Europe were attracted to the new science because it offered new ways to exploit resources for profit. Some of the early scientists made it easier for these groups to accept the new ideas by showing how they could be applied directly to specific industrial and technological needs. Galileo, for example, consciously sought an alliance between science and the material interests of the educated elite when he assured his listeners that the science of mechanics would be quite useful "when it becomes necessary to build bridges or other structures over water, something occurring mainly in affairs of great importance."

Finally, the political changes that were beginning to take place in Europe during this period may also have contributed. Many European states enlarged their bureaucratic machinery and consolidated their governments in order to collect the revenues and amass the armies needed to compete militarily with rivals. Political leaders desperately sought ways to enhance their wealth and power and grasped eagerly at whatever tools were available to guarantee their survival and prosperity.

 Why did the Scientific Revolution emerge in Europe and not in China?

was a scientific method, and it relied on an appeal to facts. A spirit of rational criticism was to be applied to everything, including religion and politics. Spanning almost a century, the Enlightenment evolved with each succeeding generation, becoming more radical as new thinkers built on the contributions of their predecessors. A few individuals, however, dominated the landscape so completely that we can gain insight into the core ideas of the philosophes by focusing on the three French giants—Montesquieu, Voltaire, and Diderot.

MONTESQUIEU Charles de Secondat (SHARL duh suh-KAHN-da), the baron de Montesquieu (MOHN-tess-kyoo) (1689–1755), came from the French nobility. His most famous

work, *The Spirit of the Laws*, was published in 1748. In this comparative study of governments, Montesquieu attempted to apply the scientific method to the social and political arena to ascertain the "natural laws" governing the social and political relationships of human beings. Montesquieu distinguished three basic kinds of governments: republic, monarchy, and despotism.

Montesquieu used England as an example of monarchy, and it was his analysis of England's constitution that led to his most lasting contribution to political thought—the importance of checks and balances achieved by means of a **separation of powers**. He believed that England's system, with its separate executive, legislative, and judicial branches that served to limit

MAP 18.1 The Enlightenment in Europe. "Have the courage to use your own intelligence!" The words of the German philosopher Immanuel Kant (i-MAHN-yoo-el KAHNT) epitomize the role of the individual in using reason to understand all aspects of life—the natural world and the sphere of human nature, behavior, and institutions.

Q *Which countries or regions were at the center of the Enlightenment, and what reasons could account for peripheral regions being less involved?*

and control each other, provided the greatest freedom and security for a state. The translation of his work into English two years after publication ensured that it would be read by American political leaders, who eventually incorporated its principles into the U.S. Constitution.

VOLTAIRE The greatest figure of the Enlightenment was François-Marie Arouet (frahn-SWAH-ma-REE ahr-WEH), known simply as Voltaire (vohl-TAYR) (1694–1778). Son of a prosperous middle-class family from Paris, he studied law, although he achieved his first success as a playwright. Voltaire was a prolific author and wrote an almost endless stream of pamphlets, novels, plays, letters, philosophical essays, and histories.

Voltaire was especially well known for his criticism of traditional religion and his strong attachment to the ideal of religious toleration (see the box "The Attack on Religious Intolerance" on p. 509). As he grew older, Voltaire became ever more strident in his denunciations. "Crush the infamous thing," he thundered repeatedly—the infamous thing being religious fanaticism, intolerance, and superstition.

Throughout his life, Voltaire championed not only religious tolerance but also **deism**, a religious outlook shared by most other philosophes. Deism was built on the Newtonian world-machine, which implied the existence of a mechanic (God) who had created the universe. To Voltaire and most other philosophes, the universe was like a clock, and God was

The Attack on Religious Intolerance

RELIGION & PHILOSOPHY

ALTHOUGH VOLTAIRE'S IDEAS ON RELIGION were not original, his lucid prose, biting satire, and clever wit caused his works to be widely read and all the more influential. These two selections present different sides of Voltaire's attack on religious intolerance. The first is from his straightforward treatise *The Ignorant Philosopher*, and the second is from his only real literary masterpiece, the novel *Candide*, where he used humor to make the same fundamental point about religious intolerance.

Voltaire, *The Ignorant Philosopher*

The contagion of fanaticism then still subsists.... The author of the Treatise upon Toleration has not mentioned the shocking executions wherein so many unhappy victims perished in the valleys of Piedmont. He has passed over in silence the massacre of six hundred inhabitants of Valtelina, men, women, and children, who were murdered by the Catholics in the month of September, 1620. I will not say it was with the consent and assistance of the archbishop of Milan, Charles Borome, who was made a saint. Some passionate writers have averred this fact, which I am very far from believing; but I say, there is scarce any city or borough in Europe where blood has not been spilt for religious quarrels; I say, that the human species has been perceptibly diminished because women and girls were massacred as well as men; I say, that Europe would have had a third larger population if there had been no theological disputes. In fine, I say, that so far from forgetting these abominable times, we should frequently take a view of them, to inspire an eternal horror for them; and that it is for our age to make reparation by toleration, for this long collection of crimes, which has taken place through the want of toleration, during sixteen barbarous centuries.

Let it not then be said, that there are no traces left of that shocking fanaticism, of the want of toleration; they are still everywhere to be met with, even in those countries that are esteemed the most humane. The Lutheran and Calvinist preachers, were they masters, would, perhaps, be as little inclined to pity, as obdurate, as insolent as they upbraid their antagonists with being.

Voltaire, *Candide*

At last [Candide] approached a man who had just been addressing a big audience for a whole hour on the subject of charity. The orator peered at him and said:

"What is your business here? Do you support the Good Old Cause?"

"There is no effect without a cause," replied Candide modestly. "All things are necessarily connected and arranged for the best. It was my fate to be driven from Lady Cunégonde's presence and made to run the gauntlet, and now I have to beg my bread until I can earn it. Things could not have happened otherwise."

"Do you believe that the Pope is Antichrist, my friend?" said the minister.

"I have never heard anyone say so," replied Candide; "but whether he is or he isn't, I want some food."

"You don't deserve to eat," said the other. "Be off with you, you villain, you wretch! Don't come near me again or you'll suffer for it."

The minister's wife looked out of the window at that moment, and seeing a man who was not sure that the Pope was Antichrist, emptied over his head a chamber pot, which shows to what lengths ladies are driven by religious zeal.

Compare the two approaches that Voltaire uses to address the problem of religious intolerance. Which do you think is more effective? Why?

Source: From *Absolutism to Revolution: 1648–1848*, 2/E by Herbert Rowen. Copyright © 1968 by Macmillan College Publishing Company, Inc.

---

the clockmaker who had created it, set it in motion, and allowed it to run according to its own natural laws.

DIDEROT Denis Diderot (duh-NEE dee-DROH) (1713–1784) was the son of a skilled craftsman from eastern France who became a writer so that he could be free to study and read in many subjects and languages. One of Diderot's favorite topics was Christianity, which he condemned as fanatical and unreasonable. Of all religions, Christianity, he averred, was the worst, "the most absurd and the most atrocious in its dogma."

Diderot's most famous contribution to the Enlightenment was the *Encyclopedia, or Classified Dictionary of the Sciences, Arts, and Trades*, a twenty-eight-volume compendium of knowledge that he edited and referred to as the "great work of his life." Its purpose, according to Diderot, was to "change

the general way of thinking." It did precisely that in becoming a major weapon of the philosophes' crusade against the old French society. The contributors included many philosophes who attacked religious intolerance and advocated a program for social, legal, and political improvements that would lead to a society that was more cosmopolitan, more tolerant, more humane, and more reasonable. The *Encyclopedia* was sold to doctors, clergymen, teachers, lawyers, and even military officers, thus spreading the ideas of the Enlightenment.

TOWARD A NEW "SCIENCE OF MAN" The Enlightenment belief that Newton's scientific methods could be used to discover the natural laws underlying all areas of human life led to the emergence in the eighteenth century of what the philosophes called a "science of man," or what we would call the

A London Coffeehouse. Coffeehouses first appeared in the major cities of the Ottoman Empire in the sixteenth century, where they were often associated with antigovernment activity. They spread quickly throughout Europe and by the beginning of the eighteenth century had become a means for spreading Enlightenment ideas. In addition to drinking coffee, patrons of coffeehouses could read magazines and newspapers, exchange ideas, play chess, smoke, and even engage in business transactions. In this scene from a London coffeehouse around 1705, well-attired gentlemen make bids on commodities.

social sciences. In a number of areas, such as economics, politics, and education, the philosophes arrived at natural laws that they believed governed human actions.

Adam Smith (1723–1790) has been viewed as one of the founders of the modern discipline of economics. Smith believed that individuals should be free to pursue their own economic self-interest. Through the actions of these individuals, all society would ultimately benefit. Consequently, the state should in no way interrupt the free play of natural economic forces by government regulations on the economy but should leave it alone, a doctrine that subsequently became known as *laissez-faire* (less-ay-FAYR) (French for "leave it alone").

Smith allotted government only three basic functions: to protect society from invasion (via an army), defend its citizens from injustice (by means of a police force), and keep up certain public works, such as roads and canals, that private individuals could not afford.

THE LATER ENLIGHTENMENT By the late 1760s, a new generation of philosophes who had grown up with the worldview of the Enlightenment began to move beyond their predecessors' beliefs. Most famous was Jean-Jacques Rousseau (ZHAHNH-ZHAHK roo-SOH) (1712–1778), whose political beliefs were presented in two major works. In his *Discourse on the Origins of the Inequality of Mankind*, Rousseau argued that people had adopted laws and governors in order to preserve their private property. In the process, they had become enslaved by

government. What, then, should people do to regain their freedom? In his celebrated treatise *The Social Contract*, published in 1762, Rousseau found an answer in the concept of the social contract, whereby an entire society agreed to be governed by its general will. Each individual might have a particular will contrary to the general will, but if the individual put his particular will (self-interest) above the general will, he should be forced to abide by the general will. "This means nothing less than that he will be forced to be free," said Rousseau, because the general will, being ethical and not just political, represented what the entire community ought to do.

Another influential treatise by Rousseau was his novel *Émile*, one of the Enlightenment's most important works on education. Rousseau's fundamental concern was that education should foster, rather than restrict, children's natural instincts. Rousseau's own experiences had shown him the importance of the emotions. What he sought was a balance between heart and mind, between emotion and reason.

But Rousseau did not necessarily practice what he preached. His own children were sent to orphanages, where many children died at a young age. Rousseau also viewed women as "naturally different" from men. In *Émile*, Sophie, Émile's intended wife, was educated for her role as wife and mother by learning obedience and the nurturing skills that would enable her to provide loving care for her husband and children. Not everyone in the eighteenth century agreed with Rousseau, however.

THE "WOMAN QUESTION" IN THE ENLIGHTENMENT For centuries, many male intellectuals had argued that the nature of women made them inferior to men and made male domination of women necessary and right. In the Scientific Revolution, however, some women had made notable contributions. Maria Winkelmann (VINK-ul-mahn) in Germany, for example, was an outstanding practicing astronomer. Nevertheless, when she applied for a position as assistant astronomer at the Berlin Academy, for which she was highly qualified, she was denied the post by the academy's members, who feared that hiring a woman would set a bad precedent ("mouths would gape"). Winkelmann's difficulties with the Berlin Academy were typical of the obstacles women faced in being accepted in scientific work, which was considered a male preserve.

Female thinkers in the eighteenth century disagreed with this attitude and offered suggestions for improving conditions for women. The strongest statement for the rights of women was advanced by the English writer Mary Wollstonecraft (WULL-stun-kraft) (1759–1797), viewed by many as the founder of modern European **feminism**.

In her *Vindication of the Rights of Woman*, written in 1792, Wollstonecraft pointed out two contradictions in the views of

The Rights of Women

MARY WOLLSTONECRAFT responded to an unhappy childhood in a large family by seeking to lead an independent life. Few occupations were available for middle-class women in her day, but she survived by working as a teacher, chaperone, and governess to aristocratic children. All the while, she wrote and developed her ideas on the rights of women. This selection is taken from her *Vindication of the Rights of Woman*, written in 1792. This work led to her reputation as the foremost British feminist thinker of the eighteenth century.

Mary Wollstonecraft, *Vindication of the Rights of Woman*

It is a melancholy truth—yet such is the blessed effect of civilization—the most respectable women are the most oppressed; and, unless they have understandings far superior to the common run of understandings, taking in both sexes, they must, from being treated like contemptible beings, become contemptible. How many women thus waste life away the prey of discontent, who might have practiced as physicians, regulated a farm, managed a shop, and stood erect, supported by their own industry, instead of hanging their heads surcharged with the dew of sensibility, that consumes the beauty to which it at first gave luster....

Proud of their weakness, however, [women] must always be protected, guarded from care, and all the rough toils that dignify the mind. If this be the fiat of fate, if they will make themselves insignificant and contemptible, sweetly to waste "life away," let them not expect to be valued when their beauty fades, for it is the fate of the fairest flowers to be admired and pulled to pieces by the careless hand that plucked them. In how many ways do I wish, from the purest benevolence, to impress this truth on my sex; yet I fear that they will not listen to a truth that dear-bought experience has brought home to many an agitated bosom, nor willingly resign the privileges of rank and sex for the privileges of humanity, to which those have no claim who do not discharge its duties....

Would men but generously snap our chains, and be content with rational fellowship instead of slavish obedience, they would find us more observant daughters, more affectionate sisters, more faithful wives, and more reasonable mothers—in a word, better citizens. We should then love them with true affection, because we should learn to respect ourselves; and the peace of mind of a worthy man would not be interrupted by the idle vanity of his wife.

 What picture did Wollstonecraft paint of the women of her day? Why were they in such a deplorable state? Why did Wollstonecraft suggest that both women and men were at fault for the "slavish" situation of females?

Source: From *First Feminists: British Women, 1578–1799* by Moira Ferguson. Copyright © 1985 Indiana University Press.

women held by such Enlightenment thinkers as Rousseau. To argue that women must obey men, she said, was contrary to the beliefs of the same individuals that a system based on the arbitrary power of monarchs over their subjects or slave owners over their slaves was wrong. The subjection of women to men was equally wrong. In addition, she argued, the Enlightenment was based on an ideal of reason innate in all human beings. If women have reason, then they should have the same rights as men to obtain an education and engage in economic and political life (see the box "The Rights of Women" above).

Culture in an Enlightened Age

Although the Baroque style that had dominated the seventeenth century continued to be popular, by the 1730s, a new style affecting decoration and architecture known as **Rococo** (ruh-KOH-koh) had spread throughout Europe. Unlike the Baroque, which stressed power, grandeur, and movement, Rococo emphasized grace, charm, and gentle action. Rococo rejected strict geometrical patterns and had a fondness for curves; it liked to follow the wandering lines of natural objects, such as seashells and flowers. It made much use of interlaced designs colored in gold with delicate contours and graceful arcs. Highly secular, its lightness and charm spoke of the pursuit of pleasure, happiness, and love.

Some of Rococo's appeal is evident in the work of Antoine Watteau (AHN-twahn wah-TOH) (1684–1721), whose lyrical views of aristocratic life, refined, sensual, and civilized, with gentlemen and ladies in elegant dress, revealed a world of upper-class pleasure and joy. Underneath that exterior, however, was an element of sadness as the artist revealed the fragility and transitory nature of pleasure, love, and life.

Another aspect of Rococo was that its decorative work could easily be paired with Baroque architecture. The palace at Versailles had made an enormous impact on Europe. "Keeping up with the Bourbons" became important as European rulers built grandiose palaces. While imitating Versailles in size, they were not so much modeled after the French classical style as they were after the seventeenth-century Italian Baroque, as modified by a series of brilliant German and Austrian sculptor-architects. This Baroque-Rococo architectural style typified eighteenth-century palaces and church buildings, and often the same architects designed both. This is evident in the work of one of the greatest architects of the eighteenth century, Johann Balthasar Neumann (yoh-HAHN BAHL-tuh-zahr NOI-mahn) (1687–1753). One

Antoine Watteau, *Return from Cythera*. Antoine Watteau was one of the most gifted painters in eighteenth-century France. His portrayal of aristocratic life reveals a world of elegance, wealth, and pleasure. In this painting, which is considered his masterpiece, Watteau depicts a group of aristocratic lovers about to depart from the island of Cythera, where they have paid homage to Venus, the goddess of love. Luxuriously dressed, they move from the woodlands to a golden barge that is waiting to take them from the island.

Vierzehnheiligen. Pictured here is the interior of the Vierzehnheiligen, the famous pilgrimage church in Bad Staffelstein, Bavaria, designed by Johann Balthasar Neumann. Elaborate detail, blazing light, rich colors, and opulent decoration were brought together to create a work of stunning beauty. The pilgrim in search of holiness is struck by an incredible richness of detail. Persuaded by joy rather than fear, the believer is lifted toward heaven on a cloud of rapture.

of Neumann's masterpieces was the pilgrimage church known as the Vierzehnheiligen (feer-tsayn-HY-li-gen) (Fourteen Saints) in southern Germany. Secular and spiritual merge in its lavish and fanciful ornamentation; light, bright colors; and elaborate, rich detail.

HIGH CULTURE Historians have grown accustomed to distinguishing between a civilization's high culture and its popular culture. **High culture** is the literary and artistic culture of the educated and wealthy ruling classes; **popular culture** is the written and unwritten culture of the masses, most of which has traditionally been passed down orally.

By the eighteenth century, the two forms were beginning to blend, owing to the expansion of both the reading public and publishing. Whereas French publishers issued 300 titles in 1750, about 1,600 were being published yearly in the 1780s. Although the majority of these titles were still intended for small groups of the educated elite, many were directed to the new reading public of the middle classes, which included women and even urban artisans.

An important aspect of the growth of publishing and reading in the eighteenth century was the development of magazines for the general public. Great Britain saw 25 different periodicals published in 1700, 103 in 1760, and 158 in 1780. Along with magazines came daily newspapers. The first was printed in London in 1702, but by 1780, thirty-seven other English towns had their own newspapers.

POPULAR CULTURE The distinguishing characteristic of popular culture is its collective nature. Group activity was especially common in the *festival*, a broad name used to cover a variety of celebrations: community festivals in Catholic Europe that celebrated the feast day of the local patron saint; annual festivals, such as Christmas and Easter, that went back to medieval Christianity; and the ultimate festival, Carnival, which was celebrated in the Mediterranean world of Spain, Italy, and France as well as in Germany and Austria.

Carnival began after Christmas and lasted until the start of Lent, the forty-day period of fasting and purification leading up to Easter. Because people were expected to abstain from meat, sex, and most recreations during Lent, Carnival was a time of great indulgence, when heavy consumption of food and drink was the norm. It was a time of intense sexual activity as well. Songs with double meanings that would ordinarily be considered offensive could be sung publicly at this time of year. A float of Florentine "keymakers," for example, sang this ditty to the ladies: "Our tools are fine, new and useful. We always carry them with us. They are good for anything. If you want to touch them, you can."[3]

Caffe Quadri, Venice, Italy/The Bridgeman Art Library

Carnival. The Carnival of Venice, Italy, depicted here in an eighteenth-century painting, was one of Europe's most elaborate festivals. In this scene from the Carnival, attendees are portrayed eating, drinking, and dancing in their finest attire and masks in the Piazza San Marco.

Economic Changes and the Social Order

 FOCUS QUESTION: What changes occurred in the European economy in the eighteenth century, and to what degree were these changes reflected in social patterns?

The eighteenth century in Europe witnessed the beginning of economic changes that ultimately had a strong impact on the rest of the world.

New Economic Patterns

Europe's population began to grow around 1750 and continued to increase steadily. The total European population was probably around 120 million in 1700, 140 million in 1750, and 190 million in 1790. A falling death rate was perhaps the most important reason for this population growth. Of great significance in lowering death rates was the disappearance of bubonic plague, but so was diet. More plentiful food and better transportation of food supplies led to improved nutrition and relief from devastating famines.

More plentiful food was in part a result of improvements in agricultural practices and methods in the eighteenth century, especially in Britain, parts of France, and the Low Countries. Food production increased as more land was farmed, yields per acre increased, and climate improved. Climatologists believe that the "little ice age" of the seventeenth century waned in the eighteenth, especially evident in moderate summers that provided more ideal growing conditions. Also important to the increased yields was the cultivation of new vegetables, including two important American crops, the potato and maize (Indian corn). Both had been brought to Europe from the Americas in the sixteenth century.

Textiles were the most important product of European industry in the eighteenth century. Most were still produced by master artisans in guild workshops, but in many areas, textile production was beginning to shift to the countryside where the "putting-out" or "domestic" system was used. A merchant-capitalist entrepreneur bought the raw materials, mostly wool and flax, and "put them out" to rural workers who spun the raw material into yarn and then wove it into cloth on simple looms. The capitalist entrepreneurs sold the finished product, made a profit, and used it to purchase materials to manufacture more. This system became known as the **cottage industry** because the spinners and weavers worked at spinning wheels and looms in the cottages where they lived.

In the eighteenth century, overseas trade boomed. Some historians speak of the emergence of a true global economy, pointing to the patterns of trade that interlocked Europe, Africa, the East, and the Americas (see Map 18.2). In one trade pattern, gold and silver flowed into Spain from its colonial American empire. Much of this gold and silver made its way to Britain, France, and the Netherlands in return for manufactured goods. The British, French, and Dutch merchants then used their profits to buy tea, spices, silk, and cotton goods from China and India to sell in Europe. The plantations of the

© 2016 Cengage Learning

MAP 18.2 Global Trade Patterns of the European States in the Eighteenth Century. New patterns of trade interlocked Europe, Africa, the East, and the Americas. Dutch, English, French, Spanish, and Portuguese colonies had been established in North and South America, and the ships of these nations followed the trade routes across the Atlantic, Pacific, and Indian Oceans.

Q *With what regions did Britain conduct most of its trade?*

Western Hemisphere were another important source of trading activity. The plantations produced coffee, tobacco, sugar, and cotton, which were shipped to Europe. In a third pattern of trade, British merchant ships carried British manufactured goods to Africa, where they were traded for cargoes of slaves, which were then shipped to Virginia and paid for with tobacco, which was in turn shipped back to Britain, where it was processed and then sold in Germany for cash.

As a result of the growth in trade, historians have argued that during the eighteenth century, England and parts of northern Europe experienced a "consumer revolution," where ordinary people partook in a large increase in the consumption of consumer goods. Expensive commodities such as Chinese porcelain became more affordable as production moved to Europe by the beginning of the eighteenth century, while imports of inexpensive Indian fabric increased the sale of clothing. By the end of the eighteenth century, most ordinary families could consume former luxury goods such as tea, sugar, tobacco, furniture, cutlery and clothing.

Commercial capitalism resulted in enormous prosperity for some European countries. By 1700, Spain, Portugal, and the Dutch Republic, which had earlier monopolized overseas trade, found

themselves increasingly overshadowed by France and England, which built hugely profitable colonial empires in the course of the eighteenth century. After the French lost the Seven Years' War in 1763, Britain emerged as the world's strongest overseas trading nation, and London became the world's greatest port.

European Society in the Eighteenth Century

The patterns of Europe's social organization, first established in the Middle Ages, continued well into the eighteenth century. Society was still divided into the traditional orders or estates determined by heredity.

Because society was still mostly rural in the eighteenth century, the peasantry constituted the largest social group, about 85 percent of Europe's population. There were rather wide differences within this group, however, especially between free peasants and serfs. In eastern Germany, eastern Europe, and Russia, serfs remained tied to the lands of their noble landlords. In contrast, peasants in Britain, northern Italy, the Low Countries, Spain, most of France, and some areas of western Germany were largely free.

The nobles, who constituted only 2 to 3 percent of the European population, played a dominating role in society. Being born a noble automatically guaranteed a place at the top of the social order, with all its attendant special privileges and rights. Nobles, for example, were exempt from many forms of taxation. Since medieval times, landed aristocrats had functioned as military officers, and eighteenth-century nobles held most of the important offices in the administrative machinery of state and controlled much of the life of their local districts.

Townspeople were still a distinct minority of the total population except in the Dutch Republic, Britain, and parts of Italy. At the end of the eighteenth century, about one-sixth of the French population lived in towns of two thousand people or more. The biggest city in Europe was London, with a million inhabitants; Paris was a little more than half that size.

Many cities in western and even central Europe had a long tradition of **patrician** oligarchies that continued to control their communities by dominating town and city councils. Just below the patricians stood an upper crust of the middle classes: nonnoble officeholders, financiers and bankers, merchants, wealthy *rentiers* (rahn-TYAYS) who lived off their investments, and important professionals, including lawyers. Another large urban group was the lower middle class, made up of master artisans, shopkeepers, and small traders. Below them were the laborers or working classes and a large group of unskilled workers who served as servants, maids, and cooks at pitifully low wages.

The Aristocratic Way of Life. The eighteenth-century country house fulfilled the desire among British aristocrats for both elegance and greater privacy. Thomas Gainsborough's *Conversation in the Park*, shown here, captures the relaxed life of two aristocrats in the park of their country estate.

Colonial Empires and Revolution in the Americas

 FOCUS QUESTION: What colonies did the British and French establish in the Americas, and how did their methods of administering their colonies differ?

In the sixteenth century, Spain and Portugal had established large colonial empires in the Americas (see Chapter 14). Portugal continued to profit from its empire in Brazil. The Spanish also maintained an enormous South American empire, but Spain's importance as a commercial power declined rapidly in the seventeenth century because of a drop in the output of the silver mines and the poverty of the Spanish monarchy. By the beginning of the seventeenth century, both Portugal and Spain found themselves facing new challenges to their American empires from the Dutch, English, and French, who increasingly sought to create their own colonial empires in the Western Hemisphere, both within the West Indies and on the North American continent.

The West Indies

Both the French and British colonial empires in the Americas ultimately included large parts of the West Indies. The British held Barbados, Jamaica, and Bermuda, and the French possessed Saint-Dominique, Martinique, and Guadeloupe. On these tropical islands, both the British and the French used African slaves to work plantations that produced tobacco, cotton, coffee, and sugar, all products increasingly in demand in Europe.

The "sugar factories," as the sugar plantations in the Caribbean were called, played an especially prominent role. By the last two decades of the eighteenth century, Jamaica, one of Britain's most important colonies, was producing 50,000 tons of sugar annually with the slave labor of 200,000 blacks. The French colony of Saint-Dominique (later Haiti) had 500,000 slaves working on three thousand plantations during the same period. This colony produced 100,000 tons of sugar a year, but at the expense of a high death rate from the brutal treatment of the slaves. It is not surprising that Saint-Dominique saw the first successful slave uprising in 1793.

British North America

Although Spain had claimed all of North America as part of its American overseas empire, other nations largely ignored its claim, following the English argument that "prescription without possession availeth nothing." The Dutch had been among the first to establish settlements on the North American continent. Their activities began after 1609 when Henry Hudson, an English explorer hired by the Dutch, discovered the river that bears his name. Within a few years, the Dutch had established the mainland colony of New Netherland, which stretched from the mouth of the Hudson River as far north as Albany, New York. Present-day names such as Staten Island and Harlem remind us that it was the Dutch who initially settled the

La Figure des Moulins a Sucre

A Sugar Mill in the West Indies.
Cane sugar was one of the most valuable products produced in the West Indies. By 1700, sugar was replacing honey as a sweetener for increasing numbers of Europeans. This seventeenth-century French illustration shows the operation of a sugar mill in the French West Indies.

Hudson River valley. In the second half of the seventeenth century, competition from the English and French and years of warfare with those rivals led to the decline of the Dutch commercial empire. In 1664, the English seized the colony of New Netherland and renamed it New York.

In the meantime, the English had begun to establish their own colonies in North America. The first permanent English settlement in America was Jamestown, founded in 1607 in what is now Virginia. The settlers barely survived, making it clear that colonizing American lands was not necessarily conducive to quick profits. But the desire to practice one's own religion, combined with economic interests, could lead to successful colonization, as the Massachusetts Bay Company demonstrated. The Massachusetts colony had 4,000 settlers in its early years, but by 1660 their numbers had swelled to 40,000. By the end of the seventeenth century, the English had established control over most of the eastern seaboard of the present United States.

British North America came to consist of thirteen colonies. They were thickly populated, containing about 1.5 million people by 1750, and were also prosperous. Supposedly run by the British Board of Trade, the Royal Council, and Parliament, these thirteen colonies had legislatures that tended to act independently. Merchants in such port cities as Boston, Philadelphia, New York, and Charleston resented and resisted regulation from the British government.

Both the North American and the West Indian colonies of Britain were assigned roles in keeping with mercantilist theory. They provided raw materials for the mother country while buying the latter's manufactured goods. Navigation acts regulated what could be taken from and sold to the colonies. Theoretically, the system was supposed to provide a balance of trade favorable to the mother country.

French North America

The French also established a colonial empire in North America. In 1534, the French explorer Jacques Cartier (ZHAHK kar-TYAY) had discovered the Saint Lawrence River and laid claim to Canada as a French possession. Not until Samuel de Champlain (sa-my-ELL duh shahm-PLAN *or* SHAM-playn) established a settlement at Quebec in 1608, however, did the French take a serious interest in Canada as a colony. In 1663, Canada was made the property of the French crown and administered by a French governor like a French province.

French North America was run autocratically as a vast trading area, where valuable furs, leather, fish, and timber were acquired. The inability of the French state to persuade its people to emigrate to its Canadian possessions, however, left the territory thinly populated. In the mid-eighteenth century, there were only about 15,000 French Canadians, most of whom were hunters, trappers, missionaries, or explorers. The French also failed to provide adequate men or money for the venture, allowing their wars in Europe to take precedence over the conquest of the North American continent. Already in 1713, by the Treaty of Utrecht, the French began to cede some of their American possessions to their British rival. As a result of the Seven Years' War, they surrendered the rest of their Canadian lands to Britain in 1763 (see "Changing Patterns of War: Global Confrontation" later in this chapter).

The American Revolution

By the mid-eighteenth century, increasing trade and industry had led to a growing middle class in Britain that favored expansion of trade and world empire. These people found a spokesman in William Pitt the Elder (1708–1778), who became prime minister in 1757 and began to expand the British Empire. In

North America, after the end of the Seven Years' War in 1763, Britain controlled Canada and the lands east of the Mississippi.

The Americans and the British had different conceptions of how the empire should be governed, however. In eighteenth-century Britain, the king or queen and Parliament shared power, with Parliament gradually gaining the upper hand. The monarch chose ministers who were responsible to the crown and who set policy and guided Parliament. Parliament had the power to make laws, levy taxes, pass budgets, and indirectly influence the monarch's ministers. The British envisioned that Parliament would be the supreme authority performing these functions throughout the empire. But the Americans had their own representative assemblies. They believed that neither king nor Parliament should interfere in their internal affairs and that no tax could be levied without the consent of their own assemblies. After the Seven Years' War, when British policymakers sought to obtain new revenues from the colonies to pay for British army expenses in defending the colonies, the colonists resisted. An attempt to levy new taxes by the Stamp Act of 1765 led to riots and the law's quick repeal.

Crisis followed crisis in the 1770s until 1776, when the colonists decided to declare their independence from the British Empire. On July 4, 1776, the Second Continental Congress approved a declaration of independence written by Thomas Jefferson (1743–1826). A stirring political document, the Declaration of Independence affirmed the Enlightenment's natural rights of "life, liberty, and the pursuit of happiness" and declared the colonies to be "free and independent states absolved from all allegiance to the British crown." The war for American independence had formally begun.

Of great importance to the colonies' cause was the support of foreign countries that were eager to gain revenge for earlier defeats at the hands of the British. French officers and soldiers served in the American Continental Army under George Washington (1732–1799), the commander in chief. When the British army of General Cornwallis was forced to surrender to a combined American and French army and French fleet under Washington at Yorktown in 1781, the British decided to call it quits. The Treaty of Paris, signed in 1783, recognized the independence of the American colonies and granted the Americans control of the territory from the Appalachians to the Mississippi River.

BIRTH OF A NEW NATION The thirteen American colonies had gained their independence, but a fear of concentrated power and concern for their own interests caused them to have little enthusiasm for establishing a united nation with a strong central government, and so the Articles of Confederation, ratified in 1781, did not create one. A movement for a different form of national government soon arose. In the summer of 1787, fifty-five delegates attended a convention in Philadelphia to revise the Articles of Confederation. The convention's delegates—wealthy, politically experienced, and well educated—rejected revision and decided instead to devise a new constitution.

The proposed United States Constitution established a central government distinct from and superior to the governments of the individual states. The central or federal government was divided into three branches, each with some power to check the functioning of the others. A president would serve as the chief executive with the power to execute laws, veto the legislature's acts, supervise foreign affairs, and direct military forces. Legislative power was vested in the second branch of government, a bicameral legislature composed of the Senate, elected by the state legislatures, and the House of Representatives, elected directly by the people. A supreme court and other courts "as deemed necessary" by Congress provided the third branch of government. They would enforce the Constitution as the "supreme law of the land."

The Constitution was approved by the states—by a slim margin. Important to its success was a promise to add a bill of rights to the Constitution as the new government's first piece of business. Accordingly, in March 1789, the new Congress enacted the first ten amendments to the Constitution, known ever since as the Bill of Rights. These guaranteed freedom of religion, speech, press, petition, and assembly, as well as the right to bear arms, protection against unreasonable searches and arrests, trial by jury, due process of law, and protection of property rights. Many of these rights were derived from the **natural rights** philosophy of the eighteenth-century philosophes and the American colonists. Is it any wonder that many European intellectuals saw the American Revolution as the embodiment of the Enlightenment's political dreams?

Toward a New Political Order and Global Conflict

 FOCUS QUESTION: What do historians mean by the term *enlightened absolutism*, and to what degree did eighteenth-century Prussia, Austria, and Russia exhibit its characteristics?

There is no doubt that Enlightenment thought had some impact on the political development of European states in the eighteenth century. The philosophes believed in natural rights, which were thought to be privileges that ought not to be withheld from any person. These natural rights included equality before the law, freedom of religious worship, freedom of speech and press, and the right to assemble, hold property, and seek happiness.

But how were these natural rights to be established and preserved? Most philosophes believed that people needed to be ruled by an enlightened ruler. What made rulers enlightened? They must allow religious toleration, freedom of speech and press, and the rights of private property. They must foster the arts, sciences, and education. Above all, they must obey the laws and enforce them fairly for all subjects. Only strong monarchs seemed capable of overcoming vested interests and effecting the reforms society needed. Reforms then should come from above (from absolute rulers) rather than from below (from the people).

Many historians once assumed that a new type of monarchy emerged in the later eighteenth century, which they called *enlightened despotism* or **enlightened absolutism**. Monarchs such as Frederick II of Prussia, Catherine the Great of Russia, and Joseph II of Austria supposedly followed the advice of the philosophes and ruled by enlightened principles. Recently, however, scholars have questioned the usefulness of the concept of enlightened absolutism. We can determine the extent to which it can be applied by examining the major "enlightened absolutists" of the late eighteenth century.

Prussia: The Army and the Bureaucracy

Frederick II, known as Frederick the Great (1740–1786), was one of the best-educated and most cultured monarchs of the eighteenth century. He was well versed in Enlightenment thought and even invited Voltaire to live at his court for several years. A believer in the king as the "first servant of the state," Frederick the Great was a conscientious ruler who enlarged the Prussian army (to 200,000 men) and kept a strict watch over the bureaucracy. The Prussian army, because of its size and excellent reputation, was the most important institution in the state. Its officers, who were members of the nobility or landed aristocracy, had a strong sense of service to the king or state. As Prussian nobles, they believed in duty, obedience, and sacrifice. The bureaucracy also had its own code in which the supreme values were obedience, honor, and service to the king as the highest duty.

For a time, Frederick seemed quite willing to make enlightened reforms. He abolished the use of torture except in treason and murder cases and also granted limited freedom of speech and press, as well as complete religious toleration. At the same time, however, he kept Prussia's rigid social structure and serfdom intact and avoided any additional reforms.

The Austrian Empire of the Habsburgs

The Austrian Empire had become one of the great European states by the beginning of the eighteenth century. Yet it was difficult to rule because it was a sprawling conglomerate of nationalities, languages, religions, and cultures (see Map 18.3). Empress Maria Theresa (1740–1780) managed to make administrative reforms that helped centralize the Austrian Empire, but they were done for practical reasons—to strengthen the power of the Habsburg state—and were accompanied by an enlargement and modernization of the armed forces. Maria Theresa remained staunchly conservative and was not open to the wider reform calls of the philosophes. But her successor was.

Joseph II (1780–1790) believed in the need to sweep away anything standing in the path of reason. As he said, "I have made Philosophy the lawmaker of my empire; her logical applications are going to transform Austria." Joseph's reform

MAP 18.3 Europe in 1763. By the middle of the eighteenth century, five major powers dominated Europe—Prussia, Austria, Russia, Britain, and France. Each sought to enhance its power both domestically, through a bureaucracy that collected taxes and ran the military, and internationally, by capturing territory or preventing other powers from capturing territory.

Q *Given the distribution of Prussian and Habsburg holdings, in what areas of Europe were they most likely to compete for land and power?*

program was far-reaching. He abolished serfdom, abrogated the death penalty, and established the principle of equality of all before the law. Joseph carried out drastic religious reforms as well, including complete religious toleration.

Joseph's reform program proved overwhelming for Austria, however. He alienated the nobility by freeing the serfs and alienated the church by his attacks on the monastic establishment. Joseph realized his failure when he wrote the epitaph for his own gravestone: "Here lies Joseph II, who was unfortunate in everything that he undertook." His successors undid many of his reforms.

Russia Under Catherine the Great

Catherine II the Great (1762–1796) was an intelligent woman who was familiar with the works of the philosophes and seemed to favor enlightened reforms. She invited the French philosophe Diderot to Russia and, when he arrived, urged him to speak frankly "as man to man." He did, outlining a far-reaching program of political and financial reform. But Catherine was skeptical about impractical theories, which, she said, "would have turned everything in my kingdom upside down." She did consider the idea of a new law code that would recognize the principle of the equality of all people in the eyes of the law. But in the end she did nothing, knowing that her success depended on the support of the Russian nobility. In 1785, she gave the nobles a charter that exempted them from taxes.

Catherine's policy of favoring the landed nobility led to even worse conditions for the Russian peasants and a rebellion. Incited by an illiterate Cossack, Emelyan Pugachev (yim-yil-YAHN poo-guh-CHAHF), the rebellion began in 1773 and spread across southern Russia. But the rebellion soon faltered. Pugachev was captured, tortured, and executed. The rebellion collapsed completely, and Catherine responded with even stronger measures against the peasantry.

Above all, Catherine proved a worthy successor to Peter the Great in her policies of territorial expansion westward into Poland and southward to the Black Sea. Russia spread southward by defeating the Turks. Russian expansion westward occurred at the expense of neighboring Poland. In three partitions of Poland, Russia gained about 50 percent of Polish territory.

CHRONOLOGY	Enlightened Absolutism in Eighteenth-Century Europe
Prussia	
Frederick II the Great	1740–1786
Austrian Empire	
Maria Theresa	1740–1780
Joseph II	1780–1790
Russia	
Catherine II the Great	1762–1796
Pugachev's rebellion	1773–1775
Charter of the Nobility	1785

Enlightened Absolutism Reconsidered

Of the rulers we have discussed, only Joseph II sought truly radical changes based on Enlightenment ideas. Both Frederick II and Catherine II liked to talk about enlightened reforms, and they even attempted some. But the policies of neither seemed seriously affected by Enlightenment thought. Necessities of state and maintenance of the existing system took precedence over reform. Indeed, many historians maintain that Joseph, Frederick, and Catherine were all primarily guided by a concern for the power and well-being of their states. In the final analysis, heightened state power was used to create armies and wage wars to gain more power.

It would be foolish, however, to overlook the fact that the ability of enlightened rulers to make reforms was also limited by political and social realities. Everywhere in Europe, the hereditary aristocracy was still the most powerful class in society. Enlightened reforms were often limited to administrative and judicial measures that did not seriously undermine the powerful interests of the European nobility. As the chief beneficiaries of a system based on traditional rights and privileges for their class, they were not willing to support a political ideology that trumpeted the principle of equal rights for all. The first serious challenge to their supremacy would come in the French Revolution, an event that blew open the door to the modern world of politics.

Robert Clive in India. Robert Clive was the leader of the army of the British East India Company. He had been commanded to fight the ruler of Bengal in order to gain trading privileges. After the Battle of Plassey in 1757, Clive and the East India Company took control of Bengal. In this painting by Edward Penny, Clive is shown receiving a grant of money for his injured soldiers from the local nabob or governor of Bengal.

British Victory in India

POLITICS & GOVERNMENT

THE SUCCESS OF THE BRITISH against the French in India was due to Robert Clive, who, in this excerpt from one of his letters, describes his famous victory at Plassey, north of Calcutta, on June 23, 1757. This battle demonstrated the inability of native Indian soldiers to compete with Europeans and signified the beginning of British control in Bengal. Clive claimed to have a thousand Europeans, two thousand sepoys (local soldiers), and eight cannons available for this battle.

Robert Clive's Account of His Victory at Plassey

At daybreak we discovered the [governor's army] moving toward us, consisting, as we since found, of about fifteen thousand horse and thirty-five thousand foot, with upwards of forty pieces of cannon. They approached apace, and by six began to attack with a number of heavy cannon, supported by the whole army, and continued to play on us very briskly for several hours, during which our situation was of the utmost service to us, being lodged in a large grove with good mud banks. To succeed in an attempt on their cannon was next to impossible, as they were planted in a manner round us and at considerable distances from each other. We therefore remained quiet in our post, in expectation of a successful attack upon their camp at night. About noon the enemy drew off their artillery and retired to their camp....

On finding them make no great effort to dislodge us, we proceeded to take possession of one or two more eminences

lying very near an angle of their camp, from whence, and an adjacent eminence in their possession, they kept a smart fire of musketry upon us. They made several attempts to bring out their cannon, but our advanced fieldpieces played so warmly and so well upon them that they were always driven back. Their horse exposing themselves a good deal on this occasion, many of them were killed, and among the rest four or five officers of the first distinction; by which the whole army being visibly dispirited and thrown into some confusion, we were encouraged to storm both the eminence and the angle of their camp, which were carried at the same instant, with little or no loss; though the latter was defended (exclusively of blacks) by forty French and two pieces of cannon; and the former by a large body of blacks, both horse and foot. On this a general rout ensued, and we pursued the enemy six miles, passing upwards of forty pieces of cannon they had abandoned, with an infinite number of carts and carriages filled with baggage of all kinds.... It is computed there are killed of the enemy about five hundred.

Our loss amounted to only twenty-two killed and fifty wounded, and those chiefly blacks.

In what ways, if any, would Clive's account likely have been different if the Battle of Plassey had occurred in Europe? According to the letter, what role did native Indians seemingly play in the battle? Why does Clive give them such little mention?

Source: From *Readings in European History*, vol. 2, by James Harvey Robinson (Lexington, Mass.: Ginn and Co., 1906).

Changing Patterns of War: Global Confrontation

The philosophes condemned war as a foolish waste of life and resources in stupid quarrels of no value to humankind. Despite their words, the rivalry among states that led to costly struggles remained unchanged in the European world of the eighteenth century. Europe consisted of a number of self-governing, individual states that were largely guided by the self-interest of the ruler. And as Frederick the Great of Prussia said, "The fundamental rule of governments is the principle of extending their territories."

By far the most dramatic confrontation occurred in the Seven Years' War. Although it began in Europe, it soon turned into a global conflict fought in Europe, India, and North America. In Europe, the British and Prussians fought the Austrians, Russians, and French. With his superb army and military skill, Frederick the Great of Prussia was able for some time to defeat the Austrian, French, and Russian armies. Eventually, however, his forces were gradually worn down and faced utter defeat until a new Russian tsar withdrew Russian troops from the conflict. A stalemate ensued, ending the European conflict in 1763.

The struggle between Britain and France in the rest of the world had more decisive results. In India, local rulers allied with British and French troops fought a number of battles. Ultimately, the British under Robert Clive won out, not because they had better forces but because they were more persistent (see the box "British Victory in India" above). By the Treaty of Paris in 1763, the French withdrew and left India to the British.

The greatest conflicts of the Seven Years' War took place in North America, where it was known as the French and Indian War. British and French rivalry led to a number of confrontations. The French had more troops in North America but less naval support. The defeat of French fleets in 1759 left the French unable to reinforce their garrisons. That year, British forces under General Wolfe defeated the French under General Montcalm on the Plains of Abraham, outside Quebec. The British went on to seize Montreal, the Great Lakes area, and the Ohio Valley. The French were forced to make peace. In the Treaty of Paris, they ceded Canada and the lands east of the Mississippi to Britain. Their ally Spain transferred Spanish Florida to British control; in return, the French gave their Louisiana territory to the Spanish. By 1763, Great Britain had become the world's greatest colonial power. The loss of France's empire was soon followed by an even greater internal upheaval.

The French Revolution

 FOCUS QUESTION: What were the causes, the main events, and the results of the French Revolution?

The year 1789 witnessed two far-reaching events, the beginning of a new United States of America under its revamped constitution and the eruption of the French Revolution. Compared to the American Revolution a decade earlier, the French Revolution was more complex, more violent, and far more radical in its attempt to reconstruct both a new political order and a new social order.

Background to the French Revolution

The root causes of the French Revolution must be sought in the condition of French society. Before the Revolution, France was a society grounded in privilege and inequality. Its population of 27 million was divided, as it had been since the Middle Ages, into three orders or estates.

SOCIAL STRUCTURE OF THE OLD REGIME The First Estate consisted of the clergy and numbered about 130,000 people who owned approximately 10 percent of the land. Clergy were exempt from the *taille* (TY), France's chief tax. Clergy were also radically divided: the higher clergy, stemming from aristocratic families, shared the interests of the nobility, while the parish priests were often poor and from the class of commoners.

The Second Estate consisted of the nobility, composed of about 350,000 people who owned about 25 to 30 percent of the land. The nobility had continued to play an important and even crucial role in French society in the eighteenth century, holding many of the leading positions in the government, the military, the law courts, and the higher church offices. The nobles sought to expand their power at the expense of the monarchy and to maintain their control over positions in the military, church, and government. Moreover, the possession of privileges remained a hallmark of the nobility. Common to all nobles were tax exemptions, especially from the *taille*.

The Third Estate, or the commoners of society, constituted the overwhelming majority of the French population. They were divided by vast differences in occupation, level of education, and wealth. The peasants, who constituted 75 to 80 percent of the total population, were by far the largest segment of the Third Estate. They owned 35 to 40 percent of the land, although their landholdings varied from area to area and more than half had little or no land on which to survive. Serfdom no longer existed on any large scale in France, but French peasants still had obligations to their local landlords that they deeply resented. These "relics of feudalism," or aristocratic privileges, had survived from an earlier age and included the payment of fees for the use of village facilities, such as the flour mill, community oven, and winepress.

Another part of the Third Estate consisted of skilled craftspeople, shopkeepers, and other wage earners in the cities. In the eighteenth century, these urban groups suffered a noticeable decline in purchasing power as consumer prices rose faster than wages. Their daily struggle for survival led many of these people to play an important role in the Revolution, especially in Paris.

About 8 percent of the population, or 2.3 million people, constituted the bourgeoisie or middle class, who owned about 20 to 25 percent of the land. This group included merchants, industrialists, and bankers who controlled the resources of trade, manufacturing, and finance and benefited from the economic prosperity after 1730. The bourgeoisie also included professional people—lawyers, holders of public offices, doctors, and writers. Many members of the bourgeoisie had their own set of grievances because they were often excluded from the social and political privileges monopolized by nobles.

Moreover, the new political ideas of the Enlightenment proved attractive to both the aristocracy and the bourgeoisie. Both elites, long accustomed to a new socioeconomic reality based on wealth and economic achievement, were increasingly frustrated by a monarchical system resting on privileges and on an old and rigid social order based on the concept of estates. The opposition of these elites to the **old order** led them ultimately to take drastic action against the monarchical **old regime**. In a real sense, the Revolution had its origins in political grievances.

OTHER PROBLEMS FACING THE FRENCH MONARCHY Although France had enjoyed fifty years of economic expansion in the first half of the eighteenth century, in the late 1780s bad harvests in 1787 and 1788 and the beginnings of a manufacturing depression had resulted in food shortages, rising prices for food and other goods, and unemployment in the cities. The number of poor, estimated at almost one-third of the population, reached crisis proportions on the eve of the Revolution.

The French monarchy seemed incapable of dealing with the new social realities. Louis XVI (1774–1792) had become king in 1774 at the age of twenty; he knew little about the operations of the French government and lacked the energy to deal decisively with state affairs. His wife, Marie Antoinette (ma-REE ahn-twahn-NET), was a spoiled Austrian princess who devoted much of her time to court intrigues (see the Film & History feature "*Marie Antoinette* (2006)" on p. 522). As France's crises worsened, neither Louis nor his queen seemed able to fathom the depths of despair and discontent that soon led to violent revolution.

The immediate cause of the French Revolution was the near collapse of government finances. Costly wars and royal extravagance drove French governmental expenditures ever higher. The government responded by borrowing. Poor taxation policy contributed to the high debt, with most of the monarchy's funds coming from the peasantry. Unlike Britain, where the Bank of England financed the borrowing of money at low interest rates, France had no central bank, and instead relied on private loans (see the box "The State of French Finances" on p. 523). By 1788, the interest on the debt alone constituted half of government spending. Financial lenders, fearful they would never be repaid, were refusing to lend additional amounts.

Marie Antoinette (2006)

The film *Marie Antoinette* (2006), directed by Sofia Coppola, is based on Antonia Fraser's interpretation of the early life of Marie Antoinette in her book, *Marie Antoinette: A Journey* (2001). The film begins with the marriage of Marie Antoinette (Kirsten Dunst), the daughter of Empress Maria Theresa of Austria (Marianne Faithful), to the dauphin Louis (Jason Schwartzman), the heir to the French throne. Four years later, in 1774, Marie Antoinette became queen of France; in 1793, she went to the guillotine. Although the Revolution and financial troubles of the monarchy briefly enter the film toward the end, the majority of the film focuses on the experiences of a young woman thrust into the court of Versailles where she faces increasing suspicion, frustration, and isolation.

Perhaps the best part of the film is the portrayal of court life at Versailles. The film depicts days filled with courtly ceremonies, daily mass, and attendance of the public at meals. Under intense scrutiny due to her Austrian heritage and unfamiliar with the protocol of life at Versailles, Marie Antoinette makes several early missteps. She refuses to speak to Louis XV's mistress, the comtesse du Barry (Asia Argento), because the comtesse threatens Marie Antoinette's position as the highest-ranking woman at court. Ignoring the king's mistress, however, places the young dauphine in the precarious position of appearing to insult the king.

In addition to her troubles at court, Marie Antoinette faces an even greater challenge: the need to secure her place by producing an heir to the French throne. But her young husband, whose interests include hunting, lock making, and reading, creates problems for the young couple. Their marriage is not consummated for seven years. During these years, Marie Antoinette faces increasing pressure from her mother, who has produced sixteen children while ruling the Austrian Empire. Bored but aware that she must remain chaste, the young dauphine turns to frivolous pursuits including games, plays, outings in Paris, decorating, gambling, and, above all, purchasing clothes. Marie Antoinette's desire for elaborate gowns is encouraged by her role as the tastemaker for the French court. In 1782, she commissions ninety-three gowns made of silk and other expensive fabrics. The scene of Marie Antoinette's twenty-first birthday is particularly effective in conveying how her frustration and boredom have led her to a life of frivolity and luxury. Sitting in her finery, she plays cards and eats sweets until the early hours of the morning.

Marie Antoinette (Kirsten Dunst) at Versailles.

Columbia/American Zoetrope/Sony/The Kobal Collection

After the birth of her children, the first in 1777, Marie Antoinette begins to withdraw from the scrutiny of the court. In 1783, she is given the keys to the Petit Trianon, a small palace on the grounds of Versailles, where she spends most of her days. Although she is spending more time with her children and less on the frivolity of her earlier days at Versailles, her increasing estrangement from the court only worsens her reputation with the French public.

Filmed at Versailles, the film captures the grandeur and splendor of eighteenth-century royal life. But the movie did not receive favorable reviews when it opened in France, in part because of its use of contemporary music by artists such as The Cure and The Strokes and the inclusion of modern products such as Converse sneakers. Although the flurry of costumes and music can be distracting, they also convey the rebelliousness of a young woman, frustrated and bored, isolated, and yet always on display.

On the verge of a complete financial collapse, the government of Louis XVI was finally forced to call a meeting of the Estates-General, the French parliamentary body that had not met since 1614. The Estates-General consisted of representatives from the three orders of French society. In the elections for the Estates-General, the government had ruled that the Third Estate should get double representation (it did, after all, constitute 97 percent of the population). Consequently, while both the First Estate (the clergy) and the Second Estate (the nobility) had about three hundred delegates each, the Third Estate had almost six hundred representatives, most of whom were lawyers from French towns.

The State of French Finances

POLITICS & GOVERNMENT

IN 1781, JACQUES NECKER (ZHAHK neh-KAIR), the assistant to Louis XVI's controller general of finance (Necker could not be named controller general due to his Swiss birth and Protestant faith), published an account of the French monarchy's finances. Although Necker denied that the monarchy was in debt and hid France's enormous interest payments, his efforts to expose the inadequacies of the monarchy's monetary policies were the first real steps toward financial reform. His efforts, however, could not prevent the financial crisis that engulfed the French monarchy.

Jacques Necker, *Preface to the King's Accounts* (1781)

Sire,

[I] offer Your Majesty … a public account of … the current state of His Majesty's finances.…

If one examines the great credit that England enjoys and which is currently its greatest strength in the war, one should not attribute that entirely to the nature of its government; because, regardless of the authority of the monarch of France, since his interests are known always to rest on the foundation of faithfulness and justice, he could easily make all forget that he has the power to dismiss those principles; it is up to Your Majesty, with his strength of character and virtue, to make this truth felt through experience.

But another cause of the great credit of England is … the public renown to which the status of its finances is subject. That status is presented to Parliament each year, and printed afterward; and thus all lenders have regular knowledge of the balance being maintained between revenue and expenditure, they are never troubled by suspicions and imaginary fears.…

In France, a great mystery is always made of the status of the finances; or, if they are occasionally discussed, it is in the preambles of edicts and always when we want to borrow; but

those words, too often the same to be true, have necessarily lost their authority and experienced men no longer believe them without the guarantee, so to speak, of the moral character of the minister of finance. It is vital to found confidence on a more solid base. I admit that, under certain circumstances, it has been possible to profit from the veil cast over the financial situation to obtain, in the midst of disorder, some mediocre credit that was not warranted; but this momentary advantage, which sustained a misleading illusion and favored the indifference of the administration, was soon followed by unhappy transactions, the memory of which lasts longer and which will take long to correct.…

The sovereign of a realm like that of France can always, when he wants to do so, maintain the balance between expenditures and ordinary revenue; the diminution of the former, always seconded by the wishes of the public, is in his hands; and when circumstances require, increasing taxes is within his power; but the most dangerous, and the most unjust of resources, is to seek momentary aid with blind confidence and take loans without insuring the interest, or to raise revenues, or to economize.

Such administration, which is seductive because it postpones the moment of difficulty, only increases ills and digs itself deeper into the hole; while another kind of conduct, simpler and more frank, multiplies the means available to the Sovereign and forever protects it from any sort of injustice.

It is thus this broad view of administration on the part of His Majesty which has permitted us to offer a public account of the state of his finances; and I hope that, for the good of the realm and his power, this happy institution will not be temporary.

 What did Necker believe were the main differences between the French and British systems of public finance?

Source: From Mason, *The French Revolution*, 1e. © 1999 Cengage Learning.

From Estates-General to National Assembly

The Estates-General opened at Versailles on May 5, 1789. It was troubled from the start with the question of whether voting should be by order or by head (each delegate having one vote). Traditionally, each order would vote as a group and have one vote. That meant that the First and Second Estates could outvote the Third Estate two to one. The Third Estate demanded that each deputy have one vote. With the assistance of liberal nobles and clerics, that would give the Third Estate a majority. When the First Estate declared in favor of voting by order, the Third Estate responded dramatically. On June 17, 1789, the Third

Estate declared itself the "National Assembly" and decided to draw up a constitution. This was the first step in the French Revolution because the Third Estate had no legal right to act as the National Assembly. But this audacious act was soon in jeopardy, as the king sided with the First Estate and threatened to dissolve the Estates-General. Louis XVI now prepared to use force.

The common people, however, saved the Third Estate from the king's forces. On July 14, a mob of Parisians stormed the Bastille, a royal armory, and proceeded to dismantle it, brick by brick. Louis XVI was soon informed that the royal troops were unreliable. Louis's acceptance of that reality signaled the collapse of royal authority; the king could no longer enforce his will.

COMPARATIVE ILLUSTRATION

POLITICS & GOVERNMENT

Revolution and Revolt in France and China. Both France and China experienced revolutionary upheaval at the end of the eighteenth century and well into the nineteenth. In both countries, common people often played an important role. At the right is a scene from the storming of the Bastille in Paris in 1789. This early action by the people of Paris ultimately led to the overthrow of the French monarchy. At the top is a scene from one of the struggles during the Taiping Rebellion, a major peasant revolt in the mid-nineteenth century in China. An imperial Chinese army is shown recapturing the city of Nanjing from Taiping rebels in 1864.

 What role did common people play in revolutionary upheavals in France and China in the eighteenth and nineteenth centuries?

At the same time, popular revolts broke out throughout France, both in the cities and in the countryside (see the Comparative Illustration "Revolution and Revolt in France and China" above). Behind the popular uprising was a growing resentment of the entire landholding system, with its fees and obligations. The fall of the Bastille and the king's apparent capitulation to the demands of the Third Estate now led peasants to take matters into their own hands. The peasant rebellions that occurred throughout France had a great impact on the National Assembly meeting at Versailles.

Destruction of the Old Regime

One of the first acts of the National Assembly was to abolish the rights of landlords and the fiscal exemptions of nobles, clergy, towns, and provinces. Three weeks later, the National Assembly adopted the Declaration of the Rights of Man and the Citizen (see Opposing Viewpoints "The Natural Rights of

the French People: Two Views" on p. 525). This charter of basic liberties proclaimed freedom and equal rights for all men and access to public office based on talent. All citizens were to have the right to take part in the legislative process. Freedom of speech and the press were coupled with the outlawing of arbitrary arrests.

The declaration also raised another important issue. Did its ideal of equal rights for "all men" also include women? Many deputies insisted that it did, provided that, as one said, "women do not hope to exercise political rights and functions." Olympe de Gouges (oh-LAMP duh GOOZH), a playwright, refused to accept this exclusion of women from political rights. Echoing the words of the official declaration, she penned the Declaration of the Rights of Woman and the Female Citizen, in which she insisted that women should have all the same rights as men (see Opposing Viewpoints "The Natural Rights of the French People: Two Views" on p. 525). The National Assembly ignored her demands.

The Natural Rights of the French People: Two Views

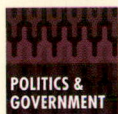

POLITICS & GOVERNMENT

ONE OF THE IMPORTANT DOCUMENTS OF THE FRENCH REVOLUTION, the Declaration of the Rights of Man and the Citizen, was adopted on August 26, 1789, by the National Assembly. The declaration affirmed that "men are born and remain free and equal in rights," that government must protect these natural rights, and that political power is derived from the people.

Olympe de Gouges (the pen name used by Marie Gouze) was a butcher's daughter who wrote plays and pamphlets. She argued that the Declaration of the Rights of Man and the Citizen did not apply to women and composed her own Declaration of the Rights of Woman and the Female Citizen in 1791.

Declaration of the Rights of Man and the Citizen

1. Men are born and remain free and equal in rights. Social distinctions can only be founded upon the general good.
2. The aim of all political association is the preservation of the natural and imprescriptible rights of man. These rights are liberty, property, security, and resistance to oppression.
3. The principle of all sovereignty resides essentially in the nation. No body or individual may exercise any authority which does not proceed directly from the nation.
4. Liberty consists in being able to do everything which injures no one else....
6. Law is the expression of the general will. Every citizen has a right to participate personally or through his representative in its formation. It must be the same for all, whether it protects or punishes. All citizens being equal in the eyes of the law are equally eligible to all dignities and to all public positions and occupations according to their abilities and without distinction except that of their virtues and talents.
7. No person shall be accused, arrested, or imprisoned except in the cases and according to the forms prescribed by law....
10. No one shall be disturbed on account of his opinions, including his religious views, provided their manifestation does not disturb the public order established by law.
11. The free communication of ideas and opinions is one of the most precious of the rights of man. Every citizen may, accordingly, speak, write and print with freedom, being responsible, however, for such abuses of this freedom as shall be defined by law.
12. The security of the rights of man and of the citizen requires public military force. These forces are, therefore, established for the good of all and not for the personal advantage of those to whom they shall be entrusted....
14. All the citizens have a right to decide either personally or by their representatives as to the necessity of the public contribution, to grant this freely, to know to what uses it is put, and to fix the proportion, the mode of assessment, and of collection, and the duration of the taxes.
15. Society has the right to require of every public agent an account of his administration.
16. A society in which the observance of the law is not assured nor the separation of powers defined has no constitution at all.
17. Property being an inviolable and sacred right, no one shall be deprived thereof except where public necessity, legally determined, shall clearly demand it, and then only on condition that the owner shall have been previously and equitably indemnified.

Declaration of the Rights of Woman and the Female Citizen

Mothers, daughters, sisters and representatives of the nation demand to be constituted into a national assembly. Believing that ignorance, omission, or scorn for the rights of woman are the only causes of public misfortunes and of the corruption of governments, the women have resolved to set forth in a solemn declaration the natural, inalienable, and sacred rights of woman in order that this declaration, constantly exposed before all the members of the society, will ceaselessly remind them of their rights and duties....

Consequently, the sex that is as superior in beauty as it is in courage during the sufferings of maternity recognizes and declares in the presence and under the auspices of the Supreme Being, the following Rights of Woman and of Female Citizens.

1. Woman is born free and lives equal to man in her rights. Social distinctions can be based only on the common utility.
2. The purpose of any political association is the conservation of the natural and imprescriptible rights of woman and man; these rights are liberty, property, security, and especially resistance to oppression.
3. The principle of all sovereignty rests essentially with the nation, which is nothing but the union of woman and man; no body and no individual can exercise any authority which does not come expressly from [the nation].

(continued)

4. Liberty and justice consist of restoring all that belongs to others; thus, the only limits on the exercise of the natural rights of woman are perpetual male tyranny; these limits are to be reformed by the laws of nature and reason....

6. The law must be the expression of the general will; all female and male citizens must contribute either personally or through their representatives to its formation; it must be the same for all: male and female citizens, being equal in the eyes of the law, must be equally admitted to all honors, positions, and public employment according to their capacity and without other distinctions besides those of their virtues and talents.

7. No woman is an exception; she is accused, arrested, and detained in cases determined by law. Women, like men, obey this rigorous law....

10. No one is to be disquieted for his very basic opinions; woman has the right to mount the scaffold; she must equally have the right to mount the rostrum, provided that her demonstrations do not disturb the legally established public order.

11. The free communication of thought and opinions is one of the most precious rights of woman, since that liberty assured the recognition of children by their fathers....

12. The guarantee of the rights of woman and the female citizen implies a major benefit; this guarantee must be instituted for the advantage of all, and not for the particular benefit of those to whom it is entrusted....

14. Female and male citizens have the right to verify, either by themselves or through their representatives, the necessity of the public contribution. This can only apply to women if they are granted an equal share, not only of wealth, but also of public administration, and in the determination of the proportion, the base, the collection, and the duration of the tax.

15. The collectivity of women, joined for tax purposes to the aggregate of men, has the right to demand an accounting of his administration from any public agent.

16. No society has a constitution without the guarantee of rights and the separation of powers; the constitution is null if the majority of individuals comprising the nation have not cooperated in drafting it.

17. Property belongs to both sexes whether united or separate; for each it is an inviolable and sacred right; no one can be deprived of it, since it is the true patrimony of nature, unless the legally determined public need obviously dictates it, and then only with a just and prior indemnity.

What "natural rights" does the first document proclaim? To what extent was this document influenced by the writings of the philosophes? What rights for women does the second document enunciate? Given the nature and scope of the arguments in favor of natural rights and women's rights in these two documents, what key effects on European society would you attribute to the French Revolution?

Sources: Excerpt from Thomas Carlyle, *The French Revolution: A History*, Vol. I, (George Bell and Sons, London, 1902), pp. 346–348. From *Women in Revolutionary Paris, 1789–1795: Selected Documents Translated with Notes and Commentary.* Translated with notes and commentary by Darline Gay Levy, Harriet Branson Applewhite, and Mary Durham Johnson. Copyright © 1979 by the Board of Trustees of the University of Illinois. Used with permission of the editors and the University of Illinois Press.

Because the Catholic Church was seen as an important pillar of the old order, it too was reformed. Most of the lands of the church were seized. The new Civil Constitution of the Clergy was put into effect in 1790. Both bishops and priests were to be elected by the people and paid by the state. The Catholic Church, still an important institution in the life of the French people, now became an enemy of the Revolution.

By 1791, the National Assembly had completed a new constitution that established a limited constitutional monarchy. There was still a monarch (now called "king of the French"), but the new Legislative Assembly was to make the laws. The Legislative Assembly, in which sovereign power was vested, was to sit for two years and consist of 745 representatives, or deputies, chosen by an indirect system of election that preserved power in the hands of the more affluent members of society. A small group of 50,000 electors chose the deputies.

By 1791, the old order had been destroyed. The new order, however, had many opponents—Catholic priests, nobles, lower classes hurt by a rise in the cost of living, peasants who remained opposed to dues that had still not been abandoned, and political clubs like the Jacobins (JAK-uh-binz) that offered more radical solutions to France's problems. The king also made things difficult for the new government when he sought to flee France in June 1791 and almost succeeded before being recognized, captured, and brought back to Paris. In this unsettled situation, under a discredited and seemingly disloyal monarch, the new Legislative Assembly held its first session in October 1791. France's relations with the rest of Europe soon led to Louis's downfall.

On August 27, 1791, the monarchs of Austria and Prussia, fearing that revolution would spread to their countries, invited other European monarchs to use force to reestablish monarchical authority in France. The French fared badly in the initial fighting in the spring of 1792, and a frantic search for scapegoats began. As one observer noted, "Everywhere you hear the cry that the king is betraying us, the generals are betraying us, that nobody is to be trusted; ... that Paris will be taken in six weeks by the Austrians.... We are on a volcano ready to spout flames."[4] Defeats in war coupled with economic shortages in the spring led to renewed political demonstrations, especially against the king. In August 1792, radical political groups in Paris attacked the royal palace, took the king captive, and forced the Legislative Assembly to suspend the monarchy and call for a national convention, chosen on the basis of universal male suffrage, to decide on the future form of government. The French Revolution was about to enter a more radical stage.

The Radical Revolution

In September 1792, the newly elected National Convention began its sessions. Dominated by lawyers and other professionals, two-thirds of its deputies were under the age of forty-five, and almost all had gained political experience as a result of the Revolution. Almost all distrusted the king. As a result, the convention's first step on September 21 was to abolish the monarchy and establish a republic. On January 21, 1793, the king was executed, and the destruction of the old regime was complete. But the execution of the king created new enemies for the Revolution both at home and abroad.

In Paris, the local government, known as the Commune, whose leaders came from the working classes, favored radical change and put constant pressure on the convention, pushing it to ever more radical positions. Meanwhile, peasants in the west and inhabitants of the major provincial cities refused to accept the authority of the convention.

A foreign crisis also loomed large. By the beginning of 1793, after the king had been put to death, most of Europe—an informal coalition of Austria, Prussia, Spain, Portugal, Britain, the Dutch Republic, and even Russia—aligned militarily against France. Grossly overextended, the French armies began to experience reverses, and by late spring, France was threatened with invasion.

A NATION IN ARMS   To meet these crises, the convention gave broad powers to an executive committee of twelve known as the Committee of Public Safety, which came to be dominated by Maximilien Robespierre (mak-see-meel-YENH

ROHBZ-pyayr). For a twelve-month period, from 1793 to 1794, the Committee of Public Safety took control of France. To save the Republic from its foreign foes, the committee decreed a universal mobilization of the nation on August 23, 1793:

> Young men will fight, young men are called to conquer. Married men will forge arms, transport military baggage and guns and will prepare food supplies. Women, who at long last are to take their rightful place in the revolution and follow their true destiny, will forget their futile tasks: their delicate hands will work at making clothes for soldiers; they will make tents and they will extend their tender care to shelters where the defenders of the *Patrie* [nation] will receive the help that their wounds require. Children will make lint of old cloth. It is for them that we are fighting: children, those beings destined to gather all the fruits of the revolution, will raise their pure hands toward the skies. And old men, performing their missions again, as of yore, will be guided to the public squares of the cities where they will kindle the courage of young warriors and preach the doctrines of hate for kings and the unity of the Republic.[5]

In less than a year, the French revolutionary government had raised an army of 650,000 and by 1795 had pushed the allies back across the Rhine and even conquered the Austrian Netherlands.

The French revolutionary army was an important step in the creation of modern **nationalism**. Previously, wars had been fought between governments or ruling dynasties by relatively small armies of professional soldiers. The new French army was the creation of a "people's" government; its wars were now "people's" wars. The entire nation was to be involved in the war. But when dynastic wars became people's wars, warfare increased in ferocity and lack of restraint. The wars of the French revolutionary era opened the door to the total war of the modern world.

REIGN OF TERROR   To meet the domestic crisis, the National Convention and the Committee of Public Safety launched the

Citizens in the New French Army. To save the Republic from its foreign enemies, the National Convention created a revolutionary army of unprecedented size. This illustration, from a book of paintings on the French Revolution by the Lesueur brothers, shows three citizens learning to drill, while a young volunteer is being armed and outfitted by his family.

"Reign of Terror." Revolutionary courts were instituted to protect the Republic from its internal enemies. In the course of nine months, 16,000 people were officially killed under the blade of the guillotine—a revolutionary device designed for the quick and efficient separation of heads from bodies.

Revolutionary armies were set up to bring recalcitrant cities and districts back under the control of the National Convention. The Committee of Public Safety decided to make an example of Lyons (LYOHNH), which had defied the authority of the National Convention. By April 1794, some 1,880 citizens of Lyons had been executed. When the guillotine proved too slow, cannon fire was used to blow condemned men into open graves. A German observed:

> Whole ranges of houses, always the most handsome, burnt. The churches, convents, and all the dwellings of the former patricians were in ruins. When I came to the guillotine, the blood of those who had been executed a few hours beforehand was still running in the street.... I said to a group of [radicals] that it would be decent to clear away all this human blood. Why should it be cleared? one of them said to me. It's the blood of aristocrats and rebels. The dogs should lick it up.[6]

EQUALITY AND SLAVERY: REVOLUTION IN HAITI Early in the French Revolution, the desire for equality led to a discussion of what to do about slavery. A club called Friends of the Blacks advocated the abolition of slavery, which was achieved in France in September 1791. However, French planters in the West Indies, who profited greatly from the use of slaves on their sugar plantations, opposed the abolition of slavery in the French colonies. When the National Convention came to power, the issue was revisited, and on February 4, 1794, guided by ideals of equality, the government abolished slavery in the colonies.

In one French colony, slaves had already rebelled for their freedom. In 1791, black slaves in the French sugar colony of Saint-Domingue (san doh-MAYNG) (the western third of the island of Hispaniola), inspired by the ideals of the revolution occurring in France, revolted against French plantation owners. Slaves attacked, killing plantation owners and their families and burning their buildings. White planters retaliated with equal brutality. One wealthy French settler reported, "How can we stay in a country where slaves have raised their hands against their masters?"

Revolt in Saint-Domingue

Eventually, leadership of the revolt was taken over by Toussaint L'Ouverture (too-SANH loo-vayr-TOOR) (1746–1803), a son of African slaves, who seized control of all of Hispaniola by 1801. Although Napoleon, the French leader, had accepted the revolutionary ideal of equality, he did not reject the reports of white planters that the massacres of white planters by slaves demonstrated the savage nature of blacks. In 1802, he reinstated slavery in the French West Indian colonies and sent an army that captured L'Ouverture, who died in a French dungeon within a year. But the French soldiers, weakened by disease, soon succumbed to the slave forces. On January 1, 1804, the western part of Hispaniola, now called Haiti, announced its freedom and became the first state in Latin America to win its independence. Despite Napoleon's efforts to the contrary, one of the French revolutionary ideals had triumphed abroad.

Reaction and the Directory

By the summer of 1794, the French had been successful on the battlefield against their foreign foes, making the Reign of Terror less necessary. But the Terror continued because Robespierre, who had become a figure of power and authority, became obsessed with purifying the body politic of all the corrupt. Many deputies in the National Convention were fearful, however, that they were not safe while Robespierre was free to act and gathered enough votes to condemn him. Robespierre was sent to the guillotine on July 28, 1794.

After the death of Robespierre, a reaction set in as more moderate middle-class leaders took control. The Reign of Terror came to a halt, and the National Convention reduced the power of the Committee of Public Safety. In addition, in August 1795 a new constitution was drafted that reflected the desire for a stability that did not sacrifice the ideals of 1789. Five directors—known as the Directory—acted as the executive authority.

Government under the Directory (1795–1799) was characterized by stagnation and corruption. The Directory faced political enemies on both the left and the right. On the right, royalists who wanted to restore the monarchy continued their agitation. On the left, radical hopes of power were revived by continuing economic problems. Battered from both sides, unable to solve the country's economic problems, and still carrying on the wars inherited from the Committee of Public Safety, the Directory increasingly relied on the military to maintain its power. This led to a coup d'état in 1799 in which a popular military general, Napoleon Bonaparte (1769–1821), seized power.

CHRONOLOGY	The French Revolution
Meeting of the Estates-General	May 5, 1789
Formation of the National Assembly	June 17, 1789
Fall of the Bastille	July 14, 1789
Declaration of the Rights of Man and the Citizen	August 26, 1789
Civil Constitution of the Clergy	July 12, 1790
Flight of the king	June 20–21, 1791
Attack on the royal palace	August 10, 1792
Abolition of the monarchy	September 21, 1792
Execution of the king	January 21, 1793
Universal mobilization	August 23, 1793
Execution of Robespierre	July 28, 1794
Adoption of the Constitution of 1795 and the Directory	August 22, 1795

Napoleon and Psychological Warfare

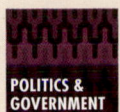

POLITICS & GOVERNMENT

IN 1796, AT THE AGE OF TWENTY-SEVEN, Napoleon Bonaparte was given command of the French army in Italy, where he won a series of stunning victories. His use of speed, deception, and surprise to overwhelm his opponents is well known. In this selection from a proclamation to his troops in Italy, Napoleon also appears as a master of psychological warfare.

Napoleon Bonaparte, Proclamation to French Troops in Italy (April 26, 1796)

Soldiers:

You have in a fortnight won six victories, taken twenty-one standards [flags of military units], fifty-five pieces of artillery, several strong places, and conquered the richest part of Piedmont [in northern Italy]; you have made fifteen thousand prisoners and killed or wounded more than ten thousand men…. You have won battles without cannon, crossed rivers without bridges, made forced marches without shoes, camped without brandy and often without bread. Only republican phalanxes, soldiers of liberty, would have been able to bear what you have borne. Thanks be to you, soldiers, for this. Your grateful country will owe its prosperity to you….

The two armies which but recently attacked you with confidence are fleeing in consternation before you. Those misguided men who laughed at your misery and rejoiced in the thought of the triumphs of your enemies have been confounded.

But, soldiers, you have done nothing as yet compared with what there still remains to do…. The greatest obstacles undoubtedly have been overcome, but you still have battles to fight, cities to capture, rivers to cross. Is there any one among you whose courage is slackening? No…. All of you are burning to extend the glory of the French people. All long to humiliate those haughty kings who dare to contemplate placing us in fetters. All desire to dictate a glorious peace, one which will indemnify our country for the immense sacrifices which it has made; all would wish, as they return to their native villages, to be able to say proudly, "I was with the victorious army of Italy!"

What themes did Napoleon use to play on the emotions of his troops and inspire them to greater efforts? Do you think Napoleon believed these words? Why or why not?

Source: From James Harvey Robinson, *Readings in European History* (Lexington, Mass.: Ginn and Co., 1906), p. 471.

The Age of Napoleon

FOCUS QUESTION: Which aspects of the French Revolution did Napoleon preserve, and which did he destroy?

Napoleon dominated both French and European history from 1799 to 1815. The coup that brought him to power occurred exactly ten years after the outbreak of the French Revolution. In a sense, Napoleon brought the Revolution to an end, but he was also its child; he even called himself the Son of the Revolution. The French Revolution had made possible his rise first in the military and then to supreme power in France. Even beyond this, Napoleon had once said, "I am the Revolution," and he never ceased to remind the French that they owed to him the preservation of all that was beneficial in the revolutionary program.

The Rise of Napoleon

Napoleon was born in Corsica in 1769, only a few months after France had annexed the island. The son of an Italian lawyer whose family stemmed from the Florentine nobility, Napoleone Buonaparte (his birth name) grew up in the countryside of Corsica, a willful and demanding child who nevertheless developed discipline, thriftiness, and loyalty to his family. His father's connections in France enabled him to study first at a school in the French town of Autun, where he learned to speak French, and then to obtain a royal scholarship to study at a military school. At that time, he changed his first name to the more French-sounding Napoleon (he did not change his last name to Bonaparte until 1796).

Napoleon's military education led to his commission as a lieutenant in 1785, although he was not well liked by his fellow officers because he was short, spoke with an Italian accent, and had little money. For the next seven years, Napoleon spent much of his time reading the works of the philosophes, especially Rousseau, and educating himself in military matters by studying the campaigns of great military leaders from the past, including Alexander the Great, Charlemagne, and Frederick the Great. The French Revolution and the European war that followed broadened his sights and presented him with new opportunities.

Napoleon rose quickly through the ranks. In 1794, at the age of only twenty-five, he was made a brigadier general by the Committee of Public Safety. Two years later, he commanded the French armies in Italy, where he won a series of victories and returned to France as a conquering hero (see the box "Napoleon and Psychological Warfare" above). After a disastrous expedition to Egypt, Napoleon returned to Paris, where he participated in the coup that gave him control of France. He was only thirty years old.

After the coup of 1799, a new form of the Republic, called the Consulate, was proclaimed in which Napoleon, as first consul, controlled the entire executive authority of government. He had overwhelming influence over the legislature, appointed members of the administrative bureaucracy, commanded the army, and conducted foreign affairs. In 1802, Napoleon was made consul for life, and in 1804, he returned France to monarchy when he crowned himself Emperor Napoleon I.

Domestic Policies

One of Napoleon's first domestic policies was to establish peace with the oldest and most implacable enemy of the Revolution, the Catholic Church. In 1801, Napoleon arranged a concordat with the pope that recognized Catholicism as the religion of a majority of the French people. In return, the pope agreed not to raise the question of the church lands confiscated in the Revolution. As a result of the concordat, the Catholic Church was no longer an enemy of the French government, and Frenchmen who had acquired church lands during the Revolution were assured that they would not be stripped of them, an assurance that made them supporters of the Napoleonic regime.

Napoleon's most enduring domestic achievement was his codification of the laws. Before the Revolution, France had some three hundred local legal systems. During the Revolution, efforts were made to prepare a single code of laws for the entire nation, but it remained for Napoleon to bring the work to completion in the famous Civil Code. This preserved most of the revolutionary gains by recognizing the principle of the equality of all citizens before the law, the abolition of serfdom and feudalism, and religious toleration. Property rights were also protected.

At the same time, the Civil Code strictly curtailed the rights of some people. During the radical phase of the French Revolution, new laws had made divorce an easy process for both husbands and wives and allowed sons and daughters to inherit property equally. Napoleon's Civil Code undid these laws. Divorce was still allowed but was made more difficult for women to obtain. Women were now "less equal than men" in other ways as well. When they married, their property came under the control of their husbands.

Napoleon also developed a powerful, centralized administrative machine and worked hard to develop a bureaucracy of capable officials. Early on, the regime showed that it cared little whether the expertise of officials had been acquired in royal or revolutionary bureaucracies. Promotion, whether in civil or military offices, was to be based not on rank or birth but on ability only. This principle of a government career open to talent was, of course, what many bourgeois had wanted before the Revolution.

© RMN-Grand Palais/Art Resource, NY

The Coronation of Napoleon. In 1804, Napoleon restored monarchy to France when he crowned himself emperor. In the coronation scene painted by Jacques-Louis David, Napoleon is shown crowning his wife, the empress Josephine, while the pope looks on. The painting shows Napoleon's mother seated in the box in the background, even though she was not at the ceremony.

In his domestic policies, then, Napoleon both destroyed and preserved aspects of the Revolution. Although equality and the opening of careers to talent were retained in the law code, the creation of a new aristocracy, the strong protection accorded to property rights, and the use of conscription for the military make it clear that much equality had been lost. Liberty had been replaced by an initially benevolent despotism that grew increasingly arbitrary. Napoleon shut down sixty of France's seventy-three newspapers and insisted that all manuscripts be subjected to government scrutiny before they were published. Even the mail was opened by government police.

Napoleon's Empire

When Napoleon became consul in 1799, France was at war with a second European coalition of Russia, Great Britain, and Austria. Napoleon realized the need for a pause and made a peace treaty in 1802. But war was renewed in 1803 with Britain, which was soon joined by Austria, Russia, and Prussia in the Third Coalition. In a series of battles from 1805 to 1807, Napoleon's Grand Army defeated the Austrian, Prussian, and Russian armies, giving Napoleon the opportunity to create a new European order.

THE GRAND EMPIRE From 1807 to 1812, Napoleon was the master of Europe. His Grand Empire was composed of three major parts: the French Empire, dependent states, and allied states (see Map 18.4). Dependent states were kingdoms under the rule of Napoleon's relatives; these came to include Spain, the Netherlands, the kingdom of Italy, the Swiss Republic, the Grand Duchy of Warsaw, and the Confederation of the Rhine (a union of all German states except Austria and Prussia).

© 2016 Cengage Learning

MAP 18.4 Napoleon's Grand Empire. Napoleon's Grand Army won a series of victories against Austria, Prussia, and Russia that gave the French emperor full or partial control over much of Europe by 1807.

Q *On the European continent, what is the overall relationship between distance from France and degree of French control, and how can you account for this?*

Allied states were those defeated by Napoleon and forced to join his struggle against Britain; these included Prussia, Austria, Russia, and Sweden.

Within his empire, Napoleon sought acceptance of certain revolutionary principles, including legal equality, religious toleration, and economic freedom. In the inner core and dependent states of his Grand Empire, Napoleon tried to destroy the old order. Nobility and clergy everywhere in these states lost their special privileges. He decreed equality of opportunity with offices open to talent, equality before the law, and religious toleration. This spread of French revolutionary principles was an important factor in the development of liberal traditions in these countries.

Napoleon hoped that his Grand Empire would last for centuries; it collapsed almost as rapidly as it had been formed. As long as Britain ruled the waves, it was not subject to military attack. Napoleon hoped to invade Britain, but he could not overcome the British navy's decisive defeat of a combined French-Spanish fleet at Trafalgar in 1805. To defeat Britain, Napoleon turned to his **Continental system**. An alliance put into effect between 1806 and 1808, it attempted to prevent British goods from reaching the European continent in order to weaken Britain economically and destroy its capacity to wage war. But the Continental system failed. Allied states resented it; some began to cheat and others to resist.

Napoleon also encountered new sources of opposition. His conquests made the French hated oppressors and aroused the patriotism of the conquered peoples. A Spanish uprising against Napoleon's rule, with British support, kept a French force of 200,000 pinned down for years.

THE FALL OF NAPOLEON The beginning of Napoleon's downfall came in 1812 with his invasion of Russia. The refusal of the Russians to remain in the Continental system left Napoleon with little choice. Although aware of the risks in invading such a huge country, he also knew that if the Russians were allowed to challenge the Continental system unopposed, others would soon follow suit. In June 1812, he led his Grand Army of more than 600,000 men into Russia. Napoleon's hopes for victory depended on quickly defeating the Russian armies, but the Russian forces retreated and refused to give battle, torching their own villages and countryside to keep Napoleon's army from finding food. When the Russians did stop to fight at Borodino, Napoleon's forces won an indecisive and costly victory. When the remaining troops of the Grand Army arrived in Moscow, they found the city ablaze. Lacking food and supplies, Napoleon abandoned Moscow late in October and made a retreat across Russia in terrible winter conditions. Only 40,000 of the original 600,000 men managed to arrive back in Poland in January 1813.

This military disaster led other European states to rise up and attack the crippled French army. Paris was captured in March 1814, and Napoleon was sent into exile on the island of Elba, off the coast of Italy. Meanwhile, the Bourbon monarchy was restored in the person of Louis XVIII, the count of Provence, brother of the executed king. (Louis XVII, son of Louis XVI, had died in prison at age ten.) Napoleon, bored on Elba, slipped back into France. When troops were sent to capture him, Napoleon opened his coat and addressed them: "Soldiers of the 5th regiment, I am your Emperor.... If there is a man among you would kill his Emperor, here I am!" No one fired a shot. Shouting "Vive l'Empereur! Vive l'Empereur!" the troops went over to his side, and Napoleon entered Paris in triumph on March 20, 1815.

The powers that had defeated him pledged once more to fight him. Having decided to strike first at his enemies, Napoleon raised yet another army and moved to attack the allied forces stationed in what is now Belgium. At Waterloo on June 18, Napoleon met a combined British and Prussian army under the duke of Wellington and suffered a bloody defeat. This time, the victorious allies exiled him to Saint Helena, a small, forsaken island in the South Atlantic. Only Napoleon's memory continued to haunt French political life.

CHAPTER SUMMARY

In the Scientific Revolution, the Western world overthrew the medieval, Ptolemaic worldview and arrived at a new conception of the universe: the sun at the center, the planets as material bodies revolving around the sun in elliptical orbits, and an infinite rather than finite world. With the changes in the conception of "heaven" came changes in the conception of "earth." The work of Descartes left Europeans with the separation of mind and matter and the belief that by using only reason they could, in fact, understand and dominate the world of nature.

Highly influenced by the new worldview created by the Scientific Revolution, the philosophes of the eighteenth century hoped that they could create a new society by using reason to discover the natural laws that governed it. They believed that education could create better human beings and a better human society. They attacked traditional religion as the enemy and created the new "sciences of man" in economics, politics, and education. Together, the Scientific Revolution of the seventeenth century and the Enlightenment of the eighteenth century constituted an intellectual revolution that laid the foundations for a modern worldview based on rationalism and secularism.

Everywhere in Europe at the beginning of the eighteenth century, the old order remained strong. Nobles, clerics, towns, and provinces all had privileges. Everywhere in the eighteenth century, monarchs sought to enlarge their bureaucracies to raise taxes to support large standing armies. The existence of these armies led to wars on a worldwide scale. Indeed, the Seven Years' War could be viewed as the first world war. Although the wars resulted in few changes in Europe, British victories enabled Great Britain to emerge as the world's greatest naval and colonial power. Meanwhile, in Europe increased demands for taxes to support these wars led to attacks on the old order and a desire for change not met by the ruling monarchs. At the same time, a growing population as well as changes in finance, trade, and industry created tensions that undermined the foundations of the old order. Its inability to deal with these changes led to a revolutionary outburst at the end of the eighteenth century that marked the beginning of the end for the old order.

The revolutionary era of the late eighteenth century was a time of dramatic political transformations. Revolutionary upheavals, beginning in North America and continuing in France, spurred movements for political liberty and equality. The documents promulgated by these revolutions, the Declaration of Independence and the Declaration of the Rights of Man and the Citizen, embodied the fundamental ideas of the Enlightenment and created a liberal political agenda based on a belief in popular sovereignty—the people as the source of political power—and the principles of liberty and equality. Liberty meant, in theory, freedom from arbitrary power as well as the freedom to think, write, and worship as one chose. Equality meant equality in rights, although it did not include equality between men and women.

CHAPTER TIMELINE

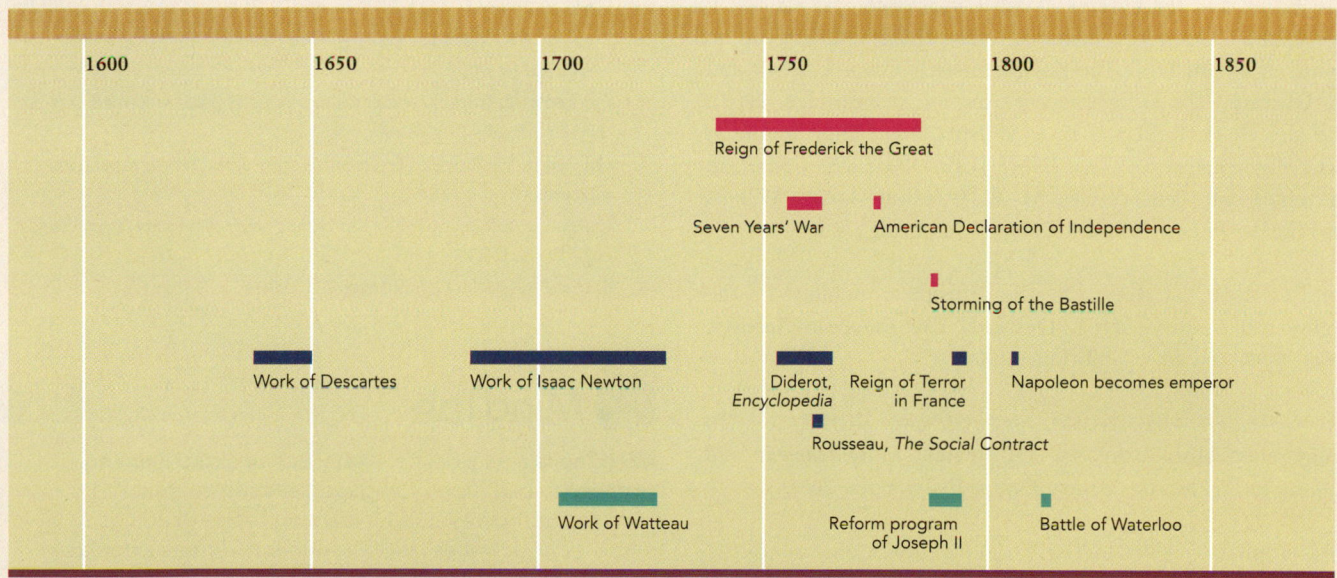

CHAPTER REVIEW

Upon Reflection

Q What was the impact of the intellectual revolution of the seventeenth and eighteenth centuries on European society?

Q How was France changed by the revolutionary events between 1789 and 1799, and who benefited the most from these changes?

Q In what ways did Napoleon's policies reject the accomplishments of the French Revolution? In what ways did his policies strengthen those accomplishments?

Key Terms

Scientific Revolution (p. 504)
geocentric theory (p. 504)
heliocentric theory (p. 504)
world-machine (p. 505)
Cartesian dualism (p. 506)
rationalism (p. 506)
Enlightenment (p. 506)
scientific method (p. 506)
philosophes (p. 506)
separation of powers (p. 507)

deism (p. 508)

laissez-faire (p. 510)

feminism (p. 510)

Rococo (p. 511)

high culture (p. 512)

popular culture (p. 512)

cottage industry (p. 513)

patrician (p. 515)

rentiers (p. 515)

natural rights (p. 517)

enlightened absolutism (p. 517)

old order (p. 521)

old regime (p. 521)

nationalism (p. 527)

Continental system (p. 532)

Suggested Reading

INTELLECTUAL REVOLUTION IN THE WEST   Two general surveys of the Scientific Revolution are **J. R. Jacob, *The Scientific Revolution: Aspirations and Achievements, 1500–1700*** (Atlantic Highlands, N.J., 1998), and **J. Henry, *The Scientific Revolution and the Origins of Modern Science***, 2nd ed. (New York, 2002). Good introductions to the Enlightenment can be found in **U. Im Hof, *The Enlightenment*** (Oxford, 1994), and **D. Outram, *The Enlightenment***, 2nd ed. (Cambridge, 2005). See also **P. H. Reill** and **E. J. Wilson, eds., *Encyclopedia of the Enlightenment***, rev. ed. (New York, 2004). On women in the eighteenth century, see **M. E. Wiesner-Hanks, *Women and Gender in Early Modern Europe*** (Cambridge, 2000).

THE SOCIAL ORDER   On the European nobility in the eighteenth century, see **J. Dewald, *The European Nobility, 1400–1800,*** 2nd ed. (Cambridge, 2004).

ENLIGHTENED ABSOLUTISM AND GLOBAL CONFLICT   On enlightened absolutism, see **D. Beales, *Enlightenment and Reform in Eighteenth-Century Europe*** (New York, 2005).

THE FRENCH REVOLUTION   A well-written, up-to-date introduction to the French Revolution can be found in **W. Doyle, *The Oxford History of the French Revolution***, 2nd ed. (Oxford, 2003). On the entire revolutionary and Napoleonic eras, see **O. Connelly, *The French Revolution and Napoleonic Era***, 3rd ed. (Fort Worth, Tex., 2000). For interesting insight into Louis XVI and French society, see **T. Tackett, *When the King Took Flight*** (Cambridge, Mass., 2003). An important work on the radical stage of the French Revolution is **D. Andress, *The Terror: The Merciless War for Freedom in Revolutionary France*** (New York, 2005). The importance of the revolutionary wars in the radical stage of the Revolution is underscored in **T. C. W. Blanning, *The French Revolutionary Wars, 1787–1802*** (New York, 1996).

THE AGE OF NAPOLEON   The best biography of Napoleon is **S. Englund, *Napoleon: A Political Life*** (New York, 2004). See **A. I. Grab, *Napoleon and the Transformation of Europe*** (New York, 2003), on Napoleon's Grand Empire. On Napoleon's wars, see **D. A. Bell, *The First Total War: Napoleon's Europe and the Birth of Warfare as We Know It*** (Boston, 2007).

Chapter Notes

1. R. Descartes, *Philosophical Writing*, ed. and trans. N. K. Smith (New York, 1958), pp. 118–119.

2. J. Locke, *An Essay Concerning Human Understanding* (New York, 1964), pp. 89–90.

3. Quoted in P. Burke, *Popular Culture in Early Modern Europe*, rev. ed. (New York, 1994), p. 186.

4. Quoted in W. Doyle, *The Oxford History of the French Revolution* (Oxford, 1989), p. 184.

5. Quoted in L. Gershoy, *The Era of the French Revolution* (Princeton, N.J., 1957), p. 157.

6. Quoted in Doyle, *Oxford History*, p. 254.

MindTap is a fully online, highly personalized learning experience built upon Cengage Learning content. MindTap combines student learning tools—readings, multimedia, activities, and assessments—into a singular Learning Path that guides students through their course.

THE PERIOD OF WORLD HISTORY from 1800 to 1945 was characterized by three major developments: the growth of industrialization, Western domination of the world, and the rise of nationalism. The three developments were, of course, interconnected. The Industrial Revolution became one of the major forces of change in the nineteenth century as it led Western civilization into the industrial era that has characterized the modern world. Beginning in Britain, it spread to the continent and the Western Hemisphere in the course of the nineteenth century. At the same time, the Industrial Revolution created the technological means, including new weapons, by which the West achieved domination over much of the rest of the world by the end of the nineteenth century. Moreover, the existence of competitive European nation-states after 1870 was undoubtedly a major determinant in leading European states to embark on their intense scramble for overseas territory.

The advent of the industrial age had a number of lasting consequences for the world at large. On the one hand, the material wealth of the nations that successfully passed through the process increased significantly. In many cases, the creation of advanced industrial societies strengthened democratic institutions and led to a higher standard of living for the majority of the population. On the other hand, not all the consequences of the Industrial Revolution were beneficial. In the industrializing societies themselves, rapid economic change often led to widening disparities in the distribution of wealth and, with the decline in the pervasiveness of religious belief, a sense of rootlessness and alienation among much of the population.

A second development that had a major impact on the era was the rise of nationalism. Like the Industrial Revolution, the idea of nationalism originated in eighteenth-century Europe, where it was a product of the secularization of the age and the experience of the French revolutionary and Napoleonic eras. Although the concept provided the basis for a new sense of community and the rise of the modern nation-state, it also gave birth to ethnic tensions and hatreds that resulted in bitter disputes and civil strife and contributed to the competition that eventually erupted into world war.

Industrialization and the rise of national consciousness also transformed the nature of war itself. New weapons of mass destruction created the potential for a new kind of warfare that reached beyond the battlefield into the very heartland of the enemy's territory, while the concept of nationalism transformed war from the sport of kings to a matter of national honor and commitment. Since the French Revolution, governments had relied on mass conscription to defend the national cause, while their engines of destruction reached far into enemy territory to destroy the industrial base and undermine the will to fight. This trend was amply demonstrated in the two world wars of the twentieth century.

In the end, then, industrial power and the driving force of nationalism, the very factors that had created the conditions for European global dominance, contained the seeds for the decline of that dominance. These seeds germinated during the 1930s, when the Great Depression sharpened international competition and mutual antagonism, and then sprouted in the ensuing conflict, which for the first time spanned the entire globe. By the time World War II came to an end, the once powerful countries of Europe were exhausted, leaving the door ajar for the emergence of two new global super-powers, the United States and the Soviet Union, and for the collapse of the Europeans' colonial empires.

Europeans had begun to explore the world in the fifteenth century, but even as late as 1870, they had not yet completely penetrated North America, South America, Australia, or most of Africa. In Asia and Africa, with few exceptions, the West-ern presence was limited to trading posts. Between 1870 and 1914, Western civilization expanded into the rest of the Americas and Australia, while the bulk of Africa and Asia was divided into European colonies or spheres of influence. Two major events explain this remarkable expansion: the migration of many Europeans to other parts of the world due to population growth and the revival of imperialism, which

was made possible by the West's technological advances. Beginning in the 1880s, European states began an intense scramble for overseas territory. This revival of imperialism—the "new imperialism," some have called it—led Europeans to carve up Asia and Africa.

What was the overall economic effect of imperialism on the subject peoples? For most of the population in colonial areas, Western domination was rarely beneficial and often destructive. Although a limited number of merchants, large landowners, and traditional hereditary elites undoubtedly prospered under the umbrella of the expanding imperialistic economic order, the majority of colonial peoples, urban and rural alike, probably suffered considerable hardship as a result of the policies adopted by their foreign rulers.

Some historians point out, however, that for all the inequi-ties of the colonial system, there was a positive side to the experience as well. The expansion of markets and the begin-nings of a modern transportation and communications net-work, while bringing few immediate benefits to the colonial peoples, offered considerable promise for future economic growth. At the same time, colonial peoples soon learned the power of nationalism, and in the twentieth century, national-ism would become a powerful force in the rest of the world as nationalist revolutions moved through Asia, Africa, and the Middle East. Moreover, the exhaustive struggles of two world wars sapped the power of the European states, and the colo-nial powers no longer had the energy or the wealth to main-tain their colonial empires after World War II. ◆

The Beginnings of Modernization: Industrialization and Nationalism in the Nineteenth Century

A gathering of statesmen at the Congress of Vienna

CHAPTER OUTLINE AND FOCUS QUESTIONS

The Industrial Revolution and Its Impact

Q What were the basic features of the new industrial system created by the Industrial Revolution, and what effects did the new system have on urban life, social classes, family life, and standards of living?

The Growth of Industrial Prosperity

Q What was the Second Industrial Revolution, and what effects did it have on economic and social life? What were the main ideas of Karl Marx, and what role did they play in politics and the union movement in the late nineteenth and early twentieth centuries?

Reaction and Revolution: The Growth of Nationalism

Q What were the major ideas associated with conservatism, liberalism, and nationalism, and what role did each ideology play in Europe between 1800 and 1870? What were the causes of the revolutions of 1848, and why did these revolutions fail?

National Unification and the National State, 1848–1871

Q What actions did Cavour and Bismarck take to bring about unification in Italy and Germany, respectively, and what role did war play in their efforts?

The European State, 1871–1914

Q What general political trends were evident in the nations of western Europe in the late nineteenth and early twentieth centuries, and to what degree were those trends also apparent in the nations of central and eastern Europe? How did the growth of nationalism affect international affairs during the same period?

CRITICAL THINKING

Q In what ways was the development of industrialization related to the growth of nationalism?

CONNECTIONS TO TODAY

Q How do the locations of the centers of industrialization today compare with those during the Industrial Revolution, and how do you account for any differences?

IN SEPTEMBER 1814, hundreds of foreigners began to converge on Vienna, the capital city of the Austrian Empire. Many were members of European royalty—kings, archdukes, princes, and their wives—accompanied by their diplomatic advisers and scores of servants. Their congenial host was the Austrian emperor, Francis I, who never tired of regaling Vienna's guests with concerts, glittering balls, sumptuous feasts, and innumerable hunting parties. One participant remembered, "Eating, fireworks, public illuminations. For eight or ten days, I haven't been able to work at all. What a life!" Of course, not every waking hour was spent in pleasure during this gathering of notables, known to history as the Congress of Vienna. These people were also representatives of all the states that had fought Napoleon, and their real business was to arrange a final peace settlement after almost a decade of war. On June 8, 1815, they finally completed their task.

The forces of upheaval unleashed during the French revolutionary and Napoleonic wars were temporarily quieted in 1815 as rulers sought to restore stability by reestablishing much of the old order in a Europe ravaged by war. But the Western world had been changed, and it would not readily go back to the old system. New ideologies of change, especially liberalism and nationalism, products of the upheaval initiated in France, had become too powerful to be contained. The forces of change called forth revolts that periodically shook the West and culminated in a spate of revolutions in 1848. Some of the revolutions and revolutionaries were successful; most were not. And yet by 1870, many of the goals sought by the liberals and nationalists during the first half of the nineteenth century seemed to have been achieved. National unity became a reality in Italy and Germany, and many Western states developed parliamentary features.

During the late eighteenth and early nineteenth centuries, another revolution—an industrial one—transformed the economic and social structure of Europe and spawned the industrial era that has characterized modern world history.

The Industrial Revolution and Its Impact

Q **FOCUS QUESTION:** What were the basic features of the new industrial system created by the Industrial Revolution, and what effects did the new system have on urban life, social classes, family life, and standards of living?

The Industrial Revolution triggered an enormous leap in industrial production. Coal and steam replaced wind and water as new sources of energy and power to drive laborsaving machines. In turn, these machines required new ways of organizing human labor as factories replaced workshops and home workrooms. During the Industrial Revolution, Europe shifted from an economy based on agriculture and handicrafts to an economy based on manufacturing by machines and automated factories.

Although the Industrial Revolution took decades to spread, it was truly revolutionary in the way it fundamentally changed the world. Large numbers of people moved from the countryside to cities to work in the new factories. The creation of a wealthy industrial middle class and a huge industrial working class substantially transformed traditional social relationships. Finally, the Industrial Revolution altered how people related to nature, ultimately creating an environmental crisis that in the twentieth century was finally recognized as a danger to human existence itself.

The Industrial Revolution in Great Britain

Although the Industrial Revolution evolved over a period of time, historians generally agree that it began in Britain sometime after 1750.

ORIGINS A number of factors or conditions coalesced in Britain to produce the Industrial Revolution. Improvements in agricultural practices in the eighteenth century led to a significant increase in food production. British agriculture could now feed more people at lower prices with less labor; even ordinary British families no longer had to use most of their income to buy food, giving them the wherewithal to purchase manufactured goods. At the same time, rapid population growth in the second half of the eighteenth century provided a pool of surplus labor for the new factories of the emerging British industry.

Britain also had a ready supply of capital for investment in the new industrial machines and the factories that were needed to house them. In addition to profits from trade and the cottage industry, Britain possessed an effective central bank and well-developed, flexible credit facilities. But capital is only part of the story. Britain had a fair number of individuals who were interested in making profits if the opportunity presented itself. No doubt the English revolutions of the seventeenth century had helped create an environment in Britain, unlike that of the absolutist states on the European continent, where political power rested in the hands of a progressive group of people who favored innovation in economic matters.

Britain also had ample supplies of important mineral resources, such as coal and iron ore, needed in the manufacturing process. It was also a small country, and the relatively short distances made transportation nonproblematic. Britain's government, too, played a significant role in the process of industrialization. Parliament contributed to the favorable business climate by providing a stable government and passing laws that protected private property.

Finally, in the course of its eighteenth-century wars and conquests, Great Britain had assembled a vast colonial empire at the expense of its leading rivals, the Dutch Republic and France. The many markets of empire gave British industrialists a ready outlet for their manufactured goods. British exports quadrupled from 1660 to 1760. A crucial factor in Britain's successful industrialization was the ability to produce cheaply the articles in greatest demand. The traditional methods of the cottage industry could not keep up with the growing demand for cotton clothes throughout Britain and its vast colonial empire. This problem led British cloth manufacturers to seek and adopt the new methods of manufacturing that a series of inventions provided. In so doing, these individuals ignited the Industrial Revolution.

CHANGES IN TEXTILE PRODUCTION The invention of the flying shuttle made it possible to weave faster on a loom, enabling weavers to double their output. This created shortages of yarn until James Hargreaves's spinning jenny, perfected by 1768, allowed spinners to produce yarn in greater quantities. Edmund Cartwright's loom, powered by water and invented in 1787, allowed the weaving of cloth to catch up with the spinning of yarn. It was now more efficient to bring workers to the machines and organize their labor collectively in factories located next to rivers and streams, the sources of power for these early machines.

The cotton industry was then pushed to even greater heights of productivity by the invention of the steam engine. In the 1760s, a Scottish engineer, James Watt (1736–1819), built an engine powered by steam that could pump water from mines three times as quickly as previous engines, thereby allowing for more coal to be extracted from the mines. In 1782, Watt developed a rotary engine that could turn a shaft and thus drive machinery. Steam power could now be applied to spinning and weaving cotton, and before long, cotton mills using steam engines were multiplying across Britain. Fired by coal, these steam engines could be located anywhere.

The boost given to cotton textile production by these technological changes was readily apparent. In 1760, Britain had imported 2.5 million pounds of raw cotton, which was farmed out to cottage industries. In 1787, the British imported 22 million pounds of cotton; most of it was spun on machines, some powered by water in large mills. By 1840, some 366 million pounds of cotton—now Britain's most important product in value—were being imported. By this time, most cotton industry employees worked in factories, and British cotton goods were sold everywhere in the world.

OTHER TECHNOLOGICAL CHANGES The British iron industry was also radically transformed during the Industrial Revolution. Britain had always had large deposits of iron ore, but at the beginning of the eighteenth century, the basic process of producing iron had changed little since the Middle Ages and still depended heavily on charcoal. A better quality of iron was developed in the 1780s when Henry Cort developed a system called puddling, in which coke, derived from coal, was used to burn away impurities in pig iron (crude iron) and produce an iron of high quality. A boom then ensued in the British iron industry. In 1740, Britain produced 17,000 tons of iron; by the 1840s, more than 2 million tons; and by 1852, almost 3 million tons, more than the rest of the world combined.

The new high-quality wrought iron was in turn used to build new machines and ultimately new industries. In 1804,

Richard Trevithick (TREV-uh-thik) pioneered the first steam-powered locomotive on an industrial rail line in southern Wales. It pulled 10 tons of ore and seventy people at 5 miles per hour. Better locomotives soon followed. Engines built by George Stephenson and his son proved superior, and it was Stephenson's *Rocket* that was used on the first public railway line, which opened in 1830, stretching 32 miles from Liverpool to Manchester. *Rocket* sped along at 16 miles per hour. Within twenty years, locomotives had reached 50 miles per hour, an incredible speed to contemporary travelers. By 1840, Britain had almost 6,000 miles of railroads.

The railroad was important to the success and maturing of the Industrial Revolution. Railway construction created new job opportunities, especially for farm laborers and peasants who had long been accustomed to finding work outside their local villages. Perhaps most important, the proliferation of a cheaper and faster means of transportation had a ripple effect on the growth of the industrial economy. As the prices of goods fell, markets grew larger; increased sales meant more factories and more machinery, thereby reinforcing the self-sustaining aspect of the Industrial Revolution—a development that marked a fundamental break with the traditional European economy. Continuous, self-sustaining economic growth came to be seen as an essential characteristic of the new economy.

THE INDUSTRIAL FACTORY Another visible symbol of the Industrial Revolution was the factory (see the Comparative Illustration "Textile Factories, West and East" on p. 541). From its beginning, the factory created a new labor system. Factory owners wanted to use their new machines constantly. Workers were therefore obliged to work regular hours and in shifts to keep the machines producing at a steady rate. Early factory workers, however, came from rural areas, where they were used to a different pace of life. Peasant farmers worked hard, especially at harvest time, but they were also used to periods of inactivity.

Early factory owners therefore had to create a system of work discipline that would accustom employees to working regular hours and doing the same tasks over and over. Of course, such work was boring, and factory owners resorted to

Railroad Line from Liverpool to Manchester. The railroad line from Liverpool to Manchester, which opened in 1830, relied on steam locomotives. As is evident in this illustration, carrying passengers was the railroad's main business. First-class passengers rode in covered cars; second- and third-class passengers, in open cars.

Textile Factories, West and East.
The development of the factory changed the relationship between workers and employers as workers were encouraged to adjust to a new system of discipline that forced them to work regular hours under close supervision. At the top is an 1835 illustration that shows men and women working in a British cotton factory. The factory system came later to the rest of the world than it did to Britain. Shown at the bottom is one of the earliest industrial factories in Japan, the Tomioka silk factory, built in the 1870s. Note that although women are doing the work in both factories, the managers are men. Although these illustrations show mostly women working in the factories, both men and women were factory workers.

Q *What do you think were the major differences and similarities between British and Japanese factories (see also the box "Attitudes of the Industrial Middle Class in Britain and Japan" on p. 547)?*

tough methods to accomplish their goals. They issued minute and detailed factory regulations (see the box "Discipline in the New Factories" on p. 542). For example, adult workers were fined for a wide variety of minor infractions, such as being a few minutes late for work, and dismissed for more serious misdoings, especially drunkenness, which set a bad example for younger workers and also courted disaster in the midst of dangerous machinery. Employers found that dismissals and fines worked well for adult employees; in a time when population growth had produced large masses of unskilled labor, dismissal could be disastrous. Children were less likely to understand the implications of dismissal, so they were sometimes disciplined more directly—often by beating. As the nineteenth century progressed, the second and third generations of workers came to view a regular workweek as a natural way of life.

By the mid-nineteenth century, Great Britain had become the world's first and richest industrial nation. Britain was the "workshop, banker, and trader of the world." It produced half of the world's coal and manufactured goods; its cotton industry alone in 1850 was equal in size to the industries of all other European countries combined.

The Spread of Industrialization

From Great Britain, industrialization spread to the continental countries of Europe and the United States at different times and speeds during the nineteenth century. First to be industrialized on the continent were Belgium, France, and the German states (see Map 19.1).

INDUSTRIALIZATION ON THE CONTINENT In 1815, Belgium, France, and the German states were still largely agrarian. Although they had experienced some developments similar to those of Britain in the eighteenth century, these countries did not move in new industrial directions in the 1770s and 1780s because they lacked certain advantages that had made Britain's Industrial Revolution possible. Lack of

Discipline in the New Factories

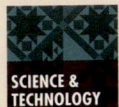

SCIENCE & TECHNOLOGY

WORKERS IN THE NEW FACTORIES of the Industrial Revolution had been accustomed to a lifestyle free of overseers. Unlike the cottages, where workers spun thread and wove cloth in their own rhythm and time, the factories demanded a new, rigorous discipline geared to the requirements of the machines. This selection is taken from a set of rules for a factory in Berlin in 1844. They were typical of company rules everywhere the factory system had been established.

Factory Rules, Foundry and Engineering Works, Royal Overseas Trading Company

In every large works, and in the coordination of any large number of workmen, good order and harmony must be looked upon as the fundamentals of success, and therefore the following rules shall be strictly observed.

1. The normal working day begins at all seasons at 6 A.M. precisely and ends, after the usual break of half an hour for breakfast, an hour for dinner, and half an hour for tea, at 7 P.M., and it shall be strictly observed....

2. Workers arriving 2 minutes late shall lose half an hour's wages; whoever is more than 2 minutes late may not start work until after the next break, or at least shall lose his wages until then. Any disputes about the correct time shall be settled by the clock mounted above the gatekeeper's lodge....

3. No workman, whether employed by time or piece, may leave before the end of the working day, without having first received permission from the overseer and having given his name to the gatekeeper. Omission of these two actions shall lead to a fine of ten silver groschen (pennies) payable to the sick fund.

4. Repeated irregular arrival at work shall lead to dismissal. This shall also apply to those who are found idling by an

official or overseer, and refuse to obey their order to resume work....

6. No worker may leave his place of work otherwise than for reasons connected with his work.

7. All conversation with fellow-workers is prohibited; if any worker requires information about his work, he must turn to the overseer, or to the particular fellow-worker designated for the purpose.

8. Smoking in the workshops or in the yard is prohibited during working hours; anyone caught smoking shall be fined five silver groschen for the sick fund for every such offense....

10. Natural functions must be performed at the appropriate places, and whoever is found soiling walls, fences, squares, etc., and similarly, whoever is found washing his face and hands in the workshop and not in the places assigned for the purpose, shall be fined five silver groschen for the sick fund....

12. It goes without saying that all overseers and officials of the firm shall be obeyed without question, and shall be treated with due deference. Disobedience will be punished by dismissal.

13. Immediate dismissal shall also be the fate of anyone found drunk in any of the workshops....

14. Every workman is obliged to report to his superiors any acts of dishonesty or embezzlement on the part of his fellow workmen. If he omits to do so, and it is shown after subsequent discovery of a misdemeanor that he knew about it at the time, he shall be liable to be taken to court as an accessory after the fact and the wage due to him shall be retained as punishment.

What impact did factories have on the lives of workers? To what extent have such "rules" determined much of modern industrial life?

Source: From *Documents of European Economic History*, Vol. I by Sidney Pollard & Colin Holmes. Copyright © Sidney Pollard and Colin Holmes.

good roads and problems with river transit made transportation difficult. Customs barriers along state boundaries increased the costs and prices of goods. Moreover, continental businessmen were generally less enterprising than their British counterparts and tended to adhere to traditional business attitudes, including an unwillingness to take risks in investment. Thus, industrialization on the continent faced numerous hurdles, and as it proceeded in earnest after 1815, it did so along lines that were somewhat different from Britain's.

Lack of technical knowledge was initially a major obstacle to industrialization. But the continental countries possessed an advantage here; they could simply borrow British techniques and practices. Gradually, the continent achieved technological independence as local people learned all the skills their British teachers had to offer. Even more important, however, continental countries, especially France and the German states, began to establish a wide range of technical schools to train engineers and mechanics.

That government played an important role in this regard brings us to a second difference between British and continental industrialization. Governments in most of the continental countries were accustomed to playing a significant role in economic affairs. Furthering the development of industrialization was a logical extension of that attitude. For example, the governments awarded grants to inventors and provided funds to

© 2016 Cengage Learning

MAP 19.1 The Industrialization of Europe by 1850. Great Britain was Europe's first industrialized country; however, by the middle of the nineteenth century, several regions on the continent, especially in Belgium, France, and the German states, had made significant advances in industrialization.

Q *What might explain why coal mining and iron industries were densely clustered in manufacturing and industrial areas?*

build roads, canals, and railroads. By 1850, a network of iron rails had spread across Europe.

A third significant difference between British and continental industrialization was the role of the **joint-stock investment bank** on the continent. Such banks pooled the savings of thousands of small and large investors, creating a supply of capital that could then be plowed back into industry. These investments were essential to continental industrialization. By starting with less expensive machines, the British had been able to industrialize largely through the private capital of successful individuals who reinvested their profits. On the continent, advanced industrial machines necessitated large amounts of capital; joint-stock industrial banks provided it.

THE INDUSTRIAL REVOLUTION IN THE UNITED STATES
The Industrial Revolution also transformed the new nation in North America, the United States. In 1800, there were no cities with populations of more than 100,000, and six out of every seven American workers were farmers. By 1860, however, the population had grown from 5 million to 30 million people, larger than Great Britain's; nine U.S. cities had populations over 100,000; and only 50 percent of American workers were farmers.

In sharp contrast to Britain, the United States was a large country. Thousands of miles of roads and canals were built linking east and west. The steamboat facilitated transportation on the Great Lakes, Atlantic coastal waters, and rivers. Most important in the development of an American transportation system was the railroad, which was needed to transport the abundant raw materials found throughout the country. Beginning with 100 miles in 1830, by 1865 the United States was crisscrossed by more than 35,000 miles of railroad track—more than three times the amount in Great Britain. This transportation revolution turned the United States into a single massive market for the manufactured goods of the Northeast, the early center of American industrialization.

Labor for the growing number of factories in this area came primarily from rural New England. Many of the workers in the new textile and shoe factories of the region were women, who often accounted for more than 80 percent of the labor force. Factory owners sometimes sought entire families, including children, to work in their mills; one mill owner ran this advertisement in a newspaper in Utica, New York: "Wanted: A few sober and industrious families of at least five children each, over the age of eight years, are wanted at the Cotton Factory in Whitestown. Widows with large families would do well to attend this notice." A growing manufacturing sector, an abundance of raw materials, and an elaborate transportation system turned the United States into the world's second largest industrial nation by the end of the nineteenth century.

Limiting the Spread of Industrialization in the Rest of the World

Before 1870, the industrialization that was transforming western and central Europe and the United States did not extend in any significant way to the rest of the world (see the Comparative Essay "The Industrial Revolution" on p. 545). Even in eastern Europe, industrialization lagged far behind. Russia, for example, was still largely rural and agricultural, ruled by an autocratic regime that preferred to keep the peasants in serfdom.

In other parts of the world, the newly industrialized European states pursued a deliberate policy of preventing the growth of mechanized industry in the areas where they had established control (see Chapter 21). India provides an excellent example. In the eighteenth century, India had become one of the world's greatest exporters of cotton cloth produced by hand labor, producing over twenty-five times as much cotton cloth per year as England. In the first half of the nineteenth century, much of India fell under the control of the British East India Company. With British control came inexpensive textiles produced in British factories. As the indigenous Indian textile industry declined, thousands of Indian spinners and handloom weavers lost their jobs, forcing many to turn to growing raw materials, such as cotton, wheat, and tea, for export to Britain, while buying British-made finished goods. The example of India was repeated elsewhere, as the rapidly industrializing nations of Europe worked to thwart the spread of the Industrial Revolution to their colonial dominions.

Social Impact of the Industrial Revolution

Eventually, the Industrial Revolution revolutionized the social life of Europe and the world. This change was already evident in the first half of the nineteenth century in the growth of cities and emergence of new social classes.

POPULATION GROWTH AND URBANIZATION The European population had begun to increase in the eighteenth century, but the pace accelerated dramatically in the nineteenth. In 1750, the total European population stood at an estimated 140 million; by 1850, it had almost doubled to 266 million. The key to the expansion of population was a decline in death rates evident throughout Europe. Wars and major epidemic diseases, such as plague and smallpox, became less frequent, which led to a drop in the number of deaths. Thanks to the increase in the food supply, more people were better fed and more resistant to disease.

However, this was not the case throughout Europe. Overpopulation, especially noticeable in parts of France, northern Spain, southern Germany, Sweden, and Ireland, magnified the already existing problem of rural poverty. In Ireland, it produced the century's greatest catastrophe (see the box "The Great Irish Potato Famine" on p. 546).

Throughout Europe, cities and towns grew rapidly in the first half of the nineteenth century, a phenomenon related to industrialization. By 1850, especially in Great Britain and Belgium, cities were rapidly becoming home to many industries. With the steam engine, factory owners could locate their manufacturing plants in urban centers, where they had ready access to transportation facilities and large numbers of new arrivals from the country looking for work.

In 1800, Great Britain had one major city, London, with a population of one million and six cities with populations between 50,000 and 100,000. Fifty years later, London's population had swelled to 2,363,000, and there were nine cities over 100,000 and eighteen with populations between 50,000 and 100,000. By 1850, more than half of the British population lived in towns and cities. Urban populations also grew on the continent, but at a less frenzied pace.

The dramatic growth of cities in the first half of the nineteenth century resulted in miserable living conditions for many of the inhabitants. Located in the center of most industrial towns were the row houses of the industrial workers. Rooms were not large and were frequently overcrowded, as a government report of 1838 in Britain revealed: "I entered several of the tenements. In one of them, on the ground floor, I found six persons occupying a very small room, two in bed, ill with fever. In the room above this were two more persons in one bed, ill with fever." Another report said, "There were 63 families where there were at least five persons to one bed; and there were some in which even six were packed in one bed, lying at the top and bottom—children and adults."[1]

Sanitary conditions in these towns were appalling; sewers and open drains were common on city streets: "In the center of this street is a gutter, into which the refuse of animal and vegetable matters of all kinds, the dirty water from the washing of clothes and of the houses, are all poured, and there they stagnate and putrefy."[2] Unable to deal with human wastes, cities in the early industrial era smelled horrible and were extraordinarily unhealthy. The use of coal blackened towns and cities with soot, as Charles Dickens described in one of his

The Industrial Revolution

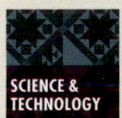

Why some societies were able to embark on the road to industrialization during the nineteenth century and others were not has long been debated. Some historians have found an answer in the cultural characteristics of individual societies, such as the Protestant work ethic in parts of Europe or the tradition of social discipline and class hierarchy in Japan. Others have placed more emphasis on practical reasons. To historian Peter Stearns, for example, the availability of capital, natural resources, a network of trade relations, and navigable rivers all helped stimulate industrial growth in nineteenth-century Britain. By contrast, the lack of an urban market for agricultural products (which reduced landowners' incentives to introduce mechanized farming) is sometimes cited as a reason for China's failure to set out on its own path toward industrialization.

To some observers, the ability of western European countries to exploit the wealth and resources of their colonies in Asia, Africa, and Latin America was crucial to their industrial success. In this view, the Age of Exploration led to the creation of a new "world system" characterized by the emergence of global trade networks, propelled by the rising force of European capitalism in pursuit of precious metals, markets, and cheap raw materials.

These views are not mutually exclusive. In *The Great Divergence: China, Europe, and the Making of the Modern World Economy*, Kenneth Pomeranz has argued that access to coal resources and to the cheap raw materials of the Americas were both assets for Great Britain as it became the first to enter the industrial age.

The Steam Engine. Pictured here is an early steam engine developed by James Watt. The steam engine revolutionized the production of cotton goods and helped usher in the factory system. Hip/Art Resource, NY

Clearly, there is no single answer to this controversy. In any event, the advent of the industrial age had a number of lasting consequences for the world at large. On the one hand, the material wealth of the nations that successfully passed through the process increased significantly. In many cases, the creation of advanced industrial societies strengthened democratic institutions and led to a higher standard of living for the majority of the population. It also helped reduce class barriers and bring about the emancipation of women from many of the legal and social restrictions that had characterized the previous era.

On the other hand, not all the consequences of the Industrial Revolution were beneficial. In the industrializing societies themselves, rapid economic change often led to widening disparities in the distribution of wealth and a sense of rootlessness and alienation among much of the population. Although some societies were able to manage these problems with a degree of success, others experienced a breakdown of social values and political instability. In the meantime, the transformation of Europe into a giant factory sucking up raw materials and spewing manufactured goods out to the entire world had a wrenching impact on traditional societies whose own economic, social, and cultural foundations were forever changed by their absorption into the new world order.

Q *What were the positive and negative consequences of the Industrial Revolution?*

---

novels: "A long suburb of red brick houses—some with patches of garden ground, where coal-dust and factory smoke darkened the shrinking leaves, and coarse rank flowers; and where the struggling vegetation sickened and sank under the hot breath of kiln and furnace."[3] Towns and cities were death traps: deaths outnumbered births in most large cities in the first half of the nineteenth century; only a constant influx of people from the country kept them alive and growing.

THE INDUSTRIAL MIDDLE CLASS The rise of industrial capitalism produced a new kind of middle class. The bourgeoisie was not new; it had existed since the emergence of cities in the Middle Ages. Originally, the bourgeois or burgher was simply a town dweller, active as a merchant, official, artisan, lawyer, or man of letters. Because many of these people lived comfortable lives, the term took on a certain cachet. And so as other people began to accumulate wealth, the term *bourgeois* came to

The Great Irish Potato Famine

FAMILY & SOCIETY

IN THE NINETEENTH CENTURY, IRELAND was one of the most oppressed areas in western Europe. The cultivation of the potato, a nutritious and relatively easy food to grow, gave Irish peasants a basic staple that enabled them to survive and even expand in numbers. Between 1781 and 1845, the Irish population doubled from 4 million to 8 million. Probably half of this population depended on the potato for survival. In the summer of 1845, the potato crop in Ireland was struck by blight due to a fungus that turned the potatoes black. More than a million people died of starvation and disease, and almost 2 million immigrated to the United States and Britain. Nicholas Cummins, a magistrate from County Cork, visited Skibbereen, one of the areas most affected by the famine, and sent a letter to the duke of Wellington reporting what he had seen. A copy of the letter was published in the London newspaper *The Times*, on Christmas Eve in 1846, and became one of the most famous descriptions of the Irish crisis.

Nicholas Cummins, "The Famine in Skibbereen"

My Lord Duke,

Without apology or preface, I presume so far to trespass on your Grace as to state to you, and by the use of your illustrious name, to present to the British public the following statement of what I have myself seen within the last three days. Having for many years been intimately connected with the western portion of the County of Cork, and possessing some small property there, I thought it right personally to investigate the truth of several lamentable accounts which had reached me, of the appalling state of misery to which that part of the country was reduced. I accordingly went to … Skibbereen, and … I shall state simply what I there saw….

Being aware that I should have to witness scenes of frightful hunger, I provided myself with as much bread as five men could carry, and on reaching the spot I was surprised to find the wretched hamlet apparently deserted. I entered some of the hovels to ascertain the cause, and the scenes which presented themselves were such as no tongue or pen can convey the slightest idea of. In the first, six famished and ghastly skeletons, to all appearances dead, were huddled in a corner on some filthy straw, their sole covering what seemed a ragged horsecloth, their wretched legs hanging about, naked above the knees. I approached with horror, and found by a low moaning they were alive—they were in fever, four children, a woman and what had once been a man. It is impossible to go through the detail. Suffice it to say, that in a few minutes I was surrounded by at least 200 such phantoms, such frightful spectres as no words can describe, either from famine or from fever….

In another case, decency would forbid what follows, but it must be told. My clothes were nearly torn off in my endeavor to escape from the throng of pestilence around, when my neckcloth was seized from behind by a grip which compelled me to turn, I found myself grasped by a woman with an infant just born in her arms and the remains of a filthy sack across her loins—the sole covering of herself and baby. The same morning the police opened a house on the adjoining lands, which was observed shut for many days, and two frozen corpses were found, lying upon the mud floor, half devoured by rats.

What was the impact of the Great Irish Famine on the Irish people?

Source: From "The Famine in Skibbereen" from *The Great Hunger* by Cecil Woodham-Smith (New York: Harper-Collins, 1962).

---

be applied to people involved in commerce, industry, and banking as well as professionals such as teachers, physicians, and government officials, regardless of where they lived.

The new industrial middle class was made up of the people who constructed the factories, purchased the machines, and figured out where the markets were (see the box "Attitudes of the Industrial Middle Class in Britain and Japan" on p. 547). Their qualities included resourcefulness, single-mindedness, resolution, initiative, vision, ambition, and often, of course, greed. As Jedediah Strutt, a cotton manufacturer said, "Getting of money … is the main business of the life of men."

Members of the industrial middle class not only sought to reduce the barriers between themselves and the landed elite, but also tried at the same time to separate themselves from the laboring classes below them. In the first half of the nineteenth century, the working class was actually a mixture of different groups, but in the course of the century, factory workers came to form an industrial **proletariat** that constituted a majority of the working class.

THE INDUSTRIAL WORKING CLASS Early industrial workers faced wretched working conditions. Work shifts ranged from twelve to sixteen hours a day, six days a week, with a half hour for lunch and dinner. There was no security of employment and no minimum wage. The worst conditions were in the cotton mills, where temperatures were especially debilitating. One report noted that "in the cotton-spinning work, these creatures are kept, fourteen hours in each day, locked up, summer and winter, in a heat of from eighty to eighty-four degrees." Mills were also dirty, dusty, and unhealthy.

Conditions in the coal mines were also harsh. Although steam-powered engines were used to lift coal from the mines to the top, inside the mines, men still bore the burden of digging the coal out while horses, mules, women, and children

Attitudes of the Industrial Middle Class in Britain and Japan

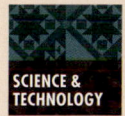

SCIENCE & TECHNOLOGY

A NEW INDUSTRIAL MIDDLE CLASS in Great Britain took the lead in the nineteenth century in creating the Industrial Revolution. Japan did not begin to industrialize until after 1870 (see Chapter 22). There, too, an industrial middle class emerged, although there were important differences in the attitudes of business leaders in Britain and Japan. Some of these differences can be seen in these documents. The first is an excerpt from the book *Self-Help* (first published in 1859) by Samuel Smiles, who espoused the belief that people succeed through "individual industry, energy, and uprightness." The other two selections are by Shibuzawa Eiichi (shih-boo-ZAH-wah EH-ee-chee), a Japanese industrialist who supervised textile factories. Although he began his business career in 1873, he did not write his autobiography, the source of his first excerpt, until 1927.

Samuel Smiles, *Self-Help*

"Heaven helps those who help themselves" is a well-worn maxim, embodying in a small compass the results of vast human experience. The spirit of self-help is the root of all genuine growth in the individual; and, exhibited in the lives of many, it constitutes the true source of national vigor and strength. Help from without is often enfeebling in its effects, but help from within invariably invigorates. Whatever is done for men or classes, to a certain extent takes away the stimulus and necessity of doing for themselves; and where men are subjected to overguidance and overgovernment, the inevitable tendency is to render them comparatively helpless....

National progress is the sum of individual industry, energy, and uprightness, as national decay is of individual idleness, selfishness, and vice. What we are accustomed to decry as great social evils, will, for the most part, be found to be only the outgrowth of our own perverted life; and though we may endeavor to cut them down and extirpate them by means of law, they will only spring up again with fresh luxuriance in some other form, unless the individual conditions of human life and character are radically improved. If this view be correct, then it follows that the highest patriotism and philanthropy consist, not so much in altering laws and modifying institutions as in helping and stimulating men to elevate and improve themselves by their own free and independent action as individuals....

Many popular books have been written for the purpose of communicating to the public the grand secret of making money. But there is no secret whatever about it, as the proverbs of every nation abundantly testify.... "A penny saved is a penny gained."—"Diligence is the mother of good-luck."—"No pains, no gains."—"No sweat, no sweet."—"Sloth, the Key of poverty."—"Work, and thou shalt have."—"He who will not work, neither shall he eat."—"The world is his, who has patience and industry."

Shibuzawa Eiichi, *Autobiography*

I ... felt that it was necessary to raise the social standing of those who engaged in commerce and industry. By way of setting an example, I began studying and practicing the teachings of the *Analects of Confucius*. It contains teachings first enunciated more than twenty-four hundred years ago. Yet it supplies the ultimate in practical ethics for all of us to follow in our daily living. It has many golden rules for businessmen. For example, there is a saying: "Wealth and respect are what men desire, but unless a right way is followed, they cannot be obtained; poverty and lowly position are what men despise, but unless a right way is found, one cannot leave that status once reaching it." It shows very clearly how a businessman must act in this world.

Shibuzawa Eiichi on Progress

One must beware of the tendency of some to argue that it is through individualism or egoism that the State and society can progress most rapidly. They claim that under individualism, each individual competes with the others, and progress results from this competition. But this is to see merely the advantages and ignore the disadvantages, and I cannot support such a theory. Society exists, and a State has been founded. Although people desire to rise to positions of wealth and honor, the social order and the tranquility of the State will be disrupted if this is done egoistically. Men should not do battle in competition with their fellow men. Therefore, I believe that in order to get along together in society and serve the State, we must by all means abandon this idea of independence and self-reliance and reject egoism completely.

What are the major similarities and differences in the attitudes toward business of Samuel Smiles and Shibuzawa Eiichi? How do you explain the differences?

Sources: Samuel Smiles, *Self-Help*, London, 1859. Shibusawa Eiichi, *The Autobiography of Shibusawa Eiichi: From Peasant to Entrepreneur, 1927* (Tokyo: University of Tokyo Press, 1994).

---

hauled coal carts on rails to the lift. Dangerous conditions, including cave-ins, explosions, and gas fumes, were a way of life. The cramped conditions in the mines—tunnels were often only 3 or 4 feet high—and their constant dampness led to deformed bodies and ruined lungs.

Both children and women worked in large numbers in early factories and mines. Children had been an important part of the family economy in preindustrial times, working in the fields or carding and spinning wool at home. In the Industrial Revolution, however, child labor was exploited more than ever. The owners of cotton factories found child labor very helpful. Children had an especially delicate touch as spinners of cotton. Their smaller size made it easier for them to crawl under machines to gather loose cotton. Moreover, children were more easily trained to do factory work. Above all, children represented a cheap source of labor. In 1821, about half of the British population was under twenty years of age. Hence, children made up an abundant supply of labor, and they were paid only about one-sixth to one-third of what a man was paid. Children as young as seven worked twelve to fifteen hours per day, six days a week, in the cotton mills.

By 1830, women and children provided two-thirds of the cotton industry's labor. Under the Factory Act of 1833, however, which prohibited employment of children under the age of nine and restricted the working hours of those under eighteen, the number of children employed declined. The new law did not end child labor, however, as many parents needed the income of working children to support the family. In 1838, children under eighteen still made up 29 percent of the total workforce. Moreover, as the number of children employed declined, their places were taken by women, who came to dominate the labor forces of the early factories. Women made up 50 percent of the labor force in textile (cotton and woolen) factories before 1870. They were mostly unskilled labor and were paid half or less of what men received.

Laws that limited the work hours of children and women also led to a new pattern of work based on a separation of work and home. Men were expected to be responsible for the primary work obligations, while women assumed daily control of the family and performed low-paying jobs such as laundry work that could be done in the home. Domestic industry made it possible for women to continue their contributions to family survival.

DID INDUSTRIALIZATION BRING AN IMPROVED STANDARD OF LIVING?
During the first half of the nineteenth century, industrialization altered the lives of Europeans, especially the British, as they left their farms, moved to cities, and found work in factories. Historians have debated whether industrialization improved the standard of living during this time. Some historians have argued that industrialization increased employment and lowered the price of consumer goods, thereby improving the way people lived. They also maintain that household income rose because multiple members of the family could now hold wage-paying jobs. Other historians argue that wage labor made life worse for many families during the first half of the nineteenth century. They maintain that employment in the early factories was highly volatile as employers quickly dismissed workers whenever demand declined. Wages were not uniform, and inadequate housing in cities forced families to live in cramped and unsanitary conditions. Families continued to spend the majority of their incomes on food and clothing. Most historians agree that members of the middle class were the real gainers in the early Industrial Revolution and that industrial workers had to wait until the second half of the nineteenth century to begin to reap the benefits of industrialization.

EFFORTS AT CHANGE
In the first half of the nineteenth century, the pitiful conditions found in the slums, mines, and factories of the Industrial Revolution gave rise to efforts for change. One of them was a movement known as **socialism**. The term eventually became associated with a Marxist analysis of human society (see "Organizing the Working Classes" later in this chapter), but early socialism was largely the product of intellectuals who believed in the equality of all people and wanted to replace competition with cooperation in industry. To later socialists, especially the followers of Karl Marx, such ideas were merely impractical dreams, and they contemptuously labeled these theorists **utopian socialists**. The term has lasted to this day.

Robert Owen, a British cotton manufacturer, was one such utopian socialist. He believed that humans would show their true natural goodness if they lived in a cooperative environment.

Women and Children in the Mines. Women and children were often employed in the factories and mines of the early nineteenth century. This illustration shows a woman and boy in a coal mine struggling to draw and push a cart filled with coal. In 1842, the Coal Mines Act forbade the use of boys younger than ten and women in the mines.

At New Lanark in Scotland, he transformed a squalid factory town into a flourishing, healthy community. But when he tried to create such a cooperative community at New Harmony, Indiana, in the United States in the 1820s, fighting within the community eventually destroyed his dream.

Another movement for change came through the formation of labor organizations to gain decent wages and working conditions. Known as **trade unions**, these new associations were formed by skilled workers in a number of new industries, including ironworkers and coal miners. Some trade unions were even willing to strike (refuse to work) to win improvements for the members of their trades. In the 1820s and 1830s, the union movement began to focus on the creation of national unions. The largest and most successful of these unions in Britain was the Amalgamated Society of Engineers, formed in 1851. Its provision of generous unemployment benefits in return for a small weekly payment was precisely the kind of practical gains that the trade unions sought.

The Growth of Industrial Prosperity

Q **FOCUS QUESTIONS:** What was the Second Industrial Revolution, and what effects did it have on economic and social life? What were the main ideas of Karl Marx, and what role did they play in politics and the union movement in the late nineteenth and early twentieth centuries?

After 1870, the Western world experienced a dynamic boom in material prosperity. The new industries, new sources of energy, and new goods of the Second Industrial Revolution led people to believe that their material progress reflected human progress.

New Products

The first major change in industrial development after 1870 was the substitution of steel for iron. New methods for shaping steel made it useful in the construction of lighter, smaller, and faster machines and engines as well as railways, ships, and armaments. In 1860, Great Britain, France, Germany, and Belgium together produced 125,000 tons of steel; by 1913, the total was 32 million tons.

Electricity was a major new form of energy that could be easily converted into other forms—such as heat, light, and motion—and moved relatively effortlessly through space by means of transmitting wires. In the 1870s, the first commercially practical generators of electrical current were developed, and by 1910, hydroelectric power stations and coal-fired steam-generating plants enabled homes and factories in whole neighborhoods to be tied in to a single, common source of power.

Electricity spawned a number of inventions. The light bulb, developed independently by the American Thomas Edison and the Briton Joseph Swan, permitted homes and cities to be illuminated by electric lights. By the 1880s, electricity-powered streetcars and subways had appeared in major European cities. Electricity also transformed the factory. Conveyor belts, cranes,

Photo courtesy private collection

An Age of Progress. The Second Industrial Revolution led many Europeans to believe that most human problems would be solved through scientific achievements. This illustration is from a special issue of the *Illustrated London News* celebrating the Diamond Jubilee of Queen Victoria in 1897. On the left are scenes from 1837, when Victoria came to the British throne; on the right are scenes from 1897. The vivid contrast underscored the magazine's conclusion: "The most striking … evidence of progress during the reign is the ever increasing speed which the discoveries of physical science have forced into everyday life. Steam and electricity have conquered time and space to a greater extent during the last sixty years than all the preceding six hundred years witnessed."

machines, and machine tools could all be powered by electricity and located anywhere. Thanks to electricity, all countries could now enter the industrial age. A revolution in communications began when Alexander Graham Bell invented the telephone in 1876 and Guglielmo Marconi (gool-YEL-moh mahr-KOH-nee) sent the first radio waves across the Atlantic in 1901.

The development of the internal combustion engine, fired by oil and gasoline, provided a new source of power in transportation and gave rise to ocean liners as well as airplanes and automobiles. In 1900, world production stood at 9,000 cars, but an American, Henry Ford, revolutionized the automotive industry with the mass production of the Model T. By 1916, Ford's factories were producing 735,000 cars a year. In 1903, at Kitty Hawk, North Carolina, brothers Orville and Wilbur Wright made the first flight in a fixed-wing airplane. The first regular passenger air service was established in 1919.

New Patterns

Industrial production grew rapidly at this time because of the greatly increased sales of manufactured goods. An increase in real wages for workers after 1870, combined with lower prices for manufactured goods because of reduced transportation costs, made it easier for Europeans to buy consumer products. In the cities, the first department stores began to sell a whole new range of consumer goods made possible by the development of the steel and electrical industries (see the box "The Department Store and the Beginnings of Mass Consumerism" on p. 551). The desire to own sewing machines, clocks, bicycles, electric lights, and typewriters was rapidly generating a new consumer ethic that has been a crucial part of the modern economy.

Not all nations benefited from the Second Industrial Revolution, however. Between 1870 and 1914, Germany replaced Great Britain as the industrial leader of Europe. Moreover, by 1900, Europe was divided into two economic zones. Great Britain, Belgium, France, the Netherlands, Germany, the western part of the Austro-Hungarian Empire, and northern Italy constituted an advanced industrialized core that had a high standard of living, decent systems of transportation, and relatively healthy and educated peoples (see Map 19.2). Another part of Europe, the backward and little industrialized area to the south and east, consisting of southern Italy, most of Austria-Hungary, Spain, Portugal, the Balkan kingdoms, and Russia, was still largely agricultural and relegated by the industrial countries to the function of providing food and raw materials.

Emergence of a World Economy

The economic developments of the late nineteenth century, combined with the transportation revolution that saw the growth of marine transport and railroads, fostered a true world economy. International trade increased dramatically between 1850 and 1914. By 1900, Europeans were receiving beef and wool from Argentina and Australia, coffee from Brazil, nitrates from Chile, iron ore from Algeria, and sugar from Java. Until the Industrial Revolution, European countries had imported more from Asia than they had exported, but now foreign countries provided markets for the surplus manufactured goods of Europe. European capital was also invested abroad to develop railways, mines, electrical power plants, and banks. High rates of return, such as 11.3 percent on Latin American banking shares that were floated in London, provided plenty of incentive for investors. With its capital, industries, and military might, Europe dominated the world economy by the beginning of the twentieth century.

The Spread of Industrialization

At the same time, after 1870, industrialization began to spread beyond western and central Europe and North America. Especially noticeable was its rapid development, fostered by governments, in Russia and Japan. A surge of industrialization began in Russia in the 1890s under the guiding hand of Sergei Witte (syir-GYAY VIT-uh), the minister for finance. Witte pushed the government toward a program of massive railroad construction. By 1900, some 35,000 miles of track had been laid. Witte's program also made possible the rapid growth of a modern steel and coal industry, making Russia by 1900 the fourth-largest producer of steel, behind the United States, Germany, and Great Britain. Russia was also turning out half of the world's production of oil.

In Japan, the imperial government took the lead in promoting industry (see Chapter 22). The government financed industries, built railroads, brought foreign experts to train Japanese employees in new industrial techniques, and instituted a universal educational system based on applied science. By the end of the nineteenth century, Japan had developed key industries in tea, silk, armaments, and shipbuilding.

Mary Evans Picture Library/The Image Works

Shopping at Le Bon Marché. Early department stores benefited from the use of steel in building construction, which allowed for large open spaces and natural lighting for the goods on display. Le Bon Marché featured wrought-iron beams, an iron and glass roof, balconies, and iron bridges that enabled customers to view the goods and the scene below. By the 1890s, between 15,000 and 18,000 people entered the department store daily.

The Department Store and the Beginnings of Mass Consumerism

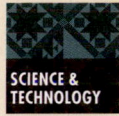

SCIENCE & TECHNOLOGY

DOMESTIC MARKETS were especially important for the sale of the goods being turned out by Europe's increasing number of industrial plants. New techniques of mass marketing arose to encourage the sale of the new consumer goods. The Parisians pioneered in the development of the department store, and this selection is taken from a contemporary's account of the growth of these stores in the French capital city.

E. Lavasseur, *On Parisian Department Stores*, 1907

It was in the reign of Louis-Philippe [1830–1848] that department stores for fashion goods and dresses, extending to material and other clothing, began to be distinguished.... These stores have increased in number and several of them have become extremely large. Combining in their different departments all articles of clothing, toilet articles, furniture and many other ranges of goods, it is their special object so to combine all commodities as to attract and satisfy customers who will find conveniently together an assortment of a mass of articles corresponding to all their various needs. They attract customers by permanent display, by free entry into the shops, by periodic exhibitions, by special sales, by fixed prices, and by their ability to deliver the goods purchased to customers' homes, in Paris and to the provinces. Turning themselves into direct intermediaries between the producer and the consumer, even producing sometimes some of their articles in their own workshops, buying at lowest prices because of their large orders and because they are in a position to profit from bargains, working with large sums, and selling to most of their customers for cash only, they can transmit these benefits in lowered selling prices. They can even decide to sell at a loss, as an advertisement or to get rid of out-of-date fashions. Taking 5–6 percent on 100 million [francs] brings them in more than 20 percent would bring to a firm doing a turnover of 50,000 francs.

The success of these department stores is only possible thanks to the volume of their business, and this volume needs considerable capital and a very large turnover. Now capital, having become abundant, is freely combined nowadays in large enterprises, although French capital has the reputation of being more wary of the risks of industry than of State or railway securities. On the other hand, the large urban agglomerations, the ease with which goods can be transported by the railways, the diffusion of some comforts to strata below the middle classes, have all favored these developments.

As example we may cite some figures relating to these stores....

Le Louvre, dating to the time of the extension of the rue de Rivoli under the Second Empire [1855], did in 1893 a business of 120 million at a profit of 6.4 percent. *Le Bon Marché*, which was a small shop when Mr. Boucicaut entered it in 1852, already did a business of 20 million at the end of the Empire [1870]. During the republic its new buildings were erected; Mme. Boucicaut turned it by her will into a kind of cooperative society, with shares and an ingenious organization; turnover reached 150 million in 1893, leaving a profit of 5 percent....

According to the tax records of 1891, these stores in Paris, numbering 12, employed 1,708 persons and were rated on their site values at 2,159,000 francs; the largest had then 542 employees. These same stores had, in 1901, 9,784 employees; one of them over 2,000 and another over 1,600; their site value has doubled (4,089,000 francs).

Did the invention of department stores respond to or create the new "consumer ethic" in industrialized societies? What was this new turn-of-the-century ethic? According to Lavasseur, what were the positive effects of department stores on Parisian society?

Women and Work: New Job Opportunities

During the course of the nineteenth century, working-class organizations persisted in the belief that women should remain at home to bear and nurture children and not be allowed in the industrial workforce. Working-class men argued that keeping women out of the factories would ensure the moral and physical well-being of families. In reality, however, if their husbands were unemployed, women had to do low-wage work or labor part-time in sweatshops to support their families.

The Second Industrial Revolution opened the door to new jobs for women. The development of larger industrial plants and the expansion of government services created a variety of service or white-collar jobs. The increased demand for white-collar workers at relatively low wages coupled with a shortage of male workers led employers to hire women. Big businesses and retail shops needed clerks, typists, secretaries, file clerks, and salesclerks. The expansion of government services opened opportunities for women to be secretaries and telephone operators and to take jobs in health and social services. Compulsory education necessitated more teachers, while the

Map legend

Railroad development
- Lines completed by 1848
- Area of main railroad completed by 1870
- Other major lines

▲ Steel
◆ Engineering
● Chemicals
■ Electrical industry

🛒 Low-grade coal
🛒 High-grade coal
⚒ Iron ore deposits
🛢 Petroleum deposits

○ Oil production

Industrial concentration:
- ▫ Cities
- ▪ Areas

MAP 19.2 The Industrial Regions of Europe at the End of the Nineteenth Century. By the end of the nineteenth century, the Second Industrial Revolution—in steelmaking, electricity, petroleum, and chemicals—had spurred substantial economic growth and prosperity in western and central Europe; it also sparked economic and political competition between Great Britain and Germany.

Q *Look back at Map 19.1. What parts of Europe not industrialized in 1850 had become industrialized in the ensuing decades?*

development of modern hospital services opened the way for an increase in the number of nurses.

Many of the new white-collar jobs were far from exciting. The work was routine and, except for teaching and nursing, required few skills beyond basic literacy. Nevertheless, these jobs had distinct advantages for many women. For some middle-class women, the new jobs offered freedom from the domestic patterns expected of them. Moreover, because middle-class women did not receive an education comparable to that of men, they were limited in the careers they could pursue. Thus, they found it easier to fill the jobs at the lower end of middle-class occupations, such as teaching and civil service jobs, especially in the post office. Most of the new white-collar jobs, however, were filled by working-class women who saw the job as an opportunity to escape from the physical labor of the lower-class world.

Organizing the Working Classes

The desire to improve their working and living conditions led many industrial workers to form socialist political parties and socialist labor unions. These emerged after 1870, but the theory

"Proletarians of the World, Unite." To improve their working and living conditions, many industrial workers, inspired by the ideas of Karl Marx, joined working-class or socialist parties. Pictured here is a socialist-sponsored poster that proclaims in German the closing words of *The Communist Manifesto:* "Proletarians of the World, Unite!"

that made them possible had been developed more than two decades earlier in the work of Karl Marx. **Marxism** made its first appearance on the eve of the revolutions of 1848 with the publication of a short treatise titled *The Communist Manifesto,* written by two Germans, Karl Marx (1818–1883) and Friedrich Engels (FREE-drikh ENG-ulz) (1820–1895).

MARXIST THEORY Marx and Engels began their treatise with the statement that "the history of all hitherto existing society is the history of class struggles." Throughout history, then, oppressor and oppressed have "stood in constant opposition to one another."[4] One group of people—the oppressors—owned the means of production and thus had the power to control government and society. Indeed, government itself was but an instrument of the ruling class. The other group, which depended on the owners of the means of production, were the oppressed.

This **class struggle** continued in the industrialized societies of Marx's day. According to Marx and Engels, "Society as a whole is more and more splitting up into two great hostile camps, into two great classes directly facing each other:

Bourgeoisie and Proletariat." Marx predicted that the struggle between the bourgeoisie and the proletariat would finally break into open revolution, "where the violent overthrow of the bourgeoisie lays the foundation for the sway of the proletariat." The fall of the bourgeoisie "and the victory of the proletariat are equally inevitable."[5] For a while, the proletariat would form a dictatorship to reorganize the means of production, and then the state—itself an instrument of the bourgeois interests—would wither away. Since classes had arisen from the economic differences that would have been abolished, the end result would be a classless society (see the box "The Classless Society" on p. 554).

SOCIALIST PARTIES In time, Marx's ideas were picked up by working-class leaders who formed socialist parties. Most important was the German Social Democratic Party (SPD), which emerged in 1875 and espoused revolutionary Marxist rhetoric while organizing itself as a mass political party competing in elections for the Reichstag (RYKHSS-tahk), the lower house of parliament. Once in the Reichstag, SPD delegates sought to pass legislation to improve the condition of the working class. Despite government efforts to destroy it, the SPD continued to grow. In the 1912 elections, it received 4 million votes, making it the largest party in Germany.

Socialist parties also emerged in other European states, although not with the kind of success achieved by the German Social Democrats. In 1889, leaders of the various socialist parties formed the Second International, an association of national socialist groups dedicated to fighting against capitalism worldwide. (The First International had failed in 1872.) The Second International took some coordinated actions—May Day (May 1), for example, was made an international labor holiday—but differences often wreaked havoc at the organization's congresses.

REVISIONISM AND TRADE UNIONS Marxist parties divided over the issue of **revisionism**. Pure Marxists believed in violent revolution that would bring the collapse of capitalism and socialist ownership of the means of production. But others, called revisionists, rejected **revolutionary socialism** and argued that workers must organize mass political parties and work together with other progressive elements to gain reforms. Having won the right to vote, workers were in a better position than ever to achieve their aims through democratic channels. Evolution by democratic means, not revolution, would achieve the desired goal of socialism.

Another force working for evolutionary rather than revolutionary socialism was the development of trade unions. In Great Britain, unions won the right to strike in the 1870s. Soon after, the masses of workers in factories were organized into trade unions in order to use the instrument of the strike. By 1900, there were 2 million workers in British trade unions; fourteen years later, there were almost 4 million. Trade unions in the rest of Europe had varying degrees of success, but by the outbreak of World War I, they had made considerable progress in improving the living and working conditions of the laboring classes.

The Classless Society

FAMILY & SOCIETY

IN *THE COMMUNIST MANIFESTO,* Karl Marx and Friedrich Engels projected that the struggle between the bourgeoisie and the proletariat would end in the creation of a classless society. In this selection, they discuss the steps by which that classless society would be reached.

Karl Marx and Friedrich Engels, *The Communist Manifesto*

We have seen … that the first step in the revolution by the working class is to raise the proletariat to the position of ruling class…. The proletariat will use its political supremacy to wrest, by degrees, all capital from the bourgeoisie; to centralize all instruments of production in the hands of the State, i.e., of the proletariat organized as the ruling class; and to increase the total of productive forces as rapidly as possible.

Of course, in the beginning, this cannot be effected except by means of despotic inroads on the rights of property, and on the conditions of bourgeois production; by means of measures, therefore, which appear economically insufficient and untenable, but which, in the course of the movement, outstrip themselves, necessitate further inroads upon the old social order, and are unavoidable as a means of entirely revolutionizing the mode of production.

These measures will of course be different in different countries.

Nevertheless, in the most advanced countries, the following will be pretty generally applicable:

1. Abolition of property in land and application of all rents of land to public purposes.
2. A heavy progressive or graduated income tax.
3. Abolition of all right of inheritance….
5. Centralization of credit in the hands of the State, by means of a national bank with State capital and an exclusive monopoly.

6. Centralization of the means of communication and transport in the hands of the State.
7. Extension of factories and instruments of production owned by the State….
8. Equal liability of all to labor. Establishment of industrial armies, especially for agriculture.
9. Combination of agriculture with manufacturing industries; gradual abolition of the distinction between town and country, by a more equable distribution of the population over the country.
10. Free education for all children in public schools. Abolition of children's factory labor in its present form….

When, in the course of development, class distinctions have disappeared, and all production has been concentrated in the whole nation, the public power will lose its political character. Political power, properly so called, is merely the organized power of one class for oppressing another. If the proletariat during its contest with the bourgeoisie is compelled, by the force of circumstances, to organize itself as a class, if, by means of a revolution, it makes itself the ruling class, and, as such, sweeps away by force the old conditions of production, then it will, along with these conditions, have swept away the conditions for the existence of class antagonisms and of classes generally, and will thereby have abolished its own supremacy as a class.

In place of the old bourgeois society, with its classes and class antagonisms, we shall have an association, in which the free development of each is the condition for the free development of all.

 How did Marx and Engels define the proletariat? The bourgeoisie? Why did Marxists come to believe that this distinction was paramount for understanding history and shaping the future?

Source: From *The Communist Manifesto* by Karl Marx and Friedrich Engels.

Reaction and Revolution: The Growth of Nationalism

 FOCUS QUESTIONS: What were the major ideas associated with conservatism, liberalism, and nationalism, and what role did each ideology play in Europe between 1800 and 1870? What were the causes of the revolutions of 1848, and why did these revolutions fail?

Industrialization was a major force for change in the nineteenth century as it led the West into the machine-dependent modern world. Another major force of change was nationalism, which transformed the political map of Europe in the nineteenth century.

The Conservative Order

After the defeat of Napoleon, European rulers moved to restore much of the old order. This was the goal of the great powers—Great Britain, Austria, Prussia, and Russia—when they met at the Congress of Vienna in September 1814 to arrange a final peace settlement after the Napoleonic wars. The leader of the congress was the Austrian foreign minister, Prince Klemens von Metternich (KLAY-menss fun MET-ayr-nikh)

(1773–1859), who claimed that he was guided at Vienna by the principle of **legitimacy**. To reestablish peace and stability in Europe, he considered it necessary to restore the legitimate monarchs who would preserve traditional institutions. This had already been done in France with the restoration of the Bourbon monarchy and in a number of other states, but it did not stop the great powers from also grabbing land to add to their states (see Map 19.3).

The peace arrangements of 1815 were only the beginning of a conservative reaction determined to contain the liberal and nationalist forces unleashed by the French Revolution. Metternich and his kind were representatives of the ideology known as **conservatism**. Most conservatives favored obedience to political authority, believed that organized religion was crucial to social order, hated revolutionary upheavals, and were unwilling to accept either the liberal demands for civil liberties and representative governments or the nationalistic aspirations generated by the French revolutionary era. After 1815, the political philosophy of conservatism was supported by hereditary monarchs, government bureaucracies, landowning aristocracies, and revived churches, be they Protestant or Catholic. The conservative forces were dominant after 1815.

One method used by the great powers to maintain the new status quo they had constructed was the Concert of Europe, according to which Great Britain, Russia, Prussia, and Austria (and later France) agreed to meet periodically in conferences to take steps that would maintain the peace in Europe. Eventually, the great powers adopted a principle of **intervention**, asserting the right to send armies into countries where there were revolutions to restore legitimate monarchs to their thrones.

Forces for Change

After 1815, conservative governments throughout Europe worked to maintain the old order. But powerful forces for change—liberalism and nationalism—were also at work. **Liberalism** owed much to the Enlightenment of the eighteenth century and the American and French Revolutions; it was based on the idea that people should be as free from restraint as possible.

Politically, liberals came to hold a common set of beliefs. Chief among them was the protection of civil liberties, or the basic rights of all people, which included equality before the law; freedom of assembly, speech, and the press; and freedom from arbitrary arrest. All of these freedoms should be guaranteed by a written document, such as the American Bill of Rights or the French Declaration of the Rights of Man and the Citizen. In addition to religious toleration for all, most liberals advocated separation of church and state. Liberals also demanded the right of peaceful opposition to the government in and out of parliament and the making of laws by a

MAP 19.3 Europe After the Congress of Vienna, 1815. The Congress of Vienna imposed order on Europe based on the principles of monarchical government and a balance of power. Monarchs were restored in France, Spain, and other states recently under Napoleon's control, and much territory changed hands, often at the expense of small, weak states.

Q *How did Europe's major powers manipulate territory to decrease the probability that France could again threaten the continent's stability?*

representative assembly (legislature) elected by qualified voters. Thus, many liberals believed in a constitutional monarchy or constitutional state with limits on the powers of government to prevent despotism and in written constitutions that would guarantee these rights. Liberals were not democrats, however. They thought that the right to vote and hold office should be open only to men who owned property. Liberals also believed in economic values based upon *laissez-faire* principles that rejected state interference in the regulation of wages and work hours. As a political philosophy, liberalism was adopted by middle-class men, especially the industrial bourgeoisie, who favored voting rights for themselves so that they could share power with the landowning classes.

Nationalism was an even more powerful ideology for change in the nineteenth century. Nationalism arose out of an awareness of being part of a community that has common institutions, traditions, language, and customs. This community constitutes a "nation," and it, rather than a dynasty, city-state, or other political unit, becomes the focus of the individual's primary political loyalty. Nationalism did not become a popular force for change until the French Revolution. From then on, nationalists came to believe that each nationality should have its own government. Thus, the Germans, who were not united, wanted national unity in a German nation-state with one central government. Subject peoples, such as the Hungarians, wanted the right to establish their own autonomy rather than be subject to a German minority in the multinational Austrian Empire.

Nationalism, then, was a threat to the existing political order. A united Germany, for example, would upset the balance of power established at Vienna in 1815. At the same time, an independent Hungarian state would mean the breakup of the Austrian Empire. Because many European states were multinational, conservatives tried hard to repress the radical threat of nationalism.

At the same time, in the first half of the nineteenth century, nationalism and liberalism became strong allies. Most liberals believed that liberty could be realized only by peoples who ruled themselves. Many nationalists believed that once each people obtained their own state, all nations could be linked together into a broader community of all humanity. In fact, the nationalism that later triumphed in the second half of the nineteenth century—a new, loud nationalism—divided people rather than unifying them as the new national states became embroiled in bitter competition.

Revolution and Reform, 1830–1832

The conservative order dominated much of Europe after 1815, but the forces of liberalism and nationalism, first generated by the French Revolution, continued to grow as that second great revolution, the Industrial Revolution, expanded and brought new groups of people who wanted change. In 1830, in France, these forces for change erupted as a revolution overthrew the Bourbon monarch and created a limited constitutional monarchy under Louis-Philippe (1830–1848), soon called the "bourgeois monarch" because political support for his rule came from the

upper middle class. Great Britain, by contrast, avoided revolutionary upheaval by passing a Reform Bill in 1832 that increased the numbers of male voters, primarily benefiting the members of the upper middle class who favored liberal ideas.

Supporters of liberalism played a primary role in the revolution in France and British reform in 1832, but nationalism was the crucial force in three other revolutionary outbursts in 1830. Belgium, which had been annexed to the Dutch Republic in 1815 to create a larger state to act as a barrier against French aggression, rebelled against the Dutch and established an independent constitutional monarchy. Two other revolutions, however, failed. Russian forces crushed the Poles' attempt to liberate themselves from foreign domination, while Austrian troops intervened in Italy to uphold reactionary governments in a number of Italian states. But the forces of liberalism and nationalism continued to grow and gave rise to new revolutions in 1848.

The Revolutions of 1848

Revolution in France was the spark for revolts in other countries. A severe industrial and agricultural depression beginning in 1846 brought hardship in France to the lower middle class, workers, and peasants, while the government's persistent refusal to extend the suffrage angered the disenfranchised members of the middle class. When the government of King Louis-Philippe refused to make changes, opposition grew and finally overthrew the monarchy on February 24, 1848. A group of moderate and radical republicans established a provisional government and called for the election by universal male suffrage of a "constituent assembly" that would draw up a new constitution.

The new constitution, ratified on November 4, 1848, established the Second Republic, with a single legislature elected to three-year terms by universal male suffrage and a president, also elected by universal male suffrage to a four-year term. In the elections for the presidency held in December 1848, Charles Louis Napoleon Bonaparte (1808–1873), the nephew of the famous ruler, won a resounding victory. Within four years, President Louis Napoleon would become Emperor Napoleon III and establish an authoritarian regime.

REVOLUTION IN CENTRAL EUROPE News of the 1848 revolution in France led to upheaval in central Europe as well (see Opposing Viewpoints "Response to Revolution: Two Perspectives" on p. 557). The Vienna settlement in 1815 had recognized the existence of thirty-eight sovereign states (called the Germanic Confederation) in what had once been the Holy Roman Empire. Austria and Prussia were the two great powers in terms of size and might; the other states varied considerably. In 1848, cries for change caused many German rulers to promise constitutions, a free press, jury trials, and other liberal reforms. In Prussia, King Frederick William IV (1840–1861) agreed to establish a new constitution and work for a united Germany.

The promise of unity reverberated throughout all the German states as governments allowed elections by universal

Response to Revolution: Two Perspectives

POLITICS & GOVERNMENT

BASED ON THEIR POLITICAL BELIEFS, EUROPEANS RESPONDED DIFFERENTLY to the specter of revolution that haunted Europe in the first half of the nineteenth century. The first excerpt is taken from a speech given by Thomas Babington Macaulay (muh-KAHL-lee) (1800–1859), a historian and a member of Parliament. Macaulay spoke in Parliament on behalf of the Reform Act of 1832, which extended the right to vote to the industrial middle classes of Britain. The revolution of 1830 in France had influenced his belief that it was better to reform than to have a political revolution.

The second excerpt is taken from the *Reminiscences* of Carl Schurz (SHOORTS) (1829–1906). Like many liberals and nationalists in Germany, Schurz received the news of the February Revolution of 1848 in France with much excitement and great expectations for revolutionary change in the German states. After the failure of the German revolution, Schurz made his way to the United States and eventually became a U.S. senator.

Thomas Babington Macaulay, Speech of March 2, 1831

My hon[orable] friend the member of the University of Oxford tells us that, if we pass this law, England will soon be a Republic. The reformed House of Commons will, according to him, before it has sat ten years, depose the King, and expel the Lords from their House. Sir, if my hon[orable] friend could prove this, he would have succeeded in bringing an argument for democracy infinitely stronger than any that is to be found in the works of Paine. His proposition is, in fact, this—that our monarchical and aristocratical institutions have no hold on the public mind of England; that these institutions are regarded with aversion by a decided majority of the middle class.... Now, sir, if I were convinced that the great body of the middle class in England look with aversion on monarchy and aristocracy, I should be forced, much against my will, to come to this conclusion, that monarchical and aristocratical institutions are unsuited to this country. Monarchy and aristocracy, valuable and useful as I think them, are still valuable and useful as means, and not as ends. The end of government is the happiness of the people; and I do not conceive that, in a country like this, the happiness of the people can be promoted by a form of government in which the middle classes place no confidence, and which exists only because the middle classes have no organ by which to make their sentiments known. But, sir, I am fully convinced that the middle classes sincerely wish to uphold the royal prerogatives, and the constitutional rights of the Peers....

But let us know our interest and our duty better. Turn where we may—within, around—the voice of great events is proclaiming to us, "Reform, that you may preserve." Now, therefore, while everything at home and abroad forebodes ruin to those who persist in a hopeless struggle against the spirit of the age; now, while the crash of the proudest throne of the Continent is still resounding in our ears; … now, while the heart of England is still sound; now, while the old feelings and the old associations retain a power and a charm which may too soon pass away; now, in this your accepted time; now, in this your day of salvation, take counsel, not of prejudice, not of party spirit … but of history, of reason, of the ages which are past, of the signs of this most portentous time. Pronounce in a manner worthy of the expectation with which this great debate has been anticipated, and of the long remembrance which it will leave behind. Renew the youth of the State. Save property divided against itself. Save the multitude, endangered by their own ungovernable passions. Save the aristocracy, endangered by its own unpopular power. Save the greatest, and fairest, and most highly civilized community that ever existed, from calamities which may in a few days sweep away all the rich heritage of so many ages of wisdom and glory. The danger is terrible. The time is short. If this Bill should be rejected, I pray to God that none of those who concur in rejecting it may ever remember their votes with unavailing regret, amidst the wreck of laws, the confusion of ranks, the spoliation of property, and the dissolution of social order.

Carl Schurz, *Reminiscences*

One morning, toward the end of February, 1848, I sat quietly in my attic-chamber, working hard at my tragedy of "Ulrich von Hutten" [a sixteenth-century German knight], when suddenly a friend rushed breathlessly into the room, exclaiming: "What, you sitting here! Do you not know what has happened?"

"No; what?"

"The French have driven away Louis Philippe and proclaimed the republic."

I threw down my pen—and that was the end of "Ulrich von Hutten." I never touched the manuscript again. We tore down the stairs, into the street, to the market-square, the accustomed meeting-place for all the student societies after their midday dinner. Although it was still forenoon, the market was already crowded with young men talking excitedly. There was no shouting, no noise, only agitated conversation. What did we want there? This probably no one knew. But

(continued)

since the French had driven away Louis Philippe and proclaimed the republic, something of course must happen here, too.... We were dominated by a vague feeling as if a great outbreak of elemental forces had begun, as if an earthquake was impending of which we had felt the first shock, and we instinctively crowded together....

The next morning there were the usual lectures to be attended. But how profitless! The voice of the professor sounded like a monotonous drone coming from far away. What he had to say did not seem to concern us. The pen that should have taken notes remained idle. At last we closed with a sigh the notebook and went away, impelled by a feeling that now we had something more important to do—to devote ourselves to the affairs of the fatherland. And this we did by seeking as quickly as possible again the company of our friends, in order to discuss what had happened and what was to come. In these conversations, excited as they were, certain ideas and catchwords worked themselves to the surface, which expressed more or less the feelings of the people. Now had arrived in Germany the day for the establishment of "German Unity," and the founding of a great, powerful national German

Empire. In the first line the convocation of a national parliament. Then the demands for civil rights and liberties, free speech, free press, the right of free assembly, equality before the law, a freely elected representation of the people with legislative power, responsibility of ministers, self-government of the communes, the right of the people to carry arms, the formation of a civic guard with elective officers, and so on—in short, that which was called a "constitutional form of government on a broad democratic basis." Republican ideas were at first only sparingly expressed. But the word *democracy* was soon on all tongues, and many, too, thought it a matter of course that if the princes should try to withhold from the people the rights and liberties demanded, force would take the place of mere petition. Of course the regeneration of the fatherland must, if possible, be accomplished by peaceable means.... Like many of my friends, I was dominated by the feeling that at last the great opportunity had arrived for giving to the German people the liberty which was their birthright and to the German fatherland its unity and greatness, and that it was now the first duty of every German to do and to sacrifice everything for this sacred object.

What arguments did Macaulay use to support the Reform Bill of 1832? Was he correct? Why or why not? Why was Carl Schurz so excited when he heard the news about the revolution in France? Do you think being a university student helps explain his reaction? Why or why not? What differences do you see in the approaches of these two writers? What do these selections tell you about the development of politics in the German states and Britain in the nineteenth century?

Sources: Thomas Babington Macaulay, Speech of March 2, 1831. From *Speeches, Parliamentary and Miscellaneous* by Thomas B. Macaulay (New York: Hurst Co., 1853), vol. 1, pp. 20–21, 25–26. From *The Reminiscences of Carl Schurz* by Carl Schurz (New York: The McClure Co., 1907), vol. 1, pp. 112–113.

male suffrage for deputies to an all-German parliament called the Frankfurt Assembly. Its purpose was to fulfill a liberal and nationalist dream—the preparation of a constitution for a new united Germany. But the Frankfurt Assembly failed to achieve its goal. The members had no real means of compelling the German rulers to accept the constitution they had drawn up. German unification was not achieved; the revolution had failed.

The Austrian Empire needed only the news of the revolution in Paris to erupt in flames in March 1848. The Austrian Empire was a multinational state, a collection of at least eleven ethnically distinct peoples, including Germans, Czechs, Magyars (Hungarians), Slovaks, Romanians, Serbs, and Italians, who had pledged their loyalty to the Habsburg emperor. The Germans, though only a quarter of the population, were economically dominant and played a leading role in governing Austria. The Hungarians, however, wanted their own legislature. In March, demonstrations in Buda, Prague, and Vienna led to the dismissal of Metternich, the Austrian foreign minister and the archsymbol of the conservative order, who fled abroad. In Vienna, revolutionary forces took control of the capital and demanded a liberal constitution. Hungary was

given its own legislature and a separate national army. In Bohemia, the Czechs began to clamor for their own government as well.

Austrian officials had made concessions to appease the revolutionaries, but they were determined to reestablish firm control. As in the German states, they were increasingly encouraged by the divisions between radical and moderate revolutionaries and played on the middle-class fear of a working-class social revolution. In June 1848, Austrian military forces ruthlessly suppressed the Czech rebels in Prague. By the end of October, radical rebels had been crushed in Vienna, but it was only with the assistance of a Russian army of 140,000 men that the Hungarian revolution was finally put down in 1849. The revolutions in the Austrian Empire had failed.

REVOLTS IN THE ITALIAN STATES Revolutions in Italy also failed. The Congress of Vienna had established nine states in Italy, including the kingdom of Sardinia in the north, ruled by the house of Savoy; the kingdom of the Two Sicilies (Naples and Sicily); the Papal States; a handful of small duchies; and the important northern provinces of Lombardy and Venetia (vuh-NEE-shuh), which were now part of the Austrian

Empire. Italy was largely under Austrian domination, but a new movement for Italian unity, known as Young Italy, led to initially successful revolts in 1848. Within a year, however, the Austrians had reestablished complete control over Lombardy and Venetia, and the old order also prevailed in the rest of Italy.

Throughout Europe in 1848, popular revolutions had led to liberal constitutions and liberal governments. Moderate, middle-class liberals and radical workers soon divided over their aims, however, and the failure of the revolutionaries to stay united soon led to the reestablishment of authoritarian regimes. In other parts of the Western world, revolutions took somewhat different directions.

Nationalism in the Balkans: The Ottoman Empire and the Eastern Question

The Ottoman Empire had long been in control of much of southeastern Europe, an area known as the Balkans. In the first half of the nineteenth century, a number of states in the Balkans sought to free themselves from the Ottomans. Serbia, for example, won its autonomy in 1817. As the Ottoman Empire began to decline and authority over its outlying territories in southeastern Europe waned, European governments began to take an active interest in its disintegration. The "Eastern Question," as it came to be called, troubled European diplomats throughout the nineteenth century. Russia's proximity to the Ottoman Empire and the religious bonds between the Russians and the Greek Orthodox Christians in Turkish-dominated southeastern Europe naturally gave Russia special opportunities to enlarge its sphere of influence. The Austrian Empire feared Russian ambitions and had its own interest in the apparent demise of the Ottoman Empire. France and Britain were interested in commercial opportunities and naval bases in the eastern Mediterranean.

In 1821, the Greeks revolted against their Turkish masters. Although subject to Muslim control for four hundred years, the Greeks had been allowed to maintain their language and their Greek Orthodox faith. The Greek revolt was soon transformed into a noble cause by an outpouring of European sentiment for the Greeks' struggle. In 1827, a combined British and French fleet went to Greece and defeated a large Turkish fleet. A year later, Russia declared war on the Ottoman Empire. In 1829, the Turks agreed to allow Russia, France,

The Balkans in 1830

The Crimean War

and Britain to decide the fate of Greece, and one year later, the three powers declared Greece an independent kingdom.

THE CRIMEAN WAR The Crimean War was another episode in the story of the Eastern Question. In 1853, war had erupted again between the Russians and Turks over Russian demands for the right to protect Christian shrines in Palestine, a privilege that had already been extended to the French. When the Turks refused, the Russians invaded Turkish Moldavia (mohl-DAY-vee-uh) and Wallachia (wah-LAY-kee-uh). Failure to resolve the problem by negotiations led the Turks to declare war on Russia on October 4, 1853. In the following year, on March 28, Great Britain and France, fearful that the Russians would gain at the expense of the disintegrating Ottoman Empire, declared war on Russia.

The Crimean War was poorly planned and poorly fought. Britain and France decided on an attack on Russia's Crimean peninsula in the Black Sea. After a long siege and at a terrible cost in troops on both sides, the main Russian fortress of Sevastopol (suh-VAS-tuh-pohl) fell in September 1855, and the Russians soon sued for peace. Under the Treaty of Paris, signed in March 1856, Russia was forced to give up Bessarabia at the mouth of the Danube and accept the neutrality of the Black Sea. In addition, the Danubian principalities of Moldavia and Wallachia were placed under the protection of all the great powers.

The Crimean War proved costly to both sides. More than 250,000 soldiers died in the war, 60 percent of them from disease (primarily cholera). Even more would have died on the British side if it had not been for the efforts of Florence Nightingale (1820–1910). Her insistence on strict sanitary conditions saved many lives and helped make nursing a profession of trained, middle-class women.

The Crimean War destroyed the Concert of Europe. Austria and Russia, the two chief powers maintaining the status quo in the first half of the nineteenth century, were now enemies because of Austria's unwillingness to support Russia in the war. Russia, defeated and humiliated by the obvious failure of its armies, withdrew from European affairs for the next two decades. Great Britain, disillusioned by its role in the war, also pulled back from continental affairs. Austria, paying the price for its neutrality, was now without friends among the great powers. This new international situation opened the door for the unification of Italy and Germany.

Florence Nightingale. Florence Nightingale is shown caring for wounded British soldiers in the military hospital at Scutari during the Crimean War. After a British journalist, W. H. Russell, issued a scathing denunciation of the quality of medical care afforded to wounded British soldiers, the British government allowed Nightingale to take a group of nurses to the Crimean warfront. Through her efforts in the Crimean War, Nightingale helped make nursing an admirable profession for middle-class women. At the right is a photograph of Nightingale. Florence Nightingale Museum, London, UK/The Bridgeman Art Library

National Unification and the National State, 1848–1871

Q **FOCUS QUESTION:** What actions did Cavour and Bismarck take to bring about unification in Italy and Germany, respectively, and what role did war play in their efforts?

The revolutions of 1848 had failed, but within twenty-five years, many of the goals sought by liberals and nationalists during the first half of the nineteenth century were achieved. Italy and Germany became nations, and many European states were led by constitutional monarchs.

The Unification of Italy

The Italians were the first people to benefit from the breakdown of the Concert of Europe. In 1850, Austria was still the dominant power on the Italian peninsula. After the failure of the revolution of 1848–1849, more and more Italians looked to the northern Italian state of Piedmont, ruled by the royal house of Savoy (suh-VOI), as their best hope to achieve the unification of Italy. It was, however, doubtful that the little state could

The Unification of Italy

Legend:
- Kingdom of Piedmont, before 1859
- To Kingdom of Piedmont, 1859
- To Kingdom of Piedmont, 1860
- To Kingdom of Italy, 1866, 1870

provide the leadership needed to unify Italy until King Victor Emmanuel II (1849–1878) named Count Camillo di Cavour (kuh-MEEL-oh dee kuh-VOOR) (1810–1861) prime minister in 1852.

As prime minister, Cavour pursued a policy of economic expansion that increased government revenues and enabled Piedmont to equip a large army. Cavour, however, knew that Piedmont's army was not strong enough to beat the Austrians; consequently, he made an alliance with the French emperor Napoleon III and then provoked the Austrians into invading Piedmont in 1859. After French armies defeated the Austrians, a peace settlement gave the French Nice (NEES) and Savoy, which they had been promised for making the alliance, and Lombardy went to Piedmont. Cavour's success caused nationalists in some northern Italian states (Parma, Modena, and Tuscany) to overthrow their governments and join Piedmont.

Meanwhile, in southern Italy, Giuseppe Garibaldi (joo-ZEP-pay gar-uh-BAHL-dee) (1807–1882), a dedicated Italian patriot, raised an army of a thousand volunteers called the Red Shirts because of the color of their uniforms. Garibaldi's forces swept through Sicily and then crossed over to the mainland and began a victorious march up the

Garibaldi and Romantic Nationalism

POLITICS & GOVERNMENT

GIUSEPPE GARIBALDI was one of the more colorful figures involved in the unification of Italy. Accompanied by only a thousand of his famous Red Shirts, the Italian soldier of fortune left Genoa on the night of May 5, 1860, for an invasion of the kingdom of the Two Sicilies. The ragged band entered Palermo, the chief city on the island of Sicily, on May 31. This selection is taken from an account by a correspondent for the *Times* of London, the Hungarian-born Nandor Eber.

Times, June 13, 1860

Palermo, May 31—Anyone in search of violent emotions cannot do better than set off at once for Palermo. However blasé he may be, or however milk-and-water his blood, I promise it will be stirred up. He will be carried away by the tide of popular feeling....

In the afternoon Garibaldi made a tour of inspection round the town. I was there, but find it really impossible to give you a faint idea of the manner in which he was received everywhere. It was one of those triumphs which seem to be almost too much for a man.... The popular idol, Garibaldi, in his red flannel shirt, with a loose colored handkerchief round his neck, and his worn "wide-awake" [a soft-brimmed felt hat], was walking on foot among those cheering, laughing, crying, mad thousands; and all his few followers could do was to prevent him from being bodily carried off the ground. The people threw themselves forward to kiss his hands, or, at least, to touch the hem of his garment, as if it contained the panacea for all their past and perhaps coming suffering. Children were brought up, and mothers asked on their knees for his blessing; and all this while the object of this idolatry was calm and smiling as when in the deadliest fire, taking up the children and kissing them, trying to quiet the crowd, stopping at every moment to hear a long complaint of houses burned and property sacked by the retreating soldiers, giving good advice, comforting, and promising that all damages should be paid for....

One might write volumes of horrors on the vandalism already committed, for every one of the hundred ruins has its story of brutality and inhumanity.... In these small houses a dense population is crowded together even in ordinary times. A shell falling on one, and crushing and burying the inmates, was sufficient to make people abandon the neighboring one and take refuge a little further on, shutting themselves up in the cellars. When the Royalists retired they set fire to those of the houses which had escaped the shells, and numbers were thus burned alive in their hiding places....

If you can stand the exhalation, try and go inside the ruins, for it is only there that you will see what the thing means and you will not have to search long before you stumble over the remains of a human body, a leg sticking out here, an arm there, a black face staring at you a little further on. You are startled by a rustle. You look round and see half a dozen gorged rats scampering off in all directions, or you see a dog trying to make his escape over the ruins.... I only wonder that the sight of these scenes does not convert every man in the town into a tiger and every woman into a fury. But these people have been so long ground down and demoralized that their nature seems to have lost the power of reaction.

This article from the London Times *is the first newspaper primary source document to appear in this textbook. How does this new source of information reflect the growth of an industrial middle class?*

Source: From *The Times* of London, June 13, 1860.

Italian peninsula (see the box "Garibaldi and Romantic Nationalism" above). Naples, and with it the kingdom of the Two Sicilies, fell in early September 1860. Ever the patriot, Garibaldi chose to turn over his conquests to Cavour's Piedmontese forces. On March 17, 1861, the new kingdom of Italy was proclaimed under a centralized government subordinated to the control of Piedmont and King Victor Emmanuel II of the house of Savoy.

The task of unification was not yet complete, however. Venetia in the north was still held by Austria, and Rome was under papal control, supported by French troops. In the Austro-Prussian War of 1866, the new Italian state became an ally of Prussia. Although the Italian army was defeated by the Austrians, Prussia's victory left the Italians with Venetia. In 1870, the Franco-Prussian War resulted in the withdrawal of French troops from Rome. The Italian army then annexed the city on September 20, 1870, and Rome became the new capital of the united Italian state.

CHRONOLOGY	The Unification of Italy
Victor Emmanuel II	1849–1878
Count Cavour becomes prime minister of Piedmont	1852
Garibaldi's invasion of the Two Sicilies	1860
Kingdom of Italy is proclaimed	March 17, 1861
Italy's annexation of Venetia	1866
Italy's annexation of Rome	1870

The Unification of Germany

After the failure of the Frankfurt Assembly to achieve German unification in 1848–1849, more and more Germans looked to Prussia for leadership in the cause of German unification. Prussia had become a strong, prosperous, and authoritarian state, with the Prussian king in firm control of both the government and the army. In the 1860s, King William I (1861–1888) attempted to enlarge and strengthen the Prussian army. When the Prussian legislature refused to levy new taxes for the proposed military changes, William appointed a new prime minister, Count Otto von Bismarck (OT-toh fun BIZ-mark) (1815–1898). Bismarck ignored the legislative opposition to the military reforms, arguing instead that "Germany does not look to Prussia's liberalism but to her power.... Not by speeches and majorities will the great questions of the day be decided—that was the mistake of 1848–1849—but by iron and blood."[6] Bismarck collected the taxes, reorganized the army anyway, and governed Prussia by simply ignoring parliament. In the meantime, opposition to his domestic policy determined Bismarck on an active foreign policy, which led to war and German unification. Bismarck has often been portrayed as the ultimate realist, the foremost nineteenth-century practitioner of *Realpolitik* (ray-AHL-poh-lee-teek)—the "politics of reality."

After defeating Denmark with Austrian help in 1864 and gaining control over the duchies of Schleswig (SHLESS-vik) and Holstein (HOHL-shtyn), Bismarck created friction with the Austrians and goaded them into a war on June 14, 1866. The Austrians were barely defeated at Königgrätz (kur-nig-GRETS) on July 3, but Prussia now organized the German states north of the Main River into the North German Confederation. The southern German states, largely Catholic, remained independent but signed military alliances with Prussia due to their fear of France, their western neighbor.

Prussia now dominated all of northern Germany, but problems with France soon arose. Bismarck realized that France would never be content with a strong German state to its east because of the potential threat to French security. In 1870, Prussia and France became embroiled in a dispute over the candidacy of a relative of the Prussian king for the throne of Spain. Bismarck manipulated the misunderstandings between the French and Prussians to goad the French into declaring war on Prussia on July 15, 1870. The southern German states honored their military alliances with Prussia and joined the war effort against the French. The Prussian armies advanced into France, and at Sedan (suh-DAHN) on September 2, 1870, captured an entire French army and Napoleon III himself. Paris capitulated on January 28, 1871. France had to pay an indemnity of 5 billion francs (about $1 billion) and give up the provinces of Alsace (al-SASS) and Lorraine (luh-RAYN) to the new German state, a loss that left the French burning for revenge.

Even before the war had ended, the southern German states had agreed to enter the North German Confederation. On January 18, 1871, in the Hall of Mirrors in Louis XIV's palace at Versailles, William I was proclaimed kaiser (KY-zur) (emperor) of the Second German Empire (the first was the medieval Holy Roman Empire). German unity had been achieved by the Prussian monarchy and the Prussian army. The Prussian leadership of German unification meant the triumph of authoritarian, militaristic values over liberal, constitutional sentiments in the development of the new German state. With its industrial resources and military might, the new state had become the strongest power on the continent. A new European balance of power was at hand.

The Unification of Germany

Prussia, 1862
United in 1866–1867 with Prussia as North German Confederation
South German Confederation
Annexed in 1871 after Franco-Prussian War

The Unification of Germany. Under Prussian leadership, a new German empire was proclaimed on January 18, 1871, in the Hall of Mirrors in the palace at Versailles. King William of Prussia became Emperor William I of the Second German Empire. Otto von Bismarck, the man who had been so instrumental in creating the new German state, is shown here, resplendently attired in his white uniform, standing at the foot of the throne.

CHRONOLOGY	The Unification of Germany
King William I of Prussia	1861–1888
Danish War	1864
Austro-Prussian War	1866
Franco-Prussian War	1870–1871
German Empire is proclaimed	January 18, 1871

Nationalism and Reform: The European National State at Mid-Century

While European affairs were dominated by the unification of Italy and Germany, other states in the Western world were also undergoing change.

GREAT BRITAIN Unlike the nations on the European continent, Great Britain managed to avoid the revolutionary upheavals of the first half of the nineteenth century. In the early part of the century, Britain was governed by the aristocratic landowning classes that dominated both houses of Parliament. But in 1832, to avoid the turmoil on the continent, Parliament passed a reform bill that increased the number of male voters, chiefly members of the industrial middle class (see Opposing Viewpoints "Response to Revolution: Two Perspectives" on p. 557). By joining the industrial middle class to the landed interest in ruling Britain, Britain avoided revolution in 1848.

Another reason for Britain's stability was its continuing economic growth. After 1850, middle-class prosperity was at last coupled with some improvements for the working classes as real wages for laborers increased more than 25 percent between 1850 and 1870. The British sense of national pride was well represented in Queen Victoria (1837–1901), whose sense of duty and moral respectability reflected the attitudes of her age, which has ever since been known as the Victorian Age (see the Film & History feature "*The Young Victoria* (2009)" on p. 564).

In the 1850s and 1860s, the British liberal parliamentary system also made both social and political reforms that enabled the country to remain stable. Although the Whigs (now called the Liberals), who had been responsible for the Reform Act of 1832, talked about passing additional reform legislation, it was actually the Tories (now called the Conservatives) who carried it through. Under the leadership of Benjamin Disraeli (diz-RAY-lee) (1804–1881), the Tory leader in Parliament, the Reform Act of 1867 added an important step in the democratization of Britain. The number of voters increased from 1 million to slightly over 2 million. At the same time, the extension of the right to vote had an important by-product as it forced the Liberals and Conservatives to organize carefully in order to manipulate the electorate. Party discipline intensified, and the rivalry between the Liberals and Conservatives became a regular feature of parliamentary life.

FRANCE Events in France after the revolution of 1848 moved toward the restoration of monarchy. Four years after his election as president, Louis Napoleon returned to the people to ask for the restoration of the empire. Ninety-seven percent responded in the affirmative, and on December 2, 1852, Louis Napoleon assumed the title of Napoleon III (the first Napoleon had abdicated in favor of his son, Napoleon II, on April 6, 1814). The Second Empire had begun.

The first five years of Napoleon III's reign were a spectacular success. He took many steps to expand industrial growth. Government subsidies helped foster the rapid construction of railroads as well as harbors, roads, and canals. The major French railway lines were completed during Napoleon's reign, and iron production tripled. In the midst of this economic expansion, Napoleon III also undertook a vast reconstruction of the city of Paris. The medieval Paris of narrow streets and old city walls was destroyed and replaced by a modern Paris of broad boulevards, spacious buildings, circular plazas, public squares, an underground sewage system, a new public water supply, and gas streetlights.

In the 1860s, as opposition to his rule began to mount, Napoleon III liberalized his regime. He gave the Legislative Corps more say in affairs of state, including debate over the budget. Liberalization policies worked initially; in a plebiscite in May 1870 on whether to accept a new constitution that might have inaugurated a parliamentary regime, the French people gave Napoleon another resounding victory. This triumph was short-lived, however. War with Prussia in 1870 brought Napoleon's ouster, and a republic was proclaimed.

THE AUSTRIAN EMPIRE Although nationalism was a major force in nineteenth-century Europe, one of the region's most powerful states, the Austrian Empire, managed to frustrate the desire of its numerous ethnic groups for self-determination. After the Habsburg rulers had crushed the revolutions of 1848–1849, they restored centralized, autocratic government to the empire. But Austria's defeat at the hands of the Prussians in 1866 forced the Austrians to deal with the fiercely nationalistic Hungarians.

The result was the negotiated *Ausgleich* (OWSS-glykh), or Compromise, of 1867, which created the Dual Monarchy of Austria-Hungary. Each part of the empire now had its own constitution, its own legislature, its own governmental bureaucracy, and its own capital (Vienna for Austria and Buda for Hungary). Holding the two states together was a single monarch—Francis Joseph (1848–1916) was emperor of Austria and king of Hungary—as well as a common army, foreign policy, and system of finances. The *Ausgleich* did not, however, satisfy the other nationalities that made up the Austro-Hungarian Empire.

RUSSIA At the beginning of the nineteenth century, Russia was overwhelmingly rural, agricultural, and autocratic. The Russian tsar was still regarded as a divine-right monarch with unlimited power. The Russian imperial autocracy, based on soldiers, secret police, and repression, had withstood the revolutionary fervor of the first half of the nineteenth century. But

The Young Victoria (2009)

Directed by Jean-Marc Vallée, *The Young Victoria* is an imaginative and yet relatively realistic portrayal of the early struggles of the young woman who became Britain's longest-reigning monarch. The film begins in 1836 when the seventeen-year-old Victoria (Emily Blunt) is the heir to the throne. Her controlling mother, the duchess of Kent (Miranda Richardson), schemes to prevent her daughter from ascending the throne by trying to create a regency for herself and her close adviser and paramour, Sir John Conroy (Mark Strong). Conroy is accurately shown trying to force the young Victoria to sign a paper establishing a regency. The mother and Conroy fail, and Victoria succeeds to the throne after the death of her uncle, King William IV (Jim Broadbent), on June 20, 1837, about one month after she turned eighteen. The movie also shows the impact that Lord Melbourne (Paul Bettany), the prime minister, had on the young queen as her private secretary and adviser. Indeed, Victoria's attachment to Melbourne led to considerable discontent among her subjects. Central to the film, however, is the romantic portrayal of the wooing of Victoria by her young German cousin, Prince Albert of Saxe-Coburg-Gotha (Rupert Friend), the nephew of the king of Belgium. The film accurately conveys the close bond and the deep and abiding love that developed between Victoria and Albert.

The film is a visual treat, re-creating the life of the young Victoria in a number of castle and cathedral settings. As a romantic dramatization of some of the main events before and after the coronation of Victoria, the film also contains some noticeable flaws. Victoria is shown painting with her right hand, although she was actually left-handed. The facts are also embellished at times in order to dramatize the story. Although there was an assassination attempt on the queen, Prince Albert was not shot while trying to protect her. Both shots fired by Edward Oxford, her would-be assassin, went wide of the mark. The character of Victoria's other uncle, King Leopold I of Belgium (Thomas Kretschmann), is also not quite accurate. He was not as selfish as he is portrayed in pushing Albert to marry Victoria. The banquet scene in which King William IV insults the duchess of Kent is quite accurate (it actually uses many of the exact words the king uttered), but its consequences were not. The duchess did not leave the room, and Victoria did not remain calm, but broke into tears. Finally, except for a passing reference to Victoria's concern for workers' housing conditions, this romantic movie makes no attempt to understand the political and social issues that troubled the British Empire of Victoria's time.

The coronation of Victoria (Emily Blunt) as queen of England

Gk Films/The Kobal Collection

---

defeat in the Crimean War in 1856 led even staunch conservatives to realize that Russia was falling hopelessly behind the western European powers. Tsar Alexander II (1855–1881) decided to make serious reforms.

Serfdom was the most burdensome problem in tsarist Russia. On March 3, 1861, Alexander issued his emancipation edict (see the box "Emancipation: Serfs and Slaves" on p. 565). Peasants were now free to own property and marry as they chose. The lands given to the peasants, however, were purchased by the state from the landlords, who kept the best parcels, leaving the Russian peasants without enough arable land to support themselves. Peasants were also expected to repay the state in long-term installments. To ensure that the payments were made, peasants were subjected to the authority of their *mir* (MEER), or village commune, which was collectively responsible for the land payments to the government. And since the village communes were responsible for the payments, they were reluctant to allow peasants to leave their land. Emancipation, then, led not to a free, landowning peasantry along the Western model but to an unhappy, land-starved peasantry that largely followed the old ways of agricultural production.

Alexander II attempted other reforms as well, but he soon found that he could please no one. Reformers wanted more and rapid change; conservatives thought that the tsar was attempting to undermine the basic institutions of Russian society. When one group of radicals assassinated Alexander II in 1881, his son and successor, Alexander III, turned against reform and returned to the traditional methods of repression.

Emancipation: Serfs and Slaves

FAMILY & SOCIETY

ALTHOUGH OVERALL THEIR HISTORIES have been quite different, Russia and the United States shared a common feature in the 1860s. They were the only states in the Western world that still had large enslaved populations (the Russian serfs were virtually slaves). The leaders of both countries issued emancipation proclamations within two years of each other. The first excerpt is taken from the imperial decree of March 3, 1861, which freed the Russian serfs. The second excerpt is from Abraham Lincoln's Emancipation Proclamation, issued on January 1, 1863.

Tsar Alexander II's Imperial Decree, March 3, 1861

By the grace of God, we, Alexander II, Emperor and Autocrat of all the Russias, King of Poland, Grand Duke of Finland, etc., to all our faithful subjects, make known:

Called by Divine Providence and by the sacred right of inheritance to the throne of our ancestors, we took a vow in our innermost heart to respond to the mission which is intrusted to us as to surround with our affection and our Imperial solicitude all our faithful subjects of every rank and of every condition, from the warrior, who nobly bears arms for the defense of the country, to the humble artisan devoted to the works of industry; from the official in the career of the high offices of the State to the laborer whose plough furrows the soil....

We thus came to the conviction that the work of a serious improvement of the condition of the peasants was a sacred inheritance bequeathed to us by our ancestors, a mission which, in the course of events, Divine Providence called upon us to fulfill....

In virtue of the new dispositions above mentioned, the peasants attached to the soil will be invested within a term fixed by the law with all the rights of free cultivators....

At the same time, they are granted the right of purchasing their close [a parcel of land], and, with the consent of the proprietors, they may acquire in full property the arable lands and other appurtenances which are allotted to them as a permanent holding. By the acquisition in full property of the quantity of land fixed, the peasants are free from their obligations toward the proprietors for land thus purchased, and they enter definitely into the condition of free peasant-landholders.

Abraham Lincoln's Emancipation Proclamation, January 1, 1863

Now therefore, I, Abraham Lincoln, President of the United States, by virtue of the power in me vested as Commander-in-Chief of the Army and Navy of the United States in time of actual armed rebellion against the authority and government of the United States, and as a fit and necessary war measure for suppressing such rebellion, do, on this 1st day of January, A.D. 1863, and in accordance with my purpose to do so, ... order and designate as the States and parts of States wherein the people thereof, respectively, are this day in rebellion against the United States the following, to wit:

Arkansas, Texas, Louisiana, ... Mississippi, Alabama, Florida, Georgia, South Carolina, North Carolina, and Virginia....

And by virtue of the power for the purpose aforesaid, I do order and declare that all persons held as slaves within said designated States and parts of States are, and henceforward shall be free; and that the Executive Government of the United States, including the military and naval authorities thereof, will recognize and maintain the freedom of said persons.

 What changes did Tsar Alexander II's emancipation of the serfs initiate in Russia? What effect did Lincoln's Emancipation Proclamation have on the southern "armed rebellion"? What reasons did each leader give for his action?

Sources: From *Annual Register* (New York: Longmans, Green, 1861), p. 207. From *U.S. Statutes at Large* (Washington, D.C., Government Printing Office, 1875), vol. 12, pp. 1268–1269.

The European State, 1871–1914

 FOCUS QUESTIONS: What general political trends were evident in the nations of western Europe in the late nineteenth and early twentieth centuries, and to what degree were those trends also apparent in the nations of central and eastern Europe? How did the growth of nationalism affect international affairs during the same period?

Throughout much of the Western world by 1870, the national state had become the focus of people's loyalties and the arena for political activity. Only in Russia, eastern Europe, Austria-Hungary, and Ireland did national groups still struggle for independence.

Within the major European states, considerable progress was made in achieving such liberal practices as constitutions and parliaments, but it was largely in western European states that **mass politics** became a reality. Reforms encouraged the expansion of political democracy through voting rights for men and the creation of mass political parties. At the same time, however, these latter developments were strongly resisted in parts of Europe where the old political forces remained strong.

Western Europe: The Growth of Political Democracy

By 1871, Great Britain had a functioning two-party parliamentary system. For fifty years, the Liberals and Conservatives alternated in power at regular intervals, although they also shared some common features. Both were dominated by a ruling class made up of a coalition of aristocratic landowners, who were also frequently involved in industrial and financial activities, and upper-middle-class businesspeople. The two parties competed with each other in supporting legislation that expanded the right to vote. By 1918, all males over twenty-one and women over thirty could vote. Political democracy was soon accompanied by social welfare measures for the working class.

The growth of trade unions, which advocated more radical change of the economic system, and the emergence in 1900 of the Labour Party, which dedicated itself to workers' interests, caused the Liberals, who held the government from 1906 to 1914, to realize that they would have to create a program of social welfare or lose the support of the workers. Therefore, they voted for a series of social reforms. The National Insurance Act of 1911 provided benefits for workers in case of sickness and unemployment, to be paid for by compulsory contributions from workers, employers, and the state. Additional legislation provided a small pension for Britons over age seventy and compensation for those injured in accidents at work. Although both the benefits of the program and the tax increases were modest, they were the first hesitant steps toward the future British welfare state.

In France, the confusion that ensued after the collapse of the Second Empire ended in 1875 when an improvised constitution established a republican form of government. This constitution established a bicameral legislature, with an upper house, the Senate, elected indirectly and a lower house, the Chamber of Deputies, chosen by universal male suffrage. The powers of the president, selected by the legislature to be the executive of the government for a term of seven years, were deliberately left vague. The premier (or prime minister) led the government, and he and his ministers were responsible not to the president but to the Chamber of Deputies.

The Constitution of 1875, intended only as a stopgap measure, solidified the Third Republic, which lasted sixty-five years. France's parliamentary system was weak, however, because the existence of a dozen political parties forced the premier to depend on a coalition of parties to stay in power. The Third Republic was notorious for its changes of government. Nevertheless, by 1914, the republic commanded the loyalty of most French people.

By 1870, Italy had emerged as a geographically united state with pretensions to great power status. Its internal weaknesses, however, gave that claim a particularly hollow ring. Sectional differences—a poverty-stricken south and an industrializing north—thwarted any sense of national unity. Chronic turmoil between labor and industry undermined the social fabric. The Italian government was unable to deal effectively with these problems because of extensive corruption among government officials and a lack of stability created by ever-changing government coalitions.

Central and Eastern Europe: Persistence of the Old Order

The constitution of the new imperial Germany begun by Bismarck in 1871 provided for a bicameral legislature. The lower house of the German parliament, the Reichstag, was elected on the basis of universal male suffrage, but it did not have ministerial responsibility. Ministers of government, among whom the most important was the chancellor, were responsible not to the parliament but to the emperor. The emperor also commanded the armed forces and controlled foreign policy and internal administration.

During the reign of Emperor William II (1888–1918), Germany continued as an "authoritarian, conservative, military-bureaucratic power state." By the end of William's reign, Germany had become the strongest military and industrial power on the continent. More than 50 percent of German workers had jobs in industry, while only 30 percent of the workforce was still in agriculture. Urban centers had mushroomed in number and size. These rapid changes helped produce a society torn between modernization and traditionalism. With the expansion of industry and cities came demands for true democracy. Conservative forces, especially the landowning nobility and representatives of heavy industry, two of the powerful ruling groups in Germany, tried to block it by supporting William II's activist foreign policy. Expansion abroad, they believed, would divert people's attention from the yearning for democracy at home.

The tensions in German society created by the conflict between modernization and traditionalism were also manifested in radicalized right-wing politics. A number of nationalist pressure groups arose to support nationalistic goals. Antisocialist and antiliberal, such groups as the Pan-German League stressed strong German nationalism and advocated imperialism as a tool to overcome social divisions and unite all classes. They also denounced the Jews as the destroyers of the German national community, fueling the flames of **anti-Semitism**.

After the creation of the Dual Monarchy of Austria-Hungary in 1867, the Austrian part received a constitution that theoretically established a parliamentary system. Emperor Francis Joseph largely ignored parliament, however, ruling by decree when parliament was not in session.

The problem of the various nationalities remained a difficult one. The German minority that governed Austria felt increasingly threatened by the Czechs, Poles, and other Slavic groups within the empire. The granting of universal male suffrage in 1907 served only to exacerbate the problem when nationalities that had played no role in the government now agitated in the parliament for autonomy. This led prime ministers after 1900 to ignore the parliament and rely increasingly on imperial emergency decrees to govern. On the eve of World War I, the Austro-Hungarian Empire was as far away as ever from solving its minorities problem.

By 1870, Russia was witnessing an increasing number of reform movements. Intellectuals known as **Westernizers** believed that Western ways were the solutions to Russia's problems and advocated the creation of parliamentary institutions and a policy of industrialization. Westernizers, however, were opposed by **Slavophiles**, who maintained that Russia's tsarist system, peasant villages, and Orthodox religious faith were superior to any Western ideals. Other Russians rejected both the Westernizers and Slavophiles and called for a more radical approach to reform. Among these were the **anarchists**, who believed that small groups of well-trained fanatical revolutionaries could perpetrate so much violence that the state and all its institutions would disintegrate. For the anarchist revolutionaries, assassination was the primary instrument of terror, and one group was successful in killing Tsar Alexander II in 1881.

This act had unexpected repercussions for the anarchists. Alexander III (1881–1894), the son and successor of the assassinated tsar, was now convinced that his father's attempts at reform had been a mistake, and he lost no time in persecuting both reformers and revolutionaries. When Alexander III died, his weak son and successor, Nicholas II (1894–1917), began his rule with his father's conviction that the absolute power of the tsars should be preserved: "I shall maintain the principle of autocracy just as firmly and unflinchingly as did my unforgettable father."[7] But conditions were changing, especially with the growth of industrialization.

Industrialization progressed rapidly in Russia after 1890, and with it came factories, an industrial working class, and the development of socialist parties, although repression in Russia soon forced the socialists to go underground and turn revolutionary. The social revolutionaries worked to overthrow the tsarist autocracy and establish peasant socialism. Growing opposition to the tsar finally exploded into revolution in 1905.

Nicholas II. The last tsar of Russia hoped to preserve the traditional autocratic ways of his predecessors. In this photograph, Nicholas II and his wife, Alexandra, are shown around 1907 with their four daughters and son on holiday on the deck of a ship.

CHRONOLOGY The European State, 1871–1914	
Great Britain	
Formation of Labour Party	1900
National Insurance Act	1911
France	
Republican constitution (Third Republic)	1875
Germany	
Bismarck as chancellor	1871–1890
Emperor William II	1888–1918
Austria-Hungary	
Emperor Francis Joseph	1848–1916
Russia	
Tsar Alexander III	1881–1894
Tsar Nicholas II	1894–1917
Russo-Japanese War	1904–1905
Revolution	1905

The defeat of the Russians by the Japanese in 1904–1905 encouraged antigovernment groups to rebel against the tsarist regime. Nicholas II granted civil liberties and agreed to create a legislative assembly, the Duma (DOO-muh), elected directly by a broad franchise. But real constitutional monarchy proved short-lived. Already by 1907, the tsar had curtailed the power of the Duma and relied again on the army and bureaucracy to rule Russia.

International Rivalries and the Winds of War

Between 1871 and 1914, Europe was mostly at peace. Wars did occur (including wars of conquest in the non-Western world), but none involved the great powers. A series of crises occurred, however, that might easily have led to war. Until 1890, Bismarck, the chancellor of Germany, exercised a restraining influence on Europeans. He realized that the emergence in 1871 of a unified Germany as the most powerful state on the continent had upset the balance of power established at Vienna in 1815 (see Map 19.4). Fearful of a possible anti-German alliance involving France and Russia and possibly even Austria-Hungary, Bismarck made a defensive alliance with Austria in 1879. Both powers agreed to support each other in the event of an attack by Russia. In 1882, this German-Austrian alliance was enlarged by the addition of Italy, angry with the French over conflicting colonial ambitions in North Africa. The Triple Alliance of 1882 committed Germany, Austria-Hungary, and Italy to unite in their defense against France. Bismarck also signed a separate treaty with Russia.

When Emperor William II cashiered Bismarck in 1890 and took over direction of Germany's foreign policy, he embarked on an activist foreign policy dedicated to enhancing German power by finding, as he put it, Germany's rightful "place in the sun." One of his changes in Bismarck's foreign policy was

MAP 19.4 Europe in 1871. German unification in 1871 upset the balance of power established at Vienna in 1815 and eventually led to a realignment of European alliances. By 1907, Europe was divided into two opposing camps: the Triple Entente of Great Britain, Russia, and France and the Triple Alliance of Germany, Austria-Hungary, and Italy.

Q *How was Germany affected by the formation of the Triple Entente?*

to drop the treaty with Russia, which he viewed as being at odds with Germany's alliance with Austria. The ending of the alliance brought France and Russia together, and in 1894, the two powers concluded a military alliance. During the next ten years, German policies abroad caused the British to draw closer to France. By 1907, a loose confederation of Great Britain, France, and Russia—known as the Triple Entente (ahn-TAHNT)—stood opposed to the Triple Alliance of Germany, Austria-Hungary, and Italy. Europe was now divided into two opposing camps that became more and more inflexible and unwilling to compromise. A series of crises in the Balkans between 1908 and 1913 over the remnants of the Ottoman Empire set the stage for World War I.

The Ottoman Empire and Nationalism in the Balkans

Like the Austro-Hungarian Empire, the Ottoman Empire was severely troubled by the nationalist aspirations of its subject peoples, especially in the Balkans. Corruption and inefficiency had so weakened the Ottoman Empire that only the interference of the great European powers, who were fearful of each other's designs on the empire, kept it alive.

In the course of the nineteenth century, the Balkan provinces of the Ottoman Empire gradually gained their freedom, although the rivalry in the region between Austria and Russia complicated the process. By 1878, Greece, Serbia, Romania, and Montenegro (mahn-tuh-NEE-groh) had become independent.

Bulgaria did not become totally independent but was allowed to operate autonomously under Russian protection. The Balkan territories of Bosnia and Herzegovina (HAYRT-suh-guh-VEE-nuh) were placed under the protection of Austria-Hungary. Austria could occupy but not annex them.

CRISES IN THE BALKANS, 1908–1913 In 1908, Austria took the drastic step of annexing the Slavic-speaking territories of Bosnia and Herzegovina. Serbia was outraged because the annexation dashed the Serbs' hopes of creating a large Serbian kingdom that would include most of the southern Slavs. But the Austrians had annexed Bosnia explicitly to prevent that eventuality. The creation of a large Serbia would be a threat to the unity of their empire with its large Slavic population. The Russians, as protectors of their fellow Slavs and also desiring to increase their own authority in the Balkans, supported the Serbs and opposed the Austrian action. Backed by the Russians, the Serbs prepared for war against

The Balkans in 1913

Austria. At this point, William II intervened and demanded that the Russians accept Austria's annexation of Bosnia and Herzegovina or face war with Germany. Weakened from their defeat in the Russo-Japanese War in 1904–1905, the Russians backed down but vowed revenge. Two wars between the Balkan states in 1912–1913 further embittered the inhabitants of the region and generated more tensions among the great powers.

Serbia's desire to create a large Serbian kingdom remained unfulfilled. In frustration, Serbian nationalists blamed the Austrians. Austria-Hungary was convinced that Serbia was a mortal threat to its empire and must at some point be crushed. As Serbia's chief supporters, the Russians were determined not to back down again in the event of a confrontation with Austria or Germany in the Balkans. The allies of Austria-Hungary and Russia were also determined to be more supportive of their respective allies in another crisis. By the beginning of 1914, two armed camps viewed each other with suspicion.

CHAPTER SUMMARY

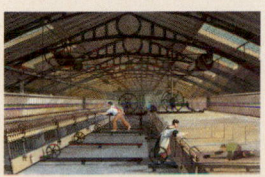

In 1815, a conservative order had been reestablished throughout Europe, but the forces of liberalism and nationalism, unleashed by the French Revolution and now reinforced by the spread of industrialization, were pushing Europe into a new era of political and social change. Industrialization spread rapidly from Great Britain to the European continent and United States. As cities grew, the plight of Europe's new working class became

the focus of new political philosophies. Utopian socialists championed better living conditions for the working poor, while the work of Karl Marx sought to liberate the oppressed proletariat. At the same time, middle-class industrialists adopted the political philosophy of liberalism, espousing freedom in politics and in economic activity. By the mid-nineteenth century, nationalism threatened the status quo in divided Germany and Italy and the multiethnic Austrian Empire.

The revolutionary waves of the 1820s and 1830s made it clear that the ideologies of liberalism and nationalism were still alive and active in the Western world. In 1848, revolutions erupted once more. A republic with universal manhood suffrage was established in France, but conflict emerged between socialist demands and the republican political agenda. The Frankfurt Assembly worked to create a unified Germany, but it also failed. In the Austrian Empire, the liberal demands of the Hungarians and other nationalities were eventually put down. In Italy, too, uprisings against Austrian rule failed when conservatives regained control.

By 1871, nationalist forces had prevailed in Germany and Italy. The combined activities of Count Cavour and Giuseppe Garibaldi finally led to the unification of Italy in 1870. Under the guidance of Otto von Bismarck, Prussia engaged in wars with Denmark, Austria, and France before it finally achieved the goal of German national unification in 1871. Reform characterized developments in other Western states. Austria created the Dual Monarchy of

Austria-Hungary. Russia's defeat in the Crimean War led to reforms under Alexander II, which included the freeing of the Russian serfs.

Between 1871 and 1914, the national state began to expand its functions by adopting such social insurance measures as protection against accidents, illnesses, and old age in order to appease the working masses. Liberal and democratic reforms, especially in western Europe, brought new possibilities for greater participation in the political process. Nevertheless, significantly large minorities, especially in the multiethnic empires controlled by the Austrians, Ottomans, and Russians, had not achieved the goal of their own national states. Meanwhile, the collapse of the Ottoman Empire caused Russia and Austria to set their sights on territories in the Balkans. As Germany's power increased, the European nations formed new alliances that helped maintain a balance of power but also led to the creation of large armies. The alliances also generated tensions that were unleashed when Europeans were unable to resolve a series of crises in the Balkans and rushed into the catastrophic carnage of World War I.

CHAPTER TIMELINE

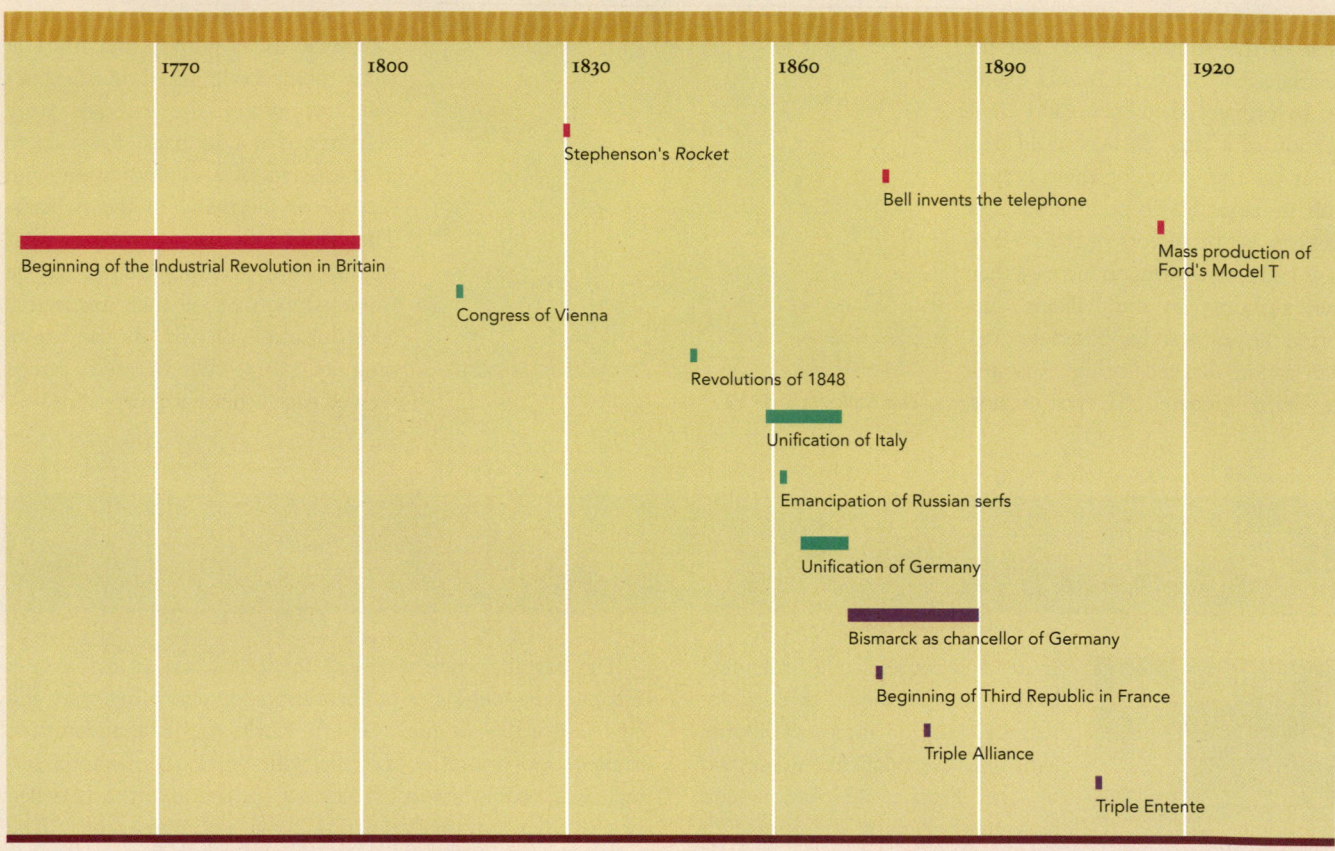

1770   1800   1830   1860   1890   1920

Stephenson's *Rocket*

Bell invents the telephone

Mass production of Ford's Model T

Beginning of the Industrial Revolution in Britain

Congress of Vienna

Revolutions of 1848

Unification of Italy

Emancipation of Russian serfs

Unification of Germany

Bismarck as chancellor of Germany

Beginning of Third Republic in France

Triple Alliance

Triple Entente

CHAPTER REVIEW

Upon Reflection

Q What are the major similarities and differences between the First and Second Industrial Revolutions?

Q What were the chief ideas associated with the ideologies of liberalism and nationalism, and how were these ideas put into practice in the first half of the nineteenth century?

Q Between 1871 and 1914, two major domestic political goals involved the achievement of liberal practices and the growth of political democracy. To what extent were these realized in Great Britain, France, Germany, Austria-Hungary, and Russia?

Key Terms

joint-stock investment bank (p. 543)
proletariat (p. 546)
socialism (p. 548)
utopian socialists (p. 548)
trade unions (p. 549)
Marxism (p. 553)
class struggle (p. 553)
revisionism (p. 553)
revolutionary socialism (p. 553)
legitimacy (p. 555)
conservatism (p. 555)
intervention (p. 555)

liberalism (p. 555)
Realpolitik (p. 562)
Ausgleich (p. 563)
mass politics (p. 565)
anti-Semitism (p. 566)
Westernizers (p. 566)
Slavophiles (p. 567)
anarchists (p. 567)

Suggested Reading

THE INDUSTRIAL REVOLUTION AND ITS IMPACT   A good introduction to the Industrial Revolution is **J. Horn, The *Industrial Revolution*** (Westport, Conn., 2007). On the role of the British, see **K. Morgan, *The Birth of Industrial Britain: Social Change, 1750–1850*** (New York, 2004). A work on female labor patterns is **J. Rendall, *Women in an Industrializing Society: England, 1750–1880*** (Oxford, 2002). For a global approach to the modern economy, see **K. Pomeranz, *The Great Deliverance: China, Europe, and the Making of the Modern World Economy*** (Princeton, N.J., 2002).

THE GROWTH OF INDUSTRIAL PROSPERITY   The impact of the new technology on European thought is imaginatively discussed in **S. Kern, *The Culture of Time and Space, 1880–1918***, rev. ed. (Cambridge, Mass., 2003). On Marx, the standard work is **D. McLellan, *Karl Marx: His Life and Thought***, 4th ed. (New York, 2006).

THE GROWTH OF NATIONALISM, 1814–1848   For a good survey of the nineteenth century, see **R. Gildea, *Barricades and Borders: Europe, 1800–1914***, 3rd ed. (Oxford, 2003). Also valuable is **T. C. W. Blanning, ed., *Nineteenth Century: Europe, 1789–1914*** (Oxford, 2000). For a survey of the period 1814–1848, see **M. Lyons, *Postrevolutionary Europe, 1815–1856*** (New York, 2006). The best introduction to the revolutions of 1848 is **J. Sperber, *The European Revolutions, 1848–1851***, 2nd ed. (New York, 2005).

NATIONAL UNIFICATION AND THE NATIONAL STATE, 1848–1871   The unification of Italy can be examined in **B. Derek** and **E. F. Biagini, *The Risorgimento and the Unification of Italy***, 2nd ed. (London, 2002). The unification of Germany can be pursued first in a biography of Bismarck, **E. Feuchtwanger, *Bismarck*** (London, 2002). Louis Napoleon's role can be examined in **J. F. McMillan, *Napoleon III*** (New York, 1991). On the Austrian Empire, see **R. Okey, *The Habsburg Monarchy*** (New York, 2001). Imperial Russia is covered in **T. Chapman, *Imperial Russia, 1801–1905*** (London, 2001). On Victorian Britain, see **W. L. Arnstein, *Queen Victoria*** (New York, 2005).

THE EUROPEAN STATE, 1871–1914   The domestic politics of the period can be examined in the general works listed above. See also **J. Sperber, *Europe 1850–1914*** (New York, 2009).

Chapter Notes

1. Quotations in E. R. Pike, *Human Documents of the Industrial Revolution in Britain* (London, 1966), pp. 314, 343.
2. Ibid., p. 315.
3. C. Dickens, *The Old Curiosity Shop* (New York, 2000), p. 340. Originally published in 1840–1841.
4. K. Marx and F. Engels, *The Communist Manifesto* (Harmondsworth, England, 1967), p. 80. Originally published in 1848.
5. Ibid., pp. 91, 94.
6. Quoted in L. L. Snyder, ed., *Documents of German History* (New Brunswick, N.J., 1958), p. 202.
7. Quoted in S. Galai, *The Liberation Movement in Russia, 1900–1905* (Cambridge, 1973), p. 26.

MindTap is a fully online, highly personalized learning experience built upon Cengage Learning content. MindTap combines student learning tools—readings, multimedia, activities, and assessments—into a singular Learning Path that guides students through their course.

The Americas and Society and Culture in the West

A portrait of Toussaint L'Ouverture, leader of the Haitian independence movement

CHAPTER OUTLINE AND FOCUS QUESTIONS

Latin America in the Nineteenth and Early Twentieth Centuries

Q What role did liberalism and nationalism play in Latin America between 1800 and 1870? What were the major economic, social, and political trends in Latin America in the late nineteenth and early twentieth centuries?

The North American Neighbors: The United States and Canada

Q What role did nationalism and liberalism play in the United States and Canada between 1800 and 1870? What economic, social, and political trends were evident in the United States and Canada between 1870 and 1914?

The Emergence of Mass Society in the West

Q What is meant by the term *mass society*, and what were its main characteristics?

Cultural Life: Romanticism and Realism in the Western World

Q What were the main characteristics of Romanticism and Realism?

Toward the Modern Consciousness: Intellectual and Cultural Developments

Q What intellectual and cultural developments in the late nineteenth and early twentieth centuries "opened the way to a modern consciousness," and how did this consciousness differ from earlier worldviews?

CRITICAL THINKING

Q In what ways were the intellectual and cultural developments in the Western world between 1800 and 1914 related to the economic, social, and political developments?

CONNECTIONS TO TODAY

Q In the late nineteenth century, new work opportunities for women emerged, but many middle- and upper-class women were still expected to remain at home. What are the new opportunities and challenges for women today, and how do they compare with those in the nineteenth century?

NATIONALISM—one of the major forces for change in Europe in the nineteenth century—also affected Latin America as the colonial peoples there overthrew their Spanish and Portuguese masters and began the process of creating new national states. An unusual revolution in Haiti preceded the main independence movements. François-Dominique Toussaint L'Ouverture (frahn-SWAH-doh-muh-NEEK too-SANH loo-vayr-TOOR), the grandson of an African king, was born a slave in Saint-Domingue (san doh-MAYNG)—the western third of the island of Hispaniola, a French sugar colony—in 1746. Educated by his godfather, Toussaint was able to amass a small private fortune through his own talents and the generosity of his French master. When black slaves in Saint-Domingue, inspired by news of the French

Revolution, revolted in 1791, Toussaint became their leader. For years, Toussaint and his ragtag army struck at the French. By 1801, after his army had come to control Saint-Domingue, Toussaint assumed the role of ruler and issued a constitution that freed all slaves.

But Napoleon Bonaparte refused to accept Toussaint's control of France's richest colony and sent a French army of 23,000 men under General Leclerc (luh-KLAHR), his brother-in-law, to crush the rebellion. Although yellow fever took its toll on the French army, the superior size and arms of the French forces enabled them to gain the upper hand. Toussaint was tricked into surrendering in 1802 with Leclerc's promise: "You will not find a more sincere friend than myself." What a friend! Toussaint was arrested, put in chains, and shipped to France, where he died a year later in a dungeon. The western part of Hispaniola, now called Haiti, however, became the first independent state in Latin America when Toussaint's lieutenants drove out the French forces in 1804. Haiti was only one of a number of places in the Americas where new nations were formed during the nineteenth century. Indeed, nation building was prominent in North America as the United States and Canada expanded.

As national states in both the Western Hemisphere and Europe were evolving in the nineteenth century, significant changes were occurring in society and culture. The rapid economic changes of the nineteenth century led to the emergence of mass society in the Western world, which meant improvements for the lower classes, who benefited from the extension of voting rights, a better standard of living, and universal education. The coming of mass society also created new roles for the governments of nation-states, which now fostered national loyalty, created mass armies by conscription, and took more responsibility for public health and housing measures in their cities. Cultural and intellectual changes also paralleled these social developments, and after 1870, Western philosophers, writers, and artists began exploring modern cultural expressions that questioned traditional ideas and increasingly provoked a crisis of confidence. ◄

Latin America in the Nineteenth and Early Twentieth Centuries

 FOCUS QUESTIONS: What role did liberalism and nationalism play in Latin America between 1800 and 1870? What were the major economic, social, and political trends in Latin America in the late nineteenth and early twentieth centuries?

The Spanish and Portuguese colonial empires in Latin America had been integrated into the traditional monarchical structure of Europe for centuries. When that structure was challenged, first by the ideas of the Enlightenment and then by the upheavals of the Napoleonic era, Latin America encountered the possibility of change. How it responded to that possibility, however, was determined in part by conditions unique to the region.

The Wars for Independence

By the end of the eighteenth century, the ideas of the Enlightenment and the new political ideals stemming from the successful revolution in North America were beginning to influence the creole elites (descendants of Europeans who became permanent inhabitants of Latin America). The principles of the equality of all people in the eyes of the law, free trade, and a free press proved very attractive. Sons of creoles, such as Simón Bolívar (see-MOHN boh-LEE-var) (1783–1830) and José de San Martín (hoh-SAY day san mar-TEEN) (1778–1850), who became leaders of the independence movement, even went to European universities, where they absorbed the ideas of the Enlightenment. These Latin American elites, joined by a growing class of merchants, especially resented the domination of their trade by Spain and Portugal.

NATIONALISTIC REVOLTS IN LATIN AMERICA The creole elites soon began to use their new ideas to denounce the rule of the Iberian monarchs and the peninsulars (Spanish and Portuguese officials who resided in Latin America for political and economic gain). As Bolívar said in 1815, "It would be easier to have the two continents meet than to reconcile the spirits of Spain and America."[1] Bolívar reflected the growing nativism among the creole elites and their resentment of the Spanish peninsulars, who dominated Latin America and drained the people of their wealth. At the beginning of the nineteenth century, Napoleon's continental wars provided the creoles with an opportunity for change. When Bonaparte toppled the monarchies of Spain and Portugal, the authority of the Spaniards and Portuguese in their colonial empires was weakened, and between 1807 and 1825, a series of revolts enabled most of Latin America to become independent.

As described in the chapter-opening vignette, the first revolt was actually a successful slave rebellion. Led by Toussaint L'Ouverture (1746–1803), the revolt resulted in the formation of Haiti as the first independent postcolonial state in Latin America in 1804.

In 1810, Mexico, too, experienced a revolt, fueled initially by the desire of the creole elites to overthrow the rule of the peninsulars. The first real hero of the Mexican independence movement, however, was Miguel Hidalgo y Costilla (mee-GEL ee-THAHL-goh ee kahs-TEE-yuh), a parish priest in a small village about 100 miles from Mexico City. Hidalgo, who had studied the French Revolution, roused the local Indians and mestizos, many of whom were suffering from a major famine in 1810, to free themselves from the Spanish: "My children, this day comes to us as a new dispensation. Are you ready to receive it? Will you be free? Will you make the effort to recover from the hated Spaniards the lands stolen from your forefathers three hundred years ago?"[2] On September 16, 1810, a crowd of Indians and mestizos, armed with clubs, machetes, and a few guns, quickly formed a mob army and attacked the Spaniards, shouting, "Long live independence and death to the Spaniards." But Hidalgo was not a good organizer, and his forces were soon crushed. A military court sentenced Hidalgo to death, but his memory lived on. In fact, September 16, the first day of the uprising, is celebrated as Mexico's Independence Day.

The participation of Indians and mestizos in the revolt against Spanish control frightened both creoles and peninsulars in Mexico. Fearful of the masses, they cooperated in defeating the popular revolutionary forces. The elites—both creoles and peninsulars—then decided to overthrow Spanish rule as a way of preserving their own power. They selected a creole military leader, Augustín de Iturbide (ah-goo-STEEN day ee-tur-BEE-day), as their leader and the first emperor of Mexico in 1821. Simón Bolívar said of Iturbide that he had become emperor "by the grace of God and bayonets." The new government fostered neither political nor economic changes, and it soon became apparent that Mexican independence benefited primarily the creole elites.

Independence movements elsewhere in Latin America were likewise the work of elites—primarily creoles—who overthrew Spanish rule and set up new governments that they could dominate. The masses of people—Indians, blacks, mestizos, and mulattoes—gained little from the revolts. José de San Martín of Argentina and Simón Bolívar of Venezuela, the leaders of the independence movement who were hailed as the liberators of South America, were both members of the creole elite.

THE EFFORTS OF BOLÍVAR AND SAN MARTÍN Simón Bolívar has long been regarded as the George Washington of Latin America. Born into a wealthy Venezuelan family, he was introduced as a young man to the ideas of the Enlightenment. While in Rome in 1805 to witness the coronation of Napoleon as king of Italy, he committed himself to free his people from Spanish control. He vowed, "I swear before the God of my fathers, by my fathers themselves, by my honor and by my country, that my arm shall not rest nor my mind be at peace until I have broken the chains that bind me by the will and power of Spain."[3] When he returned to South America, Bolívar began to lead the bitter struggle for independence in Venezuela as well as other parts of northern South America. Although he was acclaimed as the "liberator" of Venezuela in 1813 by the people, it was not until 1821 that he definitively defeated Spanish forces there. He went on to liberate Colombia, Ecuador, and Peru. Already in 1819, he had become president of Venezuela, at the time part of a federation that included Colombia and Ecuador. Bolívar was well aware of the difficulties in establishing stable republican governments in Latin America (see the box "Simón Bolívar on Government in Latin America" on p. 575).

While Bolívar was busy liberating northern South America from the Spanish, José de San Martín was concentrating his efforts on the southern part of the continent. The son of a Spanish army officer in Argentina, San Martín himself went to

The Liberators of South America. José de San Martín and Simón Bolívar are hailed as the leaders of the South American independence movement. In the painting on the left, by Theodore Géricault (zhay-rih-KOH), a French Romantic painter, San Martín is shown leading his troops at the Battle of Chacabuco in Chile in 1817. The painting at the right shows Bolívar leading his troops across the Andes in 1823 to fight in Peru. This depiction of impeccably uniformed troops moving in perfect formation through the snow of the Andes, by the Chilean artist Franco Gomez, is, of course, highly unrealistic.

Simón Bolívar on Government in Latin America

POLITICS & GOVERNMENT

SIMÓN BOLÍVAR IS ACCLAIMED as the man who liberated Latin America from Spanish control. His interest in history and the ideas of the Enlightenment also led him to speculate on how Latin American nations would be governed after their freedom was obtained. This selection is taken from a letter that he wrote to the English governor of Jamaica.

Simón Bolívar, *The Jamaica Letter*

It is … difficult to foresee the future fate of the New World, to set down its political principles, or to prophesy what manner of government it will adopt…. We inhabit a world apart, separated by broad seas. We are young in the ways of almost all the arts and sciences, although in a certain manner, we are old in the ways of civilized society…. But we scarcely retain a vestige of what once was; we are, moreover, neither Indian nor European, but a species midway between the legitimate proprietors of this country and the Spanish usurpers. In short, though Americans by birth we derive our rights from Europe, and we have to assert these rights against the rights of the natives, and at the same time we must defend ourselves against the invaders. This places us in a most extraordinary and involved situation….

The role of the inhabitants of the American hemisphere has for centuries been purely passive. Politically they were nonexistent. We are still in a position lower than slavery, and therefore it is more difficult for us to rise to the enjoyment of freedom…. States are slaves because of either the nature or the misuse of their constitutions; a people is therefore enslaved when the government, by its nature or its vices, infringes on and usurps the rights of the citizen or subject. Applying these principles, we find that America was denied not only its freedom but even an active and effective tyranny. Under absolutism there are no recognized limits to the exercise of governmental powers….

So negative was our existence that I can find nothing comparable in any other civilized society, examine as I may the entire history of time and the politics of all nations. Is it not an outrage and a violation of human rights to expect a land so splendidly endowed, so vast, rich, and populous, to remain merely passive?…

Despite the convictions of history, South Americans have made efforts to obtain liberal, even perfect, institutions…. But are we capable of maintaining in proper balance the difficult charge of a republic? Is it conceivable that a newly emancipated people can soar to the heights of liberty …? Such a marvel is inconceivable and without precedent. There is no reasonable probability to bolster our hopes.

More than anyone, I desire to see America fashioned into the greatest nation in the world, greatest not so much by virtue of her area and wealth as by her freedom and glory…. [However], I cannot persuade myself that the New World can, at the moment, be organized as a great republic. Since it is impossible, I dare not desire it; yet much less do I desire to have all America a monarchy because this plan is not only impracticable but also impossible. Wrongs now existing could not be righted, and our emancipation would be fruitless. The American states need the care of paternal governments to heal the sores and wounds of despotism and war.

What problems did Bolívar foresee for Spanish America's political future? Do you think he believed in democracy? Why or why not?

Source: From Simón Bolívar, *Selected Writings*, ed. H. A. Bierck, trans. L. Berrand (New York, 1951), pp. 106, 108, 112–114.

Spain and pursued a military career in the Spanish army. In 1811, after serving twenty-two years, he learned of the liberation movement in his native Argentina, abandoned his military career in Spain, and returned to his homeland in March 1812. Argentina had already been freed from Spanish control, but San Martín believed that the Spaniards must be removed from all of South America if any nation was to remain free. In January 1817, he led his forces over the high Andes Mountains, an amazing feat in itself. Two-thirds of their pack mules and horses died during the difficult journey. Many of the soldiers suffered from lack of oxygen and severe cold while crossing mountain passes that were more than 2 miles above sea level. The arrival of San Martín's troops in Chile completely surprised the Spaniards, whose forces were routed at the Battle of Chacabuco (chahk-ah-BOO-koh) on February 12, 1817. One of San Martín's military leaders was Bernardo O'Higgins, a fierce proponent of Chilean independence, who was now made "supreme dictator" of Chile.

In 1821, San Martín moved on to Lima, Peru, the center of Spanish authority. Convinced that he was unable to complete the liberation of all of Peru, San Martín welcomed the arrival of Bolívar and his forces. As he wrote to Bolívar, "For me it would have been the height of happiness to end the war of independence under the orders of a general to whom [South] America owes its freedom. Destiny orders it otherwise, and one must resign oneself to it."[4] Highly disappointed, San Martín left South America for Europe, where he remained until his death outside Paris in 1850. Meanwhile, Bolívar took on the task of crushing the last significant Spanish army at Ayacucho (ah-ya-KOO-choh) on December 9, 1824. By then, Peru, Uruguay, Paraguay, Colombia, Venezuela, Argentina, Bolivia, and Chile had all become free states (see Map 20.1). In 1823, the Central American states became independent and in 1838–1839 divided into five republics (Guatemala, El Salvador, Honduras, Costa Rica, and Nicaragua). Earlier, in 1822, the prince regent of Brazil had declared Brazil's independence from Portugal.

MAP 20.1 Latin America in the First Half of the Nineteenth Century.

Latin American colonies took advantage of Spain's weakness during the Napoleonic wars to fight for independence, beginning with Argentina in 1810 and spreading throughout the region over the next decade with the help of leaders like Simón Bolívar and José de San Martín.

Q *How many South American countries are sources of rivers that feed the Amazon, and roughly what percentage of the continent is contained within the Amazon's watershed?*

Simón Bolívar, who had accomplished so much as the liberator of South America, grew increasingly pessimistic about his achievements. Shortly before his death from tuberculosis in 1830, at the age of forty-seven, he wrote to one of his Venezuelan generals, "You know I have been in command for twenty years; and … I have derived only a few sure conclusions: first, [South] America is ungovernable;… fourth, this country will fall without fail into the hands of an unbridled multitude, to pass later to petty, almost imperceptible, tyrants of all colors and races."[5]

INDEPENDENCE AND THE MONROE DOCTRINE In the early 1820s, only one major threat remained to the newly won independence of the Latin American states. Reveling in their success in crushing rebellions in Spain and Italy, the victorious continental powers favored the use of troops to restore Spanish control in Latin America. This time, Britain's opposition to intervention prevailed. Eager to gain access to an entire continent for investment and trade, the British proposed joint action with the United States against European interference in Latin America. Distrustful of British motives, President James Monroe acted alone in 1823, guaranteeing the independence of the new Latin American nations and warning against any further European intervention in the Americas under what is known as the Monroe Doctrine. Even more important to Latin American independence than American words was

Britain's navy. All of the continental powers were reluctant to challenge British naval power, which stood between Latin America and any European invasion force.

The Difficulties of Nation Building

As Simón Bolívar had foreseen, the new Latin American nations, most of which began as republics, faced a number of serious problems between 1830 and 1870. The wars for independence themselves had resulted in a staggering loss of population, property, and livestock. Despite the Monroe Doctrine, fear of European intervention persisted, and disputes arose between nations over their precise boundaries. Poor transportation and communication systems fostered regionalism and made national unity difficult.

POLITICAL DIFFICULTIES The new nations of Latin America established republican governments, but they had had no experience in ruling themselves. Due to the insecurities prevalent after independence, strong leaders known as **caudillos** (kah-DEEL-yohz *or* kow-THEEL-yohz) came to power. Although caudillos could be found at both the regional and national levels, national caudillos were generally one of two types. One group, who supported the elites, consisted of autocrats who controlled (and often abused) state revenues, centralized power, and kept the new national states together. Sometimes they were also modernizers who built roads and canals, ports, and schools. Others were destructive, such as Antonio Lopez de Santa Anna (ahn-TOHN-yoh LOH-pes day SAHN-tuh AH-nah), who ruled Mexico from 1829 to 1855. He misused state funds, curtailed reforms, created chaos, and helped lose some of Mexico's territory to the United States. Caudillos were usually supported by the Catholic Church, the rural aristocracy, and the army—which emerged from the wars of independence as a powerful political force that often made and deposed governments. Many caudillos, in fact, were former army leaders.

In contrast, other caudillos were supported by the masses, became extremely popular, and served as instruments for radical change. Juan Manuel de Rosas (WAHN mahn-WEL day ROH-sas), for example, who led Argentina from 1829 to 1852, became very popular by favoring Argentine interests against foreigners. Rafael Carrera (rah-fah-EL kuh-RERR-uh), who ruled Guatemala from 1839 to 1865, supported native Indian cultures and pursued a policy of land redistribution to aid the natives. But he was disliked by the elites, who wanted to Europeanize the economy and Guatemalan culture, and his efforts were undone by his successor, Justo Rufino Barrios (HOO-stoh roo-FEE-noh BAHR-yohs) (1873–1885). A caudillo who was supported by the elites, Barrios pushed the economy to coffee production and forced the Indians to give up their lands and become wage laborers to serve the interests of large plantation owners.

ECONOMIC PATTERNS Although political independence brought economic independence, old patterns of capital flows and trade were quickly reestablished. Instead of Spain and Portugal, Great Britain now dominated the Latin American economy. British merchants arrived in large numbers, and British investors poured in funds, especially into the mining industry. Since Latin America served as a source of raw materials and foodstuffs for the industrializing nations of Europe and the United States, exports—especially wheat, tobacco, wool, sugar, coffee, and hides—to the North Atlantic countries increased noticeably. At the same time, finished consumer goods, especially textiles, were imported in increasing quantities, causing a decline in industrial production in Latin America. The emphasis on exporting raw materials and importing finished products ensured the ongoing domination of the Latin American economy by foreigners.

SOCIAL CONDITIONS A fundamental underlying problem for all of the new Latin American nations was the persistent domination of society by the landed elites. Large estates remained an important aspect of Latin America's economic and social life (see the box "A Radical Critique of the Land Problem in Mexico" on p. 578). After independence, the size of these estates expanded even more. By 1848, the Sánchez Navarro (SAHN-ches nuh-VAH-roh) family in Mexico owned seventeen haciendas (hah-see-EN-duhz), or plantations, covering 16 million acres. Governments facilitated this process by selling off church lands, public domains, and the lands of Indian communities. In Argentina, five hundred people bought 21 million acres of public land. Estates were often so large that they could not be farmed efficiently. As one Latin American newspaper put it, "The huge fortunes have the unfortunate tendency to grow even larger, and their owners possess vast tracts of land, which lie fallow and abandoned. Their greed for land does not equal their ability to use it intelligently and actively."[6]

Land remained the basis of wealth, social prestige, and political power throughout the nineteenth century. The Latin American elites tended to identify with European standards of progress, which worked to their benefit, while the masses gained little. Landed elites ran governments, controlled courts, and maintained the system of debt peonage that provided large landowners with a supply of cheap labor. These landowners made enormous profits by concentrating on specialized crops for export, such as coffee, while the masses, left without land to grow basic food crops, lived in dire poverty.

CHURCH AND STATE Conflicts between church and state were also common in the new nations. The Catholic Church had enormous landholdings in Latin America and through its amassed wealth exercised great power. After independence, clerics often took positions in the new governments and wielded considerable influence. Throughout Latin America, a division arose between liberals who wished to curtail the temporal powers of the church and conservatives who hoped to maintain all of the church's privileges and prerogatives. In Mexico, this division even led to civil war—the bloody War of Reform fought between 1858 and 1861—in which Catholic clergy and the military lined up against a liberal government.

A Radical Critique of the Land Problem in Mexico

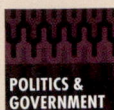

POLITICS & GOVERNMENT

THE DOMINATION OF MEXICO by elites who owned large estates remained a serious problem throughout the nineteenth century. Conservatives, of course, favored the great estates as the foundation stones of their own political power, while even liberals shied away from any extremist attack on property rights. Nevertheless, there were some strong voices of protest, as this excerpt from a speech delivered in 1857 by the social liberal Ponciano Arriaga (pahn-SYAHN-oh ah-RYAH-guh) demonstrates. Arriaga's appeal went unheeded; conservatives called him a "communist."

Ponciano Arriaga, Speech to the Constitutional Convention of 1856–1857

One of the most deeply rooted evils of our country—an evil that merits the close attention of legislators when they frame our fundamental law—is the monstrous division of landed property.

While a few individuals possess immense areas of uncultivated land that could support millions of people, the great majority of Mexicans languish in a terrible poverty and are denied property, homes, and work....

There are Mexican landowners who occupy (if one can give that name to a purely imaginary act) an extent of land greater than the areas of some of our sovereign states, greater even than that of one of several European states.

In this vast area, much of which lies idle, deserted, abandoned, awaiting the arms and labor of men, live four or five million Mexicans who know no other industry than agriculture, yet are without land or the means to work it, and who cannot emigrate in the hope of bettering their fortunes. They must either vegetate in idleness, turn to banditry, or accept the yoke of a landed monopolist who subjects them to intolerable conditions of life....

How can a hungry, naked, miserable people practice popular government? How can we proclaim the equal rights of men and leave the majority of the nation in conditions worse than those of helots or pariahs? How can we condemn slavery in words, while the lot of most of our fellow citizens is more grievous than that of the black slaves of Cuba or the United States?...

With some honorable exceptions, the rich landowners of Mexico, or the administrators who represent them, resemble the feudal lords of the Middle Ages. On his seignorial land,... the landowner makes and executes laws, administers justice and exercises civil power, imposes taxes and fines, has his own jails and irons, metes out punishments and tortures, monopolizes commerce, and forbids the conduct without his permission of any business but that of the estate. The judges or officials who exercise on the hacienda the powers attached to public authority are usually the master's servants or tenants, his retainers, incapable of enforcing any law but the will of the master.

An astounding variety of devices are employed to exploit the peons or tenants, to turn a profit from their sweat and labor. They are compelled to work without pay even on days traditionally set aside for rest. They must accept rotten seeds or sick animals whose cost is charged to their miserable wages.... They must make all their purchases on the hacienda, using tokens or paper money that do not circulate elsewhere. At certain seasons of the year they are assigned articles of poor quality, whose price is set by the owner ..., constituting a debt which they can never repay. They are forbidden to use pastures and woods, firewood and water, or even the wild fruit of the fields, save with the express permission of the master. In fine, they are subject to a completely unlimited and irresponsible power.

What serious problems for Latin American politics were created by the concentration of land ownership in the hands of the elites? How did such large estates affect the structure of Latin American societies?

Source: Excerpt from *Latin American Civilization* by Benjamin Keen, ed. (Boston: Houghton Mifflin, 1974), vol. 2, pp. 270–272.

Tradition and Change in the Latin American Economy and Society

After 1870, Latin America began to experience rapid economic growth based to a large extent on the export of a few basic items, such as wheat and beef from Argentina, coffee from Brazil, nitrates from Chile, coffee and bananas from Central America, and sugar and silver from Peru. Exports from Argentina doubled between 1873 and 1893; Mexican exports quadrupled between 1877 and 1900. These foodstuffs and raw materials were generally exchanged for finished goods—textiles, machines, and luxury goods—from Europe and the United States. With economic growth came a boom in foreign investment. Between 1870 and 1913, British investments—mostly in railroads, mining, and public utilities—grew from 85 million pounds to 757 million pounds, which constituted two-thirds of all foreign investment in Latin America. As Latin Americans struggled to create more balanced economies after 1900, they focused on increasing industrialization, especially in textiles, food processing, and construction materials.

Nevertheless, the growth of the Latin American economy continued to come largely from the export of raw materials, and economic modernization in the region simply added to its growing dependence on the capitalist nations of the West. Modernization was basically a surface feature of Latin American society, where, for the most part, old patterns still prevailed. Rural elites continued to dominate their estates and their rural workers. Although slavery was abolished by 1888, former slaves and their descendants remained at the bottom of their society. The Indians remained poverty-stricken, debt servitude was still a way of life, and the inhabitants continued to be economically dependent on foreigners. Despite its economic growth, Latin America was still an underdeveloped region of the world.

The prosperity that arose from Latin America's export-based economy had both social and political repercussions. One result was the modernization of the elites, who were determined to pursue their vision of progress. Large landowners sought to rationalize their production methods in order to increase their profits. Consequently, cattle ranchers in Argentina and coffee barons in Brazil became more aggressive entrepreneurs.

Another result of the new prosperity was some growth in the middle sectors of Latin American society—lawyers, merchants, shopkeepers, businessmen, schoolteachers, professors, bureaucrats, and military officers. These sectors, which made up only 5 to 10 percent of the population, depending on the country, were hardly large enough in numbers to constitute a true middle class. Nevertheless, after 1900, the middle sectors continued to expand. Regardless of the country, they shared some common characteristics. They lived in the cities, sought education and decent incomes, and increasingly looked to the United States as a model to emulate, especially in regard to industrialization and education.

The middle sectors in Latin America sought liberal reform, not revolution, and the elites found it relatively easy to co-opt them by giving them the right to vote. Although the middle sectors were not large and remained dependent on the agrarian sector of the economy, in some places they were able to enhance their political power. In Costa Rica, the middle sectors played an important role in maintaining a constitutional government from 1882 to 1917. An alliance of the middle sectors with the working classes won control of Chile's government in 1918. In Argentina, the extension of suffrage to the middle sectors in 1912 enabled a middle party to win power in 1916.

As Latin American exports increased, so did the working class, and that in turn led to the growth of labor unions, especially after 1914. Radical unions often advocated the use of the general strike as an instrument for change. By and large, however, the governing elites succeeded in stifling the political influence of the workers by restricting their right to vote. The need for industrial labor also led Latin American countries to encourage immigration from Europe. Between 1880 and 1914, 3 million Europeans, primarily Italians and Spaniards, settled in Argentina. More than 100,000 Europeans, mostly Italian, Portuguese, and Spanish, arrived in Brazil each year between 1891 and 1900.

As in Europe and the United States, industrialization led to urbanization, evident in both the emergence of new cities and the rapid growth of old ones. Buenos Aires (the "Paris" of

Buenos Aires. Buenos Aires is called the "Paris" of South America because of its use of neoclassical architecture influenced by European practices. The rapid urbanization of Buenos Aires is captured in this 1885 photograph of the Avenue Callao, which was designed to resemble the grand boulevards of Paris.

South America) had 750,000 inhabitants by 1900 and 2 million by 1914—a fourth of Argentina's population. By that time, urban dwellers made up 53 percent of Argentina's population overall. Brazil and Chile also witnessed a dramatic increase in their urban populations.

Political Change in Latin America

Latin America also experienced a political transformation after 1870. Large landowners began to take a more direct interest in national politics, sometimes actually becoming involved in governing. In Argentina and Chile, for example, landholding elites controlled the government, and although they produced constitutions similar to those of the United States and the European nations, they were careful to restrict voting rights to ensure that they would maintain power.

In some countries, large landowners relied on a dictator to protect their interests. José de la Cruz Porfirio Díaz (hoh-SAY day lah KROOZ por-FEER-yoh DEE-ahs), who ruled Mexico from 1876 to 1910, established a conservative, centralized government with the support of the army, foreign capitalists, large landowners, and the Catholic Church. But there were forces for change in Mexico that led to a revolution in 1910.

During Díaz's dictatorial regime, the real wages of the working class declined. Moreover, 95 percent of the rural population owned no land, while about a thousand families owned almost all of Mexico. When a liberal landowner, Francisco Madero (frahn-SEES-koh muh-DERR-oh), forced Díaz from power, he opened the door to a wider revolution. Madero's ineffectiveness triggered a demand for agrarian reform led by Emiliano Zapata (eh-mee-LYAH-noh zup-PAH-tuh), who aroused the masses of landless peasants and began to seize the haciendas of the wealthy landholders

Zapata and Land Reform

POLITICS & GOVERNMENT

EMILIANO ZAPATA WAS A SHARECROPPER on a sugar plantation in Morelos (moh-RAY-lohs), a mountainous state in southern Mexico. Using the slogan "Land and Liberty," Zapata formed a guerrilla band of Indians and led them in revolt against the haciendas of southern Mexico, burning the houses and sugar refineries. Convinced that the new president of Mexico, Francisco Madero, would not go far enough with land reform, Zapata issued his own plan, the Plan of Ayala (ah-yah-LUH), from which these excerpts are taken.

The Plan of Ayala

Liberating Plan of the sons of the State of Morelos, affiliated with the Insurgent Army which [demands] the reforms … it … believed proper to [aid] in benefit of the Mexican Fatherland.

We who undersign, constituted in a revolutionary junta to sustain and carry out the promises which the revolution of November 20, 1910, just past, made to the country, declare solemnly before the face of the civilized world which judges us … propositions which we have formulated to end the tyranny which oppresses us.…

1. Taking into account that the so-called Chief of the liberating Revolution of Mexico, Don Francisco I. Madero, through lack of integrity and the highest weakness, did not carry to a happy end the revolution which gloriously he initiated with the help of God and the people, since he left standing most of the governing powers and corrupted elements of oppression of the dictatorial government of Porfirio Díaz,… we declare the aforementioned Francisco I. Madero inept at realizing the promises of the revolution of which he was the author, because he has betrayed the principles with which he tricked the will of the people and was able to get into power.…

4. The Revolutionary Junta of the State of Morelos manifests to the Nation under formal oath: that it makes its own the plan of San Luis Potosí [Madero's revolutionary plan], with the additions which are expressed below in benefit of the oppressed peoples, and it will make itself the defender of the principles it defends until victory or death.…

6. As an additional part of the plan, we invoke, we give notice: that [regarding] the fields, timber, and water which the landlords or bosses have usurped, the towns or citizens who have the titles corresponding to those properties will immediately enter into possession of that real estate of which they have been despoiled by the bad faith of our oppressors, maintain at any cost with arms in hand the mentioned possession.…

7. In virtue of the fact that the immense majority of Mexican towns and citizens are owners of no more than the land they walk on, suffering the horrors of poverty without being able to improve their social condition in any way or to dedicate themselves to Industry or Agriculture, because land, timber, and water are monopolized in a few hands, for this cause there will be expropriated the third part of those monopolies from the powerful proprietors of them, with prior indemnization, in order that the towns and citizens of Mexico may obtain colonies and foundations for towns, or fields for sowing or laboring, the Mexicans' lack of prosperity and well-being may improve in all and for all.

8. The landlords or bosses who oppose the present plan directly or indirectly, their goods will be nationalized and the two-third parts which [otherwise would] belong to them will go for indemnizations of war, pensions for widows and orphans of the victims who succumb in the struggle for the present plan.…

Why did the hacienda system and its abuses prompt Zapata to issue the Plan of Ayala? Why did both his origins and this proposal endear him to the common people of Mexico?

Source: John Womack, *Zapata and the Mexican Revolution* (New York: Knopf, 1969), pp. 400–404.

(see the box "Zapata and Land Reform" above). The ensuing revolution caused untold destruction to the Mexican economy. Finally, a new constitution in 1917 established a strong presidency, initiated land reform policies, established limits on foreign investors, and set an agenda for social welfare for workers. The revolution also led to an outpouring of nationalistic pride. Intellectuals and artists in particular sought to capture what was unique about Mexico, with special emphasis on its Indian past. As the Mexican minister of education said, "Tired, disgusted of all this copied civilization,… we wish to cease being Europe's spiritual colonies."

By this time, a new power had begun to wield its influence over Latin America. At the beginning of the twentieth century, the United States, emerging as a world power, increasingly interfered in the affairs of its southern neighbors. As a result of

CHRONOLOGY Latin America	
Revolution in Mexico	1810
Bolívar and San Martín free most of South America	1810–1824
Augustín de Iturbide becomes emperor of Mexico	1821
Brazil gains independence from Portugal	1822
Monroe Doctrine	1823
Rule of Porfirio Díaz in Mexico	1876–1910
Mexican Revolution begins	1910

the Spanish-American War (1898), Cuba became an American protectorate, and Puerto Rico was annexed outright. American investments in Latin America soon followed; so did American resolve to protect these investments. Between 1898 and 1934, U.S. military forces were sent to Cuba, Mexico, Guatemala, Honduras, Nicaragua, Panama, Colombia, Haiti, and the Dominican Republic to protect American interests. Some expeditions remained for many years; U.S. Marines were in Haiti from 1915 to 1934, and Nicaragua was occupied from 1909 to 1933. At the same time, the United States became the chief foreign investor in Latin America.

North American Neighbors: The United States and Canada

 FOCUS QUESTIONS: What role did nationalism and liberalism play in the United States and Canada between 1800 and 1870? What economic, social, and political trends were evident in the United States and Canada between 1870 and 1914?

Whereas Latin America had been colonized by Spain and Portugal, the colonies established in North America were part of the British Empire. Although they gained their freedom from the British at different times, both the United States and Canada emerged as independent and prosperous nations whose political systems owed much to British political thought. In the nineteenth century, both the United States and Canada faced difficult obstacles in achieving national unity.

The Growth of the United States

The U.S. Constitution, ratified in 1789, committed the United States to two of the major influences of the first half of the nineteenth century, liberalism and nationalism. Initially, divisions over the power of the federal government vis-à-vis the individual states challenged this constitutional commitment to national unity. Bitter conflict erupted between the Federalists and the Republicans. Led by Alexander Hamilton (1757–1804), the Federalists favored a financial program that would establish a strong central government. The Republicans, guided by Thomas Jefferson (1743–1826) and James Madison (1751–1836), feared centralization and its consequences for popular liberties. These divisions were intensified by European rivalries because the Federalists were pro-British and the Republicans pro-French. The successful conclusion of the War of 1812 brought an end to the Federalists, who had opposed the war, while the surge of national feeling generated by the war served to heal the nation's divisions. (Over the next decades, the Republicans of this era gave rise to the Democratic Party, while a new Republican Party was formed in the 1850s as an antislavery party.)

Another strong force for national unity came from the Supreme Court while John Marshall (1755–1835) was chief justice from 1801 to 1835. Marshall made the Supreme Court into an important national institution by asserting the right of the Court to overrule an act of Congress if the Court found it to be in violation of the Constitution. Under Marshall, the Supreme Court contributed further to establishing the supremacy of the national government by curbing the actions of state courts and legislatures.

The election of Andrew Jackson (1767–1845) as president in 1828 opened a new era in American politics, the era of mass democracy. The electorate was expanded by dropping property qualifications; by the 1830s, suffrage had been extended to almost all adult white males. During the period from 1815 to 1850, the traditional liberal belief in the improvement of human beings was also given concrete expression through the establishment of detention schools for juvenile delinquents and new penal institutions; both were motivated by the belief that the right kind of environment would rehabilitate wayward individuals.

SLAVERY AND THE COMING OF WAR By the mid-nineteenth century, however, the issue of slavery increasingly threatened American national unity. Both North and South had grown dramatically in population during the first half of the nineteenth century, but in different ways. The cotton economy and social structure of the South were based on the exploitation of enslaved black Africans and their descendants. The importance of cotton is evident from production figures. In 1810, the South produced a raw cotton crop of 178,000 bales worth $10 million. By 1860, it was generating 4.5 million bales of cotton with a value of $249 million. Fully 93 percent of Southern cotton in 1850 was produced by a slave population that had grown dramatically since the beginning of the century. Although the importation of new slaves had been barred in 1808, there were 4 million slaves in the South by 1860—four times the number sixty years earlier. The cotton economy depended on plantation-based slavery, and the attempt to maintain it in the first half of the nineteenth century led the South to become increasingly defiant as the rise of an abolitionist movement in the North challenged the Southern order and created an "emotional chain reaction" that ultimately led to civil war.

The push of the nation westward was a major factor in bringing the issue of slavery to the forefront of U.S. politics. Although slavery was permitted by the Constitution, all the states in the North had abolished it. Should new states be admitted to the Union as free or slave states? The issue first arose in the 1810s as new states were being created by the rush of settlers beyond the Mississippi. The free states of the North feared the prospect of a slave-state majority in the national government. Attempts at compromise did not solve this divisive issue but merely postponed it.

By the 1850s, the slavery question had caused the Whig Party to become defunct and the Democrats to split along North-South lines. Passage of the Kansas-Nebraska Act of 1854, which allowed slavery in the Kansas and Nebraska territories to be determined by popular sovereignty, unleashed a firestorm in the North and led to the creation of a new sectional party. The Republicans were united by antislavery principles and were especially driven by the fear that the "slave power" of the South would attempt to spread the slave system throughout the country.

As the country became increasingly polarized over the issue of slavery, compromise became less feasible. When

Abraham Lincoln, the man who had said in a speech in Illinois in 1858 that "this government cannot endure permanently half slave and half free," was elected president in November 1860, the die was cast. Lincoln, the Republicans' second presidential candidate, carried only 2 of the 1,109 counties in the South; the Republican Party was not even on the ballot in ten Southern states. On December 20, 1860, a South Carolina convention voted to repeal the state's ratification of the U.S. Constitution. In February 1861, six more Southern states did the same, and a rival nation, the Confederate States of America, was formed (see Map 20.2). In April, fighting erupted between North and South—the first shots were fired at Fort Sumter in South Carolina, which fell to the Confederates on April 13.

THE CIVIL WAR The American Civil War (1861–1865) was an extraordinarily bloody struggle, a foretaste of the total war to come in the twentieth century. More than 600,000 soldiers died, either in battle or from deadly infectious diseases spawned by filthy camp conditions. The Northern, or Union, forces enjoyed a formidable advantage in numbers of troops

and material resources, but to Southerners, those assets were not decisive. As they saw it, the Confederacy only had to defend the South from invasion, whereas the Union had to conquer the South. Furthermore, the South's aristocratic landowning society had a far stronger military tradition than the business-oriented North, so many of the most promising young military officers were Southerners. Southerners also believed that the dependence of manufacturers in the North and the European countries on Southern raw cotton would lead to antiwar sentiment in the North and support abroad for the South.

All these Southern calculations meant little in the long run. Over a period of four years, the Union states of the North mobilized their superior assets and gradually wore down the Confederate forces of the South. As the war dragged on, it had the effect of radicalizing public opinion in the North. What began as a war to save the Union became a war against slavery. On January 1, 1863, Lincoln issued his Emancipation Proclamation, declaring most of the nation's slaves "forever free" (see the box "Emancipation: Serfs and

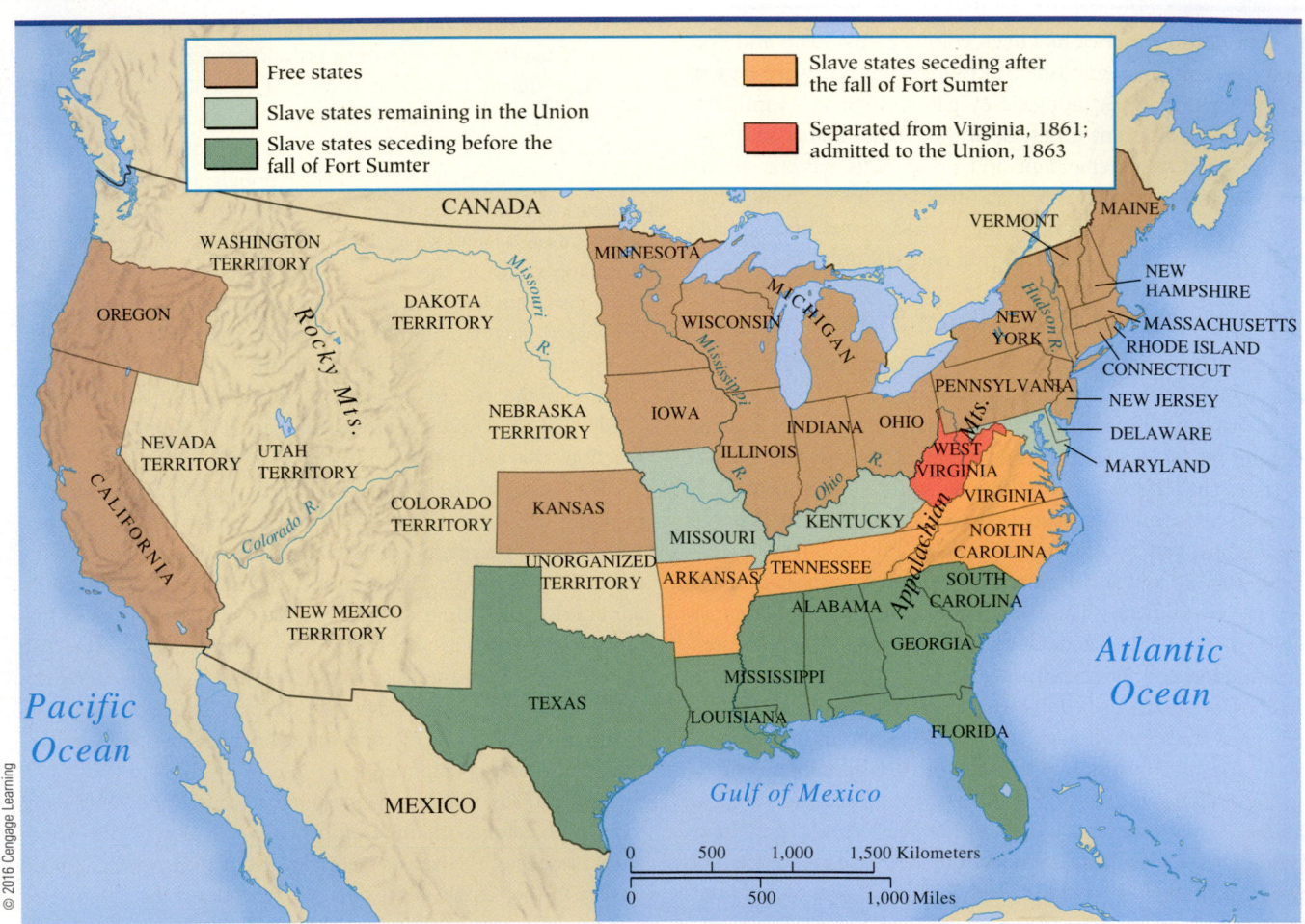

MAP 20.2 The United States: The West and the Civil War. By 1860, the North had developed an economy based on industry and commerce, whereas the South had remained a primarily agrarian economy based on black slave labor. The question of the continuance of slavery itself and the expansion of slavery into western territories led to the Civil War, in which the South sought to create an independent country.

Q *Why would its inhabitants want to create the separate state of West Virginia?*

Slaves" on p. 565 in Chapter 19). An increasingly effective Union blockade of the ports of the South, combined with a shortage of fighting men, made the Confederate cause desperate by the end of 1864. The final push of Union troops under General Ulysses S. Grant forced General Robert E. Lee's Confederate Army to surrender on April 9, 1865. Although problems lay ahead, the Union victory reunited the country and confirmed that the United States would thereafter again be "one nation, indivisible."

The Rise of the United States

Four years of bloody civil war had restored American national unity. The old South had been destroyed; one-fifth of its adult white male population had been killed, and 4 million black slaves had been freed. For a while at least, a program of radical change in the South was attempted. The Thirteenth Amendment to the Constitution formally abolished slavery in 1865, and the Fourteenth and Fifteenth Amendments extended citizenship to blacks and gave black men the right to vote. Radical Reconstruction in the early 1870s tried to create a new South based on the principle of the equality of black and white people, but the changes were soon mostly undone. Militia organizations, such as the Ku Klux Klan, used violence to discourage blacks from voting. A new system of sharecropping made blacks once again economically dependent on white landowners. New state laws made it nearly impossible for blacks to exercise their right to vote. By the end of the 1870s, supporters of white supremacy were back in power everywhere in the South.

PROSPERITY AND PROGRESSIVISM Between 1860 and 1914, the United States made the shift from an agrarian to a mighty industrial nation. American heavy industry stood unchallenged in 1900. In that year, the Carnegie Steel Company alone produced more steel than Great Britain's entire steel industry. Industrialization also led to urbanization. While established cities, such as New York, Philadelphia, and Boston, grew even larger, other moderate-sized cities, such as Pittsburgh, grew by leaps and bounds because of industrialization. Whereas 20 percent of Americans lived in cities in 1860, more than 40 percent did in 1900. Four-fifths of the population growth in cities came from migration. Eight to 10 million Americans moved from rural areas into the cities, and 14 million foreigners came from abroad.

The United States had become the world's richest nation and greatest industrial power. Yet serious questions remained about the quality of American life. In 1890, the richest 9 percent of Americans owned an incredible 71 percent of all the wealth. Workers' concerns over unsafe working conditions, strict work discipline, and periodic cycles of devastating unemployment led to the formation of unions. By the turn of the century, one national organization, the American Federation of Labor, had emerged as labor's dominant voice. Its lack of real power, however, was reflected in its membership figures. In 1900, it included only 8.4 percent of the American industrial labor force.

During the so-called Progressive Era after 1900, the reform of many features of American life became a primary issue. Efforts to improve living conditions in the cities included attempts to eliminate corrupt machine politics. At the state level, reforming governors sought to achieve clean government by introducing elements of direct democracy, such as direct primaries for selecting nominees for public office. State governments also enacted economic and social legislation, such as laws that governed hours, wages, and working conditions, especially for women and children.

The realization that state laws were ineffective in dealing with nationwide problems, however, led to a Progressive movement at the national level. The Meat Inspection Act and Pure Food and Drug Act provided for a limited degree of federal regulation of industrial practices. The presidency of Woodrow Wilson (1913–1921) witnessed the enactment of a graduated federal income tax and the establishment of the Federal Reserve System, which permitted the national government to play a role in important economic decisions formerly made by bankers. Like European nations, the United States was slowly adopting policies that broadened the functions of the state.

THE UNITED STATES AS A WORLD POWER At the end of the nineteenth century, the United States began to expand abroad. The Samoan Islands in the Pacific became the first important American colony; the Hawaiian Islands were next. By 1887, American settlers had gained control of the sugar industry on the Hawaiian Islands. As more Americans settled in Hawaii, they sought political power. When Queen Liliuokalani (LIL-ee-uh-woh-kuh-LAH-nee) tried to strengthen the monarchy in order to keep the islands for the Hawaiian people, the U.S. government sent Marines to "protect" American lives. The queen was deposed, and Hawaii was annexed by the United States in 1898.

The defeat of Spain in the Spanish-American War in 1898 expanded the American empire to include Cuba, Puerto Rico, Guam, and the Philippines. Although the Filipinos appealed for independence, the Americans refused to grant it. As President William McKinley said, the United States had the duty "to educate the Filipinos and uplift and

CHRONOLOGY	The United States and Canada	
United States		
Election of Andrew Jackson	1828	
Kansas-Nebraska Act	1854	
Election of Abraham Lincoln and secession of South Carolina	1860	
Civil War	1861–1865	
Lincoln's Emancipation Proclamation	1863	
Surrender of Robert E. Lee's Confederate Army	April 9, 1865	
Spanish-American War	1898	
Presidency of Woodrow Wilson	1913–1921	
Canada		
Rebellions	1837–1838	
Formation of the Dominion of Canada	1867	
Transcontinental railroad	1885	
Wilfred Laurier as prime minister	1896	

Christianize them," a remarkable statement in view of the fact that most of them had been Roman Catholics for centuries. It took three years and 60,000 troops to pacify the Philippines and establish U.S. control. By the beginning of the twentieth century, the United States had become another Western imperialist power.

The Making of Canada

North of the United States, the process of nation building was also making progress. Under the Treaty of Paris in 1763, Canada—or New France, as it was called—passed into the hands of the British. By 1800, most Canadians favored more autonomy, although the colonists disagreed on the form this autonomy should take. The residents of Upper Canada (now Ontario) were predominantly English speaking, whereas Lower Canada (now Quebec) was dominated by French Canadians. A dramatic increase in immigration to Canada from Great Britain (almost one million immigrants between 1815 and 1850) also fueled the desire for self-government.

In 1837, a number of Canadian groups rose in rebellion against British authority. Rebels in Lower Canada demanded separation from Britain, creation of a republic, universal male suffrage, and freedom of the press. Although the rebellions were crushed by the following year, the British government now began to seek ways to satisfy some of the Canadian demands. The U.S. Civil War proved to be a turning point. Fearful of American designs on Canada during the war and eager to reduce the costs of maintaining the colonies, the British government finally capitulated to Canadian demands. In 1867, Parliament established the Dominion of Canada, with its own constitution. Canada now possessed a parliamentary system and ruled itself, although foreign affairs still remained under the control of the British government.

Canada faced problems of national unity between 1870 and 1914. At the beginning of 1870, the Dominion of Canada had only four provinces: Quebec, Ontario, Nova Scotia, and New Brunswick. With the addition of two more provinces in 1871—Manitoba and British Columbia—the Dominion of Canada now extended from the Atlantic Ocean to the Pacific. As the first prime minister, John Macdonald (1815–1891) moved to strengthen Canadian unity. He pushed for the construction of a transcontinental railroad, which was completed in 1885 and opened the western lands to industrial and commercial development. This also led to the incorporation of two more provinces—Alberta and Saskatchewan—into the Dominion of Canada in 1905.

Canada, 1914

Real unity was difficult to achieve, however, because of the distrust between the English-speaking majority and the French-speaking Canadians, living primarily in Quebec. Wilfred Laurier (LOR-ee-ay), who became the first French Canadian prime minister in 1896, was able to reconcile Canada's two major groups and resolve the issue of separate schools for French Canadians. During Laurier's administration, industrialization boomed, especially the production of textiles, furniture, and railway equipment. Hundreds of thousands of immigrants, primarily from central and eastern Europe, also flowed into Canada. Many settled on lands in the west, thus helping to populate Canada's vast territories.

The Emergence of Mass Society in the West

 FOCUS QUESTION: What is meant by the term *mass society*, and what were its main characteristics?

While new states were developing in the Western Hemisphere in the nineteenth century, a new kind of society—a **mass society**—was emerging in Europe, especially in the second half of the nineteenth century, as a result of rapid economic and social changes. For the lower classes, mass society brought voting rights, an improved standard of living, and access to education. At the same time, however, mass society also made possible the development of organizations that manipulated the populations of the **nation-states**. To understand this mass society, we need to examine some aspects of its structure.

The New Urban Environment

One of the most important consequences of industrialization and the population explosion of the nineteenth century was urbanization. In the course of the nineteenth century, more and more people came to live in cities. In 1800, city dwellers constituted 40 percent of the population in Britain, 25 percent in France and Germany, and only 10 percent in eastern Europe. By 1914, urban residents had increased to 80 percent of the population in Britain, 45 percent in France, 60 percent in Germany, and 30 percent in eastern Europe. The size of cities also expanded dramatically, especially in industrialized countries. Between 1800 and 1900, London's population grew from 960,000 to 6.5 million and Berlin's from 172,000 to 2.7 million.

Urban populations grew faster than the general population primarily because of the vast migration from rural areas to cities. But cities also grew faster in the second half of the nineteenth century because health and living conditions were improving as reformers and city officials used new technology to improve urban life. In the 1840s, a number of urban reformers had pointed to filthy living conditions as the primary cause of epidemic diseases. Following the advice of reformers, city governments set up boards of health to boost the quality of housing and instituted regulations requiring all new buildings to have running water and internal drainage systems.

Octavia Hill and Working-Class Housing in London. Although urban workers experienced some improvements in the material conditions of their lives after 1870, working-class housing remained drab and depressing as shown in the top photograph, taken in 1912. Rows of similar-looking buildings line treeless streets in the East End of London; most of these houses had no gardens or green areas. The bottom photograph shows new cottage-style housing constructed in southern London by reformer Octavia Hill following the success of her housing project for the poor in Marylebone, London. Overlooking Red Cross Garden, Hill's small cottages offered more fresh air and light and allowed the residents to have gardens. Hill argued that these houses provided better living conditions for urban workers.

Essential to the public health of the modern European city was the ability to bring in clean water and to expel sewage. The problem of fresh water was solved by a system of dams and reservoirs that stored the water and aqueducts and tunnels that carried it from the countryside to the city and into individual dwellings. Gas heaters in the 1860s, and later electric heaters, made regular hot baths available to many people. The treatment of sewage was also improved by laying mammoth underground pipes that carried raw sewage far from the city for disposal. The city of Frankfurt, Germany, for example, began its program after a lengthy public campaign enlivened by the slogan "From the Toilet to the River in Half an Hour."

Middle-class reformers also focused on the housing needs of the working class. Overcrowded, disease-ridden slums were viewed as dangerous not only to physical health but also to the political and moral health of the entire nation. V. A. Huber, the foremost early German housing reformer, wrote in 1861, "Certainly it would not be too much to say that the home is the communal embodiment of family life. Thus, the purity of the dwelling is almost as important for the family as is the cleanliness of the body for the individual."[7] To Huber, good housing was a prerequisite for stable family life, and without stable family life, society would fall apart.

Early efforts to attack the housing problem emphasized the middle-class, liberal belief in the power of private, or free, enterprise. Reformers such as Huber believed that the construction of model dwellings renting at a reasonable price would force other private landlords to elevate their housing standards. A fine example of this approach was the work of Octavia Hill. As cities continued to grow in number and size, by the 1880s governments concluded that private enterprise could not solve the housing crisis. In 1890, a British law empowered local town councils to construct cheap housing for the working classes. Similar activity was set in motion in Germany. More and more, governments were stepping into areas of activity that they would not have touched earlier.

The Social Structure of Mass Society

At the top of European society stood a wealthy elite, constituting only 5 percent of the population but controlling between 30 and 40 percent of the wealth. In the course of the nineteenth century, landed aristocrats had joined with the most successful industrialists, bankers, and merchants (the wealthy upper middle class) to form a new elite. Members of this elite, whether aristocratic or middle class in background, assumed leadership roles in government bureaucracies and military hierarchies. Marriage also united the two groups. Daughters of business tycoons gained titles, while aristocratic heirs gained new sources of cash. When the American Consuelo Vanderbilt married the duke of Marlborough, the new duchess brought $10 million to her husband.

The middle classes included a variety of groups. Below the upper middle class was a group that included lawyers, doctors, and members of the civil service, as well as business managers, engineers, architects, accountants, and chemists benefiting from industrial expansion. Beneath this solid and comfortable middle group was a lower middle class of small shopkeepers, traders, small manufacturers, and prosperous peasants.

Standing between the lower middle class and the lower classes were new groups of white-collar workers who were the product of the Second Industrial Revolution—the salespeople, bookkeepers, bank tellers, telephone operators, and secretaries. Though often paid little more than skilled laborers, these white-collar workers were committed to middle-class ideals.

The middle classes shared a certain lifestyle and values that dominated much of nineteenth-century society. This was especially evident in Victorian Britain, often considered a model of middle-class society. The European middle classes believed in hard work, which they viewed as open to everyone and guaranteed to have positive results. They were also regular churchgoers who believed in the good conduct associated with traditional Christian morality. The middle class was concerned with propriety, the right way of doing things, which gave rise to an incessant stream of books aimed at the middle-class market with such titles as *The Habits of Good Society* or *Don't: A Manual of Mistakes and Improprieties More or Less Prevalent in Conduct and Speech*.

Below the middle classes on the social scale were the working classes, who constituted almost 80 percent of the European population. Many of them were landholding peasants, agricultural laborers, and sharecroppers, especially in eastern Europe. The urban working class consisted of many different groups, including skilled artisans in such traditional trades as cabinet-making, printing, and the making of jewelry, along with semi-skilled laborers, who included carpenters, bricklayers, and many factory workers. At the bottom of the urban working class stood the largest group of workers, the unskilled laborers. They included day laborers, who worked irregularly for very

low wages, and large numbers of domestic servants, most of whom were women.

Despite the new job opportunities, many lower-class women were forced to become prostitutes to survive (see the box "Prostitution in Victorian London" on p. 587). Employment was unstable, and wages were low. No longer protected by family or the village community and church, girls who flocked to the city from rural areas often faced one grim option—prostitution.

The Experiences of Women

In the nineteenth century, women remained legally inferior, economically dependent, and largely defined by family and household roles. Many women still aspired to the ideal of femininity popularized by writers and poets. Alfred, Lord Tennyson's poem *The Princess* expressed it well:

> Man for the field and woman for the hearth:
> Man for the sword and for the needle she:
> Man with the head and woman with the heart:
> Man to command and woman to obey;
> All else confusion.

This traditional characterization of the sexes, based on socially defined gender roles, was elevated to the status of universal male and female attributes in the nineteenth century, due largely to the impact of the Industrial Revolution on the family. As the chief family wage earners, men worked outside the home for pay, while women were left with the care of the family, for which they were paid nothing.

MARRIAGE AND THE FAMILY For most of the nineteenth century, marriage was viewed as the only honorable career available to most women. Although the middle class glorified the ideal of domesticity, for most women marriage was a matter of economic necessity. The lack of meaningful work and the lower wages paid to women for their work made it difficult for single women to earn a living. Most women chose to marry.

The most significant development in the modern family was the decline in the number of offspring born to the average woman. Although some historians attribute the decline to more widespread use of coitus interruptus, or male withdrawal before ejaculation, others have emphasized female control of family size through abortion and even infanticide or abandonment. That a change in attitude occurred was apparent in the development of a movement to increase awareness of birth control methods. Europe's first birth control clinic, founded by Dr. Aletta Jacob, opened in Amsterdam in 1882.

The family was the central institution of middle-class life. Men provided the family income, while women focused on household and child care. The use of domestic servants in many middle-class homes, made possible by an abundant supply of cheap labor, reduced the amount of time middle-class women had to spend on household work. At the same time, by having fewer children, mothers could devote more time to child care and domestic leisure.

The middle-class family fostered an ideal of togetherness. The Victorians created the family Christmas with its Yule log,

Prostitution in Victorian London

FAMILY & SOCIETY

AS CITIES GREW, many women living without family support turned to prostitution to survive. Most prostitutes were active for only a short time, usually from their late teens through their early twenties. The increase in prostitution led to the spread of venereal disease, prompting public health officials to call for laws against prostitutes. In England, the Contagious Diseases Acts of the 1860s allowed police to arrest women on suspicion of prostitution. Men who frequented prostitutes were rarely charged, however, and a public outcry against the laws led to their repeal and a more sympathetic view of prostitution by the end of the century. In the meantime, journalists such as Henry Mayhew began to interview prostitutes in an effort to understand their plight. This excerpt, which tells the story of a young London prostitute, was published in Mayhew's *London Labour and the London Poor* in 1862.

Henry Mayhew, *London Labour and the London Poor*

The narrative which follows—that of a prostitute, sleeping in the low-lodging houses, where boys and girls are huddled promiscuously together, discloses a system of depravity, atrocity, and enormity, which certainly cannot be paralleled in any nation, however, barbarous, nor in any age, however "dark." …

A good-looking girl of sixteen gave me the following awful statement:

"I am an orphan. When I was ten I was sent to service as maid of all-work, in a small tradesman's family. It was a hard place, and my mistress used me very cruelly, beating me often. When I had been in place three weeks, my mother died; my father having died … years before. I stood my mistress's ill-treatment for about six months. She beat me

with sticks as well as her hands. I was black and blue, and at last I ran away. I got to Mrs. ——, a low lodging-house. I didn't know before that there was such a place….

"During this time I used to see boys and girls from ten and twelve years old sleeping together, but understood nothing wrong. I had never heard of such places before I ran away. I can neither read nor write. My mother was a good woman, and I wish I'd had her to run away to….

"At the month's end, when I was beat out, I met with a young man of fifteen—I myself was going on twelve years old—and he persuaded me to take up with him. I stayed with him three months in the same lodging house, living with him as his wife, though we were mere children, and being true to him. At the three months' end he was taken up for picking pockets, and got six months. I was sorry, for he was kind to me; … [I] was forced to go into the streets for a living. I continued walking the streets for three years, sometimes making a good deal of money, sometimes none, feasting one day and starving the next….

"I lodged all this time at a lodging-house in Kent-street. They were all thieves and bad girls. I have known between three and four dozen boys and girls sleep in one room. The beds were filth and full of vermin…. "At the house where I am [now] it is 3*d.* a night; but at Mrs. ——'s it is 1*d.* and 2*d.* a night, and just the same goings on. Many a girl—nearly all of them—goes out into the streets from this penny and twopenny house, to get money for their favourite boys by prostitution. If the girl cannot get money she must steal something, or will be beaten by her 'chap' when she comes home."

 What role did poverty play in prostitution? Based on this account, what other options did a poor orphan girl have?

Source: Excerpt from Henry Mayhew, *London Labour and the London Poor: Cyclopedia of the Conditions and Earnings of Those that Will Work, Those that Cannot Work, and Those that Will Not Work* (London: Charles Griffin & Co., 1862) Vol. 1, pp. 458–460.

Christmas tree, songs, and exchange of gifts. In the United States, Fourth of July celebrations changed from drunken revels to family picnics by the 1850s.

Women in working-class families were more accustomed to hard work. Daughters were expected to work until they married; even after marriage, they often did piecework at home to help support the family. For the children of the working classes, childhood was over by the age of nine or ten when they became apprentices or were employed in odd jobs.

Between 1890 and 1914, however, family patterns among the working class began to change. High-paying jobs in heavy industry and improvements in the standard of living made it possible for working-class families to depend on the income of husbands and the wages of grown children. By the early twentieth century, some working-class mothers could afford

to stay at home, following the pattern of middle-class women. At the same time, working-class families also aspired to buy new consumer products, such as sewing machines, clocks, bicycles, and cast-iron stoves.

THE MOVEMENT FOR WOMEN'S RIGHTS In the 1830s, a number of women in the United States and Europe, who worked together in several reform movements, argued for the right of women to divorce and own property. These early efforts were not particularly successful, however. Women did not gain the right to their own property until 1870 in Britain, 1900 in Germany, and 1907 in France.

Divorce and property rights were only a beginning for the women's movement, however. Some middle- and upper-middle-class women gained access to higher education, while others sought entry into occupations dominated by men. The first to fall was teaching. As medical training was largely closed to women, they sought alternatives through the development of nursing. Nursing pioneers included the British nurse Florence Nightingale, whose efforts during the Crimean War (1854–1856), along with those of Clara Barton in the American Civil War (1861–1865), transformed nursing into a profession of trained, middle-class "women in white."

By the 1840s and 1850s, the movement for women's rights had entered the political arena with the call for equal political rights. Many feminists believed that the right to vote was the key to all other reforms to improve the position of women. **Suffragists** had one basic aim: the right of women to full citizenship in the nation-state.

The British women's movement was the most vocal and active in Europe. Emmeline Pankhurst (PANK-hurst) (1858–1928) and her daughters, Christabel and Sylvia, founded the Women's Social and Political Union in 1903, which enrolled mostly middle- and upper-class women. The members of Pankhurst's organization realized the value of the media and used unusual publicity stunts to call attention to their demands. Derisively labeled "suffragettes" by male politicians, they pelted government officials with eggs, chained themselves to lampposts, smashed the windows of department stores on fashionable shopping streets, burned railroad cars, and went on hunger strikes in jail.

Before World War I, the demands for women's rights were being heard throughout Europe and the United States, although only in Norway and some American states did women actually receive the right to vote before 1914. It would take the dramatic upheaval of World War I before male-dominated governments capitulated on this basic issue.

Women reformers also took on issues besides suffrage. In many countries, women supported peace movements. Bertha von Suttner (BAYR-tuh fun ZOOT-nuh) (1843–1914) became head of the Austrian Peace Society and protested against the growing arms race of the 1890s. Her novel *Lay Down Your Arms* became a best-seller and brought her the Nobel Peace Prize in 1905. Lower-class women also took up the cause of peace. A group of women workers marched in Vienna in 1911 and demanded, "We want an end to armaments, to the means of murder, and we want these millions to be spent on the needs of the people."

Bertha von Suttner was but one example of the "new women" who were becoming more prominent at the turn of the century. These women rejected traditional feminine roles (see Opposing Viewpoints "Advice to Women: Two Views" on p. 589) and sought new freedom outside the household and roles other than those of wife and mother.

Education in an Age of Mass Society

Universal education was a product of the mass society of the late nineteenth and early twentieth centuries. Education in the early nineteenth century was primarily for the elite or the wealthier middle class, but after 1870, most Western governments began to offer at least primary education to both boys and girls between the ages of six and twelve. States also assumed responsibility for better training of teachers by establishing teacher-training schools. By the beginning of the twentieth century, many European states, especially in northern and western Europe, provided state-financed primary schools, salaried and trained teachers, and free, compulsory elementary education.

Why did Western nations make this commitment to **mass education**? One reason was industrialization. The new firms of the Second Industrial Revolution demanded skilled labor. Both boys and girls with an elementary education had new possibilities of jobs beyond their villages or small towns, including white-collar jobs with railways and subways, in post offices, with banking and shipping firms, and in teaching and nursing. Mass education furnished the trained workers industrialists needed. For most students, elementary education led to apprenticeship and a job.

The chief motive for mass education, however, was political. For one thing, the expansion of voting rights necessitated a more educated electorate. In parts of Europe where the Catholic Church remained in control of education, implementing a mass education system reduced the influence of the church over the electorate. Even more important, however, mass compulsory education instilled patriotism and nationalized the masses, providing an opportunity for even greater national integration. As people lost their ties to local regions and even to religion, nationalism supplied a new faith. The use of a single national language created

A Middle-Class Family. Nineteenth-century middle-class moralists considered the family the fundamental pillar of a healthy society, and togetherness constituted one of the important ideals of the middle-class family. This painting by William P. Frith, titled *Many Happy Returns of the Day*, shows grandparents, parents, and children taking part in a family birthday celebration for a little girl. The servant at the left holds the presents for the little girl.

Advice to Women: Two Views

FAMILY & SOCIETY

INDUSTRIALIZATION HAD A STRONG IMPACT ON MIDDLE-CLASS WOMEN as strict gender-based social roles became the norm. Men worked outside the home to support the family, while women provided for the needs of their children and husband at home. In the first selection, *Woman in Her Social and Domestic Character* (1842), Elizabeth Poole Sanford gives advice to middle-class women on their proper role and behavior.

Although a majority of women probably followed the nineteenth-century middle-class ideal of women as keepers of the household and nurturers of husband and children, an increasing number of women fought for women's rights. The second selection is taken from the third act of Henrik Ibsen's 1879 play *A Doll's House*, in which the character Nora Helmer declares her independence from her husband's control.

Elizabeth Poole Sanford, *Woman in Her Social and Domestic Character*

The changes wrought by Time are many. It influences the opinions of men as familiarity does their feelings; it has a tendency to do away with superstition, and to reduce every thing to its real worth.

It is thus that the sentiment for woman has undergone a change. The romantic passion which once almost deified her is on the decline; and it is by intrinsic qualities that she must now inspire respect…. But if there is less of enthusiasm entertained for her, the sentiment is more rational, and, perhaps, equally sincere; for it is in relation to happiness that she is chiefly appreciated.

And in this respect it is, we must confess, that she is most useful and most important. Domestic life is the chief source of her influence; and the greatest debt society can owe to her is domestic comfort; for happiness is almost an element of virtue; and nothing conduces more to improve the character of men than domestic peace. A woman may make a man's home delightful, and may thus increase his motives for virtuous exertion. She may refine and tranquilize his mind—may turn away his anger or allay his grief. Her smile may be the happy influence to gladden his heart, and to disperse the cloud that gathers on his brow. And in proportion to her endeavors to make those around her happy, she will be esteemed and loved. She will secure by her excellence that interest and that regard which she might formerly claim as the privilege of her sex, and will really merit the deference which was then conceded to her as a matter of course….

Perhaps one of the first secrets of her influence is adaptation to the tastes, and sympathy in the feelings, of those around her. This holds true in lesser as well as in graver points. It is in the former, indeed, that the absence of interest in a companion is frequently most disappointing. Where want of congeniality impairs domestic comfort, the fault is generally chargeable on the female side. It is for woman, not for man, to make the sacrifice, especially in indifferent matters. She must, in a certain degree, be plastic herself if she would mold others….

Nothing is so likely to conciliate the affections of the other sex as a feeling that woman looks to them for support and guidance. In proportion as men are themselves superior, they are accessible to this appeal. On the contrary, they never feel interested in one who seems disposed rather to offer than to ask assistance. There is, indeed, something unfeminine in independence. It is contrary to nature, and therefore it offends…. A really sensible woman feels her dependence. She does what she can; but she is conscious of inferiority, and therefore grateful for support. She knows that she is the weaker vessel, and that as such she should receive honor. In this view, her weakness is an attraction, not a blemish.

In every thing, therefore, that women attempt, they should show their consciousness of dependence. If they are learners, let them evince a teachable spirit; if they give an opinion, let them do it in an unassuming manner. There is something so unpleasant in female self-sufficiency that it not unfrequently deters instead of persuading, and prevents the adoption of advice which the judgment even approves.

Henrik Ibsen, *A Doll's House*

NORA *(Pause)*: Does anything strike you as we sit here?

HELMER: What should strike me?

NORA: We've been married eight years; does it not strike you that this is the first time we two, you and I, man and wife, have talked together seriously?

HELMER: Seriously? What do you mean, *seriously*?

NORA: For eight whole years, and more—ever since the day we first met—we have never exchanged one serious word about serious things….

HELMER: Why, my dearest Nora, what have you to do with serious things?

NORA: There we have it! You have never understood me. I've had great injustice done to me, Torvald; first by Father, then by you.

HELMER: What! Your father *and* me? We, who have loved you more than all the world!

NORA *(Shaking her head)*: You have never loved me. You just found it amusing to think you were in love with me.

(continued)

(Opposing Viewpoints continued)

HELMER: Nora! What a thing to say!

NORA: Yes, it's true, Torvald. When I was living at home with Father, he told me his opinions and mine were the same. If I had different opinions, I said nothing about them, because he would not have liked it. He used to call me his doll-child and played with me as I played with my dolls. Then I came to live in your house.

HELMER: What a way to speak of our marriage!

NORA *(Undisturbed)*: I mean that I passed from Father's hands into yours. You arranged everything to your taste and I got the same tastes as you; or pretended to—I don't know which—both, perhaps; sometimes one, sometimes the other. When I look back on it now, I seem to have been living here like a beggar, on handouts. I lived by performing tricks for you, Torvald. But that was how you wanted it. You and Father have done me a great wrong. It is your fault that my life has come to naught.

HELMER: Why, Nora, how unreasonable and ungrateful! Haven't you been happy here?

NORA: No, never. I thought I was, but I never was.

HELMER: Not—not happy! …

NORA: I must stand quite alone if I am ever to know myself and my surroundings; so I cannot stay with you.

HELMER: Nora! Nora!

NORA: I am going at once. I daresay [my friend] Christina will take me in for tonight.

HELMER: You are mad! I shall not allow it! I forbid it!

NORA: It's no use your forbidding me anything now. I shall take with me only what belongs to me; from you I will accept nothing, either now or later.

HELMER: This is madness!

NORA: Tomorrow I shall go home—I mean to what was my home. It will be easier for me to find a job there.

HELMER: Oh, in your blind inexperience—

NORA: I must try to gain experience, Torvald.

HELMER: Forsake your home, your husband, your children! And you don't consider what the world will say.

NORA: I can't pay attention to that. I only know that I must do it.

HELMER: This is monstrous! Can you forsake your holiest duties?

NORA: What do you consider my holiest duties?

HELMER: Need I tell you that? Your duties to your husband and children.

NORA: I have other duties equally sacred.

HELMER: Impossible! What do you mean?

NORA: My duties toward myself.

HELMER: Before all else you are a wife and a mother.

NORA: That I no longer believe. Before all else I believe I am a human being just as much as you are—or at least that I should try to become one. I know that most people agree with you, Torvald, and that they say so in books. But I can no longer be satisfied with what most people say and what is in books. I must think things out for myself and try to get clear about them.

 According to Elizabeth Sanford, what is the proper role of women? What forces in nineteenth-century European society merged to shape Sanford's understanding of "proper" gender roles? In Ibsen's play, what challenges does Nora Helmer make to Sanford's view of the proper role and behavior of wives? Why is her husband so shocked? Why did Ibsen title this play A Doll's House?

Sources: From Elizabeth Poole Sanford, *Woman in Her Social and Domestic Character* (Boston: Otis, Broaders & Co., 1842), pp. 5–7, 15–16. From Henrik Ibsen, *A Doll's House*, Act III, 1879, as printed in *Roots of Western Civilization* by Wesley D. Camp, John Wiley & Sons, 1983.

greater national unity than loyalty to a ruler did (see the Comparative Essay "The Rise of Nationalism" on p. 591).

Compulsory elementary education created a demand for teachers, and most of them were women. Many men viewed the teaching of children as an extension of women's "natural role" as nurturers of the young. Moreover, females were paid lower salaries, in itself a considerable incentive for governments to encourage the establishment of teacher-training institutes for women. The first female colleges were teacher-training schools. It was not until the beginning of the twentieth century that women were permitted to enter the male-dominated universities.

The most immediate result of mass education was an increase in literacy. In Germany, Great Britain, France, and the Scandinavian countries, adult illiteracy was virtually eliminated by 1900. Where there was less schooling, the story was quite different. Adult illiteracy rates were 79 percent in Serbia, 78 percent in Romania, and 79 percent in Russia.

Leisure in an Age of Mass Society

With the Industrial Revolution came new forms of leisure. Work and leisure became opposites as leisure came to be viewed as what people do for fun when they are not at work. The new leisure hours created by the industrial system—evening hours after work, weekends, and later a week or two in the summer—largely determined the contours of the new **mass leisure**.

New technology created novel experiences for leisure, such as the Ferris wheel at amusement parks, while the introduction of subways and streetcars in the 1880s meant that even the working classes were no longer dependent on neighborhood facilities but could make their way to athletic games, amusement parks, dance halls, and department stores. New technology also made available more consumer goods. On evenings and weekends, urban dwellers strolled into the newly constructed department stores, where they could purchase any of the thousands of items for sale.

The Rise of Nationalism

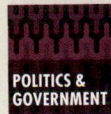

POLITICS & GOVERNMENT

Like the Industrial Revolution, the concept of nationalism originated in eighteenth-century Europe, where it was the product of a variety of factors, including the spread of printing and the replacement of Latin with vernacular languages, the secularization of the age, and the experience of the French revolutionary and Napoleonic eras. The French were the first to show what a nation in arms could accomplish, but peoples conquered by Napoleon soon created their own national armies. At the beginning of the nineteenth century, peoples who had previously focused their identity on a locality or a region, on loyalty to a monarch or to a particular religious faith, now shifted their political allegiance to the idea of a nation, based on ethnic, linguistic, or cultural factors. The idea of the nation had explosive consequences: by the end of the first two decades of the twentieth century, the three largest multiethnic states in the world—Imperial Russia, Austria-Hungary, and the Ottoman Empire—had all given way to a number of individual nation-states.

The idea of establishing political boundaries on the basis of ethnicity, language, or culture had a broad appeal throughout Western civilization, but it had unintended consequences. Although the concept provided the basis for a new sense of community that was tied to liberal thought in the first half of the nineteenth century, it also gave birth to ethnic tensions and hatreds in the second half of the century that resulted in bitter disputes and contributed to the competition between nation-states that eventually erupted into world war. Governments,

Garibaldi. Giuseppe Garibaldi was a dedicated patriot and an outstanding example of the Italian nationalism that led to the unification of Italy by 1870.

following the lead of the radical government in Paris during the French Revolution, took full advantage of the rise of a strong national consciousness and transformed war into a matter of national honor that would require the commitment of the entire population. Universal schooling enabled states to arouse patriotic enthusiasm and create national unity. Most soldiers who joyfully went to war in 1914 were convinced that their nation's cause was just.

But if the concept of nationalism was initially the product of conditions in modern Europe, it soon spread to other parts of the world. Although a few societies, such as Vietnam, had already developed a strong sense of national identity, most of the peoples living in Asia and Africa lived in multiethnic and multireligious communities and were not yet ripe for the spirit of nationalism. As we shall see, the first attempts to resist European colonial rule were often based on religious or ethnic identity, rather than on the concept of denied nationhood. But the imperialist powers, which at first benefited from the lack of political cohesion among their colonial subjects, eventually reaped what they had sown. As the colonial peoples became familiar with Western concepts of democracy and self-determination, they too began to manifest a sense of common purpose that helped knit together the different elements in their societies to oppose colonial regimes and create the conditions for the emergence of future nations. For good or ill, the concept of nationalism had now achieved global proportions. We shall explore such issues, and their consequences, in greater detail in the chapters that follow.

 What is nationalism? How did it arise, and what impact did it have on the history of the nineteenth and twentieth centuries?

By the late nineteenth century, team sports had also developed into another important form of mass leisure. Unlike the old rural games, which were spontaneous and often chaotic activities, the new sports were strictly organized with sets of rules and officials to enforce them. These rules were the products of organized athletic groups, such as the English Football Association (1863) and the American Bowling Congress (1895). The development of urban transportation systems made possible the construction of stadiums where thousands could attend, making mass spectator sports into a big business.

Cultural Life: Romanticism and Realism in the Western World

Q **FOCUS QUESTION:** What were the main characteristics of Romanticism and Realism?

At the end of the eighteenth century, a new intellectual movement known as **Romanticism** emerged to challenge the ideas of the Enlightenment. To the Enlightenment, reason was the chief means for discovering truth. Although the Romantics by no means disparaged reason, they tried to balance its use by stressing the importance of feeling, emotion, and imagination as sources of knowing.

The Characteristics of Romanticism

Romantic writers emphasized emotion and sentiment and believed that these inner feelings were understandable only to the person experiencing them. In their novels, Romantic writers created figures who were often misunderstood and rejected by society but who continued to believe in their own worth through their inner feelings.

Many Romantics also possessed a passionate interest in the past. They revived medieval Gothic architecture and left European countrysides adorned with pseudo-medieval castles and cities bedecked with grandiose neo-Gothic cathedrals, city halls, and parliamentary buildings. Literature, too, reflected this historical consciousness. The novels of Walter Scott (1771–1832) became European best-sellers in the first half of the nineteenth century. *Ivanhoe*, in which Scott sought to evoke the clash between Saxon and Norman knights in medieval England, became one of his most popular works.

Many Romantics had a deep attraction to the exotic and unfamiliar. For some, this meant a fascination with historical figures from the non-Western parts of the world, evident in Samuel Taylor Coleridge's *Kubla Khan*, a poem about the ruler who established a new Chinese dynasty in the thirteenth century. For others, this preoccupation with the exotic took an exaggerated form in so-called **Gothic literature**, chillingly evident in Mary Shelley's *Frankenstein* and Edgar Allan Poe's short stories of horror. Some Romantics even tried to bring the unusual into their own lives by experimenting with cocaine, opium, and hashish to achieve drug-induced altered states of consciousness.

To the Romantics, poetry ranked above all other literary forms because they believed it was the direct expression of the soul. Romantic poetry gave full expression to one of the most important characteristics of Romanticism: love of nature, especially evident in the poetry of William Wordsworth (1770–1850). His experience of nature was almost mystical as he claimed to receive "authentic tidings of invisible things":

> One impulse from a vernal wood
> May teach you more of man,
> Of Moral Evil and of good,
> Than all the sages can.[8]

Romantics believed that nature served as a mirror into which humans could look to learn about themselves.

Friedrich, Caspar David (1774–1840)/The Art Gallery Collection/Alamy

Caspar David Friedrich, *The Wanderer Above the Sea of Fog.* The German artist Caspar David Friedrich sought to express in painting his own mystical view of nature. "The divine is everywhere," he once wrote, "even in a grain of sand." In this painting, a solitary wanderer is shown from the back gazing at mountains covered in fog. Overwhelmed by the all-pervasive presence of nature, the figure expresses the human longing for infinity.

Like the literary arts, the visual arts were also deeply affected by Romanticism. To Romantic artists, all artistic expression was a reflection of the artist's inner feelings; a painting should mirror the artist's vision of the world and be the instrument of his own imagination.

The early life experiences of Caspar David Friedrich (kass-PAR dah-VEET FREED-rikh) (1774–1840) left him with a life-long preoccupation with God and nature. Friedrich painted landscapes with an interest that transcended the mere presentation of natural details. His portrayals of mountains shrouded in mist, gnarled trees bathed in moonlight, and the stark ruins of monasteries surrounded by withered trees all conveyed a feeling of mystery and mysticism. For Friedrich, nature was a manifestation of divine life, as is evident in *The Wanderer Above the Sea of Fog*. To Friedrich, the artistic process depended on one's inner vision. He advised artists, "Shut your physical eye and look first at your picture with your spiritual eye; then bring to the light of day what you have seen in the darkness."

A New Age of Science

The Scientific Revolution had created a modern, rational approach to the study of the natural world, but even in the eighteenth century, these intellectual developments had remained the preserve of an educated elite and resulted in few practical applications. With the Industrial Revolution, however, came a renewed interest in basic scientific research. By the 1830s, new scientific discoveries had led to many practical benefits that caused science to have an ever-greater impact on European life.

In biology, the Frenchman Louis Pasteur (LWEE pass-TOOR) (1822–1895) came up with the germ theory of disease, which had enormous practical applications in the development of modern scientific medical practices. In chemistry, the Russian Dmitri Mendeleev (di-MEE-tree men-duh-LAY-ef) (1834–1907) in the 1860s classified all the material elements then known on the basis of their atomic weights and provided the systematic foundation for the periodic law. The Briton Michael Faraday (1791–1867) put together a primitive generator that laid the foundation for the use of electricity.

The popularity of scientific and technological achievement produced a widespread acceptance of the scientific method as the only path to objective truth and objective reality. This undermined the faith of many people in religious revelation. It is no accident that the nineteenth century was an age of increasing **secularization**, evident in the belief that truth was to be found in the concrete material existence of human beings. No one did more to create a picture of humans as material beings that were simply part of the natural world than Charles Darwin.

In 1859, Charles Darwin (1809–1882) published *On the Origin of Species by Means of Natural Selection*. The basic idea of this book was that all plants and animals had evolved over a long period of time from earlier and simpler forms of life, a principle known as **organic evolution**. In every species, he argued, "many more individuals of each species are born than can possibly survive." This results in a "struggle for existence." Darwin believed that some organisms were more adaptable to the environment than others, a process that Darwin called **natural selection**. Those that were naturally selected for survival ("survival of the fit") reproduced and thrived. The unfit did not and became extinct. The fit who survived passed on small variations that enhanced their survival until, from Darwin's point of view, a new and separate species emerged. In *The Descent of Man*, published in 1871, he argued for the animal origins of human beings: "Man is the co-descendant with other mammals of a common progenitor." Humans were not an exception to the rule governing other species.

Realism in Literature and Art

The name **Realism** was first applied in 1850 to a new style of painting and soon spread to literature. The literary Realists of the mid-nineteenth century rejected Romanticism. They wanted to deal with ordinary characters from actual life rather than

Romantic heroes in exotic settings. They also sought to avoid emotional language by using close observation and precise description, an approach that led them to write novels rather than poems.

The leading novelist of the 1850s and 1860s, the Frenchman Gustave Flaubert (goo-STAHV floh-BAYR) (1821–1880), perfected the Realist novel. His *Madame Bovary* (1857) was a straightforward description of barren and sordid provincial life in France (see the box "Flaubert and an Image of Bourgeois Marriage" on p. 594). Emma Bovary is trapped in a marriage to a drab provincial doctor. Impelled by the images of romantic love she has read about in novels, she seeks the same thing for herself in adulterous love affairs but is ultimately driven to suicide.

The British novelist Charles Dickens (1812–1870) achieved extraordinary success with his novels focusing on the lower and middle classes in Britain's early industrial age. His descriptions of the urban poor and the brutalization of human life were vividly realistic.

Realism also made inroads in Latin America by the second half of the nineteenth century. There, Realist novelists focused on the injustices of Latin American society, evident in the work of Clorinda Matto de Turner (kloh-RIN-duh MAH-toh day TUR-nerr) (1852–1909). Her *Aves sin Nido* (*Birds Without a Nest*) was a brutal revelation of the pitiful living conditions of the Indians in Peru. She especially blamed the Catholic Church for much of their misery.

In art, too, Realism became dominant after 1850. Realist art demonstrated three major characteristics: a desire to depict

Gustave Courbet, *The Stonebreakers*. Realism, largely developed by French painters, aimed at lifelike portrayals of the daily activities of ordinary people. Gustave Courbet was the most famous of the Realist artists. As is evident in *The Stonebreakers*, he sought to portray things as they really appear. He shows an old road builder and his young assistant in their tattered clothes, engrossed in their dreary work of breaking stones to construct a road.

Flaubert and an Image of Bourgeois Marriage

ART & IDEAS

IN *MADAME BOVARY*, Gustave Flaubert portrays the tragic life of Emma Rouault, a farm girl whose hopes of escape from provincial life are dashed after she marries a doctor, Charles Bovary. After her initial attempts to find happiness in her domestic life, Emma seeks refuge in affairs and extravagant shopping. In this excerpt, Emma expresses her restlessness and growing boredom with her new husband. Flaubert's detailed descriptions of everyday life make *Madame Bovary* one of the seminal works of Realism.

Gustave Flaubert, *Madame Bovary*

Charles's conversation was as flat as a sidewalk, with everyone's ideas walking through it in ordinary dress, arousing neither emotion, nor laughter, nor dreams. He had never been curious, he said, the whole time he was living in Rouen to go see a touring company of Paris actors at the theater. He couldn't swim, or fence, or shoot, and once he couldn't even explain to Emma a term about horseback riding she had come across in a novel.

But a man should know everything, shouldn't he? Excel in many activities, initiate you into the excitements of passion, into life's refinements, into all its mysteries? Yet this man taught nothing, knew nothing, hoped for nothing. He thought she was happy, and she was angry at him for this placid stolidity, for this leaden serenity, for the very happiness she gave to him.

Sometimes she would draw. Charles was always happy watching her lean over her drawing board.... As for the piano, the faster her fingers flew over it, the more he marveled. She struck the keys with aplomb and ran from one end of the keyboard to the other without a stop....

On the other hand, Emma did know how to run the house. She sent patients statements of their visits in well-written letters that didn't look like bills. When some neighbor came to dine on Sundays, she managed to offer some tasty dish.... All this reflected favorably on Bovary.

Charles ended up thinking all the more highly of himself for possessing such a wife. In the living room he pointed with pride to her two small pencil sketches that he had mounted in very large frames and hung against the wallpaper on long green cords.

He would come home late, at ten o'clock, sometimes at midnight. Then he would want something to eat and Emma would serve him because the maid was asleep. He would remove his coat in order to eat more comfortably. He would report on all the people he had met one after the other,... and, content with himself, would eat the remainder of the stew, peel his cheese, bite into an apple, empty the decanter, then go to sleep, lying on his back and snoring....

And yet, in line with the theories she admired, she wanted to give herself up to love. In the moonlight of the garden she would recite all the passionate poetry she knew by heart and would sing melancholy adagios to him with sighs, but she found herself as calm afterward as before and Charles didn't appear more amorous or moved because of it.

After she had several times struck the flint on her heart without eliciting a single spark, incapable as she was of understanding that which she did not feel ... she convinced herself without difficulty that Charles's passion no longer offered anything extravagant. His effusions had become routine; he embraced her at certain hours. It was one habit among others, like the established custom of eating dessert after the monotony of dinner.

What does this passage reveal about bourgeois life in France during the mid-nineteenth century? What does the passage tell us about the roles of women during this time? How did Charles fail to live up to Emma's expectations of romantic love?

Source: From Gustave Flaubert, *Madame Bovary*, trans. by Mildred Marmur (New York: Penguin Press), 39–43.

---

the everyday life of ordinary people, whether peasants, workers, or prostitutes; an attempt at photographic accuracy; and an interest in the natural environment. The French became leaders in Realist painting.

Gustave Courbet (goo-STAHV koor-BAY) (1819–1877), the most famous artist of the Realist school, reveled in realistic portrayals of everyday life. His subjects were factory workers, peasants, and the wives of saloonkeepers. "I have never seen either angels or goddesses, so I am not interested in painting them," he exclaimed. One of his famous works, *The Stonebreakers*, painted in 1849, shows two road workers engaged in the deadening work of breaking stones to build a road. This representation of human misery was a scandal to those who objected to Courbet's "cult of ugliness."

Toward the Modern Consciousness: Intellectual and Cultural Developments

FOCUS QUESTION: What intellectual and cultural developments in the late nineteenth and early twentieth centuries "opened the way to a modern consciousness," and how did this consciousness differ from earlier worldviews?

Before 1914, many people in the Western world continued to believe in the values and ideals of the Scientific Revolution and the Enlightenment. The idea that human beings could improve themselves and achieve a better society seemed to be proved by a rising standard of living, urban comforts, and mass education. Such products of modern technology as electric lights and automobiles reinforced the popular prestige of science. It was easy to think that the human mind could make sense of the universe. Between 1870 and 1914, however, radically new ideas challenged these optimistic views and opened the way to a modern consciousness.

A New Physics

Science was one of the chief pillars underlying the optimistic and rationalistic view of the world that many Westerners shared in the nineteenth century. Supposedly based on hard facts and cold reason, science offered a certainty of belief in the orderliness of nature. The new physics dramatically altered that perspective.

Throughout much of the nineteenth century, Westerners adhered to the mechanical conception of the universe postulated by the classical physics of Isaac Newton. In this perspective, the universe was viewed as a giant machine in which time, space, and matter were objective realities that existed independently of the people observing them. Matter was thought to be composed of indivisible and solid material bodies called atoms.

These views were first seriously questioned at the end of the nineteenth century. The French scientist Marie Curie (kyoo-REE) (1867–1934) and her husband, Pierre Curie (1859–1906), discovered that an element called radium gave off rays of radiation that apparently came from within the atom itself. Atoms were not simply hard, material bodies but small worlds containing such subatomic particles as electrons and protons, which behaved in seemingly random and inexplicable fashion.

Building on this work, in 1900 a Berlin physicist, Max Planck (PLAHNK) (1858–1947), rejected the belief that a heated body radiates energy in a steady stream but maintained instead that it did so discontinuously, in irregular packets of energy that he called "quanta." The quantum theory raised fundamental questions about the subatomic realm of the atom. By 1900, the old view of atoms as the basic building blocks of the material world was being seriously questioned.

Albert Einstein (YN-styn) (1879–1955), a German-born patent officer working in Switzerland, pushed these new theories into new terrain. In 1905, Einstein published a paper titled "The Electro-Dynamics of Moving Bodies" that contained his special theory of relativity. According to **relativity theory**, space and time are not absolute but relative to the observer, and both are interwoven into what Einstein called a four-dimensional space-time continuum. Neither space nor time had an existence independent of human experience. As Einstein later explained simply to a journalist, "It was formerly believed that if all material things disappeared out of the universe, time and space would be left. According to the relativity theory, however, time and space disappear together with the things."[9] Moreover, matter and energy reflected the relativity of time and space. Einstein concluded that matter was nothing but another form of energy. His epochal formula

Marie Curie. Marie Curie was born in Warsaw, Poland, but studied at the University of Paris, where she received degrees in both physics and mathematics. She was the first woman to win two Nobel Prizes, one in 1903 in physics and another in chemistry in 1911. She is shown here in her Paris laboratory in 1912. She died of leukemia, a result of her laboratory work with radioactivity.

$E = mc^2$—indicating that the energy of each particle of matter is equivalent to its mass times the square of the velocity of light—was the key theory explaining the vast energies contained within the atom. It led to the atomic age.

Sigmund Freud and Psychoanalysis

At the turn of the twentieth century, the Viennese physician Sigmund Freud (SIG-mund *or* ZIG-munt FROID) (1856–1939) advanced a series of theories that undermined optimism about the rational nature of the human mind. Freud's thought, like the new physics, added to the uncertainties of the age. His major ideas were published in 1900 in *The Interpretation of Dreams.*

According to Freud, human behavior was strongly determined by the unconscious, by past experiences and internal forces of which people were largely oblivious. For Freud, human behavior was no longer truly rational but rather instinctive or irrational. He argued that painful and unsettling experiences were blotted from conscious awareness but still continued to influence behavior since they had become part of the unconscious (see the box "Freud and the Concept of Repression" on p. 596). Repression of these thoughts began in childhood. Freud devised a method, known as **psychoanalysis**, by which a psychotherapist and patient could probe deeply into

Freud and the Concept of Repression

SIGMUND FREUD'S PSYCHOANALYTICAL THEORIES resulted from his attempt to understand the world of the unconscious. This excerpt is taken from one of five lectures given in 1909 in which Freud described how he arrived at his theory of the role of repression. Although Freud valued science and reason, his theories of the unconscious produced a new image of the human being as governed less by reason than by irrational forces.

Sigmund Freud, *The Origin and Development of Psychoanalysis*

But I did not give [the technique of encouraging patients to reveal forgotten experiences] up without drawing definite conclusions from the data which I had gained. I had substantiated the fact that the forgotten memories were not lost.

They were in the possession of the patient, ready to emerge and form associations with his other mental content, but hindered from becoming conscious, and forced to remain in the unconscious by some sort of a force. The existence of this force could be assumed with certainty, for in attempting to drag up the unconscious memories into the consciousness of the patient, in opposition to this force, one got the sensation of his own personal effort striving to overcome it. One could get an idea of this force, which maintained the pathological situation, from the resistance of the patient.

It is on this idea of resistance that I based my theory of the psychic processes of hystericals. It had been found that in order to cure the patient it was necessary that this force should be overcome. Now with the mechanism of the cure as a starting point, quite a definite theory could be constructed.

These same forces, which in the present situation as resistances opposed the emergence of the forgotten ideas into consciousness, must themselves have caused the forgetting, and repressed from consciousness the pathogenic experiences. I called this hypothetical process "repression" and considered that it was proved by the undeniable existence of resistance.

But now the question arose: what were those forces, and what were the conditions of this repression, in which we were now able to recognize the pathogenic mechanism of hysteria? A comparative study of the pathogenic situations, which the cathartic treatment has made possible, allows us to answer this question. In all those experiences, it had happened that a wish had been aroused, which was in sharp opposition to the other desires of the individual, and was not capable of being reconciled with the ethical, aesthetic and personal pretensions of the patient's personality. There had been a short conflict, and the end of this inner struggle was the repression of the idea that presented itself to consciousness as the bearer of this irreconcilable wish. This was, then, repressed from consciousness and forgotten. The incompatibility of the idea in question with the "ego" of the patient was the motive of the repression, the ethical and other pretensions of the individual were the repressing forces. The presence of the incompatible wish, or the duration of the conflict, had given rise to a high degree of mental pain; this pain was avoided by the repression. This latter process is evidently in such a case a device for the protection of the personality.

 According to Freud, how did he discover the existence of repression? What function does repression perform?

Source: From *The American Journal of Psychology*, Vol. 21, No. 2 (April 1910), pp. 192–199.

---

the memory in order to retrace the chain of repression all the way back to its childhood origins. By making the conscious mind aware of the unconscious and its repressed contents, the patient's psychic conflict was resolved.

The Impact of Darwin: Social Darwinism and Racism

In the second half of the nineteenth century, scientific theories were sometimes wrongly applied to achieve other ends. For example, the application of Charles Darwin's principle of organic evolution to the social order came to be known as **Social Darwinism**, the belief that societies were organisms that evolved through time from a struggle with their environment. Progress came from the "struggle for survival," as the "fit"— the strong—advanced while the weak declined.

Rabid nationalists and racists also applied Darwin's ideas to human society in an even more radical way. In their pursuit of national greatness, extreme nationalists often insisted that nations, too, were engaged in a struggle for existence in which only the fittest survived. The German general Friedrich von Bernhardi (FREED-rikh fun bayrn-HAR-dee) argued in 1907, "War is a biological necessity of the first importance,… since without it an unhealthy development will follow, which excludes every advancement of the race, and therefore all real civilization. 'War is the father of all things.'"[10]

Perhaps nowhere was the combination of extreme nationalism and racism more evident or more dangerous than in Germany. One of the chief propagandists of German racism was Houston Stewart Chamberlain (1855–1927), a Briton who became a German citizen. According to Chamberlain, modern-day Germans were the only pure successors of the **Aryans**, who were portrayed as the true and original founders of Western culture. The Aryan race, under German leadership, must be prepared to fight for Western civilization and save it from the destructive assaults of such lower races as Jews, Negroes, and Orientals. Chamberlain singled out the Jews as the racial enemy who wanted to destroy the Aryan race.

ANTI-SEMITISM   Anti-Semitism had a long history in European civilization, but in the nineteenth century, as a result of the ideals of the Enlightenment and the French Revolution, Jews were increasingly granted legal equality in many European countries. Many Jews now left the ghetto and became assimilated into the cultures around them. Many became successful as bankers, lawyers, scientists, scholars, journalists, and stage performers.

These achievements represent only one side of the picture, however. In Germany and Austria during the 1880s and 1890s, conservatives founded right-wing anti-Jewish parties that used anti-Semitism to win the votes of traditional lower-middle-class groups who felt threatened by the new economic forces of the times. The worst treatment of Jews at the turn of the century, however, occurred in eastern Europe, where 72 percent of the world's Jewish population lived. Russian Jews were forced to live in certain regions of the country, and persecutions and pogroms were widespread. Hundreds of thousands of Jews decided to emigrate to escape the persecution.

Many Jews went to the United States, although some moved to Palestine, which soon became the focus of a Jewish nationalist movement called **Zionism**. For many Jews, Palestine, the land of ancient Israel, had long been the land of their dreams. A key figure in the growth of political Zionism was Theodor Herzl (TAY-oh-dor HAYRT-sul) (1860–1904), who predicted in his book *The Jewish State*, "The Jews who wish it will have their state" (see the box "The Voice of Zionism: Theodor Herzl and the Jewish State" on p. 598).

Settlement in Palestine was difficult, however, because it was then part of the Ottoman Empire, which was opposed to Jewish immigration. Despite the problems, however, the first Zionist Congress, which met in Switzerland in 1897, proclaimed as its aim the creation of a "home in Palestine secured by public law" for the Jewish people. In 1900, about a thousand Jews migrated to Palestine, and the trickle rose to about three thousand a year between 1904 and 1914, keeping the Zionist dream alive.

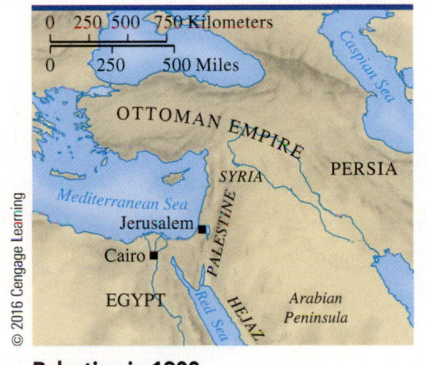

Palestine in 1900

The Culture of Modernity

The revolution in physics and psychology was paralleled by a revolution in literature and the arts. Before 1914, writers and artists were rebelling against the traditional literary and artistic styles that had dominated European cultural life since the Renaissance. The changes that they produced have since been called **Modernism**.

At the beginning of the twentieth century, a group of writers known as the Symbolists caused a literary revolution. Primarily interested in writing poetry and strongly influenced by the ideas of Freud, the Symbolists believed that an objective knowledge of the world was impossible. The external world

was not real but only a collection of symbols that reflected the true reality of the individual human mind. Art, they believed, should function for its own sake instead of serving, criticizing, or seeking to understand society.

The period from 1870 to 1914 was one of the most fertile in the history of art. Since the Renaissance, the task of artists had been to represent reality as accurately as possible. By the late nineteenth century, artists were seeking new forms of expression. The preamble to modern painting can be found in **Impressionism**, a movement that originated in France in the 1870s when a group of artists rejected the studios and museums and went out into the countryside to paint nature directly. Camille Pissarro (kah-MEEl pee-SAH-roh) (1830–1903), one of Impressionism's founders, expressed what they sought:

> Precise drawing is dry and hampers the impression of the whole, it destroys all sensations. Do not define too closely the outlines of things; it is the brush stroke of the right value and color which should produce the drawing.... Work at the same time upon sky, water, branches, ground, keeping everything going on an equal basis and unceasingly rework until you have got it.... Don't proceed according to rules and principles, but paint what you observe and feel. Paint generously and unhesitatingly, for it is best not to lose the first impression.[11]

An important Impressionist painter was Berthe Morisot (BAYRT mor-ee-ZOH) (1841–1895), who believed that women had a special vision, which was, as she said, "more delicate than that of men." She made use of lighter colors and flowing brush strokes (see the Comparative Illustration "Painting—West and East" on p. 599). Near the end of her life, she lamented the refusal of men to take her work seriously: "I don't think there has ever been a man who treated a woman as an equal, and that's all I would have asked, for I know I'm worth as much as they."[12]

By the 1880s, a new movement known as **Post-Impressionism** had emerged in France and soon spread to other European countries. Post-Impressionism retained the Impressionist emphasis on light and color but revolutionized it even further by paying more attention to structure and form. Post-Impressionists shifted from objective reality to subjective reality and in so doing began to withdraw from the artist's traditional task of depicting the external world. A famous Post-Impressionist was the tortured and tragic figure Vincent van Gogh (van GOH *or* vahn GOK) (1853–1890). For van Gogh, art was a spiritual experience. He was especially interested in color and believed that it could act as its own form of language. Van Gogh maintained that artists should paint what they feel.

By the beginning of the twentieth century, the belief that the task of art was to represent "reality" had lost much of its meaning. By that time, the new psychology and the new physics had made it evident that many people were not sure what constituted reality anyway. Then, too, the growth of photography gave artists another reason to reject Realism. Invented in the

The Voice of Zionism: Theodor Herzl and the Jewish State

POLITICS & GOVERNMENT

THE AUSTRIAN JEWISH JOURNALIST Theodor Herzl wrote *The Jewish State* in the summer of 1895 in Paris while he was covering the Dreyfus (DRY-fuss) case for his Vienna newspaper. (Alfred Dreyfus, a French army officer who was also Jewish, was accused and wrongly convicted of selling military secrets. Although he was later exonerated, the case revealed the depth of anti-Semitism in France.) In several weeks, during a period of feverish composition, he set out to analyze the fundamental causes of anti-Semitism and devise a solution to the "Jewish problem." In this selection, he discusses two of his major conclusions.

Theodor Herzl, *The Jewish State*

I do not intend to arouse sympathetic emotions on our behalf. That would be a foolish, futile, and undignified proceeding. I shall content myself with putting the following questions to the Jews: Is it true that, in countries where we live in perceptible numbers, the position of Jewish lawyers, doctors, technicians, teachers, and employees of all descriptions becomes daily more intolerable? True, that the Jewish middle classes are seriously threatened? True, that the passions of the mob are incited against our wealthy people? True, that our poor endure greater sufferings than any other proletariat?

I think that this external pressure makes itself felt everywhere. In our economically upper classes it causes discomfort, in our middle classes continual and grave anxieties, in our lower classes absolute despair.

Everything tends, in fact, to one and the same conclusion, which is clearly enunciated in that classic Berlin phrase: "Juden raus!" (Out with the Jews!)

I shall now put the Jewish Question in the curtest possible form: Are we to "get out" now? And if so, to what place?

Or, may we yet remain? And if so, how long?

Let us first settle the point of staying where we are. Can we hope for better days, can we possess our souls in patience, can we wait in pious resignation till the princes and peoples of this earth are more mercifully disposed toward us? I say that we cannot hope for a change in the current of feeling. And why not?… The nations in whose midst Jews live are all, either covertly or openly, Anti-Semitic.…

The whole plan is in its essence perfectly simple, as it must necessarily be if it is to come within the comprehension of all.

Let the sovereignty be granted us over a portion of the globe large enough to satisfy the rightful requirements of a nation; the rest we shall manage for ourselves.

The creation of a new State is neither ridiculous nor impossible. We have in our day witnessed the process in connection with nations which were not in the bulk of the middle class, but poorer, less educated, and consequently weaker than ourselves. The Governments of all countries scourged by Anti-Semitism will be keenly interested in assisting us to obtain the sovereignty we want.…

Palestine is our ever memorable historic home. The very name of Palestine would attract our people with a force of marvelous potency. Supposing his Majesty the Sultan [of the Ottoman Empire] were to give us Palestine, we could in return undertake to regulate the whole finances of Turkey. We should there form a portion of the rampart of Europe against Asia, an outpost of civilization as opposed to barbarism. We should as a neutral State remain in contact with all Europe, which would have to guarantee our existence. The sanctuaries of Christendom would be safeguarded by assigning to them an extraterritorial status such as is well known to the law of nations. We should form a guard of honor about these sanctuaries, answering for the fulfillment of this duty with our existence. This guard of honor would be the great symbol of the solution of the Jewish Question after eighteen centuries of Jewish suffering.

 Why did Herzl believe that Palestine was necessary for Jews? How does he seek to gain the acceptance of the Ottoman sultan and the Christian nations of Europe?

Source: From Theodor Herzl, *The Jewish State*, 3rd ed. Sylvia D-Anigdor, trans.

1830s, photography became popular and widespread after George Eastman created the first Kodak camera in 1888 for the mass market. What was the point of an artist's doing what the camera did better? Unlike the camera, which could only mirror reality, artists could create reality. Like the Symbolist writers of the time, artists sought meaning in individual consciousness.

By 1905, one of the most important figures in modern art was just beginning his career. Pablo Picasso (PAHB-loh pi-KAH-soh) (1881–1973) was from Spain but settled in Paris in 1904. Picasso was extremely flexible and painted in a remarkable variety of styles. He was instrumental in the development of a new style called **Cubism** that used geometrical designs as visual stimuli to re-create reality in the viewer's mind.

The modern artist's flight from "visual reality" reached a high point in 1910 with the beginning of abstract painting. A Russian who worked in Germany, Wassily Kandinsky (vus-YEEL-yee kan-DIN-skee) (1866–1944) was one of the founders of **abstract painting**. As is evident in his *Square with White Border*, Kandinsky sought to avoid representation altogether. He believed that art should speak directly to the soul. To do so, it must avoid any reference to visual reality and concentrate on line and color.

Modernism in the arts revolutionized architecture and architectural practices. A new principle known as **functionalism** motivated this revolution. Functionalism meant that buildings, like the products of machines, should be "functional" or

COMPARATIVE ILLUSTRATION

Painting—West and East. Berthe Morisot, the first female painter to join the Impressionists, developed her own unique style. Her gentle colors and strong use of pastels are especially evident in *Young Girl by the Window*, seen at the left. The French Impressionist style also spread abroad. One of the most outstanding Japanese artists of the time was Kuroda Seiki (koor-OH-duh SAY-kee) (1866–1924), who returned from nine years in Paris to open a Western-style school of painting in Tokyo. Shown at the right is his *Under the Trees*, painted in 1898, an example of the fusion of contemporary French Impressionist painting with the Japanese tradition of courtesan prints.

Q *What differences and similarities do you notice in these two paintings?*

Vincent van Gogh, *The Starry Night*. The Dutch painter Vincent van Gogh was a major figure among the Post-Impressionists. His originality and power of expression made a strong impact on his artistic successors. In *The Starry Night*, van Gogh's subjective vision was given full play as the dynamic swirling forms of the heavens above overwhelm the village below. The heavens seem alive with a mysterious spiritual force.

Pablo Picasso, *Les Demoiselles d'Avignon.* Pablo Picasso, a major pioneer and activist of modern art, experimented with a remarkable variety of modern styles. *Les Demoiselles d'Avignon* (lay dem-wah-ZEL dah-vee-NYONH) (1907) was the first great example of Cubism, which one art historian has called "the first style of [the twentieth] century to break radically with the past." Geometrical shapes replace traditional forms, forcing the viewer to re-create reality in his or her own mind. The head at the upper left of the painting reflects Picasso's attraction to aspects of African art, as is evident from the mask shown at the left.

useful, fulfilling the purpose for which they were constructed. Art and engineering were to be unified, and all unnecessary ornamentation was to be stripped away.

The United States was a leader in these pioneering architectural designs. Unprecedented urban growth and the absence of restrictive architectural traditions allowed for new building methods, especially in the relatively new city of Chicago. The Chicago School of the 1890s, led by Louis H. Sullivan (1856–1924), used reinforced concrete, steel frames, and electric elevators to build skyscrapers virtually free of external ornamentation. One of Sullivan's most successful pupils was Frank Lloyd Wright (1867–1959), who became known for innovative designs in domestic architecture. Wright's private houses, built chiefly for wealthy patrons, featured geometrical structures with long lines, overhanging roofs, and severe planes of brick and stone. The interiors were open spaces and included cathedral ceilings and built-in furniture and lighting. Wright pioneered the modern American house.

Wassily Kandinsky, *Square with White Border.* One of the originators of abstract painting was the Russian Wassily Kandinsky, who sought to eliminate representation altogether by focusing on color and avoiding any resemblance to visual reality. In *Square with White Border*, Kandinsky used color "to send light into the darkness of men's hearts." He believed that color, like music, could fulfill a spiritual goal of appealing directly to the human being.

CHAPTER SUMMARY

Since the sixteenth century, much of the Western Hemisphere had been under the control of Great Britain, Spain, and Portugal. But between 1776 and 1826, an age of revolution in the Atlantic world led to the creation of the United States and nine new nations in Latin America. Canada and other nations in Latin America followed in the course of the nineteenth century. This age of revolution was an expression of the force of nationalism, which had first emerged as a political ideology at the end of the eighteenth century. Influential, too, were the ideas of the Enlightenment that had made an impact on intellectuals and political leaders in both North and South America.

The new nations that emerged in the Western Hemisphere did not, however, develop without challenges to their national unity. Latin American nations often found it difficult to establish stable republics and resorted to strong leaders who used military force to govern. And although Latin American nations had achieved political independence, they found themselves economically dependent on Great Britain as well as their northern neighbor. The United States dissolved into four years of bloody civil war before reconciling, and Canada achieved only questionable unity owing to distrust between the English-speaking majority and the French-speaking minority.

By the second half of the nineteenth century, much of the Western world was experiencing a new mass society in which

the lower classes in particular benefited from the right to vote, a higher standard of living, and new schools that provided them with some education. New forms of mass transportation, combined with new work patterns, enabled large numbers of people to enjoy weekend trips to amusement parks and seaside resorts, as well as to participate in new mass leisure activities.

The cultural revolutions before 1914 produced anxiety and a crisis of confidence in Western civilization. Albert Einstein showed that time and space were relative to the observer, that matter was simply another form of energy, and that the old Newtonian view of the universe was no longer valid. Sigmund Freud added to the uncertainties of the age with his argument that human behavior was governed not by reason but by the unconscious. Some intellectuals used the ideas of Charles Darwin to argue that in the struggle of race and nations, only the fittest survive. Collectively, these new ideas helped create a modern consciousness that questioned most Europeans' optimistic faith in reason, the rational structure of nature, and the certainty of progress. As we shall see in Chapter 23, the devastating experiences of World War I would turn this culture of uncertainty into a way of life after 1918.

CHAPTER TIMELINE

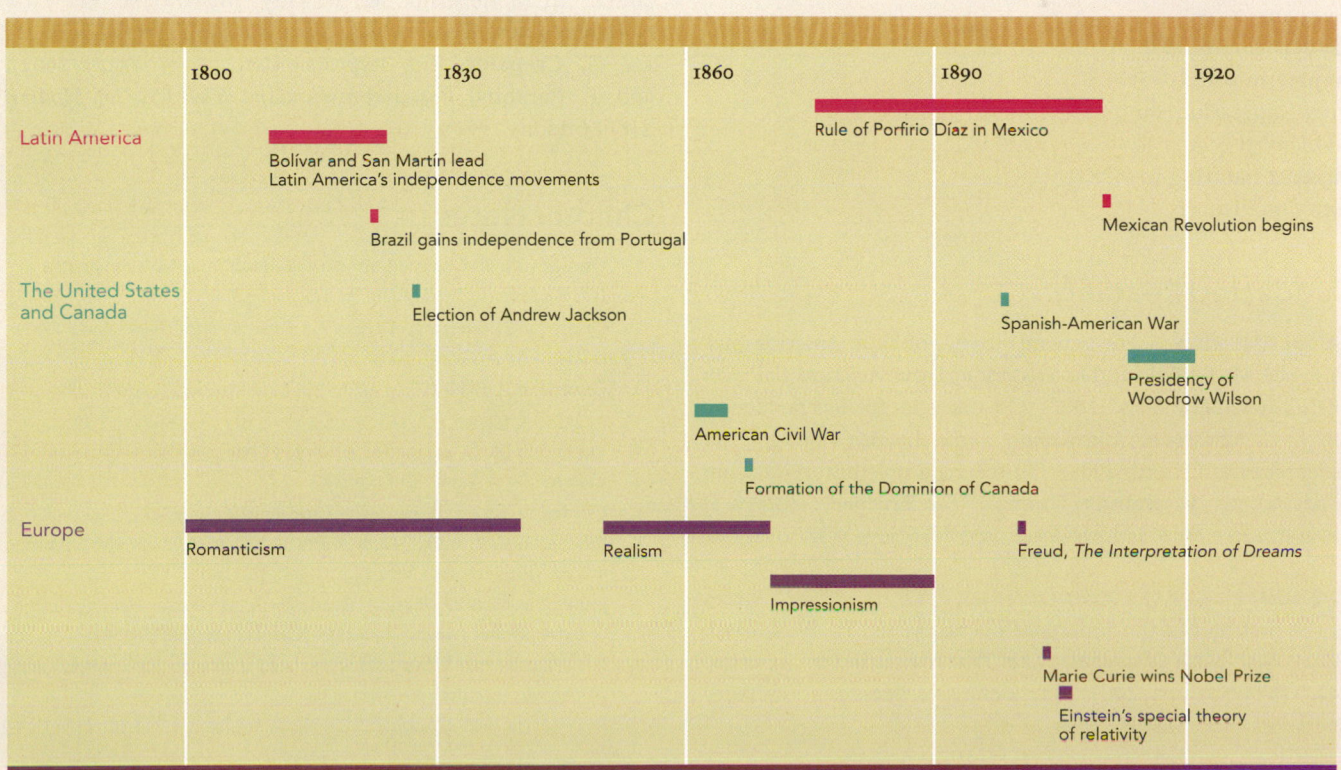

	1800	1830	1860	1890	1920
Latin America				Rule of Porfirio Díaz in Mexico	
		Bolívar and San Martín lead Latin America's independence movements			Mexican Revolution begins
		Brazil gains independence from Portugal			
The United States and Canada		Election of Andrew Jackson		Spanish-American War	
					Presidency of Woodrow Wilson
			American Civil War		
			Formation of the Dominion of Canada		
Europe	Romanticism		Realism	Freud, *The Interpretation of Dreams*	
			Impressionism		
				Marie Curie wins Nobel Prize	
				Einstein's special theory of relativity	

CHAPTER REVIEW

Upon Reflection

Q What were the similarities and dissimilarities in the development of Latin American nations, the United States, and Canada in the nineteenth century?

Q How were the promises and problems of the new mass society reflected in education, leisure, and the experiences of women?

Q How is Modernism evident in literature and the arts between 1870 and 1914? How do these literary and artistic products reflect the political and social developments of the age?

Key Terms

caudillos (p. 577)
mass society (p. 584)
nation-states (p. 584)
suffragists (p. 588)
mass education (p. 588)
mass leisure (p. 590)
Romanticism (p. 592)
Gothic literature (p. 592)
secularization (p. 593)
organic evolution (p. 593)
natural selection (p. 593)
Realism (p. 593)
relativity theory (p. 595)
psychoanalysis (p. 595)
Social Darwinism (p. 596)
Aryans (p. 596)
Zionism (p. 597)
Modernism (p. 597)
Impressionism (p. 597)
Post-Impressionism (p. 597)
Cubism (p. 598)
abstract painting (p. 598)
functionalism (p. 598)

Suggested Reading

LATIN AMERICA For general surveys of Latin American history, see **M. C. Eakin,** *The History of Latin America: Collision of Cultures* (New York, 2007). On the wars for independence, see **J. C. Chasteen,** *Americanos: Latin America's Struggle for Independence* (Oxford, 2008). On the economic history of Latin America, see **V. Bulmer-Thomas,** *The Economic History of Latin America Since Independence*, 2nd ed. (New York, 2003).

THE UNITED STATES AND CANADA On the United States in the first half of the nineteenth century, see **D. W. Howe,** *What God Hath Wrought: The Transformation of America, 1815–1848* (Oxford, 2007). The definitive one-volume history of the American Civil War is **J. M. McPherson,** *Battle Cry of Freedom: The Civil War Era* in the Oxford History of the United States series (New York, 2003). On the second half of the nineteenth century, see **L. Gould,** *America in the Progressive Era, 1890–1914* (New York, 2001). For a general history of Canada, see **S. W. See,** *History of Canada* (Westport, N.Y., 2001).

THE EMERGENCE OF MASS SOCIETY IN THE WEST For a good introduction to housing reform on the continent, see **N. Bullock and J. Read,** *The Movement for Housing Reform in Germany and France, 1840–1914* (Cambridge, 1985). There are good overviews of women's experiences in the nineteenth century in **B. Smith,** *Changing Lives: Women in European History Since 1700*, rev. ed. (Lexington, Mass., 2005). A concise and well-presented survey of leisure patterns is **G. Cross,** *A Social History of Leisure Since 1600* (State College, Pa., 1989).

ROMANTICISM AND REALISM On the ideas of the Romantics, see **M. Cranston,** *The Romantic Movement* (Oxford, 1994). For an introduction to the arts, see **I. Ciseri,** *Romanticism 1780–1860: A New Sensibility* (New York, 2003). On Realism, **J. Malpas,** *Realism* (Cambridge, 1997), is a good introduction.

TOWARD THE MODERN CONSCIOUSNESS: INTELLECTUAL AND CULTURAL DEVELOPMENTS On Freud, see **P. D. Kramer,** *Sigmund Freud: Inventor of the Modern Mind* (New York, 2006). European racism is analyzed in **N. MacMaster,** *Racism in Europe, 1870–2000* (New York, 2001). On Modernism, see **P. Gay,** *Modernism: The Lure of Heresy* (New York, 2007). Very valuable on modern art are **G. Crepaldi,** *The Impressionists* (New York, 2002), and **T. Parsons,** *Post-Impressionism: The Rise of Modern Art* (London, 1992).

Chapter Notes

1. Quoted in J. C. Chasteen, *Americanos: Latin America's Struggle for Independence* (Oxford, 2008), p. 122.
2. Quoted in H. Herring, *A History of Latin America* (New York, 1961), p. 255.
3. Quoted in P. Bakewell, *A History of Latin America* (Oxford, 1997), p. 367.
4. Quoted in M. C. Eakin, *The History of Latin America: Collision of Cultures* (New York, 2007), p. 188.
5. Quoted in Bakewell, *History of Latin America*, p. 372.
6. Quoted in E. B. Burns, *Latin America: A Concise Interpretive History*, 4th ed. (Englewood Cliffs, N.J., 1986), p. 116.
7. Quoted in N. Bullock and J. Read, *The Movement for Housing Reform in Germany and France, 1840–1914* (Cambridge, 1985), p. 42.
8. W. Wordsworth, "The Tables Turned," *Poems of Wordsworth*, ed. M. Arnold (London, 1963), p. 138.

9. Quoted in A. E. E. McKenzie, *The Major Achievements of Science* (New York, 1960), vol. 1, p. 310.

10. F. von Bernhardi, *Germany and the Next War*, trans. A. H. Powles (New York, 1914), pp. 18–19.

11. Quoted in J. Rewald, *History of Impressionism* (New York, 1961), pp. 456–458.

12. Quoted in A. Higonnet, *Berthe Morisot's Images of Women* (Cambridge, Mass., 1992), p. 19.

MindTap is a fully online, highly personalized learning experience built upon Cengage Learning content. MindTap combines student learning tools—readings, multimedia, activities, and assessments—into a singular Learning Path that guides students through their course.

The High Tide of Imperialism

Revere the conquering heroes: Establishing British rule in Africa

Mansell/Time Life Pictures/Getty Images

CHAPTER OUTLINE AND FOCUS QUESTIONS

The Spread of Colonial Rule

Q What were the causes of the new imperialism of the nineteenth century, and how did it differ from European expansion in earlier periods?

The Colonial System

Q What types of administrative systems did the various colonial powers establish in their colonies, and how did these systems reflect the general philosophy of colonialism?

India Under the British Raj

Q What were some of the major consequences of British rule in India, and how did they affect the Indian people?

Colonial Regimes in Southeast Asia

Q Which Western countries were most active in seeking colonial possessions in Southeast Asia, and what were their motives in doing so?

Empire Building in Africa

Q What factors were behind the "scramble for Africa," and what impact did it have on the continent?

The Emergence of Anticolonialism

Q How did the subject peoples respond to colonialism, and what role did nationalism play in their response?

CRITICAL THINKING

Q What were the consequences of the new imperialism of the nineteenth century for the colonies of the European powers? How should the imperialist countries be evaluated in terms of their motives and stated objectives?

CONNECTIONS TO TODAY

Q Based on the definition of imperialism contained in this chapter, do you think it is fair to conclude that the United States is an imperialist nation?

IN 1877, THE YOUNG BRITISH empire builder Cecil Rhodes drew up his last will and testament. He bequeathed his fortune, achieved as a diamond magnate in South Africa, to two of his close friends and acquaintances. He also instructed them to use the inheritance to form a secret society with the aim of bringing about "the extension of British rule throughout the world, the perfecting of a system of emigration from the United Kingdom ... especially the occupation by British settlers of the entire continent of Africa, the Holy Land, the valley of the Euphrates, the Islands of Cyprus and Candia [Crete], the whole of South America.... The ultimate recovery of the United States of America as an integral part of the British Empire ... then finally the foundation of so great a power as to hereafter render wars impossible and promote the best interests of humanity."[1]

Preposterous as such ideas sound today, they serve as a graphic reminder of the hubris that characterized the worldview of Rhodes and many of his contemporaries during the age of imperialism, as well as the complex union of moral concern and vaulting ambition that motivated their actions on the world stage.

Through their efforts, Western colonialism spread throughout much of the non-Western world during the nineteenth and early twentieth centuries. Spurred by the demands of the Industrial Revolution, a few powerful Western states—notably, Great Britain, France, Germany,

Russia, and the United States—competed avariciously for consumer markets and raw materials for their expanding economies. By the end of the nineteenth century, virtually all of the traditional societies in Asia and Africa were under direct or indirect colonial rule. As the new century began, the Western imprint on Asian and African societies, for better or for worse, appeared to be a permanent feature of the political and cultural landscape. ❧

The Spread of Colonial Rule

 FOCUS QUESTION: What were the causes of the new imperialism of the nineteenth century, and how did it differ from European expansion in earlier periods?

In the nineteenth century, a new phase of Western expansion into Asia and Africa began. Whereas European aims in the East before 1800 could be summed up in Vasco da Gama's famous phrase "Christians and spices," now a new relationship took shape as European nations began to view Asian and African societies as sources of industrial raw materials and as markets for Western manufactured goods. No longer were Western gold and silver exchanged for cloves, pepper, tea, silk, and porcelain. Now the prodigious output of European factories was sent to Africa and Asia in return for oil, tin, rubber, and the other resources needed to fuel the Western industrial machine. This relationship between the West and Asian and African societies has been called the new **imperialism** (see the Comparative Essay "Imperialisms Old and New" on p. 606).

The Motives

The reason for this change, of course, was the Industrial Revolution, which began in England in the late eighteenth century and spread to the European continent a few decades later. Now industrializing countries in the West needed vital raw materials that were not available at home, as well as a reliable market for the goods produced in their factories. The latter factor became increasingly crucial as producers began to discover that their home markets could not always absorb domestic output and that they had to export their manufactures to make a profit. When consumer demand lagged, economic depression threatened.

The relationship between colonialism and national survival was expressed directly in a speech by the French politician Jules Ferry (ZHOOL feh-REE) in 1885. A policy of "containment or abstinence," he warned, would set France on "the broad road to decadence" and initiate its decline into a "third- or fourth-rate power." British imperialists agreed, convinced by social Darwinism (the application of Charles Darwin's theory of evolution to society) that in the struggle between nations, only the fit are victorious and survive. As the British professor of mathematics Karl Pearson argued in 1900, "The path of progress is strewn with the wrecks of nations; traces are everywhere to be seen of the [slaughtered remains] of inferior races.... Yet these dead people are, in very truth, the stepping stones on which

mankind has arisen to the higher intellectual and deeper emotional life of today."[2]

For some, colonialism had a moral purpose, whether to promote Christianity or to build a better world. The British colonial official Henry Curzon (CURR-zun) declared that the British Empire "was under Providence, the greatest instrument for good that the world has seen." To Cecil Rhodes, the most famous empire builder of his day, the extraction of material wealth from the colonies was only a secondary matter. "My ruling purpose," he remarked, "is the extension of the British Empire."[3] That British Empire, on which, as the saying went, "the sun never set," was the envy of its rivals and was viewed as the primary source of British global dominance during the second half of the nineteenth century.

The Tactics

With the change in European motives for colonization came a corresponding shift in tactics. Earlier, when their economic interests were more limited, European states had generally been satisfied to deal with existing independent countries rather than attempting to establish direct control over vast territories. There had been exceptions where state power at the local level was at the point of collapse (as in India), where European economic interests were especially intense (as in Latin America and the East Indies), or where there was no centralized authority (as in North America and the Philippines). But for the most part, the Western presence in Asia and Africa had been limited to controlling the regional trade network and establishing a few footholds where the foreigners could carry on trade and missionary activity.

After 1800, the demands of industrialization in Europe created a new set of dynamics. Maintaining access to industrial raw materials such as tin and rubber and setting up reliable markets for European manufactured products required more extensive control over colonial territories. As competition for colonies increased, the imperialist powers sought to solidify their hold over their territories to protect them from attack by their rivals. During the last two decades of the nineteenth century, the quest for colonies became a scramble as all the major European states, now joined by the United States and Japan, engaged in a global land grab. In many cases, economic interests were secondary to security concerns or the requirements of national prestige. In Africa, for example, the British engaged in a struggle with their rivals to protect their interests in the Suez Canal and the Red Sea. In Southeast Asia, the United States seized the Philippines from Spain at least partly to keep them out of the hands of the Japanese, and the French took over Indochina for fear that it would otherwise be occupied by Germany, Japan, or the United States.

By 1900, almost all the societies of Africa and Asia were either under full colonial rule or, as in the case of China and the Ottoman Empire, at a point of virtual collapse. Only a handful of states, such as Japan in East Asia, Thailand in Southeast Asia, Afghanistan and Persia in the Middle East, and mountainous Ethiopia in East Africa, managed to escape internal disintegration or subjection to colonial rule. For the most part, the exceptions were the result of good fortune

Imperialisms Old and New

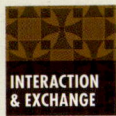

The Random House Dictionary of the English Language defines *imperialism* as "the policy of extending the rule or authority of an empire or nation over foreign countries, or of acquiring and holding colonies and dependencies." The word derives from the Latin verb meaning "to command, or rule" and has been applied to certain types of political entities since the days of the Roman Empire.

At first, the term was used in situations described by the first part of the dictionary definition. An empire was larger than a kingdom and was composed of "an aggregate of nations and peoples," all ruled by an emperor who represented one dominant ethnic or religious group within the territory under his command. The lands under imperial rule were usually, but not always, contiguous. Good examples include the Roman Empire—whose sway extended well beyond the shores of the Italian peninsula—the Chinese Empire, the Mongolian Empire in Central Asia, the empires of Ghana and Mali in West Africa, and perhaps the Inkan Empire in South America.

More recently, the second part of the definition has come to the fore. As Western expansion into Asia and Africa gathered strength during the nineteenth century, it became fashionable to call that process "imperialism" as well. In this instance, the expansion was motivated by the efforts of capitalist states in the West to seize markets, cheap raw materials, and lucrative avenues for investment in the countries beyond Western civilization. Eventually, it resulted in the creation of colonies ruled by the imperialist power. In this interpretation, the primary motives behind imperial expansion were economic. The best-known promoter of this view was the British political economist John A. Hobson, who published a major analysis, *Imperialism: A Study*, in 1902. In this influential book, Hobson maintained that modern imperialism was a direct consequence of the modern industrial economy.

As historians began to analyze the phenomenon, however, many became convinced that the motivations of the imperial powers were not simply economic. As Hobson himself conceded, economic concerns were inevitably tinged with political overtones and questions of national grandeur and moral purpose as well. To nineteenth-century Europeans, economic wealth, national status, and political power went hand in hand with the possession of a colonial empire. To global strategists, colonies brought tangible benefits in the world of balance-of-power politics as well as economic profits, and many nations pursued colonies as much to gain advantage over their rivals as to acquire territory for its own sake.

After World War II, when colonies throughout Asia and Africa were replaced by independent nations, a new term *neocolonialism* appeared to describe the situation in which imperialist nations cede a formal degree of political independence to their former colonies, but continue to exercise control by various political and economic means. Hence, in the view of many critics in the former colonial territories, Western imperialism has not disappeared but has simply found other ways to maintain its influence. We will discuss this issue further in Part V.

 What were the principal motives of the major trading nations for seizing colonies in Asia and Africa in the late nineteenth century?

Gateway to India. Built in the Roman imperial style by the British to commemorate the visit to India of King George V and Queen Mary in 1911, the Gateway to India was erected at the water's edge in the harbor of Bombay (now Mumbai), India's greatest port city. For thousands of British citizens arriving in India, the Gateway to India was the first view of their new home and a symbol of the power and majesty of the British raj.

rather than design. Thailand escaped subjugation primarily because officials in London and Paris found it more convenient to transform the country into a buffer state than to fight over it. Ethiopia and Afghanistan survived not only because of their long tradition of fierce resistance to outside threats, but also because of their remote locations and mountainous terrain. Only Japan managed to avoid the common fate through a concerted strategy of political and economic reform. By the end of the nineteenth century, Japan itself had become engaged in the pursuit of colonies (see Chapter 22).

The Colonial System

Q **FOCUS QUESTION:** What types of administrative systems did the various colonial powers establish in their colonies, and how did these systems reflect the general philosophy of colonialism?

Once they had control of most of the world, what did the colonial powers do with it? As we have seen, their primary objective was to exploit the natural resources of the subject areas and to open up markets for manufactured goods and capital investment from the mother country. In some cases, that goal could be realized in cooperation with local political elites, whose loyalty could be earned, or purchased, by economic rewards or by confirming them in their positions of authority and status in a new colonial setting. Sometimes, however, this policy of **indirect rule** was not feasible because local leaders refused to cooperate with their colonial masters or even actively resisted the foreign conquest. In such cases, the local elites were removed from power and replaced with a new set of officials recruited from the mother country.

In general, the societies most likely to actively resist colonial conquest were those with a long tradition of national cohesion and independence, such as Burma and Vietnam in Asia and the Muslim states in northern Nigeria and Morocco in Africa. In those areas, the colonial powers encountered higher levels of resistance and consequently tended to dispense with local collaborators and govern by direct means. In some parts of Africa, the Indian subcontinent, and the Malay Peninsula, where the local authorities, for whatever reason, were willing to collaborate with the imperialist powers, indirect rule was more common.

The distinctions between **direct rule** and indirect rule were not merely academic and often had fateful consequences for the peoples involved. Where colonial powers encountered resistance and were forced to overthrow local political elites, they often adopted policies designed to eradicate the source of resistance and destroy the traditional culture. Such policies often had quite corrosive effects on the indigenous societies and provoked resentment and resistance that not only marked the colonial relationship but even affected relations after the restoration of national independence. The bitter struggles after World War II in Algeria, the Dutch East Indies, and Vietnam can be ascribed in part to that phenomenon.

The Philosophy of Colonialism

To justify their rule, the colonial powers appealed in part to the time-honored maxim of "might makes right." By the end of the nineteenth century, that attitude received pseudoscientific validation from the concept of social Darwinism, which maintained that only societies that moved aggressively to adapt to changing circumstances would survive and prosper in a world governed by the Darwinian law of "survival of the fittest."

Some people, however, were uncomfortable with such a brutal view of the law of nature and sought a moral justification that appeared to benefit the victim. Here again, social Darwinism pointed the way. In that view, by bringing the benefits of Western democracy, capitalism, and Christianity to the tradition-ridden societies of Africa and Asia, the colonial powers were enabling backward peoples to adapt to the challenges of the modern world. Buttressed by such comforting theories, sensitive Western minds could ignore the brutal aspects of colonialism and persuade themselves that in the long run the results would be beneficial for both sides. Few were as adept at describing the "civilizing mission" of colonialism as the French administrator and twice governor-general of French Indochina Albert Sarraut (ahl-BAYR sah-ROH). While admitting that colonialism was originally an "act of force" undertaken for commercial profit, he insisted that by redistributing the wealth of the earth, the colonial process would result in a better life for all:

> Is it just, is it legitimate that such [an uneven distribution of resources] should be indefinitely prolonged? ... No!... Humanity is distributed throughout the globe. No race, no people has the right or power to isolate itself egotistically from the movements and necessities of universal life.[4]

The Company Resident and His Puppet. The British of the East India Company gradually replaced the sovereigns of the once independent Indian states with puppet rulers who carried out the company's policies. Here we see the company's resident dominating a procession in Tanjore in 1825, while the Indian ruler, Sarabhoji, follows like an obedient shadow. As a boy, Sarabhoji had been educated by European tutors and had filled his life and home with English books and furnishings.

Art Media · Victoria and Albert Museum, London/HIP/The Image Works

White Man's Burden, Black Man's Sorrow

ONE OF THE JUSTIFICATIONS FOR MODERN IMPERIALISM was the notion that the allegedly "more advanced" white peoples had the moral responsibility to raise "ignorant" indigenous peoples to a higher level of civilization. Few captured this notion better than the British poet Rudyard Kipling (1865–1936) in his famous poem "The White Man's Burden." His appeal, directed to the United States, became one of the most famous verses in the English-speaking world.

That sense of moral responsibility, however, was often misplaced or, even worse, laced with hypocrisy. All too often, the consequences of imperial rule were detrimental to almost everyone living under colonial authority. Few observers described the destructive effects of Western imperialism on the African people as well as Edmund Morel, a British journalist whose book *The Black Man's Burden* pointed out some of the more harmful aspects of colonialism in the Belgian Congo. The brutal treatment of Congolese workers involved in gathering rubber, ivory, and palm oil for export aroused an international outcry and in 1903 led to the formation of a commission under British consul Roger Casement to bring about reforms.

Rudyard Kipling, "The White Man's Burden"

Take up the White Man's burden—
Send forth the best ye breed—
Go bind your sons to exile
To serve your captives' need;
To wait in heavy harness,
On fluttered folk and wild—
Your new-caught sullen peoples,
Half-devil and half-child.

Take up the White Man's burden—
In patience to abide,
To veil the threat of terror
And check the show of pride;

By open speech and simple,
An hundred times made plain
To seek another's profit,
And work another's gain.

Take up the White Man's burden—
The savage wars of peace—
Fill full the mouth of Famine
And bid the sickness cease;
And when your goal is nearest
The end for others sought,
Watch Sloth and heathen Folly
Bring all your hopes to nought.

Edmund Morel, *The Black Man's Burden*

It is [the Africans] who carry the "Black man's burden." They have not withered away before the white man's occupation. Indeed … Africa has ultimately absorbed within itself every Caucasian and, for that matter, every Semitic invader, too. In hewing out for himself a fixed abode in Africa, the white man has massacred the African in heaps. The African has survived, and it is well for the white settlers that he has.…

What the partial occupation of his soil by the white man has failed to do; what the mapping out of European political "spheres of influence" has failed to do; what the Maxim and the rifle, the slave gang, labour in the bowels of the earth and the lash, have failed to do; what imported measles, smallpox and syphilis have failed to do; whatever the overseas slave trade failed to do; the power of modern capitalistic exploitation, assisted by modern engines of destruction, may yet succeed in accomplishing.

For from the evils of the latter, scientifically applied and enforced, there is no escape for the African. Its destructive effects are not spasmodic; they are permanent. In its permanence resides its fatal consequences. It kills not the body merely, but the soul. It breaks the spirit. It attacks the African at every turn, from every point of vantage. It wrecks his polity, uproots him from the land, invades his family life, destroys his natural pursuits and occupations, claims his whole time, enslaves him in his own home.

 According to Kipling, why should Western nations take up the "white man's burden"? What was the "black man's burden," in the eyes of Edmund Morel?

Sources: From Rudyard Kipling, "The White Man's Burden," *McClure's Magazine* 12 (Feb. 1899). From Edmund Morel, *Black Man's Burden*, Metro Books, 1972.

But what about the possibility that historically and culturally the societies of Asia and Africa were fundamentally different from those of the West and could not, or would not, be persuaded to transform themselves along Western lines? Was the human condition universal, or were human beings so shaped by their history and geographic environment that their civilizations would inevitably remain distinct? In that case, a policy of cultural transformation could not be expected to succeed and could even lead to disaster (see Opposing Viewpoints "White Man's Burden, Black Man's Sorrow" above).

ASSIMILATION AND ASSOCIATION In fact, colonial theorists never decided this issue one way or the other. The French, who were most inclined to philosophize about the problem, adopted the terms **assimilation** (which implied an effort to transform colonial societies in the Western image) and **association** (implying collaboration with local elites while leaving local traditions alone) to describe the two alternatives and then proceeded to vacillate between them. French policy in Indochina, for example, began as one of association but switched to assimilation under pressure from those who felt that colonial powers owed a debt to their subject peoples. But assimilation (which in any case was never accepted as feasible or desirable by many colonial officials) aroused resentment among the local population, many of whom opposed the destruction of their culture and traditions. In the end, the French abandoned the attempt to justify their presence and fell back on a policy of ruling by force of arms.

Other colonial powers expressed little interest in the philosophical aspects of the issue. The British, whether out of a sense of pragmatism or of racial superiority, refused to entertain the possibility of assimilation and treated their subject peoples as culturally and racially distinct. The United States, in formulating a colonial policy for the Philippines, straddled the issue by adopting a policy of assimilation in theory but often neglecting to put it into practice.

In reality, colonial policies varied greatly from country to country based on local conditions and the needs of the moment. In general, the French usually tried to impose a centralized administrative system on their colonies that mirrored the system in use in France, whereas the British sought to transform local aristocrats into the equivalent of the landed gentry at home in Britain. Other differences stemmed from conditions in the colonies themselves and the colonizers' aspirations for them. For instance, some Western powers believed they could obtain only limited economic benefits from some colonies and therefore treated those colonies somewhat differently than colonies where they perceived that large profits could be made.

To many of the colonial peoples, such questions must have appeared academic, since in their eyes the primary objective of all colonial officials was economic exploitation and the retention of power. Like the British soldier in Kipling's poem "On the Road to Mandalay," all too many Westerners living in the colonies viewed the Buddha as nothing but a "bloomin' idol made of mud."

India Under the British Raj

 Q FOCUS QUESTION: What were some of the major consequences of British rule in India, and how did they affect the Indian people?

By 1800, the once glorious empire of the Mughals (MOO-guls) had been reduced by British military power to a shadow of its former greatness. During the next few decades, the British sought to consolidate their control over the Indian subcontinent, expanding from their base areas along the coast into the interior. Some territories were taken over directly, first by the East India Company and later by the British crown; others were ruled indirectly through their local maharajas (mah-huh-RAH-juhs) and rajas (RAH-juhs).

Colonial Reforms

As the Indian territory under British rule expanded, British colonial officials began to initiate reforms designed to bring Indian society in line with conditions in western Europe. British governance over the subcontinent brought order and stability to a society that had been rent by civil war. By the early nineteenth century, British control had been consolidated and led to a relatively honest and efficient government that in many respects operated to the benefit of the average Indian. One of the benefits of the period was the heightened attention given to education. Through the efforts of the British administrator Thomas Babington Macaulay (muh-KAHL-lee), a new school system was established to train the children of Indian elites, and the British civil service examination was introduced. The instruction of young girls also expanded, with the primary purpose of making them better wives and mothers for the educated male population (see the box "Indian in Blood, English in Taste and Intellect" on p. 610). In 1875, a Madras (muh-DRAS or muh-DRAHS) medical college admitted an Indian woman for the first time.

British rule also brought an end to some of the more inhumane aspects of Indian tradition. The practice of *sati* (suh-TEE) was outlawed, and widows were legally permitted to remarry. The British also attempted to put an end to the endemic brigandage (known as *thuggee*, which gave rise to the English word thug) that had plagued travelers in India since time immemorial. Railroads, the telegraph, and the postal service were introduced to India shortly after they appeared in Great Britain itself. Work began on the main highway from Calcutta to Delhi (DEL-ee) in 1839 (see Map 21.1), and the first rail network was opened in 1853. A new penal code based on the British model was adopted, and health and sanitation conditions were improved.

The Cost of Colonialism

But many Indians paid a high price for the peace and stability brought by the British **raj** (RAHJ) (from the Indian *raja*, or prince). Perhaps the most flagrant cost was economic. While British entrepreneurs and a small percentage of the Indian population attached to the imperial system reaped financial benefits from British rule, it brought hardship to millions of others in both the cities and the rural areas. The introduction of cheap British textiles, for example, put thousands of Bengali women out of work and severely damaged the cottage textile industry.

In rural areas, the British introduced the *zamindar* (zuh-meen-DAHR) system (see Chapter 16) in the expectation that it would both facilitate the collection of agricultural taxes and create a new landed gentry, who could, as in Britain, become the conservative foundation of imperial rule. But many local gentry took advantage of this new authority to increase taxes and force the less fortunate peasants to become

Indian in Blood, English in Taste and Intellect

INTERACTION & EXCHANGE

THOMAS BABINGTON MACAULAY (1800–1859) was named a member of the Supreme Council of India in the early 1830s. In that capacity, he was responsible for drawing up a new educational policy for British subjects in the area. In his *Minute on Education*, he considered the claims of English and various local languages to become the vehicle for educational training and decided in favor of the former. It is better, he argued, to teach Indian elites about Western civilization so as "to form a class who may be interpreters between us and the millions whom we govern; a class of persons, Indian in blood and color, but English in taste, in opinions, in morals, and in intellect." Later Macaulay became a prominent historian. The debate in India over the relative benefits of English and the various Indian languages continues today.

Thomas Babington Macaulay, *Minute on Education*

We have a fund to be employed as government shall direct for the intellectual improvement of the people of this country. The simple question is, what is the most useful way of employing it?

All parties seem to be agreed on one point, that the dialects commonly spoken among the natives of this part of India contain neither literary or scientific information, and are, moreover, so poor and rude that, until they are enriched from some other quarter, it will not be easy to translate any valuable work into them....

What, then, shall the language [of education] be? One half of the Committee maintain that it should be the English. The other half strongly recommend the Arabic and Sanskrit. The whole question seems to me to be, which language is the best worth knowing?

I have no knowledge of either Sanskrit or Arabic—but I have done what I could to form a correct estimate of their value. I have read translations of the most celebrated Arabic and Sanskrit works. I have conversed both here and at home with men distinguished by their proficiency in the Eastern tongues. I am quite ready to take the Oriental learning at the valuation of the Orientalists themselves. I have never found one among them who could deny that a single shelf of a good European library was worth the whole native literature of India and Arabia....

It is, I believe, no exaggeration to say, that all the historical information which has been collected from all the books written in the Sanskrit language is less valuable than what may be found in the most paltry abridgments used at preparatory schools in England. In every branch of physical or moral philosophy the relative position of the two nations is nearly the same.

Q *How did Macaulay justify the teaching of the English language in India? Do you find his arguments persuasive? How might a critic respond?*

Source: From *Speeches by Lord Macaulay, With His Minute on Indian Education* by Thomas B. MacAuley. AMS Press, 1935.

---

tenants or lose their land entirely. When rural unrest threatened, the government passed legislation protecting farmers against eviction and unreasonable rent increases, but this measure had little effect outside the southern provinces, where it had originally been enacted.

In Great Britain, economic inequities were being addressed by introducing political reforms designed to provide the disadvantaged with the means of affecting legislation. British officials were dubious about the relevance of the British political system in a South Asian setting, however, and made few efforts during the nineteenth century to introduce democratic institutions or values to the Indian people. As one senior political figure remarked in Parliament in 1898, democratic institutions "can no more be carried to India by Englishmen ... than they can carry ice in their luggage."[5]

British colonialism was also remiss in bringing the benefits of modern science and technology to India. Some limited forms of industrialization took place, notably in the manufacturing of textiles and jute (used in making rope). The first textile mill opened in 1856. Seventy years later, there were eighty mills in the city of Bombay alone. Nevertheless, the lack of local capital and the advantages given to British imports prevented the emergence of other vital new commercial and manufacturing operations.

Foreign rule also had a psychological effect on the Indian people. Although many British colonial officials sincerely tried to improve the lot of the people under their charge, British arrogance and contempt for local tradition cut deeply into the pride of many Indians, especially those of high caste, who were accustomed to a position of superior status in India. Educated Indians trained in the Anglo-Indian school system for a career in the civil service, as well as Eurasians born to mixed marriages, often imitated the behavior and dress of their rulers, speaking English, eating Western food, and taking up European leisure activities, but many rightfully wondered where their true cultural loyalties lay (see the Comparative Illustration "Cultural Influences—East and West" on p. 612). This cultural collision was poignantly described in the novel *A Passage to India* by the British writer E. M. Forster, which relates the story of a visiting Englishwoman who becomes interested in the Indian way of life, much to the dismay of the local European community.

AFGHANISTAN

KASHMIR AND JAMMU

PUNJAB
Lahore ■ ■ Amritsar

TIBET

Delhi ■

RAJPUTANA
Agra ■
Lucknow ■

UNITED PROVINCES

Cawnpore ■

Ganges R.

ASSAM

Karachi ■

SIND

Indus R.

Varanasi (Benares) ■
Patna ■

BIHAR AND ORISSA

BENGAL

Calcutta ■

Arabian Sea

CENTRAL PROVINCES

BURMA

Bombay ■

BOMBAY

HYDERABAD

Bay of Bengal

Goa ■

MYSORE

Madras ■
Pondicherry ■

Cochin ■

CEYLON (CROWN COLONY)

0   250   500   750 Kilometers
0   250   500 Miles

Legend:
- Territory under British rule
- Territories permanently administered by government of India (mostly tribal)
- States and territories under Indian administration
- Portuguese enclave
- French enclave
- Hindu-majority provinces
- Muslim-majority provinces
- Area of large Sikh population

© 2016 Cengage Learning

MAP 21.1 India Under British Rule, 1805–1931. This map shows the different forms of rule that the British applied in India during the period it was under their control.

Q *Where were the major cities of the subcontinent located, and under whose rule did they fall?*

Colonial Regimes in Southeast Asia

Q FOCUS QUESTION: Which Western countries were most active in seeking colonial possessions in Southeast Asia, and what were their motives in doing so?

In 1800, only two societies in Southeast Asia were under effective colonial rule: the Spanish Philippines and the Dutch East Indies. During the nineteenth century, however, European interest in Southeast Asia increased rapidly, and by 1900, virtually the entire area had come under Western domination (see Map 21.2).

"Opportunity in the Orient": The Colonial Takeover in Southeast Asia

The process began after the Napoleonic wars, when the British, by agreement with the Dutch, abandoned their claims to territorial possessions in the East Indies in return for a free hand in the Malay Peninsula. In 1819, the colonial administrator Stamford Raffles (1781–1826) founded a new British colony on the island of Singapore at the tip of the peninsula. When the invention of steam power enabled merchant ships to save time and distance by passing through the Strait of Malacca rather than sailing with the westerlies across the southern Indian Ocean, Singapore became a major stopping point for traffic en route to and from China and other commercial centers in the region.

During the next few decades, the pace of European penetration into Southeast Asia accelerated as the British attacked lower Burma in 1826 and eventually established control over the country, arousing fears in France that its British rival might soon establish a monopoly of trade in South China. The French still maintained a clandestine missionary organization in Vietnam despite harsh persecution by the local authorities, who viewed Christianity as a threat to Confucian doctrine. In 1857, the French government decided to compel the Vietnamese to accept French protection. A naval attack launched a year later was not a total success, but the French eventually forced the Nguyen (NGWEN) dynasty in Vietnam to cede territories in the Mekong River delta. A generation later, French rule was extended over the remainder of the country. By 1900, French seizure of neighboring Cambodia and Laos had led to the creation of the French-ruled Indochinese Union.

After the French conquest of Indochina, Thailand was the only remaining independent state on the Southeast Asian mainland. Under the astute leadership of two remarkable rulers, King Mongkut (MAHNG-koot) (1851–1868) and his son, King Chulalongkorn (CHOO-luh-lahng-korn) (1868–1910), the Thai attempted to introduce Western learning and maintain relations with the major European powers without undermining internal stability or inviting an imperialist attack. In 1896, the British and the French agreed to preserve Thailand as an

COMPARATIVE ILLUSTRATION

Cultural Influences—East and West. When Europeans moved into Asia in the nineteenth century, some Asians began to imitate European customs for prestige or social advancement. Seen at the left, for example, is a young Vietnamese during the 1920s dressed in Western sports clothes, learning to play tennis. Sometimes, however, the cultural influence went the other way. At the right, an English nabob, as European residents in India were often called, apes the manner of an Indian aristocrat, complete with harem and hookah, the Indian water pipe. The paintings on the wall, however, are in the European style.

Q *Compare and contrast the artistic styles in these two paintings. What message do they send to the viewer?*

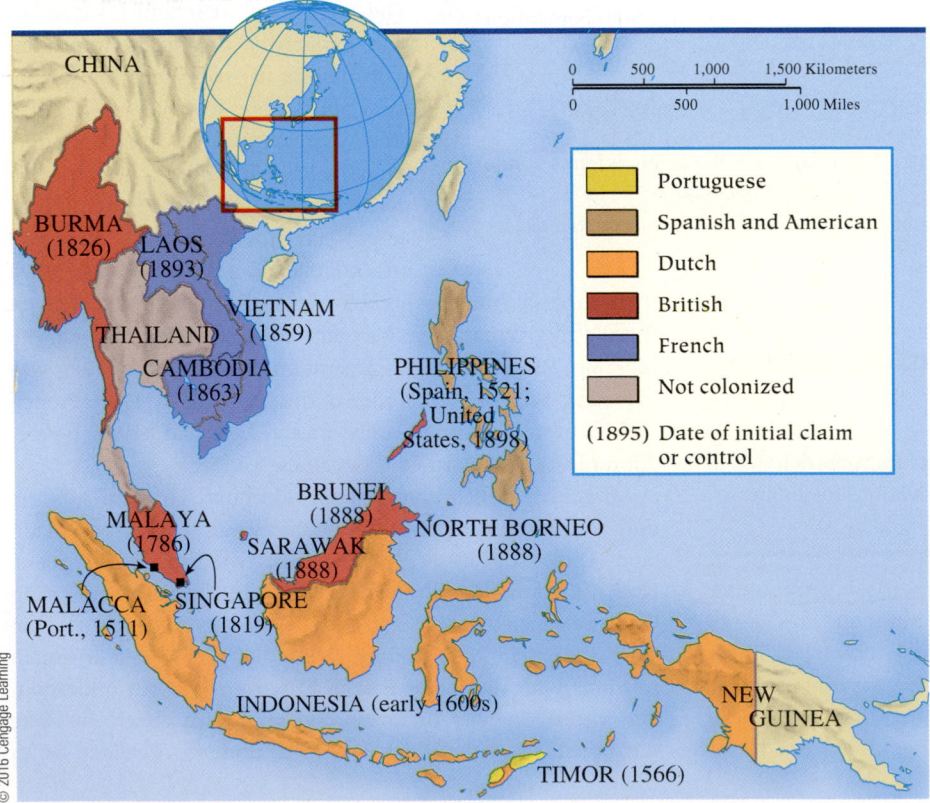

MAP 21.2 Colonial Southeast Asia.
This map shows the spread of European colonial rule into Southeast Asia from the sixteenth century to the end of the nineteenth. Malacca, initially seized by the Portuguese in 1511, was taken by the Dutch in the seventeenth century and then by the British one hundred years later.

Q *What was the significance of Malacca?*

Map legend:
- Portuguese
- Spanish and American
- Dutch
- British
- French
- Not colonized

(1895) Date of initial claim or control

CHINA
BURMA (1826)
LAOS (1893)
VIETNAM (1859)
THAILAND
CAMBODIA (1863)
PHILIPPINES (Spain, 1521; United States, 1898)
BRUNEI (1888)
MALAYA (1786)
SARAWAK (1888)
NORTH BORNEO (1888)
MALACCA (Port., 1511)
SINGAPORE (1819)
INDONESIA (early 1600s)
NEW GUINEA
TIMOR (1566)

The Harbor at Singapore. After the occupation of the strategic island of Singapore by the British in 1819, the one-time pirate haven rapidly emerged as a major transit point for British shipping between the Indian Ocean and the South China Sea. By mid-century it had become one of the most important seaports in all of Asia. In this 1850 painting by a British artist, ships from several nations anchor in the spacious harbor as they carry valuable goods between Western countries and East Asia. The modern European section of the city, with its distinctive Anglican cathedral, glimmers on the shoreline.

The French Seizure of North Vietnam. In the late 1850s, the French seized control of the southern part of Vietnam in the Mekong River delta and transformed it into the French colony of Cochin China. In the summer of 1884, the French sought to complete their conquest of Vietnam by seizing the Red River delta. In this painting by a Vietnamese artist, French troops prepare for an attack on the port city of Haiphong (Hy-PHONG) in preparation for an advance toward the Vietnamese capital of Hanoi. Eventually the entire country was occupied, and the northern part of Vietnam—renamed Tonkin—became a French protectorate.

independent buffer zone between their possessions in Southeast Asia.

The final piece in the colonial edifice in Southeast Asia was put in place in 1898, when, during the Spanish–American War, U.S. naval forces under Commodore George Dewey defeated the Spanish fleet in Manila Bay. President William McKinley agonized over the fate of the Philippines but ultimately decided that the moral thing to do was to turn the islands into an American colony to prevent them from falling into the hands of the Japanese. In fact, the Americans (like the Spanish before them) found the islands convenient as a jumping-off point for the China trade (see Chapter 22). The mixture of moral idealism and the desire for profit was reflected in a speech given in the Senate in January 1900 by Senator Albert Beveridge of Indiana:

> Mr. President, the times call for candor. The Philippines are ours forever, "territory belonging to the United States," as the Constitution calls them. And just beyond the Philippines are China's illimitable markets. We will not retreat from either.... We will not renounce our part in the mission of our

The Effects of Dutch Colonialism in Java

INTERACTION & EXCHANGE

EDUARD DOUWES DEKKER (AY-dooart DOW-uss DEK-er) was a Dutch colonial official who served in the East Indies for nearly twenty years. In 1860, he published a critique of the Dutch colonial system that had an impact in the Netherlands similar to that of Harriet Beecher Stowe's *Uncle Tom's Cabin* in the United States. In the following excerpt from his book *Max Havelaar, or Coffee Auctions of the Dutch Trading Company*, Douwes Dekker described the system as it was applied on the island of Java, in the Indonesian archipelago.

Eduard Douwes Dekker, *Max Havelaar*

The Javanese is by nature a husbandman; the ground whereon he is born, which gives much for little labor, allures him to it, and, above all things, he devotes his whole heart and soul to the cultivating of his rice fields, in which he is very clever. He grows up in the midst of his *sawahs* [rice fields] … ; when still very young, he accompanies his father to the field, where he helps him in his labor with plow and spade, in constructing dams and drains to irrigate his fields; he counts his years by harvests; he estimates time by the color of the blades in his field; he is at home amongst the companions who cut paddy with him; he chooses his wife amongst the girls of the *dessah* [village], who every evening tread the rice with joyous songs. The possession of a few buffaloes for plowing is the ideal of his dreams. The cultivation of rice is in Java what the vintage is in the Rhine provinces and in the south of France. But there came foreigners from the West, who made themselves masters of the country. They wished to profit by the fertility of the soil, and ordered the native to devote a part of his time and labor to the cultivation of other things which should produce higher profits in the markets of Europe. To persuade the lower orders to do so, they had only to follow a very simple policy. The Javanese obeys his chiefs; to win the chiefs, it was only necessary to give them a part of the gain,—and success was complete.

To be convinced of the success of that policy we need only consider the immense quantity of Javanese products sold in Holland; and we shall also be convinced of its injustice, for, if anybody should ask if the husbandman himself gets a reward in proportion to that quantity, then I must give a negative answer. The Government compels him to cultivate certain products on his ground; it punishes him if he sells what he has produced to any purchaser but itself; and it fixes the price actually paid. The expenses of transport to Europe through a privileged trading company are high; the money paid to the chiefs for encouragement increases the prime cost; and because the entire trade must produce profit, that profit cannot be got in any other way than by paying the Javanese just enough to keep him from starving, which would lessen the producing power of the nation.

According to Douwes Dekker, what was the impact of Dutch colonial policies on Javanese peasants? How might a colonial official respond to the criticism?

Source: From *Max Havelaar, or the Coffee Auctions of the Dutch Trading Company* by Multatali, translated with notes by Roy Edwards. Penguin USA, 1995.

---

race, trustee, under God, of the civilization of the world. And we will move forward to our work, not howling out regrets like slaves whipped to their burdens, but with gratitude for a task worthy of our strength, and thanksgiving to Almighty God that He has marked us as His chosen people, henceforth to lead in the regeneration of the world.[6]

Not all Filipinos agreed with Senator Beveridge's portrayal of the situation. Under the leadership of Emilio Aguinaldo (ay-MEEL-yoh ah-gwee-NAHL-doh), guerrilla forces fought bitterly against U.S. troops to establish their independence from both Spain and the United States. But America's first war against guerrilla forces in Asia was a success, and the bulk of the resistance collapsed in 1901. President McKinley had his stepping-stone to the rich markets of China.

The Nature of Colonial Rule

In Southeast Asia, economic profit was the immediate and primary aim of colonial enterprise. For that purpose, imperial powers tried wherever possible to work with local elites to facilitate the exploitation of natural resources. Indirect rule reduced the cost of training European administrators and had a less corrosive impact on the local culture. In the Dutch East Indies, for example, officials of the Dutch East India Company (or VOC, the initials of its Dutch name) entrusted local administration to the indigenous landed aristocracy, who maintained law and order and collected taxes in return for a payment from the VOC (see the box "The Effects of Dutch Colonialism in Java" above). The British followed a similar practice in Malaya. While establishing direct rule over the crucial commercial centers of Singapore and Malacca, the British allowed local Muslim rulers to maintain princely power in the interior of the peninsula.

ADMINISTRATION AND EDUCATION Indirect rule, however convenient and inexpensive, was not always feasible. In some instances, local resistance to the colonial conquest made such a policy impossible. In Burma, the staunch opposition of traditionalist forces caused the British to abolish the monarchy and administer the country directly through their colonial government in India. In Indochina, the French used both direct and indirect means. They imposed direct rule on the southern provinces in the Mekong Delta, where their economic interests were strong. In the north, however, they set up a protectorate, with the emperor retaining titular authority from his palace in Hué (HWAY). In Cambodia and Laos,

COMPARATIVE ILLUSTRATION

RELIGION & PHILOSOPHY

The Face of Christianity in Batak Country. After the Dutch began to consolidate their control over the islands of Indonesia in the eighteenth and nineteenth centuries, missionaries from the Netherlands began to evangelize among the local population. Although the majority of the population in the archipelago was Muslim and thus not receptive to conversion, the situation was different among minority populations, such as the Batak peoples, who for over two millennia have occupied upland regions in the mountains of Sumatra. Christianity has had some success among the Batak, who have combined Christian teachings with their own traditional animist beliefs. In the photo on the top, a spirit house shares the spotlight with a Christian church. Both were constructed along the lines of the traditional longhouse (bottom photo), a familiar site throughout the region.

Q Why do you think conversion to Christianity was more difficult among Muslims in the region?

where French interests were limited, local rulers were left in charge with French advisers to counsel them.

Whatever method was used, colonial regimes in Southeast Asia, as in India, were slow to create democratic institutions. The first legislative councils and assemblies were composed almost exclusively of European residents in the colony. Eventually, a few representatives from the indigenous population were admitted, but they were wealthy and conservative in their political views. When Southeast Asians complained, colonial officials reluctantly began to broaden the franchise. The French colonial official Albert Sarraut advised patience in awaiting the full benefits of colonial policy: "I will treat you like my younger brothers, but do not forget that I am the older brother. I will slowly give you the dignity of humanity."[7]

Colonial officials were also slow to adopt educational reforms. Although the introduction of Western ways was one of the justifications of imperialism, colonial officials soon discovered that educating indigenous elites could backfire. Often there were few jobs for highly trained lawyers, engineers, and architects in colonial societies, leading to the threat of an

indigestible mass of unemployed intellectuals who would take out their frustrations on the colonial regime. Educational opportunities for the common people were even harder to come by. In French-controlled Vietnam in 1917, only 3,000 of the 23,000 villages in the country had a public school. The French had opened a university in Hanoi (ha-NOY), but it was immediately closed as a result of student demonstrations. As one French official noted in voicing his opposition to increasing the number of schools in Vietnam, educating the Vietnamese meant not "one coolie less, but one rebel more."

On the other hand, Western missionaries were active in some parts of Southeast Asia where it was felt that the local population might be susceptible to the appeal of Christianity. This was especially the case among minority peoples in the mountains or on isolated islands within the region where animist beliefs continued to predominate. Missionary activity had relatively little success where great traditional religions like Buddhism, Hinduism, and Islam continued to predominate (see the Comparative Illustration "The Face of Christianity in Batak Country" above).

Colonial Regimes in Southeast Asia ■ **615**

ECONOMIC DEVELOPMENT Colonial powers were equally reluctant to take up the "white man's burden" in the area of economic development. As we have seen, their primary goals were to secure a source of cheap raw materials and to maintain markets for manufactured goods. Such objectives would be undermined by the emergence of advanced industrial economies. So colonial policy concentrated on the export of raw materials—teakwood from Burma; rubber and tin from Malaya; spices, tea and coffee, and palm oil from the East Indies; and sugar and copra (coconut meat) from the Philippines. In some Southeast Asian colonial societies, a measure of industrial development did take place to meet the needs of the European population and local elites. Major manufacturing cities such as Rangoon in lower Burma, Batavia (buh-TAY-vee-uh) on the island of Java, and Saigon (sy-GAHN) in French Indochina grew rapidly. Although the local middle class benefited from the increased economic activity, most large industrial and commercial establishments were owned and managed by Europeans or, in some cases, by Indian or Chinese merchants. In Saigon, for example, even the production of *nuoc mam* (NWAHK MAHM), the traditional Vietnamese fish sauce, was under Chinese ownership. In most cities, foreigners controlled banking, major manufacturing activities, and the import-export trade. The local residents were more apt to work in a family business, in factory or assembly plants, or as peddlers, day laborers, or rickshaw pullers—in other words, at less profitable and less capital-intensive businesses.

COLONIALISM AND THE COUNTRYSIDE Despite the growth of an urban economy, the vast majority of people in the colonial societies continued to farm the land. Many continued to live by subsistence agriculture, but the colonial policy of emphasizing cash crops for export also led to the creation of a form of plantation agriculture in which peasants were recruited to work as wage laborers on rubber and tea plantations owned by Europeans. To maintain a competitive edge, the plantation owners kept the wages of their workers at poverty level. Many plantation workers were "shanghaied" (the English term originated from the practice of recruiting laborers, often from the docks and streets of Shanghai, by unscrupulous means such as the use of force, alcohol, or drugs) to work on plantations, where conditions were often so inhumane that thousands died. High taxes, enacted by colonial governments to pay for administrative costs or improvements in the local infrastructure, were an additional heavy burden for poor peasants.

The situation was made even more difficult by the steady growth of the population. Peasants in Asia had always had large families on the assumption that a high proportion of their children would die in infancy. But improved sanitation and medical treatment, one of the salutary consequences of colonial rule, resulted in lower rates of infant mortality and a staggering increase in population. The population of the island of Java, for example, increased from about a million in the precolonial era to about 40 million at the end of the nineteenth century. Under these conditions, the rural areas could no longer support the growing populations, and many young people fled to the cities to seek jobs in factories or shops. The migratory pattern gave rise to squatter settlements in the suburbs of the major cities.

As in India, colonial rule did bring some benefits to Southeast Asia. It led to the beginnings of a modern economic infrastructure and to what is sometimes called a "modernizing elite"

The Production of Rubber. Natural rubber was one of the most important cash crops in the European colonies in Asia. Rubber trees, native to the Amazon River basin in Brazil, were eventually transplanted to Southeast Asia, where they became a major source of profit. Workers on the plantations received few benefits, however. Once the sap of the tree, called latex, was extracted, as shown on the left, it was hardened and pressed into sheets (right photo) and then sent to Europe for refining.

dedicated to the creation of an advanced industrialized society. The development of an export market helped create an entrepreneurial class in rural areas. This happened, for example, on the outer islands of the Dutch East Indies (such as Borneo and Sumatra), where small growers of rubber trees, palm trees for oil, coffee, tea, and spices began to share in the profits of the colonial enterprise.

A balanced assessment of the colonial legacy in Southeast Asia must take into account that the early stages of industrialization are difficult in any society. Even in western Europe, industrialization initially led to the creation of an impoverished and powerless proletariat, urban slums, and displaced peasants driven from the land. In much of Europe and Japan, however, the bulk of the population eventually enjoyed better material conditions as the profits from manufacturing and plantation agriculture were reinvested in the national economy and gave rise to increased consumer demand. In contrast, in Southeast Asia, most of the profits were repatriated to the colonial mother country, while displaced peasants fleeing to cities like Rangoon, Batavia, and Saigon found little opportunity for employment. Many were left with seasonal employment, with one foot on the farm and the other in the factory. The old world was being destroyed while the new one had yet to be born.

Empire Building in Africa

 FOCUS QUESTION: What factors were behind the "scramble for Africa," and what impact did it have on the continent?

Up to the beginning of the nineteenth century, the relatively limited nature of European economic interests in Africa had provided little temptation for the penetration of the interior or the political takeover of the coastal areas. The slave trade, the main source of European profit during the eighteenth century, could be carried on by using African rulers and merchants as intermediaries. Political instability, lack of transportation, and the unhealthy climate all deterred the Europeans from more extensive efforts in Africa. The situation began to change in the nineteenth century, as the growing need for industrial products, along with heightened competition from both European and African interests, created an incentive for imperialist countries to increase their economic presence in the continent.

From Slavery to "Legitimate Trade" in Africa

As the new century dawned, the slave trade was in a state of decline. One reason was the growing sense of outrage among humanitarians in several European countries over the purchase, sale, and exploitation of human beings. Dutch merchants effectively ceased trafficking in slaves in 1795, and the Danes stopped in 1803. In 1808 the slave trade was declared illegal in both Great Britain and the United States. The British began to apply pressure on other nations to follow suit, and most did so after the end of the Napoleonic wars in 1815, leaving only Portugal and Spain as European practitioners of the trade south of the equator. At first, the institution of slavery was left untouched where it already existed, but as the demand for slaves began to decline over the course of the century, by the 1880s the practice had been abolished in all major countries of the world (see the box "Tragedy at Caffard Cove" on p. 618). It continued to exist, although at a reduced rate, along the Swahili Coast of East Africa.

Economic as well as humanitarian interests contributed to the end of the slave trade. The cost of slaves had begun to rise after the middle of the eighteenth century, and the growth of the slave population reduced the need for additional labor on the plantations in the Americas. The British, with some reluctant assistance from France and the United States, added to the costs by actively using their navy to capture slave ships and free the occupants. When slavery was abolished in the United States in 1863 and in Cuba and Brazil seventeen years later, the slave trade across the Atlantic was effectively brought to an end.

As the slave trade in the Atlantic declined during the first half of the nineteenth century, European interest in what was sometimes called "legitimate trade" in natural resources increased. Exports of peanuts, timber, hides, and palm oil from West Africa increased substantially during the first decades of the century, while imports of textile goods and other manufactured products rose.

Stimulated by growing commercial interests in the area, European governments began to push for a more permanent presence along the coast. During the first decades of the nineteenth century, the British established settlements along the Gold Coast and in Sierra Leone, where they set up agricultural plantations for freed slaves who had returned from the Western Hemisphere or had been liberated by British ships while en route to the Americas. A similar haven for ex-slaves was developed with the assistance of the United States in Liberia. The French occupied the area around the Senegal River near Cape Verde, where they attempted to develop peanut plantations (see Map 21.3).

The heightened European presence in West Africa led to the emergence of a new class of Africans educated in Western culture and often employed by Europeans. Many became Christians, and some studied in European or American universities. Eventually, a few became alarmed at the exploitation suffered by their fellow Africans and began to call for efforts to defend African interests, including the formation of nation-states on the Western model.

Tragedy at Caffard Cove

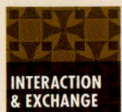

INTERACTION & EXCHANGE

THE SLAVE TRADE WAS DECLARED ILLEGAL in France in 1818, but the clandestine shipment of Africans to the Americas continued for many years afterward. At the same time, slavery was widely tolerated in the French colonies, especially in the Caribbean, where sugar plantations on the islands of Guadeloupe and Martinique depended on cheap labor for their profits. It was not until 1849 that slavery was abolished throughout the French empire.

Among the tragic events that characterized the shipment of slaves to the Americas (often called the "Middle Passage"), few are as poignant as the incident described in the passage below, which took place in 1830 on the island of Martinique. The text, which includes passages from the original official report of the incident, is taken from a memorial erected at the site many years later. Laurent Valère, a local sculptor, erected fifteen statues to commemorate the victims. The name of the ship and the name and nationality of the ship's captain, as well as the ultimate fate of the surviving victims, remain a mystery to this day.

The Caffard Memorial

Around noon on the 8th of April 1830, a sailing ship [was observed] carrying out odd maneuvers off the coast of [the town of] Diamant [on the southern coast of Martinique]; at about five P.M. [the vessel] cast anchor off the dangerous coast of nearby Caffard Cove. François Dizac, a resident of the neighborhood and manager of the Plage du Diamant, a plantation owned by the Count de Latournelle, realized that the ship's situation was perilous, but a heavy swell prevented him from launching a boat to warn the captain that the vessel was in imminent danger of running aground. He therefore sent signals that the captain either could not, or chose not, to acknowledge.

At 11 P.M. that evening, anguished cries and cracking sounds suddenly began to shatter the silence of the night. Dizac and a party of slaves from the nearby plantation rushed promptly to the scene, only to encounter a horrifying sight: the ship had been dashed on the rocks and its passengers thrown into the fury of the raging seas. The rescuers on shore then observed a large number of panic-stricken males clinging desperately to the ship's foremast, which suddenly broke in two, tossing them into the foam or onto the rocks. Broken masts lying on the rocks, fragments of torn sails floating alongside ropes caught in the reef where the ship itself lay on the rocks all provided visual evidence of the frightful incident that had just occurred.

Forty-six bodies, four of whom were white males, were lying amidst the rocks…. "I ordered the bodies of the black victims to be buried at a short distance from the shore, then directed that those of the white males be carried to the cemetery of Diamant parish, where they received a Christian burial. I was then taken to the cabin of a certain Borromé, a free man of color, where those black castaways who had been rescued from the shipwreck had been given temporary shelter. Among the victims, six were found to be in such poor condition that they could not be taken to the Latournelle plantation. The other 80 survivors were handed over to the naval authorities at Fort Royal. In all, 86 African captives, of whom 60 were women or girls, were rescued out of a ship's 'cargo' estimated at nearly 300 persons.

"I ordered the interrogation of the surviving black castaways by interpreters, and it became clear from their testimony that the ship had been at sea for four months, and that most of the white sailors on board had died during the crossing [of the Atlantic], and that an additional 70 blacks had died from illness and had been thrown overboard during the voyage. Another 260 individuals remained on the ship when it was sunk off the coast of Diamant…. Only a few males had thus survived, since all of them were shackled together in the ship's hold with irons on their feet at the time of the wreck."

At that point, a legal issue was raised: what should be done with the surviving castaways who, although they could not be classified as slaves under existing law (since they were victims of illegal trade), yet could not be considered in this colony as men and therefore couldn't be freed. In May 1830, the Privy Council of Martinique ordered that the captured Negroes were to be shipped to Cayenne [the capital of French Guiana] in order to avoid having in the [French] West Indies a special class of people who could not be classified either as slaves or as free individuals….

Thus, in July 1830, a second deportation followed the first, adding to the ordeal of the [African] slaves who had survived the shipwreck at Caffard Cove.

How were the surviving victims of the shipwreck at Caffard Cove dealt with by the government authorities in Martinique? Under what provisions of the law was the decision reached?

Source: Association de Sauvegarde du Patrimoine du Diamant. Text by Merlande, Moanda Saturnin, historian. Translation from the original French by the author.

The growing numbers of Europeans also inevitably led to increasing tensions with African governments in the area. British efforts to increase trade with Ashanti (uh-SHAN-tee *or* uh-SHAHN-tee) led to conflict in the 1820s, but nevertheless British influence in the area intensified in later decades. Most African states, especially those with a fairly high degree of political integration, were initially able to maintain their independence from this creeping European encroachment, called "informal empire" by some historians, but the prospects for the future were ominous. When local groups attempted to organize to protect their interests, the British stepped in and annexed the coastal states as the British colony of Gold Coast in 1874. At about the same time, the British extended an informal protectorate over warring ethnic groups in the Niger delta.

Imperialist Shadow over the Nile

A similar process was under way in the Nile Valley. There had long been interest in shortening the trade route to the East by digging a canal across the low, swampy isthmus separating the Mediterranean from the Red Sea. The Turks had considered constructing a canal from Cairo to Suez in the sixteenth century, as had the French king Louis XIV a century later, but the French did nothing about it until the end of the eighteenth century. At that time, Napoleon planned a military takeover of Egypt to cement French power in the eastern Mediterranean and open a faster route to India.

Napoleon's plan proved abortive. French troops landed in Egypt in 1798 and toppled the ramshackle Mamluk (MAM-look) regime in Cairo, but the British counterattacked, destroying the French fleet and eventually forcing the French to evacuate in disarray. The British restored the Mamluks to power, but in 1805, Muhammad Ali (1769–1849), an Ottoman army officer of Turkish or Albanian extraction, seized control.

During the next three decades, Muhammad Ali introduced a series of reforms to bring Egypt into the modern world. He modernized the army, set up a public educational system (supplementing the traditional religious education provided in Muslim schools), and sponsored the creation of a small industrial sector producing refined sugar, textiles, munitions, and even ships. Muhammad Ali also extended Egyptian authority southward into the Sudan and across the Sinai Peninsula into Arabia, Syria, and northern Iraq and even briefly threatened to seize Istanbul itself. To prevent the possible collapse of the Ottoman Empire, the British and the French recognized Muhammad Ali as the hereditary **pasha** (PAH-shuh), later to be known as the khedive (kuh-DEEV), of Egypt under the loose authority of the Ottoman government.

The growing economic importance of the Nile Valley, along with the development of steam navigation, made the heretofore visionary plans for a Suez canal more urgent. In 1854, the French entrepreneur Ferdinand de Lesseps (fer-DEE-nahn duh le-SEPS) signed a contract to begin construction of the canal, and it was completed in 1869. The project brought little immediate benefit to Egypt, however. The construction not only cost thousands of lives but also left the Egyptian government deep in debt, forcing it to depend increasingly on foreign financial support. When an army revolt against growing foreign influence broke out in 1881, the British stepped in to protect their investment (they had bought Egypt's canal company shares in 1875) and established an informal protectorate that would last until World War I.

Rising discontent in the Sudan added to Egypt's growing internal problems. In 1881, the Muslim cleric Muhammad Ahmad (AH-mahd) (1844–1885), known as the Mahdi (MAH-dee) (in Arabic, the "rightly guided one"), led a religious

MAP 21.3 Africa in 1914. By the start of the twentieth century, virtually all of Africa was under some form of European rule. The territorial divisions established by colonial powers on the continent of Africa on the eve of World War I are shown here.

Q *Which European countries possessed the most colonies in Africa? Why did Ethiopia remain independent?*

Possessions, 1914

- Spain
- Portugal
- Great Britain
- France
- Germany
- Italy
- Belgium
- Independent

revolt that brought much of the Upper Nile under his control. The famous British general Charles Gordon (1833–1885), who had earlier commanded Manchu armies fighting against the Taiping Rebellion in China (see Chapter 22), led a military force to Khartoum (kahr-TOOM) to restore Egyptian authority, but his besieged army was captured in 1885 by the Mahdi's troops, thirty-six hours before a British rescue mission reached Khartoum. Gordon himself died in the battle, which became one of the most dramatic news stories of the last quarter of the century (see the Film & History feature *"Khartoum* (1966)" on p. 621).

The weakening of Turkish rule in the Nile Valley had a parallel farther to the west, where local viceroys in Tripoli, Tunis, and Algiers had begun to establish their autonomy. In 1830, the French, on the pretext of protecting European shipping in the Mediterranean from pirates, seized the area surrounding Algiers and integrated it into the French Empire. By the mid-1850s, more than 150,000 Europeans had settled in the fertile region adjacent to the coast. In 1881, the French imposed a protectorate on neighboring Tunisia. Only Tripoli and Cyrenaica (seer-uh-NAY-uh-kuh), the Ottoman provinces that comprise modern Libya, remained under Turkish rule until the Italians seized them in 1911–1912.

The Suez Canal

Arab Merchants and European Missionaries in East Africa

As always, events in East Africa followed their own distinctive pattern of development. Although the Atlantic slave trade was declining, demand for slaves was increasing on the other side of the continent due to the growth of plantation agriculture in the region and on the islands off the coast. The French introduced sugar to the island of Réunion (ray-yoo-NYAHN) early in the century, importing slaves from Africa and South Asia for the purpose, and plantations of cloves (introduced from the Moluccas in the eighteenth century) were established under Omani Arab ownership on the island of Zanzibar (ZAN-zi-bar). Zanzibar itself became the major shipping port along the entire east coast during the early nineteenth century, and the sultan of Oman (oh-MAHN), who had reasserted Arab suzerainty over the region in the aftermath of the collapse of Portuguese authority, established his capital at Zanzibar in 1840.

From Zanzibar, Arab merchants fanned out into the interior plateaus in search of slaves, ivory (known colloquially as "white gold"), and other local products. The competition for slaves spread as far as Lake Victoria and the lower Sudan as traders from the north launched their own raids to obtain conscripts for the Egyptian army. The khedive sent General Charles Gordon to Uganda to stop the practice, but in the absence of alternative sources of income, local merchants could not easily be persuaded to give up a lucrative occupation.

The tenacity of the slave trade in East Africa—Zanzibar had now become the largest slave market in Africa—was undoubtedly a major reason for the rise of Western interest and Christian missionary activity in the region during the middle of the century. The most renowned missionary was the Scottish doctor David Livingstone (LIV-ing-stuhn) (1813–1873), who arrived in Africa in 1841. Because Livingstone spent much of his time exploring the interior of the continent, discovering Victoria Falls in the process, he was occasionally criticized for being more explorer than missionary. But Livingstone was convinced that it was his divinely appointed task to bring Christianity to the far reaches of the continent, and his passionate opposition to slavery did far more to win public support for the abolitionist cause than the efforts of any other figure of his generation. Public outcries provoked the British to redouble their attempts to bring the slave trade in East Africa to an

The Opening of the Suez Canal. The Suez Canal, which connected the Mediterranean and Red Seas, was constructed under the direction of the French promoter Ferdinand de Lesseps. Still in use today, the canal is Egypt's greatest revenue producer. This sketch shows the ceremonial passage of the first ships through the canal in 1869. Note the combination of sail and steam power, reflecting the transition to coal-powered ships in the mid-nineteenth century.

Khartoum (1966)

The mission of General Charles "Chinese" Gordon to Khartoum in 1884 was one of the most dramatic news stories of the last quarter of the nineteenth century. Gordon was already renowned in his native Great Britain for his successful efforts to bring an end to the practice of slavery in North Africa. He had also attracted attention—and acquired the nickname "Chinese"—for helping the Manchu Empire suppress the Taiping Rebellion in China in the 1860s (see Chapter 22). But the Khartoum affair not only marked the culmination of his storied career but also symbolized in broader terms the epic struggle in Britain between advocates and opponents of imperial expansion. The battle for Khartoum thus became an object lesson in modern British history.

Proponents of British imperial expansion argued that the country must project its power in the Nile River valley to protect the Suez Canal as its main trade route to the East. Critics argued that imperial overreach would inevitably entangle the country in unwinnable wars in far-off places. The movie *Khartoum* (1966), filmed in Egypt and London, dramatically captures the ferocity of the battle for the Nile as well as its significance for the future of the British Empire. General Gordon, stoically played by the American actor Charlton Heston, is a devout Christian who has devoted his life to carrying out the moral imperative of imperialism in the continent of Africa. When peace in the Sudan (then a British protectorate in the upper Nile River valley) is threatened by the forces of radical Islam led by the Muslim mystic Muhammad Ahmad—known as the Mahdi—Gordon leads a mission to Khartoum under orders to prevent catastrophe there. But Prime Minister William Ewart Gladstone, admirably portrayed by the consummate

General Charles Gordon (Charlton Heston) astride his camel in Khartoum, Sudan.

Cinerama/United Artists/The Kobal Collection/The Picture Desk

British actor Ralph Richardson, fears that Gordon's messianic desire to save the Sudan will entrap his government in an unwinnable war; he thus orders Gordon to lead an evacuation of the city. The most fascinating character in the film is the Mahdi himself (played brilliantly by Sir Laurence Olivier), who firmly believes that he has a sacred mandate to carry the Prophet's words to the global Muslim community.

The conclusion of the film, set in the breathtaking beauty of the Nile River valley, takes place as the clash of wills reaches a climax in the battle for Khartoum. Although the film's portrayal of a face-to-face meeting between Gordon and the Mahdi is not based on fact, the narrative serves as an object lesson on the dangers of imperial overreach and as an eerie foretaste of the clash between Islam and Christendom in our own day.

---

end, and in 1873, the slave market at Zanzibar was finally closed as the result of pressure from London. Shortly before, Livingstone had died of illness in Central Africa, but some of his followers brought his body to the coast for burial. His legacy is still visible today in the form of an Anglican cathedral that was erected on the site of the slave market at Zanzibar.

Bantus, Boers, and British in the South

Nowhere in Africa did the European presence grow more rapidly than in the south. During the eighteenth century, the Boers (BOORS *or* BORS), Afrikaans-speaking farmers descended from the original Dutch settlers of the Cape Colony, began to migrate eastward. After the British seized control of the cape from the Dutch during the Napoleonic wars, the Boers' eastward migration intensified, culminating in the Great Trek of the mid-1830s. In part, the Boers' departure

was provoked by the different attitude of the British to the indigenous population. Slavery was abolished in the British Empire in 1834, and the British government was generally more sympathetic to the rights of the local African population than were the Afrikaners (ah-fri-KAH-nurz), many of whom believed that white superiority was ordained by God and fled from British rule to control their own destiny. Eventually, the Boers formed their own independent republics—the Orange Free State and the South African Republic, usually called the Transvaal (trans-VAHL) (see Map 21.4).

Although the Boer occupation of the eastern territory was initially facilitated by internecine warfare among the local inhabitants of the region, the new settlers met some resistance. In the early nineteenth century, the Zulus (ZOO-looz), a Bantu people led by a talented ruler named Shaka (SHAH-kuh), engaged in a series of wars with the Europeans that ended only when Shaka was overthrown. The local Khoisan

MAP 21.4 The Struggle for Southern Africa. European settlers from the Cape Colony expanded into adjacent areas of southern Africa in the nineteenth century. The arrows indicate the routes taken by Afrikaans-speaking Boers.

Q *Who were the Boers, and why did they migrate eastward?*

(KOI-sahn) people also sometimes reacted with violence when the Boers attempted to drive them off their grazing lands. One Dutch official complained that the Khoisan were driving settlers from their farms "for no other reason than because they saw that we were breaking up the best land and grass, where their cattle were accustomed to graze."[8] Ultimately, most of the black Africans in the Boer republics began to be resettled in reservation-like homelands created by the white government.

The Scramble for Africa

At the beginning of the 1880s, most of Africa was still independent. European rule was limited to the fringes of the continent, such as Algeria, the Gold Coast, and South Africa. Other areas like Egypt, lower Nigeria, Senegal (sen-ni-GAHL), and Mozambique (moh-zam-BEEK) were under various forms of loose protectorate. But the pace of European penetration was accelerating, and the constraints that had limited European rapaciousness were fast disappearing.

The scramble began in the mid-1880s when several European states, including Belgium, France, Germany, Great Britain, and Portugal, engaged in a feeding frenzy to seize a piece of the African cake before the plate had been picked clean. By

1900, virtually all of the continent had been placed under some form of European rule (see Map 21.3). Only the mountainous state of Ethiopia, where an Italian effort to extend its control over the region early in the twentieth century was soundly defeated, appeared safe from Western imperialist rapacity. It was one of the more notable setbacks for European arms on the African continent.

What had happened to spark the sudden imperialist hysteria that brought an end to African independence? Although the level of trade between Europe and Africa had increased substantially during the latter part of the nineteenth century, it was probably not sufficient, by itself, to justify the risks and expense of conquest. More important than economic interests were the intensified rivalries among the European states that led them to engage in imperialist takeovers out of fear that if they did not, another state might do so, leaving them at a disadvantage. As one British diplomat remarked, a protectorate at the mouth of the Niger River would be an "unwelcome burden," but a French protectorate there would be "fatal." As occurred in Southeast Asia, as described earlier, statesmen felt compelled to obtain colonies as a hedge against future actions by rivals. In the most famous example, the British solidified their control over the entire Nile Valley to protect the Suez Canal from seizure by the French.

Another consideration might be called the "missionary factor," as European missionary interests lobbied with their governments for colonial takeovers to facilitate their efforts to convert the African population to Christianity. The concept of social Darwinism and the "white man's burden" persuaded many that it was in the interests of the African people, as well as their conquerors, to be introduced more rapidly to the benefits of Western civilization (see Opposing Viewpoints "White Man's Burden, Black Man's Sorrow" on p. 608). Even David Livingstone had become convinced that missionary work and economic development had to go hand in hand, pleading to his fellow Europeans to introduce the "three C's" (Christianity, commerce, and civilization) to the continent. How much easier such a task would be if African peoples were under benevolent European rule!

There were more prosaic reasons as well. Advances in Western technology and European superiority in firearms made it easier than ever for a small European force to defeat superior numbers. Furthermore, life expectancy for Europeans living in Africa had improved. With the discovery that quinine (extracted from the bark of the cinchona tree) could provide partial immunity from the ravages of malaria, the mortality rate for Europeans living in Africa dropped dramatically in the 1840s. By the end of the century, European residents in tropical Africa faced only slightly higher risks of death by disease than individuals living in Europe.

Under these circumstances, King Leopold (LAY-oh-polt) II of Belgium (1835–1909) used missionary activities as an excuse to claim vast territories in the Congo River basin for his own personal use—Belgium, he said, as "a small country, with a small people," needed a colony to enhance its image.[9] The royal land grab set off a desperate race among European nations to stake claims throughout sub-Saharan Africa. Leopold ended up with the territories south of the Congo River, while France occupied areas to the north. Rapacious European adventurers established plantations in the new Belgian Congo to grow rubber, palm oil, and other valuable export products. Conditions for African workers on the plantations were so abysmal that an international outcry eventually led to the formation of a commission under British consul Roger Casement to investigate. The commission's report, issued in 1904, helped to bring about reforms.

Meanwhile, on the eastern side of the continent, Germany (through the activities of an ambitious missionary and with the agreement of the British, who needed German support against the French) annexed the colony of Tanganyika (tan-gan-YEE-kuh). To avert the possibility of violent clashes among the great powers, the German chancellor, Otto von Bismarck, convened a conference in Berlin in 1884 to set

Legacy of Shame. By the mid-nineteenth century, most European nations had prohibited the trade in African slaves, but slavery continued to exist in Africa well into the next century. The most flagrant example was in the Belgian Congo, where the mistreatment of conscript laborers led to a popular outcry and the formation of a commission to look into the situation and recommend reforms. Shown here are two manacled members of a chain gang in the Belgian Congo. The photograph was taken in 1904.

Universal Images Group/SuperStock

ground rules for future annexations of African territory by European nations. The conference combined high-minded resolutions with a hardheaded recognition of practical interests. The delegates called for free commerce in the Congo—where Leopold's efforts to squeeze out foreign competition had provoked widespread opposition—and along the Niger River as well as for further efforts to end the slave trade. At the same time, the participants recognized the inevitability of the imperialist dynamic, agreeing only that future annexations of African territory should not be given international recognition until effective occupation had been demonstrated. No African delegates were present.

The Berlin Conference had been convened to avert war and reduce tensions among European nations competing for the spoils of Africa. It proved reasonably successful at achieving the first objective but less so at the second. During the next few years, African territories were annexed without provoking a major confrontation between the Western powers, but in the late 1890s, Britain and France reached the brink of conflict at Fashoda (fuh-SHOH-duh), a small town on the Nile River in the Sudan. The French had been advancing eastward across the Sahara with the transparent objective of controlling the regions around the Upper Nile. In 1898, British and Egyptian troops seized the Sudan from successors of the Mahdi and then marched southward to head off the French. After a tense face-off at Fashoda, the French government backed down, and British authority over the area was secured. Except for the Mediterranean littoral and their small possessions of Djibouti (juh-BOO-tee) and a portion of the Somali coast, the French were restricted to equatorial Africa.

Ironically, the only major clash between Europeans over Africa took place in southern Africa, where competition among the European imperialist powers was almost nonexistent. The

The Scramble for Africa. The rivalry among Western powers for territory in Africa at the end of the nineteenth century inspired much controversy in Europe between supporters and opponents of the imperialist enterprise. In this cartoon, published in the contemporary French journal *L'Assiette au Beurre* (*The Butter Plate*), the anonymous artist lampoons the struggle between the British and the French, resulting here in a torn map of Africa. Significantly, the cartoon does not take a position on the issue but implies that the results will not be beneficial for either side.

discovery of gold and diamonds in the Boer republic of the Transvaal was the source of the problem. Clashes between the Afrikaner population and foreign (mainly British) miners and developers led to an attempt by Cecil Rhodes, prime minister of the Cape Colony and a prominent entrepreneur in the area, to subvert the government in Transvaal and bring the republic under British rule. In 1899, the so-called Boer War broke out between Britain and the Transvaal, which was backed by its fellow republic, the Orange Free State. Guerrilla resistance by the Boers was fierce, but the vastly superior forces of the British were able to prevail by 1902. To compensate the defeated Afrikaner population for the loss of independence, the British government agreed that only whites would vote in the now essentially self-governing colony. The Boers were placated, but the brutalities committed during the war (the British introduced an institution later to be known as the concentration camp) created bitterness on both sides that continued to fester through future decades.

Colonialism in Africa

As we have seen, European economic interests were initially somewhat more limited in Africa than elsewhere. Having seized the continent in what could almost be described as a fit of hysteria, the European powers had to decide what to do with it. With economic concerns relatively limited except for isolated areas like the gold mines in the Transvaal and copper deposits in the Belgian Congo, interest in Africa declined, and most European governments turned their attention to suppressing continued local resistance and then to governing their new territories with the least effort and expense possible. In many cases, this meant a form of indirect rule similar to what the British used in the princely states in India.

BRITISH RULE IN NIGERIA Nigeria offers a typical example of British-style indirect rule (see the box "The British in Hausaland: A Memoir" on p. 625). British officials operated at the central level, but local authority was assigned to Nigerian chiefs, with British district officers serving as intermediaries with the central administration. The local authorities were expected to maintain law and order and to collect taxes from the indigenous population. A dual legal system was instituted that applied African laws to Africans and European laws to foreigners.

One advantage of such an administrative system was that it did not severely disrupt local customs and institutions. On the other hand, it was misleading, because all major decisions were made by the British administrators while the African authorities served primarily as a mechanism for enforcing those decisions. Among some peoples, indirect rule served to perpetuate the autocratic system in use prior to colonial takeover, since there was a natural tendency to view the local aristocracy as the African equivalent of the British ruling class. Such a policy provided few opportunities for ambitious and talented young Africans from outside the traditional elite and thus sowed the seeds for generational and class tensions after the restoration of independence in the twentieth century.

THE BRITISH IN EAST AFRICA The situation was somewhat different in Kenya, which had a relatively large European population attracted by the temperate climate in the central highlands. The local government had encouraged white settlers to migrate to the area as a means of promoting economic development and encouraging financial self-sufficiency. To attract Europeans, fertile farmlands in the central highlands were reserved for European settlement, while, as in South Africa, specified reserve lands were set aside for Africans. The presence of a substantial European minority (although in fact they represented only about 1 percent of the entire population) had an impact on Kenya's political development. The white settlers actively sought self-government and dominion status similar to that granted to such former British possessions as Canada and Australia. The British government, however, was not willing to run the risk of provoking racial tensions with the African majority and agreed only to establish separate government organs for the European and African populations.

SOUTH AFRICA The British used a different system in southern Africa, where there was a high percentage of European settlers. The situation was further complicated by the division between English-speaking and Afrikaner elements within the

The British in Hausaland: A Memoir

FAMILY & SOCIETY

MOST AFRICANS LIVING OUTSIDE THE PORT CITIES had little idea of what to expect from the arrival of the white man and the new colonial authority. Thanks to these memoirs, recounted a half-century later by Baba, an African woman from northern Nigeria, we are offered an intimate glimpse into the arrival of the British at the end of the nineteenth century. As this excerpt makes clear, reaction to the arrival of European rule varied depending on conditions in the affected area. In northern Nigeria, local Hausa (HOW-suh) trading people still harbored considerable resentment toward the Fulani (FOO-lah-nee), a predominantly pastoral people who had seized the area centuries earlier.

It is also interesting to note that slavery among Africans was still a long-established tradition in the area. In a later passage, Baba remarks that her family lost income from the flight of its slaves, but the loss was offset by a reduction in taxes that African farmers had traditionally been compelled to pay to fill the pockets of local officials and chiefs.

Baba, a Hausa Woman of Nigeria

When I was a maiden the Europeans first arrived. Ever since we were quite small the *malams* [Muslim scholars] had been saying that the Europeans would come with a thing called a train, they would come with a thing called a motor-car.... They would stop wars, they would repair the world, they would stop oppression and lawlessness, we should live at peace with them. We used to go and sit quietly and listen to the prophecies....

I remember when a European came to Karo on a horse, and some of his foot soldiers went into the town. Everyone came out to look at them.... Everyone at Karo ran away—"There's a European, there's a European!" ...

At that time Yusufu was the [Fulani] king of Kano. He did not like the Europeans, he did not wish them, he would not sign their treaty. Then he saw that perforce he would have to agree, so he did. We Habe wanted them to come, it was the Fulani who did not like it. When the Europeans came the Habe saw that if you worked for them they paid you for it, they didn't say, like the Fulani, "Commoner, give me this! Commoner, bring me that!" Yes, the Habe wanted them....

The Europeans said that there were to be no more slaves; if someone said "Slave!" you could complain to the *alkali* [judge] who would punish the master who said it, the judge said, "That is what the Europeans have decreed." ... When slavery was stopped, nothing much happened at our *rinji* [the farm where their slaves lived] except that some slaves whom we had bought in the market ran away. Our own father went to his farm and worked, he and his son took up their large hoes.... They farmed guinea-corn and millet and groundnuts and everything; before this they had supervised the slaves' work—now they did their own. When the midday food was ready, the women of the compound would give us children the food, one of us drew water, and off we went to the farm to take the men their food at the foot of a tree.

Why did the Fulani and the Habe peoples respond in different ways to the arrival of the Europeans? How did the Europeans affect the institution of slavery in the area?

Source: From Mary E. Smith, *Baba of Karo: A Woman of the Muslim Hausa* (New Haven, CT: Yale University Press, 1981), pp. 66–68.

European population. In 1910, the British agreed to the creation of the independent Union of South Africa, which combined the old Cape Colony and Natal (nuh-TAHL) with the Boer republics. The new union adopted a representative government, but only for the European population, while the African reserves of Basutoland (buh-SOO-toh-land), now Lesotho (luh-SOH-toh); Bechuanaland (bech-WAH-nuh-land), now Botswana (baht-SWAH-nuh); and Swaziland (SWAH-zee-land) were subordinated directly to the crown. The union was now free to manage its own domestic affairs and possessed considerable autonomy in foreign relations. Formal British rule was also extended to the remaining lands south of the Zambezi River, which were eventually divided into the territories of Northern and Southern Rhodesia. Southern Rhodesia attracted many British immigrants, and in 1922, after a popular referendum, it became a crown colony.

DIRECT RULE Most other European nations governed their African possessions through a form of direct rule. The prototype was the French system, which reflected the centralized administrative system introduced in France itself by Napoleon. As in the British colonies, at the top of the pyramid was a French official, usually known as the governor-general, who was appointed from Paris and governed with the aid of a bureaucracy in the capital city. At the provincial level, French commissioners were assigned to deal with local administrators, but the latter were required to be conversant in French and could be transferred to a new position at the needs of the central government.

After World War I, European colonial policy in Africa entered a new and more formal phase that specialists in African studies call "**high colonialism**." Colonial governments paid more attention to improving social services, including education, medicine and sanitation, and communications. More Africans were now serving in colonial administrations, though relatively few were in positions of responsibility. On the other hand, race consciousness probably increased during this period. Segregated clubs, schools, and churches were established as more European officials brought their wives and began to raise families in the

The Civilizing Mission in Egypt

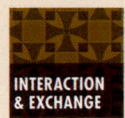

IN MANY PARTS OF THE COLONIAL WORLD, European occupation served to sharpen class divisions in traditional societies. Such was the case in Egypt, where the British protectorate, established in the early 1880s, benefited many elites, who profited from the introduction of Western culture. Ordinary Egyptians, less inclined to adopt foreign ways, seldom profited from the European presence. In response, British administrators showed little patience for their subjects who failed to recognize the superiority of Western civilization. This view found expression in the words of the governor-general, Lord Cromer (KROH-mer), who remarked in exasperation, "The mind of the Oriental, ... like his picturesque streets, is eminently wanting in symmetry. His reasoning is of the most slipshod description." Cromer was especially irritated at the local treatment of women, arguing that the seclusion of women and the wearing of the veil were the chief causes of Islamic backwardness.

Such views were echoed by some Egyptian elites, who were utterly seduced by Western culture and embraced the colonialists' condemnation of local traditions. The French-educated lawyer Qassim Amin (KAH-sum AH-meen) was one example. His book, *The Liberation of Women*, published in 1899 and excerpted here, precipitated a heated debate between those who considered Western nations the liberators of Islam and those who reviled them as oppressors.

Qassim Amin, *The Liberation of Women*

European civilization advances with the speed of steam and electricity, and has even over spilled to every part of the globe so that there is not an inch that he [European man] has not trodden underfoot. Any place he goes he takes control of its resources ... and turns them into profit ... and if he does harm to the original inhabitants, it is only that he pursues happiness in this world and seeks it wherever he may find it.... For the most part he uses his intellect, but when circumstances require it, he deploys force. He does not seek glory from his possessions and colonies, for he has enough of this through his intellectual achievements and scientific inventions. What drives the English-man to dwell in India and the French in Algeria ... is profit and the desire to acquire resources in countries where the inhabitants do not know their value or how to profit from them.

When they encounter savages they eliminate them or drive them from the land, as happened in America ... and is happening now in Africa.... When they encounter a nation like ours, with a degree of civilization, with a past, and a religion ... and customs and ... institutions ... they deal with its inhabitants kindly. But they do soon acquire its most valuable resources, because they have greater wealth and intellect and knowledge and force.... [The veil constituted] a huge barrier between woman and her elevation, and consequently a barrier between the nation and its advance.

 Why did Qassim Amin believe that Western culture would be beneficial to Egyptian society? How might a critic of colonialism have responded?

Source: From Leila Ahmen, *Women and Gender in Islam* (New Haven, CT: Yale University Press, 1992), p. 152–160.

---

colonies. European feelings of superiority to their African subjects led to countless examples of cruelty similar to Western practices in Asia. While the institution of slavery was discouraged, African workers were often subjected to unbelievably harsh conditions as they were put to use in promoting the cause of imperialism.

WOMEN IN COLONIAL AFRICA The establishment of colonial rule had a mixed impact on the rights and status of women in Africa. Sexual relationships changed profoundly during the colonial era, sometimes in ways that could justly be described as beneficial. Colonial governments attempted to bring an end to forced marriage, bodily mutilation such as clitoridectomy (clit-er-ih-DEK-toh-mee), and polygyny. Missionaries introduced women to Western education and encouraged them to organize themselves to defend their interests (see the box "The Civilizing Mission in Egypt" above).

But the colonial system had some unfavorable consequences as well. African women had traditionally benefited from the prestige of matrilineal systems and were empowered by their traditional role as the primary agricultural producers in their community. Under colonialism, the widespread conscription of males for forced labor on plantations and building projects left many woman behind to fend for their families on their own. Moreover, European settlers not only took the best land for themselves but also, in introducing new agricultural techniques, tended to deal exclusively with males, encouraging them to develop lucrative cash crops, while women were restricted to traditional farming methods. Whereas African men applied chemical fertilizer to the fields, women used manure. While men began to use bicycles, and eventually trucks, to transport goods, women still carried their goods on their heads, a practice that continues today. In British colonies, Victorian attitudes of female subordination led to restrictions on women's freedom, and positions in government that they had formerly held were now closed to them.

The Emergence of Anticolonialism

 FOCUS QUESTION: How did the subject peoples respond to colonialism, and what role did nationalism play in their response?

Thus far we have looked at the colonial experience primarily from the point of view of the European colonial powers. Equally important is the way the subject peoples reacted to the experience. In this chapter, we will deal with the initial response, which can be described in most cases by the general term "traditional resistance." Later, however, many people in the colonized societies began to turn to the concept of nationalism as a means of preserving their ethnic, cultural, or religious identity. We will deal with that stage in more detail in Chapter 24.

Stirrings of Nationhood

As noted earlier, nationalism refers to a state of mind rising out of an awareness of being part of a community that possesses common institutions, traditions, language, and customs (see the Comparative Essay "The Rise of Nationalism" on p. 591 in Chapter 20). In the nineteenth century, few societies around the world met such criteria. Even today, most modern states contain a variety of ethnic, religious, and linguistic communities, each with its own sense of cultural and national identity. To cite one example, should Canada, which includes peoples of French, English, and Native American heritage, be considered a nation? Another question is how nationalism differs from other forms of tribal, religious, or linguistic affiliation. Should every group that resists assimilation into a larger political entity be called nationalist?

Such questions complicate the study of nationalism even in Europe and North America and make agreement on a definition elusive. They create even greater dilemmas in discussing Asia and Africa, where most societies are deeply divided by ethnic, linguistic, and religious differences and the very term *nationalism* is a foreign concept imported from the West. Prior to the colonial era, most traditional societies in Africa and Asia were formed on the basis of religious beliefs, ethnic loyalties, or devotion to hereditary monarchies. Although individuals in some countries may have identified themselves as members of a particular national group, others viewed themselves as subjects of a king, members of a lineage group, or adherents to a particular religion.

The advent of European colonialism brought the consciousness of modern nationhood to many of the societies of Asia and Africa. The creation of European colonies with defined borders and a powerful central government led to the weakening of local ethnic and religious loyalties and a significant reorientation in the individual's sense of political identity. The introduction of Western ideas of citizenship and representative government—even though they usually were not replicated in the colonial territories themselves—produced a heightened desire for participation in the affairs of government. At the same time, the appearance of a new elite class based not on hereditary privilege or religious sanction but on alleged racial or cultural superiority aroused a shared sense of resentment among the subject peoples, who felt a common commitment to the creation of an independent society ruled by their own kind. By the first quarter of the twentieth century, political movements dedicated to the overthrow of colonial rule and the creation of modern nations had arisen throughout much of the non-Western world.

Modern nationalism, then, was a product of colonialism and, in a sense, a reaction to it. But a sense of nationhood does not emerge full-blown in a society. The rise of modern nationalism is a process that begins among a few members of the educated elite (most commonly among articulate professionals such as lawyers, teachers, journalists, and doctors) and then spreads only gradually to the mass of the population. Even after national independence has been realized, as we shall see, it is often questionable whether a mature sense of nationhood has been created, since local ethnic, linguistic, or religious ties often continue to predominate over loyalty to the larger community (see Chapter 29).

Traditional Resistance: A Precursor to Nationalism

The beginnings of modern nationalism can be found in the initial resistance by the indigenous peoples to the colonial conquest. Although, strictly speaking, such resistance was not "nationalist" because it was essentially motivated by the desire to defend traditional institutions, it did reflect a primitive concept of nationhood in that it aimed at protecting the homeland from the invader. After independence was achieved, governments of new nations often hailed early resistance movements as the precursors of twentieth-century nationalist movements. Thus, traditional resistance to colonial conquest may logically be viewed as the first stage in the development of modern nationalism.

Such resistance took various forms. For the most part, it was led by the existing ruling class, although in some instances traditionalists continued to oppose foreign conquest even after resistance had collapsed at the center. In India, Tipu Sultan (tih-POO SUL-tun) fought the British in the Deccan after the collapse of the Mughal Dynasty. Similarly, after the decrepit monarchy in Vietnam had bowed to French pressure, a number of civilian and military officials set up an organization called Can Vuong (kahn VWAHNG) (literally, "save the king") and continued their own resistance campaign without imperial sanction.

Sometimes traditional resistance to Western penetration went beyond elite circles. Most commonly, it appeared in the form of peasant revolts. Rural rebellions were not uncommon in traditional Asian societies as a means of expressing peasant discontent with high taxes, official corruption, rising rural debt, and famine in the countryside. Under colonialism, rural conditions often deteriorated as population density increased and peasants were driven off the land to make way for plantation agriculture. Angry peasants then vented their frustration

Vietnamese Prisoners in Stocks. Whereas some Vietnamese took up Western ways, others resisted the foreign incursion but were vigorously suppressed by the French. In this photograph, Vietnamese prisoners who had plotted against the French are held in stocks in preparation for trial in 1907.

at the foreign invaders. For example, in Burma, the Buddhist monk Saya San (SAH-yuh SAHN) led a peasant uprising against the British many years after they had completed their takeover. Similar forms of unrest occurred in various parts of India, where *zamindars* and rural villagers alike resisted government attempts to increase tax revenues. Yet another peasant uprising took place in Algeria in 1840.

OPPOSITION TO COLONIAL RULE IN AFRICA Because of the sheer size of Africa and its ethnic, religious, and linguistic diversity, resistance to the European seizure of territory in that continent was often sporadic and uncoordinated, but fierce nonetheless. The uprising led by the Mahdi in the Sudan was only the most dramatic example. In South Africa, as we have seen, the Zulus engaged in a bitter war of resistance to Boer colonists arriving from the Cape Colony. Later they fought against the British occupation of their territory and were not finally subdued until the end of the century. In West Africa, the Ashanti ruling class led a bitter struggle against the British with broad-based popular support. The lack of modern weapons was decisive, however, and African resistance forces eventually suffered defeat throughout the continent. The one exception was Ethiopia where, at the Battle of Adowa (AH-doo-wah) in 1896, the modernized army created by Emperor Menelik was able to fend off an Italian invasion force and preserve the country's national independence well into the next century.

THE SEPOY REBELLION Perhaps the most famous uprising against European authority in the mid-nineteenth century was the revolt of the **sepoys** (SEE-poiz) in India. The sepoys (from the Turkish *sipahis*, cavalrymen or soldiers) were Indian troops hired by the East India Company to protect British interests in the region. Unrest within Indian units of the colonial army had been common since early in the century, when it had been sparked by economic issues, religious sensitivities, or nascent anticolonial sentiment. Such attitudes intensified in the mid-1850s when the British instituted a new policy of shipping Indian troops abroad—a practice that exposed Hindus to pollution by foreigners. In 1857, tension erupted when the British adopted the new Enfield rifle for use by sepoy infantrymen. The new weapon was a muzzle-loade that used paper cartridges covered with animal fat and lard; because the cartridge had to be bitten off, it broke strictures against high-class Hindus' eating animal products and Muslim prohibitions against eating pork. Protests among sepoy units in northern India turned into a full-scale mutiny, supported by uprisings in rural districts in various parts of the country. But the revolt lacked clear goals, and rivalries between Hindus and Muslims and discord among the leaders within each community prevented them from coordinating operations. Although the Indian troops often fought bravely and outnumbered the British six to one, they were poorly organized, and the British forces (supplemented in many cases by sepoy troops) suppressed the rebellion.

Still, the revolt frightened the British and led to a number of major reforms. The proportion of Indian troops in the army was reduced, and precedence was given to ethnic groups likely to be loyal to the British, such as the Sikhs (SEEKS *or* see-ikhz) of Punjab (pun-JAHB) and the Gurkhas (GUR-kuhz), an upland people from Nepal (nuh-PAHL) in the Himalaya Mountains. To avoid religious conflicts, ethnic groups were spread throughout the service rather than assigned to special units. The British also decided to suppress the final remnants of the hapless Mughal Dynasty, which had supported the mutiny, and turned responsibility for the administration of the subcontinent over to the crown.

Like the Sepoy Rebellion, traditional resistance movements usually met with little success. Peasants armed with pikes and spears were no match for Western armies possessing the most terrifying weapons then known to human society. In a few cases, such as the revolt of the Mahdi at Khartoum, the local peoples were able to defeat the invaders temporarily. But such successes were rare, and the late nineteenth century witnessed the seemingly inexorable march of the Western powers, armed with the Gatling gun (the first rapid-fire weapon and the precursor of the modern machine gun), to mastery of the globe.

A British Encampment in Zululand. In 1879 British military forces launched an attack on the Zulus, a Bantu-speaking people living in the lands northeast of the Cape Colony who were resisting the extension of British rule into their territory. The first battle in the war took place at Isandlwana in January 1879, where 20,000 Zulu warriors armed with spears overwhelmed a much smaller British force possessing advanced breech-loading rifles. Casualties were heavy on both sides. Stung by the setback, the British intensified their efforts, leading to an eventual Zulu defeat in the campaign. In this illustration from 1879, British troops entered an encampment on the border of Zulu territory in preparation for the battle.

THE PATH OF COLLABORATION   Not all Asians and Africans reacted to a colonial takeover by choosing the path of violent resistance. Some found elements to admire in Western civilization and compared it favorably with their own traditional practices and institutions (see the box "The Civilizing Mission in Egypt" on p. 626). Even in sub-Saharan Africa, where the colonial record was often at its most brutal, some elites elected to support the imposition of colonial authority, as the following letter to Queen Victoria from African leaders in Cameroons indicates:

> We *wish* to have your laws in our towns. We want to have every *fashion* altered; also we will do according to your Consul's *word*. Plenty wars here in our country. Plenty murder and plenty idol worshippers. Perhaps these *lines* of our writing will *look* to you as an *idle* tale.
>
> We have *spoken* to the English consul plenty times about having an English *government* here. We never have answer from you, so we wish to write you *ourselves*.[10]

The decision to collaborate with the colonial administration was undoubtedly motivated in many cases by the desire for personal survival or self-aggrandizement. Such instances frequently aroused scorn and even hostility among the collaborators' contemporaries, and especially among those who chose to oppose the occupation by force of arms. On occasion, however, the decision was reached only after an excruciating and painful examination of equally unpleasant alternatives. Whatever the circumstances, the decision often divided friends and families, as occurred with two onetime childhood friends in central Vietnam, when one chose resistance and the other collaboration (see Opposing Viewpoints "To Resist or Not to Resist" on p. 630).

Not all colonial subjects, of course, felt required to choose between resistance and collaboration. Most simply lived out their lives without engaging in the political arena. Even so, in some cases their actions had an impact on the future of their country. A prime example was Ram Mohan Roy (RAHM moh-HUHN ROI). A *brahmin* from Bengal (ben-GAHL), Roy founded the Brahmo Samaj (BRAH-moh suh-MAHJ) (Society of Brahma) in 1828. He probably had no intention of promoting Indian independence when he created the new organization as a means of helping his fellow religionists defend the Hindu faith against verbal attacks from their British acquaintances. Roy was by no means a hidebound traditionalist. He opposed such practices as *sati* and recognized the benefit of introducing the best aspects of European culture into Indian society. But in encouraging his countrymen to defend their traditional values and institutions against the onslaught of Western civilization, he helped to promote the first stirrings of nationalist sentiment in nineteenth-century India.

The Emergence of Anticolonialism   ■   **629**

OPPOSING ✕ VIEWPOINTS

To Resist or Not to Resist

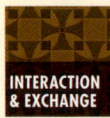

INTERACTION & EXCHANGE

HOW TO RESPOND TO THE IMPOSITION OF COLONIAL RULE was sometimes an excruciating problem for political elites in many Asian countries, since resistance often seemed futile while simply adding to the suffering of the indigenous population. Hoang Cao Khai (HWANG cow KY) and Phan Dinh Phung (FAN din FUNG) were members of the Confucian scholar-gentry from the same village in Vietnam. Yet they reacted in dramatically different ways to the French conquest of their country. Their exchange of letters, reproduced here, illustrates the dilemmas they faced.

Hoang Cao Khai's Letter to Phan Dinh Phung

Soon, it will be seventeen years since we ventured upon different paths of life. How sweet was our friendship when we both lived in our village…. At the time when the capital was lost and after the royal carriage had departed, you courageously answered the appeals of the King by raising the banner of righteousness. It was certainly the only thing to do in those circumstances. No one will question that.

But now the situation has changed and even those without intelligence or education have concluded that nothing remains to be saved. How is it that you, a man of vast understanding, do not realize this? … You are determined to do what ever you deem righteous…. But though you have no thoughts for your own person or for your own fate, you should at least attend to the sufferings of the population of a whole region….

Until now your actions have undoubtedly accorded with your loyalty. May I ask however what sin our people have committed to deserve so much hardship? I would understand your resistance, did you involve but your family for the benefit of a large number. As of now, hundreds of families are subject to grief; how do you have the heart to fight on? I venture to predict that, should you pursue your struggle, not only will the population of our village be destroyed but our entire country will be transformed into a sea of blood and a mountain of bones. It is my hope that men of your superior morality and honesty will pause a while to appraise the situation.

Reply of Phan Dinh Phung to Hoang Cao Khai

In your letter, you revealed to me the causes of calamities and of happiness. You showed me clearly where advantages and disadvantages lie. All of which sufficed to indicate that your anxious concern was not only for my own security but also for the peace and order of our entire region. I understood plainly your sincere arguments.

I have concluded that if our country has survived these past thousand years when its territory was not large, its army not strong, its wealth not great, it was because the relationships between king and subjects, fathers and children, have always been regulated by the five moral obligations. In the past, the Han, the Sung, the Yuan, the Ming time and again dreamt of annexing our country and of dividing it up into prefectures and districts within the Chinese administrative system. But never were they able to realize their dream. Ah! if even China, which shares a common border with our territory, and is a thousand times more powerful than Vietnam, could not rely upon her strength to swallow us, it was surely because the destiny of our country had been willed by Heaven itself.

The French, separated from our country until the present day by I do not know how many thousand miles, have crossed the oceans to come to our country. Wherever they came, they acted like a storm, so much so that the Emperor had to flee. The whole country was cast into disorder. Our rivers and our mountains have been annexed by them at a stroke and turned into a foreign territory.

Moreover, if our region has suffered to such an extent, it was not only from the misfortunes of war. You must realize that wherever the French go, there flock around them groups of petty men who offer plans and tricks to gain the enemy's confidence…. They use every expedient to squeeze the people out of their possessions. That is how hundreds of misdeeds, thousands of offenses have been perpetrated. How can the French not be aware of all the suffering that the rural population has had to endure? Under these circumstances, is it surprising that families should be disrupted and the people scattered?

My friend, if you are troubled about our people, then I advise you to place yourself in my position and to think about the circumstances in which I live. You will understand naturally and see clearly that I do not need to add anything else.

Q *Explain briefly the reasons advanced by each writer to justify his actions. Which argument do you believe would earn more support from contemporaries? Why?*

Sources: From Truong Buu Lam, *Patterns of Vietnamese Response to Foreign Intervention*, Monograph Series No. 11. Southeast Asian Studies, Yale University, 1967. Dist. by Celler Book Shop, Detroit, MI.

Imperialism: The Balance Sheet

Few periods of history are as controversial among scholars and casual observers as the era of imperialism. To defenders of the colonial enterprise like the poet Rudyard Kipling, imperialism was the "white man's burden," a disagreeable but necessary phase in the evolution of human society, lifting up the toiling races from tradition to modernity and bringing an end to poverty, famine, and disease (see Opposing Viewpoints "White Man's Burden, Black Man's Sorrow" on p. 608).

Critics take exception to such views, portraying imperialism as a tragedy of major proportions. The insatiable drive of the advanced economic powers for access to raw materials and markets created an exploitative environment that transformed the vast majority of colonial peoples into a permanent underclass while restricting the benefits of modern technology to a privileged few. Kipling's "white man's burden" was dismissed as a hypocritical gesture to hoodwink the naive and salve the guilty feelings of those who recognized imperialism for what it was—a savage act of rape. In the blunt words of two Western critics of imperialism: "Why is Africa (or for that matter Latin America and much of Asia) so poor? ... The answer is very brief: we have made it poor."[11]

Defenders of the colonial enterprise sometimes concede that there were gross inequities in the colonial system but point out that there was a positive side to the experience as well. The expansion of markets and the beginnings of a modern transportation and communications network, while bringing few immediate benefits to the colonial peoples, laid the groundwork for future economic growth. At the same time, the introduction of new ways of looking at human freedom, the relationship between the individual and society, and democratic principles set the stage for the adoption of such ideas after the restoration of independence following World War II. Finally, the colonial experience offered a new approach to the traditional relationship between men and women. Although colonial rule was by no means uniformly beneficial to the position of women in African and Asian societies, growing awareness of the struggle by women in the West to seek equality offered their counterparts in the colonial territories a weapon to fight against the long-standing barriers of custom and legal discrimination.

Between these two irreconcilable views, where does the truth lie? This chapter has contended that neither extreme position is justified. In fact, the consequences of colonialism have been more complex than either its defenders or its critics would have us believe. While the colonial peoples received little immediate benefit from the imposition of foreign rule, overall the imperialist era brought about a vast expansion of the international trade network and created at least the potential for societies throughout Africa and Asia to play an active and rewarding role in the new global economic arena. If, as the historian William McNeill believes, the introduction of new technology through cross-cultural encounters is the driving force of change in world history, then Western imperialism, whatever its faults, served a useful purpose in opening the door to such change, much as the rise of the Arab empire and the Mongol invasions hastened the process of global economic development in an earlier time.

Still, the critics have a point. Although colonialism did introduce the peoples of Asia and Africa to new technology and the expanding economic marketplace, it was unnecessarily brutal in its application and all too often failed to realize the exalted claims and objectives of its promoters. Existing economic networks—often potentially valuable as a foundation for later economic development—were ruthlessly swept aside in the interests of providing markets for Western manufactured goods. Potential sources of local industrialization were nipped in the bud to avoid competition for factories in Amsterdam, London, Pittsburgh, or Manchester. Training in Western democratic ideals and practices was ignored out of fear that the recipients might use them as weapons against the ruling authorities.

The fundamental weakness of colonialism, then, was that it was ultimately based on the self-interests of the citizens of the colonial powers. Where those interests collided with the needs of the colonial peoples, those of the former always triumphed. However sincerely the David Livingstones, Albert Sarrauts, and William McKinleys of the world were convinced of the rightness of their civilizing mission, the ultimate result was to deprive the colonial peoples of the right to make their own choices about their own destiny. Sophisticated, age-old societies that could have been left to respond to the technological revolution in their own way were thus squeezed dry of precious national resources under the false guise of a "civilizing mission." As the sociologist Clifford Geertz remarked in his book *Agricultural Involution: The Processes of Ecological Change in Indonesia*, the tragedy is not that the colonial peoples suffered through the colonial era but that they suffered for nothing.

CHAPTER SUMMARY

By the first quarter of the twentieth century, virtually all of Africa and a good part of South and Southeast Asia were under some form of colonial rule. With the advent of the age of imperialism, a global economy was finally established, and the domination of Western civilization over those of Africa and Asia appeared to be complete.

The imperialist rush for colonies did not take place without opposition. In most areas of the world, local governments and peoples resisted the onslaught, sometimes to the bitter end. But with few exceptions, they were unable to overcome the fearsome new warships and firearms that the

Industrial Revolution in Europe had brought into being. Although the material benefits and democratic values of the occupying powers aroused admiration from observers in much of the colonial world, in the end it was weapons, more than ideas, that ushered in the age of imperialism.

Africa and southern Asia were not the only areas of the world that were buffeted by the winds of Western expansionism in the late nineteenth century. The nations of eastern Asia, and those of Latin America and the Middle East as well, were also affected in significant ways.

The consequences of Western political, economic, and military penetration varied substantially from one region to another, however, and therefore require separate treatment. The experience of East Asia will be dealt with in the next chapter. That of Latin America and the Middle East will be discussed in Chapter 24. In these areas, new rivals—notably the United States, Russia, and Japan—entered the scene and played an active role in the process. By the end of the nineteenth century, the rush to secure colonies had circled the world.

CHAPTER TIMELINE

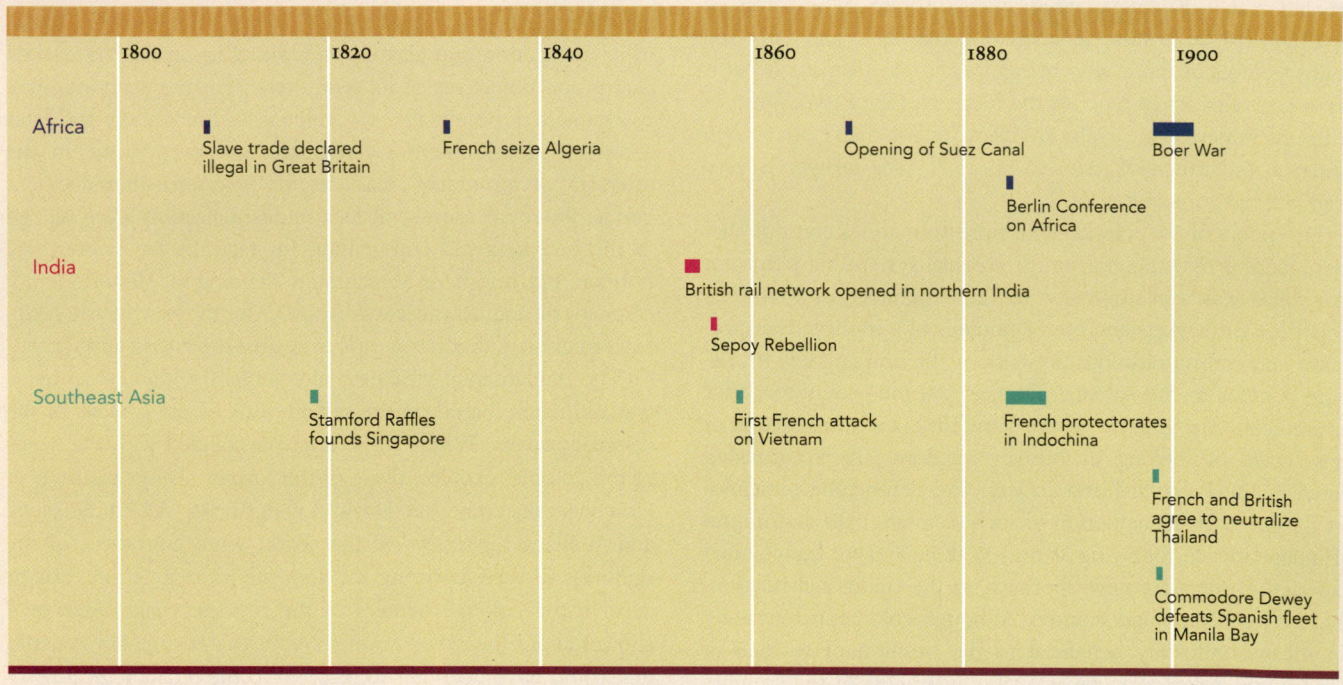

	1800	1820	1840	1860	1880	1900
Africa	Slave trade declared illegal in Great Britain	French seize Algeria		Opening of Suez Canal	Berlin Conference on Africa	Boer War
India				British rail network opened in northern India / Sepoy Rebellion		
Southeast Asia		Stamford Raffles founds Singapore		First French attack on Vietnam	French protectorates in Indochina	French and British agree to neutralize Thailand / Commodore Dewey defeats Spanish fleet in Manila Bay

CHAPTER REVIEW

Upon Reflection

Q What arguments have been advanced to justify the European takeover of colonies in Asia and Africa during the latter part of the nineteenth century? To what degree are such arguments justified?

Q The colonial powers adopted two basic philosophies in seeking to govern their conquered territories in Asia and Africa—assimilation and association. What were the principles behind these philosophies, and how did they work in practice? Which do you believe was more successful?

Q What was the purpose of the Berlin Conference of 1884, and how successful was it at achieving that purpose? What was the impact of the conference for the European powers and for Africa?

Key Terms

imperialism (p. 605)
indirect rule (p. 607)
direct rule (p. 607)
assimilation (p. 609)
association (p. 609)
raj (p. 609)
informal empire (p. 619)
pasha (p. 619)
high colonialism (p. 625)
sepoys (p. 629)

Suggested Reading

IMPERIALISM AND COLONIALISM   There are a number of good works on the subject of imperialism and colonialism. For a study that focuses directly on the question of whether colonialism was beneficial to subject peoples, see **D. K. Fieldhouse**, *The West and the Third World: Trade, Colonialism, Dependence, and Development* (Oxford, 1999). Also see **D. B. Abernathy**, *Global Dominance: European Overseas Empires, 1415–1980* (New Haven, Conn., 2000). For a defense of the British imperial mission, see **N. Ferguson**, *Empire: The Rise and Demise of the British World Order* (New York, 2003).

IMPERIALIST AGE IN AFRICA   On the imperialist age in Africa, see **B. Vandervoort**, *Wars of Imperial Conquest in Africa, 1830–1914* (Bloomington, Ind., 1998), and **T. Pakenham**, *The Scramble for Africa* (New York, 1991). The three-sided conflict in South Africa is ably analyzed in **M. Meredith**, *Diamonds, Gold, and War: The British, the Boers, and the Making of South Africa* (New York, 2007). The scandal in the Belgian Congo is chronicled in **A. Hothschild**, *King Leopold's Ghost: A Story of Greed, Terror, and Heroism in Central Africa* (New York, 1999). Also informative is **R. O. Collins, ed.,** *Historical Problems of Imperial Africa* (Princeton, N.J., 1994).

INDIA   For an overview of the British takeover and administration of India, see **S. Wolpert**, *A New History of India*, 8th ed. (New York, 2008). **C. A. Bayly**, *Indian Society and the Making of the British Empire* (Cambridge, 1988), is a scholarly analysis of the impact of British conquest on the Indian economy. Also see **A. Wild's** elegant *East India Company: Trade and Conquest from 1600* (New York, 2000). In a provocative work, *Ornamentalism: How the British Saw Their Empire* (Oxford, 2000), **D. Cannadine** argues that it was class and not race that motivated British policy in the subcontinent. In *The Last Mughal: The Fall of a Dynasty: Delhi 1857* (New York, 2007), **W. Dalrymple** argues that religion was the key issue in provoking the Sepoy Rebellion. Also see **N. Dirks**, *The Scandal of Empire: India and the Creation of Imperial Britain* (Cambridge, Mass., 2007).

COLONIAL AGE IN SOUTHEAST ASIA   General studies of the colonial period in Southeast Asia are rare because most authors focus on specific areas. For an overview by several authors, see **N. Tarling, ed.,** *The Cambridge History of Southeast Asia*, vol. 3 (Cambridge, 1992).

Chapter Notes

1. Quoted in J. G. Lockhart and C. M. Wodehouse, *Rhodes* (London, 1963), pp. 69–70.
2. K. Pearson, *National Life from the Standpoint of Science* (London, 1905), p. 184.
3. Quoted in H. Braunschwig, *French Colonialism, 1871–1914* (London, 1961), p. 80.
4. Quoted in G. Garros, *Forceries Humaines* (Paris, 1926), p. 21.
5. Cited in B. Schwartz's review of D. Cannadine's *Ornamentalism: How the British Saw Their Empire*, in *The Atlantic*, November 2001, p. 135.
6. Quoted in R. Bartlett, ed., *The Record of American Diplomacy: Documents and Readings in the History of American Foreign Relations* (New York, 1952), p. 385.
7. Quoted in L. Roubaud, *Vietnam: La Tragédie Indochinoise* (Paris, 1926), p. 80.
8. Quoted in J. Iliffe, *Africans: The History of a Continent* (Cambridge, 1995), p. 124.
9. Quoted in T. Pakenham, *The Scramble for Africa* (New York, 1991), p. 13.
10. Quoted in ibid., p. 182, citing a letter to Queen Victoria dated August 7, 1879.
11. Quoted in P. C. W. Gutkind and I. Wallerstein, eds., *The Political Economy of Contemporary Africa* (Beverly Hills, Calif., 1976), p. 14.

MindTap is a fully online, highly personalized learning experience built upon Cengage Learning content. MindTap combines student learning tools—readings, multimedia, activities, and assessments—into a singular Learning Path that guides students through their course.

Shadows over the Pacific: East Asia Under Challenge

The imperial throne room in the Forbidden City

CHAPTER OUTLINE AND FOCUS QUESTIONS

The Decline of the Manchus

Q Why did the Qing Dynasty decline and ultimately collapse, and what role did the Western powers play in this process?

Chinese Society in Transition

Q What political, economic, and social reforms were instituted by the Qing Dynasty during its final decades, and why were they not more successful in reversing the decline of Manchu rule?

A Rich Country and a Strong State: The Rise of Modern Japan

Q To what degree was the Meiji Restoration a "revolution," and to what extent did it succeed in transforming Japan?

CRITICAL THINKING

Q How did China and Japan each respond to Western pressures in the nineteenth century, and what implications did their different responses have for each nation's history?

CONNECTIONS TO TODAY

Q What lessons can developing nations today learn from the experiences encountered by China and Japan during the period covered in this chapter?

THE BRITISH EMISSARY Lord Macartney had arrived in Beijing in 1793 with a caravan loaded with six hundred cases of gifts for the emperor. Flags and banners provided by the Chinese proclaimed in Chinese characters that the visitor was an "ambassador bearing tribute from the country of England." But the tribute—as his hosts defined it—was in vain, for Macartney's request for an increase in trade between the two countries was flatly rejected, and he left Beijing in October with nothing to show for his efforts. Not until half a century later would the Qing Dynasty—at the point of a gun—agree to the British demand for an expansion of commercial ties.

In fact, the Chinese emperor Qianlong had responded to the requests of his visitor with polite but poorly disguised condescension. To Macartney's proposal that a British ambassador be stationed in the capital of Beijing, the emperor replied that such a request was "not in harmony with the state system of our dynasty and will definitely not be permitted." As for the British envoy's suggestion that regular trade relations be established between the two countries, that proposal was also rejected (see Chapter 17). We receive all sorts of precious things, replied the Celestial Emperor, as gifts from myriad nations. "Consequently," he added, "there is nothing we lack, as your principal envoy and others have themselves observed. We have never set much store on strange or ingenious objects, nor do we need more of your country's manufactures."

Historians have often viewed the failure of Macartney's mission as a reflection of the disdain of Chinese rulers toward their counterparts in other countries and their serene confidence in the superiority of Chinese civilization in a world inhabited by barbarians. If that was the case, Qianlong's confidence was misplaced, for as the eighteenth century came to an end, his country faced a growing challenge not only from the escalating power and ambitions of the West but from its own growing internal weakness as well. When insistent British demands for the right to carry out trade and missionary activities in China were rejected, Britain resorted to force and in the Opium War, which broke out in 1839, gave Manchu troops a sound thrashing. A humiliated China was finally forced to open its doors. ⇜

The Decline of the Manchus

 FOCUS QUESTION: Why did the Qing Dynasty decline and ultimately collapse, and what role did the Western powers play in this process?

In 1800, the Qing (CHING) or Manchu Dynasty appeared to be at the height of its power. China had experienced a long period of peace and prosperity under the rule of two great emperors, Kangxi (kang-SHEE) and Qianlong (CHAN-loong). Its

borders were secure, and its culture and intellectual achievements were the envy of the world. Its rulers, hidden behind the walls of the Forbidden City in Beijing (bay-ZHING), had every reason to describe their patrimony as the "Central Kingdom." But there was trouble under the surface, and a little over a century later, humiliated and harassed by the black ships and big guns of the Western powers, the Qing Dynasty, the last in a series that had endured for more than two thousand years, collapsed in the dust (see Map 22.1).

Historians once assumed that the primary reason for the rapid decline and fall of the Manchu Dynasty was the intense pressure applied to a proud but somewhat complacent traditional society by the modern West. Now, however, most historians believe that internal changes played a major role in the dynasty's collapse and point out that at least some of the problems suffered by the Manchus during the nineteenth century were self-inflicted and had little to do with the Western onslaught.

The latter explanation certainly has some validity. Like so many of its predecessors, after an extended period of growth, the Qing Dynasty at the end of the eighteenth century began

MAP 22.1 The Qing Empire. Shown here is the Qing Empire at the height of its power in the late eighteenth century, as well as its shrunken sphere of influence at the moment of dissolution in 1911.

 How do China's tributary states on this map differ from those in Map 17.2 on p. 481? Which of them fell under the influence of foreign powers during the nineteenth century?

The Roots of Rebellion in Qing China

POLITICS & GOVERNMENT

HONG LIANGJI (Hoong Lyahng-JEE) (1746–1809) was a middle-level government official serving the Qing Dynasty at the end of the eighteenth century. When the White Lotus Rebellion broke out in the central provinces in 1796 (see Chapter 17), Hong wrote a memorial to Emperor Jiaqing (Jya-CHING) contending that the uprising was not caused by disloyal elements espousing "heterodox" doctrines, but by economic hardships precipitated by corrupt local officials seeking to pad their own nests. For his audacity, Hong was forced to resign his office and submit to exile in far-off Xinjiang province, where he died a decade later. Hong is viewed today as the stereotypical upright official dedicated to governing by Confucian moral principles.

Hong Liangji, Memorial on the War Against Heterodoxy (1798)

The deterioration of the county government is a hundred times worse than ten or twenty years ago. The [county officials] have betrayed the laws of the Son of Heaven and exhausted the resources of the common people. From what I have heard, although there are heterodox sects in such places as Yichang in Hubei and Dashou in Sichuan, the people there value their lives and property and love their wives and children too much to dare to violate the law. The county officials were not able to prevent the spread of heterodoxy by exerting good influences on the people, and when sectarianism spread, the officials would use the pretext of investigating heterodoxy to make demands on the people and threaten their lives, until the people joined the rebels. I would humbly suggest that in locations where heterodox rebellions have arisen, inquiry must be made into the causes of conflict, to see whether the rebellion was precipitated by the officials, who should be punished according to the facts of each case.

County magistrates have incriminated themselves in three ways:

1. Funds authorized by the court for disaster relief were pocketed by the officials, who would declare that the funds were intended for making up deficiencies in what was due the government—in this way, the beneficence of the court never reached the people.

2. In ordinary times, the local officials would appropriate taxes and military funds [for their own use]. But when troubles arose, they would try to conceal their failure and even claim some merit. County officials would conceal the facts from the prefects and circuit intendants; prefects and circuit intendants from the governors-general and governors; governors-general and governors from even Your Imperial Majesty. Thus the sentiments of those on the lower level have no way of reaching the higher level.

3. When there is some success, even personal servants and secretaries [of the county magistrate] claim a share of the merit. But in case of failure, the blame is fixed on the good people who are in distress as roving migrants. Failure, to be sure, is not the fault of the county officials alone. High officials at the provincial level and the high military commanders and officers all behave in this way without even making a secret of it. It is no surprise that the county officials imitate them.

How might the official Hong Liangji have been inspired by reading the Confucian Analects *and other classical works from ancient China?*

Source: From *Sources of Chinese Tradition*, Vol. 2, 2e, by Wm. Theodore de Bary and Richard Lufrano. Copyright © 2000 Columbia University Press. Reprinted with permission of the publisher.

---

to suffer from the familiar dynastic ills of official corruption, peasant unrest, and incompetence at court (see the box "The Roots of Rebellion in Qing China" above). Such weaknesses were probably exacerbated by the rapid growth in population. The long era of peace and stability, the introduction of new crops from the Americas, and the cultivation of new, fast-ripening strains of rice had enabled the Chinese population to double between 1550 and 1800. The population continued to grow after 1800, placing enormous pressure on the agricultural sector to feed a population that rose to the unprecedented level of 400 million by 1900. Even without the irritating presence of the Western powers, the Manchus might have been destined to repeat the fate of previous imperial dynasties. The ships, guns, and ideas of the foreigners simply highlighted the growing weakness of the Manchu Empire and likely hastened its demise. In doing so, Western imperialism still exerted an indelible impact on the history of modern China—but as a contributing, not a causal, factor.

Opium and Rebellion

By 1800, Westerners had been in regular contact with China for almost three centuries, but after an initial period of flourishing relations, Western traders had been limited to a small commercial outlet at Canton. This arrangement was not acceptable to the British, however. Not only did they chafe at being restricted to a tiny enclave, but the growing British appetite for Chinese tea created a severe balance-of-payments problem. After Macartney's failure in 1793, another mission led by Lord Amherst arrived in China in 1816. But it too achieved little except to worsen the already strained relations between the two countries. The British solution to the problem was opium. A product more addictive than tea, opium was grown in northeastern India and then shipped to China in British ships. Opium had been grown in southwestern China for several hundred years but had been used primarily for medicinal purposes. Now, as imports increased, popular demand for the product in southern China became insatiable despite an official prohibition on its use. Soon bullion was flowing out of the Chinese imperial treasury into the pockets of British merchants.

The Qing became concerned and tried to negotiate. In 1839, Lin Zexu (LIN dzeh-SHOO) (1785–1850), a Chinese official appointed by the court to curtail the opium trade, appealed to Queen Victoria on both moral and practical grounds and even threatened to prohibit the sale of rhubarb (widely used as a laxative in nineteenth-century Europe) to Great Britain if she did not respond. But moral principles, then as now, paled before the lure of profits, and the British continued to promote the opium trade, arguing that if the Chinese did not want the opium, they did not have to buy it. Lin Zexu attacked on three fronts, imposing penalties on smokers, arresting dealers, and seizing supplies from importers as they attempted to smuggle the drug into China. The last tactic caused his downfall. When he blockaded the foreign factory (warehouse) area in Canton to force traders to hand over their remaining chests of opium, the British government, claiming that it could not permit British subjects "to be exposed to insult and injustice," launched a naval expedition to punish the Manchus and force the court to open China to foreign trade.[1]

THE OPIUM WAR The Opium War (1839–1842) demonstrated the superiority of British firepower and military tactics (including the use of a shallow-draft steamboat that effectively harassed Chinese coastal defenses). British warships destroyed Chinese coastal and river forts and seized the offshore island of Zhoushan (JOH-shahn), not far from the mouth of the Yangzi River. When a British fleet sailed virtually unopposed up the Yangzi to Nanjing (nan-JING) and cut off the supply of "tribute grain" from southern to northern China, the Qing finally agreed to British terms. In the Treaty of Nanjing in 1842, the Chinese agreed to open five coastal ports to British trade, limit tariffs on imported British goods, grant extraterritorial rights to British citizens in China, and pay a substantial indemnity to cover the costs of the war. China also agreed to cede the island of Hong Kong (dismissed by a senior British official as a "barren rock") to Great Britain. Nothing was said in the treaty about the opium trade, which continued unabated until it was brought under control through Chinese government efforts in the early twentieth century.

Although the Opium War has traditionally been considered the beginning of modern Chinese history, it is unlikely that many Chinese at the time would have seen it that way.

The Opium War. The Opium War, waged between China and Great Britain between 1839 and 1842, was China's first conflict with a European power. Lacking modern military technology, the Chinese suffered a humiliating defeat. In this painting, heavily armed British steamships destroy unwieldy Chinese junks along the Chinese coast. China's humiliation at sea was a legacy of its rulers' lack of interest in maritime matters since the middle of the fifteenth century, when Chinese junks were among the most advanced sailing ships in the world.

This was not the first time that a ruling dynasty had been forced to make concessions to foreigners, and the opening of five coastal ports to the British hardly constituted a serious threat to the security of the empire. Although a few concerned Chinese argued that the court should learn more about European civilization, others contended that China had nothing to learn from the barbarians and that borrowing foreign ways would undercut the purity of Confucian civilization.

For the time being, then, the Manchus attempted to deal with the problem in the traditional way of playing the foreigners off against each other. Concessions granted to the British were offered to other Western nations, including the United States, and soon thriving foreign concession areas were operating in treaty ports along the southern Chinese coast from Canton to Shanghai (SHANG-hy).

THE TAIPING REBELLION In the meantime, the Qing court's failure to deal with pressing internal economic problems led to a major peasant revolt that shook the foundations of the empire. On the surface, the Taiping (TY-ping) Rebellion owed something to the Western incursion. The leader of the uprising, Hong Xiuquan (HOONG shee-oo-CHWAHN), a failed examination candidate, was a Christian convert who viewed himself as a younger brother of Jesus and hoped to establish what he referred to as a "Heavenly Kingdom of Supreme Peace" in China. But there were many local causes as well. The rapid increase in population forced millions of peasants to eke out a living as sharecroppers or landless laborers. Official corruption and incompetence led to the whipsaw of increased taxes and a decline in government services; even the Grand Canal was allowed to silt up, hindering the shipment of grain. In 1853, the Taiping rebels seized the old Ming capital of Nanjing, but that proved to be the rebellion's high-water mark. Plagued by factionalism, the rebellion gradually lost momentum until it was finally suppressed in 1864, but by then it had had devastating effects on Chinese society. More than 25 million people were killed, the vast majority of them civilians.

One reason for the dynasty's failure to deal effectively with the internal unrest was its continuing difficulties in dealing with the Western challenge. In 1856, the British and the French, still

The Taiping Rebellion

smarting from Qing restrictions on trade and missionary activities, launched a new series of attacks against China and seized Beijing in 1860. To punish China for its recalcitrance, British troops destroyed the emperor's summer palace just outside the city. In the ensuing Treaty of Tianjin (TYAHN-jin), the Qing agreed to humiliating new concessions: the legalization of the opium trade, the opening of additional ports to foreign trade, and the cession of the peninsula of Kowloon (KOW-loon) (opposite the island of Hong Kong) to the British (see Map 22.2). Additional territories in the north were ceded to Russia.

Efforts at Reform

By the late 1870s, the old dynasty was well on the road to internal disintegration. In fending off the Taiping Rebellion, the Manchus had been compelled to rely on armed forces under regional command. After quelling the revolt, many of these regional commanders refused to disband their units and, with the support of the local gentry, continued to collect local taxes for their own use. The dreaded pattern of imperial breakdown, so familiar in Chinese history, was beginning to appear once again.

In its weakened state, the court finally began to listen to the appeals of reform-minded officials, who called for a new

MAP 22.2 Canton and Hong Kong. This map shows the estuary of the Pearl River in southern China, an important area of early contact between China and Europe.

Q *What was the importance of Canton? What were the New Territories, and when were they annexed by the British?*

policy of what they called **self-strengthening**, in which Western technology would be adopted while Confucian principles and institutions were maintained intact. This policy, popularly known by its slogan "East for Essence, West for Practical Use," remained the guiding standard for Chinese foreign and domestic policy for nearly a quarter of a century. Some even called for reforms in education and in China's hallowed political institutions (see Opposing Viewpoints "Practical Learning or Confucian Essence: The Debate over Reform" on p. 640). Pointing to the power and prosperity of modern European nations, the journalist Wang Tao (wahng TOW ["ow" as in "how"]) (1828–1897) called on Chinese leaders to abandon their resistance to reform. "I know," he remarked, "that within a hundred years China will adopt all Western methods and excel in them."[2] Such democratic ideas were too radical for most moderate reformers, however. One of the leading court officials of the day, Zhang Zhidong (JANG jee-DOONG), countered that "the doctrine of people's rights will bring us not a single benefit but a hundred evils … — what use will it be?"[3]

For the time being, Zhang Zhidong's arguments won the day. During the last quarter of the century, the Manchus attempted to modernize their military establishment and build up an industrial base without disturbing the essential elements of traditional Chinese civilization. Railroads, weapons arsenals, and shipyards were built, but the value system remained essentially unchanged.

The Climax of Imperialism

In the end, the results spoke for themselves. During the last two decades of the nineteenth century, the European penetration of China, both political and military, intensified. Rapacious imperialists began to bite off the outer edges of the Qing Empire. The Gobi Desert north of the Great Wall, Central Asia, and Tibet, all inhabited by non-Chinese peoples and never fully assimilated into the Chinese Empire, were gradually lost. In the north and northwest, the main beneficiary was Russia, which took advantage of the dynasty's weakness to force the cession of territories north of the Amur (ah-MOOR) River in Siberia. In Tibet, competition between Russia and Great Britain prevented either power from seizing the territory outright but enabled Tibetan authorities to revive local autonomy never recognized by the Chinese. In the south, British and French advances in mainland Southeast Asia removed Burma

and Vietnam from their traditional vassal relationship to the imperial court in Beijing. Even more ominous were the so-called "spheres of influence" in the Chinese heartland, where local commanders were willing to sell exclusive commercial, railroad-building, or mining privileges to commercial interests of a particular foreign power.

The crumbling of the Manchu Dynasty accelerated at the end of the nineteenth century. In 1894, the Qing went to war with Japan over Japanese incursions into the Korean peninsula, which threatened China's long-held suzerainty over the area (see "Joining the Imperialist Club" later in this chapter). To the surprise of many observers, the Chinese were roundly defeated, confirming to some critics the devastating failure of the policy of self-strengthening by halfway measures. China's disintegration gathered speed in 1897, when Germany, a new entry in the race for spoils in East Asia, used the pretext of the murder of two German missionaries by Chinese rioters to demand the cession of territories in the Shandong (shahn-DOONG) Peninsula. The approval of Berlin's demand by the imperial court set off a scramble for territory by other interested powers (see Map 22.3). Russia now demanded the Liaodong (LYOW-doong) Peninsula with its ice-free port at

MAP 22.3 Foreign Possessions and Spheres of Influence About 1900. At the end of the nineteenth century, China was being carved up like a melon by foreign imperialist powers. Colored areas indicate territories that had recently come under foreign influence.

Q Which of the areas marked on the map were removed from Chinese control during the nineteenth century?

Practical Learning or Confucian Essence: The Debate over Reform

POLITICS & GOVERNMENT

BY THE LAST QUARTER OF THE NINETEENTH CENTURY, Chinese officials and intellectuals had become increasingly alarmed at the country's inability to counter the steady pressure emanating from the West. Some, like the journalist Wang Tao (1828–1897), asserted that nothing less than a full-scale reform of Chinese society was required, including the adoption of the Western concept of political rights and democratic institutions. Others, like the scholar-official Zhang Zhidong (1837–1909), countered that such values and institutions would not work in China, and that the adoption of Western technology and science would be sufficient to protect the country from collapse. These two excerpts display the depth of disagreement between the two opposing views.

Zhang Zhidong, *Rectification of Political Rights*

The theory of people's rights will bring us not a particle of good but a hundred evils. Are we going to establish a parliament? Among Chinese scholar-officials and among the people there are still many today who are obstinate and uneducated. They understand nothing about the general situation of the world, and they are ignorant of the affairs of state. They have never heard of important developments concerning the schools, political systems, military training, and manufacture of machinery. Suppose the confused and tumultuous people are assembled in one house, with one sensible man there out of a hundred who are witless, babbling aimlessly, and talking as if in a dream—what use would it be? Moreover, in foreign countries the matter of revenue is mainly handled by the lower house, while matters of legislation are taken care of by the upper house. To be a member of parliament the candidate must possess a fairly good income. Nowadays Chinese merchants rarely have much capital, and the Chinese people are lacking in long-range vision. If any important proposal for raising funds comes up for discussion, they will make excuses and keep silent; so their discussion is no different from non-discussion.... This is the first reason why a parliament is of no use....

Wang Tao, *A Note on the British Government*

The real strength of England, however, lies in the fact that there is a sympathetic understanding between the governing and the governed, a close relationship between the ruler and the people.... My observation is that the daily domestic political life of England actually embodies the traditional ideals of our ancient Golden Age [lit., the Three Dynasties and earlier].

In official appointments the method of recommendation and election is practised, but the candidates must be well known, of good character and achievements before they can be promoted to a position over the people.... And moreover the principle of majority rule is adhered to in order to show impartiality.... In their treatment of the people the officials never dare to use severe punishments, heavy fines, or tyrannical and excessive taxation. Nor dare they accept any bribery ... or squeeze the blood and flesh of myriads of people in order to fill up their own pockets. The English people are likewise public spirited and law-abiding; the laws and regulations are hung up high (for everyone to see), and no one dares violate them. He who violates the law goes to the court only to have his confession taken; when the real truth has been obtained, then a verdict is made, and he is imprisoned. There has never been such cruelty as torturing and beating him by bamboos and clubs so that his blood and flesh spread all over. In prison the convict is supplied with food and clothing, so that he may not be hungry or cold. He is taught to work and not allowed to become idle. He is visited every seven days by preachers to make him repent and live a new life. He is never maltreated by those in charge of the prison. The excellence of the prison system is what China has never had since the Golden Age....

An important question is jointly discussed in the upper and lower houses of parliament, and all must agree before an action can be taken. If there is a proposal for a military expedition it is necessary to make a universal inquiry of the whole nation. When the multitude of people desire to fight, then there is a war; and when the multitude desire to cease then a truce....

The expenditure of the British ruler is a constantly fixed amount for every year; he does not dare to eat myriads of delicacies. His palaces are all very simple; he does not care for extravagance, and he has never had separate mansions and distant palaces linked with one another over scores of *li*. The king has only one queen, and besides here there is no concubine, and there has never been a multitude of three thousand beautiful women in the harem....

Q *Why does journalist Wang Tao believe that the reforms he proposes are necessary? What are Zhang Zhidong's criticisms of such reforms?*

Sources: From *Sources of Chinese Tradition*, Vol. 2, 2e, by Wm. Theodore de Bary and Richard Lufrano, pp. 178–179. Copyright © 2000 Columbia University Press. Reprinted with permission of the publisher. From Ssu-yu Teng and John K. Fairbank, *China's Response to the West: A Documentary Survey 1839–1923* (Cambridge: Harvard University Press, 1954), p. 140.

Port Arthur, and Great Britain weighed in with a request for a coaling station in northern China and, in order to obtain fresh water and agricultural produce for the growing population on Hong Kong island, obtained a hundred-year lease on the so-called New Territories, located on the mainland adjacent to the island.

The government responded to the challenge with yet another spasmodic effort at reform. In the spring of 1898, an outspoken advocate of change, the progressive Confucian scholar Kang Youwei (KAHNG yow-WAY), won the support of the young emperor Guangxu (gwahng-SHOO) for a comprehensive reform program patterned after recent measures in Japan. Without dramatic change, he argued, China would perish. During the next several weeks, the emperor issued edicts calling for major political, administrative, and educational reforms.

Not surprisingly, Kang's proposals were opposed by many conservatives, who saw little advantage and much risk in copying the West. Most important, the new program was opposed by the emperor's aunt, the Empress Dowager Cixi (TSE-shee) (1835–1908), the real power at court. Cixi had begun her political career as a concubine to an earlier emperor. After his death, she became a dominant force at court and in 1878 placed her infant nephew, the future Emperor Guangxu, on the throne. For two decades, she ruled in his name as regent. Although Cixi had been receptive to modest reforms over the past few years, and had apparently supported Zhang Zhidong's program of self-strengthening, she interpreted Guangxu's action as a British-supported effort to reduce her influence at court and promote radical changes in Chinese society. With the aid of conservatives in the army, she arrested and executed several of the reformers and had the emperor incarcerated in the palace. Kang Youwei succeeded in fleeing abroad. With Cixi's palace coup, the so-called One Hundred Days of reform came to an end.

OPENING THE DOOR During the next two years, foreign pressure on the dynasty intensified. With encouragement from the British, who hoped to avert a total collapse of the Manchu Empire, in 1899 U.S. Secretary of State John Hay presented the other imperialist powers with a proposal to ensure equal economic access to the China market for all states. Hay also suggested that all powers join together to guarantee the territorial and administrative integrity of the Chinese Empire. Though probably motivated more by the United States' preference for open markets than by a benevolent wish to protect China, the so-called **Open Door Notes** did have the practical effect of reducing the imperialist hysteria over access to the China market. That hysteria, a product of decades of mythologizing among Western commercial interests about the 400 million Chinese customers, had accelerated at the end of the century as fear of China's imminent collapse increased. The "gentlemen's agreement" about the Open Door (it was not a treaty, merely a pious and nonbinding expression of intent) served to deflate fears in Britain, France, Germany, and Russia that other powers would take advantage of China's weakness to dominate the China market.

The Empress Dowager Cixi. Portraits of ruling figures have traditionally been designed to inspire admiration or devotion and thus tend to emphasize the majestic or charismatic quality of the subject. After the disastrous Boxer Rebellion of 1900, however, the Empress Dowager Cixi sought to improve her image in the Western world and turned to the modern medium of photography as a means of doing so. In this photograph, taken in 1903, she appeared in an elaborate costume in a traditional Chinese setting, but her casual stance was apparently intended to soften her image among foreign observers.

THE BOXER REBELLION In the long run, then, the Open Door policy was a positive step that brought a measure of sanity to imperialist meddling in East Asia. Unfortunately, it came too late to stop the domestic explosion known as the Boxer Rebellion. The Boxers, so-called because of the physical exercises they performed (which closely resembled the more martial forms of tai chi), were members of a secret society operating primarily in rural areas in northern China. Provoked by a damaging drought and high unemployment

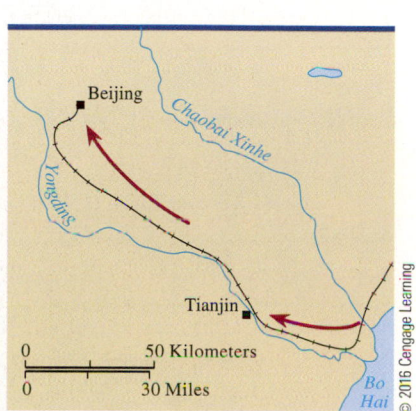

The International Expeditionary Force Advances to Beijing to Suppress the Boxers

Justice or Mercy? Uncle Sam Decides. In the summer of 1900, Chinese rebels known as Boxers besieged Western embassies in the imperial capital of Beijing. Western nations, including the United States, dispatched troops to North China to rescue their compatriots. In this cartoon, which appeared in a contemporary American newsmagazine, China figuratively seeks pardon from a stern Uncle Sam.

caused in part by foreign economic activity (the introduction of railroads and steamships, for example, undercut the livelihood of barge workers on the rivers and canals), the Boxers attacked foreign residents and besieged the foreign legation quarter in Beijing. The empress dowager, while probably uncomfortable at the sight of mobs rioting at the gates of the Imperial City, surreptitiously supported the Boxer forces as a means of fending off the aggressive actions of the Western powers. As a result, when the foreigners were rescued by an international expeditionary force in the late summer of 1900, the victorious troops destroyed a number of temples in the capital suburbs, and the Chinese government was compelled to pay a heavy indemnity to the foreign governments involved in suppressing the uprising.

The Collapse of the Old Order

During the next few years, the old dynasty tried desperately to reform itself. The empress dowager, perhaps recognizing the urgency of the situation, now embraced a number of reforms. The venerable civil service examination system was replaced by a new educational system based on the Western model. Schools for women were opened in a number of major cities. In 1905, a commission was formed to study constitutional changes; over the next few years, legislative assemblies were established at the provincial level, and elections for a national assembly were held in 1910.

Such moves helped shore up the dynasty temporarily, but history shows that the most dangerous period for an authoritarian system is when it seeks to reform itself, because change breeds instability and performance rarely matches rising expectations. Such was the case in China. The emerging provincial elite, composed of merchants, professionals, and reform-minded gentry, soon became impatient with the

The Empress Dowager's Navy. Historians have often interpreted the stone pavilion shown here as a symbol of the inability of the Qing Dynasty to comprehend the nature of the threat to its survival. At the command of Empress Dowager Cixi, funds meant to strengthen the Chinese navy against external threats were allegedly used instead to construct this stone pleasure boat on a lake at the Summer Palace west of Beijing. Whether or not the allegation is true, any woman exercising a degree of political power in China—as the ghost of the one-time Tang Dynasty concubine Yang Guifei (yahng gway-FAY) can attest (see Chapter 10)—has traditionally been viewed by Chinese historians as an incarnation of the forces of evil. Cixi was no exception to the rule. Today the lake is a popular place for Chinese tourists.

slow pace of political change and were disillusioned to find that the new assemblies were intended to be primarily advisory rather than legislative. The government also alienated influential elements by financing railway development projects through foreign firms rather than local investors. The reforms also had little meaning for peasants, artisans, miners, and transportation workers, whose living conditions were being eroded by rising taxes and official venality. Rising rural unrest, as yet poorly organized and often centered on secret societies such as the Boxers, was an ominous sign of deep-seated resentment to which the dynasty would not or could not respond.

THE RISE OF SUN YAT-SEN   To China's reformist elite, such signs of social discontent were a threat to be avoided. To its tiny revolutionary movement, they were a harbinger of promise. The first physical manifestations of future revolution appeared during the last decade of the nineteenth century with the formation of the Revive China Society by the young radical Sun Yat-sen (SOON yaht-SEN) (1866–1925). Born in a village south of Canton, Sun was educated in Hawaii and returned to China to practice medicine. Soon he turned his full attention to the ills of Chinese society.

At first, Sun's efforts yielded few positive results, but at a convention held in Tokyo in 1905, he managed to unite radical groups from across China in the so-called Revolutionary Alliance, or Tongmenghui (toong-meng-HWAY). The new organization's program was based on Sun's **three people's principles** of nationalism (meaning primarily the elimination of Manchu rule over China), democracy, and people's livelihood. It called for a three-stage process beginning with a military takeover and ending with a constitutional democracy (see the box "Program for a New China" on p. 644). Although the new organization was small and relatively inexperienced, it benefited from rising popular discontent.

THE REVOLUTION OF 1911   In October 1911, Sun's followers launched an uprising in the industrial center of Wuhan (WOO-HAHN), in central China. With Sun traveling in the

United States, the insurrection lacked leadership, but the imperial government's inability to react quickly encouraged political forces at the provincial level to take measures into their own hands. The dynasty was now in a state of virtual collapse: the empress dowager had died in 1908, one day after her nephew Guangxu; the throne was now occupied by China's "last emperor," the infant Puyi (POO-YEE). Sun's party had neither the military strength nor the political base necessary to seize the initiative, however, and was forced to turn to a representative of the old order, General Yuan Shikai (yoo-AHN shee-KY) (1859–1916). A prominent figure in military circles since the beginning of the century, Yuan had been placed in charge of the imperial forces sent to suppress the rebellion, but now he abandoned the Manchus and acted on his own behalf. In negotiations with representatives of Sun Yat-sen's party (Sun himself had arrived in China in January 1912), he agreed to serve as president of a new Chinese republic. The old dynasty and the age-old system that it had attempted to preserve were no more (see the Film & History feature "The Last Emperor (1987)" on p. 645).

Although the dynasty was gone, the rebel forces were unable to consolidate their gains. Sun Yat-sen's program was based on Western liberal democratic principles aimed at the urban middle class. That class had provided the driving force for the capitalist democratic revolutions in western Europe and North America in the late eighteenth and nineteenth centuries, but its counterpart in China was still too small to form the basis for a new political order. The vast majority of the Chinese people still lived on the land. Sun had hoped to win their support with a land reform program, but few peasants were aware of it, and rural participation in the 1911 revolution was minimal. In failing to provide a set of ideas that could arouse the active support of the majority of the population, Sun and his followers had brought about less a revolution than a collapse of the old order. Under the weight of Western imperialism and its own internal weaknesses, the old dynasty had crumbled before new political and social forces were ready to fill the void.

What China experienced in the 1911 revolution was part of a historical process that was bringing down traditional empires across the globe, both in regions threatened by Western imperialism and in Europe itself, where tsarist Russia, the Austro-Hungarian Empire, and the Ottoman Empire all came to an end within a few years after the collapse of the Qing. The circumstances of their demise were not all the same. The Habsburg and Ottoman Empires, for example, were dismembered by the victorious allies after World War I, and the fate of tsarist Russia was directly linked to that conflict (see Chapter 23). Still, all four regimes bore some responsibility for their fate in that they had failed to meet the challenges posed by the times. All had responded to the forces of industrialization and popular participation in the political process with hesitation and reluctance, and their attempts at reform were too little and too late. All paid the supreme price for their folly.

CHRONOLOGY China in the Era of Imperialism	
Lord Macartney's mission to China	1793
Opium War	1839–1842
Taiping rebels seize Nanjing	1853
Taiping Rebellion suppressed	1864
Cixi becomes regent for nephew, Guangxu	1878
Sino-Japanese War	1894–1895
One Hundred Days reform	1898
Open Door policy	1899
Boxer Rebellion	1900
Commission to study constitution formed	1905
Deaths of Cixi and Guangxu	1908
Revolution in China	1911

Program for a New China

POLITICS & GOVERNMENT

In 1905, Sun Yat-sen united a number of anti-Manchu groups into a single patriotic organization called the Revolutionary Alliance (Tongmenghui). The new organization eventually formed the core of his Guomindang (gwoh-min-DAHNG), or Nationalist Party. This excerpt is from the organization's manifesto, published in 1905 in Tokyo. Note that Sun believed that the Chinese people were not ready for democracy and required a period of tutelage to prepare them for the final era of constitutional political government. This was a formula that would be adopted by many other political leaders in Asia and Africa after World War II.

Sun Yat-sen, *Manifesto for the Tongmenghui*

By order of the Military Government, … the Commander-in-Chief of the Chinese National Army proclaims the purposes and platform of the Military Government to the people of the nation:

Therefore we proclaim to the world in utmost sincerity the outline of the present revolution and the fundamental plan for the future administration of the nation.

1. *Drive out the Tartars:* The Manchus of today were originally the eastern barbarians beyond the Great Wall. They frequently caused border troubles during the Ming Dynasty; then when China was in a disturbed state they came inside Shanhaikuan [the eastern terminus of the Great Wall], conquered China, and enslaved our Chinese people…. The extreme cruelties and tyrannies of the Manchu government have now reached their limit. With the righteous army poised against them, we will overthrow that government, and restore our sovereign rights.
2. *Restore China:* China is the China of the Chinese. The government of China should be in the hands of the Chinese. After driving out the Tartars we must restore our national state….
3. *Establish the Republic:* Now our revolution is based on equality, in order to establish a republican government. All our people are equal and all enjoy political rights….
4. *Equalize land ownership:* The good fortune of civilization is to be shared equally by all the people of the nation. We should improve our social and economic organization, and assess the value of all the land in the country. Its present price shall be received by the owner, but all increases in value resulting from reform and social improvements after the revolution shall belong to the state, to be shared by all the people, in order to create a socialist state, where each family within the empire can be well supported, each person satisfied, and no one fail to secure employment….

The above four points will be carried out in three steps in due order. The first period is government by military law. When the righteous army has arisen, various places will join the cause…. Evils like the oppression of the government, the greed and graft of officials, … the cruelty of tortures and penalties, the tyranny of tax collections, the humiliation of the queue [the requirement that all Chinese males braid their hair]—shall all be exterminated together with the Manchu rule. Evils in social customs, such as the keeping of slaves, the cruelty of foot binding, the spread of the poison of opium, should also all be prohibited….

The second period is that of government by a provisional constitution. When military law is lifted in each *hsien* [district], the Military Government shall return the right of self-government to the local people….

The third period will be government under the constitution. Six years after the provisional constitution has been enforced a constitution shall be made. The military and administrative powers of the Military Government shall be annulled; the people shall elect the president, and elect the members of parliament to organize the parliament.

 How do Sun Yat-sen's proposals compare with those advanced by Wang Tao earlier in this chapter? Can Sun be described as a Chinese nationalist?

Source: From *Sources of Chinese Tradition* by William Theodore De Bary. Copyright © 1964 by Columbia University Press. Reprinted with permission of the publisher.

Chinese Society in Transition

 FOCUS QUESTION: What political, economic, and social reforms were instituted by the Qing Dynasty during its final decades, and why were they not more successful in reversing the decline of Manchu rule?

The growing Western presence in China during the late nineteenth and early twentieth centuries obviously had a major impact on Chinese society. Hence, until recently historians routinely asserted that the arrival of the Europeans shook China out of centuries of slumber and launched it on the road to revolutionary change. As we now know, however, Chinese society was already in a state of transition when the European economic penetration began to accelerate during the imperialist era. The growth of industry and trade was particularly noticeable in the cities, where a national market for such commodities as oil, copper, salt, tea, and porcelain had developed. The foundation of an infrastructure more conducive to the rise of a money economy appeared to be in place. In the countryside, new crops introduced from abroad significantly increased food production and aided population

The Last Emperor (1987)

On November 14, 1908, the Chinese emperor Guangxu died in Beijing. One day later, Empress Dowager Cixi—the real power behind the throne—passed away as well. A three-year-old boy, to be known in history as Henry Puyi, ascended the throne. Four years later, the Qing Dynasty collapsed, and the deposed monarch lived out the remainder of his life in a China lashed by political turmoil and violence. He finally died in 1967 at the height of the Great Proletarian Cultural Revolution.

The Last Emperor (1987), directed by the Italian filmmaker Bernardo Bertolucci, is a brilliant portrayal of the experience of one hapless individual in a nation caught up in the throes of a seemingly endless revolution. The film evokes the fading majesty of the last days of imperial China but also the chaos of the warlord era and the terrors of the Maoist period, when the last shreds of the ex-emperor's personality were shattered under the pressure of Communist brainwashing techniques. Puyi (John Lone), who never appears to grasp what is happening to his country, lives and dies a nonentity.

The film, based on Puyi's autobiography, benefits from having been filmed partly on site in the Imperial City. In

Three-year-old Puyi (Richard Vuu), the last emperor of China, watches an emissary approach at the Imperial Palace.

Helmsdale Film Corp./The Kobal Collection/The Picture Desk

addition to the Chinese American actors John Lone and Joan Chen, the cast includes the veteran film star Peter O'Toole, who plays Puyi's tutor when he was an adolescent.

growth. The Chinese economy had never been more productive or more complex.

The Economy: The Drag of Tradition

Whether these changes by themselves in the absence of outside intervention would eventually have led to an industrial revolution and the rise of a capitalist economy on the Western model is a hypothetical question that historians cannot answer. Certainly, a number of obstacles would have made it difficult for China to embark on the Western path if it had wished to do so.

Although industrial production was on the rise, it was still based almost entirely on traditional methods. There was no uniform system of weights and measures, and the banking system was still primitive by European standards. The use of paper money, invented by the Chinese centuries earlier, was still relatively limited (see Chapter 10). The transportation system, which had been neglected since the end of the Yuan dynasty, was increasingly chaotic. There were few paved roads, and the Grand Canal, long the most efficient means of carrying goods from north to south, was silting up. As a result, merchants had to rely more and more on the coastal route, where they faced increasing competition from foreign shipping.

Although foreign concession areas in the coastal cities provided a conduit for the importation of Western technology and modern manufacturing methods, the Chinese borrowed less than they might have. Foreign manufacturing enterprises could not legally operate in China until the last decade of the nineteenth century, and their methods had little influence beyond the concession areas. Chinese efforts to imitate Western methods, notably in railroads, shipbuilding, and weapons manufacture, were dominated by the government and often suffered from mismanagement.

Equally serious problems persisted in the countryside. The rapid increase in population had led to smaller plots and burgeoning numbers of tenant farmers. Whether per capita consumption of food was on the decline is not clear from the available evidence, but apparently rice as a staple of the diet was increasingly being replaced by less nutritious foods, many of which depleted the soil, already under pressure from the dramatic increase in population. Some farmers benefited from switching to commercial agriculture to supply the markets of the growing coastal cities, but the shift entailed a sizable investment. Many farmers went so deeply into debt that they eventually lost their land. In the meantime, the traditional patron-client relationship was frayed as landlords moved to the cities to take advantage of the glittering urban lifestyle introduced by the West.

Some of these problems can undoubtedly be ascribed to the challenges presented by the growing Western presence. But the court's hesitant efforts to cope with these challenges suggest that the most important obstacle was at the top: Qing officials often seemed overwhelmed by the combination of external pressure and internal strife. At a time when a number of other traditional societies, such as Russia, the Ottoman Empire, and Japan, were making vigorous attempts to modernize their economies, the Manchu court, along with much of the elite class, still exhibited an alarming degree of complacency and was unable to bring the Chinese economy up to the standards being applied in the industrial world.

The Impact of Imperialism

In any event, with the advent of the imperialist era in the second half of the nineteenth century, the question of whether China left to itself would have experienced an industrial revolution became academic. Imperialism caused serious distortions in the local economy that resulted in massive changes in Chinese society during the twentieth century. Whether the Western intrusion was beneficial or harmful is debated to this day. The Western presence undoubtedly accelerated the development of the Chinese economy in some ways: the introduction of modern means of production, transport, and communications; the creation of an export market; and the steady integration of the Chinese market into the nineteenth-century global economy. To many Westerners at the time, it was self-evident that such changes would ultimately benefit the Chinese people (see the Comparative Essay "Imperialism and the Global Environment" on p. 647). In this view, Western civilization represented the most advanced stage of human development. By supplying (in the catchphrase of the day) "oil for the lamps of China," it was providing a backward society with an opportunity to move up a notch or two on the ladder of human evolution.

Not everyone agreed. The Russian Marxist Vladimir Lenin contended that Western imperialism actually hindered the process of structural change in preindustrial societies because the imperialist powers thwarted the rise of local industrial and commercial sectors in order to maintain colonies and semicolonies as a market for Western manufactured goods and a source of cheap labor and materials. Fellow Marxists in China such as Mao Zedong (see Chapter 24) later took up Lenin's charge and asserted that if the West had not intervened, China would have found its own road to capitalism and thence to socialism and communism.

Many historians today would say that the issue is too complex for such simplistic explanations. By shaking China out of its traditional mind-set, imperialism accelerated the process of change that had begun in the late Ming and early Qing periods and forced the Chinese to adopt new ways of thinking and acting. At the same time, China paid a heavy price in the destruction of its local industry while many of the profits flowed abroad. Although the Industrial Revolution was a painful process whenever and wherever it occurred, the Chinese found the experience doubly painful because it was foisted on China from the outside.

Daily Life in Qing China

At the beginning of the nineteenth century, daily life for most Chinese was not substantially different from what it had been in earlier centuries. Most were farmers, living in thousands of villages in rice fields and on hillsides throughout the country. Their lives were governed by the harvest cycle, village custom, and family ritual. Their roles in society were firmly fixed by the time-honored principles of Confucian social ethics.

The First Chinese Railroad. Few Western technological innovations were as controversial in late-nineteenth-century China as the railroad. Not only were they viewed as threats to traditional forms of transportation—the cart and the barge—but the belching steam engines and even the train tracks were believed to disturb the graves and the spirits of the ancestors. Shown here is a drawing of the first train leaving the railroad station in Shanghai, already in 1876 a city dominated by Western interests.

Liszt Collection/Alamy

COMPARATIVE ESSAY

Imperialism and the Global Environment

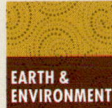

EARTH & ENVIRONMENT

Beginning in the late nineteenth century, European states engaged in an intense scramble for overseas territory. This "new imperialism," as it is termed by historians, led to the carving up of independent Asian and African states and the creation of European colonial empires. Within these empires, the new rulers exercised complete political control over the indigenous societies and redrew political boundaries to meet their needs. In Africa, for example, in drawing the boundaries that separated one colony from another (boundaries that often became the boundaries of the modern countries of Africa), Europeans ignored existing political, linguistic, or religious divisions and frequently divided distinctive communities into different colonies or included two hostile communities within the same colony.

In order to organize these new colonies to meet their own needs in the global marketplace, European colonial authorities paid little attention to the economic requirements of their colonial subjects. As a result, they often dramatically altered the local environment, a transformation that was visible in a variety of ways. Western-owned companies drilled for oil and dug mines for gold, tin, iron ore, and copper, a process that resulted in enormous profits for colonial interests but that inevitably transformed and often scarred the natural landscape.

Rural landscapes were even more dramatically altered by Europe's demand for cash crops. Throughout vast regions of Africa, Asia, and colonial territories in the Western hemisphere, woodlands were cleared to make way for plantations where crops for export could be cultivated. In Ceylon (modern Sri Lanka) and India, the British cut down vast tropical forests to plant row upon row of tea bushes. The Dutch razed forests in the East Indies to plant palm oil plantations and cinchona trees (a derivative of the bark of the latter, quinine, had been discovered to cure malaria). In Indochina, the French replaced extensive forests with rubber, tea, and coffee plantations. Local workers, who were usually paid pitiful wages by their European overseers, provided the labor for all of these vast plantations.

In many areas, precious farmland was turned over to the cultivation of cash crops, thus making it more difficult to feed growing populations. In the Dutch East Indies, farmers were forced to plow up some of their rice fields to make way for the cultivation of sugar. In West Africa, overplanting of cash crops damaged fragile grasslands and turned parts of the Sahel (suh-HAYL or suh-HEEL) into a wasteland.

During the era of new imperialism, the commercial exploitation of the Asian and African environment redounded almost entirely to the benefit of the colonial powers themselves. After the restoration of independence, however, many of the new states of Asia and Africa found it to their advantage to continue the process of extracting raw materials and cultivating cash crops as a means of improving their balance of payments. The profits from such activities are now beginning to benefit members of the local population, but the damage to the environment continues. The new enemy is thus not the imperialist powers themselves, but the industrial revolution that they unleashed over two centuries ago.

 How did the effects of imperialism on the environment in colonial countries compare with the impact of the Industrial Revolution in Europe and North America?

Picking Tea Leaves in Ceylon. In this 1900 photograph, women on a plantation in Ceylon (Sri Lanka) pick tea leaves for shipment abroad. The British cut down vast stands of tropical forests in Ceylon and India to grow tea to satisfy demand back home.

Male children, at least the more fortunate ones, were educated in the Confucian classics, while females remained in the home or in the fields. All children were expected to obey their parents, and wives to submit to their husbands.

A visitor to China a hundred years later would have seen a very different society, although still recognizably Chinese. Change was most striking in the coastal cities, where the educated and affluent had been visibly affected by the growing Western cultural presence. Confucian social institutions and behavioral norms were declining rapidly in influence, while those of Europe and North America were on the ascendant. Change was much less noticeable in the countryside, but even there, the customary bonds had been dangerously frayed by the rapidly changing times.

Some of the change can be traced to the educational system. During the nineteenth century, the importance of a

Chinese Society in Transition ■ **647**

Confucian education steadily declined as up to half of the degree holders had purchased their degrees. After 1906, when the government abolished the civil service examinations, a Confucian education ceased to be the key to a successful career, and Western-style education became more desirable. The old dynasty attempted to modernize by establishing an educational system on the Western model with universal education at the elementary level. Such plans had some effect in the cities, where public schools, missionary schools, and other private institutions educated a new generation of Chinese with little knowledge of or respect for the past.

CHANGING ROLES FOR WOMEN The status of women was also in transition. During the mid-Qing era, women were expected to remain in the home. Their status as useless sex objects was painfully symbolized by the practice of foot binding, a custom that had probably originated among court entertainers in the Tang Dynasty and later, during the Song Dynasty, spread to the upper classes and then to the common people. By the mid-nineteenth century, more than half of all adult women probably had bound feet.

During the second half of the nineteenth century, signs of change began to appear. Women began to seek employment in factories—notably in cotton mills and in the silk industry, established in Shanghai in the 1890s. Some women were active in dissident activities, such as the Taiping Rebellion and the Boxer movement, and a few fought beside men in the 1911 revolution. Qiu Jin (chee-oo JIN), a well-known female revolutionary, wrote a manifesto calling for women's liberation and then organized a revolt against the Manchu

government, only to be captured and executed at the age of thirty-two in 1907.

By the end of the century, educational opportunities for women began to appear for the first time. Christian missionaries began to open girls' schools, mainly in the foreign concession areas. Although only a relatively small number of women were educated in these schools, they had a significant impact on Chinese society as progressive intellectuals began to argue that ignorant women produced ignorant children. In 1905, the court announced its intention to open public schools for girls, but few such schools ever materialized. Private schools for girls were established in some urban areas. The government also began to take steps to discourage the practice of foot binding, initially with only minimal success.

A Rich Country and a Strong State: The Rise of Modern Japan

 FOCUS QUESTION: To what degree was the Meiji Restoration a "revolution," and to what extent did it succeed in transforming Japan?

By the beginning of the nineteenth century, the Tokugawa (toh-koo-GAH-wah) Shogunate had ruled the Japanese islands for two hundred years. It had revitalized the old governmental system, which had virtually disintegrated under its predecessors. It had driven out the foreign traders and missionaries and reduced Japanese contacts with the Western world. The Tokugawa maintained formal relations only with Korea, although informal trading links with Dutch and Chinese merchants continued at Nagasaki (nah-gah-SAH-kee). Isolation, however, did not mean stagnation. Although the vast majority of Japanese still depended on agriculture for their livelihood, a vigorous manufacturing and commercial sector had begun to emerge during the long period of peace and prosperity. As a result, Japanese society had begun to undergo deep-seated changes, and traditional class distinctions were becoming blurred. Eventually, these changes would end Tokugawa rule and destroy the traditional feudal system.

Some historians speculate that the Tokugawa system was beginning to come apart, just as the medieval order in Europe had started to disintegrate at the beginning of the Renaissance. Factionalism and corruption plagued the central bureaucracy, while rural unrest, provoked by a series of poor harvests brought about by bad weather, swept the countryside. Farmers fled to the towns, where anger was already rising as a result of declining agricultural incomes and

Private Collection/The Bridgeman Art Library

Women with Bound Feet. To ensure the best possible marriages for their daughters, upper-class families began to perform foot binding during the Song Dynasty. Eventually, the practice spread to all social classes in China. Although small feet were supposed to denote a woman of leisure, most Chinese women with bound feet contributed to the labor force, working mainly in textiles and handicrafts to supplement the family income. The two young women shown here are clearly from an upper-class family and are being taken for an outing on a rickshaw.

A Letter to the Shogun

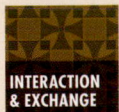

INTERACTION & EXCHANGE

WHEN COMMODORE MATTHEW PERRY arrived in Tokyo Bay on his first visit to Japan in July 1853, he carried a letter from the president of the United States, Millard Fillmore. The letter requested that trade relations between the two countries be established. The United States was already becoming a major participant in the race for the East Asian market. Little did the president know how momentous the occasion was or with what eagerness the Japanese would eventually respond to the challenge.

A Letter from the President of the United States

Millard Fillmore
President of the United States of America

To His Imperial Majesty,
The Emperor of Japan

Great and Good Friend!
I send you this public letter by Commodore Matthew C. Perry, an officer of the highest rank in the Navy of the United States, and commander of the squadron now visiting your Imperial Majesty's dominions.

I have directed Commodore Perry to assure your Imperial Majesty that I entertain the kindest feelings towards your Majesty's person and government; and that I have no other object in sending him to Japan, but to propose to your Imperial Majesty that the United States and Japan should live in friendship, and have commercial intercourse with each other. The constitution and laws of the United States forbid all interference with the religious or political concerns of other nations. I have particularly charged Commodore Perry to abstain from every act which could possibly disturb the tranquility of your Imperial Majesty's dominions.

The United States of America reach from ocean to ocean, and our territory of Oregon and state of California lie directly opposite to the dominions of your Imperial Majesty. Our steamships can go from California to Japan in eighteen days....

Japan is also a rich and fertile country, and produces many very valuable articles.... I am desirous that our two countries should trade with each other, for the benefit both of Japan and the United States.

We know that the ancient laws of your Imperial Majesty's government do not allow of foreign trade except with the Dutch. But as the state of the world changes, and new governments are formed, it seems to be wise from time to time to make new laws.... If your Imperial Majesty were so far to change the ancient laws as to allow a free trade between the two countries, it would be extremely beneficial to both....

Many of our ships pass every year from California to China; and great numbers of our people pursue the whale fishery near the shores of Japan. It sometimes happens in stormy weather that one of our ships is wrecked on your Imperial Majesty's shores. In all such cases we ask and expect, that our unfortunate people should be treated with kindness, and that their property should be protected, till we can send a vessel and bring them away....

May the Almighty have your Imperial Majesty in his great and holy keeping! ...

Your Good Friend,
Millard Fillmore

 Why did President Fillmore want to establish relations with Japan? Why were Japanese leaders reluctant to agree to his request?

Source: From Frank Hayward Severance, ed., *Millard Fillmore Papers*, Vol. 1 (Buffalo, New York: Buffalo Historical Society, 1907), pp. 393–396.

---

shrinking stipends for the samurai. Many of the samurai lashed out at the perceived incompetence and corruption of the government. In response, the *bakufu* (buh-KOO-foo *or* bah-KOO-fuh) became increasingly rigid, persecuting its critics and attempting to force fleeing peasants to return to their lands.

The government also intensified its efforts to limit contacts with the outside world, driving away the foreign ships that were beginning to prowl along the Japanese coast in increasing numbers. For many years, Japan had financed its imports of silk and other needed products from other countries in Asia with the output of its silver and copper mines. But as these mines became exhausted during the eighteenth century, the *bakufu* cut back on foreign trade, while encouraging the domestic production of goods that had previously been imported. Thus, the Tokugawa sought to adopt a policy of *sakoku* (sah-KOH-koo), or closed country, even toward many of the Asian neighbors with which Japan had once had active relations.

Opening to the World

To the Western powers, Japan's refusal to open its doors to Western goods was an affront and a challenge. Driven by the growing rivalry among themselves and convinced that the expansion of trade on a global basis would benefit all nations, Western countries began to approach Japan in the hope of opening up the kingdom to foreign economic interests.

The first to succeed was the United States. American steamships crossing the northern Pacific needed a fueling station before going on to China and other ports in the area. In the summer of 1853, an American fleet of four warships under Commodore Matthew C. Perry arrived in Edo (now Tokyo) Bay with a letter from President Millard Fillmore asking for the opening of foreign relations between the two countries (see the box "A Letter to the Shogun" above). A few months later, Perry returned with a larger fleet for an answer. In his absence, Japanese officials had hotly debated the issue. Some argued that contacts with the West would be both politically and morally

Black Ships in Tokyo Bay. The arrival of a U.S. fleet commanded by Commodore Matthew Perry in 1853 caused consternation among many Japanese observers, who were intimidated by the size and ominous presence of the American ships. This nineteenth-century woodblock print shows curious Japanese paddling out to greet the arrivals.

disadvantageous to Japan, while others pointed to U.S. military superiority and recommended concessions. For the shogunate in Edo (EH-doh), the black guns of Perry's ships proved decisive, and Japan agreed to the Treaty of Kanagawa (kah-nah-GAH-wah), which provided for the return of shipwrecked American sailors, the opening of two ports, and the establishment of a U.S. consulate on Japanese soil. In 1858, U.S. consul Townsend Harris negotiated a more elaborate commercial treaty calling for the opening of several ports to U.S. trade and residence, the exchange of ministers, and the granting of extraterritorial privileges for U.S. residents in Japan. Similar treaties were soon signed with several European nations.

The decision to open relations with the Western barbarians was highly unpopular in some quarters, particularly in regions distant from the shogunate headquarters in Edo. Resistance was especially strong in two of the key outside daimyo (DYM-yoh) territories in the south, Satsuma (sat-SOO-muh) and Choshu (CHOH-shoo), both of which had strong military traditions. In 1863, the "Sat-Cho" alliance forced the hapless shogun to promise to end relations with the West. The shogun eventually reneged on the agreement, but the rebellious groups soon learned of their own weakness. When Choshu troops fired on Western ships in the Strait of Shimonoseki (shee-moh-noh-SEK-ee), the Westerners fired back and destroyed the Choshu fortifications. The incident convinced the rebellious samurai of the need to strengthen their own military and intensified their unwillingness to give in to the West. Having strengthened their influence at the imperial court in Kyoto, they demanded the shogun's resignation and the restoration of the emperor's power. In January 1868, rebel armies attacked the shogun's palace in Kyoto and proclaimed the restored authority of the emperor. After a few weeks, resistance collapsed, and the venerable shogunate system was brought to an end.

The Meiji Restoration

Although the victory of the Sat-Cho faction had appeared on the surface to be a triumph of tradition over change, the new leaders soon realized that Japan must modernize to survive. Accordingly, they embarked on a policy of comprehensive reform that would lay the foundations of a modern industrial nation within a generation.

The symbol of the new era was the young emperor himself, who had taken the reign name Meiji (MAY-jee), meaning "enlightened rule," on ascending the throne after the death of his father in 1867. Although the post-Tokugawa period was termed a "restoration," the Meiji ruler, who shared the modernist outlook newly adopted by the Sat-Cho group, was controlled by the new leadership just as the shogunate had controlled his predecessors. In tacit recognition of the real source of political power, the new capital was located at Edo, now renamed Tokyo ("eastern capital"), and the imperial court was moved to the shogun's palace in the center of the city.

THE TRANSFORMATION OF JAPANESE POLITICS Once in power, the new leaders launched a comprehensive reform of Japanese political, social, economic, and cultural institutions and values. They moved first to abolish the remnants of the old order and strengthen executive power in their hands. To undercut the power of the daimyo, hereditary privileges were abolished in 1871, and the great lords lost title to their lands. As compensation, they were given government bonds and were named governors of the territories formerly under their control. The samurai, comprising about 8 percent of the total population, received a lump-sum payment to replace their traditional stipends, but they were forbidden to wear the sword, the symbol of their hereditary status.

Program for Reform in Japan

POLITICS & GOVERNMENT

IN THE SPRING OF **1868,** the reformers drew up a program for transforming Japanese society along Western lines in the post-Tokugawa era. Though vague in its essentials, the Charter Oath is a good indication of the plans that were carried out during the Meiji Restoration. Compare this program with the Declaration of the Rights of Man and the Citizen drafted at the time of the French Revolution and discussed in Chapter 18.

The Charter Oath of Emperor Meiji

By this oath we set up as our aim the establishment of the national weal on a broad basis and the framing of a constitution and laws.

1. Deliberative assemblies shall be widely established and all matters decided by public discussion.

2. All classes, high and low, shall unite in vigorously carrying out the administration of affairs of state.

3. The common people, no less than the civil and military officials, shall each be allowed to pursue his own calling so that there may be no discontent.

4. Evil customs of the past shall be broken off and everything based upon the just laws of Nature.

5. Knowledge shall be sought throughout the world so as to strengthen the foundations of imperial rule.

 Do all of these principles conform to the basic concepts of liberal democracy as practiced in Western societies? To what degree did the Meiji political system put them into effect? How did the Meiji Constitution differ from those in the West?

Source: From *Sources of Chinese Tradition,* by William Theodore De Bary, pp. 139–140. Copyright © 1960 by Columbia University Press. Reprinted with permission of the publisher.

Art Resource, NY

Emperor Meiji and the Charter Oath. In 1868, reformist elements overthrew the Tokugawa Shogunate in an era of rapid modernization in Japanese society. Their intentions were announced in a charter oath of five articles promulgated in April 1868. In this contemporary print, the young Emperor Meiji listens to the reading of the Charter Oath in his palace in Kyoto.

The Meiji modernizers also set out to create a modern political system based roughly on the Western model. In the Charter Oath of 1868, the new leaders promised to create a new deliberative assembly within the framework of continued imperial rule (see the box "Program for Reform in Japan" above). They also called for the elimination of the "evil customs" of the past and the implementation of a vigorous program of reform based on international practices in order to "strengthen the foundations of imperial rule." Although senior positions in the new government were given to the daimyo, the key posts were dominated by modernizing samurai, eventually to be known as the *genro* (gen-ROH *or* GEN-roh), or elder statesmen, from the Sat-Cho clique.

During the next two decades, the Meiji government undertook a systematic study of Western political systems. A constitutional commission under Ito Hirobumi (ee-TOH HEE-roh-BOO-mee) (1841–1909) traveled to several Western countries, including Great Britain, Germany, Russia, and the United States, to study their political systems. As the process evolved, a number of factions appeared, each representing different political ideas. The most prominent were the Liberal Party and the Progressive Party. The Liberal Party favored political reform on the Western liberal democratic model, with supreme authority vested in the parliament as the representative of the people. The Progressive Party called for the distribution of power between the legislative and executive branches, with a slight nod to the latter. There was also an imperial party, which advocated the retention of supreme authority exclusively in the hands of the emperor.

THE CONSTITUTION OF 1890 During the 1870s and 1880s, these factions competed for preeminence. Ito Hirobumi himself harbored doubts about the Western system of liberal democracy, fearing that it might not be appropriate for Japan. In the end, the Progressives emerged victorious. The Meiji Constitution, which was adopted in 1890, was based on the Bismarckian model with authority vested in the executive branch; the imperialist faction was pacified by the statement that the constitution was the gift of the emperor. Members of the cabinet were to be handpicked by the Meiji oligarchs. The upper house of parliament was to be appointed and have equal legislative powers with the lower house, called the Diet, whose members would be elected. The core ideology of the state, called the *kokutai* (KOH-kuh-TY), or national polity, embodied (although in very imprecise form) the concept of the uniqueness of the Japanese system based on the supreme authority of the emperor. At the suggestion of a German adviser, the ancient practice of Shinto was transformed into a virtual national religion, in imitation of the perceived role of Christianity in the states of western Europe and North America, and its traditional ritual ceremonies were performed at all important events in the imperial court.

The result was a system that was democratic in form but despotic in practice, modern in appearance but still traditional in that power remained in the hands of a ruling oligarchy. The stated goal of the new system was to achieve the slogan of *bunmei kaika* ("civilization and enlightenment"), but under the surface, its promoters argued that in actuality it represented a return to the ancient practice of imperial rule. In fact, the system permitted the traditional ruling class to retain its influence and economic power while acquiescing in the emergence of new institutions and values.

MEIJI ECONOMICS With the end of the daimyo domains, the government needed to establish a new system of land ownership that would transform the mass of the rural population from indentured serfs into citizens. To do so, it enacted a land reform program that redefined the domain lands as the private property of the tillers while compensating the previous owner with government bonds. One reason for the new policy was that the government needed operating revenues. At the time, public funds came mainly from customs fees, which were limited by agreement with the foreign powers to 5 percent of the value of the product. To remedy the problem, the Meiji leaders added a new agriculture tax, which was set at an annual rate of 3 percent of the estimated value of the land. The new tax proved to be a lucrative and dependable source of income for the government, but it was onerous for the farmers, who had previously paid a fixed percentage of their harvest to the landowner. As a result, in bad years, many peasants were unable to pay their taxes and were forced to sell their lands to wealthy neighbors. Eventually, the government reduced the tax to 2.5 percent of the land value. Still, by the end of the century, about 40 percent of all farmers were tenants.

With its budget needs secured, the government turned to the promotion of industry with the basic objective of guaranteeing Japan's survival against the challenge of Western imperialism. Building on the small but growing industrial economy that existed under the Tokugawa, the Meiji reformers supplied a massive stimulus to Japan's industrial revolution. The government provided financial subsidies to needy industries, training, foreign advisers, improved transport and communications, and a universal educational system emphasizing applied science. In contrast to China, Japan was able to achieve results with minimal reliance on foreign capital. Although the first railroad—built in 1872—was financed by a loan from Great Britain, future projects were all backed by local funds. The foreign currency holdings came largely from tea and silk, which were exported in significant quantities during the latter half of the nineteenth century.

During the late Meiji era, Japan's industrial sector began to grow. Besides tea and silk, other key industries were weaponry, shipbuilding, and sake (SAH-kee) (fermented rice wine). From the start, the distinctive feature of the Meiji model was the intimate relationship between government and private business in terms of operations and regulations. Once an individual

The Emperor Inspects His Domain. A crucial challenge for the Japanese government during the Meiji era was to increase the country's food supply by improving the productivity of agricultural workers. In this painting, Emperor Meiji inspects a flooded field where farmers are planting rice seedlings. The practice of showing the imperial face in public was an innovation introduced by Emperor Meiji that earned him the affection of his subjects.

enterprise or industry was on its feet (or, sometimes, when it had ceased to make a profit), it was turned over entirely to private ownership, although the government often continued to play some role even after it was no longer directly involved in management. Historians have explained the process:

> [The Meiji government] pioneered many industrial fields and sponsored the development of others, attempting to cajole businessmen into new and risky kinds of endeavor, helping assemble the necessary capital, forcing weak companies to merge into stronger units, and providing private entrepreneurs with aid and privileges of a sort that would be corrupt favoritism today. All this was in keeping with Tokugawa traditions that business operated under the tolerance and patronage of government. Some of the political leaders even played a dual role in politics and business.[4]

From the workers' perspective, the Meiji reforms had a less attractive side. As we have seen, the new land tax provided the funds to subsidize the growth of the industrial sector, but it imposed severe hardships on the rural population, forcing many people to abandon their farms and flee to the cities, where they provided an abundant source of cheap labor for Japanese industry. As in Europe during the early decades of the Industrial Revolution, workers toiled for long hours in the coal mines and textile mills, often under horrendous conditions. Reportedly, coal miners employed on a small island in Nagasaki harbor worked naked in temperatures up to 130 degrees Fahrenheit. If they tried to escape, they were shot.

BUILDING A MODERN SOCIAL STRUCTURE By the late Tokugawa era, the rigidly hierarchical social order was showing signs of disintegration. Rich merchants were buying their way into the ranks of the samurai, and Japanese of all classes were beginning to abandon their rice fields and move into the growing cities. Nevertheless, community and hierarchy still formed the basis of Japanese society. The lives of all Japanese were determined by their membership in various social groups—the family, the village, and their social class. Membership in a particular social class determined a person's occupation and social relationships with others. Women in particular were constrained by the "**three obediences**" imposed on their sex: child to father, wife to husband, and widow to son. Husbands could easily obtain a divorce, but wives could not (supposedly, a husband could divorce his spouse if she drank too much tea or talked too much). Marriages were arranged, and the average age at marriage for women was sixteen years. Females did not share inheritance rights with males, and few received any education outside the family.

The Meiji reformers dismantled much of the traditional social system in Japan. With the abolition of hereditary rights in 1871, the legal restrictions of the past were brought to an end with a single stroke. Special privileges for the aristocracy were abolished, as were the legal restrictions on the *eta* (AY-tuh), the traditional slave class (numbering about 400,000 in the 1870s). Another key focus of the reformers was the army. The Sat-Cho reformers had been struck by the weakness of the Japanese forces in clashes with Western powers and embarked on a major program to create a military force that could compete in the modern world. The old feudal army based on the traditional warrior class was abolished, and an imperial army based on universal conscription was formed in 1871. For many rural males, the army became a route of upward mobility.

Education also underwent major changes. The Meiji leaders recognized the need for universal education, including technical subjects, and after a few years of experimenting, they adopted the American model of a three-tiered system culminating in a series of universities and specialized institutes. In the meantime, they sent bright students to study abroad and brought foreign scholars to Japan to teach in the new schools, where much of the content was inspired by Western models. In another break with tradition, women for the first time were given an opportunity to get an education.

These changes were included in the Imperial Rescript on Education that was issued in 1890, but the rescript also placed strong emphasis on the traditional Confucian virtues of filial piety and loyalty to the state (see the box "The Rules of Good Citizenship in Meiji Japan" on p. 654). One reason for issuing the Imperial Rescript was the official concern that libertarian and individualistic ideas from the West might dilute the traditional Japanese emphasis on responsibility to the community.

Indeed, Western ideas and fashions had become the rage in elite circles, and the ministers of the first Meiji government were known as the "dancing cabinet" because of their addiction to Western-style ballroom dancing. Young people, increasingly exposed to Western culture and values, began to imitate the clothing styles, eating habits, and social practices of their European and American counterparts. They even took up American sports when baseball was introduced.

TRADITIONAL VALUES AND WOMEN'S RIGHTS Nonetheless, the self-proclaimed transformation of Japan into a "modern society" by no means detached the country entirely from its traditional moorings. Although an educational order in 1872 increased the percentage of Japanese women exposed to public education, conservatives soon began to impose restrictions and bring about a return to more traditional social relationships. As we have seen, the Imperial Rescript on Education in 1890 stressed the Confucian virtues of filial piety, patriotism, and loyalty to the family and community. Traditional values were given a firm legal basis in the Constitution of 1890, which restricted the franchise to males and defined individual liberties as "subject to the limitations imposed by law," and by the Civil Code of 1898, which de-emphasized individual rights and essentially placed women within the context of their role in the family.

By the end of the nineteenth century, however, changes were under way as women began to play a crucial role in their nation's effort to modernize. Urged by their parents to augment the family income, as well as by the government to fulfill their patriotic duty, young girls were sent en masse to work in textile mills. From 1894 to 1912, women represented 60 percent of the Japanese labor force. Thanks to them, by 1914, Japan was the world's leading exporter of silk and dominated cotton manufacturing. If it had not been for the export revenues earned from textile exports, Japan might

The Rules of Good Citizenship in Meiji Japan

POLITICS & GOVERNMENT

AFTER SEIZING POWER from the Tokugawa Shogunate in 1868, the new Japanese leaders turned their attention to the creation of a new political system that would bring the country into the modern world. After exploring various systems in use in the West, a constitutional commission decided to adopt the system used in imperial Germany because of its paternalistic character. To promote civic virtue and obedience among the citizenry, the government then drafted an imperial rescript that was to be taught to every schoolchild in the country. The rescript instructed all children to obey their sovereign and place the interests of the community and the state above their own personal desires.

Imperial Rescript on Education, 1890

Know ye, Our subjects:

Our Imperial Ancestors have founded Our Empire on a basis broad and everlasting, and have deeply and firmly implanted virtue. Our subjects ever united in loyalty and filial piety have from generation to generation illustrated the

beauty thereof. This is the glory of the fundamental character of Our Empire, and herein also lies the source of Our education. Ye, Our subjects, be filial to your parents, affectionate to your brothers and sisters, as husbands and wives be harmonious, as friends true; bear yourselves in modesty and moderation; extend your benevolence to all; pursue learning and cultivate arts, and thereby develop intellectual faculties and perfect moral powers; furthermore, advance public good and promote common interests; always respect the Constitution and observe the laws; should emergency arise, offer yourselves to the State; and thus guard and maintain the prosperity of Our Imperial Throne coeval with heaven and earth. So shall ye not only be Our good and faithful subjects, but render illustrious the best traditions of your forefathers.

According to the Imperial Rescript, what was the primary purpose of education in Meiji Japan? How did these goals compare with those in China and the West?

Source: From *Sources of Japanese Tradition*, Vol. 2., 2e, p. 780, by William Theodore de Bary, Carol Gluck, and Arthur E. Tiedemann. Copyright © 2005 by Columbia University Press. Reprinted with permission of the publisher.

---

not have been able to develop its heavy industry and military prowess without an infusion of foreign capital.

Japanese women received few rewards, however, for their contribution to the nation. In 1900, new regulations prohibited women from joining political organizations or attending public meetings. Beginning in 1905, a group of independent-minded women petitioned the Japanese parliament to rescind this restriction. Although the regulation was not repealed until 1922, movements got under way to bring about an extension of women's rights in Japanese society.

Joining the Imperialist Club

Traditionally, Japan had not been an expansionist country. As we have seen, except for sporadic forays against Korea, the Japanese had generally been satisfied to remain on their home islands and had even deliberately isolated themselves from their neighbors during the Tokugawa era. Now, however, the Japanese did not just imitate the domestic policies of their Western mentors; they also emulated the Western approach to foreign affairs. This is perhaps not surprising. The Japanese regarded themselves as particularly vulnerable in the world economic arena. Their territory was small, lacking in resources, and densely populated, and they had no natural outlet for expansion. To observant Japanese, the lessons of history were clear. Western nations had amassed wealth and power not only because of their democratic systems and high level of education but also because of their colonies.

The Japanese began their program of territorial expansion close to home (see Map 22.4). In 1874, the Japanese claimed

MAP 22.4 Japanese Overseas Expansion During the Meiji Era. Beginning in the late nineteenth century, Japan ventured beyond its home islands and became an imperialist power. The extent of Japanese colonial expansion through World War I is shown here.

Which parts of the Chinese Empire came under Japanese influence?

compensation from China for fifty-four sailors from the Ryu-kyu (RYOO-kyoo) Islands who had been killed by the local population on the island of Taiwan (TY-WAHN) and sent a Japanese fleet to Taiwan to punish the perpetrators. When the Qing Dynasty evaded responsibility for the incident while agreeing to pay an indemnity to Japan to cover the cost of the expedition, it weakened its claim to ownership of the island of Taiwan. Japan was then able to claim suzerainty over the Ryukyu Islands, long tributary to the Chinese Empire. Two years later, Japanese naval pressure forced Korea to open three ports to Japanese commerce.

Korea had long followed Japan's example and attempted to isolate itself from outside contact except for periodic tribute missions to China. Christian missionaries, mostly Chinese or French, were vigorously persecuted. But Korea's problems were basically internal. In the early 1860s, a peasant revolt, inspired in part by the Taiping Rebellion in China, caused considerable devastation before being crushed in 1864. In succeeding years, the Yi (YEE) Dynasty sought to strengthen the country by returning to traditional values and fending off outside intrusion, but rural poverty and official corruption remained rampant. A U.S. fleet, following the example of Commodore Perry in Japan, sought to open the country in 1871 but was driven off with considerable loss of life.

Korea's most persistent suitor, however, was Japan, which was determined to bring an end to Korea's dependency status with China and modernize it along Japanese lines. In 1876, the two countries signed an agreement opening three treaty ports to Japanese commerce in return for Japanese recognition of Korean independence. During the 1880s, Sino-Japanese rivalry over Korea intensified. China supported conservatives at the Korean court, while Japan promoted a more radical

faction that was determined to break loose from lingering Chinese influence. When a new rural rebellion broke out in Korea in 1894, China and Japan intervened on opposite sides. During the war, the Japanese navy destroyed the Chinese fleet and seized the Manchurian city of Port Arthur (see Opposing Viewpoints "Two Views of the World" on p. 656). In the Treaty of Shimonoseki in 1895, China was forced to recognize the independence of Korea and cede Taiwan and the Liaodong Peninsula with its strategic naval base at Port Arthur to Japan.

Shortly thereafter, under pressure from the European powers, the Japanese returned the Liaodong Peninsula to China, but in the early twentieth century, they went back on the offensive. Rivalry with Russia over influence in Korea led to increasingly strained relations between the two countries. In 1904, Japan launched a surprise attack on the Russian naval base at Port Arthur, which Russia had taken from China in 1898. The Japanese armed forces were weaker, but Russia faced difficult logistical problems along its new Trans-Siberian Railway and severe political instability at home. In 1905, after Japanese warships sank almost the entire Russian fleet off the coast of Korea, the Russians agreed to a humiliating peace, ceding the strategically located Liaodong Peninsula back to Japan, as well as southern Sakhalin (SAK-uh-leen *or* suh-khuh-LYEEN) and the Kurile (KOOR-il *or* koo-REEL) Islands. Russia also agreed to abandon its political and economic influence in Korea and southern Manchuria, which now came increasingly under Japanese control. The Japanese victory stunned the world, including the colonial peoples of Southeast Asia, who now began to realize that the white race was not necessarily invincible.

Total Humiliation. Whereas China had persevered in hiding behind the grandeur of its past, Japan had embraced the West, modernizing politically, militarily, and culturally. China's humiliation at the hands of its newly imperialist neighbor is evident in this scene, where the differences in dress and body posture of the officials negotiating the treaty after the war reflect China's disastrous defeat by the Japanese in 1895.

OPPOSING ✕ VIEWPOINTS

Two Views of the World

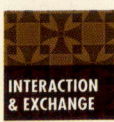

INTERACTION & EXCHANGE

DURING THE NINETEENTH CENTURY, CHINA'S HIERARCHICAL WAY of looking at the outside world came under severe challenge, not only from European countries avid for new territories in Asia but also from the rising power of Japan, which accepted the Western view that a colonial empire was the key to national greatness. Japan's first objective was Korea, long a dependency of China, and in 1894, the competition between China and Japan in the peninsula led to war. The following declarations of war by the rulers of the two countries are revealing. Note the Chinese use of the derogatory term *Wojen* ("dwarf people") in referring to the Japanese.

Declaration of War Against China

Korea is an independent state. She was first introduced into the family of nations by the advice and guidance of Japan. It has, however, been China's habit to designate Korea as her dependency, and both openly and secretly to interfere with her domestic affairs. At the time of the recent insurrection in Korea, China despatched troops thither, alleging that her purpose was to afford a succor to her dependent state. We, in virtue of the treaty concluded with Korea in 1882, and looking to possible emergencies, caused a military force to be sent to that country.

Wishing to procure for Korea freedom from the calamity of perpetual disturbance, and thereby to maintain the peace of the East in general, Japan invited China's cooperation for the accomplishment of the object. But China, advancing various pretexts, declined Japan's proposal.... Such conduct on the part of China is not only a direct injury to the rights and interests of this Empire, but also a menace to the permanent peace and tranquility of the Orient.... In this situation,... we find it impossible to avoid a formal declaration of war against China.

Declaration of War Against Japan

Korea has been our tributary for the past two hundred odd years. She has given us tribute all this time, which is a matter known to the world. For the past dozen years or so Korea has been troubled by repeated insurrections and we, in sympathy with our small tributary, have as repeatedly sent succor to her aid.... This year another rebellion was begun in Korea, and the King repeatedly asked again for aid from us to put down the rebellion. We then ordered Li Hung-chang to send troops to Korea; and they having barely reached Yashan the rebels immediately scattered. But the *Wojen*, without any cause whatever, suddenly sent their troops to Korea, and entered Seoul, the capital of Korea, reinforcing them constantly until they have exceeded ten thousand men. In the meantime the Japanese forced the Korean king to change his

system of government, showing a disposition every way of bullying the Koreans....

As Japan has violated the treaties and not observed international laws, and is now running rampant with her false and treacherous actions commencing hostilities herself, and laying herself open to condemnation by the various powers at large, we therefore desire to make it known to the world that we have always followed the paths of philanthropy and perfect justice throughout the whole complications, while the *Wojen*, on the other hand, have broken all the laws of nations and treaties which it passes our patience to bear with. Hence we commanded Li Hung-chang to give strict orders to our various armies to hasten with all speed to root the *Wojen* out of their lairs.

 Compare the worldviews of China and Japan at the end of the nineteenth century, as expressed in these declarations. Which point of view do you find more persuasive?

Sources: From MacNair, *Modern Chinese History*, pp. 530–534, quoted in Franz Schurmann and Orville Schell, eds., *The China Reader: Imperial China* (New York: Vintage, 1967), pp. 251–259.

During the next few years, the Japanese consolidated their position in northeastern Asia, annexing Korea in 1908 as an integral part of Japan. When the Koreans protested the seizure, Japanese reprisals resulted in thousands of deaths. The United States was the first nation to recognize the annexation, in return for Tokyo's declaration of respect for U.S. authority in the Philippines and Japanese acceptance of the principles of the Open Door. But mutual suspicion between the two countries was growing, sparked in part by U.S. efforts to restrict immigration from all Asian countries. President Theodore

Roosevelt, who mediated the Russo-Japanese War, had aroused the anger of many Japanese by turning down a Japanese demand for reparations from Russia. In turn, some Americans began to fear the rise of a "yellow peril" manifested by Japanese expansion in East Asia.

Japanese Culture in Transition

The wave of Western technology and ideas that entered Japan in the second half of the nineteenth century greatly altered the shape of traditional Japanese culture. Literature in particular

Commodore Perry arrives in Tokyo Bay	1853
Townsend Harris Treaty	1858
Fall of Tokugawa Shogunate	1868
U.S. fleet fails to open Korea	1871
Feudal titles abolished in Japan	1871
Japanese imperial army formed	1871
Meiji Constitution adopted	1890
Imperial Rescript on Education	1890
Treaty of Shimonoseki awards Taiwan to Japan	1895
Russo-Japanese War	1904–1905
Korea annexed by Japan	1908

was affected as European models eclipsed the repetitive and frivolous tales of the Tokugawa era. Dazzled by this "new" literature, Japanese authors began translating and imitating the imported models. Experimenting with Western verse, Japanese poets were at first influenced primarily by the British but eventually adopted such styles as Symbolism, Dadaism (DAH-duh-iz-um), and Surrealism, although some traditional poetry was still composed.

As the Japanese invited technicians, engineers, architects, and artists from Europe and the United States to teach their "modern" skills to a generation of eager students, the Meiji era became a time of massive consumption of Western artistic techniques and styles. Japanese architects and artists created huge buildings of steel and reinforced concrete adorned with Greek columns and cupolas, oil paintings reflecting the European concern with depth perception and shading, and bronze sculptures of secular subjects. All expressed the individual creator's emotional and aesthetic preferences.

Cultural exchange also went the other way as Japanese arts and crafts, porcelains, textiles, fans, folding screens, and woodblock prints became the vogue in Europe and North America. Japanese art influenced Western painters such as Vincent van Gogh, Edgar Degas (duh-GAH), and James Whistler, who experimented with flatter compositional perspectives and unusual poses. Japanese gardens, with their exquisite attention to the positioning of rocks and falling water, became especially popular in the United States.

After the initial period of mass absorption of Western art, a national reaction occurred at the end of the nineteenth century as many artists returned to pre-Meiji techniques. In 1889, the Tokyo School of Fine Arts (today the Tokyo National University of Fine Arts and Music) was founded to promote traditional Japanese art. Over the next several decades, Japanese art underwent a dynamic resurgence, reflecting the nation's emergence as a prosperous and powerful state. While some artists attempted to synthesize Japanese and foreign techniques, others returned to past artistic traditions for inspiration.

In architecture, as in painting, the tension between tradition and modernity was often on vivid display (see the Comparative Illustration "A Tale of Two Cities: Shanghai and Tokyo" on p. 658). Japan's split personality revealed itself most effectively

in the Diet building. As the home of the new Japanese parliament, it was supposed to reflect both progress and the nation and culture of Japan. For half a century, conflicting views over the priority of these concepts delayed its construction. After a number of proposals were rejected, the government held a competition in 1919, but none of the designs won general approval. Finally, in 1936 the government decided on the final design, which followed neither traditional styles nor European architecture of the period.

The Meiji Restoration: A Revolution from Above

Japan's transformation from a feudal, agrarian society to an industrializing, technologically advanced society in little more than half a century has frequently been described by outside observers (if not by the Japanese themselves) in almost miraculous terms. Some historians have questioned this characterization, pointing out that the achievements of the Meiji leaders were spotty. In *Japan's Emergence as a Modern State*, the Canadian historian E. H. Norman lamented that the **Meiji Restoration** was an "incomplete revolution" because it had not ended the economic and social inequities of feudal society or enabled the common people to participate fully in the governing process. Although the *genro* were enlightened in many respects, they were also despotic and elitist, and the distribution of wealth remained as unequal as it had been under the old system.[5]

It has also been noted that Japan's transformation into a major industrial nation was by no means complete by the beginning of the new century. Until at least the outbreak of World War I in 1914, the majority of goods produced by the manufacturing sector came from traditional cottage industries, rather than from modern factories based on the principle of large-scale output. The integration of the Japanese economy into the global marketplace was also limited, and foreign investment played a much smaller role than in most comparable economies in the West.

These criticisms are persuasive, although most of them could also be applied to many other societies going through the early stages of industrialization. In any event, from an economic perspective, the Meiji Restoration was one of the great success stories of modern times. Not only did the Meiji leaders put Japan firmly on the path to economic and political development, but they also managed to remove the unequal treaty provisions that had been imposed at mid-century. Japanese achievements are especially impressive when compared with the difficulties experienced by China, which was not only unable to realize significant changes in its traditional society but had not even reached a consensus on the need for doing so. Japan's achievements more closely resemble those of Europe, but whereas the West needed a century and a half to achieve a significant level of industrial development, the Japanese realized it in forty years.

One of the distinctive features of Japan's transition from a traditional to a modern society during the Meiji era was that it took place for the most part without violence or the kind of

Roger-Viollet/The Image Works

Art Resource, NY

COMPARATIVE ILLUSTRATION

A Tale of Two Cities: Shanghai and Tokyo. Nothing more effectively symbolizes the dramatic changes brought about by the Western penetration of East Asia than the rise of modern cities like Shanghai and Tokyo. By the end of the nineteenth century, both of these urban centers had developed an electrical grid, a fast and efficient transport system, and a manufacturing sector capable of absorbing immigrant labor from surrounding areas. There were some key differences, however. Whereas the Bund, a string of modern stone buildings in the European style along the banks of the Huangpu River in Shanghai (upper left), was constructed almost entirely by foreign interests, the Ginza (lower right), a business and mercantile sector of Tokyo shown in this 1877 woodblock print, was built almost entirely by the Japanese themselves.

 Why do you think the Japanese were able to finance their own urban development in cities such as Tokyo, rather than depending on foreign assistance?

social or political revolution that occurred in so many other countries. The Meiji Restoration, which began the process, has been called a "revolution from above," a comprehensive restructuring of Japanese society by its own ruling group.

Technically, of course, the Meiji Restoration was not a revolution, since it was not violent and did not result in the displacement of one ruling class by another. The existing elites undertook to carry out a series of major reforms that transformed society but left their own power intact. In the words of one historian, it was "a kind of amalgamation, in which the enterprising, adaptable, or lucky individuals of the old privileged classes [were] for most practical purposes tied up with those individuals of the old submerged classes, who, probably through the same gifts, were able to rise." In that respect, the Meiji Restoration resembles the American Revolution more than the French Revolution; it was a "conservative revolution" that resulted in gradual change rather than rapid and violent change.[6]

WHAT EXPLAINS JAPANESE UNIQUENESS? The differences between the Japanese response to the West and the response of China and many other nations in the region have sparked considerable debate among students of comparative history. In this and previous chapters we have already discussed some of the reasons why China—along with most other countries in Asia and Africa—had not yet begun to enter their own industrial revolutions by the end of the nineteenth century. The puzzle, then, becomes, why was Japan apparently uniquely positioned to make the transition to an advanced industrial economy?

A number of explanations have been offered. Some have argued that Japan's success was partly due to good fortune. Lacking abundant natural resources, it was exposed to less pressure from the West than many of its neighbors, and thus was able to adjust to changing conditions at its own pace. That argument is problematic, however, and would probably not have been accepted by Japanese observers at the time. Nor does it explain why nations under considerably less pressure, such as Laos and Nepal, did not advance even more quickly. All in all, the luck hypothesis is not very persuasive.

Some explanations have already been suggested in this book. Japan's unique geographic position in Asia—and the cultural attributes that flowed from this reality—was certainly a factor. China, a continental nation with a heterogeneous ethnic composition, was distinguished from its neighbors by its Confucian culture. By contrast, Japan was an island nation, ethnically and linguistically homogeneous, and had never been conquered. Unlike the Chinese or many other peoples in the region, the Japanese had little to fear from cultural change in terms of its effect on their national identity. The fact that the emperor, the living symbol of the nation, had adopted change ensured that his subjects could follow in his footsteps without fear.

In addition, a number of other factors may have played a role. The nature of the Japanese value system, with its emphasis on practicality and military achievement, may have contributed. Finally, the Meiji also benefited from the fact that the pace of urbanization and commercial and industrial development had already begun to quicken under the Tokugawa. Having already lost their traditional feudal role and much of the revenue from their estates, the Japanese aristocracy—daimyo and samurai alike—could discard sword and kimono and don modern military uniforms or Western business suits and still feel comfortable in both worlds.

Whatever the case, as the historian W. G. Beasley has noted, the Meiji Restoration was possible because aristocratic and capitalist elements managed to work together to bring about drastic change. Japan, it was said, was ripe for change, and nothing could have been more suitable as an antidote for the collapsing old system than the Western emphasis on wealth and power. It was a classic example of challenge and response.

THE FUSION OF EAST AND WEST The final product was an amalgam of old and new, Japanese and foreign, forming a new civilization that was still uniquely Japanese. There were some undesirable consequences, however. Because Meiji politics was essentially despotic, Japanese leaders were able to fuse key traditional elements such as the warrior ethic and the concept of feudal loyalty with the dynamics of modern industrial capitalism to create a state totally dedicated to the possession of material wealth and national power. This combination of *kokutai* and capitalism, which one scholar has described as a form of "Asian fascism," was highly effective but explosive in its international manifestation. Like modern Germany, which also entered the industrial age directly from feudalism, Japan eventually engaged in a policy of repression at home and expansion abroad in order to achieve its national objectives. In Japan, as in Germany, it took defeat in war to disconnect the drive for national development from the feudal ethic and bring about the transformation to a pluralistic society dedicated to living in peace and cooperation with its neighbors.

CHAPTER SUMMARY

Few areas of the world resisted the Western incursion as stubbornly and effectively as East Asia. Although military, political, and economic pressure by the European powers was relatively intense during this era, two of the main states in the area were able to retain their independence, while the third—Korea—was temporarily absorbed by one of its larger neighbors. Why the Chinese and the Japanese were able to prevent a total political and military takeover by foreign powers is an interesting question. One key reason was that both had a long history as well-defined states with a strong sense of national community and territorial cohesion.

Although China had frequently been conquered, it had retained its sense of unique culture and identity. Geography, too, was in its favor. As a continental nation, China was able to survive partly because of its sheer size. Japan possessed the advantage of an island location.

Even more striking, however, is the different way in which the two states attempted to deal with the challenge. While the Japanese chose to face the problem in a pragmatic manner, borrowing foreign ideas and institutions that appeared to be of value and at the same time not in conflict with traditional attitudes and customs, China agonized over the issue for half a century while conservative elements fought a desperate battle to retain a maximum of the traditional heritage intact.

This chapter has discussed some of the possible reasons for those differences. In retrospect, it is difficult to avoid the conclusion that the Japanese approach was the more effective one. Whereas the Meiji leaders were able to set in motion an orderly transition from a traditional to an advanced society, in China the old system collapsed in disorder, leaving chaotic conditions that were still not rectified a generation later. China would pay a heavy price for its failure to respond coherently to the challenge.

But the Japanese "revolution from above" was by no means an unalloyed success. Ambitious efforts by Japanese leaders to carve out a share in the spoils of empire led to escalating conflict with China as well as with rival Western powers and in the early 1940s to global war. We will deal with that issue in Chapter 25. Meanwhile, in Europe, a combination of old rivalries and the effects of the Industrial Revolution were leading to a bitter regional conflict that eventually engulfed the entire world.

CHAPTER TIMELINE

CHAPTER REVIEW

Upon Reflection

Q What were some of the key reasons why the Meiji reformers were so successful in launching Japan on the road to industrialization? Which of those reasons also applied to China under the Manchus?

Q What impact did colonial rule have on the environment in the European colonies in Asia and Africa during the nineteenth century? Did some of these same factors apply in China and Japan?

Q How did Western values and institutions influence Chinese and Japanese social mores and traditions during the imperialist era?

Key Terms

self-strengthening (p. 639)
Open Door Notes (p. 641)

three people's principles (p. 643)
sakoku (p. 649)
genro (p. 651)
kokutai (p. 652)
bunmei kaika (p. 652)
three obediences (p. 653)
eta (p. 653)
Meiji Restoration (p. 657)

Suggested Reading

CHINA For a general overview of modern Chinese history, see **I. C. Y. Hsu,** *The Rise of Modern China,* 6th ed. (Oxford, 2000). Also see **J. Spence's** stimulating work *The Search for Modern China* (New York, 1990).

On the Taiping Rebellion, **J. Spence,** *God's Chinese Son: The Taiping Heavenly Kingdom of Hong Xiuquan* (New York, 1996), has become a classic. Social issues are dealt with in **E. S. Rawski,** *The Last Emperors: A Social History of Qing*

Imperial Institutions (Berkeley, Calif., 1998). On the Manchus' attitude toward modernization, see **D. Pong, *Shen Pao-chen and China's Modernization in the Nineteenth Century*** (New York, 1994). For a series of stimulating essays on various aspects of China's transition to modernity, see **Wen-hsin Yeh, ed., *Becoming Chinese: Passages to Modernity and Beyond*** (Berkeley, Calif., 2000).

Sun Yat-sen's career is explored in **M. C. Bergère, *Sun Yat-sen*, trans. J. Lloyd** (Stanford, Calif., 2000). **J. Chang, *Empress Dowager Cixi: The Concubine Who Launched Modern China*** (New York, 2013), is a revisionist treatment of the once-reviled "Dragon Lady." On the Boxer Rebellion, see **D. Preston, *The Boxer Rebellion: The Dramatic Story of China's War on Foreigners That Shook the World in the Summer of 1900*** (Berkeley, Calif., 2001).

JAPAN The Meiji period of modern Japan is covered in **M. B. Jansen, ed., *The Emergence of Meiji Japan*** (Cambridge, 1995). Also see **D. Keene, *Emperor of Japan: Meiji and His World, 1852–1912*** (New York, 2000). To understand the role of the samurai in the Meiji Revolution, see **E. Ikegami, *The Taming of the Samurai: Honorific Individualism and the Making of Modern Japan*** (Cambridge, 1995). For a thoughtful overview of modern Japanese history, see **I. Buruma, *Inventing Japan, 1853–1964*** (New York, 2003).

On the international scene, **W. Lafeber, *The Clash: U.S.-Japanese Relations Throughout History*** (New York, 1997), is slow reading but a good source of information. The U.S. role in opening Japan to the West is analyzed in **G. Feifer, *Breaking Open Japan: Commodore Perry, Lord Abe, and American**

Imperialism in 1853 (Washington, D.C., 2007). On the Russo-Japanese War, **R. Connaughton, *Rising Sun and Tumbling Bear: Russia's War with Japan*** (London, 2003), is one of several good offerings. The best introduction to Japanese art is **P. Mason, *History of Japanese Art*** (New York, 1993).

Chapter Notes

1. H. B. Morse, *The International Relations of the Chinese Empire* (London, 1910–1918), vol. 2, p. 622.
2. William Theodore de Bary and Richard Lufrano, eds., *Sources of Chinese Tradition*, 2nd ed, (New York, 1999), vol. 2, p. 252.
3. Quoted in S. Teng and J. K. Fairbank, eds., *China's Response to the West: A Documentary Survey, 1839–1923* (New York, 1970), p. 167.
4. J. K. Fairbank, A. M. Craig, and E. O. Reischauer, *East Asia: Tradition and Transformation* (Boston, 1973), p. 514.
5. Quoted in J. W. Dower, ed., *The Origins of the Modern Japanese State: Selected Writings of E. H. Norman* (New York, 1975), p. 13.
6. C. Brinton, *The Anatomy of Revolution* (New York, 1965), quoted in W. G. Beasley, *The Meiji Restoration* (Stanford, Calf., 1972), p. 423.

MindTap™

MindTap is a fully online, highly personalized learning experience built upon Cengage Learning content. MindTap combines student learning tools—readings, multimedia, activities, and assessments—into a singular Learning Path that guides students through their course.

The Beginning of the Twentieth-Century Crisis: War and Revolution

British infantrymen prepare to advance during the Battle of the Somme

Universal History Archive/UIG/Getty Images

CHAPTER OUTLINE AND FOCUS QUESTIONS

The Road to World War I

Q What were the long-range and immediate causes of World War I?

The Great War

Q Why did the course of World War I turn out to be so different from what the belligerents had expected? How did World War I affect the belligerents' governmental and political institutions, economic affairs, and social life?

War and Revolution

Q What were the causes of the Russian Revolution of 1917, and why did the Bolsheviks prevail in the civil war and gain control of Russia? What were the objectives of the chief participants at the Paris Peace Conference of 1919, and how closely did the final settlement reflect these objectives?

An Uncertain Peace

Q What was the aftermath of World War I, and what problems did Europe and the United States face in the 1920s?

In Pursuit of a New Reality: Cultural and Intellectual Trends

Q How did the cultural and intellectual trends of the post–World War I years reflect the crises of the time as well as the lingering effects of the war?

CRITICAL THINKING

Q What was the relationship between World War I and the Russian Revolution?

CONNECTIONS TO TODAY

Q What lessons from the outbreak of World War I are of value in considering international relations today?

ON JULY 1, 1916, BRITISH and French infantry forces attacked German defensive lines along a 25-mile front near the Somme (SUHM) River in France. Each soldier carried almost 70 pounds of equipment, making it "impossible to move much quicker than a slow walk." German machine guns soon opened fire: "We were able to see our comrades move forward in an attempt to cross No-Man's-Land, only to be mown down like meadow grass," recalled one British soldier. "I felt sick at the sight of this carnage and remember weeping." In one day, more than 21,000 British soldiers died. After six months of fighting, the British had advanced 5 miles; one million British, French, and German soldiers had been killed or wounded.

Philip Gibbs, an English war correspondent, described what he saw in the German trenches that the British forces overran: "Victory!… Some of the German dead were young boys, too young to be killed for old men's crimes, and others might have been old or young. One could not tell because they had no faces, and were just masses of raw flesh in rags of uniforms. Legs and arms lay separate without any bodies thereabout."

World War I (1914–1918) was the defining event of the twentieth-century world. Overwhelmed by the scale of its battles, the extent of its casualties, and its impact on all facets of life, contemporaries referred to it simply as the "Great War." The Great War was all the more disturbing to Europeans because it came after what many believed to have been an age of progress. Material prosperity and a fervid belief in scientific and technological progress had convinced many people that the world stood on the verge of creating the utopia that humans had dreamed of for centuries. The historian Arnold Toynbee expressed what the era before the war had meant to his generation:

> [We had expected] that life throughout the world would become more rational, more humane, and more democratic and that, slowly, but surely, political democracy would produce greater social justice. We had also expected that the progress of science and technology would make mankind richer, and that this increasing wealth would gradually spread from a minority to a majority. We had expected that all this would happen peacefully. In fact we thought that mankind's course was set for an earthly paradise.[1]

After 1918, it was no longer possible to maintain naive illusions about the progress of Western civilization. As World War I was followed by revolutionary upheavals, the mass murder machines of totalitarian regimes, and the destructiveness of World War II, it became all too apparent that instead of a utopia, Western civilization had become a nightmare. World War I and the revolutions it spawned can properly be seen as the first stage in the crisis of the twentieth century. ◄

The Road to World War I

 FOCUS QUESTION: What were the long-range and immediate causes of World War I?

On June 28, 1914, the heir to the Austrian throne, the Archduke Francis Ferdinand, was assassinated in the Bosnian city of Sarajevo (sar-uh-YAY-voh). Although this event precipitated the confrontation between Austria and Serbia that led to World War I, underlying forces had been propelling Europeans toward armed conflict for a long time.

Nationalism and Internal Dissent

The system of nation-states that had emerged in Europe in the second half of the nineteenth century (see Map 23.1) had led to severe competition. A frenzied imperialist expansion led to rivalries over colonies and trade. This competition for lands abroad, especially in Africa, led to conflict and heightened the existing antagonism among European states (see Chapter 19). Moreover, the division of Europe's great powers into two loose alliances (the Triple Alliance of Germany, Austria, and Italy, formed in 1882; the Triple Entente of France, Great Britain, and Russia, created in 1907) only added to the tensions. The series of crises that tested these alliances in the 1900s and early 1910s had not led directly to war at the time but had left European states embittered, eager for revenge, and willing to revert to war as an acceptable way to preserve the power of their national states.

The growth of nationalism in the nineteenth century had yet another serious consequence. Not all ethnic groups had achieved the goal of nationhood. Slavic minorities in the Balkans and the multiethnic Habsburg empire, for example, still dreamed of creating their own national states. So did the Irish in the British Empire and the Poles in the Russian empire.

National aspirations, however, were not the only source of internal strife at the beginning of the twentieth century. Socialist labor movements had grown more powerful and were increasingly inclined to use strikes, even violent ones, to achieve their goals. Some conservative leaders, alarmed at the increase in labor strife and class division, even feared that European nations were on the verge of revolution. Did these statesmen opt for war in 1914 because they believed that "prosecuting an active foreign policy," as some Austrian leaders expressed it, would smother "internal troubles"? Some historians have argued that the desire to suppress internal disorder may have encouraged some leaders to take the plunge into war in 1914.

Militarism

The growth of large mass armies after 1900 not only heightened the existing tensions in Europe but also made it inevitable that if war did come, it would be extremely destructive. **Conscription**—obligatory military service—had been established as a regular practice in most Western countries before 1914 (the United States and Britain were major exceptions). European military machines had doubled in size between 1890 and 1914. With its 1.3 million men, the Russian army had grown to be the largest, but the French and Germans were not far behind, with 900,000 each. The British, Italian, and Austrian armies numbered between 250,000 and 500,000 soldiers.

Militarism, however, involved more than just large armies. As armies grew, so did the influence of military leaders, who drew up vast and complex plans for quickly mobilizing millions of men and enormous quantities of supplies in the event of war. Fearful that changing these plans would cause chaos in the armed forces, military leaders insisted that the plans could not be altered. In the crises during the summer of 1914, the generals' lack of flexibility forced European political leaders to make decisions for military instead of political reasons.

The Outbreak of War: Summer 1914

Militarism, nationalism, and the desire to stifle internal dissent may all have played a role in the coming of World War I, but the decisions made by European leaders in the summer of 1914 directly precipitated the conflict. It was another crisis in the Balkans that forced this predicament on Europe's statesmen.

As we have seen, states in southeastern Europe had struggled to free themselves from Ottoman rule in the course of the nineteenth and early twentieth centuries. But the rivalry between Austria-Hungary and Russia for domination of these new states created serious tensions in the region. By 1914, Serbia, supported by Russia, was determined to create a large, independent Slavic state in the Balkans, while Austria, which had its own Slavic minorities to contend with, was equally set on preventing that possibility. Many Europeans perceived the inherent dangers in this combination of Serbian ambition

MAP 23.1 **Europe in 1914.** By 1914, two alliances dominated Europe: the Triple Entente of Britain, France, and Russia and the Triple Alliance of Germany, Austria-Hungary, and Italy. Russia sought to bolster fellow Slavs in Serbia, whereas Austria-Hungary was intent on increasing its power in the Balkans and thwarting Serbia's ambitions. Thus, the Balkans became the flash point for World War I.

Q *Which nonaligned nations were positioned between the two alliances?*

© 2016 Cengage Learning

the Austrian government did not know whether the Serbian government had been directly involved in the archduke's assassination, it saw an opportunity to "render Serbia innocuous once and for all by a display of force," as the Austrian foreign minister put it. Fearful of Russian intervention on Serbia's behalf, Austrian leaders sought the backing of their German allies. Emperor William II and his chancellor responded with the infamous "blank check," their assurance that Austria-Hungary could rely on Germany's "full support," even if "matters went to the length of a war between Austria-Hungary and Russia." Much historical debate has focused on this "blank check" extended to the Austrians. Did the Germans realize that an Austrian-Serbian war could lead to a wider war? If so, did they actually want one? Historians are still divided on the answers to these questions.

Strengthened by German support, Austrian leaders issued an ultimatum to Serbia on July 23 in which they made such extreme demands that Serbia had little choice but to reject some of them in order to preserve its sovereignty. Austria then declared war on Serbia on July 28. Although Austria had hoped to keep the war limited to Serbia and Austria in order to ensure its success in the Balkans, these hopes soon vanished.

bolstered by Russian hatred of Austria and the Austrian conviction that Serbia's success would mean the end of its empire. The British ambassador to Vienna wrote in 1913:

> Serbia will some day set Europe by the ears, and bring about a universal war on the Continent.... I cannot tell you how exasperated people are getting here at the continual worry which that little country causes to Austria under encouragement from Russia.... It will be lucky if Europe succeeds in avoiding war as a result of the present crisis. The next time a Serbian crisis arises ..., I feel sure that Austria-Hungary will refuse to admit of any Russian interference in the dispute and that she will proceed to settle her differences with her little neighbor by herself.[2]

It was against this backdrop of mutual distrust and hatred that the events of the summer of 1914 were played out.

THE ASSASSINATION OF FRANCIS FERDINAND: WHAT WAS THE "BLANK CHECK"?

The assassination of the Austrian Archduke Francis Ferdinand and his wife, Sophia, on June 28, 1914, was carried out by a Bosnian activist who worked for the Black Hand, a Serbian terrorist organization dedicated to the creation of a pan-Slavic kingdom. Although

DECLARATIONS OF WAR Still smarting from its humiliation in the Bosnian crisis of 1908, Russia was determined to support Serbia's cause. On July 28, Tsar Nicholas II ordered partial mobilization of the Russian army against Austria. The Russian General Staff informed the tsar that their mobilization plans were based on a war against both Germany and Austria simultaneously. They could not execute partial mobilization without creating chaos in the army. Consequently, the Russian government ordered full mobilization of the Russian army on July 29, knowing that the Germans would consider this an act of war against them (see the box "'You Have to Bear the Responsibility for War or Peace'" on p. 665). Germany quickly responded with an ultimatum that the Russians must halt their mobilization within twelve hours. When the Russians ignored it, Germany declared war on Russia on August 1.

France now became involved in the war. Under the guidance of General Alfred von Schlieffen (AHL-fret fun SHLEE-fun), chief of staff from 1891 to 1905, the German General Staff had devised a military plan based on the assumption of a two-front war with France and Russia because the two powers had formed a military alliance in 1894. The Schlieffen Plan called for a minimal troop deployment against Russia while most of

"You Have to Bear the Responsibility for War or Peace"

POLITICS & GOVERNMENT

AFTER AUSTRIA DECLARED WAR on Serbia on July 28, 1914, Russian support of Serbia and German support of Austria threatened to escalate the conflict in the Balkans into a wider war. As we can see in these last-minute telegrams between the Russians and Germans, neither side was able to accept the other's line of reasoning.

Communications Between Berlin and Saint Petersburg on the Eve of World War I

Emperor William II to Tsar Nicholas II, July 28, 10:45 P.M.

I have heard with the greatest anxiety of the impression which is caused by the action of Austria-Hungary against Servia [Serbia]. The inscrupulous agitation which has been going on for years in Servia has led to the revolting crime of which Archduke Franz Ferdinand has become a victim. The spirit which made the Servians murder their own King and his consort still dominates that country. Doubtless You will agree with me that both of us, You as well as I, and all other sovereigns, have a common interest to insist that all those who are responsible for this horrible murder shall suffer their deserved punishment....

> Your most sincere and devoted friend and cousin
> (*Signed*) WILHELM

Tsar Nicholas II to Emperor William II, July 29, 1:00 P.M.

I am glad that you are back in Germany. In this serious moment I ask You earnestly to help me. An ignominious war has been declared against a weak country and in Russia the indignation which I fully share is tremendous. I fear that very soon I shall be unable to resist the pressure exercised upon me and that I shall be forced to take measures which will lead to war. To prevent a calamity as a European war would be, I urge You in the name of our old friendship to do all in Your power to restrain Your ally from going too far.

> (*Signed*) NICOLAS

Emperor William II to Tsar Nicholas II, July 29, 6:30 P.M.

I have received Your telegram and I share Your desire for the conservation of peace. However: I cannot—as I told You in my first telegram—consider the action of Austria-Hungary as an "ignominious war." Austria-Hungary knows from experience that the promises of Servia as long as they are merely on paper are entirely unreliable.... I believe that a

direct understanding is possible and desirable between Your Government and Vienna, an understanding which—as I have already telegraphed You—my Government endeavors to aid with all possible effort. Naturally military measures by Russia, which might be construed as a menace by Austria-Hungary, would accelerate a calamity which both of us desire to avoid and would undermine my position as mediator which—upon Your appeal to my friendship and aid—I willingly accepted.

> (*Signed*) WILHELM

Emperor William II to Tsar Nicholas II, July 30, 1:00 A.M.

My Ambassador has instructions to direct the attention of Your Government to the dangers and serious consequences of a mobilization. I have told You the same in my last telegram. Austria-Hungary has mobilized only against Servia, and only a part of her army. If Russia, as seems to be the case, according to Your advice and that of Your Government, mobilizes against Austria-Hungary, the part of the mediator with which You have entrusted me in such friendly manner and which I have accepted upon Your express desire, is threatened if not made impossible. The entire weight of decision now rests upon Your shoulders; You have to bear the responsibility for war or peace.

> (*Signed*) WILHELM

German Chancellor to German Ambassador at Saint Petersburg, July 31, URGENT

In spite of negotiations still pending and although we have up to this hour made no preparations for mobilization, Russia has mobilized her entire army and navy, hence also against us. On account of these Russian measures, we have been forced, for the safety of the country, to proclaim the threatening state of war, which does not yet imply mobilization. Mobilization, however, is bound to follow if Russia does not stop every measure of war against us and against Austria-Hungary within 12 hours, and notifies us definitely to this effect. Please to communicate this at once to M. Sazonoff and wire hour of communication.

How do the telegrams exchanged between William II and Nicholas II reveal why the Europeans foolishly went to war in 1914? What do they tell us about the nature of the relationship between these two monarchs?

Source: From *The Western World: From 1700 Vol. II*, by W. E. Adams, R. B. Barlow, G. R. Kleinfeld, and R. D. Smith (Dodd, Mead, and Co., 1968), pp. 421–442.

the German army would make a rapid invasion of France before Russia could become effective in the east or before the British could cross the English Channel to help France. This meant invading France by advancing through neutral Belgium, with its level coastal plain on which the army could move faster than on the rougher terrain to the southeast. After the planned quick defeat of the French, the German army expected to redeploy to the east against Russia. Under the Schlieffen Plan, Germany could not mobilize its troops solely against

Russia and therefore declared war on France on August 3 after it had issued an ultimatum to Belgium on August 2, demanding the right of German troops to pass through Belgian territory. On August 4, Great Britain declared war on Germany, officially over this violation of Belgian neutrality but in fact over the British desire to maintain world power. As one British diplomat argued, if Germany and Austria were to win the war, "what would be the position of a friendless England?" By August 4, all the great powers of Europe were at war.

The Excitement of War

POLITICS & GOVERNMENT

THE INCREDIBLE OUTPOURING of patriotic enthusiasm that greeted the declaration of war at the beginning of August 1914 demonstrated the power that nationalistic feeling had attained in the early twentieth century. Many Europeans seemingly believed that the war had given them a higher purpose, a renewed dedication to the greatness of their nations. These selections are taken from three sources: the autobiography of Stefan Zweig (SHTE-fahn TSVYK), an Austrian writer; the memoirs of Robert Graves, a British writer; and a letter by a German soldier, Walter Limmer, to his parents.

Stefan Zweig, *The World of Yesterday*

The next morning I was in Austria. In every station placards had been put up announcing general mobilization. The trains were filled with fresh recruits, banners were flying, music sounded, and in Vienna I found the entire city in a tumult.... There were parades in the street, flags, ribbons, and music burst forth everywhere, young recruits were marching triumphantly, their faces lighting up at the cheering....

And to be truthful, I must acknowledge that there was a majestic, rapturous, and even seductive something in this first outbreak of the people from which one could escape only with difficulty. And in spite of all my hatred and aversion for war, I should not like to have missed the memory of those days. As never before, thousands and hundreds of thousands felt what they should have felt in peace time, that they belonged together. A city of two million, a country of nearly fifty million, in that hour felt that they were participating in world history, in a moment which would never recur, and that each one was called upon to cast his infinitesimal self into the glowing mass, there to be purified of all selfishness. All differences of class, rank, and language were flooded over at that moment by the rushing feeling of fraternity....

What did the great mass know of war in 1914, after nearly half a century of peace? They did not know war, they had hardly given it a thought. It had become legendary, and distance had made it seem romantic and heroic. They still saw it in the perspective of their school readers and of paintings in museums; brilliant cavalry attacks in glittering uniforms, the fatal shot always straight through the heart, the entire campaign a resounding march of victory—"We'll be home at Christmas," the recruits shouted laughingly to their mothers in August of 1914.... A rapid excursion into the romantic, a wild, manly adventure—that is how the war of 1914 was painted in the imagination of the simple man, and the younger people were honestly afraid that they might miss this most wonderful and exciting experience of their lives; that is why they hurried and thronged to the colors, and that is why they shouted and sang in the trains that carried them to the slaughter....

Robert Graves, *Goodbye to All That*

I had just finished with Charterhouse and gone up to Harlech, when England declared war on Germany. A day or two later I decided to enlist. In the first place, though the papers predicted only a very short war—over by Christmas at the outside—I hoped that it might last long enough to delay my going to Oxford in October, which I dreaded. Nor did I work out the possibilities of getting actively engaged in the fighting, expecting garrison service at home, while the regular forces were away. In the second place, I was outraged to read of the Germans' cynical violation of Belgian neutrality. Though I discounted perhaps twenty percent of the atrocity details as wartime exaggeration, that was not, of course, sufficient.

Walter Limmer, Letter to His Parents

In any case I mean to go into this business.... That is the simple duty of every one of us. And this feeling is universal among the soldiers, especially since the night when England's declaration of war was announced in the barracks. We none of us got to sleep till three o'clock in the morning, we were so full of excitement, fury, and enthusiasm. It is a joy to go to the Front with such comrades. We are bound to be victorious! Nothing else is possible in the face of such determination to win.

What do these excerpts reveal about the motivations of people to join and support World War I? Do the passages reveal anything about the power of nationalism in Europe in the early twentieth century?

Sources: From *The World of Yesterday* by Stefan Zweig, translated by Helmut Ripperger. Translation copyright 1943 by the Viking. Press, Inc. Robert Graves, *Good-Bye to All That* (New York: Anchor, 1958). From *German Students' War Letters*, edited by Philipp Witkop, Translated by A. F. Wedd. Originally published in 1929 by Methuen. Pine Street Books © 2002.

The Great War

FOCUS QUESTIONS: Why did the course of World War I turn out to be so different from what the belligerents had expected? How did World War I affect the belligerents' governmental and political institutions, economic affairs, and social life?

Before 1914, many political leaders had become convinced that war involved so many political and economic risks that it was not worth fighting. Others had believed that "rational" diplomats could control any situation and prevent the outbreak of war. At the beginning of August 1914, both of these prewar illusions were shattered, but the new illusions that replaced them soon proved to be equally foolish.

1914–1915: Illusions and Stalemate

Many Europeans went to war with remarkable enthusiasm (see the box "The Excitement of War" above). Government propaganda had been successful in stirring up national antagonisms before the war. Now, in August 1914, the urgent pleas of governments for defense against aggressors found many receptive ears in every belligerent nation. Middle-class crowds, often composed of young students, were especially enthusiastic, though workers in the cities and peasants in the countryside were considerably less eager for war. Once the war began, however, most people seemed genuinely convinced that their nation's cause was just.

A new set of illusions also fed the enthusiasm for war. In August 1914, almost everyone believed that the war would be over in a few weeks. People were reminded that the major battles in European wars since 1815 had ended in a matter of weeks, thus conveniently overlooking the American Civil War (1861–1865), which was a better prototype for World War I. Both the soldiers who exuberantly boarded the trains for the war front in August 1914 and the jubilant citizens who bombarded them with flowers as they departed believed that the warriors would be home by Christmas.

German hopes for a quick end to the war rested on a military gamble. The Schlieffen Plan had called for the German army to proceed through Belgium into northern France with a vast encircling movement that would sweep around Paris and surround most of the French army. But the plan suffered a major defect from the beginning: it called for a strong right flank for the encircling of Paris, but German military leaders, concerned about a Russian invasion in the east, had moved forces from the right flank to strengthen the German army in the east.

As a result, the German advance was halted only 20 miles from Paris at the First Battle of the Marne (September 6–10). The war quickly turned into a stalemate as neither the Germans nor the French could dislodge the other from the trenches they had begun to dig for shelter. Two lines of trenches soon extended from the English Channel to the frontiers of Switzerland (see Map 23.2). The western front had become bogged down in **trench warfare**, which kept both sides immobilized in virtually the same positions for four years.

In contrast to the western front, the war in the east was marked by much more mobility, although the cost in lives was equally enormous. At the beginning of the war, the Russian army moved into eastern Germany but was decisively defeated at the Battles of Tannenberg on August 30 and the Masurian Lakes on September 15. The Russians were no longer a threat to German territory.

The Austrians, Germany's allies, fared less well initially. They had been defeated by the Russians in Galicia (guh-LISH-ee-uh) and thrown out of Serbia as well. To make matters worse, the Italians betrayed the Germans and Austrians and entered the war on the Allied side by attacking Austria in May 1915. By this time, the Germans had come to the aid of the Austrians. A German-Austrian army defeated and routed the Russian army in Galicia and pushed the Russians back 300 miles into their own territory. Russian casualties stood at 2.5 million killed, captured, or wounded; the Russians had almost been knocked out of the war. Buoyed by their success, the Germans and Austrians, joined by the Bulgarians in September 1915, attacked and eliminated Serbia from the war.

1916–1917: The Great Slaughter

The successes in the east enabled the Germans to move back to the offensive in the west. The early trenches dug in 1914, stretching from the English Channel to the frontiers of Switzerland, had by now become elaborate systems of defense. Both lines of trenches were protected by barbed-wire entanglements 3 to 5 feet high and 90 feet wide, concrete machine-gun nests, and mortar batteries, supported farther back by heavy artillery. Troops lived in holes in the ground, separated from each other by a "no-man's land."

The unexpected development of trench warfare on the western front baffled military leaders, who had been trained to fight wars of movement and maneuver. Periodically, the high command on either side would order an offensive that would begin with an artillery barrage to flatten the enemy's barbed wire and leave the enemy in a state of shock. After "softening up" the enemy in this fashion, a mass of soldiers would climb out of their trenches with fixed bayonets and hope to work their way toward the enemy trenches. The attacks rarely worked, as the machine gun put hordes of men advancing unprotected across open fields at a severe

Mary Evans Picture Library/The Image Works

The Excitement of War. World War I was greeted with incredible enthusiasm. Each of the major belligerents was convinced of the rightness of its cause, demonstrating the power of nationalism. Even socialists supported their governments rather than maintaining the solidarity of the working classes regardless of nationality. Everywhere in Europe, jubilant civilians sent their troops off to battle with joyous fervor, as is evident in this photograph of French troops marching off to war. The belief that the soldiers would be home by Christmas proved to be a pathetic illusion.

The map image with labels:

North Sea, SWEDEN, Stockholm, Saint Petersburg, RUSSIA, Baltic Sea, Moscow, Don R., GREAT BRITAIN, NETHERLANDS, GERMAN EMPIRE, (EAST PRUSSIA), Tannenberg, Masurian Lakes, London, Ypres, Antwerp, Brussels, Cologne, Warsaw, Brest-Litovsk, Calais, BELGIUM, LUX., Coblenz, Frankfurt, Le Havre, Arras, Prague, GALICIA, Kiev, Dnieper R., Paris, Luxembourg, Verdun, AUSTRIA-, Vienna, Dniester R., (UKRAINE), Seine R., Versailles, Nancy, Carpathian Mts., SWITZERLAND, HUNGARY, Budapest, TRANSYLVANIA, (CRIMEA), FRANCE, Alps, Po R., ROMANIA, Bucharest, Black Sea, Belgrade, Danube R., (BOSNIA), SERBIA, Sofia, Corsica, MONTE-NEGRO, BULGARIA, ITALY, ALBANIA, Constantinople, Sardinia, GREECE, Salonika, Gallipoli, Bosporus, OTTOMAN EMPIRE, Dardanelles

Eastern Front:
- Battle site, 1914
- Russian advances, 1914–1916
- Deepest German penetration
- Brest-Litovsk boundary, 1918

Western Front:
- Farthest German advance, September 1914
- German offensive, March–July 1918
- Winter, 1914–1915
- Armistice line

- → German advances
- ← Allied advances
- (CRIMEA) Regions of national states

MAP 23.2 **World War I, 1914–1918.** This map shows how greatly the western and eastern fronts of World War I differed. After initial German gains in the west, the war became bogged down in trench warfare, with little change in the battle lines between 1914 and 1918. The eastern front was marked by considerable mobility, with battle lines shifting by hundreds of miles.

Q *How do you explain the difference in the two fronts?*

disadvantage. In 1916 and 1917, millions of young men were sacrificed in the search for the elusive breakthrough. In ten months at Verdun (ver-DUHN) in 1916, 700,000 men lost their lives over a few miles of terrain.

Warfare in the trenches of the western front produced unimaginable horrors (see the box "The Reality of War: Trench Warfare" on p. 670 and the Film & History feature *"Paths of Glory* (1957)" on p. 671). Battlefields were hellish landscapes of barbed wire, shell holes, mud, and injured and dying men. The introduction of poison gas in 1915 produced new forms of injuries, as one British writer described them:

I wish those people who write so glibly about this being a holy war could see a case of mustard gas ... could see the poor things burnt and blistered all over with great mustard-coloured suppurating blisters with blind eyes all sticky ... and

stuck together, and always fighting for breath, with voices a mere whisper, saying that their throats are closing and they know they will choke.[3]

Soldiers in the trenches also lived with the persistent presence of death. Since combat went on for months, soldiers had to carry on in the midst of countless bodies of dead men or the remains of men dismembered by artillery barrages. Many soldiers remembered the stench of decomposing bodies and the swarms of rats that grew fat in the trenches.

The Widening of the War

As another response to the stalemate on the western front, both sides looked for new allies who might provide a winning advantage. The Ottoman Empire had already come into the

The Horrors of War. The slaughter of millions of men in the trenches of World War I created unimaginable horrors for the participants. For the sake of survival, many soldiers learned to harden themselves against the stench of decomposing bodies and the sight of bodies horribly dismembered by artillery barrages.

war on Germany's side in August 1914. Russia, Great Britain, and France declared war on the Ottoman Empire in November. Although the Allies attempted to open a Balkan front by landing forces at Gallipoli (gah-LIP-poh-lee), southwest of Constantinople, in April 1915, the entry of Bulgaria into the war on the side of the Central Powers (as Germany, Austria-Hungary, and the Ottoman Empire were called) and a disastrous campaign at Gallipoli caused them to withdraw. The Italians, as we have seen, also entered the war on the Allied side after France and Britain promised to further their acquisition of Austrian territory. In the long run, however, Italian military incompetence forced the Allies to come to the assistance of Italy.

A GLOBAL CONFLICT Because the major European powers controlled colonial empires in other parts of the world, the war in Europe soon became a world war (see the Comparative Illustration "Soldiers from Around the World" on p. 672). In the Middle East, the British officer T. E. Lawrence (1888–1935), who came to be known as Lawrence of Arabia, incited Arab princes to revolt against their Ottoman overlords in 1916. In 1918, British forces from

German Possessions in Africa, 1914

Egypt and Mesopotamia destroyed the rest of the Ottoman Empire in the Middle East. For their Middle East campaigns, the British mobilized forces from India, Australia, and New Zealand.

The Allies also took advantage of Germany's preoccupation in Europe and lack of naval strength to seize German colonies in Africa. But there too the war did not end quickly. The first British shots of World War I were actually fired in Africa when British African troops moved into the German colony of Togoland near the end of August 1914. But in East Africa, the German commander Colonel Paul von Lettow-Vorbeck (POWL fun LEH-toh-FOR-bek) managed to keep his African troops fighting one campaign after another for four years; he did not surrender until two weeks after the armistice ended the war in Europe.

In the battles in Africa, Allied governments drew mainly on African soldiers, but some states, especially France, also recruited African troops to fight in Europe. The French drafted more than 170,000 West African soldiers, many of whom fought in the trenches on the western front. African troops were also used as occupation forces in the German Rhineland at the end of the war. About 80,000 Africans were killed or injured in Europe, where they were often at a distinct disadvantage due to the unfamiliar terrain and climate.

Hundreds of thousands of Africans were also used for labor, especially for carrying supplies and building roads and bridges. In East Africa, both sides drafted African laborers as carriers for their armies. More than 100,000 of these laborers died from disease and starvation caused by neglect.

The immediate impact of World War I in Africa was the extension of colonial rule since Germany's African colonies were simply transferred to the winning powers, especially the British and the French. But the war also had unintended consequences for the Europeans. African soldiers who had gone to war for the Allies, especially those who left Africa and fought in Europe, became politically aware and began to advocate political and social equality. As one African who had fought for the French said, "We were not fighting for the French, we were fighting for ourselves [to become] French citizens."[4] Moreover, educated African elites, who had aided their colonial overlords in enlisting local peoples to fight, did so in the belief that they would be rewarded with citizenship and new political possibilities after the war. When their hopes were frustrated, they soon became involved in anticolonial movements (see Chapter 24).

In East Asia and the Pacific, Japan joined the Allies on August 23, 1914, primarily to seize control of German territories in Asia. As one Japanese statesman

The Reality of War: Trench Warfare

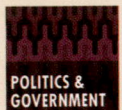

POLITICS & GOVERNMENT

THE ROMANTIC ILLUSION about the excitement and adventure of war that filled the minds of so many young men who marched off to battle quickly disintegrated after a short time in the trenches on the western front. This description of trench warfare is taken from the most famous novel that emerged from World War I, Erich Maria Remarque's *All Quiet on the Western Front*, published in 1929. Remarque had fought in the trenches in France.

Erich Maria Remarque, *All Quiet on the Western Front*

We wake up in the middle of the night. The earth booms. Heavy fire is falling on us. We crouch into corners. We distinguish shells of every calibre.

Each man lays hold of his things and looks again every minute to reassure himself that they are still there. The dugout heaves, the night roars and flashes. We look at each other in the momentary flashes of light, and with pale faces and pressed lips shake our heads.

Every man is aware of the heavy shells tearing down the parapet, rooting up the embankment and demolishing the upper layers of concrete…. Already by morning a few of the recruits are green and vomiting. They are too inexperienced….

The bombardment does not diminish. It is falling in the rear too. As far as one can see it spouts fountains of mud and iron. A wide belt is being raked….

Our trench is almost gone. At many places it is only eighteen inches high; it is broken by holes, and craters, and mountains of earth. A shell lands square in front of our post. At once it is dark. We are buried and must dig ourselves out….

Towards morning, while it is still dark, there is some excitement. Through the entrance rushes in a swarm of fleeing rats that try to storm the walls. Torches light up the confusion. Everyone yells and curses and slaughters. The madness and despair of many hours unloads itself in this outburst. Faces are distorted, arms strike out, the beasts scream; we just stop in time to avoid attacking one another….

Suddenly it howls and flashes terrifically, the dugout cracks in all its joints under a direct hit, fortunately only a light one that the concrete blocks are able to withstand. It rings metallically; the walls reel; rifles, helmets, earth, mud, and dust fly everywhere. Sulfur fumes pour in…. The recruit starts to rave again and two others follow suit. One jumps up and rushes out, we have trouble with the other two. I start after the one who escapes and wonder whether to shoot him in the leg—then it shrieks again; I fling myself down and when I stand up the wall of the trench is plastered with smoking splinters, lumps of flesh, and bits of uniform. I scramble back.

The first recruit seems actually to have gone insane. He butts his head against the wall like a goat. We must try tonight to take him to the rear. Meanwhile we bind him, but so that in case of attack he can be released.

Suddenly the nearer explosions cease. The shelling continues but it has lifted and falls behind us; our trench is free. We seize the hand grenades, pitch them out in front of the dugout, and jump after them. The bombardment has stopped and a heavy barrage now falls behind us. The attack has come.

No one would believe that in this howling waste there could still be men; but steel helmets now appear on all sides out of the trench, and fifty yards from us a machine gun is already in position and barking.

The wire entanglements are torn to pieces. Yet they offer some obstacle. We see the storm troops coming. Our artillery opens fire. Machine guns rattle, rifles crack. The charge works its way across….

We recognize the distorted faces, the smooth helmets: they are French. They have already suffered heavily when they reach the remnants of the barbed-wire entanglements. A whole line has gone down before our machine guns; then we have a lot of stoppages and they come nearer.

I see one of them, his face upturned, fall into a wire cradle. His body collapses, his hands remain suspended as though he were praying. Then his body drops clean away and only his hands with the stumps of his arms, shot off, now hang in the wire.

 What is causing the "madness and despair" Remarque describes in the trenches? Why does the recruit in this scene apparently go insane?

declared, the war in Europe was "divine aid … for the development of the destiny of Japan."[5] The Japanese took possession of German territories in China, as well as the German-occupied islands in the Pacific. New Zealand and Australia quickly joined the Japanese in conquering the German-held parts of New Guinea.

ENTRY OF THE UNITED STATES Most important to the Allied cause was the entry of the United States into the war. The impetus for American involvement grew out of the naval conflict between Germany and Great Britain. Britain used its superior naval power to maximum effect by imposing a naval blockade on Germany. Germany retaliated with a

Paths of Glory (1957)

Paths of Glory, directed by Stanley Kubrick, is a powerful antiwar film made in 1957 and based on the novel with the same name by Humphrey Cobb. Set in France in 1916, the film deals with the time during World War I when the western front had become bogged down in brutal trench warfare. The novel was based loosely on a true story of five French soldiers who were executed for mutiny. In the film, General George Broulard (Adolphe Menjou) of the French General Staff suggests to his subordinate, General Mireau (George Macready), that he launch what would amount to a suicidal attack on the well-defended Ant Hill. Mireau refuses until Broulard mentions the possibility of a promotion, at which point Mireau abruptly changes his mind and accepts the challenge. He walks through the trenches preparing his men with a stock question: "Hello there, soldier, are you ready to kill more Germans?" Mireau persuades Colonel Dax (Kirk Douglas) to mount the attack, despite Dax's protest that it will be a disaster. Dax proves to be right. None of the French soldiers reach the German lines, and one-third of the troops are not even able to leave their trenches because of enemy fire.

To avoid blame for the failure, General Mireau accuses his men of cowardice, and three of them (one from each company, chosen in purely arbitrary fashion) are brought before a hastily arranged court-martial. Dax defends his men but to no avail. The decision has already been made, and the three men are shot in front of the assembled troops. As General Broulard cynically comments, "One way to maintain discipline is to shoot a man now and then." After the execution, when General Broulard offers Dax a promotion, Dax responds, "Would you like me to suggest what you can do with that promotion?" Replies Broulard, "You're an idealist; I pity you." But Dax has the last word: "I pity you for not seeing the wrongs you have done." The film ends with the troops being ordered back to the front.

The film realistically portrays the horrors of trench warfare in World War I—the senseless and suicidal attacks through no-man's land against well-entrenched machine-gun batteries. The film is also scathing in its portrayal of military leaders. The generals are shown drinking cognac in the palaces they requisitioned for their headquarters while the troops live in the mud and filth of the trenches. Both generals are portrayed as arrogant, ego-driven individuals who think nothing of the slaughter of their men in battle. The men condemned to die for cowardice are scapegoats sacrificed to cover up the mistakes of their superior officers, who are determined to pursue "paths of glory" to advance themselves. The film's portrayal of the military executions was not accurate, however. The French army did not choose individuals at random for punishment, although it did execute some soldiers on charges of cowardice, as did the armies of the other belligerents.

This realistic indictment of war and the military elites offended some countries. French authorities saw it as an insult to the honor of the army and did not allow it to be shown in France until 1975. The military regime of Francisco Franco in Spain also banned the film for its antimilitary content. Kubrick himself went on to make two other antiwar films, capturing the Vietnam War in *Full Metal Jacket* and the Cold War in *Dr. Strangelove*.

United Artists/The Kobal Collection/Picture Desk

Colonel Dax (Kirk Douglas) begins to lead his men out of the trenches to attack Ant Hill.

counter-blockade enforced by submarine warfare. Strong American protests over the German sinking of passenger liners, especially the British ship *Lusitania* on May 7, 1915, when more than a hundred Americans lost their lives, forced the German government to suspend unrestricted submarine warfare in September 1915 to avoid further antagonizing the Americans.

In January 1917, however, eager to break the deadlock in the war, the Germans decided on another military gamble by returning to unrestricted submarine warfare. German naval officers convinced Emperor William II that the use of unrestricted submarine warfare could starve the British into submission within five months, before the Americans could act. The return to unrestricted submarine warfare brought the

POLITICS & GOVERNMENT

COMPARATIVE ILLUSTRATION

Soldiers from Around the World.
Although World War I began in Europe, it soon became a global conflict fought in different areas of the world and with soldiers from all parts of the globe. France, especially, recruited troops from its African colonies to fight in Europe. Shown in the photograph at the top are French Senegalese troops arriving in France in 1915; they would later fight in the Marne campaign on the western front. About 80,000 Africans were killed or injured in Europe. The photo at the bottom shows a group of German soldiers in their machine-gun nest on the western front.

Q *What do these photographs reveal about the nature of World War I and the role of African troops in the conflict?*

United States into the war on April 6, 1917. Although American troops did not arrive in Europe in large numbers until 1918, the entry of the United States into the war in 1917 gave the Allied Powers a psychological boost when they needed it.

The year 1917 had not been a good year for them. Allied offensives on the western front were disastrously defeated. The Italian armies were smashed in October, and in November a revolution in Russia (see "The Russian Revolution" later in this chapter) led to Russia's withdrawal from the war and left Germany free to concentrate entirely on the western front. The cause of the Central Powers looked favorable, although war weariness in the Ottoman Empire, Bulgaria, Austria-Hungary, and Germany was beginning to take its toll. The home front was rapidly becoming a cause for as much concern as the war front.

A New Kind of Warfare

By the end of 1915, airplanes appeared on the battlefront. The planes were first used to spot the enemy's position, but soon they began to attack ground targets, especially enemy communications. Fights for control of the air occurred and increased over time. At first, pilots fired at each other with handheld pistols, but later machine guns were mounted on the noses of planes, which made the skies considerably more dangerous.

The Germans also used their giant airships—the zeppelins (ZEP-puh-lins)—to bomb London and eastern England. This caused little damage but frightened many people. Germany's enemies, however, soon found that zeppelins, which were filled with hydrogen gas, quickly became raging infernos when hit by antiaircraft guns.

TANKS Tanks were also introduced to the battlefields of Europe in 1916. The first tank—a British model—used caterpillar tracks, which enabled it to move across rough terrain. Armed with mounted guns, tanks could attack enemy machine-gun positions as well as enemy infantry. But the first tanks were not very effective, and it was not until 1918, with the introduction of the British Mark V model, that tanks had more powerful engines and greater maneuverability. They could now be used in large numbers, and coordinated with infantry and artillery, they became effective instruments in pushing back the retreating German army.

The tank came too late to have a great effect on the outcome of World War I, but the lesson was not lost on those who realized the tank's potential for creating a whole new kind of warfare. In World War II (see Chapter 25), lightning attacks that depended on tank columns and massive air power enabled armies to cut quickly across battle lines and encircle entire enemy armies. It was a far cry from the trench warfare of World War I.

The Home Front: The Impact of Total War

The prolongation of World War I made it a **total war** that affected the lives of all citizens, however remote they might be from the battlefields. The need to organize masses of men and matériel for years of combat (Germany alone had 5.5 million men in active units in 1916) led to increased centralization of government powers, economic regimentation, and manipulation of public opinion to keep the war effort going.

POLITICAL CENTRALIZATION AND ECONOMIC REGIMENTATION Because the war was expected to be short, little thought had been given to economic considerations or long-term wartime needs. Governments had to respond quickly, however, when the war machines failed to achieve their knockout blows and made ever-greater demands for men and matériel. To meet these needs, governments expanded their powers. Countries drafted tens of millions of young men for that elusive breakthrough to victory.

Throughout Europe, wartime governments expanded their powers over their economies. Free market capitalistic systems were temporarily shelved as governments experimented with price, wage, and rent controls; rationed food supplies and materials; and nationalized transportation systems and industries. In effect, to mobilize all national resources for the war effort, European nations moved toward planned economies directed by government agencies. Under total war mobilization, the distinction between soldiers at war and civilians at home was narrowed. In the view of political leaders, all citizens constituted a national army dedicated to victory. As the American president Woodrow Wilson expressed it, the men and women "who remain to till the soil and man the factories are no less a part of the army than the men beneath the battle flags."

PUBLIC ORDER AND PUBLIC OPINION As the Great War dragged on and casualties mounted, the patriotic enthusiasm that had marked the early stages of the conflict waned. By 1916, there were numerous signs that civilian morale was beginning to crack under the pressure of total war. War governments, however, fought back against the growing opposition to the war. Authoritarian regimes, such as those of Germany, Russia, and Austria-Hungary, had always relied on force to subdue their populations, but under the pressures of the war, even parliamentary regimes resorted to an expansion of police powers to stifle internal dissent. At the very beginning of the war, the British Parliament passed the Defense of the Realm Act (DORA), which allowed the public authorities to arrest dissenters as traitors. Newspapers were censored, and sometimes their publication was even suspended. In 1917, government authorities in France began to suppress basic civil liberties.

Wartime governments made active use of propaganda to arouse enthusiasm for the war. At first, public officials needed to do little to achieve this goal. The British and French, for example, exaggerated German atrocities in Belgium and found that their citizens were only too willing to believe these accounts. But as the war dragged on and morale sagged, governments were forced to devise new techniques for stimulating enthusiasm. In one British recruiting poster, for example, a small daughter asked her father, "Daddy, what did YOU do in the Great War?" while her younger brother played with toy soldiers and cannons.

THE SOCIAL IMPACT OF TOTAL WAR Total war had a significant impact on European society, most visibly by bringing an end to unemployment. The withdrawal of millions of men from the labor market to fight, combined with the heightened demand for wartime products, led to jobs for everyone able to work.

The cause of labor also benefited from the war. To ensure that labor problems would not disrupt production, war governments in Britain, France, and Germany for the first time

British Recruiting Poster. As the conflict persisted month after month, governments resorted to active propaganda campaigns to generate enthusiasm for the war. In this British recruiting poster, the government encourages men to "enlist now" in order to preserve their country. By 1916, the British were forced to adopt compulsory military service.

Women in the Factories

FAMILY & SOCIETY

DURING WORLD WAR I, women were called on to assume new job responsibilities, including factory work. In this selection, Naomi Loughnan, a young, upper-middle-class woman, describes the experiences in a munitions plant that considerably broadened her perspective on life.

Naomi Loughnan, "Munition Work"

We little thought when we first put on our overalls and caps and enlisted in the Munition Army how much more inspiring our life was to be than we had dared to hope. Though we munition workers sacrifice our ease, we gain a life worth living. Our long days are filled with interest, and with the zest of doing work for our country in the grand cause of Freedom. As we handle the weapons of war we are learning great lessons of life. In the busy, noisy workshops we come face to face with every kind of class, and each one of these classes has something to learn from the others....

Engineering mankind is possessed of the unshakable opinion that no woman can have the mechanical sense. If one of us asks humbly why such and such an alteration is not made to prevent this or that drawback to a machine, she is told, with a superior smile, that a man has worked her machine before her for years, and that therefore if there were any improvement possible it would have been made. As long as we do exactly what we are told and do not attempt to use our brains, we give entire satisfaction, and are treated as nice, good children. Any swerving from the easy path prepared for us by our males arouses the most scathing contempt in their manly bosoms.... Women have, however, proved that their entry into the munition world has increased the output. Employers who forget things personal in their patriotic desire for large results are enthusiastic over the success of women in the shops. But their workmen have to be handled with the utmost tenderness and caution lest they should actually imagine it was being suggested that women could do their work equally well, given equal conditions of training—at least where muscle is not the driving force....

The coming of the mixed classes of women into the factory is slowly but surely having an educative effect upon the men. "Language" is almost unconsciously becoming subdued. There are fiery exceptions, who make our hair stand up on end under our close-fitting caps, but a sharp rebuke or a look of horror will often straighten out the most savage.... It is grievous to hear the girls also swearing and using disgusting language. Shoulder to shoulder with the children of the slums, the upper classes are having their eyes opened at last to the awful conditions among which their sisters have dwelt. Foul language, immorality, and many other evils are but the natural outcome of overcrowding and bitter poverty.... Sometimes disgust will overcome us, but we are learning with painful clarity that the fault is not theirs whose actions disgust us, but must be placed to the discredit of those other classes who have allowed the continued existence of conditions which generate the things from which we shrink appalled.

 What did Naomi Loughnan learn about men and lower-class women while working in the munitions factory? What did she learn about herself?

Source: From "Munition Work" by Naomi Loughnan in Gilbert Stone, ed., *Women War Workers* (London: George Harrap and Company, 1971), pp. 25, 35, 38.

---

allowed trade unions to participate in making important government decisions on labor matters. In return, unions cooperated on wage limits and production schedules. This opened the way to the collective bargaining practices that became more widespread after World War I and increased the prestige of trade unions, enabling them to attract more members.

World War I also created new roles for women. With so many men off fighting at the front, women were called on to assume jobs and responsibilities that had not been open to them before. Overall, 1,345,000 women in Britain obtained new jobs or replaced men during the war. Women were also now employed in jobs that had been considered "beyond the capacity of women." These included such occupations as chimney sweeps, truck drivers, farm laborers, and factory workers in heavy industry (see the box "Women in the Factories" above). In Germany, 38 percent of the workers in the Krupp (KROOP) armaments works in 1918 were women. Nevertheless, despite the noticeable increase in women's wages that resulted from government regulations, women's industrial wages were still not equal to men's wages by the end of the war.

Even worse, women's place in the workforce was far from secure. Both men and women seemed to assume that many of the new jobs for women were only temporary, an expectation quite evident in the British poem "War Girls," written in 1916:

> There's the girl who clips your ticket for the train,
> And the girl who speeds the lift from floor to floor,
> There's the girl who does a milk-round in the rain,
> And the girl who calls for orders at your door.
> Strong, sensible, and fit,
> They're out to show their grit,
> And tackle jobs with energy and knack.
> No longer caged and penned up,
> They're going to keep their end up
> Till the khaki soldier boys come marching back.[6]

At the end of the war, governments moved quickly to remove women from the jobs they had encouraged them to take earlier. By 1919, there were 650,000 unemployed women in Britain, and wages for women who were still employed were lowered. The work benefits for women from World War I seemed to be short-lived as demobilized men returned to the job market.

Nevertheless, in some countries, the role played by women in the wartime economies did have a positive impact on the women's movement for social and political emancipation. The most obvious gain was the right to vote, given to women in Germany and Austria immediately after the war (in Britain a few months earlier). Contemporary media, however, tended to focus on the more noticeable yet in some ways more superficial social emancipation of upper- and middle-class women. In ever-larger numbers, these young women took jobs, had their own apartments, and showed their new independence by smoking in public and wearing shorter dresses, cosmetics, and new hairstyles.

War and Revolution

 FOCUS QUESTIONS: What were the causes of the Russian Revolution of 1917, and why did the Bolsheviks prevail in the civil war and gain control of Russia? What were the objectives of the chief participants at the Paris Peace Conference of 1919, and how closely did the final settlement reflect these objectives?

By 1917, total war was creating serious domestic turmoil in all of the European belligerent states. Only one, however, experienced the kind of complete collapse that others were predicting might happen throughout Europe. Out of Russia's collapse came the Russian Revolution.

The Russian Revolution

After the Revolution of 1905 had failed to bring any substantial changes to Russia, Tsar Nicholas II relied on the army and bureaucracy to uphold his regime. But World War I magnified Russia's problems and severely challenged the tsarist government. The tsar, possessed of a strong sense of moral duty to his country, was the only European monarch to take personal charge of the armed forces, despite a lack of training for such an awesome responsibility. Russian industry was unable to produce the weapons needed for the army. Ill-led and ill-armed, Russian armies suffered incredible losses. Between 1914 and 1916, 2 million soldiers were killed while another 4 to 6 million were wounded or captured.

The tsarist government was unprepared for the tasks that it faced in 1914. The surge of patriotic enthusiasm that greeted the outbreak of war was soon dissipated by a government that distrusted its own people. Although the middle classes and liberal aristocrats still hoped for a constitutional monarchy, they were sullen over the tsar's revocation of the political concessions made during the Revolution of 1905. Peasant discontent flourished as conditions worsened. The concentration of Russian industry in a few large cities made workers' frustrations all the more evident and dangerous. In the meantime, Nicholas was increasingly insulated from events by his wife, Alexandra.

Tsarina Alexandra, a well-educated German-born princess, had fallen under the influence of Rasputin (rass-PYOO-tin), a Siberian peasant whom the tsarina regarded as a holy man

because he alone seemed able to stop the bleeding of her hemophiliac son, Alexis. Rasputin's influence made him a power behind the throne, and he did not hesitate to interfere in government affairs. As the leadership at the top experienced a series of military and economic disasters, the middle class, aristocrats, peasants, soldiers, and workers grew more and more disenchanted with the tsarist regime. Even conservative aristocrats who supported the monarchy felt the need to do something to reverse the deteriorating situation. For a start, they assassinated Rasputin in December 1916. By then it was too late to save the monarchy, and its fall came quickly at the beginning of March 1917.

THE MARCH REVOLUTION At the beginning of March, a series of strikes broke out in the capital city of Petrograd (formerly Saint Petersburg). Here the actions of working-class women helped change the course of Russian history. Weeks earlier, the government had introduced bread rationing in the capital city after the price of bread had skyrocketed. Many of the women who stood in the lines waiting for bread were also factory workers who had put in twelve-hour days. The Russian government soon became aware of the volatile situation in the capital. One police report stated:

> Mothers of families, exhausted by endless standing in line at stores, distraught over their half-starving and sick children, are today perhaps closer to revolution than [the liberal opposition leaders] and of course they are a great deal more dangerous because they are the combustible material for which only a single spark is needed to burst into flame.[7]

On March 8, a day celebrated since 1910 as International Women's Day, about ten thousand Petrograd women marched in parts of the city chanting "Peace and Bread" and "Down with Autocracy." Soon the women were joined by other workers, and together they called for a general strike that succeeded in shutting down all the factories in the city two days later. The tsarina wrote to Nicholas at the battlefront that "this is a hooligan movement. If the weather were very cold they would all probably stay at home." Believing his wife, Nicholas responded to his military leaders, "I command you tomorrow to stop the disorders in the capital, which are unacceptable in the difficult time of war with Germany and Austria."[8] The troops were ordered to disperse the crowds, shooting them if necessary. Initially, the troops cooperated, but soon significant numbers of the soldiers joined the demonstrators. The Duma (DOO-muh) or legislative body, which the tsar had tried to dissolve, met anyway and on March 12 declared that it was assuming governmental responsibility. It established a provisional government on March 15; the tsar abdicated the same day.

The Provisional Government, which came to be led in July by Alexander Kerensky (kuh-REN-skee) (1881–1970), decided to carry on the war to preserve Russia's honor—a major blunder because it satisfied neither the workers nor the peasants, who above all wanted an end to the war. The Provisional Government also faced another authority, the **soviets**, or councils of workers' and soldiers' deputies. The Petrograd soviet had been formed in March 1917; at the same time, soviets sprang up spontaneously in army units, factory towns, and rural areas. The soviets represented the more radical interests of the lower classes and were largely composed of socialists of various kinds. Among them was the Marxist Social Democratic Party, which had formed in 1898 but divided in 1903 into two factions known as the Mensheviks (MENS-shuh-viks) and the Bolsheviks (BOHL-shuh-viks). The Mensheviks wanted the Social Democrats to be a mass electoral socialist party based on a Western model.

LENIN AND THE BOLSHEVIK REVOLUTION The Bolsheviks were a small faction of Russian Social Democrats who had come under the leadership of Vladimir Ulianov (VLAD-ih-meer ool-YA-nuf), known to the world as Lenin (LEH-nin) (1870–1924). Trained as a lawyer, he had earlier turned into a dedicated enemy of tsarist Russia when his older brother was executed for planning to assassinate the tsar. Arrested for his revolutionary activity, Lenin was shipped to Siberia. After his release, he chose to go into exile in Switzerland and eventually assumed the leadership of the Bolshevik wing of the Russian Social Democratic Party. Under Lenin's direction, the Bolsheviks became a party dedicated to violent revolution. He believed that only a revolution could destroy the capitalist system and that a "vanguard" of activists must form a small party of well-disciplined professional revolutionaries to accomplish the task. Between 1900 and 1917, Lenin spent most of his time in Switzerland. When the Provisional Government was formed in March 1917, he believed that an opportunity for the Bolsheviks to seize power had come. Just weeks later, with the connivance of the German High Command, who hoped to create disorder in Russia, Lenin was shipped to Russia in a sealed train by way of Finland.

Lenin's arrival in Russia on April 3 opened a new stage of the Russian Revolution. Lenin maintained that the soviets of soldiers, workers, and peasants were ready-made instruments of power. The Bolsheviks must work toward gaining control of these groups and then use them to overthrow the Provisional Government (see the box "Solider and Peasant Voices" on p. 677). At the same time, Bolshevik propaganda must seek mass support through promises geared to the needs of the people: an end to the war, redistribution of all land to the peasants, the transfer of factories and industries from capitalists to committees of workers, and the relegation of government power from the Provisional Government to the soviets. Three simple slogans summed up the Bolshevik program: "Peace, Land, Bread," "Worker Control of Production," and "All Power to the Soviets."

By the end of October, the Bolsheviks had achieved a slight majority in the Petrograd and Moscow soviets. The number of party members had also grown, from 50,000 to 240,000. With Leon Trotsky (TRAHT-skee) (1877–1940), a fervid revolutionary, as chairman of the Petrograd soviet, Lenin and the Bolsheviks were in a position to seize power in the name of the soviets. During the night of November 6, pro-soviet and pro-Bolshevik forces took control of Petrograd; the Provisional Government quickly collapsed, with little bloodshed. The following night, the all-Russian Congress of Soviets, representing local soviets from all over the country, affirmed the transfer of power. At the second session, the night of November 8, Lenin

Lenin and Trotsky. Vladimir Lenin and Leon Trotsky were important figures in the Bolsheviks' successful seizure of power in Russia. On the left, Lenin is seen addressing a rally in Moscow in 1917. On the right, Trotsky, who became commissar of war in the new regime, is shown haranguing his troops.

Soldier and Peasant Voices

POLITICS & GOVERNMENT

IN 1917, RUSSIA EXPERIENCED a cataclysmic upheaval as two revolutions overthrew first the tsarist regime and then the Provisional Government that replaced it. Peasants, workers, and soldiers poured out their thoughts and feelings on these events, some of them supporting the Bolsheviks and others denouncing the Bolsheviks for betraying their socialist revolution. These selections are taken from two letters, the first from a soldier and the second from a peasant. Both are addressed to Bolshevik leaders.

Letter from a Soldier in Leningrad to Lenin, January 6, 1918

Bastard! What the hell are you doing? How long are you going to keep on degrading the Russian people? After all, it's because of you they killed the former minister ... and so many other innocent victims. Because of you, they might kill even other former ministers belonging to the [Socialist Revolutionary] party because you call them counterrevolutionaries and even monarchists.... And you, you Bolshevik gang leader hired either by Nicholas II or by Wilhelm II, are waging this pogrom propaganda against men who may have done time with you in exile.

Scoundrel! A curse on you from the politically conscious Russian proletariat, the conscious ones and not the kind who are following you—that is, the Red Guards, the tally clerks, who, when they are called to military service, all hide at the factories and now are killing ... practically their own father, the way the soldiers did in 1905 when they killed their own, or the way the police and gendarmes did in [1917]. That's who they're more like. They're not pursuing the ideas of socialism because they don't understand them (if they did they wouldn't act this way) but because they get paid a good salary both at the factory and in the Red Guards. But not all the workers are like that—there are very politically aware ones and the soldiers—again not all of them—are like that but only former policemen, constables, gendarmes and the very ignorant ones who under the old regime tramped with hay on one foot and straw on the other because they couldn't tell their right foot from their left and they are pursuing not the ideas of socialism that you advocate but to be able to lie on their cots in the barracks and do absolutely nothing not even to be asked to sweep the floor, which is already piled with several inches of filth. And so the entire proletariat of Russia is following you, but count fewer than are against you, but they are only physically or rather

technically stronger than the majority, and that is what you're abusing when you disbanded the Constituent Assembly the way Nicholas II disbanded the Duma. You point out that counterrevolutionaries gathered there. You lie, scoundrel, there wasn't a single counterrevolutionary and if there was then it was you, the Bolsheviks, which you proved by your actions when you encroached on the gains of the revolution: you are shutting down newspapers, even socialist ones, arresting socialists, committing violence and deceiving the people; you promised loads but did none of it.

Letter from a Peasant to the Bolshevik Leaders, January 10, 1918

TO YOU!

Rulers, plunderers, rapists, destroyers, usurpers, oppressors of Mother Russia, citizens Lenin, Trotsky, ... and Co. [leaders of the Bolshevik party]:

Allow me to ask you how long you are going to go on degrading Russia's millions, its tormented and exhausted people. Instead of peace, you signed an armistice with the enemy, and this gave our opponent a painful advantage, and you declared war on Russia. You moved the troops you had tricked to the Russian-Russian front and started a fratricidal war. Your mercenary Red Guards are looting, murdering, and raping everywhere they go. A fire has consumed all our dear Mother Russia. Rail transport is idle, as are the plants and factories; the entire population has woken up to find itself in the most pathetic situation, without bread or kerosene or any of the other essentials, unclothed or unshod in unheated houses. In short: hungry and cold.... You have strangled the entire press, and freedom with it, you have wiped out the best freedom fighters, you have destroyed all Russia. Think it over, you butchers, you hirelings of the Kaiser [William II]. Isn't your turn about up, too? For all you are doing, we, politically aware Great Russians, are sending you butchers, you hirelings of the Kaiser, our curse. May you be damned, you accursed one, you bloodthirsty butchers, you hirelings of the Kaiser—don't think you're in the clear, because the Russian people will sober up and that will be the end of you. I'm writing in red ink to show that you are bloodthirsty.... I'm writing these curses, a great Russian native of Orel Province, peasant of Mtsensk Uezd.

What arguments do both of the writers of these letters use against Lenin and the Bolsheviks? Why do they feel so betrayed by the Bolsheviks?

Source: From Mark D. Steinberg, *Voices of Revolution, 1917* (New Haven: Conn.: Yale University Press, 2001), pp. 291 and 302–303.

announced the new Soviet government, the Council of People's Commissars, with himself as its head.

But the Bolsheviks, soon renamed the Communists, still had a long way to go. For one thing, Lenin had promised peace, and that, he realized, was not an easy task because of

the humiliating losses of Russian territory that it would entail. There was no real choice, however. On March 3, 1918, Lenin signed the Treaty of Brest-Litovsk (BREST-li-TUFFSK) with Germany and gave up eastern Poland, Ukraine, and the Baltic provinces. To his critics, Lenin argued that it made no difference because the spread of socialist revolution throughout Europe would make the treaty largely irrelevant. In any case, he had promised peace to the Russian people, but real peace did not come, for the country soon sank into civil war.

CIVIL WAR There was great opposition to the new communist regime, not only from groups loyal to the tsar but also from bourgeois and aristocratic liberals and anti-Leninist socialists. In addition, thousands of Allied troops were eventually sent to different parts of Russia in the hope of bringing Russia back into the war.

Between 1918 and 1921, the Red (Bolshevik) Army was forced to fight on many fronts. The first serious threat to the Bolsheviks came from Siberia, where White (anti-Bolshevik) forces attacked westward and advanced almost to the Volga River before being stopped. Attacks also came from the Ukrainians in the southeast and from the Baltic regions. In mid-1919, White forces swept through Ukraine and advanced almost to Moscow. By 1920, the major White forces had been defeated and Ukraine retaken. The next year, the communist regime regained control over the independent nationalist governments in the Caucasus: Georgia, Russian Armenia, and Azerbaijan (az-ur-by-JAHN).

The royal family was yet another victim of the civil war. After the tsar had abdicated, he, his wife, and their five children had been taken into captivity. They were moved in August 1917 to Tobolsk in Siberia and in April 1918 to Ekaterinburg (i-kat-tuh-RIN-burk), a mining town in the Urals. On the night of July 16, members of the local soviet murdered the tsar and his family and burned their bodies in a nearby mine shaft.

How had Lenin and the Bolsheviks triumphed over what seemed at one time to be overwhelming forces? For one thing, the Red Army became a well-disciplined and formidable fighting force, largely due to the organizational genius of Leon Trotsky. As commissar of war, Trotsky reinstated the draft and insisted on rigid discipline; soldiers who deserted or refused to obey orders were summarily executed.

The disunity of the anti-communist forces seriously weakened their efforts. Political differences created distrust among the Whites and prevented them from cooperating effectively with each other. Some Whites insisted on restoring the tsarist regime, while others understood that only a more liberal democratic program had any chance of success. It was difficult enough to achieve military cooperation; political differences made it virtually impossible.

The Whites' inability to agree on a common goal was in sharp contrast to the Communists' single-minded sense of purpose. Inspired by their vision of a new socialist order, the Communists had the advantage of possessing the determination that comes from revolutionary fervor and revolutionary convictions.

The Communists also succeeded in translating their revolutionary faith into practical instruments of power. A policy of **war communism**, for example, was used to ensure regular supplies for the Red Army. War communism included the nationalization of banks and most industries, the forcible requisition of grain from peasants, and the centralization of state power under Bolshevik control. Another Bolshevik instrument was "revolutionary terror." A new Red secret police, known as the

CHRONOLOGY	The Russian Revolution
	1916
Murder of Rasputin	December
	1917
March of women in Petrograd	March 8
General strike in Petrograd	March 10
Establishment of Provisional Government	March 12
Tsar Nicholas II abdicates	March 15
Formation of Petrograd soviet	March
Lenin arrives in Russia	April 3
Bolsheviks gain majority in Petrograd soviet	October
Bolsheviks overthrow Provisional Government	November 6–7
	1918
Treaty of Brest-Litovsk	March 3
Murder of royal family	July 16
Civil war	1918–1921

Cheka (CHEK-uh), instituted the Red Terror, aimed at nothing less than the destruction of all opponents of the new regime. Finally, the intervention of foreign armies enabled the Communists to appeal to the powerful force of Russian patriotism. Although the Allied Powers had intervened initially in Russia to encourage the Russians to remain in the war, the end of the war on November 11, 1918, had made that purpose inconsequential. Nevertheless, Allied troops remained, and even more were sent, as Allied countries did not hide their anti-Bolshevik feelings. At one point, more than 100,000 foreign troops, mostly Japanese, British, American, and French, were stationed on Russian soil. This intervention by the Allies enabled the communist government to appeal to patriotic Russians to fight the attempts of foreigners to control their country.

By 1921, the Communists were in control of Russia. In the course of the civil war, the Bolshevik regime had also transformed Russia into a bureaucratically centralized state dominated by a single party. It was also a state that was largely hostile to the Allied Powers that had sought to assist the Bolsheviks' enemies in the civil war. To most historians, the Russian Revolution is unthinkable without the total war of World War I, for only the collapse of Russia made it possible for a radical minority like the Bolsheviks to seize the reins of power. In turn, the Russian Revolution had an impact on the course of World War I.

The Last Year of the War

For Germany, the withdrawal of the Russians from the war in March 1918 offered renewed hope for a favorable end to the war. The victory over Russia persuaded Erich von Ludendorff (LOO-dun-dorf) (1865–1937), who guided German military operations, and most German leaders to make one final military gamble—a grand offensive in the west to break the military stalemate. The German attack was launched in March and lasted into July, but an Allied counterattack, supported by the arrival of 140,000 fresh American troops, defeated the

Germans at the Second Battle of the Marne on July 18. Ludendorff's gamble had failed. With the arrival of 2 million more American troops on the European continent, Allied forces began to advance steadily toward Germany.

On September 29, 1918, General Ludendorff informed German leaders that the war was lost and demanded that the government sue for peace at once. When German officials discovered, however, that the Allies were unwilling to make peace with the autocratic imperial government, they instituted reforms to set up a liberal government. But these reforms came too late for the exhausted and angry German people. On November 3, naval units in Kiel (KEEL) mutinied, and within days, councils of workers and soldiers were forming throughout northern Germany and taking over the supervision of civilian and military administrations. William II capitulated to public pressure and abdicated on November 9, and the Socialists under Friedrich Ebert (FREED-rikh AY-bert) (1871–1925) announced the establishment of a republic. Two days later, on November 11, 1918, the new German government agreed to an armistice. The war was over.

THE CASUALTIES OF THE WAR World War I devastated European civilization. Between 8 and 9 million soldiers died on the battlefields; another 22 million were wounded. Many of those who survived later died from war injuries or lived on with missing arms or legs or other forms of mutilation. The birthrate in many European countries declined noticeably as a result of the death or maiming of so many young men.

Nor did the killing affect only soldiers. Untold numbers of civilians died from war injuries or starvation. In 1915, using the excuse of a rebellion by the Armenian minority and their supposed collaboration with the Russians, the Turkish government began systematically to kill Armenian men and expel women and children. Within seven months, 600,000 Armenians had been killed, and 500,000 had been deported. Of the latter,

400,000 died while marching through the deserts and swamps of Syria and Mesopotamia. By September 1915, an estimated one million Armenians were dead, the victims of genocide.

The Peace Settlement

In January 1919, the delegations of twenty-seven victorious Allied nations gathered in Paris to conclude a final settlement of the Great War. Over a period of years, the reasons for fighting World War I had been transformed from selfish national interests to idealistic principles.

PEACE AIMS No one expressed these principles better than U.S. President Woodrow Wilson. Wilson's proposals for a truly just and lasting peace included "open covenants of peace, openly arrived at" instead of secret diplomacy; the reduction of national armaments to a "point consistent with domestic safety"; and the self-determination of people so that "all well-defined national aspirations shall be accorded the utmost satisfaction." Wilson characterized World War I as a people's war waged against "absolutism and militarism," which could be eradicated only by creating democratic governments and a "general association of nations" that would guarantee the "political independence and territorial integrity to great and small states alike" (see Opposing Viewpoints "Three Voices of Peacemaking" on p. 680). As the spokesman for a new world order based on democracy and international cooperation, Wilson was enthusiastically cheered by many Europeans when he arrived in Europe for the peace conference, held at the palace of Versailles. Wilson's rhetoric on self-determination also inspired peoples in the colonial world, in Africa, Asia, and the Middle East, and was influential in developing anticolonial nationalist movements in these areas (see Chapter 24).

Wilson soon found, however, that more practical motives guided other states at the peace table. The secret treaties and agreements that had been made before the war could not be totally ignored, even if they did conflict with the principle of self-determination enunciated by Wilson. National interests also complicated the deliberations of the Paris Peace Conference. David Lloyd George (1863–1945), prime minister of Great Britain, had won a decisive electoral victory in December 1918 on a platform of making the Germans pay for this dreadful war.

France's approach to peace was determined primarily by considerations of national security. To Georges Clemenceau (ZHORZH kluh-mahn-SOH) (1841–1929), the feisty premier of France who had led his country to victory, the French people had borne the brunt of German aggression. They deserved revenge and security against future German encroachment.

Wilson, Clemenceau, and Lloyd George made the most important decisions at the Paris Peace Conference. Italy was considered one of the so-called Big Four powers but played a much less important role than the other three countries. Germany, of course, was not invited to attend, and Russia could not because of its civil war.

In view of the many conflicting demands at Versailles, it was inevitable that the Big Three would quarrel. Wilson was determined to create a "league of nations" to prevent future wars. Clemenceau and Lloyd George were equally determined to punish Germany. In the end, only compromise made it

CHRONOLOGY	World War I
	1914
Battle of Tannenberg	August 26–30
First Battle of the Marne	September 6–10
Battle of Masurian Lakes	September 15
	1915
Battle of Gallipoli begins	April 25
Italy declares war on Austria-Hungary	May 23
	1916
Battle of Verdun	February 21–December 18
	1917
United States enters the war	April 6
	1918
Last German offensive	March 21–July 18
Second Battle of the Marne	July 18
Allied counteroffensive	July 18–November 10
Armistice between Allies and Germany	November 11

OPPOSING ✕ VIEWPOINTS

Three Voices of Peacemaking

POLITICS & GOVERNMENT

WHEN THE ALLIED POWERS MET IN PARIS IN JANUARY 1919, it soon became apparent that the victors had different opinions on the kind of peace they expected. The first selection is a series of excerpts from the speeches of Woodrow Wilson in which the American president presented his idealistic goals for a peace based on justice and reconciliation.

The French leader, Georges Clemenceau, had a different vision. The French sought revenge and security. In the selection from his book *Grandeur and Misery of Victory*, Clemenceau revealed his fundamental dislike and distrust of Germany.

A third voice of peacemaking was heard in Paris in 1919, although not at the peace conference. W. E. B. Du Bois (doo BOYZ), an African American writer and activist, had organized the Pan-African Congress to meet in Paris during the Paris Peace Conference. The goal of the Pan-African Congress was to present a series of resolutions that promoted the cause of Africans and people of African descent. As can be seen in the selection presented here, the resolutions did not call for immediate independence for African nations.

Woodrow Wilson, Speeches

May 26, 1917

We are fighting for the liberty, the self-government, and the undictated development of all peoples, and every feature of the settlement that concludes this war must be conceived and executed for that purpose. Wrongs must first be righted and then adequate safeguards must be created to prevent their being committed again....

No people must be forced under sovereignty under which it does not wish to live. No territory must change hands except for the purpose of securing those who inhabit it a fair chance of life and liberty. No indemnities must be insisted on except those that constitute payment for manifest wrongs done. No readjustments of power must be made except such as will tend to secure the future peace of the world and the future welfare and happiness of its peoples.

And then the free peoples of the world must draw together in some common covenant, some genuine and practical cooperation that will in effect combine their force to secure peace and justice in the dealings of nations with one another.

April 6, 1918

We are ready, whenever the final reckoning is made, to be just to the German people, deal fairly with the German power, as with all others.... To propose anything but justice, even-handed and dispassionate justice, to Germany at any time, whatever the outcome of the war, would be to renounce and dishonor our own cause. For we ask nothing that we are not willing to accord.

January 3, 1919

Our task at Paris is to organize the friendship of the world, to see to it that all the moral forces that make for right and justice and liberty are united and are given a vital organization to which the peoples of the world will readily and gladly respond. In other words, our task is no less colossal than this, to set up a new international psychology, to have a new atmosphere.

Georges Clemenceau, *Grandeur and Misery of Victory*

For the catastrophe of 1914 the Germans are responsible. Only a professional liar would deny this....

What after all is this war, prepared, undertaken, and waged by the German people, who flung aside every scruple of conscience to let it loose, hoping for a peace of enslavement under the yoke of a militarism, destructive of all human dignity? It is simply the continuance, the recrudescence, of those never-ending acts of violence by which the first savage tribes carried out their depredations with all the resources of barbarism....

I have sometimes penetrated into the sacred cave of the Germanic cult, which is, as every one knows, the *Bierhaus* [beer hall]. A great aisle of massive humanity where there accumulate, amid the fumes of tobacco and beer, the popular rumblings of a nationalism upheld by the sonorous brasses blaring to the heavens the supreme voice of Germany, *Deutschland über alles! Germany above everything!* Men, women, and children, all petrified in reverence before the divine stoneware pot, brows furrowed with irrepressible power, eyes lost in a dream of infinity, mouths twisted by the intensity of willpower, drink in long draughts the celestial hope of vague expectations. These only remain to be realized presently when the chief marked out by Destiny shall have given the word. There you have the ultimate framework of an old but childish race.

Pan-African Congress

Resolved

That the Allied and Associated Powers establish a code of law for the international protection of the natives of Africa....

The Negroes of the world demand that hereafter the natives of Africa and the peoples of African descent be governed according to the following principles:

1. The Land: the land and its natural resources shall be held in trust for the natives and at all times they shall have effective ownership of as much land as they can profitably develop....

3. Labor: slavery and corporal punishment shall be abolished and forced labor except in punishment for crime....

5. The State: the natives of Africa must have the right to participate in the government as fast as their development permits, in conformity with the principle that the government exists for the natives, and not the natives for the government.

 How did the peacemaking aims of Wilson and Clemenceau differ? How did their different views affect the deliberations of the Paris Peace Conference and the nature of the final peace settlement? How and why did the views of the Pan-African Congress differ from those of Wilson and Clemenceau?

Sources: Excerpts from *The Public Papers of Woodrow Wilson: War and Peace*, edited by Ray Stannard Baker. Copyright 1925, 1953 by Edith Bolling Wilson. From Georges Clemenceau, *Grandeur and Misery of Victory* (New York: Harcourt, 1930), pp. 105, 107, 280. Excerpts from *Resolution from the Pan-African Congress*, Paris, 1919.

possible to achieve a peace settlement. Wilson's wish that the creation of an international peacekeeping organization be the first order of business was granted, and on January 25, 1919, the conference adopted the principle of the League of Nations. In return, Wilson agreed to make compromises on territorial arrangements to guarantee the establishment of the League, believing that a functioning League could later rectify bad arrangements. Clemenceau also compromised to obtain some guarantees for French security. He renounced France's desire for a separate Rhineland and instead accepted a defensive alliance with Great Britain and the United States. Both states pledged to help France if it were attacked by Germany.

THE TREATY OF VERSAILLES The final peace settlement consisted of five separate treaties with the defeated nations—Germany, Austria, Hungary, Bulgaria, and Turkey. The Treaty

The Treaty of Versailles. Shown at the left are the three most important decision makers at the Paris Peace Conference, Georges Clemenceau, Woodrow Wilson, and David Lloyd George, shortly after the signing of the Treaty of Versailles. The German reaction to what it considered a harsh and unfair peace treaty is captured on the cover of *Simplicissimus*, a German satirical magazine. A black man representing France is seen beating a German tied to a tree trunk while an Englishman looks on with a grin on his face.

of Versailles with Germany, signed on June 28, 1919, was by far the most important one. The Germans considered it a harsh peace and were particularly unhappy with Article 231, the so-called **War Guilt Clause**, which declared Germany (and Austria) responsible for starting the war and ordered Germany to pay **reparations** for all the damage to which the Allied governments and their people were subjected as a result of the war "imposed upon them by the aggression of Germany and her allies."

The military and territorial provisions of the treaty also rankled Germans. Germany had to reduce its army to 100,000 men, cut back its navy, and eliminate its air force. German territorial losses included the return of Alsace and Lorraine to France and sections of Prussia to the new Polish state (see Map 23.3). German land west and as far as 30 miles east of the Rhine was established as a demilitarized zone and stripped of all armaments or fortifications to serve as a barrier to any future German military moves westward against France.

Outraged by the "dictated peace," the new German government complained but accepted the treaty.

THE OTHER PEACE TREATIES The separate peace treaties made with the other Central Powers extensively redrew the map of eastern Europe. Many of these changes merely ratified what the war had already accomplished. Both the German and Russian empires lost considerable territory in eastern Europe, and the Austro-Hungarian Empire disappeared altogether. New nation-states emerged from the lands of these three empires: Finland, Latvia, Estonia, Lithuania, Poland, Czechoslovakia, Austria, and Hungary. Territorial rearrangements were also made in the Balkans. Romania acquired land from Russia, Hungary, and Bulgaria. Serbia formed the nucleus of a new southern Slavic kingdom, later called Yugoslavia, which united Serbs, Croats, and Slovenes under a single monarch.

Although the Paris Peace Conference was supposedly guided by the principle of self-determination, the mixtures of

© 2016 Cengage Learning

Lost immediately after World War I

- By Russia
- By Germany
- By Ottoman Empire
- By Bulgaria
- By Austria-Hungary

MAP 23.3 Territorial Changes in Europe and the Middle East After World War I. The victorious Allies met in Paris to determine the shape and nature of postwar Europe. At the urging of U.S. President Woodrow Wilson, many nationalist aspirations of former imperial subjects were realized with the creation of several new countries from the prewar territory of Austria-Hungary, Germany, Russia, and the Ottoman Empire.

Q *What new countries emerged in Europe and the Middle East?*

peoples in eastern Europe made it impossible to draw boundaries along neat ethnic lines. As a result of compromises, virtually every eastern European state was left with a minorities problem that could lead to future conflicts. Germans in Poland; Hungarians, Poles, and Germans in Czechoslovakia; Hungarians in Romania; and the combination of Serbs, Croats, Slovenes, Macedonians, and Albanians in Yugoslavia all became sources of later conflict.

Yet another centuries-old entity, the Ottoman Empire, was dismembered by the peace settlement after the war. To gain Arab support against the Ottoman Turks during the war, the Western Allies had promised to recognize the independence of Arab states in the Middle Eastern lands of the Ottoman Empire. But the imperialist habits of Western nations died hard. After the war, France was given control of Lebanon and Syria, while Britain received Iraq and Palestine (including Trans-Jordan). Officially, both acquisitions were called **mandates**. Because Woodrow Wilson had opposed the outright annexation of colonial territories by the Allies, the peace settlement had created a system whereby a nation officially administered a territory on behalf of the League of Nations. The invention of mandates could not hide the fact that the principle of national self-determination at the Paris Peace Conference was largely for Europeans.

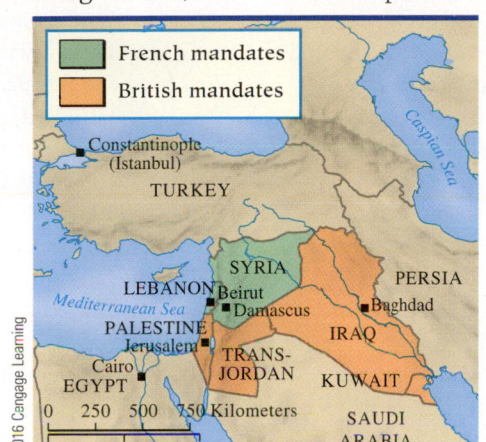

The Middle East in 1919

Map legend:
- French mandates
- British mandates

An Uncertain Peace

 FOCUS QUESTION: What was the aftermath of World War I, and what problems did Europe and the United States face in the 1920s?

Four years of devastating war had left many Europeans with a profound sense of despair and disillusionment. The Great War indicated to many people that something was dreadfully wrong with Western values. In *The Decline of the West*, the German writer Oswald Spengler (1880–1936) reflected this disillusionment when he emphasized the decadence of Western civilization and posited its collapse (see the box "The Decline of European Civilization" on p. 684).

The Impact of World War I

The enormous suffering and the deaths of almost 10 million people shook traditional society to its foundations and undermined the whole idea of progress. New propaganda techniques had manipulated entire populations into maintaining involvement in senseless slaughter. How did Europeans deal with such losses? In France, for example, probably two-thirds of the population was in mourning over the deaths of these young people.

An immediate response was the erection of war memorials accompanied by ceremonies to honor the dead. Battlefields also became significant commemorative sites with memorial parks, large monuments, and massive cemeteries, including ossuaries, vaults where the bones of thousands of unidentified soldiers were interred. Virtually all belligerent countries adopted national ceremonies for the burial of a symbolic "unknown soldier," a telling reminder of the brutality of World War I. Moreover, businesses, schools, universities, and other corporate bodies all set up their own war memorials.

It is impossible to calculate the social impact of the mourning for the lost soldiers. One French mother explained, "No matter how proud as Frenchwomen we poor mothers may be of our sons, we nevertheless carry wounds in our hearts that nothing can heal. It is strongly contrary to nature for our children to depart before us."[9] Another Frenchman wrote, "Why should the old people remain alive, when the children who might have initiated the most beautiful era in French history march off to the sacrifice?"[10]

World War I created a "lost generation" of war veterans who had become inured to violence; indeed, in the course of the war, brutality became a way of life and a social reality. As one Frenchman recounted, "Not only did war make us dead, impotent or blind. In the midst of beautiful actions, of sacrifice and self-abnegation, it also awoke in us … ancient instincts of cruelty and barbarity. At times, I, who have never punched anyone, who loathes disorder and brutality, took pleasure in killing."[11] After the war, some veterans became pacifists, but for many veterans, the violence of the war seemed to justify the use of violence in the new political movements of the 1920s and 1930s (see "Retreat from Democracy: Dictatorial Regimes" in Chapter 25). These men were fiercely nationalistic and eager to restore the national interests they felt had been betrayed in the peace treaties.

The Search for Security

The peace settlement at the end of World War I had tried to fulfill the nineteenth-century dream of nationalism by creating secure boundaries and new states. From its inception, however, this peace settlement had left nations unhappy and eager to revise it.

U.S. President Woodrow Wilson had recognized that the peace treaties contained unwise provisions that could serve as new causes for conflicts and had placed many of his hopes for the future in the League of Nations. The League, however, was not particularly effective in maintaining the peace. The failure of the United States to join the League in a backlash of isolationist sentiment undermined its effectiveness from the beginning. Moreover, the League could use only economic sanctions to halt aggression.

The Decline of European Civilization

THE DUTCH HISTORIAN JOHAN HUIZINGA was one of many European intellectuals who questioned the very survival of European civilization as a result of the crises that ensued in the aftermath of World War I. In his book *In the Shadow of Tomorrow*, written in 1936, Huizinga lamented the decline of civilization in his own age, in large part due to the impact of World War I.

Johan Huizinga, *In the Shadow of Tomorrow*

We are living in a demented world. And we know it. It would not come as a surprise to anyone if tomorrow the madness gave way to a frenzy which would leave our poor Europe in a state of distracted stupor, with engines still turning and flags streaming in the breeze, but with the spirit gone.

Everywhere there are doubts as to the solidity of our social structure, vague fears of the imminent future, a feeling that our civilization is on the way to ruin. They are not merely the shapeless anxieties which beset us in the small hours of the night when the flame of life burns low. They are considered expectations founded on observation and judgment of an overwhelming multitude of facts. How to avoid the recognition that almost all things which once seemed sacred and immutable have now become unsettled, truth and humanity, justice and reason? We see forms of government no longer capable of functioning, production systems on the verge of collapse, social forces gone wild with power. The roaring engine of this tremendous time seems to be heading for a breakdown....

The first ten years of this century have known little if anything in the way of fears and apprehensions regarding the future of our civilization. Friction and threats, shocks and dangers, there were then as ever. But except for the revolutionary menace which Marxism had hung over the world, they did not appear as evils threatening mankind with ruin....

Today, however, the sense of living in the midst of a violent crisis of civilization, threatening complete collapse, has spread far and wide. Oswald Spengler's *The Decline of the West* has been the alarm signal for untold numbers the world over.... It has jolted [people] out of their unreasoning faith in the providential nature of Progress and familiarized them with the idea of a decline of existing civilization and culture in our own time....

How naïve the glad and confident hope of a century ago, that the advance of science and the general extension of education assured the progressive perfection of society, seems to us today! Who can still seriously believe that the translation of scientific triumphs into still more marvelous technical achievements is enough to save civilization.... Modern society, with its intensive development and mechanization, indeed looks very different from the dream vision of Progress! ...

What problems are described in this excerpt from Huizinga's book? Why does he think these problems negate the prewar vision of progress?

Source: From Johan Huizinga, *In the Shadow of Tomorrow* (W. W. Norton, 1936), p. 386.

THE FRENCH POLICY OF COERCION (1919–1924) The weakness of the League of Nations and the failure of both the United States and Great Britain to honor their defensive military alliances with France left France embittered and alone. France's search for security between 1919 and 1924 was founded primarily on a strict enforcement of the Treaty of Versailles. This tough policy toward Germany began with the issue of the reparations payments that the Germans were supposed to make to compensate for war damage. In April 1921, the Allied Reparations Commission settled on a sum of 132 billion marks ($33 billion), payable in annual installments of 2.5 billion (gold) marks. The new German Republic made its first payment in 1921, but by the following year, facing financial problems, the Germans announced that they were unable to pay more. Outraged, the French government sent troops to occupy the Ruhr valley, Germany's chief industrial and mining center. If the Germans would not pay reparations, the French would collect reparations in kind by operating and using the Ruhr's mines and factories.

Both Germany and France suffered from the French occupation of the Ruhr. The German government adopted a policy of passive resistance to French occupation that was largely financed by printing more paper money. This only intensified the inflationary pressures that had begun in Germany toward the end of the war. The German mark became worthless, and economic disaster fueled political upheavals. All the nations, including France, were happy to cooperate with the American suggestion for a new conference of experts to reassess the reparations problem.

THE HOPEFUL YEARS (1924–1929) In August 1924, an international commission produced a new plan for reparations. The Dawes Plan, named after the American banker who chaired the commission, reduced reparations and stabilized Germany's payments on the basis of its ability to pay. The Dawes Plan also granted an initial $200 million loan for German recovery, which opened the door to heavy American investments in Europe that helped create an era of European prosperity between 1924 and 1929.

With prosperity came new efforts at European diplomacy. The foreign ministers of Germany and France, Gustav Stresemann (GOOS-tahf SHTRAY-zuh-mahn) and Aristide Briand (ah-ruh-STEED bree-AHNH), fostered a spirit of international cooperation by concluding the Treaty of Locarno (loh-KAHR-noh) in 1925. This guaranteed Germany's new western borders with France and Belgium. Although Germany's new eastern borders with Poland were conspicuously absent from the agreement, the Locarno pact was viewed by many as the beginning of a new era of European peace. On the day after the pact was concluded, the *New York Times* proclaimed, "France and Germany Ban War Forever," and the *London Times* declared, "Peace at Last."[12]

The spirit of Locarno was based on little real substance, however. Germany lacked the military power to alter its western borders even if it wanted to. And the issue of disarmament soon proved that even the spirit of Locarno could not bring nations to cut back on their weapons. The League of Nations had suggested the "reduction of national armaments to the lowest point consistent with national safety." Germany, of course, had been disarmed with the expectation that other states would do likewise. Numerous disarmament conferences, however, failed to achieve anything substantial as states were unwilling to trust their security to anyone but their own military forces.

The Great Depression

After World War I, most European states hoped to return to the liberal ideal of a market economy based on private enterprise and largely free of state intervention. But the war had vastly strengthened business cartels and labor unions, making some government regulation of these powerful organizations necessary. At the same time, reparations and war debts had severely damaged the postwar international economy, making the prosperity that did occur between 1924 and 1929 exceedingly fragile and the dream of returning to the liberal ideal of a self-regulating market economy merely an illusion. What destroyed the concept altogether was the Great Depression.

CAUSES Two factors played a major role in the coming of the Great Depression: a downturn in domestic economies and an international financial crisis created by the collapse of the American stock market in 1929. Already in the mid-1920s, prices for agricultural goods were beginning to decline rapidly due to overproduction of basic commodities such as wheat. Prices fell by 30 percent between 1924 and 1929. Meanwhile, an increase in the use of oil and hydroelectricity led to a slump in the coal industry even before 1929.

Furthermore, much of Europe's prosperity between 1924 and 1929 had been built on American bank loans to Germany. In 1928, American investors had begun to pull money out of Germany in order to invest in the booming New York stock market. The

crash of the U.S. stock market in October 1929 led panicky American investors to withdraw even more of their funds from Germany and other European markets. The withdrawal of funds seriously weakened the banks of Germany and other central European states. The Credit-Anstalt, Vienna's most prestigious bank, collapsed on May 31, 1931. By that time, trade was slowing down, industrialists were cutting back production, and unemployment was increasing as the ripple effects of international bank failures had a devastating impact on domestic economies.

UNEMPLOYMENT Economic depression was by no means a new phenomenon in European history. But the depth of the economic downturn after 1929 fully justifies the "Great Depression" label. During 1932, the worst year of the downturn, one British worker in four was unemployed, and 6 million workers, or 40 percent of the German labor force, were out of work. Between 1929 and 1932, industrial production plummeted almost 50 percent in the United States and nearly as much in Germany. Unemployed and homeless people filled the streets of cities throughout the advanced industrial world.

SOCIAL AND POLITICAL REPERCUSSIONS The economic crisis also had unexpected social repercussions. Women were often able to secure low-paying jobs as servants, housecleaners, or laundresses, while many men remained unemployed, either begging on the streets or staying at home to do household tasks. Many unemployed men, resenting this reversal of traditional gender roles, were open to the shrill cries of demagogues with simple solutions to the economic crisis. In addition, high unemployment rates among young males often led them to join gangs that gathered in parks or other public places, creating fear among local residents.

The Great Depression: Bread Lines in Paris. The Great Depression devastated the European economy and had serious political repercussions. Because of its more balanced economy, France did not feel the effects of the depression as quickly as other European countries. By 1931, however, even France was experiencing lines of unemployed people at free-food centers.

Governments seemed powerless to deal with the crisis. The classical liberal remedy for depression, a deflationary policy of balanced budgets, which involved cutting costs by lowering wages and raising tariffs to exclude other countries' goods from home markets, only served to worsen the economy and cause even greater mass discontent. This in turn led to serious political repercussions. Increased government activity in the economy was one reaction, even in countries like the United States that had a strong *laissez-faire* tradition. Another effect was a renewed interest in Marxist doctrines, since Marx had predicted that capitalism would destroy itself through overproduction. Communism took on new popularity, especially among workers and intellectuals. Finally, the Great Depression increased the attractiveness of simplistic dictatorial solutions, especially from a new movement known as fascism. Everywhere in Europe, democracy seemed on the defensive in the 1930s.

The Democratic States

The Great Depression had political as well as economic consequences for all of the democratic states. In some, especially the United States, it became the impetus for new social reform measures.

GREAT BRITAIN After World War I, Great Britain went through a period of serious economic difficulties. During the war, Britain had lost many of the markets for its industrial products, especially to the United States and Japan. The postwar decline of such staple industries as coal, steel, and textiles led to a rise in unemployment, which reached the 2 million mark in 1921. But Britain soon rebounded and from 1925 to 1929 experienced an era of renewed prosperity, even though unemployment remained at the startling level of 10 percent.

By 1929, Britain faced the growing effects of the Great Depression. The Labour Party, which had become the largest party in Britain, failed to solve the nation's economic problem and fell from power in 1931. A national government (a coalition of Liberals and Conservatives) claimed credit for bringing Britain out of the worst stages of the depression, primarily by using the traditional policies of balanced budgets and protective tariffs. British politicians had largely ignored the new ideas of a Cambridge economist, John Maynard Keynes (KAYNZ) (1883–1946), who published his *General Theory of Employment, Interest and Money* in 1936. He condemned the traditional view that in a free economy, depressions should be left to work themselves out. Instead, Keynes argued that unemployment stemmed not from overproduction but from a decline in demand and that demand could be increased by putting people back to work constructing highways and public buildings. Such public works should be used to stimulate the economy even if the government had to go into debt to pay for them, a concept known as **deficit spending**.

FRANCE After the defeat of Germany, France had become the strongest power on the European continent. Its greatest need was to rebuild the devastated areas of northern and eastern France, but no French government seemed capable of solving the nation's financial problems between 1921 and 1926. Like other European countries, though, France did experience a period of relative prosperity between 1926 and 1929.

Because it had a more balanced economy than other nations, France did not begin to feel the full effects of the Great Depression until 1932. Economic instability soon had political repercussions. During a nineteen-month period in 1932 and 1933, six different cabinets were formed as France faced political chaos. Finally, in June 1936, a coalition of leftist parties—Communists, Socialists, and Radicals—formed a Popular Front government.

Although the Popular Front initiated a program for workers that included the right of collective bargaining, a forty-hour workweek, two-week paid vacations, and minimum wages, its policies failed to solve the problems of the depression. By 1938, the French were experiencing a serious decline of confidence in their political system.

GERMANY After the imperial Germany of William II had come to an end in 1918 with Germany's defeat in World War I, a German democratic state known as the Weimar (VY-mar) Republic was established. From the very start, the Weimar Republic was plagued by problems. It had no truly outstanding political leaders, and in 1925, Paul von Hindenburg (POWL fun HIN-den-boork), a World War I army commander, was elected president at the age of seventy-seven. Hindenburg was a traditional military man, monarchist in sentiment, who at heart was not in favor of the republic he had been elected to serve.

The Weimar Republic also faced serious economic difficulties. Germany experienced runaway inflation in 1922 and 1923; widows, orphans, the retired elderly, army officers, teachers, civil servants, and others who lived on fixed incomes all watched their monthly stipends become worthless and their lifetime savings evaporate. Their economic losses increasingly pushed the middle class to the rightist parties that were hostile to the republic. To make matters worse, after a period of prosperity from 1924 to 1929, Germany faced the Great Depression. Unemployment increased to 3 million in March 1930 and 4.4 million by December of the same year. The depression paved the way for the rise of extremist parties.

UNITED STATES After Germany, no Western nation was more affected by the Great Depression than the United States. By 1932, U.S. industrial production had fallen to half what it had been in 1929. By 1933, there were 15 million unemployed. Under these circumstances, the Democratic presidential candidate, Franklin Delano Roosevelt (1882–1945), was able to win a landslide electoral victory in 1932. He and his advisers pursued a policy of active government intervention in the economy with a stepped-up program of public works that came to be known as the **New Deal**. The Works Progress Administration (WPA), a government organization established in 1935, employed 2 to 3 million people building bridges, roads, post offices, and airports. The Roosevelt administration was also responsible for new social legislation that launched the

American welfare state. In 1935, the Social Security Act created a system of old-age pensions and unemployment insurance.

The New Deal provided some social reform measures that perhaps averted the possibility of social revolution in the United States. It did not, however, solve the unemployment problems of the Great Depression. In May 1937, during what was considered a period of full recovery, American unemployment still stood at 7 million. Only World War II and the subsequent growth of the armaments industry brought American workers back to full employment.

Socialism in Soviet Russia

With their victory in the civil war, Bolshevik leaders could now turn to the challenging task of building the first socialist society in a world dominated by their capitalist enemies. But the civil war had taken an enormous toll of life. During the civil war, Lenin had pursued a policy of war communism, but once the war was over, peasants began to sabotage the program by hoarding food. Added to this problem was drought, which caused a great famine between 1920 and 1922 that claimed as many as 5 million lives. Industrial collapse paralleled the agricultural disaster. By 1921, industrial output was only 20 percent of its 1913 levels. Russia was exhausted. A peasant banner proclaimed, "Down with Lenin and horseflesh, Bring back the Tsar and pork." As Leon Trotsky said, "The country, and the government with it, were at the very edge of the abyss."[13]

NEW POLICIES In March 1921, Lenin pulled Russia back from the abyss by adopting his **New Economic Policy** (NEP), a modified version of the old capitalist system. Forced requisitioning of food from the peasants was halted, and peasants were now allowed to sell their produce openly. Retail stores and small industries that employed fewer than twenty people could now operate under private ownership, although heavy industry, banking, utilities, and mines remained in the hands of the government.

In 1922, Lenin and the Communists formally created a new state called the Union of Soviet Socialist Republics, known as the USSR by its initials or the Soviet Union by its shortened form. Already by that year, a revived market and a good harvest had brought the famine to an end; Soviet agricultural production climbed to 75 percent of its prewar level. Overall, the NEP had saved the nation from complete economic disaster even though Lenin and other leading Communists intended it to be only a temporary, tactical retreat from the goals of communism.

The new government also introduced a number of social changes. Alexandra Kollontai (kul-lun-TY) (1872–1952), who had become a supporter of revolutionary socialism while in exile in Switzerland, took the lead in pushing a Bolshevik program for women's rights and social welfare reforms. As minister of social welfare, she tried to provide health care for women and children by establishing Palaces for the Protection of Maternity and Children. Between 1918 and 1920, the new regime issued a series of reforms that made marriage a civil act, legalized divorce, decreed the equality of men and women, and permitted abortions. Kollontai was also instrumental in establishing an agency within the Communist Party known as Zhenotdel (zhen-ut-DEL) that sent men and women to all parts of the Russian Empire to explain the new social order. In the provinces in the east, Zhenotdel members were often brutally murdered by angry men who objected to any kind of liberation for their wives and daughters. Much to Kollontai's disappointment, many of these early communist social reforms were later undone as the Communists came to face more pressing matters, including survival of the new regime.

THE STRUGGLE FOR POWER Lenin's death in 1924 inaugurated a struggle for power among the seven members of the Politburo (POL-it-byoor-oh), the institution that had become the leading organ of the party. The Politburo was severely divided over the future direction of the nation. The Left, led by Leon Trotsky, wanted to end the NEP and launch the nation on the path of rapid industrialization, primarily at the expense of the peasantry. This same group wanted to continue the revolution, believing that the survival of the Russian Revolution ultimately depended on the spread of communism abroad. Another group in the Politburo, called the Right, rejected the cause of world revolution and wanted to concentrate instead on constructing a socialist state. The members of this group also favored a continuation of Lenin's NEP because they believed that rapid industrialization would harm the living standards of the peasantry.

These ideological divisions were underscored by an intense personal rivalry between Leon Trotsky and Joseph Stalin (1879–1953). In 1924, Trotsky held the post of commissar of war and was the leading spokesman for the Left in the Politburo. Stalin was content to hold the dull bureaucratic job of party general secretary, while other Politburo members held party positions that enabled them to display their brilliant oratorical abilities. Stalin was skilled at avoiding allegiance to either the Left or the Right faction in the Politburo. He was also a good organizer (his fellow Bolsheviks called him "Comrade Card-Index"), and the other members of the Politburo soon found that the position of party secretary was really the most important in the party hierarchy. Stalin used his post to gain complete control of the Communist Party. Trotsky was expelled from the party in 1927. Eventually, he made his way to Mexico, where he was murdered in 1940, no doubt on Stalin's orders. By 1929, Stalin had succeeded in eliminating the Old Bolsheviks of the revolutionary era from the Politburo and establishing a powerful dictatorship.

In Pursuit of a New Reality: Cultural and Intellectual Trends

  FOCUS QUESTION: How did the cultural and intellectual trends of the post–World War I years reflect the crises of the time as well as the lingering effects of the war?

Four years of devastating war left many Europeans with a profound sense of despair and a conviction that something was dreadfully wrong with Western values. The Great Depression only added to the desolation left behind by World War I.

Political and economic uncertainties were paralleled by social innovations. The Great War had served to break down many traditional middle-class attitudes, especially toward sexuality. In the 1920s, women's physical appearance changed dramatically. Short skirts, short hair, the use of cosmetics that were once thought to be the preserve of prostitutes, and the new practice of suntanning gave women a new image. This change in physical appearance, which stressed more exposure of a woman's body, was also accompanied by frank discussions of sexual matters. In 1926, the Dutch physician Theodor van de Velde (TAY-oh-dor vahn duh VEL-duh) published *Ideal Marriage: Its Physiology and Technique*. Translated into a number of languages, it became an international best-seller. Van de Velde described female and male anatomy, discussed birth control techniques, and glorified sexual pleasure in marriage.

Nightmares and New Visions

Uncertainty also pervaded the cultural and intellectual achievements of the postwar years. Artistic trends were largely a working out of the implications of prewar developments. Abstract painting, for example, became ever more popular as many pioneering artists of the early twentieth century matured (see the Comparative Essay "A Revolution in the Arts" on p. 689). In addition, prewar fascination with the absurd and the unconscious contents of the mind seemed even more appropriate after the nightmare landscapes of World War I battlefronts. This gave rise to both the Dada movement and Surrealism.

THE DADA MOVEMENT Dadaism (DAH-duh-iz-um) attempted to enshrine the purposelessness of life. Tristan Tzara (TRISS-tun TSAHR-rah) (1896–1945), a Romanian-French poet and one of the founders of Dadaism, expressed the Dadaist contempt for the Western tradition in a lecture in 1922: "The acts of life have no beginning or end. Everything happens in a completely idiotic way…. Like everything in life, Dada is useless." Revolted by the insanity of life, the Dadaists tried to give it expression by creating anti-art. The 1918 Berlin Dada Manifesto maintained that "Dada is the international expression of our times, the great rebellion of artistic movements." Many Dadaists took pieces of junk (wire, string, rags, scraps of newspaper, nails, washers) and assembled them into collages, believing that they were transforming the refuse of their culture into art.

In the hands of Hannah Höch (HURKH) (1889–1978), Dada became an instrument to comment on women's roles in the new mass culture. Höch was the only female member of the Berlin Dada Club, which featured photomontage. Her work was part of the first Dada show in Berlin in 1920. In *Dada Dance*, she seemed to criticize the "new woman" by making fun of the way women were inclined to follow fashion trends. In other works, however, she projected positive images of the modern woman and expressed a keen interest in new freedoms for women.

Hannah Höch, *Cut with the Kitchen Knife Dada Through the Last Weimar Beer Belly Cultural Epoch of Germany.* Hannah Höch, a prominent figure in the postwar Dada movement, used photomontage to create images that reflected women's issues. In *Cut with the Kitchen Knife* (1919), she combined pictures of German political leaders with sports stars, Dada artists, and scenes from urban life. One major theme emerged: the confrontation between the anti-Dada world of German political leaders and the Dada world of revolutionary ideals. Höch associated women with Dada and the new world.

SURREALISM AND MODERN ARCHITECTURE Another important artistic movement was **Surrealism**, which sought a reality beyond the material, sensible world and found it in the world of the unconscious through the portrayal of fantasies, dreams, or nightmares. Employing logic to convey the illogical, the Surrealists created disturbing and evocative images. The Spaniard Salvador Dalí (sahl-vah-DOR dah-LEE) (1904–1989) became the high priest of Surrealism and in his mature phase became a master of representational Surrealism. In *The Persistence of Memory*, Dalí portrayed recognizable objects divorced from their normal context. By placing these objects in unrecognizable relationships, Dalí created a disturbing world in which the irrational had become tangible.

The move toward functionalism in modern architecture also became more widespread in the 1920s and 1930s. Especially important in the spread of functionalism was the Bauhaus (BOW-howss) school of art, architecture, and design, founded in 1919 at Weimar, Germany, by the Berlin architect Walter Gropius (VAHL-tuh GROH-pee-uss). The Bauhaus teaching staff included architects, artists, and designers, who worked together to blend the study of fine arts (painting and

A Revolution in the Arts

The period between 1880 and 1930 witnessed a revolution in the arts throughout Western civilization. Fueled in part by developments in physics and psychology, artists and writers rebelled against the traditional belief that the task of art was to represent "reality" and experimented with innovative new techniques in order to approach reality from a totally fresh perspective. Their daring break with the past reflected both the exhilaration of an age propelled by technological discoveries and a fascination with the unconscious contents of the human mind.

From Impressionism and Expressionism to Cubism, abstract art, Dadaism, and Surrealism, painters seemed intoxicated with the belief that their canvases would help reveal the radically changing world. Especially after the cataclysm of World War I, which shattered the image of a rational society, artists sought an absolute freedom of expression, confident that art could redefine humanity in the midst of chaos. Other arts soon followed their lead: James Joyce turned prose on its head by focusing on his characters' innermost thoughts; Arnold Schönberg (AR-nawlt SHURN-bayrk) created atonal music by using a scale composed of twelve notes independent of any tonal key; and Le Corbusier (luh kor-boo-ZYAY) launched a revolution in architecture by using concrete slabs to make "machines for living."

This revolutionary spirit had already been exemplified by Pablo Picasso's canvas *Les Demoiselles d'Avignon*, painted in 1907 (see the illustration "Pablo Picasso, *Les Demoiselles d'Avignon*" on p. 600 in Chapter 20). Picasso used geometrical designs to create a new reality and appropriated non-Western cultural resources in the desire to revitalize Western art. Reflecting the prevailing European view that African masks were primitive oddities, Picasso ignored the cultural and religious significance of such carvings. Although some African observers charged that Picasso had exploited African culture just as European governments had exploited their colonies, Picasso had succeeded in helping revitalize Western art.

Another illustration of the revolutionary approach to art was the decision by the French artist Marcel Duchamp (mar-SEL duh-SHAHN) to enter a porcelain urinal in a 1917 art exhibit held in New York City. By signing it and giving it the title *Fountain*, Duchamp proclaimed that he had transformed the urinal into a work of art. His "ready-mades" (as such art would henceforth be labeled) declared that art was whatever the artist proclaimed as art. The Dadaist Kurt Schwitters (KOORT SCHVIT-urz) brought together

Kurt Schwitters, *Der Harz*. Kurt Schwitters became identified with the Dada movement when he began to create his collages. He wrote in 1928, "Fundamentally, I cannot understand why one is not able to use in a picture, exactly in the same way as commercially made color … all the old junk which piles up in closets or the rubbish heaps."

postage stamps, old handbills, streetcar tickets, newspaper scraps, and pieces of cardboard to form his works of art.

Such intentionally irreverent acts were a slap in the face of the established art world and demystified the nearly sacred reverence that had traditionally been attached to works of art. Essentially, Duchamp, Schwitters, and others claimed that anything under the sun could be selected as a work of art because the mental choice itself equaled the act of artistic creation. Therefore, art need not be a manual construct; it need only be a mental conceptualization. This liberating concept opened the floodgates of the art world, causing the new century to swim in this free-flowing, exploratory torrent.

 How was the revolution in the arts between 1880 and 1930 related to the political, economic, and social developments of the same period?

Hesse and the Unconscious

ART & IDEAS

THE NOVELS OF HERMANN HESSE made a strong impact on young people, first in Germany in the 1920s and then in the United States in the 1960s after they had been translated into English. Many of these young people shared Hesse's fascination with the unconscious and his dislike of modern industrial civilization. This excerpt from *Demian* spoke directly to many of them.

Hermann Hesse, *Demian*

The following spring I was to leave the preparatory school and enter a university. I was still undecided, however, as to where and what I was to study. I had grown a thin mustache, I was a full-grown man, and yet I was completely helpless and without a goal in life. Only one thing was certain: the voice within me, the dream image. I felt the duty to follow this voice blindly wherever it might lead me. But it was difficult and each day I rebelled against it anew. Perhaps I was mad, as I thought at moments; perhaps I was not like other men? But I was able to do the same things the others did; with a little

effort and industry I could read Plato, was able to solve problems in trigonometry or follow a chemical analysis. There was only one thing I could not do: wrest the dark secret goal from myself and keep it before me as others did who knew exactly what they wanted to be—professors, lawyers, doctors, artists, however long this would take them and whatever difficulties and advantages this decision would bear in its wake. This I could not do. Perhaps I would become something similar, but how was I to know? Perhaps I would have to continue my search for years on end and would not become anything, and would not reach a goal. Perhaps I would reach this goal but it would turn out to be an evil, dangerous, horrible one?

I wanted only to try to live in accord with the promptings which came from my true self. Why was that so very difficult?

How does Hesse's interest in the unconscious appear in this excerpt? Why was a dislike of mechanized society particularly intense after World War I?

Source: From *Demian*, by Hermann Hesse. (New York: Bantam Books, 1966), p. 30.

Salvador Dalí, *The Persistence of Memory*. Surrealism was an important artistic movement in the 1920s. Influenced by the theories of Freudian psychology, Surrealists sought to reveal the world of the unconscious, or the "greater reality" that they believed existed beyond the world of physical appearances. As is evident in this painting, Salvador Dalí sought to portray the world of dreams by painting recognizable objects in unrecognizable relationships.

Probing the Unconscious

The interest in the unconscious, evident in Surrealism, was also apparent in the new literary techniques that emerged in the 1920s. One of its most apparent manifestations was the "stream of consciousness" technique, in which the writer presented an interior monologue, or a report of the innermost thoughts of each character. One example of this genre was written by the Irish exile James Joyce (1882–1941). His *Ulysses*, published in 1922, told the story of one day in the life of ordinary people in Dublin by following the flow of their inner dialogue. Disconnected ramblings and veiled allusions pervade Joyce's work.

The German writer Hermann Hesse (hayr-MAHN HESS-uh) (1877–1962) dealt with the unconscious in a considerably different fashion. His novels reflected the influence of both the psychological theories of Carl Jung (YOONG) and Eastern religions and focused, among other things, on the spiritual loneliness of modern human beings in a mechanized urban society. *Demian* was a psychoanalytic study of incest,

sculpture) with the applied arts (printing, weaving, and furniture making). Gropius urged his followers to foster a new union of arts and crafts in order to create the buildings and objects of the future.

and *Steppenwolf* mirrored the psychological confusion of modern existence. Hesse's novels made a large impact on German youth in the 1920s (see the box "Hesse and the Unconscious" above). He won the Nobel Prize in Literature in 1946.

For much of the Western world, the best way to find (or escape) reality was in the field of mass entertainment. The 1930s represented the heyday of the Hollywood studio system, which in the single year of 1937 turned out nearly six hundred feature films. Supplementing the movies were cheap paperback books and radio, which brought sports, soap operas, and popular music to the masses.

Mass forms of communication and entertainment were not new. But the increased size of audiences and the ability of radio and cinema, unlike the printed word, to provide an immediate mass experience did add new dimensions to mass culture. Favorite film actors and actresses became stars whose lives then became subject to public adoration and scrutiny. Sensuous actresses such as Marlene Dietrich, whose appearance in the early sound film *The Blue Angel* catapulted her to fame, projected new images of women's sexuality.

CHAPTER SUMMARY

The assassination of Archduke Francis Ferdinand of Austria-Hungary in the summer of 1914 in the Bosnian capital of Sarajevo led within six weeks to a major war among the major powers of Europe. The Germans drove the Russians back in the east, but in the west a stalemate developed, with trenches defended by barbed wire and machine guns extending from the Swiss border to the English Channel. After German submarine attacks, the United States entered the war in 1917, but even from the beginning of the war, battles also took place in the African colonies of Europe's great powers as well as in the East, making this a truly global war.

Unprepared for war, Russia soon faltered and collapsed, leading to a revolution against the tsar. But the new Provisional Government in Russia also soon failed, enabling the revolutionary Bolsheviks of V. I. Lenin, to seize power. Lenin established a dictatorship and made a costly peace with Germany. After American troops entered the war, the German government collapsed, leading to an armistice on November 11, 1918.

World War I was the defining event of the twentieth century. The incredible destruction and the deaths of almost 10 million people undermined the whole idea of progress. World War I was also a total war that required a mobilization of resources and populations and increased the centralization of government power. Civil liberties, such as freedom of the press, speech, and assembly, were circumscribed in the name of national security. Governments' need to plan the distribution of goods restricted economic freedom. World War I made the practice of strong central authority a way of life.

Finally, World War I ended the age of European hegemony over world affairs. In 1917, the Russian Revolution had laid the foundation for the creation of a new Eurasian power, the Soviet Union, and the United States had entered the war. The waning of the European age was not immediately evident to all, however, for it was clouded by American isolationism and the withdrawal of the Soviets from world affairs while they nurtured the growth of their own socialist system. These developments, though temporary, created a political vacuum in Europe that all too soon would be filled by the revival of German power.

Although World War I destroyed the liberal optimism of the prewar era, many people in the 1920s still hoped that the progress of Western civilization could somehow be restored. These hopes proved largely unfounded. France, feeling vulnerable to another invasion, sought to weaken Germany. European recovery, largely the result of American loans and investments, ended with the Great Depression at the end of the 1920s. Democratic states, such as Great Britain, France, and the United States, spent much of the 1930s trying to recover from the Great Depression. In the Soviet Union, Lenin's New Economic Policy helped to stabilize the economy, but on his death a struggle for power ensued that ended with the establishment of a dictatorship under Joseph Stalin.

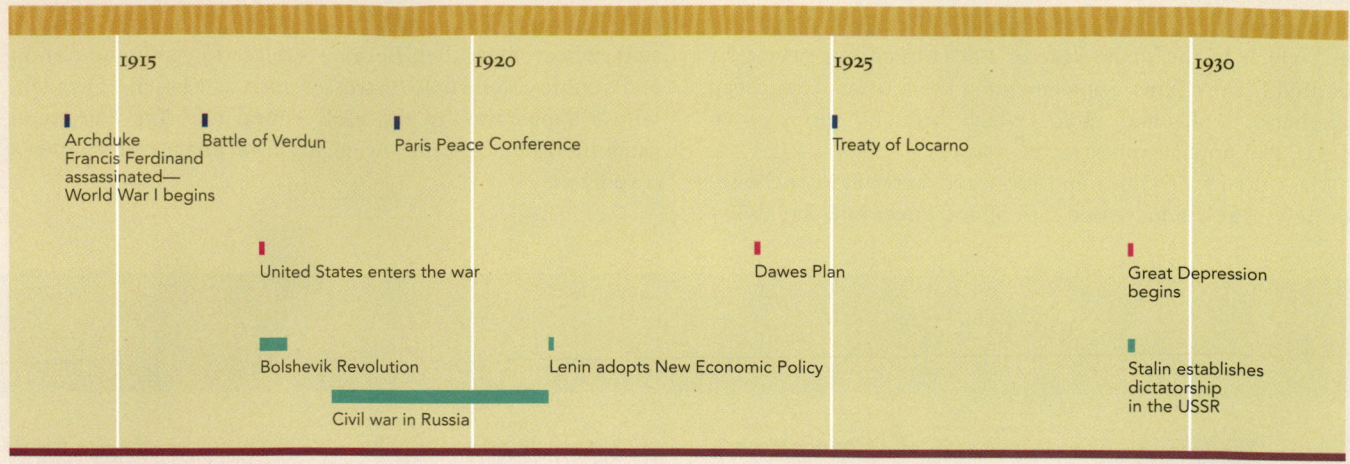

1915 — Archduke Francis Ferdinand assassinated—World War I begins

Battle of Verdun

1920 — Paris Peace Conference

1925 — Treaty of Locarno

1930

United States enters the war

Dawes Plan

Great Depression begins

Bolshevik Revolution

Lenin adopts New Economic Policy

Stalin establishes dictatorship in the USSR

Civil war in Russia

CHAPTER REVIEW

Upon Reflection

Q What nation, if any, was the most responsible for causing World War I? Why?

Q How did Lenin and the Bolsheviks manage to seize and hold power despite their small numbers?

Q What were the causes of the Great Depression, and how did European states respond to it?

Key Terms

conscription (p. 663)
militarism (p. 663)
trench warfare (p. 667)
total war (p. 673)
soviets (p. 675)
war communism (p. 678)
War Guilt Clause (p. 682)
reparations (p. 682)
mandates (p. 683)
deficit spending (p. 686)
New Deal (p. 686)
New Economic Policy (p. 687)
Dadaism (p. 688)
Surrealism (p. 688)

Suggested Reading

GENERAL WORKS ON TWENTIETH-CENTURY EUROPE A number of general works on European history in the twentieth century provide a context for understanding both World War I and the Russian Revolution. Especially valuable is N. Ferguson, *The War of the World: Twentieth-Century Conflict and the Descent of the West* (New York, 2006). See also R. Paxton, *Europe in the Twentieth Century*, 4th ed. (New York, 2004).

CAUSES OF WORLD WAR I The historical literature on the causes and background of World War I is vast. Good starting points are the works by J. Joll and G. Martel, *The Origins of the First World War*, 3rd ed. (London, 2006), and M. MacMillan, *The War That Ended Peace: The Road to 1914* (New York, 2013).

WORLD WAR I The best brief account of World War I is H. Strachan, *The First World War* (New York, 2004). On the global nature of World War I, see M. S. Neiberg, *Fighting the Great War: A Global History* (Cambridge, Mass., 2005), and W. K. Storey, *The First World War: A Concise Global History* (New York, 2009). On the role of women in World War I, see S. Grayzel, *Women and the First World War* (London, 2002).

On the Paris Peace Conference, see M. MacMillan, *Paris, 1919: Six Months That Changed the World* (New York, 2002). On the impact of Woodrow Wilson's ideas on the colonial world, see E. Manela, *The Wilsonian Moment: Self-Determination and the International Origins of Anticolonial Nationalism* (Oxford, 2007).

THE RUSSIAN REVOLUTION A good introduction to the Russian Revolution can be found in R. A. Wade, *The Russian Revolution, 1917*, 2nd ed. (Cambridge, 2005), and S. Fitzpatrick, *The Russian Revolution, 1917–1932*, 2nd ed. (New York, 2001). On Lenin, see R. Service, *Lenin: A Biography* (Cambridge, Mass., 2000).

THE 1920S For a general introduction to the post–World War I period, see M. Kitchen, *Europe Between the Wars*, 2nd ed. (London, 2006). On European security issues after the Peace of Paris, see S. Marks, *The Illusion of Peace: Europe's International Relations, 1918–1933*, 2nd ed. (New York, 2003). On the Great Depression, see C. P. Kindleberger, *The World in Depression, 1929–39*, rev. ed. (Berkeley, Calif., 1986).

Chapter Notes

1. A. Toynbee, *Surviving the Future* (New York, 1971), pp. 106–107.

2. Quoted in J. Remak, "1914–The Third Balkan War: Origin Reconsidered," *Journal of Modern History* 43 (1971), pp. 364–365.

3. Quoted in J. M. Winter, *The Experience of World War I* (New York, 1989), p. 142.

4. Quoted in Hew Strachan, *The First World War* (New York, 2004), pp. 94–95.

5. Quoted in ibid., p. 72.

6. Quoted in C. W. Reilly, ed., *Scars upon My Heart: Women's Poetry and Verse of the First World War* (London, 1981), p. 90.

7. Quoted in W. M. Mandel, *Soviet Women* (Garden City, N.Y., 1975), p. 43.

8. Quoted in M. D. Steinberg, *Voices of Revolution, 1917* (New Haven, Conn., 2001), p. 55.

9. Quoted in S. Audoin-Rouzeau and A. Becker, *14–18: Understanding the Great War*, trans. C. Temerson (New York, 2002), p. 212.

10. Quoted in ibid., p. 213.

11. Quoted in ibid., p. 41.

12. Quoted in R. Paxton, *Europe in the Twentieth Century*, 2nd ed. (San Diego, Calif., 1985), p. 237.

13. Quoted in I. Howe, ed., *The Basic Writings of Trotsky* (London, 1963), p. 162.

Nationalism, Revolution, and Dictatorship: Asia, the Middle East, and Latin America from 1919 to 1939

Nguyen the Patriot at Tours

Bibliotheque Nationale, Paris, France/Archives Charmet/The Bridgeman Art Library

CHAPTER OUTLINE AND FOCUS QUESTIONS

The Rise of Nationalism

Q What were the various stages in the rise of nationalist movements in Asia and the Middle East, and what challenges did they face?

Revolution in China

Q What problems did China encounter between the two world wars, and what solutions did the Nationalists and the Communists propose to solve them?

Japan Between the Wars

Q How did Japan address the problems of nation building in the first decades of the twentieth century, and why did democratic institutions not take hold more effectively?

Nationalism and Dictatorship in Latin America

Q What problems did the nations of Latin America face in the interwar years? To what degree were the problems a consequence of foreign influence?

CRITICAL THINKING

Q How did the societies discussed in this chapter deal with the political, economic, and social challenges that they faced after World War I, and how did these challenges differ from one region to another?

CONNECTIONS TO TODAY

Q Do nationalist movements in various parts of the world today face any of the same challenges faced by nationalist movements of the early twentieth century? If so, what are these challenges?

ON CHRISTMAS DAY IN 1920, a young Asian man in an ill-fitting rented suit stood up nervously to address the several hundred delegates of the French Socialist Party (FSP) who had gathered in the French city of Tours. The speaker called himself Nguyen Ai Quoc (Win EYE-gwok), or Nguyen the Patriot in the Vietnamese language, and he was a Vietnamese subject of the French colony of Indochina.

The delegates had assembled to decide whether the FSP would follow the path of violent revolution recommended by the new Bolshevik regime in Soviet Russia. Among those voting in favor of the proposal was Nguyen Ai Quoc, who had concluded that only the path of Karl Marx and Vladimir Lenin could lead to national independence for his compatriots. Later he would become the founder of the Vietnamese Communist Party and become known to the world by the pseudonym Ho Chi Minh (HOH CHEE MIN).

The meeting in Tours was held at a time when resistance to colonial rule was on the rise, and the decision that Nguyen Ai Quoc faced of whether to opt for violent revolution was one that would be faced by colonial peoples throughout the world. As Europeans devastated their own civilization on the battlefields of Europe, the subject peoples of their vast colonial empires were quick to recognize the opportunity to shake free of foreign domination. In the colonial territories, movements for national independence began to take shape. Some were inspired by the nationalist and liberal movements of the West, while others looked to the new Marxist model provided by the victory of the Bolsheviks in Soviet Russia, who soon worked to spread their revolutionary vision to African and Asian societies. In the Middle East, World War I brought an end to the Ottoman Empire and led to the creation of new states, many of which were placed under Western domination.

The societies of Latin America were no longer under direct colonial rule and thus, for the most part, did not face the same types of challenges as their counterparts in Asia and Africa. Nevertheless, the economies of some Latin American countries were virtually controlled by foreign interests. A similar situation prevailed in China and to a lesser degree in Japan, which had managed with some difficulty to retain a degree of political independence, despite severe pressure from the West. The political flux and economic disruption that characterized much of the world during the two decades following World War I affected Latin America, China, and Japan, leading many in these regions to heed the siren call of fascist dictatorship or social revolution. For the peoples of Africa, Asia, the Middle East, and Latin America, the end of the Great War had not created a world safe for democracy, as Woodrow Wilson had hoped, but an age of great peril and uncertainty. ❧

The Rise of Nationalism

 FOCUS QUESTION: What were the various stages in the rise of nationalist movements in Asia and the Middle East, and what challenges did they face?

World War I sundered the political and social foundations of the West and severely undermined its self-confidence. In Europe, doubts about the future viability of Western civilization were widespread, especially among the intellectual elite. These doubts were quick to reach the perceptive observers in Asia and Africa and contributed to a rising tide of unrest against Western political domination throughout the colonial and semicolonial world. That unrest took a variety of forms but was most notably displayed in increasing worker activism, rural protest, and a sense of national fervor among anticolonialist intellectuals. In areas of Asia, the Middle East, and Latin America where independent states had successfully resisted the Western onslaught, the discontent fostered by the war and later by the Great Depression led to a loss of confidence in democratic institutions and the rise of political dictatorships.

Modern Nationalism

The first stage of resistance to the West in Asia and Africa (see Chapter 21) had resulted in humiliation and failure and must have confirmed many Westerners' conviction that colonial peoples lacked the capacity, at least for the foreseeable future, to create modern states and govern their own destinies. But the process was just beginning. The next phase—the rise of modern nationalism—began to take shape at the beginning of the twentieth century and was the product of the convergence of several factors. The most vocal source of anticolonialist sentiment was a new urban middle class of westernized intellectuals. In many cases, these merchants, petty functionaries, clerks, students, and professionals had been educated in Western-style schools. A few had spent time in the West. Many spoke Western languages, wore Western clothes, and worked in occupations connected with the colonial regime. Some even wrote in the languages of their colonial masters.

The results were paradoxical. On the one hand, this "new class" admired Western culture and sometimes harbored a deep sense of contempt for traditional ways. On the other hand, many strongly resented the foreigners and their arrogant contempt for colonial peoples. Though eager to introduce Western ideas and institutions into their own societies, these intellectuals were dismayed at the gap between ideal and reality, theory and practice, in colonial policy. Although Western political theory exalted democracy, equality, and individual freedom, such concepts were virtually nonexistent in the colonies.

Equality in economic opportunity and social life was also noticeably lacking in colonial areas. Normally, members of the middle class did not suffer in the same manner as impoverished peasants or menial workers in coal mines or on sugar or rubber plantations, but they, too, had complaints. They were usually relegated to low-level jobs in the government or business and were paid less than Europeans in similar positions. The superiority of the Europeans was expressed in a variety of ways, including "whites only" clubs and the use of the familiar form of the language (normally used by adults to children) when addressing the local peoples.

Under these conditions, many members of the urban educated class were ambivalent toward their colonial masters and the civilization that they represented. Out of this mixture of hopes and resentments emerged the first stirrings of modern nationalism in Asia and Africa. During the first quarter of the century, in colonial and semicolonial societies from the Straits of Gibraltar to the shores of the Pacific Ocean, educated indigenous peoples began to organize political parties and movements seeking reforms or the end of foreign rule and the restoration of independence.

RELIGION AND NATIONALISM At first, many of the leaders of these movements did not focus clearly on the importance of nationhood but were motivated primarily to defend indigenous economic interests or religious beliefs. In Burma, for example, the first expression of modern nationalism came from students at the University of Rangoon, who protested against official persecution of Buddhist religious practices and the failure of British visitors to observe local customs in Buddhist temples, such as by not removing their footwear. As part of the protest against British arrogance and lack of respect for local religious traditions, the students adopted the title Thakin (TAHK-in)—a polite term in the Burmese language that means "lord" or "master"—thereby emphasizing their demand for the right to rule themselves. Only in the 1930s did the Thakins begin to focus specifically on national independence from British rule.

The Dilemma of the Intellectual

INTERACTION & EXCHANGE

SUTAN SJAHRIR WAS A PROMINENT LEADER of the Indonesian nationalist movement who briefly served as prime minister of the Republic of Indonesia in the 1950s. Like many Western-educated Asian intellectuals, he was tortured by the realization that by education and outlook he was closer to his colonial masters—in his case, the Dutch—than to his own people. He wrote the following passage in a letter to his wife in 1935 and later included it in his book *Out of Exile*.

Sutan Sjahrir, *Out of Exile*

Am I perhaps estranged from my people? … Why are the things that contain beauty for them and arouse their gentler emotions only senseless and displeasing for me? In reality, the spiritual gap between my people and me is certainly no greater than that between an intellectual in Holland … and the undeveloped people of Holland…. The difference is rather … that the intellectual in Holland does not feel this gap because there is a portion—even a fairly large portion—of his own people on approximately the same intellectual level as himself….

This is what we lack here. Not only is the number of intellectuals in this country smaller in proportion to the total population—in fact, very much smaller—but in addition, the few who are here do not constitute any single entity in spiritual outlook, or in any spiritual life or single culture whatsoever…. It is for them so much more difficult than for the intellectuals in Holland. In Holland they build—both consciously and unconsciously—on what is already there….

Even if they oppose it, they do so as a method of application or as a starting point.

In our country this is not the case. Here there has been no spiritual or cultural life, and no intellectual progress for centuries. There are the much-praised Eastern art forms but what are these except bare rudiments from a feudal culture that cannot possibly provide a dynamic fulcrum for people of the twentieth century? … Our spiritual needs are needs of the twentieth century; our problems and our views are of the twentieth century. Our inclination is no longer toward the mystical, but toward reality, clarity, and objectivity….

We intellectuals here are much closer to Europe or America than we are to the Borobudur or Mahabharata or to the primitive Islamic culture of Java and Sumatra….

So, it seems, the problem stands in principle. It is seldom put forth by us in this light, and instead most of us search unconsciously for a synthesis that will leave us internally tranquil. We want to have both Western science and Eastern philosophy, the Eastern "spirit," in the culture. But what is this Eastern spirit? It is, they say, the sense of the higher, of spirituality, of the eternal and religious, as opposed to the materialism of the West. I have heard this countless times, but it has never convinced me.

Why did Sutan Sjahrir feel estranged from his own culture? What was his answer to the challenges faced by his country in coming to terms with the modern world?

Source: From *Out of Exile* by Soetan Sjahrir and Charles Wolf, Jr. (New York: The John Day Company, Inc., 1949), pp. 66–68.

In the Dutch East Indies, Sarekat (SAR-eh-kaht) Islam (Islamic Association) was formed in 1911 as a self-help society among Muslim merchants to fight domination of the local economy by Chinese interests. Eventually, activist elements in the organization began to realize that the source of the problem was not the Chinese merchants but the colonial presence itself, and in the 1920s Sarekat Islam was transformed into a new organization, the Nationalist Party of Indonesia (PNI), that focused on national independence. Like the Thakins in Burma, this party would eventually lead the country to independence after World War II.

INDEPENDENCE OR MODERNIZATION? THE NATIONALIST QUANDARY Building a new sense of nationhood, however, requires more than a shared sense of grievances against the foreign invader. A host of other issues also had to be resolved. Soon patriots throughout the colonial world were engaged in a lively and sometimes acrimonious debate over such questions as whether independence or modernization should be their primary objective. The answer depended in part on how the colonial regime was perceived. If it was viewed as a source of

needed reforms in a traditional society, a gradualist approach made sense. But if it was seen primarily as an impediment to change, the first priority, in the minds of many, was to bring it to an end. Most of this first wave of nationalists were convinced that to survive, their societies must adopt some aspects of the Western way of life; yet many were equally determined that the local culture should not become a carbon copy of the West. What was the national identity, after all, if it did not incorporate national traditions?

One important reason for retaining some traditional values was to provide ideological symbols that the common people could understand and would rally around. Though aware that they needed to enlist the mass of the population in the common struggle, most urban intellectuals had difficulty communicating with the teeming population in the countryside who did not understand such complicated and unfamiliar concepts as democracy and nationhood. As the Indonesian intellectual Sutan Sjahrir (SOO-tan syah-REER) (1909–1966) lamented, many westernized intellectuals had more in common with their colonial rulers than with the rural population in the villages (see the box "The Dilemma of the Intellectual" above). As one

French colonial official remarked in some surprise to a French-educated Vietnamese reformist, "Why, Monsieur, you are more French than I am!"

Gandhi and the Indian National Congress

Nowhere in the colonial world were these issues debated more vigorously than in India. Before the Sepoy Rebellion (see Chapter 21), Indian consciousness had focused primarily on the question of religious identity. After all, the subcontinent had not been ruled by a dynasty of purely indigenous origins since the Guptas in the middle of the first millennium C.E. But in the latter half of the nineteenth century, a stronger sense of national consciousness began to emerge, provoked by the conservative policies and racial arrogance of the British colonial authorities.

The first Indian nationalists were upper class and educated. Many of them were from urban areas such as Bombay (now Mumbai), Madras (now Chennai), and Calcutta (now Kolkata). Some were trained in law and were members of the civil service. At first, many tended to prefer reform to revolution on the assumption that India needed to modernize in many ways to assist its leaders to compete in a changing world. An exponent of this view was Gopal Gokhale (goh-PAHL GOH-kuh-lay) (1866–1915), a moderate nationalist who hoped that he could convince the British to bring about needed reforms in Indian society. Gokhale and other like-minded reformists did have some effect. In the 1880s, the government introduced a measure of self-government for the first time. All too often, however, such efforts were sabotaged by local British officials.

The slow pace of reform convinced many Indian nationalists that relying on British benevolence was futile. In 1885, a small group of Indians, with some British participation, met in Bombay to form the Indian National Congress (INC). Although they hoped to speak for all India, most were high-caste English-trained Hindus, and thus had few ties to the majority of their compatriots. Like their predecessors, most members of the INC did not demand immediate independence and accepted the need for reforms to end traditional abuses like child marriage and *sati*. At the same time, however, they called for an Indian share in the governing process, more spending on economic development, and less spending on military campaigns waged along the frontier. The British responded with a few concessions, but change was glacially slow. As the more impatient members of the INC became disillusioned, a group of radicals split off from the main group and formed the New Party, which called for the use of terrorism and violence to achieve national independence.

The INC also had difficulty reconciling religious differences within its ranks. The stated goal of the INC was to seek self-determination for all Indians regardless of class or religious affiliation, but many of its leaders were Hindu and inevitably reflected Hindu concerns. In the first decade of the twentieth century, a separate Muslim League was created to represent the interests of the millions of Muslims in Indian society.

NONVIOLENT RESISTANCE In 1915, a young Hindu lawyer returned from South Africa to become active in the INC. He transformed the movement and galvanized India's struggle for independence and identity. Mohandas Gandhi (moh-HAHN-dus GAHN-dee) (1869–1948) was born in Gujarat (goo-juh-RAHT), in western India, the son of a government minister. After earning a degree in law in London, in 1893 he went to South Africa to work in a law firm serving Indian émigrés working as laborers there. He soon became aware of the racial prejudice and exploitation experienced by Indians living in the territory and tried to organize them to protect their interests.

On his return to India, Gandhi immediately became active in the independence movement. Using his experience in South Africa, he set up a movement based on nonviolent resistance—the Hindi term was *satyagraha* (SUHT-yuh-grah-hah), meaning "hold fast to the truth"—to try to force the British to improve the lot of the poor and grant independence to India. His goal was twofold: to convert the British to his views while simultaneously strengthening the unity and sense of self-respect of his compatriots. Gandhi was particularly concerned about the plight of the millions of untouchables, whom he called *harijans* (HAR-ih-jans), or "children of God." When the British attempted to suppress dissent, he called on his followers to refuse to obey British regulations. He began to manufacture his own clothes, now dressing in a simple *dhoti* (DOH-tee) made of coarse homespun cotton, and adopted the spinning wheel as a symbol of Indian resistance to imports of British textiles.

Gandhi combined his anticolonial activities with an appeal to the spiritual instincts of all Indians. Though he had been born and raised a Hindu, his universalist approach to the idea of God transcended individual religion, albeit shaped by the historical themes of Hindu belief. At a speech given in London in September 1931, he expressed his view of the nature of God as "an indefinable mysterious power that pervades everything …, an unseen power which makes itself felt and yet defies all proof."[1]

Gandhi, now increasingly known as Mahatma (mah-HAHT-muh), or India's "Great Soul," organized mass protests to achieve his aims, but in 1919 they got out of hand and led to violence and British reprisals. British troops killed hundreds of unarmed protesters in an enclosed square in the city

AFGHANISTAN • KASHMIR AND JAMMU • CHINA • Lahore • Amritsar • TIBET • Delhi • Calcutta • BURMA • Bombay • Arabian Sea • Goa • Bay of Bengal • Madras • Pondicherry • CEYLON (CROWN COLONY)

0 375 750 Kilometers
0 250 500 Miles

© 2016 Cengage Learning

■ Areas under direct British rule

British India Between the Wars

COMPARATIVE ILLUSTRATION

POLITICS & GOVERNMENT

Masters and Disciples. When the founders of nationalist movements passed leadership over to their successors, the result was often a change in the strategy and tactics of the organizations. When Jawaharlal Nehru (left photo, on the left) replaced Mahatma Gandhi (wearing a simple Indian *dhoti* rather than the Western dress favored by his colleagues) as leader of the Indian National Congress, the movement adopted a more secular posture. In China, Chiang Kai-shek (right photo, standing) took Sun Yat-sen's Nationalist Party in a more conservative direction after Sun's death in 1925.

Q How do these four leaders compare in terms of their roles in furthering political change in their respective countries?

of Amritsar (am-RIT-sur) in northwestern India. When the protests spread, Gandhi was horrified at the violence. Nevertheless he was arrested for his role in sparking the protests and spent several years in prison.

While Gandhi was in prison, the political situation continued to evolve. In 1921, the British passed the Government of India Act, transforming the heretofore advisory Legislative Council into a bicameral parliament, two-thirds of whose members would be elected. Similar bodies were created at the provincial level. In a stroke, 5 million Indians were enfranchised. But such reforms were no longer enough for many members of the INC, who wanted to push aggressively for full independence. The British exacerbated the situation by increasing the salt tax and prohibiting the Indian people from manufacturing or harvesting their own salt. Gandhi, now released from prison, returned to his earlier policy of **civil disobedience** by openly joining several dozen supporters in a 240-mile walk to the sea, where he picked up a lump of salt and urged Indians to ignore the law. Gandhi and many other members of the INC were arrested.

Indian women were also active in the movement. The first organizations to promote women's rights had been established in the early years of the century, and they quickly became involved in a variety of efforts to bring about social reforms. Women accounted for about 20,000, or nearly 10 percent, of people arrested and jailed for taking part in demonstrations during the interwar period. Women marched, picketed foreign shops, and promoted the spinning and wearing of homemade cloth. By the 1930s, women's associations were actively promoting a number of reforms, including women's education, the introduction of birth control devices, the abolition of child marriage, and universal suffrage. In 1929, the Sarda Act raised the minimum age of marriage to fourteen.

NEW LEADERS AND NEW PROBLEMS In the 1930s, a new figure entered the movement in the person of Jawaharlal Nehru (juh-WAH-hur-lahl NAY-roo) (1889–1964), son of an earlier INC leader. Educated in the law in Great Britain and a *brahmin* by birth, Nehru personified the new Anglo-Indian politician: secular, rational, upper class, and intellectual (see the Comparative Illustration "Masters and Disciples" above). With Nehru's emergence, the independence movement embarked on two paths, religious and secular, Indian and Western, traditional and modern. The dual character of the INC leadership may well have strengthened the movement by bringing together the two primary impulses behind the desire for independence: elite nationalism and the primal force of Indian traditionalism. But it portended trouble for the nation's new leadership in defining India's future path in the contemporary world. In the meantime, Muslim discontent with Hindu dominance over the INC was increasing. In 1940, the Muslim League called for the creation of a separate Muslim state of Pakistan ("land of the pure") in the northwest (see Opposing Viewpoints "Islam in the Modern World: Two Views" on p. 701). As communal strife between Hindus and Muslims increased, many Indians came to realize with sorrow (and some British colonialists with satisfaction) that British rule was all that stood between peace and civil war.

The Nationalist Revolt in the Middle East

In the Middle East, as in Europe, World War I hastened the collapse of old empires. The Ottoman Empire, which had dominated the eastern Mediterranean since the seizure of Constantinople in 1453, had been growing weaker since the end of the eighteenth century, troubled by rising governmental corruption, a decline in the effectiveness of the sultans, and the loss of considerable territory in the Balkans and southwestern Russia. In North Africa, Ottoman authority, tenuous at best, had disintegrated in the nineteenth century, enabling the French to seize Algeria and Tunisia and the British to establish a protectorate over the Nile River valley.

TWILIGHT OF THE OTTOMAN EMPIRE Reformist elements in Istanbul, to be sure, had tried from time to time to resist the trend, but military defeats continued: Greece declared its independence, and Ottoman power eroded steadily in the Middle East. A rising sense of nationality among Serbs, Armenians, and other minority peoples threatened the internal stability and cohesion of the empire. In the 1870s, a new generation of Ottoman reformers seized power in Istanbul and pushed through a constitution aimed at forming a legislative assembly that would represent all the peoples in the state. But the sultan they placed on the throne suspended the new charter and attempted to rule by traditional authoritarian means.

By the end of the nineteenth century, the defunct 1876 constitution had become a symbol of change for reformist elements, now grouped together under the common name **Young Turks** (undoubtedly borrowed from the Young Italy nationalist movement earlier in the century). They found support in the Ottoman army and administration and among Turks living in exile. In 1908, the Young Turks forced the sultan to restore the constitution, and he was removed from power the following year.

But the Young Turks had appeared at a moment of extreme fragility for the empire. Internal rebellions, combined with Austrian annexations of Ottoman territories in the Balkans, undermined support for the new government and provoked the army to step in. With most minorities from the old empire now removed from Istanbul's authority, many ethnic Turks began to embrace a new concept of a Turkish state based on Turkish nationality.

The final blow to the old empire came in World War I, when the Ottoman government allied with Germany in the hope of driving the British from Egypt and restoring Ottoman rule over the Nile Valley. In response, the British declared an official protectorate over Egypt and, aided by the efforts of the dashing, if eccentric, British adventurer T. E. Lawrence (popularly known as Lawrence of Arabia), sought to undermine Ottoman rule in the Arabian peninsula by encouraging Arab nationalists there (see the Film & History feature "*Lawrence of Arabia* (1962)" on p. 700). In 1916, the local governor of Mecca, encouraged by the British, declared Arabia independent from Ottoman rule, while British troops, advancing from Egypt, seized Palestine. In October 1918, having suffered more than 300,000 casualties during the war, the Ottoman Empire negotiated an armistice with the Allied Powers.

MUSTAFA KEMAL AND THE MODERNIZATION OF TURKEY During the next few years, the tottering empire began to fall apart as the British and the French made plans to divide up Ottoman territories in the Middle East and the Greeks won Allied approval to seize the western parts of the Anatolian peninsula for their dream of re-creating the substance of the old Byzantine Empire. The impending collapse energized key elements in Turkey under the leadership of a war hero, Colonel Mustafa Kemal (moos-tah-FAH kuh-MAHL) (1881–1938), who had commanded Turkish forces in their successful defense of the Dardanelles against a British invasion during World War I. Now he resigned from the army and convoked a national congress that called for an elected government and the preservation of the remaining territories of the old empire in a new republic of Turkey. Establishing his capital at Ankara (AN-kuh-ruh), Kemal's forces drove the Greeks from the Anatolian peninsula and persuaded the British to agree to a new treaty. In 1923, the last of the Ottoman sultans fled the country, which was now declared a Turkish republic. The Ottoman Empire had come to an end.

During the next few years, President Mustafa Kemal, now popularly known as Atatürk (ah-tah-TIRK), or "Father Turk," attempted to transform Turkey into a modern secular republic. The trappings of a democratic system were put in place, centered on an elected Grand National Assembly, but the president was relatively intolerant of opposition and harshly suppressed critics of his rule. Turkish nationalism was emphasized, and the Turkish language, now written in the Roman alphabet, was shorn of many of its Arabic elements. Popular education was emphasized, old aristocratic titles like *pasha* and *bey* were abolished, and all Turkish citizens were given family names in the European style.

Atatürk also took steps to modernize the economy, overseeing the establishment of a light industrial sector producing textiles, glass, paper, and cement and instituting a five-year plan on the Soviet model to provide for state direction over the economy. Atatürk was no admirer of Soviet communism, however, and the Turkish economy can be better described as a form of state capitalism. He also encouraged the

Lawrence of Arabia (1962)

The conflict in the Middle East produced one of the great romantic heroes of World War I. T. E. Lawrence, a British army officer popularly known as Lawrence of Arabia, organized Arab tribesmen and led them in battle against the Ottoman Turks, who had become allies of the Central Powers (Germany and its allies). Although the military significance of Lawrence's exploits was limited, their long-term implications for the region were enormous. During the peace negotiations that followed the German surrender in November 1918, most Ottoman possessions in the Middle East were replaced by British and French mandates, while the Arabian peninsula embarked on the road to independence under the tribal chieftain Ibn Saud (IB-un sah-OOD). The political implications of that settlement are still important today.

The movie *Lawrence of Arabia* (1962), directed by the great British filmmaker David Lean, won seven Oscars and made an instant star of actor Peter O'Toole, who played the eccentric Lawrence with mesmerizing perfection. The photography and the acting are both superb, and Lean's deft portrayal of the behavior and motives of all participants makes the lengthy film (more than three hours) essential viewing for those interested in comprehending the complex roots of the current situation in the Middle East.

British objectives, as voiced by the British general Viscount Edmund Allenby (played by the veteran actor Jack Hawkins), were unabashedly military in nature—use Arab unrest in the region as a means of taking the Ottomans out of the war. Arab leaders such as Prince Faisal—languidly played by the consummate actor Alec Guinness—openly sought their independence from Turkish rule, but initially appeared hopelessly divided. It was Major Lawrence who provided the spark and the determination to knit together a coalition of Arab forces capable of

Columbia/The Kobal Collection/Picture Desk

T. E. Lawrence (Peter O'Toole in white) at the head of the Arab tribes.

winning crucial victories in the final year of the war. Faisal himself would eventually be chosen by the British to become the king of the artificial state of Iraq.

Lawrence himself remains an enigma—in the movie as in real life. Combining a fervent idealism about the Arab cause with an overweening sense of self-promotion, he played to the end an ambiguous role in the geopolitics of the Middle East. Disenchanted with the postwar peace settlement, he eventually removed himself from the public eye and died in a motorcycle accident in 1935.

---

modernization of the agricultural sector by establishing training institutions and model farms, but such reforms had relatively little effect on the nation's generally conservative peasantry.

Perhaps the most significant aspect of Atatürk's reform program was his attempt to break the power of the Islamic clerics and transform Turkey into a secular state. The caliphate was formally abolished in 1924 (see Opposing Viewpoints "Islam in the Modern World: Two Views" on p. 701), and *Shari'a* (Islamic law) was replaced by a revised version of the Swiss law code. The fez (the brimless cap worn by Turkish Muslims) was abolished, and women were discouraged from wearing the traditional Islamic veil. Women received the right to vote in 1934 and were legally guaranteed equal rights with men in all aspects of marriage and inheritance. Education and the professions were now open to citizens of both sexes, and some women even began to participate in politics. All citizens were given the right to convert to another religion at will. Finally, Atatürk attempted to break the waning power of the various religious orders of Islam by abolishing all monasteries and brotherhoods.

The legacy of Mustafa Kemal Atatürk was enormous. Although not all of his reforms were widely accepted in practice, especially by devout Muslims, most of the changes he introduced were retained after his death in 1938. In virtually every respect, the Turkish republic was the product of his determined efforts to create a modern Turkish nation.

OPPOSING ✕ VIEWPOINTS

Islam in the Modern World: Two Views

POLITICS & GOVERNMENT

AS PART OF HIS PLAN TO TRANSFORM TURKEY INTO A MODERN SOCIETY, Mustafa Kemal Atatürk sought to free his country from what he considered to be outdated practices imposed by traditional beliefs. The first selection is from a speech in which he proposed bringing an end to the caliphate, which had been in the hands of Ottoman sultans since the formation of the empire. But not all Muslims wished to move in the direction of a more secular society. Mohammed Iqbal (ik-BAHL), a well-known Muslim poet in colonial India, was a prominent advocate of the creation of a separate state for Muslims in South Asia. The second selection is from an address he presented to the All-India Muslim League in December 1930, explaining the rationale for his proposal.

Atatürk, Speech to the Assembly (October 1924)

The sovereign entitled Caliph was to maintain justice among the three hundred million Muslims on the terrestrial globe, to safeguard the rights of these peoples, to prevent any event that could encroach upon order and security, and confront every attack which the Muslims would be called upon to encounter from the side of other nations. It was to be part of his attributes to preserve by all means the welfare and spiritual development of Islam....

If the Caliph and Caliphate, as they maintained, were to be invested with a dignity embracing the whole of Islam, ought they not to have realized in all justice that a crushing burden would be imposed on Turkey, on her existence; her entire resources and all her forces would be placed at the disposal of the Caliph? ...

For centuries our nation was guided under the influence of these erroneous ideas. But what has been the result of it?

Everywhere they have lost millions of men. "Do you know," I asked, "how many sons of Anatolia have perished in the scorching deserts of the Yemen? Do you know the losses we have suffered in holding Syria and Egypt and in maintaining our position in Africa? And do you see what has come out of it? Do you know?

"Those who favor the idea of placing the means at the disposal of the Caliph to brave the whole world and the power to administer the affairs of the whole of Islam must not appeal to the population of Anatolia alone but to the great Muslim agglomerations which are eight or ten times as rich in men.

"New Turkey, the people of New Turkey, have no reason to think of anything else but their own existence and their own welfare. She has nothing more to give away to others."

Mohammed Iqbal, Speech to the All-India Muslim League (1930)

It cannot be denied that Islam, regarded as an ethical ideal plus a certain kind of polity—by which expression I mean a social structure regulated by a legal system and animated by a specific ethical ideal—has been the chief formative factor in the life history of the Muslims of India. It has furnished those basic emotions and loyalties which gradually unify scattered individuals and groups and finally transform them into a well-defined people. Indeed it is no exaggeration to say that India is perhaps the only country in the world where Islam, as a people-building force, has worked at its best. In India, as elsewhere, the structure of Islam as a society is almost entirely due to the working of Islam as a culture inspired by a specific ethical ideal. What I mean to say is that Muslim society, with its remarkable homogeneity and inner unity, has grown to be what it is under the pressure of the laws and institutions associated with the culture of Islam.

Communalism in its higher aspect, then, is indispensable to the formation of a harmonious whole in a country like India.

The units of Indian society are not territorial as in European countries. India is a continent of human groups belonging to different religions. Their behavior is not at all determined by a common race consciousness. Even the Hindus do not form a homogeneous group. The principle of European democracy cannot be applied to India without recognizing the fact of communal groups. The Muslim demand for the creation of a Muslim India within India is, therefore, perfectly justified....

I therefore demand the formation of a consolidated Muslim State in the best interests of India and Islam. For India it means security and peace resulting from an internal balance of power; for Islam an opportunity to rid itself of the stamp that Arabian imperialism was forced to give it, to mobilize its law, its education, its culture, and to bring them into closer contact with its own original spirit and with the spirit of modern times.

Q *Why did Mustafa Kemal believe that the caliphate no longer met the needs of the Turkish people? Why did Mohammed Iqbal believe that a separate state for Muslims in India would be required? How did he attempt to persuade non-Muslims that this would be to their benefit as well?*

Source: From Ataturk's Speech to the Assembly, pp. 432–433. A speech delivered by Ghazi Mustafa Kemal, President of the Turkish Republic, October 1927. From *Sources of Indian Tradition*, Vol. 2, 2e, by Stephen Hay, pp. 218–222. Copyright © 1988 by Columbia University Press. Reprinted with permission of the publisher.

AP Images

Mustafa Kemal Atatürk. The war hero Mustafa Kemal took the initiative in creating the republic of Turkey. As president of the new republic, Atatürk ("Father Turk"), as he came to be called, worked hard to transform Turkey into a modern secular state by restructuring the economy, adopting Western dress, and breaking the powerful hold of Islamic traditions. He is now reviled by Muslim fundamentalists for his opposition to an Islamic state. In this photograph, Atatürk, at the left in civilian clothes, hosts the shah of Persia during the latter's visit to Turkey in July 1934.

MODERNIZATION IN IRAN In the meantime, a similar process was under way in Persia. Under the Qajar (kuh-JAHR) dynasty (1794–1925), the country had not been very successful in resisting Russian advances in the Caucasus or resolving its domestic problems. To secure themselves from foreign influence, the Qajars moved the capital from Tabriz to Tehran (teh-RAHN), in a mountainous area just south of the Caspian Sea. During the mid-nineteenth century, one modernizing shah attempted to introduce political and economic reforms but faced resistance from tribal and religious—predominantly Shi'ite—forces. To buttress its rule, the dynasty turned increasingly to Russia and Great Britain to protect itself from its own people.

Eventually, the growing foreign presence led to the rise of an indigenous Persian nationalist movement. Its efforts were largely directed against Russian advances in the northwest and the growing European influence in the small modern industrial sector, the profits from which left the country or disappeared into the hands of the dynasty's ruling elite. Supported actively by Shi'ite religious leaders, opposition to the regime rose steadily among both peasants and merchants in the cities, and in 1906, popular pressures forced the reigning shah to grant a constitution on the Western model. It was an eerie foretaste of the revolution of 1979 (see Chapter 29).

© 2016 Cengage Learning

Iran Under the Pahlavi Dynasty

As in the Ottoman Empire and Manchu China, however, the modernizers had moved too soon, before their power base was secure. With the support of the Russians and the British, the shah was able to retain control, while the two foreign powers began to divide the country into separate spheres of influence. One reason for the growing foreign presence in Persia was the discovery of oil reserves in the southern part of the country in 1908. Within a few years, oil exports increased rapidly, with the bulk of the profits going into the pockets of British investors.

In 1921, an officer in the Persian army by the name of Reza Khan (ree-ZAH KAHN) (1878–1944) led a mutiny that seized power in Tehran. The new ruler had originally intended to establish a republic, but resistance from traditional forces impeded his efforts, and in 1925 the new Pahlavi (PAH-luh-vee) dynasty, with Reza Khan as shah, replaced the now defunct Qajar dynasty. During the next few years, Reza Khan attempted to follow the example of Atatürk in Turkey, introducing a number of reforms to strengthen the central government, modernize the civilian and military bureaucracy, and establish a modern economic infrastructure. In 1935, he officially changed the name of the nation to Iran.

Unlike Atatürk, Reza Khan did not attempt to destroy the power of Islamic beliefs, but he did encourage the establishment of a Western-style educational system and forbade women to wear the veil in public. Women continued to be exploited, however. Like the textile industry in Meiji Japan (see Chapter 22), the Iranian carpet industry was based on the intensive labor of women; the carpets they produced were a valuable export—second only to oil—in the interwar period. To strengthen the sense of Iranian nationalism and reduce the power of Islam, Reza Khan attempted to popularize the symbols and beliefs of pre-Islamic times. Like his Qajar predecessors, however, he was hindered by strong foreign influence. When the Soviet Union and Great Britain decided to send troops into the country during World War II, he resigned in protest and died three years later.

NATION BUILDING IN IRAQ One other consequence of the collapse of the Ottoman Empire was the emergence of a new political entity along the Tigris and Euphrates Rivers, once the heartland of ancient empires. Lacking defensible borders and sharply divided along ethnic and religious lines—a Shi'ite majority in rural areas was balanced by a vocal Sunni minority in the cities and a largely Kurdish population in the northern mountains—the area had been under Ottoman rule since the seventeenth century. With the advent of World War I, the lowland area from Baghdad southward to the Persian Gulf was occupied by British forces, who hoped to protect oil-producing regions in neighboring Persia from a German takeover.

Although the British claimed to have arrived as liberators, in 1920 the country now known as Iraq was placed under

CHRONOLOGY   The Middle East Between the Wars

Balfour Declaration on Palestine	1917
Reza Khan seizes power in Persia	1921
End of Ottoman Empire and establishment of a republic in Turkey	1923
Rule of Mustafa Kemal Atatürk in Turkey	1923–1938
Beginning of Pahlavi dynasty in Iran	1925
Establishment of kingdom of Saudi Arabia	1932

British control as a mandate of the League of Nations. Civil unrest and growing anti-Western sentiment rapidly dispelled any immediate plans for the emergence of an independent government, and in 1921, after the suppression of resistance forces, the country was placed under the titular authority of King Faisal (FY-suhl) of Syria, a descendant of the Prophet Muhammad. Faisal relied for support primarily on the politically more sophisticated urban Sunni population, although they represented less than a quarter of the population. The discovery of oil near Kirkuk (kir-KOOK) in 1927 increased the value of the area to the British, who granted formal independence to the country in 1932, although British advisers retained a strong influence over the fragile government.

THE RISE OF ARAB NATIONALISM As we have seen, the Arab uprising during World War I helped bring about the demise of the Ottoman Empire. There had been resistance against Ottoman rule in the Arabian peninsula since the eighteenth century, when the devoutly Muslim Wahhabi (wuh-HAH-bee) sect revolted in an attempt to drive out outside influences and cleanse Islam of corrupt practices that had developed in past centuries. The revolt was eventually suppressed, but Wahhabi influence within the Arab population persisted.

World War I offered an opportunity for the Arabs to throw off the shackles of Ottoman rule—but what would replace them? The Arabs were not a nation but an idea, a loose collection of peoples who often did not see eye to eye on matters that affected their community. Disagreement over what constitutes an Arab has plagued generations of political leaders who have sought unsuccessfully to knit together the disparate peoples of the region into a single Arab nation.

When the Arab leaders in Mecca declared their independence from Ottoman rule in 1916, they had hoped for British support, but—despite the efforts of T. E. Lawrence—they were to be sorely disappointed. At the close of the war, the British and French agreed to create a number of mandates in the area

under the general supervision of the League of Nations (see Chapter 23). Iraq was assigned to the British; Syria and Lebanon (the two areas were separated so that Christian peoples in Lebanon could be placed under Christian administration) were given to the French.

In the early 1920s, a leader of the Wahhabi movement, Ibn Saud (IB-un sah-OOD) (1880–1953), united Arab tribes in the northern part of the Arabian peninsula and drove out the remnants of Ottoman rule. Ibn Saud was a descendant of the family that had led the Wahhabi revolt in the eighteenth century. Devout and gifted, he won broad support among Arab tribal peoples and established the kingdom of Saudi Arabia throughout much of the peninsula in 1932.

At first, his new kingdom, consisting essentially of the vast desert wastes of central Arabia, was desperately poor. Its financial resources were limited to the income from Muslim pilgrims visiting the holy sites in Mecca and Medina. But during the 1930s, American companies began to explore for oil, and in 1938, Standard Oil made a successful strike at Dhahran (dah-RAHN), on the Persian Gulf. Soon an Arabian-American oil conglomerate, popularly called Aramco, was established, and the isolated kingdom was suddenly inundated by Western oilmen and untold wealth.

The Impact of Oil. Oil discoveries in the Arabian peninsula and the Persian Gulf in the early twentieth century brought unimagined wealth to Western oil companies, their investors, and to elite groups throughout the region. It also distorted the local political culture in many countries and resulted in widespread foreign interference. The Middle East is still paying a heavy price for this unforeseen gift. Shown here is an oil derrick being prepared to provide "black gold" to the outside world in the desert wastes of Saudi Arabia.

Dmitri Kessel/Time Life Pictures/The LIFE Premium Collection/Getty Images

The Rise of Nationalism   ■   **703**

The Zionist Case for Palestine

POLITICS & GOVERNMENT

AFTER THE BRITISH GOVERNMENT ISSUED THE FAMOUS Balfour Declaration in 1917 recognizing the right of the Jewish people to a Jewish homeland in Palestine, the Zionist organization presented a memorandum to the delegates at the Paris Peace Conference in February 1919. The memorandum, excerpted here, sought to make the case for a Jewish home in Palestine as the Great Powers assembled to discuss the future of one-time Ottoman holdings in the Middle East.

Memorandum to the Peace Conference in Versailles

The Historic Title

The claims of the Jews with regard to Palestine rest upon the following main considerations:

1. The land is the historic home of the Jews; there they achieved their greatest development; from the centre, through their agency, there emanated spiritual and moral influences of supreme value to mankind. By violence they were driven from Palestine, and through the ages they have never ceased to cherish the longing and the hope of a return.

2. In some parts of the world, and particularly in Eastern Europe, the conditions of life of millions of Jews are deplorable. Forming often a congested population, denied the opportunities which would make a healthy development possible, the need of fresh outlets is urgent, both for their own sake and the interests of the population of other races, among whom they dwell. Palestine would offer one such outlet. To the Jewish masses it is the country above all others in which they would most wish to cast their lot. By the methods of economic development to which we

shall refer later, Palestine can be made now, as it was in ancient times, the home of a prosperous population many times as numerous as that which now inhabits it.

3. Palestine is not large enough to contain more than a proportion of the Jews of the world. The greater part of the fourteen millions or more scattered throughout all countries must remain in their present localities, and it will doubtless be one of the cares of the Peace Conference to ensnare for them, wherever they have been oppressed, as for all peoples, equal rights and humane conditions. A Jewish National Home in Palestine will, however, be of high value to them also. Its influence will permeate the Jewries of the world, it will inspire these millions, hitherto often despairing, with a new hope; it will hold out before their eyes a higher standard; it will help to make them even more useful citizens in the lands in which they dwell.

4. Such a Palestine would be of value also to the world at large, whose real wealth consists in the healthy diversities of its civilizations.

5. Lastly, the land itself needs redemption. Much of it is left desolate. Its present condition is a standing reproach. Two things are necessary for that redemption—a stable and enlightened Government, and an addition to the present population which shall be energetic, intelligent, devoted to the country, and backed by the large financial resources that are indispensable for development. Such a population the Jews alone can supply.

What are the key points included in this excerpt of a memorandum in defense of the idea of a Jewish state in Palestine?

Source: David Hunter Miller, *My Diary at the Conference of Paris* (New York, 1924), V, pp. 15–29, as printed in Akram F. Khater, *Sources in the History of the Modern Middle East*, 2nd ed. (Cengage, 2011), pp. 152–153.

THE ISSUE OF PALESTINE The land of Palestine—once the home of the Jews but now inhabited primarily by Muslim Arabs—became a separate mandate and immediately became a thorny problem for the British. In 1897, the Austrian-born journalist Theodor Herzl (1860–1904) (see Chapter 20) had convened an international conference in Basel, Switzerland, which led to the creation of a World Zionist Organization (WZO). The aim of the organization was to create a homeland in Palestine for the Jewish people, who had long been dispersed widely throughout Europe, North Africa, and the Middle East.

Over the next decade, Jewish immigration into Palestine, then under Ottoman rule, increased with WZO support. By the outbreak of World War I, about 85,000 Jews lived in Palestine, representing about 15 percent of the total population. In 1917, responding to appeals from the British chemist Chaim Weizmann (KY-im VYTS-mahn), British Foreign

Secretary Lord Arthur Balfour (BAL-foor) issued a declaration stating that Palestine was to be a national home for the Jews (see the box "The Zionist Case for Palestine" above). The Balfour Declaration, which was later confirmed by the League of Nations, was ambiguous on the legal status of the territory and promised that the decision would not undermine the rights of the non-Jewish peoples currently living in the area. But Arab nationalists were incensed. How could a national home for the Jewish people be established in a territory where the majority of the population was Muslim?

After World War I, more Jewish settlers began to arrive in Palestine in response to the promises made in the Balfour Declaration. As tensions between the new arrivals and existing Muslim residents began to escalate, the British tried to restrict Jewish immigration into the territory while Arab voices rejected the concept of a separate state. In a bid to relieve Arab sensitivities, Great Britain created the separate emirate of Trans-Jordan out of the eastern portion of Palestine. After World War II, it would become the independent kingdom of Jordan. The stage was set for the conflicts that would take place in the region after World War II.

THE BRITISH IN EGYPT The waves of nationalist agitation also lapped at the shores of North Africa. Great Britain had maintained a loose protectorate over Egypt since the middle of the nineteenth century, although the area remained nominally under Ottoman rule. London formalized its protectorate in 1914 to protect the Suez Canal and the Nile River valley from possible seizure by the Central Powers. After the war, however, nationalist elements became restive and formed the Wafd (WAHFT) Party, a secular organization dedicated to the creation of an independent Egypt based on the principles of representative government. The Wafd received the support of many middle-class Egyptians who, like Kemal Atatürk in Turkey, hoped to meld Islamic practices with the secular tradition of the modern West. This modernist form of Islam did not have broad appeal outside the cosmopolitan centers, however, and in 1928 the Muslim cleric Hasan al-Bana (hah-SAHN al-BAN-ah) organized the Muslim Brotherhood, which demanded strict adherence to the traditional teachings of the Prophet, as set forth in the Qur'an. The Brotherhood rejected Western ways and sought to create a new Egypt based firmly on the precepts of the *Shari'a*. By the 1930s, the organization had as many as a million members.

Nationalism and Revolution

Before the Russian Revolution, to most intellectuals in Asia and Africa, "westernization" referred to the capitalist democratic civilization of Western Europe and the United States, not the doctrine of social revolution developed by Karl Marx. Until 1917, Marxism was regarded as a utopian idea rather than a concrete system of government. Moreover, to many observers, Marxism appeared to have little relevance to conditions in Asia and Africa. Marxist doctrine, after all, declared that a communist society would arise only from the ashes of an advanced capitalist society that had already passed through the Industrial Revolution. Since most societies in Asia and Africa, from the perspective of Marxist historical analysis, were still at the feudal stage of development; they lacked the economic conditions and political awareness to achieve a socialist revolution that would bring the working class to power.

Finally, the Marxist view of nationalism and religion had little appeal to many patriotic individuals in the non-Western world. Marx believed that nationhood and religion were essentially false ideas that diverted the attention of the oppressed masses from the critical issues of class struggle and, in his phrase, the exploitation of one person by another. Instead, Marx stressed an "internationalist" outlook based on class consciousness and the eventual creation of a classless society with no artificial divisions

French mandates
British mandates

The Middle East After World War I

based on culture, nation, or religion. To many observers in Asia and Africa where religious faith was a fact of daily life, such views had little relevance.

For these reasons, many patriotic individuals and groups outside of Europe initially deemed Marxism both irrelevant and unappealing. That situation began to change after the Russian Revolution in 1917. The rise to power of the Bolsheviks demonstrated that a revolutionary party espousing Marxist principles could overturn a corrupt, outdated system and launch a new experiment dedicated to ending human inequality and achieving a paradise on earth. In 1920, Lenin proposed a new revolutionary strategy designed to relate Marxist doctrine and practice to non-Western societies. His reasons were not based on theoretical considerations alone. Soviet Russia, surrounded by capitalist powers, desperately needed allies in its struggle to survive in a hostile world.

LENIN AND THE EAST To Lenin, the anticolonial movements emerging in North Africa, Asia, and the Middle East after World War I were natural allies of the beleaguered new regime in Moscow. In the spring of 1913, he had written, "Was it so long ago that China was considered typical of the lands that had been standing still for centuries? Today China is a land of seething political activity, the scene of a virile social movement and of a democratic upsurge."[2] Similar conditions, he added, were spreading the revolution to other parts of Asia—to Turkey, Persia, Iraq, and British India. Since, in Lenin's view, only the ability of the imperialist powers to find markets, raw materials, and sources of capital investment in the non-Western world kept capitalism alive, if the tentacles of capitalist influence in Asia and Africa could be severed, imperialism would weaken and collapse.

Establishing such an alliance would not be easy, however. Most nationalist leaders in colonial countries belonged to the urban middle class, and many abhorred the idea of a comprehensive revolution to create a totally egalitarian society. In addition, many still adhered to traditional religious beliefs and were opposed to the atheistic principles of classical Marxism. As a result, Lenin sought a compromise that would enable Communist parties organized among the working classes in the preindustrial societies of Asia and Africa to forge informal alliances with existing middle-class parties to struggle against the common enemies of feudal reaction (the remnants of the traditional ruling class) and Western imperialism. Such an alliance, in his view, could not be permanent because many bourgeois nationalists in Asia and Africa would reject an egalitarian, classless society. Once the imperialists had been overthrown, therefore, the Communist parties would turn against their erstwhile nationalist partners to seize power on their own and carry out the socialist revolution. Lenin thus proposed a two-stage revolution: an initial "national democratic" stage followed by a "proletarian socialist" stage.

The Path of Liberation

POLITICS & GOVERNMENT

IN 1919, the Vietnamese revolutionary Ho Chi Minh (1890–1969) was living in exile in France, where he first became acquainted with the new revolutionary experiment in Bolshevik Russia. Later he became a leader of the Vietnamese Communist movement. In the following passage, written in 1960, he reminisces about his reasons for becoming a Communist. The Second International mentioned in the text was an organization created in 1889 by moderate socialists who pursued their goal by parliamentary means. Lenin created the Third International, or Comintern, in 1919 to promote violent revolution. Having rallied to Lenin's strategy at the Congress of Tours in 1920, Ho Chi Minh went to Moscow in 1923 to receive training at Comintern headquarters.

Ho Chi Minh, "The Path Which Led Me to Leninism"

After World War I, I made my living in Paris, now as a retoucher at a photographer's, now as a painter of "Chinese antiquities" (made in France!). I would distribute leaflets denouncing the crimes committed by the French colonialists in Vietnam.

At that time, I supported the October Revolution [in Russia] only instinctively, not yet grasping all its historic importance. I loved and admired Lenin because he was a great patriot who liberated his compatriots; until then, I had read none of his books.

The reason for my joining the French Socialist Party was that these "ladies and gentlemen"—as I called my comrades at that moment—had shown their sympathy toward me, toward the struggle of the oppressed peoples. But I understood neither what was a party, a trade union, nor what was Socialism nor Communism.

Heated discussions were then taking place in the branches of the Socialist Party, about the question whether the Socialist Party should remain in the Second International, should a Second-and-a-Half International be founded, or should the Socialist Party join Lenin's Third International? I attended the meetings regularly, twice or three times a week, and attentively listened to the discussion. First, I could not understand thoroughly. Why were the discussions so heated? Either with the Second, Second-and-a-Half, or Third International, the revolution could be waged. What was the use of arguing then? As for the First International, what had become of it?

What I wanted most to know—and this precisely was not debated in the meetings—was: which International sides with the peoples of colonial countries?

I raised this question—the most important in my opinion—in a meeting. Some comrades answered: It is the Third, not the Second International. And a comrade gave me Lenin's "Thesis on the national and colonial questions," published by *l'Humanité*, to read.

There were political terms difficult to understand in this thesis. But by dint of reading it again and again, finally I could grasp the main part of it. What emotion, enthusiasm, clear sightedness, and confidence it instilled in me! I was overjoyed to tears. Though sitting alone in my room, I shouted aloud as if addressing large crowds: "Dear martyrs, compatriots! This is what we need, this is the path to our liberation!"

After that, I had entire confidence in Lenin, in the Third International.

Why did Ho Chi Minh believe that the Third International was the key to the liberation of the colonial peoples? What were the essential elements of Lenin's strategy for bringing that about?

Source: From *Vietnam: History, Documents, and Opinions on a Major World Crisis*, Marvin Gentleman, ed. (New York: Fawcett Publications, 1965), pp. 30–32.

Lenin's strategy became a major element in Soviet foreign policy in the 1920s. Soviet agents fanned out across the world to carry Marxism beyond the boundaries of industrial Europe. The primary instrument of this effort was the Third International, usually known as the **Communist International**, or **Comintern** for short. Formed in 1919 at Lenin's prodding, the Comintern was a worldwide organization of Communist parties dedicated to the advancement of world revolution. At its headquarters in Moscow, agents from around the world were trained in the precepts of world communism and then sent back to their own countries to form Marxist parties and promote the cause of social revolution. By the end of the 1920s, almost every colonial or semicolonial society in Asia had a party based on Marxist principles. The Soviets had less success in the Middle East, where Marxist ideology appealed mainly to minorities such as Jews and Armenians in the cities, or in black Africa, where Soviet strategists in any case felt that conditions were not sufficiently advanced for the creation of Communist organizations (the rise of nationalist and revolutionary movements in sub-Saharan Africa will be discussed in Chapter 29).

THE APPEAL OF COMMUNISM According to Marxist doctrine, the rank and file of Communist parties should be urban factory workers alienated from capitalist society by inhumane working conditions. In practice, many of the leaders even in European Communist parties tended to be urban intellectuals or members of the lower middle class (in Marxist parlance, the "petty bourgeoisie"). That phenomenon was even more true in the non-Western world, where most early Marxists were rootless intellectuals. Some were probably drawn into the movement for patriotic reasons and saw Marxist doctrine as a new and more effective means of modernizing their societies and removing the colonial exploiters. Such was the case with the Vietnamese patriot Ho Chi Minh (see the box "The Path of Liberation" above).

Others were attracted by the message of egalitarian communism and the utopian dream of a classless society. For those who had lost their faith in traditional religion, communism often served as a new secular ideology, dealing not with the hereafter but with the here and now or, indeed, with a remote future when the state would wither away and the "classless society" would replace the lost truth of traditional faiths.

Of course, the new doctrine's appeal was not the same in all non-Western societies. In Confucian societies such as China and Vietnam, where traditional belief systems had been badly discredited by their failure to counter the Western challenge, communism had an immediate impact and rapidly became a major factor in the anticolonial movement. In Buddhist and Muslim societies, where traditional religion remained strong and actually became a cohesive factor in the resistance movement, communism had less success. To maximize their appeal and minimize potential conflict with traditional ideas, Communist parties frequently attempted to adapt Marxist doctrine to indigenous values and institutions. In the Middle East, for example, the Ba'ath (BAHTH) Party in Syria adopted a hybrid socialism combining Marxism with Arab nationalism. The Wafd Party in Egypt was less receptive to revolutionary ideals. Formed by modernist intellectuals in 1918, it focused its efforts on the creation of an independent government based on Western democratic principles and gave little thought to measures designed to alleviate problems of poverty in urban and rural areas.

In some instances, the Communists were briefly able to establish a cooperative relationship with the bourgeois parties. The most famous example was the alliance between the Chinese Communist Party and Sun Yat-sen's Nationalist Party (discussed in the next section). In the Dutch East Indies, the Indonesian Communist Party (known as the PKI) allied with the middle-class nationalist group Sarekat Islam but later broke loose in an effort to organize its own mass movement among the poor peasants. In French Indochina, a revolutionary movement organized by Ho Chi Minh sought at first to cooperate with bourgeois nationalist parties against the colonial regime. These efforts were abandoned in 1928, however, when the Comintern, reacting to Chiang Kai-shek's betrayal of the alliance with the Chinese Communist Party, declared that Communist parties should restrict their recruiting efforts to the most revolutionary elements in society—notably, the urban intellectuals and the working class. Harassed by colonial authorities and saddled with strategic directions from Moscow that often had little relevance to local conditions, Communist groups in most colonial societies had little success in the 1930s and failed to build a secure base of support among the mass of the population.

Revolution in China

 FOCUS QUESTION: What problems did China encounter between the two world wars, and what solutions did the Nationalists and the Communists propose to solve them?

Overall, revolutionary Marxism had its greatest impact in China, where a group of young radicals, including several

faculty and staff members from Peking (Beijing) University, founded the Chinese Communist Party (CCP) in 1921. The rise of the CCP was a consequence of the failed revolution of 1911. When political forces are too weak or too divided to consolidate their power during a period of instability, the military usually steps in to fill the vacuum. In China, Sun Yat-sen (SOON yaht-SEN) and his colleagues had accepted General Yuan Shikai (yoo-AHN shee-KY) as president of the new Chinese republic in 1911 because they lacked the military strength to compete with his control over the army (see Chapter 22). Moreover, many feared, perhaps rightly, that if the revolt lapsed into chaos, the Western powers would intervene and the last shreds of Chinese sovereignty would be lost. But some had misgivings about Yuan's intentions. As one remarked in a letter to a friend, "We don't know whether he will be a George Washington or a Napoleon."

As it turned out, he was neither. Showing little comprehension of the new ideas sweeping into China from the West, Yuan ruled in a traditional manner, reviving Confucian rituals and institutions and eventually trying to found a new imperial dynasty. Yuan's dictatorial inclinations rapidly led to clashes with Sun's party, now renamed the Guomindang (GWOH-min-dahng), or Nationalist Party. When Yuan dissolved the new parliament, the Nationalists launched a rebellion; it failed, and Sun fled to Japan.

Yuan was strong enough to brush off the challenge from the revolutionary forces but not to turn back the clock of history. He died in 1916 (apparently of natural causes, although legend holds that his heart was broken by popular resistance to his imperial pretensions) and was succeeded by one of his military subordinates. For the next several years, China slipped into semianarchy as the power of the central government disintegrated and military warlords seized power in the provinces.

Mr. Science and Mr. Democracy: The New Culture Movement

Although the failure of the 1911 revolution was a clear sign that China was not yet ready for radical change, discontent with existing conditions continued to rise in various sectors of Chinese society. The most vocal protests came from radical intellectuals, who opposed Yuan Shikai's conservative rule but were now convinced that political change could not take place until the Chinese people were more familiar with trends in the outside world. Braving the displeasure of Yuan and his successors, progressive intellectuals at Peking University launched the **New Culture Movement**, aimed at abolishing the remnants of the old system and introducing Western values and institutions into China. Using the classrooms of China's most prestigious university as well as the pages of newly established progressive magazines and newspapers, the intellectuals introduced a bewildering mix of new ideas, from the philosophy of Friedrich Nietzsche (FREED-rikh NEE-chuh) and Bertrand Russell to the educational views of the American John Dewey and the feminist plays of Henrik Ibsen. As such ideas flooded into China, they stirred up a new generation of educated Chinese youth, who chanted "Down with

Confucius and sons" and talked of a new era dominated by "Mr. Sai" (Mr. Science) and "Mr. De" (Mr. Democracy). No one was a greater defender of free thought and speech than the chancellor of Peking University, Cai Yuanpei (TSY yoo-wahn-PAY):

> So far as theoretical ideas are concerned, I follow the principles of "freedom of thought" and an attitude of broad tolerance in accordance with the practice of universities the world over.... Regardless of what school of thought a person may adhere to, so long as that person's ideas are justified and conform to reason and have not been passed by through the process of natural selection, although there may be controversy, such ideas have a right to be presented.[3]

The problem was that appeals for American-style democracy and women's liberation had little relevance to Chinese peasants, most of whom were still illiterate and concerned above all with survival. Consequently, the New Culture Movement did not win widespread support outside the urban areas. It certainly earned the distrust of conservative military officers, one of whom threatened to lob artillery shells into Peking University to destroy the poisonous new ideas and eliminate their advocates.

Discontent among intellectuals, however, was soon joined by the rising chorus of public protest against Japan's efforts to expand its influence on the mainland. During the first decade of the twentieth century, Japan had taken advantage of the Qing's decline to extend its domination over Manchuria and Korea (see Chapter 22). In 1915, the Japanese government insisted that Yuan Shikai accept a series of twenty-one demands that would have given Japan a virtual protectorate over the Chinese government and economy. Yuan was able to fend off the most far-reaching Japanese demands by arousing popular outrage in China, but at the Paris Peace Conference four years later, Japan received Germany's sphere of influence in Shandong (Shahn-DOONG) Province as a reward for its support of the Allied cause in World War I. On hearing that the Chinese government had accepted the decision, on May 4, 1919, patriotic students, supported by other sectors of the urban population, demonstrated in Beijing and other major cities of the country (see the Comparative Illustration "Student Demonstrations in Beijing" on p. 709). Although this May Fourth Movement did not lead to the restoration of Shandong to Chinese rule, it did alert a substantial part of the politically literate population to the threat to national survival and the incompetence of the warlord government.

The Nationalist-Communist Alliance

By 1920, central authority had almost ceased to exist in China. Two competing political forces now began to emerge from the chaos. One was Sun Yat-sen's Nationalist Party. Driven from the political arena seven years earlier by Yuan Shikai, the party now reestablished itself on the mainland by making an alliance with the warlord ruler of Guangdong (gwahng-DOONG) Province in southern China. From Canton, Sun sought international assistance to carry out his national revolution. The other was the CCP. Following Lenin's strategy, Comintern agents advised the new party to link up with the more experienced Nationalists. Sun Yat-sen needed the expertise and the diplomatic support that Soviet Russia could provide because his anti-imperialist rhetoric had alienated many Western powers; one English-language newspaper in Shanghai remarked, "All his life, all his influence, are devoted to ideas which keep China in turmoil, and it is utterly undesirable that he should be allowed to prosecute those aims here."[4] In 1923, the two parties formed an alliance to oppose the warlords and drive the imperialist powers out of China.

For three years, with the assistance of a Comintern mission in Canton, the two parties submerged their mutual suspicions and mobilized and trained a revolutionary army to march north and seize control of China. The so-called Northern Expedition began in the summer of 1926 (see Map 24.1). By the following spring, revolutionary forces were in control of all Chinese territory south of the Yangzi River, including the major river ports of Wuhan (WOO-HAHN) and Shanghai (SHANG-hy). But

MAP 24.1 The Northern Expedition and the Long March. This map shows the routes taken by the combined Nationalist-Communist forces during the Northern Expedition of 1926–1928. The blue arrow indicates the route taken by Communist units during the Long March led by Mao Zedong. Provinces mentioned in the text are indicated in capital letters on the map.

Q *Where did Mao establish his new headquarters after the Long March?*

Sovfoto/Universal Images Group/Getty Images

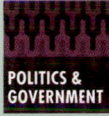

COMPARATIVE ILLUSTRATION

POLITICS & GOVERNMENT

Student Demonstrations in Beijing. On May 4, 1919, students gathered at Tiananmen Square in central Beijing to protest the Japanese takeover of the Shandong Peninsula after World War I. The protests triggered the famous May Fourth Movement, which highlighted the demand by progressive forces in China for political and social reforms. In the top photo, women students in Shanghai demonstrate for reforms in conjunction with the protests taking place in Beijing and other cities around China. Seventy years later (bottom photo), students and their supporters gathered once again in Tiananmen Square to demand democracy and an end to official corruption in China. The Heroes' Monument and Mao's mausoleum are in the background.

© William J. Duiker

 Compare and contrast the motives, participants, and consequences of the demonstrations that took place in 1919 and 1989.

tensions between the two parties now surfaced. Sun Yat-sen had died of cancer in 1925 and was succeeded as head of the Nationalist Party by his military subordinate, Chiang Kai-shek (CHANG ky-SHEK) (see the Comparative Illustration "Masters and Disciples" on p. 698). Chiang feigned support for the alliance with the Communists but actually planned to destroy them. In April 1927, he struck against the Communists and their supporters in Shanghai, killing thousands. After the massacre, most of the Communist leaders went into hiding in the city, where they attempted to revive the movement in its traditional base among the urban working class. Some party members, however, led by the young Communist organizer Mao Zedong (mow zee-DOONG ["ow" as in "how"]), fled to the hilly areas south of the Yangzi River.

Unlike most CCP leaders, Mao was convinced that the Chinese revolution must be based not on workers in the big cities but on the impoverished peasants in the countryside. The son of a prosperous farmer, Mao had helped organize a

A Call for Revolt

POLITICS & GOVERNMENT

IN THE FALL OF 1926, Nationalist and Communist forces moved north from Canton on their Northern Expedition in an effort to defeat the warlords. The young Communist Mao Zedong accompanied revolutionary troops into his home province of Hunan, where he submitted a report to the CCP Central Committee calling for a massive peasant revolt against the ruling order. The report shows his confidence that peasants could play an active role in the Chinese revolution despite the skepticism of many of his colleagues.

Mao Zedong, "The Peasant Movement in Hunan"

During my recent visit to Hunan I made a firsthand investigation of conditions.... In a very short time, ... several hundred million peasants will rise like a mighty storm, ... a force so swift and violent that no power, however great, will be able to hold it back. They will smash all the trammels that bind them and rush forward along the road to liberation. They will sweep all the imperialists, warlords, corrupt officials, local tyrants, and evil gentry into their graves. Every revolutionary party and every revolutionary comrade will be put to the test, to be accepted or rejected as they decide. There are three alternatives. To march at their head and lead them? To trail behind them, gesticulating and criticizing? Or to stand in their way and oppose them? Every Chinese is free to choose, but events will force you to make the choice quickly.

The main targets of attack by the peasants are the local tyrants, the evil gentry and the lawless landlords, but in passing they also hit out against patriarchal ideas and institutions, against the corrupt officials in the cities and against bad practices and customs in the rural areas.... As a result, the privileges which the feudal landlords enjoyed for thousands of years are being shattered to pieces.... With the collapse of the power of the landlords, the peasant associations have now become the sole organs of authority, and the popular slogan "All power to the peasant associations" has become a reality.

The peasants' revolt disturbed the gentry's sweet dreams. When the news from the countryside reached the cities, it caused immediate uproar among the gentry.... From the middle social strata upwards to the Kuomintang [Nationalist] right-wingers, there was not a single person who did not sum up the whole business in the phrase, "It's terrible!" ... Even quite progressive people said, "Though terrible, it is inevitable in a revolution." In short, nobody could altogether deny the word "terrible." But ... the fact is that the great peasant masses have risen to fulfill their historic mission.... What the peasants are doing is absolutely right; what they are doing is fine! "It's fine!" is the theory of the peasants and of all other revolutionaries. Every revolutionary comrade should know that the national revolution requires a great change in the countryside. The Revolution of 1911 did not bring about this change, hence its failure. This change is now taking place, and it is an important factor for the completion of the revolution. Every revolutionary comrade must support it, or he will be taking the stand of counterrevolution.

 Why did Mao Zedong believe that rural peasants could help bring about a social revolution in China? How does his vision compare with the reality of the Bolshevik Revolution in Russia?

Source: From *Selected Works of Mao Tse-Tung* (London: Lawrence and Wishart, Ltd., 1954), Vol. 1, pp. 21–23.

---

peasant movement in southern China during the early 1920s and then served as an agitator in rural villages in his home province of Hunan (HOO-NAHN) during the Northern Expedition in the fall of 1926. At that time, he wrote a report to the party leadership suggesting that the CCP support peasant demands for a land revolution (see the box "A Call for Revolt" above). But his superiors refused, fearing that such radical policies would destroy the alliance with the Nationalists.

The Nanjing Republic

In 1928, Chiang Kai-shek founded a new Chinese republic at Nanjing, and over the next three years, he managed to reunify China by a combination of military operations and inducements (known derisively as "silver bullets") to various northern warlords to join his movement. He also attempted to put an end to the Communists, rooting them out of their urban base in Shanghai and their rural redoubt in the rugged hills of Jiangxi (JAHNG-shee) Province. He succeeded in the first task in 1931, when most party leaders were forced to flee Shanghai for Mao's base in southern China. Three years later, using their superior military strength, Chiang's troops surrounded the Communist base in Jiangxi, inducing Mao's young Red Army (in imitation of Bolshevik experience) to abandon its guerrilla lair and embark on the famous Long March, an arduous journey of thousands of miles on foot through mountains, marshes, and deserts to the small provincial town of Yan'an (yuh-NAHN) 200 miles north of the city of Xian (SHEE-ahn) in the dusty hills of northern China (see Map 24.1). Of the 90,000 who embarked on the journey in October 1934, only 10,000 arrived in Yan'an a year later. Contemporary observers must have thought that the Communist threat to the Nanjing regime had been averted forever.

Mao Zedong on the Long March. In 1934, the Communist leader Mao Zedong led his bedraggled forces on the famous Long March from southern China to a new location at Yan'an, in the hills just south of the Gobi Desert. The epic journey has ever since been celebrated as a symbol of the party's willingness to sacrifice for the revolutionary cause. In this photograph, Mao sits astride a white horse as he accompanies his followers on the march. Reportedly, he was the only participant allowed to ride a horse en route to Yan'an.

Meanwhile, Chiang was trying to build a new nation. When the Nanjing Republic was established in 1928, Chiang publicly declared his commitment to Sun Yat-sen's "three people's principles." In a program announced in 1918, Sun had written about the all-important second stage of "political tutelage":

> China … needs a republican government just as a boy needs school. As a schoolboy must have good teachers and helpful friends, so the Chinese people, being for the first time under republican rule, must have a farsighted revolutionary government for their training. This calls for the period of political tutelage, which is a necessary transitional stage from monarchy to republicanism. Without this, disorder will be unavoidable.[5]

In keeping with Sun's program, Chiang announced a period of political indoctrination to prepare the Chinese people for a final stage of constitutional government. In the meantime, the Nationalists would use their dictatorial power to carry out a land reform program and modernize the urban industrial sector.

But it would take more than paper plans to create a new China. Years of neglect and civil war had severely frayed the political, economic, and social fabric of the nation. There were faint signs of an impending industrial revolution in the major urban centers, but most of the people in the countryside, drained by warlord exactions and civil strife, were still grindingly poor and overwhelmingly illiterate. A westernized middle class had begun to emerge in the cities and formed much of the natural constituency of the Nanjing government. But this new westernized elite, preoccupied with bourgeois values of individual advancement and material accumulation, had few links with the peasants in the countryside or the rickshaw drivers "running in this world of suffering," in the poignant words of a Chinese poet. In an expressive phrase, some critics dismissed Chiang and his chief followers as "banana Chinese"—yellow on the outside, white on the inside.

THE BEST OF EAST AND WEST Chiang was aware of the difficulty of introducing exotic foreign ideas into a society still culturally conservative. While building a modern industrial sector, he attempted to synthesize modern Western ideas with traditional Confucian values of hard work, obedience, and moral integrity. In the officially promoted New Life Movement, sponsored by his Wellesley-educated wife, Meiling Soong (may-LING SOONG), Chiang sought to propagate traditional Confucian social ethics such as integrity, propriety, and righteousness while rejecting what he considered the excessive individualism and material greed of Western capitalism.

Unfortunately for Chiang, Confucian ideas—at least in their institutional form—had been widely discredited by the failure of the traditional system to solve China's growing problems. With only a tenuous hold over the Chinese provinces (the Nanjing government had total control over only a handful of provinces in the Yangzi Valley), a growing Japanese threat in the north, and a world suffering from the Great Depression, Chiang made little progress with his program. Lacking the political sensitivity of Sun Yat-sen and fearing Communist influence, Chiang repressed all opposition and

CHRONOLOGY Revolution in China	
May Fourth demonstrations	1919
Formation of Chinese Communist Party	1921
Death of Sun Yat-sen	1925
Northern Expedition	1926–1928
Establishment of Nanjing Republic	1928
Long March	1934–1935

censored free expression, thereby alienating many intellectuals and political moderates. Since the urban middle class and landed gentry were his natural political constituency, he shunned programs that would lead to a redistribution of wealth. A land reform program was enacted in 1930 but had little effect.

Chiang Kai-shek's government had little more success in promoting industrial development. During the decade of precarious peace following the Northern Expedition, industrial growth averaged only about 1 percent annually. Much of the national wealth was in the hands of the senior officials and close subordinates of the ruling elite. Military expenses consumed half the budget, and distressingly little was devoted to social and economic development.

The new government, then, had little success in dealing with China's deep-seated economic and social problems. The deadly combination of internal disintegration and foreign pressure now began to coincide with the virtual collapse of the global economic order during the Great Depression and the rise of militant political forces in Japan determined to extend Japanese influence and power in an unstable Asia. These forces and the turmoil they unleashed will be examined in the next chapter.

"Down with Confucius and Sons": Economic, Social, and Cultural Change in Republican China

The transformation of the old order that had commenced at the end of the Qing era extended into the period of the early Chinese republic. The industrial sector continued to grow, albeit slowly. Although about 75 percent of all industrial goods were still manually produced in the early 1930s, mechanization was gradually beginning to replace manual labor in a number of traditional industries, notably in the manufacture of textile goods. Traditional Chinese exports, such as silk and tea, were hit hard by the Great Depression, however, and manufacturing suffered a decline during the 1930s. It is difficult to gauge conditions in the countryside during the early republican era, but there is no doubt that farmers were often victimized by high taxes imposed by local warlords and the endemic political and social conflict.

SOCIAL CHANGES Social changes followed shifts in the economy and the political culture. By 1915, the assault on the old system and values by educated youth was intense. The main focus of the attack was the Confucian concept of the family—in particular, filial piety and the subordination of women (see the Comparative Essay "Out of the Doll's House" on p. 713). Young people called for the right to choose their own mates and their own careers. Inspired by the American women's advocate Margaret Sanger who visited China in 1922, women began to demand rights and opportunities equal to those enjoyed by men. More broadly, progressives called for an end to the concept of duty to the

community and praised the Western individualist ethos. The popular short story writer Lu Xun (loo SHUN) criticized the Confucian concept of family as a "man-eating" system that degraded humanity. In a famous short story "Diary of a Madman," the protagonist remarks:

> I remember when I was four or five years old, sitting in the cool of the hall, my brother told me that if a man's parents were ill, he should cut off a piece of his flesh and boil it for them if he wanted to be considered a good son. I have only just realized that I have been living all these years in a place where for four thousand years they have been eating human flesh.[6]

Such criticisms did have some beneficial results. During the early republic, the tyranny of the old family system began to decline, at least in urban areas, under the impact of economic changes and the urgings of the New Culture intellectuals. Women began to escape their cloistered existence and seek education and employment alongside their male contemporaries. Free choice in marriage and a more relaxed attitude toward sex became somewhat more common among affluent families in the cities, where the teenage children of westernized elites aped the clothing, social habits, and musical tastes of their contemporaries in Europe and the United States.

But, as a rule, the new emphasis on individualism and women's rights did not penetrate to the textile factories, where more than a million women worked in slave labor conditions, or to the villages, where traditional attitudes and customs held sway. Arranged marriages continued to be the rule rather than the exception, and concubinage remained common. According to a survey taken in the 1930s, well over two-thirds of the marriages even among urban couples had been arranged by their parents (see the box "An Arranged Marriage" on p. 714), and in one rural area, only 3 out of 170 villagers interviewed had even heard of the idea of "modern marriage." Even the tradition of binding the feet of female children continued despite efforts by the Nationalist government to eradicate the practice.

A NEW CULTURE? Nowhere was the struggle between traditional and modern more visible than in the field of culture. Beginning with the New Culture era, radical reformists criticized traditional culture as the symbol and instrument of feudal oppression that must be entirely eradicated before a new China could stand with dignity in the modern world. During the 1920s and 1930s, Western literature and art became highly popular, especially among the urban middle class. Traditional culture continued to prevail among more conservative elements, and some intellectuals argued for a new art that would synthesize the best of Chinese and foreign culture. But the most creative artists were interested in imitating foreign trends, while traditionalists were more concerned with preservation.

Literature in particular was influenced by foreign ideas as Western genres like the novel and the short story attracted a

COMPARATIVE ESSAY

Out of the Doll's House

FAMILY & SOCIETY

In Henrik Ibsen's 1879 play *A Doll's House*, Nora Helmer informs her husband, Torvald, that she will no longer accept his control over her life and announces her intention to leave home to start her life anew (see Opposing Viewpoints "Advice to Women: Two Views" on p. 589 in Chapter 20). When the outraged Torvald cites her sacred duties as wife and mother, Nora replies that she has other duties just as sacred, those to herself. "I can no longer be satisfied with what most people say," she declares. "I must think things out for myself and try to get clear about them."

To Ibsen's contemporaries, such remarks were revolutionary. In nineteenth-century Europe, the traditional characterization of the sexes, based on gender-defined social roles, had been elevated to the status of a universal law. As the family wage earners, men were expected to go off to work, while women were responsible for caring for home and family. Women were advised to accept their lot and play their role as effectively and as gracefully as possible. In other parts of the world, women generally had even fewer rights than their male counterparts. Often, as in traditional China, they were viewed as sex objects.

The traditional ideal, however, did not always match the contemporary reality. With the advent of the Industrial Revolution, many women in Europe, especially those in the lower classes, were driven by the need for supplemental income to seek employment outside the home, often in the form of menial labor. Some women, inspired by the ideals of human dignity and freedom expressed during the Enlightenment and the French Revolution, began to protest against a tradition of female inferiority that had long kept them in a "doll's house" of male domination and to claim equal rights before the law.

The movement to liberate women from the iron cage of legal and social inferiority first began to gain ground in

English-speaking countries such as Great Britain and the United States, but it gradually spread to the continent of Europe and then to colonial areas in Africa and Asia. By the first decades of the twentieth century, women's liberation movements were under way in parts of North Africa, the Middle East, and East Asia, voicing a growing demand for access to education, equal treatment before the law, and the right to vote. Nowhere was this more true than in China, where a small minority of educated women began to agitate for equal rights with men.

Progress, however, was often agonizingly slow, especially in societies where age-old traditional values had not yet been undermined by the corrosive force of the Industrial Revolution. In many colonial societies, the effort to improve the condition of women was subordinated to the goal of gaining national independence. In some instances, women's liberation movements were led by educated elites who failed to include the concerns of working-class women in their agendas. Colonialism, too, was a double-edged sword, as the sexist bias of European officials combined with indigenous traditions of male superiority to marginalize women even further. As men moved to the cities to exploit opportunities provided by the new colonial administration, women were left to cope with their traditional responsibilities in the villages, often without the safety net of male support that had sustained them during the precolonial era.

Based on the information presented in this textbook, to what extent, if at all, did the imperial policies applied in colonial territories serve to benefit women's rights?

[Image caption, center:]

The Art Archive/Private Collection/CCI/Picture Desk

The Chinese "Doll's House." A woman in traditional China binding her feet.

growing audience. Although most Chinese novels written after World War I dealt with Chinese subjects, they reflected the Western tendency toward social realism and often dealt with the new westernized middle class, as in *Midnight* by Mao Dun (mow DOON ["ow" as in "how"]), which describes

the changing mores of Shanghai's urban elites. Another favorite theme was the disintegration of the traditional Confucian family—Ba Jin's famous novel *Family* is an example. Most of China's modern authors displayed a clear contempt for the past.

An Arranged Marriage

FAMILY & SOCIETY

UNDER WESTERN INFLUENCE, Chinese social customs changed dramatically for many urban elites in the interwar years. A vocal women's movement, inspired in part by translations of Henrik Ibsen's play *A Doll's House*, campaigned aggressively for universal suffrage and an end to sexual discrimination. Some progressives called for free choice in marriage and divorce and even for free love. By the 1930s, the government had taken some steps to free women from patriarchal marriage constraints and realize sexual equality. But life was generally unaffected in the villages, where traditional patterns held sway. This often created severe tensions between older and younger generations, as this passage from a novel by the popular twentieth-century writer Ba Jin (BAH JIN) shows.

Ba Jin, *Family*

Brought up with loving care, after studying with a private tutor for a number of years, Chueh-hsin entered middle school.... [H]e graduated four years later at the top of his class. He was very interested in physics and chemistry and hoped to study abroad, in Germany. His mind was full of beautiful dreams. At that time he was the envy of his classmates.

In his fourth year at middle school, he lost his mother. His father later married again, this time to a younger woman who had been his mother's cousin. Chueh-hsin was aware of his loss, for he knew full well that nothing could replace the love of a mother. But her death left no irreparable wound in his heart; he was able to console himself with rosy dreams of his future. Moreover, he had someone who understood him and could comfort him—his pretty cousin Mei, "mei" for "plum blossom."

But then, one day, his dreams were shattered, cruelly and bitterly shattered. The evening he returned home carrying his diploma, the plaudits of his teachers and friends still ringing in his ears, his father called him into his room and said:

"Now that you've graduated, I want to arrange your marriage. Your grandfather is looking forward to having a great-grandson, and I, too, would like to be able to hold a grandson in my arms. You're old enough to be married; I won't feel easy until I fulfill my obligation to find you a wife. Although I didn't accumulate much money in my years away from home as an official, still I've put by enough for us to get along on. My health isn't what it used to be; I'm thinking of spending my time at home and having you help me run the household affairs. All the more reason you'll be needing a wife. I've already arranged a match with the Li family. The thirteenth of next month is a good day. We'll announce the engagement then. You can be married within the year...."

Chueh-hsin did not utter a word of protest, nor did such a thought ever occur to him. He merely nodded to indicate his compliance with his father's wishes. But after he returned to his own room, and shut the door, he threw himself down on his bed, covered his head with the quilt and wept. He wept for his broken dreams.

He was deeply in love with Mei, but now his father had chosen another, a girl he had never seen, and said that he must marry within the year....

He cried his disappointment and bitterness. But the door was closed and Chueh-hsin's head was beneath the bedding. No one knew. He did not fight back, he never thought of resisting. He only bemoaned his fate. But he accepted it. He complied with his father's will without a trace of resentment. But in his heart he wept for himself, wept for the girl he adored—Mei, his "plum blossom."

Why does Chueh-hsin comply with the wishes of his father in the matter of his marriage? Why were arranged marriages so prevalent in traditional China?

Japan Between the Wars

FOCUS QUESTION: How did Japan address the problems of nation building in the first decades of the twentieth century, and why did democratic institutions not take hold more effectively?

During the first two decades of the twentieth century, Japan had made remarkable progress toward the creation of an advanced society on the Western model. The political system based on the Meiji Constitution of 1890 began to evolve along Western pluralistic lines, and a multiparty system took shape, while the economic and social reforms launched during the Meiji era led to increasing prosperity and the development of a modern industrial and commercial sector. Optimists had reason to hope that Japan was on the road to becoming a full-fledged democracy.

Experiment in Democracy

As the twentieth century progressed, the Japanese political system appeared to evolve significantly toward the pluralistic democratic model. In the aftermath of World War I, political parties expanded their popular following and became increasingly competitive. In 1921, Hara Kei (HA-ruh KAY), a member of the Seiyukai (SAY-you-ky) political party, became the first member of the lower house of the legislature to become prime minister. Universal male suffrage was instituted in the 1920s, and individual pressure groups began to appear in Japanese society, along with an independent press and a bill of rights. Yet the influence of the old ruling oligarchy, the *genro*, remained substantial behind the scenes, and the ideological foundation of the Meiji era, the *kokutai* (koh-kuh-TY), continued to exert considerable influence on Japanese politics (see Chapter 22).

Still, these fragile democratic institutions were able to survive through the 1920s, often called the era of **Taisho** (TY-SHOH) **democracy**, from the reign title of the ruling emperor. During that period, political parties actively competed for power, the military budget was reduced, and a suffrage bill enacted in 1925 granted the vote to all Japanese males, thus continuing the process of democratization begun earlier in the century. Women remained disenfranchised, but women's associations became increasingly visible during the 1920s, and many women were active in the labor movement and in campaigns for various social reforms. The first university for women was established in Tokyo in 1918.

But the era was also marked by growing social turmoil, and two opposing forces within the system were gearing up to challenge the prevailing wisdom. On the left, a Marxist labor movement, which reflected the tensions in the working class and the increasing radicalism among the rural poor, began to take shape in the early 1920s in response to growing economic difficulties. Government suppression of labor disturbances led to further radicalization. On the right, ultranationalist groups called for a rejection of Western models of development and a more militant approach to realizing national objectives. In 1919, the radical nationalist Kita Ikki (KEE-tuh IK-kee) called

for a military takeover and the establishment of a new system bearing strong resemblance to what would later be called National Socialism in Germany. Two years later, Prime Minister Hara Kei was assassinated for agreeing to sign a treaty limiting Japanese naval forces in the Pacific.

This cultural conflict between old and new, indigenous and foreign, was reflected in literature. Japanese self-confidence had been restored after the victories over China and Russia and launched an age of cultural creativity in the early twentieth century. Fascination with Western literature gave birth to a striking new genre called the "I novel." Defying traditional Japanese reticence, some authors reveled in self-exposure with confessions of their innermost thoughts. Others found release in the "proletarian literature" movement of the early 1920s. Inspired by Soviet literary examples, these authors wanted literature to serve socialist goals and improve the lives of the working class. While much of the country's urban youth culture was fascinated with exotic foreign ideas from such disparate thinkers as Karl Marx and Friedrich Nietzsche, some Japanese writers blended Western psychology with Japanese sensibility in exquisite novels reeking with nostalgia for the old Japan. One well-known example is *Some Prefer Nettles* (1929) by Junichiro Tanizaki (jun-ih-CHEE-roh tan-ih-ZAH-kee), which delicately juxtaposed the positive aspects of both traditional and modern Japan.

A *Zaibatsu* Economy

During the immediate postwar years, Japan continued to make impressive progress in economic development. Spurred

Geishas, Old and New. The geisha (GAY-shuh) ("accomplished person") was a symbol of old Japan. Dressed in traditional costumes, her body movements highly stylized, she served not only as an entertainer and an ornament but also as a beautiful purveyor of elite Japanese culture. That image was dramatically transformed in a new Japan that had been inundated by the influence of the modern West. In the photo on the left, geishas in early-twentieth-century Tokyo mimic Western fashions and dance positions. In the photo on the right, two young Japanese women in traditional costumes take a stroll on the grounds of the medieval castle at Himeji.

Underwood & Underwood/Historical/Corbis

© William J. Duiker

by rising domestic demand as well as continued government investment in the economy, the production of raw materials tripled between 1900 and 1930, and industrial production increased more than twelvefold. Much of the increase went into exports, and Western manufacturers began to complain about increasing competition from the Japanese.

As often happens, rapid industrialization was accompanied by some hardship and rising social tensions. In the Meiji model, various manufacturing processes were concentrated in a single enterprise, the *zaibatsu* (zy-BAHT-soo *or* DZY-bahtss), or financial clique. Some of these firms were existing merchant companies, such as Mitsui (MIT-swee) and Sumitomo (soo-mee-TOH-moh), that had the capital and the foresight to move into new areas of opportunity. Others were formed by enterprising samurai, who used their status and experience in management to good account in a new environment. Whatever their origins, these firms gradually developed, often with official encouragement, into large conglomerates that controlled a major segment of the Japanese economy. By 1937, the four largest *zaibatsu*—Mitsui, Mitsubishi (mit-soo-BEE-shee), Sumitomo, and Yasuda (yah-SOO-duh)—controlled 21 percent of the banking industry, 26 percent of mining, 35 percent of shipbuilding, 38 percent of commercial shipping, and more than 60 percent of paper manufacturing and insurance.

This concentration of power and wealth in a few major industrial combines created problems in Japanese society. In the first place, it resulted in the emergence of a dual economy: on the one hand, a modern industry characterized by up-to-date methods and massive government subsidies, and on the other, a traditional manufacturing sector characterized by conservative methods and small-scale production techniques.

Concentration of wealth also led to growing economic inequalities. As we have seen, economic growth had been achieved at the expense of the peasants, many of whom fled to the cities to escape rural poverty. That labor surplus benefited the industrial sector, but the urban proletariat was still poorly paid and ill housed. Rampant inflation in the price of rice led to food riots shortly after World War I. A rapid increase in population (the total population of the Japanese islands increased from an estimated 43 million in 1900 to 73 million in 1940) led to food shortages and the threat of rising unemployment. In the meantime, those left on the farm continued to suffer. As late as 1940, an estimated half of all Japanese farmers were tenants.

Shidehara Diplomacy

A final problem for Japanese leaders in the post-Meiji era was the familiar colonial dilemma of finding sources of raw materials and foreign markets for the nation's manufactured goods. Until World War I, Japan had dealt with the problem by seizing territories such as Taiwan, Korea, and southern Manchuria and transforming them into colonies or protectorates of the growing Japanese empire. That policy had succeeded brilliantly, although it had aroused deep hostility among the population of Korea and began to arouse the concern and in

some cases the hostility of the Western nations as well. China was also becoming apprehensive; as we have seen, Japanese demands for Shandong Province at the Paris Peace Conference in 1919 aroused massive protests in major Chinese cities.

The United States was especially concerned about Japanese aggressiveness. Although the United States had been less active than some European states in pursuing colonies in the Pacific, it had a strong interest in keeping the area open for U.S. commercial activities. In 1922, in Washington, D.C., the United States convened a major conference of nations with interests in the Pacific to discuss problems of regional security. The Washington Conference led to agreements on several issues, but the major accomplishment was a nine-power treaty recognizing the territorial integrity of China and the Open Door. The other participants induced Japan to agree to these provisions by accepting its special position in Manchuria.

During the remainder of the 1920s, Japanese governments attempted to play by the rules laid down at the Washington Conference. Known as Shidehara (shee-deh-HAH-rah) diplomacy, after the Japanese foreign minister (and later prime minister) who attempted to carry it out, this policy sought to use diplomatic and economic means to realize Japanese interests in Asia. But this approach came under severe pressure as Japanese industrialists began to move into new areas, such as heavy industry, chemicals, mining, and the manufacturing of appliances and automobiles. Because such industries desperately needed resources not found in abundance locally, the Japanese government came under increasing pressure to find new sources abroad.

THE RISE OF MILITANT NATIONALISM In the early 1930s, with the onset of the Great Depression and growing tensions in the international arena, nationalist forces rose to dominance in the Japanese government. The changes that occurred in the 1930s, which we shall discuss in Chapter 25, were not reflected in changes in the constitution or the institutional structure, which remained essentially intact, but rather in the composition and attitudes of the ruling group. Party leaders during the 1920s had attempted to realize Tokyo's aspirations within the existing global political and economic framework. The dominant elements in the government in the 1930s, a mixture of military officers and ultranationalist politicians, were convinced that the diplomacy of the 1920s had failed and advocated a more aggressive approach to protecting national interests in a brutal and competitive world.

TAISHO DEMOCRACY: AN ABERRATION? The dramatic shift in Japanese political culture that occurred in the early 1930s has caused some historians to question the breadth and depth of the trend toward democratic practices in the immediate post–World War I era. Was Taisho democracy merely a fragile attempt at comparative liberalization in a framework dominated by the Meiji vision of empire and *kokutai*? Or was the militant nationalism of the 1930s an aberration brought on by the Great Depression, which caused the inexorable emergence of democracy in Japan to stall?

Clearly, there is some truth in both contentions. A process of democratization was taking place in Japan during the first decades of the twentieth century, but without shaking the essential core of the Meiji concept of the state. Political forces deeply imbedded in Japanese culture had apprehensions about the country's effort to imitate the Western democracies and continued to believe in Japan's sacred mission in East Asia. When the "liberal" approach of the 1920s failed to solve the problems of the day, the shallow roots of the democracy movement in Japan became exposed, and the shift toward a more aggressive approach was inevitable.

Still, the course of Japanese history after World War II (see Chapter 30) suggests that the emergence of multiparty democracy in the 1920s was not simply an aberration but a natural consequence of evolutionary trends in Japanese society. The seeds of democracy nurtured during the Taisho era were nipped in the bud by the cataclysmic effects of the Great Depression of the 1930s, but in the more conducive climate after World War II, a democratic system—suitably adjusted to Japanese soil—reached full flower.

Nationalism and Dictatorship in Latin America

Q FOCUS QUESTIONS: What problems did the nations of Latin America face in the interwar years? To what degree were the problems a consequence of foreign influence?

Because most of Latin America had won its independence from European control during the nineteenth century, the issues of nationalism and political change took different forms in the years following World War I than they did in Asia and the Middle East. But the region was by no means isolated from trends occurring throughout the rest of the world. National sentiment in opposition to foreign—and especially U.S.—political and economic influence was sometimes intense, and when the Great Depression struck in the late 1920s, the political equation in Latin America was affected in profound ways.

A Changing Economy

At the beginning of the twentieth century, virtually all of Latin America, except for the three Guianas, British Honduras, and some of the Caribbean islands, had achieved independence. The economy of the region (see Map 24.2) was still based largely on the export of foodstuffs and raw materials. Some countries relied on exports of only one or two products. Argentina, for example, exported primarily beef and wheat; Chile, nitrates and copper; Brazil and the Caribbean nations, sugar; and the Central American states, bananas. A few reaped large profits from these exports, but for the majority of the population, the returns were meager.

MAP 24.2 Latin America in the First Half of the Twentieth Century. Shown here are the boundaries dividing the countries of Latin America after the independence movements of the nineteenth century.

Q *Which areas remained under European rule?*

A Pledge of Cooperation

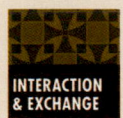
INTERACTION & EXCHANGE

DURING THE FIRST THREE DECADES of the twentieth century, the United States intervened periodically in the affairs of various countries in Latin America to protect the lives of U.S. citizens and its growing economic interests. By the late 1920s, that policy had aroused considerable resentment among governments throughout the region. U.S. President Franklin D. Roosevelt attempted to allay their concerns by announcing the Good Neighbor policy toward other nations in the hemisphere. This selection is from a speech given in August 1936, in which he discussed this policy.

Franklin D. Roosevelt's Good Neighbor Policy

Long before I returned to Washington as President of the United States, I made up my mind that ... the United States could best serve the cause of peaceful humanity by setting an example. That was why on the 4th of March, 1933, I made the following declaration:

> In the field of world policy I would dedicate this nation to the policy of the good neighbor—the neighbor who resolutely respects himself and because he does so, respects the rights of others—the neighbor who respects his obligations and respects the sanctity of his agreements in and with a world of neighbors.

In the whole of the Western Hemisphere our good neighbor policy had produced results that are especially heartening.... The American republics to the south of us have been ready always to cooperate with the United States on a basis of equality and mutual respect, but before we inaugurated the good neighbor policy there was among them resentment and fear, because certain administrations in Washington had slighted their national pride and their sovereign rights.

In pursuance of the good neighbor policy, and because in my younger days I had learned many lessons in the hard school of experience, I stated that the United States was opposed definitely to armed intervention.

We have negotiated a Pan-American convention embodying the principles of nonintervention. We have abandoned the Platt amendment which gave us the right to intervene in the internal affairs of the Republic of Cuba. We have withdrawn American marines from Haiti. We have signed a new treaty which places our relations with Panama on a mutually satisfactory basis. We have undertaken a series of trade agreements with other American countries to our mutual commercial profit....

Throughout the Americas the spirit of the good neighbor is a practical and living fact. The twenty-one American republics are not only living together in friendship and in peace; they are united in the determination so to remain.

How did President Roosevelt define the concept of a "good neighbor" in this speech? What previous U.S. policies toward Latin America does he suggest will be discarded?

Source: From Ruhl Bartlett, ed., *The Record of American Diplomacy* (New York: Knopf, 1952), pp. 551–552.

THE ROLE OF THE YANKEE DOLLAR World War I led to a decline in European investment in Latin America and a rise in the U.S. role in the local economies. By the late 1920s, the United States had replaced Great Britain as the foremost source of investment in Latin America. Unlike the British, however, U.S. investors put their funds directly into production enterprises, causing large segments of the area's export industries to fall into American hands. A number of Central American states, for example, were popularly labeled "banana republics" because of the power and influence of the U.S.-owned United Fruit Company. American firms also dominated the copper mining industry in Chile and Peru and the oil industry in Mexico, Peru, and Bolivia.

Increasing economic power reinforced the traditionally high level of U.S. political influence in Latin America. This influence was especially evident in Central America and the Caribbean, regions that many Americans considered their backyard and hence vital to U.S. national security. The growing U.S. presence in the region provoked hostility and a growing national consciousness among Latin Americans, who viewed the United States as an aggressive imperialist power. Some charged that Washington worked to keep ruthless dictators, such as Juan Vicente Gómez (WAHN vee-SEN-tay GOH-mez) of Venezuela and Fulgencio Batista (full-JEN-see-oh bah-TEES-tuh) of Cuba, in power in order to preserve U.S. economic influence; sometimes the United States even intervened militarily. In a bid to improve relations with Latin American countries, in 1933 President Franklin D. Roosevelt promulgated the **Good Neighbor policy**, which rejected the use of U.S. military force in the region (see the box "A Pledge of Cooperation" above). To underscore his sincerity, Roosevelt ordered the withdrawal of U.S. marines from the island nation of Haiti in 1936. For the first time in thirty years, there were no U.S. occupation troops in Latin America.

Because so many Latin American nations depended for their livelihood on the export of raw materials and food products, the Great Depression of the 1930s was a disaster for the region. In 1930, the value of Latin American exports fell to only half of the amount that had been exported in each of the previous five years. Spurred by the decline in foreign revenues, Latin American governments began to encourage the development of new industries. In some cases—the steel

Hipólito Irigoyen becomes president of Argentina	1916
Argentine military overthrows Irigoyen	1930
Rule of Getúlio Vargas in Brazil	1930–1945
Presidency of Lázaro Cárdenas in Mexico	1934–1940
Beginning of U.S. Good Neighbor policy	1933

industry in Chile and Brazil, the oil industry in Argentina and Mexico—government investment made up for the absence of local sources of capital.

The Effects of Dependency

During the late nineteenth century, most governments in Latin America had been increasingly dominated by landed or military elites, who controlled the mass of the population—mostly impoverished peasants—by the blatant use of military force. This trend toward authoritarianism increased during the 1930s as domestic instability caused by the effects of the Great Depression led to the creation of military dictatorships throughout the region. This trend was especially evident in Argentina, Brazil, and Mexico—three countries that together possessed more than half of the land and wealth of Latin America.

ARGENTINA By no means were all of Latin America's problems the consequence of foreign influence. Some were self-imposed. The government of Argentina, controlled by landowners who had benefited from the export of beef and wheat, was slow to recognize the growing importance of establishing a local industrial base. In 1916, Hipólito Irigoyen (ee-POH-lee-toh ee-ree-GOH-yen) (1852–1933), head of the Radical Party, was elected president on a program to improve conditions for the middle and lower classes. Little was achieved, however, as the party became increasingly corrupt and identified with the interests of the large landowners. In 1930, the army overthrew Irigoyen's government, but its effort to return to the previous export economy and suppress the growing influence of labor unions failed, and in 1946 General Juan Perón (WAHN puh-ROHN)—claiming the support of the *descamisados* (days-kah-mee-SAH-dohs) ("shirtless ones")—seized sole power (see Chapter 28).

BRAZIL Brazil followed a similar path. In 1889, the army replaced the Brazilian monarchy, installed by Portugal years before, with a republic. But it was controlled by landed elites, many of whom had grown wealthy through their ownership of vast rubber and coffee plantations. Exports of Brazilian rubber dominated the world market until just before World War I. When it proved easier to produce rubber in Southeast Asia, however, Brazilian exports suddenly collapsed, leaving the economy of the Amazon River basin in ruins.

To make matters worse, the coffee industry also suffered problems. In 1900, three-quarters of the world's coffee was grown in Brazil. As in Argentina, the ruling oligarchy ignored

The Tango, National Dance of Argentina. In the early twentieth century, the gaucho (GOW-choh), or cowboy, came to epitomize the self-image of the Argentinean people. Immigrants from southern Europe who had come to Latin America in search of work and a better life, they eventually settled in the vast grassy plains called the pampas (PAM-puhz *or* PAHM-pahs), becoming key participants in the emerging cattle industry that transformed the country into a major exporter of beef and hides. For entertainment, many visited the bawdyhouses and brothels of Buenos Aires, where the tango—a soulful and nostalgic dance based on Iberian rhythms—symbolized the hopes and frustrations of the immigrant experience. Once exported abroad, the tango became an overnight sensation in Europe and North America, where its sensuous movements aroused stern criticism in religious circles.

the importance of establishing an urban industrial base. When the Great Depression ravaged profits from coffee exports, a wealthy rancher, Getúlio Vargas (zhi-TOO-lyoo VAHR-guhs) (1883–1954), seized power and ruled the country as president from 1930 to 1945. At first, Vargas sought to appease workers by instituting an eight-hour workday and a minimum wage, but influenced by the apparent success of fascist regimes in Europe, he ruled by increasingly autocratic means and relied on a police force that used torture to silence his opponents. His industrial policy was relatively enlightened, however, and by the end of World War II, Brazil had become Latin America's major industrial power. In 1945, the army, fearing that Vargas might prolong his power illegally after calling for new elections, forced him to resign.

MEXICO After the dictator Porfirio Díaz (por-FEER-yoh DEE-ahs) was ousted from power in 1910 (see Chapter 20), Mexico entered a state of turbulence that lasted for years. The

Hulton Archive/Getty Images

The Opera House at Manaus. The discovery of rubber in the mid-nineteenth century was one of the most significant events in the history of Brazil. Derived from the sap of a tree native to the Amazon River basin, rubber became the source of great wealth for Brazilian plantation owners until the rubber boom declined after 1900. The most visible symbol of "king rubber" is the Opera House at Manaus (mah-NOWSS), the largest city on the Amazon. Built in 1896 in an opulent style including the profligate use of Italian marble, it fell into disrepair when the rubber trade moved from Brazil to Southeast Asia in the first quarter of the twentieth century. Thus, the Opera House is a vivid example of the vicissitudes that developing countries may experience as a result of economies based on exports of primary products. The building has recently been renovated and stands as a beacon of promise for one of Latin America's fastest growing regions.

ineffective leaders who followed Díaz were unable either to solve the country's economic problems or to bring an end to the civil strife. Declining real wages were squeezing the working class, while in the countryside almost all of the land was controlled by about a thousand families. In southern Mexico, the landless peasants responded eagerly to Emiliano Zapata (ee-mee-LYAH-noh zup-PAH-tuh) (1879–1919) when he called for land redistribution and began to seize the estates of wealthy landholders.

For the next several years, Zapata and rebel leader Pancho Villa (pahn-CHOH VEE-uh) (1878–1923), who operated in the northern state of Chihuahua (chih-WAH-wah), became an important political force in the country by publicly advocating efforts to redress the economic grievances of the poor (see the box "Zapata and Land Reform" on p. 580 in Chapter 20). But neither had a broad grasp of the challenges facing the country, and power eventually gravitated to a more moderate group of reformists around the Constitutionalist Party. The latter were intent on breaking the power of the great landed families and U.S. corporations, but without engaging in radical land reform or the nationalization of property. After a bloody conflict that cost the lives of thousands, the moderates consolidated power, and in 1917, they promulgated a new constitution that established a strong presidency, initiated land reform policies, established limits on foreign investment, and set an agenda for social welfare programs.

In 1920, the Constitutionalist Party leader Alvaro Obregon (AHL-vah-roh oh-bree-GAHN) assumed the presidency and began to carry out his reform program. But real change did not take place until the presidency of General Lázaro Cárdenas (LAH-zah-roh KAHR-day-nahss) (1895–1970) in 1934. Cárdenas won wide popularity with the peasants by ordering the redistribution of 44 million acres of land controlled by landed elites. He also seized control of the oil industry, which had hitherto been dominated by major U.S. oil companies. Alluding to the Good Neighbor policy, President Roosevelt refused to intervene, and eventually Mexico agreed to compensate U.S. oil companies for their lost property. It then set up PEMEX, a governmental organization, to run the oil industry. By now, the revolution was democratic in name only, as the ruling political party, known as the Institutional Revolutionary Party (PRI), controlled the levers of power throughout society. Every six years, for more than half a century, PRI presidential candidates automatically succeeded each other in office.

Latin American Culture

The first half of the twentieth century witnessed a dramatic increase in literary activity in Latin America, a result in part of its ambivalent relationship with Europe and the United States. Many authors, while experimenting with imported modernist styles, felt compelled to proclaim their region's unique identity through the adoption of Latin American themes and social issues. In *The Underdogs* (1915), for example, Mariano Azuela (mahr-YAHN-oh ah-SWAY-luh) (1873–1952) presented a sympathetic but not uncritical portrait of the Mexican Revolution as his country entered an era of unsettling change.

In their determination to commend Latin America's distinctive characteristics, some writers extolled the promise of the region's vast virgin lands and the diversity of its peoples. In *Don Segundo Sombra*, published in 1926, Ricardo Guiraldes (ree-KAHR-doh gwee-RAHL-dess) (1886–1927) celebrated the life of the ideal gaucho (cowboy), defining Argentina's hope and strength through the enlightened management of its fertile earth. Likewise, in *Dona Barbara*, Rómulo Gallegos (ROH-moo-loh gah-YAY-gohs) (1884–1969) wrote in a similar vein about his native Venezuela. Other authors pursued the theme

Struggle for the Banner. Like Diego Rivera, David Alfaro Siqueiros (dah-VEED al-FAHR-oh see-KAY-rohss) (1896–1974) decorated public buildings with large murals that celebrated the Mexican Revolution and the workers' and peasants' struggle for freedom. Beginning in the 1930s, Siqueiros expressed sympathy for the exploited and downtrodden peoples of Mexico in dramatic frescoes such as this one. He painted similar murals in Uruguay, Argentina, and Brazil and was once expelled from the United States, where his political art and views were considered too radical.

of solitude and detachment, a product of the region's physical separation from the rest of the world.

Latin American artists followed their literary counterparts in joining the Modernist movement in Europe, yet they too were eager to promote the emergence of a new regional and national essence. In Mexico, where the government provided financial support for painting murals on public buildings, the artist Diego Rivera (DYAY-goh rih-VAIR-uh) (1886–1957) began to produce monumental murals that served two purposes: to illustrate the national past by portraying Aztec legends and folk customs and to popularize a political message in favor of realizing the social goals of the Mexican Revolution. His wife, Frida Kahlo (FREE-duh KAH-loh) (1907–1954), incorporated Surrealist whimsy in her own paintings, many of which were portraits of herself and her family.

CHAPTER SUMMARY

The turmoil brought about by World War I not only resulted in the destruction of several of the major Western empires and a redrawing of the map of Europe but also opened the door to political and social upheavals elsewhere in the world. In the Middle East, the decline and fall of the Ottoman Empire led to the creation of the secular republic of Turkey. The state of Saudi Arabia emerged in the Arabian peninsula, and Palestine became a source of tension between newly arrived Jewish settlers and longtime Muslim residents.

Other parts of Asia and Africa also witnessed the rise of movements for national independence. In many cases, these movements were spearheaded by local leaders who had been educated in Europe or the United States. In India, Mahatma Gandhi and his campaign of civil disobedience played a crucial role in his country's bid to be free of British rule. Communist movements also began to emerge in Asian societies as radical elements sought new methods of bringing about the overthrow of Western imperialism. Japan continued to follow its own path to modernization, which, although successful from an economic perspective, took a menacing turn during the 1930s.

Between 1919 and 1939, China experienced a dramatic struggle to establish a modern nation. Two dynamic political organizations—the Nationalists and the Communists—competed for legitimacy as the rightful heirs of the old order. At first, they formed an alliance in an effort to defeat their common adversaries, but cooperation ultimately turned to conflict. The Nationalists under Chiang Kai-shek emerged supreme, but Chiang found it difficult to control the remnants of the warlord regime in China, while the Great Depression undermined his efforts to build an industrial nation.

During the interwar years, the nations of Latin America faced severe economic problems because of their dependence on exports. Increasing U.S. investments in Latin America contributed to growing hostility toward the powerful neighbor to the north. The Great Depression forced the region to begin developing new industries, but it also led to the rise of authoritarian governments, some of them modeled after the fascist regimes of Italy and Germany.

By demolishing the remnants of their old civilization on the battlefields of World War I, Europeans had inadvertently encouraged the subject peoples of their vast colonial empires to begin their own movements for national independence. The process was by no means completed in the two decades following the Treaty of Versailles, but the bonds of imperial rule had been severely strained. Once Europeans began to weaken themselves in the even more destructive conflict of World War II, the hopes of African and Asian peoples for national independence and freedom could at last be realized. It is to that devastating world conflict that we must now turn.

CHAPTER TIMELINE

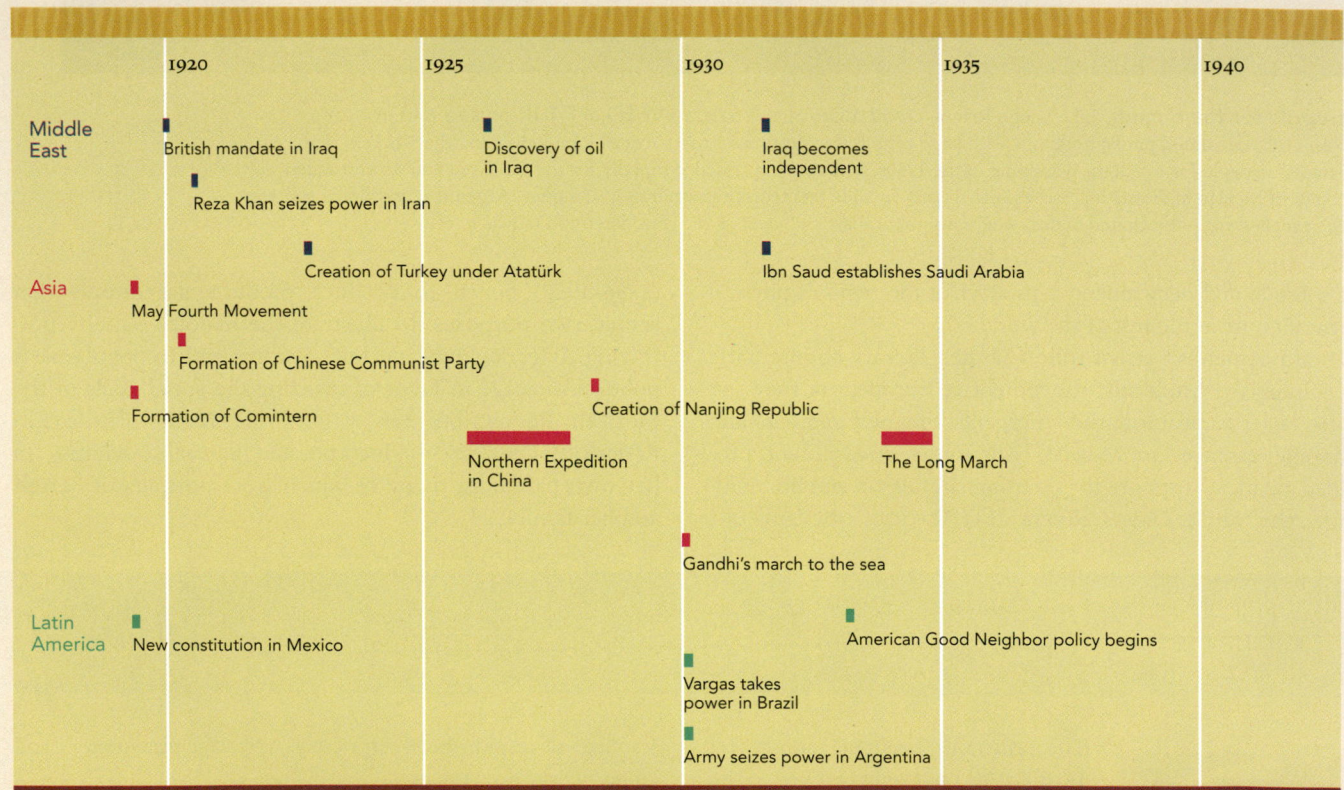

CHAPTER REVIEW

Upon Reflection

Q In what ways did Japan's political system and social structure in the interwar years combine modern and traditional elements? How successful was the attempt to create a modern political system while retaining indigenous traditions of civil obedience and loyalty to the emperor?

Q During the early twentieth century, did conditions for women change for the better or for the worse in the countries discussed in this chapter? Why?

Q Communist Parties were established in many Asian societies in the years immediately following the Bolshevik Revolution. How successful were these parties in winning popular support and achieving their goals?

Key Terms

satyagraha (p. 697)
harijans (p. 697)
civil disobedience (p. 698)
Young Turks (p. 699)
Communist International (Comintern) (p. 706)
New Culture Movement (p. 707)
Taisho democracy (p. 715)
zaibatsu (p. 716)
Good Neighbor policy (p. 718)
descamisados (p. 719)

Suggested Reading

NATIONALISM The most up-to-date survey of modern nationalism is **E. Gellner,** *Nations and Nationalism*, 2nd ed. (Ithaca, N.Y., 2009), but it has little to say about the non-Western world. For a provocative study of the roots of nationalism in Asia, see **B. Anderson,** *Imagined Communities: Reflections on the Origins and Spread of Nationalism* (London, 1983).

INDIA There have been a number of studies of Mahatma Gandhi and his ideas. See, for example, **S. Wolpert,** *Gandhi's Passion: The Life and Legacy of Mahatma Gandhi* (Oxford, 1999), and **D. Dalton,** *Mahatma Gandhi: Nonviolent Power in Action* (New York, 1995). For a study of Nehru, see **J. M. Brown,** *Nehru* (New York, 2000).

MIDDLE EAST For a general survey of events in the Middle East in the interwar era, see **E. Bogle,** *The Modern Middle East: From Imperialism to Freedom* (Upper Saddle River, N.J., 1996). For more specialized studies, see **I. Gershoni et al.,** *Egypt, Islam, and the Arabs: The Search for Egyptian Nationhood* (Oxford, 1993), and **W. Laqueur,** *A History of Zionism: From the French Revolution to the Establishment of the State of Israel* (New York, 1996). The role of Atatürk is examined in **A. Mango,** *Atatürk: The Biography of the Founder of Modern Turkey* (New York, 2000). The Palestinian issue is dealt with in **B. Morris,** *Righteous Victims: The Palestinian Conflict, 1880–2000* (New York, 2001). On the founding of Iraq, see **S. Mackey,** *The Reckoning: Iraq and the Legacy of Saddam Hussein* (New York, 2002). For a penetrating account of the fall of

the Ottoman Empire and its consequences for the postwar era, see **D. Fromkin,** *A Peace to End All Peace: The Fall of the Ottoman Empire and the Creation of the Modern Middle East* (New York, 2001).

CHINA AND JAPAN On the early Chinese republic, a good study is **J. Fitzgerald,** *Awakening China: Politics, Culture, and Class in the Nationalist Revolution* (Stanford, Calif., 1996). The rise of the Chinese Communist Party is charted in **A. Dirlik,** *The Origins of Chinese Communism* (Oxford, 1989). Also see **J. Taylor,** *The Generalissimo: Chiang Kai-shek and the Struggle for Modern China* (Cambridge, Mass., 2009). On Japan, see **J. McLain,** *Japan: A Modern History* (New York, 2001).

LATIN AMERICA For an overview of Latin American history during the interwar period, see **J. Chasteen,** *Born in Blood and Fire: A Concise History of Latin America*, 2nd ed. (New York, 2005). For documents, see **J. Wood and J. Chasteen, eds.,** *Problems in Latin American History: Sources and Interpretations*, 3rd ed. (New York, 2009).

Chapter Notes

1. Speech delivered in London, September 1931, while attending the first Roundtable Conference.
2. V. I. Lenin, "The Awakening of Asia," in *The Awakening of Asia: Selected Essays* (New York, 1963–1968), p. 22.
3. Ts'ai Yüan-p'ei, "Ta Lin Ch'in-nan Han," in *Ts'ai Yüan-p'ei Hsien-sheng Ch'uan-chi* [Collected Works of Mr. Cai Yuanpei] (Taipei, 1968), pp. 1057–1058.
4. Quoted in N. R. Clifford, *Spoilt Children of Empire: Westerners in Shanghai and the Chinese Revolution of the 1920s* (Hanover, N.H., 1991), p. 93.
5. Quoted in W. T. de Bary et al., eds., *Sources of Chinese Tradition* (New York, 1963), p. 783.
6. Lu Xun, "Diary of a Madman," in *Selected Works of Lu Hsun* (Beijing, 1957), vol. 1, p. 20.

MindTap is a fully online, highly personalized learning experience built upon Cengage Learning content. MindTap combines student learning tools—readings, multimedia, activities, and assessments—into a singular Learning Path that guides students through their course.

The Crisis Deepens:
World War II

Adolf Hitler salutes soldiers marching in Nuremberg during the party rally in 1938

Hugo Jaeger/Timepix/Time Life Pictures/Getty Images

CHAPTER OUTLINE AND FOCUS QUESTIONS

Retreat from Democracy: Dictatorial Regimes

Q What are the characteristics of totalitarian states, and to what degree were these characteristics present in Fascist Italy, Nazi Germany, and Stalinist Russia? To what extent was Japan a totalitarian state?

The Path to War

Q What were the underlying causes of World War II, and what specific steps taken by Nazi Germany and Japan led to war?

World War II

Q What were the main events of World War II in Europe and Asia?

The New Order

Q What was the nature of the new orders that Germany and Japan attempted to establish in the territories they occupied?

The Home Front

Q What were conditions like on the home front for the major belligerents in World War II?

Aftermath of the War

Q What were the costs of World War II? How did World War II affect the European nations' colonial empires? How did the Allies' visions of the postwar world differ, and how did these differences contribute to the emergence of the Cold War?

CRITICAL THINKING

Q What was the relationship between World War I and World War II, and how did the ways in which the wars were fought differ?

CONNECTIONS TO TODAY

Q In what ways are the results of World War II still having an impact today?

ON FEBRUARY 3, 1933, only four days after he had been appointed chancellor of Germany, Adolf Hitler met secretly with Germany's leading generals. He revealed to them his desire to remove the "cancer of democracy," create a new authoritarian leadership, and forge a new domestic unity. All Germans would need to realize that "only a struggle can save us and that everything else must be subordinated to this idea." Youth especially must be trained and their wills strengthened "to fight with all means." Since Germany's living space was too small for its people, Hitler said, Germany must rearm and prepare for "the conquest of new living space in the east and its ruthless Germanization." Even before he had consolidated his power, Hitler had a clear vision of his goals, and their implementation meant another war.

World War II in Europe was clearly Hitler's war. Although other countries may have helped make the war possible by not resisting Hitler's Germany earlier, it was Nazi Germany's actions that made World War II inevitable.

But World War II was more than just Hitler's war. It was in fact two separate and parallel conflicts, one provoked by the ambitions of Germany in Europe and the other by the ambitions of Japan in Asia. Around the same time that Hitler was consolidating his power in the early 1930s, the United States and major European nations raised the tariffs they imposed on Japanese imports in a desperate effort to protect local businesses and jobs. In response, militant groups in Tokyo began to argue that Japan must obtain by violent action what it could not secure by peaceful means. By 1941, when the United States became embroiled in both wars, the two had merged into one global conflict.

Although World War I has been described as a total war, World War II was even more so and was fought on a scale unknown in history. Almost everyone in the warring countries was involved in one way or another: as soldiers; as workers in wartime industries; as ordinary citizens subject to invading armies, military occupation, or bombing raids; as refugees; or as victims of mass extermination. The world had never witnessed such widespread human-induced death and destruction. ✦

Retreat from Democracy: Dictatorial Regimes

 FOCUS QUESTIONS: What are the characteristics of totalitarian states, and to what degree were these characteristics present in Fascist Italy, Nazi Germany, and Stalinist Russia? To what extent was Japan a totalitarian state?

The rise of dictatorial regimes in the 1930s had a great deal to do with the coming of World War II. The apparent triumph of liberal democracy in 1919 had proved extremely short-lived. By 1939, only two major states in Europe (Great Britain and France) and several minor ones (the Low Countries, the Scandinavian states, Switzerland, and Czechoslovakia) remained democratic. Italy and Germany had succumbed to the political movement called fascism, and Soviet Russia under Joseph Stalin moved toward repressive totalitarianism. A host of other European states and Latin American countries adopted authoritarian structures of different kinds, while a militarist regime in Japan moved that country down the path of war. What had happened to Woodrow Wilson's claim that World War I had been fought to make the world safe for democracy? Actually, World War I turned out to have had the opposite effect.

The Retreat from Democracy: Did Europe Have Totalitarian States?

The postwar expansion of the electorate made mass politics a reality and seemed to enhance the spread of democracy in Europe. But the war itself had created conditions that led the new mass electorate to distrust democracy and move toward a more radicalized politics.

Many postwar societies were badly divided, especially along class lines. During the war, to maintain war production, governments had been forced to make concessions to trade unions and socialist parties, which strengthened the working class after the war. At the same time, the position of many middle-class people had declined as consumer industries had been curtailed during the war and war bonds, which had been purchased by the middle classes as their patriotic contribution to the war effort, sank in value and even became worthless in some countries.

Gender divisions also weakened social cohesion. After the war, as soldiers returned home, women were forced out of jobs they had taken during the war, jobs that many newly independent women wanted to retain. The loss of so many men during the war had also left many younger women with no marital prospects and widows with no choice but to find jobs in the labor force. At the same time, fears about a declining population because of the war led many male political leaders to encourage women to return to their traditional roles of wives and mothers. Many European countries outlawed abortion and curtailed the sale of birth control devices while providing increased welfare benefits to entice women to remain at home and bear children.

The Great Depression served to deepen social conflict. Larger and larger numbers of people felt victimized, first by the war and now by socioeconomic conditions that seemed beyond their control. Postwar politics became more and more polarized as people reverted to the wartime practice of dividing into friends and enemies, downplaying compromise and emphasizing conflict. Moderate centrist parties that supported democracy soon found themselves with fewer and fewer allies as people became increasingly radicalized politically, supporting the extremes of left-wing communism or right-wing fascism. In the 1920s, Italy had become the first fascist state, while the Soviet Union moved toward a repressive communist state. In the 1930s, a host of other European states adopted authoritarian structures of various kinds. Is it justified to call any of them **totalitarian states**?

The word *totalitarian* was first used by Benito Mussolini (buh-NEE-toh moos-suh-LEE-nee) in Italy to describe his new fascist state: "Fascism is totalitarian," he declared. A number of historians eventually applied the term to both Nazi Germany and the Soviet Union (Fascist Italy, Nazi Germany, and the Soviet Union are discussed later in this chapter). Especially during the Cold War between the United States and the Soviet Union in the 1950s and 1960s, Western leaders were inclined to refer to both the Soviet Union and the eastern European states that had been brought under Soviet control as "totalitarian."

What did the historians who used the term think were the characteristics of a totalitarian state? Totalitarian regimes, it was argued, extended the functions and power of the central state far beyond what they had been in the past. The totalitarian state expected the active loyalty and commitment of its citizens to the regime's goals and used modern mass propaganda techniques and high-speed modern communications to conquer the minds and hearts of its subjects. The total state aimed to control not only the economic, political, and social aspects of life, but also the intellectual and cultural aspects. The purpose of that control was the active involvement of the masses in the achievement of the regime's goal, whether it be war, a socialist state, or a thousand-year Reich (RYKH). Moreover, the totalitarian state was led by a single leader and a single party and ruthlessly rejected the liberal ideal of limited government power and constitutional guarantees of individual freedoms. Indeed, individual freedom was subordinated to the collective will of the masses, organized and determined for them by a leader. Furthermore, modern technology gave these states unprecedented ability to use police controls to enforce their wishes on their subjects.

By the 1970s and 1980s, however, revisionist historians were questioning the usefulness of the term *totalitarian* and regarded it as crude and imprecise. Certainly, some regimes, such as Fascist Italy, Nazi Germany, and the Soviet Union, sought total control, but these states exhibited significant differences, and none of them was successful in establishing total control of its society.

Nevertheless, these three states did transcend traditional political labels and led to some rethinking of these labels. Fascism in Italy and Nazism in Germany grew out of extreme rightist preoccupations with nationalism and, in the case of Germany, with racism. Communism in the Soviet Union emerged out of Marxist socialism, a radical leftist program. Thus, extreme right-wing and left-wing regimes no longer appeared to be at opposite ends of the political spectrum but came to be viewed as similar to each other in at least some respects.

The Birth of Fascism

In the early 1920s, Benito Mussolini bestowed on Italy the first successful fascist movement in Europe. Mussolini (1883–1945) began his political career as a socialist, but in 1919, he established a new political group, the *Fascio di Combattimento* (FASH-ee-oh dee com-bat-ee-MEN-toh) (League of Combat), which won support from middle-class industrialists fearful of working-class agitation and large landowners who objected to strikes by farmworkers. Mussolini also perceived that Italians were angry over Italy's failure to receive

more territory after World War I. In 1920 and 1921, bands of armed Fascists called *squadristi* (skwah-DREES-tee) were formed and turned loose to attack socialist offices and newspapers. The movement gained momentum as Mussolini's nationalist rhetoric and the middle-class fear of socialism, communist revolution, and disorder made the Fascists seem more and more attractive. On October 29, 1922, after Mussolini and the Fascists threatened to march on Rome if they were not given power, King Victor Emmanuel (1900–1946) capitulated and made Mussolini prime minister of Italy.

By 1926, Mussolini had established the institutional framework for a fascist dictatorship. Press laws gave the government the right to suspend any publications that fostered disrespect for the Catholic Church, the monarchy, or the state. The prime minister was made "head of government" with the power to legislate by decree. A law empowered the police to arrest and confine anybody for both nonpolitical and political crimes without pressing charges. The government was given the power to dissolve political and cultural associations. In 1926, all anti-fascist parties were outlawed, and a secret police force was established. By the end of the year, Mussolini ruled Italy as *Il Duce* (eel DOO-chay), the leader.

Mussolini conceived of the fascist state as totalitarian: "Fascism is totalitarian, and the Fascist State, the synthesis and unity of all values, interprets, develops and gives strength to the whole life of the people."[1] Mussolini did try to create a

Mussolini, the Iron Duce. One of Mussolini's favorite images of himself was that of the Iron Duce—the strong leader who is always right. Consequently, he was often seen in military-style uniforms and military poses. This photograph shows Mussolini in one of his numerous uniforms with his Blackshirt bodyguards giving the Fascist salute.

Hugo Jaeger/Timepix/Time Life Pictures/Getty Images

The Nazi Mass Spectacle. Hitler and the Nazis made clever use of mass spectacles to rally the German people behind the Nazi regime. These mass demonstrations evoked intense enthusiasm, as is evident in this photograph of Hitler arriving at the Bückeberg (BOOK-uh-bayrk) near Hamelin for the Harvest Festival in 1937. Almost one million people were present for the celebration.

combined the symbolism of a religious service with the merriment of a popular amusement. They had great appeal and usually evoked mass enthusiasm and excitement.

The apparatus of Hitler's total state had some confusing features. One usually thinks of Nazi Germany as having an all-powerful government that maintained absolute control and order. In truth, Nazi Germany was the scene of almost constant personal and institutional conflict, which resulted in administrative chaos. Incessant struggle characterized the relationships within the party, within the state, and between party and state. Hitler, of course, remained the ultimate decision maker and absolute ruler.

In the economic sphere, Hitler and the Nazis also established control. Although the regime pursued the use of public works projects and "pump-priming" grants to private construction firms to foster employment and end the depression, there is little doubt that rearmament contributed far more to solving the unemployment problem. Unemployment, which had stood at 6 million in 1932, dropped to 2.6 million in 1934 and less than 500,000 in 1937. The regime claimed full credit for solving Germany's economic woes, and this was an important factor in convincing many Germans to accept the new regime, despite its excesses.

For those who needed coercion, the Nazi state had its instruments of terror and repression. Especially important were the *Schutzstaffel* (SHOOTS-shtah-fuhn) (guard squadrons), known simply as the SS. Originally created as Hitler's personal bodyguard, the SS, under the direction of Heinrich Himmler (1900–1945), came to control all of the regular and secret police forces. Himmler and the SS functioned on the basis of two principles: terror and ideology. Terror included

the instruments of repression and murder: the secret police, criminal police, concentration camps, and later the execution squads and death camps for the extermination of the Jews. For Himmler, the SS was a crusading order whose primary goal was to further the Aryan master race.

Other institutions, such as the Catholic and Protestant churches, primary and secondary schools, and universities, were also brought under the control of the Nazi totalitarian state. Nazi professional organizations and leagues were formed for civil servants, teachers, women, farmers, doctors, and lawyers. Since the early indoctrination of youth would create the foundation for a strong totalitarian state for the future, youth organizations—the *Hitler Jugend* (HIT-luh YOO-gunt) (Hitler Youth) and its female counterpart, the *Bund Deutscher Mädel* (BOONT DOIT-chur MAY-dul) (League of German Maidens)—were given special attention. The oath required of Hitler Youth members demonstrates the degree of dedication expected of youth in the Nazi state: "In the presence of this blood banner, which represents our Führer, I swear to devote all my energies and my strength to the savior of our country, Adolf Hitler. I am willing and ready to give up my life for him, so help me God."

The creation of the Nazi total state also had an impact on women. Women played a crucial role in the Aryan racial state as bearers of the children who would bring about the triumph of the Aryan race. To the Nazis, the differences between men and women were natural: men were warriors and political leaders, while women were destined to be wives and mothers.

Nazi ideas determined employment opportunities for women. The Nazis hoped to drive women out of certain areas of the labor market, including heavy industry or other jobs that might hinder them from bearing healthy children. Certain professions, including university teaching, medicine, and law, were also considered inappropriate for women, especially married women. Instead, the Nazis encouraged women to pursue professional occupations that had direct practical application, such as social work and nursing. The Nazi regime pursued its campaign against working women with such poster slogans as "Get hold of pots and pans and broom and you'll sooner find a groom!"

The Nazi total state was intended to be an Aryan racial state. From its beginning, the Nazi Party reflected Hitler's strong anti-Semitic beliefs. In September 1935, the Nazis announced new racial laws at the annual party rally in Nuremberg. These "Nuremberg laws" excluded German Jews from German citizenship and forbade marriages and extramarital relations between Jews and German citizens. The

Nuremberg laws essentially separated Jews from the Germans politically, socially, and legally and were the natural extension of Hitler's stress on the creation of a "pure" Aryan race.

A more violent phase of anti-Jewish activity took place in 1938 and 1939, initiated on November 9–10, 1938, by the infamous *Kristallnacht* (kri-STAHL-nahkht), or night of shattered glass. The assassination of a secretary in the German embassy in Paris became the pretext for a Nazi-led rampage against the Jews in which synagogues were burned, 7,000 Jewish businesses were destroyed, and at least one hundred Jews were killed. Moreover, 20,000 Jewish males were rounded up and sent to concentration camps. Jews were barred from all public buildings and prohibited from owning, managing, or working in any retail store. Finally, under the direction of the SS, Jews were encouraged to "emigrate from Germany."

NAZI CULTURE   In the 1920s, Weimar (VY-mar) Germany was one of the chief European centers for modern art. Hitler, however, wanted the Third Reich to stand for a new cultural model, one that embodied militarism, heroism, Aryan values, and traditional social mores. He preferred artworks that drew "the true picture of life" and that were "clear and simple in style and manner." No longer was art an expression of individual freedom but a form of propaganda. Consequently, German artists now mostly created landscape and still life paintings, portraits, and allegorical statues with themes that included animals and nature, motherhood, sports, peasant life, military life, and battle scenes.

Nazi values also affected other cultural forms. The Nazi state closely monitored literature and supported works that emphasized the values of Nazism, such as Ernest Jünger's *The Storm of Steel*, a memoir of a German soldier during World War I that stressed military service and sacrifice. In music, an emphasis was placed on "Germanic composers," such as the nineteenth-century composer Richard Wagner. A Nazi film office supported filmmakers willing to push the cause of National Socialism. The propaganda films of Leni Riefenstahl (LAY-nee REE-fuhn-shtahl), in particular *Triumph of the Will*, captured Hitler's charisma and the effect of the Nazi mass rallies of the 1930s (see the Film & History feature "*Triumph of the Will* (1934)" on p. 731).

The Stalinist Era in the Soviet Union

Joseph Stalin made a significant shift in Soviet economic policy in 1928 when he launched his first five-year plan. Its real goal was nothing less than the transformation of the agrarian Soviet Union into an industrial country virtually overnight. Instead of consumer goods, the first five-year plan emphasized maximum production of capital goods and armaments and succeeded in quadrupling the production of heavy machinery and doubling oil production. Between 1928 and 1937, during the first two five-year plans, steel production increased from 4 million to 18 million tons per year.

Rapid industrialization was accompanied by an equally rapid collectivization of agriculture. Stalin believed that the capital needed for industrial growth could be gained by creating agricultural surpluses that would be created by eliminating private farms and pushing people onto collective farms (see the box "The Formation of Collective Farms" on p. 732). By eliminating private property, a communist ideal would also be achieved.

By 1934, Russia's 26 million family farms had been collectivized into 250,000 units. This was done at tremendous cost, since Stalin did not hesitate to starve the peasants to force them to comply with the policy of collectivization, especially in Ukraine, where 2.9 million died. Stalin himself supposedly told Winston Churchill during World War II that 10 million peasants died in the artificially created famines of 1932 and 1933. The only concession Stalin made to the peasants was to allow each household to have one tiny, privately owned garden plot.

Stalin's program of rapid industrialization entailed additional costs as well. To achieve his goals, Stalin strengthened the party bureaucracy under his control. Anyone who resisted was sent into forced labor camps in Siberia. Stalin's desire for sole control of decision making also led to purges of the Old Bolsheviks. Between 1936 and 1938, the most prominent Old Bolsheviks were put on trial and condemned to death. During this same time, Stalin undertook a purge of army officers, diplomats, union officials, party members, intellectuals, and numerous ordinary citizens. One old woman was sent to Siberia for saying, "If people prayed, they would work better." Estimates are that 8 million Russians were arrested; millions died in Siberian forced labor camps. This gave Stalin the distinction of being one of the greatest mass murderers in human history. The Stalinist bloodbath made what some Western intellectuals had hailed as the "new civilization" much less attractive by the late 1930s.

Disturbed by a rapidly declining birthrate, Stalin also reversed much of the permissive social legislation of the early 1920s. Advocating complete equality of rights for women, the Communists had made divorce and abortion easy to obtain while also encouraging women to work outside the home and to set their own moral standards. After Stalin came to power, the family was praised as a miniature collective in which parents were responsible for inculcating values of duty, discipline, and hard work. Abortion was outlawed, and divorced fathers who failed to support their children were fined heavily.

The Stalinist era did witness some positive aspects in the everyday lives of Soviet citizens. To create leaders for the new communist society, Stalin began a program to enable workers, peasants, and young Communists to receive higher education, especially in engineering. There was also tremendous growth in part-time schools where large numbers of adults took courses to become literate so that they could advance to technical school or college. Increasing numbers of people saw education as the key to better jobs and upward mobility in Soviet society. One woman of peasant background recounted, "In Moscow I had a burning desire to study. Where or what wasn't important; I wanted to study." For what purpose? "We had a saying at work: 'Without that piece

Triumph of the Will (1934)

Probably the best-known films of Nazi Germany today are documentaries, in particular those of Leni Riefenstahl. Riefenstahl was an actress who turned to directing in 1932. Adolf Hitler liked her work and invited her to make a film about the 1934 Nuremberg party rally. In filming this party day of unity—as it was called—Hitler was trying to demonstrate, in the wake of the purge of the SA on June 30, that the Nazi Party was strongly united behind its leader. Hitler provided the film's title, *Triumph des Willens* (*Triumph of the Will*).

Much of the film's success was due to careful preparation. A crew of 172 people assisted Riefenstahl. Good camera work was coordinated with the physical arrangements for the rally to produce a spectacle that was manipulated for cinematic purposes from beginning to end. As one critic remarked, "The Rally was planned not only as a spectacular mass meeting, but as a spectacular propaganda film." To add to the dramatic effect, Riefenstahl used a number of techniques including moving cameras (one was even mounted on Hitler's Mercedes), telephoto lenses for unusual perspectives, aerial photographs, and music carefully synchronized with each scene. The result is an effective piece of propaganda aimed at conveying to viewers the power of National Socialism.

The movie begins with the introductory titles that are almost religious in character:

> Twenty years after the outbreak of
>   the World War,
> Sixteen years after the beginning of
>   Germany's suffering,
> Nineteen months after the beginning
>   of the rebirth of Germany,
> Adolf Hitler flew to Nuremberg to
>   review his faithful followers.

The rest of the film is devoted to scenes from the six days of the party rally: the dramatic opening when Hitler is greeted with thunderous applause; the major speeches of party leaders; an outdoor rally of Labor Service men who perform pseudo-military drills with their shovels; a Hitler Youth rally in which Hitler tells thousands of German boys, "in you Germany will live"; military exercises; and massive ceremonies with thousands of parading SA and SS men.

The film ends with Hitler's closing speech in which he reviews the struggle of the Nazi Party to take control of Germany. The screen fades to black as the crowd sings "The Horst Wessel Lied," a famous Nazi anthem.

Throughout the film, Hitler is shown in messianic terms—his descent from the clouds at the beginning, his motorcades through the streets with him standing like a god in an open car as thousands of people cheer, and his many appearances at the rally where he commands the complete adulation of the masses assembled before him. In his speeches, Hitler emphasized the power of the new German state: "It is our will that this state shall endure for a thousand years." He also stressed the need for unity: "We want to be one people, one nation, and with one leader." As Rudolf Hess, Hitler's deputy, summed up at the end of the film: "The Party is Hitler. Hitler is Germany just as Germany is Hitler."

Considerable controversy has surrounded the film. Many people accused Riefenstahl of using art to promote a murderous and morally corrupt regime. In Germany, under postwar denazification laws, the film can be shown only for educational purposes. Yet Riefenstahl always maintained, against all the evidence, that it was "a pure historical film." To a viewer today, however, the film is obviously a propaganda piece. The speeches seem tedious and the ideas simplistic, but to watch thousands of people responding the way they did is a terrible reminder of how Hitler used mass spectacles to achieve his goal of educating the German people to his new Nazi state.

Nsdap/The Kobal Collection/Picture Desk

A scene from *Triumph of the Will* showing one of the many mass rallies at Nuremberg.

The Formation of Collective Farms

FAMILY & SOCIETY

ACCOMPANYING THE RAPID INDUSTRIALIZATION of the Soviet Union was the collectivization of agriculture, a feat that involved nothing less than transforming Russia's 26 million family farms into 250,000 collective farms called *kolkhozes* (kuhl-KAHZ-zuhz). This selection provides a firsthand account of how the process worked.

Max Belov, *The History of a Collective Farm*

General collectivization in our village was brought about in the following manner: Two representatives of the [Communist] Party arrived in the village. All the inhabitants were summoned … to a meeting at which the policy of general collectivization was announced.… The upshot was that although the meeting lasted two days, from the viewpoint of the Party representatives nothing was accomplished.

After this setback the Party representatives divided the village into two sections and worked each one separately. Two more officials were sent to reinforce the first two. A meeting of our section of the village was held in a stable which had previously belonged to a kulak [wealthy farmer]. The meeting dragged on until dark. Suddenly someone threw a brick at the lamp, and in the dark the peasants began to beat the Party representatives, who jumped out the window and escaped from the village barely alive. The following day seven people were arrested. The militia was called in and stayed in the village until the peasants, realizing their helplessness, calmed down.…

By the end of 1930 there were two kolkhozes in our village. Though at first these collectives embraced at most only 70 percent of the peasant households, in the months that followed they gradually absorbed more and more of them.

In these kolkhozes the great bulk of the land was held and worked communally, but each peasant household owned a house of some sort, a small plot of ground and perhaps some livestock. All the members of the kolkhoz were required to work on the kolkhoz a certain number of days each month; the rest of the time they were allowed to work on their own holdings. They derived their income partly from what they grew on their garden strips and partly from their work in the kolkhoz.

When the harvest was over, and after the farm had met its obligations to the state … and had sold on the market whatever undesignated produce was left, the remaining produce and the farm's monetary income were divided among the kolkhoz members according to the number of "labor days" each one had contributed to the farm's work.… It was in 1930 that the kolkhoz members first received their portions out of the "communal kettle." After they had received their earnings, at the rate of 1 kilogram of grain and 55 kopecks per labor day, one of them remarked, "You will live, but you will be very, very thin." …

By late 1932 more than 80 percent of the peasant households … had been collectivized.… That year the peasants harvested a good crop and had hopes that the calculations would work out to their advantage and … strengthen them economically. These hopes were in vain. The kolkhoz workers received only 200 grams of flour per labor day for the first half of the year; the remaining grain, including the seed fund, was taken by the government. The peasants were told that industrialization of the country … demanded grain and sacrifices from them.

 What was the purpose of collectivizing Soviet agriculture? According to Belov, why did the peasants of his village assault the Communist Party representatives? What was the result of their protest?

Source: From Sidney Harcave, *Readings in Russian History* (New York: Thomas Crowell & Co., 1962), pp. 208–210.

---

of paper [the diploma], you are an insect; with it, a human being.' My lack of higher education prevented me from getting decent wages."[5]

The Rise of Militarism in Japan

The rise of militarism in Japan resulted not from a seizure of power by a new political party but from the growing influence of militant forces at the top of the political hierarchy. During the 1920s, a multiparty system based on democratic practices appeared to be emerging. Two relatively moderate political parties, the Minseito (men-SAY-toh) and the Seiyukai (say-YOO-ky), dominated the legislature and took turns providing executive leadership in the cabinet. Nevertheless, the political system was probably weaker than it seemed at the time. Both of the major parties were heavily dependent on campaign contributions from powerful corporations, and conservative forces connected to the military or the old landed aristocracy were still highly influential behind the scenes. As in the Weimar Republic in Germany during the same period, the actual power base of modern political forces was weak, and politicians unwittingly undermined the fragile system by engaging in bitter attacks on each other.

In the early 1930s, the growing confrontation with China in Manchuria, combined with the onset of the Great Depression,

Fascist Italy	
Creation of Fascist Party	1919
Mussolini is made prime minister	October 29, 1922
Establishment of Fascist dictatorship	1926
Nazi Germany	
Hitler as Munich politician	1919–1923
Beer Hall Putsch	1923
Hitler is made chancellor	January 30, 1933
Enabling Act	March 23, 1933
Hindenburg dies; Hitler as sole ruler	August 2,1934
Nuremberg laws	1935
Kristallnacht	November 9–10, 1938
Soviet Union	
First five-year plan begins	1928
Stalin's purges	1936–1938

brought an end to the fragile stability of the immediate post-war years. The depression had a disastrous effect on Japan. The value of Japanese exports dropped by 50 percent from 1929 to 1931, and wages dropped nearly as much. Hardest hit were farmers as the price of rice and other staple food crops plummeted.

During the early 1930s, civilian cabinets managed to cope with the economic challenges presented by the depression. By abandoning the gold standard, Prime Minister Inukai Tsuyoshi (ih-NOO-ky tsoo-YOH-shee) was able to lower the price of Japanese goods on the world market, and exports climbed back to earlier levels. But the political parties were no longer able to stem the growing influence of militant nationalist elements.

In May 1932, Tsuyoshi was assassinated by right-wing extremists. He was succeeded by a moderate, Admiral Saito Makoto (sy-TOH muh-KAH-toh), but extremist patriotic societies composed of ultranationalists began to terrorize opponents, assassinating businessmen and public figures identified with the Shidehara (shee-deh-HAH-rah) policy of conciliation toward the outside world (see Chapter 24). Some, such as the publicist Kita Ikki (KEE-tuh IK-kee), were convinced that the parliamentary system had been corrupted by materialism and Western values and should be replaced by a system that would return to traditional Japanese values and imperial authority. His message, "Asia for the Asians," had not won widespread support during the relatively prosperous 1920s but increased in popularity after the Great Depression, which convinced many Japanese that capitalism was unsuitable for Japan. These same people advocated the use of military force to create a self-sufficient Japan that would acquire the resources and raw materials it needed by controlling East Asia.

During the mid-1930s, the government steadily came under the influence of the military and extreme nationalists.

Minorities and left-wing elements were persecuted, and moderates were intimidated into silence. Terrorists on trial for participating in assassination attempts portrayed themselves as selfless patriots and received light sentences. Japan continued to hold national elections, and moderate candidates continued to receive substantial popular support, but the cabinets were dominated by the military or advocates of Japanese expansionism. In February 1936, junior army officers led a coup, briefly occupying the Diet building and other key government installations in Tokyo and assassinating several members of the cabinet. The ringleaders were quickly tried and convicted of treason, but under conditions that further strengthened the influence of the military.

The Path to War

 FOCUS QUESTION: What were the underlying causes of World War II, and what specific steps taken by Nazi Germany and Japan led to war?

Only twenty years after the "war to end war," the world plunged back into the nightmare. The efforts at collective security in the 1920s—the League of Nations, the attempts at disarmament, the pacts and treaties—all proved meaningless in view of the growth of Nazi Germany and the rise of Japan.

The Path to War in Europe

World War II in Europe had its beginnings in the ideas of Adolf Hitler, who believed that only so-called Aryans were capable of building a great civilization. But to Hitler, the Germans, the leading group of Aryans, were threatened from the east by a large mass of "inferior" peoples, the Slavs, who had learned to use German weapons and technology. Germany needed more land to support a larger population and be a great power. Already in the 1920s, in the second volume of *Mein Kampf*, Hitler had indicated where a National Socialist regime would find this land: "And so we National Socialists ... take up where we broke off six hundred years ago. We stop the endless German movement to the south and west, and turn our gaze toward the land in the east.... If we speak of soil in Europe today, we can primarily have in mind only Russia and her vassal border states."[6] Once Russia had been conquered, its land could be resettled by German peasants while the Slavic population could be used as slave labor to build the Aryan racial state that would dominate Europe for a thousand years. Hitler's conclusion was apparent: Germany must prepare for its inevitable war with the Soviet Union.

A DIPLOMATIC REVOLUTION: SCRAPPING THE TREATY OF VERSAILLES When Hitler became chancellor on January 30, 1933, Germany's situation in Europe seemed weak. The Versailles treaty had created a demilitarized zone on Germany's western border that would allow the French to move into the heavily industrialized parts of Germany in the event of war.

To Germany's east, the smaller states, such as Poland and Czechoslovakia, had defensive treaties with France. The Versailles treaty had also limited Germany's army to 100,000 troops, with no air force and only a small navy.

Posing as a man of peace in his public speeches, Hitler emphasized that Germany wished only to revise the unfair provisions of Versailles by peaceful means and achieve Germany's rightful place among the European states. On March 9, 1935, he announced the creation of a new air force and one week later the introduction of a military draft that would expand Germany's army from 100,000 to 550,000 troops. Hitler's unilateral repudiation of the Versailles treaty brought a swift reaction, as France, Great Britain, and Italy condemned Germany's action and warned against future aggressive steps. But nothing concrete was done.

On March 7, 1936, buoyed by his conviction that the Western democracies had no intention of using force to maintain the Treaty of Versailles, Hitler sent German troops into the demilitarized Rhineland. According to the Versailles treaty, the French had the right to use force against any violation of the demilitarized Rhineland. But France would not act without British support, and the British viewed the occupation of German territory by German troops as reasonable action by a dissatisfied power. The *London Times* noted that the Germans were only "going into their own back garden."

Meanwhile, Hitler gained new allies. In October 1935, Benito Mussolini had committed Fascist Italy to imperial expansion by invading Ethiopia. Angered by French and British opposition to his invasion, Mussolini welcomed Hitler's support and began to draw closer to the German dictator he had once called a buffoon. The joint intervention of Germany and Italy on behalf of General Francisco Franco in the Spanish Civil War in 1936 also drew the two nations closer. In October 1936, Mussolini and Hitler concluded an agreement that recognized their common political and economic interests, and one month later, Mussolini referred publicly to the new Rome-Berlin Axis. Also in November, Germany and Japan (the rising military power in the Far East) concluded the Anti-Comintern Pact and agreed to maintain a common front against communism.

By the end of 1936, Hitler and Nazi Germany had achieved a "diplomatic revolution" in Europe. The Treaty of Versailles had been virtually scrapped, and Germany was once more a "world power," as Hitler proclaimed. Hitler was convinced that neither the French nor the British would provide much opposition to his plans and decided in 1938 to move on Austria. By threatening Austria with invasion, Hitler coerced the Austrian chancellor into putting Austrian Nazis in charge of the government. The new government promptly invited German troops to enter Austria and assist in maintaining law and order. One day later, on March 13, 1938, after his triumphal return to his native land, Hitler formally annexed Austria to

Germany. Great Britain's ready acknowledgment of Hitler's action only increased the German dictator's contempt for Western weakness.

THE TAKEOVER OF CZECHOSLOVAKIA

The annexation of Austria improved Germany's strategic position in central Europe and put Hitler in position to achieve his next objective—the destruction of Czechoslovakia. This goal might have seemed unrealistic, as democratic Czechoslovakia was fully prepared to defend itself and was well supported by pacts with France and the Soviet Union. Hitler, however, was convinced that France and Britain would not use force to defend Czechoslovakia.

He was right again. On September 15, 1938, Hitler demanded the cession of the Sudetenland (soo-DAY-tun-land) (an area in northwestern Czechoslovakia inhabited largely by ethnic Germans) to Germany and expressed his willingness to risk "world war" if he was refused. Instead of objecting, the British, French, Germans, and Italians—at a hastily arranged conference at Munich—reached an agreement that essentially met all of Hitler's demands. German troops were allowed to occupy the Sudetenland as the Czechs, abandoned by their Western allies and the Soviet Union, stood by helplessly. The Munich Conference was the high point of Western **appeasement** of Hitler. When Neville Chamberlain, the British prime minister, returned to England from Munich, he boasted that the Munich agreement meant "peace for our time." Hitler had promised Chamberlain that he had made his last demand. Like scores of politicians before him, Chamberlain had believed Hitler's promises (see Opposing Viewpoints "The Munich Conference" on p. 735).

Hitler Arrives in Vienna. By threatening to invade Austria, Hitler forced the Austrian government to capitulate to his wishes. Austria was annexed to Germany. Shown here is the triumphal arrival of Hitler in Vienna on March 13, 1938. Seated beside him is Arthur Seyss-Inquart, Hitler's new handpicked governor of Austria.

OPPOSING ✕ VIEWPOINTS

The Munich Conference

POLITICS & GOVERNMENT

AT THE MUNICH CONFERENCE, THE LEADERS OF FRANCE AND GREAT BRITAIN CAPITULATED to Hitler's demands on Czechoslovakia. Although the British prime minister, Neville Chamberlain, defended his actions at Munich as necessary for peace, another British statesman, Winston Churchill, characterized the settlement at Munich as "a disaster of the first magnitude."

Winston Churchill, Speech to the House of Commons, October 5, 1938

I will begin by saying what everybody would like to ignore or forget but which must nevertheless be stated, namely, that we have sustained a total and unmitigated defeat, and that France has suffered even more than we have…. The utmost my right honorable Friend the Prime Minister … has been able to gain for Czechoslovakia and in the matters which were in dispute has been that the German dictator, instead of snatching his victuals from the table, has been content to have them served to him course by course…. And I will say this, that I believe the Czechs, left to themselves and told they were going to get no help from the Western Powers, would have been able to make better terms than they have got….

We are in the presence of a disaster of the first magnitude which has befallen Great Britain and France. Do not let us blind ourselves to that….

And do not suppose that this is the end. This is only the beginning of the reckoning. This is only the first sip, the first foretaste of a bitter cup which will be proffered to us year by year unless by a supreme recovery of moral health and martial vigor, we arise again and take our stand for freedom as in the olden time.

Neville Chamberlain, Speech to the House of Commons, October 6, 1938

That is my answer to those who say that we should have told Germany weeks ago that, if her army crossed the border of Czechoslovakia, we should be at war with her. We had no treaty obligations and no legal obligations to Czechoslovakia. When we were convinced, as we became convinced, that nothing any longer would keep the Sudetenland within the Czechoslovakian State, we urged the Czech Government as strongly as we could to agree to the cession of territory, and to agree promptly…. It was a hard decision for anyone who loved his country to take, but to accuse us of having by that advice betrayed the Czechoslovakian State is simply preposterous. What we did was to save her from annihilation and give her a chance of new life as a new State, which involves the loss of territory and fortifications, but may perhaps enable her to enjoy in the future and develop a national existence under a neutrality and security comparable to that which we see in Switzerland today. Therefore, I think the Government deserve the approval of this House for their conduct of affairs in this recent crisis which has saved Czechoslovakia from destruction and Europe from Armageddon.

 What were the opposing views of Churchill and Chamberlain on the Munich Conference? Why did they disagree so much? With whom do you agree? Why?

Sources: From *Parliamentary Debates, House of Commons* (London: His Majesty's Stationery Office, 1938), vol. 339, pp. 361–369. From Neville Chamberlain, *In Search of Peace* (New York: Putnam, 1939), pp. 215, 217.

POLAND Munich confirmed Hitler's perception that the Western democracies were weak and would not fight. Hitler was increasingly convinced of his own infallibility, and he had been pleased but by no means satisfied at Munich. In March 1939, Germany occupied all the Czech lands (Bohemia and Moravia) while the Slovaks, with his encouragement, declared their independence of the Czechs and became a puppet state (Slovakia) of Nazi Germany. On the evening of March 15, 1939, Hitler triumphantly declared in Prague that he would be known as the greatest German of them all.

At last, the Western states realized that they had to react vigorously to the Nazi threat. Hitler's unremitting aggression made clear that his promises were worthless. When he began to demand the return to Germany of Danzig, which had been made a free city by the Treaty of Versailles to serve as a seaport for Poland, Britain recognized the danger and offered to protect Poland in the event of war. At the same time, both France and Britain realized that, among the European powers, only the Soviet Union was powerful enough to counter Nazi aggression and so began political and military negotiations with Stalin. Their distrust of Soviet communism, however, made an alliance unlikely.

Meanwhile, Hitler pressed on in the belief that Britain and France would not fight over Poland. To preclude an alliance between the western European states and the Soviet Union, which would create the danger of a two-front war, Hitler, ever the opportunist, negotiated his own nonaggression pact with Stalin and shocked the world with its announcement, on

August 23, 1939. The treaty with the Soviet Union gave Hitler the freedom to attack Poland. He told his generals, "Now Poland is in the position in which I wanted her.... I am only afraid that at the last moment some swine or other will yet submit to me a plan for mediation."[7] He need not have worried. On September 1, German forces invaded Poland; two days later, Britain and France declared war on Germany. Europe was again at war.

The Path to War in Asia

In September 1931, on the pretext that the Chinese had attacked a Japanese railway near Mukden (MOOK-dun) (the "Mukden incident" had actually been carried out by Japanese saboteurs), Japanese military units seized Manchuria. Japanese officials in Tokyo were divided over the wisdom of the takeover, but the moderates were unable to control the army. Eventually, worldwide protests against the Japanese action led the League of Nations to send an investigative commission to Manchuria. When the commission issued a report condemning the seizure, Japan withdrew from the League. Over the next several years, the Japanese consolidated their hold on Manchuria, renaming it Manchukuo (man-CHOO-kwoh) and placing it under the titular authority of the former Chinese emperor and now Japanese puppet Puyi (POO-YEE). Japan now began to expand into northern China.

Not all politicians in Tokyo agreed with this aggressive policy, but right-wing terrorists assassinated some of the key critics and intimidated others into silence. By the mid-1930s, militants connected with the government and the armed forces were effectively in control of Japanese politics. The United States refused to recognize the Japanese takeover of Manchuria but was unwilling to threaten the use of force. Instead, the Americans attempted to appease Japan in the hope of encouraging Japanese moderates. As a senior U.S. diplomat with long experience in Asia warned in a memorandum to the president:

> Utter defeat of Japan would be no blessing to the Far East or to the world. It would merely create a new set of stresses, and substitute for Japan the USSR as the successor to Imperial Russia—as a contestant (and at least an equally unscrupulous and dangerous one) for the mastery of the East. Nobody except perhaps Russia would gain from our victory in such a war.[8]

JAPANESE AGGRESSION IN CHINA For the moment, the prime victim of Japanese aggression was China. Chiang Kai-shek attempted to avoid a confrontation with Japan so that he could deal with the Communists, whom he considered the greater threat. When clashes between Chinese and Japanese troops broke out, he sought to appease the Japanese by granting them the authority to administer areas in northern China. But as Japan moved steadily southward, popular protests in Chinese cities against Japanese aggression intensified. In December 1936, Chiang was briefly kidnapped by military forces commanded by General Zhang Xueliang (JAHNG

A Japanese Victory March in China. After consolidating its authority over Manchuria, Japan began to expand into northern China. Direct hostilities between Japanese and Chinese forces began in 1937. This photograph shows a Japanese victory march in Shanghai at the beginning of December 1937. By 1939, Japan had conquered most of eastern China.

scheh-LEE-AHNG), who compelled him to end his military efforts against the Communists in Yan'an and form a new united front against the Japanese. After Chinese and Japanese forces clashed at Marco Polo Bridge, south of Beijing, in July 1937, China refused to apologize, and hostilities spread.

Japan had not planned to declare war on China, but neither side would compromise, and the 1937 incident eventually turned into a major conflict. The Japanese advanced up the Yangzi River valley and seized the Chinese capital of Nanjing in December, but Chiang Kai-shek refused to capitulate and moved his government upriver to Hankou (HAHN-kow). When the Japanese seized that city, he moved on to Chongqing (chung-CHING), in remote Sichuan (suh-CHWAHN) province. Japanese strategists had hoped to force Chiang to join a Japanese-dominated New Order in East Asia, comprising Japan, Manchuria, and China. This was part of a larger plan to seize Soviet Siberia with its rich resources and create a new "Monroe Doctrine for Asia" under which Japan would guide its Asian neighbors on the path to development and prosperity (see the box "Japan's Justification for Expansion" on p. 737). After all, who better to instruct Asian societies on modernization than the one Asian country that had already achieved it?

Japan's Justification for Expansion

POLITICS & GOVERNMENT

ADVOCATES OF JAPANESE EXPANSION justified their proposals by claiming both economic necessity and moral imperatives. Note the familiar combination of motives in this passage written by an extremist military leader in the late 1930s.

Hashimoto Kingoro on the Need for Emigration and Expansion

We have already said that there are only three ways left to Japan to escape from the pressure of surplus population. We are like a great crowd of people packed into a small and narrow room, and there are only three doors through which we might escape, namely emigration, advance into world markets, and expansion of territory. The first door, emigration, has been barred to us by the anti-Japanese immigration policies of other countries. The second door, advance into world markets, is being pushed shut by tariff barriers and the abrogation of commercial treaties. What should Japan do when two of the three doors have been closed against her?

It is quite natural that Japan should rush upon the last remaining door.

It may sound dangerous when we speak of territorial expansion, but the territorial expansion of which we speak does not in any sense of the word involve the occupation of the possessions of other countries, the planting of the Japanese flag thereon, and the declaration of their annexation to Japan. It is just that since the Powers have suppressed the circulation of Japanese materials and merchandise abroad, we are looking for some place overseas where Japanese capital, Japanese skills and Japanese labor can have free play, free from the oppression of the white race.

We would be satisfied with just this much. What moral right do the world powers who have themselves closed to us the two doors of emigration and advance into world markets have to criticize Japan's attempt to rush out of the third and last door? …

At the time of the Manchurian incident, the entire world joined in criticism of Japan. They said that Japan was an untrustworthy nation. They said that she had recklessly brought cannon and machine guns into Manchuria, which was the territory of another country, flown airplanes over it, and finally occupied it. But the military action taken by Japan was not in the least a selfish one. Moreover, we do not recall ever having taken so much as an inch of territory belonging to another nation. The result of this incident was the establishment of the splendid new nation of Manchuria. The Powers are still discussing whether or not to recognize this new nation, but regardless of whether or not other nations recognize her, the Manchurian empire has already been established, and now, seven years after its creation, the empire is further consolidating its foundations with the aid of its friend, Japan.

And if it is still protested that our actions in Manchuria were excessively violent, we may wish to ask the white race just which country it was that sent warships and troops to India, South Africa, and Australia and slaughtered innocent natives, bound their hands and feet with iron chains, lashed their backs with iron whips, proclaimed these territories as their own, and still continues to hold them to this very day.

What arguments does Hashimoto Kingoro make in favor of territorial expansion? What is his reaction to the condemnation of his proposal by western European nations?

Source: From *Sources of Japanese Tradition* by William Theodore de Bary. Copyright © 1958 by Columbia University Press.

ADVANCE TO THE SOUTH During the late 1930s, Japan began to cooperate with Nazi Germany on the assumption that the two countries would ultimately launch a joint attack on the Soviet Union and divide up its resources between them. But when Germany surprised the world by signing a nonaggression pact with the Soviets in August 1939, Japanese strategists were compelled to reevaluate their long-term objectives. Japan was not strong enough to defeat the Soviet Union alone, as a small but bitter border war along the Siberian frontier near Manchuria had amply demonstrated. So the Japanese began to shift their sights southward to the vast resources of Southeast Asia—the oil of the Dutch East Indies, the rubber and tin of Malaya, and the rice of Burma and Indochina.

A move southward, of course, would risk war with the European colonial powers and the United States. Japan's attack on China in the summer of 1937 had already aroused strong criticism abroad, particularly from the United States.

When Japan demanded the right to occupy airfields and exploit economic resources in French Indochina in the summer of 1940, the United States warned the Japanese that it would cut off the sale of oil and scrap iron unless Japan withdrew from the area and returned to its borders of 1931.

The Japanese viewed the American threat of retaliation as an obstacle to their long-term objectives. Japan badly needed oil and scrap iron from the United States. Should they be cut off, Japan would have to find them elsewhere. The Japanese were thus caught in a vise. To obtain guaranteed access to natural resources that were necessary to fuel the Japanese military machine, Japan must risk being cut off from its current source of raw materials that would be needed in case of a conflict. After much debate, the Japanese decided to launch a surprise attack on American and European colonies in Southeast Asia in the hope of a quick victory that would evict the United States from the region.

Japan seizes Manchuria	September 1931
Hitler becomes chancellor of Germany	January 30, 1933
Hitler announces a German air force	March 9, 1935
Hitler announces military conscription	March 16, 1935
Mussolini invades Ethiopia	October 1935
Hitler occupies the demilitarized Rhineland	March 7, 1936
Mussolini and Hitler intervene in the Spanish Civil War	1936
Rome-Berlin Axis formed	October 1936
Anti-Comintern Pact (Japan and Germany)	November 1936
Japan invades China	July 1937
Germany annexes Austria	March 13, 1938
Munich Conference: Sudetenland goes to Germany	September 29, 1938
Germany occupies the rest of Czechoslovakia	March 1939
German-Soviet Nonaggression Pact	August 23, 1939
Germany invades Poland	September 1, 1939
Britain and France declare war on Germany	September 3, 1939

World War II

 FOCUS QUESTION: What were the main events of World War II in Europe and Asia?

Unleashing an early form of **Blitzkrieg** (BLITZ-kreeg), or "lightning war," Hitler stunned Europe with the speed and efficiency of the German attack. Moving into Poland with about 1.5 million troops from two fronts, German forces used armored columns or panzer divisions (a *panzer division* was a strike force of about three hundred tanks and accompanying forces and supplies) supported by airplanes to break quickly through Polish lines and encircle the outnumbered and poorly equipped Polish armies. The coordinated air and ground assaults included the use of Stuka dive bombers; as they descended from the skies, their sirens emitted a bloodcurdling shriek, adding a frighteningly destructive element to the German attack. Regular infantry units, still on foot with their supplies drawn by horses, then marched in to hold the newly conquered territory. Soon afterward, Soviet military forces attacked eastern Poland. Within four weeks, Poland had surrendered. On September 28, 1939, Germany and the Soviet Union officially divided Poland between them.

Europe at War

Although Hitler's hopes to avoid a war with the western European states were dashed when France and Britain declared war on September 3, he was confident that he could control the situation. After a winter of waiting (called the "phony war"), Hitler resumed his aggression on April 9, 1940, with another

Blitzkrieg, against Denmark and Norway (see Map 25.1). One month later, on May 10, the Germans launched an attack on the Netherlands, Belgium, and France. The main assault through Luxembourg and the Ardennes forest was completely unexpected by the French and British forces. German panzer divisions broke through the weak French defensive positions there and raced across northern France, splitting the Allied armies and trapping French troops and the entire British army on the beaches of Dunkirk. Only by heroic efforts did the British succeed in a gigantic evacuation of 330,000 Allied (mostly British) troops. The French capitulated on June 22. German armies occupied about three-fifths of France, while the French hero of World War I, Marshal Henri Pétain (AHN-ree pay-TANH) (1856–1951), established an authoritarian regime— known as Vichy (VISH-ee) France—over the remainder. Germany was now in control of western and central Europe, but Britain still had not been defeated.

THE PROBLEM OF BRITAIN As Hitler realized, an amphibious invasion of Britain would be possible only if Germany gained control of the air. At the beginning of August 1940, the German air force, or Luftwaffe (LOOFT-vahf-uh), launched a major offensive against British air and naval bases, harbors, communication centers, and war industries. The British fought back doggedly, supported by an effective radar system that gave them early warning of German attacks. Nevertheless, the British air force suffered critical losses by the end of August and was probably saved by a change in Hitler's strategy. In September, in retaliation for a British attack on Berlin, Hitler ordered a shift from military targets to massive bombing of British cities to break British morale. The British rebuilt their air strength quickly and were soon inflicting major losses on Luftwaffe bombers. By the end of September, Germany had lost the Battle of Britain, and the invasion of Britain had to be postponed.

At this point, Hitler pursued the possibility of a Mediterranean strategy, which would involve capturing Egypt and the Suez Canal and closing the Mediterranean to British ships, thereby shutting off Britain's supply of oil. Hitler's commitment to the Mediterranean was never wholehearted, however. His initial plan was to let the Italians defeat the British in North Africa, but this strategy failed when the British routed the Italian army. Although Hitler then sent German troops to the North African theater of war, his primary concern lay elsewhere; he had already reached the decision to fulfill his lifetime obsession with the acquisition of territory in the east.

INVASION OF THE SOVIET UNION Although he had no desire for a two-front war, Hitler became convinced that Britain was remaining in the war only because it expected Soviet support. If the Soviet Union were smashed, Britain's last hope would be eliminated. Moreover, Hitler had convinced himself that the Soviet Union, with what he contemptuously regarded as its Jewish-Bolshevik leadership and a pitiful army, could be defeated quickly and decisively. Although the invasion of the Soviet Union was scheduled for spring 1941, the attack

MAP 25.1 World War II in Europe and North Africa. With its fast and effective military, Germany quickly overwhelmed much of western Europe. Hitler had overestimated his country's capabilities, however, and underestimated those of his foes. By late 1942, his invasion of the Soviet Union was failing, and the United States had become a major factor in the war. The Allies successfully invaded Italy in 1943 and France in 1944.

Q *Which countries were neutral, and how did geography help make their neutrality an option?*

was delayed because of problems in the Balkans. Hitler had already obtained the political cooperation of Hungary, Bulgaria, and Romania, but Mussolini's disastrous invasion of Greece in October 1940 exposed Hitler's southern flank to British air bases in that country. To secure his Balkan flank, German troops seized both Yugoslavia and Greece in April 1941. Feeling reassured, Hitler turned to the east and invaded the Soviet Union, believing that the Soviets could still be decisively defeated before winter set in.

On June 22, 1941, Nazi Germany launched its attack on the Soviet Union, by far the largest invasion the Germans had yet attempted. The German force consisted of 180 divisions,

including 20 panzer divisions, 8,000 tanks, and 3,200 airplanes. German troops were stretched out along an 1,800-mile front. The Soviets had 160 infantry divisions but were able to mobilize another 300 divisions out of reserves within half a year. Hitler had badly miscalculated the potential power of the Soviets. The German troops advanced rapidly, capturing 2 million Soviet soldiers. By November, one German army group had swept through Ukraine, while a second was besieging Leningrad; a third approached within 25 miles of Moscow, the Russian capital.

An early winter and unexpected Soviet resistance, however, brought the German advance to a halt. Armor and transport vehicles stalled in temperatures of 30 degrees below zero. Hitler's commanders wished to withdraw and regroup for the following spring, but Hitler refused. Fearing the disintegration of his lines, he insisted that there would be no retreat. A Soviet counterattack in December 1941 by an army supposedly exhausted by Nazi victories came as an ominous ending to the year. Although the Germans managed to hold on and reestablish their lines, a war diary kept by a soldier in Panzer Group Three described the desperate situation: "Discipline is breaking down. More and more soldiers are heading west on foot without weapons.... The road is under constant air attack. Those killed by bombs are no longer being buried. All the hangers-on (cargo troops, Luftwaffe, supply trains) are pouring to the rear in full flight."[9] By December 1941, another of Hitler's decisions—the declaration of war on the United States—probably made his defeat inevitable and turned another European conflict into a global one.

Japan at War

On December 7, 1941, Japanese carrier-based aircraft attacked the U.S. naval base at Pearl Harbor in the Hawaiian Islands. The same day, other units launched assaults on the Philippines and began advancing toward the British colony of Malaya (see Map 25.2). Shortly thereafter, Japanese forces invaded the Dutch East Indies and occupied a number of islands in the Pacific Ocean. In some cases, as on the Bataan (buh-TAN *or* buh-TAHN) peninsula and the island

MAP 25.2 **World War II in Asia and the Pacific.** In 1937, Japan invaded northern China, beginning its effort to create a "Great East-Asia Co-Prosperity Sphere." Further expansion led the United States to end iron and oil sales to Japan. Deciding that war with the United States was inevitable, Japan engineered a surprise attack on Pearl Harbor.

Q *Why was control of the islands in the western Pacific of great importance both to the Japanese and to the Allies?*

of Corregidor (kuh-REG-ih-dor) in the Philippines, resistance was fierce, but by the spring of 1942, almost all of Southeast Asia and much of the western Pacific had fallen into Japanese hands. Japan then announced its intention to liberate the colonies of Southeast Asia from Western rule. For the moment, however, it needed the resources of the region for its war machine and placed its conquests on a wartime basis.

Japanese leaders had hoped that their lightning strike at American bases would destroy the U.S. Pacific fleet and persuade the Roosevelt administration to accept Japanese domination of the Pacific. The American people, in the eyes of Japanese leaders, had been made soft by material indulgence. But the Japanese had miscalculated. The attack on Pearl Harbor galvanized American public opinion and won broad support for Roosevelt's war policy. The United States now joined with European nations and Nationalist China in a combined effort to defeat Japan and bring an end to its hegemony in the Pacific. Believing that American involvement in the Pacific would render the United States ineffective in the European theater of war, Hitler declared war on the United States four days after Pearl Harbor.

The Turning Point of the War, 1942–1943

The entry of the United States into the war created a coalition (the Grand Alliance) that ultimately defeated the Axis Powers (Germany, Italy, and Japan). Nevertheless, the three major Allies—Britain, the United States, and the Soviet Union—had to overcome mutual suspicions before they could operate as an effective alliance. Two factors aided that process. First, Hitler's declaration of war on the United States made it easier for the Americans to accept the British and Russian contention that the defeat of Germany should be the first priority of the United States. For that reason, the United States, under its lend-lease program (which had begun before U.S. entry into the war), sent large amounts of military aid, including $50 billion worth of trucks, planes, and other arms, to the British and the Soviets. Also important to the alliance was the tacit agreement of the three chief Allies to stress military operations while ignoring political differences and larger strategic issues concerning any postwar settlement. At the beginning of 1943, the Allies agreed to fight until the Axis Powers surrendered unconditionally. Although this principle of **unconditional surrender** prevented a repeat of the mistake of World War I, which ended in 1918 with an armistice rather than a total victory, it likely discouraged dissident Germans and Japanese from attempting to overthrow their governments in order to arrange a negotiated peace. At the same time, it did have the effect of cementing the Grand Alliance by making it nearly impossible for Hitler to divide his foes.

Defeat, however, was far from Hitler's mind at the beginning of 1942. As Japanese forces advanced into Southeast Asia and the Pacific after crippling the American naval fleet at Pearl Harbor, Hitler and his European allies continued the war in Europe against Britain and the Soviet Union.

Until the fall of 1942, it appeared that the Germans might still prevail on the battlefield. Reinforcements in North Africa enabled the Afrika Korps under General Erwin Rommel (RAHM-ul) to break through the British defenses in Egypt and advance toward Alexandria. In the spring of 1942, a renewed German offensive in the Soviet Union led to the capture of the entire Crimea, causing Hitler to boast in August 1942:

> As the next step, we are going to advance south of the Caucasus and then help the rebels in Iran and Iraq against the English. Another thrust will be directed along the Caspian Sea toward Afghanistan and India. Then the English will run out of oil. In two years we'll be on the borders of India. Twenty to thirty elite German divisions will do. Then the British Empire will collapse.[10]

But this would be Hitler's last optimistic outburst. By the fall of 1942, the war had turned against the Germans.

NORTH AFRICA AND THE EASTERN FRONT In North Africa, British forces had stopped Rommel's troops at El Alamein (ell ah-lah-MAYN), Egypt, in the summer of 1942 and then forced them back across the desert. In November 1942, British and American forces invaded French North Africa and forced the German and Italian troops to surrender in May 1943. On the eastern front, the turning point of the war occurred at Stalingrad. After the capture of the Crimea, Hitler's generals wanted him to concentrate on the Caucasus and its oil fields, but Hitler decided that Stalingrad, a major industrial center on the Volga, should be taken first. Between November 1942 and February 1943, German troops were stopped, then encircled, and finally forced to surrender on February 2, 1943 (see the box "A German Soldier at Stalingrad" on p. 742). The entire German Sixth Army of 300,000 men was lost. By February 1943, German forces in Russia were back to their positions of June 1942. By the spring of 1943, long before Western Allied troops returned to the European continent, even Hitler knew that the Germans would not defeat the Soviet Union.

ASIA The tide of battle in the Far East also turned dramatically in 1942. In the Battle of the Coral Sea on May 7 and 8, 1942, American naval forces stopped the Japanese advance and temporarily relieved Australia of the threat of invasion. On June 4, at the Battle of Midway Island, American carrier planes destroyed all four of the attacking Japanese aircraft carriers and established American naval superiority in the Pacific. The victory came at high cost; about two-fifths of the American planes were shot down in the encounter. By the fall of 1942, Allied forces were beginning to gather for offensive operations in three areas: from bases in north Burma and India into the rest of Burma; in the Solomon Islands and on New Guinea, with forces under the direction of American general Douglas MacArthur moving toward the Philippines; and across the Pacific where combined U.S. Army, Marine, and Navy forces would mount attacks against Japanese-held

A German Soldier at Stalingrad

POLITICS & GOVERNMENT

THE SOVIET VICTORY AT STALINGRAD was a major turning point in World War II. This excerpt comes from the diary of a German soldier who fought and died in the Battle of Stalingrad. His dreams of victory and a return home with medals were soon dashed by the realities of Soviet resistance.

Diary of a German Soldier

Today, after we'd had a bath, the company commander told us that if our future operations are as successful, we'll soon reach the Volga, take Stalingrad, and then the war will inevitably soon be over. Perhaps we'll be home by Christmas.

July 29. The company commander says the Russian troops are completely broken, and cannot hold out any longer. To reach the Volga and take Stalingrad is not so difficult for us. The Führer knows where the Russians' weak point is. Victory is not far away....

August 10. The Führer's orders were read out to us. He expects victory of us. We are all convinced that they can't stop us.

August 12. This morning outstanding soldiers were presented with decorations.... Will I really go back to Elsa without a decoration? I believe that for Stalingrad the Führer will decorate even me....

September 4. We are being sent northward along the front toward Stalingrad. We marched all night and by dawn had reached Voroponovo Station. We can already see the smoking town. It's a happy thought that the end of the war is getting nearer. That's what everyone is saying....

September 8. Two days of nonstop fighting. The Russians are defending themselves with insane stubbornness. Our regiment has lost many men....

September 16. Our battalion, plus tanks, is attacking the [grain storage] elevator, from which smoke is pouring—the

grain in it is burning; the Russians seem to have set light to it themselves. Barbarism. The battalion is suffering heavy losses....

October 10. The Russians are so close to us that our planes cannot bomb them. We are preparing for a decisive attack. The Führer has ordered the whole of Stalingrad to be taken as rapidly as possible....

October 22. Our regiment has failed to break into the factory. We have lost many men; every time you move you have to jump over bodies....

November 10. A letter from Elsa today. Everyone expects us home for Christmas. In Germany everyone believes we already hold Stalingrad. How wrong they are. If they could only see what Stalingrad has done to our army....

November 21. The Russians have gone over to the offensive along the whole front. Fierce fighting is going on. So, there it is—the Volga, victory, and soon home to our families! We shall obviously be seeing them next in the other world.

November 29. We are encircled. It was announced this morning that the Führer has said: "The army can trust me to do everything necessary to ensure supplies and rapidly break the encirclement."

December 3. We are on hunger rations and waiting for the rescue that the Führer promised....

December 26. The horses have already been eaten.... The soldiers look like corpses or lunatics, looking for something to put in their mouths. They no longer take cover from Russian shells; they haven't the strength to walk, run away, and hide. A curse on this war!

What did this soldier believe about the Führer? Why? What was the source of his information? Why is the battle for Stalingrad considered a major turning point in World War II?

Source: From Vasili Chuikov, *The Battle of Stalingrad* (Grafton Books, 1964).

---

islands. After a series of bitter engagements in the waters of the Solomon Islands from August to November 1942, Japanese fortunes began to fade.

The Last Years of the War

By the beginning of 1943, the tide of battle had turned against Germany, Italy, and Japan. After the Axis forces had surrendered in Tunisia on May 13, 1943, the Allies crossed the Mediterranean and carried the war to Italy. After taking Sicily, Allied troops began the invasion of mainland Italy in September. In the meantime, after the ouster and arrest of Benito Mussolini, a new Italian government offered to surrender to Allied forces. But Mussolini was liberated by the Germans in a daring raid and then set up as the head of a puppet German

state in northern Italy while German troops moved in and occupied much of the rest of the country. The new defensive lines established by the Germans in the hills south of Rome were so effective that the Allied advance up the Italian peninsula was a painstaking affair accompanied by heavy casualties. Rome did not fall to the Allies until June 4, 1944. By that time, the Italian war had assumed a secondary role anyway as the Allies prepared to open their long-awaited "second front" in western Europe.

ALLIED ADVANCES IN EUROPE Since the autumn of 1943, the Allies had been planning a cross-channel invasion of France from Britain. Under the direction of the American general Dwight D. Eisenhower (1890–1969), the Allies landed five assault divisions on the beaches of Normandy on June 6,

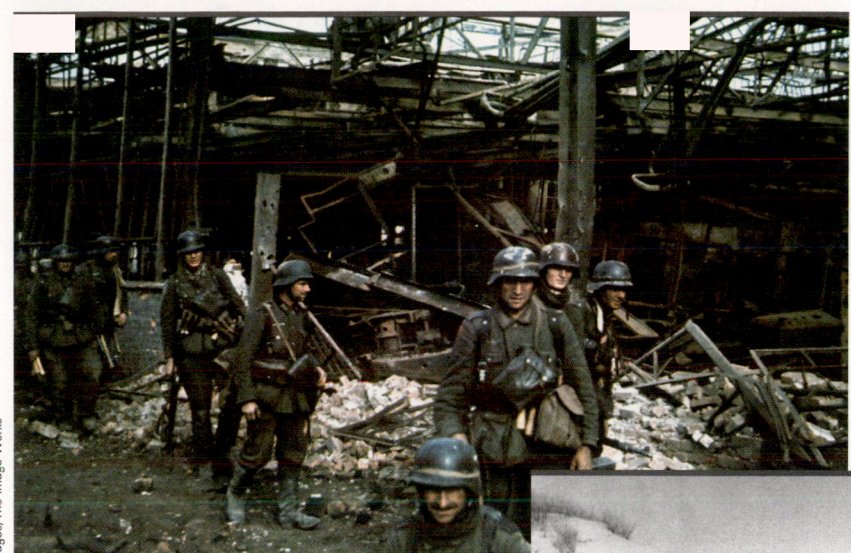

The Battle of Stalingrad. The Battle of Stalingrad was a major turning point on the eastern front. Shown in the first photograph is a German infantry platoon in the ruins of a tractor factory they had captured in the northern part of Stalingrad. This victory took place on October 15, 1942, at a time when Hitler still believed he was winning the battle for Stalingrad. That belief was soon dashed as a Soviet counteroffensive in November led to a total defeat for the Germans. The second photograph shows thousands of captured soldiers being marched across frozen Soviet soil to prison camps. The soldiers in white fur hats are Romanian. Fewer than 6,000 captured soldiers survived to go home; the remainder—almost 85,000 prisoners—died in captivity.

1944, in history's greatest naval invasion. An initially indecisive German response enabled the Allied forces to establish a beachhead. Within three months, they had landed 2 million men and a half-million vehicles that pushed inland and broke through German defensive lines.

After the breakout, Allied troops moved south and east and liberated Paris by the end of August. By March 1945, they had crossed the Rhine River and advanced farther into Germany. At the end of April 1945, Allied armies in northern Germany moved toward the Elbe River, where they finally linked up with the Soviets. The Soviets had come a long way since the Battle of Stalingrad in 1943. In the summer of 1943, Hitler had gambled on taking the offensive by making use of newly developed heavy tanks, but the German forces were soundly defeated by the Soviets at the Battle of Kursk (KOORSK) (July 5–12), the greatest tank battle of World War II. Soviet forces then began a relentless advance westward. The Soviets had reoccupied Ukraine by the end of 1943 and lifted the siege of Leningrad and moved into the Baltic states by the beginning of 1944. Advancing along a northern front, Soviet troops occupied Warsaw in January 1945 and entered

Berlin in April. Meanwhile, Soviet troops along a southern front swept through Hungary, Romania, and Bulgaria.

In January 1945, Hitler had moved into a bunker 55 feet under Berlin to direct the final stages of the war. In his final political testament, Hitler, consistent to the end in his rabid anti-Semitism, blamed the Jews for the war: "Above all I charge the leaders of the nation and those under them to scrupulous observance of the laws of race and to merciless opposition to the universal poisoner of all peoples, international Jewry."[11] Hitler committed suicide on April 30, two days after Mussolini had been shot by partisan Italian forces. On May 7, German commanders surrendered. The war in Europe was over.

DEFEAT OF JAPAN The war in Asia continued. Beginning in 1943, American forces had gone on the offensive and advanced their way, slowly at times, across the Pacific. The Americans took an increasing toll of enemy resources, especially at sea and in the air. As Allied military power drew inexorably closer to the main Japanese islands in the first months of 1945, President Harry Truman, who had succeeded to the

Refugees Flee Japanese Cities. American bombing attacks on Japanese cities began in earnest in November 1944. Built of flimsy materials, Japan's crowded cities were soon devastated by these air raids. This photograph shows refugees carrying a few belongings as they flee the city of Hakodate.

presidency on the death of Franklin Roosevelt in April, had an excruciatingly difficult decision to make. Should he use atomic weapons (at the time, only two bombs had been developed, and their effectiveness had not been demonstrated) to bring the war to an end without the necessity of an Allied invasion of the Japanese homeland? As the world knows, Truman answered that question in the affirmative. The first bomb was dropped on the city of Hiroshima (hee-roh-SHEE-muh) on August 6. Truman then called on Japan to surrender or expect a "rain of ruin from the air." When the Japanese did not respond, a second bomb was dropped on Nagasaki (nah-gah-SAH-kee). Japan surrendered unconditionally on August 14. World War II was finally over.

The New Order

 FOCUS QUESTION: What was the nature of the new orders that Germany and Japan attempted to establish in the territories they occupied?

The initial victories of the Germans and the Japanese gave them the opportunity to create new orders in Europe and Asia. Although both countries presented positive images of these new orders for publicity purposes, in practice both followed policies of ruthless domination of their subject peoples.

The New Order in Europe

After the German victories, Nazi propagandists conjured up glowing images of a **Nazi New Order** in Europe based on "equal chances" for all nations and an integrated economic community. This was not Hitler's conception of a European New Order. He regarded the Europe he had conquered

simply as subject to German domination. Only the Germans, he once said, "can really organize Europe."

THE NAZI EMPIRE The Nazi empire stretched across continental Europe from the English Channel in the west to the outskirts of Moscow in the east. In no way was this empire organized systematically or governed efficiently. Some areas, such as western Poland, were directly annexed by Nazi Germany and made into German provinces. The rest of occupied Europe was administered by German military or civilian officials in combination with varying degrees of indirect control from collaborationist regimes.

Racial considerations played an important role in determining how conquered peoples were treated. German civil administrations were established in Norway, Denmark, and the Netherlands because the Nazis considered their peoples Aryan, racially kin to the Germans and hence worthy of more lenient treatment. "Inferior" Latin peoples, such as the occupied French, were given military administrations. By 1943, however, as Nazi losses continued to multiply, all the occupied territories of northern and western Europe were ruthlessly exploited for material goods and manpower for Germany's labor needs.

CHRONOLOGY	The Course of World War II
Germany and the Soviet Union divide Poland	September 28, 1939
Blitzkrieg against Denmark and Norway	April 1940
Blitzkrieg against Belgium, Netherlands, and France	May 1940
France surrenders	June 22, 1940
Battle of Britain	Summer–Fall 1940
Nazi seizure of Yugoslavia and Greece	April 1941
Germany invades the Soviet Union	June 22, 1941
Japanese attack Pearl Harbor	December 7, 1941
Battle of the Coral Sea	May 7–8, 1942
Battle of Midway Island	June 4, 1942
Allied invasion of North Africa	November 1942
Germans surrender at Stalingrad	February 2, 1943
Axis forces surrender in North Africa	May 1943
Battle of Kursk	July 5–12, 1943
Invasion of mainland Italy	September 1943
Allied invasion of France	June 6, 1944
Hitler commits suicide	April 30, 1945
Germany surrenders	May 7, 1945
Atomic bomb dropped on Hiroshima	August 6, 1945
Japan surrenders	August 14, 1945

Hitler's Plans for a New Order in the East

POLITICS & GOVERNMENT

HITLER'S NIGHTLY MONOLOGUES to his postdinner guests, which were recorded by the Führer's private secretary, Martin Bormann, reveal much about the New Order he wished to create. On the evening of October 17, 1941, Hitler expressed his views on what the Germans would do with their newly conquered territories in the east.

Hitler's Secret Conversations, October 17, 1941

In comparison with the beauties accumulated in Central Germany, the new territories in the East seem to us like a desert.... This Russian desert, we shall populate it.... We'll take away its character of an Asiatic steppe; we'll Europeanize it. With this object, we have undertaken the construction of roads that will lead to the southernmost point of the Crimea and to the Caucasus. These roads will be studded along their whole length with German towns, and around these towns our colonists will settle.

As for the two or three million men whom we need to accomplish this task, we'll find them quicker than we think. They'll come from Germany, Scandinavia, the Western countries, and America. I shall no longer be here to see all that, but in twenty years the Ukraine will already be a home for twenty million inhabitants besides the natives. In three hundred years, the country will be one of the loveliest gardens in the world.

As for the natives, we'll have to screen them carefully. The Jew, that destroyer, we shall drive out.... We shan't settle in the Russian towns, and we'll let them fall to pieces without intervening. And, above all, no remorse on this subject! We're not going to play at children's nurses; we're absolutely without obligations as far as these people are concerned. To struggle against the hovels, chase away the fleas, provide German teachers, bring out newspapers—very little of that for us! We'll confine ourselves, perhaps, to setting up a radio transmitter, under our control. For the rest, let them know just enough to understand our highway signs, so that they won't get themselves run over by our vehicles.... There's only one duty: to Germanize this country by the immigration of Germans, and to look upon the natives as Redskins. If these people had defeated us, Heaven have mercy! But we don't hate them. That sentiment is unknown to us. We are guided only by reason....

All those who have the feeling for Europe can join in our work.

In this business I shall go straight ahead, cold-bloodedly. What they may think about me, at this juncture, is to me a matter of complete indifference. I don't see why a German who eats a piece of bread should torment himself with the idea that the soil that produces this bread has been won by the sword.

 What were Hitler's plans for the conquered eastern territories and the peoples who inhabited these lands? Concerning eastern Europeans, do you believe Hitler's statements that "we don't hate them" and "we are guided only by reason"? What motivations do you see behind this monologue?

Source: From *Hitler's Conversations*, Hugh Trevor Roper, copyright © 1953 by New American Library, published by Octagon Books, a Division of Hippocrene Books, Inc.

PLANS FOR AN ARYAN RACIAL EMPIRE Because the conquered lands in the east contained the living space for German expansion and were populated in Nazi eyes by racially inferior Slavic peoples, Nazi administration there was considerably more ruthless. Hitler's racial ideology and his plans for an Aryan empire were so important to him that he and the Nazis began to implement their race-based program soon after the conquest of Poland. Heinrich Himmler, a strong believer in Nazi racial ideology and the leader of the SS, was put in charge of German resettlement plans in the east. Himmler's task was to evacuate the inferior Slavic peoples and replace them with Germans, a policy first applied to the new German provinces carved out of western Poland. One million Poles were uprooted and dumped in southern Poland. Hundreds of thousands of ethnic Germans (descendants of Germans who had migrated decades earlier from Germany to different parts of southern and eastern Europe) were encouraged to colonize designated areas in Poland. By 1942, 2 million ethnic Germans had been settled in Poland.

The invasion of the Soviet Union inflated Nazi visions of German colonization in the east. Hitler spoke to his intimate circle of a colossal project of social engineering after the war, in which Poles, Ukrainians, and Russians would become slave labor while German peasants settled on the abandoned lands and Germanized them (see the box "Hitler's Plans for a New Order in the East" above). Nazis involved in this planning were well aware of the human costs. Himmler told a gathering of SS officers that although the destruction of 30 million Slavs was a prerequisite for German plans in the east, "whether nations live in prosperity or starve to death interests me only insofar as we need them as slaves for our culture. Otherwise it is of no interest."[12]

USE OF FOREIGN WORKERS Labor shortages in Germany led to a policy of ruthless mobilization of foreign labor for Germany. After the invasion of the Soviet Union, the 4 million Russian prisoners of war captured by the Germans along with more than 2 million workers conscripted in France became a major source of heavy labor, but it was wasted by allowing more than 3 million of them to die from neglect. In 1942, a special office was created to recruit labor for German farms and industries. By the summer of 1944, 7 million foreigners were laboring in Germany, constituting 20 percent of the nation's workforce. At the same time, another 7 million workers were supplying forced labor in their own countries on farms, in industries, and even in military camps. Forced labor, however, often proved counterproductive because it created economic chaos in occupied countries and disrupted industrial production that could have helped Germany. The brutality of Germany's recruitment policies often led more and more people to resist the Nazi occupation forces.

The Holocaust

No aspect of the Nazi New Order was more terrifying than the deliberate attempt to exterminate the Jewish people of Europe. Racial struggle was a key element in Hitler's ideology and meant to him a clearly defined conflict of opposites: the Aryans, creators of human cultural development, against the Jews, parasites who were trying to destroy the Aryans. By the beginning of 1939, Nazi policy focused on promoting the "emigration" of German Jews from Germany. Once the war began in September 1939, the so-called Jewish problem took on new dimensions. For a while, there was discussion of the Madagascar Plan, which aspired to the mass shipment of Jews to the island of Madagascar off the east coast of Africa. When war contingencies made this plan impractical, an even more drastic policy was conceived.

THE SS AND THE *EINSATZGRUPPEN* Himmler and the SS organization shared Hitler's racial ideology. The SS was given responsibility for what the Nazis called their **Final Solution** to the Jewish problem—the annihilation of the Jewish people. Reinhard Heydrich (RYN-hart HY-drikh) (1904–1942), head of the SS's Security Service, was given administrative responsibility for the Final Solution. After the defeat of Poland, Heydrich ordered the *Einsatzgruppen* (YN-zahtz-groop-un), special strike forces that he had created, to round up all Polish Jews and concentrate them in ghettos established in a number of Polish cities.

In June 1941, the *Einsatzgruppen* were given new responsibilities as mobile killing units. These SS death squads followed the regular army's advance into the Soviet Union. Their job was to round up Jews in the villages and execute and bury them in mass graves, often giant pits dug by the victims themselves before they were shot. Such constant killing produced morale problems among the SS executioners. During a visit to Minsk in the Soviet Union, Himmler tried to build morale by pointing out that "he would not like it if Germans did such a thing gladly. But their conscience was in no way impaired, for they were soldiers who had to carry out every order unconditionally. He alone had responsibility before God and Hitler for everything that was happening, … and he was acting from a deep understanding of the necessity for this operation."[13]

THE DEATH CAMPS Although it has been estimated that as many as a million Jews were killed by the *Einsatzgruppen*, this

Library of Congress Prints and Photographs Division [LC-USZ61-671]

The Holocaust: Mission of the *Einsatzgruppen*. The activation of mobile killing units known as the *Einsatzgruppen* marked the first stage in implementing Hitler's Final Solution, the mass murders of the Holocaust. This picture shows the execution of a Jew by a member of one of these SS killing squads. Onlookers include members of the German army, the German Labor Service, and even Hitler Youth. When it became apparent that this method of killing individuals one by one was inefficient, it was replaced by the death camps, where large groups could be put to death at once.

approach to solving the Jewish problem was soon perceived as inadequate. Instead, the Nazis opted for the systematic annihilation of the European Jewish population in specially built death camps. The plan was simple: Jews from countries occupied by Germany (or sympathetic to Germany) would be rounded up, packed like cattle into freight trains, and shipped to Poland, where six extermination centers were built for this purpose. The largest and most famous was Auschwitz-Birkenau (OW-shvitz-BEER-kuh-now). Medical technicians chose Zyklon B (the commercial name for hydrogen cyanide) as the most effective gas for quickly killing large numbers of people in gas chambers designed to look like shower rooms to facilitate the cooperation of the victims.

The death camps were up and running by the spring of 1942. Although the elimination of the ghettos in Poland was the first priority, by the summer of 1942, Jews were also being shipped from France, Belgium, and the Netherlands. In 1943, there were shipments of Jews from the capital cities of

Heinrich Himmler: "We Had the Moral Right"

POLITICS & GOVERNMENT

ALTHOUGH NAZI LEADERS WERE RELUCTANT to talk openly about their attempted destruction of the Jews of Europe, when they did, they had no qualms about justifying it. Heinrich Himmler, the leader of the SS, assumed responsibility for executing the Holocaust and in 1943 gave a remarkable speech to the leaders of the SS in Poznan, Poland.

Heinrich Himmler, Speech to SS Leaders

I also want to talk to you, quite frankly, on a very grave matter. Among yourselves it should be mentioned quite frankly, and yet we will never speak of it publicly. I mean the clearing out of the Jews, extermination of the Jewish race. It's one of those things it is easy to talk about—"The Jewish race is being exterminated," says one party member, "that's quite clear, it's in our program—elimination of the Jews, and we're doing it, exterminating them." And then they come, 80 million worthy Germans, and each one had his decent Jew. Of course, the others are vermin, but this one is an A-1 Jew. Not one of those who talk this way has witnessed it, not one of those who talk this way has witnessed it, not one of them has been through it. Most of you must know what it means when 100 corpses are lying side by side, or 500 or 1000. To

have stuck it out and at the same time … to have remained decent fellows, that is what has made us hard. This is a page of glory in our history which has never been written and is never to be written,…. We have taken from them what wealth they had. I have issued a strict order, … that this wealth should, as a matter of course, be handed over to [Germany] without reserve. We have taken none of it for ourselves…. We had the moral right, we had the duty to our people, to destroy this people which wanted to destroy us. But we have not the right to enrich ourselves with so much as a fur, a watch, a mark, or a cigarette or anything else. Because we have exterminated a bacterium we do not want, in the end, to be infected by the bacterium and die of it. I will not see so much as a small area of sepsis appear here or gain a hold. Wherever it may form, we will cauterize it. Although however, we can say, that we have fulfilled this most difficult duty for the love of our people. And our spirit our soul, our character has not suffered injury from it.

How does Himmler justify the Holocaust? What is wrong with his argument, and how does it demonstrate the danger of ideological rigidity?

Source: *Nazi Conspiracy and Aggression* (Washington, D.C., 1946), 4: 563–564.

Berlin, Vienna, and Prague, and from Southern France, Italy and Denmark. Even as the Allies were making significant advances in 1944, Jews were being shipped from Greece and Hungary. These shipments depended on the cooperation of Germany's Transport Ministry, and despite desperate military needs, the Final Solution was given priority in using railroad cars for the transportation of Jews to death camps.

A harrowing experience awaited the Jews when they arrived at one of the six camps. Rudolf Höss (HESS), commandant at Auschwitz-Birkenau, described it:

> We had two SS doctors on duty at Auschwitz to examine the incoming transports of prisoners. The prisoners would be marched by one of the doctors, who would make spot decisions as they walked by. Those who were fit for work were sent into the camp. Others were sent immediately to the extermination plants. Children of tender years were invariably exterminated since by reason of their youth they were unable to work…. At Auschwitz we endeavored to fool the victims into thinking that they were to go through a delousing process. Of course, frequently they realized our true intentions and we sometimes had riots and difficulties due to that fact.[14]

About 30 percent of the arrivals at Auschwitz were sent to a labor camp; the remainder went to the gas chambers. After they had been gassed, the bodies were burned in specially built crematoria. The victims' goods and even their bodies

were used for economic gain. Women's hair was cut off, collected, and used to stuff mattresses or make cloth. Some inmates were also subjected to cruel and painful "medical" experiments. Altogether, the Germans killed between 5 and 6 million Jews, more than 3 million of them in the death camps. About 90 percent of the Jewish populations of Poland, the Baltic countries, and Germany were exterminated. Overall, the Holocaust was responsible for the death of nearly two of every three Jews in Europe (see the box "Heinrich Himmler: 'We Had the Moral Right'" above).

THE OTHER HOLOCAUST The Nazis were also responsible for another Holocaust, the death by shooting, starvation, or overwork of at least another 9 to 10 million people. Because the Nazis also considered the Gypsies of Europe (like the Jews) a race containing alien blood, they were systematically rounded up for extermination. About 40 percent of Europe's one million Gypsies were killed in the death camps. The leading elements of the "subhuman" Slavic peoples—the clergy, intelligentsia, civil leaders, judges, and lawyers—were arrested and deliberately killed. Probably an additional 4 million Poles, Ukrainians, and Byelorussians lost their lives as slave laborers for Nazi Germany, and 3 to 4 million Soviet prisoners of war were killed in captivity. The Nazis also singled out homosexuals for persecution, and thousands lost their lives in concentration camps.

Japan's Plan for Asia

POLITICS & GOVERNMENT

THE JAPANESE OBJECTIVE IN WORLD WAR II was to create a vast Great East-Asia Co-Prosperity Sphere to provide Japan with needed raw materials and a market for its exports. The following passage is from a secret document produced by a high-level government committee in January 1942.

Draft Plan for the Establishment of the Great East-Asia Co-Prosperity Sphere

The Plan. The Japanese empire is a manifestation of morality and its special characteristic is the propagation of the Imperial Way. It is necessary to foster the increased power of the empire, to cause East Asia to return to its original form of independence and co-prosperity by shaking off the yoke of Europe and America, and to let its countries and peoples develop their respective abilities in peaceful cooperation and secure livelihood.

The Form of East Asiatic Independence and Co-Prosperity. The states, their citizens, and resources, comprised in those areas pertaining to the Pacific, Central Asia, and the Indian Oceans formed into one general union are to be established as an autonomous zone of peaceful living and common prosperity on behalf of the peoples of the nations of East Asia. The area including Japan, Manchuria, North China, lower Yangzi River, and the Russian Maritime Province, forms the nucleus of the East Asiatic Union. The Japanese empire possesses a duty as the leader of the East Asiatic Union.

The above purpose presupposes the inevitable emancipation or independence of Eastern Siberia, China, Indo-China, the South Seas, Australia, and India....

Outline of East Asiatic Administration. It is intended that the unification of Japan, Manchukuo, and China in neighborly friendship be realized by the settlement of the Sino-Japanese problems through the crushing of hostile influences in the Chinese interior, and through the construction of a new China.... Aggressive American and British influences in East Asia shall be driven out of the area of Indo-China and the South Seas, and this area should be brought into our defense sphere. The war with Britain and America shall be prosecuted for that purpose....

Chapter 3: Political Construction

Basic Plan. The following are the basic principles for the political construction of East Asia....

The desires of the peoples in the sphere for their independence shall be respected, and endeavors shall be made for their fulfillment, but proper and suitable forms of government shall be decided for them in consideration of military and economic requirements and of the historical, political, and cultural elements peculiar to each area.

It must also be noted that the independence of various peoples of East Asia should be based on the idea of constructing East Asia as "independent countries existing within the New Order of East Asia" and that this conception differs from an independence based on the idea of liberalism and national self-determination....

Western individualism and materialism shall be rejected, and a moral worldview, the basic principle of whose morality shall be the Imperial Way, shall be established. The ultimate object to be achieved is not exploitation but co-prosperity and mutual help, not competitive conflict but mutual assistance and mild peace, not a formal view of equality but a view of order based on righteous classification, not an idea of rights but an idea of service, and not several worldviews but one unified worldview.

What were Japan's proposals for a Japanese-led Asia? What distinction did the government committee that drafted this document draw between "Western individualism and materialism" and the "Imperial Way"? Based on this document, were individualism and materialism a part of the Imperial Way?

Source: From *Sources of Japanese Tradition*, Vol. 2, 2e, by William Theodore de Bary, Carol Gluck, and Arthur E. Tiedemann. Copyright © 2005 by Columbia University Press. Reprinted with permission of the publisher.

The New Order in Asia

Once the takeover was completed, Japanese war policy in the occupied areas in Asia became essentially defensive, as Japan hoped to use its new possessions to meet its burgeoning needs for raw materials, such as tin, oil, and rubber, and also as an outlet for Japanese manufactured goods. To provide an organizational structure for the arrangement, Japanese leaders set up the Great East-Asia Co-Prosperity Sphere, a self-sufficient economic community designed to provide mutual benefits to the occupied areas and the home country (see the box "Japan's Plan for Asia" above). The Ministry for Great East Asia, staffed by civilians, was established in Tokyo in October 1942 to handle arrangements between Japan and the conquered territories.

JAPANESE POLICIES The Japanese conquest of Southeast Asia had been accomplished under the slogan "Asia for the Asiatics," and many Japanese probably sincerely believed that their government was bringing about the liberation of the Southeast Asian peoples from European colonial rule. Japanese officials in the occupied territories quickly made contact with anticolonialist elements and promised that independent governments would be established under Japanese tutelage.

Such governments were eventually established in Burma, the Dutch East Indies, Vietnam, and the Philippines.

In fact, however, real power rested with the Japanese military authorities in each territory, and the local Japanese military command was directly subordinated to the army general staff in Tokyo. The economic resources of the colonies were exploited for the benefit of the Japanese war machine, while local peoples were recruited to serve in local military units or conscripted to work on public works projects. In some cases, the people living in the occupied areas were subjected to severe hardships. In Indochina, for example, forced requisitions of rice by the local Japanese authorities for shipment abroad created a food shortage that caused the starvation of more than a million Vietnamese in 1944 and 1945.

The Japanese planned to implant a new moral and social order as well as a new political and economic order in the occupied areas. Occupation policy stressed traditional values such as obedience, community spirit, filial piety, and discipline that reflected the prevailing political and cultural bias in Japan, while supposedly Western values such as materialism, liberalism, and individualism were strongly discouraged. To promote this New Order, occupation authorities gave particular support to local religious organizations but discouraged the formation of formal political parties.

RESENTMENT AND RESISTANCE At first, many Southeast Asian nationalists took Japanese promises at face value and agreed to cooperate with their new masters. In Burma, an independent government was established in 1943 and subsequently declared war on the Allies. But as the exploitative nature of Japanese occupation policies became increasingly clear, sentiment turned against the New Order. Japanese officials sometimes unwittingly provoked resentment by their arrogance and contempt for local customs. In the Dutch East Indies, for example, Indonesians were required to bow in the direction of Tokyo and recognize the divinity of the Japanese emperor—practices that were repugnant to Muslims. In Burma, Buddhist pagodas were sometimes used as military latrines.

Like German soldiers in occupied Europe, Japanese military forces often had little respect for the lives of their subject peoples. In their conquest of Nanjing, China, in 1937, Japanese soldiers had devoted several days to killing, raping, and looting. Almost 800,000 Koreans were sent overseas, most of them as forced laborers, to Japan. Tens of thousands of women from Korea and the Philippines were forced to serve as "comfort women" (prostitutes) for Japanese troops. In construction projects to help their war effort, the Japanese also made extensive use of labor forces composed of both prisoners of war and local peoples. In building the Burma-Thailand railway in 1943, for example, the Japanese used 61,000 Australian, British, and Dutch prisoners of war and almost 300,000 workers from Burma, Malaya, Thailand, and the Dutch East Indies. By the time the railway was completed, 12,000 Allied prisoners of war and 90,000 local workers had died from the inadequate diet and appalling working conditions in an unhealthy climate.

Such Japanese behavior created a dilemma for many nationalists, who had no desire to see the return of the colonial powers. Some turned against the Japanese, while others lapsed into inactivity. Indonesian patriots tried to have it both ways, feigning support for Japan while attempting to sabotage the Japanese administration. In French Indochina, Ho Chi Minh's Indochinese Communist Party established contacts with American military units in southern China and agreed to provide information on Japanese troop movements and rescue downed American flight crews in the area. In Malaya, where Japanese treatment of ethnic Chinese residents was especially harsh, many joined a guerrilla movement against the occupying forces. By the end of the war, little support remained in the region for the erstwhile "liberators."

The Home Front

 FOCUS QUESTION: What were conditions like on the home front for the major belligerents in World War II?

World War II was even more of a total war than World War I. Fighting was much more widespread and covered most of the planet. Economic mobilization was more extensive; so was the mobilization of women. The number of civilians killed was far higher: almost 20 million were killed from bombing raids, mass extermination policies, and attacks by invading armies.

Mobilizing the People

The home fronts of the major belligerents varied considerably, based on local circumstances.

THE SOVIET UNION World War II had an enormous impact on the Soviet Union. Known to the Soviets as the Great Patriotic War, the German-Soviet war witnessed the greatest land battles in history as well as incredible ruthlessness. To Nazi Germany, it was a war of oppression and annihilation that called for merciless measures. Two out of every five persons killed in World War II were Soviet citizens.

The initial defeats of the Soviet Union led to drastic emergency mobilization measures that affected the civilian population. Leningrad, for example, experienced nine hundred days of siege, during which its inhabitants became so desperate for food that they ate dogs, cats, and mice. As the German army made its rapid advance into Soviet territory, the factories in the western part of the Soviet Union were dismantled and shipped to the interior—to the Urals, western Siberia, and the Volga region. Machines were placed on the bare ground, and walls went up around them as workers began their work.

This widespread military, industrial, and economic mobilization created yet another industrial revolution for the Soviet Union (see the Comparative Essay "Paths to Modernization" on p. 750). Stalin labeled the war effort a "battle of machines," and the Soviets won, producing 78,000 tanks and 98,000 artillery pieces. Fully 55 percent of Soviet national income went for war matériel, compared to 15 percent in 1940. As a result of

COMPARATIVE ESSAY

Paths to Modernization

POLITICS & GOVERNMENT

To the casual observer, the most important feature of the first half of the twentieth century was the rise of a virulent form of competitive nationalism that began in Europe and ultimately descended into the cauldron of two destructive world wars. Behind the scenes, however, another competition was taking place over the most effective path to modernization.

The traditional approach, in which modernization was fostered by an independent urban merchant class, had been adopted by Great Britain, France, and the United States and led to the emergence of democratic societies on the capitalist model. In the second approach, adopted in the late nineteenth century by imperial Germany and Meiji Japan, modernization was carried out by traditional elites in the absence of a strong independent bourgeois class. Both Germany and Japan relied on strong government intervention to promote the growth of national wealth and power, and in both nations, modernization led ultimately to the formation of fascist and militarist regimes during the depression years of the early 1930s.

The third approach, selected by Vladimir Lenin after the Bolshevik Revolution in 1917, was designed to carry out an industrial revolution without going through an intermediate capitalist stage. Under the guidance of the Communist Party in the almost total absence of an urban middle class, an advanced industrial society would be created by destroying the concept of private property. Although Lenin's plans ultimately called for the "withering away of the state," the party adopted totalitarian methods to eliminate enemies of the revolution and carry out the changes needed to create a future classless utopia.

How did these various approaches contribute to the crises that afflicted the world during the first half of the twentieth century? The democratic-capitalist approach proved to be a considerable success in an economic sense, leading to advanced economies that could produce manufactured goods at a rate never seen before. Societies just beginning to undergo their own industrial revolutions tried to imitate the success of the capitalist nations by carrying out their own "revolutions from above," as in Germany and Japan. But the Great Depression and competition over resources and markets soon led to an intense rivalry

Bettmann/Corbis

The Soviet Path to Modernization. One aspect of the Soviet effort to create an advanced industrial society was the collectivization of agriculture, which included the rapid mechanization of food production. In this photograph, peasants are watching a new tractor at work.

between the established capitalist states and their ambitious late arrivals, a rivalry that ultimately erupted into global conflict.

In the first decade of the twentieth century, imperial Russia appeared ready to launch its own bid to join the ranks of the industrialized nations. But that effort was derailed by its entry into World War I, and before that conflict had come to an end, the Bolsheviks were in power. Isolated from the capitalist marketplace by mutual consent, the Soviet Union was able to avoid being dragged into the Great Depression but, despite Stalin's efforts, was unsuccessful in staying out of the "battle of imperialists" that followed at the end of the 1930s. As World War II came to an end, the stage was set for a battle of the victors—the United States and the Soviet Union—over political and ideological supremacy.

 What were the three major paths to modernization in the first half of the twentieth century, and why did they lead to conflict?

the emphasis on military goods, Soviet citizens experienced extreme shortages of both food and housing.

Soviet women played a major role in the war effort. Women and girls worked in industries, mines, and railroads. Overall, the number of women working in industry increased almost 60 percent. Soviet women were also expected to dig antitank ditches and work as air-raid wardens. In addition, the Soviet Union was the only country in World War II to use women as combatants. Soviet women functioned as snipers and also as air crews in bomber squadrons. The female pilots who helped defeat the Germans at Stalingrad were known as the "Night Witches."

Women in the Factories. Although only the Soviet Union used women in combat positions, the number of women working in industry increased dramatically in most belligerent countries. British women are shown here in a British munitions factory during World War II, probably in 1943.

THE UNITED STATES The home front in the United States was quite different from that of its chief wartime allies, largely because the United States faced no threat of war on its own territory. Although the economy and labor force were slow to mobilize, eventually the United States became the arsenal of the Allied Powers, producing the military equipment they needed.

The immediate impact of mobilization was a dramatic expansion of the U.S. economy, which ultimately brought an end to the Great Depression. Old factories were converted from peacetime goods to war goods, and many new factories were built. American industry not only supplied the American armed forces but also provided U.S. allies with the huge quantities of tanks, trucks, jeeps, and airplanes needed to win the war. During the war years, gross national product (GNP) rose by 15 percent a year. During the high point of war production in the United States in November 1943, the nation was constructing six ships a day and $6 billion worth of other military equipment a month. Airplane production increased from 6,000 in 1939 to over 96,000 in 1944.

The mobilization of the American economy created social problems, however. Boomtowns sprang up near the new factories where thousands came to work but then faced a shortage of houses, health facilities, and schools. The dramatic expansion of small towns into large cities often brought a breakdown in traditional social mores, especially evident in an increase in teenage prostitution. Economic mobilization also led to extensive movements of people, which in turn created new social tensions. Sixteen million men and women were enrolled in the military, and another 16 million, mostly wives and sweethearts of the servicemen or workers looking for jobs, also relocated. More than a million blacks migrated from the rural South to the industrial cities of the North and West,

looking for jobs in industry. The presence of blacks in areas where they had not lived before led to racial tensions and sometimes even racial riots. In Detroit in June 1943, white mobs roamed the streets attacking blacks. Many of the one million blacks who enrolled in the military, only to be segregated in their own battle units, were angered by the way they were treated. Some became militant and prepared to fight for their civil rights.

Japanese Americans were treated even more shabbily. On the West Coast, 110,000 Japanese Americans, 65 percent of whom had been born in the United States, were removed to camps encircled by barbed wire and made to take loyalty oaths. Although public officials claimed this policy was necessary for security reasons, no similar treatment of German Americans or Italian Americans ever took place. The racism inherent in this treatment of Japanese Americans was evident when the governor of California, Culbert Olson, said, "You know, when I look out at a group of Americans of German or Italian descent, I can tell whether they're loyal or not. I can tell how they think and even perhaps what they are thinking. But it is impossible for me to do this with inscrutable orientals, and particularly the Japanese."[15]

GERMANY In August 1914, Germans had enthusiastically cheered their soldiers marching off to war. In September 1939, the streets were quiet. Many Germans were apathetic or, even worse for the Nazi regime, had a foreboding of disaster. Hitler was very aware of the importance of the home front. He believed that the collapse of the home front in World War I had caused Germany's defeat, and in his determination to avoid a repetition of that experience, he adopted economic policies that may indeed have cost Germany the war.

To maintain the morale of the home front during the first two years of the war, Hitler refused to cut the production of consumer goods or increase the production of armaments. Blitzkrieg allowed the Germans to win quick victories, after which they believed they could plunder the food and raw materials of the conquered countries to avoid diverting resources from the civilian economy. After the German defeats on the Russian front and the American entry into the war, the economic situation changed. Early in 1942, Hitler finally ordered a massive increase in armaments production and in the size of the army. Hitler's architect, Albert Speer (AHL-bert SHPAYR), was made minister for armaments and munitions that year. By eliminating waste and rationalizing procedures, Speer was able to triple the production of armaments between 1942 and 1943 despite the intense Allied air raids. Speer's urgent plea for a total mobilization of resources for the war effort went unheeded, however. Hitler, fearful of civilian morale problems that would undermine the home front, refused any dramatic cuts in the production of consumer goods. A total mobilization of the economy was not implemented until 1944, when schools, theaters, and cafés were closed and Speer was finally permitted to use all remaining resources for the production of a few basic military items. By that time, it was in vain. Total war mobilization in July 1944 was too little and too late to save Germany from defeat.

The war caused a reversal in Nazi attitudes toward women. Nazi resistance to female employment declined as the war progressed and more and more men were called up for military service. Nazi magazines now proclaimed, "We see the woman as the eternal mother of our people, but also as the working and fighting comrade of the man."[16] But the number of women working in industry, agriculture, commerce, and domestic service increased only slightly. The total number of employed women in September 1944 was 14.9 million, compared to 14.6 million in May 1939. Many women, especially those of the middle class, resisted regular employment, particularly in factories. Even the introduction of labor conscription for women in January 1943 failed to achieve much as women found ingenious ways to avoid the regulations.

JAPAN In Japan, society was placed on a wartime footing even before the attack on Pearl Harbor. A conscription law was passed in 1938, and economic resources were put under strict government control. Two years later, all political parties were merged into the Imperial Rule Assistance Association. Labor unions were dissolved, and education and culture were purged of all "corrupt" Western ideas in favor of traditional values emphasizing the divinity of the emperor and the higher spirituality of Japanese civilization. During the war, individual rights were severely curtailed as the entire population was harnessed to the needs of the war effort. Traditional habits of obedience and hierarchy were emphasized to encourage citizens to sacrifice their resources, and sometimes their lives, for the national cause. Especially important was the code of Bushido (BOO-shee-doh), or the way of the warrior, the old code of morality of the samurai, who had played a prominent military role in medieval and early modern Japan. The code of Bushido was revived during the nationalistic fervor of the 1930s. Based on an ideal of loyalty and service, the code emphasized the obligation to honor and defend emperor, country, and family and to sacrifice one's life if one failed in this sacred mission. The system culminated in the final years of the war, when young Japanese were encouraged to volunteer en masse to serve as pilots in suicide missions—known as kamikaze (kah-mi-KAH-zee), or "divine wind"—against U.S. warships.

Women's rights, too, were to be sacrificed to the greater national cause. Already by 1937, Japanese women were being exhorted to fulfill their patriotic duty by bearing more children and by espousing the slogans of the Greater Japanese Women's Association. Nevertheless, Japan was extremely reluctant to mobilize women on behalf of the war effort. General Hideki Tojo (hee-DEK-ee TOH-joh), prime minister from 1941 to 1944, opposed female employment, arguing that "the weakening of the family system would be the weakening of the nation.... We are able to do our duties only because we have wives and mothers at home."[17] Female employment increased during the war, but only in areas, such as the textile industry and farming, where women had traditionally worked. Instead of using women to meet labor shortages, the Japanese government brought in Korean and Chinese laborers.

The Bombing of Cities

Bombing was used in World War II against nonhuman military targets, against enemy troops, and against civilian populations. The bombing of civilians made World War II as devastating for noncombatants as it was for frontline soldiers. A small number of bombing raids in the last year of World War I had given rise to the argument, crystallized in 1930 by the Italian general Giulio Douhet (JOOL-yoh doo-AY), that the public outcry in reaction to the bombing of civilian populations would be an effective way to coerce governments into making peace. Consequently, European air forces began to develop long-range bombers in the 1930s.

LUFTWAFFE ATTACKS The first sustained use of civilian bombing contradicted Douhet's theory. Beginning in early September 1940, the German Luftwaffe subjected London and many other British cities and towns to nightly air raids, making the Blitz (as the British called the German air raids) a national experience. Londoners took the first heavy blows and set the standard for the rest of the British population by refusing to panic. But London morale was helped by the fact that German raids were widely dispersed over a very large city. Smaller communities were more directly affected by the devastation. On November 14, 1940, for example, the Luftwaffe destroyed hundreds of shops and 100 acres of the city center of Coventry. The destruction of smaller cities did produce morale problems as rumors of social collapse spread quickly in these communities (see the Comparative Illustration "The Bombing of Civilians—East and West" on p. 753). Nevertheless, morale was soon restored. In any case, war production in these areas seems to have been little affected by the raids.

THE BOMBING OF GERMANY The British failed to learn from their own experience, however, and soon retaliated by bombing Germany. Prime Minister Winston Churchill (1874–1965) and his advisers believed that destroying German communities would break civilian morale and bring victory. Major bombing raids began in 1942 under the direction of Arthur Harris, the wartime leader of the British air force's Bomber Command, which was rearmed with four-engine heavy bombers capable of taking the war into the center of occupied Europe. On May 31, 1942, Cologne became the first German city to be subjected to an attack by a thousand bombers.

The entry of the Americans into the war produced a new bombing strategy. American planes flew daytime missions

COMPARATIVE ILLUSTRATION

FAMILY & SOCIETY

The Bombing of Civilians—East and West. World War II was the most destructive war in world history, not only for frontline soldiers but for civilians at home as well. The most devastating bombing of civilians came near the end of the war when the United States dropped atomic bombs on the Japanese cities of Hiroshima and Nagasaki. At the left is a panoramic view of Hiroshima after the bombing that shows the incredible devastation produced by the atomic bomb. The photograph at the right shows a street in Clydebank, near Glasgow in Scotland, the day after the city was bombed by the Germans in March 1941. Only 7 of the city's 12,000 houses were left undamaged; 35,000 of the 47,000 inhabitants became homeless overnight.

Q *What was the rationale for bombing civilian populations? Did such bombing achieve its goal?*

aimed at the precision bombing of transportation facilities and wartime industries, while the British Bomber Command continued nighttime saturation bombing of all German cities with populations over 100,000. Bombing raids added an element of terror to circumstances already made difficult by growing shortages of food, clothing, and fuel. Germans especially feared the incendiary bombs, which set off firestorms that swept destructive paths through the cities. Four raids on Hamburg in August 1943 produced temperatures of 1,800 degrees Fahrenheit, obliterated half the city's buildings, and killed thousands of civilians. The ferocious bombing of Dresden for three days in 1945 (February 13–15) created a firestorm that may have killed as many as 35,000 inhabitants and refugees. Even some Allied leaders began to criticize what they saw as the unnecessary terror bombing of German cities.

Germany suffered enormously from the Allied bombing raids. Millions of buildings were destroyed, and possibly half a million civilians died from the raids. Nevertheless, it is highly unlikely that Allied bombing sapped the morale of the German people. Instead, Germans, whether pro-Nazi or anti-Nazi, fought on stubbornly, often driven simply by a desire to live. Nor did the bombing destroy Germany's industrial capacity. The Allied Strategic Bombing survey revealed that

the production of war matériel actually increased between 1942 and 1944. Even in 1944 and 1945, Allied raids cut German armaments production by only 7 percent. Nevertheless, the widespread destruction of transportation systems and fuel supplies made it extremely difficult for the new materials to reach the German military.

THE BOMBING OF JAPAN: THE ATOMIC BOMB In Japan, the bombing of civilians reached a new level with the use of the first atomic bomb. Japan was especially vulnerable to air raids because its air force had been virtually destroyed in the course of the war and its crowded cities were built of flimsy materials. Attacks on Japanese cities by the new American B-29 Superfortresses, the biggest bombers of the war, began in June 1944. By the summer of 1945, many of Japan's industries had been destroyed, along with one-fourth of its dwellings. After the Japanese government ordered the mobilization of all people between the ages of thirteen and sixty into the People's Volunteer Corps, President Truman and his advisers feared that Japanese fanaticism might mean a million American casualties. This concern led them to drop the atomic bomb on Hiroshima (August 6) and Nagasaki (August 9). The destruction was incredible. Of 76,000 buildings near the center of the explosion in Hiroshima, 70,000 were flattened, and 140,000 of the city's 400,000 inhabitants died by the end of 1945. Over the next five years, another 50,000 had perished from the effects of radiation. The dropping of the first atomic bomb marked the start of the nuclear age.

After the war, Truman's decision to approve the use of nuclear weapons to compel Japan to surrender was harshly criticized, not only for causing thousands of civilian casualties but also for introducing a frightening new weapon that could threaten the survival of the human race. Some have even charged that Truman's real purpose in ordering the nuclear strikes was to intimidate the Soviet Union. Defenders of the decision argue that the human costs of invading the Japanese home islands would have been infinitely higher had the bombs not been dropped, and that the Soviet Union would have had ample time to consolidate its control over Manchuria.

Aftermath of the War

 FOCUS QUESTIONS: What were the costs of World War II? How did World War II affect the European nations' colonial empires? How did the Allies' visions of the postwar world differ, and how did these differences contribute to the emergence of the Cold War?

World War II was the most destructive war in history. Much had been at stake. Nazi Germany followed a worldview based on racial extermination and the enslavement of millions in order to create an Aryan racial empire. The Japanese, fueled by extreme nationalist ideals, also pursued dreams of empire in Asia that led to mass murder and untold devastation. Fighting the Axis Powers in World War II required the mobilization of millions of ordinary men and women in the Allied countries who rose to the occasion and struggled to preserve a different way of life. As Winston Churchill once put it, "War is horrible, but slavery is worse."

The Costs of World War II

The costs of World War II were enormous. At least 21 million soldiers died. Civilian deaths were even greater and are now estimated at around 40 million, of whom more than 28 million were Russian and Chinese. The Soviet Union experienced the greatest losses: 10 million soldiers and 19 million civilians. In 1945, millions of people around the world faced starvation; in Europe, 100 million people depended on food relief of some kind.

Millions of people had also been uprooted by the war and became "displaced persons." Europe alone may have had 30 million displaced persons, many of whom found it hard to return home. After the war, millions of Germans were expelled from the Sudetenland in Czechoslovakia, and millions more were ejected from former eastern German territories turned over to Poland, all of which seemed reasonable to

people who had suffered so much at the hands of the Germans. In Asia, millions of Japanese were returned from the former Japanese empire to Japan, while thousands of Korean forced laborers returned to Korea.

Devastation was everywhere. Most areas of Europe had been damaged or demolished, China was in shambles after eight years of conflict, the Philippines had suffered heavy damage, and large parts of the major cities in Japan had been destroyed in air raids. Millions of tons of shipping now lay beneath the seas; factories, farms, transportation systems, bridges, and dams lay in ruins. The total monetary cost of the war has been estimated at $4 trillion. The economies of most belligerents, with the exception of the United States, were left drained and on the brink of disaster.

World War II and the European Colonies: Decolonization

As we saw in Chapter 24, movements for independence had begun in earnest in Africa and Asia in the years between World War I and World War II. After World War II, these movements grew even louder. The ongoing subjugation of peoples by colonial powers seemed at odds with the goals the Allies had pursued in overthrowing the repressive regimes of Germany, Italy, and Japan. Then, too, indigenous peoples everywhere took up the call for national self-determination and expressed their determination to fight for independence.

The ending of the European powers' colonial empires did not come easy, however. In 1941, Churchill had said, "I have not become His Majesty's Chief Minister in order to preside over the liquidation of the British Empire." Britain and France in particular seemed reluctant to let go of their colonies, but for a variety of reasons both eventually gave in to the obvious—the days of empire were over.

During the war, the Japanese had already humiliated the Western states by overrunning their colonial empires. In addition, colonial soldiers who had fought on behalf of the Allies (India, for example, had contributed large numbers of troops to the British Indian Army) were well aware that Allied war aims included the principle of self-determination for the peoples of the world. Equally important to the process of **decolonization** after the war, the power of the European states had been destroyed by the exhaustive struggles of World War II. The greatest colonial empire builder, Great Britain, no longer had the energy or the wealth to maintain its colonial empire. Given the combination of circumstances, a rush of decolonization swept the world after World War II.

The Allied War Conferences

The total victory of the Allies in World War II was not followed by a real peace but by the emergence of a new conflict known as the **Cold War**, which dominated world politics until the end of the 1980s. The Cold War grew out of military, political, and ideological differences, especially between the Soviet Union and the United States, that became apparent at the Allied war conferences held in the last years of the war. Although Allied leaders were mostly preoccupied with ending the war, they were also strongly motivated by differing, and often conflicting, visions of the postwar world.

THE CONFERENCE AT TEHRAN Stalin, Roosevelt, and Churchill, the leaders of the Big Three of the Grand Alliance, met at Tehran, the capital of Iran, in November 1943 to decide the future course of the war. Their major tactical decision concerned the final assault on Germany. Stalin and Roosevelt argued successfully for an American-British invasion of the European continent through France, which they scheduled for the spring of 1944. The acceptance of this plan had important consequences. It meant that Soviet and British-American forces would meet in defeated Germany along a north-south dividing line and that eastern Europe would most likely be liberated by Soviet forces. The Allies also agreed to a partition of postwar Germany until denazification could take place.

THE YALTA CONFERENCE By the time of the conference at Yalta in southern Russia in February 1945, the defeat of Germany was a foregone conclusion. The Western powers, which had earlier believed that the Soviets were in a weak position, now faced the reality of 11 million Red Army soldiers taking possession of eastern and central Europe. Like Churchill, Stalin was still operating under the notion of spheres of influence. He was deeply suspicious of the Western powers and desired a buffer to protect the Soviet Union from possible future Western aggression. At the same time, however, Stalin was eager to obtain economically important resources and strategic military positions. Roosevelt by this time was moving away from the notion of spheres of influence toward the more Wilsonian ideal of self-determination. He called for "the end of the system of unilateral action, exclusive alliances, and spheres of influence." The Grand Alliance approved a declaration on liberated Europe. This was a pledge to assist Europeans in the creation of "democratic institutions of their own choice." Liberated countries were to hold free elections to determine their political systems.

At Yalta, Roosevelt sought Soviet military help against Japan. The atomic bomb was not yet assured, and American military planners feared the possibility of heavy losses in amphibious assaults on the Japanese home islands. Roosevelt therefore agreed to Stalin's price for military assistance against Japan: possession of Sakhalin and the Kurile Islands, as well as two warm-water ports and railroad rights in Manchuria.

The creation of the United Nations was a major American concern at Yalta. Roosevelt hoped to ensure the participation of the Big Three powers in a postwar international organization before difficult issues divided them into hostile camps. After a number of compromises, both Churchill and Stalin accepted Roosevelt's plans for a United Nations organization and set the first meeting for San Francisco in April 1945.

The issues of Germany and eastern Europe were treated less decisively. The Big Three reaffirmed that Germany must surrender unconditionally and created four occupation zones (see Map 25.3). German reparations were set at $20 billion. A compromise was also worked out in regard to Poland. Stalin agreed to free elections in the future to determine a new government. But the issue of free elections in eastern Europe caused a serious rift between the Soviets and the Americans. The principle was that eastern European governments would be freely elected, but they were also supposed to be pro-Soviet. As Churchill expressed it, "The Poles will have their future in their own hands, with the single limitation that they must honestly follow in harmony with their allies, a policy friendly to Russia."[18] This attempt to reconcile two irreconcilable goals was doomed to failure, as soon became evident at the next conference of the Big Three powers.

THE POTSDAM CONFERENCE Even before the conference at Potsdam took place in July 1945, Western relations with the Soviets were deteriorating

The Victorious Allied Leaders at Yalta. Even before World War II ended, the leaders of the Big Three of the Grand Alliance, Churchill, Roosevelt, and Stalin (shown from left to right), met in wartime conferences to plan the final assault on Germany and negotiate the outlines of the postwar settlement. At the Yalta meeting (February 5–11, 1945), the three leaders concentrated on postwar issues. The American president, who died two months later, was already a worn-out man at Yalta.

MAP 25.3 Territorial Changes in Europe After World War II. In the last months of World War II, the Red Army occupied much of eastern Europe. Stalin sought pro-Soviet satellite states in the region as a buffer against future invasions from western Europe, whereas Britain and the United States wanted democratically elected governments. Soviet military control of the territory settled the question.

Q *Which country gained the greatest territory at the expense of Germany?*

rapidly. The Grand Alliance had been a collaboration of necessity in which ideological incompatibility had been subordinated to the pragmatic concerns of the war. The Allies' only common aim was the defeat of Nazism. Once this aim had been accomplished, the many differences that antagonized East-West relations came to the surface.

The Potsdam conference of July 1945 consequently began under a cloud of mistrust. Roosevelt had died on April 12 and had been succeeded as president by Harry Truman. During the conference, Truman received word that the atomic bomb had been successfully tested. Some historians have argued that this knowledge resulted in Truman's stiffened resolve against the Soviets. Whatever the reasons, there was a new coolness in the relations between the Soviets and Americans.

At Potsdam, Truman demanded free elections throughout eastern Europe. Stalin responded, "A freely elected government in any of these east European countries would be anti-Soviet, and that we cannot allow."[19] After a bitterly fought and devastating war, Stalin sought absolute military security. To him, it could be gained only by the presence of communist states in eastern Europe. Free elections might result in governments hostile to the Soviets. By the middle of 1945, only an invasion by Western forces could undo developments in eastern Europe, and after the world's most destructive conflict had ended, few people favored such a policy.

EMERGENCE OF THE COLD WAR As the war slowly receded into the past, the reality of conflicting ideologies had reappeared.

Many in the West interpreted Soviet policy as part of a world-wide Communist conspiracy. The Soviets viewed Western, especially American, policy as nothing less than global capitalist expansionism or, in Leninist terms, economic imperialism. Vyacheslav Molotov (vyich-chiss-SLAHF MAHL-uh-tawf), the Russian foreign minister, referred to the Americans as "insatiable imperialists" and "war-mongering groups of adventurers."[20] In March 1946, in a speech to an American audience, the former British prime minister Winston Churchill declared that "an iron curtain" had "descended across the continent," dividing Europe into two hostile camps. Stalin branded Churchill's speech a "call to war with the Soviet Union." Only months after the world's most devastating conflict had ended, the world seemed once again to be bitterly divided.

CHAPTER SUMMARY

Between 1933 and 1939, Europeans watched as Adolf Hitler rebuilt Germany into a great military power. For Hitler, military power was an absolute prerequisite for the creation of a German racial empire that would dominate Europe and the world for generations to come. During that same period, the nation of Japan fell under the influence of military leaders who conspired with right-wing forces to push a program of expansion at the expense of China and the Soviet Union as well as territories in Southeast Asia. The ambitions of Germany in Europe and those of Japan in Asia led to a global conflict that became the most devastating war in human history.

The Axis nations, Germany, Italy, and Japan, proved victorious during the first two years of the war, which began after the German invasion of Poland on September 1, 1939. By 1942, the war had begun to turn in favor of the Allies, an alliance of Great Britain, the Soviet Union, and the United States.

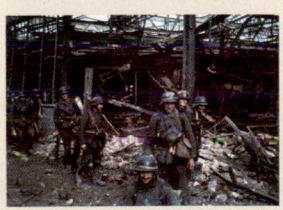

The Japanese advance was ended at the Battles of the Coral Sea and Midway in 1942. In February 1943, the Soviets won the Battle of Stalingrad and began a push westward. By mid-1943, Germany and Italy had been driven out of North Africa; in June 1944, Rome fell to the Allies, and an Allied invasion force landed in Normandy in France. After the Soviets linked up with British and American forces in April 1945, Hitler committed suicide, and the war in Europe came to an end. After atomic bombs were dropped on Hiroshima and Nagasaki in August 1945, the war in Asia also ended.

During its domination of Europe, the Nazi empire brought death and destruction to many, especially Jews, minorities, and others that the Nazis considered racially inferior peoples. The Japanese New Order in Asia, while claiming to promote a policy of "Asia for the Asians" also brought economic exploitation, severe hardship, and often death for the peoples under Japanese control. All sides bombed civilian populations, making World War II as devastating for civilians as for the frontline soldiers.

If Hitler had been successful, the Nazi New Order, built on authoritarianism, racial extermination, and the brutal oppression of peoples, would have meant a triumph of barbarism and the end of freedom and equality, which, however imperfectly realized, had become important ideals in Western civilization.

The Nazis lost, but only after tremendous sacrifices and costs. Much of European civilization lay in ruins, and the old Europe had disappeared forever. Europeans, who had been accustomed to dominating the world at the beginning of the twentieth century, now watched helplessly at mid-century as the two new superpowers created by the two world wars took control of their destinies. Even before the last battles had been fought, the United States and the Soviet Union had arrived at different versions of the postwar European world. No sooner had the war ended than their differences gave rise to a new and potentially even more devastating conflict known as the Cold War.

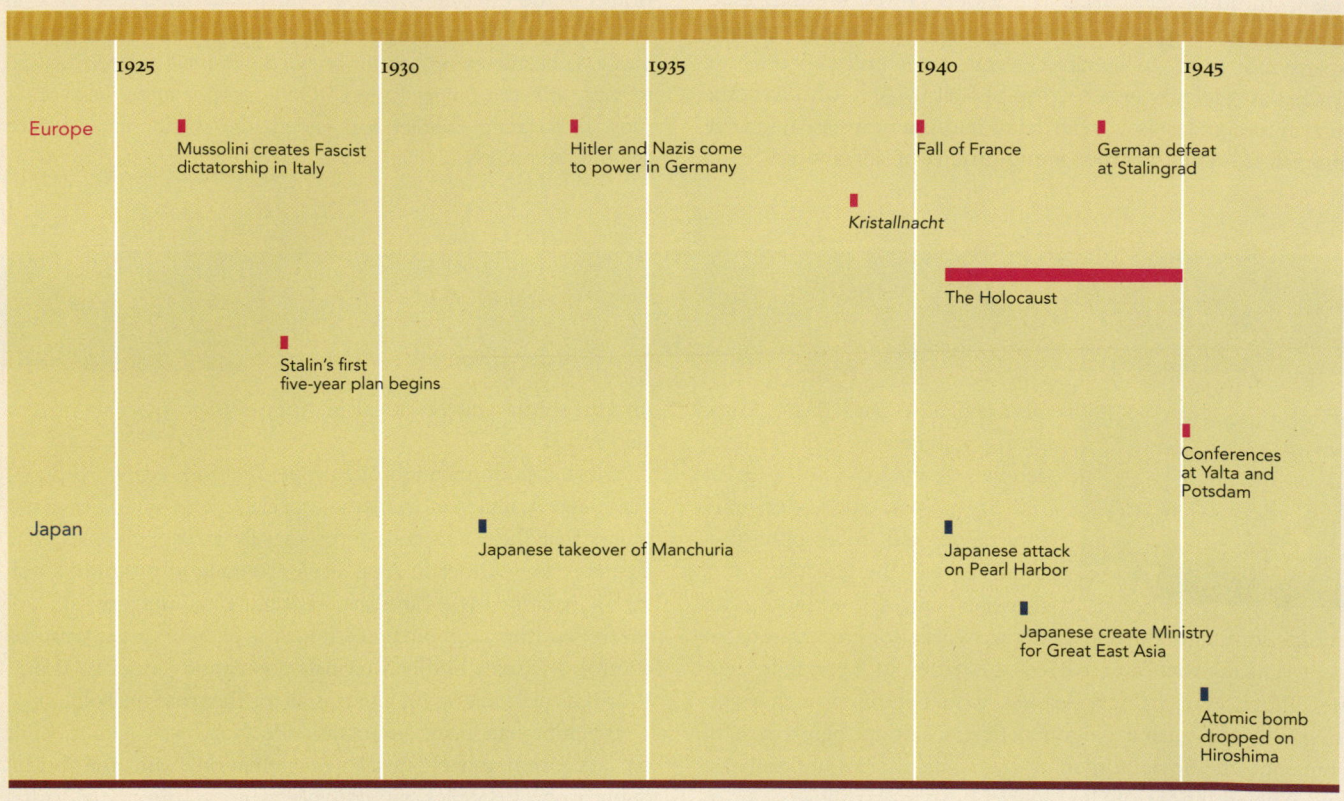

	1925	1930	1935	1940	1945
Europe	Mussolini creates Fascist dictatorship in Italy		Hitler and Nazis come to power in Germany	Fall of France	German defeat at Stalingrad

Kristallnacht

The Holocaust

Stalin's first five-year plan begins

Conferences at Yalta and Potsdam

Japan — Japanese takeover of Manchuria

Japanese attack on Pearl Harbor

Japanese create Ministry for Great East Asia

Atomic bomb dropped on Hiroshima

CHAPTER REVIEW

Upon Reflection

Q How do you account for the early successes of the Germans from 1939 to 1941?

Q How did the Nazis attempt to establish a New Order in Europe after their military victories, and what were the results of their efforts?

Q How did the attempt to arrive at a peace settlement after World War II lead to the beginnings of a new conflict known as the Cold War?

Key Terms

totalitarian state (p. 725)
squadristi (p. 726)
appeasement (p. 734)
Blitzkrieg (p. 738)
unconditional surrender (p. 741)
Nazi New Order (p. 744)
Final Solution (p. 746)
Einsatzgruppen (p. 746)
decolonization (p. 754)
Cold War (p. 754)

Suggested Reading

THE DICTATORIAL REGIMES The best biography of Mussolini is **R. J. B. Bosworth**, *Mussolini* (London, 2002). A brief but sound survey of Nazi Germany is **J. J. Spielvogel** and **D. Redles**, *Hitler and Nazi Germany: A History*, 7th ed. (Upper Saddle River, N.J., 2014). The best biography of Hitler is **I. Kershaw**, *Hitler, 1889–1936: Hubris* (New York, 1999), and *Hitler: Nemesis* (New York, 2000). On the Nazis in power, see **R. J. Evans**, *The Third Reich in Power, 1933–1939* (New York, 2005). The collectivization of agriculture in the Soviet Union is examined in **S. Fitzpatrick**, *Stalin's Peasants: Resistance and Survival in the Russian Village After Collectivization* (New York, 1995). On Stalin himself, see **R. Service**, *Stalin: A Biography* (Cambridge, Mass., 2006).

THE PATH TO WAR On the causes of World War II, see **A. J. Crozier**, *Causes of the Second World War* (Oxford, 1997). On the origins of the war in the Pacific, see **A. Iriye**, *The Origins of the Second World War in Asia and the Pacific* (London, 1987).

WORLD WAR II The best general work on World War II is **G. Weinberg**, *A World at Arms: A Global History of World*

War II, 2nd ed. (Cambridge, 2005). A good military history of World War II can be found in **W. Murray** and **A. R. Millett,** *A War to Be Won: Fighting the Second World War* (Cambridge, Mass., 2000).

THE HOLOCAUST Excellent studies of the Holocaust include **S. Friedänder,** *The Years of Extermination: Nazi Germany and the Jews, 1939–1945* (New York, 2007), and **L. Yahil,** *The Holocaust* (New York, 1990). For a brief study, see **D. Dwork** and **R. J. van Pelt,** *Holocaust: A History* (New York, 2002).

THE HOME FRONT On the home front in Germany, see **M. Kitchen,** *Nazi Germany at War* (New York, 1995). The Soviet Union during the war is examined in **M. Harrison,** *Soviet Planning in Peace and War, 1938–1945* (Cambridge, 1985). On the American home front, see the collection of essays in **K. P. O'Brien** and **L. H. Parsons,** *The Home-Front War: World War II and American Society* (Westport, Conn., 1995). The Japanese home front is examined in **T. R. H. Havens,** *The Valley of Darkness: The Japanese People and World War Two* (New York, 1978). On the Allied bombing campaign against Germany, see **R. Hansen,** *Fire and Fury: The Allied Bombing of Germany, 1942–1945* (London, 2008).

Chapter Notes

1.   Mussolini, "The Doctrine of Fascism," in A. Lyttleton, ed., *Italian Fascisms from Pareto to Gentile* (London, 1973), p. 42.

2.   Quoted in A. De Grand, "Women Under Italian Fascism," *Historical Journal* 19 (1976), pp. 958–959.

3.   Quoted in J. J. Spielvogel and D. Redles, *Hitler and Nazi Germany: A History,* 6th ed. (Upper Saddle River, N.J., 2010), p. 60.

4.   Quoted in J. Fest, *Hitler,* trans. R. Winston and C. Winston (New York, 1974), p. 418.

5.   Quoted in S. Fitzpatrick, *Everyday Stalinism—Ordinary Life in Extraordinary Times: Soviet Russia in the 1930s* (New York, 1999), p. 87.

6.   A. Hitler, *Mein Kampf,* trans. R. Manheim (Boston, 1971), p. 654.

7.   *Documents on German Foreign Policy* (London, 1956), Series D, vol. 7, p. 204.

8.   Memorandum by John Van Antwerp MacMurray, quoted in A. Waldron, *How the Peace Was Lost: The 1935 Memorandum* (Stanford, Calif., 1992), p. 5.

9.   Quoted in W. Murray and A. R. Millett, *A War to Be Won: Fighting the Second World War* (Cambridge, Mass., 2000), p. 137.

10. Quoted in A. Speer, *Spandau,* trans. R. Winston and C. Winston (New York, 1976), p. 50.

11. *Nazi Conspiracy and Aggression* (Washington, D.C., 1946), vol. 6, p. 262.

12. International Military Tribunal, *Trial of the Major War Criminals* (Nuremberg, 1947–1949), vol. 22, p. 480.

13. Quoted in R. Hilberg, *The Destruction of the European Jews,* rev. ed. (New York, 1985), vol. 1, pp. 332–333.

14. *Nazi Conspiracy and Aggression,* vol. 6, p. 789.

15. Quoted in J. Campbell, *The Experience of World War II* (New York, 1989), p. 170.

16. Quoted in C. Koonz, "Mothers in the Fatherland: Women in Nazi Germany," in R. Bridenthal and C. Koonz, eds., *Becoming Visible: Women in European History* (Boston, 1977), p. 466.

17. Quoted in Campbell, *Experience of World War II,* p. 143.

18. Quoted in N. Graebner, *Cold War Diplomacy, 1945–1960* (Princeton, N.J., 1962), p. 117.

19. Ibid.

20. Quoted in W. Loth, *The Division of the World, 1941–1955* (New York, 1988), p. 81.

MindTap is a fully online, highly personalized learning experience built upon Cengage Learning content. MindTap combines student learning tools—readings, multimedia, activities, and assessments—into a singular Learning Path that guides students through their course.

Toward a Global Civilization?
The World Since 1945

AS WORLD WAR II came to an end, the survivors of that bloody struggle felt able to face the future with a cautious optimism. There was modest reason to hope that the bitter rivalry that had marked relations among the Western powers would finally be put to an end and that the wartime alliance of the United States, Great Britain, and the Soviet Union could be maintained into the postwar era. If so, the steady march toward a more prosperous future for the world's peoples could resume.

Nearly seventy years later, these hopes have been only partly realized. In the decades following the war, the Western capitalist nations managed to recover from the economic depression that had led into World War II and advanced to a level of economic prosperity never seen before. The bloody conflicts that had erupted among European nations during the first half of the twentieth century ended, and Germany and Japan were fully reintegrated into the world community.

On the other hand, the prospects for a stable, peaceful world and an end to balance-of-power politics were hampered by the emergence of the grueling and sometimes tense ideological struggle between the socialist and capitalist camps, a competition headed by the only remaining great powers, the Soviet Union and the United States. Many observers feared that the rivalry could only end in a new and even more destructive war.

Although the Western European states made a remarkable economic recovery and reached untold levels of prosperity, in Eastern Europe, Soviet domination, both political and economic, seemed so complete that many people doubted it could ever be undone. Fortunately, communism never put down deep roots in Eastern Europe, and in the late 1980s, when Soviet leaders unexpectedly indicated that they would no longer intervene militarily to keep the Eastern European states in line, the latter were quick to embrace their freedom and adopt new economic structures based on Western models.

Meanwhile, the peoples of Africa and Asia had their own reasons for optimism as World War II came to a close. In the Atlantic Charter, reached in the summer of 1941, Franklin Roosevelt and Winston Churchill had set forth a joint declaration of their peace aims calling for the self-determination of all peoples and self-government and sovereign rights for all nations that had been deprived of them. Although some colonial powers eventually proved reluctant to divest themselves of their colonies, World War II had severely undermined the stability of the colonial order, and by the end of the 1940s, most colonies in Asia had received their independence. Africa followed a decade or two later.

Broadly speaking, the leaders of these newly liberated countries set forth three goals at the outset of independence. They wanted to throw off the shackles of Western economic domination and ensure material prosperity for all of their citizens. They wanted to introduce new political institutions that would enhance the right of self-determination of their peoples. And they wanted to develop a sense of common nationhood among their populations and establish secure territorial boundaries. Most opted to follow a capitalist or a moderately socialist path toward economic development. In a few cases—most notably in China and Vietnam—revolutionary leaders opted for the communist mode of development. Regardless of the path chosen, in the short run, the results were often disappointing. Over the next generation, much of Africa and Asia remained economically dependent on the advanced industrial nations. Some societies faced severe problems of urban and rural poverty. Others were rent by bitter internal conflicts.

What had happened to tarnish the bright dream of economic affluence? During the late 1950s and early 1960s, the dominant school of thought among many Western scholars and government officials was what is known as modernization theory. This school took the view that the problems faced by the newly independent countries were a consequence of the difficult transition from a traditional to a modern society. Modernization theorists were convinced that agrarian countries were destined to follow the path of the West toward the creation of modern industrial societies on the capitalist model but would need both time and substantial amounts of economic and technological assistance from the West to complete the journey.

Eventually, modernization theory came under attack from a new generation of scholars. In their view, the responsibility for continued economic underdevelopment in the postcolonial world lay not with the countries themselves but with their continued domination by the former colonial powers. In this view, known as dependency theory, the countries of Asia, Africa, and Latin America were the victims of the international marketplace, in which high prices were charged for the manufactured goods of the West while low prices were paid to the preindustrial countries for their raw material exports. Efforts by such countries to build up their industrial sectors and move into the stage of self-sustaining growth were hampered by foreign control of many of their resources via European- and American-owned corporations. To end this "neocolonial" relationship, dependency theory advocates argued, developing societies should reduce their economic ties with the West and institute a policy of economic self-reliance, thereby taking control of their own destinies.

Leaders of African and Asian countries also encountered problems creating new political cultures responsive to the needs of their citizens. At first, most accepted some form of the concept of democracy as the defining theme of that culture. Within a decade, however, democratic systems throughout the developing world had been found wanting and were replaced by military dictatorships or one-party governments that redefined the concept of democracy to fit their own preferences. It was clear that the difficulties in building democratic political institutions in developing societies had been underestimated.

The problem of establishing a common national identity has in some ways been the most daunting of all the challenges facing the new nations of Asia and Africa. Many of these new states were a composite of various ethnic, religious, and linguistic groups that found it difficult to agree on common symbols of nationalism or national values. The process of establishing an official language and delineating territorial boundaries left over from the colonial era created difficulties in many countries. Internal conflicts spawned by deep-rooted historical and ethnic hatreds proliferated throughout the world, causing vast numbers of people to move across state boundaries in migrations as large as any since the great migrations of the thirteenth and fourteenth centuries.

The introduction of Western cultural values and customs has also had a destabilizing effect in many areas. Though welcomed by some groups, such ideas are firmly resisted by others. Where Western influence has the effect of undermining traditional customs and religious beliefs, it often provokes violent hostility and sparks tension and even conflict within individual societies. Much of the anger recently directed at the United States in Muslim countries has undoubtedly been generated by such feelings.

Nonetheless, social and political attitudes are changing rapidly in many Asian and African countries as new economic circumstances have led to a more secular worldview, a decline in traditional hierarchical relations, and a more open attitude toward sexual practices. In part, these changes are a consequence of the influence of Western music, movies, and television. But they are also a product of the growth of an affluent middle class in many societies of Asia and Africa.

Today, we live not only in a world economy but in a world society, where a revolution in the Middle East can cause a rise in the price of oil in the United States and a change in social behavior in Malaysia and Indonesia, where the collapse of an empire in Asia can send shock waves as far as Hanoi and Havana, and where a terrorist attack in New York City or London can disrupt financial markets around the world. ◆

East and West in the Grip of the Cold War

Churchill, Roosevelt, and Stalin at Yalta

CHAPTER OUTLINE AND FOCUS QUESTIONS

The Collapse of the Grand Alliance

Q Why were the United States and the Soviet Union suspicious of each other after World War II, and what events between 1945 and 1949 heightened the tensions between the two nations?

Cold War in Asia

Q How and why did Mao Zedong and the Communists come to power in China, and what were the Cold War implications of their triumph?

From Confrontation to Coexistence

Q What events led to the era of coexistence in the 1960s, and to what degree did each side contribute to the reduction in international tensions?

An Era of Equivalence

Q Why did the Cold War briefly flare up again in the 1980s, and why did it come to a definitive end at the end of the decade?

CRITICAL THINKING

Q How have historians answered the question of whether the United States or the Soviet Union bears the primary responsibility for the Cold War, and what evidence can be presented on each side of the issue?

CONNECTIONS TO TODAY

Q Are the challenges facing the world today a product of the Cold War, or did the latter serve to distract world leaders from facing those challenges?

"OUR MEETING HERE in the Crimea has reaffirmed our common determination to maintain and strengthen in the peace to come that unity of purpose and of action which has made victory possible and certain for the United Nations in this war. We believe that this is a sacred obligation which our Governments owe to our peoples and to all the peoples of the world."[1]

With these ringing words, drafted at the Yalta Conference in February 1945, U.S. President Franklin D. Roosevelt, Soviet leader Joseph Stalin, and British Prime Minister Winston Churchill affirmed their common hope that the Grand Alliance that had been victorious in World War II could be sustained into the postwar era. Only through continuing and growing cooperation and understanding among the three Allies, the statement asserted, could a secure and lasting peace be realized that, in the words of the Atlantic Charter, would "afford assurance that all the men in all the lands may live out their lives in freedom from fear and want."

Roosevelt hoped that the decisions reached at Yalta would provide the basis for a stable peace in the postwar era. Allied occupation forces—American, British, and French in the west and Soviet in the east—were to bring about the end of Axis administration and organize the free election of democratic governments throughout Europe.

To foster mutual trust and end the suspicions that had marked relations between the capitalist world and the Soviet Union prior to the war, Roosevelt tried to assure Stalin that Moscow's legitimate territorial aspirations and genuine security needs would be adequately met in a durable peace settlement.

It was not to be. Within months after the German surrender, the mutual trust among the Allies—if it had ever truly existed—rapidly disintegrated, and the dream of a stable peace was replaced by the specter of a potential nuclear holocaust. The United Nations, envisioned by its founders as a mechanism for adjudicating international disputes, became mired in partisan bickering. As the Cold War between Moscow and Washington intensified, Europe was divided into two armed camps, while the two superpowers, glaring at each other across a deep ideological divide, held the survival of the entire world in their hands. ◄

The Collapse of the Grand Alliance

 FOCUS QUESTION: Why were the United States and the Soviet Union suspicious of each other after World War II, and what events between 1945 and 1949 heightened the tensions between the two nations?

The problems started in Europe. At the end of the war, Soviet military forces occupied all of Eastern Europe and the Balkans (except Greece, Albania, and Yugoslavia), while U.S. and other Allied forces secured the western part of the continent. Roosevelt had hoped that free elections, administered promptly by "democratic and peace-loving forces," would lead to democratic governments responsive to the local population. But it soon became clear that the Soviet Union interpreted the Yalta agreement differently. When Soviet occupation authorities began forming a new Polish government, Stalin refused to accept the Polish government-in-exile—headquartered in London during the war and composed primarily of landed aristocrats who harbored a deep distrust of the Soviet Union—and instead set up a government composed of Communists who had spent the war in Moscow. Roosevelt complained to Stalin but eventually agreed to a compromise whereby two members of the London government were included in the new communist regime. A week later, Roosevelt was dead of a cerebral hemorrhage, leaving the challenge to a new U.S. president, Harry Truman (1884–1972), who lacked experience in foreign affairs.

Soviet Domination of Eastern Europe

Similar developments took place in all of the states occupied by Soviet troops. Coalitions of all political parties (except fascist or right-wing parties) were formed to run the government but within a year or two, the Communist Party in each coalition had assumed the lion's share of power. It was then a short step to the establishment of one-party communist governments. Between 1945 and 1947, communist governments became firmly entrenched in East Germany, Bulgaria, Romania, Poland, and Hungary. In Czechoslovakia, with its strong tradition of democratic institutions, the Communists did not achieve their goals until 1948. After the Czech elections of 1946, the Communist Party shared control of the government with the non-communist parties. When it appeared that the latter might win new elections early in 1948, the Communists seized control of the government on February 25. All other parties were dissolved, and the Communist leader Klement Gottwald (KLEM-ent GUT-vald) (1896–1953) became the new president of Czechoslovakia.

Yugoslavia was a notable exception to the pattern of Soviet dominance in Eastern Europe. The Communist Party there had led the resistance to the Nazis during the war and easily assumed power when the war ended. Josip Broz (yaw-SEEP BRAWZ), known as Tito (TEE-toh) (1892–1980), the leader of the Communist resistance movement, appeared to be a loyal Stalinist. After the war, however, he moved to establish an independent communist state. Stalin hoped to take control of Yugoslavia but Tito refused to capitulate to Stalin's demands and gained the support of the people (and some sympathy in the West) by portraying the struggle as one of Yugoslav national freedom. In 1958, the Yugoslav party congress asserted that Yugoslav Communists did not see themselves as deviating from communism, only from Stalinism. They considered their more decentralized system, in which workers managed themselves and local communes exercised some political power, closer to the Marxist-Leninist ideal.

To Stalin (who had once boasted, "I will shake my little finger, and there will be no more Tito"), the creation of pliant pro-Soviet regimes throughout Eastern Europe to serve as a buffer zone against the capitalist West may simply have represented his interpretation of the Yalta peace agreement and a reward for sacrifices suffered during the war. If the Soviet leader had any intention of promoting future Communist revolutions in Western Europe—and there is some indication that he did—such developments would have to await the appearance of a new capitalist crisis a decade or more into the future. As Stalin undoubtedly recalled, Lenin had always maintained that revolutions come in waves, and he was willing to wait for the next one to come along.

Eastern Europe in 1948

© 2016 Cengage Learning

Descent of the Iron Curtain

To the United States, however, the Soviet takeover of Eastern Europe represented an ominous development that threatened Roosevelt's vision of a durable peace. Public suspicion of Soviet intentions grew rapidly, especially among the millions of Americans who had relatives living in Eastern Europe. Winston Churchill was quick to put such fears into words. In a highly publicized speech at Westminster College in Fulton, Missouri, in March 1946, Churchill said that an "iron curtain" had "descended across the Continent," dividing Germany and Europe itself into two hostile camps. Stalin responded that Churchill's speech was a "call to war with the Soviet Union." But he need not have worried. Although public opinion in the United States put increasing pressure on Harry Truman, Roosevelt's successor, to devise an effective strategy to counter Soviet advances abroad, the American people were in no mood for another war.

The first threat of a U.S.-Soviet confrontation took place in the Middle East. During World War II, British and Soviet troops had been stationed in Iran to prevent Axis occupation of the rich oil fields in that country. Both nations had promised to withdraw their forces after the war but at the end of 1945 there were ominous signs that Moscow might attempt to use its troops as a bargaining chip to annex Iran's northern territories—known as

Azerbaijan (az-ur-by-JAHN)—into the Soviet Union. When the government of Iran, with strong U.S. support, threatened to take the issue to the United Nations, the Soviets backed down and removed their forces from that country in the spring of 1946.

The Truman Doctrine

A civil war in Greece created another potential arena for confrontation between the superpowers and an opportunity for the Truman administration to take a stand. Communist guerrilla forces supported by Tito, who hoped to create a Balkan Federation under Yugoslav domination, had taken up arms against the pro-Western government in Athens. Great Britain had initially assumed primary responsibility for promoting postwar reconstruction in the eastern Mediterranean but in 1947 economic problems caused the British to withdraw from the active role they had been playing in both Greece and Turkey. President Truman, alarmed by British weakness and the possibility of Soviet expansion into the eastern Mediterranean, responded with the **Truman Doctrine**, which said in essence that the United States would provide financial aid to countries that claimed they were threatened by Communist expansion (see the box "The Truman Doctrine" on p. 765). If the Soviets were not stopped in Greece, Truman declared, then the United States would have to face the spread of communism throughout the free world. As Dean Acheson, the U.S. secretary of state, explained, "Like apples in a barrel infected by disease, the corruption of Greece would infect Iran and all the East … likewise Africa … Italy … France…. Not since Rome and Carthage has there been such a polarization of power on this earth."[2]

The somewhat apocalyptic tone of Acheson's statement was intentional. Not only were the American people in no mood for foreign adventures but the administration's Republican opponents in Congress were in an isolationist frame of mind. Only the prospect of a dire threat from abroad, the president's advisers argued, could persuade the nation to take action. The tactic worked, and Congress voted to provide the aid Truman had requested.

The U.S. suspicion that Moscow was actively supporting the insurgent movement in Greece turned out to be unfounded, however. Stalin was apparently unhappy with Tito's role in the conflict, not only because he suspected that the latter was attempting to create his own sphere of influence in the Balkans but also because it risked provoking a direct confrontation between the United States and the Soviet Union in an area that was clearly within the American sphere of influence. "The rebellion in Greece," he declared, "must be crushed."[3]

The Marshall Plan

The White House, however, was ignorant of Stalin's views in Moscow, and the proclamation of the Truman Doctrine was followed in June 1947 by the European Recovery Program, better known as the **Marshall Plan**, which provided

A Call to Arms. Within five years after the end of World War II, the Grand Alliance that had brought victory over the Axis Powers was in tatters. In March 1946, the former British prime minister Winston Churchill, in an address given at Westminster College in Fulton, Missouri, declared that Soviet occupation of Eastern Europe had divided the continent into two hostile camps. The speech is often credited with launching the first salvo in the Cold War.

AP Images

The Truman Doctrine

POLITICS & GOVERNMENT

IN 1947, THE BATTLE LINES IN THE COLD WAR had been clearly drawn. This excerpt is taken from a speech by President Harry Truman to the U.S. Congress in which he justified his request for aid to Greece and Turkey. Truman expressed the urgent need to contain the expansion of communism. Compare this statement with that of Soviet leader Leonid Brezhnev cited in the box "The Brezhnev Doctrine" on p. 785.

Truman's Speech to Congress, March 12, 1947

The peoples of a number of countries of the world have recently had totalitarian regimes forced upon them against their will. The Government of the United States has made frequent protests against coercion and intimidation, in violation of the Yalta agreement, in Poland, Rumania, and Bulgaria. I must also state that in a number of other countries there have been similar developments.

At the present moment in world history nearly every nation must choose between alternative ways of life. The choice is too often not a free one.

One way of life is based upon the will of the majority, and is distinguished by free institutions, representative government, free elections, guarantees of individual liberty, freedom of speech and religion, and freedom from political oppression.

The second way of life is based upon the will of a minority forcibly imposed upon the majority. It relies upon terror and oppression, a controlled press and radio; fixed elections, and the suppression of personal freedoms.

I believe that it must be the policy of the United States to support free peoples who are resisting attempted subjugation by armed minorities or by outside pressures.

I believe that we must assist free peoples to work out their own destinies in their own way.

I believe that our help should be primarily through economic and financial aid which is essential to economic stability and orderly political processes.... I therefore ask the Congress for assistance to Greece and Turkey in the amount of $400,000,000.

How did President Truman defend his request for aid to Greece and Turkey? What role did this decision play in intensifying the Cold War?

Source: From U.S. Congress, Congressional Record, 80th Congress, 1st Session (Washington, D.C.: U.S. Government Printing Office, 1947), Vol. 93, p. 1981.

$13 billion in U.S. assistance for the economic recovery of war-torn Europe. Underlying the program was the belief that the economic recovery of war-torn Europe would insulate the peoples of that continent against the appeal of international communism.

From the Soviet perspective, the Marshall Plan was capitalist imperialism, a thinly veiled attempt to buy the support of the smaller European countries for a U.S. effort to encircle the Soviet Union. A Soviet spokesperson described the United States as the "main force in the imperialist camp," whose ultimate goal was "the strengthening of imperialism, preparation for a new imperialist war, a struggle against socialism and democracy, and the support of reactionary and antidemocratic, profascist regimes and movements." Although the Marshall Plan was open to the Soviet Union and its Eastern European satellite states, Soviet leaders viewed the offer as a devious capitalist ploy and refused to participate. Under heavy pressure from Moscow, Eastern European governments did so as well. The Soviets were in no position to compete financially with the United States, however, and could do little to counter the Marshall Plan except tighten their control in Eastern Europe.

Europe Divided

By 1947, the split in Europe between East and West had become a fact of life. At the end of World War II, the Truman administration had favored a quick end to its commitments in Europe but fears of Soviet aims caused the United States to play an increasingly important role in Europe. In an article in *Foreign Affairs* in July 1947, George Kennan, a well-known U.S. diplomat with much knowledge of the Soviet Union, advocated a policy of **containment** against further aggressive Soviet moves. Kennan favored the "adroit and vigilant application of counter-force at a series of constantly shifting geographical and political points, corresponding to the shifts and maneuvers of Soviet policy."

When the Soviets blockaded Berlin in 1948, containment of the Soviet Union became formal U.S. policy.

THE BERLIN BLOCKADE The fate of Germany had become a source of heated contention between East and West. Aside from **denazification** (dee-naht-sih-fuh-KAY-shun)—the removal of all pro-Nazi elements from positions of influence in German society—and the partitioning of Germany (and Berlin) into four occupied zones, the Allied Powers had agreed on little with regard to the

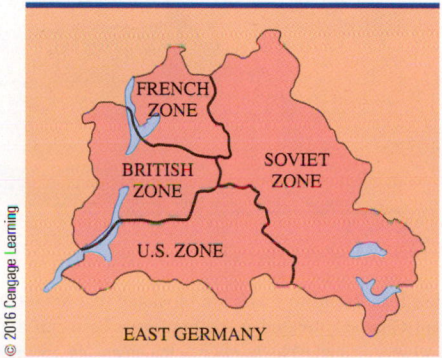

Berlin at the Start of the Cold War

conquered nation. The Soviet Union, hardest hit by the war, took reparations from Germany by booty. By the summer of 1946, nearly six hundred factories in the East German zone had been shipped to the Soviet Union. At the same time, the German Communist Party was reestablished under the control of Walter Ulbricht (VAHL-tuh OOL-brikkt) (1893–1973), and it was soon in charge of the political reconstruction of the Soviet zone in eastern Germany.

Although the foreign ministers of the four occupying powers kept meeting in an attempt to arrive at a final peace treaty with Germany, they moved further and further apart. In response, the British, French, and Americans gradually began to merge their zones economically and by February 1948 were making plans for the formation of a national government. In an effort to secure all of Berlin and to prevent the creation of a West German government, the Soviet Union imposed a blockade of West Berlin that prevented all traffic from entering the city's western zones through Soviet-controlled territory in East Germany.

The Western powers faced a dilemma. Direct military confrontation seemed dangerous, especially at a time when the U.S. military presence in Europe had been severely reduced, and no one wished to risk World War III. (All the Soviet army would need to drive all the way to the English Channel, lamented U.S. Defense Secretary Robert Lovett to an acquaintance, "was their shoes.") Therefore, an attempt to break through the blockade with tanks and trucks was ruled out. The solution was to deliver supplies for the city's inhabitants by plane. At its peak, the Berlin Airlift flew 13,000 tons of supplies daily into Berlin. The Soviets, also not wanting war, did not interfere and finally lifted the blockade in May 1949. But the blockade had severely increased tensions between the United States and the Soviet Union and brought about the separation of Germany into two states. The Federal Republic of Germany (FRG) was formally created from the three western zones in September 1949, and a month later, the separate German Democratic Republic (GDR) was established in East Germany. Berlin remained a divided city and the source of much contention between East and West.

NATO AND THE WARSAW PACT The search for security in the Cold War also led to the formation of military alliances. The North Atlantic Treaty Organization (NATO) was formed in April 1949 when Belgium, Britain, Denmark, France, Iceland, Italy, Luxembourg, the Netherlands, Norway, and Portugal signed a treaty with the United States and

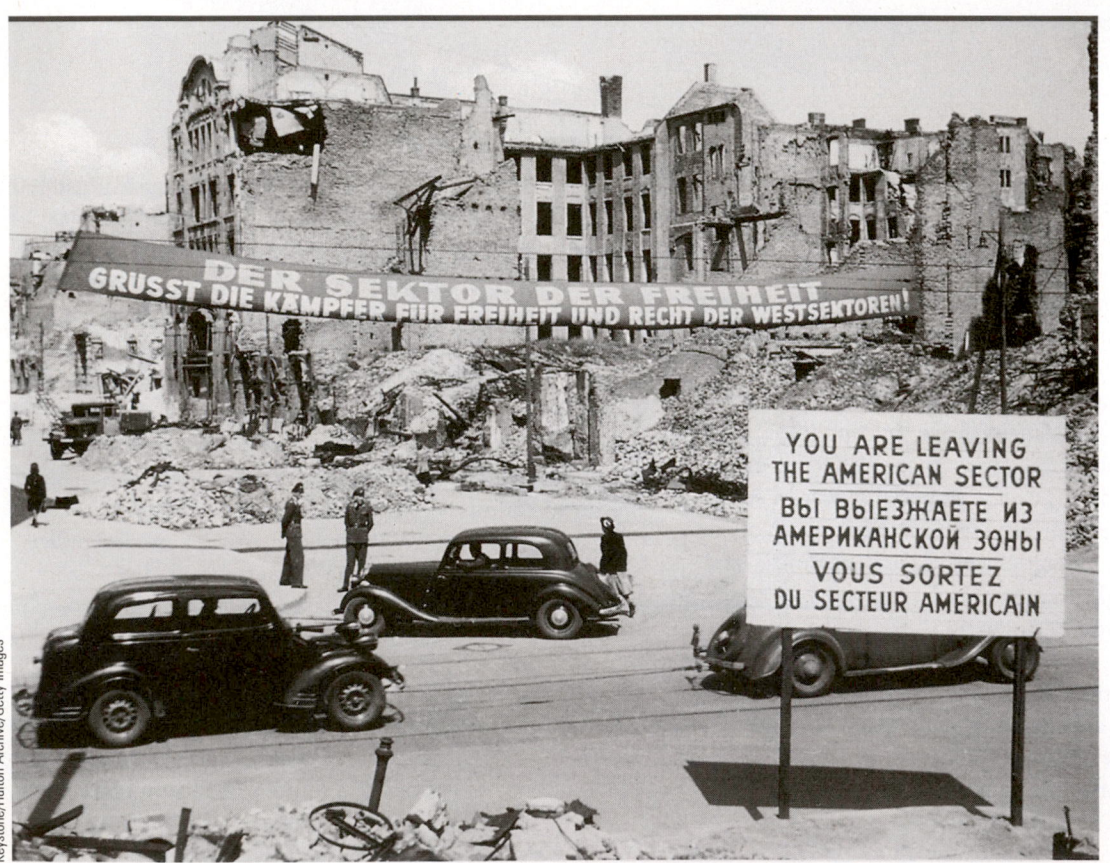

A City Divided. In 1948, U.S. planes airlifted supplies into Berlin to break the blockade that Soviet troops had imposed to isolate the city. Shown here is "Checkpoint Charlie," located at the boundary between the U.S. and Soviet zones of Berlin, just as Soviet roadblocks are about to be removed. The banner at the entrance to the Soviet sector reads, ironically, "The sector of freedom greets the fighters for freedom and rights of the Western sectors."

Canada. All the powers agreed to provide mutual assistance if any one of them was attacked. A few years later, West Germany and Turkey joined NATO. In the meantime, the United States engaged in an arms buildup aimed at preventing the further expansion of communism anywhere in the world.

The Soviet Union and its Eastern European allies soon followed suit. In 1949, they formed the Council for Mutual Economic Assistance (COMECON) for economic cooperation. Then, in 1955, Albania, Bulgaria, Czechoslovakia, East Germany, Hungary, Poland, Romania, and the Soviet Union organized a formal military alliance, the Warsaw Pact. Once again, Europe was tragically divided into hostile alliance systems (see Map 26.1).

WHO STARTED THE COLD WAR? There has been considerable historical debate over who bears responsibility for starting the Cold War. In the 1950s, most scholars in the West assumed that the bulk of the blame must fall on the shoulders of Stalin, whose determination to impose Soviet rule on Eastern Europe snuffed out hopes for freedom and self-determination there and aroused justifiable fears of Communist expansion in the West. During the next decade, however, revisionist historians in the West—influenced in part by their hostility to aggressive U.S. policies in Southeast Asia—began to argue that the fault lay primarily in Washington, where Truman and his anti-communist advisers abandoned the precepts of Yalta and sought to encircle the Soviet Union with a tier of pliant U.S. client states. More

MAP 26.1 The New European Alliance Systems During the Cold War. This map shows Europe as it was divided during the Cold War into two contending power blocs, the NATO alliance and the Warsaw Pact. Major military and naval bases are indicated by symbols on the map.

Q *Where on the map was the Iron Curtain?*

© 2016 Cengage Learning

recently, many historians have adopted a more nuanced view, noting that both the United States and the Soviet Union took some unwise steps that contributed to rising tensions at the end of World War II.

In fact, both nations were working within a framework conditioned by the past. The rivalry between the two superpowers ultimately stemmed from their different historical perspectives and their irreconcilable political ambitions. As we have seen, intense competition for political and military supremacy had long been a regular feature of Western civilization. The United States and the Soviet Union were the heirs of that European tradition of power politics, and it should come as no surprise that two such different systems would seek to extend their way of life to the rest of the world. Because of its need to secure its western border, the Soviet Union was not prepared to give up the advantages it had gained in Eastern Europe from Germany's defeat. But neither were Western leaders prepared to accept without protest the establishment of a system of Soviet satellites that not only threatened the security of Western Europe but also deeply offended Western sensibilities because of its blatant disregard of human rights.

This does not necessarily mean that both sides bear equal responsibility for starting the Cold War. Some revisionist historians have claimed that the U.S. doctrine of containment was an unnecessarily provocative action that aroused Stalin's suspicions and drove him into a position of hostility toward the West. This charge lacks credibility. Although it is understandable that the Soviets were concerned that the United States might use its monopoly of nuclear weapons to attempt to intimidate them, information now available from the Soviet archives and other sources makes it increasingly clear that Stalin's suspicions of the West were rooted in his Marxist-Leninist worldview and long predated Washington's enunciation of the doctrine of containment. As his foreign minister, Vyacheslav Molotov, once remarked, Soviet policy was inherently aggressive and would be triggered whenever the opportunity offered. Although Stalin apparently had no master plan to advance Soviet power into Western Europe, he was undoubtedly prepared to make every effort to do so once the next revolutionary wave arrived. Under the circumstances, Western leaders were fully justified in reacting to this possibility by strengthening their own lines of defense.

On the other hand, a case can be made that in deciding to respond to the Soviet challenge in a primarily military manner, Western leaders overreacted to the situation and virtually guaranteed that the Cold War would be transformed into an arms race that could conceivably result in a new and uniquely destructive war. George Kennan, the original architect of the doctrine of containment, had initially proposed a primarily political approach and eventually disavowed the means by which the containment strategy was carried out.

Cold War in Asia

 FOCUS QUESTION: How and why did Mao Zedong and the Communists come to power in China, and what were the Cold War implications of their triumph?

The Cold War was somewhat slower to make itself felt in Asia. At Yalta, Stalin formally agreed to enter the Pacific war against Japan three months after the close of the conflict with Germany. As a reward for Soviet participation in the struggle against Japan, Roosevelt promised that Moscow would be granted "preeminent interests in Manchuria" (reminiscent of the interests possessed by imperial Russia prior to its defeat at the hands of Japan in 1904–1905) and allowed to establish a Soviet naval base at Port Arthur (see Map 26.2). In return, Stalin promised to sign a treaty of alliance with the Republic of China, thus implicitly committing the Soviet Union not to assist the Chinese Communists in a possible future civil war. Although many observers would later question Stalin's sincerity in making such a commitment to the vocally anti-communist Chiang Kai-shek, in Moscow the decision probably had a logic of

MAP 26.2 The Chinese Civil War. After the close of the Pacific war in 1945, the Nationalist Chinese government and the Chinese Communists fought a bitter civil war that ended with a Communist victory in 1949. The path of the Communist advance is shown on the map.

 Where did Chiang Kai-shek's government retreat to after its defeat?

its own. Stalin had no particular liking for the independent-minded Mao Zedong (he once derisively labeled the Chinese leader a "radish Communist"—red on the outside and white on the inside) and indeed did not anticipate a Communist victory in any civil war in China. Only an agreement with Chiang could provide the Soviet Union with a strategically vital economic and political presence in northern China.

The Truman administration was equally reluctant to get embroiled in a confrontation with Moscow over the unfolding events in East Asia. Doubts about Chiang Kai-shek's political abilities ran high in Washington, and as we shall see, many key U.S. policymakers hoped to avoid a deeper involvement in China by brokering a compromise agreement between Chiang and Mao Zedong, his Communist rival. Despite such misgivings in both Washington and Moscow, the Allied agreements on China soon broke down, and East Asia was sucked into the vortex of the Cold War by the end of the 1940s. The root of the problem lay less in the agreements at Yalta than in the underlying weakness of Chiang's regime, which threatened to create a political vacuum in East Asia that both Moscow and Washington would be tempted to fill.

The Chinese Civil War

As World War II came to an end in the Pacific, relations between the government of Chiang Kai-shek in China and its powerful U.S. ally had become frayed. Although Roosevelt had once hoped that republican China would be the keystone of his plan for peace and stability in Asia after the war, U.S. officials eventually became disillusioned with the corruption within Chiang's government, as well as his unwillingness to risk his forces against the Japanese (he hoped to save them for use against the Communists after the war in the Pacific ended). Hence, China was no longer the object of Washington's close attention as the war came to a close. Nevertheless, U.S. military and economic aid to China had been substantial, and at war's end, the Truman administration still hoped that it could rely on Chiang to support U.S. postwar goals in the region.

While Chiang wrestled with Japanese aggression during the Sino-Japanese conflict, the Communists were building up their strength in northern China. To enlarge their political base, they carried out a "mass line" strategy (a term in Communist jargon that meant responding to the immediate needs and demands of the mass of the Chinese population), reducing land rents and confiscating the lands of wealthy landlords. By the end of World War II, 20 to 30 million Chinese were living under the administration of the Communists, and their People's Liberation Army (PLA), as it was now called, numbered nearly one million troops.

Chiang Kai-shek and Mao Zedong Exchange a Toast. After World War II, the United States sent General George C. Marshall to China in an effort to prevent civil war between Chiang Kai-shek's government and Mao Zedong's Communists. Marshall's initial success was symbolized by this toast between Chiang (at the right) and Mao. But suspicion ran too deep, and soon conflict ensued, resulting in a Communist victory in 1949. Chiang's government retreated to the island of Taiwan.

As the war came to an end, world attention began to focus on the prospects for renewed civil strife in China. Members of a U.S. liaison team stationed in Yenan (yuh-NAHN) were impressed by the performance of the Communists, and some recommended that the United States should remain neutral in a possible conflict between Communists and Nationalists for control of China. The White House, though skeptical of Chiang's ability to meet the challenges of the postwar era, was increasingly concerned about the spread of communism in Europe and sought to find a peaceful solution through the formation of a multiparty coalition government that would keep the Nationalists in power.

THE COMMUNIST TRIUMPH The effort failed. By 1946, full-scale war between the Nationalist government, now reinstalled in Nanjing, and the Communists resumed. Initially, most of the fighting took place in Manchuria, where newly arrived PLA units began to surround Nationalist forces occupying the major cities. Now Chiang Kai-shek's errors came home to roost. In the countryside, millions of peasants, attracted to the Communists by promises of land and social justice, flocked to serve under their banners. In the cities, middle-class Chinese, normally hostile to communism, were alienated by Chiang's brutal suppression of all dissent and his government's inability to slow the ruinous rate of inflation or solve the economic problems it caused. By the end of 1947, almost all of Manchuria was under Communist control.

The Truman administration reacted to the spread of Communist power in China with acute discomfort. Washington had no desire to see a communist government on the mainland but it had little confidence in Chiang Kai-shek's ability to realize Roosevelt's dream of a strong, united, and prosperous China. In December 1945, President Truman sent General George C. Marshall to China in a last-ditch effort to bring about a peaceful settlement but anti-communist elements in the Republic of China resisted U.S. pressure to create a coalition government with the Chinese Communist Party (CCP). During the next two years, the United States gave limited military support to Chiang's regime but refused to commit U.S. power to guarantee its survival. The administration's hands-off policy deeply angered many members of Congress, who charged that the White House was "soft on communism" and called for increased military assistance to the Nationalist government.

With morale dropping in the cities, Chiang's troops began to defect to the Communists. Sometimes whole divisions, officers as well as ordinary soldiers, changed sides. By 1948, the PLA was advancing south out of Manchuria and had encircled Beijing. Communist troops took the old imperial capital, crossed the Yangzi the following spring, and occupied the commercial hub of Shanghai (see Map 26.2). During the next few months, Chiang's government and 2 million of his followers fled to Taiwan, which the Japanese had returned to Chinese control after World War II.

With the Communist victory in China, Asia became a major theater of the Cold War and an integral element in American politics. In a white paper issued by the State Department in the fall of 1949, the Truman administration placed most of the blame for the debacle on Chiang Kai-shek's regime (see the box "Who Lost China?" on p. 771). Republicans in Congress, however, disagreed, arguing that Roosevelt had betrayed Chiang Kai-shek at Yalta by granting privileges in Manchuria to the Soviet Union. In their view, Soviet troops had hindered the dispatch of Nationalist forces to the area and provided the PLA with weapons to use against their rivals. The fall of China unleashed a period of anti-communist hysteria in the United States that was fostered in part by the demagogic claims of Wisconsin Senator Joseph McCarthy, who contended that "red agents" had systematically infiltrated the U.S. government in order to bring about the worldwide triumph of communism.

In later years, sources in Moscow and Beijing made it clear that in actuality the Soviet Union gave little assistance to the CCP in its postwar struggle against the Nanjing regime. In fact, at the close of World War II, Stalin—probably concerned at the prospect of a military confrontation with the United States—advised Mao against undertaking the effort. Although the PLA undoubtedly received some assistance from Soviet occupation troops in Manchuria, the Communist victory ultimately stemmed from conditions inside China. Nevertheless, the White House was forced to respond to its critics. During

the spring of 1950, under pressure from Congress and public opinion to define U.S. interests in Asia, the Truman administration adopted a new national security policy known as NSC-68 that declared that the United States would take whatever steps were necessary to stem the further expansion of communism in the region. Containment had come to East Asia.

The New China

In their new capital of Beijing, China's Communist leaders probably hoped that their accession to power in 1949 would bring about a reduction of tensions in the region and permit their new government to concentrate on domestic goals. But their desire for peace was tempered by their determination to erase a century of humiliation at the hands of imperialist powers and to restore the traditional outer frontiers of the Chinese empire. In addition to recovering lost territories such as Manchuria, Taiwan, and Tibet, the Chinese leaders also hoped to restore Chinese influence in former tributary areas such as Korea and Vietnam.

It soon became clear that these two goals were not always compatible. Negotiations between Mao Zedong and Joseph Stalin, held in Moscow in January 1950, were tense (see "The Sino-Soviet Dispute" later in this chapter) but led to Soviet recognition of Chinese sovereignty over Manchuria and Xinjiang (SHIN-jyahng)—the desolate lands north of Tibet that were known as Chinese Turkestan because many of the peoples in the area were of Turkic origin—although the Soviets retained a measure of economic influence in both areas. Chinese troops occupied Tibet in 1950 and brought it under Chinese administration for the first time in more than a century. But in Korea and Taiwan, China's efforts to re-create the imperial buffer zone provoked new conflicts with foreign powers.

The problem of Taiwan was a consequence of the Cold War. As the Chinese civil war came to an end, the Truman administration was determined to avoid entanglement in China's internal affairs and initially indicated that it would not seek to prevent a Communist takeover of the island, now occupied by Chiang Kai-shek's Republic of China (ROC). But as tensions between the United States and the new Chinese government escalated during the winter of 1949–1950, influential figures in the United States began to argue that Taiwan was crucial to U.S. defense strategy in the Pacific.

The Korean War

The sudden outbreak of war in Korea intensified the Cold War in East Asia. After the Sino-Japanese War in 1894–1895, Korea, long a Chinese tributary, had fallen increasingly under the rival influences of Japan and Russia. After the Japanese defeated the Russians in 1905, Korea became an integral part of the Japanese empire and remained so until 1945. Japanese rule had been deeply unpopular in Korea, and the removal of the country from Japanese occupation had been one of the stated objectives of the Allies in World War II. On the eve of Japanese surrender in August 1945, the Soviet Union and the

Who Lost China?

POLITICS & GOVERNMENT

IN 1949, WITH CHINA ABOUT TO FALL under the control of the Communists, President Truman instructed the State Department to prepare a detailed "white paper" report explaining why the U.S. policy of seeking to avoid a Communist victory in China had failed. The authors of the report concluded that responsibility lay at the door of Nationalist Chinese leader Chiang Kai-shek and that there was nothing the United States could have done to alter the result. Most China observers today would accept that assessment but it did little at the time to deflect criticism of the administration for selling out the interests of our ally in China.

U.S. State Department White Paper on China, 1949

When peace came the United States was confronted with three possible alternatives in China: (1) it could have pulled out lock, stock, and barrel; (2) it could have intervened militarily on a major scale to assist the Nationalists to destroy the Communists; (3) it could, while assisting the Nationalists to assert their authority over as much of China as possible, endeavor to avoid a civil war by working for a compromise between the two sides.

The first alternative would, and I believe American public opinion at the time so felt, have represented an abandonment of our international responsibilities and of our traditional policy of friendship for China before we had made a determined effort to be of assistance. The second alternative policy, while it may look attractive theoretically, in retrospect was wholly impracticable. The Nationalists had been unable to destroy the Communists during the ten years before the war. Now after the war the Nationalists were ... weakened, demoralized, and unpopular. They had quickly dissipated their popular support and prestige in the areas liberated from the Japanese by the

conduct of their civil and military officials. The Communists on the other hand were much stronger than they had ever been and were in control of most of North China. Because of the ineffectiveness of the Nationalist forces, which was later to be tragically demonstrated, the Communists probably could have been dislodged only by American arms. It is obvious that the American people would not have sanctioned such a colossal commitment of our armies in 1945 or later. We therefore came to the third alternative policy whereunder we faced the facts of the situation and attempted to assist in working out a modus vivendi which would avert civil war but nevertheless preserve and even increase the influence of the National Government....

The distrust of the leaders of both the Nationalist and Communist Parties for each other proved too deep-seated to permit final agreement, notwithstanding temporary truces and apparently promising negotiations. The Nationalists, furthermore, embarked in 1946 on an overambitious military campaign in the face of warnings by General Marshall that it not only would fail but would plunge China into economic chaos and eventually destroy the National Government....

The unfortunate but inescapable fact is that the ominous result of the civil war in China was beyond the control of the government of the United States. Nothing that this country did or could have done within the reasonable limits of its capabilities could have changed that result; nothing that was left undone by this country has contributed to it. It was the product of internal Chinese forces, forces which this country tried to influence but could not. A decision was arrived at within China, if only a decision by default.

How did the authors of the white paper explain the Communist victory in China? According to their argument, what actions might have prevented it?

Source: From *United States Relations with China* (Washington, D.C., Dept. of State, 1949), pp. iii–xvi.

United States agreed to divide the country into two separate occupation zones at the 38th parallel. The two countries originally planned to hold national elections after the restoration of peace to reunify Korea under an independent government, but as U.S.-Soviet relations deteriorated, two separate governments emerged in Korea, a communist one in the north and an anti-communist one in the south.

Tensions between the two governments ran high along the dividing line, and Kim Il-sung, the Communist leader in the north, asked Moscow to support his plan to unify the peninsula under his control. Stalin, however, was still unwilling to confront the United States. "If you should get kicked in the teeth," he replied, "I shall not lift a finger. You have to ask Mao for all the help."[4]

Kim Il-sung, convinced that the United States lacked the stomach for a new war on the Asian mainland, was not deterred, and on June 25, 1950, North Korean troops invaded the south. Increasingly concerned about Communist intentions in Asia, Truman immediately ordered U.S. naval and air forces to support South Korea, and the United Nations Security Council (with the Soviet delegate absent to protest the refusal of the UN to assign China's seat to the new government in Beijing) passed a resolution calling on member nations to jointly resist the invasion, in line with the security provisions in the United Nations Charter. By September, UN forces under the command of U.S. General Douglas MacArthur marched northward across the 38th parallel with the aim of unifying Korea under a single, non-communist government.

A Pledge of Eternal Friendship. After the Communist victory in the Chinese civil war, in 1950 Chairman Mao Zedong traveled to Moscow, where he negotiated a treaty of friendship and cooperation with the Soviet Union. The poster shown here trumpets the results of the meeting: "Long live and strengthen the unbreakable friendship and cooperation of the Soviet and Chinese peoples!" The two leaders, however, did not get along. Mao reportedly complained to colleagues that obtaining assistance from Stalin was "like taking meat from a tiger's mouth."

President Truman worried that by approaching the Chinese border at the Yalu (YAH-loo) River, the UN troops—the majority of whom were from the United States—could trigger Chinese intervention but MacArthur assured him that China would not respond. In November, however, Chinese "volunteer" forces intervened in large numbers on the side of North Korea and drove the UN troops southward in disarray. A static defense line was eventually established near the original dividing line at the 38th parallel (see Map 26.3), although the war continued.

To U.S. officials, the Chinese intervention in Korea was clear evidence that China intended to promote communism throughout Asia, and immediately after the invasion, President Truman dispatched the U.S. Seventh Fleet to the Taiwan Strait to prevent a possible Chinese invasion of Taiwan. Recent evidence does suggest that Mao Zedong, convinced that a new revolutionary wave was on the rise in Asia, had given his blessing to the North Korean invasion of the south. But China's decision to enter the war was probably motivated in large part by the fear that hostile U.S. forces might be stationed on the Chinese frontier and perhaps even launch an attack across the border. General MacArthur intensified such fears by calling publicly for air attacks on Manchurian cities in preparation for an attack on communist China.

The consequences were particularly expensive for China. Not only did the United States react by seeking to

MAP 26.3 The Korean Peninsula. In June 1950, North Korean forces crossed the 38th parallel in a sudden invasion of the south. Shown here is the cease-fire line that brought an end to the war in 1953.

 What is the significance of the Yalu River?

prevent a possible Chinese invasion of Taiwan but the outbreak of war in Korea hardened Western attitudes against the new Chinese government and led to China's isolation from contacts with the major capitalist powers for over two decades. The United States continued to regard the Nationalist government in Taiwan as the only legal representative of the Chinese people and to support its retention of China's seat on the UN Security Council. As a result, mainland China was cut off from all forms of economic and technological assistance and was forced to rely almost entirely on the Soviet Union.

Conflict in Indochina

During the mid-1950s, Communist leaders in Beijing began to back away from their confrontational stance toward the West and sought to build contacts with the nonsocialist world. A cease-fire agreement brought the Korean War to an end in July 1953, and China signaled its desire to live in peaceful coexistence with other independent countries in the region. But Beijing's message of peace was clouded by its role in a bitter conflict that began to intensify on China's southern flank, in French Indochina. The struggle had begun after Japan's surrender at the end of World War II, when the Indochinese Communist Party led by Ho Chi Minh (HOH CHEE MIN) (1890–1969), at the head of a multiparty nationalist alliance called the Vietminh (vee-et-MIN) Front, seized power in northern and central Vietnam. After abortive negotiations between Ho's government and the returning French, war broke out in December 1946. French forces occupied the

Ho Chi Minh Plans an Attack on the French.
Unlike many of the peoples of Southeast Asia, the Vietnamese had to fight for their independence after World War II. That fight was led by the talented Communist leader Ho Chi Minh. In this 1950 photograph taken at his secret base in the mountains of North Vietnam, Ho plans an attack on French positions. He changed the location of his headquarters on several occasions to evade capture by French forces.

AFP/Getty Images

cities and the densely populated lowlands, while the Vietminh took refuge in the mountains.

For three years, the Vietminh waged a "people's war" of national liberation from colonial rule, gradually increasing in size and effectiveness. At the time, however, the conflict in Indochina attracted relatively little attention from world leaders. The Truman administration was uneasy about Ho's long-standing credentials as a Soviet agent but was equally reluctant to anger anticolonialist elements in the region by intervening on behalf of the French. Moscow had even less interest in the issue. Stalin—still hoping to see the Communist Party come to power in Paris—ignored Ho's request for recognition of his movement as the legitimate representative of the national interests of the Vietnamese people.

But what had begun as an anticolonial struggle by the Vietminh Front against the French became entangled in the Cold War after the CCP came to power in China. In early 1950, Beijing began to provide military assistance to the Vietminh to burnish its revolutionary credentials and protect its own borders from hostile forces. The Truman administration, increasingly concerned that a revolutionary "Red tide" was sweeping through the region, decided to provide financial and technical assistance to the French while pressuring them to prepare for an eventual transition to independent non-communist governments in Vietnam, Laos, and Cambodia.

Despite growing U.S. involvement in the war, Vietminh forces continued to gain strength, and in the spring of 1954, with Chinese assistance, they besieged a French military outpost at Dien Bien Phu (DEE-en bee-en FOO), not far from

Indochina After 1954

© 2016 Cengage Learning

the border of Laos. The attack took place at a difficult time for the government in Paris. With war casualties in Indochina mounting, the French public had become increasingly tired of fighting the "dirty war" in Indochina, and the French government had just agreed to hold peace talks with the Vietminh beginning in May of 1954. On the day before the peace conference was scheduled to convene in Geneva, Switzerland, Vietminh forces overran the last French bastion at Dien Bien Phu. This humiliating defeat further weakened French resolve to maintain a military presence in Indochina, and in July, the two sides agreed on a peace settlement. Vietnam was temporarily divided into a northern communist half, known as the Democratic Republic of Vietnam (DRV), and a non-communist southern half based in Saigon (sy-GAHN) (now Ho Chi Minh City) that was soon renamed the Republic of Vietnam (RVN). A demilitarized zone separated the two entities at the 17th parallel. Elections were to be held in two years to create a unified country. Cambodia and Laos were both declared independent under their own neutral governments. French forces were withdrawn from all three countries.

China had played an active role in bringing about the settlement and clearly hoped that it would reduce tensions in the area but subsequent efforts to improve relations between China and the United States foundered on the issue of Taiwan. In the fall of 1954, the United States signed a mutual security treaty with the ROC guaranteeing U.S. military support in case of an invasion of Taiwan. When Beijing demanded U.S. withdrawal from Taiwan as the price for improved relations, diplomatic talks between the two countries collapsed.

From Confrontation to Coexistence

 FOCUS QUESTION: What events led to the era of coexistence in the 1960s, and to what degree did each side contribute to the reduction in international tensions?

The decade of the 1950s had opened with the world teetering on the edge of a nuclear holocaust. The Soviet Union had detonated its first nuclear device in 1949, and the two blocs—capitalist and socialist—viewed each other across an ideological divide that grew increasingly bitter with each passing year. Yet as the decade drew to a close, a measure of sanity crept into the Cold War, and the leaders of the major world powers began to seek ways to coexist in a peaceful and stable world (see Map 26.4).

The first clear sign of change occurred after Stalin's death in early 1953. His successor, Georgy Malenkov (gyee-OR-gyee muh-LEN-kawf) (1902–1988), openly hoped to improve relations with the Western powers in order to reduce defense expenditures and shift government spending to growing consumer needs. Nikita Khrushchev (nuh-KEE-tuh KHROOSH-chawf) (1894–1971), who replaced Malenkov in 1955, continued his predecessor's efforts to reduce tensions with the West and improve the living standards of the Soviet people.

In an adroit public relations touch, Khrushchev called for a policy of **peaceful coexistence** with the West. In 1955, he surprisingly agreed to negotiate an end to the postwar occupation of Austria by the victorious Allies and allow the creation of a neutral country with strong cultural and economic ties with the West. He also called for a reduction in defense expenditures and reduced the size of the Soviet armed forces.

Ferment in Eastern Europe

At first, Western leaders were suspicious of Khrushchev's motives, especially in light of events that were taking place in Eastern Europe. The key to security along the western frontier of the Soviet Union was the string of Eastern European satellite states that had been assembled in the aftermath of World War II (see Map 26.1). Once Communist domination had been assured, a series of "little Stalins" put into power by Moscow instituted Soviet-type five-year plans that emphasized

MAP 26.4 The Global Cold War. This map shows the location of the major military bases and missile sites maintained by the three contending power blocs at the height of the Cold War.

 Which continents were the most heavily armed? Why?

heavy industry rather than consumer goods, the collectivization of agriculture, and the nationalization of industry. They also appropriated the political tactics that Stalin had perfected in the Soviet Union, eliminating all non-communist parties and establishing the classic institutions of repression—the secret police and military forces. Dissidents were tracked down and thrown into prison, and "national Communists" who resisted total subservience to the Soviet Union were charged with treason in mass show trials and executed.

Despite these repressive efforts, popular discontent became increasingly evident in several Eastern European countries. Hungary, Poland, and Romania harbored bitter memories of past Russian domination and suspected that Stalin, under the guise of proletarian internationalism, was seeking to revive the empire of the tsars. For the vast majority of the residents of Eastern Europe, the imposition of the so-called people's democracies (a term invented by Moscow to refer to a society in the early stage of socialist transition) resulted in economic hardship and severe threats to the most basic political liberties. The first indications of unrest appeared in East Berlin, where popular riots broke out against Communist rule in 1953. The riots eventually subsided but the virus had spread to neighboring countries.

In Poland, public demonstrations against an increase in food prices in 1956 escalated into widespread protests against the regime's economic policies, restrictions on the freedom of Catholics to practice their religion, and the continued presence of Soviet troops (as called for by the Warsaw Pact) on Polish soil. In a desperate effort to defuse the unrest, the party desperately turned to Wladyslaw Gomulka (vlah-DIS-lahf goh-MOOL-kuh) (1905–1982), a popular party official who had previously been demoted for his "nationalist" tendencies. When Gomulka took steps to ease the crisis, Khrushchev flew to Warsaw to warn him against adopting policies that could undermine the political dominance of the party and weaken security links with the Soviet Union. After a tense confrontation, Poland agreed to remain in the Warsaw Pact and to maintain the sanctity of party rule; in return, Gomulka was authorized to adopt domestic reforms, such as easing restrictions on religious practice and ending the policy of forced collectivization in rural areas.

THE HUNGARIAN REVOLUTION

The developments in Poland sent shock waves throughout the region. The impact was strongest in neighboring Hungary, where the methods of the local "little Stalin," Mátyás Rákosi (MAH-tyash RAH-koh-see) (1892–1971), were so brutal that he had been summoned to Moscow for a lecture ("He distrusts everybody," remarked one Soviet official). In late October 1956, student-led popular riots broke out in the capital of Budapest and soon spread to other towns and villages throughout the country. Rákosi was forced to resign and was replaced by Imre Nagy (IM-ray NAHJ) (1896–1958), a "national Communist" who attempted to satisfy popular demands without arousing the anger of Moscow. Unlike Gomulka, however, Nagy was unable to contain the zeal of leading members of the protest movement, who sought major political reforms and the

How the Mighty Have Fallen. In the fall of 1956, Hungarian freedom fighters rose up against Communist domination of their country in the short-lived Hungarian Revolution. Their actions threatened Soviet hegemony in Eastern Europe, however, and in late October, Soviet leader Nikita Khrushchev dispatched troops to quell the uprising. In the meantime, the Hungarian people had voiced their discontent by toppling a gigantic statue of Joseph Stalin in the capital of Budapest. Statues of the Soviet dictator had been erected in all the Soviet satellites after World War II. ("W.C." identifies a public toilet in European countries.)

withdrawal of Hungary from the Warsaw Pact. On November 1, Nagy promised free elections, which, given the mood of the country, would probably have brought an end to Communist rule. After a brief moment of uncertainty, Khrushchev decided on firm action. Soviet troops, recently withdrawn at Nagy's request, returned to Budapest and installed a new government under the more pliant party leader János Kádár (YAH-nush KAH-dahr) (1912–1989). While Kádár rescinded many of Nagy's measures, Nagy sought refuge in the Yugoslav embassy. A few weeks later, he left the embassy under the promise of safety but was quickly arrested, convicted of treason, and executed (see Opposing Viewpoints "Soviet Repression in Eastern Europe: Hungary, 1956" on p. 776).

DIFFERENT ROADS TO SOCIALISM

The dramatic events in Poland and Hungary graphically demonstrated the vulnerability of the Soviet satellite system in Eastern Europe, and many observers throughout the world anticipated that the United States would intervene on behalf of the freedom fighters in Hungary. After all, President Dwight D. Eisenhower (1890–1969) and his administration had promised that they would "roll back communism," and radio broadcasts by the U.S.-sponsored Radio Liberty and Radio Free Europe had encouraged the peoples of Eastern Europe to rise up against Soviet domination. In reality, the United States was well aware that U.S. intervention could lead to nuclear war and limited its response to protesting Soviet brutality in crushing the uprising.

The year of discontent was not without consequences, however. Soviet leaders now recognized that they could maintain control over the satellites in Eastern Europe only by granting them the leeway to adopt domestic policies appropriate to local conditions. Khrushchev had already embarked on this path in 1955 when he assured Tito that there were "different roads to

AP Images/Arpad Hazafi

Soviet Repression in Eastern Europe: Hungary, 1956

INTERACTION & EXCHANGE

DEVELOPMENTS IN POLAND IN 1956 INSPIRED THE COMMUNIST LEADERS OF HUNGARY to begin to extricate their country from Soviet control. But there were limits to Khrushchev's tolerance, and he sent Soviet troops to crush Hungary's movement for independence. The first selection is a statement by the Soviet government justifying its use of troops, while the second is the brief and tragic final statement from Imre Nagy, the Hungarian leader.

Statement of the Soviet Government, October 30, 1956

The Soviet Government regards it as indispensable to make a statement in connection with the events in Hungary.

The course of the events has shown that the working people of Hungary, who have achieved great progress on the basis of their people's democratic order, correctly raise the question of the necessity of eliminating serious shortcomings in the field of economic building, the further raising of the material well-being of the population, and the struggle against bureaucratic excesses in the state apparatus.

However, this just and progressive movement of the working people was soon joined by forces of black reaction and counterrevolution, which are trying to take advantage of the discontent of part of the working people to undermine the foundations of the people's democratic order in Hungary and to restore the old landlord and capitalist order.

The Soviet Government and all the Soviet people deeply regret that the development of events in Hungary has led to bloodshed. On the request of the Hungarian People's Government the Soviet Government consented to the entry into Budapest of the Soviet Army units to assist the Hungarian People's Army and the Hungarian authorities to establish order in the town.

The Last Message of Imre Nagy, November 4, 1956

This fight is the fight for freedom by the Hungarian people against the Russian intervention, and it is possible that I shall only be able to stay at my post for one or two hours. The whole world will see how the Russian armed forces, contrary to all treaties and conventions, are crushing the resistance of the Hungarian people. They will also see how they are kidnapping the Prime Minister of a country which is a Member of the United Nations, taking him from the capital, and therefore it cannot be doubted at all that this is the most brutal form of intervention. I should like in these last moments to ask the leaders of the revolution, if they can, to leave the country. I ask that all that I have said in my broadcast, and what we have agreed on with the revolutionary leaders during meetings in Parliament, should be put in a memorandum, and the leaders should turn to all the peoples of the world for help and explain that today it is Hungary and tomorrow, or the day after tomorrow, it will be the turn of other countries because the imperialism of Moscow does not know borders, and is only trying to play for time.

How did the United States and its allies respond to the events in Hungary? Why did the United States decide not to intervene in support of the dissident forces?

Source: From *Department of State Bulletin*, Nov. 12, 1956, pp. 746–747.

---

socialism." Some eastern European Communist leaders now took Khrushchev at his word and adopted reform programs to make socialism more palatable to their subject populations. Even Kádár, derisively labeled the "butcher of Budapest," managed to preserve many of Nagy's reforms to allow a measure of capitalist incentive and freedom of expression in Hungary.

CRISIS OVER BERLIN But in the late 1950s, a new crisis erupted over the status of Berlin. The Soviet Union had launched its first intercontinental ballistic missile (ICBM) in August 1957, arousing U.S. fears of a missile gap between the United States and the Soviet Union. Khrushchev attempted to take advantage of the U.S. frenzy over missiles to solve the problem of West Berlin, which had remained an island of prosperity inside the relatively poverty-stricken state of East Germany (the GDR). Many East Germans sought to escape to West Germany by fleeing through West Berlin, a serious blot on the GDR's credibility and a potential source of instability in East-West relations. In November 1958, Khrushchev announced that unless the West removed its forces from West Berlin within six months, he would turn over control of the access routes to the East Germans. Unwilling to accept an ultimatum that would have abandoned West Berlin to the Communists, President Eisenhower and the West stood firm, and Khrushchev eventually backed down.

Despite such periodic crises in East-West relations, there were tantalizing signs that an era of true peaceful coexistence between the two power blocs could be achieved. In the late 1950s, the United States and the Soviet Union initiated a cultural exchange program. While Leningrad's Kirov Ballet appeared at theaters in the United States, clarinetist Benny Goodman and the film *West Side Story* played in Moscow.

The Kitchen Debate. During the late 1950s, the United States and the Soviet Union sought to defuse Cold War tensions by encouraging cultural exchanges between the two countries. On one occasion, U.S. Vice President Richard M. Nixon visited Moscow in conjunction with the arrival of an exhibit to introduce U.S. culture and society to the Soviet people. Here, Nixon lectures Soviet Communist Party chief Nikita Khrushchev on the technology of the U.S. kitchen. Beside Nixon at the far right is future Soviet president Leonid Brezhnev.

In 1958, Khrushchev visited the United States and had a brief but friendly encounter with President Eisenhower at the presidential retreat in northern Maryland.

Rivalry in the Third World

Yet Khrushchev could rarely avoid the temptation to gain an advantage over the United States in the competition for influence throughout the world, a posture that exacerbated the unstable relationship between the two global superpowers. Unlike Stalin, who had exhibited a profound distrust of all political figures who did not slavishly follow his lead, Khrushchev viewed the dismantling of colonial regimes in Asia, Africa, and Latin America as a potential advantage for the Soviet Union. When neutralist leaders like Nehru in India, Tito in Yugoslavia, and Sukarno (soo-KAHR-noh) in Indonesia founded the **Nonaligned Movement** in 1955 to provide an alternative to the two major power blocs, Khrushchev took every opportunity to promote Soviet interests in the Third World (as the nonaligned countries of Asia, Africa, and Latin America were now popularly called). Khrushchev openly sought alliances with strategically important neutralist countries such as India, Indonesia, and Egypt, while the United States' ability to influence events at the United Nations began to wane.

In January 1961, just as John F. Kennedy (1917–1963) assumed the U.S. presidency, Khrushchev unnerved the new president at an informal summit meeting in Vienna by declaring that the Soviet Union would provide active support to national liberation movements throughout the world. Increasingly, Washington was becoming concerned about Soviet meddling in such sensitive trouble spots as Southeast Asia, where insurgent activities in Indochina continued to simmer; Central Africa, where the pro-Soviet tendencies of radical leader Patrice Lumumba (puh-TREES loo-MOOM-buh) (1925–1961) aroused U.S. suspicions; and the Caribbean, where a little-known Cuban revolutionary named Fidel Castro threatened to transform his country into an advance base for Soviet expansion in the Americas.

The Cuban Missile Crisis and the Move Toward Détente

In 1959, the left-wing revolutionary Fidel Castro (fee-DELL KASS-troh) (b. 1926/1927) overthrew the Cuban dictator Fulgencio Batista (full-JEN-see-oh bah-TEES-tuh) and established a Soviet-supported totalitarian regime. As tensions increased between the new government in Havana and the United States, the Eisenhower administration broke relations with Cuba and drafted plans to overthrow Castro, who reacted by drawing closer to Moscow.

Soon after taking office in early 1961, Kennedy approved a plan drawn up under his predecessor to support an invasion of Cuba by anti-Castro exiles. But the attempted landing at the Bay of Pigs in southern Cuba was an utter failure. At Castro's invitation, the Soviet Union then began to station nuclear missiles in Cuba, within striking distance of the American mainland. (That the United States had placed nuclear weapons in Turkey within easy range of the Soviet Union was a fact that Khrushchev was quick to point out.) When in October 1962 U.S. intelligence discovered that a Soviet fleet carrying more missiles was heading to Cuba, Kennedy decided to dispatch U.S. warships into the Atlantic to prevent the fleet from reaching its destination.

This approach to the problem was risky but had the benefit of delaying confrontation and providing time to find a peaceful solution. After a tense standoff during which the two countries came frighteningly close to a direct nuclear confrontation (the Soviet missiles already in Cuba were launch-ready), Khrushchev finally sent a conciliatory letter to Kennedy agreeing to turn back the fleet if Kennedy pledged not to invade Cuba. In a secret concession not revealed until many years later, the president also promised to dismantle U.S. missiles in Turkey. To the world (and to an angry Castro), however, it appeared that Kennedy had bested Khrushchev. "We were eyeball to eyeball," noted U.S. Secretary of State Dean Rusk, "and they blinked" (see the Film & History feature "*Dr. Strangelove, or: How I Learned to Stop Worrying and Love the Bomb* (1964)" on p. 778).

Dr. Strangelove, or: How I Learned to Stop Worrying and Love the Bomb (1964)

In 1964, director Stanley Kubrick released *Dr. Strangelove, or: How I Learned to Stop Worrying and Love the Bomb*, a black comedy about the Cold War and nuclear weapons. The film begins when a general in the U.S. Air Force, Jack D. Ripper (Sterling Hayden), orders a nuclear attack on the Soviet Union because he believes that Communists are secretly poisoning American drinking water with fluoride. The situation becomes critical when efforts to call off Ripper's air strike fail. The Soviet Union, in an attempt to deter such an attack, has created the "Doomsday Device," a computerized defense system that will destroy the earth if triggered. This system is irreversible, so unless Ripper's men are stopped, the entire planet will be consumed by nuclear holocaust.

Numerous communications lapses occur throughout the film, as it satirizes the leadership protocol each nation has implemented to oversee its nuclear arsenal. The president of the United States (Peter Sellers) and the Soviet premier lack the means to fully prevent the pending nuclear war.

Meanwhile, the mysterious Dr. Strangelove (also played by Peter Sellers), a German physicist and adviser to the president, suggests how accidents and misunderstandings could easily cause the destruction of our planet. Even Dr. Strangelove's plan to repopulate the planet fails, as he relies on Nazi ideals and prejudices to select those who will survive.

Kubrick based the film on Peter George's 1958 novel *Red Alert*, a thriller about accidental nuclear war. Written at a time when more than 34,000 nuclear weapons existed, the film pokes fun at military and political leaders and the posturing that resulted from the Cold War arms race. Although it is a parody, *Dr. Strangelove* accurately portrayed American paranoia and policies during the Cold War. Senator Joseph McCarthy and the House Un-American Activities Committee (HUAC) sought out anyone who might be conspiring against America or promoting communist ideals, and the threat of nuclear attack prompted the creation of numerous bomb shelters and contingency plans. Schoolchildren were trained to hide under their desks in the event of a disaster, and a telephone hotline connected Moscow and Washington, D.C., to ensure communications between the two superpowers.

The military showdown in *Dr. Strangelove* paralleled actual events, in particular the Cuban Missile Crisis of 1962. In the film, General Turgidson (George C. Scott) suggests that a preemptive nuclear strike would catch the Soviets by surprise. "We would therefore prevail," declares Turgidson, "and suffer only modest and acceptable civilian casualties from their remaining force which would be badly damaged and uncoordinated." Turgidson believed that "acceptable" casualties would number "no more than 10 to 20 million killed," an irreverent jab at President Kennedy's advisers, who in 1962 recommended attacking Cuba despite the threat of nuclear missiles. The Doomsday Device of *Dr. Strangelove* also mocked the superpowers' attempts at deterrence. Nikita Khrushchev claimed that by placing missiles in Cuba, the Soviets would deter the United States from starting war, and the fictional Doomsday Device was intended to produce a similar effect. As Dr. Strangelove explained, "Deterrence is the art of producing in the mind of the enemy … the fear to attack." Hailed by one film critic as "arguably the best political satire of the century," *Dr. Strangelove* evoked the fear and anxiety of the Cold War.

General Turgidson (George C. Scott) with the president (Peter Sellers).

HAWK Films Prod/Columbia/The Kobal Collection/Picture Desk

The ghastly realization that the world might have faced annihilation in a matter of days had a profound effect on both sides. A communication hotline between Moscow and Washington was installed in 1963 to expedite rapid communication between the two superpowers in time of crisis. In the same year, the two powers agreed to ban nuclear tests in the atmosphere, a step that served to lessen the tensions between the two nations.

The Sino-Soviet Dispute

Nikita Khrushchev had launched his appeal for peaceful coexistence as a means of improving relations with the capitalist powers; ironically, one result of the campaign was to undermine Moscow's ties with its close ally, China. During Stalin's lifetime, Beijing had accepted the Soviet Union as the acknowledged leader of the socialist world. After Stalin's death, however, relations began to deteriorate. Part of the reason may have been Mao Zedong's contention that he, as the most experienced Marxist leader, should now be acknowledged as the most authoritative voice in the socialist community. But another determining factor was that just as Soviet policies were moving toward moderation, China's were becoming more radical.

Several other issues were involved, including territorial disputes along the Sino-Soviet border and China's unhappiness with limited Soviet economic assistance. But the key sources of disagreement involved ideology and the Cold War. Chinese leaders were convinced that the successes of the Soviet space program confirmed that the socialists were now technologically superior to the capitalists (the East Wind, trumpeted the Chinese official press, had now triumphed over the West Wind), and they urged Khrushchev to go on the offensive to promote world revolution. Specifically, China wanted Soviet assistance in retaking Taiwan from Chiang Kai-shek. But Khrushchev, for reasons we have discussed earlier, was trying to improve relations with the West and rejected Chinese demands for support against Taiwan.

By the end of the 1950s, the Soviet Union had begun to remove its advisers from China, and in 1961, the dispute broke into the open. Increasingly isolated in the global arena, China voiced its hostility to what Mao described as the "urban industrialized countries" (which included the Soviet Union) and portrayed itself as the leader of the "rural underdeveloped countries" of Asia, Africa, and Latin America in a global struggle against imperialist oppression. In effect, China had applied Mao Zedong's concept of people's war in an international framework (see Opposing Viewpoints "Peaceful Coexistence or People's War" on p. 780).

The Second Indochina War

In the meantime, a new source of Cold War friction was opening up in Southeast Asia with the renewal of conflict in Indochina. The Eisenhower administration had opposed the peace settlement at Geneva in 1954, which divided Vietnam temporarily into two separate regroupment zones, because the provision for future national elections risked the possibility that the entire country would come under Communist rule. But Eisenhower had been unwilling to introduce U.S. military forces to continue the conflict, and in the end, Washington promised not to break the provisions of the agreement but refused to commit itself to the results. In the meantime, the White House began to provide aid to the new government in South Vietnam, formally known as the Republic of Vietnam (RVN) and now led by the anti-communist politician Ngo Dinh Diem (NGHOH din DZEE-em) (1901–1963).

Bolstered by U.S. assistance, the RVN began to root out internal dissidents. With the tacit approval of the United States, Diem refused to hold the national elections called for by the Geneva Accords. It was widely anticipated, even in Washington, that the Communists would win such elections. In 1959, the communist government in Hanoi, despairing of the peaceful unification of the country under Communist rule, decided to unleash a new policy of revolutionary war in the south. To provide an image of political legitimacy, Hanoi sponsored the formation of a new political organization designed to win the support of a wide spectrum of the population in the south. Called the National Front for the Liberation of South Vietnam (NLF), it purported to be an independent organization representing the interests of the population in the south but was actually under the secret but firm leadership of Communist leaders in Hanoi (see Opposing Viewpoints "Confrontation in Southeast Asia" on p. 781).

By 1963, South Vietnam was on the verge of collapse. Diem's autocratic methods and inattention to severe economic inequality had alienated much of the population, and revolutionary forces, popularly known as the **Viet Cong** (Vietnamese Communists) and supported by the communist government in the north, expanded their influence throughout much of the country. In the fall of 1963, with the approval of the Kennedy administration, a military coup overthrew the Diem regime. But factionalism kept the new military leaders from reinvigorating the struggle against the insurgent forces, and the situation in South Vietnam continued to deteriorate. By early 1965, the Viet Cong, their ranks now swelled by military units infiltrated from North Vietnam, were on the verge of seizing control of the entire country. In March, President Lyndon Johnson (1908–1973) decided to send U.S. combat troops to South Vietnam to prevent the total defeat of the anti-communist government in Saigon. Over the next three years, U.S. troop levels steadily increased as the White House counted on U.S. firepower to persuade Ho Chi Minh to abandon his quest to unify Vietnam under Communist leadership.

THE VIETNAM CONFLICT IN THE COLD WAR Chinese and Soviet leaders observed the gradual escalation of the conflict in South Vietnam with mixed feelings. The former were undoubtedly pleased to have a firm communist ally—one that had in many ways followed the path of Mao Zedong—just beyond their southern frontier. Yet the Chinese—like their Soviet counterparts—were concerned that bloodshed in South Vietnam might enmesh them in an open confrontation with the United States. Beijing had a further concern that a powerful and ambitious DRV might wish to extend its influence

From Confrontation to Coexistence ■ 779

OPPOSING ✕ VIEWPOINTS

Peaceful Coexistence or People's War?

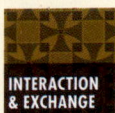

INTERACTION & EXCHANGE

THE SOVIET LEADER VLADIMIR LENIN had contended that war between the socialist and imperialist camps was inevitable because the imperialists would never give up without a fight. Joseph Stalin agreed, and told colleagues shortly after World War II that a new war would break out in fifteen to twenty years. But Stalin's successor, Nikita Khrushchev, feared that a new world conflict could result in a nuclear holocaust and contended that the two sides must learn to coexist, although peaceful competition would continue. In this speech given in Beijing in 1959, Khrushchev attempted to persuade the Chinese to accept his views. But Chinese leaders argued that the "imperialist nature" of the United States would never change, and predicted that "people's wars" in the Third World would bring down the structure of imperialism. That argument was presented in a 1966 article by Marshall Lin Biao (LIN BYOW), at that time one of Mao Zedong's (Mao Tse-tung in Wade-Giles transliteration) closest allies.

Nikita Khrushchev, Speech to the Chinese, 1959

Comrades! Socialism brings to the people peace—that greatest blessing. The greater the strength of the camp of socialism grows, the greater will be its possibilities for successfully defending the cause of peace on this earth. The forces of socialism are already so great that real possibilities are being created for excluding war as a means of solving international disputes....

When I spoke with President Eisenhower—and I have just returned from the United States of America—I got the impression that the President of the U.S.A.—and not a few people support him—understands the need to relax international tension....

There is only one way of preserving peace—that is the road of peaceful coexistence of states with different social systems. The question stands thus: either peaceful coexistence or war with its catastrophic consequences. Now, with the present relation of forces between socialism and capitalism being in favor of socialism, he who would continue the "cold war" is moving towards his own destruction....

It is not at all because capitalism is still strong that the socialist countries speak out against war, and for peaceful coexistence. No, we have no need of war at all. If the people do not want it, even such a noble and progressive system as socialism cannot be imposed by force of arms. The socialist countries therefore, while carrying through a consistently peace-loving policy, concentrate their efforts on peaceful construction; they fire the hearts of men by the force of their example in building socialism, and thus lead them to follow in their footsteps. The question of when this or that country will take the path to socialism is decided by its own people. This, for us, is the holy of holies.

Lin Biao, "Long Live the Victory of People's War"

Many countries and peoples in Asia, Africa, and Latin America are now being subjected to aggression and enslavement on a serious scale by the imperialists headed by the United States and their lackeys.... As in China, the peasant question is extremely important in these regions. The peasants constitute the main force of the national-democratic revolution against the imperialists and their lackeys. In committing aggression against these countries, the imperialists usually begin by seizing the big cities and the main lines of communication. But they are unable to bring the vast countryside completely under their control.... The countryside, and the countryside alone, can provide the revolutionary basis from which the revolutionaries can go forward to final victory. Precisely for this reason, Mao Tse-tung's theory of establishing revolutionary base areas in the rural districts and encircling the cities from the countryside is attracting more and more attention among the people in these regions.

Taking the entire globe, if North America and Western Europe can be called "the cities of the world," then Asia, Africa, and Latin America constitute "the rural areas of the world." Since World War II, the proletarian revolutionary movement has for various reasons been temporarily held back in the North American and West European capitalist countries, while the people's revolutionary movement in Asia, Africa, and Latin America has been growing vigorously. In a sense, the contemporary world revolution also presents a picture of the encirclement of cities by the rural areas. In the final analysis, the whole cause of world revolution hinges on the revolutionary struggles of the Asian, African, and Latin American peoples, who make up the overwhelming majority of the world's population. The socialist countries should regard it as their internationalist duty to support the people's revolutionary struggles in Asia, Africa, and Latin America....

Ours is the epoch in which world capitalism and imperialism are heading for their doom and communism is marching to victory. Comrade Mao Tse-tung's theory of people's war is not only a product of the Chinese revolution, but has also the characteristic of our epoch. The new experience gained in the people's revolutionary struggles in various countries since World War II has provided continuous evidence that Mao Tse-tung's thought is a common asset of the revolutionary people of the whole world.

Q *Why did Nikita Khrushchev feel that the conflict between the socialist and capitalist camps that Lenin had predicted was no longer necessary? How did Lin Biao respond?*

Sources: From G. F. Hudson et al., eds., *The Sino-Soviet Dispute* (New York: Frederick Praeger, 1961), pp. 61–63, cited in *Peking Review*, No. 40, 1959. From *Nationalism and Communism*, Norman Graebner, ed. Copyright © 1977 by D. C. Heath and Company.

OPPOSING ✕ VIEWPOINTS

Confrontation in Southeast Asia

POLITICS & GOVERNMENT

IN DECEMBER 1960, THE NATIONAL FRONT FOR THE LIBERATION OF SOUTH VIETNAM (NLF) was born. Composed of political and social leaders opposed to the anti-communist government, it operated under the direction of the Communist regime in North Vietnam and served as the formal representative of revolutionary forces in the south throughout the remainder of the Vietnam War. When, in the spring of 1965, President Lyndon B. Johnson began to dispatch U.S. combat troops to Vietnam to prevent a Communist victory there, the NLF issued the declaration presented in the first selection. The second selection is from a speech that Johnson gave at Johns Hopkins University in April 1965 in response to the NLF.

Statement of the National Front for the Liberation of South Vietnam (1965)

American imperialist aggression against South Vietnam and interference in its internal affairs have now continued for more than ten years. More American troops and supplies, including missile units, Marines, B-57 strategic bombers, and mercenaries from South Korea, Taiwan, the Philippines, Australia, Malaysia, etc., have been brought to South Vietnam....

The Saigon puppet regime, paid servant of the United States, is guilty of the most heinous crimes. These despicable traitors, these boot-lickers of American imperialism, have brought the enemy into our country. They have brought to South Vietnam armed forces of the United States and its satellites to kill our compatriots, occupy and ravage our sacred soil and enslave our people.

The Vietnamese, the peoples of all Indo-China and Southeast Asia, supporters of peace and justice in every part of the world, have raised their voice in angry protest against this criminal unprovoked aggression of the United States imperialists.

In the present extremely grave situation, the South Vietnam National Liberation Front considers it necessary to proclaim anew its firm and unswerving determination to resist the U.S. imperialists and fight for the salvation of our country.... [It] will continue to rely chiefly on its own forces and potentialities, but it is prepared to accept any assistance, moral and material, including arms and other military equipment, from all the socialist countries, from nationalist countries, from international organizations, and from the peace-loving peoples of the world.

Lyndon B. Johnson, "Peace Without Conquest"

The world as it is in Asia is not a serene or peaceful place.

The first reality is that North Viet-Nam has attacked the independent nation of South Viet-Nam. Its object is total conquest.

Of course, some of the people of South Viet-Nam are participating in attack on their own government. But trained men and supplies, orders and arms, flow in a constant stream from north to south.

This support is the heartbeat of the war.

And it is a war of unparalleled brutality. Simple farmers are the targets of assassination and kidnapping. Women and children are strangled in the night because their men are loyal to their government. And helpless villages are ravaged by sneak attacks. Large-scale raids are conducted on towns, and terror strikes in the heart of cities....

Why are these realities our concern? Why are we in South Viet-Nam?

We are there because we have a promise to keep. Since 1954 every American President has offered support to the people of South Viet-Nam. We have helped to build, and we have helped to defend. Thus, over many years, we have made a national pledge to help South Viet-Nam defend its independence.

Our objective is the independence of South Viet-Nam, and its freedom from attack. We want nothing for ourselves—only that the people of South Viet-Nam be allowed to guide their own country in their own way. We will do everything necessary to reach that objective. And we will do only what is absolutely necessary.

Q *How did the NLF justify its claim to represent the legitimate aspirations of the people of South Vietnam? What was President Johnson's counterargument?*

Sources: From *New Times* (March 27, 1965), pp. 36–40. From Lyndon B. Johnson, "Peace Without Conquest" speech, April 1965 from *Public Papers of the Presidents of the United States: Lyndon B. Johnson, 1965.* Volume I, entry 172, pp. 394–399. Washington D.C.: Government Printing Office, 1966.

throughout mainland Southeast Asia, an area that China considered its own backyard.

Both Moscow and Beijing therefore tiptoed delicately through the minefield of the Indochina conflict. As the war escalated in 1964 and 1965, Soviet leaders assured Washington that they had no interest in seeing the conflict in Indochina escalate into a Great Power confrontation. Beijing, for its part, announced its public support for the war of national liberation

War in the Rice Paddies. The first stage of the Vietnam War consisted primarily of guerrilla conflict, as Viet Cong insurgents relied on guerrilla tactics to bring down the U.S.-supported government in Saigon. In 1965, however, President Lyndon Johnson ordered U.S. combat troops into South Vietnam (top photo) in a desperate bid to prevent a Communist victory in that beleaguered country. The Communist government in North Vietnam responded in kind, sending its own regular forces down the Ho Chi Minh Trail to confront U.S. troops on the battlefield. In the photo on the bottom, North Vietnamese troops storm the U.S. Marine base at Khe Sanh (KAY SARN), near the demilitarized zone, in 1968, the most violent year of the war. Although U.S. military commanders believed that helicopters would be a key factor in defeating the insurgent forces in Vietnam, this was one instance when technological superiority did not produce a victory on the battlefield.

Q *How do you think helicopters were used to assist U.S. operations in South Vietnam? Why didn't their use result in a U.S. victory?*

AP Images

Three Lions/Hulton Archive/Getty Images

in South Vietnam but privately assured Washington that China would not directly enter the conflict unless U.S. forces threatened its southern border. Beijing also refused to cooperate fully with Moscow in shipping Soviet goods to North Vietnam through Chinese territory.

Despite its dismay at the lack of full support from its allies, the Communist government in Hanoi responded to U.S. escalation by infiltrating more of its own regular troops into the south, and by 1968, the war had reached a stalemate (see the Comparative Illustration "War in the Rice Paddies" above). The Communists were not strong enough to overthrow the government in Saigon, whose weakness was shielded by the presence of half a million U.S. troops, but President Johnson was reluctant to engage in all-out war on North Vietnam for fear of provoking a global nuclear conflict. In the fall, after the Communist-led Tet offensive undermined claims of progress in Washington and aroused intense antiwar protests in the United States, peace negotiations began in Paris.

THE QUEST FOR PEACE Richard Nixon (1913–1994) came into the White House in 1969 on a pledge to bring an honorable end to the Vietnam War. With U.S. public opinion sharply divided on the issue (see Chapter 28), he began to withdraw U.S. troops while continuing to hold peace talks in Paris. But the centerpiece of his strategy was to improve relations with China and thus undercut Chinese support for the North Vietnamese war effort. During the 1960s, relations between Moscow and Beijing had reached a point of extreme tension, and thousands of troops were stationed on both sides of their long common frontier. To intimidate their Communist rivals, Soviet sources hinted that they might launch a preemptive strike to destroy Chinese nuclear facilities in Xinjiang. Sensing an opportunity to split the two onetime allies, Nixon sent his emissary, Henry Kissinger, on a secret trip to China. Responding to assurances that the United States was determined to withdraw from Indochina and hoped to improve relations with the mainland regime, Chinese leaders invited President Nixon to visit China in early 1972. Nixon accepted, and the

A New Beginning in Sino-American Relations

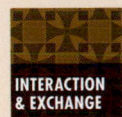

INTERACTION & EXCHANGE

ON JANUARY 1, 1979, the United States and the People's Republic of China agreed to establish diplomatic relations. It was the first time that the two countries had exchanged diplomatic representatives since 1949, when the Communist Party seized control of the mainland from Chiang Kai-shek's Nationalist government. To achieve their new relationship, both Beijing and Washington had to place several contentious issues on the back burner—notably, the continued existence of the Republic of China on the island of Taiwan. Note how the two statements carefully describe that issue to reflect their distinct points of view.

Statement of the United States of America

As of January 1, 1979, the United States of America recognizes the People's Republic of China as the sole legal government of China. On the same date, the People's Republic of China accords similar recognition to the United States of America. The United States thereby establishes diplomatic relations with the People's Republic of China.

On that same date, January 1, 1979, the United States of America will notify Taiwan that it is terminating diplomatic relations and that the Mutual Defense Treaty between the United States and the Republic of China is being terminated in accordance with the provisions of the Treaty. The United States also states that it will be withdrawing its remaining military personnel from Taiwan within four months.

In the future, the American people and the people of Taiwan will maintain commercial, cultural and other relations without official government representation and without diplomatic relations.

The Administration will seek adjustments to our laws and regulations to permit the maintenance of commercial, cultural and other non-governmental relationships in the new circumstances that will exist after normalization.

The United States is confident that the people of Taiwan face a peaceful and prosperous future. The United States continues to have an interest in the peaceful resolution of the Taiwan issue and expects that the Taiwan issue will be settled peacefully by the Chinese themselves.

The United States believes that the establishment of diplomatic relations with the People's Republic will contribute to the welfare of the American people, to the stability of Asia where the United States has major security and economic interests and to the peace of the entire world.

Statement of the People's Republic of China

As of January 1, 1979, the People's Republic of China and the United States of America recognize each other and establish diplomatic relations, thereby ending the prolonged abnormal relationship between them. This is a historic event in Sino-U.S. relations.

As is known to all, the Government of the People's Republic of China is the sole legal government of China and Taiwan is a part of China. The question of Taiwan was the crucial issue obstructing the normalization of relations between China and the United States. It has now been resolved between the two countries in the spirit of the Shanghai Communiqué and through their joint efforts, thus enabling the normalization of relations so ardently desired by the people of the two countries. As for the way of bringing Taiwan back to the embrace of the motherland and reunifying the country, it is entirely China's internal affair.

At the invitation of the U.S. Government, Teng Hsiaoping, vice-premier of the State Council of the People's Republic of China, will pay an official visit to the United States in January 1979, with a view to further promoting the friendship between the two peoples and good relations between the two countries.

 What are the key differences between these two statements with regard to the Taiwan situation? Given these differences, why did China and the United States decide to resume diplomatic relations?

Sources: U.S. statement from *Public Papers: Jimmy Carter*, 1978, p. 2266. China statement from Xinhua, Dec. 16, 1978 in Foreign Broadcast Information Service, *Daily Report: People's Republic of China*, Dec. 18, 1978, p. A2.

---

two sides agreed to set aside their differences over Taiwan to pursue a better mutual relationship.

THE FALL OF SAIGON Incensed at the apparent betrayal by their close allies, North Vietnamese leaders decided to seek a temporary settlement of the war in the south. In January 1973, a peace treaty was signed in Paris calling for the removal of all U.S. forces from South Vietnam. In return, the Communists agreed to halt military operations and to engage in negotiations to resolve their differences with the Saigon regime. But negotiations over the political settlement soon broke down, and in early 1975, the Communists resumed the offensive. At the end of April, under a massive assault by North Vietnamese military forces, South Vietnamese resistance collapsed. A year later, the country was formally unified under Communist rule.

The Communist victory in Vietnam was a severe humiliation for the United States. But its strategic impact was limited because of the new relationship with China. During the next decade, Sino-American relations continued to improve. In 1979, the two countries established diplomatic ties as the United States renounced its mutual security treaty with the Republic of China in return for a pledge from China to seek reunification with Taiwan by peaceful means (see the box "A New Beginning in Sino-American Relations" above). By the end of the 1970s, China and the United States had forged a "strategic relationship" in which they would cooperate against the common threat of Soviet hegemony in Asia.

Why had the United States failed to achieve its objective of preventing a Communist victory in Vietnam? Dean Rusk, U.S. Secretary of State during the 1960s, later commented that Washington had underestimated the determination of its adversary in Hanoi and overestimated the patience of the American people. No doubt both of these admissions are justified. Deeper reflection suggests, however, that another factor was equally important: the United States had overestimated the ability of its client state in Saigon to earn the support of the people of South Vietnam and defend it against a disciplined adversary. Although many South Vietnamese fought bravely in the effort to prevent a takeover by the DRV, their leaders in Saigon lacked the determination and the capacity to support their efforts. In subsequent years, the Vietnam War became a crucial lesson to the Americans on the perils of nation building.

An Era of Equivalence

 FOCUS QUESTION: Why did the Cold War briefly flare up again in the 1980s, and why did it come to a definitive end at the end of the decade?

When the Johnson administration sent U.S. combat troops to South Vietnam in 1965, Washington's main concern was with Beijing, not Moscow. By the mid-1960s, U.S. officials viewed the Soviet Union as an essentially conservative power, more concerned with protecting its vast empire than with expanding its borders. In fact, U.S. policymakers periodically requested Soviet assistance in seeking a peaceful settlement of the Vietnam War. As long Khrushchev was in power, they found a receptive ear in Moscow. Khrushchev was firmly dedicated to promoting peaceful coexistence (at least on his terms) and had no wish to risk a confrontation with the United States in far-off Southeast Asia.

Such was not the case with his successor. When Khrushchev was replaced in October 1964 with a new leadership headed by party chief Leonid Brezhnev (lee-oh-NYEET BREZH-neff) (1906–1982) and Prime Minister Alexei Kosygin (uh-LEK-say kuh-SEE-gun) (1904–1980), Soviet attitudes about the Cold War became more ambivalent (see Chapter 27). On the one hand, the new Soviet leaders had no desire to provoke an open military conflict with the United States. On the other hand, they were eager to take advantage of their adversary's discomfort in Southeast Asia and to protect their own interests within the socialist camp and, when possible, to expand their own influence in the world.

The Brezhnev Doctrine

One consequence of this new attitude took place in Eastern Europe, where discontent with Stalinist policies began to emerge in Czechoslovakia. The Czechs had not shared in the thaw of the mid-1950s and remained under the rule of the hardliner Antonín Novotný (AHN-toh-nyeen NOH-vaht-nee) (1904–1975), who had been placed in power by Stalin

himself. By the late 1960s, however, Novotný's policies had led to widespread popular alienation, and in 1968, with the support of intellectuals and reformist party members, Alexander Dubček (DOOB-check) (1921–1992) was elected first secretary of the Communist Party. He immediately attempted to implement what was popularly called "socialism with a human face," relaxing restrictions on freedom of speech and the press and on the right to travel abroad. Economic reforms were announced, and party control over all aspects of society was reduced. A period of national euphoria erupted that came to be known as the "Prague Spring."

It proved to be short-lived. Encouraged by Dubček's actions, some Czechs called for more far-reaching reforms, including neutrality in the Cold War and even withdrawal from the Soviet bloc. Determined to forestall the spread of this "spring fever" and convinced that the United States would take no action, Moscow ordered the Soviet Red Army, supported by troops from other Warsaw Pact states, to invade Czechoslovakia in August 1968 and crush the reform movement. Gustav Husák (goo-STAHV HOO-sahk) (1913–1991), a committed Stalinist, replaced Dubček and restored the old order, while Moscow attempted to justify its action by issuing the so-called **Brezhnev Doctrine** (see the box "The Brezhnev Doctrine" on p. 785).

In East Germany as well, Stalinist policies continued to hold sway. The ruling Communist government, led by party chief Walter Ulbricht, had consolidated its position in the early 1950s and had become a faithful Soviet satellite. Industry was nationalized and agriculture collectivized. After a workers' revolt was crushed by Soviet tanks in 1953, a steady flight of East Germans to West Germany ensued, primarily through the city of Berlin. This exodus of mostly skilled laborers, numbering an estimated three million by 1961 ("Soon only party chief Ulbricht will be left," remarked one Soviet observer sardonically), created economic problems and in 1961 led the East German government to erect a wall separating East Berlin from West Berlin (known officially in the GDR as "the democratic anti-fascist protection wall"), as well as even more fearsome barriers along the entire border with West Germany.

After building the Berlin Wall, East Germany succeeded in developing the strongest economy among the Soviet Union's Eastern European satellites. In 1971, Ulbricht was succeeded by Erich Honecker (AY-reekh HON-nek-uh) (1912–1994), a party hard-liner. Propaganda increased, and the use of the Stasi (SHTAH-see), the secret police, became a hallmark of Honecker's virtual dictatorship. Honecker ruled unchallenged for the next eighteen years.

An Era of Détente

Still, under Brezhnev and Kosygin, the Soviet Union continued to pursue peaceful coexistence with the West and adopted a generally cautious posture in foreign affairs. By the early 1970s, a new phase in Soviet-American relations had emerged, often referred to as **détente** (day-TAHNT), a French term meaning a reduction of tensions between the two sides. One symbol of the new relationship was the Antiballistic Missile (ABM)

The Brezhnev Doctrine

POLITICS & GOVERNMENT

IN THE SUMMER OF 1968, when the new Communist Party leaders in Czechoslovakia were seriously considering proposals for reforming the totalitarian system there, the Warsaw Pact nations met under the leadership of Soviet party chief Leonid Brezhnev to assess the threat to the socialist camp. Soon afterward, military forces of several Soviet bloc nations entered Czechoslovakia and imposed a new government subservient to Moscow. The move was justified by the spirit of "proletarian internationalism" and was widely viewed as a warning to China and other socialist states not to stray too far from Marxist-Leninist orthodoxy, as interpreted by the Soviet Union. But Moscow's actions also raised tensions in the Cold War.

A Letter to the Central Committee of the Communist Party of Czechoslovakia

Dear comrades!

On behalf of the Central Committees of the Communist and Workers Parties of Bulgaria, Hungary, the German Democratic Republic, Poland, and the Soviet Union, we address ourselves to you with this letter, prompted by a feeling of sincere friendship based on the principles of Marxism-Leninism and proletarian internationalism and by the concern of our common affairs for strengthening the positions of socialism and the security of the socialist community of nations.

The development of events in your country evokes in us deep anxiety. It is our firm conviction that the offensive of the reactionary forces, backed by imperialists, against your Party and the foundations of the social system in the Czechoslovak Socialist Republic, threatens to push your country off the road of socialism and that

consequently it jeopardizes the interests of the entire socialist system....

We neither had nor have any intention of interfering in such affairs as are strictly the internal business of your Party and your state, nor of violating the principles of respect, independence, and equality in the relations among the Communist Parties and socialist countries....

At the same time we cannot agree to have hostile forces push your country from the road of socialism and create a threat of severing Czechoslovakia from the socialist community.... This is the common cause of our countries, which have joined in the Warsaw Treaty to ensure independence, peace, and security in Europe, and to set up an insurmountable barrier against the intrigues of the imperialist forces, against aggression and revenge.... We shall never agree to have imperialism, using peaceful or non-peaceful methods, making a gap from the inside or from the outside in the socialist system, and changing in imperialism's favor the correlation of forces in Europe....

That is why we believe that a decisive rebuff of the anticommunist forces, and decisive efforts for the preservation of the socialist system in Czechoslovakia are not only your task but ours as well....

We express the conviction that the Communist Party of Czechoslovakia, conscious of its responsibility, will take the necessary steps to block the path of reaction. In this struggle you can count on the solidarity and all-round assistance of the fraternal socialist countries.

Warsaw, July 15, 1968.

 How did Leonid Brezhnev justify the Soviet decision to invade Czechoslovakia? To what degree do you find his arguments persuasive?

Source: From *Moscow News*, Supplement to No. 30 (917), 1968, pp. 3–6.

Treaty, often called SALT I because it emerged from the first round of Strategic Arms Limitation Talks (SALT). In the treaty, which was signed in 1972, the two nations agreed to limit the size of their ABM systems.

The U.S. objective in pursuing the treaty was to make it unlikely that either superpower could win a nuclear exchange by launching a preemptive strike against the other. U.S. officials believed that a policy of "equivalence," in which there was a roughly equal power balance between the two sides, was the best way to avoid a nuclear confrontation. Détente was pursued in other ways as well. When President Nixon took office in 1969, he sought to increase trade and cultural contacts with the Soviet Union. His purpose was to set up a series of "linkages" in U.S.-Soviet relations that would persuade Moscow of the economic and social benefits of maintaining good relations with the West.

The Helsinki Accords were a symbol of that new relationship. Signed in 1975 by the United States, Canada, and all European nations on both sides of the Iron Curtain, these accords recognized all borders in Europe that had been established since the end of World War II, thereby formally acknowledging for the first time the Soviet sphere of influence in Eastern Europe. The Helsinki Accords also committed the signatories to recognize and protect the human rights of their citizens, a clear effort by the Western states to force the Soviet Union and its allies to improve their performance in that area. Whether the effort had any effect is subject to dispute.

Renewed Tensions in the Third World

Protection of human rights became one of the major foreign policy goals of the next U.S. president, Jimmy Carter (b. 1924). Ironically, just at the point when U.S. involvement in Vietnam came to an end and relations with China began to improve, U.S.-Soviet relations began to sour, for several reasons. Some Americans had become increasingly concerned about perceived aggressive new tendencies in Soviet foreign policy. The first indication came in Africa. Soviet influence was on the rise in Somalia, across the Red Sea from South Yemen, and later in neighboring Ethiopia, where a Marxist regime took control. In Angola, once a colony of Portugal, an insurgent movement supported by Cuban troops came to power.

In 1979, attention shifted to the Middle East, when Soviet troops were sent across the border into Afghanistan to protect a newly installed Marxist regime that was facing internal resistance from fundamentalist Muslims. Some Western observers suspected that Moscow's chief motive in deciding to advance into hitherto neutral Afghanistan was to extend Soviet power into the oil fields of the Persian Gulf. To deter such a possibility, the White House promulgated the Carter Doctrine, which declared that the United States would use its military power, if necessary, to safeguard Western access to the oil reserves in the Middle East. As it turned out, Western concerns were probably exaggerated, for sources in Moscow later disclosed that the Soviet advance had little to do with the oil of the Persian Gulf but was an effort to increase Soviet influence in a region increasingly beset by Islamic fervor. Soviet officials feared that Islamic activism could spread to the Muslim populations in the Soviet republics in Central Asia and were confident that the United States was too distracted by the so-called **Vietnam syndrome** (the public fear of U.S. involvement in another Vietnam-type conflict) to respond. Such attitudes were undoubtedly also a factor in encouraging Moscow to become more aggressive in pursuing influence in Africa.

Another reason for the growing suspicion of the Soviet Union in the United States was the fear on the part of some U.S. defense analysts that Moscow had abandoned the policy of equivalence and was seeking strategic superiority in nuclear weapons. Accordingly, they argued for a substantial increase in U.S. defense spending. Such charges, combined with the evidence of Soviet efforts in Africa and the Middle East and reports of the persecution of Jews and dissidents in the Soviet Union, helped undermine public support for détente in the United States. These changing attitudes were reflected in the failure of the Carter administration to obtain congressional approval of a new arms limitation agreement (SALT II), signed with the Soviet Union in 1979.

Countering the Evil Empire

The early years of the administration of President Ronald Reagan (1911–2004) witnessed a return to the harsh rhetoric, if not all of the harsh practices, of the Cold War. President Reagan's anti-communist credentials were well known. In a speech given shortly after his election in 1980, he referred to the Soviet Union as an "evil empire" and frequently voiced his suspicion of its motives in foreign affairs. In an effort to eliminate perceived Soviet advantages in strategic weaponry, the White House began a military buildup that stimulated a renewed arms race. In 1982, the Reagan administration introduced the nuclear-tipped cruise missile, whose ability to fly at low altitudes made it difficult to detect by enemy radar. Reagan also became an ardent exponent of the Strategic Defense Initiative (SDI), nicknamed **Star Wars**. Its purposes were to create a space shield that could destroy incoming missiles and to force Moscow into an arms race that it could not hope to win. President Reagan's assumptions were correct: Soviet officials reacted with concern to the bellicose remarks and actions coming out of Washington, and began preparations for war. However, these preparations ceased later in the decade, when the White House reassured the Soviets of its peaceful intentions.[5]

The Reagan administration also adopted a more activist stance in the Third World. This activism was most directly demonstrated in Central America, where the revolutionary Sandinista (san-duh-NEES-tuh) regime had been established in Nicaragua after the overthrow of the brutal Somoza dictatorship in 1979. Charging that the Sandinista regime was supporting a guerrilla insurgency movement in nearby El Salvador, the Reagan administration began to provide material aid to the government in El Salvador while simultaneously supporting an anti-communist guerrilla movement (the **Contras**) in Nicaragua. Though the administration insisted that it was countering the spread of communism in the Western Hemisphere, its actions aroused considerable controversy in Congress, where some members charged that growing U.S. involvement could lead to a repeat of the nation's bitter experience in Vietnam.

The Reagan administration also took the

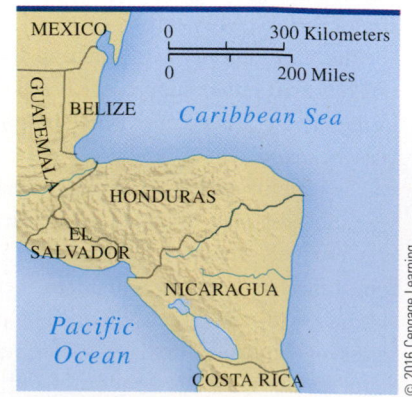

Northern Central America

CHRONOLOGY   The Cold War to 1980

Truman Doctrine	1947
Formation of NATO	1949
Soviet Union explodes first nuclear device	1949
Communists come to power in China	1949
Nationalist government retreats to Taiwan	1949
Korean War	1950–1953
Geneva Conference ends Indochina War	1954
Warsaw Pact created	1955
Khrushchev calls for peaceful coexistence	1955–1956
Sino-Soviet dispute breaks into the open	1961
Cuban Missile Crisis	1962
SALT I treaty signed	1972
Nixon's visit to China	1972
Fall of South Vietnam	1975
Soviet invasion of Afghanistan	1979

offensive in other areas. By providing military support to the anti-Soviet insurgents in Afghanistan, the White House helped maintain a Vietnam-like conflict in Afghanistan that would embed the Soviet Union in its own quagmire. Like the Vietnam War, the conflict in Afghanistan resulted in heavy casualties and demonstrated that the influence of a superpower was limited in the face of strong nationalist, guerrilla-type opposition.

Toward a New World Order

In 1985, Mikhail Gorbachev (meek-HAYL GOR-buh-chawf) (b. 1931) was elected secretary of the Communist Party of the Soviet Union. During Brezhnev's last years and the brief tenures of his two successors (see Chapter 27), the Soviet Union had entered an era of serious economic decline, and the dynamic new party chief was well aware that drastic changes would be needed to rekindle the dreams that had inspired the Bolshevik Revolution. During the next few years, he launched a program of restructuring, or *perestroika* (per-uh-STROI-kuh),

to revitalize the Soviet system. As part of that program, he set out to improve relations with the United States and the rest of the capitalist world. When he met with President Reagan in Reykjavik (RAY-kyuh-vik), the capital of Iceland, the two leaders agreed to set aside their ideological differences and seek to cooperate in several areas.

Gorbachev's desperate effort to rescue the Soviet Union from collapse was too little and too late. In 1989, popular demonstrations against communist rule broke out across Eastern Europe. The contagion soon spread eastward, and in 1991 the Soviet Union, for 70 years an apparently permanent fixture on the global scene, suddenly disintegrated. In its place arose fifteen new nations. That same year, the string of Soviet satellites in Eastern Europe broke loose from Moscow's grip and declared their independence from communist rule. The Cold War was over (for these events, see Chapter 27).

The end of the Cold War lulled many observers into the seductive vision of a new world order that would be characterized by peaceful cooperation and increasing prosperity.

An Afghan War Memorial. Moscow's failed war in Afghanistan in the 1980s cost the lives of an estimated 27,000 Soviet soldiers. Reportedly, at least half the troops lost in the war came from Belarus, once a Soviet republic and now an independent state under a dictatorial regime. A war memorial to commemorate those who died in the war was recently built in Minsk, the capital of Belarus. The bridegroom in this wedding party is from Syria, which symbolizes the multiethnic composition of contemporary Eastern Europe.

Reagan and Gorbachev in Reykjavik. With the election of Mikhail Gorbachev as party general secretary in 1985, Moscow and Washington began to explore the means to reduce tensions between the two great powers. In October of 1986, Gorbachev and U.S. President Ronald Reagan held a summit meeting in Reykjavik, the capital of Iceland, to explore issues of concern to both sides. Although no agreements resulted from the meeting, the atmospherics from the meeting resulted in a new era of good feeling, and soon led to meaningful agreements on arms control and a reduction of tensions in the Cold War.

An Era of Equivalence ■ 787

Global Village or Clash of Civilizations?

INTERACTION & EXCHANGE

As the Cold War came to an end in 1991, policymakers, scholars, and political pundits began to forecast the emergence of a "new world order." One hypothesis, put forth by the political philosopher Francis Fukuyama, was that the decline of communism signaled that the industrial capitalist democracies of the West had triumphed in the world of ideas and were now poised to remake the rest of the world in their own image.

Not everyone agreed with this optimistic view of the world situation. In *The Clash of Civilizations and the Remaking of the World Order*, the historian Samuel P. Huntington suggested that the post–Cold War era, far from marking the triumph of Western ideals, would be characterized by increased global fragmentation and a "clash of civilizations" based on ethnic, cultural, or religious differences. According to Huntington, the twenty-first century would be dominated by disputatious cultural blocs in East Asia, Western Europe and the United States, Eurasia, and the Middle East. The dream of a universal order—a global village—dominated by Western values, he concluded, is a fantasy.

Recent events have lent some support to Huntington's hypothesis. The collapse of the Soviet Union led to the emergence of an atmosphere of conflict and tension all along the perimeter of the old Soviet empire. More recently, the terrorist attack on the United States in September 2001 set the advanced nations of the West and much of the Muslim world on a collision course. As for the new economic order—now enshrined as official policy in Western capitals—public anger at the impact of globalization has reached disturbing levels in many countries, leading to a growing demand for self-protection and group identity in an impersonal and rapidly changing world.

Are we then headed toward multiple power blocs divided by religion and culture as Huntington predicted? His thesis is indeed a useful corrective to the complacent tendency of many observers to view Western civilization as the zenith of human achievement. By dividing the world into competing cultural blocs, however, Huntington has underestimated the

Ronald McDonald in Indonesia. This giant statue welcomes young Indonesians to a McDonald's restaurant in the capital city, Jakarta. McDonald's restaurant chain symbolizes the globalization of today's world civilization.

© William J. Duiker

centrifugal forces at work in the various regions of the world. As the industrial and technological revolutions spread across the face of the earth, their impact is measurably stronger in some societies than in others, thereby intensifying historical rivalries in a given region while establishing links between individual societies and counterparts in other parts of the world. In recent years, for example, Japan has had more in common with the United States than with its traditional neighbors, China and Korea.

The most likely scenario for the next few decades, then, is more complex than either the global village hypothesis or its rival, the clash of civilizations. The twenty-first century will be characterized by simultaneous trends toward globalization and fragmentation as the thrust of technology and information transforms societies and gives rise to counterreactions among societies seeking to preserve a group identity and sense of meaning and purpose in a confusing world.

 How has the recent global economic recession affected the issues discussed in this essay?

Sadly, such hopes have not been realized. A bitter civil war in the Balkans in the mid-1990s and the recent flare-up in U.S.-Russian relations over the future of Ukraine have graphically demonstrated that old fault lines of national and ethnic hostility still divide the post–Cold War world. With the end of the Cold War, other issues beyond the daily headlines—the growing threat to the global environment, the gap between rich and poor nations, and tensions unleashed by the migration of peoples—began to resurface (see the Comparative Essay "Global Village or Clash of Civilizations?" above). Then, on September 11, 2001, the world entered a dangerous new era when terrorists attacked the nerve centers of U.S. power in New York City and Washington, D.C., inaugurating a new round of tension between the West and the forces of militant Islam. These events will be discussed in greater detail in the chapters that follow.

CHAPTER SUMMARY

At the end of World War II, the two superpowers, the United States and the Soviet Union, began to compete for political domination. The ideological division began in Europe but soon spread throughout the world as the United States fought in Korea and Vietnam to prevent the spread of communism in Asia, while the Soviet Union used its influence to prop up pro-Soviet regimes in Asia, Africa, and Latin America.

The two power blocs faced each other across an ideological divide characterized by high levels of hostility and suspicion. To many contemporary observers, a nuclear confrontation appeared almost inevitable.

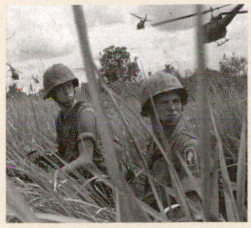

As the twentieth century wore on, however, there were tantalizing signs of a thaw in the Cold War. In 1979, China and the United States established mutual diplomatic relations, a consequence of Beijing's decision to focus on domestic reform and stop supporting wars of national liberation in Asia. Six years later, the ascent of Mikhail Gorbachev to leadership, which culminated in the dissolution of the Soviet Union in 1991, brought an end to almost half a century of bitter rivalry between the world's two superpowers.

The Cold War thus ended without the horrific vision of a mushroom cloud. Unlike the earlier rivalries that had resulted in two world wars, this time the antagonists had gradually come to realize that the struggle for supremacy could be carried out in the political and economic arena rather than on the battlefield. And in the final analysis, it was not military superiority but political, economic, and cultural factors that brought about the triumph of Western civilization over the Marxist vision of a classless utopia. The world's policymakers could now shift their focus to other problems of mutual concern. These issues will be addressed in the chapters that follow.

CHAPTER TIMELINE

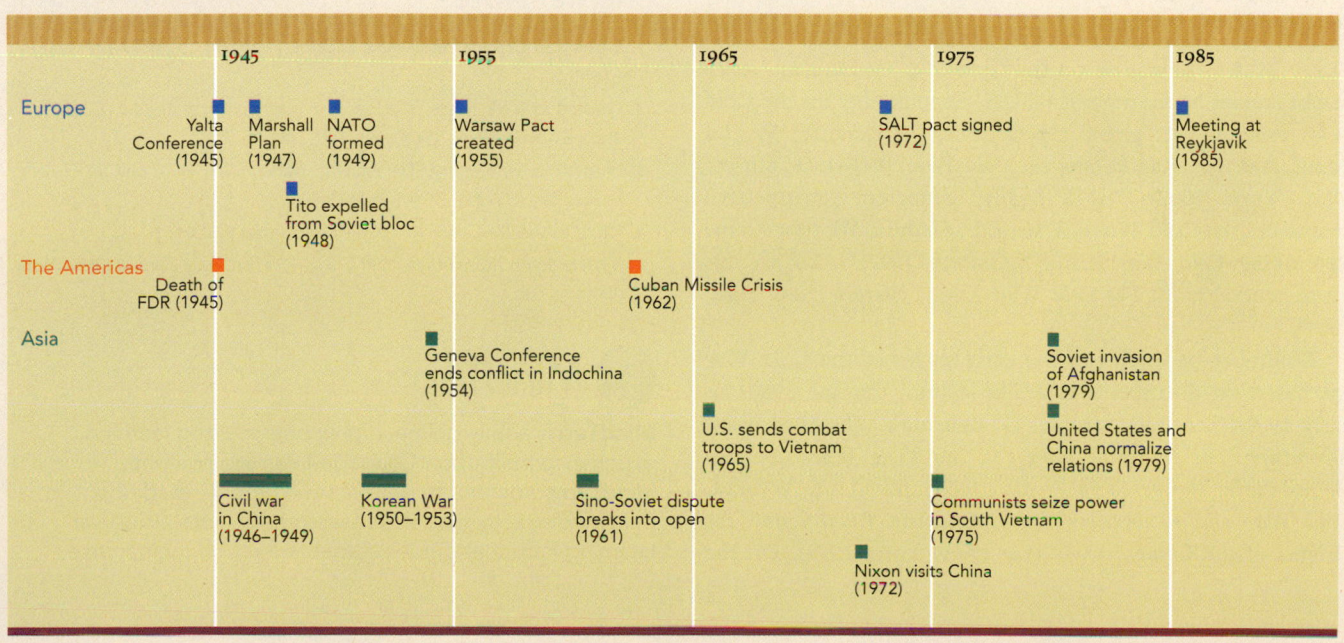

CHAPTER REVIEW

Upon Reflection

Q This chapter has described the outbreak of the Cold War as virtually inevitable, given the ambitions of the two superpowers and their ideological differences. Do you agree? How might the Cold War have been avoided?

Q What disagreements brought about an end to the Sino-Soviet alliance in 1961? Which factors appear to have been most important?

Q How did the wars in Korea and Vietnam relate to the Cold War and affect its course?

Key Terms

Truman Doctrine (p. 764)
Marshall Plan (p. 764)
containment (p. 765)
denazification (p. 765)
peaceful coexistence (p. 774)
Nonaligned Movement (p. 777)
Viet Cong (p. 779)
Brezhnev Doctrine (p. 784)
détente (p. 784)
Vietnam syndrome (p. 786)
Star Wars (p. 786)
Contras (p. 786)

Suggested Reading

COLD WAR   Literature on the Cold War is abundant. Revisionist studies have emphasized U.S. responsibility for the Cold War, especially its global aspects. See, for example, **W. La Feber,** *America, Russia, and the Cold War, 1945–1966,* 8th ed. (New York, 2002). For a highly competent retrospective analysis of the Cold War era, see **J. L. Gaddis,** *We Now Know: Rethinking Cold War History* (Oxford, 1997). Also see his more general work *The Cold War: A New History* (New York, 2005).

A number of studies of the early stages of the Cold War are based on documents unavailable until the late 1980s or early 1990s. See, for example, **G. Behrman,** *The Most Noble Adventure: The Marshall Plan and the Time When America Helped Save Europe* (New York, 2007) and **O. A. Westad,** *Cold War and Revolution: Soviet-American Rivalry and the Origins of the Chinese Civil War* (New York, 1993). On the

Korean War, see **Chen Jian,** *China's Road to the Korean War: The Making of the Sino-American Confrontation* (New York, 1994) and **S. Goncharov, J. W. Lewis,** and **Xue Litai,** *Uncertain Partners: Stalin, Mao, and the Korean War* (Stanford, Calif., 1993). For a perspective that places much of the blame for the Korean War on the United States, see **B. Cumings,** *The Korean War: A History* (New York, 2010).

CHINA   There are several informative surveys of Chinese foreign policy since the Communist rise to power. A particularly insightful account is **Chen Jian,** *Mao's China and the Cold War* (Chapel Hill, N.C., 2001). For a defense of Chiang Kai-shek's efforts to prevent a Communist takeover of China, see **J. Taylor,** *The Generalissimo: Chiang Kai-shek and the Struggle for Modern China* (Cambridge, Mass., 2011). On Chinese policy in Korea, see **Shu Guang Zhang,** *Mao's Military Romanticism: China and the Korean War* (Lawrence, Kans., 2001), and **Xiaobing Li et al.,** *Mao's Generals Remember Korea* (Lawrence, Kans., 2001). On Sino-Vietnamese relations, see **Ang Cheng Guan,** *Vietnamese Communists' Relations with China and the Second Indochina Conflict* (Jefferson, N.C., 1997).

THE COLD WAR ENDS   Two recent works that deal with the end of the Cold War are the gripping account by **M. E. Sarotte,** *1989: The Struggle to Create Post–Cold War Europe* (Princeton, N.J., 2009), and **V. Sebestyen,** *Revolution 1989: The Fall of the Soviet Empire* (New York, 2009).

Chapter Notes

1. Quoted in *Department of State Bulletin,* February 11, 1945, pp. 213–216.
2. Quoted in J. M. Jones, *The Fifteen Weeks (February 21–June 5, 1947),* 2nd ed. (New York, 1964), pp. 140–141.
3. Quoted in M. Glenny, *The Balkans: Nationalism, War, and the Great Powers* (New York, 1999), pp. 543–544.
4. Cited in the *New York Review of Books,* June 9, 2011, p. 71.
5. V. Sebestyen, *Revolution 1989: The Fall of the Soviet Empire* (New York, 2009), p. 91.

 MindTap™

MindTap is a fully online, highly personalized learning experience built upon Cengage Learning content. MindTap combines student learning tools—readings, multimedia, activities, and assessments—into a singular Learning Path that guides students through their course.

27

Brave New World: Communism on Trial

Shopping in Moscow

© William J. Duiker

CHAPTER OUTLINE AND FOCUS QUESTIONS

The Postwar Soviet Union

Q How did Nikita Khrushchev change the system that the Soviet dictator Joseph Stalin had put in place before his death in 1953? To what degree did his successors adopt Khrushchev's policies?

The Disintegration of the Soviet Empire

Q What were the key components of *perestroika*, which Mikhail Gorbachev espoused during the 1980s? Why did it fail?

The East Is Red: China Under Communism

Q What were Mao Zedong's chief goals for China, and what policies did he institute to try to achieve them?

"Serve the People": Chinese Society Under Communism

Q What significant political, economic, and social changes have taken place in China since the death of Mao Zedong? How successful have they been at improving the quality of life in China?

CRITICAL THINKING

Q Why has communism survived in China when it failed to survive in Eastern Europe and Russia? Are Chinese leaders justified in claiming that without party leadership, the country would fall into chaos?

CONNECTIONS TO TODAY

Q Do China's successes in raising the standard of living of the Chinese people over the last thirty years compensate for the continuing lack of individual freedom in the People's Republic of China today? If not, why not?

ACCORDING TO KARL MARX, capitalism is a system that involves the exploitation of man by man; under socialism, it is the other way around. That wry joke was typical of popular humor in post–World War II Moscow, where the dreams of a future utopia had faded in the grim reality of life in the Soviet Union.

For the average Soviet citizen after World War II, few images better displayed the shortcomings of the Soviet system than a long line of people queuing up outside an official state store selling consumer goods. Because the command economy was so inefficient, items of daily use were chronically in such short supply that when a particular item became available, people often lined up immediately to buy several for themselves and their friends.

Despite the evident weaknesses of the centralized Soviet economy, the Communist monopoly on power seemed secure, as did Moscow's hold over its client states in Eastern Europe. In fact, for three decades after the end of World War II, the Soviet empire appeared to be a permanent feature of the international landscape. But by the early 1980s, it had become clear that there were cracks in the Kremlin wall. The Soviet economy was stagnant, the minority nationalities were restive, and Eastern European leaders were increasingly emboldened to test the waters of the global capitalist marketplace. In the United States, the newly elected president, Ronald Reagan, boldly predicted the imminent collapse of the "evil empire."

At the time many observers questioned that prediction but it soon seemed uncannily clairvoyant. Within a span of less than three years (1989–1991), the Soviet Union ceased to exist as a nation as Russia and other former Soviet republics declared their separate independence, communist regimes in Eastern Europe were toppled, and the long-standing division of postwar Europe came to an end.

The fate of communism in China has been quite different. Despite some turbulence, the Communist Party has managed to retain power in China, even as that nation takes giant strides toward becoming an economic superpower. Yet as China's leaders struggle to bring the nation into the modern age, many of the essential principles of Marxist-Leninist dogma have been tacitly abandoned, and cynicism among the nation's youth is widespread. Whether communism will continue to provide a realistic framework for the challenges that lie ahead remains an open question. The "brave new world" forecast by Karl Marx remains but a figment of his imagination. ✦

The Postwar Soviet Union

FOCUS QUESTIONS: How did Nikita Khrushchev change the system that the Soviet dictator Joseph Stalin had put in place before his death in 1953? To what degree did his successors adopt Khrushchev's policies?

At the end of World War II, the Soviet Union was one of the world's two superpowers, and its leader, Joseph Stalin, was in a position of strength. He and his Soviet colleagues were now in control of a vast empire (see Map 27.1) that included Eastern Europe, much of the Balkans, and new territory gained from Japan in East Asia.

From Stalin to Khrushchev

World War II devastated the Soviet Union. Twenty million citizens lost their lives, and cities such as Kiev (KEE-yev), Kharkov (KHAR-kawf), and Leningrad suffered enormous physical destruction. As the lands that had been occupied by the German forces were liberated, the Soviet government turned its attention to restoring their economic structures. Nevertheless, in 1945, agricultural production was only 60 percent and steel output only 50 percent of prewar levels. The Soviet people faced incredibly difficult conditions: they worked longer hours than before the war, ate less, and were ill-housed and poorly clothed.

STALINISM IN ACTION   In the immediate postwar years, the Soviet Union removed goods and materials from occupied Germany and extorted valuable raw materials from its satellite states in Eastern Europe. More important, however, to create a new industrial base, Stalin returned to the method he had used in the 1930s—the extraction of development capital from Soviet labor. Working hard for little pay and for precious few consumer goods, Soviet laborers were expected to produce goods for export with little in return for themselves. The incoming capital from abroad could then be used to purchase machinery and Western technology. The loss of millions of men in the war meant that much of this tremendous workload fell on Soviet women, who performed almost 40 percent of the heavy manual labor.

The pace of economic recovery in the years immediately after the war was impressive. By 1947, industrial production had attained 1939 levels; three years later, it had surpassed those levels by 40 percent. New power plants, canals, and giant factories were built, and industrial enterprises and oil fields were established in Siberia and Soviet Central Asia. Stalin's new five-year plan, announced in 1946, reached its goals in less than five years.

Although Stalin's economic strategy was successful in promoting growth in heavy industry, primarily for the benefit of the military, consumer goods remained scarce, and long-suffering Soviet citizens were still being asked to sacrifice for a better tomorrow. The development of thermonuclear weapons, MIG fighter planes, and the first space satellite (*Sputnik*) in the 1950s may have elevated the nation's reputation as a world power abroad, but domestically, the people of the Soviet Union were shortchanged. Heavy industry grew at a rate three times that of personal consumption. Moreover, housing was in short supply, and living conditions were especially difficult in the overcrowded cities.

When World War II ended in 1945, Stalin had been in power for more than fifteen years. During that time, he had quashed all opposition to his rule and emerged as the undisputed master of the Soviet Union. Political terror enforced by several hundred thousand secret police ensured that he would remain in power. By the late 1940s, an estimated 9 million Soviet citizens were in Siberian concentration camps or were employed as slave laborers elsewhere in the Soviet Union.

Increasingly distrustful of potential competitors, Stalin exercised sole authority and pitted his subordinates against one another. His morbid suspicions extended to even his closest colleagues. In 1948, Andrei Zhdanov (ahn-DRAY ZHDAH-nawf), his presumed successor and head of the Leningrad party organization, died under mysterious circumstances, almost certainly at Stalin's order. Within weeks, the Leningrad party organization was purged of several top leaders, many of whom were accused of having traitorous connections with Western intelligence agencies. Stalin was especially suspicious of Jewish doctors, whom he suspected of secret ties with international Jewish organizations or even to Western intelligence agencies.

In succeeding years, Stalin directed his suspicions at other members of the inner circle, including Foreign Minister Vyacheslav Molotov. Known as "Old Stone Butt" to Western

MAP 27.1 **Eastern Europe and the Soviet Union.** After World War II, the boundaries of Eastern Europe were redrawn as a result of Allied agreements reached at the Tehran and Yalta Conferences. This map shows the new boundaries that were established throughout the region, placing Soviet power at the center of Europe.

Q *How had the boundaries changed from the prewar era?*

diplomats for his stubborn defense of Soviet security interests, Molotov had been a loyal lieutenant since the early years of Stalin's rise to power. Now Stalin distrusted Molotov and had his Jewish wife sent to a Siberian concentration camp. This intimidated virtually all of Stalin's colleagues. As Stalin remarked mockingly on one occasion, "When I die, the imperialists will strangle all of you like a litter of kittens."[1]

Stalin died—under mysterious circumstances—in 1953 and, after some bitter infighting within the party leadership, was succeeded by Georgy Malenkov, a veteran administrator and ambitious member of the Politburo (POL-it-byoor-oh), the party's governing body. Malenkov came to power with a clear agenda. In foreign affairs, he hoped to promote an easing of Cold War tensions and improve relations with the Western powers. For Moscow's Eastern European allies, he advocated a so-called **new course** in their mutual relations and a decline in Stalinist methods of rule. Inside the Soviet Union, he hoped to reduce defense expenditures and improve the standard of

living. Such goals probably had the support of the majority of the population but they did not necessarily appeal to key groups, including the army, the Communist Party, the managerial elite, and the security services (now known as the Committee on Government Security, or KGB). Malenkov was soon dismissed from his position, and power shifted to his rival, the new party general secretary, Nikita Khrushchev.

THE RISE AND FALL OF KHRUSHCHEV During the struggle for power with Malenkov, Khrushchev had outmaneuvered his rival by calling for heightened defense expenditures and a continuing emphasis on heavy industry. Once in power, however, Khrushchev showed the dexterity displayed by many American politicians and reversed his priorities. He now resumed the efforts of his predecessor to reduce tensions with the West and boost the standard of living of the Soviet people. He moved vigorously to improve the performance of the Soviet economy and revitalize Soviet society. By nature, Khrushchev was a man of enormous energy and creativity. In an attempt to release the stranglehold of the central bureaucracy over the national economy, he abolished dozens of government ministries and split up the party and government apparatus. Khrushchev also sought to rejuvenate the stagnant agricultural sector, long the Achilles's heel of the Soviet economy. He tried to spur industrial and agricultural production by increasing profit incentives and opened thousands of acres in Soviet Kazakhstan (ka-zak-STAN or kuh-zahk-STAHN) to cultivation.

Like any innovator, however, Khrushchev had to overcome the inherently conservative instincts of the Soviet bureaucracy, as well as of the mass of the Soviet population. His plan to remove the "dead hand" of the state, however laudable in intent, alienated much of the Soviet official class, and his effort to split the Communist Party angered those who saw it as the central force in the Soviet system. Khrushchev's agricultural schemes inspired similar opposition. Although the Kazakhstan wheat lands would eventually demonstrate their importance, progress was slow, and his effort to persuade Soviet citizens to eat more corn (an idea he had apparently picked up during a visit to the United States) earned him the mocking nickname "Cornman." The combination of disappointing agricultural production and high military spending hurt the Soviet economy. The industrial growth rate, which had soared in the early 1950s, now declined dramatically, from 13 percent annually in 1953 to 7.5 percent in 1964.

Khrushchev was probably best known for his policy of **de-Stalinization**. As a protégé of Stalin, he had risen rapidly in the party hierarchy but he had been deeply disturbed by his mentor's excesses and, once in a position of authority, moved to excise the Stalinist legacy from Soviet society. The campaign began at the Twentieth National Congress of the Communist Party in February 1956, when Khrushchev gave a long speech in private criticizing some of Stalin's major shortcomings. The speech apparently had not been intended for public distribution but it was quickly leaked to the Western press and created a sensation throughout the world (see the box "Khrushchev Denounces Stalin" on p. 795). During the next few years, Khrushchev encouraged more freedom for writers, artists, and composers, arguing that "readers should be given the chance to make their own judgments" about the acceptability of controversial literature and that "police measures shouldn't be used."[2] Under Khrushchev's instructions, thousands of prisoners were released from concentration camps.

Khrushchev's personality and behavior, however, did not endear him to higher Soviet officials, who frowned at his tendency to crack jokes and play the clown. Nor were the higher members of the party bureaucracy pleased when Khrushchev tried to curb their privileges. Foreign policy failures further damaged Khrushchev's reputation among his colleagues. His plan to install missiles in Cuba was the final straw (see Chapter 26). While he was on vacation in 1964, a special meeting of the Soviet Politburo voted him out of office (citing "deteriorating health") and forced him into retirement. Although a team of leaders succeeded him, real power came into the hands of Leonid Brezhnev (1906–1982), the "trusted" supporter of Khrushchev who had engineered his downfall.

The Brezhnev Years (1964–1982)

The ouster of Nikita Khrushchev in October 1964 vividly demonstrated the challenges that would be encountered by any leader sufficiently bold to try to reform the Soviet system. In democratic countries, pressure on the government comes from various sources in society at large—the business community and labor unions, innumerable interest groups, and the general public. In the Soviet Union, pressure on government and party leaders originated from sources essentially operating inside the system—the government bureaucracy, the party apparatus, the KGB, and the armed forces.

Leonid Brezhnev, the new party chief, was undoubtedly aware of these realities of Soviet politics, and his long tenure in power was marked, above all, by the desire to avoid changes that might provoke instability, either at home or abroad. Brezhnev was himself a product of the Soviet system. He had entered the ranks of the party leadership under Stalin, and although he was not a particularly avid believer in party ideology—indeed, there were innumerable stories about his addiction to "bourgeois pleasures," including expensive country houses and fast cars (many of them gifts from foreign leaders)—he was no partisan of reform.

Still, Brezhnev sought domestic stability. He and his prime minister, Alexei Kosygin, undertook what might be described as a program of "de-Khrushchevization," returning the responsibility for long-term planning to the central ministries and reuniting the Communist Party apparatus. Despite some cautious attempts to stimulate the stagnant agricultural sector, there was no effort to revise the basic system of collective farms. In the industrial sector, the regime launched a series of reforms designed to give factory managers (themselves employees of the state) more responsibility for setting prices, wages, and production quotas. These "Kosygin reforms" had little effect, however, because they were stubbornly resisted by the bureaucracy and were adopted by relatively few enterprises in the vast state-owned industrial sector.

A CONTROLLED SOCIETY Brezhnev also initiated a significant retreat from Khrushchev's policy of de-Stalinization. Criticism of the "Great Leader" had angered conservatives both within the party hierarchy and among the public at large, many of whom still revered Stalin as a hero and a defender of Mother Russia against Nazi Germany. Many influential figures in the Kremlin feared that de-Stalinization could lead to internal instability and a decline in public trust in the legitimacy of party leadership—the hallowed "dictatorship of the proletariat." Early in Brezhnev's reign, Stalin's reputation began to revive. Although his alleged shortcomings were not totally ignored, he was now described in the official press as "an outstanding party leader" who had been primarily responsible for the successes achieved by the Soviet Union. Many ordinary Soviet citizens, who had been bombarded for decades with propaganda about the achievements of their "little father," undoubtedly agreed.

The regime also adopted a more restrictive policy toward dissidents in Soviet society. Critics of the Soviet system, such as the physicist Andrei Sakharov (ahn-DRAY SAH-kuh-rawf),

Khrushchev Denounces Stalin

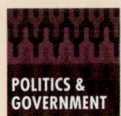

POLITICS & GOVERNMENT

THREE YEARS AFTER STALIN'S DEATH, the new Soviet premier, Nikita Khrushchev, addressed the Twentieth Congress of the Communist Party and denounced the former Soviet dictator for his crimes. This denunciation was the beginning of a policy of de-Stalinization. When it was secretly leaked to Western news organizations, it provoked excited debate in countries around the world and great consternation among conservative elements in the Soviet Union. One member of the Congress reportedly died of a heart attack shortly after the speech.

Khrushchev Addresses the Twentieth Party Congress, February 1956

A lot has been said about the cult of the individual and about its harmful consequences.... The cult of the person of Stalin ... became at a certain specific stage the source of a whole series of exceedingly serious and grave perversions of Party principles, of Party democracy, of revolutionary legality.

Stalin absolutely did not tolerate collegiality in leadership and in work and ... practiced brutal violence, not only toward everything which opposed him, but also toward that which seemed, to his capricious and despotic character, contrary to his concepts.

Stalin abandoned the method of ideological struggle for that of administrative violence, mass repressions and terror.... Arbitrary behavior by one person encouraged and permitted arbitrariness in others. Mass arrests and deportations of many thousands of people, execution without trial and without normal investigation created conditions of insecurity, fear, and even desperation.

Stalin showed in a whole series of cases his intolerance, his brutality, and his abuse of power.... He often chose the path of repression and annihilation, not only against actual enemies, but also against individuals who had not committed any crimes against the Party and the Soviet government....

Many Party, Soviet, and economic activists who were branded in 1937 and 1938 as "enemies" were actually never enemies, spies, wreckers, and so on, but were always honest communists; they were only so stigmatized, and often, no longer able to bear barbaric tortures, they charged themselves (at the order of the investigative judges-falsifiers) with all kinds of grave and unlikely crimes.

This was the result of the abuse of power by Stalin, who began to use mass terror against the Party cadres.... Stalin put the Party and the NKVD [the Soviet police agency] up to the use of mass terror when the exploiting classes had been liquidated in our country and when there were no serious reasons for the use of extraordinary mass terror. The terror was directed ... against the honest workers of the Party and the Soviet state....

Stalin was a very distrustful man, sickly, suspicious.... Everywhere and in everything he saw "enemies," "two-facers," and "spies." Possessing unlimited power, he indulged in great willfulness and choked a person morally and physically. A situation was created where one could not express one's own will. When Stalin said that one or another would be arrested, it was necessary to accept on faith that he was an "enemy of the people." What proofs were offered? The confession of the arrested.... How is it possible that a person confesses to crimes that he had not committed? Only in one way—because of application of physical methods of pressuring him, tortures, bringing him to a state of unconsciousness, deprivation of his judgment, taking away of his human dignity.

 What were the key charges that Khrushchev made against Stalin? Can it be said that Khrushchev corrected these problems?

Source: From *Congressional Record*, 84th Congress, 2nd Session, Vol. 102, Part 7, pp. 9389–9402 (June 4, 1956).

---

were harassed and arrested or, like the famous writer Alexander Solzhenitsyn (sohl-zhuh-NEET-sin), forced to leave the country. There was also a return to the anti-Semitic policies and attitudes that had marked the Stalin era. Other minorities, such as ethnic Germans and Muslims in the republics of Central Asia, suffered as well. Such indications of renewed repression aroused concern in the West and were instrumental in the inclusion by Western diplomats of a statement on human rights in the 1975 Helsinki Accords (see Chapter 26).

Free expression was also restricted. Organized religion was attacked as contrary to the principles of Marxist orthodoxy, and attendance at churches was severely discouraged. The media were controlled by the state and presented only what the state wanted people to hear. The two major newspapers, *Pravda* ("Truth") and *Izvestia* ("News"), were the agents of the party and the government, respectively. Cynics joked that there was no news in *Pravda* (PRAHV-duh) and no truth in *Izvestia* (iz-VESS-tee-uh). According to Western journalists, airplane accidents in the Soviet Union were rarely publicized, out of concern that they would raise questions about the quality of the Soviet airline industry. Shortly after the disaster at the Chernobyl (chur-NOH-buhl) nuclear plant in 1986, a Soviet official testily assured me that foreign news reports about the seriousness of the incident were just Western propaganda. He was only repeating the official line.

The government also made strenuous efforts to prevent the Soviet people from being exposed to harmful foreign ideas, especially modern art, literature, and rock music. When the Summer Olympic Games were held in Moscow in 1980, Soviet newspapers advised citizens to keep their children indoors to prevent them from being polluted with "bourgeois" ideas passed on by foreign visitors. But the latter effort proved

St. Basil's Cathedral in Moscow. Constructed in the sixteenth century at the order of Ivan the Terrible, St. Basil's Cathedral was the spiritual center of the Russian Orthodox Church until 1917, when it was converted into a state museum as part of the Soviet regime's effort to stamp out the influence of religion in Russia. For seven decades, the practice of any form of religious faith, whether Christian, Muslim, or Jewish, was stringently suppressed.

fruitless, as Soviet adolescents nonetheless became enamored of forbidden Western rock music and clothing styles.

For citizens of Western democracies, such a political atmosphere would seem highly oppressive but for the Russian people, an emphasis on law and order (*poryadok* (pohr-YA-dok) in Russian) was an accepted aspect of everyday life inherited from the tsarist period. It was firmly enshrined in the Soviet constitution, in which individual freedom was subordinated to the interests of the state (see the box "The Rights and Duties of Soviet Citizens" on p. 797). Conformity was the rule in virtually every corner of Soviet society, from the educational system (characterized at all levels by rote memorization and political indoctrination) to child rearing (it was forbidden, for example, to be left-handed) and even to yearly vacations (most workers took their vacations at resorts run by their employer, where the daily schedule of activities was highly regimented). Young Americans studying in the Soviet Union reported that their Soviet friends were often shocked to hear U.S. citizens criticizing their own president.

A STAGNANT ECONOMY Soviet leaders also failed to achieve their objective of revitalizing the national economy. Whereas growth rates during the early Khrushchev era had been impressive (prompting Khrushchev during a 1956 reception at the Kremlin to chortle to an American guest, "We will bury you"), under Brezhnev industrial growth declined to an annual rate of less than 4 percent in the early 1970s and less than 3 percent in the period from 1975 to 1980. Successes in the agricultural sector were equally meager. Grain production rose from less than 90 million tons in the early 1950s to nearly 200 million tons in the 1970s but then stagnated at that level.

One of the primary problems with the Soviet economy was the absence of incentives. Salary structures offered little reward for hard labor and extraordinary achievement. Pay differentials operated in a much narrower range than in most Western societies, and there was little danger of being dismissed. According to the Soviet constitution, every Soviet citizen was guaranteed an opportunity to work.

There were, of course, some exceptions to this general rule. Athletic achievement was highly prized, and a gymnast of Olympic stature would receive great rewards in the form of prestige and lifestyle. Senior officials did not receive high salaries but were provided with countless perquisites, such as access to foreign goods, official automobiles with chauffeurs, and entry into prestigious institutions of higher learning for their children. For the elite, it was *blat* (influence) that most often differentiated them from the rest of the population. The average citizen, however, had little material incentive to produce beyond the minimum acceptable level. It is hardly surprising that per capita productivity was only about half that realized in most capitalist countries. At the same time, the rudeness of Soviet clerks and waiters became legendary.

The problem of incentives existed at the managerial level as well, where centralized planning discouraged initiative and innovation. Factory managers, for example, were assigned monthly and annual quotas by the **Gosplan** (gaws-PLAHN)—the "state plan" drawn up by the central planning commission. Because state-owned factories faced little or no competition, managers did not care whether their products were competitive in terms of price and quality, as long as the quota was attained. One of the key complaints of Soviet citizens was the low quality of domestic consumer goods. Knowledgeable consumers quickly discovered that products manufactured at the end of the month were often of lower quality (because factory workers had to rush to meet their quotas) and sought to avoid purchasing them.

Often consumer goods were simply unavailable. Whenever Soviet citizens saw a queue forming in front of a store, they automatically got in line, often without even knowing what people were lining up for, because they never knew when that item might be available again. When they reached the head of the line, most would purchase several of the same item in order to swap with their friends and neighbors. This "queue psychology," of course, was a time-consuming process and inevitably served to reduce the per capita rate of productivity.

Soviet citizens often tried to overcome the shortcomings of the system by resorting to the black market (buying "on the left," in Soviet parlance). Private economic activities, of course, were illegal, but many workers took to moonlighting

The Rights and Duties of Soviet Citizens

POLITICS & GOVERNMENT

IN THE SOVIET UNION, and in other countries modeled on the Soviet system, the national constitution was viewed not as a timeless document, but as a reflection of conditions at the time it was framed. As Soviet society advanced from a state of "raw communism" to a fully socialist society, new constitutions were drafted to reflect the changes taking place in society as a whole. The first two constitutions of the Soviet Union, promulgated in 1924 and 1936, declared that the state was a "dictatorship of the proletariat" guided by the Communist Party, the vanguard organization of the working class in the Soviet Union. But the so-called Brezhnev constitution of 1977 described the Soviet Union as a "state of all the people," composed of workers, farmers, and "socialist intellectuals," although it confirmed the role of the Communist Party as the "leading force" in society. The provisions from the 1977 constitution presented here illustrate some of the freedoms and obligations of Soviet citizens. Especially noteworthy are Articles 39 and 62, which suggest that the interests and prestige of the state took precedence over individual liberties.

The Soviet Constitution of 1977

Chapter 1: The Political System

Article 6. The leading and guiding force of the Soviet society and the nucleus of its political system, of all state organizations and public organizations, is the Communist Party of the Soviet Union. The CPSU exists for the people and serves the people.

The Communist Party, armed with Marxism-Leninism, determines the general perspectives of the development of society and the course of the home and foreign policy of the USSR, directs the great constructive work of the Soviet people, and imparts a planned, systematic, and theoretically substantiated character to their struggle for the victory of communism.

Chapter 6: Equality of Citizens' Rights

Article 35. Women and men have equal rights in the USSR. Exercise of these rights is ensured by according women equal access with men to education and vocational and professional training, equal opportunities in employment, remuneration and promotion, and in social and political, and cultural activity, and by the special labor and health protection measures for women; by providing conditions enabling mothers to work; by legal protection, and material and moral support for mothers and children, including paid leaves and other benefits for expectant mothers and mothers, and gradual reduction of working time for mothers with small children.

Chapter 7: The Basic Rights, Freedoms, and Duties of Citizens of the USSR

Article 39. Citizens of the USSR enjoy in full the social, economic, political, and personal rights and freedoms proclaimed and guaranteed by the Constitution of the USSR and by Soviet laws. The socialist system ensures enlargement of the rights and freedoms of citizens and continuous improvement of their living standards as social, economic, and cultural development programs are fulfilled. Enjoyment by citizens of their rights and freedoms must not be to the detriment of the interests of society or the state, or infringe the rights of other citizens.

Article 62. Citizens of the USSR are obliged to safeguard the interests of the Soviet state, and to enhance its power and prestige. Defense of the Socialist Motherland is the sacred duty of every citizen of the USSR. Betrayal of the Motherland is the gravest of crimes against the people.

 Which of these provisions would seem out of place if they were to appear in the Constitution of the United States?

Source: Excerpts from *The Soviet Constitution of 1977*. Novosti Press Agency Publishing House. Moscow, 1985.

---

to augment their meager salaries. An employee in a state-run appliance store, for example, would promise to repair a customer's television set on his own time in return for a payment "under the table." Otherwise, servicing of the set might require several weeks. Knowledgeable observers estimated that as much as one-third of the entire Soviet economy operated outside the legal system.

Another major obstacle to economic growth was primitive technology. Except in the area of national defense, the overall level of Soviet technology was not comparable to that of the West or the advanced industrial societies of East Asia. Part of the problem stemmed from issues already described. With no competition, factory managers had little incentive to improve the quality of their products. But another reason was the high

priority assigned to national defense. The military sector regularly received the most resources from the government and attracted the cream of the country's scientific talent.

AN AGING LEADERSHIP Such problems would be intimidating for any government but they were particularly so for the elderly generation of party leaders surrounding Leonid Brezhnev, many of whom were cautious to a fault. Though some undoubtedly recognized the need for reform and innovation, they were paralyzed by the fear of instability and change. The problem worsened during the late 1970s when Brezhnev's health began to deteriorate.

Brezhnev died in November 1982 and was succeeded by Yuri Andropov (YOOR-ee ahn-DRAHP-awf) (1914–1984), a party veteran and head of the Soviet secret services. During his brief tenure as party chief, Andropov was a vocal advocate of reform but most of his initiatives were limited to the familiar nostrums of punishment for wrongdoers and moral exhortations to Soviet citizens to work harder. At the same time, material incentives were still officially discouraged and generally ineffective. Andropov had been ailing when he was selected to succeed Brezhnev as party chief, and when he died after only a few months in office, little had been done to change the system. He was succeeded by a mediocre party stalwart, the elderly Konstantin Chernenko (kuhn-stuhn-TEEN chirn-YEN-koh) (1911–1985). With the Soviet system in crisis, Moscow seemed stuck in a time warp. As one concerned observer told an American journalist, "I had a sense of foreboding, like before a storm. That there was something brewing in people and there would be a time when they would say, 'That's it. We can't go on living like this. We can't. We need to redo everything.'"[3]

Cultural Expression in the Soviet Union

In his occasional musings about the future Communist utopia, Karl Marx had predicted that a new, classless society would replace the exploitative and hierarchical systems of feudalism and capitalism. Workers would engage in productive activities and share equally in the fruits of their labor. In their free time, they would produce a new, advanced culture, proletarian in character and egalitarian in content.

The reality in the post–World War II Soviet Union was somewhat different. Under Stalin, the Soviet cultural scene was a wasteland. Beginning in 1946, a series of government decrees made all forms of literary and scientific expression dependent on the state. All Soviet culture was expected to follow the party line. Historians, philosophers, and social scientists all grew accustomed to quoting Marx, Lenin, and, above all, Stalin as their chief authorities. Novels and plays, too, were supposed to portray Communist heroes and their efforts to create a better society. No criticism of existing social conditions was permitted. Even distinguished composers such as Dmitry Shostakovich (dih-MEE-tree shahs-tuh-KOH-vich) were compelled to heed Stalin's criticisms, including his view that contemporary Western music was nothing but a "mishmash." Some areas of intellectual activity were virtually abolished; the science of genetics disappeared, and few movies were made during Stalin's final years.

Stalin's death brought a modest respite from cultural repression. Writers and artists banned during the Stalin years were again allowed to publish, in an era known, from the title of a contemporary novel, as "the Thaw." Still, Soviet authorities, including Khrushchev, were reluctant to allow cultural freedom to move far beyond official Soviet ideology.

These restrictions, however, did not prevent the emergence of some significant Soviet literature, although authors paid a heavy price if they alienated the Soviet authorities. Boris Pasternak (buh-REESS PASS-tur-nak) (1890–1960), who began his literary career as a poet, won the Nobel Prize in 1958 mainly for his celebrated novel *Doctor Zhivago*, published in Italy in 1957. But the Soviet government condemned Pasternak's allegedly anti-Soviet tendencies, banned the novel, and would not allow him to accept the prize. The author had alienated the authorities by describing a society scarred by the excesses of Bolshevik revolutionary zeal.

Alexander Solzhenitsyn (1918–2008) caused an even greater furor than Pasternak. Solzhenitsyn had spent eight years in forced labor camps for criticizing Stalin, and his novel *One Day in the Life of Ivan Denisovich*, one of the works for which he won the Nobel Prize in 1970, was an account of life in those camps. Khrushchev allowed the book's publication as part of his de-Stalinization campaign. In 1973, Solzhenitsyn's *Gulag Archipelago*, a detailed indictment of the whole system of Soviet oppression, was published in the West. Soviet authorities denounced Solzhenitsyn's efforts to inform the world of Soviet crimes against humanity and expelled him from the Soviet Union in the same year.

Although restrictive policies continued into the late 1980s, some Soviet authors learned how to minimize battles with the censors by writing under the guise of humor or fantasy. Two of the most accomplished and popular Soviet novelists of the period, Yury Trifonov (YOOR-ee trih-FAH-nawf) (1925–1981) and Fazil Iskander (fah-ZUHL is-KAN-der) (b. 1929), focused on the daily struggle of Soviet citizens to live with dignity. Trifonov depicted the everyday life of ordinary Russians with grim realism, while Iskander used humor to poke fun at the incompetence of the Soviet regime.

Soviet citizens did enjoy some of the many advances in modern popular culture experienced elsewhere. By the early 1970s, there were 28 million television sets in the Soviet Union, although state authorities controlled the content of the programs that the Soviet people watched. Tourism, too, made inroads into the communist world as state-run industries provided vacation time and governments established resorts for workers on the Black Sea and Adriatic coasts. Spectator sports

© William J. Duiker

Stalinist Heroic: An Example of Socialist Realism. Under Stalin and his successors, art was assigned the task of indoctrinating the Soviet population on the public virtues, such as hard work, loyalty to the state, and patriotism. Grandiose statuary erected to commemorate the heroic efforts of the Red Army during World War II appeared in every Soviet city. Here is an example in Minsk, today the capital of Belarus.

became a large industry and were also highly politicized as a result of Cold War divisions. "Each new victory," one party leader stated, "is a victory for the Soviet form of society and the socialist sport system; it provides irrefutable proof of the superiority of socialist culture over the decaying culture of the capitalist states."[4] Accordingly, the state provided money for the construction of gymnasiums and training camps and portrayed athletes as superheroes.

Social Changes

According to Marxist doctrine, state control of industry and the elimination of private property were supposed to lead to a classless society. Although that ideal was never achieved, it did have important social consequences. For one thing, traditional ruling classes were stripped of their special status, and new elites appeared to take their place. Children of manual laborers now had preference over their middle-class counterparts in competition for employment and access to higher education. As time went on, most professional occupations, such as judges, academics, and industrial managers, came from working-class backgrounds. Education, in fact, became crucial in preparing for new jobs in the communist system and led to higher enrollments in both secondary schools and universities.

By the 1970s, however, the situation began to change, as these new elites, regardless of class background, realized the importance of higher education and used their power to gain special privileges for their children. By 1971, 60 percent of the children of white-collar workers attended university, and even though blue-collar families constituted 60 percent of the population, only 36 percent of their children attended institutions of higher learning.

This shift in educational preferences demonstrates yet another aspect of the social structure in the communist world: the emergence of a new privileged class, made up of members of the Communist Party, state officials, high-ranking officers in the military and the secret police, and a few special professional groups. The new elite not only possessed political power but also received special privileges, including the right to purchase high-quality goods in special stores, paid vacations at special resorts, access to good housing and superior medical services, and advantages in education and jobs for their children. In 1980, in one Soviet province, 70 percent of Communist Party members came from the families of managers, technicians, and government and party bureaucrats.

WOMEN IN THE SOVIET UNION The system also failed to measure up in its treatment of women. Long after the Bolshevik Revolution had called for true equality of the sexes, men continued to dominate the leadership positions of the Communist Party and the government. Women did have greater opportunities in the workforce and even in the professions, however, and women comprised 51 percent of the labor force in 1980; by the mid-1980s, they constituted 50 percent of the engineers, 80 percent of the doctors, and 75 percent of the teachers and teachers' aides. But many of these were low-paying jobs; most female doctors, for example, worked in primary care and were paid less than skilled machinists. The chief administrators in hospitals and schools were still men.

Moreover, although women made up nearly half of the workforce, they were still expected to fulfill their traditional roles in the home. Most women worked what came to be known as the "double shift." After spending eight hours in their jobs, they came home to do the housework and take care of the children. They might spend another two hours a day in long lines at a number of stores waiting to buy food and clothes. Because of the scarcity of housing, they had to use kitchens that were shared by a number of families.

Nearly three-quarters of a century after the Bolshevik Revolution, then, the Marxist dream of an advanced, egalitarian society was as far off as ever. Although in some respects conditions in the Soviet Union were better than before World War II, many problems and inequities were as intransigent as ever.

Social Conditions in the Eastern European Satellites

The imposition of Marxist systems in Eastern Europe had far-reaching social consequences. Most Eastern European countries made the change from peasant societies to industrial economies. The agricultural sector was collectivized, and millions of farmers moved to the cities to obtain employment in the new state-run factories established by their regimes to provide consumer goods for a changing economy. But the lack of incentives was, as usual, a serious drawback. "We pretend to work," as the sardonic joke had it, "and they pretend to pay us."

Still, during the first decades after World War II, most Eastern European countries experienced some improvement in their standard of living as salaries rose and consumer goods became more widely available. Education became more widely available and, as in the Soviet Union, was crucial in providing trained workers for the region's new industrializing economies. To strengthen the effort to build a future classless society, preferences in employment and educational opportunities were provided to children from the lower classes of society, while members of the traditional elite in all Eastern European countries were subject to restrictions, and sometimes even exposed to punishment because of their class background.

Cultural freedoms in Eastern Europe varied from country to country. In Poland, intellectuals had access to Western publications as well as greater freedom to travel to the West. Hungary and Yugoslavia, as well, tolerated a certain level of intellectual activity that was frowned upon but not prohibited. After the Soviet invasion of Czechoslovakia in 1968, however, the local regimes followed a policy of strict control, and dissident activities were stringently prohibited. Such was also the case in Bulgaria and Romania, where Stalinist leaders maintained stringent limitations on any aspect of individual freedoms.

© William J. Duiker

Stalin's Wedding Cake. During the Stalinist era, architects in the Soviet Union and in Moscow's satellites in Eastern Europe were ordered to build grandiose public structures that represented a mixture of Classical, Gothic, and Baroque styles and reflected the hubris of the early Soviet period. One of the most notorious of such buildings was the Palace of Culture, built in the 1950s in the Polish capital of Warsaw. Local residents joked that the best view of the city could be seen from atop the palace because one could not see the building from there.

The Disintegration of the Soviet Empire

Q **FOCUS QUESTIONS:** What were the key components of *perestroika*, which Mikhail Gorbachev espoused during the 1980s? Why did it fail?

On the death of Konstantin Chernenko in 1985, party leaders selected a talented and youthful Soviet official, Mikhail Gorbachev, to succeed him. The new Soviet leader had shown early signs of promise. Born into a peasant family in 1931, Gorbachev combined farm work with education and received the Order of the Red Banner for his agricultural efforts. This award and his good school record enabled him to study law at the University of Moscow. After receiving his law degree in 1955, he returned to his native southern Russia, where he eventually became first secretary of the Communist Party in the city of Stavropol (STAH-vruh-puhl *or* stav-ROH-puhl)—he had joined the party in 1952—and then first secretary of the regional party committee. In 1978, Gorbachev was made a

member of the party's Central Committee in Moscow. Two years later, he became a full member of the ruling Politburo and secretary of the Central Committee.

During the early 1980s, Gorbachev began to realize the immensity of Soviet problems and the crucial need to transform the system. During a visit to Canada in 1983, he discovered to his astonishment that Canadian farmers worked hard on their own initiative. "We'll never have this for fifty years," he reportedly remarked.[5] On his return to Moscow, he set up a number of committees to evaluate the situation and recommend measures to improve the system.

The Gorbachev Era

With his election as party general secretary in 1985, Gorbachev seemed intent on taking earlier reforms to their logical conclusions. The cornerstone of his program was *perestroika* (per-uh-STROI-kuh), or "restructuring." At first it meant only a reordering of economic policy, as Gorbachev called for the beginning of a market economy with limited free enterprise and some private property (see the Comparative Illustration "Sideline Industries: Creeping Capitalism in a Socialist Paradise" on p. 813). Initial economic reforms were difficult to implement, however, and often led to unexpected difficulties. When the regime ended state control over the distribution of consumer goods, shortages developed and prices rose. Radicals criticized Gorbachev for his caution and demanded decisive measures; conservatives feared that rapid changes would be too painful. In his attempt to achieve compromise, Gorbachev often seemed indecisive and pursued partial liberalization, which satisfied neither faction and also failed to work, producing only more discontent.

Gorbachev soon perceived that in the Soviet system, the economy was intimately tied to the social and political spheres. Any efforts to reform the economy without political or social reform, he felt, would be doomed to failure. As a result, one of the most important instruments of *perestroika* was *glasnost* (GLAHZ-nohst), or "openness." Soviet citizens and officials were encouraged to openly discuss the strengths and weaknesses of the Soviet Union. The effects of this policy could be seen in *Pravda*, the official newspaper of the Communist Party, which began to report news of disasters such as the nuclear accident at Chernobyl in 1986 and collisions of ships in the Black Sea. This more liberal approach was soon extended to include reports of official corruption, sloppy factory work, and protests against government policy. Previously banned art works were now published, and motion pictures were allowed to depict negative aspects of Soviet life. Music based on Western styles, such as jazz and rock, could now be performed openly. Religious activities, long banned by the government, were once again tolerated.

Political reforms were equally revolutionary. In June 1987, the principle of two-candidate elections was introduced; previously, voters had been presented with only one choice. A year became increasingly skeptical of success. "Russia," one erst-while optimist lamented, "is not ready for democracy."

END OF EMPIRE One of Gorbachev's most serious problems stemmed from the nature of the Soviet Union. The Union of Soviet Socialist Republics was a truly multiethnic country, containing 92 nationalities and 112 recognized languages. Previously, the iron hand of the Communist Party, centered in Moscow, had kept a lid on the centuries-old ethnic tensions that had periodically erupted throughout the region. As Gorbachev released this iron grip, tensions resurfaced, a by-product of *glasnost* that Gorbachev had not anticipated. Ethnic groups took advantage of the new openness to protest what they perceived to be ethnically motivated slights. As violence erupted, nationalist movements surfaced in all fifteen republics of the Soviet Union. Often motivated by ethnic concerns, many of them called for sovereignty of the republics and independence from Russian-based rule centered in Moscow. The Soviet army, in disarray since the Soviet intervention in Afghanistan, appeared powerless to control the situation.

In December 1989, the Communist Party of Lithuania declared itself independent of the Communist Party of the Soviet Union. Gorbachev made it clear that he supported self-determination but not secession, which he believed would be detrimental to the Soviet Union. Nevertheless, on March 11, 1990, the Lithuanian Supreme Council unilaterally declared that the Lithuanian Soviet Socialist Republic was now the independent Lithuanian Republic. Four days later, the Soviet Congress of People's Deputies, though recognizing a general right to secede from the Union of Soviet Socialist Republics, proclaimed the Lithuanian declaration null and void, insisting that proper procedures must be followed before secession would be allowed. The Lithuanians ignored the decision.

For the next several months, Gorbachev struggled to cope with the problems unleashed by his reforms, seeking to appease conservative forces who complained about the growing disorder within the country while simultaneously trying to accommodate liberal elements who increasingly favored a new kind of decentralized Soviet federation. In so doing, he found a temporary ally in Boris Yeltsin (YELT-sun) (1931–2007), who had been elected president of the Russian Republic in June 1991.

By that time, conservatives within the army, the government, the KGB, and the military had grown increasingly worried about the possible dissolution of the Soviet Union and its impact on their own fortunes. On August 19, 1991, a group of these discontented rightists arrested Gorbachev and attempted to seize power. Gorbachev's unwillingness to work with the conspirators and the brave resistance in Moscow of Yeltsin and thousands of Russians who had grown accustomed to their new liberties caused the coup to fall apart rapidly. The actions of these right-wing plotters served to accelerate the very process they had hoped to stop—the disintegration of the Soviet Union.

Something Old, Something New. Under Soviet rule, church weddings were declared illegal, and marriage became a simple civil ceremony, lacking the ritual solemnity that religious sanctions had previously provided. With the advent of *glasnost* under Mikhail Gorbachev, many people began to return to prerevolutionary practices. These newlyweds in the Ukrainian port city of Odessa celebrate their marriage ties in the traditional manner.

later, Gorbachev called for the creation of a new Soviet parliament, the Congress of People's Deputies, whose members were to be chosen in competitive elections. When it convened in 1989, the first such meeting in the nation since 1918, one of the delegates was Andrei Sakharov, who had been released from internal exile a few months previously. As a leader of the dissident deputies, Sakharov called for an end to the Communist monopoly of power, and on December 11, 1989, the day he died, he urged the creation of a new, noncommunist party. In response, Gorbachev legalized the formation of other political parties and struck out Article 6 of the Soviet constitution, which guaranteed the leading role of the Communist Party. As the Communist Party became less closely associated with the state, the influence of the party's first secretary diminished. Gorbachev attempted to consolidate his power by creating a new state presidency and in March 1990 became the Soviet Union's first president. By now, however, his stature within the country had diminished, and reformist elements who had once welcomed his policies

Despite desperate pleas from Gorbachev, the Soviet republics soon opted for complete independence. On December 1, 1991, Ukraine voted for independence. A week later, the leaders of Russia, Ukraine, and Belarus (bell-uh-ROOSS) announced that the Soviet Union had "ceased to exist" and would be replaced by a "commonwealth of independent states." On Christmas day, Gorbachev resigned and turned over his responsibilities as commander-in-chief to Yeltsin, the president of Russia. By the end of 1991, one of the largest empires in world history had come to an end, and fifteen new nations had embarked on an uncertain future.

Eastern Europe: From Satellites to Sovereign Nations

The gradual disintegration of the Soviet Union had an immediate impact on its neighbors to the west. As before, Poland was one of the first to react to events.. In the late 1970s, high food prices led to popular protests and the emergence of an independent labor union called **Solidarity**. Led by Lech Walesa (LEK vah-WENT-sah) (b. 1943), Solidarity rode the wave of national spirit stoked by the visit of Polish-born pope John Paul II in June 1979 and rapidly became an influential force for change. Sensing a threat to its monopoly of power, the regime outlawed the union and declared martial law in 1981 but the movement continued to muster popular support, and when Mikhail Gorbachev made it clear that Moscow wouldn't bail them out, Communist leaders bowed to the inevitable and permitted free national elections to take place, resulting in the election of Walesa as president of Poland in December 1990. Moscow—inspired by Gorbachev's policy of encouraging "new thinking" to improve relations with the Western powers—took no action to reverse the verdict in Warsaw.

In Hungary, as in Poland, the process of transition had begun many years earlier. After crushing the Hungarian revolution of 1956, the Communist government of János Kádár had tried to assuage popular opinion by enacting a series of far-reaching economic reforms (labeled "communism with a capitalist face-lift"). But as the 1980s progressed, the economy sagged, and in 1989, the regime permitted the formation of opposition political parties, leading eventually to the formation of a non-communist coalition government in elections held in March 1990.

The transition in Czechoslovakia was more abrupt. After Soviet troops crushed the Prague Spring in 1968, hard-line Communists under Gustav Husák followed a policy of massive repression to maintain their power. In 1977, dissident intellectuals, inspired by the signing of the Helsinki Accords, formed an organization called Charter 77 as a vehicle for protest against violations of human rights. Regardless of the repressive atmosphere, dissident activities continued to grow during the 1980s, and when massive demonstrations broke out in several major cities in 1989, President Husák's government, lacking popular support, collapsed. At the end of December, he was replaced by Václav Havel (VAHT-slahf HAH-vul) (1936–2011), a dissident playwright who had been a leading figure in Charter 77 (see the box "Václav Havel: A Call for a New Politics" on p. 803).

But the most dramatic events took place in East Germany, where a persistent economic slump and the ongoing oppression by the Erich Honecker regime led to a flight of refugees (described by wits as the "Trabi trail" in reference to the ubiquitous Trabi automobiles manufactured in the German Democratic Republic) and mass demonstrations against the regime in the summer and fall of 1989. Capitulating to popular pressure, the Communist government opened its entire border with the West. The Berlin Wall, the most tangible symbol of the Cold War, became the site of a massive celebration; most of it was dismantled by joyful Germans from both sides of the border. In March 1990, free elections led to the formation of a non-communist government that rapidly carried out a program of political and economic reunification with West Germany.

The dissolution of the Soviet Union and its satellite system in Eastern Europe brought a dramatic end to the Cold War. By the beginning of the 1990s, a generation of global rivalry between two ideological systems had come to a close, and world leaders turned their attention to the construction of what U.S. President George H. W. Bush called the New World Order. But what sort of new order would it be?

Why Did the Soviet Union Collapse?

What caused the sudden disintegration of the Soviet system? It is popular in some quarters in the United States to argue that the aggressive defense policies adopted by the Reagan administration forced Moscow into an arms race that it could not afford and that ultimately led to the collapse of the Soviet economy. This contention has some superficial plausibility, as Soviet leaders did indeed react to Reagan's "Star Wars" program by increasing their own defense expenditures, which put a strain on the Soviet budget. And President Reagan was prescient for having pointed out the vulnerability of the Soviet system at a time when most analysts doubted that it would collapse any time in the near future.

Most knowledgeable observers, however, agree that the fall of the Soviet Union was primarily a consequence of conditions inherent in the system, several of which have been pointed out in this chapter. For years, if not decades, leaders in the Kremlin had disguised or ignored the massive inefficiencies in the Soviet economy. In the 1980s, time began to run out. The perceptive Mikhail Gorbachev tried to stem the decline by instituting radical reforms but by then it was too late. We have noted in previous chapters that repressive regimes are most vulnerable when seeking to revitalize themselves, and halfway measures are often not sufficient to halt the decline.

An additional factor should also be considered. One of the most striking aspects of the Soviet Union was its multiethnic character, with only a little more than half of the total population composed of ethnic Russians. Many of the minority nationalities were becoming increasingly restive and were demanding more autonomy or even independence for their regions. By the end of the 1980s, such demands brought

Václav Havel: A Call for a New Politics

POLITICS & GOVERNMENT

WITH THE COLLAPSE OF THE COMMUNIST REGIMES in Eastern Europe, a new generation of leaders began to call for a new political culture to replace the distorted values that had predominated under the "people's democracies." Some pointed to the need for a new perspective, especially a moral one, to face the challenges of a new era. The excerpt below is taken from a speech by Václav Havel, a playwright and a long-time critic of the Communist regime who was elected the new president of Czechoslovakia at the end of 1989.

Address to the People of Czechoslovakia, January 1, 1990

For forty years you heard from my predecessors on this day different variations on the same theme: how our country was flourishing, how many million tons of steel we produced, how happy we all were, how we trusted our government, and what bright perspectives were unfolding in front of us.

I assume you did not propose me for this office so that I, too, would lie to you.

Our country is not flourishing. The enormous creative and spiritual potential of our nations is not being used sensibly. Entire branches of industry are producing goods that are of no interest to anyone, while we are lacking the things we need. A state which calls itself a workers' state humiliates and exploits workers. Our obsolete economy is wasting the little energy we have available. A country that once could be proud of the educational level of its citizens spends so little on education that it ranks today as seventy-second in the world. We have polluted the soil, rivers and forests bequeathed to us by our ancestors, and we have today the most contaminated environment in Europe....

But all this is still not the main problem. The worst thing is that we live in a contaminated moral environment. We fell morally ill because we became used to saying something different from what we thought. We learned not to believe in anything, to ignore one another, to care only about ourselves. Concepts such as love, friendship, compassion, humility or forgiveness lost their depth and dimension, and for many of us they represented only psychological peculiarities, or they resembled gone-astray greetings from ancient times, a little ridiculous in the era of computers and spaceships. Only a few of us were able to cry out loudly that the powers that be should not be all-powerful and that the special farms, which produced ecologically pure and top-quality food just for them, should send their produce to schools, children's homes and hospitals if our agriculture was unable to offer them to all.

The previous regime—armed with its arrogant and intolerant ideology—reduced man to a force of production, and nature to a tool of production. In this it attacked both their very substance and their mutual relationship. It reduced gifted and autonomous people, skillfully working in their own country, to the nuts and bolts of some monstrously huge, noisy and stinking machine, whose real meaning was not clear to anyone....

When I talk about the contaminated moral atmosphere, I am ... talking about all of us. We had all become used to the totalitarian system and accepted it as an unchangeable fact and thus helped to perpetuate it. In other words, we are all—though naturally to differing extents—responsible for the operation of the totalitarian machinery. None of us is just its victim. We are all also its co-creators....

If we realize this, hope will return to our hearts.

Do you believe that Václav Havel's criticisms of Czech society under Communist rule have relevance to many advanced industrial nations in the world today?

Source: http://old.hrad.cz/president/Havel/speeches/1990/0101_uk.html

---

about the final collapse of the system. The Soviet empire died at least partly from imperial overreach.

The East Is Red: China Under Communism

FOCUS QUESTION: What were Mao Zedong's chief goals for China, and what policies did he institute to try to achieve them?

"A revolution is not a dinner party, or writing an essay, or painting a picture, or doing embroidery; it cannot be so refined, so leisurely and gentle, so temperate and kind, courteous, restrained, and magnanimous. A revolution is an insurrection, an act of violence by which one class overthrows another."[6] With these words—written in 1926, at a time when the Communists, in cooperation with Chiang Kai-shek's Nationalist Party, were embarked on their Northern Expedition to defeat the warlords and reunify China—the young revolutionary Mao Zedong warned his colleagues that the road to victory in the struggle to build a communist society would be arduous and would inevitably involve acts of violence against the class enemy.

In the fall of 1949, China was at peace for the first time in twelve years. The newly victorious Communist Party, under the leadership of its chairman, Mao Zedong, turned its attention to consolidating its power base and healing the wounds of war. Its long-term goal was to construct a socialist society but its leaders realized that popular support for the revolution was based on the party's platform of honest government, land reform, social justice, and peace rather than on the utopian goal of a classless society. Accordingly, the new regime temporarily set aside Mao Zedong's stirring exhortation of 1926 and followed Soviet precedent by adopting a moderate program of political and economic recovery known as New Democracy.

New Democracy

With **New Democracy**—patterned roughly after Lenin's New Economic Policy in Soviet Russia in the 1920s (see Chapter 23)—the new Chinese leadership tacitly recognized that time and extensive indoctrination would be needed to convince the Chinese people of the superiority of socialism. In the meantime, the party would rely on capitalist profit incentives to spur productivity. Manufacturing and commercial firms were permitted to remain under private ownership, although with stringent government regulations. To win the support of the poorer peasants, who made up the majority of the population, a land redistribution program was adopted but the collectivization of agriculture was postponed.

In a number of key respects, New Democracy was a success. About two-thirds of the peasant households in the country received land and thus had reason to be grateful to the new regime. Spurred by official tolerance for capitalist activities and the end of internal conflict, the national economy began to rebound, although agricultural production still lagged behind both official targets and the growing population, which was increasing at an annual rate of more than 2 percent. But not all benefited. In the course of carrying out land redistribution, thousands if not millions of landlords and well-to-do farmers lost their lands, their personal property, their freedom, and sometimes their lives. Many of those who died were tried and convicted of "crimes against the people" in tribunals set up under official sponsorship in towns and villages around the country (see the box "Land Reform in Action" on p. 805). As Mao himself later conceded, many were innocent of any crime, but in the eyes of the party, their deaths were necessary to destroy the power of the landed gentry in the countryside.

The Transition to Socialism

Originally, party leaders intended to follow the Leninist formula of delaying the building of a fully socialist society until China had a sufficient industrial base to permit the mechanization of agriculture. In 1953, they launched the nation's first five-year plan (patterned after similar Soviet plans), which called for substantial increases in industrial output. Lenin had believed that mechanization would induce Russian peasants to join collective farms, because the farms, with their greater size and efficiency, could purchase expensive farm machinery that individual farmers could not afford. But the difficulty of providing tractors and reapers for millions of rural villages eventually convinced Mao that it would take years, if not decades, for China's infant industrial base to meet the needs of a modernizing agricultural sector. He therefore decided to begin collectivization immediately, in the hope that collective farms would increase food production and release land, labor, and capital for the industrial sector. Accordingly, beginning in 1955, virtually all private farmland was collectivized (although peasant families were allowed to retain small private plots for their own use), and most businesses and industries were nationalized.

Collectivization was achieved without arousing the massive peasant unrest that had taken place in the Soviet Union during the 1930s, perhaps because the Chinese government followed a policy of persuasion rather than compulsion (Mao Zedong remarked that Stalin had "drained the pond to catch the fish") and because the Communist land redistribution program had already earned the support of millions of rural Chinese. But the hoped-for production increases did not materialize, and in 1958, at Mao's insistent urging, party leaders approved a more radical program known as the **Great Leap Forward**. Existing rural collectives, normally the size of a traditional village, were combined into vast "people's communes," each containing more than 30,000 people. These communes were to be responsible for all administrative and economic tasks at the local level, and in some cases, farm families were moved out of their houses and forced to live in large barracks—a policy designed not only to conserve resources but also to undermine the traditional family system. The party's official slogan promised "Hard work for a few years, happiness for a thousand."[7]

Some party members were concerned that this ambitious program would threaten the government's rural base of support but Mao argued that Chinese peasants were naturally revolutionary in spirit. The Chinese rural masses, he said, are

> first of all, poor, and secondly, blank. That may seem like a bad thing, but it is really a good thing. Poor people want change, want to do things, want revolution. A clean sheet of paper has no blotches, and so the newest and most beautiful words can be written on it, the newest and most beautiful pictures can be painted on it.[8]

Those words, of course, were *socialism* and *communism*.

The communes were a disaster. Administrative bottlenecks, bad weather, and peasant resistance to the new system (which, among other things, attempted to eliminate work incentives and destroy the traditional family as the basic unit of Chinese society) combined to drive food production downward, and over the next few years, as many as 35 million people may have died of starvation. Many peasants were reportedly

Land Reform in Action

FAMILY & SOCIETY

ONE OF THE GREAT ACHIEVEMENTS of the new Communist regime in China was the land reform program, which resulted in the distribution of farmland to almost two-thirds of the rural population. The program consequently won the gratitude of millions of Chinese. But it also had a dark side as local land reform tribunals routinely convicted "wicked landlords" of crimes against the people and then put them to death. The following passage, written by a foreign observer, describes the process in one village.

Revolution in a Chinese Village

T'ien-ming [a Party cadre] called all the active young cadres and the militiamen of Long Bow [village] together and announced to them the policy of the county government, which was to confront all enemy collaborators and their backers at public meetings, expose their crimes, and turn them over to the county authorities for punishment. He proposed that they start with Kuo Te-yu, the puppet village head. Having moved the group to anger with a description of Te-yu's crimes, T'ien-ming reviewed the painful life led by the poor peasants during the occupation and recalled how hard they had all worked and how as soon as they harvested all the grain the puppet officials, backed by army bayonets, took what they wanted, turned over huge quantities to the Japanese devils, forced the peasants to haul it away, and flogged those who refused.

As the silent crowd contracted toward the spot where the accused man stood, T'ien-ming stepped forward.... "This is our chance. Remember how we were oppressed. The traitors seized our property. They beat us and kicked us....

"Let us speak out the bitter memories. Let us see that the blood debt is repaid...."

He paused for a moment. The peasants were listening to every word but gave no sign as to how they felt....

"Come now, who has evidence against this man?"

Again there was silence.

Kuei-ts'ai, the new vice-chairman of the village, found it intolerable. He jumped up [and] struck Kuo Te-yu on the jaw with the back of his hand. "Tell the meeting how much you stole," he demanded....

The people in the square waited fascinated as if watching a play. They did not realize that in order for the plot to unfold they themselves had to mount the stage and speak out what was on their minds.

That evening T'ien-ming and Kuei-ts'ai called together the small groups of poor peasants from various parts of the village and sought to learn what it was that was really holding them back. They soon found the root of the trouble was fear of the old established political forces, and their military backers....

Emboldened by T'ien-ming's words, other peasants began to speak out. They recalled what Te-yu had done to them personally. Several vowed to speak up and accuse him the next morning....

On the following day the meeting was livelier by far. It began with a sharp argument as to who would make the first accusation, and T'ien-ming found it difficult to keep order. Before Te-yu had a chance to reply to any questions, a crowd of young men, among whom were several militiamen, surged forward ready to beat him.

 What was the Communist Party's purpose in carrying out land reform in China? How did the tactics employed here support that strategy?

Source: From Richard Solomon, *Mao's Revolution and the Chinese Political Culture*, pp. 198–199. Copyright © 1971 Center for Chinese Studies, University of Michigan.

---

reduced to eating the bark off trees and in some cases allowing infants to starve. In 1960, the experiment was essentially abandoned. Although the commune structure was retained, ownership and management were returned to the collective level. Mao was severely criticized by some of his more pragmatic colleagues (one remarked bitingly that "one cannot reach Heaven in a single step"), causing him to complain that he had been relegated to the sidelines "like a Buddha on a shelf."

The Great Proletarian Cultural Revolution

But Mao was not yet ready to abandon either his power or his dream of a totally egalitarian society. In 1966, he returned to the attack, mobilizing discontented youth and disgruntled party members into revolutionary units, soon to be known as Red Guards, who were urged to take to the streets to cleanse Chinese society—from local schools and factories to government ministries in Beijing—of impure elements who (in

Mao's mind, at least) were guilty of "taking the capitalist road." Supported by his wife, Jiang Qing (jyahng CHING), and other radical party figures, Mao launched China on a new forced march toward communism.

The so-called **Great Proletarian Cultural Revolution** (literally, a "great revolution to create a proletarian culture") lasted for ten years, from 1966 to 1976. Some Western observers interpreted it as a simple power struggle between Mao Zedong and some of his key rivals such as Liu Shaoqi (lyoo show-CHEE ["ow" as in "how"]), Mao's designated successor, and Deng Xiaoping (DUHNG show-PING ["ow" as in "how"]), the party's general secretary. Both were removed from their positions, and Liu later died, allegedly of torture, in a Chinese prison. But real policy disagreements were involved. Mao and his supporters feared that capitalist values and the remnants of "feudalist" Confucian ideas would undermine ideological fervor and betray the revolutionary cause. He was convinced that only an atmosphere of **uninterrupted revolution** could enable the Chinese to overcome the lethargy of the past and achieve the final stage of utopian communism. "I care not," he once wrote, "that the winds blow and the waves beat. It is better than standing idly in a courtyard."

His opponents argued for a more pragmatic strategy that gave priority to nation building over the ultimate communist goal of spiritual transformation. But with Mao's supporters now in power, the party carried out vast economic and educational reforms that virtually eliminated any remaining profit incentives, established a new school system that emphasized "Mao Zedong thought," and stressed practical education at the elementary level at the expense of specialized training in science and the humanities in the universities. School learning was discouraged as a legacy of capitalism, and Mao's famous Little Red Book (officially, *Quotations of Chairman Mao Zedong*, a slim volume of Maoist aphorisms to encourage good behavior and revolutionary zeal) was hailed as the most important source of knowledge in all areas.

The Red Sun in Our Hearts. During the Great Proletarian Cultural Revolution, Chinese art was restricted to topics that promoted revolution and the thoughts of Chairman Mao Zedong. All the knowledge that the true revolutionary required was to be found in Mao's Little Red Book, a collection of his sayings on proper revolutionary behavior. In this painting, Chairman Mao's portrait hovers above a crowd of his admirers, who wave copies of the book as a symbol of their total devotion to him and his vision of a future China.

The radicals' efforts to destroy all vestiges of traditional society were reminiscent of the Reign of Terror in revolutionary France, when the Jacobins sought to destroy organized religion and even created a new revolutionary calendar. Red Guards rampaged through the country attempting to eradicate the "four olds" (old thought, old culture, old customs, and old habits). They destroyed temples and religious sculptures; they tore down street signs and replaced them with new ones carrying revolutionary names. At one point, the city of Shanghai even ordered that the significance of colors in stoplights be changed so that red (the revolutionary color) would indicate that traffic could move. That experiment was soon abandoned.

But a mood of revolutionary ferment and enthusiasm is difficult to sustain. Key groups, including bureaucrats, urban professionals, and many military officers, did not share Mao's belief in the benefits of uninterrupted revolution and constant turmoil. Many were alienated by the arbitrary actions of the Red Guards, who indiscriminately accused and brutalized their victims in a society where legal safeguards had almost entirely vanished (see the box "Make Revolution!" on p. 807). Inevitably, the sense of anarchy and uncertainty caused popular support for the movement to erode, and when the end came with Mao's death in 1976, the vast majority of the population may well have welcomed its demise.

Personal accounts by young Chinese who took part in the Cultural Revolution show that their initial enthusiasm often turned to disillusionment. In *Son of the Revolution*, Liang Heng (lee-ahng HUHNG) tells how at first he helped friends organize Red Guard groups: "I thought it was a great idea. We would be following Chairman Mao just like the grownups, and Father would be proud of me. I suppose I too resented the teachers who had controlled and criticized me for so long, and I looked forward to a little revenge."[9] Later he had reason to repent. His sister ran off to join the local Red Guard group. Prior to her departure, she denounced her mother and the rest of her family as "rightists" and enemies of the revolution. Their home was regularly raided by Red Guards, and their father was severely beaten and tortured for having three neckties and "Western shirts." Books, paintings, and writings were piled in the center of the floor and burned before his eyes. On leaving, a few of the Red Guards helped themselves to his monthly salary and his transistor radio.

From Mao to Deng

Mao Zedong died in September 1976 at the age of eighty-three. After a short but bitter succession struggle, the pragmatists led by Deng Xiaoping (1904–1997) seized power from the radicals and formally brought the Cultural Revolution to an end. Mao's widow, Jiang Qing, and three other radicals (derisively called the "Gang of Four" by their opponents) were placed on trial and sentenced to death or to long prison terms. The egalitarian policies of the previous decade were reversed, and a new program emphasizing economic modernization was introduced.

Under the leadership of Deng Xiaoping, who placed his supporters in key positions throughout the party and the

Make Revolution!

POLITICS & GOVERNMENT

IN 1966, MAO ZEDONG UNLEASHED the power of revolution on China. Rebellious youth in the form of Red Guards rampaged through all levels of society, exposing anti-Maoist elements, suspected "capitalist roaders," and those identified with the previous ruling class. In this poignant excerpt, Nien Cheng (nee-uhn CHUHNG), the widow of an official of Chiang Kai-shek's regime, describes a visit by Red Guards to her home during the height of the Cultural Revolution.

Nien Cheng, *Life and Death in Shanghai*

Suddenly the doorbell began to ring incessantly. At the same time, there was furious pounding of many fists on my front gate, accompanied by the confused sound of hysterical voices shouting slogans. The cacophony told me that the time of waiting was over and that I must face the threat of the Red Guards and the destruction of my home....

I stood up to put the book on the shelf. A copy of the Constitution of the People's Republic caught my eye. Taking it in my hand and picking up the bunch of keys I had ready on my desk, I went downstairs.

At the same moment, the Red Guards pushed open the front door and entered the house. There were thirty or forty senior high school students, aged between fifteen and twenty, led by two men and one woman much older.

The leading Red Guard, a gangling youth with angry eyes, stepped forward and said to me, "We are the Red Guards. We have come to take revolutionary action against you!"

Though I knew it was futile, I held up the copy of the Constitution and said calmly, "It's against the Constitution of

the People's Republic of China to enter a private house without a search warrant."

The young man snatched the document out of my hand and threw it on the floor. With his eyes blazing, he said, "The Constitution is abolished. It was a document written by the Revisionists within the Communist Party. We recognize only the teachings of our Great Leader Chairman Mao." ...

Another young man used a stick to smash the mirror hanging over the blackwood chest facing the front door.

Mounting the stairs, I was astonished to see several Red Guards taking pieces of my porcelain collection out of their padded boxes. One young man had arranged a set of four Kangxi wine cups in a row on the floor and was stepping on them. I was just in time to hear the crunch of delicate porcelain under the sole of his shoe. The sound pierced my heart. Impulsively I leapt forward and caught his leg just as he raised his foot to crush the next cup. He toppled. We fell in a heap together....

The young man whose revolutionary work of destruction I had interrupted said angrily, "You shut up! These things belong to the old culture. They are the useless toys of the feudal emperors and the modern capitalist class and have no significance to us, the proletarian class.... Our Great Leader Chairman Mao taught us, 'If we do not destroy, we cannot establish.' The old culture must be destroyed to make way for the new socialist culture."

 How do the tactics of the Red Guards compare with those employed by the land reform cadres in the box "Land Reform in Action" on p. 805? To what degree did they succeed in remaking the character of the Chinese people?

Source: From *Life and Death in Shanghai* by Nien Cheng (New York: Penguin, 1986).

---

government, attention focused on what were called the **Four Modernizations**: industry, agriculture, technology, and national defense. Deng had been a leader of the faction that opposed Mao's program of rapid socialist transformation, and during the Cultural Revolution, he had been forced to perform menial labor to "sincerely correct his errors." But Deng continued to espouse the pragmatic approach, which he often likened to the Chinese aphorism "cross the river by feeling the stones." Reportedly, he also once remarked, "Black cat, white cat, what does it matter so long as it catches the mice?" Under the program of Four Modernizations, many of the restrictions against private activities and profit incentives were eliminated, and people were encouraged to work hard to benefit themselves and Chinese society. The familiar slogan "Serve the people" was replaced by a new one repugnant to the tenets of Mao Zedong thought: "Create wealth for the people."

Crucial to the program's success was the government's ability to attract foreign technology and capital. For more than two

decades, China had been isolated from technological advances taking place elsewhere in the world. Now, to make up for lost time, the government abandoned its policy of self-reliance and sought to improve relations with the rest of the world. It encouraged foreign investment and sent thousands of students and specialists abroad to study capitalist techniques. By adopting this pragmatic approach in the years after 1976, China made great strides in ending its chronic problems of poverty and underdevelopment. Per capita income roughly doubled during the 1980s; housing, education, and sanitation improved, and both agricultural and industrial output skyrocketed.

But critics, both Chinese and foreign, complained that Deng's program had failed to achieve a "fifth modernization": democracy. Official sources denied such charges and spoke proudly of restoring "socialist legality" by doing away with the arbitrary punishments applied during the Cultural Revolution. Deng himself encouraged the Chinese people to speak out against earlier excesses. In the late 1970s, with the

Punishing China's Enemies During the Cultural Revolution. The Cultural Revolution, which began in 1966, was a massive effort by Mao Zedong and his radical supporters to eliminate rival elements within the Chinese Communist Party and the government. Accused of being "capitalist roaders," such individuals were subjected to public criticism and removed from their positions. Some were imprisoned or executed. Here Red Guards parade a victim wearing a dunce cap through the streets of Beijing.

apparent tolerance of the regime, ordinary citizens pasted "big character posters" criticizing the abuses of the past on the so-called Democracy Wall near Tiananmen (tee-AHN-ahn-muhn) Square in downtown Beijing.

Yet it soon became clear that the new leaders would not tolerate any direct criticism of the Communist Party or of Marxist-Leninist ideology. Dissidents were suppressed, and some were sentenced to long prison terms. Among them was the well-known astrophysicist Fang Lizhi (FAHNG lee-JURR), who spoke out publicly against official corruption and the continuing influence of Marxist-Leninist concepts in post-Mao China, telling an audience in Hong Kong that "China will not be able to modernize if it does not break the shackles of Maoist and Stalinist-style socialism." Fang immediately felt the weight of official displeasure. He was refused permission to travel abroad, and articles that he submitted to official periodicals were rejected.

The problem began to intensify in the late 1980s as more Chinese began to study abroad and more information about Western society reached educated individuals inside the country. Rising expectations aroused by the economic improvements of the early 1980s led to increasing pressure from students for better living conditions, relaxed restrictions on study abroad, and increased freedom to select employment after graduation.

Incident at Tiananmen Square

As long as economic conditions for the majority of Chinese were improving, other classes did not share the students' discontent,

and the government was able to isolate them from other elements in society. But in the late 1980s, an overheated economy led to rising inflation and growing discontent among salaried workers, especially in the cities. At the same time, corruption, nepotism, and favored treatment for senior officials and party members were provoking increasing criticism. In May 1989, student protesters carried placards demanding "Science and Democracy" (reminiscent of the slogan of the May Fourth Movement, whose seventieth anniversary was celebrated in the spring of 1989), an end to official corruption, and the resignation of China's aging party leadership (see the Comparative Illustration "Student Demonstrations in Beijing" on p. 709 in Chapter 24). These demands received widespread support from the urban population (although notably less in rural areas) and led to massive demonstrations in Tiananmen Square (see the Opposing Viewpoints "Students Appeal for Democracy" on p. 809).

The demonstrations divided the Chinese leaders. Reformist elements around party general secretary Zhao Ziyang (JOW dzee-YAHNG) were sympathetic to the protesters but veteran leaders such as Deng Xiaoping saw the student demands for more democracy as a disguised call for an end to Chinese Communist Party (CCP) rule. After some hesitation, the government sent tanks and troops into Tiananmen Square to crush the demonstrations. Dissidents were arrested, and the regime once again began to stress ideological purity and socialist values. Although the crackdown came under widespread criticism abroad, Chinese leaders insisted that

OPPOSING ⊁ VIEWPOINTS

Students Appeal for Democracy

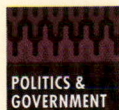

POLITICS & GOVERNMENT

IN THE SPRING OF 1989, THOUSANDS OF STUDENTS GATHERED IN TIANANMEN SQUARE in downtown Beijing to provide moral support to their many compatriots who had gone on a hunger strike in an effort to compel the Chinese government to reduce the level of official corruption and enact democratic reforms, opening the political process to the Chinese people. The first selection is from an editorial published on April 26 by the official newspaper *People's Daily*. Fearing that the student demonstrations would get out of hand, as had happened during the Cultural Revolution, the editorial condemned the protests for being contrary to the Communist Party. The second selection is from a statement by Zhao Ziyang, the party general secretary, who argued that many of the students' demands were justified. On May 17, student leaders distributed flyers explaining the goals of the movement to participants and passersby, including the author of this chapter. The third selection is from one of these flyers.

People's Daily Editorial, April 26, 1989

This is a well-planned plot ... to confuse the people and throw the country into turmoil.... Its real aim is to reject the Chinese Communist Party and the socialist system at the most fundamental level.... This is a most serous political struggle that concerns the whole Party and nation.

Statement by Party General Secretary Zhao Ziyang Before Party Colleagues, May 4, 1989

Let me tell you how I see all this. I think the student movement has two important characteristics. First, the students' slogans call for things like supporting the Constitution, promoting democracy, and fighting corruption. These demands all echo positions of the Party and the government. Second, a great many people from all parts of society are out there joining the demonstrations and backing the students.... This has grown into a nationwide protest. I think the best way to bring the thing to a quick end is to focus on the mainstream views of the majority.

"Why Do We Have to Undergo a Hunger Strike?"

By 2:00 P.M. today, the hunger strike carried out by the petition group in Tiananmen Square has been under way for 96 hours. By this morning, more than 600 participants have fainted. When these democracy fighters were lifted into the ambulances, no one who was present was not moved to tears.

Our petition group now undergoing the hunger strike demands that at a minimum the government agree to the following two points:

1. To engage on a sincere and equal basis in a dialogue with the "higher education dialogue group." In addition, to broadcast the actual dialogue in its entirety. We absolutely refuse to agree to a partial broadcast, to empty gestures, or to fabrications that dupe the people.

2. To evaluate in a fair and realistic way the patriotic democratic movement. Discard the label of "troublemaking" and redress the reputation of the patriotic democratic movement.

It is our view that the request for a dialogue between the people's government and the people is not an unreasonable one. Our party always follows the principle of seeking truths from actual facts. It is therefore only natural that the evaluation of this patriotic democratic movement should be done in accordance with the principle of seeking truths from actual facts.

Our classmates who are going through the hunger strike are the good sons and daughters of the people! One by one, they have fallen. In the meantime, our "public servants" are completely unmoved. Please, let us ask where your conscience is.

 What were the key demands of the protesters in *Tiananmen Square*? Why were they rejected by the Chinese government?

Sources: From *People's Daily* Editorial, April 26, 1989. Statement by Party Chairman Zhao Ziyang before Party colleagues, May 4, 1989. Original flyer in possession of author.

economic reforms could only take place in conditions of party leadership and political stability.

Deng Xiaoping and other aging party leaders turned to the army to protect their base of power and suppress what they described as "counterrevolutionary elements." Deng was undoubtedly counting on the fact that many Chinese, particularly in rural areas, feared a recurrence of the disorder of the Cultural Revolution and craved economic prosperity more than political reform. In the months following the confrontation, the government issued new regulations requiring courses on Marxist-Leninist ideology in the schools, sought out dissidents within the intellectual community, and made it clear that while economic reforms would continue, the CCP's monopoly of power would not be allowed to decay. Harsh punishments were imposed on those accused of undermining the Communist system and supporting its enemies abroad.

Riding the Tiger

As the new decade began, party leaders had begun to realize the complexity of maintaining control and stability in a rapidly changing society. "When you ride the tiger," goes an ancient Chinese proverb, "it's hard to dismount." In the 1990s, the government sought to nurture urban support by reducing the rate of inflation and guaranteeing the availability of consumer goods in great demand among the rising middle class. Under Deng Xiaoping's successor, Jiang Zemin (JYAHNG zuh-MIN) (b. 1926), who occupied the positions of both party chief and president of China, the government promoted rapid economic growth while cracking down harshly on political dissent. Massive construction projects, including a nationwide rail network, modern airports, and dams to provide hydroelectric power, were initiated throughout the country. That policy paid dividends in bringing about a perceptible decline in alienation among the residents of the cities. As industrial production continued to rise, living standards—at least in urban areas—soon followed, and outside observers began to predict that China would become one of the economic superpowers of the twenty-first century.

But now a new challenge arose, as lagging farm income, high taxes, increasing environmental problems, and official corruption began to spark resentment in the countryside. Highly sensitive to the historic record that suggested that peasant revolt was often the harbinger of a collapse of a dynasty, party leaders sought to contain the issue with a combination of the carrot and the stick. The problem was complicated, however, by the fact that with the rise of cell phones and the Internet, the Chinese people were becoming much more aware of events taking place around them. As the public exchange of ideas rapidly increased in the new electronic age, dissidents found a forum to voice their views, while countless ordinary people were newly enabled to exchange information on incidents and issues that official sources wished to suppress. Although the regime scrambled to arrest or intimidate key dissidents and limit public access to events taking place in China and around the world, it was, like Sisyphus pushing a stone up a mountain, facing an uphill battle.

New leaders installed in 2002 and 2003 appeared aware of the magnitude of the problem. Hu Jintao (HOO jin-TOW ["ow" as in "how"]) (b. 1943), who replaced Jiang Zemin as CCP general secretary and head of state, called for further reforms to open up Chinese society, reduce the level of corruption, and bridge the yawning gap between rich and poor. At the party's Seventeenth National Congress, held in October 2007, President Hu emphasized the importance of adopting a "scientific view of development," a vague concept calling for social harmony, improved material prosperity, and a reduction in the growing income gap between rich and poor in Chinese society. The new leadership also began to show a growing tolerance for the public exchange of ideas, although subversive thoughts and activities were still stringently suppressed.

But the new leadership did not entirely fulfill expectations. Although the economy continued to grow rapidly during the first decade of the new millennium, many of the key issues of public concern, such as corruption, income inequality, and growing environmental concerns (see "An Environmental Time Bomb" later in this chapter), remained unresolved, and as party elders gathered in the fall of 2012 to select a new slate of leaders for the next decade, signs of division had begun to appear in the form of a neo-leftist challenge led by Sichuan (su-CHWAHN) party chief Bo Xilai (Bwo SHEE-lie). Although the latter was quickly removed from office and faced charges of corruption and disloyalty, discontent with current conditions was becoming widespread, and it was clear that party unity on ideological issues could no longer be taken for granted.

In the fall of 2012, Xi Jinping (SHEE Jin-ping) (b. 1953), the son of one of Mao Zedong's closest comrades, took office as president of the People's Republic of China. As a young man, Xi had spent time in the United States and has generally been viewed as a pragmatist

Building a New Silk Road. Although the new high-speed trains running between major cities along China's eastern corridor are the envy of the entire world, an equally important project involved the construction of a dual-track rail line along the old Silk Road to Russia. Although economic considerations played a role in the project, an equally important consideration was to utilize the new transportation network to strengthen Chinese claims of sovereignty over Xinjiang province, home of China's restive Muslim minority. Shown here, a team of railroad workers (all of them Han Chinese) install a new track along the route not far from the famed grottoes of Dunhuang.

© William J. Duiker

but it was clear that he would face severe challenges in balancing the issues of economic growth and fairness during his tenure in office. Public statements suggest that he is aware of the need to control rampant corruption and open up the economy to market forces but he has also issued stern warnings against alleged threats to China's national security from hostile Western forces and ideas. Criticisms of the performance of the Communist Party, from whatever source, are dismissed as "historical nihilism" designed "to negate the legitimacy of the long-term rule of the CCP." Like his predecessors, the new president will face constant challenges as he seeks to "ride the tiger" of China's long-term growth into a major power.

Back to Confucius?

Through this period of trial and error, senior leaders have remained steadfast in their belief that the Communist Party must remain the sole political force in charge of carrying out the revolution. Ever fearful of chaos, they are convinced that only a firm hand at the tiller can keep the ship of state from crashing onto the rocks. At the same time, they have tacitly come to recognize that Marxist exhortations are no longer an effective means of enforcing social discipline. Accordingly, they have increasingly turned to Confucianism as a tool to influence political and social attitudes. Ceremonies celebrating the birth of Confucius now receive official sanction, and hallowed moral virtues such as righteousness, propriety, and filial piety are widely cited as an antidote to the growing tide of antisocial behavior. As a further indication of its willingness to employ traditional themes to further its interests, the regime has begun to sponsor the establishment of Confucian centers in countries around the world to promote its view that Confucian humanism is ultimately destined to replace traditional religious faiths in coming decades.

The regime has also begun to rely on another familiar political tactic to maintain control—stoking the fires of nationalism. In a striking departure from the precepts of Marxist internationalism, official sources in Beijing cite

Confucian tradition to support their assertion that China is unique and will not follow the path of "peaceful evolution" (to use their term) toward a future democratic capitalist society. New president Xi Jinping—who recently declared that Mikhail Gorbachev was responsible for the fall of the Soviet system by abandoning the principle of the party as the sole force in society—has reportedly visited Singapore to examine its "Singapore model" (see Chapter 30) of flexible authoritarianism.

That attitude is clearly reflected in Beijing's foreign policy, as China is playing an increasingly active role in the region. The first example of this new attitude took place as early as 1979, when Chinese forces briefly invaded Vietnam as punishment for the Vietnamese occupation of neighboring Cambodia. Then, beginning in the 1990s, China aroused concern in the region by claiming sole ownership over the Spratly (sprat-LEE) Islands in the South China Sea and over the Diaoyu (DYOW-you) Islands (also claimed by Japan, which calls them the Senkakus) near Taiwan (see Map 27.2). To buttress its claims to an active role in the region, the regime points with pride to the long-ago voyages of Admiral Zheng He to the South Seas and has made no secret of its determination to create a deep-water navy that can compete with potential rivals over influence within the region.

MAP 27.2 The People's Republic of China. This map shows China's current boundaries. Major regions are indicated in capital letters.

Q *In which regions are there movements against Chinese rule?*

To some of its neighbors, including Japan, India, and Vietnam, China's new posture is disquieting and raises suspicions that Beijing is once against preparing to flex its muscle as it did occasionally in the imperial era. Chinese leaders, however, view their actions as legitimate efforts to reassert China's rightful role in the affairs of the region. After a century of humiliation at the hands of the Western powers and neighboring Japan, the nation, in Mao's famous words of 1949, "has stood up," and no one will be permitted to humiliate it again. For the moment, at least, a fervent patriotism seems to be on the rise in China, actively promoted by the party as a means of holding the country together. The decision by the International Olympic Committee to award the 2008 Summer Games to Beijing led to widespread celebration throughout the country. The event served to symbolize China's emergence as a major national power on the world stage.

The Potala Palace in Tibet. Tibet was a distant and reluctant appendage of the Chinese empire during the Qing Dynasty. Since the rise to power of the Communist Party in 1949, the regime in Beijing has consistently sought to integrate the region into the People's Republic of China. Resistance to Chinese rule, however, has been widespread. In recent years, the Dalai Lama, the leading religious figure in Tibetan Buddhism, has attempted without success to persuade Chinese leaders to allow a measure of autonomy for the Tibetan people. In 2008, massive riots by frustrated Tibetans took place in the capital city of Lhasa (LAH-suh) just prior to the opening of the Olympic Games in Beijing. The Potala Palace, symbol of Tibetan identity, was constructed in the seventeenth century in Lhasa and serves today as the foremost symbol of the national and cultural aspirations of the Tibetan people.

Pumping up the spirit of patriotism, however, is not the solution to all problems. Unrest is growing among China's national minorities: in Xinjiang, where restless Muslim peoples are observing with curiosity the emergence of independent Islamic states in Central Asia, and in Tibet, where the official policy of quelling separatist sentiment has led to the violent suppression of Tibetan culture and an influx of thousands of ethnic Chinese immigrants. In the meantime, the growing popularity of organized religion, including Christianity and Islam as well as indigenous faiths, is an additional indication that with the disintegration of the old Maoist utopia, the Chinese people will need more than a pallid version of Marxism-Leninism or a revived Confucianism to fill the gap.

Whether the current leadership will be able to prevent further erosion of the party's power and prestige is unclear. In the short term, efforts to slow the process of change may succeed because many Chinese are understandably fearful of punishment and concerned for their careers. And high economic growth rates can sometimes obscure a multitude of problems as many individuals will opt to chase the fruits of materialism rather than the less tangible benefits of personal freedom. But the challenge to party leadership in the new electronic age is severe. Today, more people are "surfing the Net" in China than in any other country except the United States, and they are no longer totally reliant on propaganda instruments in Beijing for their information. In the long run, the party leadership must face the challenge of reducing the growing gap between urban and rural areas and resolving the contradiction between political authoritarianism and economic prosperity.

CHRONOLOGY	China Under Communist Rule
New Democracy	1949–1955
Era of collectivization	1955–1958
Great Leap Forward	1958–1960
Great Proletarian Cultural Revolution	1966–1976
Death of Mao Zedong	1976
Era of Deng Xiaoping	1978–1997
Tiananmen Square incident	1989
Presidency of Jiang Zemin	1993–2002
Hu Jintao becomes president	2002
Beijing hosts Olympic Games	2008

"Serve the People": Chinese Society Under Communism

Q **FOCUS QUESTIONS:** What significant political, economic, and social changes have taken place in China since the death of Mao Zedong? How successful have they been at improving the quality of life in China?

When the Communist Party came to power in 1949, Chinese leaders made it clear that their policies would differ from the Soviet model in one key respect. Whereas the Bolsheviks had distrusted all nonrevolutionary elements in Russia and relied almost exclusively on the use of force to achieve their objectives, the CCP initially sought to win

COMPARATIVE ILLUSTRATION

POLITICS & GOVERNMENT

Sideline Industries: Creeping Capitalism in a Socialist Paradise. In the late 1980s, Communist leaders in both the Soviet Union and China began to encourage their citizens to engage in private commercial activities as a means of reviving moribund economies. In the photo on the left, a Soviet farmworker displays fruits and vegetables on a street corner in Odessa, a seaport on the Black Sea. On the right, a Chinese woman sells her dumplings to passersby in Shandong province. As her smile suggests, the Chinese took up the challenge of entrepreneurship with much greater success and enthusiasm than their Soviet counterparts did.

 Why did Chinese citizens adopt capitalist reforms in the countryside more enthusiastically than their Soviet counterparts?

support from the mass of the population by carrying out reforms that could win popular support. Only the leading elements within the opposition were singled out for punishment. This "mass line" policy, as it was called, worked fairly well until the late 1950s, when Mao and his radical allies adopted policies such as the Great Leap Forward that began to alienate much of the population. Ideological purity was now valued over expertise in building an advanced and prosperous society.

Economics in Command

When he came to power in the late 1970s, Deng Xiaoping recognized the need to restore credibility to a system on the verge of breakdown and hoped that rapid economic growth would satisfy the Chinese people and prevent them from demanding political freedoms. Post-Mao leaders clearly placed economic performance over ideological purity. To stimulate the stagnant industrial sector, which had been under state direction since the end of the New Democracy era, they reduced bureaucratic controls over state industries and allowed local managers to have more say over prices, salaries, and quality control. Productivity was encouraged

by permitting bonuses for extra effort, a policy that had been discouraged during the Cultural Revolution. The regime also tolerated the emergence of a small private sector. The unemployed were encouraged to set up restaurants, bicycle or radio repair shops, and handicraft shops on their own initiative (see the Comparative Illustration "Sideline Industries: Creeping Capitalism in a Socialist Paradise" above).

Finally, the regime opened up the country to foreign investment and technology. Special economic zones were established in urban centers near the coast (ironically, many were located in the old nineteenth-century treaty ports), where lucrative concessions were offered to encourage foreign firms to build factories. Foreign tourists were welcomed, and some students were sent abroad to study.

The new leaders especially stressed educational reform. The system adopted during the Cultural Revolution, emphasizing practical education and ideology at the expense of higher education and modern science, was rapidly abandoned (Mao's Little Red Book was even withdrawn from circulation and could no longer be found on bookshelves), and a new system based generally on the Western model was instituted. Admission to higher education was based on success in merit examinations, and courses on science and mathematics received high priority.

AGRICULTURAL REFORM No economic reform program could succeed unless it included the countryside. Three decades of socialism had done little to increase food production or to lay the basis for a modern agricultural sector. China, with a population now numbering one billion, could still barely feed itself. Peasants had little incentive to work and few opportunities to increase production through mechanization, the use of fertilizer, or better irrigation.

Under Deng Xiaoping, agricultural policy made a rapid about-face. Under the new **rural responsibility system**, adopted shortly after Deng had consolidated his authority, collectives leased land to peasant families, who paid the collective a quota as rent. Anything produced on the land beyond that payment could be sold on the private market or consumed. To soak up excess labor in the villages, the government encouraged the formation of so-called sideline industries, a modern equivalent of the traditional cottage industries in premodern China. Peasants raised fish or shrimp, made consumer goods, and even assembled living room furniture and appliances for sale to their newly affluent compatriots.

The reform program had a striking effect on rural production. Grain production increased rapidly, and farm income doubled during the 1980s. Yet it also created problems. In the first place, income at the village level became more unequal as some enterprising farmers (known sardonically as "ten-thousand-dollar households") earned profits several times those realized by their less fortunate or less industrious neighbors. When some farmers discovered that they could earn more by growing cash crops or other specialized commodities, they devoted less land to rice and other grain crops, thereby threatening to reduce the supply of China's most crucial staple. Finally, the agricultural policy threatened to undermine the government's population control program, which party leaders viewed as crucial to the success of the Four Modernizations.

China has been seeking to limit its rate of population growth since a misguided period in the mid-1950s when Mao Zedong had argued that more labor would result in higher productivity. By 1970, that assumption had proven to be mistaken, and the government launched a stringent family planning program—including education, incentives, and penalties for noncompliance—to persuade the Chinese people to limit themselves to one child per family. The program did have some success, and population growth was reduced drastically beginning in the 1980s. It was more controversial in rural areas, however, because the rural responsibility system encouraged farm families to pay the penalties for having additional children in the belief that their labor would increase family income and provide the parents with a form of social security for their old age. Eventually, the program was relaxed, as rural families were permitted to have a second child if the first child was a girl. Today it remains in place, although further modifications reflect concern in official circles of potential labor shortages in the near future.

CHINA: THE NEW INDUSTRIAL POWERHOUSE Still, the overall effects of the modernization program were impressive. The standard of living improved for the majority of the population. Whereas a decade earlier, the average Chinese had struggled to earn enough to buy a bicycle, radio, watch, or washing machine, by the late 1980s, many were beginning to purchase videocassette recorders, refrigerators, and color television sets. Yet the rapid growth of the economy created its own problems: inflationary pressures, greed, envy, increased corruption, and—most dangerous of all for the regime—rising expectations. Young people in particular resented restrictions on employment and opportunities to study abroad. Disillusionment ran high, especially in the cities, where lavish living by officials and rising prices for goods aroused widespread alienation and cynicism and laid the groundwork for the massive protest demonstrations in 1989.

During the 1990s, growth rates in the industrial sector continued to be high as domestic capital became increasingly available to compete with the growing presence of foreign enterprises. The government finally recognized the need to close down inefficient state enterprises, and by the end of the decade, the private sector, with official encouragement, accounted for more than 10 percent of the nation's gross domestic product. A stock market opened, and with the country's entrance into the World Trade Organization (WTO) in 2001, China's prowess in the international marketplace improved dramatically. Today, China has the second-largest economy in the world and is the largest exporter of goods. Even the global economic crisis that struck the world in the fall of 2008 has not derailed the Chinese juggernaut, which quickly recovered from the sudden drop in demand for Chinese goods in countries still suffering from the economic downturn.

As a result of these developments, China now possesses a large and increasingly affluent middle class and a burgeoning domestic market for consumer goods. More than 80 percent of all urban Chinese now own a color television set, a refrigerator, and a washing machine. One-third own their homes, and nearly as many have an air conditioner. For the more affluent, a private automobile is increasingly a possibility, and in 2010, more vehicles were sold in China than in the United States.

But as Chinese leaders have discovered, rapid economic change never comes without cost. The closing of state-run factories led to the dismissal of millions of workers each year, and the private sector, although growing at more than 20 percent annually, initially struggled to absorb them. Poor working conditions and low salaries in Chinese factories resulted in periodic outbreaks of labor unrest. Demographic conditions, however, are changing. The reduction in birthrates since the 1980s is creating a labor shortage, which is putting upward pressure on workers' salaries. As a result, China is facing inflation in the marketplace and increased competition from exports produced by factories located in lower-wage countries in South and Southeast Asia.

Discontent has also been increasing in the countryside, where farmers earn only about half as much as their urban counterparts (the government tried to increase the official purchase price for grain but rescinded the order when it became too expensive). China's entry into the World Trade

The Three Gorges Dam. The damming of the Yangzi River over the past two decades is one of the most massive and ambitious construction projects in human history. Designed to increase the amount of farmland in the Yangzi River valley and enable precious water resources to be redistributed to drought-prone regions of the country, the project has also caused considerable environmental damage throughout the Yangzi River valley and displaced several million Chinese from their ancestral homes. Shown here is the famous Three Gorges Dam at Yichang (EE-CHAHNG), a modern wonder of the world.

Organization was greeted with great optimism but has been of little benefit to farmers facing the challenges of cheap foreign imports. Taxes and local corruption add to their complaints, and land seizures by the government or by local officials are a major source of anger in rural communities. In desperation, millions of rural Chinese have left for the big cities, where many of them are unable to find steady employment and are forced to live in squalid conditions in crowded tenements or in the sprawling suburbs. Millions of others remain on their farms and attempt to augment their income by producing for the market or, despite the risk of stringent penalties, by increasing the size of their families. A new land reform law passed in 2008 authorizes farmers to lease or transfer land use rights, although in principle all land in rural areas belongs to the local government.

AN ENVIRONMENTAL TIME BOMB Another factor hindering China's rush to economic advancement is its impact on the environment. With the rising population, fertile land is in increasingly short supply (China's population has doubled since 1950 but only two-thirds as much irrigable land is available). Soil erosion is a major problem, especially in the north, where the desert is encroaching on farmlands, and up to one-sixth of all arable land in the country is polluted. Water is also a problem. An ambitious plan to transport water by canals from the Yangzi River to the more arid northern provinces has run into a number of roadblocks. Another massive project to construct dams on the Yangzi River has sparked protests from environmentalists, as well as from local peoples forced to migrate from the area. Air pollution is ten times the level in the United States, contributing to growing health concerns. To add to the challenge, more than 700,000 new cars and trucks appear on the country's roads each year, and the fleet's pollution controls are not up to Western standards. To reduce congestion on roadways, China is constructing an extensive rail network for high-speed bullet trains that will connect all the major regions in the country, but a number of serious accidents have raised questions about the safety of the rail network.

Chinese Society in Flux

At the root of Marxist-Leninist ideology is the idea of building a new citizen free from the prejudices, ignorance, and superstition of the "feudal" era and the capitalist desire for self-gratification. This new citizen would be characterized not only by a sense of racial and sexual equality but also by the selfless desire to contribute his or her utmost for the good of all.

OUT WITH THE OLD: IN WITH THE NEW For Mao and his colleagues, the first order of business was to remake Chinese society as a means of creating the new citizen. Like the progressive intellectuals of the New Culture movement a generation previously, they viewed old values, old attitudes, and old customs as the foremost obstacle to their ambitious political objectives. At the root of the problem, in their view, was the time-honored Confucian emphasis on the primacy of the family, headed by the patriarch, as the key component in Chinese society. During the early 1950s, they took a number of steps to bring a definitive end to the Confucian legacy in modern China. Women were given the vote and encouraged to become active in the political process. At the local level, an increasing number of women became active in the CCP and in collective organizations. In 1950, a new marriage law guaranteed women equal rights with men. Most important, perhaps, it permitted women for the first time to initiate divorce proceedings against their husbands. Within a year, nearly one million divorces had been granted.

At first, however, the new government moved carefully on family issues to avoid unnecessarily alienating its supporters in the countryside. When collective farms were established in the mid-1950s, payment for hours worked in the form of ration coupons was made not to the individual but to the family head, thus maintaining the traditionally dominant position of the patriarch. When people's communes were established in the late 1950s, however, payments went to the individual, while children were encouraged to report to the authorities any comments by their parents that criticized the system. Such practices continued during the Cultural Revolution, when children were expected to tell on their parents, students on their teachers, and employees on their superiors. By encouraging the oppressed elements in society—the young, the female, and the poor—to voice their bitterness, Mao was hoping to break the tradition of dependency. Such denunciations had been issued against landlords and other "local tyrants" in the land reform tribunals of the late 1940s and early 1950s. Later, during the Cultural Revolution, they were applied to other authority figures in Chinese society.

The post-Mao era brought a decisive shift away from revolutionary utopianism and a return to the pragmatic approach to social engineering. With some exceptions, family relationships became once more a private affair. As with all social changes, however, the return to a more traditional approach had a price. Although in large cities attitudes toward women, marriage, and the family have evolved in line with trends in Western countries, in rural areas the old norms of filial piety and the five relationships sometimes still hold sway. Arranged marriages, nepotism, and the mistreatment of females have returned, although such behavior most likely existed under the cloak of revolutionary piety for a generation. Expensive weddings are now increasingly common, along with the payment of a dowry to the family of the groom. Prostitution and sex crimes against women appear also to be on the rise. To discourage sexual abuse, the government now seeks to provide free legal services for women living in rural areas.

Women in China today do possess some advantages compared with their Western counterparts. Because of the differential in the percentage of women to men in Chinese society (among infants, there are 118 males to every 100 females in today's China), women can afford to be more particular in selecting a husband. Young men often complain in the media that without an automobile or an apartment to offer as an incentive, they find it difficult to locate a wife. Indeed, the problem of rootless young males, often with limited employment opportunities, is an issue of increasing concern for China's leaders today (see the box "Love and Marriage in China" on p. 817).

There are other prices to pay for the trend toward privatization. Under the Maoist system, the elderly and the sick were provided with retirement benefits and health care by the state or by the collective organizations. Under current conditions, with the latter no longer playing such a social role and more workers operating in the private sector, the safety net has been removed (see the Comparative Essay "Family and Society in an Era of Change" on p. 818). The government recently attempted to fill the gap by enacting a social security law but because of the lack of funds, eligibility is limited primarily to individuals living in urban areas. Those living in the countryside are essentially unprotected, prompting legislation in 2010 to provide modest pensions and medical insurance to the poorest members of Chinese society. Yet much more needs to be done, for as the population ages, the lack of an adequate retirement system represents a potential time bomb. The regime attempted to ease the problem recently, when it promulgated a new law requiring adult children (often living in the cities) to provide occasional visits and necessary care to their aging parents in the countryside. Confucius would be pleased!

LIFESTYLE CHANGES: FROM MAO TO MOD The post-Mao era brought a decisive shift away from the puritanical ethic and embraced the ideal of material consumption. Taking advantage of slogans in the 1980s trumpeting such values as "create wealth for the people" and "to get rich is glorious," enterprising Chinese began to concentrate on improving their standard of living. For the first time, millions of Chinese saw the prospect of a house or an urban apartment with a washing machine, television set, and indoor plumbing. Young people whose parents had given them patriotic names such as "Strengthen the Country," "Protect Mao Zedong," and "Assist Korea" began to choose more elegant and cosmopolitan names for their own children. Some names, such as "Surplus Grain" or the more sexist "Bring a Younger Brother," expressed hope for the future.

The new attitudes were also reflected in physical appearance. For a generation after the civil war, clothing had been restricted to the traditional baggy "Mao suit" in olive drab or dark blue, but by the 1980s, young people craved such fashionable Western items as designer jeans, trendy sneakers, and sweat suits, or reasonable facsimiles (see the Comparative Illustration "Then and Now: Changing Clothing Styles in China" on p. 819). Cosmetic surgery to create a more buxom figure or a more Western facial look became increasingly common among affluent young women in the cities. Many had the epicanthic fold over their eyelids removed or their noses enlarged—a curious decision in view of the tradition of referring derogatorily to foreigners as "big noses." Prosperity, however, has its own price, as the problem of obesity, especially among younger Chinese, has skyrocketed in recent years. "China's waistlines," goes one recent joke, "are growing faster than the nation's gross domestic product."

The shift from Marxism toward the worship of consumerism is having another predictable effect in a growing sense of rootlessness in Chinese society, especially among the young, who did not live through the difficult years prior to the death of Mao Zedong. Incidents of random terrorism are on the rise, and many young people are openly materialistic in their attitude and correspondingly cynical about politics. The growing popularity of organized religion is undoubtedly a consequence. As the government has become more tolerant of religious belief, some Chinese have returned to the traditional

Love and Marriage in China

FAMILY & SOCIETY

"What men can do, women can also do." So said Chairman Mao as he "liberated" and masculinized Chinese women to work alongside men. Women's individuality and sexuality were sacrificed for the collective good of his new socialist society. Marriage, which had traditionally been arranged by families for financial gain, was now dictated by duty to the state. The Western concept of romantic love did not enter into a Chinese marriage, as this interview of a schoolteacher by the reporter Zhang Xinxin (JANG SHEEN-SHEEN) in the mid-1980s illustrates. According to recent surveys, the same is true today.

Zhang Xinxin, *Chinese Lives*

My husband and I never did any courting—honestly! We registered our marriage a week after we'd met. He was just out of the forces and a worker in a building outfit. They'd been given a foreign-aid assignment in Zambia, and he was selected. He wanted to get his private life fixed up before he went, and someone introduced us. Seeing how he looked really honest, I accepted him....

He went off with the army as soon as we'd registered our marriage and been given the wedding certificates. He was away three years.... Those three years were a test for us. The main problem was that my family was against it. They thought I was still only a kid and I'd picked the wrong man. What did they have against him? His family was too poor. Of course I won in the end—we'd registered and got our wedding certificates. We were legally married whether we had the family ceremony or not....

I never really wanted to take the college entrance exams. Then in 1978 the school leadership got us all to put our names forward. They said they weren't going to hold us back:

the more of us who passed, the better it would be for the school. So I put my name forward, crammed for six weeks, and passed. I already had two kids then....

I reckoned the chance for study was too good to miss. And my husband was looking after the kids all by himself. I usually only came back once a fortnight. So I couldn't let him down.

My instructors urged me to take the exams for graduate school, but I didn't. I was already thirty-four, so what was the point of more study? There was another reason too. I didn't want an even wider gap between us: he hadn't even finished junior middle school when he joined the army.

It's bad if the gap's too wide. For example, there's a definite difference in our tastes in music and art, I have to admit that. But what really matters? Now we've set up this family we have to preserve it. Besides, look at all the sacrifices he had to make to see me through college. Men comrades all like a game of cards and that, but he was stuck with looking after the kids. He still doesn't get any time for himself—it's all work for him.... I'm not going to be like those men who ditch their wives when they go up in the world.

I'm the head of our school now. With this change in my status I've got to show even more responsibility for the family. Besides, I know how much he's done to get me where I am today. I've also got some duties in the municipal Women's Federation and Political Consultative Conference. No, I'm not being modest. I haven't done anything worth talking about, only my duty....

Do you think the marriage described here is successful? Why or why not? What do you think this woman feels about her marriage?

Source: From *Chinese Lives: An Oral History of Contemporary China*, by Zhang Xinxin and Sang Ye, copyright © 1987 by W. J. F. Jenner and Delia Davin.

Buddhist faith or to folk religions, and Buddhist and Taoist temples are once again crowded with worshipers. Despite official efforts to suppress its more evangelical forms, Christianity has become increasingly popular as well; like the "rice Christians" (persons who supposedly converted for economic reasons) of the past, many now view it as a symbol of success and cosmopolitanism.

China's Changing Culture

The rise to power of the Communist Party in 1949 had a revolutionary impact on Chinese culture. Like their Soviet counterparts, Mao and his colleagues viewed culture as an important instrument of indoctrination. The standard would no longer be aesthetic quality or the personal preference of the artist but "art for life's sake," whereby culture would serve the interests of socialism.

CULTURE IN A REVOLUTIONARY ERA At first, the new emphasis on socialist realism did not entirely extinguish the influence of traditional culture. Mao and his colleagues tolerated—and even encouraged—efforts by artists to synthesize traditional ideas with socialist concepts and Western techniques. During the Cultural Revolution, however, all forms of traditional culture came to be viewed as reactionary. Socialist realism became the only acceptable standard in literature, art, and music. All forms of traditional expression were forbidden, and the deification of Mao and his central role in building a Communist paradise became virtually the only acceptable form of artistic expression.

Characteristic of the changing cultural climate in China was the experience of author Ding Ling (DING LING). Born in 1904 and educated in a school for women set up by leftist intellectuals during the hectic years after the May Fourth

Family and Society in an Era of Change

FAMILY & SOCIETY

One of the paradoxes of the modern world is that at a time of political stability and economic prosperity for many people in the advanced capitalist societies, public cynicism about the system is increasingly widespread. Alienation and drug use are at dangerously high levels, and the rate of criminal activities in most areas remains much higher than in the years immediately after World War II.

Although various reasons have been advanced to explain this paradox, many observers contend that the decline of the traditional family system is responsible for many contemporary social problems. There has been a steady rise in the percentage of illegitimate births and single-parent families in countries throughout the Western world. In the United States, approximately half of all marriages end in divorce. Even in two-parent families, more and more parents work full time, leaving the children to fend for themselves on their return from school. In many countries in Europe, the birthrate has dropped to alarming levels, leading to a severe labor shortage that is attracting a rising number of immigrants from other parts of the world.

Observers point to several factors to explain these conditions: the growing emphasis in advanced capitalist states on an individualistic lifestyle devoted to instant gratification, a phenomenon promoted vigorously by the advertising media; the rise of the feminist movement, which has freed women from the servitude imposed on their predecessors, but at the expense of removing them from full-time responsibility for the care of the next generation; and the increasing mobility of contemporary life, which disrupts traditional family ties and creates a sense of rootlessness and impersonality in the individual's relationship to the surrounding environment.

These trends are not unique to Western civilization. The traditional nuclear family is also under attack in many societies around the world. Even in East Asia, where the Confucian tradition of family solidarity has been endlessly touted as a major factor in the region's economic success, the incidence of divorce and illegitimate births is on the rise, as is the percentage of women in the workforce. Older citizens frequently complain that the Asian youth of today are too materialistic, faddish, and steeped in the individualistic values of the West. Such criticisms are now voiced in mainland China as well as in the capitalist societies around its perimeter (see Chapter 30).

In societies less exposed to the corrosive effects of Western culture, such as India, Africa, and the Middle East, traditional attitudes about the family continue to hold sway, and the tenacity of the family system should not be ignored, as Mao Zedong discovered to his dismay during the Great Leap Forward. Still, the trend toward a more individualistic lifestyle seems to be a worldwide phenomenon, as the situation in China and many of its neighbors demonstrates. As young people move into the growing cities to pursue their careers, their elderly parents living in the countryside are often left to fend for themselves, sometimes in desperate straits. No wonder Chinese leaders are resurrecting Confucius as a zealous guardian of traditional virtues!

© William J. Duiker

China's "Little Emperors." Chinese leaders have launched a massive family planning program to curtail population growth. Urban families are restricted to a single child. In conformity with tradition, sons are especially prized, and some Chinese complain that many parents overindulge their children, turning them into spoiled "little emperors."

 To what degree and in what ways are young people in China becoming more like their counterparts in the West?

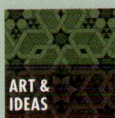
COMPARATIVE ILLUSTRATION

Then and Now: Changing Clothing Styles in China.

For the longtime visitor to China, the change in clothing styles that has taken place in China since the end of the Cultural Revolution is striking. In the illustration on the top, taken in the 1970s, a group of college students pose for a photograph in front of their classroom at the Beijing Teacher's College. The photo on the bottom shows a group of young Chinese on the Bund in Shanghai, complete with their designer handbags and their hand-held electronic devices. The forest of skyscrapers in the Pudong (Poo-DOONG) district looms in the background. As the illustration suggests, the Japanese fashion of "tea hair" (see Chapter 30) has caught on among young people in China as well.

Q *Does the apparent improvement in living conditions over the past generation suggested by these photographs justify the claim by the Chinese government that centralized leadership by the Communist Party is necessary to improve the lives of its citizens? Why or why not?*

© William J. Duiker

© Yvonne V. Duiker

Movement, she became involved in party activities and settled in Yan'an, where she wrote her most famous novel, *The Sun Shines over the Sangan River*, which described the CCP's land reform program in favorable terms. It was awarded the Stalin Prize three years later.

During the early 1950s, Ding Ling was one of the most prominent literary lights of the new China, but in the more ideological climate at the end of the decade, she was attacked for her individualism and her occasional criticism of the party's treatment of women. Although temporarily rehabilitated, during the Cultural Revolution she was sentenced to hard labor on a commune in the far north and was not released until the late 1970s after the death of Mao Zedong. Crippled and in poor health, she began writing a biography of her mother that examined the role of women in twentieth-century China, but she died in 1981. Ding Ling's fate mirrored the fate of thousands of progressive Chinese intellectuals who, despite their efforts, were not able to satisfy the constantly changing demands of a repressive regime.

ART AND ARCHITECTURE After Mao's death, Chinese culture was finally released from the shackles of socialist realism. In painting, where for a decade the only acceptable standard for excellence was praise for the party and its policies, the new permissiveness led to a revival of interest in both traditional and Western forms. Although some painters continued to blend Eastern and Western styles, others imitated trends from abroad, experimenting with a wide range of previously prohibited art styles, including Cubism and abstract painting. Some of the more avant-garde examples of contemporary art shocked the Chinese public and provoked the wrath of the party, leading the regime to declare that henceforth it would regulate all art exhibits. Since the 1990s, some Chinese artists, such as the world-famous Ai Weiwei (I WAY-WAY) (b. 1957), have aggressively challenged the government's authority. In response, the government razed Ai's art studio in Shanghai in 2011. He was subsequently taken into police custody on charges related to tax evasion. He was eventually released but the government is maintaining a close watch on his activities. Nonetheless, much contemporary Chinese art is attracting international attention and commanding exorbitant prices on the world market.

In recent years, China has invested heavily in infrastructure projects, not only in the field of transportation but also in multitudinous blocks of apartment complexes erected to house the steady stream of migrants into the cities. This has led to an explosive building boom, highlighted by the projects connected with the 2008 Olympic Games in Beijing and spreading outward to China's many megacities. At a dizzying pace, renowned architects, both Chinese and foreign, are currently executing some of the new century's most original and experimental architectural designs. The gleaming vertiginous forest of skyscrapers currently rising in Shanghai's Pudong district is only the most quintessential example (see the bottom photo in the Comparative Illustration "Then and Now: Changing Clothing Styles in China" on p. 819).

LITERATURE The limits of freedom of expression were most apparent in literature. During the early 1980s, party leaders encouraged Chinese writers to express their views on the mistakes of the past, and a new "literature of the wounded" began to describe the brutal and arbitrary character of the Cultural Revolution. One of the most prominent writers was Bai Hua (by HWA) (b. 1930), whose film script *Bitter Love* described the life of a young Chinese painter who joined the revolutionary movement during the 1940s but whose work was condemned as counterrevolutionary during the Cultural Revolution. In describing the excesses of the Cultural Revolution, Bai Hua was only responding to Deng Xiaoping's appeal for intellectuals to speak out but he was soon criticized for failing to point out the essentially beneficial role of the CCP in recent Chinese history. The film was withdrawn from circulation in 1981, and Bai Hua was compelled to recant his errors and to state that the great ideas of Mao Zedong on art and literature were "still of universal guiding significance today."[10]

As the attack on Bai Hua illustrates, many party leaders remained suspicious of the impact that "decadent" bourgeois culture could have on the socialist foundations of Chinese society. The official press periodically warned that China should adopt only the "positive" aspects of Western culture (notably, its technology and its work ethic) and not the "negative" elements such as drug use, pornography, and hedonism.

Conservatives were especially incensed by the tendency of many writers to dwell on the shortcomings of the socialist system and to come uncomfortably close to direct criticism of the role of the CCP. One such writer is Mo Yan (muh YAHN) (b. 1956), whose novels *The Garlic Ballads* (1988) and *Life and Death Are Wearing Me Out* (2008) expose the rampant corruption of contemporary Chinese society, the roots of which he attributes to one-party rule. Like Mo Yan, Yan Lianke (Yen Lyan-KUH) addresses the suffering of the Chinese peasant. In *Dream of Ding Village* (2011), which was banned by the government, he exposes the real-life AIDS epidemic that resulted from tainted blood provided by a dishonest blood donor business. Jiang Rong (JYAHNG-RONG), in his gripping novel *Wolf Totem* (2007), describes an example of rural injustice in Inner Mongolia, as traditional economical practices are sacrificed on the altar of rapid economic growth. Today, Chinese culture has been dramatically transformed by the nation's adoption of a market economy and the invasive spread of the Internet. A new mass literature, much of it written by and intended for China's new urban youth, explores the aspirations and frustrations of a generation obsessed with material consumption and the right of individual expression. Lost in the din are the voices of China's rural poor.

As in the Western world, people in China are probably more influenced by what they see in film than by the written word. Today the Chinese film industry is growing dramatically and currently rivals the United States and India for the number of films produced annually. In the past, most Chinese films were of the popular kung fu variety, and often dealt with historical subjects designed to inspire the spirit of patriotism among the audience, but in recent years, a new genre of movies has been produced—often by young directors—that

Hollywood in China. In recent years, the movie industry has become a big business in China, as box office deposits are surpassed only by those in the United States. For years, the Beijing regime has been promoting films with Chinese historical themes—often accompanied by the swashbuckling antics of kung fu adepts—as a painless way of promoting patriotism among the populace. Recently, however, a new generation of Chinese filmmakers has begun to produce films on more serious subjects, some of which are tacitly critical of conditions in today's China. Shown here, a film crew in the southern city of Guangzhou (GWAHNG-Joh) is on safer ground as it produces a typical film based on Chinese history.

focus on the lives and aspirations of young people. Some have been banned by official sources because of their emphasis on materialist and hedonistic pursuits.

Confucius and Marx: The Tenacity of Tradition

Why has communism survived in China, albeit in a substantially altered form, when it failed in Eastern Europe and the Soviet Union? One of the primary factors is probably cultural. Although the doctrine of Marxism-Leninism originated in Europe, many of its main precepts, such as the primacy of the community over the individual and the denial of the concept of private property, run counter to trends in Western civilization. This inherent conflict is especially evident in the societies of western and central Europe, which were strongly influenced by Enlightenment philosophy and the Industrial Revolution. These forces were weaker farther to the east, although they had begun to penetrate tsarist Russia by the end of the nineteenth century.

In contrast, Marxism-Leninism found a more receptive climate in China and other countries in the region influenced by Confucian tradition. In its political culture, the communist system exhibits many of the same characteristics as traditional Confucianism—a single truth, an elite governing class, and an emphasis on obedience to the community and its governing representatives. Although a significant and influential minority of the Chinese population—primarily urban and educated—finds the idea of personal freedom against the power of the state appealing, such concepts have little meaning in rural villages, where the interests of the community have always been emphasized over the desires of the individual. It is no accident that Chinese leaders now seek to reintroduce the precepts of State Confucianism to bolster a fading belief in the existence of a future communist paradise.

Party leaders today are banking on the hope that China can be governed as it has always been—by an elite class of highly trained professionals dedicated to pursing a predefined objective. In fact, however, real changes are taking place in China today. Although the youthful protesters in Tiananmen Square were comparable in some respects to the reformist elements of the early republic, the China of today is fundamentally different from that of the early twentieth century. Literacy rates and the standard of living are far higher, the pressures of outside powers are less threatening, and China has entered its own industrial and technological revolution. Many Chinese depend more on independent talk radio and the Internet for news and views than on the official media. Whereas Sun Yat-sen, Chiang Kai-shek, and even Mao Zedong broke their lances on the rocks of centuries of tradition, poverty, and ignorance, the present leaders rule a country much more aware of the world and China's place in it. Although the shift in popular expectations may be gradual, China today is embarked on a journey to a future for which the past no longer provides a roadmap.

CHAPTER SUMMARY

For four decades after the end of World War II, the two major Communist powers appeared to have become permanent features on the international landscape. Suddenly, though, in the late 1980s, the Soviet Union entered a period of internal crisis that shook the foundations of Soviet society. In 1991 the system collapsed, to be replaced by a series of independent states based primarily on ethnic and cultural differences that had existed long before the Bolshevik Revolution. China went through an even longer era of instability, beginning with the Cultural Revolution in 1966, but it managed to survive under a hybrid system that combines features of a Leninist command economy with capitalist practices adapted from the modern West.

Why were the outcomes so different? Although the cultural differences we have described were undoubtedly an important factor, the role of human action should not be ignored. Whereas Mikhail Gorbachev introduced the idea of *glasnost* to permit the emergence of a more pluralistic political system in the Soviet Union, Chinese leaders crushed the protest movement in the spring of 1989 and reasserted the authority of the Communist Party. Deng Xiaoping's gamble paid off, and today the party stands at the height of its power.

CHAPTER TIMELINE

	1945	1955	1965	1975	1985	1995	2005
Soviet Union and Russia		Death of Stalin and emergence of Khrushchev	Era of Brezhnev		The Gorbachev years	Dissolution of the Soviet Union / Yeltsin era	
Eastern Europe	Communist governments established in Eastern Europe		"Prague Spring"		Revolutions of Eastern Europe		
China		Creation of People's Republic of China / Period of New Democracy / Great Leap Forward	Great Proletarian Cultural Revolution	Death of Mao Zedong / Rise to power of Deng Xiaoping / Era of "Four Modernizations"	Tiananmen Square incident	Presidency of Jiang Zemin / Hu Jintao becomes president	

CHAPTER REVIEW

Upon Reflection

Q   How have six decades of Communist rule affected the concept of the family in China? How does the current state of the family in China compare with the family in other parts of the world?

Q   What strategies were used by the leaders of the Soviet Union and the People's Republic of China as they sought to build communist societies in their countries? In what ways were the strategies different, and in what ways were they similar? To what degree were they successful?

Q   How has the current generation of leadership in China made use of traditional values to solidify Communist control over the country? To what degree has this approach contradicted the theories of Karl Marx?

Key Terms

new course (p. 793)
de-Stalinization (p. 794)
Gosplan (p. 796)
perestroika (p. 800)
glasnost (p. 800)
Solidarity (p. 802)
New Democracy (p. 804)
Great Leap Forward (p. 804)

Great Proletarian Cultural Revolution (p. 805)
uninterrupted revolution (p. 805)
Four Modernizations (p. 807)
rural responsibility system (p. 814)

Suggested Reading

RUSSIA AND THE SOVIET UNION   For a general view of modern Russia, see **M. Malia,** *Russia Under Western Eyes* (Cambridge, Mass., 1999), and **M. T. Poe,** *The Russian Moment in World History* (Princeton, N.J., 2003). On the Khrushchev years, see **W. Taubman,** *Khrushchev: The Man and His Era* (New York, 2004). For an inquiry into the reasons for the Soviet collapse, see **R. Conquest,** *Reflections on a Ravaged Century* (New York, 1999), and **R. Strayer,** *Why Did the Soviet Union Collapse? Understanding Historical Change* (New York, 1998). For an analysis of the underlying weakness of the entire satellite system in Eastern Europe, see **S. Kotkin,** *Uncivil Society: 1989 and the Implosion of the Communist Establishment* (New York, 2010).

CHINA UNDER MAO ZEDONG   A number of useful surveys deal with China after World War II. The most comprehensive treatment of the Communist period is **M. Meisner,** *Mao's China and After: A History of the People's Republic* (New York, 1999). Also see **R. Macfarquhar, ed.,** *The Politics of China: The Eras of Mao and Deng* (Cambridge, 1997). A recent critical biography of China's "Great Helmsman" is **J. Chang** and **J. Halliday**, *Mao: The Unknown Story* (New York, 2005). The disastrous Great Leap Forward is analyzed in **F. Dikotter**, *Mao's Great Famine: The History of China's Most Devastating Catastrophe* (New York, 2010).

POST-MAO CHINA The 1989 demonstrations and their aftermath are described in an eyewitness account by **L. Feigon**, *China Rising: The Meaning of Tiananmen* (Chicago, 1990). Documentary materials relating to the events of 1989 are chronicled in **A. J. Nathan** and **P. Link, eds.**, *The Tiananmen Papers* (New York, 2001) and **Zhao Ziyang, Prisoner of the State: The Secret Journal of Chinese Premier Zhao Ziyang** (New York, 2009). Subsequent events are analyzed in **J. Fewsmith**, *China Since Tiananmen: The Politics of Transition* (Cambridge, 2001). On China's challenge from the process of democratization, see **J. Gittings**, *The Changing Face of China: From Mao to Market* (Oxford, 2005). China's evolving role in the world is traced in **S. Shirk**, *China: Fragile Superpower* (Oxford, 2007).

CHINESE LITERATURE AND ART For a comprehensive introduction to twentieth-century Chinese literature, consult **J. Lau** and **H. Goldblett**, *The Columbia Anthology of Modern Chinese Literature* (New York, 1995). On twentieth-century Chinese art, see **M. Sullivan**, *Arts and Artists of Twentieth-Century China* (Berkeley, Calif., 1996).

Chapter Notes

1. Quoted in V. Zubok and C. Pleshakov, *Inside the Kremlin's Cold War: From Stalin to Khrushchev* (Cambridge, Mass., 1996), p. 166.
2. N. Khrushchev, *Khrushchev Remembers*, trans. S. Talbott (Boston, 1970), p. 77.
3. Quoted in H. Smith, *The New Russians* (New York, 1990), p. 30.
4. Quoted in F. B. Tipton and R. Aldrich, *An Economic and Social History of Europe from 1939 to the Present* (Baltimore, 1987), p. 193.
5. Quoted in Smith, *New Russians*, p. 74.
6. "Report on an Investigation of the Peasant Movement in Hunan (March 1927)," in *Quotations from Chairman Mao Tse-tung* (Beijing, 1976), p. 12.
7. Quoted in S. Karnow, *Mao and China: Inside China's Cultural Revolution* (New York, 1972), p. 95.
8. Quoted from an article by Mao in the journal *Red Flag* (June 1, 1958), in S. R. Schram, *The Political Thought of Mao Tse-tung* (New York, 1963), p. 253.
9. Liang Heng and J. Shapiro, *Son of the Revolution* (New York, 1983).
10. Quoted in J. Spence, *Chinese Roundabout: Essays in History and Culture* (New York, 1992), p. 285.

MindTap™

MindTap is a fully online, highly personalized learning experience built upon Cengage Learning content. MindTap combines student learning tools—readings, multimedia, activities, and assessments—into a singular Learning Path that guides students through their course.

Europe and the Western Hemisphere Since 1945

Survivors in the ruins of Berlin, Germany, at the end of World War II

© SZ Photo/SV-Bilderdienst/The Bridgeman Art Library

CHAPTER OUTLINE AND FOCUS QUESTIONS

Recovery and Renewal in Europe

Q What problems have the nations of Western Europe faced since 1945, and what steps have they taken to try to solve these problems? What problems have Eastern European nations faced since 1989?

Emergence of the Superpower: The United States

Q What political, social, and economic changes has the United States experienced since 1945?

The Development of Canada

Q What political, social, and economic developments has Canada experienced since 1945?

Latin America Since 1945

Q What problems have the nations of Latin America faced since 1945, and what role has Marxist ideology played in their efforts to solve these problems?

Society and Culture in the Western World

Q What major social, cultural, and intellectual developments have occurred in Western Europe and North America since 1945?

CRITICAL THINKING

Q What were the similarities and differences between the major political, economic, and social developments in the first half of the twentieth century and those in the second half of the century?

CONNECTIONS TO TODAY

Q Since 1945, the nations of Europe and the Western Hemisphere have experienced many changes and challenges. What changes and challenges will these nations face over the next 50 years?

THE END OF WORLD WAR II in Europe had been met with great joy. One visitor in Moscow reported, "I looked out of the window [at 2:00 A.M.]; almost everywhere there were lights in the windows—people were staying awake. Everyone embraced everyone else; someone sobbed aloud." But after the victory parades and celebrations, Europeans awoke to a devastating realization: their civilization was in ruins. Almost 40 million people (both soldiers and civilians) had been killed over the last six years. Massive air raids and artillery bombardments had reduced many of the great cities of Europe to heaps of rubble. The Polish capital of Warsaw had been almost completely obliterated. An American general described Berlin: "Wherever we looked, we saw desolation. It was like a city of the dead. Suffering and shock were visible in every face. Dead bodies still remained in canals and lakes and were being dug out from under bomb debris." Millions of Europeans faced starvation as grain harvests were only half what they had been in 1939. Millions were also homeless.

Yet by 1970, Europe had not only recovered from the devastating effects of World War II but had experienced an economic resurgence that seemed nothing less than miraculous. Economic growth and virtually full employment continued so long that the first postwar recession, in 1973, came as a shock. It was short-lived, however, and economic growth resumed. Important to this economic expansion was the creation of the welfare state—a prominent social development in postwar Europe. After the collapse of communist governments in the revolutions of 1989, a number of Eastern European states sought to create market economies and join the military and economic unions first formed by Western European states.

The most significant development after 1945 was the emergence of the United States as the world's richest and most powerful nation. American prosperity reached new heights in the two decades after World War II, but a series of economic and social problems—including racial tensions and staggering budget deficits—left an imposing array of obstacles.

Latin America, to the south of the United States, had its own unique heritage. Although some Latin Americans in the nineteenth century had looked to the United States as a model for their own development, in the twentieth century many strongly criticized the United States for its military and economic domination of their countries. And even though they had escaped the turmoil of World War II, many Latin American countries struggled with economic and political instability in the postwar years.

Toward the end of the century, as the West adjusted from Cold War to post–Cold War realities, other changes were also shaping the Western outlook. The demographic face of European countries changed as massive numbers of immigrants introduced greater ethnic diversity. New artistic and intellectual currents, the continued advance of science and technology, the coming to grips with environmental problems, the surge of the women's liberation movement—all reflected a vibrant, ever-changing world. At the same time, a devastating series of terrorist attacks made the Western world vividly aware of its vulnerability to international terrorism.

Recovery and Renewal in Europe

 FOCUS QUESTIONS: What problems have the nations of Western Europe faced since 1945, and what steps have they taken to try to solve these problems? What problems have Eastern European nations faced since 1989?

All the nations of Europe faced similar problems at the end of World War II. First and foremost, they needed to rebuild their shattered economies. Remarkably, within a few years after the defeat of Germany and Italy, an incredible economic revival brought renewed growth to Western Europe.

Western Europe: The Revival of Democracy and the Economy

With the economic aid of the Marshall Plan, which provided the countries of Western Europe with 9.4 billion dollars between 1947 and 1950, recovery from the devastation of World War II took place relatively rapidly. Between the early 1950s and the late 1970s, industrial production surpassed all previous records, and Western Europe experienced virtually full employment.

FRANCE: FROM DE GAULLE TO NEW UNCERTAINTIES

The history of France for nearly a quarter-century after the war was dominated by one man—Charles de Gaulle (SHAHRL duh GOHL) (1890–1970). The founding of the Fourth Republic, with a parliamentary system based on parties that de Gaulle considered weak, led him to withdraw for a while from politics. In 1958, however, frightened by the bitter divisions within France caused by the Algerian crisis (see Chapter 29), the panic-stricken leaders of the Fourth Republic offered to let de Gaulle take over the government and revise the constitution.

De Gaulle's constitution for the Fifth Republic greatly enhanced the power of the president, who would now have the right to choose the prime minister, dissolve parliament, and supervise both national defense and foreign policy. As the new president, de Gaulle sought to return France to the status of a great power. With that goal in mind, he invested heavily in the nuclear arms race. France exploded its first nuclear bomb in 1960. Nevertheless, de Gaulle did not really achieve his ambitious goals; in truth, France was too small for such global ambitions.

During de Gaulle's presidency, the French gross domestic product experienced an annual increase of 5.5 percent, greater than that of the United States. France became a major industrial producer and exporter, particularly in such areas as automobiles and armaments. But the nationalization (government ownership) of traditional industries, such as coal, steel, and railroads, led to large government deficits. The cost of living rose faster in France than in the rest of Europe. Increased dissatisfaction led to a series of student protests in May 1968, followed by a general strike by the labor unions. Although he restored order, de Gaulle became discouraged, resigned from office in April 1969, and died the next year.

The worsening of France's economic situation in the 1970s brought a political shift to the left. By 1981, the Socialists had become the dominant party in the National Assembly, and the Socialist leader, François Mitterrand (frahnh-SWAH MEE-tayr-rahnh) (1916–1995), was elected president. Mitterrand passed a number of measures to aid workers: a higher minimum wage, expanded social benefits, a mandatory fifth week of paid vacation for salaried workers, and a thirty-nine-hour workweek. The victory of the Socialists led them to enact some of their more radical reforms: the government nationalized the steel industry, major banks, the space and electronics industries, and important insurance firms.

Charles de Gaulle. Charles de Gaulle returned to politics in 1958 in response to the crisis in Algeria. As president, he sought to revive the greatness of the French nation. He is shown here arriving in Algeria in 1958.

The socialist policies largely failed to work, however, and within three years, a decline in support for the Socialists caused the Mitterrand government to reprivatize portions of the economy. But France's economic decline continued. In 1993, French unemployment stood at 10.6 percent, and in the elections in March of that year, the Socialists won only 28 percent of the vote; a coalition of conservative parties ended up with 80 percent of the seats. The move to the right was strengthened when the conservative mayor of Paris, Jacques Chirac (ZHAHK shee-RAK) (b. 1932), was elected president in May 1995 and reelected in 2002. As high unemployment rates fueled resentment against foreign-born residents, many French voters called for restrictions on all new immigration. Chirac himself pursued a plan of sending illegal immigrants back to their home countries.

In the fall of 2005, however, antiforeign sentiment provoked a backlash of its own as young Muslims in the crowded suburbs of Paris rioted against dismal living conditions and the lack of employment opportunities for foreign residents in France. After the riots subsided, government officials promised to adopt measures to respond to the complaints, but tensions between the Muslim community and the remainder of the French population have become a chronic source of social unrest throughout the country—an unrest that Nicolas Sarkozy

(nee-kohl-AH sar-koh-ZEE) (b. 1955), elected president in 2007, promised to address but without much success.

Growing concern over Europe's financial problems led the French to move to the left and elect Socialist candidate François Hollande (frahn-SWAH oh-LAHN) (b. 1954) as president on May 6, 2012. Hollande has vowed to raise taxes on the wealthy, regulate banks, and address the economic crises.

FROM WEST GERMANY TO ONE GERMANY As noted in Chapter 26, the three Western zones of Germany were unified as the Federal Republic of Germany in 1949. Konrad Adenauer (AD-uh-now-ur) (1876–1967), the leader of the Christian Democratic Union (CDU), served as chancellor from 1949 to 1963 and became the Federal Republic's "founding hero." Adenauer sought respect for postwar Germany by cooperating with the United States and the other Western European nations.

Adenauer's chancellorship saw the resurrection of the West German economy, often referred to as the "economic miracle." Although West Germany had only 52 percent of the territory of prewar Germany, by 1955 the West German gross domestic product exceeded that of prewar Germany. Real wages doubled between 1950 and 1965. Unemployment fell from 8 percent in 1950 to 0.4 percent in 1965.

After the Adenauer era, German voters moved politically from the center-right of the Christian Democrats to center-left politics; in 1969, the Social Democrats became the leading party. The first Social Democratic chancellor was Willy Brandt (VIL-ee BRAHNT) (1913–1992), who was especially successful with his "opening toward the east"—known as *Ostpolitik* (OHST-poh-lee-teek)—for which he received the Nobel Peace Prize in 1972. On March 19, 1971, Brandt worked out the details of a treaty with East Germany (the former Russian zone) that led to greater cultural, personal, and economic contacts between West and East Germany.

In 1982, the Christian Democratic Union of Helmut Kohl (HEL-moot KOHL) (b. 1930) formed a new center-right government. Kohl was a clever politician who benefited greatly from an economic boom in the mid-1980s and the 1989 revolution in East Germany, which led in 1990 to the long-awaited reunification of the two Germanies, making the new restored Germany, with its 79 million people, the leading power in Europe.

But the excitement over reunification soon dissipated as new problems arose. All too soon, the realization set in that the revitalization of eastern Germany would take far more money than was originally thought, and Kohl's government was soon forced to face the politically undesirable task of raising taxes substantially. Moreover, the virtual collapse of the economy in eastern Germany led to extremely high levels of unemployment and severe discontent. East Germans were also haunted by another memory from their recent past.

The opening of the files of the secret police—the *Stasi* (SHTAH-see)—revealed that millions of East Germans had spied on their neighbors and colleagues, and even their spouses and parents, during the Communist era. A few senior Stasi officials were put on trial for their past actions, but many Germans preferred simply to close the door on that unhappy period in their lives and face the challenges of the future.

As the century neared its close, then, Germans struggled to cope with the challenge of building a united nation. To reduce the debt incurred for economic reconstruction in the east, the government threatened to cut back on many of the social benefits West Germans had long been accustomed to receiving. This in turn sharpened resentments that were already beginning to emerge between western and eastern Germany.

In 1998, voters took out their frustrations at the ballot box. Helmut Kohl's conservative coalition was defeated, and a new prime minister, Social Democrat Gerhard Schröder (GAYR-hahrt SHRUR-dur) (b. 1944), came into office. But Schröder had little success at solving Germany's economic woes, and as a result of elections in 2005, Angela Merkel (AHNG-uh-luh MERK-uhl) (b. 1954), leader of the Christian Democrats, became the first female chancellor in German history. Merkel pursued health care reform and new energy policies at home while taking a leading role in the affairs of the European Union. Merkel has since been reelected twice and has led the European Union (EU) nations in attempting to solve the financial problems of several EU members including Greece, Italy, Spain, and Portugal.

THE DECLINE OF GREAT BRITAIN The end of World War II left Britain with massive economic problems. In elections held immediately after the war, the Labour Party overwhelmingly defeated Churchill's Conservatives. Labour had promised far-reaching reforms, particularly in the area of social welfare, and in a country with a tremendous shortage of consumer goods and housing, its platform was quite appealing. The new Labour government under Clement Attlee (1883–1967) proceeded to turn Britain into a modern **welfare state**.

The process began with the nationalization of the Bank of England, the coal and steel industries, public transportation, and public utilities, such as electricity and gas. In 1946, the new government established a comprehensive social security program and nationalized medical insurance, thereby enabling the state to subsidize the unemployed, the sick, and the aged. The health act established a system of **socialized medicine** that forced doctors and dentists to work with state hospitals, although private practices could be maintained. The British welfare state became the model for most European nations after the war.

Continuing economic problems, however, brought the Conservatives back into power from 1951 to 1964. Although the British economy had recovered from the war, its slow rate of improvement reflected a long-term economic decline. The war had cost Britain much of its prewar revenues from abroad but left a burden of debt from innumerable international commitments. And as the influence of the United States and the Soviet Union continued to rise, Britain's ability to play the role of a world power declined substantially. Between 1964 and 1979, Conservatives and Labour alternated in power, but neither party was able to heal Britain's ailing economy.

In 1979, the Conservatives returned to power under Margaret Thatcher (1925–2013), who became the first woman prime minister in British history (see the Film & History feature "*The Iron Lady* (2011)" on p. 828). Thatcher pledged to lower taxes, reduce government bureaucracy, limit social welfare, restrict union power, and end inflation. The "Iron Lady," as she was called, did break the power of the labor unions. Although she did not eliminate the basic components of the social welfare system, she used austerity measures to control inflation. "Thatcherism," as her economic policy was termed, improved the British economic situation, but at a price. The south of England, for example, prospered, but the old industrial areas of the Midlands and north declined and were beset by high unemployment, poverty, and sporadic violence. Cutbacks in education seriously undermined the quality of British education, long regarded as the world's finest.

Thatcher dominated British politics in the 1980s. But in 1990, Labour's fortunes revived when Thatcher's government attempted to replace local property taxes with a flat-rate tax payable by every adult to a local authority. Many British citizens argued that this was nothing more than a poll tax that would allow the rich to get away with paying the same rate as the poor. In 1990, after antitax riots broke out, Thatcher's popularity plummeted, and a revolt within her own party forced her to resign as prime minister. She was replaced by John

Margaret Thatcher. Great Britain's first female prime minister, Margaret Thatcher was a strong leader who dominated British politics in the 1980s and served in the post longer than any man in modern times. This picture of Thatcher was taken during a meeting with French president François Mitterrand in 1986.

The Iron Lady (2011)

The Iron Lady, directed by Phyllida Lloyd, is a film based on the life of Margaret Thatcher, the first and only female British prime minister. In power from 1979 to 1990, she was also Britain's longest-serving prime minister. Much of the film focuses on Thatcher's later years, when she suffered from dementia. The film shows Thatcher (Meryl Streep) talking regularly to her recently deceased husband Denis (Jim Broadbent) as if he were still alive. Thatcher's early life and career as prime minister are depicted through flashbacks.

The Iron Lady is strong on presenting Thatcher's personality but weak on historical events. The film offers little to explain her development as a strongly principled conservative, other than that she was influenced by her father's conservative values as a small shop owner. She is also portrayed as a potential feminist, who sought to break away from the traditional female roles of wife and mother.

As she so aptly informs her husband-to-be in the film when he proposes marriage, she will not be a "domestic woman, silent and pretty" because she wants to "live a life that matters."

Thatcher was a divisive figure in British politics; she was loved and hated in equal measure for her policies and actions. Unfortunately, the film touches only briefly on some of the most important events in her career as prime minister: her fight for the leadership of the Conservative Party, reform of the labor unions, privatization of state-owned industries, military intervention in the Falkland Islands, and reduction in social welfare benefits. All of these deserve more time in a film about Thatcher's life.

The strength of the film is the performance by Meryl Streep, who won her third Academy Award for Best Actress. Streep prepared diligently for her role, watching films of Thatcher, talking to people who knew her, and attending sessions of Parliament to obtain background. In many ways, Streep's performance captures much of the essence of Thatcher as a person. Clearly portrayed is her ideological rigidity; Thatcher believed firmly in her principles and that she was always right: "I do what I know to be right," she says in the film. She reveled in her toughness in dealing with any situation. On the use of British forces to recapture the Falklands from Argentina, she says, "I will not negotiate with thugs. We must stand on principle. Right will triumph over wrong." Despite the reservations of her advisers, Thatcher is shown being adamant about imposing a poll tax: "You haven't got the courage to fight; you are cowards." As Streep portrays her, however, Thatcher's lack of flexibility and her conviction that she was always right turned to arrogance and led to her downfall. When members of her party turned against her over the poll tax, she had no choice but to resign as prime minister.

Prime Minister Margaret Thatcher (Meryl Streep) at a cabinet meeting.

Film 4/Kobal Collection/ Picture Desk

Major (b. 1943), but his government failed to capture the imagination of most Britons. In new elections on May 1, 1997, the Labour Party won a landslide victory. The new prime minister, Tony Blair (b. 1953), was a moderate whose youthful energy immediately instilled a new vigor on the political scene. Adopting centrist policies reminiscent of those followed by President Bill Clinton in the United States, his party dominated British politics into the new century. Blair was one of the prominent leaders who joined an international coalition against terrorism after the September 11 terrorist attacks on the United States in 2001. Four years later, his support of the U.S. war in Iraq when a majority of Britons opposed it caused his popularity to plummet, although the failure of the Conservative Party to field a popular candidate kept him in power until the summer of 2007, when he stepped down and allowed the Labour leader Gordon Brown (b. 1951) to become prime minister.

In 2010, in the wake of climbing unemployment and a global financial crisis, the thirteen-year rule of Britain's Labour Party ended when Conservative Party candidate David Cameron (b. 1966) became prime minister on the basis of a coalition with the Liberal Democrats. Cameron promised to decrease the government debt by reducing government waste and welfare benefits, cutting social services, and introducing legislation to overhaul Britain's health care system.

Welfare state emerges in Great Britain	1946
Konrad Adenauer becomes chancellor of West Germany	1949
Charles de Gaulle reassumes power in France	1958
Student protests in France	1968
Willy Brandt becomes chancellor of West Germany	1969
Margaret Thatcher becomes prime minister of Great Britain	1979
François Mitterrand becomes president of France	1981
Helmut Kohl becomes chancellor of West Germany	1982
Reunification of Germany	1990
Election of Jacques Chirac in France	1995
Labour Party victory in Great Britain	1997
Social Democratic victory in Germany	1998
Angela Merkel becomes chancellor of Germany	2005
Election of Nicolas Sarkozy in France	2007
Election of David Cameron in Britain	2010
Election of François Hollande in France	2012

Eastern Europe After Communism

The fall of communist governments in Eastern Europe during the revolutions of 1989 (see Chapter 27) brought a wave of euphoria to Europe. The new structures meant an end to a postwar European order that had been imposed on unwilling peoples by the victorious forces of the Soviet Union. In 1989 and 1990, new governments throughout Eastern Europe worked diligently to scrap the remnants of the old system and introduce the democratic procedures and market systems they believed would revitalize their scarred lands. But this process proved to be neither simple nor easy.

Most Eastern European countries had little or virtually no experience with democratic systems. Then, too, ethnic divisions, which had troubled these areas before World War II and had been forcibly submerged under Communist rule, re-emerged with a vengeance. Finally, the rapid conversion to market economies also proved painful. The adoption of "shock therapy" austerity measures caused much suffering. Unemployment, for example, climbed above 13 percent in Poland in 1992.

Nevertheless, by the beginning of the twenty-first century, many of these states, especially Poland and the Czech Republic, were making a successful transition to both free markets and democracy. In Poland, Aleksander Kwaśniewski (kwahsh-NYEF-skee) (b. 1954), a former Communist, was elected president in November 1995 and pushed Poland toward an increasingly prosperous free market economy. His successor, Lech Kaczyński (LEK kuh-ZIN-skee) (1949–2010), emphasized the need to combine modernization with tradition. In Czechoslovakia, the shift to non-communist rule was complicated by old problems, especially ethnic issues. Czechs and Slovaks disagreed over the makeup of the new state but were able to agree to a peaceful division of the country. On January 1, 1993, Czechoslovakia split into the Czech Republic and Slovakia. Václav Havel (VAHT-slahf HAH-vul) (1936–2011) was elected the first president of the new Czech Republic. In Romania, the current president, Traian Băsescu (trih-YAHN buh-SES-koo) (b. 1951), leads a country that is just beginning to experience economic growth and the rise of a middle class.

The revival of the post–Cold War Eastern European states is evident in their desire to join both NATO and the EU, the two major Cold War institutions of Western European unity (see "The Unification of Europe" later in this chapter). In 1997, Poland, the Czech Republic, and Hungary became full members of NATO. In 2004, ten nations—including Hungary, Poland, the Czech Republic, Slovenia, Estonia, Latvia, and Lithuania—joined the EU. In 2007, the EU expanded again as Bulgaria and Romania joined the union, and in July 2013, Croatia joined.

Not everyone is convinced that European integration is a good thing. Eastern Europeans fear that their countries will be dominated by investments from their prosperous neighbors, while their counterparts in Western Europe are concerned about a possible influx of low-wage workers from the new member countries. The global financial crisis of 2008–2009 also added to the economic problems of Eastern European countries.

THE DISINTEGRATION OF YUGOSLAVIA From its beginning in 1918, Yugoslavia had been an artificial creation. Strong leaders—especially the dictatorial Marshal Tito after World War II—had managed to hold together the six disparate republics and two autonomous provinces that made up the country. After Tito's death in 1980, however, no successor emerged, and eventually Yugoslavia was caught up in the reform movements sweeping through Eastern Europe.

After negotiations among the six republics failed, Slovenia and Croatia declared their independence in June 1991. Slobodan Milošević (sluh-BOH-dahn mih-LOH-suh-vich) (1941–2006), the leader of the republic of Serbia, rejected these efforts. He asserted that these republics could be independent only if new border arrangements were made to accommodate the Serb minorities in those republics who did not want to live outside the boundaries of Serbia. Serbian forces attacked both new states; although unsuccessful against Slovenia, they captured one-third of Croatia's territory.

The international recognition of independent Slovenia and Croatia in 1992 and of Macedonia and Bosnia and Herzegovina soon thereafter did not deter the Serbs, who now turned their guns on Bosnia (see the box "A Child's Account of the Shelling of Sarajevo" on p. 830). By mid-1993, Serbian forces had acquired 70 percent of Bosnian territory. The Serbian policy of **ethnic cleansing**—killing or forcibly removing Bosnian Muslims from their lands—revived memories of Nazi atrocities in World War II. This account by one Muslim survivor from the town of Srebrenica (sreb-bruh-NEET-suh) is eerily reminiscent of the activities of the Nazi *Einsatzgruppen* (see Chapter 25):

When the truck stopped, they told us to get off in groups of five. We immediately heard shooting next to the trucks.... About ten Serbs with automatic rifles told us to lie down on the ground face first. As we were getting down, they started

A Child's Account of the Shelling of Sarajevo

POLITICS & GOVERNMENT

WHEN BOSNIA DECLARED its independence in March 1992, Serbian army units and groups of Bosnian Serbs went on the offensive and began to shell the capital city of Sarajevo. One of its residents was Zlata Filipović (ZLA-ta Fi-li-PO-vich), the ten-year-old daughter of a middle-class lawyer. Zlata was a fan of MTV and pizza, but when the Serbs began to shell Sarajevo from the hills above the city, her life changed dramatically, as is apparent in this excerpt from her diary.

Zlata Filipović, *Zlata's Diary, A Child's Life in Sarajevo*

April 3, 1992: Daddy came back … all upset. He says there are terrible crowds at the train and bus stations. People are leaving Sarajevo.

April 4, 1992: There aren't many people in the streets. I guess it's fear of the stories about Sarajevo being bombed. But there's no bombing.…

April 5, 1992: I'm trying hard to concentrate so I can do my homework (reading), but I simply can't. Something is going on in town. You can hear gunfire from the hills.

April 6, 1992: Now they're shooting from the Holiday Inn, killing people in front of the parliament.… Maybe we'll go to the cellar.…

April 9, 1992: I'm not going to school. All the schools in Sarajevo are closed.…

April 14, 1992: People are leaving Sarajevo. The airport, train and bus stations are packed.…

April 18, 1992: There's shooting, shells are falling. This really is WAR. Mommy and Daddy are worried, they sit up late at night, talking. They're wondering what to do, but it's hard to know.… Mommy can't make up her mind—she's constantly in tears. She tries to hide it from me, but I see everything.

April 21, 1992: It's horrible in Sarajevo today. Shells falling, people and children getting killed, shooting. We will probably spend the night in the cellar.

April 26, 1992: We spent Thursday night with the Bobars again. The next day we had no electricity. We had no bread, so for the first time in her life Mommy baked some.

April 28, 1992: SNIFFLE! Everybody has gone. I'm left with no friends.

April 29, 1992: I'd write to you much more about the war if only I could. But I simply don't want to remember all these horrible things.

 How do you think Zlata Filipović was able to deal with the new conditions in her life?

Source: From Zlata Filipović, Zlata's Diary, A Child's Life in Sarajevo © 1994 by Fixot et editions Robert Laffont.

---

to shoot, and I fell into a pile of corpses. I felt hot liquid running down my face. I realized that I was only grazed. As they continued to shoot more groups, I kept on squeezing myself in between dead bodies.[1]

Almost eight thousand men and boys were killed in the Serbian massacre at Srebrenica. Nevertheless, despite worldwide outrage, European governments failed to take a forceful stand against the Serbs' actions, leaving the Muslim population of Bosnia in desperate straits. At long last, as the fighting spread, European nations and the United States began to intervene to stop the bloodshed, and in the fall of 1995, a fragile cease-fire agreement was reached. An international peacekeeping force was stationed in the area to maintain tranquility.

Peace in Bosnia, however, did not bring peace to Yugoslavia. A new war erupted in 1999 over Kosovo (KAWSS-suh-voh), which had been made an autonomous province within the Serbian republic in 1974. Kosovo's inhabitants were mainly ethnic Albanians. But the province was also home to a Serbian minority. In 1989, Yugoslav president Milošević stripped Kosovo of its autonomous status. Four years later, some groups of ethnic Albanians founded the Kosovo Liberation Army (KLA) and began a campaign against Serbian rule in Kosovo. When Serb forces began to massacre ethnic Albanians in an effort to crush the KLA, the United States and its NATO allies mounted a bombing campaign that forced Milošević to stop. In elections held in the fall of 2000, Milošević was ousted from power and later put on trial by an international tribunal for crimes against humanity for his ethnic cleansing policies. He died in prison in 2006 before his trial could be completed.

Troops from the European Union remain in Bosnia to keep the peace. NATO military forces were also brought into Kosovo while United Nations officials worked to set up democratic institutions there. In 2004, Yugoslavia ceased to exist when the new national government under Vojislav Koštunica (VOH-yee-slav kuh-STOO-nit-suh) (b. 1944) officially renamed the truncated country Serbia and Montenegro. Two years later, Montenegrins voted in favor of independence. Thus, by 2006, all six republics cobbled together to form Yugoslavia in 1918 were once again independent nations. Kosovo unilaterally proclaimed its independence from Serbia in 2008 and was recognized by most other world nations as the seventh sovereign state to emerge from the former Yugoslavia.

The War in Bosnia. By mid-1993, irregular Serb forces had overrun much of Bosnia and Herzegovina amid scenes of untold suffering. This photograph shows a woman running past the bodies of victims of a mortar attack on Sarajevo on August 21, 1992. Three mortar rounds landed, killing at least three people.

AP Images/Rikard Larma

The New Russia

Soon after the disintegration of the Soviet Union in 1991, a new era began in Russia with the presidency of Boris Yeltsin (YELT-Sun) (1931–2007). A new constitution created a two-chamber parliament and established a strong presidency. During the mid-1990s, Yeltsin sought to implement reforms that would place Russia on a firm course toward a pluralistic political system and a market economy. But the new post-communist Russia remained as fragile as ever. Burgeoning economic inequality and rampant corruption aroused widespread criticism and shook the confidence of the Russian people in the superiority of the capitalist system over the one that existed under Communist rule. A nagging war in the Caucasus—where the people of Chechnya (CHECH-nee-uh) sought national independence from Russia—drained the government budget and exposed the decrepit state of the once vaunted Red Army. In presidential elections held in 1996, Yeltsin was reelected, although his precarious health raised serious questions about his ability to govern.

THE PUTIN ERA At the end of 1999, Yeltsin suddenly resigned and was replaced by Vladimir Putin (VLAD-ih-meer POO-tin) (b. 1952), a former member of the KGB. Putin vowed to strengthen the role of the central government in managing the affairs of state. During the succeeding months, the parliament approved his proposal to centralize power in the hands of the federal government in Moscow.

The new president also vowed to return the breakaway state of Chechnya to Russian authority and to adopt a more assertive role in international affairs. Fighting in Chechnya continued throughout 2000, nearly reducing the republic's capital city of Grozny (GRAWZ-nee) to ruins. In July 2001,

Putin launched reforms, which included the unrestricted sale and purchase of land and tax cuts aimed at boosting economic growth and budget revenues. Although Russia soon experienced a budget surplus and a growing economy, serious problems remained.

Putin attempted to deal with the chronic problems in Russian society by centralizing his control over the system and by silencing critics—notably in the Russian media. Although he was criticized in the West for these moves, many Russians expressed sympathy with Putin's attempts to restore a sense of pride and discipline in Russian society.

In 2008, Dmitry Medvedev (di-MEE-tree mehd-VYEH-dehf) (b. 1965) became president of Russia when Putin could not run for reelection under Russia's constitution. Instead, Putin became prime minister, and the two men shared power. In 2012, despite public protests, Putin was again elected president to a six-year term.

The Unification of Europe

As we saw in Chapter 26, the divisions created by the Cold War led the nations of Western Europe to seek military security by forming the North Atlantic Treaty Organization (NATO) in 1949. The destructiveness of two world wars, however, caused many thoughtful Europeans to consider the need for some additional form of unity.

In 1957, France, West Germany, the Benelux countries (Belgium, the Netherlands, and Luxembourg), and Italy signed the Treaty of Rome, which created the European Economic Community (EEC). The EEC eliminated customs barriers for the six member nations and created a large free-trade area protected from the rest of the world by a common external tariff. All the member nations benefited economically. In 1973, Great

Britain, Ireland, and Denmark gained membership in what now was called the European Community (EC). Greece joined in 1981, followed by Spain and Portugal in 1986. In 1995, Austria, Finland, and Sweden also became members of the EC.

THE EUROPEAN UNION The European Community was an economic union, not a political one. By 2000, the EC contained 370 million people and constituted the world's largest single trading entity, transacting one-fourth of the world's commerce. In the 1980s and 1990s, the EC moved toward even greater economic integration. The Treaty on European Union, which went into effect on January 1, 1994, turned the European Community into the European Union (EU), a true economic and monetary union of all EC members. One of its first goals was achieved in 1999 with the introduction of a common currency, the euro. On January 1, 2002, the euro officially replaced twelve national currencies. By 2011, the euro had been adopted in seventeen countries and was serving approximately 327 million people; it had become the second-largest reserve currency after the U.S. dollar.

A major crisis for the euro emerged in 2010, when Greece's burgeoning public debt threatened to cause the bankruptcy of that country as well as financial difficulties for many European banks. To avert a financial disaster, other EU members, led by Germany, labored to put together a financial rescue plan. Subsequently, Portugal and Ireland also asked for assistance.

In addition to creating a single internal market for its members and a common currency, the European Union also established a common agricultural policy, under which subsidies are provided to farmers to enable them to sell their goods competitively on the world market. The end of national passports has given millions of Europeans greater flexibility in travel. The EU has been less successful in setting common foreign policy goals, primarily because individual nations still see foreign policy as a national priority and are reluctant to give up this power to a single overriding institution. Nevertheless, the EU did create a military force of 60,000, which is used chiefly for humanitarian and peacekeeping purposes, as in Bosnia where EU troops have replaced NATO forces. Indeed, the focus of the EU is on peaceful conflict resolution, not making war.

In 2009, the European Union ratified the Lisbon Treaty, which created a full-time presidential post and a new voting system that reflects each country's population size. It also provided more power for the European Parliament in an effort to promote the EU's foreign policy goals.

But as successful as the European Union has been, problems still exist. Europeans are often divided on the EU. Some oppose it because the official representatives of the EU are not democratically accountable to the people. Moreover, many Europeans do not see themselves as "Europeans" but remain committed to a national identity. The issue of bailouts has also created tensions between the bankrupt and solvent nations.

TOWARD A UNITED EUROPE At the beginning of the twenty-first century, the EU established a new goal: to incorporate into the union the states of eastern and southeastern Europe. Many of these states were considerably poorer than the current members, which raised the possibility that adding these nations might weaken the EU itself. To lessen the danger, EU members established a set of qualifications requiring candidates for membership to demonstrate a commitment both to market capitalism and to democracy, including not only the rule of law but also respect for minorities and human rights. Hence joining the EU might well add to the stability of these nations and make the dream of a united Europe a reality. In May 2004, the European Union took the plunge and added ten new members: Cyprus, the Czech Republic, Estonia, Hungary, Latvia, Lithuania, Malta, Poland, Slovakia, and Slovenia, thus enlarging the population of the EU to 455 million people. In January 2007, the EU expanded again as Bulgaria and Romania joined the union, and in July 2013, Croatia joined (see Map 28.1).

Emergence of the Superpower: The United States

 FOCUS QUESTION: What political, social, and economic changes has the United States experienced since 1945?

At the end of World War II, the United States emerged as one of the world's two superpowers. As its Cold War confrontation with the Soviet Union intensified, the United States directed much of its energy toward combating the spread of communism throughout the world. With the collapse of the Soviet Union at the beginning of the 1990s, the United States became the world's foremost military power.

American Politics and Society Through the Vietnam Era

Franklin Roosevelt's New Deal of the 1930s initiated a basic transformation of American society that included a dramatic increase in the role and power of the federal government, the rise of organized labor as a significant force in the economy and politics, the beginning of the welfare state, a grudging acceptance of ethnic minorities, and a willingness to experiment with deficit spending as a means of spurring the economy. The New Deal in American politics was bolstered by the election of Democratic presidents—Harry Truman in 1948, John F. Kennedy in 1960, and Lyndon B. Johnson in 1964. Even the election of a Republican president, Dwight D. Eisenhower, in 1952 and 1956 did not significantly alter the fundamental direction of the New Deal. As Eisenhower observed in 1954, "Should any political party attempt to abolish Social Security and eliminate labor laws and farm programs, you would not hear of that party again in our political history."

The economic boom after World War II fueled confidence in the American way of life. A shortage of consumer goods during the war left Americans with both surplus income and the desire to purchase these goods after the war. Then, too, the development of organized labor enabled more and more

MAP 28.1 European Union, 2013. Beginning in 1957 as the European Economic Community, also known as the Common Market, the union of European states seeking to integrate their economies has gradually grown from six members to twenty-seven. By 2002, the European Union had achieved two major goals—the creation of a single internal market and a common currency—although it has been less successful at working toward common political and foreign policy goals.

Q *What additional nations do you think will eventually join the European Union?*

Map legend:

- 1967: France, West Germany, Belgium, Netherlands, Luxembourg, Italy
- 1973: Great Britain, Ireland, Denmark
- 1981: Greece
- 1986: Spain, Portugal
- 1995: Austria, Finland, Sweden
- 2004: Czech Republic, Estonia, Hungary, Latvia, Lithuania, Malta, Poland, Slovakia, Slovenia, and Cyprus
- 2007: Bulgaria, Romania
- 2013: Croatia

© 2016 Cengage Learning

workers to get the wage increases that spurred the growth of the domestic market. Between 1945 and 1973, real wages grew an average of 3 percent a year, the most prolonged advance in U.S. history.

Starting in the 1960s, problems that had been glossed over earlier came to the fore. The decade began on a youthful and optimistic note when John F. Kennedy (1917–1963), age forty-three, became the youngest elected president in the history of the United States and the first one born in the twentieth century. His own administration, cut short by an assassin's bullet on November 22, 1963, focused primarily on foreign affairs. Kennedy's successor, Lyndon B. Johnson (1908–1973), who won a new term as president in a landslide in 1964, used his stunning mandate to pursue the growth of the welfare state begun in the New Deal. Johnson's programs included health care for the elderly and the War on Poverty, to be fought with food stamps and the Job Corps.

Johnson's other domestic passion was achieving equal rights for black Americans. In August 1963, the eloquent Martin Luther King Jr. (1929–1968), a Baptist minister and leader of a growing movement for racial equality, led the March on

Washington for Jobs and Freedom to dramatize black Americans' desire for treatment no different from that accorded to whites. This march and King's impassioned plea for racial equality had an electrifying effect on the American people. President Johnson pursued the cause of civil rights. As a result of his initiative, Congress enacted the Civil Rights Act of 1964, which created the machinery to end segregation and discrimination in the workplace and in public accommodations. The Voting Rights Act the following year eliminated obstacles to black participation in elections in southern states. But laws alone could not guarantee the "Great Society" that Johnson envisioned, and soon the administration faced bitter social unrest.

In the North and the West, blacks had had voting rights for many years, but local patterns of segregation resulted in considerably higher unemployment rates for blacks (and Hispanics) than for whites and left blacks segregated in huge urban ghettos. In these ghettos, the calls for militant action by radical black nationalist leaders, such as Malcolm X (1925–1965) of the Black Muslims, attracted more attention than the nonviolent appeals of Martin Luther King. In the summer of 1965, race

Bob Adelman/Historical Premium/Corbis

The Civil Rights Movement. In the early 1960s, Martin Luther King Jr. and his Southern Christian Leadership Conference organized a variety of activities to pursue the goal of racial equality. He is shown here with his wife, Coretta Scott King (right), and Rosa Parks and Ralph Abernathy (far left) leading a march in 1965 against racial discrimination. He was assassinated three years later.

of students to distant neighborhoods to achieve racial integration of the public schools had provoked a white backlash.

As president, Nixon was paranoid about conspiracies and resorted to subversive methods of gaining political intelligence on his political opponents. Nixon's zeal led to the Watergate scandal—the attempted bugging of Democratic National Headquarters, located in the Watergate apartment and hotel complex in Washington, D.C. Although Nixon repeatedly lied to the American public about his involvement in the affair, secret tapes of his own conversations in the White House revealed the truth. On August 9, 1974, Nixon resigned the presidency rather than face possible impeachment and then trial by the U.S. Congress.

After Watergate, American domestic politics focused on economic issues. Gerald Ford (1913–2006) became president when Nixon resigned, only to lose in the 1976 election to the former governor of Georgia, Jimmy Carter (b. 1924), who campaigned as an outsider against the Washington establishment. By 1980, the Carter administration faced two devastating problems. High inflation and a decline in average weekly earnings were causing a perceptible drop in American living standards. At the same time, a crisis abroad had erupted when fifty-three Americans were taken hostage by the Iranian government of Ayatollah Khomeini (ah-yah-TUL-uh khoh-MAY-nee) and held for nearly fifteen months (see Chapter 29). Carter's inability to gain the release of the American hostages led to perceptions at home that he was a weak president. His overwhelming loss to Ronald Reagan (1911–2004) in the election of 1980 brought forward the chief exponent of right-wing Republican policies.

The Reagan Revolution, as it has been called, sent U.S. policy in a number of new directions. Reversing decades of changes, Reagan cut back on the welfare state by decreasing spending on food stamps, school lunch programs, and job programs. At the same time, his administration fostered the largest peacetime military buildup in American history. Total federal spending rose from $631 billion in 1981 to over $1 trillion by 1986. But instead of raising taxes to pay for the new expenditures, Reagan convinced Congress that massive tax cuts would supposedly stimulate rapid economic growth and produce new revenues. Much of the tax cut went to the wealthy. Reagan's policies seemed to work in the short run as the United States experienced an economic upturn that lasted until the end of the 1980s. But the administration's spending policies also produced record government deficits, which loomed as an obstacle to long-term growth. In 1980, the total

riots broke out in the Watts district of Los Angeles, leading to thirty-four deaths and the destruction of more than one thousand buildings. When King was assassinated in 1968, more than one hundred cities erupted in rioting, including Washington, D.C., the nation's capital. The combination of riots and extremist comments by radical black leaders led to a "white backlash" and a severe racial division in America.

Antiwar protests also divided the American people after President Johnson committed American troops to a costly war in Vietnam (see Chapter 26). Teach-ins, sit-ins, and occupations of university buildings alternated with more radical demonstrations that increasingly led to violence. The killing of four student protesters at Kent State University in 1970 by the Ohio National Guard shocked both activists and ordinary Americans, and thereafter the vehemence of the antiwar movement began to subside. But the combination of antiwar demonstrations and riots in the cities caused many people to call for "law and order," an appeal used by Richard Nixon (1913–1994), the Republican presidential candidate in 1968. Nixon's election in 1968 started a shift to the right in American politics.

The Shift Rightward After 1973

Nixon eventually ended U.S. involvement in Vietnam by gradually withdrawing American troops. Politically, he pursued a "southern strategy," carefully calculating that "law and order" issues would appeal to southern whites. The Republican strategy, however, also gained support among white Democrats in northern cities, where court-mandated busing government debt was around $930 billion; by 1988, the total debt had almost tripled, reaching $2.6 trillion.

The inability of Reagan's successor, George H. W. Bush (b. 1924), to deal with the deficit problem, coupled with an economic downturn, led to the election of a Democrat, Bill Clinton (b. 1946), in November 1992. The new president was a southerner who claimed to be a new Democrat, one who favored a number of the Republican policies of the 1980s—a clear indication that this Democratic victory had by no means ended the rightward drift in American politics. In fact, Clinton's reelection in 1996 was due in part to his adoption of conservative policies.

President Clinton's political fortunes were aided considerably by a lengthy economic revival. A steady reduction in the annual government budget deficit strengthened confidence in the performance of the national economy. Much of Clinton's second term, however, was overshadowed by charges of misconduct stemming from the president's affair with a White House intern. After a bitter partisan struggle, the U.S. Senate acquitted the president on two articles of impeachment brought by the House of Representatives. But Clinton's problems helped the Republican candidate, George W. Bush (b. 1946), win the presidential election in 2000. Although Bush lost the popular vote to the Democratic candidate Al Gore, he narrowly won the electoral vote after a highly controversial victory in the state of Florida decided ultimately by the U.S. Supreme Court.

The first four years of Bush's administration were largely occupied with the war on terrorism and the U.S.-led war on Iraq. The Department of Homeland Security was established after the 2001 terrorist assaults to help protect the United States from future terrorist acts. At the same time, Bush pushed tax cuts through Congress that mainly favored the wealthy and helped produce record deficits reminiscent of the Reagan years. Environmentalists were especially disturbed by the Bush administration's efforts to weaken environmental laws and impose regulations that would benefit American corporations. In November 2004, after a highly negative political campaign, Bush was narrowly elected to a second term. Thereafter, Bush's popularity plummeted drastically as discontent grew over the Iraq War and financial corruption in the Republican Party, as well as the administration's poor handling of relief efforts after Hurricane Katrina devastated the city of New Orleans and other areas of Louisiana and Mississippi in 2005.

The many failures of the Bush administration led to the lowest approval ratings for a modern president and opened the door for a dramatic change in American politics. The new and often inspiring voice of Barack Obama (b. 1961), who campaigned on a platform of change "we can believe in" and ending the war in Iraq, led to an overwhelming Democratic victory in the elections of 2008. The Democrats were also aided by the dramatic collapse of the American financial system in the fall of 2008. Obama moved quickly in 2009 to deal with the worst economic recession since the Great Depression. At the same time, Obama persuaded Congress to pass a sweeping health care bill to provide most Americans with medical insurance and to enact legislation aimed at regulating the financial institutions that had helped bring about the financial crisis. He also emphasized the need to combat global warming and the decline in the educational system. Obama was reelected for a second term in 2012.

Anne Sherwood/Getty Images News/Getty Images

Presidential Candidate Barack Obama. In this photograph, Barack Obama is seen speaking to an overflow crowd of his supporters at a campaign rally in Montana on May 19, 2008. By this time, Obama was ahead of his chief opponent, Senator Hillary Clinton, and after primary victories two weeks later in South Dakota and Montana, he finally clinched the nomination. Campaigning on the slogan, "Change We Can Believe In," Obama electrified his campaign audiences.

The Development of Canada

 FOCUS QUESTION: What political, social, and economic developments has Canada experienced since 1945?

Canada's development in the postwar years has paralleled that of the United States. For twenty-five years after World War II, Canada experienced extraordinary economic prosperity as it set out on a path of industrial development. Canada had always had a strong export economy based on its abundant natural resources. Now it also developed electronic, aircraft, nuclear, and chemical engineering industries on a large scale. Much of the Canadian growth, however, was financed by capital from the United States, which resulted in American ownership of Canadian businesses. Though many Canadians welcomed the economic growth, others feared American economic domination of Canada and its resources.

A notable feature of Canada's postwar history has been its close relationship with the United States. In addition to fears of economic domination, Canadians have also worried about playing a subordinate role politically and militarily to the neighboring superpower. Canada agreed to join NATO in 1949 and even sent military contingents to fight in Korea the following year. But to avoid subordination to the United States or any other great power, Canada has consistently and actively supported the United Nations. Nevertheless, concerns about the United States have not kept Canada from maintaining a special relationship with its southern neighbor.

For three decades after 1945, the Liberal Party largely dominated Canadian politics and created Canada's welfare state by enacting a national social security system (the Canada Pension Plan) and a national health insurance program. The most prominent Liberal government was that of Pierre Trudeau (PYAYR troo-DOH) (1919–2000), who came to power in 1968. A French Canadian, Trudeau did not harbor separatist sentiments and was dedicated to Canada's federal union. In 1968, his government passed the Official Languages Act, which created a bilingual federal civil service and encouraged the growth of French culture and language in Canada. Although Trudeau's government vigorously pushed an industrialization program, high inflation and Trudeau's efforts to impose the will of the federal government on the powerful provincial governments alienated voters and weakened his government.

Economic recession in the early 1980s brought Brian Mulroney (b. 1939), leader of the Progressive Conservative Party, to power in 1984. Mulroney's government sought greater privatization of Canada's state-run corporations and negotiated a free-trade agreement with the United States. Bitterly resented by many Canadians, the agreement cost Mulroney's government much of its popularity. In 1993, the ruling Conservatives were overwhelmingly defeated, and the Liberal leader, Jean Chrétien (ZHAHNH kray-TEN) (b. 1934), became prime minister. Chrétien's conservative fiscal policies, combined with strong economic growth, enabled his government to have a budgetary surplus by the late 1990s and led to another Liberal victory in the elections of 1997. Charges of widespread financial corruption in the government, however, led to a Conservative victory early in 2006, and Stephen Harper (b. 1959) became the new prime minister. Harper's government collapsed in March 2011, but elections held in May resulted in Harper remaining as prime minister.

The government has also faced an ongoing crisis over the French-speaking province of Quebec. In the late 1960s, the Parti Québécois (par-TEE kay-bek-KWAH), headed by René Lévesque (ruh-NAY lay-VEK) (1922–1987), campaigned on a platform of Quebec's secession from the Canadian confederation. In 1970, the party won 24 percent of the popular vote in Quebec's provincial elections. To pursue their dream of separation, some underground separatist groups even used terrorist bombings and kidnapped two prominent government officials. In 1976, the Parti Québécois won Quebec's provincial elections and in 1980 called for a referendum that would enable the provincial government to negotiate Quebec's independence from the rest of Canada.

Quebec

Voters in Quebec narrowly rejected the plan in 1995, however, and debate over the province's future continues to divide Canada.

Latin America Since 1945

 FOCUS QUESTION: What problems have the nations of Latin America faced since 1945, and what role has Marxist ideology played in their efforts to solve these problems?

In many Latin American countries, the Great Depression of the 1930s had created political instability that led to military coups and militaristic regimes (see Chapter 24). But the depression also resulted in the transformation of Latin America from a traditional to a modern economic structure. Since the nineteenth century, Latin Americans had exported raw materials, especially minerals and foodstuffs, while buying the manufactured goods of the industrialized countries in Europe and the United States. As a result of the depression, however, exports were cut in half, and the revenues available to buy manufactured goods declined. This encouraged many Latin American countries to develop industries to produce goods that were formerly imported. Due to a shortage of capital in the private sector, governments often invested in the new industries, thus leading, for example, to government-run steel industries in Chile and Brazil.

Despite these developments, in the 1960s Latin American countries still found themselves dependent on the United States, Europe, and now Japan, especially for the advanced technology needed for modern industries. Because of the great poverty in much of Latin America, domestic markets were limited in size, and many Latin American countries failed to find markets abroad for their products. These failures led to instability and a new reliance on military regimes, especially to curb the power of the new industrial middle class and working classes, which had increased in size and power as a result of industrialization. In the 1960s, repressive military regimes in Chile, Brazil, and Argentina abolished political parties and repeatedly returned to export-import economies financed by foreigners. They also invited multinational companies to partake in Latin America's burgeoning growth. The companies that accepted the invitations did so primarily to take advantage of Latin America's raw materials and abundant supply of cheap labor, and thus only contributed to the ongoing dependency of Latin America on the industrially developed nations.

In the 1970s, Latin American regimes grew even more dependent, borrowing from abroad, especially from banks in Europe and the United States, to maintain their failing economies. Between 1970 and 1982, debt to foreigners increased from $27 billion to $315 billion. By 1982, a number of governments announced that they could no longer pay interest on their debts to foreign banks, and their economies began to crumble.

The debt crisis was paralleled by a movement toward democracy during the 1980s. In part, some military leaders were simply unwilling to deal with the monstrous debt problems. At the same time, many people realized that military power without popular consent was incapable of providing a strong state. Then, too, there was a swelling of popular support for basic rights and free and fair elections. By the 1980s and early 1990s, democratic regimes were in place everywhere except Cuba, some of the Central American states, Chile, and Paraguay. At the end of the twentieth century and beginning of the twenty-first, a noticeable political trend in Latin America was the election of left-wing governments, evident in the election of Hugo Chávez

South America

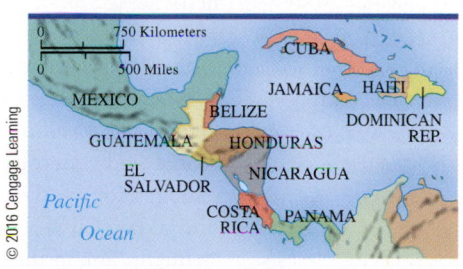

Central America

(OO-goh CHAH-vez) (1954–2013) in Venezuela in 1998, Luiz Inácio Lula da Silva in Brazil in 2002, Michelle Bachelet in Chile in 2006, and Daniel Ortega in Nicaragua in 2007.

The United States has also played an important role in Latin America since 1945. For years, the United States had intervened militarily in Latin American affairs, particularly in Central America and the Caribbean, a region it considered its "backyard" and thus of strategic importance. As Chapter 24 described, in the 1920s the United States became the leading investor in Latin America, replacing Great Britain. By investing directly in Latin American firms, Americans succeeded in gaining control of a large portion of Latin America's export industries. Thus, copper mining in Chile and Peru and the oil industry in Bolivia, Mexico, and Peru came under American control, and the American-owned United Fruit Company gained a virtual monopoly over the banana trade in a number of Central American nations, turning them into "banana republics." The control of these industries by American investors reinforced a growing nationalist sentiment in Latin America against the United States as a neo-imperialist power.

But the United States also tried to pursue a new relationship with Latin America. In 1948, the nations of the Western Hemisphere formed the Organization of American States (OAS), which was intended to eliminate unilateral interference by one state in the internal or external affairs of any other state. But as the Cold War between the United States and the Soviet Union intensified, American policymakers grew anxious about the possibility of communist regimes arising in Central America and the Caribbean and returned to a policy of unilateral action when they believed that Soviet agents were attempting to establish communist governments. Especially after the success of Castro in Cuba (see the next section), the desire of the United States to prevent "another Cuba" largely determined American policy toward Latin America until the collapse of the Soviet Union in the early 1990s. The United States provided massive military aid to anti-communist regimes, regardless of their nature.

The Threat of Marxist Revolutions

Until the 1960s, Marxism played little role in the politics of Latin America. The success of Fidel Castro in Cuba and his espousal of Marxism, however, opened the door for other Marxist movements that aimed to gain the support of

Castro's Revolutionary Ideals

POLITICS & GOVERNMENT

On July 26, 1953, Fidel Castro and a small group of supporters launched an ill-fated attack on the Moncada Barracks in Santiago de Cuba. Castro was arrested and put on trial. This selection is taken from the speech he made in his defense, in which he discussed the goals of the revolutionaries.

Fidel Castro, "History Will Absolve Me"

I stated that the second consideration on which we based our chances for success was one of social order because we were assured of the people's support. When we speak of the people we do not mean the comfortable ones, the conservative elements of the nation, who welcome any regime of oppression, any dictatorship, and despotism, prostrating themselves before the master of the moment until they grind their foreheads into the ground. When we speak of struggle, the people means the vast unredeemed masses, to whom all make promises and whom all deceive; we mean the people who yearn for a better, more dignified, and more just nation; who are moved by ancestral aspirations of justice, for they have suffered injustice and mockery, generation after generation; who long for great and wise changes in all aspects of their life; people, who, to attain these changes, are ready to give even the very last breath of their lives—when they believe in something or in someone, especially when they believe in themselves.

In the brief of this cause there must be recorded the five revolutionary laws that would have been proclaimed immediately after the capture of the Moncada barracks and would have been broadcast to the nation by radio....

The First Revolutionary Law would have returned power to the people and proclaimed the Constitution of 1940 the supreme Law of the land, until such time as the people should decide to modify or change it....

The Second Revolutionary Law would have granted property, not mortgageable and not transferable, to all planters, subplanters, lessees, partners, and squatters who hold parcels of five or less *caballerias* of land [total of 166 acres], and the state would indemnify the former owners on the basis of the rental which they would have received for these parcels over a period of ten years.

The Third Revolutionary Law would have granted workers and employees the right to share 30 percent of the profits of all the large industrial, mercantile, and mining enterprises, including the sugar mills....

The Fourth Revolutionary Law would have granted all planters the right to share 55 percent of the sugar production and a minimum quota of forty thousand *arrobas* [total of 500 tons] for all small planters who have been established for three or more years.

The Fifth Revolutionary Law would have ordered the confiscation of all holdings and ill-gotten gains of those who had committed frauds during previous regimes, as well as the holdings and ill-gotten gains of all their legatees and heirs....

Furthermore, it was to be declared that the Cuban policy in the Americas would be one of close solidarity with the democratic people of this continent, and that those politically persecuted by bloody tyrants oppressing our sister nations would find generous asylum, brotherhood, and bread in [Cuba]. Not the persecution, hunger, and treason that they find today. Cuba should be the bulwark of liberty and not a shameful link in the chain of despotism.

Q *What did Fidel Castro intend to accomplish by his revolution in Cuba? On whose behalf did he fight this revolution?*

Source: Excerpt from *Latin American Civilization* by Benjamin Keen, ed. (Boston: Houghton Mifflin, 1974), pp. 369–373.

---

peasants and industrial workers and bring radical change to Latin America.

THE CUBAN REVOLUTION A dictatorship, headed by Fulgencio Batista (full-JEN-ee-oh bah-TEES-tuh) (1901–1973) and closely tied economically to U.S. investors, had ruled Cuba since 1934. In the 1950s, Batista's government came under attack by a strong opposition movement, led by Fidel Castro (fee-DELL KASS-troh) (b. 1926) and assisted by Ernesto "Ché" Guevara (er-NAY-stoh CHAY guh-VAHR-uh) (1928–1967), an Argentinian who believed in the need for revolutionary upheaval (see the box "Castro's Revolutionary Ideals" above). When their initial assaults brought little success, Castro's forces turned to guerrilla warfare. Batista's regime responded with such brutality that he alienated his own supporters. The dictator fled in December 1958, and Castro's revolutionaries seized Havana on January 1, 1959.

Relations between Cuba and the United States quickly deteriorated early in 1960 when the Soviet Union agreed to buy Cuban sugar and provide $100 million in credits. On March 17, 1960, President Eisenhower directed the Central Intelligence Agency (CIA) to "organize the training of Cuban exiles, mainly in Guatemala, against a possible future day when they might return to their homeland."[2] As arms from Eastern Europe began to arrive in Cuba, the United States cut its purchases of Cuban sugar, and the Cuban government retaliated by nationalizing U.S. companies and banks. In October 1960, the United States declared a trade embargo of Cuba, which drove Castro closer to the Soviet Union. In December 1960, Castro declared himself a Marxist.

On January 3, 1961, the United States broke diplomatic relations with Cuba. The new U.S. president, John F. Kennedy, supported a coup attempt against Castro's government, but the landing of 1,400 CIA-assisted Cuban exiles in Cuba at the

Fidel Castro. On January 1, 1959, a band of revolutionaries led by Fidel Castro overthrew the authoritarian government of Fulgencio Batista. Castro (second from the right) is shown here in 1957, surrounded by some of his followers at a secret base near the Cuban coast.

Bay of Pigs on April 17, 1961, turned into a military disaster. The Soviets then attempted to install nuclear missiles in the country, an act that led to a showdown with the United States (see Chapter 26). As part of the bargain to defuse the missile crisis, the United States agreed not to invade Cuba.

But the missile crisis affected Cuba in another way; Castro realized that the Soviet Union had been unreliable and the security of revolutionary Cuba would necessitate social revolution in the rest of Latin America. Castro judged Bolivia, Haiti, Venezuela, Colombia, Paraguay, and a number of Central American states to be especially open to radical revolution. He believed that once guerrilla wars were launched, peasants would flock to the movement and overthrow the old regimes. Guevara began a guerrilla war in Bolivia but was caught and killed by the Bolivian army in the fall of 1967. The Cuban strategy had failed.

Nevertheless, Castro's socialist revolution proceeded within Cuba, with mixed results. The Cuban Revolution did secure some social gains for the Cuban people, especially in health care and education. The regime provided free medical services for all citizens, and the population's health improved noticeably. Developing new schools and establishing teacher-training institutes that tripled the number of teachers within ten years wiped out illiteracy. The theoretical equality of women in Marxist thought was put into practice in Cuba by new laws, such as the family code, which stated that husband and wife were equally responsible for the economic support of the family and household, as well as for child care. Such laws led to improvements but fell short of creating full equality for women.

Eschewing rapid industrialization, Castro encouraged agricultural diversification, but the Cuban economy continued to rely heavily on the production and sale of sugar. Economic problems forced the Castro regime to depend on Soviet subsidies and the purchase of Cuban sugar by Soviet bloc countries. After the collapse of these communist regimes in 1989, Cuba lost their support. Although economic conditions continued to decline, Fidel Castro remained in power until illness forced him to resign the presidency in 2008, when his brother, Raúl Castro (rah-OOL KASS-troh) (b. 1931), succeeded him.

CHILE'S MARXIST ADVENTURE   Another challenge to U.S. influence in Latin America came in 1970 when the Marxist Salvador Allende (sahl-vah-DOR al-YEN-day) (1908–1973) was elected president of Chile and attempted to create a socialist society by constitutional means. Chile suffered from a number of economic problems. Wealth was concentrated in the hands of large landowners and a few large corporations. Inflation, foreign debts, and a decline in the mining industry (copper exports accounted for 80 percent of Chile's export income) caused untold difficulties. Right-wing control of the government had failed to achieve any solutions, especially since foreign investments were allowed to expand. There was already growing resentment of U.S. corporations, especially Anaconda and Kennecott, which controlled the copper industry.

In the 1970 elections, a split in the moderate forces enabled Allende to become president of Chile as head of a coalition of Socialists, Communists, and Catholic radicals. Allende increased the wages of industrial workers and began to move toward socialism by nationalizing the largest domestic and foreign-owned corporations. Nationalization of the copper industry—essentially without compensation for the owners—caused the Nixon administration to cut off all aid to Chile, creating serious problems for the Chilean economy. At the same time, the government offered only halfhearted resistance to radical workers who were beginning to take control of the landed estates.

In response, the upper and middle classes organized strikes against the government (with support from the American CIA). Allende attempted to stop the disorder by bringing three military officers into his cabinet. They succeeded in ending the strikes, but when Allende's coalition increased its vote in the congressional elections of March 1973, the Chilean army, under the direction of General Augusto Pinochet (aw-GOO-stoh pin-noh-chet *or* pee-noh-CHAY) (1915–2006), decided on a coup d'état. In September 1973, Allende and thousands of his supporters were killed. Contrary to the expectations of many right-wing politicians, the military remained in power and set up a dictatorship. The regime moved quickly to outlaw all political parties and restore many nationalized industries to their original owners. By the mid-1980s, the regime's horrible abuses of human rights led to growing unrest against the government.

In 1989, free elections produced a new president, Patricio Aylwin (pa-TREES-yoh YL-win) (b. 1918), who advocated free market economics. Despite some economic improvement, unemployment remained high. Early in 2004, Chile entered into a free-trade agreement with the United States in the hopes of boosting economic growth. In 2006, Michelle

Bachelet (mih-SHELL BAHSH-uh-let) (b. 1951), a moderate Socialist running on a platform of increasing social welfare measures for the nation's poor, became the first woman to be elected president of Chile. In January 2010, following divisions in the Socialist Party, Chileans elected center-right National Renewal Party candidate Sebastián Piñera (say-bahs-TYAHN peen-YAIR-uh) (b. 1949). A Harvard-educated billionaire, Piñera promised to uphold the social economic policies of the Socialists, while being tougher on crime.

NICARAGUA: FROM THE SOMOZAS TO THE SANDINISTAS

During the early twentieth century, the United States intervened in Nicaraguan domestic affairs on several occasions, and U.S. marines even remained there for long periods of time. After the leader of the U.S.-supported National Guard, Anastasio Somoza (ah-nahs-TAH-see-oh suh-MOH-suh) (1896–1956), seized control of the government in 1937, his family remained in power for forty-three years. U.S. support for the Somoza military regime enabled the family to overcome its opponents while enriching themselves at the expense of the state.

Opposition to the regime finally arose from Marxist guerrilla forces known as the Sandinista National Liberation Front. By mid-1979, military victories by the Sandinistas (san-duh-NEES-tuhz) left them in virtual control of the country. Inheriting a poverty-stricken nation, the Sandinistas organized a provisional government aligned with the Soviet Union. The Reagan and Bush administrations, believing that Central America faced the danger of another communist state, financed Contra rebels in a guerrilla war against the Sandinista government. The Contra war and an American economic embargo damaged the Nicaraguan economy and undermined support for the Sandinistas. In 1990, they agreed to free elections and lost to a coalition headed by Violeta Barrios de Chamorro (vee-oh-LET-uh bah-REE-ohss day chah-MOH-roh) (b. 1929). Nevertheless, the Sandinistas remained the strongest single party in Nicaragua and finally won new elections in 2006. Daniel Ortega (dah-NYEL awr-TAY-guh) (b. 1945) became president in January 2007 and was reelected in 2011.

Nationalism and the Military: The Examples of Argentina and Brazil

The military became the power brokers of twentieth-century Latin America. Especially in the 1960s and 1970s, Latin American armies portrayed themselves as the guardians of national honor and orderly progress.

ARGENTINA Juan Perón (WAHN puh-ROHN) (1895–1974) first rose to prominence as a member of the military regime that had seized power in Argentina in 1943. As labor

secretary in the military government, he used his position to curry favor with the workers. But as Perón grew more popular, other army officers began to fear his power and arrested him. An uprising by workers forced the officers to back down, and in 1946, Perón was elected president.

To please his chief supporters—labor and the urban middle class—Perón pursued a policy of increased industrialization. At the same time, he sought to free Argentina from foreign investors. The government bought the railways; took over the banking, insurance, shipping, and communications industries; and assumed regulation of imports and exports. But Perón's regime was also authoritarian. His wife, Eva Perón (1919–1952), organized women's groups to support the government, while Perón assembled fascist gangs, modeled after Hitler's Brown Shirts, that used violence to intimidate his opponents. But growing corruption in the Perón government and the alienation of more and more people by the regime's excesses encouraged the military to overthrow him in September 1955. Perón went into exile in Spain.

Overwhelmed by problems, however, military leaders eventually decided to allow Perón to return. Reelected president in September 1973, Perón died a year later. In 1976, the military installed a new regime. Tolerating no opposition, the military leaders encouraged the "disappearance" of their opponents. Perhaps 30,000 people, including 6,000 leftists, were killed as a result.

But economic problems remained. To divert people's attention, the military regime invaded the Falkland Islands off the coast of Argentina in April 1982. Great Britain, which had controlled the islands since the nineteenth century, sent ships and

Juan and Eva Perón. Elected president of Argentina in 1946, Juan Perón soon established an authoritarian regime that nationalized some of Argentina's basic industries and organized fascist gangs to overwhelm its opponents. He is shown here with his wife, Eva, during the inauguration ceremonies initiating his second term as president, in 1952.

troops to defend the islands. When the Argentine forces surrendered to the British in July, angry Argentinians denounced the military regime. The loss discredited the military and opened the door to civilian rule. In 1983, Raúl Alfonsín (rah-OOL al-fahn-SEEN) (1927–2009) of the Radical Party was elected president and tried to restore democratic practices. In elections in 1989, the Perónist Carlos Saúl Menem (KAHR-lohs sah-OOL MEN-em) (b. 1930) won. This peaceful transfer of power gave hope that Argentina was moving on a democratic path. Despite problems of foreign debt and inflation, Argentina has witnessed economic growth since 2003, first under the government of President Nestor Kirchner (NAY-stor KEERCH-nehr) (1950–2010) and then under his wife, Christina Fernández de Kirchner (kris-TEE-nuh fehr-NAHN-des day KEERCH-nehr) (b. 1953), who in 2007 became the first woman to be elected president of Argentina.

BRAZIL After the military put an end to the authoritarian regime of Getúlio Vargas (zhi-TOO-lyoo VAHR-guhs) (1882–1954) in 1945, Brazil established a republic. Over the next two decades, various democratically elected presidents (including Vargas himself) struggled to solve Brazil's economic problems, especially its soaring inflation, but with little success. Finally, in the spring of 1964, the military decided to intervene and took over the government.

Unlike previous interventions by military leaders in politics, this time the armed forces remained in direct control of the country for twenty years. The military set course on a new economic direction, cutting back somewhat on state control of the economy and emphasizing market forces. Beginning in 1968, the new policies seemed to work, and Brazil experienced an "economic miracle" as it moved into self-sustaining economic growth, generally the hallmark of a modern economy. Economic growth also included the economic exploitation of the Amazon basin, which the regime opened to farming; some experts believe that the resulting destruction of the extensive Amazon rain forests, which is still going on, poses a threat to the ecological balance not only of Brazil but of the earth itself. Rapid economic growth had additional drawbacks. Ordinary Brazilians hardly benefited at all as the gulf between rich and poor, always wide, grew even wider. In 1960, the wealthiest 10 percent of Brazil's population received 40 percent of the nation's income; in 1980, they received 51 percent. Then, too, rapid development led to an inflation rate of 100 percent a year, while an enormous foreign debt added to the problems. By the early 1980s, the economic miracle was turning into a nightmare. Overwhelmed, the generals retreated and opened the door for a return to democracy in 1985.

The new democratic government faced herculean obstacles—massive foreign debt, runaway inflation, and a lack of social consensus. Nevertheless, by the 1990s, some stability was maintained as Brazil became committed to democratic elections. The enduring gulf between rich and poor helped lead to the election in 2002 of Luiz Inácio Lula da Silva (LWEES ee-NAH-syoh LOO-luh duh-SEEL-vuh) (b. 1945), who pursued a policy of increased trade and social reforms while continuing to increase exports. Despite economic growth, problems of crime and poor education still persisted in Brazil. In October 2010, Lula's chief of staff, Dilma Rousseff (DIL-muh ROO-seff) (b. 1947), became the first woman to be elected president of Brazil.

The Mexican Way

During the 1950s and 1960s, Mexico's ruling party (the Institutional Revolutionary Party, or PRI) focused on a balanced industrial program. Fifteen years of steady economic growth combined with low inflation and real gains in wages for more and more people made those years seem a golden age in Mexico's economic development. But at the end of the 1960s, the true nature of Mexico's domination by one party became apparent with the student protest movement. On October 2, 1968, a demonstration of university students in Tlaltelolco (tuh-lahl-teh-LOH-koh) Square in Mexico City was met by police forces, who opened fire and killed hundreds of students (see the box "Student Revolt in Mexico" on p. 842). Leaders of the PRI became concerned about the need to change the system.

The next two presidents, Luis Echeverría (loo-EES eh-cheh-vahr-REE-uh) (b. 1922), who was elected in 1970, and José López Portillo (hoh-SAY LOH-pehz pohr-TEE-yoh) (1920–2004), who was elected in 1976, introduced political reforms. Rules for the registration of political parties were eased, making their growth more likely, and greater freedom of debate in the press and universities was allowed. But

CHRONOLOGY Latin America Since 1945	
Juan Perón becomes president of Argentina	1946
Creation of the Organization of American States	1948
Castro's forces seize Cuba	1959
Bay of Pigs invasion	1961
Cuban Missile Crisis	1962
Death of Ché Guevara in Bolivia	1967
Presidency of Luis Echeverría in Mexico	1970–1976
Overthrow of Salvador Allende in Chile	1973
Perón returns to power	1973
Presidency of José López Portillo in Mexico	1976–1982
Sandinistas establish provisional government in Nicaragua	1979
Falklands War	1982
Election of Carlos Salinas in Mexico	1988
Election of Vicente Fox in Mexico	2000
Election of Luiz Inácio Lula da Silva in Brazil	2002
Election of Michelle Bachelet as the first woman president of Chile	2006
Election of Christina Fernández de Kirchner as the first woman president of Argentina	2007
Raúl Castro becomes president of Cuba	2008
Election of Dilma Rousseff as the first woman president of Brazil	2010

Student Revolt in Mexico

POLITICS & GOVERNMENT

GROWING CONFLICT between government authorities and university students in Mexico came to a violent and bloody climax on October 2, 1968, when army troops killed and wounded large numbers of students in Mexico City. This excerpt is taken from an account of the events by the student National Strike Council.

National Strike Council, Events of October 2–3

After an hour and a half of a peaceful meeting attended by ten thousand people and witnessed by scores of domestic and foreign reporters, a helicopter gave the army the signal to attack by dropping flares into the crowd. Simultaneously, the plaza was surrounded and attacked by members of the army and all police forces, using weapons of every caliber, up to 9 mm.

The local papers have given the following information about the attack, confirmed by firsthand witnesses:

1. Numerous secret policemen had infiltrated the meeting in order to attack it from within, with orders to kill. They were known to each other by the use of a white handkerchief tied around their right hands....

3. High caliber weaponry and expansion bullets were used. Seven hours after the massacre began, tanks cleaned up the residential buildings of Nonoalco-Tlaltelolco with short cannon blasts and machine-gun fire.

4. On the morning of October 3, the apartments of supposedly guilty individuals were still being searched, without a search warrant.

5. Doctors in the emergency wards of the city hospitals were under extreme pressure, being forced to forgo attention to the victims until they had been interrogated and placed under guard. Various interns who attended the demonstration for the purpose of giving medical aid had since disappeared.

6. The results of this brutal military operation include hundreds of dead (including women and children), thousands of wounded, an unwarranted search of all the apartments in the area, and thousands of violent arrests. Those arrested were taken to various illegal locations, such as Military Camp No. 1. It should be added that members of the National Strike Council who were captured were stripped and herded into a small archaeological excavation at Tlaltelolco, converted for the moment into a dungeon. Some of them were put up against a wall and shot.

7. Onesimo Mason, the general who directed the operation, praised the preparedness of his men, in contrast to the obvious lack of preparedness on the part of the students.

All this has occurred only ten days before the start of the Olympics. The repression is expected to become even greater after the Games, in view of the fact that national public opinion and the protest from the provinces are unified against a regime whose only interest lies in demonstrating its power to control.

Already individual liberties have been suspended, and restricted zones have been created where all vehicles are searched at gunpoint and personal identification is demanded. The Secretary of Defense declared that the friendly disposition of the regime will solve the conflict.

WE ARE NOT AGAINST THE OLYMPIC GAMES. WELCOME TO MEXICO.

Why did the Mexican army attack this peaceful student protest? Do you think that the timing of the Olympic Games in Mexico City was a factor? How does this event compare with what happened at Kent State University in 1970 and with the 1989 student protests in Tiananmen Square?

Source: From *Latin American Civilization* by Benjamin Keen, ed. (Boston: Houghton Mifflin, 1974), pp. 226–227.

---

economic problems continued to trouble Mexico. In the late 1970s, vast new reserves of oil were discovered. As the sale of oil abroad increased dramatically, the government became even more dependent on oil revenues. When world oil prices dropped in the mid-1980s, Mexico was no longer able to make payments on its foreign debt, which had reached $80 billion in 1982. The government was forced to adopt new economic policies, including the increased sale of publicly owned companies to private parties.

The debt crisis and rising unemployment increased dissatisfaction with the government, which was especially evident in the 1988 election, when the PRI's choice for president, Carlos Salinas (KAHR-lohs sah-LEE-nahs) (b. 1948), who was expected to win in a landslide, won by only a 50.3 percent majority. Increasing dissatisfaction with the government's economic policies finally led to the unthinkable: in 2000, Vicente Fox (vee-SEN-tay FOKS) (b. 1942) defeated the PRI candidate for the presidency. Despite high hopes, Fox's presidency failed to deal with police corruption and bureaucratic inefficiency in the government. His successor, Felipe Calderón (feh-LEE-pay kahl-duh-ROHN) (b. 1962), has made immigration reform a major priority, with little success. He has also waged war on Mexico's powerful drug cartels.

Society and Culture in the Western World

Q FOCUS QUESTION: What major social, cultural, and intellectual developments have occurred in western Europe and North America since 1945?

Socially, culturally, and intellectually, the post–World War II Western world has been marked by much diversity, and although many trends represent a continuation of prewar modern developments, they have affected society in unpredictable ways.

The Emergence of a New Society

During the first decades after World War II, such products of new technologies as computers, television, jet planes, contraceptive devices, and new surgical techniques all dramatically altered the pace and nature of human life. Scientific advances and vigorous economic growth fueled the rapid changes in society. Called a *technocratic society* by some and the **consumer society** by others, postwar Western society has been characterized by an evolving social structure and new movements for change.

European society was dramatically altered after 1945. Especially noticeable were the changes in the middle class. As large companies and government agencies began employing large numbers of white-collar supervisory and administrative personnel, people in managerial and technological occupations greatly augmented the ranks of such traditional middle-class groups as businesspeople and professionals in law, medicine, and academia. In both eastern and western Europe, the new managers and experts were very much alike. Everywhere their positions depended on specialized knowledge acquired through higher education, and everywhere they focused on the effective administration of their corporations.

A SOCIETY OF CONSUMERS Changes also occurred among the traditional lower classes. Especially noticeable was the dramatic shift of people from rural to urban areas. The number of people in agriculture declined drastically; by the 1950s, the number of farmers throughout most of Europe had dropped by 50 percent. Nor did the size of the industrial working class expand. In West Germany, industrial workers made up 48 percent of the labor force throughout the 1950s and 1960s. Thereafter, the number of industrial workers began to dwindle as the number of white-collar service employees increased. At the same time, a substantial increase in their real wages enabled the working classes to aspire to the consumption patterns of the middle class. Buying on the installment plan, introduced in the 1930s, became widespread in the 1950s and gave workers a chance to imitate the middle class by buying such products as televisions, washing machines, refrigerators, vacuum cleaners, and stereos. But the most visible symbol of mass consumerism was the automobile. Before World War II, cars were reserved mostly for the European upper classes. In 1948, there were 5 million cars in all of Europe, but by 1957, the number had tripled. By the 1960s, there were almost 45 million cars.

Rising incomes, combined with shorter working hours, created an even greater market for mass leisure activities. Between 1900 and 1980, the workweek was reduced from sixty hours to a little more than forty hours, and the number of paid holidays increased. All aspects of popular culture—music, sports, media—became commercialized and offered opportunities for leisure activities.

Another very visible symbol of mass leisure was the growth of tourism. Before World War II, most persons who traveled for pleasure were from the upper and middle classes. After the war, the combination of more vacation time, increased prosperity, and the flexibility provided by package tours with their lower rates and budget-priced accommodations enabled millions to expand their travel possibilities.

A Revolt in Sexual Mores

The **permissive society** was yet another label critics applied to postwar Europe. World War I had opened the first significant crack in the rigid code of manners and morals of the nineteenth century. The 1920s had witnessed experimentation with drugs, the appearance of hardcore pornography, and a new sexual freedom (police in Berlin, for example, issued cards that permitted female and male homosexual prostitutes to practice their trade). But these indications of a new attitude appeared mostly in major cities and touched only small numbers of people. After World War II, changes in manners and morals were far more extensive and far more noticeable.

Sweden took the lead in the propagation of the so-called sexual revolution of the 1960s, but the rest of Europe and the United States soon followed. Sex education in the schools and the decriminalization of homosexuality were but two aspects of Sweden's liberal legislation. The introduction of the birth control pill, which became widely available by the mid-1960s, gave people more freedom in sexual behavior. Meanwhile, sexually explicit movies, plays, and books broke new ground in the treatment of once hidden subjects. Cities like Amsterdam, which allowed open prostitution and the public sale of hard-core pornography, attracted thousands of curious tourists.

The new standards were evident in the breakdown of the traditional family. Divorce rates increased dramatically, especially in the 1960s, and premarital and extramarital sexual experiences also rose substantially. A survey in the Netherlands in 1968 revealed that 78 percent of men and 86 percent of women had participated in extramarital sex.

Youth Protest and Student Revolt

The 1960s also saw the emergence of a drug culture. Marijuana, though illegal, was widely used by college and university students. For young people more interested in higher levels of consciousness, Timothy Leary, who had done research at Harvard on the psychedelic effects of

The "Love-In." In the 1960s, a number of outdoor public festivals for young people combined music, drugs, and sex. Flamboyant dress, face painting, free-form dancing, and drugs were vital ingredients in creating an atmosphere dedicated to "love and peace." Shown here are "hippies" dancing around a decorated bus at a "love-in" during 1967's Summer of Love.

LSD (lysergic acid diethylamide), became the high priest of hallucinogenic experiences.

New attitudes toward sex and the use of drugs were only two manifestations of a growing youth movement in the 1960s that questioned authority and fostered rebellion against the older generation. Spurred by opposition to the Vietnam War and a growing political consciousness, the youth rebellion became a full-fledged protest movement by the second half of the 1960s (see the box "'The Times They Are A-Changin'': The Music of Youthful Protest" on p. 845).

Before World War II, higher education had largely remained the preserve of Europe's wealthier classes. After the war, European states began to foster greater equality of opportunity in higher education by eliminating fees, and universities experienced an influx of students from the middle and lower classes. Enrollments grew dramatically; in France, 4.5 percent of young people went to a university in 1950. By 1965, the figure had increased to 14.5 percent.

But there were problems. Overcrowded classrooms, professors who paid little attention to students, administrators who acted in an authoritarian fashion, and an education that to many seemed irrelevant to the modern age led to an outburst of student revolts in the late 1960s. One of the major issues that mobilized youthful European protesters was the United States' war in Vietnam, which they viewed as an act of aggression and imperialism. In 1968, demonstrations broke out in universities in Italy, France, and Britain. In part, these were an extension of the protests against the Vietnam War in American universities in the mid-1960s. In London, 30,000 demonstrators took to

the streets protesting America's involvement in Vietnam. But student protests in Europe also backfired in that they provoked a reaction from people who favored order over the lawlessness of privileged young people. As Pier Paolo Pasolini (PYER PAH-loh pah-SOH-lee-nee) (1922–1975), an Italian poet and intellectual, wrote, "Now all the journalists of the world are licking your arses … but not me, my dears. You have the faces of spoiled brats, and I hate you, like I hate your fathers.… When yesterday at Valle Giulia [in Rome] you beat up the police, I sympathized with the police because they are the sons of the poor."[3]

There were other reasons for the student radicalism besides protesting the Vietnam War. Some students were genuinely motivated by a desire to reform the university. They also attacked other aspects of Western society, such as its materialism, and expressed concern about becoming cogs in the large and impersonal bureaucratic jungles of the modern world. For many students, the calls for democratic decision making in the universities were a reflection of their deeper concerns about the direction of Western society.

Women in the Postwar Western World

Despite their enormous contributions to the war effort, women at the end of World War II were removed from the workforce to free up jobs for the soldiers returning home. After the horrors of war, people seemed willing for a while to return to traditional family practices. Female participation in the workforce declined, and birthrates began to rise, creating a "baby boom." The boost in the birthrate lasted until the early 1960s, when family size began to decline primarily because of the widespread practice of birth control. Invented in the nineteenth century, the condom was already in wide use, but the development in the 1960s of oral contraceptives, known as birth control pills, provided a reliable means of birth control that quickly spread to all Western countries.

The trend toward smaller families contributed to changes in women's employment in both Europe and the United States, mainly because women now needed to devote far fewer years to rearing children. That led to a large increase in the number of married women in the workforce. At the beginning of the twentieth century, even working-class wives tended to stay at home if they could afford to do so. In the postwar period, this was no longer the case. In the United

"The Times They Are A-Changin'": The Music of Youthful Protest

IN THE 1960s, the lyrics of rock music reflected the rebellious mood of many young people. Bob Dylan (b. 1941), a vastly influential performer and recording artist, expressed the feelings of the younger generation. His song "The Times They Are A-Changin'," released in 1964, has been called an "anthem for the protest movement."

Bob Dylan, "The Times They Are A-Changin'"

Come gather 'round people
Wherever you roam
And admit that the waters
Around you have grown
And accept it that soon
You'll be drenched to the bone
If your time to you
Is worth savin'
Then you better start swimmin'
Or you'll sink like a stone
For the times they are a-changin'

Come writers and critics
Who prophesize with your pen
And keep your eyes wide
The chance won't come again
And don't speak too soon
For the wheel's still in spin
And there's no tellin' who
That it's namin'
For the loser now
Will be later to win
For the times they are a-changin'

Come senators, congressmen
Please heed the call
Don't stand in the doorway

Don't block up the hall
For he that gets hurt
Will be he who has stalled
There's a battle outside
And it is ragin'
It'll soon shake your windows
And rattle your walls
For the times they are a-changin'

Come mothers and fathers
Throughout the land
And don't criticize
What you can't understand
Your sons and your daughters
Are beyond your command
Your old road
Is rapidly agin'
Please get out of the new one
If you can't lend your hand
For the times they are a-changin'

The line it is drawn
The curse it is cast
The slow one now
Will later be fast
As the present now
Will later be past
The order is
Rapidly fadin'
And the first one now
Will later be last
For the times they are a-changin'

 What prompted the student campus revolts of the 1960s? According to Bob Dylan, who and what are causing the problem?

States, for example, married women made up about 15 percent of the female labor force in 1900; by 1970, their number had increased to 62 percent.

But the increased presence of women in the workforce did not change some old patterns. Working-class women in particular still earned salaries lower than those of men performing equivalent work. In the 1960s, women earned only 60 percent of men's wages in Britain, 50 percent in France, and 63 percent in West Germany. In addition, women still tended to enter traditionally female jobs. As one Swedish woman guidance counselor remarked in 1975, "Every girl now thinks in terms of a job. This is progress. They want children, but they don't pin their hopes on marriage. They don't intend to be housewives for some future husband. But there has been no change in their vocational choices."[4] Many European women also still faced the double burden of earning income on the one hand and raising a family and maintaining the household on the other. Such inequalities led increasing numbers of women to rebel.

THE FEMINIST MOVEMENT: THE QUEST FOR LIBERATION

The participation of women in World Wars I and II helped them achieve one of the major aims of the nineteenth-century feminist movement—the right to vote. Already after World

War I, many governments acknowledged the contributions of women to the war effort by granting them the franchise. Sweden, Great Britain, Germany, Poland, Hungary, Austria, and Czechoslovakia did so in 1918, followed by the United States in 1920. Women in France and Italy did not obtain the vote until 1945. After World War II, European women tended to fall back into the traditional roles expected of them, and little was heard of feminist concerns. But by the late 1960s, women began to assert their rights again and speak as feminists. Along with the student upheavals of the late 1960s came renewed interest in feminism, or the **women's liberation movement**, as it was now called. Increasingly, women protested that the acquisition of political and legal equality had not brought true equality with men:

> We are economically oppressed: in jobs we do full work for half pay; in the home we do unpaid work full-time. We are commercially exploited by advertisement, television, and the press; legally we often have only the status of children. We are brought up to feel inadequate, educated to narrower horizons than men. This is our specific oppression as women. It is as women that we are, therefore, organizing.[5]

These were the words of a British Women's Liberation Workshop in 1969.

Of great importance to the emergence of the postwar women's liberation movement was the work of a Frenchwoman, Simone de Beauvoir (see-MUHN duh boh-VWAR) (1908–1986). Born into a Catholic middle-class family and educated at the Sorbonne in Paris, de Beauvoir supported herself as a teacher and later as a novelist and writer. De Beauvoir believed that she lived a "liberated" life for a twentieth-century European woman, but for all her freedom, she still came to perceive that as a woman she faced limits that men did not. In 1949, she published her highly influential work *The Second Sex*, in which she argued that as a result of male-dominated societies, women had been defined by their differences from men and consequently received second-class status (see the box "The Voice of the Women's Liberation Movement" on p. 847).

Another important influence in the growth of the women's movement in the 1960s was Betty Friedan (free-DAN) (1921–2006). A journalist and the mother of three children, Friedan grew increasingly uneasy with her attempt to fulfill the traditional role of the "ideal housewife and mother." In 1963, she published *The Feminine Mystique*, in which she analyzed the problems of middle-class American women in the 1950s and argued that women were being denied equality with men. *The Feminine Mystique* became a best-seller and made Friedan a celebrity.

TRANSFORMATION IN WOMEN'S LIVES To ensure the natural replacement of a country's population, women need to produce an average of 2.1 children each. Many European countries fall short of this mark; their populations stopped growing in the 1960s, and the trend has continued since then. By the 1990s, among the nations of the European Union, the average number of children per woman of childbearing age was 1.4. At 1.31 in 2009, Spain's rate is among the lowest in the world.

AP Photos

The Women's Liberation Movement. In the late 1960s, as women began once again to assert their rights, a revived women's liberation movement emerged. Feminists in the movement maintained that women themselves must alter the conditions of their lives. During this women's liberation rally, some women climbed the statue of Admiral Farragut in Washington, D.C., to exhibit their signs.

At the same time, the presence of women in the workforce has continued to rise. In Britain, for example, women made up 44 percent of the labor force in 1990, up from 32 percent in 1970. Moreover, women have entered new employment areas. Greater access to universities and professional schools has enabled women to take jobs in law, medicine, government, business, and education. In the Soviet Union, for example, about 70 percent of doctors and teachers were women. Nevertheless, economic inequality still often prevails; women are paid lower wages than men for comparable work and receive fewer promotions to management positions.

Feminists in the women's liberation movement came to believe that women themselves must transform the fundamental conditions of their lives. Women sought and gained a measure of control over their own bodies by seeking to legalize both contraception and abortion. In the 1960s and 1970s, hundreds of thousands of European women worked to repeal laws that prohibited contraception and abortion and began to meet with success. Even in Catholic countries, where the church remained strongly opposed to both procedures, legislation allowing contraception and abortion was passed in the 1970s and 1980s.

The Voice of the Women's Liberation Movement

SIMONE DE BEAUVOIR was an important figure in the emergence of the postwar women's liberation movement. This selection is taken from her book *The Second Sex,* in which she argued that women have been forced into a position subordinate to men.

Simone de Beauvoir, *The Second Sex*

Now, woman has always been man's dependent, if not his slave; the two sexes have never shared the world in equality. And even today woman is heavily handicapped, though her situation is beginning to change. Almost nowhere is her legal status the same as man's, and frequently it is much to her disadvantage. Even when her rights are legally recognized in the abstract, long-standing custom prevents their full expression in the mores. In the economic sphere men and women can almost be said to make up two castes; other things being equal, the former hold the better jobs, get higher wages, and have more opportunity for success than their new competitors. In industry and politics men have a great many more positions and they monopolize the most important posts. In addition to all this, they enjoy a traditional prestige that the education of children tends in every way to support, for the present enshrines the past—and in the past all history has been made by men. At the present time, when women are beginning to take part in the affairs of the world, it is still a world that belongs to men—they have no doubt of it at all and women have scarcely any. To decline to be the *Other,* to refuse to be a party to a deal—this would be for women to renounce all the advantages conferred upon them by their alliance with the superior caste. Man-the-sovereign will provide woman-the-liege with material protection and will undertake the moral justification of her existence; thus, she can evade at once both economic risk and the metaphysical risk of a liberty in which ends and aims must be contrived without assistance. Indeed, along with the ethical urge of each individual to affirm his subjective existence, there is also the temptation to forgo liberty and become a thing. This is an inauspicious road, for he who takes it—passive, lost, ruined—becomes henceforth the creature of another's will, frustrated in his transcendence and deprived of every value. But it is an easy road; on it one avoids the strain involved in undertaking an authentic existence. When man makes of woman the *Other,* he may, then, expect her to manifest deep-seated tendencies toward complicity. Thus, woman may fail to lay claim to the status of subject because she lacks definite resources, because she feels the necessary bond that ties her to man regardless of reciprocity, and because she is often very well pleased with her role as the *Other.*

Now, what peculiarly signalizes the situation of woman is that she—a free and autonomous being like all human creatures—nevertheless finds herself living in a world where men compel her to assume the status of the *Other.*

 What did Simone de Beauvoir mean by the "second sex"? By "the Other"? What is the difference between being a "thing" and having an "authentic existence"? According to de Beauvoir, how do women fall prey to the former?

As more women became activists, they also became involved in new issues. In the 1980s and 1990s, women faculty in universities concentrated on developing more enlightened cultural attitudes through the new academic field of women's studies. Such courses, which stressed the role and contributions of women in history, mushroomed in colleges and universities on both sides of the Atlantic.

Other women began to try to affect the political environment by allying with the antinuclear movement. In 1981, a group of women in Britain protested American nuclear missiles by chaining themselves to the fence of an American military base. Thousands more joined in creating a peace camp around the military compound. Enthusiasm ran high; one participant said, "I'll never forget that feeling; it'll live with me forever.... As we walked round, and we clasped hands … it was for women; it was for peace; it was for the world."[6]

Some women joined the ecological movement. As one German writer who was concerned with environmental issues said, it is women "who must give birth to children, willingly or unwillingly, in this polluted world of ours." Especially prominent was the number of women members in the Green Party in Germany (see "The Environment and the Green Movements" later in this chapter).

Women in the West have also reached out to work with women from the rest of the world in international conferences to change the conditions of their lives. Between 1975 and 1995, the United Nations held conferences in Mexico City, Copenhagen, Nairobi, and Beijing. These meetings made the differences between women from Western and non-Western countries very clear. Whereas women from Western countries spoke of political, economic, cultural, and sexual rights, women from developing countries in Latin America, Africa, and Asia focused on bringing an end to the violence, hunger, and disease that haunt their lives. Despite these differences, these meetings demonstrated that women in both developed and developing nations were organizing to increase awareness of women's issues among all people, male and female.

The Growth of Terrorism

Acts of terror by individuals and groups opposed to governments have become a frightening aspect of modern Western society. During the late 1970s and early 1980s, small bands of terrorists used assassination, indiscriminate killing of civilians, the taking of hostages, and the hijacking of airplanes to draw attention to their demands or to destabilize governments in the hope of achieving their political goals. Terrorist acts garnered considerable media attention. When Palestinian terrorists kidnapped and killed eleven Israeli athletes at the Munich Olympic Games in 1972, hundreds of millions of people watched the drama unfold on television. Indeed, some observers believe that media exposure has been an important catalyst for some terrorist groups.

Motivations for terrorist acts vary considerably. Left- and right-wing terrorist groups flourished in the late 1970s and early 1980s, but terrorist acts have also stemmed from militant nationalists who wish to create separatist states. Most prominent was the Irish Republican Army (IRA), which resorted to vicious attacks against the ruling government and innocent civilians in Northern Ireland.

Although left- and right-wing terrorist activities declined in Europe in the 1980s, international terrorism continued. Angered by the loss of their territory to Israel, some militant Palestinians responded with a policy of terrorist attacks against Israel's supporters. Palestinian terrorists operated throughout European countries, attacking both Europeans and American tourists; Palestinian terrorists massacred vacationers at airports in Rome and Vienna in 1985. State-sponsored terrorism was often an integral part of international terrorism. Militant governments, especially in Iran, Libya, and Syria, assisted terrorist organizations that launched attacks on Europeans and Americans. On December 21, 1988, Pan American flight 103 from Frankfurt to New York exploded over Lockerbie, Scotland, killing all 259 passengers and crew members. A massive investigation revealed that the bomb responsible for the explosion had been planted by two Libyan terrorists.

TERRORIST ATTACK ON THE UNITED STATES One of the most destructive acts of terrorism occurred on September 11, 2001, in the United States. Terrorists hijacked four commercial jet airplanes after takeoff from Boston, Newark, and Washington, D.C. The hijackers flew two of the airplanes directly into the twin towers of the World Trade Center in New York City, causing these buildings, as well as a number of surrounding buildings, to collapse. A third hijacked plane slammed into the Pentagon near Washington, D.C. The fourth plane, apparently headed for Washington, crashed instead in an isolated area of Pennsylvania. In total, nearly three thousand people were killed, including everyone aboard the four airliners.

Terrorist Attack on the World Trade Center in New York City. On September 11, 2001, hijackers flew two commercial jetliners into the twin towers of the World Trade Center. Shown at the left are the two towers in the New York skyline before the attack. The middle picture shows the second of the two jetliners about to hit one of the towers while smoke billows from the site of the first attack. In the scene below, firefighters are making their way through what was left of the 110-story towers after their collapse.

Jeremy Walker/Stone/Getty Images

AP Photo/Carmen Taylor

AFP/Getty Images

These coordinated acts of terror were carried out by hijackers connected to an international terrorist organization known as al-Qaeda, run by Osama bin Laden (1957–2011). A native of Saudi Arabia of Yemeni extraction, bin Laden used an inherited fortune to set up terrorist training camps in Afghanistan, under the protection of the nation's militant fundamentalist Islamic rulers known as the Taliban.

U.S. President George W. Bush vowed to wage a lengthy and thorough war on terrorism and worked to create a coalition of nations to assist in ridding the world of al-Qaeda and other terrorist groups. Within weeks of the attack on America, U.S. and NATO air forces began bombing Taliban-controlled command centers, airfields, and al-Qaeda hiding places in Afghanistan. On the ground, Afghan forces, assisted by U.S. special forces, pushed the Taliban out and gained control of the country by the end of November 2001. A democratic multiethnic government was installed but has faced problems from revived Taliban activity (see Chapter 29).

THE WEST AND ISLAM   One of the major sources of terrorist activity against the West, especially the United States, has come from parts of the Muslim world. The ongoing Israeli-Palestinian conflict, in which the United States has steadfastly supported Israel, has certainly fed anti-Western and especially anti-American feelings among many Muslims. In 1979, the revolution in Iran that led to the overthrow of the Western-oriented shah and the establishment of a new Islam-based government also stoked anti-Western sentiment (see Chapter 29).

The involvement of the United States in the liberation of Kuwait in the Persian Gulf War in 1991 also had unexpected consequences in the relationship of Islam and the West. During that war, U.S. forces were stationed in Saudi Arabia, the location of many sacred Islamic sites. Certain anti-Western Islamic groups, especially that of Osama bin Laden and his followers, considered the presence of American forces an affront to Islam. These anti-Western attitudes came to be shared by a number of radical Islamic groups, as is evident in the 2004 bombing in Madrid and the 2005 bombing on subway trains in London.

The U.S. invasion of Iraq in 2003 (see Chapter 29) further inflamed Islamic groups against the United States and the West. Although there was no evidence of a relationship between al-Qaeda terrorists and the regime of Iraqi dictator Saddam Hussein, this claim was one of the excuses used by the United States to launch a preemptive war against Iraq. Although many Iraqis welcomed the overthrow of Saddam Hussein, the subsequent deaths of innocent civilians, the torturing of Muslim prisoners by American soldiers, and the prolonged American occupation of Iraq in the heart of the Middle East served to deepen anti-American resentment throughout the Muslim world.

Guest Workers and Immigrants

As the economies of the western European countries revived in the 1950s and 1960s, a severe labor shortage forced them to rely on foreign workers. Scores of Turks and eastern and southern Europeans came to Germany, North Africans to France, and people from the Caribbean, India, and Pakistan to Great Britain. Overall, there were probably 15 million **guest workers** in Europe in the 1980s.

Although these workers had been recruited for economic reasons, their presence caused social and political problems for their host countries. The concentration of guest workers in certain cities and even certain sections of those cities often created tensions with the local native populations. Foreign workers constituted almost one-fifth of the population in the German cities of Frankfurt, Munich, and Stuttgart. Having become settled in their new countries, many were unwilling to leave, even after the end of the postwar boom in the early 1970s led to mass unemployment.

In the 1980s, there was an influx of other refugees, especially to West Germany, which had liberal immigration laws that permitted people seeking asylum from political persecution to enter the country. During the 1970s and 1980s, West Germany absorbed more than a million refugees from eastern Europe and East Germany. In 1986 alone, 200,000 political refugees from Pakistan, Bangladesh, and Sri Lanka entered the country. Other parts of Europe saw a similar influx of foreigners. Between 1992 and 2002, London and the southeast region of England witnessed an increase of 700,000 new foreigners, primarily from Yugoslavia, Southeast Asia, the Middle East, and Africa. A survey in 1998 showed that English was not the first language of one-third of inner-city children in London.

This great influx of foreigners, many of them nonwhite, has strained not only the social services of European countries but also the patience of native residents who oppose making their countries ethnically diverse. Antiforeign sentiment, increased by growing unemployment, has been encouraged by new right-wing political parties that cater to people's complaints. Thus, the National Front in France, organized by Jean-Marie Le Pen (ZHAHNH-muh-REE leh PEN) (b. 1928), and the Republican Party in Germany, led by Franz Schönhuber (FRAHNTS SHURN-hoo-bur) (1923–2005), a former SS officer, advocate restricting all new immigration and limiting the assimilation of settled immigrants. Much more frightening, however, have been organized campaigns of violence, especially against African and Asian immigrants, by radical right-wing groups.

Even nations that have been especially tolerant in opening their borders to immigrants and seekers of asylum are changing their policies. In the Netherlands, 19 percent of the people have a foreign background, representing almost 180 nationalities. In 2004, however, the Dutch government passed tough new immigration laws, including a requirement that newcomers pass a Dutch language and culture test before being admitted to the Netherlands.

Sometimes these policies have been aimed at religious practices. Another effect of the influx of foreigners into Europe has been a dramatic increase in the number of Muslims. Although Christians still constitute a majority (though many no longer practice their faith), the number of Muslims has mushroomed in France, Britain, Belgium, the Netherlands, and Germany. It has been estimated that at least 15 million Muslims were living in European Union nations at the beginning of the twenty-first century.

In some nations, concern that Muslim immigration will result in the erosion of national values has led to attempts to restrict the display of Islamic symbols. In 2004, France enacted a law prohibiting female students from wearing a headscarf (*hijab*) to school. Article 1 stated: "In public elementary, middle and high schools, the wearing of signs or clothing which conspicuously manifest students' religious affiliations is prohibited." The law further clarified "conspicuous" to mean "a large cross, a veil, or a skullcap."[7] Small religious symbols, such as small crosses or medallions, were not included. Critics of this law argue that it will exacerbate ethnic and religious tensions in France, while supporters stress that it upholds the tradition of secularism and equality for women in France (see Opposing Viewpoints "Islam and the West: Secularism in France" on p. 851).

The Environment and the Green Movements

Beginning in the 1970s, environmentalism has become a major item on the European political agenda. By that time, serious ecological problems had become all too apparent. Air pollution, produced by nitrogen oxide and sulfur dioxide emissions from road vehicles, power plants, and industrial factories, was causing respiratory illnesses and having corrosive effects on buildings and monuments. Many rivers, lakes, and seas had become so polluted that they posed serious health risks. Dying forests and disappearing wildlife alarmed more and more people. The opening of Eastern Europe after the revolutions of 1989 brought to the world's attention the incredible environmental destruction of that region caused by unfettered industrial pollution.

Environmental concerns have forced the major political parties in Europe to advocate new regulations for the protection of the environment. The Soviet nuclear power disaster at Chernobyl in Ukraine in 1986 made Europeans even more aware of potential environmental hazards, and 1987 was touted as the "year of the environment." Many European states established government ministries to oversee environmental issues.

Growing ecological awareness also gave rise to Green movements and Green Parties that emerged throughout Europe in the 1970s. Most visible was the Green Party in Germany, which was officially organized in 1979 and had elected forty-two delegates to the West German parliament by 1987. Green Parties have also competed successfully in Sweden, Austria, and Switzerland.

Although the Green movements and parties have played an important role in making people aware of ecological problems, they have not supplanted the traditional political parties, as some political analysts in the mid-1980s forecast. For one thing, the coalitions that made up the Greens found it difficult to agree on all issues and tended to splinter into different cliques. Moreover, traditional political parties have co-opted the environmental issues of the Greens. By the 1990s, more and more European governments were beginning to sponsor projects to safeguard the environment and clean up the worst sources of pollution.

GREEN URBAN PLANNING By the beginning of the twenty-first century, many European cities began to recognize the need for urban sustainability. Many cities have enacted laws that limit the amount of new construction, increase the quantity and quality of green spaces within the city, and foster the construction of new public transportation systems. The use of such alternatives as rail, metro, bus, and bicycle has created more options for public transportation (see the Comparative Illustration "Green Urbanism" on p. 853). In Stockholm, Sweden, 70 percent of all trips are made by public transit. Moreover, the emphasis on public transportation has served to limit the growth of urban sprawl. Many cities, such as Vienna, where 50 percent of the city's land is in green space, are also enacting new laws to protect urban parks and forests.

Western Culture Since 1945

Intellectually and culturally, the Western world since World War II has been notable for its diversity and innovation. Especially since 1970, new directions have led some observers to speak of a "Postmodern" cultural world.

POSTWAR LITERATURE One of the most original trends in postwar literature was known as the Theater of the Absurd. Its most famous proponent was the Irishman Samuel Beckett (1906–1990), who lived in France. In Beckett's play *Waiting for Godot* (1952), the action on the stage is not drawn from real life. Two men talk as they wait for someone with whom they may or may not have an appointment. No background information on the two men is provided. During the course of the play, nothing seems to happen. The audience is never told if the action in front of them is real or imagined. Unlike traditional theater, suspense is maintained not by having the audience wonder what is going to happen next but by having them wonder what is happening now.

The Theater of the Absurd reflected its time. The immediate postwar period was a time of disillusionment with fixed ideological beliefs in politics or religion. The same disillusionment that inspired the **existentialism** of Albert Camus (ahl-BAYR ka-MOO) (1913–1960) and Jean-Paul Sartre (ZHAHNH-POHL SAR-truh) (1905–1980), with its sense of the world's meaninglessness, underscored the bleak worldview of absurdist drama and literature. The starting point of the existentialism of Sartre and Camus was the absence of God in the universe. Although the death of God was tragic, it meant that humans had no preordained destiny and were utterly alone in the universe, with no future and no hope. As Camus expressed it:

> A world that can be explained even with bad reasons is a familiar world. But, on the other hand, in a universe suddenly divested of illusions and lights, man feels an alien, a stranger. His exile is without remedy since he is deprived of the memory of a lost home or the hope of a promised land. This divorce between man and his life, the actor and his setting, is properly the feeling of absurdity.[8]

Islam and the West: Secularism in France

FAMILY & SOCIETY

THE BANNING OF HEADSCARVES IN SCHOOLS WAS PRECEDED by a debate on the secular state in France. Secularism in France extends beyond the separation of church and state: while recognizing the right to religious expression, French law dictates that religious expression must remain in the private sphere. Before the law was enacted, President Jacques Chirac set up the Stasi Commission (named after its chair, Bernard Stasi) to interview school, religious, and political leaders on the issue. The commission decided in favor of prohibiting all conspicuous religious symbols in schools.

The first selection is taken from a speech by President Chirac, who favored the ban. The second is taken from interviews with French Muslim women, many of them from the Maghreb (the Arabic term for Northwest Africa). Many of these women questioned how the law protects their individual rights and freedom of religious expression.

French President Jacques Chirac on Secularism in French Society

The debate on the principle of secularism goes to the very heart of our values. It concerns our national cohesion, our ability to live together, our ability to unite on what is essential.... Many young people of immigrant origin, whose first language is French, and who are in most cases of French nationality, succeed and feel at ease in a society which is theirs. This kind of success must also be made possible by breaking the wall of silence and indifference which surrounds the reality of discrimination today. I know about the feeling of being misunderstood, of helplessness, sometimes even of revolt, among young French people of immigrant origin whose job applications are rejected because of the way their names sound, and who are too often confronted with discrimination in the fields of access to housing or even simply of access to leisure facilities.... All of France's children, whatever their history, whatever their origin, whatever their beliefs, are the daughters and sons of the republic. They have to be recognized as such, in law but above all in reality. By ensuring respect for this requirement, by reforming our integration policy, by our ability to bring equal opportunities to life, we shall bring national cohesion to life again. We shall also do so by bringing to life the principle of secularism, which is a pillar of our constitution. It expresses our wish to live together in respect, dialogue and tolerance. Secularism guarantees freedom of conscience. It protects the freedom to believe or not to believe.... We also need to reaffirm secularism in schools, because schools must be preserved absolutely....

There is of course no question of turning schools into a place of uniformity, of anonymity, where religious life or belonging would be banned. It is a question of enabling teachers and head teachers, who are today in the front-line and confronted with real difficulties, to carry out their mission serenely with the affirmation of a clear rule. Until recently, as a result of a reasonable custom which was respected spontaneously, nobody ever doubted that pupils, who are naturally free to live their faith, should nevertheless not arrive in schools, secondary schools or A-level colleges, in religious clothes. It is not a question of inventing new rules or of shifting the boundaries of secularism. It is a question of expressing, with respect but clearly and firmly, a rule which has been part of our customs and practices for a very long time. I have consulted, I have studied the report of the Stasi Commission, I have examined the arguments put forward by the National Assembly committee [on secularism], by political parties, by religious authorities, by major representatives of major currents of thought. In all conscience, it is my view that the wearing of clothes or of symbols which conspicuously demonstrate religious affiliations must be banned in state schools.

North African Women in France Respond to the Headscarf Ban

Labiba (Thirty-Five-Year-Old Algerian)

I don't feel that they should interfere in the private life of people in the respect that we're in a secular country; France shouldn't take a position toward one religion to the detriment of another.... I think that in a secular school, we should all be secular, otherwise we need to have religious school and then everyone is free to wear what he wants.

Nour (Thirty-Four-Year-Old Algerian)

Honestly, you know the secular school, it doesn't miss celebrating Easter, and when they celebrate Easter, it doesn't bother me. My daughter comes home with painted Easter eggs and everything; it's pretty; it's cute. There are classes that are over 80 percent Maghrebin in the suburbs, and they celebrate Easter, they celebrate Christmas, you see? And

(continued)

that's not a problem for the secular school. And I don't find that fair.

I find that when it's Ramadan, they should talk about Ramadan. Honestly, me, it wouldn't be a problem. On the contrary, someone who comes into class … with a veil, that would pose a question actually, that we could discuss in class, to know why this person wears the veil. So why punish them, amputate them from that part of their culture without discussing it? Why is it so upsetting to have someone in class who wears a veil, when we could make it a subject of discussion on all religions? Getting stuck on the veil hides the question. They make such a big deal out of it, the poor girls, they take them out of school; people turn them into extraterrestrials. In the end we turn them

into people who will have problems in their identities, in their culture and everything…. For a country that is home to so many cultures, there's no excuse.

Isma (Thirty-Six-Year-Old Algerian)

The girls who veil in France, especially the high school and junior high students, it's first of all a question of identity, because these girls are born in France to foreign parents…. At a given time an adolescent want to affirm himself, to show that he's someone, that he's an individual, so he thinks, I'd say, he thinks that it's by his clothes that he shows that he comes from somewhere, that he's from someone. So then, I think you should let them do it, and afterwards, by themselves, people come back to who they really are.

 What were the perspectives of the French president and the French Muslim women who were interviewed? How do they differ? Do you think there might be a way to reconcile the opposing positions? Why or why not?

Source: French President Jacques Chirac on Secularism in French Society. Caitlin Killian, *Gender and Society*, Vol. 17, No. 4, pp. 567–590, copyright 2003 by SAGE Publications.

According to Camus, then, the world was absurd and without meaning; humans, too, are without meaning and purpose. Reduced to despair and depression, humans have but one source of hope—themselves.

POSTMODERNISM The term *Postmodern* covers a variety of intellectual and artistic styles and ways of thinking prominent since the 1970s. In the broadest sense, **Postmodernism** rejects the modern Western belief in an objective truth and instead focuses on the relative nature of reality and knowledge.

While existentialism wrestled with notions of meaning and existence, a group of French philosophers in the 1960s attempted to understand how meaning and knowledge operate through the study of language and signs. **Poststructuralism**, or **deconstruction**, formulated by Jacques Derrida (ZHAHK DEH-ree-duh) (1930–2004), holds that culture is created and can therefore be analyzed in a variety of ways, according to the manner in which people create their own meaning. Hence there is no fixed truth or universal meaning.

Michel Foucault (mih-SHELL foo-KOH) (1926–1984) drew on Derrida to explore relationships of power. Believing that "power is exercised rather than possessed," Foucault argued that the diffusion of power and oppression marks all relationships. For example, any act of teaching entails components of assertion and submission, as the student adopts the ideas of the person in power. Therefore, all norms are culturally produced and entail some degree of power struggle.

Postmodernism was also evident in literature. In the Western world, the best examples were found in Latin America, in a literary style called *magic realism*, and in central and eastern Europe. Magic realism combined realistic events with dreamlike or fantastic backgrounds. One of the finest examples of magic realism can be found in the novel *One Hundred Years of Solitude*, written by Gabriel García Márquez (gahb-ree-EL gar-SEE-uh MAHR-kes) (1928–2014), a Colombian who won the Nobel Prize for Literature in 1982. The novel is the story of the fictional town of Macondo as seen by several generations of the Buendias, its founding family. The author slips back and forth between fact and fantasy. Villagers are not surprised when a local priest rises into the air and floats. But when wandering gypsies introduce these villagers to magnets, telescopes, and magnifying glasses, the villagers are dumbfounded by what they see as magic. According to the author, fantasy and fact depend on one's point of view.

The other center of Postmodernism was in central and eastern Europe, especially in the work of Milan Kundera (MEE-lahn koon-DAYR-uh) (b. 1929) of Czechoslovakia. Like the magic realists of Latin America, Kundera blended fantasy with realism. Unlike the magic realists, though, Kundera used fantasy to examine moral issues and remained

COMPARATIVE ILLUSTRATION

Green Urbanism. One of the ways that many cities are combating carbon dioxide emissions and promoting urban sustainability is by encouraging the use of bicycles. In Beijing (shown at the top), almost 4 million cyclists use the bicycle as their main form of transportation. In Paris, a new public bicycle program, called the *Velib*, short for "free bike," began in 2007, with 10,000 bikes and 700 rental stations. Today, the program has 17,000 bikes and approximately 1,200 rental stations where visitors and citizens can rent a bike by the hour, as shown below.

Q *How do you account for the success of the Velib program?*

optimistic about the human condition. Indeed, in his first novel, *The Unbearable Lightness of Being*, published in 1984, Kundera does not despair because of the political repression in his native land that he so aptly describes, but allows his characters to use love as a way to a better life. The human spirit can be diminished but not destroyed.

Trends in Art

Following the war, the United States dominated the art world, much as it did the world of popular culture. New York City replaced Paris as the artistic center of the West. The Guggenheim Museum, the Museum of Modern Art, and the Whitney Museum of Modern Art, together with New York's numerous art galleries, promoted modern art and helped determine artistic tastes throughout much of the world. One of the styles that became synonymous with the emergence of the New York art scene was **Abstract Expressionism**.

Dubbed "action painting" by one critic, Abstract Expressionism was energetic and spontaneous, qualities evident in the enormous canvases of Jackson Pollock (1912–1956). In such works as *Lavender Mist* (1950), paint seems to explode, enveloping the viewer with emotion and movement. Pollock's swirling forms and seemingly chaotic patterns broke all conventions of form and structure. His drip paintings, with their total abstraction, were extremely influential with other artists, and he eventually became a celebrity. Inspired by Native American sand painters, Pollock painted with the canvas on the floor. He explained, "On the floor I am more at ease. I feel nearer, more a part of the painting, since this way I can walk around it, work from four sides and be literally *in* the painting. When I am in the painting, I am not aware of what I am doing. There is pure harmony."

The early 1960s saw the emergence of Pop Art, which took images of popular culture and transformed them into works of fine art. Andy Warhol (1930–1987), who began as an

Hans Namuth/Science Source

Jackson Pollock at Work. After World War II, Abstract Expressionism moved to the center of the artistic mainstream. One of its best-known practitioners was the American Jackson Pollock, who achieved his ideal of total abstraction in his drip paintings. He is shown here painting in his Long Island studio. Pollock found it easier to cover his large canvases with spontaneous patterns of color when he put them on the floor.

advertising illustrator, was the most famous of the pop artists. Warhol adapted images from commercial art, such as cans of Campbell's soup, and photographs of such celebrities as Marilyn Monroe. Other artists drew their inspiration from comic strips. Derived from mass culture, these works were mass-produced and deliberately "of the moment," expressing the fleeting whims of popular culture.

Postmodernism's eclectic commingling of past tradition with Modernist innovation became increasingly evident in architecture. Charles Moore (1929–1993) provides one example. His *Piazza d'Italia* (1976–1980) in New Orleans is an outdoor plaza that combines classical Roman columns with stainless steel and neon lights. This blending of modern-day materials with historical references distinguished the Postmodern architecture of the late 1970s and 1980s from the Modernist glass box.

ART IN THE AGE OF COMMERCE: THE 1980S AND 1990S
Throughout the 1980s and 1990s, the art and music industries

increasingly adopted the techniques of marketing and advertising. With large sums of money invested in painters and musicians, pressure mounted to achieve critical and commercial success. Negotiating the distinction between art and popular culture was essential as many people equated merit with sales or economic value rather than aesthetic considerations.

In the art world, Neo-Expressionism reached its zenith in the mid-1980s. The economic boom and free spending of the Reagan years contributed to a thriving art scene in the United States. Neo-Expressionist artists such as Anselm Kiefer (AN-selm KEEF-uhr) (b. 1945) became increasingly popular as the art market soared. Born in Germany the year the war ended, Kiefer combines aspects of Abstract Expressionism, collage, and German Expressionism to create works that are stark and haunting.

The World of Science and Technology

Many of the scientific and technological achievements since World War II have revolutionized people's lives. During World War II, university scientists were recruited to work for their governments and develop new weapons and practical instruments of war. British physicists played a crucial role in the development of an improved radar system that helped defeat the German air force in the Battle of Britain in 1940. German scientists created self-propelled rockets as well as jet airplanes to keep Hitler's hopes alive for a miraculous turnaround in the war. The computer, too, was a wartime creation. The British mathematician Alan Turing designed a primitive computer to assist British intelligence in breaking the secret codes of German ciphering machines. The most famous product of wartime scientific research was the atomic bomb, created by a team of American and European scientists under the guidance of the physicist J. Robert Oppenheimer. Many wartime devices were created for destructive purposes, but computers and breakthrough technologies such as nuclear energy were soon adapted for peacetime uses.

The sponsorship of research by governments and the military during World War II created a new scientific model. Science had become very complex, and only large organizations with teams of scientists, huge laboratories, and complicated equipment could undertake large-scale scientific projects. The requisite facilities were so expensive that they could be provided only by governments or large corporations.

There was no more stunning example of how the new scientific establishment operated than the space race of the 1960s. The announcement by the Soviets in 1957 that they had sent the first space satellite, *Sputnik*, into orbit around the earth spurred the United States to launch an ambitious project to land a manned spacecraft on the moon within a decade. Massive amounts of government money financed the scientific research and technological advances that attained this goal in 1969.

In 2004, two vehicles sent by the National Aeronautics and Space Administration (NASA) arrived on the planet Mars. These Mars rovers, called *Spirit* and *Opportunity*, landed three weeks apart on different parts of the planet. Both contained

From the Industrial Age to the Technological Age

SCIENCE & TECHNOLOGY

As many observers have noted, a key aspect of the world economy is that it is in the process of transition to what has been called a "postindustrial age," characterized by a system that is not only increasingly global in scope but also increasingly technology-intensive. Since World War II, a stunning array of technological changes—especially in transportation, communications, space exploration, medicine, and agriculture—have transformed the world in which we live. Technological changes have also raised new questions and concerns and led to unexpected results. Some scientists have worried that genetic engineering might accidentally result in new strains of deadly bacteria that cannot be controlled outside the laboratory. Some doctors have recently raised the alarm that the overuse of antibiotics has created supergerms that are resistant to antibiotic treatment. The Technological Revolution has also led to the development of more advanced methods of destruction. Most frightening have been nuclear weapons.

The transition to a technology-intensive postindustrial world, which the futurologist Alvin Toffler has dubbed the Third Wave (the first two being the Agricultural and Industrial Revolutions), has produced difficulties for people in many walks of life—for blue-collar workers, whose high wages price them out of the market as firms begin to move their factories abroad; for the poor and uneducated, who lack the technical skills to handle complex tasks in the contemporary economy; and even for some members of the middle class, who have been fired or forced into retirement as their employers seek to reduce payrolls or outsource jobs to compete in the global marketplace.

It is now increasingly clear that the Technological Revolution, like the Industrial Revolution that preceded it, will entail enormous consequences and may ultimately give birth to a new era of social and political instability. The success of advanced capitalist states in the post–World War II era has been built on a broad consensus on the importance of two propositions: (1) the need for high levels of government investment in education, communications, and transportation as a means of meeting the challenges of continued economic growth and technological innovation and (2) the desirability of cooperative efforts in the international arena as a means of maintaining open markets for the free exchange of goods.

In the twenty-first century, these assumptions are increasingly under attack as citizens refuse to support education and oppose the formation of trading alliances to promote the free movement of goods and labor across national borders. The breakdown of the public consensus that brought modern capitalism to a pinnacle of achievement raises serious questions about the likelihood that the coming challenges of the Third Wave can be successfully met without a growing measure of political and social tension.

The Technological Age. A communication satellite is seen orbiting above the earth.

Adastra/Taxi/Getty Images

Q *What is implied by the term* Third Wave, *and what challenges does the Third Wave present to humanity?*

instruments that determine the chemical content of rocks. Based on the minerals found in Mars rocks, NASA scientists were able to conclude that the now barren planet once had generous supplies of water. NASA plans additional missions to Mars to help prepare for the eventual landing of humans on the planet.

The postwar alliance of science and technology led to an accelerated rate of change that has become a fact of life in Western society (see the Comparative Essay "From the Industrial Age to the Technological Age" above). One product of this alliance—the computer—may yet prove to be the most revolutionary of all the technological inventions of the twentieth century. Early computers, which required thousands of vacuum tubes to function, were large and hot and took up considerable space. The development of the transistor and then the silicon chip produced a revolutionary new approach to computer design. With the invention in 1971 of the microprocessor, a machine that combines the equivalent of thousands of transistors on a single, tiny silicon chip, the road was open for the development of the personal computer. By the 1990s, the personal computer had become a regular fixture in businesses, schools, and homes. The Internet—the world's largest computer network, launched in the 1980s by the U.S. government—provides millions of people around the world with quick access to immense quantities of information, as well as rapid communication and commercial transactions.

Internet growth quickly increased, with almost 500 million people using the Internet by 2000, and almost 2 billion more by 2013.

Despite the marvels produced by science and technology, some people came to question the underlying assumption of this alliance—that scientific knowledge gave human beings the ability to manipulate the environment for their benefit. They maintained that some technological advances had far-reaching side effects damaging to the environment. The chemical fertilizers, for example, that were touted for producing larger crops wreaked havoc with the ecological balance of streams, rivers, and woodlands.

Varieties of Religious Life

Existentialism was one response to the despair generated by the apparent collapse of civilized values in the twentieth century. A revival of religion was another. Ever since the Enlightenment of the eighteenth century, Christianity had been on the defensive. But in the twentieth century, a number of religious leaders attempted to bring new life to the faith.

In the Catholic Church, attempts at religious renewal came from two charismatic popes—John XXIII and John Paul II. Pope John XXIII (1881–1963) reigned for only a short time (1958–1963) but sparked a dramatic revival of Catholicism when he summoned the twenty-first ecumenical council of the church. Known as Vatican Council II, it liberalized a number of Catholic practices. The Mass was henceforth to be celebrated in the vernacular languages rather than Latin. New avenues of communication with other Christian faiths were also opened for the first time since the Reformation.

John Paul II (1920–2005), who had been the archbishop of Krakow in Poland before his elevation to the papacy in 1978, was the first non-Italian to be elected pope since the sixteenth century. Although he alienated a number of people by reasserting traditional Catholic teaching on such issues as birth control, women in the priesthood, and clerical celibacy, John Paul's numerous travels around the world helped strengthen the Catholic Church throughout the non-Western world. A strong believer in social justice, the charismatic John Paul II was a powerful figure reminding Europeans of their spiritual heritage and the need to temper the pursuit of materialism with spiritual concerns.

The global nature of the Catholic Church became apparent on March 13, 2013, with the election of a new pope. Cardinal Jorge Mario Bergoglio (HOR-hey MAH-rio Bare-GO-lio) (b. 1936), the archbishop of Buenos Aires, became the first Latin American as well as the first non-European since the eighth century to be elected pope. He chose to be called Pope Francis in honor of the humble Saint Francis of Assisi (see Chapter 12).

FUNDAMENTALISM   Despite the revival of religion after World War II, church attendance in Europe and the United States declined dramatically in the 1960s and 1970s as a result of growing secular attitudes. Yet even though the numbers of regular churchgoers in established Protestant and Catholic churches continued to decline, the number of fundamentalist churches and churchgoers has been growing, especially in the United States.

Fundamentalism was originally a movement within Protestantism that arose early in the twentieth century. Its goal was to maintain a strict traditional interpretation of the Bible and the Christian faith, especially in opposition to the theory of Darwinian evolution and secularism. In the 1980s and 1990s, fundamentalists became involved in a struggle against such nontheistic belief systems as secular humanism and communism, as well as legalized abortion and homosexuality. Especially in the United States, fundamentalists organized politically to elect candidates who supported their views. This so-called Christian right played an influential role in electing Ronald Reagan and both George Bushes to the presidency.

THE GROWTH OF ISLAM   Fundamentalism, however, was not unique to Protestantism. In Islam, the term *fundamentalism* is used to refer to a return to traditional Islamic values, especially in opposition to a perceived weakening of moral strictures due to the corrupting influence of Western ideas and practices. After the Iranian Revolution of 1979, the term was also applied to militant Islamic movements, such as the Taliban in Afghanistan, who favored militant action against Western influence.

Despite the wariness of Islamic radicalism in the aftermath of the September 11, 2001 terrorist attacks on the United States, Islam is growing in both Europe and the United States, due primarily to the migration of people from Muslim countries. As Muslim communities became established in France, Germany, Britain, Italy, and Spain during the 1980s and 1990s, they built mosques for religious worship and religious education.

The Explosion of Popular Culture

Especially since World War II, popular culture has played an important role in helping Western people define themselves. It also reflects the economic system that supports it, for this system manufactures, distributes, and sells the images that people consume as popular culture. Modern popular culture is therefore an integral part of the mass consumer society in which it has emerged.

The United States has been the most influential force in shaping popular culture in the West and, to a lesser degree, the rest of the world. Through movies, music, advertising, and television, the United States has spread its particular form of consumerism and the American dream around the globe. Already in 1923, the New York *Morning Post* noted that "the film is to America what the flag was once to Britain. By its means Uncle Sam may hope some day … to Americanize the world."[9]

Motion pictures were the primary vehicle for the diffusion of American popular culture in the years immediately following the war and continued to dominate both European and American markets in the next decades. Although developed in the 1930s, television did not become readily available until the late 1940s. By 1954, there were 32 million sets in the

United States as television became the centerpiece of middle-class life. In the 1960s, as television spread around the world, American networks exported their products to Europe and developing countries at extraordinarily low prices.

The United States has also dominated popular music since the end of World War II. Jazz, blues, rhythm and blues, rap, rock-and-roll, and hip-hop have been by far the most popular music forms in the Western world—and much of the non-Western world—during this time. All of them originated in the United States, and all are rooted in African American musical innovations. As these forms spread to the rest of the world, they inspired local artists, who then transformed the music in their own way.

The introduction of the video music channel MTV in the early 1980s radically changed the music scene by making image as important as sound in selling records. Artists like Michael Jackson and Madonna became superstars by treating the music video as an art form. Rather than merely a recorded performance, many videos were short films involving elaborate staging and special effects set to music. Technological advances became prevalent in the music of the 1980s with the advent of the synthesizer, an electronic piano that produced computerized sounds.

Sports have become a major product of both popular culture and the leisure industry. The development of satellite television and various electronic breakthroughs helped make sports a global phenomenon. The Olympic Games can now be broadcast around the world instantly from anyplace on earth. In 2010, approximately 715 million people, or one out of every ten people in the world, watched the World Cup championship match between Spain and the Netherlands. Sports have also become a cheap form of entertainment for consumers as spectators do not have to leave their homes to watch athletic competitions. As sports television revenue has escalated, many sports have come to receive the bulk of their yearly revenue from television contracts.

CHAPTER SUMMARY

Western Europe reinvented itself in the 1950s and 1960s as a remarkable economic recovery fostered a new optimism. Western European states embraced political democracy, and with the development of the European Community, many of them began to move toward economic unity. A new European society also emerged after World War II. White-collar workers increased in number, and installment plan buying helped create a consumer society. The welfare state provided both pensions and health care. Birth control led to smaller families, and more women joined the workforce.

Although many people were optimistic about a "new world order" after the collapse of communism, uncertainties still prevailed. Germany was successfully reunited, and the European Union became even stronger with the adoption of a common currency in the euro. Yugoslavia, however, disintegrated into warring states that eventually all became independent, and ethnic groups that had once been forced to live under distinct national banners began rebelling to form autonomous states. Although some were successful, others were brutally repressed.

In the Western Hemisphere, the United States and Canada built prosperous economies and relatively stable communities in the 1950s, but there, too, new problems, including ethnic, racial, and linguistic differences, along with economic difficulties, dampened the optimism of earlier decades. Although some Latin American nations shared in the economic growth of the 1950s and 1960s, it was not accompanied by political stability. Not until the 1980s did democratic governments begin with consistency to replace oppressive military regimes.

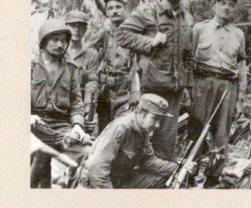

While the "new world order" was fitfully developing, other challenges emerged. The arrival of many foreigners, especially in western Europe, not only strained the social services of European countries but also led to antiforeign sentiment and right-wing political parties that encouraged it. Environmental abuses led to growing threats not only to Europeans but also all humans. Terrorism, especially that caused by some parts of the Muslim world, emerged as a threat to many Western states. Since the end of World War II, terrorism seems to have replaced communism as the number one enemy of the West. At the beginning of the twenty-first century, a major realization has been the recognition that the problems afflicting the Western world have become global problems.

CHAPTER TIMELINE

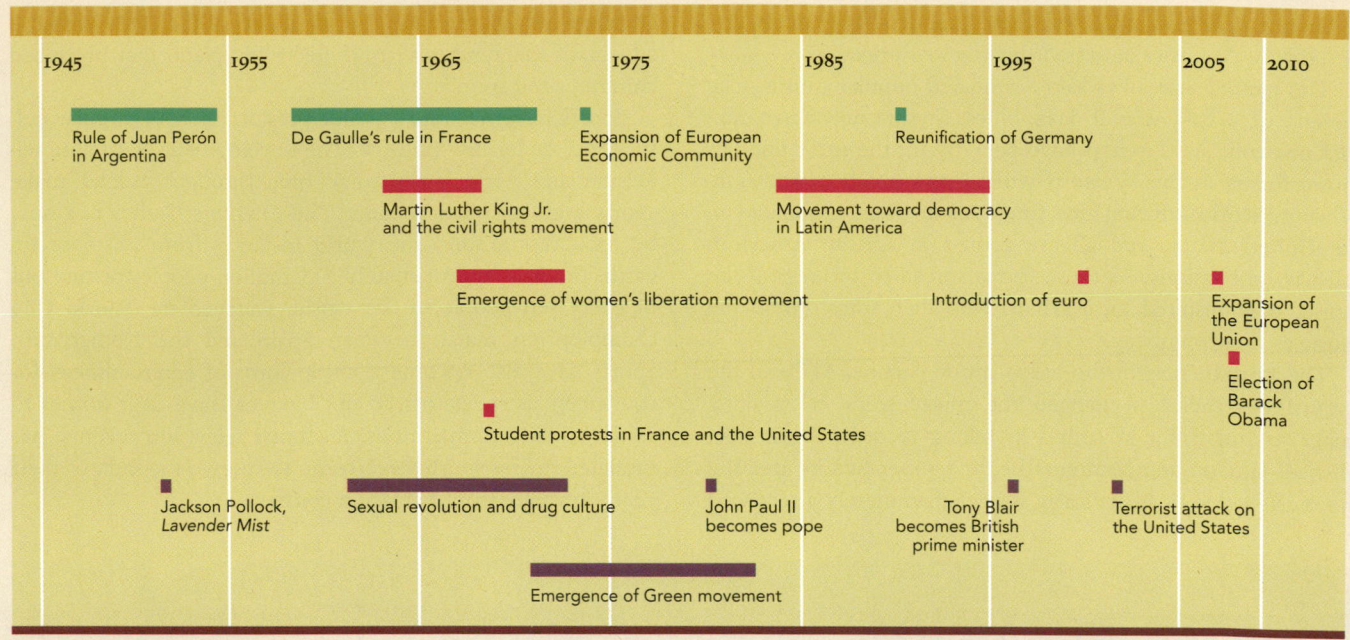

| 1945 | 1955 | 1965 | 1975 | 1985 | 1995 | 2005 | 2010 |

Rule of Juan Perón in Argentina

De Gaulle's rule in France

Expansion of European Economic Community

Reunification of Germany

Martin Luther King Jr. and the civil rights movement

Movement toward democracy in Latin America

Emergence of women's liberation movement

Introduction of euro

Expansion of the European Union

Election of Barack Obama

Student protests in France and the United States

Jackson Pollock, *Lavender Mist*

Sexual revolution and drug culture

John Paul II becomes pope

Tony Blair becomes British prime minister

Terrorist attack on the United States

Emergence of Green movement

CHAPTER REVIEW

Upon Reflection

Q What were the major successes and failures of the western European democracies between 1945 and 2010?

Q What directions did eastern European nations take after they became free from Soviet control? Why did they react as they did?

Q What role did popular culture play in the Western world after 1945?

Key Terms

welfare state (p. 827)
socialized medicine (p. 827)
ethnic cleansing (p. 829)
consumer society (p. 843)
permissive society (p. 843)
women's liberation movement (p. 846)
guest workers (p. 849)
existentialism (p. 850)
Postmodernism (p. 852)
poststructuralism (deconstruction) (p. 852)
Abstract Expressionism (p. 853)
fundamentalism (p. 856)

Suggested Reading

EUROPE SINCE 1945   For a well-written survey on Europe since 1945, see **T. Judt,** *Postwar: A History of Europe Since 1945* (New York, 2005). On the building of common

institutions in western Europe, see **S. Henig,** *The Uniting of Europe: From Discord to Concord* (London, 1997). On eastern Europe, see **P. Kenney,** *The Burden of Freedom: Eastern Europe Since 1989* (London, 2006).

THE UNITED STATES AND CANADA   For a general survey of U.S. history since 1945, see **W. H. Chafe,** *Unfinished Journey: America Since World War II* (Oxford, 2006). Information on Canada can be found in **C. Brown, ed.,** *The Illustrated History of Canada,* 4th ed. (Toronto, 2003).

LATIN AMERICA   For general surveys of Latin American history, see **M. C. Eakin,** *The History of Latin America: Collision of Cultures* (New York, 2007), and **E. Bradford Burns** and **J. A. Charlip,** *Latin America: An Interpretive History,* 8th ed. (Upper Saddle River, N.J., 2007). The twentieth century is the focus of **T. E. Skidmore** and **P. H. Smith,** *Modern Latin America,* 6th ed. (Oxford, 2004).

SOCIETY IN THE WESTERN WORLD   On the turbulent 1960s, see **A. Marwick,** *The Sixties: Social and Cultural Transformation in Britain, France, Italy, and the United States* (Oxford, 1999). On the sexual revolution of the 1960s, see **D. Allyn,** *Make Love, Not War: The Sexual Revolution—An Unfettered History* (New York, 2000).

The changing role of women is examined in **R. Rosen,** *The World Split Open: How the Modern Women's Movement Changed America* (New York, 2001). On terrorism, see **C. E. Simonsen** and **J. R. Spendlove,** *Terrorism Today: The Past, the Players, the Future,* 3rd ed. (Upper Saddle River, N.J., 2006). The problems of guest workers and immigrants are examined in **W. Laqueur, *The Last Days of Europe: Epitaph for an Old Continent*** (New York, 2007).

WESTERN CULTURE SINCE 1945   For a general view of postwar thought and culture, see **J. A. Winders, *European Culture Since 1848: From Modern to Postmodern and Beyond***, rev. ed. (New York, 2001). On Postmodernism, see **C. Butler, *Postmodernism: A Very Short Introduction*** (Oxford, 2002). On the arts, see **A. Marwick, *Arts in the West Since 1945*** (Oxford, 2002).

Chapter Notes

1. Quoted in W. I. Hitchcock, *The Struggle for Europe: The Turbulent History of a Divided Continent, 1945–2002* (New York, 2003), pp. 399–400.

2. D. D. Eisenhower, *The White House Years: Waging Peace, 1956–1961* (Garden City, N.Y., 1965), p. 533.

3. Quoted in T. Judt, *Postwar: A History of Europe Since 1945* (New York, 2005), p. 390.

4. Quoted in H. Scott, *Sweden's "Right to Be Human"—Sex-Role Equality: The Goal and the Reality* (London, 1982), p. 125.

5. Quoted in M. Rowe et al., *Spare Rib Reader* (Harmondsworth, England, 1982), p. 574.

6. Quoted in R. Bridenthal, "Women in the New Europe," in R. Bridenthal, S. M. Stuard, and M. E. Wiesner, eds., *Becoming Visible: Women in European History*, 3rd ed. (Boston, 1998), pp. 564–565.

7. Quoted in Joan W. Scott, *The Politics of the Veil* (Princeton, N.J., 2009), p. 1.

8. Quoted in H. Grosshans, *The Search for Modern Europe* (Boston, 1970), p. 421.

9. Quoted in R. Maltby, ed., *Passing Parade: A History of Popular Culture in the Twentieth Century* (New York, 1989), p. 11.

MindTap is a fully online, highly personalized learning experience built upon Cengage Learning content. MindTap combines student learning tools—readings, multimedia, activities, and assessments—into a singular Learning Path that guides students through their course.

Challenges of Nation Building in Africa and the Middle East

The face of Islamic extremism in Central Africa

AHMED OUOBA/AFP/Getty Images

CHAPTER OUTLINE AND FOCUS QUESTIONS

Uhuru: The Struggle for Independence in Africa

Q What role did nationalist movements play in the transition to independence in Africa, and how did such movements differ from their counterparts elsewhere?

The Era of Independence

Q How have dreams clashed with realities in the independent nations of Africa, and how have African governments sought to meet these challenges?

Continuity and Change in Modern African Societies

Q How did the rise of independent states affect the lives and the role of women in African societies? How does that role compare with the role played by women in other parts of the contemporary world?

Crescent of Conflict

Q What problems have the nations of the Middle East faced since the end of World War II, and to what degree have they managed to resolve them?

Society and Culture in the Contemporary Middle East

Q How have religious issues affected economic, social, and cultural conditions in the Middle East in recent decades?

CRITICAL THINKING

Q What factors can be advanced to explain the chronic instability and internal conflict that have characterized conditions in Africa and the Middle East since World War II?

CONNECTIONS TO TODAY

Q Is it in the interests of the advanced countries to provide assistance to Africa in order to manage the continent's current economic problems?

ON TAKING OVER THE CITY, they began to terrorize the inhabitants—cutting off the hands of suspected thieves, stoning adulterous couples to death, forbidding the playing of any kind of musical instrument, and desecrating the famous library and the shrines of local Sufi mystics. The invaders were fanatical tribal warriors who sought to impose their strict version of Islam on the population throughout the region. The city was Timbuktu, once a fabled caravan stop on a major trade route snaking through the Sahara and more recently a sleepy river port in the western African country of Mali. The time was January 2013.[1]

Timbuktu lies in the Sahel, a grassy region just south of the Sahara that stretches from the western tip of the African continent to the Nile River valley in the east. Historically a geographic fault line between the arid desert and the rich tropical forest lands along the Atlantic coast to the south, in recent times, the Sahel has become a political and ideological battleground as well, as

Muslim pastoralists compete with Christian and animist farmers for scarce fertile land and access to precious water reserves. The struggle has been going on for centuries but it has intensified in recent years as a result of the increasing desiccation of the region and the current tensions between the Muslim and Christian worlds today. Dealing with this issue is one challenge that many nations in Africa face today. ❖

Uhuru: The Struggle for Independence in Africa

 FOCUS QUESTION: What role did nationalist movements play in the transition to independence in Africa, and how did such movements differ from their counterparts elsewhere?

After World War II, some European governments reluctantly recognized that the end result of colonial rule in Africa would be African self-government, if not full independence. Accordingly, the African population would have to be trained to handle the responsibilities of representative government. As a result, during the 1950s, reforms were introduced into most British colonies that increased the representation of the local population in the governing process. Members of legislative and executive councils were increasingly chosen through elections, and Africans came to constitute a majority of these bodies. Elected councils at the local level were introduced in the 1950s to reduce the power of the chiefs and clan heads, who had controlled local government under indirect rule. An exception was South Africa, where European domination continued. In the Union of South Africa, the franchise was restricted to whites except in the former territory of the Cape Colony, where persons of mixed ancestry had enjoyed the right to vote since the mid-nineteenth century. Black Africans did win some limited electoral rights in Northern and Southern Rhodesia (now Zambia and Zimbabwe, respectively), although whites generally dominated the political scene.

A similar process of political liberalization was taking place in the French colonies. At first, the French tried to integrate the African peoples into French culture. By the 1920s, however, racist beliefs in Western cultural superiority and the tenacity of traditional beliefs and practices among Africans had somewhat discredited this ideal. Therefore, the French instituted a more limited program of assigning a limited number of French-educated elites as administrators at the local level as a link to the remainder of the population. The remaining European colonial powers, notably Belgium and Portugal, made little effort to prepare their subject peoples for independence.

The Colonial Legacy

As in Asia, colonial rule had a mixed impact on the societies and peoples of Africa. The Western presence brought a number of short-term and long-term benefits to Africa, such as improved transportation and communication facilities, and in a few areas laid the foundation for a modern industrial and commercial sector. Improved sanitation and medical care increased life expectancy. The introduction of selective elements of Western political systems laid the groundwork for the eventual creation of independent democratic societies.

Yet the benefits of westernization were distributed very unequally, and the vast majority of Africans found their lives little improved, if at all. Only South Africa and French-held Algeria, for example, developed modern industrial sectors, extensive railroad networks, and modern communications systems. In both countries, European settlers were numerous, most investment capital for industrial ventures was European, and whites comprised almost the entire professional and managerial class. Members of the local population were generally restricted to unskilled or semiskilled jobs at wages less than one-fifth those enjoyed by Europeans.

Many colonies concentrated on export crops—peanuts in Senegal and Gambia, cotton in Egypt and Uganda, coffee in Kenya, palm oil and cocoa products in the Gold Coast. In some cases, the crops were grown on plantations, which were usually owned by Europeans. But plantation agriculture was not always suitable in Africa, and much farming was done by free or tenant farmers. In some areas, where land ownership was traditionally vested in the community, the land was owned and leased by the corporate village. The vast majority of the profits from the export of agricultural products or of Africa's vast mineral resources, however, accrued to Europeans or to merchants from other foreign countries, such as India and the Arab emirates.

While a fortunate few benefited from the increase in exports, the vast majority of Africans continued to be subsistence farmers growing food for their own consumption. The gap was particularly wide in places like Kenya, where the best lands were reserved for European settlers to make the colony self-sufficient. As in other parts of the world, the early stages of the Industrial Revolution were especially painful for the rural population, and ordinary subsistence farmers reaped few benefits from colonial rule. To make matters worse, in some areas—notably in West Africa—the cultivation of cash crops eroded the fragile soil base and turned farmland into desert.

The Rise of Nationalism

Political organizations founded to promote African rights did not arise until after World War I, and then only in a few areas, such as British-ruled Kenya and the Gold Coast. At first, organizations such as the National Congress of British West Africa (formed in 1919 in the Gold Coast) and Jomo Kenyatta's Kikuyu Central Association focused on improving living conditions in the colonies rather than on national independence. After World War II, however, following the example of independence movements elsewhere, these groups became organized political parties with independence as their objective. In the Gold Coast, Kwame Nkrumah (KWAH-may en-KROO-muh) (1909–1972) led the Convention People's Party, the first formal political party in black Africa. In the late

1940s, Jomo Kenyatta (JOH-moh ken-YAHT-uh) (1894–1978) founded the Kenya African National Union (KANU), which focused on economic issues but had an implied political agenda as well.

For the most part, these political activities were nonviolent and were led by Western-educated African intellectuals. Their constituents were primarily urban professionals, merchants, and members of labor unions. But the demand for independence was not restricted to the cities. In Kenya, for example, the widely publicized Mau Mau (MOW MOW ["ow" as in "how"]) movement among the Kikuyu (ki-KOO-yoo) people used guerrilla tactics as an element of its program to achieve *uhuru* (oo-HOO-roo) (Swahili for "freedom") from the British. One of the primary reasons for the revolt was to protest against the unlawful seizure of African lands by European plantation owners. Although only about a hundred Europeans were killed compared with an estimated two thousand Africans who died at the hands of either Mau Mau units or the British, the specter of a nationwide revolt alarmed the European population and convinced the British government in 1959 to promise eventual independence.

In South Africa and Algeria, where the political system was also dominated by European settlers, the transition to independence was more complicated. In South Africa, political activity by local Africans began with the formation of the African National Congress (ANC) in 1912. Initially, the ANC was dominated by Western-oriented intellectuals and had limited mass support. Its goal was to achieve economic and political reforms, including full equality for educated Africans, within the framework of the existing system. But the ANC's efforts met with little success, while conservative white parties managed to stiffen the segregation laws and impose a policy of full legal segregation, called **apartheid** (uh-PAHRT-hyt), in 1948. In response, the ANC became increasingly radicalized, and by the 1950s, the prospects for violence rather than conciliation were growing.

In Algeria, resistance to French rule by indigenous Berbers and Arabs living in rural areas had never ceased. After World War II, urban agitation intensified, leading to a widespread rebellion against colonial rule in the mid-1950s. At first, the French government tried to maintain its authority in Algeria, which was considered an integral part of metropolitan France. But when Charles de Gaulle became

president of France in 1958, he reversed French policy, and Algeria became an independent republic four years later, with Ahmad Ben Bella (AH-muhd ben BELL-luh) (1918–2004) as its president. The armed struggle in Algeria hastened the transition to statehood in its neighbors as well. Tunisia won its independence in 1956 after some urban agitation and rural unrest but retained close ties with Paris. The French attempted to suppress the nationalist movement in French Morocco by sending Sultan Muhammad V into exile but the effort failed, and in 1956, he returned as the ruler of the independent state of Morocco.

Most black African nations achieved their independence in the late 1950s and 1960s, beginning with the Gold Coast, renamed Ghana, in 1957 (see Map 29.1). It was soon followed by Nigeria; the Belgian Congo, renamed Zaire (zah-EER) and then the Democratic Republic of the Congo; Kenya; Tanganyika (tang-an-YEE-kuh), later joined with Zanzibar (ZAN-zi-bar) and renamed Tanzania (tan-zuh-NEE-uh); and several other countries. Most of the French colonies agreed to accept independence within the framework of de Gaulle's

MAP 29.1 Modern Africa. This map shows the fifty-four independent states in Africa today.

Q *Why was unity so difficult to achieve in African regions?*

© 2016 Cengage Learning

French Community. By the late 1960s, only parts of southern Africa and the Portuguese possessions of Mozambique and Angola remained under European rule.

Independence thus came later to Africa than to most of Asia. Several factors help explain the delay. For one thing, colonialism was established in Africa somewhat later than in most areas of Asia, and the inevitable reaction from the local population was consequently later in coming. Furthermore, with the exception of a few areas in West Africa and along the Mediterranean, coherent states with a strong sense of cultural, ethnic, and linguistic unity did not exist in most of Africa. Most traditional states, such as Ashanti (uh-SHAN-tee *or* uh-SHAHN-tee) in West Africa, Songhai (song-HY) in the southern Sahara, and Kongo in the Congo River basin, were collections of heterogeneous peoples with little sense of national or cultural unity. Even after colonies were established, the European powers often practiced a policy of "divide and rule," and the British encouraged political decentralization by retaining the authority of the traditional local chieftains. It is hardly surprising that when opposition to colonial rule emerged, unity was difficult to achieve.

The Era of Independence

FOCUS QUESTION: How have dreams clashed with realities in the independent nations of Africa, and how have African governments sought to meet these challenges?

The newly independent African states faced intimidating challenges. They had been profoundly affected by colonial rule but the experience had been highly unsatisfactory in most respects. Although Western political institutions, values, and technology had been introduced, at least in the cities, the exposure to European civilization had been superficial at best for most Africans and tragic for many. At the outset of independence, most African societies were still primarily agrarian and traditional, and their modern sectors depended mainly on imports from the West.

The Destiny of Africa: Unity or Diversity?

Like their counterparts in South and Southeast Asia, most of Africa's new leaders came from the urban middle class (see Chapter 30). They had studied in Europe or the United States and spoke and read European languages. Although most were profoundly critical of colonial policies, they appeared for the most part to accept the Western model of governance and Western democratic values as potential models for the establishment of independent states on the African continent.

Their views on economics were somewhat more diverse. Some, like Jomo Kenyatta of Kenya and General Mobutu Sese Seko (moh-BOO-too SES-ay SEK-oh) (1930–1997) of Zaire, were advocates of Western-style capitalism. Others, like Julius Nyerere (ny-REHR-ee) (1922–1999) of Tanzania, Kwame

Nkrumah of Ghana, and Sékou Touré (say-KOO too-RAY) (1922–1984) of Guinea, preferred what was termed an "African form of socialism," which bore scant resemblance to the Marxist-Leninist socialism practiced in the Soviet Union. According to its advocates, it was descended from traditional communal practices in precolonial Africa.

At first, most of the new African leaders accepted the national boundaries established during the colonial era. This presented a problem, however, since, as we have noted, these boundaries were artificial creations of the colonial powers. Virtually all of the new states included widely diverse ethnic, linguistic, and territorial groups. Zaire, for example, was composed of more than two hundred territorial groups speaking seventy-five different languages. Such conditions posed a severe challenge to the task of forming cohesive nation-states.

A number of leaders—including Nkrumah of Ghana, Touré of Guinea, and Nyerere of Tanganyika—were enticed by **pan-Africanism**, the concept originally developed by African intellectuals living abroad of a continental unity that transcended national boundaries. Nkrumah in particular hoped that a pan-African union could be established that would unite all of the new countries of the continent in a broader community. His dream was not widely shared by other African political figures, however, who eventually settled on a more innocuous concept of regional cooperation on key issues. The concrete manifestation of this idea was the Organization of African Unity (OAU), founded in Addis Ababa (AH-diss AH-bah-buh) in 1963.

Dream and Reality: Political and Economic Conditions in Independent Africa

The program of the OAU called for an Africa based on freedom, equality, justice, and dignity and on the unity, solidarity, prosperity, and territorial integrity of African states. It did not take long for reality to set in. Vast disparities in education and wealth and the lingering effects of colonial domination made it hard to establish material prosperity in much of Africa. Expectations that independence would lead to stable political structures based on "one person, one vote" were soon disappointed as the initial phase of pluralistic governments gave way to a series of military regimes and one-party states. Between 1957 and 1982, more than seventy leaders of African countries were overthrown by violence.

THE PROBLEM OF NEOCOLONIALISM Part of the problem was the residual impact of colonialism. Most new countries in Africa were dependent on the export of a single crop or natural resource. Many of these resources were still controlled by foreigners, leading to the charge that colonialism had been succeeded by **neocolonialism**, in which Western domination was maintained primarily by economic rather than political or military means. Even when such resources were owned by local interests, exploitation was hindered by inadequate technology and the lack of an efficient transportation network. Africa's road and rail networks were grossly inadequate to

Stealing the Nation's Riches

AFTER 1965, AFRICAN NOVELISTS transferred their anger from the foreign oppressor to their own national leaders, deploring their greed, corruption, and inhumanity. One of the most pessimistic expressions of this betrayal of newly independent Africa is found in *The Beautiful Ones Are Not Yet Born*, a novel published by the Ghanaian author Ayi Kwei Armah (AY-yee KWAY AR-mah) in 1968. The author decried the government of Kwame Nkrumah and was unimpressed with the rumors of a military coup, which, he predicted, would simply replace the regime with a new despot and his entourage of "fat men." Ghana today has made significant progress in reducing the level of corruption.

Ayi Kwei Armah, *The Beautiful Ones Are Not Yet Born*

The net had been made in the special Ghanaian way that allowed the really big corrupt people to pass through it. A net to catch only the small, dispensable fellows, trying in their anguished blindness to leap and to attain the gleam and the comfort the only way these things could be done. And the big ones floated free, like all the slogans. End bribery and corruption. Build Socialism. Equality. Shit. A man would just have to make up his mind that there was never going to be anything but despair, and there would be no way of escaping it....

In the life of the nation itself, maybe nothing really new would happen. New men would take into their hands the power to steal the nation's riches and to use it for their own satisfaction. That, of course, was to be expected. New people would use the country's power to get rid of men and women who talked a language that did not flatter them. There would be nothing different in that. That would only be a continuation of the Ghanaian way of life. But here was the real change. The individual man of power now shivering, his head filled with the fear of the vengeance of those he had wronged. For him everything was going to change. And for those like him who had grown greasy and fat singing the praises of their chief, for those who had been getting themselves ready for the enjoyment of hoped-for favors, there would be long days of pain ahead. The flatterers with their new white Mercedes cars would have to find ways of burying old words. For those who had come directly against the old power, there would be much happiness. But for the nation itself there would only be a change of embezzlers and a change of the hunters and the hunted. A pitiful shrinking of the world from those days Teacher still looked back to, when the single mind was filled with the hopes of a whole people. A pitiful shrinking, to days when all the powerful could think of was to use the power of a whole people to fill their own paunches. Endless days, same days, stretching into the future with no end anywhere in sight.

 According to Ayi Kwei Armah, who was to blame for conditions in his country?

Source: From *The Beautiful Ones Are Not Yet Born* by Ayi Kwei Armah (Heinemann, 1989).

---

serve the needs of growing economies, while airplane service was still in its infancy.

World trade patterns often exacerbated these problems. Most African states had to import technology and manufactured goods from the West, and the prices of those goods rose more rapidly than those of the export products. On the other hand, many of their exports were raw materials, whose prices were often subject to rapid fluctuations.

Admittedly, the new states frequently contributed to their own problems. Treasury funds were squandered on military equipment or expensive consumer goods rather than applied to building up the infrastructure to support and sustain an industrial economy. Education was neglected, leaving much of the population of the continent, especially in rural areas, functionally illiterate. Corruption, a painful reality throughout the modern world, became almost a way of life in Africa as bribery became necessary to obtain even the most basic services (see the box "Stealing the Nation's Riches" above).

AFRICA IN THE COLD WAR Many of the problems encountered by the new nations of Africa were also ascribed to the fact that independence had not ended Western interference in Africa's political affairs. Many African leaders were angered when Western powers led by the United States conspired to overthrow the left-leaning politician Patrice Lumumba (puh-TREES loo-MOOM-buh) (1925–1961) in the Congo in the early 1960s. Lumumba, who had been educated in the Soviet Union, aroused fears in Washington that he might promote Soviet influence in Central Africa (see Chapter 26). Eventually, he was assassinated under mysterious circumstances.

The episode was a major factor influencing African leaders to form the OAU as a means of reducing Western influence on the continent but the strategy achieved few results. Although many African leaders opted to adopt a neutral stance in the Cold War, competition between Moscow and Washington throughout the region was fierce, often undermining the efforts of fragile governments to build stable new nations. To make matters worse, African states had difficulty achieving a united position on many issues, and their disagreements left the region vulnerable to external influence and conflict. Border disputes festered in many areas of the continent, and in some cases—as with Morocco and a rebel movement in the Western Sahara and between Kenya and Uganda—flared into outright war.

Even within many new African nations, the concept of nationhood was undermined by the lingering force of regionalism or ethnic rivalries. Nigeria, with the largest population on the continent, was rent by civil strife during the late 1960s when dissident Ibo (EE-boh) groups in the southeast attempted unsuccessfully to form the independent state of Biafra (bee-AH-fruh). Another force undermining nationalism in Africa was that of pan-Islamism. Its prime exponent in Africa was the Egyptian president Gamal Abdul Nasser (guh-MAHL AB-dool NAH-sur) (see "Nasser and Pan-Arabism" later in this chapter). After Nasser's death in 1970, the torch of Islamic unity in Africa was carried by the Libyan president Muammar Qaddafi (moo-AHM-ahr guh-DAH-fee) (1942–2011), whose ambitions to create a greater Muslim nation in the Sahara under his authority led to conflict with neighboring Chad. The Islamic resurgence also surfaced in Nigeria and other nations of West Africa, where divisions between Muslims and Christians began to emerge and have recently erupted into violence.

THE POPULATION BOMB Finally, rapid population growth crippled efforts to create modern economies. By the 1980s, annual population growth averaged nearly 3 percent throughout Africa, the highest rate of any continent. Drought conditions and the inexorable spread of the Sahara (technically known as *desertification*), caused partly by overcultivation of the land, led to widespread hunger and starvation, first in West African countries such as Niger and Mali and then in Ethiopia, Somalia, and the Sudan. Predictions are that the population of Africa will increase by at least 200 million over the next ten years, surpassing a total of two billion people by mid-century.

This prediction does not take into account the prevalence of AIDS, which has reached epidemic proportions in Africa. According to a United Nations study, at least 5 percent of the entire population of sub-Saharan Africa is infected with the virus, including a high percentage of members of the urban middle class. More than 65 percent of the AIDS cases reported around the world are on the continent of Africa, and the majority of cases are among the young. Although there have been some signs of progress in recent years, without further measures to curtail the effects of the disease, the grisly reality is that it could have a significant impact on the rate of population growth in several African countries.[2]

Today poverty is widespread in Africa, particularly among the three-quarters of the population still living off the land. Urban areas have grown tremendously but most are surrounded by massive squatter settlements composed of migrants from rural areas who have fled to the cities in search of a better life. The expansion of the cities has overwhelmed

© William J. Duiker

Africa's Population Boom: Cause for Concern? The rate of population growth is higher in Africa than in any other continent in the world today. With marriage-age women giving birth to an average of more than six children in many countries, the total population of Africa is expected to double by mid-century to over two billion people. By comparison, in 1950, there were three times as many Europeans as sub-Saharan Africans. By 2010, sub-Saharan Africans outnumbered Europeans by over 15 percent. When combined with high poverty rates and the growing incidence of drought in many regions of the continent, the situation is indeed highly combustible and a cause for concern. The illustration shows a crowd of happy children as they greet visitors to their village in the Gambia, one of the most densely populated countries on the continent.

fragile transportation and sanitation systems and led to rising pollution and perpetual traffic jams, while millions are forced to live without running water and electricity (see "Nigeria: A Nation Divided" later in this chapter). Meanwhile, the fortunate few (all too often government officials on the take) live the high life and emulate the consumerism of the West (in a particularly expressive phrase, the rich in many East African countries are known as *wabenzi*, or "Mercedes-Benz people").

The Search for Solutions

While the problems of nation building described here have to one degree or another afflicted all of the emerging states of Africa, each has sought to deal with the challenge in its own way, sometimes with strikingly different consequences. Some African countries have made dramatic improvements in the past two decades but others have encountered increasing difficulties. Despite all its shared problems, Africa today remains one of the most diverse regions of the globe, and generalizations are notoriously risky.

TANZANIA: AN AFRICAN ROUTE TO SOCIALISM Concern over the dangers of economic inequality inspired a number of African leaders to restrict foreign investment and nationalize the major industries and utilities while promoting democratic ideals and values. Julius Nyerere of Tanzania was the most consistent, promoting the ideals of socialism and self-reliance through his Arusha (uh-ROO-shuh) Declaration of 1967, which set forth the principles for building a socialist society in Africa. Nyerere did not seek to establish a Leninist-style dictatorship of the proletariat in Tanzania but neither was he a proponent of a multiparty democracy, which in his view would be divisive under the conditions prevailing in Africa:

> Where there is one party—provided it is identified with the nation as a whole—the foundations of democracy can be firmer, and the people can have more opportunity to exercise a real choice, than when you have two or more parties.

To import the Western parliamentary system into Africa, he argued, could lead to violence because the opposition parties would be viewed as traitors by the majority of the population.[3]

Taking advantage of his powerful political influence, Nyerere placed limits on income and established village collectives to avoid the corrosive effects of economic inequality and government corruption. Sympathetic foreign countries provided considerable economic aid to assist the experiment, and many observers noted that levels of corruption, political instability, and ethnic strife were lower in Tanzania than in many other African countries. Nyerere's vision was not shared by all of his compatriots, however. Political elements on the island of Zanzibar, citing the stagnation brought by two decades of socialism, agitated for autonomy or even total separation from the mainland. Tanzania also has poor soil, inadequate rainfall, and limited resources, all of which have contributed to its slow growth and continuing rural and urban poverty.

In 1985, Nyerere voluntarily retired from the presidency. In his farewell speech, he confessed that he had failed to achieve many of his ambitious goals to create a socialist society in Africa. In particular, he admitted that his plan to collectivize the traditional private farm (*shamba*) had run into strong resistance from conservative peasants. "You can socialize what is not traditional," he remarked. "The *shamba* can't be socialized." But Nyerere insisted that many of his policies had succeeded in improving social and economic conditions, and he argued that the only real solution was to consolidate the multitude of small countries in the region into a larger East African Federation. Today, a quarter of a century later, Nyerere's party, the Party of the Revolution, continues to rule the country. The current president, Jakaya Kikwete (jah-KAH-yah kee-KWEH-tee) (b. 1950), was reelected in 2010 by a comfortable margin, although there were charges of electoral fraud.

KENYA: THE PERILS OF CAPITALISM The countries that opted for capitalism faced their own dilemmas. Neighboring Kenya, blessed with better soil in the highlands, a local tradition of aggressive commerce, and a residue of European settlers, welcomed foreign investment and profit incentives. The results have been mixed. Kenya has a strong current of indigenous African capitalism and a substantial middle class, mostly based in the capital, Nairobi (ny-ROH-bee). But landlessness, unemployment, and income inequities are high, even by African standards (almost one-fifth of the country's 41 million

Building His Dream House. In Africa, the houses of rural people are often constructed with a wood frame, known as wattle, daubed with mud, and then covered with a thatched roof. Such houses are inexpensive to build and remain cool in the hot tropical climate. In this Kenyan village not far from the Indian Ocean, a young man is applying mud to the wall of his future home. Houses are built in a similar fashion throughout the continent, as well as in much of southern Asia.

© William J. Duiker

Meeting the Challenges of Independence

POLITICS & GOVERNMENT

TOM MBOYA (uhm-BOY-yuh) (1930–1969) was an inspiring political figure in Kenya during the era of early independence. As minister of labor during the transition to statehood, he urged his fellow Kenyans to believe in the prospect of independence, while calming the anxieties of European residents by assuring them that their lives and property would not be threatened or confiscated. This selection is from a speech he delivered in July 1962, in which he recognized the challenges of independence while expressing confidence that the experiment would inevitably succeed. In 1969, Mboya was assassinated by a political opponent.

Tom Mboya, "Kenya as a Nation," July 23, 1962

It is suggested by some people that there is no such thing as a Kenya nation. All kinds of arguments and recriminations are thrown up to try to prove that any nationalist ambitions for Kenya must encounter more difficulties than could ever be overcome. Noisy minorities in all walks of life, both here and in their contact with overseas interests, keep plugging away at their "no confidence" theme. Some people say that Kenya is heading for economic disaster and political chaos and tribal war....

When I talk now about a "Kenya nation," I am not speaking as a political romantic, but as a realist. Any sincere politician or leader must have some vision in front of him. There must be something much more than notoriety to attract him toward unceasing work, the bitterness of struggle, the temptations, and the pressures. There must be a factor of dedication, an undeniable impulse to build and to serve. In this he must satisfy himself. There are very few other rewards.

It is not only the vision of the leaders that dictates our struggle. There are the deep-rooted aspirations of our people. These people may appear simple and uneducated; they may not be articulate, but they are human beings and not stones. They have an inborn pride and a genuine desire for self-improvement and self-fulfillment. These are facts which may have dodged many people in the past but with which we all must reckon in the future. To ignore this force would be to lead to frustrations and explosions—indeed we have already had such an experience in Kenya.

It is not, however, the fear of this force that should dictate our decisions. There is the positive side of this force, namely, its ability to face the challenge of nation building. We have to release this force of our people for new and constructive purposes. We have to harness the enthusiasm for self-improvement to form the spearhead in our efforts for nation-building.

True, we have tribal differences and sensitivities. So often people point at the Congo and warn that Kenya is doomed to become another Congo. I do not share this view. We have passed the stage when this could have happened. We have passed through more trials than most African countries, and I believe we have come to appreciate freedom to a point where we would be prepared to defend it with our lives. We do not intend to exchange British colonialism for either local dictatorship or Soviet and American colonialism.

Why is the author of this document confident that the people of Kenya can surmount the challenges of nationhood?

Source: From R. Collins, ed., *African History in Documents: East African History* (Princeton, 1997), pp. 166–170, from T. Mboya, *The Challenges of Nationhood: A Collection of Speeches and Writings* (London, 1970), pp. 41–47.

---

people are squatters, and unemployment is currently estimated at 40 percent). The rate of population growth—about 2.5 percent annually—is one of the higher rates in the world. Almost 80 percent of the population remains rural, and 50 percent of the people live below the poverty line. The result has been widespread unrest in a country formerly admired for its successful development.

Kenya's problems have been exacerbated by chronic disputes between disparate ethnic groups and simmering tensions between farmers and pastoralists, leading some to question whether the country is capable of achieving political stability (see the box "Meeting the Challenges of Independence" above). For many years, the country maintained a fragile stability under the dictatorial rule of President Daniel arap Moi (ah-RHAP moh-YEE) (b. 1924), one of the most authoritarian of African leaders. Plagued by charges of corruption, Moi finally agreed to retire in 2002 but under his successor, Mwai Kibaki (MWY kih-BAH-kee) (b. 1931), the twin

problems of political instability and widespread poverty continue to afflict the country. When presidential elections held in January 2008 led to a victory for Kibaki's party, opposition elements—angered by the government's perceived favoritism toward Kibaki's Kikuyu constituency—launched numerous protests, and violent riots occurred throughout the country. A fragile truce was eventually put in place but popular anger at current conditions smolders just beneath the surface. In March 2013, another disputed presidential election resulted in a victory for Uhuru Kenyatta (b. 1961), the son of the country's first president.

SOUTH AFRICA: AN END TO APARTHEID Perhaps Africa's greatest success story is in South Africa, where the white government, which long maintained a policy of racial segregation (apartheid) and restricted black sovereignty to a series of small "Bantustans" in relatively infertile areas of the country, finally accepted the inevitability of African involvement in the political process and the national economy. A key factor in the decision was growing international pressure in the form of a campaign to persuade foreign investors to withdraw funds from the country. In 1990, the government of President F. W. (Frederik Willem) de Klerk (b. 1936) released African National Congress leader Nelson Mandela (man-DELL-uh) (1918–2013) from prison, where he had been held since 1964. In 1993, the two leaders agreed to hold democratic national elections the following spring. In the meantime, ANC representatives agreed to take part in a transitional coalition government with de Klerk's National Party. Those elections resulted in a substantial majority for the ANC, and Mandela became president.

In May 1996, a new constitution was approved, calling for a multiracial state. The National Party immediately went into opposition, claiming that the new charter did not adequately provide for joint decision making by members of the coalition. But the new ANC-dominated government won broad support from many groups within the country, and in 1999, a major step toward political stability was taken when Nelson Mandela stepped down from the presidency and was replaced by his longtime disciple Thabo Mbeki (TAH-boh uhm-BAY-kee) (b. 1942). The new president faced a number of intimidating problems, including rising unemployment, widespread lawlessness, chronic corruption, and an ominous flight of capital and professional personnel from the country. Mbeki's conservative economic policies earned the support of some white voters and the country's new black elite but were criticized by labor unions, which contended that the benefits of the new black leadership were not seeping down to the poor. The government's promises to carry out an extensive land reform program—aimed at providing farmland to the nation's 40 million black farmers—were not fulfilled, leading some squatters to seize unused private lands near Johannesburg.

In 2008, Mbeki was forced out of office by disgruntled ANC party members. A year later, his onetime vice president and rival Jacob Zuma (ZOO-muh) (b. 1942) was elected president. Zuma's party was reelected six years later amid charges of widespread corruption. Although the country faces serious challenges, South Africa remains the wealthiest and most industrialized state in Africa and the best hope that a multiracial society can succeed on the continent. The country's black elite now number nearly one-quarter of its wealthiest households, compared with only 9 percent in 1991.

NIGERIA: A NATION DIVIDED If the situation in South Africa provides grounds for modest optimism, the situation in Nigeria provides reason for serious concern. Africa's largest country in terms of population and one of its wealthiest because of substantial oil reserves, Nigeria was for many years in the grip of military strongmen. During his rule, General Sani Abacha (SAH-nee ah-BAH-chuh) (1943–1998) ruthlessly suppressed all opposition and in late 1995 ordered the execution of author Ken Saro-Wiwa (SAH-roh-WEE-wah) (1941–1995) despite widespread protests from human rights groups abroad. Saro-Wiwa had criticized environmental damage caused by foreign oil interests in southern Nigeria but the regime's major concern was his support for separatist activities in the area that had launched the Biafran insurrection in the late 1960s. When Abacha died in 1998 under mysterious circumstances, national elections led to the creation of a civilian government under Olusegun Obasanjo (ohl-OO-seh-goon oh-buh-SAHN-joh) (b. 1937).

An End to Apartheid. In 1994, Nelson Mandela, the long-time head of the African National Congress (ANC), was elected president of the Republic of South Africa and the policy of apartheid officially came to an end. Shown here in an iconic photograph, Mandela stands between his predecessor F. W. de Klerk and his chief lieutenant and eventual successor as chief of state, Thabo Mbeki. The ANC remains in power today, twenty years later.

Alexander Joe/AFP/Getty Images

Civilian leadership has not been a panacea for Nigeria's problems, however. Although Obasanjo promised reforms to bring an end to the corruption and favoritism that had long plagued Nigerian politics, the results were disappointing (the state power company—known as NEPA—was so inefficient that Nigerians joked that the initials stood for "never expect power again"). In the teeming city of Lagos (at over 15 million people, it currently ranks sixth in the world in total population), less than 1 percent of households are connected to a sanitation system. When presidential elections held in 2007 led to the election of Umaru Yar'Adua (oo-MAHR-oo YAHR-ah-doo-uh) (b. 1951–2010), an obscure member of Obasanjo's ruling political party, opposition forces and neutral observers complained that the vote had been seriously flawed. After Yar'Adua died from an illness in 2010, he was succeeded by his vice president, Goodluck Jonathan (b. 1951).

One of the most critical problems facing the Nigerian government in recent years has its roots in religious disputes. Unified in 1914 into a single colony by the British for their own convenience, since its independence, Nigeria has been faced with the uneasy reality of a Muslim north and a Christian south. In early 2000, religious tensions between Christians and Muslims began to escalate when riots broke out in several northern cities as a result of the decision by Muslim provincial officials to apply *Shari'a* throughout their jurisdictions. The crisis temporarily abated as local officials managed to craft compromise policies that limit the application of some of the harsher aspects of Muslim law but the dispute continues to threaten the fragile unity of Africa's most populous country. The election of Goodluck Jonathan, a Christian, in 2011 led to new protests among Muslims in the northern part of the country. Churches and mosques have been burned and massacres have taken place on both sides of the religious divide. The unrest has been fueled in part by the terrorist activities of Boko Haram (BOH-ko har-AHM), an al-Qaeda affiliate active in the region. Efforts by the government to quell the uprising have been hindered by reports of widespread brutality committed by Nigerian military units on the civilian population.

TENSIONS IN THE DESERT The religious tensions that erupted in Nigeria are mirrored by similar conditions in nearby states on the southern border of the Sahara, which for centuries has marked the approximate dividing line between Muslim and non-Muslim communities in the hump of West Africa. Pressure to apply *Shari'a* has recently spread to Mali, where a radical Islamic group seized power in the northern part of the country, applying strict punishments on local residents for alleged infractions against *Shari'a* law in the historic city of Timbuktu (see the opening vignette at the beginning of this chapter). French military units were dispatched to the region in early 2013 and drove the rebels out of the major population centers but the threat of Islamic radicalism has not subsided (see the Comparative Essay "Religion and Society" on p. 870).

A similar rift between farmers and herders has been at the root of the lengthy civil war that has been raging in Sudan. Conflict between Muslim pastoralists—supported by the central government in Khartoum—and predominantly Christian black farmers in the southern part of the country was finally brought to an end in 2004, and the government agreed to permit a plebiscite in the south under the sponsorship of the United Nations to determine whether the local population there wished to secede from the country. In elections held in early 2011, voters overwhelmingly supported independence as the new nation of the Republic of South Sudan but tribal disputes and tensions along the common border have led to chronic unrest in the new country.

The dispute between Muslims and Christians throughout the southern Sahara is a contemporary variant of the traditional tensions that have existed between farmers and pastoralists throughout recorded history. Muslim cattle herders, migrating southward to escape the increasing desiccation of the grasslands south of the Sahara, compete for precious land with primarily Christian farmers. As a result of the religious revival now under way throughout the continent, the confrontation often leads to outbreaks of violence with strong religious and ethnic overtones.

CENTRAL AFRICA: CAULDRON OF CONFLICT The most tragic situation took place in the Central African states of Rwanda and Burundi, where a chronic conflict between the minority Tutsis and the Hutu majority has led to a bitter civil war, with thousands of refugees fleeing to the neighboring Congo. The predominantly pastoral Tutsis, supported by the colonial Belgian government, had long dominated the sedentary Hutu population. The Hutus' attempt to bring an end to Tutsi domination initiated the most recent conflicts, which have been marked by massacres on both sides. In the meantime, the presence of large numbers of foreign troops and refugees intensified centrifugal forces inside neighboring Zaire, where General Mobutu Sese Seko had long ruled with an iron hand. In 1997, military forces led by Mobutu's longtime opponent Laurent-Désiré Kabila (loh-RAHN-DAY-zee-ray kah-BEE-luh) (1939–2001) managed to topple the general's corrupt government. Once in power, Kabila renamed the country the Democratic Republic of the Congo

CHRONOLOGY	Modern Africa	
Ghana gains independence from Great Britain	1957
Algeria gains independence from France	1962
Formation of the Organization of African Unity	1963
Biafra revolt in Nigeria	1966–1970
Arusha Declaration in Tanzania	1967
Nelson Mandela elected president of South Africa	1994
Genocide in Central Africa	1996–2000
Olusegun Obasanjo elected president of Nigeria	1999
Creation of the African Union	2001
Civil war breaks out in Darfur province in Sudan	2004
Ethnic riots in Kenya	2008
Jacob Zuma becomes president of South Africa	2009
Independence for the Republic of South Sudan	2011

Religion and Society

RELIGION & PHILOSOPHY

The nineteenth and twentieth centuries witnessed a steady trend toward the secularization of society as people increasingly turned from religion to science for explanations of natural phenomena and for answers to the challenges of everyday life.

In recent years, however, the trend has reversed as religious faith in all its guises appears to be reviving in much of the world. Although the percentage of people attending religious services on a regular basis or professing firm religious convictions has been dropping steadily in many countries, the intensity of religious belief appears to be growing among the faithful. This phenomenon has been widely publicized in the United States, where the evangelical movement has become a significant force in politics and an influential factor in defining many social issues. But it has also occurred in Latin America, where a drop in membership in the Roman Catholic Church has been offset by significant increases in the popularity of evangelical Protestant sects. In the Muslim world, the influence of traditional Islam has been steadily on the rise, not only in the Middle East but also in non-Arab countries such as Malaysia and Indonesia (see Chapter 30). In Africa, as we observe in this chapter, the appeal of both Christianity and Islam appears to be on the rise. Even in Russia and China, where half a century of communist government sought to eradicate religion as the "opiate of the people," the popularity of religion is growing.

One major reason for the increasing popularity of religion in contemporary life is the desire to counter the widespread sense of malaise brought on by the absence of any sense of meaning and purpose in life—a purpose that religious faith provides. For many evangelical Christians in the United States, for example, the adoption of a Christian lifestyle is seen as a necessary prerequisite for resolving problems of crime, drugs, and social alienation. It is likely that a similar phenomenon is present with other religions and in other parts of the world. Religious faith also provides a sense of community at a time when village and family ties are declining in many countries.

Buddhist monks worship at a temple on the island of Taiwan.

Historical evidence suggests, however, that although religious fervor may enhance the sense of community and commitment among believers, it can have a highly divisive impact on society as a whole, as the examples of Northern Ireland, Yugoslavia, Africa, and the Middle East vividly attest. Even if less dramatically, as in the United States and Latin America, religion divides as well as unites, and it will be a continuing task for religious leaders of all faiths to promote tolerance for peoples of other persuasions.

Another challenge for contemporary religion is to find ways to coexist with expanding scientific knowledge. Influential figures in the evangelical movement in the United States, for example, not only support a conservative social agenda but are also suspicious of the role of technology and science in the contemporary world. Similar views are often expressed by significant factions in other world religions. Although fear of the impact of science on contemporary life is widespread, efforts to turn the clock back to a mythical golden age are not likely to succeed in the face of powerful forces for change set in motion by advances in scientific knowledge.

 What are some of the reasons for the growing intensity of religious faith in many parts of the world today?

and promised a return to democratic practices. The new government systematically suppressed political dissent, however, and in January 2001, Kabila was assassinated. He was succeeded by his son Joseph Kabila (b. 1971). Peace talks to end the conflict began that fall but the fighting has continued, leading to horrific casualties among the civilian population, and the country is now afflicted with chronic civil conflict.

Africa: A Continent in Flux

The brief survey of events in some of the more important African countries provided here illustrates the enormous difficulty that historians of Africa face in drawing any general conclusions about the pace and scope of change that has taken place in the continent in recent decades. Progress in some areas has been countered by growing problems elsewhere, and signs of hope in one region contrast with feelings of despair in another.

The shifting fortunes experienced throughout the continent are most prominently illustrated in the political arena. Over the past two decades, the collapse of one-party regimes has led to the emergence of fragile democracies in several countries. In other instances, however, democratic governments were replaced by authoritarian leaders or erupted in civil war. One prominent example of the latter is the Ivory Coast, long considered one of West Africa's most stable and prosperous countries. After the death of President Félix Houphouet-Boigny (fay-LEEKS oo-FWAY-bwah-NYEE) in 1993, long-simmering resentment between Christians in the south and newly arrived Muslim immigrants in the north erupted into open conflict. National elections held in 2010 led to sporadic violence and a standoff between opposition forces and the sitting president, who was forced to resign the following year. Somalia, once a pawn of great power rivalries, has been racked by tribal disputes and Islamic radicalism. By contrast, in Liberia, a bitter civil war recently gave way to the emergence of a stable democratic government under Ellen Johnson-Sirleaf (b. 1938), one of the continent's first female presidents.

The economic picture in Africa has also been mixed. It is clear that African societies have not yet managed to surmount the challenges they have faced since independence. Most African states are still poor and their populations illiterate. Moreover, African concerns continue to carry little weight in the international community. A recent agreement by the World Trade Organization (WTO) on the need to reduce agricultural subsidies in the advanced nations has been widely ignored. In 2000, the General Assembly of the United Nations passed the Millennium Declaration, which called for a dramatic reduction in the incidence of poverty, hunger, and illiteracy worldwide by the year 2015. So far, however, efforts to realize these ambitious goals have been limited. At a conference on the subject in September 2005, the participants squabbled over how to fund the effort. Some delegations, including that of the United States, argued that external assistance cannot succeed unless the nations of Africa adopt measures to bring about good government and sound economic policies.

Despite the African continent's chronic economic problems, however, there are signs of hope. The overall rate of economic growth for the region as a whole is twice what it was during the 1980s and 1990s (see the Comparative Illustration "New Housing for the Poor" on p. 872). African countries were also less affected by the recent economic downturn than was much of the rest of the world. Although poverty, AIDs, and a lack of education and infrastructure are still major impediments in much of the region, rising commodity prices—most notably, an increase in oil revenues—are enabling many countries to make additional investments and reduce their national debt. One promising sign is that the African people as a whole are not about to despair. In a recent survey of public opinion throughout the continent, the majority of respondents were optimistic about the future and confident that they would be economically better off in five years.

Certainly, part of the solution to the continent's multiple problems must come from within. Although there are gratifying signs of progress toward political stability in some countries, others are still governed by brutal dictatorships or racked by civil strife. Corruption and political inexperience are serious problems as well. But many of Africa's difficulties are a consequence of interference by foreign governments and international corporations. Efforts by Western governments to protect their local farmers by providing subsidies or levying high tariffs have hurt African growers in countries where agricultural products are a major export crop. In recent years, the government of China has sponsored a number of projects in Africa. While many Africans are grateful for the infusion of investment funds in badly needed public services, some express concern that Chinese officials, like those representing other foreign corporations, often interfere in local politics and impede the normal political process, often to the detriment of local populations. Africans will need help in putting their house in order, but must take care to guarantee that the interests of their own people be protected.

THE AFRICAN UNION: A GLIMMER OF HOPE A significant part of the problem is that Africans must find better ways to cooperate with one another and to protect and promote their own interests. A first step in that direction was taken in 1991, when the OAU agreed to establish the African Economic Community (AEC). In 2001, the OAU was replaced by the **African Union**, which is intended to provide greater political and economic integration throughout the continent on the pattern of the European Union (see Chapter 28). The new organization has already sought to mediate several of the conflicts in the region.

As Africa evolves, it is useful to remember that economic and political change is often an agonizingly slow and painful process. Introduced to industrialization and concepts of Western democracy only a century ago, African societies are still groping for ways to graft Western political institutions and economic practices onto a structure still significantly influenced by traditional values and attitudes.

© William J. Duiker

© William J. Duiker

COMPARATIVE ILLUSTRATION

FAMILY & SOCIETY

New Housing for the Poor. Under apartheid, much of the black population in South Africa was confined to so-called townships, squalid slums located along the fringes of the country's major cities. The top photo shows a crowded township on the edge of Cape Town, one of the most modern cities on the continent of Africa. Today, the government is actively building new communities that provide better housing, running water, and electricity for their residents. The photo on the bottom shows a new township rising on the outskirts of the city of New London. The township has many modern facilities and even a new shopping mall with consumer goods for local residents.

 Why do you think the segregated housing facilities known as "townships" developed in the first place in South Africa? For whom were they designed?

Continuity and Change in Modern African Societies

 FOCUS QUESTIONS: How did the rise of independent states affect the lives and the role of women in African societies? How does that role compare with the role played by women in other parts of the contemporary world?

In general, the impact of the West has been greater on urban and educated Africans and more limited on their rural and illiterate compatriots. One reason is that the colonial presence was first and most firmly established in the cities. Many cities, including Dakar, Lagos, Johannesburg, Cape Town, Brazzaville, and Nairobi, are direct products of the colonial experience. Most large African cities today look like their counterparts elsewhere in the world. They have high-rise buildings, blocks of residential apartments, wide boulevards, neon lights, movie theaters, and traffic jams. Surrounding the affluent commercial sectors, however, are miles and miles of squalid tenement buildings, ramshackle roadside shops, and muddy alleyways. Beyond the city boundaries lie the countless villages, where the vast majority of the population still lives today.

Education

The educational system has been the primary means of introducing Western values and culture. In the precolonial era, formal schools did not really exist in Africa except for parochial schools in Christian Ethiopia and academies to train young males in Islamic doctrine and law in Muslim societies in North and West Africa. For the average African, education took place at the home or in the village courtyard and stressed socialization and vocational training. Traditional education in Africa was not necessarily inferior to that in Europe. Social values and customs were transmitted to the young by storytellers, often village elders, who could gain considerable prestige through their performance.

Europeans introduced modern Western education into Africa in the nineteenth century. At first, the schools concentrated on vocational training, with some instruction in European languages and Western civilization. Eventually, pressure from Africans led to the introduction of professional training, and the first institutes of higher learning were established in the early twentieth century.

With independence, African countries established their own state-run schools. The emphasis was on the primary level but high schools and universities were established in major cities. The basic objectives have been to introduce vocational training and improve literacy rates. Unfortunately, both funding and trained teachers are scarce in most countries, and few rural areas have schools. As a result, illiteracy remains high, estimated at about 70 percent of the population across the continent. There has been a perceptible shift toward education in the vernacular languages. In West Africa, only about one in four adults is conversant in a Western language.

Urban and Rural Life

The cities are where the African elites live and work. Affluent Africans, like their contemporaries in other developing countries, have been strongly attracted to the glittering material aspects of Western culture. They live in Western-style homes or apartments and eat Western foods stored in Western refrigerators, and those who can afford it drive Western cars. It has been said, not wholly in praise, that there are more Mercedes-Benz automobiles in Nigeria than in Germany, where they are manufactured.

Outside the major cities, where about three-quarters of the continent's inhabitants live, Western influence has had less impact. Millions of people throughout Africa (as in Asia) live

much as their ancestors did, in thatch huts without modern plumbing and electricity: they farm or hunt by traditional methods, practice time-honored family rituals, and believe in the traditional deities. Even here, however, change is taking place. Slavery has been eliminated, for the most part, although there have been persistent reports of raids by slave traders on defenseless villages in the southern Sudan. Economic need, though, has brought about massive migrations as some leave to work on plantations, others move to the cities, and still others flee abroad or to refugee camps to escape starvation. Migration itself is a wrenching experience, disrupting familiar family and village ties and enforcing new social relationships.

Nowhere, in fact, is the dichotomy between old and new, local and foreign, rural and urban as clear and painful as in Africa. Urban dwellers regard the village as the repository of all that is backward in the African past, while rural peoples view the growing urban areas as a source of corruption, prostitution, hedonism, and the destruction of communal customs and values. The tension between traditional ways and Western culture is particularly strong among African intellectuals, many of whom are torn between their admiration for things Western and their desire to retain an African identity.

African Women

As noted in Chapter 21, one of the consequences of colonialism in Africa was a change in the relationship between men and women. Some of these changes could be described as beneficial but others were not. Women were often introduced to Western education and given legal rights denied to them in the precolonial era. But they also became a labor source and were sometimes recruited or compelled to work on construction projects.

Independence also had a significant impact on gender roles in African society. Almost without exception, the new governments established the principle of sexual equality and permitted women to vote and run for political office. Yet as elsewhere, women continue to operate at a disability in a

Education: Preparing for the Future of Africa. Educating the young is one of the most crucial problems for many African societies today. Few governments are able to allocate the funds necessary to meet the challenge, so religious organizations—usually Muslim or Christian—often take up the slack. But much more needs to be done. Shown here, a class of students at a high school in Kenya is on a field trip to Malindi to visit a monument commemorating the departure point for the Portuguese adventurer Vasco da Gama. It was from this coastal city that da Gama's tiny fleet of three ships departed on its historic voyage across the Indian Ocean in 1498.

world dominated by males. Politics remains a male preserve, and although a few professions, such as teaching, child care, and clerical work, are dominated by women, most African women are employed in menial positions such as agricultural labor, factory work, and retail trade or as domestics. Education is open to all at the elementary level but women comprise less than 20 percent of students at the upper levels in most African societies today.

URBAN WOMEN Not surprisingly, women have made the greatest strides in the cities. Most urban women, like men, now marry on the basis of personal choice, although a significant minority are still willing to accept their parents' choice. After marriage, African women appear to occupy a more equal position than their counterparts in most Asian countries. Each marriage partner tends to maintain a separate income, and women often have the right to possess property separate from their husbands. Though many wives still defer to their husbands in the traditional manner, others are like the woman in Abioseh Nicol's story "A Truly Married Woman," who, after years of living as a common-law wife with her husband, is finally able to provide the price and finalize the marriage. After the wedding, she declares, "For twelve years I have got up every morning at five to make tea for you and breakfast. Now I am a truly married woman, [and] you must treat me with a little more respect. You are now my husband and not a lover. Get up and make yourself a cup of tea."[4]

In the cities, a feminist movement is growing but it is firmly based on conditions in the local environment. Many African women writers, for example, opt for a brand of African feminism much like that of Ama Ata Aidoo (AH-mah AH-tah ah-EE-doo) (b. 1942), a Ghanaian novelist, whose ultimate objective is to free African society as a whole, not just its female inhabitants. After receiving her education at a girls' school in the preindependence Gold Coast and attending Stanford University in the United States, she embarked on a writing career. Every African woman and every man, she insists, "should be a feminist, especially if they believe that Africans should take charge of our land, its wealth, our lives, and the burden of our development. Because it is not possible to advocate independence for our continent without also believing that African women must have the best that the environment can offer."[5]

WOMEN IN RURAL AREAS Feminism has had less impact on women in rural areas, where traditional attitudes continue to exert a strong influence. In some societies, female genital mutilation, the traditional rite of passage for a young girl's transit to womanhood, is still widely practiced. Polygamy is also not uncommon, and arranged marriages are still the rule rather than the exception. In some Muslim societies, efforts to apply *Shari'a* law have led to greater restrictions on the freedom of women. In northern Nigeria, a woman was recently sentenced to death for committing adultery. The sentence was later reversed on appeal.

The dichotomy between rural and urban values can lead to acute tensions. Many African villagers regard the cities as the fount of evil, decadence, and corruption. Women in particular have suffered from the tension between the pull of the city and the village. As men are drawn to the cities in search

Salt of the Earth. During the precolonial era, many West African societies were forced to import salt from Mediterranean countries in exchange for tropical products and gold. Today, the people of Senegal satisfy their domestic needs by mining salt deposits contained in lakes like this one in the interior of the country. These lakes are the remnants of vast seas that covered the region of the Sahara in prehistoric times. Note that women are doing much of the heavy labor while men occupy the managerial positions.

of employment and excitement, their wives and girlfriends are left behind, both literally and figuratively, in the village. Fortunately, there are some signs of change. In 2006, Ellen Johnson-Sirleaf was elected president of Liberia—the first woman to be elected chief executive of a country on the African continent.

African Culture

Inevitably, the tension between traditional and modern, local and foreign, and individual and communal that has permeated contemporary African society has spilled over into culture. In general, in the visual arts and music, utility and ritual have given way to pleasure and decoration. In the process, Africans have been affected to a certain extent by foreign influences but have retained their distinctive characteristics. Wood carving, metalwork, painting, and sculpture, for example, have preserved their traditional forms but are now increasingly adapted to serve the tourist industry and the export market.

LITERATURE No area of African culture has been so strongly affected by political and social events as literature. Except for Muslim areas in North and East Africa, precolonial Africans did not have a written literature, although their tradition of oral storytelling served as a rich repository of history, custom, and folk culture. The first written literature in the vernacular or in European languages emerged during the nineteenth century in the form of novels, poetry, and drama.

Angry at the negative portrayal of Africa in Western literature (see Opposing Viewpoints "Africa: Dark Continent or Radiant Land?" on p. 876), African authors initially wrote primarily for a European audience as a means of establishing black dignity and purpose. In response to condescending Western attitudes about African history, many glorified the emotional and communal aspects of the traditional African experience. The Nigerian Chinua Achebe (CHIN-wah ah-CHAY-bay) (1930–2013) is considered the first major African novelist to write in the English language. In his writings, he attempted to interpret African history from an African perspective and to forge a new sense of African identity. In his trailblazing novel *Things Fall Apart* (1958), he recounted the story of a Nigerian who refused to submit to the new British order and eventually committed suicide. Criticizing his contemporaries who accepted foreign rule, the protagonist lamented that the white man "has put a knife on the things that held us together and we have fallen apart."

In recent decades, the African novel has taken a dramatic turn, shifting its focus from the brutality of the foreign oppressor to the shortcomings of the new African leaders. Having gained independence, African politicians are portrayed as mimicking and even outdoing the injustices committed by their colonial predecessors. A prominent example of this genre is the work of the Kenyan Ngugi Wa Thiong'o (GOO-gee wah tee-AHNG-goh) (b. 1938). His first novel, *A Grain of Wheat*, takes place on the eve of independence. Although it mocks local British society for its racism, snobbishness, and superficiality, its chief interest lies in its unsentimental and even unflattering portrayal of ordinary Kenyans in their daily struggle for survival.

Like most of his predecessors, Ngugi initially wrote in English but he eventually decided to write in his native Kikuyu as a means of broadening his readership. For that reason, perhaps, in the late 1970s, he was placed under house arrest for writing subversive literature. There, he secretly wrote *Devil on the Cross*, which urged his compatriots to overthrow the ruling government. Published in 1980, the book sold widely and was eventually read aloud by storytellers throughout Kenyan society. Fearing an attempt on his life, Ngugi has since lived in exile.

Many of Ngugi's contemporaries have followed his lead and focused their frustration on the failure of the continent's new leadership to carry out the goals of independence. One of the most outstanding is the Nigerian Wole Soyinka (woh-LAY soh-YEENK-kuh) (b. 1934). His novel *The Interpreters* (1965) lambasted the corruption and hypocrisy of Nigerian politics. Succeeding novels and plays have continued that tradition, resulting in a Nobel Prize in Literature in 1986. In 1994, however, Soyinka barely managed to escape arrest, and he entered a self-imposed exile abroad until the Abacha regime in Nigeria came to an end. In a protest against the brutality of the regime, he published from exile a harsh exposé of the crisis. His book, *The Open Sore of a Continent*, placed the primary responsibility for failure not on Nigeria's long list of dictators but on the very concept of the modern nation-state, which was introduced to Africa arbitrarily by Europeans. A nation, he contends, can only emerge spontaneously from below, as the expression of the moral and political will of the local inhabitants; it cannot be imposed artificially from above.

A number of Africa's most prominent writers today are women. Traditionally, African women were valued for their talents as storytellers but writing was strongly discouraged by both traditional and colonial authorities on the grounds that women should occupy themselves with their domestic obligations. In recent years, however, a number of women have emerged as prominent writers of African fiction. Two examples are Buchi Emecheta (BOO-chee ay-muh-CHAY-tuh) (b. 1940) of Nigeria and Ama Ata Aidoo of Ghana. Beginning with *Second Class Citizen* (1975), which chronicled the breakdown of her own marriage, Emecheta has published numerous works exploring the role of women in contemporary African society and decrying the practice of polygamy. Ata Aidoo has focused on the identity of today's African women and the changing relations between men and women in society. In her novel *Changes: A Love Story* (1991), she chronicles the lives of three women, none presented as a victim but all caught up in the struggle for survival and happiness. Of late, two young authors have garnered great acclaim for their novels about Nigeria's political and social upheavals—Chimamanda Ngozi Adichie (chim-muh-MAHN-duh en-GOH-zee ah-DEECH-ee) (b. 1977) in *Half a Yellow Sun* (2006) and Sefi Atta (b. 1964) in *Everything Good Will Come* (2005).

MUSIC Contemporary African music also reflects a hybridization or fusion with Western culture. Having traveled to

Africa: Dark Continent or Radiant Land?

INTERACTION & EXCHANGE

COLONIALISM CAMOUFLAGED ITS ECONOMIC OBJECTIVES under the cloak of a "civilizing mission," which in Africa was aimed at illuminating the so-called Dark Continent with Europe's brilliant civilization. In 1899, the Polish-born English author Joseph Conrad (1857–1924) fictionalized his harrowing journey up the Congo River in the novella *Heart of Darkness*. Conrad's protagonist, Marlow, travels upriver to locate a Belgian trader who has mysteriously disappeared. The novella describes Marlow's gradual recognition of the egregious excesses of colonial rule, as well as his realization that such evil lurks in everyone's heart. The story concludes with a cry: "The horror! The horror!" Voicing views that expressed his Victorian perspective, Conrad described an Africa that was incomprehensible, sensual, and primitive.

Over the years, Conrad's work has provoked much debate. Author Chinua Achebe, for one, lambasted *Heart of Darkness* as a racial diatribe. Since independence, many African writers have been prompted to counter Conrad's portrayal by reaffirming the dignity and purpose of the African people. One of the first to do so was the Guinean author Camara Laye (1928–1980), who in 1954 composed a brilliant novel, *The Radiance of the King*, which can be viewed as the mirror image of Conrad's *Heart of Darkness*. In Laye's work, Clarence, another European protagonist, undertakes a journey into the impenetrable heart of Africa. This time, however, he is enlightened by the process, obtaining self-knowledge and ultimately salvation.

Joseph Conrad, *Heart of Darkness*

We penetrated deeper and deeper into the heart of darkness. It was very quiet there. At night sometimes the roll of drums behind the curtain of trees would run up the river and remain sustained faintly, as if hovering in the air high over our heads, till the first break of day. Whether it meant war, peace, or prayer we could not tell.... But suddenly, as we struggled round a bend, there would be a glimpse of rush walls, of peaked grass-roofs, a burst of yells, a whirl of black limbs, a mass of hands clapping, of feet stamping, of bodies swaying, of eyes rolling, under the droop of heavy and motionless foliage. The steamer toiled along slowly on the edge of a black and incomprehensible frenzy. The prehistoric man was cursing us, praying to us, welcoming us—who could tell? We were cut off from the comprehension of our surroundings; we glided past like phantoms, wondering and secretly appalled, as sane men would be before an enthusiastic outbreak in a madhouse.

Camara Laye, *The Radiance of the King*

At that very moment the king turned his head, turned it imperceptibly, and his glance fell upon Clarence....

"Yes, no one is as base as I, as naked as I," he thought. "And you, lord, you are willing to rest your eyes upon me!" Or was it because of his very nakedness? ... "Because of your very nakedness!" the look seemed to say. "That terrifying void that is within you and which opens to receive me; your hunger which calls to my hunger; your very baseness which did not exist until I gave it leave; and the great shame you feel...."

When he had come before the king, when he stood in the great radiance of the king, still ravaged by the tongue of fire, but alive still, and living only through the touch of that fire, Clarence fell upon his knees, for it seemed to him that he was finally at the end of his seeking, and at the end of all seekings.

Compare the depiction of the continent of Africa in these two passages. Is Laye making a response to Conrad? If so, what is it?

Sources: From *Heart of Darkness* by Joseph Conrad. Penguin Books, 1991. From *The Radiance of the King* by Camara Laye, translated from the French by James Kirkup. New York: Vintage, 1989.

the Americas via the slave trade centuries earlier, African drum beats evolved into North American jazz and Latin American dance rhythms, only to return to reenergize African music. In fact, today music is one of Africans' most effective weapons for social and political protest. Easily accessible to all, African music, whether Afro-beat in Nigeria, *rai* in Algeria, or *reggae* in Benin, represents "the weapon of the future," contemporary musicians say; "it helped free Nelson Mandela" and "will put Africa back on the map." Censored by all the African dictatorial regimes, these courageous musicians persist in their struggle against corruption, what one singer calls the second slavery, "the cancer that is eating away at the system." Their voices echo the chorus "Together we can build a nation / Because Africa has brains, youth, knowledge."[6]

What Is the Future of Africa?

Nowhere in the developing world is the dilemma of continuity and change more agonizing than in Africa. Mesmerized by the spectacle of Western affluence yet repulsed by the bloody trail from slavery to World War II and the atomic bombs over Hiroshima and Nagasaki, African intellectuals have been torn between the dual images of Western materialism and African uniqueness. For the average African, of course, such intellectual dilemmas pale before the daily challenge of survival. But the fundamental gap between traditional and modern is perhaps wider in Africa than anywhere else in the world and may well be harder to bridge.

What is the future of Africa? It seems almost foolhardy to seek an answer to such a question, given the degree of ethnic, linguistic, and cultural diversity that exists throughout the vast continent. Not surprisingly, visions of the future are equally diverse. Some Africans still yearn for the dreams embodied in the program of the OAU. Novelist Ngugi Wa Thiong'o calls for "an internationalization of all the democratic and social struggles for human equality, justice, peace, and progress."[7]

Others have discarded the democratic ideal and turned their attention to systems based on the subordination of the individual to the community as the guiding principle of national development. The growing divide between Muslim and non-Muslim states, a product partly of trends taking place elsewhere in the world, adds an additional element of complexity. Like all peoples, Africans must ultimately find their own solutions within the context of their own traditions, not by seeking to imitate the example of others.

Crescent of Conflict

 FOCUS QUESTION: What problems have the nations of the Middle East faced since the end of World War II, and to what degree have they managed to resolve them?

"We Muslims are of one family even though we live under different governments and in various regions."[8] So said Ayatollah Ruholla Khomeini (ah-yah-TUL-uh roo-HUL-uh khoh-MAY-nee), the Islamic religious figure and leader of the 1979 revolution that overthrew the shah in Iran. The ayatollah's remark was dismissed by some as just a pious wish by a religious mystic. In fact, however, it illustrates one crucial aspect of the political dynamics of the region.

If the concept of cultural uniqueness was occasionally presented as a potential alternative to the system of nation-states in Africa, a similar role has been played in the Middle East by the religion of Islam. In both regions, a yearning for a sense of community beyond national borders tugs at the emotions and intellect of their inhabitants and counteracts the dynamic pull of nationalism that has led to political turmoil and conflict in much of the rest of the world.

A dramatic example of the powerful force of pan-Islamic sentiment took place on September 11, 2001, when Muslim terrorists hijacked four U.S. airliners and turned them into missiles aimed at the center of world capitalism (see Chapter 28). Although the organizers of the attack—known as al-Qaeda—were located in Afghanistan, the terrorists themselves came from other Muslim states, primarily Saudi Arabia. In the months that followed, support for al-Qaeda and its elusive leader, Osama bin Laden (1957–2011), intensified throughout the Muslim world. To many observers, it was clear that bin Laden and his cohorts had tapped into a wellspring of hostility and resentment directed at the Western world.

What were the sources of Muslim anger? In a speech released on videotape shortly after the attack, bin Laden declared that the attacks were a response to the "humiliation and disgrace" inflicted on the Islamic world for more than eighty years, a period dating back to the end of World War I (see the box "I Accuse!" on p. 878). For the Middle East, the period between the two world wars was an era of transition. With the fall of the Ottoman and Persian Empires, new modernizing regimes emerged in Turkey and Iran, and a more traditionalist but fiercely independent government was established in Saudi Arabia. Elsewhere, European influence continued to be strong; the British and French had mandates in Syria, Lebanon, Jordan, and Palestine, and British influence persisted in Iraq, in southern Arabia, and throughout the Nile Valley. **Pan-Arabism**—the concept of the unity of all Arab peoples—was on the rise but it lacked focus and coherence.

During World War II, the Middle East became the cockpit of European rivalries, as it had been during World War I. The region was more significant to the warring powers than previously because of the growing importance of oil and the Suez Canal's position as a vital sea route. For a brief period, the German Afrika Korps threatened to seize Egypt and the Suez Canal but British troops defeated the German forces at El Alamein, west of Alexandria, in 1942. Thereafter, the entire region from the Mediterranean Sea eastward was under secure Allied occupation until the end of the war.

The Question of Palestine

The end of World War II led to the emergence of a number of independent states in the Middle East. Jordan, Lebanon, and Syria, all European mandates before the war, became independent. Egypt, Iran, and Iraq, though still under a degree of Western influence, became increasingly autonomous. Sympathy within the region for the idea of Arab unity led to the formation of the Arab League in 1945 but different points of view among its members prevented it from achieving anything of substance.

The one issue on which all Muslim states in the area could agree was the question of Palestine. As tensions between Jews and Arabs in that mandate intensified during the 1930s, the British attempted to limit Jewish immigration into the area and firmly rejected proposals for independence, despite the promise made in the 1917 Balfour Declaration (see Chapter 24).

After World War II ended, the situation drifted rapidly toward crisis, as thousands of Jewish refugees, many of them from displaced persons camps in Europe, sought to migrate to Palestine despite Arab complaints and British efforts to

I Accuse!

POLITICS & GOVERNMENT

IN 1998, OSAMA BIN LADEN was virtually unknown outside the Middle East. But this scion of a wealthy industrialist from Saudi Arabia was on a mission—to avenge the hostile acts perpetrated on his fellow Muslims by the United States and its allies. Having taken part in the successful guerrilla war against Soviet occupation troops in Afghanistan during the 1980s, Osama now turned his ire on the tyrannical regimes in the Middle East and their great protector, the United States. In the following excerpts from a 1998 interview, he defends the use of terror against those whom he deems enemies of Islam. Three years later, his followers launched the surprise attacks that led to more than three thousand deaths on September 11, 2001.

Interview with Osama bin Laden by His Followers (1998)

What is the meaning of your call for Muslims to take up arms against America in particular, and what is the message that you wish to send to the West in general?

The call to wage war against America was made because America has spearheaded the crusade against the Islamic nation, sending tens of thousands of its troops to the land of the two Holy Mosques [Saudi Arabia], over and above its meddling in its affairs and its politics and its support of the oppressive, corrupt, and tyrannical regime that is in control. These are the reasons behind the singling out of America as a target. And not exempt from responsibility are those Western regimes whose presence in the region offers support to the American troops there. We know at least one reason behind the symbolic participation of the Western forces and that is to support the Jewish and Zionist plans for expansion of what is called the Great Israel. Surely, their presence is not out of concern over their interests in the region…. Their presence has no meaning save one and that is to offer support to the Jews in Palestine who are in need of their Christian brothers to achieve full control over the Arab Peninsula which they intend to make an important part of the so called Greater Israel.

Many of the Arabic as well as the Western mass media accuse you of terrorism and of supporting terrorism. What do you have to say to that?

Every state and every civilization and culture has to resort to terrorism under certain circumstances for the purpose of abolishing tyranny and corruption. Every country in the world has its own security system and its own security forces, its own police, and its own army. They are all designed to terrorize whoever even contemplates an attack on that country or its citizens. The terrorism we practice is of the commendable kind for it is directed at the tyrants and the aggressors and the enemies of Allah, the tyrants, the traitors who commit acts of treason against their own countries and their own faith and their own prophet and their own nation. Terrorizing those and punishing them are necessary measures to straighten things and to make them right. Tyrants and oppressors who subject the Arab nation to aggression ought to be punished…. America heads the list of aggressors against Muslims. The recurrence of aggression against Muslims everywhere is proof enough. For over half a century, Muslims in Palestine have been slaughtered and assaulted and robbed of their honor and of their property. Their houses have been blasted, their crops destroyed. And the strange thing is that any act by them to avenge themselves or to lift the injustice befalling them causes great agitation in the United Nations, which hastens to call for an emergency meeting only to convict the victim and to censure the wronged and the tyrannized whose children have been killed and whose crops have been destroyed and whose farms have been pulverized….

In today's wars, there are no morals, and it is clear that mankind has descended to the lowest degrees of decadence and oppression. They rip us of our wealth and of our resources and of our oil. Our religion is under attack. They kill and murder our brothers. They compromise our honor and our dignity and if we dare to utter a single word of protest against the injustice, we are called terrorists. This is compounded injustice. And the United Nations insistence to convict the victims and support the aggressors constitutes a serious precedent that shows the extent of injustice that has been allowed to take root in this land.

 What reasons does Osama bin Laden present to justify the terrorist attacks carried out by his followers around the world? How would you respond to his charges?

Source: From Akram Khater, *Sources in the History of the Modern Middle East*, 2e. © 2011 Cengage Learning, pp. 294–295.

---

prevent their arrival (see the box "The Arab Case for Palestine" on p. 879), As violence between Muslims and Jews intensified in the fall of 1947, the issue was taken up in the United Nations General Assembly. After an intense debate, the assembly voted to approve the partition of Palestine into two separate states, one for the Jews and one for the Arabs. The city of Jerusalem was to be placed under international control.

A UN commission was established to iron out the details and determine the future boundaries.

During the next several months, growing hostility between Jewish and Arab forces—the latter increasingly supported by neighboring Muslim states—caused the British to announce that they would withdraw their own peacekeeping forces by May 15, 1948. Shortly after the stroke of midnight, as the British

The Arab Case for Palestine

POLITICS & GOVERNMENT

AS MORE AND MORE JEWS IMMIGRATED to Palestine after World War II, the world powers began to discuss how to handle the growing tensions in the area. In 1946, the Arab Office in Jerusalem issued a statement outlining its case against the Zionist proposal to transform Palestine into a Jewish state. The statement declared that any solution to the Palestinian problem "must recognize the right of the indigenous inhabitants of Palestine to continue in occupation of the country and to preserve its traditional character." Further, it stated, any representative government in Palestine "should be based upon the principle of absolute equality of all citizens irrespective of race and religion." The following selection is an excerpt from this document.

The Problem of Palestine

1. The whole Arab People is unalterably opposed to the attempt to impose Jewish immigration and settlement upon it, and ultimately to establish a Jewish State in Palestine. Its opposition is based primarily upon right. The Arabs of Palestine are descendants of the indigenous inhabitants of the country, who have been in occupation of it since the beginning of history; they cannot agree that it is right to subject an indigenous population against its will to alien immigrants, whose claim is based upon a historical connection which ceased effectively many centuries ago. Moreover they form the majority of the population; as such they cannot submit to a policy of immigration which if pursued for long will turn them from a majority into a minority in an alien state; and

they claim the democratic right of a majority to make its own decisions in matters of urgent national concern....

2. In addition to the question of right, the Arabs oppose the claims of political Zionism because of the effects which Zionist settlement has already had upon their situation and is likely to have to an even greater extent in the future. Negatively, it has diverted the whole course of their national development. Geographically Palestine is part of Syria; its indigenous inhabitants belong to the Syrian branch of the Arab family of nations; all their culture and tradition link them to the other Arab peoples; and until 1917 Palestine formed part of the Ottoman Empire which included also several of the other Arab countries. The presence and claims of the Zionists, and the support given them by certain Western Powers have resulted in Palestine being cut off from the other Arab countries and subjected to a regime, administrative, legal, fiscal, and educational, different from that of the sister-countries. Quite apart from the inconvenience to individuals and the dislocation of trade which this separation has caused, it has prevented Palestine participating fully in the general development of the Arab world.

 How did the authors of this document justify their opposition to the establishment of an independent Jewish state in Israel? What counterarguments were presented by spokespersons for the Zionist movement, as presented in the document in Chapter 24 (see the box "The Zionist Case for Palestine" on p. 704)?

Source: From Akram Khater, *Sources in the History of the Modern Middle East*, 2e. © Cengage Learning, pp. 179–190.

---

mandate formally came to a close, the Zionist leader David Ben-Gurion (ben-GOOR-ee-uhn) (1886–1973) announced the independence of the state of Israel. Later that same day, the new state was formally recognized by the United States, while military forces from several neighboring Muslim states—all of which had vigorously opposed the formation of a Jewish state in the region—entered Israeli territory but were beaten back. Thousands of Arab residents of the new state fled. Internal dissonance among the Arabs, combined with the strength of Jewish resistance groups, contributed to the failure of the invasion but the bitterness between the two sides did not subside. The Muslim states refused to recognize the new state of Israel, which became a member of the United Nations, legitimizing it in the eyes of the rest of the world. The stage for future conflict was set.

The exodus of thousands of Palestinian refugees into neighboring Muslim states had repercussions that are still felt today. Jordan, which had become an independent kingdom under its Hashemite (HASH-uh-myt) ruler, was

flooded by the arrival of one million urban Palestinians. They overwhelmed the half million Jordanians, most of whom were Bedouins. To the north, the state of Lebanon had been created to provide the local Christian community with a country of their own but the arrival of the Palestinian refugees upset the delicate balance between Christians and Muslims. Moreover, the creation of Lebanon had angered the Syrians, who had lost that land as well as other territories to Turkey as a result of European decisions before and after World War II.

Nasser and Pan-Arabism

The dispute over Palestine put Egypt in an uncomfortable position. Technically, Egypt was not an Arab state. King Farouk (fuh-ROOK) (1920–1965), who had acceded to power in 1936, had frequently declared support for the Arab cause but the Egyptian people were not Bedouins and, aside from a common commitment to Islam, shared little of the culture of the peoples across the Red Sea. Nevertheless, Farouk committed Egyptian armies to the disastrous war against Israel.

In 1952, Farouk, whose corrupt habits had severely eroded his early popularity, was overthrown by a military coup engineered by young military officers, and the monarchy was replaced by a republic. The real force behind the scenes was Colonel Gamal Abdul Nasser (1918–1970), the son of a minor government functionary who, like many of his fellow officers, had been angered by the army's inadequate preparation for the war against Israel four years earlier.

In 1954, Nasser seized power in his own right and immediately instituted a land reform program. He also adopted a policy of neutrality in foreign affairs and expressed sympathy for the Arab cause. The British presence had rankled many Egyptians for years, for even after granting Egypt independence, Britain had retained control over the Suez Canal. In 1956, Nasser suddenly nationalized the Suez Canal Company, which had been under British and French administration. Seeing a threat to their route to the Indian Ocean, the British and the French launched a joint attack on Egypt to protect their investment. They were joined by Israel, whose leaders had grown exasperated at sporadic Arab commando raids launched from the Egyptian Sinai (SY-ny) Peninsula against Israeli territory and now decided to strike back. But the Eisenhower administration in the United States, concerned that the attack smacked of a revival of colonialism, supported Nasser and brought about the withdrawal of foreign forces from Egypt and of Israeli troops from the Sinai.

THE UNITED ARAB REPUBLIC Nasser now turned to pan-Arabism. Egypt had won the admiration of other states in the area for its successful eviction of the British and the French from the Suez Canal and for its sponsorship of efforts to replace Israel by an independent Palestinian state. The Ba'ath (BAHTH) Party, which advocated the unity of all Arab states in a new socialist society, assumed power in Syria in 1957 and opened talks with Egypt on a political union between the two countries, which took place in March 1958 following a plebiscite. Nasser was named president of the new United Arab Republic (UAR).

Egypt and Syria hoped that the union would eventually expand to include all Arab states but other Arab leaders, including the kings of Jordan, Iraq, and Saudi Arabia, were suspicious. The latter two in particular feared pan-Arabism on the reasonable assumption that they would be asked to share their vast oil revenues with the poorer states of the Middle East. Indeed, in Nasser's view, through Arab unity, this wealth could be used to improve the standard of living in the area. To achieve a more equitable division of the wealth of the region, natural resources and major industries would be nationalized; central planning would guarantee that resources were exploited efficiently but private enterprise would continue at the local level.

In the end, however, Nasser's determination to extend state control over the economy brought an end to the UAR. When the government announced the nationalization of a large number of industries and utilities in 1961, a military coup overthrew the Ba'ath leaders in Damascus, and the new authorities declared that Syria would end its relationship with Egypt.

The breakup of the UAR did not necessarily end Nasser's dream of pan-Arabism. In 1962, Algeria finally received its independence from France and, under its new president, Ahmad Ben Bella, established close relations with Egypt, as did a new republic in Yemen. During the mid-1960s, Egypt took the lead in promoting Arab unity against Israel. At a meeting of Arab leaders held in Jerusalem in 1964, the Palestine Liberation Organization (PLO) was set up under Egyptian sponsorship to represent the interests of the Palestinians. According to the charter of the PLO, only the Palestinian people (and hence not Jewish immigrants) had the right to form a state in the old British mandate. A guerrilla movement called al-Fatah (al-FAH-tuh), led by the dissident PLO figure Yasir Arafat (yah-SEER ah-ruh-FAHT) (1929–2004), began to carry out terrorist attacks on Israeli territory, prompting the Israeli government to raid PLO bases in Jordan in 1966.

The Arab-Israeli Dispute

Growing Arab hostility was a constant threat to the security of Israel. In the years after independence, Israeli leaders dedicated themselves to creating a Jewish homeland. Aided by reparations paid by the postwar German government and private funds provided by Jews living abroad, notably in the United States, the government attempted to build a modern democratic state that would be a magnet for Jews throughout the world and a symbol of Jewish achievement.

Ensuring the survival of the tiny state surrounded by antagonistic Arab neighbors was a considerable challenge, made more difficult by divisions within the Israeli population. Some were immigrants from Europe, while others came from other states in the Middle East. Some were secular and even socialist in their views, while others were politically and religiously conservative. The state was also home to Christians as well as Muslim Palestinians who had not fled to other countries. To balance these diverse interests, Israel established a parliament, called the Knesset (kuh-NESS-it), on the European model, with proportional representation based on the number of votes each party received in the general election. The parties were so numerous that none ever received a majority of votes, and all governments had to be formed from a coalition of several parties. As a result, moderate secular leaders such as longtime prime minister David Ben-Gurion had to cater to more marginal parties composed of conservative religious groups.

During the late 1950s and 1960s, the dispute between Israel and other states in the Middle East intensified. Essentially alone except for the sympathy of the United States and a handful of western European countries, Israel adopted a policy of determined resistance to and immediate retaliation against PLO and Arab provocations. By the spring of 1967, relations between Israel and its Arab neighbors had deteriorated as Nasser attempted to improve his standing in the Arab world by imposing a blockade against Israeli commerce through the Gulf of Aqaba (AH-kah-buh), a move that he had attempted before in 1956.

THE SIX-DAY WAR Concerned that it might be isolated, and lacking firm support from Western powers (which had originally guaranteed Israel the freedom to use the Gulf of Aqaba), in June 1967 Israel suddenly launched air strikes against Egypt and several of its Arab neighbors. Israeli armies then broke the blockade at the head of the Gulf of Aqaba and occupied the Sinai Peninsula. Other Israeli forces attacked Jordanian territory on the West Bank of the Jordan River (Jordan's King Hussein had recently signed an alliance with Egypt and placed his army under Egyptian command), occupied the city of Jerusalem, and seized Syrian military positions in the Golan Heights, along the Israeli-Syrian border (see Map 29.2). In a war lasting only six days, Israel had mocked Nasser's pretensions of Arab unity and tripled the size of its territory, thus enhancing its precarious security. But the attack aroused even more bitter hostility among the Arabs and added one million Palestinians inside Israel's borders, most of them on the West Bank of the Jordan River.

During the next few years, the focus of the Arab-Israeli dispute shifted as Arab states demanded the return of the territories lost in the 1967 war. Meanwhile, many Israelis argued that the new lands improved the security of the beleaguered state and should be retained. Concerned that the dispute might lead to a confrontation between the superpowers, with the Soviet Union backing the Arabs, the Nixon administration tried to achieve a peace settlement. When Egyptian President Nasser died of a heart attack in September 1970, his successor,

MAP 29.2 **Israel and Its Neighbors.** This map shows the evolution of the state of Israel since its founding in 1948. Areas occupied by Israel after the Six-Day War in 1967 are indicated in green.

Q *What is the significance of the West Bank?*

The Temple Mount at Jerusalem. The Temple Mount is one of the most sacred spots in the city of Jerusalem. Originally, it was the site of the Temple built during the reign of Solomon, king of the Israelites, about 1000 B.C.E. The Western Wall of the Temple is shown in the foreground. Beyond the wall is the Dome of the Rock complex, built on the place from which Muslims believe that Muhammad ascended to heaven. Sacred to both Judaism and Islam, the Temple Mount is now a major bone of contention between Muslims and Jews and a prime obstacle to a final settlement of the Arab-Israeli dispute.

ex-general Anwar al-Sadat (ahn-WAHR al-sah-DAHT) (1918–1981), soon showed himself to be more pragmatic than his predecessor, dropping the now irrelevant name United Arab Republic in favor of the Arab Republic of Egypt and replacing Nasser's socialist policies with a new strategy based on free enterprise and encouragement of Western investment. He also agreed to sign a peace treaty with Israel on condition that Israel withdraw to its pre-1967 frontiers. Concerned that other Arab countries would refuse to make peace and take advantage of its presumed weakness, Israel refused.

Rebuffed in his offer of peace, smarting from criticism of his moderate stand from other Arab leaders, and increasingly concerned over Israeli plans to build permanent Jewish settlements in the West Bank, Sadat attempted once again to renew Arab unity through a new confrontation with Israel. On Yom Kippur (the

Jewish Day of Atonement), an Israeli national holiday, Egyptian forces suddenly launched an air and artillery attack on Israeli positions in the Sinai just east of the Suez Canal. Syrian armies attacked Israeli positions in the Golan Heights. After early Arab successes, the Israelis managed to recoup some of their losses on both fronts. As a superpower confrontation between the United States and the Soviet Union loomed, a cease-fire was finally reached.

THE CAMP DAVID ACCORDS After his election as U.S. president in 1976, Jimmy Carter began to press for a compromise peace based on Israel's return of territories occupied during the 1967 war and Arab recognition of the state of Israel. In September 1978, Sadat and Israeli Prime Minister Menachem Begin (muh-NAH-kuhm BAY-gin) (1913–1992) met with Carter at Camp David, the presidential retreat in Maryland. In the first treaty signed with a Muslim state, Israel agreed to withdraw from the Sinai but not from other occupied territories unless it was recognized by other Arab countries.

The promise of the Camp David accords was not fulfilled. One reason was the assassination of Sadat by Islamic militants in October 1981. But there were deeper causes, including the continued unwillingness of Muslim governments to recognize Israel and the Israeli government's encouragement of Jewish settlements in the occupied West Bank.

THE PLO AND THE *INTIFADA* Frustrated by the failure of their allies to resolve their concerns, the militancy of the Palestinians increased, leading to rising unrest, popularly labeled the *intifada* (in-tuh-FAH-duh) (uprising), among PLO supporters living inside Israel and in neighboring Lebanon. In the early 1990s, U.S.-sponsored peace talks took place between Israel and a number of its neighbors but progress was slow. Terrorist attacks by Palestinian militants resulted in heavy casualties and shook the confidence of many Jewish citizens that their security needs could be protected. National elections held in Israel in 1996 led to the formation of a new government under Benjamin Netanyahu (net-ahn-YAH-hoo) (b. 1949). The new government quickly adopted a tougher stance in negotiations with the Palestinian Authority under Yasir Arafat.

CHRONOLOGY The Arab-Israeli Dispute	
Formation of the state of Israel	1948
Founding of the Palestine Liberation Organization	1964
Six-Day War between Arab states and Israel	1967
Yom Kippur War between Arab states and Israel	1973
Camp David accords	1978
Israeli forces invade Lebanon	1982
Oslo Agreement	1993
Assassination of Yitzhak Rabin	1995
Peace talks between Israel and Syria begin	1999
Election of Ariel Sharon as prime minister of Israel	2000
Withdrawal of Israeli settlers from Gaza	2005
Return to office of former Prime Minister Netanyahu of Israel	2009

In 1999, a new Labour government under Prime Minister Ehud Barak (EH-hud bah-RAHK) (b. 1942) was elected to office and promised to revitalize the peace process. Negotiations with the PLO resumed but soon broke down over the future of the city of Jerusalem, leading to a dramatic increase in bloodshed on both sides.

The death of Yasir Arafat in 2004 and his replacement by the Palestinian moderate Mahmoud Abbas (mah-MOOD ah-BAHS) (b. 1935), followed by the unilateral evacuation of Israeli settlers from the Gaza Strip a year later, raised modest hopes for progress in peace talks but the victory of Hamas (HAH-mahs), a militant organization that calls for the destruction of the state of Israel, in Palestinian elections held in late 2005 undermined the search for peace. In 2006, rocket attacks launched by guerrillas from **Hezbollah** (hes-bah-LAH *or* HEZ-bull-lah), a militant Shi'ite organization and political party based in Lebanon, provoked an Israeli invasion of southern Lebanon to wipe out the source of the assault, thereby raising the specter of a wider conflict. As attitudes on both sides hardened, national elections in 2009 led to the return to office of former Prime Minister Benjamin Netanyahu amid signs that both sides had despaired of bringing an end to the conflict. As both sides hardened their stance, negotiations proposed by the Obama administration have led nowhere.

Revolution in Iran

As it intensified, the Arab-Israeli dispute sent shockwaves throughout the region. In 1960, a number of oil-producing states formed the Organization of Petroleum Exporting Countries (OPEC) to gain control over oil prices but the organization was not recognized by the foreign oil companies. During the 1973 Yom Kippur War, some OPEC nations announced significant increases in the price of oil to foreign countries. The price hikes were accompanied by an apparent oil shortage and created serious economic problems in the United States and Europe as well as in the Third World. They also proved to be a boon to oil-exporting countries, such as Libya, now under the leadership of the militantly anti-Western Colonel Muammar Qaddafi.

One of the key oil-exporting countries was Iran. Under the leadership of Shah Mohammad Reza Pahlavi (ree-ZAH PAH-luh-vee) (1919–1980), who had taken over from his father in 1941, Iran had become one of the richest countries in the Middle East. Relations with the West had occasionally been fragile, especially after Prime Minister Muhammad Mossadegh (MOH-sah-dek) (1882–1967) attempted to nationalize the oil industry in 1951. Mossadegh was overthrown in 1953 with covert U.S. assistance, and during the next twenty years, Iran became a prime U.S. ally. With encouragement from Washington, which hoped that Iran could become a force for stability in the Persian Gulf, the shah attempted to carry out a series of social and economic reforms to transform the country into the most advanced in the region.

On paper, it appeared that his efforts were succeeding. Per capita income increased dramatically, literacy rates improved, a modern communications infrastructure took shape, and an affluent middle class emerged in the capital of Tehran (teh-RAHN). Under the surface, however, trouble was brewing. An ambitious land reform program left many peasants still landless, while the urban middle class was squeezed by rising unemployment and high inflation. Housing costs had skyrocketed, in part because of a massive influx of foreigners attracted by oil money.

THE FALL OF THE SHAH Some of the unrest took the form of religious discontent as millions of devout Muslims looked with distaste at a new Iranian civilization based on greed, sexual license, and a decline in religious values. Religious conservatives opposed rampant government corruption, the ostentation of the shah's court, and the extension of voting rights to women. Some opposition elements resorted to terrorism against wealthy Iranians or foreign residents in an attempt to initiate social and political disorder. In response, the shah's U.S.-trained security police, the SAVAK, imprisoned and sometimes tortured thousands of dissidents.

Leading the opposition was Ayatollah Ruholla Khomeini (1900–1989), an austere Shi'ite cleric who had been exiled to Iraq and then to France because of his outspoken opposition to the shah's regime. From Paris, Khomeini continued his attacks in print, on television, and in radio broadcasts. By the late 1970s, large numbers of Iranians—especially Shi'ite Muslims, whose approach to religion is sometimes more mystical and messianic than that of their Sunni counterparts—began to respond to Khomeini's diatribes against the "satanic regime." Demonstrations by his supporters were repressed with ferocity by the police but workers' strikes grew in intensity, and in 1979 the government collapsed and was replaced by a hastily formed Islamic republic headed by the returning Ayatollah Khomeini. The new government, dominated by Shi'ite clergy, immediately began to introduce traditional Islamic law (see the Comparative Essay "Religion and Society" on p. 870). A new reign of terror ensued as supporters of the shah were rounded up and executed. The shah himself left Iran and died of cancer in 1980.

Though much of the outside world focused on the U.S. embassy in Tehran, where militants held a number of foreign hostages, the Iranian Revolution involved much more. In the eyes of the ayatollah and his followers, the United States was "the great Satan," the powerful protector of Israel and enemy of Muslims everywhere. Furthermore, it was responsible for the corruption of Iranian society under the shah. With economic conditions in Iran rapidly deteriorating, the Islamic revolutionary government finally agreed to free the hostages in return for the release of Iranian assets in the United States.

During the next few years, the intensity of the Iranian Revolution moderated slightly as the government displayed a modest tolerance for a loosening of clerical control over freedom of expression and social activities. In 1997, a moderate Muslim cleric, Mohammad Khatami (KHAH-tah-mee) (b. 1943), was elected president of Iran. Khatami sought to relax controls over freedom of expression and sent signals that Iran might wish to improve relations with the United States but severe pressures from conservative elements blunted many of his efforts, and a new wave of official repression soon ensued. Although student protests erupted into the streets in 2003, hard-liners continued to reject proposals to expand civil rights and limit the power of the clerics (see the Film & History feature "Persepolis (2007)" on p. 884).

In 2005, the presidential elections brought a new leader, Mahmoud Ahmadinejad (mah-MOOD ah-mah-dee-nee-ZHAHD) (b. 1956), to power in Tehran. He immediately inflamed the situation by calling publicly for the destruction of the state of Israel, while his government aroused unease throughout the world by indicating its determination to develop a nuclear energy program, ostensibly for peaceful purposes. Although Ahmadinejad was reelected in 2009, worsening conditions inside Iran eroded the government's popularity and led to the victory of a moderate candidate, Hassan Rouhani (Hah-SAHN Roh-HAH-nee) (b. 1948), in presidential elections held in 2013. With his election came a sliver of hope that the era of Iran's confrontation with the Western nations might be brought to an end.

Crisis in the Persian Gulf

Although much of the Iranians' anger was directed against the United States during the early phases of the revolution, Iran had enemies closer to home. To the north, the immensely powerful Soviet Union, driven by atheistic communism, was viewed as the latest incarnation of the Russian threat of previous centuries. To the west was a militant and hostile Iraq, under the leadership of the ambitious and brutal Saddam Hussein (sah-DAHM hoo-SAYN) (1937–2006). Iraq had just passed through a turbulent period. The monarchy had been overthrown by a military coup in 1958 but conflict within the military ruling junta led to chronic instability, and in 1979 Colonel Hussein, a prominent member of the local Ba'ath Party, seized power on his own.

THE VISION OF SADDAM HUSSEIN Saddam Hussein was a fervent believer in the Ba'athist vision of a single Arab state in the Middle East and soon began to persecute non-Arab groups in Iraq, including Persians and Kurds. He then turned his sights to territorial expansion to the east.

Iraq and Iran had traditionally suffered an uneasy relationship, fueled by religious differences (Iranian Islam is predominantly Shi'ite, while the ruling caste in Iraq was Sunni) and

Persepolis (2007)

The Iranian author Marjane Satrapi (b. 1969) has re-created *Persepolis*, her autobiographical graphic novel, as an enthralling animated film of the same name. Using simple black-and-white animation, the movie recounts key stages in the turbulent history of modern Iran as seen through the eyes of a spirited young girl, also named Marjane. The dialogue is in French with English subtitles (a version dubbed in English is also available), and the voices of the characters are rendered beautifully by Danielle Darrieux, Catherine Deneuve, Chiara Mastroianni, and other European film stars.

In the film, Marjane is the daughter of middle-class left-wing intellectuals who abhor the dictatorship of the shah and actively participate in his overthrow in 1979. After the revolution, however, the severity of the ayatollah's Islamic rule arouses their secularist and democratic impulses. Encouraged by her loving grandmother, who reinforces her modernist and feminist instincts, Marjane resents having to wear a head scarf and the educational restrictions imposed by the puritanical new Islamic regime but to little avail. Emotionally exhausted and fearful of political retribution from the authorities, her family finally sends her to study in Vienna.

Study abroad, however, is not a solution to Marjane's problems. She is distressed by the nihilism and emotional shallowness of her new Austrian school friends, who seem oblivious to the contrast between their privileged lives and her own experience of living under the shadow of a tyrannical regime. Disillusioned by the loneliness of exile and several failed love affairs, she descends into a deep depression and then decides to return to Tehran. When she discovers that her family is still suffering from political persecution, however, she decides to leave the country permanently and settles in Paris.

Observing the events, first through the eyes of a child and then through the perceptions of an innocent schoolgirl, the viewer of the film is forced to fill in the blanks, as Marjane initially cannot comprehend the meaning of the adult conversations swirling around her. As Marjane passes through adolescence into adulthood, the realization of the folly of human intransigence and superstition becomes painfully clear, both to her and to the audience. Although animated films have long been a staple in the cinema, thanks in part to Walt Disney, both the novel and the film *Persepolis* demonstrate how graphic design can depict a momentous event in history with clarity and compassion. The film had a mixed reception in Muslim countries, as some critics objected to the portrayal of Islam in the movie and sought to have it banned from appearing in local theaters.

---

a perennial dispute over borderlands adjacent to the Persian Gulf, the vital waterway for the export of oil from both countries. Like several of its neighbors, Iraq had long dreamed of unifying the Arabs but had been hindered by internal factions and suspicion among its neighbors. Then, during the mid-1970s, Iran gave some support to a Kurdish rebellion in the mountains of Iraq. In 1975, the government of the shah agreed to stop aiding the rebels in return for territorial concessions at the head of the Gulf. Five years later, however, the Kurdish revolt had been suppressed.

Saddam Hussein now saw his opportunity; accusing Iran of violating the territorial agreement, in 1980 he launched an attack on his neighbor. The war was a bloody one and lasted nearly ten years. Poison gas was used against civilians, and children were employed to clear minefields. Finally, with both sides virtually exhausted, a cease-fire was arranged in the fall of 1988.

The bitter conflict with Iran had not slaked Saddam Hussein's appetite for territorial expansion. In early August 1990, Iraqi military forces suddenly moved across the border and occupied the small neighboring country of Kuwait at the head of the Gulf. The immediate pretext was the claim that Kuwait was pumping oil from fields inside Iraqi territory. Baghdad was also angry over the Kuwaiti government's demand for repayment of loans it had made to Iraq during the war with Iran. But the underlying reason was Iraq's contention that Kuwait was legally a part of Iraq. Kuwait had been part of the Ottoman Empire until the beginning of the twentieth century, when the local prince had agreed to place his patrimony under British protection. When Iraq became independent in 1932, it claimed the area on the grounds that the state of Kuwait had been created by British imperialism but opposition from major Western powers and other countries in the region, which feared the consequences of a "greater Iraq," prevented an Iraqi takeover.

THE PERSIAN GULF WAR The Iraqi invasion of Kuwait in 1990 sparked an international outcry, and the United States assembled a multinational coalition that, under the name Operation Desert Storm, liberated the country and destroyed a substantial part of Iraq's armed forces in 1991. But the allied forces did not occupy Baghdad at the end of the war out of fear that doing so would cause a breakup of the country and operate to the benefit of Iran. The allies hoped instead that Saddam's

© 2016 Cengage Learning

- 🟧 Predominantly Sunni areas
- 🟩 Predominantly Shi'ite areas
- 🟨 Predominantly Kurdish areas

Iraq

regime would be ousted by an internal revolt. In the meantime, harsh economic sanctions were imposed on the Iraqi government as the condition for peace. The anticipated overthrow of Saddam Hussein did not materialize, however, and his tireless efforts to evade the conditions of the cease-fire continued to bedevil U.S. President Bill Clinton and his successor, George W. Bush.

Conflicts in Afghanistan and Iraq

The terrorist attacks launched against U.S. targets in September 2001 added a new dimension to the Middle Eastern equation. After the failure of the Soviet Union to quell the rebellion in Afghanistan during the 1980s, a fundamentalist Muslim group known as the Taliban, supported covertly by the United States,

The Afghan War. After the overthrow of the Taliban regime in 2002, U.S. and allied peacekeeping forces sought to prevent the Taliban from returning to power while providing a shield to enable the emergence of a more moderate government in Kabul. The results have been mixed, and by 2014 the conflict in Afghanistan earned the dubious title of the longest war in U.S. history. In this photograph, U.S. forces patrol mountainous regions in search of Taliban insurgents.

seized power in Kabul and ruled the country with a fanaticism reminiscent of the Cultural Revolution in China. Backed by conservative religious forces in Pakistan, the Taliban provided a base of operations for Osama bin Laden's al-Qaeda terrorist network. After the attacks of September 11, a coalition of forces led by the United States overthrew the Taliban and attempted to build a new and moderate government in Afghanistan. But the country's history of bitter internecine warfare among tribal groups remained a severe challenge to those efforts, and Taliban forces managed to regroup and continued to operate in the mountainous region adjacent to the Pakistani border. The terrorist threat from al-Qaeda, however, was dealt a major blow in May 2011, when Osama bin Laden was killed by U.S. special operations forces during a raid on his hideout in northern Pakistan.

After moving against the Taliban at the end of 2001 the administration of George W. Bush, charging that Iraqi dictator Saddam Hussein had not only provided support to bin Laden's terrorist organization but also stockpiled weapons of mass destruction for use against his enemies, threatened to invade Iraq and remove him from power. The White House hoped that the overthrow of the Iraqi dictator would promote the spread of democracy throughout the region. The plan, widely debated in the media and opposed by many of the United States'

traditional allies, disquieted Arab leaders and fanned anti-American sentiment throughout the Muslim world. Nevertheless, in March 2003, U.S.-led forces attacked Iraq and overthrew Saddam Hussein's regime. In the months that followed, occupation forces sought to restore stability to the country while setting out plans on which to build a democratic society. But although Saddam Hussein was captured by U.S. troops and later executed, armed resistance by militant Muslim elements continued.

When Barack Obama came into office in 2009, he ordered a gradual withdrawal of U.S. combat forces from Iraq, while training an Iraqi military force capable of defeating the remaining insurgents. Accordingly, the last remaining U.S. forces were removed on schedule in the fall of 2011. However, the government, led by the Shi'ite Prime Minister Nouri al-Maliki antagonized Sunni and Kurdish elements in the country, provoking an invasion by Sunni militants from neighboring Syria in 2014 that threatened to undermine the fragile stability of the Iraqi state.

Revolution in the Middle East

In the early months of 2011, popular protests against current conditions broke out in several countries in the Middle East. Beginning in Tunisia, the riots spread rapidly to Egypt—where they brought about the abrupt resignation of

Afghanistan and Pakistan

Claudia Wiens/Alamy

Tahrir Square: Ground Zero for the Arab Spring. When popular demonstrations broke out against the regime of Egyptian president Hosni Mubarak in early 2011, Tahrir Square, in the heart of the teeming metropolis of Cairo, was at the epicenter of the protests. For weeks, supporters and opponents of the regime clashed periodically in the square, resulting in severe casualties. After the overthrow of Mubarak, the square continued to provide a venue for public protests against the newly-elected government of President Mohamed Morsi, leader of the Muslim Brotherhood, and when public protests against the latter escalated, the army stepped in to depose President Morsi.

longtime president Hosni Mubarak (HAHS-nee moo-BAH-rahk) (b. 1929)—and then to other countries in the region, such as Syria, Libya, and Yemen, where political leaders sought to quell the unrest, often by violent means. The uprisings (dubbed by pundits the "Arab Spring") aroused hopes around the world that the seeds of democracy had been planted in a region long dominated by autocratic governments but also provoked widespread concern that unstable conditions could lead to further violence and an increase in international terrorism. In the months following the outbreak of unrest, such worries appeared to be well founded. In Libya, the bloody regime of dictator Muammar Qaddafi was overthrown by a popular revolt with the assistance of NATO air strikes, but instability continues to reign throughout the country. In Syria, popular protests have expanded into a brutal civil war that threatens to engulf the entire region into conflict.

Society and Culture in the Contemporary Middle East

Q FOCUS QUESTION: How have religious issues affected economic, social, and cultural conditions in the Middle East in recent decades?

In the Middle East today, all aspects of society and culture—from political and economic issues to literature, art, and the role of the family—are intertwined with questions of religious faith.

Varieties of Government: The Politics of Islam

To many seasoned observers, ambitious schemes drafted by outsiders to remake the Middle East in the Western liberal democratic image often appear unrealistic, since democratic values are not deeply rooted in the culture of the region. In many countries in the area, feudal rulers remain securely in power. Often they continue to govern by traditional precepts and, citing the distinctive character of Muslim society, have refused to establish representative political institutions. These rulers insist that strict observance of traditional customs be maintained. In some cases, religious police are responsible for enforcing the Muslim dress code, maintaining the prohibition against alcohol, and making sure that offices close during the time of prayer.

Even in states where traditional authority has been replaced by charismatic rulers or modernizing bureaucratic regimes, the transition to more pluralistic forms of government has been difficult. The regimes of Muammar Qaddafi in Libya, Saddam Hussein in Iraq, and Hosni Mubarak in Egypt have all been replaced as a result of the popular unrest that has occurred in recent years, but what forms of rule will eventually replace them is not yet evident. The situation in Egypt is a case in point. After national elections elevated Prime Minister Mohamed Morsi (b. 1951) of the Muslim Brotherhood to office in Cairo, opposition forces took to the streets once more in protest, leading to a takeover of power by the Egyptian army.

To be sure, there have been some tantalizing signs of change in recent years. A few Arab nations, such as Bahrain, Kuwait, and Jordan, have engaged in limited forms of democratic experimentation. Most of the region's recent leaders, however, have maintained that Western-style democracy is not appropriate for their societies, and even modernizing societies such as the United Arab Emirates (UAE) have severely repressed dissident activities. Bashar al-Assad (bah-SHAHR al-ah-SAHD) (b. 1965), the president of Syria, was probably typical when he once declared that he would tolerate only "positive criticism" of his policies. "We have to have our own democracy to match our history and culture," he said, "arising from the needs of our people and our reality."[9] President Mubarak of Egypt often insisted to foreign critics that only authoritarian rule could prevent the spread of Islamic radicalism throughout his country, and the election of the Muslim Brotherhood in 2011 appeared to prove his point.

The one major exception to the rule is Turkey, where free elections and the sharing of power have become more prevalent in recent years. For a long time, the military

Islam and Democracy

RELIGION & PHILOSOPHY

ONE OF GEORGE W. BUSH'S OBJECTIVES in launching the invasion of Iraq was to promote the emergence of democratic states in the Middle East. According to U.S. officials, one reason for the formation of terrorist movements in Muslim societies is the prevalence of dictatorial governments that do not serve the interests of their citizens. According to the author of this editorial, an Indian Muslim, the problem lies as much with the actions of Western countries as it does with political attitudes in the Muslim world.

M. J. Akbar, "Linking Islam to Dictatorship"

Let us examine a central canard, that Islam and democracy are incompatible. This is an absurdity. There is nothing Islamic or un-Islamic about democracy. Democracy is the outcome of a political process, not a religious process.

It is glibly suggested that "every" Muslim country is a dictatorship, but the four largest Muslim populations of the world—in Indonesia, India, Bangladesh, and Turkey—vote to change governments. Pakistan could easily have been on this list.

Voting does not make these Muslims less or more religious. There are dictators among Muslims just as there are dictators among Christians, Buddhists, and Hindus.... Christian Latin America has seen ugly forms of dictatorship, as has Christian Africa.

What is unique to the Muslim world is not the absence of democracy but the fact that in 1918, after the defeat of the Ottoman Empire, every single Muslim in the world lived under foreign subjugation....

The West, in the shape of Britain, France, or America, was never interested in democracy when a helpful dictator or king would serve. When people got a chance to express their wish, it was only logical that they would ask for popular rule. It was the street that brought Mossadegh to power in Iran and drove the shah of Iran to tearful exile in Rome. Who brought the shah of Iran and autocracy back to Iran? The CIA.

If Iranian democracy had been permitted a chance in 1953, there would have been no uprising led by Ayatollah Khomeini in 1979. In other countries, where the struggle for independence was long and brutal, as in Algeria and Indonesia, the militias who had fought the war institutionalized army authority. In other instances, civilian heroes confused their own well-being with national health. They became regressive dictators. Once again, there was nothing Islamic about it.

Muslim countries will become democracies, too, because it is the finest form of modern governance. But it will be a process interrupted by bloody experience as the street wrenches power from usurpers....

Democracy has become the latest rationale for the occupation of Iraq.... Granted, democracy is always preferable to tyranny no matter how it comes. But Iraqis are not dupes. They will take democracy and place it at the service of nationalism....

There is uncertainty and apprehension across the Muslim nations: uncertainty about where they stand, and apprehension about both American power and the repugnant use of terrorism that in turn invites the exercise of American power. There is also anger that a legitimate cause like that of Palestine can get buried in the debris of confusion. Muslims do not see Palestinians as terrorists.

 How does the author of this editorial answer the charge that democracy and Islam are incompatible? To what degree, in his view, is the West responsible for the problems of the Middle East?

Source: From M. J. Akbar, "Linking Islam to Dictatorship," in *World Press Review*, May 2004.

---

played the dominant role in Turkish politics, but in 1996 a Muslim political party assumed power in a coalition government and immediately adopted a pro-Arab stance in foreign affairs. Concerned that the secular legacy of Mustafa Kemal Atatürk was being eroded, military leaders forced the new government to resign under heavy pressure. But a new Islamist organization, known as the Justice and Development Party (AKP), won elections held in 2007. Under Prime Minister Recep Erdogan (b. 1954), the AKP government immediately earned broad popular support by adopting a moderate stance on religious issues and by carrying out a number of economic reforms, but charges of official corruption and the suppression of dissenting voices have recently eroded Erdogan's popularity. The latter's vision for his country's role in world affairs appears to be limitless. Under his benign gaze, the past glories of the Ottoman Empire have been revived, triggered by films on the 1453 seizure of Constantinople and a new soap opera about the life and times of Suleyman the Magnificent. Whether Turkey's recent experiment with political pluralism will succeed remains an open question.

Are the critics correct that the Middle East—with the exception of the Jewish state of Israel—is not fertile ground for the establishment of democratic institutions? Are political pluralism and the principles of human freedom Western values and truly antithetical to the culture and principles of Islam? For many years, most world leaders accepted the logic of such contentions, provoking some critics to charge that Western governments coddled Middle Eastern dictatorships as a means of preserving their access to the vast oil reserves located in the region (see the box "Islam and Democracy" above). The current wave of popular unrest has aroused hopes that a new order awaits in the wings but the immediate signs are not promising. As we await the consequences, the fate of the region hangs in the balance.

The Economics of the Middle East: Oil and Sand

Few areas exhibit a greater disparity of individual and national wealth than the Middle East. While millions live in abject poverty, a fortunate few rank among the wealthiest people in the world. The primary reason for this disparity is oil. Unfortunately for most of the peoples of the region, oil reserves are distributed unevenly and all too often are located in areas where the population density is low (see Map 29.3). Egypt and Turkey, with more than 75 million inhabitants apiece, have almost no oil reserves. The combined population of the oil-rich states of Kuwait, the United Arab Emirates, and Saudi Arabia is about 35 million people. This disparity in wealth inspired Nasser's quest for Arab unity but has also posed a major obstacle to that unity.

ECONOMICS AND ISLAM Not surprisingly, considering their different resources and political systems, the states of the Middle East have adopted diverse approaches to the problem of developing strong and stable economies. Some, like Nasser in Egypt and the leaders of the Ba'ath Party in Syria, attempted to create a form of Arab socialism, favoring a high level of government involvement in the economy to relieve the inequities of the free enterprise system. Others turned to the Western capitalist model to maximize growth while using taxes or massive development projects to build a modern infrastructure, redistribute wealth, and maintain political stability and economic opportunity for all (see the Comparative Illustration "From Rags to Riches in the UAE" on p. 889).

Whatever their approach, all the states have attempted to develop their economies in accordance with Islamic beliefs. Although the Qur'an has little to say about economics and cannot be said to be either capitalist or socialist, it is clear in its opposition to charging interest and in its concern for the material welfare of the Muslim community, the *umma*. How these goals are to be achieved, though, is a matter of interpretation.

Socialist theories of economic development such as Nasser's were often suggested as a way to promote economic growth while meeting the requirements of Islamic doctrine. State intervention in the economic sector would bring about rapid development, while land redistribution and the nationalization or regulation of industry would minimize the harsh inequities of the marketplace. In general, however, the socialist approach has had little success, and most governments, including those of Egypt and Syria, eventually shifted to a more free enterprise approach while encouraging foreign investment to compensate for a lack of capital or technology.

AGRICULTURAL POLICIES Although the amount of arable land is relatively small, most countries in the Middle East rely

MAP 29.3 The Modern Middle East. Shown here are the boundaries of the independent states in the contemporary Middle East.

Q *Which are the major oil-producing countries?*

© 2016 Cengage Learning

COMPARATIVE ILLUSTRATION

From Rags to Riches in the UAE. One of the most startling success stories in the Middle East is the transformation of the United Arab Emirates from a poverty-stricken region on the edge of the Arabian peninsula into one of the wealthiest countries—on a per capita basis—in the entire world. At the beginning of the twentieth century, Abu Dhabi and Dubai were small fishing villages inhabited by Arab tribal peoples who had migrated into the region a few generations previously (bottom photo). But the discovery of oil in the region dramatically changed the situation, and today the two cities sport gleaming skyscrapers (top photo), artificial islands built along the edge of the Persian Gulf, and glamorous resorts, shopping malls, and golf courses for the beautiful people of the world.

 Which are the wealthiest states in the region? Which are the poorest?

on farming to supply food for their growing populations. Much of the fertile land was owned by wealthy absentee landlords but land reform programs in several countries have attempted to alleviate this problem.

The most comprehensive and probably the most successful land reform program was instituted in Egypt, where Nasser and his successors managed to reassign nearly a quarter of all cultivable lands by limiting the amount a single individual could hold. Similar programs in Iran, Iraq, Libya, and Syria generally had less effect. After the 1979 revolution in Iran, many farmers forcibly seized lands from the landlords, raising questions of ownership that the revolutionary government has tried to resolve with only minimal success.

Agricultural productivity throughout the region has been plagued by overpopulation and a lack of water. With populations growing at more than 2 percent annually on average in the Middle East (more than 3 percent in some countries), several governments have tried to increase the amount of water available for irrigation. Many attempts have been sabotaged by government ineptitude, political disagreements, and territorial conflicts, however. For example, disputes between Israel and its neighbors over water rights and between Iraq and its neighbors over the exploitation of the Tigris and Euphrates Rivers have caused serious tensions in recent years. Today, the dearth of water in the region is reaching crisis proportions.

One prominent source of the region's economic difficulties is the high rate of population growth. To deal with the problem, governments in the poorer countries have encouraged emigration to oil-producing states with small populations, such as Saudi Arabia and the United Arab Emirates. Since the mid-1980s, the majority of the population in the latter has been composed of foreign nationals, who often send the bulk of their salaries back to their families in their home countries. In times of political turmoil and economic recession, however, many governments have taken measures to evict foreigners and reduce their migrant population. Today migrant workers, many of them living in substandard housing, are a volatile force in the politics of the region.

The Islamic Revival

In recent years, developments in the Middle East have often been described in terms of a resurgence of traditional values and customs in response to Western influence. Indeed, some conservative religious forces in the area have consciously attempted to replace foreign culture and values with allegedly "pure" Islamic forms of belief and behavior.

MODERNIST ISLAM Initially, many Muslim intellectuals responded to Western influence by trying to create a "modernized" set of Islamic beliefs and practices that would not clash with the demands of the twentieth century. This process was especially prevalent in Turkey, Egypt, and Iran. Mustafa Kemal Atatürk embraced the concept when he attempted to secularize the new Turkish republic. The Turkish model was followed by Shah Reza Khan and his son Mohammad Reza Pahlavi in Iran and then by Nasser in postwar Egypt, all of whom attempted to honor Islamic values while asserting the primacy of other issues such as political and economic development. Religion, in effect, had become the handmaiden of political power, national identity, and economic prosperity.

These secularizing trends prevailed among the political, intellectual, and economic elites in urban areas but had less influence in the countryside, among the poor, and among devout elements within the clergy. Many of the clerics believed that Western influence in the cities had given birth to political and economic corruption, sexual promiscuity, hedonism, individualism, and the prevalence of alcohol, pornography, and drugs. Although such practices had long existed in the Middle East, they were now far more visible and socially acceptable.

RETURN TO TRADITION Reaction among conservatives against the modernist movement was quick to emerge in several countries and reached its zenith in the late 1970s with the return of the Ayatollah Khomeini to Iran. It is not surprising that Iran took the lead in light of its long tradition of seeking ideological purity within the Shi'ite sect as well as the uncompromisingly secular character of the shah's reforms in the postwar era. In Iran today, traditional Islamic beliefs are all-pervasive and extend into education, clothing styles, social practices, and the legal system. In recent years, for example, Iranian women have been heavily fined or even flogged for violating the Islamic dress code.

The cultural and social effects of the Iranian Revolution soon began to spread. In Algeria, the political influence of fundamentalist Islamic groups enabled them to win a stunning victory in the national elections in 1992. When the military stepped in to cancel the second round of elections and crack down on the militants, the latter responded with a campaign of terrorism against moderates that claimed thousands of lives. A similar trend emerged in Egypt, where militant groups such as the Muslim Brotherhood, formed in 1928 as a means of promoting personal piety, began to engage in terrorism, including the assassination of President Anwar al-Sadat and attacks on foreign tourists, who are considered carriers of corrupt Western influence.

Even in Turkey, generally considered the most secular of Islamic societies, the victory of Islamist parties in recent

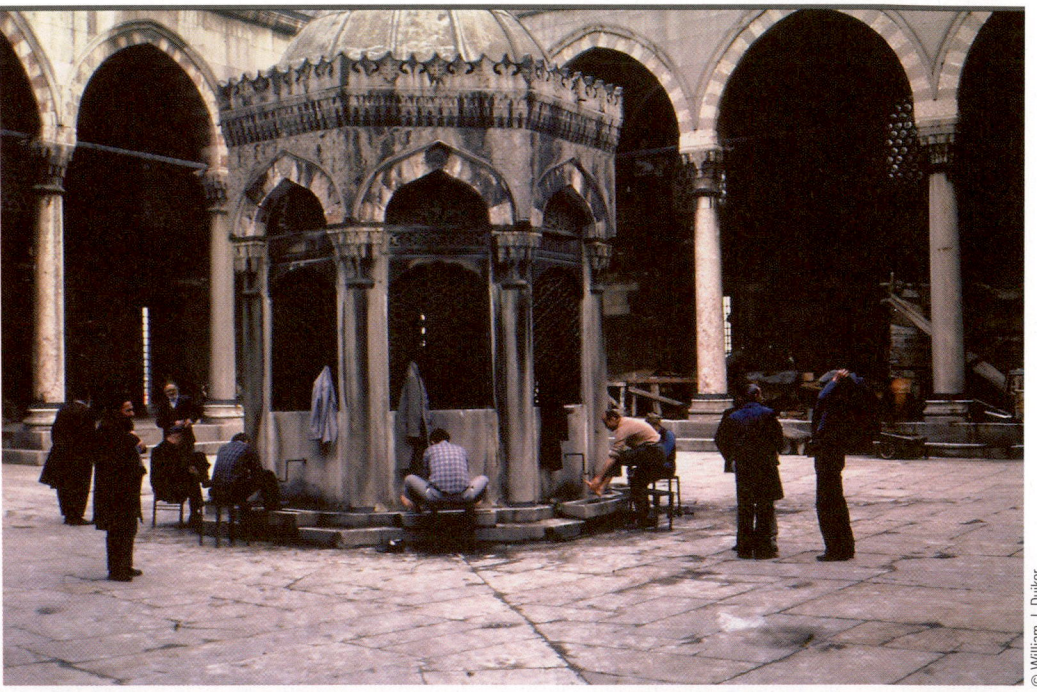

Answering the Call of the _Muezzin_. Since the establishment of the Turkish Republic in the early 1920s, Turkey has been a secular state, as Mustafa Kemal Atatürk sought to introduce the Western concept of separation of church and state to his young country. In fact, well over 90 percent of the population of Turkey today adheres to the Muslim faith, and under the current government of Prime Minister Recep Erdogan, Islam has achieved higher visibility in Turkish society. Courses on religion, which focus almost exclusively on Sunni Islam, are required subjects in Turkish schools, and Erdogan has made no secret of his desire to revive the glories of the Ottoman Empire, when Turkey was the leading force in the Middle East. In the photograph shown here, a group of Muslims prepare for prayer at the seventeenth-century Yeni Cami (New Mosque) in the heart of Istanbul.

elections has led to efforts to guarantee the rights of devout Muslims to display their faith publicly. Throughout the Middle East, even governments and individuals who do not support efforts to return to pure Islamic principles have adjusted their behavior and beliefs in subtle ways. In the United Arab Emirates, Western expatriates teaching at local universities are being replaced by academics trained in Islamic countries, while in Egypt television programs devoted to religion are officially encouraged in preference to comedies and adventure shows imported from the West. A constitution recently enacted under the government of Mohamed Morsi sought to expand the role of Islam in Egyptian society.

Women in the Middle East

Nowhere have the fault lines between tradition and modernity in Muslim societies in the Middle East been as sharp as in the ongoing debate over the role of women. At the beginning of the twentieth century, women's place in Middle Eastern society had changed little since the death of the prophet Muhammad. Women were secluded in their homes and had few legal, political, or social rights. During the first decades of the twentieth century, however, advocates of modernist views began to contend that Islamic doctrine was not inherently opposed to increased women's rights. To modernists, Islamic traditions such as female seclusion, wearing the veil, and polygamy were actually pre-Islamic folk traditions that had been tolerated in the early Islamic era and continued to be practiced in later centuries. Such views had a considerable impact in countries like Turkey and Iran, where greater rights for women were a crucial element in the social revolutions promoted by Kemal Atatürk, and Shah Reza Khan and his son granted female suffrage and encouraged the education of women. In Egypt, a vocal feminist movement arose in educated women's circles in Cairo as early as the 1920s.

In recent years, a more traditional view of women's role has tended to prevail in many Middle Eastern countries. Attacks by religious conservatives on the growing role of women contributed to the emotions underlying the Iranian Revolution of 1979. Iranian women were instructed to wear the veil and to dress modestly in public. Films produced in postrevolutionary Iran rarely featured women, and when they did, physical contact between men and women was prohibited. The events in Iran had repercussions in secular Muslim societies such as Egypt, Turkey, and Morocco, where women began to dress more modestly in public and criticism of open sexuality in the media became increasingly frequent. The contrast with the state of Israel is striking, where—except in Jewish Orthodox communities—women have achieved substantial equality with men and are active in politics, the professions, and even the armed forces. Golda Meir (may-EER) (1898–1978), prime minister of Israel from 1969 to 1974, became an international symbol of the ability of women to be world leaders.

The most conservative nation by far remains Saudi Arabia, where following Wahhabi tradition, women are not only segregated and expected to wear the veil in public but also restricted in education and forbidden to drive automobiles (see the box

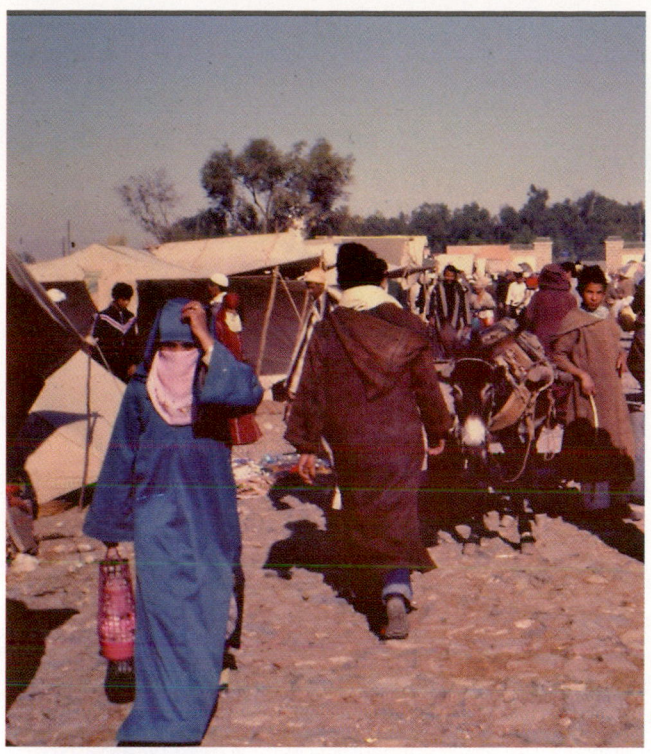

© William J. Duiker

Behind the Veil. In many Islamic countries today, women living in rural areas are much more likely than their urban counterparts to cover their faces and bodies in the traditional way. In a small Berber village in the Atlas Mountains of Morocco, this woman does her daily shopping while wearing a *chador* (a long gown covering the entire body and the head, often in blue or gray), supplemented by a veil (known as a *niqab*) to cover the lower half of her face. Women living in the cities and larger towns such as Rabat and Casablanca often wear a hair covering but leave their faces uncovered. The Berber peoples, who have lived in the mountains of North Africa for thousands of years, initially resisted the Arab conquest in the eighth century but continue to dress in traditional ways.

"Keeping the Camel out of the Tent" on p. 892). Still, women's rights have been extended in a few countries in the region. In 1999, women obtained the right to vote in Kuwait, and they have been granted an equal right with their husbands to seek a divorce in Egypt. Even in Iran, women have many freedoms that they lacked before the twentieth century; for example, they can receive military training, vote, practice birth control, and publish fiction. Most important, today nearly 60 percent of university entrants in Iran are women.

Literature and Art

As in other areas of Asia and Africa, the encounter with the West in the nineteenth and twentieth centuries stimulated a cultural renaissance in the Middle East. Muslim authors translated Western works into Arabic and Persian and began to experiment with new literary forms. Because of space limitations, we can list here only a few of the most prominent examples.

NATIONAL LITERATURES Iran has produced one of the most prominent national literatures in the contemporary Middle East. Perhaps the most outstanding Iranian author of the twentieth century was the short-story writer Sadeq Hedayat

Keeping the Camel out of the Tent

FAMILY & SOCIETY

"Almighty God created sexual desire in ten parts; then he gave nine parts to women and one to men." So pronounced Ali, Muhammad's son-in-law, as he explained why women are held morally responsible as the instigators of sexual intercourse. Consequently, over the centuries, Islamic women have been secluded, veiled, and in many cases genitally mutilated in order to safeguard male virtue. Women are forbidden to look directly at, speak to, or touch a man prior to marriage. Even today, they are often sequestered at home or limited to strictly segregated areas away from all male contact. Women normally pray at home or in an enclosed antechamber of the mosque so that their physical presence will not disturb men's spiritual concentration.

Especially limiting today are the laws governing women's behavior in Saudi Arabia. Schooling for girls has never been compulsory because fathers believe that "educating women is like allowing the nose of the camel into the tent; eventually the beast will edge in and take up all the room inside." The country did not establish its first girls' school until 1956. The following description of Saudi women is from *Nine Parts Desire: The Hidden World of Islamic Women* by the journalist Geraldine Brooks.

Geraldine Brooks, *Nine Parts Desire*

Women were first admitted to university in Saudi Arabia in 1962, and all women's colleges remain strictly segregated. Lecture rooms come equipped with closed-circuit TVs and telephones, so women students can listen to a male professor and question him by phone, without having to contaminate themselves by being seen by him. When the first dozen women graduated from university in 1973, they were devastated to find that their names hadn't been printed on the commencement program. The old tradition, that it dishonors women to mention them, was depriving them of recognition they believed they'd earned. The women and their families protested, so a separate program was printed and a segregated graduation ceremony was held for the students' female relatives....

But while the opening of women's universities widened access to higher learning for women, it also made the educational experience much shallower. Before 1962, many progressive Saudi families had sent their daughters abroad for education. They had returned to the kingdom not only with a degree but with experience of the outside world.... Now a whole generation of Saudi women have completed their education entirely within the country....

Lack of opportunity for education abroad means that Saudi women are trapped in the confines of an education system that still lags men's. Subjects such as geology and petroleum engineering—tickets to influential jobs in Saudi Arabia's oil economy—remain closed to women.... Few women's colleges have their own libraries, and libraries shared with men's schools are either entirely off limits to women or open to them only one day per week....

But women and men sit for the same degree examinations. Professors quietly acknowledge the women's scores routinely outstrip the men's. "It's no surprise," said one woman professor. "Look at their lives. The boys have their cars, they can spend the evenings cruising the streets with their friends, sitting in cafés, buying black-market alcohol and drinking all night. What do the girls have? Four walls and their books. For them, education is everything."

According to Geraldine Brooks, do women in Saudi Arabia have an opportunity to receive an education? To what degree do they take advantage of it?

Source: From *Nine Parts Desire: The Hidden World of Islamic Women*, by Geraldine Brooks (Doubleday, 1996).

(sah-DEK HAY-dy-yaht) (1903–1951). Hedayat was obsessed with the frailty and absurdity of life and wrote with compassion about the problems of ordinary human beings. Frustrated and disillusioned at the government's suppression of individual liberties, he committed suicide in 1951. Like Japan's Mishima Yukio, Hedayat later became a cult figure among his country's youth.

Despite the male-oriented nature of Iranian society, many of the country's new writers have been women. Since the 1979 revolution, the veil and the *chador* (CHUH-der *or* CHAH-der), an all-enveloping cloak, have become the central metaphor in Iranian women's writing. Those who favor body covering praise it as the last bastion of defense against Western cultural imperialism, giving Muslim women a private space where they can breathe freely, unpolluted by foreign exploitation and moral corruption. Other Iranian women, however, consider such clothing styles a "mobile prison" and an oppressive anachronism from the Dark Ages. As one writer, Sousan Azadi, expressed it, "As I pulled the *chador* over me, I felt a heaviness descending over me. I was hidden and in hiding. There was nothing visible left of Sousan Azadi. I felt like an animal of the light suddenly trapped in a cave. I was just another faceless Moslem woman carrying a whole inner world hidden inside the *chador*."[10] Whether or not they accept the veil, women writers are a vital part of contemporary Iranian literature, addressing all aspects of social issues.

Like Iran, Egypt in the twentieth century experienced a flowering of literature accelerated by the establishment of the Egyptian republic in the early 1950s. The most illustrious contemporary Egyptian writer was Naguib Mahfouz (nah-GEEB mah-FOOZ) (1911–2006), who won the Nobel Prize for Literature in 1988. His *Cairo Trilogy* (1952) chronicled three generations of a merchant family in Cairo during the tumultuous years between the world wars. Mahfouz was particularly adept at blending panoramic historical events with the intimate lives of ordinary human beings. One of the most popular current writers is Alaa-al-Aswany (ah-LAH al-as-WAH-nee) (b. 1957). In *The Yacoubian Building*, he deplores the problems of political corruption and religious fundamentalism that plagued Egypt under Mubarak's regime.

The emergence of a modern Turkish literature can be traced to the establishment of the republic in 1923. The most popular, as well as prolific, contemporary writer is Orhan Pamuk (OHR-han PAHM-ook) (b. 1952), whose novels attempt to capture Turkey's unique blend of cultures. His novel *Snow* (2002) dramatizes the conflict between secularism and radical Islam in contemporary Turkey.

Although Israeli literature arises from a totally different tradition from that of its neighbors, it shares with them certain contemporary characteristics and a concern for ordinary human beings. Early writers identified with the aspirations of the new nation, trying to find a sense of order in the new reality, voicing terrors from the past and hopes for the future. In recent years, several Israeli writers such as Amoz Oz (b. 1939), A. B. Yehoshua (b. 1936), and David Grossman (b. 1954) have taken controversial positions on sensitive national issues, such as the plight of the Palestinian people, and have thus embroiled themselves in the debate over the future of the state of Israel.

MUSIC AND POLITICS Like literature, the popular music of the contemporary Middle East has been strongly influenced by that of the modern West but to different degrees in different countries. In Israel, many contemporary young rock stars voice lyrics as irreverent toward the traditions of their elders as those of Europe and the United States. One idol of many Israeli young people, the rock star Aviv Geffen (b. 1973), declares himself "a person of no values," and his music carries a shock value that attacks the country's political and social shibboleths. The rock music popular among Palestinians, on the other hand, makes greater use of Arab musical motifs and is closely tied to a political message. One recording, "The Song of the Engineer," lauds Yahya Ayash (1966–1996), a Palestinian accused of manufacturing many of the explosive devices used in terrorist attacks on Israeli citizens. The lyrics have their own shock value: "Spread the flame of revolution. Your explosive will wipe the enemy out, like a volcano, a torch, a banner." As the Arab Spring spread from Tunisia and Egypt throughout the region, many performers were inspired to use their music for openly political purposes. One song, entitled "Come On, Bashar, Leave," became popular as a rallying cry for dissidents in Syria.

CHAPTER SUMMARY

The Middle East is one of the most unstable regions in the world today. This turbulence is due in part to the continued interference of outsiders attracted by the massive oil reserves in the vicinity of the Persian Gulf. Outside interference not only underlined the humiliating weakness of Muslim nations in their relations with the West, but it also served to identify Western policy toward the Middle East with unpopular dictators in the region. The similarities with Africa are striking, as governments in both regions have struggled to achieve regional cooperation among themselves while fending off the influence of powerful foreign states or multinational corporations.

But, as recent events clearly suggest, internal factors are equally if not more important in provoking the chronic turmoil within the region. One divisive issue is the tug-of-war

between the sense of ethnic identity in the form of nationalism and the intense longing to be part of a broader Islamic community, a dream that dates back to the time of the prophet Muhammad. Sometimes, the motive for seeking Arab unity may simply be self-aggrandizement—three such examples are Gamal Abdul Nasser, Muammar Qaddafi, and Saddam Hussein. Today it is Iran's radical ayatollahs who aspire to that position.

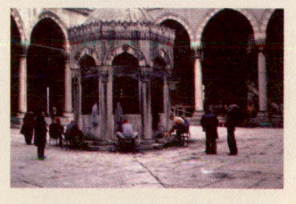

A further reason for the current unrest in the Middle East is the intense debate over the role of religion in civil society. Muslims, of course, are not alone in deploring the sense of moral decline that is perceived to be occurring in societies throughout the world today. And adherents of all faiths sometimes turn to religion as a means of reversing that trend. But in many parts of the Middle East, the effort has taken an especially extremist and violent turn. The fact is that many Muslim societies in the region have yet to come to terms with a world characterized by dramatic social and technological change. The result is the emergence of a deep-seated sense of anger and frustration, especially among the young, that is surging through much of the Islamic world today, a sense of resentment that is directed as much at the region's internal leadership as at allegedly hostile outside forces in the West. Today, the world is reaping the harvest of that bitterness, and the consequences cannot yet be foreseen.

CHAPTER TIMELINE

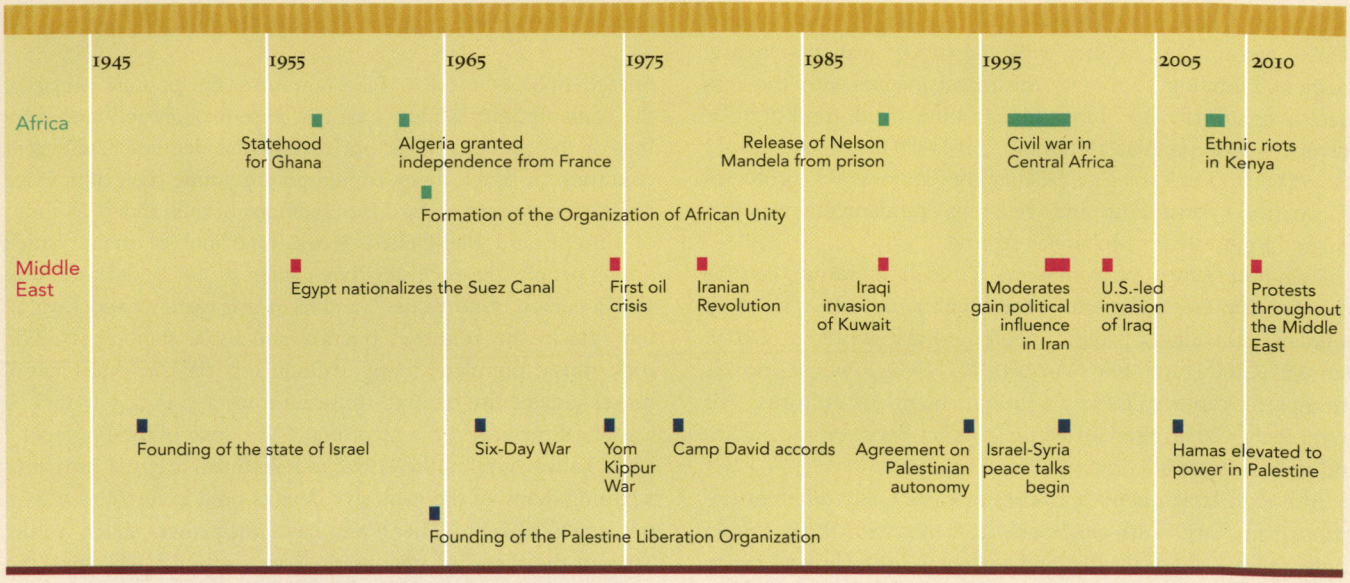

	1945	1955	1965	1975	1985	1995	2005	2010

Africa

Statehood for Ghana

Algeria granted independence from France

Release of Nelson Mandela from prison

Civil war in Central Africa

Ethnic riots in Kenya

Formation of the Organization of African Unity

Middle East

Egypt nationalizes the Suez Canal

First oil crisis

Iranian Revolution

Iraqi invasion of Kuwait

Moderates gain political influence in Iran

U.S.-led invasion of Iraq

Protests throughout the Middle East

Founding of the state of Israel

Six-Day War

Yom Kippur War

Camp David accords

Agreement on Palestinian autonomy

Israel-Syria peace talks begin

Hamas elevated to power in Palestine

Founding of the Palestine Liberation Organization

CHAPTER REVIEW

Upon Reflection

Q What are some of the key reasons advanced to explain why democratic institutions have been slow to take root in the Middle East?

Q Why do tensions between farmers and pastoral peoples appear to be on the rise in Africa today? In what parts of the continent is the problem most serious?

Q What are the main sources of discord in the Middle East today? How do they contribute to the popularity of radical terrorist organizations in the region?

Key Terms

uhuru (p. 862)
apartheid (p. 862)
pan-Africanism (p. 863)
neocolonialism (p. 863)
African Union (p. 871)
pan-Arabism (p. 877)
intifada (p. 882)
Hezbollah (p. 882)

Suggested Reading

AFRICA: GENERAL   For general surveys of contemporary African history, see **P. Nugent**, *Africa Since Independence* (New York, 2004); **M. Meredith**, *The Fate of Africa* (New York, 2005); and **H. French**, *A Continent for the Taking: The Tragedy and Hope of Africa* (New York, 2004).

AFRICAN LITERATURE AND ART   For a survey of African literature, see **A. Kalu, ed.,** *The Rienner Anthology of African Literatures* (London, 2007); **M. J. Hay,** *African Novels in the Classroom* (Boulder, Colo., 2000); and **M. J. Daymond et al., eds.,** *Women Writing Africa: The Southern Region* (New York, 2003). On art, see **S. L. Kasfir,** *Contemporary African Art* (London, 1999).

WOMEN IN AFRICA   For interesting analyses of women's issues in the Africa of this time frame, see **M. Kevane,** *Women and Development in Africa: How Gender Works* (Boulder, Colo., 2004).

RECENT EVENTS IN AFRICA   For contrasting views on the reasons for Africa's current difficulties, see **J. Marah,** *The African People in the Global Village: An Introduction to Pan-African Studies* (Lanham, Md., 1998), and **G. Ayittey,** *Africa in Chaos* (New York, 1998).

THE MIDDLE EAST   A good general survey of the modern Middle East is **A. Goldschmidt, Jr.,** and **L. Davidson,** *A Concise History of the Middle East,* 10th ed. (Boulder, Colo., 2013).

ISRAEL AND PALESTINE   On Israel and the Palestinian question, see **D. Ross,** *The Missing Peace: The Inside Story of the Fight for Middle East Peace* (New York, 2004). On Jerusalem, see **B. Wasserstein,** *Divided Jerusalem: The Struggle for the Holy City* (New Haven, Conn., 2000).

IRAN AND IRAQ   On the Iranian Revolution, see **S. Bakash,** *The Reign of the Ayatollahs* (New York, 1984). Iran's role in Middle Eastern politics and diplomacy is analyzed in **T. Parsi,** *Treacherous Alliance: The Secret Dealings of Israel, Iran, and the United States* (New Haven, Conn., 2007). The Iran-Iraq War is discussed in **S. C. Pelletiere,** *The Iran-Iraq War: Chaos* in a Vacuum (New York, 1992). The issue of oil is examined in **D. Yergin et al.,** *The Prize: The Epic Quest for Oil, Money, and Power* (New York, 1993).

For historical perspective on the invasion of Iraq, see **J. Kendell,** *Iraq's Unruly Century* (New York, 2003). **R. Khalidi,** *Resurrecting Empire: Western Footprints and America's Perilous Path in the Middle East* (Boston, 2003), is a critical look at U.S. policy in the region.

For expert analysis on the background of the situation in the region, see **B. Lewis,** *What Went Wrong? Western Impact and Middle Eastern Response* (Oxford, 2001), and **P. L. Bergen,** *Holy War, Inc.: Inside the Secret World of Osama bin Laden* (New York, 2001). Also see **M. Afkhami** and **E. Friedl,** *In the Eye of the Storm: Women in Post-Revolutionary Iran* (Syracuse, N.Y., 1994).

MIDDLE EASTERN LITERATURE   For a scholarly but accessible overview of Arabic literature, see **M. M. Badawi,** *A Short History of Modern Arab Literature* (Oxford, 1993).

Chapter Notes

1. See the report in *The New York Times*, January 24, 2013.
2. According to a report issued by the United Nations, life expectancy in Africa dropped dramatically in the first years of the new millennium because of the prevalence of AIDS. See C. W. Dugger, "Devastated by AIDS, Africa Sees Life Expectancy Plunge," in *The New York Times*, July 16, 2004.
3. Cited in M. Meredith, *The Fate of Africa* (New York, 2004), p. 168.
4. A. Nicol, *"A Truly Married Woman" and Other Stories* (London, 1965), p. 12.
5. A. Ata Aidoo, *No Sweetness Here* (New York, 1995), p. 136.
6. G. Médioni, "Stand Up, Africa!" *World Press Review*, July 2002, p. 34.
7. Ngugi Wa Thiong'o, *Decolonising the Mind: The Politics of Language in African Literature* (Portsmouth, N.H., 1986), p. 103.
8. Quoted in R. R. Andersen, R. F. Seibert, and J. G. Wagner, *Politics and Change in the Middle East: Sources of Conflict and Accommodation*, 4th ed. (Englewood Cliffs, N.J., 1982), p. 51.
9. S. Sachs, "Assad Looks at Syria's Economy in Inaugural Talk," *New York Times*, July 18, 2000.
10. S. Azadi, with A. Ferrante, *Out of Iran* (London, 1987), p. 223.

MindTap is a fully online, highly personalized learning experience built upon Cengage Learning content. MindTap combines student learning tools—readings, multimedia, activities, and assessments—into a singular Learning Path that guides students through their course.

Toward the Pacific Century?

The Petronas Towers in Kuala Lumpur, Malaysia

Buena Vista Images/The Image Bank/Getty Images

CHAPTER OUTLINE AND FOCUS QUESTIONS

South Asia

Q How did Gandhi's and Nehru's goals for India differ, and what role has each leader's views played in shaping modern India?

Southeast Asia

Q What kinds of problems have the nations of Southeast Asia faced since 1945, and how have they attempted to solve them?

Japan: Asian Giant

Q How did the Allied occupation after World War II change Japan's political and economic institutions, and what remained unchanged?

The Little Tigers

Q What factors have contributed to the economic success achieved by the Little Tigers? To what degree have they applied the Japanese model in forging their developmental strategies?

CRITICAL THINKING

Q What differences and similarities do you see in the performances of the nations of South, Southeast, and East Asia since World War II? What do you think accounts for the differences?

CONNECTIONS TO TODAY

Q What lessons do you think the so-called "Little Tigers" can provide for other nations seeking a path toward economic development and prosperity? Can such lessons be followed in other parts of the world?

FIRST-TIME VISITORS to the Malaysian capital of Kuala Lumpur (KWAH-luh loom-POOR) are astonished to see a pair of twin towers thrusting up above the surrounding buildings into the clouds. The Petronas Towers rise 1,483 feet from ground level; they were the world's tallest buildings at the time of their completion in 1998. (They have since been surpassed by other structures such as Burj Khalifa, in Dubai, and Taipei 101, in Taiwan.)

Beyond their status as an architectural achievement, the Petronas Towers announced the emergence of Southeast Asia as a major player on the international scene. It is no accident that the foundations were laid on the site of the Selangor Cricket Club, symbol of British colonial hegemony in Southeast Asia. "These towers," commented one local official, "will do wonders for Asia's self-esteem and confidence, which I think is very important, and which I think at this moment are at the point of takeoff."[1]

The sky-piercing towers in Kuala Lumpur and Taipei (TY-PAY) are not alone in signaling Asia's new prominence on the world stage in the century now unfolding. Several other cities in the region, including

Hong Kong, Singapore, Tokyo, and Shanghai, have become major capitals of finance and monuments of economic prowess, rivaling the traditional centers of New York, London, Berlin, and Paris.

That the nations of the Pacific Rim would become a driving force in global development was all but unimaginable after World War II, when the Communist triumph in China ushered in an era of intense competition between the capitalist and socialist camps. Bitter conflicts in Korea and Vietnam were visible manifestations of a region in turmoil. Yet today, many of the nations of eastern Asia have become models of successful nation building, characterized by economic prosperity and political stability. They have heralded the opening of what has been called the "Pacific Century." ⬅

South Asia

 FOCUS QUESTION: How did Gandhi's and Nehru's goals for India differ, and what role has each leader's views played in shaping modern India?

In 1947, nearly two centuries of British colonial rule came to an end when two new independent nations, India and Pakistan, came into being. Under British authority, the subcontinent of South Asia had been linked ever more closely to the global capitalist economy. Yet, as in other areas of Asia and in Africa, the experience brought only limited benefits to the local peoples; little industrial development took place, and the bulk of the profits went into the pockets of Western entrepreneurs. Nationalist forces had been seeking reforms in colonial policy and the eventual overthrow of colonial power for at least half a century but the peoples of South Asia did not attain their independence until after World War II.

The End of the British Raj

During the 1930s, the nationalist movement in India was severely shaken by factional disagreements between Hindus and Muslims. The outbreak of World War II subdued these sectarian clashes but they erupted again after the war ended in 1945. Battles between Hindus and Muslims broke out in several cities, and Muhammad Ali Jinnah (muh-HAM-ad ah-LEE JIN-uh) (1876–1948), leader of the Muslim League, demanded the creation of a separate state for each ethnic group. Meanwhile, the Labour Party, which had long been critical of British colonial policies on both moral and economic grounds, had come to power in Great Britain, and the new prime minister, Clement Attlee, announced that governing authority would be transferred to "responsible Indian hands" by June 1948.

But the imminence of independence had no effect on communal strife. As riots escalated, the British reluctantly accepted the inevitability of partition and declared that on August 15, 1947, two independent nations—primarily Hindu India and Muslim Pakistan—would be established. Pakistan would consist of the main area of Muslim habitation in the Indus River valley in the west and a separate territory in eastern Bengal, 2,000 miles to the east. Although Mahatma Gandhi warned that partition would provoke "an orgy of blood,"[2] he was by now regarded as a figure of the past, and his views were ignored.

The British instructed the rulers in the princely states to choose which nation they would join by August 15 but problems arose in predominantly Hindu Hyderabad (HY-der-uh-bahd), where the governor was a Muslim, and in the mountainous province of Jammu (JUHM-oo) and Kashmir (KAZH-meer), usually referred to simply as Kashmir, where a Hindu prince ruled over a Muslim population. After independence was declared, the flight of millions of Hindus and Muslims across the borders led to violence and the deaths of more than a million people. One of the casualties was Gandhi, who was assassinated on January 30, 1948, on his way to morning prayer (see the Film & History feature "Gandhi (1982)" on p. 898). The assassin, a Hindu militant, was apparently motivated by Gandhi's opposition to a strictly Hindu India.

Independent India

Upon independence, the Indian National Congress, now renamed the Congress Party, assumed governing responsibility under Jawaharlal Nehru (juh-WAH-hur-lahl NAY-roo), the new prime minister. The prospect must have been intimidating. The vast majority of India's 400 million people were poor and illiterate. The new nation encompassed a large number of ethnic groups and fourteen major languages. Although Congress leaders spoke bravely of building a new nation, Indian society still bore the scars of past wars and divisions.

The government's first problem was to resolve disputes left over from the transition period. The rulers of Hyderabad and Kashmir had both followed their own preferences rather than the wishes of their subject populations. Nehru was determined to include both states within India. In 1948, Indian troops invaded Hyderabad and annexed the area. India also seized most of Kashmir but at the cost of creating an intractable problem that has poisoned relations with Pakistan to the present day.

AN EXPERIMENT IN DEMOCRATIC SOCIALISM Under Nehru's leadership, India adopted a political system on the British model, with a figurehead president and a parliamentary form of government. A number of political parties operated legally but the Congress Party, with its enormous prestige and charismatic leadership, was dominant at both the central and local levels.

Nehru had been influenced by British socialism and patterned his economic policy roughly after the program of the

Gandhi (1982)

To many of his contemporaries, Mohandas Gandhi—usually referred to as the Mahatma, or "Great Soul"—was the conscience of India. Son of a senior Indian official from the state of Gujarat and trained as a lawyer at University College in London, Gandhi first dealt with racial discrimination when he sought to provide legal assistance to Indian laborers living under the apartheid regime in South Africa. On his return to India in 1915, he rapidly emerged as a fierce critic of British colonial rule over his country. His message of *satyagraha* ("hold fast to the truth"), embodying the idea of a steadfast but nonviolent resistance to the injustice and inhumanity inherent in the colonial enterprise, inspired millions of his compatriots in their long struggle for national independence. It also earned the admiration and praise of sympathetic observers around the world. His death by assassination at the hands of a Hindu fanatic in 1948 shocked the world.

Time, however, has somewhat dimmed his message. Gandhi's vision of a future India was symbolized by the spinning wheel—he rejected the industrial age and material pursuits in favor of the simple pleasures of the traditional Indian village. Since achieving independence, however, India has followed the path of national wealth and power laid out by Gandhi's friend and colleague Jawaharlal Nehru. Gandhi's appeal for religious tolerance and mutual respect at home rapidly gave way to a bloody conflict between Hindus and Muslims that has not yet been eradicated in our own day. On the global stage, his vision of world peace and brotherly love has similarly been ignored, first during the Cold War and more recently during the "clash of civilizations" between Western countries and the forces of militant Islam.

It was at least partly in an effort to revive and perpetuate the message of the Mahatma that in 1982 the British filmmaker Richard Attenborough directed the film *Gandhi*. Epic in its length and scope, the film seeks to present a faithful rendition of the life of its subject, from his introduction to apartheid in South Africa at the turn of the century to his tragic death after World War II. Actor Ben Kingsley, son of an Indian father and an English mother, plays the title role with intensity and conviction. The film was widely praised and earned eight Academy Awards. Kingsley received an Oscar in the Best Actor category.

Columbia Pictures/Everett Collection

Jawaharlal Nehru (Roshan Seth), Mahatma Gandhi (Ben Kingsley), and Muhammad Ali Jinnah (Alyque Padamsee) confer before the partition of India into Hindu and Muslim states.

British Labour Party. The state took over ownership of the major industries and resources, transportation, and utilities, while private enterprise was permitted at the local and retail levels. Farmland remained in private hands but rural cooperatives were officially encouraged. The government also sought to avoid excessive dependence on foreign investment and technological assistance. All businesses were required by law to have majority Indian ownership.

In other respects, Nehru was a devotee of Western materialism. He was convinced that to succeed, India must industrialize. In advocating industrialization, Nehru departed sharply from Gandhi, who believed that materialism was morally corrupting and that only simplicity and nonviolence (as represented by the traditional Indian village and the symbolic spinning wheel) could save India, and the world itself, from self-destruction (see Opposing Viewpoints "Two Visions for India" on p. 899).

The primary themes of Nehru's foreign policy were anticolonialism and antiracism. Under his guidance, India took a neutral stance in the Cold War and sought to provide leadership to all newly independent nations in Asia, Africa, and Latin America. India's neutrality put it at odds with the United States, which during the 1950s was trying to mobilize all nations against what it viewed as the menace of international communism. Relations with Pakistan also continued to be troubled. Nehru refused to consider Pakistan's claim to Kashmir, even though the majority of the population there were Muslims. Tension between the two countries persisted, erupting into war in 1965. In 1971, when riots against the Pakistani government broke out in East Pakistan, India intervened on the side

OPPOSING ⚔ VIEWPOINTS

Two Visions for India

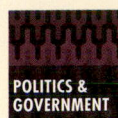

POLITICS & GOVERNMENT

ALTHOUGH JAWAHARLAL NEHRU AND MOHANDAS "MAHATMA" GANDHI agreed on their desire for an independent India, their visions of the future of their homeland were dramatically different. Nehru favored industrialization to build material prosperity, whereas Gandhi praised the simple virtues of manual labor. The first selection is from a speech by Nehru; the second is from a letter written by Gandhi to Nehru.

Nehru's Socialist Creed

I am convinced that the only key to the solution of the world's problems and of India's problems lies in socialism, and when I use this word I do so not in a vague humanitarian way but in the scientific economic sense.... I see no way of ending the poverty, the vast unemployment, the degradation and the subjection of the Indian people except through socialism. That involves vast and revolutionary changes in our political and social structure, the ending of vested interests in land and industry, as well as the feudal and autocratic Indian states system.

That means the ending of private property, except in a restricted sense, and the replacement of the present profit system by a higher ideal of cooperative service.... In short, it means a new civilization, radically different from the present capitalist order. Some glimpse we can have of this new civilization in the territories of the USSR. Much has happened there which has pained me greatly and with which I disagree, but I look upon that great and fascinating unfolding of a new order and a new civilization as the most promising feature of our dismal age.

Mohandas Gandhi, A Letter to Jawaharlal Nehru

I believe that if India, and through India the world, is to achieve real freedom, then sooner or later we shall have to go and live in the villages—in huts, not in palaces. Millions of people can never live in cities and palaces in comfort and peace. Nor can they do so by killing one another, that is, by resorting to violence and untruth.... We can have the vision of ... truth and nonviolence only in the simplicity of the villages. That simplicity resides in the spinning wheel and what is implied by the spinning wheel....

You will not be able to understand me if you think that I am talking about the villages of today. My ideal village still exists only in my imagination.... In this village of my dreams

the villager will not be dull—he will be all awareness. He will not live like an animal in filth and darkness. Men and women will live in freedom, prepared to face the whole world. There will be no plague, no cholera, and no smallpox. Nobody will be allowed to be idle or to wallow in luxury. Everyone will have to do body labor. Granting all this, I can still envisage a number of things that will have to be organized on a large scale. Perhaps there will even be railways and also post and telegraph offices. I do not know what things there will be or will not be. Nor am I bothered about it. If I can make sure of the essential thing, other things will follow in due course. But if I give up the essential thing, I give up everything.

 What are the key differences between these two views on the future of India? Why do you think Nehru's proposals triumphed over Gandhi's?

Sources: From *Sources of Indian Tradition*, Vol. 2, 2e by Stephen Hay, pp. 317–319. Copyright © 1988 by Columbia University Press, New York. From Gandhi "Letter to Jawaharlal Nehru" pp. 328–331 from *Gandhi in India: In His Own Words*, Martin Green, ed. Copyright © 1987 by Navajivan Trust. Lebanon, NH: University Press of New England.

---

of East Pakistan, which declared its independence as the new nation of Bangladesh (see Map 30.1 on p. 900).

THE POST-NEHRU ERA Nehru's death in 1964 aroused concern that Indian democracy was dependent on the Nehru mystique. When his successor, a Congress Party veteran, died in 1966, Congress leaders selected Nehru's daughter, Indira Gandhi (in-DEER-uh GAHN-dee) (1917–1984)—no relation to Mahatma Gandhi—as the new prime minister. Gandhi was inexperienced in politics but she quickly showed the steely determination of her father.

Like Nehru, Gandhi embraced democratic socialism and a policy of neutrality in foreign affairs but she was more activist in promoting her objectives than her father. To combat

rural poverty, she nationalized banks, provided loans to peasants on easy terms, built low-cost housing, distributed land to the landless, and introduced electoral reforms to enfranchise the poor. To control India's growing population she adopted a policy of enforced sterilization. This policy proved unpopular, however, and combined with growing official corruption and Gandhi's authoritarian tactics, it led to her defeat in the general election of 1975, the first time the Congress Party had failed to win a majority at the national level.

A minority government composed of procapitalist parties was formed but it was ineffective, and within two years Indira Gandhi was back in power. She now faced a new challenge, however, in the state of Punjab (pun-JAHB), located in the

MAP 30.1 Modern South Asia. This map shows the boundaries of all the states in contemporary South Asia.

 Which of the countries on this map have a Muslim majority?

© 2016 Cengage Learning

⁂ **CHRONOLOGY**   South Asia Since 1945

India and Pakistan become independent	1947
Assassination of Mahatma Gandhi	1948
Death of Jawaharlal Nehru	1964
Indo-Pakistani War	1965
Indira Gandhi elected prime minister	1966
Bangladesh declares its independence	1971
Assassination of Indira Gandhi	1984
Assassination of Rajiv Gandhi	1991
Military coup overthrows civilian government in Pakistan	1999
U.S.-led forces oust Taliban in Afghanistan	2001
Congress Party returns to power in India	2004
Assassination of Benazir Bhutto in Pakistan	2007
Terrorist attack in Mumbai	2008
Massive floods in the Indus River valley	2010
Osama bin Laden killed in Pakistan	2011

During the early 1990s, Congress remained the leading party but the powerful hold it had once had on the Indian electorate had evaporated. New parties, such as the militantly Hindu Bharatiya Janata (BAR-ruh-tee-uh JAH-nuh-tuh) Party (BJP), actively vied with Congress for control of the central and state governments. Competition between the two parties was accompanied by rising tensions between Hindus and Muslims. When a coalition government formed under Congress leadership collapsed, the BJP, under Prime Minister A. B. Vajpayee (VAHJ-py-ee) (b. 1924), ascended to power and played on Hindu sensibilities to build its political base. It also adopted an aggressive program of privatization in the industrial and commercial sectors and made a major effort to promote the nation's small but growing technological base.

But BJP leaders had underestimated the discontent of India's poorer citizens (an estimated 350 million Indians earned less than one U.S. dollar a day), and in the spring of 2004, a stunning defeat in national elections forced the Vajpayee government to resign. The Congress Party returned to power at the head of a coalition government based on a commitment to maintain economic growth while carrying out reforms in rural areas. But sectarian strife between Hindus and Muslims, as well as pervasive official corruption, continued to bedevil the government. In the fall of 2008, a terrorist attack in the city of Mumbai (MUM-bye) left nearly 200 dead and raised serious questions about the effectiveness of Indian security procedures. Indian officials charged that the inspiration for the attack came from Pakistan. The Congress Party remained in power after 2009 but economic stagnation and widespread corruption continued to erode its popularity. In national elections held in the spring of 2014, the BJP was returned to power.

The Land of the Pure: Pakistan Since Independence

When Pakistan achieved independence in August 1947, it was, unlike its neighbor India, in all respects a new nation,

border region between India and Pakistan, where militant Sikhs (SEEKS *or* SEE-ikhz) demanded autonomy or even independence from India. Gandhi did not shrink from a confrontation and attacked Sikh rebels hiding in their Golden Temple in the city of Amritsar (uhm-RIT-ser). The incident aroused widespread anger among the Sikh community, and in 1984, Sikh members of Gandhi's personal bodyguard assassinated her.

By now, Congress politicians were convinced that the party could not remain in power without a member of the Nehru family at the helm. Gandhi's son Rajiv Gandhi (rah-JEEV GAHN-dee) (1944–1991), a commercial airline pilot with little interest in politics, was persuaded to replace his mother as prime minister. Rajiv lacked the strong ideological and political convictions of his mother and grandfather and allowed a greater role for private enterprise. But his government was criticized for cronyism, inefficiency, and corruption, as well as insensitivity to the poor.

Rajiv Gandhi also sought to play a role in regional affairs, mediating a dispute between the government in Sri Lanka and Tamil rebels (known as the Elam Tigers) who were ethnically related to the majority population in southern India. The decision cost him his life: while campaigning for reelection in 1991, he was assassinated by a member of the Tiger organization. India faced the future without a member of the Nehru family as prime minister.

based on religious conviction rather than historical or ethnic tradition. The unique state consisted of two separate territories 2,000 miles apart. West Pakistan, including the Indus River basin and the West Punjab, was perennially short of water and was populated by dry crop farmers and peoples of the steppe. East Pakistan was made up of the marshy deltas of the Ganges and Brahmaputra Rivers. Densely populated with rice farmers, it was the home of the artistic and intellectual Bengalis (ben-GAH-leez).

The peoples of West Pakistan were especially diverse and included, among others, Pushtuns, Baluchis (buh-LOO-cheez), and Punjabis (pun-JAHB-eez). The Pushtuns are organized on a tribal basis and have kinship ties with the majority population across the border in neighboring Afghanistan. Many are nomadic and cross the border on a regular basis with their flocks. The Baluchis straddle the border with Iran, while the region of Punjab was divided between Pakistan and India at the moment of independence.

Even though the new state was an essentially Muslim society, its first years were marked by intense internal conflicts over religious, linguistic, and regional issues. Muhammad Ali Jinnah's vision of a democratic state that would assure freedom of religion and equal treatment for all was opposed by those who advocated a state based on Islamic principles. Even more dangerous was the division between east and west. Many in East Pakistan felt that the new country's leaders, most of whom were from the west, ignored their needs, a sentiment strengthened by the government's decision to adopt Urdu, a language derived from Hindi and used by Muslims in northern India, as the national language of the entire country. Most East Pakistanis spoke Bengali, an unrelated language. As tensions rose, in March 1971 East Pakistan declared its independence as the new nation of Bangladesh. Pakistani troops attempted to restore central government authority in the new capital of Dhaka (DAK-uh *or* DAH-kuh), but rebel forces supported by India went on the offensive, and the government bowed to the inevitable and recognized independent Bangladesh.

The breakup of the union between East and West Pakistan undermined the fragile authority of the military regime that had ruled Pakistan since 1958 and led to its replacement by a civilian government under Zulfikar Ali Bhutto (ZOOL-fee-kahr ah-LEE BOO-toh) (1928–1979). But now religious tensions came to the fore, despite a new constitution that made a number of key concessions to conservative Muslims. In 1977, a new military government under General Zia Ul Ha'q (ZEE-ah ool HAHK) (1924–1988) came to power with a commitment to make Pakistan a true Islamic state. *Shari'a* became the basis for social behavior as well as for the legal system. Laws governing the consumption of alcohol and the role of women were tightened in accordance with strict Muslim beliefs. But after Zia was killed in a plane crash, Pakistanis elected Benazir Bhutto (ben-uh-ZEER BOO-toh) (1953–2007), the daughter of Zulfikar Ali Bhutto and a supporter of secularism who had been educated in the United States. Removed from power by the military on charges of incompetence and corruption, she was reelected in 1993, only to be dismissed once again in 1997. Her successor soon came under fire for the

same reason and in 1999 was ousted by a military coup led by General Pervaiz Musharraf (pur-VEZ moo-SHAHR-uf) (b. 1943), who promised to restore political stability and honest government.

In September 2001, Pakistan became the focus of international attention when a coalition of forces occupied Afghanistan to overthrow the Taliban regime and destroy the al-Qaeda terrorist network. Despite considerable support for the Taliban among the local population, President Musharraf pledged to help bring the terrorists to justice while returning his country to the secular principles espoused by Muhammad Ali Jinnah. By then, however, problems had begun to escalate on the domestic front. As Musharraf sought to fend off challenges from radical Muslim groups—some of them allied with Taliban forces in neighboring Afghanistan—secular opposition figures criticized the authoritarian nature of his regime. When Benazir Bhutto returned from exile to present herself as a candidate in presidential elections to be held early in 2008, she was assassinated, leading to widespread suspicions of official involvement. In September 2008, amid growing political turmoil, Benazir Bhutto's widower, Asif Ali Zardari (AH-seef ah-LEE zahr-DAR-ree) (b. 1955), was elected president of Pakistan. In September 2013, he was replaced by a democratically elected successor.

Whoever holds the reins of power in Pakistan faces a number of crucial challenges in coping with the multitude of problems affecting the country today. Half of the entire population of 150 million live in poverty, and illiteracy is widespread. Massive flooding of the Indus River in 2010 killed nearly 2,000 people and left millions homeless. Plagued by the inability to resolve the Kashmir dispute, relations with powerful neighbor India are fragile, while chronic disputes among the various ethnic groups undermine the search for political stability.

In a nation where much of the rural population still professes loyalty to traditional tribal leaders, the sense of nationalism remains fragile, while military elites, who have long played a central role in Pakistani politics, continue to press their own agenda. Sympathy with the Taliban remains strong in some quarters, especially along the border with Afghanistan. The internal divisions within the country's ruling class became painfully apparent when the al-Qaeda leader Osama bin Laden was killed in a U.S. raid on his compound in the spring of 2011. The terrorist leader had been living secretly in a villa in the military town of Abbottabad, within two hours' drive of the national capital of Islamabad. Many observers suspected that elements within the Pakistan military were aware of his presence there (see the box "I Accuse!" on p. 878 in Chapter 29).

Poverty and Pluralism in South Asia

The leaders of the new states that emerged in South Asia after World War II faced a number of problems. The peoples of the region were still overwhelmingly poor and illiterate, and the sectarian, ethnic, and cultural divisions that had plagued Indian society for centuries had not dissipated.

THE POLITICS OF COMMUNALISM Perhaps the most sincere effort to create democratic institutions was in India, where the new constitution called for social justice, liberty, equality of status and opportunity, and brotherhood. All citizens were guaranteed protection from discrimination on the grounds of religious belief, race, caste, sex, or place of birth. The Congress Party sought to avoid being identified as a party exclusively for the Hindu majority by including prominent non-Hindus among its leaders and favoring measures to protect minority groups such as Sikhs and Muslims from discrimination.

In reality, a number of distinctive characteristics made it difficult for the new India to live up to its promises, for beneath the surface lay age-old ethnic, linguistic, and religious divisions. Because of India's vast size and complex history, no national language had ever emerged. Hindi was the most prevalent but it was the native language of less than one-third of the population. During the colonial period, English had served as the official language of government, and many non-Hindi speakers suggested making it the official language. But English was spoken only by the educated elite, and it represented an affront to national pride. Eventually, India recognized fourteen official tongues, making the parliament sometimes sound like the proverbial Tower of Babel.

Jawaharlal Nehru had managed to finesse the issue by applying his prestige and adept maneuvering but problems surfaced after his death, when anger at widespread corruption and the party's failure to keep its promises grew. Only the lack of appeal of its rivals and the Nehru family charisma carried on by his daughter Indira Gandhi kept the party in power. But she was unable to prevent the progressive disintegration of the party's power base at the state level, where regional or ideological parties won the allegiance of voters by exploiting ethnic or social revolutionary themes.

During the 1980s, religious tensions began to intensify. The first signs appeared when Indira Gandhi's uncompromising approach to Sikh separatism led to her assassination in 1984. Under her son Rajiv, tensions began to surface in Hindu-Muslim relations when Hindu militants at Ayodhya (ah-YOHD-yuh), a city in northern India, demanded the destruction of a mosque built on the traditional site of King Rama's birthplace, where a Hindu temple had previously existed. When Hindu demonstrators destroyed the mosque and erected a temporary temple at the site, clashes broke out between Hindus and Muslims throughout the country. In protest, rioters in neighboring Pakistan destroyed a number of Hindu shrines in that country. In 2010, an Indian court ordered that the land that had contained the mosque be divided between the Hindu and Muslim plaintiffs.

In the early years of the new century, communal divisions intensified as militant Hindu groups demanded a state that would cater to the Hindu majority, now numbering more than 700 million people. Some textbooks were rewritten to reflect a more Hindu-oriented version of history, including the contention that the Indus Valley civilization was founded by Aryan peoples, the Hindus' ancestors (see Chapter 2). In the eastern state of Orissa, pitched battles broke out between Hindus and Christians over efforts by the latter to win converts to their faith. As the fragile consensus over India's multireligious secular traditions began to unravel, Prime Minister Manmohan Singh (MUHN-moh-hahn SING) (b. 1932) lamented what he called the dangerous assault on India's "composite culture."[3]

ECONOMIC DIFFICULTIES When India became independent in 1947, much of the population of the subcontinent was afflicted with the familiar problems of illiteracy, ill health, and widespread poverty. Nehru's answer was socialism. He instituted a series of five-year plans, which led to the creation of a relatively large and reasonably efficient state-run manufacturing sector, centered on steel, motor vehicles, and textiles. Industrial production almost tripled between 1950 and 1965, and per capita income rose by 50 percent between 1950 and 1980, although it was still less than $300 (in U.S. dollars). By the 1970s, however, industrial growth had slowed. The lack of modern infrastructure was a problem, as was the rising price of oil, most of which had to be imported. The relatively weak performance of the state-owned sector, which grew at an annual rate of only about 2 percent in the 1950s and 1960s, versus 5 percent for the private sector, also became a serious obstacle.

India's major economic weakness, however, was in agriculture. At independence, mechanization was almost unknown, fertilizer was rarely used, and most farms were small and uneconomical because of the Hindu tradition of dividing the land equally among all male children. As a result, the vast majority of the Indian people lived in conditions of abject poverty. Landless laborers outnumbered landowners by almost two to one. The government attempted to relieve the problem by redistributing land to the poor, limiting the size of landholdings, and encouraging farmers to form voluntary cooperatives. But all three programs ran into widespread opposition and apathy.

Another problem was overpopulation. Even before independence, the country had had difficulty supporting its people. In the 1950s and 1960s, the population grew by more than 2 percent annually, twice the nineteenth-century rate, and straining the capacity of the new country to feed itself. Beginning in the 1960s, the Indian government sought to curb population growth. Indira Gandhi instituted a program combining monetary rewards and compulsory sterilization. Males who had fathered too many children were sometimes forced to undergo a vasectomy. Popular resistance undermined the program, however, and the goals were scaled back in the 1970s.

There have been some signs of progress in recent years. The so-called **green revolution**—involving the introduction of more productive, disease-resistant strains of rice and wheat—doubled grain production between 1960 and 1980, although it also led to an increase in rural inequality, since only wealthier farmers were able to purchase the necessary fertilizer. In addition, as a result of media popularization and better government programs, the trend today is toward smaller families. The average number of children a woman bears has been reduced from six in 1950 to three today. As has occurred elsewhere, the decline in family size began among the educated and is gradually spreading throughout Indian society. Still, India now contains well over one billion people and is on target to become the most populous nation in the world, surpassing China, by the year 2025.

After the death of Indira Gandhi in 1984, her son Rajiv proved more receptive to foreign investment and a greater role for the private sector in the economy. India began to export more manufactured goods, including computer software. The pace of change has accelerated under Rajiv Gandhi's successors, who have continued to transfer state-run industries to private hands. These policies have stimulated the growth of a prosperous new middle class, now estimated at more than 100 million. Consumerism has soared, and sales of television sets, DVD players, cellphones, and automobiles have increased dramatically. Equally important, Western imports are being replaced by new products manufactured in India with Indian brand names.

One consequence of India's entrance into the industrial age is the emergence of a small but vibrant technological sector that provides many important services to the world's advanced nations. The city of Bangalore in southern India has become an important technological center, benefiting from low wages and the presence of skilled labor with proficiency in the English language.

Nevertheless, Nehru's dream of a socialist society remains strong. State-owned enterprises still produce about half of all domestic goods, and high tariffs continue to stifle imports. Nationalist parties have played on the widespread fear of foreign economic influence to make it difficult for large multinational corporations, such as the retail giant Walmart, to break into the Indian market. A combination of religious and environmental groups attempted unsuccessfully to prevent Kentucky Fried Chicken from establishing outlets in major Indian cities (see the box "Say No to McDonald's and KFC!" on p. 904). Today, many of the most prominent international fast-food chains have established a foothold in India's major cities, although they are less common in smaller towns and rural areas.

As in the industrialized countries of the West, economic growth has been accompanied by environmental damage. Water and air pollution has led to illness and death for many people, and according to a recent report, almost half of the nation's water supply is contaminated with toxic bacteria. Some critics, reflecting the traditional anti-imperialist attitude of Indian intellectuals, blame Western capitalist corporations for the problem, as in the highly publicized case of leakage from a foreign-owned chemical plant at Bhopal (boh-PAHL). Much of the problem, however, comes from state-owned factories erected with Soviet aid. And not all the environmental damage can be ascribed to industrialization. The Ganges River is so polluted by human overuse that it is risky for Hindu believers to bathe in it (see the Comparative Essay "One World, One Environment" on p. 913).

Moreover, many Indians have not benefited from the new prosperity. Nearly one-third of the population lives below the national poverty line. Millions continue to live in urban slums, such as the famous "City of Joy" in Kolkata (Calcutta), and most farm families remain desperately poor. Despite the socialist rhetoric of India's leaders, the inequality of wealth in India is as pronounced as it is in capitalist nations in the West. Indeed, India has been described as two nations: an educated urban India of 100 million people surrounded by more than nine times that many impoverished peasants in the countryside (see the Comparative Illustration "Two Indias" on p. 905).

The enormous gap between India's rich and poor is reflected in the educational system. For the children of affluent families, parental pressure to obtain a college degree is often intense, and many students devote long hours to studying for examinations to gain entrance to the country's many institutes of higher learning. Yet only about 12 percent of India's nearly 200 million students are in college, one of the lowest ratios in the world, and illiteracy, especially in rural areas, is widespread.

Such problems are even more serious in neighboring Pakistan and Bangladesh. The overwhelming majority of Pakistan's citizens are poor, and at least half are illiterate. The recent flooding along the Indus River has had a devastating effect on people living in the region and was described by a United Nations official as the worst humanitarian crisis in the sixty-five years of the UN's existence. Prospects for the future are not bright, for Pakistan lacks a modern technological sector to serve as a magnet for the emergence of a modern middle class.

CASTE, CLASS, AND GENDER Drawing generalizations about the life of the average Indian is difficult because of ethnic, religious, and caste differences, which are compounded by the vast gulf between town and country.

Although the constitution of 1950 guaranteed equal treatment and opportunity for all, regardless of class and caste, and prohibited discrimination based on untouchability, prejudice is hard to eliminate. Untouchability persists, particularly in the villages, where *harijans* (HAR-ih-jans), now called *dalits* (DAH-lits), still perform menial tasks and are often denied fundamental human rights.

In general, urban Indians appear less conscious of caste distinctions. Material wealth rather than caste identity is increasingly defining status. Still, color consciousness based on the age-old distinctions between upper-class and lower-class Indians remains strong. Class-conscious Hindus still express a distinct preference for light-skinned marital partners, and it is normal for the prospective bride and groom to consult with their parents before deciding whether to go through with a marriage.

Marriage between individuals of different religious persuasions can be an even more sensitive issue. Although in many parts of India Hindus and Muslims live side by side in harmony, tensions between the two communities have been rising in recent years as a result of events taking place on the national and international scene. As a result, marriage between individuals of the two faiths continues

Say No to McDonald's and KFC!

INTERACTION & EXCHANGE

ONE OF THE CONSEQUENCES of Rajiv Gandhi's decision to deregulate the Indian economy has been an increase in the presence of foreign corporations, including U.S. fast-food restaurant chains. Their arrival set off a storm of protest in India: from environmentalists concerned that raising grain for chickens is an inefficient use of land, from religious activists angry at the killing of animals for food, and from nationalists anxious to protect the domestic market from foreign competition. Fast-food restaurants now represent a growing niche in Indian society but most cater to local tastes, avoiding beef products and offering many vegetarian dishes, such as the Veg Pizza McPuff. This piece, which appeared in the *Hindustan Times*, was written by Maneka Gandhi, a daughter-in-law of Indira Gandhi and a onetime minister of the environment who has emerged as a prominent rival of Congress Party president Sonia Gandhi.

Fast Food, Indian Style. Some of the popular international fast-food chains like McDonald's and Kentucky Fried Chicken have begun to make their appearance in large Indian cities like Mumbai and New Delhi, despite the criticism by some observers that they would encourage bad health habits and hurt local restaurants. Their familiar logos are rarely seen in smaller towns and in rural areas, however, where many Indians cannot afford their prices or prefer to eat at roadside stalls serving a variety of tasty local dishes, as this small restaurant in Goa attests.

© Yvonne V. Duiker

Why India Doesn't Need Fast Food

India's decision to allow Pepsi Foods Ltd. to open 60 restaurants in India—30 each of Pizza Hut and Kentucky Fried Chicken—marks the first entry of multinational, meat-based junk-food chains into India. If this is allowed to happen, at least a dozen other similar chains will very quickly arrive, including the infamous McDonald's.

The implications of allowing junk-food chains into India are quite stark. As the name denotes, the foods served at Kentucky Fried Chicken (KFC) are chicken-based and fried. This is the worst combination possible for the body and can create a host of health problems, including obesity, high cholesterol, heart ailments, and many kinds of cancer. Pizza Hut products are a combination of white flour, cheese, and meat—again, a combination likely to cause disease....

Then there is the issue of the environmental impact of junk-food chains. Modern meat production involves misuse of crops, water, energy, and grazing areas. In addition, animal agriculture produces surprisingly large amounts of air and water pollution.

KFC and Pizza Hut insist that their chickens be fed corn and soybeans. Consider the diversion of grain for this purpose. As the outlets of KFC and Pizza Hut increase in number, the poultry industry will buy up more and more corn to feed the chickens, which means that the corn will quickly disappear from the villages, and its increased price will place it out of reach for the common man. Turning corn into junk chicken is like turning gold into mud....

It is already shameful that, in a country plagued by famine and flood, we divert 37 percent of our arable land to growing animal fodder. Were all of that grain to be consumed directly by humans, it would nourish five times as many people as it does after being converted into meat, milk, and eggs....

Of course, it is not just the KFC and Pizza Hut chains of Pepsi Foods Ltd. that will cause all of this damage. Once we open India up by allowing these chains, dozens more will be eagerly waiting to come in. Each city in America has an average of 5,000 junk-food restaurants. Is that what we want for India?

Why does the author of this article oppose the introduction of fast-food restaurants in India? Do you think her complaints apply in the United States as well?

Source: From *World Press Review* (September 1995), p. 47.

COMPARATIVE ILLUSTRATION

Two Indias. Contemporary India is a study in contrasts. In the photo on the top, middle-class students learn to use a computer, a symbol of their country's recent drive to join the global technological marketplace. Yet India today remains primarily a nation of villages. On the bottom, women in colorful saris fill their pails of water at the village well. As in many developing countries, the scarcity of water is one of India's most crucial problems.

Q *In what other regions of the world is lack of water a serious problem?*

Indranil Mukherjee/AFP/Getty Images

© William J. Duiker

to be fraught with problems (see the box "A Marriage of Convenience" on p. 906).

Since independence, Congress Party leaders have sought to deal with problems caused by caste differences by providing benefits in hiring and education for applicants from the lower castes. Individuals from such castes have served in important positions in business, education, and government. Yet prejudice and inequality still exist, and in recent years, low-caste Indians (who represent more than 80 percent of the voting public) have begun to demand additional measures to expand their opportunities and give them a more equal share in the national wealth. Opponents of such measures,

however, are often not reluctant to fight back against such affirmative action programs, pointing out that those who have benefitted often come from professional families. Violent conflicts between caste groups have been on the rise in recent years, and in some areas, political parties are organized almost entirely on the basis of caste identity. The situation is different in parts of southern India, where for years members of lower castes have focused on education and economic achievement rather than on increasing their political influence in Indian society. As a result, many members of traditionally lower castes have become prominent in business, technological pursuits, and education.

A Marriage of Convenience

ART & IDEAS

ONE OF INDEPENDENT INDIA'S foremost challenges has been to realize Mahatma's Gandhi's dream of integrating the country's multiple ethnic and religious groups into a cohesive society. Among the most serious issues is the uneasy relationship between the Muslim community and the Hindu majority. In *A Suitable Boy*, author Vikram Seth (b. 1952) describes the dilemma faced by a Hindu family when a daughter wishes to marry her Muslim boyfriend. Rupa Mehra is the mother of two daughters, Savita and Lata. Savita has married Pran, a fellow Hindu, but Lata has fallen in love with Kabir, a Muslim student at her university.

In the passage presented here, the author portrays the anguish experienced by family members as they seek to resolve the problem. At the end of 1,500 pages, Lata finally agrees to follow family tradition and marry the young Hindu her mother has chosen. Although it will initially be a "marriage of convenience," she hopes that respect for her husband will eventually turn to love, as happened with her sister Savita.

A Suitable Boy

Mrs. Rupa Mehra was not more prejudiced against Muslims than most upper-caste Hindu women of her age and background. As Lata had inopportunely pointed out, she even had friends who were Muslims, though almost all of them were not orthodox at all. The Nawab Sahib was perhaps, quite orthodox, but then he was, for Mrs. Rupa Mehra, more a social acquaintance than a friend.

Source: From V. Seth, *A Suitable Boy* (New York: Harper Collins, 1993), pp. 197–198.

The more Mrs. Rupa Mehra thought, the more agitated she became. Even marrying a non-kshatriya Hindu was bad enough. But this was unspeakable. It was one thing to mix socially with Muslims, entirely another to dream of polluting one's blood and sacrificing one's daughter.

Whom could she turn to in her hour of darkness? When Pran came home for lunch and heard the story, he suggested mildly that they meet the boy. Mrs. Rupa Mehra threw another fit. It was utterly out of the question. Pran then decided to stay out of things and to let them die down. He had not been hurt when he realized that Savita had kept her sister's confidence from him, and Savita loved him still more for that. She tried to calm her mother down, console Lata, and keep them in separate rooms—at least during the day.

Lata looked around the bedroom and wondered what she was doing in this house with her mother when her heart was entirely elsewhere, anywhere but here—a boat, a cricket field, a concert, a banyan grove, a cottage in the hills, Blandings Castle, anywhere, anywhere, so long as she was with Kabir. No matter what happened, she would meet him as planned, tomorrow. She told herself again and again that the path of true love never did run smooth.

 What is the source of Mrs. Rupa Mehra's objection to her daughter's planned marriage? How does her daughter respond?

© Yvonne V. Duiker

Dhobi Ghat of Mumbai. Caste relationships are gradually eroding in contemporary India, a consequence of a changing economy and government-mandated affirmative action programs. But some Indian professions are still identified with specific caste (*jati*) groupings. Such is the case with the *dhobis*, a widespread and ethnically diverse caste whose primary occupation is the washing and dry cleaning of clothes. The *dhobi ghat* (washing place) in downtown Mumbai is the best known such establishment in India today, and the colorful sight of its extensive wash basins and lines hung with drying laundry is highly popular with visitors. Although at one time most of the clients were local residents who lacked facilities at home for cleaning their dirty linen, today the *dhobi ghat* services the laundry needs of nearby hospitals and hotels. In 2011, a film by the same name was produced by a movie company in Mumbai.

After independence, India's leaders faced an equally serious challenge in seeking to equalize treatment of the sexes. The constitution expressly forbade discrimination based on gender and called for equal pay for equal work. Laws prohibited child marriage, *sati*, and the payment of a dowry by the bride's family. Women were encouraged to attend school and enter the labor market.

Such laws, along with the dynamics of economic and social change, have had a major impact on the lives of many Indian women. Middle-class women in urban areas are much more likely to seek employment outside the home, and many hold managerial and professional positions. Some Indian women, however, choose to play a dual role—a modern one in their work and in the marketplace and a more submissive, traditional one at home. Indira Gandhi was a prominent example of a woman who combined a professional career with a more traditional position within her marriage.

Nothing more strikingly indicates the changing role of women in South Asia than the fact that in recent decades, three of the major countries in the area—India, Pakistan, and Sri Lanka—have had women prime ministers. It is worthy of mention, however, that all three—Indira Gandhi, Benazir Bhutto, and Srimivao Bandaranaike (see-ree-MAH-voh bahn-dur-uh-NY-uh-kuh)—came from prominent political families and owed their initial success to a husband or father who had served as prime minister before them.

Like other aspects of life, the role of women has changed much less in rural areas. In the early 1960s, many villagers still practiced the institution of *purdah*. Female children are still much less likely to receive an education. The overall literacy rate in India today is about 60 percent but it is less than 50 percent among women. Laws relating to dowry, child marriage, and inheritance are routinely ignored in the countryside. There have been a few highly publicized cases of *sati*, although undoubtedly more women die of mistreatment at the hands of their husband or of other members of his family. In a few instances, widows have been forcibly thrown on the funeral pyre by their in-laws.

Perhaps the most tragic aspect of continued sexual discrimination in India is the high mortality rate among girls. One-quarter of the female children born in India die before the age of fifteen as a result of neglect or infanticide. Others are aborted before birth after gender-detection examinations. The results are striking. In India, according to one recent estimate, there are only 933 females to every 1,000 males.

South Asian Literature Since Independence

Recent decades have witnessed a prodigious outpouring of literature in India. Most works have been written in one of the Indian languages and have not been translated into a foreign tongue. Fortunately for foreign readers, however, many authors choose to write in English. Known as Indo-Anglian literature, such works are written primarily for the Indian elite or for foreign audiences. For that reason, some critics charge that Indo-Anglian literature lacks authenticity.

One of the most famous Indian-born authors is Salman Rushdie (b. 1947). In *Midnight's Children*, published in 1980, the author linked his protagonist, born on the night of independence, to the history of modern India, its achievements, and its frustrations. Like his contemporaries Günter Grass and Gabriel García Márquez, Rushdie used the technique of magical realism to jolt his audience into a recognition of the inhumanity of modern society and the need to develop a sense of moral concern for the fate of the Indian people and for the world as a whole.

Rushdie's later novels have tackled such problems as religious intolerance, political tyranny, social injustice, and greed and corruption. His attack on Islamic fundamentalism in *The Satanic Verses* (1988) won plaudits from literary critics but aroused widespread criticism among Muslims, including a death sentence by Iran's Ayatollah Khomeini. *The Moor's Last Sigh* (1995) examined what Rushdie perceives as the excesses of Hindu nationalism, and *Shalimar the Clown* (2005) addressed the quagmire in Kashmir. A number of younger writers are following Rushdie's lead and are providing their own critiques of India's evolving social problems. In *The White Tiger* (2008), Indian author Aravind Adiga (AR-vind ah-DEE-gah) (b. 1974) addresses the greed and corruption among India's newly rich as he traces the darkly mordant rise of a rickshaw driver to wealthy entrepreneur.

Anita Desai (dess-SY) (b. 1937) was one of the first prominent female writers to emerge from contemporary India. Her writing focuses on the struggle of Indian women to achieve a degree of independence. In her first novel, *Cry, the Peacock*, the heroine finally seeks liberation by murdering her husband, preferring freedom at any cost to remaining a captive of traditional society. Her daughter, Kiran Desai (b. 1971), also an author, has explored the contemporary issues of globalism and immigration in *The Inheritance of Loss* (2006).

What Is the Future of India?

Indian society looks increasingly Western in form, if not in content. As in a number of other Asian and African societies, the distinction between traditional and modern, or indigenous and westernized, sometimes seems to be a simple dichotomy between rural and urban. The major cities appear modern and westernized but the villages have changed little since precolonial days.

Yet traditional practices appear to be more resilient in India than in many other societies, and the result is often a synthesis rather than a clash between conflicting institutions and values. Unlike China under Mao Zedong, India did not reject its past but merely adjusted it to meet the needs of the present. Clothing styles in the streets, where the *sari* and *dhoti* continue to be popular, religious practices in the temples, and social relationships in the home all testify to the importance of tradition—and especially of religion—in contemporary India.

One disadvantage of the eclectic approach, which seeks to blend the old and the new rather than choosing one over the other, is that sometimes contrasting traditions cannot

A Pilgrimage to the Temple. Christianity has the Holy Land and the shrine at Santiago de Compostela; Islam has the *hajj* to Mecca, a trip recommended to all good Muslims. Hinduism has its pilgrimage sites as well. One of the most popular is the magnificent Sri Meenakshi temple, located in Madurai, a major city in southern India. The current structure, with its fourteen *gopurams* (see illustration "Mohenjo-Daro: Ancient City on the Indus" on p. 39 in Chapter 2), one of the largest and most magnificent religious buildings in India, was erected in the seventeenth century, but a previous temple on the site had existed at least 1,000 years previously. Over a million Hindus from all over India visit the site annually. In this photo, a group of young Indian pilgrims dressed in the sacred colors of black and orange prepare to demonstrate their faith and pay obeisance to Parvati, wife of Lord Shiva and patron saint of the temple.

easily be reconciled. In his book *India: A Wounded Civilization*, V. S. Naipaul (NY-pahl) (b. 1932), a Trinidadian of Indian descent who received the Nobel Prize for Literature in 2001, charged that Mahatma Gandhi's glorification of poverty and the simple Indian village was an obstacle to efforts to overcome the poverty, ignorance, and degradation of India's past and build a prosperous modern society. Gandhi's vision of a spiritual India, Naipaul complained, was a balm for defeatism and an excuse for failure.

Yet the appeal of Gandhi's philosophy remains a major part of the country's heritage. In July 2006, at a time when growing despair at economic conditions in the countryside resulted in a rash of suicides by poor farmers, Prime Minister Manmohan Singh called on the Indian people to reject the American model of "wasteful" consumer spending and return to the frugal teachings and spiritual vision of Mahatma Gandhi, which were, in his words, a "necessity" for a country as poor in material goods as India.[4]

Certainly, India faces a difficult dilemma. As historian Martha Nussbaum points out in *The Clash Within: Democracy, Religious Violence, and India's Future*, much of India's rural population continues to hold traditional beliefs, such as the concept of *karma* and inherent caste distinctions, that are incompatible with the capitalist work ethic and the democratic belief in equality before the law. Yet these beliefs provide a measure of identity and solace often lacking in other societies where such traditional spiritual underpinnings have eroded.

India, like Pakistan, also faces a number of other serious challenges. The Congress Party's vision of a diverse society composed of many distinct ethnic and religious communities is increasingly at odds with the virulent spirit of nationalism and religious identity sweeping the region today. India also must cope with severe environmental difficulties, including

land erosion, overcrowding, and a scarcity of water and other vital resources, which will place severe limitations on the country's ability to transform itself into an economic powerhouse. As a democratic and pluralistic society, India is unable to launch major programs without popular consent and thus cannot move as quickly or often as effectively as an authoritarian system like China's. At the same time, India's institutions provide a mechanism to prevent the emergence of a despotic government elite interested only in its own survival. Nevertheless, whether India will be able to meet its challenges remains an open question.

Southeast Asia

 FOCUS QUESTION: What kinds of problems have the nations of Southeast Asia faced since 1945, and how have they attempted to solve them?

As we saw in Chapter 25, Japanese wartime occupation had a great impact on attitudes among the peoples of Southeast Asia. It demonstrated the vulnerability of Western colonial rule in the region and showed that an Asian power could defeat Europeans. The Allied governments themselves also contributed—sometimes unwittingly—to rising aspirations for independence by promising self-determination for all peoples at the end of the war. Although Winston Churchill later said that the Atlantic Charter did not apply to the colonial peoples, it would be difficult to put the genie back in the bottle again.

The End of the Colonial Era

Some did not try. In July 1946, the United States, whose economic interests in the area had always been less than

© William J. Duiker

other colonial powers, granted total independence to the Philippines. The Americans maintained a military presence on the islands, however, and U.S. citizens retained economic and commercial interests in the new country. The British, too, under the Labour Party, were determined to bring an end to a century of imperialism in the region. In 1948, the Union of Burma received its independence. Malaya's turn came in 1957, after a communist guerrilla movement had been suppressed.

The French and the Dutch, however, both regarded their colonies in the region as economic necessities as well as symbols of national grandeur and therefore refused to turn them over to nationalist movements at the end of the war. The Dutch attempted to suppress a rebellion in the East Indies led by Sukarno (soo-KAHR-noh) (1901–1970), leader of the Indonesian Nationalist Party. But the United States, which feared a Communist victory there, pressured the Dutch to grant independence to Sukarno and his non-communist forces, and in 1950 the Dutch finally agreed to recognize the new Republic of Indonesia.

The situation was somewhat different in French Indochina, where the Communists seized power throughout much of Vietnam in the August Revolution of 1945. After the French refused to recognize the new government and sought to reimpose their rule, hostilities broke out between the French and the Vietminh Front in December 1946. At the time it was only an anticolonial war but it would soon become much more (see Chapter 26).

In the Shadow of the Cold War

Many of the leaders of the newly independent states in Southeast Asia (see Map 30.2) admired Western political institutions and hoped to adapt them to their own countries. New constitutions were patterned on Western democratic models, and multiparty political systems quickly sprang into operation.

© 2016 Cengage Learning

MAP 30.2 Modern Southeast Asia. Shown here are the countries that comprise contemporary Southeast Asia. The names of major islands are indicated in italic type.

Q *Which of the countries in Southeast Asia have democratic governments?*

THE SEARCH FOR A NEW POLITICAL CULTURE By the 1960s, most of these budding experiments in pluralist democracy had been abandoned or were under serious threat. Some had been replaced by military or one-party autocratic regimes. In Burma, a moderate government based on the British parliamentary system and dedicated to Buddhism and nonviolent Marxism had given way to a military dictatorship. In Thailand, too, the military ruled. In the Philippines, President Ferdinand Marcos (MAHR-kohs) (1917–1989) discarded democratic restraints and established his own centralized control. In South Vietnam, under pressure from Communist-led insurgents, Ngo Dinh Diem and his successors paid lip service to the Western democratic model but ruled by authoritarian means.

One problem faced by most of these states was that independence had not brought material prosperity or ended economic inequality and the domination of the local economies by foreign interests. As in Africa, most economies in the region were still characterized by tiny industrial sectors; they lacked technology, educational resources, capital investment, and leaders trained in developmental skills.

The presence of widespread ethnic, linguistic, religious, and economic differences also made the transition to Western-style democracy difficult. In Malaya, for example, the majority Malays—most of whom were farmers and virtually all of whom were (and still are) Muslims—feared economic and political domination by the local Chinese minority, who were much more experienced in industry and commerce. In 1961, the Federation of Malaya, whose ruling party was dominated by Malays, integrated former British possessions on the island of Borneo into the new Union of Malaysia in a move to increase the non-Chinese proportion of the country's population. Yet periodic conflicts persisted as the Malaysian government attempted to guarantee Malay control over politics and a larger role in the economy.

Finally, the new nations of Southeast Asia were seeking to realize their ambitious objectives in a time of intense political turmoil throughout Asia. While their political leaders were under severe pressure to take sides in the ideological Cold War, revolutionary parties—many of them influenced by the Maoist strategy of "people's war"—operated outside the system as they sought to bring about drastic change on the model of the new China.

These revolutionary parties drew support not only from China but also from North Vietnam, where Ho Chi Minh and his colleagues openly rejected the Western model and opted for the Leninist pattern of national development based on Communist Party rule. In 1958, North Vietnamese leaders launched a three-year plan to lay the foundations for a fully socialist society. Collective farms were established, and all industry and commerce above the family level were nationalized.

SUKARNO AND "GUIDED DEMOCRACY" The most prominent example of a failed experiment in democracy was in Indonesia. In 1950, the country's new leaders drew up a constitution creating a parliamentary system under a titular presidency. Sukarno was elected the first president. A spellbinding orator, Sukarno played a major role in creating a sense of national identity among the disparate peoples of the Indonesian archipelago, although his administrative skills were minimal.

In 1959, Sukarno, exasperated at the incessant maneuvering among Muslims, Communists, and the army, dissolved the constitution and attempted to rule on his own through what he called **guided democracy**. As he described it, guided democracy was closer to Indonesian traditions and superior to the Western variety. The weakness of the latter was that it allowed the majority to dominate the minority, whereas guided democracy would reconcile different opinions and points of view in a government operated by consensus. Highly suspicious of the West, Sukarno nationalized foreign-owned enterprises and sought economic aid from China and the Soviet Union while relying for domestic support on the Indonesian Communist Party.

The army and many devout Muslims resented Sukarno's increasing reliance on the Communists, and some Muslims were further upset by his refusal to consider a state based on Islamic principles. In 1965, military officers launched a coup d'état against Sukarno that provoked a mass popular uprising, which resulted in the slaughter of several hundred thousand suspected Communists, many of whom were overseas Chinese, long distrusted by the Muslim majority. In 1967, a military government under General Suharto (soo-HAHR-toh) (1921–2008) was installed.

The new government made no pretensions of reverting to democratic rule but it did restore good relations with the West and sought foreign investment to repair the country's ravaged economy. It also sought to placate the Muslims while refusing demands for an Islamic state. In a few areas, including western Sumatra, militant Muslims took up arms against the state but without success.

On the Road to Political Reform

With the end of the Vietnam War in 1975 and the gradual rapprochement between China and the United States that followed, the ferment and uncertainty that had marked the first three decades of independence in Southeast Asia gradually gave way to an era of greater political stability. In the Philippines, the dictatorial regime of Ferdinand Marcos was overthrown by a popular uprising in 1986 and replaced by a democratically elected government under President Corazon Aquino (KOR-uh-zahn ah-KEE-noh) (1933–2009), the widow of a popular politician assassinated a few years earlier. Aquino was unable to resolve many of the country's chronic economic and social difficulties, however, and political stability remained elusive. One of the problems that she and her successors faced was in the southern island of Mindanao (min-duh-NAH-oh), where Muslim separatists carried on a terrorist campaign in their effort to obtain autonomy or independence from the predominantly Christian Philippines.

In other nations, the trends have been equally mixed. Malaysia is a practicing democracy, although a coalition of groups known as the United Malays National Organization

(UMNO) has controlled the government since independence. Blessed with rich natural resources including tin and rubber, the country has embarked on the road to economic prosperity and national development. In recent years, however, tensions between Malays and Chinese, as well as between secular and orthodox Muslims, have been on the increase, thus weakening UMNO's control over the apparatus of government.

In neighboring Thailand, a fragile democracy has functioned under the watchful eye of the military. Since 2008, however, political tensions have spilled into the streets and threatened to throw Thai society into a state of paralysis. As the situation became increasingly chaotic, the army deposed the elected government of Thailand in the spring of 2014 and imposed martial law on the country.

INDONESIA AFTER SUHARTO For years, a major exception to the trend toward political pluralism in the region was Indonesia, where Suharto ruled without restraints. But in 1997, popular anger against government corruption (several members of Suharto's family had reportedly used their positions to amass considerable wealth) led to violent street riots and demands for his resignation. Forced to step down in the spring of 1998, Suharto was replaced by his deputy B. J. Habibie (hab-BEEB-ee) (b. 1936), who called for the establishment of a national assembly to select a new government based on popular aspirations. The assembly selected a moderate Muslim leader as president, but he was charged with corruption and incompetence and was replaced in 2001 by his vice president, Sukarno's daughter Megawati Sukarnoputri (meg-uh-WAH-tee soo-kahr-noh-POO-tree) (b. 1947).

The new government faced internal challenges from dissident elements seeking autonomy or separation from the republic, as well as from religious forces seeking to transform the country into an Islamic state. Under pressure from the international community, Indonesia agreed to grant independence to the onetime Portuguese colony of East Timor, where the majority of the people are Roman Catholics. But violence provoked by pro-Indonesian militia units forced many refugees to flee the country. Religious tensions also erupted between Muslims and Christians elsewhere in the archipelago, and Muslim rebels in western Sumatra continue to agitate for a new state based on strict adherence to fundamentalist Islam. In the meantime, a terrorist attack directed at tourists on the island of Bali aroused fears that the Muslim nation had become a haven for terrorist elements throughout the region.

In direct elections held in 2004, General Susilo Yudhyono (soo-SEE-loh yood-heh-YOH-noh) (b. 1949) defeated Megawati Sukarnoputri and ascended to the presidency. The new chief executive promised a new era of political stability, honest government, and economic reform while ceding more authority to the country's thirty-three provinces. Pressure from traditional Muslims to abandon the nation's secular tradition and move toward the creation of an Islamic state continues, but the level of religious and ethnic tension has declined somewhat. In elections held in 2009, Yudhyono won a second term in office, while popular support for Islamic parties dropped from 38 percent to 26 percent. Five years later, Joko Widodo, the popular governor of Jakarta, won a sharply contested election to succeed Yudhyono as president.

ON THE MARGINS OF SOUTHEAST ASIA: VIETNAM AND MYANMAR As always, Vietnam is a special case. After achieving victory over South Vietnam with the fall of Saigon in the spring of 1975 (see Chapter 26), the Communist government in Hanoi pursued the rapid reunification of the two zones under Communist Party rule and laid plans to carry out a socialist transformation throughout the country, now renamed the Socialist Republic of Vietnam (SRV). The result

Traffic Congestion in Ho Chi Minh City. As the countries of eastern and southern Asia continue to develop advanced modern economies, vehicular traffic on the streets of their cities escalates in response. Major commercial and financial hubs like Tokyo, Shanghai, and Bangkok begin to experience massive traffic jams as the number of vehicles rapidly surpasses the capacity of the transportation network to absorb them. The first stage in the process is often the growing proliferation of scooters and motorbikes, which buzz like a swarm of bees along the city streets, scattering pedestrians and other vehicles in their wake. Such is the case here in Ho Chi Minh City (the old Saigon), where the automobile is still out of reach for the average resident. Note how many people are wearing a face mask to ward off the ubiquitous smell of engine exhaust.

was an economic disaster, and in 1986, party leaders followed the example of Mikhail Gorbachev in the Soviet Union and introduced their own version of *perestroika* in Vietnam (see Chapter 27). The trend in recent years has been toward a mixed capitalist-socialist economy along Chinese lines and a greater popular role in the governing process. Elections for the unicameral parliament are more open than in the past, and the Vietnamese economy, based on the export of tropical products, rice, and inexpensive clothing, has increasingly become integrated with that of the other states in the region. Relations with the United States have been normalized as both nations seek to cooperate in preventing greater Chinese inroads into the region. The government remains suspicious of Western-style democracy, however, and represses any opposition, whether political or religious, to the Communist Party's guiding role over the state.

Only in Burma (in 1989 renamed Myanmar), where the military has been in complete control since the early 1960s, have the forces of greater popular participation been virtually silenced. Even there, however, the power of the ruling regime of General Ne Win (NAY WIN) (1911–2002) and his successors, known first as SLORC and after 1997 as the State Peace and Development Council (SPDC), was vocally challenged by Aung San Suu Kyi (AWNG SAHN SOO CHEE) (b. 1945), the admired daughter of one of the heroes of the country's struggle for national liberation after World War II. In 2011, the SPDC was officially abolished and replaced by a new constitution and an elected president, Thein Sein (TAY-en SAY-en) (b. 1945), a retired military officer. Nevertheless, the military remains in control, and tensions among the various ethnic and religious groups have prevented the evolution of the country to greater political stability.

FINANCIAL CRISIS AND RECOVERY The trend toward more representative systems of government in the region has been due in part to increasing prosperity and the growth of an affluent and educated middle class. Although Myanmar and the three Indochinese states (Cambodia, Laos, and Vietnam) are still primarily agrarian, Indonesia, Malaysia, and Thailand have been undergoing relatively rapid economic development.

In the late summer of 1997, however, these economic gains were threatened and popular faith in the ultimate benefits of globalization was shaken as a financial crisis swept through the region. The crisis was triggered by a number of problems, including growing budget deficits caused by excessive government expenditures on ambitious development projects, and irresponsible lending and investment practices by financial institutions. An underlying cause of these problems was the prevalence of backroom deals between politicians and business leaders that temporarily enriched both groups at the cost of eventual economic dislocation.

As local currencies plummeted in value, the International Monetary Fund agreed to provide assistance but only on the condition that the governments concerned permit greater transparency in their economic systems and allow market forces to operate more freely, even at the price of bankruptcies and the loss of jobs. By the early 2000s, there were signs

CHRONOLOGY   Southeast Asia Since 1945

August Revolution in Vietnam	1945
Philippines becomes independent	1946
Beginning of Franco-Vietminh War	1946
Burma becomes independent	1948
Republic of Indonesia becomes independent	1950
Malaya becomes independent	1957
Beginning of Sukarno's "guided democracy" in Indonesia	1959
Military seizes power in Indonesia	1965
Foundation of ASEAN	1967
Fall of Saigon to North Vietnamese forces	1975
Vietnamese invade Cambodia	1978
Corazon Aquino elected president in the Philippines	1986
Vietnamese withdraw from Cambodia	1991
Vietnam becomes a member of ASEAN	1996
Suharto steps down as president of Indonesia	1998
Tsunami causes widespread death and destruction throughout the region	2004
Reelection of President Yudhyono in Indonesia	2009

that the economies in the region had weathered the crisis and were beginning to recover. The massive tsunami that struck the region in December 2004 was a setback, as well as a human tragedy of enormous proportions, but as the decade wore on, progress resumed, and today the nations of Southeast Asia, with a few exceptions, are among the fastest growing in the world.

Blessed with abundant natural resources, including oil reserves, precious metals, and a variety of tropical products, the nations of Southeast Asia have surmounted the recent global economic slowdown and currently enjoy an annual growth rate greater than most other parts of the world. Overall, its prospects are brighter than could have been anticipated a generation ago. The region continues to face a number of serious challenges, however, including urban poverty, especially in the Philippines and Indonesia, and growing environmental pollution. The latter problem is caused partly by the widespread practice of clear-cutting of rain forests in order to clear land for the cultivation of important tropical products like rubber, coffee, and palm oil. In recent years, the entire region has been blanketed with heavy smog created by man-made forest fires in the outer islands of Indonesia (see the Comparative Essay "One World, One Environment" on p. 913).

Regional Conflict and Cooperation: The Rise of ASEAN

The challenge of dealing with problems related to the environment is only one reason the nations in the region have sought ways to encourage mutual cooperation; these nations also face common threats to their peace, prosperity, and stability. Prior to the 1970s, Southeast Asian peoples had no tradition

One World, One Environment

EARTH & ENVIRONMENT

A crucial factor affecting the evolution of society and the global economy in the early twenty-first century is the growing concern over the impact of industrialization on the environment. Humans have always caused some harm to their natural surroundings but never has the ecological damage been as significant and extensive as during the past century. Chemicals and other pollutants introduced into the atmosphere or into rivers, lakes, and oceans have increasingly threatened the health and well-being of all living species.

For many years, environmental concern was focused

A Forest Fire on the Island of Sumatra. Man-made forest fires are one of the most prevalent forms of environmental pollution in Southeast Asia today, as precious rain forests are clear-cut to make room for valuable export crops like rubber, coffee, and palm oil.

on the developed countries of the West, where industrial effluents, automobile exhausts, and the use of artificial fertilizers and insecticides led to urban smog, extensive damage to crops and wildlife, and a major reduction of the ozone layer in the upper atmosphere. In recent years, the problem has spread elsewhere. China's headlong rush to industrialization has resulted in major ecological damage in that country. Industrial smog has created almost unlivable conditions in many cities in Asia, while hillsides denuded of their forests have led to severe erosion and loss of farmlands. Destruction of the rain forest is a growing problem in many parts of the world, notably in Brazil and Indonesia. With the forest cover across the earth rapidly disappearing, there is less plant life to perform the crucial process of reducing carbon dioxide levels in the atmosphere.

One positive note is that environmental concerns have begun to take on a global character. As it has become increasingly clear that the release of carbon dioxide and other gases into the atmosphere as a result of industrialization plays a significant part in producing global warming, the issue has become a source of widespread international concern. If, as many scientists predict, worldwide temperatures continue to increase, the rise in sea levels could pose a major threat to low-lying

islands and coastal areas throughout the world, while climatic change could lead to severe droughts or excessive rainfall in cultivated areas.

It is one thing to recognize a problem, however, and another to solve it. So far, cooperative efforts among nations to alleviate environmental problems have all too often been hindered by economic forces or by political, ethnic, and religious disputes. A 1997 conference on global warming held in Kyoto, Japan, for example, was marked by bitter disagreement over the degree to which developing countries should share the burden of cleaning up the environment. In 2001 U.S. President George W. Bush refused to sign the Kyoto Agreement on the grounds that it discriminated against advanced Western countries. The fact is that few nations have been willing to take unilateral action that might pose an obstacle to economic development plans or lead to a rise in unemployment. Subsequent conferences on the subject including the 2009 conference in Copenhagen, Denmark, have yielded few concrete results.

What kinds of environmental problems have recently taken place in the region of South Asia? Have they all been the result of human action?

of mutual cooperation; indeed, historical rivalries and territorial disputes had dominated the scene prior to the era of colonial rule.

After World War II, that tradition continued. In the 1960s, Indonesian president Sukarno risked a confrontation with the Federation of Malaya by contending that the Malay Peninsula had once been part of empires based on the Indonesian islands. Ethnic and linguistic ties between the two regions gave his claim some surface plausibility but the claim was contemptuously dismissed by Malaysian leaders, who saw no benefit in uniting with their more populous but poverty-stricken neighbor, and was quietly dropped after Sukarno's fall from power in 1965.

A second border dispute festered between Cambodia and its own neighbors, Thailand and Vietnam, both of which had once exercised suzerainty over Cambodian territories. During the period of colonial rule, the borders of Cambodia were drawn up by French authorities for their own convenience. After the end of the Vietnam War in 1975, a border dispute between the communist governments of Cambodia and Vietnam suddenly erupted into violence. In April 1975, a brutal revolutionary regime under the leadership of the Khmer Rouge (KMAIR ROOZH) dictator Pol Pot (POHL PAHT) came to power in Cambodia and proceeded to carry out the massacre of more than one million Cambodians. Then, claiming that vast territories in the Mekong Delta had been seized from Cambodia by the Vietnamese in previous centuries, the Khmer Rouge regime launched attacks across the common border. In response, Vietnamese forces invaded Cambodia in December 1978 and installed a pro-Hanoi regime in Phnom Penh (puh-NAHM PEN). Fearful of Vietnam's increasing power in the region, China launched a brief attack on Vietnam to demonstrate its displeasure.

The outbreak of war among the erstwhile Communist allies aroused the concern of other countries in the neighborhood. In 1967, several non-communist countries had established the Association of Southeast Asian Nations, or **ASEAN**. Composed of Indonesia, Malaysia, Thailand, Singapore, and the Philippines, ASEAN at first concentrated on cooperative social and economic endeavors, but after the end of the Vietnam War, it cooperated with other states in an effort to force the Vietnamese to withdraw from Cambodia. In 1991, the Vietnamese agreed to pull back, and a new government was formed in Phnom Penh.

The growth of ASEAN from a weak collection of diverse states into a stronger organization whose members cooperate militarily and politically has helped provide the nations of

Holocaust in Cambodia. When the Khmer Rouge seized power in Cambodia in April 1975, they immediately emptied the capital of Phnom Penh and systematically began to eliminate opposition elements throughout the country. Thousands were tortured in the infamous Tuol Sleng prison and then marched out to the countryside, where they were massacred. Their bodies were thrown into massive pits. The succeeding government disinterred the remains, which are now displayed at an outdoor museum on the site.

Southeast Asia with a more cohesive voice to represent their interests on the world stage. They will need it, for disagreements with Western countries over global economic issues and the rising power of China present major challenges to the nations in the region. The admission of Vietnam into ASEAN in 1996 provides both Hanoi and its neighbors with greater leverage in dealing with China, their powerful neighbor to the north, whose claims of ownership over tiny islands in the South China Sea have aroused widespread concern throughout the region.

Daily Life: Town and Country in Contemporary Southeast Asia

The urban-rural dichotomy we have observed in India is also found in Southeast Asia, where the cities resemble those in the West while the countryside often appears little changed from precolonial days. In cities such as Bangkok, Manila, Kuala Lumpur, and Jakarta, broad boulevards lined with skyscrapers are surrounded by a ring of muddy lanes passing through neighborhoods packed with wooden shacks topped by thatch or rusty tin roofs. Nevertheless, in recent decades, millions of Southeast Asians have fled to these urban slums. Although most available jobs are menial, the pay is better than in the villages.

TRADITIONAL CUSTOMS, MODERN VALUES The urban migrants change not only their physical surroundings but their attitudes and values as well. Sometimes the move leads to a decline in traditional religious faith. Belief in natural and ancestral spirits, for example, has declined among the urban populations of Southeast Asia. In Thailand, Buddhism has come under pressure from the rising influence of materialism, although temple schools still educate thousands of rural youths whose families cannot afford the cost of public education.

Nevertheless, Buddhist, Muslim, and Confucian beliefs remain strong, even in cosmopolitan cities such as Bangkok, Jakarta, and Singapore. This preference for the traditional also shows up in lifestyle. Traditional dress—or an eclectic blend of Asian and Western dress—is still common. Asian music, art, theater, and dance remain popular, although Western music has become fashionable among the young, and Indonesian filmmakers complain that Western films are beginning to dominate the local market.

The increasing inroads made by Western culture have caused anxiety in some countries. In Malaysia, for example, fundamentalist Muslims criticize the prevalence of pornography, hedonism, drugs, and alcohol in Western culture and have tried to limit their presence in their own country. Many Indonesians have expressed concern in recent years that English has become the language of choice among the young, undercutting the role of Bahasa Indonesia, the composite language that has been employed to bring a degree of unity to the country's 250 different ethnic groups. In Thailand, traditionalists lament the decline of Buddhist beliefs and practices, especially in urban areas, where exposure to Western secular culture has affected the young and the restless.

CHANGING ROLES FOR WOMEN One of the most significant changes that has taken place in Southeast Asia in recent decades is in the role of women in society. In general, women in the region have historically faced fewer restrictions on their activities and enjoyed a higher status than women elsewhere in Asia. Nevertheless, they were not the equal of men in every respect. With independence, Southeast Asian women gained new rights. Virtually all of the constitutions adopted by the newly independent states granted women full legal and political rights, including the right to work. Today, women have increased opportunities for education and have entered careers previously reserved for men. Women have become more active in politics, and as we have seen, some have served as heads of state.

Yet women are not truly equal to men in any country in Southeast Asia. Sometimes the distinction is simply a matter of custom. In Vietnam, women are legally equal to men, yet until recently no women had served in the Communist Party's ruling Politburo. In Thailand, Malaysia, and Indonesia, women rarely hold senior positions in government service or in the boardrooms of major corporations. Similar restrictions apply in Myanmar, although Aung San Suu Kyi is the leading figure in the democratic opposition movement.

Sometimes, too, women's rights have been undermined by a social or religious backlash. The revival of Islamic fundamentalism has had an especially strong impact in Malaysia, where Malay women are expected to cover their bodies and wear the traditional Muslim headdress. Even in non-Muslim

© William J. Duiker

A Prayer to Lord Buddha. From the standpoint of religious belief, Southeast Asia is one of the most diverse regions in the world today. Although the majority of the people living in the mainland states are Buddhists, Theravada predominates in Thailand, Burma, Cambodia, and Laos, while the Vietnamese, like their neighbors to the north, are devotees of Mahayana. In the Indonesian archipelago, the vast majority of the population follows Islam but Christianity is prevalent in the Philippines. Shown here, a member of the local ethnic Chinese community in predominantly Muslim Malaysia worships at a Buddhist temple in the old colonial port of Malacca.

© William J. Duiker

Tourism and Tradition in Bali. The influence of modern Western culture has had a corrosive effect on contemporary societies throughout Southeast Asia. Traditional forms of art and architecture, music, and film have been replaced by their modern Western equivalents. The small island of Bali in eastern Indonesia has managed to preserve much of its traditional way of life by presenting it to visitors as a tourist experience. Although the tourist district in the capital of Denpasar is overrun with modern hotels, bars, and tourist shops, residents of the island still seek to preserve elements of their heritage as an outpost of Hindu culture in a country whose citizens are over 90 percent Muslim. This photo shows Balinese actors at a theatrical performance on a familiar theme from the classical Indian repertoire. In an ironic twist, tourism in Bali helps to preserve traditional culture even as it undermines its relevance in the daily lives of the islanders.

countries, women are expected to behave demurely and exercise discretion in all contacts with the opposite sex.

Cultural Trends

In most countries in Southeast Asia, writers, artists, and composers are attempting to synthesize international styles and themes with local tradition and experience. The novel has become increasingly popular as writers seek to find the best medium to encapsulate the dramatic changes that have taken place in the region in recent decades.

The best-known writer in postwar Indonesia—at least to readers abroad—was Pramoedya Toer (PRAHM-oh-DEE-yah TOOR) (1925–2006). Born in eastern Java, he joined the Indonesian nationalist movement in his early twenties. Arrested in 1965 on the charge of being a Communist, he spent the next several years in prison. While incarcerated, he began writing his four-volume *Buru Quartet*, which recounts in fictional form the story of the struggle of the Indonesian people for freedom from colonial rule and the autocratic regimes of the independence period.

Among the most talented contemporary Vietnamese novelists is Duong Thu Huong (ZHWAHNG too HWAHNG) (b. 1947). A member of the Vietnamese Communist Party who served on the front lines during the Sino-Vietnamese war in 1979, she later became outspoken in criticizing the

party's failure to carry out democratic reforms and was briefly imprisoned in 1991. Undaunted by official pressure, she has written several novels that express the horrors experienced by guerrilla fighters during the Vietnam War and the cruel injustices perpetrated by the regime in the cause of building socialism. She has recently written a fictional biography of Ho Chi Minh entitled *The Zenith* (2012), which portrays the Vietnamese leader as having expressed disappointment at the betrayal of his teachings by his followers in the twilight years of his life.

A Region in Flux

Today, the Western image of a Southeast Asia mired in the Vietnam conflict and the tensions of the Cold War is a distant memory. In ASEAN, the states in the region have created the framework for a regional organization that can serve their common political, economic, technological, and security interests. A few members of ASEAN are already on the road to advanced development.

To be sure, there are also challenges to overcome. The global crisis that erupted in the fall of 2008 continues to test the resilience of local economies that are dependent upon robust markets for their exports. Burma is only beginning to emerge from a long period of isolation. The three states of Indochina remain potentially unstable and have not yet been fully integrated into the region as a whole. Finally, terrorist groups inspired by al-Qaeda continue to operate in the region, especially in Indonesia. All things considered, however, the situation is more promising today than would have seemed possible a generation ago. Unlike the case in Africa and the Middle East, the nations of Southeast Asia have put aside the bitter legacy of the colonial era to embrace the wave of globalization that has been sweeping the world in the post–World War II era.

Japan: Asian Giant

 FOCUS QUESTION: How did the Allied occupation after World War II change Japan's political and economic institutions, and what remained unchanged?

In August 1945, Japan was in ruins, its cities destroyed, its vast Asian empire in ashes, its land occupied by a foreign army. Half a century later, Japan had emerged as the second-greatest industrial power in the world, democratic in form and content and a source of stability throughout the region. Japan's achievement spawned a number of Asian imitators. Known as the "Little Tigers," the four industrializing societies of Taiwan, Hong Kong, Singapore, and South Korea achieved considerable success by following the path originally charted by Japan. Along with Japan, they became economic powerhouses and ranked among the world's top twenty trading nations. Other nations in Asia and elsewhere took note and began to adopt the Japanese formula. It is no wonder that observers relentlessly heralded the coming of the Pacific Century.

The Transformation of Modern Japan

For five years after the end of the war in the Pacific, Japan was governed by an Allied administration under the command of U.S. General Douglas MacArthur (1880–1964). The occupation regime—known as the Supreme Command, Allied Powers, or **SCAP**—was dominated by the United States, although the country was technically administered by a new Japanese government. As commander of the occupation administration, MacArthur was responsible for demilitarizing Japanese society, destroying the Japanese war machine, trying Japanese civilian and military officials charged with war crimes, and laying the foundations of postwar Japanese society.

During the war, senior U.S. officials had discussed whether to insist on the abdication of Emperor Hirohito as the symbol of Japanese imperial expansion but ultimately decided to agree to his retention after he agreed publicly to renounce his divinity. Although some historians have contended that Emperor Hirohito (heer-oh-HEE-toh) (1901–1989) had fully supported the war effort, others argued that as a figurehead, his role in drafting wartime strategy had been minimal. Whatever the truth of the matter, U.S. policymakers eventually decided that the imperial system—shorn of the traditional belief in the divinity of the emperor—could play a useful role in bringing about the creation of a new and more democratic Japan.

Keystone/Hulton Royals Collection/Getty Images

General MacArthur and Emperor Hirohito. After the end of World War II, U.S. General Douglas MacArthur was appointed Supreme Commander of the Allied Powers (SCAP) in Japan. In that capacity, he directed Allied policy during the occupation of Japan from 1945 to 1950. Here MacArthur stands side by side with Emperor Hirohito of Japan. Note the cultural and attitudinal differences of the two leaders as expressed by their contrasting body language. Compare this photograph with the Japanese painting (see the illustration "'Total Humiliation'" on p. 655 in Chapter 22) that portrays the negotiations between China and Japan at the end of the Sino-Japanese War in 1895.

THE MACARTHUR REFORMS Under MacArthur's firm tutelage, Japanese society was remodeled along Western lines. The centerpiece of occupation policy was the promulgation of a new constitution to replace the Meiji Constitution of 1890. The new charter, which was drafted by U.S. planners and imposed on the Japanese despite their objections to some of its provisions, was designed to transform Japan into a peaceful and pluralistic society that would no longer be capable of waging offensive war. The constitution specifically renounced war as a national policy, and Japan unilaterally agreed to maintain armed forces only sufficient for self-defense (see the box "Japan Renounces War" on p. 918). Perhaps most important, the constitution established a parliamentary form of government based on a bicameral legislature, an independent judiciary, and a universal franchise; it also reduced the power of the emperor and guaranteed human rights.

Japan Renounces War

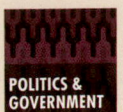

ON MAY 3, 1947, a new Japanese constitution went into effect to replace the so-called "Meiji Constitution" of 1890. The process of drafting the document had taken place under the watchful guidance of General Douglas MacArthur, the Supreme Commander of the Allied Powers (SCAP), who was determined to guarantee that the militaristic tendencies of the prewar Japanese government would not be resurrected in the postwar era. This point of view was explicitly included in the new constitution drafted under the watchful eyes of U.S. authorities. According to Article 9 of the new charter, Japan renounced war as an instrument of national policy and eventually decided only to maintain a limited number of so-called Self-defense Forces to protect itself against external attack. From that time on, Japan relied on the United States for its protection and security.

Excerpts from the Japanese Constitution of 1947

We, the Japanese people, acting through our duly elected representatives in the National Diet, determined that we shall secure for ourselves and our posterity the fruits of peaceful cooperation with all nations and the blessings of liberty throughout this land, and resolved that never again shall we be visited with the horrors of war through the action of government, do proclaim that sovereign power resides with the people and do firmly establish this Constitution. Government is a sacred trust of the people, the authority for which is derived from the people, the powers of which are exercised by the representatives of the people, and the benefits of which are enjoyed by the people. This is a universal principle of mankind upon which this Constitution is founded. We reject and revoke all constitutions, laws, ordinances, and rescripts in conflict herewith.

We, the Japanese people, desire peace for all time and are deeply conscious of the high ideals controlling human relationship, and we have determined to preserve our security and existence, trusting in the justice and faith of the peace-loving peoples of the world. We desire to occupy an honored place in an international society striving for the preservation of peace, and the banishment of tyranny and slavery, oppression and intolerance for all time from the earth. We recognize that all peoples of the world have the right to live in peace, free from fear and want.

We believe that no nation is responsible to itself alone, but that laws of political morality are universal; and that obedience to such laws is incumbent upon all nations who would sustain their own sovereignty and justify their sovereign relationship with other nations.

We, the Japanese people, pledge our national honor to accomplish these high ideals and purposes with all our resources.

Chapter I. The Emperor

Article 1. The Emperor shall be the symbol of the State and of the unity of the people, deriving his position from the will of the people with whom resides sovereign power....

Chapter II. Renunciation of War

Article 9. (1) Aspiring sincerely to an international peace based on justice and order, the Japanese people forever renounce war as a sovereign right of the nation and the threat or use of force as a mean of settling international disputes.

(2) In order to accomplish the aim of the preceding paragraph, land, sea, and air forces, as well as other war potential, will never be maintained. The right of belligerency of the state will not be recognized.

 What is the current status of Article 9 of the Japanese Constitution? Why are some observers demanding that this provision be changed?

Source: From the Japanese Constitution of 1947. Accessed at: *http://history.hanover.edu/texts/1947con.html*.

But more than a written constitution was needed to demilitarize Japan and place it on a new course. Like the Meiji leaders in the late nineteenth century, occupation administrators wished to transform Japanese social and cultural institutions and hoped their policies would be accepted by the Japanese people as readily as those of the Meiji period had been. The Meiji reforms, however, had been crafted to reflect Japanese traditions and had set Japan on a path quite different from that of the modern West. Some Japanese observers believed that a fundamental reversal of trends begun with the Meiji Restoration would be needed before Japan would be ready to adopt the Western capitalist, democratic model.

One of the sturdy pillars of Japanese militarism had been the giant business cartels, known as *zaibatsu* (see Chapter 24). Allied policy was designed to break up the *zaibatsu* into smaller units in the belief that corporate concentration not only hindered competition but was inherently undemocratic and conducive to political authoritarianism. Occupation planners also intended to promote the formation of independent labor unions, lessen the power of the state over the economy, and provide a mouthpiece for downtrodden Japanese workers. Economic inequality in rural areas was to be reduced by a comprehensive land reform program that would turn the land over to the people who farmed it. Finally, the educational system was to be remodeled along

American lines so that it would turn out independent individuals rather than automatons subject to manipulation by the state.

JAPAN IN THE COLD WAR The Allied program was an ambitious and even audacious plan to remake Japanese society and has been justly praised for its clear-sighted vision and altruistic motives. Parts of the program, such as the constitution, the land reforms, and the educational system, succeeded brilliantly. But as other concerns began to intervene, changes or compromises were made that were not always successful. In particular, with the rise of Cold War sentiment in the United States in the late 1940s, the goal of decentralizing the Japanese economy gave way to the desire to make Japan a key partner in the effort to defend East Asia against international communism. Convinced of the need to promote economic recovery in Japan, U.S. policymakers began to show more tolerance for the *zaibatsu*. Concerned at growing radicalism within the new labor movement, U.S. occupation authorities placed less emphasis on the independence of the labor unions.

Cold War concerns also affected U.S. foreign relations with Japan. On September 8, 1951, the United States and other former belligerent nations signed a peace treaty restoring Japanese independence. In turn, Japan renounced any claim to such former colonies or territories as Taiwan, Korea, and southern Sakhalin and the Kurile Islands (see Map 30.3). On the same day, Japan and the United States signed a defensive alliance and agreed that the latter could maintain military bases on the Japanese islands. Japan was now formally independent but in a new dependency relationship with the United States. Thus, by the early 1950s, Japan had regained partial control over its destiny.

POLITICS AND GOVERNMENT The Allied occupation administrators started with the conviction that Japanese expansionism was directly linked to the institutional and ideological foundations of the Meiji Constitution. Accordingly, they set out to change Japanese politics into something closer to the pluralistic model used in most Western nations. Yet a number of characteristics of the postwar Japanese political system reflected the tenacity of the traditional political culture. Although Japan had a multiparty system with two major parties, the Liberal Democrats and the Socialists, in practice there was a "government party" and a permanent opposition. With the Socialists tarnished by being identified—not always justifiably—with left-wing politics and sympathy with communism, the Liberal Democrats, who had presided over an era of growing material prosperity, were not voted out of office for thirty years. As a result, the inevitable took place, and the ruling party became increasingly complacent and corrupt. Many of the leading Liberal Democrats controlled factions on a patron-client basis, and decisions on key issues, such as who should assume the prime ministership, were reached by a modern equivalent of the Meiji oligarchs.

That tradition changed suddenly in the early 1990s when the ruling Liberal Democrats, shaken by persistent reports of

MAP 30.3 Modern Japan. Shown here are the four main islands that comprise the contemporary state of Japan.

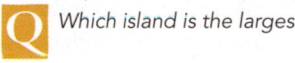 *Which island is the largest?*

corruption and cronyism between politicians and business interests, failed to win a majority of seats in parliamentary elections. A coalition government of minority parties took office but quickly split into feuding factions, and in 1995, the Liberal Democrats returned to power. When a series of governments proved unable to carry out promised reforms, in 2001 Junichiro Koizumi (joo-nee-CHEE-roh koh-ee-ZOO-mee) (b. 1942), a former minister of health and welfare, was elected prime minister. His personal charisma raised expectations that he might be able to bring about significant changes but bureaucratic resistance to reform and chronic factionalism within the Liberal Democratic Party thwarted his efforts, and in 2009, the Liberal Democrats were once again voted out of office. But the massive tsunami that struck the mainland island of Honshu in 2011 highlighted the ineptitude of the ruling Democratic Party, and in 2012 the Liberal Democrats returned to power under Prime Minister Shinzo Abe (SHIN-dzoh AH-bay) (b. 1954). The Abe government has sought to revive the lagging Japanese economy by stimulating competition and adopting tough new fiscal policies.

Tsunami! Situated on the notorious "ring of fire," a crescent-shaped line along the fringes of the Pacific Ocean that is highly susceptible to earthquakes and volcanic activity, the islands of Japan have over the years suffered innumerable earthquakes and tsunamis along their vulnerable coastline. The tsunami of January 2011—triggered by an offshore tremor in the earth's crust—was one of the worst in recent history and caused thousands of deaths along the coast of northeastern Honshu Island. The damage to a nearby nuclear reactor and the ineffective official response to the disaster shook the faith of the Japanese people in their government.

Robert Gilhooly/Alamy

JAPAN, INCORPORATED One of the problems plaguing the Japanese political system has been the centralizing tendencies that it inherited from the Meiji period. The government is organized on a unitary rather than a federal basis; the local administrative units, called prefectures, have few of the powers of states in the United States. Moreover, the central government plays an active and sometimes intrusive role in various aspects of the economy, mediating management-labor disputes, establishing price and wage policies, and subsidizing vital industries and enterprises producing goods for export.

The policy of government intervention in the economy has traditionally been widely accepted in Japan and is often cited as a key reason for the efficiency of Japanese industry and the emergence of the country as an industrial giant. In recent years, however, it has increasingly come under fire, as Japanese corporations, which previously sought government protection from imports, began to argue that deregulation was needed to enable Japanese firms to innovate in order to keep up with the competition. Such reforms, however, have been resisted by powerful government ministries in Tokyo, which are accustomed to playing an active role in national affairs.

An additional weakness of the political system is that the ruling Liberal Democratic Party has chronically been divided into factions that seek to protect their own interests and often resist changes that might benefit society as a whole. This tradition of factionalism has tended to insulate political figures from popular scrutiny and encouraged secret dealings and official corruption. A number of senior politicians, including two recent prime ministers, have been forced to resign because of serious questions about improper financial dealings with business associates.

ATONING FOR THE PAST Lingering social problems also need to be addressed. Minorities such as the *eta*, now known as the *Burakumin* (BOOR-uh-koo-min), and Korean residents in Japan continue to be subjected to legal and social discrimination. For years, official sources were reluctant to divulge growing evidence that thousands of Korean women were conscripted to serve as prostitutes (euphemistically called "comfort women") for Japanese soldiers during World War II, and many Koreans living in Japan contend that such prejudicial attitudes continue to exist. Representatives of the "comfort women" have demanded both financial compensation and a formal letter of apology from the Japanese government for the treatment they received during the Pacific War. Negotiations over the issue have been under way for several years.

Japan's behavior during World War II has been an especially sensitive issue. During the early 1990s, critics at home and abroad charged that textbooks printed under the guidance of the Ministry of Education did not adequately discuss the atrocities committed by the Japanese armed forces during World War II. Other Asian governments were particularly incensed at Tokyo's failure to accept responsibility for such behavior and demanded a formal apology. The government expressed remorse, but only in the context of the aggressive actions of all colonial powers during the imperialist era. In the view of many Japanese, the actions of their government during the Pacific War were a form of self-defense. When new textbooks were published that openly discussed instances of Japanese wartime misconduct, including sex slavery, the use of slave labor, and the Nanjing Massacre (see Chapter 25), many Japanese were outraged and initiated a campaign to delete or tone down references to atrocities committed by imperial troops during the Pacific War. Several prime ministers have exacerbated the controversy by attending ceremonies at shrines dedicated to the spirits of Japan's war dead.

The issue is not simply an academic one, for fear of a revival of Japanese militarism is still strong in the region, where

Japan's relations with other states have recently been strained by disputes with South Korea and China over ownership of small islands in the China Sea. The proper role of the military has been the subject of vigorous debate in Japan, where some influential officials, including current prime minister Abe, have argued that their country should adopt a more assertive stance toward the United States and play a larger role in Asian affairs. These concerns have increased in recent years, as the potential nuclear threat from nearby North Korea (see "South Korea: A Peninsula Divided" later in this chapter) and a more aggressive posture by powerful China have reminded many Japanese that they live in a dangerous neighborhood.

The Economy

Nowhere are the changes in postwar Japan so visible as in the economic sector, where Japan developed into a major industrial and technological power in the space of a century, surpassing such advanced Western societies as Germany, France, and Great Britain. Although this "Japanese miracle" has often been described as beginning after the war as a result of the Allied reforms, in fact Japanese economic growth began much earlier, with the Meiji reforms, which helped transform Japan from an autocratic society based on semifeudal institutions into an advanced capitalist democracy.

REFORMS DURING THE OCCUPATION As noted earlier, the officials of the Allied occupation identified the Meiji economic system with centralized power and the rise of Japanese militarism. Accordingly, they set out to break up the *zaibatsu* and decentralize Japanese industry and commerce. But with the rise of Cold War tensions, the policy was scaled back. Looser ties between companies were still allowed, and a new type of informal relationship, sometimes called the *keiretsu* (key-RET-soo), or "interlocking arrangement," began to take shape. Through such arrangements among suppliers, wholesalers, retailers, and financial institutions, the *zaibatsu* system was reconstituted under a new name.

The occupation administration had more success with its program to reform the agricultural system. Half of the population still lived on farms, and half of all farmers were still tenants. Under the land reform program, all lands owned by absentee landlords and all cultivated landholdings over an established maximum were sold on easy credit terms to the tenants. The program created a strong class of yeoman farmers, many of whom ardently supported the ruling Liberal Democratic Party, and tenants declined to about 10 percent of the rural population.

THE "JAPANESE MIRACLE" During the next fifty years, Japan re-created the stunning results of the Meiji era. In 1950, the Japanese gross domestic product was about one-third that of Great Britain or France. Thirty years later, it was larger than both put together and well over half that of the United States. Japan became the greatest exporting nation in the world, and its per capita income equaled that of the most advanced Western states.

Explanations for Japan's success tended to fall into two major categories. Some analysts pointed to cultural factors: the Japanese are naturally group oriented and find it easy to cooperate with one another. Traditionally hardworking and frugal, they are more inclined to save than to consume, a trait that boosts the savings rate and labor productivity. Like all Confucian societies, the Japanese value education, and consequently the labor force is highly skilled. The literacy rate is almost 100 percent, and a significantly higher proportion of the population graduates from high school than in most advanced nations of the West.

Other observers gave more practical reasons for Japan's success. Paradoxically, Japan benefited from the total destruction of its industrial base during World War II, in that it did not have to contend with the antiquated plants that held back many industries in the United States. Secure under U.S. protection, Japan spends less than 1 percent of its gross domestic product on national defense (by comparison, the United States spends about 5 percent on defense). In addition, the Japanese government has actively promoted business interests. Some critics have charged that Japan went beyond promotion to unfair trade practices by subsidizing exports through the Ministry of International Trade and Industry (**MITI**), dumping goods at prices below cost to break into foreign markets, maintaining an artificially low standard of living at home to encourage exports, and unduly restricting imports from other countries.

There is some truth on both sides of the argument. Many of the practical steps Japan took were possible precisely because of the cultural factors described here. The tradition of loyalty to the firm, for example, derives from the communal tradition in Japanese society. The concept of sacrificing one's personal interests to those of the state, though not necessarily rooted in the traditional period, was certainly fostered by the *genro* oligarchy during the Meiji era. On the other hand, the power assigned to MITI in managing the Japanese economy was a consequence of occupation policy, when U.S. officials believed that government intervention was necessary to balance the influence possessed by large corporations during the prewar era.

A MIRACLE TARNISHED In recent years, the Japanese economy has run into serious difficulties, raising the question as to whether the vaunted Japanese model is as appealing as many observers earlier declared. A rise in the value of the yen hurt exports and burst the bubble of investment by Japanese banks that had taken place under the umbrella of government protection. Lacking a domestic market equivalent in size to the United States, in the 1990s the Japanese economy slipped into a recession that even now has not entirely abated. Today, about 16 percent of the Japanese population lives in poverty, a figure only slightly lower than in the United States, while unemployment has been hovering around 10 percent.

These economic difficulties have placed heavy pressure on some of the vaunted features of the Japanese economy. The tradition of lifetime employment created a bloated white-collar workforce and has made downsizing difficult. Today, job security is on the decline as increasing numbers of workers are being laid off, and only about one-half of workers aged between fifteen and twenty-four years have regular jobs. A disproportionate burden of the weak economy has fallen on women, who lack seniority and continue to suffer from various forms of discrimination in the workplace. In the meantime, many older Japanese have seen their savings diminish, while retirement programs are increasingly strained by the demands of a rapidly aging population.

A final change is that Japanese consumers have become increasingly critical of the quality of some domestic products, causing one cabinet minister to complain about "sloppiness and complacency" among Japanese firms (even the Japanese automaker Toyota, whose vehicles consistently rank high in quality tests, has been faced with quality problems in its best-selling fleet of motor vehicles). The massive earthquake and tsunami that struck the coast of Japan in 2011 added to the public concern when they exposed the failure of the government to maintain proper safeguards for its nuclear plants in the vicinity. The costs of rebuilding after the disaster will pose a major challenge to Japanese leaders, who already face a crisis of confidence from their constituents.

A Society in Transition

During the occupation, Allied planners set out to change social characteristics that they believed had contributed to Japanese aggressiveness before and during World War II. Films produced under the occupation removed all references to samurai, Japan's historical traditions, and even images of Mount Fuji—once identified as a sacred spot in Shinto mythology. All things identified with the American lifestyle, including baseball, chewing gum, Coca-Cola, and even sex, were extolled. The new educational system removed all references to filial piety, patriotism, and loyalty to the emperor while emphasizing the individualistic values of Western civilization. The new constitution and a revised civil code eliminated remaining legal restrictions on women's rights to obtain a divorce, hold a job, or change their domicile. Women were guaranteed the right to vote and were encouraged to enter politics.[5]

THE PRESSURE TO CONFORM Such efforts to remake Japanese behavior through legislation have had mixed success. During the past sixty-five years, Japan has unquestionably become a more individualistic and egalitarian society. At the same time, many of the distinctive characteristics of traditional Japanese society have persisted to the present day, although in somewhat altered form. The emphasis on loyalty to the group and community relationships, for example, is reflected in the strength of corporate loyalties in contemporary Japan, although, as we have seen, the attitude has eroded in recent years.

Emphasis on the work ethic also remains strong. The tradition of hard work is taught at a young age. Japanese students attend school 240 days a year, compared with 180 days in the United States, and homework assignments tend to be more extensive. The results are impressive: Japanese schoolchildren consistently earn higher scores on achievement tests than children in other advanced countries. At the same time, this devotion to success has often been accompanied by bullying by teachers and an emphasis on conformity (see the box "Growing Up in Japan" on p. 923).

Some young Japanese find suicide the only escape from the pressures emanating from society, school, and family. Parental pride often becomes a factor, with "education mothers" pressuring their children to work hard and succeed for the honor of the family. Ironically, once the student is accepted into college, the amount of work assigned tends to decrease because graduates of the best universities are virtually guaranteed lucrative employment offers. Nevertheless, the early training instills an attitude of deference to group interests that persists throughout life.

By all accounts, however, independent thinking is on the increase in Japan. In some cases, it leads to antisocial behavior, such as crime or membership in a teenage gang. Crime rates, while well below those in the United States, have risen dramatically, leading Prime Minister Koizumi to lament in 2003 that Japan was no longer "the world's safest country." Antisocial feeling, however, is usually expressed in more indirect ways, such as the recent fashion among young people of dyeing their hair brown (known in Japanese as "tea hair"). Because the practice is banned in many schools and generally frowned on by the older generation (one police chief dumped a pitcher of beer on a student with brown hair whom he noticed in a bar), many young Japanese dye their hair as a gesture of independence. When seeking employment or getting married, however, they return their hair to its natural color.

WOMEN IN JAPANESE SOCIETY One of the most tenacious legacies of the past in Japanese society is sexual inequality. Although women are now legally protected against discrimination in employment, very few have reached senior levels in business, education, or politics. Women now comprise nearly 50 percent of the workforce but most are in retail or service occupations. Less than 10 percent of managerial workers in Japan are women, compared with nearly half in the United States. There is a feminist movement in Japan but it has none of the vigor and mass support of its counterpart in the United States.

There is no stigma attached to being a homemaker in Japan, where a woman has considerable responsibility. She is expected to be a "good wife and wise mother" and has the primary responsibility for managing the family finances and raising the children. Japanese husbands (known derisively in Japan as the "wet leaf tribe") perform little work around the house, spending (according to a recent study of social changes in Japan) an average of nine minutes a day on housework, compared with twenty-six minutes for American husbands. At the same time, Japanese divorce rates are well below those of the United States.

Growing Up in Japan

FAMILY & SOCIETY

JAPANESE SCHOOLCHILDREN are exposed to a much more regimented environment than U.S. children experience. Most Japanese schoolchildren, for example, wear black-and-white uniforms to school. These regulations are examples of rules adopted by middle school systems in various parts of Japan. The Ministry of Education in Tokyo concluded that these regulations were excessive, but they are probably typical.

School Regulations, Japanese Style

1. Boys' hair should not touch the eyebrows, the ears, or the top of the collar.
2. No one should have a permanent wave or dye his or her hair. Girls should not wear ribbons or accessories in their hair. Hair dryers should not be used.
3. School uniform skirts should be ___ centimeters above the ground, no more and no less (differs by school and region).
4. Keep your uniform clean and pressed at all times. Girls' middy blouses should have two buttons on the back collar. Boys' pant cuffs should be of the prescribed width. No more than 12 eyelets should be on shoes. The number of buttons on a shirt and tucks in a shirt are also prescribed.
5. Wear your school badge at all times. It should be positioned exactly.
6. Going to school in the morning, wear your book bag strap on the right shoulder; in the afternoon on the way home, wear it on the left shoulder. Your book case thickness, filled and unfilled, is also prescribed.
7. Girls should wear only regulation white underpants of 100% cotton.
8. When you raise your hand to be called on, your arm should extend forward and up at the angle prescribed in your handbook.
9. Your own route to and from school is marked in your student rule handbook; carefully observe which side of each street you are to use on the way to and from school.
10. After school you are to go directly home, unless your parent has written a note permitting you to go to another location. Permission will not be granted by the school unless this other location is a suitable one. You must not go to coffee shops. You must be home by ___ o'clock.
11. It is not permitted to drive or ride a motorcycle, or to have a license to drive one.
12. Before and after school, no matter where you are, you represent our school, so you should behave in ways we can all be proud of.

 What is the apparent purpose of these regulations? Why does Japan appear to place more restrictions on adolescent behavior than the United States does?

Source: From M. White, *The Material Child: Coming of Age in Japan and America* (New York: Free Press, 1993).

THE DEMOGRAPHIC CRISIS   Many of Japan's current dilemmas stem from its growing demographic problems. Today, Japan has the highest proportion of people older than sixty-five of any industrialized country—almost 23 percent of the country's total population. By the year 2024, an estimated one-third of the Japanese population will be over the age of sixty-five, and the median age will be fifty, ten years older than the median in the United States. This demographic profile is due both to declining fertility and a low level of immigration. Immigrants make up only 1 percent of the total population of Japan. Together, the aging population and the absence of immigrants are creating the prospect of a dramatic labor shortage in coming years. Nevertheless, prejudice against foreigners persists in Japan, and the government remains reluctant to ease restrictions against immigrants from other countries in the region.

Japan's aging population has many implications for the future. Traditionally, it was the responsibility of the eldest child in a Japanese family to care for aging parents but that system is beginning to break down because of limited housing space and the growing tendency of working-age women to seek jobs in the marketplace. The proportion of Japanese older than sixty-five years of age who live with their children has dropped from 80 percent in 1970 to about 50 percent today. At the same time, public and private pension plans are under increasing financial pressure, partly because of the low birthrate and the graying population.

RELIGION   When Japan was opened to the West in the nineteenth century, many Japanese became convinced of the superiority of foreign ideas and institutions and were especially interested in Western religion and culture. Although Christian converts were few, numbering less than 1 percent of the population, the influence of Christianity was out of proportion to the size of the community. Many intellectuals during the Meiji era were impressed by the emotional commitment shown by missionaries in Japan and viewed Christianity as a contemporary version of Confucianism.

Today, Japan includes almost 1.5 million Christians, along with 93 million Buddhists. Many Japanese also follow Shinto, no longer identified with reverence for the emperor and the state. As in the West, increasing urbanization has led to a decline in the practice of organized religion, although evangelical sects have proliferated in recent years. The largest and best-known sect is Soka Gakkai (SOH-kuh GAK-ky), a lay Buddhist organization that has attracted millions of followers and formed its own political party, the Komeito (koh-MAY-toh). Zen Buddhism retains its popularity, and some businesspeople seek to use Zen techniques to learn how to focus on willpower as a means of outwitting a competitor. The head of one Zen monastery, however, has publicly apologized for the sect's role in promoting fanatical patriotism in the military before World War II.

Japanese Culture

Western literature, art, and music have had a major impact on Japanese society. After World War II, many of the writers who had been active before the war resurfaced but now their writing reflected demoralization. Many were attracted to existentialism, and some turned to hedonism and nihilism. For some, defeat was compounded by fear of the Americanization of postwar Japan. One of the best examples of this attitude was the novelist Yukio Mishima (yoo-KEE-oh mi-SHEE-muh) (1925–1970), who led a crusade to stem the tide of what he described as America's "universal and uniform 'Coca-Colonization'" of the world in general and Japan in particular.[6] Mishima's ritual suicide in 1970 was the subject of widespread speculation and transformed him into a cult figure.

One of Japan's most serious-minded contemporary authors is Kenzaburo Oe (ken-zuh-BOO-roh OH-ay) (b. 1935), whose work portrays Japan's ongoing quest for modern identity and purpose. His characters reflect the spiritual anguish precipitated by the collapse of the imperial Japanese tradition and the subsequent adoption of Western culture—a trend that Oe contends has culminated in unabashed materialism, cultural decline, and a moral void. Yet unlike Mishima, Oe does not wish to reinstill the imperial traditions of the past but rather seeks to regain spiritual meaning by retrieving the sense of communality and innocence found in rural Japan.

Haruki Murakami (HAR-oo-kee moo-rah-KAH-mee) (b. 1949), one of Japan's most popular authors today, was one of the first to discard the introspective and somber style of the earlier postwar period. Characters in his novels typically take the form of a detached antihero, reflecting the emptiness of corporate life in contemporary Japan. In *The Wind-Up Bird Chronicle* (1997), Murakami highlights the capacity for irrational violence in Japanese society and the failure of the nation to accept its guilt for the behavior of Japanese troops during World War II.

Since the 1970s, increasing affluence and a high literacy rate have contributed to a massive quantity of publications, ranging from popular potboilers to first-rate fiction. Much of this new literature deals with the common concerns of all affluent industrialized nations, including the effects of urbanization, advanced technology, and mass consumption. A wildly popular genre is the "art-manga," or graphic novel. Some members of the youth counterculture have used manga to rebel against Japan's rigid educational and conformist pressures. Other aspects of Japanese culture have also been influenced by Western ideas. Western music is very popular in

KFC in Japan. Although Japan has been widely criticized over the years for its reluctance to import goods from other countries, the Japanese people were among the first to adopt many aspects of Western culture after World War II. Mickey Mouse, fashionable sneakers, and Kentucky Fried Chicken were especially popular. Their growing familiarity with the American way of life was undoubtedly heightened by the presence of U.S. occupation forces at the end of the war. This KFC outlet, complete with a statue of Colonel Sanders, appears on a downtown street in Kobe, Japan.

Japan, and scores of Japanese classical musicians have succeeded in the West. Even rap music has gained a foothold among Japanese youth, although without the association with sex, drugs, and violence that it has in the United States. No longer are Japanese authors, painters, and musicians seeking to revive the old Japan of the tea ceremony and falling plum blossoms. Raised in the crowded cities of postwar Japan, soaking up movies and television, rock music and jeans, Coca-Cola and McDonald's, many contemporary Japanese speak the universal language of today's world.

The Japanese Difference

Whether the unique character of modern Japan—a complex amalgam of traditional and modern—will endure is unclear.

Confidence in the Japanese "economic miracle" has been shaken by the long recession, and there are indications of a growing tendency toward hedonism and individualism among Japanese youth. Older Japanese frequently complain that the younger generation lacks their sense of loyalty and willingness to sacrifice. There are also signs that the concept of loyalty to one's employer may be beginning to erode among Japanese youth. Some observers have predicted that with declining job security Japan will become more like the industrialized societies in the West. Although Japan is unlikely to evolve into a photocopy of the United States, the vaunted image of millions of dedicated "salarymen" heading off to work with their briefcases and their pin-striped suits may no longer be an accurate portrayal of reality in contemporary Japan.

The Little Tigers

 FOCUS QUESTIONS: What factors have contributed to the economic success achieved by the Little Tigers? To what degree have they applied the Japanese model in forging their developmental strategies?

Postwar Japan's success in meeting the challenge from the capitalist West soon caught the eye of other Asian nations. By the 1980s, several smaller states in the region, known collectively as the Little Tigers, had embraced the Japanese example.

South Korea: A Peninsula Divided

While the world was focused on the economic miracle occurring on the Japanese islands, another miracle of sorts was taking place across the sea on the Asian mainland. In 1953, the Korean peninsula was exhausted from three years of bitter fraternal war, a conflict that took the lives of an estimated 4 million Koreans on both sides of the 38th parallel and turned as much as one-quarter of the population into refugees. Although a cease-fire was signed in July 1953, it was a fragile peace that left two heavily armed and mutually hostile countries facing each other suspiciously.

North of the truce line was the People's Republic of Korea (PRK), a police state under the dictatorial rule of the Communist leader Kim Il Sung (KIM ILL SOONG) (1912–1994). To the south was the Republic of Korea (ROK), under the equally autocratic President Syngman Rhee (SING-muhn REE) (1875–1965), a fierce anti-communist who had led the resistance to the northern invasion. But many Koreans resented Rhee's reliance on the wealthy landlord class. After several years of harsh rule, marked by government corruption, fraudulent elections, and police brutality, demonstrations broke out in the capital city of Seoul in the spring of 1960 and forced him into retirement.

THE KOREAN MODEL The Rhee era was followed by a brief period of multiparty democratic government, but in 1961, a coup d'état placed General Park Chung-Hee (1917–1979) in power. The new regime promulgated a new constitution, and in 1963, Park was elected president of a civilian government. He set out to foster recovery of the economy from decades of foreign occupation and civil war. Because the private sector had been relatively weak under Japanese rule, the government played an active role in the process by instituting a series of five-year plans that targeted specific industries for development, promoted exports, and funded infrastructure development. Under a land reform program, large landowners were required to sell all their farmland above 7.4 acres to their tenants at low prices.

The program was a solid success. Benefiting from the Confucian principles of thrift, respect for education, and hard work, as well as from Japanese capital and technology, South Korea gradually emerged as a major industrial power in East Asia. The economic growth rate rose from less than 5 percent annually in the 1950s to an average of 9 percent under Park Chung-Hee. The largest corporations—including Samsung, Daewoo, and Hyundai—were transformed into massive conglomerates called *chaebol* (jay-BOHL or je-BUHL), the Korean equivalent of the *zaibatsu* of prewar Japan. Taking advantage of relatively low wages and a stunningly high rate of saving, Korean businesses began to compete actively with the Japanese for export markets in Asia and throughout the world. Per capita income also increased dramatically, from less than $90 (in U.S. dollars) annually in 1960 to $1,560 (twice that of communist North Korea) twenty years later.

But like many other countries in the region, South Korea was slow to develop democratic principles. Although his government functioned with the trappings of democracy, Park continued to rule by autocratic means and suppressed all forms of dissidence. In 1979, Park was assassinated. But after a brief interregnum of democratic rule, in 1980 a new military government seized power. The new regime was as authoritarian as its predecessors but after widespread student protests erupted in 1987, national elections were finally held, and in 1989, South Korea reverted to civilian rule. Successive presidents sought with varying degrees of success to rein in corruption while cracking down on the *chaebols* and initiating contacts with the Communist regime in

The Korean Peninsula Since 1953

Map labels: Cease-fire line; CHINA; Yalu R.; NORTH KOREA; Korea Bay; Pyongyang; Panmunjom; Seoul; Inchon; SOUTH KOREA; Yellow Sea; Kwangju; Pusan; Sea of Japan (East Sea); Tumen R.; 38th Parallel; Korea Strait; JAPAN; 0 150 300 Kilometers; 0 100 200 Miles the PRK in an effort to seek eventual reunification of the peninsula. After the Asian financial crisis in 1997, economic conditions temporarily worsened but they have since recovered. In elections held in 2012, South Korea elected its first woman president, Park Guen-hye (Pahk Goon-heh) (b. 1952), the daughter of Park Chung-Hee.

In the meantime, however, relations with North Korea, now on the verge of becoming a nuclear power, remain tense. Multinational negotiations to persuade the regime to suspend its nuclear program have been under way for several years, so far without success. To add to the uncertainty, the regime recently faced a succession crisis, when Kim Il Sung's son and successor, Kim Jong Il (1941–2011), died suddenly in 2011 and was replaced by his inexperienced son Kim Jong Un (b. 1984). The transfer of power was accompanied by a purge of a number of senior officials in the capital at Pyongyang.

SOUTH KOREA: THE LITTLE TIGER WITH SHARP TEETH South Korea today is one of the most competitive economies in the world. Its manufactures rival in popularity those of other East Asian nations for predominance in world markets. Japanese observers complain about the country's "hungry spirit," which steals jobs from Japanese workers. Some critics inside the country, however, worry that Koreans put too much emphasis on achieving success and that many children spend so much time preparing for college entrance examinations that they are deprived of a normal childhood.

Modern Taiwan

Whether the Korean people's drive to get ahead in life is seen as a benefit or a disadvantage, there is no doubt that, as in many other East Asian countries, South Korea is changing rapidly. A predominantly rural nation at the end of World War II, it is now a manufacturing powerhouse. Though it has historically had a homogeneous population, it now hosts a growing foreign population, many of whom are low-wage workers or young women brought in from other parts of Asia to marry Koreans living in rural areas, where the shortage of marriageable Korean women is acute. The traumatic effect of the transformation of the ROK from a rural to an urban society has been ably described by author Kyung-Sook Shin (b. 1963), whose recent novel entitled *Please Look After Mom* portrays the growing gap between young middle-class urban Koreans and their aging parents living in the countryside.

Taiwan: The Other China

South Korea was not the only rising industrial power trying to imitate the success of the Japanese in East Asia. To the south on the island of Taiwan, the Republic of China began to do the same.

After retreating to Taiwan following their defeat by the Communists, Chiang Kai-shek and his followers established a new capital at Taipei. The government, which continued to refer to itself as the Republic of China (ROC), contended that it remained the legitimate representative of the Chinese people and that it would eventually return in triumph to the mainland.

Mending the Safety Net in South Korea. Until recently, it was common for South Korean parents to live with their eldest son's family in their senior years, a price that was viewed as a reward for their past sacrifices in raising their children. But with the country now transformed into an industrial and urbanized society, this social contract has eroded. As their children move into the cities to find employment, older Koreans are often left to fend for themselves in rural areas. Because the government has not yet established an adequate social security network, the elderly are often left in desperate straits. These elderly gentlemen appear to be among the more fortunate of their compatriots as they enjoy an outing at a park in the port city of Pusan.

The Nationalists had much more success on Taiwan than they had achieved on the mainland. In the relatively stable environment provided by a security treaty with the United States, signed in 1954, the ROC was able to concentrate on economic growth without worrying about a Communist invasion. First it moved rapidly to create a solid agricultural base. A land reform program led to a reduction of rents, and landholdings over 3 acres were purchased by the government and resold to the tenants at reasonable prices. At the same time, local manufacturing and commerce were strongly encouraged. By the 1970s, Taiwan had become one of the most dynamic industrial economies in East Asia. The government played a major role in the process, targeting strategic industries for support and investing in infrastructure. At the same time, as in Japan, the government stressed the importance of private enterprise and encouraged foreign investment and a high rate of internal savings.

In contrast to the Communist regime across the Taiwan Strait, the ROC actively maintained Chinese tradition, promoting respect for Confucius and its ethical principles of hard work, frugality, and filial piety. Although there was some corruption in both the government and the private sector, income differentials between the wealthy and the poor were generally less than elsewhere in the region, and the overall standard of living increased substantially. Health and sanitation improved, literacy rates were quite high, and an active family planning program reduced the rate of population growth. Nevertheless, the total population on the island increased from about 7 million in 1945 to about 20 million in the mid-1980s.

At first, increasing prosperity did not lead to the democratization of the political process, as the Nationalist government continued to rule by emergency decree and refused to permit the formation of opposition political parties on the ground that the danger of invasion from the mainland had not subsided. Some friction developed between the mainlanders, who numbered about 2 million and were dominant in the government, and the indigenous Taiwanese (mostly ethnic Chinese whose ancestors had migrated to the island during the Qing Dynasty). By the 1980s, however, these fissures in Taiwanese society had begun to diminish; by then, an ever-higher proportion of the population had been born on the island and identified themselves as Taiwanese.

After the death of Chiang Kai-shek in 1975, the ROC slowly began to move toward a more representative form of government. A national election in 1992 resulted in a bare majority for the Nationalists over strong opposition from the Democratic Progressive Party (DPP). But political liberalization had its dangers; some members of the DPP began to agitate for an independent Republic of Taiwan, a possibility that aroused concern within the Nationalist

government in Taipei and frenzied hostility on the mainland. The election of DPP leader Chen Shuibian (CHUHN SHWAY-BEE-ahn) (b. 1950) as ROC president in March 2000 angered Beijing, which threatened to invade Taiwan if the island continued to delay unification with the mainland. In 2007, the government returned to Nationalist control, a result that, at least for the time being, has eased relations with mainland China.

Whether Taiwan will remain an independent state or be united with the mainland cannot be predicted at this time. Although diplomatic ties have been severed, the United States continues to provide defensive military assistance to the Taiwanese armed forces and has made it clear that it supports self-determination for the people of Taiwan and that it expects the final resolution of the Chinese civil war to be by peaceful means. In the meantime, economic and cultural contacts between Taiwan and the mainland are steadily increasing. Nevertheless, the Taiwanese have shown no inclination to accept the PRC's offer of "one country, two systems," under which the ROC would accept the PRC as the legitimate government of China in return for autonomous control over the affairs of Taiwan.

Singapore and Hong Kong: The Littlest Tigers

The smallest but by no means least successful of the Little Tigers are Singapore and Hong Kong. Both are essentially city-states, with large populations densely packed into small territories. Singapore, once a British colony and briefly a part of the state of Malaysia, is now an independent nation. Hong Kong was a British colony for a century until it was returned to loose PRC sovereignty in 1997. In recent years, both have emerged as industrial powerhouses, with standards of living well above those of their neighbors.

The Republic of Singapore

The success of Singapore must be ascribed in good measure to the will and energy of its political leaders. When it became independent in August 1965, Singapore's longtime position as an entrepôt for trade between the Indian Ocean and the South China Sea was on the wane. With only 618 square miles of territory, much of it marshland and tropical jungle, Singapore had little to offer but the frugality and industriousness of its predominantly overseas Chinese population.

Within a decade, Singapore's role and reputation had dramatically changed. Under the leadership of Prime Minister Lee Kuan-yew (LEE kwahn-YOO) (b. 1923), once the firebrand leader of the radical People's Action Party, the government cultivated an attractive business climate while engaging in massive public works projects to feed, house, and educate its 2 million citizens. The major components of success have been shipbuilding, oil refineries, tourism, electronics, and

To Those Living in Glass Houses

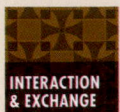

Kɪsʜoʀe Mᴀʜʙᴜʙᴀɴɪ (KEE-shore MAH-boo-bahn-ee (b. 1948) was permanent secretary in the Ministry of Foreign Affairs in Singapore from 1993 to 1998. Previously, he served as his country's ambassador to the United Nations. In this 1994 article, adapted from a piece in the *Washington Quarterly*, the author advises his audience to stop lecturing Asian societies on the issue of human rights and focus attention instead on problems in the United States. In his view, today the countries of the West have much to learn from their counterparts in East Asia. This viewpoint is shared by many other observers, political leaders, and foreign affairs specialists in the region.

Kishore Mahbubani, "Go East, Young Man"

In a major reversal of a pattern lasting centuries, many Western societies, including the U.S., are doing some major things fundamentally wrong, while a growing number of East Asian societies are doing the same things right. The results are most evident in the economic sphere. In purchasing power parity terms, East Asia's gross domestic product is already larger than that of either the U.S. or European community. Such economic prosperity, contrary to American belief, results not just from free-market arrangements but also from the right social and political choices....

In most Asian eyes, the evidence of real social decay in the U.S. is clear and palpable. Since 1960, the U.S. population has grown by 41%. In the same period, there has been a 560% increase in violent crimes, a 419% increase in illegitimate births, a 400% increase in divorce rates, a 300% increase in children living in single-parent homes, a more than 200% increase in teenage suicide rates, and a drop of almost

80 points in [SAT] scores. A clear American paradox is that a society that places such a high premium on freedom has effectively reduced the physical freedom of most Americans, especially those who live in large cities. They live in heavily fortified homes, think twice before taking an evening stroll around their neighborhoods, and feel increasingly threatened by random violence when they are outside.

To any Asian, it is obvious that the breakdown of the family and social order in the U.S. owes itself to a mindless ideology that maintains that the freedom of a small number of individuals who are known to pose a threat to society (criminals, terrorists, street gang members, drug dealers) should not be constrained (for example, through detention without trial), even if to do so would enhance the freedom of the majority.... This belief is purely and simply a gross violation of common sense.

My hope is that Americans will come to visit East Asia in greater numbers. When they do, they will come to realize that their society has swung much too much in one direction: liberating the individual while imprisoning society. The relatively strong and stable family and social institutions of East Asia will appear more appealing. And as Americans experience the freedom of walking on city streets in Asia, they may begin to understand that freedom can also result from greater social order and discipline. Perhaps the best advice to give to a young American is: "Go East, Young Man."

 What are Mahbubani's criticisms of Western civilization? How does he justify the "Asian" approach to politics?

Source: From *Far Eastern Economic Review* (May 19, 1994), p. 32.

---

finance—the city-state has become the banking hub of the entire region.

Like South Korea and Taiwan, Singapore relied on a combination of government planning, entrepreneurial spirit, export promotion, high productivity, and an exceptionally high rate of saving to achieve industrial growth rates of nearly 10 percent annually during the last quarter of the twentieth century. As in the other Little Tigers, an authoritarian political system was adopted to guarantee a stable environment for economic growth. Until his retirement in 1990, Lee Kuan-yew and his People's Action Party dominated Singapore politics, and opposition elements were intimidated into silence or arrested. The prime minister openly declared that the Western model of pluralist democracy was not appropriate for Singapore and lauded the Meiji model of centralized

development (see the box "To Those Living in Glass Houses" above). Confucian values of thrift, hard work, and obedience to authority have been promoted as the ideology of the state. Opposition voices have been harshly silenced.

In recent years, however, economic success has begun to undermine the authoritarian foundations of the system as a more sophisticated citizenry voices aspirations for more political freedoms and an end to government paternalism. Lee Kuan-yew's successor, Goh Chok-tong (GO chawk-TONG) (b. 1941), promised a "kinder, gentler" Singapore, and political restrictions on individual behavior were gradually relaxed. The process continued under Goh's successor, Lee Hsien-loong (LEE HAZ-ee-en-LAHNG) (b. 1952), the son of Lee Kuan-yew. After the new prime minister assumed office in 2004, the government announced plans to relax restrictions

National Day in Singapore. The tiny island of Singapore received its independence on August 9, 1965, when it separated from Malaysia to become an independent state. Since then, the event has been celebrated each year on what is called "National Day," with events scheduled at locations throughout the country. Because the vast majority of citizens in Singapore live in housing complexes called "estates," many of these ceremonies take place close to their place of residence. This celebration took place at the Ang Mo Kio estate and included a traditional Chinese snake dance. As a small and ethnically diverse country surrounded by more powerful neighbors, the government of Singapore places exceptional importance on instilling a sense of patriotism among its citizens.

on freedom of speech and assembly in the small island-state. Elections held in 2011 resulted in growing support for members of opposition parties.

The future of Hong Kong is not so clear-cut. As in Singapore, sensible government policies and the hard work of its people have enabled Hong Kong to thrive. At first, the prosperity of the colony depended on a plentiful supply of cheap labor. Inundated with refugees from the mainland during the 1950s and 1960s, the population of Hong Kong burgeoned to more than 6 million. More recently, Hong Kong has benefited from increased tourism, manufacturing, and the growing economic prosperity of neighboring Guangdong province, the most prosperous region of the PRC. Unlike the other societies discussed in this chapter, Hong Kong has relied on an unbridled free market system rather than active state intervention in the economy. At the same time, by allocating substantial funds for transportation, sanitation, education, and public housing, the government has created favorable conditions for economic development.

When Britain's ninety-nine-year lease on the New Territories, the food basket of the colony, expired on July 1, 1997, Hong Kong returned to mainland authority (see the box "Return to the Motherland" on p. 930). Although the Chinese promised the British that for fifty years the people of Hong Kong would live under a capitalist system and be essentially self-governing, recent statements by Chinese leaders have raised questions about the degree of autonomy Hong Kong will continue to receive under Chinese rule. In recent years, pro-democracy candidates have done well in

Hong Kong

local elections, and a vigorous protest movement seeks to pressure elected officials to resist pressures for conformity from the government in Beijing.

On the Margins of Asia: Postwar Australia and New Zealand

Geographically, Australia and New Zealand are not part of Asia, and throughout their short history, both countries have identified culturally and politically with the West rather than with their Pacific Rim neighbors. Their political institutions and values are derived from Europe, and their economies resemble those of the advanced countries of the world rather than the preindustrial societies of much of Southeast Asia. Both are currently members of the British Commonwealth and of the U.S.-led ANZUS alliance (Australia, New Zealand, and the United States).

Yet trends in recent years have been drawing both states, especially Australia, closer to Asia. In the first place, immigration from East and Southeast Asia has increased rapidly. More than one-half of current immigrants into Australia come from East Asia, and about 7 percent of the population of about 18 million people is now of Asian descent. In New Zealand, residents of Asian descent represent only about 3 percent of the population of 3.5 million, but about 12 percent of the population are Maoris, Polynesian peoples who settled on the islands about a thousand years ago. Second, trade relations with Asia are increasing rapidly. About 60 percent of Australia's export markets today are in East Asia, and the region is the source of about half of

Return to the Motherland

POLITICS & GOVERNMENT

AFTER LENGTHY NEGOTIATIONS, in 1984 China and Great Britain agreed that on July 1, 1997, Hong Kong would return to Chinese sovereignty. Key sections of the agreement are included here. In succeeding years, authorities of the two countries held further negotiations. Some of the discussions raised questions in the minds of residents of Hong Kong as to whether their individual liberties would indeed be respected after the colony's return to China.

The Joint Declaration on Hong Kong

The Hong Kong Special Administrative Region will be directly under the authority of the Central People's Government of the People's Republic of China. The Hong Kong Special Administrative Region will enjoy a high degree of autonomy, except in foreign and defense affairs, which are the responsibility of the Central People's Government.

The Hong Kong Special Administrative Region will be vested with executive, legislative, and independent judicial power, including that of final adjudication. The laws currently in force in Hong Kong will remain basically unchanged.

Source: From Kevin Rafferty, *City on the Rocks* (New York: Penguin, 1991).

The Government of the Hong Kong Special Administrative Region will be composed of local inhabitants. The chief executive will be appointed by the Central People's Government on the basis of the results of elections or consultations by the chief executive of the Hong Kong Special Administrative Region for appointment by the Central People's Government....

The current social and economic systems in Hong Kong will remain unchanged, and so will the lifestyle. Rights and freedoms, including those of the person, of speech, of the press, of assembly, of association, of travel, of movement, of correspondence, of strike, of choice of occupation, of academic research, and of religious belief will be ensured by law.... Private property, ownership of enterprises, legitimate right of inheritance, and foreign investment will be protected by law.

 To what degree are the people of Hong Kong self-governing under these regulations? How do the regulations infringe on the freedom of the population?

CHRONOLOGY	Japan and the Little Tigers Since World War II	
End of World War II in the Pacific		1945
Chiang Kai-shek retreats to Taiwan		1949
End of U.S. occupation of Japan		1950
Korean War		1950–1953
United States–Republic of China security treaty		1954
Syngman Rhee overthrown in South Korea		1960
Rise to power of Park Chung-Hee in South Korea		1961
Independence of Singapore		1965
Death of Chiang Kai-shek		1975
Park Chung-Hee assassinated		1979
Student riots in South Korea		1987
Lee Kuan-yew era ends in Singapore		1990
First free general elections on Taiwan		1992
Return of Hong Kong to Chinese control		1997
Financial crisis hits the region		1997
Chen Shuibian elected president of Taiwan		2000
Junichiro Koizumi elected prime minister in Japan		2001
Koizumi era ends in Japan		2006
Nationalist Party returns to power in Taiwan		2007
Lee Myung-bak elected president of South Korea		2007
Earthquake and tsunami in Japan		2011

its imports. Asian trade with New Zealand is also on the increase.

Whether Australia and New Zealand will ever become an integral part of the Asia-Pacific region, however, is uncertain. Cultural differences stemming from the European origins of the majority of the population in both countries hinder mutual understanding on both sides of the divide, and many ASEAN leaders express reluctance to accept the two countries as full members of the alliance. But economic and geographic realities act as a powerful force, and should the Pacific region continue on its current course toward economic prosperity and political stability, the role of Australia and New Zealand will assume greater significance.

Explaining the East Asian Miracle

What explains the striking ability of Japan and the four Little Tigers to transform themselves into export-oriented societies capable of competing with the advanced nations of Europe and the Western Hemisphere? Some analysts point to the traditional character traits of Confucian societies, such as thrift, a work ethic, respect for education, and obedience to authority. In a recent poll of Asian executives, more than 80 percent expressed the belief that Asian values differ from those of the West, and most add that these values have contributed significantly to the region's recent success. Others place more emphasis on deliberate steps taken by government and economic leaders to meet the political, economic, and social challenges their societies face.

There seems no reason to doubt that cultural factors connected to East Asian social traditions have contributed to the economic success of these societies. Certainly, habits such as frugality, industriousness, and subordination of individual desires have all played a role in their governments' ability to concentrate on the collective interest. As this and preceding chapters have shown, however, without active encouragement by political elites, such traditions cannot be effectively harnessed for the good of society as a whole. The creative talents of the Chinese people, for example, were not efficiently utilized under Mao Zedong during the frenetic years of the Cultural Revolution. Only when Deng Xiaoping and other pragmatists took charge and began to place a high priority on economic development were the stunning advances of recent decades achieved. By the same token, political elites elsewhere in East Asia were aware of traditional values and willing to use them for national purposes.

One other factor should be taken into account. Japan and the Little Tigers were operating within a regional framework highly conducive to rapid economic development. The Little Tigers received substantial inputs of capital and technology from the advanced nations of the West—Taiwan and South Korea from the United States, Hong Kong and Singapore from Britain. Japan relied to a greater degree on its own efforts but received a significant advantage by being placed under the U.S. security umbrella and guaranteed access to markets and sources of raw materials in a region dominated by U.S. naval power. In effect, the rapid rise of East Asia in the postwar era was no miracle, but a fortuitous combination of favorable cultural factors and deliberate human action.

CHAPTER SUMMARY

In the years following the end of World War II, the peoples of Asia emerged from a century of imperial rule to face the challenge of building stable and prosperous independent states. Initially, progress was slow, as new political leaders were forced to deal with the legacy of colonialism and internal disagreements over their visions for the future. By the end of the century, however, most nations in the area were beginning to lay the foundations for the creation of advanced industrial societies. Today, major Asian states like China, Japan, and India have become major competitors of the advanced Western nations in the international marketplace.

To some observers, these economic achievements have come at a high price, in the form of political authoritarianism and a lack of attention to human rights. Rapid economic development has also exacted an environmental price. Industrial pollution in China and India and the destruction of the forest cover in Southeast Asia increasingly threaten the fragile ecosystem and create friction among nations in the region. Unless they learn to cooperate effectively to deal with the challenge in future years, it will ultimately undermine the dramatic economic and social progress that has taken place.

Still, a look at the historical record suggests that, for the most part, the nations of southern and eastern Asia have made dramatic progress in coping with the multiple challenges of independence. Political pluralism is often a by-product—admittedly

sometimes delayed—of economic growth, while a rising standard of living should enable the peoples of the region to meet the social and environmental challenges that lie ahead.

CHAPTER TIMELINE

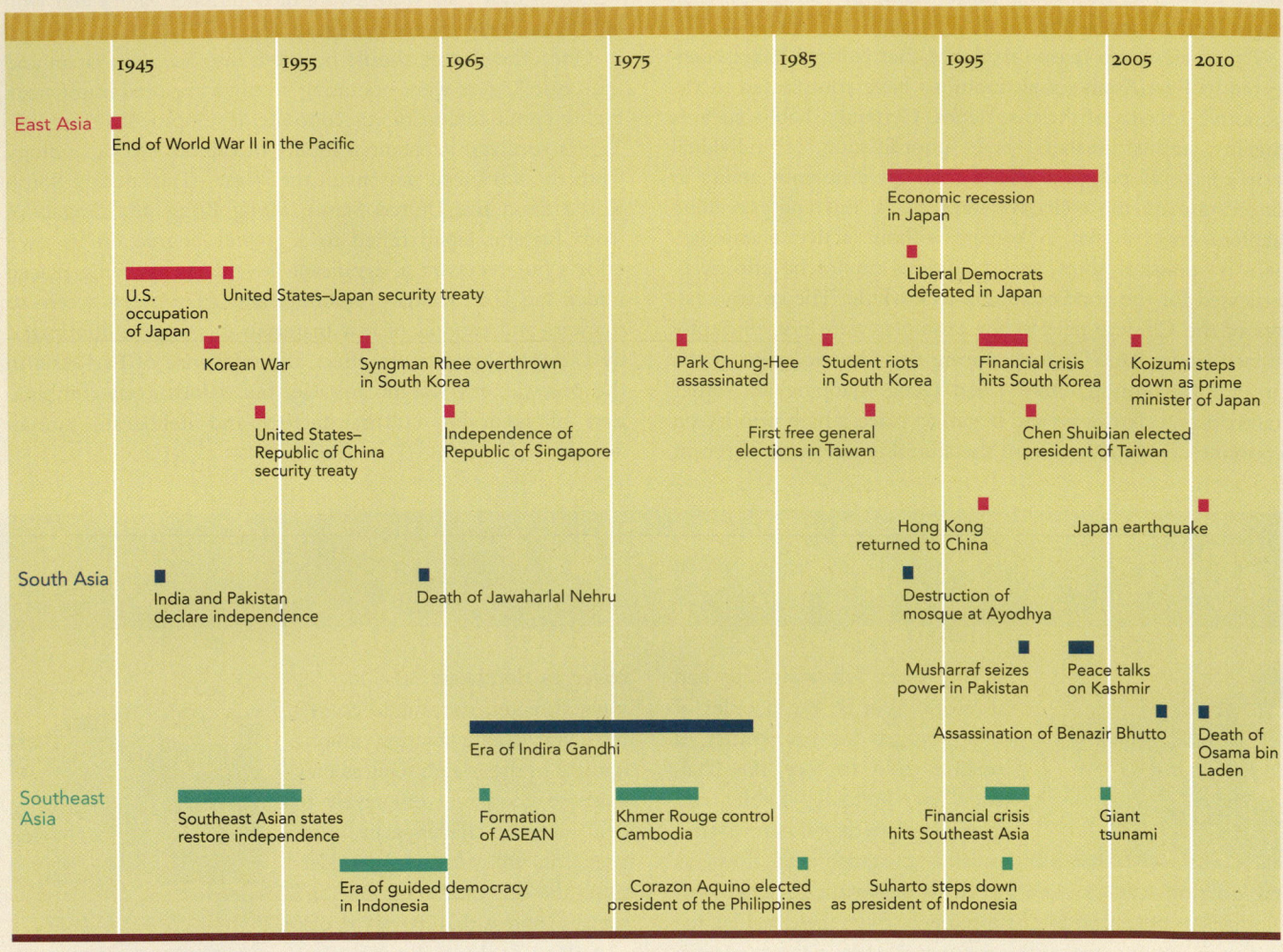

East Asia

1945	1955	1965	1975	1985	1995	2005	2010

End of World War II in the Pacific

Economic recession in Japan

Liberal Democrats defeated in Japan

U.S. occupation of Japan

United States–Japan security treaty

Korean War

Syngman Rhee overthrown in South Korea

Park Chung-Hee assassinated

Student riots in South Korea

Financial crisis hits South Korea

Koizumi steps down as prime minister of Japan

United States–Republic of China security treaty

Independence of Republic of Singapore

First free general elections in Taiwan

Chen Shuibian elected president of Taiwan

Hong Kong returned to China

Japan earthquake

South Asia

India and Pakistan declare independence

Death of Jawaharlal Nehru

Destruction of mosque at Ayodhya

Era of Indira Gandhi

Musharraf seizes power in Pakistan

Peace talks on Kashmir

Assassination of Benazir Bhutto

Death of Osama bin Laden

Southeast Asia

Southeast Asian states restore independence

Formation of ASEAN

Khmer Rouge control Cambodia

Financial crisis hits Southeast Asia

Giant tsunami

Era of guided democracy in Indonesia

Corazon Aquino elected president of the Philippines

Suharto steps down as president of Indonesia

CHAPTER REVIEW

Upon Reflection

Q What kinds of environmental problems are currently being faced by the nations of southern and eastern Asia? How have the region's political leaders sought to deal with the problems?

Q How has independence affected the role of women in southern and eastern Asia? What factors are involved?

Q How have the nations in the region dealt with the challenge of integrating their ethnic and religious minorities into their political systems?

Key Terms

green revolution (p. 902)
dalits (p. 903)
guided democracy (p. 910)
ASEAN (p. 914)

SCAP (p. 917)
Burakumin (p. 920)
keiretsu (p. 921)
MITI (p. 921)
chaebol (p. 925)

Suggested Reading

THE INDIAN SUBCONTINENT SINCE 1945   For a survey of postwar Indian history, see **S. Tharoor**, *India: From Midnight to the Millennium* (New York, 1997). A thoughtful account of India's current problems is **M. Nussbaum**, *The Clash Within: Democracy, Religion, Violence, and India's Future* (Cambridge, Mass., 2007). On India's founding father, see **J. Brown**, *Nehru: A Political Life* (New Haven, Conn., 2003). The life and career of Indira Gandhi have been well chronicled. See **K. Frank**, *Indira: The Life of Indira Nehru Gandhi* (New York, 2000). On Pakistan, see **O. B. Jones**, *Pakistan: Eye of the Storm* (New Haven, Conn., 2002).

SOUTHEAST ASIA SINCE 1945 There are a number of standard surveys of the history of modern Southeast Asia. One is **N. Tarling,** *Southeast Asia: A Modern History* (Oxford, 2002). Also see **N. Tarling, ed.,** *The Cambridge History of Southeast Asia*, vol. 4 (Cambridge, 1999) and **C. Lockard**'s more wide-ranging *Southeast Asia in World History* (Oxford, 2009).

T. Friend, *Indonesian Destinies* (Cambridge, Mass., 2003), is a fine introduction to Indonesian society and culture. The rise of terrorism in the region is discussed in **Z. Abuza, *Militant Islam in Southeast Asia: Crucible of Terror*** (Boulder, Colo., 2003). For an overview of women's issues in contemporary South and Southeast Asia, consult **B. Ramusack** and **S. Sievers,** *Women in Asia* (Bloomington, Ind., 1999).

JAPAN SINCE 1945 For a balanced treatment of all issues relating to postwar Japan, see **J. McLain,** *Japan: A Modern History* (New York, 2001). **I. Buruma,** *Inventing Japan* (New York, 2004), offers a journalistic approach that raises questions about the future of democracy in Japan.

THE LITTLE TIGERS On the four Little Tigers and their economic development, see **D. Oberdorfer,** *The Two Koreas: A Contemporary History* (Indianapolis, 1997); **Lee Kuan Yew,** *From Third World to First: The Singapore Story, 1965–2000* (New York, 2000); and **S. Rigger,** *Why Taiwan Matters: Small Island, Global Powerhouse* (New York, 2011).

Chapter Notes

1. Quoted in W. I. Hitchcock, *The Struggle for Europe: The Turbulent History of a Divided Continent, 1945–2002* (New York, 2003), pp. 399–400.
2. Quoted in L. Collins and D. Lapierre, *Freedom at Midnight* (New York, 1975), p. 252.
3. Quoted in Somini Sengupta, "In World's Largest Democracy, Tolerance Is a Weak Pillar," *New York Times*, October 29, 2008.
4. From Pankaj Mishra, "Impasse in India," *New York Review of Books*, June 28, 2007, p. 51.
5. For a lengthy discussion of occupation efforts to create a new Japanese culture, see I. Buruma, *Inventing Japan, 1853–1964* (New York, 2004), pp. 131–140.
6. Y. Mishima and G. Bownas, eds., *New Writing in Japan* (Harmondsworth, England, 1972), p. 16.

MindTap is a fully online, highly personalized learning experience built upon Cengage Learning content. MindTap combines student learning tools—readings, multimedia, activities, and assessments—into a singular Learning Path that guides students through their course.

EPILOGUE
A Global Civilization

ON A VISIT TO NUREMBERG, Germany, with his family in 2000, Jackson Spielvogel, one of the authors of this textbook, was startled to find that the main railroad station, where he had once arrived as a Fulbright student, was now ostentatiously adorned with McDonald's Golden Arches. McDonald's was the brainstorm of two brothers who opened a cheap burger restaurant in California in 1940. When they expanded their operations to Arizona, they began to use two yellow arches to make their building visible from blocks away. After Ray Kroc, an enterprising businessman, bought the burgeoning business from the brothers, McDonald's arches rapidly spread to all of the United States. And they didn't stop there. The so-called fast-food industry, which now relied on computers to maximize the automated processing of its food, found an international market. McDonald's spread to Japan in 1971 and to Russia and China in 1990; by 1995, more than half of all McDonald's restaurants were located outside the United States. By 2000, McDonald's was serving 50 million people a day.

McDonald's is but one of numerous U.S. companies that use the latest technology and actively seek global markets. Indeed, sociologists have coined the term *McDonaldization* to refer to "the process whereby the principles of the fast-food restaurant are coming to dominate more and more sectors of American society as well as the rest of the world."[1] Multinational corporations like McDonald's have brought about a worldwide homogenization of societies and made us aware of the political, economic, and social interdependence of the world's nations and the global nature of our contemporary problems. An important part of this global awareness is the technological dimension. The growth of new technology has made possible levels of world communication that simply did not exist before. At the same time that Osama bin Laden and al-Qaeda were denouncing the forces of modernization, they were promoting their message by using advanced telecommunication systems that have only recently been developed. The Technological Revolution has tied peoples and nations closely together and contributed to **globalization**, the term that is frequently used today to describe the process by which peoples and nations have become more interdependent.

Of course, as we have seen in world history, globalization is a process that is centuries old. Ever since *Homo sapiens sapiens* moved out of Africa and gradually populated the world, globalization has been occurring. During the Middle Ages, the Mongol conquests inaugurated what one scholar has called the "idea of the unified conceptualization of the globe," creating a "basic information circuit" that spread commodities, ideas, and inventions from one end of the Eurasian supercontinent to the other. Between 1500 and 1815, a

McDonald's in Japan. McDonald's has become an important symbol of U.S. cultural influence throughout the world. Seen here in a 2006 photo is a McDonald's located on a busy street in Tokyo, Japan.

maritime trade network extended throughout the entire populated world. And after 1815, the spread of Western imperialism to most parts of the world led to the domination of subject peoples but also tied the peoples of the world together in new ways. Aided by the technological advances of the twentieth and twenty-first centuries, globalization is now proceeding at an accelerated pace.

The Global Economy

Especially since the 1970s, the world has developed a **global economy** in which the production, distribution, and sale of goods are accomplished on a worldwide scale. Several international institutions have contributed to the rise of the global economy. Soon after the end of World War II, the United States and other nations established the World Bank and the International Monetary Fund (IMF) as a means of expanding global markets and avoiding dramatic economic crises such as the Great Depression of the 1930s. The World Bank is actually a group of five international organizations, largely controlled by developed countries, which provides grants, loans, and advice for economic development to developing countries. The goal of the IMF is to oversee the global financial system by supervising exchange rates and offering financial and technical assistance to developing nations. Today, 187 countries are members of the IMF. Critics have argued, however, that both the World Bank and the IMF sometimes push inappropriate Western economic practices on non-Western nations that only aggravate the poverty and debt of developing nations.

Another reflection of the new global economic order is the **multinational corporation** or **transnational corporation** (a company that has divisions in more than two countries). Prominent examples of multinational corporations include Siemens, General Electric, ExxonMobil, Mitsubishi, and Sony. These companies are among the two hundred largest multinational corporations, and are responsible for more than half of the world's industrial production. In 2000, some 71 percent of these corporations were headquartered in just three countries—the United States, Japan, and Germany. Changes in telecommunications and distribution have made it easier for corporations to be multinational. In addition, the electronics products so much in demand today, such as iPads, digital cameras, and computers, are much lighter and easier to transport than the steel, coal, and other heavy goods of earlier centuries. These supercorporations have come to dominate much of the world's investment capital, technology, and markets. A recent comparison of corporate sales and national gross domestic product found that only forty-nine of the world's hundred largest economic entities are nations; the remaining fifty-one are corporations. For this reason, some observers believe that economic globalization is more appropriately labeled "corporate globalization."

Another important component of economic globalization is free trade. In 1947, talks led to the creation of the General Agreement on Tariffs and Trade (GATT), a global trade organization that was replaced in 1995 by the World Trade Organization (WTO). Made up of more than 150 member nations, the WTO arranges trade agreements and settles trade disputes. The goal of the WTO is to open up world markets and maximize global production, but many critics charge that the WTO has ignored environmental and health concerns, harmed small and developing countries, and created an ever-growing gap between rich and poor nations.

The End of Excess

Since the 1970s, the world has developed a global economy in which the production, distribution, and sale of goods are accomplished on a worldwide scale. At the same time, international financial transactions involving financial instruments such as bonds and equities were becoming an increasingly important component of the globalized economy. Many consumers in Europe and the United States took part in the growing financialization of the economy—relaxation of mortgage lending led to a rapid housing boom in the early 2000s. By 2006, however, the low introductory mortgage rates began to expire, causing default rates to increase as a result.

The global economy experienced worldwide financial troubles beginning in 2007, following the collapse of the U.S. housing market. By September 2008, a number of large financial institutions, including insurance and mortgage companies, investment firms, and banks, were approaching or had fallen into bankruptcy. The rapid collapse of financial investments and falling housing prices caused a precipitous decline in the U.S. stock market as stocks lost almost $8 trillion in value from mid-September to November 2008.

Ultimately, the crash of the U.S. housing market led to a worldwide recession. As the American economy slowed, trade decreased worldwide because American consumers, who had been consuming because of higher home values, could no longer afford to do so. Production in Asia decreased, and prices of commodities fell, including the price of oil, which had an impact on Middle Eastern countries and Russia as well.

The United States responded to the financial crisis with an emergency program to recapitalize financial institutions and a stimulus package to support growth and reduce unemployment. In Europe, the financial fallout exposed the balance sheets of many smaller nations who had used the euro to run up large amounts of government debt. Although Europe initially faced less severe problems than the United States, several countries including Greece and Ireland have been forced to take loans from the IMF and the European Union. In return, several European countries implemented austerity measures that have reduced many social services, such as pensions and health care, in an effort to recapitalize the banks and pay off the debts incurred during the boom years. In eastern Europe, countries that only recently adopted free market economies experienced a drastic devaluation of their currencies as investors fled to the stronger dollar and euro. Many Asian nations faced a series of layoffs in the immediate wake of the crisis, although by 2010, production had begun to return to pre-crash levels. Although government measures prevented a systemic failure of the world financial system, high unemployment and weak consumption will probably plague Western nations for several years to come, as people pay off their debts from the previous era of excess.

Global Culture and the Digital Age

Since the invention of the microprocessor in 1971, the capabilities of computers have expanded by leaps and bounds, resulting in what is often called the information age or digital age. By increasing access to information, the digital age enables billions of people to communicate directly in a relatively short time, while allowing multinational corporations to make transactions from any location that has Internet access. Beginning in the 1980s, computer and software companies such as Apple and Microsoft competed to create more powerful computers. By the 1990s, the booming technology industry had made Microsoft founder Bill Gates the richest man in the world. Much of this success was due to several innovations involving computers that made them indispensable devices for communication, information, and entertainment.

Global Communication

The advent of electronic mail, or e-mail, in the mid-1990s transformed the way that people communicate. As the capacity of computers to transmit data increased, e-mail messages could carry document and image attachments, making them a workable and speedier alternative to "snail mail," as conventional postal mail came to be called. Perhaps even more transformative was the Internet, a network of smaller, interlinking Web pages with sites devoted to news, commerce, entertainment, and academic scholarship. As Web capabilities have increased, new forms of communication have emerged including Twitter, a communications platform that allows people to send instant updates from their cellphones to their friends; Facebook, a social networking site; and YouTube, an Internet site now used for international news broadcasts and for President Obama's weekly radio addresses.

Advances in telecommunications led first to cellular or mobile phones and later to smartphones, which combine many capabilities including portable media players, cameras, GPS navigation features, Wi-Fi, and mobile broadband access. Though cellular phones existed in the 1970s and 1980s, it was not until the size of the digital components of these devices was reduced in the 1990s that cellphones became truly portable. Cellphones have since become enormously important, and not only for communication. Indeed, many nations have become financially dependent on their sales for economic growth. Worldwide the number of people with access to a mobile phone increased from 12.4 million in 1990 to almost 6 billion in 2013. The ubiquity of smartphones has transformed communication into a global endeavor as users can capture video, share text messages, and place images, video, and information on the World Wide Web.

A number of the innovations that have enhanced consumers' ability to share music, read newspapers, watch movies, and search the Web were introduced by Apple, Inc., and subsequently imitated by other companies. In 2001, Apple introduced the iPod, a portable digital music player that allows users to download music from the Internet. This device revolutionized the music industry, as downloading music electronically from the Internet soon surpassed the purchasing of records (CDs, tapes, and other physical forms). CD sales declined nearly 25 percent from 2000 to 2006. Another Apple

innovation, the iPhone, enables users to connect immediately to the Internet from their phone, allowing information to be instantly updated for various telecommunication sites, such as Twitter and Facebook. Apple's most recent introduction, the iPad, a handheld tablet computer, is challenging computer sales worldwide, as almost 7.5 million iPads were sold in the first six months.

These developments in communications are also affecting current events. Smartphones and the like recently played a role in the Arab Spring. Through social networking sites such as Facebook and Twitter, protesters in Arab countries were able to inform others and organize protests.

Reality in the Digital Age

Advances in communication and information during the digital age have led many people to believe that world cultures are increasingly interdependent and homogenized. Many contemporary artists have questioned the effects of the computer age on identity and material reality. According to some, the era of virtual reality has displaced cultural uniqueness and bodily presence.

THE BODY AND IDENTITY IN CONTEMPORARY ART By focusing on bodily experience and cultural norms, contemporary artists have attempted to restore what has been lost in the digital age. Kiki Smith (b. 1954), an American artist born in Germany, creates sculptures of the human body that often focus on anatomical processes. These works, commonly made of wax or plaster, question the politics surrounding the body, including AIDS and domestic abuse, while reconnecting to bodily experiences.

Contemporary artists also continue to explore the interaction between the Western and non-Western world, particularly with the **multiculturalism** generated by global migrations (see "The Social Challenges of Globalization" later in this Epilogue). For example, the art of Yinka Shonibare (YEEN-kuh SHOH-nih-bar-eh) (b. 1962), who was born in London, raised in Nigeria, and now resides in England, investigates the notion of hybrid identity as he creates clothing and tableaux that fuse European designs with African traditions.

MULTICULTURALISM IN LITERATURE The interaction of East and West has also preoccupied numerous authors since the late 1990s. Jhumpa Lahiri (JOOM-puh luh-HEER-ee) (b. 1967) has received international attention for writings that explore contemporary Indian life. Lahiri won the Pulitzer Prize for her collection of stories, *Interpreter of Maladies* (1999), and her acclaimed first novel, *The Namesake* (2003), chronicled the lives of Indian immigrants in the United States. Both works examine generation gaps, particularly the alienation and unique synthesis that can accompany cross-cultural exchange. The success of Lahiri's work indicates how, in the digital age, there is a growing interaction between cultures and traditions. This emergence of a global culture has become part of the new globalism of the twenty-first century.

A Warning to Humanity

EARTH & ENVIRONMENT

As HUMAN THREATS to the environment grew, world scientists began to organize and respond to the crisis. One group, founded in 1969, was the Union of Concerned Scientists, a nonprofit organization of professional scientists and private citizens, now with more than 200,000 members. In November 1992, the Union of Concerned Scientists published an appeal from 1,700 of the world's leading scientists. The first selection is taken from this "Warning to Humanity."

Earlier, in 1988, in response to the threat of global warming, the United Nations established the Intergovernmental Panel on Climate Change (IPCC) to study the most up-to-date scientific information on global warming and climate change. In 2013, thousands of scientists from more than 195 countries contributed to the group's most recent report, "Climate Change, 2013: The Fifth Assessment Report," released in September 2013. The second selection is taken from the IPCC report for policymakers that summarizes the basic findings of the 2013 report.

World Scientists' Warning to Humanity, 1992

Human beings and the natural world are on a collision course. Human activities inflict harsh and often irreversible damage on the environment and on critical resources. If not checked, many of our current practices put at serious risk the future that we wish for human society and the plant and animal kingdoms, and may so alter the living world that it will be unable to sustain life in the manner that we know. Fundamental changes are urgent if we are to avoid the collision our present course will bring about. The environment is suffering critical stress:

The Atmosphere

Stratospheric ozone depletion threatens us with enhanced ultraviolet radiation at the earth's surface, which can be damaging or lethal to many life forms. Air pollution near ground level, and acid precipitation, are already causing widespread injury to humans, forests, and crops.

Water Resources

Heedless exploitation of depletable ground water supplies endangers food production and other essential human systems. Heavy demands on the world's surface waters have resulted in serious shortages in some 80 countries, containing 40% of the world's population. Pollution of rivers, lakes, and ground water further limits the supply.

Oceans

Destructive pressure on the oceans is severe, particularly in the coastal regions which produce most of the world's food fish. The total marine catch is now at or above the estimated maximum sustainable yield. Some fisheries have already shown signs of collapse.

Soil

Loss of soil productivity, which is causing extensive land abandonment, is a widespread by-product of current practices in agriculture and animal husbandry. Since 1945, 11% of the earth's vegetated surface has been degraded—an area larger than India and China combined—and per capita food production in many parts of the world is decreasing.

Forests

Tropical rain forests, as well as tropical and temperate dry forests, are being destroyed rapidly. At present rates, some critical forest types will be gone in a few years, and most of the tropical rain forest will be gone before the end of the next century. With them will go large numbers of plant and animal species.

Living Species

The irreversible loss of species, which by 2100 may reach one-third of all species now living, is especially serious. We are losing the potential they hold for providing medicinal and other benefits, and the contribution that genetic diversity of life forms gives to the robustness of the world's biological systems and to the astonishing beauty of the earth itself.

Much of this damage is irreversible on a scale of centuries, or permanent. Other processes appear to pose additional threats. Increasing levels of gases in the atmosphere from human activities, including carbon dioxide released from fossil fuel burning and from deforestation, may alter climate on a global scale.

Warning

We the undersigned, senior members of the world's scientific community, hereby warn all humanity of what lies ahead. A great change in our stewardship of the earth and the life on it is required, if vast human misery is to be avoided and our global home on this planet is not to be irretrievably mutilated.

Findings of the IPCC Fifth Assessment Report, 2013

Human Responsibility for Climate Change

The report finds that it is *"extremely likely* that human influence has been the dominant cause of the observed warming since the mid-20th century."

Warming Is Unequivocal

The report concludes that warming of the climate system is "unequivocal," and "since the 1950s, many of the observed changes are unprecedented over decades to millennia. The atmosphere and ocean have warmed, the amounts of snow and ice have diminished, sea level has risen, and the concentrations of greenhouse gasses have increased." Moreover, "each of the last three decades has been successively warmer at the Earth's surface than any preceding decade since 1850. In the Northern Hemisphere, 1983–2012 was likely the warmest 30-year period of the last 1400 years." The report also confirms that the current atmospheric concentrations of the greenhouse gases of carbon dioxide, methane, and nitrous oxide, "have increased to levels unprecedented in at least the last 800,000 years."

Additional IPCC Findings on Recent Climate Change

Rising Temperatures

- By 2100, various climate change model simulations estimate that global surface temperatures could rise from 1.5°C to 4°C.
- Since about 1950, "it is very likely that the number of cold days and nights has decreased and the number of warm days and nights has increased on the global scale."

Melting Glaciers and Snow

- The melting of ice glaciers has increased rapidly, "over the last two decades, the Greenland and Antarctic ice sheets have been losing mass, glaciers have continued to shrink almost worldwide, and the Arctic sea ice and Northern Hemisphere spring snow cover have continued to decrease in extent."

Rising Sea Levels

- "The rate of sea level rise since the mid-19th century has been larger than the mean rate during the previous two millennia."

Increasingly Severe Weather (storms, precipitation, drought)

- "It is likely, that there will be increases in intensity and/or duration of drought, and increases in intense tropical cyclone (hurricane) activity."
- "It is very likely that heat waves will occur with a higher frequency and duration."
- Storms with heavy precipitation have increased in frequency over most land areas.
- "Air quality will continue to decrease due to high carbon emissions."

 What problems and challenges do these two reports present? What do these two reports have in common? How do they differ?

Sources: From "World Scientists' Warning to Humanity," 1992. Union of Concerned Scientists. 1992. World Scientists Warning to Humanity. Excerpt. Cambridge, MA: UCS. Online at www.ucsusa.org. From "Findings of the IPCC Fifth Assessment Report, 2013." Source: http://www.climatechange2013.org/images/uploads/WGI_AR5_SPM_brochure.pdf.

Globalization and the Environmental Crisis

As many people take a global perspective in the twenty-first century, they are realizing that human beings everywhere on the planet are interdependent in terms of the air they breathe, the water they drink, the food they consume, and the climate that affects their lives. At the same time, however, human activities are creating environmental challenges that threaten the very foundation of human existence on earth (see the box "A Warning to Humanity" on p. 938).

One problem is population growth. As of January 2014, the world population was estimated at more than 7.1 billion people. At its current rate of growth, the world population could reach 12.8 billion by 2050, according to the United Nations' long-range population projections. The result has been an increased demand for food and other resources that has put great pressure on the earth's ecosystems. At the same time, the failure to grow enough food for more and more people, a problem exacerbated by drought conditions beginning to appear on several continents, has created a severe problem, as an estimated 1 billion people worldwide today suffer from hunger. Every year, more than 8 million people die of hunger, many of them young children.

Another problem is the pattern of consumption as the wealthy nations of the Northern Hemisphere consume vast quantities of the planet's natural resources. The United States, for example, which has 6 percent of the planet's people, consumes 30 to 40 percent of its resources. The spread of these consumption patterns to other parts of the world raises serious questions about the ability of the planet to sustain itself and its population. Within a few years, for example, more automobiles will be sold in China annually than in the United States.

Yet another threat to the environment is **global climate change**, which has the potential to create a worldwide crisis. Virtually all of the world's scientists agree that the **greenhouse effect**, the warming of the earth because of the buildup of carbon dioxide in the atmosphere, is contributing to devastating droughts and storms, the melting of the polar ice caps, and rising sea levels that could inundate coastal regions in the second half of the twenty-first century. Also alarming is the potential loss of biodiversity. Seven out of ten biologists believe the

The Earth. For many people in the West, as in the rest of the world, the view of the earth from outer space fostered a sense of global unity. The American astronaut Russell Schweikart wrote, "From where you see it, the thing is a whole, and it is so beautiful." In a similar reaction, Yuri Gagarin, the first Soviet cosmonaut, remarked, "What strikes me is not only the beauty of the continents ... but their closeness to one another ... their essential unity."

planet is now experiencing an alarming extinction of both plant and animal species.

The Social Challenges of Globalization

Since 1945, tens of millions of people have migrated from one part of the world to another. These migrations have occurred for many reasons. Persecution for political reasons caused many people from Pakistan, Bangladesh, Sri Lanka, and eastern Europe to seek refuge in western European countries, while brutal civil wars in Asia, Africa, the Middle East, and Europe led millions of refugees to seek safety in neighboring countries. Most people who have migrated, however, have done so to find jobs. Latin Americans seeking a better life have migrated to the United States, while guest workers from Turkey, southern and eastern Europe, North Africa, India, and Pakistan have migrated to more prosperous western European countries. In 2005, nearly 200 million people, about 3 percent of the world's population, lived outside the country where they were born.

The migration of millions of people has also provoked a social backlash in many countries. Foreign workers have often become scapegoats when countries face economic problems. Political parties in France and Norway, for example, have called for the removal of blacks, Muslims, and Arabs in order to protect the ethnic or cultural purity of their nations, while in Asian countries, there is animosity against other Asian

ethnic groups. The problem of foreigners has also led to a more general attack on globalization itself as being responsible for a host of social ills that are undermining national sovereignty.

Another challenge of globalization is the wide gap between rich and poor nations. The rich nations, or **developed nations**, are located mainly in the Northern Hemisphere. They include the United States, Canada, Germany, and Japan, which have well-organized industrial and agricultural systems, advanced technologies, and effective educational systems. The poor nations, or **developing nations**, include many nations in Africa, Asia, and Latin America, which often have primarily agricultural economies with little technology. A serious problem in many developing nations is explosive population growth, which has led to severe food shortages caused often by poor soil but also by economic factors. Growing crops for export to developed countries, for example, may lead to enormous profits for large landowners but leaves many small farmers with little land on which to grow food.

Civil wars have also created food shortages. Not only does war disrupt normal farming operations, but warring groups try to limit access to food to weaken or kill their enemies. In Sudan, 1.3 million people starved when combatants of a civil war in the 1980s prevented food from reaching them. As unrest continued during the early 2000s in Sudan's Darfur region, families were forced to leave their farms. As a result, an estimated 70,000 people starved by mid-2004.

Global Movements and New Hopes

As people have become aware that the problems humans face are not just national or regional but global in scope, they have responded to this challenge in different ways. One approach has been to develop grassroots social movements, including environmental, women's and men's liberation, human potential, appropriate technology, and nonviolence movements. "Think globally, act locally" is frequently the slogan of these grassroots groups. Related to the emergence of these social movements is the growth of **nongovernmental organizations** (**NGOs**). According to one analyst, NGOs are an important instrument in the cultivation of global perspectives: "Since NGOs by definition are identified with interests that transcend national boundaries, we expect all NGOs to define problems in global terms, to take account of human interests and needs as they are found in all parts of the planet."[2] NGOs are often represented at the United Nations and include professional, business, and cooperative organizations; foundations; religious, peace, and disarmament groups; youth and women's organizations; environmental and human rights groups; and research institutes. The number of international NGOs increased from 176 in 1910 to 40,000 in 2010.

And yet hopes for global approaches to global problems have also been hindered by political, ethnic, and religious differences. Pollution of the Rhine River by factories along its banks provokes angry disputes among European nations, and the United States and Canada have argued about the effects of acid rain on Canadian forests. Droughts in Russia and China threaten the world's food supply, while floods in Pakistan challenge the stability of Asia. The collapse of the Soviet Union and its satellite system seemed to provide an enormous boost to the potential for international cooperation on global issues, but it has had almost the opposite effect. The bloody conflict in the former Yugoslavia indicates the dangers inherent in the rise of nationalist sentiment among various ethnic and religious groups in eastern Europe. The widening gap between wealthy nations and poor nations and instability in developing nations threaten global economic stability. Many conflicts begin with regional issues and then develop into international concerns. International terrorist groups seek to wreak havoc around the world.

Thus, even as the world becomes more global in culture and interdependent in its mutual relations, centrifugal forces are still at work attempting to redefine the political, cultural, and ethnic ways in which the world is divided. Such efforts are often disruptive and can sometimes work against measures to enhance our human destiny. But they also represent an integral part of human character and human history and cannot be suppressed in the relentless drive to create a world society.

There are already signs that as the common dangers posed by environmental damage, overpopulation, and scarcity of resources become ever more apparent, societies around the world will find ample reason to turn their attention from cultural differences to the demands of global interdependence. The greatest challenge of the twenty-first century may be to reconcile the drive for individual and group identity with the common needs of the human community.

Key Terms

globalization (p. 935)
global economy (p. 935)

multinational corporation (p. 936)
transnational corporation (p. 936)
multiculturalism (p. 937)
global climate change (p. 939)
greenhouse effect (p. 939)
developed nations (p. 940)
developing nations (p. 940)
nongovernmental organizations (**NGOs**) (p. 940)

Suggested Reading

Useful books on different facets of the new global civilization include **M. B. Steger,** *Globalization: A Very Short Introduction* (New York, 2003); **J. H. Mittelman,** *The Globalization Syndrome* (Princeton, N.J., 2000); **M. Waters,** *Globalization,* 2nd ed. (London, 2001); and **P. O'Meara et al., eds.,** *Globalization and the Challenges of the New Century* (Bloomington, Ind., 2000). For a comprehensive examination of the digital age, see **M. Castells,** *The Information Age,* 3 vols. (Oxford, 1996–1998). On the role of the media in the digital age, see **J. R. Dominick,** *Dynamics of Mass Communication: Media in the Digital Age* (New York, 2006).

Chapter Notes

1. Quoted in J. N. Pieterse, *Globalization and Culture* (Lanham, Md., 2004), p. 49.
2. E. Boulding, *Women in the Twentieth Century World* (New York, 1977), pp. 187–188.

 MindTap™

MindTap is a fully online, highly personalized learning experience built upon Cengage Learning content. MindTap combines student learning tools—readings, multimedia, activities, and assessments—into a singular Learning Path that guides students through their course.

GLOSSARY

abbess   the head of a convent or monastery for women.

abbot   the head of a monastery.

absolutism   a form of government in which the sovereign power or ultimate authority rested in the hands of a monarch who claimed to rule by divine right and was therefore responsible only to God.

Abstract Expressionism   a post–World War II artistic movement that broke with all conventions of form and structure in favor of total abstraction.

abstract painting   an artistic movement that developed early in the twentieth century in which artists focused on color to avoid any references to visual reality.

African Union   the organization that replaced the Organization of African Unity in 2001; designed to bring about increased political and economic integration of African states.

Amerindians   the earliest inhabitants of North and South America. Original theories suggested migration from Siberia across the Bering Land Bridge; more recent evidence suggests migration also occurred by sea from regions of the South Pacific to South America.

anarchists   people who hold that all governments and existing social institutions are unnecessary and advocate a society based on voluntary cooperation.

anti-Semitism   hostility toward or discrimination against Jews.

apartheid   the system of racial segregation practiced in the Republic of South Africa until the 1990s, which involved political, legal, and economic discrimination against nonwhites.

appeasement   the policy, followed by the European nations in the 1930s, of accepting Hitler's annexation of Austria and Czechoslovakia in the belief that meeting his demands would ensure peace and stability.

aristocracy   a class of hereditary nobility in medieval Europe; a warrior class who shared a distinctive lifestyle based on the institution of knighthood, although there were social divisions within the group based on extremes of wealth.

Aryans   Indo-European-speaking nomads who entered India from the Central Asian steppes between 1500 and 1000 B.C.E. and greatly affected Indian society, notably by establishing the caste system. The term *Aryan* was later adopted by German Nazis to describe their racial ideal.

ASEAN   the Association for the Southeast Asian Nations, formed in 1967 to promote the prosperity and political stability of its member nations. Currently, Brunei, Cambodia, Indonesia, Laos, Malaysia, Myanmar, the Philippines, Singapore, Thailand, and Vietnam are members. Other countries in the region participate as "observer" members.

assimilation   the concept, originating in France, that the colonial peoples should be assimilated into the parent French culture.

association   the concept, developed by French colonial officials, that the colonial peoples should be permitted to retain their precolonial cultural traditions.

Atman   in Brahmanism, the individual soul.

Ausgleich   the "Compromise" of 1867 that created the dual monarchy of Austria-Hungary. Austria and Hungary each had its own capital, constitution, and legislative assembly but were united under one monarch.

bakufu   the centralized government set up in Japan in the twelfth century. *See also* shogunate system.

banners   originally established in 1639 by the Qing Dynasty, the eight banners were administrative divisions into which all Manchu families were placed. Banners quickly evolved into the basis of Manchu military organization, with each required to raise and support a prescribed number of troops.

Bao-jia **system**   the Chinese practice, reportedly originated by the Qin dynasty in the third century B.C.E., of organizing families into groups of five or ten to exercise mutual control and surveillance and reduce loyalty to the family.

bard   in Africa, a professional storyteller.

Baroque   a style that dominated Western painting, sculpture, architecture, and music from about 1580 to 1730, generally characterized by elaborate ornamentation and dramatic effects. Important practitioners included Bernini, Rubens, Handel, and Bach.

Bedouins   nomadic tribes originally from northern Arabia who became important traders after the domestication of the camel during the first millennium B.C.E. Early converts to Islam, their values and practices deeply affected Muhammad.

Berbers   an ethnic group indigenous to western North Africa.

bey   a provincial governor in the Ottoman Empire.

bhakti   in Hinduism, devotion as a means of religious observance open to all persons regardless of class.

Black Death   the outbreak of plague (mostly bubonic) in the mid-fourteenth century that killed from 25 to 50 percent of Europe's population.

Blitzkrieg   "lightning war." A war conducted with great speed and force, as in Germany's advance at the beginning of World War II.

bodhi   wisdom; sometimes described as complete awareness of the true nature of the universe.

bodhisattva   in some schools of Buddhism, an individual who has achieved enlightenment but, because of his great compassion, has chosen to renounce Nirvana and to remain on earth in spirit form to help all human beings achieve release from reincarnation.

Boers   the Afrikaans-speaking descendants of Dutch settlers in southern Africa who left the Cape Colony in the nineteenth century to settle in the Orange Free State and Transvaal; defeated by the British in the Boer War (1899–1902) and ultimately incorporated in the Union of South Africa.

bonsai   the cultivation of stunted trees and shrubs to create exquisite nature scenes in miniature; originated in China in the first millennium B.C.E. and imported to Japan between 700 and 900 C.E.

Brahman   the Hindu word roughly equivalent to God; the divine basis of all being; regarded as the source and sum of the cosmos.

Brahmanism   the early religious beliefs of the Aryan peoples in India, which eventually gave rise to Hinduism.

brahmin   a member of the Hindu priestly caste or class; literally "one who has realized or attempts to realize *Brahman*." Traditionally, duties of a *brahmin* included studying Hindu religious scriptures and transmitting them to others orally. The priests of Hindu temples are *brahmins*.

Brezhnev Doctrine   the doctrine, enunciated by Leonid Brezhnev, that the Soviet Union had a right to intervene if socialism was threatened in another socialist state; used to justify the use of Soviet troops in Czechoslovakia in 1968.

Buddhism   a religion and philosophy based on the teachings of Siddhartha Gautama around 500 B.C.E. Principally practiced in China, India, and other parts of Asia, Buddhism has 360 million followers and is considered a major world religion.

bunmei kaika   A slogan applied during the Meiji Restoration in Japan signaling the need to modernize the country to assist in competition with Western countries.

Burakumin a Japanese minority similar to *dalits* (untouchables) in Indian culture. Past and current discrimination has resulted in lower educational attainment and socioeconomic status for members of this group. Movements with objectives ranging from "liberation" to integration have tried over the years to change this situation.

Bushido the code of conduct observed by samurai warriors; comparable to the European concept of chivalry.

caliph the secular leader of the Islamic community.

calpulli in Aztec society, a kinship group, often of a thousand or more, that served as an intermediary with the central government, providing taxes and conscript labor to the state.

capitalism beginning in the Middle Ages, an economic system in which private owners invest in trade and goods in order to make profits.

caravels mobile sailing ships with both lateen and square sails that began to be constructed in Europe in the sixteenth century.

Cartesian dualism Descartes's principle of the separation of mind and matter (and mind and body) that enabled scientists to view matter as something separate from themselves that could be investigated by reason.

Catholic Reformation a movement for the reform of the Catholic Church in the sixteenth century.

caudillos strong leaders in nineteenth-century Latin America who were usually supported by the landed elites and ruled chiefly by military force, though some were popular; they included both modernizers and destructive dictators.

centuriate assembly the chief popular assembly of the Roman Republic. It passed laws and elected the chief magistrates.

chaebol a South Korean business structure similar to the Japanese *keiretsu*.

Chan Buddhism a Chinese sect (Zen in Japanese) influenced by Daoist ideas, which called for mind training and a strict regimen as a means of seeking enlightenment.

chinampas in Mesoamerica, artificial islands crisscrossed by canals that provided water for crops and easy transportation to local markets.

chivalry the ideal of civilized behavior that emerged among the European nobility in the eleventh and twelfth centuries under the influence of the church; a code of ethics knights were expected to uphold.

chonmin in Korea, the lowest class in society consisting of slaves and workers in certain undesirable occupations such as butchers; literally, "base people."

Christian humanism an intellectual movement in northern Europe in the late fifteenth and early sixteenth centuries that combined interest in the classics of the Italian Renaissance with an interest in the sources of early Christianity, including the New Testament and the writings of the church fathers.

chu nom an adaptation of Chinese written characters to provide a writing system for spoken Vietnamese; in use by the ninth century C.E.

civil disobedience the tactic of using illegal but nonviolent means of protest; designed by the Indian nationalist leader Mohandas Gandhi to resist British colonial rule. The tactic would later be adopted by nationalist and liberation forces in many other countries.

civilization a complex culture in which large numbers of humans share a variety of common elements, including cities; religious, political, military, and social structures; writing; and significant artistic and intellectual activity.

civil service examination an elaborate Chinese system of selecting bureaucrats on merit, first introduced in 165 C.E., developed by the Tang Dynasty in the seventh century C.E., and refined under the Song Dynasty; later adopted in Vietnam and with less success in Japan and Korea. It contributed to efficient government, upward mobility, and cultural uniformity.

class struggle the basis of the Marxist analysis of history, which says that the owners of the means of production have always oppressed the workers and predicts an inevitable revolution. *See also* Marxism.

Cold War the ideological conflict between the Soviet Union and the United States between the end of World War II and the early 1990s.

Columbian Exchange the exchange of animals, plants, and culture, but also communicable diseases and human populations including slaves, between the Western and Eastern Hemispheres that occurred after Columbus's voyages to the Americas.

common law law common to the entire kingdom of England; imposed by the king's courts beginning in the twelfth century to replace the customary law used in county and feudal courts that varied from place to place.

commune in medieval Europe, an association of townspeople bound together by a sworn oath for the purpose of obtaining basic liberties from the lord of the territory in which the town was located; also, the self-governing town after receiving its liberties.

Communist International (Comintern) a worldwide organization of Communist Parties, founded by Lenin in 1919, dedicated to the advancement of world revolution; also known as the Third International.

conciliarism a movement in fourteenth- and fifteenth-century Europe that held that final authority in spiritual matters resided with a general church council, not the pope. It emerged in response to the Avignon papacy and the Great Schism and was used to justify the summoning of the Council of Constance (1414–1418).

Confucianism a system of thought based on the teachings of Confucius (551–479 B.C.E.) that developed into the ruling ideology of the Chinese state. *See also* Neo-Confucianism.

conquistadors "conquerors." Leaders in the Spanish conquests in the Americas, especially Mexico and Peru, in the sixteenth century.

conscription a military draft.

conservatism an ideology based on tradition and social stability that favored the maintenance of established institutions, organized religion, and obedience to authority and resisted change, especially abrupt change.

consuls the chief executive officers of the Roman Republic. Two were chosen annually to administer the government and lead the army in battle.

consumer society a term applied to Western society after World War II as the working classes adopted the consumption patterns of the middle class and installment plans, credit cards, and easy credit made consumer goods such as appliances and automobiles widely available.

containment a policy adopted by the United States during the Cold War. It called for the use of any means, short of all-out war, to limit Soviet expansion.

Continental system Napoleon's effort to bar British goods from the European continent in the hope of weakening Britain's economy and destroying its capacity to wage war.

Contras in Nicaragua in the 1980s, an anti-Sandinista guerrilla movement supported by the U.S. Reagan administration.

Coptic a form of Christianity, originally Egyptian, that has thrived in Ethiopia since the fourth century C.E.

cottage industry a system of textile manufacturing in which spinners and weavers worked at home in their cottages using raw materials supplied to them by capitalist entrepreneurs.

council of the plebs in the Roman Republic, a council only for the plebeians. After 287 B.C.E., however, its resolutions were binding on all Romans.

creoles in Latin America, American-born descendants of Europeans.

Crusade in the Middle Ages, a military campaign in defense of Christendom.

Cubism an artistic style developed at the beginning of the twentieth century, especially by Pablo Picasso, that used geometric designs to re-create reality in the viewer's mind.

cuneiform "wedge-shaped." A system of writing developed by the Sumerians that consisted of wedge-shaped impressions made by a reed stylus on clay tablets.

Dadaism an artistic movement in the 1920s and 1930s by artists who were revolted by the senseless slaughter of World War I and used their "anti-art" to express contempt for the Western tradition.

daimyo prominent Japanese families who provided allegiance to the local shogun in exchange for protection; similar to vassals in Europe.

dalits commonly referred to as untouchables; the lowest level of Indian society, technically outside the caste system and considered less than human; renamed *harijans* ("children of God") by Gandhi, they remain the object of discrimination despite affirmative action programs.

Dao a Chinese philosophical concept, literally "the Way," central to both Confucianism and Daoism, that describes the behavior proper to each member of society; somewhat similar to the Indian concept of *dharma*.

Daoism a Chinese philosophy traditionally ascribed to the perhaps legendary Lao Zi, which holds that acceptance and spontaneity are the keys to harmonious interaction with the universal order; an alternative to Confucianism.

decolonization the process of becoming free of colonial status and achieving statehood; occurred in most of the world's colonies between 1947 and 1962.

deficit spending the concept, developed by John Maynard Keynes in the 1930s, that in times of economic depression, governments should stimulate demand by hiring people to do public works, such as building highways, even if this increases the public debt.

deism belief in God as the creator of the universe who, after setting it in motion, ceased to have any direct involvement in it and allowed it to run according to its own natural laws.

demesne the part of a manor retained under the direct control of the lord and worked by the serfs as part of their labor services.

denazification after World War II, the Allied policy of rooting out all traces of Nazism in German society by bringing prominent Nazis to trial for war crimes and purging any known Nazis from political office.

descamisados the working-class supporters of Juan Perón during his rise to power in Argentina in 1946; literally, the "shirtless ones."

de-Stalinization the policy of denouncing and undoing the most repressive aspects of Stalin's regime; begun by Nikita Khrushchev in 1956.

détente the relaxation of tension between the Soviet Union and the United States that occurred in the 1970s.

developed nations a term used to refer to rich nations, primarily in the Northern Hemisphere, that have well-organized industrial and agricultural systems, advanced technologies, and effective educational systems.

developing nations a term used to refer to poor nations, mainly in the Southern Hemisphere, that have primarily agricultural economies with little technology and serious population problems.

devshirme in the Ottoman Empire, a system (literally, "collection") of training talented children to be administrators or members of the sultan's harem; originally meritocratic, by the seventeenth century it had degenerated into a hereditary caste.

dharma in Hinduism and Buddhism, the law that governs the universe and specifically human behavior.

dictator in the Roman Republic, an official granted unlimited power to run the state for a short period of time, usually six months, during an emergency.

diffusion hypothesis the hypothesis that the Yellow River valley was the ancient heartland of Chinese civilization and that technological and cultural achievements radiated from there to other parts of East Asia. Recent discoveries of other early agricultural communities in China have led to some modification of the hypothesis to allow for other centers of civilization.

diocese the area under the jurisdiction of a Christian bishop; based originally on Roman administrative districts.

direct rule a concept devised by European colonial governments to rule their colonial subjects without the participation of local authorities. It was most often applied in colonial societies in Africa.

divination the practice of seeking to foretell future events by interpreting divine signs, which could appear in various forms, such as in the entrails of animals, in patterns in smoke, or in dreams.

divine-right monarchy a monarchy based on the belief that monarchs receive their power directly from God and are responsible to no one except God.

dyarchy during the Qing Dynasty in China, a system in which all important national and provincial administrative positions were shared equally by Chinese and Manchus, which helped consolidate both the Manchus' rule and their assimilation.

Einsatzgruppen in Nazi Germany, special strike forces in the SS that played an important role in rounding up and killing Jews.

El Niño periodic changes in water temperature at the surface of the Pacific Ocean, which can lead to major environmental changes and may have led to the collapse of the Moche civilization in what is now Peru.

emir "commander" in Arabic, a title used by Muslim rulers in southern Spain and elsewhere.

encomienda a grant from the Spanish monarch to colonial conquistadors. *See also encomienda* system.

encomienda system the system by which Spain first governed its American colonies. Holders of an *encomienda* were supposed to protect the Indians as well as use them as laborers and collect tribute but in practice exploited them.

enlightened absolutism an absolute monarchy in which the ruler follows the principles of the Enlightenment by introducing reforms for the improvement of society, allowing freedom of speech and the press, permitting religious toleration, expanding education, and ruling in accordance with the laws.

Enlightenment an eighteenth-century intellectual movement, led by the philosophes, that stressed the application of reason and the scientific method to all aspects of life.

Epicureanism a philosophy founded by Epicurus in the fourth century B.C.E. that taught that happiness (freedom from emotional turmoil) could be achieved through the pursuit of pleasure (intellectual rather than sensual pleasure).

eta in feudal Japan, a class of hereditary slaves who were responsible for what were considered degrading occupations, such as curing leather and burying the dead.

ethnic cleansing the policy of killing or forcibly removing people of another ethnic group; used by the Serbs against Bosnian Muslims in the 1990s.

eunuchs men whose testicles have been removed. Eunuchs often played an important role at court in the Chinese imperial system, the Ottoman Empire, and the Mughal Dynasty, among others.

existentialism a philosophical movement that arose after World War II that emphasized the meaninglessness of life, born of the desperation caused by two world wars.

feminism the belief in the social, political, and economic equality of the sexes; also, organized activity to advance women's rights.

fief a landed estate granted to a vassal in exchange for military services.

filial piety in traditional China, in particular, a hierarchical system in which every family member has his or her place, subordinate to a patriarch who has certain reciprocal responsibilities.

Final Solution the Nazis' name for their attempted physical extermination of the Jewish people during World War II.

Five Pillars of Islam the core requirements of the Muslim faith: belief in Allah and his prophet, Muhammad; prescribed prayers; observation of Ramadan; pilgrimage to Mecca; and giving alms to the poor.

five relationships in traditional China, the hierarchical interpersonal associations considered crucial to social order, within the family, between friends, and with the king.

foot binding an extremely painful process, common in China throughout the second millennium C.E., that compressed girls' feet to half their natural size, representing submissiveness and self-discipline, which were considered necessary attributes of an ideal wife.

Four Modernizations the radical reforms of Chinese industry, agriculture, technology, and national defense instituted by Deng Xiaoping after his accession to power in the late 1970s.

fudai daimyo during the Tokugawa Shogunate in Japan, less powerful lords who were directly subordinate to the shogunate; literally, "inside daimyo."

functionalism the idea that the function of an object should determine its design and materials.

fundamentalism a movement that emphasizes rigid adherence to basic religious principles; often used to describe evangelical Christianity as well as the practices of Islamic conservatives.

genin landless laborers in feudal Japan, who were effectively slaves.

genro the ruling clique of aristocrats in Meiji Japan.

geocentric theory   the idea that the earth is at the center of the universe and that the sun and other celestial objects revolve around the earth.

glasnost   "openness"; Mikhail Gorbachev's policy of encouraging Soviet citizens to openly discuss the strengths and weaknesses of the Soviet Union.

global climate change   the changes in climate, including an increase in the temperature of the earth's atmosphere, caused by the greenhouse effect.

global economy   an interdependent economy in which the production, distribution, and sale of goods are accomplished on a worldwide scale.

globalization   a term referring to the trend by which peoples and nations have become more interdependent; often used to refer to the development of a global economy and culture.

good emperors   the five emperors who ruled from 96 to 180 (Nerva, Trajan, Hadrian, Antoninus Pius, and Marcus Aurelius), a period of peace and prosperity for the Roman Empire.

Good Neighbor policy   a policy adopted by the administration of President Franklin D. Roosevelt to practice restraint in U.S. relations with Latin American nations.

Gosplan   in the Soviet Union, the "state plan" for the economy drawn up by the central planning commission.

Gothic   a term used to describe the art and especially architecture of Europe in the twelfth, thirteenth, and fourteenth centuries.

Gothic literature   a form of literature used by Romantics to emphasize the bizarre and unusual, especially evident in horror stories.

Grand Council   the top of the government hierarchy in the Song Dynasty in China.

grand vizier   the chief minister in the Ottoman Empire, under the sultan.

Great Leap Forward   a short-lived, radical experiment in China, started in 1958, that created vast rural communes in an attempt to replace the family as the fundamental social unit.

Great Proletarian Cultural Revolution   an attempt to destroy all vestiges of tradition in China in order to create a totally egalitarian society. Launched by Mao Zedong in 1966, it devolved into virtual anarchy and lasted only until Mao's death in 1976.

greenhouse effect   the warming of the earth caused by the buildup of carbon dioxide in the atmosphere as a result of human activity.

green revolution   the introduction of technological agriculture, especially in India in the 1960s, which increased food production substantially but also exacerbated rural inequality because only the wealthier farmers could afford fertilizer.

guest workers   foreign workers employed temporarily in European countries.

guided democracy   the name given by President Sukarno of Indonesia in the late 1950s to his style of government, which theoretically operated by consensus.

guild   an association of people with common interests and concerns, especially people working in the same craft. In medieval Europe, guilds came to control much of the production process and to restrict entry into various trades.

guru   teacher, especially in the Hindu, Buddhist, and Sikh religious traditions, where the term is an important honorific.

Hadith   a collection of the sayings of the Prophet Muhammad, used to supplement the revelations contained in the Qur'an.

harijans   a name used by Mohandas Gandhi to refer to the untouchables in India; literally, "children of God." *See also dalits*.

harem   the private living quarters of a ruler such as the sultan in the Ottoman Empire or the caliph of Baghdad; generally large and mostly inhabited by the extended family.

Hegira   the flight of Muhammad from Mecca to Medina in 622, which marks the first date on the official calendar of Islam.

heliocentric theory   the idea that the sun (not the earth) is at the center of the universe.

helots   serfs in ancient Sparta who were permanently bound to the land that they worked for their Spartan masters.

heresy   the holding of religious doctrines different from the official teachings of the church.

Hezbollah   a militant Shi'ite organization and political party based in modern Lebanon.

hieroglyphics   a highly pictorial system of writing most often associated with ancient Egypt. Also used (with different "pictographs") by other ancient peoples such as the Maya.

high colonialism   the more formal phase of European colonial policy in Africa after World War I when the colonial administrative network was extended to outlying areas and more emphasis was placed on improving social services and fostering economic development, especially the exploitation of natural resources, to enable the colonies to achieve self-sufficiency.

high culture   the literary and artistic culture of the educated and wealthy ruling classes.

Hinayana   the scornful name for Theravada Buddhism ("lesser vehicle") used by devotees of Mahayana Buddhism.

Hinduism   the main religion in India. It emphasizes reincarnation, based on the results of the previous life, and the desirability of escaping this cycle. Its various forms feature both asceticism and the pleasures of ordinary life and encompass a multitude of gods as different manifestations of one ultimate reality.

hominids   the earliest humanlike creatures. They flourished in East and South Africa as long as 3 to 4 million years ago.

Hopewell culture   a Native American society that flourished from about 200 B.C.E. to 400 C.E., noted for large burial mounds and extensive manufacturing. Largely based in Ohio, its traders ranged as far as the Gulf of Mexico.

hoplites   heavily armed infantry soldiers used in ancient Greece in a phalanx formation.

iconoclasm   an eighth-century Byzantine movement against the use of icons (pictures of sacred figures), which was condemned as idolatry.

iconoclast   a member of an eighth-century Byzantine movement against the use of icons (pictures of sacred figures), which it condemned as idolatry.

imam   an Islamic religious leader. Some traditions say there is only one per generation; others use the term more broadly.

imperialism   the policy of extending one nation's power either by conquest or by establishing direct or indirect economic or cultural authority over another. Generally driven by economic self-interest, it can also be motivated by a sincere (if often misguided) sense of moral obligation.

Impressionism   an artistic movement that originated in France in the 1870s. Impressionists sought to capture their impressions of the changing effects of light on objects in nature.

indirect rule   a colonial policy of foreign rule in cooperation with local political elites. Though implemented in much of India and Malaya and in parts of Africa, it was not feasible where resistance was greater.

indulgence   the remission of part or all of the temporal punishment in purgatory due to sin; granted for charitable contributions and other good deeds. Indulgences became a regular practice of the Christian church in the High Middle Ages, and their abuse was instrumental in sparking Luther's reform movement in the sixteenth century.

informal empire   the growing presence of Europeans in Africa during the first decades of the nineteenth century. During this period, most African states were nonetheless still able to maintain their independence.

interdict   in the Catholic Church, a censure by which a region or country is deprived of receiving the sacraments.

intervention   the idea, after the Congress of Vienna, that the great powers of Europe had the right to send armies into countries experiencing revolution to restore legitimate monarchs to their thrones.

intifada   the "uprising" of Palestinians living under Israeli control, especially in the 1980s and 1990s.

Jainism   an Indian religion, founded in the fifth century B.C.E., that stresses extreme simplicity.

janissaries   an elite core of eight thousand troops personally loyal to the sultan of the Ottoman Empire.

jati   a kinship group, the basic social organization of traditional Indian society, to some extent specialized by occupation.

jihad in Islam, "striving in the way of the Lord." The term is ambiguous and has been subject to various interpretations, from the practice of conducting raids against local neighbors to the conduct of "holy war" against unbelievers.

joint-stock company a company or association that raises capital by selling shares to individuals who receive dividends on their investment while a board of directors runs the company.

joint-stock investment bank a bank created by selling shares of stock to investors. Such banks potentially have access to much more capital than private banks owned by one or a few individuals.

justification by faith the primary doctrine of the Protestant Reformation; taught that humans are saved not through good works but by the grace of God, bestowed freely through the sacrifice of Jesus.

kami spirits worshiped in early Japan that resided in trees, rivers, and streams. *See also* Shinto.

karma a fundamental concept in Hindu (and later Buddhist, Jain, and Sikh) philosophy, that rebirth in a future life is determined by actions in this or other lives. The word refers to the entire process, to the individual's actions, and also to the cumulative result of those actions (for instance, a store of good or bad *karma*).

keiretsu a type of powerful industrial or financial conglomerate that emerged in post–World War II Japan following the abolition of the *zaibatsu*.

khanates Mongol kingdoms, in particular the subdivisions of Genghis Khan's empire ruled by his heirs.

kokutai the core ideology of the Japanese state, particularly during the Meiji Restoration, stressing the uniqueness of the Japanese system and the supreme authority of the emperor.

kowtow the ritual of prostration and touching the forehead to the ground, demanded of all foreign ambassadors to the Chinese court as a symbol of submission.

kshatriya originally, the warrior class of Aryan society in India; ranked below (sometimes equal to) *brahmins*; in modern times often government workers or soldiers.

laissez-faire French for "leave it alone." An economic doctrine that holds that an economy is best served when the government does not interfere but allows the economy to self-regulate according to the forces of supply and demand.

latifundia large landed estates in the Roman Empire (singular: *latifundium*).

lay investiture the practice in which a layperson chose a bishop and invested him with the symbols of both his temporal office and his spiritual office; led to the Investiture Controversy, which was ended by compromise in the Concordat of Worms in 1122.

Legalism a Chinese philosophy that argued that human beings were by nature evil and would follow the correct path only if coerced by harsh laws and stiff punishments. Adopted as official ideology by the Qin dynasty, it was later rejected but remained influential.

legitimacy the idea that after the Napoleonic wars, peace could best be reestablished in Europe by restoring legitimate monarchs who would preserve traditional institutions; guided Metternich at the Congress of Vienna.

liberal arts the seven areas of study that formed the basis of education in medieval and early modern Europe; consisted of grammar, rhetoric, and dialectic or logic (the *trivium*) and arithmetic, geometry, astronomy, and music (the *quadrivium*).

liberalism an ideology based on the belief that people should be as free from restraint as possible. Economic liberalism is the idea that the government should not interfere in the workings of the economy. Political liberalism is the idea that there should be restraints on the exercise of power so that people can enjoy basic civil rights in a constitutional state with a representative assembly.

limited (constitutional) monarchy a system of government in which the monarch is limited by a representative assembly and by the duty to rule in accordance with the laws of the land.

lineage group the descendants of a common ancestor; relatives, often as opposed to immediate family.

Longshan a Neolithic society from near the Yellow River in China, sometimes identified by its black pottery.

maharaja originally, a king in the Aryan society of early India (a great raja); later used more generally to denote an important ruler.

Mahayana a school of Buddhism that promotes the idea of universal salvation through the intercession of bodhisattvas; predominant in north Asia.

majlis a council of elders among the Bedouins of the Roman era.

Malayo-Polynesian a family of languages whose speakers originated on Taiwan or in southeastern China and spread from there to the Malay Peninsula, the Indonesian archipelago, and many islands of the South Pacific.

mandate of Heaven the justification for the rule of the Zhou dynasty in China. The king was charged to maintain order as a representative of Heaven, which was viewed as an impersonal law of nature.

mandates a system established after World War I whereby a nation officially administered a territory (mandate) on behalf of the League of Nations. Thus, France administered Lebanon and Syria as mandates, and Britain administered Iraq and Palestine.

Manichaeanism an offshoot of the ancient Zoroastrian religion that was later influenced by Christianity; became popular in central Asia in the eighth century C.E.

manor an agricultural estate operated by a lord and worked by peasants who performed labor services and paid various rents and fees to the lord in exchange for protection and sustenance.

mansa in the West African state of Mali, a chieftain who served as both religious and administrative leader and was responsible for forwarding tax revenues from the village to higher levels of government.

maroons camps for escaped slaves.

Marshall Plan the European Recovery Program, under which the United States provided financial aid to European countries to help them rebuild after World War II.

Marxism the political, economic, and social theories of Karl Marx, which included the idea that history is the story of class struggle and that ultimately the proletariat will overthrow the bourgeoisie and establish a dictatorship en route to a classless society.

mass education a state-run educational system, usually free of charge and compulsory, that aims to ensure that all children in society have at least a basic education.

mass leisure forms of leisure that appeal to large numbers of people in a society, including the working classes; emerged at the end of the nineteenth century to provide workers with amusements after work and on weekends; used during the twentieth century by totalitarian states to control their populations.

mass politics a political order characterized by mass political parties and universal male and (eventually) female suffrage.

mass society a society in which the concerns of the majority—the lower classes—play a prominent role; characterized by extension of voting rights, an improved standard of living for the lower classes, and mass education.

matrilinear passing through the female line—for example, from a father to his sister's son rather than his own—as practiced in some African societies; not necessarily or even usually combined with matriarchy, in which women rule.

megaliths large stones, widely used in Europe from around 4000 to 1500 B.C.E. to create monuments, including sophisticated astronomical observatories.

Meiji Restoration the period during the late nineteenth and early twentieth centuries when fundamental economic and cultural changes occurred in Japan, transforming it from a feudal and agrarian society to an industrial and technological one.

mercantilism an economic theory that held that a nation's prosperity depended on its supply of gold and silver and that the total volume of trade is unchangeable; therefore advocated that the government play an active role in the economy by encouraging exports and discouraging imports, especially through the use of tariffs.

Mesolithic Age   the period from 10,000 to 7000 B.C.E., characterized by a gradual transition from a food-gathering and hunting economy to a food-producing economy.

mestizos   the offspring of intermarriage between Europeans, originally Spaniards, and native American Indians.

Middle Passage   the journey of slaves from Africa to the Americas as the middle leg of the triangular trade.

Middle Path   a central concept of Buddhism, which advocates avoiding extremes of both materialism and asceticism; also known as the Eightfold Way.

mihrab   the niche in a mosque's wall that indicates the direction of Mecca, usually containing an ornately decorated panel representing Allah.

militarism   a policy of aggressive military preparedness; in particular, the large armies based on mass conscription and complex, inflexible plans for mobilization that most European nations had before World War I.

millet   an administrative unit in the Ottoman Empire used to organize religious groups.

MITI   the Ministry of International Trade and Industry in Japan; responsible for formulating and directing much of Japanese industrial policy after World War II.

Modernism   the artistic and literary styles that emerged in the decades before 1914 as artists rebelled against traditional efforts to portray reality as accurately as possible (leading to Impressionism and Cubism) and writers explored new forms.

monasticism   a movement that began in early Christianity whose purpose was to create communities of men and women who practiced a communal life dedicated to God as a moral example to the world around them.

monk   a man who chooses to live a communal life divorced from the world in order to dedicate himself totally to the will of God.

monotheism   having only one god; the doctrine or belief that there is only one god.

mulattoes   the offspring of Africans and Europeans, particularly in Latin America.

multiculturalism   a term referring to the connection of several cultural or ethnic groups within a society.

multinational corporation   a company with divisions in more than two countries.

mystery religions   religions that involve initiation into secret rites that promise intense emotional involvement with spiritual forces and a greater chance of individual immortality.

nationalism   a sense of national consciousness based on awareness of being part of a community—a "nation"—that has common institutions, traditions, language, and customs and that becomes the focus of the individual's primary political loyalty.

nation-state   a form of political organization in which a relatively homogeneous people inhabits a sovereign state, as opposed to a state containing people of several nationalities.

natural law   a body of laws or specific principles held to be derived from nature and binding on all human society even in the absence of positive laws.

natural rights   certain inalienable rights to which all people are entitled. They include the right to life, liberty, and ownership of property; freedom of speech and religion; and equal treatment under the law.

natural selection   Darwin's idea that organisms that are most adaptable to their environment survive and pass on the variations that enabled them to survive while less adaptable organisms become extinct; known by the shorthand expression "survival of the fittest."

Nazi New Order   the Nazis' plan for their conquered territories; included the extermination of Jews and others considered inferior, ruthless exploitation of resources, German colonization in the east, and the use of Poles, Russians, and Ukrainians as slave labor.

neocolonialism   the use of economic rather than political or military means to maintain Western domination of developing nations.

Neo-Confucianism   the dominant ideology of China during the second millennium C.E.; combined the metaphysical speculations of Buddhism and Daoism with the pragmatic Confucian approach to society, maintaining that the world is real, not illusory, and that fulfillment comes from participation, not withdrawal. It encouraged an intellectual environment that valued continuity over change and tradition over innovation.

Neolithic Revolution   the development of agriculture, including the planting of food crops and the domestication of farm animals, around 10,000 B.C.E.

new course   a short-lived, liberalizing change in Soviet policy toward eastern European allies instituted after Stalin's death in 1953.

New Culture Movement   a protest launched by students at Beijing University after the failure of the 1911 revolution; aimed at abolishing the remnants of the old system and introducing Western values and institutions into China.

New Deal   the reform program implemented by President Franklin Roosevelt in the 1930s, which included large public works projects and the introduction of Social Security.

New Democracy   the initial program of the Chinese Communist government, from 1949 to 1955, focusing on honest government, land reform, social justice, and peace rather than on the utopian goal of a classless society.

New Economic Policy   a modified version of the old capitalist system introduced in the Soviet Union by Lenin in 1921 to revive the economy after the ravages of the civil war and war communism.

new monarchies   the governments of France, England, and Spain at the end of the fifteenth century, where the rulers were successful in reestablishing or extending centralized royal authority, suppressing the nobility, controlling the church, and insisting on the loyalty of all peoples living in their territories.

Nirvana   in Buddhist thought, enlightenment, the ultimate transcendence from the illusion of the material world; release from the "wheel of life."

Nok culture   in northern Nigeria, one of the most active early iron-working societies in Africa, artifacts from which date back as far as 500 B.C.E.

Nonaligned Movement   an organization of neutralist nations established in the 1950s to provide a counterpoise between the socialist bloc, headed by the Soviet Union, and the capitalist nations led by the United States. Chief sponsors of the movement were Jawaharlal Nehru of India, Gamal Abdul Nasser of Egypt, and Sukarno of Indonesia.

noncentralized societies   societies characterized by autonomous villages organized by clans and ruled by a local chieftain or clan head; typical of the southern half of the African continent before the eleventh century C.E.

nongovernmental organizations (NGOs)   organizations that have no government ties and work to address world problems.

northern Renaissance humanism   *see* Christian humanism.

nun   a woman who withdraws from the world and joins a religious community; the female equivalent of a monk.

old regime/old order   the political and social system of France in the eighteenth century before the Revolution.

oligarchy   rule by a few.

Open Door Notes   a series of letters sent in 1899 by U.S. Secretary of State John Hay to Great Britain, France, Germany, Italy, Japan, and Russia, calling for equal economic access to the China market for all states and for the maintenance of the territorial and administrative integrity of the Chinese empire.

organic evolution   Darwin's principle that all plants and animals have evolved over a long period of time from earlier and simpler forms of life.

Paleolithic Age   the period of human history when humans used simple stone tools (c. 2,500,000–10,000 B.C.E.).

pan-Africanism   the concept of African continental unity and solidarity in which the common interests of African countries transcend regional boundaries.

pan-Arabism a movement promoted by Egyptian president Gamal Abdul Nasser and other Middle Eastern leaders to unify all Arab peoples in a single supra-national organization. After Nasser's death in 1971, the movement languished.

pantheism a doctrine that equates God with the universe and all that is in it.

pariahs members of the lowest level of traditional Indian society, technically outside the class system itself; also known as untouchables.

pasha an administrative official of the Ottoman Empire, responsible for collecting taxes and maintaining order in the provinces. Some eventually became hereditary rulers.

paterfamilias the dominant male in a Roman family whose powers over his wife and children were theoretically unlimited, though they were sometimes circumvented in practice.

patriarchy a society in which the father is supreme in the clan or family; more generally, a society dominated by men.

patricians great landowners who became the ruling class in the Roman Republic; in early modern Europe, a term used to identify the ruling elites of cities.

patrilinear passing through the male line, from father to son; often combined with patriarchy.

Pax Romana "Roman peace"; the stability and prosperity that Roman rule brought to the Mediterranean world and much of western Europe during the first and second centuries C.E.

peaceful coexistence the policy adopted by the Soviet Union under Nikita Khrushchev in 1955 and continued by his successors that called for economic and ideological rivalry with the West rather than nuclear war.

perestroika "restructuring"; the term applied to Mikhail Gorbachev's economic, political, and social reforms in the Soviet Union.

permissive society a characterization of Western society after World War II to reflect its sexual freedom and the emergence of the drug culture.

phalanx a rectangular formation of tightly massed infantry soldiers.

pharaoh the most common title used for Egyptian kings. Pharaohs possessed absolute power and were seen as divine.

philosophes intellectuals of the eighteenth-century Enlightenment who believed in applying a spirit of rational criticism to all things, including religion and politics, and who focused on improving and enjoying this world rather than on the afterlife.

plebeians the class of Roman citizens who included nonpatrician landowners, craftspeople, merchants, and small farmers in the Roman Republic. Their struggle for equal rights with the patricians dominated much of the Republic's history.

pogroms organized massacres of Jews.

polis an ancient Greek city-state encompassing both an urban area and its surrounding countryside; a small but autonomous political unit where all major political and social activities were carried out in a central location (plural: *poleis*).

polygyny the practice of having more than one wife at a time.

polytheism having many gods; belief in or the worship of more than one god.

popular culture as opposed to high culture, the unofficial written and unwritten culture of the masses, much of which was passed down orally; centered on public and group activities such as festivals. In the twentieth century, the entertainment, recreation, and pleasures that people purchase as part of mass consumer society.

portolani charts of landmasses and coastlines made by navigators and mathematicians in the thirteenth and fourteenth centuries.

Post-Impressionism an artistic movement that began in France in the 1880s. Post-Impressionists sought to use color and line to express inner feelings and produce a personal statement of reality.

Postmodernism a term used to cover a variety of artistic and intellectual styles and ways of thinking prominent since the 1970s.

poststructuralism (deconstruction) a theory formulated by Jacques Derrida in the 1960s, holding that there is no fixed, universal truth because culture is created and can therefore be analyzed in various ways.

praetorian guard the military unit that served as the personal bodyguard of the Roman emperors.

praetors the two senior Roman judges, who had executive authority when the consuls were away from the city and could also lead armies.

Prakrit an ancient Indian language, a simplified form of Sanskrit.

predestination the belief, associated with Calvinism, that God, as a consequence of his foreknowledge of all events, has predetermined who will be saved (the elect) and who will be damned.

proletariat the industrial working class; in Marxism, the class that will ultimately overthrow the bourgeoisie.

Protestant Reformation the western European religious reform movement in the sixteenth century that divided Christianity into Catholic and Protestant groups.

psychoanalysis a method developed by Sigmund Freud to resolve a patient's psychic conflict.

pueblo a three-story adobe communal house with a timbered roof. Pueblos were constructed by the Ancient Pueblo people in what is now the southwestern United States starting around the ninth century C.E.

Pueblo Bonito a large settlement built by the Ancient Pueblo people in what is now New Mexico in the ninth century C.E. It contained several hundred compounds housing several thousand residents.

puja in India, a populist tradition focused on personal worship that began to replace the Brahmanical emphasis on court sacrifice and asceticism during the early centuries of the first millennium C.E.; an aspect of the transition from Brahmanism to Hinduism.

purdah the Indian term for the practice among Muslims and some Hindus of isolating women and preventing them from associating with men outside the home.

Pure Land a Buddhist sect, originally Chinese but later popular in Japan, that taught that devotion alone could lead to enlightenment and release.

Puritans English Protestants inspired by Calvinist theology who wished to remove all traces of Catholicism from the Church of England.

quipu an Inka record-keeping system that used knotted strings rather than writing.

raj the British colonial regime in India.

raja originally, a chieftain in the Aryan society of early India, a representative of the gods; later used more generally to denote a ruler.

Ramadan the holy month of Islam, during which believers fast from dawn to sunset. Because the Islamic calendar is lunar, Ramadan migrates through the seasons.

rationalism a system of thought based on the belief that human reason and experience are the chief sources of knowledge.

Realism in medieval Europe, the school of thought that, following Plato, held that the individual objects we perceive are not real but merely manifestations of universal ideas existing in the mind of God. In the nineteenth century, a school of painting that emphasized the everyday life of ordinary people, depicted with photographic realism.

Realpolitik "politics of reality"; politics based on practical concerns rather than theory or ethics.

reincarnation the idea that the individual soul is reborn in a different form after death. In Hindu and Buddhist thought, release from this cycle is the objective of all living souls.

relativity theory Einstein's theory that holds, among other things, that space and time are not absolute but are relative to the observer and interwoven into a four-dimensional space-time continuum and that matter is a form of energy, expressed by the equation $E = mc^2$.

relics the bones of Christian saints or objects intimately associated with saints that were considered worthy of veneration.

Renaissance the "rebirth" of Classical culture that occurred in Italy between c. 1350 and c. 1550; also, the earlier revivals of Classical culture that occurred under Charlemagne and in the twelfth century.

Renaissance humanism an intellectual movement in Renaissance Italy based on the study of the Greek and Roman classics.

rentier a person who lives on income from property and is not personally involved in its operation.

reparations payments made by a defeated nation after a war to compensate another nation for damage sustained as a result of the war; required from Germany after World War I.

revisionism a socialist doctrine that rejected Marx's emphasis on class struggle and revolution and argued instead that workers should work through political parties to bring about gradual change.

revolutionary socialism the socialist doctrine espoused by Georges Sorel, who held that violent action was the only way to achieve the goals of socialism.

rhetoric the art of persuasive speaking; in the Middle Ages, one of the seven liberal arts.

Rococo a style, especially of decoration and architecture, that developed from the Baroque and spread throughout Europe by the 1730s. Though still elaborate, it emphasized curves, lightness, and charm in the pursuit of pleasure, happiness, and love.

Romanesque a term used to describe the art and especially architecture of Europe in the eleventh and twelfth centuries.

Romanticism a nineteenth-century intellectual and artistic movement that rejected the emphasis on reason of the Enlightenment. Instead, Romantics stressed the importance of intuition, feeling, emotion, and imagination as sources of knowing.

ronin Japanese warriors made unemployed by developments in the early modern era, since samurai were forbidden by tradition to engage in commerce.

rural responsibility system post-Maoist land reform in China, under which collectives leased land to peasant families, who could consume or sell their surplus production and keep the profits.

sacraments rites considered imperative for a Christian's salvation. By the thirteenth century, they consisted of the Eucharist or Lord's Supper, baptism, marriage, penance, extreme unction, holy orders, and confirmation of children; Protestant reformers of the sixteenth century generally recognized only two—baptism and communion (the Lord's Supper).

sakoku during the Tokugawa Shogunate in Japan, the policy of closing the country to foreign trade with Europe and encouraging domestic production of goods that had previously been imported.

samurai literally, "retainers"; similar to European knights. Usually in service to a particular shogun, these Japanese warriors lived by a strict code of ethics and duty.

Sanskrit an early Indo-European language, in which the Vedas were composed, beginning in the second millennium B.C.E. It survived as the language of literature and the bureaucracy in India for centuries after its decline as a spoken tongue.

sati the Hindu ritual requiring a wife to throw herself on her deceased husband's funeral pyre.

satori enlightenment, in the Japanese (especially Zen) Buddhist tradition.

satrap a governor with both civil and military duties in the ancient Persian Empire, which was divided into satrapies, or provinces, each administered by a satrap.

satrapy one of the provinces of the ancient Persian Empire, each ruled by a satrap.

satyagraha the Hindi term for the practice of nonviolent resistance, as advocated by Mohandas Gandhi; literally, "hold fast to the truth."

SCAP Supreme Command of the Allied Powers, the ruling body of the occupation forces in Japan after World War II.

scholar-gentry in Song Dynasty China, candidates who passed the civil service examinations and whose families were nonaristocratic landowners; eventually, a majority of the bureaucracy.

scholasticism the philosophical and theological system of the medieval schools, which emphasized rigorous analysis of contradictory authorities; often used to try to reconcile faith and reason.

School of Mind a philosophy espoused by Wang Yangming during the mid-Ming era of China, which argued that mind and the universe were a single unit and knowledge was therefore obtained through internal self-searching rather than through investigation of the outside world; for a while, a significant but unofficial rival to Neo-Confucianism.

scientific method a method of seeking knowledge through inductive principles; uses experiments and observations to develop generalizations.

Scientific Revolution the transition from the medieval worldview to a largely secular, rational, and materialistic perspective; began in the seventeenth century and was popularized in the eighteenth.

secularization the process of becoming more concerned with material, worldly, temporal things and less with spiritual and religious things.

self-strengthening a late-nineteenth-century Chinese policy under which Western technology would be adopted while Confucian principles and institutions were maintained intact.

senate the leading council of the Roman Republic; composed of about three hundred men (senators) who served for life and dominated much of the political life of the Republic.

separation of powers a doctrine enunciated by Montesquieu in the eighteenth century that separate executive, legislative, and judicial powers serve to limit and control each other.

sepoys local troops who formed the basis of the British Indian Army; hired by the East India Company to protect British interests in South Asia.

serf a peasant who is bound to the land and obliged to provide labor services and pay various rents and fees to the lord; considered unfree but not a slave because serfs could not be bought and sold.

Shari'a a law code, originally drawn up by Muslim scholars shortly after the death of Muhammad, that provides believers with a set of prescriptions to regulate their daily lives.

sheikh originally, the ruler of a Bedouin tribe; later, also used as a more general honorific.

Shi'ite the second largest tradition of Islam, which split from the majority Sunni soon after the death of Muhammad in a disagreement over his succession; especially significant in Iran and Iraq.

Shinto a kind of state religion in Japan, derived from beliefs in nature spirits and until recently linked with belief in the divinity of the emperor and the sacredness of the Japanese nation.

shogun a powerful Japanese leader, originally military, who ruled under the titular authority of the emperor.

shogunate system the system of government in Japan in which the emperor exercised only titular authority while the shoguns (regional military dictators) exercised actual political power.

sipahis in the Ottoman Empire, local cavalry elites who held fiefdoms and collected taxes.

Slavophiles in the nineteenth century, Russian intellectuals who believed that Russia's tsarist system, peasant villages, and Orthodox religious faith were superior to any Western ideals.

Social Darwinism the application of Darwin's principle of organic evolution to the social order; led to the belief that progress comes from the struggle for survival as the fittest advance and the weak decline.

socialism an ideology that calls for collective or government ownership of the means of production and the distribution of goods.

socialized medicine health services for all citizens provided by government assistance.

Socratic method a form of teaching that uses a question-and-answer format to enable students to reach conclusions by using their own reasoning.

Solidarity an independent labor union established in Poland during the late 1970s to fight for workers' rights against the communist regime.

Sophists wandering scholars and professional teachers in ancient Greece who stressed the importance of rhetoric and tended toward skepticism and relativism.

soviets councils of workers' and soldiers' deputies formed throughout Russia in 1917; played an important role in the Bolshevik Revolution.

squadristi in Italy in the 1920s, bands of armed Fascists used to create disorder by attacking socialist offices and newspapers.

Star Wars nickname of the Strategic Defense Initiative, proposed by President Reagan, which was intended to provide a shield that would destroy any incoming missiles; named after a popular science-fiction movie series.

State Confucianism the integration of Confucian doctrine with Legalist practice under the Han dynasty in China; became the basis of Chinese political thought until the modern era.

Stoicism   a philosophy founded by Zeno in the fourth century B.C.E. that taught that happiness could be obtained by accepting one's lot and living in harmony with the will of God, thereby achieving inner peace.

stupa   originally, a stone tower holding relics of the Buddha; more generally, a place for devotion, often architecturally impressive and surmounted with a spire.

subinfeudation   the practice in which a lord's greatest vassals subdivided their fiefs and had vassals of their own, and those vassals in turn subdivided their fiefs and so on down to simple knights, whose fiefs were too small to subdivide.

Sublime Porte   the office of the grand vizier in the Ottoman Empire.

sudras   the classes that represented the great bulk of the Indian population from ancient times, mostly peasants, artisans, or manual laborers; ranked below *brahmins*, *kshatriyas*, and *vaisyas* but above the pariahs.

suffragists   those who advocate the extension of the right to vote (suffrage), especially to women.

Sufism   a mystical school of Islam, noted for its music, dance, and poetry, which became prominent in about the thirteenth century.

sultan   "holder of power"; a title commonly used by Muslim rulers in the Ottoman Empire, Egypt, and elsewhere; still in use in parts of Asia, sometimes for regional authorities.

Sunni   the largest tradition of Islam, from which the Shi'ites split soon after the death of Muhammad in a disagreement over his succession.

Supreme Ultimate   according to Neo-Confucianists, a transcendent world distinct from the material world in which humans live but to which humans may aspire; a set of abstract principles, roughly equivalent to the Dao.

Surrealism   an artistic movement that arose between World War I and World War II. Surrealists portrayed recognizable objects in unrecognizable relationships in order to reveal the world of the unconscious.

Swahili   a mixed African-Arabian culture that developed by the twelfth century along the east coast of Africa; also, the national language of Kenya and Tanzania.

Taika reforms   the seventh-century "great change" reforms that established the centralized Japanese state.

taille   a French tax on land or property, developed by King Louis XI in the fifteenth century as the financial basis of the monarchy. It was largely paid by the peasantry; the nobility and the clergy were exempt.

Taisho democracy   the era of the 1920s in Japan when universal (male) suffrage was instituted, political parties expanded, and other democratic institutions appeared to flourish. The process of democratization proved fragile, however, and failed to continue into the 1930s.

Tantrism   a mystical Buddhist sect that emphasized the importance of magical symbols and ritual in seeking a path to enlightenment.

theocracy   a government based on a divine authority.

Theravada   a school of Buddhism that stresses personal behavior and the quest for understanding as a means of release from the wheel of life, rather than the intercession of bodhisattvas; predominant in Sri Lanka and Southeast Asia.

three obediences   the traditional duties of Japanese women, in permanent subservience: child to father, wife to husband, and widow to son.

three people's principles   the three principles on which the program of Sun Yat-sen's Revolutionary Alliance (Tongmenghui) was based: nationalism (meaning primarily the elimination of Manchu rule over China), democracy, and people's livelihood.

totalitarian state   a state characterized by government control over all aspects of economic, social, political, cultural, and intellectual life; subordination of the individual to the state; and insistence that the masses be actively involved in the regime's goals.

total war   warfare in which all of a nation's resources, including civilians at home and soldiers in the field, are mobilized for the war effort.

tozama **daimyo**   during the Tokugawa Shogunate in Japan, the larger, more independent lords who were usually more distant from the center of shogunate power in Edo; literally, "outside daimyo."

trade union   an association of workers in the same trade, formed to help members secure better wages, benefits, and working conditions.

transnational corporation   another term for a "multinational corporation," or a company with divisions in more than two countries.

trench warfare   warfare in which the opposing forces attack and counterattack from a relatively permanent system of trenches protected by barbed wire; characteristic of World War I.

Triangular Trade   a term used to describe a form of international trade taking place between three countries or regions of the world.

tribunes of the plebs   beginning in 494 B.C.E., Roman officials who were given the power to protect plebeians against arrest by patrician magistrates.

Truman Doctrine   the doctrine, enunciated by Harry Truman in 1947, that the United States would provide economic aid to countries that were threatened by Communist expansion.

twice-born   the males of the higher castes in traditional Indian society, who underwent an initiation ceremony at puberty.

tyranny   rule by a tyrant.

tyrant   in an ancient Greek *polis* (or an Italian city-state during the Renaissance), a ruler who came to power in an unconstitutional way and ruled without being subject to the law.

uhuru   "freedom" in Swahili, a key slogan in African independence movements, especially in Kenya.

uji   a clan in early Japanese tribal society.

ulama   a convocation of leading Muslim scholars, the earliest of which shortly after the death of Muhammad drew up the *Shari'a*, a law code based largely on the Qur'an and the sayings of the Prophet, to provide believers with a set of prescriptions to regulate their daily lives.

umma   the Muslim community as a whole.

unconditional surrender   complete, unqualified surrender of a nation.

uninterrupted revolution   the goal of the Great Proletarian Cultural Revolution launched by Mao Zedong in 1966.

utopian socialists   intellectuals and theorists in the early nineteenth century who favored equality in social and economic conditions and wished to replace private property and competition with collective ownership and cooperation; deemed impractical and "utopian" by later socialists.

vaisya   the third-ranked class in traditional Indian society, usually merchants.

varna   Indian classes or castes. *See also* caste system.

vassal   a person granted a fief, or landed estate, in exchange for providing military services to the lord and fulfilling certain other obligations such as appearing at the lord's court when summoned and making a payment on the knighting of the lord's eldest son.

veneration of ancestors   the extension of filial piety to include care for the deceased, for instance, by burning replicas of useful objects to accompany them on their journey to the next world.

vezir   see vizier.

viceroy   the administrative head of the provinces of New Spain and Peru in the Americas.

Viet Cong   the popular name applied to the resistance forces led by the National Front for the Liberation of South Vietnam (NLF) in South Vietnam. Literally, "Viet Communists."

Vietnam syndrome   the presumption, from the 1970s on, that the U.S. public would object to a protracted military entanglement abroad, such as another Vietnam-type conflict.

vizier   the prime minister in the Abbasid caliphate and elsewhere, a chief minister.

war communism   Lenin's policy of nationalizing industrial and other facilities and requisitioning the peasants' produce during the civil war in Russia.

War Guilt Clause   the clause in the Treaty of Versailles that declared Germany (and Austria) responsible for starting World War I and ordered Germany to pay reparations for the damage the Allies had suffered as a result of the war.

welfare state a social and political system in which the government assumes primary responsibility for the social welfare of its citizens by providing such things as social security, unemployment benefits, and health care.

well-field system the theoretical pattern of land ownership in early China, named for the appearance of the Chinese character for "well," in which farmland was divided into nine segments and a peasant family would cultivate one for its own use and cooperate with seven others to cultivate the ninth for the landlord.

wergeld "money for a man"; in early Germanic law, a person's value in monetary terms, which was paid by a wrongdoer to the family of the person who had been injured or killed.

White Lotus a Chinese Buddhist sect, founded in 1133 C.E., that sought political reform; in 1796–1804, a Chinese peasant revolt.

Westernizers in the nineteenth century, Russian intellectuals who believed that Western ways were the solution to Russia's problems.

women's liberation movement the struggle for equal rights for women, which has deep roots in history but achieved new prominence under this name in the 1960s, building on the work of, among others, Simone de Beauvoir and Betty Friedan.

world-machine Newton's conception of the universe as one huge, regulated, and uniform machine that operated according to natural laws in absolute time, space, and motion.

yangban the aristocratic class in Korea. During the Choson Dynasty, entry into the bureaucracy was limited to members of this class.

Yangshao a Neolithic society from near the Yellow River in China, sometimes identified by its painted pottery.

Young Turks a successful Turkish reformist group in the late nineteenth and early twentieth centuries.

zaibatsu powerful business cartels formed in Japan during the Meiji era and outlawed following World War II.

zamindars Indian tax collectors who were assigned land from which they kept part of the revenue. The British revived the system in a misguided attempt to create a landed gentry.

Zen (in Chinese, Chan or Ch'an) a school of Buddhism particularly important in Japan, some of whose adherents stress that enlightenment (*satori*) can be achieved suddenly, though others emphasize lengthy meditation.

ziggurat a massive stepped tower on which a temple dedicated to the chief god or goddess of a Sumerian city was built.

Zionism an international movement that called for the establishment of a Jewish state or a refuge for Jews in Palestine.

Zoroastrianism a religion founded by the Persian Zoroaster in the seventh century B.C.E., characterized by worship of a supreme god, Ahuramazda, who represents the good against the evil spirit, Ahriman.

DOCUMENTS

INDEX

German Social Democratic Party (SPD), 553, 826
Germany, 329–330, 342; African colonies of, *619*, 622, 669; after World War I, 682, *682*, 683–684; after World War II, *756*; alliances of, 663, 669, 734, 741; Allied bombings of, 752–753; anti-Semitism in, 566, 597, 727, 729–730, 743–744, 746; China and, *639*; constitution of, 566; economy in, 728, 826; European Union and, 831–832; Great Depression in, 686, 727; Green Party in, 850; Habsburgs and, 438; High Command in, 676; immigrants in, 850; imperialism by, *619*, 622; independent states in, 382; industrialization and, 541–542, 751; Luther and Lutheranism in, 418–419, 421–423; nationalism and, 597, 727; Neanderthals from, 3; occupation of, 755; partition of, 755; pogroms against Jews in, 372–374; racism in, 597; Reformation in, 421–423; reparations and, 682, 684, 755; reunification of, 766, 802, 826; Roman Empire and, 136–137; serfs in, 515; submarine warfare by, 671; trade in, 334; in Triple Alliance, 567; unification of, 562, 766, 802, 826; Versailles Treaty and, 681–682, 684; voting in, 845; women in, 751, 845; before World War I, 567. *See also* East Germany; Nazi Germany; West Germany; World War I; World War II
Germ theory, 593
Ghana, 224–226, 862; Ashanti of, 220, 411, 618, 628, 863; fall of, 225; religion in, 226; royalty in, 226
Ghazni, 247
Ghent, 334, 337
Ghettos, 746
Gia Long dynasty, 500
Giant heads of Easter Island, *265*
Gibbon, Edward, 175
Gibbs, Philip, 662
Gibraltar. *See* Straits, of Gibraltar
Gigas, Herman, 375
Gilgamesh, 13, 16
Ginza, *658*
Giovane, Palma, *371*
Giza, pyramids of, 20, *161*
Gladiator (film), 145
Gladiators, 145
Glasnost (openness), 800–801
Globalization, 931; of civilization, 935–941; digital age and, 936–937; economic, 929–930, 935–936; environmental crisis and, 939–940; society and, 940; in Southeast Asia, 896, 912, 916–917
Global trade, 157, 386. *See also* Trade
Global village, 788
Global warfare, 520–521
Global warming, 788
Glorious Revolution, 440
Goa, 394–395
Gobi Desert region, 64, *79*, *157*, 218, 283, 639. *See also* Mongols
Gods and goddesses: in Africa, 220; in Aztec society, 169–170; in Egypt, 20; in Greece, 102, 148; in India, 39, 47, 49–50, 52; in Israel, 28; in Mayan society, 163–164; in Roman Empire, 148; rulers and, 149–152; in Southeast Asia, 263; in Sumerian society, 10–11. *See also names of specific deities*; Religion
Gojoseon kingdom, 315
Gokhale, Gopal, 697
Golan Heights, 881
Gold, 67, 432; in Africa, 223, 404, 624; in Americas, *171*, 401–402; in Ghana, 225; in money economy, 334–335; trade and, 513; in West Africa, 394
Gold Coast, 394, 411, 617, *619*, 622, 861–862. *See also* Ghana

Golden Horde, 285
Golden Horn, 370, 448
Golden Pavilion, *313*
Golden Temple, 900
Gold Vase Plum (The Golden Lotus), 486
Gomez, Franco, *574*
Gómez, Juan Vicente, 718
Gomulka, Wladyslaw, 775
Goodbye to All That (Graves), 666
Good emperors (Rome), 137–138
Good Neighbor Policy, 718–719
Goods, 364. *See also* Trade
Gopuras (gate towers), 255
Gorbachev, Mikhail, 760, 787, 800–803, 811, 912
Gordon, Charles, 620–621, *621*
Gore, Al, 835
Gospels, 149–150
Gosplan, 796
Gothic cathedrals, 349–350
Gothic literature, 592
Gottwald, Klement, 763
Government: of Athens, 101–104; of Aztec society, 167–168; of Brazil, 399; of Byzantine Empire, 363, 365–368; of Canada, 584; of China, 65–71, 73, 152, 272–274, 276, 475–480, 712; in communes, 337; of Congo River region, 228; of Costa Rica, 399; of East Africa, 224, 624–625; of Eastern Woodlands peoples, 179; of Egypt, 17–19; of England, 340–341; enlightened absolutism in, 517–518; feudalism and, 331; fiefs and, 331; of France, 341, 435–438, 521–522, 527, 530–531, 686; of Germany, 566; of Ghana, 225–226; of Greece, 100; of Harappan society, 40; of Holy Roman Empire, 342–343; of India, 43–44, 462, 897–898, 908; Indian trade and, 253; industrialization and, 541–542; of Italy, 566; of Japan, 303–308, 491, 653–654, 714–715, 919; Kangxi on, 474; of Latin America, 575, 577; liberals and, 555; of Mahabharata, 43; of Mali, 225; of Medieval European cities, 337–341; Montesquieu on, 507; of Ottoman Empire, 451–453; of Pakistan, 901; of Persian Empire, 32; of Portugal, 399–402; of Rome, 128–130, 137–139, 147–148, 152; of Russia, 438–439; of Safavid society, 458–460; of Singapore, 927; of South Korea, 925; of Spain, 382, 399–402; of Sparta, 100; of Sumer, 11; of Tang China, 271; of United States, 517; of Vietnam, 321, 909, 911–912. *See also* Laws; *names of specific types of government*; Politics
Gracchus family, 131
Grain: in China, 70; Neolithic, 5; watermills for, 332. *See also names of specific types of grain*
Grain of Wheat, A (Ngugi Wa Thiong'o), 875
Granada, 198, 341
Grand Alliance (World War II), 741, *755*, 755, 762. *See also* Allies (World War II)
Grand Army of Napoleon, 531–532
Grand Canal, 269, *270*, 276, 286, 481, 645
Grand Council (China), 272
Grand Council of State (Japan), 303
Grand Duchy of Warsaw, 531–532
Grand Empire of Napoleon, 531–532
Grandeur and Misery of Victory (Clemenceau), 680
Grand National Assembly, 699
Grand vizier, 451
Granicus River, battle at, 115–116
Grant, Ulysses S., 583
Grass, Günter, 907
Grasslands, African, 213–214, 647, 869
Graves, Robert, 666
Great Altar of Pergamum, 449
Great Britain, 506. *See also* England (Britain)
Great Council (England), 341

Great Depression, *685*, 685–686, 695, 718–719, 725, 836–837
Great Divergence, The: China, Europe, and the Making of the Modern World Economy (Pomeranz), 545
Great East-Asia Co-Prosperity Sphere, 748
Greater Japanese Women's Association, 752
Great flood, 16
Great Gate, *226*
Great King (Persia), 32–33, 115
Great Leap Forward, 804, 813
Great Mosque: in Cordoba, 209; "Great peace," 491–493; in Samarra, *193*, 200, 208
Great Peloponnesian War, 104–105
Great Plains region, 159, 179
Great Proletarian Cultural Revolution, 645, 805–807, 817
Great Pyramid, 20
Great Schism, 377
Great Society, 833
Great Trek, 621–622, *622*
Great Viet. *See* Dai Viet
Great Wall, 81, *84*, 285, *288*, 639
Great War. *See* World War I
Great Zimbabwe, 212–213, 228, 234, 404, 406
Greece, 93–122, 699; alphabet in, 96; ancient, *95*; Antigonid dynasty in, 118; Archaic Age in, 98; arts in, 106–108; citizens in, 98; city-states in, 98–102; civil war in, 93, 764; classical civilization in, 102–114, 378; coins in, 49; colonization by, 98–99; conquered peoples and, *120*; culture in, 105–110, 359; Dark Age in, 96–98; European unification and, 831–832; foreign influence on culture of, 102; geography of, 94; government of, 100; Hellenistic period in, 118; Homeric, 96–98; homosexuality in, 112; independence of, 559, 567; India and, 43; Italy and, 127–128; kouros sculpture in, *102*; metalwork in, *96*; military in, 98; Minoan Crete and, 94–95; Mycenaean, 95–96; Persian Empire and, 32, 103; philosophy in, 108–110, 204; religion in, 110–111; revolt against Turks, 559; Rome and, 127, 130, 140; Sparta and, 93–94, 100; trireme in, 103; tyrants in, 99–100; warfare in, 98; World War II and, 739, 763. *See also* Hellenistic world
Greek fire, 360
Greek language, 24–25, 361
Greek Orthodoxy, 363, 559. *See also* Eastern Orthodox Christianity
Greenhouse effect, 939
Green movements, 850
Green revolution, 902
Greens (Byzantine faction), 356, 360
Gregory of Tours, 327
Gregory VII, 345
Gregory XI, 377
Gropius, Walter, 688
Grossman, David, 893
Grozny, Chechnya, 831
Guam, 583
Guangdong, 708
Guangxu, 641, 645
Guangzhou (Canton), China, 820. *See also* Canton
Guan Yin, 243, *321*
Guaraní Indians, 401, *401*
"Guardian kings," *312*, *313*, *314*
Guatemala, 158–159, 162, *166*, 575, 579, 837
Guerrilla warfare: in Afghanistan, 787; Castro and, 838–839; in Vietnam, 782
Guest workers, 849
Guevara, Ernest "Ché," 838
Guianas, *717*, *717*
Guided democracy, 910

March Revolution, 705
Marconi, Guglielmo, 549
Marcos, Ferdinand, 910
Marcus Aurelius, 145, 147
Marcus Brutus, 135
Maria Theresa, 518
Marie Antoinette, 521–522
Marie Antoinette (film), 522, *522*
Marijuana, 843–844
Maritime routes and trade. *See* Ships and shipping; Trade
Marius, 134
Markets: in Aztec society, 168; colonies as, 539; global, 388–417, 861, 904, 929–930, 935; in India, 465; slave, 408–409
Marne River, Battles of the, 667
Maroons, 408
Marrakech, 200, 225
Marriage: in 19th century, 586–587; in Africa, 874–875; arranged, 426–427, 874–875; bourgeois, 594; in China, 280–282, 485–486, 815–816, 818; in Confucianism, 293; in early modern world, 426–427; in Egypt, 22; of elites, 586–587; of Germanic peoples, 325; in Hammurabi's Code, 12; in India, 46–47, 470, 698, 903–907; in Inkan society, 177; in Japan, 309, 493–494; Luther on, 426–427; by Protestant clergy, 422; in Rome, 141–142; in Southeast Asia, 260–262; in Sparta, 100. *See also* Families; Polygamy; Polygyny
Mars (god), 148
Marshall, George C., 764, 769–770
Marshall, John, 581
Marshall Plan, 764–765
Mars (planet), 854–855
Martinique, 618
Marxism-Leninism: in Africa, 705–706; in China, 646, 808, 821
Marx (Karl) and Marxism, 552–554; capitalism and, 791; Great Depression and, 686; in Latin America, 838; as utopian idea, 705. *See also* China; Communism and communists; Soviet Union
Mary. *See* Virgin Mary
Mary I, 425
Mary II, 440
Masaccio, 378
Massachusetts colony, 402, 515
Mass consumerism, 551
Mass culture, 688
Mass democracy, 581
Mass education, 588–590
Mass leisure, 591, 843
"Mass line" policy, 769, 813
Mass politics, 565
Mass society, 584–586; education for, 588–590; leisure in, 590–591; structure of, 586; in West, 586
Mastabas, 20
"Masters of Huai Nan," 318
Masurian Lakes, Battle of, 667–668
Material goods, 8–9
Materialism, 914
Mathematical Principles of Natural Philosophy. See Principia (Newton)
Mathematics, 60; Arabic numerals and, 204; Descartes and, 506; Islamic, 156–157; Mesopotamian, 14
Matrilineal society, 230, 626
Matto de Turner, Clorinda, 593
Mauch, Karl, 212
Mau Mau movement, 862
Maurice, 364
Mauryan Empire, 118–119; carved chapels of, 61; India after, 55–56, 240, 242

Mausoleum. *See* Tombs
Max Havelaar (Doewes Dekker), 614
Maximilian, 422
Mayan civilization, 158–159, 162–167; decline of, 166–167, 174; jade in, *166*; writing of, *15*, 164–166
May Fourth Movement, 708, 808
Mayhew, Henry, 587
Mayors of the palace, 328
Ma Yuan, *296*
Mbeki, Thabo, 868, *868*
Mboya, Tom, 867
McCarthy, Joseph, 778
McDonald's: globalization of, 904, 935, *935*; in India, 904
McKinley, William, 583–584, 613–614, 631
McNeill, William, 631
Meadows of Gold (al-Mas'udi), 207
Measles, 402
Meat Inspection Act, 583
Mecca, 156, 184–185, 197, 699, 703
Medes, 28, 30
Medici, Cosimo de', 380, 380–381
Medicine, 204. *See also* Diseases; Health care
Medieval Europe. *See* Europe; Middle Ages
Medina, 187, 703
Mediterranean region: African trade and, *216*; agriculture in, 5; Arabs in, 221; Muslims and, 190–191, 197, 390–391; Ottoman Empire and, 559; Phoenicians in, 25; Rome and, 130–134, 138; Soviet expansion into, 764; trade in, 185; Turks in, 449–451; in World War II, 738. *See also names of specific countries*
Medvedev, Dmitry, 831
Megalithic structures, 23
Megasthenes, 43–44, 47, 119
Mehmet II, 371, 447–448, 451, *452*
Meiji, 650, 652, 716
Meiji Constitution, 652, 714, 917
Meiji Restoration, 650–654, *651*, 658
Mein Kampf (Hitler), 727–728, 733
Meir, Golda, 881, 891
Mekong River region, 257, 612, 614
Melanesian peoples, 264
Memoirs (Duc de Saint-Simon), 437
Memorial on the War Against Heterodoxy (Hong Liangji), 636
Memphis, Egypt, 18
Men: in Arawak society, 181; in Aztec society, 169; in China, 86, 280–282, 486; in Germanic society, 325–326; during Great Depression, 685; Neolithic, 4, 6; Paleolithic, 4; patriarchy by, 6; in Rome, 143; sexuality and, 843
Menander, 121
Mencius, 75, 82
Mendeleev, Dmitri, 593
Menelik, 628
Menem, Carlos Saúl, 841
Menes, 17
Mensheviks, 675
Mercantilism, 432, 438
Merchants: in Africa, 408–410; China and, 83, 279; in East Africa, 223; in Ghana, 225; in India, 241, 253, 469; in Japan, 493; in Ottoman Empire, 453; on Silk Road, 139
Merit system, 303. *See also* Civil service examinations
Merkel, Angela, 827
Meroë, 214–217, *215*, *222*, 234
Merovingian dynasty, 325
Meru, Mount, 263, 412
Mesa Verde, 180–181
Mesoamerica, 159–172. *See also* Central America
Mesolithic Age, 5

Mesopotamia, xxxii, 2, 7; Assyria and, 28; city-states in, 9–12; civilization in, 9–16; culture in, 13–16; empires in, 12–16; Mongols in, 196; Ottomans and, 448; Persia and, 31; Roman rule of, 138–139; society in, 12–13; trade in, 9–10, 185; writing in, 14, *14*
Message, The (Muhammad: The Messenger of God) (film), 187
Messiah, 148–149
Mestizos, 399, 573
Metal and metalwork: in Aztec society, 171; in China, 67, 67, 69, 83, 87–88; in Greece, 96; Neolithic tools, 7; in South America, 170; in West Africa, 232. *See also names of specific metals*
Metternich, Klemens von, 554–555, 558
Mexico, 159, 399; Aztecs in, 167–171; Cortes in, 392, 397; economy in, 578; government of, 720; growth of, 841–842; independence for, 573; land problem in, 578; oil in, 837, 842; reforms in, 841; revolt in, 720; social conditions in, 577; United States and, 579, 720; War of Reform in, 577; Zapotecs in, 160
Mexico City, 168, 841
Micah, 29
Michael Cerularius, 368
Michael III, 365
Michael Paleologus, 369–370
Michael Romanov, 438
Michelangelo, 379–380
Microsoft, 937
Middle Ages: agriculture in, 332–333; castles in, *195*; in Europe, 324–355; in India, 241; Italy in, 381; religious imagery in, *362*; society in, 419. *See also* Cities and towns; Trade
Middle class: after World War II, 843; in China, 710, 814; in developing world, 695; in England, 547, 558, 563; family in, 586–587; fears of working class, 558; in France, 521, 558; industrial, 545–546; in Japan, 494–497, 547; in Latin America, 579; in mass society, 586; reforms in, 587; women in workforce and, 551–552
Middle East: after World War I, 682, 683, *683*, 703, 877; agriculture in, 5; Alexander the Great and, 117; arts in, 891–893; civilizations of, 156–157; culture in, 891–893; emigrants from, 849; governments in, 886–887; Islam and, 184–211, 877; mandates in, *683*, 702–703, *705*, 877; modern, 882, 888, 890; Mongols in, 196; music in, 893; nation-state and, 861; oil in, 702–703, *703*, 764, 786, 877, 880, 882, 888–890; Ottoman Turks in, 669; plague in, 372; protests in, 885–886; rug weaving in, 208–209; at time of Muhammad, 186; trade in, 1, 387; U.S.-Soviet conflict over, 764; wealth in, 200–201; women in, 891; during World War I, 669. *See also* Arabs and Arab world; Islam and Muslims; Israel; *names of specific locations*
Middle Kingdom: Egypt, 17–19; Europe, 329
Middle Passage, 407–408
Middle Path, 52–56
Middle Stone Age. *See* Mesolithic Age
Middle way, 54
Midnight (Mao Dun), 713
Midnight's Children (Rushdie), 907
Midway Island, Battle of, 741
Migration, 219; in Africa, 873; into Americas, 159; Aryan, 42; globalization and, 940; Greek, 96, 98–99; of Jews to Palestine, 597; of Slavic peoples, 343; in Southeast Asia, 616; worldwide, 405. *See also* Immigrants and immigration
Mihrab (niche), 208
Milan, 337, 380

Militarism: Japanese, 731–732, 920–921; before World War I, 663

Military, 536–537; Abbasid, 194; American, 663; American Revolution, 516–517; Assyrian, 28, 30–31; Austrian, 663; Aztec, 168; British, 663; Byzantine, 365–368; as characteristic of civilization, 8; Chinese, 152, 477–479; Egyptian, 21; English, *376*; Ethiopian, 221; European, 435; French, *376*, 527–528; German, 663, 739; Greek, 98, 104; Hellenistic, 118; Indonesian, 910; Inkan, 177; Italian, 663; Janissary corps, 447; Japanese, 305–306, 653, 919; Latin American, 837; Mongol, 283, 285–286; Mughal, 462; Ottoman, 446; Persian, 31–32; Prussian, 438, 517; Roman, 132–134, 147–148; Russian, 663; service as vassal obligation, 331; slaves in, 231; South Korean, 927; Spanish, 382; Spartan, 100; Turkish, 451–452; weapons for, 450; before World War I, 663. *See also* Wars and warfare; Weapons

Millennium Declaration (UN), 871

Millet (administrative unit), 453

Millet (crop), 5, 48, 86

Mills: textile, 540; working conditions in, 546

Miloševic, Slobodan, 829

Miltiades, 103

Minamoto Yoritomo, 306

Mindanao, 910

Mind-body dualism, 506

Minerva, 148

Mines and mining, 547–548, *548*

Ming Dynasty, 81, 288–290, 475–479; arts of, 486–487; pottery from, *296*; society under, 288–289, 475–478

Ministry of International Trade and Industry (MITI), 921

Minoan civilization, 94–95

Minorities: in Austria-Hungary, 566; in China, 812; in Europe, 683; in India, 50, 902; in Ottoman Empire, 453. *See also* Ethnic groups; *names of specific groups*

Minos, 94–95

Min River, 70

Minute on Education (Macaulay), 610

Mir, 564

Mishima, Yukio, 892, 924

Missi dominici (messengers), 328

Missile crisis, in Cuba, 777–779, 794, 839

Missiles, 776

Missions and missionaries: in Africa, 620, 622, 625; along Silk Road, 278; in Americas, 400; in China, 475–476, 478; Christian, 326–328; in Ethiopia, 221; Hindu, 245; in Japan, 489–490, 648; Jesuit, 429; in Kiev, 344; in Korea, 499; in Latin America, 400–401; in Southeast Asia, 611; trade and, 201. *See also names of specific orders*

Mission, The (film), 401, *401*

MITI. *See* Ministry of International Trade and Industry

Mitterrand, Francois, 825, *827*

Mobility of military, 202, 449

Mobilization: in French Revolution, 527; in World War I, 664–665; in World War II, 749–752

Mobutu Sese Seko, 863, 869

Moche culture, 173–174

Moctezuma, 168

Model T Ford, 549

Modena, 560

Modern Devotion movement, 421

Modernism, 597–600

Modernization, *750*; approaches to, 761; industrialization, nationalism, and, 538–571; in Latin America, 578–579; theory of, 761; in Turkey, 699–700, *702*

Mogadishu, 223

Mohács, Battle of, 446

Mohammed. *See* Muhammad

Mohenjo-Daro, 8, 38–39, *39*, 40–41

Moi, Daniel arap, 867

Moldavia, 559

Mole sauce, 163

Molotov, Vyacheslav, 757, 768, 792–793

Moluccas. *See* Spice Islands

Mombasa, 222, 394, 404, 412

Monarchs and monarchies: absolutist, 419, 435–438; in Athens, 100–101; in Austria, 438; in England, 340–341, 439–440; in France, 521–522, 526–528; gods and, 149–152; in Hellenistic society, 118–119; in Holy Roman Empire, 343; "new monarchies" and, 419; papal, 345; in Spain, 382. *See also* Kings and kingdoms; *names of specific rulers and kingdoms*

Monasticism. *See* Monks and monasticism

Money: in Athens, 111; in China, 276; early, 49; euro, 832; wergeld, 326

Money economy, 334–335; in China, 79; in India, 47–49

Mongkut, 611

Mongol Empire, 196, 247–248, 283–287, 475

Mongols, 157, 195–196, 218, 247; attacks on Japan, Vietnam, and Indonesia, 285; in Central Asia, 196, 283–287; in China, 269, 272, 285–286; Delhi sultanate and, 247–248; historical impact of, 286–287; Islam and, 196; Japan and, 305; Korea under, 317–318; plague and, 372; in Russia, 343–344, 383; trade and, 334

Monks and monasticism, 327–328; Chinese Buddhist, 239–240, 270; Christian, 157, 326–328, 345–347; Indian Buddhist, 240–241; Japanese, 304, 312. *See also* Intellectual thought; *names of specific orders*

Monogamy: in Egypt, 21; in Southeast Asia, 260–262

Monotheism, 25; of Hebrews, 25, 27; of Islam, 187; of Zoroaster, 34

Monroe, James, 576–577

Monroe Doctrine, 576–577

Monshi, Eskander Beg, 458

Monsoons: in India, 240; trade and, 220

Montcalm, 520

Monte Alban, 160

Montenegro, 830

Montesquieu (Charles de Secondat), 507

Monte Verde, 172

Moon, 854

Moore, Charles, 854

Moors, 198

Moor's Last Sign, The (Rushdie), 907

Morality: of imperialism, 626; of Islam, 188; of Jewish law, 27; of slave trade, 409–410

Morisot, Berthe, 597, *599*

Mornington. *See* Wellesley

Morocco, 194, 198, 225, 411, 449, 607, 619, 862, 891

Morsi, Mohamed, 886

Mortality rates: Black Death, 372; in Europe, 513; for Europeans in Africa, 622; in India, 902, 907; industrialization and, 544–545; for slaves, 408

Mortgage rates, 936

Mosaics: Indian, 470; Turkish, 455, 470

Moscow, 678, 739, 795; Napoleon in, 532; princes of, 344, 383. *See also* Russia; Soviet Union

Moses, 25, 27, 186

Moslems. *See* Islam and Muslims

Mosques: at Cordoba, 208–209; at Dar es Salaam, *223*; in Mali, 234; in Ottoman Empire, 455; in Samarra, 194, 208

"Mother" statues, 6, *40*

Mound-building cultures, 180

Mount Agung, *262*

Mountains. *See names of specific mountains and ranges*

Mount Kailasa, 254

Mount Meru, 263, 412

Mount Olympus, 111

Mount Parnassus, 111

Mount Vesuvius, 146

Movable type, 294, 420

Movies. *See* Films; *names of specific films*

Mo Yan, 820

Mozambique, 406, 619, 622, 863

Mu'awiya, 190

Mubarak, Hosni, *886*, 886, 893

Muezzin (crier), 890

Mughal Empire, 248, 446, 461–471, 609–610; culture in, 470–471; Europeans in, 465–468; as "gunpowder empire," 468; society in, 468–470

Muhammad, 184–190, 703; Arab empire after, 189–199; images of, 361–362; role of, 186–189; teachings of, 187–188; trade and, 201; umma and, 200

Muhammad Ahmad, 619, 621, 628

Muhammad Ali, 619

Mukden incident, 736

Mulattoes, 399

Mulroney, Brian, 836

Multiculturalism, 937; in literature, 937

Multinational corporation, 936

Multinational states: Austrian Empire as, 558; in Europe, 558

Multiracial society, 399

Multiregional theory of human development, 3

Mumbai (Bombay), 52, 253, 394, 697, 900, *906*

Mummification: in Chile, *176*; in Egypt, 20

Mumtaz Mahal, 463–464

Munich, 727

Munich Conference, 735

"Munition Work" (Loughnan), 674

Murad I, 370, 447

Murakami, Haruki, 924

Murals, 721

Murasaki Shikibu (Lady Murasaki), 309, 311

Musa. *See* Mansa Musa

Muscovy, 438–439

Musharraf, Pervaiz, 901

Music: in Africa, 232–233, 875–876; in China, 87, 90; in India, 256; in Japan, 924; in Middle East, 893; popular, 857; rock, 857; Western, in Soviet Union, 800

Muslim Brotherhood, 705, 886, 890

Muslim League, 697, 699, 897

Muslims. *See* Arab Empire; Islam and Muslims

Mussolini, Benito, 725–726, *727*, 734, 738, 742

Mwene Metapa, 404, 411

Myanmar. *See* Burma

Mycenaean Greece, 24, 95–96

Mystery religions, 123, 148

Mysticism: in Indian poetry, 255; Sufi, 207

Myung-bak, Lee, 927

Nabobs, 612

Nagasaki, Japan, 489–490, 497, 648, 744, 753–754

Nagy, Imre, 775–776

Nahuatl language, 399

Naipaul, V. S., 908

Nairobi, 866

Namesake, The (Lahiri), 937

Namibia, 229

Nanak, 251

Nanjing, 289, *638*; Chinese republic in, 710–712, 769; Japan and, 736, 749, 920; Treaty of, 638. *See also* Nanjing Massacre

Paris Peace Conference, 679–681, 704, 708, 716
Park, Chung Hee, 925, 930
Parks, Rosa, 834
Parliaments, 341, 425, 439–440, 515–516; business and, 539; in Canada, 584; in France, 341; in Indonesia, 910; reforms by, 563
Parma, 560
Parnassus, Mount, 111
Parsis, 253
Parthenon, *108*, 108
Parti Quebécois, 836
Partitions of Germany, 755, 766
Party of the Revolution, 866
Pashas, 450, 619
Pasolini, Pier Paolo, 844
Passage to India, A (Forster), 610
Pasta, 202
Pasternak, Boris, 798
Pasteur, Louis, 593
Pastoralists, 406
Pataliputra, 43
Paterfamilias, 141
Paths of Glory (film), *671*, 671
Patriarchies, 6; in India, 46; in Mesopotamia, 12–13; in Southeast Asia, 262
Patriarchs of Constantinople, 362–363, 365. *See also names of specific patriarchs*
Patrician oligarchies, 515
Patricians: in European society, 515; in Rome, 129
Patrilineal society: in Africa, 230; in Mayan society, 163
Patriotism, 666–667, 673, 675. *See also* Nationalism
Paul III, 429
Paul of Tarsus, 150
Pax Mongolica, 287
Pax Romana, 137
Peace: after World War I, 679–683; Japanese independence and, 919; under Mongols, 287. *See also names of specific settlements and treaties*
Peaceful coexistence, 774, 776, 780, 784
Peace of Augsburg, 423
Peace of Westphalia, 434
"Peace Without Conquest" (Johnson), 781
Pearl Harbor attack, 740
Pearson, Karl, 605
"Peasant Movement in Hunan, The" (Mao Zedong), 710
Peasants, 586; in Asia, 616; Black Death and, 376; in Byzantine Empire, 368; in China, 79, 152, 477, 708, 769, 780, 804, 814; in Europe, 331, 333, 514–515; in France, 527; in High Middle Ages, 333; in Islam, 202; in Japan, 305, 494, 652; in Korea, 655; lifestyle of, 333; in Medieval Europe, 419–420; in Ottoman Empire, 453; in Rome, 134; in Russia, 565, 675, 677, 687; in Southeast Asia, 262, 614; in Soviet Union, 730. *See also* Revolts and rebellions; Serfs and serfdom
Peasant's Crusade, 351–352
Peasants' Revolt, 374
Peasants' War, 422
Peking. *See* Beijing
Peloponnesian League, 100
Peloponnesian War, 104–105
Peloponnesus region, 94, 96, 100
Pemba, 222
PEMEX, 720
Pensions, 923
"People of the Book," 186
People's Liberation Army (PLA), 769
People's Republic of China (PRC), 930. *See also* China
People's Republic of Korea (PRK). *See* North Korea

People's Volunteer Corps, 753
Pepin, 328
Perestroika (restructuring), 787, 800
Pergamum, 118, 132, *449*
Pericles, 94, 103–104
Periodicals, 512–513
Period of the Warring States, 79
Periplus (travel account), 219, 240
Permissive society, 843
Perón, Juan and Eva, 719, 840
Perry, Matthew C., 649, *650*
Persecution of Christians, 150
Persepolis, 33
Persepolis (novel and film), 884
Persia: Abbasid Dynasty and, 192–195; Arabs and, 189; Greece and, 103; Judah and, 27; literature of, 206; Mongols and, 196, 283–284; Rome and, 147; Safavids in, 448, 458–460. *See also* Iran; Persian Empire
Persian Empire, 1, 30–33; Alexander the Great and, 114; Arabs and, 360; India and, 31, 43; religion in, 33. *See also names of specific rulers*; Persia
Persian Gulf region, 222
Persian Gulf War, 849, 884–885
Persian language, 24, *463*, 471, *471*
Persian miniatures, 471
Persians, The (Aeschylus), 103
Persistence of Memory, The (Dali), *690*
Perspective in Renaissance arts, 378–380
Peru: Caral civilization in, 9, 172–173; copper mining in, 837; government of, 400; independence of, 575; Inka in, 398; Moche in, 173–176; oil in, 837; San Martín in, 575
Petain, Henri, 738
Peter, 326
Peter the Great, 438, *439*
Peter the Hermit, 351–352
Petrarch, 378
Petrograd. *See* St. Petersburg
Petronas Towers, 896
Phalanx, 98, *99*
Phan Dinh Phung, 630
Pharaohs, 18–21, 118. *See also names of specific rulers*
Philadelphia Convention, 517
Philip II Augustus (France), 341, 352
Philip II (Macedonia), 94, 114
Philip II (Spain), 430–431
Philip IV (France), 341, 377
Philip VI (France), 376
Philippines, 256, 260–261, 389; Aquino in, 910; in ASEAN, 914; Chinese trade and, 261, 475; colonialism and, 611, *612*; "comfort women" from, 749; independence of, 909; Japan and, 656, 740–741, 749; Marcos in, 909–910; Spain in, 397; U.S. and, 583, 605, 613, 656; World War II and, 740–741, 754
Philistines, 25
Philosophes, 506–511
Philosophy: in Axial Age, 109; in China, 71–78; in Greece, 108–110, *204*; in Hellenistic society, 123; of history, 207; in Islamic society, 203–205; of Locke, 506; in Safavid society, 459. *See also* Intellectual thought
Phnom Penh, Cambodia, *914*, 914
Phoenician alphabet, 96, 102
Phoenicians, 25, 130
Phonetic script, 41, 89–90, 165
Photian schism, 365
Photius, 365
Photography, 597
Physics, 60, 595
Piazza d'Italia (Moore), 854
Picasso, Pablo, 597, *600*, 600, 690

Pictographs, *15*, 41, 89; in China, 89; in Harappan society, 40
Piedmont, 560
Pilate, Pontius, 149
Pillars, 57, *59*
Pillars of Hercules, 216
Pine Forest (Tohaku), 497
Piñera, Sebastian, 839
Pinochet, Augusto, 839
Pirates, Barbary, 620
Pisa, 352, 369
Pisistratus, 102
Pissaro, Camille, 597
Pitt, William, the Elder, 516–517
Pizarro, Francisco, 398
Plague. *See* Black Death; Bubonic plague
Plains of Abraham, 520
Planck, Max, 595
Planetary motion, 504–505. *See also* Astronomy; Universe
Plan of Ayala (Zapata), 580
Plantagenets, 341
Plantation agriculture, 202
Plantations, 513; in Africa, 623, 625–626, 861; in Americas, 407, 617; environment and, 647; in Haiti, 528; slaves on, 231, 407, 617; in Southeast Asia, 412, 616; tea, 647; workers for, 616, 647
Plants, 4. *See also* Agriculture and farming; Crops
Plassey, Battle of, 465, 520
Plataea, battle at, 103
Plato, 109–110, 292
Platonic Academy, 110, 204
Please Look After Mom (Kyung-Sook Shin), 926
Plebeians, 129–130
Pliny the Elder, 84
Pliny the Younger, 144, 146, 151
PLO. *See* Palestine Liberation Organization
Plows, 332
Plutarch, 113, 135
Poe, Edgar Allan, 592
Poem, A (Du Fu), 294
Poets and poetry: Arabic, 206; Chinese, 269, 294–295; Hindu, 255; Homeric, 96–97; Indian, 471; Inkan, 179; Japanese, 313, 494–497; Roman, 140. *See also names of specific poets and works*
Pogroms, 372–374, 597
Poison gas, 668, 884
Poitiers, battle at, 191
Poland, 383; after Communism, 829; after World War I, 676, 682, *682*, 683; after World War II, 754, *763*; Christianity and, 343; in European Union, 832; Jews in, 374, 746–747; in NATO, 829; Nazi Germany and, 735–736, 738, 745–747; Russia and, 519, 556; Slavs in, 343; Solidarity in, 802; Soviet Union and, 735, 763, 767, 775–776; voting in, 845
Polis (city-state), 98
Politburo, 687, 793–794, 800
Political parties. *See also names of specific parties*: in England, 565; in Japan, 650–651, 920; in Nazi Germany, 727; socialist, 553; in Soviet Union, 797
Political structures: in Africa, 411; in Aztec society, 167–168; as characteristic of civilization, 8; in China, 65–70, 79, 81–82, 152, 269–282, 285–286; in Harappan society, 39; in Hellenistic society, 119; in Islamic society, 199–200; in Japan, 315; in Mayan society, 163. *See also names of specific types of political structures*
Politics: in Byzantine Empire, 365–368; in China, 280, 478–480; in France, 435; during German Reformation, 423; globalization and, 940; in

Quraishi clan, 186, 190
Qur'an, 184, 186–190, 199

Rabe'a of Qozdar, 206
Rabus, Ludwig, 428
Race and racism: in African colonies, 625–626,
    697; anti-Semitism, 566, 597, 727, 729–730,
    743–744, 746; color of skin in Indian society,
    44; Holocaust and, 746; imperialism and,
    625–626; Nazi Germany and, 727, 729–730,
    744–745; social Darwinism and, 596–597, 727;
    in South Africa, 861, 867–868; in United States,
    833–834. See also Slavery; Slave trade
Radar, 854
Radiance of the King, The (Laye), 876
Radiation, 595
Radicalism, 527. See also Student protests
Radical Party, 719
Radical Reconstruction, 583
Radio waves, 549
Radium, 595
Raffles, Stamford, 611
Raga (musical scale), 256
Railroads, 540; in China, 646, 810; in India, 609; in
    Japan, 652; in United States, 543
Rain forest, 913
Raj, 609–610, 897–898
Raja (prince), 48, 307, 609
Rajputs (Hindu clans), 246
Rákosi, Mátyás, 775
Rama, 57–58
Ramadan, 188
Ramayana, 57–58, 471
Ramcaritmanas, 471
Ramesses I, 15
Ramesses II, 21
Ranching in Latin America, 579
Rangoon (Yangon), 264, 616
Rann of Kutch, 253
Raphael, 379, 381
Rarotonga, 264
Rashomon (film), 310
Rasputin, 675
Rationalism, 504–506. See also Reason
Ravenna, 358
Raw materials: from Americas, 400–401;
    colonialism and, 605, 607, 616; in England, 539
Razzia (raid), 189
Re, 19
Reagan, Ronald, 786–787, 792, 802, 834, 840, 854
Reagan Revolution, 834–835
Realism: in art, 593–594; in Chinese novels, 486;
    in literature, 593–594; in Renaissance, 379
Reality, 109–110
Realpolitik, 562
Reason: in Enlightenment, 506; in Roman law,
    140–141; in scholasticism, 349. See also
    Rationalism
Rebellions. See Revolts and rebellions
Recession, 921; worldwide after 2007, 936. See
    also Great Depression
Reconquista (reconquest), 198, 341–342
Reconstruction, 583
Record keeping: Inkan, 177; Mayan, 165–166
Records of Ancient Matters (Japan), 301
Rectification of Political Rights (Zhang Zhidong), 640
Red Alert (George), 778
Red Army, 831
Red Fort, 464, 471
Red Guards, 805–807, 808
Red River region, 256, 319, 499–500
Red Sea area, 19, 185, 201, 605
Red Shirts, 560–561
Red Terror, 678
"Red tide," 773

Reform Act: of 1832, 557, 563; of 1867, 563
Reformation: Catholic, 428; in England, 425;
    Protestant, 361–362, 419–429
Reforms: in Austria, 518–519; in England, 563; in
    housing, 585; in India, 897; in Japan, 917–918,
    921; middle-class, 586; nationalism and,
    563–564; of papacy, 429; in Prussia, 518; in
    Rome, 147–148; in Russia, 519, 563–564; in
    Southeast Asia, 910–911; in United States, 583;
    by women, 587–588. See also names of specific
    reforms and reform movements
Refugees, 849
Regionalism, 912–913
Regional trade, 157
Regulation: of trade in India, 242, 244; in United
    States, 583
Reichstag, 421–422, 553, 566–567, 727
Reign of Terror, 527–528, 806
Reims, 350
Reincarnation: in Buddhism, 243; in Hinduism,
    50–52
Relativity theory, 595
Relics, 347, 421
Religion: 16th century wars of, 430; of Abbas the
    Great, 458; in Africa, 220, 869, 871; African
    education and, 871, 874; in Axum, 215; Aztec,
    169–170; Buddhism as, 244, 695; in Byzantine
    Empire, 361, 365; in Çatal Hüyük, 6; in central
    and eastern Europe, 382–383; as characteristic
    of civilization, 8, 13–14; in China, 71–78, 84,
    290–292, 806, 816–817; divisiveness of, 870;
    Egyptian, 20–21; in England, 430; English
    colonization and, 403; in Europe, 555;
    exploration and, 391–392; fundamentalism in,
    856; in German Reformation, 423; in Greece,
    110–111; of Hebrews, 25–27; Hellenistic, 123;
    imagery of, 361–362, 362; in India, 38, 50–56,
    247–251, 461, 464, 897; Indian women in, 250;
    in Indonesia, 910; in Japan, 303, 309–312, 316,
    491–492, 916–917; in Korea, 315–317, 499; in
    Latin America, 401, 870; in Mayan society,
    163–164; in Mesopotamia, 13–14; in Middle
    East, 891; in Mughal Empire, 464; nationalism
    and, 676–695, 705; Nigerian disputes over,
    865–866; in Ottoman Empire, 453; in Pakistan,
    901; pantheism and, 220; in Persian Empire,
    33; Reformation and, 419–423; in Rome,
    148–152; society and, 870; in Southeast Asia,
    262–264, 412, 695, 915–917; in Southern and
    Eastern Asia, 243; trade and, 201; in Twentieth
    Century, 856; in Vietnam, 320, 500. See also
    names of specific religions; Secularization
Religious art, 60
Religious orders: Catholic, 326–328, 345–347;
    during Reformation, 427–429. See also names of
    specific orders
Religious toleration, 517; in Mughal Empire, 461;
    Voltaire and, 508–509
Remarque, Erich Maria, 670
Reminiscences (Schurz), 557–558
Rémy, Nicholas, 432
Renaissance, 377–383; artistic, 378–380; Classical
    learning of, 420–421; intellectual, 378; printing
    in, 420; society in, 419–420; state in, 380–381,
    419–423
Renaissance humanism, 378
Rentiers, 515
Renzong, 274
Reparations: after World War I, 682, 684; after
    World War II, 755
Representation in France, 521
Repression, Freud on, 596
Republic, The (Plato), 110
Republican government in France, 566
Republican Party, 581–582

Republic of China (ROC), 930. See also Taiwan
Republic of Indonesia, 909
Republic of Korea. See South Korea
Republic of Singapore, 927
Republic of Vietnam. See South Vietnam
Republics: in England, 439–440; in France, 557.
    See also names of specific locations
Res Gestae (Augustus), 137
Resistance. See names of specific movements; Revolts
    and rebellions
Resources. See names of specific resources
Return from Cythera (Watteau), 512
Reunification of Germany, 802, 826
Revisionism, 553–554
Revolts and rebellions: anticolonial, 627–628; in
    China, 271, 477, 637–638, 803; in
    Constantinople, 357; English Peasants' Revolt,
    374; by Greeks, 559; in India, 465, 627–628; in
    Italy, 558–559; Jewish, 148–149; in Latin
    America, 573–574; by Roman slaves, 134, 144,
    148; in Russia, 439, 519; in Saint-Domingue,
    528; in Southeast Asia, 627; in Vietnam, 627;
    by White Lotus sect, 291, 479, 636. See also
    Protests; Revolutions
Revolutionary Alliance, 643
Revolutionary parties in Southeast Asia, 910
Revolutionary socialism, 553
Revolutionary War in America. See American
    Revolution
Revolutions: of 1830-1832, 557; of 1848, 557–558;
    of 1905, 675; in China, 524, 707–710, 712; in
    Cuba, 837–839; in France, 503–504, 521–528;
    Neolithic, 5; in Russia, 675; two-stage, 705. See
    also Agricultural revolution; Industrial
    Revolution; Revolts and rebellions; Scientific
    Revolution
Reykjavik, 787
Reza Khan. See Pahlavi dynasty
Rhapta, 219
Rhee, Syngman, 925
Rhetoric, 109
Rhine River region, 147, 734, 743
Rhodes, Cecil, 604–605, 624
Ricci, Matteo, 485
Rice: in China, 70, 87, 89, 276, 280, 333; Japan
    and, 652, 737; in Southeast Asia, 256–259, 737
Richard I the Lionhearted, 352
Richard II, 374
Riefenstahl, Leni, 730–731
Rigaud, Hyacinth, 436
Rights: in Greece, 98; in Russia, 567; of women,
    12, 280–282, 309, 321, 494, 510–511, 587–588.
    See also names of specific rights; Women
Rig Veda, 42, 51, 57
Rites of Zhou, 69–70, 74, 90
Rituals in Byzantine court, 363
Rivera, Diego, 721
Rivers and river regions. See names of specific river
    regions
River valley civilizations, 9. See also names of
    specific civilizations
Roads and highways: in China, 79, 81, 83–85, 130,
    276; in Inkan society, 177; in Rome, 130, 140.
    See also Transportation
Robespierre, Maximilien, 527–528
Rock art: in Africa, 215, 232; in India, 52, 246,
    254; in Sahara, 218. See also Cave art
Rock chambers, 58, 59
Rock churches, 234
Rocket (locomotive), 540
Rococo style, 511
Roger II (Sicily), 205
Roman Catholic Church, 157; in Americas, 401;
    in Austria, 519; Church of England and, 439;
    church organization and, 326–328; Clovis and,

325; Copernican system and, 504–505; corruption in, 421; decline of, 377; doctrine of, 428; in East Timor, 911; ecumenical councils and, 856; in Europe, 429; European exploration and, 391–392; in France, 430, 526, 530; Greek Orthodoxy and, 363; in Holy Roman Empire, 343; in Korea, 499; in Latin America, 401, 577, 870; in Middle Ages, 332, 343; in New World, 401; papacy and, 344; Reformation of, 427–429; salvation through relics and, 421; schism with Orthodox Church, 368; in Spain, 430; Thirty Years' War and, 434. See also names of specific orders; Papacy; Popes; Reformation

Romance of the Three Kingdoms, The (China), 85, 294

Roman Confederation, 129

Roman Empire, 126–155; Augustus in, 136–137; Britain and, 138–139, 325; Celts and, 449; Charlemagne and, 324–325; China and, 152; Christianity in, 149–150, 152; crisis in late period, 147–148; culture in, 141–142; early period in, 137–147; end of Western, 147; Greek culture in, 356; imports to, 240; Jews in, 148–149; law in, 140–141; nature of imperialism, 132–133; slavery in, 142, 144; society in, 140–147; trade and, 139–140; women in, 141–143. See also Roman Republic; Rome (ancient); Western Roman Empire

Romanesque architecture, 349

Roman History (Appian), 132

Romania: in 21st century, 829; after World War I, *682, 683*; Communism in, 763; in European Union, 832; independence of, 568–569; in Warsaw Pact, 767; during World War II, 739, 743

Romanians, 743

Roman language, 25

Roman law, 140–141, 357–359

Roman numerals, 253

Romanov family, 438. *See also names of specific individuals*

Roman Republic, 129–130; army in, 133–134; Carthage and, 132; decline and fall of, 134–136; government of, 129–130; Hellenistic world and, 132; Mediterranean region and, 130–134; Punic Wars and, 131–132; social divisions in, 129–130. *See also names of specific rulers*; Roman Empire; Rome (ancient)

Romanticism in literature and art, 592–594

Romantic nationalism, 561

Rome (ancient): Chinese silk imports, 84, 139; civil wars in, 134; colonization by, 129; economy in, 134, 140; Etruscans in, 127–129; Greece and, 127, 130, 140; legendary founding of, 126–127; military in, 133–134, 147–148. *See also* Roman Empire; Roman Republic

Rome-Berlin Axis, 734

Rome (city), 128, 142, 144; bishops of, 326; as Italian capital, 561; Treaty of, 831–832

Rommel, Erwin, 741

Romulus and Remus, 127

Romulus Augustulus, 148

Ronin (unemployed warriors), 493

Roosevelt, Franklin D.: Atlantic Charter and, 760; death of, 764; Good Neighbor Policy and, 718, 720; Great Depression and, 686; at Yalta, 762, *762, 770*

Roosevelt, Theodore, 656

Rosas, Juan Manuel de, 577

Rose Garden (Sadi), 206

Rotation of crops, 333

Rotation of earth, 121

Rousseau, Jean-Jacques, 510

Rousseff, Dilma, 841

Roy, Ram Mohan, 629

Royal Academy of Isfahan, *459*

Royalists, 528

Royal Pavilion, *470*

Royal Road, 32

"Royal Standard" of Ur, *11*

Royalty. *See* Kings and kingdoms; Monarchs and monarchies; *names of specific locations and rulers*; Queens

Rubaiyat (Omar Khayyam), 206

Rubber, 616, 616–617, 623, 737

Rubens, Peter Paul, *440, 441*

Rudra, 52

Rugs: in Middle East, 208–209; Ottoman, 455–456; Persian, 459–460

Ruhr valley, 684

Rules of Saint Benedict, 327

Rumi, 207

Runnymede, 341

Rural areas: in Africa, 625–626, 779, 861, 865, 872, 874, 874–875; in Arab world, 200; in Asia, 779; in China, 645–646, 710, 769, 780, 805, 811, 814–816; colonization and, 627–628; in India, 464; in Japan, 493, 652, 715

Rushdie, Salman, 907

Rusk, Dean, 777

Rus people, 344

Russell, Bertrand, 707

Russell, W. H., *560*

Russia, 438; in 19th century, 563–564; after Soviet Union, 802, 831; Catherine the Great in, 519; chariots in, 65; China and, 480, 656, 811; Christianity in, 365, 870; civil war in, 678; in Concert of Europe, 555; at Congress of Vienna, 554; Crimean War and, 560; economy in, 687, 831; enlightened absolutism in, 519; France and, 567–568; Germany and, 567–568; industrialization in, 550, 567–568; Jews in, 374, 597; military of, 831; Mongols in, 343–344, 383; Napoleon and, 531–532; Ottoman Empire and, 559; Poland and, 556; Polish revolution against, 556; reforms in, 831; religion in, 870; serfs in, 515; Seven Years' War and, 520; Slavs in, 343–344; socialism in, 567; society in, 831; state of, 438; Tibet and, 639; War Communism in, 678, 687; World War I and, 568, 643, 663–665, 668, 682, 682–683. *See also names of specific wars*; Russian Revolutions; Soviet Union

Russian Revolutions, 672, 675–679, 705

Russo-Japanese War, 569, 656–656

Rwanda, 406

Ryoanji temple, *314*

Ryukyu Islands, *654, 655, 811*

Saba, 215

Sacks: of Constantinople, 352, 369–370; of Delhi, 465; of Rome, 148

Sacraments, 347

Sacred Edict (Kangxi), 479, 485, 495

Sacred Way, 128

Sacrifice, 13–14. *See also* Human sacrifice

Saddam Hussein, 849, 883–886

Sadi, 206

Safavids, 446, 448, 453, 458–460

Safi al-Din, 457

Sahara Desert region, 213, 215, 863; commerce in, 411; desiccation south of, 869, 872; migration from, 218; Muslims in, 390–391; rock paintings of, 218; salt deposits in, *874*; trade in, 201, *216*, 225

Sahel, 224, 647

Saigon, 616, 773, 783–784, *911. See also* South Vietnam; Vietnam War

Saikaku, 494

Sailendra, 263

Saint Catherine, monastery of, *362*

Saint-Denis, abbey of, 350

Saint-Domingue, 528, 572. *See also* Haiti

Saint Peter's Basilica, 442

St. Petersburg, 439, 675–676. *See also* Leningrad

Saints. *See names of specific saints*

Saint-Simon, Duc de, 437

Saito Makoto, 733

Sakhalin Island, *654, 655, 919*

Sakharov, Andrei, 795, 800–801

Sakuko (closed country), 649

Saladin, 195–196, 352, 369–370

Saleh, Ghana, 225–226

Salinas, Carlos, 842

Salt: in Senegal, 874; in Timbuktu, 227

SALT I and II, 785–786

Salvation, 421. *See also names of specific religions*

Salvo, 435

Salween River region, 256–257

Samanids, 246

Samaria, 26, 27

Samarkand, 248, 284–285, 372

Samarra, Great Mosque of, 194, 208

Samoa, 264, 583

Samsung, 925

Samudragupta, 242

Samurai, 305–306, 489, 493–494, 649, 651, 659, 752

Sana, Yemen, 206

Sánchez Navarro family, 577

Sanchi, 59

Sandinistas, 786, 840

Sanford, Elizabeth Poole, 589

Sanger, Margaret, 712

Sanitation: in Harappa and Mohenjo-Daro, 39; in Paris, 563; urban, 337–338, 542, 585

San Lorenzo, Church of, 378

San Lorenzo (Olmec site), 160

San Martín, Jose de, 573, 575–576

San people, 232

Sanskrit language, 24, 42, 57, 255–256

Santa Anna, Antonio Lopez de, 577

Santa Claus, 347

Santarem, 181

San Vitale, Church of, *358–359*

Sarabhoji, *607*

Sarajevo, 663, 830

Sarda Act, 698

Sardinia, 127, 197; kingdom of, 558–559; Phoenicians in, 25

Sardis, 32

Sarekat Islam, 695–696, 707

Sargon, 11–12

Sarkozy, Nicolas, 826

Sarnath, 54; Lions of, *55*; stupa at, *54*

Saro-Wiwa, Ken, 868

Sarraut, Albert, 607, 615, 631

Sartre, Jean-Paul, 850

Saskatchewan, 584

Sassanian (Sassanid) Empire, 147, 186, 189

Satanic Verses, The (Rushdie), 907

Sat-Cho alliance, 650, 653

Satellites, 792, 855

Satellite states, 774–776, 792, 802. *See also names of specific countries*

Sati, 48, 250–251, 464, 470, 609, 629, 907

Satori (enlightenment), 312

Satrapi, Marjane, 884

Satraps and satrapies, 32

Satsuma, Japan, 650

Satyagraha, 697, 898

Saudi Arabia, 703, *705*, 888, 889, 891

Savannas, 214, 224

Savoy, house of, 558–560